Evangelical Dictionary of World Missions

A. Scott Moreau (D.Miss., Trinity Evangelical Divinity School) is associate professor of Missions and Intercultural Studies at Wheaton Graduate School. While working with Campus Crusade for Christ in Africa, he taught for eight years at the Nairobi International School of Theology and served as a Deputy Administrator for the Accrediting Council for Theological Education in Africa. Dr. Moreau has numerous publications to his credit, including several books such as *The World of the Spirits*, *Essentials of Spiritual Warfare*, and *Twentieth-Century Dictionary of Christian Biography* for which he acted as associate editor.

Harold Netland (Ph.D., Claremont Graduate School) serves as Associate Professor of Philosophy of Religion and Mission. He is also the director of Trinity's Doctor of Philosophy in Intercultural Studies Program and holds the Naomi A. Fausch Chair of Missions. Prior to coming to Trinity, Dr. Netland served for a number of years on the faculty of Tokyo Christian University. He also served as a missionary with the Evangelical Free Church of America in Japan for nine years. Among Dr. Netland's numerous published works is the book, *Dissonant Voices: Religious Pluralism and the Question of Truth*, along with many articles on mission, apologetics, and East Asia.

Charles Van Engen (Ph.D., Free University of Amsterdam) is the Arthur F. Glasser Professor of Biblical Theology of Mission at Fuller Theological Seminary. Before coming to Fuller he taught missiology at Western Theological Seminary in Michigan. Dr. Van Engen also served as president of the General Synod for the Reformed Church in America in 1997 and is widely traveled with his many responsibilities. His wide-ranging publications include *God's Missionary People*, *Mission-On-the-Way: Issues in Mission Theology*, and *Footprints of God: Mission OF, IN, and ON the Way*.

Evangelical Dictionary of World Missions

General Editor:
A. Scott Moreau

Associate Editors: Harold Netland and Charles Van Engen

Consulting Editors: David Burnett, Samuel Escobar, Paul G. Hiebert, Peter Kuzmic, Lois McKinney Douglas, Bong Rin Ro, Tite Tiénou, and Chris Wright

paternoster

Baker Books
A Division of Baker Book House Co
Grand Rapids, Michigan 49516

© 2000 by A. Scott Moreau

Published by Baker Books
a division of Baker Book House Company
P.O. Box 6287, Grand Rapids, MI 49516-6287

and

Paternoster Press
P.O. Box 300, Carlisle, Cumbria CA3 0QS
United Kingdom

Printed in the United States of America

Library of Congress Cataloging-in-Publication Data

Evangelical dictionary of world missions / general editor, A. Scott
Moreau ; associate editors, Harold Netland and Charles Van Engen ;
consulting editors, David Burnett . . . [et al.].
     p.   cm.   — (Baker reference library)
   Includes bibliographical references and index.
   ISBN 0-8010-2074-3 (hardcover)
   1. Missions—Dictionaries. 2. Missions—Theory—Dictionaries.
I. Moreau, A. Scott, 1955–   II. Netland, Harold, A., 1955–
III. Engen, Charles Edward Van. IV. Burnett, David, 1943–
V. Series.
BV2040.E92   2000
266'.003—dc21   99-044001

British Library Cataloging-in-Publication Data

A catalogue record for this book is available from the British Library.
ISBN 0-85364-995-2

For information about academic books, resources for Christian leaders, and
all new releases available from Baker Book House, visit our web site:
           http://www.bakerbooks.com

Dedicated
in loving memory of
Harvie Conn
a colleague who encouraged, inspired, and
constantly challenged the rest of us to keep
our eyes faithfully on the eternal Word as
we struggle to understand the realities of our
changing worlds

Preface

In the more than twenty-five years since the last comprehensive mission dictionary (*Concise Dictionary of Christian World Mission*, 1971) was compiled the field of mission and missiology has undergone considerable changes. One of the changes has been a strengthening of evangelical involvement not only in missionary practice but in the study of mission on the formal level. The evangelical commitment to missionary work has been supplemented by a host of evangelical scholars who are studying the missionary task in new and fresh ways, bringing better analytical tools to our task without losing sight that it is the Bible which is the foundation of our work.

In recent years a plethora of new research materials has been produced, including biographical dictionaries, handbooks of mission agencies, encyclopedias of missionary statistics, prayer guides of missionary work around the globe, and dictionaries from a broader theological spectrum. However, there has been no reference work with an admittedly evangelical orientation encompassing the issues of missionary work and reflection into a single resource, and thus the motivation for the *Evangelical Dictionary of World Missions*.

The *EDWM* was designed to provide a readily accessible overview of mission which is irenic toward differing perspectives, interdenominational in outlook, and still firmly committed to the inspiration and authority of the Bible in orienting us to the task God has entrusted to the church. This is not a dictionary *of* evangelical missions, but a dictionary on world missions *from* an evangelical perspective.

This work is intended for educated lay people, pastors, students, students, missionaries, and mission specialists. It is part of the Baker Reference Library series, which includes *The Evangelical Dictionary of Theology, The Evangelical Dictionary of Biblical Theology, Baker Encyclopedia of Psychology and Counseling, Evangelical Commentary on the Bible*, and *Baker Encyclopedia of Apologetics*. It has the same orientation, format, and style as these works.

The *EDWM* was also designed to be comprehensive without being exhaustive. Literally thousands of possible entries were initially considered for inclusion. The approximately 700 content articles finally included represent the entire discipline and practice of missions. Including the articles on people and countries, there are over 1,400 entries, with an additional 250 cross-reference listings to enable easier access to the particular topics of interest to the reader. Opinions will always vary as to which articles may have been added or removed, and the reader is humbly requested to bear in mind the impossibility of pleasing everyone with the final list.

Features to Note. For the most effective use of the *EDWM*, several features need to be understood. First, the authors were asked to stress the missiological aspect of each subject. For the theological articles, for example, they were asked not only to outline the general theological idea but also to incorporate issues, discussion, and application of mission significance. Where appropriate, critical evaluations were also to be included.

Second, to ensure access to the non-technical reader, the authors were asked to keep the language used at the popular level rather than the technical level. Our goal was that the scholar will find that what is said is fair and correct, while the lay reader will find it understandable.

Third, we worked hard to make the full breadth of the work accessible to the reader. There are three means by which this is accomplished. (A) Within each article we mark words on which entries appear elsewhere in the dictionary in Small Caps. It should be noted that we were not exhaustive in this process, assuming that readers would be aware that words such as "God," "Jesus," "Mission," "Missiology," "Islam," and so on would be found as articles elsewhere in this type of dictionary. (B) There are cross-listings at the end of many articles which are intended to supplement the use of small cap cross-references within each article. (C) Finally, we included one index (persons) as well as a complete outline of all of the content articles (i.e., non-biographical and non-geographical). It is expected that mission educators will find the outline and the index particularly helpful, as they allow the educator to read on and also readily point students to a variety of appropriate articles for use in any missions-related class.

Fourth, we intend that the work will stimulate and enable further research and reflection. Toward that end, most of the articles include short bibliographies. These are selective rather than exhaustive. As with all of the reference works in this Baker series, the publisher has chosen to limit the bibliographies to readily available English resources.

Fifth, as in any work with some 330 contributors, there will be differences of opinion and terminology. We made no effort to harmonize or force an artificial uniformity on such differences, as they are a reflection the breadth of approach of evangelicals toward mission. This applies not only to ideas but to certain terms, three categories of which should be noted. It was our decision in these cases to allow the authors latitude to use the term(s) they preferred rather than forcing an artificial uniformity. (A) Terms such as developing world, non-Western world, Third World, and Two-Thirds World, are some of the designations used to refer to African, Asian, Latin American, and Oceanic countries and cultures. (B) In missiological circles there is still some fluidity concerning "intercultural" and "cross-cultural." Technically they refer to two distinct ideas: *intercultural* generally refers to the interaction of people of diverse cultures, while *cross-cultural* refers to the study of the same phenomena in different cultures for purposes of comparison and contrast. However, these two terms are not used consistently in the missiological literature. (C) Finally, the terms *mission* and *missions* are not used uniformly in the literature. There is ongoing debate within the evangelical community as to the appropriate term to use (see the article MISSION AND MISSIONS), and we generally left the term as used by the author in recognition of that debate.

Sixth, there are 483 biographical articles scattered throughout the dictionary. To attempt to reflect the two-way flow of missions, 92 of our the subjects originated from non-Western contexts. To emphasize the role women have taken in missionary efforts, 105 are chronicled here. On a continental basis, 239 of our subjects came from Europe, 152 from North America, 48 from Asia, 22 from Africa, 12 from Latin America and the Caribbean, and 10 from Oceania. On the other end, 196 served in Asia, 94 in Africa, 66 in Europe, 53 in North America, 49 in Latin America and the Caribbean, and 25 in Oceania. In part because evangelical missiology is relatively young as a discipline, even though we consciously sought to limit the number of living people included in the Dictionary to a minimum, at the time of this writing, 52 of the subjects are still alive. To limit the proliferation, a cut-off birth year for the inclusion of living people in the Dictionary was set at 1930, with four exceptions made for particularly important non-Western leaders (Panya Baba, David Yonggi Cho, Rene Padilla, and Luis Palau).

Seventh, and finally, authors were given latitude to cover what they wanted in the country articles. Not all included statistics; and the statistical variations among the articles were not harmonized with two exceptions: (A) All population figures are taken from the United Nations 1994 projections for the A.D. 2000 populations, and (B) All country areas (square miles and kilometers) are from the *MacMillan Centennial Atlas of the World* (1997). Additionally, when countries are mentioned in non-country articles, they are generally referred to by contemporary names rather than names in history (e.g., Gold Coast is Ghana; Siam is Thailand). One exception is that of the former Zaire (now Democratic Republic of Congo), the name of which changed too late in the project to allow for name changes to be made throughout.

Acknowledgments. As with any project of this magnitude, the list of those who deserve thanks is longer than the space allowed to name them. In particular I extend my deepest gratitude to J. D. Douglas and Walter A. Elwell, both editors of numerous parallel projects, whose advice and encouragement helped throughout the years of labor this work entailed. The Associate and Contributing Editors have been invaluable resources and references throughout the life of the project. They sharpened the thinking in the beginning, helped carry the load throughout, and were essential to the success of completing this project. Special thanks go to David Barrett for the UN population statistics, and to the various graduate assistants at Wheaton whose involvement over the years of the project made things go much more smoothly than they would have otherwise: Wendy Larson, Penny Mason Gushiken, Tracy Smith, Gary Lamb, Grace Klein, Jackie Busch, Sheri Skinner, Vicki Cairns, and Nicole Feria. The people at Baker Book House, especially Jim Weaver, Maria denBoer, and Rebecca Cooper, have been particularly helpful in making important administrative decisions, keeping the project on track throughout, and encouraging me to keep to the course.

Finally I offer deep appreciation for the support and advice supplied by my colleagues in the Missions and Intercultural Studies department at Wheaton College, including John Gration, Doug McConnell (now with Pioneers), Evvy Campbell, Robert Gallagher, Alan Seaman, Cheri Pierson, and Carol Fowler. I also express my gratitude to those who provided guidance and encouragement at needed junctures, especially Ken Mulholland and Ken Gill. Finally, I would like to express my appreciation to Wheaton College and the environment of support it offers which enabled this task to be taken from the stage of a dream to the work you now hold in your hands.

Contributors

Aboagye-Mensah, Robert. Ph.D., University of Aberdeen. General Secretary, Christian Council of Ghana; Supervisory Staff, Akrofi-Christaller Memorial Centre for Mission Research and Applied Theology, Akropong-Akuapem, Ghana.

Adeney, Miriam. Ph.D., Washington State University. Research Professor of Mission, Regent College, Vancouver, Canada; Associate Professor of Cross Cultural Ministries, Seattle Pacific University, Seattle, Washington.

Akers, John N. Ph.D., University of Edinburgh. Special Assistant, The Billy Graham Evangelistic Association, Montreat, North Carolina.

Akins, Clinton M. D.Min., Southern Baptist Theological Seminary. Professor of Missiology and Religion, Indian Ocean Training Center, Madagascar.

Allison, Gregg. Ph.D., Trinity Evangelical Divinity School. Assistant Professor of Theology and Church History, Western Seminary, Portland, Oregon.

Allison, Norman E. Ph.D., University of Georgia. Director, School of World Missions, Toccoa Falls College, Toccoa Falls, Georgia.

Anderson, Gerald H. Ph.D., Boston University. Retired. Former Director, Overseas Ministries Study Center, New Haven, Connecticut.

Anderson, Justice C. Th.D., Southwestern Baptist Theological Seminary. Professor of Missions; Director, World Missions Center, Southwestern Baptist Theological Seminary, Forth Worth, Texas.

Arnold, Clinton E. Ph.D., Cambridge University. Associate Professor of New Testament Language and Literature, Talbot School of Theology, LaMirada, California.

Askew, Thomas A. Ph.D., Northwestern University. Professor and Chair of History, Gordon College, Wenham, Massachusetts.

Athyal, Sakhi. Ph.D., Fuller Theological Seminary. Free Lance Writer, Glendora, California.

Athyal, Saphir P. Ph.D., Princeton Theological Seminary. Director, Mission and Evangelism, World Vision International, Monrovia, California.

Austin, Thomas L. D.Min., Westminster Theological Seminary. Director, Africa Theological Training Resources/Mission to the World, Nairobi, Kenya.

Baker, Kenneth John. D.Miss., Trinity Evangelical Divinity School. Director, Missionary Care and Leadership Development (Niger), SIM International, Niamey, Niger.

Baker, William H. Th.D., Dallas Theological Seminary. Professor of Theology, Moody Bible Institute, Chicago, Illinois.

Barrett, David. Ph.D., Columbia University, New York. Research Professor of Missiometrics, Regent University School of Divinity, Richmond, Virginia.

Barro, Antonio C. Ph.D., Fuller Theological Seminary. President, South American Theological Seminary, Londrina, Brazil.

Baumgartner, Erich W. Ph.D., Fuller Theological Seminary. Associate Director, Institute for World Mission and Associate Professor of World Mission, Andrews University, Berrien Springs, Michigan.

Beals, Paul A. Th.D., Dallas Theological Seminary. Professor of Missiology, Grand Rapids Baptist Seminary, Grand Rapids, Michigan.

Bellingham, George Robert. D.Min., Eastern Baptist Seminary. Development Services Coordinator, World Vision of New Zealand, Auckland, New Zealand.

Bennett, Charles. M.A., Claremont Graduate School. President, Partners International, San Jose, California.

Beougher, Timothy K. Ph.D., Trinity Evangelical Divinity School. Billy Graham Chair of Evangelism, Associate Professor of Evangelism, and Associate Dean, Southern Baptist Theological Seminary, Louisville, Kentucky.

Contributors

Bevans, SVD, Steven B. Ph.D., University of Notre Dame. Director, Chicago Center for Global Ministries and Associate Professor of Doctrinal Studies, Catholic Theological Union, Chicago, Illinois.

Beyerhaus, Peter. Ph.D., Kennedy School of Missions. Professor Emeritus of Mission and Ecumenical Theology, Eberhard-Karls Univertät Tübingen, Tübingen Germany.

Bonk, Jonathan J. Ph.D., University of Aberdeen. Associate Director, Overseas Ministries Study Center, New Haven, Connecticut.

Bowers, W. Paul. Ph.D., University of Cambridge. Deputy Administrator, Accrediting Council for Theological Education in Africa (ACTEA), SIM International, Kalk Bay, South Africa.

Bradshaw, Bruce. M.A., Gordon-Conwell Theological Seminary. Director, Holistic Development Research, World Vision International, Monrovia, California.

Breshears, Gerry. Ph.D., Fuller Theological Seminary. Professor of Theology, Western Seminary, Portland Oregon.

Brewster, Elizabeth. Ph.D., University of Texas. Assistant Professor of Language/Culture Learning, Fuller School of World Mission, Pasadena, California.

Briggs, John H. Y. M.A., Cambridge. Principal, Westhill College of Higher Education, Birmingham, United Kingdom.

Brodeen, Judi. M.A., Wheaton College. Missionary, Christian and Missionary Alliance, Pasadena, California.

Broucek, David R. Ph.D., Trinity Evangelical Divinity School. Missionary Training and Research Coordinator, The Evangelical Alliance Mission, Wheaton, Illinois.

Bruce, Janet Sue. MS. Ed., Purdue University. Department Coordinator, Christian Education/Educational Ministries, Wheaton College, Wheaton, Illinois.

Buehler, Herman. Ph.D., Fuller Theological Seminary. Missionary-at-Large, West Coast and Micronesia, Liebenzell Mission of U.S.A., Glendora, California.

Bundy, David. Ph.D. Cand., Catholic University, Louvain. Associate Professor of Church History, Christian Theological Seminary, Indianapolis, Indiana.

Burnett, David. Ph.D., Bradford University. Academic Dean, All Nations Christian College, Ware, Herts, United Kingdom.

Bush, Luis. Th.M., Dallas Theological Seminary. International Director, A.D. 2000 & Beyond Movement, Colorado Springs, Colorado.

Buss, Siegfried A. Ph.D., Vanderbilt University. International Representative, Ochanomizu Christian Center, Tokyo, Japan.

Butman, Richard E. Ph.D., Fuller Graduate School of Psychology. Professor of Psychology, Wheaton College, Wheaton, Illinois.

Calenberg, Richard D. Th.D., Grace Theological Seminary. Missionary, SIM International, Jos, Nigeria.

Campbell, Evvy Hay. Ph.D., Michigan State University. Associate Professor of Missions and Intercultural Studies, Wheaton Graduate School, Wheaton, Illinois.

Carroll R., Mark Daniel. Ph.D., The University of Sheffield (England). Professor of Old Testament, Denver Seminary, Denver, Colorado.

Carson, Don A. Ph.D., Cambridge University. Research Professor of New Testament, Trinity Evangelical Divinity School, Deerfield, Illinois.

Chancellor, James Darrell. Ph.D., Duke University. W.O. Carver Professor of World Religions and Missions, Southern Baptist Theological Seminary, Louisville, Kentucky.

Chuang, Tsu-Kung. Ph.D., Trinity Evangelical Divinity School. Senior Pastor, Chinese Bible Church of Greater Boston, Boston, Massachusetts.

Clouse, Robert G. Ph.D., University of Iowa. Professor of History, Indiana State University, Terre Haute, Indiana.

Coggins, Wade T. LL.D., Nyack College. Retired Executive Director, Evangelical Foreign Missions Association, Kensington, Maryland.

Coleman, Robert E. Ph.D., University of Iowa. Director, Billy Graham Institute of Evangelism Wheaton, Illinois; Director, School of World Mission and Evangelism and Professor of Evangelism, Trinity Evangelical Divinity School, Deerfield, Illinois.

Conn, Harvie M. Th.M., Westminster Seminary. Professor of Missions, Westminster Theological Seminary, Philadelphia, Pennsylvania. Deceased.

Connor, J. Michael. Ph.D. Cand., Trinity International University. Diplomatic Representative, Christian Embassy, Washington, D.C.

Corwin, Gary Russell. M.Div. (Missions), Trinity Evangelical Divinity School. Editor, *Evangelical Missions Quarterly*, Evangelical Missions Information Service, Wheaton, Illinois.

Cotterell, F. Peter. Ph.D. Retired, former Principal, London Bible College, London, United Kingdom.

Couchell, Dimitrios G. B. A., Holy Cross Greek Orthodox School of Theology. Executive Director, Orthodox Christian Mission Center, St. Augustine, Florida.

Covell, Ralph. Ph.D., University of Denver. Senior Professor World Christianity, Denver Seminary, Denver, Colorado.

Crawford, Nancy. Psy.D., Wheaton College. Psychologist, African Inland Mission, Wheaton, Illinois.

Cruse, Richard K. Th.M., Dallas Theological Seminary. Europe Area Director, OC International, Kandern, Germany.

Crutchley, David. Ph.D., Southwestern Baptist Theological Seminary. Senior Lecturer, Baptist Theological College, Cape Town, Republic of South Africa.

Cunningham, Scott. Ph.D., Dallas Theological Seminary. Administrative Secretary for Accreditation, Accrediting Council for Theological Education in Africa (ACTEA), Charlotte, North Carolina.

Dale, Kenneth J. Ph.D., Union Seminary, New York. Professor Emeritus, Japan Lutheran Theological Seminary, Japan.

DaSilva, Jarbas. M.A., Wheaton College. Missionary, Africa Inland Mission, Sao Paulo, Brazil.

Davidson, Allan K. Ph.D., Aberdeen University. Lecturer in Church History and Pacific Studies, St. John's College, University of Auckland, Auckland, New Zealand.

Davies, Ron E. Ph.D., Fuller Theological Seminary. Associate Lecturer, All Nations Christian College, Ware, Herts, United Kingdom.

Davies, Stanley. Dip Th., London University. Executive Director, Evangelical Missionary Alliance, London, England.

Davis, Charles A. Ph.D., Trinity Evangelical Divinity School. Research Associate, The Evangelical Alliance Mission, Wheaton, Illinois.

Deiros, Pablo A. Ph.D., Southwestern Baptist Theological Seminary. Professor of Mission History, Fuller School of World Mission, Pasadena, California.

Dekar, Paul R. Ph.D., University of Chicago. Professor of Evangelism and Missions, Memphis Theological Seminary, Memphis, Tennessee.

DeVries, Sue. M.A., Wheaton College. Assistant Editor, *Kenya Church Growth Bulletin*, Africa Ministry Resources (OC International), Nairobi, Kenya.

Deyneka, Anita. M.A., Mundelein College. Director of Research, Peter Deyneka Russian Ministries, Rockford, Illinois.

DeYoung, Lee. M.B.A., University of Chicago. Vice President of Broadcasting, Words of HOPE, Grand Rapids, Michigan.

Dickerson, Lonna. Ph.D., University of Illinois. Director, Institute for Cross Cultural Training, Wheaton, Illinois.

Dollar, Harold E. Ph.D., Fuller School of World Mission. Chair of the Department of Mission, Biola University, LaMirada, California.

Douglas, J. D. Ph.D., Hartford Seminary Foundation. Author, Singapore Bible College, Singapore.

Douglas, Lois McKinney. Ph.D., Michigan State University. Emeritus Professor of Mission, Trinity Evangelical Divinity School, Deerfield, Illinois.

Dunavant, Donald R. Ph.D., Mid-America Baptist Theological Seminary. Pastor, Bartlett, Tennessee.

Durnbaugh, Donald F. Ph.D., University of Pennsylvania. Archivist, Juniata College, Huntingdon, Pennsylvania.

Dyrness, William A. D.Theol., University of Strasbourg. Dean of School of Theology and Professor of Theology and Culture, Fuller Theological Seminary, Pasadena, California.

Easterling, John. D.Miss., Trinity Evangelical Divinity School. Professor of Cross-Cultural Ministries, Northwestern College, St. Paul, Minnesota.

Eitel, Keith E. D.Theol., The University of South Africa. Professor of Christian Missions,

Southeastern Baptist Theological Seminary, Wake Forest, North Carolina.

Elliston, Edgar J. Ph.D., Michigan State University. Provost, Hope International University, Fullerton, California.

Elwell, Walter A. Ph.D., Edinburgh. Professor of Biblical and Theological Studies, Wheaton College, Wheaton, Illinois.

Enroth, Ron. Ph.D., University of Kentucky. Professor of Sociology, Westmont College.

Escobar, J. Samuel. Ph.D., Thornley B. Wood Professor of Missiology, Eastern Baptist Theological Seminary, Wynnewood, Pennsylvania.

Eshleman, Paul A. M.B.A., Michigan State University. Director, Jesus Film Project, Campus Crusade for Christ, Laguna Nigel, California.

Estep, John H. D.D., Denver Theological Seminary. Executive Director, Retired, Mission to the Americas, Glendale Heights, Illinois.

Eyring, Margot O. Ph.D., University of Tennessee at Knoxville. Adjunct Professor, American Studies Program, Washington, D. C.

Ferris, Robert Weston. Ph.D., Michigan State University. Associate Dean for Doctoral Studies, Columbia Biblical Seminary, Columbia, South Carolina.

Fiedler, Klaus. Th.D., Heidelberg University. Professor, University of Malawi, Zomba, Malawi.

Finley, Thomas John. Ph.D., University of California at Los Angeles. Professor of Old Testament and Semitics, Talbot School of Theology, LaMirada, California.

Flowers, Jamie L. M.A., Wheaton College. Freelance Writer, Chicago, Illinois.

Forgette, Adrienne M. Ph.D., Fuller Theological Seminary. Assistant Professor of Psychology, Northwestern College, Orange City, Iowa.

Freundt, Jr., Albert H. D.Min., McCormick Theological Seminary. Professor of Church History, Reformed Theological Seminary, Jackson, Mississippi.

Friesen, Paul H. Ph.D. Cand., University of St. Michaels College/Toronto School of Theology. Professor of History, Ontario Bible College, North York, Ontario, Canada.

Fryling, Robert A. M.A., Wheaton Graduate School. President, InterVarsity Press, Downers Grove, Illinois.

Fuller, Daniel. D.Theol., University of Basel. Senior Professor of Hermeneutics, Fuller Theological Seminary.

Fuller, Lois. M.A., Trinity Evangelical Divinity School. Nigerian Field Leader, World Partners of the Missionary Church, Lagos, Nigeria.

Fuller, W. Harold. D.Litt., Biola. Missions author and historian, Willowdale, Ontario, Canada.

Gailey, Charles R. Ph.D., University of South Africa. Director, School of World Mission and Evangelism, Nazarene Theological Seminary, Kansas City, Missouri.

Galadima, Bulus Y. Ph.D., Trinity Evangelical Divinity School. Academic Dean and Lecturer, Jos ECWA Theological Seminary, Jos, Nigeria.

Gallagher, Robert. Ph.D., Fuller Theological Seminary. Assistant Professor of Missions and Intercultural Studies, Wheaton College, Wheaton, Illinois.

Gensichen, Hans-Werner. D.Theol., University of Göttingen. Emeritus Professor of History of Religions and Missiology, University of Heidelberg, Heidelberg, Germany.

Gibbs, Eddie. D.Min., Fuller Theological Seminary. Professor of Church Growth, Fuller School of World Mission, Pasadena, California.

Gill, Kenneth D. Ph.D., University of Birmingham, UK. Associate Director, Billy Graham Center, Wheaton, Illinois.

Gilliland, Dean. Ph.D., Hartford Seminary Foundation. Professor of Contextualized Theology and African Studies, Fuller School of World Mission, Pasadena, California.

Ginn, Jeffery B. Ph.D., Mid-America Baptist Theological Seminary. Director and Professor of Missions, Northeast Campus of Mid-America Baptist Theological Seminary, Schenectady, New York.

Glasscock, L. E. Th.D., Grace Theological Seminary. Associate Professor, Moody Bible Institute, Chicago, Illinois.

Glasser, Arthur F. Ph.D., Union Theological Seminary (New York). Dean Emeritus of Fuller School of World Mission, Fuller School of World Mission, Pasadena, California.

Gnanakan, Ken. Ph.D. General Secretary, Asia Theological Association, Bangalore, India.

Goldsmith, Martin. M.A., Oxford. Retired Associate Lecturer, All Nations Christian College, Ware, Herts, United Kingdom.

Greenlee, David. Ph.D., Trinity Evangelical Divinity School. International Research and Strategy Associate, Operation Mobilization, Carlisle, England.

Greenway, Roger S. Th.D., Southwestern Baptist Theological Seminary. Professor of World Missiology, Calvin Theological Seminary, Grand Rapids, Michigan.

Groothuis, Douglas. Ph.D., University of Oregon. Assistant Professor of Philosophy of Religion and Ethics, Denver Seminary, Denver, Colorado.

Gross, Edward N. D.Miss., Trinity Evangelical Divinity School. Adjunct Faculty in Missions, Biblical Theological Seminary, Hatfield, Pennsylvania.

Gushiken, Penny. M.A., Wheaton Graduate School. Freelance Writer, Chicago, Illinois.

Guthrie, Stan. M.A., Columbia International University. Managing Editor, *Pulse* and *EMQ*, Evangelical Missions Information Service, Wheaton, Illinois.

Hama, Jude. M.A., Wheaton College. General Director, Scripture Union, Accra, Ghana.

Harber, Frank. Ph.D., Southwestern Baptist Theological Seminary. Evangelist and Apologist, Frank Harber Evangelistic Association, Fort Worth, Texas.

Hartford, Paul. M.A., Wheaton College. Dean of the College, Bethany College of Missions, Minneapolis, Minnesota.

Harvey, David P. D.Min., Columbia Biblical Seminary and Graduate School of World Missions. Associate Professor of Missiology, Toccoa Falls College, Toccoa Falls, Georgia.

Harvey, John. Th.D. , Toronto School of Theology. Associate Professor, Columbia Biblical Seminary and School of Missions, Columbia, South Carolina.

Harvey, Richard S. M.A., University College, London. Lecturer, All Nations Christian College, Ware, Herts, United Kingdom.

Hay, Ian M. D.Miss., Trinity Evangelical Divinity School. General Director Emeritus, SIM International, Charlotte, North Carolina.

Hayward, Douglas J. Ph.D., University of California Santa Barbara. Associate Professor, School of Intercultural Studies, Biola University, LaMirada, California.

Hedlund, Roger E. D.Miss., Fuller Theological Seminary. Professor of Mission Studies (Research), Serampore College, Madras, India.

Hertig, Paul. Ph.D., Fuller Theological Seminary. Vera B. Blinn Assistant Professor of World Christianity, United Theological Seminary, Dayton, Ohio.

Hertig, Young Lee. Ph.D., Fuller Theological Seminary. Vera B. Blinn Assistant Professor of World Christianity, United Theological Seminary, Dayton, Ohio.

Hesselgrave, David J. Ph.D., University of Minnesota. Professor Emeritus, Trinity Evangelical Divinity School, Deerfield, Illinois.

Hiebert, Paul G. Ph.D., University of Minnesota. Professor of Mission and Anthropology, Trinity Evangelical Divinity School, Deerfield, Illinois.

Hille, Rolf. Ph.D., University of Munich. Principal, Albrecht-Bengel-Haus, Tubingen, Germany.

Hoke, Stephen. Ph.D., Michigan State University. Vice President of Staff Development and Training, Church Resources Ministries, Upland, California.

Horan, Robert J. M.A., Wheaton College. Security Consultant, Crisis Consulting International, Wheaton, Illinois.

Hornberger, Andy. B.F.A., Ohio University. Public Relations Supervisor, Africa Inland Mission International, Pearl River, New York.

Howard, David M. M.A., Wheaton Graduate School. Retired; former President, Latin America Mission, Miami, Florida.

Hsu, John D. L. Ph.D., Aquinas Institute of Theology. President, Evangel Seminary and Chairman, Asia Theological Association, Hong Kong, People's Republic of China.

Hunsberger, George R. Ph.D., Princeton Theological Seminary. Professor of Missiology, Western Theological Seminary, Grand Rapids, Michigan.

Contributors

Hutchinson, Mark P. Ph.D., University of New South Wales. Director, Centre for the Study of Australian Christianity, Sydney, Australia.

Iadonisi, Joe C. M.A., Wheaton College. Missionary, Bogota, Colombia.

Inagaki, Hisakazu. Ph.D., Tokyo Metropolitan University. Professor of Philosophy, Tokyo Christian University, Tokyo, Japan.

Jackson, Eleanor M. Ph.D., Birmingham University. Senior Lecturer in Religious Studies, University of Derby, Derby, United Kingdom.

Jacobs, Donald R. Ph.D., New York University. Executive Director, Mennonite Christian Leadership Foundation, Landisville, Pennsylvania.

James, Violet. Ph.D., University of Aberdeen. Lecturer, Singapore Bible College, Singapore.

Jennings, John Nelson. Ph.D., Edinburgh University. Assistant Professor of Christian Studies, Tokyo Christian University, Tokyo, Japan.

Jensma, Jeanne L. Ph.D., Biola University (Rosemead School of Psychology). Clinical Director, Tuscarora Resource Center, Mt. Bethel, Pennsylvania.

Johnson, Todd M. Ph.D., William Carey International University. Researcher, Global Evangelization Movement, Richmond, Virginia.

Johnson, Wayne. Ph.D., Trinity International University. Academic Dean and Lecturer, Nairobi International School of Theology, Nairobi, Kenya.

Johnstone, Patrick J. B.S., Chemistry. Director for Research, WEC International, Gerrards Cross, Bucks, England.

Jørgensen, Knud. Ph.D., Fuller Theological Seminary. Director, Christian Mission to Buddhists, Oslo, Norway.

Kantzer, Kenneth. Ph.D., Harvard University. Dean Emeritus and Distinguished Professor of Biblical and Systematic Theology, Trinity Evangelical Divinity School, Deerfield, Illinois.

Kelsey, George E. M.A., Wheaton. Director, Arab Study Program, Amman, Jordan.

Kendall, Glenn. M.Div., Denver Seminary. Africa Director, CBInternational, Denver, Colorado.

Keyes, Lawrence E. D.Miss., Fuller Theological Seminary. President, OC International, Colorado Springs, Colorado.

Khai, Chin K. Th.M., International Theological Seminary. Student, Fuller School of World Mission, Pasadena, California.

King, Roberta Rose. Ph.D., Fuller School of World Mission. Missionary, CBInternational, seconded as Senior Lecturer in Ethnomusicology, Daystar University, Nairobi, Kenya.

Klaus, Byron D. D.Min., Fuller Theological Seminary. Professor of Church Leadership and President, Assemblies of God Theological Seminary, Springfield, Missouri.

Klein, Grace L. M.A., Wheaton College. Freelance Writer, Wheaton, Illinois.

Kopp, Thomas J. D.Th., University of South Africa. Professor of Missions and Intercultural Studies Department Chair, Multnomah Bible College, Portland, Oregon.

Köstenberger, Andreas J. Dr. rec. soc. oec., Vienna University of Economics; Ph.D., Trinity Evangelical Divinity School. Associate Professor of New Testament, Southeastern Baptist Theological Seminary, Wake Forest, North Carolina.

Kraft, Charles H. Ph.D., Hartford Seminary Foundation. Professor of Anthropology and Intercultural Communication, Fuller School of World Mission, Pasadena, California.

Kraft, Marguerite. Ph.D., Fuller Theological Seminary. Professor of Intercultural Studies, Biola University, LaMirada, California.

Kuzmic, Peter. Dr. Theol., Catholic Faculty of Theology. Distinguished Professor of World Missions and European Studies, Gordon Conwell Theological Seminary, South Hamilton, Massachussetts.

Lamb, Gary N. M.A., Wheaton Graduate School. Missionary, Pioneers, Orlando, Florida.

Larkin, William J. Ph.D., University of Durham (England). Professor of New Testament and Greek, Columbia Biblical Seminary and School of Missions, Columbia, South Carolina.

Larson, Wendy S. M.A., Wheaton Graduate School. Missionary, Pioneers, Sarajevo, Bosnia-Herzegovina.

Lee, David Tai Woong. D.Miss., Trinity Evangelical Divinity School. Director, Global Missionary Training Center, Seoul Korea.

Lewis, James F. Ph.D., University of Iowa. Associate Professor of Religious Studies, Wheaton College, Wheaton, Illinois.

Limpic, Ted. M.Div., Talbot Theological Seminary. Assistant Field Director, OC International, Sao Paulo, Brazil.

Lineham, Peter. D.Phil., University of Sussex. Senior Lecturer in History, Massey University, Palmerston North, New Zealand.

Ling, Samuel. Ph.D., Temple University. General Director, China Horizon, LaMirada, California.

Lingenfelter, Judy. Ph.D., University of Pittsburgh. Director, Ed.D. Program in Cross-Cultural Education, Biola University, LaMirada, California.

Lingenfelter, Sherwood. Ph.D., University of Pittsburgh. Dean and Professor of Anthropology, Fuller School of World Mission, Pasadena, California.

Lodwick, Kathleen L. Ph.D., University of Arizona. Associate Professor of Asian History, Penn State University, Allentown, Pennsylvania.

Love, Richard D. Ph.D., Fuller Theological Seminary. US Director, Frontiers, Mesa, Arizona.

Luter, A. Boyd. Ph.D., Dallas Theological Seminary. Adjunct Professor of Biblical Studies, Golden Gate Baptist Theological Seminary, San Francisco, California.

Maruyama, Tadataka. Ph.D., Princeton Theological Seminary. President, Tokyo Christian University, Tokyo, Japan.

Massaro, Dennis K. M.A., Wheaton College Graduate School. Free Lance Writer, Wheaton, Illinois.

Mathews, Edward. D.Miss., Fuller Theological Seminary. Professor of Missions, Abilene Christian University, Abilene, Texas.

Maust, John. M.A., Wheaton Graduate School. President, Media Associates International, Bloomingdale, Illinois.

McClain, T. Van. Ph.D., Southwestern Baptist Theological Seminary. Professor of Old Testament and Hebrew, Director of Library Services, Mid-America Baptist Theological Seminary, Northeast Branch, Schenectady, New York.

McConnell, C. Douglas. Ph.D., Fuller Theological Seminary. International Director, Pioneers, Orlando, Florida.

McElhanon, Ken. Ph.D., Australian National University. Missionary, Wycliffe Bible Translators and Adjunct Faculty, University of Texas, Dallas, Texas.

McGee, Gary B. Ph.D., Saint Louis University. Professor of Church History, Assemblies of God Theological Seminary, Springfield, Missouri.

McIntosh, John Alan. D.Miss., Trinity Evangelical Divinity School. Associate Professor of Missions, Reformed Theological Seminary, Jackson, Mississippi.

McKinley, Edward. Ph.D., University of Wisconsin. Professor of History, Asbury College, Wilmore, Kentucky.

McKinney, Carol V. Ph.D., Southern Methodist University. Associate Professor, Graduate Institute of Applied Lingusitics, University of Texas at Arlington; SIL International Anthropology Consultant, Wycliffe Bible Translators and the Summer Institute of Linguistics, Dallas Texas.

McQuilkin, Robertson. M.Div., Fuller Theological Seminary. General Director, Evangelical Missiological Society and President Emeritus, Columbia International University, Columbia, South Carolina.

McRay, John. Ph.D., University of Chicago. Professor of New Testament and Archaeology, Wheaton College, Wheaton, Illinois.

McReynolds, Kathy. M.A., Talbot School of Theology. Free lance writer, La Mirada, California.

Medeiros, Elias dos Santos. D.Miss., Reformed Theological Seminary. Chair and Associate Professor of Mission, Reformed Theological Seminary, Jackson, Mississippi.

Moffett, Eileen F. M.R.E., Princeton Theological Seminary. Missionary to Korea (Retired), Free-Lance Writer, Princeton, New Jersey.

Molyneux, Gordon. Ph.D., London University. Lecturer and Course Director for the Bachelor of Arts Program, All Nations Christian College, Ware, Herts, United Kingdom.

Monsma, Tim. Ph.D., Fuller Theological Seminary. Africa Director of Action International Ministries; Professor, Africa Bible College, Lilongwe, Malawi.

15

Contributors

Moreau, A. Scott. D.Miss., Trinity Evangelical Divinity School. Associate Professor, Missions and Intercultural Studies, Wheaton College, Wheaton, Illinois.

Muck, Terry C. Ph.D., Northwestern University. Professor of Comparative Religions, Austin Presbyterian Theological Seminary, Austin, Texas.

Mulholland, Kenneth B. D.Th.P., Fuller Theological Seminary. Dean and Professor of Missions, Columbia Biblical Seminary and School of Missions, Columbia, South Carolina.

Murray, Jocelyn M. Ph.D., University of California Los Angeles. Free lance writer, London, United Kingdom.

Musa, David. Ph.D. Cand., Trinity International University. Free lance writer, Zionsville, Indiana.

Nassif, Bradley. Ph.D., Fordham University. Director of Academic Programs, Fuller Seminary, Southern California Extension, Irvine, California.

Neely, Alan P. Ph.D., American University, Washington D.C. Emeritus Henry W. Luce Professor of Ecumenics and Mission, Princeton Theological Seminary, Princeton, New Jersey.

Ness, David C. Ph.D., Temple University. Christian Leadership Ministries, Campus Crusade for Christ, Austin, Texas.

Netland, Harold A. Ph.D., Claremont Graduate School. Associate Professor of Mission, Trinity Evangelical Divinity School, Deerfield, Illinois.

Neumann, Mikel. D.Miss., Fuller Theological Seminary. International Resource Consultant, CBInternational and Associate Professor, Western Seminary, Portland, Oregon.

Nyquist, John W. Ph.D., Trinity Evangelical Divinity School. Associate Professor of Mission and Evangelism, Trinity Evangelical Divinity School, Deerfield, Illinois.

O'Rear, Michael G. M.A., Wheaton College Graduate School. President, Global Mapping International, Colorado Springs, Colorado.

Olson, Laurel P. M.A., Wheaton Graduate School. Freelance Writer, Troy, New York.

Orme, John. Th.D., Dallas Theological Seminary. Executive Director, Interdenominational Foreign Mission Association, Wheaton, Illinois.

Osborne, Grant R. Ph.D., University of Aberdeen. Professor of New Testament, Trinity Evangelical Divinity School, Deerfield, Illinois.

Park, Timothy Kiho. Ph.D., Fuller Theological Seminary. Associate Professor of Asian Mission, Fuller Theological Seminary School of World Mission, Pasadena, California.

Parshall, Philip Lewis. D.Miss., Fuller Theological Seminary. Philippines Field Director, SIM International, Manila, Philippines.

Patterson, James A. Ph.D., Princeton Theological Seminary. Professor of Christian Studies, Union University, Jackson, Tennessee.

Pemberton, Sherman S. M.A., California State University (Fullerton). Inter-Cultural Studies Chair, Hope International University, Fullerton, California.

Perez, Pablo E. D.Miss., Fuller Theological Seminary. Translator, In Touch Ministries, Suwanee, Georgia.

Peterson, Douglas. Ph.D., Oxford Center for Mission Studies. President, Latin America Childcare and Director DFM, Central America Assemblies of God, San Jose, Costa Rica.

Peterson, Wendy. M.A., Providence Theological Seminary. Director, Religious Movements Resource Center, Providence College and Theological Seminary, Otterburne, Manitoba, Canada.

Pfister, Lauren F. Ph.D., University of Hawaii. Associate Professor, Religion and Philosophy Department, Hong Kong Baptist University, Hong Kong, People's Republic of China.

Phillips, James M. Ph.D., Princeton University. Associate Director, Overseas Ministries Study Center, New Haven, Connecticut.

Phillips, Timothy R. Ph.D., Vanderbilt. Associate Professor of Biblical Studies, Wheaton College, Wheaton, Illinois.

Phillips, W. Kenneth. Ed.D., University of Georgia. Professor of Christian Education/International Theological Education, Columbia Biblical Seminary and School of Missions, Columbia, South Carolina.

Pierard, Richard V. Ph.D., University of Iowa. Professor of History, Indiana State University, Terre Haute, Indiana.

Pierson, Paul E. Ph.D., Princeton. Dean Emeritus, Fuller School of World Mission, Pasadena, California.

Pierson, Steven J. Ph.D., Trinity Evangelical Divinity School. Adjunct Lecturer, Wheaton College, Illinois.

Platt, Daryl. D.Miss., Fuller Theological Seminary School of World Mission. Director of Church Growth Ministries, International Ministry Team, OC International, Colorado Springs, Colorado.

Plueddemann, James. Ph.D., Michigan State University. General Director, SIM International, Charlotte, North Carolina.

Pocock, Michael. D.Miss., Trinity Evangelical Divinity School. Professor and Department Chair of Missions and Intercultural Studies, Dallas Theological Seminary, Dallas Texas.

Pont, Arthur. Retired General Secretary, Interserve, Middlesex, United Kingdom.

Porter, David. M.A., University of Ulster. Director, Evangelical Contribution on Northern Ireland (ECONI), Belfast, Northern Ireland.

Poston, Larry A. Ph.D., Northwestern University. Professor of Religion, Nyack College, Nyack, New York.

Prasad, Andrew. M.Th., Presbyterian College and Theological Seminary, Seoul, Korea. Secretary for Personnel Resources, Council for World Mission, London, England.

Priest, Robert J. Ph.D., University of California, Berkeley. Associate Professor of Missions and Intercultural Studies, Trinity Evangelical Divinity School, Deerfield, Illinois.

Prigodich, Raymond P. M.Div., Denver Seminary. Assistant Professor of World Christianity/Department Chair, Denver Seminary, Denver, Colorado.

Rainer, Thom S. Ph.D., The Southern Baptist Theological Seminary. Dean, Billy Graham School of Missions, Evangelism and Church Growth, Louisville, Kentucky.

Ramseyer, Robert. Ph.D., University of Michigan. Emeritus Professor of Missions and Anthropology, Associated Mennonite Biblical Seminary, Elkhart, Indiana.

Rascher, Len. Ph.D., Northwestern University. Director, Practical Christian Ministry Department, Moody Bible Institute, Chicago, Illinois.

Raupp, Werner. Dr. Theol., Author and Lecturer in Church History and Philosophy, College for Social Affairs, Reutlingen, Germany.

Read, Terry. Ph.D., Trinity Evangelical Divinity School. Missionary, Church of the Nazarene, Nairobi, Kenya.

Reapsome, James W. Th.M., Dallas Theological Seminary. Retired, Former Editor *Evangelical Missions Quarterly*, Evangelical Missions Information Service, Wheaton, Illinois.

Renicks, Philip M. Ed.D., University of Alabama. Vice President, International Ministries, Association of Christian Schools International, Colorado Springs, Colorado.

Richard, H. L. B.A., Regent College, New York. Research Scholar, Delhi, India.

Richardson, Don. D.Litt., Biola University. Ambassador-at-Large, World Team, Woodland Hills, California.

Riggans, Walter. Ph.D., University of Birmingham, England. Joint Director, Prophetic World Ministries, Moggerhanger, Bedford, United Kingdom.

Riley, Terry J. B.S., Mankato State University. Associate Director, Adopt-A-People Clearinghouse, Colorado Springs, Colorado.

Ro, Bong Rin. Th.D., Concordia Lutheran Seminary. Director of Overseas Ministry, Torch Center, OMF International, Seoul, South Korea.

Robert, Dana Lee. Ph.D., Yale University. Professor of International Mission, Boston University School of Theology, Boston, Massachusetts.

Robinson, Richard A. Ph.D., Westminster Theological Seminary. Research Librarian and Web Site Coordinator, Jews for Jesus, San Francisco, California.

Rogers, Juan D. Ph.D., Virginia Polytechnic Institute. Assistant Professor, School of Public Policy, Georgia Institute of Technology, Atlanta, Georgia.

Rommen, Edward. Dr. Theol., Munich University. Deacon, Orthodox Church of America, Columbia, South Carolina.

Contributors

Roxborogh, John. Ph.D., Aberdeen. Chair, Department of Mission Studies, Bible College of New Zealand, Haitakere City, New Zealand.

Roy, Kevin. Ph.D., University of South Africa. Lecturer, Baptist Theological College, Cape Town, South Africa.

Russell, Tom. Ph.D., Vanderbilt. University Lecturer, Western Kentucky University, Nashville, Tennessee.

Sakurai, Kunio. Th.M., Fuller Theological Seminary; LL.M., University of Nagoya. Director, Kyoritu Christian Institute for Theological Studies and Mission; Associate Professor of Theology and Law, Tokyo Christian University, Tokyo, Japan.

Satyavrata, Ivan Morris. Th.M., Regent College, Vancouver, Canada. Assistant Professor; Chair, Department of Theology and Ethics, Southern Asia Bible College, Bangalore, India.

Scherer, James A. Th.D., Union Theological Seminary (New York). Professor Emeritus, World Mission and Church History, Lutheran School of Theology at Chicago, Chicago, Illinois.

Schirrmacher, Christine. Ph.D., University of Bonn. Visiting Professor of Islamics, Philadelphia Theological Seminary, Philadelphia, Pennsylvania.

Schirrmacher, Thomas. Th.D., Johannes Calvin Foundation (Theological University), Kampen/Netherlands. Professor of Missions, Philadelphia Theological Seminary and Director, Institut für Weltmission und Christliche Gesellschaft (Institute for World Mission and Christian Society), Bonn, Germany.

Schroeder, SVD, Roger. D.Miss., Pontifical Gregorian University (Rome). Assistant Professor in Cross-Cultural Studies, Catholic Theological Union, Chicago, Illinois.

Scott, Florence R. M.A., Wheaton Graduate School. Free-Lance Writer, Wheaton, Illinois.

Scott, Jr., J. Julius. Ph.D., University of Manchester. Professor of Biblical and Historical Studies, Wheaton College, Wheaton, Illinois.

Scott, Lindy. Ph.D., Northwestern University. Associate Professor of Spanish, Wheaton College, Wheaton, Illinois.

Seaman, Alan A. Ph.D., University of Virginia. Assistant Professor of TESL, Wheaton College, Wheaton, Illinois.

Seruyange, Lazarus. D.Min., Western Conservative Baptist Seminary. Principal, Nairobi International School of Theology, Nairobi, Kenya.

Sharma, Bal Krishna. M.Th., Serampore College. Minister, Assemblies of God of Nepal, Kathmandu, Nepal.

Shaw, Daniel. Ph.D., University of Papua New Guinea. Professor of Anthropology and Translation, Fuller School of World Mission, Pasadena, California.

Shaw, Mark. Th.D., Westminster Theological Seminary. Lecturer in Theology and Church History, Nairobi Evangelical Graduate School of Theology, Nairobi, Kenya.

Shenk, David D. Ph.D., New York University. Academic Dean and Professor of Theology, Lithuania Christian College, Klaipeda, Lithuania.

Shenk, Wilbert. Ph.D., Aberdeen. Associate Professor of Mission, Fuller School of World Mission, Pasadena, California.

Shepherd, David H. Ph.D., Mid-America Baptist Theological Seminary. Associate Professor of Theology/Practical Theology, Northeast Campus of Mid-America Baptist Theological Seminary, Schenectady, New York.

Showalter, Richard A. M.Div., Associated Mennonite Biblical Seminaries. President, Eastern Mennonite Missions, Landisville, Pennsylvania.

Shuster, Robert D. M.A., University of Wisconsin. Director of Archives, Billy Graham Center, Wheaton, Illinois.

Siewert, John. M.Div., North American Baptist Seminary. Director, Global Information Sharing Program, World Vision International, Monrovia, California.

Silzer, Peter James. Ph.D., Australian National University. Program Director—SIL at Biola, Summer Institute of Linguistics/Wycliffe Bible Translators, LaMirada, California.

Smarto, Don. M.A., Catholic University. Free lance writer, Wheaton, Illinois.

Smith, A. Christopher. Ph.D., Southern Baptist Theological Seminary. Vice-President for (College) Academics and Professor of Intercultural Studies, Providence College, Ottorburne, Manitoba, Canada.

Smith, Donald K. Ph.D., University of Oregon. Chair, Division of Intercultural Studies, Western Seminary, Portland, Oregon.

Smith, Ebbie C. Ph.D., Southwestern Baptist Theological Seminary. Professor of Christian Ethics and Missions, Southwestern Baptist Theological Seminary, Fort Worth, Texas.

Smith, Eric D. Th.M., Talbot Theological Seminary. Field Director, OC International, Pasig City, Philippines.

Smith, Gordon. T. Ph.D., Loyola School of Theology. Vice President, Dean and Associate Professor of Spiritual Theology, Regent College, Vancouver, Canada.

Smith, Tracy K. M.A., Wheaton Graduate School. Missionary, OC International, Kathmandu, Nepal.

Søgaard, Viggo B. Ph.D., Fuller Theological Seminary. Associate Professor of Communication, Fuller School of World Mission, Pasadena, California.

Sookhdeo, Patrick. D.D., Western Conservative Baptist Seminary. Director, Institute for the Study of Islam and Christianity, London, England.

Spindler, Marc R. Ph.D., State University of Strasbourg. Emeritus Professor of Missiology and Ecumenics, Universities of Leiden and Utrecht, Talence, France.

Spradlin, Michael. Ph.D., Mid-America Baptist Theological Seminary. President and Professor of Old Testament, Hebrew, and Practical Theology, Mid-America Baptist Theological Seminary, Northeast Branch, Schenectady, New York.

Spruance, F. David. D.Min., Denver Seminary. Retired; Adjunct Professor, International School of Theology, Manila, Philippines.

Stamoolis, James J. Th.D., Stellenbosch. Executive Director Theological Commission, World Evangelical Fellowship, Wheaton, Illinois.

Stanley, Brian. Ph.D., Cambridge University. Director of North Atlantic Missiology Project, University of Cambridge, Cambridge, United Kingdom.

Stansell, Ronald G. D.Miss., Trinity Evangelical Divinity School. Professor of Religion and Missions, George Fox University, Newberg, Oregon.

Starr, J. Barton. Ph.D., Florida State University. Chair and Professor of History, Hong Kong Baptist University, Hong Kong, People's Republic of China.

Steffen, Tom A. D.Miss., Biola University. Associate Professor of Intercultural Studies, Biola University, LaMirada, California.

Steward, John. Ph.D., Adelaide University. Development Services Manager, World Vision Australia, Warranwood, Victoria, Australia.

Steyne, Philip M. D.Miss., Fuller Theological Seminary. Professor of Missions, Columbia Biblical Seminary and School of Missions, Columbia, South Carolina.

Sywulka, Stephen R. Ph.D., Syracuse University. Director, Ration Station TGNA, Guatemala City, Guatemala.

Tallman, J. Ray. D.Miss., Trinity Evangelical Divinity School. Senior Advisor for Middle East and North Africa, OC International, Colorado Springs, Colorado.

Tan, Che Bin. Ph.D., University of Manchester. Pastor-In-Charge, River of Life Community Church, San Gabriel, California.

Tanner, John. D.Miss, Fuller Theological Seminary. Director of Missions Interlink, The Missions Commission of the Australian Evangelical Alliance, New Farm, Queensland, Australia.

Taylor, William D. Ph.D., University of Texas. Director of Missions Commission, World Evangelical Fellowship, Austin Texas.

Terry, John Mark. Ph.D., Southwestern Baptist Theological Seminary. Associate Professor of Missions, Southern Baptist Theological Seminary, Louisville, Kentucky.

Thomas, Harold. Ph.D. Cand., Fuller Theological Seminary School of World Missions. Student, Fuller School of World Mission, Pasadena, California.

Thrasher, William D. Th.D., Dallas Theological Seminary. Professor of Bible and Theology, Moody Bible Institute, Chicago, Illinois.

Tienou, Tite. Ph.D., Fuller Theological Seminary. Professor of Missions, Trinity Evangelical Divinity School, Deerfield, Illinois.

Tiersma, Judith. Ph.D., Fuller Theological Seminary. Assistant Professor in Urban Mission, Fuller School of World Mission, Pasadena, California.

Contributors

Tinder, Donald. Ph.D., Yale University. Academic Dean, Tyndale Theological Seminary, Badhoevedorp, Netherlands.

Trulear, Harold Dean. Ph.D., Drew University. Vice President, Church Collaborative Initiatives, Public/Private Ventures, Philadelphia, Pennsylvania.

Tucker, Albert Frank. Th.M., Fuller Theological Seminary. Lecturer in Missiology, Tabor College, Hove, SA, Australia.

Van der Heyden, Ulrich. Doctorate, Humboldt University, Berlin. Research Fellow, Center for Modern Oriental Studies, Berlin, Germany.

Van Engen, Charles. Ph.D., Free University of Amsterdam. Associate Professor, Fuller School of World Mission, Pasadena, California.

Van Rheenen, Gailyn. D.Miss., Trinity Evangelical Divinity School. Associate Professor of Missions, Abilene Christian University.

Vardell, Douglas J. Th.M., Dallas Theological Seminary. Chaplain, St. Luke's Hospital, Racine, Wisconsin.

Vencer, Jun. D.D., Ebenezer Bible College and Seminary. International Director, World Evangelical Fellowship, Quezon City, Philippines.

Veronis, Luke. Th.M., Fuller School of World Mission. Missionary, Albanian Orthodox Church, Tirana, Albania.

Voelkel, Jack. D.Miss., Fuller School of World Mission. Professor of Missiology and Chair, Department of Missiology, Seminario Biblico de Colombia, Medellín, Colombia.

Wagner, C. Peter. Ph.D., University of Southern California. Donald A. McGavran Professor of Church Growth, Fuller School of World Mission, Pasadena, California.

Wagner, William L. Th.D., University of South Africa. Professor of Missiology, Evangelical Theological Faculty, Leuven, Belgium.

Wagner, William Mark. Ph.D., Southwestern Baptist Theological Seminary. Pastor and Instructor, Bibelseminar, Bonn, Germany.

Wan, Enoch. Ph.D., State University of New York at Stony Brook. Professor of Missions and Anthropology. Director, Ph.D. Intercultural Studies Program, Reformed Theological Seminary, Jackson, Mississippi.

Ward, Ted W. Ed.D., University of Florida. Retired; G. W. Aldeen Professor of International Studies and Mission, Trinity Evangelical Divinity School, Deerfield, Illinois.

Warner, Timothy M. Ed.D., Indiana University. Senior Vice President for International Ministry, Freedom in Christ Ministries, Fort Wayne, Indiana.

Weber, Charles W. Ph.D., University of Chicago. Professor of History, Wheaton College, Wheaton, Illinois.

Wenzel, David R. Ph.D., Loyola College. Associate Professor of Pastoral Counseling, Western Seminary, Portland, Oregon.

White, Francis J. Ph.D., University of Maryland. Professor Emeritus of Psychological Studies, Wheaton College, Wheaton, Illinois.

Wiarda, Timothy. M.A., Wheaton College. Lecturer in Theology and Missions, Singapore Bible College, Singapore.

Wibberley, John. Ph.D., University of Reading. Visiting Fellow in Agricultural Extension & Rural Development, University of Reading; Communications Unit Coordinator of RURCON, Ryde, Isle of Wight, United Kingdom.

Wickstrom, David. Ph.D., Rosemead Graduate School of Psychology. Clinical Psychologist; Researcher with MK-CART/CORE; Adjunct Professor of Psychology and Missions, Columbia International University, Columbia, South Carolina.

Wiebracht, Dean. D.Min., Talbot Theological Seminary. Assistant Team Leader, OC International, Northern Philippines Team, Pasig City, Philippines.

Wilkins, Michael J. Ph.D., Fuller Theological Seminary. Dean of Faculty, Professor of New Testament Language and Literature, Talbot School of Theology, LaMirada, California.

Williams, Bud. Ed.D., Northern Illinois University. Associate Professor of Kinesiology, Wheaton College, Wheaton, Illinois.

Wilson, Everett A. Ph.D., Stanford University. President, Bethany College, Scotts Valley, California.

Wilson, Samuel. Ph.D., Cornell. Professor, Trinity Episcopal School for Ministry, Ambridge, Pennsylvania.

Winter, Ralph. Ph.D., Cornell. President, William Carey International University and General Director, U.S. Center for World Mission, Pasadena, California.

Wisely, Thomas N. Ph.D., Fuller Theological Seminary. Division Head, International Christian Studies, Tokyo Christian University, Tokyo, Japan.

Wong, Hoover. D.Min., Fuller Theological Seminary. Senior Associate Professor, Director of Chinese Studies, Fuller School of World Mission, Pasadena, California.

Wong, Timothy Man-Kong. Ph.D., The Chinese University of Hong Kong. Assistant Professor, Department of History, Hong Kong Baptist University, Hong Kong, People's Republic of China.

Woodberry, J. Dudley. Ph.D., Harvard University. Dean and Professor of Islamic Studies, Fuller School of World Mission, Pasadena, California.

Wright, Christopher J. H. Ph.D., Cambridge. Principal, All Nations Christian College, Ware, Herts, United Kingdom.

Yamamori, Tetsunao. Ph.D., Duke University. President, Food for the Hungry International, Scottsdale, Arizona.

Yu, Carver Tatsum. D.Phil., Oxford University. Vice President, China Graduate School of Theology, Hong Kong, People's Republic of China.

Abbreviations

ABCFM	American Board of Commissioners of Foreign Mission
ABD	*Anchor Bible Dictionary*, ed. David N. Freedman
ADLR	*Abingdon Dictionary of Living Religions*, ed. Keith Crim
AEF	African Evangelical Fellowship
AFC	*Ambassadors for Christ*, ed. John D. Woodbridge
AIM	Africa Inland Mission
ASV	American Standard Version
BaMS	Basel Mission Society
BDCM	*Biographical Dictionary of Christian Missions*, ed. Gerald Anderson
BDEB	*The Blackwell Dictionary of Evangelical Biography, 1730–1860*, ed. Donald Lewis
BEB	*Baker Encyclopedia of the Bible*, ed. Walter A. Elwell
BDT	*Baker's Dictionary of Theology*, ed. Everett F. Harrison
BibSac	*Bibliotheca Sacra*
BM	Basel Mission
BMS	Baptist Missionary Society
CCen	*Christian Century*
CDCWM	*Concise Dictionary of Christian World Mission*, ed. Stephen C. Neill, Gerald H. Anderson, and John Goodwin
CEI	*The Concise Encyclopedia of Islam*, ed. Cyril Glassé
CIM	China Inland Mission
CMA	Christian and Missionary Alliance
CMS	Church Mission Society
CT	*Christianity Today*
DAB	*Dictionary of American Biography*
DAC	*Dictionary of the Apostolic Church*, ed. James Hastings
DAWN	Discipling a Whole Nation
DBA	*Dictionary of Baptists in America*, ed. Bill J. Leonard
DCA	*Dictionary of Christianity in America*, ed. Daniel G. Reid
DCSRO	*Dictionary of Cults, Sects, Religions and the Occult*, ed. George A. Mather
DEM	*Dictionary of the Ecumenical Movement*, ed. Nicholas Lossky
DJG	*Dictionary of Jesus and the Gospels*, ed. Joel B. Green and Scot McKnight
DPCM	*Dictionary of Pentecostal and Charismatic Movements*, ed. Stanley Burgess and Gary B. McGee
DPHL	*Dictionary of Paul and His Letters*, ed. Gerald Hawthorne and Ralph P. Martin
DSCHT	*Dictionary of Scottish Church History and Theology*, ed. Nigel de S. Cameron
DWCH	*A Dictionary of Women in Church History* by Mary L. Hammack
DWME	Division of World Mission and Evangelism
EB	*Encyclopedia Britannica*
EBC	*The Expositor's Bible Commentary*
EDBT	*Evangelical Dictionary of Biblical Theology*, ed., Walter A. Elwell
EDT	*Evangelical Dictionary of Theology*, ed. Walter A. Elwell
EFMA	Evangelical Fellowship of Mission Agencies
EI	*Encyclopedia of Islam*, ed. B. Lewis, V. L. Ménage, Ch. Pellat, and J. Schacht
EJ	*Encyclopedia Judaica*
EM	*Encyclopedia of Missions*, ed. Henry O. Dwight, H. Allen Tupper, and Edwin M. Bliss
EMA	Evangelical Missionary Alliance
EMCM	*Encyclopedia of Modern Christian Missions: The Agencies*, ed. Burton L. Goddard
EMIS	Evangelical Missions Information Service
EMQ	*Evangelical Missions Quarterly*
ER	*Encyclopedia of Religion*, ed. Mircea Eliade
ERE	*Encyclopedia of Religion and Ethics*
ERT	*Evangelical Review of Theology*
ESB	*Encyclopedia of Southern Baptists*

EWM	*Encyclopedia of World Methodism*, ed. Nolan B. Harmon	NAE	National Association of Evangelicals
FJIJ	*From Jerusalem to Iryian Jaya*, Ruth Tucker	NBD	*New Bible Dictionary*, ed. J. D. Douglas
GCOWE	Global Consultation of World Evangelization	NCC	National Council of Churches
		NCE	*New Catholic Encyclopedia*
GGC	*Guardians of the Great Commission*, Ruth Tucker	NDT	*The New Dictionary of Theology*, ed. Joseph Komonchak, Mary Collins, and Dermot A. Lane
GNB	Good News Bible	NeRMs	New Religious Movements
HBD	*Harper's Bible Dictionary*, ed. Madeline Sweeny Miller	NIDCC	*The New International Dictionary of the Christian Church*, ed. J. D. Douglas
HCM	*A History of Christian Missions*, Stephen Neill	NIDNTT	*The New International Dictionary of the New Testament*, ed. Colin Brown
HEM	*A History of the Ecumenical Movement*, Ruth Rouse and Stephen C. Neill	NIDOTTE	*New International Dictionary of Old Testament Theology and Exegesis*, ed. Willem A. Gemeren
IAMS	International Association for Mission Studies	NTCERK	*The New Twentieth Century Encyclopedia of Religious Knowledge*, ed. J. D. Douglas
IBMR	*International Bulletin of Missionary Research*	NIV	New International Version
ICETE	International Council for Evangelical Theological Education	NLB	New Living Translation
		NRSV	New Revised Standard Version
ICHR	*Indian Church History Review*	ODCC	*Oxford Dictionary of the Christian Church*, ed. F. L. Cross
IDB	*Interpreters Dictionary of the Bible*, ed. George A. Buttrick	ODS	*Oxford Dictionary of the Saints*, ed. David H. Farmer
IEM	India Evangelical Mission	OMF	Overseas Missionary Fellowship
IFES	International Fellowship of Evangelical Students	OW	*Operation World*, ed. Patrick Johnstone
IFMA	Interdenominational Fellowship of Mission Agencies	PA	*Practical Anthropology*
IJFM	*International Journal of Frontier Missions*	PWCM	*Perspectives on the World Christian Movement: A Reader*, ed. Ralph D. Winter and Stephen C. Hawthorne
IMC	International Missionary Council	RSV	Revised Standard Version
IRM	*International Review of Mission*	SCM	Student Christian Movement
ISBE	*The International Standard Bible Encyclopedia*, ed. James Orr	SIM	Society for International Ministries
ISBE Rev	*The International Standard Bible Encyclopedia*, revised edition, ed. Geoffrey Bromiley	SPG	Society for the Propogation of the Gospel
JBL	*Journal of Biblical Literature*	SCM	Student Christian Movement
JETS	*Journal of the Evangelical Theological Society*	SUM	Sudan United Mission
		SVM	Student Volunteer Movement
JBP	J. B. Phillips Translation	TCDCB	*Twentieth Century Dictionary of Christian Biography*, ed. J. D. Douglas
JPC	*Journal of Psychology and Christianity*	TCKs	Third Culture Kids
JPT	*Journal of Psychology and Theology*	TDNT	*Theological Dictionary of the New Testament*, ed. Gerhard Kittel
KJV	King James Version		
LMS	London Missionary Society	TDOT	*Theological Dictionary of the Old Testament*, ed. G. Johannes Botterweck
MAF	Mission Aviation Fellowship		
MARC	Mission Advanced Research and Communication Center		
ML	*Mission Legacies*, ed. Gerald H. Anderson	TEAM	The Evangelical Alliance Mission
MS	*Mission Studies*	TEE	Theological Education by Extension

TEFL	Teaching English as a Foreign Language
TESL	Teaching English as a Second Language
TESOL	Teaching English to Speakers of Other Languages
TWOT	*Theological Wordbook of the Old Testament*, ed. R. Laird Harris
WCC	World Council of Churches
WCE	*World Christian Encyclopedia*, ed. David Barrett
WEF	World Evangelical Fellowship
WmTJ	*Westminster Theological Journal*
WSCF	World Student Christian Federation
WWCH	*Who's Who in Church History*, ed. William Pierson Barker
ZPBD	*Zondervan Pictoral Bible Dictionary*, ed. Merrill C. Tenney
ZPEB	*Zondervan Pictoral Encyclopedia of the Bible*, ed. Merrill C. Tenney

Aa

Abakua. *See* LATIN AMERICAN NEW RELIGIOUS MOVEMENTS.

Abolitionist Movement. The abolitionist movement in the United States had a great impact on the home and overseas missionary movement. During the 1820s and 1830s antislavery and proabolition activity put pressure on mission agencies to sever all relationships with slaveholders: not to appoint them as missionaries, receive their donations, place them on their boards, or receive them as members in their home mission churches. As a result, the AMERICAN BOARD OF COMMISSIONERS FOR FOREIGN MISSIONS (ABCFM) from 1840 to 1860 repeatedly was presented with petitions that called it to deal with issues of slaveholding and slaveholders in connection with its work among the Cherokee and Choctaw people in the United States. Tensions within the churches and the board itself between moderate and radical proabolition factions made it difficult for the agency to solve these disputes to everyone's satisfaction.

Such adjustments that the ABCFM and other mission agencies made did not satisfy the radical abolitionists. Therefore, the antislavery American Home Mission Society was formed in 1826, and by the early 1840s a number of "comeouter" groups separated from denominational boards. For example, the American Baptist Free Mission Society (ABFMS) was organized in 1843 and no longer worked with the Triennial Convention of northern Baptists. This society, which existed until 1868, became the means through which antislavery Baptists engaged in missions at home and abroad. During the years of their existence the ABFMS had personnel in Japan and Burma. It also agitated in Baptist state associations in the north on behalf of slaves, as well as in slaveholding areas in Kentucky and Virginia.

Similar to the ABFMS in all but a denominational name was the American Missionary Association (AMA) formed in Albany, New York, in 1846. Strongly proabolition, the AMA at its founding integrated into itself three antislavery missionary organizations—the Union Missionary Society, the Committee for West India Missions, and the Western Evangelical Society. It promoted already existing mission activities and many new ones. By 1856 it had a total of seventy-nine missionaries working among North American Indians and in Africa, the Sandwich Islands, Jamaica, Siam (Thailand), Egypt, and Canada. The AMA began work among Chinese in America in 1852, and this led to the formation of the California Chinese Mission by 1875. With the beginning of the Civil War the work of the AMA began to focus almost exclusively on the freedmen in the South, and it ceased broader missionary efforts at home and abroad. Important leaders in the work of the AMA included such evangelical abolitionists as Lewis Tappan and Joshua Leavitt.

RALPH R. COVELL

Bibliography. J. R. McKivigan, *The War against Proslavery Religion: Abolitionism and the Northern Churches, 1830–1865;* B. Wyatt-Brown, *Lewis Tappan and the Evangelical War against Slavery;* C. Whipple, *Relations of the American Board of Commissioners for Foreign Missions to Slavery;* R. Torbet, *Venture of Faith.*

Aboriginal Religions. Aboriginal religions in Australia share many similarities with other primal religions, yet they are as distinctive and as different as the variety of aboriginal languages.

In traditional aboriginal cosmology there was awareness among some tribes of a deity, such as the All Father or All Mother, although these have not generally been important. A lesser, but more significant being is the widely known Rainbow Serpent. This Rainbow Serpent and a variety of formative spirit-beings were responsible for the formation of the present world order.

The foundation for the aboriginal view of reality is the primeval, mythical epoch called the Dreaming. The Dreaming events are recounted in the aboriginal myths. In the Dreaming a variety of formative spirit-beings emerged from the earth or sea and took on part plant or animal and human forms. They moved across the featureless landscape, forming the various topographical features, plants, animals, and humans. Some of the formative spirit-beings then returned to the earth, forming various topographic phenomena that are regarded as sacred sites.

While the initial creativity of the Dreaming is complete, the Dreaming is ever present to the people through participation in ritual, ceremonies or "corroborees," art, and song. The Dreaming myths give rise to the aboriginal understanding of their relationship with the land, animals, and plant life. Aboriginal people see themselves sharing a common ancestry with the plants and animals, being of common spiritual essence. Each group is obligated to others to perform the ceremonies relevant to their particular totemic ancestors to ensure the continuity and sustenance of the species.

The main religious activity is associated with keeping alive the Dreaming creativity in the present to ensure renewal or renovation of the cosmic order. In the ritual reenactment the primordial events are made present and the performer becomes the totemic ancestor. Some rituals are solely for initiated men and held in secret; some are exclusively for women; others are shared by both genders with separate responsibilities. The Dreaming spirit-beings provided a precedent for all ceremonies and social customs as well, so all of life is seen to be sacred; their responsibility is to keep them alive and productive. To the aborigine living is a religious activity. Human life begins and ends in the spirit world.

The change brought about by acculturation and white encroachment has been cataclysmic, resulting in widespread desacralization and demoralization of society. Consequently there have been few recorded revitalization movements, yet aboriginal religions have survived and changed dramatically among the tribal people.

Whether aboriginal religious tradition is still an important reality for individuals or not, aboriginal thinking processes, basic concerns, and needs expressed in the myths remain. For this reason missions and church need to treat aboriginal religions seriously, irrespective of how their significance is understood, and assist the aborigines in recapturing the gospel that addresses their needs. There remains a great need to explore the use of indigenous art, music, and corroboree to communicate the gospel.

ALBERT F. TUCKER

SEE ALSO Primal Religions.

Bibliography. M. Charlesworth, H. Morphy, D. Bell, and K. Maddock, *Religion in Aboriginal Australia: An Anthology;* M. Eliade, *Australian Religions: An Introduction;* E. Kolig, *The Silent Revolution: The Effects of Modernization on Australian Aboriginal Religion.*

Abraham Mar Thoma (1880–1947). Indian church leader and promoter of evangelism. Pop-

ularly known in the West as Bishop Abraham, Abraham Mar Thoma was born in Kallooppara in Travancore, a state in southern India. He was raised by an uncle who belonged to the Syrian Mar Thoma Church, an indigenous denomination. He committed his life to Christ at age 13 and was ordained in 1911. After education at Madras Christian College, Toronto University, and Wycliffe College (also in Toronto), he had a parish ministry for a brief time. In 1917 he was consecrated suffragan (or assistant) metropolitan to help the head of the denomination, Titus II. The church at this time probably had a little more than one hundred thousand members. For more than a quarter of a century, the two worked together to strengthen the spiritual life of the church and to make it an active participant in the spread of the gospel. In 1924 Abraham helped formally organize the Voluntary Evangelist's Association, a lay organization that encouraged Christians to study and pray together and to go out regularly witnessing to individuals and groups. His passion for spreading the gospel was an encouragement and example to many in the church, as was his personal piety. On Titus's death in 1944, he became metropolitan. The church by the time of Abraham's death three years later had grown to about two hundred thousand members and was known for its evangelistic outreach. E. STANLEY JONES, in paying tribute to his friend, called him "the greatest Christian in India."

ROBERT SHUSTER

Abrahamic Covenant. God's initial call to Abraham to leave his family and his country in order to follow wherever the Lord would lead him and the promises God made to Abraham constitute the core of the Abrahamic covenant (Gen. 12:1–3). Throughout the story of Abraham these promises are reiterated or expanded (Gen. 12:7; 13:14–17; 15:1–21; 17:1–27; 22:15–18), and Abraham demonstrates his commitment by his obedience, culminating in his willingness to sacrifice Isaac (Gen. 22:1–18). The same promises are repeated, in whole or in part, to Abraham's descendants (Gen. 21:12, 13, 18; 25:1–6; 28:3–4, 12–15), and the covenant then becomes a central part of the rest of the Bible.

God's call of Abraham parallels his creation of humankind in his own image (Gen. 1:26–28). The first two chapters of Genesis depict a harmony between God and humanity, between man and woman, and between humanity and the rest of creation. That harmony was severed when the original pair chose the path of autonomy from God (Gen. 3:1–19), but God invited Abraham to surrender to a new path that he would mark out for him (Gen. 12:1).

The Abrahamic covenant has a key role within God's plan to get the gospel to all the world. First, God's dealings with Abraham have the seed of the gospel within it. As with his promise of salvation to all who receive the Son by faith (John 1:12), the promise to Abraham was unconditional. Abraham opened himself to God's grace, reorienting his life to God's new work on his behalf. In that act he became both an example for all future generations of believers and the channel through which God mediated his promise of reconciliation to all the world (cf. Gen. 12:3 with Rom. 4 and Gal. 3).

Second, the land that God promised to Abraham and his descendants became the central point from which the gospel would spread to the rest of the world (Acts 1:8). God created the physical world and its people with their physical bodies, and he began his plan of reconciliation with a real place.

Third, when God promised to give Abraham countless descendants, he established him as the human source of Jesus Christ, the Savior of all humanity (Matt. 1:1). Also Israel, the nation that came from Abraham, became the first of the nations that God purposed to reach with the gospel (Matt. 28:19–20; Rom. 1:16).

Fourth, God's promise to make Abraham's name great becomes an evidence of the restored relationship between God and humanity. When we try to gain a name for ourselves it results in alienation from God (Gen. 11:1–9), but when God establishes our identity for us, it results in a new life that is much better than any we could have imagined for ourselves (Matt. 19:39; Rev. 2:17).

Fifth, and finally, God promised Abraham that "all peoples on earth will be blessed through you" (Gen. 12:3). This promise moves the focus of God's plan from an individual to the entire world. God's heart was for the world, but he began with choosing one person.

THOMAS J. FINLEY

Bibliography. B. W. Anderson, *Interpretation* 42 (1988): 353–66; F. Blauw, *The Missionary Nature of the Church*; W. J. Dumbrell, *Reformed Theological Review* 41 (1982): 42–50; R. De Ridder, *Discipling the Nations*; A. Glasser, *Kingdom and Mission*; C. L. Rogers, *BibSac* 127 (1970): 241–56; J. H. Sailhamer, *The Pentateuch as Narrative*; J. M. L. Young, *CT* 13 (1968): 162–63, 165.

Abrams, Anna (c. 1858–c. 1910). American Holiness missionary in India. Daughter of a Michigan Free Methodist minister, she joined her sister, Bessie Sherman, and Charles W. Sherman in establishing the Vanguard Mission in St. Louis around 1880. It was a self-supporting enterprise developed on the model of WILLIAM TAYLOR's mission theory and described itself as a "Pauline mission" program. They established missions in American urban areas, began a training school for foreign missionaries, and sent missionaries to India. The training school also functioned as a seminary for hundreds of short-term students destined for ministry in North American Wesleyan/Holiness churches. During the Shermans' four-year mission to India, Abrams assumed leadership of all aspects of the program. Her primary tasks were financial, educational, and editorial. Her primary role outside the mission was as a mission theorist. Her missiological essays were published initially in *The Vanguard,* and then reprinted in numerous periodicals, primarily those of the smaller and more radical Wesleyan/Holiness churches. In these essays she perpetuated concerns of Taylor and other "self-supporting" missionaries, but in dialogue with the mission theory prevalent in the "mainline" churches.

A close, cooperative relationship was maintained with the Pentecost Bands (*see* WESLEYAN/HOLINESS MISSIONS) and the Free Methodist Church. The latter relationship was generally terminated after the expulsion of the Pentecost Bands from the Free Methodist Church in 1896. Abrams became involved in a struggle for control of the Vanguard Mission in 1907, when leadership was temporarily usurped by a Holiness/Pentecostal evangelist. The actuarial dates and other prosopographical data on Abrams have not been found. The archives of the Vanguard Mission were burned in 1907. Many missionaries from the Vanguard Training School served under the aegis of the Wesleyan Methodist, Pentecost Bands of the World, and Free Methodist Churches.

DAVID BUNDY

Bibliography. A. Abrams, *The Vanguard* 23:5 (1903): 1; idem, *The Vanguard* 21:18 (1903): 1; idem, *The Vanguard* 25:7 (1905): 1; idem, *The Vanguard* 26:15 (1906): 1; idem, *The Vanguard* 26:4 (1906): 8.

Abrams, Minnie F. (1859–1912). American missionary to India. Abrams had attended the Chicago Training School for Home and Foreign Missions and went to Bombay in 1887 with the Woman's Foreign Missionary Society of the Methodist Episcopal Church. She helped establish and supervise a Christian girls' school and worked with children in orphanages. In 1898 she followed the Lord's leading in becoming affiliated with the Mukti Mission, PANDITA RAMABAI's home for Indian widows, in Kedgaon.

Early in 1905 seventy volunteers at the mission responded to Ramabai's call for prayer for revival. Six months later the Spirit was poured out among them, the praying band having swelled to 550, meeting twice daily. The revival, weeping, praying, and confessing of sins continued almost uninterrupted for days, and then during the following year spread to other Indian mission sites.

In her book *The Baptism of the Holy Ghost and Fire* (1906) Abrams recorded the revival she witnessed and her own experience. With biblical references and theological explanations she described the fire accompanying (or following) the spirit baptism as a burning that brought both pain over one's sin and joy over its cleansing. The baptism was often accompanied by an urgent desire to reach souls, a boldness for service, and some gifts of the Spirit. Abrams called every Christian to seek the fire, the baptism, and continued refillings of the Spirit (Acts 4:23–31). Abrams advocated faithfulness to the Word of God as the constant in the Christian's life. Sending a copy of her book the following year to a former classmate serving in Valparaiso, Chile, greatly influenced the beginnings of the Pentecostal movement there.

After a year back in the United States, Abrams returned to India in 1910. Determined to take the gospel to unreached peoples, she led a party of seven single women missionaries to evangelize in the United Provinces, Fyzabad, and Bahraich. She died of malaria undertaking this work.

JANET BRUCE

Bibliography. G. B. McGee, *DPCM,* p. 7.

Absoluteness of Christianity. *See* THEOLOGY OF RELIGIONS.

Academic Associations of Mission. In the nineteenth century there was very little research in the field of missions and the confrontation of beliefs and cultures in the modern world. Major steps were taken following the WORLD MISSIONARY CONFERENCE at Edinburgh (1910): the launching of the *International Review of Missions* in 1912 and the founding of the Missionary Research Library in New York in 1914. These initiatives stimulated the inclusion of mission instruction in programs of theological education.

The first society to be established for the academic study of missions was German, the *Deutsche Gesellschaft für Missionswissenschaft* (GERMAN SOCIETY FOR MISSIOLOGY). Founded in 1918, it initially concentrated on publishing and on assisting the development of missiology as an academic discipline in German Catholic faculties. After the Second World War, the German Society for Missiology became more active in supporting research projects and the development of missiological documentation.

On the other side of the Atlantic, the 1920s witnessed high-quality discussion by a fellowship of leading missiologists. The Lux Mundi group on the east coast of North America broke new ground and may be said to have sharpened concepts that came to full bloom in the founding of the AMERICAN SOCIETY OF MISSIOLOGY (ASM) fifty years later.

The years after the Second World War found mission studies in deepening difficulty at academic institutions. This was the case until the early 1970s, when a renaissance in mission studies coincided with growing awareness that Christianity was becoming a predominantly non-Western religious phenomenon. Highly significant here were Olav G. Mykelbust's mid-1950s volumes on *The Study of Missions in Theological Education.* The director of the Egede Institute of Missionary Study and Research (Oslo) called for creation of an international institute of scientific mission research. This eventually led to the official founding of the INTERNATIONAL ASSOCIATION FOR MISSION STUDIES (IAMS) in 1972. The IAMS was to function as an umbrella covering a worldwide network of national and regional missiological associations.

In North America the ASSOCIATION OF PROFESSORS OF MISSIONS (APM) was formed in Louisville, Kentucky, in 1952 in the face of critical challenges to the very existence of missiological studies in the academy. Discussions ensued about the need for a new professional society to promote mission studies in the United States, a society broader, more comprehensive, and more inclusive than APM. The result was a gathering of missiologists at Nashville, Tennessee, in June 1972 to found the ASM, which would include Christian missiologists of all denominations and traditions. Its goal was to reinforce the place of missiology as a bona fide academic discipline. After much serious debate, an inaugural assembly was held in St. Louis in June 1973. A new journal, *Missiology: An International Review* (*see* JOURNALS OF MISSION AND MISSIOLOGY), was established with the editorship rotating among evangelical, conciliar Protestant, and Roman Catholic mission scholars. This reflected the tripartite, balanced nature of the association's leadership.

The ASM quickly achieved a membership of five hundred, with the result that the fledgling Association of Evangelical Professors of Missions was soon eclipsed. The AEPM had been conceived by fifteen missions professors in 1967 at the Urbana student convention. Officially formed at a meeting of the INTERDENOMINATIONAL FOREIGN MISSION ASSOCIATION (IFMA) and the EVANGELICAL FELLOWSHIP OF MISSION AGENCIES (EFMA) at Winona Lake, Indiana, in October 1968, its purpose was to provide a forum for interaction between teachers of missions in Bible schools, Christian colleges, and seminaries.

From 1974 onwards, the ASM was an affiliate member of the IAMS. Two years later, it was admitted to membership in what is now known as the Council of Societies for the Study of Religion. Following presentations by officers of the ASM, the Association of Theological Schools (ATS) in 1987 recognized the legitimacy and value of missiology as a field of learning in its own right. The

ATS proceeded to accept the doctorate of missiology as worthy of endorsement and inclusion within the roster of professional degrees. This was an important achievement.

The ASM has normally met in conjunction with the annual meetings of the APM. Since 1980, the ASM has published a monograph series through Orbis Books. Dozens of titles have been issued. In 1993 a new ASM dissertation series began in cooperation with the University Press of America.

In 1988 the IAMS Secretariat was based in Hamburg, Germany, and the journal *Mission Studies* was inaugurated. Assemblies have been held around the world every three or four years since 1972. IAMS has also sponsored international working groups and consultations on such vital issues as biblical research for mission studies (BISAM), healing and mission, and mission bibliography, documentation, and archives (DAB).

In November 1990 the AEPM broadened its base and changed its name to the EVANGELICAL MISSIOLOGICAL SOCIETY (EMS). The goal of the new organization was to serve the needs and interests of missionaries, agency executives, students, and professors of mission. It was particularly concerned to include conservative evangelical administrators and field missionaries in its membership so as to enhance communication between the academic world and the sending agencies. Its meetings synchronize with North American meetings of the Evangelical Theological Society, IFMA, EFMA, and the Association of Canadian Bible Colleges (ACBC). Proclaiming its intention to serve as a launching pad for biblical missiology in the twenty-first century, the EMS purposed from the beginning to provide avenues for publication of evangelical missiological monographs and books that otherwise might not see the light of day, such as Edward Rommen's *Spiritual Power and Missions* and David Hesselgrave's *Scripture and Strategy*. The EMS also publishes an *Occasional Bulletin* to communicate its news and views.

The British and Irish Association for Mission Studies (BIAMS), which was founded in 1990, keeps in tune with the initial vision of the IAMS. A key catalyst in this development was ANDREW F. WALLS, the founding secretary of the Scottish Institute for Missionary Studies (SIMS, 1967) and a specialist in intensive IAMS and European missiological networking. Another precedent for missiological consultation in Britain was the English-based Evangelical Fellowship for Missionary Studies, which had been founded in 1968 to provide opportunities for evangelicals working in the whole area of missionary studies and to encourage further research and publication. The EFMS was closely connected with the London-based EVANGELICAL MISSIONARY ALLIANCE (EMA).

In continental western Europe, various associations have arisen to serve mission studies.

Prominent among them are two associations of French-speaking mission scholars. The *Centre de Recherches et d'Echanges sur la Diffusion et l'Inculturation du Christianisme* (CREDIC) was founded in 1979 to provide a common forum for Catholic mission scholars and institutes. More recently, the *Association Francophone Oecuménique* (AFOM) was established in Paris in 1994 by Roman Catholic and Protestant missiologists for dialogue on the intercultural and intercontinental expressions of Christian faith in today's world. The more specialized Berlin Society for Mission History was founded in 1994.

Farther afield, it is important to recognize initiatives in Africa, Asia, and Latin America. In the Southern Hemisphere, the Southern African Missiological Society (SAMS) was founded in 1968 under the pioneer leadership of DAVID J. BOSCH. Based in the department of missiology at the University of South Africa, Pretoria, SAMS produced *Missionalia* and carried on an important abstracting service. In south Asia, the Fellowship of Indian Missiologists (FOIM), founded at Purnodaya, Bhopal, in June 1991, is worthy of note. The South Pacific Association for Mission Studies (SPAMS) was founded in Australia in the 1980s, while the *Associaçao de Professores de Missoes no Brasil*, an association of mission professors in Brazil, was founded in 1992. All of these are active in fostering and publishing scholarly research and writing in their area.

The loose network of national and international professional associations of mission has grown significantly over the last two decades. It has done much to facilitate global communication and cross-pollination in missiological thought, with the result that the field of mission studies was much stronger at the end of the twentieth century than at mid-century.

A. CHRISTOPHER SMITH

Bibliography. D. J. Hesselgrave, *EMQ* 27:2 (April 1991): 184–87; J. N. J. Kritzinger and W. A. Saayman, eds., *Mission in Creative Tension: A Dialogue with David J. Bosch*; S. Neill, in *The Mission of the Church and the Propagation of the Faith*, pp. 149–70; W. R. Shenk, *The American Society of Missiology, 1972–87*; J. A. Siewert, ed., *Directory of Professors and Schools of Mission*; A. F. Walls, *IBMR* 15:4 (1991): 146–54.

Accommodation. Missionary practice of accommodating the rituals, practices, and styles of the missionary's sending church to those of the recipient culture. It indicates what are generally conscious processes of adaptation, done with the willingness to adopt some of the forms of the receiving culture and at times to leave aside some of the prior Christian church's customs considered to be an impediment to embracing Christian faith in the receiving culture.

As a technical term within the history of mission in the Roman Catholic Church, accommodation identifies a series of specific experiments in this direction during the sixteenth through eighteenth centuries, around which a great amount of controversy gathered. Most of these were undertaken by Jesuits, the two most notable of whom were MATTEO RICCI in China and ROBERTO DE NOBILI in South India.

Ricci's efforts (from 1583 until his death in 1610) to lodge the Christian faith among people closely associated with the imperial palace led him to accommodations to Chinese practice in language (the use of the term *T'ien* ['heaven'] as a term for deity), in veneration of Confucius (considering the term applied to him, *Sheng* ['holy'], to be a term of honor for anything venerable), and in the veneration of ancestors (taken to be symbolic of the cohesion of the family and not religious worship). These issues persisted into the eighteenth century in what became known as the "Rites Controversy." In 1704, limitations were placed on the accommodations Ricci had made, but this was followed in 1720 by a number of concessions or permissions granted by a legate of Rome. Finally, in 1742 a papal bull issued by Benedict XIV swept away those permissions and required Roman practice in every detail as the law for the missions. This stood until 1938.

In the case of the work of Roberto de Nobili in South India from 1605 until his death in 1656, the controversy arose around his efforts to become as Indian as possible, adopting the lifestyle and practices of a holy man of the Brahman caste. That involved refusing customs that gave offense (such as eating meat or wearing leather shoes). It also meant not requiring converts to break with caste rules except where directly idolatrous. De Nobili's refusal to identify with the already existing church, which was viewed by Indians as the caste of the *parangi* (Portuguese), led to charges of schism. A papal bull in 1744 dictated essentially the same requirements for India as for China.

Accommodation as mission policy and strategy represented an advance over "imposition" by which the missionary church's culture entirely displaced the recipient culture in the definition of Christian life and community. But when compared with more recent notions of CONTEXTUALIZATION (a term more common among Protestants) and INCULTURATION (a term preferred among Roman Catholics) there remain inherent dilemmas. First, the missionary church remains in charge of the transaction and decides what adaptations are appropriate, this instead of the full participation of those receiving and believing the message. Second, it tends to give attention to external practices and rituals and fails to engage the more deeply felt meaning structures of the culture. Third, it leaves untouched the question of the culture of the missionary by which the Christian faith has thus far been shaped.

The notion of accommodation has re-emerged in recent missiological reflection, now more as missionary problem than strategy. In this respect, the term speaks of the way churches in the West have by stages taken into themselves post-Enlightenment culture that places a high premium on the rational, autonomous self, a belief in the inevitability of progress, and confidence in technology and technique for managing the world and constructing social order. The question arises whether, and to what extent, churches in the societies of a waning Christendom have lost their distinctive character as communities of witness by becoming overly accommodated to such a culture's assumptions, values, and instincts. This question fuels the challenge put so directly by LESSLIE NEWBIGIN to imagine what would be involved in the missionary encounter of the gospel with Western culture.

GEORGE R. HUNSBERGER

Bibliography. P. Schineller, *A Handbook on Inculturation;* S. Neill, *HCM;* W. H. Willimon and S. Hauerwas, *Resident Aliens.*

Accra Conference (1957–58). The final assembly of the INTERNATIONAL MISSIONARY COUNCIL took place in Accra in December 1957 and January 1958. In the context of the conviction that "the Christian world mission is Christ's, not ours," it was decided to recommend the integration of the work of the missionary council with that of the WORLD COUNCIL OF CHURCHES (WCC), with the intention that this would place mission, including clearly identified evangelism, at the heart of World Council life. Some missionary leaders, however, feared the marginalization of these concerns, which historically had been promoted by independent missionary agencies enjoying considerable independence from denominational bureaucracies. Two national missionary councils (Norway and Congo), in fact, did not immediately associate with the new integrated Division of World Mission and Evangelism of the WCC. Other critics have subsequently questioned whether the Accra hope has been properly fulfilled within the life of the WCC.

From the point of view of the World Council there was an issue of credibility, given its judgment that unity and disunity were essentially issues that challenged the missionary effectiveness of the church: mission and unity belonged together in one organization. There was also a need to recognize that Christian missions, whatever their origins, had established churches that might be younger than the historic churches of Western Christendom but were still churches. If they were churches, then their fellowship was needed in the World Council and as churches they, too, were called to mission. On the other hand, there were voices in the council, including those of some of the Orthodox members, mindful of what they took to be the proselytizing activities of some Protestant groups, who pointed out that the WCC was a council of *churches,* not Christian agencies, however benevolent their intention. Accra represents a turning point in the history of the ecumenical movement, for by opening the way for younger churches to join the World Council it marked the end of northern dominance in the life of that body, a change that the historic churches have sometimes been slow to recognize.

At Accra the Theological Education Fund was successfully set up. Generously endowed by J. D. Rockefeller Jr., who offered $2 million to be matched by the mission boards, the Fund has sought to remedy the grave weaknesses in ministerial formation programs evident among the younger churches.

JOHN A. Y. BRIGGS

SEE ALSO World Council of Churches Conferences.

Bibliography. L. Newbigin, *HEM,* II:181–93; R. K. Orchard, *The Ghana Assembly of the IMC, 1958;* T. Stransky, *DEM,* pp. 526–29; A. J. van Der Bent, *DEM,* pp. 325–36.

Accreditation. A procedure for certifying the appropriateness of an educational institution and its instructional programs; also, the recognition awarded to an institution or program thus certified. In missions, accreditation often refers to certification of theological education in the Third World.

A concern for appropriateness assumes both a system of values and criteria by which implementation of those values can be assessed. Theological educators often find it easier to define accreditation criteria than to clarify the qualities that distinguish appropriate ministry training.

Accreditation affords significant benefits, but also entails real dangers. Accreditation certifies the compliance of ministry training institutions and programs with assessment criteria; it facilitates communication and cooperation among similar institutions; it enables students to select appropriate programs; and it can provide a stimulus for program improvement. Nevertheless, the prestige attached to accreditation appeals almost irresistibly to elitist motives and the quest to attain and retain accreditation may tempt theological educators to compromise the contextual appropriateness of their programs. When issues of appropriateness and worth are slighted, accreditation may promote Western structures and programs without sensitivity to the non-Western church's training needs or to its economic realities.

In Europe, assurance of educational quality is entrusted to universities chartered by the national government. In the United States, accreditation is a self-monitoring function of non-governmental—but government recognized—associations of colleges and schools. In much of the world, educational quality is assured by a national "Ministry of Education," which assesses and certifies educational institutions. Because Ministries of Education in many nations view theological schools as religious (versus educational) institutions, theological educators have developed peer-accrediting structures. Since these structures lack the benefit of government sanction, their credibility depends on the appropriateness and implementation of their accrediting procedures.

In most regions, accreditation is a five-step process. (1) A national or regional agency defines the programs and awards it will accredit, and adopts standards for accrediting theological schools. When a theological school indicates its desire to seek accreditation, a review process is initiated. Normally this includes (2) institutional self-assessment on the basis of standards of the accrediting agency, plus (3) review and assessment by a panel of external visitors. The external visitors report their assessment and recommendations. (4) This report, with the institution's self-assessment, is reviewed by the agency's accrediting commission, and (5) an accreditation decision is taken—either to grant or to deny accreditation.

Two associations promote communication and coordination among regional theological education accrediting agencies. The INTERNATIONAL COUNCIL FOR EVANGELICAL THEOLOGICAL EDUCATION (ICETE) was founded in 1980 as a project of the Theological Commission of the WORLD EVANGELICAL FELLOWSHIP. Member agencies include the Accrediting Association of Bible Colleges (North America), the Accrediting Council for Theological Education in Africa, Asia Theological Association, Caribbean Evangelical Theological Association, European Evangelical Accrediting Association, the Evangelical Association for Theological Education in Latin America, and South Pacific Association of Bible Colleges. A conciliar counterpart, the World Conference of Associations of Theological Institutions (WOCATI), founded in 1989, lists twenty national and regional associations, some of which (e.g., the Association of Theological Schools in the United States and Canada) provide accrediting services.

ROBERT W. FERRIS

Bibliography. R. Kemp and P. Bowers, eds., *ERT* 19:3 (1995): 211–315.

Acculturation. *See* CULTURE LEARNING.

Acosta, José de (1540–1600). Spanish Jesuit early missiologist and missionary to Peru. Having taken Jesuit vows in 1570, Acosta arrived in

Peru in 1572, where he initially served as provincial and rector of the *Colegio* of Lima. During his tenure in Latin America he established a mission station near Lake Titicaca, was appointed the provincial superior of the Jesuits (1576), served as theologian at the important Third Provincial Council of Lima (1582–83), and traveled and observed Catholic work and local populations. In 1587 ill health forced his permanent return to Spain.

Acosta is best known for two of his works. In *De Procuranda Indorum Salute* (On How to Bring about Indian Salvation; 1588) he deals with proper ways to evangelize Indians in the New World. This was the first systematic treatment of missionary work and problems in dealing with the New World and greatly influenced Catholic missionary efforts in the Americas. In it Acosta emphasized the learning of indigenous languages, cultural adaptation, and the establishment of educational institutions. *Historia Natural y Moral de las Indias* (Natural and Moral History of the Indies; 1590) presented his systematic perspectives of the philosophical impact of the New World on the natural order of life and history. He carefully presented his observations on the environment and history of the Indians, arguing forcefully that they were just as human as the Europeans. While he did not hold their traditional religious beliefs and practices in high regard, he still respected them as people bearing God's image whose lot in life could be significantly improved through education.

Together these two books provided a formative and thorough treatment of the encounter of the church with the people of the Americas. Advanced in relation to the thinking of their times, they stand as foundations of early systematic missiological reflection.

A. Scott Moreau

Bibliography. J. Klaiber, *BDCM*, pp. 3–4; S. MacCormack, *Religion in the Andes;* L. Martin, *The Jesuit Tradition in Education and Missions*, pp. 205–14; E. O'Gorman, *NCE*, 1:88.

Acts. *See* New Testament Theology of Mission.

Adalbert of Bremen (c. 1000–1072). German promoter of mission to Nordic Europe. Born in a Saxon noble family, Adalbert became a canon in 1032 and archbishop of Bremen-Hamburg in 1045. Simultaneously aristocratic, capable, and ambitious, and prompted by a desire to establish ecclesiastical control over the northern European regions in which he, as the leading church official, would report directly to the pope, Adalbert promoted missionary work into the region to establish beachheads there. His dream of establishing a patriarchate was never realized, but his energy in mobilizing missionaries remains a legacy in the expansion of mission efforts into the Nordic countries, Scandinavia, Greenland, and Iceland.

A. Scott Moreau

Bibliography. ODCC; E. N. Johnson, *Speculum* 9 (1934): 147–79; R. Kay, *NCE*, 1:112; S. Neill, *HCM*.

Adaptation. A term belonging to a cluster of ideas linked to Contextualization, which includes concepts such as Accommodation and Indigenization as well as related ideas such as Translatability, Identification, and (in an opposing sense) Syncretism. The basic idea is that of changing the form of Christian theological ideas and practice (e.g., adaptation of the liturgy in high church contexts) so that they can be understood in a cultural context different from that of the communicator. It has as its foundation the reality of culture's role in human reasoning and actions and the resulting culture-embeddedness of religious ideas, even though theological truths are transcultural.

Adaptation and accommodation are often used interchangeably; attempting to nuance the differences between them so as to distinguish them is unacceptably stretching their use in the literature and in practice. Adaptation has typically been used more in Catholic circles than in Protestant, especially before the term *contextualization* was popularized in the early 1970s. Though proponents of contextualization sought to go beyond the other terms, the core ideas inherent in contextualization build on the previously established concepts and cannot be completely separated from them.

A. Scott Moreau

Bibliography. L. J. Luzbetak, *NCE*, 1:120–22.

Adjustment to the Field. Rapid, authentic adjustment to the field is an important key to effective cross-cultural communication of the Christian faith. During preparation, and especially on arrival, the missionary family must be aware of this challenge. The problems of adjustment must be anticipated and then positively experienced. The number one problem is Culture Shock. Basically, culture shock is an emotional and mental stalemate brought about by experiences in a culture that contrast too much with the culture a person is accustomed to. No missionary is exempt from culture shock; everyone will suffer from it to a certain extent. Like most ailments, it has its own symptoms, causes, and cures. Some never recover from it; others live in a constant state of such shock; many recover beautifully. Positive handling of culture shock is the first step toward genuine adjustment to the new field and its people.

Culture shock is precipitated by the anxiety that results from losing familiar signs and symbols of social intercourse. When the missionary enters a strange culture, all or most of these familiar cues are removed; feelings of lostness and frustration are not uncommon. Rejection and regression result and strange reactions are common. Some symptoms are excessive washing of hands; excessive concern over drinking water, food, and bedding; fits of anger over delays; refusal to learn the language; and excessive fear of being cheated, robbed, or injured. A sequence of four stages is common: curious fascination; a hostile and aggressive attitude; a superior attitude to the people; and gradual acceptance that brings enjoyment and understanding. The stage of culture shock in which the missionary family lives will have great bearing on its cross-cultural witness.

What can be done to reduce culture shock's downward spiral? Usually missiologists recommend three things: empathy, observation, and experimentation. Empathy helps missionaries get to know the people of their host culture, to feel as others feel. How missionaries relate to others is the basis of cross-cultural effectiveness. Can they trust others? Can they accept help from others? Empathy leads to a mutually dependent relationship that results in a nonjudgmental attitude. Intentional observation makes missionaries break out of their cultural cocoon and become alert to what is going on around them. Experimentation, or, in other words, "trying out something and seeing what happens!" is the way a child learns a culture, by inquiry and discovery learning. Like the child, the missionary finds out through trial and error.

Adjustment comes as the missionary family learns to cope with culture shock. Coping comes through building a knowledge background of the culture, which includes the language; through copying a reliable model in the new culture; and through creatively acting on one's best insights and making appropriate adjustments. Like any healthy learning experience, mastering culture shock is an enriching experience. It produces a deeper sense of human values; it conquers harmful ethnocentrism; it earns a freedom to constructively criticize; and it builds immunity to further serious cases. Those missionaries who have successfully passed through culture shock and have successfully adjusted to their fields of service emerge different people, in many ways healthier and better adjusted than before.

JUSTICE C. ANDERSON

SEE ALSO Culture Shock; Extent of Missionary Identification.

Bibliography. J. S. Hofman, *Mission Work in Today's World: Insights and Outlooks;* M. W. Hubbell, *Who Me? Go Where? Do What?: The Missionary and the Mission;* C. P. Wagner, *Frontiers in Missionary Strategy;* T. Ward, *Living Overseas.*

Adopt-a-People. It is difficult to sustain a mission focus on the billions of people in the world or even on the multitudes of languages and cultures in a given country. Adopt-a-people is a mission mobilization strategy that helps Christians get connected with a specific group of people who are in spiritual need. It focuses on the goal of discipling a particular people group (*see* PEOPLES, PEOPLE GROUPS), and sees the sending of missionaries as one of the important means to fulfill that goal.

Adopt-a-people was conceptualized to help congregations focus on a specific aspect of the GREAT COMMISSION. It facilitates the visualization of the real needs of other people groups, enables the realization of tangible accomplishments, develops and sustains involvement, and encourages more meaningful and focused prayer. A people group focus helps Christians to maintain an emphasis on the goal of reaching a people group and then discipling Christians from within that people. Churches in the people group are also helped to evangelize their own people and eventually to send out their own missionaries.

Adopt-a-people does not mean that a church or mission organization is adopting a group into their own organization or that no other churches or groups can work with that particular people. Rather, the goal of adopt-a-people is to be used by God to see a people adopted into his heavenly family. Thus, the implementation of the adopt-a-people concept requires maintaining a commitment until the Great Commission is fulfilled in the targeted group. In pragmatic terms, the minimal involvement for a church (or fellowship) using the adopt-a-people idea is to provide informed, dedicated prayer for the targeted people group. Other levels of involvement range from logistical or research help to financial support to short-term projects among the targeted people group and even the commissioning and support of long-term missionaries from the adopting organization.

TERRY J. RILEY

Bibliography. IJFM 12:1 (January–March 1995).

Adventist Missions. The Seventh-Day Adventist (SDA) Church is an evangelical denomination with 10 million members (1998) working in 205 countries. It is rooted in the renewal movement of William Miller, a Baptist farmer in New England, who preached the impending second advent of Christ in the 1840s.

Background. When Christ did not return by October 22, 1844, the Millerite movement disintegrated into several groups. The SDA church eventually developed from one of these groups as a missionary movement with a strongly evangelical theological core (e.g., primacy of the Scriptures, salvation through Christ), a set of distinct doctrines (e.g., seventh-day Sabbath, premillennial eschatology, spiritual gifts, tithing), and a definite lifestyle (e.g., healthful living). After a formative period under the guidance of influential leaders like James and Ellen White, Joseph Bates, and Uriah Smith, Adventists cultivated a global missionary consciousness that grew out of the Adventist understanding of biblical prophecies (cf. Rev. 14:6–12).

The SDA insistence on a healthy lifestyle that reflects personal holiness, the keeping of the seventh-day Sabbath, and the acceptance of Ellen White as a prophetic messenger to the church have sometimes caused other Christians to criticize the SDA church as a cult. But a review of SDA theology reveals that Adventists are firmly committed to the Reformation principles of *sola scriptura* and righteousness by grace through faith. Adventist practices such as Sabbath-keeping, tithing, and a commitment to world mission are understood to grow out of the believer's response to Christ's transforming grace.

Missionary Expansion. At first Adventist missionary efforts were directed largely toward those who had shared their experience in the Millerite movement. But soon Adventist immigrants in the United States were also sharing their convictions with friends and relatives, some of them on other continents. Michael Czechowski (1818–76), a former Catholic priest from Poland, eventually went back to Europe in 1864, starting SDA groups in Switzerland, Italy, and Romania. The existence of such groups led the church to send John Andrews to Europe in 1874 as the first official missionary. While Adventists were latecomers to the GREAT CENTURY OF MISSIONS, their missionaries were soon working on all continents. The SDA practice of tithing and a system of sharing financial resources upwardly throughout the organization gave mission strategists means to boldly move the church forward around the world. Today the church is organized into twelve world divisions and growing at a decadal rate of about 75 percent (lower in Western countries) with 90 percent of its members in non-Western countries. This growth testifies to a firm commitment to the task of world evangelization which is part of the Adventist identity.

Mission Practices. In addition to the strong missionary vision of the church there are several elements that have consistently contributed to the solid growth of the missionary enterprise of the SDA church, such as the church's use of media (especially publishing), a global financial and organizational structure, and a network of service and educational institutions.

The publishing work initially served to link the rather dispersed group of Adventist believers, discuss and clarify theological positions, share experiences, and unite believers. Soon it also became an effective instrument to spread the Adventist missionary vision and propagate the faith in many different settings. As of 1998 the church runs over 50 publishing houses, printing literature in almost 230 languages. It also uses radio and television to broadcast the gospel on all continents.

The backbone of the worldwide growth has been the organizational structure of the church. Early Adventists resisted formal organization. But the global mission of the church made a functional structure necessary. The first step was the creation of the General Conference (GC) of Seventh-Day Adventists in 1863. The current representative four-tier church structure (local churches, conferences, union conferences, and the general conference with twelve world divisions) goes back to 1901, when the church reorganized its administrative structure to adapt to the enormous global growth. The current departmental structure throughout all organizational levels focusing on different concerns such as Christian education, family, youth, healthful living, missionary outreach, social ministries, stewardship, and so on, was adopted at about the same time.

Another element of Adventist mission practice is the medical work and other social ministries of the church which grow out of a holistic view of the nature of human life and the lordship of Christ over all aspects of life. Adventists promote a healthful lifestyle with wholesome nutrition, abstinence from harmful substances, often vegetarianism, and a balanced life expressed through the regular keeping of a work-free Sabbath. The modern breakfast cereal industry started with a simple Adventist invention: the cornflakes of John H. Kellogg. As of 1998 the church employed over 60,000 persons in over 580 healthcare institutions. The Adventist Development and Relief Agency (ADRA) is working in 143 countries.

The constant expansion of the mission of the church also demanded the continual development of educational facilities to train men and women. Adventists believe that education should prepare students not only academically but also spiritually and practically for a life of service. The first college was established in Battle Creek in 1874. While some of its 4,400 primary schools, 975 secondary schools, and 87 colleges and universities were established through grant-in-aid programs, they were all built on an Adventist ideal that has touched millions with the transforming power of the gospel.

Current Challenges. Despite the fact that the SDA church has grown consistently for the last 150 years it is facing a number of challenges. One of them is the task to maintain unity and identity across multiple cultural barriers. Another is to resist the temptation to let the enormous institutional network absorb all available financial and human resources and neglect the millions yet unreached. In response to this pressure the church in 1990 established the office of "Global Mission" focusing on reaching unreached peoples (*see* PEOPLES, PEOPLE GROUPS) and has encouraged the emergence of Third World missions (*see* NON-WESTERN MISSION BOARDS AND SOCIETIES), other supportive ministries, and volunteer missions. The Adventist "1000 Missionary Movement" in the Philippines has sent out more than one thousand short-term missionaries (*see* SHORT-TERM MISSION) all over the world. "Adventist Frontier Missions" in Michigan, a private SDA mission agency started in 1985, focuses on planting the church in new territories. But the church is not only celebrating successes. Maybe the greatest challenge today is the church's need to reaffirm its missionary identity in the Western world where SECULARISM and POSTMODERNISM have eroded the church's traditional missionary identity.

ERICH W. BAUMGARTNER

Bibliography. E. W. Baumgartner, ed., *Re-Visioning Adventist Mission in Europe;* J. Dybdahl, ed., *Adventist Mission in the 21st Century;* G. R. Knight, *The Fat Lady and the Kingdom: Adventist Mission Confronts the Challenges of Institutionalism and Secularization;* G. Land, ed., *Adventism in America: A History;* Ministerial Association, General Conference of Seventh-day Adventists; *Seventh-day Adventists Believe . . . An Exposition of 27 Fundamental Doctrines;* G. Oosterwal, *Mission Possible.*

Aedesius (4th century). Syrian pioneer missionary to Ethiopia. Aedesius and his brother FRUMENTIUS were traveling on a ship with their father from Tyre to India when the ship was wrecked. All on board except the two brothers were killed; they were found by representatives of the Ethiopian King Ella Amida and taken into his service. Their education stood them in good stead and they introduced the king and his young son to the Christian faith. When Aeizanas, the prince, became king he and his court gave themselves to Christ. Eventually Aedesius returned to Tyre, while Frumentius was appointed bishop and returned to Ethiopia.

A. SCOTT MOREAU

Bibliography. S. C. Neill, *HCM.*

Affluence. *See* MISSIONARY AFFLUENCE.

Afghanistan *(Est. 2000 pop.: 26,674,000; 652,090 sq. km. [251,772 sq. mi.]).* The country occupies a strategic place in central Asia for the meeting of cultures and has existed as an autonomous entity since the eighteenth century. Christians entered the territory by the fourth century. A bishop from Herat attended the Council of Seleucia in 424, and a Nestorian bishop served in Kabul until the late Middle Ages. However, serious rivalry between two Christian traditions, Jacobite (monophysite) and Nestorian (dyophysite), and the rise of Islam seriously weakened Christian witness.

The name *Afghanistan* dates from 982, by which time Christian missionary activity was already in decline. With the rise of the Mogul dynasty in the sixteenth century, the area was closed to Christianity. Subsequently, no missionaries have been allowed into the country. Under Islamic law, *shari'ah*, it is a capital offense for a Muslim to convert to Christianity. As the penalty for apostasy from Islam is death, indigenous Afghan Christians tend to leave the country. A small Armenian church of about a dozen members existed in Kabul, but the church was destroyed in 1898 and the group exiled.

In this century, some Christian activity has existed. In 1933, the governments of Afghanistan and Italy signed an agreement which led to creation of the Work of Spiritual Assistance to Catholics of Afghanistan. The constitution of 1964 guaranteed non-Muslims freedom of worship, but Christian evangelization was forbidden. In July 1973, a military junta overthrew the monarchy and suspended the constitution of 1964. Among its first decrees was the provision, "Afghanistan is a republican state in accordance with the true spirit of Islam." As a result, expatriates compose the Christian community almost exclusively.

PAUL R. DEKAR

Bibliography. S. H. Moffett, *A History of Christianity in Asia;* J. Stewart, *Nestorian Missionary Enterprise. The Story of a Church on Fire.*

Africa. The growth of the church in Africa is one of the most surprising facts of twentieth-century church history. From an estimated 4 million professing Christians in 1900 African Christianity has grown to over 300 million adherents by the year 2000. What accounts for such growth? The common notion that nineteenth-century missionary efforts explain African Christianity's recent explosion is an oversimplification. The true story behind these statistics reaches back to the very earliest centuries of Christian history.

Beginnings. The roots of African Christianity are to be found in the four regional churches of Africa in the Roman era—Egypt, North Africa, Nubia, and Ethiopia. The origins of Christianity in Egypt are obscure. The first documentary evidence of the existence of an Egyptian church dates from A.D. 189 with Bishop Demetrius. Persecution in the third century caused the faith to spread down the Nile into rural Egypt among the Coptic-speaking population, where it found a new champion in Antony, the father of monasticism. After a period of syncretism in the fourth century, mature Coptic churches emerged in the fifth century under the leadership of independently minded monastic leaders such as Shenout. The signs of an indigenous Christianity rooted in the language and life of the people were everywhere evident, including Coptic-speaking clergy and Coptic liturgies together with Scripture translations.

North Africa. While Egyptian Christianity was a testimony to the importance of a contextualized Christianity, North Africa was a sober reminder of the fragility of a faith insufficiently rooted in the life of the people. The Roman segment of North Africa embraced the gospel with vigor but the Punic and Berber peoples were never adequately reached. The brilliance of North African Christianity cannot be doubted. The genius of Tertullian, Cyprian, and Augustine is well known, yet even their brilliance could not prevent the decline of a church troubled by separatism and persecution. Despite the failure of North African Christianity to contextualize the faith, Augustine's observation that the story of the African church is the story of the clash of two kingdoms, the City of God and the earthly city, continued to illuminate African church history.

Ethiopia. Solid evidence for the conversion of Ethiopia appears in 350, when King Ezana begins to ascribe his victories to the "Lord of All . . . Jesus Christ who has saved me" rather than to the traditional gods. Crucial to this change was the ministry of Bishop FRUMENTIUS, who had been commissioned by Athanasius of Alexandria as a missionary to Ethiopia. The precedent set by Athanasius became entrenched and the Ethiopian Orthodox Church continued to receive its *abun* (bishop) by appointment of the Egyptian Coptic patriarch. By Ezana's death in 400 Christianity was firmly rooted at court but had made little impact on the countryside. That changed in the sixth century with the coming of a new missionary force from Syria. The tesseatou Kidoussan ("nine saints") established monasteries in the rural areas and engaged in widespread evangelism. Linked with the Egyptian Coptic Christianity and armed with the Scriptures in the vernacular the Christians of Ethiopia entered the Middle Ages, where they "slept near a thousand years, forgetful of the world, by whom they were forgotten" (Gibbon).

Nubia. Like Ethiopia, Nubia (modern Sudan) was never part of the Roman Empire. The Christianity that infiltrated Nubia began a religious revolution in Nubia that transformed both people and prince by the sixth century. Archaeological evidence that came to light only in the 1960s has revealed the vigor of Nubian Christianity. Two sixth-century missionaries from Byzantium, Julian and Longinus, are credited with officially introducing the Christian faith, in its Monophysite form, to this kingdom along the Blue Nile.

The African Middle Ages. These four original sources of African Christianity faced their greatest challenge during the African Middle Ages. The first challenge, which inaugurated the African Middle Ages, came from a new religion—Islam. The second challenge, which brought the African Middle Ages to an end, came from the kingdoms of European Christendom represented by the Portuguese and the Dutch.

North African and Nubian collapse. The rise and spread of Islam across Africa's northern shore in the seventh and eighth centuries was followed in the tenth and eleventh centuries by a southward expansion led by the merchant and the missionary. North Africa was most dramatically affected by this expansion of Islam. The decline of North African Christianity was nearly total by the sixteenth century. Attempts by the fourth crusade (1215) to liberate North Africa politically and Franciscan attempts to revive it spiritually ended in failure. A faith only lightly rooted in the life of the people faded into memory.

Nubia proved more resistant. During the eighth through tenth centuries, while Islam continued to expand in Africa, Nubian Christianity reached its height. But in 1272 Muslim Turks sent by the legendary Saladin overthrew northern Nubia. In 1504 the southernmost kingdom, Alwa, was conquered by a tribe from the south recently converted to Islam. The last word from Nubian Christianity occurs in 1524 when they wrote to the Coptic patriarch of Egypt for help to meet their critical shortage of clergy. The lack of indigenous church leaders combined with the failure to evangelize the peoples to the south conspired to undermine Nubian Christianity.

Egyptian and Ethiopian survival. Christianity survived the onslaught of Islam but not without losses. Caliph Umar had forbidden new churches or monasteries but under the Umayyids (661–750) this law was not enforced. Other forms of pressure, however, were applied. In 744 the Muslim governor of Egypt offered tax exemption for Christians who converted to Islam. Twenty-four thousand responded. Throughout the African Middle Ages the Coptic church suffered from a lack of trained leadership, discriminatory laws, and a stagnant ritualism in worship. Nonetheless, it survived. By 1600 Egypt was a "country of dual religious cultures."

Ethiopian Christianity also followed the path of survival. After a crisis in the tenth century when the pagan Agau nearly toppled the king, Ethiopian clergy began to work for reform and revival of the national faith. One movement of renewal brought a new dynasty to the imperial throne of Ethiopia. The most popular leader of the Zagwe dynasty, Lalibela, strengthened Ethiopia's religious patriotism by building a New Jerusalem in the Ethiopian highlands and strengthening the belief that Ethiopians were the new Israel through whom God would bring light to the nations. Under the missionary monk TEKLA-HAYMANOT Ethiopian Christianity experienced revival. New missionary efforts among the Shoa of the south met with success. Emperor Zara-Yaqob (d. 1468) brought Ethiopia to new heights of glory but by 1529 the kingdom was in decline. Ahmad Gragn, a Muslim, successfully overthrew the Christian kingdom of Ethiopia but his reign was short-lived. Within a few years Christian Ethiopia was restored, this time with the help of a new player on the African stage—the Portuguese.

The Portuguese. Inspired by their visionary leader, Prince Henry, the Portuguese embarked on a campaign of aggressive expansion between 1450 and 1700. This expansion led to the European "discovery" of Africa and the establishment of a trading empire that spread from Lisbon to India. Christian communities were established in West Africa and in port cities along the southern and eastern coasts but Portuguese missions enjoyed its greatest success in the ancient kingdom of Congo, where the king Afonso I promoted the new faith aggressively. Yet the missionary efforts of the Catholic missionaries were eventually undermined by the commercial interest of Portuguese merchants who quickly saw potential for a profit in the slave trade. Hatred of the Portuguese trader soon was directed at the Portuguese priest. By the time of Livingstone's travels in the mid-nineteenth century few vestiges of Portuguese Christianity could be found.

Dutch Expansion. In 1652, one hundred representatives of the Dutch East India Company landed on Africa's southernmost tip and proceeded to establish a way station for the company ships traveling from Amsterdam to Batavia in the Pacific. From this modest beginning came Cape Town and the beginnings of the nation of South Africa. The first church established was that of the Dutch Reformed Church but by 1900 Lutherans and Moravians had also begun their work. The churches of the settlers soon came into conflict with a missionary Christianity spawned by the wave of GREAT AWAKENINGS that were sweeping North America, England, and Europe in the eighteenth century. An early representative of this new evangelical movement was the Moravian GEORG SCHMIDT, who began work among the Khoisan of the Cape in 1738. He soon came into conflict with the established church and was stopped from further mission work in 1748.

African Christianity in the Nineteenth and Early Twentieth Centuries. *The Antislavery crusade.* While Schmidt was struggling with the stubbornness of his Dutch hosts, English evangelicals began to struggle with the issue of slavery. JOHN WESLEY condemned slavery in a pamphlet of 1774, and a number of his followers took up the cause. Early opposition to slavery came from Granville Sharp, Thomas Clarkson, and William Wilberforce through the support of his upper-class evangelical friends (the CLAPHAM SECT). The first breakthrough came in 1807 with the passage of a bill prohibiting the slave trade but allowing ownership. By 1833 legislation was passed abolishing slavery everywhere in the British Empire. British evangelicals had opposed slavery both on humanitarian grounds as well as missiological ones. They realized that their desire to engage in missions in Africa would be seriously thwarted by the existence of slavery. The missionaries that English societies sent out to Africa were therefore equipped with the dual message of "Christianity and commerce." It was thought that Western-style commerce would make slavery economically unnecessary, thus permitting the message of Christianity to make its way deep into the lives of the hearers.

The growth of Christianity in Western Africa. In 1787, 411 freed blacks left London to found a community called Freetown in what is now Sierra Leone. It became a haven for freed slaves and an outpost for the spread of the gospel. Like the Puritans who settled New England, these early settlers burned with religious zeal. Freetown became a Christian commonwealth that inspired similar Christian communities farther down the coast in the Nigerian towns of Abeokuta and Badagry. "Recaptives" (slaves liberated by the British Navy) added to the population of Freetown. Many converted to the Christian faith and found an opportunity for training at Freetown's Fourah Bay college, established in 1827.

One of the most outstanding graduates of the college was a young recaptive named SAMUEL AJAYI CROWTHER. Crowther was ordained in 1843, and in 1864 became Africa's first Anglican bishop. The CHURCH MISSIONARY SOCIETY (CMS) recognized in Crowther the leader they needed to further the spread of Christianity in Africa. Under HENRY VENN, an aggressive program of Africanization was adopted that called for the immediate building of self-supporting, self-propagating, and self-governing local churches. Crowther was asked to implement this strategy in the Nigerian interior. Through the failure of some members of his team and through the hostility of white missionaries opposed to Venn's policies, Crowther was forced to resign. Leadership of the CMS work in West Africa fell into white hands. This led to a number of African-initiated churches. In addition to Nigeria, work went on in Liberia, Ghana, Cameroon, Gabon, Senegal, and Zaire, which was the main arena for Catholic missions.

Southern Africa. While West Africa was evangelized largely by Africans returning to their motherland, South Africa from the very earliest days of Christianity was dominated by the white expatriate. Despite the common denominator of white domination, there was little unity in South African Christianity, which saw three distinct and mutually hostile expressions of Christianity emerge in the nineteenth century.

The first expression was that of Afrikaner Christianity and the Dutch Reformed Church. After England gained control of South Africa in 1815, conflicts between Boer farmers and English administrators multiplied, which led to mass migrations of Afrikaner families to northeastern regions of South Africa. One small party of "voortrekkers" encountered an army of Zulu warriors. Their surprising victory at the battle of Blood River in 1838 coupled with the tradition that the trekkers had made a special covenant with God prior to the battle fueled the belief that Afrikaner Christians were an elect nation endowed by God with both a right to rule the land and a right to resist the nonelect. This religious tradition became a political and cultural force that found expression in the formation of the Afrikaner Nationalist Party.

A second expression of South African church life in the nineteenth century was that of "missionary Christianity," which made major inroads into the Xhosa community and produced outstanding believers such as the hymn writer Ntsikana and the African Presbyterian leader, Tiyo Soga. Such African leaders encouraged the missionary-dominated churches to engage in programs of training, including Lovedale College and Fort Hare University. DAVID LIVINGSTONE's fame exceeded that of all other nineteenth-century missionaries despite his failure as evangelist (he saw only one convert, who eventually fell away). His achievements as an explorer, an antislavery crusader, and missions promoter established his place in history.

Though missionary Christianity tended to emphasize an inward piety and a broadly evangelical theology that stood in contrast with the more reformed Afrikaners by the late nineteenth century, attempts were made to bridge the gap. Most successful was ANDREW MURRAY JR., moderator of the DRC and champion of both evangelical piety and missions. His emphasis on "Absolute Surrender" and the formation of new agencies such as the South Africa General Mission (now African Evangelical Fellowship) acted as a corrective to the Afrikaner Christianity.

A third expression of South African Christianity was that of the social gospel championed by people like the Anglican bishop John Colenso and John Jabavu. The emphasis of this form of Christianity was upon economic and political justice. Colenso opposed the Afrikaner and English messianic nationalism, which he saw at the root of injustice in South Africa. His clash with Bishop Robert Gray of Cape Town ended with the formation of an independent Anglican communion in South Africa. Like Colenso, John Jabavu regarded politics as an appropriate arena for Christian involvement. A tireless campaigner for African rights, he founded his own independent newspaper. This third expression of Christianity would become a major force in the years following South Africa's Sharpville massacre of 1960.

Despite the fragmented witness to the kingdom of God provided by South African Christianity, this region entered the twentieth century as one of the most Christianized regions in all of Africa. Yet white domination of the churches would eventually spawn a vigorous movement of "Ethiopianism"—separatist churches that demanded respect from the Westerner and a greater share of church leadership.

Eastern Africa. The nineteenth century witnessed the reintroduction of Christianity into the former Nubia (Sudan) and in Mombasa (Kenya). Ethiopian Christianity was also revitalized during the century. Additionally the lands of Tanzania and Uganda saw the initial introduction of this ancient African faith among their own people.

Ethiopia and Sudan. In 1830 the CMS arrived in Ethiopia. Originally working within the Coptic church, Protestant missionaries such as J. LUDWIG KRAPF clashed with Coptic church authorities, leading to expulsion in 1843. Under Emperor Menelik II, Ethiopian Christianity experienced a new surge of life and entered the twentieth century carefully guarding its dearly won political and religious independence. In Sudan, Catholic work under the leadership of the Verona Fathers was swept away by the Islamic Mahdist movement.

Kenya. Krapf began work in Kenya in 1844 after his expulsion from Ethiopia. Together with his colleague Johann Rebmann, Krapf envisioned a chain of mission stations across the continent, linking up with Freetown in West Africa. His vision would guide numerous mission agencies for the next century. Though he attempted to establish the eastern link of this chain at Rabai Mpyia, it was the later formation of Freetown in 1874 as a refuge for runaway slaves that gave Christianity its firmest foothold in British East Africa. Outstanding Christian leaders came from the community at Freetown, including David Koi, Kenya's first Protestant martyr. These missionary efforts on the coast were soon augmented by a new thrust inland. James Stewart, a Presbyterian missionary at Lovedale College, was recruited by Livingstone to establish an industrial mission in the Kenyan interior in 1891. The CMS began work among the Kikuyu of Kenya's central highlands in 1901. PETER CAMERON SCOTT and his newly founded AFRICA INLAND MISSION began churches among the Kamba people in 1895. The Holy Ghost Fathers began work in Nairobi in 1899.

Tanzania. Catholic missionary efforts centered around the formation of a "Christian Village" at Bagamoyo (1868), where three hundred freed slaves found a place of refuge. Protestant work was conducted by the Universities Mission to Central Africa (UMCA), who were vigorous in their opposition to the Arab slave trade that was decimating the inland peoples of Africa's Great lake region, where the LMS and CMS had established a presence. Through the intervention of Germany the Arab slave trade was broken and a number of German mission agencies introduced Lutheranism.

Uganda. More dramatic than in any other part of East Africa was the response to the gospel in Uganda. Christianity was introduced by the CMS in 1877 and flourished under the zealous leadership of Alexander Mackay. White Fathers introduced Catholicism in 1879. Despite the indifference of King Mutesa I and the violent hostility of his son Mwanga, Protestant and Catholic Christianity eventually produced a religious revolution in Uganda that spilled beyond the borders of the kingdom of Buganda into the smaller kingdoms that make up the modern-day nation of Uganda.

The missionary factor. The colonial era (1885–1960) brought sweeping changes to African Christianity. The most notable change was the proliferation of missionaries and agencies from the West and the corresponding growth of African Christianity. In 1900 there were an estimated 4 million Christians spread throughout the continent compared to 60 million Muslims. By the autumn of colonialism in 1950 the number of African Christians had reached 34 million.

The missionaries of the colonial era were, on the whole, a remarkable lot. Like ROWLAND BINGHAM of the Sudan Interior Mission (SIM; now SOCIETY FOR INTERNATIONAL MINISTRIES), they were a tough-minded breed who often buried their colleagues and kept going. Like GEORGE GRENFELL of the Baptist Mission Society of Congo, they were tireless explorers and enemies of the slave trade. Like ALBERT SCHWEITZER of Gabon they were often humanitarians. Like MARY SLESSOR of the Calabar mission many were single women who gave their entire lives to the work. Like P. A. Bennett, acting secretary of the CMS in Nigeria, they were sometimes incorrigible racists. But like Archdeacon Dennis, also of the CMS in Nigeria, they more often opposed racism with equal vigor. Like Father Shanahan of Nigeria they aggressively founded schools. Most important, like Carl Christian Reindorf of Ghana, they mastered the vernacular languages of the people and like GEORGE PILKINGTON of Uganda, they translated the Scriptures and trained indigenous evangelists. This last factor, vernacular translations and the training of national evangelists, accounts for the remarkable church growth that took place during the colonial decades.

Independent religious movements. One reaction to the missionary factor was the birth of the AFRICAN INITIATED CHURCH MOVEMENT. The independent churches that were founded tended to fall into distinct groupings. Some were primarily concerned with African leadership and only secondarily concerned with changing missionary theology or worship. A second grouping emphasized healing and the supernatural. Armed with Scriptures in their own languages they struck out on their own, like WILLIAM WADE HARRIS of Liberia, whose preaching in West Africa between 1913 and 1915 claimed over one hundred thousand adherents. Others like SIMON KIMBANGU of Zaire catalyzed separation from missionary churches into new denominations. In some cases these prophet churches moved clearly outside the bounds of orthodoxy. Such was the case with Isaiah Shembe and his Church of the Nazarites in South Africa. After his death in 1935 his followers proclaimed that he had risen from the dead and was in fact the true Christ for Africa. A third category covers movements of revival within established denominations. The passion in these types of movements was the discovery of a vital Christianity to replace a numbing nominalism in the church. The outstanding example of this third type of movement is the East Africa Revival that swept much of East Africa from 1930 onwards.

Christianity in Independent Africa. In 1960, fourteen African nations achieved selfhood and inaugurated a new era within African Christianity. Henry Venn's vision of an African Christianity that was self-governing, self-propagating, and self-supporting was at last realized. In denomination after denomination African leaders replaced missionaries. The new leaders faced a number of new challenges in the modern era. Five challenges in particular have dominated African Christianity in the closing decades of the twentieth century.

Church and state. The overarching fact of modern African life since the late 1960s was widespread disillusionment with the nation-state. As the promise of the new African ruling elite turned sour, criticism began to mount. The common response of the ruling elite to the growing chorus of criticism was tightened control, promotion of personality cults and messianic nationalism, and growing conflict with the church. Kwame Nkrumah's tragic rise and fall in Ghana was all too typical. Zaire's Mobutu Sese Seko, Liberia's Samuel Doe, Uganda's Idi Amin, and Ethiopia's Mengistu Haile Mariam were typical of leaders who saw the church as a dangerous independent voice. Church responses have varied from silent partnership with the ruling elite (Roman Catholicism in Rwanda, DRC in South Africa) to critical protest of state injustice (Desmond Tutu in South Africa, NCCK in Kenya). Occasionally the state has lashed out violently against the church as in the cases of the martyred Archbishop Janani Luwum of Uganda and the numerous imprisoned pastors of Mengistu's Ethiopia.

Unity and diversity. Over six thousand different independent churches were documented in Africa by the late 1960s. Organizations like the All Africa Conference of Churches (AACC), the Organization of African Instituted Churches (OAIC), and the Association of Evangelicals in Africa (AEA) have sought to bring some unity to the fractured body of Christ in Africa. A series of Pan-African Christian Leadership Assemblies (PACLA) have sought additional harmony by bringing leaders of the AACC and AEA together. Parachurch agencies have also played their part in bridging denominational dividing lines, some by working with the independent churches.

Theology and culture. In Roman Catholic as well as Protestant circles great effort has gone into the formation of a Christian theology that would adequately address the modern African context. The varieties of theologies within the African context range from theologies of identity to traditional evangelical formulations to radical liberation theology. African evangelical theology is still emerging, but important voices include Tokunboh Adeyemo, Kwame Bediako, Byang Kato, Lamin Sanneh, and Tite Tiénou.

African missions and church growth. In the 1970s Kenyan Presbyterian leader John Gatu called for a MORATORIUM on Western missionaries in order to foster "selfhood" within the church. The outcome of this debate has been a decrease in "mainline" missionaries (5,000 in 1959 to 3,000 in early 1970) At the same time there has been a resurgence of missions in three other groups. In 1974 a Synod of Bishops at Rome rejected the call for moratorium and pledged 100,000 new missionaries by the year 2000. Evangelical missionaries from the faith missions grew from 11,000 in the 1970s to over 16,000 in the late 1980s. In addition dozens of new African mission agencies emerged in the 1970s, 1980s, and 1990s. The most dramatic story of church growth in Africa, however, was the expansion of Pentecostal and charismatic preachers, evangelists, and missionaries in the closing decades of the twentieth century. The gospel of health, wealth, and wholeness accounted for much of the appeal of this form of Christianity.

Discipleship, leadership, and nominalism. The greatest challenge facing African Christian leadership was the challenge not of the unreached but of the undiscipled. If one accepts the statistics that African Christianity has grown from an estimated 4 million professing Christians in 1900 to some 300 million adherents today then one is forced to ask how these huge numbers of people can be discipled. Though the promise of African Christianity is great, the church of Africa must wrestle with the dilemma of a Christianity that

may be "expanding at the periphery" even while it is "collapsing at the center" (Roland Oliver). Leadership development and the training of the laity seem to be the crucial needs of this continent "shaped like a question mark" (Ali Mazrui).

MARK SHAW

Bibliography. J. Baur, *2000 Years of Christianity in Africa*; J. de Gruchy, *The Church Struggle in South Africa*; R. Gray, *Black Christians and White Missionaries*; C. P. Groves, *The Planting of the Church in Africa*; A. Hastings, *The Church in Africa, 1450–1950*; E. Isichei, *A History of Christianity in Africa*; L. Sanneh, *West African Christianity*; M. Shaw, *The Kingdom of God in Africa*.

Africa Evangelical Fellowship. Founded in 1889 by Martha Osborn-Howe, Spencer Walton, and ANDREW MURRAY for the purposes of spiritual renewal and missionary outreach, Africa Evangelical Fellowship (AEF) was initially known as the Cape General Mission and later the South African General Mission. The name was changed to its current designation in 1965. By the turn of the twentieth century work had expanded from South Africa to Swaziland and Zimbabwe; Malawi was entered in 1901 and Zambia in 1910. By 1930 work was present in Angola and Mozambique as well. Work presently has extended to Botswana, Namibia, Gabon, Tanzania, and the Indian Ocean islands of Reunion, Madagascar, and Mauritius. The American branch was started in 1906. AEF was loosely organized until 1941, when a constitutional organization was adopted that provided for a general director and appropriate administrative personnel. The international office is in Newbury, England, with additional branches (known as Sending Councils) in the United States, Canada, South Africa, and Australia.

An interdenominational FAITH MISSION, AEF services include the areas of education, health, and church planting. Educational ministries include Bible schools, elementary schools, correspondence courses, literacy training, and publishing work. Health ministries include a school for the blind, clinics and hospitals, and leprosaria. Currently AEF has 291 long-term and 41 short-term missionaries.

A. SCOTT MOREAU

Bibliography. G. B. A. Gerdener, *Recent Developments in the South African Mission Field*; J. Pollock, *CDCWM*, pp. 562–63; E. A. Shank, *EMCM*, pp. 3–4.

Africa Inland Mission, International (AIM). In 1895 PETER CAMERON SCOTT, a young man who had given himself fully to the task of reaching Africa for Christ, founded the Africa Inland Mission. Scott, who died in Africa only a year after his arrival, had a vision of establishing a line of mission stations from Mombasa, Kenya, up to Lake Chad in hopes of hampering the spread of

Islam to the south. Following the deaths of Scott and several of the other founding missionaries, AIM's future was in serious question. But the words of ARTHUR T. PIERSON, a council member, kept AIM pressing onward: "Gentleman," he said, "the hallmark of God on any work is death. God has given us that hallmark. Now is the time to go forward." And so they did.

Today, over one hundred years later, Scott's vision has come to fruition. AIM now has five sending councils worldwide and over eight hundred missionaries serving in fourteen African nations and in various urban centers throughout the United States. AIM's primary goal is to plant churches through the evangelization of UN-REACHED PEOPLES and effective training of church leaders. The methodology involves identifying and filling perceived needs in order to establish relationships based on trust and caring; after such relationships are established, Christ can be appropriately shared. The growth of the planted churches requires trained indigenous leaders, and Bible schools have been established to that end.

AIM offers a variety of support services such as AIM AIR, AIM TECH, and AIM SERV. They provide air transportation as well as logistical and technical assistance to both the mission body and nationals in the local church. In 1906, AIM established the Rift Valley Academy (RVA), which provides a quality education for close to five hundred students whose parents serve in ninety different mission organizations and twenty-two African countries.

Further, AIM established the Training in Ministry Outreach (TIMO) program to provide training for new missionaries. The program couples a team of new missionaries with a more experienced missionary for a period of two years. During those two years the team studies a curriculum and simultaneously puts it into practice on the field. Some of these teams have planted viable ongoing churches during their two-year ministries.

AIM also challenges its constituents to involve themselves at a deeper level by adoption of an unreached people group. The ADOPT-A-PEOPLE program encourages churches, small groups, and families to commit themselves to pray for, financially support, or even go as missionaries to one of sixty-one people groups that it identifies.

ANDY HORNBERGER

Bibliography. D. Anderson, *We Felt like Grasshoppers: The Story of Africa Inland Mission;* S. Langford, *It's a Battle;* K. Richardson, *Garden of Miracles: A History of the African Inland Mission;* M. Sywulka, *Workers Together with Him: A Short History: Africa Inland Mission, Tanganyika Terr., Africa.*

African Initiated Church Movement. Originally an unanticipated product of the modern missionary movement in Africa, the African Independent Churches (AICs) today number 55 million church members in some 10,000 distinct denominations present in virtually all of Africa's 60 countries. This title is the most frequent descriptive term in the current literature of some 4,000 books and articles describing it. However, because Western denominations and Western-mission related churches in Africa regard themselves also as "independent," African AIC members have since 1970 promulgated the terms African Instituted Churches, or African Indigenous Churches, or locally founded churches. Some Western scholars still use the older terms African Separatist Churches or NEW RELIGIOUS MOVEMENTS.

These movements first began with a secession from Methodist missions in Sierre Leone in 1817. Spreading rapidly across Africa by means of virtually unrelated but similar schisms and secessions, by 1900 there were a hundred thousand members of these churches, by 1935 two million, by 1968 six million, and by 1997 55 million. Countries most heavily involved are, in order of number of members, South Africa, Congo-Kinshasa, and Nigeria. The largest distinct denominations are: Zion Christian Church (12 million in 10 countries), Church of Jesus Christ on Earth through the Prophet SIMON KIMBANGU (8 million), Cherubim and Seraphim (3 million), Deeper Life Bible Church (2 million in 40 countries worldwide). Earlier movements closely copied their parent bodies in name, polity, titles, dogmas, liturgies, and ecclesiastical dress, and were frequently seen as merely Pentecostal imitations. But from 1980 onward, newer bodies became much more dynamic, postdenominationalist, charismatic, and apostolic, with a majority of their leaders being highly educated professionals avoiding ecclesiastical dress and similar trappings, often leading megachurches with thousands of enthusiastic young people as deeply committed members.

After decades of fruitlessly trying to join ecumenical councils of churches, evangelical councils or alliances, or Western confessional bodies, almost all of which rejected such applications, the AICs began their own conciliar movement and today have over 100 AIC councils of churches across the continent and in several cases even worldwide. In 1978 the major continent-wide body was formed, OAIC (Organization of African Independent Churches, later renamed Organization of African Instituted Churches), in collaboration with the Coptic Orthodox Church of Egypt as the original African independent church. By 1998, however, the sheer weight of numbers, Christian commitment, and credibility had become such that OAIC was invited to become, and became, an associate council of the World Council of Churches, as well as a member council of the All Africa Conference of Churches.

Bibliocentric and christocentric throughout their history, these churches are now producing radically new Christian theology and practice. A notable example is earthkeeping, a blend of theological environmentalism or caring for God's creation, especially in relation to land, trees, plants, natural resources, and in fact the whole of God's creation.

DAVID B. BARRETT

African Mission Boards and Societies. A study of the general landscape of African mission boards and societies reveals that the majority of the work to date has taken place in the Anglophone countries, particularly West Africa (Nigeria and Ghana). In Eastern and Central Africa, largely Christian churches seem to assume either that most people have already heard the gospel or that Western missionaries are the only ones to tackle the job. For the Francophone church, African missionaries crossing international boundaries in large numbers remains a dream to be fulfilled in the future.

Perhaps most notable for zeal for internal cross-cultural evangelism is Zaire, a country which could legitimately claim to be "too poor" to afford international missions. However, Christians not hindered with a vision of missions requiring a four-wheel-drive vehicle and a salary seem to be accomplishing the most for the kingdom, much of it undocumented.

As an outstanding example of an indigenous missionary movement, Nigeria's Evangelical Churches of West Africa (ECWA) church and its Evangelical Missionary Society (EMS, headed by PANYA BABA), is premier. A mighty mission force with 541 couples and 15 single missionaries, EMS has been instrumental in the growth of the church. One of the more successful campaigns of Muslim outreach is Uganda's version of Here's Life, adapted from Campus Crusade for Christ in America. In Mozambique, the Deeper Life Christian Ministry, led by Nigerians, has been especially successful. It works in thirty countries across Africa.

Chad deserves imitation for its successful implementation of saturation mission. Association of Evangelicals of Africa (AEA) Secretary for Missions and Evangelism Bayo Famonure reports that 24,000 Chadian Christians were mobilized to reach 2,193 villages in a six-day period, aiming to plant a church in every village. Costs were virtually limited to food and transport for the volunteers.

Most African mission boards are run separately from Western agencies. There seems to be space to operate without the need to cooperate, though a few boards are experimenting with partnering such as Timo Teams, jointly sponsored by Africa Inland Church (AIC) and AFRICA INLAND MISSION (AIM). Some boards are modeled after FAITH MISSIONS with no guaranteed salary or retirement fund, no special schools for their children, and no work account funds. A few, like Sheepfold, Kenya's largest interdenominational board, pool their income so that all missionaries get an equal share of whatever comes into the mission that month. Others receive directly whatever comes in from their supporters. One trend can be seen everywhere: sinking local currencies have greatly hurt development of the international element of the African missionary movement.

Generally speaking, accountability and supervision structures in African mission societies are loose. Financial support is typically low, erratic, and often based on only one or two special offerings a year. Fragmentation of efforts is the norm. Each denomination or group sets its goals without any overall plan or sometimes even awareness of where the unreached are, according to the AEA. Sometimes the dominant motivation seems to be the desire to plant a denominational church in an urban center rather than to take the gospel to those who have not yet had an opportunity to hear.

Language learning is often done informally at the destination, and with much less trauma and fuss than for Western missionaries undergoing LANGUAGE SCHOOL. Children of missionaries are educated in the local schools until high school age, sometimes to their detriment educationally.

Some mission boards and missionary training colleges belong to a particular denomination, such as the AIC Mission Board in East Africa or Nigeria's ECWA-EMS. Some denominations once had a missionary sending agency which has subsequently died out, such as the Church of the Province of Kenya (Anglican) Diocesan Mission Association. Others are interdenominational and indigenous, such as Agape Missions, Calvary Ministry (CAPRO, with over 300 full-time missionaries), and Christian Missionary Fellowship (CMF). Together, these form the three largest interdenominational mission agencies in Nigeria, but there are also seventy other smaller mission boards there (*see* NIGERIAN MISSION BOARDS AND SOCIETIES). Some African mission boards have virtually become church denominations, such as the CMF.

But probably the most remarkable contribution of Africans to the missionary movement has been the migration of Christian traders, businessmen, and professionals, such as university professors and doctors, to other countries or neighboring tribes where Christianity is not yet firmly established. These men and women leave home because of economic privations, but by the working of the Holy Spirit have become church planters in their host countries. The fellowships they end up planting are not always denominational or ethnic and become broad-based churches. Their secular jobs support them, and they have no professional missionary training apart from the modeling of healthy churches they have seen while growing up in their home country. At this time, economic translocation rather than the formation of formal mission boards appears to be the most widespread and effective means of spreading the gospel currently practiced by the African church.

Sue DeVries

See also Non-Western Mission Boards and Societies.

African New Religious Movements. *See* African Initiated Church Movement.

African Theology. The year 1956 symbolizes the official beginning of African theology, as it is usually understood. Two important publications, one Catholic and one Protestant, make that year an important milestone for African theology. The Catholic publication, entitled *Des prêtres noirs s'interrogent et suggèrent*, was the collective work of black priests from Africa and Haiti. They suggested a real africanization of the church. For the Protestants, Paul D. Fueter's article "Theological Education in Africa," published in the *International Review of Missions* (45 [1956]: 377–95), signaled the recognition of the need to develop an African expression of theology.

Recognizing 1956 as a pivotal year for African theology does not mean, however, that all discussions related to the africanization of Christianity begin with that date. It is likely that the first African converts to the Christian faith embarked on intuitive and unconscious "African theologizing" (*see* Walls). Toward the end of the nineteenth century, however, people such as Mojola Agbebi (1860–1917) were deliberately calling for the integration of Christianity and African culture. On April 7, 1889, Agbebi declared: "To render Christianity indigenous to Africa, it must be watered by native hands, pruned with the native hatchet, and tended with the native earth" (Ayandele, p. 18). Since "rendering Christianity indigenous to Africa" is an important aspect of African theology, regardless of how one defines it, Mojola Agbebi may be considered one of its precursors.

Missiologists and theologians have devoted much time and energy to defining African theology, especially in the early discussions of the subject. Noting the lack of consensus among scholars regarding the meaning of African theology, Ghanaian J. K. Agbeti suggested that "Christian Theology . . . expressed by African theologians using African thought forms" should be distinguished from "African Theology"; the latter being "the interpretation of the pre-Christian and pre-Moslem African peoples' experience of their God" (1972, p. 6). Scholars have not adopted Agbeti's distinction as a general practice. In fact Agbeti's attempt at clarification has generated confusion

and drew sharp criticism from Nigerian Byang H. Kato.

Kato pointed out, correctly, that Agbeti's definition of African theology fits African Traditional Religions better than it does Christianity. Kato contends that Agbeti's "basic concern . . . is an attempt to synthesize Christianity with African traditional religions" (*Theological Pitfalls*, p. 55). It should be noted, however, that the views of Agbeti and Kato are not as diametrically opposed as it may seem. Both agree that Christian theology should be made indigenous to Africa. When, for instance, Agbeti states that "Christianity and its theology will remain essentially the same universally, even though the expression of the faith may differ from place to place" (Agbeti, p. 7), he expresses one of Kato's basic convictions. One may also compare Agbeti's call to African Christian theologians to indigenize Christian theology with the following statement from Kato: "The noble desire to indigenize Christianity in Africa must not be forsaken. An indigenous theology is a necessity" (*Theological Pitfalls*, p. 16). It is therefore somewhat unfortunate that Kato's depiction of African theology is the basis on which many evangelicals evaluate the whole movement. Evangelicals may prefer a different terminology, such as "African Christian Theology," for example, and they should not conclude that everyone using the term "African theology" advocates Syncretism.

There may be disagreement about what name to give to the process of indigenizing Christian theology in Africa; nevertheless, the various families of the Christian faith recognize the legitimacy of seeking ways to develop Christian theologies related to African realities. This represents a major step forward in light of the dissenting voices, warning of the dangers of such a search, often heard in the 1950s and 1960s. In the broadest sense, African Christian theology "[is] done in Africa, . . . to a certain degree arises out of the identity of African people, draws on African categories of thought and speaks to the historical situation of African people" (Dickson, Kalilombe, and Presler, p. 94). Taking into account the four characteristics of locality, identity, cognition, and history in producing theology can minimize foreignness. These characteristics also provide theologians with a basis from which to generate the relevant issues.

An examination of the literature on African theology indicates that the authors tend to deal with the following major issues: culture, color, poverty, and nation building/reconstruction. The trends and contents of African theology relate to the issue chosen by the theologian and how that issue is treated. The focus on culture leads to African contextual or inculturation theologies while making color the primary concern leads to black theology. Similarly, liberation theology wrestles with the issue of poverty and the theology of reconstruction seeks Christian solutions to the present political, economic, and social crises of the continent.

Contextual or inculturation theologies represent the oldest kind of African theology. Much of the theological output in Africa can be classified in this category. Here African cultures and religions are taken seriously in the formulation of Christian theology. Mbiti's proposal that eschatology be built on an African concept of time, Sawyer's and Sundkler's focus on the African concept of the Great Family as the basis for ecclesiology in Africa, or Christology portraying Christ as Ancestor or Master of initiation (Nyamiti, Bujo, and Sanon) are all examples of this kind of theology. Evangelicals have generally expressed reservations and criticisms over some of the unbiblical excesses contained in these theologies. They are not, however, against the judicious usage of elements of African cultures, religions, and thought forms. Kato, who is often cited for his extreme evangelical negative views of African cultures, states clearly: "Every effort should be made to make the gospel indigenous in the local culture where it has been introduced. . . . I am fully in favour of the ever-abiding gospel being expressed within the context of Africa, for Africans to understand" (*African Cultural Revolution*, p. 54).

Scholars have not devoted the same time and energy to black theology, liberation theology, and the theology of reconstruction as they have given to contextual theologies. Black theology is primarily a movement in South Africa during the apartheid years and its concerns make it similar to black theology in the United States. Jean-Marc Ela, from Cameroon, has vigorously and consistently articulated an African liberation theology but liberation theology has not acquired the same status in Africa as it has in Latin America.

The theology of reconstruction is rather recent since it originated in the decade of the 1990s. Many of the proponents of the theology of reconstruction have connections with the All Africa Conference of Churches. The initial impetus was provided in essays presented at the March 1990 General Committee of the All Africa Conference of Churches. Kenyan J. N. K. Mugambi's book *From Liberation to Reconstruction: African Christian Theology After the Cold War* was published in 1995. Advocates of the theology of reconstruction also include Congolese Kä Mana and Rwandan André Karamaga. It is difficult to ascertain the specific contents of this theology. It appears to be more a program for Christian involvement in the renaissance of African nations. The theology of reconstruction will likely be the subject of much debate in the future.

Theological currents come and go in Africa as in the rest of the world. For African theology the challenge is to serve the church in Africa without being a footnote of Western theology or an exotic mixture of Christianity and African culture.

African theology is not a program or a process for crafting new Christian doctrines. It is rather an attempt to state biblical teaching and Christian doctrine in language and thought forms understandable to contemporary Africans. In that sense, African theology is not very different from efforts at contemporizing the Christian message in the world and through the generations. In their quest for securing the Christian faith firmly within African realities, African theologians have been forced to reexamine the nature of Christian theology and its purpose. In this process of reexamination, they "have recaptured the character of theology as Christian intellectual activity on the frontier with the non-Christian world, and hence as essentially communicative, evangelistic and missionary" (Bediako, p. 259). In an era of transition for both missiology and theology, this contribution of African theologians has significance for Africa and global Christianity.

TITE TIÉNOU

Bibliography. J. K. Agbeti, *Presence* 5:3 (1972); E. A. Ayandele, *A Visionary of the African Church*; K. Bediako, *Christianity in Africa: The Renewal of a Non-Western Religion*; B. Bujo, *African Theology in Its Social Context*; K. A. Dickson, P. A. Kalilombe, and T. Presler, *Mission Studies* 2:1 (1985): 93–96; R. Gibellini, ed., *Paths of African Theology*; B. H. Kato, *African Cultural Revolution and the Christian Faith*; idem, *Theological Pitfalls in Africa*; S. Ngewa, M. Shaw, and T. Tiénou, eds., *Issues in African Christian Theology*; J. Parratt, ed., *A Reader in African Christian Theology*, 2nd ed.; E. E. Uzukwu, *A Listening Church: Autonomy and Communion in African Churches*; A. F. Walls, *IBMR* 21:4 (October 1997), pp. 146–53.

African Traditional Religions. General designation for the religions of the ethnic groups of Africa. It does not describe a specific religion. It does not refer to the religious system of any particular group. By using expressions such as "African Traditional Religions," "African Primal Religions," or "African Religion," scholars seek to distinguish the indigenous religions of Africa from foreign and imported ones such as Christianity, Islam, Hinduism or Buddhism.

Scholars of religion in Africa do not agree among themselves on the use of the plural for the term chosen to group together and describe the indigenous religious beliefs of African peoples. They also disagree on the necessity of keeping adjectives like "traditional" and "primal." There is, however, near unanimity about the fact that certain terms used in the past are no longer adequate or appropriate. For example, African religions have been called primitive, savage, native, tribal, pagan, animistic, or heathen. This way of describing African religions is now found mostly in older studies. Occasionally, in polemical literature, one may still see references to idolatry and fetishism as the main characteristics of African religions. "African Traditional Religions" and "African Religion" are, nevertheless, the terms most commonly used in current studies.

The preference for African Traditional Religions, African Religion, or an equivalent term represents an important shift in understanding African religious beliefs and systems. This shift in understanding and depicting the religions of Africa is a recognition of the fact that these religions must be studied in their own right. They are not varieties of primitive religion. They must be viewed as major living religions. In that sense, African religions belong in the category "world religions." One should not think, therefore, that "traditional" in African Traditional Religions indicates that these are dead or dying religions. They are the beliefs and practices of contemporary Africans. Their present vitality is best suggested by the use of African Religions or Religion since the adjective "traditional" may imply that these religions are either "past" or practiced by "non-modern" Africans.

Should one approach the study of religion in Africa with the assumption of unity or multiplicity? Are we faced with many ethnic religions or are these religions different manifestations of a coherent African religion? If a single coherent African religion does not exist, how useful is the linking together of all indigenous African religions? These questions have fueled much debate among students of religion in Africa. There seems to be a growing consensus that unity is a better way of conceptualizing the religious beliefs and practices of Africans. One must, however, use caution in generalizing about religion in Africa. One should neither proceed too quickly to make comparisons nor refrain from noting similarities. General and comparative studies of religion in Africa are indicated when one deals with questions of religious presuppositions, worldview, and structure. This kind of study is useful in its description of broad and general characteristics which may be common to the majority of African religions. For concrete everyday religious life and practice, however, there is need to be as specific as possible: for example, one may investigate the doctrines and practices of Yoruba or Akamba religion. Numerous monograph studies of African religions by anthropologists and others are representative of this approach. These and other specific studies provide the necessary complement to general comparative descriptions of African religion. They elucidate the ethnic grounding of these religions, thereby depicting the particular African traits.

Whether one studies the religion of a particular ethnic group or attempts to understand the general characteristics of African religions, one faces an important challenge: African religions do not have known founders or sacred books preserving their teachings and doctrines. Oral narratives and rituals are therefore the main materials from which scholars derive the beliefs of African peoples.

The examination of African religious ceremonies and narratives reveals that they focus on the importance of affirming life. A basic assumption seems to be that life is essentially good and that, ideally, people should have health and prosperity and enjoy fulfillment, honor, and progeny in the world. Yet, in their experience in the world, people seldom attain this ideal good life. Evil forces tend to frustrate people's destiny or prevent the enjoyment of full life. Since evil forces, visible and invisible, destroy life, people need to find ways to protect themselves and maximize life. This seems to be one of the foundational principles undergirding African religious practices. It provides the basis for understanding the purpose of religion as the prevention of misfortune and the maximization of good fortune.

The focus on preventing misfortune and maximizing good fortune makes African religions anthropocentric; that is, a major goal of African religions is to ensure the present well-being of humans and their communities. Harmony between spiritual and physical forces, the environment, and humans is the prerequisite for the well-being of the individual and the community. God, the all-powerful Creator of all things, is believed to be benevolent. In that sense, harmony, success, and abundant life come from him. But God is rather uninvolved in the daily lives of humans. He has given the responsibility of regulating human lives to spiritual entities that can be called "minor deities." In this regard, Joseph Osei-Bonsu notes that "[t]he idea of minor deities is found among our people. These are believed to be the sons of the Supreme Being, created by him, and to whom he has delegated the supervision of the affairs of this world" (1990, 354).

Mediation between God and humans is the chief religious role of the minor deities. They share this role with the ancestors, the elders, and the various religious functionaries of African societies. Harmony in the world and all the conditions for health, prosperity, and abundant life are achieved by the mediation of these multiple intermediaries. This conception of mediation is crucial for understanding the essence of African religions. Mediation is also one of the fundamental points of divergence between African religions and Christianity since "the idea of intermediary divinities has no place in Christianity" (ibid.).

The relationship between God and the mediators, taken together with the focus on the "lesser divinities," helps explain why it is nearly impossible to solve the nature of theism in African religions. One cannot categorically state that African religions are either monotheistic or polytheistic. Belief in God, the One and Supreme High Being, is widespread. Yet, the Supreme Being may not be approached without the help of intermediaries. This means that theism in African religions can be described as ontological monotheism with liturgical polytheism. It is liturgical polytheism that makes African religions pragmatic, anthropocentric, and resilient.

The utilitarian characteristic of African religions and their anthropocentric spirituality make them appealing to many modern Africans, especially those who want to live in continuity with Africa's indigenous cultures and religions while embracing modernity. African religions have shown a remarkable ability for adapting to change. They have not disappeared in the encounter of African peoples with modernity, secularization, and missionary religions such as Christianity or Islam. The capacity for adaptation has assured survival for African religions over the years. More recently, survival has given way to resurgence. The resurgence of African religions means that they will continue to be an important dimension of the context of Christian mission in Africa for the foreseeable future. Christian missionaries, evangelists, and theologians who are interested in Africa cannot, therefore, afford to ignore or neglect the study of African religions.

TITE TIÉNOU

Bibliography. R. J. Gehman, *African Traditional Religion in Biblical Perspective;* L. Magesa, *African Religion: The Moral Traditions of Abundant Life;* J. S. Mbiti, *Concepts of God in Africa;* J. Osei-Bonsu, *AFER: African Ecclesial Review* 32:6 (December 1990): 346–58.

Aggrey, J. E. Kwegyir (1875–1927). Ghanaian educator in the United States. At the age of 13 Aggrey joined other youth and a missionary on preaching trips. A year later, he made his own decision for Christ. He began teaching first in a village and then at Wesleyan Centenary Memorial School, where he also taught Sunday school and preached. He developed as a scholar and a teacher, retranslating portions of the Fanti Bible and helping to prepare a book of Fanti hymns.

In 1898 Aggrey was asked to become headmaster, but chose instead to leave for further education in the United States. He attended Livingstone College in Salisbury, North Carolina, earning the B.A. and M.A. He also received a D.D. from Hood Theological Seminary. Years later he took another M.A. degree and completed Ph.D. course work at Columbia University.

From 1902 to 1920 Aggrey was a faculty member at Livingstone; he also took on responsibilities as a pastor from 1914 to 1920. His ability to articulate clearly African issues to white audiences led to appointment as the only nonwhite member of the prestigious Phelps-Stokes Com-

mission to study education in Africa. In 1924 he accepted an appointment as the first staff member and one of the vice-principals of Achimota College in Ghana, an institution designed to remedy the faults in African education pointed out by the Commission's report. In 1927 he returned to the United States to continue his Ph.D. work but died of meningitis before it was completed. An early African voice for recognition of African capabilities, Aggrey excelled as a scholar, professor, pastor, and international spokesman for relevant African education.

DONALD K. SMITH

Bibliography. E. C. Smith, *Aggrey of Africa.*

Agnew, Eliza (1807–83). American missionary to Sri Lanka. Born in New York City, Agnew dedicated her life to missionary service while she was still a girl, but she did not actually sail from Boston to Sri Lanka until 1839, after the death of her parents. She is believed to be the first single woman missionary to Sri Lanka.

Agnew served for forty years as principal of the AMERICAN BOARD OF COMMISSIONERS FOR FOREIGN MISSIONS' Uduville girls' boarding school. Founded in 1824, the school had ninety-five students when Agnew arrived to help overworked missionary wives. During her tenure, Agnew instructed and influenced about 1,300 young women, more than 600 of whom made professions of Christian faith. Her three and four generations of pupils often returned to their homes as Christian wives and teachers.

Agnew never left Sri Lanka. During vacations, she visited many of her former students, encouraging them in their faith. Weathering setbacks to the school prompted by the "Three Self" movement toward the indigenization of missions, Agnew retired in 1879, a stalwart supporter of female education. She died, having established a reputation as the "Mother of a Thousand Daughters" for her work in Uduville, Jaffna province.

STANLEY M. GUTHRIE

Bibliography. A. R. Gracey, *Eminent Missionary Women;* P. E. Kretzmann, *Glimpses of the Lives of Great Missionary Women.*

Agnosticism. Refusal to attempt answers to certain religious questions and specifically to the question of the existence of God. Such a perspective is usually justified by appeal to the lack of sufficient evidence on which to base a meaningful answer.

The term itself, which calls to mind the reference to the "unknown [*agnosto*] god" in Acts 17:23, appears to have been coined by Thomas Huxley in 1869. The concept was affirmed by twentieth-century logical positivism, a short-lived philosophical movement building on the empiricism of David Hume. Since it appeared to be impossible to specify a circumstance in which the religious proposition "God is love" could be falsified (an explanation could always be found for any apparent contraindication), the proposition itself was, in positivist terms, "meaningless." Friedrich Engels, in a celebrated comment, dismissed the agnostics as "shamefaced atheists."

There is, of course, a place for a thoughtful agnosticism on some religious issues, most obviously where competent theologians are themselves divided. The nature of heaven and the duration of HELL are clear examples. More radical religious agnosticism leads inevitably to the elimination of explicit doctrinal beliefs.

Agnosticism as related to belief in the existence of God, however, is a more complex matter. Muslim radical agnosticism at this point, for example, leads to a negative hypostatization: when applied to God, language is emptied of meaning. Furthermore, that the consequences of belief or unbelief are discernible both in undoubted time and in prospective eternity brings into question the very possibility of agnosticism. Our conduct unequivocally demonstrates belief or unbelief. As Blaise Pascal insisted, we began our journey in life years ago *(vous êtes déjà embarqué)* and have already been compelled to make moral and ethical decisions, and in making those decisions we have inescapably demonstrated either our belief or our unbelief.

F. PETER COTTERELL

Bibliography. R. A. Armstrong, *Agnosticism and Theism in the Nineteenth Century;* R. Flint, *Agnosticism.*

Agricultural Missions. Agriculture is the main means of livelihood for 65 percent to 90 percent of the population in most African, Asian, and Latin American countries. Even for industrialized countries such as the United Kingdom, where farmers represent less than 2 percent of the workforce, agricultural mission is vitally needed.

The practice of agriculture involves caring management or stewardship of land and natural resources in order to satisfy several objectives, including food production, maintenance of the environment (e.g., the soil and habitat), conservation of genetic resources (of both domesticated and wild species), provision of creative employment for people, sustenance of strategic stocks of food against poor harvests, and the integration with other uses of land for human welfare.

Aims of Agricultural Mission. Agricultural missionary work aims to present the good news of Jesus Christ in rural areas so that this gospel transforms not only individuals and their social relationships, but also the way they farm. In short, agricultural missions seek to promote living and farming to the glory of God. In effect,

God has provided two means of conveying how this should be done—creation and the Bible—which are perceived through the senses and conscience, and which require the motivation of the Holy Spirit to enable us to farm accordingly. The creation mandate given to humankind is expressed in Genesis 1:26–31, notably the assignment of "dominion" (meaning in Hebrew, "complete authority") and the subsequent description of plants "pleasant to the eyes and good for food" (Gen. 2:8). Wisdom and discernment are needed to pursue a course of development that is not only economic, but also social, and which addresses the whole person, body, mind, and spirit.

The right pursuit of agriculture, specific to each locality, has a crucial part to play in managing change and increasing well-being of the local people. The *local* principle is extremely important: experience is the treasure of years, and generations of local farmers have accumulated much wealth of this kind. It is the task of the agricultural missionary to learn, respect, and operate within this fund of local experience, knowledge, and wisdom, introducing new ideas from elsewhere only if technically, economically, and socioculturally appropriate. It may also be the missionary's task to help people discern local beliefs and practices that may run counter to the will and purposes of God. While some non-Christian beliefs may leave people in undeveloped bondage, uncontrolled materialism leads to overexploitation of land, plants, animals, and people. Agricultural missionaries need not only technical agricultural competence and wholistic biblical understanding, but also humility to learn from local farmers and cultural sensitivity to facilitate beneficial changes.

Activities. Agricultural missions comprise a wide variety of activities. In Latin America missions have developed demonstration farms managed at orphanages, and engage in land right work for justice and reconciliation. In many countries of Africa, farmers' savings clubs and cooperatives assist farmers financially and help train leadership. Services are also operated to enable farmers to combine responsible Christian principles in their farming practice. Additionally, rural development counseling is provided by RURCON (Rural Development Counselors for Christian Churches in Africa). In Europe, the "Farm Crisis Network" was set up to help stressed European farmers, and the Christian Farmers' Association was established for united action. In North America, agricultural communities run by Christians have been established, some of which are designed to provide a place where the needy such as ex-convicts can rehabilitate and develop marketable work skills. In countries in Asia, tree-planting services and alternative farming schemes have been established. Around the world, teaching agriculture in schools, colleges, and universities provides the opportunity to develop appropriate agricultural techniques.

Summary. In addition to the development of appropriate agricultural techniques and land stewardship, agricultural missions involve at least three critical thrusts. The first is *contextual evangelism,* communicating the gospel to and through people who live and work in an agricultural context. The second is *church growth,* seeking to help improve and manage agricultural development as part of the life and witness of local churches. Finally is *pastoral care,* which includes ministry to those engaged in agriculture, and/or agricultural ethics and assisting the application of biblical principles to farm practice and agricultural policy formulation.

JOHN WIBBERLEY

Bibliography. S. Higginbottom, *The Gospel and the Plow, Or, the Old Gospel and Modern Farming in Ancient India;* B. H. Hunnicutt and W. W. Reid, *The Story of Agricultural Missions;* I. W. Moomaw, *Deep Furrows: Goals, Methods and Results of Those Who Work Toward a Brighter Tomorrow.*

Aidan of Lindisfarne (d. 651). Irish missionary to northern Britain. Oswald, king of Northumbria, came to Christ in 634 after a vision in which COLUMBA OF IONA assured him of victory in battle. Victorious, he requested someone from the monastery at Iona to revive the faith initially established in Northumbria by PAULINUS but since lapsed. The first monk sent, traditionally named Corman, returned unsuccessful. Aidan was subsequently commissioned to the work. He walked to his assignment, evangelizing as he went. Given space on the island of Lindisfarne, he established a monastery. Aidan and his followers (WILFRED was instructed there) carried the message of Christ throughout northern England and southwest Scotland.

A. SCOTT MOREAU

Bibliography. B. Colgrave, *NCE,* 1:224; A. C. Fryer, *Aidan, Apostle of the North; ODCC;* S. Neill, *HCM.*

AIDS and Mission. *A Global Overview.* AIDS (acquired immune-deficiency syndrome), as a global pandemic, has provided a unique challenge and opportunity to the church: a challenge to deal with life's most fundamental moral and ethical issues, and an opportunity for service to those in need.

Appearing in the late 1970s, AIDS is currently one of the most critical health problems in the world. By 2020 there will be an estimated 55 million cases of HIV (human immunodeficiency virus) infection. In African countries with advanced HIV/AIDS epidemics life expectancy at birth has declined—to 37 years in Uganda, for example, the lowest global life expectancy. By 2010 a decline of 25 years in life expectancy is predicted for a number of African and Asian countries. In Zimbabwe it could reduce life expectancy from 70 to 40 years in the next 15 years. Sub-saharan Africa, with less than 10 percent of the world's population, has 70 percent of the world's population infected with HIV.

Asia, the world's most populous region, is poised as the next epicenter of the epidemic. Initially spread in the region primarily by drug injection and men having sex with men, heterosexual transmission is now the primary cause of infection. It is expected that child mortality in Thailand, where the sex-tourism industry has fueled the epidemic, will triple in the next 15 years without a sharp decline in the rate of HIV infection. Latin America and the Caribbean, with 8.4 percent of the world's population, have 11.5 percent of the HIV infection. Primarily a homosexual and bisexual epidemic initially, heterosexual contact is becoming the primary mode of transmission, with needle sharing also being common.

Of the 8,500 new cases of HIV infection which occur daily, 90 percent are in the developing world. Much of Eastern Europe and most countries in the former Soviet Union, relatively free of AIDS prior to the political shifts of the late 1980s, are in the earlier stages of the epidemic, as are Bangladesh, the Philippines, parts of China, and India.

Key Issues. The economic and social impact of AIDS in the developing world is profound because it characteristically affects adults during the most economically productive ages of 15 to 25. A Kenyan study estimated labor costs for some businesses could increase by 23 percent due to absenteeism, the cost of training new workers, death benefits, and health care costs by the year 2005. Service agencies strain to meet demands created by the epidemic, and extended family systems stagger under the burden of increased dependents and decreasing numbers of providers. In heavily affected areas of Asia and Africa 30 to 50 percent of household income is devoted to care of family members with AIDS and funeral expenses may cost a year's income.

Populations with behaviors that put them at high risk for HIV infection include prostitutes and their clients, prisoners, long-distance truckers, homosexual and bisexual men, soldiers, police officers, and migrant workers. Sexual transmission of the virus is more efficient from men to women than from women to men. Women also have higher levels of undiagnosed sexually transmitted diseases. Worldwide, these two factors mean that women are becoming infected at faster rates than men.

Wealthy countries have access to the antiretrovirals and other drugs that prolong the lives of HIV-positive individuals. Worldwide 90 percent of those infected are not aware of their infection, due to lack of access to costly AIDS tests. The rise of tuberculosis (TB) rates is directly correlated to HIV prevalence and inversely correlated with the quality of TB programs.

Responding to the AIDS Pandemic: International Agencies, Governments, Nongovernment Organizations (NGOs), and Churches. The World Health Organization's Global Program on AIDS, under the dynamic leadership of Jonathan Mann, initiated a global response to HIV/AIDS during the first decade of the epidemic. Subsequently, UNAIDS has been the United Nation's agency coordinating the global response. Ministries of Health throughout the world, often dealing with multiple discreet epidemics in their countries, have become deeply involved in responses to AIDS as their populations have been affected by the epidemic. USAID (United States Agency for International Development) has provided strategic leadership and significant funding through AIDSCAP (AIDS Control and Prevention Project). NGOs have also played a crucial role in responding to AIDS. MAP International, a Christian NGO working to build the capacity of churches in East and southern Africa, partnered with the Association of Evangelicals in Africa and the Evangelical Association of Uganda in 1994 to bring 150 participants from 28 countries for the All Africa AIDS and the Church Consultation, held in Kampala, Uganda. A powerful declaration to the church resulted from the conference, urging that AIDS issues become a priority on the agenda of the church. Local initiatives, such as the Kenya Christian AIDS Network (Kenyan CAN or KCAN), with more than 30 branches meeting regularly, sprang up within two years after the conference.

A number of Christian AIDS programs are linked to mission hospitals. Under the leadership of Major Ruth Schoch, a Swiss Salvation Army office nurse and midwife who had already served twenty years in the Republic of Zambia, a Bethany Ward for the terminally ill was established in 1987 and a significant community-based initiative addressing AIDS was initiated at the Salvation Army's Chikankata Hospital. Similarly, the Vanga Evangelical Hospital—a 400-bed hospital with eight full-time physicians under the administration of the Baptist Community of Western Zaire—offers whole-person care, including counseling, prayer, and group meetings, to those with HIV/AIDS through an HIV care program. In Nigeria the SIM AIDS Project (SIM International) is helping Christians know how to minister to those affected by AIDS and is developing biblical teachings on sexuality, marital relationships, and being made in God's image. Campus Crusade's Youth at the Crossroads has developed Life at the Crossroads, a substantial educational curriculum program that addresses AIDS from a positive biblical viewpoint.

Agencies promoting networking among the many Christian AIDS initiatives, often modest programs linked to a local church or as free-standing grass-roots organizations, have been particularly valuable in strengthening the global response of churches. AIDS Intercessors, for example, provides a monthly prayer diary with updates on the AIDS programs of more than forty Christian groups. Others agencies have multiple affiliates. AIDS Care Education and Training (ACET), based in London and started by Patrick Dixon, has prevention and care programs in Romania, Thailand, Tanzania, Uganda, and throughout the United Kingdom.

HIV/AIDS has unquestionably provided the church with one of its greatest challenges and most significant opportunities for ministry—and the church is responding.

EVVY CAMPBELL

Bibliography. G. Capdevila, *Inter Press Service English News Wire,* Nov. 28, 1997; P. Dixon, *The Truth About AIDS;* D. Dortzbach, *AIDS in Kenya: The Church's Challenge;* H. Dunphy, *The Columbian,* Nov. 3, 1997, A-2; D. E. Fountain, *Care of Persons with AIDS in a Christian Hospital;* E. B. Marks, Jr., *Life at the Cross Roads: An Educational Curriculum Program from Youth at the Crossroads.*

Aitolos, Kosmas (1714–79). Greek Orthodox missionary evangelist in the Balkans. Born in the Greek province of Aitolia, Kosmas Aitolos was raised in a poor family with no opportunity for education. Kosmas's search for an education and his thirst for God led him to the Philotheu monastery on Mount Athos in 1743. For seventeen years, Kosmas lived a life of seclusion and studied diligently. Through his study he realized that Christians should be concerned not just with their own salvation, but also with the salvation of others.

Thus motivated, Kosmas left the monastery in 1760 and became an itinerant preacher throughout northern Greece, Albania, and southern Serbia. For twenty years, he traveled from village to village preaching the gospel in a simple, contemporary form that villagers could understand. He helped found more than two hundred elementary schools and ten "higher" schools. His ultimate purpose in starting schools was for people to overcome their illiteracy and begin reading the Bible and church fathers. Kosmas's life and work are considered one of the greatest influences in helping to preserve and strengthen Christianity in the Balkans during the eighteenth century. Kosmas was martyred by hanging in the village of Kalinkontasi.

LUKE A. VERONIS

Bibliography. C. Cavarnos, *St. Cosmas Aitolos;* N. M. Vaporis, *Father Kosmas: The Apostle of the Poor;* L. A. Veronis, *Missionaries, Monks and Martyrs: Making Disciples of All Nations.*

Albania *(Est. 2000 pop.: 3,624,000; 28,748 sq. km. [11,100 sq. mi.]).* Albania, one of the poorest countries in Europe, located in the southern Balkans with a population of 3.6 million people, has experienced tremendous religious persecution in the past. Albania's political history has strongly influenced the efforts of missionaries to evangelize. In spite of a Christian presence as early as A.D. 200, prior to the communist regime, Islam was the major religion of Albania. The Orthodox and Roman Catholic Churches also had a strong presence. Overall, the country was accepting of the religious influences that existed. The tolerance level changed dramatically when the Communists took over in 1945.

Enver Hoxha, the communist dictator, began an active campaign against religious institutions. Despite the adoption of a communist constitution that guaranteed freedom of religion, he issued decrees that allowed the government to control the activities of religious institutions. Many clergy and believers were tried, tortured, and executed by the government. All formal worship was eventually eradicated.

Upon Hoxha's death in 1991, a two-party democratic form of government was elected to run the country. Ramiz Alia, the successor to Hoxha, took a tolerant stance toward religious practice. The ban on religious services was lifted and 95 percent of all mosques and churches that had been damaged during the communist rule were restored. The drastic change in attitude toward religion has been very significant for Christian mission efforts in Albania.

After the fall of communism, a number of mission agencies entered the country to evangelize and plant churches, many of which reported excellent results in their evangelistic efforts. More recently, the Christian Broadcasting Network broadcast the first programs with a Christian message over government-owned television, with a viewership of 1.8 million, over half of the population. The future of evangelical missions in Albania is questionable, however, due to the fact that the Catholics, Orthodox, and Muslims are trying to pass legislation that will not allow other religions to exist within the country. If this legislation is passed, Albania will once again return to being a country with limited religious freedoms.

MARKUS WAGNER

Bibliography. R. Peterson, *Tomorrow You Die.*

Aldersey, Mary Ann (1797–1868). English pioneer missionary to China. Born in a prosperous nonconformist family in London, she attended classes in Chinese taught by ROBERT MORRISON when he visited England in 1824–26. She made generous gifts to the LONDON MISSIONARY SOCIETY (LMS) and when she was free from family duties she went to Batavia (1837) and established a school for Chinese girls. In 1843, when the Treaty Ports were opened, she moved to Ningpo, where she continued to conduct a school until 1861. She had close links with LMS, but was never an agent of any society. Several of her teachers were the Chinese-speaking daughters of missionaries, including Maria Dyer, whose marriage to JAMES HUDSON TAYLOR she strongly opposed, and Mary Ann Leisk, who married William Russell, later bishop of North China. In 1861 she handed her school over to the CHURCH MISSION SOCIETY (CMS) and retired to Adelaide, Australia, where she lived until her death. She appears to have been the first unmarried woman missionary to have worked in China, and the first, male or female, to reach Ningpo. She worked in Malacca and Ningpo for almost twenty-four years, and ought to be remembered, not only for her differences with Hudson Taylor, but as a pioneer worker in China.

JOCELYN MURRAY

Bibliography. E. A. White, *A Woman Pioneer in China: The Life of Mary Ann Aldersey;* J. Pollock, *Hudson Taylor and Maria. Pioneers in China;* D. MacGillivray, ed., *A Century of Protestant Missions in China (1807–1907).*

Algeria *(Est. 2000 pop.: 31,158,000; 2,381,741 sq. km. [919,590 sq. mi.]).* "I see many knights going to the Holy Land beyond the seas, and thinking that they can acquire it by force of arms. . . . It seems to me that the conquest . . . ought to be attempted . . . by love and prayers, and the pouring out of tears and blood." These are the words of RAYMON LULL, who became a missionary martyr in Algeria in 1315.

Since then, the largest continuous Protestant mission effort pouring out tears and blood among the Algerians has been the North Africa Mission (now the Arab World Ministries), established in 1881 by a Briton, a Swiss, and a Druze. Other missions include the Plymouth Brethren (1885), Wesleyan Methodists (French) (1886), Algiers Mission Band (1888; merged with NAM in 1964), Rolland Mission (French) (1908), and Methodist (1908).

A Bible Society was established in 1881, and Bible reading rooms have attracted great interest when they have been allowed, though literacy is only 50 percent. Evangelizing through the desert as early as 1893, LILLIAS TROTTER reported again and again the great longing of the desert men for books. Today radio, Bible correspondence courses, the JESUS FILM in Kabyle Berber, Arabic and French languages, and locally produced music and Scripture tapes are received hungrily if clandestinely. Production cannot keep up with demand. Postal censorship is severe, however. Recipients may be interrogated by the police.

The gospel may have come to Algeria in the first century through believers in the large Algerian Jewish community. By the fourth century, North Africa had given birth to some of the finest Latin Christian theology, written by men like Augustine, Tertullian, and Cyprian. Vandals in the fifth century and Muslims in the eighth erased much of the church. Yet in the eleventh century five bishops remained. In 1645 the French Lazarists established a mission to ameliorate the suffering of the thousands of Europeans who had been captured by "Barbary pirates." By the nineteenth century, Catholic bishops, orders like the White Fathers and White Sisters, and hermits like Charles Foucauld sought to evangelize Algerians. But the French colonial government deported evangelists, removed crucifixes from mission hospitals, and forbade Muslims to enter the cathedral. During this century European Protestants immigrated in large numbers, bringing their churches and pastors. However, these showed little concern for Algerians, and departed at independence in 1962. After the bloody eight-year war for independence, Catholic and Protestant missions including the Salvation Army, Mennonites, and Friends helped rebuild the country.

In particular, the Berbers have responded to the gospel. Numbering perhaps 25 million across Africa, in Algeria Berbers may comprise 30 percent of the population. Somewhat independent in mountain villages, thousands have come to Christ. Indigenous leadership is vigorous and creative.

Since 1992 an uprising of Islamists has massacred 75,000 civilians. The outcome could significantly influence the rest of the Arab world toward radical or moderate governments. Meanwhile, as social trauma makes people more open to the gospel, believers meet in small Bible study groups. There is no seminary, though THEOLOGICAL EDUCATION BY EXTENSION is conducted.

MIRAM ADENEY

Bibliography. J. H. Kane, *A Global View of Christian Mission;* K. S. Latourette, *A History of the Expansion of Christanity;* P. St. John, *Until the Day Breaks . . . : The Life and Work of Lilias Trotter, Pioneer Missionary to Muslim North Africa;* S. Zwemer, *Raymond Lull: First Missionary to the Moslems.*

Alienation. Alienation describes the sense of deprivation and marginalization of persons who perceive that their once-fulfilled lives, or the lives to which they aspired, have lost their sense or possibility of personal fulfillment and satisfaction. Alienation may be attributed to a loss of norms, values, and a reassuring worldview, often brought about by abrupt change. This state corresponds to the condition denoted by the term ANOMIE. But alienation may also be linked to other disadvantages, including discrimination, exclusion, dislocation, the ravages of war and other human conflict, changes in technological and social organization, and oppressive political systems—which refer not just to subjective states but to concrete conditions. The concept of alienation derives from related theological and philosophical terms used from the times of Plotinus and Augustine to those of Hegel ("alienated spirit"), Feuerbach ("Man's alienation from his own material nature"), and Marx ("alienation labor").

In each case these terms carry the sense of estrangement and incompleteness resulting from one's separation from elements essential to personal realization. The cure is implied in the diagnosis: Hegel thought in terms of alienation from God, but saw religious forms and organization as themselves inhibiting spiritual wholeness; Feuerbach sought to restore humans to their rightful place in the material world; and Marx identified alienation primarily as social injustice. While evangelical use of the term "alienation" may be invested with these precedents, evangelicals generally apply alienation in the theological sense of viewing human sin (alienation from God) and redemption (reconciliation with God) as being the cause and antidote for all other human ills. People who respond to the gospel are primarily those who in some sense feel alienated—unfulfilled or dissatisfied. Evangelicalism at its roots is a promise of wholeness, LIBERATION from the bondage of sin, restitution to a community of transformed (born-again) believers, and an eschatological assurance of ultimate salvation.

DOUG PETERSEN

Bibliography. D. Lyon, *Karl Marx: An Assessment of His Life and Thought;* J. Míguez-Bonino, *Toward a Christian Political Ethic;* D. Petersen, *Not by Might Nor by Power: A Pentecostal Theology of Social Concern.*

Allan, George (c. 1870–1941). New Zealand missionary to Argentina and Bolivia and founder of Bolivian Indian Mission. Both Allan and his wife, Mary Stirling, were raised in South Otago and in Southland, New Zealand, in evangelical Presbyterian homes, and trained for missionary service at the Angus Missionary College in Adelaide, Australia. They became interested in service in South America, and were sent out to Buenos Aires in 1899 with the South American Evangelical Mission, which was based in Toronto. Allan's work took him on itinerant visits to Bolivia. His mission amalgamated with the Regions Beyond Missionary Union in 1903, but the Australasian committee and its eight workers became independent. In 1908 they formed a new body, the Bolivian Indian Mission, which was based in the small town of San Pedro.

The Allans initiated educational and evangelistic work for the Quechua and several Australians and New Zealanders joined their team of workers. The translation of the New Testament into Quechua was one of their achievements. In 1915 Allan founded a U.S. board of the mission, which resulted in a new influx of American missionaries. In 1930 the mission center was moved to Cochabamba and the work broadened to embrace Spanish-speaking Bolivians. Here Allan died, preceded by his wife in February of 1939. With quiet determination he had built a mission which later merged with SIM to create one of the great world missions.

PETER LINEHAM

Bibliography. M. A. Hudspith, *Ripening Fruit: A History of the Bolivian Indian Mission.*

Allen, Roland (1868–1947). English missionary to China and Africa and missions theorist. Roland Allen was born in England, studied at Oxford University, and was ordained in the Anglican Church in 1892. He went to China with the Society for the Propagation of the Gospel in Foreign Parts in 1895, but returned for health reasons in 1904 to serve as a parish priest. He resigned in 1907 in a dispute over baptism, but served as a chaplain on a hospital ship during World War I.

From the 1920s on he was something of an international missions consultant, working with groups trying to revive missionary vision. He visited churches in Canada, India, Kenya, Zimbabwe, and South Africa. Allen finally settled in Kenya in 1931 and lived there until he died. After observing what he considered the drawbacks of traditional missionary work, he revived the teachings of RUFUS ANDERSON and HENRY VENN and became a strong proponent of the so-called Three-Self theory, which holds that churches started by foreign agencies should become self-governing, self-supporting, and self-propagating (*see also* INDIGENOUS CHURCHES). Allen's somewhat iconoclastic approach to missions attracted wide interest among evangelical mission agencies. Largely because of his book, *Missionary Methods: St. Paul's or Ours* (1912), he ranks among the most influential when it comes to applying biblical principles to missionary work.

Allen was a prolific writer of letters and articles. His second most influential book was *The Spontaneous Expansion of the Church and the Causes Which Hinder It* (1927). There his deep commitment to the work of the Holy Spirit in missions came to full flower. He is credited with being the first to develop the connection between the HOLY SPIRIT and missions.

In that context he challenged what he saw as an overreliance on professionalism, money, and organization in mission. For example, he wrote: "There is a horrible tendency for an organization to grow in importance till it overshadows the end of its existence, and begins to exist for itself" (p. 98). This system rooted in the material and the professional actually squelches propagation of the gospel, he believed. His brief summation, *Missionary Principles,* expounds the principle that the presence of Christ in the missionary is the source from which all ministry springs. "The missionary spirit of Christ in us cannot rest until it finds an expression in some form of service," he wrote (p. 105).

Allen was an unusual blend of the pragmatist (trying to loose the church overseas from foreign control) and the preacher, driving missionary work back to first principles of biblical discipleship.

JIM REAPSOME

Bibliography. D. Paton, ed., *The Ministry of the Spirit: Selected Writings of Roland Allen;* idem, *Reform of the Ministry: A Study in the Work of Roland Allen;* H. J. B. Allen, *Roland Allen: Pioneer, Priest, and Prophet.*

Ambassador of God. A missionary's task is to represent God and his message to an alien world. This shows the special relationship between the Creator and the messenger, who is dispatched as an envoy, an ambassador of God. An ambassador is an official diplomatic agent of high rank who is sent out by a ruler or government as a public representative. A missionary is one who is sent out to work as a citizen of the KINGDOM OF GOD, representing truth and light in a world of deceit and darkness.

In the Old Testament there are numerous examples of God's ambassadors. Noah represented God's righteousness to unbelievers. Moses proclaimed God's power and justice in pharaoh's court. Joshua showed the might and strength of the Lord before the Canaanites. Both Gideon and Deborah were mediators between God and the rebellious and defeated Israelites. God's special agents, called to proclaim and to direct people to obedience, lived lives that were testimonies of faith and commitment. Daniel and Esther served in alien governments as ambassadors of God through their words and actions.

In the New Testament, Christ tells a parable of a ruler sending an emissary, a select delegation to negotiate peace (Luke 13:32). God's ambassadors are a select, chosen few who challenge the enemy and seek to negotiate eternal peace in the hearts of humanity. The apostle Paul wrote to the church at Corinth stating that "we are ambassadors for Christ, as though God were making his appeal through us" (2 Cor. 5:20). To the church at Ephesus he wrote, "I am an ambassador in chains" (Eph. 6:20). This refers to his imprisonment for openly proclaiming the good news of Jesus Christ. Paul measures himself as personally commissioned by Christ to present the gospel to the entire world. The Greek word *presbeuō* literally means a senior, one who is aged. However, Paul brings new meaning to the term. He is an elder statesperson representing the kingdom of

God before the rulers and their subjects on this earth.

Missionaries serve as ambassadors of God. They are believers in Jesus Christ to whom God imparts certain spiritual gifts, and calls and sends out to make disciples and preach the good news (Matt. 20:18–20; Rom. 10:15). As citizens of the kingdom of God, they are subject to God's laws and are under the authority of the Lord they represent before the rest of the world.

JOHN EASTERLING

American Bible Society. *See* BIBLE SOCIETIES.

American Board of Commissioners for Foreign Missions (ABCFM).

The ABCFM was the first and most important nineteenth-century American mission board. Samuel Mills, a child of the Second Great Awakening, led a group of students at Williams College to pledge themselves to missions in the "HAYSTACK PRAYER MEETING" in 1806. In 1810, as students at Andover Seminary, the group proposed to the Congregational Association of Massachusetts the formation of a foreign mission board.

In 1812 the ABCFM was incorporated, and its first five missionaries sailed for India. Out of the first group the JUDSONS and Luther Rice became Baptists, the Judsons going on to Burma (now Myanmar) while Rice returned to the United States to form the Baptist Missionary Union.

The Board's purpose was to propagate the gospel in "heathen" lands by supporting missionaries and diffusing the knowledge of the Holy Scriptures. Evangelism and church planting had the highest priority, with Bible translation important and social concerns subordinate. About half of its missionaries were Congregationalists; most of the others were Presbyterian or Reformed. The Board worked in thirty-four fields, which included indigenous Americans. When the Cherokees were expelled from their land in Georgia, two missionaries went to prison in protest; others accompanied the people on the "Trail of Tears." Traders had arrived in Hawaii by 1800; as a result, the native population had fallen by half, its culture disintegrating. In 1820 the missionaries came, and by 1840 the language was reduced to writing, most of the Bible translated, literature produced, schools established, and twenty thousand people, a fifth of the population, had become church members. The local rulers passed laws against prostitution, gambling, and drunkenness.

In the Middle East the goals were to work with Muslims, ancient Christian churches, and Jews. Success among Muslims was limited, and although the missionaries did not plan to PROSELYTIZE members of the older churches, converts to evangelical Christianity were expelled from those bodies, leading to the establishment of Protestant churches.

In Sumatra the first two missionaries were killed and eaten by the Bataks, but a church was later established among them by European missionaries.

The Bible was translated into a number of languages, many of which were first reduced to writing. Educational institutions from the primary to university levels were established, while PETER PARKER and John Scudder were acclaimed for their medical work in China and India.

RUFUS ANDERSON, a secretary of the Board from 1823 to 1866, was America's most outstanding mission leader and theoretician of the nineteenth century. He is best known for his formulation, along with HENRY VENN of the CMS, of the "THREE-SELF" formula, which stated that the goal was to establish churches that were self-governing, self-supporting, and self-propagating. He also advocated Christianization over civilization—Westernization—in an important debate.

The theological shift in New England Congregationalism in the last third of the nineteenth century greatly affected the Board and contributed to its eventual decline. But by 1959 it had sent out over 4,800 men and women. With the union of the Congregational and Evangelical and Reformed Churches in the 1950s the ABCFM became the United Church Board of World Ministries.

PAUL E. PIERSON

Bibliography. R. P. Beaver, ed., *To Advance the Gospel: Selections from the Writings of Rufus Anderson;* F. F. Goodsell, *You Shall Be My Witnesses;* C. J. Phillips, *Protestant America and the Pagan World, the American Board of Commissioners for Foreign Missions, 1810–1860.*

American Samoa

(Est. 2000 pop. 63,000; 197 sq. km. [76 sq. mi.]). American Samoa consists of five islands and two atolls, 2,300 miles south of Hawaii and 1,600 miles northeast of New Zealand. Complex rivalry between British, German, and American strategic interests in Samoa in the nineteenth century resulted in American Samoa becoming an unincorporated territory of the United States in 1900. Fifty percent of its 63,000 people are members of the Christian Congregational Church (formerly LMS), 20 percent are Roman Catholics, with Methodists and Mormons also prominent.

ALLAN K. DAVIDSON

SEE ALSO Polynesia.

American Society for Church Growth.

The American Society for Church Growth (ASCG) was founded in 1984 as the North American Society for Church Growth. C. PETER WAGNER served as the society's first president. The ASCG describes itself as "a professional association of Christian leaders worldwide whose ministry activities are based on the basic and key principles of church growth as originally developed by the late DONALD MCGAVRAN."

Membership in the ASCG includes those who specialize in monocultural contexts, as well as those who minister cross-culturally. It is open to professors, theoreticians, and practitioners, including pastors and denominational or parachurch leaders in the United States.

The ASCG's activities include an annual meeting and publication of the *Journal of the American Society for Church Growth*.

CHARLES VAN ENGEN

SEE ALSO Church Growth Movement.

Bibliography. T. S. Rainer, *The Book of Church Growth;* E. Towns, ed., *Evangelism and Church Growth: A Practical Encyclopedia;* E. Towns, J. N. Vaughan, and D. Siefert, eds., *The Complete Book of Church Growth.*

American Society of Missiology.

The American Society of Missiology is a professional association for mission studies in North America. It was founded in 1972 and grew out of a concern to provide "a community of scholarship, fellowship and mission" that would draw together not only professors of mission but mission administrators and missionaries as well. Its purpose is to maintain an interdisciplinary approach to the study of mission, giving attention to the historical, social, cultural, biblical, theological, and methodological aspects of mission. It does this within a conscious commitment to be inter-confessional, incorporating within its structures of governance a balance of representation from three major streams: Roman Catholic, conciliar Protestant, and independent/evangelical. The society's publications and presentations at its meetings reflect this tripartite constituency as well.

The society sustains publication efforts along several lines. It publishes one of the leading journals in the field of mission studies, *Missiology: An International Review,* a quarterly journal that picked up the heritage of *Practical Anthropology* when that journal ceased publication at the end of 1972 (*see also* JOURNALS OF MISSION AND MISSIOLOGY). *Missiology* continues the distinctive contributions of that prior journal within an expanded range of issues in the field of missiology. The journal represents the interdisciplinary approach of the society itself, giving attention to history, theology, anthropology, communication theory, religious encounter, ecumenics, and methodology.

In addition, monographs on critical issues in mission are published in the ASM Series, a series produced collaboratively with Orbis Books. In the first nineteen years since the initiation of the series in 1979, over twenty-five volumes appeared. In addition, another series was begun in the late 1990s to make available doctoral dissertations of importance in the field. The ASM Dissertation Series, published through University Press of America, produced its first volume in 1997.

From the outset, the ASM has maintained a close relationship with the ASSOCIATION OF PROFESSORS OF MISSION which normally holds its meetings in conjunction with those of the ASM. The ASM is a constituent society of the Council of Societies for the Study of Religion and an affiliate society in the INTERNATIONAL ASSOCIATION FOR MISSION STUDIES.

GEORGE R. HUNSBERGER

Bibliography. W. R. Shenk, *The American Society of Missiology 1972–87.*

Amerindian Religions. *See* INDIGENOUS AMERICAN RELIGIONS.

Amillennialism. As a term, amillennialism, like premillennialism and postmillennialism, was not coined until the 1840s. But, in fact, all three views are represented through the long history of the church. And they have shared much in common.

Shared Perspectives. Dominating those common features has been a confidence in the personal, visible, and glorious return of Jesus Christ to consummate his work of redemption and restoration begun with his life, death, and resurrection.

Also shared, with varieties of interpretation, has been the neo-Augustinian perception of this age stretching between the first and the second coming of Christ as a day of divine grace offered to the sinner.

In the years following the sixteenth century, that understanding combined especially with the colonialist expansion of Europe. An expanded knowledge of the world called for an expanded effort to announce that divine word of grace and forgiveness in Christ. And sadly, in that expansion, Western ethnocentrism often had difficulty in extracting "Christianizing" from "civilizing." Eschatology as Christ-centered hope too often began to look strangely like Western-centered progress.

Restraining this tendency toward the nationalization of eschatology were other beliefs shared in common by the three millennial viewpoints. The expectation of a full exhibition of the glorious reign of God on earth with Christ's appearance, of the physical resurrection from death, of the gathering in of "the fullness of the Gentiles" (Rom. 11:25), and the salvation of "all Israel" (Rom. 9:26) have had long standing in the church. These shared perspectives often create difficulties in too sharply dividing pre-nineteenth-century 'millenarianism' into specific schools (Murray, 1971, 48–49).

Missiological Trajectories. What are those particular features of amillennialism (sometimes called realized or inaugurated millennialism) that nurture the accomplishment of the missionary task?

First, the movement remains relatively unencumbered by the elaborate chronological details needed to insert a literal 1000-year period into an eschatological sequence. Its understanding of the millennium as the gospel age separating the first and second coming concentrates more on Christ as the center of history and Christ's return as the ultimate outcome of history. Its eschatological center thus tends to orbit more around Christology than around specific details immediately surrounding the second coming of the Lord.

Second, amillennialism, with postmillennialism, traces many of its theological roots to Puritanism's earlier emphasis on the sovereign rule of God in history. Missions, particularly in its Reformed expression, is then seen as still deeply *Missio Dei*.

In common with evangelical thought, late-nineteenth-century mission thinking has impacted this motivation with an additional focus on obedience to the GREAT COMMISSION (Beaver, 1968, 141–142). But the movement still clings to the union, formulated by Jonathan Edwards (1703–1758), of the themes of the divine reign of God and of the demand for regeneration, personal faith, and revival (Beaver, 1959, 67).

Third, this focus on the mission of God has made it somewhat easy for the movement to incorporate the current growing consensus in evangelical circles between missions and the KINGDOM OF GOD. In that consensus the kingdom is seen as the saving reign of God initiated by Christ's coming (the 'already') and to be consummated by his coming again (the 'not yet').

And for the amillennialist the missionary preaching of the kingdom's good news to all becomes a divine requirement given to the Christian community on its way to eschatological fulfillment (1 Cor. 9:16). Empowered by the Holy Spirit (Acts 1:8), the church is "under obligation" (Rom. 1:14) to announce that Christ has come to inaugurate the kingdom through his redemptive work (Mark 1:14–15; Luke 4:18–21).

Fourth, amillenialism sees eschatology ("the last days") as initiated by the redeeming work of Christ (1 Cor. 10:11; Heb. 1:2). This pleads for a strong element of continuity between our life in the Spirit in "the present age" and "in the age to come" (Eph. 1:21).

This continuity becomes a powerful incentive for a holistic understanding of missions as both word and deed, evangelism and socio-cultural involvement (Matt. 25:31–46). Because perfect righteousness and peace will characterize the kingdom's future we seek also their beginnings in the kingdom's present, yet imperfect, manifestation (2 Peter 3:11–14; Matt. 6:10).

Fifth, and finally, this same perception of amillennialism as missions "between the times" also underlines a sense of discontinuity. There is still the reality of sin to bar missionary enthusiasm and promote the nations' obstinate refusal of Christ. Over-optimism concerning the course of human history toward the gospel's consummation is restrained by the reality that "many are called but few are chosen" (Matt. 22:14).

History's Modifications. Amillennialism, like its counterparts, has not escaped reshaping in the history of the church. And that reshaping has not always strengthened its missionary dimensions.

Its strong emphasis on continuity and the church's eschatological role "between the times" can sometimes lead its supporters to a kind of church imperialism that blurs the line between the church and the KINGDOM OF GOD. Its sensitivity to discontinuity can find the church's missionary role reduced to that of guerrilla action within an institutional remnant. In doing so, its understanding of the presence of the kingdom in Christ can become a "world-avertive" shelter instead of a "worldformative" intrusion. And, in common with other millennial viewpoints, it can become so lost in chronological debates with those alternatives that it falls into eschatological paralysis.

HARVIE M. CONN

See also Millennial Thought.

Bibliography. R. P. Beaver, *Basileia*, pp. 60–75; idem, *Reinterpretation in American Church History*, pp. 113–51; J. DeJong, *As the Waters Cover the Sea: Millennial Expectations in the Rise of Anglo-American Missions, 1640–1810*; A. Hoekema, *The Bible and the Future;* I. Murray, *The Puritan Hope;* B. Nicholls, *In Word and Deed: Evangelism and Social Responsibility.*

Amersterdam 1983 and 1986. *See* INTERNATIONAL CONFERENCES FOR ITINERANT EVANGELISTS.

Amsterdam Assembly (1948). On August 23, 1948, the WORLD COUNCIL OF CHURCHES came into being by action of its first general assembly. This gathering, held from August 22 to September 4 in Amsterdam, culminated a process initiated in 1937 to bring together two streams of ecumenical life, the Faith and Order Movement and the Life and Work Movement, into a fully representative global assembly of churches. A total of 351 delegates from 44 nations and 147 denominations participated. The assembly adopted as its basis: "The World Council of Churches is a fellowship of churches which accept our Lord Jesus Christ as God and Savior." Deliberations focused on the church as the agency through which God would accomplish his purposes.

The theme of the Amsterdam Assembly, "Man's Disorder and God's Design," was considered in four sections: the universal church in God's design; the church's witness to God's design; the church and the disorder of society; the church and the international order. The second section in particular addressed issues related to mission and evangelism. Recognizing the existence and growth of the younger churches, it called for the whole church to set itself to the task of winning the whole world for Christ. Also, it stressed the close relationship between unity and inner renewal, and declared invalid the distinction between Christian and non-Christian nations.

The third section developed the concept of the responsible society, one which seeks to maintain the balance between justice and freedom. It critiqued the assumption of laissez-faire capitalism that justice will follow automatically the exercise of free enterprise, and the communist assumption that freedom will come once economic justice is established. Since no civilization can avoid the judgment of God's Word, none is to be accepted uncritically.

At Amsterdam, the assembly, which is the supreme legislative body of the World Council of Churches, adopted a constitution, set conditions for membership, outlined programs, defined structures and policies, made decisions about how to relate to other ecumenical bodies, established offices in Geneva, and elected a central committee, which in turn named W. A. Visser 't Hooft as the first general secretary. Apart from highlighting the vital role of the laity in the ongoing witness of the church, the Amsterdam Assembly did not contribute substantial new material to the reflection on mission. It did, however, create a new context in which common concerns could be discussed. While the World Council of Churches and the INTERNATIONAL MISSIONARY COUNCIL were considered to be in close association with each other, emphasis fell upon the essential unity of the church as distinguished from its missionary obligation.

KEN MULHOLLAND

Bibliography. R. Rouse and S. Neill, eds., *A History of the Ecumenical Movement 1517–1948;* W. A. Visser 't Hooft, *The Genesis and Formation of the World Council of Churches;* idem, ed., *The First Assembly of the World Council of Churches;* World Council of Churches, *Man's Disorder and God's Design: The Amsterdam Assembly Series.*

Anabaptist Missions. "Anabaptist" ("re-baptizer") is a cover name given to a movement of splinter groups initiated at the time of the Reformation. They denied infant baptism, instituting a restriction of baptism to believing adults. Though not thinking of themselves as *re*baptizers, this pejorative label (given by the Catholics and Reformers who persecuted them) has through historical use become the accepted term of reference.

In addition to believer's baptism, Anabaptist groups were characterized generally by personal devotion to Christ, passionate commitment to evangelism, and radical separation of church and state. Several groups also lived communally, preached eschatological urgency, and were pacifists. The blend of unswerving evangelistic fervor and persistent refusal to take oaths of loyalty to earthly rulers resulted in the perception that they were insurrectionists. They were thus outlawed almost everywhere they went.

Literally thousands were martyred, many by drowning as a cruel parody of their baptismal practice. The sheer number of martyrs, however, attests to the movement's vitality. Long before WILLIAM CAREY, and in contrast to the Reformers, Matthew 28:19–20 was a central text in Anabaptist mission motivation. A primary goal was *re*establishing the biblical model of the church, which they felt had been lost in the mixed marriage of church and state. Generally they gathered people in homes rather than ecclesiastical structures for worship, and these home groups maintained fluidity and the ability to multiply rapidly. The movement was largely lay-driven; each person responding to Christ became an active missionary, sharing Christ at home, in the market, and in vocational life. Those who fled persecution witnessed wherever they went.

Eventually the combination of constant persecution, slowing apocalyptic fervor, and loss of first-generation commitment led to withdrawal from mainstream culture and second-generation complacency. At a time when the Reformers largely ignored the need for missionary outreach, however, the Anabaptists engaged in work that remains a model still relevant today, and contemporary Mennonites carry on their legacy (*see* MENNONITE MISSIONS).

A. SCOTT MOREAU

Bibliography. H. Kasdorf, *Anabaptists and Mission,* pp. 51–60; R. L. Ramsayer, *Anabaptists and Mission,* pp. 178–78; N. van der Zijpp, *Anabaptists and Mission,* pp. 119–36.

Ancestral Beliefs and Practices. Throughout the world, cultures recognize the continuance of life after death. Wherever this is true, such recognition often results in the belief that the departed ancestors are still alive and correspondingly need to be recognized or acknowledged in some fashion. Though this basic belief is commonly found around the world, the formal manifestations and means by which this belief is acted out are represented in a staggering variety of beliefs, ethical codes, and rituals.

Beliefs and Ethics. In parts of Asia where CONFUCIANIST thinking undergirds culture, the obligation of filial piety undergirds the ethical need to respect the ancestors. Maintaining one's place in life, and (in the case of the eldest son) carrying out the role of supporting the departed in their place in ongoing life is critical. The cult of the ancestors has critical social functions, such as maintaining order in society through sustaining respect for the elders and adherence to social roles. In many parts of southern Africa no important family decision would be made without hearing from the ancestors through divination, dreams, or possession. The dead are thought of as the *living* dead, and local ethical codes demand that they be granted the same respect in death that they enjoyed as elders while alive. When times are troubling, whether from drought or disease, the ancestors may be called upon to protect the living. Among indigenous peoples of Latin America, as also in Africa, the ancestors are still seen as participating in the community of the living, even though their attention may not always be welcome. In all these contexts, failure to acknowledge the dead may result in retribution by the dead on the living. Thus, the obligation to participate in the practices and beliefs is often seen as a cultural necessity. Even in the materialistic West the popularity of attempts to reach the dead, whether through seances or mediums, shows that the need for ongoing connection with the departed remains an important felt need.

Rituals. The rituals associated with the ancestors vary widely. They include personal devotions, household rituals, rites of the extended family or clan, and rites of the whole people on behalf of all of the ancestors. Rites of transition may be necessary to ensure that the departed is accepted by the spirit realm, and great funerals may be the means by which this is done. Cyclical rites, such as recognition on the departed's birthday or death date may be needed to cement the family together. Rites of crisis enable the living to beseech the dead for protection or deliverance from their troubles. They ensure that the living do not join the dead before the appropriate time!

Missionary Response. A perplexing problem for missionaries is understanding exactly what the beliefs are, what the roles of the ancestors are, and why the living feel they need to relate to them. Initially missionaries considered the relationship to be one of worship. More recently it has been recognized that worship, in the sense of paying homage to deity, is not always an appropriate word to use and "ancestral veneration" has become the accepted term. However, the reality is that the problem is not just one of vocabulary, but of finding ways to enable Christian communities to obey the fifth commandment (honoring mother and father) in their cultural context without violating warnings against contact with the dead (e.g., Lev. 19:31; 20:6, 27; Deut. 18:9–14; 1 Sam. 28:3–20). Proposed answers have ranged from simply declaring ancestral practices Christian to abolishing them altogether. The missionary's main role is not to make decisions for the local community, but to assist that community in going to the Scriptures for guidance in evaluating the cultural beliefs and practices in light of God's revelation.

A. SCOTT MOREAU

Bibliography. R. J. Hammer, *CDCWM*, pp. 20–21; H. Hardacre, *ER*, 1:263–68; H. Kuckertz, ed., *Ancestor Religion in Southern Africa: Proceedings of a Seminar on Ancestor Belief;* J. Y. Lee, ed., *Ancestor Worship and Christianity in Korea;* A. S. Moreau, *The World of the Spirits;* M. Odell and M. Schwartzbaum, *ADLR*, pp. 30–33; B. Rin Ro, ed., *Christian Alternatives to Ancestor Practices;* M. Singleton, *Pro Mundi Vita Bulletin* 68 (September–October, 1977): 2–35; G. Van Rheenen, *Communicating Christ in Animistic Contexts.*

Anderson, Gerald H. (1930–). American missiologist, advocate, and missionary in the Philippines. After graduation from Grove City College with a degree in business administration, Anderson chose to follow God's calling to enter the ministry and pursued theological studies at Boston University School of Theology. After completion of his master's degree, and with the help of a Fulbright scholarship, his studies took him to universities in Germany, Switzerland, and Scotland. He received his Ph.D. in church history from Boston University in 1960.

His work in the Philippines was at Union Theological Seminary, where he taught church history and served as academic dean (1963–66) and director of graduate studies (1968–70) before returning to the United States to take the post of president at Scarritt College for Christian Workers (Nashville; 1970–73). After a one-year appointment as a senior research associate at Cornell University, Anderson became the associate director of the Overseas Ministries Study Center (OMSC; 1974).

The Theology of the Christian Mission (1961) was the first of more than a dozen major edited works and it exemplified both the level and breadth of scholarship which characterizes Anderson. Bringing together a spectrum of voices from conservative to liberal and engaging them in fruitful dialogue is a unique hallmark of his scholarship and ministry. This has been seen through his collaborative editorial work on books (*Concise Dictionary of Christian World Missions,* the *Mission Trends* series, *Biographical Dictionary of Christian Missions*) and the widely acclaimed *International Bulletin of Missionary Research* (1977) as well as his roles in the founding of the AMERICAN SOCIETY OF MISSIOLOGY and the INTERNATIONAL ASSOCIATION OF MISSION STUDIES and in his work as OMSC director (1976–2000). In 1995 he received an honorary D.D. degree from Moravian Theological Seminary. He retired in 2000, after 26 years at OMSC.

A. SCOTT MOREAU

Bibliography. R. T. Coote, *Toward the 21st Century in Christian Mission.*

Anderson, John (1805–55). Scottish pioneer missionary to India. Born in Galloway, Scotland, in the parish of Kilpatrick-Durham on May 23, 1805, he studied at parish schools and at age twenty-two entered Edinburgh University, where he distinguished himself as a student. He was ordained and sent as a missionary of the Church of Scotland in 1836. He devoted his work to evangelism through education of the Indians in Madras. He began his work by taking over a small school that had been started by two chaplains for the East India Company. His first priority was to move the school into the heart of Madras where it could establish an academic reputation and attract higher-caste Hindus. The school grew, but suffered setbacks because of community pressure after students came to Christ and lower-caste students were admitted. The first two to come to faith were baptized in 1836. In 1843 funds from Scotland were disrupted and the school came under the authority of the Free Presbyterian Church of Madras. Anderson did not marry until 1947, when he joined with Margaret Locher of Zurich who had come to teach the younger women. By 1850 Anderson was experiencing health problems that were severe enough that he returned to Scotland with an early convert by the name of Rajahgopal. He returned to India the next year but died only four years later on March 25, 1855. Under the direction of William Miller the school Anderson founded was developed into Madras Christian College, a school that has provided over a century of Christian witness in India.

JOHN EASTERLING

Bibliography. J. Braidwood, *True Yokefellows in the Mission Field;* H. Holcomb, *Men of Might in India Missions: The Leaders and Their Epochs 1706–1899.*

Anderson, Rufus (1796–1880). American mission theorist. Born in Yarmouth, Maine, he was educated at Bowdoin College and Andover Seminary. There he volunteered to go to India at a time when world missions was largely an afterthought in American church life.

The AMERICAN BOARD OF COMMISSIONERS FOR FOREIGN MISSIONS (ABCFM) ordained him as an evangelist. In 1826 he became assistant secretary and in 1832 he became foreign secretary, a post he held until his retirement in 1866. His influence was extended through his worldwide travels, teaching, and writing. He was probably the first person rightfully to be called a missionary statesman. He shaped the policies of his own board by strongly emphasizing that the churches established overseas should be self-governing, self-supporting, and self-propagating. (*See* INDIGENOUS CHURCHES.) This formula was soon adopted by other agencies as well.

Anderson believed that mission compounds and reliance on foreign missionaries hindered the growth of the national church. He was firmly committed to the training and ordination of national pastors. His theories were published in 1856 by the ABCFM as the *Outline of Missionary Practice.*

JIM REAPSOME

Bibliography. R. P. Beaver, *To Advance the Gospel: Selections from the Writings of Rufus Anderson.*

Anderson–Venn Formula. *See* INDIGENOUS CHURCHES.

Andorra (*Est. 2000 pop.: 81,000; 453 sq. km. [175 sq. mi.].*). Andorra is a small autonomous principality in the southern Pyrenees between France and Spain. Over 90 percent of the population is either Spaniard or Catalonian. The vast majority of these are Roman Catholic. Jehovah Witnesses number about 400 and evangelical Protestants, mainly Seventh-Day Adventists, are less than 100. Most evangelical mission work is limited to literature distribution.

TODD M. JOHNSON

Andrews, Charles Freer (1871–1950). English missionary to India. Born in Carlisle, England, son of a Catholic Apostolic Church minister, at nineteen he had an intense conversion experience. He graduated brilliantly from Cambridge, became an Anglican, worked in the London slums (1896–1900), and was vice president of Westcott House, Cambridge (1900–1904). He then went to India under the Cambridge Mission and, dismayed by British arrogance and the caste system, became a champion of the deprived classes. He counted Hindus, Muslims, and Buddhists among his dearest friends, saw "the Spirit of Christ" in those who did not call themselves Christians, and wondered whether he could draw the boundaries of Christian thought as sharply as he once did. He rejected the literal interpretation of Scripture and the damnatory clause in the Athanasian Creed. He disliked aggressive evangelism and held that Christianity was often more professed than practiced.

Invited in 1913 to help the oppressed Indian community in South Africa, he became a close friend of Mahatma Gandhi. Andrews severed his missionary connection with mutual goodwill in 1914, became chairman of the Indian Trades Union Congress, was a longtime mediator between Indians and Europeans, and spent long meditative stays at Rabindranath Tagore's ashram. He campaigned against all forms of racial prejudice, but eventually spent most of his time striving for the abolition of indentured Indian labor, a long-entrenched evil. Before the battle was finally won, he had visited South and

East Africa, Fiji, Australia, North America, and the Caribbean area.

His *What I Owe to Christ* (1932) tells how through the many difficulties and changes he had known, a simple, joyful faith in Jesus Christ was the very center of his life. Andrews wrote a biography of Sundar Singh, as well as social and humanitarian works.

J. D. Douglas

Bibliography. T. Hugh, *The Ordeal of Love: C. F. Andrews and India;* N. Macnicol, *C. F. Andrews: Friend of India;* B. Chaturvedi and M. Sykes, *Charles Freer Andrews: A Narrative.*

Anglican Missions. The Anglican Church will seem to have an eccentric history and theology of missions if it is seen only through the prism of modern Protestant denominationalism. For well documented political, religious, and cultural reasons the Roman Catholic Church in England broke communion with the pope during the continental reformations under the direction of the English king Henry VIII (1509–47). After hesitations and compromises it emerged as the Church of England under Elizabeth I (1558–1603), with the monarch as its governor and the aristocracy and gentry as its patrons. Anglicanism, then, was susceptible to Erastianism and tended strongly to Protestantism in its key theological claims and to Catholicism in regard to sacraments, sensibilities, and ecclesiastical organization. So "protestant" and "catholic" (and later conservative and liberal) Anglicans learned early to tolerate, if barely sometimes, each other's presence in the church. Anglican protestantism has given bishops significant ecclesiastical freedom in their own jurisdictions and the sometimes unwelcome political council of powerful local laity. Anglican catholicity has rendered most of its adherents respectful of sacramental acts and wary of schisms: it has also often made its missionaries hesitant to seek converts from the Orthodox and Roman Catholic Churches. These realities helped forge Anglicanism, over the years, into a network of dioceses with a shared culture and a wide tolerance. Yet it could not have been anticipated that Anglican missions would lead to an international, multilingual communion of some 60 million on all continents by the end of the twentieth century.

In the latter sixteenth century, when the Church of England first saw itself as a reformed, national church, its leaders saw its chief mission to be the spiritual care of all those subject to the English Crown, their education in Anglicanism, and the gaining of their loyalty to the established order as the ordinance of God. Yet it was only after Puritan emigration to the American colonies, a religious and political civil war in England, and the act tolerating religious "nonconformists" in the country (1689) that the limits of the mission were admitted, and its basics in any sense accomplished in England and Wales. Scotland and Ireland being extremely resistant to English power, the church planted there was far more tenuous and unpopular. Anglican clergy up to this point did not venture out of the nation as missionaries, but as chaplains to wealthy emigrant families and commercial companies.

It was 1701 before the Society for the Propagation of the Gospel in Foreign Parts (SPG), the first overseas Anglican mission, was formed. Instigated by Anglican priests, generously supported by the gentry and aristocracy, and blessed by the Anglican archbishop of Canterbury, its mission was for the most part in America. Its goal was to bring colonists back into the Anglican Church and to evangelize the native population by planting the self-sufficient parish system of the mother country. Yet even its limited success was suddenly cut short by the American Revolution. Yet there was a silver lining to the cloud. American Anglicans were urgently propelled into establishing a ground-breaking autonomous Episcopal church with its own mission (Samuel Seabury, the first American and first overseas Anglican bishop, being forced to seek consecration in 1784 at the hands of Scottish Episcopal bishops), and the SPG was pushed to take up other fields of endeavor. Both unintended consequences of the Revolution stretched the definition of Anglican missions.

Within a few years (1787) the archbishop of Canterbury consecrated the first Canadian bishop (Nova Scotia), and the pattern was set for colonial Anglicanism as Anglican missions entered the nineteenth century. Anglican missionaries went wherever the British Empire led, and began to concentrate more and more on indigenous peoples. The formation of the second Anglican mission agency, the very evangelical Church Missionary Society (CMS) in 1799, was not destructive of Anglican unity and effectiveness. Both the SPG and the CMS recruited missionary-clergymen, raised their support, and helped build independent Anglican dioceses throughout the growing British commonwealth. Markedly protestant or catholic Anglican agencies that sprouted up in the following years—the Colonial and Continental Church Society (1823), the South American Missionary Society (1844), the Universities' Mission to Central Africa (1857), and others—quarreled, but did not cause schisms. They fed their efforts into new and far-flung dioceses that were closely governed by autonomous bishops and able to function quickly as independent parts of a rapidly growing Anglican communion.

In the late nineteenth century Anglican missions were sent not only from Britain, but from American and colonial dioceses as British immigrants concentrated on natives in what was now their hinterland and on indigenous peoples in more remote British and other European possessions. Anglican missions also continued their diversifying tendencies, and began to encompass everything from direct evangelism to medical, educational, and agricultural projects, learning the value of challenging or even defying imperial authority to accomplish their mandate. But in the years following the great WORLD MISSIONARY CONFERENCE in Edinburgh (1910) in which they optimistically participated, Anglican missions met tough new challenges. The national independence movements that followed, the trend to democracy in all societal institutions, the rapid theological changes that emerged in Western theology, and the consequent plunge in missionary vocations shook their self-understanding.

But several encouraging trends have emerged. The accelerated ordination of indigenous clergy and bishops has encouraged the self-sufficiency of even more recent Anglican mission areas, and put Anglicans of European descent in the role of requested consultants. More recently, non-European Anglican missionaries have become consultants to moribund Anglicanism in Europe and North America. The episcopal system has continued to avoid schisms and it has become more responsive to the laity as a whole, which has generated its patrons and voting members for its elections and synods and has given new energy and leadership to the Anglican communion. And though theological controversy, secularism, and growing pluralism have sapped Anglican mission of much of its vitality in the West, Anglicans have become more sympathetic to their co-religionists in countries dominated by other world religions or Western economies. Finally, Anglicans responded to their predicament by supporting a communion-wide "Decade of Evangelism" (1988–98), run between its global Lambeth conferences.

PAUL. H. FRIESEN

Bibliography. C. Craston, ed., *By Word and Deed: Sharing the Good News through Mission*; H. G. G Herklots, *Frontiers of the Church: The Making of the Anglican Communion*; J. S. Higgins, *One Faith and Fellowship: The Missionary Story of the Anglican Communion*; S. Neill, *Anglicanism*; A. Nichols, *Equal Partners: Issues of Mission and Partnership in the Anglican World*; W. Sachs, *The Transformation of Anglicanism: From State Church to Global Communion*.

Angola *(Est. 2000 pop.: 13,074,000; 1,246,700 sq. km. [481,351 sq. mi.]).* Angola, a country more than twice the size of France with a population of about 13 million people, situated on the west coast of southern Africa, had its first contact with Christianity through the early Portuguese navigators who arrived in 1483. In 1491 the Portuguese established the first Catholic mission to Angola in the north. Jesuits, Capuchins, and

Carmelites were the first to evangelize the area. The church grew rapidly at first. The king of the ruling Kongo kingdom accepted Christianity, and his son became the first African bishop. This early growth, however, was not sustained. Malaria and dysentery killed many priests. Furthermore, Portugal became deeply involved in the world slave trade. Bishops and priests would baptize groups of slaves before they were shipped to foreign lands, and this involvement with the slave trade caused the people to become disillusioned with the church. It was not until the late nineteenth century that the Roman Catholic Church began to establish itself, beginning to work in the interior of Angola.

Protestant work in Angola was pioneered by the British Baptists, who arrived in 1878 to work among the Bakongo people in the north. Shortly after their arrival, the American Board Mission sent a party to work among the Ovimbundu. In 1884 the Brethren began their labors in Angola, pioneered by FREDERICK ARNOT. William Taylor brought a party from America and founded the United Methodist Church. Others followed, and some of the largest Protestant communities in Angola today are the fruit of these early pioneers.

Under Portuguese Catholic rule Protestant churches and missionaries experienced some degree of discrimination, although the Constitution allowed freedom of worship. This became worse with the onset of the struggle for independence after 1961 since the leaders of all three nationalist movements were the sons of Protestant church leaders. Many Protestant churches were closed and missionaries were expelled.

When the Portuguese formally withdrew from Angola in 1975, the MPLA, one of three main liberation movements, gained control of the central government with the assistance of Cuban troops, setting up a one-party Marxist state. In the first ten years after independence, Christians suffered considerable persecution; many pastors and believers were martyred and many churches were destroyed. Independence was also followed by almost twenty years of civil war between the MPLA government (backed by the former Soviet Union and Cuba) and UNITA (backed by the United States and South Africa). In 1988 a treaty among Angola, Cuba, and South Africa led to the withdrawal of all foreign troops, a ceasefire between the Angolan government and UNITA, and preparations for multiparty democratic elections in 1992. MPLA won the elections but civil war resumed when UNITA refused to accept the results as valid. In 1995 an agreement to bring UNITA into a government of national unity gave promise of achieving a more lasting peace.

Through all the fiery trials of decades of war, bloodshed, suffering, famine, and hardship the church in Angola has grown rapidly. Bodies include Congregationalists, Christian Brethren,

Methodists, Seventh-Day Adventists, and Assemblies of God.

KEVIN ROY

Bibliography. M. Froise, ed., *World Christianity: South Central Africa;* World Council of Churches, "Survey on Angola," *Handbook of Member Churches.*

Anguilla *(Est. 2000 pop.: 8,000; 91 sq. km. [35 sq. mi.]).* An island in the Lesser Antilles. Anguilla's population is 95 percent Afro-Caribbean. Aridity has kept this member of the British Commonwealth dependent on fishing and tourism, leaving it with one of the lowest per capita incomes in the region. The population is 96 percent Protestant, mainly Anglican and Methodist, of whom 18 percent are evangelical.

EVERETT A. WILSON

SEE ALSO Caribbean.

Bibliography. A. Lampe, *The Church in Latin America, 1492–1992,* pp. 201–15; J. Rogozinski, *A Brief History of the Caribbean: From the Arawak and the Carib to the Present.*

Animism. The term "animism" was coined by the early anthropologist E. B. Tylor and defined as belief in spiritual beings. From dreams and death early humans inferred the idea of the soul, Tylor argued. And if humans had souls, then perhaps so did animals, plants, and mountains. From the idea of a soul that survives the death of a body evolved the idea of disembodied spirits, gods, and eventually God. Animists impute human attributes to the world, and employ the same actions used to affect humans (love, gifts, threats, punishment) to affect such things as rain. But since spirits are tied to the physical world, animists also employ actions designed to manipulate the physical world to control spirits.

At one level, animism is a term linked to an outdated theory about the primordial core of religion. Yet many anthropologists still use the term. They use it, first, as a synonym for traditional, tribal, FOLK, or PRIMAL RELIGION, as opposed to major WORLD RELIGIONS. Second, they use the term where religious belief focuses on spirits that interpenetrate the physical material world, and religious practice is characterized by attempts to manipulate the physical world by recourse to spirits and spirits by recourse to the physical world.

ROBERT J. PRIEST

SEE ALSO Folk Religions; Primal Religions; Spiritism.

Bibliography. E. A. Nida, *Introducing Animism;* A. R. Tippett, *Bibliography for Cross-Cultural Workers.*

Annihilationism. Proponents of annihilationism maintain that God's JUDGMENT utterly obliterates the wicked. Recently annihilationism has made inroads among evangelicals. These annihilationists dispute the extent of punishment due the sinner. They affirm God's punishment in HELL is eternal in its effects, but not in its length. Sometimes this position is linked with an anthropological view called conditional immortality, which holds that humans have only potential immortality. The issue of annihilationism and hell's extent has occasioned much debate in recent scholarship. Four major points are in contention.

A Punishment with Eternal Results. Some annihilationists argue that when the Greek adjective for eternal, *aiōnios,* is used with nouns of action, it refers to an occurrence with eternal results, not an eternal process (Fudge). So "eternal punishment" denotes a punishment that occurs once with everlasting results. But this argument is weak. For "everlasting salvation" (Heb. 5:9) refers not simply to Christ's work long ago. Scripture describes believers, even in the age to come, as existing "in Christ" (2 Cor. 5:17; Col. 2:6, 7; 2 Tim. 2:10). So *aiōnios sōteria* refers to a salvation that is everlasting in action and its result. Similarly, "everlasting punishment" should be interpreted as everlasting in process and result. Confirming this meaning, Jesus uses the same adjective *(aiōnios)* for eternal life and eternal punishment, indicating that in his mind the extent of each future is identical (Matt. 25:46).

Destruction. Some annihilationists insist that the biblical imagery of destruction and a consuming fire implies the cessation of life (Stott). However, the Greek verb "destroy" *(apollumi)* and its cognates range in meaning from "lost" (Luke 15:8, 24) to "ruined" (Matt. 9:17). Even when referring to physical death, "destroy" does not suggest extinction; for Jesus cautions that those who kill the body cannot kill the soul (Matt. 10:28). Jesus' juxtaposing the two destinies of "life" and "destruction" (Matt 7:13–14; John 3:16) is not contrasting survival and extinction. Rather these are two qualitatively different types of life, one involving a loving communion with God and another lacking it and in a state of "ruin" (John 8:12; 10:10; 1 John 5:11–12).

The annihilationists' argument that fire totally consumes what it burns ignores that Jesus' portrayal of hell's fires are not literal descriptions. These are metaphors for God's retributive punishment (Luke 17:29) which must cohere with other biblical accounts. Elsewhere Jesus pictures hell as a place where *"their* worm does not die," suggesting that this worm is endlessly linked to the damned as their due; so "their worm" has traditionally been interpreted as the soul's internal torment (Mark 9:48). Other Scriptures explicitly teach that the wicked are punished with "everlasting torment" (Rev. 20:10, 15; 14:10–11).

Justice of God. While acknowledging God's retributive judgment, annihilationists insist that this punishment must be commensurate with the evil deed. Why should sins committed in time require torment throughout eternity? Is not everlasting torment vindictive, and incompatible with the LOVE OF GOD? The punishment due to the sinner is the central challenge of the annihilationists.

Scripture is the norm for delineating the penalty for sin, not our own self-justifying assessments. Scripture identifies Christ's priestly work of ATONEMENT as the penalty necessary for sin. For God in Christ became our substitute to bear the punishment for our sins: "He did this to demonstrate his justice . . . so as to be just and to be the one who justifies those who have faith in Jesus" (Rom. 3:21–26; 2 Cor. 5:21; 1 Peter 2:24). If Christ was only a human, his substitutionary work would suggest that the penalty is simply a finite loss. Suffering a finite penalty as extinction is consistent with that scenario. But Christ was simply not human. God himself was present at the cross establishing this RECONCILIATION by accepting the punishment due us (1 Cor. 2:8). Jesus' priestly work indicates that the penalty for sin against the Infinite is infinite. As Scripture testifies, God's punishment of the damned is infinite, and of everlasting duration.

Annihilationism's Theological Shift. Annihilationism does not simply mute hell's horror, it represents an anthropocentric reading which places in motion decisive theological changes. Denying that sin is an infinite offense against the infinite God requiring an infinite punishment undercuts the gravity of humanity's rebellion as well as God's lordship. Just because we are finite does not entail that sin is finite offense. Rather sin's gravity is established by the one to whom we are accountable, God our Creator (Rom. 2:6–16; 1 Peter 4:5). Moreover, rejecting an everlasting hell disparages the cost of our salvation. It renders the sacrifice of the God-man in and of itself unnecessary. Nor is it accidental that in mainline circles annihilationism has historically gone hand in hand with a denial of Jesus' deity (Socinianism and non-universalist liberals). But ultimately annihilationism's anthropocentric focus fails. For historically the commitment to EVANGELISM of even evangelical annihilationist institutions has faltered after the second or third generation. Underemphasizing the importance of hell tends to diminish the motivation for missions.

TIMOTHY R. PHILLIPS

Bibliography. D. A. Carson, *The Gagging of God: Christianity Confronts Pluralism*, pp. 515–36; D. L. Edwards and J. Stott, *Evangelical Essentials*, pp. 306–31; E. Fudge, *The Fire That Consumes*; S. McKnight, *Through No Fault of Their Own: The Fate of Those Who Have Never Heard*, pp. 147–57; J. I. Packer, *Reformation and Revival* 6:2 (Spring 1997): 37–51; M. R. Talbot, *Reformation and Revival* 5:4 (Fall 1996): 117–34.

Anointing. Ritual application of a substance to a person or an object. As well as having diverse secular uses (e.g., cosmetic, aesthetic, medicinal, festal) anointing is almost universal in the history of ancient and modern religions, although the substance used (usually fat, oil, or water) and the details of the cultic practice vary considerably.

In religious contexts anointing has the general purpose of symbolically transferring spiritual or divine presence or power on the anointed object or person. The more specific meaning attributed by its practicioners may be summarized in three distinct, though related, categories. (1) *Healing:* The physical healing properties of oil often cannot be separated from the magical or supernatural conceptions often associated with anointing since disease is often attributed to the power of malevolent spiritual beings. (2) *Consecration:* People or objects may be consecrated for a particular sacred purpose or task through anointing, which symbolizes the focusing of divine presence, pleasure, power, or protection. (3) *Ordination:* Anointing also occurs in many cultures when certain individuals are appointed to positions of prominence and leadership associated with sacred duty.

When used in a religious context, anointing in biblical texts generally falls into these categories. In the Old Testament anointing is at times connected with the Spirit of God (1 Sam. 16:13; Isa. 61:1) and thus the anointing of Israel's priests (Exod. 28:41), kings (1 Sam. 10:1), and prophets (1 Kings 19:16) symbolized their separation for the task and divine empowerment for it. Objects associated with the worship of Yahweh were also consecrated through anointing (Exod. 30:26–29).

The Hebrew title "messiah" (Greek, *christos*) means "anointed one" and its New Testament application to Jesus stems from the prophetic tradition associating the coming messiah with King David. Besides references to Jesus, who was anointed by the Holy Spirit (Luke 4:18), the few other religious uses in the New Testament associate anointing with divine healing (James 5:14) and anointing by the Holy Spirit which is true of every Christian (1 John 2:20, 27).

These biblical allusions to anointing have led to its diverse uses in various Christian traditions throughout history. In the Roman Catholic Church it became the sacrament known as "extreme unction" (after Vatican II, "anointing of the sick") with the intention of effecting remission of sin and restoration of bodily health. In reaction to Roman Catholic practice, Reformation churches have largely suppressed the practice.

Perhaps because of the cultural distance of the symbolism, it appears to be less common in culturally Western churches. However, it is more frequent among churches influenced by charismatic and Pentecostal traditions, which emphasize the linkage to the Holy Spirit. Christian churches in non-Western cultures may find anointing more meaningful due to its use in non-Christian religious contexts with which they are familiar as well as their appreciation of anointing in Old Testament contexts, an understanding that stems from similarities to their own cultures. In these situations caution should be exercised so that such practices as the anointing of new church leaders and the sick are biblically (and not just culturally) informed and interpreted.

SCOTT CUNNINGHAM

Bibliography. M. Dudley and G. Rowell, eds., *The Oil of Gladness: Anointing in the Christian Tradition;* G. W. Bromiley, *EDT,* pp. 114–16; *ERE,* II: 367–406.

Anomie. The concept of anomie originated in Emile Durkeim's *Suicide,* and was developed by R. K. Merton in *Social Theory and Social Structure* and later by Peter Berger and Thomas Luckman in *The Social Construction of Reality*.

Anomie has generally been described as a condition in which values, norms, and worldview that give stability to the individual and collective life break down, and people are left without a sense of self-image, dignity, and social identity. Further dislocation brought about by economic deprivation and the breakdown of traditional society culminate in the consequent loss of traditional values. Social relations and ethical norms are shattered. It has been suggested that a significant majority of the Two-Third World's poor and displaced people have experienced some degree of anomie—a social reality that leaves them bereft of any meaningful social structure. These conditions, accelerated by rapid demographic and economic change after World War II, provoked crises that forced the displaced masses to grope for solutions to an anomic existence.

There seems to be little disagreement with the concept of anomie, although the use of the term has become so accepted that it often lacks precision. Further, different contexts may allow considerable latitude in definitions. Though probable, the conclusion generally offered, namely, that anomie leads directly to loss of "self-image, dignity, and social identity," may apply more to the disintegration of society than to the pathologies of a person. Whether the majority of the world's poor have experienced anomie depends upon criteria upon which there may not be agreement. For example, many people seem to survive well in the midst of a crisis even though apparently they do not have good reason to feel confident. On the other hand, Durkeim used anomie to show how socially well-established people also suffer from rapid change when, for instance, a family suddenly comes into wealth.

However correct some scholars may have been in relating the rise of religious experience among the masses to emotional and economic crisis, their viewing of the movement as simply a reactionary crutch to deteriorating conditions—a "haven of the masses"—obscures and abuses one of its most characteristic features. Religious conversion is not a negative reaction but rather is an action that results in positive transformation—an antidote in the midst of upheaval that produces a radical shift in worldview. The experience is not a "refuge" from the world but rather a strategy by which to live successfully in the world. The secret of this religious experience in an individual is receiving divine love, resulting in empowerment. The power of love in the struggle for social transformation prompts a resocialization, an adaptation or transformation of the person. The "nonperson," who hears and receives the message of transformation, personally experiences the reality of an intimate relationship with God in his or her life. Converts are immediately thrust into a loving and caring community. Dignity, value, personal worth, and identity are collectively celebrated. Salvation within the "non-person" culminates in a radical transformation to self-acceptance and self-love. The new believer, who receives spiritual conversion, professes that he or she has been accepted by God and now *belongs* to the community of love. To be "in Christ" means not just to have received eternal life, but also to have the privilege to be a participant in a loving and caring community. By being incorporated into such a community, the believer regains dignity and self-acceptance and therefore becomes a meaningful participant in the further creation of the community both in individual and corporate terms.

DOUG PETERSON

Bibliography. E. Durkeim, *Suicide: A Study on Sociology;* R. K. Merton, *Social Theory and Social Structure;* P. Berger and T. Luckman, *The Social Construction of Reality*.

Ansgar (801–865). Early French missionary to Sweden. Known for his humility, courage, and initiative, he was born in northwestern France. Displaying serious Christian commitment at an early age, his missionary zeal came most likely from the Corbey monastery, which found spiritual roots in Columban and Irish monasticism (*see* CELTIC MISSIONARY MOVEMENT). Later he helped found a monastery in Westphalia (New Corbey) for newly converted Saxons, holding the office of preacher and first master.

Ansgar's first mission was to Denmark (c. 823), accompanying recently baptized King Harald to establish converts in Schleswig. In 829 Swedish officials arrived at the court of Louis the Pious (successor to Charlemagne) asking for missionaries. Ansgar responded, leaving Denmark. He and his companions endured hardships and piracy, eventually arriving in Birka on the island of Björkö in Lake Mälar, west of present-day Stockholm.

Among Ansgar's first acquaintances were Christian slaves, brought to Sweden from Viking raids. These and others (including members of the royal court) were organized into Ansgar's first congregation. Ansgar left Sweden to assume the archbishopric of Hamburg. His return to Sweden was delayed nearly twenty years by pagan reactions to Christianity. Upon returning, he reorganized the congregation, later abandoned when commerce moved from Birka to Uppsala. Ansgar's legacy is that of a harbinger. Although his personal efforts yielded little lasting fruit, Christianity would be established in Sweden some 250 years later with the destruction of the pagan temple at Uppsala.

STEVEN J. PIERSON

Bibliography. K. S. Latourette, *The Thousand Years of Uncertainty;* R. Murray, *A Brief History of the Church of Sweden;* Rimbert, *Anskar, the Apostle of the North.*

Anthropology, Biblical. *See* HUMANKIND, DOCTRINE OF.

Anthropology, Missiological Anthropology. The relationship between anthropology and world missions has been a long and profitable one with the benefits flowing both ways. Though for philosophical reasons recent generations of anthropologists have tended to be very critical of missionaries, much of the data used by professional anthropologists from earliest days has come from missionaries. Anthropological pioneers such as E. B. Tylor (1832–1917) and J. G. Frazer (1854–1954) in England, L. H. Morgan (1818–82) in the United States, and Wilhelm Schmidt (1868–1954) in Austria were greatly indebted to missionaries for the data from which they constructed their theories. Such early anthropological pioneers as R. H. Codrington (1830–1922), Lorimer Fison (1832–1907), Diedrich Westermann (1875–1956), H. A. Junod (1863–1934), and Edwin Smith (1876–1957) were missionaries for part or all of their careers.

The first of the numerous Protestant missionary conferences in the English-speaking world to include formal discussion of anthropological matters was the WORLD MISSIONARY CONFERENCE in Edinburgh (1910). Roman Catholics led the way on the Continent, sponsoring several workshops on missions and ethnology. A notable center for ethnological research was established in Vienna by Schmidt, who devoted his professional life to researching, teaching, and writing on languages and cultures in order to help missionaries. For this purpose he founded the journal *Anthropos* in 1906 and the Anthropos Institute in 1932.

Though the influence of professional anthropology on missionaries was small during this era, some impressive anthropological writing by missionaries emerged. Fison with A. W. Howitt published *The Kamileroi and the Kurnai*, still considered a basic work on Australian aboriginals. Codrington's *Melanesians* contributed to anthropology its understanding of *mana*. Junod's two-volume *Life of a South African Tribe* was years later still regarded as one of the finest anthropological monographs. And Schmidt's twelve-volume study of the origin of religion did much to dissuade the academic community from their commitment to an evolutionary explanation.

The most notable early British advocate for missiological anthropology was EDWIN SMITH. Born in Africa of missionary parents, Smith for three decades wrote and taught widely on African cultures. His most famous book is *The Golden Stool*. Two other British missionary anthropologists to note are W. C. Willoughby, who published *The Soul of the Bantu*, and Denys Shropshire, who wrote *The Church and Primitive Peoples*.

In America, with the exception of Hartford Seminary Foundation's Kennedy School of Missions, where Willoughby taught from 1919 and Smith lectured from 1939 to 1943, little was done to provide anthropological instruction for missionaries before World War II. Wheaton College (Illinois) had begun an anthropology department, and the WYCLIFFE BIBLE TRANSLATORS' Summer Institute of Linguistics, though primarily focused on LINGUISTICS, was serving to alert many to the need to take culture seriously.

Though Gordon Hedderly Smith had published *The Missionary and Anthropology* in 1945, it was EUGENE NIDA who sparked the movement to make anthropology a major component in missionary thinking. He used his position as secretary for translations of the American Bible Society to demonstrate to missionaries and their leaders the value of anthropological insight. His lectures on anthropological topics in the 1940s and early 1950s, published as *Customs and Cultures* in 1954, contributed greatly to an awakening within the missionary community to the need for and benefits of anthropological insight. By the mid-1950s Nida had surrounded himself at the Bible society with four very perceptive, anthropologically oriented translation consultants, W. A. SMALLEY, W. D. REYBURN, W. L. WONDERLY, and J. A. LOEWEN. As these men worked with translators around the world, they demonstrated the value of anthropology. In 1955, Smalley took over the editorship of the bimonthly journal *Practical Anthropology (PA)*, which Robert Taylor had started in 1953 at Wheaton with the aim of applying anthropology to missions. The writings of Nida, Smalley, Reyburn, Wonderly, and Loewen in *PA* were formative for a generation of anthropologically oriented missionaries working in the 1950s and 1960s.

From 1965 on, another stream of missiological anthropology was developing under DONALD MC-GAVRAN at Fuller Seminary's School of World Mission. McGavran's first faculty appointee was ALAN TIPPETT, an Australian anthropologist who had worked for two decades in Fiji. The Nida stream merged with this stream under Mc-Gavran's next two appointees, RALPH WINTER and Charles Kraft, both anthropologists strongly influenced by Nida and the other *PA* contributors. These events of the 1950s and 1960s laid the foundations for validating missiological anthropology within the professional subdiscipline of applied anthropology. Important publications of the 1960s included Nida's *Message and Mission* and LOUIS LUZBETAK's *Church and Cultures*, which focused helpfully on the dynamics of cultural change. Tippett's *Solomon Islands Christianity* showed how competent anthropology could be used to analyze Christian witness and practice. KENNETH PIKE's *Language in Relation to a Unified Theory of the Structure of Human Behavior*, though long and technical, contributed important insights concerning the relationships of language and culture. Many of the *PA* articles were collected by Smalley in *Readings in Missionary Anthropology*, which was followed by *Culture and Human Values*, a collection of perceptive articles by Loewen.

In 1973, *PA*, then edited by Charles Taber, an anthropologist teaching at Emmanuel School of Religion, was merged into *Missiology*, the fledgling journal of the newly formed AMERICAN SOCIETY OF MISSIOLOGY. Tippett became the first editor. This journal has maintained a strong focus on anthropology.

Currently, anthropology plays an important part in the majority of missionary training programs in evangelical institutions. The primary attention of missiological anthropology is directed toward understanding the nature of CULTURE and the pervasiveness of its influence on those we approach with the gospel. A second concern is to understand the influence of culture on the missionaries themselves. To this has been added the recognition that since the Bible is a cross-cultural book, those who would understand and interpret it correctly need cultural insight. The articles in *PA* provided understanding of these and many other important areas.

Over the years, missiological anthropology has sometimes followed the vogues of secular anthropology, sometimes resisted them. Missionary anthropologists have found congenial such secular anthropological insights as the focus on specific cultures, the strengths of research based on participant observation, certain aspects of the functionalist emphasis on the internal workings of culture, the dynamics of cultural change, and the necessity to understand WORLDVIEW. On the other hand, certain secular emphases have stirred up the opposition of Christian anthropologists. Among them are the overextension of evolutionary and relativistic thinking. Early on, one of Schmidt's motivations was to combat the simplistic evolutionary theory concerning the origin and development of religion. His *Origin of the Idea of God* was so successful that most secular anthropologists dropped the theory. Christians have not been so successful in convincing the anthropological establishment that though certain aspects of evolutionary and relativistic thinking make sense, they need to be balanced by the recognition that someone started things and established certain absolutes.

There are four general areas in which the insights of anthropology are enabling greater effectiveness in Christian ministry. First, the two-way flow of influence between missiological anthropology and BIBLE TRANSLATION continues to be significant, especially in the United States. Nida has had a lot to do with this. A second significant application of anthropology relates to the influences of culture on the communication process. Nida's pioneering *Message and Mission* brought this topic forcefully to our attention. MARVIN MAYERS, a Wycliffe translator who taught at Wheaton and later at Biola, both highlighted and broadened this theme in his important book *Christianity Confronts Culture*. A third important area of application is the contextualization or inculturation of Christianity. Kraft in *Christianity in Culture* creatively used linguistic and Bible translation theory as well as basic anthropology and COMMUNICATION theory to produce a cross-cultural perspective on theology. This book did much to show both that an anthropological approach can positively influence theologizing and that CONTEXTUALIZATION should be an evangelical issue, not merely an ecumenical theory. A fourth important area presently in focus is that of WORLDVIEW.

In addition, we should mention Homer Barnett's psychological anthropology and especially his ideas on cultural change, which have had a strong influence on Tippett and Luzbetak. More recently, the symbolic anthropology of Clifford Geertz and Mary Douglas has influenced the perspectives of Paul Hiebert and Sherwood Lingenfelter. Important recent books by missiological anthropologists include Tippett's *Introduction to Missiology*, Darrell Whiteman's *Melanesians and Missionaries*, Hiebert's *Anthropological Insights for Missionaries* and *Anthropological Reflections on Missiological Issues*, Daniel Shaw's *Transculturation* (1988), Lingenfelter's *Transforming Culture* (1992) and *Agents of Transformation* (1996), Hiebert and Eloise Meneses' *Incarnational Ministry* (1995) and Kraft's *Anthropology for Christian Witness* (1996). A lifetime of dealing with the Bible in cross-cultural perspective is summarized in Jacob Loewen's masterful *The Bible in Cross-Cultural Perspective* (1997).

CHARLES H. KRAFT

Bibliography. E. E. Evans-Pritchard, *Social Anthropology and Other Essays*; S. A. Grunlan and M. K. Mayers, *Cultural Anthropology: A Christian Perspective*; P. G. Hiebert, *Cultural Anthropology*; D. L. Whiteman, ed., *Missionaries, Anthropologists, and Cultural Change.*

Anthropology of Religion. The anthropological study of religion is related to the sociological, psychological, and comparative studies of religions. Its unique contribution lies in its data—mainly the study of non-Western tribal and FOLK RELIGIONS—and its use of in-depth ethnographic descriptions and cross-cultural comparisons. Anthropological studies of religion fall broadly into four periods, each characterized by particular questions and theories.

Evolutionary Theories of Religion. Like medieval Christian theologians, nineteenth- and early-twentieth-century anthropologists sought to account for religions in a single comprehensive history, but unlike theologians they did so in naturalistic terms. They postulated the evolution of religion from simple animistic beliefs and practices to the complex religions of the present. They attributed this to the growth of human rationality, and divided it into three stages—animistic, metaphysical/theological, and scientific. Central to their debate were two questions: what were the origins of religion, and what role did it play in the evolution of human thought?

E. B. Tylor (1871) attributed the origins to an early belief in spirit beings that arose when primitive humans, reflecting on the nature of dreams and death, concluded that humans have invisible souls which leave the body and wander to distant places. Later they extended this notion of spirit or soul to animals, plants, and even inanimate objects. From a belief in spirits, Tylor argued, it is only a small step to belief in the "continuance" of these spirits beyond death in an after-world, their "embodiment" in objects, their "possession" of living persons, and the existence of powerful "high gods." Robert Marett argued that belief in spirits was preceded by a stage in which humans experienced a sense of awe at the great forces of nature, and came to believe in a mysterious impersonal power or *mana*. Sir James Frazer (1922) posited that religious beliefs are rooted in prelogical beliefs in MAGIC based on two mistaken notions of causality, namely, that of similarity (pouring water produces rain), and contagion (acts performed on one part of a person's body, such as hair clippings, affects that person). Cultural evolutionists took religious beliefs seriously, but discounted these as prelogical and metaphysical attempts to understand the universe, which,

in time, would be displaced by rational, empirical science.

Opposition to evolutionary theories of religion came from two quarters. In Vienna, Father Wilhelm Schmidt of the Kulturkreis School of Anthropology showed from missionary reports that most simple societies believe in an all-powerful creator God, a belief evolutionists attributed only to advanced universalistic religions. In the United States Franz Boas and his students called for empirically based history to replace the "armchair speculation" that had characterized evolutionary theories.

The theory of cultural evolution influenced the modern mission movement in several ways. First, many missionaries assumed the superiority of Western civilization and peoples. Members of other races might share in their goodness and wisdom, but Westerners were the leaders and would remain so for a very long time. Missionaries considered their task to be to "civilize" and "Christianize" the people they served. They built schools and hospitals alongside churches, and saw science as essentially a part of the curriculum as the gospel. This equation of the gospel with Western culture made the gospel unnecessarily foreign in other cultures.

Second, many missionaries saw traditional religions, with their fear of spirits, witchcraft, and magical powers, as animistic superstitions, and assumed that these would die out as people accepted Christianity and science. They saw little need to study these religions. Consequently, many of the old beliefs went underground because the missionaries had not dealt with them or provided Christian answers to the problems these addressed. Today these underground beliefs are resurfacing around the world and creating havoc in young churches (*see also* ANIMISM).

Social-Functional Approaches to Religion. During the period between the World Wars, anthropologists were heavily influenced by sociology which held that social phenomena, like natural phenomena, obey laws discoverable by empirical observation and human reason. Emile Durkheim (1915) argued that religion plays a vital role in maintaining cohesion and moral order in a society. He saw religion as a set of symbols that refer not to supernatural beings, but to the society itself. Gods, spirits, and other religious symbols represent segments of a society, or its whole. By ordering these symbols in rituals, the social order is affirmed; and by declaring these symbols sacred, the authority of the society is validated, and the egocentric impulses of individuals that threaten to destroy it are suppressed. As individuals participate in religious rituals, they affirm their place in and subordination to the society. Religions, therefore, serve vital positive functions in maintaining societies, but their explicit beliefs cannot be taken as true statements about the nature of reality, or even of how the people view reality.

The central question social anthropologists asked was, What functions do religions serve in a society? In England A. R. Radcliffe-Brown, who studied tribal religion in Sri Lanka, R. F. Fortune, who studied sorcery among the Dubu, and Raymond Firth, who investigated the ritual cycle of the Tikopia, believed that religions help maintain social cohesion and order by declaring sacred those things that were directly or indirectly essential for their survival.

Bronislaw Malinowski (1935) went a step further. He refused to treat people as anonymous individuals trapped in social webs and their ideas as merely social projections, and recognized the importance of religious beliefs *qua* beliefs. All people, he said, have folk sciences by which they seek to meet their human needs through understandings of how the world works. Religion and magic, he noted, are rational responses to the universally experienced emotions of stress that arise when these sciences fail. The difference between religion and magic is one of purpose. Magic is utilitarian and instrumental. It is used to influence events such as unforeseen calamities that are beyond normal human control. Religion, on the other hand, is an end unto itself. It provides people with an explanation for suffering, crisis, and death, and thereby assures them that the world is indeed orderly and meaningful. Malinowski argued that we must understand the world as the people see it to understand why they act as they do.

Social anthropology has had a deep impact on missions in recent years. Earlier, mission leaders used geography to order their strategies. Missionaries went to India, Africa, or other 'countries,' and divided these into 'mission fields.' DONALD MCGAVRAN, PETER WAGNER, and the CHURCH GROWTH MOVEMENT showed how social dynamics play a major role in the growth and organization of the church. They introduced concepts such as homogeneous groups (*see* HOMOGENEOUS UNIT PRINCIPLE), people movements (*see* MASS MOVEMENTS), and RECEPTIVITY/resistance. The Unreached People movement shifted mission strategies based on geography to ones based on social organization (*see* PEOPLES, PEOPLE GROUPS). Both were in danger, however, of social reductionism, where success is based merely on understanding and applying social principles and measured largely in quantitative terms.

American Historical Approaches to Religion.

A second theoretical challenge to the theory of cultural evolution emerged in North America, and came to be known as American historicism. It was pioneered by Franz Boas (1858–1942), A. L. Kroeber (1876–1960), and their disciples. They studied the North American Indians whose cultures had been shattered and who were now living largely on reservations. Their central questions had to do with religious change, and their chief contributions were a series of historical accounts of nativistic and messianic movements that often emerge where traditional peoples are overrun by modernity. Ralph Linton studied the Ghost Dance of the North American Indians, and Glen Cochrane the Cargo Cults of Melanesia. From such studies A. F. C. Wallace (1956) developed a broad theory explaining these revitalization movements. American anthropologists were also influenced by Sigmund Freud, who saw religion as a projection of authority figures, and William James, who examined the personal emotional dimension of religion.

The American school influenced missions through the writings of ALAN TIPPETT, LOUIS LUZBETAK, JACOB LOEWEN, and other missiologists dealing with CONVERSION and religious change, and through the work of HAROLD TURNER and those studying the African Independent Churches (*see* AFRICAN INITIATED CHURCH MOVEMENT) and other new emerging religious movements (*see* NEW RELIGIOUS MOVEMENTS).

Symbolic and Cognitive Anthropology.

Before World War II, some anthropologists rejected the reduction of religion to social dynamics, and argued we must take religious beliefs seriously as beliefs because they are what people believe to be the true nature of reality. Their central question was how religions give humans a sense of meaning.

L. Levy-Bruhl (1926) saw primal religions as reflections of a "primitive mentality" which has its own rationality, one that is radically different from that of modern science. Primitive logic, he argued, is mystical, and governed by emotions, dreams, and notions about supernatural entities. JOHN TAYLOR (1963) captured this approach in his study of African religions. These scholars overestimate the rationality of Western thought, and ignore the fact that in much of their lives, all people use natural common sense.

E. E. Evans-Pritchard also moved from "function to meaning" in his study of magic and witchcraft among the Azande (1937) and Nuer (1940) of Africa. He argued that the Azande have sound empirical knowledge of nature which they distinguish from the 'mystical' workings of magic and witchcraft, and that the latter are rational systems of thought, given the assumptions the Azande have about the world. He held that cosmological beliefs provide people with their categories of thought, and noted that tribal religions are this-worldly religions concerned with "abundant life and fullness of years."

Edmund Leach, Mary Douglas, Victor Turner, and Claude Lèvi-Strauss opened the door further to cognitive structural approaches to the study of religion. Douglas (1966) argues that religions create symbolic systems about purity and pollution, sacred and profane that reflect and reinforce social orders. Victor Turner (1974) analyzed the structure of religious rituals and showed how they serve as boundary markers, setting off various types of social reality and transforming persons from one status to another (*see also* RITES OF PASSAGE). Lèvi-Strauss (1966) affirmed that behind the empirical diversity of religions, human minds are fundamentally the same everywhere. He contended that religion, like science, provides humans with a sense of meaning by mentally ordering the world in which they live, and that this meaning is generated by the universal unconscious processes of the human mind.

Social and symbolic approaches examine the underlying structures of religions, but do not study the content of their beliefs. Taking a problem-solving approach, Clifford Geertz argues that religion provides answers to three fundamental human experiences that threaten to make life meaningless: the problem of bafflement when human explanation systems fail, the problem of suffering and death, and the problem of injustice or feeling of moral disorder and chaos. Religion answers these by appealing to higher realities outside of daily experience. Robin Horton (1964) goes further and examines the content of African religious beliefs. He sees them as theoretical models of reality, like those of science, but that they transcend the everyday world of common sense. Daryl Forde, Marcel Griaule, and others show that religions are philosophical systems that shape peoples' worldviews.

Symbolic and cognitive anthropology has much to contribute to missions, most of which has yet to be mined. These approaches take traditional religions seriously, and help us to provide Christian responses to the questions FOLK RELIGIONS ask rather than ignoring them as superstitions. They help us understand the importance of rituals (*see* RITUAL AND CEREMONY) and myths (*see* MYTH, MYTHOLOGY) in religious life, and the importance for missionaries influenced by the modern denigrating of these to rediscover their importance in the life of the church. However, while taking the religious beliefs of people seriously, most intellectualists fail to raise the ontological question of the truth of these religious beliefs. It is here that Christian anthropologists must go beyond the current approaches, and lead in new ways of studying religions.

PAUL G. HIEBERT

Bibliography. M. Douglas, *Purity and Danger;* E. Durkeim, *The Elementary Forms of Religious Life;* E. E. Evans-Pritchard, *Witchcraft, Oracles and Magic among the Azande;* idem, *The Nuer;* J. G. Frazer, *The Golden Bough: A Study in Magic and Religion;* R. Horton, *Africa,* 34 (1964): 85–104; L. Lèvy-Bruhl, *How Natives Think;* C. Lèvi-Strauss, *The Savage Mind;* B. Malinowski, *Coral Gardens and Their Magic;* J. V. Taylor, *The Primal Vision;* V. Turner, *The Ritual Process;* E. B. Tylor,

Primitive Culture; A. F. C. Wallace, *American Anthropologist,* 58 (1956): 264–81.

Antigua and Barbuda *(Est. 2000 pop.: 68,000; 442 sq. km. [171 sq. mi.]).* Antigua, an arid, volcanic Caribbean island, and nearby Barbuda, a coralline island, formed a British dependency of nearly 100,000 inhabitants until it became independent in 1981. The inhabitants rely on tourism and light industry. The population of the two islands, 98 percent Afro-Caribbean, is in large part nominally Protestant, of whom 12 percent are evangelical.

EVERETT A. WILSON

SEE ALSO Caribbean.

Bibliography. A. Lampe, *The Church in Latin America, 1492–1992,* pp. 201–15; J. Rogozinski, *A Brief History of the Caribbean: From the Arawak and the Carib to the Present.*

Apartheid. *See* ETHNOCENTRISM.

Apologetics. *Definitions and Distinctions.* In a general sense apologetics (from the Greek *apologia,* "a defense") can be understood as the defense of the distinctive beliefs or practices of a particular religious tradition against criticisms from those outside that tradition. As such, apologetics can be found among a variety of religions and usually occurs when a particular religious tradition is confronted with different religious or nonreligious perspectives that call into question some of the central beliefs, values, and practices of that tradition. Although the term is usually associated today with Christianity, the history and literature of Judaism, Islam, Hinduism, and Buddhism are replete with examples of apologetics directed at alternative religious and philosophical perspectives.

Christian apologetics is the response of the Christian community to criticisms of the truth-claims about God, human beings, sin, salvation, and Jesus Christ, which are said to apply to all people in all cultures at all times. This inevitably brings Christian faith into conflict with alternative worldviews that assume quite different beliefs. The history of Christian missions is in part the story of very different peoples worldwide coming to modify their worldviews and to accept central Christian beliefs as true. An integral element in this process has been successful Christian apologetics, which helps people eliminate obstacles to belief and resolve questions of doubt.

Theoretical apologetics, or "problem solving" apologetics, is concerned with the objective justification of the Christian faith irrespective of any human response. The purpose here is to answer satisfactorily certain fundamental questions about the truth of the Christian worldview: How do we acquire religious knowledge? Can we know whether God exists, and if so, how? Are the Scriptures a reliable revelation from God? Did Jesus in fact rise from the dead? Discussion on this level involves highly technical issues in disciplines such as philosophy, history, archaeology, the sciences, biblical criticism, and so on.

Applied apologetics, or apologetics as "persuasion," is very much concerned with human response to the proclamation of the gospel. It actively seeks to persuade others to accept Christian faith as true. Applied apologetics involves appropriate and culturally sensitive justification procedures and data in the actual defense of the truth-claims of Christianity to a particular target audience. Effective applied apologetics must be creative, flexible, and sensitive to the distinctives of each audience. Applied apologetics builds on theoretical apologetics; answers to questions raised on the applied level (How can I be sure that God really exists?) are logically dependent upon answers to corresponding questions on the theoretical level (does God exist?). But applied apologetics is person- and culture-specific in a way that theoretical apologetics is not. The kinds of issues raised in an Islamic context will differ from those emerging from Buddhist or post-Christian secularist contexts. Appropriate levels of sophistication in apologetic response will vary with individuals, depending on educational background. Appropriate means of persuasion will also vary with cultures; vigorous public debates on religious issues might be acceptable in one culture but counterproductive in others.

A further distinction is often made between positive (offensive) and negative (defensive) apologetics. *Negative apologetics* is primarily concerned with responding to direct attacks on the Christian faith, showing that the criticism is unjustified. *Positive apologetics* goes beyond merely responding to attacks and attempts to demonstrate that the unbeliever also ought to accept the claims of Christianity as true. Positive apologetics tries to show that there is adequate reason or justification for accepting the truth-claims of Christianity.

Theological Guidelines. Some biblical guidelines for apologetics should be noted. Scripture teaches that the mind and thinking processes are tainted by sin, and that the mind is used to distort what we know to be true about God (Rom. 1:18–20; 1 Cor. 2:14; 2 Cor. 4:4). But the effects of sin should not be exaggerated. For even the unregenerate retain the image of God and can know some things to be true about God (Rom. 1:19–21).

Furthermore, the essential role of the Holy Spirit in effective apologetics must be acknowledged. Apologetics, just like evangelism, is ineffective apart from the work of the Holy Spirit on the heart (1 Cor. 12:3; Titus 3:5–6). It is the Holy Spirit who convicts of sin, removes spiritual

blindness, and produces new birth (John 3:3–8; 16:8–11; 1 Cor. 2:14–16). But this does not make apologetics unnecessary any more than it renders evangelism optional. Although ultimately it is the Holy Spirit who produces confidence in the truth of the gospel within the believer (Rom. 8:16; 1 John 3:24; 4:13), the Spirit uses various means in bringing about this conviction of truth. By removing obstacles to belief and also showing positive grounds for belief, apologetics can be used by the Spirit to produce confidence in the gospel.

Scripture indicates that appeal to evidential factors in support of the truth-claims of Christian faith is legitimate. The examples of the Old Testament prophets, our Lord Jesus Christ, and the apostles all illustrate appropriate use of evidential factors in support of one's claims. When challenged on his authority to forgive sins Jesus responded by providing visible evidence of his authority in healing the paralytic (Mark 2:1–12). Paul frequently appealed to various forms of evidence in support of his claim that Jesus was the Messiah (Acts 9:22; 13:16–41; 17:2–3, 22–31) and the bodily resurrection of Jesus (1 Cor. 15:3–19).

Apologetics is not the same thing as EVANGELISM. Evangelism, understood as the COMMUNICATION of the gospel of Jesus Christ, has a certain priority over apologetics. But where appropriate, evangelism should be supplemented by an informed and sensitive response to criticisms and questions, demonstrating why the unbeliever ought to accept the gospel as truth. Both apologetics and evangelism should be conducted with much prayer and conscious reliance on the Holy Spirit.

Christian theologians do not agree on the nature of appropriate Christian apologetics. Virtually all thinkers would accept that negative apologetics is appropriate and necessary; erroneous views should be refuted and specific criticisms of Christianity should be answered. But not all theologians endorse positive apologetics. For some, any attempt to demonstrate the truth of the Christian faith is to subject God and his revelation to a higher norm for truth and thus must be rejected. God's self-revelation is held to be self-authenticating and in need of no external corroboration. Others regard this position to be epistemologically confused and contend that this view ultimately reduces to a cognitive relativism that is incapable of either justifying its own claim to truth or rejecting alternative perspectives as false.

Apologetics and Missions. Apologetics has a long, if not always distinguished, history in Christian missions. The early church produced some brilliant apologists (Justin, Tertullian, Clement, and later Augustine) who effectively addressed criticisms arising from Hellenistic culture and Roman paganism. During the twelfth through fifteenth centuries writers such as Peter the Venerable and RAYMON LULL wrote significant apologetic works directed against Islam. Thomas Aquinas' enormously influential *Summa contra gentiles* was intended in part to be a training manual for Christian missionaries among Muslims in Spain. MATTEO RICCI in seventeenth-century China produced impressive and effective writings directed to the cultural elite influenced by Confucianism. Nineteenth-century Protestants such as W. A. P. MARTIN in China and Joseph Edkins in Japan wrote influential works defending Christianity and raising questions about opposing perspectives.

Some issues have been of perennial concern throughout various cultures and times. The problem of evil/suffering, for example, is a classic problem for apologetics, which finds expression in writings from ancient Hellenism as well as in Hindu, Confucian, and Buddhist critiques of Christianity. The Renaissance and Enlightenment in Europe placed a new set of issues on the table. Christian apologetics in the West in the past three centuries has been dominated by the post-Enlightenment agenda, focusing on issues such as the existence of God, faith and reason, the relation between science and Scripture, the question of miracles, the resurrection of Jesus, and the reliability of Scripture. Given the increasingly global spread of MODERNITY and SECULARIZATION, non-Western churches will need to develop appropriate responses to these issues as well. However, each culture also presents a unique set of challenges to the gospel. Thus Christian communities in various cultures will need to study their own cultures, discern the particular challenges to Christian faith that arise within those contexts, and respond in a biblically sound and culturally appropriate manner to those issues.

A particularly urgent problem facing the church worldwide is the increasingly vigorous attack on the Christian claim to the uniqueness and sufficiency of Jesus Christ as the only Savior for all humankind. Resurgence of the great religions of Islam, Hinduism, and Buddhism, combined with a sense of nationalism and anti-Western sentiment, has made the exclusive claims of Christianity highly problematical in many cultures today. The West itself is increasingly characterized by ethnic and religious diversity. Such pluralization, combined with growing disenchantment with Christianity in the West and increased relativism in ethical and religious matters, makes religious PLURALISM an extremely attractive ideology. Thus, whether in the West or in non-Western contexts, the church must be prepared to show why it can claim that in Jesus alone can we find the Way, the Truth, and the Life (John 14:6).

HAROLD A. NETLAND

Bibliography. D. Clark, *Dialogical Apologetics;* W. Craig, *Reasonable Faith: Christian Truth and Apologetics;* G. Lewis, *Testing Christianity's Truth Claims;* J. K. S. Reid, *Christian Apologetics;* P. Griffiths, *An Apology for Apologetics.*

Apostasy. The deliberate abandonment of the beliefs and practices of a religion by one who was formerly an adherent. The concept entered Christianity through Judaism, where Old Testament examples of individuals (2 Chron. 29:19) and corporate Israel (Jer. 2:1–9) turning from Yahweh are found.

The New Testament contains examples of apostasy and warnings against it. Judas is the prime example, but others are also named (1 Tim. 1:19–20; 2 Tim. 4:10). In the "warning passages" the writer of Hebrews reminds the readers of the consequences of apostasy (6:4–8; 10:26).

Missionaries today likewise reckon with the possibility of apostasy among converts, a possibility often aggravated by persecution or false teachers. In this context the church must wrestle with a number of different issues, most of which have been given a variety of instructive responses during the early history of the church.

What is essential to Christianity such that its denial indicates a denial of the faith? How far can one depart before becoming apostate? Apostasy should be distinguished from heresy in both kind and degree, although in practice the line is not always easily drawn. Heresy is denial of one or more tenets of the faith while still claiming to be Christian, whereas apostasy is a total rejection of the faith itself. Apostasy should also be distinguished from a temporary lapse in faith such as that manifested by the apostle Peter's denials (Matt. 26:31–35, 69–75).

How should apostasy be theologically understood? Is it possible for a true believer to cease to believe and fall from salvation? Calvinists point to God's purpose and power to preserve his chosen (John 6:37–39; 10:28–29) and to the eternal nature of regeneration in support of the view that the apostate has not lost his or her salvation, but was rather never genuinely saved in the first place. Apostasy reveals the unbelief earlier masked by an outward profession and association with the believing community (cf. Judas, Matt. 7:21–23; 1 John 2:19). Others point to the biblical warnings against departure, scriptural examples, and anecdotal evidence in saying that an apostate actually loses his or her salvation.

Once apostatized, is restoration possible? This question was important to the church in its first several centuries due to intense persecution and frequent apostasy. In the early church restoration was only possible beginning in the third century and then only through conditions of penitence. Before that time apostasy was usually considered unpardonable. Church leaders sometimes made distinctions among apostates, such as between those who apostatized voluntarily and those who did so under compulsion.

How should apostates be treated by the faithful? In the Reformation period both Catholics and Protestants used civil power to punish those charged with apostasy. However, it later became widely accepted that persuasion rather than coercion was the Christian ideal.

Missionaries working among Muslims give special consideration to Islam's law of apostasy in understanding the spirit of intolerance and persecution and the consequent fear of conversion to Christianity. The general dictum of Muslim tradition is, "He that adopts any other religion shall be put to death."

SCOTT CUNNINGHAM

Bibliography. ERE, I:623–26; S. M. Zwemer, *The Law of Apostasy in Islam.*

Apostle, Apostles. The numerous appearances of the word *apostle* in the New Testament compared with its relative absence from all other literary sources can be traced in part to its intimate relationship to the mission of the early church. The New Testament writers, especially Luke and Paul, picked up on Jesus' rare usage of the word to give importance to the missionary dynamic of the church. Apostle is almost synonymous with mission. The word is primarily used of the twelve men chosen by Jesus to accompany him and of Paul the missionary to the Gentiles. These, along with a small number of other apostles, were vanguard missionaries as the gospel moved from Jewish particularism to multicultural universalism.

According to the Synoptic Gospels, Acts, and the Epistles, Jesus specifically designated at least these thirteen people to be his apostles. The Twelve came out of Jesus' own sociocultural context, accompanying him on his mission to the Jews (Matt. 10:1–2; 15:24; John 20:21). One of the Twelve abandoned his apostolic office and was replaced by Matthias (Acts 1:16–26). Jesus chose a thirteenth apostle a few years after his ascension (1 Cor. 15:9). Together, they were specifically chosen to continue Jesus' mission. The Twelve functioned to authenticate Jesus' mission and message of the inclusion of the Gentiles (Gal. 2:1–10; Acts 1:16–26); Paul was chosen especially to implement and clarify the mission to the Gentiles.

Biblical Study of Apostleship. Apostle (*apostolos*) is defined by its use in the New Testament and its relationship to the three words *apostellō*, *pempō*, and the Twelve. *Apostellō* ("to send") is used frequently in the Gospels, Acts, and the Epistles when referring to an authoritative commission. John never uses the word in a formal sense; rather, he uses the words *apostellō* and *pempō* as synonymous terms describing Jesus' authoritative mission and commissioning (John 20:21).

Apostolos is used eighty times in the New Testament and rarely used outside the New Testament. Josephus used it only once in any comparative sense. Eighty-six percent of these 80 occurrences are found in the writings of Paul (35x) and Luke (34x). The 11 other uses are found throughout the New Testament.

The word *apostle* is indebted to the Hebrew term *shaliach*. A *shaliach*, as used by the Jews, was someone sent by one party to another to handle negotiations concerning matters secular (such as marriage) or matters religious (such as liturgical decisions between Jerusalem and the diaspora). But the universal mission of Jesus determined the precise New Testament definition and prominence of the term.

The New Testament use of apostle arose out of the need to authenticate a mission that reversed the particularistic nature of salvation history. This definition would stress (1) the relationship to Jesus and his incarnation, and (2) the Christian's participation in extending the mission begun by Jesus.

In its broadest sense the word *apostle* can refer to a church sending members on a mission (1 Cor. 8:23; Phil. 2:23; Acts 14:4, 14). This mission can include preaching the gospel, raising money, or ministering to another missionary. The number of those included in this broader sense are unknown.

Apostles and Mission in Paul. From a literary and theological standpoint, the first definition of apostle can be traced to Paul's writings. He uses the word throughout his writings (35x), with its usage concentrated in 23 references in Romans (3x), 1 Corinthians (10x), 2 Corinthians (7x), and Galatians (3x). Paul's polemical use of this term can be traced to his Gentile mission (Rom. 1:5; 11:13; Gal. 1–2). The radical nature of Paul's preaching elicited opposition from Jews within and outside the church. How was Paul going to legitimate his mission and message? He was compelled to clarify his own special calling and commission. Thus, Paul's use of the term *apostle* was fundamentally missiological.

Paul's nonpolemical and even general use of this term in 1 Thessalonians 2:6, when compared with its use in his other early Epistles, shows the extent to which his use of the term is tied to his need to authenticate his mission. Paul allowed for a general use of the word *apostle* while clearly defending a technical use for an exclusive few. While he calls a number of people apostles, he sees the Twelve (1 Cor. 15:3) and himself (Gal. 1:1) as apostles in a special sense.

Paul's use of apostle in his discussion of his mission to the Gentiles shows the direct relationship between apostle and mission. The Twelve and Paul were responsible for clarifying the nature of the church's mission (Gal. 2:1–10). Jesus specifically chose the Twelve to extend his mission into the Jewish world and authenticate the Gentile mission. Paul's personal mission was to implement, defend, and clarify the mission to the Gentiles. Even when Paul stresses the revelational dimensions of the word *apostle,* the missiological implications remain prominent (Eph. 3:1–13).

Apostles and Mission in Luke. Luke uniformly uses the word *apostles* (pl.) in Luke–Acts (34x). He never specifically calls any one person an apostle. In all but three occurrences (Luke 11:49; Acts 14:4, 14) it is used of the twelve apostles chosen by Jesus. He uses the word six times in his Gospel and twenty-eight times in Acts. Whereas in his Gospel Luke calls the apostles disciples, in Acts he only calls them apostles. Luke alone specifically says that Jesus called the Twelve apostles (Luke 6:13).

Luke's view of apostleship as seen in Acts is rooted primarily in his missiology and only secondarily in his ecclesiology. The decision of the 120 in choosing an apostolic replacement for Judas is the central event between the ascension and Pentecost (1:12–26). Why does this decision on an apostolic replacement occupy such a prominent place in Luke's narrative? Luke accents its importance by giving the qualification and the definition of an apostle and by recording *only* this event between the ascension and Pentecost (1:21–25). An apostle is defined as someone who has followed Jesus from the time of John the Baptist until the resurrection. Second, his function is to bear witness to the resurrection (cf. Acts 1:15–26 with 1 Cor. 9:1ff.; 15:7–11).

The following conclusions can be drawn from Acts 1:15–26. The apostles are twelve in number; they must have accompanied Jesus since the time of his baptism; and their basic function is witnessing about the resurrection. Judas' betrayal of Christ and abandonment of his office were prophesied in the Old Testament. Second, God directed the entire electoral process, even in the casting of lots (24–26). Third, Matthias is "chosen" just as the eleven were (Acts 1:2, 13). These twelve Spirit-filled apostles chosen by Jesus will extend the mission begun by Jesus.

But why is it so important that Luke establish the apostolic Twelve as a unique group and what relationship does this have to the mission to the Gentiles? Luke's definition of apostleship is found in the context of his overall purpose in writing a two-volume narrative of early Christianity. For Luke, the inclusion of the Gentiles takes place, not as an aberration involving some marginal Christians, but through an unbroken procession that begins with Jesus and continues through the Hellenists and Paul. Luke wants to establish these twelve apostles chosen by Jesus as successors of Jesus, thus legitimizing the Gentile mission.

These twelve lay the foundation of the mission in their ministry in Jerusalem. They, then, confirm the strategic ministry of the Hellenists (Acts 6:1–7; 8:14–14). Peter's paradigmatic mission to the Gentiles reflects the nature of the church (Acts 10:1–11:18; 15:1–35; 16:4). All other witnesses who come after them are part of this chain of events that results in the inclusion of the Gentiles. The apostles' strategic role in salvation history is both missiological and ecclesiological. Out of their missionary ministry arises a church whose fundamental calling is to constantly push forward into those areas where the gospel has yet to be heard.

Luke's use of the word *apostle* for Paul (14:4, 14) merits a brief comment. In both of these instances Barnabas is equally linked with Paul, and in one instance (v. 14) the order of their names is reversed. Luke, like Paul, uses apostles in a secondary sense, that is, Barnabas and Paul are apostles of the Antiochene church. Does Luke's failure to call Paul an apostle in the primary sense indicate some tension between Paul's definition and Luke's? For Luke the Twelve are unique (with this Paul agrees, 1 Cor. 15:9; Gal. 2:1–10), but Paul receives even greater prominence in Acts than do they. Paul's authority, mission, and effectiveness are, if anything, superior to those of the Twelve. But for Luke each has a special role to play in world evangelization.

Summary and Conclusion. The early church found in the word *apostle* a key concept for describing the unique nature of its mission. But it was Paul and Luke in particular who unpacked this term and left us with a rich theology of apostleship. An apostle is a person who was with Jesus during his incarnation (a Lukan concept), witnessed his resurrection, and participated in authenticating and engaging in worldwide missions.

While Paul and Luke have unique developments of apostleship, both agree that the twelve apostles chosen by Jesus became missionaries to the Jews and laid the foundation for a mission to the nations. Both Luke and Paul agree that Paul had a unique role in this mission. Paul's preference would be to use the term *apostle* to describe his authority and mission. Although Luke uses this for Paul only in a secondary sense, he would readily agree with Paul that his mission and calling are unique. The word *apostle* may be used in this secondary sense today, yet not without clarifying its meaning.

There is, then, a fundamental relationship between the concept of apostleship and the mission to the world. Any definition of the term *apostle* that neglects its missiological dimensions has missed a central ingredient, without which the term loses some of its dynamic.

HAROLD E. DOLLAR

Bibliography. F. Agnew, *JBL* 105 (1986): 75–96; F. W. Barnett, *DPHL*, pp. 45–51; A. C. Clark, *ERT* 13 (1989): 344–83; K. Lake, *Beginnings*, pp. 37–58; J. B. Lightfoot, *The Epistle of St. Paul to the Galatians*, pp. 92–101; K. H. Rengstorf, *TDNT*, 1:407–47.

Archives, Mission. *See* MISSION LIBRARIES.

Argentina *(Est. 2000 pop.: 36,648,000; 2,780,400 sq. km. [1,073,512 sq. mi.]).* A nation with a strong European culture, nominally Roman Catholic (85%), but with a sizable minority of Protestants (8%), and an important Jewish community, Argentina occupies a long stretch in South America, sharing borders with Chile (West); Bolivia and Paraguay (North); Brazil and Uruguay (Northeast).

One of the most remarkable features of Argentina's religious history has been the endurance and the stability of the Roman Catholic Church. Throughout the colonial period (to 1810), the Church remained unchallenged and monolithic in its dominance of public religion. Church officials breathed the spirit of the Roman religion into the structures of the Spanish colonial administration, and Catholic cultural hegemony became an inevitable fact of life. Three centuries thus passed between the beginning of Roman Catholic evangelization and the introduction of Protestant Christianity. Apart from isolated cases, Protestant penetration did not begin until the first third of the nineteenth century.

The advance of liberal ideas from France and the growing political and economic influence of the Anglo-American powers fostered such penetration. These liberals saw in Protestantism an ally with which to confront the regalist and clerical order inherited from Spain, and looked to the Protestant countries as their political models. With the struggles between church and state that followed independence, the power of the Roman Catholic Church began to wane and Protestantism made inroads into Argentina. During this period (1810–50), Roman Catholic relations with the state were marked by acrimony. The Church lost the support of the state, which sought to restrict the religious sphere of influence by introducing civil registration and marriage, secularized cemeteries, abolishing tithes, and expropriating the Church's lands. In spite of these troubles, however, Catholicism retained the loyalty of the masses and the Church continued to have structural links with the state.

Because it was thus planted in a culturally hostile environment, Protestantism grew very slowly during the first decades of its presence. It appeared in the country via three routes. At the beginning, it was an importation brought by European immigrants who came to the country as part of the colonizing efforts on liberal governments. Leaders such as Domingo F. Sarmiento saw in Protestantism an ally against ignorance and superstition and against the excessive power of the clergy, and welcomed European immigrants. Dozens of groups settled in Argentina: British Anglicans (1824), Scottish Presbyterians (1825), Welsh Baptists (1865), Italian Waldensians (1859), German Lutherans (1843), and Dutch Reformed. These immigrants tended to settle close to each other in order to preserve their ethnic, cultural, and linguistic identity. They generally did not engage in missionary work.

A second path of early Protestant penetration in Argentina was the work of the American and British Bible societies. Many colporteurs (*see* COLPORTAGE) traveled throughout the country following a common pattern: "First the Bible, then a convert, then a church." A third, later pattern of penetration came with missionary activity fostered by the Protestant churches of Europe and North America. Many of the missions came late to Argentina because Protestant missionary societies of the period considered the country to be already Christianized. As late as 1910, for this reason, the country as well as Latin America as a whole was not included in the agenda of the WORLD MISSIONARY CONFERENCE held in Edinburgh. The needs of the region, however, were increasingly recognized, and in 1916 the continent was officially considered to be a mission field by the Congress on Christian Work in Latin America, which met in Panama that year (*see* PANAMA CONGRESS). By then, Protestant missionary efforts in Argentina, though limited, were eighty years old.

With the work of European and especially North American missionary societies, a new phase of Protestant expansion began, through conversion rather than immigration, as first the Presbyterians and later the Methodists, Baptists, Plymouth Brethren, and Seventh-Day Adventists arrived. In this way, Protestantism gained a foothold in Argentina toward the close of the nineteenth century and, through the establishment of mission churches and institutions, began to develop and grow in size.

In the twentieth century, Protestant missionary penetration in Argentina has occurred most regularly and effectively in the urban areas. The rate of urban growth in Argentina, especially in the past fifty-five years, has been very significant. In this urban context, new evangelical denominations have found extraordinary opportunities for mission, especially the Pentecostals. Today, Pentecostal denominations represent 75 percent of the Protestants in Argentina.

Most converts to Protestantism in Argentina are nominal Roman Catholics. They integrate into congregations that will receive the generic qualification of "evangelical," in the sense of non-Catholic or Protestant. The different churches or denominations in the country generally tend to be strikingly heterogeneous and to reflect three influences: the social environment in which they are developing, their particular ecclesiastical and theological tradition, and their overseas links.

The first type corresponds to mainline Protestantism, which is also called historical Protestantism, because it is related to the churches of the Reformation. It is found in the ethnic communities of immigrant origin and in the churches founded by the missionaries of these groups, mostly from the United States and Europe, that followed the settlers. With them, the historical churches opened themselves to the native community. These churches are suffering a deep crisis of identity and mission.

However, today's most characteristic form of Argentinean Protestantism is evangelical Protestantism. Evangelicalism in Argentina corresponds to a current inside the great Protestant confessions associated with the "free church" tradition. This type includes both denominational and nondenominational missions. The majority of these ecclesiastical institutions reached Argentina through missionary work from the United States. So influential are these denominations that "evangelical" is today practically synonymous with "Protestant" in Argentina. This Protestantism is fundamentally conservative in doctrine and firmly committed to zealous evangelization.

A third expression of Argentinean Protestantism is Pentecostalism, represented either in autochthonous Pentecostal movements that emerged from the evangelical denominations or in movements that originated in the missionary work of European and American Pentecostals in the first decades of the twentieth century. In the second half of this century a new type developed, noted by the term "charismatic movement" or "charismatic renewal movement," which has drawn members from classic Pentecostalism as well as from both the historical and missionary churches. An even more recent development and in many ways the most dynamic one, is a post-denominational movement that Wagner calls the new apostolic reformation (see NEW APOSTOLIC REFORMATION MISSIONS). Interestingly, this movement is growing among the more traditional evangelical churches.

PABLO DEIROS

Bibliography. A. W. Enns, *Man, Milieu, and Mission in Argentina: A Close Look at Church Growth;* J. L. Mecham, *Church and State in Latin America: A History of Politico-eclesiastical Relations.*

Argue, Andrew Harvey (1868–1959). Canadian Pentecostal pioneer, pastor, and evangelist. Reared in a Methodist family in Ontario, he received a sixth-grade education before moving west to Winnipeg, where he became a successful realtor and a lay preacher in the Holiness Movement Church. In 1907 he went to Chicago to hear William Durham and received the Pentecostal experience. Returning to Canada he introduced others to Pentecostalism, emphasizing divine healing, the baptism of the Holy Spirit, and the premillennial return of Christ. He founded Calvary Temple in Winnipeg, which became one of Canada's largest Pentecostal churches. From this center he encouraged the establishment of other charismatic churches in the major cities of his homeland. He was also instrumental in the emergence of the Pentecostal Assemblies of Canada (1910–20). Leaving his business and ministry, he became a traveling evangelist with his daughter Zelma and his son Watson during the 1920s and 1930s. Among his many publications, the most notable was a magazine, the *Apostolic Messenger.* His preaching, leadership, church founding, and writings led to the growth of the Pentecostal movement in Canada. However, even more important than these activities was the inspiration that his children and their spouses provided for the movement of the Holy Spirit in their native land.

ROBERT CLOUSE

Bibliography. Z. Argue, *Contending for the Faith.*

Armenia (*Est. 2000 pop.: 3,813,000; 29,800 sq. km. [11,506 sq. mi.]*). Armenia is a landlocked, mountainous republic of the former Soviet Union, located in the southern Caucasus region. Armenia was evangelized during the third century and is considered to be the world's first Christian state. More than 75 percent of the population claims allegiance to the Armenian Apostolic Church, including nearly one hundred thousand people who participate in a significant autonomous evangelical movement known as the Brotherhood. Protestant evangelicals, the majority of whom are Pentecostal, are growing in numbers but make up less than one percent of the population. Few expatriate missionaries serve in Armenia.

RAYMOND P. PRIGODICH

SEE ALSO Commonwealth of Independent States.

Arminian Theology. Arminianism is an influential movement within Protestant Christianity founded by Jacobus Arminius (1560–1609), a Dutch Reformed pastor, professor, and theologian.

The Founder. Arminius lived during the revolt of the Netherlands against the domination of Spain, a conflict led by William, Prince of Orange, conducted intermittently from 1566 to 1609. During this time, the Dutch Reformation was taking shape in the Netherlands. In 1581, Leiden University sent Arminius to study in John Calvin's Academy in Geneva, at the time the principal Reformed university in Europe. Ordained a minister in the Reformed Church in Amsterdam, Arminius served as a pastor from 1587 to 1603.

In the Reformed churches in the Netherlands, Calvinism prevailed. A Presbyterian form of church government was adopted and the Belgic Confession and Heidelberg Catechism were considered to be theologically foundational, together with the Bible. However, there was also some feeling that these theological documents should be checked against the Bible as the only foundation for Christian faith. Arminius called for a free church founded only upon the Holy Scriptures, and a state that defended the opportunity for freedom of conscience.

The Remonstrants. In 1610 a group of forty-four ministers of the Dutch Reformed Church signed a theological statement known as the Remonstrants, supporting the emphases of Arminius. In 1618, representatives from most of the Reformed churches in Europe convened the Synod of Dort in Dordrecht, the Netherlands. The Synod condemned Arminianism and followers of Arminius were excommunicated. They responded immediately by establishing a new denomination known as the Remonstrant Brotherhood, with church laws based on tolerance, peacefulness, and "knowledge of the truth which accords with godliness" (Titus 1:1).

Theological Emphases of Early Arminianism. Solidly Reformed, the Remonstrants nevertheless vehemently opposed the Dutch Calvinist view of predestination that before the fall, even before creation, God had already determined the eternal destiny of each person. The Remonstrants emphasized the following five major points: (a) "that those who believe in Christ are saved and those who do not are damned, and that neither is the result of divine predestination; (b) that Christ died on the cross for the redemption of all (people), not just the elect; (c) that (humans) receive saving faith not from their own free will but from the grace of God by rebirth and renewal; (d) that all good works are solely due to the grace of God; and (e) that although humans can remain in a state of grace and will be sustained and protected by the Holy Spirit, it is possible for them, through their own negligence, to lose that state" (Lambetus Jacobus van Holk, in G. McCulloh, 1962, 28).

Wesleyan Methodism. During the next two centuries Arminianism became a primary stream in Protestantism in England, continental Europe, and North America, due especially to the work and ministry of two of the most famous Arminians, John and Charles Wesley. English Methodists regard Arminianism as their communion's special heritage.

Arminianism's Missionary Zeal. In *The Marks of a Methodist*, Methodist Bishop Gerald Kennedy writes, "Sometimes I think the GREAT COMMISSION was given with the Methodists in mind. For if there has ever been a Church with the word 'go' at the center of its life, it is the Methodist Church. . . . Any church must be missionary in spirit or it dies. But this is particularly true for Methodism because its whole spirit and polity are not proper for a finished institution. We must march or lose our life. . . . This devotion is the mark of a Methodist" (1960, 37–44).

Samuel Wesley, the father of John and Charles, was so committed to missionary zeal that in 1705 he presented Queen Anne of England a comprehensive scheme for the evangelization of the East, offering to go himself as a missionary to Abyssinia, India, or China (G. Smith, *History of Wesleyan Methodism*, I:1859, 81). It is no wonder, then, that six months after their father's death, John and Charles were on their way to the distant colony of Georgia, on the American continent. John Wesley's famous saying, "The world is my parish," expresses the missionary and evangelistic concern which was Wesley's deepest passion—a passion Wesley received from his Arminian roots (*see also* WESLEYAN/HOLINESS MISSIONS).

"The theology of Calvinism arises, naturally and properly, as a theology of the people of God within the household of God. An Arminian theology arises equally naturally and properly as a theology of mission to the unbeliever. . . . Wesley's Arminianism . . . was an Arminianism of the heart, a precondition of the missionary activity undertaken that all (people) might be saved by the power of Christ" (G. Nutall in G. McCulloh, 1962, 59–61).

Arminian Contributions to Mission Theology. Arminian thought has contributed to mission theology in at least the following five major areas. First, the insistence that Christ died for all peoples (not only the elect) has provided a fundamental and strong motivation for mission on the part of those churches grounded in Arminian theology. Second, the emphasis on the experience of conversion and a personal relationship with Jesus Christ provided a powerful impetus for evangelism, support for revivalism and a call for the transformation of all of life. Third, Arminianism's stress on prevenient grace (differing from Roman Catholic natural theology and Calvinist general revelation) emphasized that God's grace heals the disorders caused by sin and perfects everything that can be called good (in humans). Thus, all good works, without exception, are to be attributed to God alone, and to the operation of his grace. This perspective provided a remarkable openness to differing cultural forms around the world, providing a foundation for a very creative approach to cultural analysis and contextualization.

Fourth, the Arminian call for religious freedom of the church in relation to the state provided a free-wheeling, creative approach to mission that was relatively unencumbered by the control of colonial governments. Finally, the Arminian view of human freedom and responsibility in synergistic cooperation with God, coupled with Wesleyan and later Methodist emphases on disciplined Christian activism as God's agents of mission, provided the people and forms that powerfully contributed to world evangelization and social reform on every continent during the last two centuries.

CHARLES VAN ENGEN

Bibliography. C. Bangs, *Arminius: A Study in the Dutch Reformation;* G. Curtis, *Arminianism in History;* J. K. Girder, *EDT,* pp. 79–81; G. Kennedy, *The Marks of a Methodist;* A. C. Knudson, *The Doctrine of Redemption;* K. S. Latourette, *A History of Christianity;* G. O. McCulloh, ed., *Man's Faith and Freedom: The Theological Influence of Jacobus Arminius;* T. Runyon, *Wesleyan Theology Today: A Bicentennial Theological Consultation;* G. Smith, *History of Wesleyan Methodism;* W. W. Sweet, *The Story of Religion in America;* H. O. Wiley, *Christian Theology.*

Armstrong, Annie Walker (1850–1938). American missions activist. "Miss Annie" was born in Baltimore, Maryland, the fourth child of James D. and Mary E. Armstrong. Annie's father died when she was an infant; her mother's convictions about Christian missions and the influence of her pastor, Richard B. Fuller, profoundly stimulated young Annie to missions activism.

She was a uniquely successful missions mobilizer, promoter, and supporter. One historian has labeled her a "Dreamer in Action." She led in the formation of the Woman's Missionary Union (WMU) of the Southern Baptist Convention (SBC), establishing mission support networks and stimulating nationwide production of missions educational literature for local SBC churches.

Baltimore's urban plight aroused Armstrong's social involvement. She demonstrated keen leadership abilities and held several positions related to home mission causes in the Convention. Her talents were nationally recognized in 1888 when she became corresponding secretary of the Convention's newly formed Woman's Missionary Union, serving without pay until 1906.

Armstrong's lasting influence was the establishment of one-week prayer and offering emphases for foreign and home missions. CHARLOTTE MOON wrote from China requesting an offering just before Christmas to support new missionaries. The campaign succeeded largely due to Armstrong's tireless efforts and still continues among Convention churches. A similar effort was launched in 1895 to support HOME MISSIONS and is likewise still in effect. The latter bears Armstrong's name as a lasting tribute to a life well spent for mission causes.

KEITH E. EITEL

Bibliography. J. Mather, *ESB,* p. 82; B. Sorrill, *Annie Armstrong: Dreamer in Action;* idem, *Annie Armstrong: Shaper of Missions.*

Arnot, Frederick Stanley (1858–1914). Scottish missionary to Africa. Born into a Free Church family in Glasgow that later transferred to the Christian Brethren, he was converted in his teens and much influenced by DAVID LIVINGSTONE, whose family he knew. He attended Livingstone's funeral in Westminster Abbey in 1874, and was to edit his *Missionary Travels and Researches in South Africa* (1899). Arnot went to South Africa in 1881 and began the first of his many journeys into the hinterland. He was a peacemaker to King Lewanika of the Barotse, and dissuaded him from attacking the white settlers. After working in Angola he went in 1885 to the Belgian Congo, invited by King Mushidi of Garenganze (in modern Zaire), and there established a mission station.

Like Livingstone, Arnot was criticized both for his independence (he was linked to no missionary society and happily helped colleagues of other denominations) and for doubling as an explorer—which brought him a fellowship of the Royal Geographical Society. Arnot nevertheless established many mission stations, despite multiple obstacles including disease and lack of food and water. His example brought other workers, including Dan Crawford and the physician Walter Fisher, and led to the founding of the Christian Mission in Many Lands.

He published two volumes on Garenganze (1889, 1903) and wrote *Missionary Travels in Central Africa* (1913).

J. D. DOUGLAS

Bibliography. E. Baker, *The Life and Explorations of Frederick Stanley Arnot.*

Aroolappen (Arulappan), John Christian (1810–67). South Indian (Tamil) churchman and evangelist. Born in Ukirramankottah, Tinnevelly (Tamil Nadu), John Christian Aroolappen converted from Roman Catholicism to the Anglican Church under CHRISTIAN FRIEDRICH SCHWARTZ. The Aroolappen family later came under the influence of Karl Rhenius. Although trained as a catechist under Rhenius, Aroolappen by 1833 had accepted the ecclesiology and eschatology of the Plymouth (Open) Brethren through the instruction of Anthony Norris Groves.

Along with Groves, Aroolappen believed that Christians should follow the apostolic methods of evangelism portrayed in the New Testament. Furthermore, he believed that the gifts of the Holy Spirit remained available for the growth of the church. When news of spiritual awakenings in America and the United Kingdom reached Tinnevelly, Aroolappen and his followers in Christianpettah prayed for the outpouring of the Spirit (Joel 2:28–29) there as well. Revival began in March 1860 with phenomena that included speaking in tongues, prophecy, and visions. Other notable features included prayer for the sick, helping the poor, women preachers, and the evangelization of non-Christians, which Anglican missionaries noted as the first entirely indigenous effort on the part of Indian Christians. Though the revival, which peaked in 1865, was criticized by missionaries for its unusual phenomena and indigenous leadership, it did contribute to remarkable church growth in Tinnevelly.

GARY B. MCGEE

Bibliography. A. N. Groves, *Memoir of Anthony Norris Groves*, 3rd ed.; G. H. Lang, *History and Diaries of an Indian Christian*; *Church Missionary Intelligencer* 7 (August 1860): 175–89.

Art. From the time of the New Testament Christians have used the various arts to express their faith in Christ, often appropriating and —in the process—transforming art taken from the cultures where they have proclaimed the gospel, as Paul did on Mars Hill. As the church spread throughout the Roman Empire, Christians developed particularly the visual arts and architecture, and later, during the Middle Ages, music and drama. These were all vitally connected with the worship of the church and marked the Christian presence wherever it appeared. Nestorian Christianity in China in the eighth century is marked by a monument making use of fine calligraphy, and carved crosses near Peking date to the fourteenth century.

After the Reformation, Catholic missions, with their strong liturgical traditions, continued to feature the arts. MATTEO RICCI not only introduced foreign influences into Chinese indigenous arts but adapted Chinese ceremonies for Christian purposes, stimulating a debate that finally led to a papal decision against him in 1704. Christians in early-seventeenth-century Japan fashioned holy pictures to grace their homes. In Latin American and Filipino churches sculpture serves as a visual record of the spread of Christianity. Similarly, Orthodox missions have carried with them their consecrated icons that defined the sacred space of orthodox worship.

Modern Protestant missions inherited the iconoclastic and word-centered theology that stems from the Reformation. As a result, while many missionaries made use of music and some, such as WILLIAM CAREY, made special contributions to the advance of literature, the visual arts were largely undeveloped. Even the verbal arts and music were, with a few exceptions, imported from home rather than adapted from local materials— a practice that was, as often as not, encouraged by the attitudes of national Christians. This did not keep Christianity from having in many places a profound impact on indigenous art, as in the case of the so-called Hindu renaissance in India and the presence of Christian artists in most exhibits of contemporary African art.

Happily the growing understanding of culture and its role in faith and worship in our century has made many missionaries sensitive to the importance of the arts. Again the Catholic missionaries have taken the lead in founding centers and artists' guilds where the arts have flourished throughout the world, an advance that was chronicled especially between the wars in the pages of the journal *Liturgical Arts*. Notable among Protestant efforts are the Church Art Society (Episcopal) founded in Nanking, China, in 1934; the Kado Art Association founded after World War II in Japan; the Christian Literature Society in Madras; and the wonderful work of the Protestant church in Bali, Indonesia. All these efforts give promise that the younger churches and their mission activity will show us ways to bring the honor and glory of the nations into the heavenly kingdom.

WILLIAM DYRNESS

Bibliography. W. A. Dyrness, *Christian Art in Asia;* A. Lehmann, *Christian Art in Africa and Asia;* M. Takenaka, *Christian Art in Asia;* R. Taylor, *Jesus in Indian Paintings.*

Arthington, Robert (1823–1900). English missions philanthropist. Born on May 20, 1823, he gave generously to causes fostering frontier evangelistic initiatives among humanity's millions without the gospel. After his death, his estate accrued approximately £1,000,000 for mission causes. The will allowed no endowments and by 1936 his trust ceased. The impact of his giving affected evangelical mission causes throughout Africa and Asia.

Arthington inherited £200,000 from his father in 1864. He rarely engaged in business himself, relying instead on investment managers to increase his wealth. Living meagerly and alone, he became "the miser of Headingley" because of his reluctance to give to local charities.

Yet he was charitable to causes he preferred. Arthington favored evangelistic missions rather than humanitarian ones, as well as those that resisted creating social institutions in order to expedite advancing the gospel in unreached areas. While Arthington gave to various causes, the LONDON MISSIONARY SOCIETY (LMS) and the Baptist Missionary Society (BMS) received the most benefit because of their policies, not because of denominational preference.

Distinctly premillennial eschatological convictions invigorated his missiological ideas and shaped his aim of spreading the gospel among all nations to hasten Christ's return. Arthington helped form strategic policies by his giving. Policies he inspired lend credibility to the claim that some evangelical organizations tended to limit their social entrenchment and resisted aligning with secular governments that were bent on accomplishing temporal imperialistic aims. Eccentric for his day, he nevertheless was an early champion of UNREACHED PEOPLES, deinstitutionalization, interdenominational cooperation, and BIBLE TRANSLATION.

KEITH E. EITEL

Bibliography. L. Pachuau, *ICHR* 28 (1994): 105–25.

Aruba (Netherlands Autonomous Area) *(Est. 2000 pop.: 73,000; 193 sq. km. [75 sq. mi.]).* An arid, low-lying Dutch island just off western Venezuela, Aruba, together with nearby Bonaire and Curaçao, was governed as an integral part of the Kingdom of the Netherlands prior to its secession in 1986. Aruba was for a time the site of an oil refinery. Most Arubans are Antillean Creoles who speak Papismento, a Creole language that includes many Spanish, Portuguese, and Dutch words. The majority of the population is Roman Catholic; 10 percent is Protestant.

EVERETT A. WILSON

SEE ALSO Caribbean.

Bibliography. A. Lampe, *The Church in Latin America, 1492–1992*, pp. 201–15; J. Rogozinski, *A Brief History of the Caribbean: From the Arawak and the Carib to the Present.*

Asbury, Francis (1745–1816). English missionary to North America. Born to Joseph and Elizabeth Rogers Asbury in Handsworth near Birmingham, England, he had little formal education, but apprenticed himself to JOHN WESLEY. Upon arrival in America, he set himself to the task of evangelizing and establishing churches among the migrant pioneers of the emerging country. During the American War for Independence, Asbury was the only one of Wesley's missionary ambassadors to remain. Throughout his itinerant preaching ministry, he traveled the rugged regions by horse, approximately three hundred thousand miles from Canada to Georgia and the Atlantic coast to Kentucky.

In 1784 Wesley appointed both Asbury and THOMAS COKE to the office of superintendent. Soon Asbury assumed the title of bishop contrary to Wesley's wishes. His independent spirit became a hallmark of his ministry, and his single-minded mission led to the firm founding of American Methodism. In 1771, when Asbury arrived, there were approximately three hundred Methodists; by the time Asbury died in 1816, there were over two hundred thousand. Asbury contributed greatly to this amazing growth. When sailing for America, Asbury made a journal

entry pondering his motives for going to the rough frontier territory. He concluded, "I am going to live to God, and to bring others to so do." If the statistics are any indication, he certainly became the maker of a movement in his adopted land.

KEITH E. EITEL

Bibliography. F. Asbury, *The Journal and Letters;* F. Baker, *From Wesley to Asbury: Studies in Early American Methodism;* R. E. Richey, *Early American Methodism.*

Asceticism. Asceticism is a virtually universal phenomenon in world religion found in various locations and periods in both ancient and modern worlds. Its roots may be located in the earliest stages of Indian civilization, probably dating from the third millennium B.C., although some of the world's best-known ascetic traditions from this region such as Buddhism and Jainism emerged in a later period. In the Western world, Christian culture is the only one which has recognized asceticism as a legitimate way of life, Christian asceticism having had its beginnings with St. Anthony in Egypt at the end of the third century B.C.

Its varied religious and cultural expressions make asceticism a complex phenomenon difficult to define. In broad terms, however, asceticism involves rigorous self-discipline and the habitual renunciation of natural human desires in order to cultivate the spiritual life or attain a higher spiritual state. The principal traits of the alternative lifestyle which asceticism represents include withdrawal from society, mystic contemplation, and such austere practices as fasting, poverty, sexual abstinence, and self-inflicted physical or mental pain.

Throughout the history of the church Christian ascetics have usually gravitated toward ascetic communities or monastic orders, through which much of their spiritual energy has been channelled toward missionary activity and social service. While sincere seekers may be found among various groups of non-Christian ascetics, attempts to reach them are often hindered by their lack of accessibility and sense of self-sufficiency.

IVAN SATYAVRATA

Bibliography. R. L. Gross, *The Sadhus of India: A Study of Hindu Asceticism;* W. Kaelber, *ER* I:441–45; V. L. Wimbush, *Ascetic Behaviour in Greco-Roman Antiquity: A Sourcebook.*

Asia. Asia covers thirty independent nations in the vast areas of land from Japan in Northeast Asia, numerous other nations in Southeast Asia and South Asia, and up to Turkey in West Asia. Asia represents three major cultural blocs (Mesopotamia, India, and China) and the birthplaces of the major living WORLD RELIGIONS of Christianity, Islam, Hinduism, and Buddhism.

The region's population of approximately three billion represents 60 percent of the world's total population. Its five thousand years of history have made it a continent of rich cultural heritage. The major wars of the past four decades have been fought in Asia, bringing much suffering to millions of Asians but also awakening them to their need for spiritual values.

Historian Arnold Toynbee once stated, "The changing events of Asia will decide the future of the world tomorrow." With the rapid modernization and economic dynamism of Asian nations, particularly in the Asia-Pacific basin (Japan, Taiwan, Hong Kong, Singapore, and China), many are saying that "the 21st Century will be the Age of Asia."

Changing Patterns of Asian Societies: Political Changes. Politically, there are three major factors affecting Asia and the Asian church. First, every nation in Asia except Japan and Thailand have experienced bitter foreign colonial domination, especially from the Western nations. But today all nations in Asia are politically independent. National independence from political COLONIALISM has brought enormous changes in the political structures of the national governments as well as many internal conflicts and wars among different ethnic groups in many Asian nations. Related to independence and strong NATIONALISM is the withdrawal of Western powers, finalized for Britain in July of 1997 when Hong Kong reverted back to China. The mass exodus of British troops from the former colonies in South and Southeast Asia, the French defeat in former French Indo-China (Vietnam, Cambodia, and Laos), and the American military withdrawal from South Vietnam, Taiwan, and the Philippines have created a political vacuum in many regions.

In the past it was the foreigners who controlled the internal as well as foreign affairs of their colonies. The expatriates regulated missionary activities according to their own national interests. In contrast today an increasing number of Asian nations have used political pressures against foreign missionary activities in their countries, especially in the communist (China, North Korea, Vietnam, Kampuchea, and Laos) and Islamic (Indonesia, Pakistan, Bangladesh, Malaysia, and Central and Middle Eastern) nations. Hindu nations (India and Nepal) and Buddhist nations (Sri Lanka, Thailand, and Myanmar) also bring pressure against Christian activities. In 1997 more than 83 percent of the Asian population resided in countries where the acquisition of a missionary visa was very limited. A creative access strategy is needed in order to facilitate alternative ways of carrying on missionary activities (*see* CREATIVE ACCESS COUNTRIES).

Second, as a result of this self-control, Asian nations are experiencing a resurgence of nationalism and traditional values. This resurgence which derives from chauvinistic, patriotic passion has been expressed in cultural, linguistic, and religious ways. A common motto throughout Asia is "Import Western technology, but retain your own traditional culture."

Third, the rise of the communist threat was real throughout Asia during the Korean War (1950–53) and the Vietnam War (1964–75). Communist ideology still controls over two billion people in China, North Korea, Vietnam, Kampuchea, and Laos. In these countries the activities of national churches and of foreign religious workers are restricted.

Economic and Social Changes. One word that describes Asia the best is "changes," for Asia is rapidly changing in social and cultural patterns as well as in economic living standards. New building construction sites for high-rise apartments, department stores, and government offices are commonly observed in major cities of Asia. Rapid URBANIZATION, traffic congestion, air, noise, and water pollution, drugs, prostitution, and crime have marred the dreams of many Asians. The lifestyle of the urban cities is getting more materialistic, secularistic, and Westernized. However, rural people are still living as they always have for hundreds of years. There is a widening gap between urban and rural and between rich and poor. With the increase in economic power, many Christians in Asia are not only able to manage their churches financially but also to support their own missionaries within and outside their borders.

With the rise of living standards and the rapid MODERNIZATION of Asian society, Asians are facing many social and cultural changes. The influx of Western cultures into Asia through mass media by introducing Hollywood movies into theaters and TV, rock music, fashion shows, and other secular and hedonistic events along with fast food chains have made a tremendous impact upon Asian lifestyles. Consequently, there is an increasing gap between the older and younger generations. Young people today care much less about traditional culture, have no memory of the wars and the sufferings of their parents' generation, and readily accept new ideas and practices.

Religious Resurgence. There are three large non-Christian religious groups which constitute the majority of Asia's three billion people: one billion Muslims, 700 million Hindus, and 300 million Buddhists (*see* ISLAM, HINDUISM, BUDDHISM). There has been a resurgence of major religions in Asia and religions are used by the national governments to promote unity among different tribes, cultural groups, and languages. The influence of Islam, seen in the reintroduction of Shari'a and the rise of Islamic fundamentalism, is growing. Malaysia exemplifies this. The Federation of Malaysia consists of West Malaysia, Sarawak, and Sabah. It has 22.3 million people,

52.5 percent of whom are Malays, 30 percent Chinese, 8.1 percent Indians, and 8.9 percent tribals. The Federation is trying to unite these different races through the unification of language and religion. The Malaysian government enforced the Bahasa Malaysian program in which the Malay language is used, instead of the vernaculars. Consequently, there has been a gradual assimilation of the Chinese and Indians into the Malay Islamic culture.

Buddhism, too, has been revived in Thailand, Myanmar, Taiwan, Sri Lanka, and other Buddhist nations. Throughout urban cities and rural communities one can observe thousands of devout Buddhists worshiping the statues of Buddha and offering food and burning incense in Buddhist temples.

In India, Hinduism was also revived through its reform movements such as Brammo Samaj, Arya Samaj, and Rama Krishna Mission of the nineteenth century. Radical Hindu followers of the Rashtriya Swayamsevak Sangh (RSS) and the Vishwa Hindu Parishad (VHP) contributed significantly to rejuvenate Hinduism and Hindu nationalism in India and make minority communities of Muslims and Christians feel threatened and insecure by insisting that a true Indian must be a Hindu.

In Japan, there is a renewed interest in traditional religious traditions, including some signs of increasing links between the state and Shintoism. Nevertheless, with rapid church growth in many nations in Asia, there has been an increasing confrontation between Christianity and other traditional religions of Asia. Therefore, it is crucial for the Asian church to learn how to deal with the traditional religions of Asia.

Asia: The Least Evangelized Continent. Asia is the least evangelized continent in the world, with approximately 3 percent of the three billion people following Christ. Johnstone provides statistics of seven large Asian nations which have small Christian populations, including China, Taiwan, India, Pakistan, Bangladesh, Japan, and Thailand. The vast majority of the unreached people today reside in these countries.

The AD2000 and Beyond Movement has emphasized the evangelization of unreached peoples in the 10/40 WINDOW. These countries cover the whole continent of Asia from Japan to India, and from Central Asia to North Africa. The Adopt-a-People Campaign of the U.S. Center for World Mission in Pasadena reports that there are approximately two billion people in 11,000 unreached people groups (out of a worldwide total of 24,000).

The vast majority of these two billion are found in four major blocs. The Islamic world contains over one billion Muslims, most of whom reside in Asia, with over 4,000 unreached Muslim people groups in the world. The Hindu world of India and Nepal represents more than 700 million Hindus in 2,000 unreached groups. Most of the 300 million Buddhists are found in Southeast and Northeast Asia, representing approximately 1,000 unreached people groups. The Chinese in China today represent by far the largest number of unreached peoples in the world with 1.2 billion people, living in some 1,000 unreached people groups. There are millions of other people who belong to 3,000 small individual tribes. Therefore, Asia still presents the greatest challenge to Christian missions today and in the next century.

Most nations in the 10/40 WINDOW do not easily grant visas for foreign missionary work. Approximately 20 percent of the total missionary force in the world works in these restricted nations in Asia. This means that the future focus of world missions in the twenty-first century must be on the two billion unreached peoples of Asia. With the development of modern transportation and mass media through television, film, radio, telephone, fax, and e-mail service, we can now know the background of these unreached peoples in Asia (*see also* INFORMATION TECHNOLOGY, MEDIA, and MASS COMMUNICATION). The GLOBAL CONSULTATION OF WORLD EVANGELIZATION (GCOWE '95) which met in Seoul, Korea, with 4,000 participants from 186 nations in May 1995 adopted a motto, "A church for every people and the gospel for every person," and challenged all participants to pray especially for the unreached peoples of the world within the 10/40 Window.

Expansion of Christianity in Asia. The history of Christianity in Asia goes back to the first century. According to the Acts of Thomas, St. Thomas came to the Malabar coast of Kerela, South India, to preach the gospel to the Indians and became a martyr near Madras in A.D. 72. The Christian message penetrated into the regions of Media, Persia, Parthia, and Bactria (modern Iraq, Iran, and Afghanistan) by A.D. 150. According to the Nestorian Tablet which was discovered in the city of Sian in central China in 1625, a Nestorian missionary from the Syrian church, Alopen, went to China in A.D. 635. During the Mongolian Empire of the twelfth to thirteenth centuries, several Roman Catholic friars such as John of Plano Carpini, JOHN OF MONTECORVINO, and William Rubruck went to China as missionaries.

With the historic voyage of Vasco Da Gama to Capetown, South Africa, in 1498 and to Malabar, India, two years later, the Western colonial age known as "the Vasco Da Gama Age" began in Asia, Africa, and South America. FRANCIS XAVIER, a Jesuit missionary, came to Kagoshima, Japan, in 1549 and ministered to the Japanese for more than two years, moved to South China in 1552, and died there after four months. Since then, thousands of other Roman Catholic missionaries have been commissioned to Asia.

The beginning of the Protestant missions in the early eighteenth century heralded another era in Asia's mission history. In 1706 the first Protestant missionaries arrived in South India from Europe. The DANISH-HALLE MISSION sent BARTHOLOMAEUS ZIEGENBALG and Henrich Plutschau to Tranquebar to work among the Tamil-speaking Indians. In 1792 the BAPTIST MISSIONARY SOCIETY in England commissioned WILLIAM CAREY to Calcutta, India. He did missionary work in India for forty-one years. In 1807 ROBERT MORRISON of the LONDON MISSIONARY SOCIETY came to Macao and translated the Bible into the Chinese language. In 1813 ADONIRAM JUDSON from the United States arrived in Rangoon, Burma, and ministered to the Burmese for thirty-seven years. Since then, thousands of other Protestant missionaries from Europe, North America, and Australia/New Zealand have followed these pioneers to work in different parts of Asia.

Church Growth in Asia. The amazing church growth in Asia since the end of World War II has been widely reported throughout the world. Several countries have experienced dramatic rates of church growth. The Christian population in South Korea has reached 12 million Protestants (25% of the population) and 2.4 million Roman Catholics (6% of the population) among 47 million people since the arrival of the first Protestant missionaries in Korea in 1884. China, the most populous nation in the world, had never exceeded one percent Christian population until the Peoples' Republic of China was established in 1949. Since the modernization of China began in 1979, the Christian population has sharply increased. Some China watchers in Hong Kong report that there are between 50 million and 70 million Christians and 50,000 house churches (*see* CHINESE HOUSE CHURCH MOVEMENT), even though the Three Self Patriotic Movement (TSPM) and the Communist Party only acknowledge the growth of the church from one million Protestant members in 11,470 churches in 1949 to 7,000 state churches with 6 million Christians and 20,000 registered home meetings in 1995.

The Philippines, which is the only Roman Catholic nation in Asia, has a growing number of Protestant believers. Indonesia, with the largest Muslim population in the world, has also experienced rapid church growth. After the communist coup failed in Indonesia in 1966, President Suharto's government guaranteed religious freedom to five major religions (Islam, Hinduism, Buddhism, Protestantism, and Roman Catholicism) according to the "Pantasila" policy in the Constitution. Singapore, known as the crossroads of Asia with a multiracial and multireligious background, has Protestant and Roman Catholic populations of 8 percent and 5.7 percent respectively, particularly among educated Chinese and Indians. Nepal, the only Hindu kingdom in Asia, was very hostile to the gospel until a multipolitical party system developed in 1991. It has experienced remarkable church growth from only a handful of believers to over 52,000 Protestant members (0.56% of the population) and 2,100 Roman Catholics (0.02% of the population) today.

Slower growth has been seen in countries such as Japan, Taiwan, Thailand, and India. Minimal growth has been experienced in nations where there are tremendous struggles and resulting pressures from unsympathetic governmental and religious leaders, such as Pakistan, Bangladesh, Malaysia, Sri Lanka, and the Middle Eastern nations.

Seven Basic Issues of an Asian Church. Many Asian church leaders and theologians have discussed various issues of the Asian church through different consultations. With the rapid growth of the church in different parts of Asia, the Asian churches are facing seven important issues: (1) grassroots evangelism must be emphasized in order to reach the vast number of non-Christians in Asia; (2) leadership training for both full-time Christian workers and lay leaders is needed since there is a tremendous shortage of trained leaders at the local church level; (3) since lay Christians play a very important role in church growth, there has been an increasing demand for lay training programs; (4) national Christians must seriously evaluate their own contextual situation in order to find the most effective indigenous ways to communicate the gospel of Jesus Christ (*see* CONTEXTUALIZATION); (5) theological issues emerging from various kinds of ASIAN THEOLOGIES, religious DIALOGUE, RELIGIOUS PLURALISM, and HUMAN RIGHTS have created theological confusion in the Asian theological arena; (6) Christian social responsibility with its holistic approach must be emphasized to help the poor and to alleviate the suffering from social injustice and discrimination; and (7) spiritual renewal within the church is desperately needed to bring spiritual revival among the members of the church. There must be a discernible difference between the lifestyles of Christians and their non-Christian neighbors.

The Asian Missionary Movement. It is encouraging to observe that many Asian churches particularly since 1970 have been sending their own cross-cultural missionaries. Many Asian church leaders who attended the international missions congresses were deeply challenged for the task of world evangelization, and as a result organized their own national and regional evangelism congresses and missions consultations (*see* ASIAN MISSION BOARDS AND SOCIETIES).

Consequently, the Asia Missions Association (AMA) was organized in 1973 to coordinate missions agencies throughout Asia. In 1990 the First Asian Missions Congress was held in Seoul,

Korea, sponsored by the Missions Commission of the Evangelical Fellowship of Asia (EFA) with 1,200 participants from different parts of Asia. The theme of the congress was "World Missions: The Asian Challenge." The Second Asian Missions Congress was held in Pattaya, Thailand, in 1997 with 350 participants with the theme, "Into the 21st Century: Asian Churches in Missions." In 1997 approximately 30,000 Asian missionaries from India, Korea, Japan, Taiwan, Hong Kong, Singapore, Malaysia, the Philippines, Indonesia, and others joined their hands with Western missionaries for world evangelization. Two nations in Asia which sent out the largest number of cross-cultural missionaries were India and South Korea with 20,000 and 5,500 cross-cultural missionaries respectively.

Challenge of Asia to Christian Missions Today. As Paul had his missionary concern for the Jews and Gentiles in Palestine, Asia Minor, Macedonia, Achaia, and Rome in the first century, so Asian Christians today must have their deep prayerful concern to reach their own people with the gospel of Christ on the grassroots level. How Paul evangelized the largest city of Ephesus in Asia Minor in the first century provides a very significant missiological lesson to the Asian church today. There are a number of similarities between the Ephesus of Paul's time and urban cities in Asia today and between the Ephesian church then and the Asian church in our time. If Paul were to come to Asia today and walk on the streets of Bombay, Singapore, Jakarta, Bangkok, Hong Kong, Shanghai, Taipei, Seoul, and Tokyo, what kind of ministry would he launch to bring the good news of the gospel of Jesus Christ to Asians?

The city of Ephesus of the first century and Asian cities today have three main similarities. First, Ephesus, which was the largest city in Asia Minor with a population of 500,000, had a great harbor, emporium, library, commerce, education, and culture. Likewise, Asian cities are crowded with the masses of people and many high-rise buildings developed in modern surroundings. Second, as Ephesus was the religious city with the temple of Artemis (Acts 19:23–41), so is Asia today filled with spirits, idols, and superstitious beliefs of traditional religions of Hinduism, Buddhism, Taoism, Shintoism, and Islam. Third, Ephesus was a sinful city, as Paul described it as "having lost all sensitivity, they have given themselves over to sensuality so as to indulge in every kind of impurity, with a continual lust for more" (Eph. 4:19). Likewise, Asian cities are filled with sin, crime, drugs, sexual immorality, bribery, and injustice.

When Paul faced the great task of evangelizing Ephesus and many other cities in Asia Minor and Europe in his time, he concentrated on the leadership training of the Ephesian church by emphasizing the spiritual gifts: "It was he who gave some to be apostles, some to be prophets, and some to be evangelists, and some to be pastors and teachers, to prepare God's people for works of service, so that the body of Christ may be built up" (Eph. 4:11–12). There is a Chinese proverb that teaches a similar lesson, "Give a man a fish and he will eat for a day. Teach a man to fish and he will have food for a lifetime." It was imperative, therefore, for Paul to train the leaders of the Ephesian church in order that they would be able to train others to bring the gospel to 500,000 people in the city of Ephesus. Likewise, the training of national church leaders in the Asian church today is also imperative in order to reach three billion Asians with the gospel. These spiritual leaders will be able to mobilize the laity of the church at the grassroots level in order to penetrate into the non-Christian Asian society with the gospel of Christ.

Therefore, three important proposals need to be stressed for the evangelization of Asia. First, the burden of communicating the gospel and making disciples in Asia today must rest primarily with the national Christians. Therefore, the national church must implement the concept of "Christianization of the nation" among the national Christians. Second, effective church growth in Asia depends on the creative and spirit-filled leadership of pastors and lay leaders. Third, and finally, the top priority of the Asian church in the twenty-first century must be the training of national church leaders in order that they would be able to mobilize the laity of the church.

God has always worked through his chosen people in the history of redemption. Peter says in 1 Peter 2:9–10, "But you are a chosen people, a royal priesthood, a holy nation, a people belonging to God, that you may declare the praises of him who called you out of darkness into his wonderful light. Once you were not a people, but now you are the people of God; once you had not received mercy, but now you have received mercy." In centuries past God has used the churches in Europe and North America to bring the gospel to Asia, Africa, and South America. Asia, known spiritually as the darkest continent in the world with the least Christian population of any continent, is experiencing God's spiritual awakening among its peoples. God has chosen Asia and the Asian church in the twenty-first century to proclaim his wonderful light to millions of Asians and around the world.

BONG RIN RO

Bibliography. S. Athyal, ed., *Church in Asia Today;* D. E. Hoke, ed., *The Church in Asia;* S. H. Moffett, *A History of Christianity in Asia;* M. Mohamad and S. Ishihara, *The Voice of Asia;* B. R. Ro, ed., *Christian Suffering in Asia;* P. T. Welty, *The Asians.*

Asian Mission Boards and Societies. *General Description.* Though Asian missionary activity is recorded as early as 1884, it was not until the 1970s that the rest of the Christian world began to notice this activity. In 1972, there were over 100 mission agencies in Asia. Growth continued so that out of the 1,541 NON-WESTERN MISSION BOARDS AND SOCIETIES known in 1995, more than 825 were Asian. The most active countries are India (with an estimated 281 agencies in 1995), Korea (113 agencies in 1994), Japan (63 agencies in 1995), and the Philippines (20 agencies in 1995). Well-known agencies include the Indian Mission Association, which in 1995 included 81 member mission boards with some 10,000 Indian missionaries (with as many as 200 other Indian mission agencies not yet part of the Indian Mission Association). These numbers do not include workers who operate independently within their own country. In the Philippines alone, it is estimated that 2,000 nationals serve in this capacity.

Characteristics. One important characteristic of Asian missions is the phenomenon of missionaries crossing cultural boundaries within their own country. Following CASTE divisions, some estimate that India has at least three thousand PEOPLE GROUPS. The vast bulk of Indian missionary work is carried out within India. This is also seen in other major Asian missionary-sending countries such as Indonesia and Myanmar.

A second characteristic is that Asian mission boards cannot be equated with Western agencies, which have elaborate structures and management systems. Many of the Asian boards are still simple with inexpensive systems, relying more on faith than man-made management structures. This is especially true with the mission agencies that send people within their own country. Administrative overhead expenditures are therefore very low in comparison with Western agencies.

A third characteristic is that Asian boards are focusing their deployment into the 10/40 WINDOW. Indian mission boards have sent approximately five hundred missionaries into Nepal, Bhutan, and Uzbekistan. Most of the Myanmar missionaries stay within their own country, which is part of the 10/40 Window. There are exceptions, such as Korea, Japan, and Hong Kong, where the boards have greater financial resources to send missionaries into non-Asian contexts and out of the 10/40 Window.

Fourth, with some exceptions, there seems to be tremendous creativity in Asian mission boards. With very little support, for example, Korean missionaries are being sent to remote places in China. Their boards, lacking the elaborate communication and management structures of Western boards, have no choice but to allow a great deal of freedom to the missionaries. This means that the missionaries must be more able to stand on their own and be willing to suffer more than the average Western missionaries. Additionally, without senior missionaries on hand to provide supervision, oversight, and pastoral care, the new missionaries are forced to exercise great creativity sometimes just to survive the rigors of the field.

Fifth, there is a surprisingly high rate of financial autonomy among Asian mission boards. Recent estimates indicate that 91 percent of the Asian boards are funded by indigenous sources. This is particularly true of Japanese and Korean boards, and most missionaries from these countries are well supported by sponsoring churches and agencies. Missionaries from India, the Philippines, and Indonesia have generally not fared as well.

The final characteristic is the mix of denominational and parachurch sending agencies. In countries such as Korea and Japan denominational boards are the major contributors to the mission board scenario. In Korea, both Hap Dong and Tong Hap Presbyterians are the two largest sending agencies. Between them they send out more than one-fourth of the missionaries from Korea. By way of contrast, the vast majority of the members of the Indian Mission Association are parachurch organizations.

Relationships with International Agencies. Some of the early attempts to send out Asian missionaries were through indigenous mission agencies. An Indian Methodist was sent to Malaysia in 1884. The Korean Presbyterian Foreign Mission Board sent out the first team of cross-cultural missionaries to Shantung, China, in 1913. International mission agencies began to formulate sending bases in Asia during the 1960s. The CHRISTIAN AND MISSIONARY ALLIANCE (CMA) and the OVERSEAS MISSIONARY FELLOWSHIP (OMF) were pioneers in this endeavor. Pate estimates that somewhat more than 6 percent of the total Third World mission force serves with international organizations. One of the advantages of utilizing international agencies is the enjoyment of the benefit of already well-established field structures.

At the same time, however, there are prices to be paid for these inconveniences. The high cost of supporting missionaries to equalize pay scales between Westerner and non-Westerner is one. Additionally, the cultural differences within a multinational team (and organization) can be a source of problems. Finally, the fact that the non-Western missionaries often have to learn the organization's language (often English) in addition to the vernacular of their field of service raises an extra barrier to the development of true partnership.

Conclusion. The Asian missionary movement is still young. For the time being, Asian mission boards can afford to be simple without elaborate support systems, such as retirement plans, a complicated pastoral care system, and large schools for missionary children (MK). The honeymoon period, however, is rapidly disappearing. Missionaries from countries such as Korea, Japan, and India are struggling with the education of their children. The cases are so complex for Korean mission boards that it has taken almost a decade to get a consensus on the objectives for MK education. Additionally, field structures also present tremendous challenges. So far, a scattered effort without much teamwork among the Asian missionaries satisfied some Asian churches. Currently there is a need for field structures to coordinate and encourage a team effort. It will take time and effort to creatively formulate infrastructures that are new, affordable, and flexible enough for the ever-changing world.

Maintaining the momentum of the Asian missionary movement is a heavy burden that Asian mission boards must carry. Logically this burden should be borne by the Asian church. However, the Asian church is being bombarded with secularism and is threatened by major traditional Asian religions. Can the Asian mission boards still afford to do missions, even when it is becoming more costly and risky? Probably not without the initiative taken by Asian churches. The well-being of the Asian mission movement and the future of Asian mission boards will greatly depend on how the Asian church tackles these challenges.

DAVID TAI WOONG LEE

SEE ALSO Non-Western Mission Boards and Societies.

Bibliography. L. Pate, *From Every People: A Handbook of Two-Thirds World Mission with Directory/Histories/Analysis;* Korea Research Institute for Mission, *Korean Mission Handbook;* L. Keyes, *The Last Age of Missions;* H. Y. Kim, *From Asia to Asia: A Study on Mission History of the Presbyterian Church in Korea (1876–1992).*

Asian New Religious Movements. During the past 150 years, a wide variety of popular religious movements have emerged throughout Asia. In some countries, such as Japan, these appear in organized form as "new religions," but in other countries they are amorphous and unorganized. Thus, the discussion of religious phenomena in countries other than Japan must deal with popular religion in a somewhat broader sense than new religious organizations as such. "New" is relative, and must be used in contrast to the ancient established traditions of Hinduism, Buddhism, Confucianism, and so on, referring to movements mainly, but not confined to, the twentieth century.

With the exception of Japan, little literature is available on these movements in most of the Asian countries. Their newness and their fluid and changing nature makes them a difficult object of study. Also, there is a tendency on the part of most Western Christian observers to view such movements with indifference or disdain.

In Korea, popular folk religion is polytheistic, claiming eight million gods, including nature gods and the spirits of the living and dead. Divination, fortune telling, geomancy (religious significance in the orientation of buildings), ancestor worship, and shamans *(mudang)* and shamanic rituals *(kut)* with their elaborate dances and songs are all important elements in popular folk religion.

Nationalism is also a significant element. This is eminently true of the first post–Pacific War new religious group, the Tonghak (Eastern Learning) movement. Some of the new religions teach that Korea will become chief among the world's nations. Most new religions are directed toward alleviating economic and health problems; they anticipate a utopia on earth. Some new religions, such as Won Buddhism, are close to traditional Buddhism. Others, such as Sun Myung Moon's Unification Church, are similar to Christianity, yet alien to orthodox Christianity.

The South Korean government's statistics put total membership at about one million in 1983 (3% of the total population). The number of adherents has not grown greatly because, unlike neighboring Japan, Christianity has proved to be more powerful in attracting the masses.

In modern Taiwan, prior to 1949, the year of the communist takeover in mainland China, many Buddhist and Taoist clergy, including renowned leaders like the Taoist Heavenly Master, moved to Taiwan from the mainland, creating a strong Buddhist influence there. Many new temples were built and old ones refurbished.

In popular religions, belief in ghosts and worship of ancestors is the backbone. One of the most popular observances is the Pho To festival (Universal Salvation). It is so widely celebrated that it is considered to be a force of unity in the country. At this festival the suffering souls in the underworld are released to enjoy a month of freedom. People give offerings and join in celebrating the climactic "ghost-feeding" ritual, ghosts being the departed spirits of strangers.

Among the new religious groups are Li Chiao and Hsuan-yuan Chiao. One of the more aggressive Buddhist sects is Hsi Lai. It claims to be a return to the pure teachings of the Buddha. "Hsi Lai" literally means "coming to the West," and this sect has visibility on the West Coast of the United States.

In Hong Kong, as in Taiwan, Buddhist, Confucian, and Taoist influence is prevalent, but the extreme secular materialism of Hong Kong's commercialism precludes the development of influential new religious movements. Popular FOLK RELIGIONS of the common people are centered in ancestor worship, but even this is losing its religious meaning, leaving only its social significance.

Both Malaysia and Indonesia are predominantly Islamic in background, and in recent decades have seen new thrusts of "Islamization." Since Malaysia gained independence from Great Britain, there has been renewed effort to instill the ideals of Islam: peace, love, cooperation, honesty, hard work, honor, and abstinence from licentious behavior.

In Indonesia a new Islamic association, Sarekat Islam, was formed in 1912 and spread like wildfire into a million-member group which eventually came to lead a nationalist movement.

In the Philippines, tribal religion has produced many movements and cults that are separate from the mainstream of Roman Catholicism. For instance, tribes in northern Mindanao are known for their strong belief in the invisible forces of the spirit world and their peculiar rituals. In 1931 a violent anticlerical sect called Colorums of Central Luzon arose, aiming to establish an independent Philippine government.

There are numerous modern native cults in the Melanesian Islands of the South Pacific. Life here, lived in a half-way world between ancient paganism and envied modern Westernization, has given rise to some bizarre cults. For example, in 1939 a European missionary agitated for the need for a chairman and rules of procedure in formal meetings. He was misinterpreted, and a new religious movement called the "Chair and Rule Movement" arose in the Solomon Islands, which elevated a flag, a wooden chair, and a wooden ruler into a place of ritual importance.

In India, exposure to nineteenth-century British colonialism and modernization, along with Christian missions, stimulated various Neo-Hindu reform movements and new religious movements. After the introduction of Christianity by WILLIAM CAREY in 1793, there was a call for religious and ethical reform among Hindu intellectuals. This resulted in the Samaj (Society) movement. In the nineteenth century, under the leadership of Keshab Chandra Sen, there arose the Brahmo Samaj (Theistic Society), seeking a religious synthesis of Hinduism and Christianity. The Ramakrishna Mission, founded by Ramakrishna Paramahamsa, has now spread throughout India and also to 120 locations abroad. It teaches the essential unity of all religions and the potential divinity of humans (*see also* HINDU NEW RELIGIOIUS MOVEMENTS).

In Japan there have been a great number of organized modern sects technically called Shinko Shukyo (New Religions), and more recently a new phenomenon called Shin-shinko Shukyo (new New Religions, sects of the past decade, which generally focus on immediate benefits combined with mystical experience). Even under government control in the early decades of this century, the number of groups grew to 414 in 1930. The end of the Pacific War, when official state Shinto was dismantled, brought religious freedom, so by 1950 there were 742 New Religions registered with the government. This number has been greatly reduced since then.

The New Religions usually arose as a response to some kind of social crisis, the major crisis being the defeat of Japan in the Pacific War. Typically, they are founded by charismatic leaders, often a female who could be identified as a shaman. They tend toward monotheism, having one deity, one founder, and one revelation which sets the doctrine. They have a definite body of teaching, which usually takes a simplistic, optimistic view of the human situation. They are syncretistic, drawing from several strands of religion and culture, along with the worldview of Western science. They hold a this-wordly eschatology—they see that society can change toward a utopian goal. They offer concrete, material blessings and prosperity to their followers. They have an elegant sacred center, a national headquarters which functions as a foretaste of paradise for the believers who gather there. There is an emphasis on health and healing of sickness, and an emphasis on the power of positive thinking to solve life's problems. They have effective propagation methods and are easy to join, and have ways of getting sizable offerings from members once they have joined.

We may classify a few of the large representative groups in Japan into the following three categories. The *"old New Religions,"* or those founded before the Meiji Restoration, are represented by Tenrikyo (Religion of Heavenly Wisdom), founded by Miki Nakayama in 1838, who identified the deity as "God the Parent."

The Omoto Group. (1) Seicho on Ie (House of Growth), established by Masaharu Taniguchi in 1930, is a cross between Japanese spiritual tradition and American "New Thought." (2) Sekai Kyuseikyo (World Messianity), established by Mokichi Okada in 1950, focuses on the ritual of *jorei*, which channels divine light and healing through the outstretched palm of the hands. (3) Perfect Liberty Kyodan, founded by Tokuchika Miki in 1946, takes as its motto, "Life is art": live in a balanced, creative, esthetically expressive way. Sports and crafts are an important part of their religious practice.

The Nichiren Group includes the largest and strongest organizations: (1) Soka Gakkai (Value-creating Society), founded by Tsunesaburo Makiguchi in 1937, claimed to be the fastest growing religion in the world in the 1950s, numbering 750,000 households. A later leader, Daisaku Ikeda, also established a political party, Komeito (Clean Government Party), which he claimed would usher in a time of peace and plenty all over the world. (2) Rissho Koseikai, now counting more than six million members, was established through the efforts of Nikkyo Niwano and Myoko Naganuma in 1938. Their emphasis has been on happy living, taught in small groups called *hoza,* and on world peace and interreligious cooperation (*see also* JAPANESE NEW RELIGIOUS MOVEMENTS).

Although the new religious movements of Asia are too varied throughout time and culture to make any general statement, at least it can be said that they are a clear sign of the hunger of the human spirit for something beyond physical and economic life. With this comes a challenge to Christian mission to satisfy that hunger.

We also are made aware of the intricate relationship among religion, culture, politics, and superstition. To be a truly redeeming influence in this complex situation, the church must realize its own cultural biases, strive to understand the dynamics of the new spiritual phenomena into which it is thrust, and at the same time discern the essence of the Christian faith, being willing to let go of nonessentials for the sake of contextualizing the meaning of Christ in any particular cultural setting.

KENNETH J. DALE

See also New Religious Movements.

Bibliography. K. Dale, *Circle of Harmony: A Case Study in Popular Japanese Buddhism;* H. B. Earhart, *The New Religions of Japan;* J. H. Grayson, *Korea: A Religious History;* N. McFarland, *The Rush Hour of the Gods;* J. A. Saliba, *Perspectives on New Religious Movements;* F. von der Mehden, *Religion and Nationalism in Southeast Asia;* R. Weller, *Unities and Diversities in Chinese Religion.*

Asian Theologies. Asia is a complex continent with many diverse cultures. These cultures are directly linked with major religions such as Hinduism, Buddhism, and Islam as well as with a variety of animistic religions. Christianity in most parts of the continent is a minority religion although the influence of Christian missionaries has been significant. Christian theology has had to interact with these religions and their contexts and in recent decades numerous theologies have evolved.

The complexity of Asia includes more than religion. A contrast of rich and poor, rural and urban, and ancient and modern make the people a diverse mass. Within such a context, a variety of theologies have developed—some remaining local while others have made a worldwide impact. Kitamori's "pain of God theology" and Koyama's "water buffalo theology" are familiar to theologians all over the world. But there are many others that are local. Common to all these theologies is the concern that Western theological concepts are sometimes incomprehensible and irrelevant to the Asian context. They need to

be relevant and expressed in the language of the common people, addressing the situation they confront.

Poverty and suffering have been rampant in Asia. An Asian response came from the Japanese scholar Kazoh Kitamori. He wrote of the "pain of God" that heals our pains, developing his study from Jeremiah 31:20, where God speaks of his heart yearning for Ephraim. Kitamori understood the reality of God through the pain of God, which is seen to be essential as well as eternal. God's revelation of his love through Jesus Christ was the revelation of this pain. Theology in these terms certainly addresses the suffering context of Asia, but could easily tend to justify or even deify suffering.

Kosuke Koyama, a Japanese professor, after many years in Thailand, proposed "water buffalo theology." He incorporated Christian beliefs into Thai thinking by using their daily experiences with life, nature, and habits alongside teachings of Buddhism. Koyama was also concerned to communicate the gospel effectively to a people caught in a technological revolution and culture. He emphasized that God worked "slowly" and so we, too, must slow down to a walk. Only then can we hear God speaking. Koyama's theology is not systematic and needs further development. His concern for the communication of the gospel to common people in Asia is commendable but the tendencies toward SYNCRETISM and UNIVERSALISM minimize the uniqueness of the Christian gospel.

Minjung, meaning "people," is a people's theology developed in Korea (*see also* MINJUNG THEOLOGY). Like its Latin American counterparts, it is a political theology describing a struggle to free common people from the domination of the ruling class. Accordingly Minjung theologians focus on two main realities of the people—their social history and economic condition. They try to relate the gospel of Jesus to the struggles and aspirations of the people of Korea in their sociopolitical situation. There are three main sources of Minjung theology. First is the Bible and a new interpretation of the biblical truths to show how God dealt with the people. It recognizes the Deuteronomic code and the covenant code in the Old Testament were given to protect the rights of the poor people. The second source is the history of the church, noting that the early beginnings of Christianity were among people who were a minority in their own communities. The third is the people's struggle for LIBERATION.

Although lacking a sound biblical basis, theologies like Minung are taking root in other Asian countries wherever there are peoples' struggles. For instance, Aloysius Pieris of Sri Lanka, concerned for the millions of poor people on the continent and the numerous religions they belong to, affirms that Christianity must give an answer. Pieris advocates an Asian theology of liberation. Pieris' proposal is for tackling poverty within the pluralistic religious context; all religious dialogue must be in the context of the poor and oppressed. So Pieris calls for an effective marriage between DIALOGUE and liberation. Among other concerns, Pieris believes that for the churches in Asia to become churches *of* Asia the process of INCULTURATION must confront Asia's poverty. Also, interreligious dialogue has to take place at the level of human experience of suffering. "Basic human communities" instead of "basic Christian communities" must bring Buddhists and Christians together in their common struggle for liberation. This will enable an integration of Christian love with Buddhist wisdom.

There is another group of theologians who have grappled with Asia's religious context. Exclusivism belongs to colonial thinking, they say, and we need to be more open to incorporating truths from other religions. For instance, Raymondo Panikkar, a prominent Roman Catholic theologian, attempted to link Hinduism and Christianity through Jesus Christ. He proposed that Christ is present in the very core of Hinduism. This is Panikkar's *Unknown Christ of Hinduism*. He advocates a transformation of Hinduism to Christ without losing its identity. Panikkar further reconciled in the Christian Trinity the three ways of Hindu spirituality, namely, *karma marga* (action irrespective of reward), *bhakti marga* (of intense devotion), and *jnana marga* (exercise of intellect). For Pannikar, the Trinity is "the junction where the authentic spiritual dimensions of all religions meet." But with these concerns, Pannikar minimizes the uniqueness of the biblical revelation of Jesus Christ. Proclaiming the gospel also becomes unimportant.

MADATHILPARAMPIL MAMMEN THOMAS, Asia's "lay" theologian, made a significant contribution to world ecumenical theology. With very little formal theological training, he took the human situation as the starting point for all his theological reflection. Thomas acknowledges three revolutions in the world: first, the scientific and technological revolution; second, the revolution of the oppressed classes, nations, and races seeking social and international justice; and third, the revolution of secularization. The church either shunned these revolutions as demonic or became part of them blindly. Thomas recommends that we identify those values prompted by Christ such as freedom, humanness of the community, and involvement in the historical destiny of humans.

The mission of the church is to participate in these movements in such a way that we may "witness to Jesus Christ as source, the judge, and the redeemer of human spirituality." These revolutions become partial fulfillment of the KINGDOM OF GOD. Thomas advocates an open SECULARISM that will bring about a responsible world society.

Such a classless society is not possible where religion becomes a potential force for strife. Therefore interreligious dialogues are important channels for a Christ-centered SYNCRETISM, where whole religious systems and ideologies, not just individuals, are converted to Christ. The mission of the church will result in a Christ-centered Hindu church. The church's mission is primarily that of humanization and not evangelization. Although M. M. Thomas is acknowledged as an outstanding scholar and thinker, some critics show his work to be political and sociological rather than theological. His works are seldom biblical. Thomas attempted to find revelation in revolutions. Important aspects of theology dealing with God, Jesus Christ, and the Holy Spirit are undermined except with reference to human action.

Stanley Joseph Samartha is an Indian theologian of religion. He proposes that Hindus have positively responded to Christ in their own way and accordingly asks the vital question, "What does it mean to affirm that Jesus Christ is Lord and Savior today in India?" Recognizing various levels of Hindu response to Christ, Samartha says that the church needs to appreciate this fact rather than being unduly suspicious. The Hindu must be considered a fellow citizen in the commonwealth of Christ and not as a recruit to the kingdom of God. Samartha identifies the Hindu *anubhava* (experience) as the main source of knowledge and our starting point. But *anubhava* should be controlled by the historical fact of Christ and it should have a social dimension that is sustained, strengthened, and transmitted to others in the fellowship of the church. Thus, according to Samartha, Christ can be expressed as Brahman. Samartha's question is a valid starting point but like others he surrenders the UNIQUENESS OF CHRIST as portrayed in the Bible. He offers new interpretations of the cross, resurrection, deity of Christ, and the meaning and purpose of the death of Christ have little justification from the Bible.

Evangelicals in Asia have not been known for major theological contributions. Most evangelical theologians in Korea, Japan, Singapore, and India tend to follow generally Western forms of theologies that restrict mission to proclaiming the gospel. But recently people like Vinay Samuel and Ken Gnanakan have developed biblical theologies that make the Christian faith strongly relate to the Indian context. Samuel has addressed mission in terms of total transformation. Gnanakan advocates the actualization of the gospel in sociopolitical, economic, and environmental demonstrations of mission. Both maintain the uniqueness of Christ while exploring newer ways of demonstrating God's mission in Asia.

The 1980s saw the development of the so-called Dalit theology. *Dalit* is a Sanskrit word that means oppressed, broken, or downtrodden. In a broad sense it is a concern for all the oppressed sectors of people in the society, but Dalit theology is particularly concerned for a huge mass of people (about one-fifth of the total population of India) who were referred to as Harijans or "children of God" by Mahatma Gandhi. The Harijans are outside the traditional caste system of India, and are considered to be out-castes, ritually impure, and therefore untouchables. They have a long history of oppression, an unsuccessful struggle for justice, and they continue to constitute the poorest of the poor.

Many Dalits became Christians during the MASS MOVEMENTS in the nineteenth and twentieth centuries and comprise an estimated 70 percent of the Indian church. The advocates of Dalit theology strongly feel that hitherto the development of Indian Christian theology ignored this reality and wrote theologies addressing the higher castes, particularly the Brahmins. Various forms of Dalit theologies are making their mark both within ecumenical and evangelical churches, strongly underlining the need to relate theologies to the needs of these masses.

All Asian theologians have one thing in common. There is a strong desire to address the context within which their people live. There is a missiological focus in their theologies, but this focus varies with one's definition of mission. Evangelicals will stress the need to directly make known the redemptive message of Jesus Christ in the diverse context of Asia.

KEN GNANAKAN

Bibliography. T. D. Francis and F. J. Balasundaram, eds., *Asian Expressions of Christian Commitment: A Reader in Asian Theology;* K. Gnanakan, ed., *Biblical Theology in Asia;* Y. Hwa, *Theology and Mission in the Asian Church;* K. Koyama, *Water Buffalo Theology;* W. H. Lam, *Chinese Theology in Construction;* A. Pieris, *An Asian Theology of Liberation;* V. Ramachandra, *The Recovery of Mission: Beyond the Pluralist Paradigms;* S. J. Samartha, *One Christ, Many Religions: Towards a Revised Christology;* V. Samuel and C. Sugden, *Sharing Jesus in Two Thirds World;* C.-S. Song, *Christian Mission in Reconstruction: An Asian Attempt;* R. S. Sugirtharajah, ed., *Frontiers in Asian Christian Theology; Emerging Trends;* M. M. Thomas, *Salvation and Humanization: Some Crucial Issues of the Theology of Missions in Contemporary India;* A. Torrance and S. Martinez, eds., *Doing Christian Theology in Asian Ways.*

Association of Evangelical Professors of Mission. *See* EVANGELICAL MISSIOLOGICAL SOCIETY.

Association of Professors of Mission. The Association of Professors of Mission (APM) was organized in 1954 by professors who were teaching mission in seminaries in the United States. R. PIERCE BEAVER was instrumental in its formation. The purpose of the association is to promote among its members fellowship, spiritual life, and professional usefulness in the study, teaching, and mobilization of mission.

The APM normally holds one annual meeting, usually the second week of June, often scheduled to coincide with the annual meeting of the AMERICAN SOCIETY OF MISSIOLOGY (ASM). The annual meeting usually includes presentations, workshops, discussion groups, and sharing of experiences and resources related to the teaching of mission. Once every four or five years there is a presentation of the syllabi that members have developed for the teaching of mission.

Membership is open to professors of mission at member institutions of the American Association of Theological Schools and, by invitation of the executive committee, to other qualified persons. Members represent conciliar Protestant, Roman Catholic, evangelical, Pentecostal and charismatic traditions.

CHARLES VAN ENGEN

Bibliography. R. P. Beaver, *Missiology* 41:1 (1976): 75–87; W. R. Hogg, *Missiology* 15:4 (1987); 587–86; *IBMR* 56 (1967): 222ff.; N. A. Horner, *Association of Professors of Mission, 1952–1999;* J. Scherer, *Missiology* 13:4 (1985): 445–60; J. Siewert, ed., *Dictionary of Schools and Professors of Missions in the USA and Canada;* J. D. Woodberry, C. Van Engen, and E. J. Elliston, eds., *Missiological Education for the 21st Century.*

Association, the Socio-anthropology of. Of vital importance to the church's mission in general and urban missions in particular is the study of voluntary associations or common interest groups that have accompanied rapid social change and URBANIZATION. Not only should mission strategists capitalize on this, but anthropologically speaking, mission societies need to recognize that they themselves exist as part of this phenomenon.

At least thirty different disciplines, including missiology, sociology, and anthropology, currently recognize the significance of this topic. Distinct from what social scientists call primary groups or involuntary associations, which organize around such principles as age, sex, kinship, and territory, voluntary associations are secondary groupings, which organize around the principle of common interest or pursuit. In general, all of the above are subsumed under the larger subject known as social organization. Whereas involuntary groupings have existed universally as fundamental to the nature of society, voluntary groups have varied in nature and distribution depending upon the freedom of association allowed in the societies concerned (*see also* SOCIOLOGY).

Mission agencies should carefully study common interest organizations as forms of social critique or dissent. This would help to surface some key perceived needs and tensions socially existing during the lifetime of a given association. In some contexts associations will exist as political buffers mediating between governments with their demands and citizens with their common desires. In other situations common interest organizations will serve to expand services that the members deem lacking in the society and larger world. In this context it is instructive to note that social scientists often classify associations functionally as being either expressive or instrumental. The former signifies that a group exists primarily to meet felt needs common to its members. Contrastingly, the latter is more extroverted in that its mission is to influence and change the larger world outside its own membership.

Additionally, a mission body should recognize its identity as a common interest, voluntary association and as such study itself in the same way it would analyze a target affinity group. This would function to heighten its own sensitivity and discernment, thus allowing it to better identify with and serve other groups.

An "association" can be defined anthropologically as any common interest group. An adequate theory of association should at least include such areas as: (1) workable definitions allowing for wide comparative study; (2) a knowledge of the formative conditions that give rise to organizations; (3) knowledge of common types and classifications of associations; (4) organizational structures; (5) assumptions, values, and expectations; (6) functions; (7) membership recruitment process; and (8) visibility profile.

The formative conditions of modern associations are best summed up under the rubrics of rapid sociocultural change and urbanization. In urban contexts associations often reflect perceived deficiencies of city life and the desire for the continuity of rural services such as ethnic identity, mutual aid, and bereavement support of minorities, immigrants, and migrant laborers. With respect to rural communities the growth of common interest organizations often mirrors a growing awareness of the larger world outside and a desire for elements of it.

Social scientists appeal to four major criteria in setting up taxonomies of associations: cultural domain, stated purpose, practical function, and organizational structure. Under *cultural domain*, groups may be classified as being religious, economic, political, educational, recreational, and so on. Using the criterion of *manifest purpose*, we might classify them as professional, welfare, pressure, prestige, or philanthropic. *Practical function* classification involves the expressive-instrumental dichotomy. Instrumental groups may be further classified as majoral, minoral, or medial associations depending on whether they serve the major interests of society, focus on minorities, or mediate between institutions, respectively. *Organizational structure* is the final classificatory criterion. Groups may be either corporate in that they are autonomous and representative, or they are federal, operating in a centralized fashion in accordance with the sentiments of their founders. In this regard, it is interesting to note that many associations ideally claim to be the former, but in reality conform to the latter.

A study of the core values and the associated assumptions and social expectations is vital in taking one to the very heart or ethos of a common interest group. Identifying and distilling these makes explicit the driving motivations behind any association. Further, it reveals two cardinal objectives of many voluntary associations; namely, those of influencing cultural transformation and cultural transmission. These are vital in validating an organization's current existence as well as assuring its future continuity.

How associations recruit their membership and the visibility profile they maintain in the larger society are two valuable lines of inquiry. It is in this context that the subject of secret societies is often discussed. Even though the existence of secret societies is almost universal, cultures do differ as to the significance and meaning they attribute to the values of secrecy and exclusivity. Whereas in one context secrecy reveals the fear of oppression, in others it may serve to safeguard sacred cultural knowledge or to reinforce special social statuses.

Another fertile area of research is that of studying common interest groups in Scripture, such as Israel, Christ's band of disciples, and the church itself. Technically, the church, while fulfilling the criteria of a secondary or voluntary association, could also be viewed as a primary or kinship group in the sense of it being a spiritual family with a common Father and culture.

Research in this area is of vital importance to the growing field of urban missions. There is also the need to identify and understand voluntary affinity organizations in broader national and international contexts as well. The recruitment process for associations should also be examined carefully to determine how one can effectively penetrate them for the sake of God's kingdom. Manifest as well as latent values should be identified, realizing that in so doing one uncovers the objectives that serve to ensure the organization's survival and impact. Such study should enable a more relevant incarnation of the gospel. The study of guilds, clubs, and secret societies in rural or traditional settings also has value for missionaries in terms of reflecting indigenous perceptions of the home culture as well as the world outside. Valuable insights about contextualization can be gained from study of the success or failure of local citizens' attempts to organize around new ideas and activities.

DAVID A. NESS

Bibliography. W. H. Brackney, *Christian Voluntarism in Britain and North America: A Bibliography and Critical Assessment;* S. Grunlan and M. K. Mayers, *Cultural Anthropology: A Christian Perspective;* W. A. Haviland, *Cultural Anthropology;* P. G. Hiebert, *Cultural Anthropology;* E. S. Miller, *An Introduction to Cultural Anthropology; International Encyclopedia of the Social Sciences;* D. J. Publiese, *Voluntary Associations: An Annotated Bibliography.*

Assurance of Salvation. The *subjective confidence* which genuine Christians are privileged to possess that they truly belong to God as his children and heirs of eternal life. Wesleyan-Arminian theology focuses on the reality of the present state of grace of Christians and the assurance that engenders, while Calvinism adds that this assurance includes the confidence that they will continue as believers throughout their life and when they die they will certainly go to be with Christ in heaven forever.

Calvinism closely links assurance to divine election and the perseverance of the saints (or ETERNAL SECURITY). Those whom God has predestined, he also saves, and this includes the initiation, continuation, and consummation of salvation (Rom. 8:28–30). God's persevering work in the lives of all true believers powerfully keeps them through the exercise of their faith for a waiting salvation (1 Peter 1:3–9). Grateful recognition of this results in assurance.

To this may be added Christ's own pledge to protect believers (John 6:37–40; 10:27–30), biblical promises of God's faithfulness and love (Phil. 1:6; Rom. 8:31–39; 2 Tim. 1:12), and assurances that Christians are privileged to *know* that they possess eternal life (1 John 5:13; John 3:36; 5:24). Trust in this testimony of the Word of God produces assurance.

Scripture also speaks of the fruit of transformed lives that may generate confidence. Entitling this the "witness of one's own spirit" (Rom. 8:16), Wesleyan theology points to the biblical descriptions of character qualities and good works which believers are expected to manifest. These include love for one another, obedience, and the fruit of the Spirit. When believers compare their lives with these marks of authentic Christian testimony and a favorable judgment is rendered, this witness of transformed lives gives a measure of assurance. Some forms of Calvinism also embrace this introspective approach.

Romans 8:16 and Galatians 4:6 present the Holy Spirit as another source of assurance of belonging to God. Distinguishing the "witness of one's own spirit" from the "witness of the (Holy) Spirit," JOHN WESLEY affirmed this witness to be a direct testimony of the Spirit upon the hearts of believers, attesting to their being children of God.

Despite these several grounds of assurance, many Christians lack a subjective confidence. On the one hand, this may be due to persistent sin, grieving the Holy Spirit, or demonic deception; on the other hand, depression, personal anxiety, inability to appropriate the biblical promises of assurance, or simply ignorance of this scriptural teaching may result in an absence of assurance. Calvin noted that "Satan has no more previous or dangerous temptation to dishearten believers than when he unsettles them with doubt about their election." As Barth affirms, however, "There can be no doubt that the Christian can and should have assurance of his faith and salvation." Believers throughout history who have possessed a strong sense of assurance have stood fearlessly in giving testimony for Christ. Lucian, a pagan (second century), complained that Christians "have persuaded themselves that they will live forever, so they don't despise death." In Calvin's day, Geneva produced a "race of martyrs" spreading the gospel despite the threat of death. Convinced that their eternal destiny is secure, believers will forsake their comfortable and familiar life, cross into unknown cultures, adopt new languages and customs, face overwhelming confusion and stress, and even risk their lives for the sake of proclaiming the gospel of Christ. The history of Protestant mission during the last two hundred years is filled with the stories of thousands of cross-cultural missionaries whose assurance of salvation enabled them to give their lives, literally, for gospel proclamation.

GREGG R. ALLISON

Bibliography. D. Carson, *WmTJ* 54 (1992), pp. 1–29; K. Barth, *Church Dogmatics* IV/3, 565–66; J. Miley, *Systematic Theology* II:339–53.

Astrology. Form of divination that regards the stars and planets as powers that influence the lives and affairs of people and nations and seeks to predict what those influences will be. Astrology seems to have originated in Mesopotamia in the third millennium B.C., where it spread to India and appeared in Hinduism. Eventually it spread to Greece, where it reached its fullest development during the Hellenistic period. It was through Hellenistic influence that the Arab world was introduced to astrology and it persisted there in spite of the later prohibitions of the QUR'AN. Forms of astrology also appeared in pre-imperial China, probably through Arabic influences, and it existed even in meso-American Mayan and Aztec cultures, though its sources there are uncertain.

Hindu astrology was part of the ancient Vedic literature and was also a part of medicine as well as a means of plotting the soul's likely plan in the present incarnation through natal charts that represented the individual's past karmic patterns. Chinese astrology is uniquely independent from Mesopotamian influences in its different zodiac and twelve animal signs that delineate human characteristics. It was Arabic astrology that eventually spread to the Western world in spite of biblical prohibitions through the translation of some Muslim works into Latin.

Several problems with astrology can be noted: (1) people who live above the Arctic Circle (66 degrees latitude) where the zodiac is not visible, can have no horoscope and thus were astrologically never born; (2) astrology is based on pre-Copernican astronomy and thus involves an untrue conception of the solar system; (3) before A.D. 1500 several planets like Uranus were never seen; thus if planets have influence then all previous horoscopes were invalid; (4) according to astrological logic identical twins should live identical lives, but they do not; (5) if planets that are closest influence more greatly, there should be mention of planet Earth's great influence; and (6) how can people with different horoscopes all die in a mass tragedy?

WILLIAM H. BAKER

SEE ALSO Divination, Diviner.

Bibliography. J. R. Lewis, ed., *The Astrology Encyclopedia;* C. Strohmer, *What Your Horoscope Doesn't Tell You.*

Atheism. The English term "atheism" is derived from the Greek *atheos,* "without God," and refers to a position that denies the existence of God. It is to be distinguished from AGNOSTICISM, which is the view that we cannot know whether God exists. In modern Western cultures atheism usually means denial of the existence of the Judeo-Christian God. In other religious contexts atheism means denial of the prevailing understanding of deity. Thus, Christians in the Roman Empire were accused of atheism for denying Greek and Roman polytheistic views. "Informal" or "practical" atheism occurs when, although belief in God is not explicitly denied, God is not allowed a significant place in one's life.

Historically, Democritus and Epicurus advocated a form of materialistic atheism, and in modern Western thought atheism has been advanced by thinkers such as Karl Marx, Ludwig Feuerbach, Sigmund Freud, Friedrich Nietzsche, J. L. Mackie, and Antony Flew. The philosophical and scientific school of logical positivism earlier in this century embraced atheism, dismissing language about God as cognitively meaningless. Modern secular humanism is another pervasive form of atheism, at least to the extent that it finds "insufficient evidence for belief in the existence of the supernatural" and affirms that "no deity will save us; we must save ourselves" *(Humanist Manifesto I).*

Some religious traditions are atheistic as well. Theravada Buddhism, Zen Buddhism, and Jainism are atheistic in that they deny the reality of any transcendent supreme Being. Other traditions, such as some branches of Hinduism, philosophical Taoism, and certain schools of Mahayana Buddhism, view the religious ultimate in monistic or pantheistic terms. In a loose sense, these traditions can be regarded as atheistic from the perspective of monotheism.

WILLIAM H. BAKER

Bibliography. A. Flew, *The Presumption of Atheism;* A. MacIntyre and P. Ricoeur, *Religious Significance of Atheism;* G. Stein, *The Encyclopedia of Unbelief,* I:27–29.

Atheistic Humanism. *See* ATHEISM.

Atlases, Mission. *See* MISSION ATLASES.

Atonement. The biblical concept of atonement refers to a God-provided and -approved means of paying the penalty for human violations of God's law; a means which alleviates individuals from assuming that responsibility themselves. The need for atonement arises as a result of human sinfulness. Scripture teaches that all have sinned (Rom. 3:23). For that reason, human culpability is universal (Rom. 2:1). No one can claim exemption, regardless of culture, tradition, previous religious activities, or commitments. As a result, every individual ought to be made to pay the full price of her or his own sin, which is death and eternal separation from God (Rom. 6:23). However, Scripture also teaches that God has provided a way to fulfill the demands of divine justice which is reasonable and effective, but does not demand that the penalty be exacted from the individual.

The way in which God has chosen to resolve the problem of sin is by providing an alternative means of payment. In the Old Testament this was achieved primarily by means of animal sacrifice. The substitutes which will be accepted include the burnt offering (Lev. 1:4), the sin offering (Lev. 4:20; 7:7), and the offerings made on the Day of Atonement (Lev. 16:1–34). The clear teaching of the Old Testament is that unless some God-approved means of atonement is provided, individual sinners will themselves be required to pay the penalty.

In the New Testament the idea of atonement is focused on the person of Christ (Rom. 5:10). Reconciliation between God and humans is no longer achieved by animal sacrifice (Heb. 9:26; 10:4), but by the death of Christ (2 Cor. 5:19). The death of Christ was a reasonable and effective solution to the problem of human guilt because Christ was fully human and fully divine (Mark 10:45; 2 Cor. 5:21). Because Christ was fully human he was able to fully identify with the human state, was tested in every way as we are, yet without sin (Heb. 4:14–16). Because he was fully God, he was able to provide a payment

(Rom. 3:25–26) of sufficient value to cover the transgression of all humanity (Heb. 10:5–10). The two poles of God's salvific method are most evident on the cross. There he suffered death as any of us would have suffered it, and at the same time experienced a suffering of immeasurable intensity, since he, the Son of God, had never sinned, but was separated from the Father by voluntarily taking upon himself the sins of the many and turning away the wrath of God (Rom. 3:25).

There is relatively little disagreement concerning the basic principles outlined above. Any individual who expresses faith in Christ is covered by this payment. However, since Scripture does not clearly specify the scope or extent of the atonement, this issue has precipitated considerable debate. The basic question is whether the atonement should be viewed as limited to a certain subset of the human race, the elect, or whether it should be viewed as a provision intended for all of humankind.

Those who suggest that the atonement is limited do so on the basis of a combination of biblical passages and the use of logical arguments. They point out that there are some passages which do define a limited group of recipients. Christ died for his own people (Matt. 1:21), his sheep (John 10:11), the church bought with his own blood (Acts 20:28), and those whom God predestined and called (Rom. 8:28–35). Further, they argue that since God's will can never be countermanded, if he had intended for all to be saved, all would be saved. In addition, they point out that Christ did not die simply to make salvation possible, but to actually save certain individuals (Eph. 1:7; 2:8). They also fear that any other understanding of the atonement necessitates UNIVERSALISM.

The case for general atonement is made by appealing to Scripture passages and the history of doctrine. Scripture clearly states that Christ died for all and for the whole world (Isa. 53:6; 1 John 1:29; 2:2; 1 Tim. 2:1–6; 4:10, Heb. 2:4). There are no exegetical reasons for ascribing to these passages meanings other than the plain and inclusive sense they communicate. Proponents of general atonement also seek to demonstrate that it is the traditional position of the church. From the early church until today most of the fathers, reformers, exegetes, and theologians believed that Christ died for all. As for the danger of universalism, since salvation is only effective for those who express faith, suggesting that Christ made salvation possible for all in no way implies that all will be saved (John 3:16).

Whichever position is taken on the extent of the atonement, the evangelical understanding of the general principles of atonement have two significant implications for missions. First, if the problem of sin is universal then the message of atonement should be addressed to all. This pre-

sents no problem to the defenders of general atonement, but some have suggested that one of the consequences of a limited atonement would be to discourage the universal, urgent proclamation of the gospel. However, since there is no way for us to identify the elect ahead of time, the gospel message should still be addressed to all. If that is the case, we are under obligation to proclaim the message of Christ's atoning work without reservation. It is to be proclaimed to all, in all places, and at all times.

Second, the method God chose to provide atonement will cause some to stumble. The message of the cross will lead to opposition, cause offense, and even be ridiculed (1 Cor. 1:18–29). The messengers will, of course, experience resistance. Blinded by sin, many will find the notion of a substitutionary death on the cross either offensive or foolish. That cannot be avoided. No manner of CONTEXTUALIZATION, effective communication, or marketing techniques can remove the offense of the cross. However, care should be given so that any offense occasioned by the person or the work of the messenger be kept to a minimum.

EDWARD ROMMEN

Bibliography. H. Berkhof, *Christian Faith;* D. G. Bloesch, *A Theology of Word and Spirit;* G. D. Fee, *God's Empowering Presence;* T. N. Finger, *Christian Theology: An Eschatological Approach;* S. J. Grenz, *Theology for the Community of God;* S. J. Grenz, *Revisioning Evangelical Theology;* P. K. Jewett, *God, Creation, and Revelation;* G. R. Lewis and B. A. Demarest, *Integrative Theology III;* A. E. McGrath, *Christian Theology: An Introduction;* O. Weber, *Foundations of Dogmatics.*

Attributes of God. *See* DIVINE ATTRIBUTES OF GOD.

Attrition. Departure from field service by missionaries, regardless of the cause. There are two general categories. Unpreventable attrition (understandable or acceptable) includes retirement, completion of a contract, medical leave, or a legitimate call to another place or ministry. Preventable attrition occurs "when missionaries, because of mismanagement, unrealistic expectations, systemic abuse, personal failure, or other personal reasons, leave the field before the mission or church feels that they should. In so doing, missionaries may reflect negatively on themselves, but of greater concern is the negative impact on the specific mission structure and the cause of world missions" (Taylor, 1997, 18).

Attrition has been a critical issue facing the church through its history. In the New Testament, Stephen is martyred, John Mark abandons the apostolic team but is later restored to ministry through Barnabas, and Demas apparently leaves for good without known restoration. Throughout mission history, attrition has been evident, reflecting the high cost of "sending mission," whether through sickness, change of heart, inability to sustain cross-cultural ministry, or death on the field.

Facing the contemporary attrition challenges, the WORLD EVANGELICAL FELLOWSHIP Missions Commission carried out during 1995–97 a 14-nation study of attrition in 6 Old Sending Countries (OSC) and 8 New Sending Countries (NSC). This study generated significant data on attrition in 454 agencies (and some mission-sending churches) with some 23,000 long-term missionaries (one-sixth of the global missionary force, according to Patrick Johnstone). In terms of the global long-term missions force, one missionary in twenty (5.1% of the mission force) leaves the field yearly. Of these, 71% depart for preventable reasons. In other words, if we establish a global missionary force of 140,000, 5.1% overall annual attrition would be 7,140 people, and 71% of that figure suggests that 5,070 missionaries are returning home for what is called "preventable attrition."

There are at least four perspectives regarding the causes of any specific case of attrition: (1) the reasons agency and church leaders believe they have heard and understood; (2) the recorded reasons in agency files; (3) the reasons missionaries hold in private or may share with closest friends; and (4) the reasons one can live with in public knowledge. The true human picture is always complex and no single perspective will be totally accurate.

Recent studies suggest that preventable attrition may be reduced by more and/or better (a) initial screening and selection procedures, (b) appropriate pre-field equipping/training for the task, and/or (c) field-based strategizing, shepherding, and supervising. Inadequate attention in any of these areas may result in unwanted attrition or, worse, the case of missionaries who should go home, for their own good and the good of the ministry, but do not.

Reducing attrition engages seven strategic missions stakeholders: missionaries (current, previous, future); missions mobilizers (the prime motivators); church leaders (pastors and committees); missionary trainers (regardless of type, size, or level of equipping program); mission sending bodies (churches and agencies); national receiving churches (where they exist); and member care providers (pastors, medical and mental health personnel). While attrition cannot be totally eliminated, it can be significantly diminished.

WILLIAM DAVID TAYLOR

SEE ALSO Drop Out.

Bibliography. W. D. Taylor, *Too Valuable to Lose: Exploring the Causes and Cures of Missionary Attrition.*

Augustine of Canterbury (d. c. 604). Churchman and missionary to England. Augustine was prior of St. Andrews monastery in Rome when he was commissioned by Gregory the Great in 596 to convert the pagan English and "refound" the church in England. He was a reluctant missionary, but one of duty who led a band of thirty monks to England. He was well received by Ethelbert, king of Kent, whose wife was already a Christian before their marriage. Within one year of his arrival, Augustine had converted the king and many of his people. In 597 Augustine traveled to Arlis, France, to be consecrated archbishop of Canterbury. Gregory then made him metropolitan bishop of England and established England's independence from the French see. Augustine failed to regain the allegiance of the ancient Celtic church and was insensitive to local customs. He did, however, lay a firm foundation for the church in England through the establishment of the see at Canterbury and building of the monastery of Saints Peter and Paul in that city. Augustine's evangelistic effort was limited primarily to Kent and the surrounding region, but led eventually to the conversion of all England.

KENNETH D. GILL

Bibliography. Bede, *Ecclesiastical History;* M. Deanesly, *Augustine of Canterbury;* V. L. Walter, *EDT,* p. 105.

Augustine of Hippo (354–430). Seminal African theologian and apologist. Aurelius Augustine, bishop of Hippo Regius in North Africa, is the most important Latin theologian of the Roman Catholic Church and the spiritual father of all the major Reformers. In many of his voluminous writings Augustine discusses problems of significance to missions, as he was actively involved in reaching African people as well as Roman citizens. Augustine held both a strong belief in God's predestination of people and a strong conviction that it is the will of God to preach the gospel everywhere. He denied that the Great Commission was already achieved by the apostles on the basis of his personal awareness of barbarian tribes in Africa to whom the gospel had not yet been preached. He recognized that God had not promised that Abraham would be a blessing to the Romans alone, but to all the nations. Augustine held that the majority of the nations and people would become Christians before the return of Christ, a postmillennial element in his otherwise amillennial eschatology.

THOMAS SCHIRRMACHER

Bibliography. Augustine, *Confessions;* P. Brown, *Augustine of Hippo;* H. Chadwick, *Augustine;* M. Marshall, *The Restless Heart: The Life and Influence of St. Augustine;* J. J. O'Donnell, *Augustine.*

Australia *(Est. 2000 pop.: 19,222,000; 7,713,364 sq. km. [2,978,130 sq. mi.]).* Though suspected of existence since classical times, and reconnoitered in the seventeenth century, European settlement in Australia did not begin until a British penal settlement was founded at Port Jackson (Sydney) in 1788. "Almost as an afterthought," Pitt's government allowed placement of an evangelical Anglican chaplain, Richard Johnson, a nominee of the Eclectic Society and member of the CLAPHAM SECT. For the first fifty years of the colony, evangelical Anglicans would dominate the jail chaplaincy with the avowed intention of developing Australia as a base for mission. The second chaplain, SAMUEL MARSDEN, like Johnson a Yorkshireman with Eclectic links and Methodist sympathies, launched and coordinated the mission to New Zealand, from which activity he became known as the "Apostle to the Maoris." He has been less well treated by Australian historians, and it is clear that the policing functions of clergy in Australia defeated their missionary activities among the convicts.

The expulsion of LONDON MISSIONARY SOCIETY (LMS) missionaries from Tahiti (1798) greatly strengthened Marsden's hand, and the Hassall, Lawry, and Marsden families would become closely related in developing Anglican and Methodist missions to the Pacific. Marsden's granddaughter, Eliza Hassall, started the first CHURCH MISSIONARY SOCIETY (CMS) women's missionary training home in Sydney (1892), and worked closely with the British and Foreign Bible Society (BFBS) and Scripture Union. Mary Hassall married Walter Lawry, and assisted him in Tonga, New Zealand, and the Pacific for the Wesleyan Methodist Missionary Society (WMMS). Australian overseas missions were restricted from large-scale development, however, by distance, small population, lack of wealth, and (until the 1860s) rudimentary church organization. While Sydney became a major "break of bulk" port for intentional missionaries routing through to Asia and the Pacific, both internal and foreign mission was inhibited by the flow of funds and personnel from European churches to higher profile destinations in Canada, Asia, and Africa. The trickle of Australian-born missionaries tended to join international agencies, such as the WMMS, which sent John Watsford to Fiji in 1841 and commenced Pacific missions in 1855. Emphasis on "civilization before Christianization," strongly held by Marsden, also restrained early missionary development.

Internally, missions to the indigenous peoples of Australia also progressed slowly. The first mission, begun at Lake Macquarie (1825), was suspended by the LMS after an argument between the missionary, Lancelot Threlkeld, and Marsden. Though resurrected on public subscriptions and state support, and despite success of translation, it was closed in 1841 with the decimation of Aboriginal populations by white squatting and disease. Most nineteenth-century missions to Aborigines followed this pattern, though more success attended the missions run by Moravians. German missions played a major part of all evangelical attempts, including by the Presbyterians (supplied at Nundah by the Gossner Mission in Berlin), and the Anglicans (supplied by the Moravians, e.g., Lake Boga, Ebenezer, and Ramahyuck, and the Basel Mission Institute, e.g., Wellington). This played an important part in the planting of Lutheranism in Australia. It is probably true to say that, except for some individual efforts (e.g., Maloga and early Yarrabah) nineteenth-century evangelical mission to the Aborigines was a failure or at best a holding operation. Dramatic extension of Christianity among Aboriginal people only took place after revival (particularly that commencing on Elcho Island in the late 1970s) created the grounds for an indigenous church. Even then, Aboriginal Christianity suffered from the tendency of churches to contribute disproportionately to overseas as opposed to domestic causes.

The "long boom" of the 1870s and 1880s, the growth of population post–1851, and increasing church organization enabled more aggressive mission to commence in the 1870s. This is the period (1880–1920) that Piggin has called the "high noon of Australian Protestantism." Relying at first on Scots and Canadian missionaries, the Presbyterians began work in the New Hebrides (1863 for Presbyterian Church Victoria [PCV], 1867 for Presbyterian Church New South Wales [PCNSW]), slowly adopting total responsibility. The PCV sent its first missionary, J. H. Davies, to Korea (1889) and the PCNSW its first missionary, Mary McLean, to India (with Madras Zenana Mission) in 1891. Australian Baptists began sending women missionaries to India in 1882. Australians, beginning with MARY REED and Sophia Sackville Newton (CHINA INLAND MISSION [CIM]) began to supply significant numbers to international mission agencies, a trend which continues to the present. Three catalytic events in this supply were the visits of HUDSON TAYLOR in 1890, the missions led by Keswick speaker, George Grubb, from 1892, and the Chapman–Alexander campaigns (1902). All three interacted with the rise of student Christian groups, which fed powerfully into missions from 1890 onwards.

In the same period, the first indigenous Australian missions were established, including the Queensland Kanaka Mission (1886, later South Seas Evangelical Mission, 1904), Borneo Evangelical Mission (1928), and (internally) the Aboriginal Inland Mission (1905), Bush Church Aid Society (1919), Campaigners for Christ (1928), United Aborigines Mission (which emerged out of the NSW Aboriginal Mission and Australian Aboriginal Mission, 1907, to obtain its name in 1929). A variety of Church Missionary Associations, local affiliates of the CMS which were later renamed, emerged from Marsden's first attempt in 1825. In many of these, people of Brethren background, such as the Kitchens of Melbourne, the Decks and Youngs of New Zealand and Sydney, and philanthropists such as J. B. Nicholson, have had an influence disproportionate to their numbers.

In support of this upsurge of agencies, and following evangelical reactions against liberalization of theological training in university colleges, dedicated missionary training institutions arose through the 1910–40 period. Based on an earlier "Training Home for Missionaries, Kew," in 1902 the tea merchants, the Griffith family, supported the opening of the Hiawatha training college for women (1902), almost at the same time as C. H. Nash opened St. Hilda's deaconness training institute (1901), which went on to train for CMS and CIM purposes. Nash and a key circle of Melbourne evangelical businessmen were also fundamental to the opening of Ridley College (1910), Melbourne Bible Institute (1920, later BCV), and a chain of missionary agencies. In Adelaide, Angas College (1893) and Chapman-Alexander College (1913–26) trained for the CIM and interdenominational missions, a role filled in Sydney by the Sydney Missionary and Bible College (1916). These proliferated with the spread of sectarianism and the relocation of population, such that by 1990 there were some 135 colleges (including theological colleges such as Whitley and Moore Colleges) serving an Australian church-going population of no more than 3 million. Many of these operate within theological consortia, and numbers are being pressed toward merger as such realities as the aging of the evangelical population, de-denominationalism, and Pentecostalization bite into traditional arrangements.

With Canada and New Zealand, Australia has tended to be a high-level missionary sending country (per capita), though depending on the finance and organization flowing out of North America and Europe. Due to the dominance of evangelical Anglicanism in Australia, the CMS has been a particularly important agency, especially in East Africa, while Baptists have long-running work in India, and Presbyterians in Asia and the Pacific. All agencies have maintained work in New Guinea and Melanesia. Turnbull suggests that by 1990 there were over 2,700 full-time missionaries in the field, and many thousands more active in Tent Making and Short-Term Missions. Practical and down-to-earth, such missionaries have been particularly adapted to Faith Mission work, around the indigenizing principles first put into practice by William Carey. They have also shown an ability to internationalize and rise to leadership, examples being Kevin Dyer (International Teams); Colin Tilsley (Gospel Literature Outreach); Alan Adams (Operation Mobilization ship Logos); James Duffecy (Open Air Campaigners); Edward Gault (Christian Medical College, Vellore); Stacey Woods (International Fellowship of Evangelical Students); and Vincent Craven (Inter-Varsity Fellowship). Alan Tippett's missiology has also had a significant impact, particularly through Fuller Seminary.

At the close of the twentieth century, Australia's evangelical missionaries were working all around the globe, and its missions were partaking in the global trends toward mission partnerships, short-term missions, growing numbers of Pentecostal missionaries, and missionary exchange with former receiving cultures. Piggin and others have demonstrated the extent of the "reflex" impacts of missions on Australian society, seen in the importation of Solomon Islands spirituality, the growth of ethnic churches (particularly Chinese, Korean, Vietnamese, Samoan, Fijian, etc.), an increasingly pluralistic Australian culture, the training of leaders, and the development of an Australian political and economic profile in the Pacific. Missionary numbers continue to rise, suggesting a continuing influence in global evangelical missions.

Mark Hutchinson

Bibliography. B. Dickey, ed., *Australian Dictionary of Evangelical Biography;* M. Hutchinson et al., *This Gospel Shall Be Preached: Essays on the Australian Contribution to World Mission;* D. Paproth, *Failure is not Final: A Life of C. H. Nash;* G. Treloar, ed., *Furtherance of Religious Beliefs.*

Australian Evangelical Alliance. A national body designed to assist churches, associations, and individuals to share God's love for a suffering world, preach the gospel, and make disciples, the Australian Evangelical Alliance works at both national and state levels. Most of the national ministries operate through four commissions: The Evangelical Alliance Response (TEAR) Fund, Missions Interlink, the Theological Commission, and the Commission on Women's Concerns. Branches of the Alliance function in five states in the form of volunteer committees. The Alliance is a member of the World Evangelical Fellowship and regional fellowships in Asia and the Pacific.

In 1959 a coalition of one hundred leading evangelicals formed the Evangelical Alliance of Australia with the purpose of inviting Billy Graham. This organization was significant because it represented an attempt to work nationally instead of state by state. The Graham crusades made an immediate impact on Australians. A high profile was gained for evangelicals, and thousands of people were converted and joined the churches. The clergy were encouraged to preach the gospel within their churches, and so the effects of the crusades continued for a prolonged period of time. The Alliance fulfilled its objectives and, with no major task on its agenda, decided to disband.

However, some evangelicals perceived a need to work together in their home states. Ten years after the Graham visit, state evangelical alliances had been formed in New South Wales, South Australia, Tasmania, and Victoria; and evangelical missionary alliances were formed in New South Wales and Tasmania. These state organizations met in Canberra, the national capital, in May 1972 and formed the Australian Evangelical Alliance. The decision to form a national body to represent evangelicals at a time when Australians did not really possess a national mind-set either politically or ecclesiastically was both courageous and significant for the future. No structural continuity existed between the old Evangelical Alliance and the new, but many of the same people were actively involved. Howard H. E. Knight was one of the mission leaders of the day who played a significant role in the inauguration of the Alliance and the launching of TEAR Fund.

While the Alliance offers a variety of services to its members and maintains a number of projects and communications, its major contribution to the nation and the world is through its commissions. The activities of TEAR Fund in the United Kingdom inspired the establishment of a TEAR Fund in the State of Victoria in 1970. When the national Alliance was formed in 1972, the state quickly devolved the TEAR operation, recognizing that it properly belonged to the national body. The existence and operations of TEAR demonstrate that evangelicals are concerned about the welfare of the whole person. TEAR provides a credible and Christian alternative for evangelicals to channel development and relief funds to areas of great need. In recent years, TEAR has made a significant contribution by providing programs designed to educate people concerning the biblical and practical issues involved in development ministries.

The Missions Commission, now known as Missions Interlink, was not formed until January 1986. Prior to that time, a missionary fellowship had been established in New South Wales and an interdenominational missionary fellowship in Victoria. These two bodies functioned reasonably well at a state level for fifty years. However, national mission leaders and other influential Christians perceived that national and international needs were not being met. Ron Clough, the executive secretary of the Alliance, was a catalyst in bringing the New South Wales and Victoria fellowships together with other mission leaders in a national forum, where the decision was taken to form a national commission. In 1996, the membership of Missions Interlink was composed of sixty national missions, seven training institutions, and five related organizations. Ten denominational agencies were among the sixty member missions. Interlink records revealed that another thirty smaller agencies held membership in state branches but not in the national body. Member missions supported 1,850 missionaries working overseas and 1,485 home staff. The home staff included individuals working as missionaries to aboriginal people in Australia, workers among university students, and the employees of large Christian aid agencies. Since 1995, member missions have been cooperating to provide training and educational resources to the churches in an attempt to raise the level of missions awareness.

The two remaining commissions are in the early stages of their operation. The Theological Commission is cooperating with a Christian publisher to produce materials that present a biblical viewpoint on contemporary issues. The Commission on Women's Concerns has drawn together women from various Christian organizations with a view to enabling more women to become actively involved in kingdom ministry.

The evangelical movement within Australia is much wider than the Evangelical Alliance. It includes groups such as AD 2000, the Lausanne Movement, the Awakening Movement, March for Jesus, Reclaim Easter, and significant prayer and evangelism associations in all of the state capitals. Dialogue between a number of these groups may result in a grand coalition of evangelicals on a national scale. What this will mean for the Evangelical Alliance remains to be seen.

The church and community are waiting to see a united effort. At present, the church in Australia is undergoing significant change as leaders strive to make the church and its message relevant within the second most multicultural society on earth. A renewed church will emerge with fewer traditional and denominational restrictions. If the many evangelical groups can find a common purpose and integrate their valuable resources to serve the church, then we may see a repeat of the harvest times experienced when Billy Graham preached the gospel in 1959.

JOHN TANNER

Australian Mission Boards and Societies.

Overview. Australian churches have been sending and supporting missionaries for more than a century. Each of the ten evangelical denominations have mission boards and/or societies. In addition, Australia has at least ninety interdenominational agencies. Thirty of these are either new or small and are not registered as members of Missions Interlink, the national missions association.

The Australian missions family is diverse. Some missions have a long, rich heritage; others carry the zeal of a new vision. Some have strong international linkages; others have only a small local committee of volunteers. Some have more than one hundred missionaries; others support indigenous church workers. In 1995, Australian missions who were members of Missions Interlink supported 1,850 overseas workers and 1,485 home staff. These figures do not include overseas indigenous church workers who are also supported by Australian churches and societies.

The Path to the Present. Australia is an island nation. Before the days of relatively cheap and fast jet travel, most Australians did not venture out of the country. They lived in a country where the churches exercised considerable influence and where every child was taught religion in school. The Second World War ended the isolation. Young Australians fought in a war far from home. While some returned home embittered and sad, others brought with them a new understanding of the needs of the world and of other peoples and cultures. This awareness strengthened the missionary cause and resulted in a new wave of voluntarism. In the fifty years since the war, the advent of television, overseas travel, and access to modern technology have further reduced the insularity of many Australians. MODERNITY has brought a negative side as well, which hinders the efforts of both churches and mission societies.

Along the path to the present, the mission societies have been forced to change and adapt to ensure their long-term viability. Some changes have been of great significance. Formerly, missionaries received financial support by one of three methods—a salary from the mission, a share of gifts made to the general fund of the mission, or whatever the Lord supplied through churches and friends. While some denominational boards still pay salaries, most boards have introduced a system of team support for their missionaries. The change has meant a better income for most missionaries, but it has negatively impacted their time for rest during home assignment, as well as the general funds of their mission.

A second bittersweet change has been the change in relationships with emerging national churches. It has been satisfying to see the young churches come of age, but it has also been painful for the mission to deal with the transition in relationships from parent to partner. Problems have surfaced regularly around requests from the new church for workers and funding which appear to the society to be unwarranted.

Other areas of change include the struggle to keep up with available technology; the inroads of modernity; the frustration of having to process and prepare candidates who come from dysfunctional families or immature churches; the realization that the gospel has a holistic application (*see* HOLISTIC MISSION); the need for CONTINGENCY PLANS to safeguard missionaries in an increasingly hostile world; the need to prepare tentmakers for ministry in creative access countries (*see* TENTMAKING MISSION); and the urgent need to recruit people under thirty years of age as career missionaries and board members.

Contemporary Challenges. Underlying most of the contemporary challenges facing Australian mission boards and societies is the need to understand the thinking of young people under thirty years of age, in order to recruit them as long-term career missionaries and board members. Missions Interlink has set a goal of identifying one thousand young people who have decided to become missionaries in the future and to nurture them toward meaningful involvement in the missionary movement.

A second challenge relates directly to the need to recruit young people. At least 20 percent of Australian societies cannot remain viable with their current level of staff or finances. Some have reduced home staff in order to lessen expenditure. The way societies finance their operations is under review by those societies who have the expertise. The concept of team support will be challenged and reviewed. Some larger churches are challenging the concept now, by fully supporting their own workers but not allowing for the societies' costs. Some societies are in dialogue with possible compatible partners with a view to amalgamation. Unless the size of the resource base can be enlarged, it seems inevitable that some societies will soon cease to exist.

One way of increasing the level of support for the missionary task is to mount an effective education program in the churches about the biblical basis for the mission of the church and the ways in which the church can be involved in changing the world. Many pastors cannot undertake this task, so the missions must. The small number of missions who already have church education programs cannot meet the demand.

Proper care of the missionary family will be a prime responsibility, especially for the younger generations who demand this. Care begins with proper candidate processing, orientation, and training. Care continues to be a responsibility through a term of missionary service, and extends through debriefing and reentry to the home scene (*see* MEMBER CARE IN MISSIONS).

Finally, Australian boards and societies will face the dual challenges of completing the task with the churches they have already started and finding the keys to successful church planting in the more resistant Hindu, Buddhist, and Islamic cultures.

JOHN TANNER

Austria (*Est. 2000 pop.: 8,148,000; 83,853 sq. km. [32,376 sq. mi.]*). This small country in the heart of Europe, roughly the size of Maine (32,368 sq. miles) and populated by about 8 million people, has made a significant contribution to Western culture out of proportion to its size. While most Americans know the country from the movie *The Sound of Music*, several Austrians, including S. Freud, the father of modern psychoanalysis, the artists E. Schiele and G. Klimt, the composers W. A. Mozart, J. Strauss, J. Haydn, and G. Mahler, and L. Wittgenstein, one of this century's greatest philosophers who is noted particularly for his work on language, excelled in their respective fields.

History. Austria consists of nine provinces and shares borders with eight other countries: Germany, Czech Republic, Slovakia, Hungary, Slovenia, Italy, Switzerland, and Liechtenstein. The native language is German. Vienna, the country's capital since 1156, is located at the crossroads of Eastern and Western Europe. A diplomatic hub, it has been one of the permanent seats of the United Nations since 1979. The local university, one of the oldest in Europe, was founded in 1365. Once the center of the large Austro-Hungarian Empire (1867–1918), the city hosts cultural treasures in its many museums, churches, and palaces. Politically, Austria was ruled by two major dynasties: the Bavarian house of the Babenbergs (976–1282) and the Habsburgs (1282–1918). In 1919 Austria was constituted as a federal republic ("First Republic"), organized as a parliamentary democracy with a bicameral legislative body. The country was annexed by Hitler's German army in 1938 (Austria's role during World War II remains ambiguous and the subject of debate). The territory was occupied by the Allied forces from 1945 to 1955 and obtained its status as an independent nation ("Second Republic") with the obligation of permanent neutrality on May 29, 1955. The fall of the Soviet Empire in 1989 enabled Austria to join the European Union (EU) on January 1, 1995. In 1996 Austria celebrates the millennium of its existence (first extant reference to "ostarrîchi" in 996). Termed by its own inhabitants as an "island of the blessed," Austria is indeed privileged with breathtaking scenic beauty, particularly the Alps, and a rich cultural heritage. On the dark side, however, Austria has Europe's highest per capita consumption of alcohol, one of the highest abortion rates, and high instances of suicides and illegitimate births (26% in 1993).

Religion. The predominant religion of Austria is Roman Catholicism (78%), with a small contingent of Protestants of whom most are Lutheran (5%). Other legally recognized religions include various branches of the Orthodox Church, Judaism, Islam, Buddhism, the Old Catholic Church (which split from the Roman Catholic Church in 1871 over the doctrine of papal infallibility), the Methodist Church, and the Church of Jesus Christ of the Latter-Day Saints (Mormons). Among other privileges, the Austrian Constitution grants these religions the right to public worship, the right to administer their own internal affairs, and the entitlement to religious instruction at public schools. Relations between the Roman Catholic Church and the state were regulated by the Concordat of 1933–34 (renegotiated between 1957 and 1962). A similar arrangement was enacted with the Protestant Church in 1961. Evangelicals, numbering less than one percent of the population, are not officially recognized and are frequently considered to be a cult, along with the Jehovah's Witnesses and the Mormons, both of whom maintain a strong presence. The veneration of Mary continues at the many Marian shrines. A sizable number of Austrians are also involved in the occult, including white and black magic, witchcraft, fortune-telling, and other practices. The New Age movement and other esoteric involvements, likewise, exercise considerable appeal.

Mission. The gospel was first brought to the territory occupied by Austria today by Roman legionaires and merchants (Vienna's name was Vindobona). Florian and forty others were the first Austrians to suffer Christian martyrdom in Lauriacum (near Enns) during a period of persecution under Diocletian. Severin (d. 482) worked as a missionary in the Danube area during the time of great migration. Later, population shifts erased all traces of Christianity. After the migrations, the west of present-day Austria was christianized by the Bavarians. The diocese of Salzburg was founded as early as the seventh century owing to the initiative of Rupert (c. 650–718). Irish missionaries and Bavarian monks reevangelized the region during the eighth century. Increasingly, the Christian faith in Austria was tied to the pope in Rome, but in the course of the sixteenth century, the Reformation swept through Austria, and by 1570 Austria had largely become Protestant. The Habsburg Counter-Reformation, however, forcefully reconverted Austria to Roman Catholicism. At the apex of persecution in the winter of 1731, twenty thousand Protestants were driven out of the province of Salzburg. Only in 1781, Joseph II, son of the famous Austrian Empress Maria Theresa, issued an Edict of Toleration, ushering in a period of greater religious freedom. More recently, the Baptist church was founded in 1869; the Methodist church followed in 1870. The years following World War II witnessed a steady increase in evangelical missionary activity. In 1981 an Austrian Conference of Evangelical Churches (ARGEGÖ) was formed. However, this association lacks government recognition, and the Roman Catholic Church remains by far the most visible religious body in Austrian public life. While renewal (including charismatic) movements are found in parts of the Roman Catholic and Lutheran state churches, nominalism looms large, and the country is in urgent need of evangelization.

ANDREAS J. KÖSTENBERGER

Bibliography. *Austria: Facts and Figures* and *Austria Documentation: Religions in Austria; Austrian History Yearbook;* W. M. Johnston, *The Austrian Mind. An Intellectual and Social History 1848–1938;* J. J. Putman, *National Geographic,* April 1985, 410–48.

Authority (of the Bible). *See* INERRANCY.

Aviation Mission Work.

Every four minutes a small airplane takes off somewhere in the service of evangelical churches and missions. Two-thirds of these planes are operated by Mission Aviation Fellowship (MAF) and most of the rest by Wycliffe, AIM, or New Tribes. From a peak of nearly three hundred aircraft in 1985, the number of mission aircraft has slowly declined.

Two or three missionaries used airplanes briefly before World War II. After the war, Christian military pilots came together with a vision to use their skills in world evangelization. In 1945 former test pilot BETTY GREENE became the first MAF field pilot, serving Wycliffe in Mexico. By the early 1950s airplanes were serving several missions in Sudan, Central America, Amazonia, and New Guinea. A few individual missionaries flew their own planes.

Airplanes saved travel time. A one-hour flight replaced two or three weeks of land travel. Airplanes helped locate unreached jungle peoples and supported missionaries in places where they could not otherwise survive. Medical emergencies and war and famine relief have also played major roles. MAF cut costs by combining service to all the missions in a region, eventually providing regular service to over 160 different mission boards. At first airplanes primarily served Western missionaries but as the Third World church grew, service increasingly shifted to indigenous leaders.

Over half of all mission pilots and mechanics have trained at Moody Aviation, a department of Moody Bible Institute. Wild terrain, primitive airstrips, and lack of navigational aids make the work treacherous and over two dozen mission pilots have died in crashes.

Most mission aircraft are simple four- or six-passenger machines, but a few helicopters and larger planes are also being used. AirServ International, an MAF spinoff, has used huge Russian assault transports to fly thousands of tons of food to war and famine victims in Africa.

CHARLES BENNETT

Bibliography. G. Buss and A. F. Glasser, *Giving Wings to the Gospel;* T. Hitt, *Jungle Pilot: The Life and Witness of Nate Saint;* F. Robinson and J. Vincent, *A Vision With Wings: The Story of Missionary Aviation;* L. Roddy, *On Wings of Love.*

Aylward, Gladys

(1902–70). English missionary to China. A mailman's daughter born near London, she was converted at age eighteen while employed as a parlormaid, and set her heart on China. Rejected by the CHINA INLAND MISSION because of her lack of education, she slowly saved money, and in 1932 went east by the trans-Siberian railroad when Russia and China were at war, and finally joined Scottish missionary Jeannie Lawson in remote Yangcheng. Opposing the footbinding of girls, she was officially appointed footinspector, which gave her the opportunity to preach the gospel to women. Jeannie died, but Gladys with little resources used the inn they had opened to tell Bible stories to travelers and to house unwanted children. To reach people more effectively she became a naturalized Chinese citizen. In 1940 the Japanese invasion sent her on a month-long trek through the mountains, guiding nearly a hundred children to safety. From her incredible adventures Hollywood made the film *The Inn of the Sixth Happiness.* After a lengthy stay in England (1947–57) she returned to open an orphanage in Taiwan, where she died. Her career bristled with irregularities, but with Gladys it was always "Me—and God."

J. D. DOUGLAS

Bibliography. A. Burgess, *The Small Woman;* P. Thompson, *A Transparent Woman: The Compelling Story of Gladys Aylward.*

Azariah, Vedanayakam Samuel

(1874–1945). Indian missions promoter. Born to an evangelical Anglican pastor and his wife at Vellalanvillai in the Tinnevelly district of Madras state, he graduated from Madras Christian College and was appointed secretary to the YMCA of South India. In 1902 Azariah had an encounter with an indigenous mission society that convinced him that India had to take responsibility for its own evangelization. He is credited with being founder of the Indian Missionary Society of Tinnevelly in 1903 and the National Missionary Society of India in 1905.

Azariah was ordained as the first Indian bishop in the Anglican Church in 1909 and attended the WORLD MISSIONARY CONFERENCE at Edinburgh in 1910. There he made a plea for greater freedom for Indian church leaders. In 1912 he was placed in charge of the diocese of Dornakal. The six pastors under his care worked mainly with outcasts. He promoted evangelism and Christian unity in India and was determined that Indian Christianity should be indigenous. He lived to see a diocese of over one hundred thousand members where forty years before there had been only eight thousand.

Azariah participated in several international ecumenical gatherings, including the TAMBARAM CONFERENCE of 1938, where he delivered one of the major addresses. He was one of the faithful who paved the way for the formation of the United Church of South India and the WORLD COUNCIL OF CHURCHES.

KENNETH D. GILL

Bibliography. C. Graham, *IBMR* 9:1 (1985): 16–19; C. Graham, *Azariah of Dornakal;* B. Sundkler, *Church of South India.*

Azerbaijan *(Est. 2000 pop.: 7,969,000; 86,600 sq. km. [33,436 sq. mi.]).* Azerbaijan is an oil- and mineral-rich republic of the former Soviet Union located in the southern Caucasus region on the Caspian Sea. The dominant ethnic group, known as the Azeris, are a Turkic people, closely related to most of the major ethnic groups of ex-Soviet Central Asia. At least 80 percent of the people are at least nominally Muslim (70 percent Shi'a; 30 percent Sunni), and although religious freedom is officially guaranteed, foreigners are barred from engaging in "religious propaganda." Evangelicals are extremely few, probably numbering less than one thousand, most of whom are ethnic Russians.

RAYMOND P. PRIGODICH

SEE ALSO Commonwealth of Independent States.

Bb

Baba, Panya (1932–). Nigerian missions organizer and advocate. Born in Karu in north-central Nigeria of converted animist parents, he came to personal faith in Christ as an early teen. His education included study at Karu Bible Training School, Kagoro (Nigeria) Bible College, All Nations Christian College (U.K.), and Fuller School of World Mission (U.S.). Baba's many accomplishments were recognized in the rewarding of an honorary doctorate by Igbaja Theological Seminary (Nigeria).

Baba's ministry experience has included pastoral service and church administrative office, including two terms as president of Evangelical Church of West Africa (ECWA) denomination (1988–94). His primary contributions to missions have come as director of the Evangelical Mission Society of ECWA, Africa's largest indigenous mission society (1970–88), and as mission consultant and foreign missions director for ECWA (1994–). He had a major role in establishing the Nigeria Evangelical Missions Association, a coordinating body for indigenous Nigerian missions agencies, and served as its first chairman. Other international missions committee memberships have included the WEF Missions Commission, Third World Missions Advance Steering Committee, and the International Board of the AD 2000 Movement. As a respected spokesman on all aspects of cross-cultural missions, particularly African issues, he has been a primary contributor at numerous missions consultations worldwide.

Baba is an outspoken advocate of cooperation and partnership between indigenous churches and indigenous mission agencies and between Western and non-Western mission agencies. In 1996, as a direct result of his vision and initiative, twelve SIM-related national church denominations on three continents (Africa, South America, Asia) formed the Evangelical Fellowship Missions Association for the purpose of stimulating prayer and information sharing, the formation of national missionary movements, and coordinating joint mission efforts. He has helped develop cooperative strategies for the training, sending, and sponsorship of missionaries by Western and non-Western mission agencies in partnership, an important trend in evangelical missions in the future.

RICHARD D. CALENBERG

Bibliography. P. Baba, *EMQ* 26:2 (1990): 131–33.

Babel. Genesis 11:1–9 is a sharp polemic against the pretensions of the collective human self-sufficiency in rebellion against God. Its missionary and missiological relevance can be seen from noting its place in the history of God's redemptive work and revelation.

This is a representative episode of opposition to the purpose of the Lord following the judgment of the flood. The nations descended from Noah (Gen. 10) were implicitly required to disperse over the earth to fulfill the creation mandate (Gen. 1:28), reiterated in the covenant of preservation (Gen. 8:15–9:17). This was with a view to the redemptive purpose encapsulated in the prophecy of Noah (Gen. 9:25–27), to be fulfilled by the coming of Christ. But the line of Nimrod ("Let us rebel"), the descendant of Ham, founds Babel (Babylon[ia]) (Gen. 10:8–10), which meant "Gate of God" in its Babylonian form (but, mockingly, "confusion" in Hebrew).

The self-aggrandizing aim and motive of "making a name" for themselves and resisting dispersion was not only disobedience; it also implied a spurning of the promise given to Noah that the true intent of Eden would be restored. Artificial sacred mountains (ziggurats) in the Babel area, according to the later versions of Babylonian myths, aimed at idolizing humanity were the very antithesis of the goal of the city of God. Babel therefore epitomized the universal resistance of fallen humanity to God. If unthwarted it threatened to produce the demonic counterpart of the kingdom or rule of God. As by the eating of the tree of knowledge people became, in an ironic sense, like God (Gen. 3:22), so now, with equal irony, humans are potentially omnipotent, and (implicitly) evilly so (v. 6). Therefore the Lord comes in judgment, but also in grace, to confuse and disperse: he prevents any preempting triumph of self-sufficient, self-determining human society, and so averts the necessity of destroying humankind.

This common-grace restraint of sin and its effects preserves humankind for the redemption to come (v. 9).

The immediately following focus on Shem (Gen. 11:10), associated with blessing (9:26–27), and then on Terah, the father of Abraham and his kin (11:27), is not accidental: through Abraham all peoples will be blessed (12:3).

The reversal of both the confusion-scattering of Babel and its sinful human assertion is Pentecost. There the special redemptive grace, applying the work of the risen Christ, is symbolically and representatively poured out on all the nations, through the Jews and proselytes present. They are gathered, not scattered now, and all hear what God has done in Christ in the language of their own region; they repent and are baptized for the forgiveness of their sins. This prefigures the "purifying the lips of the peoples" and the "gathering" home of God's people (Zeph. 3:9, 20), of which the missionary task is the instrument.

JOHN A. McINTOSH

Bibliography. J. Blauw, *The Missionary Nature of the Church;* H. Blocher, *In the Beginning;* J. Davies, *JTS,* new series 5 (1952): 228–31; M. Kline, *Kingdom Prologue;* R. DeRidder, *Discipling the Nations;* D. Senior and C. Stuhlmueller, *The Biblical Foundation for Mission;* G. Wenham, *Genesis 1–15.*

Bachelor's Degrees in Mission. Bachelor-level educational programs served as one of the primary training grounds for missionaries in the twentieth century. Bible colleges and to a smaller extent church-related Christian colleges and universities have contributed to the stream of missiological training. North Americans and Northern Europeans dominated this training for the first three-quarters of the century. However, in the last quarter of the century the picture changed.

Raymond Windsor in the *World Directory of Missionary Training Programs* states that prior to 1975 only thirty non-Western training programs existed. However, since 1975 more than 125 new programs have emerged in the non-Western world. In 1995 at least 117 bachelor's programs in thirty-six countries were catalogued. This listing, however, while a substantial and representative sample, should not be seen as comprehensive.

Three institutions stand out among the North American options during the first half of the century. Their alumni/ae accounted for about 40 percent of the North American missionary force during that era. These three institutions include: Moody Bible Institute, Prairie Bible Institute, and Columbia Bible College (now Columbia International University).

The emergence of the importance of the Bible College movement as a significant training arena for missions coincided with the STUDENT VOLUNTEER MOVEMENT and the FAITH MISSION movement. The Student Volunteer movement served as the motivating force while the Faith Mission movement served as the receiving context for the ministries of the graduates. The Bible College movement followed the rise of the Bible Institutes of the late nineteenth century and early twentieth century, providing four essential components of their training. Kenneth Mulholland suggests that the biblical, practical, contextual, and spiritual development of these colleges served to well equip the surge of North American missionaries. Similar emphases were present in institutions in the United Kingdom as well in such institutions as All Nations Bible College, London Bible College, and Glasgow Bible College.

The multiplication of missionary training programs in the non-Western world parallels the growth of evangelical and Pentecostal churches in the same regions. Now more missionaries are being sent from non-Western missions than from Western missions. They are being sent from a correspondingly larger non-Western Christian community than is found in the West.

This brief survey has not considered the scores of postsecondary-level programs that do not necessarily eventuate in a bachelor's degree. This survey similarly has not considered the many programs offered in many universities both Christian and secular. Some secular universities have evangelical faculty who take initiatives to assist in the training of missionaries at a bachelor's level. And some colleges still offer degrees through national universities because of local governmental policies.

While other higher level educational programs including master's and doctoral programs also proliferated during the twentieth century, bachelor's degrees served as the backbone of Western missionary training through the period. It appears that given the present proliferation of non-Western bachelor's degrees in mission the trend will continue in the non-Western world in the early part of the twenty-first century.

EDGAR J. ELLISTON

Bibliography. K. Mullholland, *Missiological Educational for the 21st Century,* pp. 43–50; R. Windsor, ed., *World Directory of Missionary Training Programs.*

Baedeker, Friedrich Wilhelm (1823–1906). German-born English missionary to Russia. Baedeker was born in Witten in 1823 He lost his first wife in 1852 after a few months of married life, moved to Britain, traveled to Tasmania, then settled in Weston Super Mare in 1859, and remarried there in

1862. The Baedeckers led a respected but worldly upper-class life. Their conversion through evangelistic meetings led by Lord Radstock in 1866 drastically changed their lives.

His German background made Baedeker a transmitter of the Holiness Revival message to his native country, where he became one of the leading figures in the annual Blankenburg Alliance Conference and also one of the founders of the Alliance Bible School in Berlin (1905).

His main ministry was in the Russian Empire (1887–89) and other Eastern European countries. In St. Petersburg he was one of God's instruments in the revival among the Russian nobility. His initial intention was to reach the millions of German Russians, but his evangelistic vision expanded to include all the nationalities of the vast empire. His most intensive ministry was among prisoners, whom he visited even in the most remote locations of Siberia and Sachalin. He combined his evangelistic work with assistance to the needy, also looking after those who were imprisoned for their faith and working for religious freedom. He died in 1906 in Weston Super Mare.

KLAUS FIELDER

Bibliography. R. S. Latimer, *Dr. Baedeker and His Apostolic Work in Russia;* J. Marchant, ed., *Deeds Done for Christ.*

Baha'i. Although the Baha'i religion emerged from the Shi'ite sect of ISLAM, it has suffered more persecution from Shi'ites in Iran—especially since the 1979 Islamic revolution—than from any other group. This persecution is due largely to the fact that Baha'i believes in a later divine revelation that supersedes the QUR'AN. Baha'i has an estimated 5 million adherents, most of whom are located in Asia and Africa, and appears to be growing worldwide.

The fundamental teaching of Baha'i, from which other teachings stem, is the unity of the human race. Baha'i also teaches that, in spite of minor differences among them, all religions share a basic unity and have a common origin. All of the major religions are regarded as partial messengers of truth. Religion, science, and education should work together to produce a harmonious world in which the extremes of wealth and poverty are abolished. Baha'i is one of the few religions apart from Christianity to teach the absolute equality of the sexes. Baha'is believe that each person should search independently for truth, without influence from superstition or tradition. In addition, the emphasis upon world unity in Baha'i leads to concern for one common universal language and compulsory education for all.

Shi'ite Islam had taught that Ali, Muhammad's son-in-law and legitimate successor, was succeeded by a series of descendants, the last of whom disappeared in the ninth century A.D. It was believed that he would reappear someday as a messiah. In 1844 Ali Muhammad declared that he was the promised imam or successor of Ali and called himself Bab ud Din ("the gate of faith"). He became a reformer, advocating radical changes such as raising the status of women, which raised the ire of the political leaders in Persia. The Bab, as he was called, was executed in 1850, but before his death he predicted that another would come and establish a universal religion.

One disciple of the Bab, Husayn Ali, was imprisoned in Tehran and then exiled to Baghdad for ten years. During this time he came to the conclusion that he was the predicted founder of the new religion. He assumed the name Baha' Ullah ("the glory of God"), and surviving followers of the Bab (called Babis) became known as Baha'is. After years of being driven from one Middle Eastern city to another, the Baha'is were imprisoned in a Turkish prison at Akko, in modern Israel.

From this prison Baha' Ullah sent out missionaries to spread his teachings and wrote many books and letters before his death in 1892. His son, Abdul Baha, carried on his program and in 1908 was released from prison. He traveled widely in Europe and North America, spreading his teachings of peace, for which he received the honor of knighthood of the British Empire. Upon his death in 1921, his grandson Shoghi Effendi continued the work. Although there are no priests in Baha'i, the community builds temples in various locations for worship. The principal center is in Haifa, Israel, near the graves of Baha' Ullah and the Bab.

WILLIAM H. BAKER

Bibliography. W. S. Hatcher and J. D. Martin, *The Baha'i Faith: The Emerging Global Religion;* W. M. Miller, *The Baha'i Faith: Its History and Teachings.*

Bahamas *(Est. 2000 pop.: 295,000; 13,878 sq. km. [5,358 sq. mi.]).* An archipelago of seven hundred coral islands, the Bahamas lie between Florida and Cuba. Although there is little agricultural potential, the group's proximity to the United States has made it a useful staging area for offshore economic activities, rum-running in the 1920s, and more recently banking, oil refining, tourism, and drug trafficking. More than two-thirds of the population is Protestant, about half of whom are evangelicals.

EVERETT A. WILSON

SEE ALSO Caribbean.

Bibliography. A. Lampe, *The Church in Latin America, 1492–1992,* pp. 201–15; J. Rogozinski, *A Brief History of the Caribbean: From the Arawak and the Carib to the Present.*

Bahrain *(Est. 2000 pop.: 633,000; 678 sq. km. [262 sq. mi.]).* A group of islands twenty-five miles off the east coast of Saudi Arabia and recently connected to the mainland by a causeway comprise the country of Bahrain. The population is composed of the original Bahraini, Iraqi, Palestinian, Egyptian, and Saudi Arabian Arabs. These people make up 72 percent of the population. The rest of the inhabitants have come from Iran, India, Korea, and Western countries.

The discovery of oil changed the economy from pearl diving and fishing to one of refineries and a center for international banking. Bahrain has become the strategic center for all of Arabia.

Stewart, *The Nestorian Enterprise,* mentions that there was a bishopric in A.D. 225. In modern times the first American missionaries secured an upper room near the pearl bazaar in 1892. People were hostile at the time to all outsiders and unwilling to rent to Christians. They had no medical or surgical help. There did not appear to be any desire for progress. Stagnation reigned and self-satisfaction with Islam quenched hopes of development.

SAMUEL ZWEMER arrived in 1895 and began medical missions. He reached out from Bahrain to other parts of Arabia. The Reformed Church of America continued there, developing their Bahrain station as one of their largest outposts. It includes an excellent hospital, high standard schools, and the church founded by Zwemer. This church now hosts eight different congregations worshiping in as many languages. In the whole of the country there are now more than forty-five groups or fellowships with the majority of believers belonging to the Anglican and evangelical groups.

Among the expatriate workforce are Christian believers from Iraq, India, Egypt, Korea, and Western countries who make up the 7 percent Christian minority. With the new causeway connecting the islands with the mainland many Saudis go over to shop and enjoy entertainment in the less restrictive atmosphere of Bahrain. Many Bibles have been distributed and a large Christian bookstore affords a good selection of books in Arabic as well as other languages. Bahrain has become a center for tours into Arabia and the Gulf areas. With the large number of believers in the country and the moderate outlook of the ruling family there is a possibility of the church there being the staging area for further penetration of the peninsula.

GEORGE E. KELSEY

Bibliography. R. B. Betts, *Christians in the Arab East;* S. Moffett, *A History of Christianity in Asia;* W. H. Storm, *Whither Arabia?;* J. S. Trimingham, *Christianity Among The Arabs;* S. M. Zwemer, *Heirs to the Prophets.*

Baker, Amelia Dorothea (Kohlhoff) (1801–88). German missionary wife and widow in South India. Born in Tanjore, she was the granddaughter of a German Lutheran missionary, and married the young CHURCH MISSION SOCIETY (CMS) missionary, Henry Baker, in 1818. They served in Cottayam, in Travancore, where, in addition to bearing and bringing up a large family she commenced and managed a girls' school. In 1866, after her husband's death, she continued, now as a widow and with acknowledgment, the work she had already been carrying on for over forty years. She remained at Cottayam until her death. Her son (b. 1819) became a CMS missionary, and three daughters married CMS missionaries. Five granddaughters and a grandson also worked for the Anglican Church, and female descendants were engaged in girls' education well into the twentieth century. In addition to the great contribution made by her family, Amelia Baker deserves to be remembered as one of the many missionary widows who, continuing to work on after their husbands' death—in her case for eighteen years—proved to the missionary society the worth of a woman's contribution, and in fact opened the way for a greater use of single women.

JOCELYN MURRAY

Bibliography. CMS, *Register of Missionaries and Native Clergy, 1904;* E. Dalton, *The Baker Family in India;* E. A. Kohlhoff, comp., *Pastoral Symphony: The Family and Descendants of Johann Baltasar Kohlhoff.*

Baldwin, Mary Briscoe (1811–79). American missionary to Greece and Palestine. Though she felt that the lofty calling of becoming a missionary was one too high for her and reserved for only the most spiritual of people, God made it distinctly clear to this Virginian teenager that he had chosen her for such a task. While helping a friend investigate possible missionary openings, Baldwin discovered that the only opening, an overseas position, was one that she herself ardently desired. Having met the missionaries already working in Greece a year earlier while attending a conference, she applied and was approved to go to Greece to help educate the Greek and Cretan refugee peoples. She became the first female overseas missionary to come from Virginia.

In order to meet the physical and spiritual needs of the people, the veteran Greek missionaries envisioned an education system that would teach students both a skill and the message of Christ. Baldwin facilitated this vision by teaching a sewing class—a novelty in itself, considering there were no professional seamstresses in Athens at that time. Her enthusiasm and commitment to these women won her the title of

"Good Lady Mary" from her pupils as well as the community.

Baldwin became the legal guardian of her sister's three children. This ignited her desire to open a boarding school, especially for Cretan upper-class girls. Because the mission was unable to support such a venture financially, Baldwin used her own inheritance to start the school. While realizing her students' need for a good education, an understanding of Christ took precedence. Together with the other missionaries in the area, she opened her home to serve as a church on Sunday mornings. Later, the boarding school idea expanded to establishing district schools as well.

PENNY GUSHIKEN

Bibliography. E. R. Pitman, *Mission Life in Greece and Palestine.*

Baltic States. In the armed conflicts involving Orthodox, Catholic, and Lutheran Europe, few regions have suffered as have the Baltic states. Yet their strong commitment to ethnic identity and will to survive have allowed these peoples to endure and flourish. Finno-Ugric peoples apparently settled in Estonia and Finland in the third millennium B.C. Others of Indo-European linguistic origin settled in Latvia and Lithuania a thousand years later. Earliest accounts included Tacitus's reports of pagan "Aestii" living on the eastern shore of the Baltic. Later reports indicate formidable Baltic pirates during the early Middle Ages.

During the later Middle Ages (1147–1500), European military forces mounted unceasing attempts to establish control over the region, making the Baltics the scene of continuous armed struggle. In 1343 the final peasant rebellion in the Northern Baltics was crushed, leaving the territory under the control of German nobility. Farther south pagan Lithuania successfully resisted the Teutonic Knights in repeated engagements. By the mid-1300s, the well-organized and influential Lithuania had become the largest European state. By 1400, however, Lithuania had been incorporated into Catholic Europe, allying with Poland against the Knights. During this time, the Hanseatic League was also founded, Riga (Latvia) and Tallinn (Estonia) becoming influential member ports.

By the mid-1520s, Lutheranism was established among the ruling class in Latvia and Estonia (old Livonia). The pagan peasantry, however, was largely unaffected. In 1558 internal weakness in the ruling Liv class sparked a conflict involving Russia, Sweden, and Poland (Livonian Wars). Livonian rule decimated, the region was divided between Protestant Sweden and Catholic Poland. Hostilities continued as part of the Thirty Years War, using the Northern Baltics as a primary battleground. Even so, a time of relative prosperity known as the "good old Swedish time" was inaugurated. Swedish law prevailed, limiting the power of the nobles and elevating the status of the peasantry. Education was improved and extended to the commoners. A major university was founded in Tartu (1632).

The Treaty of Nystadt (1721) at the end of the Great Northern War ceded old Livonia to Russia. Russians reestablished the German nobility, stripping the peasants of rights gained under Swedish rule. Although repressed, the Northern Baltics experienced a time of relative peace, while in the south the Lithuanians continued their alliance with Poland and Catholic Europe. The Lithuanian alliance continued until the eighteenth century, when it was divided between Prussia and Russia.

Around 1730 MORAVIAN Pietists arrived in Riga. The movement grew among the peasants, prompting a visit in 1736 by Herrnhut founder, Count NIKOLAUS LUDWIG VON ZINZINDORF. By 1738 revival had spread throughout the northern region and the movement flourished in spite of Russian persecution. By 1748 MORAVIAN missionaries from the Baltics were sent to the New World, primarily to Pennsylvania. MORAVIAN Pietism produced significant social reforms, including friendlier relationships between the peasants and ruling Germans.

Recent history has seen a return to violence and repression, but not without hope. In 1918 Balts took advantage of a destabilized Bolshevik Russia by declaring independence. After defeating the Soviet counterattack, the Northern Baltics gained independence for the first time in nearly seven hundred years. By the late 1920s, all three nations had constitutional democracies, membership in the League of Nations, and independent currencies.

Nineteen years of freedom and relative prosperity ended in August 1939 with the Molotov–Ribbentrop Pact. This agreement sparked the German invasion of Poland and the Russian takeover of the Baltics. In the 1941 attack on the Soviet Union, German armies marched through the Baltics, welcomed by many as liberators from Stalinism. The Russian advance against the Germans in 1944–45 again brought war to the region.

Fearful of reprisals, many Balts fled during World War II. Stalin later deported, displaced, or murdered hundreds of thousands, leaving the population decimated. The Cold War years were marked by persistent attempts to "Russianize" the region through deportation of ethnic Balts and importation of Russians. The policy created a near majority Russian population in Latvia, where some fear the eventual disappearance of ethnic Latvians. Estonia increased to about 40 percent Russians (compared to 8 percent pre–World War

II), while in Lithuania, the population of Russians remained less significant.

The Baltics declared independence from the Soviet Union in 1991 and received immediate recognition by the international community. After years of repression and stagnation, Balts are eager to modernize and create healthy economies. The church finds new possibilities within its grasp but often experiences difficulties coping with rapid change. In addition, signs of a pagan revival provide cause for additional concern. The recent establishment of several theological training centers gives hope for the future health and growth of the church throughout the region.

STEVEN J. PIERSON

Bibliography. E. Christiansen, *The Northern Crusades: The Baltic and the Catholic Frontier, 1100–1525*; P. Jones and N. Pennick, *A History of Pagan Europe*; A. Lieven, *The Baltic Revolution: Estonia, Latvia, Lithuania and the Path to Independence*; V. Mezezers, *The Herrnhuterian Pietism in the Baltic: And Its Outreach into America and Elsewhere in the World*; I. A. Smith and M. V. Grunts, comp., *The Baltic States: Estonia, Latvia, Lithuania*; A. N. Tarulis, *Soviet Policy Toward the Baltic States 1918–1940.*

Bangkok Conference (1973). Taking the theme "Salvation Today," the WCC met in Bangkok in January of 1973. The three sections of the conference focused on (1) culture and identity, (2) salvation and social justice in a divided community, and (3) churches renewed in mission. Influenced by theologians committed to exploring the meaning of liberation, the conference asserted the indissolubility of the social and individual aspects of salvation. In its search for a holistic understanding of salvation, Bangkok opened itself to a charge of reductionism, supplanting biblical concepts of salvation, as one evangelical author put it, with "a secularized this-worldly version of social action as the mission of the church." The evangelical voices were not unified, however, as others found common ground between their thinking and that of the ecumenically committed. Indeed, it has been widely argued that at Bangkok there was no real polarization between those who stressed the social dimensions of salvation and those who underlined the personal.

A second source of controversy at the conference was its placing on the agenda of churches and mission agencies the confessedly radical concept of MORATORIUM, the suggestion that mission agencies in the north, as a possible strategy in certain situations, cease for a period the sending of personnel and finances to the churches of the south. Though the language at Bangkok was measured and restrained, the tone of the debate became overheated. Underlining the dramatic language was the need, in a largely

postcolonial world, to move from patterns of missionary PATERNALISM to PARTNERSHIP in mission. This new emphasis alarmed some conservative evangelicals to the extent that they called for withdrawal from ecumenical agencies. Ecumenical thinkers claimed that a new era of mission (not missions) was ushered into being at Bangkok; evangelicals made the same claims for Lausanne. Both, however, agreed that the hallmark of the new era would be a genuine partnership in world mission.

JOHN H. Y. BRIGGS

Bibliography. P. Beyerhaus, *Bangkok, 1973: The Beginning or End of World Mission*; E. Castro, *Sent Free: Mission and Unity in the Perspective of the Kingdom*; WCC, *Bangkok Assembly, 1973*; R. Winter, ed., *The Evangelical Response to Bangkok.*

Bangladesh *(Est. 2000 pop.: 134,417,000; 143,998 sq. km. [55,598 sq. mi.]).* December 16, 1971, marked a new beginning for the people of Bangladesh, who are ethnically referred to as Bengalis. They had suffered through the indignities of the colonial period which was followed by West Pakistan's domination. Only in 1971, after a bloody civil war, did the Bengalis receive their independence. Political freedom has not meant internal peace. Various intrigues have left two presidents assassinated along with an economy which is only marginally viable. Recurring floods, cyclones, and tornadoes have contributed to the ongoing sufferings of the people.

Approximately 134 million Bengalis are divided into communities of 85 percent Muslim, 14 percent Hindu, with less than one-half of one percent being Christian. The majority of these Christians are from a Hindu background. Therefore their cultural and linguistic preferences are more Hindu-influenced. This reality places a natural barrier between Bengali Christians and the majority Muslim community.

Protestant missionary work among Bengalis was pioneered by WILLIAM CAREY in the early nineteenth century. The Bible translated by Carey is still widely used today. Other Bible translations have followed, most notably the Simplified Version, as well as the popular evangelistic New Testament known as the *Injil Sharif* (Sacred Gospel). These have been produced by the Association of Baptists for World Evangelism (ABWE) in cooperation with the Bangladesh Bible Society.

ABWE's Literature Center is the leading producer of materials for Christians as well as for specialized tracts designed for the non-Christian. Another ministry of ABWE that has served the missionary and Bengali community is their well-equipped hospital in the south of the country.

Since 1971, many nongovernment organizations have worked extensively throughout Bangladesh. All mission societies are now required to engage in development work. Foreigners are not allowed to be involved in direct evangelism among Muslims. There is, however, no such restrictions placed on Bengali Christians.

In 1975, International Christian Fellowship (now SIM) pioneered a contextualized approach to presenting the gospel to Muslims. This style of outreach has been followed by various groups in Bangladesh. Results have been encouraging, with estimates of several thousands of Muslim background believers being formed into small worshiping cells. Most of these believers have remained within their communities (*see* MUSLIM MISSION WORK).

The Bangladesh Baptist Fellowship in cooperation with the American Southern Baptists, New Zealand Baptists, and Australian Baptists has significantly impacted Hindus with the gospel. Other mission agencies have been successful in evangelism among the small tribal minorities in Bangladesh.

Since 1958, the major effort in literature distribution to non-Christians has been spearheaded by SIM's Bangladesh Bible Correspondence School. Hundreds of thousands of students have first heard the Christian message through receiving these lessons. Much of the publicity of the correspondence school has been done by young Christian workers.

Aid and development projects from the West have been both a blessing and a curse to Christian Bengalis. All too often this assistance has created a dependency syndrome which has hindered spiritual growth. Another problem has been a competitive spirit among foreign agencies which has brought confusion and strife within the small body of believers.

In spite of all of the setbacks in Christian ministry in Bangladesh, there are still encouragements. More Bengalis are coming to faith in Christ than ever before in the history of this turbulent land.

PHIL PARSHALL

Bibliography. P. NcNee, *Crucial Issues in Bangladesh;* R. F. Nyrop, *Area Handbook for Bangladesh;* V. B. Olsen, *Daktar/Diplomat in Bangladesh.*

Baptism. Christian rite of initiation using water. The origin of its practice is usually traced specifically to John the Baptist and through him to Jewish practices of ceremonial washings, Qumran purification rites (initiates into the Essene sect of Judaism underwent a ritual washing), and proselyte baptism (Gentile converts to Judaism). It is almost universally practiced by Christians based on the precedent set by Christ in his own baptism (Matt. 3:11), his command to baptize (Matt. 28:19), and testimony in the Acts of the Apostles and the New Testament Epistles of its practice by the early Christian community.

Although reckoned by almost all branches of Christianity as a sacrament, its mode, subjects, and significance have historically been issues of sharp doctrinal controversy.

While some practice affusion (pouring of water) or aspersion (sprinkling), the Baptist position has generally called for immersion. This is primarily defended on the grounds that (1) the Greek word transliterated "baptize" in the New Testament means "to dip, immerse"; (2) immersion best illustrates the significance given to baptism by the apostle Paul (Rom. 6:1–11)—the believer's identification with the death, burial, and resurrection of Christ; and (3) immersion was practiced by the Jews, John the Baptist, and the early church.

However, the primary dispute of the Anabaptists with the other Reformation traditions concerned who was to be baptized. Calvin and Luther continued the Roman Catholic practice of infant baptism (although certainly with different theological justification), whereas the Anabaptists rejected this in favor of believer's baptism, that is, that personal confession of faith was a prerequisite for the one to be baptized. Thus the Baptist tradition has generally reserved this rite for individuals old enough to express conscious faith in Christ. The Reformers argued that baptism is analogous to infants receiving circumcision in the Old Testament. It is a sign of God's covenant promise and grace administered to Abraham and climaxing in the new covenant. It is not primarily a sign of faith/repentance on the part of the believer (as the Baptist position); rather it is a seal of the work of God that precedes and makes possible the person's response.

Protestants as a whole have disagreed with the sacramental significance assigned to baptism by Roman Catholics. Protestants view baptism as being an outward, visible manifestation of inward spiritual reality. For Catholics, baptism does not simply illustrate, but it actually effects that spiritual reality through its very operation. Thus, baptism infuses the grace of the new birth (hence, baptismal regeneration) even in infants.

The spiritual reality signified by baptism is itself variously interpreted and nuanced by Protestants. However, the following ideas are generally included: the cleansing from sin; union with Christ in death and resurrection and thus the death of the old self and its way of life and the rising to new life in Christ; and incorporation of the Christian into the Body of Christ.

Missionaries often must deal not only with the spiritual dimensions of baptism but also the social implications. In many societies where Christians are a distinct minority baptism is viewed with greater significance by Christians and non-Christians alike as it publicly marks the convert's decision to associate with the Christian community.

The practice of baptism has given rise to special difficulties in contexts where great value is given to family relationships and societal unity and where baptism by the established church has come to signify in practical terms the convert's repudiation of his or her previous social, political, and cultural loyalties. This misconception of the spiritual significance of baptism, it is said, has arisen from a perceived association of Christianity with Western culture as well as misguided efforts in winning individual converts even at the expense of separating them from their communities. Some missiologists have therefore suggested in view of such a misunderstanding of the true meaning of baptism by the non-Christian society that the insistence of baptism by the new convert be dispensed with in order to minimize his or her cultural dislocation and to allow the Christian to remain within his or her community while continuing to discreetly share Christ by life and witness from within it.

While recognizing the biblical mandate to baptize but in view of the difficulties of baptism as it is normally practiced, missionaries in Muslim fields have considered variations, such as the delay of baptism until a number of converts can be baptized together; secret baptism with a limited audience; self-baptism; or the substitution of a contextually appropriate initiation ceremony that would retain the biblical meaning of baptism but have a different form and thus reduce offense to the onlooking Muslim community.

SCOTT CUNNINGHAM

Bibliography. G. R. Beasley-Murray, *Baptism in the New Testament;* A. Gilmore, ed., *Christian Baptism;* M. Green, *Baptism: Its Purpose, Practice and Power;* P. Parshall, *New Paths in Muslim Evangelism: Evangelical Approaches to Contextualization.*

Baptist Missionary Society (BMS). The BMS was founded in Kettering, Northamptonshire, England, on October 2, 1792, and was the first of the missionary societies founded as a result of the Evangelical Revival. Formed by a group of Particular Baptists including ANDREW FULLER (1754–1815), who was appointed secretary, and WILLIAM CAREY (1761–1834), its original name was The Particular-Baptist Society for Propagating the Gospel among the Heathen. The original base of the society was in the Baptist churches of the East Midlands. A London office was not opened until 1819. The BMS sent its first missionaries, John Thomas and William Carey, to Bengal in 1793. With WILLIAM WARD (1769–1823) and JOSHUA MARSHMAN (1768–1837), Carey developed church, educational, and translation work based at Serampore, north of Calcutta, and expanded the mission eastward into what is now Bangladesh and up the Ganges Valley to the northwest. After the death of Andrew Fuller, relationships between the Serampore missionaries and the society at home deteriorated, so that from 1827 to 1837 the Serampore mission operated independently from the BMS. The BMS also began work in Sri Lanka (1812) and the Caribbean, beginning with Jamaica in 1814, where its missionaries, notably William Knibb (1803–45), were instrumental in securing the abolition of slavery in 1834. The Baptist cause among the former slaves flourished as a result, and black Jamaican Baptists played a key role in initiating the BMS mission in Cameroon in 1841. Following the German annexation of Cameroon, this mission was handed over to the BASEL MISSION in 1886. The Congo mission (1879) was maintained with lavish financial support from the Leeds philanthropist, ROBERT ARTHINGTON (1823–1900), for whom the rapid Baptist advance up the Congo River was part of a wider vision for the evangelization of Central Africa. The BMS began work in China in 1859, where TIMOTHY RICHARD (1845–1919) developed broadly conceived mission strategies that challenged many of the evangelical orthodoxies of the day. In 1891, the smaller General Baptist Missionary Society (formed in 1816), which worked mainly in Orissa, merged with the BMS as part of the coming together of the previously separate General (Armenian) and Particular (Calvinistic) strands of Baptist life in England. BMS missionary numbers reached their peak in 1921–22. As a result of the society's work, Baptist Christians are now particularly numerous in northeast India (Orissa and Mizoram), Jamaica, Zaïre, and Angola. The BMS also assists Baptist communities planted by other missions, as in Brazil, which it entered in 1953. Since the late 1980s, the Society has been active in a number of European countries, to the extent that Europe now accounts for 25 percent of the mission force and budget. The BMS in the twentieth century combined participation in ecumenical mission bodies with a firmer commitment to evangelistic priorities than has been true of some of the historic Protestant mission agencies. This commitment has strengthened in recent years in response to the conservative evangelical resurgence among British Baptists. The BMS remains active as a voluntary society supported by Baptists in England, Wales, and Scotland.

BRIAN STANLEY

Bibliography. E. D. Potts, *British Baptist Missionaries in India 1793–1837: The History of Serampore and its Missions;* R. M. Slade, *English-Speaking Missions in the Congo Independent State (1878–1908);* E. Stanley, *The History of the Baptist Missionary Society 1792–1992.*

Baptist Missions. Within the family of Christian denominations, Baptists have been a missions people. In spite of their theological controversies, ecclesiastical independence, and geographical provincialism, world missions has been the integrating center that has given them corporate life. All of their major unions, conventions, and parachurch entities have sprung from their commitment to world missions. Their cooperative efforts for world missions have brought them to the forefront of the modern missionary movement. The missions story of the Baptist denominations can be divided into five periods.

Early English Beginnings (1792–1814). The Baptists trace their denominational origins back to seventeenth-century English Separatism. The first Baptist congregations in England were no doubt greatly influenced by the Anabaptists of the sixteenth century on the Continent, but developed an ecclesiology that featured a moderate Calvinistic theology, baptism of believers by immersion, and a congregational polity. Their freechurch polity, reactionary attitude, dissident reputation, and sometimes hyper-Calvinism caused them to be very provincial. Although they participated in the transatlantic Concert of Prayer for world evangelization promoted by pietistic Europeans and Jonathan Edwards in the second half of the eighteenth century, their participation in world missions was unheard of until one of their humble pastors, WILLIAM CAREY (1761–1834), through study of the Bible and geography, derived a deep conviction for world evangelization.

Carey, an obscure pastor and sometime shoe-cobbler, came to the conclusion that the hyper-Calvinism of his denomination, which frowned on human instrumentality in evangelism, was spurious. He discovered the missionary mandate in the Bible and became aware of its necessity through his study of geography and Captain Cook's explorations.

Against the theological and practical thought of his own denomination, he wrote his famous treatise, *An Enquiry into the Obligation of Christians to use Means for the Conversion of the Heathens* (1792), which became the constitution of the modern missionary movement. The title indicates one of the difficulties with which Carey had to contend, namely, the hyper-Calvinism of the day had convinced many that the conversion of the heathen would be the Lord's own work in his own time, and that nothing could be done by human beings to hasten it. Carey's answer is a patient, methodical survey of the world and of the whole history of Christian efforts to bring the gospel to it. Christ, he held, has a kingdom that is to be proclaimed in its power to the ends of the earth; it is the duty of all Christians to engage in the proclamation of this kingdom in spite of the eschatological speculations of the day about God's agenda.

The appeal of his *Enquiry* was reinforced by Carey's sermon to a group of Baptist ministers at Nottingham in May 1792. Starting from Isaiah 54:2–3, "Lengthen thy cords, and strengthen thy stakes," he laid down his two great principles of action: "Attempt great things; expect great things." Four months later the Baptist Missionary Society was formed, and the Baptist denomination became truly missionary. In June 1793 Carey left for India with his family as the Society's first missionary, arriving in the Hooghly River estuary in November. As STEPHEN NEILL comments, "the day of the English-speaking peoples in overseas missions had begun."

The small Baptist beginning, with its modest, unwieldy Society, evoked an unexpected notoriety among the other English-speaking denominations. Carey's dedicated example, coupled with his prolific letter writing, stirred missions interest among the Anglicans, the Congregationalists, and even some of the Continental Protestants. The result was a proliferation of missionary societies after 1793, including the famous London Missionary Society of the Congregationalists and the CHURCH MISSIONARY SOCIETY of the Anglicans. The Baptists had unwittingly set in motion the modern missionary movement, and William Carey had unconsciously earned the title of "Father of Modern Missions."

The Baptist Missionary Society (BMS) focused on India as its principal mission field, but in 1812 sent missionaries to Ceylon (now Sri Lanka) and in 1814 to Jamaica. It was in Jamaica that the BMS missionaries, especially William Knibb, became well known for their litigation, which eventually led to the abolition of slavery in the British Empire. Since then, the BMS has increased its investment in India, Jamaica, and Sri Lanka. Subsequently, it opened work in Pakistan, the Congo, Angola, Trinidad, and Brazil. It celebrated its bicentennial in 1992.

North American Adherence (1814–45). At the beginning of the nineteenth century, the saga of Carey was well-known among Baptists and Congregationalists in the United States. Carey maintained constant correspondence with Baptist leaders such as William Staughton, a pastor in Philadelphia who had been a charter member of the BMS, and Thomas Baldwin, a pastor in Boston. Carey's letters were published in the denominational bulletins. BMS missionaries frequently spent time in New England on their way to their respective fields. Female and student societies were organized and began to pray and give to the SERAMPORE MISSION of Carey.

From this seedbed, a group of outstanding Congregationalist students at Williams College and Andover Seminary felt led to dedicate themselves to foreign missions. After many vicissitudes, they persuaded the Congregationalists to form the AMERICAN BOARD OF COMMISSIONERS FOR FOREIGN MISSIONS in 1810 and to appoint them as missionaries to India. Among them were ADONIRAM JUDSON and Luther Rice. Realizing that they would have to debate the question of infant baptism with Carey and his companions, they studied their Greek New Testaments on the long journey on separate ships. They both became Baptists by conviction and were baptized upon their arrival in India.

Luther Rice returned to America to break amicably with the Congregationalists and to seek support for the Judsons, who, due to visa problems, were forced to go to Burma (Myanmar) to work with Carey's son, Felix. Carey wrote letters of recommendation to New England Baptists, and Rice rallied the scattered Baptist congregations of the Eastern seaboard. On May 18, 1814, at the First Baptist Church of Philadelphia, thirty-three delegates met to form the General Missionary Convention of the Baptist Denomination in the United States for Foreign Missions (popularly known as the Triennial Convention). Although called a "convention," in constitution and function it was basically a society for foreign missions modeled after the BMS. Judson and his wife, Anne Hasseltine, became its first missionaries. In this indirect way, Baptists in America became a missionary denomination.

It is significant that this missionary society was the first organization of national scope for Baptists in America. It was the missionary impulse that integrated the fiercely independent and widely scattered congregations and brought into being the Baptist denomination of the United States. Practically all the present-day Baptist entities in the United States trace their history back to this original entity.

From 1814 to 1845 Baptists in America were united around the challenge of missions. A Home Missions Society was formed in 1832 and began a profitable work among indigenous Americans and pioneers on the Southwestern frontiers. The Triennial Convention continued to evolve into a foreign missions society. Two bases for Baptist missions organizations began to polarize: the society basis and the convention basis. Baptists in the North generally favored missionary societies; those in the South favored a more centralized convention of churches. All Baptists had no problem with the "why" of missions, but increasingly debated the "how" of missions.

In the meantime, a remarkable increase in funds and personnel was noted after 1826. New missions were opened in France, Germany, Greece, and China. By 1844 there were 111 missionaries—10 in Europe, 6 in West Africa, 63 in Asia, and 32 in North America, mostly among ethnic groups that continued under the foreign society.

Southern Baptists' Separation (1845–1945). Another milestone in Baptist missions history was the separation between Northern and Southern Baptists in the United States in 1845. The missions question was one of the principal causes of the separation. In fact, the new Southern Baptist Convention came into being in order to appoint southerners for home and foreign missions. The already growing polarization over missions polity in the United States was fueled by the ABOLITIONIST MOVEMENT, which later resulted in the Confederacy and the Civil War (1860). Sectional estrangement had been growing in Baptist life since the 1830s. The Northern Baptists (principally the middle states and New England) favored the society basis for missions; the Southern Baptists (Virginia to the South and West) favored the more centralized convention basis modeled by the South Carolina state convention.

The occasion for the separation was the involvement of the majority of Southern Baptists with slavery, which was the basis of the South's economy. When the Abolitionist Movement heated up and invaded the South, it added to the widening rift. In the early 1840s it permeated the missions entities and became an issue in the appointment of missionaries. The Triennial Convention, now a foreign missions society, gradually fell under northern dominance along with the Home Missions Society. Southern churches, which still contributed heavily, felt they were being neglected and that their candidates were being spurned. Leaders of the Baptist missions societies sought to work together despite their differences on slavery. In 1841 both home and foreign societies pledged to remain neutral on slavery in the interest of unity. These efforts to maintain neutrality proved fruitless.

Militant abolitionists in the North, and equally militant proslavery Baptists in South, drowned out the more moderate voices. As the rhetoric became more inflamed, cooperation became more difficult and, finally, schism became immanent. In 1844 test cases were presented to both the Home and Foreign societies by Georgia and Alabama Baptists that confirmed the fears of the South that their candidates were being rejected because of the slavery question. The Southern brethren then called for a constitutional meeting in Augusta, Georgia, in May 1845, which resulted in a new Southern Baptist Convention.

The Southern Baptist Convention justified its existence on the basis of missions. Its churches felt they were prohibited from being faithful to the GREAT COMMISSION because their candidates were being rejected by the predominantly Northern society. Therefore, they felt compelled to organize a new missionary organization. This they did. The naming of a Foreign Mission Board and a Home Mission Board was the first order of business. At the same time, they incorporated a new basis of missions organization. For some time they had been dissatisfied with the society method of the Northern churches, based on the voluntary cooperation of individuals; therefore they adopted the convention method, based on the voluntary cooperation of local churches. Thus, a new, cooperative way of missions was born.

In spite of the unseemly circumstances that occasioned the founding of the Southern Baptist Convention (SBC), an effective missions organization resulted; over the years it has produced one of the largest missions sending bodies in the history of Christianity. The new Convention languished during the Civil War years and the Reconstruction period, but began to flourish near the turn of the century.

The Northern Baptists continued their missions through the American Baptist Missionary Union and the American Baptist Home Mission Society. Although sectionally separated, Baptists in North America continued to grow in foreign and home missions through two World Wars and an economic depression. Northern Baptists organized a Convention in 1908, which they renamed the American Baptist Convention in 1949. They have gradually moved away from the societal methodology, but have not experienced growth in number or in mission advance like the Southern Baptists.

Post–World War II Growth (1945–80). Baptist mission efforts have universally burgeoned since World War II. The BMS has expanded its program at home and abroad to include work in India, Bangladesh, Sri Lanka, and the Republics of Zaire, Angola, Tanzania, Jamaica, Trinidad, Brazil, and Hong Kong. The majority of the missionaries are in Africa and Brazil. In addition to planting churches, the BMS has worked in the areas of Christian education, ministerial training, medical work, agricultural work, and other social ministries. The missionary motif spread to British Commonwealth Baptists also, and strong Baptist missions have emanated from Australia, South Africa, New Zealand, and especially Canada.

American Baptist in the United States (formerly Northern), in spite of hurtful fundamentalist controversies that brought divisions and new missions entities, continue effective missionary work through their International (BIM) and National (BNM) Boards. However, a shift in emphasis to new ministries has brought a sharp decline in their number of foreign and home missionaries.

In contrast, Southern Baptists (SBC) have experienced dramatic growth in missions involvement. In 1995 they had 4,000 foreign missionaries working in 131 countries and about 5,000 home missionaries working in the United States, which is considered to be the fourth largest mission field in the world! Although plagued by doctrinal controversy since 1979, this has not dimmed their dream of Bold Mission Thrust, which is their program to cooperate with other "Great Commission Christians" in reaching the unreached peoples of the world by the year 2000. In 1995 they joined the EVANGELICAL FELLOWSHIP OF MISSION AGENCIES (EFMA). In 1950 they had 711 foreign missionaries under appointment; by 1995 the number had increased to 4,066. As the largest Baptist group in the world, they are leading out in missionary effort and strategy.

Other large Baptist conventions and unions are found among ethnic Baptist churches in the United States. African Americans formed several conventions after the Civil War. Three of these conventions count on a total of 10 million Baptists. They, along with some 90 other ethnic Baptist groups in the United States, sponsor some modest missionary endeavors. Baptist Hispanics in the United States have remained in the Anglo conventions and have not formed their own missions. Fundamentalist and Conservative Baptist entities, results of Baptist controversies of the past, also sponsor some significant foreign and home mission efforts.

Two-Thirds World Missions (1980–). The great new fact in world missions, and especially in the Baptist world missionary enterprise, is the presence of a rapidly growing TWO-THIRDS WORLD missionary movement. These are the countries of the formerly called "third world" that were objects of the modern missionary movement from Europe and North America. Most are found in Africa, Asia, Latin America, and Oceania. They are now called "two-thirds world" by many because they approximate two-thirds of the world's territory and two-thirds of the world's population.

The Christians in these countries are no longer content to be objects of world mission; they want to be participants in mission. Many of the premier mission fields of Baptists, including Brazil, Nigeria, Korea, Taiwan, Argentina, and many others, are forming missionary societies and boards and sending out their own cross-cultural missionaries. They are targeting the unreached people groups found in the 10–40 WINDOW of the world, which spans North Africa, the Middle East, Central Asia, the subcontinent of India, and China. The internationalization of Baptist missions is taking place rapidly. Brazil would be an apt example. Several Baptist mission boards have been working in Brazil for years, and continue to work there, but Brazilian Baptists have a Home Mission Board with more than 500 missionaries and a Foreign Mission Board with over 120 missionaries working in 19 countries. These entities are growing so rapidly that missiologists are recognizing that the base for world mission is moving from the Northwest to the Southeast. The rise of these two-thirds world missions is by far the most exciting, encouraging fact in Baptist missions today.

In summary, Baptist missions, home and foreign, have had, and do have, a prominent place in the evangelical Christian missionary enterprise. If united, they would easily constitute the largest sector of that enterprise. They join with other Christians who take seriously the Great Commission in the pursuit of that elusive goal—the evangelization of the world in this generation.

JUSTICE C. ANDERSON

SEE ALSO Southern Baptist Convention, IMB.

Bibliography. B. J. Cauthen and F. K. Means, *Advance to Bold Mission Thrust;* W. R. Estep, *Whole Gospel, Whole World: The FMB of the SBC 1845–1995;* J. C. Fletcher, *The Southern Baptist Convention: A Sesquicentennial History;* A. W. Hardin, ed., *Baptists Around the World;* H. L. McBeth, *The Baptist Heritage: Four Centuries of Baptist Witness;* R. G. Torbet, *A History of the Baptists;* D. C. Woolley, ed., *Baptist Advance: The Achievements of the Baptists of North America for a Century and a Half.*

Barbados *(Est. 2000 pop.: 268,000; 430 sq. km. [166 sq. mi.]).* The most easterly of the Leeward (southern) Islands of the Caribbean, Barbados aquired its independence from Britain in 1966. Its relatively rich resources have made the island more prosperous than most. It has one of the more stable economies and one of the larger proportions of evangelical Protestants in the area (25 percent).

EVERETT A. WILSON

SEE ALSO Caribbean.

Bibliography. A. Lampe, *The Church in Latin America, 1492–1992,* pp. 201–15; J. Rogozinski, *A Brief History of the Caribbean: From the Arawak and the Carib to the Present.*

Barclay, Thomas (1849–1935). Scottish missionary to Taiwan. He was born and grew up in Glasgow, Scotland, where he attended both the University of Glasgow and the Free Church Divinity College. When sixteen years of age, he wrote a covenant of commitment to Christ, renewed annually, which guided him throughout his life. He was sent to Formosa (Taiwan) as a missionary by the Foreign Mission Committee of the Free Church in 1875 and served there until his death on October 5, 1935. His time in Formosa may be divided into three periods: 1875–92, when he learned the language, taught in the Presbyterian Theological College in Tainan, developed a romanized script for publishing literature in Taiwanese, and helped establish a boys' middle school and girls' school; 1895–1912, when he continued his teaching and helped organize the first presbytery and synod for the Presbyterian Church; 1913–35, when he translated and later helped revise both the New Testament and Old Testament, the major work of his distinguished career. He also prepared a dictionary and literature for use in the church. At the time of the Japanese conquest in 1895 his peacemaking efforts saved the city of Tainan from being bombed. He was awarded a Doctor of Divinity degree in 1919 by the University of Glasgow.

RALPH R. COVELL

Bibliography. E. Band, *Barclay of Formosa.*

Barth, Christian Gottlob (1799–1862). Early German mission thinker and promoter. A native of the city of Stuttgart from 1824, Barth acted as a Protestant pastor in the small village of Möttlingen in the Black Forest. In 1838 he moved near Calw and worked as a writer, publicist, and leader of the *Calwer Verlag,* which he founded in 1833. Versatile, talented, and energetic, Barth developed a worldwide reputation and labored tirelessly as a popular author (with no less than twelve books for young people), an enthusiastic preacher, hymn writer, and promoter of mission. He founded the widespread *Calwer Missionsblatt* (1828–1918) and also a missionary letter for children (1842–1918). His work *Barth's Bible Stories* (1832–1945) went through 483 German printings, numerous English editions, and approximately 90 translations as a worldwide best-seller. His books for adults include Bible commentaries and overviews, world and church histories, and missions treatises. He was a distinguished collector of natural history exhibits, by which he also pursued missionary aims. Rooted in the Pietism of J. B. Bengel and F. C. Oetinger, Barth's theology is characterized as an apoplytic history of salvation approach to God's kingdom.

WERNER RAUPP

Bibliography. C. G. Barth, *Christian Missions;* K. Werner, *Christian Gottlob Barth.*

Barth, Karl (1886–1968). *See* NEO-ORTHODOX THEOLOGY.

Basel Mission. With roots in early German pietism and revival movements, the Basel Mission *(Evangelische Missionsgesellschaft in Basel)* was established in 1815 out of a desire to provide training for German-speaking missionaries going abroad. Christian Blumhardt provided early leadership, opening a seminary for young missionaries in Basel in 1816, which continued until 1955. Initially missionaries with the Basel Mission (BM) served under other agencies such as the Church Missionary Society, but beginning in 1821 the BM sent out its own missionaries, starting work in southern Russia (1822), which was soon discontinued; Ghana (1825); India (1834); Hong Kong and south China (1846); Cameroon (1886), where the BM took over work from the English Baptists; North Togo (1912); Borneo (Kalimantan) (1921); North Borneo (Sabah) (1952); and among hill tribes in North Cameroon (Nigeria) (1959).

By 1914 there were 450 missionaries in five countries, but World War I caused a temporary hiatus in the work. Karl Hartenstein served as director of the BM from 1926 to 1939, when it was decided to make the Swiss home base alone responsible for the mission, in order to facilitate continued operation during World War II. In 1954 a separate German branch was established, with headquarters in Stuttgart. The BM is an integral part of the Swiss Mission Council and cooperates with the division of mission and evangelism in the WORLD COUNCIL OF CHURCHES. Through the German branch the BM is also connected with the German Mission Council.

From the beginning the BM has been nondenominational and ecumenical, drawing support from churches of Lutheran, Reformed, and Free Church traditions, and cooperating with various other missions organizations. Its support comes primarily from south Germany, German-speaking parts of Switzerland, and Austria. BM missionaries have been involved in a wide variety of ministries—from evangelism and church planting to theological education, education and literacy work, translation, medical missions, establishing orphanages, development of vocational skills, and so on.

EDITORS

SEE ALSO German Mission Boards and Societies.

Bibliography. H. Witschi, *EMCM*, pp. 271–74; W. Zumbrennen, *CDCWM*, p. 53.

Bavinck, Johan Herman (1895–1964). Dutch missiologist and missionary to Indonesia. Born to a minister's family in Rotterdam, Bavinck grew up in a deeply spiritual home. Studies at Free University and University of Erlangen (Ph.D., 1919) developed his interest and skills in the psychology of religion, an orientation he maintained throughout his life.

Bavinck's career involved pastoral duties in Sumatra (1919–21), Bandung, Java (1921–26), and Heemstede, Netherlands (1926–29). His pastoral work in Indonesia prepared him for the call to serve there as a missionary, which he did in Solo (1929–33) and at Jogjakarta (1935–39). For his final career phase he returned to the Netherlands to serve as part-time professor at Kampen Theological College and the Free University of Amsterdam (1939–55) and then full-time at the Free University until his death (1955–64).

Throughout his career Bavinck was a productive scholar. His initial focus in psychology and philosophy (e.g., *An Introduction to Psychology*, 1926) was augmented by a fascination with the mystical orientation of the Javanese (*Christ and Eastern Mysticism*, 1934) and a thorough grounding in biblical scholarship (e.g., *People around Jesus*, 1936). In missiological circles, he is perhaps best noted for his *An Introduction to the Science of Missions* (1954). Though a product of its times in terms of the one-way orientation to missionary work, it is still a masterful blend of Bavinck's psychological, biblical, and religious interests.

A. SCOTT MOREAU

Bibliography: J. A. Jongeneel, *BDCM*, pp. 48–49; J. van den Berg, *ML*, pp. 428–34; J. Verkuyl, *Contemporary Missiology: An Introduction.*

Bayne, Margaret (1795–1835). *See* WILSON, MARGARET BAYNE.

Beach, Harlan Page (1854–1933). American missionary, professor, and missions librarian. Born into a deeply religious farming family of modest means, Harlan graduated from Yale in 1878 and taught for two years at Phillips Andover before entering Andover Theological Seminary, from which he graduated in 1883. On June 29, 1883, he married Lucy L. Ward and later that year went to North China under the AMERICAN BOARD OF COMMISSIONERS FOR FOREIGN MISSIONS. Harlan was associated with a school in T'ungchow, where he founded one of the first YMCAs in China. He mastered five thousand Chinese characters and was assigned to a committee to revise the Mandarin Bible. The Beaches left China in 1889 due to Lucy's failing health.

From 1892 to 1895 Harlan was in charge of the School for Christian Workers in Springfield, Massachusetts. He was then appointed educational secretary for the STUDENT VOLUNTEER MOVEMENT. He promoted mission classes in colleges and seminaries, trained teachers, and wrote a series of simple yet accurate textbooks.

Harlan was the first incumbent of the professorship of missions at Yale Divinity School and concurrently librarian of the Day Missions Library. A major accomplishment was the development of the library into one of the two finest collections in the world on Protestant foreign missions. Another accomplishment was his statistical study of foreign missions. He produced *A Geography and Atlas of Protestant Missions* (1901–3), and co-edited *World Statistics of Christian Missions* (1910) and *World Missionary Atlas* (1925). Beach was for years considered to be the outstanding scholar in the United States on foreign missions. His primary concern in missions was world evangelization.

KENNETH D. GILL

Bibliography. R. H. Bainton, *Yale and the Ministry*; D. N. Beach, *Beach Family Reminiscences and Annals*; K. S. Latourette, *Dictionary of National Biography*, 21:62–63.

Beaver, Robert Pierce (1906–87). American missions scholar and missionary to China. Born, raised, and educated in Ohio, he went on to Cornell University and obtained a doctorate in history in 1933. After pastoring several Evangelical and Reformed churches, he and his wife, the former Wilma Manessier, went to China in 1938 under the Evangelical and Reformed Church, where he taught at the Central China Union Theological

Seminary in southern Hunan Province. This service was cut short by the Japanese invasion of China; ultimately, Beaver was interned in Hong Kong for seven months. Following his repatriation, he taught at the Lancaster Theological Seminary until 1948. Beaver's greatest contributions to missiology came from his leadership of the Missionary Research Library in New York from 1948 to 1955 and his teaching at the University of Chicago from 1955 to 1973. From these two strategic posts he gathered important mission papers and documents, created a mission research center, taught future missionaries and mission scholars, wrote on crucial mission topics, and motivated his own denomination and others to implement God's mission in the world. Following three years as director of the Overseas Ministries Study Center in Ventnor, New Jersey, he retired in 1976 to Arizona, where he died in 1987.

RALPH R. COVELL

Bibliography. R. P. Beaver, *All Loves Excelling: American Protestant Women in World Mission;* idem, ed., *American Missions in Bicentennial Perspective;* F. D. Lucking; *ML,* pp. 452–58.

Behavior Patterns. Christian missionaries have always concerned themselves with the behavior of other peoples. Disobedience to even the most basic of God's laws constitutes evidence of their sinful condition. Prescribed behavioral change affords evidence of their conversion. However, with the development of the social sciences, German missiology since the latter part of the nineteenth century and American missiology since World War II have reflected increased understanding of human behavior.

Most prominent in this matter have been the contributions of the behavioral sciences—sociology, psychology, and cultural anthropology (including linguistics and cross-cultural communication). As part of a process termed socialization by the sociologist and enculturation by the anthropologist (*see* CULTURE LEARNING), people consciously and unconsciously learn which behavioral patterns are expected and which are not acceptable in their respective cultures. It is these learned action patterns, as opposed to reflexive and instinctive patterns, that are of special importance to missiologists. Taking many of their clues from the sciences, missiologists have attempted to integrate new understandings with Scripture and the missionary experience. These attempts have not always been completely valid (indeed, social science theories themselves are in flux), but on the whole this process has resulted in insights into human behavior that have greatly enhanced missionary theory and practice.

Reacting to earlier psychological studies that emphasized the study of inner experiences or feelings by subjective methods, early in this cen-

tury John B. Watson proposed that psychologists confine their study to observable behavior that can be studied by objective procedures yielding statistically significant results. While not agreeing with Watson's reductionism, B. F. Skinner nevertheless focused on controlled experiments and postulated a type of psychological conditioning called reinforcement. Skinner's learning theory is reflected in certain aspects of THEOLOGICAL EDUCATION BY EXTENSION with its programmed textbooks and learning. Behaviorism as such, however, yielded center stage to the humanism of Abraham Maslow and others in the 1950s, and Maslow's hierarchy of needs has exerted a greater influence in mission theory.

Of greater missiological importance has been the influence of anthropologists such as Edward T. Hall and linguists such as EUGENE A. NIDA. Hall proposed that human behavior can be understood in terms of ten "primary message systems," only one of which is verbal. Hall's overall theory has not met with widespread understanding or approval, but his ideas on the "silent language" and the communicative aspects of such things as time and space have captured the attention of American missionaries for over a generation.

Among missionary theorists, Nida has perhaps exerted the most influence in recent years. In addition to his impact on the understanding of language learning and translation, Nida has written insightfully on the relationship between belief systems and behavior, the symbolic nature of religious behavior, social structure and communicative behavior, and more.

As a result of studies such as the foregoing, contemporary missionaries can be far better prepared to deal with behavioral issues encountered when working in another culture. CULTURE SHOCK can be ameliorated when the missionary is prepared for the encounter with behavioral patterns that have meanings entirely foreign to her or him. Culture change is most readily initiated by discovering what is happening at the informal "imitation of models" level of learning, bringing it to the level of awareness, and introducing change at that point. CONVERSION is best understood, not first of all as change at the behavioral outer layer of culture, but at its basic belief system or worldview inner core.

DAVID J. HESSELGRAVE

Bibliography. E. T. Hall, *The Silent Language;* D. J. Hesselgrave, *Communicating Christ Cross-Culturally;* E. A. Nida, *Message and Mission.*

Belarus *(Est. 2000 pop.: 10,069,000; 207,600 sq. km. [80,154 sq. mi.]).* Belarus is a landlocked, predominantly agricultural republic in the western region of the former Soviet Union. Its population is 98 percent Slavic, and most people speak Russian as their primary language. Belarus has suffered more than any other nation from the effects of the 1986 Chernobyl nuclear disaster. Although religious freedom is officially guaranteed, the government frequently employs legal and bureaucratic measures to restrict both foreign missionary activity and indigenous evangelistic efforts. Nearly half the population is at least nominally Orthodox, while almost a quarter is Roman Catholic. Evangelicals, while growing in number, make up just over one percent of the population, with Pentecostals slightly outnumbering Baptists.

RAYMOND P. PRIGODICH

See also COMMONWEALTH OF INDEPENDENT STATES.

Belgium *(Est. 2000 pop.: 10,248,000; 30,519 sq. km. [11,783 sq. mi.]).* Belgium, a highly industrialized and wealthy country in Western Europe, is the second most densely populated country in all of Europe and is made up of primarily the Flemish and Walloon people. The predominant religion is Roman Catholicism, with 87.3 percent membership. Of the overwhelming percentage of Roman Catholics, less than 10 percent attend Mass at least once a year. Therefore, religion is more cultural than it is a living faith in the lives of Belgians, making Belgium one of the most difficult countries in Western Europe to evangelize.

Not only has the Roman Catholic Church seen little growth, the Protestant mission efforts have also been unsuccessful with little growth in twenty years. Growth has been the greatest through the witness of BEM (the Belgium Evangelical Mission)/OM teams, Baptist, Brethren, and Pentecostals in certain areas. Charismatic groups have typically been a growing church in other parts of Europe, but they have had very little lasting effects in Belgium. Why is it that Belgium is such a spiritually dead country with resistance to mission efforts of other denominations? It is important to look at its political and spiritual history for answers.

Belgium has a long history of resistance by its political leaders to any reforms to spiritual traditions established by the Roman Catholic Church. Belgium and Holland in the sixteenth century formed seventeen provinces of the Spanish Low Countries. In the beginning of the century, Luther's new ideas came into the Spanish provinces. Luther's theses were posted in Wittenburg in 1517. Charles V, the reigning king, viewed Luther's ideas as heresy and ordered the death penalty in 1522 for those citizens who did not conform to Roman Catholic doctrinal beliefs. Calvinism began in the Low Countries in 1542 and many followers were martyred as a result of their nonconformity.

Philip II, Charles' son, boasted of his execution of more than 18,000 Protestants between 1567 and 1573. The Protestants were finally given more liberties in 1713 by Emperor Joseph II. These liberties included the right to worship. The country then experienced the French Revolution in 1789 and the reversion to Dutch control in 1815. Belgium gained its independence in 1830, and a constitutional monarchy began.

Belgium has been through a tumultuous history that has created spiritual apathy, thus leading to nominalism in religion. The political leaders forced Roman Catholic beliefs upon the people to the point of cruelty. As a result, the people lost respect for their religion and turned to atheism, fearing to be open to any other denomination. They may have kept their membership with the Roman Catholic Church as a protective measure, but many did not practice it.

WILLIAM L. WAGNER

Belief Systems. Belief systems are thought of in at least two different ways in missiological literature. First, as a level of mental construction they are understood to determine the legitimacy of questions, generate conceptual problems, and perform a constraining, heuristic, and justificatory role. Second, and more commonly, systems of belief are understood as an integral part of worldview. In this latter case, the study of *religious* belief systems has generated considerable interest among field missionaries.

Anthropologists have described two types of beliefs: instrumental beliefs, which are related to the concrete tasks necessary for survival, and transcendental beliefs, which involve states and elements of existence that cannot be learned directly from human experience. These categories are useful, but as yet anthropologists have not been able to agree on the meaning of some of the most basic concepts they use to investigate transcendental belief systems—concepts such as religion, the supernatural, magic, and witchcraft. Even though the transcendental-instrumental dichotomy seems to be derived more from the perspective of Western anthropologists than from categorical differences and distinctions made by people in actual cultural contexts, ethnographic data have been useful in the study of religious belief systems in many societies.

Culture provides learned categories, called cognitive categories, used to sort out perceptions. Culturally molded cognition enables human beings to apprehend order in the "world" of their existence. Thus, in the WORLDVIEW of a society, culture furnishes people with beliefs regarding the universe and a belief system through which they give meanings to their experiences. Belief systems deal with very particular and detailed items in the worldview of people in a given society. Religious belief systems deal with specific beliefs about meaning and destiny of life. People in various cultures accept the respective symbolic interpretations of reality because of the authority of the supernatural being(s) or powers involved. A belief system tends to make explicit the implicit assumptions of the worldview in which they are found and in which they function, and to apply these assumptions to behavior.

Each society, then, has a more or less systematically structured religious belief system that can be studied and learned. MYTHS and RITUALS have been key areas of culture studied by anthropologists, and such data have done much to enhance missiological understanding of the deep structures of religious belief systems in various cultures.

NORMAN E. ALLISON

Bibliography. C. Geertz, *Reader in Comparative Religion: An Anthropological Approach;* P. G. Hiebert, *Anthropological Reflections on Missiological Issues;* D. E. Hunter and P. Whitten, *The Study of Anthropology.*

Belize *(Est. 2000 popl.: 245,000; 22,965 sq. km. [8,867 sq. mi.]).* The country of Belize, independent since 1884, was known as British Honduras until 1973. Throughout its history, Belize has struggled with identity problems, developing more ties to the British Caribbean than to the rest of Central America. Occupied by the Mayan Indians in pre-Columbian times and explored by the Spanish conquistadors, it became a shelter for the British buccaneers who preyed upon Spanish shipping. European immigrants, Creoles of African origin, Black Caribs, and Indian and Spanish-speaking mestizos have melded to create a heterogeneous, multiethnic population. English is the primary language and Christianity is the dominant faith.

Christianity arrived with the Spaniards in the sixteenth century. The first Catholic missionaries arrived in 1851. Catholic testimony prospered chiefly among the Indian and mestizo population in rural areas. By the end of the nineteenth century (1893), the Roman Catholic Church constituted about two-thirds of the population. More recently, that has decreased to roughly 40 percent.

Protestantism came to Belize in 1638, when a group of shipwrecked English sailors (other sources read "buccaneers") settled. Under British protection, Belize became a Protestant enclave in Central America. In 1776, Robert Shaw introduced the Anglican testimony that was later continued by William Stanford. Evangelical Anglicans became influential in religious education. The Baptists began their testimony in 1822 with James Bourn and, under Alexander Henderson in the late 1840s, became an autonomous body. Methodists arrived in 1824 and grew in numbers through difficulties. By 1838 Protestant denominations claimed approximately 16 percent of the population. Church growth, however, was challenged by the prevailing differences of race and culture. Protestantism was conceived as the religion of the white people in a country where 90 percent of the population was black or colored.

Independence in 1884 meant an increasing nationalization of the Christian testimony in Belize. Spanish-speaking immigrants, with the arrival of the Jesuits in 1851, increased the numbers of Roman Catholics. The Anglicans lost their privileged position as other Protestant groups were established. By 1990, the Protestant community of Belize totaled just over 25 percent of the population. *Operation World* reported in 1993 seventeen missionaries from Belize in three agencies.

PABLO A. DEIROS

Bibliography. C. L. Holland, ed., *World Christianity,* vol. 4, *Central American and the Caribbean;* W. R. Johnson, *A History of Chr*

Bell, Lemuel Nelson (1894–1973). American medical missionary to China. Born in Virginia, he abandoned his first ambition to be a lawyer and committed himself to becoming a medical missionary. He took his training at the Medical College of Virginia in Richmond. Nelson married Virginia Leftwich in June 1916, and, shortly after, they were appointed missionaries with the Southern Presbyterian Foreign Mission Board, arriving in China later that year. Most of Bell's years as a medical missionary were spent in the Presbyterian hospital at Tsingkiangpu, along the Grand Canal in Jiangsu province. He expanded this facility by 1930 to be the largest Presbyterian hospital in the world. Beyond his medical duties, he engaged in evangelism and many church activities. Life in China was unsettled for the Bells as civil war, Japanese invaders, and communist guerrillas wracked China. This constant turmoil led to their return to America in 1941. During the next thirty years Bell continued to practice medicine, founded the *Southern Presbyterian Journal,* was active in church and mission endeavors, and served for many years as both executive editor and columnist of *Christianity Today,* a prestigious journal he had helped to found in 1956.

RALPH R. COVELL

Bibliography. J. C. Pollock, *A Foreign Devil in China.*

Bender, Carl Jacob (1869–1935). German-American missionary to Cameroon. Born in Eschelbach, Baden, Germany, in 1869, Bender emigrated with his family to the United States at age twelve and located in Buffalo, New York. He was working in a dry goods store when he was converted in an evangelical church and later joined a German Baptist church. Compelled to share his faith with others, Bender often held street meetings. He felt called to full-time ministry and at age twenty-four entered the German Baptist Seminary in Rochester, New York. Following his graduation and ordination in 1899, Bender accepted a missionary assignment to Cameroon under the German Baptist Missionary Society. He married Hedwig Klöber on May 7, 1904, during his first furlough. Bender's American citizenship allowed him and his wife to continue their mission work when all of the other German missionaries were imprisoned during World War I. In addition to successful evangelistic work, several churches and schools were started during the war years. The Benders left Cameroon after the war in 1919 when the work was taken over by the British and French. However, after many years of lobbying by Bender, the German Baptists resumed their work in Cameroon and he was allowed to return. On November 8, 1935, Carl Bender died in Soppo, Cameroon, where he was buried.

KENNETH D. GILL

Bibliography. C. F. H. Henry, *Bender in the Cameroon;* C. W. Weber, *International Influences and Baptist Mission in West Cameroon;* F. H. Woyke, *Heritage and Ministry of the North American Baptist Conference.*

Benin *(Est. 2000 pop.: 6,266,000; 112,622 sq. km. [43,483 sq. mi.]).* The Republic of Benin, whose population is comprised of fifty-seven ethnic groups, is a long, narrow country wedged between Nigeria and Togo in French-speaking western Africa. It is one of Africa's poorest nations and the world's least developed countries. The majority of the people (55 percent) practice tribal religions, while some 17 percent embrace Islam.

The Catholic Church built a chapel at Ouidah in 1680, which was served by Portuguese and French priests during the 1700s. Not until 1860, however, when the work in Dahomey was turned over to the African Missions of Lyon, did missions become active in the interior. The Methodist Church, still the largest Protestant denomination, was the first Protestant church to enter Benin, arriving in 1843. Historically, the Methodist churches in the south have struggled, but since 1987 both evangelicals and Catholics have seen rapid church growth. After gaining independence from France in 1960, and a brief affair with communism, the people of Benin now enjoy religious freedom.

Opportunities for evangelization abound. While translation teams are working in twelve languages, twenty-four languages still remain without a New Testament. Audio recordings are available in thirty-four languages for use in evangelism and teaching. There is one Christian radio station, Radio Parakou, which broadcasts the gospel daily.

GARY LAMB

Berlin Congress 1966. *See* WORLD CONGRESS ON EVANGELISM.

Berlin Mission Society. The pietism and revivals of early-nineteenth-century Switzerland and Germany produced a keen interest in missions, resulting in the formation of several new missions organizations such as the BASEL MISSION (1815). Founded in 1824 initially as a supporting agency of the Basel Mission, the Berlin Mission Society *(Berliner Missionsgesellschaft)* sent out its own missionaries beginning in 1833. In 1829 the Berlin Society established its own seminary. The first missionaries were sent to South Africa, and work in Africa has been the Society's principal focus, although missionaries were also sent to India (1842) and China (1882). The period from 1913 to 1949 was very difficult for the Society, as two World Wars disrupted the work and missionaries had to leave the fields or were interned.

From the beginning the Berlin Mission Society has been an interdenominational agency emphasizing spirituality and piety, strong lay involvement, and organizational independence from denominations. Although its support base includes Reformed and Lutheran churches, Lutheran influences remain strong within the Society. The Society's seminary has been closed since 1945, with missionaries now receiving training in church institutions. Missionaries with the Society have been involved in evangelism and church planting as well as a variety of other ministries such as education and medical ministries. The Berlin Mission Society continues as one of the largest German missionary societies.

EDITORS

SEE ALSO German Mission Boards and Societies AND Basel Mission.

Bibliography. J. Althausen, *EMCM,* pp. 76–77; H. W. Gensichen, *CDCWM,* p. 55.

Bermuda *(Est. 2000 pop.: 65,000; 54 sq. km. [21 sq. mi.]).* Unlike most of the Caribbean islands, the citizens of the Bermuda group, a British colony, enjoy prosperity. The economy is based on tourism and offshore financial activities. The per capita annual income compares favorably (126%) with that of the United States. While two-thirds of the population is Afro-Caribbean, many residents are from Britain, the United States, or Canada. In fact, one in every four Bermudans is foreign-born. The modest evangelical community (17%) is overwhelmingly Pentecostal.

EVERETT A. WILSON

SEE ALSO Caribbean.

Bibliography. A. Lampe, *The Church in Latin America, 1492–1992,* pp. 201–15; J. Rogozinski, *A Brief History of the Caribbean: From the Arawak and the Carib to the Present.*

Berntsen, Annie Skau (1911–92). Norwegian missionary in China. Born in Oslo in a secular family, as a teen Berntsen was an active leader in a Karl Marx club. Her grandmother's faith was an important element in Berntsen's conversion; she carried a vivid memory throughout her life of her grandmother praying with her for the conversion of Annie and her parents when Annie was seven years old. The prayer that Annie would come to faith was answered while she was in nursing school.

Following a call to missionary service, and having received her missionary training through CHINA INLAND MISSION, Berntsen traveled to China in 1938 and worked as a nurse in the Shensi province until 1951. After the Communists took over China and the missionaries were expelled, she worked in Hong Kong at a refugee camp. In 1955 she founded "The Hope of Heaven" hospital which served the Chinese fleeing the mainland.

Berntsen was recognized widely for her sacrificial faith and service. She received the Florence Nightingale Medal and Norway's Order of Saint Olaf and was named a member of the British Empire for her efforts in Hong Kong. She died in peaceful anticipation of her union with Christ in 1992.

A. SCOTT MOREAU

Bibliography. A. Møller and G. Møller, *Ambassadors for Christ,* pp. 196–99.

Beyerhaus, Peter (1929–). German professor, evangelical spokesman, and missionary to South Africa. Born into the home of a minister and his wife in Berlin, Germany, he felt called to the ministry and responded by studying theology at Uppsala University. While completing his doctorate, he married a Swedish woman who aspired to be a missionary. Together they worked for many years among the Black population of South Africa. Forced to return to Germany in 1965 because of his oldest daughter's ill health, Beyerhaus joined the theology faculty at Tübingen University as professor of missions and became director of its Institute of Missiology and Ecumenical Theology. Concerned about the liberal environment of the university, he helped establish the Albrecht Bengel House, a dormitory/lecture hall where Christian students could get spiritual help. He also mentored students by taking them with him on evangelistic preaching trips. Beyerhaus became an international spokesman for evangelical Christianity, opposing the drift away from the biblical mandate for world evangelism that he detected at both Tübingen and the World Council of Churches. In 1970 he was one of the chief architects of the FRANKFORT DECLARATION, a critical assessment of the situation, which became the symbol of a worldwide evangelical thrust for world evangelization. Beyerhaus has produced numerous publications in German, many of which have been translated into English.

KENNETH D. GILL

Bibliography. E. Rhoton, *AFC,* pp. 258–61; P. Beyerhaus, *Shaken Foundations: Theological Foundations for Mission;* idem, *God's Kingdom and Utopian Error.*

Bhengu, Nicholas Bhekinkosi Hepworth (1909–86). South African evangelist. Known as the "black Billy Graham," Bhengu was born in the Zulu kingdom the son of a Lutheran evangelist and grandson of a Zulu chief. He graduated in 1937 from South Africa General Mission Bible Training School in Dumisa, Natal. Called to the ministry, he became an evangelist and conducted "Back to God Crusades," having been inspired in a dream by a voice that said, "Africa must get back to God." He later joined the Assemblies of God in South Africa (AGSA).

Bhengu traveled extensively, preaching and raising funds for his evangelistic endeavors in South Africa, which proved to be quite successful. Preaching tours in 1954 and 1958 took him to the United States, Canada, Scotland, and Norway, making him a prominent figure in the Pentecostal World Conference. Eventually AGSA came to be governed by several "apostles," including Bhengu, who directed evangelism and church planting. His ministry focused primarily on individual conversion and strongly impacted the spiritual and moral values of South Africans. In 1974 he served as a Fellow at Selly Oak Colleges in England, and taught about evangelism. At his death, the nation mourned and over 20,000 people attended his internment.

GARY B. MCGEE

Bibliography. N. B. H. Bhengu, *Revival Fire in South Africa;* idem, *Decision* (October 1974): 4, and (November 1974): 10; idem, *Time* (November 23, 1959): 69–70.

Bhutan *(Est. 2000 pop.: 1,842,000; 47,000 sq. km. [18,147 sq. mi.]).* A small Buddhist kingdom in the eastern Himalayas between India and Tibet (now part of China). The capital is Thimphu, where Jigme Singye Wangchuk has reigned as king since 1972. Education is free and all schools are government-subsidized, but there is not adequate space for all the children and there are no private schools. Consequently, the literacy rate is around 18 percent. English is taught in all schools, but Dzongkha is the official language. There are eleven languages overall.

Lamaistic Buddhism was introduced in the eighth century and is the state religion. All public worship, evangelism, and proselytization by other religions are illegal. Since 1965 that has not been as strictly enforced, allowing slow growth of the church. Seventy percent of the Bhutanese are Buddhist. The second largest religion is Hinduism (24%).

Christians comprise only 0.33 percent of the population. There are seventy-two Protestant missionaries representing eleven agencies and ten Roman Catholic missionaries to the nation. Missionaries operating leprosy hospitals or involved in health, agriculture, and education programs are welcome, but evangelistic work is outlawed. Because of the evangelistic restrictions, several mission agencies have been working from just outside the country in India.

JAMIE FLOWERS

Bibliography. R. C. Dogra, *Bhutan;* P. Johnstone, *OW.*

Bible. The ultimate task of all forms of Christian missions is to tell of the Judeo-Christian God (Yahweh-Jehovah) and to report the salvation made available by his grace through the life and mission of Jesus Christ. This includes the proclamation of the call to repentance, faith for the forgiveness of sin, and life in fellowship with him. Christ's representatives also provide guidance for believers who seek to live worthy of and pleasing to him. All this information comes, not through human search or invention, but from God himself. The word "revelation," from the verb "to reveal" or "make known," names the doctrine that deals with God's showing or disclosing himself, his works, expectations, and provisions.

Theologians speak of both "general" and "special" revelation. The former refers to that knowledge of God available to all people, in all places, at all times. The latter is the knowledge of God available to only some people, in some times, and in some places.

GENERAL REVELATION consists of that which can be known about God in creation, nature, and the affairs of humans as a whole. Psalm 19:1–4 speaks eloquently of the evidence of God in nature. Romans 1:20–25 asserts that the created order demonstrates the fact of God's existence, power, and goodness. Humans, however, refused to pay heed to this evidence and did not honor him as God; they worshiped that which was created rather than the Creator. Consequently, "God gave them up to degrading passions" (1:26) and almost unspeakable degrading acts. Paul, before Athenian officials, says that God made all nations from a single ancestor; gives life, breath, and all things; allots the time and boundaries of human habitation "so that they should seek God; . . . he is not far from each one of us" (Acts 17:27). Indeed, observation of humanity itself, people created in the IMAGE OF GOD, should be a persuasive argument for the existence and power of God. Hebrews 11:6 affirms that to please God one must accept his existence and knowability; this, by implication, is available through general revelation.

Those who fail to acknowledge this message are, says Paul, without excuse (Rom. 1:26).

Special Revelation consists first of all in God's work through the nation Israel, her history and prophets. Micah calls to remembrance events of the nation's past "that you may know the saving acts of the LORD" (6:5). It should, however, be noted that God's special revelation to and work through Israel had a missionary purpose. It is through her that "all the nations of the world shall be blessed" (Gen. 12:3); as a "priestly kingdom" (Exod. 19:6) she is to mediate between God and others. In Exodus 34:10 God says, "I will do marvels, . . . and all the people among whom you are shall see the work of the LORD." Isaiah affirms that God's servant will be "a light to the nations" (49:6; cf. Acts 13:46–47). The supreme act of God's special revelation came in Jesus Christ through whom the Word "became flesh and dwelt among us, full of grace and truth; we have beheld his glory, glory as of the only Son from the Father" (John 1:14). In Jesus we become aware of the person, nature, and character of God, see him at work, learn that God loved the world so much that he gave his Son that believers might have life (John 3:16). In Christ we hear his invitation "come to me" (Matt. 11:28). God, in Jesus, shows himself as the holy and just judge of sin, the loving God, the dying-rising Savior, the King whose kingdom will never end and who one day will reign supreme over all. God's revelation in Israel and in Jesus also involves the work of God's close human associates, specially called, Spirit-filled persons, designated as "prophets" in the Old Testament and as "apostles" in the New. These were sent, commissioned, and authorized to speak for him. Their task was to report the facts of God's revelation and also to explain and show how to apply God's message in the affairs of daily life.

The doctrine of revelation must also include discussion of the Bible. The word "Bible" means "books"; it is a book composed of a collection of books. Together these comprise a religious book. Although it contains information on a number of topics and issues, its primary purpose, like that of many religious books, is to relate facts about God, the universe, and especially human beings in it, and their relationships. Christians believe that this is the only true religious book. All others speak of nonexistent deities and provide incorrect and even dangerous information.

The Bible is, above all, the record of the various forms of special revelation just described. Old Testament prophets and New Testament apostles wrote down virtually all we know of God's revealing work. This was not by human instigation. From Exodus 17:14 on we are told of God's command to "write." Because it is the usual source of information about God, this record is also revelation itself; it is the word of

God. As the word and Spirit work together, God's revelation of himself in the past is his contemporary self-disclosure and message. It is just because of its inclusion within God's revelation that missionaries have given much time and effort to make the Bible available in the languages of the peoples with whom they work.

There are a number of terms used to describe some important facts about the origin, nature, and character of the Bible. "Inspiration" or the phrase "inspired by God" occurs in 2 Timothy 3:16. Literally it means "God-breathed," hence, it came out of God. Second Peter 1:21 describes the communication and process of recording Scripture even more explicitly by stating that "holy men" were "moved," literally "borne" or "carried" along by the Holy Spirit. "Inspiration," then, affirms that Scripture originated with God, it was given to specially chosen individuals, and God, through his Spirit, remained active in the writing process.

"Canon," meaning literally "measuring rod," refers to an authoritative standard against which other things are measured. When referring to the Bible, canon designates those individual documents or books that are rightfully a part of Scripture, written authority. Protestant Christians traditionally acknowledge a total of sixty-six books—thirty-nine in the Old Testament, twenty-seven in the New. Roman Catholics, Orthodox, and Anglican Christians also include additional books, the Apocrypha or Deutero-canonical books. These writings seem to have come largely from the Intertestamental period (c. 400 B.C.–A.D. 70) and were included in the Septuagint, the Greek translation of the Old Testament, but apparently were not in the Hebrew Bible used in Palestine and Hebrew-speaking synagogues. The exact number of apocryphal books acknowledged varies among Christian groups who include them in their canon.

It is much easier to relate what the church did with regard to the canon than the basis upon which it acted. The Old Testament was taken over from Judaism. The three divisions of the Hebrew canon (Law, Prophets, and the Writings [in which division Psalms always stood first]) is implied in the words of Jesus in Luke 24:44. Early Hebrew-speaking Christians seemed to have used the shorter canon while those who read their Old Testament in Greek used the longer. Early Christian writers refer to three divisions of books which were put forward for inclusion in the New Testament: those acknowledged by all, those rejected by all, and those which were disputed. There seems to have been no question about twenty-two New Testament books. Hebrews, 2 Peter, 2 and 3 John, James, Jude, and possibly Revelation were among the books of the present New Testament canon about which questions seem to have been asked by one or another

group; the noncanonical books of Barnabas, Hermas, Didache, Gospel of the Hebrews, and the Revelation of Peter were regarded highly, if not actually regarded as canonical, by some.

Evidence for the basis of canonicity is inconclusive. Traditionally much emphasis has been put upon the assumed author of a book. The word of an authentic spokesman for God, prophet or apostle, or someone closely associated with such a person (Baruch in the Old Testament, Mark and Luke in the New) is assumed to have been regarded as inspired whether it was issued orally or in writing. Additional criteria have been set forth on the basis of later examinations of what the early church did rather than its own statement of them. Evangelical Christians assume, primarily by faith, that the same God who inspired Scripture remained as superintendent to assure the reliability of the recognition of the canon.

An important controversy centers upon the role of the church in the canonical process. It asks whether the church *authorized*, gave authority to the New Testament canon, or *recognized* the authority that is inherent within these writings because of their divine inspiration. The answer to this question must come from historical research. The practical implication is whether the church sits in judgment upon the Scriptures or the Scriptures upon the church.

The issue of canon is particularly important for missions, not only because of the claim that Scripture is the word of God, but because several groups advocate that additional material must be added to it. Islam, for example, makes this claim for the QUR'AN and Mormonism for the Book of Mormon. Christians insist that in showing himself personally in human form and by actually providing for the greatest need of humans in the ministry, death, and resurrection of Jesus, special revelation reached its climax and conclusion; nothing more can be added.

Two additional words often used in discussions of the Bible are "infallible" and "inerrant." The former designates the teachings of the Bible as absolutely authoritative and true. Inerrant means "without error," but those who use the term often disagree on whether they mean without error of any kind or in accomplishing God's purpose (*see* INERRANCY).

One final comment must be made regarding the Bible. Of almost equal importance with what one affirms about its nature is the question of how it is to be interpreted. Christendom, including its missionary endeavors, has all too often denied in practice the authority claims for Scripture by interpreting it in ways which fail to seek to grasp what the original writers (divine and human) intended and what the original readers understood. This must be a guide as one seeks to apply Scripture to the different geographical, cultural, and temporal settings of the contemporary world. Those concerned with HERMENEUTICS seek those principles involved in the art and science of making meaningful and relevant in one time and place that which was originally communicated in another time and place. This definition of hermeneutics is also a brief description of another term much used by missiologists, CONTEXTUALIZATION.

Modern missionaries, following the apostle Paul, may properly begin with general revelation and then move to special revelation. It is through these that God has made available the message, the only legitimate message, about himself, the universe, and their relationship which is at the heart of the missionary endeavor.

J. JULIUS SCOTT JR.

Bibliography. G. C. Berkhouwer, *General Revelation;* C. F. H. Henry, *God, Revelation and Authority;* L. Morris, *I Believe in Revelation;* J. I. Packer, *Fundamentalism and the Word of God;* B. B. Warfield, *The Inspiration and Authority of the Bible.*

Bible and Medical Misssionary Fellowship. *See* INTERSERVE.

Bible Societies. Organizations with the primary aim of making the Bible available to all people. The activities that Bible societies carry out today—TRANSLATION, production of Bibles, and distribution of material—have their prototypes in the ancient world. Old Testament portions were copied, stored, and distributed to Jewish synagogue leaders. In New Testament times the Gospels and the letters of the apostle Paul were copied and circulated. Through the early church ages, Christians painstakingly produced copies of the Scriptures for distribution. During the period of the Reformation, the Bible was translated, printed, and distributed in numerous European languages.

A forerunner of the Bible Society movement was the von Canstein Bible Institute of Halle, organized in 1710 to supply inexpensive Scriptures to the poor in Germany. By the end of the eighteenth century 3 million low-cost Bibles and New Testaments had been circulated.

The British and Foreign Bible Society (BFBS) was formed in 1804 with the intention to serve not only the churches in Britain, but all of Europe and the British colonies. As early as 1811, work was started in Calcutta, India. The American Bible Society, founded in 1816, worked in areas where American missionaries were serving. By the end of the nineteenth century, BFBS and ABS spanned the world with a network of agencies and associations. Many other Bible societies were founded in the nineteenth century.

The United Bible Societies (UBS) was formed in 1946 with the aim of making the Bible available in a form that all can understand and all can afford. Today UBS consists of 135 Bible societies covering more than 200 countries and territories. Apart from printed Bibles, the societies produce Scripture material on audiocassettes, in videos, and in braille. A network of highly trained consultants in the areas of translation, production, media, and marketing is available to the individual Bible societies. Translation is presently going on in over 600 languages.

In 1995 a total of 564,436,267 items (including Bibles, New Testaments, and single books thereof) were distributed all over the world by Bible societies related to the UBS. In cooperation with the Amity Press in Nanjing, more than 2 million Bibles are now printed annually in China. It is estimated that less than half the world's people are readers, so Bible societies are today making the Scriptures available on audiocassettes and in videos, and new developments are taking place with other electronic forms.

Bible societies have traditionally been supported by the Protestant churches, but a movement of biblical renewal in the Roman Catholic Church after the Second Vatican Council (1965) resulted in increasing involvement by Catholics. Relations with the Orthodox Church have also grown, and some Bible societies have Orthodox staff and board members.

Other Bible societies include the International Bible Society, which sponsored the production and distribution of the New International Version. In response to the LAUSANNE CONGRESS II ON WORLD EVANGELISM (MANILA 1989) fourteen diverse organizations formed the Forum of Bible Agencies. The aim of this new pooling of resources is the traditional goal of Bible societies worldwide, namely, making the Word more available to the world.

VIGGO SØGAARD

Bibliography. E. H. Robertson, *Taking the Word to the World: 50 Years of the United Bible Societies;* J. Roe, *History of the Britsh and Foreign Bible Society.*

Bible Translation. The primary objective of Bible translation is to make God's Word available to all the people of the world in the language they know best—their mother tongue. TRANSLATION has been central to communicating God's Word from the beginning of time.

Translation Throughout History. In the beginning God spoke, and what he said was manifest in the creation—the first translation (Gen. 1; Rom. 1). Throughout the ages, whenever God interacted with human beings, he used their language within a particular cultural context. When that language was not adequate for communication, the Word was translated so it would have maximum impact (Ezra, Nehemiah, and Acts 2). In the Greek-speaking world of the intertestamental period it became evident that the Hebrew Torah was not understood by the Jews of the Diaspora (nor by the Romans and barbarians), so the Septuagint (LXX) came into being. The necessity of understanding what God had to say was most evident in the Holy Spirit's enabling the apostles to declare the wonders of God in the languages of those who heard (Acts 2:11). Furthermore, the apostle Paul and the other New Testament writers used the language of the day not only to communicate their message to their particular audiences, but also to clarify Old Testament passages.

In the first four hundred years of Christianity, translations of the Scriptures into Syriac, Coptic, Gothic, and Latin contributed to reaching the peoples of the Near East, Egypt, northern Europe, and the Roman Empire respectively. More recently, the impact of the Reformation can be traced in part to the availability of Scripture in the languages of the people (Old English, German, French, and Italian). The concept of the translatability of Scripture is central to understanding biblical history as well as modern missions.

At the turn of the nineteenth century, WILLIAM CAREY was instrumental in the translation of Scripture into many of the languages of India. Despite incredible odds, ROBERT MORRISON was able in sixteen years to translate the entire Bible into Chinese. Bible societies were formed at the beginning of the nineteenth century to provide funds for the printing of vernacular Scriptures. Their work continued in the twentieth century under the WYCLIFFE BIBLE TRANSLATORS, an organization that has been central to the story of mission expansion to unreached peoples throughout the world. In short, translation has been part of God's communication to human beings from the time of creation. God wants all people (whom he created) to know what he says and to understand his Word within their particular context, wherever and whenever that may be (*see* TRANSLATION THEORY).

Translation as Mission Strategy. Bible translation as a mission strategy greatly impacted evangelization, church planting, and growth in both numbers and maturity during the last half of the twentieth century. In 1950, the entire Bible was available in 105 languages and the New Testament in 229. The decade of the 1960s saw the number of languages in which the whole Bible was available more than double, while the decades of the 1970s and 1980s saw a steady 50 percent increase in the number of languages into which the New Testament had been translated. By 1995 the numbers had grown to 349 and 841 respectively, with at least one book of the Bible available in 2,092 different languages.

The Growing Number of Languages with Complete Translations

Year	The Entire Bible	The New Testament
1950	105	229
1960	123	260
1970	249	329
1980	275	495
1990	318	726
1995	349	841

The availability of the Scriptures has enabled people to build the church on the foundation of God's Word, to apply it to their own theological development, and to guard against heresy in their particular context. While not a tool kit for church growth, vernacular translation does help to create an environment for church growth. Never before in the history of humankind have people had the freedom to search the Scriptures for themselves in their own language. A vernacular Scripture provides nurture and witness that impacts the way people live—it is a tool for conversion and relevant Christian living, not a colonial formula for coercion.

The Impact of Linguistics and Anthropology. During this same period, the science of LINGUISTICS and the work of anthropologists brought new insight to the translation effort. EUGENE NIDA's landmark work *Toward a Science of Translation* (1964) paved the way for the development of translation as an academic discipline in its own right. New understandings of COMMUNICATION theory and its applicability to translation theory became evident. And just as translations must "talk right" to be understood, translators came to realize that the people whose lives are presented in the translations must also "act right." Therefore, studies of the social context and cultural activity are important to translators as they seek to communicate in a particular language and culture. Studies indicate that the inferences people make about what is being said come out of their cultural expectations. Unless they are told otherwise, these basic assumptions constrain them to associate the meaning of a text with the behavioral forms therein, thereby biasing their understanding of what God intended.

The basic problem in translation throughout the colonial period was that well-intentioned missionaries brought their own theological and cultural biases to the interpretation of Scripture. Often they inadvertently passed on their misunderstanding of the original linguistic and cultural setting. This resulted in a clash of worldviews between the contexts of the Bible, the translator, and those who received the translation. In this way people came to understand God from the perspective of the missionary-translator—and Scripture, for them, was often foreign. Ironically, the majority of people around the world understand the cultural contexts in the Bible much better than do Western missionaries. Their kinship and social structures, as well as economic, political, and religious concerns, are much more similar to the biblical context than to the context of translators impacted by the ENLIGHTENMENT. The growing awareness of the importance of both language and culture raises the questions of who should be translators and what is the role of consultants in this process. There has been a rising interest in training national translators.

Translation Training. People with expertise in their own cultural context are asking to be involved in the translation process. For too long, translations have been viewed as the end product of a highly technical process that can be mastered only by linguistically and theologically trained experts. This perspective is changing to a focus on translation as being the responsibility of the church and an ongoing work in the process—a part of over four thousand years of biblical history.

With the increase in education, self-awareness, and sophistication, nationals want to be involved in the translation process to ensure local awareness of what God in fact said. On the other hand, the exegetical and linguistic skills necessary for understanding what God said in the original texts and contexts are not quickly learned and passed on. Accordingly, there is an increasing emphasis on making translation a team enterprise implemented from within the church. The Bible societies have long encouraged utilizing national translators, while missionaries supervise the projects and international consultants ensure the exegetical faithfulness of the translation. Wycliffe and other translation-oriented organizations are developing aids that will facilitate the understanding of source texts. Programs are being designed to train nationals to translate into their own languages or into another language spoken in their country. This provides opportunity for all segments of the church to contribute to the process and to collaborate to benefit the entire Christian and non-Christian community.

The Impact of Translation. With national independence, a political phenomenon throughout the world in the latter half of the twentieth century, has come a growing sense of religious independence. Rather than do things the way the colonialists did, people increasingly desire to express themselves in ways appropriate to their own values and beliefs. As they read Scripture in the major languages of the world, or a regional trade language, they may come to think of God as foreign to their vernacular context. However, when God's communication to human beings is couched in their own language and culture, its power and authority come to them directly.

Desmond Tutu maintains that the Bible is a revolutionary text because it helps people understand that God created all human beings for relationship with him and with each other. The Bible empowers the powerless and forces the powerful to recognize their own weakness before God. Such knowledge enables people to exercise personal freedom while at the same time recognizing the plurality of contexts in which God interacts—with all peoples. Hence vernacular Scripture provides people with spiritual understanding and encourages harmony. It promotes a celebration of differences rather than a focus on difference—unity in plurality, not division based on contrast (Gal. 3:28–29). Thus no people group can be truly independent, but needs to recognize its interdependence with others, even as they express mutual dependence on God. Through translated Scripture people are able to develop an awareness of God and understand their relationship to him. Because of the Word they are able to establish their own Christian priorities and responsibility for nurture, growth, and witness. No longer bound by what others say, they can develop their own theology and apply it to daily living.

Inasmuch as God speaks every language regardless of the number of its native speakers, we must apply God's message to each language and culture. Translators must utilize the entire assemblage of communication style and genres necessary for people to appreciate God's message to them. This suggests that translation must go far beyond the print media utilized by translators from the West and employ a multiplicity of media (audio, video, drama, mime, etc.) with a plurality of formats (stories, comedy, art, musical presentations and dance) recognized and used by the people of the society. External experts must combine their skills with internal experts to produce a translation that effectively communicates to a particular community. To this end translation organizations have established an international consortium with the express purpose of training translators and making God's Word available to every people group.

Once a translation is available, it takes on incarnational identity within the target community. God's truth and the truth of the culture interact to establish Christian truth for that particular context. Vernacular Scripture both affirms local behavior and traditions and critiques other behaviors and practices with which God would not be pleased in any human context. It also critiques cultural practices that the people themselves often recognize as going against their cultural conscience (Rom. 2:14–16). Jesus affirmed that he came to give abundant life (John 10:10), which is possible only as people live up to their own cultural expectations. Further, translated Scripture provides authority for Christian doctrine and the development of theology within the church and the community. It also becomes the standard for both determining appropriate discipline and avoiding heresy.

God's Word, available in the cultures and languages of the world, has resulted in changed lifestyles and new allegiance to him who created, loves, sustains, and speaks to all human beings. This provides the basis for that wonderful scene described by the apostle John: "a great multitude that no one could count, from every nation, tribe, people and language, standing before the throne and in front of the Lamb . . . And they cried out in a loud voice: 'salvation belongs to our God who sits on the throne and to the lamb'" (Rev. 7:9–10). It takes the multiplicity of views expressed in all the languages of the world to adequately give honor and praise to God. To that end may we diligently seek to make the sparks of divine truth known to the nations through the availability of translated Scripture. Through the Word made known, through creation, church history, and the application of cultural, exegetical and linguistic tools, people can grasp the significance of God in their midst and use that understanding to build his body, the church.

R. DANIEL SHAW

Bibliography. K. Barnwell, *Introduction to Semantics and Translation;* J. Beekman, J. J. Callow, and M. Kopesec, *The Semantic Structure of Written Communication;* D. S. Gilliland, *The Word among Us: Contextualizing Theology for Mission Today;* M. L. Larson, *Meaning-Based Translation;* P. Newmark, *Approaches to Translation;* E. A. Nida, *Toward a Science of Translation;* L. Sanneh, *Translating the Message;* R. D. Shaw, *Transculturation;* idem, *Notes on Translation* 8 (1994): 44–50; E. R. Wendland, *The Cultural Factor in Bible Translation;* R. Winter, *Reaching the Unreached,* pp. 17–44.

Biblical Anthropology. *See* HUMANKIND, DOCTRINE OF.

Biblical Criticism and Mission. The distinction between lower and higher biblical criticism offers a useful starting point for discussion. The term "lower criticism" is sometimes applied to the discipline of textual criticism. Textual criticism seeks to establish the text of Scripture by evaluating evidence supporting differences in wording (textual variants) in order to reconstruct the most likely original reading. It is higher criticism which, potentially, has the more significant impact on thinking about mission.

"Higher criticism" is a comprehensive term designating multiple techniques used to analyze the text of Scripture. One type (historical criticism) tests the reliability of the historical witness of Scripture. Certain types (source and form criticism) examine the background of the biblical text. Other types (redaction and rhetorical criticism) focus on the author and the circumstances of the original audience. Still others emphasize the literary techniques used to communicate the message (literary criticism) and the interpreter's response to the text (reader–response criticism). Two relatively recent methods (sociological and canonical criticism) focus on the "community of faith" that produced Scripture. There are a number of ways in which the indiscriminate use of these techniques can affect mission theory and practice.

First, historical criticism is most frequently applied to the Gospels. The result is often a reduced set of "authentic traditions" regarding the words and works of Jesus. At the least, questions are raised about the extent and purpose of Jesus' mission and about his instructions to the disciples regarding the continuation of that mission. At the worst, Jesus is portrayed as having no sense of mission and no expectation that his followers would be involved in mission.

Second, source, form, redaction, and rhetorical criticism tend to deflect the focus of interpretation away from the central missionary message of Scripture by focusing on the background of the text. Furthermore, the strong historical consciousness reflected in these techniques tends to heighten the differences between "then" and "now" and, consequently, to reduce the incentive to apply the biblical teaching on mission to today's historical setting.

Third, literary and reader–response criticism often tend toward hermeneutical relativism, in which the author's original intent is deemed to be irretrievable and the interpreter's response to the text becomes determinative. If any "coherent" interpretation of the text is acceptable, then questions about the appropriate application of the text must follow. The potential result is uncertainty about how and when the biblical teaching on mission may be applied today.

Fourth, emphasis on the way in which the early Christian community functioned (sociological criticism) or the way in which its beliefs shaped the material that is included in Scripture (canonical criticism) leads to a final product that is primarily descriptive. Not only is the focus of interpretation deflected away from the message of the text, but the extent of the authoritative teaching on mission that can be retrieved from the biblical text is minimized.

Each of the higher critical techniques sketched out above can be used constructively to sharpen the understanding of the biblical text and the factors that brought it into existence. Yet they must be brought under evangelical presuppositions regarding inspiration and inerrancy if the authoritative biblical mandate for mission is to be seen clearly.

JOHN D. HARVEY

Bibliography. C. E. Armerding, *The Old Testament and Criticism;* D. A. Black and D. S. Dockery, eds., *New Testament Criticism and Interpretation;* G. E. Ladd, *The*

New Testament and Criticism; G. Osborn, *The Herme-neutical Spiral;* R. N. Soulen, *Handbook of Biblical Criticism.*

Biblical Education by Extension. Biblical Education by Extension (BEE) was organized in 1979 in Vienna, Austria, by a number of mission organizations in Eastern Europe with the purpose of training church leaders in geographical areas where formal models of theological education were disallowed or restricted by governments hostile to the growth and spread of the Christian church. Joseph Dillow was appointed general director and Al Bridges as managing director. Fred Holland and Lois McKinney served as educational advisors.

In 1989 the name BEE was changed to BEE International to expand the BEE ministry to other countries. In 1996 BEE International became Church Leadership International with a focus exclusively on the former Soviet Union and Eastern Europe.

BEE World was launched by Jody Dillow to extend the original BEE ministry to China, Vietnam, Korea, the United States, and eventually, worldwide.

Following Theological Education by Extension (TEE) methodology, programmed instruction textbooks and workbooks were prepared over the seventeen courses that comprised the curriculum. Biblical subjects, evangelism, some methods courses, and study of the church formed the core. Western philosophical and historical understandings were purposefully replaced with culturally sensitive and contextualized forms acceptable in the "closed" countries of the world.

BEE was interdenominational from the beginning. Students from a number of constituencies were invited to participate in the classes—laypastors, teachers, elders, deacons, layleaders, and university students. Instruction was offered at the university level. Program graduates received a diploma roughly comparable to a Master of Arts in Biblical Studies.

TERRY READ

SEE ALSO Theological Education by Extension.

Biblical Theology of Mission. The only rule of faith and practice that God has given is the Bible. It has the force of law. Because mission embraces "the totality of the task he sent his church to do in the world" (Bosch, 1978), we must select a theme that is prominent in both Testaments.

That theme is the KINGDOM OF GOD. It dominated the ministry of Jesus and provides linkage to all "the many and various ways" by which God had earlier spoken to his people by the prophets (Heb. 1:1). "Missiology is more and more coming to see the Kingdom of God as the hub around which all of mission work revolves; one can almost speak of a consensus developing on this point" (Verkuyl, 1978). In our day evangelicals are finding that the biblical base for mission is far more complex than previous generations envisioned. Gone is the single focus of an overwhelming concern for the spiritual condition of "the HEATHEN." Nor can credibility be gained by supplementing this concern with appeals to the GREAT COMMISSION (e.g., Matt. 28:18–20; etc.), or by prooftexts supporting such related themes as the sending character of God, the compassionate compulsion of the Spirit, the example of the apostolic church, and the relation between missionary obedience and the second coming of Christ. These themes are important, but one cannot build a comprehensive biblical theology of mission on them. The kingdom or "rule" of God must be the dominant motif since by it God touches every aspect of the human condition: past, present, and future (*see* KINGDOM OF GOD).

When we explore the relationship of the kingdom of God to world mission, we begin with the reminder that God's kingship is both universal and covenantal. When God created the heavens and the earth by his Word and created the first human couple in his own image and likeness, it was inevitable that he would exercise a loving and preserving control over his creation and particularly over the human race. This can be described as his universal kingship. Both Old and New Testaments teach this universal kingship, but in the Old Testament we also find God's kingly rule identified with Israel, a people with whom he established a covenant relationship.

The Old Testament Contribution (*see also* OLD TESTAMENT THEOLOGY OF MISSION). In the opening chapters of the Old Testament we find the first reference to mission as defined above. God said to the first man and woman: "Be fruitful and increase in number; fill the earth and subdue it" (Gen. 1:26–30; 2:15, 18–25; Ps. 8:5, 6). This command is frequently termed "the CULTURAL MANDATE." By it God called Adam and Eve to accept responsibility for this world as his vice-regents, to serve and control it under his direction and for his glory. Its details pertained to their social existence, and mark the beginning of a stream of obligation—a mandate for family and community, culture and civilization—that widens and deepens as it courses throughout Scripture. We are not surprised to find that in the messianic age that Christ will later inaugurate, these many obligations will be made even more explicit as part of his missionary mandate that the church proclaim and demonstrate "the good news of the Kingdom" to the nations (Matt. 24:14). And such has proved to be the case. We might regard the cultural mandate as the prelude to the "Great Commission."

At the outset the expectation was that because God is sovereign, he will be obeyed. But this was not to be. Early on God imposed a moral test on Adam and Eve (the "trees"—2:16, 17). In granting them freedom of choice, God was running a great risk. Would they freely choose to remain under God's control or would they seek an existence separate from God? Sadly, they chose the latter and their fall (3:1–7) brought them under the dominance of "the tempter" and forged linkage with his hostile spirit-power and open opposition to the rule of God (*see also* FALL OF HUMANKIND). More was involved. Although they continued to carry out the cultural mandate, their obedience was now shaped by selfish impulses arising from their abdication of responsibility for the world and their surrender to the one who had now gained control of the world ("the god of this world"—John 12:21 and 2 Cor. 4:4; see also SATAN). Subsequent chapters (Gen. 4–11) record the effects of the Fall, ranging from fratricidal murder to worldwide violence; from God's judgment of all antedeluvians to the tragedy that came to the one family that was delivered (Noah's); and from human arrogance attempting to establish a universal kingdom with its defiant tower to further judgment, the linguistic confusion and scattering of the people (BABEL).

Since the cultural mandate was no longer being carried out under God's direction, God then began via DIVINE ELECTION and covenant to unfold a redemptive purpose that would deal with the problem of human rebellion and alienation from his fellowship. He called a man named Abram out of Ur within the complex of Babel, and began to train him to live by faith that through his seed (Israel), "all peoples on earth" would "be blessed" (Gen. 12:1–3; *see also* ABRAHAMIC COVENANT). His gracious desire was via Israel to bring fallen people "by repentance and faith" to break with Satan's control (1 John 5:19; Acts 26:18, etc.) as co-laborers with their Messiah, to regain control of the world and those within it who would respond to his love.

But Old Testament history records repeated failure on Israel's part. Actually, over the years only a remnant within Israel believed and obeyed God. At the same time, however, their prophets predicted that God would ultimately realize the covenant goal he had set for a believing remnant in the nation: "to restore the tribes of Jacob" and to become "a light for the gentiles" so that his "salvation" might be taken "to the ends of the earth" (Isa. 49:5, 6). The key to this total restoration will be "the Redeemer and Holy One of Israel"—strangely, the One "who was despised and abhorred by the nation" (49:7). Despite this, Israel went ever deeper into spiritual infidelity, open rebellion, and prolonged captivity, with only infrequent periods when through national repentance the blessing of God became partly evident

in the life and worship of his people. The tragedy is that in the end the various contending parties within Judaism, though often at loggerheads with one another, united to participate in the final tragedy of standing against the One who came as the self-confessed "Son of Man" of Daniel, the "Suffering Servant" of Isaiah, and the "Smitten Shepherd-King" of Zechariah.

Old Testament Axioms of Mission. Five major axioms in the Old Testament are inherent in the New Testament unfolding of the kingdom of God in relation to the church's mission to the nations. They can be traced within this tragic history of Israel's experience with God.

1. God is sovereign in his kingship. His rule over individuals and nations is always righteous and just. He is the moral Governor of the universe (Ps. 22:27, 28; Dan. 4:34, 35; *see also* SOVEREIGNTY OF GOD).
2. God seeks the personal commitment of his people. God's HOLINESS demands righteousness on the part of all Israelites who would be in covenantal relationship with him (Isa. 55:6, 7).
3. God's people are to constitute a "serving" community among the nations by example and through personal outreach. They are to oppose "by word and deed" all that demeans people (Mic. 6:8).
4. God's purpose through his people is relentlessly opposed by the inveteracy of human evil and the implacable hostility of Satan and his hosts (Job 1, 2; 2 Chron. 36:15, 16).
5. God's purpose for Israel and the nations always moves beyond present matters, and is invariably directed toward his future and ultimate triumph in history (Isa. 2:2–4; Zech. 14).

Specific Old Testament Contributions. Within the record of Israel's long history the Old Testament touches on themes that are relevant to mission outreach today: the issue of slavery and political liberation (Exodus and Ezra); the relation of God's people to secular power and secular events (Genesis and the Prophets); the mystery of suffering and redemption (Genesis, Exodus, and the Servant Songs of Isaiah); the lifestyle of God's people (Leviticus); the perils of religious pluralism (Hosea); the issue of racism and the disease of anti-Semitism (Esther); the basic problems encountered in serving God (Haggai and Zechariah); religious encounter and the non-negotiability of truth (Jeremiah); the pursuit of personal and national spiritual renewal (Nehemiah and Malachi); the role of the believing remnant within Israel (Amos and Isaiah); the possibility of becoming useless to God through ethnocentrism (Jonah); the function of wisdom literature as a bridge to the nations that know not God (Job, Proverbs, and Ecclesiastes); and the missiological implications of Israel as a diasporal people.

Although the Old Testament is replete with insightful material related to issues inherent in mission, on the one crucial issue it is silent. In the Old Testament God has not revealed "the mystery hidden for ages and generations" whereby Gentiles through the gospel would become fellow heirs with the people of God. Biblically informed Jewish people know that their future Golden Age will not take place without a massive ingathering of the nations to the worship of the God of Abraham, Isaac, and Jacob. But how this would come about remained a mystery until Jesus Christ inaugurated the messianic age (Eph. 3:3–9).

The New Testament Contribution (*see also* NEW TESTMAENT THEOLOGY OF MISSION). The unity of the Bible is nowhere more clearly seen than in the way in which the Old Testament kingdom axioms mentioned above were amplified and increased in the New Testament. With the advent of Jesus Christ these axioms are directly related to world mission.

First, God's sovereignty focuses on Christ's lordship. "We preach Jesus Christ as Lord" (2 Cor. 4:5). This is the heart of the good news of the kingdom (Rom. 10:9, 10). Through the cross he conquered all his foes and obtained salvation for his people. His present rule over the redeemed adumbrates his coming rule when "every knee" bows to him and "every tongue" confesses his lordship (Phil. 2:6–11). The worship of other gods is utterly abhorrent to him.

Second, Christ's lordship demands personal commitment. The New Testament stresses the necessity of faith, the new birth, the inner witness of the Holy Spirit, and its outward expression in love and kingdom service. Only "new creatures in Christ" shall enter the kingdom of God (John 3:5). Those who possess his lordship but whose lives do not reflect his values and perspectives are challenged to examine themselves to determine whether they are truly his (2 Cor. 13:5).

Third, the community of the King is the Body of Christ. Kingdom people, whether Jews or Gentiles, are custodians of the kingdom and share oneness in the church. Their common life is expressed through corporate WORSHIP, mutual sharing, united confession, and outgoing service. They live by PRAYER and the CONFESSION of sin. Although the CHURCH as Christ's body is of divine creation, its visible, structured presence is a flawed mixture of God's grace, human fallenness, and demonic penetration. Its only glory is the presence of Christ in its midst, realized by faith.

Fourth, the church is called to mission. Only after Christ had completed his redemptive work did he issue the call to world mission: to proclaim and demonstrate "by word and deed" the "good news of the kingdom of God." Its details strikingly endorse but significantly supplement the Old Testament injunction to "do justice, and to love kindness and to walk humbly with God" (Mic. 6:8). After he sent the Holy Spirit upon his disciples, they consciously began to sense that they possessed a universal faith for all nations and began to go beyond the bounds of Israel to Gentile peoples to proclaim this gospel. Mission's central and irreplaceable task is persuading people to become Christ's disciples and gathering them into local congregations (*see also* MISSIONARY TASK).

Fifth, obedience to mission involves SUFFERING. The New Testament is replete with the record of conflict and suffering precipitated by the advent and proclamation of gospel of the kingdom. Jesus himself experienced the world's rejection and the devil's fury, and learned obedience through what he suffered (Heb. 5:8). In much the same way the church, claiming the victory of Christ over the powers (Col. 2:15), will experience the sifting of Satan (Luke 22:31) and fiery trials (1 Peter 1:6–8) that it too might be perfected, the better to perform its mission. This process will continue and even intensify as the age draws to an end.

Sixth, the future remains bright with hope. God's redemptive purpose will be fulfilled (Acts 1:8). What he initiated will be consummated. Through the missionary obedience of his disciples God will call out a completed people from the nations. Then he will "judge the world in righteousness by a Man whom he has appointed, and of this he has given assurance to all by raising him from the dead" (cf. Acts 17:30, 31 with Matt. 25:31, 32). The climax of Christ's redemptive purpose will take place at his second coming "when all things are subjected to God. Then the Son will also be subjected to God who put all things under him that God may be everything to everyone" (1 Cor. 15:28; *see also* PAROUSIA).

Israel Confronts Her Messiah. In the Old Testament God frequently sent prophets to Israel to remind the people of their covenantal relationship to him and the service he expected of them (Jer. 7:25). And yet, God's sending of Jesus was unique. The fallen condition of humanity was so acute and the need for redemption so great that only the INCARNATION of God the Son and the ATONEMENT of the cross could avail to provide for the redemption of God's people. Previous "sendings" set the stage for this final "sending" of the Messiah to Israel. This event marks the great hinge of salvation history: the end of "the old" and the beginning of "the new."

When Jesus came to Israel he almost immediately began to question the traditional piety of the Pharisees. He also turned to the outcasts of society and set before them a quality of life dominated by the love of God. In this connection Bosch states: "It is remarkable to note how these people to whom Jesus turned are referred to in the Gospels. They are called the poor, the blind, the lame, the lepers, the hungry, sinners, those who weep, the sick, the little ones, the widows, the captives, the persecuted, the downtrodden, the least, the last, those who are weary and heavily burdened, the lost sheep" (1978). In other words he embodied the kingdom of God as a countercultural presence in society and offended the Pharisees who could only sneer and scornfully comment: "This mob that knows nothing of the law—there is a curse on them" (John 7:49). They did not sense the significance of his redemptive purpose despite their study of the Scriptures (John 5:39). The Sadducees also opposed him because they knew neither the Scriptures nor the power of God (Mark 12:24).

This redemptive purpose began with John the Baptist, the Messiah's herald ("Elijah has come!"; Mal. 4:5; Matt. 17:12) and Jesus' incarnation, baptism, and divine attestation by God as to his true identity (Matt. 1:23; 3:7). Then followed his confrontation and triumph over satanic temptation. With the execution of John, their joint ministry of renewal came to an end. From that point onward Jesus began to confront the Jewish people as their Messiah (Luke 4:16–30), gathered a community of disciples around himself (9:23), and inaugurated the kingdom of God in its initial hiddenness. He explained: "The Law and the Prophets were proclaimed until John. Since that time, the good news of the Kingdom of God is being preached, and everyone is forcing his way into it" (16:16).

Jesus' miracles should not be simply regarded as humanitarian acts of compassion. Actually, they were messianic "signs" which Isaiah had predicted (chs. 35, 61) would precede the decisive act of God in redeeming his people. They pointed to the reality of the kingdom of God as "already" in the midst of Israel by virtue of who he was and what he did. On one occasion he said, "If I drive out demons by the finger of God, then the Kingdom of God has come to you" (Luke 11:20). At first the crowds were drawn by the expectations he kindled and by his messianic signs. When he fed the multitudes they wanted to make him their king (John 6:15). But when it became apparent that his kingdom demanded moral transformation, the crowds melted and opposition grew.

After a brief ministry of three years devoted to preaching the kingdom by using parables loaded with mission insights, feeding the hungry, healing the sick, and liberating the demonized, Jesus was seized by the religious establishment, subjected to an unjust trial, condemned to death for blasphemy, and then turned over to the Roman authorities to be crucified. He died as a Redeemer "taking away the sin of the world" (John

1:29) and rose from the dead the third day as Victor over sin and death, as the Old Testament had predicted (Luke 24:44–49). In his post-resurrection ministry Christ stressed four realities: (1) his bodily resurrection (Acts 1:3); (2) himself as the key to understanding the Old Testament (Luke 24:25–27, 32); (3) his missionary mandate (lit. "when you go"—of course, you will go) "make disciples of all nations," incorporating converts into local congregations via baptism; and training them in discipleship, as he had trained them (Matt. 28:18–20); and (4) his order to remain in Jerusalem for the outpouring of the Holy Spirit, without whose power their missionary task would prove impossible to achieve (Luke 24:49 and Acts 1:8). He then ascended into heaven. This act was the final witness to his divine Sonship (Acts 1:9–11).

Mission Begins: Proclaiming the Kingdom. The Holy Spirit on the Day of Pentecost transformed mission from preoccupation with a particular people (the Jews, Matt. 10:5, 6; 15:24) to all peoples (Acts 2:17, 21, 39). But it took time for the early disciples to sense the full implications of Jesus' messianic Jewish movement being transformed into a universal faith—the beginning of a new era under the NEW COVENANT. At first, believers in Jesus were largely regarded as a messianic sect within Judaism. Their evangelistic method was deeply rooted in the Old Testament (13:14–43). But when Gentiles began to come to faith, the apostles did not feel that they should be transformed into Jews by circumcision and Law observance, according to the older pattern of Jewish proselytism. This produced a crisis that was partially resolved at a special council of "apostles and leaders" (ch. 15). This also influenced their evangelistic approach to non-Jewish people (17:16–34; 26:18). This provoked a growing consciousness, particularly among Jewish believers, that a "parting of the way" was taking place within Jewry between rabbinic Jews and those Jews who upon believing in Jesus were increasingly finding spiritual oneness with the growing number of Gentile believers.

This massive shift precipitated much theological debate. Fortunately, God's gift to the early church was his provision of a "task" theologian, through the conversion of the Apostle Paul (Acts 9; 22; 26, esp. 9:15). From that time onward Paul's missionary activities and the problem-solving letters they provoked greatly enlarged the movement's awareness of the complexity of the task of worldwide mission (*see also* PAUL AND MISSION). Notable is his letter to the vigorous, largely Gentile church in Rome that he sought to transform into a missionary base for operations in Spain, and throughout the western Mediterranean world. He began with an appalling portrayal of the abounding sinfulness of all people, whether Jews or Gentiles (1:18–3:20). He followed this with a comprehensive presentation of the abounding grace of God to all sinners through "the righteousness of God, the Lord Jesus Christ" (3:21–5:21). Justification is by grace through faith. But Paul could not stop. He had to delineate the amazing grace of God to all who had believed. Victorious living for Christians is gloriously possible through the Cross and the Holy Spirit. These resources are such that although sin is always possible, it is not necessary (6:1–8:39)! Then, Paul reviewed the tragic record of Israel's national experience. The nation was never intended by God to be an end in itself. Rather, Israel was chosen for worldwide ministry, but through its failure had to be set aside—neither totally nor permanently—for Israel shall yet enter its Golden Age through repentance and faith in her Messiah at his second coming (9:1–11:36). The final sections of this letter focused on practical matters related to Paul's concern that the church at Rome be transformed into a missionary-sending community eager to participate in mission outreach, particularly in the evangelization of Spain (12–16).

The Kingdom of God: A Sign of God's Tomorrow. The New Testament deals with many important mission matters such as insight into the validity of mobile mission teams as well as fixed church structures; the essentiality, diversity, and exercise of GIFTS OF THE SPIRIT; the issue of the POWERS in relation to spiritual conflict; the phenomena of ethnic religion and spiritual conversion; the eternal separation between the saved and the lost (*see* HELL); and the end of the age: the ultimate triumph of God.

But what should concern us particularly is to see the full significance of making the kingdom of God the dominant hub about which all mission activities are related. Ours is an age in which people all over the world are losing all sense of hope touching the future. But the reality of the kingdom means that God has a glorious future for Israel and all the nations. There is going to be God's tomorrow. And every Christian is called to be a "sign" of God's tomorrow in the world of today.

It follows then that the Christian community is to be countercultural, not captured by the status quo, by the privileged, the exploiters, the powerful. Its members march to the beat of a different drum, for they seek to embody all of the elements of the kingdom of God in their lives. Like Christ, their concern is the poor, the blind, the disadvantaged, the despised, the captives, the persecuted, the imprisoned, the downtrodden, the bearers of heavy burdens, indeed, all those unaware of God's love. They proclaim Jesus Christ as Liberator, Savior, Friend, and the One who grants forgiveness, newness of life, unspeakable joy, and hope. Their God is the One who makes "all things new." Their yearning for his "new heavens and new earth" constrains them to love and serve others on Christ's behalf. Their concept of the gospel is not confined to proclamation, for it involves both word and deed. Their struggle is to make sure that the good news of Jesus is not denied to any human. This is what mission is all about!

ARTHUR F. GLASSER

SEE ALSO Theology of Mission.

Bibliography. D. Bosch, *The Why and How of a True Biblical Foundation for Mission;* F. Hahn, *Mission in the New Testament;* G. W. Peters, *A Biblical Theology of Missions;* D. Senior and C. Stuhlmueller, *The Biblical Foundations for Mission;* H. A. Snyder, *The Community of the King;* C. Van Engen, *The Growth of the True Church;* J. Verkuyl, *Contemporary Missiology.*

Biculturalism. Ability to live comfortably in two differing cultural perspectives, crossing freely from one to the other as occasion merits. However, this ability may be conceived as ranging across a scale measuring the depth of identification. On one end, it simply indicates the ability of a person to understand both cultures, which might be termed *cognitive biculturalism.* At a second level, it refers to the ability to operate comfortably and without conscious consideration in each cultural setting. This may be called *functional biculturalism.* At the deepest level is the ability of the person to truly and naturally identify at the root level of both cultures emotionally and cognitively, which may be called *root biculturalism.*

While there is little doubt that short-term cross-cultural workers experience culture stress and some may experience changes in the way they view the world, only rarely if at all will they progress beyond cognitive biculturalism. Even though they may have many of the basic facts of the new culture, they simply do not have the time and exposure to internalize those facts as "natural" to themselves. Their biculturalism is generally limited to cognitive awareness and emotional attachment to their idealizations of the new culture, but only time and continuous exposure enable progress beyond that.

Those who grow up in a single cultural environment but who sojourn in another culture for an extended period often reach the stage of functional biculturalism. However, they can be said to be bicultural only to the extent that the new culture becomes a second "home" to them and they are able to identify with both cultures as "natural." For those who do not leave their culture until adulthood, moving beyond the functional to the deepest level of root biculturalism is unattainable simply because, as recent brain research indicates, the windows of opportunity to identify at the deepest levels linguistically, psychologically, socially, and emotionally with the new culture have passed. Their level of adaptation, which may be truly remarkable and take decades to accomplish, simply cannot match those of indigenes in the second culture.

Simply growing up in a bicultural environment, however, does not guarantee the development of root biculturalism. Children who do not grow up bilingual, for example, will miss an essential element of the culture whose language they do not speak, and will not be bicultural at the deepest level. The children of missionaries are often bicultural at the functional level, but less often at the root level. The same can be said of immigrant families, whose children likewise grow up in a family of one culture but in an environment of another. At times in searching for their own identity they struggle to amalgamate elements of both cultures into a new "third" cultural framework unique to them as individuals, giving rise to the term THIRD CULTURE KIDS (TCKs).

A. SCOTT MOREAU

SEE ALSO Culture Learning AND Extent of Missionary Identification.

Bill, Samuel Alexander (1864–1942). Irish missionary to Nigeria. Bill came to Christ as an eighteen-year-old at a D. L. MOODY crusade in his native Belfast. He received missionary training at Harley College and there, in June 1887, presented himself in response to an appeal for a missionary to work in Nigeria. Arriving in Nigeria in September, he settled along the Qua Iboe River and began learning the language among the Efik-speaking Ibuno. Archie Bailie, a childhood friend who remained at Harley and did the initial work of organizing the Qua Iboe Mission, arrived on site in 1888. Over the next fifty-five years, Bill worked faithfully in the delta area. His efforts resulted in a denomination of eight hundred churches and ninety thousand affiliated people (1980). By the early 1990s, there were only fourteen Qua Iboe Mission expatriate personnel working in Nigeria, down from almost fifty in the late 1930s, the bulk of the work being in indigenous hands.

A. SCOTT MOREAU

Bibliography. J. S. Corbett, *According to Plan;* E. A. Udo, *The History of Christianity in West Africa,* pp. 159–81; E. S. Watt, *The Quest of Souls in Qua Iboe.*

Bingham, Hiram (1789–1869). American missionary to Hawaii. Born in Bennington, Vermont, he was raised by pious Calvinist parents. During a revival in 1811, he felt called to the ministry. From 1813 to 1816, he attended Middlebury College, where he helped direct Middlebury's Concert of Prayer, an intercollegiate expression of concern for missions. While at Andover Seminary, he was challenged to become a missionary.

In the spring of 1819, Bingham was appointed to the Sandwich Islands by the AMERICAN BOARD OF COMMISSIONERS FOR FOREIGN MISSIONS. He was single, and the ABCFM insisted that missionaries to Hawaii be married. On September 19, the day of his ordination, he met Sybil Mosely, a woman who shared his call to missions. Within two weeks they were married and, with six other missionary couples, sailed to Hawaii.

Hawaiians traditionally worshiped spirits, but in the providence of God a new king had recently outlawed idolatry and human sacrifice. Politically and socially, conditions seemed ripe for the introduction of Christianity. Bingham seized the opportunity, and great numbers began to embrace Christianity. Schools and churches multiplied as Western civilization advanced together with the gospel. Due to Sybil's ill health, the Binghams left Hawaii after two decades of work, their goals largely accomplished. Hostile forces, however, were already doing damage.

Back home, Hiram wrote a history of the mission, entitled *A Residence of Twenty-One Years in the Sandwich Islands* (1847).

ROGER S. GREENWAY

Bibliography. C. Miller, *Fathers and Sons: The Bingham Family and the American Mission;* idem, *Selected Writings of Hiram Bingham 1814–1869: To Raise the Lord's Banner;* R. A. Tucker, *FJIJ.*

Bingham, Rowland Victory (1872–1942). English-born Canadian missionary statesman and co-founder of the Sudan Interior Mission (SIM). Born in East Grinstead, Sussex, England, he emigrated to Canada at age sixteen. Early ministry influences included work with the Salvation Army and a stint as pastoral assistant to Rev. John Salmon, pioneer of Christian and Missionary Alliance work in Canada.

By 1893, sensing God's call to missionary work, he linked up with Walter Gowans and Thomas Kent in an ill-fated attempt to evangelize the interior of the central Sudan (present-day Nigeria). Gowans and Kent died of fever within a year and Bingham returned to Canada in broken health. He then pastored a Baptist Church in Newburg, New York, and studied at A. B. Simpson's Missionary Training College.

In 1898 the SIM was formally reconstituted under a board and bylaws. Bingham was named its director, and remained so until his death in 1942. Under his leadership SIM (now SOCIETY FOR INTERNATIONAL MINISTRIES) became what was arguably the largest Protestant presence in Africa, with over four hundred mission members and hundreds of established churches.

Bingham's other areas of influence are no less impressive. From 1904 until his death he edited the *Evangelical Christian,* Canada's only interdenominational evangelical magazine. From this platform he not only spoke to the pressing theological issues of the day, but tirelessly promoted both foreign and domestic mission and outreach organizations. To these ends he also established Evangelical Publishers (1912) and Canadian Keswick Conference Center (1924).

GARY R. CORWIN

Bibliography. R. V. Bingham, *Seven Sevens of Years and a Jubilee;* J. H. Hunter, *Flame of Fire: The Life and Work of R. V. Bingham.*

Biographies of Missionaries. For the past 140 years, missionary biography has been a staple in the diet of information nourishing, shaping, and conditioning Western perception and practice of missions. For example, Appendix IV of the [1860] *Conference on Missions held at Liverpool . . .* consists of a 13-page bibliography of "Modern Works on Christian Mission," a significant proportion of which are autobiographical or biographical in nature. Likewise, the "Missionary Bibliography" section in the first volume of the *Report of the Centenary Conference on the Protestant Missions of the World held in Exeter Hall (June 9th–19th), London, 1888,* runs to some 40 pages in length, 37 of which are devoted to biographical or quasi-autobiographical 'travel' literature. The 28–page (double-column) bibliography prepared by Harlan Beach for the *New York Conference of 1900* is likewise strong in biography, while the 225-page bibliography included in the *Edinburgh 1910 World Missionary Conference Report* (vol. 6) lists some 400 biographies plus numerous works of an autobiographical nature.

Within the continuum encompassing nineteenth-century hagiography (in which missionaries could do no wrong) and late-twentieth-century pathography (in which missionaries could do no right), there has been produced a significant volume of healthily critical yet sensitively nuanced interpretations of missionary lives, as evidenced in the superb "Mission Legacies" series regularly featured in the *International Bulletin of Mission Research* since 1977, and published in the American Society of Missiology Series as a single volume, *Mission Legacies.*

ELISABETH ELLIOT's *Shadow of the Almighty: The Life and Testament of Jim Elliot* (1958)—the story of her husband who, along with four other young missionaries, was martyred in attempting to contact the Auca Indians—is arguably the single most significant biography published in the latter half of this century in terms of its impact on Western student mobilization for mission. Her book *Who Shall Ascend: The Life of R. Kenneth Strachan of Costa Rica* (1968) was likewise ground-breaking, marking the beginning of more realistic portrayals and assessments of missionary subjects.

Missionary biography as a genre will likely continue to undergo substantial change as the record of missionary private thought and life becomes increasingly difficult to track. Whereas Western missionaries of earlier generations routinely produced extensive personal diaries and journals, as well as remarkably complete station records and annual reports, this is no longer the case, and would-be biographers will find it increasingly difficult to do their work. Prayer letters tend to be vetted to the point where they contain little, if anything, of deep insight into the missionary himself or herself, and scarcely anyone today journals or keeps a diary. Furthermore, since information is increasingly stored electronically, and rapidly becomes technologically inaccessible, sources for the writing of biography will become increasingly problematic.

Furthermore, given the fact that a majority of successful missionaries during the second half of the twentieth century are often persons who seem to leave scarcely any paper trail, it is safe to conjecture that the future of conventional missionary biography looks dim, and the appearance of new studies on old subjects is much more likely than is the appearance of studies on new subjects. At the very least, research methods of biographers will need to change if the genre is to accurately reflect the key movers in this century's Christian expansion.

Ironically, while the names of many nineteenth-century Western missionaries are household words in Western Christian circles, scarcely anything is known about those persons most responsible for the twentieth-century expansion of Christianity in Africa, Asia, Latin America—"native evangelists"—undeniably the most effective missionaries of this century. Efforts to redress this lack are evident in such emerging endeavors as the University of South Africa's massive *Church History Database,* and in the proposed nonproprietary, electronic database of *African Christian Biography* under the direction of Jonathan Bonk.

JONATHAN J. BONK

Bibliography. G. H. Anderson, ed., *BDCM;* J. D. Douglas, ed., *TCDCB;* idem, *WWCH;* R. A. Tucker, *FJIJ;* idem, *GGC;* J. D. Woodbridge, ed., *AFC.*

Birinus (d. c. 650). Early missionary to England. Birinus, whose origin is apparently lost to history, was commissioned to work in England, having promised Pope Honorius I that he would go where no previous missionary had gone. In 634, he arrived in Wessex. Finding the West Saxon population largely pagan, he did not follow his original intention to go to remote England and settled among them. Within one year he had won the West Saxon king, Cynegils, to Christ, with many eventually following the king's lead.

A. SCOTT MOREAU

Bibliography. J. E. Field, *Saint Berin, The Apostle of Wessex;* E. John, *NCE* 2:574–75; S. Neil, *HCM; ODCC.*

Bishop, Isabella Bird (1831–1902). English traveler and missions motivator. Born into a pastor's family, she knew pain as a constant companion after removal of a spinal tumor when she was only eighteen. However, she vividly recounted medical trips to Canada and the United States in a style that established her reputation as a popular writer and speaker.

Married in 1881 and then widowed after only five years, Bishop decided to travel throughout western Asia and India. During her travels she came across a group of Syrian Christians who were faithfully enduring harsh persecution. The leaders pleaded with Bishop to send them teachers from England, and this call changed her attitude toward missions and missionaries. On her return to London, she reentered the speaking circuit with the purpose of challenging her audiences to take up the task of mission engagement. Further travels in Asia beginning in 1894 led to more challenges to her audiences. By the time a tumor finally took her life in 1902, her influence was such that she was referred to as the "Mother of Missions."

PENNY GUSHIKEN

Bibliography. F. E. Arnold-Foster, *Heralds of the Cross: or The Fulfilling of the Command;* E. C. Dawson, *Heroines of Missionary Adventure;* idem, *Missionary Heroines in Many Lands.*

Black Muslims. Popular designation used to refer to the Nation of Islam during the years following the 1961 publication of C. Eric Lincoln's *The Black Muslims in America.* Lincoln's book chronicled the development of the Nation of Islam from its beginnings in Detroit in the early 1930s. The mysterious Farrad Mohammed, also referred to as Mr. W. D. Fard, began teaching a group of black southern immigrants about the "true religion" of the black man of Asia and Africa. Terming Christianity as the religion of the white man, Fard taught his followers that whites had come to power through trickery, evil, and coercion and were to be overcome by the black race. Through their discovery of their true selves in the Nation of Islam, blacks would be prepared to take their rightful place in world history and throw off white domination.

Subsequent to the mysterious disappearance of Fard in 1934, Elijah Muhammad, Fard's chief minister, became the leader of the movement, moving to Chicago in 1936. There he established the Temple of Islam No. 2 as a new headquarters for the Nation of Islam. Muhammad taught the tripartite doctrine that Fard was "Allah himself," that God is a black man, and that he, Muhammad, was his "Messenger." In 1965 he published his *Message to the Black Man* as a principal document outlining theological and political beliefs for the Nation. He called for a separate nation for blacks, to be rid of the influence of evil whites. Whites were "devils by nature" having been created by a black scientist named Yakub as part of his rebellion against Allah. Consistent with the teaching of Fard, *Message* looked forward to the day when blacks would triumph over whites and take their rightful place in the theocracy of Allah.

Other central tenets of the nation of Islam included strict dietary laws forbidding the consumption of alcohol, drugs, and pork, and economic self-reliance. Indeed, these two ideas came together in Nation cooperative efforts in farming, the production and sale of fish and bean pies, and owning and operating numerous stores, restaurants, and bakeries in the black community. Men were known as diligent workers, always well dressed in dark suits and ties and often visible on neighborhood thoroughfares selling copies of the movement's *Muhammad Speaks* newspaper.

The Nation saw a strong period of growth, particularly among inner-city black males during the 1950s and 1960s. Much of this has been attributed to the work of chief Muhammad aide Malcolm X, who began working for the Nation subsequent to his release from prison in 1952. His conversion to the Nation was typical for his time; the Nation was especially adept at working with young men in inner-city neighborhoods and prisons, providing them with a message that spoke to their disillusionment with society and American race relations. As a symbol of the rejection of the legacy of white oppression Malcolm Little, like other converts, dropped his "slavemaster" surname and had it replaced with an "X."

Elijah Muhammad died in 1975 and was succeeded by his son, Wallace Deen Muhammad. Wallace soon changed his name to Warith Deen Muhammad and moved the movement closer to orthodox Islam, dropping the "whites as devils" doctrine and affirming the universal appeal of Islam. Three years later, Louis Farrakhan led a sectarian faction out of the newly named World Community of Islam in the West to retain the separatist views of the Nation of Islam.

The Nation of Islam still has a small, if steady following in prisons and inner cities. Many missionary organizations have followed their lead in concentrating on prisoners in their outreach. Similarly, organizations such as Project Joseph, led by Carl Ellis of Chattanooga, Tennessee, have targeted the Nation of Islam and other more orthodox forms of Islam in their own evangelistic efforts.

HAROLD DEAN TRULEAR

Bibliography. L. DeCaro, *On the Side of My People;* C. E. Lincoln, *The Black Muslims in America;* L. Mamiya, *Journal for Scientific Study of Religion* 21:2 (1982).

Black Theologies. The black theology movement gained ascendancy in the 1960s as African American theological scholars and church leaders attempted to respond to the growing black consciousness movement in the United States. While African American theologians such as Benjamin Mays, George Kelsey, Howard Thurman, and William Stuart Nelson had written a variety of theological texts that covered a wide range of theological options prior to and during the civil rights movement, the rise of Black Power gave occasion for a new group of theologians and church leaders to interpret the gospel in light of the oppression of black people in the United States.

Early attempts, such as the "Black Power and the Church" statement crafted by the National Council of Negro Churches in 1966, affirmed the congruence between the militant call for Black Power and the power of Jesus Christ to set people free from social oppression. Theologian James Cone produced the first full treatment of this new development in his book *Black Theology and Black Power,* which appeared in 1969. He developed his ideas further in *A Black Theology of Liberation* (1970) and *God of the Oppressed* (1975).

Cone relied heavily on a liberationist hermeneutic, arguing for the blackness of Jesus Christ as a matter of his identification with the poor and oppressed black people of the world. Conversation partners such as J. DeOtis Roberts and Major Jones attempted to work on issues of social justice and race as representing a more orthodox perspective, with Roberts focusing on the ideal of reconciliation and Jones building on the traditional ideal of hope within downtrodden communities.

The movement did not escape the attention of black evangelicals, as theologians such as William Bentley, Anthony Evans, and Ronald Potter began to wrestle with the issue of the CONTEXTUALIZATION of the gospel. Bentley emphasized the use of black history in black evangelical theology, while Potter pressed the issue of social oppression and black identity. Evans gave primary attention to the need for an orthodox biblical base for theology in the black church.

Such emphases created theological and philosophical space for a renewed interest on the part of black evangelicals in Africa and African missions. Organizations such as the Destiny Movement, founded by Elward Ellis in the late 1980s and the development of the Black Campus Ministries division of InterVarsity Christian Fellowship and Here's Life Black America in Campus Crusade for Christ gave particular attention to the role of African Americans in missions both in the United States and overseas.

Black theology was also challenged by women who accused black male theologians of replicating patterns of exclusion by whites against blacks by ignoring the oppression of black women in church and society. Borrowing the term "Womanist" from author Alice Walker, theologians such as Jacquelyn Grant, Katie Cannon, and Delores Williams called for a nonsexist, egalitarian view of the church in the black community. Church of God theological ethicist Cheryl Sanders has advocated a theology for the black church that also focuses on an egalitarian ethic, but is rooted in historic church orthodoxy and practice, including the central role of women in church planting and development.

HAROLD DEAN TRULEAR

Bibliography. W. Bentley, *The Meaning of History to Black Americans;* M. Chapman, *Christianity on Trial;* J. Cone and G. Wilmore, *Black Theology: A Documentary Witness;* C. Sanders, *Saints in Exile.*

Blasphemy. Sin of reviling, slandering, or mocking the name, character, and majestic glory of God. The concept of blasphemy is found in the Bible and in societies where organized religion exists, particularly in Islamic countries.

In the Old Testament blasphemy was always a direct or indirect insult of God, including cursing the sacred name (YHWH) (Lev. 24:10–16), deliberate disobedience of God's Law (Num. 15:30), idolatry being the ultimate blasphemy (Neh. 9:18, 26; Ezek. 20:27–29). Instead of fulfilling her mission calling to be a light drawing the nations to worship and honor the name of Yahweh (Isa. 9:6; Pss. 9:11; 96:3), Israel incurred God's judgment (captivity) and as a result provided cause for the name of Yahweh to be blasphemed by the pagans (Isa. 52:5; cf. Rom. 2:24).

The mission purpose of the church and the call to proclaim the message of Christ in cross-cultural settings (Matt. 28:19–20) demand that the church, and missionaries in particular, live with moral integrity and cultural sensitivity lest a cause for blasphemy of the name of Christ arise for those being reached with the Christian gospel today (1 Cor. 9:19–27).

In the New Testament, blasphemy takes on a wider meaning including slandering a human being (Matt. 15:19; Rom. 3:8; Eph. 4:31; Titus 3:2), celestial beings (2 Peter 2:10–12; Jude 8–10), and the Word of God (Titus 2:5). Jesus taught that the sin of blasphemy is forgivable but identified blasphemy against the Holy Spirit as unforgivable (Matt. 12:30–32; Mark 3:20–30). Much debate surrounds the nature of this sin and its commission outside this context. Of note is the fact that Paul, a self-confessed blasphemer (1 Tim. 1:13) who sought to make Christians blaspheme (Acts 26:11), was forgiven of this sin (Acts 22:14–16).

Paul's three-year evangelistic and church planting efforts in the religiously hostile environment of Ephesus had such an impact that mob violence resulted and a charge of blasphemy was leveled against him (Acts 19:23–41), a scenario repeated in mission history to the present.

In Pauline teaching, blasphemy was a serious offense involving rejection of the faith and violation of conscience of which two professed converts were guilty, demanding a severe apostolic censure and apostolic assignment of discipline at the hands of Satan (1 Tim. 1:19–20; 2 Tim. 2:17).

Generally, among all cultures where religion plays a significant role, blasphemy is taboo and Christian mission activity will be affected correspondingly. For example, in countries where Islamic law is influential, blasphemy is a serious problem for Christianity. Generally defined as any insult to God, the prophet Mohammed, or any part of the divine revelation, the trend among Islamic fundamentalist scholars has been to broaden the definition to include any statement contrary to *shar'ia* law or the Islamic religion itself. In some cases verbal witness is all that is needed for arrest and potential execution, the penalty for blasphemy. Several notorious and internationally publicized cases in the 1990s witness to the peril of this becoming a tool for religious persecution, a grave danger for missionaries and their converts in the Muslim world.

RICHARD D. CALENBERG

Bibliography. C. W. Ernst, *ER*, II:238–45; L. W. Levy, *Blasphemy: Verbal Offense Against the Sacred from Moses to Salmon Rushdie.*

Bliss, Daniel (1823–1916). American missionary to Syria. Born in Georgia, Vermont, he was appointed by the AMERICAN BOARD OF COMMISSIONERS FOR FOREIGN MISSIONS to service in Syria. Bliss is remembered as the founder of the Syrian Protestant College, renowned in later years as the American University of Beirut.

In the early 1860s there was a great demand for elementary education in Syria. Even more pressing was the need for Christian secondary schools, because after completing their elementary education in the mission schools, Protestant children were going on to secular institutions or in some cases to Jesuit schools. This led in 1862 to a decision by the missionaries to seek ABCFM approval to open a "collegiate literary institution" in Beirut and to nominate Daniel Bliss to serve as principal.

During the U.S. Civil War, interest in foreign mission work declined and so did finances. This made it a bad time to ask the Board for funds for a major new endeavor. In 1862, Bliss was sent to America to collect money and make other arrangements for the proposed college. After raising as much he could in America, he turned to England for additional funds. At last, on December 3, 1866, the Syrian Protestant College was opened in Beirut.

Bliss served as active president of the college for thirty-six years, followed by fourteen years as president emeritus.

ROGER S. GREENWAY

Bibliography. D Bliss, *The Reminiscences of Daniel Bliss;* H. H. Jessup, *Fifty-three Years in Syria;* A. L. Tibawi, *American Interest in Syria 1800–1901: A Study of Educational, Literary and Religious Work.*

Blyden, Edward Wilmot (1832–1912). West Indies born African scholar, diplomat, and educator. Blyden is considered to be one of the most significant African thinkers of the nineteenth century and the "Father of West African Nationalism." Although he was ordained in the Presbyterian Church in Liberia, he is best known for his work in the African political arena. His views on African unity were revolutionary for the period. He advocated a pan-African nationalism, stressing the withdrawal of all forms of European colonial efforts, the creation of a large West African nation, and the formation of an independent African church. It is with the latter that Blyden had his influence on missions.

He called for the Africanization of churches and indigenous-oriented worship. He was critical of European missionaries, accusing them of destroying African societies and customs through insisting on Western forms and leadership. Although he did not personally leave his Christian religion and convert to Islam, he believed Islam to be a better religion for Africa, at least in the beginning stages of its development. The author of several books and pamphlets, his views are summed up in the book *Christianity, Islam, and the Negro Race* (1887).

THOMAS L. AUSTIN

Bibliography. J. K. Ade Ajayi, *Christian Mission in Nigeria 1841–1891, The Making of a New Elite;* M. R. Lipschultz and R. K. Rasmusen, *Dictionary of African Historical Biography;* G. O. M. Tasie, *Christian Missionary Enterprise in the Niger Delta 1864–1918.*

Boarding Schools. See MISSION SCHOOLS.

Bolivia *(Est. 2000 pop.: 8,329,000; 1,098,581 sq. km. [424,162 sq. mi.]).* Bolivia is a land-locked country nestled in west-central South America. It shares borders with Chile, Peru, Argentina, Paraguay, and Brazil. Cultures with pre-Columbian roots comprise 59.4 percent of the population, with the Andean Quechua (34.3%) and Aymara (23.5%) dominating. It is estimated that as many as 1.35 million of the total population are Protestant evangelicals. From 1976 to 1992 the Bolivian population grew at 2.1 percent per year, while the evangelical churches expanded at a rate of more than 8.5 percent per year.

The expansion of the evangelical Bolivian churches related closely to both ethnic and social class response. The greatest response over one hundred years consistently came from Aymara populations, though Quechua response began to increase in the 1980s. These populations have made up the traditional peasantry. The next greatest response has come from the complex middle classes of *cholo* and mestizo populations of the cities. By the 1990s there were nearly equal numbers of rural and urban evangelicals.

The First Period: Expatriate Mission. Protestant missionary presence in Bolivia began after the establishment of the Republic in 1825 with British and American Bible Society COLPORTAGE. The leaders of independence reflected liberal ENLIGHTENMENT values (including individual rights, separation of church and state, and universal education), limited the role of the Catholic Church in government, and began national participation in the world economy. Together this meant gradually increasing toleration of Protestant missions as perceived carriers of these values.

Expatriate mission which resulted in established congregations began at the turn of the twentieth century with five pioneer organizations: the Methodists, the Brethren Assemblies, the Canadian Baptists, the Andes Evangelical Mission, and the Seventh-Day Adventists. Their entrance to the conservative nation was facilitated by the reascendancy of liberal Bolivian politics at the time the world market for tin began to expand. But it was not until 1906 that the Bolivian Constitution was changed to recognize religious liberty. More mission organizations entered in the periods after World War I, the Chaco War with Paraguay (1932–36), and World War II. By 1960 thirty-seven Protestant church-planting missions registered 24,000 adherents. Along with church planting and leadership training they carried on diverse programs, especially health and education, responding to social need.

The Second Period: The Bolivian Church. The rise of the Bolivian evangelical churches themselves, beginning in the 1960s, characterized the second period. This was evident in the emergence of mature Bolivian leadership and vision in the traditional denominations.

It was also evident in growing interdenominational and interchurch cooperation. Moves toward citywide cooperation began in 1955 with the formation of the United Churches of La Paz. National cooperation began with the Evangelism in Depth campaign of 1965. The year following, the more conservative missions and churches formed the National Association of Bolivian Evangelicals (ANDEB). ANDEB came to relate most closely to the Latin American Evangelical Co-Fraternity (CONELA, 1982), formed around the Lausanne Covenant of 1974. In 1995 ANDEB represented sixty-one organizations, about one-third of the various evangelical groups. Twelve Bolivian denominations and missions partnered in establishing the Bolivian Evangelical University in Santa Cruz in 1982. Ecumenical cooperation (UNELAM 1965; CLAI, 1982) did not receive wide support in Bolivia. Leaders of the rapidly growing independent Bolivian charismatic churches cooperated significantly in the past two decades. But most evangelical organizations functioned independently.

Beyond formal cooperation, the vision and leadership of the evangelical churches was also evident as Bolivians filled key positions in the increasing number of para-ecclesial organizations that stepped alongside or parallel to the churches. Their tasks included such things as Bible translation, literacy programs, university campus ministries, literature, and response to social need.

The second period of the Bolivian church and its leadership took place in a difficult but epic time in Bolivian national life. The Agrarian Reform of 1953 established the national vision of a multiethnic nation working together. Although it continued to be among the poorest countries of the Americas, its leadership produced an increasingly educated and globally aware citizenry.

The Third Period: The Bolivian Church in Mission. Bolivian evangelicals began to join the expanding worldwide movement of the Christian church in mission in the 1990s. Through denominational and interdenominational structures a growing number of Bolivian missionaries served in Bolivia itself, in Latin America, and in Africa. Denominational and cooperative programs for missionary training were moving rapidly into place in response to growing Bolivian vision.

The Bolivian evangelical church moves into the twenty-first century with critical challenges. Its increasing size means it must assume new responsibility as it becomes one of the forces shaping Bolivia itself. Its increasing diversity means it must purposefully discover and strengthen its essential unity and witness. Divine purpose must guide it.

HAROLD R. THOMAS

Bibliography. D. B. Barrett; *WCE;* H. S. Klein, *Bolivia: The Evolution of a Multi-Ethnic Society;* W. D. Smith Jr., *Toward Continuous Mission: Strategizing for the Evangelization of Bolivia;* C. P. Wagner, *The Protestant Movement in Bolivia.*

Bompas, William Carpenter (1834–1906). British missionary to Canada. Bompas was born in London to Baptist parents and later decided to pursue a career as a lawyer. But in 1958, after suffering a stress-related breakdown, he chose to enter pastoral ministry with the Church of England.

In 1862 Bompas volunteered to work among the indigenous peoples in northwestern Canada under THE CHURCH MISSIONARY SOCIETY, and he arrived at Fort Simpson on Christmas Day, 1865. Until his death forty-one years later, Bompas started churches and schools, learned Indian languages, and translated Scriptures and portions of the Anglican Book of Common Prayer and other

Christian materials into Beaver, Chipewyan, Slavi, Tukudh, and three other dialects.

In 1874 he became the first bishop of Athabasca, a post he held until 1884. In 1884 the diocese divided, and Bompas chose to oversee the more difficult northern region, known as Mackenzie River. From 1891 until his death at Carcross Mission, Bompas was bishop of Selkirk (now Yukon).

Bompas eschewed using formal ecclesiastical titles for himself. He was a conservative evangelical opposed to both Roman Catholic missions and ritualism. To maintain theological purity, he closely controlled the missionary appointments to his dioceses. He produced several books, including Bible translations and a book on the Mackenzie River diocese.

STANLEY M. GUTHRIE

Bibliography. H. Cody, *An Apostle of the North: Memoirs of the Right Reverend Bishop W. C. Bompas, D.D.*

Bonding. In order to minister effectively in another culture, one must learn to communicate well with the people of that culture. But meaningful communication requires more than simply being able to speak the language; it also implies developing meaningful personal relationships within that cultural context, and a willingness to listen and to see life from the other's point of view.

The term "bonding" was coined by Thomas and Elizabeth Brewster in 1979 to refer to a missionary's deep sense of belonging in relationships in a second culture and the community's acceptance of the newcomer as an accepted outsider. The term was developed by analogy to the bonding that takes place between an infant and its parents at the time of birth.

Bonding with a new community can be facilitated by the new missionary's immersion in the life of the new community and society—spending as much time as possible with the local people upon arrival in the community, preferably living with a local family for the first few weeks or months. In this way, the newcomer begins to enter the community and to enter into the people's thought patterns, worldview, and values. It also enables the community to begin to know and understand the newcomer.

Bonding is facilitated by entering with a learner attitude. The one who is a learner is willing to be dependent on the people of the community and to be vulnerable with them. The learner role implies the humility to make mistakes in language and culture and to receive correction.

By developing relationships and gaining an empathetic understanding of the people's feelings, desires, and fears, the new missionary can adopt habits of lifestyle and ministry that can enable him or her to be good news from the people's perspective in order to draw them into a belonging relationship with God.

Bonding is based on an earlier concept—*identification*—in which the missionary was encouraged to enter sympathetically into the lives of the people in order to understand their way of thinking, and discover ways in which the gospel could enter in and transform their patterns of life. It is also rooted in a belief that the incarnation of Christ (John 1:14) provides the model for missionary ministry.

Criticism of the bonding concept has centered around three main areas: (1) questioning whether it is necessary or even possible for the newcomer to attempt to bond with the new community; (2) dislike of the use of the term and of the analogy with parent/infant bonding; and (3) disagreement about the relative importance of living with a family in the early days in a new community.

ELIZABETH S. BREWSTER

Bibliography. E. T. and E. S. Brewster, *Bonding and the Missionary Task;* M. C. Chao, *PA* 7:1 (1960): 16–17; S. Granberg, *EMQ* 24:4 (1988): 344–50; D. N. Larson and W. A. Smalley, *Becoming Bilingual;* J. A. Loewen, *PA* 11:4 (1964): 145–60; K. McElhanon, *EMQ* 27:4 (1991): 390–93; W. F. Muldrow, *PA* 18:5 (1971): 208–21; E. A. Nida, *PA* 2:4 (1955): 90–95; L. E. Reed, *Preparing Missionaries for Intercultural Communication;* W. D. Reyburn, *PA* 7:1 (1960): 1–15; W. A. Smalley, *PA* 5:2 (1958): 83–84.

Boniface (Winfrith) (680–754). English missionary to Germany. Born in Devonshire, England, in 680 and given the name Winfrith, he became the most famous of all missionaries of the Dark Ages and one of the greatest of all times.

Ordained at the age of thirty, Boniface felt a strong compulsion to spread the gospel on the European Continent. Leaving England in 715, he arrived in Frisia in Holland, where he made little progress. After a temporary return to England, the missionary call led him back to Europe in 718. After laboring in Holland and Germany, Boniface traveled to Rome in 723, where Pope Gregory II consecrated him a missionary bishop to Germany. In 732, Boniface was made an archbishop.

Boniface's style was vigorous and aggressive. He attacked paganism head-on. His chopping down of the sacred oak tree of the Thundergod at Geismar typified his approach. Wherever he went, Boniface tore down pagan shrines, established monasteries, organized bishoprics, and laid the groundwork for training local clergy.

Toward the close of his ministry Boniface longed to return to Frisia, where his mission had started and which was still largely pagan. Having relinquished his administrative duties in Germany, he returned to Frisia in 753. There he and his companions were attacked and killed in 754 by pagan Frisians, bringing to an end his brilliant missionary career.

Roger S. Greenway

Bibliography. E. S. Duckett, *Anglo-Saxon Saints and Scholars;* D. Keep, *St. Boniface and His World: A Booklet to Commemorate the Thirteen Hundredth Anniversary of His Birth a Crediton in Devon;* T. Reuter, ed., *The Greatest Englishman: Essays on St. Boniface and the Church at Crediton;* J. C. Sladden, *Boniface of Devon: Apostle of Germany;* R. A. Tucker, *FJIJ.*

Boone, William James (1811–64).

American missionary to China. Born in South Carolina, at the time of his conversion he gave up the study of law and went on to obtain both seminary and medical degrees. He was appointed as a missionary to China by the Board of Foreign Missions of the Protestant Episcopal Church. He and his wife sailed for China in 1836, but spent their first four years in Java working with the Chinese there. In 1841 he lived in Macao and aided in the school started by the Morrison Education Society. The remainder of his ministry in China was spent in Amoy and Shanghai. After his appointment as a bishop in 1844, he represented Shanghai on the Committee of Delegates for Bible translation. He was known particularly for his vigorous advocacy of the Chinese term *shen* for God, rather than *shangdi,* the preference of British missionaries. In addition to preaching, teaching, and translating on the Delegates' Version, he also wrote catechisms and books of prayer in Chinese and translated Matthew, Mark, John, and Romans into the Shanghai dialect. He emphasized classical education, and one of the schools he founded in Shanghai later became St. John's University.

Ralph R. Covell

Bibliography. M. Boone, *The Seed of the Church in China;* A. Wylie, *Memorials of Protestant Missionaries to the Chinese.*

Booth, Evangeline Cory (1865–1950).

Fourth general of the Salvation Army. She had precisely the charisma, convictions, organizational skills, and heart needed to take command of the Salvation Army in November 1904 and guide its rapid expansion through persecution and controversy until its value was recognized. Though one of her first tasks was organizing relief after the 1906 Los Angeles earthquake, it was the daily squalor of hundreds on the streets of New York that moved her more. In many ways her life is the history of the Salvation Army, since she was born the year her father William Booth began the movement. In 1928 she came into bitter conflict with her brother Bramwell, general from 1912 to 1929, when she insisted the Army's constitution be modernized and democratized, having already defied him when he tried to transfer her from America in 1922. A thoroughgoing feminist, she created hostels for young single professional women who needed decent accommodation if they were to pursue their careers. As general (1934–38) she launched the International Torchbearers and the International Youth Movement. This brought her full circle to her early teenage efforts with Sunday school and a doll's hospital to mend the broken toys and unhappy lives of children in the East End of London. An organizer rather than an innovator, her most spectacular feat was to collect 1,200 alcoholics from New York bars and bus them to a service in the Memorial Hall on Thanksgiving Day, 1909.

Eleanor M. Jackson

Bibliography. R. Collier, *The General Next to God;* F. Coutts, *The History of the Salvation Army;* P. W. Wilson, *General Evangeline Booth.*

Booth, Joseph (1851–1932).

English missionary to Malawi. Born in Derby, England, in 1851, Booth was called to be a missionary later in his life. His wife Mary shared the call, but died of pneumonia three weeks before departure.

Booth worked in Malawi only from 1892 to 1903, but strongly influenced its religious and political history. He founded two interdenominational faith missions—Zambezi Industrial Mission (1892) and Nyassa Industrial Mission (1893)—and he started three denominational missions—Churches of Christ (1896), Seventh-Day Baptists (1898), and Seventh-Day Adventists (1902). Through his first convert, John Chilembwe, he was instrumental in founding the Providence Industrial Mission of the [black] American National Baptist Convention, Inc., in 1900.

Booth opposed colonialism on principle, and his conviction of human equality made him support the concept of "Africa for the African." His anticolonial attitudes made the Nyasaland government declare him a prohibited immigrant in 1907.

A pacifist, Booth rejected the use of force to achieve justice, but without him the only armed uprising against colonialism in Malawi (the Chilembwe Rising in 1915) would not have been possible. Wrongly implicated in the Rising, Booth and his second wife Anny were deported from Basutoland and South Africa in 1915.

His general aim then was to reach the unreached masses of Africa by innovative means, with preference for self-supporting "industrial missions" and churches led by Africans with limited African-American help.

Klaus Fiedler

Bibliography. J. Booth, *Africa for the African;* G. Shepperson, *Independent African: John Chilembwe and the Origins, Setting, and Significance of the Nyasaland Native Rising of 1915.*

Booth, William (1829–1912). English preacher, social reformer, and founder of the Salvation Army. Booth was born into poverty in Nottingham, England. At age fifteen he became a Methodist, and four years later he was ordained a minister. He served a five hundred-member, middle-class church near the slums of London. He converted numerous prostitutes and drunkards. His congregation disapproved and Booth resigned. In 1865 he formed the Christian Mission as an outreach to the downtrodden. He renamed it the Salvation Army in 1878.

According to Booth, people needed deliverance from sin and the material degradation that so often accompanied it. He organized street-corner revival meetings accompanied by a Salvation Army band. The early "campaigns" excited violent opposition. Many were fined and imprisoned. Others, including women, were brutally assaulted. Yet the operations of the Army were extended to the United States in 1880, Australia in 1881, and later to Europe, India, and elsewhere.

In 1890 Booth published *In Darkest England, and the Way Out* suggesting remedies for vice and POVERTY. His proposals struck a responsive cord. Money was liberally given and a large number of his ideas saw fruition. Opposition eventually gave way to widespread sympathy. In 1904 Booth had an audience with King Edward VII and opened a U.S. Senate session with prayer. In his waning years he became increasingly blind but continued his religious and social work until a few days before his death.

EDWARD MATTHEWS

Bibliography. R. Collier, *The General Next to God.*

Born Again. *See* CONVERSION.

Bosch, David J(acobus) (1929–92). South African mission scholar. Born in South Africa, he was a graduate of the universities of Pretoria and Basel. He was ordained in the Dutch Reformed Church and served as a missionary and seminary teacher in Transkei from 1957 to 1971. In 1972 he became professor of missiology at the University of South Africa (UNISA), Pretoria, where he served until his death in an automobile accident in South Africa. He was general secretary of the Southern African Missiological Society from its founding in 1968 and editor of its journal *Missionalia* from its inception in 1973. He also served as national chairman of the South African Christian Leadership Assembly in 1979 and as chairman of the National Initiative for Reconciliation from 1989, as part of his tireless effort to bring about reconciliation among racial, denominational, and theological groups in South Africa and across the world. Bosch was a "bridge person," respected as much in the WORLD COUNCIL OF CHURCHES as in the WORLD EVANGELICAL FELLOW-

SHIP and the Lausanne Committee for World Evangelization. His greatest influence and legacy in missiology came through his numerous publications, especially his *A Spirituality of the Road* (1979) and *Witness to the World* (1980), as well as his magisterial work *Transforming Mission: Paradigm Shifts in Theology of Mission* (1991).

GERALD H. ANDERSON

Bibliography. W. A. Saayman and J. N. J. Kritzinger, eds., *Mission in Bold Humility: A Dialogue with David Bosch; Missionalia* 18:1 (1990).

Bosnia-Hercegovina *(Est. 2000 pop.: 4,330,000; 51,129 sq. km. [19,741 sq. mi.]).* Bosnia-Hercegovina is a microcosm of the ethnic, religious, and cultural diversity found in the former Yugoslavia. Its name derives from the union of two provinces, Hercegovina representing the smaller region located in the south of the republic. After World War II it was established as one of the six constituent republics of former Yugoslavia and became an internationally recognized independent state in April 1992.

In 1991 Bosnia-Hercegovina's population was comprised of 43 percent Slavic Muslims, 31 percent Serbs (predominantly Orthodox Christians), and 17 percent Croats (mainly Catholic). These figures were radically altered by the war (1992–95) which caused extensive displacements and casualties.

The Romans occupied the area in the first century B.C. In A.D. 395 it became part of the West Roman Empire, and since the Great Schism between Western (Roman Catholic) and Eastern (Byzantine or Orthodox) Christianity in A.D. 1054 it has remained under the jurisdiction of the Roman Catholic Church. Yet due to its geographic isolation as a landlocked, mountainous region, the impact of Christianity on Bosnia was minimal until the tenth century. In the twelfth century the Bosnian sovereign "Ban" Kulin laid the foundation for an autonomous (independent of both Rome and Byzantium) Bosnian church whose adherents were known as the "Bogomils." Bogomils originated in Bulgaria as a medieval dualistic sect, actually a semi-evangelical reaction against the hierarchy and religious formalism of the Byzantine Christianity and ruling classes. They became heavily concentrated and very influential in Bosnia, which was ruled by a series of governors (bans) and kings until the Ottoman arrival in 1463.

In the fifteenth and sixteenth centuries the religious history of Bosnia-Hercegovina took another turn following its occupation by the Ottoman Turkish Empire. Widespread conversions to Islam followed, largely for economic and political reasons. In the late nineteenth century when the Turks were defeated, tensions arose between the Croats who welcomed the new Austro-

Hungarian administration in 1878 (formal annexation followed in 1908) and the Bosnian Muslims who opposed it. Tensions exploded in the Bosnian capital, Sarajevo, in 1914 when the Austrian Archduke Ferdinand was assassinated by Gavrilo Princip, a Serbian nationalist supporting Bosnia's union with Serbia. This event triggered the outbreak of World War I, after which (1918) Bosnia and Hercegovina were incorporated into the newly constituted Kingdom of Serbs, Croats, and Slovenes, later renamed "Yugoslavia."

Protestantism arrived in Bosnia with the Austrians who established the first Lutheran communities in the country in the last part of the nineteenth century. Very few believers from these communities still exist. During that time the British and Foreign Bible Society operated a Bible shop in Sarajevo and its colporteurs were the first Protestant missionary workers in the region. Bosnia's Muslims are considered one of Europe's least evangelized people groups. Prior to the recent war (1992–95) several evangelical missionaries from other parts of former Yugoslavia were active as church planters in Bosnia and Hercegovina. Their labors were brought to a halt with the outbreak of the war which resulted in major displacements of the population, with about one-third of the population driven from their homes and over two hundred thousand dead.

During the war the Croatian evangelical humanitarian organization Agape, along with several other agencies and international partners, became intensely involved in the wholistic ministry of alleviating human suffering and bringing the message of hope and life to thousands of Bosnian refugees and other victims of the war. This ministry of Christian relief workers and missionaries, mostly from Croatia and associated with the outreach of Agape and the Evangelical Theological Seminary from Osijek, led to the establishment of more than a dozen evangelical congregations, mostly Evangelical/Pentecostal and a few Baptist in various urban centers of Bosnia-Hercegovina. In 1997 the first evangelical Bible School in the country opened its classes in Mostar. Evangelical congregations are the only active interethnic communities in the country and are recognized as signs of hope and instruments of reconciliation in a land marked by violence largely based on ethnic and religious animosities.

PETER KUZMIC

Botswana *(Est. 2000 pop.: 1,718,000; 581,730 sq. km. [224,606 sq. mi.]).* Botswana is the land of Khama Boikano, considered among the greatest of all African Christian chiefs. Khama was baptized in 1862. Three years later his father Chief Sekhome drove him out from the tribe when Khama refused to take part in traditional initia-

tion ceremonies. Nevertheless, as eldest son he succeeded to the chieftainship in 1872, leading the Bamangwato people until his death in 1923. During his long reign, Khama fought strongly against alcohol, transformed fertility rites into national prayers for rain, substituted prayer for charms to protect his army in battle, and astutely preserved the land for his people despite the pressures of COLONIALISM and expansion from neighboring South Africa.

Botswana is also the land of ROBERT MOFFAT, DAVID LIVINGSTONE, and lesser-known missionary giants of the nineteenth century. The first church was established in 1829 at Kuruman, where Robert and Mary Moffat worked for fifty years, translating the Bible into Sechuana (published in 1857). The people of Botswana were the first in southern Africa to turn to Christ.

The open support of the various tribes initially appeared to further the gospel, galvanizing broad PEOPLE MOVEMENTS. But the emergence of a state church stimulated loyalty to the government more than loyalty to Christ. Khana used Christianity to legitimize the political structure. He refused to allow the Jesuits to found a station in 1879, for, as he claimed, "they will cause division among my subjects." In 1890, at the expulsion of an LMS missionary who had challenged his authority, he is reported to have said, "Now the church is mine. Let all discussion end." Decline of the Botswana church in the twentieth century appears more the consequence of a state-controlled church than of missionary liberalism.

Today, Botswana is a land of nominalism with no more than 50 percent of the population professing Christianity. Only half of those are affiliated with any church; less than 5 percent can be considered evangelical.

DONALD K. SMITH

Bibliography. R. Gray, *Black Christians and White Missionaries.*

Braden, Charles Samuel (1887–1970). American missionary in Bolivia and Chile. Born in Chanute, Kansas, Braden traveled to Bolivia in 1912 after studies at Baker University, Columbia, and Union Theological Seminary. Ordained in the Methodist Church in 1914, he moved to Chile the following year. There he was professor and president of Union Theological Seminary (Santiago) and edited *El Heraldo Christiano*. Returning to the United States in 1922, he worked for two years as assistant secretary at the Methodist Board of Foreign Missions in Chicago. After completing his Ph.D. at the University of Chicago in 1926, he took a position in the Religion and Literature of Religions Department at Northwestern University, where he served until 1954. Throughout his teaching career he continued to stimulate interest in the worldwide scope of the church, seen through such activities as founding *World Christianity—A Digest* in 1937 and writing several books of missiological interest, including *Religious Aspects of the Conquest of Mexico* (1930), *Modern Tendencies in World Religions* (1933), *These Also Believe: A Study of Modern American Cults & Minority Religious Movements* (1949), and *War, Communism, and World Religions* (1953).

A. SCOTT MOREAU

Bibliography. N. B. Harmon, *EWM*, p. 314.

Brainerd, David (1718–47). American missionary to indigenous Americans. The influence of David Brainerd's life far exceeded his brief missionary career among indigenous Americans. He was born in 1718 in Haddam, Connecticut, and began his studies at Yale College in 1739. After three years he was expelled for his criticism of a tutor, which seemed to flow from the effects of the GREAT AWAKENING on the campus. School authorities did not take kindly to the outbreaks of prayer and Bible study groups. However, at Yale Brainerd heard about missionary work among the Indians and in 1742 he investigated work under The Society in Scotland for the Propagation of Christian Knowledge. He was appointed and served in New York, Pennsylvania, and New Jersey. By 1746 he counted some 150 converts in New Jersey. By that time his health had failed and he died of tuberculosis at age twenty-nine.

Brainerd did not establish any landmarks in his work. In fact, some of his methods were criticized because he appeared to be unwilling to learn from others who had worked with the Indians. However, his lasting influence on world missions came through his deep devotional life, which inspired and motivated succeeding generations of missionaries until the mid-twentieth century. His *Life and Diary* became a standard devotional classic after it was published by Moody Press in 1949.

JIM REAPSOME

Bibliography. R. P. Beaver, ed., *Pioneers in Mission;* P. E. Howard Jr., ed., *The Life and Diary of David Brainerd.*

Brazil *(Est. 2000 pop.: 174,825,000; 8,511,965 sq. km. [3,286,470 sq. mi.]).* The fifth largest country of the world in area, Brazil occupies 47.7 percent of the land surface of South America. In its population of aboriginal Indians, Europeans, and Africans, 21 percent are Protestants, 72 percent are Roman Catholics, and the remaining 7 percent are Spiritists and members of other religions. However, more than 60 percent of the Roman Catholics are involved with African and European spiritist practices.

1500–1850. Protestant missions were initially associated with the French and Dutch invasions.

French Huguenots made their first effort to bring the Protestant Reformation to Brazil in 1555. On March 10, 1557, the Calvinist admiral Gaspar of Coligny, with the support of John Calvin, organized the first Reformed church in the Guanabara Bay, Rio de Janeiro.

In January 1558 the Roman Catholic French vice admiral Villegaignon, the new ruler of the French colony, began persecuting the Huguenots in Brazil. Villegaignon strangled three of them after forcing them to confess their Protestant faith. Jacques le Balleur escaped and preached among the Tamoios Indians for ten years. Later he was captured by the Portuguese army and condemned to death with the approval of José de Anchieta, a Roman Catholic Jesuit. In 1565 the French were expelled from Brazil.

The second attempt to establish the Protestant Church occurred during the Dutch invasion of northeast Brazil in 1630. The transplanted colonial Reformed Church was composed of employees of the Dutch West India Company, former Dutch soldiers who remained in Brazil, refugees and adventurers who were attracted by adventure and commerce, Brazilian Indians, and the new generation of Flemish Brazilians.

The Dutch Protestants in Brazil worked especially among the Indians of Paraiba and Pernambuco. Between 1630 and 1654 they organized two presbyteries with twelve churches and ten preaching outposts, and established the first synod. More than fifty Dutch *predicantes* (pastors) and 105 *consoladores* (assistant pastors) ministered in the northeast, but in 1654 the Dutch invaders were expelled. No record exists of a successful missionary attempt to plant Protestantism in Brazil during the next two hundred years.

1850–1970. From 1850 until 1970 five mainline Protestant denominations were established among the Brazilians: Congregational, Presbyterian, Methodist, Baptist, and Assembly of God.

Congregationalist. The Congregational movement started with ROBERT REID KALLEY and his wife, Sarah, who traveled from England to Brazil in 1855. Kalley was a medical doctor and an ordained minister of the Free Church of Scotland. He founded the *Igreja Evangélica* (Evangelical Church) in Brazil, using the Sunday school approach, installing the congregational system of government, and excluding infant baptism.

Presbyterian. In 1859 the American missionary ASHBEL GREEN SIMONTON arrived in the Guanabara Bay, Rio de Janeiro, and organized the first Presbyterian church in 1860. José Manoel de Conceição, a converted Brazilian Roman Catholic priest, brought great incentive to the new church. In 1865 the first presbytery was organized and the first Brazilian Presbyterian minister was ordained; in 1867 the first seminary was established. The first synod, formed in 1888, developed a plan for evangelizing the whole country, including different ethnic groups. In 1911 the Presbyterian Church of Brazil sent its first missionary to Portugal.

Methodist. In 1837 the American missionary Daniel P. Kidder and his wife traveled through São Paulo, Bahia, Pernambuco, and Pará as Bible colporteurs. The Methodist Church, however, was not established until 1876, when J. J. Ranson organized the first Methodist church in Brazil.

Baptist. The Baptist work began with the arrival of the American Baptist missionaries William and Anna Bagby in 1881 and Zachary and Kate Taylor in 1882. With the help of Antônio Teixeira de Albuquerque, a converted Roman Catholic priest, they planted the first Baptist churches and established the Baptist work in Brazil.

Assembly of God. By 1910 the first Assembly of God missionaries had disembarked in Brazil. Gunnar Vingren and Daniel Berg were Swedish, but had immigrated to the United States. They settled in Belém, North Brazil. The Assembly of God Church became the strongest and fastest-growing evangelical denomination in Brazil.

The astonishing growth of the Assembly of God and of the independent and indigenous charismatic churches was the most significant spiritual movement in Brazil between 1900 and 1970. The "accelerated growth" of the Assembly of God was particularly unusual. The charismatic churches comprise almost 90 percent of the total evangelical population of Brazil today.

The denominations involved in the Protestant missionary movement in Brazil between 1850 and 1970 had several elements in common: the expatriate missionaries were theologically conservative; they used colportage, personal and itinerant evangelism, discipleship, and church planting as mission strategies; they established educational schools and theological institutions for training nationals; and the expatriate missionaries and the national Protestant leaders viewed the Roman Catholics as their main mission field.

Between 1900 and 1970 the old-line denominations in Brazil struggled with the tensions between expatriate Protestant missionaries and the national leaders of the churches. A period of schisms and independence began among the Presbyterians in 1903, followed by the Baptists in 1922 and the Methodists in 1930.

From 1970 to Present. A renewal movement during the 1960s blossomed within the old-line denominations and led to the formation of several independent Baptist, Presbyterian, Methodist, Lutheran, and charismatic communities. Their emphasis on prayer, spiritual gifts, evangelism, and church planting led them to pray for the needs of the whole world.

The "Antioch Mission," founded in 1975 by a Presbyterian minister, established a mission-minded theological institution and began preparing candidates to be sent by the mission itself, by denominations or other missionary agencies. Indigenous charismatic churches, such as "Congregação Cristã do Brasil," "Brasil para Cristo," "God is Love," and "The Kingdom of God Universal Church," have flourished until this day. Their missionaries are working in Latin America, Africa, Europe, and North America.

The astonishing growth of evangelicals and their missionary vision among more than 250 evangelical denominations in Brazil is difficult to explain apart from the work of the Holy Spirit. From less than 100,000 in 1900 to more than 30 million affiliated members in 1995, Brazil has become the third largest evangelical community in the world (after the United States and China). According to the statistics presented at the First Brazilian National Missions Congress in 1993, between 1988 and 1993 more than 5,400 Brazilian missionaries were sent out.

Nevertheless, evangelicals in Brazil face several challenges. First is missionary attrition—"more than three thousand Brazilian missionaries returned home in less than two years," and 90 percent of them did not return to the field. Second is the need for continued interdependent cooperation between denominational mission boards and independent mission agencies for recruitment, training, deployment, and financial support of the missionaries. The third challenge is the inadequacy of cross-cultural missionary training. Finally, there is an urgent need for evangelical unity to foster fellowship and prayerful cooperation among evangelicals in Brazil.

Five Brazilian associations have been deliberating on these missiological issues in Brazil: the Cross-Cultural Brazilian Missions Association (AMTB), the Association of Professors of Missions in Brazil (APMB), the Association of Church Missionary Committees (ACMI), the Ibero-American Missionary Commission (COMIBAM), and the newly formed Evangelical Association of Brazil (AEYB).

ELIAS S. MEDEIROS

Bibliography. F. E. Edwards, *The Role of the Faith Mission: A Brazilian Case Study*; A. G. Gordon, *IBMR* 8 (1984): 12–14, 16–18; J. P. Hogan, *Brazil*; N. Itioka, *Internationalizing Missionary Training: A Global Perspective*, pp. 111–20; E. K. Long, *CCen* 84 (1967): 1298–1300; R. E. Nelson, *Missiology* 17 (1989): 39–51; P. E. Pierson, *A Younger Church in Search of Maturity: Presbyterianism in Brazil from 1910–1959*; W. L. Pitts, *Baptist History and Heritage* 17 (1982): 4–16; W. R. Read, *New Patterns of Church Growth in Brazil*; K. Yuasa, *Reformed and Presbyterian World* 29 (1966): 63–72.

Brazilian Mission Boards and Societies. Brazilian Protestants, established in the early nineteenth century, were slow to undertake mission work overseas. Brazil, with its vast territory, was seen as a mission field. There are numerous historical reasons for the lack of indigenous missionaries: churches were supported by foreign mission boards; when money was available it was enough only to pay a local pastor; there was no knowledge of mission fields outside Brazil; the missionaries failed to see the Brazilian churches as capable of participating in the missionary enterprise; some denominations were directed by missionaries and they did not see the need for sending missionaries from Brazil since their mission board at home was doing exactly that; and the thought that there were so much to be done in Brazil before venturing overseas was prevalent (and to some extent still is) among Brazilian church leaders.

The rise of indigenous missionary efforts started around 1911, when the Presbyterians sent Mota Sobrinho as their first missionary to Portugal with the intent to revitalize the Portuguese Presbyterian Church. This first effort was supported by Presbyterians from Brazil, Portugal, and Scotland. The Baptists organized their Missions Board in 1907 and Chile and Portugal were among the first counties to receive their help. The major indigenous boards and agencies among the denominations are the Assemblies of God and the Baptist Convention. They are totally supported by Brazilian funds.

FAITH MISSIONS started to appear in the late 1960s as a result of an awakening for missions, when many local churches started to have their own missions conferences. Books, articles, and many lectures were given, challenging the Brazilian churches to participate in mission. *Kairós* and *Missão Antioquia* are the major autochthonous agencies and support for their missionaries is raised in and out of Brazil.

The sending of Brazilians as missionaries into cross-cultural ministry contexts (both inside and outside Brazil) has grown rapidly in recent years. Figures from a 1998 missions census show some 2,200 Brazilians deployed in 84 counties around the world. Most consider the 1987 Ibero-American missions congress held in São Paulo (*see* COMIBAM) to be the watershed event. From that date the number of Brazilians serving cross-culturally has more than doubled, the number of Brazilian boards and agencies has significantly increased, and the Brazilian evangelical church has seen itself as a potential "mission force" rather than a "missions field."

The Structures. Brazilians are being sent by the following different types of missions structures: denominational boards (34%), interdenominational Brazilian agencies (33%), international agencies with Brazilian leadership (19%), international agencies with non-Brazilian leadership (12%), and local churches (1%). Nearly 90 percent of Brazil's missionaries are serving under Brazilian leadership.

The interdenominational Brazilian agencies have been the fastest growing over recent years. These agencies are most often simple structures; a board and an executive director. Office staffs are typically small and minimally resourced. The agencies see themselves as "servants" to the church and seek to partner with local congregations in training, deploying, and maintaining the missionaries.

Although 80 percent of the Brazilian evangelical church identifies itself as Pentecostal or charismatic, only 7 percent of the sending structures (sending 22% of the missionaries) identify themselves as such. Most Brazilians serve under structures that identify themselves as either "interdenominational" (34%) or "traditional/non-Pentecostal" (40%). Clearly the potential of the Pentecostal wing of the Brazilian church has not yet been realized in missions.

A common "meeting point" for Brazil's structures has been the AMTB (Association of Brazilian Cross-cultural Missions). This association is Brazilian-led and seeks to assist Brazil's missions by promoting consultations, missions publications, and partnerships among its constituency. With some regularity AMTB sponsors a Brazil-wide national missions congress.

Preferred Fields of Service. There are Brazilians developing all kinds of missionary work on six continents, including evangelism, theological and secular education, planting churches, and medical services. As might be expected, Brazil's younger agencies tend to begin by sending their missionaries to fields relatively close to Brazil. The great majority (64%) of Brazil's missionaries are serving in Latin America, Spain, or Portugal. However, what is surprising to note is the significant growth in the number and percentage of Brazilians serving in resistant countries and among peoples of the 10/40 WINDOW. In 1989 only 5 percent of Brazil's missions force served in the 10/40 Window. By 1998 that percentage had grown to 13 percent.

Brazil is expected, with Korea, to be one of the principal countries sending out missionaries over the next decade. Training for the missionary, his or her character, loyalty in sending the promised support, and partnership with receiving churches are areas that need attention in the future if the Brazilian churches want to grow in their ability to participate meaningfully in the missionary task.

ANTONIO C. BARRO AND TED LIMPIC

SEE ALSO Latin American Mission Boards and Societies.

Brethren Missions. Arising in Central Germany in 1708, the Brethren movement was powerfully influenced by the religious currents of Anabaptism and Pietism. Anabaptist principles were conveyed to its members by contacts with Swiss and German Mennonites; Pietist principles, by traveling evangelists. Both currents stressed personal commitment through conversion and application of faith convictions in daily life and conduct. This led to a striking level of evangelistic zeal by early Brethren witnessing to their new beliefs, despite oppressive actions by authorities who found their actions to be disruptive of societal peace.

These pressures led to emigration from Europe to North America, in groups (1719, 1729) and as families. By the early 1740s virtually all of the Brethren had transplanted themselves in the New World, principally in Pennsylvania. During the rest of the colonial period, they enlarged their numbers to perhaps five thousand in congregations stretching from New Jersey to Georgia. They were counted among the "Plain People" because of their nonconformist and largely withdrawn lifestyle and the similarity in church practice and belief with Mennonites and Quakers. After the American Revolution, with its stressful impact on the nonresistant (pacifist) Brethren, members streamed westward in the tide of inland settlement. By 1850 Brethren had relocated as far as the West Coast, in Oregon and California. Planting of new congregations during these decades had primarily occurred by division of growing churches and by colonization.

It was at midcentury that voices were first raised advocating organized mission efforts. This was originally designed to meet the religious needs of members who had moved to the West. Somewhat later, articles appeared in church periodicals that called the Brethren to follow the GREAT COMMISSION (Matt. 28:19–20) in reaching others. By the early 1870s congregations (organized after the 1866 into districts) set up district boards to pursue this activity. The first denominational-wide board (The Brethren's Church Extension Union) was attempted in 1877 but was soon disbanded under critical pressure.

Conservative elements within the German Baptist Brethren (as the church was then legally known) objected strenuously to the mission program. They contended that the Great Commission had been directed only to the apostles, who had indeed met the mandate, and was not binding on Christ's followers in later generations. The conservatives feared that organized mission activity (with boards, collections, and supported workers) would lead inexorably to salaried pastors and ecclesiastical machinery. This controversy was a precipitant of a three-way schism in 1881–83; the result was the creation of the conservative Old German Baptist Brethren, the progressive Brethren Church, and the much larger middle body, the German Baptist Brethren (known after

1908 as the Church of the Brethren), concerned for church unity and moderation.

Both of the latter two bodies enthusiastically adopted home and foreign missions. The German Baptist Brethren, through its General Mission Board, created active mission programs in India (1894), China (1908), and Nigeria (1922), in addition to supporting a district initiative in Denmark and Sweden begun in 1876, later terminated in 1947. The Board also began work in Asia Minor, France, and Switzerland without, however, lasting significance. When the Board began its work in 1884 it had less than $200 in hand; by 1913 its assets totaled more than $1 million. Among the church leaders most responsible for the tremendous growth in support for missions during this period were Daniel L. Miller (1841–1921), Charles D. Bonsack (1870–1953), and Otho Winger (1877–1946). The most zealous proponent of foreign missions at this time was Wilbur B. Stover (1866–1930), who led the first team of missionaries to India in 1894. Through indefatigable speaking and writing he urged missions as the "great first work of the church." His namesake H. Stover Kulp (1894–1964), together with Albert D. Helser (1897–1969), opened the mission field in Nigeria in 1922 and devoted his life to that cause.

Following World War II, a mission program was also created in Ecuador. The Indian, Chinese, and Ecuador churches all merged into national, ecumenical bodies. The Nigerian church *(Ekklesiyar 'Yan'uwa a Nigeria)*, which expanded rapidly in numbers after 1950, became autonomous in 1973 and cooperates with other regional church fellowships. It maintains a strong fraternal relationship with the Church of the Brethren, deploying expatriate church workers from the United States in its educational and church life. This reflected a shift in mission philosophy in Church of the Brethren after 1955 that emphasized indigenization and mutual mission.

The Brethren Church began many home missions projects after the 1883 separation. A Foreign Missionary Society created in 1900 mounted a strong effort in 1909 in Argentina with Charles F. Yoder (1873–1955) as the leading personality, and in 1918 in French Equatorial Africa (later the Central African Republic). In the latter, hundreds of congregations were founded after 1921. Early attempts in Persia and China failed to flourish.

Theological tensions within the Brethren Church led in 1939 to division and the inception of the Fellowship of Grace Brethren Churches. The mission society, the mission in Central Africa, and most of the missionaries and congregations in Argentina aligned themselves with the Grace Brethren, under the aggressive leadership of Louis S. Bauman (1875–1950) of California. Missionaries in Argentina remaining with the

Brethren Church under the guidance of C. F. Yoder developed a new program near Buenos Aires. Later Brethren Church mission work was started in India, Colombia, Malaysia, and Mexico. Some of their personnel cooperated with the Church of the Brethren mission in Nigeria. In the meantime, by 1980 Grace Brethren had initiated mission programs in Brazil, Mexico, France, Chad, and Germany. Home and foreign missions have been central to the life of the Fellowship of Grace Brethren Churches.

Church of the Brethren missions have always featured wholistic attention to amelioration of substandard material and social conditions as well as evangelism and conversion. They have been noted for creating orphanages, hospitals, schools, and vocational training. A missionary to India, Ira W. Moomaw, became widely known for his work with AGRICULTURAL MISSIONS. Courageous response to famines, pandemics, and armed conflicts in India and China brought numbers of converts. Work with lepers in Nigeria earned international attention, as did the preventive health program there known as *Lafiya* (wellness).

A characteristic of the programs of all three Brethren bodies active in missions—Church of the Brethren, Brethren Church, Fellowship of Grace Brethren Church—has been the significant role of women. In many cases they found possibilities for leadership and action in church work not readily available in their home congregations. Their achievement was great in education, health care, and work with indigenous women. Among the foremost were Dr. Florence Newberry Gribble (1879–1942) of Oubangui-Chari, Anna Crumpacker (1882–1967) of China, and Ida Shumaker (1873–1946) of India.

Although relatively late in mission involvement for theological and sociological reasons, Brethren of several denominations have been active on several continents since the late nineteenth century. The total membership of Grace Brethren congregations in the Central African Republic far outnumbers that in the United States; participants in worship services of the Church of the Brethren in Nigeria already outnumbered by 1995 those of the Church of the Brethren in the United States and, if membership trends continue, will soon outdo the membership of the mother body in North America. This rapid increase has been presented as a case study in the CHURCH GROWTH MOVEMENT.

DONALD F. DURNBAUGH

Bibliography. D. F. Durnbaugh, *Fruit of the Vine: A History of the Brethren, 1708–1995;* J. B. Grimley and G. E. Robinson, *Church Growth in Central and Southern Nigeria;* O. D. Jobson, *Conquering Oubangui-Chari for Christ;* A. T. Ronk, *History of Brethren Missionary Movements.*

Bribery. While there are eighty references to corruption and hundreds to various kinds of oppression and injustice in the Bible, there are few specific references to bribes, though the practice was clearly known throughout the Old Testament period. Samuel could claim "I took no bribes to distort justice" (1 Sam. 12:3) but his sons did not follow his example (1 Sam. 8:3). Some of David's contemporaries had "their hands full of bribes" (Ps. 26:10), Amos castigated those who "afflict the just, take a bribe and neglect the poor (5:12), and Isaiah counsels the righteous man to "shake his hands lest they contain a bribe" (33:15).

Bribery is defined as "the bestowing of money or favor upon a person who is in a position of trust in order to pervert his judgement or corrupt his conduct. It intends to make a person act illegally, unjustly or immorally." It is condemned in the law of Moses. "You shall take no bribes, for a bribe blinds the officials, and subverts the cause of those who are in the right" (Exod. 23:8; Deut. 16:19).

Sometimes, based on local custom where bribes may be tolerated, cross-cultural missionaries are tempted to offer bribes in order to achieve their goals. This practice should be constantly monitored and evaluated.

Gifts of appreciation may be given by those engaged in Christian mission after a service is provided to maintain cordial relationships. Bribes, however, may facilitate Christian service but compromise Christian witness.

ROB BELLINGHAM

Bibliography. B. T. Adeney, *Strange Virtues: Ethics in a Multicultural World.*

Bridges of God. The term is taken from *The Bridges of God,* written by DONALD A. MCGAVRAN in 1955, and considered the *Magna Carta* of the CHURCH GROWTH MOVEMENT. Indeed, the most common date used for the birth of the Church Growth Movement is 1955 because of the publication of *The Bridges of God.* The principal thesis of this book is that the mission station methodology of drawing converts from among those nationals who were attracted to the headquarters facilities of a foreign mission for any number of reasons was counterproductive. Converts in this approach were too frequently regarded by their peers as "cultural traitors." McGavran desired to replace it with what he termed "PEOPLE MOVEMENTS," an indigenous missiological approach in which converts would receive Christ and multiply churches within their cultural context so that conversion would take place without breaking or violating cultural ties in a kind of chain reaction. The book precipitated a vigorous debate among mission leaders of the time, but McGavran's thesis soon became the prevailing view of missiologists.

The Bridges of God was first published by World Dominion Press in the United Kingdom and distributed in the United States by Friendship Press of New York. A revised and enlarged edition was published in 1981.

C. PETER WAGNER

Bridgman, Eliza Jane Gillett (1805–71). American missionary to China. She was one of the few missionary women to begin her career single, prosper in it as a married woman, and bring it to a climactic close as a widow. Each stage of her life reveals a maturing faith and a deepening love for her work in Christ's name.

Gillett was born in Derby, Connecticut, and attended school in New Haven. She began a teaching career there before moving to New York, where she served for seventeen years as principal of a boarding school. Through the influence of her pastor, she began to sense God's call to the mission field. When the China Mission of the Episcopal Church was fully organized, Gillett was one of the three single women teachers recruited. In 1845 she became the first American unmarried woman sent to China.

Shortly after she arrived in Hong Kong, she fell in love with Elijah Coleman Bridgman. They married, which brought Eliza into sharp dispute with her mission board. As a result, she switched her relation to the American Board, and opened a girls' school at Wongka Moda in 1845. In 1850 it became a boarding school and was soon filled to its fifty-pupil capacity. Many girls were brought to Christ through her tireless work.

After her husband's death in 1861, she went to Peking, learned the Mandarin language, and, despite strong government opposition, opened another girls' school. To further her work, she spent most of her own income to buy land and erect buildings. In her efforts to reach young girls for Christ, she literally worked herself to death.

KATHY McREYNOLDS

Bright, William (1921–). American evangelist and founder of Campus Crusade for Christ. Born in Coweta, Oklahoma, he graduated from Northeastern State University, Tahlequah, Oklahoma. After going to California in 1944 to pursue a business career, he became a Christian under the influence of Henrietta Mears at First Presbyterian Church, Hollywood.

His vision for obeying the Great Commission began with evangelizing college students. He had begun seminary studies, but quit to launch Campus Crusade for Christ in 1951 at the University of California–Los Angeles, focusing on student leaders. He used a direct, aggressive approach to evangelism. His simple method later became his internationally circulated booklet, *Have You Heard of the Four Spiritual Laws?*

After rapid growth on U.S. campuses, Campus Crusade started overseas work in South Korea in 1958. Bright added specialized evangelistic outreach to athletes, business executives, political leaders, and diplomats. Campus Crusade grew rapidly to become one of the largest interdenominational mission agencies in the world, with some 6,000 fully supported U.S. and national workers in 152 countries.

Bright's most influential innovation in world mission was his movie about the life of Christ (the Jesus film, 1979). In his *The Secret: How to Live with Power and Purpose* (1989) he codified his teaching about the Holy Spirit. For his contributions to religion in America, Bright was honored with the prestigious Templeton Award in 1996.

JIM REAPSOME

Bibliography. R. Quebedeaux, *I Found It! The Story of Bill Bright and Campus Crusade.*

British and Foreign Bible Society. *See* BIBLE SOCIETIES.

British Virgin Islands (United Kingdom Dependent Area) *(Est. 2000 pop. 19,000; 153 sq. km. [59 sq. mi.]).* A group of some sixty islands, fifteen of which are populated. Local income is provided largely through tourism and offshore company registrations. In 1993 the population was estimated at 95.5 percent Christian (86.5% Protestant, 6.3% Catholic, and 2.7% marginal). Seventeen denominations are present, and the Methodists, who came in the late eighteenth century, have the largest number of members and congregations.

A. SCOTT MOREAU

Broadcasting. *See* RADIO MISSION WORK.

Brother Andrew (1928–). Dutch missionary to closed countries and founder of Open Doors. Known only by his pseudonym, Brother Andrew was born into a strong Protestant family in Witte, Holland. German occupation during World War II ended his formal education and initiated his involvement in the Dutch resistance movement. He joined the army as a teen and served as a commando in Indonesia. Wounded and disillusioned, he gave himself to God. Enlivened by a missionary concern for his co-workers in his hometown chocolate factory, he began formal missionary training in 1953 at the Worldwide Evangelization Crusade Missionary Training College in Glasgow, Scotland.

In 1955 he attended a communist youth festival in Warsaw, Poland. It was then that he realized his life work was to be among the suffering church in many such countries. Known behind the Iron Curtain as the "evangelist of Eastern Eu-

147

rope," "God's Smuggler" has become the most frequent description associated with him. His vision to make Bibles available where the church is restricted has expanded to over forty countries, with efforts more recently concentrated on the Middle East.

Brother Andrew is motivated by the conviction that there are no closed doors for the gospel, reflected in the name of his international mission organization, Open Doors. Educational materials and training, preaching, encouraging Christian believers, and providing material aid augment the principal objective of Bible distribution. Brother Andrew's approach to missions is aptly described as aggressive, experimental, and evangelical.

FLORENCE R. SCOTT

Bibliography. B. Andrew with J. and E. Sherrill, *God's Smuggler;* B. Andrew with D. Wooding, *God's Agent.*

Brown, Edith (1864–1956). English medical missionary and evangelist to India. After a struggle to qualify as a doctor at a time when English medical colleges were closed to women, she sailed to India on October 17, 1891, under the auspices of the Baptist Zenana Mission. In her first year in Ludhiana, Punjab, she had a vision of a medical college and teaching hospital for women, but it was not until 1893 that she was able to start implementing her plans with support from fourteen missions and encouragement from the surgeon-general of India. She began by persuading local midwives to come for training and to call her to difficult cases. The infant mortality rate plummeted, earning her the trust of the local women. A new hospital was begun in 1896, and the medical school opened in 1898. Coping with bubonic plague outbreaks, earthquakes, and famine, the institution went from strength to strength, the turning point coming when Indian Christian lady doctors could be appointed. Brown was a delegate to the WORLD MISSIONARY CONFERENCE (Edinburgh, 1910) and gained an international reputation on the subject of Christian medical missions and the needs of women.

In 1943, two years after she reluctantly retired, the hospital nearly closed because of wartime shortages of personnel. In 1947 Brown returned to assist in the aftermath of partition with a high-caste Hindu convert whose life she had saved. The Christian Medical College and Hospital, Ludhiana is now a premier institution in India and a powerful ecumenical witness known throughout the country.

ELEANOR M. JACKSON

Bibliography. F. French, *Miss Brown's Hospital.*

Brunei *(Est. 2000 pop.: 312,000; 5,765 sq. km. [2,226 sq. mi.]).* Brunei is a small Muslim sultanate on the northeast coast of Borneo facing the South China Sea. The Sultan of Brunei is one of the richest persons in the world, largely from income derived from the oil industry. Forty percent of the population is Kedayan of whom less than .5 percent are Christians. Another 10 percent is Chinese, who are about 10 percent Roman Catholic. Evangelical Protestants have made the greatest inroads among aboriginal peoples such as the Kenyah but form less than 3 percent of the total population.

TODD M. JOHNSON

Buchman, Frank Nathan Daniel (1878–1961). American faith missionary and founder of Moral Rearmament. Born in Pennsburg, Pennsylvania, he graduated from Muhlenberg College and Mount Airy Lutheran Seminary. After ordination and pastoral work he was converted at Keswick in 1908, then returned to student ministry at Penn State College. In 1921 he began a movement to "change lives and enlist life-changers" that in 1929 developed into the Oxford Group with its four absolutes: purity, honesty, unselfishness, and love. The name of the group changed in 1938 to Moral Rearmament, designed to bring people of all faiths "the next stage nearer God." Though he was often irascible, close colleagues worked with Buchman for years and for nothing. His crusade was run on FAITH-MISSION lines. After divine guidance had been given, commitments might be made without resources—and the funds arrived on time. Admirers included Harry Truman and foreign heads of state, Henry Ford, Bernard Shaw, and leading cardinals and archbishops. Detractors criticized this "Salvation Army for snobs," though Buchman never confined his outreach to the "up-and-outs." After World War II he was tireless in reconciliation efforts. Germans and Japanese were welcome at his Swiss center, when even some MRA personnel demurred.

MRA is said to have averted major strikes, thwarted a planned massacre of the British in Nigeria, boosted the morale of dockers in Rio, helped Tunisian and Moroccan leaders avoid the bloodshed that was to overtake Algeria, and mediated between warring Congolese tribes to ease the path to independence. Buchman is still to many an enigma, one who dealt in theological generalities, but there is something disarming about a leader who explained success in terms of having been "wonderfully led to those who were ready." Buchman's thinking is reflected in his *Remaking the World* (1947).

J. D. DOUGLAS

Bibliography. P. Howard, *Frank Buchman's Secret;* G. Lean, *On the Tail of a Comet: The Life of Frank Buchman.*

Buddhist, Buddhism. A religion founded by a man from Northeast India, Siddharta Gautama (c. 566–486 B.C.), who, by virtue of his religious insight, came to be known as the Buddha (Enlightened One). The Buddha's teachings *(dharma)* were rooted in the Hindu metaphysical systems of his day: a belief in the essential oneness of all being *(brahman-atman)* and the contingent nature of a phenomenal world driven by the dynamics of rebirth *(samsara)* (*see* REINCARNATION AND TRANSMIGRATION) and ethical progression *(karma)*. What came to be called Buddhism, however, distinguished itself by calling into question two key Hindu beliefs/practices: the spiritual value of the CASTE system and the divine character of the Hindu pantheon.

The Buddha himself was a member of the caste known as *kshatriya*, the second highest caste (second to the priestly caste, the *brahmins*) whose members formed what amounted to the aristocracy of fifth-century B.C. India. His father was king of an area called Lumbini on the modern border between India and Nepal. Gautama was given all the privileges of royalty, but came to see the spiritual vacuity of wealth and power. In reaction, he left home and family, and adopted a lifestyle outside of all caste, that of a wandering religious ascetic. Over time, however, diligent practice of asceticism showed him that mortification was equally vacuous. The Buddha's Enlightenment consisted of recognizing the futility of relying on either self-aggrandizement or self-denial as a path to freedom *(nirvana)*. Instead he began to teach a Middle Way, a path that consisted of moral living *(sila)* even as one learned, through mediative practice *(samadhi)*, that the highest wisdom *(panna)* is beyond all cultural and social constructs, including caste.

In order to register this implicit denial of the spiritual necessity of caste, the Buddha chose not a frontal attack, but an emphasis on the temporariness of all of life by characterizing all life as suffering *(dukkha)*. In Four Noble Truths he summarized the character, origin, and ubiquitousness of suffering. In the fourth Noble Truth, the Buddha taught a path made of moral and meditative injunctions designed to position the spiritual seeker in a lifestyle more receptive to the ultimate wisdom of Buddhist teaching. The effect of this was to move the locus of religious practice away from Vedic ritual and temple sacrifice (the traditional loci of classic forms of Hinduism and indigenous Indian religion) to a much more personal centered, interior based set of practices. Thus, in Buddhism caste moved from being the determiner of religious life (as in Hinduism) to being a temporary factor (in India, at least) of conditioned existence. The Buddha encouraged a movement already apparent in Indian religious life in general from a socially constructed religion to a readily adaptable cross-cultural religion focusing on the universal wisdom of his teaching rather than social realities.

Indian culture was apparently ready for this reform. Emphasis on caste had created a top-heavy religion of privilege (Hinduism) that made access to ritual and practice the province of high caste *brahmins* and *kshatriyas*. Lower caste Hindus and those outside of caste altogether were attracted to the Buddha's no-nonsense, meditative-practice teaching. If the Buddha's sermons *(suttas)* are any indication, he also attracted his share of high caste Hindus. His movement grew rapidly during the Buddha's 45-year itinerant ministry.

A result of this emphasis was a sharp lessening in importance of the elaborate Hindu pantheon of gods and goddesses. Although most converts to Buddhism probably did not give up their veneration of local deities altogether, the Buddha made it clear that these were penultimate in importance when compared with the importance of self-reliant spiritual searching. In the long term this change in the function of the gods and goddesses led to the shaping of different schools of Buddhism as it spread throughout Southeast Asia, China, Japan, Korea, and Tibet. In each of these situations, the Buddha's teachings proved to be adaptable to local cultures without losing their essential features. Southeast Asian THERAVADA, Chinese MAHAYANA, Japanese ZEN, and Tibetan VAJRAYANA Buddhism, in all their varieties, are distinctive *and* distinctively Buddhist.

This cultural adaptability is one of the reasons Buddhism has grown to be the world's fourth largest religion with an estimated 300 million adherents. Because the Buddha emphasized the heavy and ultimately illusory role history and culture play in the way we view the self and the self's spiritual search, Buddhism has proven to be effective in advocating itself to non-members. In Christian terms, Buddhism is a missionary religion. The Buddha, near the end of his life, encouraged his followers, especially the members of the order of monks *(Sangha)*, to go and spread his teachings to all sentient beings. This has made Buddhism a major player on the world's religious stage. It has now begun to spread rapidly in Western countries, with significant Buddhist populations in Western Europe and North America.

This growth has also made Buddhism a major competitor to Christianity both in the West and around the world. The cross-cultural adaptability of Buddhism is rivaled only by the ability of Christianity and Islam to transcend national, ethnic, and economic borders. This makes Buddhism an ideal religion in the increasingly global climate in which modern humanity finds itself. Buddhism has shown itself adept at addressing the traditionally thorny issues that arise around the interfacing of science and religion, for example. In some senses, the advantage here goes to

Buddhism (over Christianity and Islam) because of its "semi-theistic" stance toward the gods and the divine in general. Although different branches of Buddhism take different postures toward "divinities," gods and semidivine beings, in all forms of Buddhism gods of whatever sort are stages on the way, with final Enlightenment the task of the human individual in the end. The effect of this is that religion and science can be seen as fully compatible human endeavors, both extending human growth, both to eventually be transcended, as will all of *samsara* or the phenomenal world.

This same compatibility, however, creates a dilemma when it comes to ethical considerations. If all of reality is conditioned and impermanent, and the goal is to eventually supersede it with the unconditioned emptiness of Nirvana, then both the motivation and execution of ethical considerations can be problematic in a way that does not pertain for theistic religions with a supernatural mandate. Modern Buddhist scholars and practitioners, aware of the importance of this issue in a world filled with cultural injustices and oppression, are currently hard at work on developing a concept of "engaged Buddhism" that addresses the problems of social injustice without giving up on Buddhism's metaphysic.

Buddhism is also ideally positioned to address the essentially therapeutic emphases of modern life. Early Buddhist psychological analyses of the human person, especially the mental states, are perhaps the most sophisticated in all of human history. These analyses—found across the Buddhist traditions, all the way from Theravada Abhidhamma analysis to Zen Buddhist suprarationalism—all serve in the Buddhist systems to elaborate on the *anatta* or no-self teaching of Buddhism. This refers to the essential Buddhist understanding that the individual self is a construct of historical and cultural factors, a construct that must be superseded in order to achieve Enlightenment. This makes the goals of Buddhist psychology and associated spiritual practice very different from comparable Christian and Muslim analyses and practice.

But the analyses themselves are profound across religious traditions, and the resulting practices, particularly the meditative ones, extremely effective in helping achieve self-knowledge. Indeed, most Westerners who become attracted to Buddhism do so because of their interest in the spiritual meditative practices which form such a rich core of the Buddhist religious tradition. Theravada Buddhist *vipassana* practice (insight meditation) has achieved a wide following in the United States, as has Zen meditation and the Tibetan meditation practice of the numerous *dharmadhatu* centers throughout the Western world. Westerners searching for the peaceful stress reduction that such practices effectively engender are soon attracted beyond the meditative technique to the metaphysical understandings not far below the surface.

At that metaphysical core, one finds a spiritual conundrum between all forms of Buddhism and all forms of orthodox, theistic Christianity: The question of whether a single, personal, transcendent God exists in relationship with discrete, eternally real human souls. After all the analyses are done, Buddhist religious traditions do not recognize such a God, and Christian traditions cease being Christian if they fail to do so.

TERRY C. MUCK

SEE ALSO Pure Land Buddhism.

Bibliography. K. Ch'en, *Buddhism in China;* E. Conze, trans., *Buddhist Scriptures;* H. Dumoulin, *A History of Zen Buddhism;* N. Dutt, *Aspects of Mahayana Buddhism and Its Relation to Hinayana;* R. Fields, *How the Swans Came to the Lake: A Narrative History of Buddhism in America;* J. Kitagawa, *Religion in Japanese History;* W. Rahula, *What the Buddha Taught;* F. Streng, *Emptiness: A Study in Religious Meaning;* G. Tucci, *The Religions of Tibet.*

Bulgaria (*Est. 2000 pop.: 8,576,000; 110,912 sq. km. [42,823 sq. mi.]*). Bulgaria, a Balkan country bordered by the Black Sea in southeastern Europe, has a population that has been steadily declining since 1985 due to emigration. It was formerly communist (one of the most consistently pro-Soviet), but is now a constitutional republic with a democratically elected government. Engineering is the principal economic activity supplemented by agricultural products such as wheat, corn, and barley. Bulgaria is the fourth largest exporter of tobacco in the world. About 80 percent of the population is Bulgar and 10 percent Rumelian Turk. The remaining 10 percent is made up of six different Gypsies nationalities and smaller communities of Macedonians, Pomaks, Poles, and Armenians.

With most of the nonreligious and atheists returning to the church since 1989, the vast majority of the Christians (over 80 percent of the population) are Orthodox. However, there are one million Muslims (12% of the country's population). Evangelicals have tripled since 1970 (40,000 to 125,000) and are mainly represented by the Pentecostal Union, Church of God, Baptists, Christian Brethren, and Seventh-Day Adventists. The most rapid church growth since 1990 has been among Pentecostals. Evangelicals have experienced exceptional success among Turks and Gypsies.

The major evangelistic strategies being implemented are church planting, literature distribution, and radio/TV broadcasting. The churches are also investing major resources in discipleship, Bible teaching, and leadership training. Competition between the many new evangelical agencies as well as conflict with marginal Christian groups (Jehovah's Witnesses, Mormons, etc.) is a looming problem.

TODD M. JOHNSON

Bulu, Joeli (c. 1810–77). Tongan missionary in Fiji. Born in Vava'u, Tonga, he converted to Christ during the Great Tongan Awakening around 1833. Deeply burdened for Fiji at the same time that a letter came from missionary David Cargill requesting help, Bulu was sent in 1838. He first worked on learning the language, and when the missionaries set up a mission printing press, he was assigned to work there under James Calvert.

Proving to be faithful in the ministry, he began two years of missionary probation work in 1848, and in 1850 was the first South Pacific Islander to be ordained to ministry in the Methodist Church. In all, he toiled among the various islands of Fiji for thirty-nine years, often working in places too dangerous for Western missionaries.

He bridged the work between two major eras: cannibalism and acculturation (Tippett and Kanailagi, p. 114). His responsibilities ranged from assisting missionaries (e.g., LORIMER FISON) to pioneer evangelism and church planting to teaching and training local pastors to serving Fijian royalty. He braved life-threatening attacks from traditional religionists, political tensions and hostility, numerous hurricanes, and a measles epidemic that wiped out over forty thousand Fijians (a large proportion of the church—this set the indigenization process back by decades). Throughout, Bulu's cultural sensitivity and unwavering ability to trust God qualified him as an exemplar in bearing testimony to Christ among the Fijians.

A. SCOTT MOREAU

Bibliography. C. W. Forman, *BDCM*, p. 101; R. Tippett and T. Kanailagi, eds., *The Autobiography of Joeli Bulu: Tongan Missionary to Fiji.*

Burial Rites. *See* DEATH RITES.

Burkina Faso *(Est. 2000 pop.: 11,708,000; 274,000 sq. km. [105,791 sq. mi.]).* Christianity is a new religion in Burkina Faso. Roman Catholic missions began their work in the central part of the county at the end of the nineteenth century, in the wake of the establishment of French colonial rule over the Mossi Kingdom. The first evangelical Protestant missionaries arrived in 1921 with a vision to evangelize the Mossi. They were with the American Assemblies of God, and were followed by the CHRISTIAN AND MISSIONARY ALLIANCE (1923), SIM (1930), the WORLDWIDE EVANGELIZATION CRUSADE (1937), and the Evangelical Pentecostal Mission (1945).

The first five evangelical missions settled in specific areas of the country and evangelized the ethnic groups in their regions of ministry. This al-lowed evangelicals to occupy the land efficiently with the Assemblies of God working in the central region, the SIM in the east, the Christian and Missionary Alliance in the west, the Worldwide Evangelization Crusade and the Evangelical Pentecostal Mission in the south. Such cooperation among the original evangelical missions is a major reason for the growth and vitality of Christian communities throughout Burkina Faso in a relatively short time.

The participation of Burkinabé in the spreading of the gospel is an evidence of Christian vitality in Burkina Faso. Del Tarr recounts how, during his time as an Assemblies of God missionary in Burkina Faso, Jacques Kaboré, a Bible school student, was the human agent behind a three-month on-campus revival that resulted in 3,500 conversions to Christ (Tarr, p. 9). This is not an isolated case. The history of the other evangelical missions provides examples of Burkinabé Christians' involvement in evangelization even in the early years. They preached the gospel locally but they also carried it beyond the borders of their ethnic groups. They took their evangelistic zeal with them wherever migration led them.

Within Burkina Faso, migration and evangelistic zeal altered the Christian religious landscape in the 1970s. The denominations planted by the five original evangelical mission agencies became less regional as their adherents established their own kinds of churches in areas where they settled. New Protestant missions such as the Southern Baptists and the Mennonites also arrived in Burkina Faso at that time.

Migration to neighboring countries is an important factor in the life of Burkinabé. It was through migration that Burkinabé Christians became participants in cross-cultural missions. In Côte d'Ivoire, for instance, Burkinabé helped establish the Assemblies of God denomination. They were also active in Benin, Niger, Senegal, and Togo. Quite often they started by reaching Burkinabé immigrants in these countries. But they soon embarked on evangelizing other groups.

TITE TIÉNOU

Bibliography. D. Tarr, *Signs and Wonders in Ministry Today.*

Burma. *See* MYANMAR.

Burnout. The state of emotional, physical, and/or spiritual exhaustion that makes the missionary unable to carry out his or her work. While it is not normally terminal in life-and-death terms, it is often fatal to missionary effectiveness.

Potential causes of burnout are many, but overwork, undersupport, and prolonged exposure to the pressures of living and working cross-culturally are three of the most important. Learning the language and becoming bicultural can be particularly stressful to newcomers; living in the public view, facing unfulfilled expectations, and issues of self-esteem may be more important burnout issues for longer-term veterans.

Unfortunately, all these challenges are often compounded by a lack of pastoral care or by mission administrators insensitive to the psychological pressures their missionaries face. Reliable figures are hard to come by, but some estimate that between 20 percent and 50 percent of new missionaries fail to return for a second term. This attrition is seldom the result of theological difficulties or problems in communicating the gospel. It is almost always attributable, at least in part, to an inability to adapt to the kinds of issues that lead to burnout.

Increasingly, mission agencies are seeking ways to address the causes of burnout before they occur. Training seminars, mentoring programs, team-building efforts, pastoral care ministries, and more flexible schedules have all proven helpful. But the rigors of missionary life, particularly among some of the least reached peoples of the world, are still significant. And the limitations of human and material resources available to the worldwide missionary enterprise would seem to suggest that the issue of burnout will not soon pass from the scene.

GARY R. CORWIN

SEE ALSO Attrition.

Bibliography. M. F. Foyle, *Overcoming Missionary Stress;* M. Jones, *Psychology of Missionary Adjustment;* K. O'Donnell, ed., *Missionary Care: Counting the Cost for World Evangelization;* E. Schubert, *What Missionaries Need to Know about Burnout and Depression.*

Burns, William Chalmers (1815–68). Scottish missionary to China born in Dun, Scotland. His father was one of Scotland's most respected ministers and his mother was known for her piety. After a rebellious youth, Burns surprised his parents by preparing for the ministry. While studying theology at Glasgow he decided to become a missionary. He was accepted as a missionary to India by the Church of Scotland.

Before Burns could leave for India he became involved in the Scottish revival that began in 1839. God used him for eight years as a preacher and revivalist in Scotland, England, and Canada.

In 1846 Burns renewed his application to go to India, but the Foreign Missions Committee of the Free Church of Scotland was short of funds. At that time the Presbyterian Church of England was looking for someone to pioneer a new mission to China, and Burns applied. On April 22, 1847, Burns was ordained the first missionary to China of the Presbyterian Church of England.

Burns began his work in Canton; he later moved to Amoy and other places, arriving eventually in Peking. His method was to wear Chinese clothing, itinerate widely, and preach wherever possible. He opposed the opium and coolie trade and sought to raise consciences back home against these evils.

ROGER S. GREENWAY

Bibliography. A. Fulton, *Through Earthquake, Wind and Fire: Church and Mission in Manchuria 1867–1950;* S. Neill, *HCM.*

Burundi *(Est. 2000 pop.: 7,339,000; 27,834 sq. km. [10,747 sq. mi.]).* It is difficult to discuss the central African nation of Burundi independently of its northern neighbor, Rwanda. The two states, precolonial kingdoms with similar ethnic populations, who speak closely related Bantu languages, became after 1885 part of German East Africa. After World War I they were administered by Belgium as a League of Nations mandate, and after World War II as a United Nations Trust Territory, known as Ruanda-Urundi.

Both nations achieved independence in 1962, Burundi as a constitutional monarchy. It was the second most densely populated territory in Africa, and had an extremely low per capita income. Alongside this was a high rate of literacy and probably the highest percent of baptized Christians, both Catholic and Protestant, in Africa.

The people of Burundi—between six and seven million—all speak the same language, Kirundi; all share the same customs and all live side by side. They are divided, however (and this is true also of their northern neighbor, Rwanda), into a cattle-keeping aristocracy, the Tutsi (14%), the Hutu agriculturists (85%), and a tiny minority of indigenous pygmies, the Twa (less than 1%). The Tutsi warriors, who often appear physically different, are descended from an immigrant group coming from the north, probably about four hundred years ago, who subdued the peasant Hutu, making them their clients. The German and then Belgian colonial officials, and in some cases the missionaries also, favored the Tutsi as "natural leaders" and as more intelligent than the "Hutu peasants." In fact, the divisions between Tutsi and Hutu were originally flexible; there was intermarriage, and it was possible for a Hutu who acquired enough cattle to "become Tutsi." But in 1933 the Belgian administration introduced mandatory identity cards, which included the "ethnic identity" of the bearer, Tutsi, Hutu, or Twa. Legally, movement between groups was no longer possible. There was discrimination against the Hutu in education, in recruitment to the civil service, and, in particular, in recruitment to the army which, in Burundi, was almost totally Tutsi.

After independence (1962), the constitutional monarchy did not last long; it was overthrown by an army-led coup in 1965. The country's history since has been one of struggle between Tutsi and Hutu, with the almost exclusively Tutsi army giving that minority group the advantage, and with periods of ethnic genocide leading to the refugee exodus of hundreds and thousands of civilians into its eastern and western neighbors, Tanzania and Zaire. Parallel events in Rwanda have both influenced and been influenced by Burundi. There were military coups in Burundi in 1965, 1976, 1983, and 1993. Particularly low points were the overthrow (and killing) of the royal family in 1965, the assassination of the first popularly elected president (a Hutu) and many of his ministers in October 1993, only four months after his election, and the death of his successor in a plane crash in Rwanda in April 1994. The plane, which also carried the Rwandan president, was shot down by a rocket.

Tragically, Hutu and Tutsi Christians, baptized members of common congregations—for there was never any ethnic segregation—have not been able to separate themselves from the general social breakdown. This is true for Roman Catholic and all Protestant denominations, although of course there have been many individual acts of heroism and Christian compassion. But it is sadly clear that many Christians, including clergy and pastors, have participated in the murder of fellow-believers, even of innocent children. Where did missionaries and the church fail in their teaching? It will take many years for the churches to come to terms with what has happened, and rebuild a new foundation. For the Protestants there is a particular and bitter irony, since Ruanda-Urundi, from about 1930, was the cradle of the East Africa Revival. Members of this movement have testified to the breaking down of racial and ethnic barriers where the Holy Spirit's healing power was experienced. But even the Revival fellowship has not been enough to prevent the killings.

JOCELYN MURRAY

Butler, Fanny Jane (1850–89). English pioneer medical missionary to India. The eighth child of ten born to a museum curator, she grew up surrounded by good books. Intensely musical, she could read when she was three. She gave herself to Christ when she was thirteen. Meeting a CHINA INLAND MISSION couple in Birmingham, she resolved to work in China. But then Dr. Elmslie of Srinagar's dying appeal for women medical missionaries directed her to the School of Medicine for Women in London, of which she was the first student. When she qualified in Dublin in 1877, she became the first fully qualified English woman medical missionary. After study in Calcutta and language training, in 1883 she moved to Bhagalpur, where in four years she created an effective outpatient system and developed considerable pediatric skills. After a visit to see CMS work in Amritsar in 1886, she was inspired to volunteer to go to Kashmir, whence, after a short furlough, she arrived in December 1888. She organized the start of a much longed for women's hospital in Srinager but tragically died of complications from dysentery two weeks after the foundation stone was laid. A simple gospel preacher, she is probably most significant for showing what could be achieved through love in the way of preventive medicine. In 1890 a Fanny Butler Scholarship was created to train women medical missionary candidates in London.

ELEANOR M. JACKSON

Bibliography. E. M. Tonge, *Fanny Jane Butler, Pioneer Medical Missionary.*

Cc

Cable, (Alice) Mildred (1877–1952). English missionary to China. Born in Surrey, England, she qualified as a chemist, studied also in the fields of surgery and midwifery, and in 1902 was sent by the CHINA INLAND MISSION to Shansi Province, where she joined Eva and Francesca French in developing a girls' school. At heart, however, they were pioneers, and in 1923 the three moved to Suchow, whence they made many hazardous journeys through the Gobi Desert, Inner Mongolia, Sinkiang, and Chinese Turkestan, and occasionally fell into the hands of brigands or communist bands. They studied manners and customs of the people, and evangelized in the oases; Mildred recounted their experiences in such books as *Through Jade Gate and Central Asia* (with Eva French, 1927), *Something Happened* (with Francesca French, 1935), and *The Gobi Desert* (1942). Worsening political conditions compelled them to leave the area in 1936, and Mildred returned to England, where she continued to write while working for the British and Foreign Bible Society. She also produced the life stories of Percy Mather (1935) and George Hunter (1948).

J. D. DOUGLAS

Bibliography. W. C. Northcott, *Star over Gobi: The Story of Mildred Cable;* E. M. Sawyer, *Mildred Cable;* P. Thompson, *Desert Pilgrim: The Story of Mildred Cable's Venture for God in Central Asia.*

Cabrini, Frances Xavier (1850–1917). Italian-born missionary to the United States. Born Maria Francesca Cabrini in Sant' Angelo Lodigiano, Lombardy, Italy, she studied to become a teacher. Her attempts to become a religious were initially turned down due to frail health. Working at the House of Providence orphanage in Codogno, she made her vows there in 1877. Three years later, Cabrini founded the Institute of the Missionary Sisters of the Sacred Heart with seven orphan girls. After the establishment of several houses in northern Italy, the organization received papal approval in 1888. She served as its mother-general until her death.

Abandoning a desire from childhood to go as a missionary to China (anticipation of which led her to adopt the name Frances Xavier), Cabrini obeyed the request of Pope Leo XIII and accepted the invitation of Archbishop Michael Corrigan in 1889 to care for impoverished Italian immigrants in New York City. Her activities eventually expanded as she established more schools, orphanages, and hospitals in the United States, Latin America, and Europe. In 1909 she became a naturalized American citizen. Devoted to Christ and with an indomitable spirit, she triumphed over enormous challenges in her ministry to immigrants and other needy people, winning widespread respect and inspiring other women to join her.

When she died from malaria in 1917, there were an estimated 1,500 daughters in 67 religious houses. Mother Cabrini was canonized a saint by Pope Pius XII on July 7, 1946, for her heroic faith and service to humankind. She was the first American to receive this honor; her feast day is December 22. In 1950, the Catholic Church proclaimed her Patroness of Immigrants.

GARY B. McGEE

Bibliography. P. Di Donato, *Immigrant Saint: The Life of Mother Cabrini;* T. Maynard, *Too Small a World: The Life of Francesca Cabrini.*

Call, The. *See* THE MISSIONARY CALLING.

Calverley, Edwin Elliott (1882–1971). American renowned Islamics scholar and missionary in the Middle East. Born in Philadelphia, Pennsylvania, he received his education at The City's College, Princeton University, Princeton Theological Seminary, and Hartford Seminary Foundation. At the latter, he was mentored by Duncan Black MacDonald and completed a Ph.D. in Arabic and Islamics in 1923. The Philadelphia Presbytery of the Presbyterian Church (U.S.A.) ordained him in 1908. In the same year, he married Eleanor Jane Taylor, M.D., a recent graduate of the

Woman's Medical College of Pennsylvania in Philadelphia.

Joining the Arabian Mission of the Reformed Church in America in 1909, they went as missionaries to the Persian Gulf and served in Bahrain, Iraq, and Kuwait. An illness forced him to return home with his family in 1930. After recovery, Calverley then began a long and distinguished career on the faculty of the Kennedy School of Missions at Hartford Seminary Foundation. His expertise in Arabic and Islamics gained recognition from several professional organizations of which he was a member: American Council of Learned Societies, American Oriental Society, Royal Asiatic Society, and Royal Central Asian Society. In 1939, he was appointed to the Translations Committee of the American Bible Society. Calverley's books include *Arabian Primer, I and II* (1920), *Arabian Reader* (1925), *Worship in Islam* (1925), and *Islam, An Introduction* (1958). He served as co-editor of *The Muslim World* with Samuel M. Zwemer (1938–47), editor of *The Muslim World* (1948–52), and afterward as an associate editor. As a visiting professor, he taught at Columbia University, American University in Cairo, Johns Hopkins University, American University in Washington, D.C., and Boston University School of Theology.

GARY B. MCGEE

Bibliography. E. H. Douglas, *The Muslim World* 61 (July 1971): 155–58; E. E. Calverley, *The Muslim World* 61 (July 1971): 159–60.

Calvinism. A system of doctrine and an historical phenomenon. As a doctrinal system, Calvinism stresses certain truths that have a clear bearing on mission, three of which stand out.

First, Calvinism insists that the glory of God is the primary goal of all thought and action, including mission. "The chief end of man," says the Westminister Shorter Catechism, "is to glorify God and to enjoy him forever." Therefore, Calvinism opposes the common tendency to regard human beings and their happiness as the central concern of mission. While Calvinism clearly regards human well-being as important, and concern for the temporal and eternal welfare of humans motivates many kinds of mission activity, the glory of God remains the primary goal.

Calvinists find ample support for this in Scripture. Jesus summed up his work saying, "I have brought you (Father) glory on earth by completing the work you gave me to do" (John 17:4). Since Christ's mission on earth was to glorify the Father and he passed on his mission to his disciples, the primary goal of the church's mission can be none other than to glorify God. "As you (Father) sent me into the world, I have sent them into the world." "As the Father has sent me, I am sending you" (John 17:18; 20:21).

Missionaries who take as their chief goal the glory of God enjoy theological underpinnings that help them persevere when from a human standpoint the mission is impossible. Calvinists cling to the truth that whatever the immediate and visible results of their work may be, God is glorified when his servants carry out their assignments humbly, faithfully, and in accord with his Word.

Second, Calvinism stresses the all-embracing doctrine of the KINGDOM OF GOD, which was the main theme of Jesus' preaching. For Calvinists, Christ's lordship extends to every inch of the globe and to every area of public and private life. This claim is affirmed in the very preface to Christ's commission in Matthew 28:18–19: "All authority in heaven and earth has been given to me. Therefore go and make disciples of all nations, baptizing them in the name of the Father and of the Son and of the Holy Spirit, and teaching them to obey everything I have commanded you." Christ's claim to universal authority has powerful implications for mission work and discipleship.

Christ is Lord over all, Calvinists insist, and his Word speaks with authority to rich and poor, politicians and academicians, merchants and military, parents and children. The Word the church proclaims turns the searchlight of divine truth and righteousness upon every area of life and every human relationship. Nothing lies outside the boundaries of Christ's reign.

When Christian mission fails to teach and operate from this perspective, a form of Christianity develops that treats religious faith and morality as individual matters and leaves the public square unaffected. Churches may grow in size and number but if they fail to educate members to apply kingdom values to society at large, they fail in their role as lighthouses of the kingdom and they set the stage for suffering, violence, and revolution. The mission world is currently awakening to its failure to address the broader implications of Christ's kingdom for the plight of the poor, systemic injustices, racial tensions, and misuse of the ENVIRONMENT (*see* HOLISTIC MISSION).

A third major emphasis of Calvinist theology that has a bearing on mission is the doctrine of the SOVEREIGNTY OF GOD. Calvinism stresses the fact that mission work is first and foremost the Lord's work, not ours. He calls and equips his servants to co-labor with him in gathering his chosen ones from every corner of the earth.

Recognition of the sovereignty of God has the dual effect of keeping missionaries humble when their work goes especially well, and encouraging them when the opposition seems overwhelming. The Bible tells us that when Paul and Barnabas returned to their "sending" church in Antioch, "they gathered the church together and reported all that God had done through them and how he had opened the door of faith to the Gentiles" (Acts 14:27). Their summary of what had taken place is very instructive. They ascribed the glory to God by attributing the success they enjoyed to God's working through them and opening doors they never could have opened. Paul and Barnabas did not ignore what they as missionaries had done. They had preached, taken risks, faced opposition, gathered converts, and started churches. But the bottom line was that the work was the Lord's, not theirs. They made this plain when they reported to the church.

Besides humility, the truth of divine sovereignty offers encouragement to missionaries who tremble at the magnitude of the task before them. Calvinism reminds them that even the best preachers cannot reach farther than people's ear drums and God alone can cause sinners to respond to the gospel's call. God acts in saving power in accord with his sovereign and eternal will.

Paul the missionary succinctly summarizes God's sovereign activity in salvation and mission: "Those he predestined, he also called; those he called, he also justified; those he justified, he also glorified" (Rom. 8:30). Clearly, God uses missionaries as his callers, his co-workers. His eternal purpose and sovereign power make their mission possible and assure them that their work will not be in vain (Isa. 55:10–13). The open acknowledgment of this comforting truth is something Calvinism offers mission.

Historically, Calvinism has played a major role in the Protestant mission enterprise over the past two centuries. A large percentage, in some cases the majority, of missionaries serving in parts of Africa, Asia, and Latin America have been Calvinists. There are critics who argue that Calvinism's emphasis on the sovereignty of God discourages mission. And even among Calvinists there are a few who excuse their neglect of mission by arguing that divine predestination removes the need for human efforts to win the lost. Calvinism's defense lies in its submission to the Scriptures which clearly teach both divine sovereignty and Christian duty to co-labor with God in mission.

ROGER S. GREENWAY

Bibliography. J. H. Bavinck, *An Introduction to the Science of Missions;* C. E. Edwards, *The Evangelical Quarterly* 8 (January 1936): 48–51; J. D. Gort, *OBMR* 4 (October 1980): 156–60; N. M. Steffens, *The Presbyterian and Reformed Review* 18 (April 1894): 241–53; S. M. Zwemer, *Theology Today* 7 (July 1950): 206–16.

Cámara, Helder Pessao (1909–). Brazilian priest and theologian; champion of the poor. Born in Fortaleza, the twelfth of thirteen children, he was thoroughly acquainted with the rigors of poverty and its consequences. Ordained to the priesthood at twenty-two, he became active in politics, in public and religious education, as well as concern over the role the church should play to enable it to meet the needs of the people. In 1952, shortly after his consecration as a bishop, he organized the National Conference of the bishops of Brazil and was its secretary for twelve years. This became the leading force for social change in the country. Named auxiliary bishop of Rio de Janero (1952), he helped in the formation of the Council of Latin American Bishops (CELAM), serving as its vice president, 1959–65. In 1965 he was named archbishop of Olinda and Recife, where he served until his retirement in 1985. During his tenure his stand for economic development and pacifism was severely opposed by the government and he was eventually banned from speaking in public between 1968 and 1977. He countered with a strong position on nonviolence, which he parlayed in North America and Western Europe, where he received honorary degrees and his writings were in great demand. His simplicity and acclaimed saintliness have won for him a place among the defenders of the poor of the world.

PABLO E. PÉREZ

Cambodia *(Est. 2000 pop.: 11,637,000; 181,035 sq. km. [69,898 sq. mi.]).* Cambodia is bordered by Thailand, Vietnam, and Laos. It is estimated that less than 0.5 percent of its people are Christians and less than 0.1 percent Protestants, though recent growth rates have exceeded 20 percent annually.

The Khmer, the largest people group, developed a sophisticated Hindu culture in the tenth century. By the twelfth century, the kings had created Angkor Wat, a temple-like city that symbolized prosperity and invulnerability. The Angkor Empire collapsed in the fifteenth century, and for the next four hundred years Cambodia was embroiled in numerous wars with her neighbors. It was a protectorate of France from 1863 to 1945.

Cambodia became an unwilling participant in the Vietnam War when the king allowed the Viet Minh sanctuary. This resulted in U.S. bombing of Cambodia, which in turn opened the door for the Khmer Rouge, led by Pol Pot, to seize control in April 1975. Pol Pot carried out one of the bloodiest socialist revolutions in history in which one to 3 million lost their lives and hundreds of thousands fled the country.

Mission History. Roman Catholics first entered Cambodia in the sixteenth century with little results. The rulers persecuted and expelled all missionaries. It was only in the second half of the eighteenth century that mission work began to see some success among the Khmer.

During the time of French rule, the Khmer were relatively open to Christianity. Even so, conversions were still few in number. By the

1960s, there were about sixty thousand Catholics, of whom only three thousand were Khmer.

Protestant missionaries arrived in 1923 first under the Oriental Missionary Society (now OMS INTERNATIONAL) and later under the CHRISTIAN AND MISSIONARY ALLIANCE (CMA). The CMA missionaries initially made little progress due to the opposition of the French rulers. In 1965, King Sihanouk, believing Christianity to be anti-nationalistic, prohibited foreign missionaries. In 1970, when the king was deposed, foreign missionaries returned and experienced a new openness to Christ among the Khmer. Before 1970, there were roughly six hundred Protestant Christians. When the Khmer Rouge took over the country in 1975, there were over nine thousand. During the Pol Pot regime many of them died or fled the country. Today there is no record of Khmer Christians in Cambodia, although one source reports twelve small congregations of less than one hundred each in Phnom Penh.

From 1979 to 1991, the country was embroiled in civil war. Three separate parties have tried to overthrow the Vietnamese-backed regime led by Heng Samrin. With a semblance of peace due to UN efforts, many mission and social organizations are making inroads into Cambodia.

VIOLET JAMES

Bibliography. D. Chandler, *A History of Cambodia;* idem, *Facing the Cambodian Past;* F. Ponchaud, *The Cathedral of the Rice Paddy;* idem, *Cambodia Year Zero.*

Cameroon, United Republic of *(Est. 2000 pop.: 15,245,000; 475,442 sq. km. [183,568 sq. mi.]).* In 1845 Jamaican and British Baptist missionaries introduced Christianity in what is now Cameroon, at Victoria and Douala. In 1850, the Board of Foreign Mission of the Presbyterian Church-USA established a mission on the island of Corisco, forty miles north of the mouth of the Gabon River Estuary and just off the coast of Rio Muni. This served as a point of departure for evangelistic work along the coast, including what is now Cameroon. Catholics began work in 1890, while, two years later, Presbyterian missionaries moved into the southern Cameroon interior. The Bulu were among the first to respond. By 1930 the largely Bulu congregation at Elat (Ebolowa) was the largest Presbyterian Church in the world. The overwhelming majority of Christians belong to churches which owe their origins to these three traditions. Smaller numbers belong to Lutheran or various Pentecostal and African Initiated Churches.

While most of the population in southern and western Cameroon, which was turning to Christianity, observed traditional religions, Islam dominated in the north. Evangelistic outreach there began later and proved more difficult. At present, two-thirds of the population of Cameroon professes to be Christian. However, few Christians are in the north. There are over thirty denominations.

In the years leading up to national independence in 1960, the mission agencies handed power to Cameroonian bodies, including oversight of agricultural, broadcasting, educational, medical, translation, and other ministries. With limited resources, contemporary Cameroonian Christians have struggled to maintain these ministries through church planting, evangelism, and social outreach, especially in the areas of rural development and urban poverty. Cameroonian Christians have been among leaders in Africa in formulating a contextual approach to theological education and a holistic approach to mission.

At times, especially during the years immediately before and after Cameroon became independent in 1960 and in the early 1990s, church-state relations have been troubled. Conflict has arisen, in part, when Christian leaders have identified with political parties actively supporting a major political rival of the head of state. For example, in the early 1970s, the Catholic bishop of Nkongsamba, Cameroon's third largest city, was implicated in a plot against former President Ahmadou Ahidjo. More generally, the exercise of the churches' prophetic ministry has engendered tension as the churches have championed democratization, defended human rights, and challenged the government to address problems of the poor and marginalized.

PAUL R. DEKAR

Bibliography. L. E. Kwast, *The Discipling of West Cameroon: A Study of Baptist Growth.*

Camping. Temporary community living designed to enrich the Christian life. The customary focus is a camp, conference, retreat, or outdoor center. Although an urban environment is possible, a natural setting connecting campers to the powerful witness of God's creation is the usual site of organized camping. The temporary community enables people to come apart from the social pressures of their permanent communities, pressures that often hinder change, and to gain new perspectives on their lives and God. Camping is highly relational and introduces participants to a compelling community of love, fellowship, and shared experiences where Christian beliefs and values can be seen and tried under supportive leadership. The continuous day-by-day guided process of growth and the expectations of taking risks, trying new activities, and meeting new people open the participants to taking new steps of faith in the development of a Christlike character. While many institutions focus on a certain dimension of the person, camp is designed to minister to the whole person—physically, mentally, socially, and spiritually. Camping aims to provide powerful, memorable experiences that point to specific spiritual and biblical truths. The daily regimen of an isolated camp community offers a rich opportunity for development of Christian leadership for the church and society.

Although outdoor living goes back to the creation of humankind, and the Bible recounts the nomadic life of the patriarchs of the Jewish nation, the forty-year wandering of the children of Israel, and Christ's use of the out-of-doors for his ministry, historians view organized camping as a North American innovation of the late nineteenth century. They acknowledge, however, that the camp meetings of the Second Great Awakening at the turn of the nineteenth century set the pattern of future camping practices. Outdoor meeting sites drew people away from potentially harmful pursuits in the cities to do business with God as the frontier was being settled. The camp meeting was replaced by the Bible conference toward the end of the nineteenth century as organized camping grew.

Many of the early leaders of the movement were devout Christians whose zeal not only led them to create their own camping ministries, but also helped others to do likewise. Examples of this zeal are Luther Gulick and his wife Charlotte. The children of missionary parents, they started a camp for families at Gales Ferry, Connecticut, in 1887, taught at the School of Christian Workers (which later became the International YMCA College and eventually Springfield College), traveled to Europe on behalf of the international YMCA to spread ideas on camping and creation, and recruited hundreds of men and women to serve abroad as recreational workers and camp leaders. Charlotte is credited with founding the Camp Fire Girls, and Luther along with others founded the Boy Scouts of America. Christian missionaries and missionary societies along with organizations like the YMCA, the International Sunday School Association, the International Council on Religious Education, Scripture Union, and Inter-Varsity Fellowship have taken the camping movement throughout the world.

The need for mutual encouragement, fellowship, and sharing of ideas and resources drew evangelical camp leaders together simultaneously in California and New England in 1950 and in the Midwest and Canada shortly thereafter. These groups merged in 1961 as the Christian Camp and Conference Association and then became Christian Camping International (CCI) in 1963 as international camps were added to the membership. CCI is an alliance that aims to strengthen temporary community ministries worldwide.

BUD WILLIAMS

Bibliography. E. Eells, *Eleanor Eells' History of Organized Camping: The First 100 Years;* D. Klopfenstein, D. Klopfenstein, and B. Williams, *Come Yourselves Apart: Christian Leadership in the Temporary Community;* B. Williams, *Organizational History of Christian Camping International.*

Campus Ministry. *See* STUDENT MISSION WORK.

Canada *(Est. 2000 pop.: 31,029,000; 9,970,610 sq. km. [3,849,653 sq. mi.]).* Canada is the world's second largest country in size, covering five time zones. Yet it has just over 30 million inhabitants, a mosaic of over one hundred nationalities, their religions ranging from Asian shamanism to African animism to European "churchianity" and secular humanism.

However, Christian principles shaped this nation even before the Confederation in 1867. Many of the million British loyalists who headed north after the American War of Independence were devout Anglicans, Baptists, Congregationalists, Methodists, and Presbyterians. On the Prairies the subsequent influx of Anabaptists, reflecting Pietist views, mixed with other immigrants. The Quebec Act of 1774 gave the Roman Catholic Church in that province the right to act as a quasi-state.

Ambivalence and Tolerance. Eighty percent of Canada's inhabitants live within a hundred miles of the southern border, where the climate is least inhospitable, and the land is most arable. Of the world's exportable grain, Canada provides 20 percent (80% of its own production). However, the narrow ribbon of population stretches nearly four thousand miles from west to east, mostly along the southern border. There are only three cities of more than one million people: Vancouver (west coast), Toronto (heartland), and Montreal (east). Thus evangelism and missionary outreach tend to be very regional.

Many Canadians are ambivalent about their national identity, as, on the one hand, ethnic minorities celebrate their traditions, and, on the other hand, the culture and commerce of the United States flood across the world's longest unprotected border. Canada has only one-tenth the population of the United States but is its chief trading partner. The percentage of evangelicals in Canada (officially 7% but actually 14%, according to statistician George Rawlyk) is much lower than in America (over 30%). Separation of church and state has never been the issue it is in the United States, but then Canadians like to appear moderate about most issues.

What has been characteristic of Canadians is a mind-set that is, for the most part, tolerant of plurality in culture, religion, and ideology. After all, Canada became a nation only as a compromise between the English and the French. Because of provincial representation, the benevolent pacifism of Mennonites and other refugees in the three Prairie provinces (Alberta, Saskatchewan, Manitoba) influenced politics and society out of proportion to their numbers, and helped to sensitize the young nation to world need. Per capita charitable giving, including to missions, is among the highest in the world. The ratio of missionary sending to population has vied with New Zealand and Norway for top place.

Revival and Missions. Revival movements, such as "The Great Awakening" of the 1700s, made an impact on local communities and on government (*see* GREAT AWAKENINGS). The 1800s were dubbed "The Evangelical Century." On the official seal of the Dominion of Canada are words chosen from Psalm 72:8: "He shall have dominion from sea to sea."

Up to the early 1800s, most missionary work was directed from denominational headquarters in Europe. Gradually Canadian churches awakened to their own responsibilities. In the late 1800s, the STUDENT VOLUNTEER MOVEMENT motivated many men and women to become missionaries. Canada's InterVarsity Christian Fellowship, founded in 1929, held its first student missions conference in Toronto in 1946. That conference became the noted student missions recruitment convention now held in Urbana, Illinois. Canadians participate in "Urbana" but also hold their own regional student missions events, which motivate hundreds of young men and women to consider missions (*see also* URBANA MISSION CONFERENCES).

Prairie Bible Institute and Toronto Bible College (now Ontario Bible College and Theological Seminary) were among dozens of Bible schools initially established to prepare men and women for missionary service. Recruits from the vast prairies, accustomed to simple, rugged living and resourcefulness, made successful pioneer missionaries in developing countries. As a result, a century ago some British-oriented missions would accept workers from Canada but hesitated over Americans!

Religious Plurality. The ethnic mosaic has continued to expand, as the United Nations for several years named Canada the most desirable nation in which to live. The UN also lists Toronto as the most ethnically diverse city in North America. The city hosts the largest Italian and Somali communities outside of their homelands. Vancouver has the second largest community of Sikh expatriates in the world. Nationwide, the influx of Chinese and Korean Christians has spurred evangelical witness, particularly in churches that had lost their missionary vision.

Now far removed from its Christian roots, Canada's secularized society is scarred by overt immorality and radical humanism. The communications media enjoy casting churches either as irrelevant or bigoted. In a major exhibit in 1990, the Royal Ontario Museum stereotyped pioneer Canadian missionaries to Africa as adventurers, racists, and destroyers of culture, out to extend the British Empire. Yet the very missionaries the Museum cited as examples were just the opposite, as documented by their journals in the Museum archives!

Native Canadians, or First Nations members (terms preferred to "Indians"), continue to present a special need, as the news media have publicized abuses by several church boarding schools earlier in the 1900s. Meanwhile New Age views romanticize "native spirituality"—rejected by evangelical native churches.

Anglo-French tension, perpetuated by a minority of Quebec secessionists, also is part of the Canadian mosaic. Up to the late 1950s, missionaries from English-speaking Canada were pelted with stones and sometimes imprisoned for public witness; the Martin Luther film was banned. Now the power of the Roman Catholic Church is largely disregarded by Quebecois, and French-speaking evangelical churches multiply faster than the availability of trained leaders.

Canada constitutes a fertile mission field in itself, and also has the potential, in personnel and financial support, to provide missionaries within the nation and to other lands.

W. HAROLD FULLER

Bibliography. A. J. Austin, *Evangelical Studies Bulletin,* Spring 1997; J. W. Grant, ed., *The Churches and the Canadian Experience;* A. Motz, ed., *Reclaiming a Nation;* G. A. Rawlyk and M. A. Noll, *Amazing Grace;* B. C. Stiller, *From the Tower of Babel to Parliament Hill.*

Canadian Mission Boards and Societies. Samuel de Champlain, who founded Quebec city (1608), declared, "The salvation of a single soul is worth more than the conquest of an empire." He was sympathetic to the French Calvinistic Huguenots, several of whom accompanied him and settled in Acadia/Novia Scotia (1605) and Quebec (1608). However, the early influence of these Protestants was snuffed out by the Jesuits, who arrived in 1611, and gained control of "New France" by 1620, blocking further Huguenot immigration.

Jesuit, Franciscan, and other Roman Catholic missionaries suffered much physical hardship and, in some cases, torture and death at the hands of those they sought to win to the Church. Outreach to the far West was carried on chiefly by the Oblates of Mary Immaculate (OMI).

An early Protestant pioneer was Johann Christian Erhardt, a Moravian who visited Labrador in 1752 but was killed by the Inuit. Other Moravians arrived in 1764 and established self-supporting Christian settlements (*see also* MORAVIAN MISSION). English medical missionary WILFRED T. GRENFELL drew world attention to the plight of the native peoples of Labrador by his work 140 years later.

JOHN ELIOT'S 1661 translation of the New Testament for the Algonquins (who extended into Upper Canada) was the forerunner of Bible translations that spurred Protestant mission in Canada. The first non-English publication of the British and Foreign Bible Society was the Gospel of Mark, translated by a Mohawk chief (published 1804). The CHURCH MISSION SOCIETY undertook the evangelization of the west and north. A Methodist missionary invented a syllabic script for a Cree translation. Presbyterians and others joined in the outreach. By 1914 those efforts had resulted in an estimated three-quarters of native Canadians becoming Christian. However, since then, native peoples have suffered the impact of social vices and face great spiritual and physical problems. Today native churches and missions continue pastoral and missionary outreach among their own people.

Increasingly, Canadians responded to the call of missions overseas. Among the pioneers were Baptist Samuel Day (India 1835); Presbyterians GEORGE L. MACKAY (China 1888); Salvationist ROWLAND V. BINGHAM (Africa 1893); Baptists Archibald and Jean Reekie (Bolivia 1898). Pentecostal missions began developing early in the 1900s, with four Canadians taking part in a project in Liberia (1908).

Two Canadians who launched global missions were close friends and fellow gospel entrepreneurs. ALBERT B. SIMPSON began as a Canadian Presbyterian before moving to pulpits in the United States. Trainer of missionaries, editor, and author, he founded the CHRISTIAN AND MISSIONARY ALLIANCE in 1897. Bingham, Simpson's friend, pioneered the Sudan Interior Mission (*see* SOCIETY FOR INTERNATIONAL MINISTRIES) in 1893, opened Canada's Keswick spiritual life conference as a mission-sending base, and initiated a mission-focused magazine, a publishing house, and a mission to the armed forces.

In 1928, another Presbyterian minister, Oswald J. Smith, started Peoples Church, a non-denominational work that gained international missions fame. Traveling to 80 countries, Smith contributed to missiology through slogans, the "faith pledge," many of his 1200 hymns, poems, and gospel songs, and his 35 books (six million copies, 128 languages).

World War II exposed Christian members of Canada's armed forces to the spiritual and physical needs of other lands. Reports influenced groups such as the Mennonites to become active in missions and development projects. By the 1960s, Canadian foreign missionaries numbered over four thousand. The highest proportion of these came from Associated Gospel (AGC), Brethren, and Fellowship of Evangelical Baptists churches, although the majority served outside their own denominational missions—most under missions are linked with the INTERDENOM-INATIONAL FOREIGN MISSIONS ASSOCIATION (Canada Branch). Most evangelical denominational missions are linked with the EVANGELICAL FELLOWSHIP OF MISSION AGENCIES (USA) through their member bodies in America. Other global evangelistic associations registered in Canada include AD 2000, Lausanne Committee on World Evangelism (LCWE; *see* LAUSANNE MOVEMENT), and WORLD EVANGELICAL FELLOWSHIP.

As to media-related global outreach from Canada, Bible Stories Alive ("A Visit with Mrs. G.") produces and records dramatized Bible stories in 30 languages and ships tapes to 170 countries. These are also broadcast by international missionary radio stations (ELWA, FEBC, HCJB, TWR) and are on 500 radio stations in America alone. A high-tech counterpart is Galcom Inc., a radionics mission which has developed solar-powered, pocket-sized, fix-tuned radio receivers and distributes them around the world—especially significant in "limited access" countries.

In 1996 the Evangelical Fellowship of Canada revived the EFC Task Force on Missions, which works with church and agency leaders seeking to maximize the effectiveness of Canadian evangelicals in global mission. As well, EFC has recommissioned Vision Canada 2000 to promote evangelization within the nation.

Acceptability of Canadian missionaries is enhanced in certain sensitive nations, because they see it as a tolerant, conciliatory country that is not a major world power. The country's multiculturalism and pluralism have led some non-Canadian missions to use its ethnic communities as a base for orientating candidates headed for other lands. Canada's missionary heritage and its human and financial resources position it to play an active part in the cause of world missions.

W. HAROLD FULLER

Bibliography. A. J. Austin, *Evangelical Studies Bulletin.* Spring 1997; J. W. Grant, ed., *The Churches and the Canadian Experience;* A. Motz, ed., *Reclaiming a Nation;* G. A. Rawlyk and M. A. Noll, *Amazing Grace;* B. C. Stiller, *From the Tower of Babel to Parliament Hill.*

Canberra Assembly (1991). *See* WORLD COUNCIL OF CHURCHES ASSEMBLIES.

Candidacy. That time in the missions realm that parallels the engagement period in the realm of marriage. Before someone becomes part of a mission agency, both the agency and the individual must determine that compatibility exists. The period in which that is being evaluated is known as candidacy. Both the individual and the agency have expressed real interest, but neither has made a formal or final commitment.

As in an engagement period before the wedding takes place, there is a lot that happens during a time of candidacy. If this does not include a growing sense of confidence, intimacy, and affection, the "engagement" is usually broken off. The context in which the candidacy takes place includes a whole regimen of activities for the purpose of contact, communication, and examination. Some of these are handled by correspondence, some by personal interviews, but the most significant ones by spending time together during an orientation or candidate school. Issues of character and ministry skills are much less often assumed than they once were, and are given careful scrutiny along with a candidate's education and knowledge base.

Besides better acquainting the mission with the character and qualifications of the candidate, these schools also expand the candidate's understanding of the policies, practices, and ethos of the mission. Because more and more candidates come from broken homes or have suffered from other emotional traumas, over the last couple of decades personality and psychological testing has become an important addition to the standard procedures.

Strong candidacy programs include interaction with the home church of each candidate, reflecting the fact that it really is the church that sends the missionary. Many missions will not even consider a candidate who does not have an enthusiastic endorsement from their sending church base.

GARY R. CORWIN

Bibliography. R. W. Ferris, ed., *Establishing Ministry Training: A Manual for Programme Developers;* D. Harley, *Preparing to Serve: Training for Cross-Cultural Mission;* L. E. Reed, *Preparing Missionaries for Intercultural Communication: A Bicultural Approach;* W. D. Taylor, ed., *Internationalizing Missionary Training: A Global Perspective.*

Candidate Selection. Statisticians estimate that there are over 144,000 missionaries worldwide and that this number of cross-cultural Christian workers will continue to grow. They note that this burgeoning missionary force will come increasingly from non-Western countries.

Principles of candidate selection for ministry can be found in both the Old and New Testaments. Jethro advised Moses to select capable men who met certain qualifications to serve as judges (Exod. 18:21). Those selected to work on the tabernacle had to possess certain skills and abilities (Exod. 35:10, 30–35). The same was true for replacement of an apostle (Acts 1:21–22) or the institution of a new leadership role for deacons (Acts 6:3).

Candidate selection is most healthy when viewed from a systems perspective. Effective selection procedures must work in tandem with the follow-up support scaffolding of continuous training and mentoring, or approved candidates will be shortchanged in their total ministry effectiveness. Selection procedures should be considered one step in a system designed not only to re-

cruit and qualify capable candidates, but also to provide ministry-long maintenance.

Selection benchmarks should be specific to the task anticipated. What qualifies a person for missionary CHURCH PLANTING does not automatically qualify the candidate for BIBLE TRANSLATION, dorm parenting, tentmaking, or camp ministries. To assure sound selection benchmarks are in place, wise selectors will attempt to determine the minimal skills required for effectiveness for a particular position. Additionally, they must ask what commitment, competency, cultural, and character benchmarks will be required to accomplish these tasks effectively. Commitment benchmarks would include a sense of God's call to ministry and staying power, a firm grasp of Scripture, and appropriate ministry skills. Other minimal qualifications may include flexibility and empathetic contextual skills, servant-leadership and-followership, and moral purity.

The use of multiple assessment tools can provide the selectors and the candidate with a comprehensive evaluation. Many agencies use personal interviews, doctrinal statements, letters of reference, and psychological testing. Some require additional participation in simulation exercises or supervised ministry experience. Multiple assessment tools, when tied to specific future ministry tasks, can provide all parties with a comprehensive evaluation.

ATTRITION (premature departures) carries a heavy price tag: lost ministry opportunities, lost finances, family stress, and friction between institutions. While justifiable reasons for attrition exist (such as marriage, failing health, retirement, and care of parents), unjustifiable reasons also exist (such as peer conflict, moral problems, and adjustment and training issues). It therefore becomes incumbent on each agency leader in every country to track and investigate the accuracy of the reasons given for attrition. Such research, when not inhibited by pride on the part of agency leadership or the involved Christian worker, will assist selectors in the necessary adjustments of the selection and follow-up procedures.

Those involved as candidate selectors should represent the institutions who will provide the candidate future support in some manner. These institutions may include the sending churches, agencies, national churches, and training institutions. Institutional partnership in the selection process will ensure ownership and accountability. Such partnership in selection also demonstrates to the candidate the concern and credibility of each part.

TOM A. STEFFAN

Bibliography. T. Graham, *EMQ* 23:1 (1987): 70–79; C. Ridley, *How to Select Church Planters: A Self-Study Manual for Recruiting, Screening, Interviewing and Eval-*

uating Qualified Church Planters; B. Sawatsky, *EMQ* 27:4 (1991): 342–47.

Candomble. *See* LATIN AMERICAN NEW RELIGIOUS MOVEMENTS.

Canon. *See* BIBLE.

Cape Verde *(Est. 2000 pop.: 448,000; 4,033 sq. km. [1,557 sq. mi.]).* Cape Verde consists of an archipelago of ten islands and five islets in the Atlantic Ocean off the coast of West Africa. It is a former Portuguese colony that gained independence in 1975. Eighty percent of the population is Caboverdian Mestico, of whom 98 percent are Christian, the vast majority being Roman Catholic. Evangelical Protestants represent less than 4 percent of the population. The most successful has been the Church of the Nazarene, with over twenty congregations and nearly ten thousand members.

TODD M. JOHNSON

Carey, Lott (1780–1828). African American pioneer missionary to Liberia. Lott was a Baptist missionary and a respected leader of the freed African American slaves who colonized Liberia on the west coast of Africa in the early nineteenth century. After buying his freedom, Carey was converted at the racially mixed First Baptist Church of Richmond, Virginia, where he became active in ministry and was licensed to preach. Along with his mentor, William Crane, he helped form the Richmond African Missionary Society, an auxiliary to the General Missionary Convention of the Baptist Denomination in the United States of America for Foreign Missions, known as the Triennial Convention, which was organized in 1814.

Carey's interest in Baptist mission endeavors led to his personal desire to go to Africa as a missionary. In 1821 he and a small group of Baptist freed slaves sailed for Africa. Though they sailed under the auspices of the American Colonization Society, established in 1816 to facilitate the return of freed slaves to Africa, Carey's passion was missions and it was his distinction to be the first U.S. Baptist missionary to Africa.

Once in Liberia, Carey became a leader of the African American colony and actively engaged in a number of significant ministries, including the establishment of the first Baptist church in Monrovia (known as Providence Baptist Church), which he served as pastor. His concern for education led to help establish schools in and around Monrovia for settlers and for indigent children and to establish a mission school in Grand Cape Mount among the Vai people. This school was an especially satisfying project for Carey who, unlike other settlers, had a great zeal

to evangelize the indigents. In an effort to promote mission work among the indigenous tribes, Carey led in the establishment of the Monrovia Baptist Missionary Society and he was chosen its first president.

In spite of Carey's untimely, accidental death, he left a legacy of godly leadership and ministry etched in Baptist missions history in Africa and in the effort to bring both Christianity and Western civilization to Africa by colonization with freed American slaves.

RICHARD D. CALENBERG

Bibliography. M. M. Fisher, *Journal of Negro History* 7 (1922): 380–418; L. Fitts, *Lott Carey, First Black Missionary to Africa;* S. M. Jacobs, ed., *Black Americans and the Missionary Movement in Africa;* W. A. Poe, *Church History* 39 (1970): 49–61; T. W. Shick, *Behold the Promised Land: A History of the Afro-American Settlers in Nineteenth Century Liberia.*

Carey, Maude. *See* CARY, MAUDE (1878–1967).

Carey, William (1761–1834). English missionary to India. William Carey's nomination as the "Father of Modern Missions" may not be chronologically accurate (MORAVIAN missionaries crisscrossed the globe before he was born), but it is accurate in terms of what his life and ministry spawned in the ensuing years of Protestant missions in England—that is, the so-called GREAT CENTURY of missionary outreach. Carey was born into a poor family near Northampton. He became an apprentice shoemaker at age sixteen and was married in 1781. Poverty stalked the family, but Carey studied hard and became a Baptist lay preacher in 1785. He combined his biblical and geographical knowledge and soon preached that the church's primary responsibility was foreign missions. Fighting an uphill battle against the religious establishment, in 1792 he published his landmark study, *An Enquiry Into the Obligation of Christians to Use Means for the Conversion of the Heathens.* Under his influence, some Baptist ministers organized a new mission board, the Baptist Missionary Society. In 1793 Carey and John Thomas and their families sailed to India.

Despite family and economic hardships, Carey persisted in preaching, doing Bible translation work, and starting schools. However, for the first seven years at Malda there were no Indian converts.

Carey moved his base to SERAMPORE, where he ministered thirty-four years until his death. He completed translations of the Bible into Bengali, Sanskrit, and Marathi. He organized schools and started a print shop. By 1818 there were some six hundred baptized converts. The following year he began Serampore College to train pastors. However, as the mission grew, serious internal problems developed, which eventually caused a split in the mission in 1826.

Carey's wife Dorothy died in 1807 and he remarried within a year, much to the consternation of his fellow missionaries. His colleagues also felt that Carey's children suffered because of his heavy workload and the lack of discipline. Another grievous setback was the loss of his manuscripts in a fire in 1812, but he zealously plunged into his work again.

Carey's fatherhood of modern Protestant missions is seen in the fact that his basic strategies of work have been followed ever since: BIBLE TRANSLATION and production, EVANGELISM, CHURCH PLANTING, EDUCATION, and MEDICAL AND RELIEF WORK. Although Carey had a high regard for Indian culture, he fought against widow burning and infanticide. He left his mark on India, while in both Europe and North America his zeal for world missions provided the impetus for a remarkable upsurge in missionary vision, the starting of new mission societies, and the sending of thousands of missionaries.

JIM REAPSOME

Bibliography. M. Drewery, *William Carey: A Biography;* T. George, *Faithful Witness: The Life and Mission of William Carey.*

Cargill, Margaret (1809–40).

English pioneer missionary to Fiji. Born the second daughter of a naval captain, she was educated at home by her widowed mother. She proved to be an energetic, devoted, well-read Sunday school teacher. She and David Cargill were married in 1832 when he was ordained a Wesleyan missionary to Tonga. They sailed to Tonga, where he began his labors to translate the New Testament into Tongan. Later, they were sent to Lakemba, Fijian, where he began his work with Fijian dialects. Cargill herself proved to be an adept linguist, a skilled nurse (nicknamed "the lady with the gentle spirit"), hospitable, and able to adapt to privation and the hostile monsoon climate. In each station she organized educational classes for women and girls, also becoming a class leader in the Rewan congregation and a valued counselor of Christian and nonbeliever alike. Her diplomatic skills helped ensure the survival of the precarious persecuted Tongan congregations in Fiji. Though occasionally tormented by homesickness, her faith, trust, and joy, especially after the Tongan revival of 1835, enabled her to support her melancholy and introspective husband. After transfer to Rewa she succumbed to the effects of a hurricane, fever, anxieties arising from witnessing constant warfare and cannibalism, a sixth pregnancy in eight years, and dysentery. Cargill is an early example of the role independent-minded missionary wives could play as evangelists and educators in bridging the gulf between Victorian male culture and that of the host people she loved so much.

ELEANOR M. JACKSON

Bibliography. D. Cargill, *Memoir of Mrs. Margaret Cargill;* M. Dickson, *The Inseparable Grief: Margaret Cargill of Fiji;* E. R. Pitman, *Lady Pioneers in Many Lands;* G. S. Rowe, ed., *Fiji and the Fijans by Thomas Williams and Missionary Labours among the Cannibals by James Calvert.*

Cargo Cults. Cargo cults are distinctive manifestations of a cultural phenomenon indigenous to Melanesia. They share much in common with other revitalization movements and NEW RELIGIOUS MOVEMENTS (NERMS). Such movements have often posed a threat to missions and INDIGENOUS CHURCHES.

The term "cargo cult" focuses on the most notable aspect, the expectation of acquiring large quantities of material goods. The Melanesian use of the term *kago* refers to a restoration of a primeval, idyllic order. The cult anticipates a socioeconomic and spiritual renewal that involves a radical change in the existing socioeconomic order. There is an expectation of peace, health, social justice, and material prosperity that resembles the Jewish SHALOM but can also be cosmic in dimension.

Traditional MYTH provides the indigenous socioreligious ideology for many of the known movements. The relevant myth frequently expresses how there was an idyllic state in the primeval past that was destroyed or lost due to some failure on the part of the mythical ancestors. Arising from the myth there are aspirations for the primeval idyllic state to be restored in the present. Magical-literal understanding of the process of cause and effect gives the movements their particular expression while the use of rituals of analogy and reenactment is thought to bring about the desired effect. The existence of cargoistic ideology alone, however, does not always result in a cult movement. A situation of cultural stress caused by a sense of deprivation, such as may occur in the presence of a "superior" culture, is a common precursor to a movement. Then the availability of a charismatic or prophetic leader often catalyzes cargoistic ideology into a cargo movement.

The classical cargo movements have not been so common in recent years due to economic progress and acculturation. Nevertheless, the ideology and thinking processes behind them are still evident and are thought to provide the dynamic for secessionist, nationalistic, and political movements as well as community development enterprises. Under Christian influences cargoistic ideology may provide the dynamic for people movements to embrace the gospel. The ideology and thought processes may result in SYNCRETISM, spirit-revival movements within the church, and independent churches.

Missions and national churches need to take the spiritual-social aspects expressed in the movements seriously because they reflect the concerns of the practitioners. Missions and national churches should seek to ameliorate cargoistic tendencies by preaching a holistic salvation and practicing the presence of the KINGDOM OF GOD in power and lifestyle. Church and mission should also enable indigenous peoples to understand economic processes and the concept of linear history as the context of God's revelation.

ALBERT F. TUCKER

Bibliography. W. Flannery, ed., *Religious Movements in Melanesia Today*; E. Mantovani, ed., *An Introduction to Melanesian Religions*; G. Strelan, *Search for Salvation*.

Caribbean. The nations of the Caribbean have a diverse population of 40 million people who occupy twenty-five major islands and hundreds of smaller ones. The region has long been referred to as a "Naboth's vineyard," an unspoiled natural paradise whose serenity, resources, and vulnerability have led frequently to political intervention, economic exploitation, and cultural intrusion. Three hundred years of competition between the Spanish, French, Dutch, and British empires, a later hegemony by the United States, international commercial and tourist development, and ideological tensions—the most recent of which have been caused by Fidel Castro's communist Cuba—have given the Caribbean a colorful but often tragic history. The religious picture that follows from these conditions is a blurred mosaic of churches, social movements, and cults that to a large extent recapitulate the region's turbulent past.

The nature of Christianity in the Caribbean follows from three basic facts of the region's social history. First, its ethnic composition is the result of the virtual elimination of the indigenous peoples within decades of the discovery of the islands in the late fifteenth century and the introduction of perhaps as many as 5 million African slaves over a period of three centuries to support production of sugar, the region's main cash crop. Second, the Caribbean has a fragmented religious and cultural character as a result of European imperial rivalry, its proximity to mainland North and South America, and the importation of indentured workers, including East Indian laborers in the nineteenth century. Third, notwithstanding the high mortality rates in the region from endemic disease and unhygienic conditions, the Caribbean in the twentieth century had continuing appeal as a paradise, not only for tourism and commercial exploitation, but for political and social experimentation. Besides Cuban socialism, the region has had a long history of social uprisings, progressive labor unions, and populist parties, the most recent led by Maurice Bishop in Grenada and Michael Manley in Jamaica.

As a consequence, the insular Caribbean, including the Greater Antilles (Cuba, the island of Hispaniola [occupied by the Dominican Republic and Haiti], Jamaica, and Puerto Rico) and the Lesser Antilles, the archipelago that extends from the Bahamas in the north to Trinidad off the Venezuelan coast, offers a complex social profile. While the islands are distinguished by their geologic origins and their location (e.g., the northern Lesser Antilles are known as the Leeward Islands and the southern as the Windwards), more often the islands are grouped according to their former or actual colonial status: the former Spanish possessions of Cuba, the Dominican Republic, and Puerto Rico; the several British islands of Jamaica and the Lesser Antilles, the Bahamian and Cayman clusters, and Trinidad and Tobago; the French possessions of Haiti, Guadeloupe, Martinique, Saint Martin, and Saint Bathélemy; the Dutch possessions of Aruba, Bonaire, Curaçao, Saint Martin, Saba, and Saint Eustatius; and the Virgin Islands, which the United States purchased from Denmark in 1917.

The Caribbean population is ethnically 35 percent Afro-Caribbean, 31 percent Creole-mulatto, 30 percent European, and 4 percent Asian. The few thousand Amerindians who survive are the remnants of the native Carib and Arawak populations that probably numbered at least 300,000—if not as many as one million—at the time of European intrusion. Linguistically, 60 percent of the population speak Spanish, 20 percent French, 17 percent English, and 3 percent Dutch.

The Religious Profile. The religious preferences of the Caribbean peoples correspond roughly to their ethnic and national origins. Roman Catholics make up 60 percent of the population, Protestants 20 percent, spiritists 9 percent, and members of Eastern religions—HINDUS, BUDDHISTS, SIKHS, MUSLIMS, and BAHA'IS—about 3 percent. An estimated 9 percent of the inhabitants are considered nonreligious. The JEHOVAH'S WITNESSES, with some members in most of the islands, claim 50,000 in the French territories of Haiti, Martinique, and Guadeloupe.

The Roman Catholic traditions of the peoples of Cuba, the Dominican Republic, and Puerto Rico, who together account for more than half of the total Caribbean population, are a product of the early missionaries and a colonial administration that lasted in the case of Cuba and Puerto Rico for four hundred years, from 1492 to the Spanish-American War of 1898. Consequently, the Roman Catholic Church in the region benefits from deep religious loyalties, even in Puerto Rico, where an evangelical minority has assumed an important role, and in Cuba, where ATHEISM prevails officially.

The picture is quite different in the colonies and former dependencies of the British Empire, including Jamaica, the Bahamas, Bermuda, Barbados, Trinidad, and several of the Lesser Antilles. There Anglicans and Methodists, dating from British colonial days, tend to predominate. On the island of Anguilla, for example, the Protestant population reaches 90 percent, and on several others, Antigua and Barbuda, the British Virgin Islands, the Cayman Islands, Montserrat, Saint Kitts and Nevis, and the Turks and Caicos Islands, the proportion is above 80 percent. Nevertheless, observers sometimes conclude, nominal adherence with little commitment characterizes the faith of many Caribbean Protestants.

In contrast, Roman Catholic influence predominates in the island societies that formed under French cultural influence—even those like Dominica, Grenada, and Saint Lucia, which later came under British jurisdiction—although without the status and public support that the Catholic Church has enjoyed in the former Spanish possessions. Although Haiti's evangelical population is substantial—as much as a quarter of that country's 7 million—prolonged and sometimes intensive effort at Protestant evangelization has not altered the essential character of Haitian culture, and the Protestant community in the other French areas is generally much smaller, as low as only 4.1 percent of the inhabitants of Guadeloupe.

Two other patterns are observable in the Caribbean's religious configuration. In the Dutch islands of Aruba, Bonaire, and Curaçao, nominally Catholic societies, the evangelical population is quite small, as it is also in the Virgin Islands of the United States, the Cayman Islands, and the Bahamas, where also the process of SECULARIZATION is well advanced. In contrast, in Trinidad, along with the mainland states of Guyana and Surinam, substantial numbers of East Indians form Hindu and Muslim communities that retain distinctive religious practices and compete with the previously established Afro-Caribbean communities for recognition and control.

These descriptive categories, however, indicate little about the human aspirations and the religious dynamics of the area. The religious framework must be understood within the context of an exploitative slave and racial caste system, a stratified white society, large numbers of white indentured (often Irish Catholic) servants, an imposed, accommodating, dominant religion, whether Protestant or Catholic, a tradition of authoritarian government, ongoing struggles for freedom and identity, and in more recent decades considerable overpopulation and consequent emigration and, often, a sense of hopelessness and futility. The religious recourse has often been Afro-Caribbean spiritism. More than merely a personal cult or cultural relic, spiritism at times has given rise to organized political-religious movements of protest and rebellion (*see* LATIN AMERICAN NEW RELIGIOUS MOVEMENTS). On a smaller but not unimportant scale, indigenous Holiness, Pentecostal, and charismatic movements have emerged in several of the islands; and some mainland missionary ventures, notably those of the Seventh-Day Adventists, have established important religious beachheads.

The relative lack of spiritual inertia of the contemporary Caribbean region stands in contrast to the vitality of evangelical Christians in the nineteenth and early twentieth centuries. In earlier decades the Caribbean Protestant churches exhibited considerable vision for evangelizing their own peoples and sending missions to West Africa. Nowhere in the Caribbean except in Puerto Rico and Jamaica is there presently an island population whose evangelical (as contrasted with nominal Protestant) Christians demonstrate notable evangelistic fervor. In only five of twenty-six jurisdictions do evangelical Protestants account for more than a quarter of the population. In twelve of these island units the proportion is less than 15 percent. Nevertheless, on some islands the better-established churches and various Baptist, Holiness, and Pentecostal groups appear to be making headway. In several of the islands the largest or second largest Protestant group is the Seventh-Day Adventists.

Pervasive Spiritism. The mainly Afro-Caribbean and Creole-mulatto character of the island population has important religious and cultural overtones. While Europeans of Spanish descent make up substantial proportions in Cuba and Puerto Rico, the other European populations are but a small minority of their respective island societies. From the Afro-Caribbean cultural majority have emerged strong religious influences, such as Afro-Cuban Santería, Jamaican Rastafarianism, and Trinidadian Shango and Obeah. Spiritists (Voodoo, Vodun) acquired political importance in Haiti during the years of the dictator François "Papa Doc" Duvalier, and Rastafarianism, which identified in the post–World War II period with Emperor Haile Selassie, has gained support in Jamaica. These, however, are only the more formalized traditions among the many folk practices deeply embedded in the traditional culture. Not atypically, half of the people of the Dominican Republic are believed to engage in occult practices. While spiritist cults may not always be a defiant obstacle to evangelical Christianity in the region, they fortify latent resistance to forms of Christianity that were once the religion of the colonial, slaveholding European minority. Only where evangelical Protestantism has accommodated popular cultural forms has it taken root and grown, such as in the case of the nineteenth-century revivalist movement in Jamaica and twentieth-century Pentecostalism in Puerto Rico.

Scholars who have investigated spiritist movements throughout the region see them appealing not only to the Afro-Caribbean peasants and recent migrants to the cities, but to established urban residents as well. As survival mechanisms that thrive in small underground groups, they satisfy the need for reassurance in an uncertain, often hostile world. Spiritism and Christianity are not mutually exclusive for many adherents. The eclectic sponge-like quality of spiritism enables it to survive among the various competing religions, explains anthropologist Joan D. Koss. In comparing Haitian Vodun and Pentecostalism, Luther P. Gerlach finds many structural similarities between the two. Both religions conceive of a world of powerful supernatural forces and practice spirit possession. Both are characterized by tight-knit local cells linked together in polycephalous overlapping networks. This design, Gerlach argues, is eminently suited to survival. These groups keep a low profile and are tolerated by political authorities because, on the one hand, they appear to be harmless and, on the other, may be useful as a counterforce among the masses to the more powerful established religions. But despite some similarities, the two consider each other to be implacable enemies. Spiritists attempt to manipulate the spirit world, asserts Gerlach, while evangelical Protestants exorcise evil spirits and submit to the Holy Spirit.

Anthropologist William Wedenoja has pointed out that the conditions that gave rise to evangelical groups in Jamaica, notably Pentecostalism, have also produced a growth in Rastafarianism, with many of the same tendencies to individualism and egalitarianism. But Rastafarianism appeals most to the chronically unemployed black urban youth who appear to be the victims of MODERNIZATION. While the movement has heightened social consciousness and created pride in Jamaican indigenous culture, unlike Pentecostalism it does not cut across racial, class, and cultural lines.

The Evangelical Presence. Most of the evangelical missionary focus has been on the larger islands, where Protestant evangelicals remain in the minority. On a limited scale, elements within the established Protestant denominations have provided the mechanism for kindling evangelical sentiments. Often overlooked in the discussion of the Caribbean evangelical picture have been the homegrown Pentecostal groups, many of them receiving at least token support from North American denominations such as the Church of God (Cleveland, Tennessee) and the Church of God in Christ, but others like the *Iglesia de Dios Pentecostal* in Puerto Rico are essentially autochthonous religious expressions with little relation to any mainland organization. In several island societies these largely independent and often socially marginal Pentecostal and Holiness churches have provided the only assertive evangelical leadership.

The North American missionary force in the Caribbean includes 1,128 career (four years or longer) Protestant missionaries, one missionary for each 35,000 inhabitants. Europe has sent fewer than 100 Protestant missionaries. The North American denominations supporting the largest numbers of overseas personnel are the Christian Churches/Churches of Christ with 86 missionaries (with the largest contingents in Puerto Rico and Haiti) and the Southern Baptist Convention with 96 missionaries (27 in the Dominican Republic and 17 in the Trinidad and Tobago). By comparison, the Roman Catholic personnel at work in the Caribbean total 5,210 religious, five times the number of Protestant missionaries. Not to be overlooked, however, are the many missionaries sent from one Caribbean island to another, and, increasingly, the expatriate West Indians in the United Kingdom who are returning to evangelize their homelands.

An Assessment. The extremely diverse and often opposing cultural and religious traditions of the Caribbean preclude easy generalization about the spiritual needs. With the exception of several of the larger islands, the evangelical churches have not acquired the strength and autonomy that would permit them to radically influence the lives of their own peoples or send missionaries abroad. In this respect Puerto Rico and Jamaica stand apart, having developed strong evangelical communities, benefiting originally from Holiness and Pentecostal missionary efforts but now entirely independent and contextualized. It is estimated that 30 percent of the total population of Puerto Rico considers itself evangelical, the majority identified with one or another Pentecostal denomination. While 165 foreign Protestant missionaries serve in Puerto Rico, the island churches send 65 missionaries—and a number of effective short-term evangelists—abroad. In contrast, Protestants account for only 5 percent of the Dominican Republic's population of 8 million and 2.5 percent of Cuba's 11 million people.

Protestant evangelicals on Jamaica, on the other hand, make up an estimated 18 percent of the population, the Protestant churches are well established, and forty missionaries have been sent out to other countries. In the wake of Afro-Christian revival cults that emerged among the Jamaican masses from the 1860s to World War II, Pentecostalism has in the period of modernization from a peasant to an urban society, become the most dynamic Protestant movement on the island. William Wedenoja identifies several contrasting features of these groups, despite their many similarities. While for the revivalists God and the angels are key deities, the Pentecostals are christocentric; while the revivalists concentrate on the Old Testament, the Pentecostals focus on the New Testament; while revivalists tend to authoritarian structures, Pentecostals tend to be more congregational. Wedenoja found that the trends were away from large, formal, cold congregations in favor of churches that are fervent, smaller, and more intimate.

In a time of modernization and political independence, as the old values and ways of life are disintegrating, the majority of the Caribbean peoples are caught in a bewildering transition. The labor unions and populist movements that formed after World War I and the political experiments like those of Cuba, Trinidad, Grenada, and Jamaica have sometimes given island inhabitants nominal control, but with little sense of power, given the islands' spare resources, stagnant economics, and growing populations. Self-governing nations of the size of Antigua (64,000), Grenada (84,000), and Dominica (86,000) are far too small to deal with the burgeoning problems. With only Trinidad in the Caribbean producing substantial quantities of petroleum, and with their single-export (mainly sugar) economics having collapsed, these countries have turned increasingly to tourism and offshore banking—and the laundering of drug money—to support their peoples. As a result many young people have emigrated to mainland countries or, having resigned themselves to a life with little promise for the future, are living simply for the present. The high numbers of unmarried mothers and alarming increases in crime document as much. For the Caribbean peoples who have embraced it, however, evangelical Protestantism offers the spiritual resources either to ease the transition to modern life or to provide consolation for the sectors that the modern world has simply passed by.

EVERETT A. WILSON

Bibliography. L. P. Gerlach, *Religious Movements in Contemporary America*, pp. 686–96; S. D. Glazier, ed., *Perspectives on Pentecostalism: Case Studies from the Caribbean and Latin America*; P. E. James and C. W. Minkel, *Latin America*, 5th ed.; J. D. Koss, *Caribbean Studies* 16 (April 1976): 43; A. Lampe, *The Church in Latin America, 1492–1992*, pp. 201–15; J. Rogozinski, *A Brief History of the Caribbean: From the Arawak and the Carib to the Present*; W. Wedenoja, *Perspectives on Pentecostalism: Case Studies from the Caribbean and Latin America*, p. 44.

Caribbean New Religious Movements. As with the LATIN AMERICAN NEW RELIGIOUS MOVEMENTS, many of the spiritistic groups in the Caribbean can trace their origination to the atrocities of the slave trade and the need for the populations who had been forcibly removed from their homes to maintain some frame of religious identity. Often that identity was underground, and outward con-formity to colonial Christian norms served as a cover for inward nonconformity. Movements include Voodoo (Haiti); Convince, Kumina, Myal, and Rastafarianism (Jamaica); Shango and Obeah (Trinidad); Abakua and Santéria (Cuba); and Kele (St. Lucia). In this article we will describe some of the more significant groups (for a treatment of the factors involved in their development seen in light of the whole Caribbean historical experience, *see* CARIBBEAN). It should be noted that the selected groups introduced below can be characterized by the general themes described here, but within each movement there are also multiple folk-level variations maintained at the local level.

Descriptions of Selected Movements. *Convince* rituals in Jamaica combine Christian and spiritistic elements. The most utilized spirits are those of departed members, but African spirits are the most powerful. Believers, called *bongo* men, can be controlled by more than one spirit simultaneously. Their rituals (some held annually, others as need arises) include Christian prayers and Bible readings, veneration of the spirits, dancing and possession, and sacrifice.

Various *Rastafarian* groups emerged from the black population of Jamaica in the 1930s. Rastafarians venerate Haile Selassie I, the former emperor of Ethiopia, envisioning him as a black messiah who will liberate them from white oppression. The earlier emphasis on repatriation to Africa has waned in contemporary times. Rastafarians typically follow vegetarian dietary regulations, smoke marijuana, and wear their hair and beards in dredlocks. Their most prominent musician, Bob Marley, popularized reggae music as a Rastafarian style.

In Trinidad *Shango* groups honor various spiritual powers. Shango (the Yoruba god of thunder and lightning) is one of many powers which may possess adherents. These powers include other Yoruba deities as well as Christian figures. Each Shango cult center holds an annual four-day ritual for the particular spirit recognized at that center involving nightly prayer (including Christian prayers), drumming and singing, possession, and culminating with animal sacrifice.

Voodoo (or *vodun* or *vodou*) originated in Haiti in the late 1700s. Separated from their home, the slave populations fused a variety of belief systems and practices and developed a religion strong enough to withstand later French persecution. Usually centered on a temple, the ceremonies are festivals in which spirit possession is prominent. In it the spirits *(lwa)*, who range from African deities to stereotyped Christian saints, are thought to ride the participants like horses. They provide protection for the possessed, so long as the devotees maintain an appropriate schedule of sacrifices and offerings. Popularized through practices such as *zombi* (in which a living person's mind is altered so that he or she comes under the control of evil practitioners) and voodoo dolls (which are magically linked to an intended victim whose pain parallels damage done to the doll), voodoo is widely known outside of the Caribbean.

Missionary Implications. The historical connection of the spiritist religions to the trauma of the slave trade, their ability to meet important felt needs in their adherents whose lives are often bound up in oppression and poverty, the emotional ties of the followers to local leaders, the perception that Christianity and spiritistic practices can be readily mixed, and the ingrained ability to present one appearance on the surface and keep deeply held values underneath make genuine conversion to Christianity a complex issue. Missionaries working among these movements will need to consider all of these factors if they are to enable the adherents to respond fruitfully to the claims of Christ as Lord over all of life.

EDITORS

SEE ALSO New Religious Movements.

Bibliography. J. T. Houk, *Spirits, Blood, and Drums: The Orisha Religion in Trinidad;* J. D. Koss, *Caribbean Studies* 16 (April 1976); G. E. Simpson, *Black Religions in the New World;* idem, *ER* 3:90–98; L. E. Sullivan, *Icanchu's Drum.*

Carmichael, Amy Wilson (1867–1951). Irish missionary to India. Born in Northern Ireland and converted in her teens, she was briefly a missionary to Japan before going to South India in 1895. She never returned home. Her Dohnavur Fellowship at Tinnevelly was formed in 1901 to rescue little girls forced into temple prostitution. The task called for unusual and often misunderstood sacrifice. Everything was subordinated to the claims of the children, even evangelistic tours. In 1926 the Dohnavur Fellowship became an independent society of some nine hundred endangered girls and boys. The work involved long, weary trips all over India, sometimes fruitless, in search of children. Those who arrived were cared for, educated, and trained for lives of service. Carmichael exposed what the *Sunday School Chronicle* called "a wickedness and degradation so colossal and so deep-seated" that missionary efforts seemed powerless, yet it never lessened her faith. She set high spiritual standards for herself and a growing body of colleagues. Despite crippling disability after a fall in 1931, she carried on, not least in producing remarkable prose, poetry, and letters that went worldwide. Among them were *Things As They Are* (1903), *Overweights of Joy* (1906), *Gold Cord* (1932), *If* (1938), and *Rose from Brier* (1950).

J. D. DOUGLAS

Bibliography. E. Elliot, *A Chance to Die: The Life and Legacy of Amy Carmichael;* F. Houghton, *Amy Carmichael of Dohnavur: The Story of a Lover and Her Beloved;* E. Skoglund, *Amma: The Life and Words of Amy Carmichael.*

Carver, William Owen (1868–1954). American early missiologist, theologian, and educator. A native of Tennessee, Carver studied at Richmond College in Virginia and Southern Baptist Theological Seminary in Louisville, Kentucky. He joined the seminary faculty in the year of his graduation (1896) and served there until his retirement in 1943. Although he had received his doctorate in New Testament, he followed in the steps of H. H. Harris in teaching missions and in 1899 became the first professor in the newly created Department of Comparative Religion and Missions. He traveled to Europe in 1900 and 1907–8 to study missions there, and toured Baptist missions in South America and Asia in 1922–23.

Through Carver's teaching, publications, and promotion of missions he profoundly influenced the Southern Baptist Convention. He wrote twenty-one books in addition to many articles in denominational periodicals and journals. Carver contributed to the founding of the Woman's Missionary Union Training School for Christian Workers in Louisville (renamed the Carver School for Christian Work in 1953), the Southern Baptist Historical Society, and the Historical Commission of the Southern Baptist Convention. He was also a member of the American Theological Committee, a regional section of the World Conference on Faith and Order.

GARY B. MCGEE

Bibliography. H. G. Culpepper in *ML,* pp. 85–92; W. O. Carver, *Out of His Treasure: Unfinished Memoirs.*

Cary, Maude (1878–1967). American pioneer missionary to Morocco. Born on a farm in Kansas, she was converted when a traveling evangelist preached in her deeply religious home. At age eighteen she enrolled at the Gospel Missionary Union Bible Institute in Kansas City, Missouri, and in 1901 sailed for Morocco. She was to labor there for fifty years despite a disastrous initial two years when colleagues accused her of frivolity and a lack of piety. Fortunately, the mission let her stay. Her fiancé fled to the Sudan rather than admit she was not the meek missionary wife he wanted, causing her much anguish. By now fluent in Arabic and Berber, she soldiered on, taking her first furlough in 1924. By 1939 the three established stations were being run by four women; the work miraculously survived throughout World War II almost unscathed. In 1948 there were eleven missionaries, so Cary conducted the language school and at age seventy-one opened a new station at El Hajeb and a Bible institute. She needed medical treatment (1952–55) but returned as the mission blossomed in 1955 with the ending of French colonial occupation. In her final years she saw the fruit of her patient labors teaching the Bible, but in the year of her death the Moroccan government closed down all foreign missions lest they create political unrest.

ELEANOR M. JACKSON

Bibliography. E. Stenbock, *Miss Terri: The Story of Maude Cary, Pioneer CMU Missionary in Morocco;* R. A. Tucker, *FJIJ.*

Casalis, Eugene (1812–91). French pioneer missionary to Lesotho. At age twenty-one he was sent out by the PARIS EVANGELICAL MISSIONARY SOCIETY. Lesotho was selected due to South Africa's mix of European settlers, including French Huguenots as French Protestants were not welcome in French colonies. After founding a station at Morija in 1833, he established one in 1835 at Thaba-Boisu, the residence of Moshoeshoe I, the chief of the Lesotho tribe. His accomplishments over the following twenty years included translation of the Gospels, ethnographic studies, and serving as advisor to the chief in an important diplomatic role.

Furloughed over 1849–50, Casalis preached and rekindled a missionary passion across France. His success in motivating others resulted in his appointment six years later to direct the mission. He established a training program and oversaw the successful opening of new fields (Tahiti and Senegal in 1862, after unsuccessful attempts in China and Mauritius in 1860). Casalis retired in 1882 and died in 1891. He was the first Protestant missionary honored by membership in the Legion d'Honneur.

JOHN EASTERLING

Bibliography. E. Casalis, *The Basutos, or Twenty-three Years in South Africa.*

Caste. A hereditary division of any society into classes on the basis of occupation, color, wealth, or religion. More specifically, in HINDUISM, caste *(jati)* is the permanent social group into which a person is born, with social and religious obligations determined for a lifetime by one's caste.

The beginnings of the caste system in India are thought to date back to the invasion of Indo-European Aryans (or Vedic peoples) who migrated into the Indus Valley about 1000 B.C. *Varna* refers to the social divisions believed to have been characteristic of these people. One theory is that the organization of castes was based on *varna* (color). Aryans were light, while the invaded peoples were dark. Others believe stratification resulted in castes developing from social classes or other types of differences. During this early period, groups and strata of Hindu society began to form. No historical records exist for this period, but from the hymns, legends, and other accounts, it seems that the social system of the newcomers was composed of four major divisions: the *brahmana*, a sacerdotal or priestly category; the *rajanya*, a chiefly, noble, or warrior category; the *vaisya*, who were variously perceived as commoners, farmers, or merchants; and the *sudra*, a category of servants or commoners of a lower status.

Social anthropologists suggest that the persistent feature of Indian society has been the existence of endogamous descent groups (a system in which people must marry within their own group). Over time such groups were integrated into local hierarchical systems of cooperation and interdependence. The caste system typically includes the following components: (1) a local population composed of the series of mutually exclusive castes; (2) segments structured by caste in endogamous descent groups, ideally related unilineally; (3) a dominant caste with political and economic power over the others; (4) an occupational specialty related to each caste; (5) a ritual system of exchange of food, goods, and services concerned with purity and pollution as well as economics; (6) a ranking of each caste according to their respective degrees of pollution.

Various movements to reform the caste system have made some impact on the traditional structure. Buddhism, Islam, and Christianity have all made inroads into caste norms. It is significant, however, that most of the reform movements have resulted in castes of their own, evolving into exclusive, endogamous sects. Mahatma Gandhi's programs were aimed at the removal of the caste system, but the divisions persist even under modern pressures of Westernization. Since caste in India has always functioned as a powerful religious system of belief, movements to lessen the influence or abolish the caste system have so far failed.

Christian missions have for the most part ignored caste distinctions. Those who join a Christian church are compelled to join a church community outside the caste system, automatically forcing them downward from all their social and family relationships. Indications are that people would become Christians more readily if they were able to remain in their own social grouping. And yet many Christians maintain that the freedom found in new life in Christ (Gal. 3:26–29; Eph. 2) transcends the divisions of caste, and that the gospel challenges injustices associated with caste.

NORMAN E. ALLISON

SEE ALSO Association AND Kinship.

Bibliography. P. Kolenda, *Caste in Contemporary India: Beyond Organic Solidarity;* W. Matthews, *World Religions;* M. N. Srinivas, *Caste in Modern India and Other Essays;* R. D. Winter and D. A. Fraser, *PWCM,* pp. B:193–212.

Castro, Emilio (1927–). Uruguayan Methodist pastor, missiologist, and ecumenical leader. He received his theological training at Union Theological Seminary in Bueno Aires, and the University of Basel, under Karl Barth. He has held pastorates in Argentina, Bolivia, and Uruguay and served as president of the Evangelical Methodist Church of Uruguay. At the same time he held key positions as vice president of CPC (Christian Peace Conference), executive secretary of ASIT (South American Association of Theological Schools), and general secretary and coordinator of UNELAM (Commission for Evangelical Unity in Latin America). He was director of the WCC COMMISSION ON WORLD MISSION AND EVANGELISM and editor of *The International Review of Mission,* and from 1985 to 1992 served as general secretary of the WCC and editor of *Ecumenical Review,* residing in Geneva. In 1993 he returned to his native Uruguay to continue ministry as a pastor and evangelist. Many of his articles, reports, and books, in both English and Spanish, have played a key role in the development of a genuine Latin American pastoral theology, as well as made a significant contribution to the meaning of mission from his unique perspective

PABLO E. PÉREZ

Cayman Islands *(Est. 2000 pop.: 36,000; 259 sq. km. [100 sq. mi.]).* Consisting of three sparsely populated islands located just south of Cuba, the Caymans are a British Crown colony. Thirty percent of the population is from Britain, Canada, or the United States. Like the Bahamas and the neighboring Turks and Caicos groups, the thin-soiled, low-lying Cayman Islands were inhabited mainly by fishermen until offshore financial companies and tourist hotels began to proliferate. Grand Cayman quickly became second only to the Bahamas as a financial center, registering 500 banks and 18,000 other companies. The tiny islands had one-half million guests annually in the late 1980s. The population is 80 percent Protestant.

EVERETT A. WILSON

SEE ALSO Caribbean.

Bibliography. A. Lampe, *The Church in Latin America, 1492–1992,* pp. 201–15; J. Rogozinski, *A Brief History of the Caribbean: From the Arawak and the Carib to the Present.*

Cell Groups. *See* SMALL GROUPS.

The Celtic Missionary Movement. Ardently missionary, with a strong focus on Scripture and personal piety, the Celtic movement had a major impact on the evangelization of the British Isles, western Europe, and northern Europe in the fifth through tenth centuries. The founder was PATRICK, born about 389 in a Christian family in Britain, who was kidnapped as a teenager and taken to Ireland, where he was a slave for six years. After his escape he studied, was ordained a priest, and in 432, in response to a vision, returned to Ireland as a missionary bishop, where he remained until his death (c. 461). His ministry led to the conversion of thousands, the ordination of priests, and the establishment of monasteries, which became centers of evangelization, learning, and civilization.

Patrick's theology was evangelical; he quoted the Bible frequently, especially Romans. A man of deep spirituality and prayer, his greatest desire was to spread the gospel. The Irish monasteries became known as seminaries for the study of Scripture and for strict discipline, drawing students from the Continent and England. Streams of dedicated men poured from them to go on pilgrimages for Christ wherever they might feel led. In 563 COLUMBA landed at Iona in Scotland with twelve companions and established monasteries from which missionaries went to barbarian tribes, north into Scotland and south into England. They were more effective in evangelizing England than were the missionaries from Rome, led by AUGUSTINE OF CANTERBURY.

Beginning in 590 COLUMBANUS established monasteries that evangelized barbarian tribes in Burgundy while bringing a measure of renewal to the Frankish church. Expelled by the corrupt court, he established other houses in Switzerland and northern Italy.

The Celtic movement differed from the Roman church on several issues: the dating of Easter, the tonsure of the monks, and, most important, submission to the authority of Rome. But at the Synod of Whitby in 664 the movement began to come under the authority of Rome. Two of the greatest Celtic missionaries were consecrated as missionary bishops by Rome. WILLIBRORD (658–739) evangelized the Frisians, and BONIFACE became the apostle to central Germany. He was martyred in 753.

The Celtic missionaries were characterized by spontaneity, a lack of traditionalism, and rugged individualism. They went where others would not go, without credentials or material support, self-reliant, trusting in God, and accomplished much more than their numbers would warrant. Theirs was a type of monasticism that was ardently missionary; thus the monastery was not a place of retreat from the world but a place of preparation for mission. Women played an important role in the Irish church, and Boniface used communities of women in mission, perhaps for the first time. Many of the Celtic institutions and much of the movement were destroyed by the Viking invasions in the eighth and ninth centuries. Yet the vigor of the tradition continued in England to some degree. Missionaries from England coming from

Celtic roots were used to bring the Scandinavians into the Christian faith in the tenth century.

PAUL E. PIERSON

SEE ALSO Monastic Movement.

Bibliography. R. P. C. Hanson, *The Life and Writings of the Historical Saint Patrick;* L. Hardinge, *The Celtic Church in Britain;* J. T. McNeill, *The Celtic Churches, a History,* A.D. 200–1200.

Centenary Conference on the Protestant Missions of the World (London, 1888).

Meeting at Exeter Hall June 9–19, 1888, this was the largest, most representative interdenominational, international missions assembly to that date. Meant to celebrate the first 100 years of modern missions advance, the centennial name marked no specific anniversary. Present were 1,579 delegates from 139 denominations and societies representing 10 countries, including a coterie of non-Westerners. Great Britain and her colonies dominated the roster; 219 from 67 societies represented North America and 41 from 18 societies came from continental Europe. Most females attending were wives of male delegates, though a few women gave speeches.

Sixteen public assemblies surveyed the world's mission fields; more sensitive topics were addressed in twenty-two closed sessions, which discussed women's work, education, literature, medicine, native churches, polygamy, the opium and liquor trades, inter-mission competition, and other issues. Meeting at the zenith of the European imperialist era, speakers assumed Western colonialism to be advantageous for missions and the gospel as civilizer. Procedural rules prohibited the adoption of formal positions, which aided a spirit of generic evangelical comity. An attempt to launch a permanent international committee to facilitate inter-mission cooperation was unsuccessful. A postconference caucus did vote to petition governments to end the opium, liquor, firearms, and slave trades.

Though some delegates were disappointed at the lack of specific results, outcomes of the London Conference included an overall raised consciousness and support level for foreign missions; America assuming more contribution and leadership for world missions; the establishment of the World's Missionary Committee of Christian Women and what later became the Foreign Missions Conference of North America, important for the later ecumenical movement. Additionally the precedent was set for the decennial megaconferences in New York (1900) and Edinburgh (1910).

THOMAS A. ASKEW

Bibliography. T. A. Askew, *IBMR* 18 (1994): 113–16; W. R. Hogg, *Ecumenical Foundations;* J. E. Johnston, ed., *Report of the Centenary Conference on the Protestant Missions of the World,* 2 vols.

Central African Republic *(Est. 2000 pop.: 3,731,000; 662,984 sq. km. [240,534 sq. mi.]).* The Central African Republic is a landlocked state and home to over fifty tribal languages. With a broad diversity of religious groups, the Central African Republic enjoys freedom of religion with remarkable success in evangelism.

Muslims, mostly Sunnis of the Malekite rite (3.3%), are strongest among non-Africans, concentrating among nomads in the north along the Sudanese border. Tribal religions (5%) are professed by a minority within each tribe, with the exception of the Binga Pygmies (99%) and Mbimou (60%).

Catholics arrived in 1894, opening the first mission at Bangui. Elevated to a vicariate in 1937, the church now consists of five dioceses under an African archbishop. Christianity grew rapidly after territorial independence in 1959, when professing Christians grew from 42 percent Protestant to 47 percent in 1975. Catholicism saw a 4 percent rise from 28 percent, making this growth the most dramatic in Africa. The Baptist Mid-Missions arrived in 1920, followed a year later by the Church of the Brethren mission which sponsored a hospital, dispensaries, Bible schools, and a school of theology. The Sudan Mission, started by Lutherans in 1923, was later assisted by the American Lutheran Church and the Church of Norway.

The Association of Central African Evangelical Churches was organized in 1974 to facilitate cooperation between Protestant denominations. Two years later, the interdenominational Bangui Evangelical School of Theology opened, offering higher degrees in theology.

GARY LAMB

Bibliography. D. B. Barrett, *WCE.*

Ch'eng, Ching-yi (1881–1939). Chinese indigenous church leader. Son of a pastor of a church of the LONDON MISSIONARY SOCIETY, Ch'eng became pastor of the Mi Shih Street Church of Christ in China. He assisted in translating the Union Version of the Chinese Bible while in Britain in 1903, and gave a memorable speech at the WORLD MISSIONARY CONFERENCE in Scotland in 1910. He declared that Chinese Christians were not interested in Western denominations. In 1912 and 1913 he was interpreter as JOHN R. MOTT visited China on behalf of the WMC's Continuation Committee. Ch'eng served as the secretary of the China Continuation Committee (1913–22), and was instrumental in organizing the National Christian Conference in Shanghai (1922). He served as the secretary of the National Christian Council (1924–34), and from 1934 as the secretary of the Church of Christ in China, a union denomination made up of Presbyterian, Congregational, and Methodist congregations organized in 1927. Thus he embodied the movement of Chinese churches to unite the works of various missions, and to shape their own ministry and theology in the Chinese context. Ch'eng was one of the organizers of the INTERNATIONAL MISSIONARY COUNCIL (1921), and served as vice president from 1928 to 1938.

SAMUEL LING

Chad *(Est. 2000 pop.: 7,307,000; 1,284,000 sq. km. [495,752 sq. mi.]).* Chad is a land-locked country located in north-central Africa. The population is comprised of some 181 ethnic groups speaking 127 languages. Johnstone reports that it has more unreached people groups than any other African country. Under French rule and protection since 1900, Chad achieved independence in 1960. A variety of wars resulting from political infighting along religious and ethnic lines over the past thirty years and regular periods of severe drought have left the country economically devastated.

The single largest religion is Islam (almost 46%), followed by Christianity (35%) and traditional religions (19%). Islam arrived in the eleventh century, though until recently it has been confined largely to the desert-dominated north and eastern parts of the country. Of the Christians, roughly 20 percent are Catholic and 14 percent Protestant. The first Catholic missionaries arrived in the 1600s, though the first permanent station was not established until 1929 and extensive work did not commence until 1947.

The first Protestant missionaries, Rev. and Mrs. Berge Revnes with the Church of Lutheran Brethren, arrived in Chad in 1920. It took them four years to secure permission from the French to evangelize. Workers from Christian Missions in Many Lands arrived in 1921, Baptist Mid-Missions began their work in 1925, and the Sudan United Mission in 1927. By 1993, 249 Protestant missionaries representing 28 agencies were present in Chad. The vast bulk of missionary work has been confined to the non-Muslim south. Also by 1993 a reported 54 Chad nationals served as missionaries in other countries.

A. SCOTT MOREAU

Bibliography. D. W. Barrett, ed., *WCE;* P. Johnstone, *OW.*

Chalmers, James (1841–1901). Scottish missionary to the South Pacific. Born into a Scottish stonemason's home in Ardrishaig, and converted at age fourteen, he worked briefly with the Glasgow City Mission before studying for the Congregational ministry at Cheshunt College, Cambridge. Ordained in 1865, he trained further under the LONDON MISSIONARY SOCIETY, and in 1867 was sent first to Raratonga in the Cook Islands, then in 1877 to New Guinea. It was dangerous work: once Chalmers and his wife were threatened by the stark ultimatum, "Presents—or death." Slowly, however, they won the trust of the local peoples. As he furthered the work of evangelization and education Chalmers wrote, "It is not the preaching of a sermon so much as living the life that tells on the native heart." An advocate of INDIGENOUS CHURCHES who sought to preserve what was good in local customs, Chalmers set up a string of mission posts, established a training college, and shared his geographical interests in *Pioneer Life and Work in New Guinea* (1895). While pressing on into territory unknown to Europeans, Chalmers was killed on Goaribari Island, Papua.

J. D. DOUGLAS

Bibliography. D. Langmore: *Missionary Lives: Papua, 1874–1914.*

Chamberlain, Jacob (1835–1908). American medical missionary to India. Born in Sharon, Connecticut, he was educated at Western Reserve College, the New Brunswick (N.J.) Theological Seminary, and the College of Physicians and Surgeons, New York. In 1859 he sailed for India as a medical missionary to the Arcot mission in Madras under the appointment of the Dutch Reformed Board. He initially worked among the Tamils and was involved in teaching and administration at the Theological Seminary. In 1863 he was transferred to a district among people who spoke the Telugu language.

Combining his medical expertise with his evangelistic endeavors, he often took lengthy and arduous missionary journeys to places where the name of Jesus had never been heard. For many years he was the only physician in an area as large as his home state.

His literary labors included involvement in tract societies and overseeing the committee for the translation of the Bible in the Telugu language. He translated the liturgy of the Dutch Reformed Church, and also produced devotional works and a version of a hymnbook into the Telugu language. In 1900 he represented the Reformed Church at the ECUMENICAL MISSIONARY CONFERENCE in New York City. The following year he became the first moderator of the South India United Church Synod.

Chamberlain effectively used his medical and surgical work to open the way for Christian teaching. Considered one of the most enterprising of modern missionaries, he is credited in large measure for the marked success and rapid growth of the Christian church in India. His amazing experiences became the primary material for tracts and books. His works include *Religions of the Orient, The Kingdom in India, The Cobra's Den,* and *In the Tiger Jungle.*

FLORENCE R. SCOTT

Bibliography. J. C. Lambert, *Missionary Knights of the Cross.*

Chambers, Oswald (1874–1917). Scottish author, poet, and missionary to troops in Egypt. Born in Aberdeen, the eighth of nine children in a poor family serving the Baptist Church in Scotland, he received Christ as a teen while walking home after hearing Spurgeon preach.

Chambers' talents are seen in his poetic, musical, and artistic abilities. At the conclusion of his studies at the National Art Training School, he declined the offer of a two-year scholarship to study art in Europe, having observed the spiritual decline of others who followed that path. Eighteen months into a two-year art program at Edinburgh, he followed God's call to pursue ministerial training.

Throughout the rest of his life, Chambers preached, taught, and traveled (including a short trip to Japan and regular tours to teach in the United States). His last field of service was in Egypt, where, under the auspices of the YMCA, he and his family served the troops stationed there during World War I. There he died from complications after an emergency appendectomy, leaving behind his wife Gertrude (Biddy) and his daughter Kathleen.

Chambers is not remembered as much for his missionary service as he is for the inspiration he provided to countless missionaries through his book *My Utmost for His Highest*, a compilation of daily devotionals put together by Biddy after Chambers' death. Though her name nowhere appears on the book, it is to her that the body of Christ owes a debt of gratitude that can never be repaid.

A. SCOTT MOREAU

Bibliography. D. McCasland, *Oswald Chambers: Abandoned to God.*

Channel Islands. *See* UNITED KINGDOM DEPENDENT AREA *(Est. 2000 pop: 152,000; 195 sq. km. [75 sq. mi.]).*

Chapman, J. Wilbur (1859–1918). American crusade evangelist. Born in Richmond, Indiana, he studied at Oberlin College, Lake Forest University, and Lane Seminary (in Cincinnati). After his ordination in the Presbyterian Church in 1882, he served for twenty years in the American Midwest, stirring congregations to revival and becoming one of the founders of the Winona Lake Bible Conference in 1885. Appointed a full-time evangelist in 1903, he traveled internationally, conducting successful campaigns in Great Britain (1910 and 1914) and Australia (1909 and 1912). In 1917 he was elected general moderator of the Presbyterian Church U.S.A.

Influenced by D. L. MOODY and influencing BILLY SUNDAY, Chapman was among those on the forefront of the efforts at using CRUSADE EVANGELISM to reach American cities for Christ in the late nineteenth and early twentieth centuries. His own mark was the development of the use of simultaneous campaigns in which multiple events using varied means were held at the same time as the central crusade helping to ensure a metropolitan area was blanketed with the gospel. His crusades were characterized by extensive preparation, a method emulated by many crusade evangelists today.

A. SCOTT MOREAU

Bibliography. J. P. Cogdill, *A Major Stream of American Mass Evangelism: The Ministries of R. A. Torrey, J. W. Chapman and W. E. Biederwolf;* F. C. Oltman, *J. Wilbur Chapman: A Biography;* E. Reese, *The Life and Ministry of Wilbur Chapman, 1859–1918;* P. C. Wilt, *DCA,* pp. 240–41.

Charismatic Missionaries. *See* INDEPENDENT CHARISMATIC MISSIONARIES.

Charismatic Missions. The charismatic movement, also known as the charismatic renewal and Neo-Pentecostalism, is a worldwide revival movement, an extension of the Pentecostal revival that began around the turn of the century (*see* PENTECOSTAL MOVEMENT). While charismatics tend to emphasize the gifts of healing, prophecy, and words of knowledge over tongues, the distinction between the two movements remains blurred. Walter Hollenweger refers to the charismatic movement as "Pentecostalism within the churches," while his student, Arnold Bittlinger, includes Pentecostalism within his definition of charismatic. Pentecostal healing ministries active in the 1950s, such as those led by Oral Roberts, T. L. Osborn, and Jack Coe, attracted public attention and developed their following independent of the Pentecostal denominations which spawned them. They were influential along with the Full Gospel Business Men's Fellowship, International, founded by Demos Shakarian, and David Du Plessis, an ecumenical Pentecostal leader from South Africa, in bringing Pentecostalism into mainline Protestant churches. By 1975, a strong charismatic influence was present in all mainline American Protestant denominations, and the renewal was well under way within the Roman Catholic Church.

The charismatic movement grew dramatically in the 1980s and 1990s. Jimmy Swaggert, Jim and Tammy Bakker, Kenneth Copeland, Kenneth Hagen, and others were affiliated with Pentecostal denominations but maintained independent ministries which attracted charismatic audiences. They were joined by independent charismatic ministries such as the Christian Broadcasting Network, started by Pat Robertson, and the Trinity Broadcasting Network of Paul Crouch to dominate Christian media and claim the allegiance of a large part of Christian America. Renewal movements are evangelistic by nature, and most of these mega-ministries sought international visibility to extend their influence. A conservative estimate of the number of charismatics worldwide is 150 million, including more than 3,000 new denominations.

Charismatics who remained in their denominational churches had the benefit of established mission boards. As the renewal gained strength within a given denomination, the number of charismatic missionaries and mission leaders increased. Independent charismatics, on the other hand, lacked formal links to mission agencies. They sometimes joined nondenominational mission organizations but often met with suspicion due to their charismatic beliefs. There was a trend toward unity and evangelistic urgency in the 1980s and 1990s, with charismatic churches working together and forming associations of churches.

The movement had a prolonged internal focus due to the denominational structures it sought to reform. This carried over into the independent churches. When the leaders considered mission outreach, they looked for new strategies and approaches rather than relying on established agencies which were perceived as rigid and lifeless. They eschewed organizational structure yet lacked the internal structure to support missionaries.

Independent charismatic churches want direct involvement in missions. They become what are known as "sending churches," with as many as 125 missionaries receiving the majority of their support from one congregation. Effective congregations are characterized by having a missions director or pastor, missions-minded senior pastor, missions spending of over 10 percent of the budget, regular exposure of the congregation to missions, relationship to missionary structures, and contact with charismatic churches and ministries on the field.

The Vineyard Christian Fellowship, under the direction of John Wimber, introduced the concept of "power evangelism" in which a believer is instructed by the Holy Spirit to initiate contact with an unbeliever and SIGNS AND WONDERS accompany the encounter (*see also* POWER ENCOUNTER). The Vineyard is an example of an association of churches that has recently developed missions awareness and international outreach.

A few charismatic mission agencies were formed that have experienced unusual success. Youth With a Mission (YWAM), which gained its popularity as a short-term missionary venture, is the largest sending agency, with 6,000 full-time missionaries.

Its founder, Loren Cunningham, began with a vision to send young people from North America around the world but quickly expanded to include young people from every country. Another organization, Christ for the Nations, founded by Gordon Lindsay, claims to have planted over 8,500 congregations around the world.

The Association of International Mission Agencies (AIMS) provides a much-needed structure for charismatic mission outreach. Established in 1985 to link churches, mission agencies, and training institutions, AIMS facilitates cooperation among charismatic agencies. In addition to bridging diversity ranging from church planters to short-term professionals to tentmakers, the Association provides for the ongoing information needs of its constituency. Under the direction of Howard Foltz, the Association has grown to nearly 200 member organizations.

The Pentecostal World Conference, held every four or five years since 1944, attempted to unify Pentecostals/charismatics worldwide. These meetings focused on self-identification. With the rise of the renewal within the Roman Catholic Church, separate charismatic conferences were held to allow for the participation of Roman Catholics in leadership roles. These large gatherings gradually took on the evangelistic priorities of evangelical Christianity but never attained the numerical strength or broad representation of the movement that the leaders had envisioned.

The 1977 Kansas City Charismatic Conference was an ecumenical North American conference with an emphasis on the lordship of Christ. It was at this historic meeting that the three major streams of the North American Pentecostal/charismatic movement—classical Pentecostals, Protestant charismatics, and Roman Catholic charismatics—formed a coalition. Together they began to realize their responsibility to fulfill the GREAT COMMISSION.

The first North American Congress on the Holy Spirit and World Evangelization was held in 1986 in New Orleans. The second and largest of the two was held the next year, also in New Orleans. These conferences are credited with making world evangelization a central focus of the charismatic movement. The participants adopted the Lausanne Covenant and identified with the evangelistic goals of evangelical Christianity.

The 1990 North American Congress on the Holy Spirit and World Evangelization at Indianapolis, the third in the series, was held to prepare North Americans for the international meeting the following year. Enthusiasm was at a high pitch but did not translate into significant participation at Brighton the next year.

Brighton '91 was the International Charismatic Consultation of World Evangelization. With the working title "That the World Might Believe," this consultation was designed to prepare the worldwide charismatic movement for the "decade of evangelism." Although the geographical representation was uneven, this is thought to have been the first truly global meeting for world evangelization held by the movement. Many prominent American leaders were not in attendance nor did they endorse the gathering. Thus Brighton '91 symbolizes not only the lack of international unity but also the lack of cohesion among charismatics in North America. Orlando '95, the fourth North American Congress, was well attended but fell short of expectations.

It is hard to judge the impact of these congresses on the charismatic movement, yet they did serve as a visible demonstration of charismatic interest in missions. They also provided a means to inform large segments of the movement that evangelism is a priority. The movement itself, however, remains fragmented in its approach to world evangelization. By nature, the constituency is pulled in several directions. Ecclesiastical allegiance, participation in larger ecumenical networks, local priorities, special interests, and extensive diversity are just some of the factors which account for the current fragmentation.

The theoretical framework of the charismatic movement includes a working theology or theology of ministry. This in part led to an incomplete THEOLOGY OF MISSION as it was viewed as a simple extension of the local witness of the church. Prompted by an awareness of what was happening within the rest of Christendom, charismatics wanted to join in CROSS-CULTURAL EVANGELISM. Their Pentecostal heritage included an anti-intellectual bias often equating supernatural experience with sufficient preparation to be effective in a THIRD WORLD setting. Involvement of the laity is paramount as opposed to dependence on a trained clergy. These factors delayed the development of an effective mission strategy and, in the early days of the movement, produced many missionaries who lacked appropriate preparation for CROSS-CULTURAL MINISTRY. As with the Pentecostal movement, this trend has been corrected, and charismatic missiologists are poised to make a significant contribution to world evangelization in the twenty-first century.

While the actual number of charismatic Christians in the world is a source of constant debate, the fact that together with the Pentecostals they represent the largest segment of Christianity today is well documented. The flexibility of charismatic belief and practice facilitates its INCULTURATION in Third World countries. The Holy Spirit is expected to directly guide the local leadership as they establish local patterns of practice and APOLOGETICS.

Missionary churches were strongly influenced by the renewal following the assumption of control by natural leaders. Following World War II,

the transfer of control to national leadership spread rapidly throughout the countries of the Third World. Western Christian denominations realized the need to do the same within their mission churches. As the transfer of power was in progress, the influence of the charismatic movement was growing internationally. There was a new openness to the priorities of Third World Christians and recognition that the result was rapid church growth.

The renewal introduced the option for rhythmic clapping and dancing and vocal expressions during the worship service. It encouraged the use of local folk or popular music in church services. Charismatics recognized satanic forces at work in the world requiring prayer for God's supernatural intervention. They also prayed for healing and miracles, expecting God to demonstrate his power. The dramatic international growth of charismatic Christianity made a significant impact on the Western world, as it became a force too large to ignore.

While global unity has yet to be realized, the charismatic renewal has had the effect of a grassroots ecumenism. The common spiritual experience became a catalyst for a broad-based Christian unity. It contained an evangelistic thrust that assumed every Christian was a witness for Christ. Cooperative evangelistic efforts include pentecostal, neo-fundamental, Roman Catholic, and mainline Protestant Christians. Charismatic interest in world evangelization matured in the 1980s although financial support for missions remains below the average for evangelical churches. Charismatic missiologists and agencies are emerging.

Some feel the charismatic movement is God's plan to energize the church for evangelistic outreach. The belief that the gifts of the Spirit are for evangelistic purposes is especially true for Third World charismatics. Protestant charismatics are active in creating new ministries and promoting evangelistic concern. Roman Catholic charismatics have established programs to further world evangelization including the Catholic Evangelization Training Program at the Franciscan University of Steubenville (Ohio) and Evangelization 2000.

KENNETH D. GILL

See also Pentecostal Missions.

Bibliography. D. B. Barrett, *IBMR*, July 1988, pp. 119–21; A. Bittlinger, ed., *The Church is Charismatic*; W. Hollenweger, *The Pentecostals*; idem, *OBMR*, April 1980, pp. 68–75; G. B. McGee, *Toward the Twenty-first Century in Christian Mission*, pp. 41–53; idem, *OPCM*, pp. 610–25; L. G. McClung, *Pneuma*, 16 (1994): 11–21; K. Poewe, ed., *Charismatic Christianity as a Global Culture*; E. Pousson, *Spreading the Flame: Charismatic Churches and Missions Today*; D. Shibley, *A Force on the Earth: The Charismatic Renewal and World Evangelization*.

Charismatic Movement. *See* CHARISMATIC MISSIONS and PENTECOSTAL MOVEMENT.

Charles, Pierre (1883–1954). Belgian Catholic missiologist. Charles joined the Society of Jesus (the Jesuits) at age sixteen. After studying philosophy in England and Germany, he was ordained in 1910. He became fluent in five languages besides his native French, not counting Latin and Greek. Charles traveled widely during his lifetime, visiting Catholic missions in Africa and India, among other places. From 1914 until his death he was on the faculty of the Jesuit preparatory institute in Louvain, Belgium. There, influenced by the work of Robert Streit, he began in 1923 to develop a scientific theology of missions that emphasized rational preparation, the planting of the Christian church among all peoples, the adaptation of the gospel to individual cultures, and the need for indigenous clergy to take over leadership. He taught that Christians should approach evangelism with an understanding of respect for the value of non-Christian cultures and religions. He helped create the missions program at Gregorian University in Rome in 1932 and taught there, in addition to Louvain, for several years. Charles, through his instruction, students, writings, and conferences (the Semaines de Missiologie was held annually at Louvain except during World War II), had a profound influence on the theology and practice of missions throughout the Catholic Church and other Christian denominations. The documents of the SECOND VATICAN COUNCIL (1962–65) were heavily influenced by his doctrines.

ROBERT SHUSTER

Chastity. *See* SEXUAL MORES.

Chestnut, Eleanor (1868–1905). American medical missionary and martyr in China. Having qualified as a doctor, she arrived in South China in 1893 as a missionary under the auspices of the American Presbyterian Board of Missions. A woman of independent means, she built her own hospital. Such was her dedication that on one occasion she used skin from her own leg for a skin graft for a patient with severe burns. During the Boxer Rebellion she remained at her post longer than any other missionary before being evacuated. She returned only a year later. But the authorities were not yet in full control, and after her hospital was stormed by a xenophobic mob, she sacrificed her life vainly trying to rescue two newly arrived colleagues, who were also murdered.

ELEANOR M. JACKSON

Bibliography. H. Montgomery, *Western Women in Eastern Lands;* R. A. Tucker, *FJIJ.*

Chi-Oang (1872–1946). Chinese evangelist in Taiwan. Chi-Oang did not come to Christ until she was fifty-two years old. At that time her reputation was that of one who had successfully reconciled her fiercely independent mountain people, the Sediq, with the Japanese during their occupation of Taiwan. The occupation prevented mission work among any of the mountain tribes on Taiwan. As a result, at the age of fifty-eight, she was encouraged by a Presbyterian missionary couple, James and Lillian Dickson, to enter a two-year Bible training school and to work among her own people. Chi-Oang was uniquely fitted for this, enjoying freedom of movement and respect from both sides because of her previous work.

Finishing Bible school, she became a fearless evangelist and discipler, and the Japanese sought numerous times to stop her. Each time, however, she was spared arrest through God's providential oversight and the loyal help of her followers. As result of her ministry, at the end of World War II and the Japanese occupation, thousands of the Sediq descended from the mountains to be baptized. She died shortly after the churches gained their freedom, her work complete of building, sustaining, and nurturing them through this time.

A. SCOTT MOREAU

Bibliography. E. Band, ed., *He Brought Them Out: The Story of the Christian Movement among the Mountain Tribes of Formosa;* L. M. Cheng, *CDCWM,* pp. 98–99; R. Winslow, *The Mountains Sing: God's Love Revealed to Taiwan Tribes.*

Child Evangelism. Both biblical and historical records document the priority among global cultures of passing on a spiritual heritage to the next generation. While we may observe concerted efforts throughout church history to baptize, catechize, and evangelize children and youth, until recently there has been a dearth of global strategic planning to address children and youth as a particular focus of worldwide missionary efforts.

The New Testament and records of the Apostolic Fathers are quite clear when they speak of children and faith. The training of a child was a parental responsibility; failure by parents in carrying out this responsibility brought sorrow to child and parent alike. Second- and early-third-century Christians baptized neither infants nor young children, but by A.D. 250 infant baptism was practiced, particularly in North African Christianity. Cyprian of Carthage and AUGUSTINE OF HIPPO argued that original sin was the chief reason for the need to baptize infants and no one, including children, should be refused God's mercy and grace. While the Reformation produced groups with varying viewpoints on baptism of children, there did emerge a variety of catechetical approaches, which indicates the intentionality of churches born out of the Reformation to instruct and nurture children to full participation in Christian faith.

Although its impact and significance has been disputed, the Sunday school stands as a historical representation of concern for children and Christian faith. Its origins in England in the 1780s stems from efforts by Robert Raikes and others to educate marginalized poor children caught in massive changes brought about by the Industrial Revolution. The American version emerged as a pioneering-missionary vehicle with obvious shades of American revivalism. For example, the American Sunday School Union began in 1824 with the resolve to establish "Sunday schools in every destitute place in the Valley of the Mississippi."

The last half of the nineteenth century saw the Sunday school movement grow to international prominence as "uniform lessons" became a vehicle of expansion. By 1900 3 million English-speaking students used these lessons in New Zealand, Australia, Japan, Korea, China, Africa, and wherever British or American missionaries served. The uniform lessons were also translated into scores of languages that increased the influence of the Sunday school worldwide.

Evangelistic Sunday schools in the United States have gone through both growth and decline patterns during the twentieth century, but their evangelistic focus on children has remained constant. Research indicates that 85 percent of people make decisions for Jesus Christ before they reach fifteen years of age.

Recent studies support the strategic significance of evangelism to children. One-third of the world's population is under fifteen years of age, with 85 percent of those under fifteen living in the Third World. The vast group of children existing in non-Western settings are increasingly living in urban slums. Forty thousand children under five die daily and some estimate that 100 million children live or work on city streets worldwide. Exploitation of children as child laborers and sex objects is growing rapidly. Two-thirds of an estimated 130 million children worldwide with no access to basic education are girls.

This tragic present state of the world's children, particularly in non-Western settings, highlights a number of missiological implications. While children need to hear the gospel of Jesus Christ in contextualized forms that state clearly the forgiveness present in the work of Christ, missions strategists increasingly plan and implement holistic forms of ministry to children. The plight of the urban poor, where growing numbers of children can be found, requires a reevaluation of Christian mission in urban contexts. Crucial to any mission strategy to children is the growing evidence that women are the key to societal change and have the most impact on the lives of children. Mission agencies in the future will no longer be able to avoid developing strategies for ministry to children and may even have to rethink the PEOPLE GROUP concept with its priority on adults.

BYRON D. KLAUS

Bibliography. W. Barclay, *Educational Ideals in the Ancient World;* L. Hunt, *Handbook on Child Evangelism;* C. Ingle, ed., *Children and Conversion;* R. Lynn and E. Wright, *The Big Little School: Two Hundred Years of Sunday School;* B. Myers, *IBMR* 18:3 (1994); D. C. Wyckoff, ed., *Renewing the Sunday School and the CCD;* UNICEF, *Children of the Americas.*

Chile *(Est. 2000 pop.: 15,311,000; 756,945 sq. km. [292,256 sq. mi.]).* Chile is a South American republic located along the western slope of the Andes (2,600 miles long and averaging 110 miles wide), bordered by Peru and Bolivia on the north, Argentina on the east, and the Pacific Ocean on the west. Because of its length, climates vary from the hot, dry northern desert to the glaciers, stormy islands, and chilly Tierra del Fuego in the far south. Most of the population lives in a 600-mile stretch of the central valley, with the capital city, Santiago (over 5 million), as the focal point. Hydroelectric plants along the short but rapidly falling streams generate 75 percent of the nation's power. Chile's population is relatively well-educated, with a reported 94 percent literacy level. There are more than 230,000 enrolled in universities. Two of Chile's authors, Gabriela Mistral and Pablo Neruda, have won Nobel prizes for literature. Chile is a typical Latin American democracy with a successful expanding economy and the burden of a large, although shrinking, number of persons living below the poverty level. With the help of foreign investment, the economy has improved to the point where in 1995 the country became a candidate to join the North American Free Trade Act (NAFTA). The Spanish, who invaded in the sixteenth and seventeenth centuries, intermarried with the native Araucanians, which accounts for the mixed ancestry of 72 percent of the population. The total native American peoples account for nearly 7 percent of the population. Some 928,000 are Mapuche, descendants of the original Araucanians. Prior to freedom from Spain in 1810, Chile was subservient to the government and economic life of Lima, Peru. This led to a pervasive illegal trade with contraband goods. With intervals of conservative government controlled by the established and wealthy landowners *(latifundios)* and intermissions of military dictatorship, the country arrived at the middle of the twentieth century with unrealized expectations that the nation's riches in fertilizers and minerals would be shared by the disenfranchised masses. Increasing dissatisfaction with the deteriorating economic situation and strong leftist-Marxist influence on the university level and in the national congress resulted in the 1970 minority election of Salvador Allende to the presidency. Unprepared for victory and not knowing how to apply Marxist principles to an ailing economy, Allende added his own personal confusion, and the national standard of living spiraled downward. Both Roman Catholic and Protestant churches became involved in the politics and added to the confusion. After three years of the Allende government, in a bloody coup, the military installed Augusto Pinochet as president, who eventually became convinced that he was indispensable. Pinochet's success with the economy paralleled a growing unrest over his government's dictatorial ways. Pinochet lost a plebiscite in 1988, which led to the installation of a civilian government at the end of 1989 whose present administration is based on seventeen political parties.

According to some statistics as few as 60 percent or as many as 75 percent of Chileans claim to be Roman Catholic although attendance at Mass on any given weekend is more likely 15 percent. Liberation theology and the charismatic movement have had significant impact in the life of the Catholic Church. The key to understanding present Protestant churches is the impact of the 1909 Pentecostal revival within the Methodist Church, which presently has a membership estimated at over 500,000. Estimates of Protestant church membership statistics vary widely from 16 percent to 30 percent of the total population. Pentecostal church membership is variously reported to be from 80 percent to 95 percent of Protestants. Having left behind the first generation's religious enthusiasm, now that the churches are populated with second-, third-, and even fourth-generation evangelicals, by 1993 it was estimated that only 44 percent of Protestants regularly attended church. One major concern within evangelicalism is how to reach the middle-class masses in the cities. Several church groups, such as the Christian and Missionary Alliance, Presbyterians, and the Baptist Convention are giving special attention to this need and have met with moderate success. Another concern is the training of workers for the huge indigenous Pentecostal churches. An attempt is being made to solve this problem through the Pentecostal Bible Institute.

An equal challenge for the indigenous Pentecostal and other Protestant churches has to do with ministries outside the church. Social outreach is below what it could be given the size of the Chilean church. The same can be said for the relatively small number of cross-cultural missionaries sent out by Chilean churches.

DAVID SPRUANCE

Bibliography. P. E. Dostert, ed., *Latin America 1995.*

China (*Est. 2000 pop.: 1,284,597,000; 9,560,961 sq. km. [3,691,487 sq. mi.]*). The Christian faith was first brought to China in A.D. 635 by Nestorian missionaries who followed the silk trade route from their well-established church base in Syria and Persia. Their bishop, Alopen, was welcomed in Changan (now Xian) by the reigning emperor, Tang Tai Zung. The Nestorians translated parts of their Bible and other literature into Chinese, often using Taoist and Buddhist terms to convey their meaning. Although the Nestorian faith spread to several major cities in China and boasted thousands of converts, its greatest growth may have been among the foreign trading community. As a result of a severe persecution under Emperor Wu Zung in A.D. 845, it lost its foothold in China proper, but continued to exert a Christian influence among the Kerait, Ongut, and Uighurs—tribes on the northern frontier of China.

At the end of the thirteenth century, the Khubilai Khan, Mongol ruler of China, invited the pope to send "one hundred teachers of science and religion" to instruct the Chinese. A papal interregnum, difficulty of travel, and uncertainty over the nature of this invitation meant that this request never received a response. However, in 1294 JOHN OF MONTECORVINO, a Franciscan, was sent to China. Within a short time he baptized six thousand Chinese, established churches in several cities, and had the New Testament and Psalms translated into the language of the court (probably a Mongolian dialect). By the time the Yuan (Mongol) dynasty was replaced by the Ming dynasty in 1368, there may have been as many as one hundred thousand Roman Catholic Christians. From this period until the arrival of the Jesuits in China at the end of the sixteenth century, no record exists of Christian churches in China.

The Society of Jesus (Jesuits), with MATTEO RICCI as its chief China representative, entered China in 1582 from its base in the Portuguese colony of Macao. First assuming a religious role, much like Buddhist monks, and then becoming more like Confucian scholars, Ricci and his Jesuit colleagues identified with the Chinese elite. They prepared maps, practiced astronomy, constructed and repaired clocks that they gave to the emperor, and wrote treatises on Christianity that related to the Confucian worldview. By the beginning of the eighteenth century the Christian church in China numbered two hundred thousand, including scholars, urban dwellers, and rural peasants.

Unlike the later-arriving Franciscans and Dominicans who disagreed sharply with them, most Jesuits were flexible about the Chinese culture. They viewed ancestral rites as civil deference, not religious worship, described Confucius in semi-sacred terms as holy, and used indigenous terms for God. Their differences with the other orders and the Vatican over these issues resulted in the "rites controversy." This lasted from the early

1600s until 1724, when the Yung Zheng emperor proscribed the Christian faith in China. This violent ecclesiastical dispute contributed to the pope's disbanding the Jesuit order worldwide in 1773. Missionaries from other orders continued to work secretly in China, and the church went through difficult periods of persecution.

ROBERT MORRISON, an Englishman, came to Macao in 1807 as the first Protestant missionary to China. At that time foreigners were not allowed to live in China, and Morrison and others following him had to engage in trade in Canton or live and witness in other cities where there were Chinese, including Singapore, Penang, Malacca, Bangkok, and Batavia (Jakarta). The attempt of England to import opium into China resulted in the opium war of 1840. China's defeat led to a series of unequal treaties in 1842–44 and 1858–60 by the Western powers. These opened up China to trade, diplomacy, and missionary presence. Unfortunately, it put the stamp of "foreign" upon the Christian faith and caused some Chinese to protest: "You introduced two things to us by force, neither one of which we desired—opium and Christianity."

The Protestant mission in China expanded from a trickle of missionaries in 1842 to a high of nearly eight thousand by 1930. Over a period of 150 years, they engaged in all of the traditional types of ministry: production of grammars, dictionaries, Bibles, booklets, and tracts; evangelism and church planting among the Han Chinese and many minority groups; education, both general and theological, at all levels; establishment of hospitals and missions of mercy; opposition to evils such as footbinding, infanticide, and opium. Catholic missions, with their unique perspective, expanded in much the same way.

From 1840 to 1900 many "missionary incidents" occurred between the Chinese government and missionaries. These culminated in the huge antiforeign Boxer Rebellion of 1900, when many foreign missionaries and Chinese converts were killed.

From the fall of the Ch'ing dynasty (1911) until the advent of the People's Republic of China (1949), the control of churches and Christian activities increasingly was transferred from foreign mission agencies to Chinese church bodies. By 1949 there were about 750,000 Protestant Christians and probably double that number of Catholics—not very many for a country of 400 million people. Furthermore, Protestant churches were denominationally divided, generally small, and struggling to escape the epithet of "foreign."

During the past fifty years under the People's Republic of China, foreign religious workers have used nonmissionary roles to continue their Christian witness in China. More important, Protestant Chinese churches, now viewed as truly Chinese, have grown to numbers estimated at 20 to

60 million. These Protestant Christians worship and witness in three different contexts: in churches related to the China Christian Council; in autonomous Christian communities (often called house churches); and in student fellowship groups on school campuses.

Although under greater or lesser pressure from the government, the CCC and autonomous communities conduct normal church life, produce Christian literature, engage in witness, and establish training programs to develop new leaders.

RALPH R. COVELL

Bibliography. A. Hunter and K. K. Chan, *Protestantism in Contemporary China;* K. S. Latourette, *A History of Christian Missions in China;* S. Moffett, *A History of Christianity in Asia;* B. Whyte, *Unfinished Encounter: China and Christianity.*

China Inland Mission. *See* OVERSEAS MISSIONARY FELLOWSHIP.

China (Taiwan). An island that was under Japanese rule from 1895 to 1945, Taiwan is one hundred miles east of the China coast. After the fall of mainland China to the Communists in 1949, Taiwan became the refuge of the Nationalist Chinese government. More than 98% of the 21 million population are Han Chinese. Most of the them (Taiwanese 74%, Hakka 11%) immigrated to Taiwan more than two hundred years ago. The others (13%) are Mandarin-speaking refugees who came from mainland China after 1948. Although the majority speak Taiwanese, the official language and the language of education is Mandarin. The Malaya-Polynesian mountain peoples (1.7%) are divided into nine tribes.

The most popular religion in Taiwan is folk religion (70%), a combination of Buddhism and Taoism with an animistic worldview. Less than 4% of the population are Christians (1.4% Roman Catholic and 2.5% Protestant), with the Presbyterian Church of Taiwan the largest Protestant denomination (about 50% of the Protestants).

Between 1627 and 1664 the Dutch Reformed Church sent thirty-seven missionaries to Taiwan to minister to Dutch traders. They also made a major missionary outreach into the aboriginal communities. However, the missionaries were driven out after the Manchu established their control over Taiwan in 1683. In 1859, several Dominican Catholic missionaries arrived. The Protestant missionary efforts, pioneered by the English Presbyterian James Maxwell in the south (1865) and the Canadian Presbyterian GEORGE LESLIE MACKAY in the north (1872), proved difficult and dangerous.

Progress was slow in the early stages. Under the occupation by Japan, the missionaries had considerable freedom until 1940. The church grew dramatically between 1950 and 1960 because of the influx and conversion of refugees from mainland China. Roman Catholics soared from 13,000 in 1945 to 180,000 by 1960; the Protestant community shot up from 51,000 in 1948 to 220,000 by 1960. But stagnation has set in since then despite major evangelistic outreaches.

Protestants are unequally distributed among the different linguistic groups. About 23% of the mountain people are nominal Protestant as are 4.6% of the Mandarin, 1% of the Taiwanese, and 0.5% of the Hakka. More than thirty seminaries and Bible schools provide leadership training. The lack of pastors has become a serious problem.

The Year 2000 Gospel Movement set a specific and ambitious goal of 2 million believers, 10,000 churches, and 200 overseas missionaries sent out from Taiwan by the year 2000. Progress has not been very encouraging. In 1996 there were only about 490,000 Protestants and 3,361 churches. The revival of Buddhism and traditional Chinese religions is the greatest challenge to Christianity in Taiwan.

TSU-KUNG CHUANG

Bibliography. A. J. Swanson, *The Church in Taiwan: Profile 1980.*

Chinese House Church Movement.

As a form of ministry, the house church movement in China is a contextual response to political pressure. In the 1950s, after the expulsion of missionaries from China, those who refused to join the Three-Self Patriotic Movement (TSPM) were not allowed to worship in their churches; so they started a movement that recaptured the worship of the early Christians at home (Acts 2:46; 5:42; 1 Cor. 16:19). This form was viable because meetings could be moved from one place to another at any time and could not be easily detected by local authorities. During the Cultural Revolution, when all churches were closed down by the government, all Christians could meet only in Christian homes. The movement grew tremendously despite the hostile environment because it provided a true Christian community of commitment and love where many experienced the power of the Holy Spirit in miracles and radical life changes. Today the movement is massive in scope, with estimates ranging from 30 to 80 million participants as compared to a total Christian population of less than 1 million before the communist takeover in 1949.

The term "house church" refers to those who refuse to join the TSPM and to register with the government. The movement is not a denomination or ecclesiastical fellowship like what is found in the West. More accurately, it comprises individual house churches. There is no common statement of faith, no formal fellowship or denominational structures. It is, simply, a model of Christian community for places where structural expression is not possible. The most important feature of the house church movement is not a theological system, but a common stand defined by relationship to the TSPM and the Chinese government. This having been said, there are, however, certain common theological convictions among the house churches. One is obedience to the Word of God even to the point of risking one's life; another is the belief in the absolute separation of church and state, as the movement's adherents are convinced in the light of Scripture that government control is not acceptable.

CHE BIN TAN

Bibliography. D. Adeney, *China: The Church's Long March;* R. Fung, *Households of God on China's Soil;* M. D. Wong, *Spiritual Food.*

Chinese Mission Boards and Societies.

Chinese mission history on a wide scale began with the founding of the Chinese Foreign Missionary Union in 1928 by LELAND WANG. It represented an outreach to the scattered Chinese in the South Seas of Asia and to outposts including Borneo, Sarawak, Bali, Sumatra, and the Celebes. Later it expanded to include efforts in New Guinea, Fiji, Tahiti, and New Zealand. It was an indigenous faith effort focusing on church planting and church growth.

In 1947 Evangelize China Fellowship was established by ANDREW GIH. A faith mission with indigenous leadership, it labored in Hong Kong, Macao, and Taiwan, and later to the Chinese diaspora in Southeast Asia. Primary schools for girls and orphanages for the homeless demonstrated Gih's concern for the marginalized. Over fifty churches were planted as the mission reflected social and evangelistic concern.

Chinese mission activity on a broad scale shifted to the United States with the founding of the Chinese Christian Mission in October 1961, in Detroit, Michigan, under THOMAS WANG. Soon after, the mission moved to its present site (Petaluma, California) continuing its effort to reach both mainland and Chinese diaspora. Its global dimension includes work in Hong Kong, Taiwan, Singapore, the Philippines, Australia, and Canada, plus new thrusts to Siberia, Latin America, and the Chinese mainland. A staff of thirty full- and part-time workers undergird the work of twenty Chinese missionaries abroad. Its publishing house and San Francisco book room reach out to both believers and nonbelievers, contextualizing the gospel within Chinese traditional culture.

Another U.S. founded mission is Ambassadors for Christ. Established on May 6, 1963, by cofounders Ted Choy and Moses Chow, its focus is on the Chinese students. Its call was "to reach our kinsmen for Christ," with the hope that these persons might someday return to China and be "a force for the kingdom." The campus ministry centered around Bible study groups, where overseas Chinese students were won to Christ. Such students were then channeled into local Chinese churches for discipling.

Ambassadors for Christ undergirds its mission with a variety of publications to students, scholars, and believers in the Chinese churches. It provides leadership and resources for the growth of Chinese Christian families and American-born Chinese through seminars and conferences. It sponsors a triennial convention for North America, calling Chinese Christians to engage in world evangelism. The five previous conventions have seen attendees rise from an initial 300 to 1,800 in number, with hundreds having responded to the mission call. Unlike other Chinese mission efforts, which emphasized "going," Ambassadors for Christ has responded to those who have "come" to America. In this sense it has linked with the Chinese churches as a total mission force.

The Chinese Overseas Christian Mission was founded in 1950 by Stephen Y. T. Wang, then a student at Cambridge, England. His concern was directed to the four thousand Chinese in England and Europe, the primary task being evangelism and church planting. With Wang's death in 1971, Mary Wang and co-workers continued the mission. Today over thirty workers are based in the United Kingdom and Europe in over one hundred cities, ministering to over fifty churches and many more fellowships. With the opening of Eastern Europe and Russia, the mission extended its pioneering efforts.

With a population of eight hundred thousand Chinese in greater Europe today and only 2.5 percent of them reached for Christ, emphasis is directed to the huge numbers of Chinese restaurant workers. A new thrust now prevails among Chinese scholars from mainland China, Taiwan, and Hong Kong. Correspondence courses, lay seminars, and Theological Education by Extension (TEE) undergird the mission. Literature includes Chinese and English journals along with videos and cassettes.

Chinese mission history, as recounted, was indigenous and intracultural in nature, as first-generation Chinese reached out to their own. With over one thousand Chinese evangelical churches in North America alone, it appears that a steady supply of American-raised and American-born Chinese will bear the brunt of Chinese mission in the twenty-first century.

HOOVER WONG

SEE ALSO Asian Mission Boards and Societies.

Chitambar, Jashwaut Rao (1879–1940). Indian missions advocate. Chitambar was born in Allahabad, United Provinces (now Uttar Pradesh), the son of a Methodist minister father who had been disinherited by his family for converting to Christianity.

His early years of ministry were spent in the academy. Two years after graduating from Methodist Theological Seminary in Bareilly he married Viola Singh. In 1906 Chitambar was named a professor at Lucknow Christian College, where he later was named principal.

About this time Chitambar's interest in missions became evident. Along with K. T. PAUL and BISHOP AZARIAH, Chitambar founded the indigenous National Missionary Society in 1905. The society was one of the primary organizations advocating the CONTEXTUALIZATION of Christianity in India, using ashrams and brotherhoods along with the more traditional educational institutions and hospitals.

Chitambar put his knowledge to work as editor of the Hindustani Methodist periodical *Kaukab-I-Hind*, "Star of India," and as a member of the committee revising *The Standard Hindustani Dictionary*. A translator of hymns, he also wrote two biographies: *John Wesley* and *Mahatma Gandhi*. In 1931, three-quarters of a century after the advent of the Methodists to India, he was the first Indian to be elected bishop. Before India received international prominence and its independence in 1947, Chitambar was a well known and popular speaker for India in the United States and Europe. He died in Jubbulpore.

STANLEY M. GUTHRIE

Bibliography. J. Kane, *A Global View of Christian Missions;* S. Neill, *A History of Christian Missions.*

Cho, (David) Paul Yonggi (1936–). Korean pastor-evangelist of world's largest church. Cho was the oldest son of a farmer in Kyungnam province who had nine children. He graduated from the Full Gospel Theological Seminary and Kungmin University. When he became seriously sick and was on the verge of death in 1956, his future mother-in-law assisted him spiritually to experience divine healing. He also met an Assemblies of God missionary in Pusan who taught him Pentecostal doctrines and whose church he joined.

Cho started his ministry with a handful of people who helped him plant a tent ministry in the center of Seoul in 1961. This eventually resulted in Yoido Full Gospel Central Church, with over 700,000 members by 1993, including the members of the ten satellite churches scattered throughout Seoul. The Yoido Central Church sanctuary holds 20,000 people with six services on Sunday. The strength of his church is the well-organized 50,000 cell groups for Bible study and prayer.

Cho was elected to be the moderator of the Korean Assemblies of God in 1966, a position he held for over than ten years. In 1993 he was elected to be the president of the International

Assemblies of God. In 1994 he became the president of the only Christian daily newspaper in Korea. He has written numerous devotional books that have been translated into several vernacular languages. Cho's *The Fourth Dimension* explains his theology and philosophy of expectant visionary prayer, which he describes as the key to his success in ministry.

BONG RIN RO

Bibliography. S. Moffett, *TCDCB*, pp. 98–99; B. R. Ro and M. L. Nelson, *Korean Church Growth Explosion.*

Christ and Culture. *The Early Church's Interaction.* During its first sixteen centuries, the Western church's perception of cultures was borrowed from the Roman imperial view of the world. Culture was seen as a single, normative universal, a monocultural ideal to be stamped on the barbarian world outside the empire. With the collapse of Rome and the Western empire in the fifth century, the church became the custodian of that ideal.

In the Byzantine Empire of the East, and still today among the Orthodox family of churches, the pattern was different. The churches assimilated into existing ethnicities and languages: Greek, Coptic, Armenian, or Slavic.

By comparison, the Western church became the architect of a mono-ethnic church and imposed a single language (Latin) to promote it. Christendom's self-understanding as a superior world culture slowly grew to dominate Europe and beyond as the church expanded its reach. The CRUSADES against Islam, and later the brutal conquests of Latin America and the slave trade of Africa, became partial expressions of this cultural ethnocentrism.

In these earliest encounters with cultures, there were other responses. The abortive mission of the Nestorian Christians to China in the seventh and eighth centuries took a much more conciliatory approach in matters cultural and religious (*see* NESTORIAN MISSIONS). Minority voices like those of the Franciscan RAYMON LULL (c. 1235–1315) pled for compassion and educated understanding in dealing with Islam. From that Muslim world Western Christendom even borrowed ideas in philosophy, science, and mathematics. But these exceptions created no breaches in the prevailing and naive assumption that non-Western culture was largely an inventory of pagan items.

Iberian Expansion and the Counter-Reformation. The colonial advances of Spain and Portugal in the New World (1450–1760) brought Christendom's first large-scale contact with non-Western cultures. Secular power and coercion allied itself with persuasion. The combined motivations of "God, gold, and guns" reinforced earlier Western hostilities to "other cultures" as

"HEATHEN," a term carrying sociocultural and political connotations as weighty as theological ones.

Again, there were notable modifications of such attitudes. Bartolomé de las Casas (1474–1566) spent a lifetime protesting the colonialists' treatment of the indigenous peoples of Latin America.

Others were to press for more compassion and dignity. In China MATTEO RICCI (1552–1610) and his fellow Jesuit missionaries saw the culture not as an obstacle but a door for Christian penetration. His approval of the cult of Confucius and of ancestral rituals represented new ways to accommodate Christianity to the culture. Those accommodations would help stir what came to be called the Rites Controversy in the church (*see* ROMAN CATHOLIC MISSIONS).

The founding of the Sacred Congregation *de Propaganda Fide* in 1622 created a centralized organ for Catholic missionary activity that pled for evangelization by peaceful, not violent, means. It tended to encourage respect for the cultural way of life of other peoples and to oppose wholesale cultural domination. The Congregation introduced a rule-of-thumb distinction between the religious and secular aspects of culture. "Secular culture was not to be touched, but whatever did not conform to Catholic faith and morals was to be uprooted" (Shorter, 1992,144).

The distinction opened the door for those like the Jesuit missionary in south India, ROBERTO DE NOBILI (1577–1656). He sought a measure of legitimacy for Hindu institutions and customs, such as caste. Similar to Ricci, de Nobili could argue such customs were those of secular culture. They were therefore as compatible with the Catholic faith as those of ancient Rome.

Ultimately, however, these experiments were seen as dangerous, especially in view of the earlier COUNTER-REFORMATION decisions of the Catholic Church's Council of Trent (1545–63). In opposing the growing Protestant threat and its commitments to national and cultural pluralism on a formal church level, the Council hardened its monocultural perspectives, tragically at the very time when new cultures were being "discovered." Sweeping and rigid standardization of liturgy and theology closed the door for some time to future efforts like those of de Nobili and Ricci.

The Reformation Interlude. The beginnings of Protestantism in the sixteenth century did little of a practical sort to shift perceptions of culture as a monolith. It lacked the stimulus of global interaction and colonial power that the Catholic Church enjoyed until the end of the eighteenth century. Protestantism's attention was fixed on European Christendom as its mission field and its interests in culture were largely formed around institutional issues of church and state.

At the same time, theological paradigms and practices were being formed that would play a part in later modifications. Both Luther and Calvin rejected the Catholic view of ACCOMMODATION to culture that saw grace building on nature by way of divine modification. They affirmed the radical and extensive impact of SIN on human society while defending the exercise of the Christian's liberty in local political, cultural, or ecclesiastical customs.

They parted company in their perceptions of how the tensions between these two realities of sin and liberty could be resolved. Luther viewed the tension as one of Christ and culture in paradox, enduring one kingdom in the expectation of another more trans-historical kingdom. Calvin saw Christ as the transformer of humanity within culture and society, not apart from it. And, unlike both, the Anabaptist movement saw the community of God's people as more hostile to culture, to humanity's autonomous settings of values.

The Protestant insistence on the translation of the Bible would eventually help to break the monolithic paradigm of culture. Though not always clearly recognized, the genie of cultures was to spring out of its vernacular language bottle. BIBLE TRANSLATION would divinely validate the cultures of later converts throughout the world. It would help to change "culture" from a singular to a plural noun.

Initial Protestant Encounters with Cultures.
By the end of the eighteenth century, reversals were taking place in mission history. Catholic mission interest and efforts, after a flourishing century and a half, were in serious decline and Protestant efforts were growing. Protestant England and Holland replaced Catholic Spain and Portugal as colonial powers.

But Europe's sense of racist superiority continued to promote colonial expansion and its right and duty to rule the "inferior" cultures it dominated. Even the United States, though a latecomer to expansionist policies, was infected by its concept of "Manifest Destiny."

Protestantism's newly found vigor did not always free itself from those homeland self-perceptions of cultural superiority. In relative innocence, it had few doubts about either the wholesale depravity of cultural life in non-Western societies or Western culture as the culmination of human development.

Humanitarian motives quickly linked evangelization with "civilizing" (understood as Westernization). And the question, debated through much of the nineteenth century, became, Should one precede the other or were the two processes simultaneous?

Though disagreements were intense, either-or choices were rare in the early years (Hutchison, 1987,12). In America JOHN ELIOT (1604–90) withdrew Native American Christians from their cultural connections into Westernizing "praying towns." Fellow Puritan Cotton Mather (1663–1728) would add later, "The best thing we can do for our Indians is to Anglicize them" (Bosch, 1991, 260).

With the expansion of Protestant missions, doors opened for a wide variety of social services. The formation of the China Medical Missionary Society in 1838 gave medical missions a wide legitimacy. In India ALEXANDER DUFF (1806–78) touted the superiority of Western education as preparation for the gospel. His support for the use of English as the medium of instruction flowed from his hopes for an intellectual Anglicization to promote conversions.

Protestant Shifts in Understanding.
Not everyone shared completely the simplistic views of "barbaric" indigenous cultures that demanded Westernizing. German missiologist GUSTAV WARNECK (1834–1910), influenced by a national romanticism that glorified the *Volk* (the 'people'), saw cultures as gifts of God to be affirmed and preserved. And missionaries like BRUNO GUTTMANN (1876–1966) in Tanzania and CHRISTIAN KEYSSER (1877–1961) in Papua New Guinea created strategies to implement these convictions. Guttman resisted Western civilizing as an instrument that would destroy the peoplehood of traditional cultural patterns. Keysser supported "tribal conversions" and the building of the structures and leadership of the emerging church on clan and tribal foundations.

Meanwhile, others were questioning the traditional connections of civilizing and Christianizing as a growing "native church" demanded a shift in leadership from mission to national church. The old policies, built on skeptical disregard for human cultures, stood in the way of that transition.

Mission administrators HENRY VENN (1796–1873) of England's CHURCH MISSIONARY SOCIETY and RUFUS ANDERSON (1796–1880) of the AMERICAN BOARD OF COMMISSIONERS FOR FOREIGN MISSIONS led the way in such a shift. They called for "indigenous churches" of self-support, self-propagation, and self-government. And behind it lay their relative confidence that churches built on "native" culture could thrive with integrity and independence.

To that end Venn supported the training of "native clergy" and opposed Duff's promotion of education in the English language. And Anderson questioned repeatedly the legitimacy of "civilizing" or social transformation as an aim of missions. That would come, he argued, as a consequence of gospel impact and the "native" church's leavening of cultures.

Dissenting views also began to appear as a growing theological gulf sharply divided liberal from conservative. The difference widened into the twentieth century, shaping attitudes on evangelization and civilization into an almost either-or choice.

The earlier millennial optimism shared by British and American missions had seen the extension of Anglo-Saxon civilization as the extension of the KINGDOM OF GOD. Under the impact of liberalism, especially in its social gospel forms, millennialism took a revisionist shape. "Civilizing" and social service took priority over evangelization (*see* MILLENNIAL THOUGHT).

On the conservative side, the rise of the interdenominational FAITH MISSIONS from the 1860s and the growth of premillennialism shifted the focus to evangelization. Henry Frost of the CHINA INLAND MISSION wrote, "While it is always true that Christianity civilizes, it is never true that civilization Christianizes." Medicine and education were seen as "supportive" ministries. Cultural adaptations of a superficial sort were promoted for pragmatic reasons (Taber, 1991, 81). The American appearance of fundamentalism in the early twentieth century sharpened the differences even more.

From Culture to Cultures. Missionary optimism regarding the ultimate triumph of "Western civilization" dimmed severely with the participation of the "Christian" West in World War I and the global aftermath of the Great Depression. The political breakup of the Western colonial empires following World War II reinforced a worldwide awareness that culture was plural, not a singular.

Advancing this weariness with culture as a monolith was the growing discovery of SOCIOLOGY and CULTURAL ANTHROPOLOGY as tools for missions. In earlier decades outstanding ethnographies had been written by missionaries like R. H. CODRINGTON and Henri Junod. The research of Father Wilhelm Schmidt (1868–1954) in the global spread of cultures was an early influence in Catholic circles.

But not until the mid-1930s and the co-creation of Wycliffe Bible Translators, International and the Summer Institute of Linguistics did the full usefulness of these fledgling disciplines begin to impact the church both Protestant and Catholic. Through the early leadership of linguists like Kenneth Pike and Eugene Nida, missions began to see slowly that culture was not an abstract concept.

Under the impact of functionalism, the dominant anthropological school of the day, cultures were seen as discrete, bounded units. In their diverse forms, they became collective shapes of the ideas, values, and meanings of societies and peoples. They provided explanations, stability, and adaptive skills to understand oneself, God, and the world. Missionary anthropology was born.

In the last three decades, these insights have provoked new explorations. Evangelical authors like ALAN TIPPETT, Charles Kraft, and Paul Hiebert and Catholic scholars like LOUIS LUZBETAK have wrestled deeply with the implications of anthropological insights for Christian missions. Others like Robert Schreiter and Charles Taber have joined them in the dialogue over the Christian faith, cultures, and the shaping of theology (labeled CONTEXTUALIZATION among Protestants and INCULTURATION among Catholics).

The bulk of scholarship until now has focused on the missionary impact of Christianity on cultures. The impact of cultures on the formation of Christian theology and missions is still in its developmental stages.

A Summary Review of Historical Paradigms. Using the typology of H. Richard Niebuhr (1956), five paradigms of the Christian attitude to cultures have appeared in the church's history. On opposite ends of the alternatives are the paradigms of *Christ Against Cultures* and *Christ of Cultures*.

The paradigm of *Christ-Against-Cultures* has appeared when one sees culture only as a monolithic whole, without nuance or particulars. Cultures then become largely hostile threats to the gospel, especially when the culture observed is not one's own. Mission dominated by Western ethnocentrism has often moved in this orbit in the past.

The opposite paradigm of *Christ of Cultures* asks us not to fight cultures but to join them. Theological liberalism has been comfortable here. The Laymen's Inquiry, released in a one-volume version titled *Rethinking Missions* (1932), typified this mood. It saw the missionary as an ambassador more than a soldier and called not for evangelization but for social reconstruction.

Within the Roman Catholic Church, the paradigm of *Christ Above Cultures* remains secure. Modifying the earlier view of grace supplementing nature and the examples of Ricci and de Nobili, it has called for building Christianity on the incompleteness of cultures. Since the SECOND VATICAN COUNCIL (1962–65), it has been more aware of the deepening levels in human cultures and of cultural pluralism. The traditional model of ACCOMMODATION is now questioned as too superficial and haphazard, too limited to the institutional. Inculturation is heralded as recognizing more culture's integrative level, culture as a dynamic, systematic whole (Luzbetak, 1988, 76–83). But the two-tiered nature/grace paradigm remains in place.

The paradigm of *Christ and Cultures in Paradox* continues to see a distinction between the two kingdoms of church and cultures, and views culture's many forms and meanings as more neutral items of "adiaphora" than of hostility. This has allowed some like Warneck to commend a long period of toleration before abolishing the Indian caste system and polygamous marriages. For others like Guttmann it has meant seeing Africa's "primordial ties" of clan, neighborhood, and age grouping as ties linked to the creation itself.

Calvin's view of *Christ the Transformer of Cultures* has undergone modifications. But its basic thrust remains that of penetrating and "taking possession of" culture's sin-infected meanings for Christ's glory. Missions theorists like J. H. Bavinck (1895–1964) plead for perceiving the vestiges of God's presence in culture's many-layered diversity while avoiding the fabrication of some international super-culture. Culture is religion made visible but not indivisible. Even under divine judgment, its creational structures and values must be renewed in Christ.

HARVIE M. CONN

SEE ALSO Gospel and Culture.

Bibliography. J. H. Bavinck, *An Introduction to the Science of Missions*; H. Conn, *Eternal Word and Changing Worlds: Theology, Anthropology, and Mission in Trialogue*; W. Hutchison, *Errand to the World: American Protestant Thought and Foreign Missions*; C. Kraft, *Christianity in Culture*; R. H. Niebuhr, *Christ and Culture*; L. Sanneh, *Translating the Message*; A. Shorter, *Toward a Theology of Inculturation*; C. Taber, *The World is too Much With Us: "Culture" in Modern Protestant Missions.*

Christ. See JESUS; *also* CHRISTOLOGY.

Christian and Missionary Alliance Missions. The Christian and Missionary Alliance resulted from the merger of the Christian Alliance, founded in 1887 by ALBERT B. SIMPSON as a North American nondenominational fellowship, and the Evangelical Missionary Alliance, founded the same year as the missionary arm of the Christian Alliance. The year 1887 also saw the ordination and sending of William Cassidy, the new agency's first missionary, who tragically died en route to China. Between 1887 and 1890, a total of nineteen missionaries were sent out, beginning a movement that grew rapidly in both size and influence. By 1893, 180 missionaries were at work on forty stations in twelve fields. As the EMA grew to become larger than its parent, the two were combined to form a single organization in April 1897, the same month that the cornerstone was laid for the Missionary Training Institute building in Nyack, New York (now Nyack College). Headquarters for the agency remained in New York City until 1974, at which time they were transferred to suburban Nyack. In 1989, they were moved to Colorado Springs, Colorado.

From the beginning, Alliance missions has emphasized PIONEER MISSION activity. Simpson developed six guiding principles, which more than a century later still form the core of the organization's missionary philosophy. Included among these principles was the ethos of the missionary activity— "evangelistic and aggressive rather than educational and institutional"—as well as the overall goal: "our chosen fields are the [by missionaries] unoccupied portions of the heathen world." Economy and sacrifice were two important themes as well; the expenses of the home administration were kept to "the lowest possible figure" and missionaries were promised allowances to cover their expenses instead of regular salaries.

Throughout the twentieth century the Alliance progressively developed its overseas thrust. Having assumed denominational status in 1974, it finds itself today in the somewhat unique position of having approximately three-quarters of its church membership overseas. As a reflection of this state of affairs, the Alliance World Fellowship was established in May 1975, with seventy-four representatives from thirty-four nations joining to produce an exemplary church-mission agreement emphasizing full partnership between churches in North America and those abroad. The regular meetings of the AWF are only one of many measures implemented to keep the denomination from succumbing to the dangers of an ingrown institutionalism.

Today 1,108 Alliance missionaries are currently active in forty-six different countries, while Alliance churches exist in an additional dozen lands. The CMA is a strong proponent of the UNREACHED PEOPLES concept and conceives of itself as an agency whose chief focus is evangelism, disciplemaking, and church planting. While a relief and development arm (CAMA Services) and a TENTMAKING arm (the International Fellowship of Alliance Professionals) have been added in recent years, the denomination's missionary philosophy shows unwavering commitment to full-time, career-oriented missionary personnel involved in the establishment of God's church among those peoples who have not yet had the opportunity to hear the Good News regarding salvation in Christ.

LARRY POSTON

Bibliography. R. L. Niklaus, L. J. Sawin and S. J. Stoesz, *All for Jesus: God at Work in the Christian and Missionary Alliance Over One Hundred Years.*

Christian Church (Denominational) Missions. While claims of interest in world evangelism were present among Christian Churches from about 1800, the initial sending of missionaries did not actually begin until 1849. Significant commitment was not seen until one-quarter of a century later with the formation of the Foreign Missionary Society and the Women's Christian Missionary Society. The mission history of the movement may be divided into two historic streams: agency-based missions and "direct support" missions. The issues dividing these two streams have roots in the writings of Thomas and Alexander Campbell around the question of the application of biblical authority. The Restoration Movement has been significantly divided over these two approaches to mission activity. Commitments to mission and the means of carrying out mission have led to divisions in both the movement and local churches from the earliest days until the present.

In his early writings Alexander Campbell advocated the conversion of the world to Jesus Christ and the use of appropriate means to do that. However, he opposed some of the practices of contemporary agencies and strongly maintained that the local congregation is the only God-given institution for world evangelism. Later, in 1849, apparently changing his attitude, he founded and served as life-long president of the American Christian Missionary Society. This agency provided the first organized approach to world missions of the Christian Churches. The formation of this agency reflected some changes in the broader theological and political climate of the times.

Campbell suggested four primary functions for a mission agency: (1) selecting and appointing evangelists, (2) preaching and making converts, (3) gathering converts into congregations, and (4) organizing these converts under the care and nurture of elders and deacons. Often not aware of the historic roots of mission in the movement, both direct support and agency-supported missionaries have continued to focus on these functions.

The contemporary picture of Christian Church missions includes both direct support missionaries and missionaries who are sent by mission agencies. By 1995 missionaries were listed as serving in more than seventy countries in at least 157 different incorporated Christian Church agencies or under local congregational supervision. The actual number of missionaries sent by the Christian Churches is difficult to ascertain because of differences in defining the term. Questions of geography, nature of the ministry, and time commitment cloud the issue. Illustrating this, different denominational directories list differing numbers of missionaries, though it should be noted that in both directories the listing is voluntary. With only a few exceptions these figures do not include the many people who are serving cross-culturally with interdenominational missions, such as WYCLIFFE BIBLE TRANSLATORS, Campus Crusade, Food for the Hungry, World Vision, and Missionary World. Only a few who have a significant support base in the United States are listed. Some bivocational missionaries are listed, but the majority remain unlisted. These figures do not include short-term missionaries. Many churches recruit, support, and supervise short-term missionaries who may serve from a few weeks to two years. Since no centralized reporting structure exists among Christian Churches, it is impossible to know how many missionaries are actually serving at any given time.

Missions among the independent Christian Churches/Churches of Christ range across what is found in other evangelical missions. When one looks at the principal commitments of various Christian Church missions, the following are commonly found: evangelism and church planting, relief and development, leadership development and theological education, benevolence, Bible translation and literacy, short-term missions, and small-scale publishing.

Some agencies specialize to serve wide sectors of this fellowship of churches. For example, Team Expansion, Amor Ministries, and Christ in Youth serve largely in short-term missions. IDES and FAME serve in relief and development. Pioneer Bible Translators serves in Bible translation. Other missions serve a wider range of ministry concerns such as Christian Missionary Fellowship and African Christian Mission, whose focus is in evangelism and church planting, but who engage in medical work, education, theological education, literacy, and other kinds of ministries.

The majority of missionaries with the Christian Churches, however, serve in small direct support agencies that may include only one or two families. These agencies have been formed in many cases in the context of a local congregation to provide legal status for the mission and supervision by people who are particularly interested in that ministry. In a number of cases these small missions cooperate in field operations, as seen in Indonesia. In most cases they work independently on a given field. The National Missionary Convention meets annually and about every five years meets with the North American Christian Convention as a joint convention. The National Missionary Convention provides an opportunity for churches, mission agency personnel, and individual missionaries to meet and informally address missional issues of the Restoration Movement. Leaders from local congregations, direct support missionaries, mission agencies, and many other parachurch agencies set up booths, conduct workshops, plan corporate worship, and meet informally for about three days. This convention is normally attended by about five thousand to seven thousand depending upon its location. When combined with the North American Christian Convention, the two conventions together normally have registrations exceeding forty thousand. Mission funding and supervision remain thorny issues for Christian Churches. Some churches will only support missionaries affiliated with agencies who have acceptable boards and regular supervision. Other churches prefer to provide financial and ministry supervision from within their congregations or supervised by local congregations. Local funding within congregations reflects the same kind of ambiguity that is common to the broader denomination. Some churches raise funds through a unified budget while others depend on either designated giving or a separate mission budget. This approach to a separate mission budget is based on a "faith" commitment of an individual or family to give a certain amount for a specified time for missions. No unified denominational appeals are made since the churches are congregationally governed and no "official" mission or other denominational structures exist.

EDGAR J. ELLISTON

Bibliography. Directory of the Ministry: A Yearbook of Christian Churches and Churches of Christ 1995; D. Filbeck, *The First Fifty Years: A Brief History of the Direct-Support Missionary Movement;* L. Garrett, *The Stone-Campbell Movement: The Story of the American Restoration Movement;* J. B. North, *Union in Truth: An Interpretive History of the Restoration Movement;* D. Priest Jr., ed., *Unto the Uttermost: Missions in the Christian Churches/Churches of Christ.*

Christian Walk and Work in Mission. The tension between what they are and what they have been called to do has frustrated missionaries of all times and countries. This article addresses two things: (1) the connection between character and work; and (2) some character-based problems that hinder missionary work with suggested solutions.

Character-Ministry Relationship. A definitive statement about true religion was made when God told Samuel, "The LORD does not look at the things man looks at. Man looks at the outward appearance, but the LORD looks at the heart" (1 Sam. 16:7). The religion of the Bible stresses the danger of outward worship and service apart from a devout heart (Prov. 15:8; John 4:24). Solomon taught that character affects life when he wrote, "Above all else, guard your heart, for it is the wellspring of life" (Prov. 4:23). If this is true of Christianity in general it is especially true of those who seek to spread the faith around the world. Missionaries should never allow themselves to minister as mere professionals. Their character impacts their ministry. What they *are* determines the level of their effectiveness (2 Chron. 16:9).

It is of vital importance that missionaries remember this. Ignored or unconfessed sin hinders their ministries and, therefore, impacts everyone with whom they come in contact. Paul warned, "Watch your life and doctrine closely. Persevere in them, because if you do, you will save both yourself and your hearers" (1 Tim. 4:10). Truly, all the success that missionaries enjoy depends on the assisting work of the *Holy* Spirit (Acts 1:8). Yet sin can "grieve" and "put out the Spirit's fire" in their lives (Eph. 4:30; 1 Thess. 5:19). Missionaries cannot afford to have their work abandoned by the blessing and power of the Holy Spirit. Carefully guarding and developing character is of utmost importance.

Character-Based Missionary Problems and Proposed Solutions. Numerous surveys have shown that "the greatest problem among missionaries is relational breakdowns among themselves" (Elmer, 1993, 33). Two great needs, then, are for missionaries to cultivate love for others and effective interpersonal skills. Without these characteristics missionaries forget the real enemy and turn on each other. SPIRITUAL WARFARE is supplanted by petty infighting. Everyone is affected and the whole work weakened. Jesus linked Christian love and unity with effective evangelism (John 17:20–21). Especially when working in other cultures the spirit of teamwork is essential for missionary work (*see* TEAMS IN MISSION). Missionary agencies and churches would do well to demand that all missionaries study conflict resolution before leaving their homelands (*see* CONFLICT). Missionaries must also be reminded of the indispensable quality of love for their lives and work. Without love all service and sacrifice are "nothing" (1 Cor. 13:1–3).

Many missionaries' careers have been ruined by their inability to adapt to other cultures and other people (*see* ADJUSTMENT TO THE FIELD). "The two most valuable assets a missionary can possess are versatility and adaptability" (Kane, 1980, 93). These characteristics are developed by the Spirit in the soil of humility and servant-mindedness. Missionaries need to ask God for the grace to "become all things to all people so that by all possible means [they] might save some" (1 Cor. 9:22).

They should also realize that studying cultural ANTHROPOLOGY from a Christian perspective is an effective way to learn of their own subtle ETHNOCENTRISM and better prepare them for the life of constant adaptation that constitutes missionary living. Such study also leads to an understanding of WORLDVIEWS. Too few Christians have a well-developed biblical worldview with the lordship of Christ at its center. Not having thoroughly analyzed their own culture by Scripture, they are poorly equipped to counsel people of other cultures to follow Christ within that culture. Devotion to Christ as Lord and courage to follow him whatever the cost within their own cultures are important characteristics for missionaries.

Another problem that missionaries face is selfishness. This is especially true of many Westerners who have not forsaken the idol of materialism as a part of their conversion to Christ. Missionaries do not always leave their love of things behind when they go to serve abroad. No one has done a better job analyzing this than missiologist Jon Bonk in his book *Missions and Money* (*see also* MISSIONARY AFFLUENCE). A propensity for selfishness affects many missionaries' approach to evangelism and discipleship. These have become things to be done rather than an integral part of their lives. A credibility gap often occurs when missionaries share the gospel but do not share themselves with their hearers. Then the flaw of selfishness appears.

Many missionaries have hurt their families and testimonies by their lack of parenting skills and their blind devotion to ministry (*see* FAMILY LIFE OF THE MISSIONARY). Strong character is developed through the daily responsibilities and trials of raising a Christian family (see Gross, 1995). A missionary's credibility in public ministry is often lost by failure in the private ministry of his own family (1 Tim. 3:4–5; Titus 1:6). Much can be learned by reading the heartbreaking lament of a missionary child who was raised at the expense of the family (Van Reken, 1988; *see* MISSIONARY CHILDREN).

The Missionary Research Library in New York has discovered another missionary problem. They report that "ill health is the greatest single cause of missionary dropouts. Physical health problems account for 20.3% and mental health problems for 5.6%, making a total of 24.9%" (Kane, 1980, 105). Missionaries need the determination to cultivate the mind and the body as well as the soul. Maintaining a hobby, reading interesting books and magazines, exercising, eating well, developing recreational interests all help in preserving personal well-being (*see* MEMBER CARE).

As important as these areas are, Paul said, "physical training is of some value, but godliness has value for all things" (1 Tim. 4:8). Godliness is indispensable for the Christian. To be godly is to be like God, to follow God. Missionaries must remember that in making disciples they must not cease being disciplined followers of Christ every day. Praying, Bible reading, praising God, and sharing his Word should be as natural as eating and breathing. And of all the inner character to be developed, two traits should be constantly cultivated: *faith* that works through *love* (Gal. 5:6; 1 Thess. 1:2–3).

A personal walk with God determines the effectiveness of work for God. Christlike character is greatly needed. But the character needed comes only by grace. It is the FRUIT OF THE SPIRIT, not the effect of human determination. It is best sought by humble prayer to a heavenly Father who desires to give the best of his gifts to his children.

EDWARD N. GROSS

Bibliography. R. Bakke, *The Urban Christian: Effective Ministry in Today's Urban World;* J. Bonk, *Missions and Money: Affluence as a Western Missionary Problem;* C. Bridges, *The Christian Ministry;* D. Elmer, *Cross-Cultural Conflict: Building Relationships for Effective Ministry;* E. Gross, *Will My Children Go To Heaven? Hope and Help for Believing Parents;* S. Grunlan and M. Mayers, *Cultural Anthropology: A Christian Perspective,* 2nd ed.; J. H. Kane, *Life and Work on the Mission Field;* idem, *Wanted: World Christians;* D. Palmer, *Managing Conflict Creatively: A Guide for Missionaries and Christian Workers;* R. Sider, *Cup of Water, Bread of Life: Inspiring Stories about Overcoming Lopsided Christianity;* R. Van Reken, *Letters Never Sent.*

Christianization. *See* COLONIALISM.

Christlieb, Theodor (1833–89). Early German missiologist and missions apologist. He is remembered as the foremost promoter of the reevangelization of Germany after industrialization. He became the father of the Westgerman Evangelical Alliance in 1880 and the Gnadauer Fellowship Movement in 1888, the latter remaining the largest evangelical lay movement in the German Protestant state churches. Christlieb was one of the few Lutheran professors who favored a pietistic outlook. He was also influenced by British-American revivalism through his personal contacts during his pastoral work in London from 1858 to 1865.

Christlieb's missiological thinking paralleled that of his associate GUSTAV WARNECK. He was also influenced by RUFUS ANDERSON. He met the latter in 1873 at the International Conference of the Evangelical Alliance in which he was a major speaker. He then introduced Anderson's thinking to the German-speaking world. In 1874 he and Warneck started and edited the first journal to explore missiology as a science. In 1879 he produced the first survey of Protestant world missions entitled *Protestant Foreign Missions: Their Present State: A Universal Survey.* This six hundred-page volume went through several editions and was printed in all the major European languages, as were several of his works, including *The Indo-British Opium Trade and Its Effect* (ET 1879) and *Modern Doubt and Christian Belief* (ET 1874). Christlieb served from 1869 until his death as an outstanding professor of practical theology at Bonn University. From his first year at the university until his death on August 15, 1889, he incorporated missiology within his work on practical theology, and was thus one of the earliest German professors to continually integrate missiology into his teaching at the highest academic level.

THOMAS SCHIRRMACHER

Christmas Island (Australian States and Territories) *(Est. 2000 pop.: 1,000; 135 sq km. [52 sq. mi.]).* Christmas Island is a territory of Australia in the Indian Ocean south of Java, Indonesia. Half of the population is Han Chinese and another 35 percent is Malay. The predominant religions are Chinese folk-religion and Islam. Only 13.6 percent are Christians. Most of the Evangelicals are Anglicans, Methodists, and a few other Protestants.

TODD M. JOHNSON

Christo-Paganism. Christo-paganism is a kind of SYNCRETISM that exists and persists where the process of evangelization has been defective and incomplete, leaving the pre-Christian animistic belief-system and practices virtually intact but fused with some Christian elements.

The Australian anthropologist-missiologist ALAN TIPPETT has vividly described his own careful observation of the phenomenon in parts of Mexico and Guatemala. In these nominally Christian communities Tippett saw stark evidence of the old animistic belief-system and associated practices in the devotion of Catholic Indians of Mayan descent. He watched them on their knees approaching shrines "more Aztec than Christian," and "others putting paper or cloth under their bloodstained [sic] knees get charged with power for magical or healing purposes," all being done as Christian ceremony.

Tippett also discovered "Christian strands of thought" in the "dominantly animistic context," which he found to be typically portrayed in the native Mexican autobiography, *Juan the Chamula.* Juan, who saw himself as a faithful Catholic, believed, among other things,

> that the Savior watches over people on the road. He died on a cross to save the wayfarer from the Jews, whom he equates with devils, and who were supposedly cannibalistic.
>
> Originally the sun was cold as the moon, but it grew warmer when the Holy Child was born. He was the son of a virgin among the Jews, who sent her away because they knew the child would bring light. St. Joseph took her to Bethlehem, where the Child was born. The sun grew warmer and the day brighter. The demons ran away and hid in the mountain ravines. (pp. 21–22)

Christo-paganism may manifest a variety of elements: the survival of discrete cultural complexes; the persistence of the old mythical belief-system; the demand for a therapeutic system; and a vivid notion of the living dead. Many cases could be cited from various parts of the world, both Protestant and Catholic. Many Catholics are intensely aware of the problem; not all instances are as extreme as those mentioned above, but resemble more what DAVID HESSELGRAVE calls "multireligion." For example, some Batak Protestant Christians in Indonesia visit the gravesites of important ancestors at Easter; they make food and other offerings to them and seek their blessing on the temporal affairs of their descendants. Those Bataks from the more profoundly converted regions shun such things. Tippett observed a vivid example of Christo-paganism in Australia: aboriginal dreamtime paintings displayed behind the Communion Table.

Such phenomena are the very antithesis of *possessio,* which is the investing of an existing practice with specifically and exclusively Christian significance. They represent an ANIMISM merely submerged, not replaced. The indigenous pagan culture has been suppressed by an external cultural power, not converted. The pagan worldview has been neither adequately critiqued nor displaced by a Christian one; the old associated practices have been neither converted to authentically Christian use nor supplanted by appropriate functional substitutes.

JOHN MCINTOSH

Bibliography. J. Bavinck, *Introduction to the Science of Missions;* D. Hesselgrave, *Communicating Christ Cross-Culturally;* P. Hiebert, *Anthropological Insights for Missionaries;* L. Luzbetak, *The Church and Cultures;* W. Madsen, *Christopaganism: A Study of Mexican Syncretisms;* A. Tippett, *Christopaganism or Indigenous Christianity?,* pp. 13–34.

Christological Controversies. Owing to the central place of Christ in Christian thought (quite different from, say, the place of Buddha in Buddhist thought), there has always been controversy over his person and work. The early centuries witnessed the rise and virtual demise of several Christological heresies which in their day threatened the developing stream of orthodoxy. The Ebionites thought of Jesus Christ as a human, Jewish Messiah, to the neglect of his divinity. The Gnostics argued that the "incarnation" was a temporary donning of human flesh, for appearance's sake, by some deity less than the high God. The Arians conceived of the Son of God as a lesser deity. Denying the two natures, they argued that the nature of the Son took the place of the human soul in the historical Jesus Christ. By contrast, Apollinarius, while agreeing with the Arians that Christ had but one nature, held that nature to be thoroughly divine, displacing any human soul, such that the "human" properties of Christ were nothing more than the animal elements found in human nature. Monarchianism, in both its forms, preserved the unity of the Godhead by embracing merely functional distinctions between the Father and the Son, effectively denying the Son's subsistence as God. The Nestorians, eager to preserve Christ's human experience, effectively divided his humanity and divinity so sharply that it was difficult to see how they avoided embracing two persons.

Some of these heresies have resurfaced in new forms during the last one hundred years or so. Arianism, for instance, lies at the heart of the Christological convictions of the Jehovah's Witnesses; some forms of New Age thought seem remarkably similar to some features of ancient Gnosticism. The reason for the chasms that divide people with one set of Christological convictions from those with a quite different set is that all sides have insisted that Christology matters. It matters, finally, for how one understands Christianity, and thus salvation itself—and therefore the church's mission. The same sorts of things could be said about the more radical of the assorted Christologies generated by skeptical application of the historical-critical method during the last two centuries (cf. Henry; Runia).

But the most recent Christological controversies have been generated not so much by alternative interpretations of the sacred text, as by constructions that simultaneously recognize the validity of many elements of orthodox Christology while setting it in a framework that relativizes it. Thus Panikkar argues that, while Christ is incarnated in Jesus, Christ cannot be identified with Jesus: Christ is always more than Jesus. Christianity may have a monopoly on Jesus, but not on Christ. God has disclosed himself in Christ, and doubtless for Christians the historical connection is Jesus. But for Hindus, Christ has manifested himself in a different form appropriate to that religious structure. Thus there is a "cosmic Christ." Rahner would add that this means there are "anonymous Christians," people who are Christians without ever having heard of Christ, or even in some cases who have repudiated Christianity as they have experienced it while accepting the (unrecognized) "Christ" in their own religious heritage.

Something similar is done with some forms of *Logos-Christologies.* If the "Word" is the light that enlightens every person (John 1:9), then it would be wrong to insist that Christianity has some decisive advantage. In an alternative construction, Hick argues that the only way genuine pluralism can prevail among the religions is to postulate that there is an ultimate Reality (not even "God," since some religions have more to do with ritual and veneration of ancestors than with any deity) that stands more or less equivalently behind all religions. Thus it is entirely appropriate for Christians to worship within the framework of Christian theology; it is inappropriate for them to tell others that they ought to do so too.

In this way, some positions espoused in the most recent Christological controversies wipe out the sense of mission, classically conceived, in which Christian believers share and proclaim the good news that in Christ God is reconciling to himself a people from every tongue and people and tribe and nation. That is now likely to be dismissed as cultural imposition or, worse, colonial manipulation. The only Christological heresy left is the view that there is such a thing as Christological heresy. You may believe what you will, but you must never say that the eternal salvation of anyone is in any way tied to belief in a particular Jesus Christ.

The issues at stake are extraordinarily complex. Here it is enough to say that the exclusive claims advanced by and in behalf of Christ cannot be so easily dismissed. Despite protests, Christians who ostensibly believe in the Christian Christ while adhering to the views of Panikkar or Hick are not believing the Christian Christ at all. Some of the erroneous views are deeply rooted in demonstrably false exegesis. More importantly, "Christ" is not a cipher or an abstract notion that can be dropped into any religious structure. Jesus Christ belongs to the pattern of redemptive history that is reflected in the Bible's plot-line. Within the meta-narrative of Scripture the biblical Christ has a coherent place. Remove him from this plotline, and it is not the same Christ. To put it another way, one cannot properly appreciate the biblical Christ (whether to accept or reject him) *apart* from a firm grasp of the Bible's story-line in which he is embedded. In that case the urgency of mission is retained.

One must also say that many Christological controversies around the world at first glance seem less traumatic, since they have to do with the attempt to anchor gospel presentation of Christ in the Scriptures while finding lines of burning relevance to local hearers. If the appeal for relevance is primary, however, the Christ we present may become domesticated to the culture. On the other hand, every generation, every culture, needs to continually ask the foundational questions regarding who Christ is, as the Bible portrays him. It is not surprising that poor believers in forsaken barrios fasten on Jesus' sensitivity to the poor and his striking calls for justice. It is not surprising that African believers note the emphasis on the corporate nature of the people of God. It is not surprising that zealous believers in the Western tradition are struck by Jesus' urgent calls to active mission. This may be all to the good. The test in every case is whether some elements of biblical Christology are being blown out of proportion while others are ignored. The final synthesis needs to be recognizably the Christ of the Bible. Alternatively, even if the emphases are different, there must be a humble pursuit of biblical balance in the efforts of every generation and culture of believers to articulate who Jesus Christ is, as he is disclosed in Scripture. Christological controversy that is seeking to recover the holism of biblical Christology in a world that constantly veers toward assorted reductionisms is a healthy thing.

Donald A. Carson

See also Uniqueness of Christ.

Bibliography. R. F. Berkey and S. A. Edwards, eds., *Christology in Dialogue;* L. Boff, *Jesus Christ Liberator;* J. M. Bonino, ed., *Faces of Jesus: Latin American Christologies;* H. O. J. Brown, *Heresies: The Image of Christ in the Mirror of Heresy and Orthodoxy From the Apostles to the Present;* D. A. Carson, *The Gagging of God;* S. T. Davis, ed., *Encountering Jesus: A Debate on Christology;* S. Escobar, *Missiology* 19 (1991): 315–32; C. F. H. Henry, *Scripture, Tradition, and Interpretation,* pp. 216–33; J. Hick, *The Metaphor of God Incarnate: Christology in a Pluralistic Age;* P. Jones, *The Gnostic Empire Strikes Back;* K. Koyama, *Missiology* 12 (1984): 435–47;

L. Newbigin, *SJT* 31:1 (1978): 1–22; R. Panikkar, *The Unknown Christ of Hinduism*; J. Parratt, *Reinventing Christianity: African Theology Today*; K. Runia, *The Present-Day Christological Debate*; S. J. Samartha, *One Christ—Many Religions: Toward a Revised Christology*; E. B. Udo, *Guest Christology: An Interpretative View of the Christological Problem in Africa*.

Christology . Every facet of biblical Christology could be tied to mission, in that the biblical plotline that sets out God's mission to redeem from a lost race a vast number from every tongue and tribe and people and nation is focused on Jesus Christ, without whom the missionary plotline would be incoherent.

On the basis of John 20:21, a substantial amount of contemporary mission literature conceives of the task of mission in terms of incarnation (*see* INCARNATIONAL MISSION). The Gospel of John is perhaps the clearest in enunciating the doctrine of incarnation, and here too the resurrected Jesus tells his disciples, "As the Father has sent me, I am sending you."

In general terms (i.e., apart from the meaning of this verse), a link between the incarnation and mission is valuable on two fronts. Christologically, it focuses on the unique humility of the eternal Son in becoming a human being in order to perform his Father's will, accomplish his mission, and rescue God's guilty image bearers from sin and death. Metaphorically, it is a suggestive model of our mission: as the eternal Son entered our world to accomplish his mission, so Christ's disciples in mission must, as it were, "incarnate" themselves into the worlds they are called to serve and evangelize.

On the other hand, it is doubtful that John 20:21 can responsibly be called on to support this emphasis. As Köstenberger has shown in exhaustive exegesis, the analogical argument in that verse draws in a major theme in the Fourth Gospel: the sending of the Son, the sending of the disciples, with entailments in the authority of the "sender" and the obedience of the one sent. John's Gospel does not set forth our going as an "incarnation." The observation is more than a narrow point of picky exegesis: under the guise of the "incarnation" model of Christian mission some now so focus on "presence" and identification with those being served that the proclamatory, kerygmatic, "good news" elements are largely suppressed.

More broadly, the biblical Christology that depicts Christ as both divine and human develops an awareness of the wholeness of Christian mission. This mission is *God's* initiative; it is undertaken with *God's* sovereign authority. Yet this mission signals more than divine presence, more than information graciously provided about this God; it signals the Son's costly adoption of our nature, living our life and dying our death. In this

light, the many chapters of the canonical Gospels that describe Jesus' ministry during the days of his flesh betray a daunting concern for the whole human being. Addressed are questions of health, justice, integrity, marriage, generosity, family, priorities, humility, truth-telling, death, compassion, and much more. Nor is this the exclusive preserve of the Gospels. Elsewhere, for instance, Jesus' identity with the human race not only qualifies him to be our priest and our substitute, but ensures that his own strong cries and tears make him uniquely fitted to empathize with ours, and thus also to save to the uttermost all who come to God by him (Hebrews).

Nevertheless, the wide embrace of Jesus' concerns for broken human beings must never obscure the fact that such concerns are set within a plotline that takes him to the cross. His social and humanitarian passions cannot legitimately be given independent standing. They are tied to the dawning of the kingdom, whose consummation awaits his return, and entry into which is finally secured by the new birth (John 3:3, 5), itself predicated on the cross. The Son of Man did not come to be served, but to serve, and to *give his life a ransom for many* (Mark 10:45). Moreover, substantial elements in the ethics of Jesus turn on the critical importance of living with eternity's values in view. Thus Christian mission, while properly being wholistic, must focus on the promulgation of the good news that men and women can be accepted by God, both now and forever, because of what God has done in Christ Jesus.

Genuine Christian mission is impossible apart from genuine Christian love, and genuine Christian love is both modeled and impelled by the Father's sending of the Son out of love for this lost world, and by the Son's willing sacrifice on our behalf. If we are all by nature children of wrath (Eph. 2:3), God's love for us is not a function of how lovable we are, but of how loving he is. Insofar as Christians learn to receive that love, and learn to measure their poor love by his great love, so also they begin to learn that the love that impels Christian mission grows from within (cf. 2 Cor. 5:14–15). That is precisely the reason why Paul thought of himself as a debtor to all (Rom. 1:14): always there is the debt of love to be paid, for Christ has paid it for us.

This elementary but fundamental Christology has a direct bearing on Christian mission. This is not sentimentalism, as if the cross of Christ were a symbol of love and nothing more. If Jesus' sacrifice did not in fact aim to achieve something, then far from being an effective example of self-sacrificial love, it reduces to sheer insanity. But in fact it did achieve something: the reconciliation to God their Maker and Redeemer of a vast number of God's image bearers, otherwise lost in pathetic and evil rebellion. In that framework,

Christ's self-sacrifice is the most staggering instance of love conceivable, both the means of our redemption and the model for our living. If that model increasingly constrains Jesus' followers, mission is inevitable.

One of the great Christological themes of the New Testament, especially strong in Hebrews 5:7, pictures Jesus as the high priest par excellence. At one level this theme is associated with the story-line of redemptive history. The Levitical priesthood is displaced by the Melchizedekian, and Jesus' priesthood is of the latter order. But if the Levitical priesthood is rendered obsolete, so also is the law-covenant that bases itself upon this priesthood (Heb. 7:11–12; cf. 8:13). Thus there is a forward movement within the biblical narrative itself.

Nevertheless, the structure of priestly service, complete with tabernacle/temple, articulated in the law-covenant is certainly not obsolete in every respect. It serves as a shadow, a model, a type of the heavenly reality (Heb. 10:1ff.). What is required for a guilty people to be acceptable to and enter the presence of a holy God is depicted in gripping, symbol-laden ritual, which in turn prophetically announces the ultimate fulfillment of the reality to which it points. The priesthood of Jesus is pictured in these transcendent terms. Precisely because it is tied to Melchizedek and not to Levi, however, its relevance is not limited to the people of the Mosaic covenant. It is also in principle open to people from every tribe and tongue.

One of the major strands of New Testament Christology pictures Jesus as the One who emptied himself, humbled himself, served obediently all the way to the ignominy of the cross—and was triumphantly vindicated (e.g. Phil. 2:6–11). The ultimate vindication occurs when Jesus returns at the end of the age. This schema provides a goal, a philosophy of history (with Jesus at the crucial midpoint and returning at the end), a telos to which history rushes. Not only is it appointed to us to die and face judgment, but there is a final and irrevocable judgment at the end of the age (Heb. 9:27–28; Acts 17:31; Rev. 22:10–11). History is not simply spinning in circles, nor are we dipping in and out of it in successive cycles of reincarnated existence.

These realities not only lend a certain urgency to the task of mission, they also provide a model: self-denial and willing self-death now, final vindication later. Effective mission can only be sustained when both of these elements prevail.

One of the core Christological confessions is that Jesus is Lord. Regrettably, this may become the merest cliché, with no discernible content to "Jesus" and nothing more than religious sentimentalism connected with "Lord." But in the New Testament, heart-belief in this truth, coupled with oral confession of it, are tied to salvation (Rom. 10:9). To confess that Jesus is Lord is, implicitly, to deny lordship to all others (cf. 1 Cor.

8:4–6; 12:1–3). In the light of Septuagint usage of "Lord," it is also to confess the deity of Jesus Christ. One cannot responsibly confess Jesus as Lord and then deny the uniqueness that he claims for himself and that his earliest followers assigned him. Further, it is a public commitment of covenantal allegiance and loyalty to Jesus and to his teaching (for how can one responsibly call him "Lord! Lord!" and fail to do what he says?), and thus not only to enjoy the salvation he alone graciously gives but also to participate joyfully in his final and GREAT COMMISSION.

DONALD A. CARSON

See also Uniqueness of Christ.

Bibliography. D. M. Baillie, *God Was in Christ;* M. J. Erickson, *The Word Became Flesh;* A. Fernando, *The Supremacy of Christ;* A. J. Köstenberger, *Mission in the Fourth Gospel;* P. Lewis, *The Glory of Christ;* G. Mar Osthathios, *Mission Studies* 12 (1995): 79–94; R. J. Schreiter, *Missiology* 18 (1990): 429–37; John R. W. Stott et al., *Christ the Liberator;* D. F. Wells, *The Person of Christ: A Biblical and Historical Analysis of the Incarnation.*

Church. One way to define the church has been to do a word study of *ekklēsia*, the word used at least seventy-three times in the New Testament to refer to the church. "The word is derived from *ek* and *kaleō* and (speaks of) the assembly of free citizens in the Greek city-states who through a herald were 'called out' of their homes to the marketplace. In ordinary usage the word denoted 'the people as assembled,' 'the public meeting'" (Berkhof, 1986, 343). The term *ekklēsia* indicated the self-consciousness of the early Christians, who saw themselves as the continuation of what God had begun in the wilderness with the nation of Israel, called together by the proclamation of the gospel for the purpose of belonging to God through Christ by the power of the Holy Spirit (see, for example, Acts 19:39). Yet a word study of *ekklēsia* tells us little about the reason for which the group is called, the purposes and goals of the group, or the parameters that determine who is part of the group.

A second way to describe the church is by crafting a propositional definition. How we would love to have the confidence of Martin Luther who said, "Thank God a seven-year-old child knows what the church is, namely holy believers and sheep who hear the voice of their shepherd (John 10:3). So children pray, 'I believe in one holy Christian Church.' Its holiness . . . consists of the Word of God and true faith" (*Luther's Works,* vol. xi). Hendrik Kraemer came close to Luther's simple definition: "Where there is a group of baptized Christians, there is the Church" (*The Missionary Obligation of the Church,* 40). However, a purely propositional definition is not enough to show us the church's structure, purpose, destiny, or mission. In fact, the New Testament gives us no formal definition of the church.

A third way to define the church was used by Jesus and the New Testament writers: metaphors of the church. Paul Minear demonstrated that there are at least ninety-six different images of the church in the New Testament. We are familiar with many of these, like body, temple, building, household, family, saints, New Israel, new creation, and branches of the vine. These rich images express what the church is and serve also to show what the church should become. They call the members of the church to see themselves in a new light, challenging them to become more like the pictures offered.

These images are metaphors of the church in mission. Almost all the images of the church in the New Testament are not still photographs but rather moving pictures, dynamic videos of the church living out its witness in the world. For example, the church is the salt of the *earth*. It is the light *of the world*. As the Body of Christ, it is the physical presence of Jesus *in the world*. As a royal priesthood (1 Peter 2) the church is a priest *for the Gentiles*, who see the good works of the church and glorify God.

The church soon found that it needed a way to bring all the pictures together in a simple description. Shortly after the apostolic era, the church followed a fourth way to define itself by using three words that appeared in the Apostles' Creed, with a fourth added soon thereafter and institutionalized at Chalcedon. All the subsequent ecumenical creeds adopted these four marks or notes (from the Latin *notae*) about the church. "I believe . . . the holy catholic church, the communion of saints," is accepted by all major Christian traditions, on all continents, in all the languages of the church.

The four creedal marks of the church have tended to be understood as static adjectives modifying the church. As such, they have fostered institutionalization, maintenance, and decline in the church. Hans Küng and G. C. Berkouwer emphasized that the four marks are not only gifts but also tasks facing the church. Moltmann saw the four as descriptive of the church's solidarity with the poor. C. Van Engen and D. Guder have suggested we think of the four marks as adverbs modifying the missionary action of the church. As such, they call the church to be the unifying, sanctifying, reconciling, and proclaiming presence of Jesus Christ in the world, challenging local congregations to a transformed, purpose-driven life of mission in the world, locally and globally.

A fifth method of defining the church involves affirming a series of seemingly contradictory characteristics. When we try to describe the church we are immediately caught in a tension between the sociological and theological views of the church. The church is both divine and human, created by the Holy Spirit yet brought about by gathering human beings. The tension can be illustrated by mentioning five complementary couplets. The church is not either one or the other of these—it is both, simultaneously.

1. The church is both form and essence. What we believe to be the "essence" of the church is not seen in its forms. We believe the church to be one, yet it is divided; to be holy, yet it is the communion of sinners. We believe the essence of discipleship is love, yet we experience actions in the church that are far from loving.

2. The church is both phenomenon and creed. The church is to be believed. But what is believed is not seen. That which is perceived as a phenomenon of the visible world does not present itself as the object of our faith. The church is too often not believable. We could also use the words "Real-Ideal" or "Relevance-Transcendence" to represent this seeming contradiction. We cannot be members of an "ideal" church apart from the "real" one. The real must always be challenged and called by the ideal; the ideal must be understood and lived out in the real world.

3. The church is both institution and community; organization and organism. During the Middle Ages, the exclusively institutional view of the church took on its most extreme form. In reaction, the sixteenth-century Reformers emphasized the church as fellowship and communion. Many people feel today that we need to seek to keep both elements in equal perspective, especially when it comes to missionary cooperation between churches and mission agencies. The church is both institution and community. The community invariably, and necessarily, takes on institutional form; the institution only exists as the concrete expression of the communion of persons.

4. The church is both visible and invisible. The visible-invisible distinction has been used as a way to get around some of the difficulties involved in the first three paradoxes presented above. The visible-invisible distinction, though not explicitly found in the New Testament, was proposed in the early centuries of the church's life. The visible-invisible distinction is with us because of the reality of the church as a mixture of holiness and sinfulness. (For example, see the parable of the tares in Matt. 13:24–30, 36–43.) The distinction is important, but perhaps it must be remembered that there is one church, not two. "The one church, in its essential nature and in its external forms alike, is always at once visible and invisible" (Berkhof, 1986, 399).

5. The church is both imperfect and perfect. Luther spoke of the church as *"simul justus, simul peccator,"* seeing it as simultaneously just and sinful, holy and unrighteous, universal and particular. But the church is not, therefore, justified to remain sinful, divided, and particular. "Faith in the holiness of the church," Moltmann

said, "can no more be a justification of its unholy condition than the justification of sinners means a justification of sin" (Moltmann, 1977, 22–23). The local congregation derives its essential nature only as it authentically exhibits the nature and characteristics of the universal church. And, the universal church is experienced by women and men, witnesses to the world who give observable shape to the church only as it is manifested in local churches.

Hendrikus Berkhof called for a special visibility to see and recognize the church. The church, he said, has a threefold character, being related (1) to God as the new covenant community of the Holy Spirit, (2) to the believers as the communion of saints, and (3) simultaneously as the apostolic church sent to the world (Berkhof, 1986, 344–45). The missionary movement has been the arena where this threefold character has been given concrete shape as the church has spread over the globe, comprising now around one-third of all humanity.

A sixth way to define the church involves the actual shape which the church has taken throughout its missionary expansion around the world. During the last five hundred years there have been four major paradigms of the church in mission: colonial expansion, three-self churches, indigenous national churches, and partner churches in mission.

1. From the early 1500s to the middle of the 1800s the principal paradigm of the church in mission involved the churches of Western Europe and North America "planting" the church in Africa, Asia, and Latin America. With notable exceptions, this era could be described as a colonial competition in church cloning by Western forms of Christendom. GISBERT VOETIUS (1589–1676) described this perspective well when he spoke of the goal of mission being (1) the conversion of people, (2) the planting of the church, and (3) the glory of God. But Voetius was a child of his time. That which was planted was mostly carbon copies of the Western forms of ecclesiastical structures, Orthodox, Roman Catholic, and Protestant.

2. A second paradigm emerged around the middle of the 1800s when HENRY VENN and RUFUS ANDERSON proposed the THREE-SELF FORMULA as a way for the church in Africa, Asia, and Latin America to become autonomous and independent. Dominating mission theory and practice for the next hundred years, the formula stated that churches were maturing when they became self-supporting economically, self-governing structurally, and self-propagating locally. With heavy stress on institution and organization, the formula unfortunately tended to produce self-centered, self-preoccupied national churches that often turned in upon themselves and demonstrated little commitment or vision for world evangelization.

3. This tendency toward introversion of three-self churches fueled the search for what became a third major paradigm of the church's self-understanding: indigenous national churches in mission. Beginning with ROLAND ALLEN's call for the spontaneous expansion of the church, churches all around the globe began to see themselves as equal partners whose essential purpose was mission. In the 1920s the term "daughter churches" was used to refer to the churches in Asia, Africa, and Latin America. By 1938 at the INTERNATIONAL MISSIONARY COUNCIL (IMC) meeting in Tambaram, Madras, India, the "older" churches and "younger" ones stressed a mission-oriented view of the church. The record of this conference, *The World Mission of the Church*, shows the delegates wrestling with the intimate relationship of church and mission (*see also* TAMBARAM CONFERENCE [1938]). That same year HENDRIK KRAEMER called for churches to move from missionfield to independent church. JOHN NEVIUS, MEL HODGES, DONALD McGAVRAN, and others began calling for INDIGENOUS CHURCHES, communions, organisms, and fellowships that would be culturally appropriate to their contexts.

Along with indigeneity, the missionary nature of the church was increasingly being emphasized. Those attending the 1952 IMC meeting in Willingen, Germany, affirmed that "there is no participation in Christ without participation in his mission to the world" (*The Missionary Obligation of the Church*, 3 [*see also* WILLINGEN CONFERENCE (1952)]). The most complete development of this view was Johannes Blauw's *The Missionary Nature of the Church*, published in 1962, one year before the newly formed COMMISSION ON WORLD MISSION AND EVANGELISM of the WORLD COUNCIL OF CHURCHES met in Mexico City, emphasizing "mission on six continents" (*see also* MEXICO CITY CONFERENCE [1963]). The 1960s was a time of the birth of nations, particularly in Africa, terminating colonial domination by Europe. These movements began to recognize that the "national churches," the churches in each nation, had a responsibility to evangelize their own nations. The church was missionary in its nature and local in its outreach.

4. In the subsequent forty years, the world has changed as has the world church. The fourth paradigm reflects the fact that today over two-thirds of all Christians live south of the equator. Christianity can no longer be considered a Western religion. Western Europe and North America are increasingly seen as mission fields. Nominalism and secularization contributed to these formerly mission-sending areas becoming mostly post-Christian. Meanwhile, mission-sending from the south has been increasing to such an extent that today more cross-cultural missionaries are being sent and supported by the churches in Africa, Asia, and Latin America than from Europe and

North America. Thus since the 1970s the missionary nature of the church has meant that churches and mission agencies are called to partner together in a reciprocal flow of world evangelization that crisscrosses the globe. Thus the church's nature and forms of existence have been radically reshaped by mission.

Although we know that the ideas are distinct, it is impossible to understand church without mission. Mission activity is supported by the church, carried out by members of the church, and the fruits of mission are received by the church. On the other hand, the church lives out its calling in the world through mission, finds its essential purpose in its participation in God's mission, and engages in a multitude of activities whose purpose is mission. "Just as we must insist that a church which has ceased to be a mission has lost the essential character of a church, so we must also say that a mission which is not at the same time truly a church is not a true expression of the divine apostolate. An unchurchly mission is as much a monstrosity as an unmissionary church" (Newbigin, 1954, 169).

CHARLES VAN ENGEN

Bibliography. R. Allen, *The Spontaneous Expansion of the Church;* K. Barth, *Church Dogmatics,* vol. IV; H. Berkhof, *Christian Faith,* 339–422; G. C. Berkouwer, *The Church;* J. Blauw, *The Missionary Nature of the Church;* D. Bonhoeffer, *The Communion of the Saints;* S. Grenz, *Theology for the Community of God,* 601–742; D. Guder, ed., *Missional Church;* H. Küng, *The Church;* P. Minear, *Images of the Church in the New Testament;* J. Moltmann, *The Church in the Power of the Spirit;* S. Neill, *CDCWM,* pp. 109–10; L. Newbigin, *The Household of God;* A. Schmemann, *Church, World, Mission;* C. Van Engen, *The Growth of the True Church;* idem, *God's Missionary People.*

Church and State. The expression "church and state" refers to the relationship between two sets of authority structures that have shaped human existence. The concern of the state is temporal life whereas the church's concern is spiritual life. The question as to what is the most desirable relationship between the two has been a persistent theme throughout history. The following discussion will present an overview of these historic tensions and their influence on the expansion of Christianity.

In Matthew 22:21 Jesus taught that the two structures are separate. The statement "render therefore to Caesar the things that are Caesar's and to God the things that are God's" distinguishes the responsibilities between church and state, but does not detail the obligations. Paul followed with instructions to Christians to "be subject to the governing authorities" (Rom. 13:1) unless the submission contradicted the Scriptures (Acts 5:29). The Pax Romana of the Roman Empire with its peace and ease of travel together with Alexander's legacy of the Koine Greek language allowed the gospel to spread quickly over large areas. Formal missionary bands spontaneously spread the faith into Asia Minor, Mesopotamia, India, Armenia, Rome, Gaul, Britain, and North Africa. These advances were met by local and sporadic persecution by Decian (249–251), Valerian (257), and Diocletian (303), who saw the church as politically subversive.

It was not until Christianity became a state religion in the fourth century that scholars began to grapple with a clearer definition of the relationship between church and state. In 313 Christianity became an officially recognized religion and Emperor Constantine became responsible for directing the church. The temptation for the church was to lose evangelistic fervor and conform to culture rather than continuing to penetrate culture. In 330 with the division of the empire into East and West came also two different approaches to church–state relations. In the Byzantine Empire the secular ruler held absolute authority over both the church and the state whereas in the Western Empire the church had more freedom to direct its own affairs. By the fifth century the Roman popes took responsibility for civil justice and military matters.

During the Dark Ages the idea of a society with two realms of responsibility, one over spiritual and the other over temporal matters, became clearer. God ordained the state to strengthen and propagate the faith, and to protect the church against heretics. However, the tension over supremacy was always a struggle. It was during this time that monasticism responded to the increasing institutionalization and nominalism of the church. By secluding themselves for prayer and devotion lay people sought life consistent with the gospel. Committed communities formed and unintentionally produced the majority of missionaries for the next thousand years (*see* MONASTIC MOVEMENT). Monks like Benedict of Nursia preserved ancient learning and raised the level of civilization and Christian understanding in Western Europe. Beginning as peripheral renewal movements many of these monastic orders eventually became centers of power and lost sight of their original vision. Alongside the Western monastics were the Celtic missionaries. Persons like PATRICK, COLUMBA, COLUMBANUS, WILLIBRORD, and BONIFACE evangelized Ireland, Great Britain, and much of northwestern Europe and established important centers of biblical learning. These two great missionary movements were largely independent of both the institutional church and government.

After the sixth century the popes increased their power in both the spiritual and temporal spheres. Then in 800 Pope Leo III crowned Charlemagne as emperor and the event revived the centuries-old debate between church and state. Did the emperors receive their crowns from the papacy, or was it the emperors who approved the election of the popes?

By the eleventh century the confrontation between the two structures reached a zenith. In 1075 Pope Gregory VII decreed that he had the divine power to depose Emperor Henry, thus declaring that secular authorities had no jurisdiction to appoint ecclesiastical positions. Although a compromise came in 1122, the issue faded only with the gradual dominance of the papacy. By the end of the reign of Pope Innocent III (1198–1216) the issue had arrived at a solution—royal power was under submission to the authority of the church. The thirteenth century saw papal power in supreme control over the state, but this was to change soon as the European monarchs strengthened their national supremacy.

The REFORMATION brought fresh challenge to the authority of the papacy both spiritually and politically, and further diminished the church's control. Martin Luther did not consider ecclesiastical administration important, so many of the Lutheran states had rulers that controlled the church. John Calvin clearly differentiated between church and state by declaring that governments were to protect the church and manage society by following biblical principles. On the other hand, the Anabaptists believed that Scripture indicated the need for a complete separation of church and state, and subsequently suffered intense persecution. They believed that secular government had no authority over the religious beliefs of people and therefore the church had no right to claim financial assistance from the state. Their political views influenced other related movements in the seventeenth and eighteenth centuries, such as the Baptists and Quakers.

During the ENLIGHTENMENT of the eighteenth century John Locke and others propagated the concept that secular government was a matter for society rather than God. Thus the institutional church gradually became dominated by rising national powers and lost much of its voice in political affairs. In the United States the founding government separated church and state to protect RELIGIOUS FREEDOM from state intervention and to protect the state from the dominance of the church. Religion was a private matter between an individual and God, yet religion remained a part of national life. This strict separation of the two institutions was the commonly held view among Western nations of the nineteenth century.

From the beginning of this century Western countries have experienced increased social pressure to exclude anything religious from national life. They have secularized governments that want to severely restrict the influence of religion on political affairs. The influx of diverse ethnic and religious groups together with the erosion of Judeo-Christian values has amplified this call for a secularized society. On the other hand, most of the non-Western nations have not had to struggle with the theory of separation of church and state. For instance, Islam, Hinduism, and other religions dominate many nations which desire to protect their faith from secular contamination.

For modern missions the answer as to what is the most desirable relationship between church and state may be glimpsed in church history. The institutional church has always had struggles between itself and the state. Nonetheless, there is the government of God and then that of the state and the church. How that triad of tension plays out in life is sometimes difficult to determine and will vary depending on the historical and cultural context. However, the growth of the KINGDOM OF GOD over the ages has largely been achieved through a remnant of believers on the periphery of power regardless of their political or ecclesiastical status. It is in this position of faithfulness and obedience to the Lord of the church that future missionary endeavors will continue to see the expansion of Christianity.

ROBERT GALLAGHER

SEE ALSO Human Rights AND Ideologies.

Bibliography. S. Escobar and J. Driver, *Christian Mission and Social Justice;* E. L. Frizen and W. T. Coggins, *Christ and Caesar in Christian Missions;* K. S. Latourette, *A History of the Expansion of Christianity,* 7 vols.; S. Neill, *Colonialism and Christian Missions;* P. Niles, *Resisting the Threats to Life;* L. Pfeffer, *Church, State and Freedom;* L. Pfeffer, *God, Caesar and the Constitution;* A. P. Stokes, *Church and State in the United States,* 3 vols.; D. Tutu, *Crying in the Wilderness;* J. E. Wood, *Religion and the State;* A. J. Van der Bent, *Between Christ and Caesar;* M. A. C. Warren, *The Functions of a National Church.*

Church Development. Evangelical missions have always emphasized personal evangelism and starting churches (congregations) as their basic purpose. This dual purpose was formalized, and technically analyzed, in the 1960s by the appearance of what came to be known as the CHURCH GROWTH MOVEMENT, initiated and pioneered by DONALD ANDERSON MCGAVRAN. A science of church planting and church development resulted that has complemented the perennial emphasis of missions on personal evangelism. Church growth theory says that personal evangelism is incomplete if it does not gather the converts in congregations which, in turn, know how to multiply themselves. Therefore, the multiplication of churches (local congregations) is the best, and fastest, way to evangelize the world.

"CHURCH PLANTING" became the technical term used to describe this category of evangelism. Mission societies and boards began to appoint "church planters" and "church developers." Mission statements incorporated the goal of planting and developing churches in every socioeconomic and ethno-linguistic group in the world. "A church for every people" became the motto. As the missiological science developed, a concomitant emphasis emerged. How do you develop the congregation once it is planted? How do you ensure its continuing growth? How do you prevent a plateau after several years? Research, surveys, and study of these questions became a part of the church growth theory. Planting churches and developing them were seen as interdependent disciplines in the study of missiology.

As the Church Growth Movement developed and tested its theory, the term "church growth" came to mean a process of planting, developing, and multiplying churches. This process has become a unit of study in most missiological curriculums. The Church Growth Movement has had a significant, and somewhat controversial, impact on general missiology, especially in the evangelical wing of the modern missionary movement.

A perusal of the church growth literature on this subject, written by both those who espouse the movement and those who oppose it, reveals five dimensions of genuine, integral church development.

Internal church development means that the organized church has body life. The members will be growing in grace, in knowledge of the faith, in Bible study, and in Christian living. The church will be in a constant state of edification. Love, fellowship, and cooperation will be characteristics common to the church. The church will be a warm center in the community that radiates Christian love, service, and concern. Spiritual gifts will be emphasized, discovered, and used for the collective edification of all. Spiritual growth in discipleship will be evident. Worship and praise will be fleshed out in sacrificial service and stewardship. This internal growth is a sine qua non for the other dimensions of development.

Centripetal church development means the church is reaching out to its community. The members will be trained to witness as individuals, and collectively, to the nonchurched of the community. Evangelistic activities will be perennial. People will be added regularly to the membership not only by transfer, or by biological growth, but by conversion. A constant numerical growth will be expected and experienced. In other words, people will be attracted to the church by its reputation of internal growth and by its intentional efforts to reach them with the gospel. The internal growth will not lead to spiritual introversion, but will be a catalyst to numerical growth. Nongrowth will be a curable disease.

Centrifugal church development means that the church will try to reproduce itself, or multiply itself. It will try to become the mother of another church. It will extend itself into other areas of its field, and use its membership to start missions in sectors of its society unreachable by its normal program. It will even be willing to sacrifice some of its own members to form a nucleus for a new congregation. A really growing church will not be content to just grow larger; it will try to give birth to other churches. This multiplication principle will many times prevent the customary "plateau syndrome," experienced by so many congregations after ten or twelve years of life.

Cross-cultural church development means that the church that tries to multiply itself in a pluralistic world will inevitably confront the cross-cultural challenge. A sector of the field of the church will be the home of a different socioeconomic, or ethno-linguistic people group. The church will want to penetrate that group and try to start a church within it. The pluralistic nature of most communities today guarantees this encounter. The church will seek the means to evangelize within the other culture.

If there is no cross-cultural group in the area, then the church will want to seek ways to create world awareness among its members. Each local congregation should be aware that it is a part of the universal church of Jesus Christ and his world mission. It will initiate activities that will involve it in the world mission of its denomination. It will participate through missionary education, prayer, sacrificial giving to missions causes, and cooperation in world missions projects. In this way the church will avoid ETHNOCENTRISM and see itself as a part of the universal community of Christ.

Influential church development means that the church growing in the four dimensions will be able to have a greater impact on the larger society in which it operates. A loving, caring, growing church will demonstrate the characteristics of Christ's kingdom and will gain the favor of the community. In this way it, and its members, can have a more positive influence on the political, economic, and social aspects of its field of service.

In summary, authentic church development will be integral, involving simultaneous growth in all five dimensions. Any church that continues to grow bigger without at the same time growing better by expanding its base to care for the numerical increase will face serious consequences. Balance is basic for genuine church development.

JUSTICE C. ANDERSON

Bibliography. V. Gerber, *God's Way to Keep a Church Going and Growing;* M. Hodges, *Growing Young Churches;* D. A. McGavran, *How Churches Grow;* idem, *Understanding Church Growth;* D. Miles, *Church Growth: A Mighty River;* E. C. Smith, *Balanced Church Growth.*

Church Discipline. The practice of church discipline is mandated in the New Testament teaching of Christ and modeled in Acts and the Epistles. Inherent in the implications of the commission to "make disciples of all nations," church discipline is the responsibility and ministry of the local church body to its members. Whether the gentle admonition of an erring Christian brother (Gal. 6:1) or the dramatic action of excommunication of a persistently unrepentant member from the fellowship of a local church, the need for the church to monitor and care for its own is clearly taught. While formal disciplinary procedures become the responsibility of the church gathered, church discipline begins with a direct and personal appeal of a Christian brother by another who has been sinned against. Christ's teaching recorded in Matthew 18:15–17 outlines the procedures to be followed in the process of confronting a fellow believer. It should be noted that this passage allows the use of a mediator for the private confrontation in cultures where mediators are a necessity in conflict resolution. If a personal and private appeal goes unheeded, it is to be followed by the direct confrontation by the personal testimony of one or two other witnesses. In the case of continued refusal to acknowledge wrongdoing, a public exposure before the gathered church is to culminate in exclusion from the worship and fellowship of the body.

Biblical examples of discipline are found in churches planted by Paul and in the exercise of his apostolic authority. The specific offenses mentioned include blatant moral sin (1 Cor. 5:1–13), idleness and disregard of apostolic instruction (2 Thess. 3:6), and doctrinal deviation (1 Tim. 1:19; 2 Tim. 2:17–18). The purpose and goal is always the full restoration of the sinning member and the purity of the church (1 Cor. 5:6–8; 2 Cor. 2:6–8).

Church discipline is a doctrine difficult to teach and practice, especially in cross-cultural or multi-cultural mission contexts. Theological, cultural, and practical issues and problems must be considered when seeking to teach and implement the biblical principles and practice of discipline.

The problems of nominalism, SYNCRETISM, and CHRISTO-PAGANISM which have plagued the Christian church wherever it has been planted, are directly addressed by the practice of church discipline. New converts who have been properly taught and held accountable by other mature and consistent Christians and church leaders are generally more likely to make a break from past non-Christian practices. But the practical matter of who should be considered a "member" of a local flock and thus subject to the privileges and responsibilities of church fellowship, including submission to church discipline, has proven to be problematic in many instances. An observed trend in contexts where different denominational churches have been planted is for converts under discipline in one church to escape to another

rival fellowship which may have a very different view of church discipline.

Teaching church discipline in a cultural context in which well defined TABOOS exist can prove to be both a help and a hindrance in teaching biblical church discipline. While the idea of being responsible to the community for one's actions is understood, problems may arise in understanding the biblical concepts of SIN and the related purposes of church discipline.

The punishment and payment demanded for breaking a taboo must be distinguished from the restorative purpose of church discipline based on the biblical doctrines of sin, atonement, justification, and sanctification. Any prevailing notion of payment of a penalty to restore harmony or work of penance for an offense must be countered in teaching the biblical purpose and practice of church discipline.

In cultures where face saving is a high value, confrontation about sin becomes a serious breach of cultural values and is often avoided at all costs, especially in the case of another tribesman or a leader. In such cases cultural values dictate that GUILT before God is not as important as the potential of SHAME before people, even for leaders of the church who may have misused their authority and committed sins demanding the imposition of church discipline. In many of these cultures, a hierarchical leadership style is customary and the leader, including the pastor or church authority is to be highly honored and implicitly obeyed. Cases of the misuse of church discipline for the purpose of manipulation, control, imposing authority, and forcing submission on the flock are not uncommon in such situations. Abuses of ecclesiastical power, especially in the use of church discipline, are not new, as a study of church history reveals. The truth of the corporate nature of official church discipline usually is lost in such cases.

For many churches in Africa, the problems of adultery and polygamy are prevalent and yet are extremely difficult to adjudicate in reference to church discipline. Cultural marriage customs (e.g., levirate marriage, *see* MARRIAGE; MARRIAGE PRACTICES) may create situations which demand wisdom and skill to determine a resolution which will maintain the integrity and purpose of the practice of church discipline (as do divorce cases in other settings). The practice of some churches is to exclude from the rite of communion disciplined members discovered to have sinned and then restore them after one month of probationary observation and abstinence from the forbidden activity. The propensity of this procedure to lead to legalism has prompted one veteran missionary in Africa to call the practice of church discipline "the first really significant heresy which the African churches are in a position to produce" (Trobisch).

Some of the problems experienced in the implementation of church discipline in mission contexts may be a result of the culturally conditioned practices of sending churches, missionaries, and sending agencies. A failure by sending churches to model church discipline at home or with erring missionaries has caused confusion for the younger churches. Reluctance of some early church planting missionaries to entrust the function of church discipline to national leaders of the churches they planted has been misunderstood and resented. Yet experience in places like New Guinea has shown that biblically trained and spiritually mature leaders of the indigenous church are often more discerning than the expatriate missionaries of the cultural, theological, and practical issues in cases needing discipline and wisdom in the application of the biblical injunctions. Teaching biblical truths concerning church discipline is the function of the church, not an individual. Understanding that church discipline is a means of preserving and protecting the purity of the body can help ensure appropriate application of this crucial doctrine, in every cultural context in which the Christian church is planted.

RICHARD D. CALENBERG

Bibliography. J. R. Davis, *PA* 13:5 (September–October, 1966): 193–98; D. Elmer, *Cross-Cultural Conflict;* W. Trobisch, *The Complete Works of Walter Trobisch.*

Church Growth Movement. Church growth is that discipline which investigates the nature, expansion, planting, multiplication, function, and health of Christian churches as they relate to the effective implementation of God's commission to "make disciples of all peoples" (Matt. 28:19–20). Students of church growth strive to integrate the eternal theological principles of God's Word concerning the expansion of the church with the best insights of contemporary social and behavioral sciences, employing as the initial frame of reference the foundational work done by DONALD MC-GAVRAN.

This is the classical definition of church growth, although it has been altered and adapted by several leaders since it was first formulated and incorporated into the by-laws of the AMERICAN SOCIETY OF CHURCH GROWTH. It is important to note that the defining focus of the church growth movement is evangelization. The most restrictive clause, which separates the church growth movement from other affinity groups, is the explicit recognition of the founder, Donald A. McGavran. Not all church growth advocates adhere to the entire corpus of McGavran's teaching, but all work out of the research paradigm that he established.

Donald McGavran, after spending thirty years as a field missionary to India with the India Mission of the United Christian Missionary Society (related to the Disciples of Christ), experienced a growing frustration with the progress of the missionary enterprise as he was able to observe it. He was appalled, for example, when he reviewed the records for his mission in the early 1950s and found that they had spent $125,000, but they had added only a total of fifty-two members to the churches. He began to think that there must be a better way to do missionary work.

After a vigorous process of research and analysis, McGavran published *The Bridges of God* in 1955 (*see* BRIDGES OF GOD), which became the *Magna Carta* of the church growth movement. Its empirical background had been initiated by Methodist Bishop Wascom Pickett's research on what were called in those days "Christian mass movements" in India. McGavran was the person who used the label "church growth" to describe the missiological paradigm he was developing. The accepted date for the beginning of the church growth movement is 1955, the year of the publication of *The Bridges of God.*

Over the next fifteen years (1955–70), McGavran took several very important steps to solidify the movement. (1) He entered into voluminous correspondence with the leading missiologists of the day, dialoguing in depth on the cutting edge missiological issues of the day. (2) He continued his research and published the first edition of *Understanding Church Growth* with Eerdmans in 1970. This remains an irreplaceable textbook for serious study in the field of church growth, and it is already acclaimed as a missions classic. Eerdmans published a revised edition in 1980, and in 1990 the current edition, revised and updated by McGavran's disciple, C. PETER WAGNER, was published. It has been in print for almost thirty years. (3) McGavran relocated from India to the United States and engaged in extensive itinerant teaching, communicating the principles of church growth to thousands of leaders. (4) Recognizing that an educational institution would be necessary to solidify the movement, McGavran founded the Institute of Church Growth in 1961 at Northwest Christian College in Eugene, Oregon. By 1965 McGavran and his church growth movement had been so widely recognized as a historic innovation in missiological principles and practice, that he was invited to become the founding dean of the Fuller Theological Seminary School of World Mission and Institute of Church Growth in Pasadena, California. Fuller Seminary, therefore, became the institutional center of the movement, with the missiological base being the School of World Mission and the application to American churches in the church growth major of the Fuller Doctor of Ministry program initiated by Wagner in 1975.

The major contributions of the church growth movement to twentieth-century missiology can be summarized under four sets of principles.

Theological Principles. McGavran's field experience came at a time when liberal Christianity was in its heyday. Mission was seen as fulfilling the CULTURAL MANDATE, giving a cup of cold water in the name of Jesus, promoting social justice, and helping Muslims and Buddhists to become better citizens. Advocating CONVERSION to Christianity was widely frowned upon as being manipulative PROSELYTISM. McGavran countered this by advocating that the central purpose of missions was to be seen as God's will that lost men and women be found, reconciled to himself, and brought into responsible membership in Christian churches. Evangelism was seen not just as proclaiming the gospel whether or not something happened, but as making disciples for the Master.

Ethical Principles. McGavran's results-oriented approach provided fodder for debate on a number of ethical issues, some of which continue today. He became alarmed when he saw all too many of God's resources—personnel and finances—being used without asking whether the KINGDOM OF GOD was being materially advanced by the programs they were supporting. McGavran demanded more accountability in Christian stewardship. He wanted efforts evaluated by their results. His attitude reflects these words of Wascom Pickett: "It is disturbing to read book after book about modern missions without finding so much as a hint about either what helped or what hindered church growth. In many books the author seems eager to prove that the missionaries have done everything according to God's leading and that if no church has come into being it means only that God's time for saving souls has not come." 'The disciples' duty is to sow the seed and leave it to God to produce." How different this is from the command of Jesus, "Make disciples of the nations!"'

Missiological Principles. McGavran's major missiological principle is people movement theory (*see also* PEOPLES, PEOPLE GROUPS and PEOPLE MOVEMENTS). Before the days of the conscious application of CULTURAL ANTHROPOLOGY to MISSIOLOGY, McGavran intuitively recognized the fact that DECISION-MAKING processes are frequently quite different from one culture to the next. Whereas most Western missionaries and their converts were preaching an individualistic gospel and expecting unbelievers to come to Christ one by one against the social tide, McGavran concluded that this was not the way that multitudes could or would come to Christ. Important decisions, according to the WORLDVIEW of many non-Westerners, were community decisions. Therefore, the best way to approach many of the world's people with the gospel had to be through the encouragement of multi-individual, interdependent conversions whereby members of families, extended families, clans, villages, and tribes would often become Christian at the same time. This process was labeled a "people movement" (*see* MASS MOVEMENTS). An important corollary of McGavran's people movement theory is the HOMOGENEOUS UNIT PRINCIPLE.

Procedural Principles. The distinction between what McGavran called "discipling" and "perfecting" is his key procedural principle. He observed that discipling is best seen methodologically as a distinct stage of Christianization as over against perfecting. While the terminology has been updated by some, the principle remains intact. Discipling brings an unbelieving individual or group to initial commitment to Christ and commitment to the body of Christ, which is the church. Perfecting is the lifelong process of spiritual and ethical development in the lives of believers (called "discipleship" by some). McGavran warned that too many mission activities had been diverted to perfecting when the original mission charter demanded discipling. He never tired in pointing out that a full 70 percent of the world's population had not been discipled, and he constantly urged Christian churches worldwide to get on with sending out more laborers into the harvest fields.

The church growth movement has spread worldwide through McGavran's disciples and through the graduates of the Fuller Seminary School of World Mission where courses in church growth have been mandatory. Courses in church growth are now taught at major institutions where evangelistically oriented missiology is a major component of the curriculum.

C. PETER WAGNER

Bibliography. D. A. McGavran, *Understanding Church Growth*, 3rd ed.; J. W. Pickett, *Christian Mass Movements in India*; T. S. Rainer, *The Book of Church Growth: History, Theology, and Principles*; W. R. Shenk, ed., *Exploring Church Growth.*; C. P. Wagner, *Church Growth and the Whole Gospel.*

Church Leadership. See LEADERSHIP.

Church Mission Society (CMS). Major evangelical Anglican missionary society. Founded under the name of "the Society for Missions in Africa and the East," it officially became the Church Missionary Society in 1812, and took its present name in 1995. Set up by members of the Established Church of England (Anglican), its first field was Sierra Leone and its first missionaries German Lutherans, recruited through the Swiss BASEL MISSION (because no ordained Englishmen offered) and sent there in 1804. In 1809 English laymen sailed to New Zealand. In 1814 German and English workers were sent to South India, and the first ordained British missionary arrived in Malta.

By the 1850s CMS missionaries had gone to some fifteen territories, although in some (such as Canada) this was for limited periods. In many cases British colonies were the chosen fields, and Sierra Leone and Nigeria in West Africa and Uganda and Kenya in East Africa, with India and Ceylon, became and have remained main areas of concentration. China, Japan, and Middle East nations also received CMS missionaries, and in New Zealand it provided most of the ordained clergy for the Anglican Church that developed there. In almost all these areas diocese were set up and episcopalian churches established, their first bishops usually former CMS missionaries. The first non-Western bishop in a CMS area was SAMUEL ADJAI CROWTHER of Western Equatorial Africa (Nigeria), consecrated in 1864. Unlike a number of missionary societies, CMS had no founding figure among its overseas personnel; its general or clerical secretaries probably exercised the greatest influence, and the names of Reverend Josiah Pratt (1802–24), Reverend HENRY VENN (1846–72), and in this century Canon MAX WARREN (1942–63), and Reverend JOHN V. TAYLOR (1963–74) are especially remembered.

In 1921 a new venture, which became the CMS Ruanda General and Medical Mission (now Mid-Africa Ministry), emerged as a daughter society, and in 1922 after long discussions and negotiations a more theologically conservative group broke away and founded the Bible Churchmen's Missionary Society (now Crosslinks). CMS, however, began and has continued as a specifically Evangelical Anglican sending society.

In the mid-1900s, as it approached its bicentenary, the British Church Mission Society had more than two hundred men and women serving abroad. There were daughter sending societies in Ireland, Australia, and New Zealand. The greatest areas of concentration have been Nigeria, East Africa, and Pakistan; newer work is in eastern Zaire, Nepal, and Eastern Europe. Mid-Africa Ministry (CMS) has over forty personnel serving in Uganda, Rwanda, Burundi, and Zaire. In recent years much emphasis has been placed on bringing national workers to Britain for further education and training.

As a society CMS sent single women abroad comparatively early; the first long-serving woman went to Calcutta in 1822. By the end of its first century, 1899, 550 women had gone abroad, compared with 1,556 men; this of course does not take wives into account. The present general secretary is a woman.

JOCELYN MURRAY

Bibliography. E. Stock, *The History of the Church Missionary Society: Its Environment, Its Men and Their Work;* G. Hewitt, *The Problems of Success: A History of the Church Missionary Society, 1910–1942;* J. Murray, *Proclaim the Good News: A Short History of the Church Missionary Society.*

Church Missionary Society. *See* CHURCH MISSION SOCIETY.

Church Missions Conferences. The widespread sponsorship of mission conferences by local churches reflects the significant role played by the local church in world missions. Although the primary purpose of church mission conferences is educational, they are also used as a catalyst for increasing prayer and financial support for missionaries.

The essential character of church mission conferences has changed little since the nineteenth century. Although there is some variation among denominations, most conferences feature (1) one or more speakers, often furloughed missionaries; (2) meals that include an inspirational or educational program focused on missions; (3) a mission-related children's program; (4) a pledge drive for the church's yearly missions budget; and (5) a motivational call to support missionaries through prayer or to volunteer for missionary service.

In the decades following the Second World War, North American churches such as The People's Church of Toronto and the Park Street Congregational Church of Boston were notable for sponsoring large-scale mission conferences lasting a week or more and involving speakers and exhibits from a wide variety of missionary agencies. These influential conferences provided a prototype for other evangelical churches. Also helpful was the establishment of the Association of Church Missions Committees (ACMC, now Advancing Churches in Mission Commitment) in 1974, which led to the publication of materials that outlined a systematic approach to planning and implementing mission conferences. In recent years, church-sponsored conferences have also been influenced by innovations in electronic media and communications technology. Contemporary mission conferences may include feature-length films, videotapes of missionaries at work, computer-generated presentations, and live telephone or video links with missionaries on the field.

Church mission conferences vary in size and duration, from the annual weekend conference in a single church to larger conferences involving a network of churches in a geographical area. In the round-robin model, a group of churches alternate the leadership of the conference with the site changing from year to year. The Concerts of Prayer movement has stimulated interdenominational collaboration among churches, with emphasis on prayer for missionaries in particular areas of the world.

The manner in which financial support is raised for missions also varies. In churches where missions are included in the overall budget (or in a larger denominational budget), the primary goal of the conference is often to educate the congregation about how finances are spent and to stimulate prayer for missionaries. In contrast, the faith-promise model of giving separates the church's missions budget from the regular budget. Churches following the faith-promise model often use an annual mission conference to challenge embers to give to missions in excess of their regular church pledge. A third approach is the single offering, exemplified by the Southern Baptists' annual Lottie Moon Offering, which raises support for the denominational mission budget. In some churches, the mission conference may include a single offering for one or more missionaries serving with FAITH MISSIONS or for a specific mission-related project.

As the primary means of contact between missionary candidates or furloughed missionaries and the average church attender, church mission conferences play an understated but critical role in contemporary world evangelization.

ALAN A. SEAMAN

Bibliography. M. Collins and C. Blackburn, *Missions on the Move in the Local Church;* ACMC, *Your Church: Planning a Missions Conference.*

Church of Jesus Christ Latter Day Saints. *See* MORMONS.

Church Planting. Church planting has become the most frequently used term for starting new churches. By definition church planting can be described as the effort to bring men and women to faith in Christ and incorporate them into growing, reproducing Christian fellowships. Far from denominational aggrandizement, church planting seeks to extend God's kingdom through starting multitudes of local congregations.

The Importance of Church Planting. Christian missions has no more productive method than starting new churches. PETER WAGNER calls church planting the world's single most effective evangelistic method. DONALD A. McGAVRAN contends that the only way Christian missions can meet the expanding needs of the fantastically mounting populations of the world is by providing fantastically multiplying churches. Church planting's importance rests on several foundations. It reflects biblical patterns. Luke recorded the amazing expansion of the New Testament churches, moving from recounting the increase in numbers of members to the fact that the number of congregations "multiplied" (Acts 9:31). The Bible, in both direct teaching and overall principles, includes teaching on both the why and the hows of church planting.

Church planting also augments evangelism and church growth. Studies show that new congregations evangelize more effectively than older congregations, as new congregations put more energy into growth and less into maintenance.

Additionally, church planting promotes geographical and PEOPLE GROUP expansion. New churches are demanded to reach both geographical regions and people groups. New housing areas and underchurched regions demand new churches. It becomes increasingly clear that the churches of the fathers do not always reach the sons and daughters. The present diversity of people (and peoples) demands a diversity of churches; this diversity can only be provided by the unlimited multiplication of churches.

Church planting also satisfies critical needs. Some declare that we already have enough churches and rather than starting new congregations we should build up the existing groups. The truth is that seldom are there enough churches to meet community needs. Most often, differing groups of people cannot be adequately served by existing churches.

Finally, church planting strengthens Christian witness. Starting new churches not only helps Christianity progress; the ministry contributes to the spiritual progress of existing Christians. Opportunities for spiritual ministry expand with the starting of new congregations.

Obviously, church planting is an imperative action for effective church or denominational growth.

The Methods of Church Planting. Study of church planting demands attention both to why and to how—considering the types of and the direct steps to new churches.

Church planting models can follow either the modality type or the sodality type. Modality models involve a local church giving birth to a new congregation. The church plant might be accomplished by sending out a group of members to become the nucleus of the new group. This model, sometimes called colonization, usually achieves extension growth. Extension growth usually reaches the same type of people served by the parent church.

Sodality models involve church starts by an agency other than a local church. The planting agency might be a parachurch organization, a church-planting team, or an individual church planter. Sodality models may produce a congregation much like the founding entity, but might result in bridging growth, which produces a congregation for a different kind of people, such as a congregation for persons of different ethnic groups or socioeconomic strata.

Church planting generally follows a pattern of *persuading, preparing,* and *producing.* The first step of church planting, *persuading*, consists of convincing churches and persons that planting is called for. Persuading begins with spiritual dynamics of prayer, God's will and call. Church planting, a spiritual undertaking, requires the power of the Holy Spirit.

A second phase in persuading for church planting relates to creating a climate for church planting. Not every Christian or every church member is convinced of the need for or advisability of new churches. Every church, denomination, or other church-planting entity should have some group that will lead the entity in extension efforts. This group, which may be a missions committee, a church-planting task force, or a planning committee, guides the church-planting entity in committing resources to starting new churches.

The second step of the church planting process, *preparing*, begins the actual process of starting the church. A first phase of the preparing step relates to establishing goals. Goals relate not just to the determination to start churches, but include plans for specific kinds of churches. Goals also consider the areas for new churches. These plans should be based, when available, on the soundest data from demographic research materials.

The study of the areas for the new church seeks to ascertain the need for and possibilities of a new church. The area must be cultivated, that is, contacts made with the people in the community to ascertain needs and make known the nature of the new congregation. Meeting places should be sought.

The third step in church planting, *producing*, relates to actually beginning the church. Bible study groups and evangelistic efforts instigate the actual meetings of the church.

The producing step must lead to establishing the church both in the eyes of the members themselves and of the community. Eventually, the church will have to secure facilities. Care must be taken, however, so that provision of facilities does not consume the time and energy of the new congregation that should be expended in continuing growth. The church-planting effort includes care for achieving continuing growth. New churches should continue to grow in number of members, quality of life, and eventual reproduction.

Conclusion. Church planting remains a central interest and activity in missions. Almost every community in the world needs more churches. To remain faithful to the Lord of the Harvest, churches must emphasize vast efforts toward forming new congregations. The GREAT COMMISSION demands the constant provision of churches into which disciples can be incorporated and developed.

EBBIE C. SMITH

SEE ALSO Church Growth Movement; Saturation Church Planting.

Bibliography. C. Brock, *Indigenous Church Planting;* C. L. Chaney, *Church Planting at the End of the Twentieth Century;* D. J. Hesselgrave, *Planting Churches Cross-Culturally: A Guide for Home and Foreign Missions;* P. B. Jones, *Understanding Church Growth and Decline;* J. Redford, *Planting New Churches;* D. W. Shenk, *Creating Communities of the Kingdom: New Testament Models of Church Planting;* C. P. Wagner, *Church Planting for a Greater Harvest.*

Church Polity. Missiologists have noted that in one way or another Christians in every generation have debated the relationship of church government structure and mission. As A. F. GLASSER notes, the question at issue is, "What is the relation between the church's structured congregations, ruled by its ecclesiastical authorities, and those mission structures within its life directed by others, whether voluntary or authorized, whereby the gospel is shared with non-Christians and new congregations are planted?"

The three basic understandings of church polity are the episcopal, presbyterian, and congregational forms. There are some shared aspects, or factors of overlap, among these three approaches. In addition, it should be realized that there are hybrid understandings employed by some smaller groupings or individual congregations.

From the standpoint of the practical implementation of mission, the key issue is where the authority resides. Is it concentrated in a centralized agency, with final funding authority, or is the impetus with a local congregation or congregations, with local authority and financial support?

In the episcopal form of church government, the key office is the bishop (the traditional English rendering of the Greek *episkopos*, though it has been translated "overseer" in several more recent versions). Episcopal polity draws a distinction between the bishop and the New Testament office of elder or presbyter *(presbuteros)*, even though certain passages appear to use the terms interchangeably (Acts 20:17, 28; Titus 1:5, 7).

Adherents to the episcopal form of government primarily appeal for support to the tradition of distinguishing the offices of bishop and elder that developed during the earlier centuries of church history. There is also no clear New Testament basis for the position of archbishop (or, in the polity of the Roman Catholic Church, cardinal or pope).

In episcopal polity, all major authority is held by the bishopric. Hence, decisions on missionary personnel and programs are ultimately under the control of the church hierarchy. Financial support is undertaken from a centralized fund. A notable exception has been the CHURCH MISSIONARY SOCIETY, which has operated as a semiautonomous mission agency within the purview of the Church of England.

In the presbyterian form of church polity, the focal office is the elder. In many churches with presbyterian polity, there is also the office of deacon *(diakonos)*, with different service functions.

The group of elders (1 Tim. 4:14) is sometimes called the presbytery (more commonly, the session). Usually, though, the presbytery speaks of the meeting of a group of pastors and elders from churches within a limited region, a meaning that is plausible in 1 Timothy 4:14.

Presbyterian polity grants the major authority to the church session and presbytery. Thus, even though there is a hierarchical element in making decisions related to mission, the authority resides closer to the local church with presbyterian churches. Support generally goes through a less centralized common funding agency than under the episcopal structure.

In congregational churches, each local congregation is ultimately only responsible for itself. Though congregations often cooperate in many diverse program, the overall program (or denomination) does not have the final say. The key officials are usually the deacon (Phil. 1:1; 1 Tim. 3:8, 12) and the pastor (who is often thought of as a single elder or overseer). Based either on one way of understanding 1 Timothy 3:8 and Romans 16:1 or instances in church history, many churches also have the office of deaconness.

Under congregational polity, each local church appoints missionaries and provides direct (or earmarked) support for the mission candidates. Even though some congregational circles have very large centralized candidating, training, and funding agencies, such as the Southern Baptist Foreign and Home Missions Boards, participation is not mandatory for each local church body.

Perhaps the best way to gain insight regarding the relationship between church polity and mission, however, is to observe the unfolding of these themes side by side in the New Testament. Foundationally, in Matthew 16:18 the Lord Jesus made his epochal promise "I will build my church." Then, the capstone of Matthew's Gospel is the Lord's missionary command to "make disciples of all nations" (28:19).

At first glance, the nature of the relationship between the church and mission is not transparent. However, in the Book of Acts, "church" and "disciples" become basically interchangable terms. Also, the only New Testament use of "make disciples" *(mateteuō)* outside Matthew's Gospel is in Acts 14:21, strongly implying that, for Paul and his missionary colleagues, making disciples (v. 21), then organizing churches (v. 23), were two sides of the same coin.

There is another sense in which this largely overlooked passage is crucial. Elders are the only church officers mentioned in the new churches founded near the end of the first missionary journey (Acts 14:23). This same single-level approach to church government in newer congregations is also in evidence in Titus 1:5–9, in the churches on the island of Crete (v. 5).

On the other hand, older (and presumably larger) churches in the New Testament appear to have a two-level church polity. Both the Philippian church and the church at Ephesus that Timothy ministered to had been in existence for a decade or more and were led by both overseers (elders; Acts 20:17, 28) and deacons (Phil. 1:1; 1 Tim. 3:1–13).

Thus, it seems that as the New Testament churches grew from newer and smaller congregations to much larger, more mature ones, there was not one static, monolithic understanding of church government. Rather, there was the flexibility in polity to accommodate such growth, as well as to continue to stimulate further healthy growth.

The dynamic of EVANGELISM and CHURCH PLANTING and ensuing growth, which has emerged as a strong missiological emphasis in the past decades, is clearly at the very heart of mission. Therefore, questions related to church polity must never be divorced from carrying out Christ's Commission (Matt. 16:18; 28:19–20).

A. BOYD LUTER

Bibliography. A. F. Glasser, *Missiology* 6:3–10; A. F. Johnson and R. Webber, *What Christians Believe: A Biblical and Historical Summary;* A. B. Luter, *BibSac* 137 (1980): 267–73; idem, *ABD*, II:1090–91; L. Morris, *EDT*, pp. 238–41.

Church/Mission Relations. As old as the Acts of the Apostles, relational issues between the church local and the church itinerant (missions) have been an important focus in Christian history. Acts 13–15 includes seminal passages describing the commissioning and ministry of Paul and Barnabas as missionaries sent out by the church at Antioch. The passage describes the supremely important Council at Jerusalem, which set the pattern for addressing cultural issues in the ever-increasing expansion of the church. The key issues of "Who sends the missionary?" and "What kind of accountability of them is appropriate?" find their answers in these passages.

Paul and Barnabas, the archetypal first missionaries sent out by the postresurrection church, provide a pattern that is most instructive. On the issue of sending, it is clear from Acts that they received both an internal and an external call to itinerant cross-cultural ministry to Gentiles. The elders in Acts 13 conclude "It seemed good both to the Holy Spirit and to us" to commission Paul and Barnabas for this ministry. And so they did. And as Paul and Barnabas went they kept in mind the importance of their sending and prayer base, and the need to be accountable to it. Their return visits and reports (Acts 14 and 18) are clear testimony to this. At the same time, they functioned quite independently under the Holy Spirit's guidance in determining both the itinerary and methods of their missionary work.

The tensions that have existed in the modern period in church–mission relations have centered primarily on these same ancient issues, "Who sends the missionary?" and "What constitutes an appropriate system of accountability?" For some, the issue is described in strictly theological terms: local churches ought to send missionaries, and the only reason mission agencies even exist is because the churches fell down on the job. For others, the issue is more complex. While agreeing with the principle that the local church is the sender of missionaries, some point out that agencies are the necessary bridge to doing that with accountability and effectiveness. Were there no agencies, they argue, the churches would just have to invent them again. Both logistics and appropriate accountability require it, they say.

Supporters of the agency model point out that Paul and Barnabas were their prototype, sent out by the local church but self-governing under the leadership of the Holy Spirit in both their strategy and methodology. Accountability consisted in reporting back, not in getting prior approval. While faxes and the internet did not yet exist, it seems unlikely that on-the-spot decision making would have been overruled in any case. They seemed to operate on the assumption that the church itinerant is also part of the universal church, even if it is not everything that the church in its local manifestation encompasses. That is, rather, a transcultural bridge, in symbiotic relationship with the local church of the present, but also with the local church of the future. The fact that they appointed elders as they went certainly seems to indicate as much.

Most notable among those advocating the "two-structure" approach has been missiologist RALPH WINTER, whose 1974 modality/sodality framework is the most extensive treatment of this subject. Bruce Camp, writing in 1995, provides a rare theoretical challenge to this view.

Our own day has seen a number of new entities and models directly relevant to church and mission relations. The ministry of ACMC (Advancing Churches in Mission Commitment, originally the Association of Church Mission Committees) over the last two decades has been a strategic attempt to help local churches take their responsibility in the world mission enterprise more seriously. It has done much to enable them to become more than simply disbursers of money. Other entities, such as the Antioch Network, have endeavored to link churches in mission, particularly the plethora of burgeoning new mega churches. At the same time, progressive

agencies are working hard to genuinely serve the churches, recognizing that effective communication has sometimes broken down and an unwholesome dichotomy has developed.

The turn of the twenty-first century will be an interesting time for discerning how church and mission relations in North America ultimately evolve. New models and hybrids of models are almost certain to emerge.

GARY R. CORWIN

Bibliography. R. Allen, *The Spontaneous Expansion of the Church;* B. K. Camp, *Missiology* 23:2 (1995): 197–209; S. F. Metcalf, *EMQ* 29:2 (1993): 142–49; C. Van Engen, *God's Missionary People: Rethinking the Purpose of the Local Church;* R. D. Winter, *PCWM,* pp. B:45–57.

Circumcision. *See* INITIATION RITES.

Clapham Sect. A group of wealthy Anglican evangelicals who lived in a suburb of London in the late eighteenth and early nineteenth centuries. Influenced by the evangelical revivals, they worked for the extension of evangelical Christianity throughout the world and labored for social reform in England. John Venn was their rector; their best known lay leader was William Wilberforce. They helped establish the CHURCH MISSIONARY SOCIETY in 1799 and the British and Foreign Bible Society in 1804.

The group cooperated with dissenting or non-Anglican evangelicals in establishing chapels in many parts of England and helped fund the training of pastors. Wilberforce led the campaign in Parliament that abolished the slave trade in 1807 and ended slavery in the British Empire in 1833. Their projects for social reform included the regulation of factory conditions, the improvement of treatment of the mentally ill, sailors, chimney sweeps, the unemployed, and individuals who had been imprisoned for small debts. They promoted schools for the poor and provided funds for Sunday schools. They inspired a later generation of nineteenth-century reformers, including Lord Shaftesbury, WILLIAM BOOTH, and Florence Nightingale. They integrated their evangelical faith, their commitment to mission, and their concern for social reform.

PAUL E. PIERSON

Bibliography. N. Scotland, *Themelios* 18 (1992): 16–20.

Clark, Charles Allen (1878–1961). American missionary to Korea. Born in Spring Valley, Minnesota, he was educated at the University of Minnesota, Macalaster College, McCormick Theological Seminary, and the University of Chicago. He was sent to Korea by the Presbyterian Church U.S.A. after his ordination in 1902. With Seoul as the center of his labors until 1922, he studied Korean, worked in a hospital, did bookkeeping, wrote tracts, taught school, managed property, and pastored the Central Church. Following the principles laid out by JOHN NEVIUS, the church grew rapidly, and he opened several preaching stations. He once had charge of forty-five country churches as well as his city church. In 1908 he also began to teach homiletics and pastoral theology in the new Pyeongyang Seminary. He served as a pastor and continued to itinerate even after moving to Pyeongyang in 1922. He was president of the seminary (1933–39) when it was closed due to a Shinto shrine controversy. He continued to teach and to preach until he returned to the United States in 1941. Back home he revitalized six churches in Oklahoma and became pastor of three of them. He was a prolific writer and translator, producing seven of his own books in English and forty-two in Korean. An extraordinarily effective missionary, he baptized over three thousand persons, planted fifty-three churches, and helped give the Korean church its constitution, conservative theology, and evangelistic zeal.

ALBERT H. FREUNDT JR.

Bibliography. A. D. Clark, *History of the Korean Church;* C. A. Clark, *The Korean Church and the Nevius Method, Religions of Old Korea.*

Clough, John Everett (1836–1910). American missionary to India. Born near Frewsberg, N.Y., he spent his youth in Illinois and Iowa where he graduated from Burlington Institute and Upper Iowa College. Converted to Christ while in Burlington, he later received ordination as a Baptist minister in 1864. A year later, he arrived in south India as an ABFMS missionary to the Telugu people.

Clough began his ministry at Ongole in present-day Tamil Nadu. During his long tenure, the Baptist mission, previously considered a failure, experienced remarkable growth. The conversion of a low caste leather worker led to over 3,000 converts by 1867, mostly among the outcaste Madigas. A major turning point for the mission came with the famine of 1876–78. Participating in a government relief project for the suffering, Clough gained permission from British authorities to oversee construction of four miles of the Buckingham Canal. Giving hiring preference to Christians, they also helped supervise the more than six thousand workers. During this time, he refused to baptize new believers lest their conversions be for the wrong reasons. He changed this policy in July 1878 and in a single day, 2,222 were baptized and received into church membership. A MASS MOVEMENT had begun and within months thousands of converts had been baptized; the total reached 21,000 by 1883. At his final departure from India in 1910, the Baptist mission to the Telugus had 60,000 members.

GARY B. MCGEE

Bibliography. J. E. Clough, *Social Christianity in the Orient;* H. W. Hines, *Clough: Kingdom Builder in South India;* H. C. Mabie, *MRW* 24 (February 1911): 103–10.

Cocos Islands. (Australian States and Territories) *(Est. 2000 pop.: 1,000; 14 sq. km. [5 sq. mi.]).* Cocos (Keeling) Islands is Australian territory comprised of a group of twenty-seven islands in the Indian Ocean. Sixty-five percent of the inhabitants are Malay in origin and another 20 percent are Anglo-Australian. The majority are Muslims and about 24 percent are Christians. Evangelicals are limited to a small number of Anglicans. No other Protestants work on the islands.

TODD M. JOHNSON

Codrington, Robert Henry (1830–1922). English missionary to Melanesia. Codrington was an outstanding example of the nineteenth-century scholar missionary. Born in Wroughton, Wiltshire, England, Codrington studied at Charterhouse and Wadham College, Oxford, graduating B.A. 1852, M.A. 1857, and Hon. D.D. 1885. He was ordained an Anglican priest in 1857 and worked in the diocese of Nelson, New Zealand (1860–64). Bishop PATTESON encouraged him to transfer to the Melanesian mission, and in 1867 he became headmaster of St. Barnabas's School on Norfolk Island, which served as the central training institution for the mission. After Patteson's death in 1871 Codrington declined the invitation to become bishop, serving as acting head of the mission until 1877. Described as genial and erudite, Codrington won the friendship and respect of the Melanesian students and learned a great deal from them about their beliefs and customs. His pioneering linguistic and anthropological writings, *The Melanesian Languages* (1885) and *The Melanesians* (1891), reflected his systematic scholarship and his desire to understand Melanesian society from within. He expounded the classical concept of *mana.* Codrington was influenced by the High Church Anglican tradition and believed that all religions had some truth. While he was critical about aspects of Melanesian customs, he adopted a sympathetic and respectful approach to them. He produced *A Dictionary of the Language of Mota* (1896), and in 1912 completed the translation of the Bible into *Mota,* which served as the mission's *lingua franca.* In 1887 he retired as a missionary and worked in the diocese of Chichester in England.

ALLAN K. DAVIDSON

Bibliography. D. Hilliard, *God's Gentlemen: A History of the Melanesian Mission 1849–1942.*

Coillard, Francois (1834–1904). French pioneer missionary to southern Africa. His father died when Coillard was only five, but his resourceful mother became a housekeeper for several years to earn enough and keep the family together. At the age of eight he entered a Protestant school in preparation for ministry. Monsieur Ami Bost, his pastor, kindled Coillard's two great passions—church music and missions. After seven years of formal education at Strasbourg University, followed by seminary in Paris and eight months of training at *La Maison de Missions* in Paris, Coillard became burdened to go where no one ever wished to go. Since French Protestants were unwelcome in French colonies, the PARIS EVANGELICAL MISSION SOCIETY had only one field in the yet uncolonized Basutoland, where Coillard would serve for the next two decades (1857–77).

Prior to his departure to Africa, he met a young woman from Scotland, Christina Mackintosh, who was instantly drawn to him and his deep calling to missions. She followed him to South Africa, where they were married on February 26, 1861, in Cape Town.

In 1866 the Boer wars forced the Coillards' expulsion from Basutoland, but eventually they returned. Inspired by Livingstone, he set out in 1878 to explore and evangelize in the region of the Zambesi River. In 1889 the Coillards and their entourage journeyed to Zambesi and established several missionary stations. They encountered witchcraft, slave traders, and many other hardships. Madame Coillard died on October 28, 1891, after thirty years of marriage. Coillard served in the region of the Upper Zambesi until his death.

JOHN EASTERLING

Bibliography. C. W. Macintosh, *Coillard of the Zambesi.*

Coke, Thomas (1747–1814). Welsh pioneer of Methodist missions. Born in Brecon, Wales, into a well-respected family, he received a doctorate in civil law from Oxford. A sincere Anglican churchman, Coke came to realize that religion had to do with the heart as well as the mind. The new fervor that resulted brought about his dismissal, and he joined the Methodists, becoming JOHN WESLEY's closest associate. Coke assisted Wesley in preaching, visiting Methodist societies in England, Scotland, and Ireland, presiding over conferences, and giving legal assistance to the Methodist movement. As his focus upon the world enlarged, so did his fire for missions. In 1783 he helped draw up the first plan for organizing a missionary society in Britain. "Set apart" by Wesley, he was sent to America as cosuperintendent of the growing Methodist Church there. He continued his involvement in mission within the British Isles, oversaw personally the mission work in the West Indies, and carried on adminis-

trative and literary work and preaching. His missionary vision stretched beyond western continents to Africa and the Far East, and during the final decade of his life new fields of missionary activity opened up in these areas. In 1814, while leading a missionary band on a voyage to India and Ceylon, he died and was buried at sea.

Coke was not only a preacher of missions, but poured his own financial assets and very life into the endeavor. Long known as the "father of missions" within the Methodist movement, his influence upon American Methodism is second only to that of FRANCIS ASBURY, with whom he cofounded the Methodist Episcopal Church of America. Next to John Wesley, he is considered the most significant and formative figure in Methodism's first hundred years.

FLORENCE R. SCOTT

Bibliography. J. Vickers, *Thomas Coke, Apostle of Methodism;* C. Davey, *Mad About Mission: the Story of Thomas Coke;* W. C. Barclay, *History of Methodist Missions, I: Missionary Motivation and Expansion.*

Collectivism. *See* INDIVIDUALISM and COLLECTIVISM.

Colombia *(Est. 2000 pop.: 37,822,000; 1,138,914 sq. km. [439,735 sq. mi.]).* Colombia, the fourth largest country in South America, is located in the northwest corner of the continent with coasts on both the Pacific Ocean and the Caribbean Sea. It is bounded by the Andes Mountains in the west; plains and forests in the east. Of its population of 37.8 million, 98.6 percent speak Spanish. The indigenous Amerindians, speaking some 65 languages in 12 language groups, form .78 percent of the general population. Urbanization is over 70 percent.

The Roman Catholic Church. Following the period of the Spanish military conquest (1500–50), a series of papal pronouncements delegated spiritual responsibilities to the Crown. Several Spanish clergy, including St. Luis Beltrán and St. Pedro Claver, attempted to protect both Indians and black slaves from cruel treatment. During the colonial era (1550–1810), the Spanish established parishes, provided education for the upper classes, and founded universities and hospitals. Little attempt was made to translate the Bible into indigenous languages and, until recently, its use among the laity was not encouraged by the clergy. From 1610 the Inquisition effectively prevented the development of non-Catholic religions.

Colombia established its independence from Spain in 1819. Internal political struggles between the anticlerical Liberals (who favored a more open society) and Conservatives (supporters of the Catholic Church) spawned a period of civil wars between 1853 and 1866. They ended with a Conservative victory and the pro-clerical Constitution of 1886. The Church signed a concordat between Colombia and the Vatican and enjoyed great political and spiritual advantage until 1930, when Liberals regained power. The Catholic charismatic movement emerged and peaked in the 1970s, with an emphasis on spiritual renewal and Bible study. The Church today claims 93 percent of the population, though statistics reveal that 70 percent never attend Mass.

The Evangelical (Protestant) Churches. After independence (1819), the Inquisition was abolished. Itinerant Bible sellers (colporters; *see* COLPORTAGE) entered, the most notable being JAMES THOMSON who founded a chapter of the Bible Society in Bogotá in 1825. Formal Protestant ministry began with the arrival of a North American Presbyterian missionary, Henry B. Pratt, in 1856. Early Protestant efforts faced great resistance from the dominant Catholic milieu. Strategies included wide Bible distribution and the founding of schools.

After the turn of the century, the Presbyterians were joined by new entities such as the Gospel Missionary Union (1908), The Bible Society (1912), the Christian Missionary Alliance (1923), and the Cumberland Presbyterians (1927). In 1930 a Liberal government was elected and a widely read publication described Colombia as the least evangelized South American country. Response to both opportunity and challenge brought 20 groups between 1930 and 1948, including the Assemblies of God (1932), World Evangelization Crusade (1933), Plymouth Brethren (1933), the Latin America Mission (1937), the Southern Baptists (1941), and the Interamerican Mission (OMS; 1943).

Continual Catholic opposition culminated in the terrible years of *La Violencia* (1948–58), in which the "evangelicals" (as most Protestants are called) were identified with the Liberals and suffered vast destruction of church and school property. Some 120 were killed, and many had to flee for their lives. The evangelical church was purified, strengthened in its resolve to evangelize, grew in numbers, and experienced deep unity. For mutual support and protection, the evangelicals formed the Evangelical Confederation of Colombia (CEDEC—now known as CEDECOL), which at present embraces over fifty denominations.

In 1968, 80 percent of the evangelicals united in a year-long outreach known as Evangelism-in-Depth, which combined evangelistic efforts in the local church plus large united campaigns. Church planting in Colombia has included social, medical, and educational ministries in both rural and urban areas. Evangelicals sustain several printing houses, indigenous publications, radio stations, and more recently, high quality programs on national television.

The Wycliffe Bible translators and New Tribes Mission have pioneered work among the Indian communities, though their efforts are greatly hindered by the ubiquitous presence of guerrillas. During the 1980s and 1990s, several missionaries were killed.

Bible institutes and nonformal training opportunities are multiplying. The Biblical Seminary of Colombia (Medellín) and the Baptist Seminary (Cali) are the best known institutions that provide theological education at the university level.

The Pentecostal and charismatic movements have grown notably and count among their numbers the largest denominations and churches. Large independent congregations flourish, some attracting thousands. Increasingly churches are found among the middle and even upper classes. Almost exclusively national figures have replaced missionary leadership.

From 1958 to the late 1990s evangelicals grew eightfold. Approximate calculations indicate an evangelical presence of about 5 percent in Colombia distributed among 150 denominations and over 5,000 congregations. About 1,000 foreign missionaries serve in the country. Some 600 pastors meet in over 50 church associations.

Colombian mission agencies have also merged, including COMIBAM (Latin American Missionary Committee in Colombia). Together, they promote the involvement of nationals in cross-cultural missionary efforts. At present evangelicals support thirty-four missionaries outside of Colombia and eighteen cross-cultural workers within the country.

Colombia, at the turn of the century, finds itself in the grip of violence, with guerrilla, para-military groups, and the army in frequent combat. The drug trade continues. The government is plagued with corruption. New Age ideas attract the middle class; Satanism and witchcraft is rife. While old traditions are fast falling, it is a time of unprecedented openness to the gospel.

JACK VOELKEL

Bibliography. P. Johnstone, *OW;* R. Wheeler and W. Browning, *Modern Missions on the Spanish Main.*

Colonialism and Missions. Some have accused the missionary movement of simply serving as the religious side of nineteenth-century colonialism, as an attempt to impose "Western religion" on Asia and Africa along with political and economic domination. But the truth is far more complex. At times missionaries arrived before the colonists, at times with them, and at times later. But it is clear that the missionary movement lived in uneasy tension with colonialism, having very different goals. Hence, at times missionaries found themselves in conflict with European settlers or colonial governments; at other times they believed that European control brought the best hope for peace, stability, and protection of the native populations.

The missionary movement had its roots in the eighteenth- and nineteenth-century revivals. Consequently, its primary concern was evangelism, but it also had a powerful humanitarian focus, with especially strong opposition to slavery (*see* ABOLITIONIST MOVEMENT). At the same time the revivals affirmed the values of liberal democracy and Western culture, seeing them as basically Christian, and believing with most Europeans and Americans that the tide of history was taking Western institutions to the rest of the world. Thus most missionaries, even the most vociferous critics of the abuses of colonialism, believed the system to be consistent with the Christian faith. In this they shared the naiveté of their contemporaries.

The complexity of the relationship may be seen in the case of WILLIAM CAREY, ADONIRAM JUDSON, and the East India Company. The Company denounced Carey's venture in the British Parliament and refused him residence in Calcutta, forcing him to live in Serampore, a Danish colony. When Judson was not allowed to remain in Calcutta he went to Burma, where after a few years he was imprisoned during the Anglo-Burmese War as an English spy. Thus the missionary was often caught between two opposite forces, distrusted by both.

Two dominant motifs appear in this complex relationship. First, to the missionaries, evangelism was most important. This concern for the advance of the gospel determined varying political responses by the missionaries in widely different contexts: sometimes they favored colonialism, sometimes they did not, depending on what seemed to be most advantageous for their mission. Second, most missionaries defended the indigenous peoples against the exploitation of European commercial and political forces. This, too, led them to a variety of attitudes in different situations. But it is clear that colonial governments and European settlers were interested in stability and profits, while the missionaries had different goals. To further complicate the picture, at times the European traders and settlers were at odds with their own governments, which in some cases attempted to curb the worst exploitation of indigenous populations. And often different mission groups found themselves on opposing sides of issues. For example, Anglicans, coming from the established church in England, were more apt to favor imperialism than were English nonconformists. American missionaries, espousing the separation of church and state, were often naive in thinking they were nonpolitical. They usually supported American policies, especially in the Philippines after the Spanish American War, despite the brutality against the Filipino independence movement. But they often encouraged the aspirations of nationals for independence in colonial lands. In India the British required American missionaries to sign a pledge promising no involvement in Indian political affairs.

The attitudes of colonial governments varied. The British refused to allow missionaries to work in northern Nigeria, fearing it would antagonize the Muslim rulers. The Dutch encouraged mission work among animists in parts of Indonesia (hoping it would aid in their control) but refused to allow work among Muslims in Java. On the other hand, the British gave grants for education in India and nearly every mission school benefited.

The clash between colonialism and missions can be seen in the case of India. When Carey campaigned against infanticide and suttee, the Hindu practice of burning widows with the bodies of their husbands, the East India Company opposed him, believing that interference with such customs would threaten stability and put profits in peril. Other missionaries criticized the British government for collecting taxes from Hindu pilgrims, which were then used to support Hindu temples. But the ambiguity of the relationship is seen in the fact that Carey eventually accepted an appointment to lecture in Indian languages at the Company's college, using the income to support BIBLE TRANSLATION and distribution. When direct British control was substituted for Company rule the Serampore missionaries and others expressed their belief that it would bring great temporal benefits. The fact that it opened India to evangelization and Western education and ended certain inhumane practices were no doubt factors in this evaluation.

Baptist missionaries to Jamaica were told to have nothing to do with political affairs (i.e., slavery) but their experience with the plantation system led them to call it the "offspring of the devil." Thus the planters perceived the evangelical missionaries as a threat to the stability and power of their society. Missionary Christianity was a challenge to colonial oppression. Some missionaries urged slaves to be obedient to their masters, believing that the progress of Christianity would lead to the end of slavery. But after a slave revolt, Baptist missionary John Smith was blamed and condemned to death on scanty evidence, dying in prison before a pardon from the king arrived. The situation became worse and in 1832 fourteen Baptist and six Methodist chapels were destroyed by enraged whites over the issue.

The ambiguity may be seen further in Central Africa, where missionaries encouraged British control, believing it was the greatest protection against the slave trade by Arabs, Portuguese, and others. LIVINGSTONE's belief in "commerce and Christianity" represented an antislavery ideology, the hope that commerce would introduce prosperity and thus end the slave trade. In the 1820s LMS missionary John Philip, working in a context of violence between settlers and native peoples, became an advocate of the Xhosas, his influence being decisive in a reform giving them legal status. This incurred the rage of both English and Boer settlers. The Wesleyans had different views at some points but both missionary groups wanted British rule because they believed it would bring security and the benefits of British law to the native peoples. In midcentury another LMS missionary, John Mckenzie, working farther north, advocated British rule because he believed it to be better than either of the possible alternatives in that fluid and chaotic situation: white supremacist Boer rule or the imperialism of Cecil Rhodes.

At times the missionaries expressed strong opposition to colonial policies. At the turn of the century two American Presbyterians published articles condemning the exploitation of African rubber workers in the Congo, calling it "twentieth century slavery." The case brought international attention, the missionaries were sued for libel, and the suit was finally dismissed. Some improvement in the treatment of the African resulted, but the case created tension between the Belgian and American governments. After World War I, with nearly all the land in Kenya in the hands of English settlers, Africans were forced to work two months each year on settler lands, leaving their own crops unattended and families unprotected. While some missionaries believed the Africans should be compelled to work as part of the "civilizing" process, others disagreed. Strong protests came from two Anglican bishops and the Church of Scotland mission, reinforced by J. H. OLDHAM, a leader in the INTERNATIONAL MISSIONARY COUNCIL, who denounced the practice as immoral. As a result the government order on native labor was withdrawn in 1921. Two years later, Oldham's influence was decisive in a declaration of the Colonial Office, that the "interests of the African natives must be paramount," over against settler demands. Yet Oldham and others were not opposed in principle to white rule or settlement, but idealistically if naively believed the empire could be justified on the basis of a harmonious partnership between all groups. In contrast, the Scottish mission in Malawi worked for its independence, and was noted by an African writer as perhaps the only case of pursuit of equity in a colonial cause by a group who were members of the imperial power.

The case of the "Opium Wars" with China also illustrates the ambiguity. The opium trade and the two wars of economic aggression (1839–42 and 1858–60), were strongly criticized by the missionary community as unjust. Yet when China was opened to Europeans, and thus missionary residence, as a result, and Christians were promised protection, nearly all missionaries saw this as a providential act of God, who had used the "wrath of man" for his purpose. They naturally believed that the greatest blessing that

could come to China was the gospel and soon sent large numbers of missionaries under the umbrella of the "unequal treaties" which had been imposed on the Chinese.

Thus it is clear that most missionaries supported colonialism even as they fought against its abuses. They recognized its achievements. One wrote, "Gone is the slave trade and intertribal wars. A new era of civilization has dawned for Africa." But if they often failed to see the negative aspects of colonialism, they contributed to its destruction by refusing to accept the idea that non-Westerners were genetically inferior, believing there was no obstacle to their reaching the standards of any other people if evangelical Christianity was accepted. And the liberal education and new ideas introduced in mission schools were an important factor in generating nationalistic movements in a number of Asian and African countries, leading to their independence and thus, the end of colonialism.

PAUL E. PIERSON

Bibliography. S. C. Neill, *Colonialism and Christian Missions;* B. Stanley, *The Bible and the Flag.*

Colportage. The practice of selling or giving away small portions of Scripture or gospel tracts. The idea (and word) comes from France, where *col* (neck) and *porter* (to carry) were combined to refer to peddlers who carried packs of their wares for sale around the countryside. According to the *Oxford English Dictionary,* the term was used in English by 1796. Providing an alternative to those who had no access to bookstores or other outlets for religious literature, colporteurs were employed by missionary agencies (especially Bible Societies) and traveled mostly rural areas selling or trading for their products.

In the United States, the main promoter of colportage was the American Tract Society, which began colportage work in 1841 with two men in Indiana and Kentucky. Just a decade later, over 500 were employed by the ATS in colportage work, most of it in the American west and south. However, as towns and churches were developed, the need for colportage in the United States diminished, and the work dried up there shortly after the turn of the century.

While the need for colportage was diminishing in the United States, however, it was peaking in many other parts of the world, where access to printed literature was limited. At its height, the British and Foreign Bible Society listed some 55 countries where colportage was used as a means of Scripture distribution. Colportage was used widely in Latin America, China, the Middle East.

Colporteurs, mostly males, were hard-working and firmly committed individuals who were willing to walk seemingly endless miles and face severe persecution in the hope of bringing the printed Scriptures to people who otherwise would never have access to them. While more technologically advanced means now enable greater distribution by one person in one day than was previously possible in a month by a walking colporteur, Christian missions still owes a great debt of gratitude to those dedicated individuals who took the Scriptures in printed form to literally millions of people around the world.

A. SCOTT MOREAU

Bibliography. H. K. Moulton, *CDCWM*, pp. 122–23; D. P. Nord, *DCA*, p. 300.

Columba of Iona (521–597). Irish missionary to Scotland. Columba was born in Ireland of royal lineage through both parents. In accordance with his royal status, he benefited from the care of a priest and was brought up in the Christian faith. As a young man he entered a monastery; he was ordained a deacon and later a priest. Between 545 and 562 Columba founded numerous churches and monastic societies, the chief centers of education. Legends and traditions surround much of Columba's life, including his departure from his homeland at the age of forty-two. Whatever the actual precipitating circumstances, he, with twelve Irish monks, settled on the small island of Iona, where he established his headquarters for the missionary work to which he devoted his remaining years. There he founded a monastic community, an Order not for solitaries but one that provided training for evangelists sent to preach the gospel, build churches, and establish other monasteries. Securing good relations with King Brude enabled the Ionian community to work among pagans in the western highlands of Scotland.

Of equal concern to the Ionian Christians was the copying of Scripture. Columba himself is said to have written out over three hundred copies of the Vulgate and the Psalter. Only a few hours before his death, at the age of seventy-six, he was engaged in copying the Psalter.

The influence of the founding abbot of Iona and his community spread beyond Scotland to many parts of the British Isles, Europe, and Iceland. Columba, known as "the Apostle of the Western Isles," has also been called "the Moses of Iona" because, like Moses, he refused to take his place among royalty and chose rather the call of service to a higher King. One biographer claims that one cannot truly understand the history of the Scots without knowing something of the man Columba. *Life of Columba*, written by Adamnan, his eighth successor in the abbacy of Iona, is considered more of a hagiography than a biography.

FLORENCE R. SCOTT

Bibliography. R. B. Hale, *The Magnificent Gael*; F. MacManus, *Saint Columban*; L. Menzies, *St. Columba of Iona*.

Columbanus (c. 543–615). Irish monastic missionary to Europe. Though little is known of his early life, Columbanus was purportedly a strong, good-looking man who may have entered monastic life in part to escape the temptations of the flesh. He actually called himself Columba, but historians often refer to him by the Latin spelling to avoid confusing him with the earlier Irish missionary by the same name. He was one of the most important missionaries in the CELTIC MISSIONARY MOVEMENT. His efforts, coming after Ireland and Scotland had been reached and the Anglo-Saxon work was well established, focused on the areas that were to become France, Switzerland, and Italy. They had been reached for Christ once before, but had reverted to paganism. Though foundations of Christian influence still survived, those foundations were in desperate need of shoring up.

Columbanus is perhaps best remembered for founding influential monasteries and developing a strict set of monastic rules that affected monasteries throughout France for centuries. The first monastery he founded was in Luxeuil in the northeast part of the country. He lived there from the time of its founding (c. 590) until 610, when he was expelled by political leaders whose goal was to deport Columbanus and his twelve Irish companions back to Ireland. The boat that was to take them to Ireland, however, ran aground before they were picked up. Departing from Luxeuil, the company traveled through northern France, then along the Rhine River, down through western Switzerland (where GALL parted from the company because of illness and later founded his own significant monastery), and finally into northern Italy, where Columbanus established another monastery at Bobbio that in the Middle Ages became a center of scholarship.

A. SCOTT MOREAU

Bibliography. W. H. Marnell, *Light from the West: The Irish Mission and the Emergence of Modern Europe.*

COMIBAM. This is the acronym for COOPERACIÓN MISIONERA IBEROAMERICANA (Ibero-American Missionary Cooperation), a cooperative network among the various national missionary movements that exist in Latin America. Most of these are integrated by Christians committed to the evangelization of unreached peoples. The objective of COMIBAM is "to glorify God in awakening and developing the missionary vision and action to all the nations in the local churches of Ibero-America [Latin America and Spain], and to serve as a link of cooperation between the different missionary efforts."

A significant element in COMIBAM is the goal of having in each Spanish- or Portuguese-speaking country a contextualized missionary movement with its own specific characteristics. The organization was the result of the First Ibero-American Missionary Congress, held in São Paulo (Brazil), in November 1987. In the 1980s a growing number of evangelical churches began to be more aware of and active in intercultural and transnational missions. The idea, however, was not to develop a mere extension of the work that established denominations were already doing around the world, but to promote the Christian testimony to unreached countries and peoples.

As an expression of this movement and as a way to promote its growth, a group of leaders met in Mexico City, summoned by CONELA (Latin American Evangelical Confraternity), with the purpose of organizing the first Ibero-American Misssionary Congress. From its beginning, COMIBAM was more than an event. It was a movement that fostered vision and challenge for the involvement of Ibero-Americans in world missions. About 3,300 persons registered in this Congress, coming from twenty-five Ibero-American countries and thirty-five other countries in the world. The emphasis of COMIBAM is not so much on evangelization inside one's own culture, as on intercultural evangelization. COMIBAM has already produced an important amount of literature on intercultural missions and has organized several missionary congresses and conferences at national, regional, and continental levels, particularly in Latin America.

PABLO DEIROS

SEE ALSO Latin American Mission Boards and Societies.

Comity. A concept derived from the general principle that mission groups ought not to compete with one another. The method used to promote this concept was to make one agency responsible for evangelism in a particular territory or among a particular people. Double occupancy of a region, with the exception of big cities, was to be avoided.

Historically the term owes its origin to the late-nineteenth-century missionary conferences (for and by missionaries, with some nationals participating as guests) that took place first in Asia, and then in a less extensive fashion in parts of Africa and Latin America. The first such conference, the "General Conference of Bengal Protestant Missionaries," took place in Calcutta in 1855, and was followed by numerous regional and national conferences over the next half century, leading up to the great WORLD MISSIONARY CONFERENCE in Edinburgh (1910). The establishment of the principle of comity in missions was one of the most outstanding results of these early conferences.

The need for comity arose because missions entered many territories in a rather haphazard

fashion, with frequent chaos and overlap. The resulting waste of limited resources was widely abhorred, as was the confusion caused to those newly receiving the gospel. Because the good stewardship of personnel and money was a universal ideal among the various societies, the principle of comity quickly gained broad acceptance. Verbal and personal agreements among missionaries became the order of the day, with missions agreeing not to open up work in areas where another mission was already established.

While this approach led ultimately to what mission historian R. PIERCE BEAVER called "denominationalism by geography," there was a general expectation that many emerging churches would likely join together after the missionaries moved on to other regions. This has, in fact, often happened. At the same time, the levels of cooperation comity required often spilled over into other mission spheres as well.

On the whole, the system worked well as long as people stayed where they were. However, as greater mobility for purposes of work and education became the norm, the system increasingly showed its limitations. Its chief legacy in evangelical missions circles is in the courtesy and cooperation shown among agencies in discussing future plans and in not duplicating existing efforts.

GARY R. CORWIN

Bibliography. R. P. Beaver, *PWCM*, pp. B:58–72; S. Neill, *HCM*.

Commission on World Mission and Evangelism. At its ACCRA 1958 meeting the INTERNATIONAL MISSIONARY COUNCIL voted for integration with the WCC. The hope was that this action would put mission at the center of the WCC agenda. A primary motivation for merger was that many member organizations of the IMC, though founded as missions, were now freestanding church bodies in their own right that wished to relate to other churches as churches and not through mission agencies. Moreover, insofar as the original vision for unity was driven by a missionary imperative, it was logical that concerns for mission and unity be combined within one body. The union of the two bodies took place at the NEW DELHI ASSEMBLY of the WCC in 1961.

To further the work of mission, the Commission on World Mission and Evangelism (CWME) was established. Its mandate was "to further the proclamation to the whole world of the Gospel of Jesus Christ, to the end that all men may believe in Him and be saved." There was particular emphasis on the need for outreach evangelism by the local church. The commission was to assist churches throughout the world to "bring the Gospel to bear upon situations where there is no effective witness to Christ," and to secure coop-

sionaries) and Odessa Theological Seminary in Ukraine and, in Russia, St. Petersburg Christian University and the Russian-American Christian University in Moscow (focusing on the preparation of Christians for involvement in secular society).

The Fragmentation of the Church. Until the 1990s, divisions among evangelicals were relatively few. Under communist oppression, they tended to preserve unity as much as possible. Now, however, older denominations have begun to experience a measure of fragmentation, while both nationals and foreign missionaries have established scores of new church bodies. There has been considerable debate between those Westerners who advocate coming alongside the existing churches and those who argue that because the traditional churches are sometimes legalistic and out of step with contemporary culture, new wine should be poured into new wineskins.

Relations with Russian Orthodoxy. Western evangelicals working in the CIS are sharply divided as to the appropriate stance to be taken toward Russian Orthodoxy. The majority eschew any cooperation with the Orthodox Church, arguing, among other things, that Russian Orthodoxy seems to teach salvation by works and that it is dominated by ritualism and even superstition. However, a sizable minority of evangelicals working in the CIS argue that a renewed Orthodoxy is, in fact, the best hope for evangelizing that vast region. The Orthodox Church itself is ambivalent about any sort of cooperation with evangelicals. Most Orthodox reject Protestant Christianity out of hand as being heretical and incompatible with Slavic culture, but some Orthodox leaders have been more open to evangelical offers of cooperation and assistance.

Cooperation with Westerners. National believers tend to be quite ambivalent in their attitude toward Western missionaries serving in the CIS. While appreciating some of the resources and new ideas Westerners bring, nationals understandably resent the tendency of many Westerners to want to dominate the work in which they are involved. Nationals want partners, not parents. And again and again national believers have lamented the tendency of Westerners to stay for too short a time, to be woefully ignorant of the local language and culture, to fail to contextualize their message, and to pay insufficient attention to existing national church structures and leaders.

Threats to Religious Liberty. Although the Russian Constitution guarantees religious liberty, Orthodox leaders have repeatedly called for severe restrictions on the activities of both foreign and indigenous Protestant organizations, and in several regions of the Russian Federation local governments have unilaterally begun to suppress evangelical activities. Religious liberty has been

more consistent in Ukraine but is limited or non-existent in most of the other CIS republics.

RAYMOND P. PRIGODICH

Bibliography. M. Bourdeaux, *The Gospel's Triumph over Communism;* D. B. Clendenin, *From the Coup to the Commonwealth: An Inside Look at Life in Contemporary Russia;* K. R. Hill, *The Soviet Union on the Brink: An Inside Look at Christianity and Glasnost;* N. C. Nielsen Jr., *Christianity After Communism: Social, Political, and Cultural Struggle in Russia;* W. Sawatsky, *Soviet Evangelicals Since World War II.*

Communication. Communication is the missionary problem par excellence. The word comes from the Latin word *communis* (common). In order to fulfill the GREAT COMMISSION a "commonality" must be established with the various peoples of the world—a commonality that makes it possible for them to understand and embrace the gospel of Christ. Accordingly, when HENDRICK KRAEMER sought to place questions having to do with the missionary task in a "wider and deeper setting" than that afforded by alternative words, he chose the word "communication."

From very early days the progress of the gospel has been aided by the communication skills of its proponents. One thinks immediately of John the Baptist's preaching in Judea, Peter's sermon on Pentecost, and Paul's ministry to the Gentiles. Jesus was a master communicator. However, a tension is introduced at this point because the New Testament makes it clear that human wisdom and communication skills are not sufficient to draw people to Christ and advance his kingdom (cf. 2 Cor. 2:1–6). Though the Lord Jesus commissioned the apostles to disciple the nations by preaching and teaching, he commanded them to stay in Jerusalem until empowered by the Holy Spirit (Acts 1:8). ELENCTICS, the "science of the conviction of sin" (Herman Bavinck), deals with this tension between human and divine components in Christian communication and is a pivotal, though often neglected, concern in missiology.

AUGUSTINE was perhaps the first to introduce secular communication theory to the church in a systematic way. Called as a young man to be the *rhetor* (legal orator) of Milan, Italy, he was profoundly impressed by the eloquence of the renowned preacher of Milan, Ambrose. Converted and baptized in 387, he returned to Hippo in North Africa where he became bishop in 396. Augustine questioned the Christian use of the rhetorical knowledge and skills he and various other church leaders of the time had mastered at the university. Taking his cue from the experience of the Israelites who were commanded to take clothing, vases, and ornaments of silver and gold with them upon their exodus from Egypt, he concluded that "gold from Egypt is still gold." Profane knowledge and communication skills can be used in kingdom service. Augustine then proceeded to write *On Christian Doctrine*, Book IV, which has been called the first manual of Christian preaching.

Augustine's work constituted an auspicious beginning, but only a beginning. Down through the centuries and especially for post-Reformation British and then American clergy, classical rhetorical theory informed homiletical theory and preaching methodology. Influential pulpits have been occupied by great orators familiar with the likes of Plato, Aristotle, Quintilian, Cicero, and Fenelon. Only recently has the *summum bonum* of ancient classical education, rhetoric, been downplayed to the point that the very word has lost its original meaning and connotes flowery (and empty?) speech. Historically, both church and mission have profited greatly from a knowledge of classical rhetoric.

It must be admitted, however, that "Egyptian gold" came with a price. Ethnocentric rhetoricians of ancient times believed that if foreign audiences did not think and respond as Athenians and Romans did, they at least should be taught to do so. Until comparatively recently, Western clergy and missionaries alike have tended toward the same provincialism. With global exploration and then the dawn of the electric age, however, change became inevitable. In modern times monoculturalism has been replaced by multiculturalism; "new rhetoricians" speak of "multiple rhetorics"; speech theory has been eclipsed by communication theory; and communication theory takes into account not only face-to-face or INTERPERSONAL COMMUNICATION, but MASS COMMUNICATION and cross-cultural, INTERCULTURAL COMMUNICATION as well.

As concerns the Christian mission, post–World War II years especially have witnessed great strides forward in this regard. First came the unparalleled number of cross-cultural contacts occasioned by the war itself. This was attended by numerous writings on culture, language, and communication. Among secular writings, *The Silent Language* and other works by Edward T. Hall had the greatest impact. But earlier contributions of Christian scholars such as HENDRICK KRAEMER and the postwar writings of Jacob Loewen, William D. Reyburn, William Samarin, EUGENE A. NIDA, and others also bore fruit. Nida's *Message and Mission: The Communication of the Christian Faith*, first published in 1960 and then revised, augmented, and republished in 1990, has perhaps been most influential in shaping missionary theory and practice. Authors of widely used texts such as Charles Kraft and David Hesselgrave readily acknowledge their debt to Nida. Written from his perspective as a marketing specialist, James F. Engel has contributed a comprehensive text highlighting audience analysis and media communication. At a popular level, Don Richardson's account of how the gospel was com-

municated to the West Irian Sawi tribespeople has had a significant impact.

Most widely used to illustrate and examine the communication process are cybernetic models based on electronic media. Thus classical categories (speaker, speech, audience) have largely given way to new categories and nomenclature such as source, message, respondent, channel, encode, decode, noise, feedback, and the like. One or another version of Nida's three-culture model of intercultural missionary communication is widely used to introduce important cultural components and highlight the relationship among cultures of Bible times, the missionary source, and target culture respondents.

For many years theorists and practitioners alike have discussed issues such as the best starting point for gospel communication (the nature and attributes of God or the person and work of Christ) and the establishment of common ground with the hearers. Current issues also have to do with the interanimation among language, cognition, and WORLDVIEW; the relationship among form, meaning, and function; the role of culture in special revelation and BIBLE TRANSLATION, interpretation, and application; and the relative importance of respondent understandings and preferences in CONTEXTUALIZING the Christian message. The significance accorded to the findings of the various sciences in these discussions, as well as in missionary communication theory and practice in general, serves to indicate that Augustine's "profane knowledge" problem is a perennial one. That being the case, contemporary theorists stand to benefit not just from his insight that Egyptian gold is still gold, but also from his reminders that biblical knowledge is to be considered superior both qualitatively and quantitatively, and that secular approaches are to be used with moderation.

DAVID J. HESSELGRAVE

Bibliography. J. F. Engel, *Contemporary Christian Communications;* E. T. Hall, *The Silent Language;* D. J. Hesselgrave, *Communicating Christ Cross-Culturally;* H. Kraft, *Communication Theory for Christian Witness;* E. A. Nida, *Message and Mission;* D. Richardson, *Peace Child.*

Communism/Marxism. Any social system advocating common ownership of property rather than private property. However, the term is primarily associated with the economic, social, and political views of Karl Marx (1818–83) and Friedrich Engels (1820–95) and their followers. Just seventy years after the death of Marx, roughly one-third of the world was dominated by economic and political systems shaped by Marx's thought.

Marx understood history to be the product of an ongoing dialectic of opposing material forces shaping the economic conditions of human social existence. Ideas then are simply the manifestations of the material conditions at work in the societies in which the ideas emerge. Marx is especially remembered for his critique of capitalism and his view that future societies would see the eventual abolition of classes and of private ownership of the means of production, and the development of a communist society in which all of the systemic causes of social alienation and exploitation of humankind are eliminated. Marxism has tended to emphasize both the inevitability of social evolution toward a classless society and the necessity of violent revolution and class conflict in the transition from one stage to another. Marx was an atheist and held that humankind tries to realize through the illusions of religion what is denied them in reality. Rather than positively working to change contemporary problems, religion is a deluded attempt to escape the misery of the present world. Thus it is the "opium of the people" and must be opposed.

Although Marx's thought has undergone significant revisions by later thinkers, his views exerted enormous influence upon twentieth-century societies worldwide. Such diverse revolutionaries as V. Lenin and J. Stalin in the Soviet Union, Mao Zedong in China, Fidel Castro in Cuba, Ho Chi Minh in Vietnam, and Pol Pot in Cambodia, as well as a host of lesser figures, have claimed the authority of Marx for their repressive social and political agendas. Marxism, with its trenchant critique of Western capitalism, was especially attractive to many in the non-Western world during the 1960s and 1970s. Marxist themes, combined with the emerging nationalistic fervor of the postcolonial era and a reaction against Western economic exploitation of non-Western nations, produced powerful revolutionary movements in Latin America, Africa, and Asia. Marxist themes have also been prominent in some of the leading Roman Catholic and Protestant liberation theologians in Latin America, although most were careful to distance themselves from the atheistic and deterministic assumption of Marxism (*see* LIBERATION THEOLOGY MISSIOLOGY).

The Christian church has generally been tightly controlled and persecuted in Marxist societies. Contrary to Marx's predictions, however, religion has not withered away; indeed the Christian church remained strong in the former Soviet Union and actually grew dramatically in communist China. With the dismantling of the Berlin Wall in 1989 and the collapse of the former Soviet Union, the most visible attempts to implement the agenda of Marxism have been exposed as dismal failures. Marxism has consequently lost much of its appeal throughout the world, although it still retains considerable influence in some sectors.

HAROLD A. NETLAND

SEE ALSO Ideologies.

Bibliography. K. Bockmuhl, *The Challenge of Marxism;* J. A. Kirk, *Theology Encounters Revolution;* K. - Korsch, *Marxism and Philosophy;* D. McLellan, *Marxism After Marx;* D. McLellan, *Marxism and Religion.*

Comoros *(Est. 2000 pop.: 778,000; 1,862 sq. km. [719 sq. mi.]).* The Comoros are a group of three volcanic islands in the northern entrance of the Mozambique Channel about halfway between Madagascar and the African mainland. The nearby island of Mayotte is geographically part of the group but administratively under France. Over 90 percent of the population are ethnic Comorians who speak three distinct Swahili languages. Most are Muslims and the Christian presence is very small, representing just over one percent of the population. Most of these are Roman Catholics. Evangelicals are represented by the AFRICAN INLAND MISSION, whose churches are growing at over 5 percent per year, and a few other Protestants.

TODD M. JOHNSON

Comparative Religion. The comprehensive study of religions as phenomena using both historical and systematic methodologies, as far as possible without dogmatic presuppositions, comparing and contrasting both universal and particular features of these religions.

The study of religion as a Western academic subject is a relatively new discipline. Prior to the mid-nineteenth century, when one studied "religion," the subject matter was one's own religion with occasional thoughts on how other religions compared with *my* religion. The study of religion, in other words, was synonymous with theology. In the mid-nineteenth century, several trends gave these occasional and dogmatic thoughts about other religions a new, distinctive character. One trend, ironically, was the Christian missions movement, which was reaching the peak of several centuries of development and was supplying Western scholars with a wealth of material on non-Christian religions. Second, at this same time anthropologists and archaeologists were studying non-Western cultures and sending back an avalanche of data on cultural and religious practices from Asia, Africa, and Micronesia. Third was the full flowering of a way of looking at such data in a way that emphasized human rationality, as opposed to divine agency. This Enlightenment viewpoint was tailor-made for attempts to make some sense of this body of religious information.

This early science of religion produced scholarly works of two types. One is typified by the work of a man often called the father of religious studies, Max Müller (1832–1930). Müller, using data obtained through his linguistic studies, traced the history of religious systems and then wrote comparative studies that made "religion" the underlying category of study rather than a specific religion. The second is typified by the work of James George Frazer (1854–1941), who took the catalog approach to making sense of this deluge of religious information. His twelve-volume *Golden Bough* is organized according to cross-religious categories, such as MAGIC, TABOO, and TOTEMISM, with religious data from different religious traditions filed under the appropriate heading.

One can see in this early work the influence of a positivistic approach to data—in short, the scientific model. The task of the scientist of religion was to gather as much data as possible, and then do theory construction that attempted to explain the data in wider and wider circles of inclusivity, with the goal not of discovering metaphysical truth but of describing accurately and meaningfully the religious phenomena of the world in which we live. Given this reliance on the scientific model (in an attempt to distinguish this study from theology), it is not surprising to find that when the prevailing scientific theory of the nineteenth century changed, the study of comparative religion began to change.

In some ways, Charles Darwin's theory of evolution was a godsend for comparative religionists. One effect of Darwin's explanatory thesis was to remove the need for periodic or constant divine intervention in human affairs in order to explain why things happen as they do. Divine intervention, of course, was a staple of premodern explanatory theses. By making it scientifically respectable to offer secular explanations for human phenomena, evolutionism opened up a whole new arena of activity for the fledgling science of religion. Sociologists, psychologists, and philosophers quickly filled this new arena with huge explanatory theses that attempted globally to describe the origins and development of all religion in comprehensive schemata.

This was the age of the great sociologists of religion, Emile Durkheim (1858–1917) and Max Weber (1864–1920). A uniquely American contribution to the discipline was offered by the psychologists of religion, typified by William James (1842–1910) and his *Varieties of Religious Experience*. Perhaps more than any other, the philosophers of religion began to produce systematic philosophies of the development of religious consciousness, such as that produced by Teilhard de Chardin (1881–1955).

This ferment of scholarly activity in kindred disciplines encouraged the carving out of methodologies designed specifically for the study of religion. Objective histories of specific religious traditions began to appear from the studies of scholars like Nathan Soderblom (1886–1931) and William Brede Kristensen (1867–1953). Other scholars, in the cataloging tradition of Frazier, adapted a methodology loosely related to Edmund Husserl's philosophical phenomenology and began to develop cross-religious categories in order to better compare and contrast religious traditions. Gerardus van der Leeuw (1890–1950) and Rudolf Otto (1869–1937) published works in the PHENOMENOLOGY OF RELIGION tradition, which relied on a method that advocated a temporary suspension of one's own beliefs *(epoche)*, in order to clearly identify the unique character of religious phenomena *(sui generis)*, with the goal of understanding only *(verstehen)*. These two approaches to the data of religious studies, the longitudinal, historical study and the cross-sectional phenomenological study, have been dominant methodologies in comparative religion.

In other ways, Darwin's theory of evolution sent the discipline of religious studies down a dead-end road. The search for a common origin and developmental pattern to all religion proved to be a remarkably contentious and ultimately frustrating enterprise. The data of religions from around the world proved to be elastic in the extreme when it came to theory shaping. Some of the developmental schemes posited all religions coming from animistic roots where all being is invested with spiritual power (*see* ANIMISM), moving toward a more well-defined POLYTHEISM and finally the great monotheistic religious traditions (*see* MONOTHEISM). Others of the developmental schemes took roughly the same material and posited theories that taught exactly the opposite: that the original conceptions of God were of high gods, monotheisms that over time devolved into polytheistic and then spiritist religions, with more and more layers of gods between humans and the high gods. And as more and more of the world's religious systems were studied, they proved as a group to be less and less amenable to step-by-step developmental patterns.

In most academic circles, the recognition that these essentially Western-based universal categories and developmental patterns do not necessarily fit other cultures led to a move toward cultural RELATIVISM, which argued that no generalizations are possible from culture to culture (*see also* PLURALISM). Each must be studied totally on its own terms. This move matched some of the insights of phenomenologists regarding the subjectivity of the religious scholar himself or herself, but went beyond those insights by suggesting that suspension of one's own point of view might be a chimera, that relativity extended not only to cultures but also to cultural observers. Many scholars began to see in cultural relativism a dead end as pronounced as the one faced by evolutionists—in this case, a dead end leading to an inability to have any kind of cross-cultural (and cross-religious) communication at all. This gave rise to two middle roads between universalism and particularism. The first came to be called functionalism, a view that did not find the core of religion in truth-claims of the gods or the gods' representatives, nor in the unconnected, conditioned realities of discrete cultures, but in the function religion performed in addressing personal and societal needs. The needs that functionalists identified as "religious" varied. But for all functionalists, "religion is as religion does." Functionalist theories of religion are among the most widely used in religious studies today, and in one sense may be seen as extensions of Emile Durkheim's pioneering work. It is particularly useful to sociologists of religion such as Wach (1898–1955) and Robert Bellah (b. 1927), and anthropologists Mary Douglas (b. 1921) and Clifford Geertz (b. 1926).

A second middle road between universalism and particularism is structuralism. With roots in the work of linguist Ferdinand de Saussure (1857–1913), and given methodological form by social anthropologist Claude Levi-Strauss (b. 1908), structuralists see the use of language and language systems as the mediator between universals and particulars. Religions and cultures came to be viewed as analogous to languages. Each language (or religion), is different with its own vocabulary and grammatical rules. Each language (or religion), however, also has structural features in common that seem to run across all languages or religions. Structuralists say these features allow people of one religious tradition to recognize themselves in another person's religious tradition, but to preserve the otherness of that tradition because those features' full meaning resides more in the holistic pattern of that religious tradition than in the content of a particular belief. The recognition of these common structural features allows empathy that may lead to understanding, but not to understanding itself. Structuralism is on the cutting edge of approaches to religion being explored by scholars today. History of religions and phenomenological methodologies still provide much of the on-the-ground content and data of religious studies, but those data are increasingly filtered through the lens of structuralist forms.

Evangelical Christians can make good use of these different approaches to the study of religion so long as they are seen as useful tools in gathering and handling data of a very specific nature and not as normative methodologies over against theological and revelatory ones. They become problematic for evangelicals when these theories begin to claim for themselves absolute status, replacing propositional and ethical absolutes with methodological ones.

TERRY C. MUCK

SEE ALSO Religion; World Religions.

Bibliography. W. Capps, *Religious Studies: The Making of a Discipline;* T. Muck, *The Mysterious Beyond: A Guide to Studying Religion;* E. Sharpe, *Comparative Religion: A History.*

Computers. *See* TECHNOLOGY.

Conference. *See* CHURCH MISSIONS CONFERENCE.

Confession. In biblical usage, confession in both Hebrew *(yâdâ)* and Greek *(homologeō)* has the general sense of acknowledgment. While it is not necessarily oral, it usually involves verbalization. Two complimentary orientations of confession are found: acknowledging our faith in God and acknowledging our sin.

Confessing Faith. In the Old Testament, Israel's confession of faith is intimately tied to the praise of God and acknowledgment of his greatness. Solomon mentions the need of God's people to confess his name and turn from their sins in his prayer of dedication of the Temple (1 Kings 8:33, 35; 2 Chron. 6:24, 26), linking confessing God and confession of sin together. Nehemiah also shows the connection in leading the people in admission of sin followed by confession and worship of God (Neh. 9:2, 3).

In the New Testament the confession of faith in God is more prominent. John the Baptist admitted that he was not the Christ (John 1:20) and the Pharisees were afraid to confess their faith publicly (John 12:42). Positively, it is verbal confession of Christ which identifies a Christian (Rom. 10:9–10; 2 Tim. 2:19; Heb. 3:1). This confession, however, must be matched by a lifestyle which honors the one confessed (2 Cor. 9: 13; 1 Tim. 6:12). Though not all will become Christians, Paul tells the Philippians that every tongue will eventually confess that Jesus is Lord (Phil. 2:11).

In the historical development of the term two important nuances were added after the New Testament: confession as the testimony to Christ given by a martyr at the time of his or her death (*see also* MARTYRDOM and WITNESS), and a confession as a summary statement of belief to which a body of Christians subscribes. Such statements have been seen throughout the history of the church from the Apostles' Creed to the Lausanne Covenant. Traditionally, however, the term "confession of faith" refers to the types of statements of doctrinal beliefs and distinctives which were developed during and since the time of the Reformation.

These statements are typically attempts to clarify the Christian faith in light of cultural, social, or religious circumstances. While there are universals inherent in confessing Christ (e.g., his Deity), there are also particulars of faith which may be confessed in one context without being addressed in another context. They thus have an occasional orientation and are seen as human formulations of belief in contrast to the eternal truths conveyed in the Scriptures. Some, such as the Apostles' and Nicene Creeds, are almost universally acknowledged in the church. "Creed" is usually used to refer to the statements of the early centuries of the church now seen by the universal church to be essential for all Christians. Other confessions either were developed or have been used to give a sense of denominational identity (The Augsburg Confession for Lutherans and The Westminster Confession for Presbyterians), to declare the church's stance in difficult social circumstances (The Barmen Declaration in Nazi Germany) or to define particular biblical and theological orientations (The Lausanne Covenant for evangelicals). The Lausanne Covenant has been given a particularly important place in contemporary evangelical missions, having been translated into more than twenty languages and having many evangelical mission organizations and fellowships using it as their statement of common faith (see also LAUSANNE MOVEMENT).

Missiological Implications of Confessing Faith. The content of a personal confession of faith will of necessity have certain universal elements (see also PROFESSION OF FAITH). Personal acknowledgment of sin and submission to God through Christ are two indispensable ones. Also seen often in church history is some type of renunciation of Satan and his works in the new convert's life. In cross-cultural settings, the missionary must be aware that other renunciations of importance to the local context are often added. The Kimbanguists in Zaire, for example, ban eating monkey meat and dancing naked. Some conservative evangelical institutions in the United States prohibit drinking or social dancing; many churches in Japan do not allow participation in ANCESTRAL PRACTICES. While none of these prohibitions are universal or necessary for genuine conversion, they do show the diversity of cultural or subcultural emphases in the church and the need for missionary sensitivity to avoid taking prohibitions from the missionary's culture and naively insisting on them as elements of genuine conversion in another (Priest 1994).

Since its inception the church and its local manifestations in cultures around the world has been a confessing church. While these confessions may not always be written or explicit, they are still present in the essentials of Christian practice adhered to by local assemblies and organizations. There is no reason to believe that this will not continue to be the case. As long as the confessions or statements of faith are seen as human products and not replacements for God's Word, there will be a place for their development in every culture. While all such statements must conform to Scripture, their occasional nature will necessitate different emphases and orientations in them.

Confession of Sin. More prominent in the Old Testament than confessing faith in God is confessing sin. This is to be done individually (Lev. 5:5; Ps. 32:5; Prov. 28:13) and corporately (Lev. 26:40; Neh. 9:2). Leaders of God's people confess both personal and corporate sins (Neh. 1:6; Dan. 9:20). In the New Testament, those who were baptized by John had to confess their sins (Matt. 3:16). In response to a botched exorcism which generated the fear of God in the hearts of Ephesian Christians, they openly (publicly) confessed their sins (Acts 19:18). James commanded the church to confess sins to one another (probably in private, though public confession cannot be ruled out; James. 5:16). John gives a promise which many Christians through the centuries have found comforting: if we confess our sins, God is sure to forgive them (1 John 1:9).

Confession in Cultures and Religions. Confessing sin is not limited to Western culture or to Christianity. Cultures and religions around the world recognize the need to find absolution for wrongs committed, and have appropriate rituals which enable the confession of transgressions (see also RITUAL AND CEREMONY). In collective cultures, confessions are often heard publicly among the collective of the transgressor. Since individual sin may bring SHAME or judgment not just on the individual but on the entire ingroup, the ingroup has a moral obligation to ensure the confession of wrongdoing and often participates in that confession in some way to demonstrate solidarity with the transgressor and agreement over the impropriety of the violation (see also INDIVIDUALISM AND COLLECTIVISM).

Confession in other cultures and religions may come as part of rituals of transition in which ritual purity is a necessary precondition for successful transition from one phase of life to another (from singleness to marriage, from child to adult, from neophyte to religious leader). They may also come in times of crisis, whether already present (e.g., drought) or anticipated (e.g., preparing to go to war or impending death). They typically involve admission of wrongs done and may be accompanied by appropriate acknowledgment symbols. For example, the Huichol of Mexico tie a knot in a piece of string for each sin committed. Symbols of receiving absolution of forgiveness may also accompany the confession, such as the Huichol practice of burning the knotted string to demonstrate that the transgressions have been forgiven.

Missiological Implications of Confessing Sin.
While certainly every confession of sin must ultimately be before God, no universally normative
commands or restrictions are given in Scripture
as to the public extent of the confession or what
rituals may be involved with it. Protestants in individualistic cultures tend to emphasize private
confession before God rather than before a
priest. One of the hallmarks of the East African
Revival, however, was the public confession of
sins among believers.

Study and understanding of rituals of confession which already exist in cultures will provide
missionaries with tools which may help them develop appropriate Christian rituals. However,
care must be taken not to simply import traditional rituals wholesale into the church lest SYN-
CRETISM become a problem.

A recent development in mission circles is that
of identificational repentance (*see* POWERS, THE)
in which individuals or small groups of Christians confess on behalf of larger groups of people
(organizations, ethnic groups, nations). Justification for this practice is found in the example of
Nehemiah (1:6).

Confession of sins is a mark of a Christian, but
the method used may legitimately borrow from
cultural values and symbols so that they remain
relevant in their context.

A. SCOTT MOREAU

Bibliography. U. Bianchi, *ER*, 4:1–7; D. J. Moo,
BDET, 111–14; M. Noll, *EDT*, pp. 262–66; R. J. Priest,
Missiology 22:3 (July 1994): 291–315.

Confucianism. A system of social, political, ethical, and religious thought based upon the teachings of Confucius (c. 552–479 B.C.) and his disciples. For over the past two thousand years
Confucianism in its various forms has been influential in shaping the cultures of China, Taiwan, Hong Kong, Singapore, Korea, Vietnam,
and Japan.

Confucius (from *K'ung Fu-Tzu*, "Master K'ung")
was born into a family of lower nobility. According to tradition, after serving in various minor
posts in the state of Lu, at the age of fifty Confucius attained a relatively high rank but became
disillusioned with the lack of interest in his social
ideas. Retiring from public service, Confucius
spent some thirteen years traveling from state to
state in an effort to inspire social and political reforms. He then returned to the state of Lu to concentrate upon teaching his disciples and, according to tradition, to edit the Confucian classics.

Confucianism looks to the Five Classics—the
Book of Poetry (*Shih Ching*), the Book of Rites
(*Li Ching*), the Book of History (*Shu Ching*), the
Spring and Autumn Annals (*Ch'un Ch'iu*), and
the Book of Changes (*I Ching*)—as authoritative.
Following his death, the teachings of Confucius
were collected in the Analects (*Lun Yü*), probably
compiled in the third century B.C. In addition to
the Five Classics are the Four Books—which include the Anlects, the Great Learning (*Ta Hsüeh*),
the Doctrine of the Mean (*Chung Yung*), and the
book of Mencius—which form a smaller corpus
of authoritative texts.

Traditionally the family has been the center of
Chinese social life. This is reflected in the classical Confucian emphasis upon the Five Relationships, namely, the relationships between father
and son, elder brother and younger brother, husband and wife, elders and juniors, and rulers and
subjects. Hierarchical relationships, with carefully defined reciprocal obligations for all parties,
provided for order and stability, not only in the
family but in society at large. Confucius emphasized the virtue of filial piety (*hsiao*), or respect
and honor for one's parents. The duty of the son
is to obey his father in all things while he lives
and to honor and continue to obey him after he
is dead. Filial piety thus came to be closely identified with the ancient cult of ancestral veneration, through which the continuity of familial ties
were reinforced (*see* ANCESTRAL PRACTICES). In
turn, the father has a great responsibility for the
well being of the family.

Another central virtue for Confucius was *jen*,
often translated as "benevolence" or "humane-
ness." *Jen* might be regarded as the ideal embodiment of moral virtue, combining both righteousness (*i*) and propriety (*li*). Confucius developed the
notion of *li* (often translated "ritual," "propriety,"
"principle," or "order") into a moral and religious
concept. *Li* contains both an external and internal
sense. Externally *li* refers to proper patterns of behavior which, when performed correctly, express
and reinforce harmony among the various hierarchically ordered elements of the family, society,
and cosmos. *Li* also includes the idea of right
moral attitude and motivation in actions.

Mencius (c. 371–289 B.C.) and Hsün Tzu
(c. 298–238 B.C.), two of the most influential
teachers after Confucius, offered strikingly different analyses of human nature. Mencius held
that human nature is essentially good and that
humanity's task is to uncover and cultivate this
inherent goodness, thereby realizing the congruence of human nature with the way of Heaven
(*Tien*). Hsün Tzu, by contrast, while acknowledging the perfectability of humanity, stressed the
evil aspect in human nature. Strict controls in the
form of laws and education are necessary for an
ordered and harmonious society.

During the Han dynasty (206 B.C.–A.D. 220),
Confucianism became recognized officially as
state orthodoxy, the Confucian canon was for-
malized, and the beginnings of a religious cult of
Confucius emerged. Although attempts to deify
Confucius were initially rejected, sacrifices to
Confucius were practiced by the literati and

eventually such sacrifices were included among the state sacrifices performed by the emperor. In A.D. 630 an imperial decree called for establishment of a state temple to Confucius in every prefecture, in which sacrifices to the sage could be regularly offered. In later centuries there were attempts to purify the increasingly elaborate cult of Confucius by restoring his image as "The Perfectly Holy Teacher of Antiquity" as well as countermovements to recognize sacrifices to Confucius as equal in standing to those offered to Heaven and Earth. However, with the revolution of 1911 the cult of Confucius languished in China, although it has continued to flourish among the Chinese diaspora in Hong Kong, Taiwan, and Singapore.

Is Confucianism primarily a social ethic or a religion? Scholars are divided on the question of Confucius's own views on religion. Some see him as essentially agnostic, a social and ethical humanist who was primarily concerned with "this worldly" relationships. When asked about death Confucius replied that he knew nothing of life; how could he know about death (*Analects*, XI. 11)? When asked about the spirits he said one should respect them but keep them at a distance (VI.20). On the other hand, Confucius placed great value on proper performance on the ancestral rites (III.12), an activity with clear religious overtones. He claimed the authority of Heaven (*Tien*) for his views: "Heaven is the author of the virtue that is in me" (VII.23).

Christianity has had an ambivalent relationship with Confucianism. Some Christians, as for example MATTEO RICCI in the sixteenth century, saw in classical Confucianism much which could be adopted and utilized in establishing Christianity in the Chinese context. Ricci saw commonality between Christianity and Confucianism particularly in ethical teachings and what Ricci saw as a primitive monotheism in early Confucianism. Others regard this as a misinterpretation of Confucianism and stress the discontinuities between the systems. Given the enduring influence of Confucianism in many Asian societies, the church in Asia must continue to engage in a serious manner the themes and values of Confucianism. Fundamental questions for Christian CONTEXTUALIZATION concern the Confucian understandings of the religious ultimate (Heaven, Lord on High) and the spirits of the deceased, assumptions about the inherent goodness of human nature, and the relation between Confucianism and ancestral veneration rites.

HAROLD A. NETLAND

Bibliography. J. Ching, *Confucianism and Christianity*; R. Covell, *Confucius, the Buddha, and Christ*; H. G. Creel, *Confucius and the Chinese Way*; H. Fingarette, *Confucianism: The Secular as Sacred*; W. Liu, *A Short History of Confucian Philosophy*; L. G. Thompson, *Chinese Religion: An Introduction*, 4th ed.

Congo (*Est. 2000 pop.: 2,970,000; 342,000 sq. km. [132,046 sq. mi.]*). Located on the west coast of Central Africa and sharing borders with Zaire, Central African Republic, Cameroon, and Gabon, the Republic of Congo's population is comprised of some 75 ethnic groups. An estimated 85 percent are Christians (50 percent are Catholic, 22 percent are Protestant, and 14 percent are indigenous independent groups). Independence from France was achieved in 1960, with a Marxist-style government ruling from 1968 to 1991. Disillusionment with a failing economy resulted in constitutional reform and the adoption of democracy, with elections being held in 1992 and 1993.

Congo was initially exposed to the gospel through Portuguese missionaries who arrived in 1491, nine years after Portuguese explorers reached the coast. The king, Nzinga Nkuvu, and his son Alfonso were baptized on May 3, 1491. Alfonso ascended to the throne in 1506 and moved to establish a Christian presence in every locality in the kingdom. His son, Henrique, became the first contemporary African-born Catholic bishop. The Capuchins, an Italian order, sent some 440 missionaries between 1645 and 1835, but eventually the church deteriorated through a combination of withdrawal of missionaries by Portugal, syncretistic religiosity, and the ravages of the slave trade. Catholic work was renewed in 1883 when the Holy Ghost priests arrived, and continues strong today.

Protestant missionary work began in 1909 when the Swedish Evangelical Mission expanded their work from Zaire. Since its inception, Protestant work has been strongly affected by several indigenous movements, most notably Kimbanguism, from Zaire. The Evangelical Church, the largest Protestant denomination, achieved independent status in 1961. The Salvation Army also has a strong presence.

During the 23 years of Marxist rule missionary activity was suppressed. After the constitutional reform and elections, however, the doors opened to missionary work. In 1993 it was estimated that there were almost 120 missionaries serving in Congo representing some 15 agencies, with Scandinavians and Americans the bulk of the workers.

A. SCOTT MOREAU

Bibliography. D. Barrett, *WCE*; J. Baur, *2000 Years of Christianity in Africa*; A. Hastings, *The Church in Africa 1450–1950*; M. Shaw, *The Kingdom of God in Africa*.

Congress on the Church's Worldwide Mission (Wheaton Congress, 1966). With the merger of the INTERNATIONAL MISSIONARY COUNCIL into the WORLD COUNCIL OF CHURCHES in 1961, conservative American mission executives, missionaries, and missiologists perceived a need for a distinctly evangelical congress to address ongoing issues of theological and practical concern. Jointly sponsored by the EFMA and IFMA, the congress was held in Wheaton, Illinois, in April of 1966. The seven-day congress comprised five missions-oriented biblical expositions, ten major study papers (on topics like SYNCRETISM, UNIVERSALISM, evangelical unity, PROSELYTISM, changes in the Catholic Church), and area reports. The 938 registered delegates represented some 258 mission boards and agencies, interest groups, and educational institutions from 71 countries in every part of the world.

The conference was framed to respond to the challenges of the conciliar movement by reaffirming fundamental convictions in an atmosphere of evangelical ecumenicity. The pre-congress statement noted that there was greater missionary strength in the IFMA-EFMA affiliation than in the WCC. Thus it was felt that the time had come for this segment of the total mission force to clearly state its own convictions.

Among the papers that emerged from the congress was the Wheaton Declaration. Initially drafted by ARTHUR GLASSER, it was revised in several committees and finally adopted by the delegates. The declaration begins by affirming the need for certainty, commitment, discernment, hope, and confidence in the midst of the hardening social, religious, and political climates of the times. It confesses the failures of evangelical missions in the light of scriptural standards, and presents an evangelical consensus on the authority of the Bible and the central concern of evangelism in mission. Finally, it addresses selected crucial issues of the day (the issues studied in the major papers).

The Wheaton Congress garnered enough attention to merit the publication of the declaration in *IRM*, though there was relatively little impact in ecumenical circles. Even so, the Wheaton Congress stands as an important evangelical milestone in that it was one of the definitive steps that eventually resulted in the LAUSANNE MOVEMENT.

A. SCOTT MOREAU

Bibliography. H. Lindsell, ed., *The Church's Worldwide Mission.*

Conscience. A term traditionally understood to refer to the part of a person which distinguishes right and wrong. Paul wrote about the reality of all humans having a conscience "now accusing, now even defending them" (Rom. 2:15). The Old Testament has no specific references to conscience. However, the foundation of the concept lies in God's knowing judgment of our actions and the consequent responsibility of the follower of God to be able to evaluate his or her actions and attitudes (e.g., 1 Sam. 24:5; 2 Sam. 24:10; Job 27:6; Jer. 17:9–10). While in the Old Testament conscience is seen more in the collective context

of a covenant community, a more individualized and autonomous perspective appears in the New Testament, where conscience is considered a foundational part of every human being. Paul sought to keep his conscience clear (Act 24:16; 2 Cor. 1:12) and commended this as an example to others (1 Tim. 1:5; 3:9) even though ultimately it is God who is Paul's judge and not only Paul's conscience (1 Cor. 4:4). Some people have weak consciences and this must be recognized (1 Cor. 8 and 10:23–11:1). Others, however, have seared (1 Tim. 4:2) or corrupted (Titus 1:15) their consciences through willful participation in sin (see also Eph. 4:19).

The well known idea that Gentiles have the law of God written on their hearts (Rom. 2:14–15) does not refer as much to *content* as to *function*. Paul argues that the Gentiles' pagan laws functioned better (by both accusing and excusing them) than God's own law did in the hearts of the Jews (who only used it to excuse themselves). Here we see that conscience is not focused on content (*what* the rules are) as much as it is application of value judgments on actions and attitudes (*how* the rules are applied). Conscience "merely monitors the worldview that exists in our internal conversation" (Meadors, 114). Conscience, in this sense, acts as a moral restraint among all peoples, hindering a movement toward pure lawlessness, preventing cultures, peopled by sinful and selfish humans, from self-destructing. While the form and means of functioning of conscience will vary with the WORLDVIEW of the people, the fact of the presence of a conscience is a universal human quality.

What is the source of conscience in humanity? Sharing the IMAGE OF GOD, we are all born with the need and capacity to develop a sense of right and wrong. All humans, through the process of ENCULTURATION, are given the rules their consciences require to distinguish right and wrong, albeit within the framework of their own cultural constructs. Conscience is thus a natural gift from God in all people and does not require a special work of the Spirit to be operative. Being part of the human makeup, it can be studied in its personal, familial, and cultural contexts.

The conscience has the function of producing GUILT or SHAME when we have violated cultural norms. Though an oversimplification, it is not inappropriate to say that in an individualistic setting, *guilt* tends to be more operative—the conscience is internal, and produces guilt when one violates a norm whether or not others know what has been done. In a collective setting, *shame* is more operative—one shames the group and self through transgressions of group norms.

While no culture corresponds uniformly to God's kingdom values, every culture has vestiges of those values embedded within the rules, mores, and laws it maintains (*see also* ETHICS). Human beings are not born with the values of God *already* in their hearts; they are born with a need for such values and the capacity to grow in appreciating them. As they grow, they are taught elements of God's values, together with cultural rules and regulations (*see also* MORAL DEVELOPMENT). These become the values which are applied by our consciences in evaluating our actions.

The concept of conscience appears in many of the major religions of the world, but conscience as an internal, universal human component appears to be unique to Christianity (Despland, 50). During the early stages of the modern missionary period, Christians observing other peoples and religions sometime disparaged them because of the perceived lack of conformity to the Western concept of an internal, individual conscience. This was built on the assumption that the development of such a conscience conformed to the biblical picture and was the hallmark of civilization. Western missionaries tended to assume that their consciences were advanced beyond that of local peoples, who they felt had little if any sense of right and wrong. They took on themselves the task of teaching moral scruples, all too often imposing new cultural (rather than biblical) values and belittling or trampling on local values in the process.

To understand the cultural forms of conscience is of critical importance in missionary work. It carries implications for ELENCTICS (the conviction of sin) as well as cross-cultural ethics. When we feel that another does not have a proper conscience, we are tempted to develop one that matches ours. When we develop ethical systems, they tend to blend our cultural values together with biblical values, and may not make sense to our target population. In fact, in promulgating our ethical and moral systems rather than enabling the development of contextualized ones based on the local culture's reading of the Word of God, we develop a dependence mentality and inhibit spiritual growth, as Robert Priest aptly points out.

An approach to conscience which is biblical and culturally sensitive recognizes that (1) conscience is universal, (2) the indigenous conscience operates well, (3) it functions in its own context and in light of indigenous values, and (4) part of the missionary task is not to attack local value systems but to introduce people to the Word of God in such a way that they can see for themselves God's view of their culture through the eyes of Scripture. It is built on trust that God is at work in any people who call on his name; and that when they enter into a covenant relationship with him he is committed to enabling their growth as a body of believers into the likeness of Jesus (Eph. 4:7–16).

A. SCOTT MOREAU

Bibliography. B. Adeney, *Strange Virtues: Ethics in a Multi-Cultural World;* M. Despland, *ER,* 4:45–52; G. T. Meadors, *EDT,* pp. 113–15; R. J. Priest, *Missiology* 22:3 (July 1994): 291–315.

Constantine. *See* CYRIL (826–869).

Consultation on the Church in Response to Human Need. *See* WHEATON '83.

Consultation on the Relationship Between Evangelism and Social Responsibility (CRESR '82). CRESR '82 was a gathering of fifty evangelists, mission leaders, theologians, and missiologists at Reformed Bible College in Grand Rapids, Michigan, June 19–26, 1982. It continued the debate within evangelical circles over the broadening of the traditional understanding of mission as evangelism to include social responsibilities. There were five major sections in the discussion: (1) Church history and modern theology of salvation; (2) How broad is salvation in Scripture? (3) The kingdom in relation to the church and the world; (4) History and eschatology; and (5) Conclusions.

Prompted by a shift in John Stott's thinking to include social responsibilities as an integral component of mission between the BERLIN CONGRESS (1966) and the LAUSANNE CONSULTATION (1974) and Arthur Johnston's response to that shift in *The Battle for World Evangelism,* the participants at CRESR '82 also wrestled with the spectrum of social responsibilities in which we might be involved (from relief work to structural change). The resulting consultation statement, *Evangelism and Social Responsibility: An Evangelical Commitment,* has been well received over the years as an evangelical approach to the questions raised during the Consultation. While all agreed that our Christian responsibilities include engagement in meeting social responsibilities, the question as to whether this is integral to mission was not resolved to everyone's satisfaction.

A. SCOTT MOREAU

Bibliography. Consultation on the Relationship between Evangelism and Social Responsibility, *Evangelism and Social Responsibility: An Evangelical Commitment;* T. Sine, ed., *The Church in Response to Human Need;* J. R. W. Stott, *Transformation* 1:1 (1984): 21–22; *Trinity World Forum* 8:2 (Winter 1983).

Consumerism. Consumerism is frequently associated with the movement sparked by Ralph Nader aimed to inform and protect consumers. The term is also used as a rough synonym for American-style capitalism and materialism. Modern marketing, with its focus on consumers' needs and the development of sophisticated advertising techniques, has had a powerful impact on people's purchasing patterns. The segmentation of markets into smaller units has enabled companies to achieve greater distribution of their products. Consumerism is also an American export to many other parts of the world, where marketing fosters the transition to capitalist, consumption-oriented economies. This phenomenon frequently submerges local traditional beliefs and customs in favor of American popular culture.

Both marketing and consumerism are elements of a capitalist, materialistic system that is largely humanistic and devoid of ethical or spiritual values. American popular culture, including television, clothing fashions, movies, fast food, sports, and music, is thoroughly materialistic and consumption-oriented. The spirit of consumerism leads people to tie their identity and status to their spending. Moreover, the American economy is consumption-driven to the extent that any significant decreases in spending would result in an immediate recession. In contrast to this materialistic mind-set, Jesus taught that one's life does not consist of the multitude of one's possessions, cautioning people against greed that causes them to accumulate material possessions they cannot take with them when they die (Luke 12:15–21). Their treasure should be where their heart is (Matt. 6:21 par. Luke 12:34). Jesus expected his followers to be prepared to renounce all their possessions, to give generously to others (Matt. 19:21; Luke 14:33; 19:8), and to consider their belongings as resources entrusted to them by God to further his kingdom (Matt. 24:45–51; 25:14–30; Luke 12:41–48; 16:1–13, 19–25). Paul, likewise, preached modesty and contentment (Phil. 4:10–13; 1 Tim. 6:7–8).

Generally, consumerism has led to greater personal debt (see DEBT) and thus decreased missionary giving and deployment in recent years. As people are enculturated from childhood to expect a high level of physical comfort, they are more likely to give priority to meeting their own lifestyle needs than to sacrificing a substantial portion of their income for the cause of world evangelization. In response to changing patterns of giving, some groups have begun to accentuate single-project over long-term giving. The high cost of Western-style missions also raises the issue of efficiency in the way modern mission is conducted. In order to stem the pervasive influence of materialistic values in contemporary Western culture, it seems imperative to return to a rhythm of life that seeks to balance work with worship, prayer, rest, and time for relationships and to emulate the attitudes toward material possessions urged by Paul and Jesus.

ANDREAS J. KÖSTENBERGER

SEE ALSO Economics.

Bibliography. J. Bonk, *Missions and Money: Affluence as a Western Missionary Problem;* R. S. Greenway, *EMQ* 28 (1992): 26–32; K. P. Yohannan, *Why the World Waits: Exposing the Reality of Modern Missions.*

Contextualization. The term "contextualization" first appeared in 1972 in a publication of the Theological Education Fund entitled *Ministry in Context.* This document laid out the principles which would govern the distribution of funds for the Third Mandate of the TEF. The scholarships were awarded for the graduate education of scholars in the international church. Contextualization was described as "the capacity to respond meaningfully to the gospel within the framework of one's own situation." A precedent for the new term, "contextual theology," resulted from a consultation held in Bossey, Switzerland, in August 1971. The Ecumenical Institute of the WORLD COUNCIL OF CHURCHES had sponsored that earlier discussion under the theme "Dogmatic or Contextual Theology."

The lament behind the Third Mandate of the TEF was that "both the approach and content of theological reflection tend to move within the framework of Western questions and cultural presuppositions, failing to vigorously address the gospel of Jesus Christ to the particular situation." Further, it was declared that "Contextualization is not simply a fad or catch-word but a theological necessity demanded by the incarnational nature of the Word."

While the document had a limited purpose, the implications coming from it resulted in a movement which has had an impact on the theory and practice of mission. The contextualization concept was a timely innovation. New nations were struggling for their own life. The mission enterprise needed new symbols to mark a needed separation from the colonialistic, Western-dominated past (see COLONIALISM).

There is no single or broadly accepted definition of contextualization. The goal of contextualization perhaps best defines what it is. That goal is to enable, insofar as it is humanly possible, an understanding of what it means that Jesus Christ, the Word, is authentically experienced in each and every human situation. Contextualization means that the Word must dwell among all families of humankind today as truly as Jesus lived among his own kin. The gospel is Good News when it provides answers for a particular people living in a particular place at a particular time. This means the WORLDVIEW of that people provides a framework for communication, the questions and needs of that people are a guide to the emphasis of the message, and the cultural gifts of that people become the medium of expression.

Contextualization in mission is the effort made by a particular church to experience the gospel for its own life in light of the Word of God. In the process of contextualization the church, through the Holy Spirit, continually challenges, incorporates, and transforms elements of the culture in order to bring them under the lordship of Christ. As believers in a particular place reflect upon the

Word through their own thoughts, employing their own cultural gifts, they are better able to understand the gospel as incarnation.

The term "contextualization" is most commonly associated with theology, yet given the above definition, it is proper to speak of contextualization in a variety of ways encompassing all the dimensions of religious life. For example, church architecture, worship, preaching, systems of church governance, symbols, and rituals are all areas where the contextualization principle applies. Context, on which the term is based, is not narrowly understood as the artifacts and customs of culture only, but embraces the differences of human realities and experience. These differences are related to cultural histories, societal situations, economics, politics, and ideologies. In this sense contextualization applies as much to the church "at home," with all its variations, as it does to the church "overseas."

In mission practice the more visible aspects of contextualization were closely related to older terms such as ACCOMMODATION, ADAPTION, INCULTURATION, and INDIGENIZATION. Issues such as forms of communication, language, music, styles of dress, and so on had long been associated with the so-called three-self missionary philosophy which was built around the principle of indigenization. Indigeneity often was understood as "nativization," in that the visible cultural forms of a given people would be used in expressing Christianity. In going beyond these more superficial expressions, the new term "contextualization" tended to raise the fear of SYNCRETISM. This would mean the "old religion" would become mixed in with the new biblical faith and that culture would have more authority than revelation. Some felt, therefore, that the older concept of indigenization should not be changed but, rather, broadened to cover more adequately the field of theology.

In addition to giving greater attention to the deeper levels of culture, the new term "contextualization" became distinguished from indigenization in other ways. Indigenization always implied a comparison with the West, whereas contextualization focuses on the resources available from within the context itself. Indigenization was static while contextualization is dynamic, as a still photograph might be compared to a motion picture. The older indigenization was more isolated while contextualization, though locally constructed, interacts with global realities.

The fact that the early documents about contextualization were formulated in offices related to the World Council of Churches also made the concept difficult to accept in the nonconciliar circles. The heavy emphasis on justice and social development left little, it seemed, for evangelism and conversion. Scholars in Latin America were among the earliest to write about what they saw as an appropriate theology for their context. The direction this new theology took alarmed many evangelicals.

LIBERATION THEOLOGY became almost as a household word in the 1970s and 1980s. Evangelicals felt it demonstrated an inadequate use of the Bible and relied too heavily on a Marxist orientation. This was difficult for North American conservatives to accept. Even before his book, *Ministry in Context*, GUSTAVO GUTIÉRREZ had already written his *Theology of Liberation* (1971). Soon afterward J. MIGUEZ BONINO followed with *Doing Theology in a Revolutionary Situation* (1978). These major innovations opened up further thinking on contextualization. They followed closely the volatile 1960s in the United States. Ideas about contextualization in the United States first became associated with the controversial issues raised by the Vietnam War and American racism. "Black Power," as advocated by James Cone (1969), had become a popular application of what contextualization is.

Because of this ferment HERMENEUTICS quickly became the central point of contention among evangelicals. The question was asked whether truth is derived primarily from human experience or from REVELATION. At first there was little consensus among evangelicals about the role of CULTURE and social issues, especially in theology. The contextualization debate made serious new thinking possible, especially with regard to culture and the way in which it connects to the biblical record.

Throughout the 1970s the writing and discussion on contextualization began to clarify directions that evangelicals should take. A Lausanne-sponsored gathering at Willowbank (Bermuda) in 1978 adopted the theme "Gospel and Culture." The conference took seriously the role of the cultural context of the believer as well as the biblical text in defining evangelization and church development. The late 1970s also saw the rise (and demise) of the quarterly, *The Gospel in Context*. The journal's brief life demonstrated how creative and stimulating worldwide contextualization could be.

The decade of the 1970s also brought remarkable progress in finding ways to carry out contextualization. Each of the ways, or "models," as they are called, carries certain epistemological assumptions, as well as philosophical ideas about truth. While the models each have their differences, they also have several features that they share in common. Some are more centered on human experience while others show a greater dependence on widely accepted teachings of the church and the Bible. Thus, the assumptions undergirding some of these models make them less acceptable to evangelicals. Variations exist within a given model and certain features of more than one model may be combined. A brief review of the models will show how diverse the approaches to contextualization are.

Adaptation model: One of the earliest approaches was to make historical-theological concepts fit into each cultural situation. Traditional Western ideas are the norm. These are brought to the local culture. What is irrelevant may be set aside and what must be modified can be changed. The faulty assumption here is that there is one philosophical framework within which all cultures can communicate, assuming that other forms of knowledge are not legitimate.

Anthropological model: The beginning point is to study the people concerned. The key to communication and pathways to the human heart and spirit lies in the culture. The assumption is that people know best their own culture; worldview themes, symbols, myths are repositories of truth for all people. While this is true, unless discernment about a culture is brought to the Word for affirmation or judgment the contextualization exercise can become distorted and misleading.

Critical model: The critical aspect of this approach centers on how features of traditional culture—rituals, songs, stories, customs, music—are brought under the scrutiny of biblical teaching. Here the culture and the Scriptures are evaluated concurrently in the search for new ways to express belief and practice. One must ask who will carry out the process, and how accurate are the meanings derived from both customs and the Scripture.

Semiotic model: Semiotics is the science of "reading a culture" through "signs" (*see* Symbol, Symbolism). This comprehensive view of culture interprets symbols, myths, and the like that reveal the past as well as studying "signs" that indicate how the culture is changing. These realities are compared with church tradition in a process of "opening up" both the local culture and Christian practice. To master the complicated method would tend to separate an indigenous researcher from the people and the context.

Synthetic model: Synthesis involves bringing together four components: the gospel, Christian tradition, culture, and social change. These elements are discussed together using insights offered by the local people. Also there must be a recognition of sharing insights with "outsiders." Each contributes to the other, while each maintains its own distinctives. The openness and legitimacy given to all views would tend toward ambiguity and a kind of universalism.

Transcendental model: This model does not concentrate on the impersonal aspect of theology, that is, to prove something "out there," but is primarily concerned with what any truth means to the subject and to members of the subject's community. Likewise revelation is understood as the active perception or encounter with God's truth. Much criticism can be raised. How can one be an authentic believer without objective context and why is such Western sophistication necessary?

Translation model: Based on translation science, the nearest possible meanings of the original text are sought out in the receiving culture. Exact forms may not be possible, but expressions and forms that are equivalent are introduced. Attempts were made to identify the "kernel" or core of the gospel which then would apply to all cultures. The problem of subjectivity in selecting forms is a risk, as is separating the Word from what is culturally negotiable.

In contextualization, evangelicals have a valuable tool with which to work out the meanings of Scripture in the varieties of mission contexts and in conversations with the churches of the Two-Thirds World. A built-in risk of contextualization is that the human situation and the culture of peoples so dominate the inquiry that God's revelation through the Bible will be diminished. To be aware of this danger is a necessary step in avoiding it. Contextualization cannot take place unless Scripture is read and obeyed by believers. This means that believers will study the Scriptures carefully and respond to their cultural concerns in light of what is in the biblical text. Culture is subject to the God of culture. Culture is important to God and for all its good and bad factors, culture is the framework within which God works out God's purposes. Some indications of the gospel's presence in the soil may be evident, but Scripture is something that is outside and must be brought into the cultural setting to more fully understand what God is doing in culture, and to find parallels between the culture and the Bible.

The strength of contextualization is that if properly carried out, it brings ordinary Christian believers into what is often called the theological process. Contextualization is not primarily the work of professionals, though they are needed. It is making the gospel real to the untrained lay person and the rank-and-file believer. They are the people who know what biblical faith must do if it is to meet everyday problems. The term "incarnational theology" is another way of speaking about contextualization (*see* Incarnational Mission). This means that Christian truth is to be understood by Christians in the pews and on the streets. The objective of contextualization is to bring data from the whole of life to real people and to search the Scriptures for a meaningful application of the Word which "dwelt among us" (John 1:14). The missiological significance for contextualization is that all nations must understand the Word as clearly and as accurately as did Jesus' own people in his day.

Dean Gilliland

See also Gospel and Culture.

Bibliography. S. B. Bevans, *Models of Contextual Theology;* D. S. Gilliland, *The Word Among Us: Contextualizing Theology for Mission Today;* D. J. Hesselgrave and E. Rommen, *Contextualization: Meaning and Methods;* W. A. Dyrness, *Learning About Theology from the Third World;* R. J. Schreiter, *Constructing Local Theologies.*

Contingency Plans. As commercial and governmental communities protect themselves against Terrorism, the evangelical mission community has become a preferred target for terrorist threats, kidnapping, and extortion demands. Contingency planning is a process by which these potential risks are identified and prioritized as to possibility and consequence. It is a technical term asking the question, "What if?" and then answering it.

The objectives of a good contingency plan include identifying mitigation steps, incorporating applicable policy guidelines, exploring alternatives, and evaluating consequences and risks. The process begins with a risk assessment and then identification of any actions that can be taken before the crisis occurs to reduce its probability or the consequences. While God is sovereign, there is a human responsibility for practices that contribute to safety.

The purpose of an effective contingency plan is to provide "step-by-step" guidelines for managing a crisis. The plan should always be based on the worst-case scenario and be as thorough as circumstances allow. The wording and organization of the plan should be user-friendly. It should include the information that needs to be obtained, notifications that need to be made, and actions that need to be taken.

In the mission community contingency planning falls into two broad categories. The first is planning for individuals and families, which should include action plans specific to the local situation. These are normally developed in the field. The second is organizational planning that is done in conjunction with the development of corporate-wide policies. Policies are not contingency plans but broad guidelines that define the organization's specific direction and apply to all members of the organization.

Good contingency planning allows for time to assimilate information from a variety of sources; to evaluate, in a controlled environment, the benefits and risks of various response plans; and to provide a foundation and structure for crisis response.

Robert J. Horan

Bibliography. F. Fink, *Crisis Management: Planning for the Inevitable;* R. Klamser, *EMQ* 24:1 (1988): 30–37; K. N. Myers, *Total Contingency Planning for Disasters: Managing Risk . . . Minimizing Loss . . . Ensuring Business Continuity.*

Controversies in Contemporary Evangelical Mission Theory. In spite of the clarity of New Testament teaching concerning the world mission of the church, controversies have marked the modern missions movement from its inception. Of the many that could be discussed, this essay describes five significant controversies that currently have the attention of evangelical missiologists.

Some missiological controversies relate directly to biblical revelation and the history of the church, while others are procedural in nature as mission is carried out today. While in this article we present opposing perspectives, it should be recognized that they represent positions on spectrums of views rather than the only alternatives seen in evangelical missiology.

The Destiny of the Lost. *Literal View of Hell.* Those who hold to explicit faith in Jesus Christ as Savior as necessary for salvation appeal to the teaching of Scripture, such as Acts 4:12; Romans 10:13, 14; 1 John 5:11, 12; John 14:6, and the general tenor of Christological teaching throughout the Bible.

The traditional position gives credence to progressive revelation throughout both Old and New Testaments as related to the redemptive mandate. This position gives strong urgency to the church's world mission, since the destiny of humankind is dependent on their explicit faith in Christ. The argument is that people are lost because they are sinners, not because they have not heard the gospel.

Four major reasons given for this position are: (1) the universal sinfulness and lostness of all humankind, (2) the necessity of Christ's redemptive work for salvation, (3) the necessity of personal faith in Christ, and (4) the necessity of hearing the gospel in order to be saved. James A. Borland summarizes the position: "To hold out the possibility of any other way of salvation does not add to God's greatness but depreciates his Word and the work of the church through the ages. To teach any other way of salvation for the heathen diminishes missionary zeal and leaves the helpless hopeless" (p. 11).

Alternate Views of Hell. A number of theologians have objected to the teaching of the eternal damnation of the lost. At least three other positions currently vie for attention. The first of these views, prevalent in the Roman Catholic Church, understands purgatory to be "the state, place, or condition in the next world between heaven and hell" where purifying suffering takes place. "Purgatory is understood to continue in existence until the last judgment, at which time there will be only heaven and hell" (Hayes, 1992, 93).

Second, the metaphorical position holds that "the Bible does not support a literal view of a burning abyss. Hellfire and brimstone are not literal depictions of hell's furnishings, but figurative expressions warning the wicked of impending doom" (Crockett, 1992, 44). Those who hold to the metaphorical view believe in a real hell that is a place of judgment, but that we do not know precisely what that punishment will be like (Crockett, 1992, 49).

The third view of hell in opposition to the literal position is the conditional immortality, or annihilationism (*see* ANNIHILATION). Again this is not a denial of the reality of hell or suffering in it. Clark H. Pinnock states that "it is more scriptural, theologically coherent, and practical to interpret the nature of hell as the destruction rather than the endless torture of the wicked." He holds that the "ultimate result of rejecting God is self-destruction, closure with God, and absolute death in body, soul, and spirit" (Pinnock, 137).

Spiritual Warfare. SPIRITUAL WARFARE is a biblical concept derived from the fall of humankind. The battle was intensified by Christ's first coming that brought into focus the reality of demonization and demon-deliverance. Today there are two major views of spiritual warfare (*see also* POWER ENCOUNTER and TERRITORIAL SPIRITS).

The Classic View. Those who take this position rely on the teachings of the Word of God (Eph. 6:10–20), the power of God, and believing prayer. No biblical evidence can be found that believers can be "demonized" or "have" a demon, terms reserved in Scripture for the unregenerate. Victory in spiritual warfare for the believer centers on claiming Christ's past victory on the cross over Satan and demons (Col. 2:15; Heb. 2:14; 1 John 3:8; Rev. 12:11), claiming the believer's union with Christ (Rom. 6:1–4; Gal. 2:20), claiming the believers' position as believer priests (1 Peter 2:9), claiming the present work of the Holy Spirit (John 16:13; Eph. 5:18), winning back influence from Satan (Eph. 4:27), putting on the whole armor of God (Eph. 6:13–17), praying when we are under pressure (Phil. 4:7–7), presenting our whole being to God (Rom. 6:11–13), and resisting the devil for daily victory (James 4:7; 1 Peter 5:8–9).

The Demon-Deliverance View. This approach to spiritual warfare features actively and directly casting out demons by Christians who have the appropriate gifts for this ministry. It has been described as the "*ekballistic* mode of ministry" or EMM (*ekballō*, meaning to cast out; Powlison, 1995, 28). Those who hold to EMM say that "Christians and non-Christians often require an 'ekballistic encounter' to cast out inhabiting demons that enslave us in sexual lust, anger, low self-esteem, fascination with the occult, unbelief, and other ungodly patterns" (ibid., 29). Adherents of demon-deliverance ministry hold that non-Christians and Christians alike can be demonized and require the ministry of exorcism. Powlison states, "In sum, ekballistic spiritual warfare envisions the warfare of Christians as a battle against invading demons, either to repel them at the gates or eject them after they have

taken up residence" (ibid.). A counseling process is then put in place to encounter and cast out the demon(s).

Third Wave Theology. Since the mid-1970s the present-day controversy is heightened with the advent of what some have called the Third Wave of the Holy Spirit, a term used to refer to the rise of non-Pentecostal evangelicals who feel that the whole range of spiritual gifts is still available in the church. This is commonly associated with the Signs and Wonders movement, though the latter also includes Pentecostals and charismatics. Adherents hold the view that our work in ministry is a type of power encounter between Christ's and Satan's kingdoms, which center in healings and exorcisms of demons.

The Church Growth Movement. Church growth concepts find their origin in the New Testament. The last four decades have seen an explosion of interest in church growth thinking initiated by the work and writings of DONALD MCGAVRAN in the 1950s.

Definition of Church Growth. Church growth is "that discipline which seeks to understand, through biblical, sociological, historical, and behavioral study, why churches grow or decline. True church growth takes place when 'Great Commission' disciples are added and are evidenced by responsible church membership" (Rainer, 1993, 21; *see also* CHURCH GROWTH MOVEMENT). This perspective on church growth theory was developed by McGavran in his writings, principally in his best-known work, *Understanding Church Growth*.

Advocates of Church Growth Theory. Supporters of church growth theory hold the following tenets: (1) that numerical church growth is crucial, (2) that the church should concentrate on responsive peoples groups, (3) that people movement conversions should be encouraged, and (4) that anthropological factors should be recognized in determining a people's responsiveness (McQuilkin, 1974, 19–66).

Advocates point out three sources of church growth, namely, biological growth (children born to church members), transfer growth (people moving from one church to another), and conversion growth (when a person commits to Christ as Savior and Lord).

Opposition to Church Growth Theory. While expressing appreciation for the contributions of church growth thinking, some opponents warn of its shortcomings. Opponents of church growth object to the priority assigned by church growth to numerical growth, resulting in weak support of other goals in mission. Opponents also point to the alleged ecclesio-centrism of church growth, its results-orientation, and its over-emphasis on prioritizing so-called responsive groups.

Again, since church growth theory emphasizes a church-centered theology, some have expressed that the centrality of Christ is eclipsed. Christ-centered theology is foundational to the church's mission.

The flash point of opposition, however, centers on the HOMOGENEOUS UNIT PRINCIPLE advocated by many church growth theorists. McGavran first made the observation that "people like to become Christians without crossing racial, linguistic, or class barriers and that social dislocation should be held to a minimum" (McGavran, 1990, 163). In application, some call for the development of ethnic churches so as to minimize the amount of social dislocation experienced by people coming to Christ. Wagner states that "this principle has become the most controversial of all church growth principles because critics have interpreted it as classist or racist" (ibid., x). Wagner explains, however, that "the homogenous unit principle is an attempt to respect the dignity of individuals and allow their decisions for Christ to be religious rather than social decisions (ibid.).

Western Support of Third World Missions. Should sending money replace sending missionaries from the West? Will sending money rather than missionaries strengthen INDIGENOUS CHURCHES? Does the spread of the gospel depend on money? Will Western support enhance the missionary spirit of national churches? What is the testimony of history to outside support of national churches? Did Paul take financial support to the churches he planted? Discussion flows pro and con along both sides of these questions (*see also* FOREIGN FINANCING OF INDIGENOUS WORKERS).

Proponents of Traditional Missionary Presence. Those who defend the cross-cultural sending of Western missionaries rather than money hold the following positions: (1) that it is a fallacy to assume that the spread of the gospel can be accomplished only with money, that is, the Great Commission should not be held captive to fund raising; (2) that outside funds can create DEPENDENCY in national churches; (3) that a mercenary spirit among national leaders can be created by too strong an influx of Western funds; (4) that employing national workers will not necessarily lead to more effective ministry; (5) that sending money instead of missionaries compromises the Great Commission.

Proponents of Western Monetary Support. Those in favor of Western financial support of Third World missions, rather than sending missionaries, advance their reasoning with the following propositions: (1) Western missionaries are too expensive; (2) Western believers should multiply the effectiveness of their earnings at home by supporting national missionaries in their own countries; (3) Western missionaries spend too much time and money on social ministries; (4) the presence of Western missionaries has a negative effect in poverty-stricken areas; (5) educational preparation for Western missionaries is too time consuming and cost prohibitive.

Holistic Mission. "Holism" as it relates to Christian mission means that the church's mission in the world includes not only gospel proclamation but also sociopolitical, economic, and health dimensions. Those who hold this position believe that mending social ills and alleviating political injustices are integral to Christian mission (*see* HOLISTIC MISSION).

The Holistic View of Mission. A growing number of evangelicals defend holistic mission. JOHN R. W. STOTT articulated this position in his book, *Christian Mission in the Modern World.* Stott holds that John 20:21 is the basic statement of the Great Commission: "As the Father has sent me, I am sending you."

In addition to this position on the GREAT COMMISSION, Stott also champions the GREAT COMMANDMENT, namely, Christ's instruction to "love your neighbor as yourself." According to this view, these two commands constitute the Christian mission in the world. Stott explains that "if we love our neighbor as God made him, we must inevitably be concerned for his total welfare, the good of his soul, his body, and his community" (Stott, 1975, 30). Also according to this view, the Christian mission should include a political dimension in an effort to bring about structural social change.

This concept of mission "describes . . . everything the church is sent into the world to do. 'Mission' embraces the church's double vocation of service to be 'the salt of the earth' and 'the light of the world.' For Christ *sends* his people into the earth to be its salt, and *sends* his people into the world to be its light (Matt. 5:13–16)" (ibid., 30–31, emphasis his). In Stott's expression of this view, evangelism and social action are considered equal partners in mission and mutually integral to each other (*see also* EVANGELISM AND SOCIAL RESPONSIBILITY).

The Traditional View of Mission. Those who oppose the concepts of holistic mission distinguish between the CULTURAL MANDATE and the redemptive or evangelistic mandate in Scripture. The traditional view holds that the cultural mandate is addressed to people as persons (Gen. 1:28; 2:15; 9:1, 7), while the redemptive mandate is addressed to those who become members of the people of God. The cultural mandate is fulfilled by qualitative and quantitative improvement in culture; it is preservative in a fallen world; and it is nonredemptive. The redemptive mandate is fulfilled by obedience in proclaiming the gospel to a lost world; it offers hope to a fallen race; and it is redemptive and transformational.

Some question the use of John 20:21 as the basic statement of the Great Commission. They contend that this violates the hermeneutical principle of using the more complete and less obscure passages to understand the less complete and more obscure passages, in this case Matthew 28:19–28; Luke 24:47 (Hesselgrave, 1990, 3). Also, they argue that the sociopolitical action advocated by proponents of holistic mission is contrary to the examples of Christ and the early church. Opponents to the holistic mission position believe that using the so-called Great Commandment as a part of Christian *mission* is unmerited. Loving one's neighbor is the *duty* of the individual believer (Gal. 6:10) and not a part of Christian *mission* as such (ibid., 4).

In summarizing this position of the twofold mandate, Peters stated, "Only the second mandate [the redemptive mandate] is considered missions in the strict biblical sense. The first mandate [the cultural mandate] is philanthropic and humanitarian service rendered by man to man on the human level and as from members of the same 'family' (Gal. 6:10, Luke 10:25–27)" (Peters, 1972, 170).

PAUL A. BEALS

SEE ALSO The Missionary Task

Bibliography. J. A. Borland, *JETS* (March 1990): 3–11; D. Hesselgrave, *EMQ* 35:3 (1999): 278–84; idem, *Trinity World Forum,* Spring (1990), pp. 1–7; T. Ice and R. Dean, *A Holy Rebellion: Strategy for Spiritual Warfare;* D. McGavran, *Understanding Church Growth;* J. R. McQuilkin, *Measuring the Church Growth Movement;* B. Myers, *EMQ* 35:3 (1999): 284–87; C. Ott, *EMQ* (1993): 286–91; C. Pinnock, *A Wideness in God's Mercy;* R. Powlison, *Power Encounter: Reclaiming Spiritual Warfare;* T. Rainer, *The Book of Church Growth: History, Theology, and Principles;* J. Sanders, ed., *What About Those Who Have Never Heard?;* J. Stott, *Christian Mission in the Modern World;* J. Walvoord, W. Crockett, Z. Hayes, and C. Pinnock, *Four Views of Hell.*

Conversion. The relationship between conversion and mission is foundational to missiology, because the conversion of sinners is central to the fulfillment of the Great Commission. In one sense, the goal of the mission—conversion—is simple. But understanding the process of conversion is a complex missiological subject. We must analyze the concept of conversion from three perspectives: the biblical, the psychological, and the sociological.

The Biblical Dimension of Conversion. Biblically, the term "conversion" centers around a number of words. *Epistrephō* (turn) and *metanoia* (repentance) are two of the most frequently used terms to describe conversion. The Bible speaks about conversion as turning away from wickedness (2 Tim. 2:19) turning to God from idols (1 Thess. 1:9), or turning from darkness to light and from the dominion of Satan to God (Acts 26:18).

This call to conversion is an important part of gospel proclamation. We not only preach the Good News of Christ's death and resurrection, but we must also persuade persons to repent and believe in the gospel. Evangelicals have rightfully stressed the importance of faith as a key component of conversion but have generally minimized the importance of REPENTANCE.

The call to repentance, however, echoes throughout the New Testament. John the Baptist, Jesus, Peter, and Paul all include repentance in their preaching (Mark 1:4, 15; Acts 2:38; 3:19; 20:21; 26:20). Moreover, the church is commissioned to preach "repentance for forgiveness of sins . . . to all nations" (Luke 24:47; cf. Acts 17:30). Consequently, repentance is a crucial dimension of good missions practice. Perhaps one reason many ministries struggle with ongoing sin in the church is because repentance is not an important element in the original proclamation of the gospel. An initial, watered-down presentation of the Good News will ultimately lead to bad news—unhealthy churches and unholy people.

Therefore, we must call sinners to repentance. Conversion is thus both the duty of the evangelist and the demand of the sinner. This is the humanward aspect of conversion.

But there is also a deeper, more fundamental aspect of conversion. While we call men and women to repentance, only God can bring about conversion. We preach the gospel to people who are dead in their sins (Eph. 2:1–3). Because of this, God's Spirit must bring people to life. This is the Godward dimension of conversion, known as "regeneration" (Titus 3:5) or more popularly known as being "born again" (John 3:1–8). Hence, conversion is not just a duty or a demand. It is a gift—a supernatural and instantaneous work of God.

The Godward and humanward dimensions of conversion are both taught in the New Testament. But the Godward work of God's grace in the human heart through the Holy Spirit is primary. As Peter says in his report to the church in Jerusalem, "God has granted even the Gentiles repentance unto life" (Acts 11:18). Luke's description of Lydia's conversion also underscores the priority of God's gracious initiative in conversion: "The Lord opened her heart to respond to Paul's message" (Acts 16:14).

The Psychological Dimension of Conversion. The psychological dimensions of conversion must be understood if we are to communicate Christ effectively. The ENGEL SCALE describes a step-by-step process whereby a person who knows nothing about God is led to a true knowledge of God. Engel highlights the fact that conversion is a process, not simply a crisis. While it leads to an event, a climactic turning to Christ, it also usually involves a gradual change in the thinking of the person being converted.

While not a major theme, the psychological dimension of conversion is nevertheless implicit in the Gospels. The conversion of the apostles takes place gradually as they live and interact with Jesus. First they understand him as an authoritative teacher, one who casts out demons with a mere command (Mark 1:27). Next, they see him as a healer, as one who has authority over sickness (Mark 2:1–12). Then, they wrestle with the fact that he has authority over creation. "Who is this? Even the wind and the waves obey him!" (Mark 4:41). Finally, after considerable time, Peter makes his famous confession: "You are the Christ" (Mark 8:29).

People repent and believe in the gospel after hearing and understanding crucial truths about God, sin, and salvation. While the essence of the gospel is unchanging, we proclaim Christ in radically different contexts (see CONTEXTUALIZATION). Because of this, certain dimensions of the gospel are more relevant in particular contexts and the process of conversion varies with the people being converted. Muslims must know different things about God than Hindus. A secular American needs to understand different aspects of truth than an African animist. Because of this, we must study the people we are called to reach, so that we can speak to their unique needs and address their particular problems.

The Sociological Dimension of Conversion. The sociological (or cultural) components of conversion must be addressed. Western culture and evangelicals in general have viewed conversion in individual terms. But the Bible describes both individual and group conversions. The baptisms of extended households in the New Testament highlight the more community-oriented nature of Greco-Roman culture (Acts 10:44–48; 16:15, 34; 18:8). Similar to Greco-Roman culture, people in many cultures today do not make decisions as individuals; they make decisions as groups.

Therefore, as Harvie Conn wisely concludes, we "must continue to stress the necessity for a personal relationship to Christ as an essential part of conversion. But it must also be recognized that in the world's cultures such personal relationships are entered into not always by isolated 'individual' decisions in abstraction from the group but more frequently, in multi-personal, infra-group judgments. 'Personal' cannot be equated with 'individual'" (Conn, 1979, 103–4).

Missiologically this means that it is often wise to evangelize people in groups, in their natural social networks rather than as individuals. We should target families and friends in our evangelism. Whenever possible, our goal should be on reaching groups, that will lead ultimately to the establishment of new churches.

This is especially important among unreached peoples where the conversion of an isolated individual can lead to severe social ostracizing or even death in some cases. Understanding this sociological (or cultural) dimension of conversion

will make us more sensitive to culture and more fruitful in ministry.

RICHARD D. LOVE

See also Sociological Barriers.

Bibliography. H. M. Conn, *The Gospel and Islam*, pp. 97–111; J. Engel and H. W. Norton, *What's Gone Wrong with the Harvest?*; P. Hiebert, *The Gospel in Context*; C. B. Johnson and H. Newton Malony, *Christian Conversion: Biblical and Psychological Perspectives*; D. McGavran, *Bridges of God*.

Conviction of Sin. *See* ELENCTICS.

Cook Islands (*Est. 2000 pop.: 20,000; 236 sq. km. [91 sq. mi.]*). The Cook Islands consist of fifteen Pacific islands located between Samoa in the west and French Polynesia in the east. They are divided into the northern atolls and the southern group. A self-governing state since 1965, its population hold citizenship rights in New Zealand nearly 1,900 miles to the southwest. Some 70 percent belong to the Cook Island Christian Church (formerly the LMS), and 15 percent are Roman Catholics.

ALLAN K. DAVIDSON

See also Polynesia.

Bibliography. Richard Gilson, *The Cook Islands 1820–1950*.

Coppin, Fanny Jackson (1837–1913). American educator, missionary leader, and missionary in Africa. Born a slave in Washington, D.C., and purchased by an aunt who freed her, Coppin was sent to New Bedford, Massachusetts. At the age of fourteen, she found employment as a domestic worker in Newport, Rhode Island. In 1865 she graduated from Oberlin College, at that time the only college to accept African American women. From 1865 until 1902 she worked at the Institute for Colored Youth in Philadelphia, initially as a teacher and later as principal. During this time she developed a reputation as a respected teacher and lecturer.

Coppin was also active in missionary promotion. As president of the Women's Home and Foreign Missionary Society of the AME Church (1883–92), she traveled to England to represent the society and address the assembly at the CENTENARY CONFERENCE ON THE PROTESTANT MISSIONS OF THE WORLD (LONDON MISSIONARY CONFERENCE, 1888).

It was not until 1902, after thirty-seven years in education, that Coppin received her opportunity for overseas missionary service when her husband, Levi J. Coppin, was assigned to South Africa as a bishop of the AME Church. Together he and Fanny served the region of southern Africa until 1904, traveling as far as Bulawayo in their responsibilities. Throughout their stay, Fannie promoted the education and development of women in Africa as she had done in the United States.

After their return to Philadelphia in 1904, she devoted her remaining years to writing and promoting missionary work by African Americans in Africa.

A. SCOTT MOREAU

Bibliography. F. J. Coppin, *Reminiscences of School Life, and Hints on Teaching;* S. M. Jacobs, *Women in New Worlds,* 2:268–80.

Coppock, Grace Lydia (1882–1921). American YWCA missionary in China. From the small farming community of Superior, Nebraska, Coppock felt called by God to foreign missions during her last year at University of Nebraska. In October of 1906 she sailed for Shanghai to work with the YWCA. From the very beginning, Coppock sought to train nationals to lead the YWCA; she refused to begin work until a Chinese associate was found for her. Coppock was appointed General Secretary in 1913. By 1914, the Chinese YWCA Board of Directors consisted entirely of Chinese women who accepted full responsibility for the organization, including finances. This was a time of political turmoil in China with famines and a revolution that ended Imperial rule in China. Along with political revolution came social revolution, particularly for women. National Association women were already speaking out against the practices of footbinding and the use of opium; Coppock also opposed these practices. Coppock was committed to a social gospel; just prior to her death in October of 1921, she deviated from usual YWCA work with university students to institute industrial programs in response to the emerging needs of women in industry. Two years after Coppock's death, the first Chinese General Secretary of YWCA was appointed to replace her.

GRACE L. KLEIN

Bibliography. M. C. Ponto, *The Search for Grace in China.*

Corruption. In 1996 a new ranking of all the countries of the world was produced by the United Nations Organization based on how corrupt their economies were. New Zealand achieved the honor of being the most transparent economy in the world. In most countries corruption was considered to be a major problem, hindering economic progress and slowing the move toward the globalization of trade. Most mission activity takes place in the context of corrupt economic and political systems, which poses an ethical challenge to the presentation of the gospel and the expression of kingdom lifestyles.

There are three key reasons why corruption must be challenged and reduced. First, corruption serves the interests of the rich and powerful and disadvantages the poor for whom the Bible declares God has a special concern. Second, it breeds inefficiency. Where services are only rendered after the payment of bribes or business can only be transacted with "under the table" payments, time is wasted, bureaucracies proliferate, and costs escalate. Third, money gained by corrupt means is not taxed, is often spent on ostentatious luxury items, may finance criminal activities, or may be diverted into foreign bank accounts. The proceeds of corruption seldom serve national interests or the social good and often work directly against them.

The Bible contains ten Hebrew words and nine Greek words and their derivatives in eighty references to describe corruption. Some refer specifically to decay of the body, usually after death, others to breaking God's Law (Neh. 1:7) and lack of social morality. In Genesis 6:11, 12, God sends the flood because, from his viewpoint, all were corrupt or corrupted. In the Sermon on the Mount Jesus asserts that on earth "a corrupt tree (person) cannot produce good fruit" and "moth and rust corrupt earthly treasures" (Matt. 6:19, 43). God looks for an uncorrupted heart (1 Peter 3:4) and promises a time and kingdom, inaugurated by the resurrection, when there will be no more corruption of any kind (Matt. 6:20; 1 Cor. 15:53, 54).

Democracies are based on the utilitarian principle of "the greatest good for the greatest number." Corruption and BRIBERY, motivated by greed and self-interest, are a clear violation of this principle. The dilemma faced in many underdeveloped countries is that official wages are low, so government and private employees seek to supplement their incomes. Honest means, even if difficult, do exist, however, and corruption is not the only option. The compounding issue is that the individual has little power to change systemic corruption.

Missions face corruption in several ways. Some take an absolute stand and refuse to pay bribes of any kind. The cost can be long delays and extra expense waiting for services. Others engage local agents to handle business where bribes are demanded and serve to pay the often unitemized or vaguely worded bill. In some cases mission personnel may accept or benefit from corruption.

The case for an absolutist stance is based on the need for the means of mission to be consistent with the ends of mission. Maintenance of personal integrity and avoidance of compromise create opportunities for the God of justice to show his grace and power.

ROB BELLINGHAM

SEE ALSO Ethics.

Bibliography. B. T. Adeney, *Strange Virtues: Ethics in a Multicultural World.*

Cosmology. A term reserved primarily for the scientific study of the universe considered as a whole. Metaphysics is concerned with studies into the basic kinds of things and properties that make up the entire cosmos. Traditionally, metaphysics is subdivided into two branches: ontology and cosmology. Ontology deals with questions about the ultimate nature of things: whether a thing is one or many, or of what kind. Cosmology considers how the world is organized, and is also related to the specific view of images concerning the universe held in a religion or cultural tradition. It is in this latter usage that cosmology is related to religious BELIEF SYSTEMS. Christian anthropologists are concerned with cosmological issues both in the area of WORLDVIEW and religious belief systems. From this perspective worldview is understood as the term for a more general, less precisely delineated, set of ideas concerning life and the world. Cosmology refers to more conscious images, doctrines, and views concerning the universe. In religious belief systems, the most common source of cosmology is in the MYTHS of creation and the origin of the universe. SYMBOLISM and myths depict cosmology in the world of people, and nearly always imply an ethical concern. The behavior required of people in religious cosmologies is often described or implied in the account of the world's structure.

An understanding of the cosmology implicit in a particular worldview can be of great benefit to the missionary attempting to communicate the gospel to those within that worldview.

NORMAN E. ALLISON

See also Religious Ultimacy.

Bibliography. M. Eliade, *Myth and Reality*.

Costa Rica (*Est. 2000 pop.: 3,798,000; 51,100 sq. km. [19,730 sq. mi.]*). A Central American republic, Costa Rica, which is Iberian in heritage, has enjoyed a long history of democratic government. Evangelicalism began slowly in this traditionally Catholic nation, but in recent years has flourished at an astonishing rate.

Protestant groups established themselves in Costa Rica first by migration in the nineteenth century and only later by denominational and FAITH MISSIONS. Many of the first groups had little interest in PROSELYTISM, focusing instead on the maintenance of their own religious communities. Protestant missionaries intent on evangelism did not arrive in Costa Rica until 1891. In 1894 a Baptist church was established in Puerto Limón, and Methodists and Anglicans had organized churches in Costa Rica by 1894 and 1896 respectively. The early Protestant missionaries in Costa Rica, as in most of Latin America, basically targeted the lower middle class in urban settings.

Many of the churches established by evangelicals were of an independent and foreign nature. Fired with a desire to evangelize, missionaries involved with these endeavors invested heavily in support of pastors and auxiliary programs, but few traces of their efforts remain. Though fifty mission boards established some sense of presence in Costa Rica, by 1960, the number of communicant members numbered only a few thousand.

As in many other Latin American countries, the emergence of Pentecostalism dramatically changed the religious landscape. From extremely humble beginnings prior to World War II, its rapid growth—exceeding any correlation to the resources of the sending agencies—clearly indicated that the new groups were essentially of a grassroots nature. Pentecostalism is characterized not only by specific beliefs and practices (glossolalia and faith healing), but by essentially popular, self-sustaining churches. These churches have nationally directed administrative systems with legal constitutions, elected executive officers, and salaried members who oversee the operation and expansion of specialized educational and mission programs for women, youth, and children. These national organizations are supporting a myriad of personnel in a variety of missionary projects both within and beyond Latin America. Further, these groups, in large measure having emerged from the marginalized sectors of society (though recently they have encompassed all economic segments of the country), have from the beginning implemented an impressive social policy. With their emphasis on freedom of expression in worship and affirmation of the individual's worth within the community, Pentecostals have easily adapted to Costa Rica's variety of cultures and social classes.

La Federación Alianza Evangélica (the Evangelical Fellowship of Churches) lists 100 different organized church bodies among its membership. Research estimates 2,640 evangelical congregations, a community of 396,000 people constituting 12 percent of the population. If the evangelical presence in Costa Rica is in some sense assured, it is also precarious. Unable to gather a large following several decades ago, evangelicals must now demonstrate continuing leadership in resolving severe human problems. Only appropriate and effective application of their energies and resources can sustain the dynamic structure forged when they moved into the leadership vacuum.

DOUG PETERSEN

Bibliography. P. Johnstone, *OW*; D. Petersen, *Not by Might Nor by Fire: A Pentecostal Theology of Social Concern*.

Costas, Orlando E. (1942–87). Puerto Rican churchman, missiologist, and missionary to

Costa Rica. Converted at the 1969 Billy Graham Crusade in New York City, Costas obtained his doctorate in missiology under JOHANNES VERKUYL at the Free University of Amsterdam.

Ordained by the American Baptist Convention, Costas pastored congregations in Puerto Rico and Milwaukee prior to missionary service, first with the Latin America Mission, and later with the United Church Board for World Ministries. Assigned to Costa Rica, he served with the Institute of In-Depth Evangelization and the Latin American Biblical Seminary. He founded and directed the Latin American Evangelical Center for Pastoral Studies, and promoted the Latin American Theological Fraternity. He returned to the United States in 1979 to Eastern Baptist Theological Seminary. In 1984, he moved to Andover Newton Theological Seminary, occupying the Adoniram Judson Chair of Missiology.

Active in denominational life and ecumenical circles, Costas made significant contributions to missiological literature. He wrote over a hundred books and articles and contributed to more than thirty volumes edited by others. A radical evangelical, Costas advocated a holistic gospel of the kingdom, yet emphasized the unique role of the church. Although he moved beyond the separatist fundamentalism of his youth, Costas retained his evangelical identity as he interacted extensively with conciliar and liberation theologies.

KEN MULHOLLAND

Bibliography. O. E. Costas, *The Church and Its Mission: A Shattering Critique from the Third World;* idem, *The Integrity of Mission;* idem, *Christ Outside the Gate: Mission beyond Christendom;* idem, *Liberating News: A Theology of Contextual Evangelization.*

Côte d'Ivoire (Ivory Coast) *(Est. 2000 pop.: 16,761,000; 322,463 sq. km. [124,503 sq. mi.]).* Situated on the southern shore of the great African bulge, the Republic of Côte d'Ivoire, West Africa (popularly known as Ivory Coast in the United States) boasts a population of more than 16 million inhabitants.

The rain forests that once blanketed the country exist today only in the southern third of the republic. Much of the country, particularly in the north, is made up of savanna grasslands. More than sixty ethnic groups populate Côte d'Ivoire, with the Baoulé tribe being the largest people group and Dioula the most widely spoken language. French is the official language.

Followers of indigenous religions make up 25 percent of the population. Those calling themselves Christian now number more than 12 percent, while the Muslim population is now placed at approximately 60 percent of the country's inhabitants.

The country's president maintains an open philosophy in regard to religion. Freedom of choice in terms of religious preference is guaranteed by the Constitution. The first missionary visits were made by French Catholics in 1637, though they did not stay very long due to difficult circumstances. It was not until 1843 that missionaries returned to Côte d'Ivoire. Not until the turn of the twentieth century was the gospel proclaimed there with any consistency.

WILLIAM HARRIS of Liberia, known as the "black prophet," felt called of God to preach along the west coast of Africa, moving from the Gold Coast (presently Ghana) to Côte d'Ivoire in the early twentieth century. People burned their fetishes and were baptized in the name of the Trinity as Prophet Harris, as he was known, exhorted his followers to believe the message of those who would be coming with "the black Book." The Harris (or Harrist) Church Movement resulted from his ministry and many of his followers were found worshiping in Methodist churches on the coast and later in Christian and Missionary Alliance churches in the interior (Baouké).

Many evangelical groups that entered the country in the 1920s and 1930s profited from the preaching of Prophet Harris. The Assemblies of God, Mission Biblique, and World Evangelism Crusade entered the country during these decades followed by a host of other missions, many of them after 1960.

Most evangelical agencies have witnessed a positive response to the gospel though much of this response was found among animistic and non-Muslim peoples. Two major trends have dominated the past decade: the evangelization of the major cities of Abidjan, Yamossoukro, and Bouaké, where churches and mission agencies are seeking converts among Muslims using medical, educational, traditional, and nontraditional ministries; and efforts to reach UNREACHED PEOPLES in Côte d'Ivoire and beyond. The use of friendship evangelism, videotapes, drama, bookstores/literature, cell groups, THEOLOGICAL EDUCATION BY EXTENSION, MASS EVANGELISM, broadcast media, SIGNS AND WONDERS, and the JESUS FILM are some of the means and methods being used to proclaim Christ.

DAVID P. HARVEY

Bibliography. N. O. King, *Christian and Muslim in West Africa;* G. M. Haliburton, *The Prophet Harris;* W. J. Platt, *An African Prophet: The Ivory Coast and What Came of It.*

Council for World Mission (CWM; formerly The London Missionary Society). *The Origin.* The modern missionary movement in Britain had its foundations in "the evangelical revival" of the late eighteenth century. A group of Christians met in Baker's Coffee House in central London, and with prayer and planning decided to form a missionary society to "spread the knowledge of Christ among heathen and other unenlightened nations." Thus, in 1795 one of the pioneering societies, the Missionary Society was born. In 1818 it was renamed London Missionary Society (LMS) as numerous missionary societies had come into existence. While the BMS (1792) and many other societies were formed strictly on a denominational basis, the LMS was founded on a nondenominational principle. It was created, led, and supported by the Episcopalians, Methodists, Presbyterians, and Independents (Congregationalists).

Mission Expansion. The LMS expanded its mission in the South Pacific, southern Africa, Asia, and the Caribbean. The mission attempts of the first twenty-five years include many places such as France, the United States, Canada, Russia, Malta and Greek Islands, Mongolia, China, North and South India, Ceylon, Jamaica, Guyana, Tobago, Trinidad, Java, Amboya, Malacca, Singapore, Madagascar, Malawi, Zimbabwe, Zambia, Cook and Gilbert Islands. The first batch of thirty missionaries was sent to Tahiti in 1796. The first missionaries to India arrived in Tranquabar soon after the new Charter of 1813 permitted missionaries to enter the British territories. WILLIAM MORRIS was the founding missionary of the LMS mission in China. The well known church historian K. S. LATOURETTE also worked for LMS in China. Famous names like DAVID LIVINGSTONE and ROBERT MOFFATT are linked with the LMS mission in southern Africa. The LMS enjoyed a high profile in Britain and overseas for a long time. However, after a hundred years of activity, the work slowed down and decreased due to many factors such as lack of personnel, lack of funds, and the changing political context in the world.

Principles and Characteristics. The LMS, from its origin, had two principles at heart, the *Nondenominational* and the *Fundamental Principles*. Over the years various denominations created their own missionary societies and the LMS was left to be supported by the Independent (Congregational) churches. However, the LMS constitutionally remained a nondenominational society. The "fundamental principle" stated that "its [LMS] design is not to send Presbyterianism, Independency, Episcopacy, or any form of Church Order and Government . . . but the glorious Gospel of the blessed God, to the Heathen; and that it shall be left . . . to the minds of the persons whom God may call . . . to assume for themselves such form of Church Government as to them shall appear most agreeable to the Word of God." The LMS had recognized the importance of ecumenism and CONTEXTUALIZATION from its early days.

Other characteristics of the society were that it tended to pioneer the mission work in new territories. It developed indigenous leadership to be sent as missionary preachers and teachers to new territories within the same continent. For example, Tahitians and Samoans were used to spread the gospel in Tuvalu, Papua New Guinea, and other islands. It adopted at an early stage the principle of the THREE-SELF FORMULA: self-supporting, self-governing, and self-extending (self-propagating). As early as 1915, local churches in Samoa were paying the salary of all white missionaries working in Samoa as well as contributing to the central funds of the LMS. The LMS encouraged women and lay persons to be missionaries. The LMS reviewed its mission at five-year intervals, which later helped it to adapt to new changes. Christian missions generally worked closely with colonial, imperial, and commercial authorities. However, there is some evidence to show that the LMS missionaries in many cases stood against them.

Mission in Partnership. Under the influence of the ECUMENICAL MOVEMENT in the twentieth century, the LMS went through major changes in 1966 and again in 1977. The society became a council of churches that were engaged in mission as mission was perceived to be the responsibility of the whole church and not of mission enthusiasts alone. In 1966, it merged with the Common Wealth Missionary Society, and became the Congregational Council for the World Mission (CCWM). The formation of the United Reform Church in the United Kingdom (1972) brought the overseas work of the Presbyterians into the fold of the LMS/CCWM. The radical shift came in 1977, when the old LMS/CCWM was transformed and the new 'Council for World Mission' (CWM) was inaugurated. The old divisions of younger and older, donor and recipient, North and South, constituent and partner churches disappeared. The CWM consists of thirty-two churches across Asia, southern Africa, the Caribbean, Europe, and the Pacific. All member churches are represented on the Council as equal partners and participate in decision making at all levels. All assets of the CWM are owned by all. All partners together share responsibilities of the mission work of the Council. The CWM believes in mutual sharing, support, and challenge to enable all to participate in God's mission.

ANDREW PRASAD

Bibliography. N. Goodall, *A History of the London Missionary Society, 1895–1945;* R. Lovett, *The History of the London Missionary Society, 1795–1895;* B. Thorogood (ed.), *Gales of Changes, Responding to a Shifting Missionary Context. The Story of the London Missionary Society 1945–1977.*

Counseling, Cross-Cultural. *See* CROSS-CULTURAL COUNSELING.

Counseling of Missionaries. Deliberate and intentional investment of resources by mission agencies, churches, and other mission organizations for the nurture and development of missionary personnel comprises the essence of the facet of missions known as MEMBER CARE. One vital aspect of member care is counseling of missionaries and their families during the prefield, on-field, and postfield stages of missionary life. Counseling may provide the missionary an avenue of growth in areas important for effective CROSS-CULTURAL MINISTRY: working well with others; giving and receiving forgiveness; trusting God in the face of disappointment and the ongoing presence of human pain; seeking accountability and personal growth; and availing oneself of supportive resources as needed. These crucial areas of competence are developed and played-out within the entire family unit. Awareness of how one family member affects all other family members is critical in understanding and helping any family; however, it may be more so in the missionary family. Unlike many types of life-work, missions inevitably involve all of the family, even if just one or both of the parents are the identified missionaries (see also FAMILY LIFE OF THE MISSIONARY).

Most counseling with missionaries and their families is apt to be primarily short-term, and focused on prevention or resolution of problems. As such, counseling within missions takes on many forms, including seminary and retreat speakers, itinerant mission pastors and counselors, crisis teams, counselors-in-residence at MK schools, and help offered at on-field counseling centers.

Many of the challenges and struggles throughout the life stages of missionaries and their families are not unique. However, there are aspects of counseling that are unique to missionaries during the prefield, on-field, and postfield stages of their lives.

Prefield. Mission boards' common use of counselors and psychological assessment tools to provide feedback regarding a candidate's strengths and potential problem areas (see CANDIDATE SELECTION) can determine the prognosis for success in a cross-cultural situation and provide a basis for matching personnel to field placements and job assignments. Placing individuals in an environment in which they are apt to function well, or avoiding placement in situations that are likely to induce overwhelming distress both within the missionary and between the missionary and others is good stewardship.

A good rule-of-thumb to follow in deciding missionary placement is "the best predictor of future behavior is past behavior." Issues that are troubling for missionaries in their home culture will not only continue to be troubling in their new culture, but are likely to be exacerbated due to the added stresses of transition and cross-cultural living. The more the struggles can be re-

solved before going to the field, the less the potential harm to the missionaries and families themselves, their mission board, their supporters and home church, and their co-workers—both expatriates and nationals.

On-Field. Generally, counseling on the mission field will look much like counseling anywhere, especially in terms of the kinds of struggles that people have. In particular, missionaries are not immune to guilt, depression, grief, anger, moral failure, and crises. Two special challenges on the field are separation and trauma.

The pain, grief, and anxiety that accompany separation from important people, places, and things are not uncommon to human experience. Understandably, missionaries and their children are particularly vulnerable to separation and its accompanying anxiety and fear. Although all the incidences of mobility and transition of missionary life (home assignments, new assignments, etc.) involve separation, one of the most significant experiences occurs when the children of missionaries go to boarding schools. The manner in which separation is handled by families, boarding school personnel, and mission administrators will make a pivotal impact on the child and the family's ability to minister effectively. Counselors at MK schools can be of invaluable assistance to families who are negotiating significant transitions several times a year as children leave home and return to school (see also MISSION SCHOOLS).

Pain, grief, and anxiety also accompany trauma, which is almost a given for missionary life. The impact of trauma can go very deep, be very far-reaching, and last for a long time. When this impact is misunderstood and mismanaged, the person may be further harmed by ignoring the significance of the trauma or by attempting to deal with the pain and sadness in a destructive manner. Increasingly mission boards are establishing, enabling, and training crisis teams that can reach the victims within the crucial twenty-four to seventy-two-hour window after the traumatic event. Effective debriefing involves discussions of the traumatic events covering the facts of the crisis, the thoughts and emotional reactions to it, and the symptoms experienced during and after the event.

Postfield. Two interrelated aspects of postfield life that are likely to be difficult for missionaries and their families are reacculturation and retirement. When missionaries return to their sending countries, they are likely to grieve over the loss of the meaningfulness they had experienced in their work as missionaries and to experience stress as they adjust to a culture that was anticipated to be familiar. Often missionary families experience a decline in family cohesiveness and greater emotional dependence of the husband on the wife. Tension is apt to be present between children and parents due to adjustments to new roles and expectations. A growing number of missionary retreat centers are offering counseling, often in an educational format, for those going through this transition (*see also* REVERSE CULTURE SHOCK).

Sometimes counseling may be required as a condition for a missionary's return to the field, or may aid the missionary in moving on to meaningful work and ministry in the sending country. Counselors affiliated with the mission may provide better help to the troubled member; however, in the case where the difficulty arose between the member and the mission, a non-mission-affiliated counselor is apt to be preferred by the missionary.

Counseling, as a pillar of member care, has become an increasingly important aspect of obeying Christ's command to tell the nations the news of the kingdom. As an important resource for the lives of missionaries and their families, counseling will hopefully become more accessible to those serving in remote and hostile areas.

NANCY A. CRAWFORD

See also Psychology.

Bibliography. M. D. Bullock, *JPT* 21:1 (1993): 37–44; K. F. Carr, *Proceeding from the 17th Annual Mental Health and Missions Conference, 1996;* K. S. O'Donnell, *JPT* 25:1 (1997): 143–54; J. Powell, *Missionary Care*, pp. 123–35; C. H. Rosik, *JPT* 21:1 (1993): 159–64; E. M. Stringham, *JPT* 21:1 (1993): 66–73.

The Counter-Reformation. More than an anti-Protestant movement, the Counter-Reformation was a readjustment by the Catholic Church to meet the changing conditions of the early modern period, partially in reaction against the Protestant Reformation. It also reflected a cry for change, which began a century and a half earlier.

The primary vehicles were the Council of Trent, which ran sporadically from 1545 to 1563, and the monastic orders led by the Jesuits. Trent cut off all possibility of reconciliation with Protestants, stating Catholic dogma in a manner that defined Protestant doctrines as heretical. Authority in the Church was defined as tradition plus the Scriptures (including the Apocrypha), but it was clear that no one could interpret the Bible contrary to the Church.

Justification by faith alone was rejected, and the PRIESTHOOD OF THE BELIEVER was denied. The seven medieval sacraments were asserted to be necessary for salvation, and through them grace was conferred by the act performed (*ex opere operato*). There was a degree of moral and administrative reform, the authority of the pope was strengthened, corruption decreased greatly, and better training of the clergy and more preaching were required. The Inquisition was strengthened, especially in Spain, and was used against anyone suspected of having Protestant ideas as well as against Jews.

The Jesuit order led by IGNATIUS LOYOLA became the primary vehicle of mission, along with Franciscans and Dominicans. After a period of intense spiritual conflict, Loyola formed the nucleus of the Society of Jesus at the University of Paris in 1534, and the order was officially recognized by Rome in 1540. They took vows to obey the pope "for the good of souls and the propagation of the faith in whatever countries he might send them." By 1556 they had one thousand members.

The greatest of their early missionaries, FRANCIS XAVIER, planted the Catholic Church in India, the East Indies, and Japan, and died seeking entrance to China. Catholic missionaries accompanied the explorers to Latin America, where the indigenous peoples were baptized *en masse,* often thousands in one day, even as they were terribly exploited and cruelly treated. By 1559 nine million had been baptized in Mexico alone. Some of the missionaries raised strong protest against such treatment. Among them were Antonio Montesinos and Bartholomew de Las Casas, who argued that Indians should have the same rights as any other Spanish citizens.

ROBERT DE NOBILI went to India in 1605, mastered Sanskrit, adopted Indian dress and customs, and won a number of Brahmins; and MATTEO RICCI went to Peking in 1600, adopted Chinese customs, and won a number of converts in the court and beyond.

While some priests and friars, especially in Latin America, were unworthy, others showed great dedication and courage, a number suffering martyrdom. The major defects of early Roman Catholic missions lay in the long delay before ordaining indigenous priests and the high degree of SYNCRETISM with pagan customs. Such syncretism and the shortage of priests still plague the church in Latin America.

PAUL E. PIERSON

See also Roman Catholic Missions.

Bibliography. S. Neill, *HCM;* P. W. Searle, *The Counter Reformation.*

Cragg, Albert Kenneth (1913–). English pastor, bishop, and scholar of the Middle East and Islam. Ordained to the Church of England priesthood in 1936, Kenneth Cragg served as Canon of St. George's Cathedral, Jerusalem; Honorary Canon of Canterbury Cathedral; and assistant bishop of the Anglican see of Jerusalem, residing in Cairo. When Egypt gained diocesan status in the Anglican communion, he relinquished this position in favor of an Egyptian bishop and returned to Yorkshire, where he ministered to immigrant Muslims. He taught at the American University of Beirut in Lebanon during World War II; Hartford Seminary Foundation in Hartford, Connecticut; as faculty and subsequently Warden of St. Augustine's College, Canterbury, where he developed two major missionary study programs; Ibadan University, Nigeria; Sussex University; and Oxford University. Since his retirement in 1981, he has lived in Oxfordshire, where he lectures and writes. Author of more than thirty books and many articles, Cragg was editor of *Muslim World*. Cragg has sought to interpret Islam through insiders' eyes, to bridge the gap in understanding between Muslims and Christians, and to discern positive significance in Islam for Christian purposes.

PAUL R. DEKAR

Bibliography. P. R. Dekar, *Muslim World* 83 (1993): 177–91; G. W. Braswell, Jr., *Perspectives in Religious Studies* 8 (1981): 117–27; R. J. Jones, *IBMR* 16, no. 3 (1992): 105–10.

Crawford, Daniel (1870–1926). Scottish missionary to Zaire and Zambia. Born in Gourock, Renfrewshire, he was converted at seventeen in a Plymouth Brethren assembly. Though his early education had been restricted he was selected for the party that accompanied fellow countryman F. S. ARNOT to Central Africa in 1889. Serving originally in Katanga (modern Zaire), he traveled extensively. He settled in 1895 at Luanza (now in Zambia), and this was to be his base for the rest of his life. His only furlough (1911–15) included visits to North America and Australia. Like his mentor Arnot and his other exemplar DAVID LIVINGSTONE, Crawford was both pioneer and strong individualist, but he never lost sight of missionary priorities: setting up a string of churches, preaching the need for conversion, and teaching and translating the Bible. The New Testament in Luba was published in 1904; the Old, in 1926.

In a book that came to be recognized as a Christian classic, *Thinking Black* (1913), Crawford showed a remarkable understanding of the mind and culture of Africans. They came to regard him with deep affection, and he encouraged many of them as co-workers in ministry. Crawford's published work included *Back to the Long Grass* (1923).

J. D. DOUGLAS

Bibliography. J. J. Ellis, *Dan Crawford of Luanza*; A. R. Evans, *Dan Crawford*; G. E. Tilsley, *Dan Crawford: Missionary and Pioneer in Central Africa*.

Crawford, Isabel Alice Hartley (1865–1961). Canadian-born missionary to indigenous Americans. Born in Cheltenham (near Toronto) to the family of a Baptist minister and teacher, Crawford graduated from the Baptist Missionary training school in Chicago in 1893, having served as a missionary in the slum districts of Chicago as a student.

Though she was interested in overseas work, Crawford was sent in 1883 as part of a team by the Woman's American Baptist Home Mission Society (WABHMS) to Elk Creek, Oklahoma, to serve the Kiowas. Transferred to Saddle Mountain after two years in Elk Creek, she caused a stir by assisting an unordained interpreter in serving communion. The controversy resulted in her resignation from Saddle Mountain in 1906. She began to lecture and teach, promoting Indian rights and Baptist missions as a WABHMS representative until 1918, when she moved to the Allegheny Indian Reservation in New York State. Again she was involved in a dispute, this time championing the Indian desire to stop the transfer of Red House Church from the Baptists to the Presbyterians.

She returned to the lecture circuit until her retirement in 1930. Even in retirement she remained active, still speaking and advocating. After her death at the age of ninety-six, she was buried in the Saddle Mountain reservation, the epitaph on her tombstone reading, "I dwell among mine own people."

A. SCOTT MOREAU

Bibliography. C. Blevins, *DBA*; S. Mondello, *Foundations: A Baptist Journal of History and Theology* 21 (October 1978): 322–39; idem, *Foundations: A Baptist Journal of History and Theology* 22 (January 1979): 28–42; idem, *Foundations: A Baptist Journal of History and Theology* 22 (April 1979): 99–115.

Creation. The fact that biblical revelation begins with the creation account demonstrates the foundational importance of the creation doctrine to all other biblical doctrines, including redemption. The divine design and majestic glory of the created order witness to the character, sovereignty, and lordship of the Creator (Ps. 19:1–6), which are critical issues in the outworking and understanding of his mission purpose *(MISSIO DEI)*. Humankind, as male and female, uniquely created in the image of the Creator, is seen to be the apex of creation and focus of this purpose. To humankind is given the right to rule over and subdue the earth and its creatures and to tend and take care of their natural environment, responsibilities for which they are still accountable (Gen. 1:26–30; 2:15; Ps. 8:3–8).

The FALL OF HUMANKIND through the temptation of another created being (Satan) radically impacted all of creation and defined the mission of God for human history. Redemption of elect humanity and the restoration of the Creator's glory in them constitute the ultimate divine purposes, as decreed before the creation itself (Eph. 1:4–14; Rev. 13:8). An age-long conflict with Satan, the rebellious archenemy of his sovereign Creator, is the context for *missio Dei*. In his passionate efforts to steal glory from the Creator, including God's exclusive right to be worshiped, and to usurp God's place of authority over the created order, the enemy seeks to seduce humankind to worship other beings and objects in the created order. Such idolatry and the moral and spiritual perversions which accompany it, are the ultimate manifestation of humanity's depravity and need for the redemption and regeneration offered in the gospel (Rom. 1:18–32; 3:9–31).

The redemptive purposes of God include not only humankind but also the created order. Cursed as a result of the fall (Gen. 3:17–18), yet still an object of his care and concern (Jon. 4:11), creation is described as groaning and eagerly expecting the final redemption of humankind. The curse will be removed "at the renewal of all things" and creation itself will fulfill its divine purpose (Rom. 8:18–25; Matt. 19:28). Ultimately, the present created order will be cleansed, providing the perfect eternal abode for the redeemed to live in the presence of their Creator and redeemer forever (Isa. 65:17; 66:22; 2 Peter 3:10–13; Rev. 21:1).

An understanding of the biblical doctrines of creation, man and woman, and *missio Dei* is essential to the communication and reception of the gospel of redemption. However, the historical development of distinctive human cultures and worldviews has demonstrated the rejection of revealed truth about God, including the revelation in creation itself (Rom. 1:18–25). The result is evident in a plethora of grossly inaccurate cosmogonies, from fanciful myths about capricious deities to atheistic dialectical materialism.

In some cultural contexts, a good starting point of contact for the gospel is the doctrine of creation. Paul's address to the pagan philosophers in Athens (Acts 17:24–31) is a classic biblical case. Contemporary missionaries working among animistic tribal groups have demonstrated the effectiveness of starting with the creation account in building a foundation for the gospel. The monistic pantheism of the Hindu-Buddhistic worldview and the pantheistic naturalism and world consciousness of the Chinese worldview, especially Taoism, demand a careful explanation and understanding of the nature and purpose of creation and humanity's role and relationship to it and to a personal Creator and Redeemer.

In the latter half of the twentieth century certain exponents of liberation theology sought to integrate creation and mission around an ecological and political agenda leading to a radical redefinition of the church's mission. Rooted in the premise that creation presupposes salvation, the church's task is to seek the liberation of the earth from the oppressive policies of Western industrialization and the liberation of the poor from political oppression and economic deprivation. Creation and salvation have been merged into a struggle for political justice, economic equality, and ecological responsibility.

A comprehensive, biblically informed mission theology will include a clearly defined doctrine of creation, including a doctrine of stewardship of the earth and its resources. But mission is not ultimately informed by or subservient to the creation doctrine. Mission flows from a biblical understanding of the Creator's purposes for his creation and proclaims his sovereign lordship over his creation. The biblical mandate is to preach the good news to all creation (Mark 16:15), resulting in a body of regenerated human beings who are newborn creations in Jesus Christ (Heb. 12:23; 2 Cor. 5:17) and who live in the expectation of a new creation to the glory of the Creator (Rev. 21:1–4).

RICHARD D. CALENBERG

Bibliography. W. A. Dyrness, *Let the Earth Rejoice!: A Biblical Theology of Holistic Mission;* J. J. Kritzinger, *Missionalia* 19:1 (April 1991): 4–19; Choan-Seng Song, *Christian Mission in Reconstruction: An Asian Analysis;* P. M. Steyne, *In Step With the God of the Nations: A Biblical Theology of Missions;* D. C. van Zyl, *Missionalia* 19:3 (November 1991): 203–14.

Creative Access Countries. Sovereign governments, regimes, or territories that deny, or severely limit, long-term presence for foreigners engaging in Christian missionary or evangelistic activities. Such countries have one or more large population segments that are historically resistant to Christianity. Laws restraining Christian activities reflect the controlling influence of religio-social groups antagonistic to Christianity. Especially suspect are Christian endeavors done with or by foreign mission agencies. The sociological causes for such restrictive measures are numerous. Yet perceived threats to historic religious practices, distinct ethnic identities, or nationalistic reactions to Western colonial encroachments help explain some of the prohibitions.

At the dawn of the modern missions era, there were few restrictions on missionary activities. Those that existed were usually because of European rivalries rather than indigenous religious conflicts. Missionaries were often the first Westerners in what are now Third World countries or they entered later under the auspices of colonial governments. Since the end of World War II, Western colonial rule has given way to rising nationalistic movements.

At the end of the colonial era, the Western missionary's role grew dubious in the minds of many national leaders. Where a sizable or influential Christian presence had developed, there usually were provisions made by the emerging regimes for continuation of Western missionary presence. Where a weak Christian church existed, leaders of dominant religious groups influenced the fledgling regimes to restrict Christianity's growth and development, particularly by diminishing its foreign sustenance. A simple way to enact such restrictions was to deny visas and residence permits to those foreigners known to work with Christian elements in the country. Creative strategic initiatives, like the NONRESIDENTIAL MISSIONARY model, now enable Christian missions and missionaries to penetrate existing barriers in the traditional homelands of antagonistic blocs of Hindu, Buddhist, Islamic, tribal, and more recently communist people groups located within the political boundaries of countries resistant to Christian influence.

KEITH E. EITEL

Bibliography. D. B. Barrett and T. M. Johnston. *Our Globe and How to Reach It: Seeing the World Evangelized by A.D. 2000 and Beyond;* V. D. Garrison, *The Nonresidential Missionary: A New Strategy and the People It Serves;* idem, *IJFM* 9 (1992): 67–69.

Creed. *See* CONFESSION.

CRESR '82. *See* CONSULTATION ON THE RELATIONSHIP BETWEEN EVANGELISM AND SOCIAL RESPONSIBILITY.

Croatia *(Est. 2000 pop.: 4,433,00; 56,538 sq. km. [21,829 sq. mi.].* Croatia (with provinces of Croatia proper, Dalmatia, Istria, and Slavonia) is a crescent-shaped country bounded by Slovenia, Hungary, Yugoslavia, and the Adriatic Sea. It declared its independence from Yugoslavia in 1991, which resulted in intense warfare between the two countries, creating a major humanitarian crisis and Serbian control of one-third of Croatian lands. The country was internationally recognized in 1992 and regained full control over all its territories by 1998. The ethnic composition of the country before the war in 1991 was 77.9 percent Croats, 12.2 percent Serbs, and 9.9 percent others. This has been seriously disrupted by the expulsion of more than one hundred thousand Serbs in 1995 and due to the large influx of Bosnian refugees, both Muslim and Croat.

The region was part of the Western Roman Empire's province of Illyricum. Christianity was introduced to this area as early as the first century through the missionary travels of the apostle Paul and his co-workers (Illyricum is mentioned in Rom. 15:19, and Dalmatia in 2 Tim. 4:10). Croats who are of South Slavic origin settled in the areas of present-day Croatia and Bosnia in the seventh century A.D. Their arrival was followed by conversion from the old Slavic nature-god religions to Roman Catholicism. Since that time and following the schism in 1054 between Eastern and Western Christianity, Croatia has remained almost exclusively Roman Catholic. The peculiarity of Croatian Catholicism through the centuries has, however, been the rare permission to celebrate liturgy in its own ancient language with the use of Glagolithic script.

Croatia's statehood goes back to the year 925, when under King Tomislav and with the blessing of the pope it became an independent kingdom. In the twelfth century the Croats united in one state with the Hungarians, another Catholic nation. Over the following centuries Croatia was ruled by Venetians, the Ottoman Empire, and the Habsburgs. In the sixteenth and seventeenth centuries the Austrians created a military frontier against the Turks in southeast Croatia settled mostly by Orthodox Serbs who were fleeing the Ottoman territories. Since that time Catholic Croatia has had a large Orthodox minority.

Protestant efforts to extend influence in Croatia in the sixteenth century were initially very successful although soon brutally eradicated through the COUNTER-REFORMATION. The most prominent Croat Protestant theologian was Matthias Flacius Illyricus (1520–75), a student of Luther, prolific writer, and polemicist, considered by many to be the father of modern biblical HERMENEUTICS. Protestants Jurij Dalmatin and Konzul Istranin worked on the first Croatian translation of the Bible. With the forceful resurgence of Roman Catholicism, Protestantism was in subsequent centuries confined to minorities of Hungarians, Slovaks, and Germans.

Croatia became part of Yugoslavia in 1918, first named the Kingdom of Serbs, Croats, and Slovenes. During World War II the so-called Independent State of Croatia, which also included Bosnia, operated as a Nazi puppet state. After the war, under the rule of Tito, Croatia became one of the six republics of communist Yugoslavia. Croatian struggles against foreign domination through the centuries forced about 25 percent of the population to leave for other countries. This emigration was caused by a combination of economic and political circumstances, including periods of Turkish rule, Hungarization attempts, oppression by the Habsburgs, Serbian dictatorship in the Kingdom of Yugoslavia, and the communist totalitarianism. Many of the more recent immigrants returned following the creation of an independent Republic of Croatia in 1991.

The religious situation in today's Croatia is characterized by a revival of traditional Roman Catholicism, the influx of large numbers of Bosnian Muslim refugees, and a sudden decrease of Serbian Orthodox Christians. All Protestants together constitute only 0.6 percent of the population, and evangelicals only 0.2 percent. After years of stagnation Lutheran, Baptist, and Pentecostal churches in particular have begun to experience growth. Despite their small numbers, evangelicals have during the recent wars in Croatia and neighboring Bosnia made a significant effort to assist refugees and displaced people, to maintain church unity across ethnic divides, and to participate in the peacemaking efforts within the country. The Evangelical Theological Seminary (ETS) in Osijek (founded 1972) has trained most of the younger Christian leaders of various denominations and its graduates have pioneered in areas of university ministries, Christian publishing, broadcasting, prison ministries, and cross-cultural evangelism. Dozens of young Croats and other graduates of ETS have been sent as church-planting missionaries to Bosnia and to other post-communist nations.

PETER KUZMIC

Bibliography. S. Gazi, *A History of Croatia;* I. Nizich, *Civil and Political Rights in Croatia;* S. P. Ramet, *Balkan Babel: Politics, Culture, and Religion;* R. Stakkaerts and J. Laurens, *Historical Dictionary of the Republic of Croatia;* M. Tanner, *Croatia: A Nation Forged in War.*

Cross. *See* ATONEMENT.

Cross-Cultural Communication. *See* INTERCULTURAL COMMUNICATION.

Cross-Cultural Competency. *See* INTERCULTURAL COMPETENCY.

Cross-Cultural Counseling. Cross-cultural counseling, often referred to as multicultural, intercultural, transcultural, or ethnic counseling, occurs when the counselor's basic background differs from that of the counselee's. Prior to the 1970s most counselor training programs, primarily Western value-laden, paid little attention to cultural awareness, thereby increasing the risk of culturally inappropriate interventions in the few cases where such counseling took place.

Interest in cross-cultural counseling in America received its impetus from the vast demographic shifts brought about by the rising prominence of ethnic groups, to a lesser extent by the increasing number of university-level international students, and the growing number of international government, UN, and business projects. Missionaries further realized the need for cross-cultural counseling skills because of the growing refugee population, the fairly recent multicultural composition of missionary personnel, and the struggles of citizens of changing developing countries who were struggling with the accompanying problems that exposure to a more technological socioeconomic world brings. Rather suddenly missionaries were faced with the need for counseling skills to help fellow missionary personnel, displaced persons, and nationals cope with the stresses that cultural change tends to produce.

Missionaries wanting counseling preparation can benefit by the (1) increasing number of cross-cultural courses offered in training sites, (2) growing research on cross-cultural counseling reported in journals, and (3) expanding number of books being written, all with the aim to improve the quality of help for culturally different populations. Although ideally each culture would be served by its own members, the initial training will need to be given by those who have had access to a solid background in counseling.

The following guidelines are a summary of the salient emphases in the current Christian and secular literature that apply to cross-cultural counseling and are particularly relevant to the missionary-counselor. The assumption is that general counseling principles, strategies, and techniques are well understood.

Guidelines for the Cross Cultural Missionary-Counselor. All the literature stresses the imperative for the counselor to become culturally aware. Understanding one's own culture as well as the folkways, communication styles, traditions, belief systems, mores, and values of the other culture allows missionary-counselors to maintain their own identity while interpreting behavior and planning interventions in terms of the other culture.

Counselors can offer the most extensive help by training members of a particular culture to be counselors to their own people. Introducing basic pastoral counseling courses in seminaries and Bible schools, holding on-going seminars for church leaders, and selecting a discerning national to work by their side to interpret cultural issues could greatly reduce the chance of missionaries making ethnocentric misjudgments. For example, the family therapy concept of individuation and enmeshment differs from culture to culture, requiring a discerning national's input on what constitutes dysfunction. Meeting regularly with national counselors for mutual help whereby the counselor guides the trainee to employ appropriate interventions and the national-counselor gives feedback on how a concept or technique manifests itself in that milieu could alleviate the missionary-counselor's workload. At the same time, the counselor has the opportunity to reproduce skills in others.

Missionary-counselors must listen and listen again and again. They must *hear* the nationals' stories and experience them both cognitively and affectively from their framework without the interference of their own cultural assumptions. To assume correctly that they are understanding from the other culture's perspective, the helper constantly needs to clarify meanings in ways that are acceptable for that culture (repetition, reflection, questions, etc.).

The effective missionary-counselor gradually learns to discriminate between normal situational responses in a given culture and responses that are pathological. For example, in cultures where persecution or discrimination has existed an individual's comments may seem somewhat paranoid. This could well be a learned response to actual negative experiences. Rather than assume a deeper problem the counselor might aim to enable the person to relinquish the hurt, humiliation, anger, or fear that the situation has produced.

Goals, strategies, and techniques need to be congruent with the cultural norms, even if they are not part of the traditional repertoire of the discipline. For example, members of most cultures are sociocentric rather than egocentric (*see* INDIVIDUALISM AND COLLECTIVISM). They therefore often respond better when extended families or church leaders or even clan members are included as part of problem resolution. Also, a weekly fixed time in the missionary's office rather than the village or church may seem artificial to them. Or, counseling that too directly plunges the counselee into personal issues may increase resistance. A "tea time" of small talk frees certain cultural groups to relax and talk more freely. Each culture has its own idiosyncratic approaches and effective methods that maintain the delicate balance between manipulative informality and effective professionalism that has to be reframed for each situation.

Although counseling may enable a national to take a more active role in facilitating changes in his or her milieu, the socioeconomic-political situations are not the foreigner's domain per se. One of the goals of missionary-counselors is to let the Lord work through them to empower the counselee to function as healthily and comfortably as possible regardless of the environmental circumstances. The missionary is in a unique position to present the transcendent peace and hope of a sovereign God. Guiding what may well be victimized people to appropriate the immanent grace of the Lord, including the power to forgive, can superhumanly free them from the inner chains of hurt, despair, and anxiety that hinders healthy functioning.

Since the concept of the supernatural is prominent in many cultures, incorporating spiritual issues into the counseling process would offer a more holistic and contextual approach. To do this sensitively, wisely, and biblically, counselors must, first, clarify their own beliefs in this area. Second, they must make every effort to understand the way the worldview of the culture in which they work perceives the supernatural. Third, they need to grasp how it plays itself out in the daily affairs of the people. Fourth, counselors must carefully observe how the culture's views contribute positively or negatively to the health of the people. Nor can the role of the demonic, so real to many cultures, be ignored (*see also* POSSESSION PHENOMENA). In approaching the more mystical aspects of a culture, diagnostic skill that distinguishes among psychological, social, and spiritual events is essential. The counselor must be prepared to use God's Word with integrity, conviction, and trust in its power.

Most authors on cross-cultural counseling stress the importance of maintaining a balanced emphasis between human universals and cultural uniqueness. An appreciation for the commonalities stemming from the human race's God-relatedness can be a link to any culture. However, overemphasis on similarities could reduce cultural sensitivity and detract from efforts to differentiate that which is different as a result of their frame of reference and what is maladaptive in that particular culture. On the other hand, too much emphasis on the uniqueness of a culture can lead to stereotypes and blind counselors to the individual differences. Cultural factors do not provide all the answers to dilemmas that a person faces. Foremost the uniqueness of the individual must be considered.

Conclusion. Counseling is a relatively new phenomenon in many countries. Yet throughout the world there is a global cry for help to deal with the emotionally painful effects of the undue stresses produced by the innumerable, often unprecedented, and many times unpredictable changes taking place. Christians tend to seek support from their church leaders, more often than not, the pastors. Pastors are often in a quandary to know how to deal with the issues.

The need to develop counseling training programs to impart the necessary skills to church leaders has become an imperative. An increasing number of seminaries and Bible schools are offering at least basic counseling skills to pastors. However, the initial training must be done by those who come from countries, generally the Western ones, where they have been able to avail themselves of more in-depth training in counseling. Often they are missionaries who face the formidable challenge of acquiring cultural awareness profound enough to be able to develop strategies and techniques congruent with the given culture's way of functioning The above guidelines give a glimpse of the complexity of the task.

Missionaries trained in counseling generally have some cross-cultural training and a degree of experience in another culture. They already have a sense of call to deal in an in-depth fashion with people in order to guide them to better glorify the Lord. It seems fitting that they fill the need to acquire the necessary skills to train nationals to counsel their own people.

FRANCES J. WHITE

SEE ALSO Psychology.

Bibliography. *American Psychologist* 48:1 (1993): 45–48; J. F. Aponte, R. Y. Rivers, S. J. Wohl, *Psychological Interventions and Cultural Diversity;* D. Augsberger, *Pastoral Counseling Across Cultures;* D. J. Hesselgrave, *Counseling Cross-Culturally;* K. Lloyd, T. D. Bhugra, *Cross-Cultural Aspects of Psychotherapy* 5 (1993): 291–304; M. McGoldrick, J. K. Pearce, J. Giordano, *Ethnicity and Family Therapy;* P. P. Pedersen, J. G. Draguns, W. J. Lonner, J. E. Trimble, *Counseling Across Cultures;* P. P. Pedersen, *Handbook of Cross-Cultural*

Counseling and Psychotherapy; D. W. Sue, *Counseling the Culturally Different.*

Cross-Cultural Evangelism. In one sense any EVANGELISM involves crossing a cultural divide, since the evangelist must communicate spiritual truth to spiritually dead people who in their natural state are unable to comprehend it. Cross-cultural evangelism, however, has the added challenge of communication between people of different WORLDVIEWS and BELIEF SYSTEMS. As such, it is more often considered true missionary witness (whether geographical distance is involved or not) than is evangelism between members of the same culture.

CULTURE, of course, is generally seen as a society's folkways, mores, language, art and architecture, and political and economic structures; it is the expression of the society's worldview. Worldview has been described as the way a people looks outwardly upon itself and the universe, or the way it sees itself in relationship to all else.

For the cross-cultural evangelist, WITNESS involves a thorough understanding of one's own culture, the biblical context in which God's Word was given, and the culture of those among whom evangelism is being done. The message must be tailored or contextualized in such a way as to remain faithful to the biblical text while understandable and relevant to the receptor's context.

The late twentieth century has seen, along with widespread acceptance of anthropological insights, a flowering of respect for culture in missions and evangelism. James Engel devised a scale to measure people's understanding of the gospel and their movement toward Christ. It can be used to gauge the spiritual knowledge and involvement of both individuals and groups. At one end of the ENGEL SCALE are those with no awareness of Christianity (-7), followed by those aware of the existence of Christianity (-6), followed by those with some knowledge of the gospel (-5). Conversion is numerically neutral on the Engel Scale. At its far end are incorporation of the believer into a Christian fellowship (+2) and active gospel propagation by the believer (+3). Bridging the knowledge gap often, but not always, involves cross-cultural evangelism.

At the LAUSANNE CONGRESS ON WORLD EVANGELISM (1974), RALPH WINTER argued that 2.7 billion people cannot be won to Christ by "near-neighbor evangelism" since they have no Christian neighbors. Winter said evangelists must cross cultural, language, and geographical barriers, learn the languages and cultures of these unreached peoples, present the gospel to them, and plant culturally relevant churches among them. Winter delineated three kinds of evangelism: same culture (E-1), culture closely related to one's own (E-2), and culture different than one's own (E-3). Winter's emphasis on crossing cul-

tural boundaries to reach other cultural groups laid the foundation for the unreached peoples movement and the AD 2000 and Beyond Movement. Winter clearly distinguishes between evangelism (presenting the gospel to one's own people) and missions (crossing cultural boundaries).

At the 1978 Lausanne Committee consultation on "Gospel and Culture," thirty-three missions leaders and theologians drafted The Willowbank Report, which set down a detailed acknowledgment of the critical role of culture in missionary communication. Included in the document were evangelical understandings of culture, Scripture, the content and communication of the gospel, witness among Muslims, a call for humility, and a look at conversion and culture. The authors asserted that conversion should not "de-culturize" a convert (*see also* CULTURAL CONVERSION). They also acknowledged the validity of group, as well as individual, conversions (*see also* PEOPLE MOVEMENTS). Participants noted the difference between regeneration and conversion, the dangers of SYNCRETISM, and the church's influence on culture (*see also* GOSPEL AND CULTURE).

As evangelical understanding of culture has progressed, a number of innovative evangelism methods have been advanced. Noting that the theology of the Bible is often encased in stories, Tom Steffen of Biola University and others argue that STORYTELLING can be more effective in oral cultures than the Western-style cognitive teaching approach. Baptists working among the Muslim Kotokoli people of Togo have found that storytelling can lower cultural barriers to the gospel.

Use of Western forms of communication may stigmatize the gospel as alien in some cultures. A cross-cultural approach advocated for SHAME cultures—some Islamic societies, for example—is to emphasize the gospel as the answer for defilement and uncleanness rather than sin and guilt. J. Nathan Corbitt distinguishes between hard media (media more concrete in format and presentation, such as books and films) and soft media (media allowing flexibility during its creation and use, such as storytelling, drama, music, and conversation). Corbitt says that to communicate across cultures, evangelists must "soften" their media—using local people and focusing on the process of Christianity rather than its specific products—to spark the greatest amount of understanding and communication within a community.

Some critics have questioned the effectiveness of popular evangelism tools such as the JESUS FILM and Evangelism Explosion when used apart from an adequate understanding of the culture. Steffen argues that before the Jesus film is shown, the audience's worldview must be known, the presenters must earn the right to be heard, the film must be seen first by the community's information gatekeepers, the presenters must grasp how the community makes decisions and must know how to incorporate converts into healthy churches, and the audience must have a significant foundation for the gospel. Not to have these cultural prerequisites in place, he and others argue, is to invite nominalism or syncretism with our evangelism.

STANLEY M. GUTHRIE

Bibliography. J. N. Corbitt, *EMQ* 27:2 (April 1991): 160–65; D. J. Hesselgrave, *Communicating Christ Cross-Culturally;* T. Steffen, *EMQ* 32:2 (April 1996): 178–85; idem, *EMQ* 29:3 (July 1993): 272–76; B. Thomas, *EMQ* 30:3 (July 1994): 284–90; R. D. Winter, and S. C. Hawthorne, eds., *Perspectives on the World Christian Movement.*

Cross-Cultural Ministry. The theological basis for cross-cultural ministry lies in its examples within both Old and New Testaments, coupled with the universal nature of the Christian faith and the Lord's Commission to "disciple the nations." It may be further argued that the incarnation of Christ demands that we take culture seriously in ministry, because it is in the realities of the cultural context that the gospel is manifested (*see* INCARNATIONAL MISSION). Thus Gitari has written, "Jesus did not become a Jew as a convenient illustration of general truths. He came into real problems, debates, issues struggles and conflicts which concerned the Jewish people." The gospel requires specific cultural contexts in which to be manifested.

The missionary expansion of the church from its earliest days is evidence of the seriousness with which Christians have grasped and implemented cross-cultural ministry. In recent times the SOCIAL SCIENCES have contributed to the conscious acknowledgment of the importance of culture in relation to this missionary endeavor. EUGENE A. NIDA's *Customs and Cultures* stated that "Good missionaries have always been good 'anthropologists' . . . on the other hand, some missionaries have been only 'children of their generation' and have carried to the field a distorted view of race and progress, culture and civilization, Christian and non-Christian ways of life."

The context for much nineteenth-century Protestant missions was that of European colonial expansion and this resulted in examples of the export of European culture and expressions of Christianity alongside the gospel (*see* COLONIALISM). The twentieth century witnessed first the increasing American missionary endeavor and the rise of Two-Thirds World missions (*see* NON-WESTERN MISSION BOARDS AND SOCIETIES). As a result of the internationalizing of missions and the GLOBALIZATION of communications (with its own consequences in terms of cultural change), the issues of CULTURE and mission are today even more complex. Complementing the recognition of the importance of culture in missionary communication has been an examination of culture itself from a Christian and biblical perspective. In the New Testament we find that Paul's willingness to lay aside personal freedoms and status for the sake of the gospel (1 Cor. 8:9–13; 9:22; Phil. 3:8) illustrate the primacy of the gospel over the messenger's attitudes and behavior.

Bishop STEPHEN NEILL has asserted that there are some customs which the gospel cannot tolerate, there are some customs which can be tolerated for the time being, and there are customs which are fully acceptable to the gospel. The Lausanne Covenant affirmed that "Culture must always be tested and judged by Scripture. Because man is God's creature, some of his culture is rich in beauty and goodness. Because he is fallen, all of it is tainted with sin and some of it is demonic." Bishop David Gitari has welcomed this emphasis that "*all* cultures must always be tested by the scriptures."

The relativization of the cultural expressions of the Christian faith has resulted in the popular acceptance within missions of the concept of CONTEXTUALIZATION, which aims to be faithful to Scripture and relevant to culture. Such an approach intends to apply the absolutes to which Scripture refers within a plurality of culturally appropriate forms. However, disquiet at the prominence currently given to contextualization in missiology was expressed by Christians with a Reformed perspective at a Caucus on Mission to Muslims held at Four Brooks Conference Centre in 1985.

The practical expression of the Christian faith in a culture is a pioneer venture which is liable to the criticism that the true nature of the gospel may become distorted by SYNCRETISM or compromise. In the West there has been a debate between evangelicals and liberal Christians over how best to represent Christianity within a modern scientific culture. In the Muslim world, Phil Parshall's *New Paths in Muslim Evangelism* laid out the contextualization of Christian mission among Muslims (*see* MUSLIM MISSION WORK). This not only covered issues of COMMUNICATION, "theological bridges to salvation," but also the forms and practices of a culturally relevant "Muslim-convert church." Others have argued that the creation of separate convert churches and the Christianization of Muslim devotional means in "Jesus Mosques" (such as the position of prayer or putting the Bible on a special stand) fall short of the requirements for Christian unity in Muslim lands where historic Christian communities exist. This debate is a reminder that Christian mission needs to be sensitive to a broader range of issues than the culture of the unevangelized.

PATRICK SOOKHDEO

Bibliography. D. Gitari, *Proclaiming Christ in Christ's Way—Studies in Integral Evangelism*, pp. 101–21; C. H.

Kraft, *Christianity in Culture;* Lausanne Committee for World Evangelisation, *The Lausanne Covenant—An Exposition and Commentary by John Stott.* idem, *The Willowbank Report—Gospel and Culture;* H. Niebuhr, *Christ and Culture;* E. A. Nida, *Customs and Cultures;* P. Parshall, *New Paths in Muslim Evangelism.*

Cross-Cultural Research. Cross-cultural research forms an essential base in missiological research. Whether one is researching a church context or a non-Christian context across cultural boundaries, several concerns apply: an appropriate research design, valid and reliable methods of data collection and analysis, and appropriate application.

The research design may depend on a single disciplinary perspective such as anthropology or cross-cultural communication. More often it will depend on the integration of several different disciplines, such as theology, ANTHROPOLOGY, COMMUNICATION, SOCIOLOGY, political science, and LEADERSHIP THEORY. For the design to provide trustworthy results the cultural perspectives of both the researchers and the community being studied must be brought in focus. Furthermore, one should review the WORLDVIEW assumptions of the theory being used to structure the design because every theory and its development come out of a cultural context. No theory is "culture-free." The theory undergirding the design must allow the explanations of the data to address categories of thinking in the situation being studied. For example, if one's research assumptions preclude the possibility of the miraculous, a study of the religious experience of new churches in Argentina would not produce trustworthy results from the perspective of Argentine Christians.

Data collection and analysis methods often require multiple perspectives to see clearly across cultural boundaries. Like looking into a house, it is helpful to look through several windows in order to gain an understanding of what is inside. The view from a single window may help with one room, but will not provide access to other parts of a house. Similarly, when seeking to do cross-cultural research, the use of more than one perspective may not just be helpful; it may be essential. Even when researchers have used multiple perspectives, their own cultural biases will tend to condition the processes of data collection, analysis, and application.

When crossing cultural boundaries the definition of what is regarded as true and ethical may differ. In more oral-based traditions or strongly patriarchical settings what the older and respected "authorities" have said will take on a larger significance. Whereas in one culture, what is in print may be seen as "public domain," in another culture use of the same data may lead to charges of plagiarism. What is accepted as a method of data collection in one setting may either be unknown or mistrusted in another. Trustworthy methods often require a pilot test to identify what will produce valid and reliable results. The outsider will look from a different perspective (etic) from the insider (emic) to both describe and explain what is observed in terms of either experience or documents. An outsider may observe phenomena that appear to be significant, but are not significant to the insider. For example, while using phonetics one may distinguish different sounds in the ways that different people say the same words. The sounds may be consistently different, but insignificant and meaningless to the insider. Or, the outsider may simply miss what is considered significant by the insider. For example, in doing research into public health matters in northwest Kenya, a Western researcher may simply miss the issues of cursing. What the people believe and practice about cursing deeply influences public health from the perspective of the Turkana. The Western researcher, even if informed of its local significance, may dismiss the issue as irrelevant superstition and fail to address issues considered to be very significant among the Turkana. Traditional Turkana people often ask "who" caused an illness rather than "what" caused it.

To apply research findings collected across cultural boundaries requires great care. Worldview differences expressed in values, categories, perceptual styles, assumptions, and local expressions in both action and language all present serious stumbling blocks to the normal constraints of generalizability. Any well-designed research project will have a defined scope and further constraints imposed by the parameters of the specific methods of data collection and analysis. However, to apply the research across cultural barriers presents another set of applicational constraints. One cannot assume that what is perceived as true or believable in one culture, will necessarily be perceived that way in another culture. Nor can one assume that what would be an appropriate application in one setting will necessarily be appropriate in another.

Cross-cultural research, then, should always take into account the cultures of the researcher, the research subjects, and the theory that may be used in the research design.

EDGAR J. ELLISTON

SEE ALSO Ethnographic Research; Research.

Bibliography. H. R. Bernard, *Research Methods in Cultural Anthropology;* J. Kirk and M. L. Miller, *Reliability and Validity in Qualitative Research.*

Crowther, Samuel Adjai (c. 1808–91). Nigerian explorer and missionary statesman. The son of a royal Yoruba family in what is now Nigeria, Crowther was taken as a slave when a youth. Freed by the British, he was settled in Sierra

Leone and learned Christianity from the missionaries there.

After studies in England, Crowther was among the first to enroll at and graduate from Fourah Bay College in Freetown. He was ordained in the Anglican Church in 1843.

Crowther's name is intimately associated with the Niger River, first as an explorer and then as leader of the mission efforts of the CHURCH MISSIONARY SOCIETY (CMS). He represented the CMS on three expeditions up the Niger sponsored by the British.

It soon became clear that the Niger River was deadly for Europeans, who were not resistant to tropical diseases. Thus, HENRY VENN sponsored the idea of an all-African team of missionaries to work in the Niger River area.

Crowther was installed as bishop of the Niger territories and sent on his way together with assistants from Sierra Leone. The initial work was slow and difficult because of poor communication, pagan persecution, incompetent assistants, and the criticisms of ethnocentric missionaries from England. But Crowther was a man of sterling character who continued the work until he died in his early eighties. His career is a lasting reminder of what Africans accomplished for God during the nineteenth century.

TIMOTHY MONSMA

Bibliography. J. Du Plessis, *The Evangelization of Pagan Africa;* P. Falk, *The Growth of the Church in Africa;* S. C. Neill, *HCM.*

Crusade Evangelism. Modern crusade evangelism began in the eighteenth century when a mighty movement of God was birthed in North America and Europe. This movement in America, known as the GREAT AWAKENING, was the catalyst for thousands coming to a saving faith in Jesus Christ. The major personalities of this time were GEORGE WHITEFIELD in North America and JOHN WESLEY in England. Their dynamic preaching attracted some of the largest crowds ever to hear the gospel.

Whitefield developed the practice of preaching in the open fields in England when he was not allowed to preach in many of the English pulpits. From this practice an evangelistic ministry surfaced that took Whitefield across the face of England and up the Atlantic Coast in America. A process was begun in which masses of people would gather to hear the Bible preached and seek spiritual renewal. This planned process of revivalism became a major evangelistic tool for reaching the lost.

Wesley soon joined Whitefield in his practice of open-air preaching. Crowds of over thirty thousand flocked to hear Wesley preach. Receiving great opposition from the clergy, he declared that the world was his parish. As the demand for preaching grew, Wesley began to appoint laity to preach. He soon developed routes for his circuit preaching evangelists to travel. Wesley spent the rest of his life organizing the converts into Methodist societies.

The First Great Awakening set the stage for the planned revivalism of the nineteenth century. During the Second Great Awakening, frontier camp meetings were held in which thousands of people, of many different denominations, would come to hear gospel preaching. The camp meetings came to be held annually and took the form of protracted meetings. A starting date was planned but no conclusion.

Many notable evangelists arose during the nineteenth century. The first evangelist of great significance was CHARLES FINNEY (1792–1875). Finney instituted innovative methods called New Measures, which encouraged persons under conviction to come forward and seek salvation. Finney's New Measures included anxious meetings in which the anxious could come to a reserved section and be led immediately to Christ. Finney is remembered as the "Father of Modern Evangelism."

The year 1875 marked the last year of Finney's ministry and the first major American evangelistic campaign of D. L. MOODY (1835–99). Moody and his musician, Ira Sankey, led major crusades in England and America. Moody concentrated his efforts in the cities, believing that if he could reach the cities, he could better impact the country. He repeatedly filled the auditoriums of America's largest cities, regularly preaching to crowds up to 15,000. Moody traveled over one million miles and spoke to over one hundred million people.

A contemporary of Moody was Sam Jones (1847–1906). Whereas Moody focused on regeneration, Jones focused on reformation. He maintained a close connection between conversion and moral issues. He averaged nearly two thousand conversions per crusade, recorded over five hundred thousand professions of faith, and spoke to well over twenty-five million people.

R. A. TORREY (1856–1928) was one of the great early evangelists of the twentieth century. Torrey and his music assistant Charles Alexander were welcomed as Moody and Sankey's successors. Torrey believed that he was the divinely appointed successor to Moody and prayed that the Lord would send him around the world with the message of salvation. He held crusades across the world with notable crusades in Australia, India, and a four-year campaign in Britain, which claimed over one hundred thousand converts. His American crusades were highly successful as he gained notoriety for challenging atheists and was successful in refuting prominent Universalists and Unitarians.

D. L. Moody referred to J. WILBUR CHAPMAN (1859–1918) as the greatest evangelist in the country. Chapman became widely known for his use of the simultaneous crusade. He would divide cities into districts; evangelists would hold meetings that preceded the main crusade. He also utilized various specialists whom he believed would appeal to specific groups. His specialists included social activists, athletes, representatives of the various denominations, children's specialists, and reformed alcoholics and gamblers.

Wilbur Chapman left evangelism in 1895 for the pastorate and was succeeded by his crusade director BILLY SUNDAY (1862–1935). Sunday was a former professional baseball player for the Chicago White Stockings. His preaching style was dramatic and included acrobatics and theatrics. Sunday erected giant wooden tabernacles, some holding up to twenty-five thousand, to accommodate the crowds. Those who responded to Sunday's invitation were called "trail hitters," reflecting Sunday's key phrase in the invitation to "hit the sawdust trail." In all, Sunday preached to over one hundred million people and led over a million persons to faith in Christ.

During the twentieth century many notable crusade evangelists engaged successfully in crusade evangelistic efforts around the world. Prominent Africa-American crusade evangelists include Howard Jones and Ralph Bell. American Pentecostals who conducted massive healing crusades include Oral Roberts, Kathryn Kuhlman, and Benny Hinn. In Latin American contexts LUIS PALAU and Carlos Anacondia stand out. In Africa, Nigerian Benson Idahosa, Ugandan FESTO KIVENGERE, and Zambian Nevers Mumba are well known. Additionally, Pentecostals such as American T. L. Osborne and German Reinhard Bonnke have conducted large-scale crusades across the continent. Prominent Asian crusade evangelists include Indians Abdiyah Akbar Abdul-Haqq, Robert Cunville, and Ravi Zacharias as well as Sri Lankan Ajith Fernando. In the South Pacific, Australian Bill Newman is well known.

Perhaps no evangelist of any century, however, has had the impact of BILLY GRAHAM. Born in 1918, Graham was converted under the preaching of Evangelist Mordecai Ham. As a young minister, Graham received much notoriety as the key speaker for Youth for Christ in rallies across the country. However, it was his 1949 crusade in Los Angeles that launched his ministry into the greatest crusade ministry in revival history. Like many great evangelists before him, Graham preached numerous crusades overseas, including major efforts in Australia, England, China, Eastern Europe, and the former Soviet Union.

Over the years crusade evangelistic efforts have had their share of detractors. Controversies over excessive lifestyles and integrity issues have exposed those who have engaged in crusade ministry for personal gain. They have also resulted in better accountability structures among those who might be tempted to move in such a direction. In any event, however, there is no doubt that the varied forms of crusade evangelism have played, and will continue to play, a vital role in mission and world evangelization.

FRANK HARBER

Bibliography. E. E. Cairns, *An Endless Line of Splendor: Revivals and Their Leaders from the Great Awakening to the Present;* S. Huston, *Crusade Evangelism and the Local Church;* B. R. Lacy, Jr., *Revivals in the Midst of the Years;* W. L. Muncy, Jr., *History of Evangelism in the United States;* P. Scharff, *History of Evangelism: Three Hundred Years of Evangelism in Germany, Great Britain, and the United States of America;* M. Taylor, *Exploring Evangelism: History, Methods, Theology.*

Crusades, The. Military expeditions against various enemies of the medieval church, especially the campaigns that tried to free the Holy Land from the Muslims. Christians had gone on pilgrimages to the Holy Land during much of the medieval period, but with the arrival of the Seljuk Turks their travels were hampered. These invaders also pressured the Eastern Empire to such an extent that the emperor contacted the pope and other leaders of Western Europe to send mercenaries to help defend the Byzantine Empire. Pope Urban II responded to this appeal by proclaiming the First Crusade in a sermon at Clermont (1095). The primary reason for the Crusades was religious, for they constituted a holy war, and following Urban's appeal there was an outpouring of religious enthusiasm. In addition, the pope saw in the Crusades an outlet for the energies of the warring nobles of Europe. The First Crusade, consisting of about five thousand fighting men, moved overland to Constantinople and proceeded to conquer territory in Asia Minor and the Levant. The conquest of Jerusalem was accompanied by a frightful slaughter of the inhabitants. The Crusaders did not drive the Turks from the Middle East, but they established several states that resulted in a balance of power among them, the Byzantines, and the Muslims. When the Crusader states were endangered, Bernard of Clairvaux organized the Second Crusade (1147), which was defeated. A Third Crusade (1189–92) resulted in a three-year truce and the granting of free access to Jerusalem for Christian pilgrims. This arrangement collapsed and further Crusades were necessary. The few knights who answered Innocent III's call to the Fourth Crusade (1202–4) were unable to pay the passage charges demanded by the Venetians. This led the two groups to strike a bargain and agree to attack Constantinople. After conquering and sacking the city, the Crusaders set up the Latin Empire of Constantinople and forgot about recovering the Holy Land. During the thirteenth century there were more Crusades such as the Children's Crusade, the Sixth Crusade led by the excommunicated Frederick II, and the Seventh Crusade of Louis IX. Each of these failed in its efforts to shore up the Latin crusading kingdoms and in 1291 Acre, the last stronghold of the Christians in the Holy Land, fell to the Muslims. Despite the loss of the Middle Eastern territories the Crusades did not end. Along the Baltic the Teutonic knights conquered the Prussians and the Balts and fought the Poles and the Russians. The military orders of the Mediterranean fought several crusades as did the rulers of the Balkans during the fourteenth and fifteenth centuries.

The Crusades, although credited with reviving Europe economically and commercially, were actually a failure. They poisoned relations between the Eastern Orthodox and Western church and increased Islamic hatred of Christianity. The faith had been perverted by vicious knights and greedy merchants who inflicted terrible suffering on thousands of Muslims, Jews, and Christians.

ROBERT G. CLOUSE

Bibliography. E. Christiansen, *The Northern Crusades: The Baltic and the Catholic Frontier;* N. Housley, *The Later Crusades, 1274–1580;* B. Z. Kedar, *Crusade and Mission: European Approaches Toward the Muslims;* S. Runciman, *A History of the Crusades;* K. M. Setton, *A History of the Crusades.*

Cuba *(Est. 2000 pop.: 11,385,000; 110,861 sq. km. [42,803 sq. mi.]).* Cuba's religious disposition has been strongly conditioned by its close ties with Spain. With a large European population and its status as a Spanish dependency until 1898, the island had a well-entrenched Roman Catholic establishment existing side by side with a well-developed tradition of SECULARISM. Neither of these ideological orientations filtered down to the level of the typical rural Cuban, whose devotion to the church was limited and whose personal beliefs were likely to be those of Afro-Caribbean folk culture. Students of Cuban development recognize that institutional religion itself was weak. Protestant churches were largely urban in an agricultural society, and both the Protestant and Catholic churches were perceived as being foreign-based institutions. The Protestant presence was the result of the religious pluralism and anticlericalism that were part of the struggle for Cuban independence prior to 1898, as well as the increased mainland influence from expatriate Cubans and Protestant missionaries.

Despite the current absence of a foreign missionary force, reports of religious revival in Cuba indicate that evangelical Christianity remains hardy. Presently there are a reported 150,000 active evangelicals in Cuba, representing dozens of denominations, among them various Baptist and Pentecostal bodies.

EVERETT A. WILSON

See also Caribbean.

Bibliography. A. Lampe, *The Church in Latin America, 1492–1992,* pp. 201–15; J. Rogozinski, *A Brief History of the Caribbean: From the Arawak and the Carib to the Present.*

Cults, Cultism. Cults and new religious movements tend to emerge during times of social change and cultural upheaval. Whether the locale is North America or in a developing nation, cults are most successful when people experience alienation, rootlessness, and uncertainty as a result of rapid social change. When people experience a dislocation from previously stable social structures, they often question the efficacy and relevance of traditional social institutions like the family, government, and conventional religion. From the perspective of biblical Christianity, the new cultic movements are viewed as spiritual counterfeits and their leaders as false prophets.

It is imperative that Christians involved in missions be aware of the intrusion of these groups into mission fields around the globe. Cult missionaries can be found in virtually every country where evangelicals are ministering. In those countries where Christianity is not the dominant religion, indigenous populations are often unable to distinguish between legitimate Christian witness and the outreach of cultists because the latter often claim to be Christian and invoke the Bible as a source of their authority. It is essential, therefore, that Christian missionaries work to develop discernment skills among the people they are attempting to disciple.

The need to "guard the gospel" is illustrated by an event experienced a few years ago by a young couple involved in missionary service in Martinique, a French island in the West Indies. There they led a church-planting ministry that required heavy investment in personal evangelism and community outreach. From their labors there emerged a tiny church that gradually grew to the point of self-sufficiency. But while the missionaries were away on a leave of absence, the infant church was invaded by JEHOVAH'S WITNESSES. When they returned, they discovered that many of the members, including some of the leaders, had been influenced by the teachings of that cult and had joined with them.

This scenario is repeated over and over worldwide. New Christians, lacking a solid foundation in the faith and knowing little about the strategies and hallmarks of cults and aberrational Christian groups, are caught in a snare of deception and false teaching. It has been said that because of the enormous recent increase of cultic missionary activity overseas, missionaries today are often as likely to confront someone from an American-based cult as they are someone from another world religion. The missionary zeal of the cults in many instances surpasses that of Christian denominations.

There are several ways to define cultism and to understand how cults work. It is possible to analyze cults from sociological, psychological, and theological perspectives. For the Christian, it is important to consider the truth-claims of any religious group. God's objective truth, as revealed in Scripture, is the standard for evaluating all belief and practice. Therefore, any group, movement, or teaching may be considered cultic to the degree that it deviates from the Holy Scriptures as interpreted by orthodox, biblical Christianity and as expressed in such statements as the Apostles' Creed.

The majority of people who join cults are consciously or unconsciously embarked on a spiritual search. Some converts to NEW RELIGIOUS MOVEMENTS are vulnerable because they have no formal religious affiliation whatsoever and therefore lack the necessary discernment skills to evaluate the many religious groups that beckon. Someone has said that "nature abhors a vacuum." It is especially during times of cultural upheaval that people, uprooted from traditional ways of thinking, are susceptible to the influx of new ideas. G. K. Chesterton once remarked that when people cease to believe in God, they do not believe in nothing. They believe in anything.

What is an appropriate response for the Christian missionary to the cultists who are engaged in real spiritual competition for the souls of searching individuals? First, we must recognize that to reject the cultic alternatives to Christianity is not to suggest that there is no truth in them. Error is always built on a foundation of half-truths. Spiritual counterfeits often contain an element of the real thing. Until we identify the web of error that characterizes all groups which depart from the baseline of truth found in the Bible, we have only partially understood the dynamics of the cults and new religions. When missionaries encounter members of cults and new religious movements, they can affirm the cultists' spiritual search while at the same time refuse to accept the presuppositions they may hold. We should seek to establish a common ground rather than attempt to win an argument. Many cultists, for example, share the Christian's concern for the environment, world peace, and alleviating hunger. Seeking common ground with the cultist will provide an opportunity to introduce the claims of Jesus Christ.

It goes without saying that missionaries (or any serious Christian) attempting to reach cultists for Christ must be sure of their own faith and be able to give a reason for the hope that is in us. In the final analysis, the clash between Christianity and the cultic ways of understanding reality results from differences in worldviews. The Christian missionary must be prepared to present an alternative model of spirituality, an alternative WORLDVIEW that is centered on biblical

faith and the person of Jesus Christ. All believers are necessarily engaged in the task of APOLOGETICS, or defending the Christian faith.

Cultic movements gain most of their converts not from other WORLD RELIGIONS but from the ranks of Christians who are lacking a solid biblical foundation for their faith and who are naive regarding the recruitment tactics of cults. Therefore, it is imperative that mission agencies and non-Western church leaders give priority to the task of educating new Christians about the dangers of false teaching and demonstrating how to effectively respond to the cultic challenge. In short, while evangelizing cults and new religions may be part of the missionary's opportunity to share the gospel of Christ, more attention should be given to the task of equipping local believers to become grounded in the faith so that they can discern truth from error and therefore avoid cultic entrapment.

Just as missionaries must be familiar with the culture and religion of the people they want to reach, they must also attempt to learn as much as possible about the cult or new religious movement that is often seeking to proselytize nonbelievers and immature Christians. It is also important to identify the reasons why people are attracted to cults. It is easy to overlook the fact that theological and doctrinal attractions are often secondary to personal and social reasons. People find cults appealing because the groups meet basic human needs: the need to be affirmed, the need for community and family, the need for purpose and commitment, and the need for spiritual fulfillment.

The tragedy is that cults often exploit the significant human and spiritual needs that are going unmet in today's world. As missionaries approach the task of equipping local Christians, they must first examine their own commitment to the truth of the gospel and to the authority of God's Word. Once we understand that the gospel is really true and stands up to the most difficult scrutiny, our own faith is enlarged and we become more eager to encourage the faith of others. We all need to develop a firm framework of truth by which to evaluate the claims of other groups.

From that framework, the missionary can help young Christians to understand two core characteristics of all cultic teachings: (1) *A false or inadequate basis of salvation.* The apostle Paul made a distinction that is basic to our understanding of truth when he wrote, "For it is by grace you have been saved, through faith—and this not from yourselves, it is the gift of God—not by works, so that no one can boast" (Eph. 2:8–9). All cultic deviations tend to downplay or distort the finished work of Christ on the cross and emphasize the role of earning moral acceptance before God through our own righteous works as a basis of salvation. (2) *A false basis of authority*. Biblical Christianity by definition takes the Bible as its yardstick for determining truth, whether in matters of faith or in practice. Cults, on the other hand, commonly resort to extra-biblical revelation as the substantial basis of their theology (e.g., Unificationists rely on the *Divine Principle* of Rev. Moon, the MORMONS cite *The Book of Mormon*).

Just as Christian believers in the West have historically been involved in and supportive of overseas or "foreign" missions, we must also be sensitive to the fact that cults are expanding their influence worldwide. The cults are *coming*, but equally important is the reality that *the cults are going*. Are we prepared for the inevitable spiritual and human casualties that such movements leave in their wake?

RONALD ENROTH

Bibliography. R. Abanes, *Cults, New Religious Movements, and Your Family: A Guide to Ten Non-Christian Groups Out to Convert Your Loved Ones;* R. Enroth, ed., *A Guide to Cults & New Religions;* R. Rhodes, *Reasoning From the Scriptures With the Mormons;* idem, *Reasoning From the Scriptures With the Jehovah's Witnesses;* idem, *The Heart of Christianity;* M. T. Singer, *Cults in Our Midst.*

Cultural Anthropology. *See* ANTHROPOLOGY.

Cultural Conversion. Conversion of a people from one culture to another. It is contrasted by Charles Kraft with "Christian conversion," defined as the biblically advocated yet culturally appropriate conversion of persons from their old allegiance to an allegiance to Christ.

Most of the early advocates of Christianity understandably felt that true Christianity could only be properly expressed in the cultural forms in which they had received it. They, therefore, sought to convert Gentiles both to Christ and to Jewish culture. But God insisted on granting the Holy Spirit even to Gentiles on the basis of faith alone without the necessity of converting to Jewish culture. In agreeing with God's approach, the early church strongly asserted in Acts 15 that Christian witnesses were not to require Gentiles to convert to Jewish culture in order to be acceptable to God. They thus established the principle of faith-only in place of the faith-plus-culture requirement for conversion.

The church has, however, gone back on that agreement constantly throughout history when taking the gospel to other societies. Both Roman Catholics and Protestants have been guilty of requiring conversion to the specific cultural forms of their home denomination in order to be truly Christian. Sometimes missionaries have even resorted to providing food, money, or political favors to win converts to their way of doing things.

Such tactics led to the label "rice Christians" for those who converted merely for what they could gain culturally.

The missionary cry of the late nineteenth century, "civilize in order to evangelize," was one of the more blatant calls to cultural conversion, making as it did at least a partial conversion to Western culture a requirement for entrance into Christianity. The assumption that people had to become Westerners culturally in order to be truly Christian provided the motivation for approaches to mission in non-Western societies that emphasized the setting up of Western-style schools, churches, and other institutions.

The CONTEXTUALIZATION movement, as advocated by evangelicals (in contrast to a liberal approach), is an attempt to rectify this cultural and theological fallacy. Its aim is to enable the people of each society to experience a genuine and growing relationship with Jesus Christ in a biblically sound yet culturally understandable and appropriate manner.

CHARLES H. KRAFT

Bibliography. C. H. Kraft, *PA* 10 (1963): 179–87; idem, *Christianity in Culture.*

The Cultural Mandate. The expression "cultural mandate" refers to God's command to Adam and Eve to "rule over" creation (Gen. 1:28), meaning to share with God in the management of all that he had made. This mandate was issued before the Fall occurred (Gen. 3), and obviously it predates the missionary mandate (the GREAT COMMISSION; Matt. 28:18–20). The cultural mandate remains in force and its implications for Christian mission are important.

The cultural mandate has several parts. The first is the command to "be fruitful, increase in number, and fill the earth" (Gen. 1:28). This is the basic command to build community with the building blocks of marriage and family (Gen. 2:24). Here lies the foundation of human society.

The second part has to do with the naming of the animals (Gen. 2:19–20), where Adam's mental and aesthetic gifts along with his decision-making capacity were called into action. Implied in the command to name the animals is humankind's responsibility to study the universe, unlock its secrets, use judiciously its potential, and glorify God for the beauty and variety of creation.

The third part of the cultural mandate appears in Genesis 2:15, where Adam and Eve are placed in a bountiful garden and told to "work it and take care of it." Properly tended, the garden would provide amply for their physical needs and those of their descendants. Implied in this command is our responsibility for the natural environment, the air, soil, water, plants, and minerals, which must be diligently cared for and never exploited or misused.

Fourth, the cultural mandate includes the elements of reflection and celebration. This is implied by the fact that when he had finished creating, God evaluated what he had made, declared it to be "good" (Gen. 1:31), and set aside a day to celebrate and enjoy the fruit of his work (Gen. 2:1). So important to God was this element of rest, reflection, and celebration that he explicitly set aside one day in seven in the Ten Commandments given to Israel (Exod. 20:8).

The FALL OF HUMANKIND occurred (Gen. 3), and since that time members of the human race individually and collectively have transgressed the cultural mandate in every imaginable way. Yet its basic precepts remain intact, and the consequences of disregarding them are visible everywhere. To a bewildered and suffering world Christian mission points back to Genesis, to our first parents' rebellion and to the transgression of God's original mandate, to explain the source of the evils that now plague humanity.

There is still more to the cultural mandate so far as mission is concerned. Serious reflection on the cultural mandate enlarges the Christian message so that it addresses everything that God made, sin corrupted, and Christ makes new. It propels Christian activity into every area of human life and every corner of the world to combat evil and falsehood and promote mercy, righteousness, and truth.

The cultural mandate calls for an approach to education that begins with the presupposition that the world belongs to God and he has mandated how humans should relate to one another and treat his whole creation. Reflection on the cultural mandate leads Christians to see that their responsibilities before God are not limited to activities in the institutional church, nor to personal and private spirituality. They include all the arenas of life, the social, economic, political and scientific. In each of these arenas they honor God as they promote truth and mercy and apply scriptural principles to the affairs of life.

Tension has sometimes developed between those who stress the cultural mandate with its broad implications for Christian involvement and those who stress the missionary mandate (Matt. 28:18–20) that emphasizes preaching, making disciples, and establishing churches. The following clarifications and distinctions need to be made.

First, in a fallen world, people need to hear the gospel of Jesus Christ more than they need anything else. Therefore the missionary mandate takes precedence over the cultural mandate. But this does not mean that the missionary mandate replaces or swallows up the cultural mandate. Christians are obliged to obey both mandates, though in the order of missionary activity the proclamation of the gospel to the unsaved is primary.

Second, the witness of Christian lives in which Christ is honored as Lord over all affairs is highly important for the advance of the gospel. Likewise, deeds of mercy to the suffering and needy bear eloquent testimony to God's mercy in Christ. But our best works are flawed by imperfections and can never substitute for the word-proclamation of the gospel of God's grace in Christ. The Christian life may give "flesh" to the word, but the Word is always necessary because it points beyond human imperfections to the perfect Savior Jesus Christ.

Third, churches as institutions ought to focus on the task of proclaiming the gospel and discipling believers. Church members, acting in conjunction with the broader Christian community, should be taught and encouraged to apply the teachings of the gospel to social, cultural, and political issues. Even when the Christian community as a whole is derelict in its cultural obligations, it is unwise and inappropriate for organized churches to plunge into matters that are not their primary responsibility, because the specific task of churches is defined by the missionary mandate rather than the cultural mandate.

Christian day schools and colleges play a vital role in educating succeeding generations of children and youth to enter life with a conscious recognition of their calling to be salt and light in all spheres of life (Matt. 5:12–16). Christian education's primary responsibility lies in the area of the cultural mandate. Nevertheless, Christian education takes place in the New Testament age which is dominated by the missionary mandate. For that reason, Christian teachers should impress upon students the missionary claims of the gospel and the urgency of world evangelization.

ROGER S. GREENWAY

See also Evangelism and Social Responsibility.

Bibliography. J. H. Bavinck, *An Introduction to the Science of Missions;* J. Bolt, *Christian and Reformed Today;* D. Bosch, *Transforming Mission: Paradigm Shifts in Theology of Mission;* N. Carr, *The Origins and Purpose of Life: Genesis 1–11;* D. J. Hesselgrave, *Communicating the Gospel Cross-Culturally.*

Culture. The word "culture" may point to many things—the habits of the social elite; disciplined tastes expressed in the arts, literature, and entertainment; particular stages of historical and human development. We use the term "culture" to refer to the common ideas, feelings, and values that guide community and personal behavior, that organize and regulate what the group thinks, feels, and does about God, the world, and humanity. It explains why the Sawi people of Irian Jaya regard betrayal as a virtue, while the American sees it as a vice. It undergirds the Korean horror at the idea of Westerners' placing their elderly parents in retirement homes, and Western horror at the idea of the Korean veneration of their ancestors. It is the climate of opinion that encourages an Eskimo to share his wife with a guest and hides the wife of an Iranian fundamentalist Muslim in a body-length veil. The closest New Testament approximation for culture is *kosmos* (world), but only when it refers to language-bound, organized human life (1 Cor. 14:10) or the sin-contaminated system of values, traditions, and social structures of which we are a part (John 17:11).

Cultures are patterns shared by, and acquired in, a social group. Large enough to contain subcultures within itself, a culture is shared by the society, the particular aggregate of persons who participate in it. In that social group we learn and live out our values.

The social and kinship connections that shape a group of people vary from culture to culture. Americans in general promote strong individualism and nuclear families, usually limited tightly to grandparents, parents, and children. Individual initiative and decision making are encouraged by the belief in individual progress. By comparison, Asians and Africans as a rule define personal identity in terms of the family, clan, or kinship group. Families are extended units with wide connections. And decision making is a social, multipersonal choice reflecting those connections: "We think, therefore I am."

Cultures are not haphazard collections of isolated themes. They are integrated, holistic patterns structured around the meeting of basic human needs. Their all-embracing nature, in fact, is the assumption behind the divine calling to humankind to image God's creative work by taking up our own creative cultural work in the world (Gen. 1:28–30; *see* CULTURAL MANDATE). Eating and drinking and whatever cultural activities we engage in (1 Cor. 10:31)—all show the mark of interrelationship as God's property and ours (1 Cor. 3:21b–23). Thus the Dogon people of central Mali build their homes, cultivate their land, and plan their villages in the shape of an oval egg. This represents their creation myth of the great placenta from which emerged all space, all living beings, and everything in the world.

Among the ancient Chinese the cosmic pattern of balance and harmony, the yin and the yang, was to be re-created again and again in daily decisions. The yin was negative, passive, weak, and destructive. The yang was positive, active, strong, and constructive. Individuality came from these opposites. The yin was female, mother, soft, dark; the yang was male, father, hard, bright. The decisions where to live and where to be buried were made by choosing a site in harmony with these opposites.

The anthropological theory of functionalism underlined this holism; subsequent studies, however, have introduced modifications. Functionalism tended to assume that cultures were fully integrated and coherent bounded sets. Later scholarship, wary of the static coloring, admits that this is only more or less so. Cultures are neither aggregates of accumulated traits nor seamless garments. There is a dynamic to human cultures that makes full integration incomplete; gaps and inconsistencies provide opportunities for change and modification, some rapid and some slow.

The Dimensions of Culture. All cultures shape their models of reality around three dimensions: the cognitive (What do we know?); the affective (What do we feel?); the evaluative (Where are our values and allegiances?). The cognitive dimension varies from culture to culture. Take, for example, the view of time. In the West time is a linear unity of past, present, and infinite future; in Africa time is basically a two-dimensional phenomenon, with a long past, a present, and an immediate future. Similarly, cultures differ in their conceptions of space, that is what they consider to be public, social, personal, and intimate zones. For an American, the personal zone extends from one foot to three feet away, the intimate zone from physical contact to a foot away. For Latin Americans the zones are smaller. Thus when an Anglo engages a Latino in casual conversation, the Latino perceives the Anglo as distant and cold. Why? What for the Anglo is the social zone is for the Latino the public zone.

Affective and evaluative dimensions also differ from culture to culture. Beauty in the eye of a Japanese beholder is a garden of flowers and empty space carefully planned and arranged to heighten the deliberative experience. To the Westerner a garden's beauty is found in floral profusion and variety.

Whom can we marry? In the West that is an individual decision; in clan-oriented societies the kinship group or the family decides. Among the Dogon a man's wife should be chosen from among the daughters of a maternal uncle; the girl becomes a symbolic substitute for her husband's mother, a reenactment of mythical incest found in the Dogon account of the creation of the universe. Among the kings of Hawaii and the pharaohs of Egypt, brother-sister marriage was practiced to preserve lineal purity and family inheritance.

The Levels of Cultures. Cultures are also multilayered models of reality. Like a spiral, they move from the surface level of what we call customs through the cognitive, affective, and evaluative dimensions to the deep level of WORLDVIEW. To illustrate, the Confucian ethic of moral etiquette consists largely in making sure that relationships properly reflect the hierarchical scale. In China and Korea, where cultural backgrounds are shaped deeply by the Confucian ethic, the idea of *Li* (righteousness) makes specific demands at different cultural levels: different forms of speech in addressing people on different levels of the social scale; ritual practices; rules of propriety; observance of sharply defined understandings of the relationships of king to subject, older brother to younger brother, husband to wife, father to son. And linking all these together is the religious perception of their specific places, in the *Tao* (the Way, the rule of heaven).

In this process, cultural forms (e.g., language, gestures, relationships, money, clothing) are invested with symbolic meanings conventionally accepted by the community. They interpret the forms and stamp them with meaning and value (*see* SYMBOL, SYMBOLISM). Each cultural form, ambivalent by itself, thus becomes a hermeneutical carrier of values, attitudes, and connotations. Clothing can indicate social status, occupation, level of education, ritual participation. Foot washing in ancient Hebrew culture became an expression of hospitality (Luke 7:44). In Christian ritual it became a symbol of humble service (John 13:4–5).

This symbolic arbitrariness can either help or hinder communication between persons and groups. Jesus' reproof of hypocrites as a generation of vipers (Luke 3:7) would be a great compliment to the Balinese, who regard the viper as a sacred animal of paradise. On the other hand, his rebuke of the cunning Herod as that fox (Luke 13:32) would make good sense to the same Balinese, in whose fables the jackal plays a treacherous part. The Korean concept of *Li* (righteousness) can be a point of contact with the Bible, but also a point of confusion, as the Confucian focus on works confronts the Pauline focus on grace.

At the core of all cultures is the deep level where worldviews, the prescientific factories and bank vaults of presuppositions, are generated and stored. Here the human heart (Prov. 4:23; Jer. 29:13; Matt. 12:34), the place where our most basic commitments exist, responds to those divine constants or universals that are reshaped by every culture (Rom. 2:14–15). Twisted by the impact of sin and shaped by time and history, those internalizations produce cultures that both obey and pervert God's demands (Rom. 1:18–27). In some cultures, for example, murder is condemned, but becomes an act of bravery when the person killed belongs to a different social group. Other peoples view theft as wrong, but only when it involves the stealing of public property. Thus Native Americans, who see the land as a common possession of all, as the mother of all life, view the white intruders with their assumption of private ownership as thieves. When the Masai of Africa steal cattle, they do not regard the act as theft, for they see all cattle as their natural possession by way of gift from God.

Besides reflecting and reshaping God's demands, cultures are also the means of God's common grace. Through his providential control God uses the shaping of human cultures to check the rampant violence of evil and preserve human continuity. They provide guidelines to restrain our worst impulses, sanctions of SHAME or GUILT to keep us in line. Cultures and worldviews, then, are not simply neutral road maps. Created by those who bear the IMAGE OF GOD (Gen. 1:27–28), they display, to greater or lesser degree, both the wisdom of God and the flaws of sin.

RELIGION, given this understanding, cannot be, as functionalism argues, simply one of many human needs demanding satisfaction. As the human response to the revelation of God, it permeates the whole of life. It is the core in the structuring of culture, the integrating and radical response of humanity to the revelation of God. Life is religion.

In the building of culture, worldview or religion is the central controlling factor: (1) it explains how and why things came to be as they are, and how and why they continue or change; (2) it validates the basic institutions, values, and goals of a society; (3) it provides psychological reinforcement for the group; (4) it integrates the society, systematizing and ordering the culture's perceptions of reality into an overall design; (5) it provides, within its conservatism, opportunities for perceptual shifts and alterations in conceptual structuring. This fifth characteristic of worldview, that is, susceptibility to change, opens the door for the transforming leaven of the gospel. The coming of Christ as both Savior and judge takes every thought captive (2 Cor. 10:5). When that divine work is initiated, people, under the impulse of the Spirit, begin to change their worldview and, as a result, their culture.

In the language of CULTURAL ANTHROPOLOGY, the change wrought by the gospel is a threefold process: reevaluation (a change of allegiance), reinterpretation (a change of evaluative principles), and rehabituation (a series of changes in behavior). With regard to the change in the individual, the Bible speaks of repentance (Luke 5:32) and conversion (Acts 26:20). With regard to the wider social world, it speaks of the new creation (2 Cor. 5:17); the age to come, which has already begun in this present age (Eph. 1:21); and the eschatological renewal of all things (Matt. 19:28), the beginnings of which we taste now in changed behavior (Titus 3:5).

Peripheral changes run the risk of encouraging CULTURAL CONVERSION rather than conversion to Christ. The goal of missions must be larger, to bring our cultures into conformity with the KINGDOM OF GOD and its fullness. The whole of cultural life ought to be subjected to the royal authority of him who has redeemed us by his blood (Matt. 28:18–20).

HARVIE M. CONN

SEE ALSO Gospel and Culture.

Bibliography. E. Hall, *Silent Language;* P. Hiebert, *Anthropological Insights for Missionaries;* C. Kraft, *Christianity in Culture;* S. Lingenfelter, *Transforming Culture: A Challenge for Christian Mission;* J. Loewen, *Culture and Human Values;* L. Luzbetak, *The Church and Cultures: New Perspectives in Missiological Anthropology;* E. Nida, *Customs, Culture, and Christianity;* B. Ray, *African Religions: Symbol, Ritual, and Community;* J. Stott and R. Coote, eds., *Down to Earth: Studies in Christianity and Culture.*

Cultural Learning. The intercultural worker who desires to become competent in the culture of ministry must commit to intentional activities and to a lifestyle that results in cultural learning (*see also* INTERCULTURAL COMPETENCY). The best time to engage in intentional cultural learning is during the first two years of ministry (*see* BONDING). If the intercultural worker establishes good habits of intentional learning, those habits will carry on throughout the life of one's ministry and make a person much more effective. This brief essay highlights seven significant steps in the cultural learning process. Each can be accomplished within the first two years of living and working interculturally.

Language Learning. (*See* SECOND LANGUAGE ACQUISITION.) Language learning is essential to the whole cultural learning process. Individuals who choose to minister interculturally and do not learn language will always be excluded from a deep understanding of the local culture. While some cultural practices can be picked up through observation of behaviors, the meaning of those practices can only be understood through the language of the local people. In many social settings in the world people speak more than one language. Intercultural workers may be tempted to learn a national language and then presume that this is enough to work among a local people. While the national language is important, the deeper understanding of a local culture requires learning the local language as well. The best way to learn a local language is to employ a local language speaker who has some training in teaching that language and who is willing to teach on an intensive daily basis for a period of at least six months. If such a person is not available, then Brewster and Brewster (1976) have provided a handbook of activities that the learner can use to pick up the local language. While some people find this method very helpful and easy to use, others find it quite difficult. Whatever method you choose, learning the local language is central to deeper cultural understanding.

Economic Relations. Since all intercultural ministry involves working with people, understanding the organization of labor, cultural conceptions of property, and social expectations for payment, borrowing, and exchange is essential to effective ministry activities. These activities are best learned by participant observation in the daily economic activities of people, and by interviewing the people, seeking their explanation of how and why they do what they do. Participant observation can be done while learning language. Inquiry into economic activities, which are daily and ordinary, provides opportunity for developing one's vocabulary and deepening one's understanding of the daily life of people. Lingenfelter (1996, 43–96) provides a series of research questions that are useful in the collection of data on property, labor, and exchange, and in the analysis and comparison of those data with one's home culture.

Social Relations. Every community structures its social relations in accord with principles of kinship, marriage, interest, and other kinds of associations (*see* ASSOCIATION, SOCIOANTHROPOLOGY OF). Understanding the nature of authority in family and community is crucial to framing ministry activities and working in effective relationships with leaders in the community. Several anthropological tools are very helpful in understanding the structure of social relations. Making maps and doing a census of a particular section of the community will help one learn who is who in a community and how they are connected (or not) to one another. Doing genealogies of selected members in the community provides a conceptual map of how people think about their relationships with reference to kinship ties. The map and the census become extremely useful to intercultural workers because it provides for them names and locations of people with whom they are certain to interact during the ministry. Lingenfelter (1996, 97–143) provides questions on family and community authority that help the researcher understand the structure of authority relationships and compare them with one's home culture and commitments.

Childrearing. At first glance intercultural workers might wonder if observing childrearing practices has any relationship to intercultural ministry. What they fail to realize is that the children are the most precious resource in any community, and that the parents of children invest much time and effort in transmitting their cultural values and coaching the next generation to become mature and effective adults in the community. Childrearing practices provide direct insight into the deeper values and commitments that are crucial for acceptance and effectiveness in the wider society. It is helpful for the intercultural worker to have intimate relationships with two or three families with children in which they may observe and with whom they may dialogue about the process of raising children. Because children have unique and distinctive personalities, the childrearing process also helps the intercultural worker learn how people in the culture deal with distinctive personalities. This can be most useful when one engages these distinctive personalities as adults. Recording case studies of how parents deal with a particular child over a period of time can be a very useful form of observation and learning. Interviewing the parents about their intentions in the process can illuminate further cultural values and understanding. Spradley (1979) provides very helpful insights on structuring interviews, and collecting and analyzing interview data.

Conflict and Conflict Resolution. The careful study of CONFLICT is one of the most fruitful areas for research on a culture. In situations of conflict people engage in heated exchanges that focus around issues that are of extreme importance to them. An effective cultural learning program includes the careful recording of case studies of conflict, and the interviewing of participants in the conflict to understand what people are feeling, what they value, why they are contesting with each other, and what their hopes are with regard to resolution. In addition, careful analysis of the social processes that people employ for the resolving of conflict is very important. Inevitably each intercultural worker will experience interpersonal conflict with national co-workers. Understanding local processes for conflict resolution will enable that person to proceed with wisdom and with support in the local cultural setting (*see* Lingenfelter, 1996, 144–68, and Elmer).

Ideas and Worldview. Because Christian intercultural workers are interested in sharing the gospel with other peoples, they must seek to understand the ideas and WORLDVIEW of the people with whom they work. These ideas are best understood by careful research in the language, by recording and studying the stories, and by observing and understanding the significant life cycle rituals of the local community. Research on funerals is probably one of the most profitable activities that the intercultural worker can do for an understanding of the ideas and deeper values of the local culture (*see also* DEATH RITES). Funerals engage the widest circle of family and friends of any particular individual. At these events people discuss issues of life and death, and act together on the beliefs that they hold with regard to the causes of death and the transition from life to after life. Other life cycle activities such as marriage, naming, and birth of children provide similar fruitful insights into the belief system of a culture (*see* Lingenfelter, 1996, 165–205, and Elmer 1993).

Application for Ministry. Cultural learning for its own sake is interesting and helpful, but for the intercultural worker it is important to practice the discipline of application. Each of the areas outlined above provides very useful information that the intercultural worker may apply to build more effective ministries. However, application must be learned and practiced. The application of cultural learning to ministry typically works through analogy. One finds a particular structure of authority and organization in a community, and thinks about the analogy of that structure to a growing body of believers. One observes patterns of learning among children and draws analogies to learning among adults who are involved in community development or other ministry programs. Learning to think analogically about cultural learning and ministry is crucial for ministry effectiveness. Paul Hiebert and Eloise Meneses (1995) provide very helpful guidelines for application in the ministries of church planting. Marvin Mayers (1987) provides valuable insight into the application of cultural learning for interpersonal relationships and other kinds of intercultural relationships.

SHERWOOD LINGENFELTER

SEE ALSO Extent of Missionary Adjustment.

Bibliography. E. T. Brewster and E. Brewster, *Language Acquisition Made Practical;* D. Elmer, *Cross-Cultural Conflict;* P. G. Hiebert and E. H. Meneses, *Incarnational Ministry: Planning Churches in Band, Tribal, Peasant, and Urban Societies;* S. G. Lingenfelter, *Agents of Transformation: A Guide for Effective Cross-Cultural Ministry;* M. K. Mayers, *Christianity Confronts Culture;* J. P. Spradley, *The Ethnographic Interview.*

Culture Shock. The concept of culture shock was brought into prominence in missionary circles by the reprinting in the journal *Practical Anthropology* of Kalervo Oberg's pioneering articles entitled, "Cultural Shock: Adjustment to New Cultural Environments." In this article the condition is described as the result of "losing all our familiar signs and symbols of social intercourse" as we interact in a foreign cultural environment. Culture shock is the condition, experienced by nearly everyone at the start of life in a different culture, in which one feels off balance, unable to predict what people's reactions will be when one does or says something. It is a real psychological response to very real perceptions and must be taken seriously.

Though the condition can be serious to the extent of debilitation, it is an overstatement to label it "shock" (in the medical sense), as if every case were crippling. Many prefer the term "culture stress" with the recognition that serious cases can approach a condition similar to that labeled shock by the medical profession. The good news is that most people can survive long enough in another society to overcome at least the worst features of culture stress if they are determined enough and work hard at adapting to the new cultural world they have entered.

Four major stages have been identified as reactions to culture stress in the adjustment process. The first of these may be labeled the honeymoon or "I love everything about these people" stage. This period may last from a few weeks to several months if the person stays in the foreign environment. This is a good time to commit oneself to a rigorous program of language and culture learning, before the realities of the new situation thrust one into the next stage. Unfortunately, many return home before this period is over and write and speak very positively about an experience that was quite superficial.

If they stay, they are likely to enter the second stage which can last from months to years. This is the period in which the differences and the insecurities of living in an unpredictable environment get on their nerves, sometimes in a big way. For some this is an "I hate everything" stage. People in this second stage of culture stress are often overly concerned about cleanliness, food, and contact with those around them. They often have feelings of helplessness and loss of control, may become absent-minded, and frequently develop fears of being cheated, robbed, or injured. Not infrequently physical and spiritual problems can accompany these psychological difficulties and the cross-cultural worker's life becomes very difficult.

As Oberg points out, "this second stage of culture shock is in a sense a crisis in the disease. If you overcome it, you stay; if not, you leave before you reach the stage of a nervous breakdown." Or, as many have done, you stay but spend all your time with your kind of people, effectively insulating yourself against the people that surround you and their culture. Unfortunately, many mission compounds and institutions have provided just such a refuge for missionaries who never got beyond this stage of culture stress. To survive this stage you need to feed your determination, force yourself to be outgoing, in spite of many embarrassing situations, and plug away at your language and culture learning even though nothing seems to be coming together.

Those who survive the second stage begin to "level off," accepting that things are going to be different and difficult to predict while they are beginning to be able to function in the language and culture. They develop an ability to laugh at themselves and to endure the frequent embarrassing situations in which they don't understand what is going on. They begin to recognize that the people they are living among and their way of life are neither totally good nor totally bad but, like their own people and their way of life, some of each. By this time a person has attained enough facility in the language to function reasonable well in several situations so that sometimes, at least, things look hopeful.

Even with this improvement in attitude, however, discouragement may take over and lead to a kind of truce with the cross-cultural situation that issues in a "plateauing" or holding pattern rather than continuing growth and adaptation. Many stop at this point, having learned to function reasonably in most social situations, especially those they can control, and having learned to assert and maintain control regularly.

With developing facility in the language and culture, however, and an increasing sense of belonging, one may move to the fourth or "adjusted" stage. Though many of the problems of the third stage may remain, the determination to succeed and to master the language and culture coupled with encouraging success enable one to keep growing without giving in to discouragement. The key is to continue learning and growing, accepting the fact that you are attempting to learn in a few years a whole way of life that has taken the insiders many years to learn. Curiosity, a learning attitude, enjoyment of the process, and just plain determination are your best allies as you give yourself to the task.

Some (e.g., Dodd, 1995, 213–16) have seen the whole spread of reactions observed among humans under stress in the way different people go about the process of adapting to a new culture. Especially in stage two, they note that some dissolve in fright and never get over it. Others react by flight and return home. Still others develop one or another filter approach by moving into the escapism posture in which they resort to unhealthy attitudes such as denying differences, living in exaggerated memories of their home culture or going native. Others are determined to fight and may do this constructively, conquering the obstacles, or destructively by developing a negative, belligerent attitude toward the new culture. Those with constructive, fighting determination, however, learn to flex by accepting, learning and growing into effective functionaries in the new cultural world. These are the ones who succeed.

CHARLES H. KRAFT

SEE ALSO Adjustment to the Field.

Bibliography. C. H. Dodd, *Dynamics of Intercultural Communication;* A. Furnham and W. J. Lonner, *Culture Shock;* K. Oberg, *PA* 7 (1960): 177–82.

Curse, Curses. A curse is an utterance in which a person calls on supernatural power to bring harm to the one cursed. Curses are the opposite of blessings, usually making use of satanic power rather than, as with blessings, employing the power of God. Though words are usually used, the power is not in the words but flows from the supernatural being who empowers them.

The Bible takes curses and cursing seriously, assuming that people have the authority to invoke supernatural power in this way. The words are used about 200 times in the Scriptures. The term *anathema* (1 Cor. 16:22), often seen as a powerful curse in Scripture, is instead a formula of excommunication with which a person is turned over to God for punishment.

The authority Christians have to curse is neither to be taken lightly (James 3:8–10) nor to be abused. Indeed, both Jesus (Luke 6:28) and Paul (Rom. 12:14) admonish us to bless rather than to curse those who hurt us. The Jews who participated in the crucifixion called down on themselves a very powerful curse when they said, "Let the punishment for His death fall on us and our children!" (Matt. 27:25 GNB).

Cursing seems to be very much alive today. Missionaries from various parts of the world report situations in which parcels of land, buildings, artifacts, and missionaries themselves and/or their family members have had negative words directed at them that were followed by strange occurrences. Several instances have been reported of illness or other misfortune affecting everyone who lived in mission homes built on land the people consider cursed. In many cases, the situation has been alleviated through claiming the authority of Christ to break the apparent curses. In addition, those involved in praying with people for inner healing report great change when certain negative emotional and spiritual symptoms are dealt with by claiming the authority of Christ to break curses.

CHARLES H. KRAFT

See also Spiritual Warfare.

Bibliography. H. Aust and D. Müller, *NIDNTT* I:413–15; W. Mundle, *NIDNTT,* I:415–17; C. H. Kraft, *Defeating Dark Angels.*

Customs. *See* CULTURE.

Cyprus *(Est. 2000 pop.: 777,000; 9,251 sq. km. [3,572 sq. mi.]).* No modern nation outside Israel holds a more ancient claim to the presence of its sons and daughters among the early Christians than does the little island of Cyprus in the northeastern Mediterranean. It was a Levite from Cyprus named Joseph, but better known as Barnabas, who distinguished himself in the earliest Christian community by selling a field and placing the proceeds at the feet of the apostles (Acts 4:36).

It was this same Barnabas who was sent by the Jerusalem apostles to nurture the new Gentile outreach at Antioch (Acts 11:22) and who promptly brought Saul from Tarsus to help him. It was no accident that later when Barnabas, Saul, and John Mark set off on their first apostolic mission from Antioch, they went first to Salamis in Cyprus (Acts 13:5), probably Barnabas's home community. It is recorded that they traveled "through the whole island" (Acts 13:6), no doubt preaching everywhere they went.

Later, Barnabas took John Mark on a second journey back to Cyprus (Acts 15:39). Though no additional information is given, it seems logical to assume that on this occasion Barnabas and John Mark simply continued the work begun during the first visit of Barnabas and Paul to Cyprus. It is possible that Barnabas spent the rest of his life there. The traditional site of his tomb is still marked by a small Greek Orthodox church near the ruins of Salamis in the vicinity of Famagusta, a small Turkish town in eastern Cyprus. The modern Christian community of Cyprus quite naturally still looks back to Barnabas and Saul as its founders.

The culture of modern Cyprus was shaped by its Byzantine Christianity, conspicuously represented by the churches and monasteries dotting its picturesque mountains and plains. Though Cyprus was incorporated into the Muslim Ottoman Empire, its strong Christian community continued to dominate the local life of the island, and its British colonization in the dying years of the Ottoman Empire assured that it was not merged into the new Turkish nation-state after World War I.

As a result of its Ottoman period, however, there remained a conglomerate of majority Greek and minority Turkish villages scattered across the island landscape during the British colonial period, extending up until the early 1960s. Then as the British gave Cyprus its sovereignty as a tiny nation-state, they attempted to create a Constitution that would honor the citizenship of both Greeks and Turks with their vastly different cultures and histories, one Byzantine Christian and the other Muslim.

This attempted political solution lasted for only a decade. In 1974, amid increasing tensions between Greek and Turkish villages, the Turkish army invaded Cyprus and stimulated a population exchange that placed the vast majority of the Cypriot Turkish population in the northern third of the island while the Cypriot Greek population was now placed in the southern two-thirds. In the years following, a United Nations peace-keeping force patrolled the "green line" between the Turkish north and the Greek south, with no commerce or communication between the two. This military "solution" was undertaken against strong protests by the international community, but the Turkish army has made, and kept, its point.

In the tiny northern state called the Turkish Republic of northern Cyprus, Cypriot Turks maintain a universal, though largely secular, Islamic culture. More recent immigrants from Turkey, bolstered by Arab Muslim oil wealth, are helping reintroduce a more orthodox strain of Islam. Stimulated by evangelical Christian tentmakers, a small group or two of Cypriot Turkish believers struggle to take hold, and British remnants of their colonial period still meet to worship as Anglicans in the coastal town of Kyrenia.

In the Greek south, where the northern Turkish nation-state is not recognized, the nation of Cyprus continues its uneasy existence. Dozens of evangelical Christian "off-shore companies" focusing on mission to the Muslim world have made southern Cyprus their headquarters. Here they are tolerated as long as they do not challenge the dominant Greek orthodox culture of southern Cyprus itself. Very small groups of evangelical Cypriot Greek Christians, however, do exist.

RICHARD SHOWALTER

Cyril (826 or 827–869). Greek missionary to the Slavic people. Christened Constantine, he was born in Thessalonica (Saloniki), the youngest child of a Byzantine official. When he was fourteen Constantine went to Constantinople to study. He excelled and soon was teaching philosophy at the university. After 855, he retired to live and study at the Mount Olympus monastery (where his brother METHODIUS was a monk). Because of his fame as a teacher, he and his brother were made part of delegation sent in 860 to present Christianity to the Khazar people. They met with little lasting success. The Slavic ruler, Rastislav, asked the patriarch of Constantinople for Greek priests in 862. Constantine and Methodius were selected. In preparation, the brothers translated the Gospels and prepared a liturgy. In 863 they traveled to Rastislav's court and began preaching and started a seminary for Slavic priests. Opposition developed from the Frankish missionaries, and in 868, they went to Rome to defend their work. Pope Hadrian II approved their liturgy and had Methodius and three of the Slavic priests ordained. The pope also intended to consecrate Constantine as archbishop of Moravia. However, Constantine died in Rome on February 14, 869, after becoming a monk and taking the name of Cyril. The ministry of Cyril and Methodius is traditionally regarded as the major means by which the gospel was brought to the Slavic people.

ROBERT SHUSTER

Bibliography. F. Dvornik, *Byzantine Missions Among the Slavs: SS. Constantine-Cyril and Methodius.*

The Czech Republic and Slovakia *(Combined est. 2000 pop.: 15,814,000; 127,899 sq. km. [49,382 sq. mi.]).* The modern state of Czechoslovakia was created in 1918 out of the dismembered and defeated Austro-Hungarian Empire. Protestant churches, and the pre-Reformation Hussite movement with its development in the *Unitas Fratrum,* were always under pressure or at times outright persecution at the hands of the favored Roman Catholic Church. The *Unitas Fratrum* had both an ecumenical as well as a missionary vision, especially with leaders such as Jan Amos Comenius (1592–1620), although external circumstances never made practical implementation of the vision possible. The Renewed Moravian Church, comprising refugees from Moravia who were given sanctuary in Herrnhut by the German nobleman NICHOLAS VON ZINZENDORF, were the trailblazers of the modern Protestant missionary movement (*see also* MORAVIAN MISSIONS). They sent out hundreds of missionaries all over the world, beginning in 1732. The Protestants who remained in the Habsburg domains concentrated on survival rather than foreign mission. In 1918 the Czech and Slovak peoples achieved their independence, which sadly lasted for only twenty years. Even after the Second World War, they soon became part of the Soviet bloc and only achieved true national independence in 1989 with the "Velvet Revolution." Some missionary interest and awareness were sustained over the years of foreign domination (a number of courageous Czech pastors smuggled Bibles and Christian literature into the Soviet Union even in the dark days of communist domination), but it is only in the past ten years that there has been any real possibility of Czech and Slovak Christians being involved in cross-cultural missionary activity. This is now taking place as individuals are feeling the call of God. A few students from the Evangelical Seminary in Prague are already serving in Asia. With encouragement, the trickle could develop into a flood.

RONALD DAVIES

Czech Republic. *See* CZECH REPUBLIC AND SLOVAKIA.

Dd

Damnation. *See* JUDGMENT.

Danish Mission Boards and Societies. In 1706 the first missionaries from a Lutheran land arrived in the Tranquebar region of southeast India, sent out by what became known as the DANISH-HALLE MISSION. The Danish king, Frederick IV, had been especially eager to spread the faith by sponsoring this initiative. But in fact the first missionaries were Germans, as were most of the several dozen sent to India throughout the rest of the century. (However, the number of Danes, six or so, who went probably was the right proportion compared to the far more numerous German population.) A missionary college was founded in Denmark in 1714 to further this and other ventures. By the beginning of the nineteenth century, this early Danish-Halle thrust had been overwhelmed by a rationalistic spirit.

A new beginning occurred in 1821 with the founding of the Danish Missionary Society. It has always functioned as a voluntary society within the framework of the national Lutheran Church, to which almost all Danes nominally belong. Financial support is provided by contributions rather than through the taxes that have provided for buildings and clergy salaries. This society, like many of the other early ones around Europe, initially sent workers through the auspices of older ones, such as the BASEL MISSION, before sending missionaries on its own. Eventually the Danish society had up to seventy missionaries at a time in China. But by the 1960s there were only about eighty-five missionaries total, two-fifths each in Africa and India, the rest in Taiwan and Japan.

Meanwhile, many other societies emerged within the national Lutheran Church, eventually numbering sixteen or seventeen, mostly small and focusing on one or two fields. The only other one with more than a score of workers is a "Sudan" Mission, begun in 1911 for work in what is now Nigeria, and which reported sixty-six missionaries by 1970. Among the smaller Lutheran ones are the "Santal" dating from 1867 for work in India and a Lutheran Missionary Association begun in 1868 with work in Tanzania and Surinam.

In 1912 a national missionary council was formed, as in so many other countries in the wake of the 1910 Edinburgh WORLD MISSIONARY CONFERENCE. Initially it had twelve member societies, all Lutheran. Fifty years later the number of agencies had doubled and included four non-Lutheran ones.

As in the rest of Scandinavia, the Danish "free churches" are very small. The membership total for all of the congregations in each denomination is still only a few thousand. This has nevertheless not kept them from concern for foreign missions, and proportionately they send out far more than the societies within the national church. Their small size means that this yields only one or two dozen missionaries from each denomination. They differ from the main body also in that the denomination as a whole generally takes responsibility for the missions work. The Danish free church missions have mostly worked in Africa. One example are the Baptists who, beginning in 1928, served in the Central African countries of Rwanda and Burundi.

In the early 1970s there were about 330 Danish Protestants serving abroad with twenty-eight boards and societies in thirty countries, as well as a dozen or so Roman Catholic and Jehovah's Witness missionaries. Twenty years later the number of Protestant missionaries had risen to about 350, but mergers had reduced the agencies to eighteen.

DONALD TINDER

Danish-Halle Mission. King Frederick IV of Denmark, unsuccessful in finding Danish missionaries to work at the outpost at Tranquebar on the south coast of India, turned to the German Pietists at Halle under August H. Francke. In response, Francke sent BARTHOLOMAUS ZIEGENBALG and Henry Plütschau as the first missionaries to Tranquebar. They arrived as the first Protestant missionaries in India on July 9, 1706. Five principles characterized their work: (1) education and Christianity go together, as Christians must be able to read God's Word; (2) the Word must be available in the local language (Tamil) as quickly as possible; (3) preaching and teaching must be based on accurate insight into the WORLDVIEW of the local population; (4) the goal of the missionary work is personal conversion; and (5) an INDIGENOUS CHURCH must be started as quickly as possible.

The work at Tranquebar was a pioneer model of cooperation on an international and interconfessional scale in the missionary venture. The early missionaries came predominately from Germany, but also from Denmark and Sweden, with money and a printing press coming from England. The use of the printing press in missionary work was pioneered by Ziegenbalg at Tranquebar. After the first generation, the most famous of the Tranquebar missionaries was CHRISTIAN F. SCHWARTZ. Even though the work had all but collapsed by the turn of the nineteenth century, the mission methodology at Tranquebar set the stage for much of the missionary work in India and still remains a model of solid philosophy undergirding quality practice and cooperation.

A. SCOTT MOREAU

Bibliography. H. W. Gensichen and M. Bauer, *EMCM*, pp. 214–15; A. Lehman, *CDCWM*, pp. 159–60; S. C. Neill, *HCM*.

Das, Rajendra Chandra (1887–1976). Indian evangelist and indigenizer. Rajendra Chandra Das was born in East Bengal (now Bangladesh) in 1887. After nearly embracing the Brahmo Samaj he was baptized in Dacca in 1908. After higher education in Calcutta, he taught in Christian colleges for some years before becoming a full-time evangelist.

Das was a critic of Western methods of ministry among Hindus. From the time of his conversion he experimented with indigenous methods of worship and service. In 1930 he left Bengal to join the newly born Benares United City Mission (1929–46) in holy Benares (Varanasi) on the Ganges. This effort of seven Protestant mission societies remains the only concerted mission focus on orthodox Hindus in the history of Protestant missions. The mission never amounted to much more than Das himself. The Christian Society for the Study of Hinduism (1940–57) extended the mission's influence across India.

Changing attitudes toward the fundamental meaning of mission and evangelism, along with conservative reactions to Das's criticisms of traditional church and mission structures and programs undermined his influence and led to the closure of the mission and society.

H. L. RICHARD

Bibliography. R. C. Das, *How to Present Christ to a Hindu*; idem, *Convictions of an Indian Disciple*; H. L. Richard, ed., *R. C. Das: Evangelical Prophet for Contextual Christianity*.

DAWN. *See* DISCIPLING A WHOLE NATION.

de Nobili, Robert. *See* NOBILI, ROBERT DE.

Death. Humans, like animals, die. Unlike animals, humans know they will die. They confront ahead of time the disturbing fact of mortality. They may do this through actually witnessing the death of others, or simply through hearing stories of such. People anticipate their own death in imagination when they experience presages of death in illness, suffering, bodily aging and decay, or in the malevolent sentiments or explicit threats leveled against them by others.

People respond in diverse ways to consciousness of their mortality. Some embrace hedonism. "The most obvious way of reconciling oneself to death is to make sure of enjoying life before death snatches it from us" (Toynbee, 69). Paul acknowledges the logic of this response: "If death ends all, let us eat, drink, and be merry for tomorrow we die" (1 Cor. 15:32). Nonetheless the purposeless pursuit of pleasure is essentially escapist—repressing awareness of a problem that will not go away.

Others embrace pessimism and stress that life is so bad that death can be welcomed as a lesser evil. The Buddha, for example, stressed that "life and suffering were synonymous. Not death, but rebirth, is the arch-ordeal for a human being" (Toynbee, 71). The goal is to extinguish desire and thus extinguish the self in nirvana.

Others seek immortality by winning fame—by attempting to ensure that at least their memory will live on. Some pour themselves into their offspring, attempting somehow to live on in and through them. And of course many hold out some kind of hope in a future joyous afterlife. But ideas on this matter differ markedly and, from the human standpoint, epistemological obstacles to mapping such an afterlife seem insurmountable. While everyone crosses the river of death, the traffic is one-way.

Death presents a fundamental problem for humans—one might even say *the* fundamental problem. When Christian missionaries preach the gospel, it is a message of "good news" about that fundamental problem. This message is not the result of human speculations, or of humans reaching out with their might to penetrate the impenetrable. Rather God took the initiative in breaking into space-time history in the person of his Son, providing answers that we could not provide for ourselves. Because Jesus Christ crossed the river of death and returned to tell about it, we have a glorious gospel. We now know what caused death, wherein lies life, and what comes after death. Missionaries must never forget that their message, above all, is a message of resurrection life.

But missionaries must not only attend to their message. They must attend to the psychological, cultural, and religious responses to the awareness of death of the people to whom they minister. And this must inform the way in which they proclaim the gospel of resurrection life. The follower of the Buddha will take little comfort in a message which stresses eternal life as life which goes on and on and on. The hedonist and the pessimist cannot be approached in the same fashion.

Finally, since funerals (*see* DEATH RITES) invariably require rituals which affirm truths about life and death, missionaries must give attention to helping fledgling churches develop meaningful and appropriate Christian funeral liturgies.

In conclusion, it should be stressed that there has been remarkably little missiological writing and reflection on death, either in relation to communication of the gospel message or in relation to developing culturally and biblically appropriate Christian funerals. More is needed.

ROBERT J. PRIEST

Bibliography. A. Toynbee, *Man's Concern with Death.*

Death Rites. Death is not only a biological event that requires the disposal of a corpse, but also an occasion for questions about the meaning of life, social organization, and inheritance. All societies commemorate the event with ritual forms called RITES OF PASSAGE, symbolic acts that provide a bridge for the social transition from one status to another. Death rites provide not only the means of disposing of the corpse, but also channels for grief; they deal with questions about death and often with the social dislocation that has resulted.

Many traditional societies distinguish between a good death and a bad death. Dying at an old age with many children and grandchildren around is a good death. In contrast, dying violently, away from home, or unexpectedly as in childbirth is bad. A bad death raises questions of its cause and in some traditional societies requires interrogation of the deceased. Among the Diola of Senegal, for example, the corpse is tied to a bier supported by four men. People take turns asking the body questions; a movement of forward or backward indicates an affirmative or negative response. This custom provides an opportunity for confession, and sometimes punishment, which allows the deceased to depart.

Death rites must deal in an appropriate manner with biological decay. Burial in a wooden coffin is common to the north European people, while Muslims use a cotton shroud to wrap the body. Within Islam, proper disposal of the body is a matter of divine obligation, so many mosques are equipped with facilities to wash and prepare the body for burial. Decay may be retarded as by the mummification practiced by the ancient Egyptians. In marked contrast, decay may be accelerated as in the Indian tradition where the corpse is cremated and the skull broken to release the soul (Atman) to be reborn. In the ZOROASTRIAN tradition the corpse was considered utterly impure and could not be allowed to pollute the earth, water, or fire. Placed in a special enclosure called a tower of silence, the corpse was thus exposed to birds of prey.

In many societies the corpse is openly displayed, and people are expected to demonstrate their grief. Where wakes are the norm, the extended family and friends may stay with the relatives of the deceased for several nights. This contrasts with the practice of north Europe, where the body is quickly removed from sight and members of the family show only restrained emotions. Mourning is expressed in various ways, depending upon one's closeness to the deceased. Traditional Chinese culture has a complex system of mourning involving the extended family. In the West, public mourning has almost fallen into disuse except for the wearing of black at the ceremony.

Feasting is a common element based on the practical necessity that those who have come on a long journey to honor the dead need to be fed. The feast may be of such social importance that it is deferred for days or weeks after the actual disposal of the corpse. The elaborateness of the ritual often depends upon social status. The ceremony for a newborn baby may be slight, or there may be none at all, while for a respected leader there will be great ceremony. Sometimes food and artifacts are placed with the corpse for the journey to the next life. Among the Asante, slaves were executed so that the king would not lack for servants in the afterlife. Sometimes additional rituals are performed long after the death. This is notable in parts of Asia where ancestor veneration is an important element in daily life.

DAVID BURNETT

SEE ALSO Ancestral Practices.

Debt. Personal debt, incurred through the rising cost of education, consumer spending, or other means (*see* CONSUMERISM), has become a serious obstacle to missionary recruitment and deployment in North America in recent years. While Scripture, contrary to the claims of some, does not forbid entering into debt altogether, it does warn against the bondage that may result from debt (Prov. 22:7). Indeed, excessive debt presents a major barrier, impeding people's ability to serve God and to do his work, including mission.

Christians have already been forgiven the ultimate debt they owe—sin against God (cf. esp. Matt. 6:12 par. Luke 11:4; also Luke 7:41–43;

16:1–13). Believers are called to wise stewardship of their financial and other resources. Their faithfulness or negligence will result in heavenly reward or loss (Matt. 16:27; Eph. 6:8). Moreover, Christians' "debts" include obligations in marriage (1 Cor. 7:3; Eph. 5:28), as citizens (Rom. 13:7), in the preaching of the gospel (Rom. 1:14), and in love and service of other believers (John 13:14; Rom. 13:8; 1 John 3:16; 4:11).

The rising level of monetary debt on the part of missionary candidates mirrors a general trend in the U.S. economy, which is characterized by escalating federal budget deficits, record credit card debts, and consumer spending increases without corresponding raises in salaries. Some mission agencies currently allow a portion of missionaries' support to be devoted to the remission of debt. Other groups permit their staff to remain on support while upgrading their education. Generally, the church should act redemptively where significant debt has been incurred and preemptively wherever possible to prevent prospective Christian workers from entering into excessive financial debt.

ANDREAS J. KÖSTENBERGER

Bibliography. J. Engel, *Finances of Missions;* J. E. Hartley, *ISBE,* 1:905–6.

Decision-Making. A decision begins with an unmet need, followed by the (1) *awareness* that there is an alternative to the situation, an (2) *interest* in the alternative, and (3) *consideration* of the alternative. This consideration reviews both utilitarian and nonutilitarian issues involved. A (4) *choice* is made, and (5) *action* must follow to implement the decision. Action will require (6) *readjustment.* That, in turn, may create the awareness of further necessary changes, and the decision cycle is repeated.

Decision-making in practice, however, seldom happens in a simple, circular fashion. There are pauses and rapid skips forward and backward. There is no clear beginning or end in the decision process. Each of the identified stages must be expanded to gain a clear picture of the complexity of decision-making.

Improving Quality of Decisions. A Decisional Balance Sheet lists all known alternatives with the anticipated positive and negative consequences of each. The Decisional Balance Sheet will lead to improved decisions when seven criteria for information processing are met:

1. Consider a wide range of alternatives.
2. Examine all objectives to be fulfilled by the decision.
3. Carefully weigh the negative and positive consequences of each alternative.
4. Search thoroughly for new information relevant to each alternative.
5. Assimilate and use new information or expert judgment.
6. Reexamine all known alternatives before making a final decision.
7. Make careful provision for implementing the chosen decision.

Personality and Decisions. Individuals have been categorized as *sensors* or *intuitors* in their decision-making approaches. Sensors analyze isolated, concrete details while intuitors consider overall relationships. Intuitors have been found to have better predictive accuracy in decisions.

Other studies have suggested four personality styles in decision-making:

Decisive, using minimal information to reach a firm opinion. Speed, efficiency, and consistency are the concern. *Flexible,* using minimal information that is seen as having different meanings at different times. Speed, adaptability, and intuition are emphasized. *Hierarchic,* using masses of carefully analyzed data to reach one conclusion. Association with great thoroughness, precision, and perfectionism. *Integrative,* using large amounts of data to generate many possible solutions. Decisions are highly experimental and often creative.

It cannot be assumed, however, that individual decisions are the fundamental level of decision-making. In most societies of Central and South America, Africa, and Asia, no significant decision (individual or group) is reached apart from a group process to achieve consensus. In the more individualistic orientation of North American and European societies, group decision is often achieved through a process of argumentation and verbosity, with the sum of individual decisions expressed in a vote.

Group Decisions. A group decision is reached by accumulating emotional and factual information in a cyclical fashion. Beginning with a position accepted by consensus, new possibilities are tested. If accepted, those ideas become the new "anchored" (consensus) position; if rejected, the group returns to the original position, reaching out again as new possibilities emerge. The final stage of group decision is the members' public commitment to that decision—the essence of consensus.

Group judgment is not better than individual judgment, unless the individuals are experts in the area under consideration. Ignorance cannot be averaged out, only made more consistent. A lack of disagreement in group discussion increases the possibility of "groupthink" (an unchallenged acceptance of a position). A lack of disagreement may be construed as harmony, but contribute to poorer-quality decisions.

Higher-quality decisions are made in groups where (1) disagreement is central to decision-making, (2) leaders are highly communicative, and (3) group members are active participants.

Clearly, achieving social interdependence in the group is prerequisite to quality decisions. However, mere quantity of communication is not sufficient; the content of intragroup communication affects the quality of decision. The more time spent on establishing operating procedures, the lower the probability that a quality decision will result. Gaining agreement on the criteria for the final decision and then systematically considering all feasible solutions increases the probability of a good decision.

Consensus decision-making groups show more agreement, more objectivity, and fewer random or redundant statements than nonconsensus-seeking groups. Achievement of consensus is helped by using facts, clarifying issues, resolving conflict, lessening tension, and making helpful suggestions.

Cultural Effects on Decision-Making. A group must have decision rules, explicitly stated or implicitly understood, to function. These rules vary with culture; thus a decision model effective in societies of an American or European tradition will probably not function well in Asian or African groups. For example, probability is not normally seen as related to uncertainty in some cultures. For these cultures, probabilistic decision analysis is not the best way of aiding decision-making.

Perception of the decision required by the decision-maker must be considered. What is perceived depends on cultural assumptions and patterns, previous experience and the context. The problem as presented is seldom, if ever, the same as the perception of the problem. The greater the differences in culture, the greater the differences in perception.

DONALD E. SMITH

Bibliography. R. Y. Hirokawa and M. S. Poole, *Communication and Group Decision-Making;* I. L. Janis and L. Mann, *Decision Making: A Psychological Analysis of Conflict, Choice, and Commitment;* D. K. Smith, *Creating Understanding;* G. Wright, ed., *Behavioral Decision Making.*

Degrees in Mission and Missiology. Many missionaries never undertook formal studies in mission or missiology and yet were effective. Many, however, also proved ineffective and even destructive to the life of the church. While formal preparation for cross-cultural ministry does not guarantee future effectiveness, it does provide an opportunity for growth in knowledge and experience, hopefully to avoid the mistakes of the past and to prepare for the ever-changing future. The sending church wants well-qualified and effective representatives. The receiving church expects expatriates to contribute positively to its life. Frontier missionary activity demands the highest of qualifications. The Christian who wants to invest his or her life in world evangelism should seek adequate preparation, in many cases formal studies in an undergraduate or graduate program in mission(s)/missiology.

Theological Frameworks within which Modern Missiological Training Takes Place. Missiologists bring their own particular understandings of mission and missiology to the purpose and content of their programs. Programs in "mission(s)" or "missiology" reflect the theological commitments of those that teach and of their institutions, their understanding of the very nature of mission, and geographical and cultural approaches to education in general, and theological education in particular.

Broadly speaking, missiological training takes place within the frameworks of Roman Catholic, Conciliar Protestant, Non-Conciliar Evangelical, Orthodox, or Third World theologies. James Scherer suggests,

> It seems clear that conciliar missiologists tend to place the emphasis in mission teaching at the seminary level mainly on MISSIO DEI [the mission of God, God's abiding outreach to all] concerns and tasks of the ecumenical Christian community. Preparation for specific cross-cultural ministries, by contrast, seems to remain the preferred option among evangelical missiologists. Roman Catholic missiologists, based on ecclesiological positions taken at Vatican II, appear to lean toward the ecumenical position while still making room for cross-cultural preparation (1985, 451–52).

Among the Orthodox, salvation is a communal process of being in a right relationship with God, neighbor, and the created order. Missionary preparation includes study of the Scriptures, church history, patristics, and the language and culture of target groups, with the goal that the gospel be incarnated in each locality. Some Third World programs for missionary preparation put considerable emphasis on contextualization of the Christian message in light of non-Christian religious thinking, as well as on liberation.

Geographical Dispersion of Missiological Training and Levels of Degrees Available. Missiological training takes place around the world and across the educational spectrum, from nonformal missionary training centers offering certificates to universities and seminaries offering doctoral programs in mission(s)/missiology.

In the United States and Canada, in addition to nondegree training programs, Bible colleges, Christian liberal arts colleges, and denominational or nondenominational universities offer undergraduate majors related to missions, under various designations. Some of the bachelor's degree programs are entitled "Missions," "World Mission(s)," "Evangelism and Mission(s)," "Religion, Culture and Mission," "Intercultural Studies," "Cross-Cultural Studies/Ministry," "Global Studies/Ministry," and "Urban Studies/Ministries." Seminaries and university graduate schools offer various masters degree programs (Master of Arts—MA, Master of Arts in Religion—MAR, Master of Theological Studies—MTS, Master of Arts in Evangelism—MAEv, Master of Divinity—MDIV, Master of Theology—ThM) or doctoral degree programs (Doctor of Ministry—DMin, Doctor of Missiology—DMiss, Doctor of Theology—ThD, Doctor of Philosophy—PhD) with concentrations or specializations related to missions. Again, these programs are identified in various ways, such as "Missions/Missiology," "Intercultural Studies," "Cross-Cultural Mission/Studies," "Mission(s) and Evangelism," "World Mission and Evangelism," "Evangelism, Church Growth, and Mission," "Religion and Culture," "Urban Ministry," "Christianity and Culture," "Mission, Ecumenics, and World Religions," and "Religions of the World/Comparative Religion." A few graduate programs offer specializations for ministry with particular ethnic or geographical groups, such as "Chinese Ministry and Mission" or "Muslim/Islamic Studies" or in a particular professional preparation, such as TESOL/TEFL/TESL.

In Europe much of the preparation for missionary service is through nonformal or formal missionary training institutes, evangelical Bible institutes/colleges, and state- or church-sponsored universities. Academic degrees comparable to those offered in the United States and Canada are available through some programs. Myklebust indicated that "in respect of efforts, at university level, to promote missiological teaching and research, West Germany and Netherlands are leading the continent" (1989, 92), though most other countries also have state- or church-related universities with a chair of missiology.

Asia, Central America, and South America are growing centers for missionary training and sending. Asia is comparable to the United States in the emphasis on missions in the theological institutions, especially in India and South Korea, according to Myklebust. In Latin America "as a result of the explosive growth of Protestant/Evangelical Christianity theological schools have increasingly interested themselves in mission, but this interest has chiefly manifested itself at undergraduate level" (1989, 91). He concluded that there exist five Bible schools for every regular theological school. Among the forty-one theological schools he surveyed, thirty-six recognized missiology as a separate subject, with an assigned professor of missiology.

In general in Africa Bible institutes and colleges provide formal missionary training. Undergraduate and graduate programs in missions are most abundant in South Africa with some in Kenya, Nigeria, and the Central African Republic.

Areas to Look for in Programs. All programs are not created equal, either theologically or in the depth and breadth of the preparation they provide. The learning environment is a "hidden curriculum" that can prepare the missionary for effective ministry. Courses should be part of a well-integrated curriculum. Practical ministry is essential. The wise student will look for as many of the following features as possible in the program of choice.

The Learning Environment. The global church is valued and modeled through learning with and from those of other cultures. In addition, the training center or school demonstrates partnership with the church within and outside of the United States, to provide educational opportunities that minimize taking people out of their countries and fields of service. The leadership, teachers, and staff model a passion for God and for the lost. The teachers demonstrate a desire to learn from their colleagues and from the students. The teachers attempt to integrate the study of theology, missions, and the social sciences. Leadership development and spiritual formation are integrated within the community life, classroom, and field experiences. The community models and fosters positive approaches to conflict resolution. The learner learns how to be a self-directed learner *and* how to learn in collaboration with others. A counterculture response to the prevailing society is present, to challenge the learner to live the simple lifestyle, for the sake of social action and world evangelism.

Areas of Study. Adequate biblical and theological foundations are critical. A survey of missions would include a broad and accurate awareness of the present state of the church's ministry around the world. Theology and history of missions seek to understand the present situation in light of biblical norms and past history. Cross-cultural studies will include cultural anthropology and cross-cultural communication. Comparative religion/folk religion/non-Christian religions will be studied to enable the missionary to understand the worldview of the people with whom the gospel is shared. Missions strategies would include conceptual and practical learning of evangelism, church planting, urban ministry, and church growth principles. Missions leadership would enable knowing how to transmit the Christian faith to another generation through discipleship and leadership development of others.

Ministry Experience. The student must demonstrate minimal ministry experience prior to acceptance. Field-based experience as a "learner" in another's culture is required, to permit practice and reflection, under the guidance of more experienced leaders. The local church is involved in the process of preparing the future missionary, in partnership with the training center or school.

W. KENNETH PHILLIPS

SEE ALSO Bachelor's Degrees in Mission; Master's Degrees in Mission; Doctoral Degrees in Mission.

Bibliography. W. R. Hogg, *Missiology* 15 (1987): 487–506; H. Kasdorf, *Reflection and Projection: Missiology at the Threshold of 2001*, pp. 219–38; L. J. Luzbetak, *The Church and Cultures: New Perspectives in Missiological Anthropology;* O. G. Myklebust, *Mission Studies* 6 (1989): 87–107; J. Scherer, *Missiology* 13 (1985): 445–80; idem, *Missiology* 15 (1987): 507–22; W. R. Skenk, *Missiology* 24 (1996): 31–45; T. Steffen, *EMQ* 29 (1993): 178–83; N. E. Thomas, *Missiology* 18 (1990): 13–23.

Deism. The word *deism* is derived from *deus,* the Latin word for god, and thus was originally equivalent to *theism.* In the seventeenth and eighteenth centuries, however, the term was identified with a kind of theism based upon reason and natural religion and which rejected divine special revelation. Deists held that the universe was created by God but that it operated according to immutable natural laws with no significant divine intervention.

Deism flourished in England during the seventeenth and eighteenth centuries, with leading representatives including Lord Herbert of Cherbury, John Toland, and Matthew Tindal, who wrote what became known as the "deist's bible," *Christianity as Old as the Creation.* Continental thinkers who were also deists included Jean-Jacques Rousseau, Voltaire, and Immanuel Kant (who rejected the label). Some founding fathers of the United States, such as Benjamin Franklin, Thomas Paine, and Thomas Jefferson, were also deists.

Although there was some diversity among deists, many accepted belief in a supreme being; the obligation to worship this being; the obligation of ethical conduct; belief in divine rewards and punishments, in this life and beyond; a rational approach to religion that denied miracles and traditional Christian beliefs such as the Trinity, the incarnation, and the atonement.

Although the term itself has fallen into disuse, the fundamental worldview of deism is still very much alive, especially within the more liberal segment of Christianity, which has little place for special revelation and the miraculous and which regards Christianity largely in ethical categories.

WILLIAM H. BAKER

Bibliography. J. Collins, *God in Modern Philosophy;* J. Leland, *A View of the Principal Deistic Writers . . . ,* 3 vols; E. G. Waring, *Deism and Natural Religion: A Source Book.*

Democratic Republic of Congo (D.R.C.; formerly Zaire) *(Est. 2000 pop.: 51,136,000; 2,344,858 sq. km. [905,350 sq. mi.]).* A decade before Columbus discovered the New World, Portuguese explorer Diego Cao located the mouth of the Congo River in 1482, and established the first tenuous European contact with that part of the African continent. Prior to this, the area now known as D.R.C. had its own history of political organization in powerful kingdoms (e.g., Luba, Yaka, and Kongo) and innumerable small ethnic groupings. Within ten years of Diego Cao's expedition, Catholic missionaries arrived and before long the king of the influential Kongo tribe had been baptized along with many of his subjects. The initially successful Catholic movement declined through compromise with the flourishing Portuguese slave trade. It was only in the seventeenth century that there was a resurgence of Catholic missionary activity in the Kongo region. Although this contact was to have a profound impact (Gray, 1990) it, in turn, was to pass, and by the early nineteenth century little trace of living Christianity was to be found in the region.

Modern Missionary Period. By the time the Congo Free State had been created and granted personally to King Leopold II of Belgium by the European powers at the Berlin Conference (1884–85), Holy Ghost priests were once again established in the Boma area of the Lower River. The earliest Protestant mission agencies to work in the Congo included the Livingstone Inland Mission (1878), the BAPTIST MISSIONARY SOCIETY (1878), and the Garanganze Evangelical Mission (1886). In the northeast the AFRICA INLAND MISSION (1912) was one of the pioneer Protestant agencies. From the beginning of the colonial period (official control began in 1908) the Catholic Church enjoyed special powers and privileges in the Congo. This began to lessen, at least officially, with the extension of school subsidies to Protestant schools (1946) and the opening of state schools (1954). Although the mutual mistrust between Catholics and Protestants has abated, there is still relatively little cooperation between them.

As early as the 1902 General Conference of Missions in Leopoldville (Kinshasa), the need for cooperation was seen within the Protestant missionary movement. The Congo Protestant Council (CPC) was created in 1928, not only to facilitate COMITY between missions but also to have a single voice before the colonial government. During this period, the leadership of the church in D.R.C. was largely still an expatriate missionary affair, but in 1960 the CPC voted to transfer its administrative responsibility into national hands and for missionaries to assume the role of advisors and technicians.

Shortly after, the church in D.R.C. experienced traumatic years of independence (granted June 30, 1960) and "the Rebellion" (1963–65). In both, the church was targeted by antigovernment forces as well as opportunist gangs. Many hundreds of national believers were put to death, and dozens of missionary personnel were brutally killed. Those dark years resulted in a deepening spiritual life and maturity of the national leaders who learned how to stand without missionary assistance.

Increasingly as the 1960s drew toward a close, missions in D.R.C. recognized the maturity and responsibility of the national church. This was accelerated by the government's refusal to recognize a church body unless its founding mission had ceded to it autonomous legal standing. In 1970, the CPC (until then a group of separate churches) became the national Protestant Church of Zaire (ECZ), with each former church body a member Communaute of the whole. The government recognizes only four Christian groups: the ECZ, the Catholic Church, the Greek Orthodox Church, and the Kimbanguist Church (an independent African church, revering the founder SIMON KIMBANGU). Relations between the national government led (since 1965) by President Mobutu Sese Seko and the church (especially Roman Catholic) have often been strained, not least during the period of rigorous reaffirmation of traditional African cultural and religious values in the 1970s.

Challenges Facing the Church. D.R.C. is one of the world's poorest nations. While famine does not threaten as in some areas, the struggle for survival affects the vast majority. The downward economic spiral in this potentially wealthy country affects almost every part of the infrastructure. The church has sought to do what it can, often with little or no help from the government. The deteriorating economic situation sparked rioting in the early 1990s, which in turn led to a withdrawal of expatriate mission personnel from some parts of the country. In the east, some of the largest refugee camps result from the ethnic strife in Rwanda. Mobutu's government was overthrown by Laurent Kabila's troops in 1997 and the country's name was changed from Zaire to the current Democratic Republic of Congo.

Despite these problems, the vitality of the church sets it within the top ten non-Western nations sending out their own missionaries (Pate, 1989) for cross-cultural ministry both within and beyond their borders. While the response to the Christian message continues to be high, the greatest need is for training of national Christians in order to deepen the knowledge and spiritual life of the numerically large church which has sometimes been criticized for not influencing as it should such endemic evils as corruption.

Time and again during its turbulent history in D.R.C., the church has ridden the storm. As the church enters its second century, nominalism and formalism within the church and materialism, secularism, and proliferation of sects outside the church, will challenge again the vision and vitality of the people of Christ in D.R.C.

GORDON R. MOLYNEUX

Bibliography. J. R. Crawford, *Protestant Missions in the Congo, 1878–1969;* R. Gray, *Black Christians and White Missionaries;* C. Irvine, *The Church of Christ in Zaire;* A Handbook of *Protestant Churches, Missions, and Communities, 1878–1978;* D. McGavran and N. Riddle, *Zaire: Midday in Missions;* L. D. Pate, *From Every People: A Handbook of Two-Thirds World Missions with Directory/Histories/Analysis.*

Demon, Demonization. While Scripture does not present a clear picture of their origin, demons are generally recognized by Christians as angels who fell with Satan and are now agents seeking to work on his behalf on earth. In the Old Testament, demons (or evil spirits) do not receive a great deal of attention. Generally, they are portrayed as malicious spirit beings who are used to bring God's judgment (e.g., 1 Sam. 16:14; Judg. 9:22–24) and are connected with idols and idolatry (Deut. 32:17; Ps. 106:37, 38). While we get one glimpse of some hierarchy of demonic powers (Dan. 10:13, 20), that glimpse is left undeveloped (*see* TERRITORIAL SPIRITS).

The New Testament picture is clearer. At least five types of demonic activity can be seen. Under Satan's control, they unsuccessfully resist Jesus and try to expose his identity during his ministry (Mark 1:23–27), blind unbelievers (2 Cor. 4:3–4), engage believers in warfare (Eph. 6:10–18), wreak great destruction on earth as part of the end times (Rev. 9), and entice governments and nations to rebel against God (Rev. 16:12–16).

The Gospels present seven encounters of Jesus with demons during his three years of public ministry: the Gerasene demoniac (Mark 5:1–20 and parallels); the boy with seizures (Matt. 17:14–20 and parallels); three instances of people being healed from specific demonic-caused diseases (Matt. 9:32–33; Matt. 12:22–23 and parallel; Luke 13:10–17), and two cases where Jesus silences the spirits (Mark 1:23–27 and parallel; Matt. 8:16 and parallels). In every example we see Jesus' direct engagement of demons to set people free. Their freedom came through the exercise of his authority (Mark 1:27–28), in contrast to the rituals of the exorcists of his day.

In the thirty plus years covered in Acts, only five statements of distinct demonic encounters are found (Acts 5:15–16; 8:6–7; 16:16–18; 19:11–12; 19:13–17). As with Jesus, the apostles exercise authority over demons to set people free. The relative lack of examples from Acts appears to underscore that demons are to be confronted but are not to be given preeminent attention.

In the epistles we find important teachings on demons and their work. They are the powers behind idols (1 Cor. 10:19–21); we engage them in war (Eph. 6:10–18), humbly submitting to God and resisting Satan (James 4:7; 1 Peter 5:8–9; *see also* SPIRITUAL WARFARE); they subvert people through false doctrines (1 Tim. 4:1–4); and we are to test the spirits (1 John 4:1–4). Concerning their character and tactics, they know the truth and shudder (James 2:19), and, following Satan, they masquerade as angels of light (2 Cor. 11:2–15).

In Revelation we see demons characterized as Satan's host encamped against God. They lead the nations astray (Rev. 16:12–16) and bring destruction on earth (Rev. 9). Though the final picture is not one of battle but slaughter (Rev. 19:19–20), their power on earth over unbelievers, under God's sovereignty, is mentioned throughout Revelation.

Demonic Attack. With more than thirty terms used (many of them in the Gospels), the range of vocabulary of demonic attack against people is rich. However, it all points in one direction: demons desire to destroy the host by deception and distortion of our very humanity (seen clearly in the Gerasene demoniac; Mark 5:1–20). In terms of control, demons *indwell* people (Matt. 12:43–45); people may have spirits *in* them (Mark 1:23); be *with* a spirit (Mark 5:2); or *have* spirits (Matt. 11:18). The strongest term of demonic control is *daimonizomai*, often translated "demon-possessed." The English connotations of "possession," however, cloud the meaning. Christians cannot be "possessed" in the sense of *ownership*, since they belong to Christ. The NRSV frequently uses "demoniac" and the Amplified renders it "under the power of demons," both of which better express the idea of control than ownership. Though the term is not used after the Gospels, if this type of control over Christians were not possible, the continual warnings against demonic infiltration in the epistles would serve no purpose. Just as we can be "controlled" by false teachers, cult leaders, and so on, we can be "controlled" by demons, a fact that has long been acknowledged both by those who minister to the demonized and in non-Western contexts.

Missiological Issues. It is important for the missionary to understand the biblical teaching on demons as well as be effectively trained in dealing with demons as they manifest themselves. As is seen in Acts, however, our focus on the demonic should be selective. Paying too much attention to demonic activity can be just as bad as ignoring it. Missionaries may face either of two extremes: SECULARISM which denies demons and ANIMISM which sees demons as the source of every problem. In many Western urban settings influenced with NEW AGE thinking the two opposites can be curiously intertwined in a form of spiritistic SYNCRETISM. Many worldviews acknowledge the spirit realm and contain a variety of beliefs and rituals for handling spirits and their activities (*see* EXORCISM). The missionaries must come to grips not only with their own WORLDVIEW, but also that of the Bible and the host culture.

On a practical level, what can the missionary expect? In the New Testament, a demon drove a fortune teller to harass Paul and his missionary band so much that he had to deal with it (Acts 16:16–18). Satan repeatedly thwarted Paul's missionary plans (1 Thess. 2:17–18), and he persevered in his missionary labors despite a Satanic-given thorn in the flesh (literally "angel of Satan") by focusing on God's power and grace (2 Cor. 12:1–9). The young churches Paul planted were in danger of falling prey to Satanic deception (e.g., 2 Cor. 11:2–15) and had to put on spiritual armor (Eph. 6:10–18). Contemporary missionaries must be prepared to face all of these situations. We should also note that Satan is not limited to the particular tactics employed in the Bible. Just as human society grows and changes, so may demonic attacks (*see* POSSESSION PHENOMENA). However, the central core strategies of deception, blinding, and movement toward destruction are constant themes whatever the culture. In light of this, a crucial missionary task involves working with the local community to develop a clear biblical perspective on the demonic and to couple this with contextualized ministry methodologies which maintain biblical fidelity and, as far as possible, cultural sensitivity.

A. SCOTT MOREAU

Bibliography. C. Arnold, *Three Crucial Questions about Spiritual Warfare;* M. Kraft, *Understanding Spiritual Power;* A. S. Moreau, *The World of the Spirits;* S. Page, *Powers of Evil;* D. Powilson, *Power Encounters;* G. Van Rheenen, *Communicating Christ in Animistic Contexts.*

Denmark *(Est. 2000 pop.: 5,207,000; 43,077 sq. km. [16,632 sq. mi.]).* Denmark is the smallest of the Scandinavian nations other than Iceland. It lies between the North Sea on the west and the Baltic Sea on the southeast. The Jutland, which is the long peninsula, comprises 70 percent of Denmark's land area. The rest consists of over five hundred nearby islands, only one hundred of them inhabited. The Faeroe Islands and Greenland are self-governing units within the nation of Denmark. Denmark shares a border with Germany, thus being influenced in part by the Germans. The population is made up of primarily Nordic Scandinavians with a minority of Germans in the south. Approximately 97 percent are Danish and 3 percent foreigners. The literacy rate is almost 100 percent due to a compulsory education system in place since 1814.

The economy of Denmark is largely driven by agricultural and industrial exportation, giving the country one of the highest standards of living in the world. Its government is considered to provide the world's most advanced welfare and social service system. However, in the 1980s, concern about the costs making up 30 percent of the national budget forced the government to put restrictions on the social benefits for individuals. Currently, Denmark is a constitutional monarchy headed by Margaret I, queen since 1972. There are four principal political parties.

The religion of the people is evangelical Lutheran. Christianity was first introduced in 826 and became widespread during Canute's reign in the eleventh century. During the reign of Christian III (1534–59), the Reformation brought the establishment of a national Lutheran Church. The state supports the church, which was established in 1536, and 95 percent of the population today are members. However, it has been estimated that only about 3 percent of those members attend church services. This signifies that religion is more a part of the culture and heritage than a personal faith.

Many people are turning to the Eastern religious movement and Christian sects to find spiritual answers, thus implying further that the state church is not meeting the spiritual needs of the Danes. The biggest problem is that the evangelical witness within and outside of the state church is very weak. A major reason for the external problem is the difficulties foreign missionaries face in obtaining visas. There was a decline in missionaries since 1970 and today officially there are only 31 present (the ratio of missionaries to Danes is only 1:165,000). As long as there are visa restrictions in Denmark, evangelism will have to come primarily from the native Christians. Foreign missionaries just do not have access to the people of Denmark as their own Christian organizations and churches do. Regarding the state churches, liberal theology has infiltrated many of them. However, there are two conservative Lutheran free theological facilities in the country. These facilities are expanding and enrolling more students. This, of course, is a positive development for the future of Christianity in Denmark, but unfortunately not enough to reach the majority of Danes. Revival in the Lutheran churches or within other native Christian groups is desperately needed.

WILLIAM L. WAGNER

Bibliography. J. T. Addison, *The Medieval Missionary: A Study of the Conversion of Northern Europe;* E. H. Dunkley, *The Reformation in Denmark;* P. Hartling, ed., *The Danish Church;* C. H. Robinson, trans., *Anskar, the Apostle of the North, 801–865.*

Dependency. Dependence is a necessary part of life, an inborn tendency which cultural, social, and psychological conditions shape. The real problem of dependence is not its existence or nonexistence, but the manner of being dependent.

Overdependency of any kind (financial, physical, emotional, or intellectual) may result in erosion of self-respect, inhibiting initiative in using existing resources and leading to imitative behavior that destroys cultural integrity. But dependency also may build relationships and knit a society together, strengthening individual and group security and sense of identity.

One-way dependency is negative, ultimately destroying healthy relationships. The person or society depended upon feels exploited, and the dependent individual or group grows to resent the other.

Such dependency reduces self-respect because of an apparent inability to do anything other than receive. Lacking self-respect, the receiver may reject familiar cultural patterns and imitate the person or group that is the source of help. The consequent change is often not appropriate, creating a need for more help. A downward spiral results that leads to psychological or social dysfunction. The group helped is crippled in their ability to care for their own affairs.

One-way dependency is an addictive process in which participants become co-dependents who are unable or unwilling to see people and things realistically. The addictive process takes control of participants, pushing participants to think and do things inconsistent with their values, including deceptive behavior, in the attempt to justify dependency and yet maintain the illusion of independence.

As with any addiction, everything comes to center around satisfying a craving. More and more is needed to create the desired effect, and no amount is ever enough. Perception of information is distorted and relationships become subservient to the addiction. There is an awareness that something is wrong, but addictive thinking says that it is somebody else's fault. No responsibility is accepted. Addicts tend to be dependent and to feel increasingly powerless. The idea that they can take responsibility for their lives is inconceivable to them.

This pattern of thinking is equally applicable to individuals and groups. Either can be addicted to dependency systems (economic, structural, and psychological) as strongly as to drugs.

Economic dependency has been shown to inhibit national development, yet economic dependency has been repeated in church-mission relationships. Both national and church dependency are characterized by a very few sources investing/giving heavily through an indigenous controlling elite. Fundamental decision-making is implicitly the prerogative of the donor not the recipient. Foreign assistance is large relative to the receiving economy. A large proportion of its university students and leadership are trained in a few foreign sites, and a considerable portion of the aid is spent on purchases from abroad. The economic top 20 percent receive most of the funds, which reinforces their position, and the bottom 40 percent almost none.

Christian ministries unwittingly perpetuate economic dependency when they plead "just send money," separating funds from fellowship contrary to the example and teaching of 2 Corinthians 8 and 9. "It continues to make the national church dependent. . . . It often robs the national church of its natural potential. When easy money . . . is available, very few want to explore indigenous ways of fund raising."

Dependency is also created by imported structures, methodologies, and institutions that are suitable for churches of one culture but not for another area. By placing inappropriate and even impossible demands on the churches, those churches become dependent on the guidance of outsiders who understand the imported system. A form of Christianity is created that cannot be reproduced. Paternalism and its mate, dependence, thus may grow from the very structures of mission and church, not from some weakness in either the new believers or the missionaries.

In cultures of North America and Europe independence is considered an absolute good. A central therapeutic assumption in Euro-American psychology is that healthy behavior is self-reliant, self-sufficient, and independent. The in-born tendency to dependency, either individually or in the social structure, is to be removed as quickly as possible.

Very different assumptions are present in many cultures of Asia, Africa, and South America concerning dependency. It is two-way, part of mutual support, obligation, and reciprocity that binds the society by building relationships of interdependency. Life requires cooperation at every point. Dependency is not weakness but a part of the natural order where help always moves in circles, not in a straight line. What is given will return.

In a basic way, most of the world's people are dependent. Peoples as widespread as the Japanese, American Indians, Matabele (Zimbabwe), and the Malagasy (Madagascar) all accept dependency as necessary and positive. A reward is expected for relying on another, because you have given by receiving. *Amae* is a fundamental concept in Japanese social psychology, an automatic good expressed supremely in the role of the emperor who depends on others to rule and carry out every task yet is honored as the ultimate expression of the nation. Dependency is pivotal in the WORLDVIEW that underlies Malagasy society, and the dependency systems of India affect nearly every transaction.

Missions function within these two opposing concepts of dependency. Euro-American missionaries tend to regard all dependency as bad, and Asian-African-South Americans regard it as necessary and good. Failure to recognize these fundamental differences in attitudes to dependency leads to misunderstanding and alienation.

Gurian and Gurian provide a model that describes destructive extremes and the desirable balance. They note that a one-way dependency may result in entrapment, enslavement, helplessness, suppression, surrender, submission, and submergence. Total independency, on the other hand, can result in abandonment, estrangement, selfishness, narcissism, withdrawal, alienation, and isolation. True interdependency, a position in tension between the two poles of dependency and independency, can lead to continuity, bonding, reciprocity, mutual and healthy obligation, trust, commitment, and involvement.

Scriptures teach the interdependence of believers within the Body of Christ, not crippling dependency nor extreme individualism. Christian workers from every cultural heritage are obligated to build that interdependence within the international church, avoiding patterns that lead to either extreme.

DONALD F. SMITH

SEE ALSO Foreign Financing of Indigenous Missions; Partnerships; Paternalism.

Bibliography. M. P. Gurian, and J. M. Gurian, *The Dependency Tendency;* W. Lustbader, *Counting on Kindness: The Dilemmas of Dependency;* A. W. Schaef, *When Society Becomes an Addict;* G. Schwartz, *EMQ* 27:3 (1991): 238–41; R. Wood, *Mission Frontiers,* 19:1 (1997): 7.

Depravity of Humankind. Depravity refers to the extensiveness, or "depth dimension," of SIN. To the question, How far does the corrupting influence of sin extend to a person's being? the doctrine of *total depravity* responds that such corruption is all-pervasive, affecting every part of a person's nature, including the body, mind/intellect/reason, emotions, will, motivations, and so on. Thus, there is no spiritual good in people at all that could merit God's grace nor any human inclination to make a move toward God for salvation. Contrast this with other views (e.g., semi-Pelagianism) which deny that sin's depravity is total and maintain that some aspect of a person's being (e.g., the will or reason), while weakened by the corrupting influence of sin, retains sufficient ability to set in motion the pursuit after salvation through cooperation with divine grace.

While depravity is pervasive, the IMAGE OF GOD in humanity has not been completely effaced. CONSCIENCE or an innate awareness of good and evil remains, and corrupted people may still demonstrate a sensitivity for right and wrong. Will, the power to choose, continues, and sinful people may still engage in natural, civil, and even externally religious good. Thus, depraved people are not as evil as they possibly could be, constantly indulging in every kind of sin. They possess both depravity and dignity.

Scriptural support for depravity includes both general statements about the all-pervasive corrupting influence of sin on humanity (Gen. 6:5; Rom. 3:9–18; 7:18; Eph. 2:1–3) as well as specific statements of sin's depraving impact on the various aspects of human nature such as the mind (Eph. 4:17–18; Rom. 8:6–7), the heart (Jer. 17:9), the conscience (Titus 1:15), the "inner being" (Mark 7:20–23), and the body (Rom. 6:12–13; 8:10). The biblical evidence points not only to *deprivation* (the absence of good) but to *depravation* (total corruption resulting in evil) as the thoroughgoing problem of humankind.

The implications of depravity for missions are several: (1) Personal awareness of our own human perversity propels us to seek out the divine solution in Jesus Christ. (2) "The deeper the sense of sin, the more thorough is the moral recovery and the intenser the spiritual life" (Miley). (3) As those rescued from miserable ruin, we express our thankfulness by no longer living for ourselves, but for him who saved us. This entails commitment to the ministry of reconciliation as ambassadors for Christ (2 Cor. 5:14–21). (4) Because of the universal all-pervasiveness of sin, God justly condemns the entire world to eternal punishment (*see also* HELL). This desperate plight of our fellow human beings challenges us to embark on the missionary enterprise. The message of salvation which we carry worldwide is the profound answer corresponding to the depth dimension of human sin. It renews the mind (Rom. 12:1–2), changes the heart (Ezek. 36:26), cleanses the conscience (Heb. 9:14), transforms the "inner being" (Eph. 3:16; Col. 3:10), and redeems the body (Rom. 8:13; 1 Cor. 6:12–20). The fullness of deliverance from our depravity awaits the return of Jesus Christ.

GREGG R. ALLISON

Bibliography. J. Calvin, *The Institutes of the Christian Religion*, 2.1.8–11; J. Miley, *Systematic Theology* I:441–533; M. Erickson, *Christian Theology*, 621–39.

Deputation. In the deputation process initial missionary appointees visit churches and other gatherings of Christians to present their ministry for the purpose of developing prayer and financial support to underwrite missionary endeavors. This procedure is found in independent missions and many evangelical denominations in contrast to denomination mission boards that are usually funded through a unified budget not requiring missionaries to raise their own support. There are certain variations. The CHRISTIAN AND MISSIONARY ALLIANCE requires missionaries to minister in churches and district conferences to help raise funds for the mission, but not for personal support. OVERSEAS MISSIONARY FELLOWSHIP asks appointees to seek out prayer support but not to ask for funds. The origin of this term is related to the appointment of deputies (assistants) to stand in with the sheriff and his posse to accomplish a task, just as the supporters choose to stand in prayer and financial commitment to assist in the missionary's ministry.

The process of deputation has several drawbacks: different personalities can work for or against the candidate; one's personal network can be well developed or very limited; the costs of missionary support have risen with inflation (often equivalent to public school teacher's salaries), and the time factor has steadily increased from one to two years with certain high cost-of-living countries taking even three years of this procedure; the constant displacement of a missionary's family can create hardship; and there are often significantly different levels of personalized help in fundraising. The often overlooked aspect of deputation is the opportunity to share the appointee's passion and testimony with other potential missionaries. Historically deputation developed in the nineteenth century with the birth of interdenominational mission societies, but today the majority of North American Protestant missionaries are supported through this system.

JOHN EASTERLING

SEE ALSO Fund Raising; Furlough.

Bibliography. B. Barnett, *Friend-Raising: Building a Missionary Support Team That Lasts;* J. H. Kane, *Understanding Christian Mission.*

Deutsche Gesellschaft für Missionwisenschaft. *See* GERMAN SOCIETY FOR THE STUDY OF MISSIONS.

Devanandan, Paul David (1901–62). Indian theologian, educator, and churchman. Born in Madras, India, the son of devoted Christians, he was greatly influenced by his mother, who studied the Bible in the Tamil, Telugu, and Urdu languages. After earning degrees from universities in India and the United States (Nizam College, Madras University, Pacific School of Religion, and Yale Divinity School), he taught religion at the Union Seminary of Bangalore for seventeen years and served as director of the Christian Institute for the Study of Religion and Society from 1956 until his death. He had a great impact in India through the books and articles he wrote and edited and as a teacher and a man. He combined a personal faith in Christ as his Savior and conservative theological beliefs with an ability to encourage dialogue between people of different faiths. In his native India, overwhelmingly Hindu, this was a major step in equipping his students to minister outside the rather clannish Christian community. One of his best-remembered addresses was on the Christian mission in the world, entitled "Called to Witness," which he gave to the 1961 Assembly of the World Council of Churches in NEW DELHI. Russell Chandran, principal of the United Theological College, said of Devanandan, "No one in the Indian church has had so many friends among non-Christian scholars and thinkers and few Indian Christians have been held in so high a regard by non-Christians."

ROBERT SCHUSTER

Development. In terms of missionary activity and mission strategy, *development* usually denotes an inclusive process in which the physical and social needs of persons and groups are given attention alongside their spiritual needs.

Development is a general word, commonly used with reference to such diverse matters as fundraising, improvement of property or resources, increased effectiveness and profitability of a business or social enterprise, expansion and fulfillment of complex mental capacities, physical maturation—especially of children, and spiritual deepening across a lifetime.

Developmentalism, a closely related term in the field of psychology and social psychology, emphasizes the built-in characteristics of the organism, the person, or the social enterprise. A developmental viewpoint assumes that changes in the maturing human being or in a developing society represent an emergence of the patterns and characteristics that are psychogenetically predisposed and patterned—built into the organism or system. The writings of Piaget and Kohlberg, for example, assume that development is not something that the parent or teacher causes but rather participates in. Developmentalism does not deny the influences of environment, but it avoids assuming that the environment or any outside agents are the singular explanation for all outcomes in the development of a person or of a society. From a developmental perspective, development is defined in terms of the processes through which maturing persons or emergent societies lose the limitations that have characterized their previous condition.

The major obstacles to social development include (1) *defeatism*, in which people see no possibilities beyond the conditions and restrictiveness with which they are currently most familiar, (2) *dependency*, an actual condition or a mental state in which people assume that they are not adequate apart from significant help and resources from the outside, and (3) *pride*, through which people become self-sufficient and resistant to encouragements and assistance from outsiders.

The role of the outsider, whether teacher, parent, missionary, agriculturalist, or health worker, is a matter of assisting, stimulating, encouraging, and providing access to the resources essential to development. Thus, such outsiders could be better described as development technicians. The activity in which outsiders provide valuable services

within contemporary church ministries and evangelism in many places is *development assistance.*

Development assistance has become an increasing emphasis within missions in recent years. Although the concern for the well-being of human beings has been a facet of deliberate Christian missions all through the modern missionary era, conservative and narrow views of missions took a toll during the middle of the twentieth century. Defining missions as verbal proclamation of the gospel makes people more enthusiastic about building schools than about building hospitals. Since development assistance is usually a slow and rather costly investment in people, the threat to other missionary activity has created a substantial schism. For evangelicals and conservatives, especially for fundamentalists, meeting spiritual needs is arguably more important than attending to physical or socio-political matters.

In missiological debates development assistance often is seen as competing for resources that would otherwise be invested in spiritual matters, especially verbal evangelization. The argument usually springs from the fear that if resources are committed to the purposes of social development the emphasis on verbal proclamation of the gospel will suffer. Some have argued that this position is based on the curious assumption that God's capacities and resources are limited.

Another argument against expending Christian resources for physical, social, and economic development is based upon the view that the primary task of God's people is to act upon Christ's primary motive: "to seek and to save . . . the lost." This position arises from the view that God is honored as his people use resources wisely and in a manner disciplined to the priorities of the KINGDOM OF GOD. The conclusion one reaches will depend on how these priorities are understood (*see also* MISSIONARY TASK).

Whatever the argument against the church's participation in development assistance, the example provided by Jesus Christ's engagement in whole-person ministry stands clearly as the most valid precedent. Strategically, as well, current evidence in the field strongly suggests that large-scale evangelization of communities and large extended families often follows closely the offering of development assistance provided in the name of Jesus Christ. This recognition has led to yet another view: legitimization of development assistance because of its pragmatic value as a tool of evangelization.

Although parachurch organizations such as Food for the Hungry and World Vision have emerged largely to balance the church's mid-century denial of the importance of the physical and social needs of people, especially the poor in underdeveloped regions, there is still no consensus on the place of development assistance within Christian missions.

The local church, as a community of faith, is an especially appropriate context for community development. In regions where the church is well-planted, participation of Christians in the social welfare of their communities often provides the incentive and motivational core for substantial development process. Thus the churches of the world are increasingly providing the leadership and community resource-centers for social change.

Relief activities are substantially different from development assistance (*see also* RELIEF WORK). Although relief is a more common response to human need and is widely supported by Christians as a reflection of Jesus' teaching about the contrast between sheep and goats in Matthew 25 and his teaching about responsibilities to one's neighbor in the "good Samaritan" story, relief tends toward counter-developmental interventions and outcomes. Necessary as it is to save lives and to reduce suffering, delivering food and medical supplies can soon lead to a dependent condition, especially if delivered overmuch or overlong. The tendency to think of development as a sort of companion of relief often leads to confusion. Indeed, it is easier to solicit funds and elicit sympathy for relief needs, but relief rarely leads to making the necessary changes in sociopolitical structure, productivity, lifestyle, and culture. A Chinese proverb is used to sum up this problem: *Give a man a fish and he eats today; teach a man to fish and he eats for a lifetime.*

Development assistance requires the participation of those being assisted. The one who assists must first listen and learn, resisting the temptation to exert undue influence through one's expertise and outside leverage. Development assistance requires great patience and appropriate creativity. The primary goal is to encourage people to accept the possibility of bettering their conditions through self-help.

The major obstacle to effective development assistance is the difficulty of bringing into harmony the motives of insiders and outsiders. Views of the appropriate conditions of life, degrees of willingness to accept change, personal and community dignity and pride all must be considered. Who decides what goals are worthy? Who decides how hard and how fast to work? Who decides the best use of resources? Ordinarily, the perverted golden rule prevails: Those who hold the gold make the rules. The influence of well-intentioned outsiders, while important in the short-run, commonly becomes the undermining destructive force in many development projects.

Another common obstacle is disagreement on the scope of the problem being addressed by the development effort. Even MOTHER TERESA of Calcutta was persistently criticized for not addressing the underlying socio-political problems that produce India's poverty. Instead, she defined her mission in terms of treating symptoms, not causes. Arguments about how large to draw the target can cause development activities to bypass the most basic of human needs: the need to be directly involved in the quest for change.

In recent years the emphasis on development has waned, among missionary efforts and in regard to international assistance in general. The results of development activity have been uneven and often disappointing. Particularly among those who describe themselves as "doing development" and, worse yet, "delivering development," effectiveness typically has been minimal. Human groups simply cannot be pushed into development by outside efforts. Broad-scale community participation and altruistic local initiatives are essential, and they must arise out of what PAULO FREIRE called conscientization, more thoughtful awareness of the conditions in which people find themselves, coupled with a heightened sense of moral responsibility and initiative.

TED WARD

SEE ALSO Evangelism and Social Responsibility, Holistic Mission, AND Transformational Development.

Bibliography. E. J. Elliston, ed., *Christian Relief and Development;* D. C. Korten, *Getting to the 21st Century—Voluntary Action and the Global Agenda;* J. M. Perkins, *Beyond Charity: The Call to Christian Community Development;* T. Yamamori, B. Myers, et al., *Serving with the Poor in Asia;* idem, *Serving with the Poor in Africa;* idem, *Serving with the Poor in Latin America.*

Devil. See SATAN.

Deyneka, Peter, Sr. (1897–1987). Russian-American missionary evangelist and founder of the Slavic Gospel Association. Born in the Russian province of Grodno, he immigrated to the United States at the age of sixteen to lift his family out of debt. While working in Chicago, he drifted from his Russian Orthodox moorings and became an activist and atheist. He came to Christ through contact with Moody Memorial Church and numerous Christian individuals. After attending classes at Moody Bible Institute, he continued his education at St. Paul Bible School (Minnesota) and developed his gift for evangelism among Russian immigrants in the region.

In 1925 Peter made his first of several trips back to Russia and became the first person ever to preach the gospel of Jesus Christ in his home village. Significant also was his marriage to Vera, a young Russian Christian woman. During the following decade Deyneka was associated with the All-Russian Evangelical Christian Union and Worldwide Christian Couriers respectively. Extensive evangelistic preaching tours in the Soviet Union and around the world convinced him of the need to organize missionary outreach among Slavic people. In 1934 "The Russian Gospel Association," later expanded to "The Slavic Gospel Association" (SGA), was founded. Radio programming (see RADIO MISSION WORK) became one of SGA's largest and most effective mediums of evangelism and theological education. Other major thrusts include distribution of Bibles and Christian literature and relief work among Slavic refugees. Deyneka's booklet "Much Prayer— Much Power" illustrates his conviction that prayer is the modus operandi of missionary outreach. Deyneka remained SGA's general director until his retirement in 1975.

FLORENCE R. SCOTT

Bibliography. N. B. Rohrer and P. Deyneka, Jr., *Peter Dynamite;* P. Deyneka, *When a Russian Found Christ.*

Dialogue. The subject of vigorous discussion, dialogue seems to defy definition. Most agree, however, that dialogue includes face-to-face conversations involving persons who have fundamentally different religious convictions for the purpose of understanding and growth. In the debate on religious PLURALISM and dialogue, convictions on its nature and use appear to settle into three positions. The position held by pluralists rejects traditional views on biblical revelation, proclaiming interreligious dialogue as a new epistemology; extreme conservatism calls for the rejection of dialogue in favor of proclamation; a more centrist view affirms dialogue as a means of understanding and communication without rejecting biblical revelation.

Ontological and epistemological relativism form the basis for pluralist dialogue. Within this framework, dialogue is seen as a primary avenue toward universal religious truth. Through interfaith discussion under an attitude of equal respect for person and faith, dialogue may reveal supreme truth that transcends various religious traditions: the ultimate truth behind all cultural expressions of religious experience, whether that experience finds expression through Hinduism, Islam, Buddhism, or Christianity. Important aspects include entering dialogue with little or no predetermined expectations, complete honesty, openness, and willingness to change, even concerning important theological issues. Thus, through interfaith dialogue, the Christian may convert from Christianity, the non-Christian may convert to Christianity, or both may become agnostic. Adherents to this position include John Hick, Paul F. Knitter, John R. Cobb, Raimundo Panikkar, and Leonard Swidler.

This position, however, views RELATIVISM as a universally accepted paradigm, possibly creating a naiveté concerning the willingness of other parties to agree to the relativistic preconditions and the possibility that such dialogues become limited to other pluralists from various faiths. This position also evidences a lack of attention to smaller religious movements in the pluralist literature. Little space is given to dialogue between Christians (even liberal) and Satanists, to give an extreme example.

The opposite view may be called the antidialogue position; it is held by D. Martyn Lloyd-Jones, among others. Drawing presuppositions from conservative Christian tradition and nineteenth-century positivism, this position assumes an absolute, complete, and accurate comprehension of biblical truth as expressed in evangelical orthodoxy, forming "an exact correspondence between theology and Scripture" (Hiebert, 1985, 7). Any dialogue that contains the possibility for theological change is often perceived as a threat. Accordingly, as JOHN STOTT points out, proclamation commands the central element of this position. Careful attention is given to the presentation of the message in monologue form with less attention to surrounding beliefs or circumstances. Dialogue with non-Christians is often considered to involve compromise with anti-Christian forces, violating 2 John 7–11. Preaching in monologue style seeks to accurately communicate propositional truth, thus safeguarding the purity and integrity of the biblical message.

Weaknesses include substantial evidence of cultural and subjective bias in biblical interpretation, undermining the presupposition of exact correspondence. Accordingly, adherents may experience difficulty discerning and respecting differences in conservative biblical interpretation that stem from divergent worldviews. In addition, greater possibilities exist for insensitive presentations that can hinder comprehension of central biblical issues. For example, cultures that value relationships and conversation more than preaching may find difficulty in responding to the message.

The third position seeks to affirm both the understanding and communication aspects of dialogue without surrendering biblical absolutes, the latter being a crucial distinction from the pluralist definition of dialogue. This position, combining critical realism with theological conservatism, is held by (among others) Stott, E. STANLEY JONES, KENNETH CRAGG, Carl F. H. Henry, and Bishop STEPHEN NEILL. Through interpersonal dialogue, one listens and learns as well as shares scriptural truth. Biblical evidence for this position includes examples from the ministry of Christ (John 3–4; Luke 18:18–29), the ministry of Peter (Acts 10:27–48), Paul (Acts 13:8–18; 17:16–34; 19:8–10; 20:6–7), and the common sense of Proverbs 18:13. Stott summarizes his argument by stating that true biblical dialogue reflects authenticity, humility, integrity, and sensitivity—all without relinquishing essential biblical mandates for salvation. The position calls for careful discernment between people who are valued by Christ and religious systems that oppose him, and it is the position generally practiced by evangelical missionaries.

The weaknesses of this position include possible difficulties in maintaining a balance among interpersonal relationships, biblical truth, and resulting psychological equilibrium. Additionally, losing biblical perspective may also lead toward SYNCRETISM. However, the strengths of this approach far outweigh the weaknesses.

STEVEN J. PIERSON

Bibliography. P. J. Griffiths, *An Apology for Apologetics;* J. Hick and P. F. Knitter, eds., *The Myth of Christian Uniqueness;* P. Hiebert, *Theological Students Fellowship Bulletin* 8 (1985): 5–10; P. F. Knitter, *No Other Name?;* D. M. Lloyd-Jones, *Preaching and Preachers;* T. C. Muck, *JETS* 36 (1993): 517–29; H. A. Netland, *Dissonant Voices: Religious Pluralism and the Question of Truth;* E. Rommen and H. Netland, eds., *Christianity and the Religions: A Biblical Theology of World Religions;* J. R. W. Stott, *Christian Mission in the Modern World;* L. Swidler, *After the Absolute: The Dialogical Future of Religious Reflection.*

Diaspora(s). The role of the Jewish diaspora is seen clearly in the Acts of the Apostles. Stephen, Philip, Barnabas, and Paul were all Jews of the diaspora who were at home in both Jewish and Greek culture. And it is clear that the first to preach the gospel to Gentiles were such bicultural Jewish followers of Christ. The first specific mission to the Gentiles was called out from the Antioch church which included both Gentile and diaspora Jewish believers. Acts tells us that the nucleus of the churches planted in the Roman Empire came from diaspora Jews and "God fearers." The Syriac-speaking church in the East which took the gospel to India and, through the Nestorians, to China probably had its beginning in synagogues of the diaspora in Mesopotamia.

Through the centuries Christians have been scattered in other diasporas because of religious or political persecution or to seek economic opportunities and political freedom. The Waldensian movement arose in Lyon, France, in the twelfth century and spread across southern and central Europe, only to suffer PERSECUTION and MARTYRDOM. Some Waldensians joined remnants of the Hussite movement which arose in Bohemia and Moravia in the fifteenth century to form the *Unitas Fratrum*. It was a few members of that group who became the nucleus of the Moravian movement which became a major catalyst of the modern Protestant missionary movement (*see* MORAVIAN MISSIONS).

The Mennonites are the primary heirs of the sixteenth-century Anabaptist movement. They have been scattered through a number of European countries as well as North and South America at first because of persecution by the state churches and also in an attempt to preserve their sense of community and their pacifism (*see* PACIFIST THEOLOGY). While in some cases their communities have turned inward, in others they have reached out in mission (*see* MENNONITE MISSIONS). Part of the evangelical movement in Russia has its roots in the Mennonites.

The Puritans came to North America in diaspora and it was a latter-day Puritan, JONATHAN EDWARDS, who played a key role in the first GREAT AWAKENING which laid the foundation of the American missionary movement. Swedish Baptists and other free churches persecuted by state churches in Europe came to the United States seeking religious freedom and economic opportunity. Such groups have made a contribution to missions far beyond the proportion of their numbers. For example, the Covenant Church, of Swedish origin, was originally the Mission Covenant Church.

In the twentieth century the Chinese have established churches in at least thirty-three countries, probably more. Koreans began to flee from their homeland after 1910 and established churches in Siberia and China. It is estimated that there are two million Koreans in China, and that at least 12 percent are Christians. The more recent Korean diaspora has taken them to 170 countries, and they have established churches in at least 150 nations. In some cases they are reaching out to non-Koreans. That has no doubt been a factor in the growing Korean missionary movement. Now many of the second-generation, bicultural youth are showing interest in missions. Like the first cross-cultural Christian missionaries who were Hellenistic Jews at home in two languages and cultures, bicultural Christians today, Koreans, and others, have great potential for missions.

PAUL E. PIERSON

Bibliography. R. DeRidder, *Discipling the Nations;* F. Gibson, ed., *You Are My Witnesses, The Waldensians across 800 Years;* W. Shenk, ed., *Anabaptists and Mission.*

Dictionaries of Mission(s). Over the past two centuries several significant dictionaries of mission(s) have been published as tools to assist in the missionary task. This article will be limited to English-language resources. For the purposes of organizing this discussion, we do not distinguish encyclopedias from dictionaries, and we divide the available resources into four separate categories: (1) general mission(s) dictionaries and encyclopedias, (2) biographical dictionaries, (3) theological dictionaries, and (4) dictionaries which are not directly on mission(s) but which are of mission-related significance (e.g., dictionaries of denominations, religions, etc.). Within each category we start by listing dictionaries specifically limited to mission(s) and then give examples of broader dictionaries which include mission(s) discussion. Within the categories each work is listed by first edition date.

General Mission(s) Dictionaries. Dictionaries which cover the broad scope of missions include perhaps the earliest missionary dictionary to appear: *An Alphabetical Compendium of the Various Sects Which Have Appeared in the World* (H. Adams, 1784), later republished as *A Dictionary of all Religions and Religious Denominations, Jewish, Heathen, Mahometan and Christian* (1817). Nineteenth century works included *A Cyclopedia of Missions* (ed. H. Newcomb, 1854), *Encyclopedia of Religious Knowledge* (ed. J. N. Brown, 1858), *The Missionary World* (ed. A. D. F. Randolph, 1872), and *The Encyclopedia of Missions* (ed. E. Bliss, 1891 and revised by E. Bliss, H. A. Tupper and H. Dwight in 1904). The most recent general dictionary of mission, before this volume, is *Concise Dictionary of the Christian World Mission* (ed. S. Neill, G. H. Anderson, and J. Goodwin; 1971). In addition to these specific mission(s) dictionaries, a number of general resources contain articles on mission-related topics. For example, these include the nineteenth-century work Fessenden & Co's *Encyclopedia of Religious Knowledge* (ed. B. B. Edwards, 1835) and the contemporary works *Oxford Dictionary of the Christian Church* (3 editions: 1957, 1974, and 1997), *New International Dictionary of the Christian Church* (ed. J. D. Douglas, 1974, revised 1978), and *New 20th-Century Encyclopedia of Religious Knowledge* (ed. J. D. Douglas, 1991).

Biographical Dictionaries. Of the biographical dictionaries, several denominationally or geographically focused works have appeared, including *Bibliographic Record of the Pastors, Missionaries and Prominent Laymen of the United Lutheran Church Mission and the Andhra Evangelical Lutheran Church* (R. D. Augustus; 1938, revised 1955), *A Century of Missions of the African Methodist Episcopal Church, 1840–1940* (L. L. Berry, 1942), *Negro Baptists and Foreign Missions* (C. C. Adams, 1944), and *Biographical Dictionary of Methodist Missionaries to Japan* (ed. M. Ida, T. Kega, and J. W. Krummel; 1993). The most significant mission biographical dictionary to date, however, is *Biographical Dictionary of Christian Missions* (ed. G. H. Anderson, 1997), which gives over 2,400 biographies ranging over the full spectrum of ecclesiastical and geographic boundaries. In addition to these dictionaries, many broader biographical works have significant numbers of articles on missionaries and Third World people: *The Oxford Dictionary of Saints* (2 editions: 1978 and 1987), *A Dictionary of Women in Church History* (Mary L. Hammack, 1984), *Who's Who in Christian History* (ed. J. D. Douglas and P. W. Comfort, 1992), *Twentieth-Century Dictionary of Christian Biography* (ed. J. D. Douglas, 1995), and

The Blackwell Dictionary of Evangelical Biography: 1730–1860 (ed. D. M. Lewis, 1995).

Theological Dictionaries. There are two recent dictionaries which focus on theological and historical perspectives and issues in mission: *Philosophy, Science, and Theology of Mission in the 19th and 20th Centuries* (J. A. B. Jongeneel; 2 vols.; 1995 and 1997) presents missiology in outline form with extensive integrated bibliographies, and *Dictionary of Mission. Theology, History, Perspectives* (ed. K. Müller, SVD, T. Sundermeier, S. B. Bevans, SVD, R. H. Bliese, 1997), a translation and English adaptation of the 1987 German dictionary *Lexikon Missionstheologischer Grundbegriffe*. General theological dictionaries which contain significant missiological discussion include *Evangelical Dictionary of Theology* (W. A. Elwell, 1984, rev. 1998), *New Dictionary of Theology* (S. B. Ferguson and D. F. Wright, 1988) and *Dictionary of Scottish Church History and Theology* (N. M. de S. Cameron, D. F. Wright, D. C. Lachman, D. E. Meek, 1993).

Other Missions-Related Dictionaries. There are numerous dictionaries which cover specific facets of missions-related topics, including dictionaries organized around denominations or ecclesiastic organizations, agencies, geographic information, and world religions. Denominational or ecclesiastically oriented dictionaries deal with broader issues in denominations and theologically oriented movements. The following have significant articles on mission related topics and people: *The Mennonite Encyclopedia* (1955–59), *New Catholic Encyclopedia* (1967–79), *Encyclopedia of World Methodism* (N. B. Harmon, 1974), *Dictionary of Pentecostal and Charismatic Movements* (S. M. Burgess and G. B. McGee, 1988), and *Dictionary of the Ecumenical Movement* (ed. N. Lossky, J. Bonino, J. Pobee, T. Stransky, G. Wainwright, P. Webb; 1991).

In addition to the recent DIRECTORIES OF MISSIONS, *The Encyclopedia of Modern Christian Missions: The Agencies* (B. L. Goddard, 1967) provides articles covering the history and development of 1,400 Protestant mission organizations. The nineteenth-century forerunner of today's geographically-based dictionaries was *The Missionary Gazetteer* (C. Williams, 1832).

The recent massive *World Christian Encyclopedia* (ed. D. Barrett, 1982, revised 2000) provides detailed statistical analysis of the Christian church in global context as well as historical summaries of mission and church history for every country of the world. *Operation World* (ed. P. Johnstone), while not a dictionary, is updated regularly and provides statistical summaries as well as issues for prayer for each country. A dictionary which focuses on a specific aspect of mission is *Evangelism and Church Growth: A Practical Encyclopedia* (ed. E. L. Towns, 1995). It presents an evangelical perspective on contemporary thinking related to evangelism.

Dictionaries of religion, while not directly focusing on missionary issues, also provide invaluable introductory background of significance in missionary research. A few of the representative titles include *A Dictionary of Non-Christian Religions* (G. Parrinder, 1971), *Abingdon Dictionary of Living Religions* (ed. K. Crim, 1981), *The Encyclopedia of Religion* (M. Eliade, 1987), *Concise Dictionary of Religion* (I. Hexham, 1993), and *Dictionary of Cults, Sects, Religions and the Occult* (G. A. Mather and L. A. Nichols, 1993). In addition to these, there are many dictionaries which specialize on particular religions.

The most recent development in tools for missionary research are electronic in nature, most specifically CD-ROMs on which are stored massive amounts of data accessible through a computer. Global Mapping's *20:21 Library* contains Bibles in six translations, nine commentaries, *Operation World*, a language encyclopedia, several bibliographies, three mission directories, and two major statistical databases on one disk. A second disk has the Geographic Information System which incorporates the mapping of statistical data in ways which enable mission agencies to plan and make decisions. Another Global Mapping tool, the *African Proverbs: Collections, Studies, Bibliographies* (ed. Stan Nussbaum), has 27,000 proverbs, 23 books, 42 maps, and two annotated bibliographies dealing with African proverbs on a single CD-ROM disk. Appearing almost daily on the World Wide Web, newer resources facilitate the development of missionary research.

Conclusion. Never before in history have so many resources for missionary research been so readily available to so many people. While the reality of an information gap is an issue that persists and must be addressed, the availability and accessibility of such significant resources has put us in the position as individuals and agencies of being without excuse when it comes to doing basic research on topics, people, areas of the world, theological issues, and trends.

A. Scott Moreau

Diffusion. *See* Culture.

Directories of Mission. Mission directories help Christians understand the various mission boards, agencies, and other entities involved in world mission. A missions directory brings together information about those who have been sent to "make disciples of all nations" and information about the sending support bodies.

Some local churches publish a directory of the supported missionaries and other mission projects. These usually have more personal information than would be found in directories published for broader audiences.

Many mission organizations publish a directory with the names, addresses, and so on of their missionaries, usually in a country-by-country order. Such directories are often designed to facilitate prayer support.

A more comprehensive directory is the type that includes all the mission boards and agencies based in a country. Besides the basic directory information, it may include expanded statistical information about the individual organizations, various overall summary totals, indexes, and other information. For the United States and Canada the most comprehensive directory is the *Mission Handbook: U.S. and Canadian Ministries Overseas,* initiated in 1953 as an ongoing series by the Missionary Research Library and published since 1968 by the MARC Division of World Vision International.

In the United Kingdom the *UK Christian Handbook,* edited by Peter Brierley, has an overseas missions section along with sections on other organizations and services. Non-Western countries such as Brazil, Korea, India, and Singapore have produced mission or broader Christian directories, with some available in multiple languages.

Directory sections of non-Western cross-cultural sending missions have been included in some publications. *From Every People: A Handbook of Two-Thirds World Missions with Directory/Histories/Analysis* (1989) by Larry Pate followed earlier publications of the same nature by Marlin Nelson and Lawrence Keyes.

From time to time helpful specialized mission directories have appeared. In conjunction with the Lausanne Congress on World Evangelization (1974), Edward Dayton led a team that produced the *Unreached Peoples Directory,* which in turn stimulated further research and other publications regarding unreached people groups. The Missions Commission of the World Evangelical Fellowship sponsored the *World Directory of Missions Research and Information Centers* (1989) and the *World Directory of Missionary Training Programs* (1995).

Comprehensive world surveys initiated by the International Missionary Council in 1925 and 1936 provided directory information that appeared in related publications. In the following decades, the *World Christian Handbook* (1949, 1952, 1962, 1968), edited by Kenneth Grubb and others, included directory and statistical sections for national churches and mission societies. The most comprehensive world mission directory published to date is *The Encyclopedia of Modern Christian Missions: The Agencies* (1967), with Burton Goddard as editor. It includes historical, descriptive, and statistical (including financial when available) data for more than 1,400 Protestant foreign missionary and related agencies.

A limited amount of mission directory materials have been placed on the World Wide Web. This will most likely increase as the Web continues to develop as a publishing medium.

JOHN A. SIEWERT

Disaster Response. Disaster may be defined as a sudden turn of events (from natural or human causes) which brings about or threatens injury or death to a great number of people, disrupting normal life and requiring immediate action.

Luke 21:9–11 (LB) predicts natural disasters such as earthquakes, famines, epidemics, and "terrifying things happening in the heavens," perhaps like cyclones and hurricanes. It also warns of human-made disasters such as revolutions and wars "for nation shall rise against nation and kingdom against kingdom." Millions of people are affected annually by natural disasters. People, caught in war or civil strife, seek asylum as refugees, and their number is on the rise. Studies describe the world of tomorrow to be more susceptible to all kinds of disturbances than the world of today. Both biblical prophecy and the empirical data affirm the need to anticipate coming disasters.

Responding to disaster is not the responsibility of Christians only. It is the responsibility of every compassionate person. Yet, Christians have a good reason to be involved in disaster response. The GREAT COMMANDMENT (Matt. 22:37–39) dictates that the people of God love him and their neighbors as themselves. All humans are created in the image of God and, therefore, each life is precious—each person one for whom Christ died. All the victims of disaster, natural or human-made, should be treated with dignity and respect.

The Book of Acts gives an example of how Christians should act in response to a disaster. One of the prophets named Agabus predicted a great famine coming upon the land of Israel (which later came to pass during the reign of Claudius). "So the believers [in Antioch] decided to send relief to the Christians in Judea, each giving as much as he could." Their gifts were consigned to Barnabas and Paul, and they were delivered to the elders of the church in Jerusalem (Acts 11:27–30).

In Capernaum Jesus, turning to his enemies, asked, "Is it all right to do kind deeds on Sabbath days? . . . Is it a day to save lives or to destroy them?" No response! Jesus "was deeply disturbed by their indifference to human need" (Mark 3:1–5 LB). Elsewhere we are admonished to "stop just saying we love people," but to "really love them, and show it by our actions" (1 John 3:17–18). In implementing disaster relief, we must work closely, whenever and wherever possible, with existing churches and missions in order that we might help enhance their ministry.

All disasters create concomitant needs for the afflicted. They will need such items as food, shelter, medicine, clothes, and blankets. In a disaster, we must do all we can to provide these basic needs. In every case, food assistance is paramount.

Finally, we must remember that the most basic human need is beyond the physical—to be reconciled to God and to have fellowship with him (2 Cor. 5:18). The Lord God says in Amos 8:11: "The time is surely coming . . . when I will send a famine on the land—not a famine of bread or water, but of hearing the words of the Lord."

TETSUNAO YAMAMORI

SEE ALSO Relief Work.

Disciple, Discipleship. During Jesus' earthly ministry, and during the days of the early church, the term most frequently used to designate one of Jesus' followers was "disciple." A central theme of Jesus' earthly ministry, discipleship likewise is a central theme that is to occupy the mission of the church throughout the ages as they make disciples of all the nations (Matt. 28:18–20) and then help new disciples advance in their discipleship in following Jesus.

Disciple. In the ancient world the term "disciple" was used generally to designate a *follower* who was committed to a recognized leader or teacher. In Jesus' day several other types of individuals were called "disciples." These disciples were similar to, yet quite different from, Jesus' disciples.

The "Jews" who questioned the parents of the man born blind (John 9:18ff.) attempted to scorn the blind man by saying that, although he was a disciple of Jesus, they were "disciples of Moses" (John 9:28). They focused on their privilege to have been born Jews who had a special relation to God through Moses (cf. John 9:29). The "disciples of the Pharisees" (Mark 2:18; Matt. 22:15–16) were adherents of the Pharisaic party, possibly belonging to one of the academic institutions. The Pharisees centered their activities on study and strict application of the Old Testament, developing a complex system of oral interpretations of the Law. The "disciples of John the Baptist" (John 1:35; Mark 2:18) were courageous men and women who had left the status-quo of institutional Judaism to follow the prophet.

What then is different about Jesus' disciples? Jesus' disciples were those who heard his invitation to begin a new kind of life, accepted his call to the new life, and became obedient to it. The center of this new life was Jesus himself, because his disciples gained new life through him (John 10:7–10), they followed him (Mark 1:16–20), they were to hear and obey his teachings (Matt. 5:1–2), and they were to share in Jesus' mission by going into all of the world, preaching the gospel of the kingdom and calling all people to become Jesus' disciples (Luke 24:47; Matt. 28:19–20). In the Gospels the disciples are with Jesus, the religious leaders are those who are against Jesus, and the crowds or multitudes are those who are curious, but have not yet made a commitment to Jesus. The word "disciple" when referring to Jesus' followers is equivalent to "believer" (cf. Acts 4:32; 6:2) and "Christian" (Acts 11:26).

We should distinguish between the disciples in a narrow and broad sense. In the narrow sense we recognize especially those twelve who literally followed Jesus around and later became the apostles. We also recognize a broader group of Jesus' disciples which was composed, among others, of the large group of people who had become Jesus' followers (Luke 6:13), a variety of individual men and women (Luke 8:2–3; 23:49, 55; 24:13, 18, 33), tax-collectors (Luke 19:1–10), scribes (Matt. 8:18–21), and religious leaders (John 19:38–42; Matt. 27:57). The term "disciple" designates one as a believer in Jesus; all true believers are disciples (cf. Acts 4:32 with 6:2). The Twelve were distinguished from the larger group by a calling to become "apostles" (Luke 6:13). The Twelve were both disciples (i.e., believers) and apostles (i.e., commissioned leaders) (Matt. 10:1–2).

Discipleship. The initiative of discipleship with Jesus lies with his call (Mark 1:17; 2:14; Matt. 4:19; 9:9; cf. Luke 5:10–11, 27–28) and his choice (John 15:16) of those who would be his disciples. The response to the call involves recognition and belief in Jesus' identity (John 2:11; 6:68–69), obedience to his summons (Mark 1:18, 20), counting the cost of full allegiance to him (Luke 14:25–28; Matt. 19:23–30), and participating in his mission of being a "light to the Gentiles" (Acts 13). His call is the beginning of something new; it means leaving behind one's old life (Matt. 8:34–37; Luke 9:23–25), finding new life in the family of God through obeying the will of the Father (Matt. 12:46–50), and being sent by him to the world as the Father had sent Jesus (John 20:21).

When Jesus called men and women to follow him, he offered a personal relationship with himself, not simply an alternative lifestyle or different religious practices or a new social organization. While some of the sectarians within Judaism created separations between the "righteous" and the "unrighteous" by their regulations and traditions, Jesus broke through those barriers by calling to himself those who, in the eyes of sectarians, did not seem to enjoy the necessary qualifications for fellowship with him (Matt. 9:9–13; Mark 2:13–17). Discipleship means the beginning of a new life in intimate fellowship with a living Master and Savior. Thus discipleship also involves a commitment to call others to such a relationship with Jesus Christ.

Jesus' gracious call to discipleship was accompanied by an intense demand to count the cost of discipleship (cf. Luke 9:57–62; 14:25–33). The demand to count the cost of discipleship meant exchanging the securities of this world for salvation and security in him. For some this meant sacrificing riches (Matt. 19:16–26), for others it meant sacrificing attachment to family (Matt. 8:18–22; Luke 14:25–27), for still others it meant abandoning nationalistic feelings of superiority (Luke 10:25–37). For all disciples it means giving of one's life for gospel proclamation in the world.

Jesus declared that to be a disciple is to become like the master (Matt. 10:24–25; Luke 6:40). Becoming like Jesus includes going out with the same message, ministry, and compassion (Matt. 10:5ff.), practicing the same religious and social traditions (Mark 2:18–22; Matt. 12:1–8), belonging to the same family of obedience (Matt. 12:46–49), exercising the same servanthood (Mark 10:42–45; Matt. 20:26–28; John 13:12–17), experiencing the same suffering (Matt. 10:16–25; Mark 10:38–39), and being sent in the same way to the same world (John 20:21). The true disciple was to know Jesus so well, was to have followed him so closely, that he or she would become like him. The ultimate goal was to be conformed to Jesus' image (cf. Luke 6:40; Rom. 8:28–29; 2 Cor. 3:18; Gal. 4:19) and then live out a life of witness in word and deed to the world that Jesus is Lord.

John's Gospel carries three challenges of Jesus to his disciples. These challenges offer the means by which a disciple grows in discipleship to become like Jesus. First, true discipleship means abiding in Jesus' words as the truth for every area of life (cf. John 8:31–32). Abiding in Jesus' words means to know and to live in what Jesus says about life. Instead of listening to the world's values, disciples must listen to what Jesus says. This begins with salvation (cf. Peter's example in John 6:66–69), but involves every other area of life as well (Matt. 28:19–20). Second, true discipleship also means loving one another as Jesus loved his disciples (John 13:34–35). Love is a distinguishing mark of all disciples of Jesus, made possible because of regeneration—where a change has been made in the heart of the believer by God's love—and because of an endless supply of love from God, who is love (cf. 1 John 4:12–21). Third, Jesus also said that the true disciple will bear fruit: the fruit of the Spirit (Gal. 5:22–26), new converts (John 4:3–38; 15:16), righteousness and good works (Phil. 1:11; Col. 1:10), and proclamation witness to the world (John 20:21).

No matter how advanced Jesus' disciples would become, they would always be disciples of Jesus. In other master-disciple relationships in Judaism the goal of discipleship was one day to become the master. But disciples of Jesus are not simply involved in an education or vocational form of discipleship. Disciples of Jesus have entered into a relationship with the Son of God, which means that Jesus is always Master and Lord (Matt. 23:8–12). Therefore, this relationship with Jesus is a wholistic process—involving every area of life as the disciple grows to become like Jesus—and it lasts throughout the disciple's life.

The church therefore is a community of disciples, the family of God (cf. Matt. 12:46–50), composed of all those who have believed on Jesus for salvation. In our day we have lost that perspective. Often people of the church feel as though discipleship is optional, that perhaps it is only for those who are extremely committed, or else it is for those who have been called to leadership or ministry. We must regain the biblical perspective: to believe on Jesus draws a person into community, a community which defines its expectations, responsibilities, and privileges in terms of discipleship.

Mission and Discipleship. We have seen above that a primary goal of discipleship is becoming like Jesus (Luke 6:40). This is also understood by Paul to be the final goal of eternal election (Rom. 8:29). The process of becoming like Jesus brings the disciple into intimate relationship with the Lord Jesus Christ, and, as such, is the goal of individual discipleship. But discipleship is not simply self-centered. In a classic interaction with two of his disciples who were seeking positions of prominence, Jesus declares that servanthood is to be the goal of disciples in relationship to one another (Mark 10:35–45). The reason that this kind of servanthood is possible is because of Jesus' work of servanthood in ransoming disciples. He paid the price of release from the penalty for sin (cf. Rom. 6:23), and from the power of sin over pride and self-centered motivation. The motivation of self-serving greatness is broken through redemption, and disciples are thus enabled to focus upon others in servanthood both in the church and, with other Christians, servanthood in the world. This is very similar to Paul's emphasis when he points to Jesus' emptying himself to become a servant: Jesus provides the example of the way the Philippian believers are to act toward one another (Phil. 2:1–8).

Through his final GREAT COMMISSION Jesus focuses his followers on the ongoing importance of discipleship through the ages, and declares the responsibility of disciples toward the world: they are to make disciples of all peoples (Matt. 28:16–20). To "make disciples" is to proclaim the gospel message among those who have not yet heard the gospel of forgiveness of sins (cf. Luke 24:46–47; John 20:21). The command finds verbal fulfillment in the activities of the early church (e.g. Acts 14:21), where they went from Jerusalem to Judea, to Samaria, to the ends of the earth proclaiming the gospel of the kingdom and calling the peoples of the world to become disciples of Jesus Christ. In the early church, to believe in the gospel message was to become a disciple (cf. Acts 4:32 with 6:2). To "make disci-

ples of all the nations" is to make more of what Jesus made of them.

A person becomes a disciple of Jesus when he or she confesses Jesus as Savior and God and is regenerated by the Holy Spirit (cf. John 3:3–8; Titus 3:5). The participles "baptizing" and "teaching" in Matthew 28:18 describe activities through which the new disciple grows in discipleship. Growth includes both identification with Jesus' death and resurrection (baptism) and obedience to all that Jesus had commanded the disciples in his earthly ministry (teaching). Baptism immerses and surrounds the new believers with the reality and presence of the Triune God as they dwell within the church. Obedience to Jesus' teaching brings about full Christian formation for disciples.

Jesus concludes the Commission with the crucial element of discipleship: the presence of the Master— "I am with you always, to the very end of the age" (Matt. 28:20). Both those obeying the command and those responding are comforted by the awareness that the risen Jesus will continue to form all his disciples. The Master is always present for his disciples to follow in their mission to the world throughout the ages.

MICHAEL J. WILKINS

Bibliography. D. Bonhoeffer, *The Cost of Discipleship;* A. B. Bruce, *The Training of the Twelve;* J. D. G. Dunn, *Jesus' Call to Discipleship;* M. Hengel, *The Charismatic Leader and His Followers;* R. N. Longenecker, ed., *Patterns of Discipleship in the New Testament;* D. Müller, *NIDNTT,* 1:483–90; K. H. Rengstorf, *TDNT,* 4:415–61; F. F. Segovia, ed., *Discipleship in the New Testament;* G. Theissen, *Sociology of Early Palestinian Christianity;* M. J. Wilkins, *The Concept of Disciple in Matthew's Gospel: As Reflected in the Use of the Term Mathetes;* idem, *Following the Master: A Biblical Theology of Discipleship;* idem, *Reflecting Jesus.*

Discipling a Whole Nation (DAWN). Discussed as an effective evangelistic method since the mid-1960s, the first major attempt to systematically implement this strategy on a nationwide level occurred in the Philippines in the early 1970s. Jim Montgomery, one of the early proponents, founded Dawn Ministries to sharpen and to communicate the DAWN vision for reaching the world.

DAWN seeks to mobilize the whole body of Christ (local churches, denominations, parachurch organizations) in a nation in a determined effort to complete the Great Commission in that country. The goal is to provide an evangelical congregation for every rural village and urban neighborhood in the country. This approach is based on the conviction that the GREAT COMMISSION is not merely about people coming to faith in Christ. Rather, it is about the establishing of local congregations where evangelism and responsible discipleship can occur.

The DAWN strategy presupposes that the local church, as Jesus Christ incarnate in a geographical area, plays the key role in evangelizing peoples and nations. Subsequently, DAWN works for the multiplication of local churches (*see* SATURATION CHURCH PLANTING) as the "penultimate" step to world evangelization. Finally, it presupposes that a geo-political nation with an evangelical church for approximately every 300 people (in rural areas) to 1000 people (in urban areas) can be considered "reached" in that every person has geographic and cultural access to a church.

RICHARD CRUSE

Bibliography. J. H. Montgomery, *DAWN*.

Dispensationalism. An approach to Holy Scripture which sees God's revelation unfolding through various stages. Throughout Scripture, God reveals his missionary purpose. GEORGE PETERS showed that this purpose was generally "centripetal" in the Old Testament, that is, nations learned of God by coming to Israel. In the New Testament, mission is predominantly "centrifugal," that is, the church moves out to all nations with the gospel (1972, 21).

The modern missionary movement parallels the emergence of dispensationalism. WILLIAM CAREY, who went to India in 1793, is often mentioned as the father of modern evangelical missions, although there were earlier groups, such as the Moravians (*see* MORAVIAN MISSIONS).

Around the same time, John Nelson Darby (1800–1882) founded both the Plymouth Brethren and dispensationalism. It is clear from the beginning that personal piety, church purity, and missions, together with a dispensational orientation, were the ongoing marks of the Brethren movement. Darby, Groves, Mueller, and a host of others testify to this union of biblical method and missions (Coad, 1968, 16, 28, 37).

Nondispensational pietists, Reformed, Arminians, postmillennialists, and amillennialists have all had an honored part in the expansion of the gospel during the modern missions era. Yet George Ladd, himself not a dispensationalist, affirmed the following about dispensational leaders:

It is doubtful if there has been any other circle of men who have done more by their influence in preaching, teaching, and writing to promote a love for Bible study, a hunger for the deeper Christian life, a passion for evangelism, and zeal for missions in the history of American Christianity (1952, 49).

Dispensationalists, especially in North America, have had a great impact on missions through the Bible College movement. Graduate schools of theology like Dallas Theological Seminary have also played a key role in the development and teaching of dispensationalism. Nondispensa-

tional Bible colleges have also sent many graduates into missions. But the missionary impact of dispensational Bible colleges can be seen in the fact that Moody Bible Institute, founded in 1886, alone, has sent out over 6,600 missionaries, of whom almost 3,500 are serving cross-culturally today.

A number of dispensational missiologists have contributed to missions thinking. Among them are George W. Peters, J. HERBERT KANE, DAVID HESSELGRAVE, and Edward Pentecost. What are the distinctives of a dispensational approach to missions?

The Urgency of Missions. George Peters emphasized that missions is a response to an emergency (1972, 15). The crisis is the sinfulness of humanity, which, apart from an intervention of God, will be visited with judgment. God provided Jesus Christ who offered himself on the cross for the sin of the world (John 3:16–17; 2 Cor. 5:19; 1 John 2:2). In Christ, God was offering Israel their Messiah and the beginning of the millennial kingdom. But in their rejection and crucifixion of Christ, God provided for the salvation of the world (John 1:12; 3:16). This should not have been surprising; Jesus said that his Father had always been concerned for the Gentiles (Luke 4:24–27). But there was a new dimension to this era. The saved of all nations would be united in one body, the church. Paul called it a mystery not previously revealed as it was through his ministry (Eph. 3:1–13). This Good News directed to all the world is critically urgent to share.

Missions also derives urgency from the fact that Christ is the unique solution to humanity's dilemma (Acts 4:12). Dispensationalists are Christocentric with an evangelistic priority. People who die without conscious faith in Christ have no hope of salvation (Heb. 9:27). Christ may return at any moment (Matt. 25:36–44). Believers stand instructed by Scripture (2 Peter 3:8–15) to pay attention to personal holiness, understanding that time goes on because of God's concern for the lost. Time, then, is missionary in purpose.

This sense of urgency coupled with the belief in a future "postponed" millennial reign of Christ on earth could diminish a dispensationalist's interest in working toward present social improvement (*see also* MILLENNIAL THOUGHT AND MISSION). But this is denied by more progressive dispensationalists (Blaising and Bock, 1992, 14), as well as by many who are more traditional. Hundreds of hospitals, community development projects, and literacy endeavors conducted by both dispensational and nondispensational missionaries testify to an equal interest in HOLISTIC MISSION.

Closure Strategy. Linked to the matter of urgency is that of actually finishing the task of world evangelism. Late-twentieth-century mission leaders emphasized finishing world evangelism by the year 2000. This is similar to what occurred at the close of the last century in the STU-DENT VOLUNTEER MOVEMENT.

Focus on closure has had a tremendous effect on mission. The great evangelical advances in Latin America, Korea, and the Philippines occurred almost entirely in this century. Many cite Matthew 24:14 as the basis for their concern to finish the work of missions: "This gospel of the kingdom will be preached in all the world as a testimony to all nations, and then the end will come." Perhaps believers today can facilitate the return of Christ.

Dispensationalists agree that all peoples will, in fact, be evangelized (though not all saved) before the end of time, but they consider the "end" as the end of the great tribulation period referred to in both Daniel 9:25–27 and Revelation 7:9–17. Most dispensationalists believe that Christ will come for his saints prior to "The Great Tribulation" and they do not believe they will be involved in the final consummation of the missionary task. A final and comprehensive job of world evangelization will be done during the tribulation, possibly by witnesses who are Jewish people converted during those days (Rev. 7:4–8).

Dispensationalism and missions have had a long and rich connection. As a movement committed to the Word of God, the presence and power of Christ and his Spirit, and preaching the riches of God's incomparable grace, dispensationalists are motivated to engage in the work of missions until he comes!

MICHAEL POCOCK

Bibliography. C. A. Blaising and D. F. Bock, eds., *Dispensationalism, Israel and the Church;* F. R. Coad, *A History of the Brethren Movement;* J. N. Darby, *Synopsis of the Books of the Bible,* 5 vols.; G. E. Ladd, *Crucial Questions About the Kingdom of God;* E. C. Pentecost, *Issues in Missiology;* G. W. Peters, *A Biblical Theology of Missions;* C. C. Ryrie, *Dispensationalism;* R. D. Winters, *Perspectives on the World Christian Movement,* pp. B33–B44.

Divination, Diviner. Divination is the practice of seeking secret knowledge, usually of the future, by occult means. A wide variety of techniques are used, with the expectation that insight will be provided by supernatural beings or power. Divination is and has always been a widespread practice among non-Christian peoples and, unfortunately, among many who call themselves Christians.

Diviners are specialists in using the techniques of divination to discover the information sought by their clients. The power to gain such information is assumed to be obtained by either directly petitioning a spirit or magically through the correct performance of given rituals. Most of those who specialize in working with satanic power combine divination with their other activities. SHAMANS, spirit mediums, priests of various cults, witches, sorcerers, witch doctors, and the like usually practice divination in addition to whatever else they do.

Among the techniques used are dreams, horoscopes, and astrological tables, water witching, examination of entrails or tea leaves, observing the activities of birds or other animals, the positions of coals or stones, cards, dice, crystals, and palmistry. In Scripture we find reference to divination through examining a dead animal's liver (Ezek. 21:21), throwing down arrows (Ezek. 21:21), using a cup (Gen. 44:5), casting lots (Jonah 1:7), astrology (Isa. 47:13), and consulting the dead (Lev. 19:31; Isa. 8:19). God's disapproval of the use of such techniques to gain information from evil spirits (Lev. 20:6) is to be carefully distinguished from his willingness to use casting lots under his guidance to discern his will (Josh. 18:6, 8, 10; Acts 1:26).

A specialized form of divination, trial by ordeal, is used in many societies to discover secret information regarding the guilt or innocence of a person accused of a crime. Ordeals may involve such things as forcing accused persons to dip their hands in hot oil, swallow poison, have a hot knife pressed against their bodies, or some other act with the understanding that if they are harmed they are guilty. In Numbers 5:11–31, Moses is commanded to instruct the Israelites to use an ordeal involving an oath and the drinking of "bitter water" to discern the guilt or innocence of a wife suspected of adultery.

Divination remains common today. The techniques used are empowered by demons with very real results. Diviners are able to use Satan's communication system to find things that have been lost, make predictions concerning the future that, if believed, bear startling fruit, and to thoroughly impress those who know no greater power. Those who would present Christianity in a way that is attractive to the majority of the peoples of the world need to take such manifestations of satanic power seriously. Jesus came into a power-oriented world (like ours) and showed us how to use God's power and passed on his authority and power to us (Luke 9:1; John 14:12) to enable us to confront and defeat the enemy in contexts where he is influencing people through divination.

CHARLES H. KRAFT

SEE ALSO Shaman, Shamanism.

Bibliography. D. Burnett, *Unearthly Powers;* A. C. Lehmann and J. E. Myers, *Magic, Witchcraft and Religion.*

Divine Attributes of God. Throughout the centuries the Christian world mission has been seen as an enterprise arising from the nature of God himself. On the basis of what evidence is this claim made? Which aspects of divinity are seen in the biblical plan for missions? In his *Systematic Theology,* Louis Berkhof divides the attributes of God into the *incommunicable* aspects of his nature, which emphasize the absolute Being of God, and the *communicable* attributes, which stress the fact that he enters into relationships with his creatures. While at first glance the latter category would appear to be more essential to the missionary program, it is the incommunicable attributes that form a foundation on which the communicable aspects rest. Therefore we begin with God's incommunicable qualities.

First, God is *self-existent*. He does not need human companionship, and rather than being obligated to his creation in any way, he would actually be justified in extinguishing the human race for its collective rejection of him. The plan of redemption, then, arises out of a free choice by God to dispense his grace to individuals (John 1:13; Rom. 9:16–22), and, in imitation of his example, the biblical motivation for missions is just such a free choice on the part of missionary agents (1 Cor. 9:19–23).

God is also *immutable*—he cannot change (*see* IMMUTABILITY OF GOD). This means that his choice to dispense grace to humankind cannot be reversed, since this choice is rooted in his unchanging nature. His acceptance of Christ's atonement for sin, his election and calling, his provision of regeneration for those who respond to the gospel, his work of sanctification, and his provision of an eternal home for the redeemed are all assured (Eph. 1:3–14). The missionary offers to unbelievers a plan for salvation that is guaranteed by an unchanging God, and those who have been regenerated can rely on God's power to preserve them throughout their mortal lives (Phil. 1:6).

The fact that God is *infinite*, or *omnipresent*, gives assurance that since he inhabits all times and places simultaneously, he is able to carry out effectively all of the operations connected with salvation, and is able to do so for all persons with whom he chooses to deal (Eph. 3:11) (*see* OMNIPRESENCE OF GOD). Thus the gospel may be preached in full confidence that God will be present to hear any sinner's prayer of repentance.

The fact of God's *unity* implies that there is no sundering of purpose within the Godhead. There are no conflicting desires with regard to God's intent to offer salvation to humans. Each of the members of the Trinity is involved in the missionary enterprise: the Father has chosen individuals for salvation and provides for their regeneration by a free act of his grace (Eph. 2:8–9; 2 Thess. 2:13); the Son has provided the substitutionary atonement for sin and has delegated to his church the task of missions (Matt. 28:18–20; Heb. 10:10); and the Holy Spirit convicts the world of sin and accomplishes the work of regeneration (John 3:3–8; 16:7–11).

Secondly, with regard to God's communicable attributes, the first is *spirituality*, meaning that he is immaterial. He is not limited by flesh and blood, and consequently is above the foibles of humanity (John 4:23–24). Missionary agents can be assured that they are participants in a program whose Designer is not subject to human frailty. He makes no mistakes due to physical exhaustion or emotional imbalance, and he is completely capable of carrying out all his intentions, even when his co-laborers succumb to human weaknesses (2 Cor. 12:10).

His *intellectual* qualities are three: *knowledge, wisdom,* and *veracity*. His knowledge, or *omniscience*, indicates that he knows all things both actual and possible (*see* OMNISCIENCE OF GOD). Thus his strategies and methodologies for mission are efficacious and his timing without flaw. While missionary theologians have always had to wrestle with difficult issues such as the fate of those who have never heard the gospel, we can be assured that God is cognizant of these issues and deals with them in accordance with his perfect knowledge (Rom. 8:29–30; 1 Peter 1:1–2). Since God also possesses wisdom, he does not simply know about things in a theoretical sense. He acts on his knowledge, and his actions produce the gracious ends he intends (Eph. 1:7–8). Therefore missionaries go forth in full confidence that their participation in the GREAT COMMISSION is not in vain but is a wise pursuit (Prov. 11:30).

God is also characterized by *veracity;* he has spoken the truth concerning all that he has chosen to reveal to humankind. The Good News is reliable: Christ's death has been accepted as a substitutionary atonement for sin and humans may attain justification through submission to Jesus as Lord of their lives and belief in his resurrection (Rom. 10:9–10). Thus the missionary can proclaim the gospel boldly, assured that it accurately reflects the way things really are (1 John 5:20).

The *moral* attributes of God are also three. First, there is God's *goodness*, which includes his *love, grace, mercy,* and *longsufferingness*. The LOVE OF GOD empowers missionary agents to overcome their innate selfishness and reach out to others across cultural barriers (John 3:16; Rom. 5:8). The GRACE OF GOD—his "unmerited favor"—extends salvation to those whom he chooses (Eph. 2:8–9), and the MERCY OF GOD permits him to accept Christ's substitutionary atonement for the sins of humankind (Titus 3:4–5). His longsufferingness allows him to tolerate even for a short period of time the sins of humankind, and this enables the missionary enterprise to go forward, for otherwise his wrath would blot out all sin by erasing humankind from the earth (2 Peter 3:9).

The *HOLINESS* of God—his separateness from sin—makes the Christian world mission necessary, for his holiness stands as an impenetrable barrier to a relationship of either temporal or eternal duration with sinful creatures (Heb.

12:14). Only through submission to the gospel message can salvation from sin be attained and the way opened to enter into fellowship with God (1 John 1:5–9).

God's *righteousness*—his absolute *justice*—also makes mission necessary (*see* JUSTICE OF GOD). Unless one can fully satisfy the absolute legal standards and expectations imposed by the justice of God on his creatures, he remains unapproachable. But missionary agents proclaim the Good News that these legal requirements have been met through Christ's sinless life and sacrificial death and that one may appropriate a new legal standing in order to enter into the presence of God (Rom. 8:1–4).

Finally, God's *sovereignty*, or *omnipotence*, implies that he has both the authority and the power to do what he has said he will do (*see* SOVEREIGNTY OF GOD). He authorized Christ's atoning death, accepted its substitutionary efficacy, will apply its effects to those whom he chooses, will regenerate them, will sustain them throughout their mortal lives, and will establish them in an eternal residence with him. God's sovereignty assures that the activity of the missionary will succeed in the measure that he allows (Gal. 6:7–8). His authority has been delegated to Christ, who in turn delegates it to his disciples, empowering them for the work of the Great Commission (Matt. 28:19–20). Thus we conclude that there is no aspect of God that is not in some way involved in the outworking of the Christian world mission, and it is our privilege to participate as co-laborers with him (1 Cor. 3:9).

LARRY POSTON

See also Immanence of God; Providence of God; Transcendence of God; Wrath of God.

Bibliography. J. H. Kane, *Christian Missions in Biblical Perspective;* G. W. Peters, *A Biblical Theology of Missions.*

Divine Deliverance. Christ sets captives free. Missions is proclaiming Christ—who liberates from darkness and ignorance, from oppression and injustice, from sin and its vicious hold on every aspect of human life, and from death.

The deliverance motif runs throughout the whole story of God's redemptive work. The exodus is the defining event of the Old Testament. The people of Israel were a people set free through the merciful intervention of God; this is a recurring theme in the Psalms.

We also see deliverance in the ministry of Jesus. He announced a kingdom and viewed his mission as one of liberation, through word and deed, from the forces, spiritual and otherwise, that oppressed his hearers. And he called his followers to participate, in word and deed, in this cosmic agenda.

In the writings of Paul, we see that it is centrally through the cross that Christ brings deliverance. The cross was propitiation—a sacrificial guilt-offering. In the cross was manifested the reconciling love of God. But the cross was also the triumph through which Christ brought deliverance. Christians think of the resurrection as a great victory, and it was. But Scripture portrays the cross as the actual point of encounter between Christ and evil, when the powers of darkness were defeated and humanity, indeed the whole cosmos, was delivered from sin, the law, and death (*see* ATONEMENT).

Christ demonstrated God's justice, giving himself as a ransom—not to Satan, but to the Father. Thereby, Christ triumphed over the powers of darkness (Col. 2:13–15; Heb. 2:14–15). It was not an encounter of power with power so much as it was a freedom to let sin meet judgment. Christ triumphed by submitting to death. He defeated death by his own death.

The missionary task announces and participates in the triumph of God and divine deliverance. The announcement points to the triumph of Christ on the cross; the participation comes not by the triumph of Christians or the church, but by suffering (as identification with the cross).

For some, the primary manifestation of God's deliverance is freedom from oppressive social and economic systems. LIBERATION THEOLOGY contends that God brings deliverance through sociopolitical upheaval that leads to justice. Missions is participation in this process. But while all Christians are called to be catalysts of justice, a true social transformation will only come when the human heart is liberated from sin. The fundamental human problem is bondage, yes, but it is a bondage to sin of which the social and economic inequity in human systems is but a symptom.

For others, divine deliverance speaks of SPIRITUAL WARFARE, God's power confronting invisible forces of evil and darkness, an encounter fueled by focused intercessory prayer. Behind this lies the recognition that spiritual forces are at work in every aspect of human life and society and that divine deliverance will only come when these spiritual forces are defeated.

But a cautionary note must be raised. It is possible to overspiritualize the forms of bondage or to overstate the extent to which Satan is himself actively involved in holding people and human systems in bondage. Often the work Christians are called to do includes both prayer and acts of kindness, mercy, and justice—to do what is right in the midst of wrong. If we overspiritualize the bondage, it is easy to assume that if there is sufficient prayer or faith the bondage will be eliminated. In fact, however sincere our faith and well-intentioned our prayers, the full and final deliverance of God will not come until the consummation of Christ's kingdom.

And then also, for others, the divine deliverance is fundamentally for emotional and physical wellness. Sin has left a profound mark of dislocation and inner pain on individuals who have experienced the horrifying effects of wrongdoing. Perhaps they are the children of alcoholic parents; perhaps they experienced physical and emotional abuse. Freedom for them is deliverance that includes physical and emotional healing.

From every angle, we must remember that ultimately the whole creation is in bondage (Rom. 8:19–20) and looks forward to the day of its redemption. This reminds us that bondage is cosmic, not merely individual, and further that ultimate deliverance awaits Christ's return.

Consequently, we maintain a biblical perspective on divine deliverance when we affirm (1) that it is both individual and cosmic; (2) that it has present manifestations, but will only be complete at the return of Christ; (3) that it is fundamentally a spiritual matter, but one that has visible manifestations in every aspect of human life and society; and (4) that deliverance comes not so much through a show of force but by suffering in Jesus' name.

GORDON T. SMITH

SEE ALSO Miracles in Mission.

Bibliography. T. Oden, *The Word of Life;* E. Rommen, ed., *Spiritual Power and Missions: Raising the Issues.*

Divine Election. Divine election is part of God's work of *predestination,* his decree regarding the eternal destiny of human beings. The issue of *election* is: Does God choose certain individuals out of the entirety of humanity to be recipients of his gift of salvation in Jesus Christ, thereby assuring that they will enjoy eternal life? If so, by what manner? A corollary issue, called reprobation, is this: Does God also pass over certain individuals, in sorrow leaving them in their sins and to their eternal condemnation? If so, by what manner?

Various responses to these questions have been offered and are summarized here in six general categories.

Calvinism affirms divine election and specifies that God's choice of some for eternal life is *unconditional,* not based on any human merit or a positive response of faith to the gospel as foreseen by God. Rather, election was God's sovereign will and good pleasure purposed before the creation of the world (Eph. 1:3–14; Rom. 9:14–18) and is immutable, necessary (given the utter sinfulness of people), and efficacious. The elect will certainly embrace the salvation offered them in Jesus Christ and continue in that faith until the end (Acts 13:48; Rom. 8:28–30).

Some Calvinists, in addition to embracing election, also affirm divine *reprobation.* This view, called *double predestination,* holds that God not only chooses some for eternal salvation, but also passes over others, in sorrow deciding not to save them but to allow the sentence of eternal death to fall upon them. These people are "vessels of wrath made for destruction" (Rom. 9:14–23); the stumbling of the disobedient is the tragic end to which they were appointed (1 Peter 2:6–10; Jude 4).

A compatibilist approach underscores the causal differences between election and reprobation. In the former case, God *causes* the salvation of the elect, mercifully giving to them what they do not deserve: grace leading to salvation. This is not without genuine human response, however: divine election is ordained by God and comes about through the willing appropriation of the gospel by faith (2 Thess. 2:13–14). In the latter case, God *does not cause* the damnation of the reprobate, but justly gives to them what they deserve: condemnation due to sin and willful disobedience to the gospel (2 Thess. 1:6–10).

Pelagianism denies both election and reprobation. Divinely gifted with freedom of choice and the ability to respond to God without a work of grace upon their souls, people do not have a penchant for sin. Thus, there is no need to be predestined in any way, but people are capable of fulfilling God's purposes and are held fully responsible to do so.

Arminianism/Wesleyanism affirms divine election and specifies that such election is *conditional.* Since God does "not wish for any to perish but for all to come to repentance" (2 Peter 3:9; 1 Tim. 2:3–4) and makes universal appeals for all to embrace his offer of salvation (Matt. 11:28; Isa. 55:1), then all people must be able to meet the terms of salvation. This is made possible by *prevenient grace,* a divine work in all people everywhere which overcomes the corruption due to sin and which restores the ability to respond positively to the gospel. Election is based on God's *foreknowledge* of this positive response (Rom. 8:28–30; 1 Peter 1:1–2); thus, it is conditioned upon foreseen faith in Jesus Christ. Double predestination is denied.

Karl Barth's doctrine of election focuses attention on Jesus Christ, who is both the *elected man* and the *electing God* (this, for Barth, is double predestination). As the *elected man,* Jesus is central to the work of salvation and demonstrates that God is for humankind in election and not against humankind in reprobation. God's will from all eternity is the election of Jesus Christ. As the *electing God,* Jesus willingly elected to become man and to undergo reprobation for himself so that the entire world would be elect in him. The elect community—the church—preaches to the world, proclaiming to all this universal election by God in Jesus Christ.

A Calvinistic perspective is often seen as a deterrent to missions, for the following reasons. If

God has already elected certain individuals to salvation, then why engage in missionary work—praying, going, giving, and preaching the gospel—since those individuals will be saved anyway? This objection overlooks the fact that God not only ordains the salvation of the elect, but also ordains that their salvation will come only through hearing the gospel and appropriating this provision of forgiveness by faith and repentance (2 Thess. 2:13–14). Thus, a human response to the Good News is essential and the Missionary Task is imperative, being the divinely commanded means of linking the elect with the gospel (Rom.10:5–15). Another key to consider is the fact that divine election is a secret decree and thus not revealed to us; thus, we must engage in missions without the knowledge of whether the individuals to whom we minister are elect or not. Finally, since God's election is efficacious, missionaries may be encouraged that their labors in preaching and teaching Christ will be fruitful (Acts 18:9–10).

From an Arminian/Wesleyan perspective, if election is conditioned upon the response of individuals to the gospel, then it is imperative to engage in the missionary enterprise. Again, God alone foreknows who will respond positively to the Good News, so the gospel must be indiscriminately preached to all who will listen.

Karl Barth does not distinguish between the elect and the reprobate, since all people have been elected. However, not all people live as elect; rather, many live as reprobate. The Christian mission, therefore, consists of proclaiming to all people that they are elected by God in Jesus Christ, enabling those who do not realize this fact to be aware of their election so as to live in the light of this magnificent work.

Whether we are elected unconditionally (Calvinism), conditionally (Arminianism), or universally (Barth), all who are the elect of God have the responsibility of praying, going, giving and proclaiming Jesus Christ as part of the missionary enterprise.

Gregg R. Allison

Bibliography. J. Calvin, *The Institutes of the Christian Religion*, 3.21–24; J. Arminius, *Examination of Perkins' Pamphlet and Declaration of Sentiments;* K. Barth, *Church Dogmatics* II/2; C. Pinnock, ed., *Grace Unlimited* and *The Grace of God, the Will of Man: A Case for Arminianism;* T. Schreiner and B. Ware, *The Grace of God, the Bondage of the Will: A Case for Calvinism.*

Divine Initiative. The Scriptures present God as the one ultimate and Supreme Being in the universe. Before anything else existed, God eternally "was." It was within the depths of his Being that the idea of what would exist arose and when it pleased him those ideas took concrete external shape at the word of his command. God created the supernatural world and the physical world in which the human race would be placed. This is the import of Genesis 1:1, which says, "In the beginning God created the heavens and the earth" and all of this speaks to the question of God's initiative. If God had not taken the initiative there would have been no reality external to himself. He conceived, developed, and executed the plan that gave reality to what we now experience as our universe and our place in it.

The initiative of God did not end when he had accomplished the initial creation of all things. By a continuous act of his power God sustains everything in existence. Created, contingent being has no power to keep itself in existence; were it not for the sustaining word and will of God, all that is would lapse back into its primal nonexistence and be no more. In addition to this God has retained his right to intervene creatively in his universe for the governance and good of his creation. He does this by sometimes working through the orderly structures he has established and sometimes by contravening them for a higher good (*see* Miracles). After all, the orderly structures (the so-called natural laws) are all part of a larger moral order and subserve those higher purposes. So God's intervention in his own universe is not a violation of independently functioning laws but rather a rearranging of those orderly structures to serve a higher end. The Deists of the eighteenth century down to and including the liberal theologians of our own day deny that God (if there is a personal God) would do this sort of thing. They assert that after the world was established, God left it to work out its own purposes, especially the purposes of human beings, who now have the ultimate initiative. Scripture does not teach this. It allows that human beings do exercise initiative and may genuinely act as responsible beings, but it is all within the matrix of God's overall sustenance and management (providence). We may exercise initiative, but not ultimately.

Scripture is replete with examples of God's taking the initiative. God made the world; God said "Let the land produce vegetation" (Gen. 1:11) and it obeyed him. God created the human pair and established his relationship with them, setting limits upon them. God judged them when they failed. The overwhelming number of times God's initiative is spoken of in Scripture has caused some modern theologians actually to *define* God as a "God who acts" (as opposed to the pagan gods who could do nothing) and the Bible as the "Book of the Acts of God" (G. Ernest Wright; R. H. Fuller).

From a missiological point of view, the concept of the divine initiative most directly relates to God's self-disclosure with a view to bringing fallen humans into a redemptive relation with himself. God has called his people to share this good news of redemption with every living soul.

God took the initiative in seeking out the lost progenitors of our race and all of their descendants. He established a plan of salvation that we may enter into, he commissions people to proclaim this message, he works on the hearts of the unredeemed to awaken a sense of need, and he regenerates those who believe. The apostle Paul worked out an entire philosophy of history based on this conception of God, as he explained to the Athenian philosophers in Acts 17. God made the world and everything in it (17:24); he needs nothing, "because he himself gives all men life and breath and everything else" (17:25); he made all nations from one person "and determined the times set for them and the exact places where they should live" (17:26); and he "did this so that men would seek him and perhaps reach out for him and find him, though he is not far from each one of us" (17:27). Paul sees the redemptive purposes of God at work everywhere and himself as an AMBASSADOR OF GOD calling everyone, everywhere to repentance and conscious faith in Jesus Christ. He also sees it as the task of the church to share in this ministry and proclaim the saving message of the gospel to those who are lost (*see* MISSIONARY TASK).

Those who proclaim the gospel may be sure that God has gone before them. He who made and sustains this universe and who initiated the plan of salvation for lost humanity did not suddenly stop working and leave it all up to human efforts. He certainly includes those efforts, but, thankfully, they are within the context of his own creative involvement and activity. In the end, it is not "he who plants nor he who waters [who] is anything, but only God who made it grow" (1 Cor. 3:7). We are fellow-workers with God (1 Cor. 3:9).

God has gone before us in at least four ways and those who go out to labor in God's field may be certain that God has been there first—and is still there at work (1 Cor. 3:9; Matt. 9:38). First, God has preceded us by making a knowledge of himself available to everyone (Pss. 19:1–4; 22:27, 28; 48:10; John 1:1–5, 9; Rom. 1:18, 19, 28). Second, God has revealed significant aspects of his nature through GENERAL REVELATION, such as his righteousness (Rom. 1:32), his kindness (Matt. 5:45; Acts 14:17), his power (Ps. 29:3–10; Rom. 1:20), his majesty and glory (Ps. 8:1–4; 19:1), and his truth (Rom. 1:21, 25). Third, God has written his moral requirements into the human heart and no matter how badly they may be distorted by sin, they are still there and may be appealed to. C. S. Lewis called these "the Tao" in *The Abolition of Man* and finds the basis for all natural forms of religion in them. These moral requirements include the need to worship (Acts 17:22, 23), the need to seek God (Acts 17:27), fundamental moral principles (Matt. 5:47; Rom. 2:13–16), and a sense of impending judgment

upon wrongdoing (Rom. 1:21–25, 32). Finally, God's *will* to save is also made known, although, rather obviously, the *facts of salvation* are not. They may only be known through special revelation (Acts 17:27; Rom. 2:5–11; Titus 2:11; 2 Peter 3:3; 5:4, 8, 9).

The command to proclaim the gospel is a universal one (Matt. 28:19, 20; Acts 1:8) and we may confidently build upon what we know God has been doing before our arrival. Sometimes it is just a general work that God has been doing and we must labor hard in the face of ridicule and rejection, as Paul did in Athens (Acts 17:32, 33). Sometimes God has been preparing the ground very specifically and our call may be to a specific area (Macedonia, Acts 16:10) or a specific individual (Cornelius, Acts 19:19–22). Either way the divine initiative precedes ours and assures us that our labors will not be in vain.

WALTER A. ELWELL

Bibliography. A. D. Clarke and B. W. Winter, eds., *One God, One Lord;* B. Demarest, *General Revelation;* C. S. Lewis, *The Abolition of Man;* L. Newbigin, *The Gospel in a Pluralist Society;* B. G. Nicholls, ed., *The Unique Christ in Our Pluralist World;* G. E. Wright and R. H. Fuller, *The Book of the Acts of God.*

Divorce. God's ideal for marriage remains one man and one woman for life in a one-flesh relationship. Divorce, for whatever reason, violates this intended union both for marriage in general and for each affected marriage in particular (Gen. 2:18–24; Mark 10:2–12). Though a violation of God's will and therefore sinful, divorce, like other sins, can be forgiven and persons involved cleansed "from all unrighteousness" (1 John 1:9).

Divorce impacts missions in at least three ways. Cross-cultural ministry must address the place in the churches of persons divorced either before or after conversion. Are divorced persons to be admitted fully into church membership? Each church group will of necessity decide and make clear its convictions. In no way should divorced persons be made to feel that they are second-class members in the church. Remembering that divorce can be forgiven and repentant sinners cleansed, perhaps missionaries should consider that those whom God has brought into the kingdom should likewise be admitted to the churches.

A second impact of divorce on missions relates to the place of divorced persons (national and missionary) in church leadership. Many missionary agencies do not appoint divorced persons as missionaries and some churches do not allow divorced persons to serve in church leadership. This conviction is often based on 1 Timothy 3:2 and 12. A grammatical parallel is found in 1 Timothy 5:9, where a widow can be "put on the list" or cared for only if she is sixty years of age and the "wife of one husband." It is possible that the phrase "husband of one wife" and "wife of one husband" focus on marital fidelity rather than continuing status. If so, these verses, of themselves, do not prohibit divorced persons from church leadership.

A third impact of divorce on mission relates to the need for strengthening marriages—both missionary and national. Marriage counseling to prevent divorce often comes too late. Churches must extend every effort to help couples reach toward God's ideal for marriage and maintain God-intended relationships.

Divorce wrecks God's intent for marriage and affects God's work in every country. Missionary and church leadership must address and seek to correct the problems associated with divorce.

EBBIE C. SMITH

Djibouti *(Est. 2000 pop.: 645,000; 23,200 sq. km. [8,958 sq. mi.]).* Djibouti is a small nation on the Red Sea coast of the Horn of Africa. Nearly half of the people are Somalis with an additional 35 percent of Afar background. Ninety-three percent of the country's population are Muslim, with a small Christian population of about 5.6 percent. The vast majority of the Christian community are French-speaking Roman Catholics and Orthodox from Greece and Ethiopia. Evangelical Protestants are found among Ethiopian Protestants and the Red Sea Mission Team.

TODD M. JOHNSON

Dober, (Johann) Leonhard (1706–66). First Moravian missionary and mission promoter. Born in Münchsroth, Wüttemberg, Germany, and a potter by trade, he arrived at Herrnhut in the late 1720s and rapidly became a leading figure in the newly reconstituted "Unity of the Brethren" or Moravian church. When in 1731 Count ZINZENDORF returned to Herrnhut from Copenhagen with the vision of a mission to the Danish West Indies, Dober volunteered to go. He left on August 21, 1732, with the carpenter DAVID NITSCHMANN to travel to St. Thomas, Virgin Islands, to evangelize African slaves. This marked the beginning of the famous Moravian foreign mission enterprise. He worked alone as a lay preacher, as Nitschmann returned home after five months to take up another assignment. After a year and a half of labor Dober had made only one convert, an orphan boy named Carmel Oly, whom he took to Herrnhut in 1734 when eighteen new missionaries arrived and he was recalled to become chief elder of the community. In Europe he performed administrative functions and engaged in evangelistic activities, including work among the Jews of Amsterdam. He gave up the chief elder position in 1741 but was ordained bishop in 1747. The most distinguished of

Zinzendorf's co-workers, Dober traveled incessantly around Europe to maintain contacts among the scattered Moravian churches. He died in Herrnhut.

RICHARD V. PIERARD

Doctoral Degrees in Missiology. Seminaries and universities are granting a wide range of doctoral degrees related to missiology. Such areas as the history of mission, contextualization, theology of mission, mission strategies, Bible translation, Christian leadership development for mission, ethnographic studies that serve as bases for missiological strategy planning, and studies of Christian relief and development illustrate the breadth of the range of missiological studies. The lines that delimit missiological studies from church history, ethics, theology, evangelism and other topics of the theological curriculum focus on the issue of crossing boundaries. However, they remain fuzzy.

Missiological studies are being conducted at doctoral levels from a variety of academic disciplinary perspectives, including missiology, theology, ethics, church history, anthropology, sociology, leadership, political science, economics, education, communications, community development, comparative religion, linguistics, and music. Very often missiological studies are multidisciplinary, drawing on two or more academic disciplines. Multidisciplinary approaches in missiology allow researchers to gain multiple perspectives on complex issues.

The range of doctoral degrees in missiology is also wide and complex. In a search of titles and abstracts listed with University Microfilms, Inc. from 1988 to 1996, sixteen doctoral degree names can be found. The most common related to missiology include the Ph.D., D.Min., D.Miss., Th.D., and Ed.D. Each of these degrees has a related set of names depending on the degree-granting university or seminary. All four types of degrees are commonly granted by seminaries and university divinity schools. However, the Ph.D. and Ed.D. are the most common.

Doctoral degrees related to missiology differ in purpose and content. The Doctor of Ministry degree assumes a prerequisite M.Div. plus three years of post-M.Div. ministry experience. The degree is a ministry-focused degree with the person studying while in service. The 1996 Association of Theological Schools in the USA (ATS) standards describes the purpose of the D.Min. as "to enhance the practice of ministry for persons who hold the M.Div. degree and have engaged in ministerial leadership." The D.Min. degree requires one year of academic work beyond the M.Div. including significant peer learning, integrative and interdisciplinary activities, personal and spiritual growth, and a doctoral level project or dissertation. It is designed to take between three and six years to complete.

The 1996 ATS *Bulletin of Procedures, Standards, and Criteria for Membership* states that the Doctor of Missiology is "a professional degree which is designed to prepare persons for denominational/interdenominational leadership roles in specialized cross-cultural ministries both in North America and around the world, as well as for teaching. While the primary thrust of the program is professional, it should include theological and theoretical foundations as well as training in research skills." The D.Miss. has an M.Div. as a prerequisite and two years of ministry experience. Language requirements normally include a field language other than English and such other languages as would be needed to complete the research. The requirements of the degree normally include at least two years of full-time study in missiology beyond the M.Div. plus a dissertation. The D.Miss. is normally an interdisciplinary degree with significant studies in the social sciences to supplement the theological component.

Neither a Ph.D. nor Ed.D requires a prerequisite theology degree and so both are granted not only by seminaries, but universities as well. The requirements for a Ph.D. or Ed.D. with a focus in a missiological topic vary widely. Normally, one would expect at least three years of post-bachelor's study plus a research-based dissertation. However, in some seminaries, the Ph.D. follows an M.Div. equivalence with three years of study and research. A Ph.D. is seen as a degree based on research and aimed at equipping a person for teaching in a specialized area. An Ed.D. will normally require a significant focus in education.

The difference between the D.Miss. and the Ph.D. may be seen by an analogy from medicine. The D.Miss. is to missiology what the M.D. is to medicine or an Ed.D. is to education. It is designed for the professional practitioner who can apply the theory to a concrete situation. Similarly, the Ph.D. is to missiology what the Ph.D. is to medicine. Both are related to theory development and application. A person with a Ph.D. in biochemistry will instruct the person seeking the M.D. A person with a Ph.D. related to missiology may be a practitioner, but will be expected to develop the theory for the person with the D.Miss. to use in field practice.

Other related doctoral degrees such as the Th.D. focus on their primary theological purpose while incorporating missiological studies. The Ph.D. in missiology, for example, requires an M.Div. plus at least one additional year of theological study as part of the doctoral program. The D.Min. may relate to missiology, but has no specific accreditation related requirements in missiology.

Universities granting missiologically related degrees include private Christian universities, state universities, private "secular" universities, and royal chartered universities. The faculties within these universities who grant missiologically related degrees range across a broad spectrum of disciplines as mentioned above. The search of UMI documentation identified 130 institutions which have granted more than 550 doctoral degrees related to mission over the past six years. Ten institutions accounted for approximately two-thirds of the doctoral degrees.

EDGAR J. ELLISTON

SEE ALSO Degrees in Mission and Missiology.

Doing Theology. *See* THEOLOGICAL METHOD.

Doke, Clement Martyn (1893–1980). South African educator, scholar, and missionary. He came from a distinguished missionary lineage. WILLIAM CAREY was an ancestor through his mother Agnes. His father, Joseph J. Doke, had been a Baptist pastor, missionary, social activist, and church leader in many countries, including South Africa, where he had been a friend of M. K. Gandhi. In 1913 Clement accompanied his father on a mission to the Lamba people at Kafulafuta, in what is now Zambia. J. J. Doke died before the end of the year, but the work he started was continued by the South African Baptist missionary society, including his daughter Olive, Clement, and Clement's wife Hilda. They went on preaching treks throughout the area and helped lay the foundations of a church. In 1919 malaria brought the treks of Doke and his wife to a close. He completed degrees in languages at universities in the Transvaal and England and began lecturing on Bantu studies at the University of Witwatersrand in 1932. Soon he was acknowledged as an authority on Bantu and other southern African languages. Perhaps his crowning scholarly achievement was the preparation, with assistance from other scholars, of Zulu and Lamba dictionaries and grammars. But much of his effort went into a translation of the Bible in Lamba, which he completed, with his sister's help, in 1959. He was also a leader in the Baptist church. Posts he held included editor of *South African Baptist* from 1923 to 1932, president from 1949 to 1950 of the Baptist Union of South Africa (as his father had been), and the first principal of the Baptist Theological College in Johannesburg in 1951.

ROBERT SHUSTER

Bibliography. C. M. Doke, *Trekking in South-Central Africa, 1913–1919;* P. C. Stine, *BDCM*, p. 181.

Dominica *(Est. 2000 pop. 71,000; 751 sq. km. [290 sq. mi.]).* A former French colony, Dominica was acquired by Britain in 1759 and gained its independence in 1978. The rugged, mountainous island is set between the French islands of Guadeloupe and Martinique. The population is almost entirely Afro-Caribbean, with a tiny minority of Caribs, a remnant of the indigenous peoples. Although English is the official language, the island's cultural heritage is reflected in the French Creole commonly spoken by most citizens and their adherence to Roman Catholicism (75 percent of the population). Evangelical Protestants make up fewer than 10 percent of the residents.

EVERETT A. WILSON

See also Caribbean.

Bibliography. A. Lampe, *The Church in Latin America, 1492–1992,* pp. 201–15; J. Rogozinski, *A Brief History of the Caribbean: From the Arawak and the Carib to the Present.*

Dominican Republic *(Est. 2000 pop.: 8,495,000; 48,734 sq. km. [18,816 sq. mi.]).* Occupying the eastern two-thirds of the island of Hispaniola, the Dominican Republic is more than 90 percent Roman Catholic. Less than 5 percent of the people are evangelical. The mainline denominations have had less success here than in several other Caribbean societies, with Seventh-Day Adventists constituting the largest non-Catholic church. Dominican Pentecostals are also a significant minority. Other Protestant bodies with some representation are the Church of the Nazarene and the Free Methodists.

EVERETT A. WILSON

See also Caribbean.

Bibliography. A. Lampe, *The Church in Latin America, 1492–1992,* pp. 201–15; J. Rogozinski, *A Brief History of the Caribbean: From the Arawak and the Carib to the Present.*

Doremus, Sarah (1802–77). American urban missionary and mission activist. Born into a wealthy New York City family, she spent the majority of her life building on the benevolent Christian foundation she had been given. In 1828, seven years after marrying a man of substantial wealth, Thomas Doremus, and becoming the mother of nine children, she began her first organized benevolent work among Greek women. In the early 1830s, she instigated church services in the New York City prison and later formed the Women's Prison Association for discharged prisoners. Her other efforts include manager of the New York City and Tract Mission; manager of the City Bible Society; founder of the House and School of Industry, the Nursery and Child's Hospital, and the Women's Hospital; and organizer of the Presbyterian Home for Aged Women. Although she was an active member of the South Reformed Church, this denominational affiliation was no barrier to her breadth of service nor did it prevent her from launching the effort for which she is most remembered, the Women's

Union Missionary Society of America, in February 1861. Having long supported foreign missions, it was no surprise that she was called on to organize an interdenominational society geared specifically for sending single women missionaries. Although subjugated at the hands of strong male opposition in the 1830s, when it was first suggested, it took off under Sarah's leadership thirty years later when the opposition had decreased. The organization thrived under her presidency and continued on as an inspiration to other denominational women's organizations long after her death. Her entire consecration to the Lord's service truly makes her one of the most significant women of nineteenth-century American Protestantism and a true pioneer of urban mission efforts to help women, children, and the poor.

WENDY S. LARSON

Bibliography. R. P. Beaver, *American Protestant Women in World Mission;* P. R. Hill, *The World Their Household;* R. A. Tucker, *GGC;* N. Hardesty, *Women Called to Witness;* A. Brouwer, *Reformed Church Roots.*

Doubt. The mission Christ has given to his church is to disciple the nations (Matt. 28:18–20). This commissioning involves evangelizing the world (Luke 24:47), equipping the saints (Eph. 4:12–16), and training qualified leaders (2 Tim. 2:21). It is to be done in loving obedience to Christ and in faith.

Doubt may be defined as a state of uncertainty regarding God, his Word, and his works. The mission of the church demands faith in God's ability to guide, provide, and protect. It demands faith in his Word that is displayed by obedience to his commissioning command. It also demands faith in his accomplished work of salvation and his continual works of convicting, regenerating, and empowering. There is clearly a distinction between permanent unbelief as illustrated by Judas and doubts that find resolution in lives such as Job, John the Baptist, Peter, and Thomas. However, since faith involves one's mind, emotions, and will, one may intellectually believe and still be characterized by unbelief (James 2:19).

The lexical basis for the scriptural understanding of doubt revolves around the various negations of *'aman* and *batah* in the Old Testament and *pisteuō* in the New Testament. *Apistos* refers to the faithless and unbelieving. *Apisteō* has the nuance of "to be unfaithful" and "to refuse to believe." *Apistia* means "unfaithfulness" and is closely related to disobedience. *Oligopistos* refers to the lack of faith and occurs exclusively in the Gospels.

Throughout Scripture Satan's warfare tactics are waged against faith (*see* SPIRITUAL WARFARE). In the temptation of Eve, the serpent raises doubt in God's character and his Word (Gen. 3:1–5). In

Jesus' interpretation of the parable of the sower, he stated that the devil seeks to hinder belief in God's Word (Luke 8:12). He also told the Pharisees that their unbelief in his Word demonstrated that the devil was their spiritual father (John 8:44–47). The Apostle Paul related Satan's temptation as being aimed at his converts' faith (1 Thess. 3:5). For example, pride is the root cause of sin and was the sin of the devil (1 Tim. 3:6) and Jesus clearly taught that pride hinders faith (John 5:44; 12:42–43). Likewise, Jesus called the devil the father of lies (John 8:44), and it is the acceptance of wrong doctrine that upsets faith (2 Tim. 2:18).

Faith is the means by which one becomes God's child, whereas permanent unbelief results in God's condemnation (John 3:18; 8:24). The unbelieving find their place in the lake of fire (Rev. 21:8), but the one who has placed his faith in Christ has been delivered from this consequence. However, Scripture is clear on the effects of unbelief even in the life of a Christian. Since a lack of trust is seen as the root of sin and rebellion (Deut. 9:23; 2 Kings 17:14), an unbelieving heart is also called a sinful or evil heart (Heb. 3:12).

Unbelief is evidenced in God's people as a hesitancy to act in obedience to God and a lack of conviction (Deut. 1:26–33). Unbelief does not please God (Heb. 11:6); it is sin (Rom. 14:23). It hinders the prayer life of God's people (James 1:6–8; cf. Matt. 21:21; Mark 11:23–24). Whereas faith leads to worship (John 9:38), doubt hinders worship (Matt. 28:17).

The character of unbelief is to turn away from God (Heb. 3:12) and look to something else. To refuse to trust the true God is to commit spiritual adultery (Jer. 3:6, 8) and opens one up to falsehood and deception (2 Thess. 2:11–12). No other object of faith puts one on stable ground whether it be possessions (Prov. 11:28), another person (Jer. 17:5), or oneself (Prov. 28:26). A refusal to believe God dishonors his trustworthy name (1 John 5:10). Unbelief grieves the heart of Christ (Matt. 17:17), who longs to satisfy the thirsts of all who continually look to him (John 6:35; 7:37–39).

God graciously works in response to faith in his truth (Gal. 3:5). While faith opens the door to the release of God's power (Matt. 17:20; Mark 9:23; John 14:12), unbelief hinders the working of God (Matt. 13:58) and quenches God's Spirit. The individual Christian and the life of the church are greatly affected by the sin of unbelief. It opens the door to anxiety (John 14:1; Matt. 6:30) and fear (Matt. 8:26; 14:30–31). It makes one unstable (James 1:6–8) and fails to deliver one from dismay (Isa. 28:16), disappointment (Rom. 9:33), and corruption (Titus 1:15).

Since it is faith in God's revelation that opens the door to true understanding (Heb. 11:3), a lack of faith hinders spiritual discernment (Matt. 16:8). The naive or simple lack discretion in knowing what to believe and are contrasted with the prudent (Prov. 14:15). Since the shield of faith is an important protective piece of the Christian's armor, unbelief makes one vulnerable in spiritual battles (Eph. 6:16).

Unbelief never catches God by surprise (John 6:64); and it cannot and does not alter or change his perfect faithfulness (Rom. 3:3; 2 Tim. 2:13). It is the Holy Spirit's role to convict the world of sin, but the unbelief of the church grieves or quenches this convicting work and invites the Lord's loving discipline (John 16:9). The Scriptures are full of examples of objects of God's discipline such as the nation of Israel (Num. 14:11–23; Ps. 106:24–27; Jude 5), Moses (Num. 20:12), and Zechariah (Luke 1:20).

God desires merciful support to be shown to the doubting (Jude 22). He also desires that his people encourage each other's faith (Rom. 1:12). He uses his servants and trials to strengthen our faith (Acts 16:5; Jon. 11:15). He does not belittle cries for help in our unbelief (Mark 9:24) and gives enabling grace to believe (Acts 18:27; Phil. 1:29). Thomas (John 20:27) and Abraham (Rom. 4:20) are examples of those who received God's aid to believe. As Jesus prayed that Peter's faith would not fail (Luke 22:32), he lives today to intercede for the faith of his church (Heb. 7:25).

While God rebukes unbelief (Mark 16:14), he invites the repentant to return to him (Jer. 3:12) and let him heal their unfaithfulness. In light of the church's large measure of unresponsiveness to its mission this provision needs to be taken seriously.

WILLIAM D. THRASHER

SEE ALSO Assurance of Salvation.

Bibliography. R. Bultmann, *TDNT*, VI:174–228; O. Becker, *NIDNTT*, I:587–93; O. Michel, *NIDNTT*, I:593–606.

Dreams and Visions. Dreams and visions are common universal phenomena, neither restricted to particular peoples nor historical eras. Technically, dreams are related to the state of sleep, while visions occur in trance-like states when people are awake. However, because of their often ecstatic nature and revelatory character, dreams and visions function in much the same manner. They are both important mediums of divine revelation in Scripture. In fact, they are explicitly mentioned or alluded to almost two hundred times in the Bible. Thus, dreams and visions play an important role in the drama of redemption.

Dreams and visions were prevalent throughout antiquity. For example, the royal courts of both Mesopotamia and Egypt had wise men who were professional interpreters of dreams. In the Greek world, sophisticated systems of interpretation were developed as well. Overall, there was an excessive preoccupation with dreams and visions in the Ancient Near East and the Greco-Roman world.

This is the not the case in Scripture, however. The elements that dominated the dream world of antiquity—the riotous superstition, perversion, curiosity, and obsession with one's fate—are lacking in the Bible. When viewed in this light, the biblical description of dreams and visions, while pervasive, is restrained and sober.

The Bible emphasizes that dreams and visions are typical mediums of divine revelation: "When a prophet of the Lord is among you, I reveal myself to him in visions, I speak to him in dreams" (Num. 12:6; cf. 1 Sam. 3:1; 28:6, 15; Hos. 12:10). The prophets usually received their messages through dreams or visions (Isa. 1:1; Ezek. 1:1; Daniel).

In the New Testament, dreams and visions are described as characteristic of the age of the Spirit. The apostle Peter, quoting the fulfillment of Joel's prophecy of the outpouring of the Spirit, notes that the church is to be a prophetic community, a community where "young men will see visions . . . old men will dream dreams" (Acts 2:17).

This emphasis on dreams and visions is outlined in Acts. Luke gives numerous illustrations of visions in the early church. Ananias receives a vision regarding Paul (9:10). Paul is converted through a vision (26:19). Through visions, God prepares the Gentile Cornelius to receive the gospel and prepares the Jew, Peter, to preach the gospel (chaps. 10–11). The famous Macedonian call comes through a vision (16:9). And at Corinth, Paul is encouraged by God to keep preaching the gospel through a vision (18:9–10).

What do these data suggest? What are the missiological implications of the Bible's teaching on dreams and visions? While not a normal part of the Western evangelical experience, dreams and visions are biblical and play an important part of life for people in the Two-Thirds World. Only someone with an extreme anti-supernatural bias would deny their relevance to missions.

Second, dreams and visions are mediums of revelation. God speaks through dreams and visions to convert sinners (Paul and Cornelius) as well as to encourage and guide his people (Ananias, Peter, Paul). He does the same today. Even the most conservative branches of Christianity are reporting the use of dreams and visions in the conversion of the unreached. Just as God used a vision to convert Paul, in like manner he is revealing himself to Muslims, Hindus, and Buddhists. Just as God prepared Cornelius to hear the gospel through dreams, so too is God preparing a multitude of unreached peoples to respond to his Good News.

As a missionary God, God's method of communication is incarnational. He enters into our world to communicate his message. His revelation is contextual (see CONTEXTUALIZATION) and thus he meets people where they are. Because many of the unreached are beyond the reach of the gospel and because much of the world is illiterate, dreams and visions are particularly relevant. Moreover, similar to the case of Cornelius, dreams or visions about Jesus often prepare the way for the message of the evangelist.

God is sovereign and never limited to human agency. He uses and will continue to use dreams and visions to fulfill his GREAT COMMISSION. Nevertheless, his use of dreams and visions in mission in no way minimizes the role of missionaries. Visions and missionaries were involved in the conversion of both Paul and Cornelius (Ananias and Peter). Whether God communicates supernaturally through dreams and visions or not, missionaries are always needed.

To affirm the reality and even need of dreams and visions to help fulfill the Great Commission in no way deprecates the priority and centrality of the Word of God. The Bible is the exclusive medium of special revelation, whereas dreams and visions are at best only supplementary and secondary.

Moreover, dreams or visions are not always divinely inspired. They can also be psychologically or satanically inspired. Because of this, new converts must be taught discernment. They must learn to examine their dreams and visions in light of Scripture. They also need to submit their dreams and visions to the leaders of their churches who will help them determine if God is speaking.

The Bible is God's full and final revelation in written form, our highest objective authority. We must examine all things by the Word of God. Moreover, Jesus primarily speaks to us through the Bible. However, he is not bound to the Bible alone. He also speaks to and guides his church through dreams and visions. To deny this supplementary and secondary form of revelation (dreams and visions), is to deny teaching of our primary medium of revelation, the Bible!

RICHARD D. LOVE

Bibliography. D. E. Aune, *ISBE* Revised, IV:993–94; R. J. Budd, *NIDNTT*, I:511–12; M. Kelsey, *God, Dreams, and Revelation;* A. Oepke, *TDNT*, V:220–38; J. H. Stek, *ISBE* Revised, I:991–92; J. G. S. S. Thompson, *NBD*, p. 1239; J. G. S. S. Thompson and J. S. Wright, *NBD*, pp. 289–90.

Dropout. Typically used of an unnecessary premature departure from a missionary assignment. The term's roots can be found in an earlier time and mind-set, a time in which ministry "calling" had a profound and almost eternal ring to it. Originally, the concept of "calling" was an important Reformation insight that affirmed the worth of all ethical vocations as reflections of God's providential plan to bring himself glory through the unique giftedness of individuals.

In later adaptations of the concept of "calling," however, all spiritual vocations, and the missionary vocation in particular, were viewed differently from other vocations. They were generally understood as life-long commitments of the self for service. Missionary candidates were not normally accepted without reference to a divine call in their life, a proper standard that should have been, but seldom was, equally applied to other vocations as well. Those who entered vocational ministry and later departed, therefore, generally bore alone the stigma of those who had "put their hands to the plow and then looked back."

A shifting of generational perspectives, however, has diminished both the popularity and usage of the term "dropout." Younger baby boomers and the generations that have followed them tend to see God's calling more in terms of a progressive revelation that may require different responses at various points in one's life. They are much less likely than earlier generations to equate God's calling with any particular job, location, or organizational affiliation.

All of the above is not to minimize issues of ATTRITION (the loss of active missionaries from an agency's ranks), which are being examined more thoroughly and with a greater sense of urgency than perhaps at any other time in history. If in a previous day "attrition" was almost automatically assumed to be the result of spiritual or character weakness (hence "dropouts"), the more recent trend has been to recognize the myriad of personal, organizational, and contextual reasons that keep missionaries from returning to their fields of service and to address those that are preventable.

GARY R. CORWIN

SEE ALSO Adjustment to the Field; Attrition.

Bibliography. M. F. Foyle, *Overcoming Missionary Stress;* K. O'Donnell, ed., *Missionary Care: Counting the Cost for World Evangelization;* E. Schubert, *What Missionaries Need to Know about Burnout and Depression;* M. Jones, *Psychology of Missionary Adjustment.*

Dualism. Dualism can be understood in at least two distinct senses: (1) views that see the cosmos as a battleground between opposing (and more or less equal) forces of good and evil; and (2) views that see a sharp division of human nature into spirit and matter. There are, of course, many varieties within each category. An example of an influential dualistic perspective from the second category would be R. Descartes' dichotomy between the mind and the body.

Dualism of the first category can be divided into *radical* and *moderate* dualisms. Radical dualism postulates two original coequal and coeternal principles, while moderate dualism holds to only one original principle with a second that derives from the first. Zoroastrianism from the Middle Ages is an example of the radical form, and some forms of ancient gnosticism, with their supreme God and the created devil who in turn creates the material world, are examples of moderate dualism.

Among living religions, Zoroastrianism is dualistic with its good god, Ahura Mazda, who is opposed by the evil god, Angra Mainyu. Ahura Mazda is said to have created the world as a battleground in which to overcome Angra Mainyu and eventually thus to destroy all evil. From a very different tradition, the notion of Yin and Yang in Chinese thought, with the idea of opposing forces producing harmony when in proper balance and evil when not in proper alignment, is another form of cosmic dualism. Among ANIMISTS, the Pueblo Indians of the southwestern United States define the cosmos as a dualistic sacred world, with the more profane world being the one into which people have emerged. Also, the Navajos hold that the totality of phenomena fall into two parts—the good and bad, positive and negative, male and female—all of which complement each other in a fashion not unlike the Yin and Yang in Chinese thought.

From a Christian perspective, while there are certainly aspects of dualistic thought that can be embraced, Christians must challenge any form of cosmic dualism that compromises the biblical understanding of God as the supreme power and authority over all that exists or which limits God's control over the forces of evil.

WILLIAM H. BAKER

Duff, Alexander (1806–78). Scottish missionary to India. Born in Scotland's Perthshire Highlands, he studied at St. Andrews under Thomas Chalmers, whose strong educational policies he espoused. Ordained in 1829, Duff sailed for Calcutta (surviving two shipwrecks), and opened a school where the higher classes studied the Bible and all true knowledge. A general government decree ordained that higher education teaching should be in English and should promote European literature and science. Soon Duff's College (as it came to be known) was the largest mission school in India, causing anxiety among Hindu leaders. Poor health forced Duff to temporarily return home (1835–39); then, in 1843, Chalmers led evangelicals in forming the Free Church, and Duff (who approved) had to vacate the Church of Scotland's Indian property and seek new accommodations.

Duff co-founded and edited (1845–49) the *Calcutta Review* before returning to Scotland, where he was his church's moderator in 1851. A missions-promotion tour of North America followed in 1845. In a gripping address to the British Evangelical Alliance in 1855 Duff condemned worldliness in the churches and called on Christendom "to remember the perishing nations." SYNCRETISM to Duff was anathema; HINDUISM was a "stupendous system of error." His college's enrollment rose to over 1,700. Duff had provided the role model that led to the establishment of other colleges for the training of Indian evangelists, and was a prime mover in founding the University of Calcutta. When ill health finally compelled him to leave India in 1867, he became professor of theology at New College, Edinburgh, but remained a tireless promoter of missions. Among his numerous works was *Missions the Chief End of the Christian Church* (1839).

J. D. DOUGLAS

Bibliography. A. A. Millar, *Alexander Duff of India;* W. Paton, *Alexander Duff: Pioneer of Missionary Education;* G. Smith, *The Life of Alexander Duff, D.D., L.L.D.*

Dutch Mission Boards and Societies. Though Dutch Protestants initially took the lead in missions work, by the twentieth century the contribution had become overwhelmingly from the Catholic portion of the population despite the large Protestant presence at home and in commerce. The Catholic population has remained comparatively large and stable, being almost 40 percent in 1830 and the same 40 percent in 1970. By the 1990s, Catholics had dropped to about a third of the population, and the proportion of those who attended Mass regularly had plummeted. But in the early 1970s, even though the number had started declining, it is noteworthy that of some 12,300 Dutch priests, fully 30 percent of them were still serving as missionaries overseas. They were joined by many more brothers, sisters, and lay workers, so that in total there were over 7,600 missionaries. At the same time there were only some 350 Dutch Protestant missionaries, less than 5 percent as many missionaries as the Catholics were sending.

In the 1970s, this declining but still formidable Catholic missionary force of 7,600 was widely dispersed. There were no significant indigenous Dutch sending agencies, so instead some three dozen international agencies or orders were used, the largest number being with the Mill Hill Fathers, the White Fathers, the Spiritans, and the Franciscans. However, those four still comprised less than one-fifth of the total force. As to area of service, roughly one-third were in Africa. They were scattered, with Congo's 450 being the largest contingent. Another third were in Asia, of whom four-fifths were quite understandably in Indonesia, the former Dutch East Indies. The final third served in the Americas, the Pacific Islands, and even some in Europe, chiefly Scandinavia. Brazil, the largest Catholic country, received more than one thousand Dutch missionaries. But about 630 were serving in the small Netherlands Antilles or in the sparsely populated South American Dutch possession which did not gain independence as Suriname until 1975. However, by the early 1990s, the number of Catholic missionaries had continued to fall to less than five thousand.

The trend for Protestantism is quite different. Their percentage of the population in the homeland has dropped sharply, so that by 1970 slightly fewer Dutch people identified themselves as Protestants than as Catholics, and by the 1990s they comprise even nominally only about one-fourth of this Protestant-founded nation. That makes the recent significant increase in Protestant missionaries even more interesting, showing that there is no simple correlation between overall church attendance and missionary effort.

Dutch ministers had been working abroad since the early 1600s, when the small Dutch nation started becoming a major global trading and colonizing power. Though they lost what became New York in 1664, various waves of Dutch immigration to North America before and since, and the corresponding effort to minister to the immigrants and their descendants, have probably diverted overseas efforts that might otherwise have gone to non-Christian areas. On the other hand, as the Dutch integrated into North America society, they became major participants, not just in ethnic churches, but in church life generally, including the missionary effort from North America. The colonial Great Awakening began among the Dutch before leaping to English-speaking settlers. In the twentieth century, Dutch entrepreneurs led the evangelical book publishing industry.

The first major Dutch Protestant mission society was founded in 1797, alongside of, but not controlled by or limited to, the Reformed Church. It understandably concentrated its efforts in Indonesia, where the Netherlands had already replaced Portugal as the leading commercial power and gradually extended its political control outward from Java. Theological controversies in the homeland were also reflected in new mission societies (within the main church) and new denominations (generally with their small mission efforts being part of their official church structure) being formed throughout the nineteenth century. These new agencies generally occupied different areas of the vast East Indies. In the twentieth century most began cooperating more closely, and the societies (except one) of the main church finally in 1951 united as an official arm of it. Most of the older mission efforts, including those of the older (and very small) non-Reformed churches, are represented in a Missions Council, are more theologically diverse, and their missionaries are decreasing and have disbursed from their original concentration in Indonesia. From about 350 in the early 1960s, their numbers had decreased more than 60 percent to under 140 by the early 1980s.

By contrast, the newer non-Reformed churches, though still relatively small at home, and joined by some of the Reformed, are sending forth an increasing number of missionaries, often through small Dutch branches of the denominational and interdenominational societies that have become such a key part of the evangelical movement in the twentieth century. The Evangelical Missionary Alliance included forty such agencies with almost 180 missionaries in the early 1980s, but by the mid-1990s there were about eighty agencies in the Alliance (none very large) and they comprise the great majority of the approximately 1,200 Dutch Protestant missionaries.

DONALD TINDER

Dynamic Equivalence. Label for meaning-based or thought-based (as opposed to word-based) Bible translations. Though this kind of translation was first done (and theorized) in English by J. B. Phillips (1958), the label "dynamic equivalence" was coined by EUGENE A. NIDA to contrast with the term "formal correspondence," Nida's term for literal translations. A literal translation attempts to move from the word forms and grammatical structures of the original language as directly as possible into the corresponding words and structures of the receiving language, often without adequate concern for the impact such awkwardness of language will have on the receptors as they strive to determine the meaning. English examples of formal correspondence translations are KJV, ASV, RSV, and NIV.

A dynamic equivalence translation, however, seeks to live up to Phillips' ideal that a translation should not sound like a translation but an original work in the language. The translator(s) thus seek to recreate in the receptor language "the closest natural equivalent" to the source-language message with a view toward stimulating receptors to understand the original meanings and to respond to those meanings as the original hearers would have (Nida and Taber 1969). This approach takes seriously, in a way impossible for literal translations, the large differences between the conceptual worlds languages represent and the structures by which they represent them. The translator employing this approach, then, will choose words and structures in the receiving language that may differ markedly from the corresponding forms in the source language in order to get across to receptors in a different conceptual and linguistic world the meanings intended by the original authors. English translations produced according to this approach are JBP, GNB, CEV, and NLT.

This concept of translation has created a revolution in the way Bible translation is carried out (*see* TRANSLATION THEORY). Translation organizations such as The United (including American) Bible Societies and WYCLIFFE BIBLE TRANSLATORS have long since converted to this approach. Though biblical scholars often hold out for more literal renderings, those with actual expertise in translating virtually all subscribe to a dynamic equivalence approach, though they sometimes use other names for it (e.g., thought for thought, meaning based).

Charles Kraft, in *Christianity in Culture* (1979), broadened the application of dynamic equivalence to apply to a series of missiological topics in addition to translation. He advocates "dynamic equivalence churches" as the contextualization model we should strive for. An appropriate church, he suggests, should express itself, including its theology, preaching and approach to conversion in ways that look just as much a part of their culture as a dynamic equivalence Bible translation looks and sounds in its language. Whenever a church (or a theology or a Bible translation) looks like literal Bible translations, they are not true to the aims of the God who seeks to be known by every people in terms they can understand. In order to be properly biblical, Kraft contends, churches need to be both appropriate in cultural form and equivalent to apostolic ideals in function and dynamic within their own culture. Just as the early church decided in Acts 15 to refrain from imposing Jewish cultural forms on Gentiles, encouraging them to develop their own cultural expressions of Christianity, so we should aim at churches that grow from biblical seed in ways appropriate to their culture.

CHARLES H. KRAFT

SEE ALSO Bible Translation.

Bibliography. C. H. Kraft, *Christianity in Culture;* E. A. Nida, and C. R. Taber, *The Theory and Practice of Translation;* J. B. Phillips, *The New Testament in Modern English.*

Ee

Ecology, Ecological Movement. Clearly a crisis of degradation is enveloping God's earth. Environmental destruction includes the transformation of forest and field into concrete and pavement, the extinction of entire species, the alteration of earth's energy exchange systems, and the toxification of the atmosphere, land, and water systems of the world. Industrial development and consumerism exploit whole cultures. Advanced nations work violence against nature and all its forms of life for economic profit, worshiping the god Mammon rather than the God who created all things.

That Christianity is the main source of environmental ruin seems axiomatic to many environmentalists, who feel that the command to subdue and have dominion over the earth (Gen. 1:28; Ps. 8:5–6) gave Christians a theological sanction for destroying both earth and ENVIRONMENT. Indeed, evangelicals appear guilty as charged when they describe creation as "the late, great planet earth" that God will destroy with fire and dismiss attempts to redeem it as futile efforts to do God's work by human means. We unwittingly appear to believe the chief value of the earth is to fuel human industry.

The Biblical-Theological Foundation. The reasons for environmental involvement are strong. "We who bring the good news of God's love for the cosmos (John 3:16) and of Jesus Christ's work as Creator, Sustainer and Reconciler (John 1; Col. 1; Heb. 1) cannot be complicit bystanders or participants in the degradation and defilement of the world God loves, sustains and reconciles" (DeWitt and Prance, 1992, viii). Meeting human needs without caring for the earth is not only impossible, but unbiblical. But the focus cannot be "nature" or "resources" or "the environment," but God's creation. Earthkeeping must be a worshipful activity, an act of praise to the Creator. Reverence for God must include appreciation of all his creation.

Both humans and the earth are part of God's creation. They are deeply interlinked realities. God placed humans in the garden and told them to till and care for it (Gen. 2:15; *see also* CULTURAL MANDATE). Stewardship of God's creation is implicit in the IMAGE OF GOD and explicit in this commandment. We bless and keep God's creation as he blesses and keeps us. The capability and responsibility to affect, modify, and control many aspects of the ecosphere is called STEWARDSHIP.

If we are responsible caretakers of God's creation, then we must use the earth, the atmosphere, the land, the water so as to maintain their purity and to conserve and renew their systems as intended by God. The earth is not a commodity to be bought and sold to fulfill sinful greed and exploitation.

There is much commonality between humans and other living beings. God filled the seas and the land with living souls, the common designation for both the living beings of the seas (Gen. 1:20) and the land (1:24) as well as humans (Gen. 2:7). The commonality as creatures has been obscured in most English versions because these terms are translated with different words (e. g., living creature vs. living beings, NIV). God formed Adam's body out of the dust (Gen. 2:7) in a way similar to how he formed animals out of the earth (1:24). Creation was subjected to frustration and decay, and groans as a result of human sin (Gen. 3:17–19; Rom. 8:20). Human sin continues to impact the land (Num. 26:19–22; Lev. 18:28; Deut. 11:17; 28:1–68). We share a common, interlinked creatureliness.

But humans are also different from the other animals and the rest of creation, being created in God's image and given dominion over the rest of creation (Gen. 1:28; Ps. 8:5–6) and the command to till and care for the garden (2:15). Only humans dwell in communion with God and live responsibly under his command. Only we can sin in the proper sense of the term. This SIN impacted all of creation; stewardship continues, but it will be accomplished only with toil and struggle.

It is important to notice that the mandate for earth-keeping stems from CREATION, not from ATONEMENT. Jesus did not die for the earth. But it will be liberated from that bondage and share the glorious redemption of humanity (Rom. 8:19–23) when Christ, the Lord of all creation, restores the whole cosmos. Ultimately, salvation is cosmological in scope, leading to fellowship with God, community with other humans, and unity with all of creation (Eph. 1:22; Col. 1:18–20).

Currently we experience only the firstfruits of this salvation, an inheritance that extends to Christ's lordship over all creation (Eph. 1:22; Col. 1:18–20). The people of God, as a part of their obedience to the Lord of the earth, must restore earthkeeping as a part of the stewardship of his creation. The church should be the salt of the earth, calling all humans to righteousness, including faith in Jesus Christ, justice in a deteriorating society, and caretaking of an ailing environment.

Dangers to Be Avoided. We must be aware of potential dangers involved in environmental involvement. Missions could fall prey to a compromise of priority. EVANGELISM and CHURCH PLANTING are the substance of the GREAT COMMISSION. Environmental and social concerns are always secondary to the priority of bringing people into relationship with God (*see also* EVANGELISM AND SOCIAL RESPONSIBILITY). To reverse these would be to deny the heart of the gospel, which is reconciliation with God, justification by grace alone through faith alone. But to refuse to speak to environmental issues flowing out of obedience to our Creator and Redeemer out of fear of compromise is a grave danger as well.

One can be drawn into the kind of PANTHEISM found in New Age religions or idolatry such as Israel wrestled with in the ancient pagan religions. New Age philosophies err by locating the fundamental problems of humanity in ignorance or the dichotomy between material and spiritual rather than in sin that separates us from God, other humans, as well as creation (*see also* NEW AGE MOVEMENT). Our beliefs, ceremonies, and practices must honor God (YHWH) rather than a "god" who is the living force behind the universe. This earth is not God's body in which he is incarnate, but God's creation in which he manifests himself. Neither is it a divine being nor identified directly with God's power. The living triune personal God is distinct and transcendent as well as involved by choice in his creation.

We affirm that the earth is the Lord's, not that the earth is the Lord. We must never reduce the distinction between God and humans. Christians cannot be involved with those who believe created humans can create a utopian world through our own power. While the church is the primary means through with God works his redemption today, salvation is God's work.

We must proclaim Jesus Christ and never move toward a Christ who is little more than the principle of interconnectedness within all of nature. He alone is the way to salvation. The real human predicament is solved by the Cross, not by biology or environmental engineering.

Evangelicals must reject the claim that any attempt to deem humans more valuable than any other animal or plant is a form of bigotry. We must maintain a unique role for human beings as made in God's image and the focus of creation, sin, and redemption. Humans have a unique spiritual nature, a personal relatedness and responsibility to God that is found nowhere else in creation. Of course this does not mean affirming sinful human nature with its greed and selfishness and insensitivity, but the human as responsible steward as image and likeness of the living God.

Conclusion. If we really believe the environment we inhabit is the handiwork of God and that we have been given responsible stewardship for it, then we will be zealous to protect and preserve what the Creator has put in our trust. We will see ourselves as God's stewards rather than owners. We will proclaim a theology that includes personal justification by grace alone through faith alone, but also includes a corporate life of promoting obedient living in every part of our life.

Because we believe both justification and sanctification, we will proclaim a gospel of personal salvation leading to a God-honoring life that includes environmental righteousness. We will forsake selfishness in favor of the benefit of fellow humans and the environment because we care for the creation out of our love for the Creator.

Mission that includes care for creation is not a new emphasis. WILLIAM CAREY was not only the father of modern missions, but also founded the agricultural and horticultural society of India and was a conservationist, calling for forest conservation in 1811. Many missionaries have followed his example; may we also follow him in recognizing our God-given responsibilities as stewards of his creation.

GERRY BRESHEARS

Bibliography. C. DeWitt and G. Prance, *Missionary Earthkeeping;* W. Granberg-Michaelson, *Ecology and Life;* B. R. Reichenbach and V. E. Anderson, *On Behalf of God: A Christian Ethic for Biology;* F. Schaeffer, *Pollution and the Death of Man;* L. Wilkenson, ed., *Earthkeeping in the 90's.*

Economics. Economics deals with the allocation of limited resources. Mission, in a Christian context, entails the church's modeling and propagation of the gospel message. Economics and mission intersect at many crucial junctures. We first look at mission-economic highlights in biblical history before discussing the contemporary economic implications for mission.

Scriptural Foundation. From the earliest days of God's dealings with his people, it is clear that God's call ought to take priority over an individual's loyalties. Abraham, the father of believers, was called to leave his home, even to sacrifice his son; the other patriarchs, likewise, were enjoined to live by faith (Heb. 11:8–22). Moses, too, chose to renounce his earthly possessions (Heb. 11:24–28), and the abandonment of self-pursuits was required of the Old Testament prophets. The same principle is reflected in the New Testament in Christ's own self-emptying (Phil. 2:7), his selfless service (Mark 10:45; John 13:1–15), and his becoming poor to make believers rich (2 Cor. 8:9). Such sacrifice also became the requirement for discipleship (Luke 9:57–62; Jesus' stewardship parables).

Of the four Evangelists, it is Luke who shows the greatest interest in economic issues. Luke's account of the life of the early church in Acts provides an eschatological foretaste of kingdom living (Acts 2:44–45; 4:32–37). Paul, likewise, emulated self-sacrifice in his own life and ministry, calling believers to the sharing of resources with those in need (esp. the collection for the Jerusalem church: Rom. 15:25–27; 1 Cor. 16:1–4; 2 Cor. 8–9), contentment with life's necessities (Phil. 4:11–12; 1 Tim. 6:6–8), a disinterested attitude toward worldly possessions (1 Cor. 7:30–31), and hospitality (Rom. 12:13).

Believers were to extend hospitality to missionaries and itinerant preachers of the gospel (Matt. 10:10–15; Heb. 13:2; 2 John 10–11; 3 John 5–8). Fundamental to missions is the acknowledgment that Christians are merely resident aliens and that this world is not their permanent abode (Phil. 3:20; 1 Peter 1:1, 17; 2:11). The love of money is the root of all types of evil (1 Tim. 6:10; cf. Mark 4:18–19; 1 Tim. 3:3; 2 Tim. 3:2), no one can serve two masters, God and Money (Matt. 6:24), and rich persons will enter the kingdom only with great difficulty (Mark 10:23–31; Luke 12:16–21; 16:19–31; 19:1–10; 1 Tim. 6:17–19; James 5:1–6). In the seer's apocalyptic vision, Babylon the Great, with its excessive reliance on her own wealth, has fallen (Rev. 17–18).

Contemporary Relevance. Economics and mission interface at several crucial junctions. Relevant issues include: (1) the general economic environment for mission (Bonk) and the question of which economic system is most compatible with biblical principles (Chewning, Smith); (2) the economic situation of missionaries, including the raising of funds, "tentmaking," the problem of fluctuating currency exchange rates, the problem of financial indebtedness of missionary candidates (*see* DEBT), and the issue of greater cost efficiency of national missionaries (Yohannan); (3) the economic circumstances of the target cultures of mission, raising issues such as the need for community DEVELOPMENT AND RELIEF WORK, sociological barriers between the missionary and nationals, the need for economic support of new converts ostracized from their socioeconomic community, and

the problem of INDIGENOUS CHURCHES' dependence on foreign funds.

Of contemporary movements, it is particularly LIBERATION THEOLOGY that focuses on economic issues, usually in terms of Marxist economic analysis. The following factors, however, appear to contradict this approach (France): first, Jesus conceived of his own role not in terms of political or national liberation but of the restoration of an individual's personal relationship with God; he explicitly rejected a political role, stressing rather love and forgiveness even of one's enemies, an element frequently missing in radical movements; second, liberation in the New Testament almost always pertains to liberation from sin; third, Jesus does not present a program for achieving the redistribution of wealth or other socioeconomic reforms; liberation theology concentrates on the symptom of socioeconomic justice while neglecting to deal with the root cause, the fallenness of human nature, which produces the twisted values of selfish materialism.

A sensitivity to economic issues is vital for the church's effective ministry. The world's rapid URBANIZATION, the evolution of modern technologies creating a new information elite, the increasing gap between rich and poor countries, and many other factors affect the church's ministry at home and abroad in many ways. Evangelical spokesmen such as R. Sider and T. Campolo have called for a more simple, radical life-style on the part of Christians for the sake of missions. It has been the subject of considerable debate in evangelical circles over the past decades to what extent social and economic concerns are to be part of the missionary enterprise (*see* GREAT COMMANDMENT). Some advocate the priority of evangelism and church planting, while others favor a holistic approach that also incorporates social and economic issues. Many favor an approach that is patterned after the model of Christ's incarnation and service.

The following implications for modern missions emerge from these considerations: (1) biblical discipleship, the prerequisite for missions, entails a disinterested attitude toward worldly possessions; (2) material resources are to be used for the spreading of God's kingdom (Jesus' kingdom and stewardship parables); (3) solidarity is called for between believers of different means in local churches and across cultures, leading to a sharing of resources; (4) the ultimate issues in missions are spiritual, but economic and social factors may provide barriers to effective evangelization (Bonk); (5) all missions work takes place in a political, economic, and social environment, and these factors influence the accomplishment of the missionary task (Clouse).

ANDREAS KÖSTENBERGER

Bibliography. J. J. Bonk, *Missions and Money: Affluence as a Western Missionary Problem;* R. C. Chewning, ed., *Biblical Principles and Economics: The Foundations;* R. G. Clouse, ed., *Wealth and Poverty: Four Christian Views;* P. H. Davids, *DJG,* pp. 701–10; R. T. France, *Evangelical Quarterly* 58 (1986): 3–23; I. Smith, *God and Culture,* pp. 162–79; K. P. Yohannan, *Why the World Waits: Exposing the Reality of Modern Missions.*

Ecuador *(Est. 2000 pop.: 12,646,000; 283,561 sq. km. [109,483 sq. mi.]).* Ecuador, so named because it straddles the equator, is located in the northwest corner of the South American continent with the Amazon jungle in the east, the high Andean Sierra in the center, and a fertile coastal plain on the Pacific Coast. The Galapagos Islands lie 1,000 kilometers to the west. Just under 57 percent of the 12.6 million people speak Spanish. The indigenous Amerindians, speaking 22 different languages, form 42 percent of the population. Urbanization is over 50 percent.

The Roman Catholic Church. What is now Ecuador at one time formed part of the ancient Inca Empire with its capital in Cuzco (Peru). The Spanish invaded and conquered the native peoples in 1534. During the colonial era the Spanish established parishes, provided education for the upper classes, and founded universities and hospitals. Little attempt was made to translate the Bible into indigenous languages and, until recently, its use among the laity was not encouraged by the clergy.

After gaining independence from Spain in 1822, the Conservatives signed a Concordat with the Vatican (1863). Its provision included the establishment of the Catholic religion as the only one of the state, the prohibition of other faiths, placed the church as responsible to supervise public education, and required the state to pay for the propagation of the Catholic faith.

Today Roman Catholics represent 93.3 percent of the population. In recent years a small charismatic movement has offered opportunities for more personal spiritual experience and Bible study.

The Evangelical (Protestant) Churches. The first evangelical (Protestant) efforts in Ecuador were pioneered by agents of the Bible Society, JAMES THOMSON (1824) and FRANCISCO PENZOTTI, whose religious activities were limited to the sale of the Scriptures.

In 1895, the liberal general, Eloy Alfaro, led a political insurrection. In 1896, three young Americans of the Gospel Missionary Union, George Fisher, J. A. Strain, and F. W. Farnol, arrived in Ecuador, had an audience with General Alfaro, and received his support. In the same year, the CHRISTIAN AND MISSIONARY ALLIANCE sent Charles Chapman and Charles Polk (from the United States) and Zebulun Yates (from Jamaica). In 1897 Alfaro revoked the Concordat and established freedom of worship, which enabled the entrance of Protestant missions.

In 1902, Julia Anderson Woodward (GMU) initiated work with the Quichuas in Caliata, Chimborazo. The Adventists entered in 1904 to develop their ministry of evangelism and to establish schools and clinics.

In 1931 Clarence Jones and Reuben Larson of World Missionary Fellowship founded HCJB, "The Voice of the Andes," in Quito. HCJB's programming now includes educational and nonpolemic religious broadcasting 900 hours weekly in 17 languages and 23 Quichua dialects internationally, as well as extensive national transmission including a color television station.

The Lutherans entered Ecuador in 1942, followed by the Andean Indians Mission (1945), the Plymouth Brethren (1946), and the Covenant Church (1947). In 1956, five missionaries were martyred while attempting to reach the Auca (Waorani) Indians on the Curaray River. Their deaths challenged many young people, especially in the United States, to foreign missionary service.

By 1993 over 83 agencies fielding more than 1,000 missionaries were in Ecuador. Unity among evangelicals has been promoted by the Ecuadorian Evangelical Fellowship (1964), the Union of Evangelical Ecuadorian Women (1968), and the Ecuadorian Evangelical Missionary Association (1968). In 1969 the program of Evangelism-in-Depth united almost all the evangelicals in a year-long evangelistic effort.

In 1960, the percentage of evangelicals in Ecuador was Latin America's smallest; during the last 30 years there has been a twentyfold increase. The reasons are varied, including physical disasters and the breakdown of the old feudal structures, both of which have made the Ecuadorians more receptive. In the 1960s, Pentecostal groups entered the country. Following widely publicized miraculous healings in a Foursquare Gospel church in 1964, 2,300 converts were reported and 15 new churches opened. As in all of Latin America, the Pentecostal phenomenon has positively influenced the numerical growth of the evangelical churches. At the present time evangelicals and Pentecostals represent about 8 percent of the population.

Indian work progressed very slowly at first but by 1993, 10 percent of the 3 million native peoples in Chimborazo Province had become evangelicals. The publication of a Quichua New Testament (1954), increasing participation of lay leaders, and the establishment of two Quichua language radio stations influenced this growth. Another factor was land reform which during this period gave Indians new experience in the freedom of personal choice. In spite of intense anti-missionary propaganda from some anthropologists, traders, and agitators, the WYCLIFFE BIBLE TRANSLATORS have nearly reached their goal of making the New Testament available in all the Indian languages of Ecuador.

Four agencies have recently sent out from Ecuador three foreign workers; three cross-cultural missionaries serve within the country. Goals for national evangelism are being projected. In 1996, the Ecuadorian Evangelical Confraternity, which brings together the majority of Ecuador's Protestant churches, launched an outreach called "100 towns, 100 churches." Their goal: to take the gospel to previously untouched cities and communities by the year 2000.

JACK VOELKEL

Bibliography. E. Elliot, *Through Gates of Splendor;* P. Johnstone, *Operation World;* J. Maust, *New Song in the Andes.*

Ecumenical Missionary Conference (New York, 1900).

Though not widely known, the Ecumenical Missionary Conference held in New York City, April 21–May 1, 1900, may be the largest 10-day event in American religious history; 170,000 to 200,000 persons gathered at its numerous sessions in various churches. Headquarters and principal speeches were located at the 4,000-seat Carnegie Hall. The word "ecumenical" in its title indicated global coverage rather than representation from all Christian traditions. Accorded extensive press coverage, the conference featured former President Benjamin Harrison as honorary chair and addresses by President William McKinley and governor of New York, Theodore Roosevelt.

The New York conference demonstrates the impact the foreign missions movement had on the popular imagination. Invitations were sent to all known missionaries, but only 2,500 served as official "members," with delegations from 162 mission boards apportioned by the size of their budgets. Like the CENTENARY CONFERENCE ON THE PROTESTANT MISSIONS OF THE WORLD (London, 1888), New York 1900 was inspirational and informative rather than a working conference to legislate policy priorities. A vast agenda was covered, including medicine, evangelism, education, native churches, non-Christian religions, and a country-by-country survey. Women in missions were highlighted, and a scattering of non-Westerners addressed sessions.

Prominent participants included J. HUDSON TAYLOR, Bishop JAMES M. THOBURN, JOHN G. PATON, JOHN R. MOTT, A. T. PIERSON, and ROBERT E. SPEER.

A postconference caucus called for the formation of a permanent international missions coordinating committee, but the project never materialized. The Ecumenical Missionary Conference did, however, pave the way for the WORLD MISSIONARY CONFERENCE (Edinburgh, 1910) with its more significant outcomes.

THOMAS A. ASKEW

Bibliography. Ecumenical Missionary Conference New York, 1900, 2 vols.; W. R. Hogg, *Ecumenical Foundations: A History of the International Missionary Council and Its Nineteenth Century Background.*

Ecumenical Movement.

The word "ecumenical" comes from the New Testament word *oikoumenē,* which meant either the whole world or the Roman Empire. In the fourth century the term was used to describe the whole church, and referred to those church councils recognized as authoritative by the undivided church. Thus the first seven councils, called to resolve doctrinal issues mainly concerning Christology (*see also* CHRISTOLOGICAL CONTROVERSIES), are called the ecumenical councils. They took place before the division of the Eastern and Western churches and so included all Christians. The final division of the Roman Catholic and Eastern Orthodox churches in 1054 created the ecumenical problem for all churches, which, up to that point, had understood the church as one.

The Protestant Reformation exacerbated the problem. Even though Luther wished only to reform the Western church with no thought of establishing a different church, the sixteenth century saw massive fragmentation of the Body of Christ in the West, leaving groups ranging from Roman Catholic to Anglican, Lutheran, Reformed, and various Anabaptist communities. Despite the ecumenism of Calvin, Bucer, and others, who longed for the unity of Protestants, most were denouncing each other as apostates by the seventeenth century.

While it is clear in the New Testament that there is only one church and that the unity of all believers is an objective fact based on the work of Christ, the modern ecumenical movement finds its major biblical basis in John 17, where Jesus prayed that all who believed in him would be one so that the world might believe. Thus unity would be linked to mission. And in fact the historical roots of ecumenism are found in movements of renewal and mission beginning with PIETISM and Moravianism in the eighteenth century (*see* MORAVIAN MISSIONS). An example was the correspondence among Francke, the Lutheran Pietist in Germany; Mather, the Congregationalist in New England; Chamberlyne and Newman, the secretaries of the Society for the Propagation of Christian Knowledge; Boehm, the court chaplain at St. James Chapel; and ZIEGENBALG, the Lutheran missionary in India in which they sought greater unity in order to carry out the missionary task. Later, Anglicans cooperated with Lutherans in the mission in India. And because of his desire to work for renewal, unity, and mission together, ZINDZENDORF would be called an "ecumenical pioneer."

The revivals on both sides of the Atlantic brought other manifestations of ecumenism. In North America, GEORGE WHITEFIELD, an Anglican; JONATHAN EDWARDS, a Congregationalist; and

Gilbert Tennent, a Presbyterian, cooperated in the first GREAT AWAKENING. And in England the revival saw cooperation among Anglicans and dissenters. Members of different denominations corresponded, encouraged each other, and read each other's works. Carey would be partly motivated in his missionary vocation through reading DAVID BRAINERD and the Moravians. The modern Protestant missionary movement, which stemmed from the revivals, saw further steps in cooperation. Most of the early missionaries of the Anglican CHURCH MISSIONARY SOCIETY were German Lutherans, influenced by pietism. The LONDON MISSIONARY SOCIETY included Congregationalists, Presbyterians, and Anglicans, while the British and Foreign Bible Society and the Religious Tract Society found support among all evangelical groups. In an early and visionary attempt at greater unity, Carey proposed "a general association of all denominations of Christians, from the four quarters of the world," to be held in Capetown in 1810 or 1812, "to enter into one another's views."

While Carey's dream would not become a reality until a century later, missionaries of various denominations began to meet in 1825 in Bombay to promote Christian fellowship and exchange ideas. At a similar meeting in 1858 an Anglican stated that while denominational controversies may elicit truth in the West, elsewhere they produce nothing but evil, adding his hope that God would produce a church in India different in many aspects from those in Europe or America. Western denominational divisions seemed to make no sense in Asia or Africa and were often a scandal. They seemed to deny a basic aspect of the faith. In December 1862, another conference prefaced its report with the prayer, "that they all may be one," and discerned a pattern of "the united action of Christian men who pray, confer, and work together, in order to advance the interests of their Master's kingdom." In the same meeting, Anglicans, Presbyterians, Methodists, and Baptists took Communion together. Similar conferences took place in Japan, China, Africa, Latin America, and the Muslim world.

The most prominent focus in these conferences was UNITY, which was a result of both the common commitment to mission and the experience of working and praying together. Many recognized that their unity was much deeper than differences in CHURCH POLITY or style of worship, and was based on a common devotion to Christ and his mission. But not all took part. The High Church Anglicans at one extreme, and some FAITH MISSIONS on the other, stayed away. But at this point there was still a broad consensus among the great majority about the nature and purpose of mission.

An additional and related factor was the Evangelical Alliance, formed in 1846. It sought to unite in fellowship all who believed in the full authority of the Bible, the incarnation, atonement, salvation by faith, and the work of the Holy Spirit. Its monthly journal, *Evangelical Christendom*, brought news of missionary work all over the world, and was avidly read by missionaries as well as those at home. This strengthened the vision of missionary cooperation.

Missionary conferences overseas had their counterparts in Europe and North America. In 1854 ALEXANDER DUFF spoke in New York at a meeting open to friends of mission from "all evangelical denominations," to consider eight key questions about world evangelization. Many similar meetings were held during the last half of the century in various parts of Europe as well as the United States. A new and important step was ECUMENICAL MISSIONARY CONFERENCE held in New York in 1900. Nearly two hundred thousand people attended its various sessions, and it was opened with an address by President William McKinley. The word "ecumenical" was used in its title "because the plan of campaign which it proposes covers the whole area of the inhabited globe." Thus the original dimension was brought again to the meaning of the term. Now it referred, not only to the whole church and thus to unity and cooperation, but to the worldwide scope of the missionary task.

Along with the revivals and the missionary movement the nineteenth-century student movements formed a third stream contributing to the ecumenical movement. The Intercollegiate YMCA existed on 181 campuses by 1884, emphasizing Bible study, worship, and personal evangelism. In 1880 the Interseminary Missionary Alliance was formed by students from thirty-two seminaries to encourage focus on the missionary task. Through these two organizations mission became the primary feature of the student movement. The STUDENT VOLUNTEER MOVEMENT, formed in 1886, carried the emphasis further. Student Christian movements were organized in a number of countries, and these were brought together in the World Student Christian Federation in 1895 under the leadership of JOHN R. MOTT. Its founders saw the need for greater unity at home if their goal of world evangelization was to be realized. In England, for example, it brought together Free Church, Evangelical, and Anglo Catholic students to promote missionary zeal. The Federation sought to promote the spirit of unity for which the Lord longed, and to emphasize the efficacy of prayer, the saving work of Christ, and the "energizing power of the Spirit and the Word of God."

These powerful streams came together in the Edinburgh MISSIONARY CONFERENCE in 1910. Many of those who planned it came from the Student Christian movement. A number of them would become leaders in the formation of the

WORLD COUNCIL OF CHURCHES in midcentury. John R. Mott, the chairman, was the most visible leader of the SVM and probably the most important symbol of the growing ecumenical movement. Three topics of the conference were "Carrying the Gospel to all the World," "The Church on the Mission Field," and "Cooperation and the Promotion of Unity." However, in order to ensure the participation of the High Church Anglicans and continental Lutherans, the conference limited participants to those involved in mission to "non-Christians." Consequently those involved in mission to traditionally Roman Catholic Latin America were excluded. This would create barriers between Latin American evangelicals and the conciliar ecumenical movement later on. On the other hand, neither Roman Catholics nor Orthodox were invited.

Edinburgh's most important achievement was the formation, in 1921, of the INTERNATIONAL MISSIONARY COUNCIL (IMC) which promoted international missionary cooperation. However, it was also uniquely responsible for the formation of the World Council of Churches. It did so by bringing the younger churches into the thinking of the older churches, helping to recognize them as an essential part of the world Christian community. Even though the organizers had agreed not to discuss matters of theology and polity, some in attendance saw the need to do so and, as a result, the Faith and Order Movement was initiated in 1927. The influence of the Student Movement and Edinburgh was also important in the formation of the Universal Christian Council for Life and Work, established in 1925. Bishop Soderblom of Sweden who had been influenced by D. L. MOODY and Mott, established the council to seek cooperative action on common problems. Faith and Order and Life and Work would become the parent movements of the World Council of Churches (WCC), organized in 1948 (*see* AMSTERDAM ASSEMBLY). For the older denominations it has been the primary institutional expression of the ecumenical movement.

When the IMC became a part of the WCC in 1961 some hoped it would place mission at the heart of the Council. Others feared the move would result in a decline in mission. The latter proved to be right as a combination of theological liberalism, which seemed to doubt the importance of evangelism and maintained a primary focus on social issues, led to a great decrease in missionary activity by most conciliar churches in Europe and North America. Thus the WCC has not succeeded in fulfilling the goal of its early proponents, unity so that the world might believe. Its member churches seem to be playing an ever decreasing role in world evangelism. This can be seen in statistics from the United States. In 1918, 82% of the missionary force came from the "mainline" churches, most likely to be members of the WCC today. In 1966, only 6% of American missionaries served under those boards.

Other manifestations of ecumenism are councils of churches in many countries and mergers of various denominational traditions in some nations. The United Church of Canada was formed in 1925 by Methodists, Congregationalists, and some Presbyterians with the hope of more effective outreach in the West. However, the result has been disappointing and decline rather than growth has been the result. The Church of Christ in China was formed in 1927 by Presbyterians, United Brethren, the United Church of Canada, and some Baptists and Congregationalists. Under the communist regime it became the parent body of the current "Three-Self Church," sanctioned by the government. The Church of South India was formed in 1947 and included Anglicans, the first time they had been drawn into communion with Presbyterians, Methodists, and others. In 1941 most Protestants in Japan, under government pressure, formed the Church of Christ in Japan, but Anglicans, Lutherans, and some others withdrew from it after the war. In 1948 the United Church of Christ in the Philippines was established. It appears that most of these united churches, with the exception of the Church in China, are not growing as rapidly as many of the newer groups.

The early ecumenical movement was based on a theological consensus which was solidly evangelical and breathed missionary passion. To the extent that agencies lost either or both of these, they declined. But after midcentury a new evangelical ecumenism arose. This is probably the most important manifestation of the ecumenical movement today. In the first half of this century fundamentalists and evangelicals tended to focus more on the issues which separated them from each other than on their common faith and task. But in 1966 the CONGRESS ON THE CHURCH'S WORLDWIDE MISSION at Wheaton and the WORLD CONGRESS ON EVANGELISM in Berlin began to overcome the separatism. Those meetings were succeeded by the INTERNATIONAL CONGRESS ON WORLD EVANGELISM, held at Lausanne in 1974. The stature of BILLY GRAHAM helped greatly in bringing together men and women from diverse traditions and many nations, while the theological insights of JOHN STOTT contributed to the formulation of a statement of faith that laid the foundation for a more adequate understanding of mission. The formation of the Lausanne Committee on World Evangelization (LCWE) worked to bring about greater cooperation in the evangelistic task in a number of areas. Those involved included a wider spectrum than ever before, ranging from Anglicans to Pentecostals. At the same time the insights and concerns of Christians from Asia, Africa, and Latin America contributed to deeper understanding of the Gospel and the missionary task by those in the West (*see* EVANGELICAL MOVEMENT).

The second congress of the LCWE, held in Manila in 1989, was probably the most inclusive Christian gathering in history up to that time (*see* LAUSANNE CONGRESS II). Four thousand evangelical Christians from 150 countries gathered for a week. They included over sixty from the former Soviet Union, while others came from obscure countries like Chad in Central Africa. The goal was that half the delegates come from Asia, Africa, and Latin America. Pentecostals were included among the speakers. So were women. Thus the whole church was represented to an extent not previously seen. The focus recaptured the ecumenical ideal: the whole church, taking the whole gospel, to the whole world. And while Manila did not contribute the kind of significant theological reformulation done at Lausanne, it seemed to provide additional impetus to the goals of cooperation in mission.

While the LCWE has been the most visible symbol of the new evangelical ecumenism, there are many others. The AD 2000 Movement, led, not by a European or North American, but by an Argentine, the GLOBAL CONSULTATION on WORLD EVANGELIZATION held in Korea ('95) and South Africa ('97), the Latin American mission conferences (*see* COMIBAM) held in 1987 and 1997, and the internationalization of the missionary movement, are all aspects of ecumenism. While there is still much to be done, the evangelical movement is now more genuinely ecumenical than ever before, as men and women from many races, languages, cultures, and nations seek to discover how they can demonstrate our unity in Christ so that the world might believe.

PAUL E. PIERSON

Bibliography. J. Hoekstra, *The World Council of Churches and the Demise of Evangelism;* W. R. Hogg, *Ecumenical Foundations;* LCWE; The Lausanne Covenant; K. S. Latourette, *A History of Christianity;* S. Neill and R. Rouse, *A History of the Ecumenical Movement.*

Educational Mission Work. Mission work is inherently educational. The GREAT COMMISSION, the mandate and charter of Christian missions, is a command to "make disciples" and to "teach"— both explicitly educational activities. Despite the misguided efforts of some in church history, Christian ETHICS (and the biblical view of persons that underlies it) preclude any attempt to make converts by force or deception. Informing others of gospel truth, clarifying their understanding of the truth and its implications, and calling for decision is the task of missions (*see* MISSIONARY TASK).

Modern missionaries pursue that task through a wide variety of educational means. Preaching may have a persuasive intent, but its method is educational. Home Bible studies and "one-on-one" encounters are the stock in trade of missionary evangelists and church planters the world over; in each case the method is to witness to and nurture understanding of biblical truth. Bible correspondence courses (*see* BIBLE EDUCATION BY EXTENSION), explicitly educational in their design, have been effectively used as evangelistic tools in many cultures, especially in Muslim lands.

Among resistant people groups and in CREATIVE-ACCESS COUNTRIES, educational services can afford an entree that does not otherwise exist. The twentieth-century emergence of English as the language of international commerce has created an enormous demand for teachers of English as a second language, many of whom are Christians who serve with explicitly missionary intent (*see* TEACHING ENGLISH TO SPEAKERS OF OTHER LANGUAGES). DEVELOPMENT workers and AGRICULTURAL MISSIONS also offer educational services as a means of incarnating Christian compassion and winning a hearing for the gospel. Radio, television, and literature ministries are likewise intentionally educational (*see* MASS MEDIA). It is COMMUNICATION of (i.e., instruction in) Christian truth that renders any ministry "missionary."

Educational ministries are also prevalent in the church. Discipleship programs are designed to cultivate Christian understanding and habits among the recently converted, and catechism or baptismal classes are common in most traditions. In addition to teaching that occurs in regular preaching services, church education programs, such as Sunday school and neighborhood or SMALL GROUP Bible studies provide important stimulus for growth in grace. Nonformal evening, weekend, or seasonal training programs provide additional instruction for believers, including formal and informal church leaders.

Theological education entails training for Christian ministry. Bible schools, seminaries, and THEOLOGICAL EDUCATION BY EXTENSION (TEE) receive high priority in the work of missions. In several regions of the world, "pastors' conferences" offer a unique opportunity for both trained and untrained church leaders to receive stimulus and instruction aimed at developing their ministries.

Educational mission work also includes training missionaries and their children. Schools for MISSIONARY CHILDREN exist in every region of the world, enabling parents to provide quality education for their families in proximity to their area of service. Although missionary training schools in the West may not be considered part of the global missionary endeavor, training missionaries called and sent from churches in the non-Western world is an urgent and strategic aspect of educational mission work. Likewise, on-field professional development of the missionary force is a responsibility of mission leadership critical to each missionary's continuing vitality and effectiveness.

Schools have held a central role in the modern Protestant missionary enterprise from its very inception. The case of missions in India is instructive. After arriving in India in 1793, WILLIAM CAREY set immediately to learning and to translating the Bible into several Indian languages, but he also established schools for instruction in these languages. In 1819, Carey founded Serampore College. Just eleven years later, in 1830, ALEXANDER DUFF arrived in Calcutta with a vision of reaching India's upper castes through European secondary schools and universities using the English language. Briefly, the debate between "vernacularists" and "Anglicists" raged, but Duff's vision won the day and mission-founded English-language schools spread across the subcontinent. In 1859, when the English colonial government addressed the education of its Indian subjects, the decision was taken to provide grants-in-aid to agencies operating schools and colleges that would agree to adhere to government standards, to include specified courses in their curriculum, and to submit to government inspection. This came as an enormous boon to the founding missions. With the increasing influx of missionary personnel, the government's policy led to a rapid multiplication of mission schools, which remained strong until a national education program was established following independence in 1947.

Mission schools were similarly significant in China during the nineteenth and early twentieth centuries. In Japan, education was the only type of mission work permitted prior to 1873. In the Middle East, mission-founded universities won high regard. In sub-Sahara Africa, "bush schools" (led by indigenous pastors or catechists) and mission schools (nearly all at the primary level) were the principal sources of education well into the 1960s.

Three factors account for the commitment of mission personnel and financial resources to schooling. As a religion of the Book, LITERACY is vitally important to the Christian mission. A somewhat fuller understanding of Christian truth, furthermore, is important to the development and exercise of LEADERSHIP within the Christian community. Finally, at least since Alexander Duff, Christian missionaries have sought through schooling to engender a social transformation which, even among non-Christians, is congenial to Christianity and its values. Constitutional government, legal assurance of egalitarian human rights, capitalistic economies, and modern technologies were viewed as fruits of Christianity in the West, which were to be shared through mission schools.

In light of the immense investment of mission resources in schooling—perhaps more than any other kind of mission work—it is appropriate to review the benefits realized. Most observers acknowledge that the evangelistic effect of mission schools is minimal. Sometimes (as in Japan and the Middle East) educational work has provided access to populations otherwise inaccessible, but the close linkage between mission schools and colonial powers also proved problematic as nationalism grew in Africa and Asia (see NATION, NATION-BUILDING, NATIONALISM, and COLONIALISM). Nationalism of mission schools has greatly diminished their missionary role and significance today. With respect to social transformation, few (if any) societies are congenial to the church or to Christian values. Nevertheless, it can be argued that mission schools and colleges have helped shape the world on which the twenty-first century dawns. How the benefits of mission schooling square with the task and goal of Christian missions is an issue on which all Christians should prayerfully reflect.

ROBERT W. FERRIS

Bibliography. R. Allen, *Education in the Native Church*; W. H. T. Gairdner, *Edinburgh 1910*; IMC, *The Life of The Church*; J. H. Kane, *Life and Work on the Mission Field*; S. C. Neill, *Colonialism and Christian Missions*; World Missionary Conference, *Report of Commission III: Education in Relation to the Christianization of National Life*.

Edwards, Jonathan (1703–58). Prominent American philosopher-theologian and missionary to indigenous Americans. Gifted with one of the best theological minds in America (graduating from Yale at the age of seventeen), his reflections on the nature of genuine religion and advocacy for experiential Calvinism influenced generations of Christians. An intellectually vigorous preacher who aroused deep emotional response in his audience, his sermons were pivotal in the outbreak of the first GREAT AWAKENING beginning in 1739. In 1741 he preached "Sinners in the Hands of an Angry God," perhaps the best known sermon in American history.

Accepting a position in 1727 at the First Congregational Church in Northampton, Massachusetts, under his grandfather Solomon Stoddard, Edwards took over the pastorate after Stoddard's death in 1729. Ousted from the church in 1750 after controversy over his strict Communion standards, he accepted an invitation to work with the Mohawk and Housatonnoc Indians in Stockbridge, Massachusetts, a mission he had helped to found in 1734. He served there from 1751 until 1758, during which time he produced his most mature reflections (for example, *Freedom of the Will*, 1754; *The Great Christian Doctrine of Original Sin*, 1758). In 1758, he reluctantly accepted a call to the presidency of the College of New Jersey (now Princeton), dying several weeks later from the effects of a smallpox inoculation.

His legacy of advocacy in missionary efforts, including leadership in the Great Awakening, the work of putting into publishable form the diary of DAVID BRAINERD, and his influential arguments that the GREAT COMMISSION was still relevant (in contrast to the Reformed theology of the time) as well as efforts in preaching the gospel across cultural barriers make him one of the most significant forerunners of the modern missionary movement.

A. SCOTT MOREAU

Bibliography. R. E. Davies, *IBMR* 21:2 (1997): 60–66; C. Mitchell, *WWCH*, pp. 224–26; I. Murray, *Jonathan Edwards: A New Biography;* H. S. Stout, *BDCM*, p. 195.

EFMA. *See* EVANGELICAL FELLOWSHIP OF MISSION AGENCIES.

Egede, Hans Povelsön (1686–1758). Norwegian missionary to Greenland. Egede was born in northeastern Norway. After graduating from the University of Copenhagen in 1705, he was ordained a Lutheran minister and became a pastor. Egede learned about the old Norse Christian settlements in Greenland that had been out of contact with Europe since 1410. He tried to interest bishops and the Danish king in a mission to Greenland, but received only lukewarm support. Eventually he helped found a company to start trading posts on Greenland and support missionary endeavors. He sailed for Greenland in 1722, with his family and a small group to start a Danish colony.

Egede found no Norse communities but rather the Eskimo people, who were the sole inhabitants. He attempted to learn their language and present the gospel to the people, but had limited success. He became a great believer in training indigenous preachers. In 1733 a smallpox epidemic killed thousands. Egede's care of the sick won him great respect among the Greenlanders. His son Paul, who had grown up among the Eskimos and spoke their language, began preaching and won many to Christ. MORAVIAN missionaries arrived in 1733 and also experienced great success, although they were in frequent conflict with Egede. In 1736 he left, returned to Denmark, where he became superintendent of a missionary school for Greenland and wrote books on the island's history, folklore, geography, and language. He and Paul translated the New Testament and other works into the Eskimo language. Thanks largely to his efforts and those of the Moravians, all the inhabitants of Greenland became members of Christian churches.

ROBERT SHUSTER

Bibliography. L. Bobe, *Hans Egede: Colonizer and Missionary of Greenland.*

Egypt (*Est. 2000 pop.: 69,146,000; 1,001,449 sq. km. [386,660 sq. mi.]*). Egypt holds a prominent place in both secular and biblical history, presenting the longest-lasting civilization and one of Christianity's most enduring churches. Recorded history dates back to the twenty-third century B.C. and leaves an impressive record of both divine and human activity. In the fourth century B.C. Alexander the Great captured the Nile Valley and established the city of Alexandria, which continues today as the second largest city in Egypt. Macedonian Ptolemy rule maintained control from 306 B.C. to 30 B.C., when Augustus Caesar made Egypt a province, which lasted until A.D. 395. At that time the Byzantines took control.

By A.D. 639 the Arab Muslim invasions led to the decline and entrenchment of the Coptic Orthodox Church. The establishment of a series of Arab dynasties then followed until Egypt became part of the Ottoman Empire in A.D. 1517. The eventual decline of the Ottoman Empire led to the establishment of British control in A.D. 1801 and then to a protectorate status in A.D. 1914. Eight years later independence was declared and a constitutional monarchy established. By 1953 Egypt became a republic and continues as such.

The history of Christianity in Egypt is equally impressive, tracing its roots to the preaching of Mark in A.D. 50, as recorded by Eusebius. The Coptic Church is one of the autocephalous (self-governing) Oriental Orthodox Churches (non-Chalcedonian) and represents the largest single Christian population in the Middle East. Though strongly affected today by emigration trends, reflecting Middle Eastern political instability, Egyptian Copts still represent 11 percent to 15 percent of the population. Desert monasticism, following the rules of St. Anthony and St. Pachomeus, established Coptic Christian predominance in Egypt and enhanced African missionary successes in Nubia, Sudan, and Ethiopia. Pope Shenouda III, current patriarch of the Copts, has led the church in significant social programs and spiritual renewal in recent years.

The Coptic Church has persevered through the centuries in spite of its minority environment, demonstrating Christian stability in a predominantly Muslim society. The church is marked by the competing values of "a remnant of the faithful" mind-set, ecumenical objectives for removing schism within the worldwide Christian church, and a commitment to spiritual renewal.

Though smaller in numbers, the evangelical churches and the Roman Catholic Church are also present in Egypt. Among the 46 denominations present in Egypt, the Presbyterians and Anglicans are the largest. Christian witness is most commonly provided through Bible and Christian literature distribution and more recently through Christian broadcasts on satellite television. Christian outreach to Muslims is severely restricted. The distribution of ethno-linguistic groups in Egypt is represented by Egyptians (86.4%), Arabs

(6.%), Nubians (3%), Gypsies (2%), and Berbers (2%). The predominant religions represented are Islam (85.4%) and Christianity (14.2% with Coptic Orthodox representing 13%). The literacy rate is 49%. Two world-class cities, Cairo (14,000,000) and Alexandria (4,034,000), are notable centers of Egyptian life and influence.

The situation for Christian mission is seriously affected by two issues. First is the issue of religious tolerance. Jewish tolerance has been moderate, with Egypt being the first Arab state to give official recognition to Israel. This occurred in 1979 by the courageous act of Egypt's president Anwar Sadat, who signed a peace treaty with Israel. This alienated the majority of Arab countries who had less tolerance for a Jewish state and eventually led to the expulsion of Egypt from the League of Arab States and Sadat's assassination in 1981 by extremists. This also provided impetus to developing Islamic fundamentalism accompanied by cries of Jihad.

Tolerance for the Christian minority in Egypt and freedom for Christian expression has also been severely limited. Accounts of numerous HUMAN RIGHTS abuses continue to be recorded in Egypt. The second and related issue is the rise of Islamic fundamentalism, which originates from Egypt in association with the rise of Muslim Brotherhoods.

Egypt is considered the intellectual center of Islam with its history rooted in the ancient and still influential Al Ahzar University. This prominent center has spawned many religious and political parties, among which are several of fundamentalist orientation. Though Qur'anic law (Shariah) is not the political framework of the Republic, there is considerable pressure to make it so. Both of these issues make the climate for Christian witness by nationals and expatriates a difficult endeavor.

Nevertheless, some of the most significant growth of the church in the Middle East is found in Egypt and it is recognized that Egypt is strategically important to the mission of the church. The future of Christian witness, though sensitive, is of high priority. The biblical promise of "blessing to all nations" through the seed of Abraham must eventually return to the household of Hagar, the Egyptian slave, and her descendants. Egypt retains an important place in biblical history and prophecy, intricately situated in relation to the GREAT COMMISSION.

J. RAY TALLMAN

Bibliography. *Turning Over a New Leaf: Protestant Missions and the Orthodox Churches of the Middle East: The Final Report of a Multi-mission Study Group on Orthodoxy;* B. Lewis, *The Middle East;* I. Nafi, *The Religious Situation in Egypt: A Report, 1996;* N. Jabbour, *The Rumbling Volcano: Islamic Fundamentalism in Egypt.*

El Salvador *(Est. 2000 pop.: 6,425,000; 21,041 sq. km. [8,124 sq. mi.]).* Bordering Guatemala and Honduras and facing the Pacific Ocean, El Salvador is the smallest of the five Central American republics. The language is Spanish, with only 5 percent of the people of Indian descent. The capital city is San Salvador (metropolitan area of 1.5 million). Both nation and capital are globally unique for they are named after Christ the Savior.

El Salvador elects a head of state for a five-year term. The economy is focused on agricultural exports (coffee, cotton, sugar—utilizing 40% of the labor force) and other industries (textiles for export and chemicals).

It gained its independence from Spain in 1821, and in 1839 it withdrew from the Central American Federation. Historically, the absence of a democratic social foundation generated a series of strong political/military leaders, and a number of internal revolutions and regional struggles. Its power structure has been dominated by a small land-owning oligarchy. Inevitable social inequities in this century have led to clashes and violent military encounters, including the 1934–35 massacre by the military of some 30,000 peasants accused of communism. The 1969 battle with Honduras over the presence of some 300,000 Salvadoran workers in Honduras left some 2,000 dead.

Latin American Marxist guerrilla movements, supported by Russia and Cuba, during the 1960s and 1970s encouraged a full-scale insurrection which fractured the nation. The United States countered with countless millions of dollars in military and economic assistance. During the conflict at least 75,000 people lost their lives—with violence by both extreme right and left. Catholic priests and nuns, as well as some evangelical leaders were martyred. The twelve-year civil war ended with the UN-brokered January 1992 formal peace treaty. The expected "peace dividend" has not yet generated economic prosperity due to the political and financial cost of reforms and national infrastructure, the problem of retraining thousands of demobilized soldiers and guerrillas, the challenge of an 80 percent poor population.

Historically and culturally, El Salvador is a Roman Catholic nation, and hence 97.5 percent call themselves Christian: Catholic 75 percent, growing at an annual rate of 0.8 percent; Protestant/Evangelicals (with some 64 denominations), 20.6 percent, (2.3% in 1960) of which 80 percent are Pentecostal/charismatic, growing at an annual rate of 5.9 percent; the remaining 4.4 percent covers other religious groups and the non-religious.

Protestantism arrived in El Salvador in 1896 through Samuel A. Purdie (Central American Mission) and his family, influenced by the great colporteur, FRANCISCO PENZOTTI. In 1996 the Centennial of the Gospel was celebrated through the efforts of an interdenominational evangelical coalition, involving Pentecostal and non-Pentecostal leadership as well as national mission agencies and parachurch organizations.

Evangelical spiritual harvest has impacted all strata of society, in spite of violence, poverty, and structural injustice. Church leaders now face the challenge of a fluid postmodern world as they disciple young believers, and create new church and leadership training models. Significantly, Salvadoran evangelicals are committed to their own global missionary responsibility and have sent out scores of missionaries through their own agencies.

WILLIAM DAVID TAYLOR

Bibliography. Economist Intelligence Unit, *Country Profile: Guatemala, El Salvador* (4th Quarter, 1996–97); O. Johnson, ed., *1997 Almanac: Atlas and Yearbook;* P. Johnstone, *OW;* E. A. Núñez, and W. D. Taylor, *Crisis and Hope in Latin America: An Evangelical Perspective.*

Election, Divine. *See* DIVINE ELECTION.

Elections. *See* POLITICAL ELECTIONS.

Elenctics. J. H. BAVINCK refers to elenctics as a missionary science which asks the question, "What have you done with God?" The term comes from the Greek word *elenchō*, which means to reprove, to rebuke, to convince, to convict. Most specifically, it refers to the work of the Holy Spirit in convicting people of SIN as seen in John 16:8. Thus the Holy Spirit is the agent of elenctics in that he is the one who convicts of sin. According to Bavinck, elenctics is "the science which is concerned with the conviction of sin. It is the science which unmasks to heathendom all false religions as sin against God, and it calls heathendom to acknowledge the only true God." Thus it presumes the falsehood of all other religions against the truth of Christianity. It does not compare religions or enter into "DIALOGUE" as if all religions including Christianity were neutral and contained necessary religious truths to be discovered and believed. Rather, it is apologetic in nature in that it defends the Christian faith as the only true faith and accuses all other religions as rebellion against God (*see* APOLOGETICS).

Elenctics takes humankind back to the Fall of Genesis 3, to our original sin, and calls us to repentance, to turn away from our sin to faith in Christ and to serve the only true God. Therefore, elenctics takes sin very seriously, as well as the need for repentance. Thus it is of necessity evangelistic, confrontational, and directive. It evangelizes by proclaiming the whole counsel of God, the gospel, as it is presented in Scripture, God's revelation to us. It confronts the non-Christian with his or her sin and the resulting separation from God and warns of the wrath to come. And it directs the listener to repent and to believe Christ as the only hope for salvation and eternal life with God.

Bavinck explains that the basis of elenctics is God's revelation in Jesus Christ and a strong trust in the work of the Holy Spirit, who alone convicts of sin and brings to faith in Christ. He gives several considerations to support this. God manifests himself through his GENERAL REVELATION in culture and in individuals even before the missionary makes any contact. He also points out that there may appear to be similarities between Christianity and other religions but that these perceptions fail to plumb the depths of either religion and may lead one to make serious errors in faith. Again, the Holy Spirit is the only agent of elenctics, and he alone convicts of sin and calls to repentance. The missionary is only the means by which the Spirit works. Finally, our philosophical reasoning and argument may cause an adherent to renounce his or her non-Christian faith, but that is useless unless the person puts his or her faith in Jesus Christ as Lord and God.

Therefore elenctics is seen as an approach theory in missions. It refuses to accept that there is God's special revelatory truth in non-Christian religions and, in appropriate ways, confronts these religions in order to call their adherents to repentance. Thus it is important that missionaries have knowledge of religions, but even more important that they have a deep knowledge of the Word of God and a strong faith in Jesus Christ. For it is only through God's truth that error can be discerned and true faith built.

Harvie Conn provides five characteristics of elenctics: (1) It is personal in that it approaches individuals in relationship. (2) It is holistic in that it approaches in deeds as well as words. This means that the missionary becomes a part of the community and deals with people in community. (3) It is contextual in that it approaches people where they are in their culture, in their belief system. This means that the missionary must be knowledgeable about the culture and sensitive to the needs of people within that culture and belief system. (4) It is verdict-oriented in that its goal is to bring a person to a personal relationship with Jesus Christ as Lord and God. This of course requires that a person be confronted with the claims and demands of Jesus Christ and be called to repentance. Finally, (5), it is God-centered in that it seeks primarily to convince people to be reconciled to God. It does not seek to improve systems or lifestyles but to fill the earth with worshipers for God.

It is crucial for missionaries involved in elenctics to be correctly informed of the context of their ministry—the culture in which they seek to do elenctics, that is, the receptor culture. They not only must understand and believe their own faith, but also understand the beliefs and faith of the receptor culture so as to facilitate true communication of the meaning of the gospel using the proper cultural language, forms, values, and symbols. Without this there will be misunderstanding and SYNCRETISM among those hearing the message.

Because elenctics seeks primarily to convict of sin (i.e., to awaken and charge the conscience with the seriousness and guilt of sin), it is most important that missionaries understand what sin is in their own culture, in the biblical culture, and in the receptor culture. With this understanding missionaries are enabled to engage as God's instruments in the conviction of sin and the call to repentance for offenses which are considered sin in the receptor culture and which are truly sin, because they are declared sin in Scripture. Robert Priest explains that unless people are convinced of their sin from their own cultural understanding and definitions, there will be no conviction or repentance of sin. Therefore, as he explains, in the initial stages of evangelism, missionaries should concentrate the proclamation of sinfulness, guilt, and repentance on the common agreement of these between the receptor culture and the biblical definitions. As missionaries preach sin in the forms and behaviors of the culture, which are also in agreement with the biblical view of sin, the Holy Spirit will convict of sin, and the people will hear and understand the call to repentance.

As the Holy Spirit begins to work on persons in the elenctic process, the missionary will need to know how sensitively and correctly to proclaim the gospel and to counsel the persons in terms of GUILT, in terms of fear as they are confronted with a just God who judges sin, and in terms of SHAME as they are confronted with a holy God whom they have greatly offended. Then as the Holy Spirit completes his saving work through convicting of sin, repentance, and effectual call, missionaries must be able to counsel the person regarding God's forgiveness and eternal love.

Elenctics as practical theology and as an approach theory in missions has become more significant in recent years due to the problems of syncretism in missions and to issues related to the CONTEXTUALIZATION of theology. The church is growing rapidly in many parts of the world, but in some cases the fruits of repentance and holiness of life are not evident. Elenctics refuses to allow syncretism and its related errors and demands repentance of sin as explained in Scripture and turning to Christ as Lord and God.

THOMAS L. AUSTIN

Bibliography. J. H. Bavinck, *An Introduction to the Science of Missions;* D. J. Hesselgrave, *Missiology* 11:4 (October 1983): 461–83; R. J. Priest, *Missiology* 22:3 (July 1994): 291–315; F. Turretin, *Institutes of Elenctic Theology,* vol. 1.

Eliot, John (1604–90). English missionary to Indigenous Americans. Eliot was born in 1604 in Widford, England. After receiving an A.B. from Jesus College at Cambridge in 1622, he worked at a school headed by Thomas Hooker, who influenced him to adopt Puritan beliefs. Because of the anti-Puritan policies of the Church of England, Eliot emigrated to Massachusetts Bay in 1631. The Puritans had done little to evangelize the Indigenous Americans and there was little support for such work. But Eliot felt a call to reach these neighbors with the gospel. He learned some Algonquin from a neighbor's servant and, in 1646, began preaching in Algonquin in tribal villages. Slowly he made converts. Opposition came not only from tribal sachems, but also from colonists. But Eliot persisted and his reports led in 1649 to the founding in England of the Society for the Propagation of the Gospel in New England. Eliot believed converts should be separated from the associations of tribal life, so he organized the settlement of towns, where the "Praying Indians" could live close to English communities and adopt the English lifestyle. The first of fourteen such settlements was in 1651 at Natick. Eliot prepared a catechism in 1653 as part of his continuing effort to train indigenous American lay leaders and ministers. He published in 1663 his translation of the entire Bible in Algonquin, one of the first achievements of American scholarship. In 1671 he distributed dialogues in English that provided vivid pictures of the means he and his Indian associates used to communicate the gospel in meaningful terms. By 1674 there were almost 4,000 Praying Indians, led by twenty-four indigenous ministers, about 1,100 in Eliot's settlements. Disaster came in 1675. As a result of the so-called King Philip's War in 1675, the Praying Indians were rounded up and eventually sent to a small island, where harsh conditions and the shock of betrayal killed some and broke the spirit of more. Eliot tried to protect them, but was largely ineffectual. After the war ended in 1676, the remaining Praying Indians could return home, but only enough for four small settlements came back. Eliot continued to labor among them, but few other English or Algonquin-speaking people took up his work. He died on May 21, 1690, but his example was a strong influence on future American missionary efforts.

ROBERT SHUSTER

Bibliography. H. W. Bowden and J. P. Ronda, *John Eliot's Indian Dialogues: A Study in Cultural Interaction;* O. E. Winslow, *John Eliot: "Apostle to the Indians."*

Elliot, Elisabeth Howard (1926–). American lecturer, author, and missionary to Ecuador. Elliot was born of missionary parents in Brussels, Belgium. Her father, Philip E. Howard Jr., later became the editor of the *Sunday School Times.*

She and her five siblings, all of whom entered Christian ministry, were exposed regularly to missionary guests in their home.

After graduating from Wheaton College in 1948, Elliot went to Ecuador in 1952, working initially among the Colorado Indians. In 1953 she married Jim Elliot and joined him among the Quichua Indians. In 1956 Jim and four companions were speared to death in an attempt to reach Auca Indians.

In 1958 Elisabeth and her three-year-old daughter, Valerie, with Rachael Saint, went by invitation to live among the Aucas, where she learned the language and began translation work. In 1963 she returned to the United States.

She was married in 1969 to Addison Leitch, who died of cancer in 1973. She married again in 1977 to Lars Gren. A popular speaker to students, women, and others, she produces a daily radio broadcast, *Gateway to Joy,* heard nationwide and a bimonthly newsletter. She has written more than two dozen books, many of which have been best-sellers and have stimulated great interest in missions.

DAVID M. HOWARD

Bibliography. E. Elliot, *The Savage, My Kinsman;* idem, *Passion and Purity;* idem, *The Shaping of a Christian Family.*

Elliot, Philip James (1927–56). American missionary martyr in Ecuador. Elliot was born to godly parents in Portland, Oregon. He graduated from Wheaton College in 1949, having been a champion wrestler and campus leader as president of the Student Foreign Missions Fellowship. He began keeping a personal journal in 1948, parts of which have been widely quoted because of his keen spiritual insights.

Elliot went to Ecuador in 1952 to work among the Quichua Indians. In 1953 he married Elisabeth Howard in Quito.

Burdened for unreached tribes, he and companions Nate Saint and Ed McCully searched for the Aucas, which they discovered in September 1955. For three months they dropped gifts weekly from the air to the Aucas. In January 1956, with two more companions, Roger Youderian and Peter Fleming, the five established a beachhead on the Curaray River near the Auca territory. One friendly contact with three Aucas took place at their river encampment. Then on January 8, 1956, they were attacked and speared to death by the Aucas. The story of Jim Elliot and his companions has continued to motivate Christians all over the world for commitment to missionary service.

DAVID M. HOWARD

Bibliography. E. Elisabeth, *Through Gates of Splendor;* idem *Shadow of the Almighty,* idem (ed.), *The Journals of Jim Elliot.*

Emde, Johannes (1774–1859). German pietist missionary in Indonesia. A naval officer with the Dutch East India Company, Emde is regarded as a cofounder (along with C. L. Coolen) of the Protestant church in East Java. Retiring from his naval career, Emde settled in Surabaya, East Java, and married a Javanese woman. In spite of two centuries of Dutch presence in Java, the Javanese were still unreached with the gospel. Working as a watchmaker, Emde established contacts with the Javanese, preaching the gospel to them and distributing portions of Scripture in their language.

Eventually two Christian groups arose among the Javanese in Surabaya—one around Emde and his friends and the other around Coolen, a Christian working for the Dutch government. In 1837 under Coolen's leadership a group of Javanese Muslims responded positively to the gospel of Jesus Christ. After guiding the new converts for several years, Coolen sent them on to Emde, where they joined his growing community. Out of the Emde and Coolen groups came Christian communities with membership eventually numbering about 19,000. Emde and Coolen had rather different views on how the Christian converts should relate to Javanese culture. Coolen was more accepting of Javanese customs whereas Emde expected the people to make a clean break with the culture, adopting Western dress and ways. Later, under the leadership of the Dutch missionary Jelle Jellesma, the Javanese Christians adopted a more balanced perspective toward indigenous cultural ways.

HAROLD NETLAND

Enculturation. Learning of a culture through growing up in it. Enculturation is the process that begins from the moment of birth in which the cultural rules and pathways, values and dreams, and patterns and regulations of life are passed on from one generation to the next. Every human being is born without culture but with the innate need to learn how to live as a member of a culture. Learning how to communicate, the rules and regulations of social behavior, evaluating events and values as positive or negative, as well as connecting to God (or the transcendent) are all part of the enculturation process.

The chief means of enculturation are the normal everyday patterns of life, which every person observes, interprets, and internalizes while growing up. The way our parents raise us, the way siblings respond to us, our spiritual and physical environments, the values we see in relationships and social institutions, and the media to which we were exposed were all factors in our own enculturation processes.

Missionaries have the tendency to forget their own enculturation and how deeply their own cultural values are embedded in them, and they are tempted to criticize inappropriately the process of enculturation as they observe it in a new culture, often because what they see does not "feel" right to them. Understanding the enculturation process is important for successful CONTEXTUALIZATION, for it provides crucial insights needed for success in the process of helping people of a new culture understand the message of the gospel.

A. SCOTT MOREAU

Bibliography. S. Grunlan and M. K. Mayers, *Cultural Anthropology: A Christian Perspective;* L. J. Luzbetak, *The Church and Cultures.*

End Times. A primary scriptural impetus for the global missionary enterprise is the GREAT COMMISSION statement crowning the First Gospel: "go and make disciples of all nations. . . . I am with you to the very end of the age" (Matt. 28:19–20). Jesus makes it clear that the urgent emphasis of mission must not be simply to "disciple" the world, but to continue to do so until the culmination of the end times events.

Relatedly, the Savior had already spoken to the heart of the issue in the Olivet Discourse, Jesus' sermon on the end of the age. Assurance that the global evangelistic task will be completed can be drawn from Matthew 24:14: "And this gospel of the kingdom will be preached in the whole world as a testimony to all nations, and then the end will come." Unfortunately, this passage does not elaborate on how this climactic proclamation will come about or who will accomplish it, nor does it address other questions that divide evangelical Bible scholars and missiologists.

Nor are these the only key passages that relate mission to the end times. For example, in Acts 2:17 the apostle Peter relates the phenomena going on around him on the Day of Pentecost to "the last days," citing Joel 2:28–32, which is there linked to the "day of the Lord" (Acts 2:20), a great theme of Old Testament eschatology. These references added urgency to Peter's appeal to his hearers: Call on the name of the Lord and be saved (v. 21) before it is too late for you to do so (v. 20)!

This passage also reveals the balancing perspective that "the last days" actually began in earnest with the inbreaking of the new age of the Spirit at Pentecost. This understanding is shared by the description of Christ being revealed in "these last days" in Hebrews 1:2. Relatedly, Paul speaks of ungodly behavior characterizing "later times," which seems to include his own day (1 Tim. 4:1).

On the other hand, Paul also looks ahead to absolutely "terrible times in the last days" (2 Tim. 3:1), though still times in which the God-breathed Scriptures will bring hearers to salvation (3:15–4:5). Of that latter-day period, Peter reminds his readers that the Lord wants "everyone to come to repentance" (2 Peter 3:9), urging

a blameless lifestyle that will be a crucial aspect of attracting unbelievers to salvation (vv. 14–15).

Unfortunately, to this point, evangelicals have not sufficiently probed the Book of Revelation for specifics with regard to the completion of the Great Commission. Recently, however, R. Bauckham's programmatic discussion of the "conversion of the nations" in regard to the Apocalypse has served to stimulate fresh discussion in this area.

For example, it is quite likely that "a great multitude that no one could count, from every nation, tribe, people and language" (Rev. 7:9) standing before the heavenly throne is to be linked to the Matthean Commission. This vast throng from "all the nations" (Matt. 28:19), whether martyrs or not, are the end times fruit of the Great Commission.

Also, the references to "the eternal gospel to proclaim to those who live on the earth, to every nation, tribe, language and people" (Rev. 14:6–7) and the group of martyrs standing on the glassy sea (15:2) apparently are the fulfillment of the promise of the age-concluding preaching of the gospel described in Matthew 24:14. That understanding becomes even more likely when one sees that this use of "gospel" in 14:6 is its lone inclusion in the Book of Revelation.

Further, the two-sided harvest of Revelation 14:14–19 reflects strikingly similar imagery and terminology to Christ's parable of the wheat and the weeds (Matt. 13:24–30, 36–43). Since it speaks of the judgment at the "end of the age" (vv. 39–40), in which the children of the kingdom and the children of the evil one are separated to their ultimate destinies, there are important missiological implications.

So, if nothing else, recent study of the Book of Revelation has located several passages that seem to detail the completion of the Great Commission in the end times. It remains for further exegetical and theological study to clarify important details that will inform the theory and practice of the evangelical missionary enterprise in the crucial time ahead.

With the new millennium, there is great curiosity about the possible arrival of the "end times." From the standpoint of mission, there has been much creative strategizing and sending, including hundreds of strategies aimed toward the goal of completing the global imperative by the turn of the century.

Since there is still much uncertainty attached to the specific impact of these efforts with respect to God's plan and timing, encouragement should be drawn from joyfully remembering the promise of the risen Lord, in the context of the carrying out of the Great Commission: "I am with you always, to the very end of the age" (Matt. 28:20).

On the other hand, God's sovereignty must never be an excuse for irresponsibility or complacency. Employing imagery with overtones of the end times, the apostle Paul laid out the practical urgency of "understanding the present time. The hour has come for you to wake up from your slumber, because our salvation is nearer now than when we first believed. The night is nearly over; the day is almost here" (Rom. 13:11–12).

A. BOYD LUTER

SEE ALSO Millennial Thought and Mission.

Bibliography. R. Bauckham, *The Climax of Prophecy, The Theology of the Book of Revelation,* BEB, II:1310–11; A. Johnson and R. Webber, *What Christians Believe: A Biblical and Historical Summary;* A. B. Luter and K. McReynolds, *Disciplined Living: What the New Testament Teaches about Recovery and Discipleship.*

Engel Scale. A model that illustrates the spiritual decision process has become known as the *Engel Scale.* The idea behind the model or scale is to indicate that a decision for Christ is not just one event, but a journey or series of events that will lead toward spiritual maturity.

The scale was developed through cooperation between James F. Engel and Viggo Søgaard. A rudimentary model was first published by Viggo Søgaard *(Everything You Need to Know for a Cassette Ministry).* The model was titled *Total Program Principles,* indicating the total program needed to carry out the GREAT COMMISSION. It was designed for strategic application and to assist in comparative media decisions. Biblical background was seen from the parable of the sower, and from Paul's illustration of one who planted and another who watered (1 Cor. 3:6).

Engel refined the model, adding significant thinking from secular behavioral science. To a large extent, Engel follows the paradigm of a linear approach to DECISION MAKING as seen in a consumer behavior model: knowledge-belief-attitude-intention-behavior. On such a model, both cognitive and affective dimensions are united on one linear dimension. A similar approach has been followed by Rogers in *Diffusion of Innovations.*

In *Contemporary Christian Communication,* Engel gives a full description of the scale and its implications for the church and its mission. The scale shows the various stages in the decision-making process, starting from initial exposure for those who have no awareness of the Christian faith, through conversion, and a lifelong pattern of growth and maturity. Everyone is somewhere on this scale.

The model was quickly adopted by teachers and became a primary model for many organizations, with significant adaptations.

One drawback of the scale is the fixed linear approach. The sequence of elements needs to be flexible, allowing for different ordering of the events. For some the spiritual journey begins with information and knowledge, but for others it may start through a power encounter which has caused attitude change. For most people there will be concurrent processes of cognitive and affective changes toward spiritual maturity.

A revised version, utilizing a two-dimensional model, separating cognitive and affective processes, was published by Viggo Søgaard in 1986 *(Applying Christian Communication).* Based on the conviction that conversion is not an entirely cognitive process, the affective dimension has been added. The affective dimension will primarily be a person's feelings toward the gospel, the church, and Christ.

Cognitive changes are illustrated as an upward move, while affective responses can fluctuate between positive and negative attitudes. The model (or scale) provides a grid for illustrating and evaluating strategies, and as such provides a way to analyze evangelistic and nurture ministries in the light of a decision-making process. Questions needing research include: Are we aiming where the audience is? Do the translated materials really fit? How does this ministry relate to that which was done before? How does it relate to that which follows?

VIGGO B. SØGAARD

Bibliography. J. F. Engel and W. H. Norton, *What's Gone Wrong With the Harvest?;* J. F. Engel, *Contemporary Christian Communication, Its Theory and Practice;* E. M. Rogers, *Diffusion of Innovations,* 3rd ed.; V. B. Søgaard, *Everything You Need to Know for a Cassette Ministry;* idem, *Applying Christian Communications.*

England. *See* UNITED KINGDOM.

English Mission Boards and Societies. The two oldest English mission agencies predate the Evangelical Revival. The Society for Promoting Christian Knowledge was established in 1698 to provide schooling and Christian literature in both Britain and North America. Connections with German Pietists also led the Society in 1710 to adopt the Danish Lutheran mission at Tranquebar, the first Protestant missionary venture in India. The Society for the Propagation of the Gospel in Foreign Parts was founded in 1701 primarily to provide Anglican pastoral ministry to settlers in the British North American colonies. Although the Society's royal charter made implicit reference to the needs of the indigenous American peoples, the SPG remained almost entirely a colonial church society until the 1830s.

These two religious societies were not dedicated exclusively to overseas mission. The first English society founded specifically for this purpose was the Particular Baptist Society for Propagating the Gospel among the Heathen, founded in 1792 by the Particular (Calvinistic) Baptists. The Baptist Missionary Society (BMS), as the

Society became known, sent WILLIAM CAREY to Bengal in 1793. Other denominations similarly touched by the Evangelical Revival soon followed suit. In 1795 evangelicals from various churches formed "The Missionary Society" in an united endeavor to send the gospel to the "heathen," leaving the converts to decide their own form of church government. This dream of evangelical ecumenism proved hard to sustain once different denominations had their own missionary bodies. The name was changed to the LONDON MISSIONARY SOCIETY in 1818. The LMS became chiefly identified with the Congregational denomination. Among its missionaries were ROBERT MORRISON, ROBERT MOFFAT, and DAVID LIVINGSTONE. Evangelicals in the established Church of England formed their own missionary society in 1799: the "Society for Missions to Africa and the East" or "CHURCH MISSIONARY SOCIETY." The CMS grew over the course of the nineteenth century into the largest of the English societies. From the ranks of its secretaries came two of the most influential missionary thinkers in recent Christian history: HENRY VENN and MAX WARREN. JOHN WESLEY's new "Methodist" movement within the Church of England was also actively involved in foreign mission from 1786, when the first Methodist missionary arrived in the West Indies. However, the formal organization of the Wesleyan Methodist Missionary Society took place only after 1813, when different Methodist districts established their own missionary societies, which came together in one national body in 1818. Unlike the BMS, LMS, or CMS, the WMMS was not a voluntary society separate from denominational structures, but an integral part of the Methodist connectional machinery.

Nevertheless, the English mission agencies in the nineteenth century shared an essentially common evangelical theology and similar approaches to fundraising at home and policy on the field. As the century proceeded, three developments occurred that diversified this picture. First, the revival of High Churchmanship within the Anglican Church expressed in the Oxford Movement first transformed the SPG into an effective missionary agency, and then, in 1857, led to the formation of a new mission, the Universities' Mission to Central Africa. Although owing much to the ideas of Livingstone, the new mission also embodied the distinctively Anglo-Catholic principle that missionary ventures should be pioneered by "missionary bishops." The focus was shifting from voluntary society to church. Second, JAMES HUDSON TAYLOR's formation of the CHINA INLAND MISSION in 1865 marked an alternative and distinctively evangelical departure from the voluntary society ideal. The CIM repudiated the idea of a society run by an elected committee and responsible to its subscribers, and introduced instead the model of

nondenominational "faith mission," directed on the field by a spiritually gifted leader, with the domestic emphasis falling less on fundraising than on prayer. This ideal became international in scope during the 1880s and 1890s, but also spawned other faith missions in England such as the Regions Beyond Missionary Union (whose origins go back to 1878) or the Sudan United Mission (1904). Third, in the final years of the century strains began to appear within English missions over theological issues, particularly in relation to biblical criticism and attitudes to Indian religions. By the early 1920s these strains had become acute, issuing, for example, in the secession of some conservatives from the CMS in 1922 to form the Bible Churchmen's Missionary Society (now known as Crosslinks).

In terms of size of missionary force and levels of popular support the older denominational societies reached their peak between the World Wars. After 1945 these societies, under the leadership of mission statesmen such as Max Warren, began to revise their policies in response to the growth of nationalism in the non-Western world and the beginnings of decolonization. Their approaches were also affected in varying measure by the increasing theological doubts about the appropriateness of seeking to convert people of other faiths to Christianity. Some of the older societies changed their names or even dissolved themselves in favor of new bodies that expressed ideals of global Christian partnership rather than mission in the traditional sense of a one-way flow of personnel and funds from the West. Between 1966 and 1977 the LMS was transformed into a global partnership body, the Council for World Mission. Less radically, the CMS in 1995 changed its name to the Church *Mission* Society, reflecting an understanding that mission is a broader process than the sending of missionaries. In 1965 the SPG and the UMCA had merged to form the United Society for the Propagation of the Gospel (USPG).

In England, as elsewhere, the newer faith missions have continued to stress the priority of initiating evangelistic expansion to unreached populations. However, by the 1990s they too were struggling to maintain their levels of support, as the younger generation of English evangelicals appeared less acutely concerned than their forebears about the spiritual condition of non-Western peoples. To some extent evangelicals in England have followed the more liberal sections of the English churches in focusing their overseas concerns on Christian relief agencies such as TEAR Fund, set up by the Evangelical Alliance in 1968. Young people in England have nonetheless been attracted to a third generation of mission agencies, such as Operation Mobilisation (1957) or Youth With a Mission (1960), which have encouraged short-term service and vacation mission opportunities for students.

BRIAN STANLEY

SEE ALSO Scottish Mission Boards and Societies.

Bibliography. J. Murray, *Proclaim the Good News: A Short History of the Church Missionary Society;* B. Stanley, *The Bible and the Flag: Protestant Missions and British Imperialism in the Nineteenth and Twentieth Centuries;* idem, *The History of the Baptist Missionary Society 1792–1992;* H. P. Thompson, *Into All Lands: The History of the Society for the Propagation of the Gospel in Foreign Parts 1701–1950;* B. Thorogood, ed., *Gales of Change: Responding to a Shifting Missionary Context. The Story of the London Missionary Society 1945–1977;* A. F. Walls, *DSCHT,* pp. 567–94.

Enlightenment. Surely one of church history's more intriguing ironies is the fact that the modern Protestant missionary movement, which began in the late eighteenth century, came out of an environment that was strongly influenced by the philosophy of the Enlightenment.

Often explicitly anti-Christian in outlook, Enlightenment philosophers not only attacked traditional Christian beliefs but propounded ideas that called into question the need for evangelism and missions. In its own way, however, the Enlightenment both prepared the way for the new missionary initiatives and influenced their direction.

Building on the humanistic foundations of the Renaissance and seventeenth-century rationalism, eighteenth-century Enlightenment philosophers as diverse as Rousseau, Voltaire, Lessing, Kant, Paine, and Hume asserted the autonomy of the individual and the ability of unaided human reason to discover truth. They therefore rejected reliance on any external source of truth in philosophy and religion, including divine revelation and the authority of religious institutions. The attitude of many Enlightenment philosophers toward religion is well summarized in the title of Immanuel Kant's 1793 essay *Religion Within the Bounds of Reason Alone.*

Most Enlightenment philosophers did not deny God's existence, but were Deists who believed that God was distant and uninvolved in human affairs, and had left it to human reason to discover the path to happiness, morality, and truth. Their focus, therefore, was on nature and on human experience, and by exalting human reason as the arbiter of what was ethical or true they affirmed the innate goodness and potential of the individual. They therefore rejected the Christian belief in the DEPRAVITY OF HUMANKIND or the need for spiritual conversion—and thus evangelical missionary activity.

Christians who retained their orthodox convictions reacted sharply against Deism and other aspects of Enlightenment philosophy. On a theological level, Bishop Joseph Butler's *The Analogy of Religion* (1736) was apparently intended as a point-by-point refutation of the writings of the noted Deist Matthew Tindal; it became the most widely used theological work of the eighteenth century. Although Butler is usually remembered as a philosophical theologian, one of his printed sermons supported the cause of foreign missions.

On a practical level, evangelists such as JOHN WESLEY and GEORGE WHITEFIELD crisscrossed the British Isles (and in Whitefield's case the American colonies) proclaiming the Bible's message to large crowds. Most of their hearers were ordinary people, but Whitefield's *Journals* are sprinkled with accounts of encounters with Deist intellectuals. "I fear Deism has spread much in these parts," he wrote during a 1739 trip through Maryland.

When WILLIAM CAREY, the father of modern foreign missions, catalogued the religious state of the nations of the world in his influential tract *An Enquiry into the Obligation of Christians to use Means for the Conversion of the Heathen* (1792), he noted that France consisted of "Catholics, Deists, and Protestants" and added that "Various baneful, and pernicious errors appear to gain ground, in almost every part of Christendom; the truths of the gospel, and even the gospel itself, are attacked." Although urging the cause of foreign missions, Carey realized that so-called Christian countries could not be excluded from missionary activity.

Nevertheless the Enlightenment significantly influenced the spirit of eighteenth-century society, and as such had an indirect but definite impact on the beginnings of modern Protestant foreign missions, particularly in England.

Enlightenment thinkers unintentionally encouraged foreign missions, for example, through their attempt to find a common natural religion throughout the world. The age of exploration had opened up new vistas for studying diverse human societies, and as they looked beyond superficial cultural differences Enlightenment scholars concluded that human nature was basically the same everywhere. As David Hume declared in 1748, "It is universally acknowledged, that there is a great uniformity among the acts of men, in all nations and ages, and that human nature remains still the same." In Christian eyes this reinforced the conviction that the gospel was equally valid for all humanity, and that no culture should be excluded from its message.

The scientific and experimental methodology of the Enlightenment also influenced the growth of missions. As eighteenth-century evangelicals moved away from Puritanism, with its preoccupation with inward-looking piety as the test of conversion, they embraced immediate religious experience as the basis of their assurance of salvation. In so doing they were mirroring the Enlightenment's method of seeking truth through immediate experience. This in turn encouraged a new activism in evangelism and missions, since CONVERSION could be immediately experienced.

In other ways the Enlightenment spurred the growth of an activist spirit in Western society as a whole, which in turn influenced evangelical Christianity. Enlightenment ideas gave impetus to a new spirit of optimism and progress in society, for example, and a determination not to be bound by the past. While at times this could take radical directions (as indeed happened in the French Revolution), in a more general way this progressive attitude encouraged the development of new approaches to old problems and new ways of looking at the world. This in turn made Christians more open to new directions in their work—including foreign missions.

In a similar way the Enlightenment opened the door to a new wave of pragmatism and a willingness to experiment with new methodologies. Evangelicals embraced this attitude with enthusiasm. The field preaching of Wesley and Whitefield is one example of this; another is the growth in lay witness and work. The explosion in evangelical foreign mission societies (as well as voluntary societies devoted to a host of other religious and social causes) in the late eighteenth and early nineteenth centuries owed far more to lay activists than to ordained clergy.

The Enlightenment unquestionably laid the foundations for much modern secular thinking, and as such continues to challenge contemporary Christians. Even in modern missions its continuing influence can be detected among those who deny the need for overt evangelism and reduce missions solely to humanitarianism. Nevertheless, without the Enlightenment the emergence of the modern missionary impulse would have been seriously hampered.

JOHN N. AKERS

Environment. While various social structures, including business and government, are increasingly concerned about environmental problems—pollution, exploding population, famine, vanishing resources—evangelical missions often reflect the general evangelical trend to leave such concerns to secular groups. This attitude comes from a hierarchical, Platonic view of life, which makes caring for the physical world less urgent than the salvation of souls. The fear that faith in God might be taken over by the concern for nature is ever present. As a consequence, lamented FRANCIS SCHAEFFER, an evangelistic opportunity is being lost; for while modern young people have a real sensitivity to nature, most Christians do not care about the beauty of nature or nature as such. Another consequence of the evangelical perspective and activities on the mission field is that they often pave the way for self-interested enterprise, ignorance, and greed, which lead to environmental degradation.

Christians can no longer avoid seeing that the environmental damage brought by war, multinational companies, and modern technology conflicts with human survival needs and the long-term intentions of a compassionate God who created a world in which every part waits for its redemption (Rom. 8:21). An organic or holistic view of life will bring many insights to challenge Christians (*see also* HOLISM, BIBLICAL); for example, the links between population growth, environmental destruction, and social conflict; the irresponsibility of powerful groups' accumulating wealth through mining and industry without taking thought for the associated environmental damage or the suffering of disadvantaged people (the loss of land in order to build factories, the industrial pollution of rivers); the rise of Gaia-consciousness in the New Age movement.

Such challenges, when contrasted with kingdom insights about the rule of God over all creation (Isa. 11:9; 65:25), have led some missions to think about environmental issues. For God's mission in redemption cannot be separated from his mission in creation. While limits of time, energy, skill, and finance must confine the scope of missionary concern about nature, environmental degradation so affects people that caring for their spiritual welfare cannot be separated from caring for creation. This in effect reinterprets the biblical concept of stewardship—not dominion and control, but responsibility and accountability to the Lord of creation.

The gospel has environmental, as well as eternal, imperatives (Eph. 1:10; Col. 1:19–20). "You have placed humankind in charge of everything you made; everything is put under their authority" (Ps. 8:6). Part of the image of God is the responsibility of stewardship over the earth. But many Christians have misunderstood stewardship as ownership or exploitation rather than trusteeship, and live in such a way that their central purpose seems to be consumption.

The Christian ethic is the world's only hope of averting environmental disaster. This requires a transformation of attitudes, which is most effectively achieved by the regeneration of human hearts. Evangelism is, then, an essential part of ECOLOGY, a fact that few missions have realized. Balance will be recovered only as we study and adopt the integrated view of life reflected in Hebrew thought, the theology of FRANCIS OF ASSISI, and Eastern Orthodoxy rather than the Western individualism that has held sway since the Reformation.

When we seek the KINGDOM OF GOD, environmental issues will assume their full significance as part of a larger structure of rightness and integrity. We will take note that most of the growth in world POPULATION is concentrated in the poorest and most environmentally degraded countries, and that there is a global increase in environmental refugees who are being displaced because of drought, soil erosion, and flooding. The perspective of many of these people is such that organic and ecological models and metaphors can be used to explore with them the deep issues of life.

Environmental issues suggest various ways in which mission in the twenty-first century can be made more effective. We should study biblical holism and the role of stewardship in God's plan for both urban and rural situations. Courses in the THEOLOGY OF MISSION should incorporate environmental concerns. We can analyze case studies of how mission grows out of the work of Christians with a holistic worldview (e.g., Peter Harris in Portugal). We can make the good news real for powerless people by challenging evil structures and working to reverse the pollution of their air, water, and soil. Organic metaphors and models of appropriate lifestyles can be used to communicate the gospel. Missions can involve themselves in environmental issues that relate to human survival—population, land ownership and use, relationships between the powerful and the marginalized. Mission work must take these issues seriously as part of the challenge of the whole gospel for the whole world.

JOHN STEWARD

Bibliography. W. D. Roberts, *Patching God's Garment*; C. DeWitt, *The Environment and the Christian*; P. Harris, *Under the Bright Wings*; H. Snyder, *Earthcurrents*; L. Wilkinson, *Earthkeeping in the Nineties*; F. Schaeffer, *Pollution and the Death of Man.*

Episcopalian Mission. *See* ANGLICAN MISSION.

Equatorial Guinea *(Est. 2000 pop.: 452,000; 28,071 sq. km. [10,838 sq. mi.]).* The people of Republic of Equatorial Guinea speak seventeen languages. Tribal religionists account for less than 5 percent of the population, in large part due to the country's long-standing association with Catholicism. Catholicism arrived in the fifteenth century and existed under European colonial administration prior to independence in 1968.

Baptist missionaries first arrived from the West Indies in 1841 but were expelled by the Spanish administration in 1858. In 1870 the English Methodist Church sent missionaries in response to an appeal from the Fernando Poo Protestant community. The Methodists were allowed to remain in 1870 only through the British consul's intervention. Methodism remains the largest Protestant body on the island.

The principal evangelical body on the mainland of Rio Muni is the Evangelical Church, which receives support from the United Presbyterian Church and since 1970, the Worldwide Evangelization Crusade of UK. The Presbyterian Church began on the island of Corisco in 1850, reaching the mainland in 1865. Five years later the first African pastor was ordained and within ten years an African missionary had been sent to Cameroon. WEC INTERNATIONAL entered Rio Muni in 1933, merging its work with that of the Presbyterians to form the Evangelical church in 1970.

President Macias Nguema came to power at independence in 1968 and subjected the country to a reign of terror until he was overthrown and executed in 1979. Protestant buildings were confiscated, foreign missionaries expelled, and local clergy suffered imprisonment and torture. During his despotic reign tens of thousands of Guineans were victims of political assassinations.

GARY LAMB

Eritrea *(Est. 2000 pop.: 4,025,000; 124,000 sq. km. [47,876 sq. mi.]).* Eritrea, until 1993 a northern province of Ethiopia, is an independent state on the Red Sea. Seventy-five percent of the population are Tigrai and Tigre. Eritrea is 41 percent Christian and the Orthodox represent 75 percent of the total number of Christians. Lutheran Evangelicals number more than 20,000 and are active in evangelization.

TODD M. JOHNSON

Eschatology. One of the striking characteristics of the evangelical missionary enterprise is the optimism with which it is being pursued. There appears to be little, if anything, that can shake its advocates' belief that the GREAT COMMISSION can and soon will be fulfilled. It has been suggested that the worldwide church is on the threshold of unprecedented growth. It is said that this will involve a near universal hearing of the gospel accompanied by successful CHURCH PLANTING among every ethnic group. This success will signal the final epoch of missions and inaugurate the end of this age.

This confident outlook is based on an eschatological orientation, in which the inexorable implementation of God's salvific plan is followed from his promise to Abraham (Gen. 12:1–3), through the sending of the Son (Gal. 4:4), and on to the yet outstanding parade of the nations to Zion (Zech. 8:20–22). This air of anticipation is not generated by the calamitous state of the world, but by the present state of missionary advance. Jesus said (Matt. 24:14) that before he would return the gospel would have to be preached to the whole world, to every nation, tribe, and language. For the first time in history this appears to be a real possibility. In light of the progress that has been made and technological advances at our disposal, it is reasonable to believe that every people can hear the gospel and have the church planted in it. We just might be able to complete the task within this generation.

Of course, few dare to suggest particular dates. Neither is there agreement on the details of the eschatological timetable. But that our Lord will return, of that there is little evangelical doubt. This, more than anything, has contributed to an atmosphere of heightened eschatological anticipation. There seems to be a general consensus that we are not only in or near the final stage of history, but that we are also close to reaching the ultimate goal of salvation history, the full reinstatement of the KINGDOM OF GOD.

The key biblical text in this regard is Matthew 24:14. To the degree that this text is accepted as a promise of Christ's return, it yields several consequences of decisive import for the missionary enterprise.

First, it states the content of the missionary message in terms of the gospel of the kingdom of God. The purpose of Jesus' ministry is to announce and offer God's salvation to all of humanity. He does not speak of vengeance, but rather salvation, especially for sinners. It is a message of salvation, peace, and hope, which is offered even to publicans and prostitutes (Mark 2:15ff.). Of course, the availability of salvation both now and in the future depends on an individual's present attitudes (Luke 19:42). Since he offers immediate forgiveness of sin (Mark 21:1–12) it is an announcement of salvation as something already present and operative. However, the reign of which Christ speaks, although inaugurated in the present, will not be completed until the parousia. It will not be fully and perfectly realized until Christ returns. Yet, it does provide the missionary with a message of present significance. We really do have something of immediate benefit to proclaim.

Second, this passage is an eschatologically irrevocable announcement of divine intent. Jesus does make reference to human responsibility. We are to pray for it (Matt. 6:10), implore God for it (Luke 18:7), strive to get in (Luke 12:31), hold ourselves ready for it (Matt. 25:44). But human agency cannot bring it into existence. No more than it can hasten, delay, or hinder it. God alone gives it (Luke 12:32) and disposes it (Luke 22:29). Jesus promises it (Matt. 5:3) and grants or denies admittance (Matt. 8:11). What the kingdom is, is necessarily linked to the person of Christ, who determines its contents in terms of his own sending. He is Savior and Victor. He will bring ultimate victory of truth over all contradicting human ideologies, of justice in the struggle between right and wrong, of healing of all wounds, and love and reconciliation over all revengeful justice. These images portray a kingdom which God alone can and will institute. From this it becomes clear that history is indeed moving toward its God-appointed end. Christ will be victorious over death, sin, and Satan. Knowing that gives

the missionary movement the confidence needed for bold and aggressive world evangelization.

Third, the text speaks of a specific commission or task, that is, proclaiming this message to all peoples. Since this is given in the context of the eventual completion of salvation history, this part of it also takes on eschatological significance. The messengers, those converted, and the concrete structures that result, the ever expanding people of God, are a sure sign of the coming kingdom.

Fourth, this text provides a powerful motivation for missions. God has commissioned his people with the implementation of the decisive and final stage of salvation history. Although this does not necessarily mean that the missionary work will hasten the return of Christ, some evangelicals do believe that the timing of Christ's return depends on the pace of our work; the sooner we complete our commission, the sooner he can return.

The most important thing in this text is not the controverted specifics of chronological sequence but rather the motivational value of the delay in Christ's return. How close are we to completing our missionary task? When will Christ return? God alone knows (Acts 1:7). But we do know that he has not yet returned and until he does, our work is not finished. This should cause us to view missionary work with sobriety, realism, and confidence. We will not be spared opposition and disappointment. The last days will be characterized by heightened activity on the part of the forces of darkness. But the end will come. The missionary task will be completed and therein lies the actual motivation, our confidence. The hope of Jesus' return is an essential element in an evangelical theology of mission.

EDWARD ROMMEN

SEE ALSO Millennial Thought and Mission.

Bibliography. H. Berkhof, *Christian Faith*; D. G. Bloesch, *A Theology of Word and Spirit*; G. D. Fee, *God's Empowering Presence*; T. N. Finger, *Christian Theology: An Eschatological Approach*; S. J. Grenz, *Revisioning Evangelical Theology*; idem, *Theology for the Community of God*; P. K. Jewett, *God, Creation, and Revelation*; G. R. Lewis and B. A. Demarest, *Integrative Theology*; A. E. McGrath, *Christian Theology: An Introduction*.

Estonia (*Est. 2000 pop.: 1,495,000; 45,100 sq. km. [17,413 sq. mi.]*). Pagan Finno-Ugric peoples from Western Asia arrived on the Baltic in the third millennium B.C. Christian forces conquered the region in the early 1200s, beginning a seven hundred-year period of foreign occupation. German nobility ruled until the early 1500s. Reformation Swedish control brought educational and social improvements. Russian domination (1721–1920) reversed many reforms but saw significant revival among the commoners. After 50 years of Soviet repression (1940–91), new religious freedoms introduced significant challenges to the church as well as in economy and industry.

STEVEN J. PIERSON

SEE ALSO Baltic States.

Bibliography. A. Lieven, *The Baltic Revolution: Estonia, Latvia, Lithuania and the Path to Independence;* V. Mezezers, *The Herrnhuterian Pietism in the Baltic: And its Outreach into America and Elsewhere in the World.*

Eternal Life. The Apostles' Creed closes with the words "I believe . . . in the resurrection of the body and the life everlasting." Although anticipated in the Old Testament (Isa. 26:19; Dan. 12:2), the concept of "eternal" or "everlasting" (KJV) life is more fully developed in the New Testament, particularly in the Johannine literature.

Eternal life is more than mere continuing existence. It is qualitative in nature as well as unending in duration (John 10:10). It is the divine life which is present in God and Christ and bestowed as a gift upon the believer through the Holy Spirit (John 1:4; 1 John 1:1–2; 5:11). The life of the Christian is not his or her own life; it is the life of Christ who lives in his followers (Gal. 2:20; Phil. 1:21).

Although unending existence is encompassed within the concept, eternal life is essentially relational. In his high priestly prayer, Jesus describes it as knowing God and having fellowship with him through his Son, Jesus Christ (John 17:3). Christianity is unique among the world's religions in the nature of the claims it makes about its founder, claims derived from the words and actions of Jesus himself (John 11:25; 14:6; *see also* UNIQUENESS OF CHRIST).

Because it is imparted at the moment of regeneration, eternal life begins in the present life and is not affected by physical death. Those possessing eternal life are declared to be saved and are promised that they shall never perish (John 3:15–16, 18, 36; 5:24; 10:9). To be absent from the body is to be present with the Lord (2 Cor. 5:8). The gift of eternal life is received by faith so that those who believe have already passed from death to life (John 5:24; 1 John 3:14) and have the life which is in the Son (1 John 5:12), a life which expresses itself in victory (1 John 3:8–9), love (John 15:9–17), and joy (John 16:20–24).

The New Testament uses the figures of new birth and spiritual resurrection to describe eternal life. First, the new birth (John 1:12, 13; 3:3) relates the believer to the family of God. Second, the reception of eternal life is described as spiritual resurrection. Having been "raised together with Christ" (Col. 3:1), the believer now enjoys being "alive from the dead" (Rom. 6:13). The concept of spiritual resurrection, however, does not negate the New Testament teaching regarding physical resurrection, developed most fully in 1 Corinthians 15.

Because the biblical teaching regarding eternal life stands in stark contrast with the teaching of other major world religions regarding life after death, it has received great emphasis in missionary proclamation, particularly among Muslims, Hindus, and Buddhists.

Like the Bible, Islam teaches eternal personal existence (Sura 3:103; 9:21; 15:48; 18:2; 56:31, 32) in heaven (Sura 55:26–27) or hell (Sura 37:22–23; 55:44; 67:7–10). Hell is the abode of the wicked (Sura 70:15). Allah will fill Gehenna with men and "jinn" (Sura 11:120).

Islam views death not as a punishment for sin, but the natural termination of life. It is to be followed on the Day of Resurrection by judgment resulting in admission to Paradise or assignment to hell based upon the works done in this life (Sura 3:185). However, ultimately, it is Allah's will which determines one's eternal destiny. Muslims have no assurance of ultimate salvation (*see also* SOTERIOLOGY IN NON-CHRISTIAN RELIGIONS).

Although the primary purpose of life is to walk in God's path, abide by his laws, and secure his pleasure, Islam is devoid of the concept of eternal life as a present reality during this life. Rather the Qur'an contrasts sharply this life with the life to come (Sura 4:77).

In its description of heaven, the Qur'an says little about the worship of God or relationship with him. Rather, heaven is depicted as physical and sensual, as a beautiful garden filled with tasty fruits (Sura 55:48–60). Men are promised unending opportunity to consort with multiple beautiful, wide-eyed maidens. Little is said about the women apart from those who serve in the role of physical partners for men. This stands in sharp contradiction to Jesus' teaching that men and women will neither marry nor be given in marriage in the hereafter (Matt. 22:30).

Christian proclamation to Muslims with regard to eternal life, while affirming the continuity of personality beyond the grave and the reality of heaven and hell, stresses the present reality of eternal life, the assurance of salvation, the relational and spiritual character of heaven, and the equal status of men and women before God.

Since Hinduism does not distinguish between the Creator and the creation, the concept of absorption into the Divine implies the ultimate loss of personal identity. The self is viewed as uncreated and distinct from the physical body. Salvation, likened to a drop of water merging into the sea, comes at the conclusion of a long series of reincarnations, sometimes referred to as "the wheel of existence" (*see also* REINCARNATION AND TRANSMIGRATION). This cycle of multiple births and deaths continues until a true understanding of the self brings it to an end. Inherently connected to the belief in reincarnation is the doctrine of karma, the accumulation of merit and demerit, whereby each person experiences the consequences of his or her past and present lives.

With reference to eternal life, Christian proclamation in Hindu contexts has emphasized the continuing personal identity of the believer in relationship with a truly compassionate personal God, the assured hope of salvation, the reality of a qualitatively superior life in the present, and the experience of forgiveness that brings freedom from bad karma and escape from the wheel of existence. Christians, referring to Hebrews 9:27, testify with assurance that this is their first and last earthly lifetime!

The Buddhist understanding of eternal life is conditioned by the experience of Buddha Gautama, who set out on a spiritual journey for the purpose of overcoming and transcending the old age and sickness that lead to the agony of dying. Although Buddhism adopted many of the Hindu views regarding karma and reincarnation, it developed many of its own unique concepts as found in the four noble truths, the eightfold path, and the twelve steps of interdependency. Since suffering is caused by desire, freedom from desire leads to Nirvana, a state which is in essence nonbeing. Buddhists do not hold to the permanence of the self.

The concept of karma leads to the desire to acquire merit in order to improve one's position in future lives. The fatalism implicit in the Buddhist concept of karma leaves no room for the possibility of divine forgiveness.

Christian proclamation in Buddhist contexts emphasizes continuing personal identity that transcends death, the legitimate desire for and reality of eternal fellowship with a personal God, eternal life as a gift from a loving and gracious Heavenly Father to be received by faith, and a lifestyle of love as a response to God's forgiveness and his gift of the Holy Spirit through Jesus Christ.

KENNETH B. MULHOLLAND

Bibliography: H. Cower, ed., *Life after Death in World Religions*.

Eternal Security. Eternal security, also known as the *perseverance of the saints*, refers to the *continuation* of the work of God in the life of a true believer. To the question "Will the operation of divine grace begun in a true believer's life certainly continue and be brought to completion such that a genuine Christian can never completely fall away from Christ and fail to obtain eternal salvation?", two different answers—one positive, one negative—have historically been offered, by Calvinism and Arminianism respectively.

The Calvinist doctrine of perseverance is expressed by the *Westminster Confession of Faith* (17.1): "They, whom God has accepted in his Beloved, effectually called, and sanctified by his Spirit, can neither totally nor finally fall away from the state of grace, but shall certainly persevere therein to the end, and be eternally saved." Key points include: (1) This does not apply to everyone who professes faith, but only to those whom God has elected and saved. (2) These true believers, though they may fall into sin temporarily, will certainly persist in exercising faith and engaging in good works in the midst of temptations and attacks. This refutes "a common caricature of this doctrine which describes it as teaching that believers are certain to be saved no matter how they live" (Hoekema). (3) Perseverance is a continuing work of God and hence the security of these true believers does not ultimately rest on their ability to withstand assaults and maintain themselves in Christ. But this persevering power does not operate apart from the believers' faith which is the means by which God preserves them. (4) This faith includes perseverance as a constitutive element: "genuine faith, by definition, perseveres; where there is no perseverance, by definition the faith cannot be genuine" (Carson).

Scriptural support for the Calvinist position includes promises stressing divine power and faithfulness to protect believers (1 Peter 1:3–9; Phil. 1:6; Rom. 8:31–39; 1 Cor. 1:8–9; 1 Thess. 5:23–24), passages presenting God's purposes for believers as being all of a piece (Rom. 8:28–30), Christ's own pledges to guard believers (John 6:37–40; 10:27–30), and assurances of eternal life (John 3:36; 5:24; 1 John 5:13). The Spirit's ministry of regenerating and sealing people (John 3:3–8; Eph. 1:13–14; 4:30) is the guarantee of their ultimate salvation. The intercessory work of Christ ensures complete salvation (Heb. 7:23–25; John 17:24). The reality of being part of the New Covenant—providing believers with a new heart (Ezek. 36:25–27), transforming power (2 Cor. 3), and union with Christ (1 Cor. 1:30; Eph. 1:1–12)—enables them to persevere in faith and holiness. Perseverance is also linked with divine election and irresistible grace. This theological outlook has meant that Calvinist missions have tended to emphasize personal conversion, the organization and structure/development of the church, and the transformation of society, especially through education, health, and agriculture. Once people come to faith, since their salvation is secure, they are to live in ways that contribute positively to changing their context.

Contrast this with Arminian theology. While stressing that provision of persevering grace has been made for the church, it considers this grace to be conditional with respect to each individual Christian. The believer is protected by God's power, but this grace can be resisted. Ultimate salvation is thus contingent on the believer persevering in the faith. Thus, "there is no way of telling whether a given person in the Church will persevere to the end; the fact of his perseverance at any given moment is shown in the fact that he is persevering" (Marshall). Although some Arminians consider apostasy by true believers only a possibility, others affirm that falling away does occur.

Scriptural support for the conditionality of individual salvation includes warnings against apostasy (Heb. 2: 1–3; 3:12; 10:26–31; 2 Peter 3:17) and exhortations to remain firm in the faith until the end (Col. 1:21–23; Heb. 3:14–15; John 15:1–7; Matt. 10:22) Such instructions would appear superfluous if true believers could not fall away but are guaranteed eternal salvation. Also, cases of actual apostasy are presented as evidence that falling away does indeed occur (Heb. 6:4–6; 1 John 2:18–19; 2 Peter 2:1–2; Judas; Acts 5:1–11; 1 Tim. 1:19–20; 2 Tim. 2:16–18; 4:10). Objecting to the Calvinist viewpoint, Arminianism finds eternal security to be inconsistent with human free will and claims that it leads to complacency and moral laxity.

This outlook has generally worked itself out in Arminian missions through an emphasis on personal conversion followed by Christian discipleship, growth in spiritual maturity, and continual need for revival and increased holiness of the converts. Education, health, agriculture, and other social emphases have tended to be downplayed, compared with the importance of growth in the personal and corporate holiness, worship, spirituality, and devotion of the churches and their leaders.

A compatibalist approach to this doctrine encourages responsible integration of the passages stressing God's continuing work of preservation with those emphasizing the believer's responsibility to persevere in the faith. Acknowledging the difficulty of knowing if some people are genuine believers, it admits that some non-believers give startling evidence of conversion (Heb. 6:4–6; Mark 4:1–20; 1 John 2:18–19; Matt. 7:21–23) yet turn away, not from saving faith, but from the religious position they once held. True believers, however, always continue in grace until ultimate salvation, and the ground of this perseverance is God's sustaining power which works through their persistent faith. One means of encouraging such abiding faith is the above-mentioned scriptural warnings and exhortations.

ASSURANCE OF SALVATION is the legitimate and comforting result of this doctrine. This subjective confidence paves the way for believers to face difficulties, persecutions, and even threats of death without fear of being separated from God. This engenders boldness and dedication to the cause of Christ worldwide.

GREGG R. ALLISON

Bibliography. J. Calvin, *The Institutes of the Christian Religion,* 3.24.6–11; G. C. Berkouwer, *Faith and Perseverance;* D. Carson, *WmTJ*54 (1992): 1–29; A. Hoekema, *Saved by Grace,* pp. 234–56; W. Pope, *A Compendium of Christian Theology,* 3.131–47; I. H. Marshall, *Kept By the Power of God.*

Ethics. Christians can all agree, at least in a general sense, to the notion that ethics are in some way important for theological reflection and mission. Confusion can arise, however, as to what some key fundamental terms mean and to how discussions on ethics should be articulated. A brief introduction to the nature of ethical discourse, therefore, can provide a framework for a more informed exploration into the relationship of ethics to both Christian mission in general and cross-cultural missionaries in particular.

Basic Definitions and General Orientation. In popular parlance, often no distinction is drawn between morality and ethics. Within the academic discipline of ethics, however, these two terms are not synonymous, although they are related. The first concerns the concrete manner in which people act and order their lives; the second, on the other hand, refers to articulating the explanations and justifications of why and how people do what they do. To speak of "ethics in mission" is to deal with both of these aspects— that is, with the mundane realities of human existence and the theoretical foundations of behavior and values. This opening part of the discussion will focus on the insights that philosophical and theological ethics can offer into the nature of ethical reasoning. These might serve missiological reflection and missionaries facing complex ethical quandaries by helping to specify the nature of the issues at stake and by identifying at what point dialogue (or disagreement) and resolution (or confrontation) can be expected. They can also aid ethical discussions through fomenting more careful analysis of different points of view and solutions.

To begin with, ethicists differentiate among four levels of ethical discourse. These range from the spontaneous human responses to given situations (level one) to accepted cultural mores and unquestioned socialized patterns (level two), and on to more reflective debate on ethical principles (level three). Lastly, there is the meta-ethical level, which posits an answer to the ultimate question "Why be ethical?" Christians, for instance, in certain situations might react in similar patterns to others within their context (levels one and two). They may or may not hold to broadly held views of justice or compassion and make common cause on individual issues (e.g., abortion, POVERTY), even though the principles underlying their opinions and actions would be grounded in their faith (level three). Christians will necessarily part with others over the most fundamental grounding of ethical behavior (level four). For them, the person of God and the demands of the gospel provide unique motivations for individual and corporate life. Ethical interaction with those of different commitments becomes increasingly difficult as one moves up these four levels.

Philosophical ethics traditionally has categorized ethical reasoning according to a few classical approaches (Fairweather and McDonald). Deontology (from the Greek *dei*, "it is necessary") focuses on duty and making correct decisions in accordance with transcendent principles. Teleological (from the Greek *telos*, "the end") ethics focuses on consequences and desires to seek the greatest good. In contrast, virtue ethics centers not so much on the decision-making process, but on the character of the person or community; it highlights the nurture and formation of moral people. Each of these ways of formulating ethics finds echoes in the Bible and defenders among Christian ethicists. A comprehensive ethic would need to incorporate the contributions of each emphasis.

What is more, all ethical persuasions utilize a variety of sources (Verhey, 1984, 159–97; Wright, 1995, 11–178). All usually appeal in some fashion to human reason, conscience, and experience. Christian ethics do also, although the understanding and evaluation of these potential sources for ethics is influenced by belief in the CREATION, the FALL OF HUMANKIND, and REDEMPTION. Ethical stances can be linked as well to traditions of particular communities, which attempt to train their members to conform to certain values and lifestyle models. The church, of course, would be the locus for a specific set of traditions and provide the communities for the Christian. The conviction that God has revealed himself in word and deed argues for two other sources for ethical direction: the Bible and the Holy Spirit of God. These general affirmations, however, in no way should minimize the fact that Christians differ over the viability and use of these multiple sources. For example, disagreements surface over the ability of the CONSCIENCE to discern right from wrong, the nature of biblical authority, the relationship between the two Testaments, and the means by which the Spirit guides believers. A Christian ethic must be conscious of the breadth of theological formulations that would comprise a coherent and comprehensive ethical stance.

This list of theological issues, and the options taken on each one, are inseparable from a final factor to take into account: the impact of theological frameworks on ethical discussion. The three major theological streams that flow out from the REFORMATION—Lutheranism, Calvinism, Anabaptism—have developed different ethical visions. Over the centuries and around the world each has generated different kinds of societies and Christian communities. Each as well has

proposed views which have determined how Christians have perceived their identity and their mission in the world. The positions developed vis-à-vis, for instance, the responsibility of the Christian and the church to the state, the essence of Christ's work on the cross, the relevance of the theme of the KINGDOM OF GOD today, and the use of violence, all inevitably help shape how missiology and individual missionaries comprehend ethical problems, conceive of what sources to appeal to in their ethical thinking, and decide among possible courses of action (*see also* CHRIST AND CULTURE). More recently, LIBERATION THEOLOGY has proffered a new paradigm of reflection and PRAXIS: the partial realization of the kingdom in the achievement of justice in oppressive situations. This theological construct, that begins from the perspective of the preferential OPTION FOR THE POOR, is now suggesting different slants to those crucial theological issues that must occupy any serious ethical reflection (Schubeck).

Missionary Cross-Cultural Ethics. In addition to the aforementioned philosophical and theological topics that demand thoughtful consideration, missionaries working in a cross-cultural setting can face the additional obstacles of having to deal not only with ethical issues alien to their own experience, but also with a context that might define and solve problems from another vantage point. A sort of "cultural-ethical" shock can result. Hence, the need for greater missionary self-awareness of cultural makeup and differences.

Missionaries should be cognizant of how their background and the host culture in which they labor compare concerning items such as the significance of time, the importance of social STATUS AND ROLE, GENDER ROLE differences, the role of GUILT AND SHAME, and the meaning of success. Each culture has its own orientation to life and structures the many institutions of its society accordingly. Missionaries can reject, substitute for their own, add to or synthesize with their own, the new ethical values and positions they encounter. The descriptive task of properly understanding this different ethical world, when joined with the virtue of humility, is the solid first step before any missionary attempt at prescriptive words or actions. The subsequent challenges are multiple. Legal implications for those missionaries who are foreigners are unavoidable, and wrestling with the possibilities and the right to act within the limits set for those from outside can be a source of tension. Missionaries must strive to be true to their faith and the biblical witness; they must be willing to listen and learn, to admit to inappropriate behavior and change biblical interpretations if warranted, and to have the courage and wisdom sometimes to take uncomfortable ethical stands. In sum, missionaries are called to cultural sensitivity and realism and Christian integrity, even as they try to avoid slipping into ethical relativism (Adeney, 1995; Carroll R., 1986, 1994; Mayers, 1987, 241–63).

An orientation to cross-cultural ethics that adds another dimension to the thrust of these comments is suggested by the science of ELENCTICS (Priest). This term (from the Greek *elenchō*, "to convict, rebuke"), coined by the missiologist J. H. BAVINCK, points to the issues of human conscience and guilt. The conscience is operative in all human beings (e.g., Rom. 2:1–15; 2 Cor. 4:2), but is greatly influenced by cultural norms, values, and ideals. The variability of conscience holds true for the believer and non-believer alike. Therefore, missionaries should be careful not to uncritically identify the content of their conscience with the divine will and to quickly condemn others whose conscience does not respond in the same way to similar situations. Once more, the necessity of self-awareness and the priority of the descriptive task over the prescriptive are apparent. The New Testament teaches that God appeals to the conscience to convict humans of their sin; after salvation, the Scriptures and the Spirit of God work together to correct and renew the conscience of all who believe. Missionaries, then, should partner with God in touching the conscience of those who need to respond to the gospel message and endeavor to help believers to mature in their faith so that they might live with a sanctified conscience.

Social Ethics in Context. The distinction between individual ethics and social ethics for missiology and missionaries can frequently be a false one, even though the differentiation might prove to be theoretically helpful. Personal experience can bring one in touch with dangers of wider import. Good examples are the problems of BRIBERY, the experiences of women, and PEACE. Attempts to seek resolution and redress can lead into the labyrinth of government corruption, the ugliness of some manifestations of gender inequality, and the abuse of political power. All of these items demand not only theological clarity, but also wisdom and valor in the meeting of the pragmatic challenges that they force on those desiring to obey the will of God (Adeney, 1995, 142–62, 192–250).

The phrase "social ethics" many times is associated with certain kinds of issues that impact the broader body politic. If the phrase, though, is defined simply as the shared moral values and behavior of a specific context, then it ties back into the earlier part of the discussion. For believers, identity and duty are linked with Christian faith, tradition, and community, even as they are inseparable from the life of other human beings around them. The continual struggle for Christians and the church is to balance being faithful to their particularity and sensitive to the realities of their cultural setting and environment (Carroll R., 1994).

Another understanding of "social ethics" would relate the phrase to issues of social structures and processes. The focus is now on more global items, like how societies are put together and function economically and socially (*see* ECONOMICS). Interest is no longer limited to individuals—how they should respond to different social pressures or certain demands. Rather, concern is directed especially at identifying, analyzing, and evaluating the policies and practices of institutions, then proposing alternative schemes that might better conform to certain ethical standards. Topics include justice, equity, and HUMAN RIGHTS. Each touches the gamut of human communities, from the family to governments bound together by treaties in the international arena.

Regarding justice, debates revolve around whether it should be distributive (so that all get an equal share—an ideal of socialism) or productive (all have equal opportunity—an ideal of capitalism); whether the achievement of justice (however defined) for the whole can legitimate the possible deprivation of justice of particular individuals or groups; and whether and to what degree the state can intervene in the life of citizens to attain greater justice for everyone or for particular groups. Equity raises questions, at one level, of how the government carries out its duties and apportions benefits; it also concerns the call to the individual not take unfair advantage of others in, for example, work and judicial settings. The concept of human rights posits certain inalienable and irrevocable rights possessed by all human beings, regardless of the rulings and practices of any government. These rights have been inscribed in international agreements and are used to evaluate states which are thought to be suspect in their observance.

The scope and the obvious complexity of these social issues are indeed daunting. They require an informed and interdisciplinary approach: a sagacious and educated utilization of the social sciences and a thoroughly biblical and theological orientation. The SOCIAL SCIENCES stand as an unexplored and untapped source for ethics for many evangelicals. On the other hand, the Reformation traditions alluded to earlier, from the pens of their founders to the present day, have striven in different times and places to respond theologically to human realities. At least in many North American evangelical circles, a related quality of missiological reflection to meet the larger crises of modern life has not emerged. For several decades, some evangelicals have manifested a reluctance to entertain issues of systemic and global justice and human rights for fear of diverting attention away from evangelism and church planting (*see* JUSTICE OF GOD). Some also would warn of the possible danger of an interest in the social sciences replacing a commitment to the Bible as the final authority in ethical thinking. However one might appraise liberation theologies, that theological current has seriously dealt with these problems at a communal, national, and international level and places the theme of justice as the foundational criterion for all ethical reflection and PRAXIS.

Any evangelical missiological entrance into these sometimes explosive issues will require a mature evaluation and acceptance of pertinent elements of the Reformation heritage, as well as interaction with the insights from philosophical ethics. Contextual awareness and sensitivity must also not be forgotten, as missiologists and missionaries attempt to grapple with specific problems in the warp and woof of daily life in other socio-cultural settings.

M. DANIEL CARROLL R.

Bibliography. B. T. Adeney, *Strange Virtues: Ethics in a Multicultural World*; M. D. Carroll R., *JETS* 29:3 (1986): 307–15; idem, *Themelios* 19:3 (1994): 9–15; I. C. M. Fairweather and J. I. H. McDonald, *The Quest for Christian Ethics: An Inquiry into Ethics and Christians Ethics*; M. K. Mayers, *Christianity Confronts Culture: A Strategy for Cross-cultural Evangelism*; R. J. Priest, *Missiology* 22:3 (1994): 291–315; T. L. Schubeck, *Liberation Ethics: Sources, Models, and Norms*; A. Verhey, *The Great Reversal: Ethics and the New Testament*; Christopher J. H. Wright, *Walking in the Ways of the Lord: The Ethical Authority of the Old Testament*.

Ethiopia (*Est. 2000 pop.: 63,785,000; 1,221,900 sq. km. [471,776 sq. mi.]*). Christianity in Ethiopia began in the fourth century with the coming of two Syrian Christians, FRUMENTIUS and AEDESIUS, to the ancient capital of Ethiopia at Aksum. Frumentius was responsible for the conversion of the future emperor Ezana in 328, thus marking the beginning of Ethiopian Christianity. Frumentius, though granted his freedom, returned to Ethiopia in A.D. 340 newly consecrated by Athanasius of Alexandria as the first bishop of Ethiopia. The coming of the "nine saints," monks from Syria, in the fifth century transformed Christianity from a court religion to a grassroots faith.

The rise of Islam in the seventh century was the beginning of over a millennium of isolation for Ethiopia. A strong nationalistic Christianity emerged during these centuries that enabled the kingdom to survive a long series of challenges from within and from without. At the heart of this nationalism was the legend of Solomon and Sheba. As recorded in the thirteenth-century Kebra-Negast (Book of Kings), the Solomonic dynasty begins with Menelik I, son of Solomon and Sheba, who returned to Ethiopia with the ark of the covenant and turned Ethiopia into a new Israel. With the acceptance of Christ as Lord in the fourth century, Ethiopia became even more the true Israel and its capital the new Jerusalem. The fifteenth century emperor Zara-Yaqob used this civil religion to lead the nation to new heights.

This nationalistic mythology served Ethiopia well during its brief conquest by Muslim forces in the sixteenth century. With the help of the Portuguese, the Solomonic leadership was restored.

Ethiopia in the nineteenth century reached a low point under Tewodros II, whose rash imprisonment of English missionaries led to a British invasion and a humiliating defeat in 1868 at Maqdala. In a sharp reversal of fortune the next emperor, Menelik II, renewed Ethiopian self-confidence and won the admiration of the world for his victory over Italian invaders at Adowa in 1896. In an Africa cruelly partitioned by European rivals, the picture of an independent Christian kingdom conquering a colonial power was not forgotten by African leaders. The concept of "Ethiopianism" helped transform missionary Christianity into something more connected with the African past.

Ethiopia lumbered into the twentieth century as a largely feudal kingdom ill-equipped to face the modern world. In 1930 Haile Selassie ascended to the throne and slowly moved his nation forward. His successful defense of Ethiopia during its war with Italy (1935–41) furthered his program of reform. His impact on the church was profound, leading ultimately to the independence of the Ethiopian Orthodox Church from the Coptic Church of Egypt in 1959, ending a dependency that began in 340.

In 1974 Haile Selassie was overthrown by a military coup. In 1984 Colonel Haile Mengistu Miriam seized power from the ruling military council. His ideological Marxism meant the seizure of church property and the imprisonment of many church leaders. In 1991, Mengistu was overthrown and religious freedom restored under Prime Minister Meles Zenawi. On April 27, 1993, Eritrea declared independence after a referendum was passed by a landslide vote, ending years of bitter conflict with Ethiopia.

The decade of the 1990s saw Christianity in all its wide variety expand in Ethiopia. Though Muslims composed 35 percent of Ethiopia's 56 million citizens, Christianity remained the dominant faith. The Ethiopian Orthodox Church (Tewahido) had upwards of 25 million members. Roman Catholicism (both Latin and Alexandrian rites) remained under one million. Protestant groups composed 14 percent of the population. Fastest growing were the evangelical churches, with the Kale Heywet Church (SIM related) numbering approximately two million members and the Mekane Yesu Church (Evangelical Lutheran) estimated at 400,000.

MARK R. SHAW

Bibliography. J. Bonk, *An Annotated and Classified Bibliography of English Literature Pertaining to the Ethiopian Orthodox Church*; D. Crummey, *Priests and Politicians: Protestant and Catholic Missions in Ortho-*

dox Ethiopia, 1830–1868; T. Tamrat, *Church and State in Ethiopia: 1270–1527.*

Ethnicity. Classification of a person or persons into a particular group based on factors such as physical characteristics (e.g., skin color, facial characteristics, body shape); cultural identity (e.g., language or dialect, religion), or geographic origin. Since the founding of the church, ethnicity has been a fundamental reality of missions.

For example, wherever intercultural evangelists have gone they sought to translate the gospel into the local language. They knew that the gospel had to be understood in local terms, they also knew that the gospel had to be lived in the local milieu. Jesus was the model. Even though he was God, he took upon himself a human body and was shaped in a particular cultural context—he was a Galilean Jew. That is the way God enters cultures and saves people. God takes CULTURE very seriously. So should intercultural evangelists. The gospel affirms culture in general terms. As the gospel enters culture as salt and light it actually enhances culture.

Needed: A Theology of Ethnicity. Missiologists have developed theologies of "ethnic evangelism," but few missiologists are developing a theology of "ethnicity" itself. This task is becoming increasingly urgent because the demands of ethnicity will probably dominate the world's agenda at least in the opening decades of the new millennium.

Lessons might be learned from the history of northern Europe, which was torn apart by ethnic struggles for centuries. In the process of time the problem was sorted out to some degree by simply drawing national boundaries around ethnic realities—Germany for the Germans, Holland for the Dutch, France for the French, Italy for the Italians, and so forth. This did not solve all the problems as recent events in the Balkans have shown. But it did have a salutary effect of stressing nation over tribe (ethnic entity). It seemed a bit more civil to be a nationalist than a "tribalist." But history has shown that the two are essentially the same.

Ethnicity and the State Today. Several factors have served to mitigate the impact of ethnicity on world history in recent years. First is the phenomenon of COLONIALISM. By exerting powerful influence the colonial powers sought to suppress ethnic feelings so that the rule of colonial law could be upheld. Second, strong nations have emerged where the aboriginal population was either displaced or suppressed by immigrant peoples from a variety of cultures. This was the case in much of South, Central, and North America along with Australia and New Zealand. Third, ideological hegemony was exercised by some states such as totalitarian socialism or communism. In these systems there was simply no opportunity for authentic ethnic expression. Ethnicity was treated as a thing of the past or as an ornament which could be worn on occasion if it did not interfere with the march of the totalitarian state.

Two of those factors are almost gone—structural colonialism is no more and ideological totalitarianism is in shreds. Under the facades of these two systems ethnicity not only survived but flourished, awaiting the moment when once again ethnicity could be claimed, admired, and expressed. That is the case today. Where these two systems reigned, now ethnicity has emerged as a major factor. As the breakup of the former Yugoslavia shows, however, this is not always a positive thing.

The Role of Ethnicity in Society. Ethnicity has a positive and a negative side. Through genetics we inherit many things, but we do not inherit culture; that we learn. Our cultures give us specific ways of viewing the world, as well as how to interact with other persons, how to survive and prosper. Cultures provide identity and a place to belong. The process of ENCULTURATION which begins at birth provides the individual with a way to be human. Alone, newly born human beings have no hope of survival. Culture shapes the person. The formative role of culture or ethnicity is profound and pervasive. This is the positive side. The harmful effects of ethnicity appear when ethnocentrism takes the upper hand in cases where one group imposes its will on another or when a group fears this will happen.

So much interethnic hostility exists in the world today that the word itself has begun to take on a negative meaning. This bodes ill for the opening decades of the twentieth century because ethnicity is on the rise.

The Gospel and Ethnicity. The gospel is very clear with regard to ethnicity. The KINGDOM OF GOD is not a new "generic" culture, but a family which includes people from a great variety of cultures. The unity of the Christian church has nothing to do with culture, yet it affirms all cultures. Believers are "one" because they love the same Lord and are redeemed by the one Lamb of God. Their unity is the result of the love which they receive as a fruit of the Holy Spirit. In the Body no one culture dominates nor dictates to another. Everyone stands humbly before God, in their culture but not of that culture. The culmination of world history will be when the followers of Christ will join the multiethnic choir—out of every tribe and nation and tongue, praising God forever and ever (Rev. 7).

DONALD R. JACOBS

SEE ALSO Minority, Minority Populations.

Bibliography. J. Hutchinson and A. D. Smith, eds., *Ethnicity;* D. Kecmamovic, *The Mass Psychology of Ethnonationalism;* M. E. Marty and R. S. Appleby, eds., *Religion, Ethnicity, and Self Identify: Nations in Turmoil;*

D. McGavran, *Understanding Church Growth;* D. P. Moynihan, *Pandemonium, Ethnicity in International Politics;* W. Pfaff, *The Wrath of Nations;* L. O. Sanneh, *Translating the Message: The Missionary Impact on Culture;* W. A. Van Horne, ed., *Global Convulsions: Race, Ethnicity and Nationalism at the End of the Twentieth Century.*

Ethnocentrism. The term "ethnocentrism" may simply be defined as the belief that one's own people group or cultural ways are superior to others. An ethnocentric person generally has an attitude/opinion of prejudice (prejudging others as inferior). This internal orientation may be manifested in individual action or institutionalized policy toward others as in the case of anti-Semitism, apartheid, bigotry, fascism, and racism.

Prejudice or discrimination in a scientific sense can be both positive and negative. However, in the social sciences, including missiology, the terms are generally used with a negative connotation. It is necessary to distinguish between the two: prejudice is an attitude; discrimination is action or social interaction unfavorable to others on the basis of their religious, ethnic, or racial membership.

Prejudice is the subjective prejudgment of others to be inferior, whereas ethnocentrism is the subjective presumption that one's own people-group or cultural ways are superior. Bigotry (i.e., narrow-mindedness or intolerance due to differences between self and others) and racism (i.e., the presumed cultural superiority or inferiority as caused by genetically inherited physical characteristics such as facial feature, skin color, etc.) are two general forms of prejudice.

Institutionalized manifestation of ethnocentrism and prejudice can be found in specific cases historically. Fascism (i.e., authoritarian nationalism) of Benito Mussolini, which emerged in the 1920s in Italy, and Adolf Hitler's control of Germany in the 1930s are cases in point. Hitler's belief in the superiority and purity of his own kind gave impetus to anti-Semitic measures that led to the holocaust of the Jews. The black and white racial conflicts in the United States and South Africa are examples of institutionalized manifestation of ethnocentrism and prejudice.

Ethnocentrism is Contrabiblical to Mission. Mission is the divine design of bringing spiritual blessings to all nations, reflected in God's covenant with Abraham (Gen. 12) and Christ's Great Commission to bring the gospel to all nations. God's desire is that none should perish but all should come to repentance (2 Peter 3:9).

Ethnocentric pride of many Jews prevented them from performing their duties as God's choice instruments of grace to the nations (Rom. 7–9). The apostles had difficulty in following the resurrected Christ's command to bear witness to the nations (Acts 1:9) Even during persecution they persisted in evangelizing only their own kind (Acts 11:19).

The detailed description of the Holy Spirit's directing Peter toward the Roman official Cornelius in Acts 10 is very telling regarding ethnocentrism and mission. The Holy Spirit prepared Peter personally by leading him to lodge at Simon's house (cf. the Jewish ceremonial law of Lev. 11) prior to giving visions and directions to both Peter and Cornelius. Later Peter came to a new understanding: "I now realize how true it is that God does not show favoritism and accepts men from every nation" (Acts 19:34–35). When witnessing the "Gentile pentecost," the Jewish Christians "were astonished that the gift of the Holy Spirit had been poured out even on the Gentiles" (10:44–45).

Ethnocentrism is Counterproductive in Missions. "Missions" are the ways and means whereby the Christian church fulfills its mission of world evangelization. Intercultural Communication, Cross-Cultural Ministry, and Church Planting are parts of the process of world evangelization. At any of these points ethnocentrism can curtail or cripple efforts in missions.

Persons with an ethnocentric orientation have difficulty developing a genuine social relationship with members outside their group. While we must recognize that no one is entirely without prejudice or ethnocentrism of some kind, ethnocentrism in the Christian inhibits obedience to the Great Commandment ("love your neighbor as yourself") and the Great Commission. Ethnocentrism is a significant obstacle to missionaries serving as messengers of the "gospel of reconciliation" (2 Cor. 5).

The ethnocentric Western Christian has the tendency to presuppose a "guilt feeling" in the audience in talking about justification, atonement, and so on. People from a shame culture (*see* Shame; avoid embarrassment and "losing face" at all cost and acquire honor and "save face" by all means) may be more ready to appreciate and accept Christ as the "Mediator, Shame-bearer, Reconcilor" (Rom. 5; 2 Cor. 5; Eph. 2; Heb. 9; etc.)

Some Western Christians are predisposed to the use of informational/impersonal evangelistic means of the technological society as compared to oral and mostly relational cultures of the target group. The understanding of "limited cultural relativism" (viewing cultural ways as relative, an antidote to "ethnocentrism") will enable Christians to adapt to new cultural contexts with the relevant gospel message and flexible evangelistic methods.

Ethnocentrism Still Inhibits Missions. Martin Luther despised the Book of James as "the straw epistle" and preferred Romans and Galatians. This is a historical example showing the power of prejudice. His pattern of preferential treatment of different books of the Bible can still be found in modern missions in prioritizing Bible books for translation. In a similar manner, cross-cultural church planters may disregard the cultural context of the target ethnic groups and persist in imposing their own Christian tradition on new converts in terms of worship and preaching style, discipleship programs, and church policy.

At a personal level, missionaries may not be completely free from ethnocentrism in their attitude, etiquette, and action. All missionaries must be willing to ask themselves on a regular basis if they are displaying ethnocentric attitudes in what they communicate by the very way they live.

ENOCH WAN

Bibliography. W. Allport, *The Nature of Prejudice;* J. D. Dovidio and S. L. Gaertner, *Prejudice, Discrimination, and Racism;* P. Jackson, ed., *Race and Racism: Essays in Social Geography;* D. Kitagawa, *Race Relations and Christian Mission;* R. A. LeVine and D. T. Campbell, *Ethnocentrism: Theories of Conflict, Ethnic Attitudes, and Group Behavior;* V. Reynolds, et al., eds., *The Sociobiology of Ethnocentrism.*

Ethnographic Research. Ethnography is the task of describing a culture from the perspective of the people for whom it is a way of life. The ethnographer learns from people by participating in their lives and observing their world while carefully recording his or her observations. Ethnographic research is the systematic study of culture using the methodology of ethnography.

The Ethnographic Method. The ethnographic method begins with an ethnographer choosing a cultural context in which to study. In selecting a context, careful consideration should be given to the accessibility of the activities and people who form the basis of the study. The ethnographer must balance the issues of personal interest with the needs of others who are working in the area. The overall concern is protecting the integrity of the work while avoiding spoiling the field. Missiological concerns will inevitably guide the selection process.

Another aspect of the selection criteria is the central focus or research problem that determines the direction of the study. The research problem may be chosen prior to entering the context through a survey of the literature or in dialogue with others who have similar research interests. The research problem may also arise out of the preliminary work done in the context of the study. In either case, the research problem articulates the focus of the study as a manageable unit and provides the basis for the critical questions that the ethnographer seeks to answer. Ethnographic research is most useful when the ethnographer has a good working knowledge of the local language.

After selecting the context, the ethnographer begins the process of participant observation.

Participant observation, a cognate term for ethnography, is the process of identifying with the people through participation in their activities, events, and conversations while observing the interactions. The degree of participant observation may range from a person who is completely involved in the process to a person who is primarily an observer. The initial work of the ethnographer is to make observations of the place, activities, and actors in a given social situation in an effort to describe the setting. Early observations should include a record of (1) the use of space and time, (2) artifacts that are present in the social situations, (3) descriptions of the people including their physical characteristics and the language(s) used, and (4) structural observations of both the material objects and the social relationships.

As the participant observation process continues, the ethnographer moves beyond initial observations to more focused observations and specific observing and informal conversations of interviews, the most productive ethnographic technique. Interviews may be structured (such as questionnaires or surveys), informal (which appear to be natural conversations), or retrospective (which asks an informant to reconstruct the past by recalling information about a person or event). Interview quality is dependent on the preparation and mental alertness of the interviewer and the willingness and ability of the informant. The ethnographer must develop the skill of interviewing both to ensure a culturally acceptable form and to exercise a degree of control over the direction of the interview. In the case of ethnographers who are learning the language, interviews provide useful exercises for both data collection and language practice, but are hard to direct. At the heart of the interview is respect for the person(s) being interviewed and a willingness on the part of the ethnographer to explore the world through the eyes of the informant. Central to the entire observational process is the written record.

Observational data are recorded in a written account known as fieldnotes. Types of fieldnotes include the condensed account, the expanded account, and the fieldwork journal. The purpose of the condensed account is to record exact statements, words, and observations as they are heard to ensure accuracy and exactness. The expanded account is the record that is kept in its complete form, including the transcription and expansion of the notes from the condensed account. The third form is the journal, in which the ethnographer keeps a record of feelings, personal observations, and activities that help provide insight into the process and account for the attitudes of the individual.

The usefulness of fieldnotes depends on the objectivity of the record. Although there is debate over the issue of objectivity, there are a number of methodological conventions that reduce observer bias. The first area deals with three principles for language recording. The language identification principle requires the ethnographer to clearly identify the language for each fieldnote entry. The verbatim principle addresses the need to make an accurate verbatim record of the content of interaction and conversations. The last principle is that of using concrete language to ensure that as much detail as possible is recorded without the inevitable condensing and summarization that characterize the majority of formal note taking.

Another area of concern for objectivity involves the issues of reliability and validity of the measurement. The ethnographer must develop a procedure for data collection that employs different techniques. Reliability is the extent to which these techniques or the measurement procedures provides the same answer every time it is used. If a measure is reliable, another person may use the method and come up with comparable results. The second issue is that of validity, which determines the extent to which the procedure gives the correct answer. Validity may be approached in two ways: respondent validation and triangulation. Respondent validation seeks to check the accuracy of the accounts of the attitudes and beliefs with the key respondents from whom the account was taken. Triangulation is the process of checking all sources of data with a minimum of two other sources to ensure that it is not idiosyncratic in nature. The ethnographer triangulates all of the significant input to ensure that inaccuracies, either through misunderstandings or intentional misleading, are removed from the record.

Analyzing the data is an ongoing element of the research from preentry through each phase of the observational process. The ethnographer begins to explore hunches and assumptions in the early phase moving on to a more formal level of analysis as the data are recorded in the fieldnotes. In addition to the components of objectivity, the ethnographer analyzes phenomena observed in the research and recorded in the fieldnotes to discover key terms and concepts that provide insights into the cultural context. The ethnographer must be thoroughly familiar with the data in order to compare the terms and concepts in a move toward categories of meaning that can be further triangulated to ensure validity. This process requires both analysis and further observations at an increasing level of specificity. Due to the cyclical nature of the analysis and observational process, the ethnographer is directed by the questions emerging from the analysis. It is essential that the ethnographer maintain a constant interaction among observation, recording, and analysis in order to ensure that the research remains focused. As the research nears completion, the analysis will produce a number of cultural categories that are further compared, leading eventually to the discovery of typologies, models, themes, or theories that are grounded in the data.

The final phase of the ethnographic research process is the writing of the description as a document known as an ethnography. While it appears tedious, the formal writing provides an irreplaceable opportunity to synthesize the data into a systematic description that becomes a useful document to the community at large.

Missiological Implications. The potential contribution of ethnographic research to our understanding raises the following issues: (1) an increasing number of missionaries must be competent in ethnographic research methodology; (2) ethnographies should be included in the preparation of missionary candidates; (3) ethnographic research is crucial to the ongoing process of CONTEXTUALIZATION, especially with the problem of nominalism; (4) ethnographic research should be encouraged to provide comparative data for the development of strategies employed by missions; and (5) mission leaders should incorporate ethnographic research as a useful method of gaining understanding as the internationalization of missions continues both at the level of field ministries and in developing multicultural leadership.

C. DOUGLAS MCCONNELL

SEE ALSO Qualitative Research.

Bibliography. M. H. Agar, *Speaking of Ethnography;* H. R. Bernard, *Research Methods in Cultural Anthropology;* D. M. Fetterman, *Ethnography Step by Step;* B. Glaser and A. Strauss, *The Discovery of Grounded Theory;* M. Hammersley and P. Atkinson, *Ethnography: Principles and Practice;* J. Kirk and M. L. Miller, *Reliability and Validity in Qualitative Research;* M. Punch, *The Politics and Ethics of Fieldwork;* J. P. Spradley, *Participant Observation.*

Ethnography. A methodology that looks for significant patterns of behavior in social contexts and seeks to interpret them according to the insider's perspective. This type of QUALITATIVE RESEARCH, involving "participant observation," was brought to popular consciousness by Margaret Mead (1928) and Oscar Lewis (1963). The researchers immerse themselves in a given social context as participants, making detailed observations that they convert to written data for analysis. Some researchers attempt to become one with the social group and make their observations from the inside (the emic perspective); others join the social group as outsiders (the etic perspective) and seek to confirm their findings through open-ended interviews with its members.

Ethnography is particularly useful for missionaries because it provides them with the tools they need to study any given cultural situation within its own context. As students of mission have become increasingly sensitive to the need to contextualize the biblical message, ethnography has helped them describe accurately the cultural context to which the message must be adapted. In addition, in an age when cultural contexts are constantly changing and no two contexts are precisely alike, ethnography allows the student of mission to make disciplined assessments of any current cultural grouping, to focus on and define what may be available only in a general form in the literature.

Ethnographical attempts to understand the complexity of human behavior begin with general observations in the field. The ethnographer attempts to observe as much as possible, noting, for instance, the use of space, objects, acts, activities, events, time, actors, goals, and feelings. This all-encompassing survey avoids the trap of looking for something specific. Often the richest insights and understandings result from observation of patterns that the ethnographer did not expect to find or did not understand at the beginning of research. All of these observations are converted into written data, which are then analyzed and coded. This cycle is repeated until a complex set of patterns begins to emerge in the observations and analysis. Interview protocols are then developed to explore the meaning of these patterns from the point of view of the members of the group. The interviews are often carried out with open-ended (no specific answer) and indirect (what would other people say?) questions, a technique that allows the interviewees to reveal what otherwise would be unknown to the interviewer. These data are likewise analyzed and coded into a "grounded theory." The findings are then transformed into a readable report known as an ethnography.

Ethnography as a research method should not be confused with QUANTITATIVE RESEARCH. Quantitative research breaks down and interprets surveys through statistical analysis. In contrast, as ethnography attempts to discover and describe complex human behavior, it develops the questions that may later be used for quantitative research. Ethnography freely admits that qualitative research is a subjective approach, but asserts that with proper techniques the researcher can compensate for personal bias.

CHARLES A. DAVIS

Bibliography. O. Lewis, *The Children of Sanchez: Autobiography of a Mexican Family;* M. Mead, *Coming of Age in Samoa;* J. P. Spradley, *Participant Observation;* A. L. Strauss, *Qualitative Analysis for Social Scientists.*

Ethnomusicology. Ethnomusicology is an academic discipline emerging in the twentieth century. It grew out of the tension posed by the adage, "Music is a universal language," and the discovery of great varieties of music never previously observed as a result of nineteenth-century explorations into various parts of the world. With its roots dating back to the 1880s in the field of comparative musicology, the term "ethnomusicology" was first coined in 1958 by Jaap Kunst. As a discipline, ethnomusicology has grown from initial "arm-chair" observations of music collected by explorers to active analysis, documentation, and participant-observation research of the ever-burgeoning musics of the world's cultures. Ethnomusicology is interdisciplinary, drawing from ANTHROPOLOGY, LINGUISTICS, and musicology. A major goal of ethnomusicologists today is to understand the music of the world's peoples.

Traditionally, ethnomusicology includes the study of folk and traditional music, contemporary music in oral tradition, and Eastern art music. It involves the study of conceptual issues such as the origin of music, musical change, composition and improvisation, music as symbol, universals in music, the roles and functions of music in society, the comparison of musical systems, and the interrelationships of music in multimedia events with drama and dance. Although research methodologies can apply to any musical culture, ethnomusicologists most often study cultures other than their own.

Historically, ethnomusicologists have debated the philosophical and methodological foundations of the discipline. The great divide falls between anthropological and musicological approaches to music. Alan Merriam's thinking evolved from seeing ethnomusicology as "the study of music in culture" (1960), to "the study of music as culture" (1973), to the assertion that "music is culture and what musicians do is society" (1975). Musicological approaches, on the other hand, kept their focus on the transcription and analysis of the world's musics.

Despite this conflict in approaches, ethnomusicologists today generally agree on five main characteristics of the field. First, they recognize similarities and universals in music and musical behavior over against an appreciation for the plethora of musical styles worldwide. Second, they agree that personal research must be carried out in the field. Drawing from anthropological methodologies, field research includes the gathering of data about music, the collecting of music, participant-observation techniques, the audio-videorecording of music events, the collection of song texts and musical instruments, the investigation of concepts about musical sound and musical behavior, and learning to perform the music under investigation. Third, ethnomusicologists generally agree that music can be written down and analyzed from a visible format. They seek solutions that go beyond the adaptation of Western musical notation. Fourth, ethnomusicologists investigate music as a phenomenon of culture. They insist that music has roles and functions within the wider cultural organization of societies, and that the study of music within its cultural context produces a true, genuine understanding of that music. Finally, ethnomusicologists extend their interests to the processes of musical change, the ways in which music remains stable, grows, and disappears. They interest themselves in the music of a culture as a whole, in the individual song or piece, and in the life of an individual or group.

Ethnomusicology and Mission. Historically, music and ethnomusicology played only a minor role when it came to doing the task of mission. Parallel to academia, most missionaries viewed music as "a universal language" that required the translation of Western hymns into local dialects for new converts. However, current research shows that the discipline of ethnomusicology can greatly impact the task of missions. Two major approaches help accomplish this. First, ethnomusicology, through the study of a culture's music and song texts, can bring a deeper dimension in cultural understandings of the people with whom a cross-cultural worker is ministering. Second, it can help make the gospel more relevant by working within the indigenous communication systems inherent within a culture. The development of culturally appropriate songs and music for evangelism, discipleship, and worship makes a major contribution to creative contextualization of the gospel.

Within contemporary missions, ethnomusicology is receiving a more recognized role for making Christ known among the nations. Vida Chenowith, a pioneer in ethnomusicology for mission as a professional musician and Bible translator, has combined linguistic methodologies, ethnomusicological concerns, and her desire to provide indigenous songs for worship. Roberta King, who focuses on music as communication, seeks to encourage the development of culturally relevant and meaningful songs for communicating the gospel that are readily acceptable to and understood by the receiving culture. The process includes working with indigenous Christian musicians in setting Scripture to song; the approach leads to creative contextualization of the gospel. James Krabill has studied the growth and theological development of an indigenous church, the Harrists of Côte d'Ivoire, through the study of their song texts. The Southern Baptists and Christian Missionary Alliance also pursue various approaches to incorporating ethnomusicology in mission. Newer missions, such as Frontiers, are sending teams to areas of the world where music and dance are major channels of communication and encouraging them to develop evangelistic methods based on the "arts."

Ethnomusicology can and should be integrated into every level of the missionary task. The missionary-ethnomusicologist's major work is to develop mission approaches and methods that are meaningful and helpful to the church, that are readily understood by missionaries as being highly effective, that are in agreement with national church leaders' goals and concerns for the church, and that are readily accessible to Christian workers. Ethnomusicology for missions is more than the mere development and collection of indigenous hymns, although this is important in itself. Rather, in addition, it seeks to contribute to the overall increased effectiveness of making Christ known through the study of a culture's musical genres, the learning of a people's worldview through the study of song texts, the identification of the role and function of music for developing methods in the use of music for evangelism, music for making disciples, and music for training leaders. Finally, the development of meaningful songs for worship that lead people to an encounter with God is an ultimate goal.

ROBERTA R. KING

Bibliography. V. Chenowith, *Melodic Perception and Analysis;* J. R. Krabill, *The Hymnody of the Harrist Church among the Dida of South-Central Ivory Coast (1913–1949): A Historico-Religious Study;* A. Merriam, *The Anthropology of Music;* Helen Myers, ed., *Ethnomusicology: Historical and Regional Studies;* B. Nettl, *The Study of Ethnomusicology: Twenty-nine Issues and Concepts.*

Ethnopsychology. *See* CROSS-CULTURAL COUNSELING.

Ethnotheologies. Ethnotheology is a recent word in mission vocabulary. Achieving prominence in the 1970s, it has grown out of a new reality—the cross-cultural diffusion of the gospel into every corner of the world. The Christian faith has been rooted in Africa, Oceania, and various parts of Asia. Latin America is reformulating its centuries-old dialogue with the faith into something that is more than "borrowed" from Iberian or Anglo-Saxon churches. Voices in the United States—African-American, Asian, and Hispanic, for example—silenced by their minority status, are speaking loudly. A new day for missions has dawned—a demographic shift in the ecclesiastical center of gravity from north to south, from west to east, from majority to minority.

With that shift comes a new opportunity for theological cross-fertilization beyond those traditional geographical, social, and ethnic barriers, and new reflections on the meaning of Christianity in new contexts. The reading list of the world church has expanded past the names of Calvin and Wesley, Hodge and Packer. To it has been added names of Elizonelo and Kim, Mbiti and Cone.

Terminology. No single term has yet emerged to describe this new situation. "Indigenous theology" was an early term that is still in use in some places. But its colonialist ring and its attachment to missionary sources sound too much like an "outsider's" imposition. "Contextual theology" draws attention to role of context and setting in doing theology. But some evangelicals, for that very reason, are hesitant to give it full support; they fear an overemphasis on context and an underemphasis on biblical text. "Local theology" is popular among some Roman Catholic missiologists (Schreiter, 1985, 6).

"Ethnotheology" has found wide, but not widespread, acceptance in evangelical Protestant circles. Its strengths lie in its focus on the specificity of theology for a given socio-cultural area and its support from linguistics and cultural anthropology (Kraft, 1979).

One common danger may be lying behind all these terms. It is the hidden, parochial assumption that real theology, theology without an adjective, is what has been done in the Anglo-Saxon world. And that those developing theologies variously called indigenous, local, contextual, or ethnic are mere addenda to this generic universal. A true terminological breakthrough will not come until we can speak easily of all particular theologies as ultimately contributions, northern and southern, to mutual enrichment and self-criticism.

The Contributions of Ethnotheologies. In this new global mission setting ethnotheologies are prodding theological reflection in directions new and old. They are underlining again the missiological dimension of all theology past and present. Paul's theology was that—a task theology whose map found its orientation point in missions. And the early church that followed him did not lose that dimension (Conn, 1990, 51–63).

Through the years, however, the missiological dimension has moved to the periphery. Theology has made itself comfortable in the Western world of Christendom, the *corpus Christianum*. It "occupies itself with the missionary enterprise as and when it seems to it appropriate to do so" (Bosch, 1991, 494).

Ethnotheologies, however, do not flow out of a world where the church is in a majority. They must define the faith in a non-Christian world where theirs is a minority voice. In this setting, whether post- or pre-Christian, ethnotheologies are recovering the missionary obligation of all theology. The gospel's connection to the world demands the service of more than simply theologians; evangelicals are calling for mission theologians (Branson and Padilla, 1986, 311–23).

Ethnotheologies are expanding the global interests of theology. Anglo-Saxon theology, for example, has explored Christology in terms of the traditional titles of Jesus as the Lord, Son of God, Son of Man, Jesus as prophet, priest, and king. African theologians are turning to their own cultural designations. Can we speak of Jesus as the master of initiation, as chief, as ancestor and elder brother, and as healer (Schreiter, 1991)?

In an Asian context where the world's major religions predominate, how do we confess Christ in an Islamic setting? Who is Jesus for Asian women? In a Korean context of suffering and repressed anger, how does Jesus speak for the people (the minjung)? In a Hindu setting, is he Avatar or more (Sugirtharajah, 1993)?

Ethnotheologies are widening theology's context in a more holistic direction. For a millennium and a half, Western European theology increasingly found its dominant dialogue partner in philosophy. Its concerns turned to more abstract issues of ontology and epistemology. The secularist worldview of the Enlightenment turned theology to issues of faith and reason. And the rise of the university gave both skepticism and religious studies a home, further compartmentalizing life into separate categories of the public and the private, theology and ethics, knowledge and virtue. In a world now seen as governed by human reason and natural law, Western European theology found itself asking, "Where is the God of truth in a world of science?"

The ethnotheologies of a new day are driven by other contextual interests. In a political world of power versus powerlessness, they cross the boundary between theology and ethics. BLACK THEOLOGIES in the United States and South Africa and LIBERATION THEOLOGIES in Latin America ask, "Where is the God of righteousness and justice in a world of injustice?" Often the theological formulations are THEODICY questions. Western European theologies ask, "Does God exist?" Black theology and FEMINIST THEOLOGIES ask, "Does God care?"

Issues of traditional culture dominate the black African theological agenda: What should our attitude be to AFRICAN TRADITIONAL RELIGIONS? What is our relation as African Christians to Africa's past (*see* AFRICAN THEOLOGIES)? And in Asia ethnotheologies are formed particularly in dialogue with the world's major religions. Theology there resembles religious apologetics (*see* ASIAN THEOLOGIES).

Emerging Concerns. In this explosion of creative theologizing, evangelicals remain concerned about the balance between text and context. "Theology must undoubtedly always be relevant and contextual, but this may never be pursued at the expense of God's revelation" (Bosch, 1991, 187). In the hermeneutical process of theology Christians must take seriously the normative priority of their classical text, the Scriptures. But, with a general weakness of biblical exposition in many ethnotheologies (Dyrness, 1990, 195), at least two particulars threaten this balance.

First, when does sensitivity to context become SYNCRETISM (Conn, 1984, 176–205)? The 1982 gathering of Third World evangelical theologians reflected this concern. "Ethnotheologies are often politically motivated and do little or no justice to the Scriptures. Syncretistic theologies often accommodate biblical truth to cultural variables. Several liberation theologies have raised vital questions which we cannot ignore. But we reject their tendency to give primacy to a PRAXIS which is not biblically informed in the doing of theology. Likewise we object to their use of a socioeconomic analysis as the hermeneutical key to the Scriptures" (Ro and Eshenaur, 1984, 23–24).

Second, can the particularism of ethnotheology lose its connection to the universal gospel? Where is the continuity between the theological formulations of the past and the emerging ethnotheologies of the present? How do we relate new understandings to the church's theological heritage of the past?

And how do we do it without assuming that there is some grand cookie-cutter pattern—a kind of universal theology that will apply in every context without nuance? How do we deal with discontinuities between Western European and other theologies? Where is the line between *semper reformanda* and *semper imitanda?* These are the contemporary questions that surround ethnotheology and its ongoing development.

HARVIE M. CONN

Bibliography. D. Bosch, *Transforming Mission;* M. L. Branson and R. Padilla, eds., *Conflict and Context: Hermeneutics in the Americas;* H. M. Conn, *Eternal Word and Changing Worlds;* idem, *WTJ* 52:1 (Spring 1990): 51–63; W. Dyrness, *Learning About Theology from the Third World;* C. H. Kraft, *Christianity in Culture;* B. R. Ro and R. Eshenaur, eds., *The Bible and Theology in Asian Contexts: An Evangelical Perspective in Asian Theology;* R. Schreiter, *Constructing Local Theologies;* idem, ed., *Faces of Jesus in Africa;* R. S. Sugirtharajah, ed., *Asian Faces of Jesus.*

Europe. Mission in Europe, as also in Africa and Asia, must start with the biblical record: thus the importance for Europeans of the Syrophonecian woman in Mark's Gospel who used Jesus' sense of humor to secure the healing of her daughter, and the Greeks in John's Gospel "who would see Jesus." Building on this the record indicates European participation in the Pentecostal experience: Peter's direction by vision to accept Cornelius as a fellow follower of the Way, and the Macedonian appeal to Paul to render help to the youthful churches of Europe. Thus bound up with the early history of Europe is the growth of the early Christian community, the story of how it came to define its core beliefs in relation to incipient heresy, and how from being a persecuted sect it became the state religion of the Roman Empire. This process was not all gain, for with it, as Eusebius (c. 260–340), the church's first historian, observed, there came social advantage in adopting the Christian faith, whose adherents came to represent a range of motivations from continued faithfulness to more pragmatic reasons ("the hypocrisy of people who crept into church" with an eye upon securing imperial favor).

With the Christianization of the Roman world, the expansion of the empire itself came to have mission implications. Some have suggested that the expansion of Christianity among the Teutonic peoples pressing on the borders of the empire was in the first place a product of Christians who had been taken prisoner by, for example, the marauding Goths. Franks and Celts were to follow in accepting the Christian faith and among them some remarkable early missionaries responded to the missionary call to evangelize the continent: receiving cultures soon became also sending cultures, seen, for example, in the lives of COLUMBANUS (c. 543–615) and BONIFACE (680–764) (*see also* CELTIC MISSIONS). Later the missionary endeavors in the East of two Greek brothers, CYRIL (826–869) and METHODIUS (c. 815–885), saw the gospel taken in 862 to Moravia, where Cyril's educational activities led to the invention of the Cyrillic alphabet, which it is claimed became the foundation of all Slavonic languages. The Eastern Church's use of the vernacular in early missionary activities was in marked distinction to the Western Church's concentration on Latin.

In the fifteenth century the missionary endeavors of a reinvigorated Catholic Church were more obvious than the outreach of Protestantism, which remained confined to Europe. In the West the sending of priests alongside the *conquistadores* to colonize the new world that Columbus had "discovered" was seen as simply a continuation of the Christianization of the Iberian peninsula, or *Reconquista,* the driving of the Moors out of Spain. Columbus's famous journey and the fall of Granada both occurred in 1492. At the same time militant Islam, in the form of the Ottoman Turks, was pressing the Christian East with great ferocity until 1683, when Vienna in the center of Christian Europe came under siege by these alien forces. The most remarkable missionary story of the sixteenth century was that of the Jesuit, FRANCIS XAVIER (1506–52), who in the last decade of his life undertook a formidable program of evangelization starting in Goa. From there he traveled to Sri Lanka and the islands of Indonesia, going as far east as Japan and founding a church there before continuing his mission work in China. In the process he was surprised to find a Christian presence already in India in the form of the Malabar Christians whom he thought most dreadfully ignorant. MATTEO RICCI (1552–1610), born in the year of Xavier's death and also a Jesuit, won the trust of the Chinese court through his demonstrated mastery of science and technology and exploited this for missionary purposes.

In the Protestant world it was not until the era of PIETISM had succeeded that of the REFORMATION that the churches began to look to wider missionary horizons. In England the SOCIETY FOR THE PROPAGATION OF THE GOSPEL IN FOREIGN PARTS was founded in 1701. Although much of its work was among European ex-patriots it did provide a mechanism to evangelize non-Christian populations, a theme that in continental Europe came to be championed by Count VON ZINZENDORF (1700–1760) and the MORAVIANS. By the end of the eighteenth century, Protestants, under the influence of Calvinism modified by the experience of the Evangelical Revival inaugurated what LATOURETTE has called 'THE GREAT CENTURY' of missionary endeavor. The BAPTIST MISSIONARY SOCIETY was formed in 1792, with the LONDON MISSIONARY SOCIETY following in 1795 and the CHURCH MISSIONARY SOCIETY in 1799. In Europe, where Bremen led the way with the founding of a new missionary society in 1819, Hamburg followed in 1822; the BASEL MISSION was established in 1815, the Rhineland Society in 1828, and the BERLIN SOCIETY in 1824, two years after French Protestants had formed the PARIS EVANGELICAL MISSIONARY SOCIETY.

MISSIOLOGY in such a context was born out of shared experiences and soon implanted within the university curriculum with the establishment of the Halle chair of mission studies in 1896. Missiological scholars networked with one another and with practitioners through the activities of the INTERNATIONAL MISSIONARY COUNCIL, itself a child of the historic WORLD MISSIONARY CONFERENCE meeting in Edinburgh in 1910, which played such a crucial part in bringing the ECUMENICAL MOVEMENT to maturity. Consent between Christians on the style and content of Christian mission was not easily obtained and was not resolved by the integration of the IMC into the work of the WORLD COUNCIL OF CHURCHES in 1961.

Already, by the second half of the nineteenth century, denominational endeavors were supplemented by interdenominational initiatives in which a new kind of missionary society was born, of which HUDSON TAYLOR'S CHINA INLAND MISSION of 1865 was archetypal. The new FAITH MISSIONS did not overtly solicit funds from supporters, who no longer controlled policy, for decision making was now invested in the hands of missionaries to identify with those to whom they ministered in dress and culture.

The century which followed that of Europe's unstinted investment of human resources and finances in both home and foreign missions, has been a century of SECULARIZATION. Fundamentally, it was the fruits of ENLIGHTENMENT thinking as well as scientific advances which, for many of Europe's citizens, in a century of troubled political and economic development, pushed matters of faith to the margins of life and concern. In the East the legacy of the years of Marxist constraint and persecution is still painfully present. Regrettably the relationships between evangelical minorities and state orthodoxy have all too often deteriorated since the end of the Cold War, while in the former Yugoslavia, as in the island of Cyprus, ethnic tensions and conflict have all too often set Christians against their Islamic neighbors.

In the West, folk or national churches still claim large baptismal memberships and maintain an excellent range of worship buildings and ancillary facilities, even though regular worshipers form only a small percentage of secular Europe's population. Europe hardly needed the reminder of the MEXICO CITY CONFERENCE ON WORLD MISSION in 1963 that witness was to take place in all six continents. Those who had been sending nations now desperately needed to receive something of the buoyancy and hope of the churches of the south. Many North American missionary societies increasingly saw Europe as a mission field needing urgent attention.

In its turn this has led to a new relationship between mission agencies and the churches which had been born out of the labors of their missionaries. First, within the ECUMENICAL MOVEMENT younger mission-founded churches sought recognition as churches in their own right, not to be represented by proxy through mission boards. Second, questions were raised about missionary structures and some of the old societies chose to reconstruct themselves more into mission partnership organizations. Perhaps the classic transformation was the way in which the London Missionary Society became first the Congregational Council for World Mission in 1966. This body was in turn fully internationalized as the COUNCIL FOR WORLD MISSION in 1977. The new council, it was hoped, recognizing a diversity of leadership through equality of presence around a single partnership table, would combine a commitment to unity with a commitment to mission. In Europe, the PARIS EVANGELICAL MISSIONARY SOCIETY went through a similar change in 1971 when it became the *Communaute Evangelique d'Action Apostolique* (CEVAA). Other societies were reluctant both to unite home and foreign mission and to replace the societal model by one of world PARTNERSHIP.

Europe has seen the uniting of some churches, especially within the Methodist and Reformed traditions, the continuation of large national churches though with serious loss of membership, and the revival of orthodoxy in the context of political freedom but economic constraint. The Roman Catholic Church at the end of the century recognizes other Christians in a way that would have seemed impossible at its beginning. In some countries it has joined national ecumenical bodies as an equal partner, and there are good relationships between the Conference of European Churches and the Conference of European Bishops, so that they are able to have joint continent-wide celebrations. Moreover, the influence of the CHARISMATIC MOVEMENT among Roman Catholic laity and clergy has opened up new and fruitful lines of communication, but a reluctance to go further still emanates from the Vatican on such issues as the recognition of non-Roman orders and the possibilities of shared communion. Undoubtedly, a major aspect of the century has been both the growth of Pentecostalism alongside historic Protestantism and the wide impact of the Charismatic movement both within the mainstream churches and the new house and community churches. Together, these have contributed to growth in Christian witness in Europe.

JOHN H. Y. BRIGGS

Evangelical Fellowship of Mission Agencies. The Evangelical Fellowship of Mission Agencies (EFMA) is a voluntary association of more than one hundred missionary agencies. It is composed of both denominational and nondenominational missions from a wide variety of evangelical traditions.

History of the EFMA. The EFMA was formed in the 1940s as part of a larger evangelical resurgence in the United States. The advance of theological liberalism as represented in the old Federated Council of Churches (predecessor of the National Council of Churches) and its missions arm, the Division of Foreign Missions (predecessor of the Division of Overseas Ministries), had given rise to concerns for developing evangelical missions.

Efforts to present an evangelical voice were hampered by continued divisions in outlook and strategy. The moderate voice that developed was called the National Association of Evangelicals (1943), rallying around leaders such as Harold Ockenga and Clyde Taylor.

In 1945 Taylor issued a call for evangelical missions, both denominational and nondenominational, to come together under the aegis of the NAE to deal with missions-related problems. Fourteen of the missions agencies that gathered for this purpose became charter members and launched the EFMA. Taylor served as executive director of the EFMA until 1975. The organization was led by Wade Coggins from 1975 to 1990, and by Paul E. McKaughan from 1990. The EFMA broke new ground by pulling together evangelicals from various traditions, ranging from Baptist to Reformed, Mennonite, Holiness, and Pentecostal. As a variety of evangelical denominations, missions and service agencies, and student ministries joined the association, the EFMA experienced rapid growth.

One of the first moves by the EFMA was to establish a presence in Washington, D.C., so as to represent the concerns connected with the surge in evangelical missionary activity following World War II. For example, the EFMA has intervened to enable evangelical missionaries to obtain passports more easily, and has worked with the U.S. Department of State and with foreign embassies in Washington to provide, where necessary, certification of the reliability of member missions agencies and churches. This has eased the process of obtaining visas for missionaries serving under organizations affiliated with the EFMA.

Already on the scene since 1917 was the INTERDENOMINATIONAL FOREIGN MISSION ASSOCIATION (IFMA), which served non-Pentecostal missions groups including the historical "FAITH MISSIONS." In the early days of the EFMA, relations between the EFMA and the IFMA were tense, but by the 1960s an era of cooperation began. The two associations formed a joint Latin America Committee that continued until the 1990s. In 1964 they formed the Evangelical Missions Information Service (EMIS) and began publishing the *Evangelical Missions Quarterly* (EMQ). In the late 1950s Wade Coggins joined Clyde Taylor in the work of EFMA, and in the 1960s E. L. Frizen Jr. became the director of the IFMA. Coggins, Taylor, and Frizen were the architects of many cooperative efforts between the IFMA and the EFMA. At various times, as needed, there have been joint committees related to Africa, Latin America, Asia, Personnel, Publication, Church Growth, and Theological Education by Extension (TEE).

Through the 1950s the number of missionaries being sent out by the EFMA and the IFMA agencies increased while those related to the National Council of Churches of Christ (NCCC) declined. By 1960 it was noted by missiologists that the combined number of missionaries of EFMA and IFMA agencies was greater than those of the NCC-related groups.

One significant example of EFMA–IFMA cooperation was joint sponsorship in 1966 of the CONGRESS ON THE CHURCH'S WORLDWIDE MISSION, which came to be known as "Wheaton '66." Meeting on the campus of Wheaton College, it gathered together hundreds of missions leaders to hear the challenge of reaching the world with the gospel of Jesus Christ. The Congress issued a statement called the WHEATON DECLARATION, which stated the continuing call to the church to acknowledge the lostness of humanity and the need to take the gospel to all the earth.

EFMA has been a major proponent and supporter of the WORLD EVANGELICAL FELLOWSHIP (WEF), an association of more than 120 national organizations of evangelicals worldwide. These national units—variously known as evangelical fellowships, associations, federations, alliances, or councils—frequently have within their membership the churches that have grown out of the work of EFMA and IFMA missions.

EFMA Distinctives. The EFMA is a nonprofit membership organization that provides many services to its members and to the larger evangelical community. In many ways it parallels a trade or professional association. The EFMA concentrates on the needs of its members, seeking to enhance their work and to make the leadership of member organizations more effective in their respective tasks.

While retaining solid commitment on the evangelical theological essentials, member agencies represent a wide range of doctrinal distinctives within the broader evangelical family. Membership is divided almost evenly between denominational and nondenominational groups. They come from traditions including Wesleyan, Reformed, Pentecostal/Charismatic, Baptist, Presbyterian, Lutheran, Mennonite, and Brethren. While denominational groups provided important momentum for the EFMA, independent missions have also been a significant part of the association from the beginning. Missions with specialized ministries and service organizations are also an integral part of the EFMA.

The EFMA has maintained a fundamental commitment to cooperation, a stance that has characterized its philosophy and activity. It has sometimes found itself caught between the broader ecumenical movement and the more separatist evangelicals and fundamentalists. During the years of its ascendancy, the separatist American Council of Churches made vicious attacks on the NAE and EFMA because of their more moderate stance. In time, the EFMA became the largest association of missionary agencies.

Identification and authentication are very important components of EFMA's ministry. Through its membership standards it provides individuals and churches with a way to recognize missions agencies that conform to specific doctrinal and financial standards.

Strategic planning is another significant role, with the EFMA often serving as a kind of "think tank," providing opportunities for missions leaders to wrestle with ideas and strategies. Through such forums various missions strategists have launched major new missions concepts and initiatives.

An important channel of catalytic ministry was the formation and development, with the IFMA, of the EMIS. Under the leadership of James Reapsome, *EMQ* and *World Pulse* contribute significantly to the distribution of news and ideas about missions. The EMIS has also sponsored significant strategy conferences and seminars.

As a cooperative effort with the IFMA, the annual Personnel Workshop has stimulated significant advances in how missions deal with personnel concerns. Subjects addressed by the workshop include recruitment of missionaries, orientation, training, evaluation, compensation, retirement, pensions, children's education, and pastoral and psychological care.

The Church Growth Movement was given prominence as an academic discipline and missions strategy through EFMA-sponsored workshops by Donald McGavran during the 1960s. Through the ministry of the EMIS, Church Growth seminars were conducted by international teams (often including McGavran) and local leaders worldwide. Having served as a catalyst in this area, the EFMA left the development of programs and training to others. The Disciple a Whole Nation (DAWN) strategy, for example, has its roots in the Church Growth seminars held in the Philippines.

The EFMA also had a significant role in the development and dissemination of Theological Education by Extension (TEE). Through its joint (with IFMA) subsidiary Committee to Assist Ministry Education Overseas (CAMEO), EFMA supported seminars for missionaries in the preparation of TEE materials. In turn, TEE programs around the world have impacted thousands of lives and provided theological training for church leaders. CAMEO, led by Raymond Buker and later Lois McKinney, also gave important leadership in developing improved curricula for all levels of leadership training worldwide.

Focus/listening groups constitute another method of strategic planning. EFMA convenes such groups at various locations across the United States, bringing together people from the missions community such as missions executives, pastors, academic leaders, and specialized ministry representatives. Such gatherings provide opportunities for creative thinking and planning as issues and opportunities confronting missions in the coming decades are considered.

Although not without its problems, the EFMA has served a vital role in the task of world evangelization during the past half century. As the church moves into the twenty-first century it will confront an increasingly complex world with a fresh set of opportunities and challenges, and the EFMA can be expected to continue to provide leadership to member groups as they work together to make disciples of Jesus Christ among all nations.

Wade T. Coggins

Bibliography. W. T. Coggins and E. L. Frizen, *EMQ* 20:2 (1984): 118–27.

Evangelical Missiological Society (EMS).

A North American organization that brings together professors of missiology and related disciplines, missionaries/missiologists, and missions administrators for the purpose of encouraging fellowship and professional stimulation in the common commitment to carrying out the GREAT COMMISSION. Regional and annual meetings provide forums for discussion of missiological issues facing evangelicals in their missions endeavors. Members share a common evangelical theological framework as expressed in the doctrinal statements of the INTERDENOMINATIONAL FOREIGN MISSION ASSOCIATION (IFMA), the EVANGELICAL FELLOWSHIP OF MISSION AGENCIES (EFMA), and the Fellowship of Frontier Missions.

Due in large measure to the vigorous leadership of DONALD MCGAVRAN and DAVID J. HESSELGRAVE, the EMS was officially established in November 1990 through a reorganization of the already existing Association of Evangelical Professors of Mission (AEPM). Several factors led to the formation of EMS. First, there was a perceived need for a missiological society composed solely of evangelicals who were committed both to the full authority of Scripture and to the priority of EVANGELISM and CHURCH PLANTING in mission. The already existing AMERICAN SOCIETY OF MISSIOLOGY, with its broader membership base (which includes Roman Catholics and conciliar Protestants) and interests, did not fit this expectation. Second, since membership in the AEPM was restricted to professors of mission, it was felt that a new society was needed that included not only classroom professors but also field practitioners and missions administrators with missiological interests. Third, there was a perceived need for closer ties between the evangelical missions community and the broader evangelical theological world. Through regular joint meetings with the Evangelical Theological Society (ETS), the IFMA, and the EFMA, the EMS was expected to represent evangelical missions interests within the broader evangelical community. Annual meetings of the EMS are held in conjunction with the ETS and, every third year, the IFMA and EFMA.

In addition to its national and regional meetings, the EMS has also sponsored numerous monographs and publications addressing critical missiological issues from an evangelical perspective. The first executive director of the EMS was David Hesselgrave, under whose leadership society membership increased dramatically.

HAROLD A. NETLAND

SEE ALSO Academic Associations of Mission.

Bibliography. EMQ 27 (1991): 184–87.

Evangelical Missionary Alliance (EMA). The

EMA, an evangelical missions association in the United Kingdom, aims to resource, equip, represent, and network its members to promote the cause of global mission. The roots of the EMA can be traced to 1941, when the Fellowship of Interdenominational Missionary Societies (FIMS)

was founded. EMS was a prayer fellowship that disbanded in 1957 prior to the 1958 formation of EMA.

The EMA incorporated into its membership both interdenominational and denominational organizations. Its first secretary was Gilbert Kirby, who was then also the secretary of the Evangelical Alliance UK. In 1966, Ernest Oliver was appointed secretary and carried this responsibility in a part-time capacity in addition to being first secretary of Regions Beyond Missionary Union and later a director of Tear Fund. His distinguished work at EMA in 1966–82 provided the foundation for further development in recent years. In 1983 Stanley Davies, the current general secretary, was appointed.

There are four members of staff, including the general secretary. Additionally, a council of twenty-six elected persons is responsible for establishing policy, approving budgets, and appointing senior staff. It is also a forum for debating current missiological issues in the United Kingdom. An appointed executive committee of nine provides guidance for senior staff regarding EMA work.

The EMA has acted as an information service on all aspects of world mission, monitoring world developments, brokering relationships, and advising members on a wide range of issues (financial, legal, technical, training, and missiological). It convenes various continental and functional working groups (e.g., Africa, radio, short-term mission) and consultations of specific regions and issues; it holds specialist seminars and courses (e.g., for missionaries on home assignment, promotion, and publicity for mission). It also convenes an annual conference that addresses key missiological issues. It helps in developing and facilitating youth involvement in mission, and initiates new ventures that raise the profile of world mission in the United Kingdom by encouraging and fostering partnership in all aspects of Christian mission. From time to time, it also provides representation to government and media publishing material.

EMA Cooperation. While the EMA is a separate organization with its own constitution and council, it has a partnership relationship with the Evangelical Alliance UK. The two organizations are committed to working together in mobilizing churches for mission involvement through their joint World Mission Project. Another joint project is the Commission on Unreached Peoples, which aims to foster pan-evangelical reflection and action, evaluate strategic initiatives, and comment on trends and issues requiring action (*see also* PEOPLES, PEOPLE GROUPS).

The EMA also works with other bodies. It cooperates with Churches Commission on Mission (CCOM), the ecumenical mission network in the United Kingdom, on a number of joint initiatives such as the Personnel Officers Group and The Mission Finance Officers Group. It also has worked with CCOM health-related issues such as AIDS consultations.

The EMA also cooperates with the European Evangelical Missionary Alliance (EEMA), a network of national missionary associations across Europe. The EEMA holds an annual meeting that is hosted by one of its national member associations. It occasionally calls a Europe-wide consultation on a particular topic, such as EURO-COMET '92, a consultation on the care and education of MISSIONARY CHILDREN. Currently the EMA UK office services the EEMA network.

Finally, the EMA is represented on the WORLD EVANGELICAL FELLOWSHIP Missions Commission by its general secretary, who is a member of the executive committee. The EMA is committed to the goals of the commission, and participates in its programs.

Membership. There are three categories of EMA membership. First, *corporate membership* is for organizations that send missionaries into cross-cultural work, agencies that support the cause of world mission in different ways, and organizations that train people for cross-cultural mission. Corporate membership requires members to meet and maintain certain standards with regard to publicity, finance, and relationships. In 1996, there were over 140 corporate members, representing nearly six thousand serving missionaries and staff. This represents over 60 percent of all Christian missionaries, of all denominations, sent from the United Kingdom. Second, *affiliate membership* is open to non-U.K. originated agencies that work cross-culturally in the United Kingdom. Third, *personal membership* is available for individuals committed to global mission.

Vision. The EMA vision for the decade from 1995 to 2005 is that it will be a dynamic catalyst, impacting local, national, and global Christian organizations in the education and implementation of world mission. It will be recognized as the key network of successful cooperation for world mission, enabling all U.K. evangelicals to contribute to the goal of a church for every people and promoting missiological reflection and application among colleges, agencies, and churches. It will serve as the primary U.K. voice of evangelical missions in representing, encouraging, educating, and enabling them in effective world mission, and in working with the EMA so that world mission will be high on the agenda of local churches.

STANLEY DAVIES

Evangelical Missions Conferences. Represented by a broad spectrum of types, evangelical missions conferences have typically shared the common purpose of furthering the worldwide Christian movement. While they have taken a variety of forms, most have tended to fall within one of two main categories. They generally exist either as "think-tanks" for discussing missions strategies, programs, and policies, or as inspirational meetings to rally the Christian public. The latter seek to inform and inspire people in the pews to contribute their prayer and financial support, as well as to send forth their sons and daughters (and increasingly themselves, as short-term and second-career missionaries) to engage directly in the great missionary task.

The most common variety of the inspirational type conferences have been those held annually in local churches (*see* CHURCH MISSIONS CONFERENCES). These have followed a wide variety of schedules and patterns during their lengthy history, but the long-popular pattern of week-long conferences with nightly meetings has largely given way in our overly programmed and frenetic age to weekend conferences or month-long mission emphases with special events and speakers taking center stage over several weeks of regular meeting times. The common features generally include displays and reports from furloughing missionaries and mission agencies that the church supports as well as messages from one or more gifted speakers.

A related but largely fading tradition among fundamentalist and evangelical Christians is the Bible and missions conference centers, which combine rustic vacation and recreational opportunities with Bible teaching and missionary reports and challenges. While these were very popular during the late nineteenth century and much of the twentieth, they have not fared as well in recent decades with an increasingly affluent and harried American evangelical population. Even where these centers have continued with relative success, the missions emphasis has become much less pronounced.

In terms of perennial conferences, there can be little doubt that the triennial URBANA MISSION CONFERENCES are among the most famous and long-lasting. This massively attended event (close to 20,000 in 1996) has been held over the Christmas break since 1948 at the University of Illinois at Urbana, but its roots go all the way back to the quadrennial student conventions begun by the STUDENT VOLUNTEER MOVEMENT in 1891. Those gatherings continued until 1936, but ended as the clouds of war gathered. The model was again picked up in 1946 in Toronto by the InterVarsity Christian Fellowship, which had recently merged with the Student Foreign Missions Fellowship. The gatherings today at Urbana, which combine large doses of both inspiration and information, attract hundreds of mission agencies and thousands of students, missionaries, and others.

Conferences devoted to discussing strategic missions policies, programs, and plans have played an influential role in shaping the North American evangelical missionary movement through the years. Over the last three decades or so, they have been doing the same internationally as well. On the domestic North American scene, a long-standing and influential place has been held by the annual conferences sponsored by the INTERDENOMINATIONAL FOREIGN MISSIONS ASSOCIATION (since 1917), and the EVANGELICAL FELLOWSHIP OF MISSION AGENCIES, the missionary wing of the National Association of Evangelicals, formerly known as the Evangelical Foreign Missions Association (since 1945). Supplementing their annual meetings, these two associations have also met jointly on a triennial basis since 1963, when their momentous first meeting together gave birth to the Evangelical Missions Information Service. Others among their meetings have also been of weighty importance. Their meeting together at Green Lake, Wisconsin, in 1971, for example, was a pivotal event in the history of evangelical mission and church relationships, providing as it did a strategic examination of both overseas and domestic issues.

Other important issues-oriented missions conferences that take place annually or periodically in North America would include the meetings of groups like the AMERICAN SOCIETY OF MISSIOLOGY, the EVANGELICAL MISSIOLOGICAL SOCIETY, the International Society for Frontier Missions, AIMS (Association of International Mission Services), and ACMC (Advancing Churches in Missions Commitment).

There are in addition periodic scholarly conferences devoted to missions topics, generally sponsored by evangelical seminaries and graduate studies programs. An important example would be the June 1986 conference held at Wheaton College, "A Century of World Evangelization: North American Evangelical Missions, 1886–1986." More regular but smaller study conferences are also sponsored by the Overseas Ministries Study Center, a center for missions scholarship which publishes the *International Bulletin of Missionary Research*.

On a wider and usually international front, there is a long tradition of the great conferences, some of which would be claimed by both evangelical Christians and others, and some of which would be far less international than others. The earliest of these would include gatherings such as the UNION MISSIONARY CONVENTION (NEW YORK MISSIONARY CONFERENCE, 1854), the CENTENARY CONFERENCE ON THE PROTESTANT MISSIONS OF THE WORLD (LONDON MISSIONARY CONFERENCE, 1888), the ECUMENICAL MISSIONARY CONFERENCE (New York, 1900), the PANAMA CONGRESS (1916), and most notable of all, the WORLD MISSIONARY CONFERENCE (EDINBURGH, 1910).

In recent decades a new wave of self-consciously evangelical international conferences have taken place. Beginning in 1966, with the twin events of the CONGRESS ON THE CHURCH'S WORLDWIDE MISSION (Wheaton, 1966) and the WORLD CONGRESS ON EVANGELISM (BERLIN CONGRESS 1966), evangelicals of many stripes, and from around the world, have gathered together in events like these to declare their commitment to global mission in the face of theological, cultural, and pluralistic challenges to its legitimacy. Subsequent global conferences over the period have maintained this emphasis while building on it in various ways.

The most significant of these more recent conferences was the first LAUSANNE CONGRESS ON WORLD EVANGELIZATION (1974). Besides being the most representative global conference up to that time, it was pivotal in at least two ways: First, it refocused in a very important way the attention of the evangelical missions community on the most neglected segment of the world's population, unreached peoples. Second, through the instrumentation of the Lausanne Covenant, it enhanced the status of social concern ministry as an integral part of gospel witness. Other conferences that followed built on these foundations.

These included the LAUSANNE CONGRESS II ON WORLD EVANGELISM held Manila in 1989, a fact indicating perhaps better than anything else the enduring legacy of Lausanne I. It clearly was a watershed event, having produced in its wake a movement with the same name.

The other really significant series of global conferences that followed in the train of Lausanne I, albeit with a less churchly and more specifically missions-oriented clientele, were the Global Consultations on World Evangelization held in Singapore in 1989, in Seoul in 1995 (*see* GLOBAL CONSULTATION OF WORLD EVANGELIZATION [GCOWE 95]), and in Pretoria in 1997 (*see* GLOBAL CONSULTATION OF WORLD EVANGELIZATION '97 [GCOWE II]). This series of conferences has been particularly significant in mobilizing national evangelical leadership in various countries to the task of reaching the unevangelized peoples and corners of their own land with the gospel, as well as in stirring up a passion for engaging in mission beyond their own borders.

Finally, mention should be made of the WORLD EVANGELICAL FELLOWSHIP and its network of associations and commissions that sponsor global, regional, and national conferences that serve over 100 million evangelicals globally every year. A significant portion of these have a profound missions impact.

GARY R. CORWIN

Bibliography. J. D. Allan, *The Evangelicals: An Illustrated History;* J. D. Douglas, ed., *Let the Earth Hear His Voice: International Congress on World Evangelization, Lausanne, Switzerland;* idem, *Proclaim Christ Until He Comes: Lausanne II in Manila;* D. M. Howard, *Student Power in World Evangelization;* H. Lindsell, ed., *The Church's Worldwide Mission;* D. McGavran, ed., *The*

Conciliar-Evangelical Debate: The Crucial Documents 1964–1976; J. M. Phillips, and R. T. Coote, eds., *Toward the 21st Century in Christian Mission;* J. Stott, ed., *Making Christ Known: Historic Mission Documents from the Lausanne Movement, 1974–1989;* T. Wang, ed., *Countdown to AD 2000: GCOWE in Singapore. The AD 2000 Movement.*

Evangelical Movement. In the broadest sense, an "evangelical" movement comprises persons who believe in salvation by faith in Jesus Christ and present the gospel to others. In the context of North America, the term denotes a twentieth-century movement committed to the historic doctrines of the Christian faith, the supreme authority of Scripture in faith and practice, the need for personal conversion, and the imperative of world evangelization. In global Christianity, "evangelicalism" encompasses a broad scope of Christians, movements, and organizations which transcend confessional and ecclesiastical lines.

In the sixteenth century, an early evangelical movement appeared among Roman Catholics in Spain and Italy (e.g., Juan de Valdes) who wished to bring about reform in the institutional church through a more biblically based faith than that of the late medieval church. Much more prominently, however, "evangelical" described the faith of Martin Luther and his followers who initiated the Protestant Reformation. Along with justification by faith, he taught the priesthood of all believers, thereby replacing a sacred hierarchy with a community of faith in which all believers serve as priests before God. Gradually, the term embraced the "Reformed" churches originating with Huldrych Zwingli and John Calvin. It also described the faith of Mennonites and Swiss Brethren in the Radical Reformation, as well as English Separatists and Baptists. Beginning in the seventeenth century, renewal movements changed the landscape of Protestant Christianity. Puritanism, already a force for Reformed theology in the Church of England, sought to bring about the restoration of New Testament Christianity and a Christian society. Its influence extended to the pietist movement in Germany and the later evangelical revival in England. Celebrated Puritan leaders included Richard Baxter and John Owen; in America, Puritanism reached its peak in the spiritual and theological writings of JONATHAN EDWARDS.

In continental Europe, PIETISM emerged in the Lutheran and Reformed churches. Though faithful to Luther's teaching on justification, it focused on the believer's need of regeneration. Lutheran Pietists Philipp Jakob Spener and August Hermann Francke emphasized a "heartfelt" conversion, individual and family prayers, devotional study of the Bible with applications for the Christian life, hope for the world as expressed in Christian social action, and foreign missions. The

movement soon spilled over into Mennonite, Brethren, and Quaker churches. Jansenism and quietism in the Roman Catholic Church were part of the larger spiritual awakening at the time associated with Pietism.

The mass evangelism of Charles and JOHN WESLEY and GEORGE WHITFIELD advanced the evangelical revival in eighteenth-century England. In 1738, at a Moravian meeting on Aldersgate Street in London, John Wesley found new meaning in the doctrine of justification by faith when he received personal assurance of his own salvation. While the "Methodists," as their converts were called, eventually left the Church of England, Anglican evangelicalism continued, led in part by Charles Simeon and William Wilberforce. Across the Atlantic, stirred by revivalists like Jonathan Edwards and George Whitfield, the GREAT AWAKENING secured for evangelicals an important role in the development of the United States. In nineteenth-century America, evangelical Christianity reigned as the dominant faith and forged the nation's values and religious consciousness. Revivalism, promoted by evangelists such as CHARLES G. FINNEY, offered hope for a spiritual awakening that would eliminate social evils and bring about the establishment of a Christian republic. African-American churches guided by leaders Richard Allen (African Methodist Episcopal Church), Thomas Paul (Baptist), and others, also taught evangelical doctrine. Social activists, represented by the later Ida B. Wells-Barnett (Methodist), found strength for their struggles for racial equality in a deep evangelical faith.

The Wesleyan holiness movement, fired by the teachings of John Fletcher, PHOEBE PALMER, and William Arthur, highlighted the postconversion experience of "entire sanctification" for the perfection of the believer and purification of society. Reformed revivalists DWIGHT L. MOODY, Hannah Whitall Smith, and speakers at the annual KESWICK CONVENTIONS in England viewed this second experience of grace as the beginning of the "Higher Life," a fully consecrated life empowered for Christian service. Both holiness camps referred to this as baptism in the Holy Spirit.

From the holiness taproot grew the PENTECOSTAL MOVEMENT shortly after the turn of the twentieth century. It originated with a revival at Charles F. Parham's Bethel Bible School in Topeka, Kansas, in 1901. The movement became worldwide several years later as a result of the interracial Azusa Street revival (1906–9) in Los Angeles, California, led by the African-American William J. Seymour. With scores of succeeding revivals in North America and Europe, a new diaspora of missionaries left for the mission lands. Concurrent with the Azusa Street revival, a Pentecostal revival commenced in India in 1906.

Between the Civil War and World War I, the hegemony of evangelical Christianity declined due to rapid changes in the culture. Waves of immigration brought large numbers of Roman Catholics, Eastern Orthodox Christians, and Jews to the American shores that threatened evangelical dominance. Prompted by the religious skepticism of the ENLIGHTENMENT, Darwinian evolution, and the radical higher criticism of the Bible coming from German and English academic circles, questions arose about the ultimate claims of the Christian faith. These challenges appeared to undermine the historical integrity of Scripture, creationism, miracles, and the divinity and resurrection of Christ. Furthermore, the growing appeal of the social gospel convinced numerous evangelicals that social action was now replacing the priority of personal conversion in some church bodies. Many were influenced by dispensational PREMILLENNIALISM with its negative assessment of human progress and warning of the imminent return of Jesus Christ and impending judgment on the wicked. In response to these assaults on traditional Christian beliefs, conservatives in mainline churches sought to preserve theological orthodoxy by controlling denominational structures and seminaries. This agenda consequently led to the fundamentalist-modernist controversy that peaked in the 1920s. Modernists endeavored to reconcile Christian beliefs with scientific discoveries and higher criticism, and concentrated their energies on the social applications of the gospel. Some endorsed forms of religious PLURALISM. Fundamentalists, as the conservatives were called, coming largely from the Reformed sector of evangelicalism, denied the Enlightenment notion of the innate goodness of humankind and fought modernist tenets. Losing the battle in their denominations, fundamentalists like the New Testament scholar J. Gresham Machen, Carl T. McIntire, founder of the American Council of Christian Churches, and the Canadian Baptist T. T. Shields, encouraged conservatives to separate from them.

Fundamentalists resisted changes that imperiled their vision of a Christian society, the truth claims of non-Christian religions, scientific arguments against biblical teachings on the origins of life, as well as the ECUMENICAL MOVEMENT and the Pentecostal movement. After the famous "Monkey Trial" in 1925 at Dayton, Tennessee, in which John T. Scopes was convicted of illegally teaching evolutionary theory in a public school, the public viewed fundamentalism as antiscientific and obscurantist.

By the 1940s, conservatives J. Elwin Wright, Harold J. Ockenga, Carl F. H. Henry, BILLY GRAHAM, and others rejected the denominational separatism and intellectual and cultural isolationism of fundamentalism and became the spokesmen for the "New Evangelicals." The evangelistic crusades of Billy Graham, which first gained national attention in 1948, played a crucial part in

the shaping of "neo-evangelicalism." Key institutions also served the new movement: among them, the National Association of Evangelicals (NAE [1943]), Wheaton College (1869), Fuller Theological Seminary (1947), and *Christianity Today* magazine (1956). These and similar institutions fostered a "renaissance" of evangelical biblical and theological scholarship beginning in the 1950s. The elections of evangelicals as presidents of the United States in recent decades has not only marked the resurgence of evangelicalism, but signaled widely different political orientations within.

The organization of the National Black Evangelical Association (1963), and to the north, the Evangelical Fellowship of Canada (1964), represented other notable milestones. While the NAE preempted the term "evangelical," many evangelicals remained within their denominations, most of which were constituent members of the National Council of Churches (NCC) and the World Council of Churches (WCC). Three large evangelical denominations—the Lutheran Church–Missouri Synod, Wisconsin Evangelical Lutheran Synod, and the Southern Baptist Convention—have chosen to remain outside conciliar bodies.

Modern evangelicalism now encompasses an almost unbridgeable diversity of Christians, all loyal to the gospel message, but with varying theological and spiritual orientations. Major groupings consist of Lutherans, Presbyterians, Anglicans, Pentecostals, Baptists, Wesleyans, Mennonites, Brethren, Churches of Christ, and others in the Restoration Movement. To these can be added Messianic Jews, nondenominational Christians, and constituents of parachurch agencies (e.g., Campus Crusade for Christ). Although controversial, some observers have listed Seventh-Day Adventists; and "Jesus Name" or Oneness Pentecostals belong.

The CHARISMATIC MOVEMENT has magnified evangelical witness in the mainline denominations, highlighted the ministry of the Holy Spirit in the life of the believer, and notably influenced contemporary Christian music and worship styles across a wide range of churches. Noted leaders included Dennis Bennett (Episcopal Church), Larry Christenson (Evangelical Lutheran Church in America), Demos Shakarian (Full Gospel Business Men's Fellowship International), and David J. du Plessis (Assemblies of God). In a significant development, some charismatics in the Roman Catholic Church have identified themselves as "evangelical Catholics."

In England, the perceived new threat of Roman Catholicism and the decline of evangelical doctrine led to the founding of the Evangelical Alliance in 1846 to sponsor conferences and promote biblical Christianity, an international week of prayer, aid to Protestant minorities, and the evangelization of the world. A century later, it became a founding member of the WORLD EVAN-GELICAL FELLOWSHIP (1951). Anglican Evangeli-calism advanced under the tutelage of JOHN R. W. STOTT, James I. Packer, and Anglicans in other countries such as FESTO KIVENGERE in Uganda and Leon Morris in Australia.

Protestant missions began as a result of renewal movements subsequent to the Reformation. While the Reformers exhibited little interest in evangelizing non-Christians (*see* REFORMATION AND MISSION), the rediscovering of the gospel and the value placed on the translation of the Scriptures into the vernacular languages made a profound impact on the course of the missions movement. Indicative of the complex origins of Protestant missions, early efforts varied from chaplains working for the Dutch East India Company, to Puritan missions to Native Americans in New England, and in England the founding of the Society for Promoting Christian Knowledge (1698–99) and the SOCIETY FOR THE PROPAGATION OF THE GOSPEL IN FOREIGN PARTS (SPG) (1701). From Germany came the DANISH-HALLE MISSION (1705) and MORAVIAN MISSIONS (1732), the latter under the leadership of the pietist NIKOLAUS LUDWIG VON ZINZENDORF.

Missions gained more ground with the publication of WILLIAM CAREY's *Enquiry into the Obligations of Christians to Use Means for the Conversion of the Heathen* and the organization of the BAPTIST MISSIONARY SOCIETY, both in 1792. Many more societies emerged, including the LONDON MISSIONARY SOCIETY (1795), the CHURCH MISSIONARY SOCIETY (1799), the AMERICAN BOARD OF COMMISSIONERS FOR FOREIGN MISSIONS (1810), the Wesleyan Methodist Missionary Society (1813), African Baptist Missionary Society (1815), Presbyterian Board of Foreign Missions (1831), Woman's Union Missionary Society (1861), and the Woman's Foreign Missionary Society of the Methodist Episcopal Church (1869). The evangelical unity of these agencies and the several hundred mission societies that followed laid the theological basis for COMITY agreements in the nineteenth century and the international missionary conferences (e.g., CENTENARY CONFERENCE ON THE PROTESTANT MISSIONS OF THE WORLD [LONDON MISSIONARY CONFERENCE, 1888]).

University and college students were inspired to dedicate their lives to foreign missions at Dwight L. Moody's Northfield Conference in Massachusetts in 1886. At the gathering, ARTHUR T. PIERSON, an ardent evangelical and later editor of the *Missionary Review of the World*, challenged the students with the watchword, "The evangelization of the world in this generation." From this event arose the STUDENT VOLUNTEER MOVEMENT FOR FOREIGN MISSIONS (SVM) and leaders such as JOHN R. MOTT (World Student Christian Federation) and Robert P. Wilder (SVM traveling secretary).

As the missions movement progressed, practices that centered on establishing schools and charitable institutions came under fire from critics who favored apostolic methods (e.g., Matt. 10:7–10). Usually impelled by premillennial eschatology and dissatisfied with the slow rate of conversions, independent FAITH MISSIONS (e.g., CHINA INLAND MISSION founded by J. Hudson Taylor in 1865) aimed their attention primarily at direct evangelism. Radical evangelicals like A. B. SIMPSON, founder of the CHRISTIAN AND MISSIONARY ALLIANCE (1881), anticipated that in the end-times the outpouring of the Holy Spirit (Joel 2:28–29) would bring miraculous SIGNS AND WONDERS (Acts 5:12) that would once more accompany gospel proclamation. A novel approach to training unfolded with "Bible institutes," which prepared ministers and missionaries for the FAITH MISSIONS. Early schools included the Missionary Training Institute (Nyack College) founded by Simpson in 1882; Chicago Evangelization Society (Moody Bible Institute) by Dwight L. Moody in 1889; Boston Missionary Training Institute (Gordon College and Gordon-Conwell Theological Seminary) by A. J. GORDON in 1889; and Toronto Bible Training School (Tyndale College and Seminary) by Elmore Harris in 1894.

In the twentieth century, doubts about the need for sending missionaries took a heavy toll on Protestant missions and after midcentury, the number of missionaries in most of the older denominations declined. In contrast, the missions that remained conservative in theology grew. Networking among them resulted in the formation of the INTERDENOMINATIONAL FOREIGN MISSION ASSOCIATION (1971) and the EVANGELICAL FELLOWSHIP OF MISSION AGENCIES (1945), an NAE affiliate. Subsequent efforts at cooperation have included the CONGRESS ON THE CHURCH'S WORLDWIDE MISSION (WHEATON CONGRESS, 1966), WORLD CONGRESS ON EVANGELISM (BERLIN CONGRESS, 1966), LAUSANNE CONGRESS ON WORLD EVANGELISM (1974), and International Conference for Itinerant Evangelists (1983). Regional networks have been formed to further evangelism and achieve other objectives (e.g., theological education, social action, relief work).

In addition to nondenominational faith missions, a variety of parachurch organizations have extended vital services. Along with the contributions of the United Bible Societies (1946), WYCLIFFE BIBLE TRANSLATORS (1934) has trained workers to reduce languages to writing, produce grammars, and translate the Scriptures. Continuing the tradition of the SVM, Inter-Varsity Christian Fellowship (1936) and its triennial URBANA MISSION CONFERENCES in the United States have inspired thousands of students to become missionaries. Youth With a Mission (YWAM [1960]) has created opportunities for youth to evangelize overseas. Mission Aviation Fellowship

(1944) has provided air transport and communications assistance for missionaries. World Vision (1950) has focused on relief and development activities. Others have engaged in publishing ventures, and radio and television evangelism. The INTERNATIONAL COUNCIL FOR EVANGELICAL THEOLOGICAL EDUCATION (ICETE) (1980) has encouraged the upgrading of standards in Bible colleges and seminaries and promoted regional accrediting associations.

Pentecostalism ushered in a new pattern in missions, based on the radical expectancy of miracles in ministry (e.g., physical healings, deliverance from chemical addictions), glossolalia and the gifts of the Holy Spirit for spiritual empowerment, and the encouragement of INDIGENOUS CHURCHES. Embracing many of the same beliefs, the charismatic movement influenced missions in church bodies connected to NCC and WCC. Independent charismatics have found assistance for their missions in the Association of International Mission Services (1985). Believing that supernatural interventions and "power encounters" will help bring closure to the GREAT COMMISSION before the imminent return of Christ, "Third Wave" and "New Apostolic Reformation" mission endeavors have grown under the tutelage of John Wimber, Charles H. Kraft, and C. Peter Wagner (*see also* NEW APOSTOLIC REFORMATION MISSIONS).

Evangelical Christianity has grown significantly outside of North America and Europe in the last half-century. Major advances have taken place in Latin America, sub-Saharan Africa, Asia, and Oceania. Christians in these areas, the majority of whom now exhibit features of Pentecostal/charismatic spirituality and are vibrantly concerned for world evangelization. They have begun sending out their own missionaries in one of the momentous developments in modern Christianity (*see also* NON-WESTERN MISSION BOARDS AND SOCIETIES).

GARY B. MCGEE

Bibliography. D. W. Bebbington, *Evangelicalism in Modern Britain: A History for the 1730s to the 1980s;* D. G. Bloesch, *The Evangelical Renaissance;* J. A. Carpenter and W. R. Shenk, eds., *Earthen Vessels: American Evangelicals and Foreign Missions, 1880–1980;* M. Dieter, *The Holiness Movement of the Nineteenth Century;* K. A. Fournier with W. D. Watkins, *A House United? Evangelicals and Catholics Together;* R. A. N. Kydd, *Healing Through The Centuries: Models For Understanding;* G. M. Marsden, *Fundamentalism and American Culture;* idem, *Reforming Fundamentalism;* G. A Rawlyk, ed., *The Canadian Protestant Experience, 1760–1990;* G. A. Rawlyk and M. A. Noll, eds., *Amazing Grace: Evangelicalism in Australia, Britain, Canada, and the United States;* M. C. Sernett, *Black Religion and American Evangelicalism;* F. E. Stoeffler, ed., *Continental Pietism and Early American Christianity;* V. Synan, *The Holiness-Pentecostal Tradition: Charismatic Movements in the Twentieth Century.*

Evangelical Theology. The basic relationship between missions and evangelical theology can be defined in terms of two doctrines: bibliology and soteriology.

Evangelicals' view of Scripture is characterized by a strong commitment to divine inspiration, inerrancy, and the grammatical-historical method of exegesis. But more than any other factor, it has been the evangelicals' unyielding adherence to the unconditional authority of Scripture that has shaped their approach to mission. Evangelicals view the BIBLE as a reservoir of divinely revealed truth, its authority being traced back to the absolute authority of God himself. That being the case, all prescriptive statements of Scripture must be followed to the letter.

This conviction naturally leads to an emphasis on obedience as a motivation for service. Compliance with God's own commission to make disciples of all nations (Matt. 28:19) is a theme that has echoed down through every epoch of the modern missionary movement and has repeatedly loosed new waves of activity. The STUDENT VOLUNTEER MOVEMENT is a good example of this. Between 1890 and 1920 the movement was able to motivate upwards of 1,800 volunteers by appealing to the Christian's responsibility to go. Typical of this are the words of one of the movement's leaders. According to ROBERT E. SPEER, "everyone of us rests under a sort of obligation to give life and time and possessions to the evangelization of the souls everywhere that have never heard of Jesus Christ, and we are bound to go, unless we can offer some sure ground of exemption" (Wallstrom, 16). He firmly believed that the only thing that could prevent successful evangelization of the world was the Christian's disobedience.

The same motive, obedience, still characterizes much of evangelicalism's recruitment of new missionaries. And the case is almost exclusively based on Christ's authoritative command as recorded in Matthew 28:19–20.

Soteriology is the other doctrine that has shaped the evangelical approach to mission. According to evangelical understanding of salvation, the necessity of mission arises, on the one hand, out of the spiritual need of humanity, and on the other hand, out of the redemptive work of Christ. As a result of the fall into sin human beings are alienated from God, live under his anger, and will suffer eternal damnation. However, Jesus' vicarious death and resurrection achieved a basis for justification. This basic soteriological orientation has been applied to the missionary task in two ways.

First, every individual who has not accepted the message of God's grace by faith is lost. There are no exceptions, since Scripture clearly expresses the fact that all have sinned (Rom. 3:23), that all sinners are subject to God's wrath (Eph. 2:3). Of course, it has become especially difficult for moderns to accept the idea that people who through no fault of their own have not heard will be damned. Recently there have been several attempts to reevaluate or soften the impact of these verses. Nevertheless, the lostness of the unevangelized has been and remains the position of most evangelicals (*see also* ANNIHILATION and UNIVERSALISM).

Second, the offer of salvation is addressed to all of humanity. Perhaps it is because of the uncomfortable consequences of the previous thesis that some seek a way out by interpreting passages like 2 Corinthians 5:18 in a universalistic way. But, whatever discomfort or reservations they might have, most evangelicals strictly reject all forms of universalism, since the salvation which has been made available to all can only be appropriated by means of an individual act of faith. As a result, evangelical missionary efforts have been consistently driven by a desire to reach everyone with the gospel message. This has been done under the banner of slogans such as "evangelize the world in this generation." And a great deal has been made of statistics that show the disproportionate relationship between the Christian missionary force and that part of the world's population that remains UNEVANGELIZED.

Combined with the emphasis on the necessity of individual faith, this global outreach places the personal act of the will at center stage. All other responses (e.g., good works or general religiosity) are rejected as false or misleading and are in all likelihood some form of SYNCRETISM, in which case, the essential element of the gospel, the necessity of CONVERSION, is lost. There is no way around personal faith in Christ and this message of salvation must be offered to all.

All of this has had a pronounced and sometimes stifling effect on the level of theological activity among evangelicals engaged in mission. The basic theological framework described above is so widely accepted that one may indeed speak of a consensus. This is borne out by the documents produced by various conferences convened by evangelicals, which reflect a high degree of theological commonality. But one of the unintended results is that many within the evangelical missiological community have assumed that because there is general agreement on basic theological issues we should focus our resources exclusively on the practical contingencies of completing that task. Driven by a desire for achievement, they have abandoned theological reflection and have turned to the secular marketplace in search of methodological guarantors of success. Encouraged by the prospect of new levels of productivity, they uncritically apply social scientific or managerial techniques to essentially theological issues (*see also* SOCIAL SCIENCES).

Unfortunately, this tends to obviate the advantages of consensus, by allowing activism to blind us to the theologically fluid nature of missionary encounter. For example, the ongoing encounter with non-Christian religions generates a steady stream of theological questions. Theological consensus does not obviate the need for what might be called dynamic field theologizing, since problems of a primarily theological nature do not yield to nontheological (social scientific) solutions.

This form of theological atrophication would not be so difficult to overcome if it had not been replaced by other, nontheological paradigms. Perhaps it is the elevation of pragmatism to the status of a missiological norm that has led to an uncritical acceptance of applied social science. This trend has continued unabated during the last few years. There can be little doubt that the insights and techniques of social science are useful. Nevertheless as Os Guinness observes, "it is distressing to witness the lemming-like rush of church leaders who forget theology in the charge after the latest insights of sociology—regardless of where the ideas come from or where they lead" (Guinness, 157).

Just where have these ideas led? To a missionary enterprise in which there is little place for God and his enabling Spirit. The often stunning effectiveness of these methodologies has deceived some into thinking that (or acting as though) ministry can be managed quite nicely without God. If human agency is viewed as the primary engine of missions, it should come as no surprise that theology has been neglected. But if the majority of missiological problems are actually theological in nature, theological skills will have to be recultivated and reasserted in every area of mission.

EDWARD ROMMEN

Bibliography. H. Berkhof, *Christian Faith;* D. G. Bloesch, *A Theology of Word and Spirit;* G. D. Fee, *God's Empowering Presence;* T. N. Finger, *Christian Theology: An Eschatological Approach;* O. Guinness and J. Seel, *No God But God;* S. J. Grenz, *Revisioning Evangelical Theology;* idem, *Theology for the Community of God;* P. K. Jewett, *God, Creation, and Revelation;* G. R. Lewis and B. A. Demarest, *Integrative Theology;* A. E. McGrath, *Christian Theology: An Introduction;* E. Rommen and H. Netland, eds., *Christianity and the Religions: A Biblical Theology of World Religions;* J. Sanders, *No Other Name;* C. Van Engen, *Mission on the Way;* T. Wallstrom, *The Creation of a Student Movement to Evangelize the World;* O. Weber, *Foundations of Dogmatics.*

Evangelism. Evangelism announces that salvation has come. The verb "evangelize" literally means to bear good news. In the noun form, it translates "gospel" or "evangel." The angels' proclamation of Christ's birth is typical of the more than 130 times the term in its various forms occurs in the New Testament: "Behold, I bring you good tidings of great joy, which shall be to all people. For there is born to you this day in the city of David a Savior, who is Christ the Lord" (Luke 2:10–11).

The Hebrew term translated in the Septuagint by the same word appears in the writings of Isaiah: "How beautiful upon the mountains are the feet of him that brings good news . . ." (Isa. 52:7). Again, speaking of the ministry of the coming Messiah, the prophet writes, "The Spirit of the LORD God is upon Me; because the LORD has anointed Me to preach good tidings . . ." (Isa. 61:1, 2).

Jesus interpreted his mission as fulfillment of this promise (Luke 4:18, 19). He saw himself as an evangelist, announcing the coming of the KINGDOM OF GOD. This message was to be proclaimed in the context of demonstrated compassion for the bruised and forgotten people of the world.

At this point, there is often confusion among Christians today. Some contend that evangelism involves only the gospel declaration, while others identify it essentially with establishing a caring presence in society or seeking to rectify injustice.

It should be clear that both are necessary. One without the other leaves a distorted impression of the good news. If Jesus had not borne the sorrows of people and performed deeds of mercy among them, we might question his concern. On the other hand, if he had not articulated the gospel, we would not have known why he came, nor how we could be saved. To bind up the wounds of the dying, while withholding the message that could bring deliverance to their souls, would leave them still in bondage. Mere social concern does not address the ultimate need of a lost world (*see also* EVANGELISM AND SOCIAL RESPONSIBILITY).

A Revelation of God. What makes the announcement so compelling is its divine source. Contrary to the opinion of popular humanism, evangelism does not originate in the valiant groping of persons seeking a higher life. Rather, it comes as a revelation of God who is ever seeking to make a people to display his glory.

The deposit of this divine quest is the canon of inspired Scripture. As the Word of God, "without error in all that it affirms" (The Lausanne Covenant, Section 2) the BIBLE is the objective authority for the gospel. To be sure, it does not pretend to answer every curious question of humankind, but what is written does show God's way of salvation to an honest heart. Not surprisingly, then, theological systems that compromise Scriptural verities do not produce evangelism.

The revelation makes us see how we have all turned to our own way. Such arrogance cannot be ignored by a just God, since it is an affront to his holiness. Inevitably, then, the sinner must be separated from God. Furthermore, his wrath upon iniquity cannot be annulled as long as the cause of evil remains. Since life is unending, all the spiritual consequences of sin continue on forever in HELL.

Knowing, therefore, what is at stake, evangelism strikes at the heart of SIN. Though the disclosure of human rebellion and its result may be bad news, still the gospel shines through it all, for God judges so that he might save.

Incarnate in Christ. The redeeming work of the Trinity focuses in the person of the Son. In Jesus Christ evangelism becomes incarnate. Jesus is not God apart from the human, nor the human apart from God; he is God and mankind united in one Personality. In this perfect union of eternal consciousness, Christ becomes the reconciling center of the gospel. All that took place in salvation before his coming was in anticipation of him. All that has taken place since his coming is accomplished in his Name—the only "Name under heaven given among men by which we must be saved" (Acts 4:12).

The apostolic gospel does not minimize the exclusive claims of Christ. He alone is Lord, and with "all authority" (Matt. 28:18), he stands among us, and says, "I am the way, the truth, and the life. No one comes to the Father except through me" (John 14:6).

His mission reaches its climax on the hill of Calvary. There in the fullness of time Jesus bore our sins in his own body on the cross, suffering in our stead, "the just for the unjust, that he might bring us to God" (1 Peter 3:18).

Christ's bodily resurrection and subsequent ascension into heaven bring the cross forcibly to our attention. For when one dies who has the power to rise from the grave, in all honesty we must ask why he died in the first place. To this penetrating question the gospel unequivocally answers, "Jesus . . . was delivered for our offenses, and was raised again for our purification" (Rom. 4:24, 25).

Experiencing Grace. In confronting the reality of the cross, we are made supremely aware of God's love. It is "not that we loved God, but that he loved us," and "gave himself" for us (1 John 4:10; Gal. 2:20). Perhaps we could understand one giving his life for a righteous person, or for a friend, but "God demonstrates his own love toward us, in that while we were still sinners, Christ died for us" (Rom. 5:8).

Heaven is the wonder of the gospel. Nothing deserved! Nothing earned! In our complete helplessness, bankrupt of all natural goodness, God moved in and did for us what we could not do for ourselves. It is all of GRACE—unmerited love. From beginning to end, salvation is the "gift of God" (Eph. 2:8).

The invitation is to all. "Whosoever will may come" (Rev. 22:17). Though the enabling power to believe is entirely of grace, the responsibility to respond to God's word rests upon the sinner. We must receive the gift in true repentance and faith.

It means that we choose to turn from the pretense of self-righteousness, and with a broken and contrite spirit, trust ourselves unto the loving arms of Jesus. Until there is such a CONVERSION, no one can enter the kingdom of heaven (Matt. 18:3).

Through this commitment, the believer is introduced to a life of forgiveness, love and true freedom. "Old things have passed away; behold, all things have become new" (2 Cor. 5:17). There is an actual partaking of the divine nature, so that a regenerated person begins to live in the Savior. It is this inward dynamic of sanctification that makes Christianity a saving force for holiness in the world. Out of it flows compassionate deeds of mercy and bold evangelistic outreach.

A Ministering Church. Faithful witness of the gospel calls forth the church. All who heed the call and live by faith in the Son of God—past, present, and future—become part of this communion of the saints.

As the church is created by evangelism, so it becomes the agent of God in dispensing the gospel to others. Unfortunately, our mission to the whole world may be forgotten, and we accept the same delusion as did the self-serving religious community of Jesus' day. Their attitude was seen in bold relief at the cross when they said in derision, "He saved others; himself he cannot save" (Mark 15:31). What they failed to realize was that Jesus had not come to save himself; he came to save us; "The Son of Man did not come to be served, but to serve, and to give his life as a ransom for many" (Mark 10:4); he came "to seek and to save that which was lost" (Luke 19:10).

Those who take up his cross, as we are bidden, enter into this mission. In this service, whatever our gifts, every person in the church is "sent" from God, even as we are called into Christ's ministry (John 17:18; 20:21).

Underscoring this mission, before returning to the Father in heaven, Jesus commanded his church to "go and make disciples of all nations" (Matt. 28:18). The GREAT COMMISSION is not some special assignment for a few clerical workers; it is a way of life; it is the way Jesus directed his life with a few disciples while he was among us, and now the way he expects his church to follow.

Wrapped up in this lifestyle is his plan to evangelize the world. For disciples—learners of Christ—will follow him, and as they learn more of him, they will grow in his likeness, while also becoming involved in his ministry. So they, too, will begin to make disciples, teaching them in turn to do the same, until, through the process of multiplication, the whole world will hear the gospel.

Bringing people to Christ is not the only expression of the church's ministry, of course. But it is the most crucial, for it makes possible every other church activity. Without evangelism the church would soon become extinct.

The Way of the Spirit. Let it be understood, however, that this work is not contrived by human ingenuity. God the Holy Spirit is the enabler. What God administers as the Father and reveals as the Son, he accomplishes as the Third Member of the Trinity. So the mission of Christ through the church becomes the acts of the Spirit. He lifts up the Word, and as Jesus is glorified, convicted men and women cry out to be saved. Evangelism is finally God's work, not ours. We are merely the channel through which the Spirit of Christ makes disciples.

That is why even to begin the Christian life one must be "born again" (John 3:3). "It is the Spirit who gives life; the flesh profits nothing" (John 6:63). Likewise, it is the Spirit who sustains and nourishes the developing relationship. He calls the church to ministry. He leads us in prayer. He dispenses gifts for service. Through the Spirit's strength faith comes alive in obedience and by his impartation of grace, we are being conformed to the image of our Lord.

Everything, then, depends upon the Spirit's possession of the sent ones, the church. Just as those first disciples were told to tarry until they received the promised power, so must we (Luke 24:49; Acts 2:4). The spiritual inducement at Pentecost, by whatever name is called, must be a reality in our lives, not as a distant memory, but as a present experience of the reigning Christ. Hindrances that obstruct his dominion must be confessed, and our hearts cleansed so that the Spirit of holiness can fill us with the love of God. Though we can never contain all of him, he wants all of us—to love and adore him with all that we are and all that we hope to be. Any evangelistic effort that circumvents this provision will be as lifeless as it is barren. The secret of New Testament evangelism is to let the Holy Spirit have his way in our lives.

The Glorious Consummation. Whatever may be our method of presenting the gospel, and wherever God may place us in his service, we labor in the confidence that his world mission will be finished. Evangelism, as the heartbeat of Christian ministry, simply directs our energy to that goal toward which history is moving, when the completed church will be presented "faultless before the presence of his glory with exceeding joy" (Jude 24).

Indeed, in Christ the KINGDOM OF GOD is already present in the hearts of those that worship him, and the day is hastening when his kingdom will come to fruition in the new Jerusalem. The church militant, like an ever-advancing army, will at last shatter the principalities of Satan and storm the gates of hell. In the councils of eternity the celebration has already begun (Rev. 7:9, 10: 11:15). Anything we do which does not contribute to that destiny is an exercise in futility.

Our work now on earth may seem slow, and sometimes discouraging, but we may be sure that God's program will not suffer defeat. Someday the trumpet will sound, and the Son of Man, with his legions, shall descend from heaven in trailing clouds of glory, and he will reign over his people gathered from every tongue, every tribe, every nation. This is the reality which always rings through evangelism.

The King is coming! While it does not yet appear what we shall be, "we know that, when he is revealed, we shall be like him" (1 John 3:2). And before him every knee shall bow and "every tongue confess that Jesus Christ is Lord, to the glory of God the Father" (Phil. 2:11).

ROBERT E. COLEMAN

SEE ALSO Cross-Cultural Evangelism; Cross-Cultural Ministry; Crusade Evangelism; Lifestyle Evangelism; Presence Evangelism; AND Proclamation Evangelism.

Bibliography. R. E. Coleman, *The Master Plan of Evangelism*; J. I. Packer, *Evangelism and the Sovereignty of God*; E. L. Towns, *Evangelism and Church Growth: A Practical Encyclopedia*; *Equipping for Evangelism*.

Evangelism and Social Responsibility.

Over the past two centuries the modern Protestant movement has planted vibrant churches around the world. Today, the center of Christianity is moving to these younger churches. But this growth is not without its problems. One area of deep concern in many evangelical circles is the division between evangelism and social concerns. Despite many efforts to present a whole gospel, the effects of this dualism in missions and churches are still apparent.

The roots of this division go back to medieval Europe, where churches and monasteries were centers of worship, evangelism, literacy, relief, medicine, and agriculture. The WORLDVIEW of the Middle Ages, rooted in biblical thought, divided reality between the Creator and the creation. In this view God was intimately involved in all of his creation, and all creation, including both heavenly and earthly concerns, was one. That same unity is evident in the ministry of Jesus, which reflects a wholism that does not seem natural today.

By the eighteenth century, the church felt called to worship and to mission, but education, medicine, and agriculture became the domains of science and the modern nation-state. The shift was due mainly to the rediscovery of Greek thought, especially Greek dualism, which separated spirit and matter, supernatural and natural, and heavenly and earthly affairs. The absorption of dualism theologically was formalized by Thomas Aquinas. The result was the increasingly sharp distinction between religion and science, or between eternal and earthly needs.

On the surface, the modern mission movement began in the nineteenth century with a whole gospel. Missionaries planted churches, and established schools, hospitals, handicraft projects, and agricultural centers. They cared for the starving during times of famine, and called for social justice. Underneath these activities, however, the dualistic perspective persisted. It did not help that missionaries often cooperated with the colonial agenda, the goal of which was "civilizing" their new territories. Evangelism and church planting were seen as the marks of Christianity. Education, medicine, and agriculture were signs of civilization. In many cases, however, people accepted science, technology, and other manifestations of modern rational thought introduced by the missionaries, but rejected the gospel they proclaimed. That is why some observers conclude that Christian missionaries have unwittingly been a force for SECULARIZATION worldwide.

A second consequence of this dualism was that missions organized schools, hospitals, and agricultural projects based on Western models that did not fit local contexts. The operation of these institutions reflected the division between evangelism and social concern. Specialists provided services in a compartmentalized way that communicated something less than an integrated gospel. Furthermore, these institutions required large amounts of money and Western-style organizational skill, most of which had to be imported from outside. Later, when missions began handing over the administration of the institutions to local churches, local leaders often saw them as heavy burdens which their churches could not easily sustain.

The division between evangelism and social concern reached its peak in the early twentieth century in the battles between liberals and fundamentalists over the emerging Social Gospel movement. Liberal churches virtually abandoned aggressive evangelism in favor of relief and development ministries of all kinds. Conservative churches increasingly focused their attention on evangelism and church planting, and left relief and development tasks to parachurch agencies. That emphasis has created the impression in many parts of the world that the church deals with ultimate concerns, but has little to contribute to the urgent needs of the contemporary world.

In recent years there have been efforts in evangelical circles to restore a holistic understanding of the gospel. In 1966 the CONGRESS ON THE CHURCH'S WORLDWIDE MISSION was held at Wheaton, Illinois, sponsored by the Evangelical Foreign Mission Association (now the EVANGELICAL FELLOWSHIP OF MISSION AGENCIES) and the INTERDENOMINATIONAL FOREIGN MISSION ASSOCIATION, agencies that represented at that time 102 mission boards and 30,000 missionaries. The congress, which was comprised of nearly 1,000 delegates from 71 countries, wrote *The Wheaton Declaration*, in which they called on the church to address contemporary issues such as racism, war, the population explosion, poverty, and the disintegration of the family. This growing concern for a Christian response to social problems was due, in part, to the influence of the large number of participants from outside the United States whose churches could not ignore the social evils around them. Also in 1966, the WORLD CONGRESS ON EVANGELISM gathered in Berlin, sponsored by *Christianity Today*. That congress reaffirmed the importance of proclaiming the gospel, but in the closing statement condemned racism and called for repentance and unity among Christians in addressing the world's desperate needs. In the regional congresses that followed (Singapore, Minneapolis, Bogota), the involvement of the church in social issues was a recurring theme. In 1973, the Workshop on Evangelicals and Social Concern drafted the *Chicago Declaration of Evangelical Social Concern* which represented another attempt to transcend the traditional dichotomy between evangelism and social responsibility.

The LAUSANNE CONGRESS ON WORLD EVANGELIZATION (1974) took a major step toward resolving the tension between these two concerns by affirming that both evangelism and social responsibility are essential to the mission of the church. The Lausanne Covenant stated that "The message of salvation also implies a message of judgment upon every form of alienation, oppression, and discrimination, and we should not be afraid to denounce evil and injustice wherever they exist" (section 5). The plea to keep evangelism and social concerns together was strengthened by a statement of support that was signed by some five hundred Lausanne participants. This effort to bring evangelism and social responsibility together generated sharp criticisms on the part of some mission leaders in North America. But, particularly for those in the Two-Thirds World, it was an invitation to proclaim a whole gospel. That conviction was validated again at the All India Conference on Evangelical Social Action (1979), the Second Latin American Congress on Evangelism (1979), and the Consultation on Simple Lifestyle (1980) sponsored by the Lausanne Committee and the WORLD EVANGELICAL FELLOWSHIP. Although attempts were made at the WORLD CONSULTATION ON WORLD EVANGELIZATION (Pattaya, 1980) to focus exclusively on world evangelism, many delegates called for the inclusion of social issues in the conference statement.

The need to clarify the relationship between evangelism and social responsibility led to the CONSULTATION ON THE RELATIONSHIP BETWEEN EVANGELISM AND SOCIAL RESPONSIBILITY (Grand Rapids, 1982) sponsored by the Lausanne Committee for World Evangelization, and the CONSULTATION ON THE CHURCH IN RESPONSE TO HUMAN NEED (Wheaton, 1983) sponsored by the World Evangelical Fellowship. Both affirmed that evangelism cannot be divorced from meaningful involvement with people in all their needs. In recent years, Christian agencies such as World Vision International, Food for the Hungry, the Mennonite Central Committee, and the Adventist Development and Relief Agency have initiated theological and administrative reflections on how to implement the proclamation of the whole gospel (*see also* HOLISM, BIBLICAL).

It is clear that as long as evangelism and social concern are seen as two separate entities that need to be integrated, the dualism that has weakened missions will remain. Some will reduce one to the other: conservatives will see social ministries as means to evangelistic ends and liberals will see social ministries as ends in themselves. Others will try to balance the two by claiming that one is more important than the other, with many conservatives arguing that evangelism is the top priority while liberals counter that the church must concentrate on other, more pressing needs. Both approaches fail to integrate the different strands of the gospel into a single whole.

We will proclaim a whole gospel only when we reject the dualism between supernatural and natural realities, religion and science, and evangelism and social concerns. Many young churches in other cultures have taken a step in this direction by making no distinction between the spiritual and the material, or between supernatural and natural realms. Many of them model integrated ministries to whole persons and societies. Evangelical mission agencies and churches are catching on as well. In partnership with younger churches, they are beginning to focus on people more than tasks, on holistic development more than relief, on transformation more than the simple delivery of services (*see also* TRANSFORMATIONAL DEVELOPMENT), and on the formation of living communities of faith rather than bureaucratic institutions. Some agencies are backing away from the overspecialization that characterizes Western approaches to life and are offering a more generalized sort of training with holistic ministry in mind (*see also* HOLISTIC MISSION).

The push for holism draws strength from the rediscovery of the church as a healing community where Christians gather to WORSHIP, to bear WITNESS to the world, and to minister healing, in the fullest sense of the term, to people. It is also fueled by a renewed emphasis on a theology of the kingdom of God, within which evangelism, church, ministry, and prophetic witness are parts of the whole. This kingdom, however, cannot be defined by theories of modern utopias, as in Marxism and capitalism. It is defined by Christ, its King. He and his incarnation as a human unite God's concerns for all creation, now and for eternity. His salvation includes not only eternal life in the presence of God, but also a new earth characterized by righteousness, peace, justice, and fullness of life. In a word, Shalom is the ideal to which individual Christians as well as the corporate church aspires. As Dan Fountain points out, "God's plan for the world is this: that all persons everywhere, in every nation, know God's saving health and be delivered from disobedience, disruption, despair, disease and all that would destroy our wholeness."

PAUL G. HIEBERT AND MONTE B. COX

Bibliography. B. Bradshaw, *Bridging the Gap: Evangelism, Development and Shalom;* E. J. Elliston, ed., *Christian Relief and Development: Developing Workers for Effective Ministry;* R. Greenway, *Together Again!;* B. J. Nicholls, *Word and Deed: Evangelism and Social Responsibility;* C. R. Padilla, *Transformation* 2:3 (1985): 27–32; E. Ram, ed., *Transforming Health: Christian Approaches to Healing and Wholeness;* T. Sine, ed., *The Church in Response to Human Need;* C. Van Engen, *Mission on the Way.*

Evangelist. The term "evangelist" is used three times in the New Testament: Acts 21:8 refers to Philip as the evangelist; Ephesians 4:11 refers to the evangelist as a gift or office of the church; and in 2 Timothy 4:5 Timothy is exhorted to do the work of an evangelist. These references indicate that the evangelist is a divinely gifted specialist in the work of the church.

During the second century, evidence indicates that there were great numbers of Christians who became full-time wandering evangelists. As missionaries they set out on long journeys endeavoring to preach the gospel to those who had never heard.

The evangelist in many ways parallels the APOSTLE. The apostle is described in the *Didache* as a wandering missionary. Such a close association has led scholars, such as Adolf Harnack, to conclude that there was little distinction between apostles and evangelists. Because the apostles were known as those who preach the gospel (Gal. 1:8; outside of the New Testament, *see* 1 Clem. 42.1; Polycarp, Ep. 6:3; and Barn. 8:3), the evangelists were closely linked with them. A frequently quoted dictum was, "Every apostle is an evangelist but not every evangelist is an apostle." The evangelist continued the work of the apostles long after the technical sense of an apostle as one who was an eyewitness of Jesus' earthly ministry (Acts 1:21–22) ceased.

Evangelists also served as apologists, giving able defenses of the faith to the secular world. Quadradus has been thought by many to be the earliest Christian apologist. The historian Eusebius refers to him as an evangelist who wrote a defense against the false charges of the heathen in order to defend his fellow Christians. He addressed his defense of Christianity to the Emperor Hadrian.

Other early evangelists served in the missionary capacity such as PANTAENUS, who took the gospel as far as India. Pantaenus was the founder and first teacher of the theological school in Alexandria around A.D. 180. He was primarily a missionary theologian. When he arrived in India, he discovered that many people had a copy of the Gospel of Matthew. Eusebius notes that these copies had been left by the apostle Bartholomew during a preaching tour through India.

From the beginning of Christianity, the evangelist has played an important role in reaching the non-Christian population. As missionaries, apologists, and theological educators, evangelists have played vital roles in the growth of the church.

In contemporary times, evangelists have been particularly effective through the medium of mass evangelism (*see also* MASS COMMUNICATION). Evangelists such as BILL BRIGHT, BILLY GRAHAM, LUIS PALAU, and Ravi Zacharias have seen great impact in reaching people through specialized tools (e.g., tracts), mass media (radio, television, the JESUS FILM), crusades (*see* CRUSADE EVANGELISM), and other significant evangelistic methods.

FRANK HARBER

Bibliography. J. D. Douglas, ed., *The Work of an Evangelist;* idem, ed., *The Calling of the Evangelist;* M. Green, *Evangelism in the Early Church.*

Evangelistic Mandate. *See* GREAT COMMISSION.

Evangelization, Measurement of. A major biblical concept standing for human response and responsibility with regard to the implementation of God's mission to the world. The term can be defined as the whole process of spreading the Good News of the KINGDOM OF GOD, the extent to which the Good News has been spread, the extent of awareness of Christianity, Christ, and the gospel. It is based on the central biblical verb *euangelizō*, which with its immediate cognates occurs 25 times in the Greek Old Testament (Septuagint) and 132 times in the New Testament, with its meaning similar to the English transliteration *evangelize*. The Greek verb means to spread the good news of the gospel, with signs following, in both supernatural power and compassionate deed; to preach, to persuade, to call to faith in Christ. The Greek verb has 42 synonyms in biblical Greek, and the English verb has 700 synonyms in current English, which can be reduced to 400 distinct and different dimensions of evangelization.

Evangelization can be seen as obedience to the seven mandates of Christ's GREAT COMMISSION: Receive (the Spirit)! Go! Witness! Proclaim! Disciple! Baptize! Train! The church's endeavors to obey this Commission have resulted in some 45 major types or varieties of Christian ministry and outreach. Down through the centuries, the church's concern with evangelization has resulted in over 1,400 distinct global plans to evangelize the world, some 300 of which are still being energetically implemented today.

In order to keep track of the status of evangelization and progress with its implementation, the world's churches and missions spend about U.S. $750 billion each year on their annual censuses. This status is measured and enumerated for individuals, for peoples, for language speakers, for cities, for countries, for continents, or for the entire world. It enables the computation, for any specific population, of the number of evangelistic opportunities people receive, per year per capita. It also enables the trichotomy to be formed whereby the world and its populations can be categorized as either World A (the unevangelized, being populations with individuals numbering less than 50% evangelized, but with church members less than 60%), and World C (the Christian world, with church members numbering more than 60%). This enables mission planners to see clearly the distinction between, on the one hand, the world's 4 billion non-Christians, as priority target for the sharing of all the benefits of Christ and his kingdom, and on the other hand, the world's already heavily Christianized populations with strong enough home ministries to not require foreign missionary resources.

Evangelization is widely recognized as dangerous business. Throughout 20 centuries and 70 generations of Christian mission, 60 million Christians have become martyrs for Christ—believers who have lost their lives, prematurely, in situations of witness, as a result of human hostility. Every day around 500 Christians scattered across 100 countries are murdered because of their faith. Inevitably, persons at highest risk are those implementing evangelization—bishops, evangelists, colporteurs, and foreign missionaries. MARTYRDOM has thus become, empirically, the major single factor involved in world evangelization.

DAVID B. BARRETT

SEE ALSO Quantitative Research.

Evans, Helen E. (1930–). American missionary to Vietnam and Indonesia. Educated at Wheaton College (Illinois) (B.A., 1946) and the Nyack Missionary Training College (New York) (1949), she served as a rural Bible teacher under the New England Fellowship of Evangelicals (1946–48, 1950). She was sent by the CHRISTIAN AND MISSIONARY ALLIANCE (CMA) to French Indo-China in 1951 after French-language studies in Paris.

After learning the language of the Koho, a mountain dwelling people in the Central Highlands near Dalat, Vietnam, she served there twenty-three years as a teacher, translator, and youth worker. She was a regular faculty member at the Koho Bible Institute, which was established in the 1930s by Herbert Jackson, Helen's uncle. She was a primary contributing translator for the Koho New Testament (published 1967) and translated hymns and choruses for the Koho church hymnal. Alongside her academic and translation work her weekends were devoted to taking Koho youth in her Land Rover into the surrounding mountain villages for services in Christian villages and for witness to non-Christians. Due to the Vietnamese communist revolution of 1975 she relocated to Indonesia, where from 1977 to 1986 she learned the Indonesian language and taught theology at the CMA Bible School in Makale, South Sulawesi, Indonesia. In 1986 her mission reassigned her to assist immigrant tribal refugees from Vietnam's Central Highlands resettle in Charlotte, North Carolina, where she resides.

JAMES F. LEWIS

Evans, James (1801–46). English missionary to Canada and linguist. Born in England, Evans traveled to Canada in 1823 and taught at the Rice Lake Indian Mission School. He was ordained a Methodist minister in 1833 and went to work among the Ojibwa people. Evans was appointed general superintendent of Northwest Indian Missions in 1840, based in northern Manitoba. He had already prepared a grammar for the Ojibwa language and now started work on a written language for the Cree Indians. He invented a syllabic alphabet of simplicity and eloquence that was adopted by the Crees and is still in use today among many of the Indian people of northwest Canada. In 1841, using ingenuity and the materials at hand, he printed a hymnal in Cree, possibly the first book printed in the Canadian northwest. By this time he had made enemies in Hudson Bay Company, which was the political power in the area. Evans taught his converts to rest on Sunday and this slowed down fur trade. Company officials accused him of immorality and murder. Although cleared of all charges, the struggle broke his health and heart and he returned to England to die in 1846. But he trained a group of translators to succeed him and in 1861 they published the entire Bible in the Cree language, using his alphabet.

ROBERT SHUSTER

Bibliography. P. R. Dekar, *BDCM*, pp. 203–4; N. Shipley, *The James Evans Story*.

Evanston Assembly (1954). *See* WORLD COUNCIL OF CHURCHES ASSEMBLIES.

Evil Spirit. *See* DEMON, DEMONIZATION; *also* POSSESSION PHENOMENA.

Exegesis. Exegesis, from the Greek word *exegeomai* meaning "to lead out" or "explain," "interpret," or "describe," has come to refer to the act and process of determining the meaning of a text, particularly a biblical text. In the broader field, HERMENEUTICS (the principles and theory of the art and science of interpretation), modern students may include such goals as discovering the author's experience and person at the moment of writing or the reader's authentic selfhood. Traditional exegesis seeks to discover as precisely as possible the meaning and intent of the original author. Hence, it is assumed that, with the possible exception of predictive prophecy, the correct interpretation of a passage must be something the author could have intended and the first hearer/readers understood.

The careful exegete will employ a number of steps included in what is often called "the grammatical-historical method." These include: (1) *What did the writer write?* Answering this question includes consideration of textual criticism, seeking that which is most likely what the writer wrote when there are differences in the wording among ancient manuscripts linguistic study of the words and grammatical structure of the original language if possible; and the nature and wording of translations (literary, dynamic equivalent, paraphrase). (2) *What was the literary setting?* Here one seeks to identify the *genre* or literary form (narrative, poetry, history, prophecy, wisdom, apocalyptic, gospel, epistle, etc.) in order to employ the methods appropriate for understanding it. Consideration of the literary context enables the student to see the implications for interpretation of what comes just before and after the passage under consideration as well as its relation to the book as a whole, all books by the same author, its position within the Testament, Old or New, within which it appears, and in the Bible as a whole. (3) What were the *"introductory" matters* of the identity of the writer and *recipients*, their situation, when and where the document was written, the *purpose,* and the writer's *sources* of information? (4) What were the elements of the *historical situation*, including the influences of geography, politics, philosophy, the social, religious, and cultural context of the day, as well as the intellectual and current events of the writer's time? It is important to note that different parts of the BIBLE often have their distinct historical-cultural settings within which each must be considered.

The exegete may also find help in seeing how others have dealt with the passage. An examination of the history of its interpretation will provide both positive and negative examples. Consulting commentaries may furnish information and insights one might otherwise miss. However, neither of these should substitute for the interpreter's personal struggling with the passage.

These steps provide the raw data, the original meaning of the passage. Theological exegesis seeks to understand what it teaches about God, God's view of human persons, God's expectations from those who confront his revelation, and examples of God's dealing with people. The careful exegete is aware of basic spiritual and moral principles, rooted in the nature of God, which are revealed in the Bible. Occasionally these are stated plainly, more often they are revealed through the situations related in the Bible. These principles should be identified in individual passages and in Scripture as a whole. These revealed principles comprise the teachings, the doctrines, of Scripture which were applied in the ancient world and now must be implemented in very different situations of the modern world.

Exegesis is important for missions at a number of points. It is the biblical message that the missionary proclaims; exegesis is essential to ensure it is indeed that message which is declared. Exegesis is imperative to understand properly the nature and parameters of the missionary commission lest we undertake a human rather than the divine agenda.

Careful exegesis must distinguish between the basic principles of Scripture and the adaptation and application of them in specific cultural settings. Contemplation of the essential truths of the faith and their cultural adaptations in Scripture must be the basis for legitimate CONTEXTUALIZATION. This helps guard against letting the modern culture pour its message into the Bible rather than making the divine revelation understandable and adaptable to the modern world. This is essential in conveying the gospel and its implications in the culture and setting of people groups addressed by missions, avoiding unnecessarily transporting forms, emphases, traditions, and values from the missionaries' own culture. The cultural awareness which is a part of the missionary-interpreter's responsibilities is also essential to avoid literalistic or legalistic interpretations and applications which miss the author's (divine and human) intent.

All biblical translation should be based upon solid exegesis. As important as it is to put as quickly as possible the Scriptures in the language of groups among which missions work, the translator must, by careful exegesis, be sure that the translation conveys the same message to the mind of the modern recipient as it did to the original recipients. Exegesis must assure that the translator has done this as closely as possible before work is begun on transferring the message into the new setting (*see also* BIBLE TRANSLATION).

J. JULIUS SCOTT, JR.

Bibliography. G. Bray, *Biblical Interpretation Past and Present*; G. D. Fee and D. Stuart, *How to Read the Bible For All Its Worth*; G. D. Fee, *New Testament Exege-*

sis, A Handbook for Students and Pastors; W. J. Larkin, *Culture and Biblical Hermeneutics. Interpreting and Applying the Authoritative Word in a Relativistic Age;* M. Larson, *Meaning Based Translation;* A. B. Mickelsen, *Interpreting the Bible;* G. Osborne, *The Hermeneutical Spiral: A Comprehensive Introduction to Biblical Interpretation;* D. Stuart, *Old Testament Exegesis.*

Exodus, The. *See* OLD TESTAMENT THEOLOGY OF MISSION.

Exorcism. To exorcize is to charge under oath (e.g., in Matt. 26:63 Jesus is "adjured" to tell the truth about his messianic status). The term also refers to the expelling of a spirit or spirits by means of ritual(s). Such rituals involve oaths; they may also include the use of magical formulas and secret incantations. Though widely used today of Christian work in expelling demons, the term "exorcism" is not used in the New Testament to describe Jesus' or his disciples' ministry. Rather than relying on ritual, they cast out demons by verbally exercising God's authority (*see* DEMON, DEMONIZATION). The noun occurs only in Acts 19:13 of Jewish exorcists who used the name of Jesus in a botched exorcism.

Rituals of exorcism are found in every world religion and especially in FOLK RELIGIONS. Four components are almost universally involved: the exorcist, the victim, the community, and the ritual. The exorcist is seen as a person with special powers. The victim may be troubled because of personal, clan, or tribal TABOO violations or relational breakdowns. Anthropologists note that the victim is often a scapegoat for the community. In spite of this, the community still lends support to the exorcistic process, especially when community participation is required for restoration. The ritual is the actual ceremony in which the spirits are expelled. The variations are many, though they generally focus on the release of spiritual power. This may be accomplished by torture to make the victim an uninhabitable host for spirits; the application of specially prepared herbs; the use of magical formulas, chants, and incantations; an offering; or some type of animal sacrifice. The help or advice of friendly spirits may be enlisted through mediumistic channeling to deal with the spirit tormenting the victim. Understanding the functions of such rituals and the way they act as a social glue in the community is important for the missionary. If they are discarded by the missionary and the social functions that they serve remain unmet, the practices may simply go underground.

A variety of formalized exorcism ceremonies have existed inside the church from early on. In the second and third centuries, rituals of exorcism were a common part of the baptismal process. The Catholic Church has a well-established ritual. Lutherans and Anglicans once had exorcism ritu-

als, but abandoned or issued strict controls over them by the 1600s to prevent abuses. Among some contemporary Christian groups the form of demonic confrontation, the use of religious paraphernalia (water, oil, crucifixes), prayer and fasting, and repetitive reading of key Bible passages all with the extensive use of formulaic language point to a ritual orientation even though no formalized procedure is being followed.

It is important for the missionary to understand the function of exorcism in the local community. The fact that we are privileged to call on Christ's authority in dealing with spirits in a POWER ENCOUNTER is often recognized by the local community as God's work among them, and thus provides an evangelistic breakthrough. A danger to be noted is that if missionaries present a ritual-dependent Christian authority over the demonic, they may be opening the door to the rise of SYNCRETISM in the form of Christian magical thinking.

A. SCOTT MOREAU

SEE ALSO Demons, Demonism AND Possession Phenomena.

Bibliography. F. Goodman, *How about Demons? Possession and Exorcism in the Modern World;* M. Kraft, *Understanding Spiritual Power;* S. Moreau, *The World of the Spirits.*

Extended Family. *See* KINSHIP.

Extent of Missionary Identification. Missionary identification pervades all levels of the missionary task. A complex concept, effective missionary identification lies at the heart of making Christ known across cultures and involves all that we are as human beings. A superficial missionary identification merely imitates the local customs of a people hoping to gain access for a hearing of the gospel. With time, however, the receiving culture will recognize such identification as a gimmick. As Nida notes, the goal is not to "propagandize people into the kingdom" but to identify with them so as to communicate more clearly with them. This can only come about by being with them where they are and working *with* them rather than *for* them.

Historically rooted in anthropological research techniques where the researcher studied his or her "subjects" in their own context, identification was recognized as a means of increasing insights, sympathy, and influence among the people under study. The sensitive missionary, however, goes further and benefits more deeply by becoming subjectively involved with the people among whom he or she ministers. Recognizing that the final decision for Christ lies with the hearer, not the advocate, early concepts for missionary identification called for the missionary to work in light of human social institutions and the associated means to make decisions in the local setting when presenting the gospel.

Contemporary missiology presents missionary identification based on an incarnational model for ministry (*see* INCARNATIONAL MISSION). The model functions within three main arenas: the life of the missionary, the message itself, and the medium or forms that convey the message.

The first arena, the missionary's lifestyle, fosters the most powerful means of identification. The missionary seeks to become a full participant in the host society. Recognizing the reality of misunderstanding, the missionary enters the new culture as a learner rather than teacher. He or she is open to genuinely sharing his or her own cultural background. Thus, the missionary becomes a type of culture-broker living between two worlds, transmitting information from one to the other, bringing the gospel from without and giving from one cultural context to contemporary yet culturally different recipients. The goal of identification is to achieve a cross-cultural understanding in order to effectively communicate the message of Christ. The result of participating deeply in another culture forces one to think in new ways and recognize differing views of reality. In doing so, the missionary becomes a "bicultural" person with a broader vision that enables the ability to pull away from the home culture and work meaningfully in the new one (*see* BICULTURALISM). Incarnational missionaries thus develop a new cultural framework based on the two cultures known to them, allowing more effective ministry in the host culture. Additionally, they often find new perceptions about their home culture.

Inherent to the goal of living in two worlds as a bicultural person is the danger of rejection of one of our two worlds. We may either reject the culture in which we are ministering or reject our own culture by "going native." Neither of these options is helpful to the missionary personally or professionally. The first option denies the validity of the people with whom we are ministering. The second option denies the fact that we will always be seen as outsiders. Our goal is to learn to accept what is true and good in *all* cultures and to critique what is false and evil in each of them based on deeply rooted biblical truth.

The practice of incarnational missionary identification functions on three levels: (1) lifestyle—external identification in terms of language, dress, food, patterns of courtesy, use of local transportation, and housing; (2) willingness to serve alongside and eventually under a local leader; (3) inner identification, the deepest of all levels. Attitudes of dignity, respect, and trust speak of our genuine love for the people with whom we minister. Genuinely deep love forms both the foundation and capstone for all levels of identification.

The second arena for missionary identification deals with the content and presentation of the message. Drawing from COMMUNICATION theory, the missionary is encouraged to adopt the receptor's frame of reference where one becomes familiar with the conceptual framework of the receptor and attempts to fit communication of the message within the categories and felt needs of the receptor's WORLDVIEW. Thus, the message is presented in a way that "scratches where the hearer itches." Jesus demonstrated this when he spoke to the woman at the well about living water and her background. He also dealt with Nicodemus on his own Pharasaic terms. He interacted differently with Zacchaeus (Luke 19:1–10), the rich young ruler (Mark 10:21), and the demoniac (Luke 8:38–39). Furthermore, the apostle Paul followed Jesus' example when he determined to be Jewish or Greek depending on his audience (1 Cor. 9:19–22), clearly seen in his address to the Athenians (Acts 17:22–31).

The third arena for missionary identification lies in the development of the forms and media for conveying the gospel message. The missionary who has not learned the beliefs, feelings, and values of a culture will often fail to recognize the most appropriate methods for communicating Christ. There is the continued danger of simple translation of Western books, songs, drama, and films. As Tippett suggested, "the first step in identification is to accept as many indigenous forms and procedures as can legitimately be retained as Christian." Although the cost in time and effort to pursue such CONTEXTUALIZATION of the gospel is great, it does not match the cost and threat of miscommunicating the gospel. A syncretistic acceptance of the gospel and stilted or stunted churches easily result from lack of identification on this level.

Missionary identification today is not an option: it is an imperative. Historically, one of the results of poor missionary identification has been the national outcry of "Missionary go home!" We must learn from our mistakes and move ahead with greater determination, especially in light of modernity's more complex degree of multiculturalism. In spite of our tendency to work at external identification, people still need to experience love on deeper levels. Missionaries must incarnate themselves by recognizing and working within the individual needs and social contexts of peoples.

ROBERTA R. KING

SEE ALSO Bonding; Culture Learning; Culture Shock.

Bibliography. K. Bediako, *Christianity in Africa: The Renewal of a Non-Western Religion;* P. Hiebert, *Anthropological Insights for Missionaries;* C. H. Kraft, *Christianity in Culture;* E. Nida, *Message and Mission: The Communication of the Faith;* P. Parshall, *New Paths in Muslim Evangelism;* A. Tippett, *Introduction to Missiology.*

Ff

Fads in Missions. When an innovation begins to take hold, we would like to know if it is going to endure. One way is to ask how biblical the innovation is: Does it aim at reinforcing some biblical mandate or principle, or recovering one that has been neglected?

For example, when RALPH WINTER rocked the LAUSANNE CONGRESS ON WORLD EVANGELIZATION in 1974 with his vision of "hidden people," it was not a fad. Recognizing Christ's mandate to reach every nation, the unreached of the world became the focal point of evangelical missions. Thus, toward the end of the twentieth century a plethora of innovations aimed in the same direction: the 10/40 WINDOW concept, the AD 2000 Movement, identifying the "gateway" cities or peoples, for example, all target the least reached. Are they fads? Time will tell.

Another innovation which has endured is the "indigenous" methodology developed in the nineteenth century by JOHN NEVIUS—that the goal of missions is to establish self-governing, self-supporting, self-propagating churches (*see* INDIGENOUS CHURCHES). The Third-World missions movement has grown from the "self-propagating" or GREAT COMMISSION mandate, an enduring "new" development. But fads often seem to accompany biblical innovation. For example, the self-support principle became, "let the nationals do it," and let the West pay for it (*see* FOREIGN FINANCING OF INDIGENOUS WORKERS). These are fads that will pass because they violate basic biblical principles. We can never buy our way out of personal responsibility, nor assign world evangelism to others so long as half the world has no Christian "nationals," because peoples live out of reach of present gospel witness.

DONALD MCGAVRAN's themes of concentrating on responsive peoples and targeting homogenous units for evangelism are certainly far less popular than they once were. This should come as no surprise regarding the HOMOGENEOUS UNIT PRINCIPLE, since it is extra-biblical (though not demonstrably anti-biblical, at least in the way McGavran advocated it). But concentration on responsive people is clearly biblical, the way God himself operates. Nevertheless, this concept does not have the strength the innovation once knew, so may prove to be a fad.

Two of the strongest emphases in the last quarter of the twentieth century were SHORT-TERM MISSION and TENT-MAKING MISSIONS. These cannot be considered fads since they have always been with us, but unrealistic expectations for these approaches may pass since they lack biblical mandate or principle.

Holy Spirit power is essential for missionary success, but the innovations accompanying the POWER ENCOUNTER movement at the end of the twentieth century—prayer walks, spiritual mapping, confronting an identifiable demonic prince that reigns over a city or region (*see* TERRITORIAL SPIRITS), and many others—may prove to be fads because the biblical foundation is at least problematic.

Innovation is essential for the cause of missions and this will bring genuine biblical advance, but inevitably it will bring passing fads as well. The way of confidence is to evaluate each new idea at the bar of Scripture.

ROBERTSON MCQUILKIN

SEE ALSO Controversies in Contemporary Evangelical Missions.

Faeroe Islands (Denmark Autonomous Area) *(Est. 2000 pop. 47,000; 1,399 sq. km. [540 sq. mi.]).* A small group of eighteen islands off the coast of northern Europe between Iceland and Scotland populated primarily by Faeroese (of Scandinavian descent) who are largely dependent on fishing for their livelihood. In 1993 the population was estimated at 93.4 percent Christian (93% Protestant, 0.1% Catholic, 0.3% marginal), though they are generally nominal. The Evangelical Lutheran Church, thought to be present since the mid-eighth century, is the largest denomination, followed by the Christian Brethren.

A. SCOTT MOREAU

Faith. Faith is both proposition and practice, creed and conduct, belief and behavior. Hebrews 11 describes what faith is and what faith does. James warns that faith that does not work is no faith at all. Throughout Scripture, faith is not only revealed in terms of what to believe, the object of faith, God himself, but it is also that which works in the human mind, heart, and will to bring people to saving trust in the living God.

Although the word "faith" does not stand out boldly in the Old Testament, the stories of God's people are replete with belief, trust, and hope. For example, the deeply introspective psalms reveal how intense personal faith is. To these writers, faith stands out like a life preserver. Trust in God, rather than self, is proposed as the only way to salvation and wholeness, whether the enemies be internal or external. Old Testament persons did not have the advantage of hearing Jesus or reading Paul, but they clearly understood what God required of them in terms of obedient faith, trust, and hope.

Faith blossoms like a spring rose in the New Testament. Taken together, in its verb, noun, and adjectival forms, the basic Greek word *pistis* occurs more than three hundred times. The object of such faith is God's saving work in his Son, the Lord Jesus Christ. Faith is a personal relationship. People of faith relinquish their own efforts to be good enough to please God. Instead, they trust completely in Christ and in him alone for salvation, forgiveness, righteousness, and wholeness (*see also* SHALOM).

Although intimately relational, New Testament faith is rooted in certain historical facts. People who come to faith believe the testimony, or the record, about Christ's life, death, resurrection, and ascension. The only valid repository of faith is the Lord Jesus Christ himself, not a set of facts about him, not the Bible, not the church, but a living person. Saving faith does not require a complete understanding of biblical theology, but it does require knowing why Jesus came to earth, died, and rose again.

Subjective faith begins with a conviction of the mind based on adequate evidence. It grows in the confidence of the heart, or emotions, based on the conviction of the mind. Faith is crowned in the consent of the will, by means of which conviction and confidence are expressed in conduct. The will acts in response to what God has done in Christ. The will says "Yes" to Jesus Christ. This combination of the elements in human personality involves a moral decision, according to Paul (1 Thess. 1:9) and Peter (1 Peter 2:25). Jesus described that "Yes" in many different ways, as receiving him, trusting him, believing in him, welcoming him, drinking of him, eating of him, loving him, and obeying him (*see also* CONVERSION).

New Testament stories and dogma emphasize that the Son of Man who came to redeem people from sin also came to live in them, to direct and control their lives, to be the object of their worship, love, obedience, and service. Therefore, people of faith confess Christ as Savior and Lord. They commit themselves without reservation to do his good and perfect will.

From this obedient faith springs the New Testament pattern for mission. Faith is not a passing phase; it is a continuing walk of obedience to the Lord's commands, including his GREAT COMMISSION.

Church history reveals remarkable exploits of what we call "faith" to evangelize the unbelieving world. Unfortunately, too often these heroines and heroes of faith were loners, isolated from the larger institutional churches because they dared to go against the grain. While church hierarchies and public opinion argued otherwise, these missionary pioneers abandoned their comfort zones to enter uncharted waters, where the name of Jesus was not known or confessed.

These people believed God not for salvation alone but also for overcoming horrendous obstacles. In that sense, they discovered a realm of faith often described by Jesus. For example, he said, "Everything is possible for him who believes" (Mark 9:23). He promised great results from faith that was as small as a grain of mustard seed (Matt. 17:20; Luke 17:6).

The story of the expansion of Christianity is filled with exploits that would qualify for inclusion in Hebrews 11. At the same time, not all of those people were delivered from great tribulation, neither were many missionary pioneers who laid the foundation for the worldwide church today. In fact, missionary martyrs are many, and it is important to recognize not only the obedience of their faith, but also the costliness of it. Having confessed Christ, they put their lives on the line for him (*see* MARTYRDOM).

Mission board archives are crammed with stories showing that for many missionaries faith was defined as obedience, courage, trust, hope, and a willingness to die for the sake of planting the church. Perhaps this quote from LOTTIE MOON, a nineteenth-century missionary to China, says it best: "If I had a thousand lives, I would give them all for the women of China."

To look at mission from the other side, it is safe to say that apart from this kind of faith, the church would never have advanced anywhere. But somehow the mission of the church exploded because a minority of Christians took their cue from the faith they saw exercised by the early believers in the Book of Acts. Those Christians not only confessed personal faith in Christ, but they either went themselves or sent others to declare Christ's lordship throughout the Roman Empire and into Africa and Asia. Their successors took Christ's name throughout Eastern and Western Europe.

Faith is the key to personal salvation and to missionary obedience. Faith links people to God through Jesus Christ; faith engages them wholeheartedly in God's worldwide mission. Faith has been God's instrument for building his universal church.

JIM REAPSOME

Faith Missions. With the beginning of the modern missionary movement in the last years of the eighteenth century, several types of mission agencies emerged. The earliest agencies, such as the AMERICAN BOARD OF COMMISSIONERS FOR FOREIGN MISSIONS and the LONDON MISSIONARY SOCIETY were interdenominational. In the early years of the nineteenth century denominations organized their own boards of missions; and even as late as 1925, 75 percent of American missionaries were affiliated with denominational boards.

Faith mission societies, often also referred to as independent, interdenominational, or nondenominational, developed in the latter half of the nineteenth century. At the present time they have many more missionaries under appointment than do the denominational agencies. These types of mission agencies appeared first in Great Britain, the best known being the CHINA INLAND MISSION in 1865. Some of the early faith missions in the United States were the CHRISTIAN AND MISSIONARY ALLIANCE (1887), the Evangelical Alliance Mission (1890), the SUDAN INTERIOR MISSION (1893), and the AFRICA INLAND MISSION (1895).

Several interrelated factors led to the development of faith mission societies. First was the conviction that the denominational agencies were not reaching the unevangelized areas of the world—they were not penetrating the interiors or frontiers of many countries. The terms "interior" and "inland" in the names of these new agencies testified to this fact. Among the unreached in many countries were women. This led to the first American faith mission, the Woman's Union Missionary Society (1860).

A second major issue was theological. Christian leaders were alarmed at the growth of what they perceived to be liberalism in many denominations and wished to found agencies that were fully committed to the authority of Scripture and had an evangelistic fervor to reach the lost. These new agencies were connected with the fundamentalist movement, were theologically conservative, and usually separated themselves from the mainline denominations. They tended to be opposed to the conciliar ECUMENICAL MOVEMENT, believing that many of its leaders were liberal and that it was more committed to social issues than to evangelism.

A third factor for the establishing of the independent mission agencies was financial. Denominational agencies often had insufficient funds to send out missionaries. The new boards, operating on the faith principle, believed that God would provide even when it appeared that no money was available. This made it possible for them to continue to send out new missionaries. At the beginning, societies like the China Inland Mission instructed their missionaries not to ask for money nor to tell anyone but God about their specific financial need. At present, most of the faith agencies ask for money or in some way make their financial needs known.

As concerned Christian leaders assessed the spiritual needs of the world, they formed a number of specialized mission agencies that can also be considered faith or independent societies. Among these were Mission Aviation Fellowship, Far Eastern Broadcasting Company, Gospel Recordings, and WYCLIFFE BIBLE TRANSLATORS.

The formation of these new agencies came in a period at the end of the nineteenth century when mission interest was stirred to new heights by many mission conferences both in England and in America. Among these were international conventions held in Cleveland, Detroit (1894), and Liverpool (1896) by the STUDENT VOLUNTEER MOVEMENT FOR FOREIGN MISSIONS. Another series of important annual conferences was promoted, beginning in 1893, by the Interdenominational Conference of Foreign Missionary Boards and Societies in the United States and Canada. The most international and interdenominational of all these conferences was the ECUMENICAL MISSIONARY CONFERENCE held in New York in 1900.

From the beginning, the faith mission societies derived their finances and personnel from independent Bible and community churches. Most of their missionaries were trained in Bible schools founded in the last two decades of the nineteenth century, such as Nyack (1882), Moody (1886), Ontario (1894), and Barrington (1900). Gradually, many of these schools added liberal arts courses to their curriculum and became Bible colleges granting the B.A. degree. Most candidates for faith missions continue to come from these schools.

Many faith mission agencies that were based originally only in the United States or England have now established centers in other countries, even in Asia, Latin America, and Africa. Thus they have become international societies, sending missionaries from six continents to six continents.

The theologically more inclusive nature of the WORLD MISSIONARY CONFERENCE at Edinburgh in 1910, the growth of liberalism in mainline denominations, and the antipathy of denominational boards to the faith mission agencies contributed to the founding in 1917 of the INTERDENOMINATIONAL FOREIGN MISSION ASSOCIATION of North America. Boards formerly a part of the Foreign Mission Conference of North America, such as the Africa Inland Mission, Central American Mission, China

Inland Mission, Sudan Interior Mission, South Africa General Mission, Inland South America Missionary Union, and the Woman's Union Missionary Society joined forces to form this new association of interdenominational or faith missions societies. Today a total of seventy-two agencies belong to the IFMA.

The IFMA does not include denominational, Pentecostal, or holiness groups, even though it is willing to work with them in cooperative endeavors. So in 1945 a group of mission executives related to the National Association of Evangelicals formed the Evangelical Foreign Missions Association (EFMA), now renamed EVANGELICAL FELLOWSHIP OF MISSION AGENCIES. It includes many agencies that are not members of the IFMA.

RALPH R. COVELL

SEE ALSO Independent Non-Denominational Mission Agencies.

Bibliography. E. L. Frizen Jr., *75 Years of IFMA 1917–1992*; J. H. Kane, *A Concise History of the Christian World Mission.*

Falkland Islands [Islas Malvinas] (United Kingdom Dependent Area) *(Est. 2000 pop.: 2,000; 16,300 sq. km. [6,293 sq. mi.]).* The Falkland Islands consist of two main islands and over 100 smaller ones in the South Atlantic Ocean off the coast of Argentina. It is a colony of the United Kingdom and its residents enjoy all civil and political rights. Nearly all residents are British in background. Most of these are Christians but there is a growing movement among the nonreligious. Evangelicals are found among the Anglicans and the Free Church.

TODD M. JOHNSON

Fall of Humankind, The. The biblical teaching concerning the fall of humankind is found in Genesis 3; Romans 5:12–19; 1 Corinthians 15:21–22; and 1 Timothy 2:12–13. Genesis 1 and 2 record the conditions of the "golden age" when humans, created in the image of God with mandates for dominion over and stewardship of creation (Gen. 1:26–28), were given only one limitation. "You are free to eat from any tree in the garden; but you must not eat from the tree of the knowledge of good and evil, for when you eat of it you will surely die" (Gen 2:16–17). God sets the prohibition in the context of his limitless provision and gives no rationale other than a declaration of the consequences: death.

The narrative of temptation and sin (Gen. 3:1–6) introduces Satan as the "crafty" tempter, the serpent. He leads Eve to doubt God's goodness and truthfulness, to allow her appetites to transgress God's law limits, and to act on her desires in willful rebellion against God. She further

compounds her sin by persuading her husband to sin (1 Tim. 2:12–13).

The immediate consequences of sin were entry of sin and guilt into the formerly perfect world. The couple experiences guilt, when their eyes are opened, they know shame, and they hide from the presence of God (Gen. 3:7–11). Immediately they "die" spiritually and in old age they will die physically. In fact, the whole creation becomes subject to frustration and decay (Rom. 8:20–22). As a result, a mitigated but real curse falls on Adam and Eve and all humankind. There is multiplied pain in child bearing and a constant tension in Eve's relation to her husband. She will desire to master him, but his role will be to have the leadership in the home (Gen. 3:16). The man will only by much toil wrest a living from the soil, a task of doubtful meaningfulness, since his end is physical death, in which he returns to the same soil from which he was taken.

The greatest consequence, however, is the introduction of original sin into human history (Rom. 5:12–19; 1 Cor. 15:21–22). Each succeeding generation will be born spiritually dead, lacking original right standing with God, charged with the guilt of the first human's sin, with a sin nature driving them toward a life of sin, and with only one prospect for eternity: eternal condemnation (Gen. 4:1–8, 19; 6:2, 5; Ps. 51:5; Jer. 17:9).

The account of the fall of humankind does offer a glimmer of hope, however. The "seed of the woman" would be final victor in the continuing spiritual battle with the serpent's seed. Addressing the serpent God declares the offspring of the woman will "crush his head" (Gen. 3:15). The rest of biblical revelation reveals that Jesus Christ is that offspring and in his death and resurrection he won the victory everyone who believes may claim as his or her own.

ANIMISM, as well as a number of the world's great religions, have myths of origin that include an account of the fall of humankind. These accounts to a greater or lesser extent agree in detail with the Genesis account. The student of comparative religion may posit "nostalgia for the beginning of things" as a "permanent part of man's collective memory." He or she will conclude that humans in many cultures "once positing it as a golden age" will then have to "explain the accident that produced the present situation" in which there is both physical and moral evil (Ries, 1987, 267). Since Genesis 1–3 presents itself not as a religiously generated myth but as a historical account of beginnings, it is better to explain all the similarities between Genesis and religious mythology as evidence of humankind's common historical memory, which under the influence of the fall yields a variety of versions of what actually happened. The early chapters of Genesis then provide the missionaries with both opportunity and challenges as they approach other cultures and religions with the gospel. The opportunity is "bridge building" to the culture by dealing in the area of origins from Genesis 1–3. The challenge is to effectively correct the religionist's views on these matters so that clearer understanding of the truth of biblical revelation results.

Among animists many narratives of the fall may be found. These often stress the closeness of God and humanity in the "golden age," a theme congruent with that of Genesis. The "accident," which introduces death into the world, though sometimes a sin, in many instances is not. What brings the fall may be disturbing the gods with the noise of grinding millet (the Dogon of Mali) or an accident like falling asleep (Aranda of Australia). It may be a matter of an original archetypal message of immortality being changed in transmission or not passed on by the messenger (Ashanti of Ghana). It may occur because of human frailty. A Maasai myth tells of a package that humans are given by God and forbidden to open. However, their curiosity drives them to open it. In all these instances, biblical revelation's moral and salvation history framework for the fall must be a necessary corrective.

Hinduism knows no definite occasion on which the fall of humankind occurred, only a gradual decline in the second of four ages of humankind's history. The imputation of guilt from the first human to all succeeding generations is similar in principle to the concept of *samsara* and karma, though the difference is very important. In Scripture, it is only the guilt of Adam's sin, not effects of the sinfulness of each succeeding generation, which is imputed to the individual. Neither Buddhism nor Chinese traditional thought contains myths of the fall of humankind. Islam's Koran follows Genesis 1–3 fairly closely. It does provide an explanation for why Satan *(Iblis)* fell: his refusal to bow to Adam. While the guilt for the fall is imputed to the devil, humans only experience the sanctions and consequences. Original sin is minimized to the level of weakness, the habitual.

WILLIAM J. LARKIN JR.

See also Sin.

Bibliography. M. Eliade, *Myths, Dreams, and Mysteries;* J. Ries, *ER,* 5:256–67; G. G. Van Groningen, *EDBT,* pp. 240–41.

Family Life of the Missionary. With the generational shift in evangelical missions, the family life of missionaries has become a crucial topic. Earlier volumes on Christian mission generally did not address the issue. In the age of rugged individualism it simply would not have occurred to people. That is not to say that missionaries in the past did not marry and have families, but it does recognize that the reduced life expectancy of missionaries in the nineteenth century made the subject somewhat moot, particularly since the children of missionaries most often remained in the home country for their education and safety. As the twentieth century progressed, children did go overseas with their parents, but usually spent most of their time in the protected and often insulated enclave of the missionary school.

In the mid-twentieth century, family issues began to receive expanded attention in missionary circles. This has had both positive and negative effects. On the positive side, it opened up a discussion of very real issues that impact both the effectiveness and longevity of missionaries. On the negative side, an almost idolatrous fixation on family needs has at times undercut the purposes for which missionaries go forth in the first place.

This is in many respects a time of transition in the way agencies and churches respond to issues of family life among missionaries. Most agencies today are highly aware that family issues are among the most important factors impacting both missionary recruitment and attrition. Woe to the agency that has not developed policies and made suitable provision. Perhaps chief among the issues is the education of children. Gone are the days when missionaries happily sent their children off to boarding school; most want multiple options.

A related issue of great importance is the status of the missionary wife. Here, too, maximum flexibility is desired and often demanded. For some the issue is finding a satisfying ministry niche, which may or may not parallel that of the husband. For others the primary issue is the freedom not to have significant responsibilities outside the home, particularly if there are children whom the couple desire to homeschool. Whatever the particular issue, maximum flexibility with understanding and encouragement is necessary. This can provide no small challenge to agencies and churches seeking to maintain cost-effective, accountable, and equitable policies. The good news is that significant research and many broadly based efforts and organizations have emerged to address such family issues as care for MISSIONARY CHILDREN, reentry into the home culture (*see* REENTRY SHOCK), and retirement planning.

GARY R. CORWIN

Bibliography. P. Echerd and A. Arathoon, eds., *Understanding and Nurturing the Missionary Family;* B. J. Kenney, *The Missionary Family;* R. J. Rowen and S. F. Rowen, *Sojourners: The Family on the Move.*

Farrar, Cynthia (1795–1862). American missionary to India. She was born in Marlborough, New Hampshire. When she was twenty years old she made a profession of faith and immediately joined the Congregational Church. After completing her studies at Union Academy in Plainfield, New Hampshire, she applied her teaching skills both in New Hampshire and later in Boston, Massachusetts. It was during this time that the Marathi Mission in western India requested that the AMERICAN BOARD send an experienced single woman educator to their school. It was the belief of the mission that they needed expert and continual supervision that no one caring for a family and a husband could provide. Farrar received and accepted the challenge in May 1827, and sailed for India on June 5, 1827, becoming the first unmarried American woman to be sent overseas as a missionary by any American agency. During her thirty-four years with the Marathi Mission she successfully educated many young women who formerly were not allowed an education by their Hindu fathers. She gained the respect of the higher castes, the support of some prominent British residents, including the governor, and later, Bishop Carr provided her with funds to establish additional schools. In 1839, she was transferred to Ahmednagar, where she organized new schools that attracted the attention of some of the high-caste men who asked that she establish two schools for their daughters. Unfortunately the sponsors closed these schools when one of the Brahmin teachers employed by Farrar became a Christian. Shunning discouragement, she continued to direct mission schools and later a primary and secondary school before her death.

WENDY S. LARSON

Bibliography. R. P. Beaver, *All Loves Excelling;* R. C. Brouwer, *New Women for God: Canadian Presbyterian Women & India Missions 1876–1914.*

Farrow, Lucy F. (b. c. 1852). African American pastor, evangelist, and missionary to Liberia. Born in slavery in Norfolk, Virginia, Farrow was a niece of the abolitionist and journalist Frederick Douglass. She came in contact with Pentecostal evangelist Charles F. Parham in 1905 while pastoring a small Holiness church in Houston, Texas. By now a widow, she served for a brief time as a governess in the Parham household.

Farrow introduced William J. Seymour, a member of her congregation, to the Pentecostal movement and then arranged for him to attend Parham's Houston Bible School, where he accepted the latter's Pentecostal doctrine. In early 1906, Seymour traveled to Los Angeles, California, where he played a major role in the internationally significant Azusa Street Revival (1906–13). Farrow followed and ministered there, praying for seekers to receive the baptism in the Holy Spirit with speaking in tongues. Beginning in August 1906, she traveled across the country holding evangelistic meetings and four months later went as a missionary to Monrovia, Liberia, returning to Los Angeles in 1907. Farrow's con-

tributions include her encouragement of Seymour to enter the Pentecostal movement, interracial ministry, and service in the vanguard of Pentecostal missions.

GARY B. MCGEE

Bibliography. J. R. Goff Jr., *Fields White Unto Harvest: Charles F. Parham and the Missionary Origins of Pentecostalism;* C. M. Robeck Jr., *Initial Evidence and Spirit Baptism.*

Fearing, Maria (1838–1937). African American missionary to Zaire. Maria Fearing was one of the few single African American women to ever become a missionary. Through her hard work and dedication to the missionary efforts in Africa she became known as a "Mother to African Girls." One of the most intriguing things about her was that her personal efforts to get to Africa were just as noteworthy as the work she accomplished while she was there.

She was born a slave in Gainsville, Alabama. Sometime during her childhood, she developed a desire to go to Africa. At thirty-three, she completed the ninth grade at Talladega College, where she also served as assistant matron.

At fifty-six, she volunteered for the Congo Mission of the Presbyterian Church. However, because of her age, the Committee for Foreign Missions turned her down. But that did not stop her. She sold her house, withdrew her savings, and applied again to the committee, offering to pay her own expenses.

The committee then agreed to accept her. She went to the Congo Mission in May 1894. Because of her hard work and devotion, within two years she was appointed a missionary with full support. She founded the Pantops Home for orphaned girls and was the director there until 1915.

She then returned to Gainsville, where she died in 1937. Perhaps one of her greatest legacies was that she did not let her age become an obstacle. Nor did she let the opinion of others hinder her from obeying Christ's call to the mission field. As a result, many orphaned girls gained a "Mother in Africa."

KATHY MCREYNOLDS

Bibliography. S. M. Jacobs, *Black Americans and the Missionary Movement,* pp. 155–76.

Feminist Theologies. Although it can be argued that there is no such thing as feminist theology, only feminist *theologies,* this is only a response to the diversity of the women theologians engaged in the debate. This ignores the fact that there is an underlying common approach and agenda which is shared by women of other faiths, especially Jewish women. Consequently feminist issues have proved a fruitful ground for interfaith dialogue, as some of the titles below indicate. The literature in the field is now so vast that only a few titles representative of the different insights and disciplines involved can be given.

Feminist theology is of necessity highly contextual. It addresses the factors governing women's existence from a woman's perspective. Women feel marginalized from the conduct of worship, from the decision-making processes of their faith community, and from professional training and the creation of academic theology and a living spiritual tradition. In some denominations, the study of theology may be restricted to those involved in the training for male-ordained ministry. However, this situation may be due to a lack of opportunity for women to take advantage of higher education in some countries, discrimination against single mothers in the wider society, and so on.

Feminist theologians have increasingly listened to their non-Western sisters and perceived that the dignity of women is indissolubly linked to HUMAN RIGHTS, POVERTY, and deprivation. They have appropriated the feminist concept of the patriarchy to locate the socioeconomic and religious causes of this. They criticize the traditions that depict women as Eves, temptresses, those who at best load men down with domestic duties that distract them from salvation, or who at worst are responsible for leading them into sin. Together with secular feminists, feminist theologians object to women's inferior status and to the cult of Mary exalting motherhood in the abstract while mothers are oppressed. They scrutinize the underlying issues of ritual purity which bar women from approaching the sacred, or exclude them from their own households during menstruation and childbirth, but reject the pro-abortion stance of secular feminists.

In feminist theology the sacred Scriptures are reclaimed for study, and reinterpreted both to retrieve women's contributions as, for example, that of Miriam, Moses' sister, of charismatic leaders such as Deborah, or of the founders of early Christian communities. Texts are also reinterpreted to address contemporary situations. Religious language is made 'inclusive,' feminine epithets and similes applied to God, and liturgy rewritten while theology is restructured and a new image of God created. Fresh translations of the original Hebrew Scriptures have revealed a male bias which cannot be justified in terms of accuracy or theology.

Feminist theology seeks the liberation of women and men, but is not linked so closely to analysis of a particular political ideology as liberation theology is. Such earnest and thorough-going study of the Scriptures and the early fathers (or their equivalent in Judaism and Islam) and such openness to the moving of the Spirit can only benefit the tradition as a whole. It underlines the truth that to be effective a theology of mission must be fully contextual.

In many cultures the coming of the gospel meant education and liberation, and as Ruth Brouwer shows, missionary societies offered women meaningful service, lifetime careers, and management experience. Yet, ironically, since 1914 women have increasingly felt oppressed by evangelical structures. There are disproportionately few women missiologists compared with other theological disciplines and too often in evangelical congregations they are expected to keep silent. A radical reappraisal of all Christian traditions is necessary if the flow of women out of the churches into goddess worship, alternative communities, and Neo-Buddhism is not to become a flood tide.

ELEANOR M. JACKSON

Bibliography. R. C. Brouwer, *New Women for God. Canadian Presbyterian Women and India Missions, 1876–1914;* M. Grey, *Redeeming the Dream: Feminism, Redemption and Christian Tradition;* D. Hampson, *Theology and Feminism;* L. Hogan, *From Women's Experience to Feminist Theology;* R. Holloway, ed., *Who Needs Feminism? Men Respond to Sexism in the Church;* A. Joseph, ed., *Through the Devil's Gateway: Women, Religion and Taboo;* U. King, ed., *Women and Religion;* J. Plaskow, *Standing Again at Sinai. Judaism from a Feminist Perspective.*

Festivals, Religious. Religious festivals are cyclic phenomena in most, if not all, religious traditions. They are extremely varied in form and function. Such festivals include the Jewish Passover; the Christian Christmas; the Hindu Deepâval, Dasara, and Kubha Mela; the Xocoth Huetzi of the Aztecs; the New Yam festival of the Igbo; and the Muslim Ramadan. Religious festivals are fundamentally rites of symbolic, expressive communication and religious celebration. All religious festivals fulfill some of the social, psychic, and spiritual needs of the people who practice them, reflecting a universal, inner human quest to relate to the transcendent.

In the social dimension religious festivals function as significant means of informal socialization and contribute to a sense of corporate identity, thus promoting social cohesion. There is an aspect of gaiety and flexibility in the format of festivals, but where these elements are replaced by rigid formalism the rituals easily become a burdensome, legalistic ritualism. Ritualism destroys the very re-creative purpose of the festivals. This will only continue to be the case as these festivals can withstand the threat of SECULARIZATION through tourism and CONSUMERISM. Taking a wider perspective, some religious festive cycles have been shown to be important as socioreligious mechanisms in maintaining a dynamic balance between consumption and conservation in the environment.

From a religious perspective, festivals establish and strengthen the link between the sacred and the profane; the temporal existence and the experience of the eternal. They renew and transform the profane and affirm the essential goodness of life, while at the same time they critique its destructive elements. Festivals interrupt the mundaneness and profanity of life. Religious festivals raise the level of consciousness of the continuity of life by allowing participants to withdraw temporarily from profane time into sacred time while also bringing a measure of sacredness to all of life.

A religious festival often involves reenactment of historical or mythical events, making the sacred past present in experience or the benefits of the event made a present reality. It can also be a medium to communicate the experience of thanksgiving, atonement, redemption, and hope. The uniqueness of Christian festivals lies in their source in divine revelation of God and in the ritual meaning and perception of the participant's role. Christians not only celebrate the past and present, but also anticipate a future life in the consummated kingdom of God. Christian celebrations involve reenactments that do not renew the initial redemptive act, but the benefits of that act are made present. The Christian is an observer and recipient of the divine act, not a participant in the divine act.

The Christian engaging in cross-cultural ministry must consider making use of the ritual symbolism to communicate the gospel to avoid a foreign message or SYNCRETISM. Religious festivals reveal the significant religious concerns of the practitioners and have an important social and possibly an ecological function. For these reasons Christians also need to consider the use of functional substitutes that are both indigenous and Christian to fulfill at least the social (and environmental) needs.

ALBERT F. TUCKER

SEE ALSO Burial Rites, Rites of Passage.

Bibliography. R. L. Browning, *Religious Education* 75 (1980): 273–81; M. Eliade, *The Sacred and the Profane: The Nature of Religion.*

Fetish. *See* MAGIC, MAGICK, MAGICAL BELIEFS AND PRACTICES.

Field Appointment. The designation of missionaries to particular fields is both the work of divine sovereignty and of personal choice. The apostle Paul's calling was to the Gentiles (Acts 9), but he and Barnabas chose to visit Cyprus and Asia Minor (Acts 13) on the first missionary journey. J. HERBERT KANE cites four aspects of making a choice for missionary service: the mission, the country, the people, and the vocation. These four factors are not presented in a fixed order, but the secret is to focus upon one of them and get clear guidance, then wait on the Lord for his leading on the other three. Today many mission agencies provide considerable counsel, advice, and the use of various forms of testing, including psychological inventories and language aptitude exams, prior to appointing a candidate to a designated field (*see* CANDIDACY). It is necessary to carefully consider the gifts, the abilities, the background, and even the candidate's personality in making a field appointment. By contrast many early societies offered much less help in this process and gave the missionaries total freedom without adequate accountability. Ultimately both the mission agency and the missionary need to arrive at a consensus of field appointment that could possibly include a designated PEOPLE GROUP and also a well-thought-out job description.

JOHN EASTERLING

Bibliography. J. H. Kane, *Life and Work on the Mission Field.*

Field Responsibilities. A missionary's lifestyle and field of service involve several parties: sending church, mission agency, co-workers, and nationals (including leaders and national churches). Field responsibilities include at least six areas: personal and family welfare, interpersonal relationships, effective communication, witness and evangelism, planting and/or development of the church, and leadership preparation. The personal needs of the missionary include spiritual growth, physical care, intellectual stimulation, and needs of the spouse and children. When these needs are adequately met, the missionary can then minister with greater freedom and success. Interpersonal relationships must start in the home as a foundation (*see* FAMILY LIFE OF THE MISSIONARY). The missionaries need to work as team members with an interdependent spirit of humility and love (*see* TEAMS IN MISSION). Missionaries need to develop a servant attitude in working with others. The open lines of communication among missionaries, mission administrators, and nationals create the basis of trust and a sense of concern. SECOND LANGUAGE ACQUISITION and cultural understanding are necessary for identifying with the nationals and reaching out to those who do not know Christ. The development and planting of churches give permanence and stability to the emerging Christian community. The final goal of the missionary is selectively training local leaders who are spiritually mature and gifted (*see* LEADERSHIP). The end result will be INDIGENOUS CHURCHES, churches that are strong and ultimately independent from missionary leadership. Each field responsibility needs to be kept in balance with others to avoid BURNOUT and to maximize the missionary's effectiveness.

JOHN EASTERLING

Bibliography. P. A. Beals, *A People for His Name.*

Field, Adele Marion (1839–1916). American pioneer Baptist missionary to Thailand (1867–72) and China (1873–90). Raised a universalist, Field graduated from the State Normal School at Albany, New York, and taught school. Having converted to her fiancé's Baptist belief, she sailed for 149 days to Hong Kong only to learn of her fiancé's death. Another 34-day voyage took her to Bangkok. The only single woman at the Thai (Siamese) mission, she was criticized for socializing (playing cards, dancing, and reportedly smoking opium) with diplomats and businessmen. En route home after colleagues insisted she be recalled, she stopped in Amoy where the missionaries begged her to stay since she spoke the dialect. In China she began the much copied practice of training Bible women; worked on an Amoy dictionary published under the mission's name; and was one of the few women to attend the 1877 Shanghai Missionary Conference.

Although not wealthy, just prior to retirement Field resigned so as not to receive her pension, declaring that she had never believed Baptist teachings. Once home she reported on anti-Semitic pogroms in Russia. In New York as a suffragette she organized the League for Political Education. She wrote books about China and articles about politics and her biological studies, particularly on ants. After a decade in New York she moved to Seattle, where she was instrumental in establishing the political processes of referendum and recall.

KATHLEEN L. LODWICK

Bibliography. H. N. Stevens, *Memorial Biography of Adele M. Fielde, Humanitarian;* F. B. Hoyt, *Historian* 44 (May 1982): 318–22; R. A. Tucker, *GGC.*

Fiji *(Est. 2000 pop.: 845,000; 18,274 sq. km. [7,056 sq. mi.]).* Fiji comprises a group of some 330 volcanic islands in the South Pacific. Originally a British territory, Fiji's population bears the impress of its colonial history. The British imported over 60,000 indentured Indian laborers between 1879 and 1916 to work in the sugarcane fields. The descendants of these laborers constitute a numerical majority on the islands, while the native Fijians constitute a minority. Fiji is 54.5% Christian (43% Protestant) and 35.5% Hindu. Evangelicals are found in all of the Protestant denominations but the Assemblies of God have been the most successful with over 32,000 members.

TODD M. JOHNSON

Financial Support. *See* DEPUTATION.

Financing Missions. *Biblical Models.* Three biblical models of financing missionary efforts are found in the life of Paul. He wrote to the Philippians that he had learned to trust God in all circumstances to provide his needs (Phil.

4:12–14). A tentmaker by trade (Acts 18:3), he mentioned to the Ephesians and the Thessalonians that he provided his own needs through his labor (Acts 20:34 and 1 Thess. 2:9). TENT-MAKING MISSION, as it is known today, is named after this practice. In writing to the Corinthians, however, Paul directly urged them to give generously (2 Cor. 8–9). His flexibility for financing missionary work illustrates a general principle that any method which is ethically sound and God-honoring may be considered acceptable.

Types of Missionary Support. The most common method of mission funding has long been the voluntary contribution of members of local churches, though there are multiple means used to channel what is given to where it is needed. Some denominational missions assess member churches on a per capita basis to fund the denominational mission efforts, while others allow each church to develop its own mission budget and give money as it sees fit. Non-denominational mission agencies also serve as administrative conduits through which money is collected and distributed (*see also* FAITH MISSIONS). Many agencies require each missionary to raise his or her own individual support, while others form a central pool for which every missionary raises money and out of which all salaries and project funding comes.

Following Paul's example (Acts 18:3), many continue to engage in tent-making mission. This is perhaps the most common method of financing Third-World missionaries, whose churches and agencies often do not have the financial capability to underwrite international travel or urban mission work among the economic elite in the major cities of the world.

Since the dawn of political states looking favorably on Christianity, missions have also been financed out of state treasuries, including financial grants, land grants, and imperial patronages. During the colonial era, many Protestant efforts were financed by colonial grant-in-aid deals which mutually benefited missionary and colonial enterprise. The resulting entanglements of church and state, however, often left a mixed perception on the part of both missionaries and the national churches, with the latter seeing the former as agents of the supporting state rather than ambassadors of Christ.

Finally, contemporary economic trends in the West have enabled the development of numerous private foundations and trust funds, many of which underwrite projects and otherwise finance Christian charitable work as well as direct evangelistic endeavors.

Issues in Financing Mission. Recently, however, several issues of significance for future mission financing have been raised. First, at least in North America, mission giving has largely come out of discretionary income, which has been dry-ing up over the last few decades. While a wealthy generation that is now in process of dying has been leaving large gifts to missionary work in wills and trust funds, such giving is generally not projected to extend beyond this generation.

Second, many Western churches and agencies have begun to build giving policies around the financing of Third World missionaries, who are significantly cheaper than Western missionaries. In general this emphasis, based on new thinking of global partnership and cost-effectiveness, is a welcome change. Unfortunately, however, for some it has become an inappropriate vehicle to call for a cessation of supporting Western missionaries altogether (*see also* FOREIGN FINANCING OF INDIGENOUS WORKERS).

Third, some rightly question the amount that Western missionaries feel they must raise, which often adds up to many thousands of dollars per month to finance family travel and lifestyles which are often well above the level of indigenous populations along with benefits such as health insurance and retirement income. The implications of this for giving patterns and priorities is now being felt in churches, mission agencies, and on the various fields of service (Bonk; *see also* MISSIONARY AFFLUENCE).

Fourth, control of money and exercise of power cannot be separated as easily as we might like. This is especially significant when foreign funds have been used to initiate and preserve large missionary institutions (e.g., schools, and hospitals) which the local economy could not support unaided. Such institutions have tended to foster dependence rather than PARTNERSHIP in missionary efforts.

Finally, alarms over future Western missionary funding has begun to sound in many quarters. Models that have become traditional in the West, such as the mission agency relying on local churches to passively and unquestioningly give whenever approached, no longer hold. Discretionary finances in the consumer-driven Western cultures appear to be dwindling, as in commitment to traditional mission fund-raising techniques.

In light of these factors, it will be increasingly important in the future to find new and appropriate ways to creatively trust God to supply the necessary means for engaging in the missionary task. However, since it is God's intention to see the whole world reached, it does not seem unreasonable to assume that he will continue to provide the means to do so, though not necessarily in the ways we expect and not without our taking seriously our responsibility to the GREAT COMMISSION.

A. SCOTT MOREAU

Bibliography. J. Bonk, *Missions and Money: Affluence as a Western Missionary Problem;* L. Bush, *Funding Third World Missions; CDCWM*, pp. 208–9; J. F. Engel, *A Clouded Future: Advancing North American World Missions;* J. Ronsvale and S. Ronsvale, *Behind the Stained Glass Windows.*

Finkenbinder, Paul Edwin (1921–). American missionary evangelist. Born in Santurce, Puerto Rico, of missionary parents, he was bilingual in Spanish and English from an early age. After finishing his education in the United States and pastoring briefly a church in New Mexico, he and his wife Linda went to El Salvador in 1943 as Assemblies of God missionaries. People in El Salvador began calling him Hermano Pablo (Brother Paul) because they could not pronounce "Finkenbinder." In 1955 he began broadcasting a five-minute radio program that eventually became known as *Un Mensaje a la Conciencia* (A Message to the Conscience). The program was especially aimed at the machismo of non-Christian men who considered religion womanly. In 1960 he began preparing television broadcasts as well. The Finkenbinders moved to Costa Mesa, California, in 1964 and that has been the base of Hermano Pablo Ministries ever since. By 1995 Finkenbinder's programs were broadcast over 1,911 radio and 317 television stations in 28 countries. His column was carried in 179 papers. Besides being one of the leading Protestant broadcasters in Latin America, he led city crusades, pastor seminars, and university meetings and produced Christian dramatic films based on the Bible. His broadcasts and films have won numerous awards from Christian organizations.

ROBERT SHUSTER

Bibliography. S. R. Sywulka, *TCDCB*, p. 142.

Finland (*Est. 2000 pop.: 5,201,000; 338,145 sq. km. [130,558 sq. mi.]*). Finland is the fifth largest country in Europe (exclusive of the Russian federation). Although Finland is so vast, its population is only about one-third as large as that of the Netherlands. The industrialized southern section of the country is the most densely populated with about eight times as many people per square mile as in the northern two-thirds of the country. Finland is one of the leading manufacturers and exporters of timber and paper products. The economy depends heavily on the forestry industry.

Finland borders Norway on the north, the Russian federation on the east, the Gulf of Finland on the south, and the Gulf of Bothnia and Sweden on the west. The hostility of their neighbors has frequently forced the Finnish people to defend themselves. There have been battles with Russia and Sweden throughout the ages for control of the land. During the eighteenth century a growing separatist movement in Finland demanded independence. Independence was declared on December 6, 1917. As a result of the war of 1808–9, Sweden surrendered Finland to Russia. Russia allowed the Finns to retain their old Constitution. Finland continued to battle Russia for the Karelian territories, however. Finally, a peace treaty was signed in 1947.

Upon conquering Finland in the twelfth century, Sweden introduced Christianity. In the sixteenth century, as Sweden consolidated its authority in Finland, Lutheranism was proclaimed the official religion. Currently, the Lutheran and Orthodox churches are recognized as official state churches. The Finnish Constitution, adopted in 1919, allows freedom of worship.

Today, the Evangelical Lutheran Church claims 88.4 percent of the population of 5.2 million; the Orthodox Church, 1.1 percent; the Roman Catholic Church, 0.1 percent; and other denominations, 0.8 percent; 9.6 percent have no church affiliation. The Lutheran churches that are evangelical have been fairly successful with revivals and fellowship meetings. The attendance at their Sunday services is very low, however (4 percent). This may indicate that the traditional services are not meeting the needs of the members, while the more casual and personal fellowship meetings are fulfilling spiritual and relational needs. The free churches, which tend to be less traditional in their forms, are growing; and groups that target youth are proving successful. Given the economic recession that followed the collapse of the Soviet Union (unemployment in Finland has run as high as 18 percent) as well as other challenges of daily living, alcoholism has become a problem and provides a further challenge for Christian evangelism in Finland. Some Finnish Christians have chosen to focus on evangelizing their neighbors. The collapse of communism in Russia has provided others with an opportunity to share the gospel with the Russian people and to be a support to the Christians in Estonia.

MARKUS WAGNER

Finney, Charles Grandison (1792–1875). American evangelist, theologian, and educator. Born in Warren, Connecticut, he received little religious instruction and only brief formal education. He was practicing law when converted on October 10, 1821. He was licensed to preach in 1823 and ordained as an evangelist in 1824. His meetings in western New York began drawing large crowds and strong responses. Finney preached in a simple, lawyerly, unsentimental way to convince people of their sin and need for deliverance. His "new methods" were based on New School Presbyterian beliefs that put greater emphasis on a sinner's ability to choose redemption. Soon he was preaching in the largest cities of the North. From 1832 until 1837, he was a pastor in New York City. Men and women converted or influenced by Finney became leaders in antislavery, temperance, anti-Mason, and home and foreign mission movements. Finney joined the Congregational church in 1836. The next year he became professor of theology at Oberlin College (Ohio), where he taught until his death. He also served as president from 1851 until 1866. He regularly held revival meetings in urban settings (twice in England) until 1860. His meetings, classes, and books shaped generations of church leaders, and the mission movement in the United States was spurred on by his emphasis on the need for sinners to accept Christ and for Christians to preach salvation.

ROBERT SHUSTER

Bibliography. C. G. Finney, *Revivals of Religion;* idem, *The Memoirs of Charles G. Finney: The Complete Restored Text;* K. Hardman, *Charles Grandison Finney 1792–1875: Revivalist and Reformer.*

Finnish Mission Boards and Societies. Finland became independent only in 1917, after a century of Russian czarist rule and, before that, seven centuries of Swedish domination. The oldest and, until recently, largest sending agency, the Finnish Missionary Society, was founded in 1959 and traditionally was organizationally independent of, but closely linked with, the Lutheran Church. It sent out its first missionaries in 1870 to the northernmost region (Ovamboland) of what is now Namibia and a strong Lutheran Church eventually resulted in what remained its main receiving field. In 1901, missionaries were sent to China. After World War II they were withdrawn, but work, usually cooperating with other agencies, was begun in Tanzania, Taiwan, Pakistan, and Jerusalem. By the mid-1960s there were nearly two hundred missionaries with this agency, representing more than 90 percent of the national church's total force, and supported by voluntary contributions rather than official church funds.

There are a few other small sending societies working within the national church. Mention should be made of the Lutheran Evangelistic Association, which began in 1873 for home mission work as part of a revival movement, but since 1900 has often supported around a dozen missionaries at a time in Japan in association with the Lutheran Church there.

The total of all Protestant free church adherents in Finland is probably under 3 percent of the population and is divided into several denominations, most of which have Swedish- and Finnish-speaking sections (which usually have separate mission programs). The Pentecostals apparently have more members than the combination of all the rest (Adventist, Baptist, Free Church Methodist, Salvation Army, etc.) In general, the small free church denominations take responsibility as a whole for their missionaries rather than through separate organizations. These missionaries often work in cooperation with international agencies, so that it is hard to identify a mission church of specifically Finnish free church origin.

However, the free churches as a whole, and the Pentecostals in particular, contribute quite disproportionately to the total missionary force from Finland. In the early 1970s there were over five hundred Finnish missionaries and this was a doubling of the figure from a decade before. The Pentecostals were sending more than a third of them (and they were going to many different fields, especially in Asia). By the early 1990s, the total of missionaries had grown to over 1,300, serving with some twenty-two agencies, six of which work within the national church. Operation Mobilization has been especially successful in recruiting Finns to serve abroad, most commonly for shorter periods of service.

DONALD TINDER

Fisk, Pliny (1792–1825). American missionary to the Middle East. Born in Massachusetts, he was educated in New England. In 1818 he and Levi Parsons were sent to the Middle East by the AMERICAN BOARD OF COMMISSIONERS FOR FOREIGN MISSIONS to determine its desirability as a field for American missionaries. All this area—Greece, Asia Minor, Palestine, Syria, and Egypt—was then under the actual or nominal control of the Ottoman Empire. They arrived in Smyrna in 1820 and stayed in that area for the next two years, studying the languages, preaching, and distributing tracts. Fisk sent back reports on the spiritual condition of the region to the *Missionary Herald*. In 1822 they traveled to Egypt, where Parsons died. Fisk continued his travels. Although he hoped to base his work on reviving the existing churches, rather than creating new ones, his preaching and distribution of tracts and the Bible offended Muslim government officials, Catholic priests, and the Maronite patriarch. By 1825, he joined three missionary recruits in Beirut, where a mission was started. He died in October of that year, just after finishing his Arabic-English dictionary. His efforts marked the beginning of American Protestant missionary work in the region. His niece Fidelia (1816–64) was, in the next generation, an influential missionary among the women of Persia.

ROBERT SHUSTER

Fiske, Fidelia (1816–64). American pioneer missionary to Turkey. Raised in Massachusetts in a strong Christian family that traced its American immigrant roots to 1637, Fiske made public confession of faith in Christ at the age of fifteen, and at the age of twenty-three began attending Mount Holyoke Seminary. After graduating, she taught at the seminary until compelled to go to Persia (now Turkey) by the request for help from a visiting missionary. She arrived in the small Nesto-

rian Community in Urumiah, Persia, in 1842. Fiske saw that one way of raising the value of women in Persian Nestorian society was to educate them. Her task was difficult, for education was not valued in Persia and the Nestorian community, though viewed as heretical in the rest of the world, considered itself Christian. She enjoyed a great deal of success, watching several of her students mature into godly Christian women and providing a model for other girls' seminaries which opened in cities throughout Persia. When forced by illness to return to America in 1858, she wrote the book *Woman and Her Savior in Persia*. After teaching for a year at Mount Holyoke Seminary, she died in the summer of 1864.

GRACE L. KLEIN

Bibliography. E. C. Dawson, *Missionary Heroines of the Cross*; P. Kretzmann, *Men and Missions: Glimpses of the Lives of Great Missionary Women*; D. L. Robert, *BDCM*, p. 213.

Fison, Lorimer (1832–1907). English missionary to Fiji. Born in Suffolk, England, he attended Caius College, Cambridge, but was suspended. He went to the goldfields in Australia in the 1850s. Following his conversion in 1860 at an open air Methodist service, he began to preach. He was appointed as a Methodist missionary to Fiji and served there 1863–72 and 1875–84. Fison was the outstanding scholar missionary in Fiji during the nineteenth century and recognized as an authority on Fijian society. He strongly supported Fijian land rights and influenced government policy in this area. In the face of the exploitation of Pacific laborers he made strong representations on their behalf. While he championed the rights of Fijian ministers he adopted a gradualist approach toward the independence of the Fijian church. As principal of Navuloa Theological Institution (1877–84) he provided valuable resources for Fijian students. His breadth of religious outlook was seen in his condemnation of the Methodist-Catholic conflict at Rotuma. His pioneering anthropological work was recognized by honorary degrees and a Civil List pension. In 1884 he returned to Australia, where he edited the Methodist paper, *The Spectator* (1888–1905), and published *Tales of Old Fiji* (1907).

ALLAN K. DAVIDSON

Bibliography. A. H. Wood, *Overseas Missions of the Australian Methodist Church*, vol. 2, Fiji.

Fjellstedt, Peter (1802–81). Swedish missionary to India and Turkey and pioneer missions promoter in Sweden. Born in Varmland, Sweden, he was a shy but very intelligent young man who changed his name to Fjellstedt at age sixteen. After completing his studies, he joined the BASEL MISSION SOCIETY (BaMS) in 1827 because the Church in Sweden had no structures for sending their own missionaries. Prior to departure for India, BaMS required that he return to his homeland to help foster interest in missions. His preaching inspired the formation of the Swedish Missionary Society in 1829. Six years later, a society of the same name but national in its scope was established. After a four-year term in India and another in Smyrna, Turkey, he returned to Europe, where he became a traveling preacher to promote mission interest across the Continent. His sweeping success in addition to his commitment to educating missionaries in biblical and theological studies led to the formation of the first mission institute in Sweden in 1846. As director of the Lund Institute he not only saw to the grounding of the students in the fundamentals; he also launched *Lunds Mission-Tidning*, a newspaper created solely for the purpose of informing people about the newly formed Lund Missionary Society and to stimulate more interest in the cause of missions. It is fair to say that, before his death, he had succeeded in making missions an important imperative in the life of the Swedish church.

WENDY S. LARSON

Bibliography. E. E. Eklund, *Peter Fjellstedt: Missionary Mentor to Three Continents*; C. F. Hallencreutz, *CDCWM*, p. 210.

Flaw of the Excluded Middle. A concept developed by missiologist Paul Hiebert in an article in *Missiology* 10:1 (January 1982, pp. 35–47) and later reprinted in *Anthropological Reflections on Missiological Issues.* Hiebert observed that the Western two-tiered view of the universe typically left out an entire dimension seen quite readily by people of non-Western cultures. Hiebert built his analysis on a two-dimensional matrix. The first dimension is that of three worlds or domains: (1) a seen world (that which is of this world and seen), (2) the unseen of this world (that which is of this world but not seen), and (3) an unseen transempirical world (that which pertains to heavens, hells, and other worlds). The second dimension is that of two types of analogies people use to explain the powers around them: (1) an organic analogy (powers are personal, e.g., gods and spirits) and (2) a mechanical analogy (powers are impersonal, e.g., gravity and electricity). Combining the seen/unseen/transempirical worlds and organic/mechanical analogies into a matrix, Hiebert's model highlighted the difference between Westerners, who tend to see only two worlds (the seen world and the transempirical world) and many non-Westerners who recognize the middle world, comprised of unseen powers (magical forces, evil eye, mana) and spirits that are very much a part of everyday human life (e.g., a person is ill because of a curse or a spirit

attack). The blind spot in the Western worldview Hiebert labeled the flaw of the excluded middle.

His model was quickly picked up by missionaries and missiologists working among non-Western populations, especially those working in areas such as SPIRITUAL WARFARE. It was used to give legitimacy to demonic and spiritual explanations of phenomena that had been previously overlooked by Western theology, anthropology, and missiology, all of which tended to look for so-called natural explanations for the observed phenomena. As a tool it named an area many evangelical missionaries had missed in their training and identified the sources of their discomfort in finding ways to contextually address middle world issues in non-Western cultures.

For some, however, the pendulum has swung so far that the danger is a flaw of an *expanded* middle in which every strange event is thought to have a middle domain explanation; this is especially significant in the contemporary discussion of TERRITORIAL SPIRITS. Using the middle domain to explain all such events is taking Hiebert's analytic model beyond its intention, which was to address the ways events are explained in differing cultures rather than to give an ontological picture of the explanations behind such events.

A. SCOTT MOREAU

SEE ALSO Folk Religions.

Flynn, John (1880–1951). Australian Presbyterian minister, missionary, and founder of Australian Inland Mission. Developing a passion for Australian outback while on shearer's missions and teaching, Flynn used his church contacts to mobilize Presbyterian and wider church interest in the largely uncared-for outback. First through his highly successful publication *Bushman's Companion* (1910), then through the Oodnadatta Nursing Hostel (1911) Flynn began a long career of developing services and ministry to bush dwellers. The Oodnadatta institution developed along the lines of Flynn's vision for a "Mantle of Safety" into a chain of hostels, hospitals, and chaplaincies, followed by the foundation of the AIM Aerial Medical Service (AMS, a.k.a. Flying Doctor Service). Services were soon also extended to the aboriginal populations of the bush, though his care for indigenous people was long questioned by Charles Duguid. The AMS relied heavily on contact, leading Flynn to champion the use of radio in remote stations, leading to considerable technological advance. His ceaseless advertisement of his programs and his energetic apologetic for the bush caused him to become a key government advisor on services to the outback. The AMS was nationalized and became the Flying Doctor Service of Australia after 1942 (later "Royal"). Flynn was internationally recognized for his work, receiving an OBE and a number of honorary doctorates. He became the symbol of Christian involvement in national affairs, later appearing on the Australian $20 bill. Too activist and incarnational to be evangelical in his theology, Flynn was influenced in younger life by German romanticism and idealism. Long, thin, and given to drawling sermons, which told a story without "religious tags" or "emotional blackmail of any sort," he suited the outback better than the polish required in the city. At his request, he was buried at the foot of Mount Gillen, outside Alice Springs, central Australia.

MARK HUTCHINSON

Bibliography. G. Bucknall, *Australian Dictionary of Biography,* vol. 8; M. McKenzi, *Fred McKay: Successor to Flynn of the Inland;* W. S. McPheat, *John Flynn: Apostle to the Inland.*

Folk Religions. Most scholars trained in Western schools define religion in terms of the formal, institutionalized religions such as Christianity, Judaism, Islam, Hinduism, Buddhism, and Sikhism, most of which claim universal application. These have sacred texts and commentaries, philosophical traditions and orthodoxies, professional leaders and schools, and organized churches, temples, and mosques.

During the age of exploration, travelers, missionaries, and colonial administrators encountered a great many oral religions around the world. These centered around rituals, myths, ancestors, spirits, witchcraft, and magic, and were particularist in nature. Each tribe and people group had its own gods, and did not seek to convert other peoples to its beliefs.

The initial response of Western scholars was to see these oral religions as superstitions based on prelogical thought. They called these 'ANIMISM,' in contrast to 'religions,' which they believed were logical and true. They assumed that when the high religions came, the people would abandon their superstitions. Consequently, Christian missionaries rarely took time to study the traditional religions or to deal with them.

As missionaries and anthropologists began to study traditional religions, they found that underlying these are sophisticated conceptual systems that can be articulated by the philosophers in these societies. Moreover, they found that when traditional religionists became Christians, Hindus, or Muslims, they did not abandon their old ways, but added high religious beliefs over the old leading to two-tiered religious systems. While the leaders might be committed wholly to Islam or Hinduism, the common folk went to the mosque or temple to answer some questions, and to the shaman and witch doctor to answer other ones. Most converts were folk Muslims or folk Hindus. Christian missions faces the same problem of split-level religion. Lay Christians around

the world go to churches on Sunday, but to traditional healers, exorcists, diviners, and priests during the week. To understand this religion of the common folk, we need to examine the nature of formal and informal religion.

Formal religions deal with ontological questions regarding the ultimate origins, meaning, and end of this world, of humankind, and of individual persons, which they affirm are universally true for all people. Most of the leaders are literate and develop sophisticated philosophical systems based on sacred texts to answer these questions, and are concerned that the laypeople learn and accept these truths. Formal religions have local traditions—the local gatherings of lay followers who live their lives out in the world, and have little knowledge of or time for the theological debates of the great tradition. They provide the people with a sense of the cosmic story and their place in it as they participate in the prescribed rituals.

But high religions often leave unanswered the existential questions ordinary people face in their everyday lives. What is the meaning of life here on earth when I am caught in meaningless drudgery to make a living? How can I prevent calamities such as illnesses and crop failures? Why did my child die so suddenly, leaving no one to care for me in my old age? People know that they need to care for their bodies to be healthy, and to plant and tend their fields to get crops, but when their folk sciences fail, what do they do? If their formal religion provides no answers, they turn to animistic practices—to magic, spirits, ancestors, divination, and other local religious practices.

Folk religions are ad hoc mixtures of local expressions of formal religions and local animistic beliefs and practices. They are sets of loosely related practices, often mutually contradictory, used not to present a coherent true view of reality but to produce immediate results. They provide answers to the existential questions of everyday life. One is the meaning of life here on earth, and an explanation of death, not for those who die, but for those who remain behind and must deal with the grief and loss. A second is the desire for a good life, and the need to deal with the constant crises of life such as illness, spirit possession, droughts, famines, and defeats in battle. A third is the need to make everyday decisions regarding marriage, farming, business, hunting and raids, and the problem that much is unknown. A fourth is the desire for justice and social order, and the constant experiences of injustice, offense, and pollution. Folk religions provide various courses of action to those facing illnesses, bad fortunes, sudden deaths, failure in love and marriage, and guidance for those making important decisions.

The relationship between the leaders of formal religions and the animistic practices of their followers is an uneasy one. In many cases, such as in Islamic fundamentalism, the leaders condemn them as heretical and seek to stamp them out, often by force. In other cases, such as in Hinduism, formal and local folk beliefs and rites are interwoven in complex accommodations. Tribal and local gods are absorbed into Hinduism by identifying them as incarnations of one of the high Hindu deities. Local rites are embedded in orthodox rituals, and goddesses and local spirits are enshrined under the trees and on the edges of Hindu temples.

Given this difference in focus, it should not surprise us that Christian missionaries and leaders trained in formal Christianity called people to eternal salvation, and often failed to address the everyday problems the people were facing. Consequently the people continued to go to traditional healers and diviners. In many cases, new converts knew that the leaders objected to their old ways, so they continued these practices in secret. Animistic beliefs and practices did not disappear, nor were they stamped out. They simply went underground. The notable exception are the independent churches arising around the world, which often seek to provide answers to the problems of everyday life (*see* AFRICAN INITIATED CHURCH MOVEMENT).

Dealing with folk religious beliefs and practices remains an unfinished task in the CONTEXTUALIZATION of the gospel in churches around the world, young and old. They often have few answers to the questions of sickness, spirits, witchcraft, ancestors, and guidance, so Christians turn to their old ways for answers, even as they go to church for forgiveness and fellowship with God.

There is a growing awareness of the need for the church to provide a whole gospel that addresses both the ultimate and existential questions the common people face. It must present the Good News of forgiveness, salvation, and reconciliation with God. It must also show that this Good News answers the everyday questions of the people. If it does not proclaim a whole gospel, lay folk will continue to come to the church for eternal salvation, but turn elsewhere to deal with the spiritual problems of everyday life. The result will continue to be a two-tiered Christianity, which, in the long run, will make Christianity marginal in their lives, or turn it into CHRISTO-PAGANISM in which the gospel becomes captive to the local culture and its worldview.

PAUL G. HIEBERT

Bibliography. P. Hiebert, D. Gilliland, and T. Tienou, *Folk Religions;* A. C. Lehmann and J. E. Myers, *Magic, Witchcraft and Religion: An Anthropological Study of the Supernatural;* G. Van Rheenen, *Communicating Christ in Animistic Contexts.*

Folklore. A wide range of stories, traditions, beliefs, and practices that have been preserved by a people but not accepted as part of the official religion. The church has regarded such traditions as mere superstitions, and the Enlightenment philosophers attacked them as unscientific and worthless. The first steps to study religious folklore were taken by the Grimm brothers, who were part of the nineteenth-century Romantic movement. The Grimms claimed that there was a direct relationship between ancient MYTH and modern fairy tales, which the folklorist should bring to light.

Much folklore is connected with the calendar or stages in the life cycle—birth, marriage, and death. Because a newborn child and its mother are especially exposed to danger, precautions must be taken. A common story is that the fairies may try to steal the baby and replace it with one that is deformed. Brides are encouraged to wear something borrowed and something blue. At a funeral the curtains of the house may be kept closed and the mourners dress in black. Many European people still touch wood for luck.

Folklore is particularly rich among children: studies have shown that they may retain elements that have passed out of use among adults. They have songs and rhymes addressed to ladybirds, butterflies, snails, the first tooth, and the new month. The sun may be asked to shine, and the rain to go away and come another day. Regional repertories are extensive, and though social mobility has increased, many of the stories remain.

DAVID BURNETT

Foreign Financing of Indigenous Workers.
Nineteenth-century missionaries often employed local personnel as evangelists, pastors, and Bible women, but eventually they came to realize that unhealthy DEPENDENCY and "rice Christian" attitudes often resulted from this employer-employee relationship. In reaction to this problem, mission theorists insisted that churches and ministries in the non-Western world should be totally self-governing, self-propagating, and especially self-supporting (*see* INDIGENOUS CHURCHES). By the early twentieth century many missions had established firm policies against any mission pay or subsidy for local pastors and evangelists.

However, some people believed that insisting on full self-support was an overreaction. Instead, they advocated careful financial partnership with indigenous ministries, treating them as equals rather than employees. Partners International (then CNEC) was founded in 1943 for that express purpose. Among the most vocal advocates of financial support for indigenous workers were Robert Finley, founder of International Students, Inc. and Christian Aid; his brother Allen, president of

CNEC/Partners International; and Ian North, Australian founder of Ambassadors for Christ.

As Western colonialism dissolved, between 1946 and 1960, European and American mainline denominations quickly handed over leadership of the churches and institutions their missionaries had established in former colonies. To symbolize this new relationship, American Presbyterians even began to call their missionaries "FRATERNAL WORKERS."

Theologically conservative missions were slower to change but as the churches in the Third World increased rapidly in size and maturity, attitudes among leaders of evangelical missions began to shift. In 1972 the Latin America Mission granted full autonomy to all its field ministries and openly espoused continual financial partnership with them. To a lesser degree, other missions began to follow suit.

Around 1980 two new evangelical partnering agencies were formed, Gospel for Asia and Overseas Council for Theological Education. By the late 1980s partnership with indigenous ministries as equals had become almost a watchword. Scores of new organizations were formed for the express purpose of supporting indigenous workers and ministries in the Third World, instead of sending out missionaries from the West. By 1996 there were more than 110 such organizations in North America alone. In October of that year the leaders of more than fifty of these new support missions met together at the Billy Graham Center in Wheaton, Illinois, for the first "Consultation on Support of Indigenous Ministries."

The two most common questions that arise when considering foreign financing of indigenous workers are:

1. How can you give them financial assistance without creating unhealthy dependency?
2. How can you assure financial accountability and proper use of funds if you have no direct control over them?

Advocates of financial assistance for indigenous workers insist that interdependency between different parts of the Body of Christ is both biblical and healthy. Unhealthy dependency develops when one partner tries to exercise too much control. Usually it is the provider of financial resources that does so.

If most of the funding comes from a foreign source, then the recipients will feel they cannot risk offending that source. But if the vision, control, and a majority of the funding is indigenous and an open trust relationship exists between the two parties, then foreign funding can leverage and multiply the effectiveness of indigenous ministries without creating unhealthy dependency.

Accountability is greatly enhanced by funding only ministry teams that are organized and have governing boards or similar accountability structures. Giving funds to indigenous workers who are "lone rangers" is always fraught with danger, however effective or charismatic the leaders may be. It is perfectly proper to require regular financial reports by the recipients and even external audits where possible. However, the key to success is to have open trust relationships in a partnership between equals.

CHARLES BENNETT

SEE ALSO Globalization.

Bibliography. L. Bush and L. Lutz, *Partnering in Ministry;* A. Finley and L. Lutz, *The Family Tie;* J. H. Kraakevik, ed., *Partners in the Gospel;* D. Rickett and D. Welliver, eds., *Supporting Indigenous Ministries;* W. Taylor, ed., *Kingdom Partnerships for Synergy in Missions.*

Foreign Missions Inquiry, Laymen's. Interdenominational endeavor that grew out of the concern of a number of Baptist laymen, including John D. Rockefeller, over the difficulties that foreign missions were encountering in securing support from contributors and young people. A committee was formed with a membership from seven denominations, including the Northern Baptists, Congregational, Methodist Episcopal, Presbyterian Church in the USA, Protestant Episcopal, Reformed Church in America, and United Presbyterian to try to formulate an effective approach to missions in the modern world. Each of these churches was informally represented by five individuals who made up the Directors of the Inquiry.

In the fall of 1930 three teams of carefully selected research workers, "fact finders," were sent out to survey the missions of these denominations in India, Burma, China, and Japan. Their work was placed at the disposal of a fifteen-member commission of appraisal headed by the distinguished philosopher WILLIAM E. HOCKING. They spent about nine months visiting the countries surveyed and writing the report, *Re-Thinking Missions* (1932). A vigorous debate resulted, concentrating on the liberal theological convictions found in the document. The Christian message, the report explained, had passed beyond arguments "over details of the mode of creation, the age of the earth, the descent of man, miracle and law, to the state of maturity in which there is little disposition to believe that sincere and aspiring seekers after God in other religions are to be damned: it has become less concerned in any land to save men from eternal punishment than from the danger of losing the supreme good" (p. 19). It advocated that missionaries should cooperate with the good in other religions and cultures to secure social justice and to purify unhealthy religious practices, and that the ultimate goal should be the emergence of the various faiths out of their isolation into a world fellowship of religion. It also noted that the great dangers with which all religions had to deal were communism and secularism.

The report was widely criticized, especially in Europe, for its abdication of the basic MISSIONARY TASK of proclaiming the gospel. However, subsequent to the report, it proved impossible for the major Protestant denominations to return to missions with the same assurance of the WORLD MISSIONARY CONFERENCE (EDINBURGH 1910). Despite the controversy surrounding the Inquiry's conclusions, the wealth of information found in the "fact finders" reports published in the supplementary volumes continue to be valuable.

ROBERT G. CLOUSE

Bibliography. W. E. Hocking, *Re-Thinking Missions, A Laymen's Inquiry After One Hundred Years;* K. A. Latourette, *IRM* 22 (1933): 153–73; idem, *IRM* 46 (1957): 164–70; *Laymen's Foreign Missions Inquiry, Supplemental Series* (7 vols.).

Foreknowledge. *See* DIVINE ELECTION.

Forgiveness of Sins. The forgiveness of sins is at the very heart of the Christian message. It is a profoundly complex doctrine that ultimately includes our idea of God, of God's relation to the world, of the nature of humankind, of sin, of the incarnation, death, and resurrection of Jesus, of the last judgment, and of our eternal state in heaven or hell. The concept of forgiveness was at the core of Israel's worship in both tabernacle and temple, centering upon sacrifices—some even being named sin-offering, trespass-offering, and peace-offering. These offerings dealt with the problem of sin and restored peace with God by affirming the reality of forgiveness through a God-appointed religious practitioner.

But forgiveness of sin is not just a national or a theological issue. It is also a very personal issue, lying deep within the human heart. We all struggle with the realization that something is drastically wrong that we cannot put right. We have offended God and his moral laws and justly deserve judgment. Yet also deep within us we know that God can forgive us our sins, so we cry out to him for that remission. In the New Testament, the message of forgiveness was brought by John the Baptist (Luke 3:3), by Jesus in his earthly life (Mark 2:5, 7, 10) and in his post-resurrection state (Luke 24:45–47), by Peter at Pentecost (Acts 2:38), and by Paul as he traveled on his missionary journeys (Acts 13:38, 39). In the Book of Revelation the redeemed of God are those who conquered through the blood of the Lamb (Rev. 5:9; 7:14; 12:11) and Jesus is symbolically seen as the triumphant slain Lamb who can unfold the destiny of the nations and is wor-

thy of all praise (Rev. 5:6–10). The Christian message is a message of forgiveness and the redeemed who spend their eternity with God are those who have been forgiven of their sins.

The Biblical Doctrine of Forgiveness. Theologically speaking, there are three basic components to the doctrine of forgiveness: the nature of humankind, the nature of God, and the provision that God has made to restore the broken relationship between himself and his fallen world.

The Fallen Nature of Humankind. It is not necessary to consider every aspect of the human person in order to discuss the nature of forgiveness; one alone is necessary, the fact of human sinfulness (*see* SIN). It is this negative quality, oddly enough, that lifts us most clearly above the rest of our earthly, created order and shows us most decisively what we are not to be, even though that is what we are. This is true because sin is a moral category and only moral, responsible beings may sin. And because guilt attends our sin, we are painfully aware that sin ought not to be there even though it is and it is unquestionably ours; we cannot honestly blame anyone else. All the major religions of the world have concepts of morality, sin, guilt, and responsibility (*see also* HUMAN CONDITION IN WORLD RELIGIONS). The Bible, in particular, speaks with great force and clarity here, emphasizing the *inherent* nature of our sinfulness, its gravity, and its consequences. Sin is not simply something that we have done wrong or some hurt we have inflicted upon someone else; sin is an offense against God and God's moral requirements, requirements that derive from his very nature. Were the moral nature of the universe simply the result of God's decisions, they would not have ultimate ontic reality and could be changed at will. Rather, the moral categories—the violation of which makes sin sinful—are expressions of the very nature of reality as God has created it, with ourselves as God intended us to be, and with God himself as he eternally is (*see* DIVINE ATTRIBUTES OF GOD). Hence, David cries out, "I know my transgressions and my sin is always before me. Against you, you only have I sinned and done what is evil in your sight" (Ps. 51:3, 4). As the contemporary psychologist Karl Menninger puts it, sin is "An implicitly aggressive quality—a ruthlessness, a hurting, a breaking away from God and from the rest of humanity, a partial alienation, or act of rebellion. . . . Sin has a willful, defiant or disloyal quality. *Someone* is defied or offended or hurt" (*Whatever Became of Sin?* p. 19)—and that someone is God. The Bible presents an unremitting picture of universal human sinfulness, surrounded by the apostle Paul in Romans 3:10–18, concluding with "All have sinned and fall short of the glory of God" (Rom. 3:23).

Among the many dire consequences of sin, the most devastating is alienation from God, which results in eternal condemnation. The sinful mind is hostile to God (Rom. 8:7), sinners are the enemies of God (Rom. 5:10), we are dead in our trespasses and sins (Eph. 2:1), the wrath of God abides upon us (John 3:36), and sinners will not inherit the kingdom of God (1 Cor. 6:9) but "will be punished with everlasting destruction and shut out from the presence of the Lord and from the majesty of his power" (2 Thess. 1:8).

The radical nature of our sinfulness renders us incapable of rectifying the situation. We are incapable of bringing anything of sufficient value or ultimacy to God of such a nature as to atone for our sins. We are, in fact, lost in our sins and totally unable to find a way out of our hopeless situation.

The Nature of God. As has already been seen, sin is, in essence, a violation of the nature of God, but what is it in God that is violated? Scripturally speaking, it is the totality of God's infinite perfections or attributes. All that God is recoils from that which is less than morally perfect and the attempt to single out one attribute or another that is most offended by sin would be to slice God up into categories as though God were some internally unrelated collection of qualities, rather than a unified, personal Being. Having said that, however, the holiness of God does stand out as the quality most obviously violated when human beings sin (Josh. 24:19; Pss. 5:4; 92:15; Hab. 1:13; Rev. 6:10). The Bible is replete with affirmations of God's holiness and of the demand that we be holy (Exod. 15:11; Lev. 11:44, 45; Isa. 6:3; 1 Peter 1:15) and when we fail to live up to God's standards we fall under the just judgment of God. God's justice and impartiality decree that everyone be treated fairly and equally, which translates into everyone being equally under the judgment of God, since every one of us has violated God's commands.

Were this the end of the story, humankind would be in a sorry state, for there could be no such thing as forgiveness. However, God's love and his mercy work alongside his holiness and justice in such a way that all aspects of his being are satisfied. The Scriptures reveal a God, who although he is holy, also delights in mercy and forgiveness (Deut. 4:31; Neh. 9:31; Ps. 78:38; Isa. 55:7; Dan. 9:9; Luke 6:35). "Who is a God like you?" asks Micah, "Who pardons sin and forgives the transgression of the remnant of his inheritance?" Who, indeed? There is no other God who can forgive the sins of lost humanity.

The Provision of God for Forgiveness. There was only one way that the totality of God's being could be satisfied that the demands of his holiness and justice be met while at the same time expressing God's love and mercy. To do that God devised a plan of salvation that met his infinite demands and offered full salvation to the lost, at no cost to them, since they were in no position to pay anything. No human being could do such a

thing, yet it had to be done on the human plane, because it was for the sake of human beings. The infinite demands of God could only be met by the infinite God himself. This line of reasoning underlies the New Testament's doctrine of the incarnation, death, and resurrection of Christ. Only God could meet the demands of God, so the second person of the Trinity became one of us in order to pay the price of sin, freeing God up to offer forgiveness of sin to the lost (2 Cor. 5:21). As Paul put it, "God was in Christ, reconciling the world unto himself" (2 Cor. 5:19). In this way God could be both just and the One who justifies the person who has faith in Jesus, because all the requirements of his holiness, justice, love, and mercy have been met (Rom. 3:25, 26). Specifically, the redemptive work of God is the death of Jesus Christ on the cross. There the punishment due us was paid for by God himself in the person of his Son (Rom. 5:6–10; 1 Cor. 15:3; Gal. 1:4; Eph. 2:13). Jesus ties the forgiveness of sins directly to his coming death, when at the last supper he says, "This is my blood of the covenant, which is poured out for many for the forgiveness of sins" (Matt. 26:28).

The Missiological Implications of Forgiveness. When considering the missiological implications of forgiveness, what stands out most prominently in the New Testament is the UNIQUENESS OF CHRIST, who he is and what he has done. Because there is only one God, there is only one Son of God, who died for sin once for all. There is only one plan of salvation and one Savior who must be proclaimed to all the earth for "Salvation is found in no one else, for there is no other name under heaven given to men by which we must be saved" (Acts 4:12). The fact of Christ's uniqueness and that forgiveness of sin may be found nowhere else lays a moral imperative upon the church to make his name known. There are not many saviors for many people, but only one savior for all peoples and that is the incarnate Son of God who died and rose again. It is this fact that underlies the command of God himself to us that repentance and forgiveness of sins be preached in Jesus' name to all nations (Luke 24:47). Where else can salvation be found except in Jesus? Because of this, those who had experienced the forgiveness of their sins were to be empowered by the Holy Spirit and then become "witnesses in Jerusalem, and in all Judea and Samaria, and to the ends of the earth" (Acts 1:8). Peter began this on the day of Pentecost in Jerusalem offering his countrymen forgiveness of their sins in Jesus' name (Acts 2:38), continuing this to the Gentile Cornelius in Caesarea (Acts 10:43), then reaching others in Asia Minor (1 Peter 1:1, 2), ultimately giving his life for the gospel in Rome during the Neronian Persecution. Others went elsewhere. Paul traveled extensively across the Roman world, John went to Ephesus,

Titus went to Crete, Mark went to Egypt, and Thomas, according to some records, went to India.

What motivated these early believers was certainly the uniqueness of their message, coupled with the command of God, but they had also experienced the love of God in their own forgiveness and hence wished to share that sense of release with others (2 Cor. 5:14). For whatever reason, the early church realized that the forgiveness of sins must be at the heart of their message (Acts 10:43; 13:38, 39; 26:17, 18), just as it must be today.

WALTER A. ELWELL

SEE ALSO Confession of Sin.

Bibliography. E. M. B. Green, *The Meaning of Salvation*; H. D. McDonald, *The Atonement of the Death of Christ*; H. R. Mackintosh, *The Christian Experience of Forgiveness*; K. Menninger, *Whatever Became of Sin?*; H. Vorländer, *NIDNTT* 1:697–703; J. R. W. Stott, *The Cross of Christ*, pp. 87–110; V. Taylor, *Forgiveness and Reconciliation*; W. Telfer, *The Forgiveness of Sins*.

Forman, Charles W. (1916–97). Indian-born American missionary scholar and missionary in India. Despite being born in a family of Presbyterian missionaries that spanned three generations, Forman did not consider missionary work until he was an adult. While in seminary at Union (New York), already having completed a Ph.D. (history) at the University of Wisconsin, it suddenly dawned on him that he could teach seminary in an overseas setting. In 1945 he moved to the North India United Theological College in Saharanpur, where he taught until 1950. Three years after returning to the United States he succeeded KENNETH SCOTT LATOURETTE at Yale University, where he taught for the next thirty-four years.

Deeply involved from the beginning in the Theological Education Fund of the WCC, his extensive travels in the late 1950s provided exposure to the development of educational facilities in the South Pacific that were largely unknown in the West. The lack of available research and the indigenous nature of the churches and institutions motivated him to concentrate his study and research in that part of the world. This led to positions such as chair of the Foundation for Theological Education in Southeast Asia from 1970 to 1989, publications such as *The Voice of Many Waters: The Story of the Life and Ministry of the Pacific Conference of Churches* (1982), and international recognition as an authority on the church in the South Pacific.

A. SCOTT MOREAU

Bibliography. G.H. Anderson, *BDCM*, pp. 218–19; C.W. Forman, *Christianity in the Non-Western World*; idem, *IBMR* 18 (1994): 26–28; idem, *The Island Churches of the South Pacific*; idem, *The Nation and the Kingdom*.

Forsyth, Christina nee Moir (1844–1918). Scottish missionary to South Africa. In her own words, she described herself as "a watcher for souls." Her desire was to proclaim Christ not to the masses, but to the individual. She wholeheartedly believed that through the individual she could reach the masses. Her life was a paragon of her philosophy. For thirty years, she ministered single-handedly in the remotest part of Fingoland, South Africa.

She was born in Scotland. She grew up in a Christian home, raised by parents who were deeply devoted to Scripture. At the age of fourteen, she had a religious experience after which she fully surrendered her life to Christ.

She had a desire to become a missionary and was particularly interested in South Africa. She offered herself to the Mission Board of the United Presbyterian Church in Scotland and worked in South Africa for three years. When her work was complete, she returned to Scotland and married Allan Forsyth. After his untimely death one year later, Christina returned to South Africa. She requested to work in Xolobe, the remotest part of Fingoland. Many attempts had been made by missionaries to reach the Fingos, but to no avail. All that remained in Xolobe was a deserted mission house. The Lord gave Christina a vision of Xolobe won for Christ and she never wavered from it. At forty-six years of age, she moved into the mission house, established a Sunday school, and brought many people to Christ. For thirty years, she never left the region. She worked alone, toiling in the backwoods of South Africa and scarcely ever seeing a white face. Today, Xolobe has a fully organized mission station, complete with a church building and a day school.

KATHY MCREYNOLDS

Bibliography. A. C. Ross, *BDCM*, p. 219.

France (*Est. 2000 pop.: 59,024,000; 543,965 sq. km. [210,025 sq. mi.]*). One of the largest countries in Western Europe and one of the ten wealthiest countries in the world, France has often been referred to as the "eldest Daughter of the Church" when reflecting on its rich Roman Catholic heritage, but since the Revolution of 1789, the society has become a hardened, secular state.

History of Christianity in France. The gospel was brought to France by the end of the first century A.D. via Italy and was firmly established in Lyons and Arles in the second century. The church father, Irenaeus, was consecrated the bishop of Lyons in A.D. 180 as he ministered among both the Greek-speaking community and in the vernacular. Serious persecution is recorded in A.D. 171 in both Lyons and Vienne. Further persecution under the Emperor Decius (A.D. 249–251) brought on the martyrdom of St. Denis, the Bishop of Paris, and Saturnin of Toulouse. By

A.D. 312 Christianity became the official religion of France and gained further control of the society. The conversion of Clovis, the king of the Franks, on Christmas Day in A.D. 496 marked the beginning of the strong ties of the church and state. COLUMBANUS (c. 543–615) and BONIFACE (680–754), early missionaries from the British Isles, journeyed through France.

The ties of church and state were strengthened under Charlemagne of the Holy Roman Empire in A.D. 800. The CRUSADES to recapture the Holy Land were first preached in A.D. 1095 by Bernard de Clairvaux. The church's power and intolerance grew and forced movements of laity that emphasized personal piety and the translation of the Bible into the vernacular. At the height of the Reformation the Protestants and their sympathizers were estimated to encompass nearly a quarter of France's population. This posed a tremendous threat to the monarchy and the Roman Catholic Church and ultimately led to a war of religion that drained France of many of her educated literate artisans and others. Many lost their lives and hundreds of thousands left France for Switzerland, Germany, South Africa, and even the American colonies. By the time of the French Revolution, the Protestants found more freedom but had little strength. Over the nineteenth century while the Roman Catholics sought in vain to regain their former strength and power over French society, missionaries/pastors from Scotland (Haldane) and England (Baptists and Methodists) established a foothold. In the early twentieth century the Salvationists and the Welsh Revival made their mark.

In terms of France's mission outreach, the French have played a significant role in Catholic missions. In addition to the work of the PARIS EVANGELICAL MISSION SOCIETY, other smaller French Protestant mission societies have been active over the past two centuries (*see also* FRENCH MISSION BOARDS AND SOCIETIES).

People of France. There are growing ethnic minorities due to naturalization and immigration. The ethnic French are 74.7 percent with regional minorities including the Breton, Alsatian, Flemish, Basque, Corsican, and Catalan. National minorities include the Jews, West Indian Antilleans, Gypsies, and Reunionese. North Africans and Middle Easterners comprise 7.3 percent of the country but are nearly 50 percent of the population of Marseilles. Asians, coming from Vietnam, China, Laos, Cambodia, India, and Sri Lanka account for 1.3 percent of the population. Africans from the former colonies are less than 1 percent.

Religion of France. Since 1905 there has been a separation of church and state. The nonreligious are currently estimated at just over 19 percent; almost 8 percent are Muslim. Though over 70 percent claim to be Christian, the church attendance rate is only 13 percent. Less than 2 percent are Protestant, just over half of which are evangelical.

There are numerous missionaries serving in France from North America, the United Kingdom, Holland, Germany, Scandinavia, and Switzerland. Many of the newer evangelical churches in the metropolitan areas are being founded with help from missionaries.

France is described as an ideological vacuum and has become a mission field for Christians, both Protestant and Roman Catholics, as well as Muslims, Buddhists, and the cults.

JOHN EASTERLING

Bibliography. J. Ardagh, *The New France: A Society in Transition;* C. Dubois, *France in Perspective;* F. Orna-Ornstein, *France: Forgotten Mission Field.*

Francis, Mabel (1880–1975). American missionary to Japan. Of the many things that could be said about Mabel Francis, the one statement at the top of the list is that she loved her enemies. She was an American missionary to Japan during World War II. At a time when the United States and Japan were waging war against each other, Francis was sharing the gospel of reconciliation.

Francis was born in Corinth, New Hampshire, where she was raised. She started teaching school at age 15. Soon thereafter, she began to feel a conviction from the Lord about her failure to preach the gospel. So she began holding Sunday afternoon church services in the schoolhouse. Revival broke out in that New England community, even among the most resistant people.

At age 19, Francis responded to God's call to missionary service in Japan. She began her ministry there in 1909 and remained in Japan for fifty-six years. When the missionaries were called to return to the United States during the 1930s, she decided to remain with the Japanese people.

She was deeply devoted to them and could not bear to leave them during their greatest trials. Due to the lack of financial support from the United States and the Great Depression, both she and the Japanese people suffered greatly. However, because of her courage, love, and consistency in preaching the gospel, many Japanese people were brought to the Lord.

KATHY MC REYNOLDS

Bibliography. M. Francis with G. B. Smith, *One Shall Chase a Thousand.*

Francis of Assisi (c. 1182–1226). Italian founder of the Franciscan Order. Francis worked in his father's textile trade until a serious illness brought him to a deep internal struggle. This conflict and a vision in 1205 led him to dedicate himself to a life of prayer and ministry among the poor. After a pilgrimage, during which he traded clothes with a beggar and personally experienced poverty, he broke from his father and turned to work with beggars and lepers.

In 1209, responding to another visionary call, he discarded the last of his worldly possessions and began evangelizing. A small band gathered around him, and he drew up a simple set of rules for living. They traveled throughout France and Spain evangelizing, though his hope to reach Africa went unfulfilled due to illness. Papal permission to establish the Order of Friars Minor was granted in 1209. In 1212, during the Fifth Crusade, Francis and some followers traveled to eastern Europe and Egypt. In his absence, leadership of the Order passed to others and he never sought to regain it. The rest of his life was spent preaching, writing circular letters to and admonishing members of his Order, and taking repeated breaks for solitary retreats.

A. SCOTT MOREAU

Bibliography. D. W. H. Arnold, *Francis: A Call to Conversion;* M. Bishop, *Saint Francis of Assisi;* G. K. Chesterton, *St. Francis of Assisi;* M. A. Habig, ed., *St. Francis of Assisi: Writings and Early Biographies: English Omnibus of the Sources for the Life of St. Francis;* L. Hardick, *NCE,* 6:28–31; *ODCC.*

Frankfurt Declaration on the Fundamental Crisis in Christian Mission.

Among evangelical efforts to redress the significant shifts in mission theology seen in the ECUMENICAL MOVEMENT was the Frankfurt Declaration. The flash point was the preconference document "Renewal in Mission," prepared for the WCC Uppsala Assembly in 1968. PETER BEYERHAUS felt that the document represented a serious disruption of the whole tradition of missiological thinking. DONALD MCGAVRAN's parallel response led to correspondence between the two in which McGavran urged Beyerhaus to pen a statement similar to the Wheaton Declaration (*see* CONGRESS ON THE CHURCH'S WORLDWIDE MISSION), but dealing with the recent WCC documents and thinking. The Theological Convention, a group of fifteen German theologians, echoed McGavran's urging. Beyerhaus drafted the declaration, and after discussion and revision the group signed it on March 4, 1970.

The single goal of the Frankfurt Declaration was to reaffirm the biblical basis of mission. Beyerhaus listed seven indispensable elements of mission, each of which specifically refuted a trend seen in the WCC: (1) the foundation for mission is found solely in the New Testament; (2) the primary goal is to glorify and proclaim God's name throughout the world; (3) Jesus alone is the basis, content, and authority of mission; (4) mission is the church's presentation of salvation appropriated through belief and baptism; (5) the primary visible task is to call out from among all people those who are saved and to incorporate them into the church; (6) salvation is

found only through faith in Christ; and (7) mission is God's decisive activity that will continue until the return of Christ.

Reaction among German scholars tended to be either strongly in favor of or strongly against the declaration. It received significant attention in American evangelical circles through the efforts of McGavran and Harold Lindsell, who published it in *Christianity Today.* Interestingly enough, ecumenical leadership publicly ignored it in spite of the fact that it received international acceptance within evangelicalism.

A. SCOTT MOREAU

Bibliography. P. Beyerhaus, *Shaken Foundations;* idem, *Missions: Which Way? Humanization or Redemption;* D. McGavran, *Eye of the Storm.*

Franson, Fredrik (1852–1908). Swedish-born American founder of TEAM. Born in Nora, Sweden, in 1852, Franson immigrated to the United States at age seventeen with his mother and stepfather and settled in Nebraska. A profound conversion experience at age nineteen left him an intensely committed disciple of Jesus Christ. In 1875 he moved to Chicago and joined Moody Church, which commissioned him to conduct evangelistic campaigns among the Scandinavian immigrants in the United States.

Ordained in the Evangelical Free Church in 1881, Franson continued to minister around the country. In 1890 he organized a missionary training course in Brooklyn and a mission board in Chicago. Having been heavily influenced by GEORGE MÜLLER and HUDSON TAYLOR, his was a mission based on prayer, faith in God's provision, and an evangelistic focus. In the years that followed, hundreds of missionaries were sent out to China, Japan, India, and Africa under the Scandinavian Alliance Mission of North America.

From the founding of the mission until he died in 1908, Franson traveled the globe preaching the imminent return of Christ and encouraging his fellow missionaries. The legacy of this man of faith, prayer, and unwavering commitment to his Savior continues today as his mission, which is now known as THE EVANGELICAL ALLIANCE MISSION (TEAM), fearlessly proclaims the truth of Jesus Christ around the world.

WENDY S. LARSON

Bibliography. D. B. Woodward, *Aflame for God;* E. Torjesen, *Fredrik Franson: A Model for Worldwide Evangelism;* idem, *BDCM,* p. 223.

Fraser, Donald (1870–1933). Scottish missionary to Malawi. Missionaries influenced the parents of Donald Fraser, who was dedicated for ministry at birth. While a theology student, Fraser helped organize an international missionary conference entitled, "The Evangelization of the World in This Generation." In 1896 the Scottish Free Presbyterian Church sent him to Nyasaland to serve with the Livingstonia Mission. During furlough (1901) he married Agnes Renton Robson, a physician, who also had a mission call. She was active in the work, teaching women, giving medical care, and writing. They had five children; one died at birth.

Fraser served in a large area where the British government did not have influence. His responsibilities included evangelization, leadership training, and overseeing a system of village schools. His writings show his obvious love of the Word and the people. His missiological principles included the following: use local customs to build biblical knowledge; dreams, knowledge of the spirit world, and group loyalty are important evangelism factors; evangelism is best done by local people; local elders must be involved in all church decisions; village schools are to be built and financed by the villages; Christians should be involved in ministry; and Africans should send missionaries. Fraser wrote several books and articles about Africa and how to reach Africans with the gospel.

MIKEL NEUMANN

Bibliography. A. R. Fraser, *Donald Fraser;* D. Fraser, *IRM* 15 (1926): 438; idem, *Winning a Primitive People,* J. Thompson, *ML,* pp. 166–72.

Fraternal Workers. Fraternal workers, a term used by denominations and mission agencies since the 1960s, refers to long- and short-term cross-cultural missionaries.

In the 1960s, the term "national church" was used to refer to the churches of Africa, Asia, and Latin America. Calls for a MORATORIUM on sending missionaries from Europe and North America, and cries such as "missionary go home," gave rise to the thinking behind "MISSION ON SIX CONTINENTS" at the 1963 CWME MEXICO CITY CONFERENCE.

Mission on six continents called for new ways to refer to missionaries and their roles, especially among mainline churches of the United States and state churches in Europe, resulting in concepts like "mutual sharing of resources" and "partnership in mission." Protestants and Roman Catholics rediscovered the local church as the primary mission agent, leading to a new view of the purpose and role of missionaries and mission agencies. An integral response to this was to refer to missionaries as "fraternal workers."

"Fraternal workers" meant that missionaries were accountable to leaders in the receiving churches in an equal, cooperative relationship. Missions as organizations of expatriate missionaries were dissolved, recognizing the authority of the national churches. Mission agendas and projects were to be set by the receiving churches with specific goals and time lines. The "fraternal workers" became employees of the sending denomi-

nation or mission agency, transferred to work for the receiving church.

Although the motives behind using fraternal worker were well-intentioned, the results were mixed. The unique call, authority, giftedness, and leadership of the long-term cross-cultural missionary were undermined. The significance and contribution of long-term missionaries in CONTEXTUALIZATION of the gospel and in providing new vision and direction in world evangelization were diminished. The term lowered the motivation of churches and individuals in the West to support mission efforts financially and structurally, and its use in ecumenical and mainline Protestant circles paralleled their dramatic decline in mission funding and sending.

CHARLES VAN ENGEN

Bibliography. D. Bosch, *Transforming Mission: Paradigm Shifts in Theology of Mission;* O. Costas, *Christ Outside the Gate: Mission Beyond Christendom;* R. T. Parsons, *CDCWM,* p. 217; B. Sundkler, *The World of Mission;* J. Verkuyl, *Contemporary Missiology: An Introduction.*

Freedom. *See* RELIGIOUS FREEDOM.

Freeman, Thomas Birch (1806–90). English missionary to West Africa. The son of a black African father and a white English mother, he was born in England two years after the slave trade had been abolished. A Wesleyan Methodist shoemaker led him to Christ. His African roots gave him an interest in African missions.

Freeman sailed for the Gold Coast in 1837 under the Wesleyan Methodist Missionary Society. This portion of West Africa (Ghana, Togo, Benin, and Western Nigeria) was known to the outside world for the brutal slave trade and the short life of white missionaries. His new bride died within two months of their arrival. His second wife died in 1841 after less than seven months in Africa. His ill health, discouragement of losing his wives, and lack of funds did not deter him from his work. In 1854 he married an educated African Christian. They had four children.

Freeman was instrumental in starting churches and schools throughout two great African kingdoms, the Ashanti and the Dahomey, where the gospel was unknown. While he never learned the local language, he made friends of powerful Africans who said, "He understands our customs." He was the first missionary to visit the great cities of gold. He also observed the brutal atrocities of the slave trade that he fought. He was a peacemaker among Africans and between England and African kingdoms.

MIKEL NEUMANN

Bibliography. A. Birtwhistle, *Thomas Birch Freeman, West African Pioneer;* T. B. Freeman, *Journal of Various*

Visits to the Kingdoms of Ashanti, Aku, and Dahomi; F. D. Walker, *Thomas Birch Freeman: The Son of an African.*

Freire, Paulo Reglus Neves (1921–97). Brazilian educator and theorist. Born in northeastern Brazil on September 19, 1921, Paulo Freire's early life was a journey from childhood poverty into secondary school teaching, adult literacy efforts, and political activism, culminating in a professorship at the University of Recife. There, along with students, he developed a highly effective literacy program which gained the support of the government and rapidly grew into a national movement.

The Revolution of 1964 forced Freire into exile. He first went to Chile where he worked in agrarian reform and wrote Spanish and Portuguese editions of his two most significant works, *Education for Critical Consciousness* and *Pedagogy of the Oppressed.* Later, he taught at Harvard University (1959) and served as a consultant with the WORLD COUNCIL OF CHURCHES in Geneva (1970–79).

When he returned to Brazil in 1980, Freire became involved in the *Partido de Trabalhadores* (Workers' Party), in base ecclesial communities within the Roman Catholic Church, and in a spectrum of other teaching, consulting, and writing activities. He died May 2, 1997.

For Freire, the major problem of society is that the masses live in a culture of silence, dominated and oppressed by higher classes. Nondialogic or "banking" education, with its emphasis on depositing information in the minds of passive students, is a principal instrument of oppression. Education which liberates must be dialogic, problem-posing, and consciousness-raising (conscientizing).

Freire's thought has had a global impact on adult education, international development, religious education, and missiology. His influence is seen in the writings of liberation theologians and in documents from the Second Latin American Episcopal Conference (Medellín, 1968). Evangelical appraisals of Freire's contributions appear in publications of the Latin American Theological Fraternity. His ideas are also evident in Catholic and Protestant base ecclesial communities, in renewal movements in international theological education, and in the PRAXIS elements of THEOLOGICAL EDUCATION BY EXTENSION.

LOIS MCKINNEY DOUGLAS

Bibliography. J. L. Elias, *Paulo Freire, Pedagogue of Liberation;* P. Freire, *Education for a Critical Consciousness.* idem, *Pedagogy of the Oppressed.*

French Guiana *(Est. 2000 pop.: 179,000; 91,000 sq. km. [35,135 sq. mi.]).* French Guiana or Guyane is located on the northeast coast of South America, east of Suriname and with Brazil to the east and south. The name "Guiana" means "Land of Many Waters," and was known as Cayenne in colonial times. The country continues to be dependent on France although it is an Overseas Department of France. It is known for its famous former penal colony of Devil's Island.

The region was visited by the Spanish explorers early in the sixteenth century, who did not settle down because there was no gold. The British tried to take possession of the territory in 1654. Guyane became a French colony in 1667. Except for a Dutch attack in 1676, it remained undisturbed until 1809, when it was seized by an Anglo-Portuguese naval force. In 1814, France regained control until 1946 when the Colony of French Guiana became the Department of Guyane.

The predominant religion of Guyane is Roman Catholicism, although the majority of the population are nominally Roman Catholic. The first missionaries were Jesuits, followed by the Holy Ghost Fathers and other European orders. The Roman Catholic testimony spread among the maroons or Bush Negroes (descendants of escaped slaves). The work among the Djuka was especially successful. During the 1820s a colony was founded by Mother ANNE MARIE JAVOUHAY, Superior of the Sisters of St. Joseph Cluny, for the freed slaves. In 1848 slavery was irrevocably abolished. French Guiana comprises the single diocese of Cayenne, suffragan to the archdiocese of Fort-de-France, Martinique.

Protestant testimony has not been in significant in the country. The local Anglican Church forms part of the diocese of Guyana, with the bishop residing in Georgetown. Other Protestant communities are the Seventh-Day Adventists and the Assemblies of God.

PABLO A. DEIROS

Bibliography. R. Price, ed., *Maroon Societies: Rebel Slave Communities in the Americas.*

French Mission Boards and Societies. France has been a mission field since the beginning of Christianity. Paul's disciple Crescens possibly reached Gaul (2 Tim. 4:10 according to ancient manuscripts). The first congregations were Greek-speaking. Latin became common until French was shaped and established itself as a religious language. Worship in French became the rule in the sixteenth century in the emerging churches of the Reformation. The Roman Catholic Church of France followed suit only after the SECOND VATICAN COUNCIL allowed local languages to be used in the Mass liturgy (1963). Sermons, however, were always delivered in French. The level of language is differentiated according to educational, social, and geographical backgrounds. BIBLE SOCIETIES produce several translations from basic to literary French.

France today is both a mission field and a sending country. Home and foreign missions (based mostly in America, England, Holland, and Germany) are approaching secularized French populations and also linguistic minorities settled in France in growing numbers (North and West Africans, Asians, Eastern Europeans). A striking development was the creation of the Evangelical Gypsy Church in France through the ministry of Clément Le Cossee and some American missionaries. This church was received in 1975 as a full member of the Federation of Protestant Churches in France. Similarly, some missionary groups are targeting so-called NOMINAL CHRISTIANS. Many scattered Pentecostal, Baptist, and independent evangelical congregations and networks have emerged mainly in the cities, either spontaneously or through the ministry of evangelists and missionaries.

While the consolidated Protestant population in France oscillates between 2 and 5 percent, Roman Catholic tradition is cherished by about two-thirds of the population. This includes a strong foreign missionary commitment, which interfered with French foreign policy in the nineteenth and the beginning of the twentieth centuries, when France officially protected Roman Catholic missions in China and the Pacific.

There are about 300 Roman Catholic missionary orders and congregations in France; among them at least 210 women's congregations of French origin. But most of them have become international groups due to the Vatican strategy of centralization since 1922, and to international recruitment. At this time most of originally French Catholic foreign missions have moved their headquarters to Rome: the Oblates of Mary Immaculate, founded in 1816 by Eugéne de Mazenod; the Holy Ghost Fathers, refounded by François Libermann in 1848; the White Fathers, founded by Charles Lavigerie in 1868; the Christian Brothers, the Sisters of St. Joseph of Cluny, the Daughters of Charity of St. Vincent de Paul, among many others. Until the decline of missionary vocations in the 1960s, France and the Netherlands had the highest ratio of missionaries in the world. Roman Catholic missions are supported by a worldwide fund established in Rome since 1922, but fund raising is also operated by local and regional missionary networks.

The internationalization of the Protestant missionary movement is probably even more evident. The PARIS EVANGELICAL MISSIONARY SOCIETY (1822–1971) always recruited its staff from many European countries and worked in close cooperation with the LONDON MISSIONARY SOCIETY, the BASEL MISSION, and the Methodist Mission. This mission board was restructured in 1971 as the French Evangelical Department of Apostolic Action (DEFAP). It recruits missionaries and volunteers on behalf of almost all denominations (Reformed, Lutheran, Moravians, Baptists, Mennonites, Free Churches). Other French evangelical missions are associated with Swiss, Dutch, German, English, and American mission boards. Significant organizations in France are *Action Chrétienne en Orient* Fellowship (founded in 1922 by Paul Berron in Strasbourg, restructured in 1995), the Baptist branch of the European Baptist Union, the French branch of the Evangelical Leprosy Mission, the French branch of the Evangelical Mission in Côte d'Ivoire, the International Association for the Albert Schweitzer Hospital at Lambarene, Gabon.

When the churches in the mission fields became autonomous bodies in the 1950s and 1960s, mainline mission boards merged into the synodal structure of the French churches. This so-called churchification of missions led to the creation of a new intercontinental and interchurch body, the Apostolic Community for Apostolic Action (CEVAA) (1971), which presently operates on behalf of forty-seven churches worldwide, with headquarters in Paris. Its first executive secretary was Victor Rakotoarimanana, of the United Reformed Church of Madagascar. This body is directly supported by church synods, according to the respective financial capacities of the member churches. Swiss and French contributions make up 90 percent of the budget.

Relationships between Roman Catholic and Protestant missions used to be tense and even hostile until the SECOND VATICAN COUNCIL (1962–65) articulated a new theology of ecumenism. There have been many successful experiments in forms of common witness. Two ecumenical associations of missiologists have been established (1979 for mission history, 1994 for mission theology).

A puzzling development is the multiplication of highly profiled nongovernmental organizations in the field of development and relief, relying upon secular funding. Many of them have a Christian background, but are reluctant to cooperate with established churches and mission boards.

MARC R. SPINDLER

Bibliography. P. King, ed., *French Christian Handbook.*

French Polynesia (*Est. 2000 pop.: 242,000; 4,000 sq. km. [1,544 sq. mi.]*). French Polynesia consists of some 130 islands in five groups located in the western Pacific halfway between Australia and South America. The French protectorate declared in 1842 was extended over the whole group by 1901. The country is an overseas territory of France with its people having French citizenship, representation in the French parliament, and their own Territorial Assembly. Nearly half the population are members of the Evangelical Church; one-third are Roman Catholics; and

Mormons, Seventh-Day Adventists, and Jehovah's Witnesses are significant minorities.

ALLAN K. DAVIDSON

SEE ALSO Polynesia.

Freytag, Walter (1899–1959). German theologian and missiologist. He served as professor of missions and ecumenical studies at the University of Hamburg until his death in 1959, having graduated from Tübingen, Marburg, and Halle Universities and receiving his doctorate in psychology and education from the University of Hamburg in 1925.

One year after receiving his doctorate, Freytag became the director of the German Missionary Council. He led this ecumenical group of thirty missionary societies for thirty-three years. He assumed an important role at the organizing and founding of the WORLD COUNCIL OF CHURCHES in Amsterdam in 1948. He also helped organize the East Asia Christian Conference in Indonesia in 1957.

Missiological interest and ecumenical involvement carried Freytag to the major INTERNATIONAL MISSIONARY COUNCIL meetings in Jerusalem, India, Canada, Germany, and Ghana. At his death, Freytag was vice chairman of the International Missionary Council and chairman of the Division of Studies of the World Council of Churches.

Freytag's missionary research in the 1930s carried him to New Guinea, Indonesia, and China to study the impact of Christianity upon those cultures. He published his conclusions in his book *The Spiritual Revolution in the East.*

DAVID H. SHEPHERD

Friends Missionary Prayer Board. The outgrowth of prayer bands started by Tamil young men in 1958, FMPB became a missionary sending agency in 1967 when its first missionaries were sent to Dharmapuri District. The mission expanded to North India in 1972. By 1978 there were 119 missionaries including wives. In 1987, 274 were reported, and 423 in 1992. By 1997 FMPB had a total of 620 missionaries and 120 field stations in 17 states. 300 local evangelists (converts) were trained as leaders in about 1,600 congregations begun by the mission.

FMPB is a lay Christian movement with an efficient organizational structure supported by prayer group members. Recruitment is through district "Gideonite Meets," area-wide "Challenge Meets," and prayer cell meetings where a missionary challenge and call for volunteers is given. Leadership carefully screens applicants. A rigid spiritual discipline is demanded. Candidates are sent for a year of training at Bethel Bible Institute, Danishpet, and other exposures. The first year in the field is considered probationary.

The major emphasis is on evangelism and church planting. Various social ministries are carried on providing needed health care, hygiene, water, child care, education, and other services. FMPB has experienced considerable group conversion in Gujarat and Bihar.

ROGER E. HEDLUND

Bibliography. R. E. Hedlund and F. Hrangkhuma, eds., *Indigenous Missions of India;* L. J. Joshi, *Evaluation of Indigenous Missions of India;* L. Lazarus, ed., *Proclaiming Christ: A Handbook of Indigenous Mission in India;* M. A. Nelson and C. Chun, *Asian Mission Societies: New Resources for World Evangelization.*

Friends (Quakers) Missions. One of the great puzzles of English church history is why the Friends (Quaker) missionary movement, which broke like a sunburst into the British and American scene about 1650, so quickly receded to a footnote in missions history. While Quakerism continued to claim an influence out of proportion to its numerical size, its missionary impact was muted by the Quietistic era from 1700 to 1850. A second burst of missions came between 1850 and 1900, particularly propelled forward by evangelical and Wesleyan revivals. It produced small but permanent works in Mexico, Japan, Jamaica, Palestine, India, China, Alaska, and Cuba. A third round of new activity followed in the early 1900s, especially in Africa and Latin America. After 1975 a number of new fields were opened by evangelical American and non-Western Friends in a fourth wave of missionary energy with more interest in Asia.

After 1927, British Friends mostly ceased a sense of active conversion evangelism, but continued peace and service efforts and loose ties with mission-founded groups of Friends in Africa, India, and elsewhere. The Quaker Peace and Service Committee is one of the visible heirs to the earlier British Quaker missionary concerns.

Initially, American Friends Yearly Meetings (regional conferences) were the missionary sending bodies, with each Yearly Meeting developing its own area of world interest. From 1900, shifting patterns gradually sorted American Quakers into three major alliances: Friends United Meeting, based in Richmond, Indiana; Evangelical Friends International/North America with a missions office in Denver, Colorado; and the more theologically liberal Friends General Conference, clustered in the eastern United States. Friends General Conference does not look favorably on conversion evangelism, and limits its international work to social development, humanitarian relief, and promotion of sociopolitical justice issues. Both FUM (Friends United Meeting) and EFI (Evangelical Friends International) actively combine conversion evangelism and social service in their programs of world missions. Evangelical Friends Mission (EFM) is the missionary arm of EFI/North America and after its formation in 1975 became the most active Friends agency in establishing new churches among unreached peoples.

Friends United Meeting. Friends United Meeting (FUM) maintains missionary and fraternal church ties in East Africa (Kenya, Uganda, and Tanzania), Cuba, Jamaica, Belize, Palestine (Ramallah Friends School and Monthly Meeting), Mexico, and Native American missions in the United States. New works in the 1990s include contacts in Moscow, Russia, and in Tecuci, Romania.

The overwhelmingly largest of FUM church plants is in Kenya, where perhaps more people call themselves Quaker than in any other nation. Roughly one hundred thousand adherents are now divided among a number of autonomous Yearly Meetings. The original "Friends Africa Industrial Mission" was begun about 1900 and promoted by the missionary efforts of three students from what is now Malone College in Ohio. In the beginning, it was a blend of technical training, medical ministry, founding of schools, and evangelistic church planting. One of the three students eventually left the Friends mission and paved the way for the large and prosperous work of World Gospel Mission, a phenomenon repeated by other Friends pioneers in Bolivia, Honduras, and elsewhere. Another started a new work in Burundi, later related to EFI.

Evangelical Friends Mission. Evangelical Friends Mission represents a fourth wave of Friends missions, beginning in 1975 in Mexico City. Other new missions started by EFM include a Muslim student ministry, the Philippines, Friends of Garhwal (North India), Nepal, Rwanda, and Siberia, Russia. After 1975, EFM also became a missions network for the member yearly meetings of Alaska, Evangelical Friends Church—Eastern Region, Northwest, Rocky Mountain, and Friends Church Southwest. These older missions and national churches include Bolivia, Peru, Guatemala, Honduras, and El Salvador, Bundelkhand province of India, Taiwan, Burundi, and Rough Rock Indian Mission in Arizona. The largest membership block of evangelical Friends work exists in Latin America, with perhaps fifty thousand calling themselves Friends (including Central Friends in Bolivia). New works were started in the late 1980s and 1990s in Indonesia, Cambodia, and Jamaica. The national churches of these Friends were loosely organized worldwide by the Evangelical Friends International Council with Regional Directors in Africa, Asia, Latin America, and North America.

Nonaligned but evangelical Central Yearly Meeting (Indiana) pursued a separate mission in Bolivia, with as many as five spinoff Yearly Meetings within that nation. Other individual Yearly Meetings cared for smaller and scattered missions efforts.

The close of the twentieth century found the two American Friends missions agencies (FUM and EFM) phasing out of older fields and passing into new ones. Missionaries like Everett and Catherine Cattell (India), Charles and Leora DeVol (China and Taiwan), Roscoe and Tina Knight (Latin America), and Arthur and Edna Chilson (Africa) represent a distinguished and vigorous history of cultural sensitivity, interdenominational leadership, and spiritual zeal. Their wholistic ministries stressed conversion evangelism and church planting along with education, human equality, women in ministry, and the guidance of the Holy Spirit in worship and service. Strong national leadership arose in East and Central Africa, Central and South America, and Taiwan. Were it not for twentieth-century missions, Quakerism would have nearly disappeared from the picture of world Christianity. Instead, the majority of Quakers are now non-Western evangelical Christians who have joined the missionary sending movement by commissioning workers to Nepal, Nicaragua, Peru, the Philippines, Siberia, and Zaire.

RONALD G. STANSELL

Bibliography. E. L. Cattell, *Christian Mission: A Matter of Life;* C. Jones, *American Friends in World Missions;* H. Smuck, *Friends in East Africa;* D. E. Trueblood, *The People Called Quakers;* C. P. Wagner, *The Protestant Movement in Bolivia;* W. R. Williams, *The Rich Heritage of Quakerism.*

Friendship Evangelism. Evangelism that emphasizes the crucial role that relationships play in constructing a platform from which the gospel can be communicated effectively. In this approach, friendships are not conceived of as supplanting the gospel. They are bridges over which the gospel may be delivered and received.

This approach is also commonly known as LIFESTYLE EVANGELISM. It highlights the necessity of living out the Christian life in a consistent and winsome manner in the context of family and friendships. This is foundational to the companion step of proclaiming the gospel. A living demonstration of the gospel must go together with its proclamation. This is particularly true in friendship evangelism. The foundational premise is that a lifestyle of obedience to the lordship of Christ makes one's verbal witness credible.

The biblical basis for sharing the gospel along lines established by friendships and intimates is strong. The example of Jesus is instructive. He was known as a friend of sinners (Matt. 11:19). Yet for that reason the multitudes heard him gladly. The earliest disciples of Jesus were won along such webs of relationships. John the Baptist pointed two of his disciples and friends to the

Lord. One of these, Andrew, immediately sought his brother, Peter. Philip, a likely friend of Andrew and Peter, was the next convert. In turn, Philip found his friend Nathanael and brought him to the Lord (John 1:35ff.). After Jesus had healed the Gadarene demoniac he instructed him, "Go home to your family, and tell them how much the Lord has done for you, and how he has had mercy on you" (Mark 5:19 [NIV]). In the Book of Acts the account of the Gentile centurion Cornelius illustrates this same principle. This seeker gathered together his extended family and close friends to hear the message that Peter was commissioned to share with him (Acts 10:24).

The advantages of friendship evangelism are significant. First, it makes use of the most natural avenue for the spread of the gospel. The close emotional and physical proximity of unbelieving intimates provides ample opportunities for witness. Second, the unbeliever who has observed a wholesome Christian witness from a personal friend is much more likely to receive the message of salvation and become a disciple.

Dangers are also inherent in this method. It is possible to allow the friendship factor to supplant a clear presentation of the demands of the gospel. A good testimony, as invaluable as it is, can never take the place of the gospel message in the process of salvation (Rom. 1:16). Also, one might be tempted to neglect strangers or slight acquaintances who need the gospel in favor of investing exclusively in closer friends.

The Christian has no right to limit obedience to the GREAT COMMISSION to a select circle. Nevertheless, believers should be cognizant of their responsibility to share the gospel with their friends and intimates. Even more, Christians of all cultures should be intentional in cultivating genuine friendships with unbelievers.

JEFFERY B. GINN

Bibliography. J. Aldrich, *Life-Style Evangelism: Crossing Traditional Boundaries to Reach the Unbelieving World;* D. Owens, *Sharing Christ When You Feel You Can't: Making It Easier to Tell Your Friends and Family about Your Faith in Christ;* T. Stebbens, *Friendship Evangelism by the Book;* C. Van Engen, *You Are My Witnesses.*

Frontier Mission Work. *See* PIONEER MISSION WORK.

Frontier Peoples. *See* PEOPLES, PEOPLE GROUPS; UNREACHED PEOPLES.

The Fruit of the Spirit. The fruit of the Spirit as found in Galatians 5:22–23 is often contrasted with the gifts of the Spirit and made to say something quite different than originally intended. As Paul argues for a new kind of spirituality, so those who study this text today may find themselves arguing for a spirituality that differs sharply from that found in the church today.

The Context: Particularism or Universalism. The Book of Galatians can be seen as a sustained argument by one missionary for a universalist perspective against other missionaries arguing for a particularist viewpoint. Gentile Christians are being urged to embrace circumcision and the Law as a means of sanctification. Paul argues from his own experience (Gal. 1:1–2:14) and from the Scriptures (2:15–5:12) that God wills salvation for Gentiles and Jews through free grace, apart from the Law. This freedom can only be maintained by the Holy Spirit (5:13–6:10).

Flesh or Spirit. The most pervasive of several antithetical arguments in Galatians is that of flesh/law, related to Spirit. Paul asks: "Did you receive the Spirit by doing the works of the *law* or by believing what you heard? Are you so foolish? Having started with the Spirit, are you now ending with the *flesh?*" (3:2–3, NRSV).

Individual Spirituality or Community Spirituality. Paul accents community spirituality in Galatians. This becomes clear in his "one another" exhortations (5:13, 15, 26; 6:2); "let us" challenges (5:25, 26; 6:9, 10); and warnings about "biting and devouring" and "competing against one another" (5:15, 26). Individually each Christian "lives by the Spirit," having "crucified the flesh," (5:16, 24). Paul views Christians living out this new way of life in community (5:13–15, 26; 6:1, 2, 10). The Spirit empowers relationships in community.

The Meaning of Flesh and Spirit. One's understanding of flesh and Spirit is crucial in interpreting the fruit of the Spirit in Galatians. Interpretations of flesh *(sarx)* vary widely. The NIV translates *sarx* as "human nature" in most places in Galatians while the NRSV retains the word "flesh." The NIV translation conforms to the common evangelical view of the Christian life as a struggle between two entities in the person with the Christian caught in the middle, as in Galatians 5:17. This interpretation must be rejected.

Paul's usage of flesh and Spirit in Galatians is rooted in his eschatological view of salvation history. For Paul salvation history divides between two aeons, with the death of Christ and the coming of the Holy Spirit marking this division. He reminds the Galatians that *"the Lord Jesus Christ . . . gave himself for our sins to rescue us from the present evil age"* (1:3) and recounts their salvation experience with the Holy Spirit (3:2). The flesh and Law dominates one aeon and the Spirit the other. To walk by the Spirit is to experience the empowering age to come (5:16, 18, 25).

Christ and Holy Spirit (two kingdom promises) introduce a new way of salvation. The crucified Christ and the empowering Spirit determine the nature of the universal gospel and the Spirit-empowered nature of the people of God. Particularism (flesh and Law) characterizes the old aeon. Seeking holiness without the enabling Spirit fulfills the desires of the flesh and puts one under the Law (5:16, 18, 19–21). The Spirit of Christ empowers Christians to experience the "already" of God's kingdom.

Fruit versus Works. The agricultural metaphor of fruit can be found throughout Scripture. Jesus uses this metaphor to show the results of one's relationship to God (John 15). Paul uses the metaphor to describe the life of the Christian (Rom. 6:22; Eph. 5:9; Phil. 1:11; 4:17). Paul contrasts the fruit of the Spirit (5:22–23) with the works of the flesh (5:19–21). Producing fruit through the empowering Spirit is not a passive experience, but a dynamic interaction between being led by the Spirit (the indicative) and walking by the Spirit (the imperative). Fruitbearing calls for disciplined obedience to the Holy Spirit, recognizing his presence in the community.

The word "fruit" may be considered plural or singular. Lists of vice and virtues are common in both biblical and extrabiblical literature. None of these lists are meant to be exhaustive. For example, this list leaves out such virtues as forgiveness and compassion. This list is guided by the personal needs of the church. That the vice list includes enmities, strife, jealousy, anger, quarrels, dissensions, factions, and envy points toward community needs (5:15, 26). The virtues listed almost uniformly apply to community life.

The Fruit. *Love*—Christ, Paul, and John stress love as the foundational virtue. God is love. Christ's love for marginals in society distinguished him. Love calls us to place priority on people. Love fulfills the Law (5:14).

Joy—Joy is the keynote of Christianity. The Spirit's manifest presence in the church will be evidenced by joy.

Peace—Modern life brings deep personal anxieties, robbing people of peace. Personal peace flows from and into community. The Holy Spirit can enable diverse people to experience and maintain peace.

Patience—Also translated longsuffering. Living in community calls for an ability to put up with the foibles and idiosyncrasies of others. Without Spirit-produced longsuffering there will be anger and quarrels (5:20).

Kindness—Kindness manifests itself in the words we speak and the acts we engage in when in community. Kindness manifested strengthens those benefited.

Goodness—Not found in extrabiblical literature. Being generous or good is a quality of moral excellence. This word is used for God (Luke 18:18–19). It is the opposite of envy.

Faithfulness—This word *pistis* occurs twenty-two times in Galatians, normally translated faith. Faithfulness is perhaps correct here. The spiritual quality of loyalty, commitment, and stead-fastness in our relationships in the body of Christ is the idea.

Gentleness—Perhaps the most difficult of the virtues to translate into English. At one time the English word "meekness" was a good translation. Because many people are opinionated, gentleness will curb inclinations to run roughshod over others.

Self-control—This could be one of the virtues whose primary application is individual, although certainly needed in relationships. Our passions must be brought under the control of the Spirit. Self-control is needed to avoid such sins as fornication, impurity, and drunkenness (5:19–21).

Application. Spirituality is determined by the empowering presence of the eschatological gift of the Spirit. Never before in the history of Christianity has this message been more needed than today. Missionaries establishing churches by preaching a gospel of grace may be tempted to introduce "law" for daily Christian living. For instance, missionaries in Africa confronted by polygamous marriages are tempted to lay down the law of monogamy. Dependence on anything except the Spirit leads to walking in the flesh. "Those who belong to Christ Jesus have crucified the flesh with its passions and desires" (5:24). Christianity as a way of life calls for the enabling power of the Holy Spirit.

For Western Christians this message is especially applicable. Modern evangelicalism, influenced by a highly technological society, is advocating a "technique" spirituality. Self-help and "how to" advice dominates. This new legalism characterizes Western spirituality. Paul calls for an abandonment of the flesh in all of its forms. Walk by the Spirit. Love, joy, peace, patience, kindness, goodness, faithfulness, gentleness, and self-control characterize the community of faith when the crucified Christ and the empowering Spirit are present.

HAROLD G. DOLLAR

SEE ALSO Conscience, Ethics, AND Moral Development.

Bibliography. J. M. G. Barclay, *Obeying the Truth: Paul's Ethics in Galatians;* J. D. G. Dunn, *The Epistle to the Galatians;* G. D. Fee, *God's Empowering Presence: The Holy Spirit in the Letters of Paul,* pp. 367–471; R. Y. K. Fung, *The Epistle to the Galatians;* G. W. Hansen, *Galatians;* W. Russell, *WmTJ* 57 (1995): 333–57; S. F. Winward, *Fruit of the Spirit.*

Frumentius (c. 300–380). Pioneer missionary to Ethiopia. Greek and Roman historians recount how the youthful Frumentius and his brother Edesius on a voyage from Tyre about 330 were shipwrecked on the Ethiopian coast and captured. They subsequently impressed the royal court at Axum so much that they were allowed to preach the gospel—a work continued by Frumentius after Edesius had returned to Tyre. About 339 Frumentius went to Alexandria, where Bishop Athanasius consecrated him as bishop and arranged for missionaries to join Frumentius in Ethiopia whose future church heads were known as "Abuna" ("Our Father").

J. D. DOUGLAS

Fuller, Andrew (1754–1815). English founder of the Baptist Missionary Society. Born in Wicken, Cambridgeshire, Fuller joined the Soham Baptist Church at the age of sixteen. Though lacking formal theological training, he was called to be their minister in 1775. Seven years later he moved to Kettering, Northamptonshire, where he served until his death.

Fuller began to promote the missionary endeavors of the Baptist Church in about 1784. The Baptists of his time tended to push the tenets of Calvinism to the extreme belief that since God would call his elect, there need be no invitation to salvation through presentation of the gospel. After searching the Scriptures and studying authors like JONATHAN EDWARDS, Fuller published an opposing view in 1785: *The Gospel Worthy of All Acceptance, or the Obligation of Men Fully to Credit and Cordially to Approve Whatever God Makes Known*. This book helped to ignite the fire of evangelism and missions among the Free Churches in England. It greatly impacted WILLIAM CAREY (1761–1834), who became the first missionary of the Baptist Missionary Society, which was founded in 1792 at Kettering. Fuller served as its first home director.

Fuller was given D.D. degrees by Princeton and Yale in recognition of his contributions. His complete works were first published in 1838 and have been reprinted several times.

GARY LAMB

Bibliography. T. E. Fuller, *A Memoir of the Life and Writings of Andrew Fuller*; A. G. Fuller, *The Principal Works and Remains of the Rev. Andrew Fuller*.

Fuller, Charles E. (1887–1968). American radio evangelist and founder of a school of missions. Having been influenced by A. B. SIMPSON, Charles Fuller's father, Henry Fuller (1846–1926) set aside monies from his orange groves in Redlands, California, for the advance of foreign missions. Then in 1945 Charles Fuller, internationally known from his weekly hour-long broadcast (1937–67), felt God's call to use this money to found a theological seminary with a zeal for missions.

Fuller asked Harold J. Ockenga to organize such a school because he both pastored a church in Boston supporting many missionaries and had the academic credentials needed. Fuller Theological Seminary (named after Henry Fuller) opened in Pasadena in 1947. The seminary's missionary emphasis led 20 percent of its graduates from 1950 to 1960 to go into foreign missions.

In 1964, at age seventy-seven, Charles Fuller mandated David Hubbard, the seminary's third president, to organize a school of world mission. It opened in 1965 with DONALD MCGAVRAN as dean. His church growth principles, developed as a lifelong missionary in India, shaped its curriculum and faculty selection. Since then over 1,800 students who serve in more than 150 countries have graduated with mission degrees from Fuller.

DANIEL P. FULLER

Bibliography. D. P. Fuller, *Give the Winds a Mighty Voice*; G. M. Marsden, *Reforming Fundamentalism*.

Fund Raising. Missionary enterprises require adequate financial underwriting. Missions attached to mainline denominations may use special offerings (Southern Baptists) or assessments per church member (Presbyterian Church [U.S.A.]) to supply the needs. The missionary may have little to do in this process or may have only a catalytic role (CHRISTIAN AND MISSIONARY ALLIANCE) speaking at district missions conferences. For a growing number of evangelical denominational missions (Evangelical Free) and for all independent societies (AIM, SIM), fund raising is a task shared by the agency and the individual missionary. Churches may partner with a mission agency to help in underwriting the support of individuals, mission-run institutions, and special projects. These funds may (Overseas Missionary Fellowship) or may not (The Evangelical Alliance Mission) be pooled by the agency to underwrite the general needs of the mission.

The mission may provide significant help, training, and guidance for those raising funds, but many agencies rely on the individual to follow up contacts and raise one's own support. The administrative cost of fund raising varies a great deal. In some cases there is practically no overhead because of volunteers in the home office (World Prayer League); in other cases it is a fixed percentage of all income (e.g., CBInternational—15 percent). Missions with a higher cost may often have greater benefits for their missionaries than do those with little or no administrative costs.

JOHN EASTERLING

Bibliography. B. Barnett, *Friend Raising: Building a Missionary Support Team That Lasts*.

Fundamentalisms. Certain dynamic and popular religious movements that have been a significant feature within WORLD RELIGIONS during the twentieth century. Part of their power and appeal lies in their claim to rediscover religious authenticity and divine purpose amidst the confusions of modern life by attempting a retrieval of the original doctrines and practices of their particular religion. Such fundamentals in an unchanged form are regarded as being the answer to the needs of humankind in every age and context.

Despite this focus on the past, fundamentalism is itself a product of the modern era. The history of the particular religion is seen as a record of general decline and compromise. The fundamentalist response to MODERNITY stands as an alternative to the liberal approach, which sees the history of religion as progress and is willing to review religious doctrine in the light of modern knowledge as a means of achieving contemporary relevance.

The origins of the term "fundamentalism" in Christian circles are usually associated with the publication of a series of tracts entitled *The Fundamentals* (1909–15), which defended certain tenets of biblical orthodoxy as literally true. These included creation in six days, the virgin birth, the physical resurrection and bodily return of Christ. The fundamentalists affirmed the inerrancy of Scripture (including its descriptions of supernatural events) in contrast to the more liberal approach to the Bible, which was based on historical and source criticism and scientific opinion.

In the United States the fundamentalists became associated with revivalist movements and dispensationalism. Some fundamentalists in their opposition to modernity separated from denominations that included modernists, while others (including Carl Henry) led the way for the evangelicals, Bible-believing Christians within many traditions who were more open to a cultural engagement with modernity.

Fundamentalist tendencies may be detected in other world religions (e.g., within Hinduism in the nationalist political forms of Shiv Sena and the Bharatiya Janata Party). However, the word "fundamentalism" has been more popularly associated with certain modern reform movements within Islam, although Muslim fundamentalists themselves prefer to be described as Islamists rather than fundamentalists. It may be argued that the origins of the present fundamentalist movements in Islam can be traced back to the Wahhabi movement in Arabia, the *Ikwan al Muslimun* in Egypt and Syria, and the *Jama'at-i-Islami* in India and Pakistan. These drew in part from existing thought within Islam (e.g., from Ibn Taymiyah, d. 1328) and articulated a powerful message of religion, patriotism, and revolution. In the context of the decline of Islam (associated in part with the Western colonial era) they advocated a return to the roots of the faith. What was needed was not less Islam or adulterated Islam, but original and genuine Islam. The vitality of the fundamentalist agenda continued in the postcolonial era in opposition both to Western interference and to the secularist rulers in independent Muslim nations who misjudged the religious sentiments of the masses.

The central question is whether traditional Islamic institutions and law are now outdated and need to be modernized. Islamic fundamentalists believe that the relevance of the traditional sources of Muslim faith and practice was not limited to seventh-century Arabia, but that in their original form they are still suited to the modern era. Thus fundamentalists call for the implementation of Islamic law *(shari'a)* in such detail as the veiling of women, the prohibition of banking interest, certain forms of criminal punishment, and the execution of apostates.

PATRICK SOOKHDEO

Bibliography. M. A. Noll, *Between Faith and Criticism*; H. Küng and J. Moltmann, *Fundamentalism as an Ecumenical Challenge*; M. E. Marty and R. S. Appleby, eds., *Fundamentalism Project Series*; M. Nazir-Ali, *Islam: A Christian Perspective*; W. M. Watt, *Islamic Fundamentalism and Modernity*.

Fundamentalist Denominational Missions. Many fundamentalist mission agencies emerged in the context of ecclesiastical controversy during the early twentieth century. Since most fundamentalist denominations are inherently separatistic, their approach to foreign missions has been very different from that of mainline Protestant denominations. Fundamentalists reacted to what they perceived as theological laxity and overly centralized bureaucratic structures in traditional Protestantism. In establishing alternatives to denominational mission boards, fundamentalists made concerted efforts to avoid these alleged pitfalls; hence, the relationships between fundamentalist denominations and the mission enterprises that they have supported have frequently been indirect and deliberately decentralized. In fact, very few fundamentalist denominations have mission agencies that are integrally or officially incorporated into a denominational framework.

Some of the earliest denominational missions of a fundamentalist cast resulted from the Landmark controversy in the Southern Baptist Convention, which began in earnest around 1850. Landmarkers believed that mission work was the responsibility of the local church, so they generally opposed the organized efforts of societies or denominational boards, including the SBC's Foreign Mission Board. Conflicts surrounding Landmarkism were the most intense in Arkansas and Texas during the late nineteenth and early twentieth centuries, eventually leading to the rise of two Landmark denominations, which are now known as the American Baptist Association and the Baptist Missionary Association of America. The Missionary Committee of the ABA, based in Texarkana, Texas, serves as a support agency that assists local churches in sending out missionaries who are engaged in church planting, theological education, evangelism, and literature distribution in Latin America, Europe, Africa, Asia, and Oceania. The BMAA, headquartered in Little Rock, Arkansas, reports itself as "a denominational sending agency," an apparent shift from strict Landmark principles. It supports church planting, Bible distribution, theological education, and evangelism in Latin America, Europe, and Asia. Both Landmark denominational programs are small, with a combined overseas missionary corps of less than fifty.

The fundamentalist-modernist controversy of the 1920s and 1930s produced several fundamentalist quasi-denominational agencies. Fundamentalists, particularly in the Northern Baptist Convention (now the American Baptist Churches in the U.S.A.) and the Presbyterian Church in the U.S.A. (northern), grew increasingly disillusioned with their denominational boards and turned instead to nondenominational faith missions, some of which predated the fundamentalist-modernist conflicts, or to new organizations that offered a denominational focus without being part of the mainline establishment. Overall, Baptist and Presbyterian fundamentalists wanted mission agendas with greater emphases on evangelism and doctrinal orthodoxy.

As early as 1920, Baptist fundamentalist William C. Haas, who earlier had worked with the AFRICA INLAND MISSION and the Heart of Africa Mission, set up the General Council of Co-operating Baptist Missions of North America in Elyria, Ohio. This agency became one of the endorsed missions of the General Association of Regular Baptist Churches, a fundamentalist denomination that resulted from a Northern Baptist schism in 1932. The GCCBMNA eventually expanded its ministry beyond Africa to include Latin America, Asia, and Oceania, and was renamed Baptist Mid-Missions in 1953. Currently based in Cleveland, Ohio, BMM's more recent projects have centered on church planting, Bible translation, broadcasting, camping, correspondence courses, theological education, evangelism, literature production, literacy work, medical missions, relief aid, and aviation services. One of the larger fundamentalist agencies, BMM employs more than 600 overseas personnel.

Raphael C. Thomas, a former American Baptist Foreign Mission Society medical missionary in the Philippines, established the Association of Baptists for Evangelism in the Orient in 1927 after disputes with the ABFMS regarding doctrine and evangelism. This organization, renamed the Association of Baptists for World Evangelism in 1939, likewise received the accreditation of the GARBC. Its work has grown to include other parts of Asia, Latin America, Europe, Africa, and Oceania. With headquarters in Harrisburg, Pennsylvania, the ABWE focuses

today on church planting, evangelism, Bible translation, medical work, theological education by extension, and aviation services. Like BMM, the ABWE supports in excess of 600 overseas missionaries. These two agencies represent the bulk of foreign mission endeavor that is related to the GARBC.

One additional organization that emerged out of controversy in the Northern Baptist Convention was the Conservative Baptist Foreign Mission Society. The creation of CBFMS in 1943 pointed to continuing fundamentalist concerns about the NBC's missionary program. The founders hoped to create a channel for NBC churches that wanted to support conservative evangelical missionaries, but they were not allowed to function under the NBC umbrella and thus formed the Conservative Baptist Association in 1947. The CBFMS, now called CBInternational, has been the main missionary arm of the CBA. Although established in the waning stages of the fundamentalist-modernist disputes, CBInternational now is considered part of the American evangelical mainstream, unlike BMM and the ABWE.

The most significant fundamentalist Presbyterian missionary society to appear during a period of conflict was the Independent Board for Presbyterian Missions, founded in 1933 by J. Gresham Machen. Machen had accused the Presbyterian Board of Foreign Missions of harboring modernists in its missionary corps, and wanted a missions alternative for conservatives in the Presbyterian Church. His involvement with the Independent Board led to his defrocking and the formation in 1936 of what was eventually named the Orthodox Presbyterian Church. Carl McIntire, a dissident who once was allied with Machen, subsequently gained control of the Independent Board and made it the virtual foreign missions department of his Bible Presbyterian Church. Today it is a very small agency, based in Philadelphia, with work in evangelism, church planting, theological education, and literature distribution. With the loss of the Independent Board to McIntire, the Orthodox Presbyterian Church launched its Committee on Foreign Missions in 1937. Headquartered in Willow Grove, Pennsylvania, this committee supervises less than twenty missionaries who are engaged in evangelism, church planting, theological education, literature distribution, and support of national churches in six foreign countries, most notably in Japan.

Along with several other independent organizations in the Baptist tradition, these fundamentalist missions have consistently maintained evangelism and church planting as missionary priorities. They also have contributed to the overall diversity of the American Protestant missions movement. At the same time, many of them have shown a divisive spirit and a marked unwillingness to cooperate with other evangelical agencies.

JAMES A. PATTERSON

Bibliography. J. A. Patterson, *Earthen Vessels: American Evangelicals and Foreign Missions, 1880–1980,* pp. 73–91; J. A. Siewert and J. A. Kenyon, eds., *Mission Handbook: 1993–95 Edition;* J. A. Siewert, ed., *Mission Handbook: Directory Edition 1996;* T. P. Weber, *DCA,* pp. 461–65.

Funerals. *See* DEATH RITES.

Furlough. The period of time when the missionary is home from the field for a set period of rest, reentry (adjustment to the changes in one's home country), taking care of personal and family needs, and giving reports to supporters. Since the 1980s, the word "furlough" has been replaced with the term "home assignment," for the missionary is still on active duty while at home.

Missionaries are often assigned a percentage of time to spend in active ministry in churches. Certain missions with denominational underwriting (Southern Baptists) make this time strictly a period of rest and retooling, but most missions require missionaries to spend time visiting supporters. A furlough was often set on a four-to-one ratio—four years on the field and one year on furlough. However, medical, educational, and financial needs often required an extension to meet the personal situation of the missionary.

With the advent of inexpensive international travel, a greater percentage of missionaries are moving to summer furloughs every two or three years so as to not leave their ministry for an entire year nor to interrupt the educational programs of their children.

JOHN EASTERLING

Gg

Gabon *(Est. 2000 pop.: 1,517,000; 267,667 sq. km. [103,346 sq. mi.]).* Gabon is one of the most Christianized nations in Africa. Over 90 percent of the Gabonese population professes Christian faith.

The American Board of Commissioners was the first mission agency to send missionaries to Gabon. The missionaries arrived in Baraka, near present-day Libreville, in 1842. Thus began the evangelization of northern Gabon. American Presbyterian missionaries had been active on the island of Corisco, off the coast of Gabon, since 1849. The American Board of Commissioners joined the Presbyterian Mission in 1870. This led to the opening of the first Presbyterian mission stations around Lambaréné in 1874.

American Presbyterian missionaries had to curtail their activities, however, as France extended its colonial rule over Gabon toward the end of the nineteenth century. They sought cooperation with the PARIS EVANGELICAL MISSIONARY SOCIETY as a way of gaining protection from French authorities. The Franco-American cooperation in missions lasted from 1888 to 1892. In 1892, the Presbyterians ceded their work in Gabon to the Paris Evangelical Missionary Society and transferred their missionaries to Cameroon.

Over the years, schools and other forms of social work became the focus of the Paris Evangelical Missionary Society. The Lambaréné Hospital, founded by the Mission in 1913, is the best known example. It was directed by ALBERT SCHWEITZER from 1913 until his death.

When the CHRISTIAN AND MISSIONARY ALLIANCE established its first mission station in Bongolo in 1934 it found Protestants well established in the northern part of the country. It concentrated its efforts on southern Gabon. Eventually the Alliance extended its work nationwide. There are at least two factors behind that decision. First, Christians from Alliance churches moved to Libreville and other major urban centers in northern Gabon. Second, the churches of northern Gabon were increasingly less evangelical.

As the only major evangelical church in Gabon, the Alliance enjoys significant growth. It must deal, however, with nominal Christianity fueled by the respectable and politically powerful Catholic Church and Protestant Church of northern Gabon. It must also contend with Islam and a variety of cults. The missiological challenge in Gabon is one of reevangelization.

TITE TIÉNOU

Gairdner, William Henry Temple (1873–1928). Scottish missionary to Egypt. Born in Ayrshire, Scotland, at Oxford University he received his call to missionary service through contacts with the KESWICK and STUDENT VOLUNTEER movements. In 1899 he joined Douglas Thornton in Cairo, Egypt, to begin ministry with the CHURCH MISSIONARY SOCIETY, and in 1901 was ordained in the Church of England. In 1902 he married Margaret Mitchell, who bore him five children.

Gairdner and Thornton established a reading room and bookstore, learning from patrons the arguments of Muslims against Christianity. Gairdner spoke of his frustration with these "masters of the art of disputing," preferring instead everyday conversation with individuals or small groups. In 1910 he studied Islam under Duncan Black MacDonald and Ignaz Goldziher, but felt that his goal of becoming a missionary scholar of Islam could not be realized due to the extensiveness of his ministry. However, in addition to administrative responsibilities, he taught classes on the Arabic language, published the journal *Orient and Occident*, wrote several book-length treatises on Islam, and developed dramatic productions for use in outreach ministry.

Convinced that inter-mission cooperation was necessary to erase the stigma of sectarianism, he participated in several ecumenical conferences and developed a relationship with the Coptic Church of Egypt.

LARRY POSTON

Bibliography. C. E. Padwick, *Temple Gairdner of Cairo.*

Gall (c. 560–645). Irish missionary to Switzerland. Gall, a gifted linguist and significant participant in the CELTIC MISSIONARY MOVEMENT, began his missionary career as one of twelve companions of COLUMBANUS, the Irish abbot who traveled throughout Europe to reach the peoples there for Christ. During the journey, Gall became ill, and Columbanus, who was determined to continue to northern Italy and reach the Lombards, was forced to leave him behind.

Having recovered from his illness, Gall was convinced that God had called him to serve where he was. He was given permission to set up his own very modest living accommodations, and, after some exploration, found the type of place he sought. It was here that the famous nighttime encounter with a bear (commemorated in the trademarks of St. Gallen) took place.

Gall is also remembered as a competent exorcist, and was reportedly given the land grant on which the monastery bearing his name sits by Sigebert after he cast demons out of the king's daughter. Over the thirty-five years of his ministry, Gall acquired substantial prestige, seen in nominations to become bishop of Constance and abbot of Luzeuil. His commitment to a simple lifestyle, however, compelled him to turn both down. While there is little written evidence of his own personal evangelistic activity, he is known today as the apostle of Switzerland because of the evangelistic work of his followers. Gall died from illness on October 16, 645.

A. SCOTT MOREAU

Bibliography. W. H. Marnell, *Light from the West: The Irish Mission and the Emergence of Modern Europe.*

Gambia *(Est. 2000 pop.: 1,291,000; 11,295 sq. km. [4,361 sq. mi.]).* The Republic of Gambia is surrounded on three sides by Senegal, with the Atlantic as its western border. Originally a British dependency, Gambia became a separate colony in 1888 and gained independence in 1965. In this predominantly Muslim country (85% of the population), mosques are found in the majority of towns and villages where the majority are Sunnis of the Malekite rite. African tribal religionists comprise 11 percent of the population and are strongest among the Serer, Diola, Pacari, and Bassari peoples. The Constitution of 1970 guarantees freedom of thought, religion, public manifestation, and propagation.

The first permanent missionary was an Anglican chaplain who arrived in 1816, followed five years later by the British Methodists. While Catholicism touched Gambia through Portuguese traders around 1445, the first Catholic mission was not founded until 1849. The first Protestant group was WEC INTERNATIONAL, which sent missionaries in 1966. With only 3 percent of the population professing Christianity, it is evident that none of these organizations have been successful in attracting members. By 1982, both the Anglican and Methodists had indigenous and expatriate clergy while there were no indigenous Catholic priests. There is one diocese responsible directly to the Holy See.

The Gambia Christian Council, comprising Catholics, Anglicans, and Methodists, was founded in 1963 to cooperate in joint services and the production and distribution of literature. Radio Gambia also rotates among these three churches, broadcasting an epilogue every Sunday.

GARY LAMB

Bibliography. D. B. Barrett, *WCE.*

Gardiner, Allen Francis (1794–1851). English missionary in South Africa and South America. Born in a Christian family in the quiet Berkshire village of Basildon in 1794, Allen Gardiner became a restless adolescent and joined the British Navy at the age of fourteen. The death of his mother, a narrow escape from drowning off the Peruvian coast, and observing the lives of Christians in Tahiti seem to be the main factors leading up to his conversion to Christ. He was tempted to exchange his sailor's garb for the minister's gown but the words of the Apostle Paul, "Let every man, wherein he is called, therein abide with God," convinced him to serve the Lord upon the seas, which he did for several years.

Throughout the 1830s he was used by God to initiate the gospel among the Zulus in South Africa. His stubborn perseverance finally won over the Zulu king Dingarn. But his heart was set on South America, especially the Patagonians of the southern cone. In 1838 he tried to reach them overland via Mendoza, Argentina, but this and following attempts failed. He returned to England in 1843 to try to persuade the CHURCH MISSIONARY SOCIETY to open Patagonia to the gospel. Having received a negative response from the society, Gardiner himself organized some backers. In 1850, together with a small band of committed Christians, he made one last attempt to reach the Patagonians by sea. Evangelistic encounters with the Patagonians did not produce the desired response. Sickness, scurvy, inclement weather, and a lack of food caused the members of the missionary band to die off one by one. Gardiner was the last one to perish, leaving behind only his journal. But it was the discovery and later publishing of that journal in *Hope Deferred, Not Lost* which stirred the hearts of many Christians around the world. The following year a vessel, the *Allen Gardiner,* carried new missionaries to evangelize the Patagonians. Thus was born the South American Missionary Society which for over a century has proclaimed the Word of God throughout Latin America.

LINDY SCOTT

Bibliography. P. Thompson, *An Unquenchable Flame: The Story of Captain Allen Gardiner, Founder of the South American Missionary Society.*

GCOWE. *See* GLOBAL CONSULTATION OF WORLD EVANGELIZATION '95 (GCOWE 95).

GCOWE II. *See* GLOBAL CONSULTATION OF WORLD EVANGELIZATION '97 (GCOWE II).

Geddie, John (1815–72). Scottish-born Canadian Presbyterian missionary in New Hebrides (Vanuatu) and founder of the New Hebrides Mission. Son of a Congregationalist elder in Banff, Geddie joined the Scots diaspora to Canada in 1816 and settled in Pictou, Nova Scotia. He was active in Bible and Missionary Societies, in support of LONDON MISSIONARY SOCIETY (LMS), and with others prompted the establishment of the Synod of Nova Scotia mission to Polynesia in 1844. An experienced cabinet-maker, Geddie saw printing and medicine as essential aids in mission, to gain the "good favour" of Polynesians and to make the gospel available. He departed Halifax in November 1845 and was eventually assisted by the LMS in establishing a mission on Aneitum, where he produced an alphabet and within six weeks was able to preach in dialect.

Printing of elementary school books, Scripture portions, and finally the entire New Testament in Aneityumese (1863) followed, which was to have profound effects on the development of Vanuatan culture and nationality. Though obstructed by fever, storm, indigenous opposition, traders, extension of French imperialism, and Catholic missionaries, the LMS/Nova Scotian group extended around the island. Geddie was able to use the visits of G. A. SELWYN and others to develop international support, a status developed by JOHN G. PATON into an international movement dependent during Geddie's life largely on Scots-Canadian Presbyterian missionaries, such as J. Inglis (1852), George Gordon (1857), J. Matheson (1858), and others.

The mission extended to other islands in the group, such that after his death it was said of Geddie that "When he landed in 1848 there were no Christians here, and when he left in 1872, there were no heathen." Less imperially minded than Paton, Geddie led opposition to the indentured labor trade, and to the use of British military force in reprisals against aggressive indigenes. He made the most of and fostered Australia's growing interest in missions and Pacific expansion, overseeing cooperative work between the Canadian and Australian Presbyterian churches. Wiry, intelligent, practical yet spiritual, Geddie was of the finest type of colonial Scot,

producing a missionary church of lasting integrity and influence.

MARK HUTCHINSON

Bibliography. R. S. Miller, *Misi Gete: John Geddie, Pioneer Missionary to the New Hebrides;* J. Garrett, *To Live Among the Stars.*

Gender Roles. The term "gender" refers to the nonbiological, social, cultural, and psychological aspect of being male or female. Gender roles reflect the cultural norms of the society and can be defined as the learned or socialized differences in behavior between male and female. Society's definition of feminine and masculine gender role expectations has changed throughout history and there continues to be pressure for the redefining of gender roles. Few areas of inquiry are so fraught with personal biases as the gender-role related characteristics of men and women. Though formerly research in this area was done primarily by men, a large number of research-trained women are now involved and new insights have resulted.

All societies provide institutionalized gender-appropriate roles. In some societies moving into womanhood requires special ritual and celebration for girls, often perceived as preparation for marriage. Gilmore (1990), who has researched the approved way of being an adult male in many societies around the world, sees manhood as generally needing to be achieved. It is a precarious state that boys must win against powerful odds and that can be diminished or lost as well. It involves conceptually separating adult males from the women and girls in society. Womanhood, in contrast, he sees as a natural condition that happens through biological maturation and is culturally refined or augmented through body ornamentation or cosmetic behavior.

Though male domination is a universal with men filling the positions of authority and power, women have great influence. Men and their values, status, and work, tend to be "in focus" while women have much responsibility and work hard in the background, more "out of focus." In many societies a woman's status depends on her husband's status in society. In others, a woman's status depends almost totally on her position among the other women. Another way of contrasting men's and women's status is to see men's position as "public" and women's as "private" (in the home). Men are most often seen as protectors and providers and women as childbearers and nurturers, both being necessary for the well-being of society.

The Bible clearly states that all humans are created in God's image, both male and female (Gen. 1:27). Furthermore, humans, both male and female, have been given salvation and made ambassadors for God (2 Cor. 5:17–20). However, there are a variety of interpretations of what the Bible teaches concerning the relationships of men, women, and God. On the one hand, a hierarchical arrangement is perceived with woman under man who is under God (Mickelsen, 1983). On the other hand, equality between male and female is perceived with both being equally responsible to God (Spencer, 1985). Yet another interpretation focuses on complementarity with male and female using their God-given strengths for honoring and serving God (Hull, 1987).

The institutionalized Western church has generally reserved the positions of authority, decision making, and top leadership for males. However, from the very beginning of the modern mission movement women have played an active role. Besides providing home-front support, they responded to God's call and went to the field, first as wives and mothers but later as teachers, nurses, and nannies. Once on the field they became church planters, evangelists, preachers, and administrators. Their choice to become missionaries reflected their deep Christian commitment and their search for a structure that would allow them to unite the spiritual with practical needs in the world. In the early decades of the twentieth century women outnumbered men on the mission field by a ratio of more than two to one. They have been the "guardians of the great commission" (Tucker, 1988). Though there were forty-four women's missionary boards sending both men and women to the field in 1910, today the authority structure and decision-making power in mission organizations is mostly in male hands.

It is important for missionaries to understand the fact that differences in gender roles are socially defined. In cross-cultural work the tendency is to impose the cultural patterns of the carrier of the gospel on the assumption that they are biblical without even investigating what it means to be male or female in the receptor society. The Bible, however, shows God working according to the gender role definition of each biblical society. In divided societies where women function in the women's world and men in the men's world, it is usually best that the carrier of the gospel be the same sex as the hearer. Women need to reach the women and the men the men in such a society. If one gender creates and sings the songs of the society, then that sex should be tapped as a key resource for that role in the church. Division of labor according to gender as prescribed by the society does not have to change when people become Christian. Leadership training in the church for males and females should be related to the roles they play in society. Brusco (1995) has done an excellent anthropological study on the effect of conversion to evangelical Protestantism on gender roles in Colombia. Her work shows how allegiance to Christ brings gender role changes.

Dealing with these and other changes is important to crosscultural communicators of the gospel. Often legislation allows for change long before there is a change in attitude and practice. For instance, in areas where the women's role has been traditionally in the home and then they are given the option of training for a career, when they are working outside the home they continue to be unconsciously evaluated by society on how well they run their homes. New technologies, urbanization, education, war, and industrialization all result in subtle changes in gender roles. There needs to be sensitivity not just to the logistics of what is happening, but to the meaning of what is happening to both genders. Changes affecting the women also bring change for the men, and vice versa. All of these changes influence the structure and program of the church and development programs. Often a different approach is needed to reach those choosing to retain traditional role definition from those who choose change.

MARGUERITE G. KRAFT

SEE ALSO Women in Mission.

Bibliography. E. E. Brusco, *The Reformation of Machismo: Evangelical Conversion and Gender in Colombia*; D. D. Gilmore, *Manhood in the Making: Cultural Concepts of Masculinity*; G. G. Hull, *Equal to Serve: Women and Men in the Church and the Home*; A. Mickelsen, *Authority and the Bible*; A. B. Spencer, *Beyond the Curse: Women Called to Ministry*; R. A. Tucker, *GGC*; M. S. VanLeeuwen, *Gender and Grace: Love, Work, and Parenting in a Changing World*.

General Revelation. *See* REVELATION, GENERAL.

George, Eliza Davis (1879–1979). American missionary to Liberia. Growing up in Texas during the late nineteenth century, Eliza George faced severe obstacles to her call to missions. Her vision of telling her brothers and sisters in Africa that Christ has died for them met with two major stumbling blocks. As a "black woman" she was told that she did not "have to go over there to be a missionary—we have enough Africa over here"; nor was she capable of pioneering work since an African American woman had never previously served as a foreign missionary. Yet she became "the first black woman from Texas to go to Africa as a missionary"—a pioneer missionary with remarkable accomplishments.

George arrived in Liberia in 1914, immediately establishing a Bible Industrial Academy for the training of fifty boys. Her great love became the holding of revivals in churches and in regions without churches. After fifty-five years of service in Africa in the face of continuing set-backs, "Mother" George left a legacy of the establishment of the Elizabeth Native Interior Mission with four substations, the founding of eight schools, and the planting of over one hundred churches in cooperation with local Christian leaders.

ROBERTA R. KING

Bibliography. L. Lutz, *Born to Lose, Bound to Win: The Amazing Journey of Mother Eliza George;* R. A. Tucker, *GGC.*

Georgia *(Est. 2000 pop.: 5,527,000; 69,700 sq. km. [26,911 sq. mi.]).* Georgia is a predominantly agricultural republic of the former Soviet Union, located in the southern Caucasus region on the Black Sea. Ethnic Georgians make up about two-thirds of the population, with most claiming allegiance to the Georgian Orthodox Church. This church, whose roots go back to the early centuries of the Christian era, is largely lacking in spiritual vitality today. There is also a sizable Muslim minority representing over 20 percent of the population. Less than one percent of the population is evangelical—mostly Baptists, with some Pentecostals. Despite Orthodox intimidation and opposition, which have led to restrictions on evangelism and the construction of new church buildings, evangelicals are increasing in number.

RAYMOND P. PRIGODICH

SEE ALSO Commonwealth of Independent States.

German Mission Boards and Societies. The German missions are children of revivals, and they differ depending from which revival they come. After an unsuccessful attempt by Justinian von Welz (1664), the first two German missions, the DANISH-HALLE MISSION (India, 1706) and the worldwide MORAVIAN MISSION (Herrnhut, 1732), were born in the pietistic revival (*see* PIETISM). Herrnhut managed to withstand the ENLIGHTENMENT and provided spiritual and organizational links to the classical missions of the GREAT AWAKENING, which came over to the Continent from Britain. Basel, through the *Christentumsgesellschaft,* served as a center of revival and missions for both Germany and German-speaking Switzerland. Several of the Basel auxiliaries developed into missions of their own. The first set of these Protestant classical German missions (BASEL, 1815; BERLIN, 1824; Barmen, 1828, Bremen, 1836) was interdenominational, based on Lutheran and Reformed churches, but not dependent on them. The second set of classical missions came from the more definitely Lutheran wing of the Great Awakening in Germany: Leipzig (1836), *Neuendettelsau* (1841), Hermannsburg (1849), and Breklum (1876). The power of the classical missions lay in their revival spirituality, lay involvement, and organizational independence. Both groups together form today the ecumenical missions and are largely integrated into the German Lutheran/Presbyterian territorial churches.

Next came the FAITH MISSIONS, originating in the Holiness revival (1859) which also came from Britain: *Neukirchen* (1880), *Allianz Mission* (1889), CHINA INLAND MISSION, German Branch (1896, later Liebenzell), Marburg (1899/1909), Sudan Pioneer Mission (1900), *Mission für Söd-Ost-Europa* (1903), and *Licht im Osten* (1920). The German faith missions originally followed the concepts of the British faith missions, but increasingly modified them to better suit the ecclesiastical environment. The only major mission then of the German "Free Churches" was the Baptist Mission (1890).

The Pentecostal revival (1907), not being strong in Germany, still produced some foreign mission work, starting with Velbert (1931). The Catholic missionary revival started after the Great Awakening, with major centers in France, Belgium, and Holland. Catholic missionary work relies heavily on missionary orders (Society of the Divine Word, Steyl, 1875, the Mission Benedictines of St. Ottilien, 1887, and the White Fathers of Trier, 1894, being the first in Germany) and supporting societies (*Franziskus Xaverius Verein,* 1832, *Kindheit-Jesus-Verein,* 1843). Women far outnumber men as Catholic missionaries (Servants of the Holy Spirit, Reichenbach, 1887, the first German female missionary order). Though women also provided the larger numbers in the Protestant missionary force, they developed few women's missionary societies (*Deutscher Frauenmissionsgebetsbund,* 1899).

The First World War disrupted German foreign missionary work severely, and the years between the wars were, as in other countries, years without revivals, when few new missions were founded. However, in the Third Reich the German Protestant missions as a whole took the side of the Confessing Church against the state-supported German Christians. Nazi rule and ideology did affect their work. The period after the Second World War saw a strong renewal of the efforts of the classical missions in a new ecumenical setting. A missiological reorientation connected with the NEW DELHI ASSEMBLY (1961) led to a closer integration of the classical Protestant missions into the territorial (mainline) churches, and to a reliance more on funds allocated by the churches than on funds collected by the missions.

During the same time the evangelical missions experienced a major expansion. The fact that over the decades most of the early German faith missions had become closely related to one or several fellowship movements within the territorial churches created room for new interdenominational missions. Many of them were German branches of interdenominational faith missions like WEC INTERNATIONAL, OVERSEAS MISSIONARY FELLOWSHIP, and Sudan United Mission. Taking ideas from the faith missions and from the

Brethren missions, ERNST SCHRUPP developed *Missionshaus Bibelschule Wiedenest*, which had originated in an effort to evangelize in Eastern Europe (Alliance Bible School Berlin, 1905) into a major evangelical mission with a strong congregational base. The Baptist mission was reorganized as European Baptist Mission, and a good number of new evangelical missions came into being (like *Deutsche Indianer Pionier Mission* or *Kindewerk Lima*). A new departure was the founding of the *Deutsche Missionsgemeinschaft* (1951), also *Vereinigte Deutsche Missionshilfe* (1961), designed to send German missionaries to many international faith missions. The majority of the German missions and missionaries are now evangelical. The charismatic revival, which reached Germany in 1963, was slow in developing its own missions, but is now increasingly doing so, with the missions often being based in or almost identical with a local congregation. A new development is the transformation of the *Vereinigte Evangelische Mission* (Barmen/Bethel) into a worldwide fellowship of [equal] churches in mission (United Evangelical Mission, 1996).

In Germany the classical (ecumenical) missions cooperate in the *Evangelisches Missionswerk* (1975, successor to *Deutscher Evangelischer Missionstag*, 1922), the evangelical missions cooperate in the *Arbeitsgemeinschaft Evangelikaler Missionen* (1969, with the *Freie Hochschule für Mission*), and the Pentecostal and charismatic missions in the *Arbeitsgemeinschaft Pfingstlich-Charismatischer Missionen* (1993).

KLAUS FIEDLER

German Society for Missiology. *Deutsche Gesellschaft für Missionswissenschaft,* founded at Berlin in 1918, was the first body of its kind in the world. It was designed "to promote the scholarly treatment of the history and theory of the Christian mission." From the outset membership was, and still is, by election only. No fees are charged, and there are no restrictions in terms of gender, origin, or confession. For financial support the society has depended on grants from German churches and mission bodies. Activities of the society include publication of books and a periodical on missiology, promotion of research projects, and the granting of scholarships to deserving students. While the society is unable to endow chairs of mission in universities, it exerts influence in providing adequate representation of mission studies in theological education. In the 1960s and 1970s the society sponsored a series of consultations which resulted in the inauguration of the INTERNATIONAL ASSOCIATION FOR MISSION STUDIES in 1972. Currently membership of the German Society for Missiology is two hundred members, half of them from outside of Germany.

HANS-WERNER GENSICHEN

Germany *(Est. 2000 pop.: 81,700,000; 356,974 sq. km. [137,828 sq. mi.]).* Christianity reached German territories when large parts still belonged to the Roman Empire. Professing Christians were among the Roman and Greek soldiers in the military strongholds at Trier, Cologne, Mainz, and Augsburg. Christianization started from outside, when whole tribes—Gotes in the East and Franconians in the West—corporately accepted the new faith. Missionary work proper was introduced by Iro-Scottish (COLUMBANUS) and Anglosaxon monks, particularly BONIFACE, the "Apostle of the Germans." Under Charlemagne and Otto the Great, Christianity was enforced on still resistive tribes within Germany (e.g., Saxonians) and beyond its eastern borders (e.g., Wends). The power of the sword was mitigated by the preaching and educating ministry of Benedictine and Cistercian monks, whose monasteries became centers of evangelistic, pastoral, and cultural activities. In medieval times German Christendom was characterized by the synthesis between imperial and ecclesiastic authority, some archbishops acting as secular princes in personal union. Thus the Christian religion was rather legalistic and superficial, permeated with pagan residues.

The REFORMATION brought a spiritual revolution, the impacts of which shaped German Christian culture for three centuries. Although historical circumstances impeded foreign mission ventures, the tenets of Luther's theology dynamized the Protestant faith with evangelistic force. His rediscovery of the priesthood of all baptized paved the way for the laity becoming involved in domestic and foreign missions. It was, however, only by the breakthrough of PIETISM around 1700 that the evangelistic potential of Lutheranism was fully realized. Because of the imperial reconquest of Reformed provinces to the Catholic faith, Germany was eventually divided into equal territories, in which either the Protestant or the Catholic faith became the established religion, the rights of which were guaranteed by the Treatises of Augsburg (1555) and Osnabrück (1668) after extended religious and political wars. No provision was made to tolerate the ANABAPTISTS, many of whom eventually emigrated to America. Only after the ENLIGHTENMENT did the religious climate change toward tolerance (and relativism), thereby facilitating the founding of religious societies and free churches under American and English influence in the middle of the nineteenth century.

The main impact of the Enlightenment and the French Revolution (1789–93), however, was the undermining of belief in the supernatural, the inauguration of an age of secularization, and the emergence of humanistic ideologies with atheistic tendencies. Church attendance dropped steadily in many regions, and whole sections of the population became nominal Christians. The two World Wars and the reign of anti-Christian totalitarian ideologies caused spiritual blackouts. In the eastern federal counties, only 32 percent of the population still hold at least nominal church membership (compared to 84 percent in the West).

Reevangelization. In view of the alarming process of de-Christianization, pietistic leaders assembled in 1888 in the Moravian colony of Gnadau and formed the German Association for Fostering Fellowship and Evangelization, shortly called *"Gnadauer Verband."* In 1848, Hinrich Wichern called Germans to meet the growing social and spiritual needs of the uprooted classes by engaging in a joint venture for "Inner Mission," which combined charity work with pastoral and evangelistic care. HOME MISSIONS were inaugurated to reach a variety of social segments. The evangelistic branch of the Inner Mission was called *Volksmission.* In order to ensure the spontaneous support of the believers, the Inner Mission maintained its independent status in close cooperation with church authorities. After World War II, however, the official churches acknowledged the diaconal and evangelistic functions as their own responsibility and integrated them into their structure. The Gnadau Association and the German Evangelical Alliance, however, continued to operate through their own agencies. In the wake of the LAUSANNE CONGRESS ON WORLD EVANGELISM (1974), new initiatives were taken to unite all existing forces toward a new evangelization of the country. The following years saw several projects initiated, including the declaration of 1980 as "Missionary Year" and a "Year with the Bible" later on. The visits of BILLY GRAHAM to stage telecasted campaigns like *Euro'70* and *ProChrist* proved to be inspirational for similar initiatives by German evangelical leaders. Large-scale Bible study meetings (*Gemeindetage;* Ludwig-Hofacker-Conferences) and national youth rallies (*Christival*) have attracted tens of thousands of participants.

Missiology. The German contribution to the development of missiology as a basically theological subject with interdisciplinary complementation is outstanding. The seminaries of German mission societies contributed much to produce generations of well-educated missionaries, committed to biblical doctrines and sensitive to communicate them transculturally. German missionaries did outstanding work in reducing vernaculars to writing, creating an indigenous literature, and publishing substantial volumes of anthropological research. The oldest chair of mission studies still in existence is the one established for GUSTAV WARNECK (1834–1910) in Halle in 1896. Chairs for missiology were also instituted at other theological faculties (e.g., Berlin, Tübingen, Heidelberg, Hamburg) and seminaries. Ever since the historical WORLD MISSIONARY CONFERENCE in Edinburgh in 1910, German mission thinkers tried to make their char-acteristic contribution to the proceedings of the meetings of the INTERNATIONAL MISSIONARY COUNCIL and the COMMISSION ON WORLD MISSION AND EVANGELISM. The German emphasis was on the concept of *Heilsgeschichte* (salvation history), which stressed the eschatological orientation of the church's mission. Accordingly, they criticized all tendencies in ecumenical theology to interpret the KINGDOM OF GOD in terms of an ideological utopia. Outstanding spokesmen for this view were Karl Hartenstein, WALTER FREYTAG, and Georg Vicedom. When in Uppsala 1968 the WCC's theology of mission appeared to have substituted the horizontal for the vertical dimension of salvation, a group (*Theologischer Konvent*) of theologians who were in sympathy with the new Confession Movement "No Other Gospel" (1966) issued the FRANKFURT DECLARATION ON THE FUNDAMENTAL CRISIS OF MISSIONS. German missiologists organized in the GERMAN SOCIETY FOR THE STUDY OF MISSIONS (1918) and the Working Group for Evangelical Missiology (initiated by GEORGE W. PETERS in 1977). Missionaries do their professional studies either in the seminaries of their societies or centrally at the *Freie Hochschule für Mission* in Korntal, which is now a branch of Columbia International University. Spiritual discernment with regard to heretical and syncretistic influences in missions continues to be a main function of the *Theologischer Konvent* in close cooperation with the International Christian Network (established in 1978 in London).

PETER BEYERHAUS

Bibliography. R. H. Bainton, *Here I Stand. A Life of Martin Luther;* P. Beyerhaus and H. Lefevre, *The Responsible Church and the Foreign Mission;* P. Beyerhaus, *Shaken Foundations: Theological Foundations for Mission;* idem, *God's Kingdom and the Utopian Error;* K. Fiedler, *Christianity and African Culture: Conservative Protestant Missionaries in Tanzania 1900–1940;* H. W. Gensichen, *Living Mission: The Test of Faith;* G. Vicedom, *A Prayer for the World;* J. Warneck, *The Living Forces of the Gospel;* D. Zeisberger, *Diary of D. Z.: A Moravian Missionary amongst the Indians of Ohio.*

Ghana *(Est. 2000 pop.: 20,172,000; 238,533 sq. km. [92,098 sq. mi.]).* Located on the west coast of Africa, Ghana is home to over fifty-seven indigenous language groups, with Akan, Ewe, and Ga being the three major ones. Ghana is primarily an agricultural country, with over 65 percent engaging in subsistence farming.

Formerly called the Gold Coast, Ghana received its current name when it became the first sub-Saharan country in Africa to gain independence from Britain under the leadership of Kwame Nkrumah in 1957. Ghana's post-Independence political history has been a checkered one. Nkrumah was overthrown by the military in 1966, followed by five military regimes and three short-lived civilian governments. Multiparty democratic elections were held in 1992.

The first recorded contact of the church with Ghana came in 1471 through Roman Catholic priests who were chaplains to the Portuguese traders working in Ghana. The first Protestants were the Moravians who arrived in 1737 and 1770 and among whom eleven died in thirty-five years of work. In 1828 the BASEL MISSION started work in the southeast among the Ga- and Twi-speaking people. The Methodist Church, Ghana, came into being through the instrumentality of a group of Ghanaian Christian young men led by de Graft, who requested Bibles from Britain through Captain Porters. In response, the British Methodist Church sent a missionary and some Bibles in 1835. Six of the first seven Basel missionaries and all three of the first Methodists died, and more missionaries were sent. Those who survived planted the church in Ghana. The Bremen Mission started work in 1847 among the Ewe in the German colony of Togoland. Catholic missionary work began again in the south in 1881 and the north in 1906. Near the turn of the century the African Episcopal Zion (1898), Seventh-Day Adventists (1898), and the Society for the Propogation of the Gospel (1904) began work. To facilitate social synchrony with the nationals, the Basel missionaries brought in six West Indian Christian families to augment their team. THOMAS BIRCH FREEMAN, an English Methodist of African descent, was the first missionary to reach the Asante (Kumasi) in 1839. The pioneer Basel and Bremen missionaries, J. G. Christaller and B. Schlegel, translated the Bible into the local languages and produced vernacular primers, grammars, and dictionaries for literacy work and evangelism. They also taught crafts and improved methods of agriculture.

We can trace the movement of independent African churches in Ghana to the visit in 1914 by WILLIAM WADE HARRIS to southwest Ghana. Harris turned thousands away from fetishism in the Nzema area. The Assemblies of God was the first Pentecostal mission that came to Ghana through the northern borders from Burkina Faso in 1931. The genesis of the work that later developed into the Christ Apostolic Church, the Apostolic Church, and the Church of Pentecost was the efforts of indigenous preachers in the Asamakese area. They were later served by James McKeown (from 1937).

The Christian Council of Ghana launched the Ghana Evangelism Committee (GEC) New Life for All (NLFA) outreach in 1974, mobilizing churches for aggressive evangelism. The work of Bible translation, Scripture Union in schools, and the NLFA campaign resulted in many thousands coming to Christ, and enabled renewal in the churches. From 1977 to 1986 church growth in Ghana exploded. The Presbyterian Church grew 211 percent, the Evangelical Presbyterians grew 500 percent, the Ghana Baptist Convention

169 percent, the Assemblies of God 550 percent, and the Church of Pentecost 200 percent. While today 64 percent of the population claims to follow Christ, 40 percent of these have a church affiliation and only 12 percent attend church regularly. Thus, there is still work to be done in reaching Ghana for Christ.

JUDE HAMA

Ghanaian Mission Boards and Societies. Ghanaians have been active in missionary work ever since PHILIP QUAQUE (c. 1741–1816) was first engaged by the Anglican Church to reach people from his own country. The Presbyterian Church of Ghana and the Evangelical Presbyterian Church in Ghana were planted by German mission agencies, and became the first self-governing non-Western churches in Ghana after World War I. By 1980, there were 23 active mission agencies in Ghana. In 1993 it was estimated that over 670 Ghana missionaries had been sent out by some 44 agencies. The Church of Pentecost has placed workers in several African countries as well as in Europe and North America. Christian Outreach Fellowship, founded by William Ofori Atta, deploys cross-cultural missionaries to unreached people groups. Pioneers Africa, headed by Solomon Aryeetey, works among Muslims in Mali and has focused on unreached peoples in Africa.

BIBLE TRANSLATION and Christian literature distribution have been important facets of Ghanian mission endeavor. The growth of Bible translation work in the local languages is closely related to the story of the growth of missions in Ghana. The work of the Ghana Institute of Linguistics, Literacy, and Bible Translation (GILLBT) is recognized by both the church and the state. The use of the JESUS FILM in local languages is helping Ghanians reach unreached peoples within Ghana's borders.

There are several parachurch organizations that actively utilize Ghanian staff to reach Ghana and other countries for Christ. Gottfried Osei-Mensah was the first executive director of the Lausanne Committee for World Evangelization. Theophilus B. Dankwa headed IFES-Africa and Sam Atiemo Youth for Christ. Isaac Ababio pioneered the Hour of Visitation Evangelistic Association. Florence Yeboah's GHACOE Women's Ministry is engaged in holistic mission. Scripture Union (SU) had been active in Ghana since the early 1950s, and many of the current Ghanian church leaders came to Christ through the SU efforts.

As a result of the Ghana Church Survey published by the Ghana Evangelism Committee in 1989 and a subsequent national mission consultation in 1993, Ghana's most neglected mission fields have become the target of pioneer outreaches by denominations, mission agencies, and individual churches; more cross-cultural missionaries have been sent out and an Association of Evangelical Missions has been formed.

Theological education and training for missions remains a challenge. Christian G. Baeta, Kwesi Dickson, and John Pobee have made significant contributions. Kwame Bediako and the Akrofi-Christaller Memorial Centre for Mission Research and Applied Theology are also making fresh strides in mission training and research.

Ghana has sent missionaries around the world. In the past twenty years, these have included a new wave of missionaries—"economic missionaries." They are comprised of committed believers who have been spread out from Ghana because of harsh national economic pressure on them at home. They mostly serve as professionals in their new host countries, but diligently work as members of God's kingdom on his business of telling others about Christ. They are on every continent and in every ideological and religious region around the world.

ROBERT ABOAGYE-MENSAH
AND JUDE HAMA

SEE ALSO African Mission Boards and Societies.

Gibraltar (United Kingdom Dependent Area) *(Est. 2000 pop.: 28,000; 7 sq. km. [3 sq. mi.]).* Gibraltar is a British territory located on a peninsula six square kilometers in area that extends five kilometers into the Mediterranean Sea from southeastern Spain and dominates the Strait of Gibraltar, which connects the Mediterranean to the Atlantic Ocean. The peninsula consists of the Rock of Gibraltar, a high ridge of limestone and shale rising 426 meters above the sea level, and a low-lying isthmus connecting it to the mainland.

The domination of Gibraltar by the Moors began with their invasion in A.D. 711 under Tarik Ibn Zeyad. They constructed a mosque, defenses, and an elaborate system of reservoirs at the northern end of the Rock. The territory remained in Arab hands until a surprise attack by the Spanish in 1309. The brief Spanish occupation ended in 1333 when Sultan Abul Hassan of Fez took over. Most of the extant Moorish structures were built in the ensuing years. In August 1462 the Moors were finally driven out by the Spanish, who over the next 240 years fortified the Rock and developed Gibraltar as a naval base from which they sailed against the Mediterranean and Barbary pirates. Gibraltar was captured in August 1704 by a combined Anglo-Dutch fleet, and British sovereignty was formalized in 1713 by the Treaty of Utrecht.

Gibraltar's current population of roughly 30,000 includes some 20,000 Gibraltarians, 6,000 British expatriates, and 4,000 Moroccans. Spiritually, there is religious freedom. Approximately 87 percent of the population is Christian. The Spanish influence brought with it the Roman Catholic faith practiced by the majority. The Moroccans brought the Muslim religion, which is practiced by 10 percent of the population.

MARKUS WAGNER

Gifts of the Spirit. The twentieth century witnessed an explosion of interest in the person and work of the Holy Spirit. The impact of this upon the growth and expansion of the church, especially in the non-Western world, has been almost universally acknowledged. The phenomenal growth of churches which have emphasized the Spirit's work in their worship and witness has drawn attention to the many ways the Holy Spirit influences the quality of life and the growth of the church. Although a considerable output of literature dealing with the gifts of the Spirit in recent years has emphasized its importance, confusion continues regarding this subject.

Of the several terms used to indicate the gifts of the Spirit in the New Testament, the two words of most significance are *pneumatika* and *charismata*, both distinctively Pauline terms. As used by Paul (Rom. 15:27; 1 Cor. 2:13; 9:11; 12:1; 14:1), the term *pneumatika* denotes that which belongs to, or pertains to, spirit. Since the word *pneuma* in Paul primarily refers to the Holy Spirit, *pneumatika* refers literally to the things of the Spirit, which in certain contexts is appropriately rendered spiritual gifts (1 Cor. 12:1; 14:1). The word *charismata* is also frequently translated spiritual gifts, although the term itself lacks any direct reference as such to the Spirit. Derived from *charis* (grace), *charismata* broadly signifies the various expressions of God's grace concretely manifested in the form of gracious bestowals. It is only by its application in specific contexts (Rom. 1:11; 1 Cor. 1:4–7; 12:4, 9, 28–31) that the term *charismata* acquires the meaning "gifts of the Spirit"—gracious manifestations of the Spirit in the life of the Christian community.

The key texts concerning spiritual gifts are 1 Corinthians 12–14, Romans 12:6–8, Ephesians 4:11, and 1 Peter 4:10–11. A major difficulty in any effort to define or categorize the gifts of the Spirit is that nowhere in the New Testament do we find systematic instruction on the gifts. This difficulty is further compounded by the realization that no New Testament lists are identical, with no exhaustive listing of the gifts. While some scholars have distinguished a cumulative total of twenty gifts in these passages (apostles, prophets/prophecy, evangelists, pastors, teachers/teaching, service, exhortation, giving, leadership, mercy, wisdom, knowledge, faith, healing, miracles, distinguishing of spirits, tongues, interpretation of tongues, helpers, and administrators), others have added to this list from references or allusions in other New Testament texts (celibacy, voluntary poverty, martyrdom, hospitality, missionary, intercession, and exorcism), arriving at a total of twenty-seven spiritual gifts.

Among the various attempts to classify the gifts, the most plausible analysis distinguishes three categories: service gifts, miraculous gifts, and utterance gifts. *Service gifts* include a broad range of Spirit-inspired activity, such as giving, showing mercy, serving, helping, leading, and administering, designed to strengthen and deepen interpersonal relationships within the church community. *Miraculous gifts,* such as faith, healings, and miracles, are associated with manifestations of the Spirit's power. *Utterance gifts,* which include the message of wisdom, the message of knowledge, prophecy, teaching, tongues, interpretation of tongues, and exhortation, are forms of oral expression inspired by the Holy Spirit. While the significance and value of the gifts specifically mentioned in Scripture must not be undermined, the lack of any exhaustive listing indicates the possibility that the Spirit may supply other gifts in response to specific needs at any given time and place.

While research has proved that charismatic gifts have never been altogether absent through the history of the church, there has perhaps never been a time in the postapostolic period when the exercise of spiritual gifts has been as widespread and as integral a part of the church's experience as today, although not without controversy. One question concerns the relationship of the gifts to an important Pentecostal distinctive: Are the gifts of the Spirit contingent on and a consequence of the baptism in the Holy Spirit, a special endowment of the Spirit subsequent to conversion? A significant segment of charismatic Christians remain convinced that the gifts can be appropriated apart from the Pentecostal belief in a subsequent experience. This view has gained increasing acceptance and popularity among evangelicals, largely as a result of the influence of a relatively small but influential movement of so-called THIRD WAVE evangelicals.

Another issue stems from a cessationist view of the *charismata* that limits supernatural manifestations of the Spirit to the apostolic age. Although the cessationist view is no longer widely held, it is nonetheless influential, due to its impressive theological pedigree and sophistication. In continuity with the position adopted by the Protestant Reformers, and essentially rehearsing the theological position of the great Princeton theologian, B. B. Warfield, a significant group of dispensationalist and Reformed evangelicals maintain that the spiritual gifts had only temporary significance and purpose: to authenticate the apostles as trustworthy authors of Scripture. Now that we have a complete and closed canon of Scripture, the gifts have fulfilled their function, and are no longer necessary nor to be found in the postapostolic age. In recent years, however, some persuasive scholarly responses have challenged the cessationist position. The debate continues.

A third question has to do with whether the gifts of the Spirit are to be understood in essentially natural or supernatural terms. Thus while some view the gifts primarily as natural abilities or talents dedicated to the Lord, others have emphasized the supernatural element to an extreme, denying the role of human faculties in the exercise of gifts. The biblical teaching seems to point toward a balanced incarnational understanding of the gifts, with an interpenetration of the divine and the human, the supernatural and the natural. The gifts of the Spirit are not just the wise stewardship of natural gifts and abilities, but the result of the immediate working of the Spirit in the life of the believer. A natural talent only becomes a gift of the Spirit when it is yielded to the Holy Spirit and used by the Spirit.

The New Testament clearly witnesses to the close relationship between Pentecost and the missionary witness of the church, a fact made particularly explicit in the Book of Acts (John 15:26–27; 20:19–23; Acts 1:8; 2:4ff; 11:28; 13:2, 4; 19:6; 21:4, 11). For the first-century church, the Spirit was the fulfilled eschatological promise of God, experienced personally and corporately in powerful and visible ways, especially through the Spirit's gifts. In contrast to the experience of the church through most of its history, the New Testament seems to treat the manifestation of spiritual gifts as part of the normal life of the Christian community. The life and growth of the early church can be properly understood only when viewed in terms of a community of Spirit-filled Christians exercising their spiritual gifts.

The gifts of the Spirit impact the mission of the church in at least two significant ways. The first and less obvious way in which the gifts of the Spirit facilitate the church's mission is by equipping the believer for ministry within and to the church, strengthening the church, deepening its fellowship, and enriching the quality of its life. Effective Christian witness is only possible when there is a healthy church base experiencing genuine *koinonia* and manifesting authentic signs of kingdom life. The gifts of the Spirit constitute the basic divine equipment for mission and service. The New Testament promises of spiritual power and spiritual gifts are frequently linked to the worldwide mission mandate of the church (Mark 16:15–17; Luke 24:47–49; Acts 1:8).

Apart from specific gifts such as that of the evangelist or missionary, several other power gifts have been used in various evangelism and church planting efforts in recent years, especially in Two-Thirds World contexts such as Africa, Latin America, and Asia. Called POWER ENCOUNTER by many, this process signifies the use of different miraculous gifts, such as exorcism, healing and prophetic revelation to visibly demonstrate the power of Jesus Christ over spirits, powers, or false gods which hold the allegiance of an individual or people group. Exercise of the gifts of the Spirit thus announces the reality of the kingdom's arrival in Christ, and confirms the truth of the gospel message proclaimed.

The gifts of the Spirit are not to be viewed as optional appendages to the life of the church. They are neither temporally nor culturally bound, and their cross-cultural validity makes their presence a vital and necessary component of the church's cross-cultural witness.

IVAN SATYAVRATA

Bibliography. D. A. Carson, *Showing the Spirit;* J. Deere, *Surprised by the Power of the Spirit;* G. D. Fee, *God's Empowering Presence: The Holy Spirit in the Letters of Paul;* M. Green, *I Believe in the Holy Spirit;* D. Lim, *Spiritual Gifts: A Fresh Look;* J. R. Michaels, *DPCM,* pp. 332–34; E. F. Murphy, *Spiritual Gifts and the Great Commission;* H. A. Snyder, *The Problem of Wine Skins,* J. G. S. S. Thomson and W. A. Elwell, *EDT,* pp. 1042–46; C. P. Wagner, *Your Spiritual Gifts Can Help Your Church Grow;* J. R. Williams, *Renewal Theology,* vol. 2.

Gih, Andrew (1901–85). Chinese evangelist and founder of Evangelize China Fellowship. Born in Shanghai, China; he committed his life to Christ at age twenty-two and entered the ministry at age twenty-five. He organized the Bethel World Wide Evangelistic Band and conducted crusades to many parts of China.

In 1947 Gih founded the Evangelize China Fellowship to address the needs of a China devastated by external invasion and internal suffering. Organized in Shanghai as a FAITH MISSION and interdenominational in character, the mission was expanded to Hong Kong, Macau, and Taiwan. Ensuing years saw the work extended throughout Asia.

Primary and high schools for girls and orphanages remain today as a testimony to Gih's compassionate concern for the marginal Chinese. Bible schools and colleges along with over fifty indigenous churches mark his commitment to personal redemption and renewal.

Gih was a traveler and preacher of international stature, circling the globe and building a global network of prayer and concern for the social and spiritual needs of Asia. His focus was one of wholistic ministry and indigenous effort. He was a visionary and missionary who could galvanize others into corporate action and service. He is a model and stimulant for indigenous outreach among the Chinese today.

HOOVER WONG

Gilmour, James (1843–91). Scottish missionary to Mongolia. Born near Cathkin, Scotland, he received an M.A. from Glasgow University. Accepted as a student by the LONDON MISSIONARY SOCIETY, he went to Chestnut College in London for two years' education, during which time he was assigned to the Mongol mission, unstaffed since 1845. Well-known for his sense of humor, he sailed for China in 1870 and, "with only a few sentences of Chinese, two of Mongol and none of Russian," set off with some Russians for Kalgan and Kiakhta. He acquired proficiency in Mongolian and produced several tracts and a catechism. He spent the winter of 1871–72 in Peking, returning to Mongolia in the spring (this set a pattern he would follow for many years). His eleven-year marriage to the sister of a colleague produced three sons. His only furlough was in 1882, and from 1883 to 1885 he served Mongols living in Peking. His first book, *Among the Mongols* (1883), received a rave review in the *Spectator,* where it was compared to *Robinson Crusoe;* one of his colleagues stated, "If you have not read the book, read it, there is a treat in store for you." His second book was *More About the Mongols* (1893). He died in Tientsin on May 21, 1891.

KATHLEEN L. LODWICK

Bibliography. J. T. Mueller, *Great Missionaries to China;* W. P. Nairne, *Gilmour of the Mongols.*

Glasser, Arthur F. (1914–). American mission theologian, educator, and missionary to China. Glasser studied at Cornell and Faith Theological Seminary. A Marine chaplain during World War II, he served in China with his wife Alice, from 1947 to 1951. Expelled in 1951, he taught at Columbia Bible College and then became the North American director of China Inland Mission (now OVERSEAS MISSIONARY FELLOWSHIP).

Glasser reflected on several vital issues—better missionary training, encouragement of national leadership, a positive approach to non-Western cultures, and the social concerns of the gospel. In 1970 he began to teach theology of mission at Fuller Seminary's School of World Mission, where he served as dean from 1971 to 1980.

Glasser's theology focused on the KINGDOM OF GOD, a framework that entailed evangelism and social concerns. His leadership in the broader missionary community included participation in both evangelical and ecumenical consultations. Solidly evangelical in his own faith, he sought to be a bridge builder. He helped establish the AMERICAN SOCIETY OF MISSIOLOGY and the Zwemer Institute for Muslim Studies. Special evangelistic concerns have been the Chinese and the Jews. His extensive writings have been primarily in the form of journal articles.

PAUL E. PIERSON

Bibliography. C. Van Engen, D. S. Gilliland, and P. Pierson, eds., *The Good News of the Kingdom: Mission Theology for the Third Millennium.*

Glegg, [Alexander] Lindsay (1882–1975). British evangelist. Lindsay Glegg was possibly the best known British evangelist of the twentieth century. His father, Sir Alexander Glegg, was a leading London Congregationalist, but Lindsay was always interdenominational in his contacts and sympathies. As a young man, he was attracted for a time to the "New Theology" of R. J. Campbell, but at the KESWICK CONVENTION in 1905 he discovered a new commitment to Christ and repudiated liberalism. Like his father, he was an engineer and company director, but spent his spare time from 1917 as lay pastor of Down Lodge Hall, a mission hall in Wandsworth in South London, and in conducting some forty evangelistic campaigns throughout the British Isles. Glegg was involved in an extraordinarily wide range of evangelical organizations, including the Scripture Union, Christian Endeavour, and the Evangelical Union of South America, of which he was chairman for many years. He was a regular speaker at the KESWICK CONVENTION. In 1931 he was co-founder, with Thomas Cochrane, the former China medical missionary, of the Movement for World Evangelization. In 1955 he instituted the annual Christian Holiday Crusade held at Butlin's holiday camp at Filey in Yorkshire. In later life Glegg was a close friend of BILLY GRAHAM. He continued preaching into his nineties.

BRIAN STANLEY

Bibliography. J. D. Douglas, *Completing the Course: The Story of Lindsay Glegg.*

Global Consultation on World Evangelization (GCOWE '95).

A global-strategy consultation held in Seoul, South Korea, on May 17–26, 1995. Sponsored by the AD 2000 and Beyond Movement, GCOWE '95 is believed to be the largest and most representative such gathering in history, with 4,000 delegates representing more than 180 nations.

GCOWE '95 focused on "an in-process review/assessment of the unfinished task of the GREAT COMMISSION," emphasizing UNREACHED PEOPLES, uncharted areas, and countries within the 10/40 WINDOW. Six notable marks of the consultation facilitated movement toward the stated goal of "a church for every people and the gospel for every person by the year 2000": prayer was frequent, both planned and spontaneous as the Spirit led; reconciliation and bonding occurred between individuals, ethnic groups, mission agencies, denominations, and countries; partnerships were formed as delegates shared mutual interests and discussed specific plans for world evangelization; strategic planning was pursued as conferees laid out agendas to reach their own countries and tried to cooperate in missionary-sending efforts targeting the 10/40 Window; empowerment developed as women delegates and representatives from traditional mission fields recognized their opportunity and responsibility for world evangelization; mobilization of both people and resources was identified as the next step, and an estimated 70,000 Korean young people dedicated their lives to world mission.

LUIS BUSH

Global Consultation on World Evangelization '97 (GCOWE II).

A follow-up conference to GCOWE '95, the Global Consultation on World Evangelization '97, held June 30 to July 5, 1997, drew some 4,000 delegates from 133 countries to Pretoria, South Africa. Sponsored by the global AD 2000 and Beyond Movement, GCOWE II's main focus was on assessing how many of the movement's 1,739 designated "people groups" had been "adopted" for church-planting efforts by missions agencies and churches. After the conference, about 90 percent of the 1,739 groups in the "Joshua Project 2000" list were reported to have a church-planting "movement" (however large or small) or a commitment to mobilize a team of church starters.

As with GCOWE '95, less emphasis was placed on meeting AD 2000's goal of "a church for every people and the gospel for every person by the year 2000." The AD 2000 Movement was launched in 1989 at the Lausanne II conference in Manila. By 1997 many leaders were speaking of the year 2000 as a kind of springboard for a new century of outreach, rather than as a deadline to "finish the task" of world evangelization. In Pretoria missiologist RALPH WINTER urged that a more contextualized, de-Westernized gospel be presented to the huge and largely unreached blocs of Hindus, Muslims, and Buddhists.

Some observers said the movement was embracing a broader mission for the church beyond short-term evangelism and church planting. Ten consultations were convened during GCOWE '97, including ones for business executives, African initiatives, local pastors, children's concerns, the poor, and the performing arts. Racial reconciliation, appropriate to the South African venue, was another major theme.

STANLEY M. GUTHRIE

Bibliography. B. Nickles, *Pulse*, August 1, 1997; P. Ulrey, *Pulse*, January 3, 1997; S. R. Sywulka, *Pulse*, July 7, 1995; J. Reapsome, *Pulse*, August 25, 1989.

Globalization.

In the Bible God anticipated and commanded the globalization, or worldwide spread, of biblical faith. In the Old Testament, God blessed Abraham and promised that "all peoples on earth will be blessed through you" (Gen. 12:3). The people of God were told to "Declare his glory among the nations, his marvelous deeds among all peoples" (Ps. 96:3). The covenant community was open not just to Jews but to all who would follow Yahweh, such as Ruth of Moab. God's grace and compassion reached even the wicked people of Nineveh through Jonah and Naaman the Syrian. The Servant of the Lord, fully realized in Christ, was to be "a light for the Gentiles, that you may bring my salvation to the ends of the earth" (Isa. 49:6).

In the New Testament, Jesus Christ told the disciples, "And this gospel of the kingdom will be preached in the whole world as a testimony to all nations, and then the end will come" (Matt. 24:14). After the resurrection, he commissioned them to reach beyond the Jews and "go and make disciples of all nations" (Matt. 28:19). Just before his ascension the Lord told them, "But you will receive power when the Holy Spirit comes on you; and you will be my witnesses in Jerusalem, and in all Judea and Samaria, and to the ends of the earth" (Acts 1:8). Acts chronicles the beginning of this expansion. The Bible assures us that at the end of history there will be "a great multitude that no one could count, from every nation, tribe, people and language, standing before the throne and in front of the Lamb" (Rev. 7:9).

Globalization of the Church. Christianity has advanced unevenly around the globe during most of its first twenty centuries, with the church often slow to remember its evangelistic mandate. Despite occasional periods of persecution, until A.D. 313, when Constantine issued the Edict of Milan, the church exploded across the Roman Empire. For the next three centuries, the Christian faith continued to spread via monks and bishops into Ethiopia, India, Ireland, Britain, and along the trade routes toward Central Asia.

The coming of Islam brought a series of reversals. Lost to the Muslim invaders were the holy lands, North Africa, Asia Minor, and Persia. The church, however, continued to spread across Europe, to what are now Belgium, Germany, and the Netherlands. Russia also became Christianized. NESTORIAN Christianity made its way into China but did not last. Later, the Dominicans, Franciscans, and Jesuits brought Christianity into Central Asia, China, Africa, and Latin America.

Protestants, inspired by the example of DAVID BRAINERD among the Indians of the New World and the MORAVIANS of Germany, began to remember their missionary responsibilities. But not until 1792, with the spark provided by WILLIAM CAREY, did the Protestant Church begin large-scale outreach to other lands. The 1800s, sometimes called the GREAT CENTURY OF MISSIONS, saw the proliferation of missionary societies, aided by the expansion of the great colonial powers into India, China, and Africa.

The advance of the gospel has been remarkable in the twentieth century, particularly the latter half. In 1960, an estimated 58 percent of the world's Christians were Westerners; in 1990, only 38 percent were. Latin America's evangelical presence exploded from a mere 50,000 in 1900 to 40 million in 1990. Today, with about one-third of the earth's approximately 6 billion people, Christianity is present in every nation-state. Most of the growth has come in the former "mission fields" of Asia, Africa, and Latin America. From 1960 to 1990, the number of evangelicals in the West grew from 57.7 million to 95.9 million, while evangelicals outside the West multiplied from 29 million to 208 million. About three in four of the world's evangelicals are non-Westerners. However, despite this growth, many people in the world's vast Muslim, Hindu, and secularized blocs remain relatively untouched by the gospel.

Globalization of the Missionary Task. As Christians in the former missionary "receiving" countries have realized their responsibilities to be "senders," the globalization of the missionary enterprise has begun to track the globalization of the church. The number of Protestant missionaries from the United States and Canada has declined, from 50,500 in 1988 to 41,142 in 1992, according to the fifteenth edition of *Mission Handbook.* South Korea and India each boast 4,000 missionaries, and their numbers continue to grow. Nigeria's Evangelical Missionary Society sends about 950. While the precise figures are in dispute, the numbers of non-Western missionaries are certainly growing substantially faster than their Western counterparts (*see* NON-WESTERN MISSION BOARDS AND AGENCIES). Some experts believe that Western missionaries will be numerically eclipsed by the turn of the century.

With the shifting balance of missions power have come calls for Western churches to stop sending missionaries and instead—or predominantly—send money to support "native missionaries" (*see* FOREIGN FINANCING OF INDIGENOUS WORKERS). These are said to be cheaper and more effective than Westerners. Such calls have been especially attractive to Western Christians, who find themselves increasingly inward-looking and financially pressured. While applauding the energy, vision, and commitment of the younger missionary movement, missions experts caution against idealizing the non-Westerners as without problems. They acknowledge weaknesses in the non-Western sending, training, and shepherding bases as well as dangers in sending money only— both for recipients and for senders. Non-Western churches and mission agencies are sometimes better at sending people out than keeping them there, they say. Much effort is being expended to shore up the training of non-Westerners in order to keep them in their assignments.

Most of the discussion about the relationship of Western and non-Western missions focuses on discarding old roles and developing partnerships in the common task of world evangelization. While PARTNERSHIP most often refers to Western missionaries and non-Western "nationals" working one on one as equals, it can have a more structural meaning for missionary organizations. Agencies that cross ethnic or national lines to work together are said to be internationalized. Four types of internationalized organizations have been identified: cooperative (through informal sharing, such as the Missions Advanced Research and Communication Center), task-oriented partnerships (spearheaded by groups such as Gospel for Asia and Interdev that bring several organizations together), international agencies (such as WEC INTERNATIONAL and the SOCIETY FOR INTERNATIONAL MINISTRIES, which operate in many nations or have multinational leadership), and international movements in pursuit of a common goal or strategy. The AD 2000 and Beyond Movement, with its emphasis on "unreached peoples," is an example of the latter. Such movements are effectively reaching across national, denominational, and ethnic boundaries and presenting a clearer picture of the globalization of missions at the dawn of the twenty-first century.

STANLEY M. GUTHRIE

Bibliography. D. Hicks, *Globalizing Missions;* L. Pate, *From Every People;* J. A. Siewert and J. A. Kenyon, eds., *Mission Handbook;* W. D. Taylor, ed., *Internationalizing Missionary Training;* R. D. Winter and S. C. Hawthorne, eds., *PWCM;* J. D. Woodbridge, ed., *AFC.*

Gloukharev, Makarius (1792–1847). Russian Orthodox missionary to Siberia. Makarius Gloukharev was a missionary monk who served fourteen years in the Altai Mountains of Siberia. He was also one of the first missiologists to formulate a theology of missions for the Russian Orthodox Church. Makarius was born in the province of Smolensk in 1792. In the early 1820s, he retreated into the monastery caves of Kiev for a life of solitude. There he received his missionary calling.

Makarius traveled to the mountainous Altai region of Siberia in 1829, where 40,000 people lived. Early on he translated parts of the Bible and liturgical services into the indigenous language. He emphasized a long catechism before baptism, but his solid pioneer work led to the eventual baptism of over 25,000 Altai.

In 1843, Makarius left Siberia but continued his missionary effort by writing a challenging book entitled *Thoughts on the Methods to be Followed for a Successful Dissemination of the Faith among Muhammadans, Jews and Pagans in the Russian Empire.* Makarius understood that the best way to motivate the believers was to guide them in study of the Holy Scriptures. Since only a Slavonic text of the Bible existed, he began translating the Old Testament into vernacular Russian. In the midst of this final task, Makarius died.

LUKE A. VERONIS

Bibliography. N. Struve, *IRM* 54 (4): 308–14; L. A. Veronis, *Missionaries, Monks, and Martyrs: Making Disciples of All Nations.*

Gobat, Maria (1813–79). Swiss missionary to Jerusalem. Born in Zofingen, Switzerland, she helped her father, who was a director of schools and founder of a home for orphaned children. She served these destitute children throughout her youth. In May 1834 she married Rev. Samuel Gobat. Soon after the wedding, they left for Abyssinia, where Samuel had been working. Their journey was filled with such difficulty and hardship that their arrival in Abyssinia was delayed by two years. After the Gobats established their work in Abyssinia, they were forced to leave prematurely due to Samuel's continuing health problems. Their journey back to Europe proved to be more treacherous; their newborn daughter died along the way.

Through a series of events, Samuel was nominated by Frederick William IV of Prussia to the see of Jerusalem. The Gobats served the people of Jerusalem, especially the children, for many years. Maria worked faithfully and diligently in all the schools and missions founded by her husband until her death, exactly twelve weeks after her husband's.

KATHY MCREYNOLDS

God. The relationship between the Christian doctrine of God and mission is best explored within the context of salvation history. By tracing that path we see that mission is in fact God's gracious, loving response to the problem of human SIN. Every cardinal attribute of God is brought to bear on the problem of sin (*see also* DIVINE ATTRIBUTES OF GOD).

We begin with an attempt to assess the range or scope of God's salvific desire. Using only the New Testament, we would have no difficulty concluding that God's desire is universal (1 Tim. 2:1–6). He has acted to reconcile the world to himself (2 Cor. 5:19) and has gathered a people for himself from among the Gentiles, that is, from all nations (Acts 15:14). Most of the Old Testament, however, seems to be the history of God's dealings with but one special people, Israel. Nevertheless, God's desire to save all people of all nations can be argued from several Old Testament perspectives (*see also* OLD TESTAMENT THEOLOGY OF MISSION).

First, it should be noted that God's involvement in human affairs has not been limited to any one part of the race. This unlimited scope of God's interaction with humankind is evident in several aspects of CREATION. Scripture clearly portrays

God as the Creator and Sustainer of the world and in particular the human race (Gen. 1:1–2:19; 14:19; Isa. 40:28). The intent of the command to be fruitful and multiply (Gen. 1:28; 9:1) is obviously universal as were the results of obedience. Thus, the repeated affirmation of his ownership of creation is justified (1 Sam. 2: 1–10; Ps. 24:1; Ps. 50). All peoples are his. All depend upon his custodial activity, that which sustains existence as we know it (Ps. 104:14).

The unlimited scope of God's dealings with humanity can also be seen in his sweeping and universal judgment of sin. The effects of Adam and Eve's fall were not limited to one people or ethnic group. As humankind began to spread out across the face of the earth, the effects of sin were carried with them and intensified (Gen. 3:1–7; 4:1–12; 6:5–8). At each stage of this devolution, God's response in judgment matched the range of sin's pandemic spread. In Genesis 3:14–19 judgment was meted out to each participant: the serpent, Eve, and Adam. Similarly, the flood brought divine wrath to bear on all sinners (Gen. 6:5–6). God's response is no less inclusive when sin once again engulfs humankind, as reported in Genesis 10–11.

But God's promises and implementation of restoration are also universal. In concert with each wave of judgment, God keeps hope alive with the promise of reconciliation. After the fall, in the midst of God's condemnation of the initial sin, there is a promise of the Seed, a descendent of the woman who would "crush the head of the serpent." Many have referred to Genesis 3:15 as the first statement (protevangelium) of God's ultimate answer to sin, anticipating Christ's redemptive work on the cross. After the flood, God reestablishes his relationship to humans by entering into a covenant with the whole of humanity (Gen. 9:9–17). That the covenant with Noah has universal implications can be seen from the inclusive language (*every* living creature, all generations). After the affair at Babel, God calls out Abraham and promises that through him *all* nations will be blessed.

Thus, we see that the pattern established by God's general intercourse with humanity also applies to his judgment of sin. God's concern for reconciliation extends to every people (Pss. 67:4; 82:8; 96:10; Isa. 2:4; Joel 3:12; Mic. 4:3).

God not only desires salvation universally, he has taken concrete, practical steps to accomplish that. From the Old Testament perspective this is reflected primarily in the election of Israel (*see also* DIVINE ELECTION). God enters a covenant with one person and his descendants. However, these developments alter nothing with respect to God's universal salvific will. In fact, the election of Israel is best viewed as a continuation of God's interaction with all nations. Each of the promises given in response to the first two stages of sin's spread, although universal in scope, do anticipate narrower foci of implementation (Gen. 3:15, the seed; Gen. 9:26, the blessing of Shem).

The *locus classicus* for the concept of election is Deuteronomy 7:6–8 (see also 9:4–6; 10:14ff.; 14:2). Here we see that in being chosen Israel is called a holy people and treasured possession. This description gives us significant insight into the nature of the election.

No human standard was applied and used as the basis for election. We see that Israel is not chosen on the basis of special social characteristics or cultic and moral integrity. In fact, we are told that they were the least among the nations. We know that they were just as vulnerable to the effects of sin as other peoples. So it is wholly because of God's love and grace that Israel is afforded such a privileged position. And yet, they were also not the only people to be favored by God. The nations remain in the purview of election. Deuteronomy 7:8 links election to the promise given to Abraham and with that to the universal scope of God's redemptive purpose.

The purpose of election also rests squarely within the context of God's universal design. The intended result was for Israel to be a blessing and a light for the nations (Gen. 12:3; 18:18; Gal. 3:8). Election does not only imply privilege, but also responsibility. The history of Israel is an extension of God's dealings with the nations to which Israel is to be light (Exod. 19:5–6).

Thus, it comes as no surprise that others were allowed to participate in the benefits of that privilege (Gen. 14:19, Melchizedech; Gen. 16:13, Hagar [Egyptian]; Exod. 12:38, 'mixed multitude'; Deut. 31:12 'foreigner'). In fact, there is so much material of this sort that many have inferred that Israel clearly understood the universal salvific implications of its election.

As we continue to follow the course of salvation history, we recognize that the developments described in the New Testament are largely the result of God having completed his plan of redemption. With the coming of Christ, we have the concretization of salvation, a new covenant, and a new people. Christ fulfills the promise made by God, initiates a new covenant, calls into existence a new people of God, and inaugurates the Christian mission (activation of witness).

In Galatians 4:4 we are told that when the "fullness of time had come, God sent forth his Son . . . to redeem those who were under the law." The idea here is not that time has simply run its course, but that an appointed time or the fulfillment of the promise had arrived. God himself initiates the final stage in redemption history by sending his Son into the world.

The context for our understanding of these events is the one already established by the Old Testament, namely, that of the Abrahamic promise, the covenants, and the anticipated blessing of all nations (*see also* ABRAHAMIC COVENANT). This is exactly the approach taken by Paul in Galatians 3. In Galatians 3:1–5 he raises the fundamental question of just how they received the gift of redemption (which is now a concrete reality). Their own experience provided an obvious answer. They received the gift of the Spirit as a result of their obedient response to the message of faith. In Galatians 3:6–9 Paul supplements this line of argument by appealing to Scripture (Gen. 15:6), showing that it was Abraham's willingness to have faith in God's plan and not some level of religious performance, which led to God declaring him righteous. That leads to the conclusion that the true children of Abraham are those (any, including the Gentiles) who have faith (Gen. 17:7; Rom. 9:6ff.).

The promise made to Abraham is referred to here as the gospel (Gen. 12:3; 18:18; 22:18; 26:4; 28:14). So it is faith, not ethnicity or keeping the law (3:10ff.), which leads to redemption. The law did not change the conditions of the promise (Gal. 3:15), it only revealed sin as sin. The object of faith is Christ, God's plan, as accomplished by Christ (Gal. 3:10–14), which is precisely what the promise envisioned. This fact is established by highlighting the singular of the word "seed." The promise was not intended to include all the descendants of Abraham, but *the* descendant, Christ (Gal. 3:16) and all those who are in him (Gal. 3:26–29). As in the Old Testament, the scope of the promise is universal (Gal. 3:8).

The Book of Acts picks up the theme of unrestricted mission. In 1:8 we see Jesus diverting attention from the question of time and placing it on the disciples' responsibilities. These included worldwide outreach. Consider the similarities to the GREAT COMMISSION passages.

But not only has God kept his promise by sending the Son, he also enables the new people of God to fulfill their responsibility by sending the Spirit. Even a cursory reading of the Book of Acts impresses one with the prominence and importance of the HOLY SPIRIT. And here we see how the work of the Spirit relates to that of the other members of the Godhead.

The Holy Spirit generates the missionary spirit. The drive toward spontaneous expansion comes only after Pentecost. The missionary spirit is first and foremost the spirit of sacrifice. The early Christians were willing to put their very lives on the line (Acts 15:26), give up everything familiar, family, homes (Acts 13:3), rather than retain the best for themselves, as is often the case today.

The missionary spirit is also a spirit of courage. Consider the way in which the apostles faced imprisonment, beatings, and a host of other dangers. The challenges were, of course, not just physical. They were willing to challenge existing paradigms and power structures (Acts 4:31; 21:3). Are we any less in need of courage?

The missionary spirit is the spirit of love. First Timothy 1:5 teaches that the sum of all teaching is love—unconditional love for all.

The Holy Spirit guides the missionary outreach of the early church. This was done in several ways. First, the Holy Spirit is presented as the initiator of missionary outreach (Acts 13:1ff.). Second, the Spirit inspires the proclamation of the gospel (Acts 10). Third, the Spirit guides the course of missions (Acts 16:9–10).

The Holy Spirit achieves the results. In John 16:8 Jesus teaches that it is the Spirit who opens the eyes of the world to its own sinfulness. There is no natural awareness of guilt. Consider the sermons given in Acts. They reflect a dependence on the Spirit in that (1) they call for a decision (Acts 2:28), (2) they promise forgiveness (Acts 2:28), and (3) they warn about the coming judgment.

Having followed the implementation of God's plan of salvation, we conclude that it is God himself who has been and is engaged in missions. Several decades ago Georg Vicedom popularized the term MISSIO DEI in a book with that title published in 1961. In it he suggested that he was using the phrase in order to underscore the fact that mission is above all God's work, that is, God is the active subject of mission. In that case mission is actually an extension of God's salvific desire and activity. Vicedom goes on to challenge his readers by suggesting that if our assumption that God desires mission because he is himself involved in mission is correct, then the church can be God's instrument and tool only if it allows itself to be used by him (p. 13). This may well be a needed reminder at the beginning of the twenty-first century. God, and not human agencies, is in charge of the mission of the church.

EDWARD ROMMEN

Bibliography. H. Berkhof, *Christian Faith*; D. G. Bloesch, *A Theology of Word and Spirit*; J. Carpenter and W. Shenk, eds., *Earthen Vessels*; G. D. Fee, *God's Empowering Presence*; T. N. Finger, *Christian Theology: An Eschatological Approach*; A. Glasser, *Kingdom and Mission*; S. J. Grenz, *Revisioning Evangelical Theology*; S. J. Grenz, *Theology for the Community of God*; P. K. Jewett, *God, Creation, and Revelation*; G. R. Lewis and B. A. Demarest, *Integrative Theology*; A. E. McGrath, *Christian Theology: An Introduction*; C. Van Engen, D. S. Gilliland, and P. Pierson, eds., *The Good News of the Kingdom: Mission Theology for the Third Millennium*; O. Weber, *Foundations of Dogmatics*.

Gods and Goddesses. People have always considered everyday life to be closely associated with the sacred which is encountered in the form of powers and divine beings. Concepts of gods and goddesses have developed as answers to fundamental human questions of how one can cope in an uncertain world. This topic most aptly fits those religious systems classified as POLYTHEISM, where the divine is perceived as many distinct entities. Gods and goddesses have been perceived in every conceivable expression: the sun and moon, earth and sky, climatic phenomena, animals, heroes, and various aspects of human life.

In ancient agricultural societies the earth goddess was an important deity regarded as the giver of life and of fertility. Often seen as Mother Earth, in ancient Mesopotamia she was commonly known as Ishtar or Ashtoreth. She was known to the Israelites through the Canaanites, and many turned to worship her soon after arriving in the Promised Land (Judg. 2:13; 10:6). The goddess was also known in the ancient civilization of the Indus Valley prior to the Aryan migration from the north. Frequently the moon is associated with the goddess of fertility because she seems to relate to the rhythms of life. The rhythm of fertility is also symbolized by deities depicted as dying and then rising. The modern pagan movement in the West has sought to recover the worship of the Earth Mother, who is variously spoken of as Gaia or The Lady, and is considered in the threefold form of young maid, mother, and old crone.

Often associated with the earth goddess was the sky god who brings rain, which fertilizes the earth that produces the harvest. For example, in the ancient Middle East the goddess Ashtoreth was associated with the god Baal. The fertility rituals associated with these deities took place at mountain shrines spoken of as high places in the Old Testament (1 Kings 14:23). The Baals were often considered to be the lords of particular areas, so they had appropriate surnames, for example, Baal-Peor (Num. 25:3). Baal was the great fertility god of the Canaanites whose worship throughout Israelite history was a continual challenge to the worship of Yahweh.

In the more complex civilizations of the ancient world, the pluralism of divinities was considered to operate as a pantheon, a community of gods and goddesses. The pantheon was based on a complex system of MYTHS and legends that gave an explanation of the nature of the sacred in every area of social life. There was often a senior god conceived of as the father of the gods, a supreme being associated with the sky. For example, Zeus was the high god of the Greeks, Jupiter for the Romans, and Odin for the Vikings. Sometimes this supreme deity was regarded as old or remote, so that the real powers were with the more immanent and vigorous gods. In other cases, one god ruled, and the others performed the basic functions that maintained life and order. These gods married and had offspring, fought wars or made peace.

Civilizations like those of the city-states of Egypt, Mesopotamia, Greece, and the Aztecs had a hierarchical pantheon governing through a human ruler. A close relationship was sometimes conceived between a particular god and the po-litical might of a city. Thus the Babylonians would take the idols of conquered nations back to their temples in Babylon as symbols of Babylonian domination.

Many gods had their own special domain. Those who displayed great physical powers often functioned as gods of protection and war. The Vedas of ancient India spoke of the storm god Indra, and Thor was the storm god of the Viking people. Mars was the Roman god of war protecting the state. Often the king was considered an embodiment of such a god. An example was the Japanese emperor, who was regarded as the sun god. Other deities were associated with the arts and technology. Thoth was the Egyptian god of wisdom, and Njord was the Scandinavian patron of shipping. Ogun was the Yoruba god for all those who worked with iron, the blacksmith, the goldsmith, the hunter, and even the taxi driver in modern times. The Greek god Hades, Seth of the Egyptians, and Ereshkigal of Mesopotamia received the dead into their abode. Thus there was a great variety of religious expression relating to state cults, local cults, and occupational cults. A deity might with time grow or decline in importance, so even within ancient societies there was continual change, making it difficult to draft simple typologies.

Scholars have attempted to distinguish between gods and ancestors, or between divinities and lesser spirits. An ancestor is usually a deified human, a cultural hero who through great exploits has risen to the status of a god (*see* ANCESTRAL PRACTICES). The famous Chinese general Kuan-ti was deified as the warrior protector of the empire. Although these distinctions may be useful, they can mislead, and it is usually best to begin with the categories that the particular society has set up. The Lugbara of Africa, for example, distinguish between ancestors and *adro* spirits. Ancestors remain close to the image of human beings, while the *adro* do the reverse of normal human behavior: they are cannibalistic, incestuous, and walk upside down. The ancestors express the pattern of the human world with its social order, while the *adro* represent the dangerous world of the bush. This contrast of opposites explains the perplexing features of life.

Gods and spirits are often believed to be able to reveal themselves or express their will to humans. A common manner is through DREAMS, especially those that are vivid or unusual. People ponder these dreams and ask others to help interpret whether they are warnings or promises. Another means of divine revelation is through a trance; a person possessed by a deity. In these cases the god is believed to speak directly and express his will through the mouth or the actions of the individual (*see* POSSESSION PHENOMENA).

In return gods and goddesses require homage and SACRIFICES. These are usually offered at special times of the year in order to give thanks. Among the Ga of Ghana the great annual festival is *hummowo* ("hunger-hooting"), when all the corn remaining from the previous season is cooked and presented at the shrine of the gods and ancestors. Then the first of the new corn is offered to the deities, after which the people have a time of feasting and license. Sacrifices can also be required to make atonement for violations of rules and TABOOS, to remove evil or sickness from a person or a community. Most Hindus perform simple rituals of *puja* in which vegetables, fruits, and flowers are offered to the image of a deity. RITUALS, however, often become elaborate, so that only religious specialists (priests) are able to perform them correctly. Among the Aryans the Brahmin priests came to dominate the religious ritual because of their knowledge of the Vedic hymns and the complex ceremonies, which required years of study.

Monistic religious traditions assume that the whole of reality is divine, but even here gods and goddesses can be an important feature, regarded as manifestations of the one divine reality. Within the Hindu tradition the *bhakti* way *(bhaktimarga)* is a type of devotion that leads to liberation. The worship of Vishnu in the form of Krishna or Rama is very popular in India, as is the worship of Shiva and his consort Sakti. *Bhakti* reflects not only a special relationship to a particular form of deity, but also the mood of the devotee. It is characterized by chanting of the sacred name, reciting and acting the great stories of the deity, and singing hymns of praise. Various combinations of human relationships have been used to depict this devotion to the deity: servant to master, child to parent, friend to friend, lover to beloved.

DAVID BURNETT

Goforth, Jonathan (1859–1936). Canadian missionary to China. First and last a soul-winner, Jonathan Goforth was born on a farm in rural Ontario, the seventh of eleven children. Converted at age eighteen, he soon influenced a high school teacher and an entire class to follow Christ.

Reading the memoirs of Robert Murray McCheyne, Jonathan caught the vision for a life of ministry and dedicated himself to foreign missions just before attending Knox College (Toronto). He married Rosalind Bell Smith in 1887 and was appointed by the Presbyterian Church of Canada to China, arriving there in 1888. Goforth's first focus was the North Honon Province, at that time a dangerous territory for foreigners. Given Jonathan's energetic and inspired commitment to soul-winning and to establishing a witness in new areas, the Goforths immersed themselves in the culture. Despite many setbacks and trials, including the deaths of several of their children, their first decade saw

the cultivation of indigenous Bible teachers and evangelists.

The Goforths escaped with their lives during the 1900 Boxer Rebellion, although Jonathan was nearly killed. After a brief furlough in Canada they returned to China in 1901. Grief over modernism in the homeland churches and the powerlessness of the small satellite churches in China moved Jonathan to hunger and plead with God for revival. Jonathan personally witnessed the great Korean revival in 1907 and returned to China with the burning desire to see God's spiritual blessing fall there. On a speaking tour of established churches throughout Manchuria, Jonathan's desire was realized as the spirit of revival began to take hold. A preliminary pattern was soon established: deliberate and faithful prayer, clear testimony of revival in another place, preaching of the Word, and an invitation to confess sins and pray. Churches were revitalized and thousands of new converts were baptized between 1908 and 1913.

Holding to the absolute authority of the Word of God, the Goforths carried the message of salvation to the remote areas of Manchuria. They called on mission and denominational leaders there and in the homeland to forsake the compromise of modernism. Winsome and tireless, they continued in the ministry until 1934, when failing health led them to return to Canada. During their forty-six years of faithful ministry, God raised up over sixty Chinese evangelists and Bible teachers and established thirty new mission stations.

JANET BRUCE

Bibliography. J. Goforth, *By My Spirit;* J. and R. Goforth, *Miracle Lives of China;* R. Goforth, *Goforth of China,* 6th ed.

Goforth, Rosalind Bell Smith (1864–1942). Canadian missionary to China. When Rosalind and Jonathan Goforth lost all their worldly possessions in a fire during their first year of marriage and ministry in China, Rosalind felt God weaning her soul decisively from the past to their calling among the Chinese. The Goforths prayed earnestly for converts from the very first, and God answered. As a means of breaking into a foreign culture, they opened their first home in North Honan Province for daily tours and hundreds of local villagers responded. The visitors were ushered through the house in small groups and were given a short introduction to the God of the Bible and the Lord Jesus Christ.

Rosalind bore eleven children, five of whom died in China. An educated and capable woman, she managed the household details for her large family and frequently the mission bookkeeping and correspondence as well. She had a special role in evangelizing women and training some as Bible teachers. Following Jonathan's lead, she submitted her own will to God to leave the security of the home mission station and go with her husband and children to evangelize in distant areas. Bearing up under often primitive living conditions and difficult, dangerous travel, they believed and proved together that the safest place for them and their family was the path of duty. God raised up converts and discipled thousands through their obedience and faithfulness.

In their later years, Rosalind was Jonathan's eyes and he her ears as their health began to fail. They returned to Canada in 1934 and were able to record the essence of their lifework in several books before Jonathan's passing in 1936 and Rosalind's in 1942. Rosalind's *How I Know God Answers Prayer* merited numerous reprintings and has influenced a generation of Christians to commit their lives to God and his blessing.

JANET BRUCE

Bibliography. R. Goforth, *Climbing: Memories of a Missionary's Wife;* L. Dorsett, *AFC,* pp. 180–91.

Gordon, Adoniram Judson (1836–95). American Baptist missions promoter. Born in New Hampton, New Hampshire, educated at Brown University (B.A., 1860) and Newton Theological Institution (B.D., 1863), Gordon championed the cause of missions during his pastorate of Boston's Clarendon Street Baptist Church from 1869 to 1895. He joined the Executive Committee of the American Baptist Missionary Union in 1871, and became chair in 1888. In 1884 he negotiated the ABMU takeover of the faltering British Congo River Livingstone Inland Mission. In 1889 he established the Boston Missionary Training School, which welcomed female students, sent out fifty missionaries in its first decade, and later developed into Gordon College and Gordon-Conwell Theological Seminary.

Through extensive speaking and writing, Gordon promoted missions across denominational and international boundaries. In 1886 he helped launch what became the STUDENT VOLUNTEER MOVEMENT. At the 1888 LONDON CENTENARY CONFERENCE on the Protestant Missions of the World he emerged as an international missions advocate. A premillennialist, Gordon did not conflate Christianity and Western culture, or favor the civilizing incremental missiology typical of the imperialist era. His views on world evangelization were articulated in *The Ship Jesus* (c. 1884), *The Holy Spirit in Missions* (c. 1893), his journal *The Watchword,* and the *Missionary Review of the World,* of which he became associate editor in 1890. Gordon is also remembered as a hymn writer, poet, educator, and social reformer.

THOMAS A. ASKEW

Bibliography. E. B. Gordon, *Adoniram Judson Gordon: A Biography with Letters and Illustrative Extracts;* D. L. Robert, *IBMR* 11 (1987): 176–81; G. M. Rosell,

ed., *The Vision Continues: Centennial Papers of Gordon-Conwell Theological Seminary.*

Gorham, Sarah (1832–94). American missionary to Sierra Leone. She was born in Fredericksburg, Maryland. Little is known about her childhood or educational background. About 1880 she visited some relatives in Liberia. Deeply moved by the appalling living conditions she observed, she traveled about comforting those who were in need.

She returned to the United States and settled in Boston, Massachusetts. Shortly thereafter, she joined the Charles Street AME Church and became involved in humanitarian work. In 1888 she felt God's call to the mission field and volunteered for the AME Liberian Mission.

She planned to go to Liberia, the place she had previously visited, but was moved by the Reverend Frederick to join him in Sierra Leone. At fifty-six years of age, Gorham became the first woman missionary appointed to a foreign field.

After her arrival in Sierra Leone, she moved to Magbelle, a town on the banks of the Scarcies River. She was very active in the Allen AME Church and also founded the Sarah Gorham Mission School. The school, which trained both boys and girls in religion and industry, was highly successful. By 1899, 250 to 300 pupils were enrolled.

Gorham worked with extraordinary fervor and dedication. In a letter dated May 28, 1894, she wrote: "With all I am suffering and all I am enduring I would not give up this work under any condition." Indeed, she did not give up her work until she was forced to.

In July 1894 she fell ill with fever and died on August 10. Like her Lord Jesus Christ, she literally gave her life for the work of the gospel.

KATHY MCREYNOLDS

Bibliography. S. M. Jacobs, *Women in New Worlds,* 2:268–80.

The Gospel and Culture. The GOSPEL is God's gift to humankind. CULTURE is a human creation. However, the gospel is expressed within culture and communicated through culture. "The Word became flesh [incarnation] and made his dwelling among us [enculturation]" (John 1:14a).

We create cultures because humans are created in God's image (Gen. 1:26–31) (*see* IMAGE OF GOD). God creates; humans make artifacts. God speaks; humans develop languages. God is a covenant being; humans create social institutions. God is righteous; humans develop systems of mores. Religion develops out of human yearning for a relationship with the other dimensions of existence. Artifacts, languages, social institutions, mores, and religion are some dimensions of human culture.

Cultures are organized. Like an artichoke, cultures have a core with layers encircling that core.

The WORLDVIEW is the cultural core—the understanding of the meaning of the universe and the person's place within the universe. Moving outward from the core other layers include power, values, practices, and artifacts. The core fundamentally informs each of the other layers.

All cultures possess indications of truth and graciousness. For example, most AFRICAN TRADITIONAL RELIGIONS assumed some form of life after death; there was a hint of gospel-like truth in that perception. Children were valued; the mother carried the newborn baby on her back for many months. Children grew up secure. Such indications of image-of-God-like truth and goodness are present in all cultures (Rom. 1:20; 10:8; Acts 17:22–23, 28).

All cultures also possess the imprint of evil and distortions of truth (Rom. 1:18–32). When Adam and Eve turned away from God, they did so because they wanted to "be like God" (Gen. 3:1–11). This declaration of independence from our Creator is universal. We ourselves and our cultures become our ultimate loyalty, rather than our Creator. Consequently, the gods we worship become the psychoprojection of our cultures. In various ways religions everywhere are inclined to become the mirror image of respective cultures; the gods of culture rarely call people to repent (Jer. 10:1–16).

The Bible pronounces the gods of culture as false. It is for this reason that repentance is the essential response of all who embrace biblical faith. God the Creator confronts the gods of culture. God calls people to repent, to turn away from the gods of culture they have created and worship rather the God who has created them (Exod. 20:3).

Jesus Christ is the supreme clarification event. As "God With Us," he entered and lived within a particular culture with relevant, disturbing, revolutionary, life-giving power. Jesus is unprecedented. No human culture, religion, philosophy, or speculation ever imagined the possibility of Jesus Christ (Matt. 16:13–18). Jesus is the gospel. He is God's salvation gift to humanity (John 3:16), and transformation gift to culture (Matt. 13:33).

Through the Holy Spirit, Jesus Christ seeks to make his home within the worldview and power centers of every culture (Matt. 5, 6, 7, 24:14). Missiologists refer to this as CONTEXTUALIZATION. The gospel should become relevant and revolutionary good news within every cultural context. The Dyak of Petussibau in West Kalimantan, who traditionally feared birds as omens of the gods, can discover that Jesus frees from bondage to squawking birds. However, a Harvard University astronomer would be quite amused if a Christian student were to tell him that Christ can free him from the fear of squawking crows. The cultural contexts in Boston and Petussibau are exceedingly different!

The church within every society needs to discern the aspects of the culture that the gospel blesses, and those dimensions that the gospel critiques and transforms. Acts 15 describes a conference in Jerusalem that convened to address such issues. Persons representing Jewish and Greek cultures participated. They heard accounts of what the Holy Spirit was doing in transforming lives, they searched the Scriptures for guidance, they listened to the counsel of the Holy Spirit, and in counsel together they bound some practices and loosened others.

This remarkable Jerusalem council affirmed salvation in Jesus Christ as the center of the church's faith in every culture, but also freed the church to embrace cultural diversity. Consequently the global church can celebrate astonishing cultural diversity while enjoying unity in Christ.

The gospel is always clothed within the idioms of culture. That is the nature of the Bible and the church. Consequently, Christian missionaries carry both their culture and the gospel with them when they move from one culture to another. However, whenever a people receive Jesus Christ, they are empowered and freed by the Holy Spirit and the Scriptures to evaluate and critique both their own culture and that of the missionary. The presence of Jesus Christ within any culture is life-giving empowerment (John 8:31–36).

DAVID W. SHENK

SEE ALSO Christ and Culture.

Bibliography. P. Hiebert, *Anthropological Insights for Missionaries;* T. Hopler, *A World of Difference;* C. H. Kraft, *Christianity and Culture;* E. A. Nida and W. D. Reyburn, *Meaning Across Cultures;* D. Richardson, *Eternity in Their Hearts;* L. Sanneh, *Translating the Message: The Missionary Impact on Culture;* D. W. Shenk, *Global Gods, Exploring the Role of Religions in Modern Societies.*

The Gospel and Our Culture Network. The Gospel and Our Culture movement began in the United Kingdom in the early 1980s under the influence of LESSLIE NEWBIGIN's challenge to the churches of the West to engage what he called the most important missionary challenge of the latter part of the twentieth century—the missionary encounter of the gospel with Western culture. His book *The Other Side of 1984* sparked the movement in Britain, which first took the form as the Gospel and Our Culture Programme of the British Council of Churches. That programme later merged with the C. S. Lewis Society to form Gospel and Culture, which subsequently was taken under the wing of the British and Foreign Bible Society.

In North America, the Gospel and Our Culture Network formed in the late 1980s under the influence of Newbigin and others as an effort to engage the same challenge within the specific context of the United States and Canada. Coordinated by George R. Hunsberger, the network sustains a quarterly newsletter, an annual consultation, and a program of research, publication, and education for the purpose of providing useful research for the encounter of the gospel with North American culture and encouraging local action toward the transformation of the life and witness of the churches. *The Church Between Gospel and Culture* and *Missional Church*, the first two volumes in the network's Gospel and Our Culture Series, lay out the essential agenda for Western churches as one engaged in "assessing our culture, discerning the gospel, and defining the church" and call the churches to embody their essential missional character.

Parallel movements have emerged in other Western societies, most notably the Gospel and Cultures Trust in New Zealand, founded and led by HAROLD TURNER. In addition, an international project led by Wilbert R. Shenk has begun producing a body of research and literature on the theme of a MISSIOLOGY of Western culture.

GEORGE R. HUNSBERGER

Bibliography. D. L. Guder, ed., *Missional Church;* G. R. Hunsberger and C. Van Gelder, eds., *The Church Between Gospel and Culture;* L. Newbigin, *The Other Side of 1984;* idem, *Foolishness to the Greeks*, W. R. Shenk, *Write the Vision.*

Gospel, The. The gospel *(euangelion)* or "good news" has been entrusted to the church to proclaim to all peoples. It is variously described as an "eternal gospel" (Rev. 14:6), "the gospel of peace" (Eph. 6:15), "the gospel of Christ" (1 Cor. 9:12), "the gospel of the grace of God" (Acts 20:24), and "the gospel of the kingdom" (Matt. 24:14). These different designations do not mean different gospels, for there is only one gospel (Gal. 1:8). This word is also associated with the synonym *kerygma*, a noun used eight times in the New Testament to focus particular attention on the proclamation of the precise content of the gospel. These two words are identical in their definition of the gospel and both stress the fact that in essence the gospel concerns an event of surpassing uniqueness. Prior to the consummation of human history, when God shall "bring all things in heaven and on earth together under one head, even Christ," it is his will that this gospel "must first be preached to all nations" (Eph. 1:10; Mark 13:10).

Although the uniqueness of this gospel event is clearly and frequently referred to in the New Testament as the sum total of the redemptive work of Christ, its full meaning is beyond human comprehension. When he embraced the cross this involved not only taking to his innocency the totality of human SIN and SHAME in order to make it his own responsibility, but also included the curse of sin as well, which is death (2 Cor. 5:21;

Gal. 3:13). He had to invalidate the claim and power of sin by entering into the death that is its ultimate penalty. His object thereby was to destroy it, for death is Satan's greatest weapon (Heb. 2:9, 14, 15). In so doing he "disarmed the powers and authorities" under Satan's dominion in order that he might send sin back to its demonic author. He thereby broke its tyranny and destroyed its power, and by this means removed its curse (Col. 2:15). Hence, the gospel is equated with this unique once for-all-time event: the death, burial, and RESURRECTION OF CHRIST, followed by his subsequent exaltation to the right hand of God, where he was gloriously acclaimed and "made both Lord and Christ" (Acts 2:36). "The reason the Son of God appeared was to destroy the devil's work" (1 John 3:8).

On this basis the people of God, in response to their Lord's GREAT COMMISSION to "make disciples of all nations," have but one way to demonstrate their obedience to him. They are to confront the human race with the divine command: "Repent and be baptized, every one of you, in the name of Jesus Christ for the forgiveness of your sins. And you will receive the gift of the Holy Spirit. The promise is for you and your children and for all who are far off—for all whom the Lord our God will call" (2:38, 39). From this it follows that the call to REPENTANCE and FAITH, with its promise of divine intervention, is of the very essence of God's plan for the redemption of his people from the nations of the earth.

When one examines the total usage of the word "gospel" in the Scriptures the impression quickly grows that "preaching the gospel" cannot be confined to the mere recitation of the actual facts of Christ's atoning and saving work. To the apostles all that he did was "in accordance with the Scriptures" (1 Cor. 15:3, 4). This meant nothing less to them than that the coming of Christ into the world ("when the time had fully come" Gal. 4:4) represented the central event in "salvation history." It was almost of the order of an eschatological event at a critical juncture in the biblical record of Israel's long and troubled history. Indeed, it also marked a distinctly new era in the fortunes of the nations, for by the gospel nothing less than "the KINGDOM OF GOD is being preached" (Luke 16:16). Since this would involve the reclamation of this fallen world from Satan's control, the proclamation of the gospel from then on attained the order of something special in God's dealings with not only Israel but with the Gentile world as well. This brought a sense of uniqueness to the calling of those who would go forth to the nations with this gospel. Indeed, Paul would speak of Christ having given to him "the ministry of reconciliation," a ministry so sublime in his eyes that it was nothing less than "God making his appeal through us" (2 Cor. 5:18–20). All those who proclaim this gospel can truthfully though humbly state that they are "God's fellow workers" (6:1). In their preaching of the gospel, what they share is "not the word of men, but as it actually is, the word of God" (1 Thess. 2:13). As a result their preaching was making actual and available to their hearers the very reality of God's salvation.

This brings up another point of far-reaching significance. The apostles unitedly and fiercely opposed any thought that the achievement of the world's reconciliation by Christ alone through his solitary cross was somehow incomplete. How could it be otherwise when at its heart was nothing less than God himself in his Son "reconciling the world to himself" (2 Cor. 5:19). As a result only human arrogance would dare to challenge its perfection by claiming that any human activity was needed to bring it to completion. The Christians at Ephesus were pointedly told: "It is by GRACE you have been saved, through faith—and this not from yourselves, it is the gift of God—not by works, so that no one can boast" (Eph. 2:8, 9). Indeed, no person can make himself or herself fit for God's Presence, much less enter into personal relationship with him. The preaching of the gospel has solely to do with the person of Christ and must be kept free from all reference to legalistic Judaism or any other form of what has been popularly termed "works-righteousness." The followers of Christ in Crete were told: "When the kindness and love of God our Savior appeared, He saved us, not because of the righteous things we had done, but because of His mercy" (Titus 3:4, 5).

When Saul the Pharisee was confronted by the Lord on the road to Damascus, he not only had a vision of the risen, glorified Christ. Through repentance and faith the persecutor of the people of God found himself graciously called to the fellowship and service of the One whom he had so persistently and hatefully opposed (Acts 26:12–18). As the apostle to the Gentiles he was given a fivefold task (v. 18, *see also* PAUL AND MISSION). He was "to open their eyes," for people by nature and satanic influence "cannot see the light of the gospel of the glory of Christ, who is the image of God" (2 Cor. 4:4). Paul was then to "turn them from darkness to light," for people in their fallenness are not facing this Christ, the Light of the World, who alone can meet their need. But before they can effectually reach out to the Savior, they must turn "from the power of Satan to God." This is absolutely crucial, for it involves the conscious repudiation of all that has previously controlled their lives. The early church encouraged would-be followers of Jesus to renounce by solemn oath "the devil and all his works." It was felt that only then would they be able to commit their lives to the control of the Lord. And once this change of allegiance takes place they will be able by faith to "receive the forgiveness of sins"

and subsequently "a place among those who are sanctified in Christ" (i.e., gain incorporation into a local congregation of fellow believers through baptism). Central in this evangelistic sequence is the fact that the gospel is a Person. To receive him (John 1:11, 12) involves consciously submitting to a new authority over one's life, even to Christ the Lord.

ARTHUR F. GLASSER

Bibliography. E. Bruner, *The Mediator;* L. Morris, *The Apostolic Preaching of the Cross;* L. Newbigin, *The Gospel in a Pluralist Society.*

Gossner, Johannes Evangelista (1773–1858).

German founder of the Gossner Mission Society. Born at Hausen in Bavaria, Gossner studied at Augsburg, Dillingen, and Ingolstadt. While studying, he was influenced by Johann Sailer, a pietist professor. Consecrated as a Roman Catholic priest in 1796, he served his first year as an assistant at Neuburg. As cathedral chaplain at Augsburg (1797–1804), his evangelistic views brought him into conflict with Catholic authorities. He had contact with both the Catholic and Protestant revival movements and belonged to a group of converted priests and laypeople that was suspended by the Inquisition in 1802.

Banished from Bavaria, Gossner answered a call from Czar Alexander I to Saint Petersburg in 1820 but was expelled in 1824. He formally left the Roman Catholic Church in 1826 and was ordained a Lutheran minister. While serving as pastor of the Bethlehem Church in Berlin (1829–46), he developed a vision for missions. Gossner founded a children's nursery in 1834, the Gossner Mission Society in 1836, and the Elizabeth Hospital in 1837. Over the next twenty years Gossner trained and sent out 140 missionaries around the world. He resigned from the pastorate in 1846 to devote his time to the hospital, counseling, and preaching. Among Gossner's publications were a German translation of the New Testament, a commentary on the New Testament, and a missionary journal *Die Biene auf dem Missionsfeld* (The Bee on the Mission Field).

GARY LAMB

Grace of God.

The mission of God (*MISSIO DEI*) flows directly from God's gracious, merciful love for rebellious, sinful humans who deserve justice rather than mercy. "For the wages of sin is death, but the grace/gift of God is eternal life in Christ Jesus our Lord" (Rom. 6:23). Traditionally, the grace of God has been understood to mean God's loving initiative in bestowing unmerited favor on humankind through Jesus Christ. The biblical idea of grace is foundational for the mission of the church.

First, grace is an attribute of God's being. In the Bible, God is known most essentially as "The

Lord, the compassionate and gracious God, slow to anger, abounding in love and faithfulness, maintaining love to thousands and forgiving wickedness, rebellion and sin" (Exod. 34:6; see also Exod. 22:27; 33:19; Num. 14:18 Deut. 4:31; 2 Chron. 30:9; Neh. 9:17; Pss. 111:4; 86:15; 102:8; 112:4; 145:8; Jonah 4:2; Joel 2:13; Rom. 9:15). God's grace derives from God's love (see LOVE OF GOD). John says that "God is love" (1 John 4:8). In his freedom, God "so loved the world that he gave his only begotten son" (John 3:16). Paul's missionary vision was motivated by this love: "For Christ's love compels us" (2 Cor. 5:14, 20). God's grace and mercy toward those who "like sheep have gone astray" (Isa. 53:6) motivates the church to mission.

Second, the grace of God takes two forms: common or general grace directed toward all creation and special grace in relation to God's covenant children. In the Sermon on the Mount, Jesus affirmed God's common grace, saying: "(Your Father in heaven) causes his sun to rise on the evil and the good, and sends rain on the righteous and the unrighteous" (Matt. 5:45). Common grace points the church to a wholistic, KINGDOM OF GOD orientation in mission that is concerned with all of God's creation. Common grace also provides the space for missionary CONTEXTUALIZATION, based on general revelation (Rom. 1), recognizing that in all cultures God has "endowed human beings with some inbuilt sense or presentiment of the divine existence. It is as if something about God has been engraved in the heart of every human being" (A. McGrath, p. 160, citing John Calvin, *Institutes*). This is what Don Richardson called REDEMPTIVE ANALOGIES, allowing for the possibility of conceptual bridges to those who do not yet know Jesus Christ, without going so far as to affirm the revelational stature of "natural theology" against which Karl Barth spoke so vehemently (cf. e.g., K. Barth, II:1, 134–78; D. Bloesch, 1992, 141–83; Berkouwer, 1955, 21–47).

Calvinist Reformed theology maintains a distinction between common or general grace and God's special grace that happens supremely in Jesus Christ through faith, brought about by the work of the Holy Spirit. In contrast, ARMINIAN THEOLOGY would affirm *prevenient* grace. Prevenient grace was taught by Jacobus Arminius (1560–1609) and was elaborated later by the Wesleys and Methodists. They affirmed that God's assistance is freely and graciously given to humans prior to their having saving faith and gives humans the inclination and ability to accept God's salvation in Jesus Christ. They saw "grace as a seamless garment; no difference exists between general and special grace. (Prevenient) grace provides for basic human needs, restrains evil, maintains civil justice, removes the guilt and penalty of original sin, implants the first wish to please God,

convicts of sin, and grants all people the power to turn to God in faith" (Lewis and Demarest, 22–23; cf. also S. Grenz, 259; A. McGrath, 378).

Third, God's grace takes place fully and completely by God's sending his only Son, Jesus Christ. This truth keeps common grace or general revelation from becoming inclusivist or pluralist in relation to the religions. It keeps God's grace focused in the fact that it is unmerited, a merciful response to judgment. In Jesus Christ, God's grace abounds for our salvation. "God demonstrates his own love for us in this: While we were still sinners, Christ died for us" (Rom. 5:8). The Bible emphasizes this active, direct, redemptive grace by stressing God's mercy—mercy that is not merited by human creatures (Deut. 4:31; 2 Sam. 24:11; 1 Chron. 21:13; Neh. 9:3, 31; Ps. 25:6; Jer. 9:12; Dan. 9:9, 18; Hos. 6:6; Amos 5:15; Mic. 6:8; 7:18; Luke 1:50; Eph. 2:4; 1 Peter 1:3). Paul stressed the inseparable connection of grace with the incarnation in Jesus Christ, by saying repeatedly, "the grace of our Lord Jesus Christ" (Rom. 3:24; 16:20; 1 Cor. 1:4; 16:23; Gal. 2:16; Eph. 2:5–8; Philem. 25; cf. also John 1:14, 17; Acts 15:11; Rev. 22:21).

Fourth, the church is the community of love, mercy, and grace. "As the Father has sent me," Jesus told his disciples, "I am sending you" (John 20:21). Mission in grace means that the church is to be a "koinonia" fellowship of grace, mercy, and love (C. Van Engen, 90–92). "As I have loved you, so you must love one another. By this (everyone) will know that you are my disciples, if you love one another" (John 13:34–35). Jesus told his disciples to "be merciful, just as your Father is merciful" (Luke 6:36). Paul encouraged the church in Ephesus to "be compassionate with one another" (Eph. 4:32). Peter wrote to the churches, "Finally, all of you, live in harmony with one another; be sympathetic, love as brothers, be compassionate (merciful) and humble" (1 Peter 3:8). The preaching of the Word and the administration of the sacraments are means of grace not only for church members but through the church in evangelical proclamation of the gospel to the world.

Fifth, the mission of the church is itself a work of grace whereby the disciples of Jesus Christ participate in God's gracious initiative in showing mercy to the world. So Jonah was called to have compassion on Nineveh as God has compassion. In Acts, STEPHEN, one of the first deacons, was said to be "a man full of God's grace and power" (Acts 6:8). The disciples of Jesus share Christ's love, compassion, and commitment for all those who will come to faith. They commit themselves to world evangelization because "The Lord . . . is patient, not wanting anyone to perish, but everyone to come to repentance" (2 Peter 3:9). The grace of God means, therefore, that mission is not optional or extra to the life of the church; it is essential and integral to its very being. The church is God's gracious missionary people, agents of God's mercy, calling women and men to become disciples of Jesus Christ and responsible members of Christ's church.

CHARLES VAN ENGEN

SEE ALSO Divine Election.

Bibliography. K. Barth, *Church Dogmatics*; H. Berkhof, *Christian Faith*; G. C. Berkouwer, *General Revelation*; D. Bloesch, *Theology of Word and Spirit*; J. Calvin, *Institutes of the Christian Religion*; S. Grenz, *Theology for the Community of God*; idem, *Revisioning Evangelical Theology*; G. R. Lewis and B. A. Demarest, *Integrative Theology*; A. McGrath, *Christian Theology*; S. Neill, *CDCWM*, pp. 233–34; C. Van Engen, *God's Missionary People*; O. Weber, *Foundations of Dogmatics*.

Graham, William Franklin (1918–). American evangelist and Christian statesman. Reared on a dairy farm in Charlotte, North Carolina, he was converted in 1934 through the ministry of evangelist Mordecai Ham. He studied at Florida Bible Institute and then at Wheaton College (Illinois) where he met his future wife, Ruth Bell. Upon graduation he joined Youth for Christ and preached throughout the United States and Europe. The 1949 Los Angeles crusade placed Graham in the national spotlight and the following year the Billy Graham Evangelistic Association was formed. The London crusade of 1954 brought him international prominence. He has since preached in over 185 countries and territories of the world.

In his role as a Christian statesman he has counseled numerous United States presidents and world leaders. His impact on the evangelical world has been enormous, from his part in founding *Christianity Today* and Gordon-Conwell Theological Seminary, to his bringing together mission-minded groups at conferences such as the LAUSANNE CONGRESS ON WORLD EVANGELIZATION (1974). He has preached the gospel to more people in live audiences than anyone else in history, estimated at over 210 million people. Hundreds of millions more have been reached through his use of radio, television, video, film, and print media.

TIMOTHY K. BEOUGHER

Bibliography. B. Graham, *Just As I Am*; W. Martin, *A Prophet with Honor: The Billy Graham Story*; J. Pollock, *Billy Graham, Evangelist to the World: An Authorized Biography of the Decisive Years*.

Grand Rapids Consultation (1982). See CONSULTATION ON THE RELATIONSHIP BETWEEN EVANGELISM AND SOCIAL RESPONSIBILITY.

Graul, Karl (1814–64). German pioneer missiologist and missionary to India. Graul is regarded as one of the leading German missiological thinkers of the nineteenth century. He uniquely combined linguistic skills with the ability to integrate a broad range of knowledge in service of missions. He advocated the need for theologically trained missionaries at a time when such were hard to find. He pioneered thinking on indigeneity for mission-planted churches, emphasizing that they must be independent and intimately grounded in the cultural characteristics of the people among which they were planted. Core to his concept of indigeneity was the idea that those things which are morally neutral, including most of the cultures' social order, need not be changed. This included, for example, the CASTE system, which Graul felt should be allowed in the Indian church with the hope of eventual change.

Graul, a staunch Lutheran, directed the LEIPZIG MISSION from 1844 to 1860. As director, he moved to Tamil where he lived for four years. Gifted in languages, in that short period he was able to learn Tamil well enough to establish himself as an expert in the language. He wrote extensively on Tamil, Vedanta Hinduism, and missionary principles and work. He was among the first to seek to establish a chair of missions at the university level in Germany. Though successful in setting up the opportunity, he died before he was able to assume the position.

A. SCOTT MOREAU

Bibliography. A. Lehmann, *CDCWM*, pp. 234–35; G. Myklebust, *The Study of Missions in Theological Education*.

Great Awakenings. The term "Great Awakenings" refers to a series of movements in western Europe and North America that began around 1725 and extended to the late nineteenth century. In generally accepted terminology, REVIVALS occurred within the church, bringing Christians to deeper personal faith and devotion, while awakenings resulted from revivals as the church moved powerfully into the world in evangelism, social transformation, and mission. But the two cannot be separated. Most scholars list three major awakenings during the period, even though the chronological boundaries cannot always be easily defined, and vary from area to area. The movements had their roots in English Puritanism and German pietism, while MORAVIANISM, which was part of the first awakening, was a catalyst in the wider church, especially in missions.

The First Awakening began in North America in the 1720s, led by Theodorus Frelinghuysen and Gilbert Tennent. Tennent's father William was an Irish immigrant who established a "log college" to prepare ministers who were spiritually alive as well as theologically orthodox. Influenced by pietism, they preached the necessity of conversion to Frelinghausen's Dutch parishioners and Tennent's Presbyterians. The movement spread, and the revivalists began to itinerate. In 1741 Presbyterians in the middle colonies divided over the issues of pastoral training, itineration, and the emphases of the revival. When they reunited in 1758, the revivalist group had tripled in number, while the anti-revivalist group had dwindled.

In 1734–35 Jonathan Edwards, a Congregationalist, led a revival in Northampton, Massachusetts, and neighboring towns. In 1740–42 the movement spread across much of New England and eventually across the American colonies as GEORGE WHITEFIELD became the major figure. Formerly a member of the "Holy Club" at Oxford, he had experienced an evangelical conversion in 1735. On his second trip to America in 1739–40 he preached to large crowds in the middle colonies and New England in a unique display of interdenominational cooperation. Crowds flocked to hear him; thousands were converted and joined the churches. When Congregationalists in New England split over the revival, some became Baptists and later went to Virginia and the Carolinas, where their churches grew primarily among the poor. A spontaneous movement also began in Hanover County, Virginia, as lay persons came together to read the sermons of Whitefield and writings of Luther. Thousands came, special buildings were constructed, and Presbyterian churches were eventually established. The democratizing influence of Presbyterians and Baptists would bring change in the rigid social order of Virginia.

The focus of preaching in the awakenings was the necessity of conversion, personal faith in Jesus Christ that went beyond mere assent to orthodoxy to include personal assurance of salvation, and the call to a Christian lifestyle. Opposition arose, primarily for two reasons. Some, for reasons of spiritual complacency or theology, did not believe in the validity of the movement or its necessity. Others rejected it because of the excesses and fanaticism of some revivalists or because of preaching by laymen.

In Britain, praying societies similar to pietist groups in Germany were precursors. In Wales, Daniel Rowland, an Anglican vicar, and Howell Harris, a layman, were converted in 1735 and began itinerant preaching. In 1736 Whitefield began to preach widely and with great effect. He and his friends began a daily prayer meeting in 1737 for the renewal of the church. The following year John and Charles Wesley, already zealous in their religious devotion, came to personal assurance of salvation. JOHN WESLEY'S preaching on the new birth and the radical nature of discipleship soon resulted in his exclusion from most churches. He joined Whitefield in a pattern he would follow until his death in 1791—traveling four thousand to five thousand miles per year and preaching fifteen to eighteen times per week in streets, fields, and Methodist societies. The two eventually split because of Whitefield's acceptance of Calvinism and Wesley's rejection of predestination and acceptance of the doctrine of perfection. The bishop of London sharply criticized Wesley's movement, saying it drew "to itself the lowest and most ignorant people."

The awakening gave birth to the Methodist Church, while thousands joined Presbyterian, Congregationalist, and Baptist churches. The successful antislavery movement in England found its roots here. Missionary work like that of DAVID BRAINERD among "Indians" was stimulated. Brainerd's *Journal* would be powerfully used in subsequent missionary motivation. The awakening also produced a number of colleges, including Princeton and Dartmouth. It hastened separation of church and state in America and to some degree contributed to the American Revolution. Women played a role in the Wesleyan movement as preachers and class leaders.

The awakening died down in the 1760s and 1770s with the American Revolution and the growth of rationalism. In 1784 John Erskine of Edinburgh republished Edwards' *Call to Prayer for a Revival*. Soon concerts of prayer were held across Britain and on the Continent. The directors of the newly formed LONDON MISSIONARY SOCIETY recommended that one meeting a month focus on prayer for missions.

By 1795 concerts of prayer had spread among churches of most evangelical denominations in the eastern United States, and three years later the awakening became widespread.

Revival came to Yale in 1802 under the presidency of Timothy Dwight, Edwards' grandson, and one-third of the students professed conversion. The HAYSTACK PRAYER MEETING in 1806 at Williams College resulted in the beginning of the American overseas missionary movement. The revival was orderly in the East, but in the West and Southwest it was accompanied with many unusual manifestations. A camp meeting was held in 1800 in Kentucky with services held in the open air; families came from a distance. In 1801 the Cane Ridge Meeting was organized in Kentucky, which lasted six days and was attended by around 12,500. Hundreds were held the following years, and the camp meeting became an important method of evangelism in the southern United States, led first by Presbyterians and later by Baptists and Methodists. The latter two groups grew very rapidly to become the largest Protestant denominations in the United States, largely because of the awakening and because of their flexibility in ordaining pastors with little or no training and establishing churches quickly. Other results of this phase of the Second Awakening in the United States were the formation of the AMERICAN BOARD OF COMMISSIONERS FOR FOREIGN MISSIONS in 1810, the Baptist Foreign Missionary Society in 1814, and the

Methodist Episcopal Foreign Missionary Society in 1819.

After the War of 1812 the awakening continued. Its most prominent exponent was CHARLES FINNEY, a Presbyterian who rejected the older Calvinist theology and adopted new techniques designed to lead people to conversion. In his 1830 campaign in Rochester 10 percent of the 10,000 citizens professed conversion and 450 joined the Presbyterian churches; other churches grew as well. This phase of the American awakening produced a number of interdenominational voluntary societies to promote educational and social reform and missions. At Oberlin College Finney encouraged the ministry of women. A strong antislavery movement developed in the North but not in the South.

In England the Methodists saw their total membership grow from 72,000 in 1791 to nearly a quarter of a million within a generation. Other churches also grew. The Protestant missionary movement, with roots in the earlier awakening, was launched. WILLIAM CAREY's Baptist Missionary Society was formed in 1792, the interdenominational London Missionary Society in 1795, and the Anglican CHURCH MISSIONARY SOCIETY in 1799. Other societies were formed in Scotland and on the Continent. The evangelical movement was greatly strengthened in the Church of England, led especially by Charles Simeon, who was also a strong advocate for foreign missions. The CLAPHAM SECT comprising Anglican evangelicals successfully implemented a number of social reforms, including the ABOLITION of slavery. The Religious Tract Society (1799) and the British and Foreign Bible Society (1804) were established. Evangelicals sought to work out Christian principles in society. These included Robert Raikes and Hannah Moore, who founded the Sunday School movement; Elizabeth Fry, the prison reformer; and later the Earl of Shaftsbury, who campaigned for improvement of inhuman factory conditions. The Scot, Robert Haldane, used his wealth to establish a Society for the Propagation of the Gospel at home, which sent out over one hundred catechists and missionaries, and personally financed the training of three hundred students in a missionary training institute. Eventually he ministered effectively in Switzerland and France. In Norway a movement developed through the itinerant preaching of Hans Hauge, a lay preacher who traveled widely for eight years before being imprisoned for ten years. His societies remained in the Lutheran Church.

In Scotland the evangelical party maintained Sunday schools, protested against the exploitation of the poor, and promoted popular education. Its greatest leader, Thomas Chalmers, instituted an ingenious plan for the church to care for the poor.

Similar movements in Switzerland, France, Holland, and Germany resulted in philanthropic social action, Sunday schools, Bible distribution, and mission to the Jews.

The Second Awakening had significant results in the shape of the church in the United States. Baptists and Methodists became the major denominations. Evangelical Protestantism became a significant force at every level in Great Britain and North America, and the awakening provided the foundation for the overseas mission thrust of the second half of the century.

The Third Awakening began in 1857 in the United States, when Presbyterians, Baptists, and Methodists began meeting for prayer and discussion on the need for revival and awakening. That year Jeremiah Lamphier, a lay missionary in downtown New York for the Dutch Reformed Church, started a weekly noonday prayer meeting. Beginning with six men, within six months 10,000 businessmen were meeting daily to pray in 150 different groups. Similar prayer meetings began to spring up in other cities. A financial crisis had occurred shortly after he began, but there is evidence that the revival had begun prior to the crisis.

This Third Awakening saw laymen play a much stronger role. D. L. MOODY began his Christian work in 1858 and two years later gave up his business interests to concentrate full time on Sunday schools and the YMCA, which had grown out of the Second Awakening. News from America reached the British Isles. Others began to pray, and increasingly people were converted. Twenty thousand met in the open air in Ulster, while in Scotland much of the northeast was affected, and the movement spread into the whole country. The revival began in Wales in 1858, reaching its height the two following years. Phoebe and Walter Palmer visited Newcastle in England in 1859, and the awakening began to increase in strength. WILLIAM BOOTH, joined in preaching by his wife Catherine, began an itinerant ministry, which led to the formation of the SALVATION ARMY. Theaters were used for Sunday evening services, which were attended by large crowds who would not have entered a church. The Salvation Army, the Keswick movement, Christian Unions in universities, and the growth of the Sunday School movement all resulted. A large number of itinerant evangelists came to prominence in the revival, the best known of whom was Moody.

The missionary movement received new impulses. J. HUDSON TAYLOR organized the China Inland Mission in 1865. Moody's Cambridge Mission in 1882 resulted in a number of conversions, including the Cambridge Seven, who went to China as missionaries. They powerfully influenced other students. Among the 251 in attendance at Moody's student conference in 1886, 100 volunteered for mission, and the STUDENT VOLUNTEER MOVEMENT for Foreign Missions was formed. Under its auspices 20,500 young people from Europe and North America eventually went to Asia, Africa, and Latin America as missionaries. It also led to the formation of the World Student Christian Federation.

In the last third of the century "revivals" began to lose their character of widespread movements, becoming primarily mass evangelism, a technique for reaching people that was much less concerned with changing society. This was accentuated by the rise of theological liberalism and the social gospel.

Nevertheless, the Third Awakening, building on the previous two, shaped Anglo-American Protestantism and the missionary movement during the first half of the twentieth century, and provided most of its significant leaders.

PAUL E. PIERSON

Bibliography. A. Brouwer, *Reformed Church Roots;* R. E. Davis, *I Will Pour Out My Spirit;* J. Edwards, *Works,* vol. 4, *The Great Awakening;* E. S. Gaustad, *The Great Awakening in New England;* E. H. Maxson, *The Great Awakening in the Middle Colonies;* J. E. Orr, *The Light of the Nations;* idem, *The Second Evangelical Awakening;* T. Smith, *Revivalism and Social Reform;* J. Wesley, *Journal.*

Great Britain. *See* UNITED KINGDOM.

Great Century of Missions (A.D. 1792–1910). The "great century" is considered to have begun with WILLIAM CAREY and the organization of the BAPTIST MISSIONARY SOCIETY in England in 1792. Carey is properly called the "Father of the Modern Protestant Missionary Movement," because of his leadership in initiating this new and greatly expanded phase. But he was not the first Protestant missionary. Puritans had worked with Native Americans in New England in the seventeenth century, German pietists had gone to India early in the eighteenth, and Moravians had gone to at least twenty-eight countries in that century.

The movement had its roots in the spiritual dynamic of the first and second GREAT AWAKENINGS on both sides of the Atlantic, and resulted in the organization of a large number of other missionary societies. In England they included the LONDON MISSIONARY SOCIETY (LMS, 1795), primarily by Congregationalists and Presbyterians, the CHURCH MISSIONARY SOCIETY (CMS, 1799) by evangelical Anglicans, and the British and Foreign Bible Society (1804) by evangelicals of various denominations. In the United States the AMERICAN BOARD OF COMMISSIONERS FOR FOREIGN MISSIONS (ABCFM, 1810) and the American Baptist Society (1814) were established. Others were organized in Scotland and on the Continent.

The first area of service was India, followed in 1813 by Burma (Myanmar). Beginning in 1796 LMS missionaries did heroic work in the South Sea Islands, where a number were killed. In 1820 JOHN WILLIAMS went to Samoa with eight Tahitian teachers, and in a few years the Samoan church had sent missionaries to a number of other islands. ABCFM personnel arrived in Hawaii in 1820. Anglicans, Presbyterians, and Congregationalists arrived in Iran in 1811, Egypt in 1818, and Syria, Lebanon, and Turkey shortly afterward. The CMS began sending personnel to Sierra Leone in 1804, where in twenty years over fifty missionaries died of disease. But others took their places. The BASEL MISSION began work in Ghana in 1828, the Scottish Presbyterians went to Calabar (Nigeria) in 1846, and the LMS entered South Africa in 1799. DAVID LIVINGSTONE, who arrived there in 1841, went north into Central Africa with the twofold goal of evangelizing and ending the slave trade. When Anglicans entered Uganda, Bishop James Hannington was speared to death, and later thirty-five Christian martyrs were burned alive by the chief of the Buganda people. But within a few years Buganda Christians were taking the gospel to traditional enemies, and one of them, APOLO KIVEBULAYA, won the trust of pygmies, learned their language, and translated the Gospel of Mark.

China prohibited the residence of foreigners until forced by the West to allow them to live in five ports after the treaty ending the first Opium War in 1842. The treaties after the second Opium War forced the government to allow Christians access to all of China after 1856. This resulted in a massive influx of missionaries by the end of the century, led by the CHINA INLAND MISSION, organized in 1865. Four American societies entered Japan from 1859 to 1869, and American Presbyterians and Methodists arrived in Korea in 1884 and 1885. Protestant work began in the Philippines shortly after the Spanish American War. Permanent Protestant work began in Latin America after midcentury, when Presbyterians, Baptists, and Methodists arrived in Brazil, which enjoyed a measure of religious liberty. Work in other countries followed. Thus by 1910 several thousand Protestant missionaries were at work in Asia, Africa, and Latin America.

Carey's goals, which most others accepted, were first, to preach the gospel by every possible means; second, to support the preaching by the distribution of the Bible in the languages of the people; third, to establish the church; fourth, to study the background and religious thought of the peoples; and finally, to train indigenous ministers. The nineteenth-century movement accomplished all of these objectives to some degree, although different missions and their workers varied in their emphases.

In the words of two of the greatest mission leaders of the century, HENRY VENN of the CMS, and RUFUS ANDERSON of the ABCFM, the goal was to establish churches which would be "self-supporting, self-governing, and self-propagating." An important assumption, with roots in the revivals which gave birth to missions, was that the preaching of the gospel would be accompanied by works of compassion and lead to positive changes in the societies where the church was planted. Naturally, in the minds of most missionaries those changes would include Western-style education, literacy, health care, and better treatment of women. Even though many of the changes looked very Western, that was not entirely negative. Carey worked, successfully, to end infanticide and *suttee* (the burning alive of widows with the bodies of their husbands) in India; Scottish Presbyterians were the first to speak out against female genital mutilation in Kenya; while others worked to end the painful and crippling practice of foot binding in China.

Thus, along with the preaching of the gospel, clinics, hospitals, and eventually medical schools were established along with facilities to care for marginalized people, the blind, lepers, and orphans. Missionaries established schools, seminaries, and universities. They did so, first, to train the children of new Christians and prepare church leadership, but they had other goals in mind: to raise the social and economic level of the people, and to win students and their families to the faith (*see also* EDUCATIONAL MISSION WORK). By 1826 the ABCFM had established twenty-six schools in Hawaii with sixty-six indigenous teachers and twenty thousand students. Projects to improve agriculture were initiated in several countries (*see also* AGRICULTURAL MISSIONS). Members of the Swiss Basel Mission introduced the cultivation of Cacao into Ghana. Industrial schools and Western technology were also introduced.

LITERACY, BIBLE TRANSLATION, and the production of literature were important. Many unwritten languages were learned, reduced to writing, and part or all of the Scriptures translated. By 1873 the Hawaii mission had published 153 different works plus thirteen magazines and an almanac in the local language which missionaries had reduced to writing. At the end of the century, the entire Bible had been translated into over one hundred languages, the New Testament into 120, and parts of the Bible into three hundred more.

Early in the century women began to seek a greater role in the missionary enterprise (*see also* WOMEN IN MISSION). First, they organized themselves to raise funds, to pray, and to encourage their children and churches in mission. When the male leaders of the boards were unresponsive to their desire for a greater role, women's missionary societies were organized. These, along with the older agencies, sent out many women who often did work in Asia and Africa denied to them at home. Eventually, nearly one-third of the missionary force would be single women and one-third married women. They pioneered in education and medical care for girls and women, while some itinerated as evangelists. CHARLOTTE "LOTTIE" MOON became one of the best known of all Southern Baptist missionaries because of her vision, compassion, and ability to communicate with the church back home. CLARA SWAIN, who arrived in India in 1870, was the first woman medical missionary appointed by any board. She was the first of many who not only treated women, whom men were not permitted to see, but pioneered establishing nursing and medical schools, opening these professions to women. When the first missionaries arrived in Korea, a woman had no status outside her home except for functions in traditional shamanism. But by the middle of this century, HELEN KIM was president of Ehwa, the largest women's university in the world, established by Methodists. She was also a leader in evangelism.

Shortly before the end of the century the evangelical consensus in Protestantism in general, and thus the missionary movement, began to break down. That consensus included four points: the assertion that the supreme aim of missions was to make Jesus Christ known as Savior and Lord, and to persuade persons to become his disciples and gather them into churches; allegiance to the uniquely divine nature of Jesus Christ; the willingness to defend the social dimensions of missions; and a pragmatic ecumenism. The advent of Darwinism and the undermining of biblical authority brought confidence in progress, a more optimistic view of human nature, and a lower Christology on the one hand, while the movement which would be known as fundamentalism adopted premillennialism, the view that only when Christ returned would the millennium be established and that thus the only important activity was evangelism (*see* MILLENNIAL THOUGHT).

In this context two new movements arose. The first, the STUDENT VOLUNTEER MOVEMENT FOR FOREIGN MISSIONS began among students at a conference led by D. L. MOODY in 1886. Before its decline in the 1920s it had motivated the vocations of over 20,500 missionaries, most of whom served under the older boards. The other development was the rise of the FAITH MISSIONS, beginning with the CHINA INLAND MISSION in 1865. It was soon followed by the SUDAN INTERIOR MISSION, the Central American Mission, the AFRICAN INLAND MISSION, and others. These were fundamentalist in theology, interdenominational, some led by laymen, and many of their personnel were graduates of the newly formed Bible institutes instead of universities and seminaries. This development of the fundamentalist and evangelical missions, along with the beginning of the PENTE-

COSTAL MOVEMENT in 1906 would eventually change the face of the missionary enterprise. At the same time, liberals and fundamentalists alike assumed that Western culture was Christian and superior to all others, and thus normative for all Christians, believing that the entire world would eventually adopt that culture.

Even though there were large people movements among some groups of animistic background (Karens in Burma, Mizos and Nagas in Northeast India, untouchables in other parts of India, some African tribes and especially South Pacific peoples) most of the churches formed were still small. In Korea a revival from 1903 to 1907 laid the foundation for remarkable growth later. But even though most wanted only to preach a nondenominational "pure gospel," as the LMS had urged, the churches established were similar to those from which the missionaries came. The Anglican Bishop Tucker serving in Uganda at the turn of the century wanted to see a church in which missionaries and Africans served side by side in a spirit of equality, but most churches were still dominated by Westerners. And while there were some exceptions in Korea and elsewhere, inadequate attention was given to preparing national leadership. In some areas, China and Africa especially, breakaway churches which sought to be more culturally indigenous, would later grow rapidly.

The climax of the "Great Century" came with the Edinburgh WORLD MISSIONARY CONFERENCE in 1910. Over 1,200 delegates from various mission agencies came together; however, all but eighteen were Westerners. It was a time of optimism as they planned for greater unity and advance. There was reason for celebration. For the first time in history, the Christian faith was now worldwide. The church, along with educational and medical institutions, had been planted in many countries. A growing number of national leaders was being prepared, establishing a foundation for growth in the future. The missionary movement had made a significant contribution in works of compassion with women and marginalized people, and had introduced such concepts even among some who did not accept the Christian faith. But there were also problems, some of which were seen, others not. The theological consensus regarding the nature and purpose of mission was ending. Western Christendom still failed to see the beam in its own eye: COLONIALISM, ETHNOCENTRISM, and feelings of superiority. The church still looked very foreign in many cultures. And few if any realized that four years later Western Christendom would be plunged into one of the most meaningless and bloody wars in history. That would bring the end of confidence to much of the West and would raise a whole new set of problems for the missionary movement in the new century.

PAUL E. PIERSON

Bibliography. R. P. Beaver, *All Loves Excelling;* J. Carpenter and W. Shenk, eds., *Earthen Vessels;* W. Hutchison, *Errand to the World;* S. A. Neill, *History of Christian Missions.*

Great Commandment. When considering missions, it is usually not the "Great Commandment" (Mark 12:28–34 par. Matt. 22:34–40; cf. Luke 10:25–28) but the "GREAT COMMISSION" (Matt. 28:16–20; Luke 24:46–49) that takes center stage. Arguably, however, the Great Commandment provides a crucial foundation for the Great Commission, and a unilateral emphasis on the latter creates an imbalance that may render the church's mission ineffective. We will first discuss the scriptural foundation for the Great Commandment and subsequently deal with its contemporary relevance for mission.

Scriptural Foundation. The Great Commandment, according to Jesus, is the Old Testament command to love God with all of one's heart, soul, mind, and strength (Deut. 6:4–5), together with the injunction to love one's neighbor as oneself (cf. Lev. 19:18b; on the question of who is one's "neighbor," cf. Lev. 19:34; Luke 10:25–27; and Matt. 5:43–48). To call this commandment the *Great* Commandment is to follow Matthew's terminology (Matt. 22:36: "great"; 22:38: "great and first"), where "great" is probably used with elative force to denote what is "greatest" or "most important." Mark simply numbers the commandments as "first" and "second" (Mark 12:38, 41; cf. Matt. 22:38). In Luke, the lawyer's question is, "Teacher, what shall I do to inherit eternal life?" (Luke 10:25), raising the question of whether Luke's account refers to a different event altogether, especially since, in Luke, it is not Jesus who is speaking but the lawyer (Luke 10:27).

The question of what constituted the heart of the Law was an issue widely discussed in rabbinic circles in Jesus' day. Jesus' emphatic statement, only found in Matthew, that the entire Law and the Prophets depend on the Great Commandment, is therefore of utmost significance (Matt. 22:40). Unlike the Decalogue, which is mostly given in the form of prohibitions, Jesus states this injunction in a positive way (cf. Matt. 7:12). By expressing the commandment in an absolute and categorical rather than a relative and limited fashion, Jesus stresses the priority of the inward disposition over the outward action. In keeping with Old Testament prophetic tradition, Jesus requires heart religion, not merely formalistic legalism. At the same time, it is not his desire to use this commandment to relegate every other obligation of the believer to the point of irrelevance.

What is the relationship between the Great Commandment and the Great Commission in Matthew's Gospel? Since Matthew presents discipleship as the way of righteousness (cf. Matt. 5:6,

10, 20; 6:33), and since the Great Commission entails the teaching of converts to obey everything Jesus commanded, it is clear that the keeping of the Great Commandment is a prerequisite for the fulfillment of the Great Commission. Moreover, the latter entails, not mere EVANGELISM in modern parlance, where the term usually refers merely to the bringing of a person to the point of conversion, but the grounding of Christian converts in the way of righteousness, including the observance of the Great Commandment (and, ultimately, once again the Great Commission!). Finally, the concept of righteousness in Matthew, while possessing a spiritual core, is not limited to the religious domain but also has social and economic dimensions. In these ways Matthew lays a crucial foundation for the understanding of the relationship between the Great Commandment and the Great Commission in contemporary discussion.

Contemporary Relevance for Mission. Historically, Anglo-Saxon Protestant missionary thought has emphasized the Great Commission, while the latter task never occupied an equally central position among Christians on the European Continent. The issue of the relationship between the Great Commission and the Great Commandment caused considerable discussion at the LAUSANNE CONGRESS ON WORLD EVANGELISM in 1974. While in the final conference document evangelism was named as the primary mission of the church, this drew the criticism of a significant number of participants, including JOHN STOTT, R. Sider, and others. After a reaffirmation of the primacy of evangelism by the Consultation on World Evangelization (COWE) in Pattaya, Thailand, in June 1980, the question was taken up again by the Consultation on the Relationship between Evangelism and Social Responsibility held in Grand Rapids, Michigan, in June 1982, an effort co-sponsored by the WORLD EVANGELICAL FELLOWSHIP (WEF) and the Lausanne Committee for World Evangelization (LCWE) (*see* LAUSANNE MOVEMENT). This conference identified three kinds of relationships between EVANGELISM AND SOCIAL RESPONSIBILITY: (1) social responsibility as a *consequence* of evangelism; (2) social action as a *bridge* to evangelism; and (3) social concern as a *partner* of evangelism. The delegates advocated a holistic approach to mission, since "[s]eldom if ever should we have to choose between satisfying physical hunger and spiritual hunger, or between healing bodies or saving souls, since an authentic love for our neighbor will lead us to serve him or her as a whole person" (*see* HOLISTIC MISSION).

The key questions addressed at the 1982 consultation were the following: What is mission? How broad is salvation in Scripture? What is the relationship between the church and the kingdom? What is the church's mandate for social justice? R. Sider and J. I. Packer, in contrast to

the WORLD COUNCIL OF CHURCHES (WCC) at its BANGKOK CONFERENCE (1973), argued for a narrow use of salvation language, restricting salvation "to the sphere of conscious confession of faith in Christ." A. Johnston, D. McGavran, P. Wagner, P. Beyerhaus, K. Bockmühl, and H. Lindsell joined in affirming this position against those who sought to define salvation more broadly. This latter group contended that salvation has not only personal but also social and cosmic dimensions, so that socioeconomic improvements should be described as an aspect of salvation, pointing also to Luke 4:16–21 (cf. Isa. 61:1–2). It was further argued that the lordship of Christ extends over all demonic powers of evil that "possess persons, pervade structures, societies, and the created order."

How does Scripture adjudicate between these two positions? On the one hand, it cautions against a reductionistic focus on people merely as "souls" that need to be saved, so that the church's task should not be conceived in merely "religious" terms. On the other hand, Scripture does affirm the primacy of a person's spiritual dimension, so that the effort of leading unbelievers to a Christian conversion rightly belongs at the heart of the church's mission. As noted, read in the context of Matthew's entire Gospel, the fulfillment of the Great Commission entails a "commitment to both the King and his kingdom, to both righteousness and justice" (Bosch), while the making of disciples also involves teaching them to obey Jesus' teachings which include loving God and one's neighbor. Hence love for God and others ought to be the driving motivation for mission (*see* MOTIVE, MOTIVATION), since, in love, God sent his Son; in love, Jesus gave his life for others; and by our love, the world will know that we are his disciples.

ANDREAS J. KÖSTENBERGER

Bibliography. D. J. Bosch, *IRM* 73 (1984): 17–32; D. A. Carson, *EBC*, 8:463–66; P. A. Deiros, *Faith and Mission* 2 (1985): 42–49; R. H. Fuller, *Essays on the Love Commandment*, pp. 97–121; A. P. Williamson, *CT* 26, no. 19 (1982): 32–36.

Great Commission. The term "Great Commission" is commonly assigned to Christ's command to his disciples as found in Matthew 28:18–20, Mark 16:15–16, Luke 24:46–49, John 20:21, and Acts 1:8. It is sometimes referred to as the "Evangelistic Mandate" and distinguished from the "Cultural" and/or "Social Mandate" found in Genesis 1:28–30 and Genesis 9:1–7 (*see* CULTURAL MANDATE). The prominence accorded to the Great Commission in the past two hundred years is not apparent in previous church history. The early church made remarkable progress in spreading the faith throughout the Mediterranean world by virtue of the witness of dispersed Christians and the missionary journeys of the apostle Paul and others. However, there is no clear indication in the Book of Acts that this effort was motivated by explicit appeals to the Great Commission. Rather, after Pentecost the Holy Spirit both motivated and orchestrated the missionary effort in accordance with that Commission. Similarly, throughout the early centuries when both the Eastern and especially Western branches of the church were expanding significantly, the Great Commission as such does not appear to have been a decisive motivating or defining factor.

In REFORMATION times concerns and controversies relating to the Great Commission had to do with its applicability. In 1537 Pope Paul III emphasized the importance of the Great Commission and said that all people are "capable of receiving the doctrines of the Faith." However, sixteenth-century Catholic theology applied the text to the Church with its episcopacy, not to the individual Christians as such. The Reformers generally taught that the Great Commission was entrusted to the apostles and that the apostles fulfilled it by going to the ends of their known world. This is not to say that they had no missionary vision. Hadrian Saravia (1531–1613) and Justinian von Welz (1621–61) found reason enough to write treatises in which they urged Christians to recognize their responsibility to obey the Great Commission and evangelize the world. Nevertheless, it remained for WILLIAM CAREY (1761–1834) to make one of the most compelling cases for the applicability of the Great Commission to all believers. The first section of his treatise *An Inquiry into the Obligations of Christians to Use Means for the Conversion of the Heathens* (published in 1792) made a concerted argument that individual Christians should join together in an effort to take the gospel to the HEATHEN (at that time the common designation for the unevangelized) in obedience to the Great Commission. Some historians have concluded that *An Inquiry* rivals Luther's Ninety-five Theses in terms of its influence on church history.

By the middle of the nineteenth century a consensus on the *applicability* of the Great Commission had emerged but this consensus paved the way for differences as to its *application*, particularly in America. Not everyone agreed with the interpretation and approach of A. T. PIERSON and others who, in the 1880s and 1890s, pressed the completion of world evangelization by the year 1900 "in obedience to the Great Commission." The organizers of the great Edinburgh Conference of 1910 attempted to avoid controversy concerning the requirements of the Great Commission and the nature of mission by taking the position that the Great Commission is "intrinsic" rather than "extrinsic" (James Scherer's words) to the church and its missions. In other words, it is not so much an exterior law that sits in judgment upon the missionary activities of the church, but an inner principle of church faith and life allowing for freedom in the way churches and missions interpret and carry it out.

Subsequent history has revealed how diverse and divisive such interpretations can be. The twentieth century gave rise to a number of significant points of departure in understanding. First, upon a review of history and the biblical text, some (e.g., Harry Boer) have concluded that, in the process of convincing Christians that the Great Commission applied to them, proponents unwittingly contributed to the idea that the validity of Christian mission rested primarily upon that command. This led to a corresponding neglect of the missionary role of the Holy Spirit and the missionary thrust of the whole of biblical revelation. Second, perhaps responding to the emphasis on the social task of the church in the WCC and especially at the 1968 General Assembly in Uppsala, some evangelicals (e.g., JOHN STOTT) revised their thinking on the Great Commission and now argue against the generally accepted position that the statement in Matthew 28:16–20, being the most complete, possesses a certain priority. Their revised position is that the statement in John 20:21 ("As the Father has sent me, so send I you") takes priority and makes the Lord Jesus' earthly ministry as outlined in Luke 4:18, 19 a model for modern mission. This interpretation opens the way for sociopolitical action as an integral part of biblical mission. Third, many Pentecostals and charismatics have given a certain priority to the Markan version of the Great Commission with its emphasis on the "signs following" conversion and faith—casting out demons, speaking in new tongues, handling snakes, drinking poisonous liquids without hurt, and healing the sick (Mark 16:17–19). This approach is generally dependent upon a consideration of the manuscript evidence relating to the shorter and longer endings of Mark's Gospel. Fourth, some exegetes (e.g., Robert Culver) point out that the Matthew 28:18–20 text does not support the commonly understood interpretation with its overemphasis on "going" into all the world in obedience to Christ. Rather, the main verb and imperative is "make disciples." The other verbs (in English translations) are actually participles and take their imperitival force from the main verb. In descending order of importance the verbs are "make disciples," "teach," "baptize, and "go." The text would be better translated "Going . . ." or "As you go . . ." and understanding enhanced by giving more attention to the grammatical construction of the original text. Fifth, DONALD MCGAVRAN held that there is a clear distinction between disciple-making and teaching in fulfilling the Great Commission. The former has to do with people of a culture turning from their old ways, old gods, and old holy books or myths to the missionary's God, the Bible, and a new way of living. The latter has to do with "perfecting" as many as will take instruction and follow the "new way" more closely. In obeying the Great Commission, "discipling" new peoples should never be discontinued in an effort to "perfect" a few. Though comparatively few agreed with McGavran early on, in recent years there has been a somewhat wider acceptance of certain aspects of his thesis. Sixth, Church Growth advocates generally and proponents of the AD 2000 and Beyond Movement especially (e.g., RALPH WINTER) have placed great emphasis on the phrase *panta ta ethnē* in Matthew 28:19 and have insisted that this is best understood as having reference to the various "people groups" of the world (*see* PEOPLES, PEOPLE GROUPS). Originally Donald McGavran identified endogamy as a primary characteristic of a "people group" but subsequently other characteristics such as a common worldview, religion, ethnicity, language, social order, and self-identification have been emphasized. This understanding lends itself to a program of world evangelization whereby people groups are identified and "reached" by planting viable, New Testament churches that become the primary means of evangelizing the group socially to the fringes and temporally into the future. Seventh, in recent years a growing number of missiologists (e.g., Trevor McIlwain) have advocated a missionary approach that gives more serious attention to the Great Commission requirement to teach all that Christ commanded. To many missions people this has seemed altogether too encompassing and demanding. They have preferred to communicate basic truths about human spiritual need and the way in which the Lord Jesus has met that need by means of his death and resurrection. In a way the tension between these two approaches reflects a classic missions controversy as to whether missionaries should first communicate truths about the nature of God and his requirements as revealed in the whole of Scripture or are better advised to begin with the New Testament account of Jesus' teaching and ministry. What is distinctive about the recent emphasis, however, is that its proponents usually link "all I [Christ] have commanded" in Matthew 28:20 with John 5:39 and a chronological teaching of the Bible as redemptive history.

However one may assess the foregoing (among other) responses to the requirements of the Great Commission, it seems apparent that, unlike the first two hundred years of Protestantism, during the nineteenth and twentieth centuries the Great Commission came to play an extremely important role in missions and missiology. In fact, the authors of the FRANKFURT DECLARATION of 1970 placed it first in their list of "seven indispensable basic elements of mission." In a way this growing appreciation for the Great Commission was re-

flected in the changed thinking of even the early-twentieth-century liberal scholar Adolf von Harnack. At first he concluded that the words of 28:18–20 probably constituted a later addition to the Gospel of Matthew. In later life he found it to be not only a fitting conclusion to that Gospel, but a statement so magnificent that it would be difficult to say anything more meaningful and complete in an equal number of words (see Bosch, 1991, 56–57).

DAVID J. HESSELGRAVE

Bibliography. D. J. Bosch, *Transforming Mission: Paradigm Shifts in Theology of Mission;* H. R. Boer, *Pentecost and Missions;* R. D. Culver, *A Greater Commission: A Theology for World Missions;* D. A. McGavran, *The Bridges of God.*

Greece *(Est. 2000 pop.: 10,573,000; 131,990 sq. km. [50,961 sq. mi.]).* Bordered by Turkey, Bulgaria, Albania, and the former Yugoslav Republic of Macedonia, Greece forms a geographical and cultural bridge between Europe and the Middle East. Of the more than 2,000 islands, only 169 are inhabited.

Paul was the first Christian missionary to Greece, establishing churches in Philippi, Berea, Athens, and Thessalonica (Acts 16–17). From the time of Constantine, Christianity has played a dominant role. Today some 16,500 Greeks attend churches of various Protestant traditions, most being Pentecostals. JEHOVAH'S WITNESSES have nearly twice as many adherents. It is the Eastern Orthodox Church which dominates, officially and culturally, this nation of 10.5 million. The common perception is that to be Greek is to be Orthodox. Although Greece formally adheres to international declarations on religious liberty, in practice non-Orthodox, and especially those who engage in active evangelism, face significant pressures. Too often, evangelical churches are perceived by Greeks as being foreign and unattractive.

Missionaries to Greece face the challenge of nationalism coupled with a strong group (as opposed to individual) orientation, both reinforcing the Orthodox identity of the people. Some evangelicals among the large Greek diaspora have been active in outreach to their homeland and should be encouraged to do more. Missionaries to Greece, whatever their national origin, should be prepared to cooperate with the existing evangelical entities—the two hundred congregations are already divided among forty denominations! Cooperation might both increase the effectiveness of witness and cut back the missionary attrition rate, reported at over 70 percent within the first four years.

Greece has an advantageous location for mission outreach to Muslims from the Middle East and the Balkans. Some outreach has been reported among Albanians, both in Greece and in

Albania, as well as among transient and resident Middle Easterners. But animosity resulting from centuries of Turkish domination constitutes a barrier to outreach among Turks, whether in Greece or in Turkey. Other ethnic minorities, such as the Vlach and Bulgarian-speaking Pomaks, are officially ignored by the government and may require special missionary strategies. Further, hundreds of towns and villages, especially in the north, and most of the islands have no permanent evangelical witness.

Greek evangelical missionaries currently number only a handful. While facing the challenge of their own country, they could also make a significant contribution in needy neighboring countries.

DAVID GREENLEE

Bibliography. R. Clegg, *Concise History of Greece;* T. Ware, *Introduction to the Orthodox Church,* rev. ed.

Greene, Elizabeth "Betty" (1921–97). American missionary aviation pioneer. Born in 1921, she learned to fly at the age of sixteen. A member of the Women's Air Forces Service Pilots during World War II, Greene performed high-altitude test flights, towed targets for live-fire gunnery practice, and flew a number of military aircraft, including the four-engine B-17 Flying Fortress.

Greene opened the Christian Airmen's Missionary Fellowship (CAMF) office in Los Angeles in 1944 as the designated secretary-treasurer. Colaborer with Jim Truxton, she quickly became a major driving force behind the new organization. Greene worked with Truxton, Parrott, and Buyers on the incorporation papers for CAMF, which later became Mission Aviation Fellowship (MAF). She served both on the first board of directors and on the first executive committee. In 1946, Greene became CAMF's first field pilot, flying a plane to SIL's Jungle Camp in Mexico, MAF-US's first foreign field. During her thirty-year career with MAF, Greene flew all over the globe, becoming the first woman to fly over the Andes. She also flew missionary tours in Nigeria, Sudan, Ethiopia, Uganda, Kenya, the Congo (Zaire), and Dutch New Guinea (Irian Jaya). On the forefront of promoting prayer for MAF, she launched a newsletter in 1945, "Wings of Praise and Prayer," distinguishing herself as MAF's prayer secretary.

GARY LAMB

Bibliogaphy. D. G. Buss, and A. F. Glasser, *Giving Wings to the Gospel: The Remarkable Story of Mission Aviation Fellowship;* R. A. Tucker, *FJIJ.*

Greene, Mary Jane Forbes (1845–1910). American missionary to Japan. Having spent her young adulthood in Westborough, Massachusetts, Mary Jane Forbes both attended and taught at Mount Holyoke Female Seminary. Five months after her 1869 marriage, she arrived with her husband, Daniel Crosby Greene, in Yokohama to cofound the Japan mission of the AMERICAN BOARD OF COMMISSIONERS FOR FOREIGN MISSIONS. This undertaking became the most active Protestant mission in Japan during the Meiji era.

Returning to the United States for only four brief furloughs in forty-one years, the Greenes lived in Yokohama, Kobe, Tokyo, and Kyoto. During those years they saw Japan embrace both Western technology and ideology; the response to Christianity ranged from enthusiastic embrace to indifference. When religious freedom was declared in the 1889 Meiji Constitution, the interest in Christianity began to wane.

Mary Jane's life in Japan revolved around her home, family, and mission networks. Her home, the Wayside Inn, was known for its hospitality to missionaries, expatriates, and the Japanese community. Her public missionary role included church and women's work, with her most distinctive contributions coming in the areas of teaching and music performance. She suffered two bouts with cancer and died in Tokyo in 1910.

TRACY K. SMITH

Bibliography. M. Kilson, *Mary Jane Forbes Greene (1845–1910), Mother of the Japan Mission: An Anthropological Portrait.*

Greenland (Danish Autonomous Area) *(Est. 2000 pop.: 60,000; 2,176,000 sq. km. [840,154 sq. mi.]).* Most of Greenland, the world's largest island, is glacial icecap. Approximately 80 percent of the inhabitants are Inuit Eskimos, most other residents being Danes. The island nation enjoys autonomy as a home-ruled government within the Danish kingdom. Official languages are Greenlandic, also known as Inupik, and Danish.

Greenlanders trace their history to the early Thule culture of about A.D. 900. Migrants from neighboring regions introduced new hunting and gathering techniques which enabled development of permanent settlements. Other changes in the methods of subsistence living led to the emergence of the Inussuk culture. Norsemen of the Viking cultures settled in Greenland's eastern sector about 985. In the final waves of polar Eskimo immigration in the eighteenth and nineteenth centuries from Canada and Alaska, the Inughuit settled in Avanersuaq (Thule).

The first Christians arrived with the medieval explorer Leif Eriksson about A.D. 990. Lutheran missionaries came in 1721; their work waned by 1860. The Moravians came in 1733; by 1900 they gave way to the Church of Denmark.

Measuring the exposure to the gospel, researchers conclude that Greenland is fully Christianized. Yet there is a high degree of SECULARIZATION in this modern arctic society. Like Europe and North America, there is a rapidly emerging postmodern culture. Greenland has a need for

415

fresh methods of spiritual renewal, and even new life, amid its mix of post-Christian cultures.

KEITH E. EITEL

Gregg, Jessie (1875–1942). English missionary to China. Having been accepted by the China Inland Mission, Gregg spent two years in training and six months at the women's language school at Yangchow before being assigned to Hwailu. During the Boxer Rebellion the station was destroyed, and she and her colleagues, Mr. and Mrs. C. H. S. Green, hid in a Buddhist temple and then a cave before being captured and severely beaten. After a short furlough in England she returned to China in 1901 and began actively pursuing her lifelong interest in women's work. She spent the next fifteen years in almost constant travel from Chihli to Shensi and Kansu and south to Hunan and Hupeh. She was a skilled storyteller and an excellent teacher; and although many men heard her, she insisted that she had come only to teach women and that men should listen to a male evangelist. Her five-day mission schools for women were well attended, sometimes attracting several hundred. On a number of occasions she reported that half her hearers were ready to stand up for Christ at the conclusion of her teaching.

KATHLEEN L. LODWICK

Bibliography. M. Broomhall, *The Jubilee Story of the China Inland Mission;* P. Thompson, *Each to Her Post;* R. A. Tucker, *GGC.*

Gregory the Illuminator (c. 240–332). Founder of the Armenian Church. Born in Armenia, he fled to Cappadocia when Persian rulers temporarily took control of Armenia. In Cappadocia he received Christian instruction. Returning home once Armenian king Tiridates gained power, he faced persecution after refusing to participate in a pagan ritual. Eventually, however, Tiridates came to Christ and declared Christianity the official religion. Neill relates that this is the first clear historical example of a whole country won to Christ through the conversion of the king, and Gregory is consequently remembered as the "Apostle to Armenia." Throughout the rest of his life, Gregory continued the work of evangelizing Armenia and the surrounding regions, baptizing four other kings in the process.

A. SCOTT MOREAU

Bibliography. F. X. Murphy, *NCE,* 6:790–91; S. Neill, *HCM; ODCC.*

Grenada (*Est. 2000 pop.: 94,000; 344 sq. km. [133 sq. mi.].*). The southernmost of the Windward Islands of the Lesser Antilles, Grenada came to world attention when American President Ronald Reagan authorized an armed invasion in 1984. Grenada thereafter received sufficient foreign aid for its economy to rebound from the rapid deterioration of the early 1980s. A reported 60 percent of the population is Roman Catholic, with a third nominally Protestant. In the early 1990s six evangelical missions had two dozen missionaries on the island.

EVERETT A. WILSON

SEE ALSO Caribbean.

Bibliography. A. Lampe, *The Church in Latin America, 1492–1992,* pp. 201–15; J. Rogozinski, *A Brief History of the Caribbean: From the Arawak and the Carib to the Present.*

Grenfell, George (1849–1906). English missionary to Cameroon and Zaire. George Grenfell grew up in Birmingham, England. Excellent spiritual mentors influenced his life after his conversion in a Baptist chapel at age fifteen. He apprenticed in the machine and tool industry and edited *Mission Work* magazine before attending Bristol Baptist College, where he prepared for mission service.

The Baptist Missionary Society appointed Grenfell to Cameroon in 1875. His bride, Mary Hawkes, died shortly after their arrival. He was one of two men who opened the Congo (modern Zaire) for missionary work in 1877. He married his second wife, Rose Patience Edgerley, in 1878. He buried several small children on the field. One daughter, who returned to work with him in Congo, died of fever in 1898.

He is best known for the steamship *Peace,* which he helped design and shipped unassembled to Congo. The engineers sent to help in the reconstruction died. From 1884 until 1907, he sailed the *Peace* the three thousand miles of the Congo River, opening new areas for mission work. The many converts positively impacted the area.

Cannibalism, slavery, virulent disease, war, and an antagonistic Belgian colonial regime were among the major obstacles Grenfell dealt with during his life in Congo. He was known as a peacemaker who believed that Bible translations in local languages and educational work were essential for a successful missionary effort.

MIKEL NEUMANN

Bibliography. S. J. Dickins, *Grenfell of the Congo;* H. L. Hemmens, *George Grenfell, Pioneer in Congo;* H. Johnston, *George Grenfell and the Congo.*

Grenfell, Sir Wilfred Thomason (1865–1940). English missionary to Labrador. Born near Chester, England, he graduated with a degree in medicine after studying at Oxford and London. Converted at a D. L. Moody mission service in London in 1885, he joined the Royal National Mission to Deep Sea Fishermen in 1889. He fitted out the first hospital shop for North Sea fishermen, and established homes for their use. In 1892 Grenfell began his four decades of service to the scattered communities of Labrador, himself raising most of the funds, which from 1912 were channeled through the International Grenfell Association. He operated medical ships, and had hospitals and nursing stations located at strategic points along the desolate coast of Labrador, about which he provided valuable geographical data. He also set up orphanages, schools, cooperative stores, and other institutions designed to help the fisherfolk and their families. He fought unfair traders and liquor dealers. His enterprise was backed financially by friends in Britain and North America, some of whom came to give practical help. He received fellowships from both the Royal (British) and the American College of Surgeons, a knighthood from King George V (1927), and the first honorary doctorate in medicine bestowed by Oxford. Students of St. Andrews University in Scotland elected him as their rector.

Grenfell retired in 1935 and died in Charlotte, Vermont. He was author of some two dozen books, among them the autobiographical *A Labrador Doctor* (1922) and *Forty Years for Labrador* (1932).

J. D. DOUGLAS

Groves, Anthony Norris (1795–1853). English missionary to Iraq and India. Born in Newton, Hants, England, Groves worked professionally as a dentist in Plymouth, then Exeter. In 1816, he married Mary Bethia Thompson. They had two sons who wrote histories of the Plymouth Brethren that identify Groves as an early proponent of the movement.

In an influential book *Christian Devotedness* (1825) Groves repudiated institutional mission societies. Relying on prayer, the indwelling of the Holy Spirit, Christ-centeredness, and personal holiness, Groves pioneered the TENT-MAKING approach typical of FAITH MISSIONS. From 1829 to 1833, he served as a missionary in Baghdad, where his wife and infant daughter died. Subsequently, apart from two short visits to England, Groves served in South India with his second wife, Harriet Baynes, who in 1856 published a *Memoir of A. N. Groves.*

Groves deplored as "fallen" the state of the ancient Christian churches of India. He stressed church planting, self-support, and cultural sensitivity. Plymouth Brethren missionaries and his Indian disciple, JOHN CHRISTIAN AROOLAPPEN (1810–67), adopted this approach.

PAUL R. DEKAR

Bibliography. G. H. Lang, *Anthony Norris Groves. Saint and Pioneer;* idem, *The History and Diaries of an Indian Christian (J. C. Aroolappen);* H. W. Rowdon, *BDCM,* pp. 264–65; W. T. Stunt, et al., *Turning the World Upside Down. A Century of Missionary Endeavor.*

Grubb, Sir Kenneth George (1900–1980). British missionary statesman and missionary to Latin America. Kenneth Grubb (younger brother of Norman P. Grubb) was one of the most influential British missionaries and ecumenical statesmen of the mid-twentieth century. He was converted after the end of the First World War, following prayer on his behalf by Norman. Soon afterwards, he was accepted by WEC INTERNATIONAL to travel in Amazonia and compile a linguistic schedule of the Indian peoples of the Amazon basin. This was published in 1927. Feeling somewhat constricted within WEC, he left to join the research staff of the Survey Application Trust, for whom he worked throughout the 1930s producing a series of volumes surveying Christian prospects in Latin America. With the outbreak of war imminent, he was recruited by the British government as a Latin American specialist, and was promoted rapidly to become overseas controller of publicity within the Ministry of Information. In 1944 he became president of the CHURCH MISSIONARY SOCIETY (CMS), an office he held for twenty-five years. Working closely with MAX WARREN, Grubb presided with a firm hand over the transition of the CMS into the postcolonial era. He was also an active, but not uncritical participant of the postwar ecumenical movement, serving for twenty-three years as the first chairman of the Churches' Commission on International Affairs. For many years he edited the *World Christian Handbook.* He received his knighthood in 1953.

BRIAN STANLEY

Bibliography. K. Grubb, *Crypts of Power: An Autobiography.*

Grubb, Wilfred Barbrooke (1865–1930). Scottish missionary to Latin America. Born in Edinburgh, into a medical family, Grubb was known as the "Livingstone of South America." After joining the Edinburgh Medical Mission in 1881, he sought to take part in an expedition to Africa but was thought too young. DWIGHT MOODY and Ira Sankey challenged Grubb to commit his life to missions in 1884. He was accepted by the South American Missionary Society (SAMS) at nineteen and left in 1886 for the Falkland Islands. He soon volunteered as a pioneer missionary and was appointed to work among the people of the Paraguayan Chaco in 1889.

Penetrating the interior of the Chaco, Grubb won the confidence of the Lengua Indians. Grubb strove for a holistic ministry incorporating education, medicine, and evangelism. He translated hymns, prayers, and a large portion of the New Testament into Lengua. The quality of his work and reputation prompted the Paraguayan government to appoint him as commissioner for the Chaco. Out of a desire to provide industrial training and work for the neglected Lengua, he formed the Chaco Indian Association in 1900.

In 1914 Grubb joined an effort to initiate a similar mission in the Argentine Chaco. Having returned to England in 1921 with double pneumonia, he undertook deputation work for SAMS until his death in 1930.

GARY LAMB

Bibliography. W. B. Grubb, *A Church in the Wilds;* R. J. Hunt, *The Livingstone of South America.*

Guadeloupe (French Overseas Department) *(Est. 2000 pop.: 462,000; 1,781 sq. km. [688 sq. mi.]).* A former French colony, Guadeloupe had been an overseas department of France since 1946. The island's residents are 85 percent Roman Catholic and 5 percent Protestant. After a stormy history of slave revolts, emancipation, and schemes to integrate the black citizens, the planters of Guadeloupe in the second half of the nineteenth century imported East Indian workers. This community presently makes up 10 percent of the population.

EVERETT A. WILSON

SEE ALSO Caribbean.

Bibliography. A. Lampe, *The Church in Latin America, 1492–1992,* pp. 201–15; J. Rogozinski, *A Brief History of the Caribbean: From the Arawak and the Carib to the Present.*

Guam (United States Dependent Area) *(Est. 2000 pop.: 164,000; 549 sq. km. [212 sq. mi.]).* Guam is the largest and most southerly island of the northern Marianas Archipelago, to the west of the Philippines in the eastern Pacific Ocean. It is administered as an unincorporated territory of the United States and the economy is based on financial services and the military installations. Nearly half of the population are Chamorro-speaking. Although 80 percent of the population is Roman Catholic, many evangelical groups are active in Guam, including Assemblies of God, Baptists, and Seventh-Day Adventists.

TODD M. JOHNSON

SEE ALSO Micronesia.

Guatemala *(Est. 2000 pop.: 12,222,000; 108,889 sq. km. [42,042 sq. mi.]).* A Central American country bordering Mexico, Belize, Honduras, and El Salvador, Guatemala has a population of more than 12 million, which is about 55 percent of Mayan origin. This is divided into twenty-one language groups, some with several dialects. The majority of the people live in the mountainous central highlands. The economy is largely agricultural, with coffee, sugar, bananas, beef, and cardamom the chief exports. Tourism and textiles are also important.

Guatemala has been traditionally Roman Catholic (with significant syncretistic elements of Mayan ANIMISM) since the Spanish conquest in 1524. While a few Spanish priests like Fray Bartolomé de las Casas, later bishop of Chiapas, Mexico, sought to win converts by use of local languages and gentle persuasion, the church was overwhelmingly identified with the oppressive power structures that enslaved and decimated the Indians and tried to stamp out their culture.

Early Protestant missionary efforts, including those of British colporteur Frederick Crowe (1843–46), were unsuccessful due to opposition by Catholic clergy, but sowed seeds for the liberal reforms of President Justo Rufino Barrios, who promulgated freedom of religion in 1873 and later personally invited the Presbyterian Board of Foreign Missions to open work in Guatemala. As a result, the Rev. John C. Hill arrived in November 1882, with Barrios's entourage and his support.

The Presbyterians were followed by the Central American Mission (CAM) in 1899, the Church of the Nazarene in 1901, and the Friends in 1902. These, with the Primitive Methodists (1922), adopted a comity agreement. In 1935 the five missions and their associated national churches formed the Evangelical Synod of Guatemala, precursor of the present Evangelical Alliance of Guatemala.

Progress was initially slow, but by 1982 evangelicals comprised nearly 20 percent of the population, and some seven hundred thousand gathered for a centennial rally. Explosive church growth in the 1970s was fueled by several factors: a proliferation of agencies and independent national churches, mass evangelism, the devastating earthquake of 1976, and political violence that claimed one hundred thousand lives over twenty-five years. Despite predictions evangelicals would be a majority by 1990, church growth leveled off in the mid-1980s and in 1995 evangelicals were about 24 percent of the population.

There are some 200 denominations with 16,000 local churches in Guatemala; over half of all evangelicals belong to the six largest groups: Prince of Peace Church, Church of God (Cleveland, Tenn.), Assemblies of God, Central American Evangelical Churches (CAM), Calvary Churches, and Elim Christian Mission. About two-thirds of the Protestants are Pentecostal.

Six seminaries, some twenty-five Bible Institutes, and various TEE programs provide leadership training, while fifteen evangelical radio and two television stations broadcast both evangelistic and teaching programs. Christian schools, many operated by local churches, are widespread.

Translation of the Bible and other materials into local dialects, along with cassettes and radio, has been a major factor in Mayan church growth; in 1995 four complete Bibles and fifteen New Testaments had been published, with work underway in nineteen additional dialects. Five radio stations broadcast primarily in Mayan languages.

Some 650 foreign missionaries serve with ninety agencies in the country, while two national agencies and several churches have sent about forty Guatemalans into transcultural ministries.

STEPHEN R. SYWULKA

Bibliography. C. L. Holland, ed., *World Christianity: Central America and the Caribbean.*

Guilt. Guilt refers both to an objective reality (of moral, sinful culpability) and to a subjective reality (a subjective perception and experience of oneself as culpable, a feeling of guilt). Both are relevant to missions.

Sinful human beings violate moral law(s)—both human and divine. They violate other persons—both human and divine. And they fail to exemplify and be characterized by the moral sentiments, character traits, and virtues called for by human conscience and by the God who created them in his own image. Objectively, then, all are guilty sinners deserving of death and judgment. It is this objective reality that explains both the need for Christ's work on the cross and the need for missions. And it is this objective reality of human sin and guilt that is a critical component of the missionary's message.

The call for repentance and faith is a call for an inner response in which one's subjective experience and perceptions are congruent with objective realities. The Bible itself (Romans 2) indicates that there is within each individual a set of inner perceptions and judgments (conscience) that does in fact ratify the biblical message of sin and guilt. Yet missionaries frequently complain that those to whom they proclaim the objective reality of sin and guilt do not subjectively perceive and experience themselves as sinful and guilty. In some contexts there seems to be no inner assent of conscience and soul to the message of sin, guilt, and judgment and the need for forgiveness and salvation.

In part, this is because missionaries often fail to understand subjective guilt, as it varies from culture to culture, and missiologists fail to address methodologically how objective guilt and subjective guilt should be brought together in the presentation of the gospel message.

No society can afford to affirm unbridled evil in all directions. All societies work to inculcate moral norms, interpersonal moral obligations, and personal character ideals in their members. Some cultures place formal moral codes, moral prohibitions, at the center of their moral system, carefully delineating the line at which an infraction occurs and punishment can be meted out. The transgressor in such a culture is likely to feel "law-guilt." Other cultures put the moral focus on interpersonal sensitivity and obligation. Here transgression is against persons. The transgressor feels "person-guilt." Still other cultures emphasize moral ideals in a model identity characterized by correct moral sentiments, character traits, and virtues. When self-identity is seen to fall short of model identity, "shame-guilt" is felt.

Western missionaries historically come from backgrounds stressing law-guilt, and tend to emphasize selectively the corresponding biblical imagery (sin as crime, as transgression of the law; guilt as formal pronouncement of a judge in a court of law, as deserved punishment; grace as justification, canceling of deserved punishment). When they go to Tahiti or Japan, where person-guilt and shame-guilt are stressed, they generally fail to utilize the appropriate corresponding biblical imagery (with person-guilt: sin as rebellion, ingratitude, personal harm; guilt as alienation, as debt requiring restitution; grace as restored relationship, canceled debt, redemption; or with shame-guilt: sin as falling short; guilt as nakedness, filthy uncleanness, dishonor, desire for concealment; grace as sins covered and forgotten, regeneration, a new self, glorification). Instead they retain imagery focusing on law-guilt. As a result their message of an objective guilt and preferred salvation fails to resonate with their hearers.

Furthermore, such norms, personal obligations, and ideals involve a curious mixture of conventional elements and universal moral elements, and thus vary from one culture to another. The issues here are complex, and missiology needs to go much further in generating understandings of sin, guilt, and conscience in relationship to culture, the gospel message, and missionary methodology.

ROBERT J. PRIEST

SEE ALSO Shame.

Bibliography. T. W. Dye, *Missiology* 4 (1976): 27–41; R. J. Priest, *Missiology* 22 (1994): 291–315.

Guinea (*Est. 2000 pop. 7,759,000; 245,857 sq. km [94,925 sq. mi.]*). In 1919 the CHRISTIAN AND MISSIONARY ALLIANCE opened its first mission station in French West Africa as Baro, in present-day Guinea. The group of missionaries, led by Robert Sherman Roseberry (1883–1976), was conscious of the strategic importance of this new work. For them Baro was to be the beachhead for the evangelization of the vast territory then colonized by France. Just the year before, the French government had agreed to open its West Africa colony to Christian missionaries from other Western nations. This was one of the results of the 1918 Saint Germain Treaty. For Edith Roseberry this was providential in "opening French territories to the preaching of the gospel" (E. Roseberry, 1957, 39).

Though evangelical missionaries entered Guinea only in 1919, the Christian faith had a longer history in that part of the world. In 1804, the Anglicans began work among the Susu of Guinea, and in 1861 West Indian Christians established the Pongas Mission in Conakry, present capital of Guinea. Neighboring Sierra Leone has had a vibrant and active Christian community since the eighteenth century. As African borders were still being drawn, the Christians from Sierra Leone carried the gospel to some of the people of the country we now call Guinea. Indeed, the Christian and Missionary Alliance entered Guinea from Sierra Leone. Yet little remains from the earliest Christian mission endeavors in Guinea. Today the Roman Catholic Church, the Christian and Missionary Alliance, and, to some extent, the Anglicans, are the only Christian communities with a continuous presence in Guinea since the beginning of their evangelistic efforts.

In 1967, Sékou Touré, then president of the country, decreed to expel all foreign Catholic and Protestant missionaries. This political decision may explain the privileged status enjoyed by the Catholic Church and the church related to the Christian and Missionary Alliance, the *Eglise Protestante Evangélique de Guinée*. The resilience of these two churches may be due to the fact that Guineans were their leaders and active agents. Early in its work, the Christian and Missionary Alliance opened and operated a Bible school in Baro. It is remarkable that already in the 1930s there was a Guinean teacher at Baro, Jean Kéita, who had a great influence on the students.

Mission agencies such as the Open Bible Standard, the PARIS EVANGELICAL MISSIONARY SOCIETY, and the United World Mission terminated their activities in Guinea in 1967. The Christian and Missionary Alliance was allowed to keep a few missionaries in selected areas and ministries. Only after Sékou Touré's death in 1984 did Guinea open its doors widely to foreign Christian missionaries. Evangelical missionaries, in particular, built on the foundations laid by Guinean Christians during the twenty-year ban on foreign missionaries. The story of missions in Guinea thus provides a laboratory for testing the claim that "no heathen land will ever become Christian as long as its Christianity is exotic, propagated by foreigners and dependent upon them" (Brown, 310).

TITE TIÉNOU

Bibliography. A. J. Brown, *The Foreign Missionary Yesterday and Today;* R. S. Roseberry, *Training Men for God in French West Africa;* E. Roseberry, *Kansas Prairies to African Forests.*

Guinea Bissau *(Est. 2000 pop.: 1,192,000; 36,125 sq. km. [13,948 sq. mi.]).* Located on the west coast of Africa, Guinea Bissau is surrounded by Senegal and Guinea. The almost 1.2 million inhabitants are comprised of some 27 ethnic groups. Roughly 48 percent are traditional religious adherents, 44 percent Muslims, and just under 8 percent Christians (7 percent Catholic and 1 percent Protestant). Devastated by civil war since independence was gained in 1974, Guinea Bissau remains one of the world's least developed countries. Johnstone reported in 1993 that the public debt per person was $479 while the income was only $180.

The first Catholic missionaries arrived in 1462, though progress in the work was so slow that more than two centuries later there were only 2,000 known believers. By 1929, only one priest was present in the area. In 1940, Franciscans were given oversight of the work, and by the time of independence there were some 50,000 Christians.

Catholic influence made it difficult for Protestant efforts to begin, with visa restrictions on Protestant missionaries not easing until 1990. In 1993 Johnstone estimated that there were 71 Protestant missionaries working there. Protestant labors began in 1939 with the arrival of WORLDWIDE EVANGELISTIC CRUSADE. The only large Protestant church (*Igreja Evangélica da Guiné;* Evangelical Church of Guinea, with an estimated 8,000 believers in some 60 congregations) grew out of their work. Also present are the Assemblies of God and Seventh-Day Adventists.

A. SCOTT MOREAU

Bibliography. D. Barrett, *WCE;* J. Baur, *2000 Years of Christianity in Africa;* P. Johnstone, *OW.*

Guinness, Henry Grattan (1835–1910). Irish evangelist and mission organizer. Born in Dublin, Guinness went to sea at seventeen only to return home a year later and experience a conversion at the age of twenty. With a vision for missions and a passion for evangelism, he left New College, London, without completing his training and became an itinerant international evangelist. Despite poverty and persecution, he was ordained an evangelist in 1857 and preached to thousands throughout the British Isles and the United States during the great revival.

After visiting France in 1865, Guinness founded the McAll Mission. In 1873, he opened the East London Institute for Home and Foreign Missions at Harley House. Guinness's influence also led to the founding of the North Africa Mission in 1881 and the Livingstone Inland Mission in 1887, which began in the Congo and expanded to South America and North India, eventually becoming part of the Regions Beyond Missionary Union in 1899. He encouraged the establishment of training centers in Boston and Minneapolis in 1889, which by 1910 had sent hundreds of graduates into the missionary endeavor. That same year Guinness received a D.D. from Brown University.

Guinness wrote two books that stirred international evangelical interest: *The Approaching End of the Age* (1886) and *Light for the Last Days* (1888). He believed that the world would end in 1919, but died without knowing that he was wrong.

GARY LAMB

Bibliography. S. D. Walters, *Asbury Theological Journal* 44 (Spring 1989): 29–50.

Guru. A commonly used word in much of South Asia, particularly in the HINDU tradition, referring to teachers and spiritual leaders. Its etymology is uncertain. In ancient India instructions in the Hindu sacred scriptures were orally passed on to people through an unbroken chain of gurus. A guru's house was called the academy, and his followers learned as they lived with their teacher in a strong bond of love and submissive obedience to him. He was considered to be the embodiment of his spiritual instructions, and was idealized as representing the deity.

Gurus were typically ascetics who were single, having no particular qualifications other than that of charisma in leadership. In the SIKH religion, however, the title "guru" refers particularly to the ten great original teachers and founders of the faith.

Since the 1960s, in the face of the emptiness of materialism and secularism, a great many people around the world, especially Western youth, turned to Eastern mysticism. In this context many gurus popularized the Hindu concept of salvation for individuals, communities, and nations. The lifestyles of these modern gurus are widely varied. Some are materialistic, distorting the Hindu faith and mixing religion and sex for their personal gains in the West. Others, however, are giants of religious philosophy and Eastern spirituality.

In the communication of the Christian gospel to the Hindus and the Sikhs the concept of guru as associated with Christ and the evangelist or discipler is both relevant and effective.

SAPHIR ATHYAL

Bibliography. V. Mangalwadi, *The World of Gurus;* K. Singh, *Gurus, Godmen and Good People.*

Gutiérrez, Gustavo (1928–). Peruvian systematic theologian of Latin American LIBERATION THEOLOGY. Gutiérrez's seminal work, *A Theology of Liberation,* has been translated into many different languages and still serves as the best introduction to that theological and pastoral current. A revised edition, with a substantial new introduction detailing Gutiérrez's theological pilgrimage, was published to coincide with his sixtieth birthday and the fifteenth anniversary of the Bishops' Conference at Medellín, Colombia, on which he had a profound influence. In this ground-breaking book, he discusses the foundational themes of liberation theology, which he further explores in later writings. These themes include the nature of the theological task, the contribution of the social sciences (in particular, Marxism) to the doing of theology, the mission of the (Roman Catholic) church in light of the problematic sociopolitical context of Latin America, the work of God in historical struggles of liberation, and the characteristics of a new spirituality concerned about the suffering and hopes of the poor.

Gutiérrez later focused his research and writing on a Dominican friar from the time of the Spanish conquest of the Americas, Bartolomé de las Casas (1474–1566). In this tireless defender of the indigenous peoples Gutiérrez observes a precursor of liberation theology who opposed the injustices of those in power and tried to understand the person and message of Jesus Christ in light of the needs of the oppressed.

M. DANIEL CARROLL

Bibliography. R. A. Brown, *Gustavo Gutiérrez: An Introduction to Liberation Theology;* G. Gutiérrez, *The Power of the Poor in History; We Drink from Our Own Wells; The Spiritual Journey of a People; On Job: God-Talk and the Suffering of the Innocent; Las Casas: In Search of the Poor of Jesus Christ;* B. Nickoloff, *Gustavo Gutiérrez: Essential Writings;* E. A. Núñez, *Liberation Theology;* E. A. Núñez and W. D. Taylor, *Crisis and Hope in Latin America: An Evangelical Perspective,* rev. ed.

Gutmann, Bruno (1876–1966). German mission scholar and missionary to Tanzania. Born in Dresden, Saxony, into a family of humble circumstances, he entered the Leipzig Mission Seminary in 1895 and worked from 1902 to 1938 as a missionary on the slopes of Kilimanjaro in northern Tanzania, mostly in the Old Moshi (Kidia) congregation. As a missionary, he showed deep interest in Chagga culture, which resulted in both publications and the collection and preservation of the Chagga "tribal teachings" connected to the various transition rites so relevant in Chagga society.

Because of his many writings reflecting the work of the church in Old Moshi and beyond, he became one of the best known German missiologists before World War II. Gutmann's aim was to root the church deeply in Chagga society, by basing the church's work on the three primal ties of kinship, neighborhood, and age-group. These he considered to be part of the image of God and therefore valid not only for the Chagga but for all of humankind.

Gutmann is sometimes seen as an archconservative, which he was not, as his work in Old Moshi congregation and his support for the mission's progressive educational system, based on Marangu, shows. His missionary approach, based on Lutheran premises, was very effective in coping with the quickly rising number of Christians, but when he tried to solve moral problems by making use of traditional Chagga concepts, he was often not supported by the Chagga Christians themselves.

KLAUS FIELDER

Bibliography. K. Fielder, *Christianity and African Culture: Conservative German Protestant Missionaries in Tanzania, 1900–1940;* E. Jäeschke, *ML,* pp. 173–80.

Gützlaff, Karl Friedrich August (1803–51). German missionary linguist in China. Gützlaff has been called the "Apostle of China." He was born in Pyritz, Prussian Pomerania; he died in Hong Kong. In 1821, he began study at a mission school in Berlin established by Johann Jaenicke, a devout Moravian pastor. The Netherlands Missionary Society sent Gützlaff to Batavia, the capital of Java, in 1827. There he married Miss Newell, the first self-supporting woman missionary in Java. Sadly, his wife died soon after their marriage.

Gützlaff was an outstanding linguist who published sixty-one books in various languages, including several translations of the New Testament. Although China restricted missionary work, Gützlaff made at least three voyages as surgeon and interpreter along the coast to China, Korea, and Japan, preaching and leaving tracts to nobility and peasant alike. He was employed by the East India Company, and self-funded much of his work. His attempt to utilize indigenous evangelists in China was not successful, but later missionaries learned from him. Gützlaff can be credited for helping lay the foundation for larger missionary work after his death. The greatest missionary contribution of Gützlaff was probably his inspirational example of holy consecration, sacrifice, love, eloquence, and zeal.

T. VAN MCCLAIN

Bibliography. E. L. Lueker, ed., *Lutheran Cyclopedia,* rev. ed.; J. T. Mueller, *Great Missionaries to China.*

Guyana *(Est. 2000 pop.: 883,000; 214,969 sq. km. [83,000 sq. mi.]).* Located on the north coast of South America, between Venezuela and Surinam, Guyana became a Dutch possession in the early seventeenth century. Sovereignty passed to Britain in 1814. In 1831, the three counties of Demerara, Essequibo, and Berbice were united into one colony, British Guiana. With its capital city in Georgetown, Guyana has a population of over seven thousand people. East Indians constitute the majority of the population (51%), followed by black and mixed (43%), and Amerindians (4%).

The Moravian Brethren were the first to do missionary work among the Arawak Indians in Berbice, in 1738. In 1763 an insurrection of slaves moved the missionaries to Demerara, and by the end of the century their mission was abandoned. The LONDON MISSIONARY SOCIETY began its work in 1807 among the plantation slaves, with John Wray (d. 1837). Difficulties arose when the colonial government issued a proclamation prohibiting the slaves from assembling, even for religious purposes. By 1826 there was a congregation in Georgetown, and by 1835 there were three missionary stations in Demerara. The English Methodist Missionary Society sent missionaries from other colonies to Demerara in 1815. A congregation was organized, mostly of black slaves.

The CHURCH MISSIONARY SOCIETY began its work in 1829. They worked among the seventy thousand slaves (African and Creoles) that were in Demerara-Essequibo. Their efforts were also successful among the Indians of the Essequibo and Potaro rivers. However, the work was given up in 1856. The Society for the Propagation of the Gospel began its work among the slaves in 1835. Churches and schools were erected. Other denominations came later: Plymouth Brethren, Salvation Army, Church of the Nazarene (1945), and Southern Baptists (1966). Roman Catholics constitute a minority.

After a compensated emancipation of the blacks in 1834, the freed slaves refused to work on the plantations. Only by the importation of East Indian indentured servants was the plantation system preserved. The bond servant migration ended in 1917. However, ethnic tensions have affected political life and the Christian testimony in Guyana through the years. The country became independent on May 26, 1966. Evangelization has proven to be difficult because of the various cultures, religions, and languages represented.

PABLO DEIROS

Bibliography. P. Blanshard, *Democracy and Empire in the Caribbean Area;* R. V. Long, *We Can, We Will;* T. B. Neely, *South America: Its Missionary Problems.*

Hades. *See* HELL.

Haining, Jane Mathison (1897–1944). Scottish missionary to Hungary. Born to a farming family near Dunscore, Dumfriesshire, she was educated at Dumfries Academy and was very successful as a secretary for Coats thread business. At that time, she attended a meeting in Glasgow of the Church of Scotland Jewish missions. She sensed the Lord's leading and, after further training, offered herself to the Church of Scotland's Jewish missions. In 1932 she took up her post as matron of the girls' home of Jewish missions in Budapest, Hungary.

When World War II broke out, Haining was on leave in Scotland. When she learned that Hitler had invaded Poland, she hurried back to the girls' home in Budapest. Shortly thereafter, because of the growing tensions in Europe, the Church of Scotland recalled their missionaries.

But Haining refused to leave her girls in their time of need. By that time, there was hardly any food or water available and the girls' home was in desperate need of repairs. Nonetheless, to the best of her ability, Haining provided for and comforted those who were in her care.

In May 1944 German authorities arrested Haining on suspicion of espionage. She was immediately taken to Auschwitz, where she was gassed, probably on July 17, 1944. She was the only Scot killed in a Nazi concentration camp.

Haining lived and died with those she came to serve. Her home church in Glasgow dedicated two stained glass windows in memory of her. They are fittingly named *Service* and *Sacrifice*.

KATHY McREYNOLDS

Haiti (*Est. 2000 pop.: 7,959,000; 27,750 sq. km. [10,714 sq. mi.]*) Haiti has had a tragic history since it became the first of the Caribbean states to gain independence and the first black republic to come into existence. By the 1920s, Haiti acquired its present character as a nation of peasant landowners raising food crops on their own small plots. The country soon developed a caste system of rural African peasants and light-skinned, urban elites who controlled government, the professions, and life in the capital.

While three-quarters of all Haitians are considered to be Roman Catholic, an equal proportion are considered spiritists. The proliferation of evangelical groups in Haiti has produced a combined community of more than 20 percent of the population. The Seventh-Day Adventists are the largest non-Catholic group, with Baptist and Holiness churches making up a significant proportion of the total.

EVERETT A. WILSON

SEE ALSO Caribbean.

Bibliography. F. J. Conway, *Perspectives on Pentecostalism: Case Studies from the Caribbean and Latin America;* L. P. Gerlach, *Religious Movements in Contemporary America;* A. Lampe, *The Church in Latin America, 1492–1992;* J. Rogozinski, *A Brief History of the Caribbean: From the Arawak and the Carib to the Present.*

Hamer, Lilian (1912–59). English missionary to China and Thailand. She started out as a mill worker in Lancashire, England. At twenty-one years of age, she announced to her father that she was taking a nurse's training course to prepare for missionary service. Her father was so enraged that he asked her to leave home. Though she was devastated by her father's decree, she finished her nursing training and applied to the CHINA INLAND MISSION. Much to her dismay, CIM did not accept her. However, her first priority was to serve God; so she applied to the Red Cross and was accepted.

After she had fulfilled her obligation to the Red Cross in China, she reapplied to the China Inland Mission and, this time, was welcomed into the fold. In 1951 she was forced to leave China because of the communist takeover. But she returned to the Far East a year later to work among the tribes of Thailand. It was there that she specialized in the treatment of opium addicts. She would relieve their physical symptoms

423

by use of medicine and then tell them that true freedom was found in Christ alone. An addict from the Lisu village was so impressed by her treatment that he had his kinsmen invite her to live among them.

From that time forward she lived among the Lisu people, faithfully ministering to the addicts and preaching the gospel of Christ. Sadly, in 1959, she was attacked and killed while walking in the jungle alone. Years later it was discovered that a witch doctor bribed an opium addict to commit the murder.

Despite this heinous crime, the work among the Lisu people continued. A church was built not far from where she was killed.

KATHY MCREYNOLDS

Bibliography. A. Crane, *Fierce the Conflict: The Story of Lilian Hamer.*

Han, Chul-la (1924–). Korean professor and mission advocate. Born in Pyung Yang province in North Korea, he was educated at Seoul National University, Westminster Theological Seminary, and Union Theological Seminary in Virginia. He also did graduate studies at the Ecumenical Institute in Geneva, Earlangen Universitat, and Westminister College in England. Han is president (1982–98) and professor of systematic theology at the Asian Center for Theological Studies and Mission (ACTS) in Seoul, Korea, which was founded in 1974. Prior to coming to ACTS, he was the dean of the Graduate School of the Presbyterian Theological Seminary (Tong Hap) in Seoul (1964–74).

His significant contributions to the churches in Korea and Asia are twofold. First, he has developed evangelical theological education in both Korea and Asia. One of the well-respected evangelical theologians in Korea and an ordained Presbyterian minister in the Presbyterian Church of Korea (Tong Hap), he has trained thousands of Korean pastors, parachurch organizational leaders, and theologians as well as hundreds of other Asian, African, and South American students who studied at ACTS. Second, he is a mission-minded theologian who has promoted "the evangelization of Asia" through his ACTS ministry and trained many Korean missionaries to serve overseas.

Han has written numerous books and articles, but is best known for *Asian Christian Thought* (1990).

BONG RIN RO

Bibliography. S. H. Moffett, *TCDCB*, p. 167.

Han, Kyung-Chik (1902–). Korean pastor and mission advocate. Han is pastor emeritus of the Young Nak Presbyterian Church (Tong Hap denomination) in Seoul, Korea, which he started with twenty-seven North Korean refugees before the Korean War. This church now has 60,000 members and is the largest Presbyterian church in the world.

When the Communists took over North Korea right after World War II, Han was pastoring in North Pyung Yang province of North Korea. He and other church leaders organized the Christian Socialist Democratic Party in September 1945, but he had to flee to South Korea to avoid communist persecution. He became one of the best known pastors in South Korea for his vision for evangelism, missions, education, and social concern. Over a thirty-year period, his Young Nak church has started more than 350 churches and sent out missionaries to serve in 21 countries. He is the only Korean pastor who received the prestigious Templeton Award in 1993.

He was educated at Soong Sil (Union Christian) College in Pyung Yang, North Korea, Emporia College in Kansas, and Princeton Theological Seminary. He has served as a board member for many Christian institutes and organizations.

BONG RIN RO

Bibliography. C. C. Ok, *BDCM*, p. 278; S. H. Moffett, *TCDCB*, pp. 167–68.

Harris, William Wade (1865–1929). Liberian evangelist and missionary in West Africa. Known as Prophet Harris, he was a Liberian (Grebo/Kru) Anglican catechist. Jailed twice in Liberia for anti-government activity, during his second imprisonment he had a vision of the angel Gabriel calling him to be "a prophet, to preach a gospel of repentance, to destroy 'fetish' worship, and to baptize those who obeyed." In 1913, he began preaching in Côte d'Ivoire (Ivory Coast) and Gold Coast (Ghana) that Jesus Christ must reign, and that Harris was his prophet. He proclaimed a political vision that would bring all nations under the earthly rule of Jesus. Colonial authorities were condemned as "Satan." Harris preached belief in one God, destruction of fetishes, observance of Sunday as a day of rest, and prohibition of adultery and alcohol. He stressed the "incomparable importance" of the Word of God.

Harris told those he baptized to build churches and wait for teachers who would come and give them fuller instruction. An estimated 100,000 Ivorians believed before French authorities deported Harris in 1915.

In 1923, a missionary of the English Methodist Society found 45,000 people faithful to Harris's teaching. In Ghana, Wesleyans increased sevenfold between 1912 and 1929, largely through the preaching of Harris. He continued preaching in Liberia until his death in 1929.

DONALD K. SMITH

424

Bibliography. G. M. Haliburton, *The Prophet Harris;* D. Shank, *Prophet Harris, the 'Black Elijah' of West Africa;* S. S. Walker, *The Religious Revolution in the Ivory Coast: The Prophet Harris and the Harrist Church.*

Harvey, Esther Bragg (1891–1986). American missionary administrator in India. Born in Port Huron, Michigan, Harvey attended Presbyterian and Methodist churches before joining a local Pentecostal church, where she testified to physical healing. Called to India as a missionary, Harvey enrolled at the Bible and Missionary Training School in Norwalk, Ohio, in 1911 directed by Etta Wurmser, sometime member of the Christian and Missionary Alliance. Ordained there in 1913, she soon left for India as an independent missionary. At the Pentecostal mission in Nawabganj, United Provinces, she met missionary James Harvey, a former soldier in the British Indian Army. After their marriage in 1914, they became affiliated with the Assemblies of God.

The Harveys renamed their mission the Sharannagar Mission ("place of refuge"), and initially focused on evangelism; as needs arose they added a boys' school (present-day James Harvey Memorial School) and homes for widows and orphans. Remarkable answers to prayer characterized their ministry. After James' death in 1922, Esther continued to promote and direct the mission. While on furlough in 1940, she married Sidney Grimmette, who subsequently died in Japan while en route to India. Harvey's fruitful ministry in evangelism, education, and compassion represents the dedicated service of early Pentecostal women missionaries.

GARY B. McGEE

Bibliography. E. B. Harvey, *The Faithfulness of God.*

Haygood, Laura Askew (1845–1900). American missionary to China. Born in Watkinsville, Georgia, she was brought up in Atlanta, where her mother was an administrator of a school. Her brilliance was seen in that she graduated from Wesleyan Female College after only two years of study. She taught for one year at Palmer Institute at Oxford and then returned to Atlanta after the Civil War. In 1872 she became a teacher at Girls' High School, and in 1877 was appointed principal. Her passion was to train teachers. Besides her administrative duties and teaching responsibilities at the high school, she trained Sunday school teachers for several denominations.

Haygood sensed the call to the mission field when Young J. Allen of China Mission asked her to locate an educator to develop the work among women and children in China. She sensed this to be a personal call and offered herself for duty. In November 1884 she arrived in Shanghai and took charge of the Women's Board.

Haygood was actively involved at the Clopton Boarding School for Girls and eventually merged it with Mary Lambuth School at Soochow. Throughout all her endeavors, she stressed teacher training. She raised up an army of teachers and imparted to them the same passion for teaching.

Her greatest achievement was the opening of McTyeire, a high school for girls and home and training school for new women missionaries to China. The school opened in March 1892 and became the most prominent private girls' high school in the Shanghai region.

After a long furlough in Atlanta, Haygood returned to China in 1896 and became the director of the Woman's Board for the entire Shanghai region. Despite her overwhelming administrative duties, she renewed an interest in evangelism by establishing two Bible schools for women at Soochow and Sungkiang.

KATHY McREYNOLDS

Haystack Meeting. The first American mission board to spread the gospel outside the United States was the AMERICAN BOARD OF COMMISSIONERS FOR FOREIGN MISSIONS (ABCFM). The impetus to found this society came from a group of students at Andover Theological Seminary. The leader of this group was SAMUEL MILLS, who, touched by the Second Great Awakening in New England, had received a call to missions and gone for training to Williams College in Massachusetts. Here several like-minded students, among them Luther Rice, joined with him to form the Society of Brethren, a group that met in a grove of maples near the campus for prayer and discussion about missions. One day going to their time of prayer, they were caught in a violent thunderstorm and took refuge in a nearby haystack. After an intense time of prayer, they took a pledge to devote their lives to missionary service.

After their graduation from Williams College, several of these students went to Andover Seminary, where they were joined by ADONIRAM JUDSON from Brown, Samuel Newell from Harvard, and Samuel Nott Jr. from Union College. They formed a Society of Inquiry on the Subject of Missions and in June 1810 appeared before the General Assembly of Congregational Churches, where they offered themselves for missionary service. This led to the formation of the ABCFM, with themselves as the first appointees.

RALPH R. COVELL

Bibliography. J. H. Kane, *A Concise History of the Christian World Mission.*

Healing. *See* MIRACLES IN MISSION.

Health Care and Missions. In the 1970s it became clear that the traditional pattern of health care delivery in medical missions, that of medical institutions staffed by trained medical professionals, was inadequate. Institutions were unable to cure the number of sick who came and had done little to improve the health of the majority of people in the communities they served. A variety of global health agencies and Christian groups addressed this issue, with significant leadership for the Christian community coming from the Christian Medical Commission in Geneva. Historic mission involvement in schools, agriculture, evangelism, and church planting—as well as hospitals and clinics—reflected a genuine, though often unarticulated, concern for social and economic transformation as well as for spiritual development. The legacy of the 1970s was to focus attention on community participation in health care, the responsibility of governments in health care, the relationship between health and DEVELOPMENT, training personnel for primary care, using appropriate technology in health care, and providing essential affordable drugs.

The World Health Organization definition of health includes physical, mental, and social well-being, but the biblical concept of SHALOM moves beyond that, encompassing the welfare, health, and prosperity of both the person and persons-in-community. Around the globe there have emerged many models of integrated holistic ministry that promote health. They are diversely sponsored by mission agencies, churches, development agencies, grassroots organizations, and combinations of those groups.

Model Programs. Parachurch organizations, such as the Luke Society and Campus Crusade for Christ, have made significant contributions in the area of Christian health ministries. The Luke Society, working in the Ashanti province of Ghana since 1989, founded twenty-two community health centers with trained workers as part of a larger program that also included evangelism, church planting, and income-generation projects. Community Health Evangelism, originally a program of Life Ministry Africa (Campus Crusade for Christ), was conceived to help the church meet both the physical and spiritual needs of the people. Community health evangelists teach health workers, who in turn train others in disease prevention, health promotion, and how to have an abundant Christian life through a personal relationship with Christ.

Traditional mission agencies working in partnership with local churches have developed strong programs as well. In the Republic of Congo, the Vanga Evangelical Hospital under the leadership of Dan Fountain developed in three decades from a rural hospital with two dispensaries to a 300-bed referral hospital with five physicians and a network of 50 primary health care centers, working in partnership with the Baptist Church of Western Zaire. There has been a significant impact on morbidity and mortality in its catchment area of 200,000 people.

The flexible, community-oriented initiatives, which began in the 1970s, have proliferated in subsequent years. Documentation of these initiatives has been undertaken by MARC, a division of World Vision International, in a series of publications by Ted Yamamori and colleagues entitled *Serving with the Poor in Africa, Serving with the Poor in Asia,* and *Serving with the Poor in Latin America,* making engaging reading on Christian social transformation, integrated development, and health care that ministers to both physical and spiritual needs.

EVVY CAMPBELL

SEE ALSO Medical Mission Work.

Bibliography. C. Bellamy, *The State of the World's Children 1996;* B. Bradshaw, *Bridging the Gap: Evangelism, Development and Shalom;* D. M. Ewert, *A New Agenda for Medical Missions;* E. Ram, *Transforming Health: Christian Approaches to Healing and Wholeness;* S. B. Rifkin, *Community Health in Asia;* E. H. Patterson and S. B. Rifkin, *Health Care in China: An Introduction;* D. Van Reken, *Mission and Ministry: Christian Medical Practice in Today's Changing World Cultures.*

The Heathen. In missions, the term "heathen" refers to "those who have never heard the good news that God offers sinful humanity divine forgiveness on the ground of the substitutionary death of Christ" (Henry, *Through No Fault of Their Own,* p. 246). The scriptural development of the term "heathen" centers around the words "Gentiles," "nations," and "peoples." The primary Hebrew words are *goy and 'am.* The primary Greek words are *ethnos* and *laos.*

The scriptural emphasis behind the term "heathen" is rooted in the doctrine of the sinful state of the human race. Jesus taught that slavery to sin leads to self-centeredness (Matt. 5:47), indulgence in self-centered materialistic and temporal pursuits (Matt. 6:32), abuse of relational responsibilities (Matt. 20:25), and misunderstanding of true prayer (Matt. 6:7). The apostle Paul affirmed this doctrine in a very systematic way (Rom. 1:18–3:20).

God's desire to reach all nations is clearly embedded in his covenant with Abraham (Gen. 12:1–3). The chosen nation was to be God's instrument to reach the heathen. While Israel was to be set apart from all nations (Lev. 11:43–47), it was also to be a kingdom of priests to represent the true God to the nations (Exod. 19:6). Christ reiterated God's desire to reach the world when he gave his final commission to his disciples (Matt. 28:18–20).

Scripture presents Christ as the light of the world and its only hope (John 8:12) The Book of Acts gives the historical outworking of God giving the Holy Spirit (Acts 10:48), his Word (Acts

11:1), repentance (Acts 11:18), faith (Acts 14:27), and conversion (Acts 15:13) to the Gentiles. Today God is calling Gentiles or heathen (Rom. 9:24), and taking from among them a people for his name (Acts 15:14). One day the fullness of the Gentiles will be complete, which speaks of the total number that God will save (Rom. 11:25).

The apostle Paul's response to the heathen's spiritual condition is reflected in his desire to preach the gospel where it had never been preached (Rom. 15:20–21). While all Christians are not called to be pioneer missionaries, all are called to live distinct lives (Eph. 4:17; 1 Thess. 4:5), and to obey Christ's command to disciple the nations (Matt. 28:18–20).

The classical answer to the persistent question of the spiritual state of one who has never heard the gospel is found in the early chapters of Romans. The answer is that God has spoken to all people through creation (Rom. 1:19–20; cf. Ps. 19:1–6). The revelation of God's moral law is also written on every person's conscience (Rom. 2:14–15). All persons will be judged according to the light they have received (Rom. 2:11–12). Such revelation is said to leave the heathen with no excuse (Rom. 1:20). The pattern given in Romans is a pattern of rejecting God's revelation in creation and conscience.

A recent flurry of articles and books address the issue of the heathen. Some argue that since many evangelicals make room for the salvation of infants, is not there a case for salvation of heathen apart from explicit faith in Christ? Of course, it must be noted that the infant is not guilty of volitionally rejecting GENERAL REVELATION in the same way that the heathen are.

Some argue for a UNIVERSALISM that states all will be saved. The supposed scriptural basis is rooted in God's universal desire (1 Tim. 2:4; 2 Peter 3:9), his universal provision (John 12:32), and the future universal acknowledgment of Christ (Phil. 2:9–11). The clear biblical teaching on judgment, the necessity of personal faith in Christ, and the separation of the lost and the saved appear to clearly negate this teaching that has been espoused by such ancients as Origen, who saw hell as remedial and the threat of an eternal hell as only hortatory. The related question of the nature and duration of divine punishment is outside the scope of this present article (see ANNIHILATION).

There are a number of theories that do not embrace universalism but do espouse a wider hope (see also PLURALISM). They tend to give some hope to the heathen by giving various ways that one might be saved without explicit faith in Christ. Some theorize that God will expose everyone to the gospel after they die. There appears to be no clear evidence for this position. The "spirits in prison" in 1 Peter 3:18 are probably best taken as angelic beings and the "dead" in 1 Peter 4:6 probably refers to martyred Christians who heard the gospel while they were alive.

Another theory is that the sincere seeker can be saved even apart from faith in Christ. Is it true that "God cares about the direction of the heart and not the content of theology" (Pinnock, *A Wideness in God's Mercy*, p. 158)? Roman Catholic theology, according to Vatican II, teaches that those who are guiltlessly ignorant of Christ's gospel and sincerely seek God can achieve eternal salvation. Cornelius is used as an illustration of this theory. Acts 10:35 does teach that Gentiles such as Cornelius are suitable candidates for salvation, but Acts 11:14 says he was not saved until he heard the gospel.

The theory that God will save those who respond to general revelation of creation and conscience is set forth by Justin Martyr, Chrysostom, Zwingli, Wesley, Augustus Strong, and more recently by Clark Pinnock. In one of JOHN STOTT's earlier writings he called the issue of those who have never heard a "perplexing problem." He also encouraged the Christian not to "preoccupy oneself with such speculative questions" (Stott, *Christian Counterculture*, p. 196). Jesus encouraged us to focus not on speculation but on our responsibility (Luke 13:23–24).

The emphasis in Scripture is on the necessity of human agents to bring the gospel to a lost world (Rom. 10:14–15). Scripture gives only one clear way to escape God's judgment and that is through faith in Christ. The heathen are responsible to God based on general revelation. There is a provision for all people's salvation in Christ. The church's responsibility is to declare this message to all. The Christian is not to be arrogant but rather to honor all people (1 Peter 2:17). However, there is no greater honor one gives to another than humbly sharing Jesus, the light and hope of the world.

McQuillkin considers any theory that gives hope to the unevangelized as dangerous (McQuillkin, *The Great Omission*, p. 50). Nash states his similar concerns regarding any theory that espouses that the preaching of Christ is not necessary for salvation (Nash, *Is Jesus the Only Saviour?* p. 126). Kantzer is probably correct in stating that "God does not want us to spend enormous amounts of time investigating things about which we can do absolutely nothing" (Kantzer, *Through No Fault of Their Own*, pp. 14–15). We do know that God will enable and reward every effort to reach the heathen with the gospel. We also know that our just God can never do anything that is not perfectly righteous. It is probably better, as Phillips says, to err on the side of safety than gamble on speculative leniency (Phillips, 154).

WILLIAM O. THRASHER

See also Unevangelized, the.

Bibliography. W. Crockett and J. Sigountos, eds., *Through No Fault of Their Own;* L. Dixon, *The Other Side of the Good News;* W. G. Phillips, *BibSac* 154 (1994): 140–54; J. Sanders, *No Other Name;* E. Rommen and H. Netland, eds., *Christianity and the Religions.*

Hell. Place of God's final retributive punishment for the wicked. In the Old Testament souls of the dead face a shadowy existence in Sheol (Job 10:21; Ps. 88:12; Isa. 14:10; Eccles. 9:10). Since death is not God's original intent but results from the fall, the Old Testament confidently awaits God's demonstration of his lordship by raising the righteous to life (Gen. 2–3; Pss. 16:10, 49:15; Isa. 25:8; Hos. 13:14). Occasionally it suggests a future retribution for the wicked (Pss. 21:10; 34:15–16, 140:11; Dan. 12:2; Mal. 3:18–4:2). Jesus further develops this framework, teaching that at the final judgment, Satan, his demons, and the wicked will be thrown into hell, bringing an end to evil's free ways (Matt. 25:41). His standard term for hell is *Gehenna,* referring to the valley of Hinnom outside Jerusalem, a place notorious for evil deeds and God's fiery Judgment (Jer. 7:31ff.; Isa. 30:33; 66:24).

The Biblical View of Hell.
Jesus is most responsible for defining the biblical concept of hell, which includes the following integral features.

Place of Irretrievable Bondage. The wicked are imprisoned in a "furnace" (Matt. 13:42, 50), a "lake of fire" (Rev. 20:10, 14–15; 21:8), a "prison" (Matt. 5:22–26; 18:34–35; Jude 6) and so separated from the righteous (Luke 16:26).

Place of Retribution. Jesus' image of fire portrays God's searing holiness exacting retribution for evil deeds (Luke 17:29–30). Here the wicked are punished and "paid back with harm for the harm they have done" (2 Peter 2:13; Matt. 16:27; Jude 7; Rev. 14:9–11).

Penalties of Loss. The grave's maggots (Mark 9:48; Isa. 14:11) and darkness (Matt. 8:12; Ps. 88:12) were common images of a ruined and despairing existence without hope, and thus separated from God's loving presence (Matt. 25:30).

Penalties of Torment. The pictures of "gnashing teeth," "beatings," and "fire" suggest that hell's punishment includes physical affliction (Matt 13:42; Mark 9:48–49; Luke 12:47). Since these images are often at odds with each other—darkness and fire, or never-dying worms in an unquenchable fire—they should not be interpreted literally but as metaphors for punishment.

Degrees of Punishment. Punishment varies so that those who were "entrusted with much" are more responsible (Luke 12:48).

Hell Exists Forever. Jesus' picture of hell as a place where "the fire is never put out" (Mark 9:48) reflects what Scripture clearly states elsewhere: punishment is "forever and ever" (Rev. 20:10; 14:11; Matt 25:46).

Justice and Hell.
Hell answers the perennial cry for justice. The Holocaust and ethnic cleansing haunt us with the question, "When will the wicked be judged?" These pangs of morality reflect the way God made us as accountable to him, the Moral Judge of the cosmos (Rom. 2:15–16). Scripture's ultimate answer to the problem of evil is that God, the holy Judge of all the earth, calls every human to account on the Day of Judgment for his or her life (Matt. 12:36; Ps. 31:18; Rom. 2:6–11). Hell is the horrific and tragic place where God will pay back the wicked for their evils and reestablish his righteous rule even over the reprobate (Matt. 16:27; 25:31–46; Rom. 12:19; 1 Cor. 15:24–25; 2 Cor. 5:10).

However, the fact that God will punish all sin defines the human predicament. Although created for God, humans proclaimed their independence, resulting in history's tragedy of hatred, deceit, and neglect. As a result, each sin is first and foremost an offense against the infinite God against whom "all have sinned" (Rom. 8:7; 3:23). Scripture reveals that the penalty required for sin is hell. Jesus repeatedly warns of sin's heinous nature and dreadful consequence: "If your eye causes you to sin, gouge it out. . . . It is better for you to enter life with one eye than to have two and be thrown into the fire of Hell" (Matt. 18:9).

Hell and the Proclamation of the Gospel.
How is it possible for God the Holy Judge to be merciful to sinners? The biblical answer is that the personal, infinite God has substituted himself for us. The gospel is the good news that God in Jesus Christ has come to this rebellious world and suffered the judgment for those who have "faith in Christ's blood" (Rom. 3:25; 2 Cor. 5:21). Except for God's awesome love, everyone would lack hope! If one fails to trust in Jesus, hell is the awful consequence (Luke 12:8–9; Acts 4:12; Rom. 10:9–15). So hell is both the presupposition for the gospel as well as the consequence of its rejection.

Challenges to Hell.
In view of the integral link between the gospel and the judgment for sin, revisions to the doctrine of hell have direct and even devastating implications for the proclamation of the gospel. Revisionist eschatology, Universalism, and Annihilationism pose significant challenges to concepts of hell and may result in changes to the biblical understanding of the gospel.

Revisionist Eschatology. Many have abandoned Jesus' bodily resurrection and any personal life after death, interpreting heaven and hell as simply mythological expressions of a first-century faith. Not only does this view demolish the gospel's promised hope but it also undermines life's moral significance. In this view justice cannot be established.

Universalism. Universalists insist that God will eventually transform everyone into Christ's image, even if it requires remedial punishments after death. How, they ask, could a loving God reject forever the creature he loves? Note that this question elevates humanity as God's highest good! But God is self-sufficient; his goodness and love are completely grounded in himself (Acts 17:25). Humanity exists to glorify God (Ps. 73:24–26; 1 Cor. 10:31; Col. 1:16). Because God's goodness is self-grounded, anything contrary to his will is evil and retribution reflects God's goodness. In view of Jesus' own concept of hell, universalism also attacks his character. For it must treat Jesus as ignorant of God's moral character or as intentionally misleading his hearers.

Not only does universalism dispute God's revelation in Jesus Christ, its insistence that God's eternal pursuit will bring everyone to salvation undermines the moral seriousness of our present life. By contrast Jesus stresses the urgency of a decision in the present life (Matt. 25:13; Mark 13:32–37) precisely because God's gracious offer is not eternal (Matt. 25:41). This present life is decisive for our future (Heb. 9:27). Moreover, universalism's view that those who die outside of Christ are not lost eliminates the need for evangelism. Historically universalism has subverted mission institutions into becoming merely social and political agencies.

Annihilationism. Annihilationists acknowledge the necessity for retribution, but insist that the wicked are obliterated by God's wrath and not punished forever and ever. The punishment due for sin is the crucial issue. Scripture's answer focuses on Christ's death. At the cross God in Christ became our substitute to bear the punishment for our sins so as "to be just and the one who justifies the man who has faith in Jesus" (2 Cor. 5:21; Rom. 3:21–26; 1 Peter 2:24). The fact that only God the Judge, the "Lord of glory himself" (1 Cor. 2:8), could pay the penalty due us, suggests that the penalty for sin against the Infinite is infinite. Annihilationism fails to take seriously the infinite penalty that God in Jesus Christ paid for us. Moreover, hell marks the gravity of humanity's rebellion. Diminishing hell means the horrific nature of sin begins to be lost.

Conclusion. Many questions remain. While Scripture does not answer all our questions, we know that the Lord of all the earth will do right (Gen. 18:25). Just as Christ cried over Jerusalem's fate (Luke 19:41), we can only speak of God's final damning punishment with tears as we respond to a lost world as did our Savior, who humbled himself to our condition, suffered, and died for the wicked. This destiny should impel the church to follow Christ in sacrificially proclaiming the gospel in word and deed to the lost.

TIMOTHY R. PHILLIPS

Bibliography. A. A. Hoekema, *The Bible and the Future*, pp. 265–73; C. S. Lewis, *The Problem of Pain;* J. I. Packer, *Evangelical Affirmations*, pp. 107–36; T. R. Phillips, *Through No Fault of Their Own: The Fate of Those Who Have Never Heard*, pp. 47–59; W. G. T. Shedd, *The Doctrine of Endless Punishment;* J. F. Walvoord, W. Crockett, Z. Hayes, and C. H. Pinnock, *Four Views on Hell.*

Henotheism. The term "henotheism," from the Greek *henos* (one) and *theos* (god), was introduced into the study of religion by F. Max Müller, and refers to the practice of worshiping one particular deity without necessarily denying the reality of other gods. Müller observed that in the Vedas, the oldest Indian religious literature, deities are invoked by a variety of names, but that to the particular supplicant each god is for that person or group the real divinity, absolute and supreme. Throughout Hindu religion, there is the tendency for various groups to give special place and devotion to specific deities—Shiva, Brahma, Vishnu—without necessarily denying the reality of other deities. A biblical example of henotheistic practice might be found in Canaanite religion, such as the example of the Philistines, who regarded Dagon as their superior deity while also recognizing the power of Yahweh when they captured the ark (1 Sam. 4).

Although distinct from them, the concept of henotheism overlaps to some extent with other categories for the study of religion, such as MONOTHEISM (belief in one God, excluding the very possibility of other gods), POLYTHEISM (belief in a plurality of gods), and monolatry (the exclusive worship of a deity by a certain social group). Furthermore, discussions of henotheism have frequently been plagued by rather dubious assumptions of the allegedly evolutionary development of human religion. The challenge for Christian missions is to encourage people to move from henotheistic tendencies to a full acceptance of the biblical God as the only God and Creator, who forbids the worship or acknowledgment of any other deities.

WILLIAM H. BAKER

Bibliography. R. Mackintosh, *ERE* VIII:810–11; F. M. Müller, *Lectures on the Origin and Growth of Religion;* R. Pettazoni, *Essays on the History of Religions.*

Hepburn, James Curtis (1815–1911). American missionary to China and Japan. A second-generation missionary sent to China, the first by the American Presbyterians, James C. Hepburn later became most notable for his work in Japanese languages. His Japanese-English dictionary was an internationally acclaimed work, employed extensively in the late nineteenth and early twentieth centuries.

After completing medical work in the United States, Hepburn and his wife were first assigned to Singapore and later, under the Medical Missionary Society, to the China port city of Amoy. Due to his wife's unstable health, the Hepburns returned to North America in 1845. Maintaining his Asian interests, Hepburn in 1859 was once more commissioned by the Presbyterian Church for a lifelong career in Kanagawa, Japan (1859–92).

Little is known about his medical practice there, but his missionary sensitivities drove him to emphasize educational work and the compiling of extensive notes on the rapid changes in Japanese language during the burgeoning decades of the progressive Meiji imperial era. His dictionary's first edition appeared in 1867; the third edition was republished numerous times as the standard work in the field. This extensive knowledge he applied to an early translation of the Japanese Bible.

LAUREN PFISTER

Bibliography. J. C. Hepburn, *A Japanese-English and English-Japanese Dictionary;* S. Kaiser, ed., *The Western Rediscovery of the Japanese Language;* A. Wylie, *Memorials of Protestant Missionaries to the Chinese.*

Herman of Alaska (1756–1837). Russian Orthodox missionary to Alaska. Herman was one of ten Russian Orthodox monks who took part in the first Christian mission to Alaska in 1794. He remained there for forty-three years, faithfully serving the Alaskan natives and proclaiming the gospel of Christ.

Herman was born in a little town outside Moscow. At the age of sixteen, he entered the monastery. Although he never envisioned the life of a missionary, after twenty years in the monastery he volunteered to join the first overseas mission team of the Russian Church. They arrived in Kodiak, Alaska, on September 24, 1794.

The mission thrived during the first five years despite great obstacles from Russian explorers and hunters. The missionaries baptized more than seven thousand people and established a strong foundation for the new church. Over a short period of time, however, three of the original missionaries drowned at sea, a fourth was martyred, and another five returned to Russia. Herman remained alone.

For the remaining thirty-eight years of his life, he continued to preach and protect the indigenous peoples from Russian traders. Herman's legacy best represents the Orthodox Church's understanding of "passive missions," where holy people preach the gospel more with their life than with their actual words.

LUKE A. VERONIS

Bibliography. G. Afonsky, *A History of the Orthodox Church in Alaska (1794–1917);* M. Oleksa, *Alaskan Missionary Spirituality;* idem, *Orthodox Alaska.*

Hermeneutics. Science, art, and spiritual act of interpreting the Scriptures. Presupposed is the view that the Bible is the inspired, inerrant Word of God (*see* INERRANCY). There is not just an author of the biblical books but a divine Author communicating eternal truth through the human authors. The basic dilemma in interpretation is the author-text-reader problem. An author writes a text with an embedded message. A reader studies the text in order to "understand" it, but what access do readers have to the author's intended meaning? In the case of the Bible, the authors have been dead over two millennia, and the cultures within which the Bible was written no longer exist. Is it possible to understand and contextualize the Bible in a set of cultures so far removed from the original setting? That is the basic problem.

Philosophical and literary developments, from Freud to Heidegger, Gadamer to Derrida, led to the dominant movement of the 1990s, POSTMODERNISM. In the philosophical arena, it is deconstruction; in the literary field, it is reader–response criticism; in the religious sector it is radical PLURALISM and UNIVERSALISM; in culture it is tolerance and relativism. In each of its guises postmodernism means the rejection of absolute TRUTH and the replacement of God with socio-historical forces as the deterministic forces in society. Truth is as you make it, and the only arbiter is culture or the needs of the group.

There is an answer. There is one final proof of absolute truth; and while it is grounded in rational evidence (see Osborne, ch. 1), it must in the end be accepted by faith: the Bible is the Word of God. In his Word, God has spoken, and all truth is linked to that one distinct fact. On the hermeneutical side, there are many arguments on behalf of the viability, indeed the necessity, of seeking the author's intended meaning of the text. First, God is behind it and expects the reader to ascertain and then obey his message, not some reader-oriented perspective. There is an ethical responsibility demanded of all readers to let the text guide their understanding to its meaning. This is especially true of the Bible, for authors often (see Paul's use of the rhetorical question in Romans) try to clear up any possible misunderstanding on the part of the reader. Thiselton argues (1992, 611–19) that if there was no intended meaning in the biblical text, it would lose its transforming function. It is certainly true that scholars continually debate and often fail to agree on the meaning of a particular text, but that does not mean there is no correct meaning. In fact, the ability of communities of readers to challenge each other's interpretations draws the student back to the text and produces a greater openness to its meaning. Our preunderstanding (views inherited from tradition and community) has enormous influence but does not have to *determine* our understanding. The hermeneutical process elucidated below can enable us to go beyond the interpretation mandated by our Reformed or Anabaptist or dispensational background and let the text guide us to its own meaning.

Hermeneutical Principles. There are two primary aspects to interpretation theory, which might be labeled meaning and significance (drawing from Hirsch). However, these are not distinct but part of a single process. Still, meaning refers to the search for the author's original message, and significance to the contextualization of the message for the various cultural contexts of the current age. There are three primary components of meaning—context, exegesis, and biblical theology. There are two components of significance—systematic theology and contextualization. All of these interact in the process of moving from text to context.

The Meaning of the Text. The context of a text is the literary world surrounding it. In other words, what does it add to the surrounding context? One of the major hermeneutical axioms is the realization that no word, sentence, or paragraph has meaning apart from a context. "Take out the trash" means something different if it is embedded in an editorial choice for removing a section of an article or a domestic choice for placing the garbage on the curb. So the first step is to note what kind of literary context surrounds a passage.

The exegetical task has four aspects—grammar, semantics, syntax, and backgrounds (*see also* Ex-EGESIS). Grammar studies the building blocks of language, noting how the words in a sentence relate to one another in communicating their meaning. For instance, consider the phrase "the love of God." Does it mean "God's love," "divine love," "love from God," "God loves me," "I love God," or "the church's community love that God makes possible"? All are viable, and only the larger context can decide. The tense or mood of the verb, the case of the noun, the place of prepositions or infinitives or participles, all are determinative for interpreting a passage properly. Grammar is not inconsequential but essential in hermeneutics. Of course, there are questions, such as in the current debate on traditional versus aspect theory in studying the tense of the verb. However, in the end these enhance rather than obscure grammatical knowledge. The important thing to remember is that every grammatical option makes possible a different translation.

Semantics is closely connected to grammar. The meaning of a particular term is dependent on the impact of the surrounding words in the sentence. The key again is context. No term has meaning in and of itself but draws its meaning from the larger communication unit in which it is embedded. There are three rules to follow: (1) determine the semantic range of the term; (2) allow the context to choose which of the meaning possibilities best fits the passage; (3) study the semantic field (the different terms or phrases that could have been used to communicate that meaning) to deepen the understanding of its use in the context. Note Philippians 2:7 as an example. The thrust of *ekenōsen* ("emptied") has been debated for centuries, and the "kenotic school" developed from the belief that Jesus "emptied himself" of his divinity at his incarnation. However, it has been realized recently that the verb only means "emptied" when it is transitive, that is, when the contents that have been "emptied" are mentioned. When it is intransitive, as here, it means "to make yourself low" or "humble yourself."

Syntax does not refer just to grammar but to a broader concept—tracing the interrelationships in the passage to determine the meaning of the whole. This is critical in order to counter the major failure of most commentaries—centering upon isolated words and phrases without developing the meaning of the whole. It must always be kept in mind that the structure of the whole always determines the meaning of the parts and that the value of any particular statement is entirely in its contribution to the whole message. For instance, Gospel pericopes are part of a larger pattern called "story time," namely, the developing message of the Gospel as a whole. In Mark the feeding of the five thousand and the walking on the water are a single story, concluding with the startling "their hearts were hardened." Yet they are also part of a larger unit, 6:30–8:21, centering on discipleship failure surrounding the two feeding miracles (6:30–44, 8:1–10, with the message "God will provide") and contrasting the failure of the disciples with the faith of the "little people" (7:24–37). Each episode in this section of Mark contributes to this basic message.

Finally, background analysis traces the shared assumptions between the author and original readers regarding the customs and culture behind the text. There are two approaches—social description, in which we study the text in terms of the sociological details that help us understand it more deeply; and sociological interpretation, in which we apply current models to re-create the social dynamics that led to the creation of the text. The problem with the latter is that it tends to be speculative and reductionistic. We must allow the text to drive our theory and not force our theory upon the text. Therefore, social description is far more helpful. In this we study parallels in the intertestamental world of Judaism, Qumran, and the Hellenistic world that fit the situation behind the text (*see also* INTERTESTA-MENTAL STUDIES). We consider geographical, material, everyday life, or religious customs and their impact on interpreting the text.

Biblical theology studies the developing theological message of the text by tracing the primary themes of the book as they emerge from the text. This is determined by allowing the themes to emerge and interact with one another as one exegetes the developing text. For instance, there are two major themes in the Book of Revelation (the sovereignty of God and the perseverance of the saints) with several subthemes (the unity of God and the Lamb, the conflict with Satan, the eschaton, etc.). One determines this by studying the interdependence of these themes through the progressive unfolding of the book. Biblical theology emerges from the exegetical analysis of individual passages and then the collation of the theological themes emerging from the passages first in terms of individual books, then in authors, then in the Testaments, and finally in the Bible as a whole.

The Significance of the Text. It must be stressed that this is not a separate aspect of hermeneutics but is part of the meaning of the text. Readers do not artificially determine the objective meaning of the text and only then contextualize that meaning for today. The very exegetical questions we ask come from the modern context. However, it is still a helpful metaphor to think in terms of meaning and significance.

SYSTEMATIC THEOLOGY (ST) is actually a contextualization of biblical theology (BT) in light of the models provided by the history of dogma. There are four components of theological formulation—Scripture, tradition, community, and experience. Scripture, particularly BT, provides the content of ST. The other three together make up our preunderstanding, the set of beliefs we bring to the task. We make theological decisions on the basis of the ecclesiastical tradition we have accepted and the particular formulation of that system in our particular church community. The question is how much influence our inherited system has on us as we rework our beliefs in light of the scriptural data. Theoretically, our preunderstanding should be influential but not decisive; it should be brought to the surface and placed on the examining table to be reworked on the basis of the biblical data. This process will take several steps: the Bible will first be studied inductively to discover all the passages that address the issue. Each passage will be exegeted and the theological message determined. The texts will next be collated on the basis of the aspect of the issue addressed by each, and a preliminary model of the doctrine as it emerges from the biblical teaching will be constructed. The understanding of the doctrine through history will then be consulted, and the model will be reworked in light of that data so that a covering model for today can be erected. This model is heuristic, continually reconsidered in light of the biblical data.

CONTEXTUALIZATION in essence refers to the cross-cultural application and communication of biblical and theological truths. The true goal of hermeneutics is not the learned essay but the sermon, not the commentary but the missiological adaptation of Christianity in the diverse cultures of the world. Biblical truth is meant not just to be studied but more to be applied in life-changing

ways. It must be practical and not just academic. This began with the Bible itself, as the early church moved from a Jewish to a Hellenistic-Jewish to a Hellenistic cultural base. In each new cultural center, from South Galatia (Galatians) to North Galatia (1 Peter) to the province of Asia (Ephesians, Revelation), a new set of cultural problems emerged, and Christianity had to be recontextualized. This dynamic process must be carefully controlled, as all too easily the culture rather than the Word of God can become the determining factor. If the Bible is indeed the Word of God, it must provide the content for all contextualization. In a DYNAMIC EQUIVALENCE approach, whenever the receptor culture controls the process, RELATIVISM and SYNCRETISM result. At the same time, however, the form that this content will take is determined by the cultural context. Form and content provide the matrix of contextualization. The Bible is the norm, but the current culture provides the arena within which the biblical truths are reformulated. We must allow the divine truths to adapt to those aspects of culture that we might call REDEMPTIVE ANALOGIES but at the same time challenge and transform those aspects that are contrary to Scripture. We need to exegete the culture as carefully as we do the Bible, and to understand the people anthropologically and sociologically very deeply as we contextualize, lest we misapply the Word to our world.

GRANT R. OSBORNE

Bibliography. P. Cotterell and M. Turner, *Linguistics and Biblical Interpretation;* D. J. Hesselgrave and E. Rommen, *Contextualization: Meanings, Methods, and Models;* P. Hiebert, *IBMR* (1987), pp. 104–12; E. D. Hirsch, *Validity in Interpretation;* G. R. Osborne, *The Hermeneutical Spiral: A Comprehensive Introduction to Biblical Interpretation;* idem, *Three Crucial Questions about the Bible;* M. Silva, *God, Language, and Scripture: Reading the Bible in the Light of General Linguistics;* A. C. Thiselton, *New Horizons in Hermeneutics: The Theory and Practice of Transforming Biblical Reading.*

Hesselgrave, David (1924–). American missiologist and missionary to Japan. Born in Wisconsin, Hesselgrave trusted Christ as a boy. God called him to pastoral ministry, then missions, the preparation of missionaries, and guidance of the missionary enterprise.

Married to Gertrude in 1944, he prepared for ministry at Trinity Seminary and at the University of Minnesota. There he earned a B.A. in philosophy, M.A. in speech, and Ph.D. in rhetoric emphasizing cross-cultural communication. He was ordained by the Evangelical Free Church of America with whom he served five years in a pastorate and twelve years (1950–62) in Japan.

After returning to the United States, he joined the faculty of Trinity Evangelical Divinity School (TEDS) in 1965, inaugurating the School of World Missions and Evangelism and the doctoral programs in missiology at TEDS in 1976. He served at TEDS until retirement in 1991.

A significant contribution in addition to 10 books and 140 articles on missions was the calling of several missions consultations. These brought together biblical scholars, theologians, and missiologists. Hesselgrave has always been concerned to keep the missions movement grounded in Scripture and sound theology, emphasizing this through teaching and lecturing worldwide and through active membership in several professional societies (e.g., AMERICAN SOCIETY OF MISSIOLOGY and the Evangelical Theological Society), and the directorship of the EVANGELICAL MISSIOLOGICAL SOCIETY from 1991 to 1992.

MICHAEL POCOCK

Hewat, Elizabeth G. K. (1897–1968). Scottish missionary to China. Born in Scotland, she was one of four daughters of the renowned historian and minister Kirkwood Hewat of Prestwick, Ayrshire. In 1926 she was one of the few women to graduate from Edinburgh University with a double degree in history and philosophy.

During her years at Edinburgh, she was on staff at St. Colm's, the Women's Missionary College. Afterwards, she joined her sister, Helen, in China, where they engaged in medical missionary work for several years.

Out of that experience came the material for her Ph.D. thesis in which she compared Hebrew and Chinese wisdom literature. She returned to Scotland and became assistant at the North Merchiston Church in Edinburgh.

After six months, Hewat left Edinburgh and took up the post of professor of history at Wilson College, Bombay. She stayed in that position for twenty years, from 1935 to 1955. During that time, she taught Scripture at the Women Student's Hostel and became an elder in the United Church of North India.

When she returned to Scotland, she was a strong advocate of the opening of both eldership and the ministry of the Church of Scotland to women. With her credentials and achievements, there is little doubt that she made a lasting impact both on the mission field and in the Church of Scotland.

KATHY MCREYNOLDS

Bibliography. L. O. Macdonald, *DSCHT*, p. 402.

Heyling, Peter (1607/8–52). German pioneer missionary theologian in Ethiopia. A native of the Hanseatic city of Lübeck in Germany, Heyling studied law and theology in Paris (1628–32) and was influenced by Huigh Groot (1583–1645). Together with some fellow students from Lübeck he made a decision to "reawaken the ruined churches of the Orient to a genuine evangelical life." After a stay in Egypt for one year, where he lived in monasteries in the desert to learn the Coptic and Arabic languages, he reached Ethiopia in 1634. Here, he became an influential minister, teacher, and doctor at the court of King Fâsilidas (1632–67). Eagerly he also attempted to bring about a reforming renewal in Coptic Christianity. This resulted not only in unproductive christological disputes, but also in an Amharic translation of the New Testament. John's Gospel, in particular, was widely distributed. He is also said to have compiled a collection of legislation taken from Roman and civil law. According to an unsecured tradition Heyling was extradited from the country and died in Suaqin (Sudan, at the Red Sea) as a martyr. His missionary work left its traces in the Ethiopian Evangelical Church Mekane Yesus (founded in 1959).

WERNER RAUPP

Bibliography. W. Raupp, *BDCM*, p. 292.

Hicks, Tommy (1909–73). American missionary evangelist. Little is known of Hicks' background except that he was from Lancaster, California, and served as a Baptist minister prior to becoming Pentecostal. As an independent evangelist in the healing movement of the 1950s and 1960s, his crusades were sponsored by the Full Gospel Business Men's Fellowship International.

Hicks held meetings in the United States and many foreign countries, but his claim to fame came from his meetings in Buenos Aires, Argentina. At the invitation of Assemblies of God missionaries and pastors from twelve denominations, his "Salvation-Healing Campaign" lasted from April to June 1954. The crowds grew so large that the meetings were moved from the Atlanta to the Hurucan stadium with the blessing of Juan Peron; there, nightly attendance exceeded 110,000. Driven by reports of dramatic healings and conversions, the aggregate attendance reached 2 million. As the largest evangelical gathering in Argentine history at the time, it resulted in significant Pentecostal and evangelical church growth.

Hicks' overseas ministry continued but not without controversy over his lifestyle and fundraising methods. His books include, among others, *Capturing the Nations in the Name of the Lord* (1956) and *Millions Found Christ* (1956), the latter his account of the Buenos Aires campaign.

GARY B. MCGEE

Bibliography. A. W. Enns, *Man, Milieu and Mission in Argentina;* L. W. Stokes, *The Great Revival in Buenos Aires;* "But What About Hicks?" *CCen* 71:27 (July 7, 1954): 814–15.

Hidden Peoples. *See* PEOPLES, PEOPLE GROUPS; UNREACHED PEOPLES.

Higginbottom, Sam (1874–1958). English agricultural educator and missionary in India. Higginbottom worked tirelessly at improving agricultural productivity in India. Raised in England, he moved to Boston, Massachusetts, for studies at Amherst College, Princeton, and Ohio State University. Responding to a strong call to missionary service, he left for India under the Presbyterian Board of Foreign Missions in 1903. The following year he married Jane E. Cody in Bombay, India; they later had six children.

After six years of teaching at Allahabad Christian College, Higginbottom became convinced of the need to minister to the Indian people through agriculture. In 1911 he founded the Allahabad Agricultural Institute, where research and experimental methods were used to adapt modern techniques to the particularities of Indian farming. The Institute met with great success, and grew to become India's finest agricultural college. Higginbottom also succeeded in attracting a great deal of financial assistance and trained personnel to the Institute. He taught and ministered in Allahabad until his retirement in 1944. Higginbottom served on many Indian governmental boards concerned with rural affairs. He received the Kaiser-I-Hind Gold Medal in 1924 in addition to five honorary doctorates from universities in the United States.

J. MICHAEL CONNOR

Bibliography. G. R. Hess, *Sam Higginbottom of Allahabad, Pioneer of Point Four to India;* S. Higginbottom, *Sam Higginbottom, Farmer: An Autobiography.*

Hill, David (1840–96). English missionary to China. Arriving in Shanghai in 1865 following the downfall of the Taiping revolution, David Hill prepared himself for evangelistic ministry with the Wesleyan Mission in the Hubei Province. Son of a wealthy alderman of Yorkshire in England, Hill was a self-supporting missionary who aspired to live a relatively ascetic celibate life, one which many considered exceptional and saintly. This he did to be free to preach to the widest range of Chinese people.

Believing prayer to be the mightiest tool of mission strategy, Hill maintained spiritual disciplines, including extensive daily intercession. He advocated missionary prayer unions in England, later promoted and established lay missions in China, and became known as a biblically styled apostle to the Chinese. Over thirty years his mission strategies changed from a singular emphasis on preaching in country circuits to a multifaceted plan, including medical work, schools, publishing, and charity.

Involved in famine relief in Shanxi province in 1878 and 1879, Hill from that time on dressed in Chinese attire and developed extensive ministries to the poor. From 1885 he was chairman of the Wesleyan Central China Mission, and in 1890 was designated the English president of the General Missionary Conference. He died from typhus contracted while distributing funds for the poor entrusted to him by mandarins.

LAUREN PFISTER

Bibliography. W. T. A. Barber, *David Hill: Missionary and Saint;* H. B. Rattenbury, *David Hill, Friend of China: A Modern Portrait.*

Hinderer, Anna (Martin) (1827–70). English pioneer missionary to Nigeria. Born in Norfolk, she lost her mother early and was largely brought up in the home of the Anglican rector of Lowestoft, where she assisted in work in the parish. In October 1852 she married David Hinderer, a German clergyman serving under the CHURCH MISSIONARY SOCIETY in Yoruba country (Nigeria), and they sailed almost immediately for Lagos.

Hinderer, originally at Abeokuta, near the coast, had started work at Ibadan, farther inland, and they traveled there early in 1853. Accommodation was primitive; they were both frequently ill, but Anna at once began to visit the town, and soon had a school in her home. Childless herself, she became a mother to many. After leave (1856–58) they found their Yoruba assistants had carried on well, and there were many baptisms. But in 1860 an ongoing feud between two sections of the Yoruba people came to a head, and for the next five years they lived in a state of siege. Not until April 1865 were they relieved and able to visit Britain again. They returned to Ibadan at the end of 1866 and found the work progressing well, but their health was worse and in 1869 they were forced to leave. David Hinderer resigned from the CMS and took a parish at Martham, Norfolk, where Anna died in June 1870.

The memoir her husband compiled has kept her memory fresh. She represents the sacrificial band of wives without whose help the new communities of Christians could not have developed.

JOCELYN MURRAY

Bibliography. A. Hinderer, *Seventeen Years in the Yoruba Country: Memorials of Anna Hinderer, Wife of the Rev. David Hinderer, C.M.S. Missionary in Western Africa, Gathered from Her Journals and Letters;* J. Murray, *Proclaim the Good News: A Short History of the Church Missionary Society.*

Hindu, Hinduism. "Hindu" is a term originally used by Muslim conquerors of India to refer to the indigenous peoples of North India whom they subjected in the second millennium A.D. Later "Hinduism" came to be used by British colonizers for the religion of these Hindus without initially realizing how diverse and distinct the religious communities among the Hindus were. Today, both terms are used popularly by both

Hindus and others to refer to their religious life, but at best these terms serve only to distinguish Hindus from other religious groups such as Muslims and Christians. "Hinduism" is useful only generally to refer to a cluster of mutually distinct beliefs and related practices ranging from animism to Tantric occultism to polytheism to theism and impersonal monism. These typically have warrant in Hindu texts which provide a rich treasury of symbols that are understood, combined, and used very differently. Though there is no unified religious entity that corresponds to the term "Hinduism," one can speak intelligently of Hindu traditions. What follows is a description of the history and development of those traditions.

Vedic Texts. Most Hindu traditions draw selectively upon a body of authoritative religious texts called Vedas which were written down in the 1500–300 B.C. period by the priests of warlike and nomadic Aryans from Eastern Europe who conquered and settled in the Indus River Valley of present-day Pakistan. These texts in four parts (Samhitas, Brahmanas, Aranyakas, and Upanishads) express their early beliefs and practices (Rig Veda) as well as later changes that occurred as they reinterpreted and modified traditional sacrifices to the deities and speculated about the primary source of life and experience (Brahman). The Vedas are known as *shruti* (that which is heard) to distinguish from later literature, also authoritative to many, called *smriti* (that which is remembered). Examples of smriti include some or all of the Ramayana and the Mahabharata.

The Vedas give evidence of an enduring Brahman priestly class assisted by other ritualists who made offerings to deities who inhabited earth, sky, and deep space. Some of these deities continue today to be addressed in worship such as Agni and Soma. Vedic Rudra is known today as Siva who along with deities such as Vishnu, Krishna, and Rama, are widely popular with Hindus. The priests also officiated at the observance of more than forty *samskaras* or RITES OF PASSAGE such as birth, initiation, marriage, and death. Though the number of these rites has diminished in modern times, they are vital to the life cycle of Hindus. CASTE, the stratification of society into classes of people who observe common rituals and taboos, is rooted in the Vedas (Rigveda 10:90) and serves to distinguish Hindus from one another socially and often religiously. The Indian Constitution prohibits civil discrimination on caste lines but the private lives of Hindus continue to be significantly governed by caste rules governing social contact, family life, and marriage.

The Upanishads, last of the Vedas, introduce concepts that pervade formal Hindu thought and mass consciousness. Reincarnation, (*see also* REINCARNATION AND TRANSMIGRATION) not known in the Rigveda, emerges as the notion that the atman (soul) continues existence after death according to conditions determined by karma. Karma is the belief that every act, thought, and attitude has its consequences for good or bad either in this life, the life to come, or both. This law is inexorable in that it affects all persons and cannot be set aside or its operation countered. Reincarnation and karma emerge as enduring notions for Hindus and are basic in revised forms in many other Indian religious communities such as Jains, Buddhists, and Sikhs.

Shastras. The Shastras are additional supplemental literature seen as authoritative though not all are universally recognized by Hindus. The epics of the Mahabharata and the Ramayana were probably composed some time at the end of the Vedic period and narrate myths and legends, some with possible historical footings. The Ramayana is a favorite for its story of Rama who seeks to recover his wife Sita from Ravana, the demon king of (Sri) Lanka. With the kindly help of the monkey deity Hanuman, Sita is rescued; the couple are reunited and serve as models of the ideal Hindu couple. The Mahabharata, larger than the Ramayana at well over 90,000 stanzas of 32 syllables each, contains the Bhagavad Gita (Song of God) whose impact on Hindu traditions is profound and, other than the Vedas, probably unequaled.

The Bhagavad Gita tells the story of relatives who find themselves in opposing armies on a battlefield in north India. The dilemma of the Pandava warrior, Arjuna, is similar to that of cousins in the American Civil War who faced one another across the firing line. Arjuna's servant-cum-chariot driver reasons with him that it is required of a warrior to do his duty and leave the consequences aside. This reflects a widely held view, reinforced in later Hindu literature, that the way to liberation is to perform socially required acts without attachment to their merits and consequences. Karma in the Bhagavad Gita has as one of its notions the idea that acts done with detachment do not have bad effects. Arjuna is finally convinced he should do his duty but the text shifts the reader's attention from the battlefield issue to a startling revelation that the chariot driver is in reality Krishna, the Supreme Lord and God of the universe. His message to Arjuna and the reader is that liberation *(moksha)* is possible by the grace of Krishna for those who worship him in self-surrender. Thus the Bhagavad Gita, which comingles several religious themes, subordinates them all to the doctrine of *bhakti* (devoted surrender).

Bhakti. For most Hindus, bhakti (devotion or surrender to a personal deity) is a daily experience in either the home or the temple and is expressed as *puja* (worship, adoration) in song, prayer, flowers, incense, fruit, and money before a symbol or image of the deity. Popular deities such as Vishnu, Krisha, Rama, Shiva each have wives and mounts such as a bull (Shiva) to transport them. Stories of their lives and exploits are told in Puranas (Old Stories) which were written from A.D. 500–1500. Bhakti is considered of two kinds, perfect and imperfect. Perfect bhakti is when the devotee worships the deity selflessly and without ulterior motives. This is thought to be impossible without the aid of a GURU (spiritual guide) who may himself be regarded as an *avatar* (descent) of the deity. Further, the grace of the deity is necessary for such pure devotion. Imperfect bhakti entails worship that is mixed with personal petitions and requests. Bhakti has inspired a rich body of music and hymns in the vernacular languages of India. Bhajans (hymns sings) and kirtans (musical performances) are an essential part of bhakti piety. Historic temples for major deities are found in such cities as Calcutta (Kali), Puri (Vishnu, Jagganath), Mathura (Krishna), and Madurai (Minakshi, Shiva). Deities have sometimes been combined into a single form and name as in the case of Trimurthi, which combines Vishnu, Shiva, and Brahma. Many deities have fascinating biographies and mythologies. Krishna is known in the Bhagavad Gita as Supreme Deity but in the Puranas as mischievous prankster and womanizer. Vishnu has ten avatars, including the Buddha and Krishna. Siva is known for his fierce demeanor against opponents as well as his generative powers symbolized by the *lingam* (stone phallic shaft). Shiva's wife Parvati (also Durga, Uma, Kali) has her own following centering in a widely celebrated festival called Durga Puja. Many Hindus worship more than one of the many regional and pan-India deities with no sense of impropriety or contradiction since each has special qualities and appeal.

Hindu Religious Thought. While the alleged 330,000,000 gods of India defy easy classification and comprehensive study, Hindu thinkers have systematized in logical and defensible terms the meaning they derive from their religious literature. Thus, Hindu thinkers and their followers established unique positions, debated their merits with each other, and further competed with highly refined proposals of others such as Buddhists and Jains. There are many significant religious systems among which are Advaita Vedanta, Vishishtadvaita, Dvaita, Yoga, Carvaka.

Advaita Vedanta was proposed by Shankara (A.D. 788–820) to resolve unsystematic Upanishadic passages that affirmed views of both theism and monism. Advaita (non-dual) Vedanta is one of several Vedantic systems, each of which claims to authentically interpret the last book of the Vedas and to identify the goal toward which they point (Vedanta). Based upon one of the major themes of the Upanishads, Shankara regarded highest reality (Nirguna Brahman) as non-dual, without attributes, and impersonal which, through *maya* (occult power) the universe was mysteriously created. The misinformed ignorantly *(avidya)* take Brahman as a personal deity (Ishvara, Saguna Brahman) which is a useful position until one discovers highest reality. Shankara thus accommodates bhakti while pointing seekers beyond it to the higher goal of moksha (liberation) through an intuitive and unmediated apprehension of reality, thus ending samsara (the rounds of birth and death due to reincarnation). Moksha is the unitary experience by which the soul is made one with Brahman much as a drop of water is dropped into the ocean.

Vishishtadvaita (qualified non-dualism) was Ramanuja's (A.D. 1017–1073) rejection of Advaita and constitutes a defense of bhakti since he refused to regard Ishvara, which for him was Vishnu, as something to be sublated through a non-dual experience. The world was created by a personal god who had qualities which included maya (power to create) through which matter (prakriti) and souls were formed. The world and souls are real yet derived and dependent, having no existence independent of Brahman. He spoke of Brahman as the soul of the world and the world as the body of Brahman. Liberation was possible by meditation and the grace of the deity, thus ending samsara. The soul, like fish in water, is enveloped in and totally surrounded by the deity but not identical to Brahman as in Shankara.

Dvaita (dualism) is the third of these above Vedantic positions and as proposed by Madhva (thirteenth century) takes the position that the correct synthesis of shruti and smriti is that highest reality (Vishnu, Narayana), the material world, and innumerable souls are all independent realities. Thus, the central problem of all Hindu thinkers which is to solve the relation between identity/the one and difference/the many is resolved by affirming a difference among five eternally distinct realities: Brahman and souls, Brahman and world, world and souls, souls and souls, and the finite objects of the world themselves. Brahman is thus absolutely independent though it sustains a relationship with other entities not as cause but as source since the qualities found in other entities in limited ways are found perfectly in Brahman. Souls at liberation remain distinct, contrary to Ramanuja who taught that they become indistinguishable in their purity. Madhva is unique in Hindu thought by teaching that heretics and sinners who reject his truth will suffer in hell eternally. The usual notion is that hell is not an irreversible state but given time and good karma one can escape it through the operation of samsara.

YOGA is based upon the Yoga Sutra of Patanjali (second century B.C.). Though the meditative techniques and postures of yoga have in the past and present been adopted to reach very diverse religious goals, Patanjali used it to achieve a distinct religious aim: distinguish within oneself *pu-*

rusha (changeless self) from *prakriti* (changing matter). The truth about these two eternal realities is that there is no connection. But one is falsely led to believe that when change occurs it is the self (purusha) that changes when in fact is only mind (citta, prakriti). Moksha is achieved when through meditation one ceases to confuse the changeless with the changing and experiences the absolute identity of the self and Purusha. The steps toward this goal, ideally guided by a guru, begin with ethical restraint followed by proper postures, controlled breathing, and restricted sense-awareness so as to ultimately still the mind allowing purusha to shine unhindered. The cessation of mental modifications means that the self is known to be unchanging, thereby eliminating the possibility of karmic action leading to reincarnation.

Carvaka is the system defending the belief that perception is the only valid source of knowledge about the real. It is sometimes called Lokayata, meaning only the visible world is real. The world is made up of a complex of four elements: earth, water, fire, and air. There is no place given to the time-honored notions of atman (soul) or Brahman nor to the traditional practices of bhakti, which does puja and requires the services of priests and temple functionaries. Thus, Carvaka is iconoclastic and, in contemporary terms, thoroughly secular. While it has had its historic advocates, many modern Hindus today whose education leads to a materialistic worldview, would find themselves in significant agreement with Carvaka's tenets. This fact alone is enough to warn Westerners against facile comparisons between a "spiritual" India and a "secular" West.

Hindus in the Modern Era. The nineteenth and twentieth centuries have seen Hindu reforms as well as renaissance. Reform societies such as the Brahma Samaj spoke against practices deemed cruel and offensive. The Arya Samaj launched a defense of Hindu ways as a counterattack to Christian critiques. The establishing of independent India as a secular state introduced controls on Hindus and others in the name of public order and morality. Since the 1960s the Western world has seen the introduction of the Krishna Consciousness society, Transcendental Meditation, and groups led by gurus such as Sai Baba and Bhagavan Rajneesh. Thus Hindu traditions have been both constricted and advanced by the cross-currents of the modern world.

JAMES F. LEWIS

Bibliography. R. D. Baird, ed., *Religion In Modern India;* A. Fernando, *The Christian's Attitude Toward World Religions;* G. J. Larson, *India's Agony Over Religion;* J. F. Lewis and W. G. Travis, *Religious Traditions of the Word;* R. Minor, *Modern Indian Interpreters of the Bhagavad Gita;* S. Radhakrishnan and C. A. Moore, eds., *A Sourcebook in Indian Philosophy.*

Hindu New Religious Movements. In nineteenth-century India a variety of forces led to the emergence of new Hindu groups. The Brahmo Samaj (Theistic Society, 1828), a Hindu social and religious reform movement, sought to end offensive Hindu practices such as widow burning *(sati)* and temple prostitution *(deva-dasi).* The Arya Samaj (Society of Aryans), established in 1875, supported some reforms but reacted defensively by claiming the superiority of the Hindu tradition. The Ramakrishna Mission seeks today to advance Hindu social and religious concerns through its many chapters located throughout the subcontinent and the world. The Vedanta Society, now found in many cities of Europe and America, traces its origins to the charismatic efforts of Swami Vivekananda, who effectively represented Hindu beliefs at the 1893 Chicago World's Parliament of Religions.

With the countercultural movement of the 1960s Hindu beliefs, practices, and groups began further advances in the Western world. Strengthened by increased immigration from India, Hindu temples and organizations flourished. Swami Bhaktivedanta Prabupada began to attract celebrities in New York City in the 1960s, leading to the establishing of the Krishna Consciousness Society based upon the teachings of the Bhagavad Gita. Transcendental meditation, with origins in the Hindu thought of Maharishi Maheshyogi, sought to mainstream meditation and mantra through marketing the "science of creative intelligence." Other gurus such as Bhagavan Rajneesh and Sai Baba gained followers. Hindu texts, meditative practices, and rituals have been a deep well from which diverse NEW AGE thought has drawn. However, as seen by many Hindus on the subcontinent itself, these represent less than an authentic continuation of Hindu traditions. But Hindu thought has a history of adapting to the changing religious landscape, which is precisely what is observed at the beginning of the twenty-first century.

JAMES F. LEWIS

SEE ALSO New Religious Movements.

Bibliography. R. D. Baird, *Religion in Modern India,* 2nd rev. ed.; D. K. Clark, and N. L. Geisler, *Apologetics in the New Age;* J. N. Farquhar, *Modern Religious Movements in India;* E. B. Rockford Jr., *Hare Krishna in America.*

Hinz, Hansina (1867–96). German missionary to Greenland. Born in far northern Germany on June 25, 1867, Hansina Christina was the fifth child of a humble farmer. Like her siblings, she was required to go into domestic service. During her years of service, she came into contact with the Moravians, whose simple and Christ-devoted lives led her to call upon Jesus to redeem her as well. Her heart, now seized by grace, was available for service anywhere. Her call to missionary service came via a letter from the Moravian board asking that she go to Greenland to wed a young missionary who was seeking a godly wife. Having determined that this was the call of God, she took to the stormy and ice-laden seas in March 1895, to meet her future husband.

Arriving with only the clothing on her back, Hansina met and married Johannes Hinz. Over the next year, Hansina served her husband and the people with a generous and loving heart. This service was short-lived, however, as she fell ill after the birth of their daughter and died eight days later. While her contribution was limited in duration, Hansina's life is a testimony of "that right missionary stuff" that relies completely on the grace and strength of God and goes where he wills in order to win victories in the most remote and seemingly unhopeful fields.

WENDY S. LARSON

Bibliography. E. C. Dawson, *Heroines of Missionary Adventure;* H. G. Schneider, *Hansina Hinz: A True Story of the Moravian Missions in Greenland.*

Hispanic Evangelical Theologies. The Iberian Christianization of the Americas after 1492 was carried on as part of the military conquest, within the frame of a political theology inherited from the medieval schools and the COUNTER-REFORMATION. Missionaries allied with secular power were able to coerce the people they were evangelizing instead of persuading them. A feudal social order, justified by theological discourse, was transplanted to the Americas. So the first original theological work in the continent was the critical missiology of the Dominican Bartolomé de las Casas and of Jesuit JOSÉ DE ACOSTA. The latter's book *De procuranda indorum salute* is a theological reflection about the best way to evangelize the indigenous peoples.

After independence from Spain (1810–24) Protestant missionaries who carried out Bible distribution and evangelism through the nineteenth century had an evangelical pietist outlook. Their basic Protestant tenets were strengthened by the debate with established Catholicism and, because of the declining Christendom situation in which they worked, Christology became the first privileged theme demanded by their missionary theology. The work of four generations may be recognized.

First were the *Pioneers*, basically missionaries. A lasting contribution because of his contextual frame and evangelistic thrust came from Scottish Presbyterian JOHN ALEXANDER MACKAY (1889–1983). A missiological exploration around the theme of Christ in Latin American culture was the central concern in his classic work *The Other Spanish Christ* (1933). He analyzed the popular images of Jesus as either an infant child in his big mother's arms or a bleeding victim and concluded that it was basically a docetic Christ. Mackay's missiological agenda was designed as an evangelical response at the top of which was Christology, an effort to proclaim the Jesus of the Gospels in a contextual way, and to stress Jesus as the resurrected Lord and the consequent ethical demands of faith in him.

Next was the generation of *Founders*, Latin American evangelical thinkers such as Gonzalo Báez-Camargo and Alberto Rembao whose works were journalistic and homiletical in style but embodied a rich biblical Christology, emphasizing the humanity of Jesus Christ.

After World War II a new generation of *Ecumenical Thinkers* developed. They participated in the growing ecumenical movement and were influenced by European and American mainline Protestantism. Men such as EMILIO CASTRO, Mortimer Arias, and José Míguez Bonino were influenced theologically by Karl Barth but never lost the evangelical thrust received from previous generations. Their reflection focused on the mission of the church in a changing continent. When liberation theologies developed within Catholicism, these theologians adopted it with a measure of criticism but they did not make any specific Protestant contribution to the debate. Their influence was limited to mainline churches, the smaller and less evangelistic within Latin American Protestantism.

Within the social tensions of the 1960s, Protestantism in Latin America became sharply divided and within the more conservative camp rose a new generation of *Evangelical Thinkers*. Their work developed within the frame of evangelistic and missionary conferences such as the Bogota Congress on Evangelism (CLADE I, 1969) in which the first steps were taken to found the Latin American Theological Fraternity in 1970. Thus theological work has had a basically missiological agenda.

Evangelical theologians worked first in a *critical task*, which included an ongoing debate with the liberation theologies that dominated the theological scenario in the 1970s and 1980s. A systematic critical approach was developed by Andrew Kirk, EMILIO A. NÚÑEZ, and Samuel Escobar. Daniel Schipani gathered several other contributions in a collective volume from an Anabaptist perspective. What is distinctive of the evangelical stance is an emphasis on the primacy of biblical authority in theological method and the demand to keep evangelistic activity at the center of the mission of the church. Their critical task has also included a consistent debate against the theological assumptions of Church Growth missiology (*see also* CHURCH GROWTH MOVEMENT).

The *constructive task* of this generation has been the development of a theology of mission that expresses the dynamic reality and the missionary thrust of the Latin American Evangelical churches, in order to provide a solid biblical basis for new contextual patterns of evangelism and discipleship. They have worked on the assumption that commitment to biblical authority is more than paying lip service to it. Rather it requires a fresh exploration into the depths of the biblical text, with the questions raised by the Latin American context, not limiting itself to the area of soteriology but to fresh explorations into a biblically based social ethics.

An example of this twofold approach is found in the work of RENÉ PADILLA that offers a missiological reflection based on detailed EXEGESIS of the biblical text. He takes liberation themes but works with them, incorporating the missionary thrust and the evangelistic passion of the evangelical perspective. Valdir Steuernagel works in the development of a more systematic missiology. Orlando Costas' approach was less polemical against liberation theologies, and more pragmatic about Church Growth missiology, in a continuous dialogue with missiology and ecclesiology from ecumenical theologians. Along similar lines Guillermo Cook has worked in ecclesiology. A growing number of Pentecostal theologians such as Norberto Saracco and Ricardo Gondim are contributing to the ongoing reflection.

The themes and style of this Latin American evangelical theology are related to the daily pastoral and evangelistic practice of these thinkers more than to the demands of academic debate in the European or North American settings. The urgency of the questions is also determined by the need for a radical departure from the Constantinian pattern of a missionary enterprise that relied on military power, economic conquest, and technological prowess, and in its stead a fresh look at the biblical pattern for mission. Their search coincided with the rediscovery of the Johannine pattern for mission to which JOHN STOTT contributed since the WORLD CONGRESS ON EVANGELISM (BERLIN CONGRESS 1966). This explains also the contribution of Latin Americans such as Samuel Escobar and René Padilla to the theological work of the LAUSANNE MOVEMENT after 1974. Other foci for their global dialogue have been the Theological Commission of the WORLD EVANGELICAL FELLOWSHIP and the International Fellowship of Evangelical Mission Theologians (INFEMIT). In the case of Latin America most of the contributors to this dialogue have come from the Latin American Theological Fraternity. A new and important expression of Hispanic theologies comes from the Hispanic minority in the United States. Outstanding theological work has been done in historical theology by Justo L. González and in spirituality and social ethics by Eldin Villafañe.

SAMUEL ESCOBAR

Bibliography. M. Arias, *The Great Commission;* G. Cook, *The Expectation of the Poor;* O. E. Costas, *Theology of the Crossroads in Contemporary Latin America;* idem, *Christ Outside the Gate;* idem, *Liberating News;* W. A. Dyrness, *Emerging Voices in Global Christian Theology;* S. Escobar, *Liberation Themes in Reformational Perspective;* J. L. Gonzalez, *Mañana Christian Theology from a Hispanic Perspective;* J. A. Kirk, *Liberation Theology;* D. Kirkpatrick, ed., *Faith Born in the Struggle for Life;* J. A. Mackay, *The Other Spanish Christ;* J. Míguez Bonino, *Faces of Latin American Protestantism;* E. A. Núñez, *Liberation Theology;* C. R. Padilla and L. B. M. Branson, eds., *Conflict and Context. Hermeneutics in the Americas;* C. R. Padilla, *Mission Between the Times;* V. Samuel and C. Sugden, eds., *Sharing Jesus in the Two Thirds World;* D. Schipani, ed., *Freedom and Discipleship;* V. R. Steuernagel, *The Theology of Mission in Relation to Social Responsibility Within the Lausanne Movement;* E. Villafañe, *The Liberating Spirit.*

History of Missions. *The Apostolic Age.* The story of how the followers of a first-century itinerant Jewish preacher spread his message of God's kingdom to the entire world is amazing. The initial conquest of the Roman Empire and the subsequent planting of the Christian church around the earth were the result of the witness of countless believers. A great number of these missionaries are known, but there is an even greater number whose names are unknown to subsequent generations. This lack of a complete history forces us to recognize that God empowered ordinary believers to carry out the missionary task. While Jesus limited his ministry to the areas of Judea and Galilee, with occasional forays into non-Jewish territory, he gave his disciples specific instructions to be his witnesses in "Jerusalem, Judea, Samaria and even to the remotest parts of the earth" (Acts 1:8). The Acts of the Apostles is organized along that plan, with the gospel emanating in an ever-increasing circle. With the coming of the Holy Spirit on the day of Pentecost, the gospel was preached in Jerusalem to Jews and proselytes "from every nation under heaven" (Acts 2:5).

The first persecution that dispersed the church after the stoning of STEPHEN (Acts 7) resulted in the scattering of the believers throughout Judea, Samaria (Acts 8:1), Phoenicia, Cyprus, and Antioch (Acts 11:19–20). It is noteworthy that the movement commanded by Jesus to disciple the nations only commenced with PERSECUTION. This theme of God's using what seemed like tragic events to propagate the gospel is repeated throughout history. The bringing of the gospel to the Samaritans bridged two major hurdles, religion and culture. The first recorded preaching to Gentiles is Peter's interaction with Cornelius (Acts 10). Some of those who were scattered because of persecution went to Antioch, where they shared the message with Gentiles (Acts 11:20). Since these Gentile converts were not proselytes, it is not strange that the disciples were first called Christians in Antioch to distinguish them from a sect of Judaism (Acts 11:26). The missionary journeys of Paul originated from this church, the Holy Spirit directing the sending of Paul and Barnabas (Acts 13:2ff.), indicating where Paul and his team were forbidden to preach the gospel (Acts 16:6–10). At the end of Acts Paul is in Rome preaching Christ unhindered while awaiting the disposition of the charges against him.

The early expansion of the church is a paradigm for understanding how the gospel traveled around the world in the succeeding two millennia. Under the *Pax Romana* the gospel spread rapidly in the major centers of commerce and government. Even during Jesus' ministry, the gospel had penetrated government circles (cf. Luke 8:3, where Joanna, the wife of Chuza, Herod's steward, is numbered among the circle that traveled with Jesus). Paul can write from Rome that the reason for his imprisonment is well known in the palace (Phil. 1:13). This interest in Christianity by the ruling authorities is indicative of the interaction that the gospel would have throughout history. Up through the twentieth century, the conversion of a ruler often meant gaining at least the nominal adherence of that ruler's subjects to Christianity. The close connection between the ruler's religion and the subjects' adherence is particularly pronounced through to the sixteenth century in Europe, and it is always common in close knit societies.

The interaction of the gospel with commerce is something that is seen in Acts and has been repeated in various periods of missionary work. At times the gospel was bad for business (Acts 16:19; 19:23ff.). The commercial motive drove the sponsors of both Catholic and Protestant missions. Another theme that is repeated is the interaction of the gospel with other religions. The main rivals of the Christian faith in the first century were the mystery religions; elements of these religions addressed similar questions answered in the Christian gospel. There was a spiritual hunger that the gospel could meet. However, the pagan religions did not give in easily, necessitating POWER ENCOUNTERS such as those in Acts (e.g. 6:8; 8:9ff.; 13:6ff.; 16:16ff.)

The First 500 Years. As we do not know the identity of the disciples who first preached to the Gentiles in Antioch, so we do not know who first preached the gospel in Rome. But Paul found believers there to welcome him. The earliest converts were most likely from the lower classes. However, during the persecution under the emperor Domitian (c. A.D. 96), a cousin of the emperor was put to death and his wife banished because of "sacrilege," the usual charge against Christians. Some take this as an indication of the penetration of the gospel to the highest reaches of society. At the end of the first century and throughout the second century, severe persecutions arose against Christians because of their refusal to pay homage to the Roman gods. Their loyalty to Christ alone as God earned them the name atheists since they would not acknowledge the Roman pantheon of deities. Justin Martyr (c. 100–165) was one of the early apologists who sought to defend the Christian faith against misrepresentation. By the year 251, there is an estimate of the Christian population in Rome numbering thirty thousand. The persecution did not eliminate the church, as the clear testimony of the martyrs often bore eloquent witness to the reality of the Christian faith. Because of their courageous witness, Tertullian (c. 160/70–c. 215/20) could write that the blood of the martyrs is the seed of the church (*see also* MARTYRDOM).

The gospel entered Egypt at an early date, though again the original missionaries are not known. Alexandria became a major Christian center with teachers like Clement (c. 150–215) and Origen (c. 185–254) holding firmly to the biblical revelation but also recognizing Greek philosophy as a preparation for the gospel. This is the first example of discerning the seeds of a pre-gospel understanding in a people's culture as a forerunner to evangelization. The results of both the Alexandrian model and applications of the same principle throughout the history of the church have been debated. The danger of SYNCRETISM is ever present in such formulations.

Christianity spread quickly across Roman North Africa among the educated colonial classes. These were the first Latin-speaking churches in the world. There was some use of the Punic language, brought by the Phoenicians who had colonized Carthage, but it is not clear that the church ever penetrated to the Berber vernacular of the villages and nomads. By not using the heart language of the peasant population, it was assured that these groups would turn to Islam in the seventh century. The major lesson learned from the experience in North Africa is that the church needs to penetrate the common language of the people. While the church in this area produced outstanding theologians, including the key figure in Western theology, AUGUSTINE OF HIPPO, the theological formulations did not stop the rapid spread of Islam.

The Donatist controversy, which revolved around what was to be the church's stand toward those who deny the faith during times of persecution, further weakened the church of North Africa. Nevertheless, from a missiological perspective it is sobering to note the absence of Christianity today in what had been an influential center.

The earliest Christian kingdom was Edessa, which was one of the sources for the spread of the gospel in Armenia, the second Christian kingdom. Tradition tells of the visit of the apostle Thomas to India. Such a voyage would have been possible; Roman coins found in India indicate a trading pattern. The Mar Thoma (St. Thomas) Christians regard their origin in the ministry of the apostle. The church certainly was in India in the first centuries of the Christian era.

The conversion of the emperor Constantine dramatically changed the picture for the developing church. From a persecuted minority, the church became legal and then socially acceptable. The peace of the church from external persecution provided the opportunity to solve its theological disputes, a process in which the emperors from Constantine on took part. The trinitarian and christological disputes gave rise to what are sometimes called the Oriental Eastern churches, which adopted a doctrinal stance different from the Chalcedonian formulas. These churches were missionary centers, with the NESTORIAN MISSION movement reaching into China.

Even before Christianity became recognized as the official religion of the Roman Empire (A.D. 333), the gospel had penetrated the western and northern provinces of the empire. Irenaeus (c. 130–c. 200), bishop of Lyons, writes of using Celtic as well as Latin in the church, which signifies the presence of the church among the less educated population. When Christianity became the religion of the empire, more direct assaults could be made against paganism. However, the gain in legitimacy was at the expense of an increasing nominalism. Monasticism was in part a reaction to the lower standard of Christianity.

PATRICK (c. 389–461) was captured by Irish raiders from his home in England as a youth. After six years, he escaped and entered a monastery in France. Persistent visions led him to return to Ireland at the age of forty-three, where he labored until his death. When he began his work, Ireland was nearly entirely pagan but by the time he died, Ireland was largely Christian. Later Celtic monks would be responsible for evangelizing large parts of Europe (see CELTIC MISSIONARY MOVEMENT).

One of the turning points in Europe was the baptism of Clovis, king of the Franks. He had married (in 493) a Christian princess, Clotilda of Burgundy, who did her best to convert him. Clovis vowed if the Christian God would help him defeat his enemies, the Alemanni, he would convert. On Christmas day 496 he was baptized along with three thousand of his soldiers. Other rulers had converted, but Clovis was the first to accept, to the extent he understood, the Catholic faith instead of Arianism.

The Dark Ages, 500–1000. The classical world was passing. The barbarians pouring out of the Central European plain overran western Europe. The Vikings raided as far as Constantinople and terrorized Britain and northern Europe. Centers of learning were special targets because they were wealthy, yet even the horrors of these encounters presented an opportunity for the gospel.

These five hundred years were the time when the church attempted to tame the barbarians and make their conversion more than nominal. The three key factors in this period were royal patronage, martyrdom, and monasticism (*see also* MONASTIC MOVEMENT).

Another challenge to Christendom came from Arabia, where Muhammad gathered his followers and provided them with a sense of unity and mission. They swept over Christian lands and within a hundred years of Muhammad's death, all of North Africa and most of Spain, as well as Palestine and Syria were under Muslim control. Checked for the first time by Charles Martel at Tours in 732, Muslims still sacked Rome in 846. Sicily was a Muslim country by 902. Finally in 1453, Constantinople itself fell to the Muslims, ending over a thousand years of primacy in Christendom.

Yet in spite of perilous times, the church continued to be found in new places. Irish missionaries established monasteries on the rugged Scottish coast and evangelized Britain. At the same time a mission was sent by Pope Gregory the Great to the Anglo-Saxons who had supplanted the native Britons. In 596 Augustine and a party of monks made their way to Kent, where Ethelbert (c. 560–616) was king. He had married Bertha, a Christian princess from Gaul and by the end of the year, Ethelbert and ten thousand Saxons were baptized. The Celtic missionaries had slightly different customs which had been preserved in their more isolated settings. While these differences seem insignificant to modern readers, it raised the question that reappears in other ages: Who has the right to resolve differences? In the end Rome prevailed, which set a pattern that endured until the REFORMATION.

The advance of the church was not without compromise, exemplified by Pope Gregory, who advised his missionaries to reconsecrate the pagan temples, destroying only the idols in them. Likewise, pagan festivals were remade into Christian holy days and traditional religious customs baptized as Christian symbols. The origins of the Christmas tree, the Yule log, and even the traditional date of Christmas are examples of this ACCOMMODATION.

There were POWER ENCOUNTERS between the missionaries and the indigenous people. BONIFACE, apostle to the Germans, felled the sacred oak of Thor in Hesse. The gospel made a slow, steady advance through Europe, though it is doubtful that the pagan influences were ever fully rooted out, surfacing again in folk stories of trolls and fairies, with syncretism affecting church life. Some peoples were more resistant to the gospel and many monks were martyred.

The schism between the church in the eastern and western halves of the Roman Empire was not official until the bull of excommunication of

1054 and even then it was only the hierarchies that were excommunicated. However, the drift can be detected earlier in the different theological foci that were developing. The importance for missions is that the eastern church did not insist on the same linguistic unity that the western church did. It is significant that ULFILAS (c. 311–383), the missionary bishop who translated the Bible for the Goths, was consecrated at Constantinople, though his Arianism keeps him from being claimed by the Eastern Orthodox. In the eighth century when CYRIL and METHODIUS undertook missionary work among the Slavic-speaking Moravians, they were opposed by missionaries connected with the pope because of their translation work. The three principles that these two brothers from Thessalonica put forward were the use of the vernacular in worship, the employment of indigenous clergy, and the eventual selfhood of the church. They traveled to Rome, where they were able to celebrate the Slavonic liturgy in the pope's presence. However, when Methodius returned to Moravia as a bishop, he faced opposition and eventual expulsion. Their disciples spread throughout the Slavic lands, giving rise to the circumstances that led to the conversion of Vladimir in 988. PRINCE VLADIMIR, who was descended from Vikings, used his authority to force his followers into the fold of the church, thereby setting one of the patterns for successive rulers of Russia. In spite of its beginnings, the church in Russia has endured for more than a thousand years, at times under repressive rulers who tried to control it.

The Medieval World, 1000–1500. As the Christian church entered its second millennium, it was a mainly European phenomenon. Vestiges of the ancient churches existed in Muslim-controlled territory, the church had a foothold in India and Ethiopia, but the Nestorian work in China had been suppressed. The Scandinavian peoples were initially resistant to the gospel, but by the late twelfth century, the church had been planted in the Nordic lands. The paganism that had been the religion was hard to suppress and still carries on in Nordic folklore.

The CRUSADES are perhaps the least likely vehicle for missionary expansion in the history of the church. Conceived as an attempt to wrest control of the Holy Land from the Muslims, the military adventures spanned two hundred years and resulted in thousands of lives lost. The attempt to use force to convert unbelievers, while it had a seven-hundred-year tradition in the church, was a failure, in part because the Crusaders found it easier to kill the infidels than reason with them. The attempts to witness to Muslims by the humble FRANCIS OF ASSISI (1181–1226) and the scholarly RAYMOND LULL (c. 1235–1315) are bright spots on an otherwise bleak landscape. Lull was martyred in North Africa. Francis managed to preach before the Sultan of Egypt, who is reported to have said, "If I meet any more Christians like you I will become one myself." The lasting legacy of the Crusades is enmity between Muslims and Christians that exists to this day.

The rumored existence of a Christian kingdom to the east of the Muslim-dominated lands prompted speculation. Several expeditions were undertaken to the Mongols, with varying degrees of success. The Christian kingdom was not found. However, the Mongols who ruled Central Asia threatened the Muslim Empire, capturing and destroying Baghdad in 1258 and reaching Damascus two years later. The Nestorian church enjoyed a favorable position under the Mongols it had not known before. But in the end the Mongols came under the Muslim culture and the opportunity was lost to bring them into the realm of the church.

The traveler Marco Polo brought back tales of the Chinese Empire and a request from the Kublai Khan for one hundred scholars to debate the virtues of the Christian faith. JOHN OF MONTECORVINO (c. 1247–1328), a Franciscan, undertook the journey, reaching Beijing in 1294. By the time of his death (1328), he had been joined by three other Franciscans and had been appointed archbishop by the pope. John had baptized several thousand people; however, after his death, the church in China declined because more missionaries were not sent.

The Age of Discovery, 1500–1600. The Crusades fueled a desire to reach the East by circumventing the lands under Muslim control. Voyages of exploration were undertaken to reach the East Indies to secure a trade route for the spices of the East and to attempt to find allies in the continuing crusade against Islam. Prince Henry the Navigator (1394–1460) had sent crews down the coast of Africa. Christopher Columbus tried to reach the East by sailing west and desired to bring the benefits of Christianity as well as securing lands and riches for his patron, Isabelle, queen of Spain. In 1493, to settle a dispute between two Catholic sovereigns, the pope divided the world between the nations of Spain and Portugal with the commission to bring the true faith to the lands that they conquered. All the lands west of the line were to belong to Spain, those to the east to Portugal. When the line was moved to the west a year later, Brazil came under Portugal. The conquest of the New World was accomplished with considerable violence by the *conquistadors.* Some of the missionaries to Spanish America became vocal champions of the Indians. The best known was Bartholomew de Las Casas (1474–1566), who petitioned the Spanish throne for fair treatment of the Indians. Pedro Claver (1581–1654), a Jesuit, devoted his life to ministering to the African slaves brought to work the plantations. It is said he baptized over three hundred thousand slaves.

When in 1534 IGNATIUS OF LOYOLA gathered with his six friends to form the Jesuits, a potent missionary force was launched. This new order was subject to the pope and devoted to the reconversion of heretics and the conversion of pagans to the Catholic faith. By 1640 Jesuit missionaries had been in most of the then known world. One of the original six, FRANCIS XAVIER, was not only to become a famous Catholic missionary, but arguably one of the greatest missionaries of all time. Xavier first worked among the illiterate fisherfolk in India, but news of the potential for evangelism in Japan led him there. One of Xavier's lasting contributions to missionary thinking arose out his experience in Japan. His previous ministry among low-caste people did not prepare him for the advanced culture and traditions of the Japanese. Rather than tear down everything in the culture, Xavier sought to refine and re-create elements of tradition. In some ways, this is an extension of the policy carried out during the evangelization of Europe when pagan customs were incorporated into the faith. It was to have great consequences and some controversy in the missionaries who followed Xavier.

Another great innovative Catholic missionary was MATTEO RICCI (1552–1610), who labored in China. An expert clockmaker, he presented clocks as gifts to the Chinese and when the clocks needed to be wound he used the opportunity to preach. He dressed as a Confucian scholar and allowed his converts to observe the rites that honored Confucius and the family. Ricci's principle was to make the gospel as acceptable as possible to the Chinese and, judging by the number of converts of high rank, he was successful. The question of accommodation, however easy to enunciate, is extremely difficult to practice without compromising the gospel.

Roman Catholic Missions, 1600 to 1800. The advantages of the Padroado, which divided the world between Spain and Portugal, meant that the missionaries could count on support, if not overly generous, from the colonial authorities. But it broke down because Portugal, whose population at the time was around one million, could not fulfill the missionary mandate. Thus in 1622 Pope Gregory XV established the Sacred Congregation for the Propagation of the Faith to assume the missionary task. Francesco Ingoli, the first head of the Propaganda, was a remarkable missionary statesman. Ingoli pushed for the rapid development of indigenous clergy and the freeing of Christian work from colonial attachments. In 1659 the Propaganda issued instructions to the vicars apostolic (heads of missionary regions) not to attempt to change customs of indigenous peoples unless these practices were distinctly non-Christian. "What could be more absurd than to transport France, Spain, Italy or some other European country to China."

In India ROBERT DE NOBILI (1577–1656) followed the methods of Ricci by adapting his method of presentation to Brahman customs. While he gained some success with the upper castes, he faced opposition from other European missionaries who accused him of theological compromise. It was only when the lower castes were the target of missionary work that what might be termed a MASS MOVEMENT occurred.

With the decline of Spain and Portugal, France became the great Roman Catholic missionary source. French expeditions had priests with them who journeyed with the explorers into the interior of North America, establishing missions among the indigenous populations. In France a nun of the Ursuline order, Mary of the Incarnation, had a vision of missionary work in Canada. Arriving in Montreal in 1639, the first six members of the order were the forerunners of the considerable involvement of nuns in missionary work. In Paraguay Jesuits established self-sufficient villages or *reductiones* in which they gathered their Indian converts. These were places of safety to protect the converts from hostile tribes and the colonial slave traders. While the church was the center of the community life, from the standpoint of expansion of the church, the work among the Guaraní was a failure because while the Jesuits conducted their mission for more than a century, they brought no candidate for the priesthood forward from the Indians.

The second half of the eighteenth century saw the eclipse of Roman Catholic missions. Among the reasons for this change was the evolving political situation with Protestant nations becoming world powers. In some countries a reaction against Christianity set in and many missionaries were martyred. The final blow was the suppression of the Jesuits by Pope Clement XIV in 1773. The loss of their missionaries and influence was at that time irreplaceable.

Eastern Orthodox Missions. After the Great Schism (1054), the histories of the Western and Eastern branches of Christianity drifted even farther apart. The Tartar invasion was the crucible that forged the Russian nation but it also hindered evangelism. However, there were notable missionary heroes of the Orthodox Church, all of whom shared the same concern for the Bible and liturgy to be in the language of the people. STEPHEN OF PERM (1340–96) evangelized the Zyrians, reducing their language to writing. MAKARIUS GLOUKAREV (1792–1847) worked in the Altai Mountains, incorporating education and health care into his missionary work and being one of the first to see the ministry of women. Nicholas Illiminiski (1821–91) was a linguist who became a brilliant missionary strategist. While he was never a missionary in the traditional sense, he discovered that the use of Arabic script was reinforcing the Tartars' allegiance to Islam rather than instructing them in Christianity. Illiminiski reduced the Tartar language to writing using Russian script and promoted the use of vernacular languages to teach Christian truth. INNOCENT VENIAMINOV (1797–1878) answered the missionary call to Russian Alaska, planting the church among the Aleuts. He also adopted the use of the vernacular and was proficient in navigating his kayak around his island parish. After his wife died, he became a monk, taking the name Innocent, and was made a missionary bishop for the vast territory of Siberia. He ended his service to the Church by occupying the highest office, metropolitan of Moscow. One of the missionaries that he influenced was NICOLAS KASATKIN (1836–1912), who pioneered the Orthodox Church in Japan. Kasatkin's method of making each believer responsible to teach another person mobilized the Japanese.

The common elements in these examples were the use of the vernacular and the creation of an indigenous clergy.

The Beginnings of Protestant Missions. At the time of the Protestant Reformation, the countries that embraced the Reformation were not the world's dominant powers. Furthermore, internal squabbles as well as pressure from the Catholic Church made missions impossible. The response of the Reformers was to teach that the obligation for missionary work had ceased with the apostles (*see also* REFORMATION AND MISSION). There were notable exceptions, such as Justinian von Welz (1621–68), who advocated missionary work. When Holland became a world power, chaplains were sent to its colonies. However, any missionary effort was to come after their primary task of meeting the needs of the colonists.

The discovery of America prompted a new interest in reaching the Native American population. The charter of the colony of Massachusetts included the statement that the principal purpose of the plantation was to convert the natives to Christianity. The first successful attempt was by JOHN ELIOT (1604–90), who learned the language of the Pequots and organized his converts into "Praying Towns" so they could live Christian lives. He is remembered for his Bible translation into the Indian language. DAVID BRAINERD (1718–47), a close friend of JONATHAN EDWARDS, also labored among the Indians. When he died, exhausted by his labors, he left behind a diary that influenced both WILLIAM CAREY and HENRY MARTYN.

The European missionary enterprise had its start in the movement known as PIETISM. *Pia Desideria* written by Philip Jakob Spener outlined the necessity for personal conversion, holiness, fellowship, and witness. As the movement grew in the churches, King Frederick IV of Denmark decided that he should send missionaries to his tiny colony of Tranquebar. He turned to the center of pietism in Halle in Germany for recruits. August Hermann Francke (1663–1727) selected two men, BARTHOLOMAEUS ZIEGENBALG and Henry Plüschau, who arrived on the field in 1706, the first non-Roman Catholic missionaries in India. Ziegenbalg (1683–1719), with no precedence to guide him, unerringly made the right choices and the best of missionary work followed the principles he laid down for Bible translation, an accurate understanding of local culture, definite and personal conversion, and development of indigenous clergy as quickly as possible. He saw the potential of using education to spread the gospel because Christians must be able to read the Word of God.

Another missionary leader influenced by pietism was Count NICOLAUS LUDWIG VON ZINZENDORF, who had welcomed the Brethren of the Common Life who had been exiled from Moravia to settle on his estate at Herrnhut. Hearing that the Danish mission to Greenland would likely be abandoned, he proposed that the Moravians undertake the mission. August 21, 1732, is celebrated by the Moravian churches as the beginning of their missionary work. In addition to the work in Greenland, the Moravians sent missionaries to the West Indies and Surinam (*see also* MORAVIAN MISSIONS).

The Great Century of Missions. The explosion in Protestant missions coincided with the European mastery of speed in the form of the steamship and power in the form of the steam engine. As the European powers scrambled to carve out colonies in the rest of the world, so missionary interest in the spiritual welfare of these peoples increased. The voyages of Captain Cook stirred WILLIAM CAREY, whose *An Enquiry into the Obligations of Christians to use Means for the Conversion of Heathens* (1792) was a stirring call to missions. Carey challenged the generally accepted theological notions that the missionary mandate had ceased. Carey (1761–1834) was a shoemaker and schoolteacher. A self-taught man, he is sometimes referred to as "the father of modern missions." This is not accurate, as Carey knew about the work of previous missionaries. However, Carey's importance was as a forerunner in the English-speaking world which has produced in the time since Carey the overwhelming majority of Protestant missionaries. Landing in India in 1793, he worked as a plantation manager for five years. With the arrival of more Baptist missionaries in 1799, the missionary work progressed.

Carey was persuaded to join JOSHUA MARSHMAN (1768–1837), a schoolteacher, and WILLIAM WARD (1769–1823), a printer, in establishing a station at the Danish enclave of Serampore, sixteen miles from Calcutta. They established a Baptist church and engaged in preaching tours. Their great work was in translation. In thirty years, six whole Bibles, twenty-three complete New Testaments, as well as Bible portions in ten additional languages were printed. They were students of Indian culture, with Ward publishing a book on Hindu culture in 1811.

While the SERAMPORE TRIO had education as one of their goals, it was ALEXANDER DUFF (1806–78) who opened the first English-speaking institution of higher education in India. Duff's aims were both educational and evangelistic and while he only saw thirty-three converts in eighteen years, these were solid conversions. Duff's methods were widely copied in other areas.

ADONIRAM JUDSON (1788–1850) was the pioneer in Burma (Myanmar). ANN HAZELTINE JUDSON (1789–1826) was one of the first missionary heroines, literally keeping her husband alive during his captivity in the Anglo-Burmese war. Judson's work lived on in his translation of the Bible into Burmese. But a greater legacy was to be found in one of his converts, KO THA BYU, who brought the gospel to his own Karen people. The Karens had a tradition of a Creator God whom they had displeased because of their sin. The gospel told them of a Savior who paid the price of their sin. A mass movement occurred among the Karens.

By no means the first missionary to Africa, DAVID LIVINGSTONE (1813–73) is known for his explorations and opposition to the slavery. Son-in-law to ROBERT MOFFAT (1795–1883), who served for forty-eight years among the Tswana people of Southern Africa, Livingstone was not content to stay in one place. Beckoned on by "the smoke of a thousand villages" that had never heard the gospel, he explored the interior. It was his conviction that only as Africa became Christian and developed economically could the horrors of the slave trade be stopped.

Christianity's entrance into China was with the accompaniment of commercial interests. The first Protestant missionary in China was ROBERT MORRISON (1782–1834). He arrived when it was illegal for missionaries to preach the gospel and was compelled to live in hiding. However, his fluency in Chinese was so great that he became a translator for the East India Company. The trade in tea was causing an imbalance of payments for the British as the Chinese demanded silver for their tea. The answer for the British, who controlled the areas that produced opium, was to force China to allow trade in the narcotic. Two opium wars opened China to trade and allowed the residence of foreigners in China and transferred Hong Kong to Britain. KARL F. A. GÜTZLAFF (1803–51) envisioned a grand strategy for evangelizing the interior of China by employing native agents as colporteurs (see COLPORTAGE) and evangelists. Unfortunately, his agents were not always trustworthy and did not carry out the missionary work for which they were paid. However, Gützlaff's work was not in vain as he made the outside world aware of the provinces. Another result of the opium trade and the entrance of missionaries was the T'ai P'ing rebellion. Hung Hsiu-Ch'uan (1814–64) had received Christian literature from Liang Fah (1789–1855), the first ordained Chinese Protestant pastor. Through a series of dreams he conceived of his destiny to reform China through Christian principles as he understood them. The extent of his sect's orthodoxy is debated, but he used the Lord's Prayer and the Ten Commandments, with the fifth enhanced to include filial piety and the seventh to prohibit opium use. This peaceful movement was transformed between 1848 and 1853 into a revolutionary army that had its goal of overthrowing the Manchu dynasty. Nanking was captured by the rebels in 1853 and for eleven years was the capital of Hung's dynasty. The imperial forces assisted by the Western powers crushed the revolt. Ironically Charles Gordon, the British Army officer who commanded the imperial troops, was as much a Bible reader as Hung, whose printers had been distributing Morrison's translation at a great rate.

The great visionary for China was JAMES HUDSON TAYLOR, who founded the CHINA INLAND MISSION to place missionaries in the interior of China. His workers wore Chinese dress and adapted as much as possible to the Chinese way of life. Taylor accepted missionaries who had little formal education, which was a change from the societies that were growing more professional. In most cases his recruits were fine missionaries and many became superior linguists. He also had the mission headquarters in China so that the work could be directed by those who knew the local situation.

The gospel had some success in China so that by the end of the nineteenth century there were about half a million adherents, but it also spawned fear and resistance. China was still in turmoil, with foreign nations making more demands and in some cases occupying territory. Opposition to foreigners and Christians exploded in 1900 with the formation of Righteous Harmonious Fists (Boxers), supported by the empress dowager. The Boxers killed Chinese Christians and missionaries and destroyed mission property. It was the greatest loss of missionaries' lives to that time. A military force from the Western powers finally suppressed the rebellion.

Missionary work in the twentieth century expanded dramatically. The Bible was translated into more languages. As the Bible was made available in Africa, the phenomenon of separatist churches erupted. The result of a vision of their founder, such as the Church of SIMON KIMBANGU, these groups which are variously called Zionist or Ethiopian are conveniently referred to as African Independent Churches to indicate their nonmissionary origin. Their doctrines are typically a mixture of traditional African cultures and the biblical revelation. These indigenized forms of Christianity engaged the concerns of the people and provided an answer to a population transitioning to the pressures of the modern world (*see* AFRICAN INITIATED CHURCH MOVEMENT).

The twentieth century was also marked by a worldwide charismatic phenomenon, that grew out of the Holiness movement. This renewal, which resulted in the formation of Pentecostal denominations, provided a fresh impetus for missionary work. The outbreak of charismatic activity in the older traditional denominations has prompted a new interest in spreading a gospel of power encounters with the forces of evil (*see also* PENTECOSTAL MISSIONS).

In this survey of expansion of the church, several themes have reappeared. The Bible, in the vernacular of the people, is a powerful force for transformation of societies. Empowerment of converts, either by recognizing them as leaders through ordination or through separatist movements, is the way the church grows in a culture. The contagious sharing of what has been experienced in Christ empowered by the Holy Spirit, either by missionaries or converts, is the key to church growth.

JAMES J. STAMOOLIS

Bibliography. J. Beeching, *An Open Path: Christian Missionaries 1515–1914*; S. Bolshakoff, *The Foreign Missions of The Russian Orthodox Church*; A. J. Broomhall, *Hudson Taylor and China's Open Century*; J. Du Plessis, *A History of Christian Missions in South Africa*; F. Dvornik, *Byzantine Missions Among The Slavs*; H. M. Goodpasture, *Cross and Sword: An Eyewitness History of Christianity in Latin America*; C. P. Groves, *The Planting of Christianity in Africa*; M. Jarrett-Kerr, *Patterns of Christian Acceptance: Individual Response to the Missionary Impact 1550–1950*; S. Neill, *Colonialism and Christian Missions*; idem, *A History of Christian Missions*; K. S. Latourette, *A History of the Expansion of Christianity*; idem, *Christianity in a Revolutionary Age: The 19th and 20th Centuries*; S. H. Moffett, *A History of Christianity in Asia*; D. Roberts, *American Women in Mission*; E. Smirnoff, *A Short Account of The Historical Development And Present Position of Russian Orthodox Missions*; B. Stanley, *The Bible And The Flag: Protestant Missions and British Imperialism in the Nineteenth and Twentieth Centuries*; R. A. Tucker, *FJIJ*; idem, *GGC*; A. F. Walls, *The Missionary Movement in Christian History*; M. Warren, *The Missionary Movement from Britain in Modern History*.

Hocking, William Ernest (1873–1966). American professor of philosophy at Harvard University and missions researcher. Well known for his works on the philosophy of religion, in missions he achieved fame as chair of the Commission on Appraisal of the Laymen's Foreign Missions Inquiry. In this capacity he traveled throughout Asia in 1931–32 to study American Protestant missionary work. He edited the findings of that commission, published as *Re-thinking Missions* (1932), and wrote the chapter on "General Principles." This chapter proved quite controversial because Hocking wrote that every religion contains a germ of religious truth and that world religions and Christianity should stimulate each other in religious growth. Hocking's views prompted Hendrik Kraemer to write *The Christian Message in a Non-Christian World* in rebuttal. In later years Hocking tried to clarify his views on the relationship of Christianity to world religions in his books, *Living Religions and a World Faith* (1940) and *The Coming World Civilization* (1956). In these books he stated that he believed Christianity was the best suited to be the world religion.

JOHN MARK TERRY

Bibliography. W. E. Hocking, *Re-thinking Missions: A Laymen's Inquiry After One Hundred Years*; K. S. Latourette, *CDCWM*, p. 254.

Hodges, Melvin Lyle (1909–88). American missionary to Nicaragua and El Salvador. Hodges' name is synonymous with missiology done from a Pentecostal perspective. His classic work, *The Indigenous Church*, published in 1953, was the first booklength volume on missiology published by a Pentecostal.

Hodges received missionary appointment as an Assemblies of God missionary in 1935. He spent his missionary career in Central America working primarily in Nicaragua and El Salvador. *The Indigenous Church* is a clear missiological reflection deeply influenced by the writings of ROLAND ALLEN and clearly Pentecostal in its understanding of the role of the Holy Spirit and missionary activity. The significant growth of Pentecostals in Central America during the last decades of the twentieth century must acknowledge Hodges' efforts to champion strong evangelistic churches whose capability to indigenize their Pentecostal faith has been central to their vitality and continued growth.

Recognition of Hodges' missiological contribution by those outside Pentecostal ranks was exemplified in a 1963 invitation by DONALD MCGAVRAN to be part of the first Church Growth lectures sponsored by the Institute of Church Growth.

Retiring from full-time missionary service in 1973, Hodges became professor of missions at the Assemblies of God Theological Seminary where he served until 1986.

BYRON D. KLAUS

Bibliography. G. B. McGee, *BDCM*, p. 296.

Hoekendijk, Johannes Christiaan (1912–75). Indonesian-born Dutch missiologist. Hoekendijk spent his early years in western Java, where his father served as a missionary. At the age of eighteen, he attended missionary training school in Oegstgeest in the Netherlands followed by doctoral studies at the State University of Utrecht (1936–41). His goals of finishing his dissertation and serving as a missionary in Indonesia were interrupted by World War II. In 1940, he married and, though appointed as a missionary, had to wait out the war to travel to his assignment. In the meantime, he served the Dutch resistance movement. In 1945 he arrived in Indonesia, but, to his lasting disappointment, ill health forced his return to Holland in 1946.

Hoekenjijk is remembered as an ecumenical theologian who made proposals with a secularizing focus in the 1950s and 1960s. He opposed centering our view of God's work in the world through the church ("ecclesiocentrism" or "church-ism"), instead postulating that we should focus on the secular world as the place of God's action. He did this by calling for a shift in focus from the church to a world in need of SHALOM. He did not think that the church was unimportant, but rather that it was only an instrument of God instead of *the* focus of God's attention.

A. SCOTT MOREAU

Bibliography. B. Hoedemaker, *IBMR* 19:3 (1995): 166–70.

Holiness. In Scripture, the term "holiness" most commonly derives from the Hebrew word *qadash* or the Greek word *hagios*. The issue of holiness, however, must begin with understanding the holy God who determines the standard for holiness. The concept of holiness is to be developed via the self-revelation of God's character and nature (*see* DIVINE ATTRIBUTES OF GOD). In conveying the idea of holiness in missions, it must be supposed that some cultures may not think of moral and ethical issues by the norms assumed by the missionary (*see* ETHICS) and therefore the concept of holiness must be introduced by understanding and imitating the holiness of God. It is for this reason Peter reminds the church of the same responsibility which Israel had, that is, all of God's people are to be like God in holiness: "You shall be holy for I am holy" (1 Peter 1:16; Lev. 11:44).

In the New Testament, the Greek *hagios* occurs more than 200 times and has as its basic meaning "separation." A cognate word, *hagiazō*, used 25 times in the New Testament, often means to purify or to cleanse. This can be seen in the Old Testament *qadash* as well. Israel is told to be holy because God is holy, and they were therefore to be separate from the practices and attitudes of the Canaanite people around them. Thus it must be assumed that the basic concept behind holiness is separation from those things which God has determined to be impure or those things which God has separated out for his own use. In

Scripture, a great variety of items can be holy: cities (Matt. 4:5); ground (Acts 7:33); buildings (1 Kings 8:6–11); created beings (Mark 8:38); humans (2 Peter 1:32); the law (Rom. 7:12); and bodies of believers (Rom. 12:1). It would appear that any object, place, person, or act can be holy when used in the purpose of God.

Holiness is also a quality of character. It implies a disposition and attitude toward those things consistent with the nature of God. Believers are commanded to be holy like God himself (1 Peter 1:15) and therefore holiness is the norm for standard of conduct. Holiness, however, must never be confused with religiousness or self-righteousness.

In mission, the focus on holiness has two equally significant dimensions. On the one hand, missionaries must protect themselves from impurities which will affect the way they are seen by the people who are being reached. Since the missionaries represent God to the people to whom they are ministering, lifestyle and attitude are to be compatible with God. This may require special sensitivity toward particularly offensive practices in each culture.

A significant danger for missionaries is that one must be careful that the holiness presented is according to God's definition and character and not according to one's own culturally conditioned assumptions (*see* GUILT). Jesus shocked his generation by being a "friend of sinners" (Matt. 11:19). This judgment against him was based upon culturally defined religious values and not by God's heart and will for lost people. Jesus kept himself pure from immorality and did not sin in any fashion, but he also kept himself pure from the religious hypocrisy of his day.

The second dimension of missiological holiness is separation from cultural influences in the field of service. There are always dangers related to striving for acceptance by the people to whom one is ministering, especially in a foreign culture (*see* EXTENT OF MISSIONARY IDENTIFICATION). Missionaries are trained and conditioned to be culturally relevant. This could possibly lead to unknowingly compromising the holy standards of God in order to be admitted into the new community. God's standards and character must always be in focus and the missionary must be able to evaluate each situation to guard God's holiness. The highest goal is not to be accepted by the new culture, but to correctly demonstrate God's holy character to those who must understand God's message of sin and salvation.

L. E. GLASSCOCK

Bibliography. B. A. Demarest, *BEB*, I:984–85; E. Russell, *ZPBD*, pp. 357–58; A. J. Saldarini, *HBD*, pp. 264–65; H. Seebass, *NIDNTT*, II:223–38; R. H. Strachan, *DAC*, 1:566–71; W. I. Thomas, *The Mystery of Godliness*.

Holiness Missions. *See* WESLEYAN/HOLINESS MISSIONS.

Holism, Biblical. Holism is the philosophy that the whole is greater than the sum of its parts. In reaction, holism, explained biblically, has been claimed as a unifying concept within the Christian worldview.

The Greek word *holos,* meaning whole, wholly, or complete is used by Matthew (5:29–30), Luke (Acts 3:16), John (9:34), James (1:4), and Paul (1 Thess. 5:23). Jesus (John 7:23) and Peter (Acts 3:16) are quoted using it. The English "wholly" and "holy" (Greek *hagios*), frequently confused, are not the same, although the latter is impossible without the former. The Hebrew word closest to *holos* is possibly *shalom.*

Biblical holism is based on Christ's lordship over every part of life—where people who are in right relationship with God and one another (relationship), are responsibly managing the resources entrusted by him (stewardship), in ways that show that those resources belong to God (ownership).

Sin also affects life holistically: relationships are broken, stewardship is affected, and God's ownership is ignored or usurped (Gen. 3:1–10). Every part of life shows the pain of the fall (Gen. 3:14–24). Redemption is about reversing the effects of the fall; it is multidimensional (Isa. 42:6–7).

God called the community of Israel to a shalom life (Mic. 6:8) that G. E. Wright sees as a paradigm or model for the holistic kingdom living of the New Testament community. The promises of a redeemed humanity and a new heaven and earth (Rom. 8:18–23; Rev. 21:1–5) reflect God's desire for the ultimate wholeness in the creation. If God acts holistically from Genesis to Revelation, dare we do less than that?

Mission is then no longer seen in terms of priorities, but as parts of a whole. "The scope of the gospel is the same as the scope of sin and its effects. Because sin is holistic, it is imperative that the gospel be holistic" (Athyal).

We discover three dimensions of the whole gospel: words proclaim the truth of God (the traditional focus of evangelicals); signs proclaim the power of God (most loved by Pentecostals and charismatics); and deeds proclaim the love of God (a strength of liberals and social activists). Each is a part of the Good News, but the gospel is not fully proclaimed until all three dimensions are experienced and understood; it is "both the truth and love and the power of God" (Hathaway).

Any of the three dimensions is an appropriate starting point for mission: word is for those who need to know, deed is for those who need to have, sign is for those who need to experience the power of God. Since we live in a world full of un-wanted words, the starting point is often deed or sign. Both deed and sign need explaining; in this way the Word that brings faith is received (Rom. 10:17).

There is room for all the gifts of the Spirit in holistic mission. The best missionary teams are groups of diversely gifted people representing the three dimensions of mission. "The Christian community is to be a sign of the kingdom in which evangelism, social action and the Spirit are present and inseparably related" (McAlpine).

As a result, a new focus is needed in training. This focus involves an orientation to kingdom wholeness, giving as much weight to sign and deed as to Word.

Finally, biblical holism in mission is a call to re-hearing Scripture in community, putting process before program, people before structure, context before tradition, and having a commitment to continual learning. Wherever this is happening people are entering the kingdom of Christ.

JOHN STEWARD

SEE ALSO Evangelism and Social Responsibility.

Bibliography. B. Bradshaw, *Bridging the Gap*; D. J. Hesselgrave, *EMQ* 35:3 (1999): 278–84; T. McAlpine, *By Word, Work and Wonder*; B. Myers, *EMQ* 35:3 (1999): 285–87; J. Steward, *Where God, People and Deeds Connect.*

Holistic Mission. Holistic mission is concerned with ministry to the whole person through the transforming power of the gospel. While holistic mission affirms the functional uniqueness of evangelism and social responsibility, it views them as inseparable from the ministry of the kingdom of God. Therefore, holistic mission is the intentional integration of building the church and transforming society.

Scriptural Foundation. Holistic mission begins with creation in perfect harmony under the lordship of God (Gen. 1–2) and humans in relationship with their Creator as stewards of his creation (Gen. 1:27–30). The entry of sin and consequent judgment affected every aspect of creation (Gen. 3; Rom. 3:23; 6:23), yet God did not abandon humankind but sought to redeem them by calling out a people for himself (Gen. 12:1–3; Exod. 15:2–13). His people were to be an obedient and holy nation (Exod. 19:5–6), living as stewards of the land he gave them (Deut. 4:1–8, 32–40), so that in obedience they might "enjoy long life" (Deut. 6:1–3). The law prescribed the theological, social, and economic dimensions of God's rule, symbolized by the Hebrew word SHALOM (Mal. 2:5).

The record of God's people is one of struggle and failure to maintain their allegiance, resulting in judgment (2 Kings 17:7–20; 2 Chron. 36:15–19). During this period, the prophets denounced Israel for her sins (Isa. 5:1–7; Amos

2:6–16), calling her to live according to God's will (Jer. 22:3–5; Hos. 6:6; Mic. 6:8). The failure that resulted in judgment also held the promise that a redeemer would come who would establish the kingdom characterized by *shalom* (Isa. 2:4; 9:6–7; 42:1–4; Jer. 31:31–34).

Throughout his ministry, Jesus announced the kingdom (Mark 1:15; Luke 16:16). As the fulfillment of the prophetic hope, Jesus brought *shalom* (Luke 1:32–33, 79; 2:14), which includes reconciliation with God through repentance (Matt. 4:16) leading to salvation (John 1:1–18; 3:16) and transformed relationships (Matt. 5–7; Luke 6; John 13:34–35). In establishing the kingdom, Jesus reclaimed that which was lost in the fall (Matt. 13:31–33) and called his followers to do the same (John 20:21). The church, as the community of God's redeemed people (Matt. 18:20; Rom. 12:5–8; 1 Cor. 12; Eph. 4:1–16; 1 Peter 4:10–11), is called to fulfill the mission of Christ in creation (Eph. 1:20–23; 3:10–11).

Holistic mission is the commitment to all that the church is called to do, which includes the GREAT COMMISSION (Matt. 28:18–20) and the GREAT COMMANDMENT (Matt. 22:37–40).

Critical Issues. Central to the concerns of holistic mission is the relationship between evangelism and social responsibility. The contemporary concern arose out of the fundamentalist and liberal movements of the early twentieth century. The liberal movement moved toward a conciliar position with other religions and away from the issue of conversion, emphasizing cooperation on issues of social concern. In a strong reaction against the social gospel, evangelical missions emphasized the UNIQUENESS OF CHRIST as the only way of salvation and made evangelism the primary emphasis of the MISSIONARY TASK.

Evangelical concern over the relationship between evangelism and social concern has contributed to the multiplication of specialized organizations. This dichotomy has been reflected in the traditional evangelical missions emphases on evangelism and church planting despite their widespread involvement in education, health, and development. Growing out of the concerns for social needs, evangelical relief and development organizations have multiplied. Unlike traditional missions, the relief and development groups have concentrated on physical and social needs, cooperating with other groups in their efforts (*see also* DEVELOPMENT).

In the past two decades a shift has occurred, which is evident by comparing the Lausanne Covenant (1974) with the Manila Manifesto (1989). Both documents focus on evangelism, yet the latter emphasizes the issue of the whole gospel, demonstrating the wide acceptance of social concern as an integral part of the Good News of Christ.

Current literature is exploring the biblical nature of transformation, the effects of differing worldviews, and the church's role in development. The internationalization of missions (*see* GLOBALIZATION) and the increased cooperation among organizations have functionally expanded the view of the church's role in the world and the necessity for a greater understanding of holistic mission.

DOUGLAS MCCONNELL

Bibliography. B. Bradshaw, *Bridging the Gap: Evangelism, Development and Shalom;* T. H. McAlpine, *By Word, Work and Wonder;* J. Matthews, *EMQ* 35:3 (1999): 290–98; D. Miller, *EMQ* 35:3 (1999): 299–302; A. Nichols, ed., *The Whole Gospel for the Whole World;* R. J. Sider, *One-sided Christianity? Uniting the Church to Heal a Lost and Broken World;* J. Steward, *Biblical Holism*: *Where God, People and Deeds Connect;* T. B. Yamamori, B. Myers, and D. Conner, eds., *Serving with the Poor in Asia*: *Cases in Holistic Ministry;* C. J. H. Wright, *Living as the People of God.*

Hollenweger, Walter Jacob (1927–). Swiss theologian, missiologist, and dramatist. Born in Antwerp into a Swiss family, Hollenweger was raised in Zurich. Though she was Swiss Reformed, his mother attended the Swiss Pentecostal Mission, where Hollenweger met his future wife. In 1948–49 he attended the International Bible Training Institute at Leamington Spa, England. A successful Pentecostal pastor and evangelist, he saw his congregation increase from 300 to 1,500 members, but left in 1958 because he disagreed with the narrow teachings of the denomination. Following theological studies at the University of Zurich, he was ordained in the Swiss Reformed Church.

In 1965 Hollenweger was appointed secretary of evangelism for the WCC, and in 1966 received a Th.D. from the University of Zurich for his survey of the worldwide Pentecostal movement. In 1971 he became the first occupant of the chair of mission studies at the University of Birmingham and the Selly Oak Colleges. His approach to theology combined critical thinking with narrative forms from oral cultures, which included theological stories, plays, and musicals. Considered a world authority on the Pentecostal movement and intercultural theology, Hollenweger created and coedited the series *Studies in the Intercultural History of Christianity*. With numerous books and articles to his credit, he devoted his retirement to writing theological plays and musicals.

KENNETH D. GILL

Bibliography. W. J. Hollenweger, *IRM* 75 (Jan. 1986): 3–12; idem, *The Pentecostals;* J. A. B. Jongeneel, ed., *Pentecost, Mission, and Theology.*

Holy See (*Est. 2000 pop.: 1,000; 0.44 sq. km. [0.17 sq. mi.]*). The world's smallest country, the Holy See (Vatican City) is located within Rome,

Italy. Established in 1929 by the signing of the Lateran Agreements with Italy, the Holy See was created to ensure the continuing existence of a geographic base from which international sovereignty of the Roman Catholic Church could be exercised. Its citizens are almost exclusively Catholic hierarchical figures.

EDITORS

Holy Spirit. The Spirit of God appears in Scripture from creation (Gen. 1:2) to re-creation (Rev. 22:17); from the Old Covenant (Exod. 31:3) to the New Covenant (Acts 2:1–4; Titus 3:5); and, wherever he appears he is the creative, dynamic life force of the Triune God. Who he is and how he functions becomes progressively known in the unfolding of salvation history. Throughout salvation history the Spirit empowers the people of God in making God known and experienced. The New Testament makes clear his deity and co-equality with the Father and Son (Matt. 28:19; Eph. 4:4–6).

The word *ruah* appears some 377 times in the Old Testament and can refer to breath, wind, or spirit while the word *pneuma* appears some 387 times in the New Testament and can be translated by the same words. Approximately 350 times these words refer to the Holy Spirit with slightly less than 100 of these occurring in the Old Testament. The Holy Spirit is especially prominent at redemptive and revelational moments. He gives skill in building the tabernacle (Exod. 31: 1–5); inspires national and prophetic leaders (Num. 11:24–26; 1 Sam. 16:13; Ezek. 2:2); anoints Jesus for his mission (Luke 4:18); and empowers the apostles in proclamation of the gospel to Jews and Gentiles (Acts 2:14–21; 13:1–4).

The Spirit of God in the Old Testament. The Spirit makes his presence manifest during Israel's movement into nationhood, in clarifying and applying the Law, and as the promised Spirit who will empower God's Messiah and make the New Covenant possible.

God's command that Israel build a tabernacle brings forth the Spirit's creativity and power for skill in workmanship and wisdom in interpreting and applying the Law (Exod. 31:3; Num. 11:16). The Spirit is actively involved as Israel attains nationhood. The Spirit of the Lord *came upon* Othniel, Gideon, Jephthah, and Samson, enabling them to deliver Israel from the oppression of the nations (Judg. 3:10; 6:34; 11:29; 14:19). The Spirit of the Lord came upon Saul with power and he prophesied (1 Sam. 10:5–11). The Spirit later humiliates him when Saul strips off his clothes and prophesies (1 Sam. 19:23–24). The Spirit came upon David with power (1 Sam. 16:13). When David sins he pleads: "Do not . . . take your Holy Spirit from me" (Ps. 51:11).

The prophets are keenly aware of the role of the Spirit as they call Israel to holiness. But the prophets are especially sensitive to the Spirit's work during the age to come of which they often prophesy. The Servant of the Lord, who will usher in this age, will be filled with the Spirit to accomplish a worldwide mission (Isa. 11:1: 42:1; 61:1). The Spirit will give God's people a new heart and empower them (Ezek. 18:31; 36:26; Joel 2:28–32).

The Holy Spirit in the New Testament. The sharp sense of discontinuity felt when moving from the Old Testament to the New Testament is alleviated somewhat by the role of the Holy Spirit in the life of Jesus. The degree to which the Holy Spirit appears in the life of the early church, in Paul's letters, and in all parts of the New Testament is truly impressive. Jesus made it clear that his departure would be advantageous over his personal presence (Luke 24:49; John 16:5–15; Acts 1:8). The Spirit of God in the Old Testament quickly becomes known as the *Holy* Spirit in the New Testament. He is the gift of the Father, also called the Spirit of God, the Spirit of Jesus, or the Spirit of the Lord. The New Testament writers can refer to the Holy Spirit on a par with the Father and Son without any need of explaining this as a radical idea. The Holy Spirit is the sine qua non of the Good News (Acts 2:38; Gal. 3:2).

Jesus and the Spirit. Jesus' mission cannot be explained apart from the Holy Spirit. The Spirit launches Jesus into mission, leads him, fills him, anoints him, and gives him joy (Mark 1:10, 12; Luke 4:1, 18; 10:21). The Spirit's presence in his life cannot be measured (John 3:34). All the Gospel writers stress the empowering presence of the Holy Spirit in Jesus' ministry of preaching, healing the sick, casting out demons, and relieving suffering. The Spirit's presence in the life of Jesus confirms for John the Baptist his messiahship (John 1:33). John, as well as Jesus, stresses the importance of the Holy Spirit in the apostles' mission (Luke 3:16; John 20:22; Acts 1:8).

The Holy Spirit as the Missionary Spirit. Mission as glorifying God through reconciliation places the Spirit at the center of salvation history. The statement that "the Spirit of the LORD came upon David in power" (1 Sam. 16:13) clarifies David's statement to Goliath: "I'll strike you down and cut off your head . . . the *whole world will know* that *there is a God* in Israel" (1 Sam. 17:46).

The Spirit comes upon, falls on, clothes and enables judges, prophets, and kings to lead, war, prophesy, and make God known to the world. The new age will be characterized by God's empowering presence through the Spirit. The Messiah, the apostles, and all post-Pentecost disciples are people of the Spirit. While the entire New Testament is Spirit-imprinted, John, Paul, and Luke have the most profound pneumatology.

John: The Spirit as Jesus' Presence. Without question John's pneumatology is the most complex, rich, and exact of all the Gospel accounts. In John's theology the Holy Spirit is the "other" Jesus (14:16–17, 26). The Holy Spirit will replace Jesus, giving an even greater sense of God's presence, teaching the disciples and giving them divine illumination (16:4–15).

While John's pneumatology informs mission, three passages in particular provide a clear view of the relationship of the Spirit and mission. John the Baptist sees Jesus anointed for mission during his baptism and God reveals to him that Jesus will be known as "he who baptizes with the Spirit" (1:33). When giving the apostles the GREAT COMMISSION, Jesus "breathed on them, and said, 'Receive the Holy Spirit' (20:22). Just as God breathed into Adam the breath of life, so Jesus breathes on his disciples. The most detailed outline of the Spirit's ministry in the lives of those hearing the gospel is outlined by John in 16:8–11. The Spirit "will convict the world of guilt in regard to sin and righteousness and judgment." These three themes—sin, righteousness, and judgment—find a significant place in John. John's designation of the source of this conviction as the world indicates the mission application of this passage.

Paul: The Spirit as the Eschatological Gift. Paul is the theologian of the Holy Spirit. His letters are saturated with references to the Holy Spirit. Most of Paul's 145 uses of *pneuma* refer to the Holy Spirit. Paul uses the name *Holy* Spirit about sixteen times. His favorite word is Spirit, leading to some doubt on how best to translate some of his references. For example, the NIV translators see the Holy Spirit in Romans 1:4 and 2:29, but the majority of the NRSV translators see spirit here.

For Paul the Spirit is God's eschatological gift, who cannot be understood apart from the Good News. The Spirit initiates a person into Christ through regeneration (Titus 3:5), seals the person until the day of redemption (Eph. 1:13), assures the Christian of family life (Rom. 8:14), and enables the Christian to live the Christian life (Gal. 5:16, 22, 25). The church is the temple of the Holy Spirit, receives gifts from the Holy Spirit (1 Cor. 12), and makes Jews and Gentiles one body (Eph. 2:19–22).

But some find Paul's rich theology of the Spirit incomplete or inadequate on mission. Why does Paul say so little about the Spirit's missionary role? Is the Spirit a missionary Spirit for Paul? Paul's call and commission comes from a revelation (Gal. 1:16). Paul's theological center can be found in eschatology. For Paul this new age has dawned through the resurrection of Christ and the coming of the Holy Spirit (Gal. 1:1–5; 4:4–7). Paul's conversion and call to mission, coming apocalyptically through his post-Easter experience with the risen Jesus, cannot be distinguished (Gal. 1:11–17). Paul's personal call to mission cannot be traced to the Spirit, but the Spirit is an eschatological gift, who longs for the conversion of the Gentiles (Rom. 15:8–22). Paul emphasizes the power of the Holy Spirit in his mission (1 Thess. 1:5–6). It is the Holy Spirit's power manifested by signs and wonders that confirms his apostleship and authenticates his mission (2 Cor. 12:12). The Holy Spirit gives gifts to every Christian, enabling each to minister for God (1 Cor. 12:7).

Luke: The Spirit as the Missionary Spirit. Whatever other contributions Luke makes, he is a missionary theologian and the centerpiece of his missionary theology is the Holy Spirit. Luke's focus on the Holy Spirit as the missionary Spirit begins with the announcement of John's birth to Zechariah (1:13–16). While the full manifestation of the Holy Spirit awaits Pentecost, an unprecedented outburst of charismatic activity occurs at the birth and launching of Jesus' mission. Zechariah, Elizabeth, John the Baptist, Simeon, and Jesus are all filled with the Holy Spirit (1:41, 67; 2:26–27). Mary, Zechariah, Simeon, and Anna manifest the presence of the Holy Spirit by prophetic activity (1:45, 67; 2:28–32, 38).

In Jesus' life "the Holy Spirit descended on him in bodily form" as he was praying after his baptism (3:21–22). He returns from the Jordan "full of the Spirit" and "was led by the Spirit in the desert," (4:1). After defeating the devil and defining the nature of his mission, he "returned to Galilee in the power of the Spirit" (4:14). In the synagogue of Nazareth, Jesus took the scroll of Isaiah and read these words: "The Spirit of the Lord is on me, because he has anointed me to preach the good news to the poor" (4:18).

Concluding his mission through death and resurrection, Jesus commands his disciples to remain in Jerusalem for the empowering they would need to fulfill his worldwide mission (24:49; Acts 1:4–5, 8). Pentecost comes ten days after Jesus' ascension with mighty signs from heaven, enabling all those present to witness powerfully and persuasively. Peter's words from Joel emphasize the eschatological nature of this outpouring. The Holy Spirit has now been poured out on all of God's people, giving them the ability to prophesy, leading people to "call upon the name of the Lord" (Acts 2:17–18, 21).

The Holy Spirit is the missionary Spirit, sent from the Father by the exalted Jesus, empowering the church in fulfilling God's intention that the gospel become a universal message, with Jews and Gentiles embracing the Good News. The Spirit leads the mission at every point, empowering the witnesses and directing them in preaching the gospel to those who have never heard, enabling them with signs and wonders.

Conclusion. Scripture is clear and emphatic: The Holy Spirit is God the missionary Spirit. He broods over emptiness and formlessness. Whether in the life of Israel, Jesus, or the church, the Spirit empowers the people of God in proclaiming and witnessing to the nations. He is the eschatological gift of God, enabling Christians to experience the "already" of the kingdom of God while living in the present evil age. The Spirit constantly motivates and empowers the church in reaching the unreached.

HAROLD G. DOLLAR

SEE ALSO Fruit of the Spirit; Gifts of the Spirit.

Bibliography. H. Boer, *Pentecost and Mission;* C. Brown, *NIDNTT,* III:689–709; F. W. Dillistone, *The Theology of the Christian Mission,* pp. 69–80; G. D. Fee, *God's Empowering Presence: The Holy Spirit in the Letters of Paul;* G. W. H. Lampe, *Studies in the Gospels: Essays in Memory of R. H. Lightfoot,* pp. 159–200; R. Menzies, *The Development of Early Christian Pneumatology: With Special Reference to Luke–Acts;* R. Stronstad, *The Charismatic Theology of St. Luke;* B. B. Warfield, *Biblical and Theological Studies,* pp. 127–56.

Home Assignment. *See* FURLOUGH.

Home Missions. The distinction between home and foreign missions is primarily that of distance and travel. Unfortunately, the distinction too often involved philosophy, qualifications, finances, and sense of importance. For these reasons, missions in America has had an interesting past and now has a most intriguing future.

For the first two hundred years, most home mission activity in the United States was directed toward Native Americans and black slaves. In the early 1800s, Bible societies began printing and distributing tracts in rural and frontier regions. Sunday schools and new churches were begun in these same rural and frontier areas by both denominational and independent organizations. Later in that century rescue missions, missions for lumberjacks, Jewish missions, missions to Catholics, ministry in Appalachia, orphanages, hospitals, nursing homes, and other singly focused missions came on the scene. The Great Depression and World War II brought major changes to society in general and to the cause of Christian missions in particular. Following the war, an explosion of activity on behalf of foreign missions and a lesser but significant thrust for home missions occurred.

With the building of tract houses, the phenomenon of totally new communities coming into being overnight underscored the need for churches in such communities. Congregations faced the difficult decision whether to stay, move, or help new churches become established. Churches that chose to stay in their old urban communities were forced to operate their programs with fewer people and less resources. Congregations which voted to move lost some of the faithful and their giving, and had to deal with the difficulty of breaking established emotional ties and setting down roots in a new community. Local churches, denominations, and independent organizations began concentrated programs for starting new churches. Unfortunately, these programs were confined primarily to white, middle-class, English-speaking communities.

As home missions took on new life with the challenge of starting congregations in the suburbs, the downside was that a whole new mission field was created in the cities. With so many people leaving the urban centers, churches that remained dwindled in size until many closed their doors and others became shadows of the past.

Even as the vacuum of evangelical witness increased in size, the urban mission field was growing and changing. Houses and apartments that previously held one family of five or six people became home for three or four families with twenty or more people. The sounds of different languages were heard. Cultural interests and practices changed. Old businesses relocated, with new and different businesses replacing them. While new life was burgeoning in the community, church buildings stood dark and empty.

Other changes in home missions taking place during the postwar era included growing ministries such as college/university, high school, and Christian camping. At the same time, two factors reduced or eliminated many social programs which had been part of home missions. These were (1) the increasingly stringent governmental regulations on such subjects as child care, serving of food, and medical care and (2) government programs providing for these same needs.

Three major challenges face home missions in the United States for the twenty-first century. The first is to make the church inclusive. The world has come to our doorstep, with immigrants bringing a great diversity of languages, cultural, social, and religious practices. In addition, many of the poor and disenfranchised of our society do not feel welcome and in fact are not welcome in many of churches. Congregations need to break their present comfort zones to allow the church to be biblically inclusive.

The second challenge is for the church to be creative in adopting ways to reach changing communities. Gated communities prevent initial contacts with people and then control the sale and use of all property. Churches are seen as outsiders and are often not welcome. Self-contained high-rise communities present similar challenges. Gentrification produces new communities within cities and is responsible for dramatically increased property costs. Where property is difficult to acquire or too expensive, house churches and cell churches may become necessary. In contrast to these growing areas, people are leaving small towns and rural America, reducing financial support for pastors, programs, and church buildings. Home missions must promote bivocationalism, multiparish ministries, sister church support, and other ways to ensure a strong witness in these locations.

The third challenge is for the church to be the church in an increasingly pagan society. The church must minister where society is secular and hostile, local ordinances are restrictive, and court decisions are anti-biblical.

As a nation with the third largest number of non-Christians, with ethnically diverse people, and a society that is plagued with racism, materialism, violence, and abuse, America must be seen not as a Christian nation but as a major mission field. Never has effective home missions in the United States been needed more.

JACK ESTEP

Home Schooling. Home education has a rich heritage and is an expression of the historical practice of home- and family-centered learning. Five World War II leaders were schooled at home: Franklin Roosevelt, Winston Churchill, Konrad Adenauer, Douglas MacArthur, and George Patton. Many Western MISSIONARY CHILDREN in the modern missions era have been home-schooled. A whole generation of missionary children grew up under the Calvert School correspondence course.

Home schooling currently takes a variety of forms: correspondence education through an established correspondence course, home school as a satellite of a day school or residence school, in-home tutors, home education under the supervision of a traveling teacher who chooses the curriculum and evaluates the students on a regular basis, cooperative home schooling among various families, and home-based education that is parent-designed and -led.

Some missionary families educate their children at home due to a lack of financially or geographically accessible alternatives. Other parents home school a child because of the particular needs and personality of that child. For others the decision to home school is based on a commitment to an educational philosophy; many home-schooling parents share the belief that the education of children is primarily the responsibility and right of parents. (Mary Hood described four educational philosophies that can motivate home schooling—essentialism, progressivism, perennialism, and existentialism.) Since no single schooling option is best for all families, for all children, or even for all stages in a given child's life, home schooling will not be ideal for every family.

Home schooling, however, offers some distinct advantages, including the following: the individualized instruction can take into account a pupil's learning styles and interests; self-directed learning is encouraged; learning takes place in a secure environment; there is more adult–child interaction than in a large classroom; the flexible schedule can take advantage of the richness of the unique learning environment; the student can have an opportunity to become bilingual and bicultural and to know and appreciate people of the local culture; the child can be involved in ministry along with the parents; family closeness is facilitated and enhanced; the young person tends to be less peer-dependent and less susceptible to peer pressure; in a multinational mission the instruction can be conducted in the family's native language.

In the majority of research studies the educational learning outcome of home-schooled children has been found to be highly positive. Ray, in a study of 4,600 children in the United States, found that home-educated children averaged at or above the 80th percentile on standardized achievement tests in all academic subject areas: language, mathematics, reading, listening, science, and social studies. Home-educated learners have also generally been found to do well in measures of social and emotional adjustment.

ELIZABETH S. BREWSTER

Bibliography. P. Echerd and A. Arathoon, eds., *Understanding and Nurturing the Missionary Family;* J. A. Holzmann, *Helping Missionaries Grow: Readings in Mental Health and Missions;* M. Hood, *Home School Reseacher* (1991): 1–8; E. K. McEwan, *Schooling Options;* R. Moore and D. Moore, *Home Style Teaching;* P. Nelson, *EMQ* 24 (1988): 126–29; D. C. Pollock, *IBMR* 13 (1989): 13–19; B. D. Ray, *Marching to the Beat of Their Own Drum!—A Profile of Home Education Research;* B. A. Tetzel and P. Mortenson, eds., *International Conference on Missionary Kids 1984;* T. E. Wade Jr., *The Home School Manual.*

Homiletics. The term "homiletics" is derived from homily (i.e., a sermon), from the Greek *homilia*, meaning conversation or instruction. Homiletics is the field of theological training dealing with the preparation and presentation of sermons.

The intent of the discipline of homiletics is not just to train preachers, but to prepare them to be as effective in their presentation as possible. Thus, the proper and creative linking of biblical interpretation, writing and speaking skills, and even "body language" is necessary.

Homiletics is an important skill on the mission field. However, it is further complicated by the need to deliver the sermon with cross-cultural awareness and, often, in a language or dialect other than that normally spoken by the preacher.

If anything, skill in homiletics is becoming even more crucial as media technology becomes ever more sophisticated, yet, at the same time, available to the masses. The expectation of being entertained and the shortening attention span make it difficult to reach and impact the mass audience that desperately needs to hear the gospel message and related biblical truth that can transform lives.

In the midst of an increasingly secular society, it may seem to some that homiletics and preaching are outmoded. However, Jesus himself indicates that homiletics and mission will continue hand-in-hand until the end of the age: "This gospel of the kingdom will be preached in the whole world as a testimony to all nations, and then the end will come" (Matt. 24:14).

So, there can be no question that preaching must take place in connection with mission. John the Baptist was involved in such preaching (Matt. 3:1), as was Jesus (4:17). The explosive birth of the church at Pentecost is the direct effect of Peter's preaching (Acts 2:14–41). The overflow of Paul's preaching and teaching in Ephesus spread to the entire Roman province of Asia (southwestern Turkey today; Acts 19:8–10).

The apostle to the nations clarifies the cruciality of preaching by asking, "How can they believe in the one in whom they have not heard? And how can they hear without someone preaching to them?" (Rom. 10:14). It stands to reason, then, that, if the whole world is to hear about Jesus before the end of the age, a virtual army of workers must be sent out into the harvest (Matt. 9:37–38). The training of such workers must include at least basic homiletics.

In spite of the clearcut necessity of preaching and doing so effectively, potential concerns exist in regard to homiletics. For example, from the earliest chapters of rhetoric and oratory, there has been the tendency for golden-tongued speakers to manipulate audiences. By sheer eloquence, or attractiveness, it is not uncommon for a communicator to mold his or her hearers to draw conclusions or take action that is, in a very real sense, against their will. Similarly, the stirring of emotions in seeking a specific audience reaction is frequently manipulative.

Such manipulative behavior cannot be justified, even in the name of the GREAT COMMISSION-based aim of converting the masses of the world to saving faith in Jesus Christ. No matter how laudatory or pious-sounding the end, it does not justify the means.

Preachers involved in the missiological enterprise need to hear and heed the apostle Paul's ringing rebuke of rhetorical slickness and manipulation to the Corinthian church, which was apparently quite susceptible to such skills: "When I came to you, brothers, I did not come with eloquence or superior wisdom as I proclaimed to you the testimony about God. For I resolved to know nothing while I was with you except Jesus Christ and him crucified. . . . My message and my preaching were not with wise and persuasive words, but with a demonstration of the Spirit's power, so that your faith might not rest on men's wisdom, but on God's power" (1 Cor. 2:1–5).

A related tendency in regard to homiletical training is seen in Paul's words. There is a subtle temptation to trust in communication technique, even for those who are committed to the gospel and the divine design of global mission.

However, it is clear scripturally that it is the Holy Spirit that convicts a lost and dying world of its sinfulness and need for redemption (John 16:7–11). It is the Spirit that gives spiritual freedom (2 Cor. 3:17). That being the case, it becomes clear that the preacher testifies as a teammate of the Holy Spirit (John 15:26–27), whose witness is primary and decisive.

Another significant concern of mission in regard to homiletics has to do with what has been called "putting the cookies on the lower shelf." This refers to speaking with simplicity and clarity. Just as it is very common for preachers to add unnecessary complexity to their presentations of the gospel, there is the opposite tendency to oversimplify. It should be remembered, though, that there is a bedrock historical basis for the gospel (1 Cor. 15:1–5) that is true (and, hence, must be articulated and believed) or "our preaching is useless and so is your faith" (v. 14).

There is a related tendency in cross-cultural mission that can short-circuit the gospel message. In attempting to find common ground between the missionary's cultural background and the culture of the hearer, it is entirely possible to grasp for a "lowest common denominator" that over-generalizes or distorts the gospel. This is not to discount the kind of cultural key provided by the "peace child" understanding of Don Richardson, or similar examples (see REDEMPTIVE ANALOGIES). It is only to caution that CONTEXTUALIZATION of the gospel taken too far can blur the timeless gospel in favor of a supposed timely culture-friendly message.

Beyond all these important considerations of technique and strategy, there is still the factor of faithfulness. As Paul admonished his younger associate Timothy, homiletical skill will not always be appreciated by those who need to hear and respond to the gospel: "Preach the Word; be prepared in season and out of season; correct, rebuke and encourage with great patience and careful instruction. For the time will come when men will not put up with sound doctrine" (2 Tim. 4:2–3). Even in the face of such utterly discouraging results, the homiletical practitioner is urged to tenaciously pursue the goal of the Great Commission by continuing to "do the work of an evangelist" (v. 5).

A. B. LUTER, JR.

Bibliography. C. Bugg, *Handbook of Contemporary Preaching*, pp. 474–83; K. Hemphill, *Handbook of Contemporary Preaching*, pp. 518–29; D. L. Larsen, *The Joy-*

ful Sound: Evangelistic Preaching Today; J. Piper, *The Supremacy of Christ in Preaching*; I. Pitt-Watson, *A Primer for Preachers*; H. W. Robinson, *Biblical Preaching*; J. R. W. Stott, *Between Two Worlds*.

Homogeneous Unit Principle. The homogeneous unit principle is a derivative of one of the more significant advances in missiological thinking over the past century: Donald A. McGavran's people movement theory (*see* Church Growth Movement and People Movements). McGavran's most frequently cited statement of the homogeneous principle is, "People like to become Christians without crossing racial, linguistic, or class barriers" (McGavran, 1970, 163). McGavran argued that conversion should occur with a minimum of social dislocation. The homogeneous unit principle has become perhaps the most controversial of all church growth principles because some critics have interpreted it as having racist or classist overtones. Nothing could have been further from McGavran's mind, however. The homogeneous unit principle is a serious attempt to respect the dignity of individuals and the social units to which they belong, and to encourage their decisions for Christ to be religious decisions rather than social decisions. McGavran said, "It may be taken as axiomatic that whenever becoming a Christian is considered a racial rather than a religious decision, there the growth of the church will be exceedingly slow. As the church faces the evangelization of the world, perhaps its main problem is how to present Christ so that unbelievers can truly follow him without traitorously leaving their kindred" (ibid., 155). And in a related statement, he added, "The great obstacles to conversion are social, not theological. Great turning of Muslims and Hindus can be expected as soon as ways are found for them to become Christian without renouncing their loved ones, which seem to them to be a betrayal" (ibid., 156).

A more contemporary term for the homogeneous unit principle is "the people approach to world evangelization." It is now widely recognized and accepted as a primary starting point for missiological strategy. Ralph D. Winter, while still a member of Donald McGavran's original faculty in the Fuller Seminary School of World Mission, gave the concept worldwide exposure through his plenary address at the Lausanne Congress on World Evangelism (1974). When the Lausanne Committee for World Evangelization was subsequently formed, its Strategy Working Group, led by C. Peter Wagner and Edward R. Dayton, published a series of annual directories called *Unreached Peoples*. The AD 2000 and Beyond Movement was initiated in 1989, instituting an Unreached Peoples Track as one of its principal building blocks. The Joshua Project 2000 of the AD 2000 Movement has compiled a list of 1,739 significantly large unreached people groups as primary targets for world evangelization. The AD 2000 motto, "A church for every people and the gospel for every person by the year 2000," is rooted in the homogeneous unit perspective.

What is a homogeneous unit? McGavran's brief definition is: "The homogeneous unit is simply a section of society in which all the members have some characteristics in common" (ibid., 69). A more precise definition was later forged through discussions among missiologists over the years, and now it is generally accepted, using the term "people group" instead of "homogeneous unit": "A people group is a significantly large sociological grouping of individuals who perceive themselves to have a common affinity for one another. From the viewpoint of evangelization, this is the largest possible group within which the gospel can spread without encountering barriers of understanding or acceptance." The "common affinity" can be based on any combination of culture, language, religion, economics, ethnicity, residence, occupation, class, caste, life situation, or other significant characteristics which provide ties which bind the individuals in the group together (*see also* Peoples, People Groups).

The homogeneous unit principle assumes that the focus and presentation of the gospel which has reaped an evangelistic harvest in a given people group might not have the same effect on other people groups, not because of the theological core of the gospel message, but because of irrelevant cultural trappings often attached to the gospel message by missionaries. Missionaries untrained in cultural anthropology tend to imagine that churches planted in any culture will look and sound and act like their own churches. The disastrous results of such cultural nearsightedness are extensively chronicled in missiological history. Many cases are recorded in which the gospel presented by white American missionaries has been rejected by those of other people groups because the nationals' culture was denigrated and ridiculed rather than respected. In the minds of some of the nationals, the missionary was asking them to become Americans, for example, in order to become Christians. The application of the homogeneous principle to correct and prevent such cases is a facet of Contextualization. Although there are differences of opinion about degrees and certain forms of contextualization, the principle itself is accepted as an axiom of contemporary missiology.

C. Peter Wagner

Bibliography. D. A. McGavran, *Understanding Church Growth*; C. Peter Wagner, *Our Kind of People: The Ethical Dimensions of Church Growth in America*.

Homosexuality. *See* Sexual Mores.

Honda, Koji (1912–). Japanese evangelist. Koji Honda grew up in a small town in Fukui Prefecture. Overcoming parental opposition, he was baptized when seventeen and in 1934 enrolled at the Kansai Bible School. During World War II his spiritual convictions often brought him into conflict with the authorities. In 1944 he was drafted into the military. After the war Honda supported his family for a while as a cobbler. In 1946 it was possible to return to the ministry, and a tent erected in the midst of the rubble of Kobe served as a meeting place. In 1947 churches in America supplied a Quonset hut. This was the beginning of the Kobe Central Church, which grew rapidly under Honda's leadership. In 1956 God used missionaries and his Word to challenge Honda to become an evangelist. The same year the Honda crusades began. In 1966 the Hondas with their six children moved to Tokyo and the Honda crusade became the Japan Gospel Crusade. In 1967 Honda joined other church leaders to establish the Evangelism-in-Depth Movement *(Sodoin Dendo)* and served on the executive committee of Billy Graham's Tokyo crusade. When Graham returned for crusades in 1980 and 1994, Honda was elected chairman and honorary chairman respectively.

Honda has played leading roles in many Christian organizations, among them the Pacific Broadcasting Association, Ochanomizu Christian Center, the Association of Evangelists, and the Association of Para-Ministries. In international relations, Honda has played a major role in bringing about reconciliation between the Christians of Korea and Japan.

There is good reason for describing Honda as the Billy Graham of Japan. Honda has conducted over four hundred crusades during the past forty years; he has proclaimed Christ before 1.4 million in Japan and thirteen other countries. His servant leadership was recognized by Biola University in 1988 with an honorary doctorate. Honda in 1995 was also a recipient of Japan's Senior Citizen Distinguished Christian Service Award.

SIEGFRIED A. BUSS

Honda, Yoichi (1847–1912). Japanese church planter and leader. Born in Hirosaki, Japan, of samurai (warrior) lineage, as a young man he was involved in the political struggles that followed the Meiji Restoration of the emperor's authority. In 1870 he went to Yokohama at clan expense and studied English under S. R. Brown and J. Ballagh, American missionaries from the Dutch Reformed Church. Impressed by their piety, he studied the Bible, and was baptized in 1872 as a member of the Yokohama Band of Christians. Returning to Hirosaki in 1874, he became a school principal, and worked with Methodist missionary John Ing in his school in evangelistic activity. He was ordained a Methodist minister. Honda and Ing founded the Hirosaki Church, the first Methodist church in Japan. In time over a hundred Japanese Methodist missionaries were sent out from this church. Honda was appointed president of a Tokyo school that eventually became Aoyama Gakuin. He also pastored the Aoyama [Methodist] Church.

During a period of study in America, Honda wrestled with whether he should go into politics as a member of the first Imperial Diet (parliament), but decided instead to return to his Christian work as president of Aoyama Gakuin School. When three Methodist denominations in Japan united in 1907, Honda accepted appointment as the first bishop of the newly organized Japan Methodist Church. He was also active in the YMCA and other Christian organizations, and represented Japanese Christians abroad at meetings in America and Europe. In 1912, while on the way to a Methodist Conference, he suddenly became seriously ill and died. His legacy was as a statesman, not in politics, but for the Christian community in Japan.

JAMES M. PHILLIPS

Bibliography. R. H. Drummond, *A History of Christianity in Japan,* N. Ebizawa, *Japanese Witnesses for Christ,* C. W. Iglehart, *A Century of Protestant Christianity in Japan.*

Honduras *(Est. 2000 pop.: 6,485,000; 112,088 sq. km. [43,277 sq. mi.]).* Honduras, a Central American republic, was a major center of Mayan culture. In about 1550, Franciscan missionaries began to spread the Roman Catholic faith. Although freed from Spanish rule in 1821, Honduras did not become an independent nation until 1838. It was plagued by more than a hundred revolutions prior to 1932 and has experienced military rule for much of this century. Next to Haiti, it is the poorest country in the Western Hemisphere. Although the Roman Catholic Church is officially sanctioned, there is separation of church and state, and religious freedom does exist.

Protestant missionary penetration did not begin until the latter part of the nineteenth century. By 1859, Anglicans were working on the Bay Islands off the Caribbean coast. By 1891, Seventh-Day Adventists had established work there as well. In July 1896, the Central America Mission became the first Protestant group to initiate organized activity on the mainland when four missionaries arrived in Santa Rosa de Copán. The Plymouth Brethren established work in San Pedro Sula in 1898. By 1911, the work of the Friends had spread from Guatemala to Honduras. Although the PANAMA CONGRESS (1916) assigned Honduras to the Northern Baptists, the first denominational mission to enter was the Evangelical Synod of North America, which began ministry in San Pedro Sula in 1921. The Evangelical and Reformed Church of Honduras emerged from that work. In 1931, the Moravians extended their work with the Miskito Indians from Nicaragua into Honduras.

In 1937, the first Assemblies of God missionaries entered from nearby El Salvador. Then, in 1940, indigenous Pentecostal churches sought the support of the Assemblies of God in the United States to reinforce their work. Subsequently, other Pentecostal groups have entered the country, the most numerous of which is the Church of God (Cleveland, Tennessee).

Because of the isolation caused by mountainous terrain, COMITY agreements continued to be observed until after World War II, when many new evangelical missions entered Honduras. Early progress was slow, but then accelerated dramatically after 1970. Massive outreach through evangelism, Scripture distribution, literature, and radio replaced earlier dependence on educational and medical ministries. Natural disasters as well as migrations and social upheavals occasioned both by the Honduras–El Salvador 100-hour "futbol" war in 1969 and subsequent guerrilla activity in Nicaragua have increased receptivity. Currently about 10 percent of the population is affiliated with an evangelical church.

Although most of the work has been nationalized, paternalism, poverty, denominational competition, and illiteracy have retarded the development of mature leadership. Amerindian ministries have been fruitful, though limited. Most Hondurans are mestizos, and most Indians have somewhat assimilated into the Latin culture. However, some indigenous groups such as the Miskito, Garifuna, Suma, and Tol have retained their cultural identity to a large extent. Outreach to Arabs, Chinese, and other ethnic minorities is limited or nonexistent. However, cross-cultural mission vision is growing.

KEN MULHOLLAND

Bibliography. W. M. Nelson, *Protestantism in Central Ameirca;* C. Alvarez, *People of Hope: The Protestant Movement in Central America.*

Honesty. The issue of honesty and mission calls for a critical look at two sets of relationships. First of all, it needs to be understood in the relationships involving the missionary, the mission, and the donor. Second, it needs to be understood in the relationship between the missionary and the host culture.

In today's missions, when the amount of financial support available for a particular ministry or project is often tied proportionately to the level of productivity, what is communicated to donors or potential donors about the ministry's level of success or failure may prove to be the deciding factor in whether the support, and possibly the ministry, is continued or not. Under such circumstances, honesty in communication becomes a very important factor between the missionary and his or her mission and donors and also between the mission and its donors. Honesty becomes an issue of Christian conscience in being straightforward in these relationships, and it becomes an issue of faith in our sovereign Lord who is in complete control and who is building his church. Missionaries must always remember that they cannot serve God and mammon, regardless of the noble reasons for trying.

As in many such issues, the understanding of honesty will vary from culture to culture. Therefore it is very important that the missionary be sensitive to the cultural definitions and to the standards of honesty in culture. In order to do this, the missionary must have a clear understanding of this issue within the three cultural horizons of missions: the biblical culture, his or her own culture, and the host culture. In the study of Scripture, the missionary will gain a Christian ethic with a biblical understanding of honesty. This may not be as easy as it seems when one considers God's blessing of the Hebrew midwives for lying to Pharaoh about the Hebrew women giving birth in Exodus 1:15–21; or of God caring for Rahab because she lied to protect the two spies as seen in Joshua 6:25. With this biblical understanding of honesty, the missionary must judge his or her own culture. The missionary may find that he or she is laboring under misconceptions of true honesty.

Having done this, cross-cultural missionaries are able to look more fairly at the host culture. The missionary must be able to answer cultural questions related to honesty such as ownership of property or work ethic or what is considered polite. They must gain an understanding of community and of what is considered proper within the host culture. Every culture has an understanding of what is honest and what is dishonest. The missionary must always let Scripture be the judge of whether that understanding is correct or incorrect. As the Holy Spirit sharpens the CONSCIENCE of the people and as the Scriptures inform them of their cultural inconsistencies, they will develop a more biblical understanding of honesty (as well as other moral issues) and their application of it. In this way the culture will move toward a Christian culture in context, rather than a missionary culture.

THOMAS L. AUSTIN

SEE ALSO Ethics AND Guilt.

Bibliography. R. J. Priest, *Missiology* 22:3 (1994): 291–316.

Hong Kong *(Est. 2000 pop.: 5,968,000; 1,061 sq. km. [410 sq. mi.]).* Since Hong Kong became a British colony in 1842, there has been a never-ending influx of missionaries from European, American, and Asian nations. In addition to preaching and establishing churches, there have been several outstanding missionaries who also served as the cultural bridges between China and the West. JAMES LEGGE was a distinguished translator of Chinese Classics. Karl Ludvig Reichelt (1877–1952) was likewise a well respected student of Chinese MAHAYANA BUDDHISM. He constituted interfaith dialogue at the Tao Fung Shan Ecumenical Center. More important, many missionaries and Chinese Christians were founders and collaborators of a variety of social institutions. Christian schools constitute the largest share of Hong Kong's educational system, and missionary participation in education can be traced to the first decade of British rule. The Hong Kong Chinese Christian Churches Union and the Hong Kong Christian Council, instituted in 1915 and 1954, respectively, were developed to enable better communication among different denominations and to support mission work. The BILLY GRAHAM crusades in Hong Kong in 1975 and 1990 stand as examples of collaboration among denominations and Christian organizations.

In addition to such efforts, there are a number of Christian organizations that carry out their mission by meeting the immediate needs of the community. The rehabilitation of narcotic addicts, such as Jackie Pullinger's programs and the Wu Oi Fellowship, deserve special mention.

Hong Kong has played a vital role in Christian missions to China. Between August 22 and September 4, 1843, missionaries to China from several denominations met to improve the translation of the Bible. Although its role as a Chinese Bible printing center was temporarily superseded by other Chinese cities like Shanghai, Hong Kong resumed its importance after the Communists took over China in 1949. In addition to Bible translation, missionaries and Chinese Christians extended their work in Guangdong province, through which a strong reinforcement for Christian missions between Hong Kong and China became possible. The earliest example was in the 1860s, when the LONDON MISSIONARY SOCIETY Hong Kong Mission established its outstations in Boluo and Foshan. These stations, in turn, became sources of converts, support personnel, and pastors. As a result, the To Tsai Church, the Chinese congregation of the London Missionary Society in Hong Kong, achieved independence in 1886.

Between the late 1940s and 1950s, a large number of missionaries, Chinese Christians, and Chinese church leaders moved to Hong Kong, resulting in a significant growth in both number and quality of converts. Leung Siu-choh (1889–1967), once the leader of the YMCA in Guangdong and Shanghai, became the first chairman of the Church of Christ in China Hong Kong Council when it registered with the Hong Kong government in 1957. Another noteworthy page was marked in the history of missions in Hong Kong in 1974, when the Chinese Coordination Center of World Evangelism was inaugurated. Not only did it affirm the role of Hong Kong as a center for Christian missions in China, but it also extended its commitment to other Chinese communities abroad.

With the return of Hong Kong to the People's Republic of China, many questions about the future remain unanswered. The ongoing commitment of Hong Kong's churches to Christ, however, will play a pivotal role in the continuing advance of the gospel in China.

TIMOTHY MAN-KONG WONG

Bibliography. L. Chee-kong, *Stories of Churches in Hong Kong;* J. Pullinger, *Chasing the Dragon;* C. T. Smith, *Chinese Christians: Elites, Middlemen, and the Church in Hong Kong;* D. W. Vikner, *The Role of Christian Missions in the Establishment of Hong Kong's System of Education;* L. Yuet-sang, *A History of Christianity in Hong Kong.*

Hoover, James Matthew (1872–1935). American missionary to Malaysia. On March 13, 1899, following God's prompting after nine years of elementary schoolwork, Hoover applied for and was accepted to serve as a Methodist teacher-missionary in contemporary Malaysia. He arrived in Penang, Malay, on September 9. In 1903, he was transferred to Sibu, Sarawak, where he worked with the Foochow Chinese Colony. This colony had been established for Chinese émigrés, many of them Christians escaping from the Boxer Rebellion. He helped them settle along the lush Rejang River and worked tirelessly on their behalf. Known as "Tuan Hoover of Borneo," over the course of his ministry he planted more than forty churches and helped thousands gain a new opportunity for life.

A. SCOTT MOREAU

Bibliography. T. T. Brambauagh, *CDCWM,* p. 259; F. T. Cartwright, *Tuan Hoover of Borneo;* N. B. Harmon, *EWM,* 1:1154–55.

Hoover, Willis Collins (1856–1936). American missionary to Chile. Born in Freeport, Illinois, he studied medicine. Not wishing to pursue a medical career, he volunteered to work under Methodist WILLIAM TAYLOR in Chile. In 1902, Hoover became pastor of the church in Valparaiso.

Early on, he expressed interest in the manifestations of the Holy Spirit and Pentecostal revivals. After a conference several board members were challenged to "repent and get right with God [even] if it takes all night" (Hollenweger, 172). Several did, and then initiated all-night prayer vigils every Saturday, during which Pentecostal manifestations of the Spirit were witnessed. The Methodists were not pleased, objecting to such practices as "antimethodist." This led to a heresy trial in which Hoover was found guilty of teaching false doctrines, specifically concerning charismatic manifestations of the Holy Spirit. Hoover lost Methodist support and income but stayed at the request of his congregation. The controversy led to the formation of the Methodist Pentecostal Church (IMP), which Hollenweger calls the "first theologically and financially self sufficient church in the Third World" (169). The IMP and a later splinter group, the Evangelical Pentecostal Church, are today the largest non-Catholic denominations in Chile.

JOE IADONISI

Bibliography. W. J. Hollenweger, *Methodist History*, 20 (1982): 169–82; C. E. Jones, *DPCM*, p. 445.

Hope. The expectation engendered by faith in God's promises of salvation provides part of the theological foundation of mission, and helps define its nature, message, means, goal, and motivation.

In the Old Testament, the hope is in God as Creator, who in the face of human disobedience retains his purpose for creation (Gen. 8:22), makes his promise for all the nations (Gen. 12:3), and chooses Israel to be blessed and to be a blessing, as reflected in the Davidic covenant (2 Sam. 7:19) and Solomon's prayer (1 Kings 8:43, 60). The prophetic outlook (e.g., Isa. 11:10; Zech. 8:22–23) is of a future great ingathering of the Gentiles to join *with* Israel in her promised inheritance.

The New Testament takes up such promises (e.g., Matt. 8:11–12; Luke 2:30–32), which become the foundation of the command to disciple *"all* the nations" (i.e., Gentiles as well as the Jews, Matt. 28:19–20). This is connected with the rule of God, the complete restoration of all creation.

The coming of the Spirit (Acts 2) is a sign of the last days and of the new messianic people, which includes believing Samaritans (Acts 8:17) and Gentiles (Acts 10:44–46; Gal. 3:2; 4:6), without their having to become Jewish (cf. Acts 15). The hope of Jew and Gentile alike, as forgiven sinners who rejoice in suffering in this age (Rom. 5:1–5), is Christ's coming in glory at the resurrection (Phil. 2:11; 1 Thess. 1:10; etc.). Paul sees himself as called to the realization of this hope for the Gentiles (Rom. 1:5; 15:12; Gal. 2:7); Peter, for the Jews. Peter places the same stress on the hope (Acts 2:34–35; 1 Peter 1:3–5).

The *nature* of mission must therefore include the communication of the *message*, which includes and holds out this hope to all who will turn in faith to the Lord, for his coming will bring in the kingdom of God (1 Cor. 15:22–24). The immediate *goal* of mission is beseeching all to receive the reconciliation achieved in Christ.

By this they become already the "new creation" (2 Cor. 5:17), which is also the future hope. The goal also includes their being gathered as the church. Further, the goal is that the glory of God will be revealed in the fulfillment of his promises to all the nations. The *motivation* therefore includes this hope of the glory of God. The *means* of mission will include not only the ministry of the Word, but also the fruit of the Spirit, evident in deeds of compassion and in the life of the church. This, with all that it entails by way of social concern and involvement, is sign and evidence of the full realization to come, if it is clearly associated with the message and the church.

The postmillennial and amillennial hopes have been associated with a comprehensive missionary approach in modern times, for which conversion to Christ has always been the indispensable aim, as also for the premillennial hope. The latter tended to avoid the method of planting Christian institutions in foreign mission fields, without, however, rejecting social concern, until this century. When the hope stresses the betterment of conditions in this present world only, as in realized or in existentialist eschatology, then the emphasis is on sociopolitical action.

JOHN A. MCINTOSH

SEE ALSO Millennial Thought.

Bibliography. R. H. Boer, *Pentecost and Missions*; J. M. Everts, *DPHL*, pp. 415–17; J. Moltmann, *The Theology of Hope*; D. Senior and C. Stuhmueller, *The Biblical Foundations to Mission*.

Hospital Mission Work. *See* MEDICAL MISSION WORK.

Hoste, Dixon Edward (1861–1946). English missionary to China. Born into a military family and initially an officer in the British Royal Artillery, Dixon Hoste became the second director (1900–1935) of the CHINA INLAND MISSION (CIM). Converted in 1882 at evangelistic meetings, Hoste transferred his military discipline into his Christian faith.

In 1884 he joined the China Inland Mission. After initial language training in Shanghai in 1885 Hoste was sent to the southern part of Shanxi province, working there under the first CIM-ordained Chinese pastor, Pastor Hsi (d. 1896). Working among young churches and the opium refuges established by Hsi, Hoste became known for his willing submission to Hsi and his personal disciplines in prayer and cultural adaptation. These experiences formed the basis for the missiological convictions in Hoste's later career as an administrator. In 1893 he married Hudson Taylor's niece, Gertrude Broomhall (d. 1944), and so naturally became closer to the director, whom he referred to as "Uncle." Hoste was made acting director in 1900, and became the second director in 1902.

If Hudson Taylor was the charismatic leader of CIM, then Dixon Hoste was the institutionalizing genius. During his directorate the number of CIM missionaries rose from 780 to 1,360, Chinese churches from 364 to over 1,200, "outstations" from below 400 to over 2,200, and yearly baptisms from 1,700 to 7,500. Hoste was an insightful analyst of human character, a reliable source in judging missionary leadership, a consistent advocate for indigenizing the Chinese church leadership, and a model of intercessory prayer. Hoste survived Japanese internment beginning in 1943, dying in 1946 after returning to England.

LAUREN PFISTER

Bibliography. D. E. Hoste, *The Chinese Recorder* 46 (1915): 760–63; idem, *The Chinese Recorder* 48 (1917): 349–58; P. Thompson, *D. E. Hoste, "A Prince with God": Hudson Taylor's Successor as General Director of the China Inland Mission, 1900–1935.*

House Church Movement. *See* CHINESE HOUSE CHURCH MOVEMENT.

Household Responsibilities. How does the ministry-burdened person balance outreach and basic living necessities? Historically, most missionaries, husband and wife or single, were expected to be full-time servants of the Lord. Today more missionary parents have the option to home school or to educate their children in the towns or situations where they live. It is more common to find only one parent in full-time ministry while the other parent cares for the children and household chores.

The standard at which a missionary chooses to live greatly impacts the household responsibilities. The missionary who chooses to live more or less at a Western standard in a developing economy may spend more time in acquiring and maintaining possessions. Missionaries who choose to live with fewer possessions may relate better economically to surrounding nationals but may spend much more time in providing for themselves than if they had more modern conveniences (*see also* EXTENT OF MISSIONARY IDENTIFICATION).

Ministry goals also impact household responsibilities. The missionary who focuses on translation, health care needs, school teaching, or other institutional ministries may have complete ministry contact outside the home. The institutional missionary's home might be their refuge or occasionally a place for minimal outside contact.

But the missionary focusing on evangelism, church planting, and leadership training may, as part of normal household responsibilities, need to have a very open home. It is not the possessions, or lack thereof, that create an effective church planter or evangelist. Rather, it is the attitude toward spending time with nationals. If household work or possessions get in the way of spending time with nationals, ministry will be negatively impacted. The most effective evangelistic and church planting/discipling missionaries tend to have an ability to keep household chores and responsibilities to a minimum, while balancing ministry from the home and visits outside the home. Balance, openness, love and caring are much more important ingredients than the actual amount of time spent on household responsibilities.

GLENN R. KENDALL

SEE ALSO Family Life of the Missionary.

Howard, David Morris (1928–). American missionary statesman and president of Latin America Mission. Born in Philadelphia, Pennsylvania, he was the son of Philip E. Howard Jr., who was editor of the *Sunday School Times.* He received his education at Wheaton College (BA, 1949; MA, 1952) in Illinois.

Howard began his distinguished career as a missionary to Colombia and Costa Rica with the Latin America Mission (1953–68) as assistant general director. He followed this in 1968–77 as missions director and assistant to the president of InterVarsity Christian Fellowship (and director of Urbana '73 and '76); director of consultation on World Evangelization, Pattaya, Thailand (1977–80); international director of the WORLD EVANGELICAL FELLOWSHIP (1982–92); and senior vice president of Cook Communications Ministries International (1993–95). In November 1995, Howard was appointed as the sixth president of the Latin America Mission, the organization where he began his ministry.

Howard has written eight books, including *Student Power in World Missions, By the Power of the Holy Spirit,* and *The Great Commission for Today.*

WALTER A. ELWELL

Huey, Mary Alice (1877–1960). American missionary to China. Born in Jefferson County, Alabama, she was educated at Judson College and in 1904 became one of the first students at the training school for women at Louisville, Kentucky (later known as the Woman's Missionary Union Training School).

In 1907 she heard God's call to the mission field. Later that year she was appointed by the FOREIGN MISSION BOARD OF THE SOUTHERN BAPTIST CONVENTION to serve in Laichow, China.

Huey became the principal and Bible teacher at a girls' school and diligently worked with the Laichow women and children for nearly twenty years. In 1926 she returned to the United States for a brief period of time to care for her ailing parents.

In 1932 she returned to China to carry on her work. However, her efforts were cut short when circumstances surrounding World War II forced her to leave Laichow in 1940. But these trials did not discourage her—nor did they diminish her missionary zeal.

In 1941 Huey transferred to the Hawaiian Mission at Honolulu, where she carried on evangelistic work until she retired in 1946. Through all circumstances, she proved herself to be a competent leader and dedicated missionary.

KATHY MCREYNOLDS

Bibliography. T. L. Scales, *DBA*, pp. 147–48.

Human Condition in World Religions. Common to most religions is the notion that human beings—and, in many cases, the cosmos at large—suffer from some kind of undesirable condition. Violence, murders, and wars; natural disasters such as earthquakes and floods; the inability of people to get along with each other; illness and death; a sense of anxiety and alienation—all of these indicate that something is seriously amiss in our world. A sense of longing for the transcendent suggests a reality beyond the world of ordinary experience, and religions characteristically hold that our ultimate well-being is linked to this transcendent realm.

However, in spite of these common themes the various religions offer quite different diagnoses of the human predicament. Monotheistic religions generally regard the problem in terms of an unsatisfactory relationship between God the Creator and his creatures. Central to Christianity, for example, is the idea of SIN as deliberate rejection of God and his righteous ways. The biblical view of sin must be understood with reference to a holy and righteous God to whom human beings are morally accountable. Sin includes not only individual acts that transgress God's righteous standard but also a condition or state of rebellion against God, resulting in alienation from God. The original sin of Adam and Eve resulted in a condition of sinfulness that has been passed on to all humanity (*see also* FALL OF HUMANKIND). The suffering and evils we experience are all due ultimately to sin and its tragic consequences.

JUDAISM, rooted in the Hebrew Scriptures, has focused extensively on the PROBLEM OF EVIL and suffering. Although it acknowledges the heart of the problem as human moral failure in committing sins against God, Judaism generally does not share Christianity's belief in original sin and total depravity. Rather, a more optimistic view of human nature stresses original virtue and the capacity, with God's gracious help, of working toward progressive moral development.

ISLAM holds that human beings have erred by straying from the right path of obedience to Allah. But sin in Islam is more a weakness or deficiency in human character rather than the radical corruption of human nature. People are subject to temptation from Iblis (the devil), but it is within their power to resist and remain faithful to Allah. The suffering and trials we encounter in this life are regarded not only as punishment for individual sins but also as Allah's way of testing the sincerity and faithfulness of his followers.

Quite different views of the human predicament are found in religious traditions originating in the Indian subcontinent. Here the problem is *samsara,* the wearisome and repetitive cycle of rebirths through which one transmigrates in accordance with *karma.* Birth leads inevitably to death. Death in turn inevitably results in rebirth in another body, and it is the impersonal cosmic law of *karma* that determines the conditions of each existence. HINDUISM, BUDDHISM, and JAINISM, although differing in certain key respects, all accept the framework of *samsara* and *karma,* and thus the religious goal came to be identified with liberation from *samsara* by rendering ineffective the principle of *karma.*

In spite of this common framework, however, various traditions within Hinduism and Buddhism give different views on the nature of the problem. Often the root problem is identified with ignorance *(avidya),* or holding false views about reality resulting in *samsara.* But even here various differences emerge. In Advaita Vedanta Hinduism *samsara* arises from and is rooted in false views about the nature of Brahman and the relation of the self to Brahman; in Theravada Buddhism, by contrast, it is the false belief in an enduring, substantial self *(atman)* which, when combined with desire and craving, results in suffering and rebirth. Buddhism identifies the human predicament with the claim that all existence is characterized by pervasive suffering, dissatisfaction, and impermanence.

In Chinese religious traditions, or at least non-Buddhist traditions, the human predicament is not understood in terms of the cycle of rebirths so much as failure to attain the proper balance and harmony within the social nexus, which in turn is patterned after the cosmic harmony of Heaven and the Tao. Proper alignment and harmony—within the person, the familial and social contexts, the realm of ancestors and spirits, nature, and the cosmos at large—result in human flourishing. Disharmony on any level can result in the suffering and problems encountered in ordinary life. TAOISM in particular emphasizes balance and proper alignment with the Tao, the Way or eternal principle immanent within the cosmos. Problems in society are due to the imposition of artificial constraints that prohibit the free expression of life in accordance with the Tao. CONFUCIANISM, by contrast, has been concerned with cultivating proper relationships and order within society based on virtue and moral character. With Mencius, and later Chu Hsi, Confucianism has emphasized the inherent goodness of human nature; evil results from corrupt external influences. On a popular folk level, the reality of the spirit world and the importance of proper alignment with spiritual powers is indicated by widespread practices of divination, ancestral rites, and recognition of a vast array of deities, spirits, and demons that can influence life in this world for good or ill.

Animistic traditions and primal religions, which do not make a sharp distinction between the world of ordinary experience and a transcendent spiritual world, attribute problems in everyday life such as illness, death, natural disasters, wars, and infertility to various spiritual powers believed to be capable of impacting affairs in this life. Thus, great care is taken to maintain proper rituals through which the many ancestors, demons, spirits, and gods who hold such power can be appeased.

The recognition that something is profoundly wrong with the way things are can be a point of contact between the Christian gospel and followers of other traditions. Augustine captured this sense of alienation well in his statement at the beginning of the *Confessions:* "You [God] have made us for yourself, and our hearts are restless and will find no rest until they rest in you."

HAROLD A. NETLAND

Bibliography. J. Bowker, *Problems of Suffering in the Religions of the World;* S. G. F. Brandon, *Man and His Destiny in the Great Religions;* H. Netland, *Dissonant Voices;* D. Noss and J. Noss, *A History of the World's Religions.*

Human Rights. It is commonly accepted in modern Western thought that human beings, by definition, are entitled to basic human rights. There are several presuppositions in this worldview: the inviolability of each person as a person; the right to freedom from restrictions of one's rights; the equality of each person in dignity and law; and the right to participate in decisions that affect one's life and livelihood.

Though both Luther and Calvin played significant parts in the development of the notion of fundamental dignity and freedom, the contemporary commitment to human rights is mostly the result of a momentum that has built up since the seventeenth century, when people became sick of the years of religious and ideological intolerance that followed the Reformation.

People lost respect for any rhetorical authority imposed by those who represented either church or state. They began to insist that reason, experiment, and the inherent dignity of the human being should be the arbiters of all truth. Between 1689 and 1789 the West saw these presuppositions and rationalizations enshrined in national declarations of human rights in England, the U.S., and France.

Western culture now seems fully committed to adopting this overall perspective.

Such a development, however, was only possible in a culture that had grown out of a Judeo-Christian tradition. Therefore in many cultures there is no comparable commitment. In a real sense, Christian mission is the parent of the human rights movement. There are several biblical principles that have profoundly influenced Western societies in this context: The Bible teaches that all of humanity is made in God's image; the incarnation and passion of Jesus demonstrate the value of each person to God; God challenges us to work for a society characterized by righteousness, justice, and peace; he commands us to care for the weak and disadvantaged in society; Jesus calls us to love even those whom we might consider enemies.

This modern commitment to the dignity of every human being has influenced the theology and PRAXIS of mission to a great extent. Many Christians ask: "Surely loving our fellow human beings involves defending their basic dignity under God?" Mission is therefore seen as a participation in the struggles of life alongside the oppressed. If we are distant or afraid, then we lose the credibility of the gospel message of Jesus, who gave his life for the poor and oppressed.

Other Christians believe that this commitment to "rights" is essentially a humanistic endeavor, reflecting a worldview that is at odds with the gospel. People should be giving themselves to God, trusting in his goodness for their lives. Mission is seen therefore to consist in helping people so to trust God that their focus shifts from their daily needs to their eternal destiny. Evangelism, with the hope of conversion, is the proper aim of mission, as they see it.

It would not be an exaggeration to say that a critical issue in modern missiology is precisely the dialogue between these two views.

WALTER RIGGANS

See also Enlightenment; Liberation Theology; Human Justice.

Bibliography. H. Kung and J. Moltmann, eds., *The Ethics of World Religions and Human Rights;* J. Moltmann, *On Human Dignity: Political Theology and Ethics;* Studia Missionalia, *Human Rights and Religions.*

Humanitarianism. *See* RELIEF WORK.

Humankind, Doctrine of. The Bible gives clear teaching on humankind's origin, nature, and destiny (Gen. 1–2; Ps. 8; Acts 17:16–31; Rev. 5:9; 7:9; 20:1–6). Humans are the result of a direct act of divine creation in which God declares they have been made in his image (Gen. 1:26–27). The IMAGE OF GOD involves humans relating to the earth as vice-regents, just as God is sovereign over the entire universe; relating to God as children in filial fellowship, expressing a family likeness in righteousness, holiness, and integrity (Ferguson, 1988, 329). Humankind's position in creation is unique, a "little lower than the angels," yet with dominion and stewardship of all the rest of creation (Ps. 8).

From one human being God created every culture of humans to dwell on the face of the earth in a harmonious patchwork of cultural diversity (Gen. 1:28; Deut. 32:8; Acts 17:26). Humankind in its origin is one, from one set of human parents, and that unity is more basic to the Scripture's understanding of humankind than the equally God-ordained cultural diversity.

Though after the fall and flood God left humans in cultures to go their own ways and did not punish them in each generation for their waywardness, still they are responsible to him, for he did not leave himself without a witness to his divine nature, power, and goodness (Acts 14:15–17; Rom. 1:19–20). His desire was always for humankind to seek him, find him, thank him, and worship him (Acts 17:27; Rom. 1:21). But because of sin, all humankind's religiosity is only blind groping and an ignorant, rebellious substitution of idolatry for the worship of the one true God (Acts 17:27–30; Rom. 1:21–32). So extensive have the effects of the fall been, that, left to themselves, humans do not seek God (Rom. 3:9–20) (*see also* FALL OF HUMANKIND).

Humankind's destiny is twofold. Those human beings, some from every tribe, language, people, and culture, to whom Christ has applied salvation from sin and who have responded in faith to the saving good news, will enjoy an eternity at the end of time in the glorious presence of their Savior (Rev. 5:9). Those who continue, without repentance, in their blind rebellion against the one true God will experience the eternal punishment that such sin requires (Matt. 25:41, 46; Rev. 20:15).

The biblical teaching on humankind challenges the WORLDVIEWS molded by the WORLD RELIGIONS. While Islam does follow the Genesis creation account in its understanding of the origins of the human race (Koran 15:29; 32:9; 38:72), the monisms of Hinduism and Buddhism, and the interpenetration of matter and spirit in Chinese thinking do not. Their systems cannot accommodate a Creator God who stands over against his creation, particularly its crown: human beings.

Christian teaching uniquely espouses a personal relationship between God and human beings made in his image. Human beings' position as vice-regents and stewards of all creation, with which Islam strongly concurs, stands against the passivity, the harmonious fitting into nature, which Eastern religions encourage.

The concepts of the image of God in humans and the basic unity of humankind provide a fruitful perspective for WITNESS. If all fallen human beings have the faint glimmers of the "family likeness," then as Paul at Lystra, the witness can appeal to common humanity as a means to overcome the ignorant rebellion of non-Christian religions (Acts 14:15). If what humans have in common is more basic than what divides them, then thoroughgoing cultural relativism as a barrier against CROSS-CULTURAL COMMUNICATION of the gospel is effectively dismantled. At the same time, if God's original design was for the earth to be filled with humankind living in a harmonious patchwork of diverse cultures, then ETHNOCENTRISM is effectively dealt with.

Today there is a call from inside and outside evangelicalism to somehow qualify the exclusive claims of Christ as unique Savior who must be particularly, explicitly owned as Savior and Lord by those who would be saved. But Scripture is unequivocal. Jesus is the only way salvation is accomplished (John 14:6; Acts 4:12). Explicit faith in him is the only way it is applied to humans (Rom. 10:13–17) (*see also* UNIQUENESS OF CHRIST).

Two passages capture the key concepts of biblical anthropology in their interrelationships (Gen. 2:7; 6:17). "And the Lord God formed man from the dust of the ground and breathed into his nostrils the breath of life, and man became a living being [*nephesh*—soul] . . . every creature [*kalbasar*—all flesh] that has the breath [*ruach*—spirit] of life in it." Because of the range of meaning of the terms and their juxtaposition in various passages, there is an ongoing debate about whether the biblical view of the constituent elements of a human being is trichotomous (body, soul, spirit, 1 Thess. 5:23) or dichotomous (body and soul or spirit). If Genesis 2:7 and 6:17 may be taken as guides, together with other Scriptures, then the dichotomous approach seems best. Humans have a material component: flesh (a body) and spirit (an immaterial component). The soul refers to the whole person, though in various relationships.

The biblical teaching on the material component has both a positive and a negative aspect. Positively, though taken from the dust and in frailty returning to dust, a human's body is part of a good creation (Gen. 1:31; Isa. 40:6). Indeed, it is destined for resurrection as a glorified spiritual body (1 Cor. 15:44). Negatively, since the fall, the flesh, the body of death, has been the seat of the sin principle, which works its will out through the misuse of the body's appetites, the lusts of the flesh (Rom. 7:14, 18, 24; Gal. 5:16–24).

The immaterial or animating component of our constitution is spirit (Heb. *ruach;* Gk. *pneuma*). In the Bible the vocabulary can refer to breath (Gen. 6:17); the vital powers that sustain a person alive (45:26–27); and an aspect of the inner life, whether a disposition (Job 21:4; Ezek. 3:14) or the seat of cognition (Exod. 28:3) and will (Num. 14:24; Isa. 29:24). Scripture knows of nonhuman spirits, incorporeal, intelligent, feeling beings. Normally, this designates members of the demonic hierarchy (Luke 4:33; Acts 19:12–16). It can speak of a human's spirit, not only as that dimension of the person that relates to God (Rom. 8:16; cf. 1:9). The Scriptures also use it to refer to a human's mode of existence in a disembodied state, whether in this life (2 Cor. 12:12; cf. 1 Cor. 5:3; Col. 2:5) or after death in the intermediate state (Eccles. 12:7; Luke 24:37–39; 2 Cor. 5:1–5; Heb. 12:23).

The biblical terminology for soul (Heb. *nephesh,* Gk. *psychē*) participates in much of the same range of meaning as spirit, but with some significant differences. Soul can refer to breath (Ps. 107:5) and life (Gen. 9:5) or seat of life (Mark 8:35), but it does so in an extensive way. The term embraces the whole person, either in the sense of physical existence (Matt. 6:25; Luke 12:19; John 10:11; Acts 2:27); or being a living being (Gen. 2:7); or individuality as a self (Ps. 7:2), even to the human with powers of reason, emotion, and will (Col. 3:23; 1 Thess. 2:8; Heb. 6:19). Although Scripture first and foremost views the human being as a unity, it presents every person as having a spirit, in or which animates, a physical body. But it describes each of us as a soul.

It is true that soul sometimes refers to the inner person, both in terms of desires and inclinations (Prov. 23:2; Jer. 2:24), including religious ones (Deut. 6:5). Humans relate to God and experience final salvation or condemnation. Does this mean that the Scriptures also participate in Greek thought, seeing humans as possessing an immortal soul? The biblical evidence as a whole points in another direction, having to do with eschatological and soteriological matters in which the soul stands for the person and any immortality is contingent, dependent on God who sustains persons in ETERNAL LIFE.

Biblical anthropology also challenges other religious wordviews. Since Islam builds its understanding on the same Genesis passages, it participates in the same radical distinction between the material and nonmaterial in humans as Christianity does. It equates the concepts of "soul" and "spirit" and differs from biblical teaching only in its view of the effects of the fall on the human race: the guilt is imputed to Satan, the sanctions and consequences to humankind.

Hindu thought from one standpoint views the *atman* (soul) as a distinct entity being reincarnated from life to life according to accumulated karma. From another, however, it participates in a monistic subjective ontology: all is soul. The macrocosm of *paranatman* (the universe in its true essence as Supreme Soul) is viewed as essentially identical with the microcosm of *atman* in the individual. True enlightenment and release come when persons lose their identity in the universal consciousness (Supreme Soul) and are united with it in universal Bliss. Biblical thought challenges this monism as idolatry: deification of

the human soul. It presents a solution to the problem of sin and suffering that is holistic, life-affirming, fully satisfying for the whole self.

In Buddhist thought the ontological soul is nonsubstantial and illusory. The most troublesome, but, when properly understood, most promising statement according to Buddha is "I have no soul." The trouble comes from realizing the soul does not exist. The liberation comes from realizing that "I" also does not exist. The embracing of radical nonexistence is Buddhism's way of dealing with the pain of illusory reality. Christians have hope for Buddhists for they declare that pain can be reckoned with, if we embrace an ontology with a transcendent, gracious, Creator God at the center guaranteeing the reality of and basic goodness of created existence. He created humans in his image as living souls, with the purpose that they relate to him forever in love and worship.

Animistic thought posits a world full of souls, understanding the world within the framework of immanent power. The vital principle inhabits whatever moves and lives. For humans there is an internal soul, soul-substance, which animates the body and temporarily resides in vital centers or products related to them (saliva, sweat, blood, sperm, tears). This is not a distinct entity, but an animating power made known through functional props (heart, brain), images (shadow, ghost), symbols (name, character sign), or its activities. There is an external soul, powers of the soul located outside the body. Here animists speak of the ability to leave the body and the fact of animal (totem) and human (shadow) doubles. Souls whether malevolent or benevolent may be manipulated, and must be appeased.

Chinese thought participates in this animistic thinking through its conception of the interpenetration of the material and nonmaterial aspects of the human. By linking the two souls of humans, *po* (spirit of the physical nature) and *hun* (a person's vital force: consciousness, intelligence), with the two essential components of the universe, yin and yang, the former acquire the same quality of interpenetration as the latter have. The vital force principle, *chi,* endows some with pure *po* and others with an admixture of evil. By education, the soul becomes an increasingly refined vital force that mediates between the human world and the spiritual realm. With "soul force" humans can be in touch with the dead and the highest spiritual realm: heaven. The soul helps the human achieve harmony with nature and to enter communion with the universe.

Biblical teaching, while concurring with the reality of the spiritual realm, presents a much simpler and unified view than animism does. By seeing humans as being a soul with body and spirit, made in God's image with dominion over creation, the fear engendered by a false enchantment of reality through multiple souls, inhabiting multiple phenomena, may be overcome. Again biblical teaching has good news for Chinese thought. Humans are not under an ontological bondage to evil, which is inextricably mixed with the good in the soul. Rather, there are such distinctions between the Creator and the creature, humans made in God's image, yet fallen, that salvation can be achieved through the Creator God's atoning sacrifice of his Son. True harmony is reconciliation with God the Creator in Christ.

WILLIAM J. LARKIN JR.

SEE ALSO Anthropology.

Bibliography. J. Ching, *Confucianism and Christianity: A Comparative Study;* S. B. Ferguson, *NBD,* pp. 328–29; D. C, Fredericks, *NIDOTTE,* 3:133–34; *The Hindu World: An Encyclopedic Survey of Hinduism.* 2:250–52, 425–26; C. Riviere, et al., *ER* 13:426–31; 438–43; 447–50; 460–65; C. Schultz, *EDBT,* pp. 602–04; M. Van Pelt, W. C. Kaiser Jr., and D. I. Block, *NIDOTTE,* 3:1073–78.

Hungary *(Est. 2000 pop.: 9,940,000; 93,032 sq. km. [35,920 sq. mi.]).* The life and witness of the Hungarian churches, including their missionary vision and activity, have inevitably been affected by the political and social condition of the nation. From 1951 to 1989 communist domination meant that all foreign mission activity was impossible. However, unlike some other Central and Eastern European countries, which were also under Soviet control, Hungary had a longer history of precommunist mission activity, and memories of this survived even during the worst years of the Cold War. In fact, through a kind of anomaly a representative of the Leprosy Mission continued to operate in Hungary for the whole of that time! During the same time, there was evangelical work among students, originally of an unofficial nature, but officially registered even before the demise of Soviet domination. Together, these ministries fostered missionary interest, prayer, and concern among Christian students. In at least some of the churches today there is the beginning of a genuine missionary movement.

The fascinating history of the Hungarian Protestant missionary movement from 1756 until 1951, especially in the Reformed and Lutheran churches, has been chronicled by Anne Marie Kool, who heads up a Protestant Institute for Mission Studies in Budapest. She shows how such diverse factors as the presence of the Czech Brethren bishop Jan Amos Comenius in Hungary in the seventeenth century, the Moravian influence in the eighteenth, revival impulses and the presence in Budapest of the Scottish Mission in the nineteenth, and the Student Volunteer Movement and Christian Endeavor at the turn of the nineteenth and twentieth centuries, all con-

tributed to the missionary movement in Reformed and Lutheran circles before the First World War, between the two Wars, and up to 1951. Hungarian missionaries worked among Jews and Muslims in the Balkans, as well as in Africa, China, Indonesia, and elsewhere. The numbers were never large, but had the communist period not cut it short it could have grown and developed significantly. Kool is currently involved in developing missionary interest anew in churches and among theological students in Hungary. Missionary interest in Baptist, Methodist, Brethren, and Pentecostal churches suffered similarly under Marxist rule but is also recovering and being developed with help and encouragement from Western Christian agencies.

RONALD DAVIES

Hunger. In accepting the presidency of the United States in 1960, John Kennedy stated, "We have the capacity to solve the problem of hunger in the world. What we need is the will." Decades later the problem still exists.

What Is Hunger? There are five types of hunger. Undernutrition is where people have consumed insufficient food over an extended period of time. Malnutrition is caused by not enough nutrients in the food consumed. Some people also suffer from malabsorption when their bodies are unable to utilize the food eaten, often due to the presence of intestinal parasites. Seasonal hunger occurs in some rural communities where the food supply runs out before the next harvest is gathered. Finally, famine occurs when crops fail and food runs out.

Who Are the Hungry? The United Nations calculates that there are up to one billion hungry people in the world, approximately 20 percent of the total population. Up to 35,000 of these die each day from hunger and POVERTY-related causes, three-quarters of them children. Most of these people live in tropical countries with high populations or low and variable rainfall. According to Susan George, the hungry are people in poor countries, where governments have not made food for all a priority, mostly in rural areas, among the lower social classes, especially women and female children, and newborns and fetuses.

The Hunger Cycle. Hunger especially impacts children. In infancy many children are born underweight to overworked, underfed mothers. During childhood they ingest inadequate quantities or quality of food. In adolescence they are poor learners with low energy levels and during adulthood they usually earn only low wages, have little capital, and survive on an inadequate diet.

Myths about Hunger. Some believe that, like the poor, the hungry will always be with us. Myths about hunger include:

1. *There is not enough food.* Actually there is plenty of food. It is more a problem of distribution and purchasing power.
2. *Nature causes hunger.* This is sometimes true but most hunger is due to human actions.
3. *There are too many people in the world.* Scientists suggest the world could grow enough food for up to fifteen billion people.
4. *More food aid will solve the problem.* It is more important to support local production and pay adequate prices for farmers' crops.
5. *Large farms are more productive.* No so, except for a few crops. Small owner-operated, labor-intensive farms will feed more people.

Solutions to Hunger. The hunger project suggests four actions must be taken. First, eliminating hunger must become a priority. Second, population growth should be slowed through the education and empowerment of women. Third, environmentally sustainable, appropriate food-growing technologies should be pursued. Fourth, more power and profit should be channeled into farmers' hands. These actions will benefit everyone, rich and poor, well-fed and hungry.

The Bible and Hunger. The Bible describes hunger often—for example, in Egypt and the Negev wilderness, for David and his men and Jerusalem under siege. David (Ps. 146:7) and Mary (Luke 1:53) declare that God feeds the hungry, and we must also, for feeding the hungry is a mark of true religion (Isa. 58:7) and is to be extended even to enemies (Rom. 12:20). It is a factor in the judgment (Matt. 25:35–44). In the context of a hungry world Christians must respond to the immediate needs of malnourished or starving people and seek to change the structures which cause hunger.

ROB BELLINGHAM

Bibliography. R. Sider, *Rich Christians in an Age of Hunger;* T. Yamamori, B. Myers, K. Bediako, and L. Read, eds., *Serving With the Poor in Africa.*

Hunt, John (1812–48). English missionary to Fiji. Born in Hykeham Moor near Lincoln, England, he had very limited schooling and worked as a farm laborer. Following his conversion at age seventeen he became a Methodist local preacher. Largely self-educated, he went to Hoxton Theological Institution in 1835, developing considerable abilities in theology, Greek, and Hebrew. He married Hannah Summers and in 1838 they went to Fiji. The Fijian mission was still in its pioneering period and faced considerable opposition. Hunt, first at Somosomo and then at Viwa from 1842, made a notable contribution to the acceptance of Christianity through his translation work. He combined Methodist hymns with the use of Fijian chants for tunes. His translation of the New Testament, completed in 1847, helped standardize the Fijian language. He became the mission's chairman in 1842. In the face of continuing opposition he drove himself, physically weakening his health but winning the admiration of friends and enemies alike for his saintliness. He was noted for his preaching, the centrality he gave to worship, his encouragement of revival, and the training he gave to Fijian teachers. His *Letters on Entire Sanctification* (1853) were an expression of his lifelong search for personal holiness.

ALLAN K. DAVIDSON

Bibliography. A. Birtwhistle, *In His Armour: The Life of John Hunt of Fiji;* A. H. Wood, *Overseas Missions of the Australian Methodist Church,* vol. 2, *Fiji.*

Hyde, John (1865–1912). American man of prayer and missionary to India. Born in a Presbyterian minister's family, Hyde's call to mission work was confirmed while at McCormick Seminary after a night of prayer. He sailed for India in 1892.

Prayer was the defining quality of Hyde's life, initiated in response to a disturbing letter he read en route to India. In India, a scarcity of results eventually led to an immersion in prayer. He invested thirty days and nights in prayer in preparation for the first Siaklot Convention, organized in the fall of 1904 to refresh missionaries and national workers spiritually. The success of these world-renowned conventions was attributed largely to Hyde's prayer. Later biographers appropriately dubbed him "The Apostle of Prayer."

Hyde displayed a tenacious desire to reach people for Christ. His prayer, "O God, give me souls or I die," inspired missionaries around the world. Through prayer in 1908 God gave him the goal of seeing one person per day come to Christ. This number rose to four per day by 1910.

After the 1910 Sialkot Convention, a doctor told Hyde to give up his exhausting prayer schedule or he would die within six months. Hyde chose prayer. His health failing, he left India in 1911. Once home, an operation to ease his severe headaches revealed cancer, to which he succumbed on February 17, 1912.

A. SCOTT MOREAU

Bibliography. E. G. Carré, ed., *Praying Hyde: A Challenge to Prayer;* F. McGaw, *John Hyde: The Apostle of Prayer.*

Ii

Ibiam, (Sir Francis) Akanu (1906–55). Nigerian medical missionary and church leader. Ibiam was the first African student at the University of St. Andrews (Scotland) medical school (1927–35), then a missionary doctor in Nigeria with the Church of Scotland. He founded the Abiriba hospital (1936).

He was an educational leader, becoming principal of the Hope Waddel Training Institute. Knighted by the British government in 1951, he was later appointed governor of his home region. He chose to stay with his Ibo people during the Biafran war, renouncing his knighthood and acting as a roving ambassador to gain aid. Following exile, he was honorably restored to Nigerian public life, becoming active in reconstruction and reconciliation efforts.

His own distinguished service gave weight to his criticism of missionaries as he observed them in mid-century. He felt they were "guardians of white supremacy" who did not "visit the homes of African Christians, much less the homes of non-Christians." Despite resentment at his comments, he was elected one of the six presidents of the WORLD COUNCIL OF CHURCHES in 1961. Ibiam also served as President of the Christian Council of Nigeria, the All Africa Conference of Churches, established the SCM (Student Christian Movement) in Nigeria, was a founder of the Bible Society of Nigeria, and chaired the council of the United Bible Societies. He became a respected traditional ruler, Eze Ogo Isiala I of Unwana and Osuji of Uburu.

DONALD K. SMITH

Bibliography. D. C. Nwafo, *Born to Serve, The Biography of Dr. Akanu Ibiam.*

Iceland (*Est. 2000 pop.: 282,000; 103,000 sq. km. [39,768 sq. mi.]*). The Republic of Iceland is a large volcanic island in the North Atlantic. It is famous for its Viking founders (A.D. 874) and the world's oldest parliament, the Althing (A.D. 930). While the first inhabitants of Iceland may have been Irish monks around 740, the Lutheran Church is officially recognized as the state church, with 95 percent of Icelanders claiming membership. The year 2000 marks one thousand years of Christianity. However, the majority of Icelanders are nominally Christian with little vision for missions; less than 10 percent regularly attend church. Prosperity, secularism, occultism, and New Age philosophies are working together to dechristianize Iceland. Currently, seven agencies have sent fourteen missionaries to Iceland, while only a handful of Icelandic missionaries are serving overseas.

GARY LAMB

Identification, Missionary. *See* EXTENT OF MISSIONARY IDENTIFICATION.

Identificational Repentance. *See* POWERS, THE.

Identity Movements. *See* PROPHETIC AND IDENTITY MOVEMENTS.

Identity. *See* ETHNICITY.

Ideologies. The term "ideology," derived from the Greek *idea* and *logos,* literally means "knowledge or science of ideas." In a general sense ideology refers to a particular set of ideas or beliefs that distinguish a given group or perspective. In modern times the term has assumed various pejorative connotations and is used to refer to a collection of beliefs and values held by a particular group for certain "hidden" motives or for other than purely epistemic reasons. Thus ideologies are typically regarded as sets of ideas used by particular groups in support of certain economic, political, or social agendas. With K. Marx and F. Engels the term took on a specific meaning, referring to a set of beliefs presented as objective whereas in actuality they merely reflect the material conditions of society and the interests of the ruling classes. Thus the dominant ideas of any era not only reflect the views of the ruling classes but also serve their interests. More recently, the Frankfurt School, associated with J. Habermas, has developed the notion of ideology as a set of ideas and communicative structures inherently distorted by power relations.

Some examples of modern ideologies include political liberalism, Marxism, democratic socialism, nationalism, and fascism. Political liberalism, as found in the writings of Locke, Rousseau, Mill, and Rawls, teaches that personal liberty is a fundamental good and that the ideal society is one in which individual liberty will be maximized. Intrinsic to liberalism is confidence in individual autonomy and the right of the individual to think for himself or herself. This, in turn, tends to make the liberal very suspicious of any claims to absolute authority, including any claims to religious authority rooted in God and the Bible. Christian mission, which is based on belief in the authority of Scripture and a divine mandate to make disciples of Jesus Christ of all nations, will characteristically be viewed by liberalism as a direct threat to individual liberty through the imposition of some divine mandate for society.

Marxism (as developed by Marx, Engels, and Lenin) is an economic theory advocating the ownership of all property by the community as a whole. Intrinsic to Marxism is confidence in the basic goodness and productivity of human beings as well as a denial of the existence of God. Thus Christianity's belief in human depravity and the sovereignty of God will be met with staunch resistance, since such religious beliefs are perceived to be serving the interests of the dominant classes by suppressing the lower classes and obstructing the progress of communism.

Democratic socialism, although similar to Marxism in some respects, is a theory of what is wrong with society and how these ills can be remedied through production and distribution by society as a whole rather than through private individuals. Contrary to this, the Bible advocates (notwithstanding some misinterpretations of Acts 2) responsible stewardship of property by the individual. Christianity is perceived as the sponsor of capitalism in spite of the fact that historically Christianity has existed in virtually all forms of society and is nonpolitical in its biblical form.

Nationalism is the belief that a nation exists more in terms of a given group of people than in terms of political boundaries, and that a nation's peculiar interests and security are more important than international interests and welfare. The primary virtues thus are patriotism and pride in a given nation's customs, language, or traits. In view of such attitudes as these, the Christian mission may be perceived (and historically this has unfortunately sometimes been the case) as an attempt to colonize and subjugate others in the name of a foreign religion.

Fascism stands in contrast to liberalism in its denial of the value of individual freedom. It is a system of government in which there is a rigid one-party dictatorship characterized by forcible suppression of anything that opposes it, such as unions, other political parties, and minority groups. Fascism is closely related to Nazism, but fascism originated in Italy in 1922 and Adolf Hitler later incorporated much of its ideology. These forces were defeated in World War II, but some extremist groups that are fascist in nature still exist. Their glorification of war, racist sentiments, and despotic tendencies are in direct conflict with evangelical Christianity, which is biblically required to avoid war if possible, to be indifferent to race and ethnic origin, and to respect incumbent governments regardless of their nature.

Conservatism in its purest form is the rejection of ideology. Whereas ideology is concerned with the rethinking of political and social systems, conservatism (as its name implies) seeks to conserve or maintain what it regards as good in the past and to uphold tradition. In this sense, biblical, evangelical Christianity is "conservative," for it consists in preserving intact the apostolic message from one generation to another.

If ideologies oppose the Christian mission it is in part because in the past some forms of Christianity forgot their true mission and took on political ambitions or at least unwittingly served in aiding political causes by exporting aspects of foreign cultures. This poses an obstacle that Christian mission must overcome through disassociation as it seeks to make disciples of all nations.

WILLIAM H. BAKER

Bibliography. P. Corbett, *Ideologies;* G. Graham, *Politics in Its Place;* K. Mannheim, *Ideology and Utopia: An Introduction to the Sociology of Knowledge;* M. Seliger, *Ideology and Politics.*

Idolatry. Idolatry is a major concern in both the Old and New Testaments. In the Old Testament alone there are twelve different words relating to idols or idolaters. In the New Testament, idol (*eidōlon*—or one of its cognates) is used almost thirty times. Under the old covenant, idolatry was strictly forbidden (Exod. 20: 4–5; Lev. 26:1; Deut. 5:8–9) and in the new, believers are warned to avoid any participation with the practices associated with idol worship (1 Cor. 8:7–12; 10:7; 1 John 5:21).

According to some historians, idolatry had its origin in the ancient kingdom of Babylon. This would seem logical in that it is the area of one of the oldest civilizations in recorded history. However, idolatry is instinctive in the heart of fallen people (Rom. 1:21–23) and could probably be assumed to have existed long before recorded civilization. There were at least two major forms of idolatry in the ancient Near East which influenced Israel: the worship of false gods through images and ceremony; and the false worship of the true God by means of images and pagan-influenced ceremony.

The basic concept behind idolatry is assigning divine attributes to some power other than the true God. Images are used as representations of the force or personality being worshiped and often reflect the divine attribute most coveted by the worshiper. For this reason, in paganism, multiple gods are represented because it is inconceivable that one being could possess all of the forces and mysteries witnessed by humans.

Israel, like all of fallen humanity, fell into idolatry because they sought a god with whom they could identify. The true God of Israel was invisible, mysterious, transcendent, and required behavior consistent with his own nature. Idols could be seen, designed to meet human expectations, and manipulated. They were morally weak like the humans who served them. Thus, the natural instinct was to gravitate toward that which was more consistent with human ideas and standards. The divine self-revelation given to Israel was so far beyond human design and concepts that Israel was easily seduced by the pagan ideas and religions which surrounded them.

Likewise, New Testament believers, most of whom had come from pagan lifestyles before their conversion, would be prone to return to the comforts of the familiar and humanly conceived. New Testament writers often warned of the dangers of the surrounding new religious systems which practiced idolatry in many forms. Paul implied that idolatry was more than just having an image before which to bow. In Ephesians 5:5, he stated that a covetous man is an idolater. Covetousness is the improper desire of some material object or place of power. In this sense, materialism can be identified as idolatry. Many Christians who would scoff at the idea of bowing before a statue or image are none the less prone to covet material goods. It is not uncommon to hear of Christians who have replaced dedication to God with the pursuit of money, career, entertainment, or other things of only temporal value.

For missionaries, idolatry can come in two forms. On the one hand, they will confront cultures (especially Hindu and Buddhist cultures) which openly participate in idol worship through images and ceremonies. Learning to communicate the invisible, transcendent, omnipotent, and sovereign God to those who are conditioned to relate to hundreds of deities is a significant challenge. It must be remembered that these missionaries do not have the luxury of the Old Testament prophets who lived in theocratic Israel. They cannot march into these foreign lands and chop down idols. They must convey the true and

living God in a manner consistent with the New Testament commission.

The other form of idolatry may come from within their own hearts. Missionaries often sacrifice material goods, family, comforts, and human securities. In this sacrificial lifestyle, the temptation to become covetous or to substitute God's work for more humanistic ideals of living is a serious enticement. Looking to medical doctors, savings accounts, or human advice in place of looking to God is idolatry. It needs to be remembered that God may use any of these human tools to bless and encourage his servants but they are no substitute for God himself.

L. E. GLASSCOCK

SEE ALSO Gods and Goddesses; Worship.

Bibliography. G. Bacon, *EJ*, 8:1227–38; S. Barabas, *ZPBD*, pp. 368–70; C. E. DeVries, *BEB*, I:1014–16; R. D. Knudson, *NDT*, pp. 329–30; G. W. Peters, *A Biblical Theology of Missions*.

IFMA. *See* INTERDENOMINATIONAL FOREIGN MISSION ASSOCIATION.

Ignatius of Loyola (c. 1491–1556). Spanish founder of the Jesuits. Born in the Basque region of Spain, until 1521 he pursued a military career but during convalescence from a wound he was converted to Christ through reading devotional books. His resolve to change his life led him to write the *Spiritual Exercises,* a program designed to produce mastery of the will. A pilgrimage to the Holy Land in 1523 was intended to become a permanent mission to the Muslims of the Middle East and North Africa, but Christians in the area deterred him. He returned to study at the universities of Barcelona, Alcala, Salamanca, and Paris, at each place introducing students to the *Spiritual Exercises.* In 1540 he and six companions received papal permission to found The Society of Jesus. Ignatius trained his Jesuits for social service and missionary work, with special emphasis given to the establishment of educational institutions.

From 1547 until his death, he oversaw the expansion of the order throughout Europe, Asia, and the Americas. His *Constitutions of the Society of Jesus* outlined the educational philosophy of the order; it is still used in its original form today. The combination of spiritual devotion, academic rigor, and missionary fervor that came to characterize the Jesuits has been inspirational to Catholics and Protestants alike.

LARRY POSTON

Bibliography. C. De Dalmases, *Ignatius of Loyola, Founder of the Jesuits;* G. E. Ganss, *Ignatius of Loyola: Spiritual Exercises and Selected Works.*

Illiteracy. It has been the contention of modern missions that people need to read the Bible. As a result, literacy programs have played a major part in Christian mission, and in some places LITERACY has been a requirement for baptism and church membership.

In spite of enormous efforts, both by Christian groups and by secular and government agencies, present literacy figures are rather startling. About 1.3 billion people are termed illiterates, but because many of those who enter school leave before they have fully acquired reading skills, many more are functionally illiterate. It is estimated that less than half the world's population are readers. Among some groups, in particular the poor and the outcast, literacy levels are as low as 1 percent. In some developing countries, women are illiterate and most girls are not in school.

It has been pointed out that only about 5 percent of Christ's audiences were literate, and that in New Testament times people were evangelized and leaders were trained without a written Bible. Such achievements would seem impossible today given the modern world's devotion to the printed text.

The need today is twofold. First, we need to encourage literacy programs so that as many as possible will learn to read and write. Power is associated with the printed page. The task is becoming increasingly difficult as people would rather watch television or listen to the radio. Second, we need to develop alternatives to print media. The fact is that hundreds of millions living today will never learn to read. We need to communicate the gospel to them in a form that is appropriate, and for most that means oral communication. The STORY-TELLING tradition among many people is as it was in New Testament times, well suited to communicating the Scriptures to those who cannot read.

VIGGO B. SØGAARD

SEE ALSO Educational Mission Work.

Bibliography. H. Box, *Communicating Christianity to Oral, Event-Oriented People;* H. V. Klem, *Oral Communication of the Scripture: Insights from African Oral Art;* V. B. Søgaard, *Audio Scriptures Handbook;* H. W. Weber, *The Communication of*

Image of God. "Imaging God" means showing God's attributes in actions and attitudes, words and works. God designed humans to fellowship with him, obey him, administer for him, and imitate him, including procreating more images, naming, prophesying, and influencing for righteousness. Thus work of all types, "secular" and "sacred," images God, especially when energized with the Spirit's loving power that brings all things into submission to Christ (Ps. 8:4–6; Col. 1:15–20).

God created humans as his images or "royal representatives" to glorify him. "Image" implies an audience, so imaging God was in itself a missionary endeavor. God assigned his royal priestly representatives to spread out and subdue the earth, including all the wilderness outside the Garden and the rebellious creature who would tempt the new couple to sin (Rom. 16:19–20).

God instituted the family as imaging procreation and organization, relating creatively and ruling beneficently. From the very beginning God designed individuals and families to glorify him as ambassadors, royal priests and prophets, "missionaries." The only thing that changed through time under Israel and then via the GREAT COMMISSION was the specificity of the message God's people were to take to the world. The core message has always been "follow the true God like we do, and let us show you the way."

Image as a Missionary Polemic against IDOLATRY. This missionary message directly conflicted with the message of the images of other nations. Images from wood, clay, and metal conveyed the message, "worship our gods." The creation account displays the superiority of persons as God's living images over Baal's lifeless images. Worshiping God with manufactured idols was futile (Exod. 20:4–5). The polemical intent of Genesis 1:26–28 may be paraphrased: People make images of Baal. Can you show me an image Baal has made of himself? God made humans as images of himself, so far superior to images of Baal as God himself is superior to Baal! Individually and corporately, in words and works, we show what God is like. This is our responsibility. Don't reduce your beautiful complexity to a statue! How can an idol ever replace you: living, breathing, walking, talking, authoritative representatives of our God?!

The polemic continues in Genesis 5:1–3, when God's image procreates in its own image—what image of Baal can do that? And in Genesis 9:6 the Lord states his justice in a manner the surrounding nations could easily understand: "If you attack the image, you attack God." When asked to summarize righteousness, Christ essentially asserts the converse, "If you love the image, you love God" (Matt. 22:37–40; 1 John 4:20–21).

The biblical basis of civil government rests on the foundation that we each represent God to one another. Every person continuously images God in basic minimal ways: God's breath blows through our being; God's life flows in our blood; God's light shines in our eyes. Every person must be treated with dignity as valuable to God. From the preborn to the terminally ill, from the profoundly handicapped to the profoundly rebellious, every person images God and may not be violated with impunity (James 3:9; *see also* PERSON, PERSONHOOD).

The prophets expand this polemic, insisting that individually and corporately Israel is God's image, welded together by God's strength, held upright by his power, decorated by his glory, enlivened by his Spirit-breath. When the nations bow before their images seeking guidance and power, their images remain silent. But when the nations listen to believers (God's living images), through those royal representatives God guides the nations and promises to bless their obedience to his Word with the protection and provision, fecundity and fertility their gods fail to provide them (Isa. 40:18–31; 41:7–10; 41:22–42:1; 57:13–16; Jer. 16:18; Hab. 2:17–19).

Israel images God as children image their parents (e.g., Exod. 4:22; Deut. 32:5–6, 15–20). Israel glorifies God as a missionary to the nations in the same way a good servant accurately represents (glorifies) his or her master (Isa. 44:21–26; 49:3–6). On the other hand, when Israelites worship the images of the nations' gods, they become like those images. The prophets describe an Israel which had become like the idols she worshiped: deaf, dumb, and unclean. Eventually God will cleanse Israel of the idols, removing hearts of stone, and breathing his Spirit into them: a recreation of Adam, a renewal of God's image (Ezek. 36:25–27; cf. Ps. 115).

Transformed into the Image. Today the church images God corporately and individually, as God's Spirit transforms believers into Christ's image. Moses implied that a person fully images God by keeping God's Law (e.g., Deut. 13:17; 14:2). In the New Testament, Christ "is the true image" (2 Cor. 4:4), in part because he perfectly kept the Law. We all are created "as God's image," for the purpose of representing God by fulfilling the Law of Christ.

Because the Spirit writes the Law in our hearts, we have the opportunity to represent God in a more complete way than could persons prior to the NEW COVENANT (Eph. 4:23–24; 2 Cor. 4:1–6). Believers become God's images more fully by Christ's righteousness judicially applied to us and by the Spirit's empowering us to live out Christ's righteousness. In this way we display God's glory shining through our holy love (2 Cor. 3:18; Eph. 3:10).

Being conformed to the image of Christ is inherently evangelistic and missionary (Phil. 1:27–2:16). As we act more every day like a child of our Father, a brother of our Lord, our family resemblance works itself out in all relationships, all activities, undergirding and enabling our witness.

Children Image Parents. Imitating God, Adam and Eve procreated a son in their own likeness, as their image (Gen. 5:1–3; Luke 3:38). Children represent their parents by being like them in many ways: physical appearance, values, and will. Believers carry on this responsibility by speaking and acting on God's behalf, sharing his goals and values, mirroring his mighty abilities (Isa. 43:6–7). Our goal is to represent our loving Father perfectly (Matt. 5:45, 48). Our Lord repeatedly said that to look at him was to look at his Father, to honor him was to honor his Father

(John 5:19–27; 14:9). Hebrews emphasizes the parent-child relationship as central to the concept of image: "The Son is the radiance of God's glory and the exact representation of his being" (Heb. 1:2–5; 2:6–13). In loving actions we honor our Father; in unrighteous actions we dishonor him by grotesque caricature (1 John 4:12, 20). Persons who behave in an anti-Christ manner may be labeled "children of your father the devil" (John 8:44).

Corporate Representation. We image God by functioning together as men and women (Gen. 1:27–28; 1 Cor. 11:7). Every individual represents God at some level, but corporately we image more fully and clearly. A single man and woman working in godly cooperation with one another more fully represent God than either working alone. The two married and parenting godly offspring represent God even more fully. A gathering of godly individuals and families into God's Family, Christ's Body and Bride, shows a watching universe even more fully and clearly what God is like (1 Cor. 12:27; Eph. 3:6, 9–11; 5:1ff.; Rev. 22:17).

DOUGLAS J. VARDELL

SEE ALSO Humankind, Biblical Doctrine of.

Bibliography. N. T. Anderson and R. L. Saucy, *The Common Made Holy: Being Conformed to the Image of God;* G. W. Bromiley, *ISBE Revised,* 2:803–5; G. Edwards, *The Divine Romance: The Most Beautiful Love Story Ever Told;* M. J. Erickson, *Christian Theology;* idem, *Readings in Christian Theology,* vol. 2, *Man's Need and God's Gift;* R. S. Greenway and T. M. Monsma, *Cities: Missions' New Frontier;* R. E. Hedlund, *The Mission of the Church in the World: A Biblical Theology;* C. F. H. Henry, *EDT,* pp. 545–48; D. J. Hesselgrave, *Communicating Christ Cross-Culturally,* 2nd ed.; idem, *Counseling Cross-Culturally;* M. G. Kline, *Images of the Spirit;* idem, *Kingdom Prologue;* J. D. Levenson, *Creation and the Persistence of Evil: The Jewish Drama of Divine Omnipotence;* C. G. Olson, *What in the World is God Doing?;* A. P. Ross, *Creation and Blessing.*

Immanence of God. The immanence of God is more than a theological dogma. It is a biblical reality which affects one's view of natural phenomena, human events, and perspectives on value and responsibilities. Immanence primarily deals with God's presence and activity within the realm of the created world and human activity. Particularly for mission efforts in a context of traditionally pantheistic cultures, the missionary must be cautious in expressing God's immanence. However, this must be done without excluding the Lord of the universe from personal involvement with his created order.

Beginning with Genesis 1:2, "the Spirit of God was hovering over the waters," Scripture emphasizes the Creator's intimate connection with his creation. Genesis 2:7 demonstrates that his connection with the creature made in his own image is even more intimate. God infused his very breath into humankind to make humans to be living creatures unlike any other creature in God's created system.

Unlike PANTHEISM, which teaches that everything is God or a part of God, or what Tillich called PANENTHEISM, meaning that God is not everything but is in everything (God is not a tree, but is in the tree), immanence is the view that creation is distinct from God and always dependent upon God. God is above his creation (transcendent to it) yet constantly involved with it. In Jeremiah 23:23–24, God declares that he is near to his creature and that he fills the heavens and earth. God's immanence flows out of his permeation of the created universe. His knowledge and his power saturate the entire creation, but his essence is not contained in the material world. Thus the mission of the church involves participation with God in compassion and care of God's creation.

In some cultures, the pantheistic view of God will confuse many and the Christian view must be clear in separating the material creation from the essence of God. Missionaries have confronted this problem for decades, but there is a new form which influences even Western societies. Some believe that God's presence is within nature, including human nature, and therefore being an extreme environmentalist or active social revolutionary can be seen as worshiping God. Whereas some of these causes may be noble and demonstrate a respect for God's creation, it is incorrect to assume that God's presence is in the material world. There must be a distinction between God at work in and through nature, and God being in nature.

In relation to the human race, the immanence of God teaches that he is actively involved with and near to his fallen creatures, "having determined their appointed times and the boundaries of their habitation, that they should seek God, if perhaps they might grope for him and find him, though he is not far from each of us" (Acts 17:26–27). The human race is dependent upon God and intuitively senses God's essence in the universe, "for in him we live and move and exist" (Acts 17:27; Rom. 1:19–21). Thus, one asset to missions is the reality that God is ever present with his servants and all his creatures made in his image. For this reason, classical Christian mission has always stood for early preservation and improvement of human life.

A message to the world in this age of environmental concerns and promotion of human rights is that God is truly concerned about these same issues (Matt. 6:26–30; 9:35–36; 10:29). God is a God who works through the natural world to provide for his creation (Matt. 5:45). The missionary must never make this truth the focus of mission to the point of confusing the gospel, but must show the world that God is near and concerned.

D. E. GLASSCOCK

SEE ALSO Divine Attributes of God.

Bibliography. W. Grudem, *Systematic Theology*, pp. 267–71; H. Berkhof, *Christian Faith*, pp. 119–26; K. Barth, *Church Dogmatics*, II, 1:335–45.

Immutability of God. Immutability refers to the unchangeableness of God. God claims this quality for himself, "For I, the LORD, do not change . . ." (Mal. 3:6). This truth does not, however, imply that God is a stagnant being frozen in an inflexible pose. The unchangeableness has to do with God's character, essence, goals, and promises. For those who have learned of God in one culture, it may be important to understand this truth when moving into another environment where one encounters different understandings of the divine. God is the same regardless of the environment in which we may find ourselves.

Though God cannot change in character, he is changeable in replication or willingness to respond to a proper response to his Word. Jonah 3:4 records the words of God's prophet: "yet forty days and Nineveh will be overthrown." The prophet was saying what God had already declared, and he was confident that Nineveh would be destroyed. Yet, in verse 10, we are told that when God saw the repentance of the people, "God relented concerning the calamity which he had declared he would bring upon them." God often works within contingencies and is "changeable" when circumstances are altered to comply with his conditions.

The divine constancy of God is both quantitative (he cannot increase in any attribute) and qualitative (he cannot improve in any area). God, in his attributes, nature, or promises, does not experience any sense of modification or variance. For the minister in a cross-cultural situation, it is important to keep this focus while attempting to communicate God's truth. God cannot be altered to suit a particular ethnic group, generation, or race. God is God regardless of the cultural biases of any target group. For many Americans, the idea of a God who will judge and condemn the unregenerate was too primitive; thus, many liberal theologians created the conceptions of the Old Testament god who was warlike and bloody and the New Testament god who was loving and giving. Such theology is not biblical—the Lord who loved enough to die is the same God who created the worlds (John 1:1–14), and that God has not changed in his essence or attitude toward sin and judgment.

Being immutable does not imply that God does not understand and work within sequential events and logical order to bring about his plans. Within his constant program, he works through progressive revelation and in differing contexts having unique features. What may appear to be a change from a human perspective is no more than the next phase of the continuum of his redemptive plan, which when viewed biblically is consistent with his nature and revealed will.

A key verse in understanding the immutability of God and its practical application is found in James 1:17: "with whom there is no variation, or shifting shadow." This verse addresses God's goodness in bestowing gifts to his creatures and is intended to give comfort to believers who are facing trials (vv. 12–17). Regardless of the circumstances, because God has been, is, and always will be a bestower of good things, one may have confidence in him. The assurance of the believer that God will fulfill his promises and complete the salvation he has promised is based upon the immutability of God. The God of Abraham, Isaac, and Jacob, who has not forgotten the remnant and who will fulfill all the covenant promises, will keep his word because he does not change in the things he has promised. The prophet Malachi proclaims God's own claim to the nation of Israel: "For I, the LORD, do not change; therefore you, O sons of Jacob, are not consumed." The context goes on to point out that Israel had failed to honor God's word and did not obey him. But God did not destroy them because he had made a covenant with Abraham, Isaac, and Jacob, and he will honor it. If God were to alter his character, his attributes, or his promises, then there would be no assurance of his promises. He is immutable and therefore trustworthy.

L. E. GLASSCOCK

SEE ALSO Divine Attributes of God.

Bibliography. H. Berkhof, *Christian Faith*, pp. 111–18, 140–47; K. Barth, *Church Dogmatics*, II, 1:491–522; T. Aquinas, *Summa Theologica*; J. Calvin, *Institutes of the Christian Religion*; W. Grudem, *Systematic Theology*, pp. 163–68.

In-Service Education. Efforts by mission agencies, training schools, and churches to provide in-service education for their missionaries are poorly documented. Even so, the scattered information which is available reveals some encouraging trends.

Cooperative models are beginning to emerge. AVANTE mission in Brazil is combining its resources with those of missions schools and churches into an extended training program which begins with initial orientation and field experience, continues through advanced missiological studies, and culminates in a supervised term of service in a team situation in another country (Neuza Itioka in Taylor, ed., 111–20). North American agencies and schools are beginning to work together in helping missionaries to pursue a substantial portion of a master's degree on the field.

Some in-service efforts are consciously adopting adult education methods (Brewer). A PRAXIS model which integrates new learnings with life experience is being employed. Times and places are flexible. Formal, nonformal, and informal delivery modes are all used. Missionaries are encouraged to pursue their individual goals within cooperative learning communities.

Agencies, churches, and schools are increasingly realizing that in-service education continues beyond the first term and home assignment. Ministries change and expand. Transfers to new geographical locations occur. Children no longer require full-time care (Taylor, 9, 10). Even retirement does not lessen the missionary's educational needs.

A growing concern for the care and SPIRITUAL FORMATION of missionaries can also be discerned. At least one agency offers a "mental health checkup" to returning missionaries. Mental health professional and mission leaders in the United States and Canada are convening conferences to explore issues related to missionary care (*see* MEMBER CARE).

Many church pastors are visiting fields to provide counseling and spiritual encouragement for their missionaries. Churches are also helping with funds for study programs, books, and journals. Others are initiating missiological dialogues with missionaries on e-mail. A few larger churches are offering their own courses and seminars for missionaries.

The explosion of resources for in-service education has also been encouraging. On HOME ASSIGNMENT, and often on the field as well, missionaries are being helped to network with formal study options in seminaries, graduate schools, and universities; with nonformal opportunities at seminars, conferences, and institutes; and with informal possibilities through the resources of libraries, book stores, newspapers, radio, and television. In addition, computer technology is increasingly making bibliographic databases, independent study courses, missiological forums, and other resources available through CD-ROMs, the internet, and the World Wide Web.

In the midst of these encouraging trends, there are causes for concern: the gap between prefield orientation programs and the missionary's initial field experience is sometimes wide and deep; continuing education can be haphazard, rather than planned and purposeful; the resources of national churches are seldom used effectively.

Missionaries are far more than human resources to be developed for missions. They are persons created in God's image, growing in Christ-likeness, and infinitely more valuable than any task they may perform. When all is said and done, in-service education is ongoing disciple-making, encouraging Christ's intercultural servants to keep learning from him.

LOIS MCKINNEY DOUGLAS

SEE ALSO Training.

Bibliography. M. Brewer, *ERT* 14 (July 1990): 154–279; M. S. Knowles, *The Modern Practice of Adult Education: From Pedagogy to Andragogy,* rev. ed.; *EMQ* 24 (October 1988); W. D. Taylor, ed., *Internationalizing Missionary Training.*

Incarnational Mission. The dramatic opening of John's Gospel is foundational for understanding the meaning and implications of "incarnational mission." "In the beginning was the Word," the apostle wrote, "and the Word was with God, and the Word was God. . . . And the Word became flesh and lived among us . . ." (1:1, 14). The fuller context of the passage suggests that in Jesus, God identified thoroughly with humankind, and that God came in Jesus for the express purpose of disclosing not only God's love but also God's salvific intent for the world (3:16–17).

However the Gospel writer may have understood the nature of Jesus, the church has steadfastly regarded the incarnation to mean that God was "enfleshed" in Jesus. All the Gospels bear witness to the fact that Jesus was born in a specific time and place, into a particular culture, and that he lived, matured, worked, ministered, and died as a human being. In Jesus—who came to be called "the Christ" or the Messiah—God was thereby revealed as love, self-giving love, love vulnerable to the exigencies of human life including the assault of evil and death. Yet evil was not victorious. It was instead inexorably defeated in Christ's death and resurrection. God became a human being to redeem all humankind from the destructive power of sin and to reconcile and transform the whole of creation.

Belief in the incarnation raises profound questions about the nature of God and about the nature of Jesus Christ. Yet, from the earliest attempts to grapple with and understand who Jesus was, the incarnation—God's assuming humanness—has been pivotal in comprehending the Christian faith. The earliest church councils discussed, debated, and concluded that the "God was *in Christ*" affirmation (2 Cor. 5:19) means that Jesus was fully human and fully divine. Explications (or the theology) of the incarnation are found not only in Scripture, but also in a succession of creeds. Three branches of Christianity, especially the Orthodox, as well as Roman Catholic and Anglo-Catholic, customarily give more attention and emphasis to the doctrine of the incarnation than do Protestants. In fact, some evangelical theologies tend to accentuate the divinity of Christ so disproportionately that the ultimate result is a kind of Christological docetism in which the human nature of Jesus is virtually eliminated or is little more than a facade for his divinity. Maintaining theological balance has never been easy, as any comprehensive survey of the history of theology reveals. Yet when either the divinity or the humanity of Jesus is over-emphasized, the outcome is a distortion of the nature of Jesus as represented in the New Testament. Mainstream Christianity has been unwilling to relinquish either the divine or the human nature of Jesus, though some theologians have given more attention to the meaning of the incarnation than others. Grassroots believers, meanwhile, appear to be satisfied to confess that in Jesus Christ God was uniquely revealed in history, and that in Jesus Christ the divine intent for humanity was definitively imaged. That there is mystery here no one denies. As Archbishop William Temple put it, anyone who professes to understand the relationship of the divine to the human in Jesus Christ simply demonstrates that he or she has failed to understand the significance of the incarnation (p. 139).

To refer to the incarnation as mystery, however, is not to suggest that it is "beyond us" or a kind of theological icon. Quite the contrary. As Donald Baillie said, the mystery will always be mystery, but the mystery is lessened once we realize that believing in the incarnation means accepting a paradox "which can to some small measure be understood in the light of the 'paradox of grace'" (p. 131). For the incarnation was not and is not primarily a doctrine. It was and is an event. It was a life lived, and it is a life to be lived. "He was made what we are," declared Irenaeus, "that He might make us what He is Himself" (*Adv. Haer.,* Bk. v. Pref. cited by Baillie, ibid.). Thus Paul could make the staggering claim, "For me to live is Christ" (Phil. 2:21). So committed was the apostle to the Christ who summoned, transformed, and "missioned" him, and so determined was Paul to communicate the same good news Jesus fleshed-out, that he could say, "I have been crucified with Christ, and it is no longer I who live, but it is Christ who lives in me" (Gal. 2:19–20). In these words believers find the most significant implication of the incarnation, namely, that Jesus Christ can be fleshed out in the lives of those who follow in Jesus' steps (1 Peter 2:21). In essence, therefore, this is the mission of Jesus' followers, to walk in Jesus' steps.

Common in Catholic theological tradition is the idea that the incarnation of Christ is the link between God and the institutional church, or, even more specifically, it is the link between God and the sacraments by which believers become "partakers of Christ." It is a short step, therefore, from seeing the SACRAMENTS administered by the church as means of grace to regarding the *plantatio ecclesiae* as extending the incarnation.

In 1838, with the publication of his *Kingdom of Christ,* British theologian Frederick D. Maurice went beyond the conventional Anglo-Catholic understanding of the incarnation by positing specific social and political implications. In a sense, Maurice anticipated the approach to the life of Jesus developed by many liberation theologians during the last quarter of the twentieth century. For in terms of the social and political significance of the incarnation, it has been the liberation theologians who expounded the relationship of the incarnation in the world today. Jesus, they underscore, was born in a religio-political context of suffering, oppression, and injustice. He was counted not among the rich or the powerful but rather among the common, the nondescript folk from the hill country of Galilee. To inaugurate his mission, nonetheless, Jesus made an astonishing association: "The Spirit of the Lord is upon me, because he has anointed me to bring good news to the poor. He has sent me to proclaim release to the captives and recovery of sight to the blind, to let the oppressed go free, [and] to proclaim the year of the Lord's favor" (Luke 4:18–19).

His mission, as he described it, was to liberate the impoverished, the imprisoned, the sightless, and the oppressed. As it turned out, it was these kinds of people who became Jesus' principal followers—the poor, the sick, the disabled, the despised, the marginalized, and the alienated—women, tax collectors, prostitutes, and others whom society scorned. Moreover, it was from these that Jesus chose his disciples whom he declared were "the salt of the earth" and the "light of the world" (Matt. 5:1: 13, 14).

In the late 1960s and early 1970s, Latin American liberation theologians, following the lead of the SECOND VATICAN COUNCIL, began asking what the incarnation of Jesus implied in a world beset with injustice, hatred, poverty, exploitation, premature death, and hopelessness. Though their response to the question incited intense debate—and more resistance than support from "officialdom"—the basic question they asked still begs to be answered. Jesus, liberation theologians said, indisputably sided with the hurting, exploited, and abused of his day. This was his mission, and anyone who presumes to incarnate Christ's mission today will likewise stand with the suffering peoples of the world whether they are in America, Europe, Asia, or Africa (see LIBERATION THEOLOGIES).

Standing with the poor and oppressed does not mean ignoring or neglecting the mission of evangelization, but, as Mortimer Arias notes, evangelization can never be merely "verbal proclamation." Authentic evangelization will be also "the incarnation of the gospel" in the lives of Christ's people, Christ's community (p. 107).

Reflection on the meaning of "incarnational mission" can be found also in the writings of certain ecumenical and evangelical theologians. For J. R. Chandran of India, an incarnational view of mission means INDIGENIZATION. For Nigerian Emefie Ikenga-Metuh, it means CONTEXTUALIZATION for "God has always been incarnate in human cultures." For former World Council of Churches general secretary W. Visser 't. Hooft, it meant a holistic ministry. Other more recent examples are John S. Pobee's insightful *Mission in Christ's Way* and Jonathan J. Bonk's disturbing *Missions and Money*. Pobee, an African on loan to the World Council of Churches, spells out in detail the dimensions of an incarnational mission, while Bonk, a former Mennonite missionary and now associate director of the Overseas Ministries Study Center in New Haven, Connecticut, addresses the crucial issue of missionary prosperity, saying that economically affluent missionaries can never engage in incarnational mission for what they model is an "inversion of the Incarnation." Their prosperity makes it impossible for them to "identify with the life situations of the poor" to whom the gospel is addressed (p. 61).

Nearly a half-century ago one of the most respected and effective mission leaders among Southern Baptists, M. Theron Rankin, then the executive secretary of the Foreign Mission Board, envisioned a model of incarnational mission. "If God could have saved the world by remoteness," and achieved the divine purpose while remaining detached from humanity, Rankin asked, would there have been the incarnation? Then he added, the most effective witness the church makes will always be in the lives of those who in Christ's name bury themselves in the lives and struggles of another people, missionaries who serve the people, learn to speak their language, develop the capacity to feel their hurt and hunger, and "who learn to love them personally and individually."

ALAN NEELY

Bibliography. A. Mortimer, *Announcing the Reign of God;* D. M. Baillie, *God Was in Christ;* J. J. Bonk, *Missions and Money;* J. R. Chandran, *Student World* 51 (1958): 334–42; E. Ikenga-Metuh, *Mission Studies* 6 (1989): 5–12; F. D. Maurice, *Kingdom of Christ;* J. S. Pobee, *Mission in Christ's Way;* T. M. Rankin, *The Commission* 15 (June 1952): 9; W. Temple, *Christus Veritas;* W. A. Visser 't. Hooft, *The Uppsala Report,* pp. 317–20.

Inculturation. Modeled on the anthropological term ENCULTURATION, inculturation has been used regularly in Catholic discussion since the 1970s as a parallel to CONTEXTUALIZATION. The core idea is found in the widely quoted statement from Pedro Arrupe, the former superior general of the Jesuits, in a letter to the Society (Schineller, 1996, 109): "Inculturation is the incarnation of Christian life and of the Christian message in a particular cultural context, in such a way that this experience not only finds expression through elements proper to the culture in question, but becomes a principle that animates, directs and unifies the culture, transforming and remaking it so as to bring about "a new creation."

Just as contextualization went beyond ADAPTATION, so inculturation goes beyond ACCOMMODATION. Rather than translating the concepts of the gospel in a new cultural setting by outsiders, it refers to the insiders of the culture integrating at the root of their culture the values, ideals, teachings, and orientation of the gospel and church tradition (see Luzbetak, 1988, 82–83).

While the general sense of inculturation so closely parallels contextualization that Protestants have little trouble with it, the emphasis on church tradition as parallel to the gospel in authority is a point of contention for Protestants who do not ascribe the same authority to church tradition as Catholic teaching does.

A. SCOTT MOREAU

Bibliography. S. J. Bevans, *The Japan Christian Review* 62 (1996): 5–17; M. Dhavamony, *Studia Missionalia* 44 (1995): 1–43; P. Divarkar, *A New Missionary Era,* pp. 169–73; M. P. Gallagher, *IRM* 85 (1996): 173–80; L. J. Luzbetak, *The Church and Cultures;* P. Schineller, *IBMR* 20 (1996): 109–10, 112.

Independent Charismatic Missionaries.

Charismatics, those Christians emphasizing the use of spiritual gifts, have been active in world mission for centuries but their specific contribution in the twentieth century came in three major waves. The first wave came with the formation of Pentecostal denominations, such as the Assemblies of God, at the beginning of the century (*see* THE PENTECOSTAL MOVEMENT). The second wave were charismatics who remained in mainline denominations, such as Anglicans, Lutherans, Presbyterians, Catholics, Methodists, and Baptists. Today, large numbers of missionaries from these two waves serve in nearly every country of the world.

The third wave are the independent charismatics who have formed their own churches and quasi-denominations. The first of these arose in Africa as prophets, pastors, and evangelists who broke off from existing traditions. These movements were normally evangelistic, so they supported a large number of evangelists and missionaries. Evangelists, preaching the gospel among their own people, were the most numerous but African indigenous missionaries, those who went to preach the gospel among other peoples and languages, were a significant force and today represent some six thousand cross-cultural missionaries.

Another significant independent charismatic movement is the CHINESE HOUSE CHURCH MOVEMENT. However, most of the Christian workers from this tradition are not cross-cultural missionaries, but pastors, teachers, and evangelists among the majority Han Chinese.

The bulk of the independent charismatic missionary force is sent out from the Western world. At least thirty thousand are sent out from churches in the West. Most of these are sent directly from their churches or through emerging quasi-agencies. Unfortunately, the vast majority have found the most fertile soil among Christians of other traditions, especially among Roman Catholics and Protestants in Latin America and sub-Saharan Africa, as well as, more recently, among the Orthodox in Eastern Europe and the former Soviet Union. Nonetheless, today's fifty thousand independent charismatic missionaries represent one of the fastest-growing segments of the global missionary force and are likely to contribute new and innovative approaches to world mission well into the twenty-first century.

TODD M. JOHNSON

SEE ALSO Charismatic Movement.

Independent Nondenominational Mission Agencies.

Being similar to "independent, nondenominational colleges," the strength and weakness of an independent, nondenominational mission agency is that it does not depend for its existence or its priorities upon the outcome of the majority vote of any denomination or churchwide consensus, but rather upon the usually stricter scrutiny of supporters who take a special interest in its mission.

These characteristics are quite visible in the area of global Christian mission activity. For most of Christian history "missionary outreach" has rarely been the result of either local or denominational communities of believers making a decision as a whole to reach out in mission. Rather, minority enthusiasts within such communities have taken organized initiatives without waiting for a 51 percent majority vote of the entire group, be it local or denominational.

We can think of the case of WILLIAM CAREY as a classical example of a mission endeavor lacking the majority vote of an ecclesiastical body. His board was a highly committed minority or subgroup of his Baptist friends who only much later were backed by a denomination. By contrast, his student followers in Massachusetts—the young men in the so-called HAYSTACK PRAYER MEETING—were able with the help of some seminary professors to get official ecclesiastical encouragement to form the AMERICAN BOARD OF COMMISSIONERS FOR FOREIGN MISSIONS, which then went on for quite a few years to function as the first major "interdenominational" mission in America. But because it was officially tied to a specific denomination it eventually became exclusively denominational and its work today is minimal. By contrast, the young men who organized the World Mission Prayer League within the Lutheran sphere never did get official denominational backing, although they tried, but the WMPL is thriving to this day.

Minority initiatives have resulted in deeply dedicated people going out individually, like SAMUEL ZWEMER, or in an organized team, often at great personal risk. This is not merely a modern phenomenon. The Celtic *Peregrini*, who were one of the most powerful forces for the taming of Europe, the Roman Catholic Orders, and the early Protestant missionary societies such as the Society for the Proclamation of the Gospel, the LONDON MISSIONARY SOCIETY, or the CHURCH MISSIONARY SOCIETY were all minority initiatives. Until about 1870 mission organizations almost never resulted from the central initiative of ecclesiastical structures.

In America, where the concept of a "denomination" was first developed (implying that more than one church tradition can be legitimate), dozens of "nondenominational" mission thrusts took place long before the idea gained favor within the denominations themselves to establish foreign mission departments or boards. But around 1870 missions for a brief but important period became a denominational priority. Virtually every self-respecting denomination in America felt the tug as a denomination to become involved in its own name in world mission efforts. The same thing happened later in the century with the newer, small, strictly evangelical denominations.

The idea of official denominational initiative became so strong that soon it was widely assumed that denominational mission boards were not only the best way to go but the only theologically legitimate methodology of mission. What about the older well-respected "nondenominational" boards like the London Missionary Society (in England) and the American Board of Commissioners for Foreign Missions? They had been serving valiantly for over fifty years. By 1870 these two began to discover that their denominational sources withdrew as denomination after denomination began to establish its own mission board. Denominational leaders quite often suggested—maybe even demanded—that their members no longer support "nondenominational" (or "interdenominational") missions.

Thus, when the Foreign Mission Conference of North America (FMCNA) was formed in 1891, most of the board secretaries who met together were by that date denominational mission secretaries. By that time the American Board of Commissioners for Foreign Missions, for example, was no longer an interdenominational agency but simply the denominational board of the Congregational (eventually the United Church of Christ) tradition. That is, all other denominations had pulled out. Not only that, but the FMCNA would gradually ease out the few interdenominational boards that had attended its meetings. The China

Inland Mission (now the OVERSEAS MISSIONARY FELLOWSHIP) was welcome to participate in the early period of the FMCNA, but there came a time when only strictly denominational boards were allowed a vote. By 1917 in America it behooved the interdenominational missions to form their own association, called the INTERDENOMINATIONAL FOREIGN MISSION ASSOCIATION (IFMA).

Meanwhile, the FMCNA went on through various mutations to become the Division of Overseas Ministries of the National Churches of Christ in the USA, while the IFMA, holding on tightly to its interdenominational character, gave reason for the appearance in 1945 of the EFMA (by 1995 called the EVANGELICAL FELLOWSHIP OF MISSION AGENCIES) which specifically included the newer, generally smaller, and distinctively evangelical denominational mission boards of the member denominations of the National Association of Evangelicals.

The 1890s, however, was a period of great enthusiasm for global involvement in America, and consequently denomination-wide consensus in mission effort was reasonable and relatively easy. Because the Civil War had killed so many men in a key age bracket, women took over farms, businesses, banks, and founded what would later become elite women's colleges like Wellesley and Bryn Mawr. Their efforts led to the formation of the highly mission-minded youth movement, Christian Endeavor, which is still the world's largest Christian youth movement, and which in turn fueled the Student Foreign Mission movement, whose followers eventually moved into denominational leadership, greatly expanding denominational missions. By 1925 three-quarters of all American missionaries were sent out by the mission boards of what we think of today as the older denominations.

Unfortunately, the denominational boards of the major denominations found that while they had been successful in branding the interdenominational mission societies as second-class citizens, they were unable successfully to maintain their own steam as the interests of the majority of their members gradually turned elsewhere. Dozens of newer denominations, such as the Mission Covenant (now Evangelical Covenant), the Assemblies of God, and the Baptist General Conference tended to pick up the slack, but even greater compensatory growth came from the older interdenominational agencies, mostly in the IFMA, as well as completely independent agencies like WYCLIFFE BIBLE TRANSLATORS. Three of the five agencies in the original group forming the IFMA—the China Inland Mission (now Overseas Missionary Fellowship), the Sudan Interior Mission (now SOCIETY FOR INTERNATIONAL MINISTRIES INTERNATIONAL, working all over the world), and the AFRICA INLAND MISSION, INTERNATIONAL—became large and competent organizations, each with thousands of churches on the field as fruit of their labor.

By 1970 the involvement of older denominations in mission had shrunk back from 75 percent of all American missionaries (in 1925) to less than 5 percent. By the end of the century the larger part of the foreign mission burden was again carried by organizations supported by the "mission minority" which runs throughout virtually all denominations as well as independent congregations.

Granted, the first half of the twentieth century was dominated by the mission boards of denominations, and their contribution around the world is still a major gift to the global church. But the second half of the century, following the Second World War, saw a return to dominance by mission agencies not dependent on the majority of any one denomination.

Thus, the interdenominational or nondenominational mission boards have sprung up to make major contributions and continue to be significant mission structures. What would have happened if Wycliffe Bible Translators had not emerged to rally the troops to the difficult task of BIBLE TRANSLATION? By the end of the twentieth century few denominations showed either the interest or the expertise to make strong contributions in PIONEER MISSION WORK. By that time they were mainly content to focus on the relationships and well-being of their own overseas constituencies.

It seems on the face of it quite logical for there to be "interdenominational" colleges, seminaries, Bible societies, publishers, and mission agencies. What if the Billy Graham Evangelistic Association had bowed to the questionable ethnological case against Christian organizations not directly controlled by local or denominational church structures? Churches have found it possible to cooperate at the top level in the National Council of Churches and the National Association of Evangelicals, but those organizations have never functioned as "ecumenically" as the marvelous tapestry of collaboration by the agencies we see on the mission fields.

For example, once the WORLD COUNCIL OF CHURCHES swallowed up the INTERNATIONAL MISSIONARY COUNCIL, this allowed no room in that body at the global level for either the Billy Graham Evangelistic Association or Wycliffe Bible Translators (or any of the hundred agencies of the IFMA).

Worse still, in many of the strongly evangelical churches in the so-called mission lands the idea that only denominational structures are legitimate has gravely delayed the sponsoring of missionary activity by the overseas churches. In a replay of the American experience we once again find minority, interdenominational initiatives leading the way against the current of opinion.

Note the case of the two largest non-Western mission agencies: the Evangelical Missionary Society in Nigeria is the result of the work of an interdenominational board, SIM International; while the FRIENDS MISSIONARY PRAYER BAND in India derived from a "Daily Vacation Bible School" movement that was interdenominational.

RALPH D. WINTER

SEE ALSO Faith Missions.

Bibliography. E. L. Frizen, *75 years of Service, the History of the IFMA*.

India (*Est. 2000 pop.: 1,022,021,000; 3,287,590 sq. km. [1,269,339 sq. mi.]*). India's inhabitants represent one-sixth of the people of the world and a population equal to that of all the countries of the continents of Africa and South America combined.

There was a thriving civilization in northwest India as early as 2500 B.C. which paralleled the ancient civilizations of Mesopotamia and Egypt. Aryans moved into India in the middle of the second millennium B.C. After the periods of the Maurya and Gupta empires and centuries of conflicts among many smaller kingdoms, the Mughal empire was established by the middle of the sixteenth century A.D.

European interest in India began with the coming of the Portuguese in the fifteenth century. By 1858 the British Crown took control of India. After many decades of largely nonviolent struggle for independence, India became a free country on August 15, 1947. Mahatma M. K. Gandhi and Jawaharlal Nehru were the two most influential leaders in this process.

India has remained a secular country. It upholds democracy and socialism, and in its foreign policy nonalignment. It has waged two wars with Pakistan and one with China over border disputes. There continues to be intense local struggles on religious and regional issues especially in Kashmir, Punjab, and northwest India. It is often a coalition of political parties that rules both the central and the state governments. What is amazing is that in spite of great diversities of races, cultures, languages, and religions, India remains relatively unified.

There are no legal restrictions in gospel work in the country as its Constitution grants freedom "to profess, practice, and propagate" any religion. Yet, there is strong opposition from militant Hinduism and often discriminatory actions of local officials which discourage evangelistic activity and conversion to Christ.

India's People. The people of India belong primarily to the Aryan and Dravidian races, though roughly five thousand ethnolinguistic people groups have been identified. There are fifteen official languages in addition to English (taught in all schools), and also about five hundred local dialects. Caste distinctions are basic to the Hindu view of social structures, though caste discrimination is prohibited by the country's Constitution. There are roughly six thousand subcastes under the four main castes.

About three-fourths of the population live in some six hundred thousand villages and depend upon agriculture for their livelihood. Yet urban and industrial centers are mushrooming. India has twenty-three cities with over a million inhabitants each. About 40 percent of the population live in dire poverty while 10 percent of the people hold 75 percent of the total wealth. Recent economic reforms and liberalization have strengthened a fast-growing middle class.

India's Religions. India's people are generally religious, and every major world religion is found there. Eighty percent are Hindu which is itself a mosaic of religions and more a cultural way of life than a religious system following specific beliefs and worship practices. Hinduism accommodates in itself obvious contradictory doctrines. While Hindus revere Jesus Christ as a great guru and show interest in the gospel, they abhor any idea of salvation through him only.

About 12 percent belong to Islam which was introduced in India in the eighth century A.D. About two-thirds are Sunni and the rest Shi'ite. One-tenth of the world's Muslim population is here without any legal restrictions to reaching them with the gospel.

Buddhism, which Gautama Buddha started in India in the sixth century B.C., almost disappeared by the seventeenth century A.D. However, many low caste people have recently been accepting the faith en masse.

Sikhism, founded in the fifteenth century A.D., is a syncretistic religion combining the best features of Hinduism and Islam, and claims 2 percent of India's population. Finally, there are numerous other religious orientations, including some forty million adherents of animistic traditional religions.

Christians in India number roughly 3 percent and fall into four main categories: Roman Catholics, Orthodox, Protestant, and independent indigenous. About 75 percent of Christians live in the four southern states of India (with a heavy concentration in Kerala), 15 percent in the northeastern states, and 10 percent scattered through much of the central and north India.

Church in India and Its Mission. Some significant evidence points to the existence of an established church in South India as early as the second century A.D. A very credible oral tradition maintains that the apostle Thomas came to India in A.D. 52, founded seven churches, and was martyred in Madras. Also, there were two major migrations of Syrian Christians to south India.

For centuries, the church was under the jurisdiction of Syrian authorities. Toward the end of the thirteenth century European missions began to work in India. The sixteenth century brought the Portuguese, followed by the Dutch, the Danish, the French, and the British missions along with the trading interest and political ambitions of their respective countries. The Roman Catholics vainly tried to assimilate the Syrian Christians.

The major thrust of the Protestant missions started with the arrival of WILLIAM CAREY in Bengal in 1793. Since then numerous European and American missions have done extensive work. Association with them brought about a renewal to the Syrian Christians, especially the Mar Thoma Church, and their new commitment to mission.

Christian missions in general engaged themselves in evangelistic, medical, educational, philanthropic, and related social services. They particularly excelled in education and medical work. They raised the status and condition of the lowest classes of people and gave particular focus to girls and women.

India's independence in 1947 hastened the need for the church to be independent of Western patronage and develop its indigenous administration, support, and theology. Presently, there are several hundred mission agencies with several thousand missionaries doing cross-cultural ministries primarily among the unreached peoples and the tribals. INDIA EVANGELICAL MISSION, Gospel for Asia, India Evangelical Team, and FRIENDS MISSIONARY PRAYER BAND are some of the larger ones. Most of the denominational agencies are from northwest India and most of the parachurch ones from Kerala, Tamil Nadu, and Andhra (*see also* INDIAN MISSION BOARDS AND AGENCIES).

In evangelism and church planting the church in India has fared poorly. The basic reasons include general apathy, nominalism, and lack of mission commitment. Too much energy and money are wasted in court cases over church property. To date, its own theology and systems of leadership training are largely imported from the West and theologically liberal in orientation.

Much of the life and activities in relation to the work of the gospel seem to be with those who utilize their time and resources for ministries outside the institutionalized classical churches of which they are members. Recently the charismatic and independent churches are growing in numbers and initiating new and vibrant ministries. While most of India remains unreached with the gospel at this time, there continues to be hope that God will move in mighty ways in the future.

SAPHIR ATHYAL

Bibliography. S. Athyal, ed., *India Christian Handbook;* C. B. Firth, *An Introduction to Indian Church His-*

tory; *History of Christianity in India,* 5 vols.; F. A. Hrangkhuma, *Church in Asia, Challenges and Opportunities,* pp. 393–434.

Indian Evangelical Mission (IEM).

Founded in 1965 as the indigenous missionary agency of the Evangelical Fellowship of India, the Indian Evangelical Mission grew from 5 missionaries in 1968 to 41 in 1976. In 1978, there were 88 missionaries in the field, a number that increased to 151 in 1987 and 310 in 1992. Missionaries under appointment roughly doubled every five years. By 1997 there were 430 missionaries and 15 overseas associate missionaries serving among 68 people groups at 87 mission stations. About 95 percent of all financial support comes from within India; most of it raised by honorary area secretaries through prayer groups.

Candidates are recruited through national and state missionary conventions and promotional meetings in churches. Those selected are sent to the Training Institute at Dharmapuri in Tamil Nadu. Courses include linguistics, anthropology, evangelism, religions, village health care, bookkeeping, and other practical skills. The first year is probationary for all missionaries. The IEM engages in evangelism, teaching, medical ministry, and church planting. In addition to overseeing tribal children's hostels and various development projects, the IEM is translating the Bible into 11 languages.

ROGER E. HEDLUND

Bibliography. R. E. Hedlund and F. Hrangkhuma, eds., *Indigenous Missions of India;* L. J. Joshi, *Evaluation of Indigenous Missions of India;* M. A. Nelson and C. Chun, *Asian Mission Societies: New Resources for World Evangelization.*

Indian Mission Boards and Agencies.

Thousands of Indian missionaries are presently serving under some two hundred indigenous mission organizations. Indigenous Christian missions are not new to the Indian context. Early indigenous agencies still active include the Mar Thoma Syrian Evangelistic Association (organized in 1888), the Indian Missionary Society of Tirunelveli (1903), and the National Missionary Society (1906). The India Missions Association (IMA), created in 1977 to coordinate the activities of the various indigenous missions, in 1994 claimed 75 member mission agencies having about 9,000 missionaries. In 1996 this had increased to 87 members and 14,000 Indian missionaries. The Indian Evangelical Team (IET) was the largest, with 1,032 pioneer missionaries in fourteen states. Many other mission organizations are not members of IMA. It is difficult to ascertain the number. A 1992 study identified 275 agencies engaged in cross-cultural and other direct missionary activity. An index included 103 agencies, 76 of which listed pioneer evangelism. Tamil Nadu has the largest number of mission headquarters, followed by Kerala and Andhra, Pradesh.

What precisely is an indigenous Indian mission? Definitions vary, but Indian mission boards and agencies may be delineated in terms of missionary work that is rooted in the Indian churches and has an Indian identity. They are not a copy or continuation of the foreign missions that worked in India over the past two centuries, but are a genuine expression of the missionary spirit of Indian churches and Christians.

India has two main types of mission boards. One is church-based and denominational. Examples include the Mission Board of the Presbyterian Church of North East India, the Zoram Baptist Mission of Mizoram, the Nagaland Missionary Movement, the Mar Thoma Syrian Evangelistic Association, and the various diocesan mission boards. This pattern prevails in northeast India. The other is the nondenominational or interdenominational mission. Examples include the National Missionary Society, INDIAN EVANGELICAL MISSION, FRIENDS MISSIONARY PRAYER BAND, and various independent agencies. This pattern predominates in the south. Yet this is only part of the picture.

Mission is not the exclusive domain of the mission societies. Churches and denominations themselves are also vehicles for missionary outreach. This is especially true of the rapidly expanding Pentecostal movement in India. At Madras the New Life Assembly of God sends and supports its own missionaries to other parts of India. In another instance an entire new field has been opened by missionaries sent from one local congregation at Chrompet, Madras, which also functions as a mission society (GEMS—Gospel Echoing Missionary Society). Further, independent workers have had an important role in penetrating new areas and establishing Pentecostal churches and agencies.

Roman Catholic missionary orders have not been included in most studies of indigenous missions, probably because little distinction is made between indigenous orders and those of non-Indian origins. The latter are thoroughly indigenized in personnel and management. The Catholic contribution is in fact enormous.

Indianized international Protestant agencies include Inter-Serve (India), Operation Mobilization, and Youth With a Mission. Various specialized social ministries—drug rehabilitation, education, literature, medicine, projects with youth, the poor, the destitute, and slums—also form part of the missionary edge of the Indian churches.

ROGER E. HEDLUND

SEE ALSO Asian Mission Boards and Societies.

Bibliography. R. E. Hedlund and F. Hrangkhuma, eds., *Indigenous Missions of India;* Indian Missions Association, *Languages of India: Present Status of Christian Work in Every Indian Language;* L. J. Joshi, *Evaluation of Indigenous Missions of India;* S. Lazarus, ed., *Proclaiming Christ: A Handbook of Indigenous Mission in India;* L. D. Pate, *From Every People: A Handbook of Two-Thirds World Missions.*

Indigenization. In the broadest sense, indigenization is a term describing the "translatability" of the universal Christian faith into the forms and symbols of the particular cultures of the world. Still widely accepted among evangelicals, the word validates all human languages and cultures before God as legitimate paths for understanding his divine meanings.

Indigenization provided the freedom for the Greek translators of the Hebrew Old Testament (the Septuagint) to take a word like *theos* from the idolatrous world of polytheism and use it to describe the only Creator of heaven and earth, the God *(theos)* and Father of our Lord Jesus Christ.

Indigenization enabled first-century Christian Jews in Gentile-dominated Antioch to cross a massive cultural barrier and begin preaching to the Greeks (Walls, 1996, 17). They knew that their time-honored word *Christ* would mean little to their neighbors. So they used another name to identify their Messiah in this new cultural setting: "the Lord Jesus" (Acts 11:20).

The same process of indigenization allowed freedom for the emerging churches of the world to wrestle with infusing traditional cultural and social practices with new Christian meaning. Patterns of worship and music, of initiation, marriage, and funeral rites, even of church structure and leadership could be adapted or transformed by the gospel.

The Boundaries of Indigenization. Indigenization is born out of the tension created by two realities. One is the recognition that Christians bring with their faith the particulars of their culture and social group and best appropriate that faith in terms of those particulars. The other is the recognition that this new Christian faith brings with it a universalizing factor that extends the Christian community past the particular borders of culture and group.

Indigenization as a process asks, How can the church be a universal, global Christian community and also a particular community, shaped within its own culture and society? How can the gospel flower be planted in new soil without also planting the foreign flower pot?

Working within these boundaries is not easy. How do the churches keep the balance between freedom to develop on their own path and allegiance to the transcultural gospel uniting all the churches? What should be the relation of a Christian church to its non-Christian past? When does indigenization in the name of Christian liberty slip into over-indigenization or SYNCRETISM? When does hesitation over indigenization slip into legalism and traditionalism?

Toward a Biblical Framework. The legitimacy of this process flows from the "accommodations of God himself" (Battles, 1977, 19–38). Revelation itself comes with a sensitivity to the time, place, culture, and literary genres of its receptors but never with capitulation to error. There is a history to special revelation; the condescending Father communicates truth to us in a form suited to our particular human situations (*see* BIBLE; Vos, 1948, 11–27).

Out of the reservoir of ancient Near Eastern metaphors God paints himself as the divine warrior (Exod. 15:1–3) come to deliver his people from Egypt. He reshapes the treaty language of the ancient Hittite codes from their polytheistic connections to draw a picture of the covenant made between Creator and creature, Redeemer and redeemed (Exod. 20:1–17). He encloses his eternal Word in the limiting wrappings of the Hebrew language, his own coming in the God-man Jesus Christ, the Word of God incarnate as a first-century Palestinian Jew.

In the fullness and power of his Holy Spirit he breaks through that Hebrew sociocultural world to proclaim Christ both across and within the global borders of cultural diversities and linguistic expressions (Acts 1:8). Pentecost transforms the Babel curse of diversity into global blessing; we are called to be all things to all people in order to save some at any cost (1 Cor. 9:23). The world's cultures become home where the gospel takes root. And the gospel becomes the leaven in which those cultures are judged, transformed, and liberated.

The Rocky Road of Indigenization. This apostolic balance did not always appear in the centuries that follow. Within the Roman Catholic Church, ACCOMMODATION grew as a middle ground of gradualism. The imperfections of the pagan world of nature were to be supplemented by the perfections of grace. Thus, in the seventh century Pope Gregory the Great could advise Augustine, his evangelist laboring in England, "to destroy the idols, but the temples themselves are to be sprinkled with holy water, altars set up, and relics enclosed in them."

Later Jesuit experiments particularly in China moved in a similar direction. MATTEO RICCI saw the Chinese homage to Confucius and to the ancestors as ritual expressions of gratitude not inimical to the Christian faith. He "found in Confucius the natural theology, the *preparatio evangelica,* of China as his theological training had given him this for the West in Aristotle" (Allen, 1960, 39).

In Europe observers often matched Jesuit enthusiasm. The philosopher Leibnitz could argue, "I almost think it necessary that Chinese missionaries should be sent to us to teach us the aim and practice of natural theology, as we send missionaries to them to instruct them in revealed religion."

In the face of mounting opposition by the Dominicans, confusion, and misunderstanding, in 1744, the papacy said enough was enough. Such experiments in accommodation were condemned and Roman Catholic missionary churches found themselves required to reflect in every detail the Catholic customs of the moment. Not until 1938 was that ban lifted. And not until the years following the SECOND VATICAN COUNCIL (1962–65) did Roman Catholic missiology seek to reclaim and correct features of the accommodation model in what is now called INCULTURATION (Luzbetak, 1988, 82–83).

Protestant models in the nineteenth century promised more freedom but often practiced a similar reluctance toward indigenization. There were many reasons for the hesitancy: a long history of ETHNOCENTRISM that identified things Christian with the superiority of things Western; the shaping role played by the missionary "outsider" in the receptor culture; the sense that the "native church" was still too immature to be "let go"; the emerging national churches' own identification of the shape of Christianity with its European models.

The promotion of the "indigenous church formula" (*see* INDIGENOUS CHURCHES) in the latter half of the nineteenth century began to break through those patterns. Developed by the missionary community to identify the emerging church, the "three-self" understanding of the church as self-governing, self-propagating, and self-supporting became a stepping stone to other questions that would expand into the twentieth century.

The indigenous church began to ask, What were the implications of selfhood beyond the "three-selfs"? Could the local church possess all three selves and still look and sound "foreign"? The recall of foreign missionaries during World War II and the breaking up of Western COLONIALISM gave the global church the long promised freedom to press these questions.

Indigenization became the slogan word under which such questions were asked. How could the church now be itself, responsible to the Lord and to its own cultural world (Beyerhaus and Lefever, 1964)? How could the church now planted on six continents be a viable, prophetic force in its own culture, reflecting the full power of the gospel in every part of its social context?

Since the 1970s the term CONTEXTUALIZATION has also been used to include these discussions and to add other topics. What of the self-theologizing of the global church? Indigenization is being seen as more than what is happening on "the mission field out there." It is a reflection process that does not exempt the West from self-analysis. Indigenization/contextualization now

places the burden of initiative and responsibility "squarely on Christians in the local context" (Taber, 1991, 177).

HARVIE M. CONN

Bibliography. E. L. Allen, *Christianity Among the Religions;* F. Battles, *Interpretation* 31 (1977): 19–38; P. Beyerhaus and H. Lefever, *The Responsible Church and the Foreign Mission;* V. Cronin, *The Wise Man From the West;* L. Luzbetak, *The Church and Cultures;* C. Taber, *The World is Too Much with Us;* G. Vos, *Biblical Theology;* A. Walls, *The Missionary Movement in Christian History.*

Indigenous American Religions. It is somewhat difficult to apply the term "religion" to the indigenous peoples of America. Some Native American peoples have neither the word nor the concept of religion in their language. For them the entire life experience is an integrated set of belief and behavior that includes everything that is physical, social, emotional, cultural, political, material, non-material, spiritual, secular, supernatural, and mystical.

Also, it must be pointed out that there is no single dominant religion among Native Americans. Each group has a religious tradition that is unique to its own heritage. Native Americans do, however, share certain common religious characteristics. Some of these are to live in harmony with nature and the universe; respect for "Mother Earth"; belief in spirits; the practice of communicating with the powers of nature; shamanism; ritualism; and creation stories.

A large number of American Indians are involved today in practicing and adhering to the religious traditions of their ancestors. Also, it is to be noted that in Native American communities all across America there is a revived interest on the part of many to return to the heritage and traditions of their fathers and grandfathers.

The intrusion of outside religious concepts and practices have had an impact on many of the tribal traditions, causing considerable opposition and/or change. There are at least four major influences today that are affecting the religious thinking and practice of American Indians. These are: pan-Indianism; the NEW AGE MOVEMENT; The Native American Church; and Christianity.

Although the term "pan-Indian" has a considerably broader definition, it is used here specifically to describe the practice of an Indian from one group borrowing and adopting the religious beliefs and practices from another Indian that were not necessarily a part of his/her own group's tradition. This phenomenon occurs frequently at pow wows where Native Americans are dressed in "traditional," fancy-dance, or grass dance and jingle dress costumes that are not particularly a part of their own tribal tradition. For many Indians the pow wow is much more a social event than a religious one, but for some participating in the pow wow is very much a religious experience. A number of Indians have found a source of "Indian identity" in the pow wow and have adopted much of what is associated with the pow wow as the expression of their personal religion. Some of the religious customs that have been exchanged between different tribes include the use of the pipe, sweat baths, the use of sweet grass, smudging, vision questing, and songs.

A second influence that today is impacting American indigenous religions is the New Age Movement. This movement is bringing Indians and non-Indians together in a somewhat strange way in which a number of non-Indians have adopted so-called Indian religious traditions. They are practicing various aspects of tribal religion having been taught these "ways" by a number of self-proclaimed and self-appointed Native American religious leaders. Some who have joined the New Age Movement because of environmental interests have been attracted to American Indian religion because of its closeness to and its respect for nature. It is the desire of these proselytes to Indian religion to somehow protect the environment by means of association with Indians and their religious beliefs and practices.

The Native American Church is an indigenous Indian religion that makes use of a cactus plant that grows wild in the Rio Grande Valley. It is best known by the name "peyote" from the Aztec word "Peyotl." It is classed as one of the hallucinogens and contains the drug mescaline. Apparently the use of peyote in religious rites came to the Native Americans of North America out of Mexico. It was first discovered among Indian tribes of Oklahoma in the late 1800s. By 1906 the use of peyote had spread from Oklahoma to Nebraska. The Native American Church was incorporated in Oklahoma in 1918. In 1944 the Oklahoma articles of incorporation were amended and the organization was named the "Native American Church of the United States." The peyote religion has made considerable inroads on Indian reservations and among Indian communities all across North America. Because of its spread into Canada the organization was once again renamed in 1955 as the Native American Church of North America. Today the Native American Church claims several hundred thousand members. While the religion is not native to North American Indian tribes it is Indian. White men do not control or dominate this religion and Indians are not converted to it by white missionaries. Different tribes have combined the use of peyote buttons with certain traditional religious practices as well as with the use of some Christian beliefs to form a religion which is both indigenous and significantly Indian.

The influence of Christianity on Native Americans has had considerable impact on the practice of indigenous religions throughout the entire history of Indian-White relations. Many of the atrocities perpetrated against Indians by the dominant White society were unfortunately carried out in the name of Christianity. This is an aspect of history for which White America has yet to accept responsibility and for which it needs to seek repentance and forgiveness. While a number of Indians have converted to the "Jesus Way" over the past several hundred years, Christian missionaries, governmental officials and U.S. military personnel have done much to curtail and even prohibit Indians from practicing their tribal rites and ceremonies. Today Indians are granted much more freedom to practice their indigenous religions than in previous times. Many Indians today are rejecting any attempt to "Christianize" them while at the same time others are converting to the Christian message. Perhaps the greatest impact that Christianity is having among Indians today is that which is promoted and propagated by Christian Indians themselves rather than by non-Indian missionaries. It is estimated that between 2 and 10 percent of Native Americans are classified as evangelical Christians.

LEONARD RASCHAR

Indigenous Churches. The term "indigenous" comes from biology and indicates a plant or animal native to an area. Missiologists adopted the word and used it to refer to churches that reflect the cultural distinctives of their ethnolinguistic group. The missionary effort to establish indigenous churches is an effort to plant churches that fit naturally into their environment and to avoid planting churches that replicate Western patterns.

Missionary efforts to establish indigenous churches are attempts to do missions as the apostle Paul did. A brief recital of Paul's missionary methods demonstrates this fact. Paul served as an itinerant missionary, never staying more than three years in any city. Paul's approach to evangelizing regions was to plant churches in cities from which the gospel would permeate the surrounding areas. He never appealed to the churches in Antioch or Jerusalem for funds with which to support the new churches. Rather, he expected the churches to support themselves. Paul appointed and trained elders to lead all the churches he planted. He gave the churches over to the care of the Holy Spirit, but he also visited them and wrote to them periodically.

HENRY VENN (1796–1873) of the CHURCH MISSIONARY SOCIETY and RUFUS ANDERSON (1796–1880) of the AMERICAN BOARD OF COMMISSIONERS OF FOREIGN MISSIONS first used the term "indigenous church" in the mid-nineteenth century. They both wrote about the necessity of planting "three-self" churches—churches that would be self-supporting, self-governing, and self-propagating (Venn used the term "self-extending"). They exhorted missionaries to establish churches that could support themselves, govern themselves, and carry out a program of evangelism and missions. They cautioned missionaries about becoming absorbed in pastoring and maintaining churches, insisting that the missionary's primary task must be planting new churches that would be "self-reliant" and "purely native." They instructed their missionaries to train national pastors and hand the care of the churches over to them at the earliest opportunity. Venn coupled the concept of indigenous churches with euthanasia in missions. By euthanasia he meant that missionaries should plant churches, train leaders, and then move on to new, unevangelized regions. Henry Venn believed that missionaries should always be temporary workers, not permanent fixtures.

JOHN L. NEVIUS (1829–93), a Presbyterian missionary to China, built on Venn and Anderson's indigenous principles in his classic work, *Planting and Development of Missionary Churches*. Nevius developed a set of principles that came to be called "The NEVIUS PLAN": (1) Christians should continue to live in their neighborhoods and pursue their occupations, being self-supporting and witnessing to their co-workers and neighbors. (2) Missions should only develop programs and institutions that the national church desired and could support. (3) The national churches should call out and support their own pastors. (4) Churches should be built in the native style with money and materials given by the church members. (5) Intensive biblical and doctrinal instruction should be provided for church leaders every year. In his writings Nevius criticized the heavily subsidized work that most missions carried on in China. Nevius's principles had little impact in China, but when the American Presbyterians began their work in Korea, the new missionaries invited Nevius to advise them. They adopted his plan and enjoyed great success.

ROLAND ALLEN (1868–1947), an Anglican priest, served as a missionary in China with the SOCIETY FOR THE PROPAGATION OF THE GOSPEL IN FOREIGN PARTS from 1892 until 1904. Like Nevius, he criticized the methods employed by most missions in China. He wrote several books, but expressed his philosophy of indigenous missions in *Missionary Methods: St. Paul's or Ours?* (1912) and *The Spontaneous Expansion of the Church* (1927).

Allen emphasized the role of the Holy Spirit in missions and encouraged missionaries to work in itinerant church planting, trusting the Holy Spirit to develop the churches. Allen's main principles are these: (1) All permanent teaching must be intelligible and so easily understood that those who receive it can retain it, use it, and pass it on. (2) All organizations should be set up in a way that national Christians can maintain them. (3) Church finances should be provided and controlled by the local church members. (4) Christians should be taught to provide pastoral care for each other. (5) Missionaries should give national believers the authority to exercise spiritual gifts freely and at once. Allen's principles have influenced many twentieth-century missiologists, most prominently DONALD MCGAVRAN.

MELVIN HODGES (1909–86), a missionary and mission administrator with the Assemblies of God, wrote *The Indigenous Church* (1953). Widely used in missions courses, this book expressed the ideas of Venn, Anderson, Nevius, and Allen in an updated, popular format. Hodges acknowledged the difficulty missionaries experience in changing a field from a subsidy approach to an indigenous approach. He also emphasized training national workers and giving them responsibility for the care of the churches, freeing the missionaries to concentrate on starting new churches.

In his book, *Verdict Theology in Missionary Theory*, ALAN TIPPETT (1911–88) updated the three-self formula of Henry Venn. Tippett served on the faculty of the School of World Mission at Fuller Seminary and was a member of Donald McGavran's inner circle. The writings of Tippett, McGavran, and others show that the CHURCH GROWTH MOVEMENT accepted and built on the work of the earlier proponents of indigenous missions.

In *Verdict Theology* Tippett proposed a sixfold description of an indigenous church: (1) Self-image. The church sees itself as being independent from the mission, serving as Christ's church in its locality. (2) Self-functioning. The church is capable of carrying on all the normal functions of a church—worship, Christian education, and so on. (3) Self-determining. This means the church can and does make its own decisions. The local churches do not depend on the mission to make their decisions for them. Tippett echoes Venn in saying that the mission has to die for the church to be born. (4) Self-supporting. The church carries its own financial burdens and finances its own service projects. (5) Self-propagation. The national church sees itself as responsible for carrying out the GREAT COMMISSION. The church gives itself wholeheartedly to evangelism and missions. (6) Self-giving. An indigenous church knows the social needs of its community and endeavors to minister to those needs.

Tippett summarizes his understanding of the indigenous church with this definition: "When the indigenous people of a community think of the Lord as their own, not a foreign Christ; when they do things as unto the Lord, meeting the cultural needs around them, worshiping in patterns they understand; when their congregations function in participation in a body which is structurally indigenous; then you have an indigenous church" (136).

In recent years some missiologists have suggested adding a seventh mark to Tippett's list—

self-theologizing. They believe a truly indigenous church will develop its own theology, expressed in culturally appropriate ways. These theologies would affirm the central doctrines of the Christian faith, but they would express them using metaphors and concepts that reflect their own unique cultures.

Missionaries who seek to establish indigenous churches should keep these principles in mind as they begin their work: (1) Missionaries should plant churches with the goal in mind. This means that the desired outcome—an indigenous church—should influence the methods employed. (2) There will always be a dynamic tension between supracultural doctrines and variable cultural traits. (3) Church planters should expect the churches to support themselves from the beginning. (4) Bible study groups should be encouraged to make basic decisions even before they organize as churches. (5) Missionaries should encourage new congregations to evangelize their communities and seek opportunities to begin new churches. (6) Missionaries should always use reproducible methods of evangelism, teaching, preaching, and leadership. (7) Missionaries should give priority to developing nationals to serve as church leaders. (8) Missionaries should view themselves as temporary church planters rather than permanent pastors. (9) Missionaries should resist the temptation to establish institutions and wait for the national church to take the initiative. (10) Missionaries must allow the national churches to develop theologies and practices that are biblical yet appropriate in their cultural settings.

JOHN MARK TERRY

Bibliography. R. Pierce Beaver, ed., *To Advance the Gospel: Selections from the Writings of Rufus Anderson;* M. L. Hodges, *The Indigenous Church;* J. L. Nevius, *Planting and Development of Missionary Churches;* A. Tippett, *Verdict Theology in Missionary Theory;* M. Warren, ed., *To Apply the Gospel: Selections from the Writings of Henry Venn.*

Individualism and Collectivism. A minority of the world's peoples live in cultures where individual interest (individualism) prevails over group interest (collectivism). Individualism is strong in the United States, Canada, Great Britain, Australia, New Zealand, Italy, and Western European societies. Collectivism dominates elsewhere. However, even in predominantly collectivist nations exposure to Western individualist-oriented media may shift urban groups toward individualism.

Individualism assumes that a person is the essential unit of society; collectivism assumes that a group is the basic unit. Ties between individuals are loose in an individualist society, but in a collectivist society people are woven into a cohesive unit to which they give lifelong loyalty.

A person has significance in a collectivist society only as a member of a group. In contrast, one person in an individualist culture has significance that is expressed through individual choices and actions with only secondary reference to the group.

The "group" in a collectivist society may be the extended family, the work group, caste, or entire tribe. Whatever the particular group, its survival is paramount. Group goals control social behavior, and loyalty to that group is fixed. Loyalty means the sharing of resources, whether for living expenses or for special group efforts. It is expressed and reinforced in obligatory participation in funerals, weddings, and other ritual occasions as well as in group crises.

On the other hand in an individualist society, the group is used to achieve individual objectives. There is a loose loyalty to the group, which may be disavowed if individual preferences seem to be better served elsewhere. Sharing of resources is not expected, since individuals are responsible for meeting their own needs and desires. Participation in ritual occasions is expected, but not compulsory, to maintain good standing in the group.

Variation along this individualism—collectivism continuum is perhaps the single most significant dimension of culture differences. It is related to major differences in cultural values and patterns, social systems, morality, religion, and economic development.

Leadership and Change. In a collectivist society the leader often "embodies" the characteristics of the group. The group identifies with the leader, so that the character, beliefs, wealth, and power of the leader are seen as an expression of the group. When the leader changes, the group changes.

Change in a collectivist society may also come when a large part of the group changes, catalyzing change in the remainder of the group. Decision is reached by consensus rather than by voting, which is the sum of individual choices (*see* DECISION-MAKING). Group opinion is dominant, and personal opinions either do not exist or are not tolerated. The person who does not speak or act in harmony with group opinion is considered to have a bad character.

To understand an individualist culture, study of individual beliefs and values gives the best picture. Leaders may reflect opinions and beliefs of a majority of members in an individualist society, but their authority rests on gaining or losing support of individual members. The leader's view does not necessarily express the views of the society as a whole.

Authoritarian behavior is more acceptable in collectivist cultures, and a greater social distance exists between leaders and those they lead. In contrast, individualists are most comfortable in horizontal relationships with minimal social distance between employer and employee, or leaders and group members. Individualists will seek to reduce social distance, often only reluctantly recognizing vertical relationships, while collectivists are more likely to increase social distance and reinforce a higher status for leaders (vertical relationships).

Cooperation and Confrontation. Within the in-group of a collectivist society, cooperation is extensive. Confrontation is unacceptable. Members will often mediate any conflict within the group that threatens group stability and harmony. Any perceived threat to the group's existence is dealt with severely by the power of the group, rejecting the person or cause of the threat. Loss of group membership is similar to exile, being made a non-person without rights or essential support for survival.

In an individualist society, individuals compete with and confront other individuals. Status is achieved through individual accomplishments, rather than by group membership. Confrontation is encouraged to achieve understanding and clarify the rights and limits of individuals. Group membership is relatively unimportant, allowing great freedom for a variety of individual choices.

Communication. Collectivist societies utilize their total context for communication—including space, time, body motion, objects, taste and smell, touch—giving a strong emotional content to acts of communication. The verbal content is of less importance and silence can be satisfying. Group togetherness is of greater importance than anything that might be spoken.

In comparison, individualist societies are highly verbal, avoiding silence as empty, even hostile. Content must be specifically stated because the group's relative unimportance makes communicating through the context much less certain.

Inter-group Relationships. Relationships with outsider groups are primarily competitive in collectivist cultures, even confrontational and often marked by distrust and hostility. Support of the in-group is considered necessary in dealing with outsiders, an "us against them" approach. The factionalism that fragments some nations originates in the collectivist cultures of their many constituent groups and tribes.

The individualist is expected, in contrast, to be able to function independently. Children are taught to observe, think, and act by themselves. Depending on others is considered a weakness, reducing the need for a strong supportive group. Outsiders are not normally treated with suspicion simply because the distinction between insider and outsider is much less important. Consequently, cooperation with other groups is relatively easy if that cooperation is seen to benefit individual members.

Values. Harmony, family relationships, equality in use of wealth, and modesty are high-values in collectivist societies. The possibility of bringing SHAME to the group is a strong control on behavior. The shame is in others knowing, not in the action itself. It is very important to meet the expectations of others, thus maintaining "face." Education concentrates on preparation to be a good group member, so it emphasizes tradition, rote memory, and the ability to quote respected scholars.

Freedom, self-fulfillment, recognition, honesty, and distribution of wealth according to individual effort are high values among individualists. Rather than group-centered shame, the individual feels individual GUILT when standards are violated. Education is valued when it enables individuals to cope with demands, be productive, and maximize individual abilities.

Business Dealings. Among collectivists, personal relationships are essential. Business is conducted by first establishing a social relationship, then proceeding to details of the task, and the exchange of goods, services, and money. Legal contracts are secondary to knowing the groups involved and establishing rapport and trust. Management focuses on groups as the basic unit. It is almost compulsory that persons in the in-group be given advantages in hiring, assignment of jobs, and other realms of business. Failing to do this is considered disloyalty to the group.

Individualist societies approach social and business relationships in an impersonal, factual manner that centers on the task to be accomplished. Knowing and liking among the participants is secondary to agreements carefully drafted to specify each party's obligations. Business is primarily controlled by law; personal relationships are secondary. Management focuses on individuals as the basic unit. Rewards are distributed according to the work completed, independently of personal relationships. To act otherwise is considered unfair and even dishonest.

Some Implications for Missions. Contemporary evangelical missions have predominantly originated in individualist societies, and gone to collectivist societies. Differing assumptions and expectations have led to frequent misunderstandings and antagonism. The continuing resistance of some people groups to the Christian message may well be a serious consequence.

Individualist–oriented missionaries have expected individual acceptance of the gospel, overlooking the value of a favorable group response before individuals are discipled. Antagonism and resistance often come from a perceived threat to stability and security of the group. Anything that would fragment the group is not acceptable, allowing no place for individual choice where survival of the group is thought to be involved. An individual who responds apart from group approval is a threat to unity, who must be dealt with by social exile or even death.

Missionary focus must be on the group in a collectivist culture, rather than attempting to "extract" individuals from the group. The result of an "extraction" approach is most likely to be the creation of a new group which will be considered an "out-group" by the main society. Thus, the new Christian group is to be confronted and opposed. Potential ministry bridges to the larger society are destroyed.

In a collectivist society, the pastor and church authorities are much more likely to be authoritarian, with considerable social distance between themselves and their congregations. Selection of leadership often depends more on group affiliation than on objective criteria, coming through discussion and agreement rather than election. Following the biblical pattern to become servant-leaders is a major challenge within a collectivist society.

DONALD K. SMITH

Bibliography. G. Hofstede, *Cultures and Organizations: Software of the Mind;* idem, *Culture's Consequences: International Differences in Work-Related Values;* S. Lingenfelter, *Agents of Transformation: A Guide for Effective Cross-Cultural Ministry;* H. C. Triandis, R. W. Brislin, and C. H. Hui, *Intercultural Communication: A Reader,* pp. 370–82.

Indonesia *(Ext. 2000 pop.: 212,731,000; 1,904,569 sq. km. [735,354 sq. mi.]).* Independent since 1945, Indonesia's population spans some 3,000 islands and is of great ethnolinguistic diversity. The largest groups are the Javanese (38.7%), the Sundanese (15.9%), and the Madurese (6.4%). Government statistics show Muslims at 87 percent, Christians at 9.6 percent (church statistics at 12.5%), Hindus at 1.9 percent, and tribal religionists at one percent. Professing Christians are about three-to-one Protestant (regional and ethnolinguistically based churches plus many others, including Pentecostal) to Roman Catholic.

Portuguese trading posts in the Moluccas, Suluwesi, and East Timor brought Christianity to their immediate vicinities in the sixteenth century. The work mainly of FRANCIS XAVIER and other Jesuits and Dominicans from 1562 resulted in thousands of baptisms and not a few martyrdoms.

Dutch trading incursion from 1590 ended further Roman Catholic work for two hundred years, except in Flores (and Portuguese Timor). Against the background of the Netherlands attaining freedom from Spanish and Portuguese domination, though still at war with both powers, the Dutch East India Company took over the Portuguese territories, resulting in the Catholic converts having to become Protestants.

Some of the early pastors sent out by the Company were also zealous and effective missionaries. However, they were few, and subordinate to the Company, whose commercial interests did not coincide with evangelism. Moreover, apart from the sub-Christian behavior of many of the Company's employees, there was another critical lack: the failure to instruct the Indonesian church members and church leaders, or appoint more than three indigenous pastors in the two hundred years of the Company's rule. The number of baptized had gone from 40,000 in 1600 to only 55,000 by 1800.

The new government of the Indies turned the existing regional Protestant groups into state churches. This made the ministers virtually civil servants of the religiously "neutral" government and crippled outreach. Nevertheless the pietist revival in the Netherlands and elsewhere and the resurgence of Reformed doctrine made the nineteenth century one of effective evangelism and laid the foundation of the church as it is now.

There were three groups of churches that resulted: the state churches, people-movement churches, and minority churches. Outstanding among state church efforts was the work of the Moravian-influenced Joseph Kam, sent by the Netherlands Missionary Society in 1814. He worked with the church of the Moluccas, reaching out to Minahasa and West Timor.

Notable of the people-movement churches was the German LUDWIG NOMMENSEN, who led the planting of the church in North Sumatra from 1861. This work became a people-movement, and by 1917 the Batak church numbered 180,000.

The minority East Java Christian Church was begun in defiance of the government of the Indies, and was initially torn by polar-opposite attitudes toward Javanese culture. It had reached a middle way by the time the government permitted the Netherlands Missionary Society to send J. E. Jellesma (1851) to assist in its development and outreach.

From the turn of the nineteenth century the government was more supportive of missionary work, which it saw as advantageous to itself. When the Japanese invaded in 1942, however, the churches found themselves in a newly hostile environment and many Christians suffered. On the positive side, the churches were suddenly self-standing.

Christians (and missionaries) supported Indonesian independence from the Netherlands after World War II. The repression of suspected communist sympathizers following the attempted overthrow of the government in 1965 led to thousands joining the church, especially in Java.

The Roman Catholic work, after a fall-off in effort during the eighteenth century, was renewed and became effective again after 1850, when the government of the Indies gave more freedom to missions. They moved into every region. Like the Protestants, however, they were prohibited from working in strongly Muslim areas, and were not supposed to overlap with Protestant areas.

Since the incorporation of East (Portuguese) Timor in 1975 (then mostly tribal religionist) the small minority of Roman Catholics there has become the large majority, and a small percentage has become Protestant.

In Irian Jaya people-movements have brought most of the 275 tribes to Christianity, about a quarter of the Christians being Roman Catholic. About 10 percent still remain tribal religionists, and coastal immigrants comprise the 17 percent who are Muslims in the region.

The problem of GOSPEL AND CULTURE, present from the beginning, continues in all three groups of churches: How far can the gospel shed its Western garb, and how far can it then be joined to the culture of a people to be evangelized? Syncretism, or at least dual-religion, exists widely.

Although Christians are a minority and subject to the impact on their areas of transmigration, Muslims feel like a minority over against Christians in the spheres of education, newspapers, and hospitals, and so press for more influence and status. Christians easily overreact, and so far they have engaged in little dialogue with Muslims.

The dynamism of the Indonesian churches could well lead to effective outreach beyond their own country. In a small way the Batak Protestant Church has already done this (in West Malaysia).

JOHN ALAN McINTOSH

Bibliography. H. Kraemer, *From Missionfield to Independent Church*; K. A. Steenbrink, in *Missiology: An Ecumenical Introduction*.

Inerrancy. Along with "verbal" and "plenary," both "inerrant" and "infallible" are terms the church has employed to indicate the divine truth and authority of the BIBLE. Each term carries a slightly different connotation. Verbal emphasizes that every word of Scripture is divinely authored and therefore carries God's authority; plenary notes that the divine authority is full and complete; infallible, that Scripture is incapable of mistake; and inerrant, that Scripture never wanders from the divine truth.

In the ancient church Irenaeus and Augustine represented the position of the churches of their day and handed this view on to the medieval and modern church (see the extensive list of citations in William Lee; *Inspiration*, Appendix G). At the time of the Reformation, the inerrancy of Scripture was embedded in the teaching of the Council of Trent (1545–63) and reaffirmed in the first Vatican Council (1869–70).

Luther and Calvin followed Augustine in defense of scriptural inerrancy. In the early Protestant confessions the emphasis lay on the full authority of Scripture, but this rested on the divine authorship and inerrant truth of Scripture. For Luther this is evident in his unequivocal endorsement of Augustine's doctrine of scriptural inerrancy ("*Holy Scripture cannot err*"—Luther, *Luthers Deutsche Schriften*, XXVII, 33); and from the fact that he found it necessary to expunge the Book of James from the canon of Scripture because he believed he had found an error in it (see the introduction to his *Commentary on Genesis* written in 1545 just before his death; and William Barclay, *The Letters of James and Peter*). Similarly Calvin charged Servetus with holding to a geographical error in the Bible, and the charge was dropped only when Servetus claimed not to have written or been responsible for that statement. Wesley argued that if we found but one error in the Bible, we could never trust it as the Word of God (see *Works of John Wesley*, 8:45–46).

In holding to inerrancy the church has with rare exceptions argued that the method by which God secured an infallible Bible was certainly not dictation (in spite of the charges made by their opponents). If the Latin word *dictare* was employed to refer to Scripture (so Calvin, for example), the point was explicitly made (as by Calvin) that this was not a literal dictation. Human authors of Scripture reflected their own personality and employed their own vocabulary (see, for example, Luke 1:1–4 and John 20:30, 31).

The case for biblical infallibility has always rested firmly on the teaching of our Lord and of the Scripture itself about its divine truth. How, after all, could finite humans know the Bible was infallible as to heavenly reality and the prophetic future? If Jesus Christ is truly divine, then he is our divine Lord; and we must trust him in all he taught, including what he taught about the infallible authority of Holy Scripture (see, for example, Matt. 5:17–21; 19:3–9; Mark 7:6ff.; Luke 16:17; 24:25, 44, 45; and John 10:34, 35). Likewise, if we accept the divine commission of the prophets and apostles to speak the Word of God, we cannot consistently reject their authority when they teach the necessity of believing and obeying Scripture (see, for example, Pss. 19 and 119, especially vv. 60 and 160–168; 1 Cor. 2; 2 Peter 1:19–21; and 2 Tim. 14–17).

In recent years, though rarely in earlier centuries, some evangelicals have defended a limited infallibility or limited inerrancy of Scripture. Usually this takes the form of limiting scriptural infallibility to its ethical or theological teaching. Naturally we must not take every scriptural instruction given to an individual or a group in a specific situation as necessarily a divine command to be obeyed in the same way in all circumstances (*see also* HERMENEUTICS). What is right in one instance may be quite wrong in a very different context. Inerrancy should not be understood as an excuse to take texts out of context. Yet all Scripture is profitable for every child of God, and God never commands and expects us to do what is truly wrong in the specific situation he addresses (see Gen. 22:2; 12).

Neither does the Bible speak in scientific language. Nor does it seek to provide us with a neutral scientific history of Israel or of the life and teaching of our Lord. Nor does the Bible always speak in precise and exact language. Nor does the New Testament invariably quote the Old Testament the way a twentieth-century biblical scholar would exegete the Scripture in a university classroom. But, when properly understood, it always tells the truth; and it never teaches what, as a matter of fact, is not so.

Finally, it must be noted that the contemporary theological battleground over Scripture has shifted significantly in the latter half of the twentieth century. In the nineteenth and early twentieth centuries the threat to biblical authority came from the disciplines of history, biblical criticism, and natural science. Not so today! The issue evangelicals most acutely face today is not, "Is the Bible objectively true?" More frequently it is likely to be, "Is objective nonrelative truth possible for finite human beings?" All TRUTH is relative, so it is argued; and I as a human being can possess only truth relative to me. And truth for me, as John Dewey and early pragmatists argued, is only what I as an individual hold to be true to enable me to adjust more comfortably to my environment.

While there are humbling lessons we need to learn from such relativists, Augustine, and before him, Aristotle, gave us an appropriate answer to such a position. To say one knows nothing is a fundamental nonsensical contradiction. If someone claims that he or she really does not know whether or not he or she exists, we can wash our hands of such a being and walk away realizing that such a being is functioning only as an animal, not as a human person. Such a view is as devastating to basic Christianity and to the essential gospel as it is to the infallibility of Scripture. And that is where the consistent evangelical wishes to stand.

Basic Christianity, the fundamental Christian gospel, the Lordship of Jesus Christ, and the divine authority and infallible truth of Holy Scripture—all hold together in a unity of truth. Trusting Scripture follows irresistibly from trusting Jesus Christ as Lord.

KENNETH S. KANTZER

Bibliography. J. Barr, *The Scope and Authority of the Bible;* D. A. Carson and John D. Woodbridge, eds., *Scripture and Truth;* H. M. Conn, ed., *Inerrancy and Hermeneutic;* N. Geisler, ed., *Inerrancy;* B. B. Warfield, *The Inspiration and Authority of the Bible;* N. Wolterstorff, *Divine Discourse.*

Infallibility (of the Bible). *See* BIBLE; INERRANCY.

Information Technology. With the dramatic growth in the worldwide use of the Internet, using the tools of information technology (IT) is routine today. IT here refers to electronic computing and communication systems employing digital technology, which started with the digital computer in the late 1940s and developed into computer-based internetworking by the 1970s.

In 1960, Joseph E. Grimes used a computer to do language analysis in Bible translation work in Mexico. Other mission specialists also used computers to analyze sociological and church statistics and other data in studying religious movements and church growth trends. David B. Barrett, a missionary to Kenya doing graduate studies in New York, used a computer to analyze the data he and others had collected on more that six thousand African independent church and renewal movements (*see* AFRICAN-INITIATED CHURCH MOVEMENT). Results were used in Barrett's 1968 book, *Schism and Renewal in Africa.* Also in 1968, data from the survey of mission agencies in North America were entered into a computer under the direction of Edward R. Dayton and camera-ready pages generated for the *North America Protestant Ministries Overseas Directory.*

In 1974, information on unreached peoples was gathered from seventy-three countries for the LAUSANNE CONGRESS ON WORLD EVANGELISM. This was stored on a computer from which an *Unreached Peoples Directory* was printed and distributed to Congress participants as a work-in-progress to be refined and expanded. Data about the languages of the world published in the *Ethnologue* by WYCLIFFE BIBLE TRANSLATORS were placed on a computer so subsequent editions could be more easily updated and analyzed.

With the proliferation and the growing capacity of personal computers and networks, IT supported activities in missions have become widespread. Bible translators continue to enhance specialized software used on portable computers to speed the work of translation. Electronic mail is used for instant communication in many parts of the world by missionaries, national workers, mission executives, and those supporting missionaries. Mission information about unreached peoples and other aspects of missions is available on various Internet Web sites. One can link to many of these from the Global Mapping International Web address (www.gmi.org) or the Wheaton College Missions Department address (www.wheaton.edu/missions).

The Internet's electronic mail and conferencing capabilities also provide a way for those concerned about various people groups to share information and ideas in an open networking mode. One of the most popular of these is the Brigada Network (www.brigada.org) with more than six thousand participants receiving the weekly *Brigada Today* newsletter as well as being involved in related online conferences of their specific missions interest.

The Internet can also expand and extend participation in mission conferences and other mission-related activities. During InterVarsity's 1996 Urbana world mission convention for students, background information and daily summaries appeared on the Web, including audio and video segments, for those who were not among the 19,300 onsite delegates. This has been continued to help a new generation of students anticipate the triennial convention in 2000 (www.urbana.org).

JOHN SIEWERT

SEE ALSO Technology.

Initiation Rites. These communal rituals, which are RITES OF PASSAGE, mark changes in social status or position which an individual undergoes by passing through culturally recognized life phases. Rites are generally connected with pregnancy and childbirth, transition from puberty to adulthood, betrothal, marriage, death and funerals, and in some societies associated with formal training of craftspersons (or professionals), religious specialists, and warfare. Initiation rites are the process by which individuals are made to be, and taught to function as, recognized members of society. These rites constitute some of the most significant educational experiences in the life of an individual by dramatizing and reinforcing the values of a given society as the initiate internalizes the knowledge, feelings, and aspirations of the social system. They serve to establish the function of the individual in his or her responsibility to the whole society and the society to the individual. The rites help achieve competence and the psychological growth necessary for healthy human functioning as well as safeguarding the cultural system.

In each case the rites involve three stages: (1) separation—the person is removed from normal routine and sometimes also regular social associates; (2) LIMINAL period—the in-between stage where physical and symbolic rituals are taken to extinguish the old status; during this stage there may be physical hardship, such as circumcision, incision, and/or other physical scarification, and the transmission of rules, goals, activities, folk lore, values, beliefs, and so on; (3) incorporation—the public acknowledgment of the new status. Ceremonial recognition of the changed social status legitimizes the permanently altered status with all its rights and obligations to the larger society.

The attendant rituals reflect a symbolic enactment of death and rebirth. The physical distress (frequently physical mutilations) of the initiation rites makes a difference between the old and the new life. Thus male or female (clitoridectomy) circumcision is quite common. The more painful the ritual, the more a person values the new status. There may be universal symbolism to genital operations—a ritual slaying with a rebirth into a new status. The bloodletting is an attempt to initiate, and thus participate in life-creating powers, quite common in FOLK RELIGION. Initiation rites are often associated with Third World societies which seem to place greater emphasis on the formal recognition of physiological and social changes, rituals which Western societies have supposedly outgrown. This is not so. There may be no single set of ceremonies marking transitions, only a confusion of rites which mark greater independence. However, note the customs or rites which accompany pregnancy, birth, christening/baptism, coming of age, marriage, and death/funerals in the West. Because some rites also have educational functions in which the initiate must learn and demonstrate knowledge and skills consistent with the behavior appropriate to the new status graduation ceremonies from educational institutions, religious ordination, military bootcamp, entry into new professions, and so on, serve the same purpose.

PHILIP M. STEYNE

SEE ALSO A. VAN GENNEP, *THE RITES OF PASSAGE;* C. LANE, *RITES OF RULERS.*

Inspiration of the Bible. *See* BIBLE; INERRANCY.

Institutionalization. "The development of orderly, stable, socially integrating forms and structures out of unstable, loosely patterned or merely technical types of action" (Broom and Selznick, 1968, 215). A dynamic process that continually changes over time, institutionalization involves at least four processes within a social group, such as a church or mission. Each process can be measured along a continuum.

The formalization process involves roles within the organization. These roles usually begin as voluntary, nonformalized roles in a newer mission and proceed to more structured and formalized roles in an established mission. The final stage in this institutional process is ossification. In the process, efficiency is increased, but ability to change becomes more difficult.

In the beginning everyone in a new mission is equal and all are focused on the primary purpose. There is little organized authority, but soon participants and leaders see the need for self-maintenance, a structure to maintain the mission vision and purpose. Often a constitution is adopted and purpose becomes clearer when structure supports that purpose. A danger is that the mission might become an end in itself no longer focused on the original purpose. Extreme institutionalization leads to processes and methods taking precedence over the original purpose.

A group's social base usually begins with people brought together by a common cause or through a charismatic leader. At one end of the continuum the social criteria for membership in the group are minimal. Gradually, criteria proceed from flexibility, to stability, and finally to criteria that are rigidly proscribed at the other end of a continuum. At this end, rigidity may result in a "we–they" confrontational style.

Positive Aspects of Institutionalization. Stability is necessary for the functioning of efficient and flexible organizations. Unformalized organizations, being unfocused and unwieldy, require much time and energy to function. Formalization brings greater efficiency while maintaining flexibility, as long as formalization does not become too rigid.

Groups, including mission groups, tend to decline over a period of time. Institutional structures and processes can aid in an organization's long-term survival. Institutionalization can bring order out of chaos. Using the organization's structure as a means to an end, having members who enlist new members in the group's cause, strong and renewed leadership, and a specific purpose that challenges the members are all factors in the long-term survival and balanced institutionalization of a mission organization.

Some degree of structure is necessary to purposefully plan and expedite a given task. This is most readily seen in the hundreds of plans developed over the twentieth century to fulfill the GREAT COMMISSION. The purpose must be seen as having value if people are to be drawn to its accomplishment. For missions and churches, both the purpose and the procedure to accomplish the purpose should have Scripture-based value.

Attaining a group's purposes requires mobilization of human and material resources. Institutional processes show the need for continual development of LEADERSHIP. The institutional process deals with leaders who are faithful to the group's purpose and direct their efforts to its accomplishment.

Organizational structure is a product of institutionalization. Besides the benefits already mentioned, predictability is an important feature. Knowing what to expect and being able to predict events contribute to a person's comfort with and support of an organization, especially in cultures that do not allow for ambiguity.

Negative Aspects of Institutionalization. Structure replaces purpose when the group has turned totally inward and has lost its vision and purpose. The mission's structure has become an end in itself. Parkinson notes, "Work expands to fill the time available for its completion. . . . The number of officials and quantity of work are not related to each other at all. . . . Administrators are more or less bound to multiply" (1957, 11, 12, 15).

Transference is the process whereby the seeds of death in the institutionalization process are transferred to other missions or churches. Because social structures are organic in nature, the factors that cause the demise of one organization can be commuted to related organizations.

Resources, time, personnel, and material are expended on minor issues that do not contribute to the group's stated purpose. Huge amounts of time in discussion and funds may go into a trivial project having little to do with the group's stated purpose. War stories of church committee battles over the proposed color of the sanctuary carpet exemplify the result of lost balance.

The process of institutionalization may continue past the stability stage, causing the mission to become rigid and inflexible. Inflexibility causes an organization to lose its ability to objectively evaluate itself.

When a mission begins to die it may be due to excessive emphasis upon programs rather than focusing on the people. Missions which have maintained the same membership for long periods of time, where people know each other well, may end up focusing on programs rather than people. Extreme institutionalization, with its inward focus, often ignores new people and their potential.

Normally, we think of too much structure as the problem but inadequate structure can also be a problem. "The most fundamental function of institutions is probably to protect the individual from having to make too many choices" (P. Berger, 1976, 187). Too little institutional structure can be the cause of instability.

Conclusion. Institutionalization is a process that can contribute to or detract from a mission's vision and purpose. Negatively, the final stages of the process of institutionalization lead to rigidity, detraction from the purpose, deterioration in the leadership processes, and death. Rightly implemented, processes of institutionalization in mission can lead to fulfilled purpose, efficiency, flexibility, and dynamic leadership. The mission in which institutional structure focuses on purpose and people, promotes leadership renewal, and encourages membership participation will find the group's purposes enhanced.

MIKEL NEUMANN

SEE ALSO Association, Socio-Anthropology of.

Bibliography. P. Berger, B. Berger, and H. Kellner, *The Homeless Mind*; L. Broom and P. Selznick, *Sociology*; P. Heibert, *Exploring Church Growth*, pp. 157–67; C. N. Parkinson, *Parkinson's Law*.

Interagency Cooperation. While the days of mission agencies acting as lone rangers continue to diminish, there is still progress to be made. A number of external factors will continue the push toward cooperation: the dwindling number of full-time missionaries; the increase of short-termers; churches doing their own selecting, training, sending, and mentoring; the diminishing appreciation for denominations; ministry overlap between agencies (reduplicating support personnel); the difficulty of fundraising for workers and agency maintenance. More by necessity than design, interagency cooperation provides a solution for survival and ministry.

Interagency cooperation includes a number of risks for those who wish to participate. Agency boards, leaders, and personnel will worry about a number of issues: Will they lose the agency's distinctive for existence? Will the agency's mission statement and core values be compromised? How can the different philosophies of ministry be unified? Should they? If certain positions in the agency are no longer necessary, what happens to those who filled them? What energy costs will be necessary to maintain productive cooperation? Who funds what? And of deeper concern, will their agency die?

The trust factor figures large in interagency cooperation. To offset some of the above concerns, courting should precede the wedding contract. When they eventually say, "I do," they say "yes" to commitment, character, a common vision, costs, cooperation, and communication over concerns, and "no" to competition and comparison.

The rewards of interagency cooperation must move beyond survival. And they can. From the perspective of agency personnel, the pooling of personnel and finances can meet their needs from recruitment to retirement much more adequately. From the perspective of ministry projects and programs, interagency cooperation can expand the kingdom of God in ways no single agency can. Some of these efforts may be short-term, some long-term. But all processes should be driven by the unity–diversity of the participants, thereby glorifying the creative God behind them.

TOM A. STEFFEN

SEE ALSO Globalization; Partnership.

Bibliography. L. Bush and L. Lutz, *Partnering in Ministry; The Direction of World Evangelism, IJFM* 11:1 (1994); J. H. Kraakevik and D. Welliver, eds., *Partners in the Gospel: The Strategic Role of Partnership in World;* W. Sandy, *Forging the Productivity Partnership;* W. D. Taylor, ed., *Kingdom Partnerships for Synergy in Missions.*

Intercession. *See* PRAYER.

Intercultural Communication. Interaction among people of diverse cultures. Since cultures have different symbols, different contexts, different social rules, and different expectations, development of shared understanding is often exceedingly difficult. Thorough study of COMMUNICATION patterns to identify these differences and adapt to them is the foundation of effective CROSS-CULTURAL MINISTRY.

Intercultural communication is distinct from cross-cultural communication, which compares a particular behavior or behaviors in differing cultures. International communication deals with comparative mass media communication in different nations and to communication between nations. Global communication is a term usually limited to the technology and transfer of information without regard to national borders.

Two general categories of communication models, mechanistic and humanistic, are useful to more fully understand the dominant, but differing, approaches to intercultural communication,

Mechanistic Models. Mechanistic models are most clearly seen in the development of "information theory" used in telephones, computers, and related devices. The behavioristic perspective (from behavioristic psychology) stresses stimulus and response. The transmissional perspective (Berlo and DeVito) suggests ten components of communication: source, encoding, message, channel, noise, receiver, decoding, receiver response, feedback, and context.

Use of a mechanistic model has led to emphasis on sending out a message without great attention to who is actually receiving and comprehending the message. It has also stimulated development of electronic translation units that are said to make intercultural communication possible. Equivalent words from one language are given in a second language. Applied to intercultural communication, a mechanistic model frequently overlooks significant areas, such as cultural assumptions, context, and experience. Though frequently followed in intercultural ministry, mechanistic approaches to communication have little, if any, biblical support as a pattern for either evangelism or discipling.

Humanistic Models. Humanistic models emphasize the human element in communication. The transactional view of communication recognizes that knowledge of the receiver or listener is part of shaping the message form. Communication is seen as sharing. Symbols are used to stimulate the formation of meaning in another person, and consequently the sharing of meaning through a context-sensitive process. The interactional approach recognizes the reciprocal nature of communication, in which a circle that includes feedback and alteration represents the communication process. Both the transactional and interactional views of communication are consistent with biblically based INCARNATIONAL MISSION. A Christian view of communication must also recognize the presence and work of the Holy Spirit in the communicative process.

Most humanistic models developed in the Western world assume that sharing of information is the primary aim of communication. However, East Asian societies that are deeply influenced by Confucianism (China, Korea, Japan especially) view communication as primarily to establish and maintain harmony. Balance and harmony in human relationships are the basis of society. Interpersonal communication is guided by social rules specific for each situation, depending on age, status, and intimacy. Thus, communication is an "infinite interpretive process" (Jandt, 1995, 29) where everyone concerned seeks to develop and maintain a social relationship. Communication is a way to seek consensus, not essentially to transmit information. Difficulties in intercultural communication will arise from the fundamentally different purposes in communicating between East and West, as well as from the more obvious differences in style, context, and vocabulary.

Communication and Culture. Is communication synonymous with culture, or an aspect of culture? CULTURE is a code we learn and share, and learning and sharing require communication. Every act and every cultural pattern involve communication. It is not possible to know a culture without knowing its communication, and communication can only be understood by knowing the culture involved. If culture existed without communication, culture would be unknowable. Communication, on the other hand, functions only as an expression of culture. Culture and communication are inseparable, This fundamental level is implicit to communication. It is a part of being alive, of being in any kind of community.

Communication arts focuses on specific communication modes such as graphic and fine arts, drama, music, journalism, and literature. Specific ways a particular mode (communication art) is developed depends on the purpose and cultural context. This is explicit or utilitarian communication, a skill to be acquired and used for particular purposes.

Problems in intercultural communication occur at both implicit and explicit levels of communication. It is difficult implicitly because of differing assumptions about God, humanity, the world, and the nature of reality as well as different values and different experiences, When these differences are ignored, assuming similarity instead of difference, communication across cultural boundaries will be ineffective or even negative in its effects.

Eastern Perspectives. The Eastern perspective on communication is historically based on the goal of achieving harmony between humanity and nature. Through communication the individual seeks to rise above personal interests to become one with the "universal essence" by use of ritual, meditation, and myth. Today's patterns of communication used in Eastern nations as different as communist China, Japan, and Korea derive from this common background. Kincaid and Cushman point out three characteristics shared by Eastern social and political systems: (1) subordination of the individual to a strong hierarchical authority, (2) a subjugation maintained by

a symbolic perception of harmony, and (3) a belief that events have meaning as evidences of universal principles. An Eastern view of communication emphasizes the implicit aspect.

Western Perspectives. By contrast, the Western perspective on communication emphasized its role in establishing and maintaining individual political, social, and economic freedom. Communication is used to manipulate circumstances and people so that personal goals can be achieved. Communication is utilized to reach personal or group goals, the explicit or utilitarian approach.

Intercultural communication is difficult at the explicit or utilitarian level because of language difference, nonverbal misinterpretations, and personal attitudes. These problems can be identified and overcome, but mature understanding may still not be achieved. Effective intercultural communication demands recognizing and overcoming difficulties at both the explicit and implicit levels.

Signal or Symbol System. Twelve systems of signals are used by every culture. In fact, almost all of human communication occurs by use of one or more of the twelve systems: verbal (or spoken language), written, numeric, pictorial, artifactual (three-dimensional representations and objects), audio (including silence), kinesic (what has been called "body language"), optical (light and color), tactile (touch), spatial (the use of space), temporal (time), and olfactory (taste and smell).

Even though the same signal systems are used in every culture, the many significant differences in their usage make clarity of understanding between members of different cultures difficult to achieve. One culture may emphasize the importance of the verbal (the spoken word), while another emphasizes the unspoken use of body language, the kinesic system. Another culture may have highly developed pictorial communication, while still another has an intricate system of communication involving numbers. The individual signals may have totally different signification in different cultures, for example, a gesture may mean approval in one culture and be considered obscene in another or a word may indicate appreciation in one setting but rejection in a different culture. Effective intercultural communication at the explicit-utilitarian level demands learning both the relative importance of the various signal systems in different cultures as well as learning the meaning intended by various signals.

In summary, intercultural communication is a process depending on increasing involvement of the parties seeking to communicate. Only through involvement can both implicit and explicit communication contribute to shared understanding. Such involvement is demonstrated in the life of Christ, who became flesh and lived among us (John 1:14). It is also the pattern for missionary service (John 17:18). Paul clearly modeled this kind of intercultural communication as he explains in 1 Corinthians 9:19–23.

DONALD K. SMITH

SEE ALSO Interpersonal Communication.

Bibliography. W. B. Gudykunst and Y. Y. Kim, *Communicating with Strangers An Approach to Intercultural Communication;* G. Hofstede, *Cultures and Organizations: Software of the Mind;* F. E. Jandt, *Intercultural Communication: An Introduction;* D. L. Kincaid, *Communication Theory: Eastern and Western Perspectives;* L. A. Samovar and R. E. Porter, *Intercultural Communication A Reader;* D. K. Smith, *Creating Understanding: A Handbook for Christian Communication Across Cultural Landscapes.*

Intercultural Competency. To live and work effectively interculturally, a person must engage in CULTURAL LEARNING with the goal of becoming effective in the broad range of behaviors that are part of becoming competent in any culture. Since the members of a culture have a whole lifetime in which to learn its inner workings and complexities, an intercultural worker will never have the competency of someone born in that culture. Yet, with careful and intentional learning, a missionary can master a broad range of skills required for effective COMMUNICATION, interpersonal relationships, and continuous learning in a ministry setting.

The goal of intercultural competency is to gain sufficient understanding of the broad range of required cultural behaviors so that one is sensitized to intercultural tensions, aware of cultural expectations and practices, and continually learning the finer points of communication in each area of cultural practice.

There are seven distinctive areas in which a cross-cultural worker should seek to achieve competence in any culture.

Language Fluency. The mastery of a language of a culture is essential to effective communication. Intercultural workers should master the grammatical structures of the local language, and vocabulary in all the areas of communication that are essential to their work.

Understanding the Rules of Labor and Exchange. Every culture has adopted economic practices and values that govern the organization of labor and exchange within a community. Since all intercultural workers are involved in some form of labor and exchange relationships with people in the community, understanding their rules and values with regard to work are essential for effective intercultural service.

Understanding Authority Relations in Family and Community. Every community defines structures to govern relationships between individuals and groups. The intercultural worker should seek to understand the rules and roles that are significant in family and community

structures, and know how these are practiced by members in the indigenous community.

Mastering the Basics of Conflict Resolution. Conflict is inevitable in any kind of community. Every community also has its basic assumptions and requirements for conflict resolution. An intercultural worker cannot hope to be effective unless she or he masters the patterns of conflict resolution that are practiced within the local community.

Understanding Basic Values and Personality. The bringing up of children is one of the most important activities in any culture. Through this process adults impart to children the basic values that are essential in the cultural setting, and channel the unique personalities of children into proper cultural behaviors. Understanding this process of shaping children into mature adults is crucial for competency in a culture (*see* ENCULTURATION). Learning the values that parents impart to their children and the process through which they channel unique personalities into appropriate adult behavior is crucial for effective cultural learning.

Understanding Beliefs and Worldview. All human beings actively reflect on their cultural experience and articulate the meaning of these experiences in their beliefs and WORLDVIEW. Once an intercultural worker has a good working knowledge of the language, and has acquired competencies in the other aspects of culture above, then exploration of beliefs and worldview is essential to gaining a whole picture of culture.

Effective Communication and Contextualization of Work and Ministry. The desired outcome of intercultural competency is effective communication in every area of culture. The goal of cultural competency is to contextualize work and ministry in the cultural system that is known and practiced by people in the local community. The intercultural worker must intentionally frame communication and ministry within the cultural systems available to local cultural participants. This requires that intercultural workers rethink what they do and how they do it, and reframe it into the language, economic, social, and value systems of the local culture.

Many missiologists define cultural competency with reference to incarnational ministry (*see* INCARNATIONAL MISSION). The example for incarnational ministry is the Lord Jesus Christ. In Philippians 2:6–7, Paul speaks of Jesus as being "in very nature God," yet not clinging to that identity, but "taking the very nature of a servant, being made in human likeness." Lingenfelter and Mayers (1986, p. 15) characterize Jesus as a "200% person." They then draw the analogy that the intercultural missionary must become at least a 150% person—ideally, retaining their own cultural identity at least at the level of 75%, and yet adding a new identity of 75% of the culture in which they serve. The challenge of incarnational ministry is becoming more than we are, and learning and incorporating the culture of our hosts into our lives, and participating effectively in ministry within their cultural context. Yet incarnational ministry is not enough. As Christians we are engaged in lives of pilgrimage; as Peter says, "as aliens and strangers in the world, . . . live such good lives among the pagans that, though they may accuse you of doing wrong, they may see your good deeds and glorify God on the day that He visits us" (1 Peter 2:11–12).

SHERWOOD G. LINGENFELTER

SEE ALSO Cross-Cultural Ministry.

Bibliography. P. G. Hiebert, *Anthropological Insights for Missionaries*; S. G. Lingenfelter and Marvin K. Mayers, *Ministering Cross-Culturally: An Incarnational Model for Personal Relationships*.

Interdenominational Foreign Mission Association of North America (IFMA).

In March of 1917, Paul Groef, a Wall Street broker and member of the board of the South Africa General Mission, called together leaders of key faith missions for the purpose of strengthening effectiveness and outreach. Representatives of the South Africa General Mission (now AFRICA EVANGELICAL FELLOWSHIP), The China Inland Mission (now OVERSEAS MISSIONARY FELLOWSHIP or OMF International), the Central American Mission (CAM International), and the AFRICA INLAND MISSION organized the Interdenominational Foreign Mission Association (IFMA) to enable missions leaders to get together for prayer, fellowship, and the exchange of ideas and information. The other charter members were the Sudan Interior Mission (now the SOCIETY FOR INTERNATIONAL MINISTRIES), the Inland South America Missionary Union (South America Indian Mission), and the Women's Union Missionary Society of America.

From the 1920s to the 1950s, roughly ten new agencies were added to the IFMA each decade. From the 1950s to the 1980s, the number increased to fifteen per decade. From 1981 to 1991, the number jumped by thirty-five members. Current membership comprises over one hundred agencies, representing over ten thousand missionaries sent from North America. Another five thousand from other countries are affiliated with the member agencies.

Mission agencies can maintain one of four levels of relationship with the IFMA: (1) *Association* is reserved for member agencies, with membership requirements including agreement with the basic historical fundamentals of conservative evangelical Christianity and with the IFMA Confession of Faith. Additionally, member agencies are expected to maintain a noncharismatic orientation. (2) *Cooperation* is the level of relationship for all nonmember groups which share the IFMA doctrinal and operational commitment. (3) *Fellowship* is maintained with evangelical groups whose doctrinal or operational stances make cooperation difficult. (4) *Communication* is maintained with groups whose doctrinal stances (such as the inclusivism of the WORLD COUNCIL OF CHURCHES) make fellowship impossible.

Nondenominational, interdenominational, or independent missions have been popularly called FAITH MISSIONS because their financial structures are based on prayer and trust in God to supply financial needs. There is no guaranteed salary for missionaries in faith missions. Most member missions have adopted the principle of "full information without solicitation." While some IFMA members do solicit funds, the IFMA requires of them active faith in God for the provision of needs without strong fund solicitation.

The primary concern of the original founding members of IFMA (e.g., SUD, AIM, CIM) was the unreached inland peoples. Throughout IFMA history, member agencies have been innovative in their efforts to evangelize the HIDDEN PEOPLES of the world; they have pioneered and specialized in such ministries as education, medicine, radio and television, gospel recording, Bible translation, and aviation. The IFMA has focused internally on the need for closer cooperation of the nondenominational mission agencies in these endeavors and externally on presenting a unified front against the encroachment of various forms of theological liberalism.

The first full-time executive officer of IFMA, John Percy, was elected to the office of general secretary in 1956. He was succeeded by Edwin Frizen Jr. in 1963, who was in turn succeeded by John Orme in 1991. The official board has no administrative authority over member missions, but does elect fifteen board members for the purposes of accreditation, networking for special projects, and coordination between churches, schools, and mission agencies.

Among member agencies, the direction of the work in the field is done from the field, not by home directorates or executive staff. Thus individual missionaries have not only a voice, but also a vote in the organization and conduct of mission affairs. In some agencies the missionaries themselves elect the general director and other officers. In others, the board of directors elects the general director.

Nondenominational missions characteristically have been open to cooperation with like-minded evangelical missions. In a number of instances, cooperation has led to mergers. Every three years the IFMA meets with the EVANGELICAL FELLOWSHIP OF MISSION AGENCIES (EFMA) in a joint leadership gathering. The two associations jointly sponsor the annual IFMA/EFMA Personnel Seminar. From 1964 to 1997, the two associations cosponsored the *Evangelical Missions Quarterly* and *Pulse*. In 1966, they cosponsored the CONGRESS ON THE CHURCH'S WORLDWIDE MISSION. Through the executive director of IFMA, communication and relationships are also maintained with the National Association of Evangelicals (NAE), the WORLD EVANGELICAL FELLOWSHIP (WEF), and other major entities working in world evangelization.

Through their history, the IFMA members have considered both husband and wife as full missionaries. This is in contrast with some boards that have appointed only the husband as a missionary. Among IFMA mission agencies, single women have pioneered in many ministries, including EVANGELISM and CHURCH PLANTING.

Headquartered in Wheaton, Illinois, the IFMA supplies personnel staffs with the know-how for missionary recruitment, selection, and professional development, and business and financial staffs with refresher seminars in management, taxes, and accounting. Other offerings include conferences and small group seminars that enhance leadership and management skills as well as forums enabling mission leadership to stay abreast of world issues and current theological and missiological trends.

JOHN ORME

Bibliography. E. L. Frizen Jr., *75 Years of IFMA: 1917–1992;* J. H. Kane, *Faith Mighty Faith: A Handbook of the Interdenominational Foreign Mission Association;* M. Rupert, *The Emergence of the Independent Missionary Agency as an American Institution, 1860–1917.*

International Association for Mission Studies (IAMS).

This association describes itself as "an international, interconfessional, and interdisciplinary professional society for the scholarly study of Christian witness and its impact in the world." Olav Myklebust in Norway first proposed such an organization in 1951. After preliminary meetings of European and North American missiologists in Birmingham, England, in 1968, and Oslo, Norway, in 1970, the IAMS was inaugurated in 1972 at Driebergen, The Netherlands. In 1996, when its ninth international conference met in Buenos Aires, Argentina, the association had 465 individual members and 75 corporate members, of which approximately 200 were from Asia, Africa, Latin America, and the Pacific region.

Stated objectives of the association are "to promote the scholarly study of theological, historical and practical questions relating to mission; to disseminate information concerning mission among all those engaged in such studies and among the general public, and to publish the results of biblical research; to relate studies in mission to studies in theological and other disciplines; to promote fellowship, cooperation and mutual assistance in mission studies; to organize international conferences of missiologists; to encourage the creation of centers of research; and to stimulate publications in missiology." The IAMS journal, *Mission Studies*, is sent to all members and other subscribers twice each year. The association also sponsors four study projects that are carried on by work groups: biblical studies and mission; documentation, archives, and bibliography; healing and mission; and patristics and mission. The IAMS is not a sending or promotion agency, but an association for the study of mission. Its major achievement has been to create a global network for the advancement of scholarship among individuals, organizations, and centers engaged in the study of world mission and Christianity in the non-Western world. Offices of the general secretariat are in Hamburg, Germany.

GERALD H. ANDERSON

Bibliography. G. H. Anderson, *MS* 1 (1984): 2–3; G. H. Anderson and A. Camps, *MS* 12 (1995): 3–4; O. G. Myklebust, *MS* 3 (1986): 4–11; *Introducing IAMS* (promotional brochure).

International Conferences for Itinerant Evangelists (Amsterdam 1983, 1086).

An amazing step of faith on the part of BILLY GRAHAM, the conference for itinerant evangelists was fully sponsored and well organized by hundreds within the circle of the evangelistic association that bears his name. Graham, however, was not at all sure of the outcome of a conference designed solely to minister to the coming generation of itinerant evangelists worldwide. When it was first conceived, no one was even certain of their numbers, much less how to contact them. Werner Burklin, the German executive of Youth for Christ, was assigned the task of tracking them down by visiting numerous countries and interviewing all sorts of church leaders—always with the request for information on promising young evangelists, women as well as men, who would be most likely to profit from such a gathering. At first, the response was slow, but it gathered momentum and in the end 3,827 came from 133 countries, largely (70 percent) from the non-Western world. More than half were without formal training, and for the majority the conference was their first exposure to evangelists from other countries. It was later discovered that there were at least 10,000 such itinerant workers serving throughout the world.

At the opening session Graham, while promising to avoid heavy theology, set forth four specific goals for the individual conferees: (1) maintenance of the purity of the gospel; (2) adherence to biblical ethics in home life, personal morality, and financial accounting; (3) cooperation with local churches; and (4) effectiveness in giving evangelistic invitations. From July 12 to 21, 1983, there were two plenary sessions daily, and a myriad of workshops. One warning was blunt: "Avoid being self-appointed gurus, sent by nobody and accountable to nobody." Since the sixth Assembly of the WORLD COUNCIL OF CHURCHES was meeting almost concurrently in Vancouver, Graham's closing address pointedly called on WCC leaders to renew their commitment to biblical evangelism and world mission. Then he turned to the Amsterdam delegates and stressed the indispensables to effective evangelism: a robust prayer life and an unrelenting devotion to Bible study. He confessed that the greatest failure in his life was that he had "spoken too much, studied too little." Hardly had the conference ended when the full-time convention staff began interviewing delegates to conserve the evident gains of this costly venture ($8.7 million). Many called for a repeat in the near future, and a second conference was convened in 1986.

Having been forced to turn away some 6,000 possible participants at Amsterdam '83, the capacity for Amsterdam '86 was expanded to include 8,160 evangelists and 2,000 other participants. They came from 173 countries, more than any other conference in history at that time. Simultaneous translation was made available in 25 languages, enabled by a team of 112 translators. The primary purpose of Amsterdam '86 was "to encourage, to equip, and to motivate the evangelists of the world" (*CT*, 1986, 41). In light of the goal, it was appropriate that 78 percent of the participants came from Two-Thirds World countries. The total conference cost was $21 million, paid for by contributions raised through the Billy Graham Evangelistic Association. In the late 1990s, the BGEA began planning for a final Amsterdam Conference to take place in August of 2000 with an estimated budget of some $35 milllion.

ARTHUR F. GLASSER

Bibliography. Christianity Today 27 (June 17, 1983): 46–47; (Sept. 2): 28–31, 42–46; 30 (Sept. 5, 1986): 41–43; D. Foster: *Billy Graham, A Vision Imparted: Amsterdam 83, A Pictorial Report.*

International Council for Evangelical Theological Education (ICETE).

In a little noticed phenomenon of modern global Christianity, in most parts of the Two-Thirds World the evangelical theological schools have taken the initiative to link themselves in vigorous indigenously directed alliances. Such alliances first began to emerge in the 1960s and early 1970s. In 1980 these continental movements organized themselves into a global federation, now known as the International Council for Evangelical Theological Education (ICETE, formerly ICAA). ICETE functions under the auspices of the WORLD EVANGELICAL FELLOWSHIP (WEF). Its constituency includes continental alliances of theological institutions representing all major regions of the world.

In response to the strongly felt needs of their constituencies, most ICETE associations began with, or early developed, accreditation schemes to facilitate academic recognition for their member schools. Most also developed a range of support services, and promoted contact and cooperation among member schools. Most ICETE associations have also embraced nonformal and extension theological education. ICETE itself adopted the "Manifesto on the Renewal of Evangelical Theological Education" (1983, 1990) to encourage fresh approaches. A principal achievement of ICETE since its inception has been the lively intercontinental dialogue fostered through a sequence of international consultations: Hoddesdon, England (1980); Chongoni, Malawi (1981); Seoul (1982); Wheaton (1983); Katydata, Cyprus (1984); Unterweissbach, Germany (1987); Wheaton (1989); London (1991); Bangkok (1993); and Sopley, England (1996). The papers of several of these gatherings are published in an ICETE monograph series, *Evangelical Theological Education Today.*

Evangelical schools in Africa first established an alliance in 1966 under the acronym AEBICAM. In 1970 the Asia Theological Association was formed, and in 1973 what is now the Caribbean Evangelical Theological Association was founded. In 1976 AEBICAM was superseded by the Accrediting Council for Theological Education in Africa (ACTEA), and in 1979 the European Evangelical Accrediting Association was established. In March 1980 these bodies joined with the older (1947) Accrediting Association of Bible Colleges (North America) to form ICETE. Subsequently ICETE has been joined by the South Pacific Association of Bible Colleges (founded 1969) and the Association for Evangelical Theological Education in Latin America (AETAL; founded in 1992 as the successor to AETTE, which was founded in 1968). The first general secretary of ICETE was Paul Bowers from ACTEA. He was succeeded by Robert Youngblood, who was in turn followed by Roger Kemp of Australia.

PAUL BOWERS

Bibliography. W. P. Bowers, ed., *Evangelical Theological Education: An International Agenda,* 2nd ed.; R. Kemp, *ERT* 19:3 (July 1995): 314–15; idem, ed., *Text and Context in Theological Education.*

International Council of Accrediting Agencies (ICAA). *See* INTERNATIONAL COUNCIL FOR EVANGELICAL THEOLOGICAL EDUCATION.

International Fellowship of Evangelical Students (IFES).

The International Fellowship of Evangelical Students was founded in August 1947 at the Phillips Brooks House in Harvard University. Representatives of ten countries (Australia, Britain, Canada, China, France, Holland,

New Zealand, Norway, Switzerland, United States) committed themselves to creating a network of indigenous university student movements that would have the primary purpose of "seeking to awaken and deepen personal faith in the Lord Jesus Christ and to further evangelistic work among students throughout the world." To help accomplish this, the IFES stated their desire to strengthen existing national evangelical student groups and provide for fellowship through international conferences on a regional and worldwide basis.

As of 1996, the IFES had expanded to 134 countries with another 36 countries identified for pioneering work in the future. Most of the remaining countries are in the Islamic world of North Africa, the Fertile Crescent, and the Republics in Central Asia. There are more than three hundred thousand students worldwide that are associated with IFES, with the largest student movement being the Nigerian (NIFES) movement with more than thirty thousand students involved in their discipleship and evangelistic ministries.

Because the IFES is committed to indigenous national leadership, a key strategy is the development of national staff workers in each country. As of the 1995 quadrennial *World Assembly* of the IFES only 27 countries of the 134 did not have some national staff workers. These developing student movements are frequently assisted in their ministry by staff from other countries until they can support their own staff personnel.

The IFES also seeks to strengthen its movements through intentional training strategies, literature, and media resources. Regional training personnel are appointed to serve various language and geographical groupings through specific training conferences for both staff and student leaders. Publishing houses and the development of national authors for Bible studies and books are major dimensions of a strategic and growing literature ministry.

Perhaps the most significant emphasis within the IFES is the ever present pioneering and missionary endeavors. The North American URBANA missions conference sponsored by IFES member movements, InterVarsity USA and InterVarsity Canada, has challenged nearly 200,000 delegates during its triennial conventions with the call of God to the world mission of the church. Similar conventions have taken place in Taiwan, Nigeria, Kenya, India, and Australia. These conventions not only raise missionary concerns and vision for the delegates but they provide opportunities for evangelical missionary agencies and church groups to work together in helping college and university students find their role in world missions.

Because student groups within the IFES carry out their ministry among the top educational institutions within their countries, their influence is often very significant among future national leaders in government, business, and the professions. Since students in IFES movements are given opportunities to develop their own spiritual leadership gifts while in school they are also well equipped to provide leadership within their own church context and frequently become leaders of other missionary endeavors as well.

The first elected leader (general secretary) for the IFES was the Australian C. Stacey Woods, who served for twenty-eight years in that capacity. He was followed by Chua Wee Hien from Singapore until 1991. The current general secretary is Lindsay Brown from Wales. The IFES office is located in Harrow, England.

ROBERT A. FRYLING

Bibliography. D. Johnson, *A Brief History of the International Fellowship of Evangelical Students;* P. Lowman, *The Day of His Power.*

International Missionary Council (IMC). The International Missionary Council was an outgrowth of the WORLD MISSION CONFERENCE at Edinburgh in 1910. Organized in 1921 under the leadership of JOHN R. MOTT, JOSEPH H. OLDHAM, and A. L. Warnshuis, its purpose was to encourage and assist churches and mission societies in their missionary task, understood as sharing with people everywhere the transforming power of the gospel of Jesus Christ. It hoped to bring about united efforts wherever possible.

Its membership consisted mainly of national and regional interdenominational mission organizations, such as the Committee of German Evangelical Missions and the Foreign Mission Conference of North America. It encouraged the development of national Christian councils in Asia, Africa, and Latin America, in which the churches eventually played a stronger role than the mission organizations. Thus the churches became the centers for planning, rather than the mission structures. It eventually grew to include thirty-eight such councils. The IMC saw itself as a center of information and consultation, thought, and study, holding conferences where the results of research could be shared. It also published the *International Review of Missions.*

At its first meeting in JERUSALEM in 1928, half of the 231 delegates came from Asia, Africa, and Latin America. Some called it the first truly global meeting in history. Its message was basically optimistic despite growing secularism. Theological divergence was evident as the concern for social issues caused some anxiety among conservatives, but its final word was "Our message is Jesus Christ. He is the revelation of what God is and what man through Him may become. In Him we find God incarnate." Seeking to move beyond paternalism, Jerusalem recognized the equality of the "younger churches," a term then coming into use. It also established an international committee on the Christian approach to the Jews.

The 1938 meeting brought 471 delegates, including 77 women, from 70 nations, to TAMBARAM, India, near Madras. A major issue was the relationship of Christianity to non-Christian religions. HENDRIK KRAEMER wrote his preparatory volume, *The Christian Message in a Non-Christian World*, stressing discontinuity between Christianity and other faiths against those who saw value in non-Christian religions as a preparation for the gospel. Resisting some calls for SYNCRETISM, the council reaffirmed the authority of Scripture and the truth and grace of God in Jesus Christ. Other issues addressed were the need to improve the preparation of leadership for the younger churches, and the challenges of communism, nationalism, and secularism. During World War II, the IMC did a magnificent job of gathering resources to care for orphaned European missions in various parts of Asia and Africa, cut off from their homelands and support, making possible their continued ministry. The WHITBY, Ontario meeting in 1947 was an opportunity for the renewal of fellowship after the war and called all churches to rediscover the nature of their obedience in proclaiming the gospel to a broken and revolutionary world. The slogan "Partners in Obedience" was adopted; it was intended to symbolize the full equality of older and younger churches, to overcome paternalism and dependency, and stress unity.

At WILLINGEN, Germany, in 1952, new theological winds were blowing amidst growing pessimism about the church and its mission in a revolutionary age. The question was asked, What was to be the nature of the missionary obligation of the church as many traditional mission fields were closing and the churches in the West were increasingly aware of the role of churches in mission?

At the 1958 GHANA meeting the Theological Education Fund was launched to upgrade institutions in Asia, Africa, and Latin America. But the most important issue was the decision to merge with the WORLD COUNCIL OF CHURCHES (WCC). JOHN MACKAY and others believed the merger would put mission at the very heart of the WCC. Others, especially MAX WARREN of the CHURCH MISSION SOCIETY, spoke strongly against it. He said that while mission calls for almost infinite flexibility and a readiness to take initiative, official bodies have great hesitation about taking risks. Thus he predicted that the voluntary principle that was so important in missions would be lost with the merger. But WCC leaders promised that mission and evangelism would be central to its life and work. Consequently, in 1961 the IMC became the COMMISSION ON WORLD MISSION AND EVANGELISM (CWME) of the World Council of Churches. Its stated purpose was "to further the proclamation to the whole world of the gospel of Jesus Christ to the end that all men may believe and be saved."

However, for reasons having to do both with structure and theology, the CWME disappeared in the 1990s, becoming a subunit in Programme Unit No. 2 (Churches in Mission, Health, Education, and Witness) of the WCC. The CWME, the successor to the IMC, no longer exists as a separate entity.

PAUL E. PIERSON

SEE ALSO Ecumenical Movement.

Bibliography. H. Hoekstra, *The World Council of Churches and the Demise of Evangelism;* R. W. Hogg, *Ecumenical Foundations;* S. Neill, and R. Rouse, eds., *A History of the Ecumenical Movement;* R. K. Orchard, ed., *The Ghana Assembly of the IMC, 1957–58;* C. W. Ranson, *Renewal and Advance.*

Internet. *See* INFORMATION TECHNOLOGY and TECHNOLOGY.

Interpersonal Communication. Though communication may be intrapersonal (talking to oneself), it is usually interpersonal communication (communication between persons) that we refer to when we speak of "communication." Whether the communication is between members of the same family or between those of different language communities (INTERCULTURAL COMMUNICATION), it always involves persons and thus is interpersonal. Even public communication, such as lectures or sermons, can be seen as interpersonal, since they consist of a large number of one-to-one (i.e., speaker to each listener) interactions. Though communication via electronic or print media is not usually seen as interpersonal, there are important interpersonal aspects to these forms as well, especially if the receptors know the communicator(s) personally.

Since EUGENE NIDA first introduced the concept into missiology in *Message and Mission* (1960, rev. ed. 1990), it has been customary in missiological circles to speak of communicational interaction as consisting of a *source* (or communicator) conveying a *message* to one or more *receptors*. This is often referred to as the S-M-R theory of communication. The key insights brought by this perspective concern the place of the receptor in the communication process.

All interpersonal communication involves gaps between people and the techniques used to bridge those gaps. Traditional approaches to communication have tended to focus attention either on the source of messages or on the vehicles used to convey them. The primary vehicle, of course, is LANGUAGE, and much attention has been devoted to the place of language in the communication process, as if words contained the meanings people attempt to communicate. But, as Berlo and others have demonstrated, meanings reside neither in the external world nor in language or other vehicles we use in the communication process. Though we can pass messages from person to person, meanings reside only in persons, never in the vehicles used to convey the messages. Meanings are created by receptors on the basis of their perceptions of what the communicator intends by the messages he or she is sending.

What goes on within the receptor(s) mind is, therefore, the most important part of any communicational interaction. Once the communicator has spoken or written a message, it is up to the receptor(s) to interpret the meaning. And this interpretation is done on the basis of the receptor's own understandings, whether or not these correspond with the understanding of the source. This fact creates difficulties in interpersonal communication, even between people who live in the same culture and speak the same language. It is, however, complicated greatly when the source and the receptor(s) are from different cultures. For people's patterns of perception and interpretation are strongly affected by their culture. Intercultural communication is a form of interpersonal communication, for it always involves one or more communicators attempting to convey messages to one or more receptors from another culture.

This understanding of communication has enormous implications for the communication of the gospel and the CONTEXTUALIZATION of Christianity. It means that we need first to learn as much as possible about how our receptors are perceiving the messages we are attempting to communicate. Then we need to do our best to formulate our messages in such a way that the receptors can perceive and interpret what we are saying accurately and reconstruct the meanings appropriately. Failures in this area have led to heretical understandings of Christian doctrines even though the missionaries were orthodox and doing their best to speak the truth.

Missionary history is full of examples of messages that were spoken accurately in terms of the communicator's perspective but were perceived inaccurately by the receptors. When missionaries to India, for example, invited people to be "born again," they were not heard accurately by people who are seeking to escape from the endless cycle of rebirth. Nor are those in Asia for whom the number "four" is TABOO attracted to a message that focuses on "four spiritual laws." Latin American CHRISTO-PAGANISM, Melanesian CARGO CULTS, many AFRICAN-INITIATED CHURCH MOVEMENT doctrines, and a plethora of other aberrant forms of Christianity are the products of receptor understandings of missionary messages that did not correspond with what was intended by the communicators.

On the other hand, exciting PEOPLE MOVEMENTS have often resulted when messages of God's love and power have been presented in ways that were accurately interpreted by the receptors from within their frame of reference.

CHARLES H. KRAFT.

Bibliography. D. K. Berlo, *The Process of Communication;* J. F. Engel, *Contemporary Christian Communications;* C. H. Kraft, *Communicating the Gospel God's Way;* idem, *Communication Theory for Christian Witness;* E. A. Nida, *Message and Mission;* D. K. Smith, *Creating Understanding;* V. Søgaard, *Media in Church and Mission.*

Interserve. Interserve is an international, interdenominational, and evangelical association of mission boards in a dozen sending countries that was founded in 1852. It emerged from the concern of some visionary Victorian women in London for the oppressed women in India. They founded The Indian Female Normal School and Instruction Society, with a vision: "If we can give the women of India the power to read, and the Book to read, God will bless his word." In 1873, at a time when there were only two qualified female doctors in England, they extended the work to include medical as well as literacy work in the *zenanas* (enclosed female quarters in India), and the name was changed to the Zenana Bible and Medical Mission. For many years it remained an entirely women's mission to women (men were admitted to ZBMM only in 1950) and registered remarkable achievements.

In a century and a half it has grown to encompass four hundred cross-cultural missionaries from many nations. It entered Nepal in 1954, Pakistan in 1958, and is now working in sixteen countries stretching from North Africa to Bangladesh and northward to the Central Asian Republics and eastward to China and Mongolia. The society became internationally structured in 1967 with its headquarters no longer in London, but in Delhi and later in Cyprus, and with national sending councils as far apart as Ireland and Korea. In India, the first "receiving" country now became a "sending" country, the wheel has come full circle.

Though originally a medical mission, and from 1957 known as the Bible and Medical Missionary Fellowship (BMMF), the society has become a general mission including not only doctors, nurses, and paramedics, but also teachers, engineers, foresters, administrators, children's workers, theologians, pastors, and those working among the handicapped and underprivileged. For this reason another name change, from BMMF to Interserve (short for International Service Fellowship), took place in 1987.

The society does not start its own churches or form a denomination from among those converted through its ministry. It works with and through other churches in the area or helps pioneer new congregations where none exist, but always in co-operation with others. It has been a pioneer in forming multi-mission "umbrella" consortia for work in many areas, including the United Mission to Nepal (UMN) in 1954, the International Assistance Mission (IAM) in Afghanistan in 1966, HEED (Health, Education and Economic Development) in Bangladesh in 1974, and Joint Christian services (JCS) in Mongolia in 1994.

Interserve was one of the first missions to inaugurate a short-term volunteer program in 1969, now successfully adopted by many missions. It was considered an "expensive soft option" when first introduced and likely to divert people from serious long-term commitment. Many who go overseas, however, use it as a test run before making a longer commitment. Believing that mission must serve all six continents not just "from the West to the rest," the society adopted a policy of mission in its home-based countries, particularly among ethnic minorities. This has been particularly successful in the United Kingdom, where a team of forty mission partners works in the program Ministry to Asians in Britain (MAB), making it the largest team to engage in this ministry to those of other faiths in Britain.

ARTHUR PONT

Bibliography. K. Makower, *Widening Horizons: The Story of INTERSERVE;* J. C. Pollock, *Shadows Fall Apart: The Story of the Zenana Bible and Medical Mission.*

Intertestamental Studies (also Second Temple or Commonwealth Jewish era). Investigation of the period between the Old and New Testaments. Technically the period dates from the destructions of Jerusalem and its temple by the Babylonians in 586 B.C. and by the Romans in A.D. 70. This places the first part of the Post-Exilic period as both the last of the Old Testament era and the beginning of the Second Temple Judaism.

During this time the Hebrews were ruled successively by the Persians, the Greeks under Alexander the Great, Ptolemies (from Egypt), and the Seleucids (from Syria), by their own Maccabean or Hasmonean rulers, and finally, beginning in 63 B.C., the Romans. The major sources of information—the Old Testament Apocrypha, Pseudepigrapha, the Dead Sea Scrolls, Jewish writers such as the historian Josephus and Philo the philosopher, the New Testament, and Greco-Roman writers—provide data about the historical events, religious beliefs and practices, cultural situation, as well as challenges, sufferings, hopes, and aspirations of the times immediately preceding and contemporary with the New Testament.

With the recent discovery and study of the new data of the period, especially the Dead Sea Scrolls (c. 1947), the investigation of this period has received new information, perspectives, and impetus. Of particular interest is the reinforced understanding of the distinction between this period and that which preceded and followed it, the diverse nature of the Jewish society, faith and culture of the time, the expectation of the imminent arrival of the Final Age (the last period of human history), and the complex elements of nationalism, religion, and culture, that interplayed with each other. Of particular importance were the effects upon Judaism of the various reactions to such crises as the defeat and deportation by the Babylonians, the entrance of Hellenistic (Greek) culture, and Roman domination. One also must note the nature and importance of the Greco-Roman culture, the dominant force of the civilized world at that time.

Cross-cultural missionaries live among peoples they hope to reach for the gospel in order to understand their LANGUAGE, CULTURE, and WORLDVIEWS and thus be able to communicate accurately with them. Similarly, growing familiarity with the intertestamental world, both Jewish and Greco-Roman, is essential for a better understanding of the New Testament. It is particularly important for the Bible translator who needs to know the culture and society of the biblical world even as he or she seeks to learn those of the people for whom the translation is intended (*see* BIBLE TRANSLATION).

In seeking to familiarize oneself with the New Testament world it is imperative to be aware of the distinct nature of its faith, institutions, and life. Documents which come from after the New Testament period, "Rabbinic Judaism," such as the Mishnah, Talmud, Midrashim, should be recognized as later compilations and used only with great care as sources for information about the intertestamental period (this includes the frequently consulted works of Alfred Edersheim).

Modern missiology properly places great emphasis on the challenge of ministry in unfamiliar settings; hence, the importance of cross-cultural CONTEXTUALIZATION. Intertestamental studies remind us that the deportation of the Hebrews to Babylon in the sixth century B.C. and the confrontation with Hellenistic culture in the fourth century B.C. required the intertestamental Jews to wrestle with the same sort of problems. Early Christianity also faced these issues as it moved from a wholly Jewish environment into the Greco-Roman world. An understanding both of the successes and failures in meeting the cross-cultural challenges in the intertestamental period could be of considerable value for those facing similar issues today.

J. JULIUS SCOTT, JR.

Invitation. Beginning with God's "Where are you?" (Gen. 3:9) and ending with "The Spirit and the bride say[ing], Come!" (Rev. 22:17), the Trinitarian God persistently invites those he created to return to their Creator and Redeemer. His invitation comes to people in a multitude of ways, such as dreams, visions, proclamation, calamity, testimony, and ultimately in his very incarnation. He will pursue, chastise, hide, and wait, in order to get a response.

God is an inviting God. Those who respond to his invitation in return invite others. But some are especially called to invite others. He sent Abraham to Canaan and the world. He sent Moses to tell Pharaoh and his court that Yahweh was the living God. He sent the prophets to announce to Israel and the nations that God was just and compassionate. He sent his only Son into the world, making all these invitations possible. He sent his Holy Spirit upon his awaiting disciples, empowering them to invite their families and friends to repent and turn to the living God. He sent his apostles to the nations to invite all peoples to come and feast at his eschatological banquet.

God's invitation always has specific content. Abraham believed that his seed would be as numerous as the stars in heaven (Gen. 15:6). Israel was to renounce all allegiances to other gods (Exod. 20:1–3; Josh. 24:15). According to Paul, the Christian invitation must explicitly announce that Jesus Christ died and was raised again (1 Cor. 15:1–3). Those who turn to the living God must then declare their allegiance through Christian baptism and obedience (Matt. 28:19).

Although there are continual attempts to state explicitly how one responds to God's invitation, ultimately, the response remains a mystery. Abraham responded to God's invitation and obeyed him by leaving his home, land, and family. Ruth would not leave Naomi, declaring her allegiance to Naomi and her God. Paul responded to a vision of the risen Christ by becoming an apostle. While Scripture gives many other examples of individuals and groups responding to God's invitation, there seems to be a reluctance on the part of the biblical writers to give any clear guidelines on how people should respond. While not detailing the how, John's Gospel stresses the what. Each respondent is to confess that Jesus is the Christ. Luke gives many case studies of preaching and response in Luke–Acts. The content of the invitation to turn to God is clear, along with specific calls for the listeners to repent and be baptized in the name of Jesus. But, apart from these general statements, there is little information on the response. Sometimes Luke talks about believing and baptism; sometimes he simply says, "they followed" Paul (Acts 2:38ff.; Acts 13:43).

Throughout history, and especially in its Western tradition, the church has often fallen into the trap of giving specific guidelines on how conversion should take place. Methods of issuing God's invitation and outlining specific steps of response multiplied during the twentieth century. This tendency can be traced in part to a scientific world-view that tends to superimpose method on content and relationships. When this how-to thinking shapes the Christian invitation some of the power and mystery of our relationship to God is lost. The human response to God cannot be shaped by technique. But certainly all responses to God are influenced by culture and tradition.

God, the Creator and Redeemer, is the seeking God. He invites all of humankind to return to him. His invitation extends throughout time and to all the peoples of the earth (Matt. 28:18–20; 2 Peter 3:9).

HAROLD E. DOLLAR

Bibliography. D. J. Bosch, *Transforming Mission;* W. Conn, *Christian Conversion;* V. J. Donovan, *Christianity Rediscovered;* J. H. Kroeger, *Missiology* 24:3 (1996): 369–81; T. Presler, *Missiology* 18:3 (1990): 267–78; D. Teeter, *Missiology* 19:3 (1990): 305–13; A. Tippett, *Let the Earth Hear His Voice,* ed., J. D. Douglas; D. Watson, *I Believe in Evangelism.*

Iran *(Est. 2000 pop.: 74,644,000; 1,648,000 sq. km. [636,293 sq. mi.]).* The Islamic Republic of Iran is home to over sixty-five different ethnic groups speaking approximately fifty different languages. About 99 percent of the population profess Islam. The official state religion is the Ithna-Ashariya branch of Shiism, making Iran the world center for Shiite Islam, to which 89 percent of the people adhere.

Only 0.4 percent of the population is affiliated with Christianity. The Orthodox churches are the oldest and largest in Iran. The Armenian Apostolic Church traces its founding back to the first-century apostles Thaddaeus and Bartholomew. The Ancient (Assyrian) Church of the East traces its origin to the era before Nestorius. The Russian Orthodox Church, whose projects in Tehran include a school, library, and club, was established in 1863. The Greeks came to Iran between 1917 and 1936, worshiping originally with the Russian Orthodox until a separate church was established in Tehran in 1943.

Roman Catholic missions began with the Chaldean Catholic Church, which gained its first converts in 1552; today it is the largest of the Catholic churches with about 65 percent of the Catholic population. The Latin Church missionaries arrived in Iran in the 1200s and 1600s, followed by the Armenian Catholic Church, which dates its first venture in Iran to 1605 and now numbers approximately two thousand.

Reformed, Presbyterian, and Congregationalist missionaries of the American Board of Commissioners of Foreign Missions (ABCFM), the first Protestant group in Iran, organized the Mission to the Nestorians in 1834. Resistance from the Nestorian Church turned the missionaries' attention to the Assyrians, who were more willing to convert, resulting in the Evangelical Church (1855). They, along with the Assemblies of God, who were active in 1924 and again in 1966, are the two largest Protestant churches in the country.

There are reports that more Iranians have come to Christ since the Islamic revolution of 1979 than in the years prior to it. All such deviations or defections are liable to persecution, even though constitutional rights are guaranteed for Christians, Zoroastrians, and Jews. Protestant churches tend to be small, and since the end of the war with Iraq, pressure on the evangelical Christians has increased.

GARY LAMB

Iraq *(Est. 2000 pop.: 23,753,000; 438,317 sq. km. [169,234 sq. mi.]).* In the earliest days of the church, Christian missionaries from Edessa, the crossroads of the old Silk Road east to China and south to Egypt, moved down the Euphrates River. A large Christian population prospered from the second century. Mawiyya, the first Christian Arab queen, was leader of the Tunukh tribe in 373. The whole tribe had become Christian through contact with monks who dwelt in the desert. Around 340 during the persecutions of Shapur II, waves of refugees poured into Iraq from Persia and they moved down the Arab side of the Arab Gulf and established missionary monasteries.

The Nestorian Creed first reached the Arabs through the settled communities in Mesopotamia at about 410 when a Nestorian bishop used Hirta on the east of the Euphrates as his center. Converts, known as the Ibad, spread to the settled Lakhmid nation of al Hira, whose members were fully Christianized by the seventh century. In Mesopotamia, the Nestorian population, though tolerated by the Persians, felt the heavy hand of religious and racial discrimination from the imperial government of the Sassanids. Nestorian theology was condemned by the Council of Chalcedon in 451. The Nestorians provided some of the finest scholars, scientists, and surgeons in the earliest years of their presence. They sent out missionaries from the eighth to fourteenth centuries, who carried the gospel east and south and nearly converted the Mongol nation (*see also* NESTORIAN MISSIONS). However, they did not manage to evangelize Turkistan and this led to their collapse.

Iraq's political control is in the hands of the minority Sunni Muslims. Kurdish people make up about 20 percent. The form of socialism in Iraq today is more important than religion. The Constitution of Iraq guarantees complete freedom of religion and worship as well as the legal right to register a change of religion. This has not trickled down to the masses yet. Three percent are Christians and now there are nearly forty groups in twelve denominations.

In 1886 the Archbishop of Canterbury established his mission to the Assyrian population in the north who had suffered greatly at the hands of both Kurds and Turks. In 1891 SAMUEL ZWEMER with James Cantine of the Reformed Church in America chose the southern port city of Basra as their first station and started a school and medical work. They later expanded north to Asmara and then to other parts of Iraq. Toward the end of the twentieth century, films, satellite TV, radio, and tons of Bibles and Christian books shipped in from Jordan were used by the Holy Spirit to encourage a vibrant and revived evangelical movement. Iraq is experiencing an exodus of many of the small Christian minorities from Iraq to all parts of the world. However, a good number of keen young people are studying in seminaries in Jordan and Egypt and have plans to return to Kirkuk, Baghdad, and Basrah. Many of the people displaced after the Gulf War have been converted in Jordan and many of these will return to Iraq. Such events are a harbinger of an expected expansion of the gospel in this land.

GEORGE E. KELSEY

Bibliography. R. B. Betts, *Christians in the Arab East;* S. Moffett, *A History of Christianity in Asia;* W. H. Storm, *Whither Arabia?;* J. S. Trimingham, *Christianity Among The Arabs;* S. M. Zwemer, *Heirs to the Prophets.*

Ireland *(Est. 2000 pop.: 3,616,000; 70,284 sq. km. [27,137 sq. mi.]).* The Christianity that took root in Ireland in the fifth century owed much to the character of both its messenger and the indigenous people. PATRICK arrived in 432 with a Christian message that did not carry the price of Romanization. The early Celtic church was fiercely independent, eschewed the authoritarian Roman approach, and promoted an incarnational theology in its spirituality and mission (*see also* CELTIC MISSIONARY MOVEMENT).

With the collapse of the Roman Empire, the Irish church became the guardian and vanguard of the gospel in a fragmented Europe. The exploits of its missionaries and monasteries served to establish the island's reputation as the land of saints and scholars. Foremost among these early missionaries were Columcille or COLUMBA OF IONA (to Scotland in 557) and COLUMBANUS (to Gaul in 590).

When Columcille died on Iona in 597, Augustine had just arrived in England. Celtic and Roman approaches came into confrontation. In 1170, Henry II authorized the Norman invasion from England, having secured a mandate from Pope Adrian IV, the only English pope! Faced with a weakened Celtic church, Rome's lordship was finally established in Ireland. Medieval Christendom, as with the CRUSADES, again acted on a coercive model of mission that has left a bitter legacy.

There was no indigenous Reformation in Ireland. Under Henry VIII the government of both church and state became Protestant (Anglican) and loyalty to the Roman church became part of the people's defiance of their English rulers. Protestantism took root through settlements, especially the seventeenth-century plantation of Ulster from England and Scotland.

Protestant ascendancy followed victory in the Glorious Revolution of 1688 and was strengthened by penal laws, which kept non-Anglicans out of government and most positions of influence. Religion and political power were now inseparable.

In the eighteenth century many Protestant Dissenters moved to America. There the Ulster Scots made a significant contribution to the religious life of the New World. The Anglicans turned to evangelizing their Irish Catholic neighbors. Catholic Ireland, concerned with its own survival, had itself played no part in the Roman church's missionary enterprise since the early medieval period. Emancipation, famine, and revival brought change that would impact the missionary endeavor throughout the nineteenth century.

With emancipation the Catholic Church saw tremendous growth in all kinds of vocations, including the missionary orders. The great famine of 1845–94 produced massive Catholic emigration and the church took seriously the need to provide spiritual support throughout the Irish diaspora. These developments have been well documented, unlike the Protestant missionary endeavor from this period.

The Protestant churches were quick to identify with the missionary movement. Some, like the Irish Presbyterians in India and Manchuria, established their own missionary enterprise. All found it necessary to forge links with denominational missions in the rest of Britain who were quick to form Irish auxiliaries.

Since then thousands of Irish missionaries have contributed to mission throughout the world. The Ulster Revival in 1859 contributed to the unity and growth of evangelicalism in Ireland and a consequent interest in the new faith missions. With the partition of Ireland in 1921 the contribution of the Protestant church has been mainly from Northern Ireland, known for its evangelical vigor. Irish evangelicals have also founded missions such as SAMUEL BILL (1863–1942), the Qua Iboe Mission in Nigeria (1887) and AMY CARMICHAEL (1867–1951) and the Donhnavur Fellowship in India (1927).

At the end of the twentieth century, churches in both parts of Ireland faced decline. The majority of the population in the Republic of Ireland is under age twenty-five. In Northern Ireland the ongoing conflict has eroded the church's credibility. Both parts of Ireland face the economic and social deprivation of urban poverty. In the desire to make their witness relevant, Irish churches are increasingly aware of what can be learned from the global church. While there are few Christians from other countries working in Ireland, many who have returned from overseas are now transferring their skills and experience to the task of mission in their home country.

DAVID PORTER

Bibliography. E. M. Hogan, *The Irish Missionary Movement: A Historical Survey 1830–1980;* N. W. Taggart, *The Irish in World Methodism, 1760–1900;* J. Thomson, ed., *Into All the World: A History of the Overseas Work of the Presbyterian Church in Ireland 1840–1990.*

Isaiah. *See* OLD TESTAMENT PROPHETS.

Islam, Muslim. Islam is the largest non-Christian religion in the world. It is the only faith to supplant Christianity in large geographical regions, and has proved the most resistant to Christian missions since its rise in the early seventh century. Although the Arab world remains the heartland, a majority of Muslims lives in Asia—the largest numbers in Indonesia, Bangladesh, Pakistan, India, and Central Asia.

Early Development. Muhammad (A.D. 570–732) was born in Mecca, a commercial and religious center of Arabia, where he reacted against the polytheism and injustices of his day and received what Muslims believe were revelations from God, later recorded in the QURAN ("the Recitation").

The faith that emerged incorporated elements from local Judaism, Christianity, and Arabian monotheism. In addition, much of the pagan pilgrimage to the Ka`bah sanctuary in Mecca was incorporated after the idols of tribal patron deities were removed and only references to Allah ("the god") remained.

Muslims came to understand their faith as the original revelation that had been given through a series of "prophets," including Moses and Jesus, and finally through Muhammad, whose revelation corrected any corruptions that had affected Jewish and Christian beliefs and practices.

The "five Pillars" of Muslim practice include first the confession of faith: "There is no god but God, and Muhammad is the apostle of God." The first half links Muslim and Christian, as the second half divides them. The second, the ritual prayer, borrows its name *(salat)*, ablutions, postures, and much of its content (with the exception of brief references to Muhammad) from Jewish and Christian sources. The original Muslim orientation of prayer was toward Jerusalem like the Jews, before it was directed instead toward Mecca.

The third, almsgiving, is designated by an Aramaic loan word *zakat*, which the Jewish rabbis used for charitable gifts. Likewise, the fourth, fasting, is indicated by a Judeo-Aramaic loan word, *sawm.* The practice of abstaining from eating and drinking in the daytime but not at night was a Jewish practice. Apparently the fast originally coincided with the Jewish fast before the Day of Atonement, but then it was changed to replace the pre-Islamic Arab sacred month of Ramadan.

Although the fifth pillar, the yearly pilgrimage to Mecca, was the adoption and reinterpretation of a pagan practice (*see also* PILGRIMAGES), it incorporates some elements that God used in his schoolhouse for the children of Israel. Its name, *hajj*, is the same word the Israelites used for a festival in Jerusalem in Psalm 81:4 (3 in English). The circumambulation of the sanctuary replicates the Feast of Tabernacles (cf. Ps. 26:6). The wearing of special garments and the prohibition of the cutting of hair while in a consecrated state follow biblical practices (e.g., Lev. 16:4; Num. 6:5).

Varieties of Expression. Muslims developed a strong sense of community governed by divine law *(Shari'ah)*, which in both its quranic form and subsequent development resembled Jewish oral Torah and rabbinic law. It developed to include all human duties to God and society from religious observances to family, penal, and international law.

An Islamic law developed to guide the outer paths of Muslims duties; mysticism (*see* SUFI, SUFISM) developed to guide the inner path of piety, with emphasis on the experience and devotional love of God. Being more inclusive in nature, it borrowed freely from Christians and Hindus and others and facilitated the spread of Islam from North Africa to Southeast Asia through a network of orders or brotherhoods. Its expressions range from devotional dimensions of many orthodox (or orthoprax) Muslims, to beliefs and practices of some orders that are removed from formal Islam.

In the latter cases it blends into "folk Islam," that mixture of indigenous animistic elements into the beliefs and practices of many who consider themselves to be Muslims. This modifies the traditional bridges and barriers to Christian mission among Muslims.

The major division within formal Islam is between the Sunnis (85 percent worldwide; *see* SUNNI, SUNNISM) and the Shi'is (15 percent worldwide; *see* SHI'ITE, SHI'ISM). It was occasioned by differences over who should lead the community after the death of Muhammad. The Sunni majority followed the Arabian pattern for choosing a chief: the elders elected a caliph as a political leader. The Shi'ites, reflecting ideas closer to those of divine kingship of the previous empires of West Asia, believed leadership should pass to the senior male of Muhammad's family, called an imam. He was not only to be a political leader like the Sunni caliph, but also a religious leader as a vehicle of divine guidance.

Various trends have been discernible in the Muslim community up to the present day. One is the adaptionists, who have advocated a process of Islamic acculturation. They include today's modernists who advocate religious, legal, educational, and social reforms. The second are the conservatives, who feel that the boundaries of legitimate religious interpretation ceased in the ninth century after the four orthodox schools of Sunni law were established.

Finally, there are the fundamentalists, who reject the accretions of Islamic history and seek to return to the fundamentals of the Quran and practice of Muhammad (Sunna), believing that they exhibit a pattern of values and law adequate for modern life. They do not reject modern technology but only the secular values that frequently accompany it. Some have radical social programs and others, conservative. Some are militant while others support the status quo. Yet at the threshold of the third millennium many of the expressions of Islam are experiencing resurgence.

Spread. Islam has been spread by both peaceful and militant means. On the one hand, the Quran states that there is no compulsion in religion (2:256/257) and enjoins witness in a kind manner (2:143/137; 16:125/126). On the other hand, it calls Muslims to fight against polytheists and hypocrites (9:5, 38–52) and even Jews and Christians until they submit and pay tribute (5:29), after which the latter two are to be protected.

A distinction needs to be made between the expansion of military and political power and conversion, which involves spiritual allegiance. The conversion of conquered people, if it occurred, was often a slower process. The adoption of Islam ranged from total conversion, to allegiance for expediency because of its advantages, to forced submission.

One hundred years after Muhammad's death in 632, the Muslim Arab armies had conquered North Africa, Spain, Syria, and the Persian (Sassanian) Empire. By 870, Islam had become the dominant integrating faith of a vast empire of many cultures extending from North Africa into Central Asia. During this period the basic Shari'ah law developed, to which many Muslims have turned, up to the present day.

Between 870 and 1041, various regions of the empire assumed a measure of independence. Islamdom continued to expand partly by military means but more often by trade. Berbers in North Africa became at least nominally converted to Islam and, through their caravan trade across the Sahara, provided the means for Islam's penetration into black Africa. On the eastern side of the Muslim lands the Muslim Ghaznavids in the Afghan mountains conquered northwestern India.

From 1041 to 1405, the Turkic Seljuqs and Mongols invaded the Islamic lands from Central Asia. The CRUSADES also took place during this period. Though they have poisoned Muslim attitudes ever since, they were initially a response to the Byzantine emperor's request for help against the expansion of the Seljuk Turks into Western Anatolia as the Kipchak Turks in the Ukraine had cut off Christian Russia from them.

The Islamic empires continued to expand and consolidate between 1405 and 1683. The Ottomans captured Constantinople and ended the Byzantine Empire but were not able to capture Vienna in 1683. Islam continued to follow the trade routes into Sub-Saharan Africa, especially through traders who were also teachers.

In the subsequent centuries there has been Muslim activism and revival and great biological growth. The major expansion into new areas has been in Africa and the West. In Africa, Islam and Christianity continue to grow rapidly southward by conversion growth at the expense of AFRICAN TRADITIONAL RELIGIONS. Islam has become a significant presence in Europe and North America through immigration. In the African American community in the United States where it has grown—sometimes in modified form—it has provided a vehicle of ethnic pride and social betterment.

Contemporary Muslim mission has been organized both to win converts and to counteract Christian missionary efforts. The conferees at the Muslim World League Conference in Mecca in 1974 called for the government takeover of mission hospitals, schools, and orphanages, the banning of Christian literature in Muslim countries, and cutting off financial support from countries allowing missionaries to Muslims. On the other hand, Muslim missionaries are being trained at centers like al-Azhar in Cairo. Saudi Arabia's King Fahd bin Abdul Aziz Koran Printing Complex is printing millions of Qurans in various languages for free distribution. The Organization of the Islamic Conference has expended billions for Islamic institutions around the world. Other organizations like the Islamic Society of North America include among their goals and those of their member organizations propagating the faith by various means.

Christian Missions. Muslims have been the most resistant faith community to Christian evangelism for a number of reasons (*see also* MUSLIM MISSION WORK). Aside from the spiritual obstacles, the hindrances are first, sociological: group solidarity leads to family and community ostracism and persecution of the convert. The Law of Apostasy can lead to death.

Second, they are theological: since Islam is the only world religion to rise after Christianity, Muslims believe that all that is of value in Christianity is already in Islam, and they commonly hold that the Bible has been corrupted. (The Quran is understood to deny the Trinity and Christ's incarnation, sonship, and crucifixion.)

Third, the obstacles are political: since Islam applies to every area of life including the political, non-Muslims are normally considered second-class citizens whereas Muslims are a majority. Despite the ancient churches in many Muslim lands, Muslims commonly associate Christianity with the West.

Fourth, the frequent association of Christianity with the West has often raised cultural barriers: Western forms of worship and church structure have been utilized without the realization that almost all Muslim forms of worship have been adopted or adapted from Jews and Christians. Finally, the barriers are historical: much of the contact between Muslims and Christians militarily, politically, and religiously has been hostile.

J. DUDLEY WOODBERRY

SEE ALSO Black Muslims AND Islamic New Religious Movements.

Bibliography. K. Cragg, *The Call of the Minaret;* K. Cragg and M. Speight, *Islam from Within: Anthology of a Religion;* B. D. Kateregga and D. Shenk, *Islam and Christianity: A Muslim and a Christian in Dialogue;* I. M. Lapidus, *A History of Islamic Societies;* B. Musk, *The Unseen Face of Islam: Sharing the Gospel with Ordinary Muslims;* A. Shimmel, *Mystical Dimensions of Islam;* I. I. van der Werff, *Christian Mission to Muslims: The Record (Anglican and Reformed Approaches in India and the Near East 1800–1938);* J. O. Voll, *Islam: Continuity and Change in the Modern World;* R. V. Weekes, *Muslim Peoples: A World Ethnographic Survey;* J. D. Woodberry, ed., *Muslims and Christians on the Emmaus Road.*

Islamic New Religious Movements. New Religious Movements (NERMs) is not an Islamic term, but like other clearly defined religious traditions, Islam has experienced frequent movements of renewal and innovation. These movements generally push some principal tenet or doctrine of Islam to the outer edges of acceptable interpretation. They most often center on a key figure who claims to have received or embodied new religious insight. Sufi (mystical) Orders have occasionally moved in this direction. Shi'ite Islam, with an inherently strong emphasis on the special spiritual state and insight of the Imams, is particularly productive soil for the growth of Islamic NERMs. Islamic NERMs often develop out of attempts to synthesize orthodox Islam with indigenous ethnic, cultural, and folk religious values and practices.

Often such movements develop so distinctly that they abandon their Islamic identity completely. The Druzes, a closed community of some six hundred thousand persons living in Israel, Lebanon, and Syria, began as a twelfth-century Islamic NERM within the Fatimid Isma'ili sect of Cairo. Druze beliefs are characteristically gnostic. With the claim of divinity for the founder, its own line of prophets, and distinct sacred literature, the Druzes stand well outside the broad Islamic tent. More recently, a mid-nineteenth-century reform movement of Shi'ite Islam in Iran developed into the modern BAHA'I faith. The sect claimed special spiritual status for the founder, Baha' Ullah, and quickly left behind all traditional Islamic religious identity.

Two of the more significant contemporary movements that maintain an Islamic self-identity are the Ahmadiyyah and The Lost Found Nation of Islam (Black Muslims). The Ahmadiyyah was founded by Mirza Ahmad in late-nineteenth-century India in response to the political, economic, and religious imperialism of the Christian West. Mizra Ahmad developed his own distinct doctrines of Jesus, claimed that contemporary Christianity was the apocalyptic Antichrist, and finally claimed that he was the Mahdi and the Second Coming of Jesus. The Ahmadiyyah adopted aggressive missionary techniques and are stridently anti-Christian. There are approximately 500,000 Ahmadis worldwide, with the greatest strength in Pakistan and West Africa. They view themselves as the true Muslims, but are regarded by the vast majority of Sunni Muslims as heterodox.

Ahmadiyyah missionaries to American inner cities in the 1920s and 1930s had some influence in the emergence of a distinctly African American Islamic NERM, the BLACK MUSLIMS. Elijah Muhammad (Elijah Poole) began the movement in Detroit sometime in the mid-1930s. The movement was primarily a black separatist one with many doctrines and practices that were not only outside Islamic norms, but seem to have little connection to Islam at all. Clergy were termed "ministers" and houses of worship were called "temples" rather than mosques. On the death of Elijah Muhammad in 1975, his son assumed leadership and gradually directed the Nation to abandon most of its eccentric doctrines and adopt more authentic Islam. Most African American Muslims moved in this direction and the movement has continued to grow, now numbering over one million. Louis Farrakhan led a smaller faction that retained the name "Nation of Islam" and many of its heterodox beliefs. This continuation of the original movement is quite small, numbering under fifty thousand. The Black Muslim movement has had some success outside the United States, particularly in Trinidad.

Islamic NERMs continue to arise, but due to the intense social and religious pressure of Islamic societies and occasional political pressure from sympathetic governments, most either remain small and underground, move completely outside the Islamic context, or die out rather quickly.

JAMES D. CHANCELLOR

SEE ALSO New Religious Movements.

Bibliography. C. Glasse, ed., *The Concise Encyclopedia of Islam;* Y. Y. Haddad, *The Muslims of America.*

Isle of Man (United Kingdom Dependent Area) *(Est. 2000 pop. 79,000; 588 sq. km. [227 sq. mi.]).* Located in the Irish Sea between Great Britain and Ireland, the inhabitants rely on offshore banking, manufacturing, and tourism for their livelihood. The population was Christianized before A.D. 600, probably by missionaries from Iona. During the English Reformation, most of the Christian community (almost 99% of the population in 1980) came under the Anglican Church. The second largest Protestant group are the Methodists, who trace their origin to visits by JOHN WESLEY in the late eighteenth century.

A. SCOTT MOREAU

Israel *(Est. 2000 pop.: 6,062,000; 21,056 sq. km. [8,130 sq. mi.]).* When the church begins to think theologically and missiologically about herself, her origin, nature, vocation, and relationship to the world around her, then it is inevitable that she think about Israel and the church's relationship to the Jewish people. The church's search for self-identity cannot bypass an examination of Israel's identity, since their roots are intertwined.

The church was not planted on earth in a vacuum—she exists in a context. The first context is that of the loving purposes of God himself, since our life and mission flow from him. God began his particular work of creating a people to be his special servants not with John the Baptist, but with Abraham. Christians have interpreted this relationship in different ways.

The maximalist view, associated particularly with Covenant theologies, speaks of the "Old Testament church" just as confidently as it does of the New Testament church. There is no essential difference between Israel and the church, and the focus is on historical and theological continuity. The radically minimalist view, associated with the theology of Arius, denies that Israel has anything to do with the church. The Christian church has totally replaced Israel in the heart and plans of God.

Along the continuum between these two extremes lie various other views. One of these would affirm that Israel is indispensible for the church. If God had left the Hebrew slaves in Egypt, not only would there have been no Israel and Passover celebration, nor would there have been any church and Easter. Our very vocabulary is that of Israel's relationship to God. Non-Jews need to learn the meaning of terms like Messiah, election, and covenant in their Israelite and Old Testament context. The same is true of the images used of the church in the New Testament (e.g., chosen race, holy nation, remnant), which come from the context of Israel.

Another view, in the various forms of DISPENSATIONALISM, claims that the church only began on the Day of Pentecost, although it was always

507

a part of God's historical and missiological purpose, and that it will cease from its historical function at the rapture. Before and after this period of history, God's primary dealings were and will be with and through Israel. There are, in effect, two servant peoples of God in this view, both serving within a covenant relationship with God. Ultimately, though, Israel will come to recognize Jesus as her Messiah.

Contemporary Christian scholarship is faced with another version of this view which holds that there are these two peoples of God, but that there are two distinct convenants (*see* Two-Covenant Theory). According to this position, Israel will never acknowledge Jesus as Messiah, and rightly so, since her way with God is established independently of Jesus. This view, which is growing rapidly in certain church quarters, presents a strong challenge to Christian missiology.

To return to what might be considered a consensus about biblical teaching concerning Israel, the choice of Israel was to serve God's purposes for all of his creation and to help bring about the redemption of creation. By definition this made Israel a special people, being God's representative and messenger on earth, and her relationship with God was paradigmatic for the offer of God to all nations. The church carries on this call as the assembly of people, Jewish and non-Jewish, who have welcomed and committed themselves to Jesus of Nazareth as God's unique servant—indeed God's own Son. Christian mission has been founded on the conviction that God's purposes always centered on the coming of the Son of God.

This is what lies behind Paul's anguish in Romans 9–11. The most "natural" person to be in the kingdom of God should be the Jewish person. There is something especially tragic when the very people of God don't recognize God's greatest gift and challenge to them to go on as the ministers of God's grace to the world.

On the other hand, only Israel can, and does, claim priority over the church in matters of biblical theology: Israel asserts that she knew God first, that she produced and preserved the foundational Scriptures of the church, that she learned and passed on the central perspectives and principles that emerge in the New Testament, that she taught the world about the need for the coming Messiah, and that, in short, she is the "mother" of Christianity.

What has happened historically is that in reacting against this claim to priority by Israel, Christians by and large have forgotten that their proper root is nonetheless in Israel; they have been embarrassed at Israel's refusal to acknowledge that Jesus is her long-awaited Messiah; they have developed a theology that discards Israel from the plans of God; they have allowed that theology to support a view that saw God's own love for Israel replaced with contempt; they have actively shared in that contempt; and they have

finally allowed that attitude to degenerate even further into actual persecution of Jewish people.

Neither Israel nor the church can claim to be identical with the kingdom of God, which is greater than both, and Paul's metaphor of the olive tree (Rom. 11:16–24) shows that Christ is the all-important root of the life and destiny of both. The church's relationship to Israel is sui generis, and both are irrevocably linked within the one missionary movement of God to the world. Christians cannot, therefore, relate to Jewish people in the same way that they do to any other people. The church has no vocation apart from that of Israel and the New Testament has no identity apart from the Old Testament.

Therefore, even in maintaining that the church is distinct from Israel, and that the church is the central agent in God's mission to the world today because of the centrality of Jesus in God's purposes, it remains a major task of missiology to wrestle with the fact that the essential calling and nature of the church cannot contradict that of Israel.

Walter Riggans

Bibliography. R. R. De Ridder, *Discipling the Nations*; S. Motyer, *Israel in the Plan of God: Light on Today's Debate*; M. J. Pragai, *Faith and Fulfilment: Christians and the Return to the Promised Land*; W. Riggans, *Towards an Evangelical Doctrine of the Church: The Church and Israel*; D. W. Torrance, ed., *The Witness of the Jews to God*.

Israel's Role. "Israel" in the Old Testament refers to the patriarch Jacob (Gen. 32:28), to the nation God founded at the exodus from Egypt (Hos. 11:1; Amos 3:1), or to the northern kingdom that split off from Judah after the death of Solomon (1 Kings 12). Here the "role of Israel" will refer to how God's call of the descendants of Jacob to be a holy nation contributed to God's plan for world evangelization.

The Old Testament teaches that God is the Lord of all the earth, not of only one nation. He created all things (Gen. 1; Isa. 40:28) and sustains his world daily (Ps. 104:10–30; cf. Heb. 1:3). As the owner of the earth, the Lord distributed it to all the nations, but he set aside Israel as his own portion (Deut. 32:8–9). This did not mean that Israel was more worthy than any other nation; God's sovereign choice of Israel was based on his promise to Abraham and the patriarchs (Deut. 7:6–8).

How does God's choice of Israel relate to his desire to bring salvation to the world (see Isa. 2:2–4; 19:18–25; 25:6–8; 55:1–7)? When the Lord established the covenant at Sinai, he selected Israel to be his "treasured possession . . . a kingdom of priests and a holy nation" (Exod. 19:3–6). The covenant with Moses linked with the Abrahamic Covenant in that the Lord was ready to establish a nation in the land he promised to Abraham (Gen. 15:13–21). The Lord began his work of reconciling the nations by choosing one nation who would be his people, and he would be their God (Exod. 6:7).

Many have debated whether Israel's responsibility to the nations was to be accomplished passively by obedience to the terms of the covenant or actively by spreading the truth of God throughout the world. The designation "kingdom of priests" might seem to imply a more active role, but even Israel's priestly role may be viewed as primarily her obedient service (Exod. 19:5) to the Lord. The nations would see God's acts of justice and mercy in his people and recognize him as the Lord of all the earth (see Deut. 4:5–8; Ps. 98). The prophets stressed Israel's failure to obey the Lord and its consequences for his reputation among the nations. When the Lord drove Israel out of the land, his holy name was profaned among the nations where Israel had gone (Ezek. 36:22). His name will be vindicated when he fulfills his promise to gather all Israel back to the land and give them a "new heart" (Ezek. 36:22–32).

Israel's role in God's plan was not entirely passive, however. First, resident aliens were granted the right to become a part of the covenant community (Exod. 12:48–49). Even those who did not choose to identify with Israel's religion were still to be treated justly and fairly (Exod. 22:21). Ruth, despite her Moabite background (cf. Deut. 23:3), was incorporated into the people of God (Ruth 4:11–12).

Second, individuals within the nation might find themselves in situations where, like the Israelite slave of Naaman's wife, they could direct others to the source of salvation (2 Kings 5:1–4, 15–19). Some, like the prophet Jonah, were even called to deliver God's message directly on foreign soil (Jonah 1:1–2; cf. 1 Kings 17:8–24).

Third, the prophet Isaiah pointed to the ministry of the "Servant of the Lord" or the Messiah, who would fulfill all that Israel failed to be (42:1–7; 49:1–9; 50:4–9; 52:13–53:12). The Servant was not only to bring Israel back to the Lord and atone for sin through his own death (Isa. 53:6); he was also to be a "light to the nations," taking the salvation of the Lord "to the ends of the earth" (Isa. 49:6).

The Lord called Israel to be his holy people, representing his name among all the nations of the earth. They failed in that role, but God's plans were not thwarted. His written Word, the Scriptures, came to the world through Israel (see Rom. 3:1–2), and also the living Word of God, Jesus Christ, had his physical origins through that nation (Matt. 1:1–17; Luke 3:23–38).

THOMAS J. FINLEY

SEE ALSO Old Testament Theology of Mission.

Bibliography. A. T. M. Cheung, *JETS* 29 (1986): 265–75; A. R. Cole, *Exodus: An Introduction and Commentary;* R. DeRidder, *Discipling the Nations;* D. Sheriffs, *Themelios* 15 (1990): 49–60.

Italy *(Est. 2000 pop.: 57,254,000; 301,268 sq. km. [116,320 sq. mi.]).* The Italian Republic occupies a long, mountainous peninsula in the Mediterranean Sea, and also includes the islands of Sardinia and Sicily. Given its rich political, cultural, and religious heritage—exemplified not only in the earlier Roman Empire but also in the influence of Rome, Milan, and Florence in medieval and modern European history—Italy has been a dominant force in shaping Western culture. Italy was united as a single state in 1870 and has been a republican democracy since 1946. The mountainous terrain has helped preserve regional differences within the peninsula, with the wealthier and more liberal segments of the population in the north and the poorer and more conservative groups located in the south. Roughly 67% of Italy is urbanized, with Rome having a population of 3.5 million.

When the apostle Paul arrived in Rome in A.D. 60 he found Christian believers already there (Acts 28:13–15). It is unclear who first brought the gospel to Rome. In the ensuing centuries, however, given its link to the apostle Peter, the church at Rome was to exert increasing influence upon the Christian movement. The bishop of Rome came to be recognized by the Western Church (which officially split with the Eastern Church in 1054) as having special authority, culminating in the papacy of the Roman Catholic Church.

Roman Catholicism has been closely identified with Italian history and culture. Although it is an autonomous state, the HOLY SEE, the headquarters of worldwide Roman Catholicism, is located in Rome. Roman Catholicism ceased to be the state religion in 1984, but it remains enormously influential in Italy today. Ninety-nine percent of the population are baptized Roman Catholics and the cultural identification with Catholicism remains strong. Yet there is growing ambivalence as well, as increasingly people dissociate themselves from the established church (David Barrett reports that only 6% of the population take communion every Sunday, 50% of the children are given no catechetical instruction, and 30% of the people do not receive the sacrament of extreme unction before death).

The earliest Protestant presence in Italy was the Waldensian church, inspired by Peter Waldo in the twelfth century. The Evangelical Waldensian Church is the oldest Protestant denomination in Italy. Methodist missionaries to Italy arrived in 1859, with Baptists arriving in 1863 and other groups following soon after. The Assemblies of God arrived in 1908 and experienced significant growth. Today they constitute the largest Protestant church in Italy. Recent decades have seen many other missions organizations working in Italy. However, Protestant evangelicals today comprise only about 1% of the total population.

Although overt persecution of Protestants (once not uncommon) is decreasing, the public perception of Protestant churches as "sects" or "cults" remains strong. Evangelicals must contend not only with the influence and prestige of the Roman Catholic Church, but also with the increasing influences of Secularization and the growing fascination of the occult.

Editors

Itinerant Mission. Itinerant mission work is usually done for short periods and rapidly changes its mode of operation. Because of various handicaps, an itinerant missionary likely has a short-term presence in the targeted context and works until interrupted by government intervention or the realization of the mission's objectives. The roving nature of the work mitigates against establishing institutions and requires focused evangelistic and mission goals.

The apostle Paul engaged in itinerant mission work. He went to specific locations to accomplish the clear objectives of proclaiming the gospel and establishing new churches. He was usually "on the move" and his tasks required him to appoint leaders and then set out for new territories and regions beyond those where he had already worked (Rom. 15:20; 2 Cor. 10:16).

Historically, itinerant types of mission and evangelism result from various sociopolitical restrictions. As migrant Christians rove throughout the world and engage in witnessing, they perform unintentional itinerant mission work. Intentional itinerant mission efforts may result when people migrate into new geographic areas. In the pioneer sections of the United States during the eighteenth and nineteenth centuries, circuit-riding preachers did itinerant ministries to service areas where there were not enough gospel laborers for the rising population. At the same time, itinerant work was necessary for those opening up frontier missions in the interior sections of Latin America, Africa, and Asia. Pioneering situations normally require self-imposed itinerant mission work because of limited personnel and resources.

Since World War II, new pioneer situations have emerged that are based on political circumstances rather than geographical ones. Independent nations born in the aftermath of the European colonial era established laws regulating foreign nationals in their countries. Often significantly sized population segments or people groups within these countries were historically resistant to Christian influence, especially if it seemed to be controlled by foreign agencies. These governments tended to repeal or restrict visas and residence permits that had been issued to those suspected to be foreign Christian missionaries.

Doing mission in these new types of frontier territories requires utilization of short-term visa options or seeking long-term visas under the auspices of secular humanitarian, disaster relief, or international commercial enterprises (*see* Creative Access Countries). "Tentmaking" describes the way the apostle Paul supplemented his income while doing itinerant mission work (Acts 20:33–34). Modern tentmakers employ their skills and talents to achieve as permanent a status as possible in politically restricted countries by working for these secular enterprises. Often they draw their livelihood from their secular work, though this is not inherent to the tentmaking concept. Because their visa status is still short-term, the duration of the work is equally short. Itinerant missionaries must achieve their evangelistic, discipling, and church-planting objectives with optimum results in as expeditious a manner as possible.

Keith E. Eitel

See also Nonresidential Missionary.

Bibliography. R. Allen, *Missionary Methods St. Paul's or Ours*; D. Barrett and T. M. Johnston, *Our Globe and How to Reach It*; V. D. Garrison, *The Nonresidential Missionary*.

Ivory Coast. *See* Côte d'Ivoire.

Jackson, Sheldon (1834–1909). American pioneer missionary and mission organizer to the American West and Alaska. Born to a newly converted Presbyterian family, Jackson came to faith early in life. Graduating from Princeton Seminary, he was ordained in 1858. Rejected from foreign missions for medical reasons, he accepted a home mission assignment at a Choctaw school in Spencer, Oklahoma. After one year he accepted an assignment as a church planter and organizer in Minnesota, where he served, with the exception of a two-month stint among the Union forces in the Civil War, until 1869. His nine years in Minnesota included constant travel and organizational work, a hallmark of his life and ministry.

Taking latitude with the nature of a new assignment which included much of the Rocky Mountain area, Jackson pioneered the work for the Presbyterian Church in Alaska, for which he was called the "Apostle of Alaska." Over the course of his life he traveled well over one million miles by foot, horse, stagecoach, and ship.

The same spirit that made him tireless in his travels also led to a life of controversy. Serving in dual capacity as a missionary and educational representative of the U.S. government, Jackson faced constant battles in both circles. He is remembered by early biographers for actions which fended off the extinction of indigenous peoples in Alaska through projects such as reindeer importation and planting churches and educational institutions which continue to this day.

A. SCOTT MOREAU

Bibliography. R. L. Stewart, *Sheldon Jackson;* J. A. Lazell, *Alaskan Apostle: The Life Story of Sheldon Jackson.*

Jaeschke, Heinrich Augustus (1817–83). German missionary linguist in India. Jaeschke's forebears migrated from Moravia (the modern Czech Republic). In Herrnhut (lit. "The Lord's Watch") they maintained their Moravian faith under the protection of Count ZINZENDORF.

Jaeschke taught in the boys' academy in Christiansfeld, Denmark, and was soon preaching in Danish. By 1842 he was teaching languages at the pedagogium at Niesky, Germany (near modern Poland). Besides fluency in German, Danish, and Greek, he soon learned Sanskrit, Persian, Arabic, Hungarian, Bohemian, Polish, and Swedish. He wrote his diary in seven languages.

In 1856 Jaeschke traveled to India to work with Tibetan refugees. He translated most of the New Testament, several books, and tracts into Tibetan. His German-Tibetan and English-Tibetan dictionaries became standard works. The Tibetan grammar in English he prepared was used by numerous missionaries working among the Tibetan people.

Failing health brought Jaeschke back to Germany in 1868. Much of his writing and translation work was completed during his final years in Herrnhut. His *Heimgang* (lit. "Home going") occurred in 1883. Jaeschke epitomizes the Moravian focus of missionary effort to downtrodden people. He stands as a brilliant linguist who did not waste his talents but who used them for the glory of God.

MICHAEL SPRADLIN

Bibliography. J. T. Hamilton and K. G. Hamilton, *A History of the Moravian Church;* A. H. Frank, *BDCM,* pp. 326–27.

Jaffray, Robert (1873–1945). Canadian missionary to China and Indonesia. A missionary strategist and statesman, he used his father's Canadian newspaper experience to develop mission stations. Through his monthly *Bible Messenger* Jaffray disseminated training materials for Cantonese Christian workers and later produced other colloquial-language versions. While superintending CHRISTIAN AND MISSIONARY ALLIANCE work in the troubled Guangxi province in China, Jaffray also established new mission work in

French Indo-China and later in the Dutch East Indies.

Arriving in Guangxi in 1897 Jaffray was soon appointed to Wuzhou city, his missionary base for over thirty years. Convinced that the power of the gospel had no cultural limits, Jaffray sent Christian messengers among primitive tribes as well as civilized peoples. Workers stayed in an area until a church was functioning, and then set up local Bible schools and presses so that Christian life could expand in that cultural setting. By this means an indigenized and independent church quickly developed. This strategy produced startling results in evangelism throughout Guangxi and Indo-China.

In 1931 Jaffray moved to Makassar in the Celebes to open new fields in the East Indies. Here for the first time he employed Chinese workers as foreign missionaries. As in the case of Indo-China, encounters with many peoples including the Dyaak headhunters were accompanied by unusual events of apostolic character. This ministry also grew until the Japanese invasion in 1942, when many missionaries were imprisoned, and Jaffray himself died as a war prisoner in 1945.

LAUREN PFISTER

Bibliography. A. W. Tozer, *Let My People Go!—The Life of Robert A. Jaffray.*

Jain, Jainism. Jainism is the religion of the Jain community and describes the way of life of those who follow the *Jina* (spiritual victors), human teachers who have attained infinite knowledge and preach the doctrine of *moksha* (liberation), also called *tirthankaras* (builders of the bridge across the road of suffering). One of India's most ancient non-Vedic traditions, widely regarded as the earliest heterodox offspring of HINDUISM, Jainism is often confused with BUDDHISM with which it bears some superficial similarities. Down through the centuries the Jains, however, have succeeded in maintaining their distinctive identity and the integrity of their belief system and way of life within the highly accommodative climate of Hinduism.

Although the beginnings of Jainism are commonly associated with Vardhamana Mahavira, who lived in the sixth century B.C., the Jain literature does not recognize him as founder or prophet, but as the twenty-fourth *tirthankara.* Jains today have deified him as the last and greatest savior with ideas of sinlessness and omniscience attributed to him. As a religious movement, Jainism seems to have arisen as a reaction to Brahminical Hinduism, and due to its rejection of the authority of the Vedas, is often perceived as a heresy of Hinduism. The Jaina system is opposed to the idea of God as a supreme personal being. The universe itself is regarded as un-created and eternal, made up of eternal souls *(jivas)* and eternal elements *(ajivas).*

Jainism shares with Hinduism belief in *karma* (moral retribution) and *samsara* (transmigration of the soul), although these concepts are interpreted in highly fatalistic terms within the theoretical pessimism integral to the Jaina system. It thus posits a very negative view of life in which humanity is trapped within an essentially painful and evil cycle of human existence. *Moksha* (liberation) from bondage to this cycle of birth and death is through a process of fourteen stages of spiritual evolution, involving rigid, self-denying ascetic practices. The five great *vratas* (vows) prescribing these ascetic practices are: not to kill, not to lie, not to steal, to abstain from sexual intercourse, and to renounce all worldly attachments.

Ahimsa (nonviolence) is one of the central beliefs and practices of Jainism. This cardinal principle of Jainism received worldwide attention as the essential ethical basis of the Indian movement for national independence as articulated and practiced by its chief architect, Mahatma Gandhi, who was himself deeply influenced by Jain thought and values. The deep reverence for life among the Jain community is reflected in a lifestyle which includes strict vegetarianism and noninvolvement in vocations such as farming, cattle breeding, and the armed forces. Large numbers of them have thus turned to careers in finance, commerce, and banking, making them one of the wealthiest and most influential communities in India.

Although Jainism has a very limited following of about 4.5 million adherents and the vast majority of them live in India, its influence has been powerful and far-reaching. The latter half of the twentieth century witnessed the emergence of an enterprising and influential Jain diaspora in North America, Britain, Africa, and the Far East. The Jain concern for peace, vegetarianism, and the environment contributes to the movement's universal appeal. The opportunity that Jainism presents for Christian missions is highlighted by the fact that there appears to be no specific Christian ministry directed toward the Jain community to date.

IVAN SATYAVRATA

Bibliography. C. Caillat, *ER,* VII:507–14; P. S. Jaini, *The Jaina Path of Purification;* S. Stevenson, *Heart of Jainism;* M. Tobias, *Life Force: The World of Jainism.*

Jamaica *(Est. 2000 pop.: 2,543,000; 10,990 sw. km. [4,243 sq. mi.])* While a reported 70 percent of Jamaicans are at least nominally Protestant, the island's rich cultural texture is reflected in its religious heterogeneity. A largely (93%) Afro-Caribbean society, in David Martin's opinion, found expression for its inherent diversity in a variety of religious movements. These reflect significant social class differences between the traditional Anglican, Methodist, and Moravian churches and more popular Baptist, Holiness, and Pentecostal groups. Included also are Seventh-Day Adventists, the largest Protestant community, a large Roman Catholic minority (10%), and powerful spiritist movements. The largest of these, the Rastafarians, has a larger following (80,000 adherents)—and a larger political role—than all but the largest Christian denominations.

EVERETT A. WILSON

SEE ALSO Caribbean.

Bibliography. A. Lampe, *The Church in Latin America, 1492–1992;* D. Martin, *Tongues of Fire: The Explosion of Protestantism in Latin America;* J. Rogozinski, *A Brief History of the Caribbean: From the Arawak and the Carib to the Present;* W. Wedenoja, *Perspectives on Pentecostalism: Case Studies from the Caribbean and Latin America.*

Japan *(Est. 2000 pop.: 126,472,000; 377,801 sq. km. [145, 869 sq. mi.]).* Christian mission, which has made a substantial impact upon Japan, began in 1549 when Jesuit missionary FRANCIS XAVIER landed in Kagoshima. In the 450 years since then, generally speaking, Christianity in Japan saw marked growth during transitional periods and exerted considerable influence upon the formation of society. Subsequently, its growth was curtailed when the society gained stability and traditional culture and religious powers began to counter the Christian influence. Furthermore, it has remained a minority religion of foreign origin.

Roman Catholic Mission (1549–1639). Historians often call the 1549–1639 period "the Christian Century of Japan." This period between Xavier's arrival and the beginning of the National Seclusion (1639–1854) was turbulent, yet it witnessed the emergence of new national expectations for a unified state, accumulation of capital, rational and scientific thinking, the importance of the individual, and a worldwide vision beyond the national boundary. Christianity satisfied some of these expectations and recorded a remarkable expansion. The number of "Kirishitan" (Christians) was estimated at about 300,000 by the end of the sixteenth century.

Xavier's initial ministry, which resulted in 2,000 Christians, was followed by other Jesuit missionaries, and many Christian communities sprang up in Kyushu and Chugoku, as well as in the capital, Kyoto. In 1563 the first Christian baron, Omura Sumitada, received baptism and was followed by half a dozen more barons and many of their subjects, thus adding considerable impetus to the Christian cause. As Christianity became a significant movement, the successive line of leaders aspiring to unite the country, like Oda Nobunaga, Toyotomi Hideyoshi, and Tokugawa Ieyasu, initially showed great interest in the new faith, but they soon began to fear it as a foreign ideology and a disruptive order of organized religion. In 1587 Hideyoshi abruptly issued a decree to expel all missionaries from Japan and finally in 1614, the Tokugawa government proscribed Christianity altogether. Suppression, persecution, and martyrdoms followed. The "Twenty-six Martyrs" of 1597 and the "Great Martyrdom" of 51 Christians in 1622, both in Nagasaki, were but a few examples. The Shimabara Uprising of 1637–38, when about 40,000 were massacred, marked the end of the "Christian Century."

The Modern Imperial State (1868–1945). The reintroduction of Christianity occurred at the end of the Tokugawa regime when Western powers broke Japan's seclusion policy and won commercial treaties. One outcome was the presence of foreign residents in Japanese ports, among them pastors and chaplains to serve the religious needs of the expatriates. Notable figures were such missionaries as J. C. HEPBURN (Presbyterian), G. H. F. VERBECK (Dutch Reformed), B. T. Petitjean (Catholic), and Nicolai (Russian Orthodox). Hepburn, serving as medical doctor, distinguished himself in the Japanese language and Bible translation and later founded a Christian school. Petitjean of the Paris Foreign Missionary Society met a group of the self-proclaimed Christians in 1865 and this incident led to the so-called rediscovery of about 60,000 "Hidden Christians" (Kakurekirishitan). They had long survived the government sanction and kept the faith of their seventeenth-century forefathers.

The Meiji Restoration of 1868, which restored the political power of the emperor and lifted official sanctions against Christianity in 1873, opened a new era for Christian mission. Both Roman Catholic and Russian Orthodox missions were well organized and successful. In 1912 there were about 66,000 Catholic and 32,000 Orthodox Christians in Japan. On the other hand, Protestant Christianity marked dynamic inroads into Japan and counted nearly 90,000 members in 1913. In its formative stage, many of its Japanese leaders, such as Uemura Masahisa, Uchimura Kanzô, and Nitobe Inazô coming from the former warrior class, were characterized as intellectual, independent, non-denominational, and Bible-oriented. Indeed, the first Protestant church, formed in 1872 by the early converts, was named "the Church of Christ in Japan," thus avoiding any denominational character of the Western missionaries. Uchimura's "NON-CHURCH" MOVEMENT (Mukyokai) idea was another unique but extreme example.

While a Christian influence was widely felt upon the society, by far the most noticeable area was that of education. Missionaries and national leaders considered education an effective means of evangelism and schools known as "Mission Schools" flourished. But the rise of nationalism and the religious revival of Confucianism and Shintoism turned the tide. The promulgation of the Constitution (1889) which made Shinto the state religion and the Imperial Rescript of Education (1890) forced Christian schools to reorient their education. A more decisive blow to them was Directive No. 12 of the Education Ministry (1899) which prohibited religious education and worship "even as extracurricular activities" in schools under government accreditation.

Nationalism also challenged Christianity on the issue of the imperial cult of Shintoism as a test of loyalty to the State. Since 1890 the Catholic Church had permitted Christians to participate in patriotic rites at the Shinto shrines and the Protestant churches followed. In 1941 some 30 Protestant churches were forced by the government to form the United Church of Christ in Japan.

After World War II (1945–   ). The crushing defeat of Japan brought a drastic change in the religious scene, and Christianity experienced a period of resurgence. Shinto ceased to be the state religion, and the new Constitution (1946) guaranteed freedom of religion to all. As General MacArthur of the Occupation authorities called for "1,000 missionaries" U.S. foreign missions of various church backgrounds poured their missionaries into Japan. Consequently more than 200 Protestant denominations were established.

Two distinctive features characterized post–World War II Christianity in Japan, namely ecumenism and internationalism. The formation of the WORLD COUNCIL OF CHURCHES in the AMSTERDAM ASSEMBLY (1948) incited many ecumenical concerns and movements in the mainline Protestant Churches under the National Council of Churches. On the conservative side of Protestantism, evangelical churches in Japan took an active part in the LAUSANNE CONGRESS ON WORLD EVANGELIZATION (1974) and have since followed its ecumenical guidelines. Roman Catholicism's SECOND VATICAN COUNCIL (1962–65), which faced the challenging issues of the modern world, has influenced the Catholic Church in Japan in such areas as interreligious DIALOGUE and fellowship with Asian churches.

To all appearances, the dawn of the twenty-first century still finds Christianity in Japan in dispersion and on the periphery of Japanese society. According to the 1997 Japan Christian Yearbook, the number of Christians was 1,084,737, only 0.862% of the total population. Although Christian influence in Japan goes far beyond the boundaries of the church, the reality surrounding Christianity in Japan is not bright, yet its challenging, as well as promising, future may life ahead.

TADATAKA MARUYAMA

Bibliography. O. Cary, *A History of Christianity in Japan;* N. S. Fujita, *Japan's Encounter with Christianity: The Catholic Mission in Pre-Modern Japan;* C. W. Iglehart, *A Century of Protestant Christianity in Japan;* J. Phillips, *From the Rising of the Sun: Christians and Society in Contemporary Japan.*

Japanese Mission Boards and Societies. Japan's Christian missionary outreach—surprisingly substantial for a country whose Christian population remains at about 1 percent of the total—can be connected to its historical position in relation to other countries. In the pre–World War II period Japanese Christian missionaries went out to various colonies within the expanding Japanese Empire (e.g., Taiwan) after its 1894–95 victorious war with China, to Korea after its annexation in 1910, then to protectorates granted by the League of Nations after World War I (e.g., parts of Micronesia). In other words, Japanese churches sent missionaries to work within Japanese-controlled domains.

The current period of missionary outreach is very much associated with Japan's postwar economic growth, beginning in the 1960s. The United Church, Overseas Medical Co-operative Service, Holiness Church, and Evangelical Missionary Society spearheaded the earlier postwar efforts. Much of this outreach was to Japanese people living abroad. Currently there is more of an international quality to the missions movement, in terms both of the sending-equipping agencies in Japan and of the places in which the 269 (1993) missionaries from Japan are working. Various international mission boards and societies have offices in Japan (e.g., Wycliffe) for raising up personnel, finances, and prayer support. There are organizations for coordinating communication between mission agencies and throughout the Christian community in Japan. There are interdenominational missionary training centers (e.g., Immanuel Bible Training College in Yokohama), at least one of which is associated with an accredited university (Tokyo Christian University in Chiba). Some boards and societies partner with churches in specific areas (e.g., Africa, the Philippines, Australia). Some focus on ecumenical partnership, while others emphasize social issues such as peace and hunger.

J. NELSON JENNINGS

Bibliography. L. M. Douglas, ed., *World Christianity: Oceania; OW;* J. H. Kane, *A Global View of Christian Missions: From Pentecost to the Present;* R. V. J. Windsor, ed., *World Dictionary of Missionary Training Programs,* 2d ed.

Japanese New Religious Movements. The modern era has seen the emergence of a large number of NEW RELIGIOUS MOVEMENTS in Japan which, although heavily influenced by the traditional Japanese religions, are manifestly different from SHINTO, BUDDHISM, and CONFUCIANISM. Development of these new movements falls into three distinct stages: the period of social upheaval during the late nineteenth and early twentieth centuries following modernization and the Meiji Restoration of 1868; the immediate aftermath of World War II; and the period beginning in the 1970s and continuing to the present.

During the first period new religious movements such as Tenrikyo, Kurozumikyo, and Omotokyo appeared, whose founders tended to be shamanistic figures drawing heavily on the Shinto tradition. Prior to World War II, however, their activities were severely restricted by the Japanese government, which had established Shinto as the state religion with the emperor as the supreme figure. Omotokyo, for example, was heavily persecuted because of its claims that its shamanistic leader, Degushi Onisaburo, was a living god whose authority outranked even the emperor's.

The founders of the new religions that came into prominence after World War II were mostly Buddhist laymen and laywomen who advanced their own novel interpretations of Buddhist teachings. The postwar Japanese Constitution guaranteed complete freedom of religion, providing these Buddhistic offshoots the social space in which to grow. These groups emphasized earthly prosperity based on the ritual of ancestor worship (*see* ANCESTRAL PRACTICES). Soka Gakkai, one of the most successful of these movements, claims over ten million adherents and exerts considerable political influence.

Japan was undergoing rapid modernization during the first two stages. Japanese society faced significant changes in social values and mores. The new religions addressed the very real concerns of poverty, disease, and social unrest with practical and tangible answers. In the third stage, beginning about 1970, Japanese culture expressed a new fascination with mystical and occult phenomena. Some profound transformations in Japanese society led to these new religious quests.

By 1980 Japan had emerged as a postindustrial society characterized by the revolution in information technology. As the rapid economic growth of the postwar era began to slow down people began to discover that simple acquisition of material goods did not satisfy. Their country having achieved the goal of becoming an economic superpower, the Japanese people found they had no clear purpose in life. In an effort to fill the spiritual vacuum many people began to experiment with YOGA, mystical meditation, and the OCCULT. Furthermore, the intense pressures faced by young people as well as adults fostered widespread disillusionment with life. A rigorous and highly competitive educational system, with little sympathy for those less gifted, often left students emotionally spent and empty. Japan's "economic miracle" had been achieved at tremendous cost, as company employees had to spend long hours on the job, usually at the expense of their families and their own health. These conditions produced deep frustrations for everyone—for the men who become known as "workaholic," their wives who were often left alone to raise the family, and the children who tried to cope with new family structures as well as school pressures. Across the social spectrum, then, there was a widespread search for meaning and fulfillment.

The religious movements of this third stage, such as Agonshu, AUM Shinrikyo, and Shuukyo Mahikari Kyodan, tried to fill this spiritual void. Many of these groups combine mystical experience, occult practice, and a pseudoscientific perspective. The most famous movement, AUM Shinrikyo, was founded in 1984 by Shoko Asahara, who imitated the style of a Tibetan guru and attracted many young people with his unique mixture of meditation, mystical experience, and utopian eschatology. In accordance with this unusual eschatology, in March 1995 cult members diffused highly toxic sarin gas into the subways of Tokyo, killing twelve people and injuring six thousand.

Unfortunately the Christian church in Japan has not been particularly effective either in responding to the widespread frustration and sense of spiritual emptiness in contemporary Japanese society or in reaching those involved in new religious movements. Japanese Christians must develop a deeper understanding of Japan's particular social context and its own religious traditions, which are quite different from those of the West.

HISAKAZU INAGAKI

Bibliography. H. Hardacre, *Kurozumikyo and the New Religions of Japan;* H. MacFarland, *The Rush Hour of the Gods;* S. Murakami, *Japanese Religion in the Modern Century;* C. Offner and H. Van Straelen, *Modern Japanese Religions: With Special Emphasis upon Their Doctrines of Healing.*

Javouhey, Anne Marie (1779–1851). French missionary to Africa and Latin America. Born in Jallanges, France, she was a devout Catholic and made it her life mission to care for the poor and to educate children. That ambition moved her beyond church walls into the mission field.

Her journey took her to several religious communities, but she found their way of life incompatible. Finally, Augustine Lestrange, a Cistercian, urged her to found her own congregation.

On that advice, in 1812 Javouhey bought a former Franciscan friary at Cluny and the Congregation of St. Joseph of Cluny was born. She quickly opened a school in Paris. In 1817 she founded a missionary school for native children on the island of Reunion.

In 1828 the French government asked Javouhey to oversee the colonization of Mana in Guyana; in 1834 she was again asked by the French government to educate six hundred Negro slaves about to be freed.

Her dedicated and innovative work in Guyana sparked international interest. In 1843 she left Guyana to further the work of her congregation in other parts of the world. By the time of her death, she had at least nine hundred blue-robed Sisters of St. Joseph all over the globe.

Anne Marie Javouhey's life mission was to minister to the poor and needy. Through that ambition, the world became her mission field.

KATHY MCREYNOLDS

Bibliography. M. Mott, *BDCM*, p. 330.

Jehovah's Witnesses. The Watch Tower Bible and Tract Society (WTBTS), more commonly known as Jehovah's Witnesses (JWs), was founded by Charles Taze Russell in 1884. Headquartered in New York City, it has grown to over 13 million adherents in 232 countries. In 1995 over 5 million active "publishers" (proselytizers) invested 1.15 billion hours witnessing. Growth fluctuates between 5 percent and 7 percent annually, with the greatest gains in predominately Roman Catholic countries and the former Soviet Union. The key to WTBTS growth is the constant emphasis on the imminence of the world's end.

Based on the presupposition that God has always worked through an organization and that WTBTS has been chosen for this age, all other faiths are deemed false religions, soon to be destroyed. The organization, designated "mother," is as essential to spiritual life as God the Father. Although JWs profess to hold to scriptural inerrancy, much of the New Testament is applied solely to the "anointed" class (the 144,000 [Rev. 7:4] who will spend eternity in heaven). The organization alone has authority to interpret Scripture, assigning itself the central role in prophecy.

Primary teachings of WTBTS include an aggressively anti-trinitarian stance, annihilationist position on hell, rejection of all national or religious celebrations, extreme pacifism, refusal of blood transfusions, and the kingdom of God as a divinely instituted government headed by Christ and the organization. Their Christology begins with the creation of Michael the Archangel who incarnated as Jesus of Nazareth, died on a torture stake, rose spiritually, returned to heaven as Michael, and mediates only for the 144,000.

The WTBTS continues to evolve doctrinally in order to avoid problems related to false prophecies and to expedite the transition of leadership from the elderly anointed class to those who will reside on earth forever, "the great crowd."

JWs constantly challenge the church to more effectively teach church history and theology, thereby equipping Christians to respond to those who come bearing a different gospel.

WENDY PETERSON

See also Cults, Cultism.

Bibliography. R. M. Bowman, Jr., *Jehovah's Witnesses, Jesus Christ, and the Gospel of John*; R. Franz, *Crisis of Conscience*; D. A. Reed, *How to Rescue Your Loved Ones from the Watch Tower.*

Jerusalem Conference (1928). The 1928 Jerusalem Conference of the INTERNATIONAL MISSIONARY COUNCIL, the first major meeting of the IMC after its foundation at Lake Mohonk seven years earlier, marked a considerable widening of the missionary agenda. Here missionary agencies sought to respond to the challenges of an increasingly secular and pluralist world, albeit from a thoroughly christological perspective. This is clearly demonstrated by the concerns of the seven sections of the conference: (1) the Christian message in relation to non-Christian systems of thought and life; (2) the relationship between younger and older churches (for the younger churches were swiftly emerging with competent leadership anxious to press their own points of view); (3) religious education; (4) Christian mission in relationship to racial conflict (on which J. H. OLDHAM, one of the IMC secretaries, had written four years earlier in *Christianity and the Race Problem*); (5) Christian mission and industrial difficulties; (6) Christian mission and rural problems; and (7) international missionary cooperation. Through these sections the conference emphasized a strong call to Christian service.

Several new organizations emerged out of the Jerusalem Conference. The Department of Social and Economic Research and Counsel sought to follow up on issues interfacing Christian mission and industry. The International Committee on the Christian Approach to the Jews, a first initiative in DIALOGUE, was founded in 1930; while an American expert on rural problems, K. L. Butterfield, sought by his travels to follow up on issues of rural mission, realizing that the overwhelming majority of humanity lived in rural communities. Farther afield, the Jerusalem Conference helped stimulate evangelistic endeavors such as the Kingdom of God Movement in Japan, and the Five Year Forward Movement in China.

JOHN A. Y. BRIGGS

See also World Council of Churches Conferences.

Bibliography. Conference Papers: Report of the Jerusalem Meeting of the IMC; B. Mathews, *Roads to the City of God: A World Outlook from Jerusalem, 1928*; K. S. Latourette, *HEM*, I:366–69; P. A. Potter, *DEM*, pp. 690–93; T. Stransky, *DEM*, pp. 526–29; A. J. van Der Bent, *DEM*, pp. 325–36.

Jessup, Henry Harris (1832–1910). American missionary to Lebanon. Born in Montrose, Pennsylvania, he was educated at Yale College and

Union Theological Seminary. He was ordained in the Presbyterian Church in 1855. While at Yale he became interested in missions, and traveled to Beirut in 1856 to begin service with the AMERICAN BOARD OF COMMISSIONERS. In 1857 he married Caroline Bush, who died in 1864, leaving three children. His second wife, Harriet Dodge, passed away in 1882, leaving five children. He then married Theodosia Lockwood.

Jessup's writings reveal that at a time when most missionaries to the Middle East were ignoring Muslims and evangelizing non-Protestant Christians, he and his colleagues accepted the more difficult challenge of bringing the gospel to the followers of Muhammad. For thirty years he was the pastor of the Syrian Church of Beirut and superintendent of its school. He served as the secretary for the Asfuriyeh Hospital for the Insane, and was editor of the Arabic journal *Al-Nashrah*. He was one of the founders of the Syrian Protestant College, which eventually became the American University of Beirut. Perhaps his most notable achievement was the founding of the Beirut Female Seminary, the first of its kind and a true venture of faith, since no one on either side of the Atlantic would support female education. He died April 28, 1910, and was buried in Beirut.

LARRY POSTON

Bibliography. H. H. Jessup, *Fifty-Three Years in Syria.*

Jesuit Orders. *See* ROMAN CATHOLIC MISSIONS.

Jesus and Mission. The concept of mission is central to an understanding of Jesus because Jesus and his mission are virtually synonymous. So identified was Jesus with his mission that it became his very life. "My food," said Jesus, "is to do the will of him who sent me and to finish his work" (John 4:24).

Jesus' Sense of Calling to Mission. Any discussion of Jesus' understanding of mission must begin with Jesus' own profound sense of calling. There is no indication in Scripture that Jesus ever struggled with what he should do with his life or that he tried various options before settling on his chosen path. From the very beginning, he was committed to the will of God as revealed directly to him and mediated through his reading of the Old Testament. Matthew sees this as operative even before Jesus' birth in the words of the angel to Joseph, "You are to give him the name Jesus, because he will save his people from their sins" (Matt. 1:21). The only episode recorded in our Gospels from Jesus' first thirty years shows his early sense of calling. Just before he entered into adult life, Jesus knew what he was to do: "Didn't you know I had to be in my Father's house?" (Luke 2:49). At his baptism, Jesus told John it was necessary in order to fulfill all righteousness. That act of acceptance by Jesus of

God's will was ratified by the voice from on High, "This is my Son whom I love; with him I am well pleased," accompanied by the descent of the Spirit of God (Matt. 3:13–17). After calling four fishermen to ministry, he began his next day in a solitary place, while it was still dark, in prayer. His disciples wondered why he was there and said everyone was looking for him. His reply was, "Let us go somewhere else—to the nearby villages—so I can preach there also. That is why I have come" (Mark 1:35–39). Later he would say, "the Son of Man did not come to be served, but to serve, and to give his life as a ransom for many" (Mark 10:45) and "the Son of Man came to seek and to save what was lost" (Luke 19:10). This sense of calling finds expression in the graphic words of Luke, "as the time approached for him to be taken up to heaven, Jesus resolutely set out [literally, set his face] for Jerusalem" (Luke 9:51). And what sustained Jesus in those last terrible hours on earth was his determination that the will of God be done (Matt. 26:39–44). Jesus' realization that he was to be the Savior of the world and his sense of calling to that task as the will of God for him is what gave shape to his life and ministry up to the very end.

Elements Shaping Jesus' Concept of Mission. There is no reasonable way that we can probe the mind of Jesus to determine exactly how this realization took precise shape, but we can look at three elements that went into the idea itself. The first of these is Jesus' understanding of the nature of God. For Jesus, God is compassionate, merciful, and loving. God is repeatedly called "Heavenly Father" and all that is best in fatherhood is to be found in God. Our Heavenly Father knows our deepest needs and is seeking to meet them (Matt. 6:25–32). And if human fathers, evil as they are, know how to give good gifts to their children, "how much more will your Father in heaven give good gifts to those who ask him!" (Matt. 7:11). The parable of the prodigal son, in which the father is really the key figure, pictures him as never giving up on the lost son and seeing him while still far off and lovingly welcoming him home. This love of God prompted him to send his own Son into the world so that the world might be saved (John 3:16, 17). The theme that God sent the Son is repeatedly emphasized by Jesus in the Gospel of John (5:36; 6:57; 7:29; 8:42; 11:42; 17:3, 8, 21, 23). The very essence of love is to give. God, as love, sent his Son as a gift to the world to provide the gift of salvation to those who will believe. Because Jesus understood God as love and himself as the expression of that love, he saw his mission as being sent by God to be the Savior of the world. So the nature of God as love shaped Jesus' understanding of his mission as the embodiment of God's loving purpose on earth.

The second idea that shaped Jesus' understanding of mission was his identification with the people of Israel. One aspect of God's original covenant with Israel was that Israel should be a blessing and that all the peoples of the earth should be blessed through her (Gen. 12:2, 3). Although this was interpreted by Israel essentially to mean that Gentiles who desired salvation could attain it by becoming a part of her, there were glimmers of a concept that Israel should go to the other nations taking the message to them. Jonah is an example of that, as is the message of Amos to the surrounding nations (Amos 1:9, 11, 13; 2:1). In large part, however, universal salvation was seen as eschatological, when Israel's God would be properly acknowledged as supreme over all the earth. It was this point Jesus picked up on in his correlation of eschatology and mission by postulating both a present and a future dimension to the kingdom. Inasmuch as the eschatological reality was present in and through his own earthly ministry, future reality was being brought to bear on the present. The knowledge of God which, in the future, will cover the earth like the waters cover the sea (Hab. 2:14) is now beginning its coverage in the mission of Jesus and will continue in the extension of that mission through his followers. Hence, the task of the church is to reach the ends of the earth and then the end will come when God draws history to a close in his own predetermined way (Matt. 24:14).

An aspect of Jesus' identification with Israel that is often overemphasized and sometimes misunderstood is his apparent confinement of his earthly mission to Israel alone (Matt. 10:6; 15:24). But this must be seen in the light of his prophetic mission of judgment to Israel. He was offering them their final call that in the mystery of God was to be rejected and from which would come the salvation of the world (Rom. 11:7–10, 25–36). This is seen most clearly in Jesus' explanation of his parables. Drawing upon Isaiah's call to make the heart of Israel calloused and their ears dull (Isa. 6:9, 10), Jesus said his teaching was to have this effect also (Matt. 13:10–15). What he was doing fulfilled Isaiah's prophecy, but its ultimate fulfillment was to be that blessedness had arrived which the prophets foresaw as eschatological salvation, including the Gentiles (Matt. 13:16, 17). Hence, Jesus could also minister to the Gentiles as well, without any contradiction of his being sent to the lost sheep of the house of Israel (Matt. 15:24).

The third idea that specifically influenced Jesus' concept of mission was that of the Suffering Servant as found in the Book of Isaiah. There is a collection of prophetic psalms in Isaiah (42:1–7; 49:1–7; 50:4–9; 52:13–53:12; 61:1–3; see also Mark 10:45; Luke 24:26) that speaks of God's righteous Servant who would bring redemption to the world. These prophecies were partially fulfilled by Israel, who was also God's servant, but ultimately by Jesus who was to the highest degree both Israel and Servant. The Servant as portrayed by Isaiah was to suffer for the sins of the world, establish justice, provide salvation for the nations, be a light to the Gentiles, give sight to the blind, proclaim the truth, be a covenant to the world, dispense God's Spirit, make intercession for sinners, and make peace for all people. Here in prophetic word is the mission of Jesus made plain, as he himself knew. When he began his ministry in Galilee, in his hometown of Nazareth, he selected Isaiah 61:1–2 to read in the synagogue. After reading the passage he said, "Today this Scripture is fulfilled in your hearing" (Luke 4:20, 21). The whole of Jesus' life was lived out in fulfillment of the prophesied mission of God's Suffering Servant.

Jesus' fundamental mission on earth was redemptive and revelatory of God's saving will for the world. He embodied and revealed the loving nature of God that graciously gives. He also took up into himself the covenant made with Israel, fulfilling Israel's task of mediating God's salvation to the world and came as God's specially anointed Servant, the sin-bearer for all.

Jesus' Mission and His Followers. Jesus knew that the task of mission was not his alone, but was to be transmitted to his followers. In fact, he says it was necessary for him to depart so that they, through the Holy Spirit, could reach their own full potential (John 14:12; 16:7). This inclusion of his followers may be seen in Jesus' ministry from the very beginning. Jesus' first formal calling of the future leaders of his movement (Peter, Andrew, James, and John) was specifically to mission—"I will make you fishers of men" (Matt. 4:19). When he finally settled on twelve to represent and lead the group that followed him, he named them "apostles"—those who are sent (Mark 3:14)—emphasizing the nature of their calling. Their ultimate mission was not to stay indefinitely with him, but to go and proclaim the Good News of the kingdom (Luke 9:2). Indeed, the choice of twelve to lead was in itself a statement regarding mission. Jesus was establishing a New Israel and with that a renewed focus on Israel's place in the history of salvation, the historical mediator of God's salvation to the world. When the training of the twelve was sufficient, Jesus sent them in his own name (and power) on missions of their own, duplicating his own work (Matt. 10:1–7, 8). That was in Galilee. Later, in Judea, seventy-two were sent out in similar fashion (Luke 10:1). After Jesus' resurrection, the apostle John epitomizes this concept of mission in Jesus' own words, "As the Father has sent me, I am sending you" (John 20:21), where a double sense of mission is emphasized. Jesus had been sent by the Father and he sends out his followers to fulfill the mission the Father had given to him. The Gospel story ends in the words of the so-called GREAT COMMISSION, "Go and make disciples of all nations" (Matt. 28:19).

It would be fair to say that the major focus of Jesus, in his relation to his disciples, was to prepare them for mission. This idea was enunciated over one hundred years ago by A. B. Bruce in *The Training of the Twelve*, where he saw the whole of Jesus' life as being directed to that end and more recently by Rainer Riesner in *Jesus als Lehrer*. The disciples sought to follow Jesus as far as was humanly possible and he set the example for them.

Conclusion. Jesus' sense of urgent divine mission penetrates the New Testament from beginning to end and ultimately goes back to Jesus himself. He was imbued with a sense of divine calling, he gathered his followers to support him in that mission, he commissioned them to proclaim the good news that he was bringing, he sent them out on preaching missions in his name, he accomplished the task given to him by his Father and left the fledgling church with the formidable task of going into all the world with the gospel, promising to be with them to the end of the age.

WALTER A. ELWELL

See also Christology.

Bibliography. A. B. Bruce, *The Training of the Twelve;* R. E. Coleman, *The Master Plan of Evangelism;* idem, *The Mind of the Master;* F. Hahn, *Missions in the New Testament.*

Jesus Film. In recent decades the Jesus film has emerged as one of the primary tools for evangelism throughout the world. The film is a two-hour motion picture based on the Gospel of Luke. A vision of Campus Crusade for Christ founder BILL BRIGHT, it was developed in cooperation with the Genesis Project and produced by John Heyman in 1978.

The initial theatrical release was handled by Warner Brothers. Having opened in 2,000 theaters in North America, the Jesus film was soon sold to television cable networks throughout the world. By 1998 it had already been dubbed in more than 450 languages spoken by 85 percent of the world's population. Another 200 versions were in process. The eventual goal of over 1,000 languages will potentially allow over 98 percent of the world to hear the gospel in their mother tongue.

The Jesus Film Project, a ministry of Campus Crusade for Christ, coordinates showings in more than 220 countries. A variety of methods are used, including 35-millimeter showings in commercial theaters; 16-millimeter showings in rural areas when portable screens, projectors, and generators need to be provided; national, regional, and local television releases; and videocassettes placed in rental shops and libraries or delivered home to home by church workers. Distributed by more than 700 ministries and church agencies, the film has been seen by over one billion people. At showings where an invitation to receive Christ could be offered, 50 million decisions had been indicated by 1997.

The widespread acceptability of the film to the Christian community is probably due to its scriptural base. Jesus speaks no words outside of those found in the Bible. A related factor is the film's accuracy. Five years of research went into the preparation for the production. More than four hundred scholars evaluated the script. Each scene was filmed as close as possible to the location where the original action took place two thousand years ago. The biblical approach and the selection of the actor to portray Jesus were of primary importance. After scores of screen tests Brian Deacon, a Christian Shakespearean actor from England, was selected for the role of Jesus. All of the remaining actors came from Israel, where the film was made.

The enthusiastic acceptance of the film by so many viewers from such diverse cultures is due to four primary factors. First, the film is a docudrama of first-century Palestine. Many relate to this presentation because they live in that rural type of culture where people still fish and farm for a living. Second, the film reaches people who cannot read. Third, that many people have never seen a film in their own language gives the film a strong impact. Fourth, most non-Westerners are concrete thinkers. They receive Jesus not only because he is the Savior, but because he has power over nature, evil spirits, sickness, and death.

PAUL E. ESHLEMAN

Bibliography. P. E. Eshleman, *I Just Saw Jesus;* idem, *The Touch of Jesus.*

Jew, Judaism. Judaism, the religion of the Jewish people, includes the totality of Jewish life and thought. As a religious civilization Judaism embraces the historic and cultural experience of the Jewish community from earliest times to the present. Judaism has significantly influenced the formation of both Christianity and Islam.

The terms "Hebrew," "Israelite," and "Jew" come from the Jewish Scriptures, which Christians read as the Old Testament. God calls the first Jew, Abraham, promising him offspring, land, and blessing (Gen. 12:1–3; see ABRAHAMIC COVENANT). This covenant has universal significance for the nations, and particular relevance to Abraham's physical descendants. Under Moses, the Hebrews were redeemed from slavery in Egypt and called into a covenant relationship at Sinai that embraced personal and social ethics as a reflection of their spiritual relationship with Yahweh. The election of Israel has a missionary dimension in that Israel is called to be a priestly people and a light to the nations as she bears witness to God.

Biblical Israel's identity developed in reaction to the idolatry and polytheism of her neighbors. Yet the history of the Jewish people shows how failure to live according to the covenant led to destruction and the loss of the ten northern tribes (722 B.C.). Judah, the remaining tribe, gave its name to the southern kingdom. After the exile (586 B.C.) the term "Jew" *(Yehudi)* referred to subjects of the Babylonian/Persian province of Judah. Judaism survived in exile and restoration by becoming a religion of the book, the Torah, a concept wider than that of "law," with a more general sense of "revelation" and "instruction." Transmission and application of the Torah, especially as found in Pentateuch, were reinforced by the development of the synagogue as an institution for prayer, study, and community life.

By the time of Jesus the Jewish people had fragmented into a variety of groups (Pharisees, Sadducees, Zealots, Essenes), with a majority living outside the land of Israel. After the destruction of the temple (A.D. 70) the successors of the Pharisees, the rabbis, had a normative influence on the development of later belief and practice. They codified the laws of the Pentateuch into the Mishnah ("repetition," c. A.D. 200) and reformulated the religion without direct need of temple, land, or sacrifice. The term "Judaism" *(ioudaismos)* signifies the self-definition of Jewish groups in their struggle against the influence of Hellenism.

In the period of rabbinic Judaism (A.D. 200–500) Judaism became a religion of the dual Torah, the written and oral law, culminating in the completion (c. A.D. 500) of the Talmud ("teaching"), an extended commentary and discussion of the laws *(halachah)*. The sages distanced the religion from that of the Jewish Christian sects (Ebionites, Nazarenes) by inserting the *Birkat Haminim* ("Blessing of Heretics") into the synagogue liturgy (c. A.D. 110), forcing Jewish Christians to identify themselves or withdraw.

In the medieval period the Jewish people developed strategies for survival in the frequently hostile environments of Islam and Christianity (the CRUSADES). Attempts at conversion led to public disputations over messianic prophecies, such as that between Nachmanides and Paulo Christiani in Spain (1263). Such encounters were often held under duress, and with an agenda of forced conversion. Jewish mysticism *(Kabbalah)* thrived, with a resurgence of messianic expectation (Shabbetai Zevi 1665).

In the period of emancipation (1700–1900) rationalism and humanism enabled Jews who came out of the ghettos to be actively involved in European society. Thinkers such as Spinoza, Lessing, Marx, Freud, and Einstein, often influenced by their Jewish backgrounds, made significant contributions to secular knowledge. Others distanced themselves in ultraorthodoxy (Hasidism). Reform and Liberal Judaism developed alternative patterns of liturgy, belief, and lifestyle. Patterns of emigration at the beginning of the twentieth century led to increased assimilation. ZIONISM, a secular nationalism with religious aspects, was motivated by European and Russian anti-Semitism. It became a viable project that resulted in the formation of the state of Israel (1948). Eligibility for citizenship in Israel has been challenged in a number of cases of Jewish believers in Jesus, giving rise in a secular context to the traditional "Who is a Jew?" question.

More than anything else Zionism has provided an antidote for the effects of anti-Semitism (Nazism) and the trauma of the Holocaust. However, the Jewish community today is characterized as much by "post-Holocaust disillusionment" as by a vibrant faith in the God of Israel. From a Christian perspective the creation of the state of Israel (1948) renewed the eschatological hopes of many premillennialists, and the renewed use of Hebrew as a spoken language provided new impetus for literature production and the development of worship resources.

Theology. While Judaism has always avoided credal formulation, stressing orthopraxy over orthodoxy, the ethical and religious values of Judaism can be summarized in the Ten Commandments and the Thirteen Principles of Faith of Maimonides (1135–1204), which gave Judaism a credal form in the "Thirteen articles of faith," combining a biblical theism with Aristotelian philosophy. The identity markers of Sabbath, circumcision, and the food laws *(kashrut)* have continued to be important distinctives of the Jewish people, as have celebration of the Jewish festivals, especially Passover and the Day of Atonement *(Yom Kippur)*. In recent years women have taken a more active role, with the ordination of women rabbis in the Reform and Liberal synagogues, but the traditional model of the woman's role is still the most common.

Judaism revolves around the core themes of God, Israel, and the Torah, as summarized in the *Shema*, the confession of faith of Deuteronomy 6:4. A further central topic is that of the land, *Eretz Israel*. Belief in the coming of the Messiah, while one of Maimonides' principles, is interpreted in various ways, but generally with the conclusion that Jesus was not the Messiah because he failed to fulfill the required messianic prophecies, though it may be argued that the concept of the Messiah was redefined by Judaism to specifically rule out the radically new formulation of the messianic program given by Jesus. The additional social cost of becoming a Christian has prevented many Jewish people from accepting Jesus with a willing heart. Memories of the medieval forced conversions (Inquisition) make it especially painful for Jewish people to think of "betraying their people" through conversion.

Mission. From its beginnings Christianity has defined itself and its mission in response to its Jewish origins, in proclamation of its Jewish Messiah, Jesus. In the patristic and medieval periods, debates between Jews and Christians on the messianic prophecies were frequent, but they often degenerated into polemics fed by the anti-Judaism (loosely referred to as "anti-Semitism") derived from a misreading of the New Testament and fed by the institutional aims of the church. With lamentably few exceptions the Jewish people were despised, rejected, and persecuted by the church, and the "teaching of contempt," the idea that the suffering of the Jews is due to their rejection of Jesus, has continued to feed both religious and secular forms of racial prejudice.

In the light of this some Christians have renounced the call to evangelism, seeing their mission to Israel today as one of support and reconciliation, with DIALOGUE rather than evangelism as the method (*see also* JEWISH MISSIONS). Following the proposal of Franz Rosenzweig that Jesus brought the new covenant for Gentiles (non-Jews) but that Jewish people already have a revelation of God in the Torah, some have adopted a TWO-COVENANT THEORY with a necessary redefinition of Christology, seeing the uniqueness of Christ as an anti-Semitic formulation untenable by Christianity today.

Despite this an increasing number of Jewish people have become believers in Jesus in recent years. Jewish attitudes to Jesus have changed from antipathy to a desire for a "Jewish reclamation of Jesus," a significant factor in the increasing understanding of the Jewish context of the New Testament and Jesus himself. Also, the efforts at CONTEXTUALIZATION of the gospel have seen much fruit, as the growing number of messianic synagogues and organizations like Jews for Jesus have successfully challenged the notion that you cannot be Jewish and believe in Jesus. The network of mission agencies and others involved in Jewish evangelism has been strengthened by the work of the Lausanne Consultation on Jewish Evangelism (LCJE). Today, perhaps more than at any time in the past two thousand years, it can be said that Jewish people are coming to know their Messiah.

RICHARD S. HARVEY

Bibliography. I. Epstein, *Judaism, A Historical Presentation;* C. D. Harley, *Christian Witness to the Jewish People;* L. Jacobs, *Encyclopaedia Judaica,* 10:383–97; J. Jocz, *The Jewish People and Jesus Christ;* P. Johnson, *A History of the Jews;* D. Stern, *Messianic Jewish Manifesto.*

Jewish Missions. Christians endeavor to bring Jews to faith in Christ. The apostles first proclaimed the messiahship of Jesus to their own Jewish people. Paul, the apostle to the Gentiles, evangelized in the synagogues first in each city on his itinerary. As the number of Gentile Christians grew, the Jewishness of Jesus and the gospel was ignored by the church or transformed so that no one could recognize the Jewish nature of Christianity. There arose a common teaching that the Jews were rejected by God and the church alone was the heir to all the covenant promises. Despite the hostile climate, some Jews continued to find their way to Christ in all ages.

The medieval disputations cannot properly be called "missions." Though arguments from Old Testament messianic passages were presented that are still used in Jewish apologetics to this day, much of the case presented by the Christians was to deny the validity of the Jews as the chosen people of God.

The first period of modern Jewish missions was from 1790 to 1914. Beginning with the Pietists of eighteenth-century Germany, there was a considerable amount of interest in Jewish missions in the Protestant church. Jewish mission organizations were established in the Lutheran, Anglican, Baptist, and Presbyterian churches, as well as through independent mission societies. These groups worked among the Jews of Europe and (what was then called) Palestine. By the end of the nineteenth century, American Jewish missions came into their own.

The distinctives of Jewish missions in this first period were: (1) Jewish missions were regarded in the church as a valid endeavor; (2) the method of outreach was through literature distribution, reading rooms, door-to-door visitation, and converts' homes, schools, and hospitals; (3) the apologetic was based on Old Testament prophecy and sometimes employed rabbinic literature, but little actual contextualization took place.

Two key changes took place in Jewish missions in the twentieth century. First, between the two World Wars and increasingly after the Holocaust, a weakening of evangelical theology led many denominations to replace the concept of mission with that of "dialogue." Significant exceptions were the Lutheran Church–Missouri Synod, the Presbyterian Church in America, and, most recently, the Southern Baptist Convention.

The second change was in the approach of Jewish missions. Jewish people in the Western nations were no longer poor immigrants nor were they mostly religious. But not until 1970 did Jewish missions change accordingly. Moishe Rosen, who went on to found the Jews for Jesus organization, pioneered a new methodology that included (1) the use of contemporary literature oriented to the secular Jewish person; (2) greater visibility and boldness in approach; (3) a heightened contextualization in outreach as Jewish Christians expressed their faith in a Jewish frame of reference.

In response, countermissionary organizations were formed, most notably Jews for Judaism.

Though their successes in winning Jews away from Christ were few, they succeeded in creating a climate of hostility toward Jewish missions and messianic Jews. Nevertheless, their efforts for the most part helped focus attention on the issue.

The heart of Jewish missions remains the example and teaching of the New Testament. This core is best encapsulated by the apostle Paul in Romans 1:16 and Romans 9–11. Since 1970, Jewish people have been coming to Christ in record numbers. Today it is estimated that between 0.5 percent and one percent of Jewish people are Christians. Recent happenings of note include the indigenous work being done in Israel by Jewish believers and increased access to Russian Jews with many opportunities to tell the gospel.

RICH ROBINSON

Bibliography. W. T. Gidney, *The History of the London Society for Promoting Christianity Amongst the Jews, From 1809 to 1908*; A. Huisjen, *The Home Front of Jewish Missions*; M. Rosen and W. Proctor, *Jews for Jesus*; A. E. Thompson, *A Century of Jewish Missions*.

John, Griffith (1831–1912). Welsh missionary to China. A Welsh Congregationalist associated with the LONDON MISSIONARY SOCIETY, Griffith John worked for fifty years in Central China, living to see the fall of the Qing dynasty. Noted for stirring preaching and missionary travels into dangerous areas, John also was a prolific writer and notable Bible translator.

Arriving in Shanghai in 1855, John and several other missionaries later had direct contact with ill-fated Taiping leaders. Before the Taiping insurgents were destroyed, John moved into Hankou City of Hubei province in 1861. A courageous itinerant evangelist, he risked his life numerous times in preaching to Chinese crowds and selling Chinese tracts he and others had authored.

In 1875 John experienced a personal spiritual renewal. He later countered vicious anti-Christian pamphleteering by Hunan literati with his own writings, literature distributions, and personal evangelism. He lived to see the opening of that province to numerous stable Chinese congregations. During the 1880s he translated portions of the Bible into Mandarin in a popular literary style. Well known across China for his Chinese pamphlets and books, he received an honorary degree from Edinburgh and a special interview with the famous Chinese statesman, Zhang Zhidong (1837–1909), before returning to England because of a fatal illness.

LAUREN PFISTER

Bibliography. N. Bitton, *Griffith John: The Apostle of Central China*; R. W. Thompson, *Griffith John: The Story of Fifty Years in China*.

John of Montecorvino (c. 1247–1330). Italian Franciscan missionary to Persia and China. Born in Montecorvino in southern Italy, John was a Franciscan missionary to Persia prior to his path-breaking missionary work in China. In 1270, after the opening of China to trade with the West, the Mongol emperor, Kublai Khan, asked the pope to send a hundred missionaries. Although conflict within the papacy delayed the response to this remarkable request, in 1289 John of Montecorvino started his journey to Peking with a letter from the pope to Kublai Khan. During his journey, John preached for a year in India before traveling up the coast of China and arriving in Peking in 1294. By 1300 he had learned the Chinese language and had established a thriving church. A 1305 letter describing his work caused widespread excitement in the West. In 1307, Pope Clement V named John the archbishop of China and dispatched several bishops to join him.

During his successful thirty-five years of service in China, John translated the New Testament and Psalms into the Mandarin language and gained thousands of converts. His ministry also involved repeated conflicts with the Chinese Nestorian Christians, whose church he did not recognize (*see* NESTORIAN MISSIONS). In view of the arduous journey from Europe to China, few European missionaries were able to join him, and the churches he established were destroyed after the emergence of the Ming Dynasty in 1368.

ALAN SEAMAN

Bibliography. J. Zubal, *The Catholic Missions in China during the Middle Ages*.

John XXIII (1881–1963). Italian pope and convener of Vatican II. Born in northern Italy, he was ordained in 1904, became a doctor of theology, and served in the Vatican diplomatic corps (1925–53) before becoming cardinal and patriarch of Venice, and then an unexpected choice as pope. The self-styled "pope who keeps pressing on the accelerator" convened the SECOND VATICAN COUNCIL (1962–65) to address the church's strategy in meeting the needs of the modern world. He jarred long-entrenched prejudice against non-Catholic Christians, inviting them to send observers to the Council. He made post-Reformation history by welcoming to the Vatican the archbishop of Canterbury. He capitalized on his earlier sojourns in eastern European capitals by improving relations with communist states and with the Eastern Orthodox Church, and showed himself to have a marked social concern. John's *Journal of a Soul* was translated into English in 1965.

But while he sent a breath of fresh air sweeping through conservative circles and initiated dialogues which are still continuing, the pontiff's tolerance did not take in major changes in his church's basic theological doctrines.

J. D. DOUGLAS

Bibliography. P. Hebblethwaite, *Pope John XXIII: Shepherd of the Modern World;* G. Zizola, *The Utopia of Pope John XXIII.*

Johnson, Richard (1755–1827). English missionary to Australia. Born in Yorkshire, England, Johnson studied at the Hull Grammar School and the University of Cambridge. He was ordained by the Church of England as a deacon (1783) and priest (1784), and served as a curate in two parishes. The influence of William Wilberforce and John Newton led to Johnson's appointment in 1787 as chaplain to a convict fleet that was sent to a penal colony in New South Wales (Australia). Although his role was never clearly defined, he ministered to both convicts and British military personnel. As an evangelical Anglican, he sometimes clashed with high church government officials, particularly over the efficacy of attempting to convert the indigenous population. In addition to being the only chaplain for several years, Johnson also functioned as a magistrate and schoolmaster. He left his mark as a pioneer missionary in a very difficult setting. He showed an evangelistic burden and genuine love for the aborigines, even if he was not always sensitive to their culture. Health problems forced Johnson to return to England in 1800. Following curacies in Norfolk and Essex, he finished his career with a seventeen-year stint (1810–27) as rector of the combined parish of St. Antholin's and St. John the Baptist church in London.

JAMES A. PATTERSON

Bibliography. N. K. Macintosh, *Richard Johnson, Chaplain to the Colony of New South Wales: His Life and Times, 1755–1827.*

Jonah. The Book of Jonah makes its point through interaction and dialogue between the prophet and the Lord rather than through direct statements of prophecy or theology. It concerns more than simply a prophet who ran from God's call or the miraculous mass repentance of the city of Nineveh. Certainly it is greater in scope than the miracle of the big fish that swallowed Jonah, even though that incident sometimes attracts more attention from those who study it than even the main theme of the book.

Jonah ran from God's call, something that was meant to make the reader wonder why he would do it. The answer surprises modern readers: It was because Jonah was afraid that the Ninevites would take the message of judgment seriously and repent (4:1–2). To the original readers, though, Jonah's line of reasoning may not have seemed strange.

Assyria was the major imperial power of Jonah's day (approximately the first half of the eighth century B.C.), and it was feared throughout the ancient world. For nearly a century, the Assyrian kings had been sending troops into the northern areas of Syria–Palestine and demanding that the local populations submit to Assyrian sovereignty and pay a heavy tribute. Refusal to do so often resulted in the destruction of cities and even nations, with many cruel acts of terror and havoc that devastated the populations. Knowing this, it does not seem so strange that Jonah at first tried to escape the call of God to preach repentance to such a cruel people. The intensity of Jonah's feelings becomes clear later when he overtly expressed his anger at God for having mercy on the dreaded enemy, even to the point that he asked the Lord to take his life (4:3).

The irony of Jonah's bitterness, though, stands out even stronger when the reader considers that the Ninevites were not the only object of the Lord's mercy. God had previously spared Jonah from the belly of the great fish, and Jonah concluded his prayer of thanksgiving with the words, "Salvation comes from the LORD" (2:9). Jonah could be grateful for his own salvation, but he could not accept that God would grant salvation to his bitterest enemy.

The Lord then tried to show Jonah the incongruities of his viewpoint through the lesson of the vine (4:6–11). Jonah cared about the vine because of how it involved him personally, so wouldn't it be reasonable for God to be concerned in a personal way about a great city with many innocent people and animals in it (4:11)?

We do not learn Jonah's opinion about God's rhetorical question, but our responses to that same question will indicate something about our attitude toward God's plan to bring his salvation to the ends of the earth. First, are we self-centered in our faith? Are we concerned only about ministry that will have some relationship and benefit to us personally? Will it reach the racial or ethnic group that we identify with? Will it improve our life? Will it avoid our having to express love for a group that we would rather hate? Second, an underlying question is even more pressing: To what extent have we opened our lives to the grace, compassion, and love of God ourselves if we are unwilling to love those who can do nothing for us in return or who have offended us deeply? Ultimately, the Book of Jonah and Jesus' parable of the unforgiving servant (Matt. 18:23–35) are hauntingly similar.

The human heart is unlike the heart of God. That is the message of the Book of Jonah. Jonah recognized that the Lord is "a gracious and compassionate God, slow to anger and abounding in love, a God who relents from sending calamity" (4:2). But Jonah could not express that same love himself. He knew the gospel and had experienced it for himself, but his heart remained closed to his enemies. He was the reluctant missionary who preached and saw results (chaps. 1 and 3), but only because God's Word is effective to accomplish its purpose (Isa. 55:11).

The reader also notices Jonah's blindness to God's grace in his own life. In his grace, God has chosen to work through human instruments to carry out his plan for proclaiming the gospel throughout the world. Jonah should have been grateful that God chose to involve him, but he could see no further than the limits of his own provincial outlook.

The example of Jonah calls us to expand our thinking about missions. If Jonah could be effective even in his closed-heartedness, how much more effective he could have been if he had been more open to God's work of love? To the extent that we see ourselves in the proud and bigoted Jonah, we can begin to appreciate more the miracle that God has been gracious to us. Also we can begin to pray that God will change our hearts so that we will have his heart for the world rather than our own.

THOMAS J. FINLEY

Bibliography. T. D. Alexander, *Jonah: An Introduction and Commentary;* J. Baldwin, *The Minor Prophets: An Exegetical and Expository Commentary,* II:543–90; J. R. Kohlenberger, *Jonah and Nahum;* J. Walton, *Jonah;* J. Verkuyl, *Contemporary Missiology.*

Jones, David (1707–1841). Welsh missionary to Madagascar. Born in Cardiganshire, South Wales, he was educated in his homeland at Neuaddlwyd and Gosport. He was ordained as an Independent in 1817 and appointed by the LONDON MISSIONARY SOCIETY to sail for Madagascar in 1818 with Thomas Bevan, a fellow student. During the initial foray into Madagascar a fever killed most of the party, including Jones' wife, and seriously weakened his own health. Following recuperation and remarriage in Mauritius, Jones returned to Madagascar in 1821 to establish schools and reduce the Malagasy language to writing. David Griffiths and he developed a phonetic system using Roman characters that allowed the Malagasy to write their own language. Despite resistance to this by some English colonists, Jones persisted in his work and eventually gained many converts. He and his colleagues also successfully translated the Bible into Malagasy. Antiforeign uprisings and persecution forced Jones to furlough in Great Britain in 1830. Later attempts to reestablish his work in Madagascar met with opposition from local rulers. He died in Mauritius following an accident, but the church survived, thanks in part to copies of Jones' translation of the Bible that were hidden during the intense persecution of the 1830s and 1840s.

JAMES A. PATTERSON

Bibliography. E. H. Hayes, *David Jones, Dauntless Pioneer: An Epic Story of Heroic Endeavor in Madagascar.*

Jones, Eli Stanley (1884–1973). American missionary to India. Born in Maryland, Jones went to India under the Methodist Missionary Board in 1907. By 1930 his appointment was expanded to "evangelist-at-large for India and the world." Following his initial service as pastor of an English-speaking congregation in Lucknow and then work among the outcastes, Jones changed his focus to evangelizing the upper-caste intellectuals. It was in this context that he emerged as a leading advocate of indigenizing, or Indianizing, the gospel message. For Jones this involved both de-Westernizing the gospel and immersing it in Indian cultural and philosophical forms and structures. He drew a sharp distinction in his view of evangelism between the message of Christ and the Western institutional church. His first book, *The Christ of the Indian Road* (1925), expounded the need to present Christ in an Indian setting—to give Christ to India and India to Christ. Two of his notable adaptations for indigenized evangelism were the Round Table philosophical discussions with Indian intellectuals and the establishment of Christian ashrams (adapted from the Hindu communities or "families"). During his missionary career, Jones' view of evangelism evolved from the individualistic-conversion emphasis of his Wesleyan-Holiness heritage to a blend of individual conversion and the redemption of social, economic, and political structures. Thus, E. Stanley Jones' missionary legacy is that of an ardent evangelist, a protoliberationist, a vocal ecumenist, and an innovative indigenizer.

DONALD R. DUNAVANT

Bibliography. E. S. Jones, *The Christ of the Indian Road;* idem, *Christ at the Round Table;* R. W. Taylor, *The Contribution of E. Stanley Jones.*

Jones, Lina Maude (1890–1979). New Zealand missionary in the Solomon Islands. Born on March 2, 1890, Jones was the daughter of a Methodist fitter and turner who had come to New Zealand from England and based himself in the Railway Workshops in Christchurch. Lina, the fourth of five children and an enthusiastic athlete, was trained as a teacher. In 1923, inspired by a letter from a Methodist missionary read to an Easter Bible Class camp, she volunteered to the Foreign Mission Board of the Methodist Church. She was sent to the Western Solomon Islands where the opinionated and able Australian, John F. Goldie, controlled a mission supervised by New Zealand. Based in Munda and Bilua, in 1924 she began junior classes called "kinda" at Kokeqolo. It was the first provision of general education in the Solomons. She became active in mission administration, and was the first woman to attend the Annual Synod. Strong and determined, conservative in outlook, she was committed to improving conditions for the Islanders. The missionaries were evacuated during World War II, and Lina worked in the Foreign Missions Office in Auckland. She returned to the Solomons in 1945, and helped in the translation of the New Testament and a dictionary into Rovianan. Retiring to Auckland, New Zealand, in 1950, she worked constantly to increase interest in foreign missions, until her death on June 11, 1979. Within the limits permitted to women in denominational missions she exercised a broad influence.

PETER LINEHAM

Bibliography. D. N. Beniston, *The Call of the Solomons: The New Zealand Methodist Women's Response;* G. G. Carter, *Valuable-Beyond-Price: The Story of Sister Lina M. Jones 1890–1979.*

Jordan *(Est. 2000 pop.: 6,407,000; 91,861 sq. km. [35,468 sq. mi.]).* The Hashemite Kingdom of Jordan is an Arab nation located in the northwest corner of the Arabian Peninsula. About 6 percent of the land area of Jordan is arable, and more than 90 percent is desert. Village life in Jordan dates from at least 8000 B.C. at Jericho. The area was a frequent invasion route for Assyrians, Egyptians, Babylonians, and Persians. The Ottoman Turks conquered the area in 1517, and imposed a social structure that forms a strong cultural element even today.

More than 96 percent of the population are Arabs. The bulk of the population is descended from Bedouin ancestry. Islam is the state religion, almost entirely Sunni Muslims. The Christians are less than 5 percent, the majority from the Greek Orthodox community.

The history of missions in Jordan is varied. Political divisions have changed and are still changing, thus the beginnings of modern Protestant mission work in Jordan dates back to the time when the area was known as Palestine. Great Britain has played an important political and religious role in the area for over a century. The Anglicans entered Palestine in 1860 and continue to have a strong work. The Evangelical Church of the C&MA is the national church resulting from the work of the Christian and Missionary Alliance beginning in 1890, and becoming more firmly established in the 1920s. Assemblies of God began working in 1929, and several other boards and denominations began work after 1940. Today there are an estimated 103 Protestant missionaries in Jordan from approximately 20 denominations and agencies.

Although Islam is the state religion, Christians have been granted a greater degree of freedom than in most dominant Muslim countries. Even though the majority of missionary efforts have been focused on the revitalization of Orthodox and Roman Catholic minorities, there has been an increasing interest and openness among Jordanians and refugees from the Gulf War (1991) crisis. The vast majority of the population is still classified as unreached with the gospel.

NORMAN E. ALLISON

Bibliography. J. H. Kane, *A Global View of Christ Missions: From Pentecost to the Present;* W. F. Smalley, *Alliance Missions in Palestine, Arab Lands, Israel, 1890–1970.*

Joseph, Justus (c. 1835–87). Indian churchman and prophet. Born in Travancore Kerala into a devout Hindu Brahmin home, Justus Joseph together with his family converted to Christianity and was baptized by Joseph Peet in 1861. The family adopted Christian names: the father, Venkateswara Bhagvathar, became known as Justus Cornelius, and his eldest son Raman as Justus Joseph. Spotting the young man's leadership potential, CHURCH MISSION SOCIETY (CMS) missionaries trained him for the ministry; Peet taught him English and Greek. Ordained by the Anglican bishop of Madras in 1868, he became vicar at Kannit.

Beginning in 1873, a spiritual awakening occurred among CMS and Syrian congregations. Two evangelists from Tinnevelly (Tamil Nadu), followers of JOHN CHRISTIAN AROOLAPPEN, introduced Joseph and his brothers to the teachings of the Plymouth Brethren. Features of the revival that followed included intense conviction of sin, visions, speaking in tongues, indigenous Christian music, rejection of caste, and the restoration of apostles and prophets. In the belief that the Holy Spirit had commissioned him to herald Christ's coming within six years, Joseph left the Anglican Church in 1875. With several thousand followers, he founded the Revival Church, better known as the Six Years' Party. Missionaries sharply denounced its excesses and nonconformity. Although discredited in 1881 when the prophecy failed, Justus Joseph had contributed to church growth. His activities reflected the struggle of indigenous Christians for leadership in mission churches.

GARY B. MCGEE

Bibliography. W. J. Richards, *Church Missionary Intelligencer and Record* 7 (Nov. 1882): 660–67; *Indian Evangelical Review* 4 (April 1874): 397–410.

Journals of Mission and Missiology. A wide range of periodical literature reports on and informs of the missionary activity of the Christian Church. Virtually all mission boards and agencies publish newsletters to keep their missionaries and supporters informed of their activities. These newsletters can be found in library collections of related schools or mission libraries (*see* MISSION LIBRARIES.) They are listed in publications such as the *Mission Handbook*.

Several bulletins inform the Christian community of newsworthy events and trends related to mission. *Mission Frontiers,* published by the U.S. Center for World Mission, emphasizes the cutting edge of missionary activity. *Pulse,* published by the Evangelism and Missions Information Service of the Billy Graham Center, provides articles and news items on topics that impact missionary work. The Lausanne Committee for World Evangelization communicates with the members of its network through *LCWE Newsletter.* The *AD 2025 Global Monitor,* produced by Global Evangelization Movement Research in the United States, attempts to measure the progress of world evangelization. The Christian Research Association in the United Kingdom provides a similar service through *Quadrant.*

The WORLD COUNCIL OF CHURCHES maintains the oldest English language missiological journal, *International Review of Missions.* Other major English language journals published by institutions include the *International Bulletin of Missionary Research* by the Overseas Ministries Study Center (OMSC), *Evangelical Missions Quarterly* by the Evangelism and Missions Information Service of the Billy Graham Center (EMIS), *Exchange* by the Interuniversity Institute for Missiological and Ecumenical Research (IIMO), *Mission Focus* by the Mission Training Center, Associated Mennonite Biblical Seminary, and the *Bulletin of the Scottish Institute of Missionary Studies* by the Institute. A title which attempts to investigate new trends in world evangelization is the *International Journal of Frontier Missions.*

Several journals are produced by scholarly societies and reflect the specific perspective of each society. The American Society of Missiology (ASM) produces *Missiology.* The International Association of Mission Studies (IAMS) publishes *Mission Studies. Missionalia* is the product of the Southern African Missiological Society (SAMS). *Missio Apostolica* is the journal of the Lutheran Society of Missiology.

A number of non-English journals are important for mission studies. *Norsk Tidsskrift for Misjon* is produced by the Egede Institute. *Perspectives Missionnaires,* the work of several organizations, is published in Switzerland. *Svensk Missionstidskrift* is the publication of the Svenska Institutet für Missionsforskning. *Zeitschrift für Mission* is published by the Deutschen Gesellschaft für Missionswisenschaft and the Basler Mission.

Some publications are dedicated to informing their own tradition. *Mission Bulletin,* produced by The Reformed Ecumenical Council, contains information about Reformed missions. *Anvil: An Anglican Evangelical Journal for Theology and Mission* focuses on Anglican missions.

Some denominations report missionary activities in their general publications. This is especially common for younger churches. *Advent Christian Witness* is the official publication of the Advent Christian General Conference of America. *Alliance Life* is published by The Christian & Missionary Alliance. The *Covenant Companion* is produced by the Evangelical Covenant Church. *The Evangelical Beacon* is published by the Evangelical Free Church of America. *Foursquare World Advance* is published by the International Church of the Foursquare Gospel. *Light & Life* is the official publication of the Free Methodist Church of North America. *The Messenger* is produced by the Evangelical Mennonite Conference.

Several Roman Catholic journals are produced in various parts of the world. *Indian Missiological Review* is published by the Sacred Heart Theological College in Indore. The *Japan Mission Journal* is produced at the Oriens Institute for Religious Research in Tokyo. The Instituto Español de Misiones Extranjeras (IEME) publishes *Misiones Extranjeras* in Madrid. *Neue Zeitschrift für Missionswissenschaft = Nouvelle Revue de Science Missionaire* is published at the Missionshaus Bethlehem, Immensee, Switzerland. *Spiritus,* the responsibility of several organizations, is published in Paris. And finally, *Zeitschrift für Missionswissenschaft und Religionswissenschaft* is the publication of the Internationalen Instituts für missionswissenschaftliche Forschungen (IIMF).

Major historical journals regularly carry articles on the history of mission. The *American Baptist Quarterly, Anglican and Episcopal History, The Journal of Imperial and Commonwealth History, The Journal of Presbyterian History, The Mennonite Quarterly Review, Methodist History,* and *Restoration Quarterly* are some examples.

Two major publications focus on ecumenical studies: *The Ecumenical Review,* published by the World Council of Churches, and *The Journal of Ecumenical Studies,* published by Temple University and sponsored by a number of ecumenical societies.

There are several related areas of study that are important to missiology. The social sciences, especially ANTHROPOLOGY, provide the background to understand specific cultures. The field of COMMUNICATION is essential to understand the impact of both written and oral transmission of the gospel message. General education and Christian education in particular have always been vital parts of Christian outreach. Theology began in the context of evangelism and missions, and continues to have an important role as Christianity develops within the diverse cultures of the world. World events and POLITICS are especially important to understand how local events have impacted missionary activity. WORLD RELIGIONS and NEW RELIGIOUS MOVEMENTS provide the religious context for the mission activity of the church. A large number of popular and scholarly periodicals related to these areas of study are available.

Keeping up with the literature of mission studies is a challenge for all missiologists. There are three major ways that journal publications assist the specialist in this task. First, most journals include book review sections complete with a list of books received but not reviewed. *Missiology, International Review of Mission, International Bulletin of Missionary Research, Evangelical Missions Quarterly,* and *Missionalia* carry the largest number of reviews. They rely on the community of mission scholars and practitioners to review all of the major works in the field.

A second type of assistance is comprehensive bibliography. Several major journals intentionally provide this service. *Missiology* and *International Review of Mission* contain classified annotated bibliographies of new publications in each issue. While *Missiology* covers only books, other journals include articles in their coverage. Some bibliographies are published as separate titles. *Bibliographia Missionaria* is an annual published by the Pontifical Missionary Library of the Congregation for the Evangelization of Peoples, and *Literaturschau zu Fragen der Weltmission* is an annual supplement of the *Zeitschrift für Mission.*

The third type of guide to the literature indexes current periodicals. *Missionalia* has long been an important guide to periodical literature. *Theology in Context,* published in both German and English editions, attempts to provide access to the literature of the Third World. As with all areas of religious studies, the *Religion Indexes* published by the American Theological Library Association provide the most comprehensive subject index to the literature of mission studies.

KENNETH D. GILL

Bibliography. G. H. Anderson, *CDCWM,* pp. 312–13; *Mission Handbook.*

Joy. A state of mind that accompanies any pleasurable experience. Scripture acknowledges this natural joy as well as a supernatural joy. The latter can be defined as a delight in life that runs deeper than pain or pleasure. This kind of joy is not limited by or tied solely to external circumstances. It is not a fleeting emotion but a quality of life that can be experienced in the midst of a variety of emotions.

Joy is described as a gift of God (Neh. 12:43; Eccles. 5:20; 8:15; Gal. 5:22; 1 Thess. 1:6). It is a natural outcome of fellowship with God (Ps. 16:8–9). It can be experienced in sorrow and trials (Hab. 3:17–19; Rom. 5:3; 2 Cor. 6:10; 1 Peter 1:6).

The joy that God gives is described as great (Jude 24), unspeakable (1 Peter 1:8), continual (1 Thess. 5:16), full (John 16:24), increasing (Isa. 9:3), and eternal (Isa. 51:11; 61:7; John 16:22). It is to be a part of true worship (Ps. 100:2), service

(Deut. 28:47), giving (2 Cor. 9:7), prayer (Phil. 1:4), obedience (Isa. 64:5; Luke 19:6; Heb. 13:17), witnessing (Acts 24:10), sacrifice of ourselves for others (Phil. 2:17–18), and our routine activities such as eating and drinking (Eccl. 9:7).

The mission of the church is to lead the nations to the Source of true joy. God is the joy of the whole earth (Ps. 48:2). He is the proper object of all appropriate rejoicing (1 Sam. 2:1) because he is the ultimate source of every good and perfect gift (James 1:17). Just as believers love in response to God's love for them (1 John 4:19), so they rejoice in God because God rejoices first in doing good to them (cf. Jer. 31:4; Isa. 62:5; Zeph. 3:17).

The church is to present to the world a God of joy. The tendency of sin leads people to rejoice in the work of their hands (Acts 7:41). True and lasting joy is found by rejoicing in the work of God's hands. Ultimately only what he does will last for all eternity (Ps. 127:1–2; John 15:5). The truth that joy can be found in God's person, work, provisions, rule, and presence is to be shared with the world.

A life of joy is a preoccupation with God who alone gives meaning and purpose to all of life and every task and relationship (2 Cor. 3:18). One cannot experience fullness of joy if he or she is preoccupied with security, pleasure, or any other self-interest. All blessings are to lead us back to the ultimate source (James 1:17; cf. Phil. 4:10).

How is the church to carry out its mission so as to reflect joy? Practicing God's presence (Ps. 16:8–9) and abiding in Christ (John 15:11) are the divine means. This involves the experience of answered prayer (John 16:24) and telling others how to fellowship with God (1 John 1:4). It involves the continual seeking of God's rule (Matt. 6:33) and Person (Ps. 40:16; 70:4; 105:3) as well as responding to his discipline (Ps. 90:15). It also involves an outlook of faith during trials (Matt. 5:12; 2 Cor. 12:9; Heb. 10:34) as well as a perspective of hope (Rom. 12:12). As one imitates Jesus in loving righteousness and hating lawlessness (Heb. 1:9) joy is a by-product. Fellowship with other believers is an aid to joy (Rom. 12:15; 1 Cor. 12:26) as well as true ministry to others (Prov. 12:20). Suffering need not hinder one's joy. In fact, suffering for Christ can even be a cause for rejoicing (Acts 5:41).

Our chief joy is to be a vital interest in God's purposes, program, and presence (Ps. 137:6). Today it is the building of his church (Matt. 16:18). Our chief responsibility is to exalt Christ and let him have the preeminence (John 3:29; Col. 1:18). In Christ the God of joy can be known and enjoyed.

WILLIAM D. THRASHER

Bibliography. J. Piper, *Let the Nations Be Glad.*

Judaism. *See* JEW, JUDAISM.

Judgment. Even in the postmodern relativistic West, where judgment is repugnant, the chilling details of ethnic cleansing or child abuse haunt us with the questions, "When will the wicked be judged? Will justice ever be established?"

Sin and Justice. Created for God, humanity proclaimed its autonomy. This rebellion against God is the root of human evil and injustice to others (Rom. 1:20–32; 8:7). History is the narrative of human deceit, treachery, and persecution. Perhaps our actions are not so obviously wicked, but are hidden behind false smiles and vain civility. Or maybe we were like those who were unwilling to defend Jesus publicly when the crowd called for his crucifixion. Sins of commission as well as omission have just as deadly repercussions in society. So history prompts the constant refrain, "Where is the God of justice?" (Mal. 2:17).

God made us accountable to himself, the Moral Judge of the cosmos (Rom. 2:15–16). We know wrongs must be righted. Even without considering restitution, we have a sense of what is necessary to begin righting a wrong. The offender should be forced to suffer this wrong in order to recognize the full depth of this injury. That is the purpose of retributive punishment as expressed in the Old Testament law of retaliation: those who injure their neighbor, whatever they have done must be done to them: fracture for fracture, eye for eye, tooth for tooth (Lev. 24:19–20).

The Final Judgment. Scripture's ultimate answer for evil is that God, the holy Judge of all the earth, will call every human to account for his or her life on the Day of Judgment (Pss. 5:4–6; 31:18; Matt. 12:36; Rom. 2:6–11; 1 Peter 4:5). This life has grave moral significance! Nothing can be hidden from God, not even our secret thoughts (Rom. 2:16). Every deed will be declared, from idle words to the failure to help the hungry (Matt. 16:27; 25:31–46; Rev. 22:12). We all face a future judgment of either exoneration or condemnation, receiving a welcome to heaven or the sentence of Hell.

But all have sinned (Rom. 3:23; *see also* Depravity of Humankind). So God's judgment will fall on all, except those saved by Jesus' work. For Christ, the final Judge, has already suffered the judgment for those who have "faith in Christ's blood" (John 3:18; 5:24; Rom. 3:25; 2 Cor. 5:21). And what God has already forgiven, he will not recall (Jer. 31:34; Isa. 43:25). So those in Christ will stand without accusation (Rom. 8:33–34; Eph. 5:27). It is precisely the gospel's offer of Reconciliation with God that occasions missions.

God's Judgment of Those He Loves. Scripture also teaches that God uses contemporary circumstances to test our hearts, discipline us, and direct us toward his righteous ways (Deut. 8:1–5; 1 Cor. 11:29–32; Heb. 12:5–17; Rev. 3:17–19). God will not let his people continue in Sin without judgment. So failures and persecutions should be catalysts for self-reflection and spiritual growth into Christ's image (2 Thess. 1:3–5; Col. 3:10). God's present judgment is not simply directed toward individuals (Rev. 2:5; 3:15–21). Believers need to attend to God's chastisement of every Christian institution, even the missions movement, so that we learn to embody Christ's humility (2 Cor. 6:2–11; 1 Cor. 4:9–16).

The Christian's Judgment of Others. The proclamation of God in Jesus Christ necessarily carries judgment against sinners. Furthermore, correction is essential to forming a church where the fellowship of believers self-consciously build up each other into Christ's body (Eph. 4:16). When preaching is easily turned aside, believers are obliged to help other believers recognize their sinfulness (Matt. 18:15–17; Gal. 5:26–6:2). When Jesus cautions, "Do not judge, or you too will be judged," he is not precluding preaching or reproof (Matt. 7:1–4). However correction must be in his name, so that even the admonisher remains subject to his Lord. Believers must never attempt to impose God's final judgment, but to overcome evil with good (Rom. 12:19–21). For God alone is the holy Judge.

Timothy R. Phillips

See also Church Discipline; Providence of God.

Bibliography. L. Morris, *The Biblical Doctrine of Judgment;* T. C. Oden, *Pastoral Theology: Essentials of Ministry,* pp. 206–19; D. M. Paton, *Christian Missions and the Judgment of God;* M. R. Talbot, *Reformation and Revival* 5:4 (Fall 1996): 117–34.

Judson, Adoniram (1788–1850). American missionary to Myanmar. Born in Malden, Massachusetts, and one of America's best known missionaries, he and his wife, Ann Hasseltine Judson (1789–1826), sailed for India from Salem, Massachusetts, on February 19, 1812, with the first American foreign missions contingent. Though sponsored by the Congregationalist American Board of Commissioners for Foreign Missions, the Judsons became Baptists while en route to Asia. This decision led to their founding the first mission to Burma (now Myanmar) and the formation of what became the American Baptist Missionary Union to support them and other missionaries.

Gifted linguistically, Judson labored to learn Burmese, a complex language. In 1834 he completed the Burmese Bible and his *Dictionary, English and Burmese* in 1849. A church was established despite Judson's horrendous seventeen-month imprisonment, the death of his first wife (1826) and child (1827), the death of Sara Boardman Judson (1845), his second wife, and his own persistent ill health. Returning to America in 1845, Judson advanced the expanding foreign missions movement. In 1846 he married Emily Chubbeck, a novelist, and returned to Burma. On a voyage to improve his health he died near the Andeman Islands on April 12, 1850, and was buried at sea.

The son of a Congregationalist clergyman, alumnus of Brown University (B.A., 1807) and Andover Seminary (B.D., 1810), Judson is remembered for a Burmese church of seven thousand members at his death, his translation work, and his contribution to the launching of American foreign missions.

THOMAS A. ASKEW

Bibliography. C. Anderson, *To the Golden Shore: The Life of Adoniram Judson;* R. Torbet, *Venture of Faith;* F. Wayland, *A Memoir of the Life and Labors of the Rev. Adoniram Judson, DD.*

Judson, Ann Hazeltine (1789–1826). American pioneer missionary in Myanmar. Judson was truly a lady of firsts: the first American woman missionary, the first missionary wife who felt her own call to missions, the first woman missionary who wrote on missionary life and the conditions of mission work (and who became the leading female missionary author of the early nineteenth century), the first missionary woman who addressed the specific concerns of women, and the first wife of Adoniram Judson.

The Judsons sailed to India thirteen days after their marriage in 1812, and eventually established mission work in Burma. Ann learned the language quickly and began a women's Sunday class to study the Scriptures that her husband was translating. The difficult living conditions contributed to constant illness, and she was forced to leave Burma on several occasions for medical reasons. Her first child, a son, died at seven months of age. Her courage was sorely tested when war broke out between England and Burma, and Adoniram was imprisoned. Pregnant and alone, she got food and clothing through to him and kept him alive. When Adoniram was sent on a death march, Ann followed, carrying her newborn, and eventually became so ill that guards allowed Adoniram to care for her and the baby. The British liberated the Judsons in 1826, but both Ann and the baby girl died soon afterwards.

JUDITH LINGENFELTER

Bibliography. B. Miller, *Ann Judson: Heroine of Burma;* H. M. W. Morrow, *Splendor of God.*

Justice of God. The evangelistic commitment of evangelical missions has continuously stressed the centrality of the cross of Jesus Christ as payment for the penalty for sin. This atoning work satisfies the requirements of the justice of God for eternal life. The Bible reveals, however, that the justice of God encompasses more than the spiritual dimension. His demands extend into the concrete realities of human social existence. For the last several decades this aspect of the justice of God and the relevance of this justice to the world-wide mission of the Christian church has generated vigorous debate within evangelical circles.

Opinions differ over whether social justice issues should be strictly distinguished from the mandate to evangelize the lost and instead be considered by individual Christians subsequent to conversion; whether social action should be understood as providing a bridge to evangelism by presenting opportunities for the verbal proclamation of the gospel of eternal salvation; or lastly, should the concern for social justice be seen as an integral part of the broader mission of the church in the world. In other words, is social justice the *by-product* of the mission of evangelism, the *means* toward accomplishing that foremost task of evangelism, or a *legitimate goal* of mission?

Background to the Debate. Evangelical missions historically have demonstrated an interest in matters of social import. Mission activity, at least to some degree, has been directed at the eradication of personal vices, the establishment of hospitals and orphanages, the promotion of literacy, and the provision of emergency relief from natural disasters. Critics, however, would suggest that these laudable efforts are but gestures of charity, which focus on the individual and ignore the systemic realities that perpetuate social ills. They posit that such endeavors also are limited by a missiological perspective that is condemnatory of society and wary of close contact with a fallen world. Many locate the seedbed of this reticence to engage the larger context in the fundamentalist-modernist controversies of the early part of the twentieth century.

Nevertheless, in some evangelical circles there has been a broadening of the theology of mission over the last fifty years to embrace a more holistic framework (Van Engen; *see* HOLISTIC MISSION). This development represents a recuperation of evangelical roots in, for example, the influence of JOHN WESLEY (1703–91) and Methodism on English society, the successful efforts by William Wilberforce (1759–1833) and others to abolish the slave trade in the British Empire, and the two GREAT AWAKENINGS in the United States in the eighteenth and nineteenth centuries which were concerned with improving the moral life of believers and fomenting Christian education and anti-slavery sentiments (*see* ABOLITIONIST MOVEMENT).

This debate concerning the relationship of justice issues to mission can also be placed within a wider global discussion. In the first place, reflection on the topic can be set against the backdrop of the history of missions around the globe. Some missiologists denounce what they consider to be the complicity of mission agencies with the European colonization of the TWO-THIRDS WORLD and the surfacing of contemporary North Atlantic economic neo-colonial attitudes in mission structures and operation (Costas). More nuanced approaches would suggest a chronological convergence and some ideological affinities of early missions with that colonizing activity and do recognize certain theological limitations. These responses offer a more positive evaluation of pioneer and modern missionary efforts (Escobar and Driver; Scott; Sanneh; Núñez and Taylor).

Second, the relationship between justice and mission has received attention at several international evangelical congresses. An increasing awareness of Christian social responsibility has been encouraged by these gatherings, beginning with Wheaton and Berlin in 1966, through Lausanne (1974) to Manila (1989). The WORLD EVANGELICAL FELLOWSHIP has sponsored various consultations and regional congresses to wrestle with justice. These meetings have witnessed the growing input of theologians from developing countries, who daily face the harsh realities of poverty and war, and of those whom some label "radical" evangelicals (e.g., Ron Sider and Jim Wallis). Several recently published missiology texts underscore the centrality of the justice of God for mission (Scott; Dyrness; Bosch). For certain missiologists this trend is cause for alarm, because the primacy of evangelism is perceived to be under threat. They liken this direction in missiological reflection to some of the theological options taken by the WORLD COUNCIL OF CHURCHES since its watershed assembly at Uppsala of 1968 (Beyerhaus).

Foundational Biblical and Theological Themes. The following brief survey establishes that the demand for justice, both spiritual and social, is dear to the heart of God. This all-encompassing justice should be central to the mission of the people of God in the world and incarnated within the community of faith. Different missiological positions, of course, will appreciate this mandate in their own particular ways.

The Fall and spread of sin. God announces in the garden that to eat the forbidden fruit will bring death (Gen. 2:16–17). Later revelation indicates that transgression brought spiritual death (Rom. 5:12–21), and the provision of covering through the death of an animal (Gen. 3:21) foreshadows the Law's sacrifices for sin and ultimately the sacrifice of the Lamb of God, Jesus Christ (e.g., Isa. 53:7–13; John 2:9; Heb. 9–10; Rev. 5:6–14). The first human death recorded after the Fall in Genesis 3 is fratricide. Cain kills Abel. Later, Lamech boasts of his intention of uncontrolled revenge (Gen. 4:2–9, 23–24). Cain is judged by God, and the impetuosity of Lamech is contrasted with calling on the name of the Lord (Gen. 4:10–16, 26; cf. 5:24). The Lord condemns the pervasive violence with a universal Flood (Gen. 6:11) but afterward delegates the authority to maintain justice to human agents and structures (Gen. 9:5–6; Rom. 12:17–13:5). These early chapters of the first book of the Bible disclose

that, even as sin has both vertical and horizontal dimensions, the justice of God involves every dimension of human existence.

The call of Abram. The divine commitment to the various spheres of justice reflected in Genesis 1–11 serves as the framework for the call of Abram. Part of this charge is that he be a channel of blessing to the world (Gen. 12:3). This blessing involves worship and confession of the true God, as well as trusting obedience (e.g., Gen. 12:7–8, 14:18–24, 15:6, 18:17–19; *see* ABRAHAMIC COVENANT). The patriarchal accounts in Genesis demonstrate that the notion of blessing has a social dimension grounded in the character of God. For instance, Abraham intercedes for Sodom on the basis of divine justice (Gen. 18:22–32), a justice which demands chastisement, but that is tempered by mercy.

The exodus and Sinai. God responds to the cry of the Israelites in Egypt because of God's covenant, but action on their behalf also is motivated by compassion for their suffering of cruel infanticide and oppressive labor (Exod. 2:23–25). While they are miraculously delivered in part to be free to worship the Lord (Exod. 5:3), they are called as well to create a new type of society in the Promised Land. The Law given at Sinai (Exod. 20–40) and presented in the rest of the Pentateuch reveals that God is founding an alternative community with a different kind of spiritual ethos and social ethic. The Lord desires justice among his own people, and their laws are to be a model and testimony to the surrounding nations (Deut. 4:5–8).

The Servant Songs of Isaiah. The themes of salvation and justice are repeated throughout these messianic passages (Isa. 42:1–9; 49:1–13; 50:4–11; 52:13–53:12). The ministry of the Servant will be to establish a reign of righteousness and peace in faithfulness to the God of Israel, a striking antithesis to the idolatry, war, and oppression that serve as the backdrop to this portion of Isaiah. This hope embraces all the nations of the earth and is secured by the voluntary self-sacrifice of the Servant.

Luke 4:16–20. This inaugural sermon of Jesus' ministry is based on Isaiah 61:1–2a (and 58:6b). That Isaianic passage, which describes a messianic jubilee for the nation of Israel, is now given a richer significance, even as Jesus declares its fulfillment. On the one hand, the mention of the poor, prisoners, the sick, and the oppressed anticipates the special targets of his ministry. A closer look at Lucan theology indicates that these terms have spiritual implications, too. His deeds and words are good news to those who are open to God and his Christ (6:20–26), whose bondage can be demonic (4:33–35; 9:1, 37–43; 11:14–28) and their blindness spiritual (1:79; 7:47; 24:47). His person and work exemplify the grace and exigencies of divine justice, and in his death it finds propitiation (Rom. 3:25–26; Heb. 2:17; 1 John 2:2, 4:10).

John 20:21. Some propose that the words of Jesus in John 20:21 (cf. John 17:18; Mark 12:28–31 and parallels) should be taken as the commission which defines Christian mission: the life and ministry of Jesus are a paradigm to be imitated (Stott). This perspective does not devalue evangelistic proclamation, which others consider the defining prescription in the other GREAT COMMISSION passages (Matt. 28:18–20; Mark 16:15–18; Luke 24:45–49), but argues rather for a more comprehensive understanding of mission—a holistic vision which would incorporate both the spiritual and social spheres of God's justice.

Finally, mention should be made of the theme of the KINGDOM OF GOD. The dynamic rule of God is inseparable from the justice of his character. Throughout history he expresses the demand for justice and intervenes to effect it in the various spheres suggested in the preceding survey. The future establishment of a kingdom of justice, in all of its breadth, is an integral part of the biblical hope.

M. Daniel Carroll R.

Bibliography. M. Arias and A. Johnson, *The Great Commission: Biblical Models for Evangelism*; P. J. Beyerhaus, *God's Kingdom & the Utopian Error*; D. J. Bosch, *Transforming Mission: Paradigm Shifts in Theology of Mission*; O. E. Costas, *Christ Outside the Gate: Mission Beyond Christendom*; W. A. Dyrness, *Let the Earth Rejoice: A Biblical Theology of Holistic Mission*; S. Escobar and J. Driver, *Christian Mission and Social Justice*; E. A. Núñez, C. and W. D. Taylor, *Crisis and Hope in Latin America: An Evangelical Perspective* (rev. ed.); L. Sanneh, *Encountering the West: Christianity and the Global Cultural Process*; W. Scott, *Bring Forth Justice: A Contemporary Perspective on Mission*; J. R. W. Stott, *Christian Mission in the Modern World*; C. E. Van Engen, *Earthen Vessels: American Evangelicals and Foreign Missions, 1880–1980*, pp. 203–32.

Justification. Justification is primarily a forensic term implying the results of God's work of declaring his elect to be righteous. The terms justification and righteousness are related in that they are both from the root *dikai*, having to do with both penalty (or punishment) and justice. Justification is a primary topic in the writings of Paul, who discusses the issue more than any other writer in the New Testament. Paul's mission was to preach the gospel to the peoples of the earth with a view to their being justified by grace through faith in Jesus Christ (Rom. 1:17).

There is both a generic use of the term justification and a technical use. Basically, the idea of justification is to be set right or to pronounce just. Thus, people may be justified among themselves as in James 2:21, "was not Abraham our father justified by works?" James is not declaring that Abraham was righteous before God because

of works, but that from the human perspective, he was shown to be a righteous man (justified) by his works. The works were a result of his faith in God. His faith justified Abraham (Gen. 15:6; Rom. 4:1–3), his works openly demonstrated that faith, and therefore, in the eyes of people he was shown to be righteous (justified, James 2:21; see also, e.g., Deut. 25:1).

There is also a technical sense of the word in theological propositions. This is the forensic or legal declaration of one being declared just before God. Paul is the primary theologian of this doctrine in the New Testament. He begins by pointing out that "the doers of the law shall be justified" (Rom. 2:13). The context is that it was not enough to *claim* to do the law, one must *do* the law to be justified before God. He continues his argument by pointing to the condemnation of the whole human race (both Jews who trusted in their ability to do the law, and Gentiles who did not have the law) because "there is none righteous (in God's sight), . . . none who does good (by God's standard)" (Rom. 3:10–18). Therefore, "by the works of the law no flesh will be justified in His sight" (Rom. 3:20; Gal. 3:2, 16; 3:11). However, there was one Man who did keep the law, fulfilling its every demand. This law doer was Jesus Christ, the Second Adam, God who became man (Rom. 5:15–19). In this sense, justification is recognition of fulfilling the requirements of the law and is an actualization of justice in declaring him righteous.

Theologically speaking, justification as it applies to other humans must be imputed because it cannot be earned and is not intrinsic to human nature. It is given as a gift to those who believe (Rom. 3:28) and this gift is available only by God's grace (Rom. 3:24). It is a divine act with a purely legal nature and not an infusion of moral quality into the character of the one justified. As the first Adam sinned and brought condemnation to the human race (Rom. 5:12–14), the second Adam lived righteously and provides justification for those who trust in him (Rom. 5:18–19). The fact that the Righteous One died in the place of unrighteous humankind (Rom. 5:6–9) provided the way in which God could declare righteous his fallen creatures yet remain righteous in himself. Thus, he is both just and the justifier of the one believing (Rom. 3:26). Thus Paul calls Christians to mission and gospel proclamation. "How can they learn without someone preaching to them? And how can they preach unless they are sent?" (Rom. 10:14–15).

The status of being justified does not in any manner assume that the one justified will cease from sin or that his or her character has become intrinsically righteous. Sinlessness is no more possible after being justified than before. When sin does arise in the life of a believer, the Father will discipline his children (Heb. 12) but it does not affect his or her justification because it was attributed upon faith not works. Paul raises the rhetorical question as to who could bring charges against the elect since "God is the one who justifies" (Rom. 8:33). If God has declared the sinner righteous, no one can bring condemnation to him or her. Justification is based upon the death and resurrection of Jesus and one's personal faith in that provision (Rom. 5:1, 9; 4:25).

For those carrying the message of justification to the world, the key elements must not be lost. The sin and darkness of the lost is well documented in both Scripture and the human condition. The need of the lost is to understand their insufficiency and God's gracious provision of justification by grace through faith. The bad news is that all have sinned (Rom. 3:23) and that the wages of that sin is death (Rom. 6:23). The good news (gospel) is that God has provided for sinners by his own grace and righteousness (Rom. 5:8–9). The church seems at times to have forgotten the message of justification and has set out to conform the world to standards they neither understand nor appreciate. It is typical of many Christians to stand back and condemn the lifestyles of the unregenerate and the social evils in the world without understanding that that is all non-Christians know. In this open depravity, the wickedness of humankind has highlighted the helpless condition of fallen humans. This provides a powerful environment for those who have experienced the grace of God to declare the love and provision of God. The Word of God offers a solution to the helplessness of humankind. The mission of the church is to proclaim this opportunity to be set right with God (justification).

ED GLASSCOCK

Bibliography. P. Enns, *The Moody Handbook of Theology;* R. W. Lyon, *BEB* 2:1252–54; L. M. Peterson, *ZPEB*, 3:764–73; G. Schrenk, *TDNT;* D. W. Simon, *DoB,* 2:826–29.

Kk

Kagawa, Toyohiko (1888–1960). Japanese evangelist and social activist. Born in Japan as the illegitimate son of a nobleman, Kagawa became a Christian through the friendship of two Presbyterian missionary families. As a seminary student in Kobe, he moved into the city's Shinkawa slum district to live and work with its people. His novelistic account of this experience, *Crossing the Death Line* (1920), gained him fame.

After completing his B.D. at Princeton Theological Seminary, Kagawa returned to minister at a church in Kobe. He also encouraged the organization of labor unions to meet the needs of Japanese laborers and the formation of farmers' and consumers' cooperatives. After the great 1923 Tokyo earthquake, he and his family moved to Tokyo to continue his ministries from there. He carried out evangelistic campaigns, and in 1930 started the Kingdom of God Movement to reach groups that had hitherto been unevangelized.

As Japan entered into military conflict with China in 1931, Kagawa's pacifism repeatedly got him into trouble with the government. Hostilities with America beginning in 1941 saddened him further. After Japan's defeat, he declined a role in politics, and despite ill health, continued in his pastorate and kept writing books and articles on the relation of the Christian faith to many topics. Controversies arose over his wartime radio broadcasts and his disparaging comments about Japan's outcaste community. He carried on with his pastoral and evangelistic work until his death. Often better known abroad than in Japan, his legacy combines ministry, evangelism, and social action, and continues to challenge Christians in many countries.

JAMES M. PHILLIPS

Bibliography. C. H. Davey, *Kagawa of Japan;* T. Kagawa, *Before the Dawn;* R. Schildgen, *Toyohiko Kagawa: Apostle of Love and Social Justice.*

Kairos Document. A political and theological commentary on apartheid in South Africa first published in 1985. The country was under a state of emergency which allowed the government to suspend certain civil rights. A second edition, more widely distributed, was published one year later with a significant revision of the fourth chapter on "prophetic theology." A grassroots influenced document, it contrasts "state theology" (which is a defense for the status quo of racism, capitalism, and totalitarianism) and "church theology" (which is critical of apartheid in a limited manner) with "prophetic theology" which is a call to confrontation and action. The document reflects the concern of LIBERATION THEOLOGY and PRAXIS as the sign of the reality of the gospel. There was a worldwide response and reaction from Christian groups critical of apartheid. A measured response came from a group of evangelicals *(Evangelical Witness . . .)* who appreciated the concerns but questioned the legitimacy of violence to overthrow the apartheid regime. The *Karios Document* itself was critical of what it termed "church theology's" condemnation of violence to oppose apartheid while ignoring the violence done by the government on a daily basis in support of apartheid. The document highlights the difficulty Christians have had throughout the ages deciding when rebellion is appropriate.

JAMES J. STAMOOLIS

Bibliography. *The Kairos Document: Challenge to the Church,* rev. ed.; *Evangelical Witness in South Africa: A Critique of Evangelical Theology and Practice by Evangelicals Themselves.*

Kalley, Robert Reid (1809–88). Scottish pioneer missionary in Madeira and Brazil. Born to a wealthy family in Glasgow, Kalley's agnosticism gave way to conversion in 1834. Initially he was accepted to work with the LMS in China; however, his marriage to Margaret Crawford violated mission policy and he resigned from the society before setting sail. In 1838, he and his wife went instead to Madeira, a Portuguese island in the Atlantic Ocean. His evangelistic strategy there included medical work, school development, and preaching. Many came to Christ, but the island's

Catholic officials, threatened by Kalley's success, expelled him in 1846.

Some two thousand of those who had come to Christ migrated from Madeira, and over the next several years Kalley visited among them in the Caribbean, the United States, Europe, and the Middle East. He also worked in southern Ireland, Malta, and Lebanon. After the death of his first wife, he remarried (Sarah Wilson) in 1852. The couple later settled in Brazil (1855), where he developed a COLPORTAGE work, compiled a hymnal, planted churches, and worked to establish freedom of religion in the Brazilian Constitution. In 1858, he established *Igreja Evangélica Fluminese*, considered the oldest Protestant church in Brazil. In 1876 they retired to Edinburgh, where he continued to serve evangelical causes until his death in 1888.

A. SCOTT MOREAU

Bibliography. W. B. Forsyth, *The Wolf from Scotland*; idem, *DSCHT*, p. 451; W. Mitchell, *BDCM*, pp. 351–52; H. C. Moore, *Through Flood and Flame: Adventures and Perils of Protestant Heroes*.

Kane, J. Herbert (1910–92). American missiologist and missionary to China. Born in Canada and later naturalized as an American citizen, Herbert Kane graduated from Moody Bible Institute in 1935. He and his wife Winifred went to China in 1935 with the CHINA INLAND MISSION (CIM). After language study, the Kanes were assigned to Fouyang in Anhui province where they spent most of their missionary career. Under Kane and his missionary and Chinese colleagues Fouyang became one of the most spiritually productive areas of the CIM work. The Kanes remained in China during much of the Japanese occupation, but were finally evacuated in 1945. They returned to China in 1946, but again needed to evacuate in 1950 after nineteen months under communist domination.

After his return from China, Kane received further education (B.A. Barrington College; M.A. Brown University) and then began a career teaching missiology at Barrington College (1951–63), Lancaster Bible College (1963–67), and Trinity Evangelical Divinity School (1967–80). Barrington College conferred the honorary degree of Doctor of Humane Letters on him in 1971.

Kane served as president of the AMERICAN SOCIETY OF MISSIOLOGY (1976) and authored over ten books on missions, the most noted being *Understanding Christian Missions*. These activities and his teaching expertise led his colleagues to describe him as having "an encyclopedic knowledge of missions."

RALPH R. COVELL

Bibliography. J. H. Kane, *IBMR* 11:3 (July 1987): 129–32; idem, *Twofold Growth*.

Kardecism. Kardecism is one of the most important popular religions in Brazil with an estimated 20 million followers, including 7 million regularly involved in spiritistic activities in the nearly three thousand spirit centers all over the nation. The founder of Kardecism was Hippolyte Leon Denizard Rivail. Rivail was born in France on October 3, 1804. After studying in Switzerland under the auspices of Pestalozzi, he returned to Paris and started a primary school, applying Pestalozzi's pedagogy. After an initial period of investigating the so-called rotating tables phenomenon, which had caused much controversy in the nineteenth century in the United States, he came to have his first spiritistic experiences in his own home. With the participation of his two daughters as mediums he commenced his contacts with the spirit world. The spirit he contacted told Rivail that at his incarnation, he was a druid called Allan Kardec, from which name the term "Kardecism" is derived.

Despite being baptized in the Catholic faith and having been in contact with liberal Protestantism, Kardec was unprepared to deal with and discern the spirits that from then on would be delivering their deceiving messages. On March 25, 1856, while in a trance, he started receiving revelations from a spirit called "The Spirit of Truth," which claimed to be the fulfillment of John 16:12–13. Kardec was informed that his mission was to be the codifier of the final revelation given by God to humankind. After Moses and Jesus, God has finally sent his *Spirit*. With the assistance of ten mediums he could receive the messages that came to be part of the Kardecist corpus, including the book of *Spirits*, the book of the *Mediums*, and, the most widely known among them, the *Gospel according to Allan Kardec*.

The main beliefs of Kardecism are the possibility and importance of communicating with the spirits of the dead (necromancy); the belief that by the process of reincarnation each person progresses in the spiritual realm; and the belief that once someone has achieved a higher stage of spiritual development, he or she passes into another spiritual sphere in another world. By practicing charity and accepting suffering as a purging element necessary for spiritual growth, each human being should reach progressively higher stages of maturity—hence the heavy emphasis on good works for the salvation of the soul in Kardecist spiritism. This emphasis is reflected in the numerous orphanages and philanthropic centers all over Brazil. God is seen as a distant being accessible only through his agents, the spirit guides. The Bible has to be correctly interpreted. Jesus is seen as a spirit who has reached the highest position in the development scale. The revelation brought to Kardec by the self-entitled *spirit of truth* is claimed to be the fulfillment of Jesus' promises in the Gospel of John. The devil and his demons do not exist. The universe is inhabited by millions of spirits in different stages of spiritual development. By contact between the living and the dead and the process of reincarnation, human beings will finally achieve their salvation. The long journey of spiritual transformation obviously presupposes the existence of good and bad spirits, but this fact is to be understood as a normal situation that reflects the constant evolutive state of this planet and its inhabitants.

Kardecism has a tremendous appeal to the Brazilian people. The daily socioeconomic struggles and the tragedies of life are readily understood by them as an inevitable and necessary product of the karma process of soul development. Also, the overlapping of two worlds, the visible and invisible, implies the presence and interference of good and bad spirits in human life. Through a message that demands a lifestyle of charity combined with interacting with the good spirits of the dead, Kardecists hope to achieve salvation in the sense of spiritual development. Kardecism is an important and growing religious force in Brazilian society, having nominal Catholics as the main source of new followers. The evangelical church in Brazil has so far been the only force to successfully oppose Kardecism's growing influence.

The church in Brazil as well as missionaries who serve there face a great challenge in reaching the millions involved in this spiritistic practice. Those seeking to reach Kardecists for Christ should be aware of the distortions in Kardec's teaching about reincarnation taken from the books of Isaiah, Malachi, and John. More important, however, the church must recognize Kardecists as people who are sincere seekers of truth. Thus, Christians should pay special attention to engaging in pragmatic expressions of love, all of which are to be done in the power of the Holy Spirit girded with a deep prayer commitment for those they are seeking to reach.

JARBAS DA SILVA

SEE ALSO Latin American New Religious Movements.

Karma. *See* SOTERIOLOGY IN WORLD RELIGIONS.

Kasatkin, Nicholas (1836–1912). Russian Orthodox missionary to Japan. Kasatkin was born in the Smolensk province of Russia. Graduating at the top of his class, he was urged by his superiors to pursue a life in academia. He chose instead to go as the first Russian Orthodox missionary to Japan, arriving there on June 2, 1861.

The first seven years of ministry proved frustrating as Nicholas struggled with the Japanese language and customs, the xenophobia and persecution of the government, and the failure to baptize even one convert. Things began to change, however, when he baptized three men, including a Shinto priest, in 1868. With these three men as a foundation, the church began to grow. By 1880, the Russian Church elevated Nicholas as bishop of Japan for the almost 5,000 believers he had baptized. Although no other Russian missionaries had come to help, by 1896 the Orthodox Church had grown to over 23,000. By the fiftieth anniversary of his arrival in Japan, the church consisted of 33,017 Christians in 266 communities, 43 clergy, 121 lay preachers, 200 teachers, a seminary with 94 students, and 2 girls' schools with 80 students.

Together with his astounding accomplishments as a missionary and bishop, his other main contribution was the translation of the entire New Testament and most of the Old Testament, as well as many liturgical services into Japanese.

LUKE A. VERONIS

Bibliography. N. Gorodetzky, *IRM* 31(4): 400–411; I. Kondrashov, *Theological Journal of the Moscow Patriarchate* 11 (1–2): 69–73, 72–76; L. A. Veronis, *Missionaries, Monks, and Martyrs: Making Disciples of All Nations.*

Kato, Byang Henry (1936–75). Nigerian evangelical church leader. Born in Kwoi, Nigeria, and raised in traditional religion, Kato became a Christian under the influence of a local African teacher. After theological training in Nigeria, he received a B.D. from the University of London in 1966, and was elected general secretary of his denomination, the Evangelical Churches of West Africa. In February 1973 Kato was chosen to head the Association of Evangelicals of Africa (AEA). Nearly three years of whirlwind activity followed, throughout Africa and internationally, including a Th.D. from Dallas Theological Seminary, a major address at the LAUSANNE CONGRESS ON WORLD EVANGELIZATION (1974), election as vice president of the WORLD EVANGELICAL FELLOWSHIP (WEF), and appointment as chairman of the WEF Theological Commission. All this was suddenly cut short by Kato's accidental death in December 1975, at the age of thirty-nine.

While Kato spoke and wrote prodigiously, he remains best known for his monograph *Theological Pitfalls in Africa,* which called for a Christianity that would be both truly African and truly biblical. Kato's continental influence stemmed not least from his articulate affirmation of African identity, combined with his evident commitment to a centrist evangelical theology. As the first African to lead the alliance of evangelicals in Africa, Kato infused that community with a vitalizing sense of identity and direction, encouraged relevant theological engagement, and through his vision and wide personal contacts formatively impacted the following generation of African evangelical leadership.

PAUL BOWERS

Bibliography. P. Bowers, *ERT* 1 (April 1981): 35–39; C. Breman, *The Association of Evangelicals in Africa;* B. Kato, *African Cultural Revolution and Christian Faith: Biblical Christianity in Africa.*

Kazakstan *(Est. 2000 pop.: 17,694,000; 2,717,300 sq. km. [1,049,150 sq. mi.]).* Containing massive oil and mineral reserves, Kazakstan is, geographically, the largest of the Central Asian republics of the former Soviet Union. During Soviet times, Kazakstan's population was almost evenly divided between Slavic and Turkic peoples, but since independence in 1991 many Slavs have left; ethnic Russians, however, still dominate the north. While most ethnic Kazaks profess nominal allegiance to Islam, the majority are more animistic than Muslim. Evangelical Christians make up less than one percent of the population, and nearly all are Slavic or German, although by the late 1990s there were at least 2,500 known Kazak believers and 16 predominantly Kazak congregations. There is a measure of religious liberty, and many churches have experienced significant growth.

RAYMOND P. PRIGODICH

SEE ALSO Commonwealth of Independent States.

Keller, Mirian Wittich (1889–1953). Canadian missionary to Africa. Born Marian Weller in Parry Sound, Ontario, she graduated from Normal Training School and later from Toronto Business College. After returning home, Keller attended Pentecostal meetings, where she was baptized in the Holy Spirit in 1909. Called to missions, she moved to the United States to attend the Rochester (N.Y.) Bible Training School. There she met Karl Wittich, a Baptist minister; following their marriage in 1913 they went to German East Africa (present-day Tanzania) as independent Pentecostal missionaries.

Karl died within months of their arrival; Marian, nonetheless, persevered four more years before going back to Canada. Returning to British East Africa (present-day Kenya), she met and married Otto Keller, an American Pentecostal missionary, in 1918. Together they pioneered the Nyangori Mission Station at Kisumu. By 1923 when they affiliated with the Pentecostal Assemblies of Canada (PAOC), they had established twenty-five district schools. When Otto died in 1942, three mission stations had been established with two hundred branch churches and over five hundred national ministers. The pioneering efforts of the Kellers and other PAOC missionaries laid the foundation for the Pentecostal movement in Kenya and in particular the now sizable Pentecostal Assemblies of God, Kenya, with its elementary and secondary school system and ministerial training schools.

GARY B. MCGEE

Bibliography. M. Keller, *Twenty Years in Africa;* T. W. Miller, *Canadian Pentecostals: A History of the Pentecostal Assemblies of Canada.*

Kentigern (c. 518–603). Celtic missionary in Scotland. The grandson of a pagan king, Kentigern was born at Culcross in Scotland and was educated at the monastery there. Around the year 550 he founded the diocese at Glasgow, where he served as bishop. Kentigern was driven from Scotland during the persecution after the fall of the Christian king Rhydderch. He went to Wales, where he founded a monastery at Llanelly and was instrumental in many conversions. When Rhydderch was restored to his throne in 570, Kentigern returned to Scotland, leaving the work in Wales to his assistant Asaph, who became the first bishop of the Welsh see.

During the remainder of his life, Kentigern is said to have established several churches in the kingdom of Strathclyde, founded a college of monks, and sent out numerous missionaries. Known widely in Scotland as Saint Mungo (Celtic for "my dear friend"), Kentigern is the patron saint of Glasgow, where he is reputed to be buried in the Cathedral of Saint Mungo. Although the details of his life were recorded much later in twelfth century hagiographies, it is clear that Kentigern was an energetic evangelist and church planter who did much to establish Celtic Christianity in southwest Scotland.

ALAN SEAMAN

Bibliography. A. Forbes, *Lives of S. Ninian and S. Kentigern;* J. Shepard, *Introduction to the History of the Church in Scotland.*

Kenya *(Est. 2000 pop.: 32,577,000; 580,367 sq. km. [224,080 sq. mi.]).* Kenya's Christian history began in 1498, when the Portuguese explorer Vasco da Gama landed in the East African coastal city of Malindi. By the sixteenth century Augustinian friars had carved out a Christian community of nearly six hundred African converts in Mombasa and Malindi. This work was destroyed in 1631 by a resurgent Islam.

The modern history of Christianity in Kenya dates from 1844 with the coming of the CMS missionary J. LUDWIG KRAPF and slightly later J. Rebmann. Building on that foundation were the Methodists (1862), Church of Scotland Mission (1891), and African Inland Mission (1895). The Holy Ghost Fathers arrived in 1883.

The years of COLONIALISM (1896–1963) were a time of growth for the mission-related churches such as the Presbyterian Church of East Africa, the Anglican Church of the Province of Kenya, and the Africa Inland Church, but equally as significant was the emergence of African independent churches. A new emphasis on education of the local population led to the formation of Alliance High School (1962), which in turn led to a flood of similar institutions around the country. Within these schools a conflict arose between missionaries and Kikuyu Christians in 1929 over female circumcision. In the wake of this crisis a number of Kenya's independent churches were born. By the late 1990s Kenya contained well over two hundred independent churches claiming 11 percent of the population. The African Independent Pentecostal Church and the African Orthodox Church, both centered among the Kikuyu of Central Kenya, constituted the largest of the indigenous churches (*see also* AFRICAN INITIATED CHURCH MOVEMENT).

In the 1950s yearnings for political independence expressed itself in the Mau Mau rebellion. The Revival Brethren opposed the Mau Mau and brought added vitality to the historic churches in a difficult time. The rebellion alerted both colonial powers and church leaders that the time for African leadership in church and state had arrived. A new emphasis on theological education was one response of the churches to this new political climate.

After independence from Britain in 1963, church growth escalated. The percentage of Christians in Kenya jumped from an estimated 50 percent of the population in the 1960s to approximately 80 percent in the early 1990s, though SYNCRETISM remains a concern. Organizations such as the Evangelical Fellowship of Kenya and the National Council of Churches of Kenya (NCCK) sought to unite churches for evangelism, social action, and political justice. In urban areas like Nairobi (2 million in 1995) new Christian movements of a strong charismatic nature arose in the 1990s to challenge both historic churches and African independent churches.

MARK SHAW

Kerygma. *See* THE GOSPEL.

Keswick Convention. An annual gathering in England begun modestly in the 1870s by evangelicals concerned about their increasing polarization, even bitter controversies, at a time when liberalism and AGNOSTICISM were making serious inroads into their churches. More, they were encouraged by the unexpected national impact of the first (1874) Moody/Sankey revival meetings in London coupled with the public cry for more authenticity in evangelical Christian living. The decision was taken to convene a conference that would seek to "promote Scriptural holiness" under the banner "All One in Christ Jesus." The underlying conviction of Keswick's founders was that through the gospel Christ offered his people the possibility of living victoriously by his indwelling presence and power. In their eyes Scripture held out the prospect of Christians' enjoying unbroken fellowship with God and victory over all known sin. Sin was always possible, but not necessary. The biblical themes that were felt to need wide promotion were personal surrender to Christ and buoyant faith in his Word.

The first gathering took place in 1875 at Keswick in England's Lake District. From the outset the conventions attracted hundreds despite the sharp criticisms they provoked among some prominent evangelical theologians ("Keswick promotes sinless perfection!"). For twelve years Keswick excluded all reference to missions despite the growing evidence that when young Christians deliberately surrendered themselves to Christ, they increasingly sensed a drawing to missionary service in the world for which he died. Fortunately, when this was officially recognized, a portion of each convention, usually the morning of the closing day, was devoted to missionaries and overseas nationals speaking to "the claim of Christ to his people's willing service in the cause of the evangelization of the world." Over the years Keswick's influence on missions has been enormous, particularly on the STUDENT VOLUNTEER MOVEMENT and on the WORLD MISSIONARY CONFERENCE at Edinburgh (1910).

Through promotion by such prominent Christians as Bishop G. Handley Moule, J. HUDSON TAYLOR, G. Campbell Morgan, DWIGHT L. MOODY, ROBERT E. SPEER, JOHN R. MOTT, ARTHUR T. PIERSON, Donald Grey Barnhouse, BILLY GRAHAM, and many others, and through the proliferation of conventions throughout the world, Keswick has gained and retained high regard among evangelicals. It began the pattern of sending "missioners to missionaries" to bring them spiritual renewal while on the field; even today Keswick speakers continue to minister regularly in many parts of the world. Current activities include the publishing of annual reports, the radio broadcast of "Keswick Week," a tape library service for national churches, and a hospitality fund to enable furloughed missionaries and overseas nationals to attend conventions in the United Kingdom. In 1892 Keswick sent out AMY CARMICHAEL, its first missionary, and thereby inaugurated a pattern of supporting workers serving in a wide range of societies overseas. Indeed, for almost a century Keswick represented evangelical ecumenicity at its best, although at present it does not command its former dominant position. This is doubtless due to the emergence of more contemporary renewal movements and to the change in style among evangelicals through the dynamism and growth of the charismatic and "house church" movements, particularly in England.

ARTHUR F. GLASSER

Bibliography. J. C. Pollock, *The Keswick Story;* C. F. Harford, ed., *The Keswick Convention.*

Keysser, Christian (1877–1961). German missionary to New Guinea. Born in Bavaria, Germany, Keysser attended high school in Nuremberg and the Missionary Institute in Neuendettelsau. In 1899 he sailed for New Guinea, where he was based primarily at the Lutheran mission station in Sattelberg. Keysser remained there for over twenty years as a church planter, linguist, and encourager of indigenous Christian music. At times he also served as a botanist, zoologist, ethnographer, geographer, and explorer. Difficulties with the government in New Guinea caused him to return to Germany in 1920. In his homeland he taught missions at Neuendettelsau, completed a dictionary of the Kate language (1925), earned a Ph.D. at the University of Erlangen (1929), and wrote voluminously on missionary principles and practices. He contributed significantly to the field of missionary anthropology by focusing on the tribal mind in New Guinea and advocating group conversion and discipleship. His ethnic unit approach emphasized that evangelization should bring minimal cultural disruption and should create genuine Christian communities with a burden for missions. Keysser's missiological theories provoked a wide-ranging debate. On one side was JOHANNES HOEK-ENDIJK, who extensively criticized Keysser. On the other, DONALD MCGAVRAN openly acknowledged Keysser's importance for his own thinking about church growth.

JAMES A. PATTERSON

Bibliography. D. McGavran's preface to the English translation of Keysser's *A People Reborn*.

Kil, Sun-Joo (1869–1935). Korean revivalist. Kil was born in South Pyung Yang province in North Korea and grew up during a very critical period of Korean history. After Japan defeated China in the Sino-Japanese War (1894–95) over the control of Korea, the Koreans knew that it was a matter of time before Japan would annex Korea. As a young man Kil was very interested in religion, and studied Confucianism and Buddhism extensively. In 1892 he entered the Anguk-Sa Buddhist monastery for three years for prayer and meditation but found no solution to his spiritual longing until he met a missionary named James Lee, who led him to Christ in 1895.

Kil made contributions to the church and the country largely in three areas. First, he was one of the seven graduates of the first graduating class of the Presbyterian Seminary in Pyung Yang. He became the first installed Korean pastor of a Korean church, the historic Chang Tae Hyun Presbyterian Church in Pyung Yang. He led many revival meetings in different parts of the country in spite of his poor eyesight and persecution. He preached over 13,600 times during this thirty-five-year ministry and became one of the key spiritual leaders for the first Great Revival of 1907.

Second, in 1907 he started the early dawn prayer meeting every day for the troubled country and the church. This early dawn prayer meeting in every Korean church has continued until today and has been instrumental in the rapid growth of the Korean church over the years.

Third, he was one of thirty-three Korean patriots who signed the Declaration of Independence on March 1, 1919, in Seoul against the Japanese annexation of Korea and was imprisoned for three years. He died in the pulpit while he was preaching.

BONG RIN RO

Bibliography. S. H. Moffett, *TCDCB*, pp. 201–2.

Kim, Helen (1899–1968). Korean evangelist and missions advocate. Kim, former president of Ewha University (1939–61), was the best recognized Christian woman educator in Korea in the past generation. After graduating from Ewha University in 1918, she began to teach there and served for the university for fifty years, training thousands of young women with Christian principles. She was the first Korean woman to receive a Ph.D. degree, awarded by Columbia University in New York in 1931.

She also served the country as a diplomat for Korea at the United Nations and a roving ambassador for many years. During the Korean War years, President Syngman Rhee asked her to be in charge of administration for the Red Cross and later of the Office of Public Information. She received many honorary awards, including the Ramon Magsaysay Award for Public Service (the Philippines), the Certificate of Order of Cultural Merit of the Republic of Korea, the Upper Room Citation for Leadership in World Christian Fellowship, the Order of Diplomatic Merit, First Class for her contribution to educate "more women better."

Kim was a dynamic spiritual leader with a tremendous emphasis on evangelism, social concern, and missions. After attending the World Student Christian Federation Conference in Peking in 1922, she was used as an instrument to start the Korean YWCA. In 1961 Ewha University sent three graduates as the first women missionaries to Pakistan. After her retirement, she spent her energy for the evangelization of Korea.

BONG RIN RO

Bibliography. S. H. Moffett, *TCDCB*, p. 202; C. C. Ok, *BDCM*, p. 364.

Kim, Joon-Gon (1925–). Korean evangelist and missions advocate. His Christian testimony during the Korean War has touched many lives around the globe. When he was the chaplain and principal of Soongsil High School (1951–56) in Kwangju City, North Korean communist soldiers captured the city in the summer of 1950 and killed his wife and father in front of his eyes and severely beat him. Later, he led the murderer to Christ.

He has been recognized by the Korean church for organizing a number of mass Christian gatherings in Korea. In 1974 he organized Explo '74 at Youido Plaza in Seoul, August 13–17, when 700,000 people gathered at the opening night to hear BILL BRIGHT. He was also the chairman for the 1980 World Evangelization Crusade August 11–15 with 2.7 million people on August 14. Under his leadership 3,000 Koreans traveled on a short-term mission project in Manila in 1990. When the GLOBAL CONSULTATION OF WORLD EVANGELIZATION '95 (GCOWE) was held at the Torch Center in Seoul, May 17–26, with 4,000 participants from 185 countries, he served as the chairman of the Korean Preparation Committee.

Under Kim, Campus Crusade has conducted the annual "Jesus Jamboree" for university students during the summer at which over 10,000 young people camp out for spiritual training at the Taechon beach. His Korean staff of over 350 works on different university campuses, and he is known as "the father of Korean Christian student movement."

He is a man of vision for evangelism, church growth, missions, and social concern. His contribution to the Christian student movement in Korea has inspired many other countries. He received his education from Chosun University, Fuller Theological Seminary, and Chun Buk University.

BONG RIN RO

Bibliography. S. H. Moffett, *TCDCB*, pp. 202–3.

Kimbangu, Simon, (1889–1951). Zairian Independent church founder. The Church of Jesus Christ on Earth though the Prophet Simon Kimbangu (EJCSK), largest of the several thousand AFRICAN INITIATED CHURCHES, is the result of only three months of public ministry by Simon Kimbangu. A Baptist catechist and evangelist when God called him to a healing ministry, Kimbangu initially resisted and fled from his home to Kinshasa. Through circumstances God drew Kimbangu back to his home area, and in 1921 again called him to heal. This time Kimbangu responded, and was promptly accused of being a sorcerer by a woman he had healed. Changing her mind after hearing his explanation of what had happened, she helped spread the news of what God had done. Within two months people were coming by the thousands, leaving jobs, emptying hospitals, and even bringing bodies of the dead to be raised.

While missionaries on the scene reported few genuine healings, within three months of the initial healing the Belgian authorities were so worried about the crowds that they issued a warrant for Kimbangu's arrest. Kimbangu eluded them for three months before giving himself up. His initial death sentence was commuted to life imprisonment in part at the urging of missionaries. Kimbangu spent the rest of his life as a model prisoner, dying in 1951. The EJCSK, not officially recognized until 1959, is estimated to be over 5 million strong. It is led by Kimbangu's youngest son, and is an example of a contextualized denominational framework that missionaries would do well to study.

A. SCOTT MOREAU

Bibliography. M. L. Martin, *Kimbangu: An African Prophet and His Church;* G. Molyneux, *African Christian Theology: The Quest for Selfhood.*

Kingdom of God. *Terminology.* No explicit use of the precise phrase "kingdom of God" occurs in the Old Testament, but if one looks at the Old Testament prophets through the teaching of Jesus and the totality of New Testament faith, one finds it is predicted as a future reality (the messianic age) in the ongoing redemptive purpose of God. In contrast, the New Testament uses this term or its equivalent (kingdom of heaven) more than a hundred times. This was the dominant theme in the ministry of Jesus and his use of the term seems to have oscillated between the primary concept of the rule or reign of God and the secondary sense of the realm over which he will exercise this rule (Luke 17:21 and Mark 14:25). Jesus on no occasion intimated that the kingdom actually existed prior to the beginning of his ministry (Luke 16:16). God's kingship is not unlike his providential care of his total creation: "Dominion belongs to the Lord and he rules over the nations" (Ps. 22:28). But his kingship is also eschatological: "In the time of those kings" (i.e., at a certain juncture in history) "the God of heaven will set up a kingdom that will never be destroyed . . . it will itself endure forever" (Dan. 2:44).

Old Testament History and Eschatology. God's kingship is identified with Israel, a people with whom he established a covenantal relationship that also involved a redemptive purpose: "All peoples on earth will be blessed through you [Jacob] and your offspring" (Gen. 28:14). Israel is to be "a light to the nations" within the sequence of history, extending the knowledge of God's salvation "to the ends of the earth" (Isa. 42:6; 49:6). In order that God might accomplish this he promised a NEW COVENANT that guaranteed Israel an imperishable communal existence (Jer. 31:31–37) and a messianic hope that would make possible the realization of her redemptive mission (33:14–22; Isa. 42:1–9). Israel's obedience in history will be related to the establishment of an eschatological order beyond history— "the age to come"—in which God's kingly rule will be fully manifested (Hab. 2:14) and in which his new order will bring perfection to all creation.

Messianic Hope. This involves three separate and specific strands of prophetic expectation, and all three are related to God's redemptive purpose for the nations. First, a distinctly earthly kingdom shall arise within history through a "Messiah"—a physical descendant of David who will bring renewal to Israel and to all the world (Isa. 9:6, 7; 11:1–12:7). Second, this kingdom will also come as an abrupt intrusion into history, not unlike an apocalyptic visitation accompanied with cosmic upheaval. The key personage is likewise a "Messiah" and is described as "one like a Son of Man" possessing "authority, glory, and sovereign power." His kingdom "will never be destroyed." He will be worshiped by "all peoples, nations, and men of every language," and will bestow on "the saints of the Most High" this "everlasting kingdom" to be theirs "forever and forever" (Dan. 7:13, 14, 18, 22). The third strand focuses on a Servant of the Lord, neither openly messianic nor evidently supernatural, but one who is an innocent, willing person who vicariously suffers without protest and dies in order to make his people righteous. The Old Testament does not conflate these strands of prophetic revelation, hence an aura of incompleteness characterizes the Old Testament and inevitably arouses anticipation of more to follow (Luke 2:25, 38). But it must never be forgotten that in essence God will visit his people, and his kingdom will not be the result of historical forces, such as human achievement.

New Testament: The Gospels. The ministry of Jesus in the New Testament began in the context of John the Baptist's renewal movement in Israel. Expectations were aroused by his announcement of the coming of the kingdom and of One who would baptize "with the Holy Spirit and with fire" (Matt. 3:1–12). Then Jesus came forward and publicly identified with Israel through submitting to John's baptism. During this act of obedience he was both approved by his Father and anointed for ministry by the Holy Spirit (Mark 1:9–11). Almost immediately thereafter the Holy Spirit "sent him out into the desert" to confront and demonstrate his superiority over the devil (1:12, 13). In the months that followed his ministry was virtually identical with that of John; both spoke of the coming kingdom. The Baptist's imprisonment brought this renewal ministry to an abrupt end. From that time on Jesus went to Galilee and preached: "The time has come. The kingdom of God is near. Repent and believe the good news" (Mark 1:14). By this he was announcing the glorious fact that the kingdom of God was now accessible to all those who would submit themselves to his rule. And since Jesus immediately thereafter began to call people to discipleship and his service ("I will make you fishers of men"), it follows that involvement in the kingdom of God (living under his rule) includes public proclamation and evangelism (Mark 1:16–20).

When Jesus returned to Galilee "news about him spread throughout the whole countryside" (Luke 4:14). His earlier renewal ministry in Judea had opened synagogues to him. "Everyone praised him" (v. 15). But when he began to identify himself with the Servant role prophesied by Isaiah and intimated that the gospel of the kingdom was also for non-Israelites, he encountered violent opposition (vv. 16–30). From this time on, whereas the "common people heard him gladly," the religious leaders became increasingly hostile, a hostility that culminated in his being turned over to the Romans for crucifixion.

The good news of the kingdom that Jesus preached and expounded is admittedly complex, since it represented movement toward the fulfillment of the Old Testament redemptive purpose in "the present age" as well as a radical reinterpretation of that hope with reference to "the age to come." In the present age, despite their rebellion against God, sinful human beings through repentance to God and surrender to Jesus' rule, can experience the new birth and enjoy a foretaste of the liberating kingdom. This included the forgiveness of sin, peace and acceptance with God, vital linkage with the Holy Spirit, valid insight into the Word of God, and joyous anticipation of "the powers of the coming age" (1 Cor. 2:12–15; Rom. 5:1, 2; 8:1–5, 35–39; Heb. 6:4, 5).

Even so, it is significant that Jesus never defined explicitly the term "kingdom of God." When he spoke of the kingdom as having "drawn near," he was affirming that it was an earthly rule in the world and its ongoing history. But when he stated that the kingdom is dynamically moving through human history and sweeping over people violently, he seemed to imply that it is something more than God's personal reign over individuals (Matt. 12:28; 11:12). He appeared to be referring to a new world, a new state of affairs, a new community that finds concrete expression in the world, even though it is both transcendent and spiritual. It is also political in that its full realization puts it on a collision course with all human rule and authority.

This note of spiritual conflict must not be regarded lightly. Satan is determined to thwart the progress of the kingdom. Jesus calmly asserts, however, that divine authority and rule have been given him by the Father (Luke 10:32; Matt. 11:27; 28:18). Furthermore, he will exercise this rule until Satan, sin, and death are brought to a complete end (Mark 9:1; 13:26; 14:62 with Luke 11:20–22).

The mystery of Jesus' person and the spiritual nature of his kingdom were so new and revolutionary that he could only disclose these realities gradually. To most Jews the kingdom of God would come as a stone that would shatter all godless nations (Dan. 2:44). But Jesus did not preach judgment and separation; these were eschatological realities. He came as a sower scattering the "good news of the kingdom" and looking for receptive people. He spoke in parables. These tantalized his hearers and compelled them to come to a full stop, then reflect and ask questions. The more his disciples began to discern who he was, the more they began to understand his teaching. Conversely, the more people resisted him, the more his teaching reduced itself in their minds to "hard sayings" devoid of significance (John 6:60). All they heard were stories, riddles, and paradoxes (Mark 4:11, 12).

The parables speak of the nature, growth, and value of the kingdom, largely under the theme of mission. There are the "growth" parables in which the parable of the sower is so central that Jesus pointed out that failure to understand this parable would render a person unable to understand any parable (Mark 4:13). Then follows a parable of the growth process in the hearts of those who respond to the message of the kingdom (4:26–30). This process eludes understanding and external control. When spiritual maturity begins to manifest itself the parable of the wheat and the weeds brings to the fore a "second sowing" (Matt. 13:36–43) so important that the Lord himself is the only "Sower." This follows because "the field is the world" and the distribution of his servants in it is a responsibility he grants to no other. This implies a deliberate surrender of oneself to him, a willingness to be sent into the locale and ministry that he has appointed.

The kingdom is like a buried treasure and its acquisition merits any cost or sacrifice (Matt. 13:44–46). Its form is hidden, representing the hiddenness of God, working in the hearts of his people scattered throughout the world. Although insignificant in its beginnings (a mustard seed or bit of leaven), on the day of history's consummation it will be like a great tree or a bowl of dough fully leavened. The kingdom represents Jesus' present invasion of Satan's kingdom to release people from bondage (Luke 11:14–22). He desires that they enjoy in part a foretaste of the age to come, as they enter into the life he imparts to them (John 3:3). This includes the forgiveness of their sins (Mark 2:5) and the gift of God's righteousness (Matt. 5:20). The only acceptable response that a person can make is to put oneself deliberately under Christ's rule by repentance, faith, and submission.

Jesus also intimated that the kingdom would be consummated in power and glory, and instructed his disciples to pray for that Day when the will of God would be carried out on earth even as it is in heaven (Matt. 6:10). Because the kingdom had already truly come, Jesus' disciples should manifest the "signs" that confirmed its presence. This is as urgent as the final apocalyptic display of power that will compel "every knee" to bow and "every tongue" to confess that Jesus is Lord (Phil. 2:10, 11).

Although the kingdom is wholly of God, he is pleased to share "the keys of the kingdom" with his people that under his direction their preaching of its "good news" might be determinative of those who participate in his eschatological harvest (Matt. 16:19). Because the kingdom tends through its proclamation to draw into its midst both the good and the bad, the eschatological judgment will separate the wicked from the righteous (the parable of the net; Matt. 13:47–52). On this basis the Lord distinguished the church from the kingdom (Matt. 16:18).

At the Last Supper when Jesus instituted the Eucharist, he gave his disciples a cup he identified as "my blood of the covenant, which is poured out for many" (Mark 14:24), thereby establishing linkage between that supper, the new covenant, and the coming kingdom. In this fashion he established the necessity of his death "as a ransom for many" (Mark 10:45). It was his death that made the coming apocalyptic kingdom dependent upon what would take place in history. "God did not abandon history; the eschatological kingdom invaded history in Jesus' life-death-resurrection and continues to work in history through the people of the kingdom" (Matt. 24:14; Mark 13:10; Ladd).

Acts. The resurrection of Jesus gave to his disciples—the believing remnant in Israel—a new sense of their oneness as they received further instruction in the kingdom and awaited its coming (Acts 1:3, 6). Peter's Pentecost sermon reinterpreted the Old Testament hope by speaking of Jesus' exaltation, confirming him as "Lord and Messiah" (2:30–36). In the Book of Acts the "signs" of the kingdom are everywhere present: Jesus by his Spirit is in the midst of his people, the gospel is proclaimed, signs and wonders accompany the witness, evil spirits are exorcised, conversions are frequent, and much suffering is experienced as a result of efforts to do God's will in a world that rebels against him (Matt. 5:10).

Pauline Epistles. Paul builds on Peter's reinterpretation of Jesus' messianic reign and describes it as a present relationship (Col. 1:13) and a spiritual experience (Rom. 14:17), as well as an eschatological inheritance (1 Cor. 6:9–11; Eph. 5:5). Jesus "must reign until he has put all his enemies under his feet" and destroy death, "the last enemy" (1 Cor. 15:25, 26). The end will only come "when he hands over the kingdom to God the Father after he has destroyed all dominion, authority and power" (v. 24). His ultimate goal is that "God may be all in all" (v. 28).

Revelation. The final revelation of God concerning his kingdom is of its eschatological consummation with the devil finally consigned to the lake of fire (Rev. 20:10). Just prior to this we find reference to the second coming of Christ with its rapid sequence of his total triumph over all his foes, his binding of Satan, the resurrection of his saints, his millennial reign, and the final consummation of human history (19:11–20:15). Rather than detail the elements of this controversial section, the Spirit presses on to the portrayal of God's ultimate goal: the age to come with its new heaven and new earth, and his redeemed people from all the families, tribes, languages, and peoples at long last seeing his face (21:1–4; 22:1–5).

ARTHUR F. GLASSER

Bibliography. G. R. Beasley-Murray, *Jesus and the Kingdom of God*; J. Bright, *The Kingdom of God*; A. F. Glasser, *Kingdom and Mission*; G. E. Ladd, *Jesus and the Kingdom*; H. Ridderbos, *The Coming of the Kingdom*.

Kinship. Kinship relations have long been a major part of anthropological study. For kinship (interpersonal) relations and social (intergroup) relations combine with the economic, political, and religious aspects of culture to structure human behavior. The relative importance people from different cultures (kinship, peasant, industrial, and postindustrial) place on these relations will vary widely and impact their behavior.

Despite this diversity, all human relationships can be understood within a framework of identity, STATUS, and role. *Identity* is specified by the use of a kinship term to designate particular individuals—the term serves as their identity. *Status* relates to the cultural expectations associated with particular identities—how people expect those so identified to behave. *Role* is the actual behavior of people with a particular identity; this behavior reflects the basic nature of the relationship. Thus kinship terms define cultural sets of rights and duties that are acted out in real life through specific behavior patterns.

By fitting into relationships with people on the basis of cultural expectations, missionaries serving in a particular society may be able to remove much of the mystery associated with their presence. By adapting to local cultural expectations, outsiders can learn much about appropriate behavior and use that knowledge to build relationships that may serve as a launching pad for communicating the gospel. In kinship societies, with their focus on close egalitarian relationships, outsiders must build intragenerational relationships with members of the society and use that bonding to communicate. In peasant societies relationships are more hierarchical and intergenerational, often resembling a family structure. In industrial societies, which focus on individuals, communication often springs from the interaction between individuals—friends, business associates, people with common interests. Postindustrial societies, with an emphasis on team building, demand complementary skills; each person contributes to the whole, which may be a neighborhood, club, association, or group bound by occupation.

Similarly, an appreciation for the nature of groups within a society can be utilized in presenting the gospel and assisting church growth within a cultural context. Each group has its own criteria for membership. These are often based on kinship (nuclear family, extended family, clan), territory (neighborhood, city, state), economic position (caste, occupation), or language (dialect, tribe). As with kinship relations, each group has an identity (terminologically defined), a status (set of expected behavior patterns), and roles (the actual patterns of the group's behavior). A group's understanding of themselves and others—how far the boundaries extend before others are recognized as being outside the group—can be of great assistance to missionaries attempting to discover how many translations of Scripture should be made within a particular region or which groups will interact with a newly founded church.

To build an effective missiological strategy, it is important to determine whether a given society places greater value on individual or group identity. One should also analyze whether the society is tightly or loosely structured. Societies fall into four general categories: (1) authoritarian—individual-oriented and tightly structured; (2) individualist—individual-oriented and loosely structured; (3) hierarchist—group-oriented and tightly structured; and (4) collectivist—group-oriented and loosely structured. Determining the nature of a particular society is vital for sound development and implementation of an evangelistic strategy. Should the approach focus on individuals or whole groups (*see* INDIVIDUALISM AND COLLECTIVISM)? And if groups, which ones would make the most appropriate targets, and why? Should Christianity be presented as a means for people to relate more effectively with other groups or as a means of building interpersonal relationships?

An understanding of relationships will also give insight into the nature of LEADERSHIP patterns within a society. What determines who is to be a leader—a general election, appointment (and by whom?), or a birthright? How is leadership expressed? What are the responsibilities of leaders within the group and beyond? How do leaders actually perform their duties? The framework of identity, status, and role is once again helpful for understanding rights and duties as people exercise leadership. Is leadership the prerogative of an individual, such as a judge, or is it delegated to a group, such as the panchayat under an Indian banyan tree or a palaver in Africa? Understanding the leadership patterns within a society is crucial as a church selects a pastor or gives responsibilities to a group of elders. What gives them the right to serve, and what are the implications of following cultural patterns in contrast to ignoring them?

Throughout Scripture there are many patterns of kinship and social interaction as well as expressions of leadership. Therefore we should not argue that there is a biblical pattern since there are many. Rather, Scripture can be brought to bear (both positively and negatively) on the status and roles of individuals and groups within each cultural context. Clearly research in the area of kinship and social structure is important for the introduction of the gospel and its ongoing impact as the church develops and grows.

R. DANIEL SHAW

Bibliography. T. Brewster and B. S. Brewster, *Bonding;* M. Douglas, *In the Active Voice,* pp. 183–254; W. H. Goodenough, *The Relevance of Models for Social Anthropology;* S. Lingenfelter, *Transforming Culture: A Challenge for Christian Mission;* R. D. Shaw, *Missiology* 18 (1991): 291–304.

Kinsolving, Lucien Lee (1862–1929). American missionary to Brazil. Born in Middleburg, Virginia, Kinsolving attended the Episcopal High School of Virginia where his gift for speaking was developed. Upon graduation he accepted appointment to a church school in a wild portion of Kentucky, birthing his vision for mission. After two years at the University of Virginia, he transferred to the Virginia Theological Seminary where he was ordained a deacon in 1889. The seminary sent him during the summers to lead Episcopal churches in Upper Virginia where his earnest preaching crowded the churches with eager congregations.

Stirred by the seminary's deep interest in Brazil, Kinsolving was ordained and sent through the American Church Missionary Society to Brazil in 1889. Within six months he was conducting services in Portuguese. After his marriage to Alice Brown in 1891, he became rector of the Church of our Savior in Rio Grande do Sul. Eloquent and far-sighted, Kinsolving was a respected leader among the Brazilians. Under his leadership, the Episcopal church became a self-supporting congregation led by an indigenous clergy. Elected to the bishopric by the independent Egreja Episcopal Brasilera, Kinsolving was consecrated in the U.S. and took charge of the Brazil mission in 1899.

Kinsolving was prevented from returning to Brazil after suffering a stroke. He died in 1929 at the age of sixty-six.

GARY LAMB

Bibliography. A. B. Kinsolving, *Lucien Lee Kinsolving, Missionary Bishop of Brazil.*

Kiribati *(Est. 2000 pop.: 87,000; 726 sq. km. [280 sq. mi.]).* Located in Oceania, and formerly the Gilbert Islands, Kiribati gained independence from Britain in 1979. The first Protestant missionary, HIRAM BINGHAM of the ABCFM, began work in Abaiang in 1856. As of 1993, the population was over 97 percent Christian, including 51.5 percent Catholic, 44 percent Protestant, and 2.1 percent marginal Christian groups. It is estimated that evangelicals comprise just over 6 percent. Protestant churches present include Kiribati Protestant (Congregational) Church, Church of God (Cleveland), Seventh-Day Adventist, and Assemblies of God.

A. SCOTT MOREAU

SEE ALSO Micronesia.

Kivebulaya, Apolo (1864–1933). Ugandan pioneer missionary. Apolo Kivebulaya is revered in the Church of Uganda (Anglican) as an example par excellence of the African evangelists who ministered during the colonial period. He was from a rural Baganda family in northwestern Uganda. Kivebulaya spent his younger years in various kinds of military service under the British administration, including pacification efforts into the Toro Kingdom, where afterward he took up residence.

Kivebulaya took the name Apolo when he was baptized by an Anglican missionary in 1895 in Kampala. He resided in Toro and ministered there as a church teacher which included literacy as well as instruction in the catechism. The town of Mboga became his evangelistic headquarters. From there he made excursions across the border into the former Belgian Congo. While continuing this mission he also ministered to the small congregation at Mbogo. His second missionary venture was from 1897 to 1899 to the pygmy people who live in the Ituri forest.

Apolo's sincere commitment to evangelism is one reason why he never married. Having been ordained a deacon in 1900 and priest in 1903, Apolo Kivebulaya was further honored in 1922 by being appointed to office of canon. In this way the Anglican Church recognized his long and faithful ministry, which was an example for all national evangelists, especially those who extend the gospel beyond the areas of their own ethnic origins.

DEAN S. GILLILAND

Bibliography. D. B. Barrett, *CDCWM,* p. 325; A. Luck, *African Saint: The Story of Apolo Kivebulaya.*

Kivengere, Festo (1919–88). Ugandan evangelist, church leader, and missionary in Tanzania.

Born in southwestern Uganda, Kivengere came to Christ in January 1935 through the influence of CMS missionaries. He was educated at Mukono Teachers' College (1936–39), London University Institute of Education (1957–59), and Pittsburgh Theological Seminary (1964–67). After his training at Mukono, he taught and led local evangelistic teams on weekends and through these efforts emerged as a powerful preacher.

In 1945 he responded to a call and went to Tanzania as a tent-maker for thirteen years. In 1962, he started a free-lance evangelistic ministry and traveled widely around the world. In 1971, with Michael Cassidy, he formed Africa Evangelistic Enterprise.

Kivengere was ordained in the Church of Uganda in 1966 and consecrated bishop on May 5, 1972. He was courageous and direct with both church and state issues. He opposed the growing state oppression of the church, his courage being seen in his stance against Ugandan Presidents Amin and Obote for their atrocities. He was the recipient of several of international awards including The International Peace Prize (1977) and The Cross of St. Augustine (Anglican).

Kivengere's writings include: *When God Moves* (1973); *The Spirit Is Moving* (1976); *I Love Idi Amin* (1977); *Revolutionary Love* (1983); and *Hope for Uganda and the World* (1980). He died of leukemia on May 18, 1988, and was given a state funeral in Uganda.

LAZARUS SERUYANGE

Bibliography. A. Coomes, *The Authorized Biography of Festo Kivengere.*

Ko Tha Byu (1778–1840). Myanmar evangelist. Ko Tha Byu was the first convert to Christianity among the Karen people of Burma (now Myanmar). Born in a village near Bassein in southern Burma, he led a violent life as a young man and, by his own admission, had committed about thirty murders prior to his conversion. Under the influence of ADONIRAM JUDSON, he was dramatically converted and his life transformed.

From 1828 to 1831 Ko Tha Byu accompanied George Boardman, an American Baptist missionary, in his ministry among the Karen people in the villages around Tavoy, in southern Burma. He was baptized by Boardman during this time. Boardman died in 1831, but not before seeing the beginnings of a mass movement among the Karens toward Christianity. Ko Tha Byu continued evangelistic ministry among the Karen villages until his death. He proved to be a highly effective evangelist, carrying the Christian faith into the areas around Rangoon and Bassein. The Karens were largely ANIMISTS (although they did believe in the Creator God and had a story about

a fall through which they became alienated from God) and were despised by the Buddhist majority. In some ways they were uniquely prepared for the gospel, and under the ministry of Ko Tha Byu and others hundreds soon came to Christ. By 1856 over 11,000 church members were reported. Ko Tha Byu is revered today as a fiery evangelist and pivotal leader in the mass movement among the Karens to Christianity. A special day in the Karen church calendar honors his memory.

HAROLD A. NETLAND

Bibliography. F. Mason, *The Karen Apostle: Or Memoir of Ko Tha-byu;* J. Robbins, *Boardman of Burma;* M. Wylie, *The Gospel in Burmah.*

Koran. *See* QUR'AN.

Korea, North (The Democratic People's Republic of Korea) *(Est. 2000 pop.: 25,979,000; 120,538 sq. km. [46,540 sq. mi.]).* Korea was partitioned into two sections at the Yalta Conference in 1945. North Korea was to be controlled by the Russians and South Korea by the United States until the time a joint election was held which would unite the divided country. To date, however, this joint election has not taken place. In the meantime North Korea established the Democratic People's Republic of Korea (DPRK) under communism, while South Korea established the Republic of Korea (ROK). Kim Il-Sung ruled 23 million people in North Korea from its inception until his death on July 8, 1994. He was succeeded by his son, Kim Jung-Il.

The earliest mission efforts in Korea are reported to have been by Koreans who, after visiting China and being exposed to Catholic influences, returned with the gospel to their homes. The first missionary priest to enter Korea was James Choo, a Chinese worker who arrived in 1794. Catholic mission work suffered persecution and martyrdom until the signing of the Korean Treaty with the United States in 1882. Protestant mission work did not begin until 1884 with the arrival of Horace N. Allen. At the time of the communist takeover, however, the church in Korea was the second largest in Asia, eclipsed only by the church in the Philippines, with two-thirds of the total Christian population residing in the north. Prior to 1945, among the Protestant churches, the Presbyterians had the strongest presence, followed by the Methodists, Salvation Army, and Seventh-Day Adventists.

After being established in power, the government in North Korea adopted a policy of gradual extermination of all religions. Although religious freedom was guaranteed in the Constitution, government persecution against the Christian church was so severe that all public churches were closed until 1988, when permission was given to build Bong Soo Church, the first Protestant church to be built in Pyongyang since the inception of North Korea. In 1992 another Protestant church, Ban Sock Church, was erected in memory of Mrs. Kang Ban-Sock (deaconess), who was Kim Il-Sung's mother, at the location which she used as the site of a daily dawn prayer meeting. The government also allowed the Roman Catholics to build Chang Choong Catholic Cathedral in Pyongyang. Kang Yang-Sup, Chairman of the North Korean Christian Federation, stated in early 1997 that there were about 520 house churches with 12,000 Protestant Christians and one Roman Catholic cathedral with 800 members in North Korea, though many question the reliability of these statistics.

Though politically divided, North and South Korea are still deeply emotionally and religiously tied. For example, the North Korean Church Reconstruction Department of the Korean Christian Council in South Korea launched a nationwide prayer movement to reconstruct over 2,000 disbanded churches in North Korea by encouraging each local church in South Korea to adopt a disbanded church in the north. Through this adoption the South Korean Christians pray for the restoration of the adopted church in the north and designate portions of their offerings for the reconstruction of that disbanded church until the hoped for reunification between north and south can take place.

BONG RIN RO

Bibliography. W. J. Kang, *Christ and Caesar in Modern Korea;* H. S. Kim, ed., *North Korean Church History Since the Liberation of Korea* (in Korean); B. R. Ro and M. L. Nelson, eds., *Korean Church Growth Explosion.*

Korea, South *(Est. 2000 pop.: 47,149,000; 99,263 sq. km. [38,325 sq. mi.]).* Since 1970, South Korea has been known as a "nation of economic miracles in Asia" or "a nation of church growth explosion in modern times" and has drawn the attention of many nations of the world. In fact, many church leaders in South Korea believe that the Koreans are a "chosen people" (1 Peter 1:9) for God's redemptive purpose today.

A tragic partition of Korea at the 38th parallel was drawn by the super powers at the Yalta Conference in 1945. South Korea established the Republic of Korea (ROK) on August 15, 1948 with Dr. Syngman Rhee as the first president. The Korean War, which started on June 25, 1950, when North Korean soldiers invaded South Korea, lasted for over three years and resulted in half a million deaths and millions of casualties. As a result of the war, South Korea

became "a beggar nation" of the world. Since the Korean Armistice Agreement was signed to end the war on July 27, 1953, Pammunjoon has become the focal point of dialogue between North and South Korea.

After the fall of Syngman Rhee's government precipitated by the student demonstrations throughout South Korea on April 19, 1960, the country was ruled by three military generals: Park Chung-Hee (1962–79), Chun Doo-Hwan (1980–87), and Ro Tai-Woo (1988–93). The civilian government of President Kim Young-Sam (1993–98) replaced the military regime in 1993.

The rapid economic development in South Korea began at the end of the Vietnam War. The per capita GNP grew explosively over that time, from $105 in 1965 to $10,076 in 1995. This economic growth and resulting prosperity has brought enormous changes in the lifestyle of the people. Sexual revolution, divorce, drugs, and crime are more rampant than before, especially among the younger generation.

The rapid church growth in Korea has been so well known throughout the Christian world that the Korean church has become a model for church growth in other countries. The first American Protestant missionaries came to Korea in 1884; there were approximately 12 million Protestant Christians and 38,000 churches in South Korea in 1997. In Seoul alone there were 6,800 churches in 1995, and 23 out of 50 megachurches in the world are found in South Korea. In the mid-1970s six new churches were planted in Korea daily. During the Billy Graham Crusade in Seoul in May 1973, more than 1.1 million Christians met together at one time at the Yoido Plaza in Seoul. A still larger crowd of Christians met again for the World Evangelization Crusade in August 1980 in Yoido Plaza.

Many church leaders around the world have asked why the Korean church has grown so much and so rapidly. There are both historical and spiritual factors for the rapid growth of the church. Historically, Korea, which had been colonized by the Japanese Empire for 36 years (1910–45), wished to get her political independence from Japan. The Koreans welcomed the Western powers into Korea to drive out Japanese imperialism. Therefore, the Korean gentry readily accepted Western influences and the Christian message which Western missionaries brought to Korea. The political situation in Korea was just the opposite of that of China where Western powers, including "Western Christianity," were rejected. Western missionaries in Korea also brought new Western medicine and popularized education by establishing schools for the lower class of people using the simple Korean script rather than the difficult Chinese characters.

There are a number of spiritual factors for the explosive growth of the Korean church: (1) strength of the local church by Spirit-filled and hard-working pastors; (2) strong emphasis of prayer through daily early dawn prayer meetings, all night prayer meetings, and prayer mountains for the spiritual renewal of Christians; (3) grass-roots evangelism organized by the local churches to achieve the "Christianization of Korea"; (4) well-organized cell group Bible studies; (5) abundant supply of Christian workers through theological education; (6) rising number of Korean cross-cultural missionaries; (7) faithful stewardship in tithes and personal service for the church; and (8) innovative contextual expressions of Christian faith to make Christianity be a national religion.

The Korean church hosted the First Asian Missions Congress in August 1991 in Seoul with 1,300 participants from all over Asia, and the GLOBAL CONSULTATION ON WORLD EVANGELIZATION (GCOWE 95) with 4,000 participants at the Torch Center in Seoul in May 1995. These missions meetings enlarged the vision of the Korean church for world evangelization, particularly for the evangelization of the UNREACHED PEOPLES in 10/40 WINDOW countries of the world. The number of Korean missionaries has sharply increased since 1979, when there were 93 missionaries, to 1996 with an estimated 4,402 missionaries working in 138 nations (*see also* KOREAN MISSION BOARDS AND AGENCIES). The prayer target of the Korean church is to send 10,000 Korean missionaries (including 1,000 second-generation Korean missionaries sent out by over 3,000 Korean churches in North America) by A.D. 2000.

BONG RIN RO

Bibliography. W. J. Kang, *Christ and Caesar in Modern Korea*; J. T. Kim, *Protestant Church Growth in Korea*; B. R. Ro and M. L. Nelson, eds., *Korean Church Growth Explosion*.

Korean Mission Boards and Societies.

The story of church growth in Korea has been well known throughout the world, but its missionary work has not been as widely reported. From the beginning, the Korean church has been a missionary church, particularly since the Presbyterian Church in Korea was set up as a self-governing, independent church in 1907. As of March 1998, there were over 5,800 Korean missionaries in 152 countries (Kim, 1988, 6).

Rise of the Missionary Movement in the Korean Church.

In 1907, during the culmination of Korea's first great awakening, seven men were ordained by the first Presbyterian Church in Korea and one of them, Ki-Poong Yi, was sent as a missionary to the Island of Quelpart (Chaejudo) in 1907. In 1909, Suk-Jin Han was sent to Japan, and three ordained missionaries were sent to Shantung, China in 1913 (Rhodes, 1934, 392–95): Tai-Ro Park, Pyung-Soon Sa, and Young-Hoon Kim. Also, the Korean church did the work of missions in such places as Siberia, Hawaii, Mexico, Mongolia, Manchuria, and America, working with both the Korean diaspora and the nationals, in spite of losing their sovereignty, language, and names and suffering severe persecution under Japanese Colonial Rule (1907–45). From 1902 to 1945, the Korean church sent a total of 120 missionaries.

The contemporary face of the Korean church and its involvement in missions has gone through a drastic change from those early days. The Korean War (1950–53) divided Korea and the strength of Korean Christianity moved from North to South. Samuel I. Kim has noted that from 1953 to 1976 there were a total of 234 missionaries sent from South Korea, working in Thailand, Taiwan, Japan, Vietnam, Hong Kong, Indonesia, Pakistan, Nepal, Ethiopia, Okinawa, Brazil, Mexico, Argentina, Brunei, and America (1976, 124). But it was not until the early 1980s that there was an explosive increase in the number of Korean Christians sent as missionaries. The *Antioch News* documents the explosion of numerical growth of Korean missionaries sent by denominations, local churches, and para-church and mission organizations (excluding those sent to America; Kim, 1998, 6). The numbers increased from 323 in 1982, to 1,645 in 1990, 3,272 in 1994, and 5,804 in 1998.

With this rapid growth has come the dilemma of how Koreans can most effectively be trained and enabled to work with other missionaries for the kingdom and the task of world evangelization.

Issues of Concern and the Korean Missionary Effort.

There is no doubt that Korean Christians have a strong evangelistic spirit. They want to plant churches and do missions. But too often their understanding of missions is limited to "soul saving" and the ministry of the Word. Korean missionaries need a better balance of both the ministries of the word and deed, without making a sharp separation between the two. But to do this requires that Koreans think again about the place of God in missions, or the theology of missions.

Second, with the explosion of growth in numbers of Korean missionaries since the early 1980s, too many missionaries have been sent without being properly selected or trained. There is an urgent need to give immediate attention to this deficiency in working with missionary candidates, moving them from their monocultural background to being cross-cultural people.

Third, it is sad to see how the abundance of finances has kept many Korean Christians from a childlike dependence on God in their ministry and from cooperating with other missionaries, denominations, and churches in their missionary efforts. Korean missionaries tend to use their finances to recruit nationals and new converts to work together in evangelizing and planting churches. However, they may do so at the cost of corrupting these "innocent" people, a reality observed earlier by JOHN L. NEVIUS in China and more recently seen in the Philippines.

Finally, the early Korean missionaries cooperated and worked together with the Western missionaries and the host churches as partners. Presently, however, there are a growing number of Korean missionaries who work independently with little or no consultation with other missionaries and national churches in their location of ministry. Missionaries of all nations need each other, and Korean missionaries in particular must learn (or perhaps relearn) to partner and to work cooperatively for the kingdom.

The Korean church, as a missionary church, can make great and unique contributions to the missionary movement of the church in the twenty-first century if it can solve these dilemmas.

TIMOTHY KIHO PARK

Bibliography. C. K. Kim, ed., *Antioch News*, 3:22 (March 1988); S. I. Kim, *New Forces in Missions*, pp. 121–30; H. A. Rhodes, ed., *History of the Korea Mission: Presbyterian Church U.S.A. 1884–1934.*

Kraemer, Hendrik (1888–1965). Dutch ecumenical leader, missiologist, and missionary to Indonesia. Born in the Netherlands, Kraemer lost both parents by the age of twelve and was raised in an orphanage. Through independent Bible study he experienced a personal conversion to Christ, and at sixteen decided to become a missionary. After study in Egypt, he served with the Dutch Bible Society in Indonesia.

Kraemer returned to accept a position at the University of Leiden (1937–47). During this period he was very active in Dutch church life, to the point of being a hostage under the Nazi occupation. Later he became the first director of the Ecumenical Institute in Bossey (near Geneva). After his retirement he was guest lecturer at Union Theological Seminary in New York for a year (1956–57).

Kraemer is remembered both as a pioneer with a vision and as a scholar. His book *Christian Message in a Non-Christian World* had profound influence on twentieth-century missiology. Although he was a true scholar in the fields of Eastern languages, Islam, and the history of religions, his legacy is as a missionary and a missionary theologian whose awareness of the problematic nature of present and future Christian missions and interfaith dialogue was sharper and far more advanced than that of his contemporaries.

STEPHEN HOKE

Bibliography. L. A. Hoedemaker, *ML*, pp. 508–15; H. Kraemer, *From Missionfield to Independent Church; Ecumenical Review* 18 (Jan. 1966): 96–99.

Krapf, Johann Ludwig (1810–81). German pioneer missionary in Ethiopia and Kenya. Born and educated in the German village of Derendingen, Krapf joined the CHURCH MISSIONARY SOCIETY (CMS) in 1838 after spending a brief period as a Lutheran pastor. His first assignment was in Ethiopia (Abyssinia). Fascinated by the Galla (Oromo) tribe of southern Ethiopia, he called them the Germans of East Africa. His controversial support of British intervention in Ethiopia led to his departure in 1843. In that same year Krapf married. After he and his wife Rosine were refused admittance into Ethiopia in 1844, they sought to reenter East Africa through the gateway of Mombasa. Soon after receiving permission from the sultan of Zanzibar to begin work among the non-Muslim tribes of the coast, tragedy struck with the death of his wife and newborn child. Krapf persevered and concentrated his energies on the study of Swahili.

In 1846 Johannes Rebmann arrived and assisted Krapf in establishing the first CMS station in what is now Kenya. Krapf envisioned this center at Rabai, among the Giriama, as the first link in a chain of mission stations that would reach across Africa and connect with the West African Christian communities of Freetown, Badagri, and Abeokuta. Pursuing this vision, Krapf explored the interior of East Africa into the geographical heart of Tanzania and Kenya. His reports of snowcapped mountains on the equator were met with derision in Europe.

Following a furlough in 1850, Krapf returned to Rabai, but ill health forced his permanent return to Germany in 1853. Though he later visited East Africa briefly in 1861 (to help Thomas Wakefield establish a Methodist station at Ribe, north of Mombasa) and in 1867 joined Robert Napier's punitive expedition to Ethiopia as an interpreter, his missionary work in East Africa was over. A brilliant linguist who published a Swahili New Testament, grammar, and dictionary, Krapf is best remembered for his book *Travels, Researches and Missionary Labors in Eastern Africa* (1860), which is the principal source for his life and work.

MARK A. SHAW

Krishna Pillai, H. A. (1827–1900). Indian contextualizer and poet. Born in a village near Palayamcottai in South India, he was raised in an orthodox Vaishnavite family. He strictly observed the caste rituals, was thoroughly versed in Vaishnavite literature, learned Sanskrit, and studied Tamil prose. By age eighteen he had memorized major portions of the Ramayana.

Appointed Tamil pandit in the Mission College at Sawyarpuram in 1852, Krishna Pillai for the first time came in close contact with Christians and began to read the Bible. Previously he had opposed Christianity. On March 29, 1858, he "trusted Christ alone." In his own words, "on that very day the old signs on my forehead were cleared off. The laws of jati (caste) . . . I snapped." He was baptized on April 18, 1858.

Krishna Pillai was a gifted poet. He adapted Hindu myths and symbols to communicate the biblical concept of God's salvation through Christ. His epic poem "Rakshanya Yathirigam" (comparable to Bunyan's *Pilgrim's Progress*) expresses the Christian faith in classic Tamil form.

Krishna Pillai brought to the service of Christ his deep knowledge of the HINDU background and of the great Tamil culture in which he had grown up. His published Tamil works include *The Pilgrimage of Salvation* (epic), *The Joy of Salvation* (a collection of prayers), and *The Assurance of the Religion of Salvation* (a Christian apologetic).

ROGER E. HEDLUND

Bibliography. A. J. Appasamy, *Tamil Christian Poet: The Life and Writings of H. A. Krishna Pillai;* D. D. Hudson, *Indian Church History Review* 2 (1968): 15–43; idem, *Indigenous Responses to Western Christianity.*

Kropf, Albert (1822–1910). German missionary to South Africa. Born in Potsdam in 1822, he decided to become a missionary due to the influence of pietists' literature and preaching. He studied at the Berlin Mission's seminary and in 1845 took up an assignment at its station Bethel in British Kaffraria (now Ciskei) in the Eastern Cape. He ministered among the Xhosa for sixty-one years, was superintendent of the Berlin Mission's Kaffrarian synod for forty-three of these, and also pastored a congregation of German settlers in Stutterheim for many years. He translated the entire Bible, a hymn book, Luther's Shorter Catechism, and other works in Xhosa, penned a major anthropological treatise in 1889 which is an indispensable historical source on the Xhosa, and a decade later produced the *Kaffir-English Dictionary*, which remained for decades the standard Xhosa dictionary. A determined and uncompromising confessionalist Lutheran, Kropf demanded careful instruction of potential Christians before baptism and intense catechizing and preparation for confirmation, and so the number of converts was not many.

ULRICH VAN DER HEYDEN

Bibliography. G. Pakendorf, *Missionalia* 21 (1993): 229–35.

Kuhn, Isobel (1902–57). Canadian missionary to China and Thailand. Perched on steep mountains extending from Tibet into southwestern China, Isobel Kuhn spent her mature life with her family in missionary outreach to the Lisu tribespeople in Yunnan province. Her gift of writing poignant spiritual lessons from candid illustrations describing the impoverished Lisu, their Christian culture, and their sacrificial lives greatly influenced evangelical audiences in the 1950s.

An English literature student before conversion, the Canadian Kuhn attended Moody Bible Institute before traveling to China with the China Inland Mission (now OVERSEAS MISSIONARY FELLOWSHIP). She learned Chinese before trekking over dangerous mountain paths to the Salween valley Lisu villages in 1934.

Following the precedence of J. O. Frazer, the Kuhns always sent out trained Lisu evangelists and Bible teachers first into new areas to secure spiritual footholds. In this way the Lisu Christians quickly indigenized their faith. Lisu peoples in Burma (now Myanmar) and Thailand were also reached by this means, the latter field becoming the Kuhns' home after the 1949 Maoist revolution in China. Before dying of cancer Kuhn wrote extensively about the Lisu, not living to see the full Lisu Bible published in 1962.

LAUREN PFISTER

Bibliography. I. Kuhn, *Nests above the Abyss;* idem, *Stones of Fire;* idem, *By Searching.*

Kumm, Karl Wilhelm (1874–1930). German-born British missionary to Egypt and founder of Sudan United Mission. Karl Kumm was one of the great faith mission pioneers in the interior of Africa. His first wife Lucy (d. 1906), daughter of Fanny and Grattan Guinness, had followed her mother in using her literary talent to further the cause of the "regions beyond" (Congo, South America, India). Karl, born in the (former English) German territory of Hannover, attended the East London Training Institute and joined the North Africa Mission in 1898 to work in Egypt, where he married Lucy in 1900. The Kumms took up Grattan Guinness' vision to reach the Sudan Belt stretching from Dakar to Khartoum, founding the Sudan Pioneer Mission, based in Eisenach, Germany. After disagreements they moved to Britain and started the Sudan United Mission in 1904 to reach the Sudan Belt from Nigeria. The SUM became one of the largest faith missions, with the unusual feature of combining interdenominational and denominational branches. Twelve churches resulting from the SUM in Nigeria, Cameroon, Chad, and Sudan count more than 3 million members. Kumm established home bases in Denmark, South Africa, New Zealand, and Australia, where he married Gertrud Cato. A British citizen from 1910, Kumm moved to the United States in 1914 to lead the SUM branch there.

KLAUS FIEDLER

Bibliography. G. Grattan, *Lucy Guinness Kumm, Her Life Story;* K. Kumm, *From Hausaland to Egypt through the Sudan;* P J. Spartalis and K. Kumm, *Last of the Livingstones: Pioneer Missionary Statesman.*

Kunst, Irene (1869–1934). German-born Hungarian missionary to China. Kunst was the only daughter of a marriage of German and Swedish heritage (though her parents divorced while she was a child). She came to Christ through the preaching of Andrew Moody, but her desire to join the foreign mission movement was suspended so that she could care for her blind mother.

After her mother's death in 1903, Kunst was invited by a CIM missionary to apply to the mission school at Liebenzell. She was appointed to China in 1904, and thereby became the first Hungarian woman missionary. During her first ten-year term in China, she worked at a school for the blind, becoming director of the school in 1913. Home on furlough when World War I broke out, she stayed in Budapest and ministered to Chinese refugees until 1921. During her second term, she planted and cared for eight mission stations. She died of typhoid while serving her third term.

Throughout her missionary career, Kunst fanned the flame of revival and missions commitment in Hungary. In one of her last letters she penned, "The Lord has led me in a wonderful way: I was born in Germany, Hungary became my homeland, I was newly born as a Lutheran; I wanted to go to Africa and the Lord led me to China."

A. SCOTT MOREAU

Bibliography. A. M. Kool, *God Moves in a Mysterious Way: The Hungarian Protestant Foreign Mission Movement (1756–1951).*

Kuwait (*Est. 2000 pop.: 1,818,000; 17,818 sq. km. [6,880 sq. mi.]*). Home to no indigenous Christian community after the Arab conquest of the seventh century, Kuwait was one of the cities visited by the important twentieth-century North American missionary to Muslims, SAMUEL MARINUS ZWEMER (1867–1952), of the Dutch Reformed Church in the United States, and his wife Amy Wilkes (d. 1939). Under auspices of the Arabian Mission, they first entered Kuwait in 1903. They visited on other occasions. In 1949 Zwemer spoke in Kuwait at the sixtieth anniversary of the society. He went on to other cities in the region. After a visit to the graves of missionaries and

their children, Zwemer observed, "If we should hold our peace, these very stones would cry out for evangelization of Arabia!"

Subsequently, development of the region's oil fields has attracted large numbers of Christian immigrants to Kuwait and the other Persian Gulf principalities. Eastern rite Catholics (Marconites, Melkites, Chaldeans, and others) compose the largest single Christian community, followed by various Orthodox bodies and non-Chalcedonian Christians, including Armenians and Indian Mar Thomists. After Iraq's invasion of Kuwait in 1990, many were expelled. At the time of writing, exact figures of their strength are unavailable; Christians may number over 100,000, or just over 5 percent of Kuwait's estimated 1.8 million people.

Constitutionally, Kuwait guarantees religious freedom. By implicit agreement with the Kuwaiti authorities, the Christian churches make no overt attempt to convert Muslims. Christians exercise influence through the Council of Churches of Kuwait, founded in 1960, and private schools, seven of which are under Christian management.

PAUL R. DEKAR

Bibliography. R. Betts, *Christians in the Arab East. A Political Study;* A. Horner, *A Guide to Christian Churches in the Middle East;* J. Wilson Jr., *IBMR* 10:3 (1986): 117–21.

Kuyper, Abraham (1837–1920). Dutch theologian and political leader who influenced missiological reflection. Kuyper's multifaceted life was a major influence in the political and ecclesiastical life of the Netherlands. During his first pastorate in Beesd, he moved from the theological liberalism of his university training to an orthodox Calvinism. In 1880 he founded the Free University of Amsterdam to be a center of higher education, especially for the clergy, and to be true to conservative Calvinism. He founded the Reformed Free Church of the Netherlands in 1886 and developed a Dutch neo-Calvinism. Kuyper maintained that divine sovereignty must be exercised over three realms—state, society, and church. His promotion of a "Christian democracy" immersed him in the political life of Holland, first as a member of Parliament and then as prime minister from 1901 to 1905. The Kuyperian model of integrating divine sovereignty over the three realms can be seen, for example, when as a member of Parliament he demanded, as both a statesman and a churchman, that Holland christianize its colonial holding, the Dutch West Indies, through the promotion of Christian missions, churches, and Christian schools. As a result, mission schools multiplied and Christians sought, with a measure of success, to compel the government to provide greater opportunity for missionaries and to apply the principles of the faith to the administration of the colonies.

DONALD R. DUNAVANT

Bibliography. F. Vandenberg, *Abraham Kuyper.*

Kyrgyzstan *(Est. 2000 pop.: 5,143,000; 198,500 sq. km. [76,641 sq. mi.]).* Kyrgyzstan is a mountainous Central Asian republic of the former Soviet Union, bordering China. While nearly three-quarters of the population is of Turkic origin, a sizable but shrinking Slavic minority remains. Although most Kyrgyz claim nominal allegiance to Sunni Islam, the folk Islam they practice has strongly animistic overtones. Evangelicals make up less than 0.25 percent of the population, the overwhelming majority being Slavs and Germans. Growing numbers of Kyrgyz have been coming to Christ, however, resulting in the establishment of several ethnic Kyrgyz congregations. Religious liberty has been declining, making evangelism increasingly difficult and necessitating creative strategies.

RAYMOND P. PRIGODICH

SEE ALSO Commonwealth of Independent States.

Ll

Land, Land Reform, Land Rights. The subject of land is an underrated issue in mission; it is hardly mentioned in textbooks and is largely ignored in training courses.

Historically, missionaries from the West often associated with the powerful and privileged in order to get permission to stay in a country. This agreement was often conditioned by an expectation of noninvolvement in questions of power and land ownership. The colonial mentality of missions in the early part of the twentieth century meant that missionaries were more identified with the conquerors and exploiters than the struggling classes. In the words of Desmond Tutu of South Africa: "Before the missionaries came they had the Bible and we had the land. They said 'Let us pray,' and when we opened our eyes, we had the Bible and they had the land!"

Many missions purchased land for cathedrals and churches, schools, hostels, and hospitals as the physical base to reach people. Missionary compounds, by contrast, have often been places of privacy and protection that conflict with a genuinely incarnational ministry. The need for land as a base for mission consumes energy and money. The complexities of foreigners buying land, with payoffs to power holders and traditional owners, established patterns for later dealings. Regular payments for maintenance and labor can reinforce the perception that missionary groups are powerful and patronizing.

This perception affects how the gospel is received. Land ownership by missions can contribute to a mentality that isolates national Christians from the common life of their community; to become a Christian is thus to become an alien. And when the mission passes ownership of their land to the national church, this may become a millstone around the neck, the opposite to the experience of the early church (Acts 4:34–35).

In contrast to the relative wealth of traditional missions, millions of landless people have little time to consider the gospel in their daily struggle to survive. About one out of every five human beings in the world lives in the city in significant poverty. These people are internally displaced or refugees because of regional, racial, and religious conflict, natural calamity, or the effects of industrial development, the Green Revolution, and urbanization.

One of the happiest experiences in the Old Testament was the equitable division of land within Israel, to be passed down the family line in perpetuity (Num. 26:52-56; 33:54; Ezek. 47:14). Several biblical ethicists suggest that a key human right God desires is for every household not to be permanently deprived of land.

Few evangelicals have a gospel that would resolve conflict between warring factions or resettle the homeless after a major disaster. Fewer express Good News to the poor by confronting the injustices of wealthy landowners and huge agribusiness that make peasant farmers or freeholders into day laborers on what was once their own land. Niall O'Brien calls this "land reform in reverse."

Evangelical missions have not given sufficient attention to issues of justice and righteousness as they pertain to questions about land. This is especially urgent since land reform efforts continue to fail because of the obstruction of powerful, vested interests. Even where missionary agriculturalists have made an impact working with farmers to reclaim marginalized land, the incentive to do this is restricted by the awareness that too much improvement may draw fresh interference from the rich.

Landless people in the cities are a greater challenge. They live in vulnerable places along expressways, river banks, and canals, where the "haves" would not reside. Resettlement is rarely satisfactory because it takes the urban poor away from the locations in the city where they survive on what the wealthy discard.

One recent hopeful shift in mission is the movement toward incarnation, the willingness of evangelical Christian groups to live in urban slums and shanty towns. Serving the poor by identifying in their daily struggle has brought hope that people on the margins of life can meet a Jesus who is not confined to temples made by human hands or the white washed sectors of the city.

Many tribal people groups will only be reached by the love of Christ as unresolved questions about their traditional lands are taken seriously. This, and the global increase in refugees who are landless for reasons of drought, desertification, war, or floods presents great challenges for mission in the twenty-first century.

Evangelicals need a biblical worldview that relates land rights and land reform to the Good News of God's kingdom. The drawback is that good news about land to the poor and vulnerable is often bad news to the rich and powerful.

JOHN STEWARD

Bibliography. J. Bonk, *Missions and Money;* M. Duncan, *Costly Mission;* S. Mott, *Biblical Ethics and Social Change;* N. O'Brien, *Revolution from the Heart;* H. Snyder, *Earthcurrents;* C. Wright, *Living as the People of God: An Eye for an Eye.*

Language. Learned system of arbitrary symbols (verbal or manual) used by a society to communicate and to express their identity. Language is distinctly human; animal communication systems are typically random sounds (bird calls) or set analogs (the dance of bees). Language is acquired through interaction with other people, but is based on what appear to be innate patterns in the human brain.

Language is marked by structure and pattern. Language consists of units within layers of larger units. Each language employs a small subset of the total possible sounds and combinations of sounds to create words which follow a relatively small number of phrase and clause patterns, yet is capable of expressing an infinite set of utterances. These patterns facilitate communication between speakers of the language and can aid outsiders seeking to learn a second language.

The ability to use language is common among all people and can be seen as one aspect of being created in God's image. People use language to convey, receive, and record information. Language also encodes the physical environment (Gen. 2:19) and social culture, providing important insights for mission workers. Language differences can be used to include or exclude others. Humans have typically used these distinctions for ungodly purposes (Judg. 12:5–6; 2 Kings 18:26–28; Matt. 26:73). Genesis 11 illustrates how even language unity can be misused. In Acts 2 God miraculously overcame language barriers, setting a pattern of using language as a missionary tool.

God used language in creation (Gen. 1), sent the Word to live as a human (John 1), and empowers his Word to change lives (Heb. 4:12). God revealed himself through human language and repeatedly commissioned written records of his words (Exod. 17:14; Deut. 6:9; Jer. 30:2). He inspired the authors of Scripture to preserve his message in three particular languages (Hebrew, Aramaic, Koine Greek). That God saw fit to use languages as different from each other as Hebrew and Greek demonstrates the innate ability of human language to express the essence of God's revelation. While no human words can fully describe God, God used ordinary languages to describe himself. God's use of Hebrew, Aramaic, and Greek appears to have less to do with the wonders of those particular languages than with the fact that the audience he wanted to address understood them. When people understood more than one language, God chose the language of hearth and home over that of the classroom and book learning (Acts 26:14), the language of the homeland over the language of formal religion (Acts 2:5–12). The Scriptures provide numerous instructions on the godly use of language (Exod. 20:16; Josh. 1:8; 1 Tim. 4:12–13).

There are over 6,500 distinct languages spoken in the world today, with countless more dialects of these languages. Paul used several languages in his ministry (Acts 21:37–22:1). Missionaries still need to overcome language barriers to communicate the gospel. Agencies such as the Summer Institute of Linguistics focus on the study of language and provide training to help missionaries learn and analyze languages.

PETER JAMES SILZER

SEE ALSO Linguistics; Sociolinguistics.

Bibliography. L. K. Pike, *Linguistic Concepts;* M. Silva, *God, Language and Scripture;* C. A. Wilson and D. McKeon, *The Language Gap.*

Language Learning. See SECOND LANGUAGE ACQUISITION.

Language Schools. Language schools have performed a great service to the missionary cause, facilitating many new missionaries' acquisition of language (*see* SECOND LANGUAGE ACQUISITION). Some smaller schools primarily offer access to trained tutors. Larger schools provide teachers, a curriculum, a means of evaluation of progress, and a camaraderie in the learning among the students.

In evaluating a language school, the new missionary can take into account the learning philosophy of the school, the curriculum, the training and experience of teachers, the teachers' patience and attitudes, the medium of instruction, the class size, the learning ethos, the emphasis placed on conversation and communication, the attention given to culture learning and involvement, the location of the school, the dialect being taught, the dialect commonly used in the locality of the school, the expected outcomes, the reputation of the school, the flexibility in dealing with differences in ability levels and learning styles of students, the training given to learners to enable them to continue learning independently after completion of the course, the intensity (number of contact hours, length, and extent) of the course, and the cost (tuition, books, living expenses, transportation).

In order to achieve the greatest benefit from the course, students must remain fully engaged in the learning process both in and out of the classroom. This engagement includes active participation in the classroom, willingness to try, willingness to be corrected for mistakes, discipline, and ample investment of time and energy. In addition, the learner should also regularly spend time outside the classroom relating to people in the language group. By daily involvement in the community, listening to people, and talking with them, the learner will reinforce the things learned in the classroom and make them his or her own. Immersion in the language and culture can be further enhanced by living with a local family who speak the language in their home.

The new missionary's careful attention to language learning will lay a foundation for effectiveness in ministry for years to come.

BETTY SUE BREWSTER

Bibliography. H. D. Brown, *Breaking the Language Barrier;* J. D. Brown, *The Elements of Language Curriculum: A Systematic Approach to Program Development;* E. A. Nida, *Learning a Foreign Language;* L. J. Dickerson, ed., *Helping the Missionary Language Learner Succeed—Proceedings from the International Congress on Missionary Language Learning.*

Laos *(Est. 2000 pop.: 5,602,000; 236,800 sq. km. [91,429 sq. mi.]).* Bordered by Thailand, Cambodia, Vietnam, China, and Myanmar, Laos is comprised of four major ethnolinguistic groups (*Ethnologue* lists ninety-two distinct languages). While animistic beliefs are widespread across the population, Theravada Buddhism (59%) and traditional religions (33%) dominate the overall religious adherence of the people, with Christians numbering less than 2 percent of the population. After the Communists took over with Vietnamese help in 1975, more than 10 percent fled the country to Thailand. Many of those have since emigrated to North America, Europe, Australia, or New Zealand. This former French colony (1890 to 1953) is currently governed by a single-party communist regime, the Lao People's Revolutionary Party.

Recent historical events include the killing of more than 2 million by the Khmer Rouge government under Pol Pot's leadership. As much as two-thirds of the church fled or was martyred (including more than 90% of the trained leadership). Many more have lost their faith. Even though economic restrictions have been eased

somewhat in recent years, political control remains tight and the church is closely monitored. In spite of the economic liberalization begun in 1986, the country remains one of the world's poorest, with an estimated annual income per person in 1993 of roughly $295 (though growing at almost 5% per year).

The first missionary to reach Laos was Jean deLeria, a Jesuit, who came from Cambodia in 1642. He was forced to leave after five years of work and no results. Unsuccessful attempts were made again in 1683 and 1866, but it was not until 1878 that a mission was developed in the northwest part of the country. It ended when twelve priests were martyred in 1884. From then until 1940, missionaries came from neighboring Thailand and worked in the south along the Mekong River. In 1950, owing to a general lack of success, attention was given over to tribal peoples in the mountains.

The first Protestant missionary to reach Laos was Daniel MacGilvary, a Presbyterian who made itinerant evangelistic trips from Thailand. Gabriel Contesse of the Swiss Brethren was the first Protestant missionary to settle in Laos, arriving in 1902 and concentrating his efforts in the south. After initial attempts at widespread evangelization, he and his successors changed their focus to literature development and translating the Bible into Lao, which was completed in 1932. G. Edward Roffe of THE CHRISTIAN AND MISSIONARY ALLIANCE arrived in 1929, focusing his efforts largely in the north. A dramatic people movement took place there in 1950 when a thousand Meo, a northern hill people, came to Christ over a period of several weeks. This laid the foundation for what became the Evangelical Church of Laos, the largest Protestant denomination in the country. OMF missionaries arrived in 1957 and worked alongside the Swiss Brethren. Though Protestants generally have had limited success among the majority Lao people, they have seen results from working with the refugees who were forced to flee in the face of the genocidal persecution of the mid-1970s.

EDITORS

Bibliography. D. Barrett, *WCE;* H. Cordell, *Laos;* P. Johnstone, *OW;* G. E. Roffe, *The Church in Asia,* pp. 391–409; H. Toye, *Laos: Buffer State or Battleground.*

Las Casas, Bartholmew de (1474–1566). Spanish missionary to Latin America. The son of a merchant who had traveled on Columbus's second voyage, Las Casas himself arrived in the Caribbean in 1502 and after a return to Spain and further studies, was ordained in 1507. Initially serving as an *encomendero* (recipient of a grant which gave control over Indians who were to provide labor and goods in exchange for protection and religious instruction) in Spain's colonial encomienda system, a conversion experience in August of 1514 led him to work for reform. Freeing his own slaves, he returned to Spain in 1515 to advocate for the Indians. He then launched a lifetime of attempts to initiate projects which would foster peaceful colonization, with varying success. He joined the Dominican Order in 1523.

His projects mostly met with opposition and failure, but his powerful and fertile writings were far more successful and the chief source of lasting influence. His thinking shaped the papal bull *Sublimis Deus* (1537), which recognized the Indians as rational beings with the same rights as Europeans. He also played a key role in the development and passing of a set of laws in 1542 which, among other things, limited the power of the encomenderos and prohibited slavery of the indigenes.

After retirement and final return to Spain in 1547, Las Casas engaged in major debates with Juan Ginés de Sepúlveda over the legitimacy of the Spanish conquests in the New World (1550–51). One of his most significant contributions was in developing the discussion on what would become the contemporary concept of HUMAN RIGHTS.

A. SCOTT MOREAU

Bibliography. G. Gutiérrez, *Las Casas: In Search of the Poor of Jesus Christ;* J. Klaiber, *BDCM*, p. 384; H. R. Parish and H. R. Wagner, *The Life and Writings of Bartolomé de las Casas;* A. Saint-Lu, *NCE*, 8:394-5.

Latin America. This continent must be studied in light of its unique geography, historical development, peoples, religions, and cultures, as well as its current, changing social environment. Only from that perspective can one fully understand the Latin spiritual mosaic, in particular, its vibrant evangelical Christianity. Latin America is very diverse, with each country displaying its own unique features.

Geography and Population. Latin America (Spanish- and Portuguese-speaking) is composed of nineteen nations, having 15 percent of the world's land mass and about 8 percent of the global population. Starting with Mexico's northern border, one travels 7,000 miles down to the bottom tip of Chile, just north of Antarctica, and at its widest 3,200 miles from Peru's Pacific coast eastward through Brazil to the Atlantic. Two of the nineteen countries are found in the Caribbean (Cuba and the Dominican Republic), while the other island nations enjoy their different heritages—English, French, and African. Puerto Rico is a North American Commonwealth island, and while it shares many historical, religious, and cultural values with the other nations it must be studied within its own Caribbean and U.S. realities. On the northern flank of South America are two na-

tions that identify more with the CARIBBEAN—Suriname, Guyana, and the French colony, Guyane.

The races and peoples within each country are also very diverse. The original tribal peoples whom the Europeans met over 500 years ago still compose a significant percentage of the population. Called "Indians" (so named by mistake, because Columbus concluded erroneously that he had arrived in India) pre-Columbian (before Columbus) peoples are found primarily in Mexico (11% of 102 million people), Guatemala (50% of 12.2 million), Peru (45% of 26 million), Ecuador (21% of 12.6 million), Bolivia (55% of 8.3 million), and Chile (9% of 15.3 million). The black people (originally coming as African slaves and later as Caribbean immigrants) form a significant percentage of Latin America, particularly in the Caribbean and in a "black ribbon" on the Pacific Ocean coast, as well as in Brazil (6% black and 38% mulatto). People of pure European and Asian blood live in all the nations. However, most of the population is a mixture of the races, called "mestizos."

Over 160 million Brazilians speak Portuguese, a result of the colonization by Portugal. Most of the remainder of 312 million people in the other eighteen nations speak Spanish, either as mother or trade tongue. But millions of Latin American pre-Columbian peoples also speak their historic language.

Latin America's population is growing at the annual rate of 1.8 percent per year, and will double in 38 years. By the year 2010 it is projected to have some 589 million people and by the year 2025 the estimate surges to 691. In 1997, 72 percent of the continent was considered urban; 34 percent under the ages of 15 years and only 5 percent over age 65. It is helpful to compare Latin America's annual GNP of $3,310 to that of the less developed world ($1,120), the more developed world ($19,310), and the entire world ($4,920).

A Historical Panorama. Modern Latin America must be understood from the perspective of its particular history and its four major time segments: (1) pre-Columbian times (ancient past to 1492); (2) the conquest and colonization (1492–1821); (3) the genesis and crisis of the new nations (1821–1930); and (4) the modern period (1930–92).

The demarcation date for the mutual discovery is 1492, when the Latin/European history begins in this newly discovered (for the Europeans) world. Evidence points to a crossing of the Bering straits some time prior to 20,000 B.C., and gradually the population moved down the continent. Vast civilizations had come and gone by the time Columbus landed, but in 1492 three major ones remained: the Aztecs in Central Mexico, the Maya in southern Mexico and Guatemala, and the Inca in the Andean region. Estimates of the

Indian population in 1492 range widely between 15 million to an unrealistic 100 million.

The colonial history produced a mixed legacy. On the positive side the Europeans brought a system of education; they introduced new technology; they transferred two major languages—Spanish and Portuguese; they "evangelized" bringing a new religion—Roman Catholic Christianity; they introduced an entire social structure to organize and expand Spanish culture and society. On the negative side, the Spanish have been criticized severely for social and cultural evils inherent in the conquest and colonization. Europeans delivered diseases against which the Indians were defenseless and which killed millions, and brutal slave labor wiped out uncounted numbers. Early on there was a battle to determine whether these "primitive peoples" had souls or not. If not, then they were a higher level of animals for slave work. In Mexico alone, one estimate states that the Indian population dropped from 16,871,408 to 1,069,255 between 1532 and 1608. A few valiant priests defended the Indians, such as BARTHOLOMEW DE LAS CASAS, who battled until the Indians were declared to be human. Unfortunately, this humanity did not extend to Africans, who were then imported as slaves to work the colonial economy.

Following independence from both Spain (between 1820 and 1821) and Portugal (independence in 1822; with Brazil becoming a federal republic in 1889), the new nations struggled for viability and political/economic development from 1824 to 1880. It was relatively easy to defeat Spain and gain autonomy, but nearly impossible to organize and administrate stable republics. The map was redrawn, but the nations were in crisis, with political foundations unprepared for Western democracy. Into that leadership/power vacuum emerged the dictators, who took personal charge of their nations from the early nineteenth century even into the mid-twentieth century.

The 1880–1930 period was marked by relative peace and limited national development, with social positivism experiments (Brazil and Mexico are case studies) with its "scientific technocracy." National infrastructure was developed, the armies grew stronger, and central governmental control extended. During this period the controversial role of the United States emerged as the Western Hemisphere's superpower—generating an ongoing love–hate relationship between Latin America and the United States.

The modern period, starting in 1930, gradually increased social and political stability. During the 1960s and 1970s the right-wing military controlled most of the nations, with democracy fading even as violence and poverty increased. Fundamental political and economic structures did not begin to change substantially until the late 1980s and into the 1990s. By 1995, all but one country (Cuba) had voted for some form of democratically elected government. The 1990 collapse of Russian and European Marxism robbed the intellectual left of socialist/Marxist political models, which contributed to the 1990 electoral defeat of the Nicaraguan Sandinistas. Peace accords have been signed in El Salvador and Guatemala, and political stability has even opened space for former Marxists to run for and win public office.

Much faith continues to be placed in the hands of the new political technocrats, the market economy, privatization, microeconomic development, and growing stability of trade agreements within Latin America as well as with the United States and Pacific Rim nations. The military have currently retreated to their barracks. But dark signs loom over the continent: endemic corruption, the violent drug industry, political systems drastically needing overhaul, the uncontrolled growth of poverty, the breakdown of the family, and the fragmentation of fragile human social systems. The privatization of former state industries is creating immediate high unemployment, as are the cuts in traditional social programs and services. New liberationists and leftist intellectuals severely criticize the extremes of this "neo-liberalism."

The Spiritual Mosaic. Latin America is historically and nominally Roman Catholic and Rome still considers Latin America within its religious world, which in 1900 was almost entirely Catholic. The continent has a general concept of God and the Bible, of the Virgin Mary, and of Jesus Christ (particularly his passion story). With certain notable exceptions, such as Uruguay and Argentina, Latin America is God-conscious and favorable to Christianity in the broad sense of the word.

However, probing deeper into the worldview, most Latins are presuppositionally spiritistic. This is particularly true of the pre-Columbian peoples, who for centuries worshiped their nature gods. Even with nominal conversion to Catholicism, their basic WORLDVIEW is spirit-controlled. Africa-originated spiritism is widespread, but in particular most visible in the Macumba and Umbanda cults of Brazil (*see also* LATIN AMERICAN NEW RELIGIOUS MOVEMENTS). Some 35% of Brazilians are active spiritists, and partial practitioners raise that population to 60%. Whether they come from the lowest social class or the movie stars or leading politicians, spiritism attracts Brazilians. Anyone in Latin American Christian ministry must understand this worldview and be equipped to minister in the context of POWER ENCOUNTER—both evil and Triune God-provided.

Another aspect of the cultural and spiritual mosaic is the continental spirit of "Indianism," currently on a continental rise. On the positive ledger, it celebrates the God-given values and cultures of these pre-Columbian peoples, recognizing their ethnic riches as well as their economic and political power in partial counteraction to centuries of abuse. Yet there are warning signs also, particularly the revival of traditional spiritism and pre-Columbian nature-worshiping religions.

Contemporary Latin Catholicism reveals a broad diversity of streams: the historic, traditional sacramentalist, hierarchy-ruled, in some nations allied with the oligarchy; a progressive wing with socialist to Marxist sympathies, attempting to articulate a new theology of liberation; a biblical studies circle that has generated solid Scripture resources; the charismatic "renewed" Catholics (many drawn back into Catholic mysticism but others still related to charismatic evangelicals); the large majority of Catholics who would practice some form of popular religiosity, converging traditions, personal emotions, and syncretistic folk religious practices; nominal Catholics who are simply that because of family tradition but the underlying value system is secular. Many evangelicals have interfaced with the more biblical and charismatic sectors. Liberation theology was primarily conceived, birthed, and given life within Latin Catholicism, generating a vast amount of publications and influencing global theology. Since the collapse of Russian and European Marxism, liberation theology is a movement seeking new articulation. Evangelicals would be wrong to dismiss it, for as long as a majority of people live in poverty, Christians of all stripes will attempt to speak for the poor.

Latin Catholic leaders are grappling with the new rules on an open religious playing field, a new experience for them. While Catholicism in Europe and North America has lively religious pluralism, this is not yet the case in Latin America. Pope John Paul II has made twelve trips to the region, has labeled evangelicals as "sects," and has challenged his Church to affirm Catholic doctrine and reevangelize the continent.

The Evangelicals. The Protestant gospel arrived in Latin America in five movements. The first wave came with the new settlers in the early nineteenth century from northern Europe: Germany, Holland, France, and Britain. A short-lived Lutheran Welser colony settled in Venezuela from 1528 to 1546, and French Huguenots tried to establish from 1555 to 1557 a Brazilian base. These colonists brought their Protestant faith, but largely kept it to themselves, and tended to worship in their European language within the immigrant and trade communities. Even some "Protestant pirates" got involved and helped settle what became the three Guianas. Early in the nineteenth century Moravians immigrated to this New World and established churches and communities. We honor the great Bible colporteurs, such as JAMES DIEGO THOMSON, Joseph Monguiardino, and FRANCISCO PENZOTTI, agents of the British and American Bible Societies, for their unique ministry, which for some meant MARTYRDOM.

The second wave began in the early to mid-nineteenth century, when the major denominations from Britain and the United States established churches and educational/social institutions throughout the continent. During this period the Latin political context was changing, the religious influence of Spain diminishing, and commerce with England and northern Europe growing stronger. All of this favored a new religious opening, though in some countries persecution was experienced.

Europeans focused primarily on the Southern Cone nations, but the United States denominations spread throughout the region. Early on the COMITY agreements guided territorial expansion. Churches were established in every country. However, some of these denominations gradually developed a primary social and educational emphasis, and today these historic denominations represent classic Latin Protestantism, but their churches are not growing.

The third wave came with the arrival of North American and European FAITH MISSIONS. Even D. L. MOODY and Ira Sankey ministered in Mexico City in 1894. These new societies sent thousands of cross-cultural missionaries with evangelistic and church-planting passion as early as 1890; Bible institutes were started to train pastors and evangelists; Christian radio and publishing ministries expanded. The churches grew with vibrancy in almost every nation, and today they represent the majority of non-Pentecostal/charismatic evangelicals on the continent.

The fourth wave came shortly after the Asuza Street Revival (1906), for inherent in that Spirit movement was its empowered commitment to world evangelization with new distinctives. Pentecostal denominations arrived and grew, and some of the historic churches were swept into these new movements—Chilean Methodists split and the Methodist Pentecostal Church of Chile was formed. Every Pentecostal denomination in the United States established its Latin counterpart, although some of them may now be larger than the "parent" body. In Brazil alone there are over 15 million affiliated with the Assemblies of God.

Today we witness the fifth wave of Latin American evangelical, autochthonous churches. A good number are massive, but most are smaller in size. They are autonomous, contextualizing theology and missiology, with most forming their own national and international denominations. It might be safe to estimate that they represent 30 percent of all Latin evangelical churches. In Mexico City they represent 55 percent of the churches, in Lima 37 percent, and in Guatemala 25 percent of all churches. Mostly independent Neo-Pentecostal (charismatic) churches, they are generally led by strong centralizing leaders who have emerged from the ranks of committed laity. The focus is on emotional, celebratory worship and preaching, with a strong emphasis on evangelism and church planting even beyond national borders. They have been charged with being a Protestant version of Latin popular religiosity. Undoubtedly, they challenge all other variants of Latin evangelicalism.

Growth in Numbers. How much have Latin American evangelical-Protestant churches grown in recent years? One measure comes from comparing data in the 1993 edition of Patrick Johnstone's *Operation World* with those from the 1986 edition. But it is impossible to justify all terms and statistics. Essentially the Protestant churches have grown from a total community of roughly 50,000 in 1900 to an estimated 64 million in 1997 (see also Núñez and Taylor).

Data from 1993 reveal the diversity of evangelical strength in these 19 nations, with numbers in percentage of total population: Argentina, 7.5 percent; Bolivia, 8.5 percent; Brazil, 18.9 percent; Chile, 27.1 percent; Colombia, 3.4 percent; Costa Rica, 9.8 percent; Cuba, 2.7 percent; Dominican Republic, 5.8 percent; Ecuador, 3.7 percent; El Salvador, 20.8 percent; Guatemala, 22.1 percent; Honduras, 10.1 percent; Mexico, 5.1 percent; Nicaragua, 16.3 percent; Panama, 16.1 percent; Paraguay, 5.5 percent; Peru, 6.8 percent; Uruguay, 3.5 percent; Venezuela, 5.1 percent. For the continent the total is 11.1 percent. Using the 1997 population total of 472 million, the estimated 15 percent of evangelicals generates a force of some 64 million believers.

A measured guess suggests there are some 300,000 evangelical churches in Latin America. Perhaps only 25 percent of them have a formally trained pastor-leader. Some 75 percent of the churches are Pentecostal-charismatic, and 25 percent non-Pentecostal/charismatic. But churches of both categories are growing as long as they evangelize actively. The largest percentages of evangelical populations are found in Guatemala, Chile, Brazil, and El Salvador; the lowest in Mexico, Colombia, Cuba, Ecuador, Uruguay, and Paraguay.

Some Clarifying Items Regarding Religious Terminology. In Latin America the words "Protestant" and "evangelical" are generally used interchangeably, with preference for the latter. The terms "Pentecostal" and "charismatic" sometimes describe the same reality, but at other times "Pentecostal" is used more of the older denominations, like Assemblies of God or Church of God. "Charismatic" has a broad use that runs from Spirit-filled Catholics to independent churches of Pentecostal persuasion. Perhaps 75 percent of all Latin evangelicals would consider themselves charismatic or Pentecostal. But all Latin charismatics consider themselves also "evangélicos!" The concept of "renewal" or of a "renewed church" seems to apply to the charismatic theology and practice that is moving through non-Pentecostal denominations—

such as Baptist, Methodist, Brethren, and independent non-Pentecostal. It is fair to state that Latin evangelical churches characterized as "practicing supernaturalists" are the ones demonstrating growth and vibrancy. Their worship is strong, utilizing the spectrum of instruments, with words and music now primarily written by Latins.

Whither Latin American Evangelicals? This is a unique continent-wide moment for Latin evangelicals, attempting to speak for transcendental absolutes in a world of RELATIVISM, political neoliberalism, philosophical POSTMODERNISM, and moral deconstructionism. While Latin evangelical leaders rejoice in their numerical growth, they also express profound concern about its health, citing shallow ethical depth, the moral relativism, the emphasis on emotional celebration more than authentic community, and the growth of biblical illiteracy in both pew and pulpit with devalued biblical study and exposition. Here is a series of issues in dialectical tension that will mark the future of Latin evangelicals.

First, the battle between profound renewal and maturity versus nominalism and cultural evangelicalism. Numerical growth is thrilling to many, encouraging to all, even though statistics are imprecise. But the hard questions must be asked: "What is church?" "What is growth?" "What about the problem of 'former evangelicals'?" Internal weaknesses and open heresies—from other regions as well as Latin species—seep into the churches and sap their vitality. The churches must face head-on the crisis of the disintegrating Latin family structure and articulate better answers in light of urbanism and modern lifestyles. The Spirit of God must renew stagnant evangelical churches. Studies in Costa Rica and Chile have documented the disturbing percentage of "former evangelicals." Some have returned to the Catholic fold and others have moved into privatized religion or even nonbelief.

Second, the struggle between evangelical mutual acceptance and interdependency versus isolationism and critical divisionism. A limited sense of unity in the Latin churches is manifested locally, nationally, and continentally. Whether subtle or open, it pits Pentecostal against Pentecostal, charismatic against charismatic, Pentecostal against charismatic, and non-Pentecostal versus charismatic, non-Pentecostal against non-Pentecostal, traditional denomination against Third Wave church. CONELA (The WORLD EVANGELICAL FELLOWSHIP related regional body) has the potential to unite evangelicals on a continental basis, but it awaits visionary leadership that understands the nature and influence of national and regional fellowships and will provide crucial services to the churches. Meanwhile, a few national movements will increasingly and effectively impact their nations.

Third, the tension between relevancy and biblical CONTEXTUALIZATION versus the superspiritualization of the faith. A hermeneutical struggle is found in every Christian community: How is Scripture to be applied and experienced in a radically changing Latin American society? Christians must be equipped to face the insidious enemies filtering in through SECULARISM (the rejection of a theistic point of reference); materialism (consumer society and massive debt); MODERNITY (glorification of technology and "progress"); and now the surprisingly rapid invasion of postmodernity with its deconstructionist influences (questioning of technology and "progress," the newer religious pluralism, rejection of transcendental truth).

Latin theological leaders, pastors, and those preparing for ministry must be equipped for the challenge of ongoing contextualization in light of historical needs and the new ideological face of Latin America. The Latin American Theological Fraternity has done a valiant job in this area. All leaders and believers must be equipped to confront the evil powers of the occult, so openly and influentially influencing the entire spectrum of society.

Fourth is the effective equipping of leadership for ministry versus informal volunteerism. Most Latin formal educational delivery systems are costly to create, fund, staff, and produce graduates. They do have their strategic place but need serious self-examination. Few formal institutions offer program degrees beyond the master's degree. Most Latins travel to the United States or Europe for doctoral study. In this critical time for the Latin churches, women and men with the highest credentials and strongest gift mix are needed. Formal schools serve a very small segment of church needs, and in the gap more and more smaller programs or training alternatives are emerging. There are two major entry points to ministry in Latin America; one coming through formal theological study and the other emerging "on the march" of regular lay ministry. How these two currents relate to and influence each other in the future will profoundly shape the Latin churches.

The fifth tension is the involvement in the crises of society and political governance versus forms of spiritualized isolationism. For decades evangelicals eschewed political involvement as part of the devil's work. This has radically changed, with a number of evangelicals now in the political arena. But the jury is mixed on this involvement, for some Christian politicians have sold their integrity and yet crassly serve their denominational interests. Some Latins want to establish evangelical parties, though these have no hope of winning elections. Too many evangelicals in politics are naive, have been manipulated, or lost their spiritual convictions while in power. In part this has come from the absence of spiritual accountability as well as inadequate pastoral ministry to public servants.

Sixth is the polarized polemics between Catholics and evangelicals versus mutual respect. Catholic leaders know they are losing influence and space in Latin America, and this has created an internal crisis for the hierarchy. The Roman Church is adjusting to the new religious pluralism. And some evangelicals still suffer from the ghetto mentality of a persecuted minority. But the fact is that evangelicals are still being persecuted for their faith, whether the Chamula Indians of southern Mexico (religious persecution) or the Quechua believers in Peru (political persecution). The spiritual/social value called *hispanidad* (which identifies Latins intrinsically as Catholics) has created other conflicts on the continent.

North Europeans and North Americans must not confuse their Catholicism with that of Latin America. These are two different models, and to impose experience and expectations of the first upon Latin evangelicals is wrong.

Seventh is the tension between monocultural evangelization versus cross-cultural mission, whether national or international, continental or intercontinental. The number of evangelical churches with cross-cultural vision is still low. This must change as they are challenged biblically and then mobilized to broader mission. In Latin America, church-based missions will continue to carry the day, but leaders must break old molds and attitudes. Missiological literature must be developed by Latin writers and theologians, as well as by the practitioners.

Latin-driven movements and organizations, such as COMIBAM (Cooperation of Missions of Iberoamerica), must be supported as they mobilize beyond emotionalism and create the imperative missions infrastructure for the movement to be truly visible and viable. This challenge focuses on three areas: the precandidate phase of screening, primarily by the local church; the prefield training (informal and formal) phase; and the field ministry phase, which requires adequate supervision, shepherding, and strategizing.

Eighth, and finally, is the spirit of interdependent partnership versus control and neopaternalism by expatriate organizations. Many international organizations have vested interests in Latin America, whether they be funding bodies, denominations, parachurch organizations, or foreign mission agencies. Control must pass to Latin grassroots, and decisions must be made by those directly affected by the decisions. On the continent more and more expatriate missionaries serve under Latin leadership. Expatriate missionaries from all nations continue to be welcomed, provided they come with the genuine spirit of servanthood and serve where they are truly needed in light of global missiological priorities. The fact is that many international mission organizations are searching for their identity and role in Latin America today, particularly with the emphasis on the non-Latin unevangelized nations and people groups.

Summarizing. Latin America is a multihued continent facing an uncertain future in the global and borderless economy. Its God-given vast natural and human resources have yet to be developed and wisely utilized, although political conditions are healthier today than ever before. National, regional, and continental development will take place as genuine political reform is institutionalized in a way that truly grapples with the causes and characteristics of an ever-prevalent poverty and social crises. Within this textured context we find the evangelical churches and leadership facing unique challenges, and empowered by the Spirit they will impact their world.

WILLIAM DAVID TAYLOR

Bibliography. M. Berg and P. Pretiz, *Spontaneous Combustion: Grass-Roots Christianity Latin American Style;* E. L. Cleary, and H. Stewart-Gambino, eds., *Conflict and Competition: The Latin American Church in a Changing Environment;* E. Dussell, ed., *The Church in Latin America, 1492–1992;* The Economist Intelligence Unit, *Economist Country Profiles;* G. Gustavo, *A Theology of Liberation: History, Politics and Salvation;* rev. ed. P. Johnstone, *OW;* D. Martin, *Tongues of Fire: The Explosion of Protestantism in Latin America;* E. A. Núñez and W. D. Taylor, *Crisis and Hope in Latin America: An Evangelical Perspective,* rev. ed.; D. Stoll, and V. Barrard-Burnett, eds., *Rethinking Protestantism in Latin America.*

Latin American Mission Boards and Societies.

Very early after the arrival of evangelicals in Latin America a missionary impulse among Latin Americans took them as missionaries to remote areas of their countries as well as to other countries and continents. The roots of missionary work in pietist and revivalist movements emphasized the priesthood of all believers and created structures that facilitated it, in open contrast to the priest-centered life of predominant Roman Catholicism. There are records of spontaneous missionary activity of Chileans from the Methodist Pentecostal revival of 1911, going as missionaries to Argentina beginning in 1925. Argentinean Baptists sent Maximino Fernández as a missionary to start work in Paraguay in 1919. Puerto Rican Baptists sent Santiago Soto-Fontánez as a missionary to El Salvador, and Eduardo Carlos Pereyra from Brazil crusaded for the cause of missions among Presbyterians in his country. These cases are examples of two missionary patterns that originated in Latin America. First, the migration pattern to and from neighboring countries became a vehicle used by tentmakers as a way of carrying on missionary work. This has developed significantly in recent years, when for political or economic reasons thousands of Latin Americans have emigrated to North America, Europe, and Australia, or have gone as technicians and professionals to work in the Muslim world. There are thousands of evangelicals from Latin America working in Japan, many of whom get involved as missionary volunteers in that country. Second, organized denominational mission boards following the model of North American missions developed especially in Argentina, Puerto Rico, Mexico, and Brazil. Mainly denominations that were financially strong and well organized have managed to continue this model.

After World War II, a large number of conservative evangelical faith missions came to Latin America and some of them created a third pattern for the channeling of missionary vocations among Latin Americans. Organizations such as the Latin America Mission, Wycliffe Bible Translators, Operation Mobilization, and Youth with a Mission incorporated Latin Americans into their international mission force, generally relying on North American or European funds and leadership. Student movements associated with the International Fellowship of Evangelical Students (IFES) pioneered missionary conventions to challenge students to become involved in missions in their own countries or abroad. The First Latin American Missionary Congress gathered five hundred university students and graduates from all over Latin America in Curitiba, Brazil, in January 1976. Sponsored by the IFES related *Alianza Bíblica Universitaria do Brasil* (Inter Varsity of Brazil), this congress produced the "*Declaracao de Curitiba*" (a missiological manifesto) and several of the participants volunteered for missionary service in rural Latin America, Angola, and Italy. Operation Mobilization was also active in providing vision and missionary education to Latin American young people, recruiting selected volunteers for work and travel in the ships *Doulos* and *Logos.* Mexican university graduates related to these movements started "*Proyecto Magreb,*" later on "PM International," to reach the Muslim world from a base in Spain. In July 1987, several organizations and individuals sponsored COMIBAM in São Paulo, Brazil. COMIBAM and the Latin American Theological Fraternity are working successfully to bring missiological components into theological education. Even churches and countries that went through critical days because of political violence have been the source of a missionary thrust such as AMEN (Evangelical Association for Mission to the Nations) in Peru, an indigenous faith mission that sent missionaries to England and France in the 1970s and used "Kerygma"—a folk music team—to generate interest and funds for their venture. Indigenous sending agencies have also developed in Costa Rica and Guatemala. In this fourth pattern, leadership, funding, and management is entirely in Latin American hands though funds may also be raised from churches planted by its missionaries in North America and Europe. There are an increasing number of Latin American missionaries going to Spain either to work there or to use it as a base and training ground to prepare missionaries to Muslim countries of North Africa and Central Asia. Research completed in late 1977 shows a total of four hundred Latin American mission sending agencies and approximately four thousand missionaries.

In recent years Roman Catholics have intensified the promotion of missionary vocations through Missionary Congresses that meet every other year. This has been coordinated by DEMIS, the Missions Department of the Conference of Latin American Bishops (CELAM). Among Catholic missiologists there is concern because while almost 50 percent of the Catholics of the world live in Latin America, only 2 percent of their total missionary force comes from that region. The Comboni order from Italy has been the most active in missionary education and promotion. Some of the problems of channeling missionary fervor into action that Protestants face are solved among Catholics through the traditional missionary orders such as Jesuits, Franciscans, and Dominicans. These are truly international in membership, leadership, and fund raising, and facilitate the inclusion of Latin Americans in their ranks, in order to do missionary work in other parts of the world.

SAMUEL ESCOBAR

Bibliography. W. D. Taylor, ed., *Internationalizing Missionary Training*; J. D. Woodberry, C. Van Engen, and E. J. Elliston, eds., *Missiological Education for the 21st Century.*

Latin American New Religious Movements.

Across Latin America widely diverse religious groups have proliferated over the past century. In addition to the significant growth of evangelical and Pentecostal forms of Christianity, there has also been substantial non-Christian or syncretistic religious renewal in three forms: (1) the resurgence in popularity of indigenous religions, (2) the incursion of North American cults into Latin contexts (e.g., MORMONS and JEHOVAH'S WITNESSES), and (3) the rise of syncretistic spiritualist groups. It is the final form which is most important in terms of NEW RELIGIOUS MOVEMENTS in Latin America, encompassing the greatest number of people and ranging from Afro-Cuban Akabua and Santería to Brazilian KARDECISM and Umbanda. There are parallel movements in the Caribbean such as Trinidadian Shango, Haitian Voodoo (or vodun), and Jamaican Rastafarianism (*see* CARIBBEAN NEW RELIGIOUS MOVEMENTS). Typical of each is the amalgamation of beliefs and practices from indigenous American, African, and European spiritistic belief systems.

The African Influence. Though pervasive among the spiritistic groups, in many cases the African influence on Latin American religion is subtle and African rites and symbols are usually combined with other belief systems. The disruption brought about by the slave trade, the trauma of abuse, and the lack of written religious doctrinal systems resulted in many of the African populations dislocated into Latin contexts borrowing from other cultures and adding new religious practices as a means of dealing with their overwhelming and tragic circumstances. So it comes as no surprise that in the new world, both Christian (Protestant and Roman Catholic) and indigenous American religious practices would to varying degrees be amalgamated with their own, seen in such systems as Kardecism and Santería and the pervasiveness of mediums, shamans, and priests across the various groups.

On a country by country basis, by far the greatest impact of African religion is found in Brazil. The earliest Afro-Brazilian movements to be identified were the Candomblé in the northeast and the Macumba in the southeast. More recently groups known as Xangô, Tambor de Mina, and Nagô in the northeast, and Pajelança, Catimbó, and Batuque in the northeastern and central regions have been described. All exhibit particular cultural traditions which indicate that they started with African slaves brought into local settings.

Details of the origin and development of the Afro derived groups are typically scarce but they have some elements in common. Cultic rituals are performed at centers named after West African deities. There is typically a hierarchical structure with an "overseer" who has authority over the others. Mediums consecrated to the deities offer assistance to those who need help from the deity. This help sometimes involves POSSESSION PHENOMENA and rituals. Finally, animal sacrifices are performed in some of the groups.

Examples of Significant Spiritistic Movements. While a large number of the newer spiritistic religious movements exist in Latin America, four may be noted as examples: Abakua, Santería, Candomblé, and Umbanda (the latter two under the umbrella term Macumba). In most of these groups the members consider themselves Christians. Their syncretistic approach allows them to keep their feet planted in two worlds: Christian teachings meet their ultimate concerns, while spiritistic practices are geared to meet the daily realities of life (both achieving success and warding off disasters).

Abakua is one of four main African-derived Cuban movements (others are Santería, Mayombe, and Regla de Arara). It originated in 1834 and is named after its founder. Adherents follow patterns of secret societies, with two main branches (one of which excludes Caucasians from membership). Elements derived from Yoruban tradition include possession dances; Christian elements include crucifixes and pictures of Christ and Mary. Abakua influence has spread through Cuban emigration to Miami and New York City.

Santería (or *Lucumí*) originated in Cuba and has spread widely among Hispanic populations in Miami, New York, and Los Angeles. It is yet another example of the blend of Christianity and West African religions, along with recognition of a supreme being which embraces belief in a multitude of *lower* saints or spirits who interact with humans. Santería is well known for its emphasis on magic. Rhythmic drumming, possession phenomena, divination, and animal sacrifices characterize the religious ceremonies.

Macumba is a cover term used for two Brazilian spiritistic movements, Candomblé and Umbanda. Both can trace their origin from African slaves brought into Brazil in the 1550s. Candomblé is the largest of the Macumba cults, a secretive combination of Yoruban religious tradition, Roman Catholicism, and European culture. Patterned in fashion similar to many Latin American movements, Candomblé includes lengthy initiation rites involving animal sacrifice, possession phenomena, and appeals to the spirits *(orixa)* for protection and retribution against one's enemies. It is especially prominent in the Brazilian state of Bahia.

Umbanda is the most widespread form of spiritism and has its largest membership in Brazil. It arose in Rio de Janeiro in the 1920s and spread quickly throughout the country. There is no official organization to join and most Umbandists consider themselves members of the Roman Catholic Church in good standing. Catholic saints are given the names of African deities so an outsider cannot know if an adherent is praying to the saint or the African deity. The movement is actively opposed by the Church.

Missiological Implications. Since many of the followers of Latin American spiritistic religious movements consider themselves Christians, reaching them for Christ is a complex process. Helping them see the implications of Christ's lordship over the spirit realm and finding new ways to deal with oppressive circumstances in life is difficult at best, and simplistic solutions which deny the power of their spiritistic practices will only continue to keep such practices underground. The sensitive missionary will work to understand the role of the spiritistic practices in meeting the social, physical, emotional, and religious needs of the adherents. As a result, he or she will attend not only to issues of ultimacy but also to the pragmatic issues of daily living in helping believers engage Christ's power over all areas of life.

EDITORS

Bibliography. R. Bastide, *The African Religions of Brazil;* C. L. Berg and P. E. Pretiz, *The Gospel People of Latin America;* J. J. Considine, M.M., *The Religious Dimension in the New Latin America;* Y. Maggie, *ER,* 1:102–5; E. Nida, *PA* 13:4 (1966): 133–38; W. R. Read, V. M. Monterroso, S. Rostas, and A. Droogers, eds., *The Popular Use of Popular Religion in Latin America;* G. E. Simpson, *Black Religions in the New World;* L. E. Sullivan, *Icanchu's Drum;* H. W. Turner, *Bibliography of New Religious Movements in Primal Societies,* vol. 5, *Latin America.*

Latourette, Kenneth Scott (1884–1968). American church historian of global Christianity and missionary to China. Born in Oregon City, Oregon, Latourette received his B.A. and Ph.D. from Yale University. While at Yale he joined the STUDENT VOLUNTEER MOVEMENT and the Yale Mission, to which he committed himself for missionary service in China. He served in China from 1910 until 1912, at which time he was invalided home. After teaching at Reed College and Denison College, Latourette returned to Yale in 1921, succeeding H. P. BEACH as the D. Willis James Professor of Missions. He served Yale over the next thirty-two years, retiring in 1953.

Among his many professional activities Latourette served as president of the American Society of Church History, the American Historical Association, the American Baptist Convention, and the Association for Asian Studies. Additionally, he was an active participant in ecumenical affairs.

Latourette's greatest legacy was a single idea, controversial at the time, that Christianity was a multicultural global movement continuing to grow and expand in the midst of the secularism of the modern world. Latourette was a pioneer of a truly global approach to church history. He sought to develop his ideas in a series of publications. His three hundred articles and thirty books, including two multivolume histories, established Latourette as one of the most prolific church and mission historians of the twentieth century.

MARK SHAW

Bibliography. W. R. Hogg, *ML,* pp. 416–27; K. S. Latourette, *The History of Christian Missions in China;* idem, *History of the Expansion of Christianity,* 7 vols.; idem, *Beyond the Ranges: An Autobiography.*

Latvia (*Est. 2000 pop.: 2,471,000; 64,600 sq. km. [24,942 sq. mi.].*). Commanding a major East–West trade route, the Indo-European Latvians have been a target of numerous conquering armies. Medieval Germans built the Hanseatic city of Riga on the Dvina River. Christianity came with the Germans, but probably did not reach the peasants until eighteenth-century Herrnhut revivals. Twentieth-century Soviet policies made Latvia a Soviet military center, bringing severe persecution to many evangelicals. Independence (1991) has opened new doors but also brought considerable challenges to modernize industry, the economy, and the church.

STEVEN J. PIERSON

SEE ALSO Baltic States.

Bibliography. A. Lieven, *The Baltic Revolution: Estonia, Latvia, Lithuania and the Path to Independence;* V. Mezezers, *The Herrnhuterian Pietism in the Baltic: And Its Outreach into America and Elsewhere in the World.*

Laubach, Frank Charles (1884–1970). American literacy pioneer and missionary to the Philippines. Born on September 2, 1884, in Benton, Pennsylvania, Laubach was baptized as a Methodist at age ten. He was educated at Princeton University and Union Theological Seminary, and in 1915 graduated from Columbia University with a Ph.D. in sociology. Ordained as a Congregationalist minister, Laubach then served as a missionary to the Philippines from 1915 to 1931. In 1929 he experienced a spiritual recommitment which led to a keen interest in evangelizing the Islamic Moro people of Mindanao.

Laubach is best known for his pioneering work in LITERACY, which involves a technique he developed while working among the Moros in 1930. The Laubach literacy method uses simple illustrated charts that associate sounds with phonetic symbols, primers to encourage facility in reading, and an "each one teach one" approach to develop indigenous instructors. During the remainder of his life, Laubach made yearly tours that eventually provided literacy materials for 235 languages in over one hundred countries. He established a nonprofit organization, Laubach Literacy, Inc., and authored thirty-five books. Throughout his career, Laubach continued to focus on literacy as a means for evangelism among the vast number of illiterates, whom he termed "the silent billion."

ALAN SEAMAN

Bibliography. D. Mason, *Apostle to the Illiterates;* H. Roberts, *Champion of the Silent Billion.*

Lausanne Congress II on World Evangelization (Manila, 1989). Three thousand five hundred and eighty-six church and mission leaders from 190 countries gathered in Manila, the Philippines, in July 1989, for Lausanne II, the second International Congress on World Evangelization convened by the Lausanne Committee for World Evangelization. Compared to Lausanne I, participants at Manila tended to be younger (over half were under forty-five years of age) and included more women (25 percent). For most participants, it was their first international congress.

However, many of the fundamental issues discussed at Lausanne I were also discussed at Lausanne II. For example, reaching the poor; internationalization of cross-cultural ministries; universalism in a pluralistic society; the nature of the gospel and social concern.

Lausanne II was strongly influenced by politics in China and Russia in ways that were not present at Lausanne I. Seventy Russians and other leaders from Central Europe were full of optimism about the work of the gospel in their countries. On the other hand, the Chinese delegates were represented by a section of empty chairs. At the last minute, China had refused papers for 300 pastors to visit Manila. Lausanne II produced a declaration on the "Beijing Massacre."

Another strong emphasis at Lausanne II was the presence of the "AD 2000 Movement," leaders of which predicted that 50 national "AD 2000 Plans" would emerge from the congress, and 100 such plans by 1995. At the same time, congress participants discussed the hurdles standing in the way of world evangelization: lack of workers, lack of prayer, government pressures, war, suffering, poverty, traditional religions, illiteracy, and animism.

There were 53 major speeches and 450 workshops on the program, plus countless video presentations. In addition to plenary sessions, there were 90 special interest tracks, plus country and regional meetings. Participants were asked to sign "The Manila Manifesto" at the conclusion of the congress. This document largely reflected the earlier Lausanne I document, "The Lausanne Covenant."

JIM REAPSOME

Lausanne Congress on World Evangelization (1974). The First International Congress on World Evangelization convened in Lausanne, Switzerland, in July 1974. For ten days, 2,430 participants and 570 observers from 150 countries studied, discussed, and fellowshiped around the church's evangelistic and missionary mandate. Invitations were extended on the basis of seven for every one million Protestants in the country, plus two for every ten million unreached people in the country. For example, India received seventy invitations in the first category and 150 in the second. The United States had by far the largest representation (more than 500), plus innumerable American missionaries representing countries where they worked.

The Congress Convening Committee included 168 men and 5 women from 70 countries. Each country had its own national advisory committee to select participants. They were approved by the Congress Planning Committee, made up of 28 men and one woman from 17 countries (10 of them from the U.S.). Officially invited visitors included some Roman Catholics and administrators from the WORLD COUNCIL OF CHURCHES. The congress operated on a $3.3 million budget. Evangelist BILLY GRAHAM put his prestige, influence, and organization behind the congress.

Participation began months before the congress convened. Eleven major papers were circulated in advance and comments solicited. Those who gave papers responded in their presentations. Small group discussions were organized under four major divisions: (1) national strategy groups; (2) demonstrations of evangelistic methods; (3) specialized evangelistic strategy groups; and (4) theology of evangelization groups.

The plenary program was built on seven "Biblical Foundation Papers" and five "Issue Strategy Papers." There were seven other major addresses, three panels, two special multimedia programs, and a closing communion service. Among the major speakers were Billy Graham, JOHN R. W. STOTT, Susumu Uda, DONALD MCGAVRAN, Harold Lindsell, RENÉ PADILLA, Michael Green, GEORGE PETERS, RALPH WINTER, Gottfried Osei-Mensah, PETER BEYERHAUS, Samuel Escobar, Malcolm Muggeridge, FRANCIS SCHAEFFER, Henri Blocher, and E. V. Hill.

Participants were asked to sign a 3,000-word document, "The Lausanne Covenant." Early on, it had been submitted in draft form and revisions requested. Hundreds of submissions were made by individuals and delegations. By adjournment, 2,200 participants had signed it. A poll of participants showed that 86 percent of the 1,140 who responded favored post-congress fellowship, and 79 percent favored the appointment of a "continuation committee" of 25 people. This committee evolved into The Lausanne Commmittee for World Evangelization.

JIM REAPSOME

Lausanne Covenant. *See* LAUSANNE MOVEMENT.

Lausanne Movement. The Lausanne Committee for World Evangelization (LCWE) was organized following the LAUSANNE CONGRESS ON WORLD EVANGELIZATION in Lausanne, Switzerland, in 1974. It is an international movement committed to encouraging Christians and churches everywhere to pray, study, plan, and work together for the evangelization of the world.

The congress in Lausanne was called by American evangelist BILLY GRAHAM. Some 2,300 Christian leaders from 150 nations, representing a wide cross-section of denominational affiliations, attended the congress. The congress produced an influential document, "The Lausanne Covenant," and authorized the Lausanne Continuation Committee to continue the work begun at the congress. This committee became the Lausanne Committee for World Evangelization. Subsequently, LCWE

convened another consultation in Pattaya, Thailand, in 1980, and held "Lausanne II" in Manila in 1989.

LCWE believes that: (1) cooperation and sharing are better than competition; (2) the whole gospel includes demonstration by deeds as well as proclamation by words; (3) biblical theology and mission strategy must be consistent; (4) its own neutrality creates space for all evangelicals to work together, regardless of their church or faith tradition.

LCWE is a volunteer network of individuals and groups that affirm "The Lausanne Covenant," and are committed to support the work of world evangelization, wherever it is done in a way that is true to the Bible. Its network includes some thirty committees in different countries and regions of the world. It is supported financially by people in its network, and by the gifts of those who believe in its work.

LCWE organizes small international consultations on subjects that are critical to completing the task of world evangelization. More than thirty such consultations have brought together key people to achieve an approach that is both biblical and strategic. More than fifty regional, national, and international conferences have been held in response to expressed needs.

Publications have included a number of papers and books on subjects pertinent to world evangelization, as well as a quarterly magazine, *World Evangelization* (now discontinued), which includes news and analyses of current issues arising for those who want to make Christ known to the world. *Making Christ Known. Historic Mission Documents from the Lausanne Movement, 1974–1989*, edited by JOHN STOTT, was published in 1997.

More recently, LCWE sees itself as the "Barnabas factor" in the church. As such, it encourages churches to (1) trust new and younger leaders; (2) undertake work among people different from themselves; and (3) stay with people who have different ideas until they find each other in a new way.

The long-term staying factor in the movement has been "The Lausanne Covenant." It has been translated into more than twenty languages. It has been adopted by hundreds of churches and parachurch agencies as their basis of operations and cooperation. It has led to the formation of a number of national and regional movements in Europe, Asia, Australia, Africa, North America, and Latin America. It has stimulated many cooperative movements, mostly ad hoc, short-term, and noncompetitive. It has spun off related movements such as the Lausanne Consultation on Jewish Evangelism and the Chinese Coordinating Committee for World Evangelization. It has been the basis for a variety of consultations, the findings of which have been published as "Lausanne Occasional Papers."

The issues addressed by the covenant in 1974 are still very much alive in the world of church and missions at the end of the century. For example: (1) the relationship of evangelism and social concern; (2) unity, diversity, and cooperation among Christians; (3) the uniqueness of Christ; (4) the validity of missions; (5) the work of the Holy Spirit in evangelism; (6) religious liberty and human rights; (7) the relationship of the gospel to culture.

LCWE's organizational structure is made up of what it calls" the current partners of the Lausanne Movement." This international grassroots committee includes members from Argentina, Asia, Australia, Bulgaria, Canada, Denmark, England, Estonia, Europe, Finland, France, Germany, Ireland, Italy, Kenya, Korea, the Netherlands, Nigeria, Norway, Scotland, Spain, Sweden, the United States, and Wales.

International structures include the Chinese Coordinating Committee for World Evangelization, the Health and Healing Network, the Jewish Committee, and the Tentmakers Exchange. Special interest members include the Intercession Working group, the Theology and Strategy Working Group, and groups focusing on disabled people, women, strategic evangelism partnerships, research, tentmakers, and information technology (www.lausanne.org).

JIM REAPSOME

Lavigerie, Charles Martial Allemand (1825–92). French cardinal, founder of the White Fathers, and missionary to Africa. Lavigerie was ordained as a priest in 1849 and took two doctorates (1850 and 1853) before teaching at the Sorbonne. While there he also accepted the directorship of the Oeuvre des Ecoles d'Orient. His travels in that capacity providing disaster relief in Lebanon and Syria in 1860 solidified in him a heart for missionary work.

On November 11, 1866, while serving as bishop of Nancy, Lavigerie dreamed he was in a strange land with dark-skinned people speaking a language he did not understand. One week later he received a request to allow his name to be submitted for the vacant archbishopric of Algiers. He agreed, was appointed to the post, and installed in 1867. Immediately he instituted a policy of the regeneration of Africa by Africans. His African work was characterized by vision, energy, and drive. In 1868 he founded the White Fathers and in 1869 the Missionary Sisters of Our Lady of Africa as missionary societies to carry out his African vision. He was elevated to the position of cardinal in 1882, and given the title archbishop of Carthage and primate of Africa in 1884. In this capacity he waged a vigorous inter-national campaign against slavery until his death on November 26, 1892.

A. SCOTT MOREAU

Bibliography. A. Hastings, *BDCM*, p. 387; F. Renault, *Cardinal Lavigerie, Churchman, Prophet, and Missionary.*

Law, Legal Thought. If we think of law broadly as those binding expectations or rules which govern behavior within a particular society, then it is clear that every society has some notion of law. Without it society could not exist. Such regulations might be explicit and codified in written form, as in many Western societies, or they might be implicit and passed on as oral tradition, as in many non-Western societies.

Further cultural differences concern the understanding of the nature of law itself. As in many Western societies, law might be regarded as an expression of an objective, universal norm which applies to everyone, including all government officials (e.g., even the king was subject to the Persian law in Esther 8:8). In many non-Western cultures the law is understood in less objectivist ways, so that the law becomes a tool which the ruler can use and manipulate to enforce his or her will upon the people.

Not only must the missionary understand how moral and legal norms are understood and enforced within a particular culture, but he or she must also understand the biblical-theological concepts associated with law. Many terms with strong legal implications are used in Scripture—covenant, law, testament, sin, redemption, reconciliation, atonement, righteousness, judge, court, engagement, marriage, adoption, succession, endorsement, seal, deed, and so on. Theological concepts and doctrines in Western theology have been influenced by Roman jurisprudence. Thus some understanding of the ideals of Roman jurisprudence is necessary for grasping biblical theology.

Problems of understanding can arise when biblical concepts are communicated in cultures which lack the basic assumptions behind certain biblical terms. For example, the biblical notion of "covenant" is problematic in some Asian Buddhist cultures, in which love is understood in terms of a warm but quite ambiguous relationship. The covenant of salvation may be misunderstood in terms of the religious commandments of Buddhism, and the love of God may be thought of as a kind of Buddhist magnanimity or benevolence. Similar problems attend the judicial elements of the concepts of sin and salvation.

It is important that as part of their cross-cultural preparation missionaries include the study of comparative law and legal thought. Based upon this, and with a good understanding of biblical teachings, missionaries can explore creative ways of communicating the truth about God's law in particular cultural contexts.

KUNIO SAKURAI

Lawes, William George (1839–1907). English pioneer missionary to Niue and Papua New Guinea. Born in Aldermaston, Berkshire, England, Lawes attended a village school. After studies at Bedford College he was ordained a Congregational minister in 1860. He married Fanny Wickham in 1860 and in 1861 they went to Niue, where he developed centralized political structures, started a training institution, and contributed to the translation of the New Testament. He was joined in 1868 by his brother Frank, who worked at Niue until 1910. After furlough (1872–74), Lawes went to Port Moresby in Papua, where he was the first European resident missionary on the mainland. He worked closely with his colleague and friend JAMES CHALMERS in extending the mission, although teaching and translation increasingly occupied him. In 1882 he began training Papuans as teachers and in 1894 established the Vatorata Training College. An able linguist, he championed the use of the Motu language and completed the translation of the New Testament in 1890. He opposed colonization and reluctantly assisted the British annexation in order to protect Papuans against exploitation. Glasgow University awarded him an honorary D.D. in 1895 and he was a Fellow of the Royal Geographical Society. He retired to Australia in 1906.

ALLAN K. DAVIDSON

Bibliography. J. King, *W. G. Lawes of Savage Island and New Guinea;* D. Langmore, *Missionary Lives: Papua, 1874–1914.*

Laws, Robert (1851–1934). Scottish missionary to Malawi. Born in Aberdeen and apprenticed to his cabinetmaker father, his aim to follow in DAVID LIVINGSTONE's footsteps led to successful study in arts, theology, and medicine, and ordination in the United Presbyterian Church. Ordained in 1875, he joined a mission to Central Africa in an area later known as Livingstonia, and began work near remote Lake Nyasa. Laws was woodcutter, physician, builder, stoker on the mission boat, and peacemaker. He founded mission stations at strategic lakeside and interior sites, and (a strong advocate of education) opened his first school in 1876; by the time he left Africa (1927), there were over seven hundred primary schools plus facilities for further education in theology, medicine, agriculture, and technical subjects—and a Christian community of sixty thousand with thirteen ordained African pastors.

Finding that traders and tribal chiefs did a thriving business in which guns and gunpowder were exchanged for elephant tusks and human bodies ("black and white ivory"), Laws used Livingstone's remedy: development of healthy trade. Scottish supporters of the mission formed the Central African Trading Company, which began operations in the region in 1878.

Laws' educational, humanitarian, and (later) political contributions were many, but he never lost sight of his main task. He came to see that if Africa were to be won for Christ it would be won by the Africans themselves. By 1897 huge congregations gathered once or twice a year for four or five days to hear the gospel.

Laws visited North America, Germany, and Nigeria, was United Free Church moderator in 1908, and (so highly was he regarded) served on the legislative assembly of Nyasaland (now Malawi).

J. D. DOUGLAS

Bibliography. W. P. Livingstone, *Laws of Livingstonia: A Narrative of Missionary Adventure and Achievement;* H. McIntosh, *Robert Laws: Servant of Africa.*

Leadership. The history of Christian missions is replete with examples of key people appointed by God to carry the gospel to the unreached. It is natural to look for these people in any given period and to consider their leadership as normative. However, the study of leadership in missions has revealed a number of patterns of leadership that go beyond the role of an individual person or group. Leadership is a process in which leaders influence followers in given contexts to achieve the purposes to which they were called. The unique aspect of leadership and mission is the nature of their interaction under the guidance of the Holy Spirit in understanding and obedience to the MISSIO DEI.

History. Beginning with the apostolic leadership at Pentecost (Acts 2), God has raised up people to lead his work "to the ends of the earth" (Acts 1:8). With authority delegated by the Lord Jesus Christ (Matt. 28:18), the first missions were loosely organized bands, both apostolic and lay, driven by a deep commitment to Jesus and a lifestyle that stood in contrast to the decaying culture around them. Although there are notable examples of individual leaders, no formal leadership structures existed apart from those of the growing church.

With the emergence of monasticism (*see* MONASTIC MOVEMENT) in the fourth century, the majority of missionaries came from the ranks of devout monastics following the patterns of leadership established in the monasteries. Characteristic of these missionaries was their strict vows and obedience, which spread by establishing new monasteries, the dominant form of missions through the seventeenth century. By the eighteenth century, the Protestant REFORMATION had given birth to new patterns of leadership in mission, including a return to an emphasis on the role of laity. Four major types of leadership characterized the emerging Protestant missions:

(1) the educated and ordained clergy of the major Protestant church traditions, such as Episcopal, Presbyterian, and Congregational; (2) the eldership or council rule of the pietists and Anabaptists; (3) the new leadership models of the renewal movements such as the Methodists, Baptists, and various independent groups; and (4) visionary individuals whose commitment to the task and charismatic personalities drew others to follow.

The fourth type of leadership often led to another Protestant innovation, the interdenominational missionary society. During the so-called GREAT CENTURY OF MISSION (1792–1914), there was an explosion of voluntary societies that brought together both clergy and laity. The dominant leadership characteristic of the new societies was the pragmatic concern for the spread of the gospel, which stood in contrast to the carefully defined roles of traditional church structures. As the movement grew and new societies emerged, the influential leadership positions were filled by clergy and lay leaders who had previously held no significant positions in their churches. These voluntary societies also set themselves apart from the church structures by the appointment of leaders from specialized fields, such as medicine, or individuals whose strong commitment to the cause distinguished them as proponents. Another departure from the church structures was the openness to women in positions of leadership.

Mission leadership continued to change and adapt during the twentieth century as the end of the colonial era spread. The success of interdenominational missions in the establishment of churches and ministries, particularly in the Southern Hemisphere, created a multiplicity of national church and parachurch leadership roles. Leadership began to transition from the hands of expatriate missionaries to those of the national leaders, leading to an era of integration and nationalization. The shift in the roles of the field councils and field leaders, while often difficult, resulted in the emergence of partnerships between national church leaders and mission liaison officers. A similar trend toward nationalization was widespread among parachurch ministries, often leading to increased pressure to recruit leadership from within the national church structures. Finally, denominational and renewal movements have also flourished and moved toward nationalization following the same patterns as their mission counterparts. The result of this shift has been a major focus on global leadership development at the end of the twentieth century.

Mission and Church Leadership. Critical issues emerged as the four major types of missions began to plant churches, especially for the interdenominational societies. The first was the nature of leadership in the church. Denominational missions planted churches based on their home countries, providing both structure and models for leadership. The movement toward seminaries and the recruitment of faculty ensured a direct correspondence with the theological distinctives of the denomination. The second group, those whose polity was based on eldership, were in many ways able to include growing Christian leaders in their fellowships based on a mentoring model supplemented by Bible schools. Their commitment to community gave a rationale for training that included both practical and theological aspects. The groups that emerged from the revivals, such as the Methodists, began with a direct correlation to the selection and training of leadership that grew out of their movements. The churches planted by the interdenominational societies have a variety of leadership models based on both denominational and indigenous traditions. A wide variety of selection and training models have been used; however, Bible schools that served the missions became major contributors to leadership development.

Churches that grow out of mission societies struggle with the issues of CULTURE and leadership. The more individualistic missionaries tend toward the selection and training of individuals to fill the roles. By initially working under the direction of the missionary, in either practical or church-related work, the local leader is then educated through mission schools and Bible colleges (*see* THEOLOGICAL EDUCATION IN NON-WESTERN CONTEXTS). Due to the affiliation with the expatriate missionary, the ascribed STATUS of the national pastor is often a new form within the culture. The issues of power and function become significant in the growing role of church leadership. Often misunderstandings arise between the local community and the mission and church, based on the lack of credible models within the culture coupled with the external resources provided by the missions. Unwittingly, missions create a powerful new model for leadership, which becomes a much-sought-after role. The irony is that among interdenominational missions particularly, the lay people who brought the gospel end up creating a clergy-dominated church, struggling with the role of the laity.

A concomitant to the issue of culture is the emergence of indigenous forms and functions of church leadership. Collectivist societies have a more contextualized form of leadership involved in all aspects of life. One result of this view of leadership is the involvement of clergy in politics, even to the point of holding elected offices and engaging in business. As churches grow and continue to influence society, leadership either takes on new areas of influence or becomes increasingly irrelevant within the context.

As national churches have worked through the issues of independence and interdependence, a growing realization of the responsibility for world mission has impacted them. Not only have non-Western churches taken the responsibility for selection and training of church workers, but also a growing number have assumed the role of missionary sending churches. The missions vary in leadership approaches, although the movements are often tied to renewal within the church, making the dominant model that of visionary leaders.

Contemporary Issues. The central concern of mission leadership has always been the ability to prayerfully understand and obey the mission of God. It is not surprising that this essentially theological task is at times pressured by the complexities of managing the multicultural organizations that have emerged. The pragmatic concern for the spread of the gospel that led to the creation of mission societies continues to be the dominant characteristic of mission leadership. This raises some of the greatest opportunities and challenges today, especially in the relationships between missions and churches.

It was inevitable that the growth of mission societies would lead to increasing pressures on leadership, both internally and externally. Internal concerns focus primarily on the recruitment, preparation, support, supervision, and care of missionaries. As missions have grown numerically, their structures diversify to cope with the range of issues, establishing a need for expertise in each of these primary areas. In tension with these internal issues are the external concerns of building and maintaining a supportive constituency, locating and establishing ministry with all the concomitant relational and resource issues, and developing strategies appropriate to the political, social, cultural, and spiritual context. A necessary characteristic of mission leadership continues to be the ability to assess the changing world situation and move toward the future while retaining the unique vision God has given.

As the complexities of missions have grown so has the range of solutions, to the point where new specialized roles and organizations have emerged to cover many of these challenges. The development of leadership to meet the increasing demands, including selection and training, remains a major challenge for missions. Despite the changing times, the need for spiritual leaders remains the same throughout the ages. It is the duty of those in authority to identify people for positions of leadership who have been prepared by God to influence missions with all their complexities, toward the purposes of God. A study of the patterns by which leadership emerges reveals three essential areas of development: the spiritual formation of the individual (*see* SPIRITUAL FORMATION), the formation of knowledge through the education process, and the formation of necessary skills through experiential learning. Both formal and nonformal programs to address these areas proliferated at the end of the twentieth century. Perhaps the most encouraging development has been the rediscovery of the role of mentoring in the development of leadership, a realization with antecedents in the early monastic period.

As has been the case in every major epoch of missions history, the need for innovative leadership is vital. A theologically appropriate response to the challenges of diverse colleagues, constituencies, and contexts remains the task of leadership and missions at the beginning of the twenty-first century.

DOUGLAS McCONNELL

SEE ALSO Leadership Theory.

Bibliography. J. R. Clinton, *The Making of a Leader*; R. L. Hughes, R. C. Ginnett, and G. J. Curphy, *Leadership: Enhancing the Lessons of Experience*; K. S. Latourette, A *History of Christianity*, 2 vols.; S. Lingenfelter, *Transforming Culture*; S. Neill, *A History of Christian Missions*; D. Robert, *American Women in Mission: A Social History of their Thought and Practice*; J. O. Sanders, *Spiritual Leadership*; H. A. Snyder, *The Radical Wesley and Patterns for Church Renewal*; R. A. Tucker, *Guardians of the Great Commission: The Story of Women in Modern Missions*; A. F. Walls, *The Missionary Movement in Christian History*.

Leadership Theory. Leadership poses a central issue for mission because a primary focus of the MISSIO DEI is influencing people to submit to the lordship of Christ. Leadership is primarily an influence process. Clinton expands on this: "Leadership is a dynamic process over an extended period of time, in various situations in which a leader utilizing leadership resources, and by specific leader behaviors, influences the thoughts and activity of followers, toward accomplishment of person/task aims, mutually beneficient for leaders, followers and the macro context of which they are a part" (Clinton, 25).

In a multi- or cross-cultural context two additional sets of variables arise, such as WORLDVIEW (of the leader, followers, and the community) and the interaction of key leadership variables (e.g., the leader, followers, situation, kinds and uses of power and values).

Christian leadership shares much with local secular leadership in terms of cultural values and patterns. However, it clearly differs from secular, business, or political leadership in terms of its biblical value base, the use of spiritual power, accountability to Christ, and goal in the *missio dei*.

An understanding of leadership serves several key functions. It at least provides a way to explain the influence process; a way to predict what is likely to occur; a basis for action; and the foundation for the means to develop more leaders.

Western leadership theories are useful in mission. However, as with all culturally based theories, any leadership theory may have a limited usefulness because the undergirding values, assumptions, and worldview may not be appropriate either biblically or contextually. Theories based on Western conceptions of motivation and aimed at capitalistic production may not fit in more communally oriented non-Western ministry settings. Many Western theories depend on perspectives that do not include issues of spiritual power or differences in worldview.

However, at least four different theoretical approaches may help improve patterned leadership behaviors (leadership styles): (1) *leadership perspectives* from the traditions built on the Ohio State University research around a leadership grid (e.g., Hersey and Blanchard, *Management of Organizational Behavior*); (2) *personality profiling* using insights from psychology (e.g., the Meyers-Briggs Test and the Personality Profiles test commonly known as the DiSC test; see Voges and Braund); (3) using *metaphors* to describe patterned leadership behavior (e.g., Bennett, *Metaphors for Ministry*); and (4) using *values* as the key guides or constraints for leadership behavior.

Each perspective provides a different view of basic leadership functions such as envisioning, motivating, coordinating, decision making, problem solving, task structuring, encouraging, and other leadership functions.

Western leadership theory has been undergoing continuous development through the last two centuries. Through the nineteenth century the "Great Man" theories emerged in which leaders were thought to be "born to be leaders" or "emerge out of the demands of the social context." However, through the twentieth century attention to traits, leadership behavior, interaction with followers, broader contextual issues, and values all served to show the complexities involved.

Christian leaders involved in mission should be especially careful not to naively adopt local non-Western indigenous models of leadership or management. As with Western models they typically contain assumptions which may run counter to biblical values. However, the local leadership perspectives should serve to inform the development of contextually appropriate Christian leadership patterns.

EDGAR J. ELLISTON

Bibliography. D. Bennett, *Metaphors for Ministry*; J. R. Clinton, *Handbook I: Leaders, Leadership and the Bible*; P. Hersey, K. Blanchard, and D. Johnson, *Management of Organizational Behavior*; K. Voges and R. Braund, *Understanding How Others Misunderstand You*.

Learning Theories. Among the many learning theories that have been developed by psychologists and educators, three stand out as particularly relevant to missiologists and intercultural educators: those related to adult learning, cognitive styles, and MORAL DEVELOPMENT. This article deals with the first two.

Adult Learning Theories. Carl Rogers (1969), Malcolm Knowles (1980), and PAULO FREIRE (1981) have developed interrelated theories of adult learning. Rogers focused on learning in which

> the whole person in both his feeling and cognitive aspects [is involved] in the learning event. *It is self-initiated. It is pervasive. It is evaluated by the learner.* He knows whether it is meeting his need, whether it leads toward what he *wants to know,* whether it illuminates the dark area of ignorance he is experiencing (p. 5).

Later Rogers (pp. 188–202) applied these principles in a concrete teaching situation by describing "a revolutionary program for graduate education." Students are selected because of their problem-solving ability, empathy, spontaneous curiosity, and originality. After being introduced to the institution's resources, they choose a sponsor and additional faculty members to consult with them regarding their work. Though most of their activity is carried on through independent study, they are able to join student/faculty encounter groups. As the program progresses, students submit cumulative evidence that they are competent and well informed in their fields. Finally, a decision regarding fitness to receive a doctoral degree is made by a committee of scholars and professionals from inside and outside the university. Although Rogers' illustration focuses on advanced graduate study, he believes his learning principles are applicable to other levels and contexts as well.

Malcolm Knowles developed an "andragogical" approach to learning in which adults have a felt need to learn. Trusting and free environment is created, and progress toward mutual goals is made as learners actively share their discoveries and life experiences (pp. 57, 58). These conditions of learning are created through successive planning and decision making phases: (1) the establishment of a climate conductive to adult learning; (2) the creation of an organizational structure for participative planning; (3) the diagnosis of needs for learning; (4) the formulation of directions of learning objectives; (5) the development of a design of activities; (6) the operation of the activities; (7) the rediagnosis of needs for learning (evaluation) (p. 59).

Brazilian educator Paulo Freire (1971) adds a communal and societal dimension to adult education. He sees learning as a process of "conscientization" that frees persons to reflect on their cultural situation and engage in social action to transform it. Freire describes this kind of education in a letter to coordinators of community study groups (cultural circles) in Chile:

> A cultural circle is not a school, in the traditional sense. In most schools, the teacher, convinced of his wisdom, which he considers absolute, gives classes to pupils, passive and docile, whose ignorance he also considers absolute.
>
> A cultural circle is a live and creative dialogue in which everyone knows some things, and does not know others; in which all seek, together, to know more (p. 61).

When self-actualizing, andragogical, and conscientizing principles of adult learning are transformed into action, they can contribute to both methodological and structural renewal of the programs and institutions in which they minister. This makes them especially applicable in missions contexts where a primary agenda is individual and social change.

Cognitive Style Theories. Differences in thinking and learning styles have been observed both within and across cultures. Some persons have a greater tendency toward global, intuitive, and visual thinking. Others prefer linear, analytic, and verbal modes.

These contrasts extend across centuries and across disciplinary boundaries. Some biblical scholars see cognitive style contrasts in Hebrew and Greek thought. Contemporary neurophysiologists have observed specialized functions of the right and left hemispheres of the brain. Thought patterns of left-brain dominant persons tend to be verbal and structured, while those with right-brain dominance are likely to be visual and fluid. Learning theorists such as David Kolb (1984) see learning styles "not as fixed personality traits but as possibility-processing structures resulting from unique individual programming of the basic but flexible structures of human learning" (pp. 95–97). H. A. Witkin and other cross-cultural researchers attribute cognitive style differences to factors in the physical and social environment such as childrearing practices and demands for sensitivity to visual or kinesic cues (see Bowen and Bowen).

Concerns about thinking styles overflow into broader considerations of cognition and culture. Edward T. Hall contrasts *monochronic* cultures, characterized by linear thought patters and doing one thing at a time, with *polychronic* cultures, where thought patterns are holistic and people attempt to do several things at once (see Dodd, 87–89). Hall also describes differences between high-context cultures, in which procedures and rules are made explicit, and low-context cultures, in which persons expect to be told what to do in a given situation (see Dodd, 89–92). Paul G. Hiebert (pp. 107–36) links thinking styles to WORLDVIEW differences in his contrasts between American and Indian cultures in relation to "bounded" set and "fuzzy" set categories.

Peter Chang applies cognitive style theories to missiological issues. He challenges the imposition of Western, linear thought patterns in non-Western contexts. He asks whether the observation/interpretation/application cycle of inductive Bible study and grammatical-historical exegesis, with their embodiment of Western scientific principles, are the only valid approach to achieving biblical understanding. He also questions whether abstract, technical, and depersonalized theologies add to the understanding of the Bible stories from which they are distilled.

Chang sees implications in learning style theories for theological education. Typically, theological schools are compartmentalized into Old Testament, New Testament, theology, and practical theology departments, where courses are taught by disciplinary specialists. These persons are not always qualified to prepare the general practitioners needed in ministry. Chang also observes contrasts between American and Chinese sermon organization along linear and nonlinear dimensions: American sermons are like steak, potatoes, and peas served in separate piles on a plate; Chinese sermons are like chop suey, with everything mixed together. Chang concludes, "Our exegesis, theology and theological education are reflecting the . . . dominance of [the] left hemisphere [of the brain]. It is high time that we should appreciate and exercise more non-linear thinking to upset the lopsidedness and work out a more balanced approach" (p. 286).

LOIS MCKINNEY DOUGLAS

Bibliography. E. Bowen and D. Bowen, *Internationalizing Missionary Training: A Global Perspective*, pp. 206–16; P. Chang, *ERT* 5:2 (1981): 279–86; C. D. Dodd, *Dynamics of Intercultural Communication*; P. Freire, *Convergence*, 1:61–62; P. G. Hiebert, *Anthropological Reflections on Missiological Issues*; M. S. Knowles, *The Modern Practice of Adult Education: From Pedagogy to Andragogy*, rev. ed.; D. A. Kolb, *Experiential Learning*; C. R. Rogers, *Freedom to Learn*.

Lebanon *(Est. 2000 pop.: 3,289,000; 10,400 sq. km. [4,015 sq. mi.]).* Lebanon is a war-torn country in the Middle East. While Lebanon (4,015 sq. mi.) borders Israel to the south and the Mediterranean Sea to the west, it is truly engulfed by Syria. Not only surrounded by Syria geographically to the north and east, this tiny country is also dominated by Syria's military presence.

Historically the church has been present in Lebanon since the first century. A wide variety of Christians are found in Lebanon, including six types of Catholics, the Orthodox, the Nestorian, and various Protestant denominations. Since civil war broke out in 1975, almost one-third of the population has been lost either through death or emigration, the latter composed primarily of

Christians. As a result, the country's former majority of Christians has now become a minority to the Muslim population.

Protestant work began in Lebanon in 1823 under the leadership of PLINY FISK, who was sent out by the AMERICAN BOARD OF COMMISSIONERS FOR FOREIGN MISSIONS (ABCFM). Today the work is carried out by many Protestant bodies, including Adventists, Armenians, Baptists, Christian and Missionary Alliance, and various Pentecostal groups.

Lebanon maintains freedom of religion and is a sending point for mission organizations into other Middle Eastern countries. This once diverse and tolerant nation is now a land of division and intolerance, facing an uncertain future in light of a violent past.

JAMIE FLOWERS

Bibliography. H. G. Dorman, Jr., *CDCWM*, pp. 340–41; *Lebanon: A Country Study*; G. Otis, *Strongholds of the 10/40 Window.*

Lee, Calvin (1897–1987). Chinese church planter and orphanage founder. Born in a village outside Guangzhou, China, he accepted Christ as a teenager in high school. From there he studied at Lingnam University in Guanzhou, and later graduated from Wheaton College. He also attended Princeton Seminary, majoring in biblical languages. He then served the Chinese church, teaching at the Bible Institute of Changsha, the Alliance Bible Institute in Wuzhou, and the Canton Bible Institute in Guangzhou. As pastor of the Wanshan Church in Guangzhou, he established both an elementary school and a high school, from which a significant number eventually entered the ministry. During the Japanese occupation in World War II, seeing the suffering of the homeless youth, Lee established the Morning Star Orphanage, meeting the needs of over five hundred.

With the fall of China to the Communists in 1949, Lee resided in Hong Kong as writer and editor of the *Life Bimonthly* magazine, as well as planting four churches in Kowloon and Hong Kong. Lee's mission focus was demonstrated in teaching, writing, and establishing schools and churches. His holistic commitment and breadth was amply demonstrated by his arduous efforts in ministering to the homeless, the discouraged, and the sick. His vision, concern, and relating of theology with praxis are the lasting highlights of his life and ministry.

HOOVER WONG

Legge, James (1815–97). Scottish missionary to China. He was a second-generation Chinese missionary in Malacca (1839–43), Hong Kong, and Guangdong province, China (1843–73). Legge entered Highbury College in England to prepare for a Chinese missionary career. Soon after marrying Mary Isabella Legge (1817–52), they left London in early 1839 to work at the LONDON MISSIONARY SOCIETY's Anglo-Chinese College (1818–56). There Legge became intimately familiar with the Chinese classical traditions, resulting in the publication of *The Chinese Classics* (1861–73) at the mission press in Hong Kong. This monumental work included lengthy prolegomena reflections on comparative religion, ethics, and philosophy as well as Christian apologetic evaluations of Confucian traditions. Later made the first university professor of Chinese at Oxford (1876–97), Legge produced six other volumes of Confucian and Taoist texts (1879–91) for F. Max Muller's larger Sacred Books of the East series.

Legge's approaches to Chinese translation and missionary strategy anticipate culturally sensitive methods, but it was derided as accommodating to non-Christian culture. "Leggism" consequently became a standard nineteenth-century term in Chinese missionary literature for missionary strategies seeking religious and cultural bridges within Chinese literature. A missionary agitator against the sale of opium and British militarism in China, Legge also promoted general education for both sexes in Hong Kong and Oxford.

LAUREN PFISTER

Bibliography. N. Girardot and L. Pfister, *The Whole Duty Of Man: James Legge and the Victorian Translation of China*; J. Legge, *The Confucian Classics with a Translation, Critical and Exegetical Notes, Prolegomena, and Copious Indexes*; idem, *The Religions of China.*

Leprosy Mission Work. Leprosy (Hansen's disease) affects an estimated 10 to 15 million people worldwide, though the World Health Organization (WHO) reported in 1994 that the numbers of people afflicted with this disease had dwindled to 2.5 million. It occurs mainly in tropical, subtropical, and temperate regions of Southeast Asia, Africa, and South America. Most newly diagnosed victims are recent immigrants from Asia and South America.

The infectious bacilli, *Mycobacterium leprae*, is of the same family that causes tuberculosis. It is thought to be transmitted by skin-to-skin contact and nasal discharges. Only about 5% of the persons exposed to the bacterium contract the disease, so it is not considered highly contagious.

Two main forms of the disease are known: tuberculoid and lepromatous. The tuberculoid form mainly involves the skin and nerves. The lepromatous form is a more generalized infection that involves skin, mouth, nasal passages, upper respiratory tract, eyes, nerves, adrenal glands, and reproductive organs. Various skin eruptions may cover the entire body, but numbness is more patchy and less severe than in tuberculoid leprosy. In advanced stages, however, lepromatous leprosy can cause ulcers, eyebrow loss, collapse of the nose, enlarged earlobes and facial features, and blindness.

Equally devastating to the person who contracts the disease is the social stigma that accompanies it. Not surprisingly people fear what they cannot control or understand. The practice of isolation was the most convenient way of dealing with leprous people until the mid-twentieth century, though it was also dehumanizing.

Jesus' love for and ministry to people with leprosy is documented in the Bible and illustrates the strongest motivation for helping people with this disease (Luke 17). Organized missionary work among leprous people was motivated by Jesus' example since the fourth century.

Important missiological issues developed among mission groups in the late 19th and 20th centuries, particularly among Protestant mission organizations. Missionaries, especially in Asia and Africa, witnessed the terrible plight of people afflicted with leprosy and were moved with compassion for them. The "lostness" of their "souls" was of primary importance, so strategies of evangelism developed to win them to Christ and to establish churches. Among the strategies employed was the practice of holding medical clinics to detect and treat the disease. One exemplary issue that arose was whether to hold general meetings for evangelistic purposes first and then conduct medical clinics. Such strategies were efficient for evangelistic purposes but often seen as manipulative or coercive.

It spite of such issues missionary work among people with leprosy continued. Hospitals were built and research conducted in India, Thailand, and Africa. New methods of reconstructive surgery were learned and new and more effective drugs developed. The former social stigma of the disease has become less in developing regions of the world as people have learned more about the disease and have seen that it can be treated and controlled. Governments, observing the selfless work of Christian missionaries, were influenced to change official policies of exclusion and adopt more humane treatment of their own people afflicted with this disease.

THOMAS N. WISELY

Lesotho *(Est. 2000 pop.: 2,338,000; 30,355 sq. km. [11,720 sq. mi.]).* Lesotho (formerly Basutoland) is a landlocked, mountainous constitutional monarchy entirely surrounded by the Republic of South Africa. Its 2.3 million people include 90 percent Sotho, about 7 percent Zulu and Xhosa, with tiny White and Asian populations. There are two official languages, Sesotho and English. Literacy is nearly 75 percent. The almost total lack of resources and resulting poverty force roughly 60 percent of the men to become migrant laborers in the South African mines, contributing approximately 45 percent of total domestic income.

The great Basotho leader, Moshesh, requested missionaries after his people fled into the Drakensberg Mountains for refuge from the Zulu conqueror, Chaka. The PARIS EVANGELICAL MISSIONARY SOCIETY responded, beginning work among the Basotho in 1833 at Morija, where a printing press was established in 1841, then a girls' school, industrial school, and a Bible school by 1880. The Basuthos were receptive to the gospel, assuming responsibility for the churches in 1865 and cooperating effectively in evangelism with the Paris Mission. By 1880, there were nearly 6,000 members. By 1990, the Basotho church sought other unreached areas and began a mission among the Barotse in present-day Zambia. The Lesotho Evangelical Church (a result of the Paris Mission) today includes nearly 30 percent of the population. It is an active member of the All Africa Conference of Churches and the WORLD COUNCIL OF CHURCHES.

Roman Catholic missionaries came in 1862. Today, Catholics are nearly 45 percent of the total population. The Catholic Church currently emphases institutional development, including a political party.

The third largest group is the Church of the Province of South Africa (Anglican) that began work in 1875, today including about 10 percent of the people. African indigenous churches are also about 10 percent and traditional religionists about 2 percent of the population. Methodist, Dutch Reformed, and Pentecostal groups also work in Lesotho.

Missionaries counseled Moshesh to request British protection following conflict in 1858, 1864, and 1867 with white settlers (Afrikaaners) moving north. Great Britain granted independence to Lesotho on October 4, 1966.

From the beginning, the Paris Mission stressed indigenous leadership, identifying strongly with the Basotho nation. Preservation of their territory, development of a strong church and educational system, a SeSotho (the language) literature beginning with the Bible and hymnal, and a country that claims 98 percent of its people to be professing Christians, are visible results of Moshesh's request for missionaries.

DONALD K. SMITH

Bibliography. V. F. Ellenberg, *A Century of Mission Work in Basutoland: 1833–1933;* K. W. Latourette, *A History of The Expansion of Christianity, The Great Century The Americas, Australasia and Africa.*

Lew, Timothy Tingfang (Liu Tinfang) (1890–1947). Chinese educator and indigenous church leader. Lew was born in Wenchou, China, and attended St. John's University in Shanghai. Missionaries sponsored him to go to the United States, and he attended the University of Georgia and Columbia University. Upon receiving his Ph.D. in 1920, he returned to China to teach in three universities. Outgoing, Westernized, and energetic, Lew was a leader in the Yenching (University) Christian Fellowship, a group of Chinese church leaders exploring indigenous church life and theology. Lew edited *Life Journal* for the fellowship (1920–24), and translated many hymns into Chinese. He edited *Hymns of Universal Praise* (1936), a milestone in Chinese hymnody. His slogan was "catholic appreciation," maintaining numerous contacts in both Christian and secular circles.

SAMUEL LING

Liberal Theology. In the nineteenth century, some European and American Protestants responded to the intellectual challenges of the ENLIGHTENMENT, BIBLICAL CRITICISM, and Darwinianism by calling for significant readjustments of traditional Christian doctrines. The resulting liberal paradigm included (1) a stronger emphasis on God's IMMANENCE; (2) a more optimistic assessment of human nature and technology; (3) a greater skepticism about many elements of Christian supernaturalism; (4) a marked propensity to subordinate dogmatic concerns to the pragmatic demands of building the KINGDOM OF GOD on earth; and (5) a greater willingness to accommodate the Christian message to modern culture. This new theological agenda sparked intense controversy and sounded alarms about the loss of Christian distinctives. H. Richard Niebuhr eventually challenged the liberal credo by characterizing it as "a God without wrath bringing man without sin to a kingdom without judgment through a Christ without a cross."

By the late nineteenth century, the impact of theological revisionism began to penetrate the missionary enterprise. In particular, a conflict among American Congregationalists concerning the eternal destiny of the unevangelized led some to modify claims about the absoluteness and finality of the Christian faith. A new interest in COMPARATIVE RELIGIONS, epitomized by the Chicago meeting of the WORLD'S PARLIAMENT OF RELIGIONS in 1893, further reinforced this development. In addition, some advocates of a social gospel critiqued the individualistic methods of traditional missiology and urged an approach more in line with liberal concepts of corporate salvation.

William Newton Clarke, professor at Colgate Theological Seminary, was one of the first to articulate an explicitly liberal approach to foreign missions. In *A Study of Christian Missions* (1900), Clarke sensed a looming crisis in the missionary movement that precluded naive hopes for immediate world evangelization. He still spoke of Christianity displacing other religions, but this was relatively subdued in comparison to his embrace of Darwinianism and cultural relativism. For Clarke, GENERAL REVELATION in nature and history assumed an ascendancy over special revelation through Christ and the Bible.

By the 1920s, the missiological consequences of liberalism became more visible and widespread, especially in American Protestant circles. While theological moderates dominated most denominational mission boards, liberal concepts of mission gained strength in nondenominational agencies like the STUDENT VOLUNTEER MOVEMENT and the Young Men's Christian Association. On the theological front, Daniel Johnson Fleming, a missions professor at Union Theological Seminary in New York, advocated a "fulfillment" theory that called on missionaries to adopt a "sharing and listening" strategy toward other religions. Although he recognized the validity of evangelism, Fleming appeared to place a higher priority on the practice of consistent Christian ethics for commending the gospel.

At several points, Fleming anticipated the conclusions of the Laymen's Foreign Missions Inquiry, which investigated the Protestant missionary enterprise in the early 1930s. This project, funded by John D. Rockefeller, Jr., was divided into a team of fact-finders and a Commission of Appraisal under the leadership of Harvard philosopher WILLIAM ERNEST HOCKING. The Commission dropped a theological bombshell with the publication of *Re-Thinking Missions* in 1932.

Re-Thinking Missions suggested many practical changes in the field operations of foreign missions, but controversy centered primarily on the first four chapters, which were penned by Hocking. In essence, he proposed a radical restructuring of the missionary enterprise's doctrinal base. A liberal perspective clearly surfaced in his syncretistic outlook on the issue of Christianity and other faiths, his ambiguous CHRISTOLOGY, and his reinterpretation of the evangelistic mandate. In short, Hocking and his Commission contended that the aim of missions was "to seek with people of other lands a true knowledge and love of God, expressing in life and word what we have learned through Jesus Christ, and endeavoring to give effect to his spirit in the life of the world."

The liberalism that emanated from the Laymen's Inquiry did not immediately sway the missions movement. The AMERICAN BOARD OF COMMISSIONERS FOR FOREIGN MISSIONS endorsed many of the Hocking Commission's prescriptions, but most mainline denominational boards joined fundamentalist and evangelical agencies in attacking the theological shortcomings of *Re-Thinking Missions*. Archibald Baker, of the University of Chicago, and some missionaries enthusiastically supported Hocking's ideology, but they apparently represented a minority viewpoint. In fact, a neo-orthodox surge in Europe produced deep skepticism about *Re-Thinking Missions*, seen most notably in HENDRIK KRAEMER's *The Christian Message in a Non-Christian World* (1938), which he prepared for the INTERNATIONAL MISSIONARY COUNCIL's meeting in TAMBARAM, India, in 1938.

After World War II, the ecumenical missionary movement increasingly manifested the impact of a Hocking-style liberalism. These trends accelerated with the absorption of the International Missionary Council by the WORLD COUNCIL OF CHURCHES in 1961. Since that time, several WCC conferences have revealed the triumph of a liberal mission theology, even as the actual contribution of ecumenical denominations to world missions has waned considerably.

In 1968 the WCC held its Assembly in Uppsala, Sweden. The writings of JOHANNES HOEKENDIJK, a Dutch missiologist, profoundly influenced the deliberations of this gathering. A strong critic of traditional church structures, Hoekendijk had previously called for a new conception of evangelism that focused on social engagement and transformation. In turn, Uppsala essentially jettisoned personal evangelism, redefining "mission" to include "humanization" and a wide range of secular activities. Ecumenical missiology had openly embraced the notion that the world sets the agenda for the church.

Similarly, conferences of the WCC's COMMISSION ON WORLD MISSION AND EVANGELISM further demonstrated just how far liberal missiology had veered from more evangelical models. CWME sessions in MEXICO CITY (1963), BANGKOK (1973), MELBOURNE (1980), SAN ANTONIO (1989), and SALVADOR, Brazil (1996), set forth the following tenets: (1) the priority of orthopraxis over orthodoxy (*see* PRAXIS); (2) a this-worldly understanding of salvation as the liberation of the poor and oppressed from all forms of injustice; (3) the validity of interreligious DIALOGUE as a form of witness; (4) the necessity of CONTEXTUALIZATION and a more dialogical relationship to culture; and (5) the further widening of the scope of mission to include feminist concerns (*see* FEMINIST THEOLOGIES) and ecological awareness (*see* ECOLOGY, ECOLOGICAL MOVEMENT). While the continuities with the older liberalism are unmistakable, these more recent developments point to the increasingly radical agendas of contemporary ecumenical missiology (*see* ECUMENICAL MOVEMENT).

JAMES A. PATTERSON

Bibliography. D. J. Bosch, *Transforming Mission: Paradigm Shifts in Theology of Mission;* A. Glasser et al., eds., *Crucial Dimensions in World Evangelization;* H. Hoekstra, *The World Council of Churches and the Demise of Evangelism;* W. R. Hutchison, *Errand to the World: American Protestant Thought and Foreign Missions;* A. P. Johnston, *World Evangelism and the Word of God;* D. McGavran, ed., *Crucial Issues in Missions Tomorrow;* G. Wacker, *Earthen Vessels: American Evangelicals and Foreign Missions, 1880–1980,* pp. 281–300; T. Yates, *Christian Mission in the Twentieth Century.*

Liberation. Originating in Latin American Roman Catholic circles, discussion on the meaning of liberation after Vatican II shifted from the eternal destiny of a person to the sociopolitical context. The exodus event in which God freed Israel from slavery is seen as the archetype event governing the Old Testament. In it God liberated Israel and showed himself to be a liberating God. The announcement of Jesus that he has come to preach to the poor, to proclaim release to the prisoners, and to free the oppressed (Luke 4:18–20) is seen as the corresponding New Testament archetype. Liberation in this context has taken on a specific orientation: it is the struggle on the part of the oppressed or marginalized for their own freedom once they have become aware of their bondage and the role the oppressors play in the maintenance of that bondage. The forms of bondage may be political, economic, social, racial, or gender related, and a host of liberation theologies call those who are oppressed to rise up and engage in the process of attaining their own freedom and dignity. It is maintained that while the oppression may be personal, it will always require redressing structural issues, since the very fabric of human societies tends to engender inequities and injustices. A significant driving biblical metaphor energizing the sociopolitical liberation motif is the establishment of the KINGDOM OF GOD as a liberating force in oppressive societies and situations; the resulting focus is often on the horizontal level (among people) rather than the vertical one (people with God). In this struggle it is assumed that God is on the side of the oppressed.

As developed over the decades since the SECOND VATICAN COUNCIL (1962–65) in Roman Catholic and ecumenical Protestant circles, most of the reflections on and praxis toward liberation were reactions to understandings of DEVELOPMENT, political environments, and the theological ideologies of the past. Often, though not always, oriented in Marxist thought, the tools for understanding liberation are not limited to theology but include ANTHROPOLOGY, ECONOMICS, and SOCIOLOGY. *Development*, it is noted, maintains or even exaggerates the gap between the rich and the poor. Further, it is typically the "developed" who set the agenda rather than those who are marginalized. This, it is maintained, is not genuine liberation but only a continuing form of oppression. *Political struggles* against Western hegemony in COLONIALISM were perceived to be struggles for liberation, but all too often the new regimes which arose in Third World settings after independence simply kept the old inequities intact. Liberation struggles that began initially against colonial rulers have slowly begun to turn against the new oppressive regimes that are often backed by one or the other competing global powers, unconcerned with the masses. Even so, new forms of economic colonialism in which the West economically dominates other countries still require liberation efforts, such as the call for forgiving all Third World international debt. *Theologically* it was noted that any system which did not attack the oppressive status quo was ideologically suspect in and of itself, as it did not embody the aim of true liberation, which is a holistic release of people from all oppression and injustice.

This orientation toward liberation was built in several new theological directions. First, the development of an OPTION FOR THE POOR was a conscious decision to see the poor as the favored of God who are to be the architects of their own liberation and who enjoy a privileged position in part because their WORLDVIEW is not tainted by the desire to remain in power. Second, the sociopolitical liberation of Israel through exodus was a paradigm of God's liberating desire for humankind (though consideration of Israel's conquering actions in entering Canaan are rarely entertained in the discussions). Third, SIN was defined in social terms and not limited to personal, individual rebellion toward God. In parallel fashion, SALVATION was defined as redemption of the whole person rather than some isolated interior "soulish" element of the person, and human beings are to take responsibility for their own liberation. Additionally, because of the violence waged against the poor by oppressors, it was asserted we cannot automatically rule out violence in overcoming them in the struggle for liberation. Finally, true Christian praxis was defined in terms of a lifestyle of moving peoples and societies toward justice for all members, and mission was recast as committed solidarity with the oppressed in their struggle.

Evaluation. The very fact that evangelical missiology has moved in a more holistic direction in recent years is evidence that some of the critique brought by liberation theologies and the paradigm of liberation has forced evangelicals to turn to the Scriptures for deeper examination and recognition of their own ideological biases in approaching the Bible (*see also* HOLISTIC MISSION). In this sense evangelicals have gained significant insights on liberation from its advocates.

In spite of this, important considerations weigh against taking the contemporary liberation paradigm wholesale. Many who chose to focus on the socioeconomic and political arenas did so because of an incipient or even an outright UNIVERSALISM in regard to salvation. Those who advocated radical VIOLENCE in the struggle for liberation tended to downplay the reality that violence often leads only to more violence rather than genuine liberation. The collapse of Marxism as a political ideology in Europe demonstrated that despite the rhetoric, under Marxist regimes the general population was often worse off than under free market economies. Liberationists also tended to place sole responsibility on the efforts of people in the struggle for dignity and freedom in part because they disregarded the continuing and pervasive effects on sin both in the individual and in cultures and political systems. Political structures established and carried out by fallen humans will always move in the direction of dehumanization, and thus God's desire to create new people, new heavens, and a new earth as part of his redemptive program. Human work toward liberation, while laudable and potentially serving as a type of firstfruits of which God will ultimately accomplish, will always fall short of God's ultimate goal of SHALOM, which will only be established when God finalizes his kingdom.

Paul's picture in Romans 6 is that we are slaves who can choose to serve sin or God. The picture is a dichotomistic one in which economic or political liberation is not our ultimate goal. Instead, our ultimate goal is freedom from sin because of our choice to become slaves to the Master of the universe. Jesus said that those he set free were truly free. This freedom is not a type of antinomian libertarianism, but freedom gained through holding to his teaching and knowing the truth as a result (John 8:31–36). Liberation in this sense is not an abandonment of obligations to serve our Creator, but freedom from the oppression and degradation of sin in our lives and freedom to proclaim that release to others as well.

A. SCOTT MOREAU

Bibliography. K. C. Abraham, *DEM*, pp. 604–6; G. Gutierrez, *A Theology of Liberation*; J. A. Kirk, *Liberation Theology*; A. Nuñez, *Liberation Theology*; J. Pixley and C. Boff, *The Bible, the Church and the Poor*.

Liberation Theologies. Any attempt to provide an overview of liberationist missiology must recognize the variety of movements labeled under that rubric. Each broad category of liberation "theology"—Latin American, African, Asian, or North American Black, Hispanic, or Feminist—also manifests internal diversity among its leading exponents and practitioners and has its own history of development. In addition, different movements of liberation theology have been openly critical of one another, pointing to perceived limited perspectives and commitments. The questioning of Latin American and Black liberation theology's sensitivity to gender issues by feminist and womanist theologians is an example of this mutual challenging. This diversity does not negate, however, the reality of a significant degree of commonality among liberation theologies (Hennelly). The following discussion will focus primarily on Latin American liberation theology as representative to some degree of the larger concerns of these several movements.

Fundamental Commitments. To comprehend the particular orientation and contributions of liberationist missiology requires an appreciation of its fundamental commitments. Above all else, liberation theologies highlight systemic issues of injustice and attempt to speak for the oppressed within a given context. The particular issues and groups, of course, are defined by the brand of liberation theology under discussion; accordingly, concern can center on socio-economic class, race, and/or gender. In Latin America, special attention has been given to the first of these.

The serious consideration of the Latin American social context for missiological reflection and action has sought to provide a comprehensive framework from which to define and evaluate the mission of the church. For example, the histories of the Roman Catholic Church and Protestant denominations and missions are located within the economic and political trajectories of Latin America in order to discover either complicity and oppressive regimes and systems or the models of service to the masses of the poor (Dussel; *see* POVERTY). The social sciences (including diverse elements of certain types of MARXISM) assume an important role in the analysis of the Latin American context and in the articulation of visions of an alternative social and ecclesiastical reality. In contrast to more traditional approaches, the doing of liberation theology begins from the perspective of the weak. This starting point from the "underside of history" and the "preferential OPTION FOR THE POOR" determines how the mission of the people of God is subsequently defined and evaluated (Ellacuria and Sobrino).

Key Themes. A particular interpretation of the concept of the KINGDOM OF GOD is foundational to liberationist missiology. The kingdom is an eschatological hope of total liberation that is realized in part today within history, wherever some sort of freedom from oppression is concretely achieved. The interpretation of other theological and biblical items coheres with this point of view. The historical Jesus is the basis of the PRAXIS of mission: his preaching of the kingdom of God, his earthly ministry to the marginalized (*see* MARGINAL, MARGINALIZATION), his death and resurrection are pointers to the virtue of self-sacrifice and the divine vindication of his solidarity with the poor. The mission of the church, then, has the example of Jesus to follow in its own striving to proclaim and incarnate the good news of God's commitment to the poor. The church, although it is not itself the kingdom, must be both the place where the reign of God is visible, as well as an active participant with other human beings in the partial realization of that kingdom in the here and now. In other words, the church is to be both its sign and servant.

The concentration on the context has not meant an abandonment of the mystical elements of Christian faith or of the issue of the eternal fate of the human soul. Yet, these topics are redefined in line with liberation theology's social and ecumenical orientation. Evangelization is linked to the sharing of the liberating word and life of God's kingdom of justice.

The Scope of Mission. According to liberation theology, the mission of the people of God must begin within the church. The church needs to be evangelized by the poor in the sense that it should judge whether its ethos, message, liturgy, and structures reflect the divine obligation to society's exploited. In Latin America, especially in Roman Catholic circles, this liberationist concept of the nature of the church generated a new formulation of Christian communion, the base ecclesial communities. This way of being the church was to be the catalyst for fulfilling the calling to be the instrument of the kingdom of God within the world (Boff; Cook, 150–56). Mission, therefore, is all-encompassing. The church is to reshape itself even as it reaches into the surrounding society.

The Future of Liberation Theologies. Much has changed in Latin America over the last decade, causing liberation theologians to reassess their understanding of the context and the church's mission. The failure of the Sandinistas to rebuild Nicaragua, the inability of the continent's other revolutions to establish a different socio-economic reality, and the global collapse of Marxism are among a number of factors that have forced liberationists to reconsider the church's task in the world.

On the one hand, some liberationists claim that the emerging capitalist hegemony underscores even more the themes that liberation theology has always championed, even if socialism no longer appears to be a viable option (*see also* ECONOMICS). The poor are becoming poorer, and the powerful nations continue to take advantage of the less fortunate. In addition, these circumstances provide the opportunity to probe other dimensions of mission (such as popular or FOLK RELIGION, ECOLOGY, and indigenous rights), as well as to join with other groups who are being pushed to the periphery in the global economy (Cook, 245–76; Irarrazaval).

Nevertheless, others are less sanguine about the future. Berryman details how liberation hopes in Central America broke down. He discloses how insignificant were the numbers of those actually involved in the base communities and admits that this minority voice, though important, tended to be elitist and idealistic and misread the heart of the poor. What remains for mission in the new situation are more limited pastoral projects of solidarity among those who suffer (Berryman, 1994). At the same time, Berryman studies the phenomenon of the burgeoning evangelical presence in Latin America. While critical of some of what he sees, Berryman recognizes that evangelicalism has been able to tap into the deeply felt needs of the masses and sometimes exhibits some of the same social concerns as liberation theology, even if these are manifested differently. Any rethinking of liberationist missiology cannot ignore this evangelical component of Latin American religious life (Berryman, 1994, 145–218; 1996).

M. DANIEL CARROLL R.

Bibliography. P. Berryman, *Stubborn Hope: Religion, Politics, and Revolution in Central America;* idem, *Religion in the Megacity: Catholic and Protestant Portraits from Latin America;* L. Boff, *Church: Charism and Power—Liberation Theology and the Institutional Church;* G. Cook, ed., *New Face of the Church in Latin America: Between Tradition and Change;* E. Dussel, ed., *The Church in Latin America, 1492–1992;* S. Escobar, *Themelios* 19:3 (1994): 15–17; I. Ellauria and J. Sobrino, eds., *Mysterium Liberationis: Fundamental Concepts of Liberation Theology;* A. T. Hennelly, *Liberation Theologies: The Global Pursuit of Justice;* D. Irarrazaval, *Missiology* 25:1 (1997): 61–68.

Liberia

Liberia *(Est. 2000 pop.: 3,565,000; 111,369 sq. km. [43,000 sq. mi.]).* Located on the west coast of Africa between Sierra Leone and Côte d'Ivoire, Liberia ("Land of Freedom") is home to some sixteen major ethnic groups (speaking thirty-four distinct languages) and a minority population of descendants from American freed slaves repatriated to Liberia as settlers.

Initially intended to be a resettlement colony for ex-slaves from the United States modeled after Britain's experiment in Freetown (Sierra Leone), Monrovia (named after American President James Monroe) proved to be an extremely unhealthy location. Many of the early settlers succumbed to tropical diseases. The first group to arrive came in 1820 under the auspices of the American Colonization Society (chartered in 1816). The first two black American missionaries, Baptists LOTT CAREY and Colin Teague, arrived in 1821. Several settlements were eventually established and joined together as a nation in 1847, giving Liberia the distinction of being the first African country south of the Sahara to achieve independence. Joseph Jenkins Roberts (1809–76), a settler from Virginia, was elected as the first president. Politically, Liberia was led by the minority Americo-Liberians until the coup which put Samuel Doe in power in 1980.

Many of the several thousands of colonists who arrived over the following decades were already affiliated with denominations and joined or established their own denominational churches in the new settlement. Church work focused on the settlers, and, unfortunately, through the first half of the 19th century, little attention was paid to evangelizing the indigenous peoples.

Methodists were among the settlers who arrived in 1822, though the first Methodist missionary (Melville B. Cox) did not come until 1833; the Basel Evangelical Society sent missionaries in 1828 (who departed in 1832), the Presbyterians and Congregationalists arrived in 1833, the African Episcopal Church in 1835, the (American) Episcopal Church in 1836, and the Lutherans began work among the Loma and Kpelle along the St. Paul River in 1860. Roman Catholics went through three failed attempts (1842, 1884, 1903) before establishing an enduring mission in 1906. Progress among the indigenous peoples did not come until the last part of the 1800s, when a fresh wave of African Americans arrived after the American Civil War and the emancipation of slaves in the United States. For example, two American black denominations, African Methodist Episcopal Church (1873) and AME Zion Church (1876), sent missionaries. Pentecostal missionaries first came in 1908 and worked extensively among Grebo peoples of the interior, developing three Bible schools to train indigenous pastors. The Seventh-Day Adventists initiated work in 1927, Baptist Mid-Missions in 1931, and WEC International in 1938 (founding the Liberia Inland Mission church). In 1954 the Sudan Interior Mission (SIM) founded ELWA (Eternal Love Winning Africa), the first mission radio station in Africa. Prior to being destroyed twice in the recent civil wars, it offered broadcasts in 44 languages to all of Africa and the Middle East.

Prominent Liberian Christians include WILLIAM WADE HARRIS, the charismatic West African evangelist whose primary work was outside of his own country and EDWARD W. BLYDEN, one of the most significant pioneers in African Christian theology. Today it is estimated that Liberia is roughly 37 percent Christian (8% evangelical) and 13 percent Muslim with roughly 49 percent following traditional religions. Traditional adherents focus attention on ANCESTRAL PRACTICES and affiliation as the core of their religious system. WITCHCRAFT and SORCERY are also prominent, and associated practices have been exacerbated by the recent ethnic conflicts.

The multiple civil wars which have plagued Liberia through the 1990s resulted in an estimated 750,000 fleeing for refuge in neighboring countries, potentially destabilizing the larger region. The economy has been devastated, and with the vast bulk of the business people fleeing the country the ability to rebuild economically once the instability ends looks bleak.

A. SCOTT MOREAU

Bibliography. D. Barrett, *WCE;* P. Falk, *The Growth of the Church in Africa;* P. Gifford, *Christianity and Poli-*

tics in *Doe's Liberia;* S. Jacobs, ed., *Black Americans and the Missionary Movement in Africa;* P. Johnstone, *OW.*

Libraries, Mission. *See* MISSION LIBRARIES.

Libya *(Est. 2000 pop.: 6,387,000; 1,759,540 sq. km. [679,358 sq. mi.]).* Libya is one of the least evangelized countries. The Sahara Desert consumes 90% of the land area. However, because a great reserve of oil was discovered in 1959, Libya's per capita income is higher than that of most of its neighbors. This enables Libya to import 75% of its food and to provide subsidies and handouts to its citizens. Wealth also attracts large numbers of foreign laborers and professionals. Possibly as many as 30% of Libya's 6.4 million people are expatriate.

No Christian witness to Libyans is allowed. A militant Muslim reform order founded in 1842, *Sanusiya* (Malikite rite), has influenced the ruling junta in the direction of passionate fundamentalism in belief and austere simplicity in lifestyle. "Islam is the religion of the state," according to the Constitution of 1970. *Allah Akbar* (God is great) is the national anthem. Islamic social theory is seen as a necessary antidote to communism and capitalism. In a 1971 decision, the government decreed that all laws are to be subordinated to the *Sharia* (Muslim religious law) even if that means suspending existing laws. The *Jamiat al-Dawah al-Islamiah* is the government-sponsored department that fosters Islamic missions internationally.

In 1829 the London Society for Promoting Christianity among the Jews began Bible distribution in the large Jewish community in Tripoli. In 1889 the North Africa Mission established a small dispensary to serve Muslims. This was shut down by the Italian colonial government in 1936, reopened in 1945, and terminated in 1969 when the present government came to power. Since then, neither Catholic nor Protestant missionaries have been permitted, although a few Catholic nuns are allowed to work in hospitals.

In this restricted context, ministry through radio, printed and audio and video material, and frienship with Libyans overseas takes on new importance. Radio companies beaming a Christian message to Libya include the Far East Broadcasting Company, Trans-World Radio, and High Adventure (Lebanon). One of the most useful programs is produced by the Radio School of the Bible. Incorporated in France, this is the media ministry of the Arab World Ministries. Besides radio programs, this ministry creates and coordinates publications, Bible correspondence courses, and THEOLOGICAL EDUCATION BY EXTENSION curricula.

Possibly one hundred fellowship groups meet in Libya today, largely serving Korean, Filipino, Pakistani, and European expatriates. Some are organized by homesick nominal Christians. Corporate worship must be very discrete.

MIRIAM ADENEY

Bibliography. P. Johnson, *OW;* D. Barrett, *WCE;* K. S. Latourette, *A History of the Expansion of Christianity.*

Liddell, Eric Henry (1902–45). Olympian and Scottish missionary to China. Born in Tientsin, China, in 1902 to missionary parents Liddell came to epitomize "muscular Christianity" when he won two gold medals at the 1924 Olympics. He refused to participate in the 100-meter race because it was held on a Sunday, so he ran the 400-meter instead and won. The 100-meter race having proved inconclusive, was rescheduled and once again he won.

Educated at Blackheath and Elthan College, Heriot-Wall College for Science, and Edinburgh University, Liddell received a bachelor's degree in chemistry, physics, and mathematics. In 1925 he went to China to teach at the Anglo-Chinese College, in Tientsin. In 1930, feeling a great call to mission work in China, he applied to the LONDON MISSIONARY SOCIETY. He was accepted, but remained at the college to replace a colleague who had died. He found his theological studies constantly interrupted by numerous invitations to speak to Christian youth groups, but was finally ordained in 1938 during his first furlough from China. Friends reported that he rarely spoke of his Olympic victories, but he did once tell a friend in China that he had had to leave Europe because the adulation he received there would have turned any man's head. In 1943 he was interned at Weihsien, Shantung, where he died in 1945 of either a brain tumor or a cerebral hemorrhage.

KATHLEEN L. LODWICK

Bibliography. S. Magnusson, *The Flying Scotsman;* C. M. Swift, *Eric Liddell.*

Liechtenstein *(Est. 2000 pop.: 33,000; 160 sq. km. [62 sq. mi.]).* The principality of Liechtenstein is one of the smallest independent states in the world. This territory received its name in 1719 when Prince John of Liechtenstein purchased and united the Lordship of Schellenberg and the County of Vaduz. Surrounded on three sides by Switzerland, it is not surprising that Liechtenstein's six parishes were from the start in 451 a single deanery under the diocese of the Church in Switzerland. While sweeping political changes such as the Reformation brought great reform to Switzerland, it did not affect Liechtenstein which remains 87 percent Catholic today.

Liechtenstein's major Protestant Church is the Interdenominational Evangelical Church formed in 1881 by immigrating textile workers from Lutheran or Reformed Churches. The church entered a patronage agreement with the Protestant church in Switzerland in 1954, the same year that a Lutheran congregation was formed belonging to the Association of Evangelical Lutheran Churches in Switzerland and the Principality of Liechtenstein.

While freedom of religion is guaranteed to all under the Constitution of 1921, the Roman Catholic Church is the State Church and thus enjoys the full protection of the State. Under this guarantee, the state supervises religious education.

GARY LAMB

Bibliography. R. A. Meier, *Liechtenstein, World Bibliographical Services,* V. 159; *WCE.*

Lifestyle Evangelism. "You're the only Jesus some will ever see." "People don't care how much you know until they know how much you care." "You have to 'earn' the right to be heard." These sample statements help explain the evangelistic strategy known as lifestyle evangelism. Advocates argue that EVANGELISM must be seen as a process of planting the seeds of the gospel through verbal WITNESS, watering and cultivating through Christian example and lifestyle, and finally reaping the harvest of new converts.

Great emphasis is placed on the role of the witness's life in the evangelism process. Proponents point to the incarnation as an illustration of the importance of this approach to ministry. When God wanted to communicate with humans, they argue, God did not send tracts from heaven. Instead, God communicated with us by becoming a person and living among us (John 1:7).

The focus of lifestyle evangelism, then, is using the channels of relationships to share the gospel through both words and deeds. The latest phase of the movement, stimulated by Steve Sjogren's *Conspiracy of Kindness,* emphasizes utilizing acts of service to give an opportunity for verbal witness of salvation in Jesus Christ.

While not the first book to appear on the topic, Joseph Aldrich's book *Lifestyle Evangelism* has popularized the concept of lifestyle evangelism in American evangelicalism. Related terms used by other proponents include friendship evangelism, incarnational evangelism, and relational evangelism. Since the early 1980s numerous books have been written and witnessing programs developed around the basic concept of lifestyle evangelism. Jim Peterson, missionary to Brazil, argued in 1980 for the importance of lifestyle evangelism on the mission field. He emphasized a twofold missionary strategy: (1) the proclamation of the gospel to nonbelievers; (2) the affirmation of the gospel, which involves a process of modeling and further explaining the Christian message. Peterson found that in his mission field context, deeds of love helped clarify the gospel message to those he was trying to reach.

This emphasis on affirming the gospel mirrors the often-practiced strategy of using social ministry as a bridge to share the gospel. Social ministry can help break down suspicion, open doors for ministry in closed countries, and provide a hearing for the gospel. The construction of dams by the Basel missionaries in northern Ghana provided an opportunity for the gospel to be shared to the people there. Other missionary efforts through medicine, agriculture, engineering, nutrition, and education have illustrated this principle.

Proponents cite many benefits to utilizing the approach of lifestyle evangelism. They note there is a greater possibility for on-going follow-up, not only in continually clarifying the gospel message over a period of time but also in discipling persons who trust Christ as their Savior. Lifestyle evangelism advocates also argue that a consistent Christian lifestyle helps break down the accusation of "hypocrisy" and encourages nonbelievers to consider the reality of Christ, noting how recent visible scandals in the Christian community have caused many people to wonder: "Does Christ really make a difference? Is there any substance to all this talk?"

While affirming the benefits of a "lifestyle" approach, some people caution against letting the pendulum swing too far away from an emphasis on verbal witness. They warn against the danger of lifestyle evangelism becoming all lifestyle and no evangelism, all deeds and no words. They are concerned that Christians following a lifestyle evangelism approach may place great effort in building relationships with nonbelievers but never get around to sharing the gospel verbally. Some are concerned that an overemphasis on deeds could lead in the direction of the social gospel of the 1920s, where an emphasis on repentance and faith might be lost altogether. Perhaps the strongest critique of the lifestyle evangelism movement has come from Mark McCloskey, in *Tell it Often—Tell it Well.* McCloskey notes that while lifestyle evangelism certainly has strengths, the New Testament would seem to point toward a more comprehensive approach to evangelism, including taking the initiative to share the gospel message with persons with whom you have no prior contact. He argues that there are too many lost people to depend primarily on evangelism which is relational in approach. Not everyone has Christian friends or neighbors who can live out the message in deeds as well as share with words. Therefore, he advocates a comprehensive evangelistic strategy that includes witnessing through existing relationships but that goes beyond them to include any person with whom we might come into contact.

To summarize, the lifestyle evangelism movement has reminded the church of the importance of living a Christian life before others, that the walk of believers matters as well as their talk. Concerns raised by friendly critics need to be heard as well, in that Christians should guard against overstressing the walk whereby they become "silent witnesses." Some have taken the principles of lifestyle evangelism to an extreme, saying "I just let my life do the talking." A Christian's life can only reinforce the message; it cannot substitute for it. Verbal witness gives clarity to believers' walk by pointing people past them to their Savior, the Lord Jesus Christ. Christians cannot expect the nonbeliever to know that Christians are a reflection of the good news until they know what the good news is. As Paul affirmed, "For we do not preach ourselves, but Jesus Christ as Lord, and ourselves as your servants for Jesus' sake" (2 Cor. 4:5). If believers do not point people toward Christ, they are only calling attention to themselves. Overall, the lifestyle evangelism movement has helped provide an apologetic for Christianity to an increasingly secular world, thus following the command of Christ in Matthew 5:16, "let your light shine before men, that they may see your good deeds and praise your Father in heaven."

TIMOTHY K. BEOUGHER

Bibliography. J. Aldrich, *Life-Style Evangelism;* J. Peterson, *Evangelism as a Lifestyle;* C. Van Engen, *You are My Witnesses.*

Liminality. Derived from the Latin word *limen,* liminality suggests a threshold, chasm, or margin. Anthropologists utilize the term to refer to an ambiguous phase that is uncharacteristic of the past and future states; it is a state of "inbetweenness," a transitional stage of life in which one is torn away from familiarity. The liminal state has been likened to invisibility, ambiguity, darkness, death, limbo, and being in the womb. French folklorist and ethnographer Arnold van Gennep speaks of three different stages of passage in the life cycle: preliminal rites of separation, liminal rites of transition, and postliminal rites of incorporation.

Some anthropologists have observed a sacred dimension of liminality that compensates for the lack of secular power. The liminal severance from STATUS and authority, the exclusion from a social structure dominated by power and control, require sacred power. So within the placeless, timeless, nonclassifiable milieu of liminality emerge such major categories of culture as MYTH, SYMBOL, and RITUAL. Liminality is therefore a state of both transition and potentiality.

In tribal societies liminality is often characterized by a homogeneous *communitas,* a nonstructural equality among those involved. However, such homogeneity is not found in the complex urbanized world. The multiple states of liminality caused by race, class, and gender differences make *communitas* a difficult challenge today. While many in modern and postmodern society undergo liminality in terms of alienation because of fast-paced changes, this fragmented, individualized liminality lacks the power to create *communitas.*

On the other hand, it has been suggested that the concept of liminality can be used to develop a contemporary, multicultural theology of marginality. Liminal agents can be viewed as a creative minority in God's plan of salvation, and the church can become in part a marginal community of liminality and a creative agency for transforming the world. This powerful ideal must, however, be informed by the significant distinction between voluntary and involuntary liminality. For example, missionaries voluntarily choose a liminal state, while their children experience the liminal state involuntarily. Likewise, the first and second generations of immigrant families suffer from the conflicting dynamics of voluntary and involuntary liminality.

Crucial missiological questions arise here: How do cross-cultural missionaries who choose liminality through missionary zeal process liminality in the midst of an intense phase of transformation on the field? In contrast, how do their children process their involuntary liminality to become voluntary creative agents of transformation? Finally, how in this complex urban world does one's liminal experience form *communitas* as a creative force of transformation?

The answers to all three questions are inherent in the questions themselves. Sorting out the diverse experiences of liminality is the key to processing and maximizing it. While embracing the call of all Christians to the sojourning state of liminality, an understanding of its diverse contexts furthers the challenge of generating a creative minority full of potential to transform a dehumanizing world. By acknowledging the commonalities and multiplicities of liminality, Christianity can strengthen its missionary calling to the world. Thus, liminality becomes not merely a state of transition, but a state of potentiality as well.

YOUNG LEE HERTIG

Bibliography. A. van Gennep, *The Rites of Passage;* J. Y. Lee, *Marginality: The Key to Multicultural Theology;* V. Turner and E. Turner, *Image and Pilgrimage in Christian Culture.*

Linguistics, Linguistic Theory. Linguistics, also called linguistic science, is concerned with the study of human LANGUAGE. Linguists are not necessarily polyglots—persons who are fluent speakers of several languages. Rather, they are specialists whose goals are to discover the rules of language structure, the regularities relating languages both past and present, patterns in the acquisition of languages, and principles underlying the use of languages by their speakers.

Linguists whose focus is on language structure examine aspects such as grammar, vocabulary, and pronunciation in order to develop an increasingly adequate understanding of the nature of all human language. Those investigating the relationship among languages explore topics ranging from features that occur in all living languages (language universals) to the classification of related languages into groups or families. While some specialists in language acquisition focus on the cognitive processes employed by children as they acquire their native tongue, others examine the psychological and linguistic processes of children and adults engaged in learning additional languages. Those who research language use observe the roles language plays in human interaction, such as differences between male and female speech, the importance and functions ascribed to national languages versus regional and minority languages, and attitudes of speaker toward non-native use of their language.

The discipline of linguistics traces its roots to the third and fourth centuries B.C. when Plato, Socrates, and Aristotle dialogued about the nature of human language. The Greek philosophers of this era are credited with establishing many of the grammatical categories that are still used in descriptions of modern-day languages, such as nouns and verbs as well as verb tenses such as past, present, and future. Until the past one hundred years, however, the focus of linguistic inquiry was almost entirely on the written form of the language. This emphasis changed in the twentieth century, when anthropologists began to study the conversational use of American Indian languages, thus laying the foundation for much missionary activity in linguistics and language learning. More recently, linguistics has become a highly respected academic discipline studied in universities and colleges throughout the world (Finegan and Besnier, 1989).

The field of linguistics contains a number of somewhat overlapping subfields, and new ones continue to develop. These include *historical linguistics* (the study of how languages change over time, including the present-day relationships among languages), *psycholinguistics* (the study of the psychological processes involved in language use and the study of the how first and second languages are acquired), *anthropological linguistics* (the study of the relationship between language and culture), SOCIOLINGUISTICS (the study of how people use language in social interaction), and *applied linguistics* (the application of linguistic insights to practical concerns such as language learning/teaching methods and procedures, translation and literacy, the diagnosis and treatment of language disorders such as dyslexia, and the development of computerized speech production) (Crystal, 1987).

While each of these subfields has contributed to the area of missions, the greatest impact has been that of applied linguistics. Insights from this area have been of particular value in dealing with real-world issues in BIBLE TRANSLATION, LITERACY work including the development of new alphabets, and missionary language learning (*see* SECOND LANGUAGE ACQUISITION).

A number of twentieth-century theoretical and applied linguists have made significant contributions to missions. Referring to the founder of the Summer Institute of Linguistics (SIL) and WYCLIFFE BIBLE TRANSLATORS, Ruth Tucker (p. 351) notes that "The one individual most responsible for the twentieth century surge in Bible translation work has been WILLIAM CAMERON TOWNSEND." Following Townsend's early lead, SIL continues to be at the forefront of applied linguistics in the areas of translation and literacy work. SIL personnel are currently deployed in over fifty countries, where much of their work is with lesser known language and people groups and with previously unwritten languages.

Other highly respected scholars in Bible translation include KENNETH L. PIKE, EUGENE A. NIDA, and WILLIAM A. SMALLEY. Spanning decades of involvement in missions, these pioneers have written numerous books and articles in the areas of linguistics, cultural anthropology, and translation theory and practice. In addition, they have served as translation consultants for many hundreds of projects throughout the world. Their contributions, however, extend well beyond the missions community to the broader field of general linguistics.

Pike, Nida, and Smalley have also had a major influence on missionary language learning through their many publications as well as through the development and administration of prefield training programs for missionary candidates. Other prominent applied linguists include Donald N. Larson and E. Thomas and Elizabeth S. Brewster. These specialists have shaped our view of on-the-field language acquisition and provided tools to help missionaries become more effective self-directed learners. They have also written textbooks for missionary language learners, conducted prefield training programs, and worked as language- and culture-learning consultants for mission agencies, language schools, and individuals in many countries of the world.

LONNA DICKERSON

Bibliography. D. Crystal, *The Cambridge Encyclopedia of Language;* E. Finegan and N. Besnier, *Language: Its Structure and Use;* R. A. Tucker, *FJIJ.*

Literacy, Literature Mission Work. Literacy is a threshold to another world. The printed page can communicate to hundreds of millions of people. Accordingly, in the world of missions, numerous organizations have been established to focus on literature. There are more than 300 significant literature organizations at national and international levels. An example of an international agency is the Christian Literature Crusade with bookstores around the world. OVERSEAS MISSIONARY FELLOWSHIP has publishing houses in several countries. Christian Communications Limited operates several bookstores in Hong Kong and has expanded into other countries where Chinese churches exist.

Books have a long history. Clay tablets the size of shredded-wheat biscuits were used in Babylon as far back as 2400 B.C.; papyrus was used in Egypt as early as 4000 B.C. The single most important development for book publishing was the invention of the printing press with movable type. Recently, a major step has been taken as personal computers become desktop publishing machines.

Print is the oldest mass medium and has been used in all aspects of Christian work. Indeed, it seems impossible to imagine Christian mission without printed material. Our teaching is presented in books, magazines, and pamphlets. Follow-up to evangelistic crusades and mass media programs are primarily done by letters and packages of printed material. The quarterly magazine *Interlit* helps missions use literature more effectively.

More than 22,000 new Christian book titles are published each year, and there are more than 23,000 periodicals. The great majority of books published by Christians are for Christians; only a small portion are suitable for evangelistic use. Of course, the Bible is by far the world's number one best-seller.

Of special interest are magazines published for evangelistic purposes. For example, *Breakthrough*, a Chinese magazine published in Hong Kong, reaches the young. In the Middle East, *Magalla* reaches Arabic-speaking people in several countries. *Step*, published in Nairobi, has a higher circulation than any other magazine in Africa.

Several organizations are devoted to the publication of tracts, which have had extensive use. The use of tracts has declined in the West over the last few years, though recently comics have been produced for similar purposes. In the West the usual perception is that comics are for children, but in many countries they are widely used by adults. Various BIBLE SOCIETIES have produced whole series of Bible comics for semiliterates.

Mission agencies also use literature extensively for promotional purposes. A forerunner to direct mail was the missionary prayer letter, which was sent to supporters. During the last few years, direct mail has become a major fund-raising method for Christian organizations.

In comparison to other MEDIA, literature makes big demands: one must be able to read, which takes years of learning and practice. Because the Bible is often the first book to be printed in a language, many missions have focused on literacy as a primary aim. Governments make huge investments in schools and literacy programs to help people to read. Even so, it is estimated that less than half the world's people are readers. The nonliterate are usually the poor and less privileged; but even in countries with high literacy, reading is decreasing because of television.

Among the literacy methods used by mission organizations we can mention the Laubach method (*see* LAUBACH, FRANK CHARLES), which could be called a disciple-making model. It is also known as the "each one teach one" method. The Gudaschinsky method, widely used by WYCLIFFE BIBLE TRANSLATORS, could be called the "reading to learn" method. The Freire method aims at consciousness raising (*see* FREIRE, PAULO REGLUS NEVES). Each of these methods reflects the background in which it was first developed. Today other methods are being introduced, including the use of audiocassettes as the teacher.

VIGGO SØGAARD

SEE ALSO Illiteracy.

Bibliography. J. Chaplin, *Adventure with a Pen; Training Exchange: A Resource Directory for People in Publishing;* R. E. Wolseley, *Still in Print: Journey of a Writer, Teacher, Journalist.*

Literature Mission Work. *See* LITERACY, LITERATURE MISSION WORK.

Lithuania *(Est. 2000 pop.: 3,692,000; 65,200 sq. km. [25,174 sq. mi.]).* Originally settled by Indo-Europeans, Lithuania became the largest European state of the Middle Ages. Among the last of the pagan nations, Christianity officially arrived through an alliance with Poland in 1386. By the seventeenth century, Vilnius had become a major Jewish center. In 1795 Lithuania was given over to Russia. German occupation in World War II devastated both Lithuania and the Jewish population. More recently, Lithuania led the successful 1991 Baltic independence movements. The church in Lithuania has remained predominately Catholic since the Middle Ages.

STEVEN J. PIERSON

SEE ALSO Baltic States.

Bibliography. E. Christiansen, *The Northern Crusades: The Baltic and the Catholic Frontier, 1100–1525;* P. Jones and N. Pennick, *A History of Pagan Europe;* A. Lieven, *The Baltic Revolution: Estonia, Latvia, Lithuania and the Path to Independence.*

Little, Paul E. (1928–75). American evangelist. Born in Philadelphia, Pennsylvania, he graduated from the University of Pennsylvania (1950) and joined InterVarsity Christian Fellowship to work with students on campuses in Illinois. He soon developed a special interest in international students and moved to New York City to develop a ministry there.

Later, he was promoted to serve as regional director of InterVarsity in Dallas, Texas, and then he became InterVarsity's national director of evangelism. During this time he was best known as a campus evangelist, but world missions and overseas evangelism attracted him as well. He spoke on more than two hundred campuses in the United States, Canada, Latin America, Europe, and Africa. He was program director of the International Congress on World Evangelization, Lausanne, Switzerland, in 1974, and directed InterVarsity's student missions conference at URBANA, Illinois, in 1970. He taught evangelism at Trinity Evangelical Divinity School, Deerfield, Illinois, from 1964 until his death in an automobile accident in Ontario, Canada. Based on his considerable experience as a campus evangelist, he wrote *How to Give Away Your Faith* (1966), *Know Why You Believe* (1967), and *Know What You Believe* (1970). Still in print, his books have been published in more than twenty languages.

JIM REAPSOME

Bibliography. J. W. Reapsome, *BDCM*, p. 404.

Liverpool Missionary Conference (1860). In the wake of the revival of 1858–60 in England, a few earnest Christians unrelated to missionary societies called for a conference of mission leaders. The concern was that all Christians of the United Kingdom be stirred up to greater zeal in the work of the Lord. Fortunately, the London Secretaries Association responded to the challenge and appointed one of its members to plan such a gathering. Somehow this man was able to persuade the missionary societies to support the project, and from March 19 to 23, 1860, Liverpool was the venue of a conference of 126 mission members, of whom 37 were field missionaries.

The high percentage of mission directors who attended this conference devoted their time to policy discussion and produced not a few recommendations that significantly shaped mission relationships for years to come. Papers were read on missionary recruitment, the training of converts, and the planting of native churches under native leaders. They called for the establishment of a journal to treat Christian missions at large and for a new cadre of missionaries drawn from the sons of the wealthy and learned. Large crowds attended the evening meetings, which were opened to the public. Lord Shaftesbury, who chaired the final session used the word "ecumenical" to describe it. Something was beginning to catch on! Liverpool 1860 is of significance in that it initiated the pattern of world missionary conferences that continues today.

ARTHUR F. GLASSER

Bibliography. W. R. Hogg, *Ecumenical Foundation;* K. S. Latourette, *A History of the Expansion of Christianity,* vol. 4, *The Great Century.*

Livingstone, David (1813–73). Scottish pioneer missionary and explorer in Africa. Born in Blantyre, Scotland, he left school at age ten, but a profound spiritual experience made him resolve to become a medical missionary, convinced that the God who had called him would see him past all the daunting obstacles. He qualified in medicine, trained in theology, and in 1840 set out for South Africa under the LONDON MISSIONARY SOCIETY. Aiming to reach "the smoke of a thousand villages" where no missionary had ever been, he penetrated ever farther north, beyond the Kalahari Desert. There the only foreigners were Arab and Portuguese traders, and Boers who believed the Africans had no souls and exploited them mercilessly. Livingstone had to contend with drought, fever, wild animals, superstition, and slavery, which he called the open sore of Africa and helped stamp out. He learned languages, treated medicine men with courtesy as having something to teach him, got to know the African mind as few did, and recommended the training of national workers to relinquish their dependence on Europeans.

In 1852 he began a six-thousand mile journey that took nearly four years. He headed the government's Zambesi Expedition (1868–74), after which he advocated the use of Lake Nyasa in honorable trade to make slave dealing unprofitable. On furlough in 1867 he electrified a distinguished Cambridge audience. "I direct your attention to Africa," he said, "I go back . . . to try to make an open path for commerce and Christianity. Do you carry out the work I have begun." From this developed the Universities' Mission to Central Africa—an Anglo-Catholic society that owed much to a Scottish Congregationalist. His explorations brought him both secular acclaim and criticism from some missionary circles, but whether explorer or missionary Livingstone always had right priorities. The Lord's "Lo, I am with you alway" was "the word of a gentleman of the most sacred and strictest honor." When Livingstone died in what is now Zambia his attendants bore his body 1,500 miles to the sea, and one of them was present at the funeral in Westminster Abbey.

J. D. DOUGLAS

Bibliography. W. G. Blaikie, *The Personal Life of David Livingstone;* T. Jeal, *Livingstone;* C. Northcott, *David Livingstone: His Triumph, Decline, and Fall;* A. C. Ross, *Livingstone: The Scot and the Doctor;* G. Seaver, *David Livingstone: His Life and Letters.*

Loewen, Jacob A. (1922–). Russian-born Canadian linguist and missionary in Colombia,

Panama, and Africa. Born in Russia to a German-speaking family which immigrated to Canada in 1930, Loewen grew up exposed to both cultural variations and a strong Mennonite faith. He attended Missionary Medical Institute (1942–43) and the SIL institute in Briarcrest, Saskatchewan (1943), after which he served as a home missionary under the West Coast Children's Mission in British Columbia. After his marriage to Anne Enns in 1945, he attended Tabor College and they were sent to Colombia with the Mennonite Brethren to develop a written language for the Waunana (1947–57). Religious persecution resulted in his move to complete his Ph.D. in linguistics at the University of Washington. Accepting a position at Tabor College in 1959, he continued his linguistic and church development work intermittently over the next twenty-five years working on Bible translation in Panama with the ten dialects spoken by the various groups of Choco.

Loewen joined the American and United Bible Societies in 1964, as a translation consultant responsible for South America (1964–70), and West Africa (1979–84). He focused on research and writing after his retirement in 1984.

Loewen brought a solid commitment of applying anthropological insights to understanding people as a foundation in the missionary task. His voluminous writings have significantly influenced missionary ANTHROPOLOGY and COMMUNICATION, especially the importance of understanding and utilizing BELIEF SYSTEMS and MYTH in the CONTEXTUALIZATION of the Christian message.

A. SCOTT MOREAU

Bibliography. J. A. Loewen, *Culture and Human Values;* idem, *IBMR* 22:2 (1998): 69–72.

Logos Christology. *See* CHRISTOLOGICAL CONTROVERSIES.

London Missionary Society. *See* COUNCIL FOR WORLD MISSION.

Lost, the. *See* UNEVANGELIZED.

Love. Biblical love is often a concept that has been confused with cultural views of "love." In Scripture, love is a description of God, a sacrificial act toward the undeserving, a fulfillment of the Law, and the trademark of a true disciple of Christ. Love should be characteristic of Christian mission. The Old Testament word is ·*ahab*. In the New Testament, two major concepts of love are expressed in two different words: *philos* and *agapē*.

Philos expresses fondness or an attraction to someone or something. It is a highly emotive word which is similar to the English terms fondness or appreciation or affection. Older women are to teach (or train or advise) younger women to be "husband lovers" *(philandrous)* and children lovers *(philoteknous)* indicating that affection toward the husband and children was to be developed and thus was to exceed the conditional type of emotion related to familial relationships. Scripture declares that the Father loved the Son in this way (John 5:20) and believers are to love in this same affectionate manner (John 16:27). *Philos* is not a lesser type of love than *agapē* but is of a different nature. It entails feeling good toward another person or a thing. One may be fond of someone or something and it can be a healthy and wholesome sentiment. It expresses joy in being with or involved with someone or something.

In *agapē* the idea of sacrifically giving oneself on behalf of another is the primary emphasis. This form of love is not an emotional response to a person, place, or thing, but rather a volitional act toward a person or group of persons who may or may not be lovely. This is the word used to describe God's attitude toward the world (John 3:16) and toward the sinners whom he redeemed (1 John 4:9). The love was not simply a verbal expression but a dramatic demonstration of selfless giving on behalf of those who were cut off from God and even declared to be his enemies (Rom. 5:8). This love is beyond human capacity but is to be exhibited by those who call God Father (1 John 4:7). Jesus also indicated that this love would fulfill all the law when exercised toward God with all of one's heart, soul, and mind, and toward one's neighbor (Matt. 22:36–40; Gal. 5:14). The reason for this sweeping statement is that if one is sacrificially giving himself/herself to God and neighbor, then one's acts would not do anything offensive or harmful. This fits within the intent and heart of what the law was all about.

In missions, the declaration of God's love must be demonstrated and not just verbalized. Whether in wholesome affection or sacrificial giving, the message of God's character and action toward sinful humankind must be demonstrated. Those who carry God's love must illustrate this through acts consistent with the loving behavior of the culture in which the message is being presented.

Since Jesus placed the act of loving one another as living testimony to identify the true disciples, those in ministry must protect the love relationship among fellow workers. Interpersonal relationships among missionaries are certainly observed by those hearing the message of John 3:16 and Romans 5:8. But if those who proclaim the message do not reflect such attitudes among themselves, the verbal witness can be undermined. Since loving one another is a command (John 15:17), it is evident that it is not left to human emotions nor is it merely a good thing. It is a moral obligation to give of oneself to others. To do this is to be a witness of one's connection with Jesus and to verify that one is truly on a mission for Jesus Christ who came as a demonstration of God's love for sinners. This love, however, is not from human effort but flows from a Spirit-filled life (Rom. 5:5; Gal. 5:22).

ED GLASSCOCK

Bibliography. J. P. Baker, *NDT,* pp. 398–400; W. Günthern and H.-G. Link, *NIDNTT,* 2:538–51; G. B. Funderburk, *ZPEB; 3:*989–96; J. Stott, *The Mark of the Christian;* C. Van Engen, *God's Missionary People.*

Love of God. The Christian mission stems from the saving love of God for humanity. This divine love is to be associated with the related concepts of his compassion, mercy, blessing, and grace, especially as revealed in Christ.

Since God is love (1 John 4:8) both within himself in the intra-trinitarian self-giving and in his special revelation, his love must be reflected in the act of creation, especially of human beings. Humans were originally God's priest-kings (Gen. 1:26–28; 2:9–17). Their task was to consecrate their assigned rule and realm to him in loving obedience, with a view to realizing God's ultimate eschatological goal for his creation (Dumbrell, 1994).

Their rebellion neither frustrated the divine plan for the world nor negated his love for humanity, his image in the world. Even at the point of excluding them from Eden, the realm of divine blessing, he extended hope for salvation (Gen. 3:16). When the necessity of a general judgment was typified by the Flood, the Lord graciously preserved a remnant. He also promised that his covenant of creation would stand (Gen. 6:18; 8:17–9:17), thereby also expressing his love (Matt. 5:45; Acts 14:17).

From among the disobedient nations, but in the chosen line of Shem (Gen. 9:26–27; 11:20–27), Abraham was chosen both to receive blessing and to be a blessing (Gen. 12:1–3), ultimately through Christ (Gal. 3:8) (*see also* ABRAHAMIC COVENANT). In fulfillment of this promise of blessing to humanity, and with a view to bringing his creation to its goal, God delivered Israel from Egypt. Redeemed Israel's vocation may also be called her mission, for she is called with the world in view (Exod. 19:5). Her role as a priestly kingdom and holy nation is to bear witness to the true and living God by her distinctiveness in worship and moral life as a community under the Law or Mosaic covenant. Chosen Israel was thus called to model for the nations the blessings of the divine love experienced through obedience to Yahweh as king (Exod. 19:5b–6a; cf. 1 Peter 2:9). At best Israel fulfilled this calling very imperfectly, but at certain high points, like Solomon's dedication of the temple (1 Kings 8:41–43, 60) Israel was keenly aware of her proper, Abrahamic role in the world. Only the Messiah (Christ), however, would per-

fectly manifest the love of God in himself and the divine intention of blessing for the nations.

God's love for sinful humanity resulted in his giving/sending the eternal Son to become the promised Messiah (John 3:16). Jesus expressed this love of God for fallen humanity by his own loving obedience to the Father (John 14:31; Phil. 2:5–8), showing compassion for the hungry, the sick, the demonized, and the tax-collectors and "sinners." To them he brought relief from their suffering and forgiveness of their sins through faith in him. This was a sign and foreshadowing of the future reign of God in blessing, power, and righteousness. His atoning death, "a ransom for many" (Israelites and Gentiles alike), was the crowning expression of God's love for sinners. His resurrection guaranteed the final fruition of this love in the full implementation of the reign (kingdom) of God at his PAROUSIA. That age (or world) to come will be the final realization of his purpose for creation; then it will be fully subdued under his vice-regent, Jesus Christ, and his Body, the church.

The interim between his resurrection and his coming is the appointed time for the Christian mission—the sending of the apostles and others bearing the gospel to all the nations till the close of the age (Matt. 28:16–20; Luke 24:46–48; Acts 1:8). This fulfills the promise to Abraham (Gen. 12:3) in accordance with the love of God expressed in the giving of the Son (John 3:16).

In this way the risen Christ builds the community which has experienced God's love in him through the Spirit (Rom. 5:5–8). Described in bridal imagery (Eph. 5:21–33; Rev. 21:2, 9) the church is not only the creation, through world mission, of God's saving love; it is also the community reflecting this love in its life (e.g., Phil. 2:1–8; 1 Peter 1:22; 1 John 3:11–24; 4:7–12). As such it is the global fulfillment of Israel's vocation—a living sign of the scope of God's saving love and its instrument, embracing men and women of all peoples and legal statuses (Phil. 2:14–16a; 1 Peter 2:9–12, 17; Gal. 3:28).

The final destiny of those who respond to the reconciling love of God made known to them by the Christian mission is the enjoyment of the final issue of this love for the creation: the life of the world (age) to come, the reign (kingdom) of God in all the fullness of his blessing. This will be creation perfected at last—life in all its fullness where the bride of the Lamb "who loves us and frees us by his blood," will see the face of him who is now also on the throne (Rev. 1:5, 6; chs. 21, 23).

The love of God revealed on the cross has been the core of the message and a fundamental motive for the Christian mission from the time of the apostles (2 Cor. 5:14–21) until the present day.

JOHN A. MCINTOSH

SEE ALSO Kingdom of God.

Bibliography. B. C. Berkouwer, *The Church;* W. J. Dumbrell, *The Search for Order: Biblical Eschatology in Focus;* A. Glasser, *Crucial Dimensions in World Evangelization;* H. N. Ridderbos, *Paul;* C. Van Engen, *Growth of the True Church.*

Loyola, Ignatius. *See* IGNATIUS OF LOYALA.

Luce, Alice Eveline (1873–1955). English missionary to India and the United States. Born in Cheltenham, England, into the home of an Anglican vicar, she was educated at the Cheltenham Ladies' College and London Bible College. She received further training in nursing and became competent in five languages. In 1896 she sailed to India and served as a missionary for sixteen years under the CHURCH MISSIONARY SOCIETY.

Her identification with the Pentecostal movement began in India when, convinced of the authenticity of the baptism of the Holy Spirit, she prayed until she received it (about 1910). Two years later illness forced her to return to homeside work in England and Canada; she resigned from CMS for medical reasons. She then began work among Hispanics in Mexico, Texas, and later California, and was ordained in 1915 by the Assemblies of God (AoG). In 1926 she founded the Berean Bible Institute of San Diego (now the Latin American Bible College) for training pastors and evangelists and served there until her death.

Luce's pioneering work of training an indigenous clergy for the evangelization of the Hispanic population provided the way for many young people to minister effectively to their own people. Author of several books, including *The Messenger and His Message* (1925) and *The Little Flock in the Last Days* (1927), she also prepared curricular materials for the Bible Institute and contributed regularly to various AoG publications. Her work laid the foundation for AoG missionary strategy and largely explains their successful Hispanic evangelism in the United States.

FLORENCE R. SCOTT

Bibliography. V. De Leon, *The Silent Pentecostals;* G. B. McGee, *AG Heritage* 5 (1985).

Lucifer. *See* SATAN.

Lull, Ramon (c. 1235–1315). Missionary to North Africa. Ramon Lull was born on the island of Majorca. A dissolute early life was followed by marriage to Blanca Picany, who bore him two children, but not until the age of thirty did he give his life to Christ after seeing visions of the crucifixion.

The conversion of infidels became his passion. He spent nine years at the University of Palma studying Arabic, disputing with Jews and Mus-

lims, and producing the earliest works of his prolific career. He believed that opponents of Christianity must eventually succumb to the arguments he painstakingly developed.

Another passion was the establishment of missionary training colleges, the first being founded on Majorca in 1276. After teaching for several years at the University of Paris, he made his first missionary journey to Tunis in 1292. He was almost immediately arrested and expelled, but in 1307 he returned to North Africa, only to be imprisoned for six months in Bugia. His third tour was in 1314–15, again to Bugia, but after producing at least five influential converts he was stoned to death by an angry crowd.

Besides his literary output of apologetical and devotional works—estimated at more than 250—Lull is notable for being among the first to advocate the conversion of Muslims as opposed to military crusades against them.

LARRY POSTON

Bibliography. E. A. Peers, *Ramon Lull: A Biography.*

Lutheran Mission. Lutheran world mission as an empirical fact began with the sending of Lutheran missionaries to Tranquebar, South India, by the DANISH-HALLE MISSION (1706). This marked the first recorded sending of Protestant missionaries to a non-Western nation. Important antecedents are found in the work of Martin Luther and the sixteenth-century Reformation. Several periods of Lutheran mission activity must be distinguished.

Although GUSTAV WARNECK (1834–1910), the father of nineteenth-century continental missiology, criticized Luther as being indifferent to mission because the Reformer had not supported regular overseas mission endeavors, later scholars demonstrated that Luther's theology and understanding of church and kingdom were thoroughly missionary. For Luther, mission meant reestablishing the church on its true evangelical foundation in Jesus Christ and the gospel. Always the work of the Triune God, the goal of mission is the coming of the kingdom. God's dynamic Word penetrates every barrier of culture, religion, or geography and awakens faith. The church, missionary in its very nature, is God's instrument sending out his Word into the world. Every baptized believer has both a right and a duty to witness to Christ.

For Luther, God's mission continues through the apostles and the church to the ends of time and space, resulting in universal proclamation though not world conversion. Because of the cross and the opposition of Satan, true believers will always remain a minority. The community of believers, proclamation of the gospel, baptism, the Lord's Supper, lay witness, and a regular ministry are central features of this understanding of mission. No special missionary office is needed.

A highly restricted view of mission prevailed during the period of Lutheran orthodoxy (1580–1675). Lutheran rulers were obligated to evangelize their non-Christian subjects (Jews, Muslims, pagans), but any wider applicability of the GREAT COMMISSION was in effect denied. The Lutheran theological faculty at Wittenberg in 1651 maintained that Lutherans had no obligation to send missionaries beyond their territories to convert the heathen, as Jesuits and other Catholics had done. A Lutheran layman, Justinian Welz (1621–68), who proposed a new Protestant society for sending missionaries overseas, was condemned as a heretic.

Lutheran pietism, under the leadership of Philipp Spener (1645–1705), introduced profound changes into Lutheran missionary thinking, reaffirming the universal validity of the Great Commission and recognizing the need for special agents to carry out mission in non-Christian lands. At the University of Halle, August Francke (1663–1727) recruited two dedicated theology students—BARTHOLOMAEUS ZIEGENBALG and Heinrich Plütschau—as missionary pastors for the Danish crown colony of Tranquebar under the sponsorship of King Frederick IV. Thus were laid the foundations for the first overseas Protestant mission venture. Ziegenbalg, a gifted Scripture scholar, translated Luther's Small Catechism and the New Testament into Tamil, researched the customs and beliefs of South Indian Hinduism, and engaged in dialogue with Hindu and Muslim holy men. The Lutheran mission soon became a joint ecumenical venture with the Society for Promoting Christian Knowledge (Anglican), transcending both nation and denomination.

Contemporaneous with the Danish-Halle Mission, but different in emphasis, were missions of the Moravian Brethren under the leadership of Count NICHOLAS LUDWIG VON ZINZENDORF (1700–1760) at Herrnhut (see MORAVIAN MISSIONS). Lutheran in background and trained at both Halle and Wittenberg, Zinzendorf opposed introduction of Western ecclesiastical norms and warned Moravian missionaries not to judge converts by the standards of Herrnhut. He hoped that the Brethren might act as a midwife to inclusive unity among Christians of all confessions, but failed to realize this goal.

The ENLIGHTENMENT of the eighteenth century and the French revolutionary movement had devastating consequences for missions, undercutting theological clarity and motivation. But among Lutheran pietists and Moravian circles commitment to mission endured and blossomed anew in the evangelical awakening of the late eighteenth and nineteenth centuries. Lutheran and Reformed Christians joined hands in forming evangelical mission societies for recruiting, training, and sending missionaries to Asia and Africa. The BASEL (1815) and RHENISH (1828) mission societies were typical. After 1840, however, Lutherans in Europe and North America began organizing mission work on strictly confessional lines with the aim of propagating pure Lutheran doctrine, ministry, and sacraments overseas. The Dresden (later Leipzig) Lutheran mission was an early example.

Some Lutherans (e.g., BRUNO GUTMANN in Tranzania, CHRISTIAN KEYSSER in Papua New Guinea, and Johannes Warneck in Indonesia) developed Lutheran mission concepts that combined the gospel, social structures, and indigenous cultural forms. Lutheran missions in the late nineteenth century reflected a mixture of Lutheran confessional piety and student volunteer enthusiasm. European COLONIALISM and America's ascendancy as an imperial power also contributed to popular support for Lutheran mission around 1900.

With the outbreak of World War I, Lutheran world missions faced a crisis—the wartime separation of Lutherans into opposing camps. German Lutheran missionaries working in British colonial territories were interned, with the result that their fledgling mission communities were orphaned. North American and Swedish Lutheran mission groups, working closely with the Continuation Committee of the EDINBURGH MISSIONARY CONFERENCE (1910), later the INTERNATIONAL MISSIONARY COUNCIL (1921), managed to save German orphaned missions from seizure as wartime booty. Lutherans raised large sums of money and assumed trusteeship responsibilities for these missions affected by war.

This inter-Lutheran rescue operation, with its parallel in World War II, became a primary inspiration for international Lutheran cooperation. It led to the formation of the Lutheran World Convention (1923) and the Lutheran World Federation (1947), uniting more than 120 member churches encompassing 60 million Lutherans on six continents. The policies of the LWF Commissions on World Mission (1952) and Church Cooperation (1970) called for formation of united Lutheran churches in mission areas, autonomy and representation for all member churches—small or large—in the world body, internationalization of the missionary force, and sharing of international resources for cooperative programs of mission, service, training, and development.

Western Lutheran churches and mission societies maintain both bilateral and multilateral relationships with partner churches in Asia, Africa, Oceania, and Latin America. Lutherans tend to favor integration of missions into the life of the church, though some independent mission societies still exist. In Germany and Scandinavia, formerly independent mission societies are now the mission departments of regional or national churches. The ECUMENICAL MOVEMENT has compelled Lutherans to rethink earlier attitudes of confessional exclusiveness. While supporting ecumenical ventures, Lutherans remain divided in their views about church unity and inclusive church fellowship.

World Lutherans, after nearly three centuries of global mission effort, remains predominantly a Western phenomenon with 37 million Lutherans in Europe and nearly 9 million in North America. Between 1950 and 2000, however, there was astonishing growth in the Two-Thirds World: 8 million in Africa, slightly less than 5 million in Asia, and 1.4 million in Latin America. The largest of the younger Lutheran churches are found in Indonesia, Tanzania, Ethiopia, Madagascar, India, Brazil, Papua New Guinea, South Africa, and Namibia. The participation of these bodies in the Lutheran world communion, and in LWF international programs for mission, service, development, theological study, and interfaith dialogue, has altered the historically Western character of Lutheranism and raised anew the question of Lutheran identity amid change and diversity.

JAMES A. SCHERER

Bibliography. E. T. Bachmann and M. B. Bachmann, eds., *Lutheran Churches in the World: A Handbook;* D. J. Bosch, *Transforming Mission: Paradigm Shifts in Theology of Mission,* chap. 8; H. W. Gensichen, *Living Mission: The Test of Faith;* J. A. Scherer, *Gospel, Church and Kingdom: Comparative Studies in World Mission Theology;* idem, *Justinian Welz: Essays by an Early Prophet of Mission;* idem, *Mission and Unity in Lutheranism.*

Luxembourg *(Est. 2000 pop.: 425,000; 2,586 sq. km. [998 sq. mi.]).* The Grand Duchy of Luxembourg is an independent European country bordered by Belgium, Germany, and France. Its large iron and steel industry has produced a very high standard of living. Because of its central location Luxembourg has been subject to foreign invasions and domination for much of its history, which includes periods of Burgundian, Spanish, French, Austrian, and Prussian control. In 1815, it regained national independence and, after its autonomy was strengthened, developed democratic institutions. Luxembourg was declared a neutral country until giving up its neutrality to join various economic, political, and military organizations in 1948. Having already formed a close economic union with Belgium in 1921, Luxembourg became one of the founding members of the European Economic Community. With many offices and banks of that organization being located in Luxembourg, one-quarter of the working population are foreigners.

Luxembourg's native population is primarily of French and German descent. The predominant spoken language is Letzeburgech, which is a mixture of German and French. In fact, it is such a mixture that neither French nor German natives can understand it. The people of Luxembourg wanted something distinctly their own. Both German and French are official languages, so most of the 425,000 nationals have learned at least two languages.

There is freedom of religion in Luxembourg. The Roman Catholic Church is the state church, with a membership of approximately 97 percent of the population. Protestants are a minority making up just over 1 percent of the population, most of them foreign. The foreigners seem to be hard to reach because of their mobility and lack of interest in spiritual things. Next to the Catholics, the largest group among the national population is the JEHOVAH'S WITNESSES.

MARKUS WAGNER

Luzbetak, Louis J. (1917–). American missiological anthropologist and missionary to New Guinea. Born in Joliet, Illinois, to a devout Catholic family which had emigrated from Slovakia, Luzbetak knew early in life that the mission of Christ was his only option. He entered the Divine Word Seminary at Techny, Illinois, as a freshman in high school, and over the next fourteen years (until his ordination), this group became a second family to him.

After two years of theological studies in Gregorian University (Rome), he was asked to study anthropology at the University of Fribourg under WILHELM SCHMIDT, who assigned him to research the Caucasus region in the southwestern Soviet Union. Because of the Cold War, Luzbetak was unable to enter the Caucasus for his fieldwork, and consequently went to New Guinea, where he worked from 1952 to 1956.

There he observed that the gospel did not reach the people's hearts because it lacked cultural relevancy. He dedicated himself to bring anthropological insights to the missionary task to make the gospel/culture encounter more significant. This dedication profoundly influenced his teaching career.

Luzbetak's service was rich in ecumenical exposure; his gracious spirit accommodating him across evangelical, ecumenical, and Catholic contexts. He taught at the Catholic University and Georgetown University, served as president of Divine Word Seminary (Epworth, Iowa), director of the Center for Applied Research in the Apostolate (CARA) and editor of *Anthropos* (Germany). He was an official Catholic observer at Lausanne (1974) and the Willowbank Consultation, as well as the second president of the AMERICAN SOCIETY OF MISSIOLOGY. His most widely recognized books are *The Church and Cultures: An Applied Anthropology for the Religious Worker* (1963) and *The Church and Cultures: New Perspectives in Missiological Anthropology* (1988).

A. SCOTT MOREAU

Bibliography. L. J. Luzbetak, *IBMR* 16:3 (1992): 124–28.

Mm

Mabille, Adolphe (1836–94). Swiss missionary in Lesotho. Born in Switzerland into the family of a teacher who was active in the Free Church of the Canton of Vaud, he studied at Yverdon and Basel and worked as a French teacher in the Netherlands and then England where he was converted and decided to become a missionary. In 1856–59 he studied theology in Paris in preparation for service with the PARIS EVANGELICAL MISSIONARY SOCIETY in its work in Lesotho. Before leaving he married Adèle Casalis (1840–1923), the daughter of Eugène Casalis, founder of the Lesotho mission and at the time the society's director. Born in Africa, she taught him the language while they were traveling to the field. At the society's Morija station he worked as an evangelist, opened a Bible school to train indigenous catechists (the first missionary to do so in southern Africa), and directed a publishing enterprise that brought out the Sotho Bible he had translated as well as a dictionary, hymnbook, and numerous tracts. He served as an adviser to the paramount chief Moshoeshoe (Moshesh) I and mediated conflicts between the Sotho and Boers (Afrikaners) who were encroaching on their territory. This eventually led to the establishment of the British protectorate of Basutoland in 1868. A totally committed laborer, he died of exhaustion at Morija in 1894

ULRICH VAN DER HEYDEN AND RICHARD V. PIERARD

Bibliography. E. W. Smith, *The Mabilles of Basutoland* (1939).

Macau (Portuguese District/Region) *(Est. 2000 pop.: 45,000; 16 sq. km. [6 sq. mi.]).* The island of Macau lies on the southeastern coast of China. It has been under Portuguese administration since the sixteenth century, and was an important trading port for southern China until the British established Hong Kong in 1841. Due to the recent influx of Chinese immigrants, which have more than doubled the population in a decade, Macau has been revitalized.

The total area of Macao is roughly six square miles, and the population is comprised of 95 percent Chinese, 3 percent Portuguese and other Europeans, and 2 percent other Asian. Portuguese and Chinese are the two official languages, and the Cantonese dialect is by far the predominant spoken language. In 1999 its sovereignty reverted back to China, two years after a similar arrangement for Hong Kong. The church has remained small through the years. Roughly 80 percent of the population is Buddhists and 6 percent Roman Catholic, while Protestants number less than 1 percent.

The Roman Catholic Church established work in Macau in the mid-sixteenth century. By 1576 the first bishop, Melchoir Carneiro, was installed to oversee the parish. Originally the church was primarily for the Portuguese population, but it opened its doors to the Chinese in the nineteenth century. The church experienced rapid growth after 1949 when many Catholic refugees came from China for safe haven. It was at St. Paul Seminary of Macau that MATTEO RICCI, the pioneer Roman Catholic missionary, received his training. There are now about twenty churches serving the Catholic community in Macau.

In 1807 the LONDON MISSIONARY SOCIETY sent ROBERT MORRISON, the first Protestant missionary to China. He was stationed in Macau, concentrating on language acquisition and the translation of the Bible into the Chinese language. He gave his life for the sake of the gospel and was buried in Macau. There are now fifty-five Protestant churches of various denominations. The majority of the believers are grassroots people. The church faces a critical need for leadership in both the clergy and the laity. In addition, there is a high turnover rate among the pastors since very few are home grown. The majority come from neighboring Hong Kong. In 1982 the Macau Bible Institute was established to meet this critical need.

In recent years many mission agencies, both Chinese and Western, have made a renewed effort to reach the masses, especially new immigrants. The results have been steady but slow.

JOHN D. L. HSU

Bibliography. R. D. Crement, ed., *Macau: City of Commerce & Culture*; G. Law, *Chinese Churches Handbook*.

Macedonia *(Est. 2000 pop.: 2,247,000; 25,713 sq. km. [9,928 sq. mi.]).* Macedonia, a former province of Yugoslavia, is a landlocked country in the Balkans surrounded by Greece, Albania, Serbia, and Bulgaria. Over 50 percent of the people are ethnically Macedonian and 20 percent are Albanian. Sixty-three percent of all Macedonians are Christian while 30 percent are Muslims. The vast majority of the Christians belong to the Orthodox Church. The largest of the Evangelical groups are the Methodists (3,000 members) and the Gypsy Evangelical Movement with over 1,000 adherents.

TODD M. JOHNSON

Mackay, Alexander Murdock (1849–1890). Scottish pioneer engineer-missionary to Uganda. Son of a Free Church of Scotland minister, Mackay resisted the pressure to follow in his father's footsteps and trained as an engineer in Edinburgh and Berlin. In 1876 he left for East Africa as part of a CMS group sent in response to information that King Mutesa of Buganda was willing to receive missionaries.

After three years Mackay was the only survivor in an area where tribal differences were being reinforced by Protestant and Catholic missions and Arab and Western politics. He developed good relationships at court, translated Matthew's Gospel into Luganda, and worked with Africans to build roads, houses, machinery, and boats. He opposed Catholic missions, and encouraged British intervention. After the death of King Mutesa in 1884 and the martyrdom of Catholic and Protestant Christians in 1886, he was forced to move to the south of Lake Victoria where he died at Usambiro.

Mackay's spiritual depth and practical skills were popularized by his sister's biography and admired for generations.

JOHN ROXBOROGH

Bibliography. J. W. Harrison, *The Story of the Life of Mackay of Uganda*.

MacKay, George Leslie (1844–1901). Canadian missionary to China. Arguably one of the most successful Chinese missionaries in the nineteenth century, G. L. MacKay worked out of Tamsui in northwestern Formosa, now called Taiwan. An indefatigable promoter of indigenous clergy and medical outreach, he supported cultural awareness while challenging spiritism with scientific knowledge and methods. His pioneering work among Chinese lowlanders and tribal highlanders involved active missionary apprenticeship of Chinese and Malay tribal students.

The first missionary sent by Canadian Presbyterians, MacKay settled in Tamsui in 1872 after graduating from Princeton University and studying theology in Edinburgh under ALEXANDER DUFF. Breaking with many missionary conventions, MacKay married a Formosan woman, maintained training schools for boys, girls, and women, and established a hospital and scientific-cultural museum.

His regular strategy was for a group to enter a village temple compound, gather a crowd by singing hymns, follow it by dental work, and then preach. Once a congregation was established, national preachers and Bible-women were employed rather than foreign missionaries. Before dying of throat cancer MacKay saw sixty chapels established in northern Formosa, leaving behind an encyclopedic knowledge of the peoples yet to be reached.

LAUREN PFISTER

Bibliography. G. L. MacKay, *Chinese Recorder* 23 (1892): 524–29; idem, *From Far Formosa*: *The Island, Its People and Missions*.

Mackay, John Alexander (1889–1983). Scottish missionary to Peru and Mexico; ecumenical leader. Born in Inverness, Scotland, he was seriously convicted of the correlation between his academic preparation and God's call to be a Christian missionary. He studied in Scotland, the United States, Spain, Peru, and Germany. "At the core of my movement from one academic center to another," Mackay wrote, "I sought the cultural preparation that seemed most expedient to equip me for effective missionary service."

After their marriage on August 16, 1916, Mackay and his bride, Jane Logan Wells, sailed for Lima, Peru, as the first missionaries sent by the Free Church of Scotland to Latin America. There they ministered from 1916 to 1932—nine years in Lima and seven years in Montevideo and Mexico City. Afterwards, Mackay served as president of Princeton Theological Seminary and became a central figure in the founding of the WORLD COUNCIL OF CHURCHES.

As a "Christian traveler on the road," his discovery of "the incarnational approach to the human situation" based on John 1:14 became the core of his missionary legacy and to this approach he dedicated his entire life and missionary work among academic audiences. He theorized: "I learned early in my career . . . that if I was to be taken seriously and to succeed in influencing others in the direction of the Christian faith, it was essential to establish close ties of friendship with them, and learn to understand their cultural background and aspirations."

ELIAS S. MEDEIROS

Bibliography. S. Escobar, *IBMR* 16:3 (1992): 116–22; H. M. Goodpasture, *Journal of Presbyterian History* 48 (1970): 265–92; J. A. Mackay, *CT*, January 2, 1970, 3–5.

Macomber, Eleanor (1801–40). American pioneer missionary to Myanmar (formerly Burma). Her first missionary venture came in 1830 when she was sent by the Baptist Missionary Board of America as a teacher among the Ojibwas in Michigan. After nearly four years her health failed and she was forced to return to New York. In 1836 she became associated with the Burma Mission. In the autumn of that year she was appointed to Dong Yhan to work among the Karens. Her strategy was to begin immediately the worship of God in their midst. With little knowledge of the language, she gathered people on the Sabbath to hear the gospel. Weekdays she invited people for morning and evening prayers, often asking questions at the close. She soon had a school of a dozen pupils, and a church was formed in less than one year. With a select group of converts, she traveled widely to other villages. While away from her remote post she became ill and died nine days later. She left behind a band of disciples well grounded in the Christian faith.

Macomber was one of very few single women sent to a foreign mission field in her era. She ventured beyond the limited role for women and, in her relatively short tenure, laid the foundation for a permanent Christian presence among Burmese tribes.

FLORENCE R. SCOTT

Bibliography. D. C. Eddy, *Heroines of the Missionary Enterprise*; R. P. Beaver, *All Loves Excelling: American Protestant Women in World Mission.*

Macumba. *See* LATIN AMERICAN NEW RELIGIOUS MOVEMENTS.

Madagascar *(Est. 2000 pop.: 17,259,000; 587,041 sq. km. [226,657 sq. mi.]).* Larger than France and Belgium combined, Madagascar, located off Africa's southeastern coast and the world's fourth largest island, is nearly 1,000 miles long and 350 miles wide. The more than 17 million people and their culture are of Indo-Malaysian origin with later African, Arab, and Western influences.

After failed Protestant and Catholic mission attempts in the sixteenth century, the first enduring Christian work began on August 18, 1818, when David Jones and Thomas Bevan, LONDON MISSIONARY SOCIETY (LMS) missionaries, arrived in Tamatave. Within six months the Bevans and Jones' wife and child died. Jones began work in the interior Merina kingdom under King Radama I, who desired to modernize his kingdom.

Bible translation (completed in 1835) and printing were given highest priority although the mission built schools and churches. People were attracted by the sermons and singing, both traditional Malagasy cultural forms, but seven years passed before a convert was baptized.

After Radama I's death in 1828, traditionalists took power and a great persecution ensued until 1863. Bibles were destroyed, missionaries were banned, and Christians were martyred. The church grew tenfold with indigenous leadership; the martyrs' faithful witness partially accounted for this growth.

Queen Ranavalona II came to power in 1869. She destroyed the national idols and invited the missionaries to return. The next thirty years saw some of the fastest church growth in mission history as much of the nation came into the church. The LMS returned, took over the churches from local leadership, and invited the Quakers to join their work in 1867. By the early twentieth century the church was nominal.

The SOCIETY FOR THE PROPAGATION OF THE GOSPEL began in 1864. The Norwegian Mission arrived in 1866, and the American Lutherans as a branch of the Norwegians in 1888. The Lutheran Church today is a large nationwide church.

The French conquered the nation in 1896. The French Reformed Church took up the slack of the British missionaries as the French colonial government forced them out. During the period of French rule (1896–1958) the Roman Catholic Church, the only official church, gained strength.

Beginning in the south, the area of Lutheran work, in 1894 and continuing to the present, revival movements have been characteristic of the Malagasy church. The revival encompasses parts of all major denominations today.

In 1960 the LMS, Quakers, and French Reformed combined to become the United Church of Madagascar, an influential church today. Several smaller churches began in the twentieth century: Seventh-Day Adventists (1926), Malagasy Baptists (1932), Evangelical Mission of Tananarive (1952), Jesus Saves (1962), and the United Pentecostal Church (1969).

From 1972 until 1991, the nation was under a strong socialist government that sent thousands of young people to socialist nations, the Soviet Union in particular, for military and university education. Many came to Christ in those nations and returned with a strong witness that contributed to revival.

Since 1991, many evangelical organizations, both Western and indigenous, have opened work in Madagascar. Malagasy Christians have served as missionaries in North and South Africa and in Europe. Many have taken significant leadership roles in the Lutheran World Federation, The All Africa Council of Churches, and the World Council of Churches.

MIKEL NEUMANN

Bibliography. H. Brandt, comp., *Madagascar;* M. Brown, *Madagascar Rediscovered;* B. A. Gow, *Madagascar and the Protestant Impact;* M. Neumann, *Factors Underlying Accelerated Growth Trends as Reflected in the History of the Malagasy Baptist Church;* J. B. Vigen, *A Historical and Missiological Account of the Pioneer Missionaries in the Establishment of the American Lutheran Mission in Southeast Madagascar, 1887–1911.*

Magic, Magick, Magical Beliefs and Practices.

Magic refers to RITUAL strategies people use to control unknowable supernatural forces. White magic is used for good and black magic for evil purposes. Magical practices involve the use of rituals—the right chant or words recited, the right sign used, the right object worn—inducing supernatural powers to respond in expected ways, much like a scientist controls chemical reactions. Magic is used where uncertainty, the elements of chance, and anxiety pervade. Usually the rituals employed grow out of exceptionally good previous performances. Magic has a utilitarian value available to all who know the right rituals. "Magick" is used by religious practitioners of the art to distinguish their form of practice from sleight of hand. In magic the techniques are believed to harness supernatural powers in charms, fetishes, and other direct attempts to achieve success. The belief is in forces which may be controlled through other supernatural forces in ritually prepared objects, or specific spiritual powers invited to take up "residence" in prepared objects, such as fetishes. Magic objects may be secured from persons of high social status, superior physical and/or spiritual power, a powerful animal, or some object which appears unnatural. There are several forms of magic but primarily two are widely used. *Homeopathic* or *imitative* magic—like produces like—is built on the idea that two things which resemble each other in one way will also resemble each other in other ways. The desired end is depicted or acted out and is magically transmitted to the intended target, as in the use of effigies. *Contagious* magic assumes that things once associated with each other continue the relationship after separation. Any substance or material object previously in contact with an individual, when subjected to magical rituals, is believed to act upon the person in a similar way, whether to injure, seduce, or secure success. The use of shorn hair, fingernail clippings, waste, or clothing may thus be used to inflict injury upon a person.

The concept of *mana* is part of the worldview of societies which accept magic as an effective way to deal with the uncertainties and anxieties of life. Mana, a Tahitian term, refers to an impersonal, extranatural force which permeates all things to varying degrees and may magically flow from one object or person to another, much like electricity flows through cables, to effect a desired intention.

Mana is closely related to energy fields as defined by the NEW AGE MOVEMENT and as practiced by some healers in physical therapy. Mana is innate in an object or person and works apart from human expertise. It accounts for successes or lack thereof. It can be controlled by the right rituals but is dangerous to the ignorant. Charms, which attract beneficial supernatural forces, and amulets which ward off evil supernatural influences, are thought effective because they are invested with concentrated mana. Many societies prefer to think of mana as life-force, a personal power which may be transmitted magically to another in very much the same way as mana flows from one object to another. Magical practices and beliefs are found in all societies. Among others, even Western sportsmen practice magical rituals to ensure success over their rivals. Frequently societies influenced by concepts of magic and mana transfer these concepts to Christian practices such as Communion, ordination, healing, speaking in tongues, liturgies, and holy places, resulting in syncretistic beliefs and practices.

PHILIP M. STEYNE

SEE ALSO Occult, Occultism.

Bibliography. B. Malinowski, *Magic, Science and Religion;* M. Bouisson, *Magic: Its Rites and History;* P. M. Steyne, *Gods of Power.*

Mahayana Buddhism.

Form of Buddhism dominant in China, Japan, Korea, and Vietnam. It arose between 150 B.C. and A.D. 100 in reaction against THERAVADA BUDDHISM for its literal interpretation of Buddha's teachings as well as its narrow concern for personal salvation through strenuous monastic disciplines achievable only by a few. The term "Mahayana" (Greater Vehicle) expresses the ideal of universal enlightenment in contrast to "Hinayana" (Lesser Vehicle), which aims at salvation for oneself. Its followers thus have a deep sense of mission. Even as they seek their own salvation, they do so mainly for the sake of others. Mahayana represents a radical reinterpretation of the most fundamental concepts in Buddhism—the concepts of Buddha, Arhant, Emptiness, and Nirvana.

In Theravada, the Buddha is regarded merely as the historical human sage who attained his own enlightenment, the merits of which cannot be transferred. However, in Mahayana, the concept of the Buddha becomes that of the absolute Being embodying ultimate truth and infinite compassion. The historical Sakyamuni was thought of as nothing but one of the many earthly appearances of the transcendent Buddha. There were Buddhas before and after him. Amitabha is an example. Thus Mahayanists do believe in a divine Being, faith and devotion to whom constitutes an essential part of salvation. While Theravada emphasizes self-effort for liberation, Mahayana emphasizes the gift of merit from Buddha. Thus the idea of grace is implicit.

Equally important is the idea that Buddhahood is attainable by all. Mahayana teaches that every human person possesses the Buddha nature. With proper help, one is capable of becoming a Buddha. This leads to the development of the idea of Bodhisattva in the place of the Theravada Arhant. An *arhant* is "the worthy one" who has achieved enlightenment for himself or herself, ready to be released from the cycle of rebirth to enter into *nirvana*. A Bodhisattva has likewise achieved liberation from rebirths, has even achieved transcendence, but puts off *nirvana* in order to remain in the world for the sake of delivering others. The merits of his or her virtues and wisdom can be transferred. A Bodhisattva has to go through ten stages of purification to become a Buddha. However, once the seventh stage is reached, he or she has already assumed a true Buddha nature. Progress to Buddhahood is then irreversible and sacrificial benevolence for others is spontaneous. A Bodhisattva may be regarded as the agent of salvation to those who have faith in him or her. This explains the rise of the cult of various Bodhisattvas. The cult of Avalokitesvara ("Kuan-yin" for the Chinese, and "Kannon" for the Japanese) is a good example. Self-reliance for salvation in Theravada is thus transformed into salvation through faith in a transcendent agent in the Mahayana.

Mahayanists on the one hand regard all empirical phenomena, including their constitutive elements, as void and empty; on the other, however, they affirm the reality of the indescribable Absolute. Only the Absolute is real, all empirical entities are illusions. The Madyamika School (founded by Nagarjuna, circa A.D. 15–250) follows the Middle Way. They first expose the "selfhood" of all things as void or "empty." All phenomenal entities are like shadows without substance of their own. There is no coming into being or disappearing, no differentiation or identification. However, they do not therefore affirm absolute nothingness. They affirm the reality of the Absolute. The Yogacara School (founded by the brothers Asanga and Vasubandu in the fifth century A.D.) affirms the reality of the Absolute Mind. Only Consciousness is real. All appearances of external reality are nothing but false imaginations of the mind. All of these can be eradicated only by rigorous meditation. For both schools, *nirvana* is therefore complete identification with the Absolute. Once this is achieved, one sees that the only reality is the Absolute; all the rest is revealed to be nonreality. Since the Absolute is indescribable, true knowledge is therefore unutterable. All knowledge that can be conceptualized and expressed must also be empty. Even the principle of *sunyata* (emptiness) itself is empty. Nonattachment is the ultimate principle for salvation.

Buddhism spread to China in the first century A.D. It first encountered stiff resistance. For more than two centuries, Buddhism remained foreign. Kumarajiva (A.D. 344–413) and his followers made significant contributions in the indigenization of Mahayana Buddhism in China. They used the best literary style and the most prominent philosophical ideas of the time for the propagation of Buddhism. Translation of carefully selected Buddhist texts proved to be highly significant. Mahayana Buddhism took on a distinctively Chinese character and evolved into several schools such as the T'ien Tai, Hua-yuen, Pure Land, and Ch'an. Taoist influence is quite evident. Buddhism was introduced into Japan from China, and it began to prosper there in the seventh century A.D. PURE LAND BUDDHISM and ZEN BUDDHISM became most prominent. Whether in China or Japan, it is the practical aspects of Buddhism that seem to be most emphasized.

CARVER YU

SEE ALSO Buddhism.

Bibliography. K. K. Chen, *Buddhism, the Light of Asia;* idem, *Buddhism in China;* E. Conze, *Buddhist Thought in India;* W. T. De Bary, ed., *The Buddhist Tradition in India, China and Japan;* D. T. Suzuki, *Outlines of Mahayana Buddhism.*

Malawi *(Est. 2000 pop.: 12,144,000; 118,484 sq. km. [45,747 sq. mi.]).* A century of missionary work by Malawians and foreigners made Malawi a Christian country. Islam, which came to Malawi twenty years earlier (c. 1840), became a minority (17%). Traditional religion, though much of it is still an everyday option for Muslims and Christians, is no longer an organized religion (5%). Even the officials at the territorial rain shrines are usually Christians or Muslims.

Malawi was first put on the Christian map by DAVID LIVINGSTONE (1858), who also settled the first mission (Universities' Mission to Central Africa) at Magomero in 1861. This Anglican mission could not stay long, but returned to Malawi from Zanzibar (1882). Early missionary work in Malawi was dominated by Presbyterians (Free Church of Scotland, Livingstonia, 1875; Church of Scotland, Blantyre, 1876; Dutch Reformed Church, South Africa, Nkhoma, 1889). These churches formed the Church of Central Africa Presbyterian (1926).

With Malawi being seen as a Presbyterian/Anglican territory, evangelical and Catholic missions were seen as intruders. The early evangelical missions (except South Africa General Mission, 1900) all go back to JOSEPH BOOTH, a Baptist from Melbourne: Zambezi Industrial Mission, 1892; Nyassa Industrial Mission, 1893; Churches of Christ, 1896; Seventh-Day Baptists,

1900; Seventh-Day Adventists, 1902 (now the third largest denomination).

In the early years black missionaries from Lovedale (South Africa) played a role (William Koyi, pioneer among the Ngoni), as did black Americans (like Thomas Branch and his daughter, Mabel, in Malamulo). Both groups were eventually phased out due to changing racial concepts.

As elsewhere in Africa, the schools were the greatest single mission attraction, with Overton Institution, Livingstonia (ROBERT LAWS and his wife Margaret), providing the highest education in the region. Next in attractiveness came the medical services, most missions developing at least one major hospital and a number of dispensaries. Medical work offered specific scope for women like Pauline Murray of Nkhoma. Originally almost all medical work and training was provided by the missions, and even today the churches do a third of all medical work. Animated by Livingstone's concept of opening up the interior of Africa to Christianity and commerce to fight the slave trade, Scottish Christians established the African Lakes Company, and missions like Blantyre, Livingstonia, and Nkhoma emphasized the teaching of "industrial" skills. Very soon much of the missionary work was done by Malawians, like Albert Namalambe, the first Livingstonia convert in Cape Maclear, or Mungo Chiuse of Blantyre Print, or Sara Nabanda at Mvera Hospital, along with teachers, evangelists, women leaders, and church elders. While the UMCA granted ordination to Malawians very early (1898), the first ordinations in the Presbyterian missions took place in 1912, 1914, and 1925, the Seventh-Day Adventists ordained Kalinde Malinki in 1928, and the first Catholic priest (Cornelius Chitsulo) was ordained in 1938.

The time between the wars saw a slowdown of mission expansion, with some new missions like African Methodist Episcopal Church and Apostolic Faith Mission coming in through Malawian initiative. Though the number of Christians was still small, it was clear by then that Christianity had won much of Malawi. The time after the war was marked by the independence of the "old" mission churches and the coming in of new missions like Baptists, Free Methodists, and Lutherans, and a growing number of African Instituted Churches (AIC; see AFRICAN INITIATED CHURCH MOVEMENT). Almost all churches continue to grow (through population growth and Christianization of the remaining non-Muslims), with about 30 percent of Christians being Catholics, 20 percent Presbyterians, 15 percent evangelical, and 15 percent belonging to various AICs. Women play a major role in the churches with organizations like Mvano, Chigwirizano, and Dorika. But very few churches ordain women. AIC missions started in 1900 (Chilembwe). Charles Domingo began the Seventh-Day Baptists (1910). The years between

the wars saw splits from Livingstonia Mission like Blackaman's Church. Other AICs developed from the evangelical churches and some were the result of individual efforts. Since 1980 around 50 charismatic churches (like Living Waters) arose.

Malawians have early been missionaries outside Malawi, like Grace and Lewis Mataka Bandawe (Mihecani, Mozambique), Leonard Kamungu (Anglican priest in Zambia), and Leonard Muocha to Mozambique. Christianity strongly influenced political developments. Without Blantyre Mission protesting against British plans to make the South Portuguese, Malawi would not exist in its present shape. Joseph Booth was a missionary who not only criticized aspects of COLONIALISM, but refuted the whole concept (*Africa for the African*, 1897), demanding independence for Malawi by 1920, John Chilembwe, who founded Providence Industrial Mission of the American National Baptists Inc. (1900), staged an armed uprising against colonial rule in 1915. Missions supported and criticized the colonial authorities. Many churches supported the struggle for independence (and some of the dictatorships that followed). In 1992 the Catholic bishops published their Lenten pastoral letter, starting the demise of the one-party system.

KLAUS FIEDLER

Bibliography. H. Langworthy, *"Africa for the African": The Life of Joseph Booth, Blantyre*; I. and J. Linden, *Catholics, Peasants and Chewa Resistance in Nyasaland, 1889–1939*; J. McCracken, *Politics and Christianity in Malawi 1875–1940: The Impact of the Livingstonia Mission in the Northern Province*; I. A. Phiri, *Women, Presbyterianism and Patriarchy: Religious; Experience of Chewa Women in Central Malawi*; H. Reijnaerts, A. Nielson, and M. Schoffeleers, *Montfortians in Malawi: Their Spirituality and Pastoral Approach*; A. C. Ross, *Blantyre Mission and the Making of Modern Malawi*; R. K. Ross, *Christianity in Malawi: A Source Book*; G. Shepperson and T. Price, *Independent African: John Chilembwe and the Origins, Setting and Significance of the Nyasaland Native Rising of 1915*.

Malaysia (*Est. 2000 pop.: 22,299,000; 329,758 sq. km. [127,320 sq. mi.]*). Early Christian presence may be traced to Nestorians and to traders in Melaka prior to the Portuguese conquest in 1511. The British acquired Penang in 1786, and in 1795 took over Melaka, which had been conquered by the Dutch in 1641. Roman Catholic priests from Thailand established the Major Seminary in Penang in 1810. The LONDON MISSIONARY SOCIETY (LMS) was based in Melaka and Penang from 1815, but most Protestant missions collapsed after 1842 when it became possible to enter China. Catholic leadership remained, but was divided between Portuguese and French. Open Brethren ministry dates from 1860 and Methodist from 1885. Presbyterianism grew through Chinese churches in Johore and expatriate congregations in Penang, Ipoh, and Kuala Lumpur. Missions to Sengoi indigenous people began in 1932. Pentecostalism became a larger influence through the CHARISMATIC MOVEMENT of the 1970s, but North American and Ceylonese Pentecostal missionaries had been active from 1935.

Migration was an important factor in church growth. In Sabah, the BASEL MISSION began work among migrant Hakka Chinese in 1882, many of whom were Christian. Tamil migrants to Malaya included Catholics, Lutherans, Anglicans, and Methodists. Migration increased after the Boxer Rebellion, particularly to Sitiawan and Sibu, still strong Chinese Methodist centers. Mar Thoma and Syrian Orthodox Churches were established in the 1930s following migration from the Kerela Coast of India.

In Sarawak the rule of Rajah Brooke included support for an Anglican ministry from 1847 and Catholics were later admitted. In 1828 the Australian Borneo Evangelical Mission began work with modest resources which nevertheless resulted in the largest indigenous church in Malaysia today, the SIB.

World War II saw the removal of expatriate leadership and a path toward INDIGENOUS CHURCHES was more clearly set. The Malayan Christian Council (MCC), founded in 1948, coordinated mission groups during the Malayan Emergency. Chinese relocated into "New Villages" were served by missionaries, some formerly in China, who worked alongside local Christians in social and medical work. However, after independence in 1957, many churches became overly dependent on expatriates. In the 1970s churches developed structures independent of Singapore as well as of overseas support. Recent growth in independent churches is another sign of a desire to establish a Malaysian Christian identity.

Christian commitment to education has been strong through Anglican, Catholic, and Methodist schools, now part of the government education system. Social concern is expressed through medical work, and organizations such as Malaysian CARE. The Salvation Army and YMCA/YWCA make distinctive contributions.

Since 1983 the National Evangelical Christian Fellowship (NECF) has provided a focus for evangelical and independent congregations. The Christian Federation of Malaysia incorporating the Christian Council of Malaysia (formerly MCC), Roman Catholics, and the NECF was formed in 1986. The Sabah Council of Churches and Association of Churches of Sarawak fulfill similar functions in East Malaysia.

Malaysia is a multi-religious context where Western theological preoccupations are not always relevant. Lay leadership has developed strongly in most churches. Although there are many challenges through changing political and economic circumstances, like Malaysia itself, the churches are beginning to see that they have a contribution to make on a larger stage.

JOHN ROXBOROGH

Bibliography. D. Ho, *Church in Asia Today: Challenges and Opportunities*, pp. 226–98; R. Hunt, L. K. Hing, and W. J. Roxborogh, eds., *Christianity in Malaysia. A Denominational History*; W. J. Roxborogh, *A Bibliography of Christianity in Malaysia*; G. Saunders, *Bishops and Brookes: The Anglican Mission and the Brooke Raj in Sarawak 1848–1941.*

Maldives *(Est. 2000 pop.: 297,000; 298 sq. km. [115 sq. mi.]).* The archipelago called the Republic of Maldives, which lies 450 miles southwest of Sri Lanka, with its unique flora and fauna, is an almost perfect tropical oasis. However, some environmentalists are predicting a greenhouse deluge by the year 2020 that will completely cover the 1,192 islands, none of which rise more than three meters above sea level.

Inhabited by Sri Lankans from 500 B.C. on, there is an ancient tradition about a people called the Redin, a sun-worshiping people whose pagan heritage of beliefs and customs involving spirits, or jinnis, is still evident today. The Redin, who may have arrived in 2000 B.C., supposedly left the islands about 500 B.C. or were absorbed by Buddhists from Ceylon and by Hindus from India. Later, the Maldivians converted to Sunni Islam. Because the islands were so small and building materials were limited, each subsequent people group built its important structures on the foundations of the previous inhabitants—this explains why many Maldivian mosques face the sun and not Mecca.

The government is based on Islamic law and uses its authority to enforce religious and civil Islam in order to promote national unity. We know of no officially recognized Maldivian Christians. Although restricted and unreceptive to the gospel thus far, Maldivians have made significant contacts with Christians through international commercial and sports events (e.g., the 1990 Indian Ocean Island Games in Madagascar). These contacts should be pursued by culturally sensitive Christians who can use such meetings as opportunities to help the Maldivians go beneath the surface of Islam and consider biblical answers to questions and fears stemming from their animistic background.

CLINT AKINS

Bibliography. C. Maloney, *People of the Maldive Islands.*

Mali *(Est. 2000 pop.: 12,559,000; 1,240,192 sq. km. [478,838 sq. mi.]).* Mali, the seventh largest country in Africa, is located in West Africa. Its population of over 12 million is comprised of thirty-three ethnic groups. Although the official language is French, the trade languages of Bambara, Fufulde, and Songhai are most commonly used. The economy is based on agriculture, which involves 80 percent of the population and is dependent on exports of cotton, peanuts, and cattle. While a mere 2 percent of the land is arable, 66 percent of the country is covered by the ever-encroaching Sahara Desert, which is spreading southward at a rate of eighty miles per year.

Although now one of the poorest countries in the world, Mali has a rich heritage. In the fourteenth century, the borders of its vast and enormously wealthy empire stretched inland from the Atlantic coast to the famed desert cities of Gao and Timbuktu. Colonized by France in the late 1800s, Mali became part of the French Sudan. Following independence in 1960, the country was governed by presidents under one-party rule until a 1991 coup d'état overthrew the regime in power and multiparty democracy was instituted.

Islam penetrated the land through a combination of economic and military persuasion. At times it waxed fervent, as during the Fulbe jihads of the 1800s, but for the most part was simply accepted and adapted to the existing culture. The Islamic sociopolitical system extolled by North African reformers has generally been given a lukewarm reception by the more ethnically diverse sub-Saharan nations. However, pressure has been increasing in recent years, as money and arms are offered by oil-rich Islamic nations in an attempt to convince governments to institute *sharia* (Islamic law) or to finance rebel groups that seek to overthrow the existing government in order to establish an Islamic state. Several attempts have been made in Mali, but Malian presidents, both past and present, have resisted, reaffirming the freedom of religion that is guaranteed by the country's Constitution.

Protestant missionary efforts in Mali began in 1919 with the entry of the Gospel Missionary Union, followed by the Christian and Missionary Alliance in 1923. In the early 1950s they were joined by the Evangelical Baptists and the United World Mission. In 1980 other mission organizations began entering the country, and by 1993, 309 missionaries from 35 different agencies were ministering in Mali.

The growth of Christianity has been steady, and a significant response has been seen among the Dogon, the Bwa, and other groups. Drought and desertification, with the subsequent increase of disease due to inadequate nutrition, lack of potable water, illness triggered by dust and heat, and decreased economic stability, have significantly impacted the church. These circumstances make it difficult to support pastors and ministry projects, and tend to promote dependence on outside sources. Nevertheless, a new vision is rising among Christians—a sense of urgency to bring the gospel message to the unreached of every ethnic group. This new commitment was clearly demonstrated by the scores of young people who dedicated themselves to full-time Christian service during a Youth Congress held in the capital city, Bamako, in 1995.

The 1995 organization of a Malian mission agency, Cidenya Komite, and the commissioning of a Malian couple as missionaries to a presently unreached people group, signifies the movement of the evangelical church of Mali from a body that receives missionaries to one that is participating in the fulfillment of the Great Commission by sending missionaries themselves to those who are unreached.

In expressing their concerns for the future, national church leaders see an urgent need for programs that will provide well-trained leaders capable of guiding the growing numbers of fledgling Christians to spiritual maturity, practical development projects that can assist people to regain economic stability, and health-care projects that provide medical assistance and basic teaching, giving evidence of Christian love and concern for those in need.

There has been a notable sense of disillusionment with Islam and an increasing openness to the gospel at the grassroots level of the populace since the drought years of 1973–87. Some have attributed this to a lack of response by the Islamic nations to the people's desperate plight, while Christian organizations poured in relief grain by the hundreds of tons. Nevertheless, Islam remains firmly entrenched at levels of authority, and opposition to Christianity, though not always overt, is staunch. Property and positions easily obtained by Muslims are often "unavailable" when sought by Christians. It is expected that as the Malian church grows in strength, such opposition will increase. Nevertheless, the church has been encouraged by the open atmosphere in the new democratic state, and looks to the future with hopeful anticipation.

JUDI BRODEEN

Bibliography. K. Shillington, *History of Africa;* L. Vanderaa, *A Survey for Christian Reformed World Missions of Missions and Churches in West Africa.*

Mallory, Kathleen (1879–1954). American missions promoter and leader. She grew up in a Christian home of Southern Baptist parents in Selma, Alabama, and was educated at Woman's College of Baltimore. Her engagement to a young physician ended with his death of tuberculosis. While attending the Alabama Baptist Convention (1908) with her father she was awakened to world missions. Her work began with the various women's auxiliaries to the Southern Baptist Convention of Alabama. In 1912 she was elected the corresponding secretary of the denomination-wide Woman's Missionary Union, headquartered in Baltimore, later in Birmingham (1921).

Kathleen's organizational and business acumen was reflected in the performance of her multitudinous tasks, including increasing organizational efficiency, establishing policy, raising funds for special causes, taking care of voluminous correspondence, and traveling widely. She edited the monthly magazine *Royal Service* and wrote numerous publications.

Under her leadership the Union expanded in the Orient, South America, Europe, and Africa. She encouraged its counterpart among African Americans in the National Baptist Convention. Over the years she was the recipient of numerous honors. Her legacy among Baptist women was to keep the Great Commission at the forefront through her emphases upon Christian stewardship.

FLORENCE R. SCOTT

Bibliography. A. W. Ussery, *The Story of Kathleen Mallory.*

Malta *(Est. 2000 pop.: 377,000; 316 sq. km. [122 sq. mi.]).* Island republic in the Mediterranean between Italy and Tunisia, and the site of the apostle Paul's famous shipwreck (Acts 28–29). It was also the home of the Hospitallers or "Knights of Malta" (1530–1798). One-tenth the size of Rhode Island and with a population of some 334,000, Malta won independence from Britain in 1964. About 97 percent of its indigenous people are Roman Catholics, most of whom attend Mass, and community and cultural life center around the national church. A challenge to this rigid regime was made by the Labour Party in the immediate post-independence years, and perhaps also by Vatican II reforms, but the Maltese church remains one of the most conservative in the world, disallowing both divorce and civil marriage.

The country's Constitution guarantees freedom of worship to other religions, but the latter effectively serve only the expatriate community. Scope for evangelistic outreach is in practice severely limited and even tacitly discouraged by mainline Protestant bodies themselves.

J. D. DOUGLAS

Bibliography. B. Bluet, *The Story of Malta.*

Malvinas. *See* FALKLAND ISLANDS.

Man, Isle of. *See* ISLE OF MAN.

Man. *See* HUMANKIND, DOCTRINE OF.

Mana. *See* MAGIC, MAGICK, MAGICAL BELIEFS AND PRACTICES.

Management. Global mission in the post–World War II world has increasingly taken on strategic forms. David Barrett and others have documented the exponential growth of world evangelization plans featuring closure strategies. With increased specialization in global mission has come the use of resources from the world of organizational studies in an attempt to maximize the efforts of missionaries and sending agencies.

Current research does provide specificity in the use of terms. LEADERSHIP and management are words that are often used interchangeably, but these functions have specific though interrelated character. Leadership focuses on doing the right things while management focuses on doing things right. Leadership motivates people to want to do while management focuses on getting people to do.

The application of management principles to mission agencies necessitates the facilitation organizationally of at least three questions that form an integrated system. First, Who are we? As a mission agency, organizational identity is crucial to long-term effectiveness. Second, What is our business? What are the definable features of the mission agency and the parameters of the activities that provide uniqueness for the agency? Lastly, How do we get our "business" done? What particular tasks are chosen to fulfill our "business"? Management of the tasks/functions that flesh out these three questions constitutes a stewardship of ministry that facilitates mission efforts.

Particular management tasks provide cohesiveness to this integrated system of evaluative questions. The task of formulating mission statements gives the management of a mission organization self-identity and purpose. The task of strategic planning functions to enflesh the mission statement with specific goals that best focus the agency's purpose. The task of personnel management is an ongoing function. Starting with CANDIDATE and continuing with LANGUAGE and CULTURE training, pre-field and reentry preparation, the management of personnel in mission organizations is increasingly complex. Management of on-field funding, children's education, health, and safety issues is continuous. Conflict management is a task that finds necessary usage among missionary personnel, agency leadership, and mission–national relationship.

The "how" function of any mission agency necessitates the organizing task, which arranges the work of the organization in ways most likely to bring about desired results. In Western agencies, organizational flow-charts, job-ministry descriptions, and levels of personnel participation all become part of the ongoing management scheme. The controlling function of managing organizations requires proper measurements statistically and fiscally. Controlling informational feedback is necessary to most efficiently carry out the purposes of the mission agency.

Current research is highlighting the need to become a learning organization. To remain efficient in managing the purposes that the agency has defined for itself, mission efforts must implement processes of continuous improvement. Mission agencies must continually commit themselves to being organizations of life-long learning seeking to implement an ongoing facilitation of the plan, do, check, and act cycle, so that change can be effected smoothly and maximum efficiency of the stated mission of the agency can continue at optimum levels.

BYRON D. KLAUS

SEE ALSO Institutionalization; Planning.

Bibliography. D. Augsburger, *Conflict Mediation Across Cultures;* E. Dayton and D. Fraser, *Planning Strategies for World Evangelization;* P. Drucker, *Managing the Non-Profit Organization;* P. Hersey and K. H. Blanchard, *Management of Organizational Behavior;* K. O'Donnell, ed., *Missionary Care, Counting the Cost of World Evangelization;* P. Senge, *The Fifth Discipline: The Art and Practice of Organizational Learning.*

March for Jesus. Modeled after the biblical image of Jesus' triumphal procession into Jerusalem, the first prayer and praise marches were organized to take worship experiences into the streets. In May of 1987, several groups joined together to organize a rally in London. In spite of inclement weather, some 15,000 turned out. The following year saw 55,000 join in, and the organizers, including song-writer Graham Kendrick, developed plans for multiple marches throughout Britain. Marches for Jesus were held in 45 cities in 1989, and over 600 in 1990. That same year, the first Marches for Jesus were held in the United States in Austin, Texas, with some 1,500 participating. The following year two marches were held in Texas (Austin and Houston) where 22,000 were involved. The organization went nationwide, and on May 23, 1992, there were some 142 marches around the United States. Internationally there were 25 marches in European countries. The movement became a global event in 1993 when, on June 12, an estimated 1.7 million Christians in some 850 cities participated in every continent. The largest single march was in Sao Paulo, where some 300,000 took part. June 25, 1994, was the first official global March for Jesus, with 10 million in 178 nations participating. In 1996, an estimated 2 million took part in the march in Sao Paulo alone.

The tone of the marches has been typically that of love and unity across denominational barriers and a focus on worship. Rather than confronting non-Christians, the marchers seek to celebrate the reality of their love for Jesus in a tangible and positive way. As a display of Christian unity and statement of Jesus' kingship over all the earth, Marches for Jesus stand as significant events in mission at the end of the twentieth century.

A. SCOTT MOREAU

Bibliography. S. Hawthorne and G. Kendrick, *Prayer-Walking: Praying on Site with Insight;* "March for Jesus" Web site (http://www.mfj.org).

Marginal, Marginalization. Marginalization is the process by which individuals and groups come to live on the margin of a culture, not fully able to participate in its socioeconomic, political, or religious life, due to cultural, political, religious, or socioeconomic differences. The process of marginalization may be the result of historic injustices that have developed over a protracted period of time. These injustices are usually produced by a dominant group or ideology that is systematically and intentionally exclusive. Medieval Europe is an example of a time and context that manifested marginalization in interwoven patterns of socioeconomic, political, and religious life. To be outside the dominant group/ideology was to be systematically excluded from any kind of voice or alternative to the place/purpose assigned by the dominant group. Seventeenth-century England, the entire history of Latin America and the Caribbean, colonial histories on all continents, apartheid in South Africa, immigration histories in the United States, and even the current struggles in the Mexican state of Chiapas all reveal the realities of the intentional marginalization of groups and individuals.

Marginalization is the most negative result of shifting cultural contexts. The failure of assimilation stimulates the development of marginalization. In assimilation the goal is not to maintain an isolated cultural identity, but to establish and maintain relationship with other groups. When this course is freely chosen, it creates the archetypal "melting pot." If a dominant group forces assimilation, it is termed a "pressure cooker." Variant forms of marginalization include separation. Willful separation from a dominant culture, such as that practiced by the Amish or Hutterrites, has generally been respected. However, if separation is initiated and controlled by a dominant society, the situation is termed segregation. The results of such a cultural dissonance may include an inferiority complex, ambivalence, moodiness, lack of self-confidence, and disconnectedness. These characteristics can be experienced individually or corporately.

The classic definition of marginality maintains a strict separation between dominant and subordinate where unity is a goal between the groups living in a region. The dominant group uses the goal of unity for control of the subordinate group. This process of reaching unity progresses through four stages. The first stage is contact, in which the minority or possibly immigrant group experiences being truly marginalized and alien and may even experience this initial contact in the form of racism. The second stage of the process is competition, in which new or immigrant groups threaten the position of already arrived and more established groups. For example, in U.S. history, immigration of Chinese and Irish laborers in the nineteenth century created competition and great animosity between dominant and subordinate groups. The third stage is accommodation, in which education, socialization, and intermarriage tend to soften the sharp lines between dominant and subordinate groups. The fourth and final stage is called total assimilation, where it is anticipated that the subordinate group will be fully assimilated in the dominant group.

Many marginalized groups increasingly reject the melting pot ideal because the retention of one's cultural heritage becomes limited. Robert E. Park's classic theory on assimilation of the races is being replaced by the belief that eventual assimilation of the races and cultures is not possible or even desirable. Assimilation is increasingly viewed as an ideal only for homogenous national groups (for example, on the European Continent). The viewpoint of those previously marginalized is now being taken into consideration and particularly focused around racial and gender categories. In other words, who defines the "marginal" has great impact on how that group acts out its understanding.

Marginalized groups have continually produced revolutionary leaders like Karl Marx who proposed explanations of the evil of marginalization that incited millions to revolution. Given the debilitating dynamics of the process of marginalization that have systematically stripped dignity from people, it is understandable why violence has so often been a response.

Christian history is replete with examples of theologians who have addressed the impact of marginalization on peoples. FRANCIS OF ASSISI, Martin Luther, and August Francke would be representative of such persons. Recent examples would include contextual theologians like GUSTAVO GUTIÉRREZ who championed theology from the underside in response to a dominant theological perspective that has been perceived to have grown insensitive to the interconnectedness of gospel and culture in concrete ways (see GOSPEL AND CULTURE). The contextual theologies have critiqued the perceived abstract theologies of the West (north) (see LIBERATION THEOLOGIES). The alternative theological systems have attempted to bring dignity to those on the underside (subordinate groups) by speaking of God's interaction with humanity in concrete ways such as caring for the poor or the overthrow of unjust systems.

Non-Western scholars like PAULO FREIRE have argued for responding to historical examples of marginalization with new models of cultural identity for the "marginalized." They offer a definition of marginal that has a new identity. The "new marginal person" overcomes marginality without ceasing to be a marginal person. The new marginal person transcends and lives "in but beyond." In such a model, the once negative word becomes a symbol of a creative nexus that joins diverse and often contradictory worlds together and creates a mosaic rather than a melting pot. Such a reshaping of an understanding of marginalization assumes the reality of a pluralistic world. If we use the shifting cultural context in the United States as an example of the new understanding of "marginal," we would find that "Anglo-American" does not necessarily mean a white person. True Americans in a pluralistic world are more than black, red, brown, or white. To be American is to be part of a whole as a distinct, identifiable, indispensable section of a beautiful mosaic. All Americans bring their ethnic backgrounds, whether from the majority or minority perspective, to the whole. Every American can be viewed as a marginal person who lives in multiple worlds as a part of a pluralistic society. The new marginality transcends the historic understanding of marginalization as it strives to be truly in both or in all worlds as a unique entity culturally.

BYRON D. KLAUS

Bibliography. L. Boff and V. Elizondo, *Option for the Poor: Challenge to the Rich Countries;* G. Cook, *The Expectation of the Poor;* C. Dodd, *Dynamics of Intercultural Communication;* J. Ellul, *Jesus and Marx;* J. Y. Lee, *Marginality: The Key to Multicultural Theology;* J. Martin and T. Nakayama, *Intercultural Communication in Contexts.*

Marks, John Ebenezer (1832–1915). English missionary to Myanmar (formerly Burma). Born in London to a family with Jewish roots, Marks launched a career in education as a schoolmaster in Hackney, England. The SOCIETY FOR THE PROPAGATION OF THE GOSPEL (SPG) appointed him as a missionary to Burma, where he arrived in 1860 after a difficult voyage. He began his overseas ministry at an Anglican boys' school in Moulmein. In 1863 he was ordained as a deacon and transferred to Rangoon, where he opened another boys' school that eventually became known as St. John's College. The blessing of the king of Upper Burma assisted Marks's efforts to establish another school in Mandalay in 1869, although the monarch's support proved to be short-lived. In addition, Marks founded schools at some of the SPG river stations (1867–68) and St. Michael's School in a Rangoon suburb (1878). Although he helped translate the Book of Common Prayer into Burmese and also served as a chaplain, his major achievements were in educational missions. Utilizing the English public school as his model, Marks influenced 15,000 schoolboys over a thirty-five-year period. Poor health forced his retirement from educational pursuits in 1895 and a return to England in 1898, where he promoted the SPG.

JAMES A. PATTERSON

Bibliography. J. E. Marks, *Forty Years in Burma.*

Marriage, Marriage Practices. Marriage is a nearly universal cultural institution. Marriage practices, forms, and rituals are also universal concerns. In considering this topic, therefore, it is particularly important to begin with a biblical understanding of marriage.

What Is Biblical Marriage? The creation account culminates in God's creation of human beings in his own image (Gen. 1:27). This initial creation of man and woman together as the embodiment of the IMAGE OF GOD functions as the foundational paradigm of marriage.

God's creation, humankind, is first spoken of singularly and inclusively, "him," this "him" meaning both man and woman. But "him" gives way to "them," a plural which unites and distinguishes "them" as "male" and "female." These few words eloquently describe human beings as creatures made in God's own image, as alike and similar ("him") and as unique and individual ("male" and "female"). A biblical understanding of marriage addresses each of these aspects.

God blesses and provides for the man and woman, and pronounces his work to be "very good." The instruction to be fruitful presupposes the sexual union of the man and the woman and the complementary nature of "maleness" and "femaleness." Alone, neither the man nor the woman accomplishes the apparent intentions of God in creation. It is together that they are blessed and together that they are commissioned for productivity in raising children and working in God's world. This point is reinforced in Genesis 2, where God explicitly pronounces, "It is not good that the man should be alone." The creation of woman completes the creation of humankind and cannot be separated from the creation of the man. The man and woman are joined; they are "one flesh." They are created in relationship and for relationship.

What Went Wrong? God's ideal for a harmonious relationship for man and woman, however, quickly broke down through the fall (*see also* FALL OF HUMANKIND). The initial and fundamental sin in Genesis 3, involving a declaration of independence from God, set off a cycle of human power struggles. It resulted in the eviction from an ideal community and the introduction of conflicting hierarchy replacing complementary harmony.

The difficulty of marital relationships, therefore, along with other human relationships, began with the loss of the ultimate community. A marital relationship cannot occur in isolation from the community at large.

Therefore, some missiological questions arise concerning marriage and marriage practices. How can we recover the ideals of marital relationship without the ideal community of Eden? What interplay takes place between the biblical text and culture? How may members of one culture interact meaningfully about marriage practices with members of another culture?

Biblical Marriage in Contemporary Settings. The biblical paradigm of marriage from the creation account is the ideal to which all marriage practices ought to be compared. It is the ideal par excellence. But the ideal was disrupted by the fall. Therefore, against the ideal of relationship, partnership, oneness, and difference, are the real-life crises which confront modern marriages.

Three basic patterns of marriage are recognized by anthropologists: monogamy, polygyny (commonly called polygamy), and polyandry. A fourth pattern is finding acceptance in limited communities, that of same-sex marriage.

Monogamy, the marriage of one man and one woman, with an exclusive sexual relationship, is the most common idealized form of marriage. Cultural variations of its enactment include religious rituals, civil ceremonies, and common law acceptance. The choice of partner may be up to the individual or at the discretion of the extended family. Monogamy is generally recognized to uphold the creation model of one husband and one wife restated by Jesus (Matt. 19:4–6). Polygamy, one man with two or more wives, is attested to in the Old Testament and continues to be practiced in some cultures today. Polyandry, one woman with two or more husbands, is the least common of the traditional marriage patterns. Same-sex marriages, involving two males or two females, have recently been suggested as analogous to monogamous relationships, though there is no biblical support for this type of marital union.

Several principles can be offered as foundations for the challenges related to marriage and the diversity of marriage practices found in the world today.

1. An initial acceptance of observed marriage patterns. The monogamous standard of Western culture has not always existed and is currently threatened by high divorce rates and multiple marriages resulting in what some have called serial polygamy. Previously accepted marriage patterns in the West have included polygamy, arranged marriages, common-law marriages, and marriages of convenience. It is important to remember that God works over time in the transformation of all cultures and their practices.

2. Understanding. The marriage practices of a culture have a significance for that culture which must be understood if that culture is to be fully understood. How men and women relate to one

599

another, and the meaning of their interactions provide important insights about individuals as well as cultures (*see* GENDER ROLES). It is likely that some aspects of the relationships we observe will be useful in evaluating and critiquing our own relationships and practices. We must learn before we would be teachers.

3. Issues of justice and mercy. In understanding and appreciating expressions of marital commitment in our culture as well as in other cultures, we must not overlook the critical issues of justice and mercy. We must remain sensitive to the fact that around the world women tend to be oppressed by men. The gospel is liberating good news of God's justice to those who are oppressed.

Mercy recognizes that change is difficult, and often can occur only slowly with much hardship. When practices must be changed in order to conform to the creation ideal, then special care must be taken to protect those who might be injured or experience hardship as a result. Established families should never be divided. Rather, we should enable change to occur over generations and with the full knowledge, consent, and participation of those affected.

Missionaries working within polygamous contexts have learned this lesson over the years, many times through trial and error. For example, when a man with many wives becomes a Christian, what direction does the missionary provide concerning the man's many wives (*see* POLYGAMY AND CHURCH MEMBERSHIP)? The issues are exceedingly complex, and missionaries must be patient and loving in processing these and other related issues.

ADRIENNE FORGETTE AND YOUNG LEE HERTIG

Bibliography. J. Chittister, *There is a Season.*

Marsden, Samuel (1764–1838). English chaplain and missionary to Australia and New Zealand. Born in Yorkshire, England, he was profoundly impacted by Charles Simeon during his studies at St. John's College, Cambridge. Samuel Marsden and his young family arrived in Sydney on March 10, 1794. Marsden, "Australia's second preacher," began his influential ministry in Sydney and Parramatta, founding the first permanent church building in Australia: St. John's, Parramatta (1803). A tireless worker, Marsden was involved in farming, magisterial duties, education for orphans, and supervision of a factory for female convicts. The tragic loss of two of his children and an attempt on his life by an angry convict did not supplant Marsden's missionary vision for the Pacific. On his only furlough to England, Marsden shared his burden for New Zealand, recruiting lay workers to join him. Undaunted by the stories of violent encounters, Marsden, accompanied by eight Maoris and three English missionary families, arrived in Whangoroa, New Zealand, in 1814. On Christmas Day, Marsden proclaimed the "glad tidings" from Luke 2:10 in what was the first Christian service in New Zealand. Marsden, "the Apostle to New Zealand," made seven journeys to New Zealand and witnessed a mighty work of God.

DOUGLAS MCCONNELL

Bibliography. I. H. Murray, *Australian Christian Life from 1788: An Introduction and Anthology.*

Marshall Islands (*Est. 2000 pop.: 63,000; 181 sq. km. [70 sq. mi.]*). A group of 34 atolls with 1,156 islands in Oceania halfway between Hawaii and Papua New Guinea, the Marshall Islands became a constitutional government in free association with the United States following the Compact of Free Association enforced as of October 21, 1986. In 1993 the population was estimated to be 94 percent Christian (80.3% Protestant, 10% Catholic, and 3.7% marginal, including Mormons and Jehovah's Witnesses), of which some 35 percent was evangelical. The largest Protestant denominations are the Assemblies of God, the United Church of Christ, and Reformed Congregational.

A. SCOTT MOREAU

SEE ALSO Micronesia.

Marshman, Joshua (1768–1837). English missionary to India. Born in Westbury Leigh, Wiltshire, Marshman apprenticed briefly with a bookseller in London, and then worked in his father's weaver shop. Despite limited formal education, he moved to Bristol in 1794 to teach at the Broadmead School and study at the Bristol Academy. Accounts of WILLIAM CAREY's mission efforts in India inspired Marshman to consider a missionary call, and he volunteered for appointment by the Baptist Missionary Society (BMS). In 1799 he and his wife, Hannah, along with WILLIAM WARD and others, arrived at the Danish trading colony of Serampore, near Calcutta. As one of the famed SERAMPORE TRIO, Marshman contributed significantly to educational endeavors, in spite of some resistance from the BMS. He and his wife founded boarding schools to serve both Europeans and Indians. In 1818 Marshman established Serampore College, which he hoped would aid in the development of indigenous churches by training native pastors. He also devoted countless hours to Bible translation projects in several languages, including Bengali, Sanskrit, and Chinese. Although not esteemed as a great preacher, Marshman itinerated in areas beyond Serampore and organized several mission stations. He also wrote for the *Friend of India* on doctrinal and social issues.

JAMES A. PATTERSON

Bibliography. E. D. Potts, *British Baptist Missionaries in India, 1793–1837;* A. C. Smith, *The Mission Enterprise of Carey and His Colleagues.*

Martin of Tours (316–97). Early French monastic missionary. Born into a pagan military family, Martin became a Christian at an early age and received instruction and preparation for baptism. He entered the army in his teens but obtained his discharge after a night in Amiens when, as a vision instructed him, he divided his coat with a beggar. Martin traveled with his friend Hilary to try to convert his parents. After entering monastic life in Milan, he rejoined Hilary and settled in Tours as a hermit, eventually founding the monastery at Ligugé. In 372 he was tricked into becoming the Bishop of Tours. He refused to sit on the bishop's throne, but chose a crude stool and continued to live as a hermit in a cell outside the city, then founding another monastery in Marmoutier. Sulpicius Severus wrote of many miracles attributed to Martin. The bishop was active in winning non-Christians and traveled extensively outside his diocese on various errands in the interests of the faith. He introduced a parochial system. Although impeccably orthodox, he protested against the persecution of heretics and raised important issues regarding church-state relations.

JOHN EASTERLING

Bibliography. S. Severus, *Life of St. Martin;* J. H. Corbett, *Journal of Medieval History* 7 (1981): 1–13.

Martin, Walter R. (1928–89). American apologist, evangelist, and author. Martin became a Christian under the ministry of Frank Gaebelein at the Stony Brook School and received a bachelor's degree from Shelton College and a master's degree from New York University and Biblical Seminary. Widely considered the father of the American countercult movement, in the 1950s Martin almost single-handedly challenged evangelical Christians to develop biblically faithful and apologetically solid approaches to those involved in cults, non-Christian religions, and the occult. Toward this goal he founded the Christian Research Institute in 1960.

Martin's first book, *Jehovah of the Watch Tower* (1953), was followed by many other books, booklets, and tapes, including the standard reference work *The Kingdom of the Cults* (1965), which remains in print in a revised edition. It has sold over 500,000 copies. Martin was also well known for his call-in radio program *The Bible Answer Man,* which began in 1965. An outgoing and articulate defender of the faith, he impacted world missions through his trips to Africa, Europe, Latin America, Australia, New Zealand, and the Far East to warn of the challenges of cults.

DOUGLAS GROOTHUIS

Martin, William Alexander Parsons ("Wap" Martin, 1827–1916). American missionary to China. Born in Livonia, Indiana, on April 10, 1827, Martin was raised in a family with a strong missionary zeal. In his last year at New Albany Theological Seminary he decided to be a missionary to China. In 1849, he was accepted as a missionary of the Presbyterian Board of Foreign Missions.

Martin's first publication was his translation of the Bible into the dialect of Ningbo. His *Evidence of Christianity* proved to be a popular religious text in China, Japan, and Korea. Realizing that the Qing officials and Chinese literati needed to know international law to restrain continuing European encroachment, Martin translated and published Henry Wheaton's *Elements of International Law* (1864). Between 1869 and 1894 he taught at and administered the Tong Wen College, an advanced institute for the study of Western knowledge. From 1872 to 1875 he also edited the *Zhongxi Wenjianlu,* a monthly magazine introducing modern science and technology. Among his works on Chinese culture and contemporaneous events are the *Hanlin Papers: Essays on the History, Philosophy, and Religion of the Chinese* (1880, 1881, 1894) and *The Awakening of China* (1907). Through his life and work, Martin established himself not only as a missionary, but also as a source of reform ideals for the Chinese gentry. He died in Beijing at the age of eighty-nine after sixty-six years of service for the Chinese.

TIMOTHY MAN-KONG WONG

Bibliography. R. Covell, *W. A. P. Martin: Pioneer of Progress in China;* W. A. P. Martin, *A Cycle of Cathay,* 3d ed.

Martinique (French Overseas Department) *(Est. 2000 pop.: 397,000; 1,091 sq. km. [421 sq. mi.]).* The northernmost Windward Island whose population consists almost entirely (93%) of Afro-Caribbean descendants of African slaves. Its geographical distinctive is the volcano Pelée, whose eruption in 1902 killed 30,000 inhabitants of Saint Pierre. As on its companion island of Guadeloupe, the population is 85% Roman Catholic and incorporated into French life as an overseas department of France. Evangelical Christians make up about 5% of the population, with Seventh-Day Adventists reporting the largest Protestant membership.

EVERETT A. WILSON

SEE ALSO Caribbean.

Bibliography. A. Lampe, *The Church in Latin America, 1492–1992,* pp. 201–15; J. Rogozinski, *A Brief History of the Caribbean: From the Arawak and the Carib to the Present.*

Martyn, Henry (1781–1812). English missionary to India and Iran. Born in Cornwall, England, he graduated from Cambridge. After rebelling against God, he followed in the train of DAVID BRAINERD and WILLIAM CAREY. Their missionary work motivated him to launch a brief but highly significant career in India and Iran. He emulated Brainerd's deep levels of piety and Carey's hard labor in Bible translation. Martyn fell madly in love, but maintained his vow of celibacy for the sake of becoming a missionary. After becoming an Anglican priest, he signed on with the East India Company as a chaplain and went to India in 1805. There he met Carey, who started him in Bible translation work. He had to serve the workers and their families for his employer, but he fervently pursued preaching at military posts—which included Indians—starting schools, and translating the New Testament into Arabic, Persian, and Urdu, the three primary languages of the Muslim world.

Although he was not in good health, he sailed to Iran to do further translation work. He tried to make it back to England overland, but died in Turkey. His model of sacrificial devotion, and his journal, inspired many students and missionaries in the nineteenth and twentieth centuries.

JIM REAPSOME

Bibliography. D. Bentley-Taylor, *My Love Must Wait: The Story of Henry Martyn.*

Martyrdom. The role of martyrdom in the expansion of the church is the common thread that links the church of all ages with its suffering Savior. Tertullian, third-century leader in the church of North Africa, wrote to his Roman governors in his *Apology,* "As often as you mow us down, the more numerous we become. The blood of the Christians is seed." But martyrdom is not unique to Christianity. People have sacrificed their lives throughout the ages for a variety of reasons. To define the distinctive meaning of Christian martyrdom requires investigation of the Bible and church history.

Definition. The word *martyr* is an English word transliterated from its Greek equivalent *(martyrus).* It is closely associated with the word *witness* as used in the Scriptures. The Old Testament Hebrew equivalent is *moed,* which is used in reference to the place where God establishes his covenant with his people.

In the New Testament, the ideas of truth and Scripture are integrated into the verb form *martureō.* Jesus uses it to establish his witness as truth (Matt. 26:65; Mark 14:63; Luke 22:71). John the Baptist links Jesus, truth, and Scripture. Luke speaks of witness to the whole world (Acts 1:8).

The word *martyr* also extends its meaning to include Christ-like values, such as faithfulness, truth, witness, and lifestyle. Eventually, even "death-style" is subsumed. The first Christian-era martyr known is Stephen (Acts 7) who, interestingly, was put to death by "witnesses" for his witness. In Revelation 3:14, the last word is given concerning Jesus Christ who is "the faithful and true witness." The word does away with any distinction of what a true believer might live and die for. Death does not stop the witness given. It merely adds an exclamation point of truth, faithfulness, and love for the glory of God. It is the supreme witnessing act. Neither personal gain nor personal opinion provides the motive for such a death.

Church Growth and Martyrdom. Tertullian also wrote, "For who, when he sees our obstinacy is not stirred up to find its cause? Who, when he has inquired, does not then join our Faith? And who, when he has joined us, does not desire to suffer, that he may gain the whole grace of God?" Current estimates are that roughly 150,000 Christians are martyred each year, down from a peak of 330,000 prior to the demise of communist world powers. Some project that the numbers will increase to 600,000 by A.D. 2025, given current trends in human rights abuses and growth of militant religious systems.

Those inflicting contemporary Christian martyrdom include political regimes with counter-Christian agendas (e.g., official atheistic powers, such as China and the former Soviet Union); sociopolitical regimes enforcing religious restrictions (e.g., Egypt, Sudan); ethnic tribal regimes bent on eliminating minorities (e.g., Sudan, Rwanda, and Burundi) and religious regimes (e.g., Muslim countries in which *Sharia* is the official legal system).

Conclusion. Martyrdom will continue to be associated with the progress of gospel proclamation until the KINGDOM OF GOD is established. Jesus said, "Do not suppose that I have come to bring peace to the earth. I did not come to bring peace, but a sword" (Matt. 10:34). The sword was not to be used by his disciples against others, but could be expected to be used against them. Paul said, "All this is evidence that God's judgment is right, and as a result you will be counted worthy of the kingdom of God, for which you are suffering" (2 Thess. 1:5). Finally, as Augustine wrote in *City of God:* "Despite the fiercest opposition, the terror of the greatest persecutions, Christians have held with unswerving faith to the belief that Christ has risen, that all men will rise in the age to come, and that the body will live forever. And this belief, proclaimed without fear, has yielded a harvest throughout the world, and all the more when the martyr's blood was the seed they sowed."

J. RAY TALLMAN

SEE ALSO Persecution.

Bibliography. R. Daniel, *This Holy Seed;* S. Bergman, *Martyrs: Contemporary Writers on Modern Lives of Faith;*

J. Hefley and M. Hefley, *By Their Blood: Christian Martyrs of the Twentieth Century; WCE.*

Marxism. *See* COMMUNISM, MARXISM.

Mass Communication. It has been said that the Reformation would have been impossible without Gutenberg's invention of printing with movable type, which made literature available to the common person. The various forms of mass MEDIA also seem to have been providentially provided by God for world evangelization, and have played a major role in modern missions.

Print. The "father of modern missions," WILLIAM CAREY, set the tone with his emphasis on publication and distribution of the Scriptures and other literature. He and his colleagues produced nearly 40 translations of the Bible or portions thereof in languages of South Asia, along with a great number of tracts and other Christian materials. A fellow member of the "SERAMPORE TRIO," WILLIAM WARD, was an experienced printer and newspaper editor who operated a mission press.

Similarly, other pioneers saw BIBLE TRANSLATION and literature distribution as a key to reaching the masses for Christ (*see* LITERACY, LITERATURE MISSION WORK). ROBERT MORRISON, who arrived in Canton, China, in 1807, not only translated the entire Bible into Mandarin, but also published the Shorter Catechism and part of the Book of Common Prayer, along with a number of pamphlets. Two of Morrison's colleagues were printers, and one, William Milne, set up a press in Malacca.

Early efforts to evangelize the Middle East included a printing press in Malta, donated in 1822 by the Old South Church of Boston, to publish tracts and Scriptures for distribution in the region. Similar stories could be told of almost every place in the world.

By 1921, according to Arthur J. Brown, some 160 presses run by Protestant missions were churning out 400 million pages per year. Today there are major Christian publishing houses in almost every corner of the globe. Most missions and national churches use literature extensively for evangelism as well as education of believers. Books, periodicals, Sunday school materials, pamphlets, and tracts continue to be published by the millions in hundreds of languages. Missionary organizations which work primarily with the printed page include Christian Literature Crusade, Every Home for Christ, Operation Mobilization, the various BIBLE SOCIETIES, and many more. Among many recent innovative efforts is Amity Press, set up by the United Bible Societies in China with government approval, which has printed over seven million Chinese Bibles and New Testaments. Also, several evangelistic magazines such as *Step* and *African Challenge* in Africa and *Prisma* in Mexico are reaching the secular market.

Desktop publishing and computer typesetting have revolutionized literature production, especially in non-Western alphabets.

Electronic Media. Radio began as "wireless telegraphy" at the turn of the century, with the first commercial audio broadcasts in the U.S. starting in 1919. Only ten years later, Ruben Larson and Clarence Jones began efforts to use the fledgling medium to reach the world with the gospel (*see also* RADIO MISSION WORK). Against the best technical advice at the time, which said radio would not work in the mountains or near the equator, they were led to locate in Quito, Ecuador, where the Voice of the Andes, HCJB, went on the air on Christmas Day, 1931. It became a voice heard literally around the world. Today HCJB and its affiliated stations broadcast in 39 languages, reaching Europe and the Far East as well as Latin America. In addition to the outreach within and from Ecuador, World Radio Missionary Fellowship (WRMF), HCJB's parent organization, operates a string of stations along the Texas border which reach the northern areas of Mexico, one of the few Latin American countries that restricts gospel broadcasting.

A second missionary radio giant began just after World War II. John Broger, a former Navy officer, and Robert Bowman and William Roberts, both involved in pioneer radio ministries in the U.S., formed the Far East Broadcasting Company (FEBC) in December 1945. Although they had planned to set up a station in China, the Lord directed them to Manila, where DZAS, "The Call of the Orient," began transmitting in 1948. Today FEBC and its associate organization, FEBA (Far East Broadcasting Associates), operate over 30 stations in the Philippines, Saipan, South Korea, the Seychelles, and other locations, broadcasting in some 100 languages.

Trans World Radio, founded by Dr. Paul Freed, grew out of a vision for reaching Spain with the gospel via radio. Freed was able to lease a frequency in the international city of Tangier, in North Africa. The Voice of Tangier went on the air in 1954 with a 2500-watt war surplus transmitter, broadcasting to Europe. With Morocco's independence in 1959, operations were moved to Monte Carlo. Today TWR broadcasts from high-power stations in Monaco, Guam, Bonaire, Swaziland, Cyprus, Sri Lanka, and Albania, as well as leasing time on commercial stations in various countries. Recording studios all over the world provide programming in over 90 languages.

Other major international radio ministries include ELWA, in Liberia, West Africa, founded in 1954 by SIM International; IBRA (Sweden); and Voice of Hope in Lebanon. Another high-power international station in Africa, RVOG, the Radio Voice of the Gospel, operated by the Lutheran

World Federation, was confiscated by the revolutionary government of Ethiopia in 1977, after 14 years of outreach and a $2 million investment. Also in 1977 the government of Burundi closed Radio Cordac, a joint effort of several missions. The recent civil war in Liberia resulted in major damage to equipment and forced temporary evacuation of ELWA staff.

In addition to the large international and multi-lingual radio ministries, an estimated 3,200 local stations worldwide are operated by missions, local churches, or lay Christians. Thousands of hours of gospel programming also go out each week on secular stations. Recent political changes in both western and eastern Europe have opened new doors for local gospel broadcasting in many countries where a few years ago it was totally impossible.

One new thrust in international radio outreach is "The World by 2000," a joint project of WRMF/HCJB, FEBC, TWR, and ELWA, whose purpose is to provide programming in the language of every major unreached people group. The initial goal was 144 new languages. Satellite networks like the HCJB/TWR ALAS (WINGS) make programming available to local Christian and secular stations. If and when direct satellite broadcasting becomes feasible, missionary broadcasters will undoubtedly be at the forefront.

Missionary radio pioneer HCJB also built the first missionary television station (see also TELEVISION EVANGELISM). The Window of the Andes went on the air in Quito in 1961. Latin America, with relatively free access, has seen a proliferation of Christian TV channels, while in parts of Africa and Europe evangelicals have been able to get time, sometimes free of charge, on government stations. Organizations like the U.S.-based Christian Broadcasting Network (700 Club) buy time on hundreds of TV outlets and cable services worldwide. Evangelists such as BILLY GRAHAM and LUIS PALAU have held continent or worldwide media crusades; the Graham one-hour program, "Starting Over," aired in April 1996, was seen by an estimated 2.5 billion people in over 200 countries, using 48 languages.

Radio and television are powerful tools which have taken the gospel to hundreds of millions of people, many in limited-access countries or isolated locations. The estimated total of 1.2 billion receivers means radio has the potential of reaching well over 90 percent of the world's population. The widespread use of radio by the governments of countries like Russia and China for internal communications has paved the way for missionary broadcasts to those peoples.

Nevertheless, like all media, radio and TV have their limitations. "Potential audience" is usually very different from actual listeners. The effectiveness of short-wave has declined as local stations become more widespread. Further, atmospheric conditions can severely affect propagation, and ever more powerful transmitters are required to keep up with the competition.

Perhaps an even greater challenge is to provide attractive, culturally relevant programming, particularly with television, where dubbed versions of U.S. shows have more often than not been the norm. Keeping the home constituency satisfied may conflict with ministry effectiveness; witness dictation-speed Bible readings for people learning English—in the King James Version.

Recordings. Gospel Recordings was founded in 1941 by JOY RIDDERHOF, a former missionary to Honduras, to let people throughout the world hear God's Word in their own language. By 1955 over one million 78 rpm records have been produced. Victrola-type players were simplified to the finger-operated, cardboard "Cardtalk" which required no batteries or repair parts. The vinyl record has been largely replaced by cassettes, and there are now gospel recordings in over four thousand languages.

Cassettes are being used in many areas of the mission field for both evangelism and teaching, particularly in areas of low literacy. Unlike radio, the message can be listened to repeatedly and at any hour. Rugged, hand-cranked players are available for remote areas.

Film. The lantern slides used by missionaries in the early part of the century were replaced by 16mm films and then video. Moody Science films and dramatic movies produced by groups such as Billy Graham have been widely translated and distributed. There has been some effort toward culturally relevant productions using Third World artists and settings. Cinema vans draw large open-air crowds in Africa, Latin America, and other parts of the world. Deserving special mention is the JESUS FILM, the most widely seen movie in cinematic history, which has been dubbed into more than 450 languages and seen by more than one billion people.

STEVE SYWULKA

Bibliography. B. Armstrong, *The Electric Church;* B. Siedell, *Gospel Radio;* V. B. Søgaard, *Everything You Need to Know for a Cassette Ministry.*

Mass Evangelism. See CRUSADE EVANGELISM; MASS COMMUNICATION; and TELEVISION EVANGELISM.

Mass Movements. See PEOPLE MOVEMENTS.

Master's Degrees in Missions and Missiology. In this day of increasing specialization in ministry, many individuals choose to study on the master's level in missions or missiology, either as part of their prefield preparation or as one facet of their continuing development as practicing missionaries.

In the North American context, the Association of Theological Schools (ATS) recognizes three kinds of master's degree programs that include specializations or special emphases in missions or missiology: basic programs oriented toward ministerial leadership (M.Div., M.A. in [specialization]), basic programs oriented toward general theological studies (M.A. [academic], M.A.R., M.T.S.), and advanced programs primarily oriented toward theological research and teaching (Th.M./S.T.M.). The M.Div. is a three-year program, built on the undergraduate degree. M.A. in (specialization) programs are often two years in length. The academic M.A. generally requires two years of full-time study, with advanced standing if the applicant holds an undergraduate degree in Bible/theology/missions. In some schools the length of the degree is reduced to a one-year program by such advanced standing. The Th.M. generally requires twenty-four to thirty-two semester hours of study, plus thesis, beyond the M.Div.

In Europe the master's degree is a specialization built on an undergraduate degree in a related area. Generally, schools in non-Western countries have developed their programs of study to reflect their connections with Europe or North America, as well as the standards of the educational systems and accrediting agencies of their regions.

As in all theological education, denominational distinctives are present in master's-level programs in missions and missiology. Some seminaries or graduate schools give more emphasis to the social sciences and their relation to intercultural understandings. Others place a stronger emphasis on the biblical and theological foundations for missions, with less attention given to the social sciences and their integration into the missionary effort. Some schools provide studies of a more theoretical nature while others offer extensive practical ministry experience. Most schools, however, attempt to maintain a balance with the integration of biblical truth and social science research with theoretical studies and ministry practice. Program concentrations are variously entitled Missions, Missiology, World Mission, Cross-Cultural Studies, Inter-Cultural Studies, Missions and Evangelism, Urban Ministry, or Church Growth. A few specialized programs exist in Muslim or Chinese Studies, as well as TESOL/TOEFL/TESL and Inter-Cultural Studies.

The Association of Theological Schools permits seminaries to admit as many as 10 percent of the students in the M.Div. and M.A. in (specialization) professional master's degrees without possession of the baccalaureate degree or its educational equivalent if their life experience is adequate to prepare them for graduate theological study. This provision might open doors of opportunity for older missionaries or missionary candidates.

Some seminaries have developed schools of world missions or missions departments with specialized faculty assigned to these administrative structures. Other schools have elected to integrate their specialized missions faculty with the other theological faculty to minimize separation of the missions emphasis from the rest of the school. In some cases seminary leadership has chosen teachers with extensive cross-cultural experience for most of the basic biblical, theological, and ministry-centered areas in order to provide the maximum integration of the missions focus into the life of the school and its curriculum.

The wise applicant will study catalogues from a variety of denominational and nondenominational schools to appreciate the differences and to choose the best program in light of present and future ministry responsibilities.

In North America the three-year M.Div. program (typically ninety to ninety-six semester hours) gives general preparation for local church and parachurch ministries, with strong emphasis on Bible, theology, and ministry-related coursework (evangelism, discipleship, preaching, teaching, counseling, pastoral duties, etc.). Some seminaries offer a missions track in the M.Div. Typical programs would include courses in Evangelism, Survey of Missions, Biblical Theology of Missions, History of Missions, Cultural Studies [Cultural Anthropology, Cross-Cultural Communication], Church Growth or Church Planting, plus electives in missions. Generally the M.Div. program includes a practicum or internship in cross-cultural ministry.

The two-year M.A. in (specialization) (typically sixty to sixty-four semester hours) provides a missions or missiology emphasis generally comparable to the M.Div. missions track programs. Programs vary in their admissions and graduation requirements, though. A few accept only those with previous cross-cultural experience. Some stipulate a working knowledge of a second language. All have a required theological and biblical core, plus stipulated courses as part of the missions/missiology concentration. All require some kind of integrative experience at the end of the program: practicum or internship, comprehensive exams, or thesis, or a combination of two of the three.

The academic master's degree (M.A., M.A.R. M.T.S.) (typically forty to seventy-two semester hours) is similar to the professional M.A. in (specialization). However, the applicant must hold the bachelor's degree (in North America). Generally this program does not have a practicum or internship. The integrative exercise is a thesis (preferably) with possible substitution of extra coursework and comprehensive exams for the thesis.

The Th.M./S.T.M. degree tends to permit greater flexibility in the choice of coursework in missions or missiology. The thesis and comprehensive exams assure that the graduate has competence in both content and research methodology. Many excellent seminaries or graduate schools around the world provide specializations in missions or missiology. Never before in the history of missions have there been so many opportunities for quality and variety in graduate level preparation for cross-cultural ministry.

W. KENNETH PHILLIPS

SEE ALSO Degrees in Mission and Missiology.

Bibliography. V. Hiscock, *Directory of Evangelical Bible Schools and Theological Seminaries in Europe;* W. R. Hogg, *Missiology* 15:4 (1987): 487–506; O. G. Mykleburst, *Mission Studies,* 6 (2), 87–107; idem, *The Study of Missions in Theological Education;* J. Scherer, *Missiology* 13:4 (1985): 445–60; idem, *Missiology* 15:4 (1987): 507–22; J. A. Siewert, *Directory of Schools and Professors of Mission in the USA and Canada;* T. Steffen, *EMQ,* 29 (2), 178–83; *Theological Education,* 32 (2), 16–93; R. N. Windsor, *World Directory of Missionary Training Centres.*

Mauritania *(Est. 2000 pop.: 2,580,000; 1,025,520 sq. km. [395,953 sq. mi.]).* The 99 percent Muslim majority of Mauritanians are mostly Sunnis of the Malekite rite who follow Qadiriya (Sufi) Maraboutism. Mauritania is inhabited by the Berbers, an indigenous people converted to Islam in the tenth century; the Arabs, who arrived in the fifteenth century; and blacks in the southern region. The Constitution protects Islam as the state religion and as such prohibits conversion from Islam. The country is united by Islam although some Mauritanians do follow pre-Muslim customs.

The Roman Catholic Church arrived in Mauritania at the turn of the century and remains the only organized Christian body. Almost all of the Roman Catholics are foreigners, the majority of which are transitory French government officials. Mauritania comprises the single diocese of Nouakchott, which in 1992 held approximately 4,500 adherents, the majority of which ere non-nationals. The bishop also participates in conferences of Senegal, Cape Verde, and Guinea Bissau. Due to the Islamic majority, most mission efforts are directed toward immigrant workers from other African countries.

While Protestants have attempted works in Mauritania, the last group, WEC International, withdrew in 1965. The small congregation that does exist is comprised of expatriates in the capital.

GARY LAMB

Bibliography. D. B. Barrett, *WCE; The Europa World Yearbook.*

Mauritius *(Est. 2000 pop.: 1,179,000; 2,040 sq. km. [788 sq. mi.]).* Mark Twain said that God made Mauritius so that we could have a glimpse of heaven. Much, but not all, of Mauritius's population would likely share Twain's observations. Mauritius boasted one of the most successful African economies in the 1980s, making a transition from an agricultural economy (sugar) to an industrial/commercial one (textile and tourism). Although the structural transition between these two types of economies may have taken place with relative ease, the fact that most of the older churches (Catholic and Anglican) have been in decline indicates that a socioreligious transition may not have supported the economic shift. Churches may want to reassess their role in this society moving from a traditional to modern structure. This reassessment may have a bearing on church growth and the reformulation of missiological questions for outreach to sociologically "displaced" Mauritians.

Even though only 27 percent of the Mauritian population would class themselves in the "Creole" ethnic grouping, the Creole language of Mauritius is the native language of the vast majority of the Mauritian people, and Creole is the first language of over half of the almost 1.2 million people who inhabit this volcanic island situated east of Madagascar in the Indian Ocean. This Creole ethnic/language situation points to two opposing missiological concerns revolving around "Creole" dominance. (1) Unfortunately, few of the 161 missionaries (including Catholic and Protestant) speak or minister in Creole, thus diminishing the prospect of incarnational ministry in the largest linguistic group of the island. (2) A significant degree of sensitivity should be shown to the Hindu population (65% of the national population) who often feel that one must "become a Creole" in order to become Christian. Despite this disparagement the Assemblies of God have seen a significant number of Hindus come to Christ.

Missiological thinking for Mauritius can be enhanced by examining the writings of the great Mauritian writer, Malcolm de Chazal (1902–81). One needs to ask how much de Chazal's technique of corresponding between words and things, and between language and nature deal with the real spiritual questions being asked by the Mauritian people. ("Flowers are both knowing and innocent, with experienced mouths but childlike eyes. They bend the two poles of life into a divinely closed circle," *Sens-Plastique,* p. 7.)

CLINT AKINS

Mayers, Marvin Keene (1927–). American mission scholar and missionary to Guatemala. Mayers began his career translating the Bible for the Pocomchi of Guatemala, Central America, under the Summer Institute of Linguistics. Since 1965, he has taught anthropology, intercultural communication, and linguistics to thousands of missionaries. He chaired the department of sociology and anthropology at Wheaton College (1968–74), served as director of Texas Summer Institute of Linguistics (1976–82), and was the founding dean of the School of Intercultural Studies, Biola University (1983–89).

Mayers developed three anthropological concepts that have been incorporated into the academic world: "biculturalism," "trust bond," and "basic values." Biculturalism is working in two different cultures at the same time (one's own and that of the host country) seeing both cultures as valid before God. The trust bond is the foundation for building cross-cultural relationships, asking, "Is what I am doing, thinking, or saying building or undermining trust?" The basic values concept blends biblical principles with those from the behavioral sciences.

Mayers introduced a course into the academic community based on "activity oriented learning" that has become a model for such courses throughout Christian higher education.

Among his writings, *Christianity Confronts Culture* has been recognized as one of the major contributions to missions in the past century and *Ministering Cross-Culturally* has become a standard reference book for alerting North American Christians to cross-cultural differences in their own communities.

MARGUERITE KRAFT

Bibliography. M. K. Mayers, *Christianity Confronts Culture: A Strategy for Crosscultural Evangelism;* M. K. Mayers and S. A. Grunlan, *Cultural Anthropology, A Christian Perspective;* M. K. Mayers and S. G. Lingenfelter, *Ministering Cross-Culturally: An Incarnational Model for Personal Relationships.*

McDougall, Francis Thomas (1817–86). English missionary to Borneo. Born in Sydenham, England, McDougall studied medicine at the universities of Malta and London. Later, in 1842, he completed a B.A. at Oxford, where he was profoundly affected by a campus revival. After a three-year stint as an ironworks superintendent in South Wales, he was ordained to the Anglican priesthood in 1845 and served three short curacies.

In 1847 McDougall accepted an appointment with the Borneo Mission Society for a pioneer ministry in North Borneo. There he conducted evangelistic, medical, and educational efforts, primarily among native Dyaks and immigrant Chinese. In 1853 he arranged for the transfer of his work to the SOCIETY FOR THE PROPAGATION OF THE GOSPEL. He was appointed bishop of Labuan and Sarawak in 1855, and became the first Anglican bishop to be consecrated in Asia. In addition to administrative duties, he prepared a prayerbook and catechism for the churches of his diocese. He and his wife persevered valiantly through the loss of five children and their own physical ailments.

In 1868 poor health forced McDougall's return to his homeland, where he served the Church of England for eighteen more years as vicar, canon, and archdeacon.

JAMES A. PATTERSON

Bibliography. C. J. Runyon, *Memoirs of Francis Thomas McDougall, D.C.L, F.R.C.S., Sometime Bishop of Labuan and Sarawak, and of Harriette His Wife.*

McGavran, Donald A. (1897–1991). American missionary to India and founder of the CHURCH GROWTH MOVEMENT. McGavran was born in India of missionary parents. Influenced by the STUDENT VOLUNTEER MOVEMENT, he returned to India in 1924 to serve with the Disciples of Christ in a variety of missionary capacities: educator, field executive, hospital administrator, evangelist, Bible translator, church planter, and researcher. Passionately interested in the causes of church growth, McGavran studied this issue first in India, then in a variety of other places.

Returning to the United States in 1957, McGavran established the Institute of Church Growth in Eugene, Oregon, where he was joined by Australian anthropologist ALAN TIPPETT. From 1964 to 1980, he published his ideas in the *Church Growth Bulletin,* which he founded. In 1965, he became founding dean of the School of World Mission of Fuller Theological Seminary, which provided a forum to popularize his ideas. McGavran advocated a return to classical mission with its stress on evangelism and church planting. He underscored the importance of employing the social and behavioral sciences as missiological instruments. Many of the theses written by his students were published and disseminated widely among the mission community.

In his writings, McGavran sought to identify the factors that facilitate and those that impede church growth. Investigating various PEOPLE MOVEMENTS within society, he used his findings to identify principles for church growth. McGavran also emphasized the importance of allowing persons to become Christian without forcing them to cross cultural barriers (*see* HOMOGENEOUS UNIT PRINCIPLE). He was committed to the establishment of a church movement within every segment of the human mosaic.

McGavran was also instrumental in restructuring the EVANGELICAL MISSIOLOGICAL SOCIETY. He continued to teach on a reduced schedule and to write extensively until the end of his life.

KEN MULHOLLAND

Bibliography. D. A. McGavran, *The Bridges of God;* idem, *Why Churches Grow;* idem, *Understanding Church Growth,* 3rd ed.

McGeorge, Mary (1850–92). Irish missionary to India. Born in Newry, County Down, Ireland, her home and school life prepared her well for a university career. Her call to serve the Zenana missions in India came through the urging of an Irish Presbyterian minister-friend who recognized in her the qualifications for such a task. From 1879 to 1884 she studied medicine at the London School of Medicine for Women. While waiting for her licentiateship and overseas appointment, McGeorge gained valuable experience as house surgeon. In late 1885 she sailed to Bombay.

She lived in the manufacturing city of Ahmedabad, where her medical work focused on the needs of women and children. Assisted by a national, she saw scores of patients at the dispensary on a daily basis. She was able to visit numerous outlying villages where she found many neglected, diseased, and suffering people. She believed that her dispensary work opened the hearts of the women to listen to the gospel as nothing else could.

In 1890 McGeorge left India for furlough in England. She devoted her time to promoting the interests of Zenana missions and preparing for a lifelong missionary tenure. On her return voyage to India in October 1892, her ship was wrecked during a storm. McGeorge and another missionary were among those who lost their lives.

Though there were few outward results from her labor, McGeorge left a growing group of believers. She also foresaw the time when indigenous workers would do the work that foreign missionaries were doing. Her life was an example of one whose early Christian nurturing through home and church reaped great benefits for the missionary enterprise.

FLORENCE R. SCOTT

Bibliography. C. R. Pitman, *Missionary Heroines in Eastern Lands: Woman's Work in Mission Fields.*

McLaren, Agnes (1837–1913). Scottish medical missionary pioneer in Pakistan. Born and raised in Edinburgh, even membership in an influential Liberal family could not secure McLaren admission to medical school in Scotland. Therefore, she pursued training in France. McLaren was the first female medical graduate in Montpellier and received licensure for the United Kingdom. She then practiced in Nice. Upon her conversion to Roman Catholicism in 1898 at age 60, she became a Dominican tertiary.

McLaren developed a vision to provide professional medical services for women in India through religious physicians. Her proposal to the Vatican for developing a community of women medical missionaries was denied approval five times. In 1910, McLaren founded St. Catherine's Hospital for women in Rawalpindi, Pakistan (near the border of India). She recruited female staff, including Anne Dengel, an Austrian physician. This particular sponsorship resulted in the establishment of a group of lay associates who

later became the Medical Mission Sisters. They implemented McLaren's vision and became an established community of medical missionaries after the ban against priests and nuns participating in medical work was revoked in 1936. Roman Catholics acknowledge McLaren as the one who began medical missions in their denomination. The Medical Mission Sisters currently have over 700 members in more than thirty countries.

MARGOT EYRING

Bibliography. M. Cavanagh, *DSCHT*, p. 526; J. H. Aherne, *Encyclopedic Dictionary of Religion*, 2:2202.

McPherson, Aimee Semple (1890–1944). American Pentecostal evangelist. Born in 1890, at the age of eighteen Aimee fell in love with both God and Robert Semple, the Pentecostal evangelist who led her to the Lord. After marriage both were ordained and in 1910 they left for missionary service in Hong Kong. Within weeks of their arrival, Robert contracted malaria and died, leaving Aimee a very young, pregnant widow. She returned to the United States and worked with the Salvation Army where she met and wed Stewart McPherson in 1912. They had a son, but Aimee's growing preaching ministry took a toll on her marital relationship, and she and Stewart divorced in 1921. She endured much controversy in later years over her personal life, and died in 1944.

Her accomplishments are many: she was a prolific writer, the first woman to receive an FCC license to operate a radio station, the founder of the International Church of the Foursquare Gospel, the builder of Angelus Temple in Los Angeles, and the founder of the Lighthouse for International Foursquare Evangelism (L.I.F.E.) Bible College. Her Angelus Temple Commissary met the physical needs of over 1.5 million people during the Depression, and she was a tireless fighter on behalf of the poor. A gifted communicator, she instilled in her followers a strong vision for evangelism.

JUDITH LINGENFELTER

McQuilkin, Robert C. (1886–1952). American educator and missions promoter. McQuilkin was born to Irish immigrant parents of Presbyterian heritage. His only attempt to enter missionary service was frustrated when the ship on which he was scheduled to sail caught fire in the Philadelphia harbor and sank.

In 1923, McQuilkin accepted a position as dean of the newly founded Southern Bible Institute in Columbia, South Carolina, and later became its first president, a position which he held until his death in 1952. Under his leadership the school became Columbia Bible College. In 1936, the college added a graduate division, the first evangelical graduate school of missions.

McQuilkin played a key role in encouraging students to form the Student Foreign Missions Fellowship. In 1940, he founded Ben Lippen School, a college preparatory boarding school that served many missionary families. All five of McQuilkin's children served as missionaries. His son Robertson, after twelve years in Japan, served as president of Columbia Bible College and Seminary from 1969 to 1990.

McQuilkin's emphasis on victorious Christian living and world missions was epitomized in the motto, "To know Him and to make Him known." Under his leadership Columbia became a leader in training evangelical missionaries.

KEN MULHOLLAND

Bibliography. M. McQuilkin, *Always in Triumph.*

Mears, Henrietta Cornelia (1890–1963). American Christian educator, publisher, and missions motivator. Born in Fargo, North Dakota, Mears grew up in Minneapolis. After completing a degree in education at the University of Minnesota and working as a high school teacher, she moved to California in 1928 to accept a position with the First Presbyterian Church of Hollywood. For over thirty years she served as the church's director of Christian education, developing a large and influential Sunday school program. In 1933 Mears founded Gospel Light Publications, which became one of the largest publishers of biblically based material for Sunday schools. She also established the Forest Home Camp Grounds as a conference center in the late 1930s and co-founded the National Sunday School Association in 1946.

Although not a missionary herself, Mears influenced world missions in a variety of ways. The widespread use of Gospel Light materials overseas led her to found Gospel Light International in 1961 to assist missionaries with obtaining and publishing Christian education materials in foreign languages. In addition, her emphasis on leadership training brought a sense of professionalism to nonformal Christian education programs in the United States and abroad. Mears frequently traveled internationally to speak and conduct training seminars, and encouraged over four hundred young people into full-time Christian service, including many who became missionaries.

ALAN A. SEAMAN

Bibliography. E. Baldwin and D. Benson, *Henrietta Mears and How She Did It;* E. Roe, ed., *Dream Big: The Henrietta Mears Story.*

Mecca. *See* PILGRIMAGES.

Media. The media play a significant role in Christian mission, and several mission organizations are built around specific media. The all-pervasive influence of the media challenges Christians to investigate and use the media effectively in mission. Attitudes to Christian use of media span from almost uninhibited praise to nearly total rejection.

Media Classification. In popular usage the term "media" refers to the whole complex of broadcasting, particularly television, and its many uses. Marshal McLuhan defined media as extensions of the human body, the microphone becoming an extension of the voice and the camera an extension of the eye.

Media can be classified according to the context of use. *Personal media* are media used by a single person or in an interpersonal situation. *Group media* signify media that are used to enhance or stimulate interaction with or among a group of people. *Mass media* are understood as media that aim at communicating with multiple audiences at the same time.

Media Types and Ministries. *Printed media* include books, newspapers, magazines, brochures, and anything using the alphabet. In the past, print media have been chosen by churches and missionary organizations as their primary communication tools, and worldwide literature organizations such as David C. Cook have been established. Magazines such as *Breakthrough* in Hong Kong and *Step* in East Africa have extensive readership. Today, however, print is increasingly being challenged by the electronic media.

Audio media include radio, cassettes, records, CDs, and any other media that use sound only. Radio has been used extensively by churches and missions around the world and it demonstrates many possibilities for evangelism and Christian nurture. Major international radio organizations include Far Eastern Broadcasting Company, Trans Word Radio, and HCJB (*see* RADIO MISSION WORK). The use of audiocassettes includes possibilities for this unique and versatile medium that are possibly greater than any other medium available for Christian mission. *Hosanna* in the U.S. produces several million cassettes a year that are increasingly used in Christian mission.

Video media include television, film, slides, video, and DVD (Digital Video Disk). The video medium is having an enormous impact on societies around the world. It is changing entertainment patterns as well as family life, and it is impacting classroom instruction and educational methods. We could argue that video has caused a communication revolution that may be on the same level as that experienced at the invention of the printing press.

Television has an all-pervasive influence and the extensive use of television makes it one of the strongest forces in society. The average person in the industrialized world spends several hours in front of the television set each day. Christian leaders need to be aware of both the possibilities of using television in Christian ministry, but also the possible dangers that extensive exposure to television can have on church, society, and family life.

Film is a medium with unique possibilities in Christian mission. Few media are more persuasive than film. A prime example of film use is the JESUS FILM. Video is challenging or replacing film as movies are recorded on video cassettes and made available for home use.

Computer media. The computer is impacting all media, but its specific uses for E-mail and the internet have changed the way people stay in touch, advertise their services, and get their entertainment. Many Christian ministries are using web pages on the internet for church activities, counseling services, and marketing products. For those with access to computers, this medium will increase in significance in the decades to come (*see also* INFORMATION TECHNOLOGY).

Drama and art. Music, painting, and dance-drama all deserve much more extensive treatment. We cannot envision a radio or television program without music. Music is central to church services and evangelistic approaches. The artist is important in all media work. Dance-drama and other folk media are today being rediscovered by many churches, and we are experiencing exciting new uses of drama and traditional music (*see also* ETHNOMUSICOLOGY).

Media People. Different groups of people are involved in media. There are *media theorists* who study the theological, missiological, and theoretical basis for Christian use of the media. *Media strategists* define and plan the use of a medium in the total context of a local church or mission enterprise. There are also *artists* and *media specialists* who produce programs. Finally, the *media users* or *generalists* distribute and use the programs for a given audience.

Media Research. There has been relatively little in-depth study of the effects of media in mission, and few controlled experiments. This is in sharp contrast to secular use of media, where huge sums of money are used on research, and where a significant body of material is available. The lack of research in Christian media has resulted in counting media activities rather than measuring media results.

Marketing organizations will collect extensive data on the availability and usefulness of individual media channels in a given context. Diffusion studies have, likewise, analyzed the effects of various media. Christian communicators can use the available methods for testing media products.

Christian Media Organizations. Media users have established associations where their special interests are treated. Among the organizations with cross-media and global perspectives are the International Christian Media Commis-

sion (ICMC) which has evangelical roots, and the World Association of Christian Communication (WACC), which was formed on an ecumenical basis and covers organizations and churches from around the world. The National Religious Broadcasters is a major organization in the U.S.

Issues: Media and God's Communication Approach. The challenge for the future is to make the use of media in church and mission conform to patterns that are consistent with Scripture. From the creation of the world God has communicated to humanity. Passages such as Romans 1:20 and Psalm 19:1–4 speak of God's communication through creation. In the New Testament, we see God revealing himself through his Son (John 1:14: Heb. 1:1–3a).

A study of God's communicational activities yields significant guidelines for media use. God uses communication symbols that are understood by us within our specific cultural contexts. He uses language, culture, and human form. He is working for an interactive relationship. Our use of media must follow similar patterns, and media programs need format, music selections, content, and form of presentation that are appropriate for the intended audience.

Specific Challenges to Media Users. As in all aspects of Christian mission, *the commission to communicate is the mandate*. There is a clear goal of being prophetic and to present the gospel in such a way that people will want to listen, understand, follow, and commit themselves.

Christian communication is person-based. Jesus showed us the example by becoming a real human being, participating in our affairs (Phil. 2:7; John 1:14). In him, the message and the medium became one. This person-centeredness must be carefully guarded in media communication. Credibility of a piece of literature is associated with the way it is distributed and with the person who is giving it out. We need to make our use of media be person-centered.

The audience (receptors) has priority, and media programs need to be receptor-oriented. Jesus illustrated receptor orientation by creating parables out of everyday life of the listeners. In a parable, the audience become players, and as such each one discovers new truths and principles.

There must be a *close relationship with the local church*. It is the local church that provides permanent structures for effective communication. If churches are to function as a base for media strategies and have a sense of ownership, they need to be involved in the decision-making with respect to media employment and program design.

The effective use of media is *based on the principle of process*. COMMUNICATION itself is a process, but the listener will also be living through an ongoing DECISION-MAKING process. During this process the needs of the audience will change and the communicator must adapt his or her programs and use of media accordingly.

Good information is mandatory if effective communication through media is to take place. Research provides us with information on which decisions can be based, and it makes media communication possible. The main concern is not the number of research methods used, but the fact that the needs of the audience have been studied and that products (radio programs, brochures, books, videos, etc.) are adequately tested before broadcasting or distribution.

Finally, media use needs to be rooted in *the cultural context* of the audience. As the gospel is clothed in the new culture it penetrates that culture with the true life of Christ. Then, from within that culture, it blooms to new tunes and new instruments. An intercultural understanding will lead us to investigate local and traditional media and art forms. A number of groups in Asian countries, such as India, Thailand, and Indonesia, have demonstrated the viability of using traditional forms of dance and drama in evangelism. The Balinese church has incorporated local cultural themes in the architecture of church buildings. These are helpful examples of developing appropriate media within a culture to communicate the gospel more effectively.

VIGGO B. SØGAARD

SEE ALSO Mass Communication.

Bibliography. J. F. Engel, *Contemporary Christian Communication: Theory and Practice*; C. H. Kraft, *Communication Theory for Christian Witness*, rev. ed.; M. McLuhan, *Understanding Media: The Extensions of Man*; D. K. Smith, *Creating Understanding Across Cultural Landscapes*; V. B. Søgaard, *Everything You Need to Know for a Cassette Ministry*; idem, *Media in Church and Mission: Communicating the Gospel*.

Medical Mission Work. The term "medical mission" originally referred to a medical post, such as a clinic or dispensary for the poor, which was supported by a Christian congregation. By the middle of the nineteenth century, the meaning of the term had broadened, referring primarily to the medical branch of Protestant overseas missions which paralleled the rapid growth of medical science (Grundmann, 1997, 184).

The literature of medical missions, including the publications of the mission societies which proliferated during the nineteenth century, was dominated by biographical accounts of physicians and nurses who were compelled by the urgency of human suffering and the desire to fulfill the GREAT COMMISSION. John Thomas joined WILLIAM CAREY in India in 1773 and fought the practices of abandoning sick babies to death by exposure and the burning of Hindu widows on the funeral pyres of their dead husbands. The first American medical missionary, John Scudder, was a minister of the

Reformed Church in America as well as a physician. His granddaughter, IDA SCUDDER, one of 42 missionaries in four generations of that family who collectively contributed more than eleven hundred years of missionary service, founded the Vellore Medical College in India in 1900. Edith Brown, an Englishwoman, laid the foundation for the first Asian women's medical school, Ludhiana Christian Medical College, and Peter Parker, the first American missionary to China in 1834, started a modern teaching hospital. By 1933 six of China's twelve medical schools were financed by missionary societies.

In the mid-twentieth century there were many prominent missionary physicians, particularly in Africa. HELEN ROSEVEARE served with the WORLDWIDE EVANGELIZATION CRUSADE in the Congo and during the bloody civil war was raped and beaten repeatedly by Simba Rebels who occupied the Nebobongo mission compound where she worked. Paul Carlson, who worked at the Wasolo mission station in the Ubangi Province of Congo, was captured and tortured before being killed in the streets of Stanleyville. Carl Becker, who spent nearly fifty years in the Congo under the Africa Inland Mission, was perhaps best known for his compassionate treatment of four thousand resident patients at an 1100-acre leprosy village in the early 1950s. Stanley Browne, a boy with an encyclopedic memory from a modest south London home, became one of the world's leading specialists in leprosy control and prevention. The Salvation Army Nurses' Fellowship, born out of the blitz in bomb-scarred London during the Second World War, rapidly grew to become an international organization. Their midwives traveled by bicycle or paddle-boat or trudged on foot. Payment for services might be "a love-gift of an egg, or a posy of wild flowers, or maybe a handful of grain" (Carr, 1978, 30). Between 1850 and 1950 there were more than 1,500 medical missionaries from Britain alone serving in the developing world (Aitken, Fuller, and Johnson, 1984, 158).

Issues in Medical Missions. The place of medical missions in the larger context of world missions has been repeatedly examined. Mission societies, particularly those formed by churches in Great Britain and Europe in the nineteenth century, had as their highest priorities spreading the gospel through evangelism and educating indigenous populations through schools. Medical missionaries were "to be first preachers, then medical men, if time remained for that" (Gelfund, 1984, 19). Nevertheless, a characteristic feature of this evangelical movement became the establishment of health services where none existed. The 1928 INTERNATIONAL MISSIONARY COUNCIL meeting in Jerusalem clearly stated that "Medical work should be regarded as in itself an expression of the spirit of the Master, and should not be thought of as only a pioneer of evangelism or as merely a philanthropic agency" (Lowe, 1886, 18). More recently compassionate ministries, such as medical missions, have been described as part of holistic ministry which "defines evangelism and social action as functionally separate, relationally inseparable, and essential to the total ministry of the Church" (Yamamori, 1997, 7; *see also* HOLISTIC MISSIONS).

Financially maintaining institutions built in the pioneering phase of medical missions has been increasingly difficult. Mission hospitals accepting government subsidies forfeited in principle their religious freedom and ability to operate autonomously. National churches and governments, however, have often not been able to assume the burden of these institutions, particularly that of paying staff salaries.

Adequate staffing for hospitals has been a perennial concern. Frenetic levels of activity in overcrowded facilities have often characterized mission hospitals and dispensaries because of the pressing human need they address with limited resources. Predictably, there is a high level of exhaustion, burnout, and turnover among the staff due to the medical work, staff experience frustration at the lack of time for spiritual ministry, family priorities, and personal rejuvenation.

The appropriateness of technology for health care services is a key issue. Remote hospitals with irregular power supplies often seek and request sophisticated medical equipment for radiology services, surgery, intensive care units, and laboratories. Government and mission funds disproportionately support institutions rather than health promotion at the community level. Additionally, physicians functioning as surgeons or family practitioners soon come to realize that the sicknesses they are treating could be better addressed through adequate sanitation, a clean water supply, and good nutrition.

Political instability, antagonistic postures toward Christian ministries by governments and religious groups such as Islam, the inability of institutions to significantly impact morbidity and mortality rates in their areas of service, and difficulties in integrating health ministries with affiliated local churches are all significant issues in medical missions (Van Reken, 1987, 16–19).

Directions and Trends in Medical Missions.
An important influence on medical missions was the International Conference on Primary Health Care, held in the former U.S.S.R. in 1978 at Alma-Ata, which focused global attention on health care at the community level. It defined primary health care as that which is accessible, acceptable, affordable, and linked to community initiatives. Further, primary health care included preventive, promotive, curative, and rehabilitative aspects and focused on clean water, adequate sanitation, immunization programs, maternal/child health, promotion of food supply and proper nutrition,

prevention and control of endemic diseases, and education. Emphasis was placed on coordinating efforts with other sectors of community and national development that impact health, such as housing, communications, public works, and agriculture. MAP International, a Christian relief and development organization, and the Christian Medical Society led missions and medical ministries policymakers in the development of a declaration identifying how the Alma-Ata conference might affect the structure of Christian health care ministries. This facilitated the movement of the medical missions community away from hospital-based ministries and toward community-oriented ministries. The Christian Medical Commission in Geneva, through its influential *Contact* magazine, encouraged the development of holistic integrated health programs throughout the world.

David Van Reken has described the progression of medical missions as moving from the pioneer *doing* phase through a *teaching* era in which training schools were founded, and into an *enabling* period. In this final phase *doing* and *teaching* continue, but goals of community development, national rather than mission ownership and leadership, collegial rather than teacher-student relationships, and sustainable indigenous growth are emphasized (Van Reken, 1987, 6).

Another trend is an increase in short-term medical missions with agencies such as Medical Group Missions, in which participants provide service in their areas of specialization or as educators. Early retirement and mid-career job changes have also resulted in professionals pursuing second careers as medical missionaries. TENT MAKING MISSION, receiving compensation for work done in the field, is also a trend, as are group practices for physicians in the U.S. which are structured to encourage their staff to engage in medical missions. Board certification is increasingly normative, as is a master's degree in public health. Continuing education conferences are provided annually by the Christian Medical and Dental Society, alternately held in Malaysia and Africa.

The future of medical missions increasingly lies in partnering with the church, as God's chosen channel for the restoration of wholeness and the transformation of society, and in promoting effective community-based health care, grounded in the discipline of public health, which genuinely impacts morbidity and morality rates while encouraging positive health behaviors.

EVVY CAMPBELL

SEE ALSO Health, Health Care and Missions.

Bibliography. J. T. Aitken, H. W. C. Fuller, D. Johnson, *The Influence of Christians in Medicine*; S. G. Browne, *Heralds of Health: The Saga of Christian Medical Initiatives*; I. Carr, *Tender Loving Care: The Salvation Army Nurses' Fellowship at Work*; Y. Cheung, *Mission-*

ary Medicine in China: A Study of Two Canadian Protestant Missions in China Before 1937; D. E. Fountain, *Health, the Bible, and the Church;* C. Grundmann, *DMTHP,* pp. 184–87; M. Gelfund, *Christian Doctor and Nurse: The History of Medical Missions in South Africa from 1799–1976;* J. C. Hefley, *The Cross and the Scalpel: New Directions and Opportunities for Christian Health Care Ministries: A Declaration and Study Guide;* J. Lowe, *Medical Missions: Their Place and Power;* R. A. Tucker, *FJIJ;* M. Yates, *In Central America and the Caribbean with Medical Group Missions: Mission-Dollar Vacations;* D. E. Van Reken, *Mission and Ministry: Christian Medical Practice in Today's Changing World Cultures;* WHO/UNICEF, *Primary Health Care: Report of the International Conference on Primary Health Care Alma-Ata, USSR, 6–12 September 1978;* T. Yamamori, *Furthering the Kingdom Through Relief and Development: Where and How Is It Happening?*

Medium. *See* SHAMAN, SHAMANISM.

Melanesia. Melanesia, MICRONESIA, and POLYNESIA are the three major groupings of islands in the Pacific. The islands of Melanesia from east to west include Norfolk Island; Fiji; Vanuatu; New Caledonia and the Loyalty Islands; the Solomon Islands and the Santa Cruz Islands; New Guinea (Papua New Guinea and Irian Jaya), the Admiralty Islands, and the Bismarck and Louisiade archipelagos. The year 2000 estimated combined population of the islands exceeds 6 million.

Due to the rugged terrain of many of the islands and the vast distances of water between them, Melanesia is one of the most diverse regions in the world. It is estimated that in excess of a thousand languages exist in the New Guinea region alone. Melanesian societies are based on kinship and by comparison to other areas of the world, are small-scale, ranging from as few as seventy on the smaller islands to several thousand in the New Guinea Highlands. Traditional economies were based on rudimentary agriculture, hunting, fishing, and indigenous wealth which included primarily pigs and portable valuables. Trade networks were established between the islands by means of deep sea canoes which navigated the Pacific and through inland waterways and bush tracks linking the populated areas.

The diversity of Melanesia encompasses their traditional religious beliefs and practices. In general, however, Melanesian religions are theistic in that they emerge from a belief in a god. One overall effect of the widespread theistic religions with their solid commitment to the centrality of relationships was that Christianity spread rapidly.

Although some contact with Western explorers took place prior to the second half of the eighteenth century, the major movement was a direct result of the voyages of the British explorer, Captain James Cook from 1772 to 1779. With the opening of Australia as a colony, the expansion of the British Empire brought the predictable wave of settlers driven by commerce and opportunity. A surprising outcome of Cook's exploration of Australia, New Zealand, and the islands of the Pacific came in response to his journals which became the reading material for a generation of young Christians destined to be part of the GREAT CENTURY OF MISSIONS. The earliest missionaries to the South Pacific were part of the LONDON MISSIONARY SOCIETY (LMS) group arriving in Tahiti in 1797. One of the young Christians who studied Cook's journals was JOHN WILLIAMS, a man destined to impact not only the islands of Polynesia, but to take the gospel as far as Vanuatu in Melanesia. Williams' commitment to including indigenous missionaries in his outreaches characterized Melanesian missions in the early days.

Following the early thrust of the LMS in Melanesia were the English Methodists who entered Tonga and Fiji in the mid-1820s. Methodism spread rapidly through Tonga and Fiji initially and from there to other islands of Melanesia. The Roman Catholic missions arrived in Tahiti in 1836 and in the Melanesian islands of Fiji and New Caledonia in the years from 1840 to 1851. Another thrust of missions came from the Anglicans in New Zealand and the work of GEORGE SELWYN, the first Anglican bishop and founder of the Melanesian Mission. Other missions appeared in Melanesia during this period including the Presbyterians who primarily focused on Vanuatu. By the decade of the 1870s, New Guinea became a significant target for a host of missions beginning with the LMS in 1871 and the Sacred Heart Fathers from France in 1884. Within a few years, the Neuendettelsau Mission (1886) and the RHENISH MISSIONARY SOCIETY (1887) established works in the northern part of the island which was under German rule. Missions to The Solomon Islands appeared during this same period. One of the significant missions to reach the Solomon Islands was the South Seas Evangelical Mission (formerly the Queensland Kanaka Mission).

The period from 1900 to 1942 was one of significant expansion of missions in Melanesia. Major efforts were launched by Protestant groups including the Lutherans, Anglicans, Methodists, and Congregationalists as well as new works by interdenominational faith missions such as the Unevangelized Fields Mission and the German Liebenzell Mission. The Roman Catholic missions continued to expand and develop throughout the region. The Seventh-Day Adventists entered Melanesia establishing works in a number of islands. The end of this period of active expansion coincided with the war in the Pacific.

Following the war, news of the isolated islands full of unevangelized peoples reached the ears of the churches in the West. The result was a resurgence of new missions, particularly those of the specialized ministries such as Missionary Aviation Fellowship and the Summer Institute of Linguistics. Smaller independent missions also dotted the Melanesian landscape, particularly those from North America. This growth and expansion of missionary efforts continued through the early 1980s. The early characteristic of a partnership between indigenous and expatriate missionaries was less a feature of the rapidly expanding missions in the twentieth century. One important attempt at greater cooperation in missions was the formation of the Evangelical Alliance which established combined works in education, medicine, and the Christian Leaders Training College in Papua New Guinea.

The growth of churches in Melanesia paralleled the periods of missionary expansion. The beginnings of church independence were seen in Tonga and Samoa as early as 1885, but did not reach Melanesia until the Methodist Church worked through the issues of finance and control in Fiji during the first decade of the twentieth century. Other churches followed a similar process of growth and independence.

A number of challenges and opportunities face the churches and missions of Melanesia at the end of the twentieth century. The more serious challenges include widespread nominalism, a lack of adequate resources to deal with the challenges of modernity, particularly among the youth; tribalism which undermines the church's ability to demonstrate reconciliation; and a need to develop more leaders to address the theological issues unique to Melanesia. As with any period of great challenge, great opportunities are also present. One of the most dynamic situations is the resurgence of interest in missions among the evangelical churches of Melanesia. This movement began in the early 1980s and culminated in a South Pacific missions conference held in Suva, Fiji, in 1989. One result of the conference was the launch of "The Deep Sea Canoe," a combined mission movement designed to bring Melanesians back into an active role in world missions.

DOUGLAS MCCONNELL

Bibliography. C. W. Foreman, *The Island Churches of the South Pacific*; D. Hilliard, *God's Gentlemen: A History of the Melanesian Mission, 1849–1942*; K. S. Latourette, *A History of the Expansion of Christianity*, vol. 5; Melanesian Institute, *Point*; G. W. Trompf, *Melanesian Religion*; C. J. Upton, *EB*, 5:864–70; D. L. Whiteman, *Melanesians and Missionaries*.

Melbourne Conference (1980). The theme of the conference was not a doctrinal affirmation but a prayer, "Your Kingdom Come." Its four sections focused on: (1) Good News to the Poor; (2) the Kingdom of God and Human Struggles; (3) The Church Witnesses to the Kingdom; and (4) Christ—Crucifed and Risen—Challenges Human Power. One of the images central to the conference was that of the Christ who is at the center of all things, and who is crucified "outside the gate." This emphasized the movement of grace from the center to the periphery, and thus the significance of the poor in any evangelistic strategy, for the situation of the poor is no longer "a social ethics question; it is a gospel question" (EMILIO CASTRO).

Melbourne also developed the concept of the poor being, as others also, not only sinners, but also "the sinned against." That is, the poor are those whose essential humanity is threatened and indeed compromised by the social political and economic forces that challenge the god-like image within them: "the destroyer of the body may not be able to kill the soul, but it can, and too often does, rape and maim the soul" (Raymond Fung). Putting "sinned-againstness" on the evangelistic agenda enables human sinfulness to be addressed anew.

Clark Pinnock, after pressing the evangelical claim for an urgent proclamation of the message of salvation to all peoples in the power of the Spirit, admitted the great value of evangelicals sharing in ecumenical discussions: "The unreached peoples are in large part also the poor of the earth which forces the evangelical agenda and the ecumenical agenda together. I believe that Melbourne has bridged the gap between Bangkok 72 and Lausanne 1974 to an important degree" (*International Review of Missions*, July 1980, 348). Many of the evangelicals present shared that perspective, but others were critical of a lack of doctrinal precision within the conference proceedings, especially with regard to the atonement. Some were also critical of a perceived lack of evangelistic urgency in a conference that all too easily took on the form of a mini WCC Assembly.

JOHN H. Y. BRIGGS

SEE ALSO World Council of Churches Conferences.

Bibliography. *Your Kingdom Come—Mission Perspectives: Report on the World Conference on Mission and Evangelism, Melbourne, Australia, 12–15 May, 1980.*

Member Care in Missions. The concept of member care—that mission members need to be cared for in important ways—has its roots in the New Testament. The GREAT COMMISSION was given alongside the GREAT COMMANDMENT, with love for one another being the hallmark of Christian discipleship (John 13:34–35). Scores of "one another" injunctions in the New Testament summon Christians to demonstrate this care for other believers, including care for missionaries, in many ways. Even Jesus, the missionary prototype, indicated that he needed caring companionship when he said, "My soul is overwhelmed with sorrow to the point of death. Stay here and keep watch with me" (Matt. 26:38). And the apostle Paul was fervent in expressing his gratitude for having been refreshed by the ministry of Onesiphorus (2 Tim. 1:16–18).

Today's missionaries need care as well. The sending church, mission administrators, and field colleagues are all responsible to provide quality care for the missionary—whether at home or abroad, frontliner or support staff, adult or child or perhaps even adult MK—from the missionary family's first days with the mission through retirement or termination of service (and sometimes beyond). Often member care specialists are utilized: pastoral counselors or mental health professionals with specialized interest and experience in caring for missionaries; specialists from either inside or outside the mission. These caregivers target the physical, psychological, and spiritual well-being of missionaries, seeking to promote overall health and wholeness (and, concomitantly, greater effectiveness in ministry as well).

Member care generally begins with assessment to help missions select, prepare, and place missionaries with a view toward maximizing the fit between the missionary and his or her tasks, team mates, and host culture (*see also* FIELD ADJUSTMENT). Member care goes on to offer prefield and FURLOUGH seminars on topics such as educational options for MISSIONARY CHILDREN, stress management, BURNOUT prevention, conflict resolution, and coping with transition. Member care includes training missionaries to support one another on the field. Reentry debriefing at the beginning of furlough can help missionaries make the most of furlough. Reentry seminars for MKs transitioning into college is another facet of member care. So is providing on- or off-field counseling for missionaries for preventive reasons or in times of crisis, difficult transitions, or burnout. Helping missionaries exit the mission with grace is a "must" of caring for the missionary at retirement or service termination.

Member care is an emerging specialized interdisciplinary field with a constantly expanding network of professionals, organizations, care centers, literature, and research. Standards of care and professional ethics have yet to be developed, as does the development of training models and good training opportunities. More robust research is needed. Also needed is greater internationalization, developing better and more culturally appropriate member care for missionaries of the newer sending countries. O'Donnell aptly summed up the standing and significance of this young interdisciplinary field when he wrote, "Member care has grown in prominence and is now generally understood to be a biblical responsibility and a central component of mission strategy."

JEANNE L. JENSMA

Bibliography. L. M. Gardner, *JTP* 15 (1987): 308–14; K. S. O'Donnell, *JTP* 25 (1997): 143–54; idem, *Missionary Care: Counting the Cost for World Evangelization.*

Mennonite Missions. Mennonites trace their spiritual ancestry and the origins of their concern for mission to the Anabaptist wing of the Reformation in sixteenth-century Europe. These Anabaptists had a deep sense of the responsibility of all Christians to evangelize, to share their new-found faith spontaneously in voluntary witness (*see* ANABAPTIST MISSIONS). Already in 1527, Anabaptist leaders met in Augsburg and appointed missionaries to go out by twos and threes across central Europe. As they were driven in ever widening circles by their sense of God's call and by increasingly ruthless persecution, these Anabaptists began new congregations wherever they went. Within these congregations members were taught that the GREAT COMMISSION was Christ's command to all believers at all times and they acted accordingly. They also believed that in the suffering of their church in persecution God authenticated their missionary witness. However, when most of the early leaders died as martyrs and the later church discovered that it would only be tolerated by the authorities if it was silent and abstained from mission activity, Mennonites turned their attention inward, content to practice their faith as the "quiet in the land," living as much as possible separate from the society around them, passing on their faith only to their own children.

Only in the nineteenth century did Mennonites recover their concern for mission, this time through contact with Christians from other traditions rather than from a recovery of the missionary zeal which had been at the core of the Anabaptist faith. For example, early in the nineteenth century Mennonites in Europe were major supporters of the English Baptist Mission in Serampore, India. When Mennonites themselves became missionaries, their understanding of mission was like that of evangelical Protestants of that era and the churches which they planted were indistinguishable from the Protestant churches around them.

In 1847 Mennonites in the Netherlands organized their own Sending Society and in 1851 sent Pieter Jansz to Java as the first Mennonite to serve overseas in mission. He was soon followed by other Dutch Mennonites and then, in 1871, the Sending Society opened a new field in Sumatra, which was staffed with workers from the Mennonite settlements in Russia. Although direction of the Society remained in the Netherlands, in later years the major financial support for its work came from Russian Mennonites. Abraham Friesen of the Mennonite Brethren in Russia went to Hyderabad, India, under the American Baptist Mission Union in 1889 and began what became the Mennonite Brethren Church in India.

Among North American Mennonites interest in missions grew under the influence of the Evangelical Awakening and was a major concern in the formation of the General Conference Mennonite Church in 1860. At the founding sessions both home and foreign missions were commended to the congregations and three treasuries were set up to receive funds. The candidacy of Samuel S. Haury resulted in the formation of a mission board which commissioned him to work among the Arapahoe in Oklahoma in 1880. The first North American Mennonite to serve overseas was Eusebius Hershey of the Mennonite Brethren in Christ Church (now part of the Missionary Church), who went to Sierre Leone in 1890.

Concern for mission among North American Mennonites accelerated rapidly near the close of the nineteenth century. Mission committees and boards were organized in the various Mennonite denominations, and by the early years of the twentieth century missionaries sent out by Mennonite sending agencies were at work in India, China, and the African continent. Also in this same period, Mennonites, who were almost entirely a rural people in North America, organized urban missions in a number of major North American cities. In addition to denominational missions, Mennonites also organized mission agencies which included more than one Mennonite denomination. Most notable among these were the China Mennonite Mission Society organized for work in Shandong in 1901, and the Congo Inland Mission (now the Africa Inter-Mennonite Mission) which began work in what is now Zaire in 1911. By 1957 there were 638 missionaries working under North American Mennonite mission boards in 28 countries around the world.

After the close of World War II, Mennonite concern for and involvement in worldwide mission grew rapidly. While between 1850 and 1939 Mennonites had established only 24 mission programs, in the 1940s they established 18 more, in the 1950s 42, in the 1960s 17, in the 1970s 28, and between 1980 and 1986 15 more.

In addition to more traditional mission sending agencies, North American Mennonite churches also work together in the Mennonite Central Committee, an agency formed in 1920 for famine relief in Russia. After World War II, Mennonite Central Committee ministries expanded rapidly with emergency relief aid and then development aid in many parts of the world. Now known as a relief, service, and development agency for ministry in the name of Christ, the Mennonite Central Committee had over one thousand volunteers serving in fifty countries in 1987.

Globally, Mennonite churches are loosely organized into the Mennonite World Conference. According to the 1990 *Mennonite World Handbook*, in that year there were 856,000 Mennonites worldwide organized into 171 church conferences or denominational bodies in 61 countries. Of these, 449,100 or 52 percent were found in North America and Europe, the countries where the traditional "mission fields" were located. This compares with 67 percent in Europe and North America and 33 percent in the rest of the world as recently as 1978.

In addition to cooperative mission projects among Mennonite denominations in Europe and North America, cooperation among these denominations and churches and sending agencies in Africa, Asia, and Latin America for new mission efforts beyond their own church areas has increased greatly since the 1970s. During this same period Mennonites have also worked closely with so-called indigenous churches (churches which are not the direct result of Western mission activity) in Africa and Latin America in helping them to train leaders, particularly for Bible teaching. What real "partnership" means in these various settings is a major agenda item for Mennonites in mission at the end of the twentieth century.

The second half of the twentieth century has been a time of intense Mennonite theological interest in the sixteenth-century Anabaptists and their understanding of what it means to follow Christ. In the process there has come a new appreciation for the centrality of mission in the Anabaptist faith and a new concern for making that faith central to Mennonite mission. As a result, Mennonites have come to an awareness that they may have something important to contribute in worldwide mission discussions and are playing an increasingly active role in such conferences and study groups.

ROBERT L. RAMSEYER

Bibliography. Mennonite Encyclopedia, D. G. Lichdi, ed., *Mennonite World Handbook;* W. A. Shenk, *Anabaptism and Mission.*

Mentoring. *See* DISCIPLE, DISCIPLESHIP.

Mercy of God. The English word for mercy is a translation of several different Hebrew and Greek words. For our study, three Greek words are of primary importance: *eleos, oiktirmon,* and *splanchna.* These three terms fall within the general semantic range of the English word "mercy" and hence can be visualized as a group of overlapping linguistic circles variously translated as mercy, compassion, or pity.

The biblical concept of mercy is both a feeling and an action. It refers to the deep feelings of pity and the practical rendering of aid. Indeed, it might be more accurate to say that mercy is a feeling that leads to action.

The mercy of God is related to mission in at least three ways. It is an integral part of the message we proclaim; it provides motivation for our service; and it describes the manner in which we carry out the GREAT COMMISSION.

First of all, God's mercy is an integral part of our message. The gospel describes the breaking in of the divine mercy into the world of human misery in the person of Jesus of Nazareth. His mercy is the basis of our salvation. "He saved us, not because of the righteous things we have done, but because of his mercy" (Titus 3:5).

The Bible describes God as "rich in mercy" (Eph. 2:4) and "full of mercy" (James 5:11). He is "the Father of compassion and God of all comfort" (2 Cor. 1:3). It is because of "his great mercy" (1 Peter 1:3) that we are saved. Thus, the mercy of God underlies the whole message of the Bible.

Second, mercy provides motivation for our ministry. Paul appeals to God's mercy as the basis for service. It is the experience of mercy that keeps us pressing on in the work. To the church at Rome he says, "I urge you, brothers, in view of God's mercy, to offer your bodies as living sacrifices" (Rom. 12:1). To the church at Corinth he writes, "Therefore, since through God's mercy we have this ministry, we do not lose heart" (2 Cor. 4:1).

Third, mercy describes the manner in which we carry out the Great Commission. Jesus is our model of mercy ministry. He felt deep compassion both for those who were spiritually lost and for those who were physically needy (Matt. 9:36; 20:34). But these deep feelings of compassion (literally, "moved in his bowels"—what today would be called the heart) always led Jesus to action. It was his mercy that moved him to heal the sick and feed the hungry (Matt. 14:14; 15:32). Through word and deed, Jesus engaged in holistic ministry, meeting the full range of human needs. He was not just a teacher or an evangelist. His was a life poured out in deeds of mercy, ministering to the whole person.

Jesus also taught about the importance of mercy. In the parable of the good Samaritan, Jesus illustrates the meaning of the second great command to "love your neighbor as yourself." He describes the compassionate ministry of the Samaritan as an act of mercy. He then concludes this parable with the command, "go and do likewise" (Luke 10:37). Thus, mercy ministry is a command for the entire church.

The ministry of mercy is primarily a ministry of deeds, focused on meeting the physical needs of humanity. Because of this, it is often contrasted with evangelism. EVANGELISM is seen as the spiritual work of the church while mercy ministry is merely physical. It can be cogently argued that evangelism has a logical priority over mercy ministry because of the eternal consequences of rejecting the gospel. But this is an unhelpful and unnecessary bifurcation (*see also* HOLISTIC MISSION).

Mercy ministry was a significant part of Christ's earthly ministry and remains an important aspect of the church's mission. In fact, Jesus has given numerous "deed" gifts to the church that are explicitly related to mercy ministry: service, giving, mercy, helps and administration (Rom. 12:6–8; 1 Cor. 14:28; 1 Peter 4:10–11). Jesus expects his ministry of mercy to continue through his church. Both word and deed, evangelism and mercy ministry are emphasized in Scripture. They are like the proverbial two wings of an airplane.

However, mercy ministry does not just seek the interdependence of word and deed. It also addresses one's attitudes. On two occasions, after seeing the critical and condemning attitudes of the Pharisees, Jesus rebukes them by quoting from the Old Testament: "I desire mercy, not sacrifice" (Matt. 9:13; 12:7). The scrupulously legalistic Pharisees were preoccupied with external religious rituals but knew little of God's tender mercy or heartfelt compassion.

Furthermore, Jesus contrasts mercy with a judging, condemning, and unforgiving spirit. "Be merciful, just as your Father is merciful. Do not judge, and you will not be judged. Do not condemn and you will not be condemned. Forgive and you will be forgiven" (Luke 6:36–37). Thus, mercy is an attitude that describes how we are to carry out our mission. In the words of James, "mercy triumphs over judgment!" (James 2:13).

RICHARD D. LOVE

Bibliography. E. R. Achtemeier, *IDB,* III:352–54; H. H. Esser, *NIDNTT,* II:593–601; J. W. L. Hoad, *NBD,* p. 761; T. J. Keller, *Ministries of Mercy.*

Merensky, Alexander (1837–1918). German missionary in South Africa. The son of a Prussian forest administrator, Merensky was born in Panten near Liegnitz in Silesia (Germany) in 1837 and studied at the BERLIN MISSIONARY SOCIETY's seminary. In 1859 he was posted to South Africa and undertook a new work in the Transvaal (South African Republic) among the Pedi, a Northern Sotho people who lived north of Pretoria. In 1864 a conflict among the indigenous tribes forced him to relocate and establish a new station, Bothshabelo near Middelburg, which became the center of Berlin's Transvaal mission. As the field director he developed workshops to train craftsmen, a printing plant, schools, hospitals, and a seminary to train African evangelists. He mastered several African languages, studied the history, culture, and religion of the people and published the results in Europe, and took part in geographical research expeditions. Forced to leave the South African Republic after the British defeat in 1882, he became one of the leading advocates for German colonial expansion. In

1891 he led an expedition into southern Tanganyika which opened the way for the Berlin Mission to develop a field there. In his later years he continued his scholarly works, was showered with honorary degrees and scholarly society membership, and moderated his enthusiasm for colonial missions.

ULRICH VAN DER HEYDEN

Metachurch. *See* SMALL GROUPS.

Methodist Missions. The Board of Global Ministries of the United Methodist Church resulted from the union of the Methodist Church and the Evangelical United Brethren Church that took place in 1968. To understand mission in this denomination the mission histories of the two streams need to be accounted for.

Mission from England gave birth to the Methodist Church, when from 1768 to 1774 JOHN WESLEY sent eight missionaries to America to promote and nurture the new Methodist movement. For years following the America Revolution the American frontier itself became a mission field for Methodist itinerants. The church followed the expansion to the west and an official Missionary Society was formed in 1819. Soon afterwards evangelists took the gospel into Canada and Nova Scotia.

Mission into the world was taking place when stress arose within the Methodist Episcopal Church in the United States. A schismatic problem over the episcopacy led to the formation of the Methodist Protestant Church (1830). Soon afterwards, a second division around the issue of slavery resulted in the formation of the Methodist Episcopal Church (South), while the original M.E. Church continued in the north. These lines of American Methodism pursued their separate mission programs until 1939, when union brought the three branches together, combining missionary operations under the Board of Missions of the reorganized Methodist Church.

Before the division, the Methodist Episcopal Church commissioned Melville R. Cox to Liberia. He became the first official missionary (1833). Soon afterward, work was opened up in Argentina, Brazil, and Texas (which in 1837 was still Spanish/Mexican territory). M.E. Church missions developed quickly after this time in China, Korea, India, Burma, Singapore, Malaya, and the Philippines as well as in Europe, the Baltic States, and Latin America, including Cuba, Brazil, Mexico, and Puerto Rico. The African work, which had begun in Liberia, expanded to Algeria, Tunisia, Angola, Rhodesia, Mozambique, and the Congo.

The Methodist Protestant Church, the earliest of the schismatic groups, established a Board of Foreign Missions at their first General Conference (1834). Most of the effort was in HOME MISSIONS for fifty years, with work opening up in Japan and China toward the end of the century. Second in the three-way split was the Methodist Episcopal (South), which formed its own Missionary Society in 1844 in Louisville. This board worked in home missions, not retaining any work overseas that had begun before separation. It was fifty years before mission was launched in Japan, followed by China and Korea. By 1920, the Missionary Society had work in the Congo, in Europe, Mexico, and Brazil. At the time of union M.E. (South) had 169 missionaries. However, the mission enterprise of the M.E. (North) was the largest, including all the fields mentioned above. Missionary work of the three groups, both home and foreign, was organized into one at the time of union (1939), as the Board of Missions and Church Extension. In 1952 this became the Board of Mission of the Methodist Church with three divisions: The World Division, the National Division, and the Woman's Division.

Church union between the Evangelical United Brethren Church and the Methodist Church took place in 1968. This further widened the mission areas of the newly organized United Methodist Church. The Department of World Mission, and the Woman's Society of World Service of the E.U.B. denomination had work in China, Japan, Hong Kong, Philippines, Brazil, Ecuador, Nigeria, Sierra Leone, and Europe. This presented a challenging, sometimes difficult task of reorganization, not only for the new denomination, but also for ecumenical relationships among the overseas churches.

Following the union, mission administration was finally reconstituted as the Board of Global Ministries. The structures followed primarily the Methodist patterns, as the size of the Methodist Church at the time of union was nearly ten times greater than that of the E.U.B. The total missionary force was well over one thousand in 1968. Since then, because of transfer of authority to national churches and changes in missionary roles, the number of overseas missionary personnel has been greatly reduced.

The contributions of women in all stages of mission history of the United Methodist Church are of inestimable importance (*see* WOMEN IN MISSION). The divided Methodist Church (until 1939), with their own separate boards of missions, were also organized into separate women's organizations. The Woman's Foreign Missionary Society of the Methodist Episcopal Church had 473 missionaries and a budget of $1 million when union was achieved in 1939. The Woman's Missionary Society of the M.E. Church (South), organized in 1878, brought 169 missionaries and $400,000 into the union. The Methodist Protestant Church was smaller and its Woman's Foreign Missionary Society worked more jointly with the M.P. Church's Board of Missions. Equally effective in fostering missionary education and in the raising of funds were the women's agencies of the two churches that formed the Evangelical United Brethren Church in 1946. The United Brethren Church had officially recognized their Woman's Missionary Society in 1875. The W.M.S. is remembered for beginning the earliest African mission at Totifunk in Sierra Leone. The Evangelical Association was greatly helped by the Woman's Missionary Society, formed in 1883. This Society functioned as a supportive Society rather than setting up their separate mission programs. After the merger in 1968, the Woman's Society of World Service of the E.U.B. Church was integrated with the Woman's Division of the Methodist Church.

United Methodist mission work cannot be fully appreciated without recognizing the closely allied United Methodist Committee on Relief. This is the arm of the United Methodist Church that responds by a diversity of programs to crisis situations as well as those that call for longer commitment, such as community development, agriculture, and humanitarian services. UMCOR maintains a separate program and budget, even though the kinds of projects carried out by the Board of Global Ministries and UMCOR are often very closely related.

In 1984, a second mission agency was formed as a voluntary association carrying the name The Mission Society for United Methodists. The purpose of the new society is to emphasize evangelism in the tradition of John Wesley and promote the centrality of the GREAT COMMISSION as the basis for mission. With headquarters in Atlanta, the MSUM carries on its work separately from the denominational Board. Missionary personnel of the society are United Methodists who work directly with the MSUM or are seconded to other mission agencies. This additional feature of joining with other mission organizations has resulted in a diversity of ministries in South and Central America, Central and Southeast Asia, Africa, North America, and in the new states of the former Soviet Union.

DEAN S. GILLILAND

Bibliography. W. C. Barclay, *History of Methodist Missions*, vols. 1–3; J. B. Behny and P. Eller, *The History of the Evangelical United Brethren*; J. Cannon, *History of Southern Methodist Missions*; J. T. Copplestone, *History of Methodist Missions*, vol. 4; B. L. Goddard, *The Encyclopedia of Modern Christian Missions*.

Methodius (c. 815–885). Greek missionary to the Slavic people. Born in Thessalonika (Saloniki) in the Byzantine Empire, he took the name of Methodius upon becoming a monk at the Mount Olympus monastery, where his younger brother Constantine (later to take the name of CYRIL) joined him after 855. The work for which they are known began in 682 when Rastislav of Moravia requested Greek priests to teach the Slavic people in their own language. They traveled to Rastislav's court and began training Slavic priests. They ran into increasing opposition from the Bavarian Catholic missionaries there. They traveled to Rome in 868 to confer with the pope, who approved the work of the brothers and the Slavic liturgy they created. Methodius was ordained, and eventually consecrated as archbishop of Pannonia and Moravia, which was removed from the authority of the Franks (Germans). This produced a violent reaction among Frankish secular and religious leaders and in 870 King Louis the German imprisoned Methodius in Swabia. Pope John VIII secured Methodius's restoration in 873, although apparently only after a promise that use of the Slavic liturgy would be curtailed. The conflicts, however, continued. Methodius returned briefly to Constantinople (881–882) to complete the translation of the Bible he and Cyril had begun. He died in Moravia on April 6, 885. After his death, his followers were forced out of Moravia, with the result that they began evangelistic work among the Poles, Bulgars, Bohemians, and other Slavic peoples. The ministry of Cyril and Methodius is traditionally regarded as the major means by which the gospel was brought to the Slavic people.

ROBERT SHUSTER

Bibliography. F. Dvornik, *Byzantine Missions Among the Slavs: SS. Constantine-Cyril and Methodius.*

Mexico City Conference (1963). The first world conference of the newly created Division of World Mission and Evangelism, brought into being through the integration of the INTERNATIONAL MISSIONARY COUNCIL into the life of the WORLD COUNCIL OF CHURCHES, was held in Mexico City in December 1963. Under the title of "Witness in Six Continents" its four sections focused on: (1) the witness of Christians to those of other faiths; (2) the witness of Christians to people living in a secular world; (3) the witness of the congregation in its neighborhood; and (4) the witness of the Christian church across national and confessional boundaries. Taken together these clearly set the missionary task in the context of what God was doing in the secular world, with less emphasis on the nature of the church itself. Mexico City abandoned the geographical concept of Christendom because "The missionary frontier runs around the world: it is the line that separates belief from unbelief, the unseen frontier which cuts across all other frontiers and presents the universal church with its primary missionary challenge." It was the first mission conference at which the Orthodox were formally present.

Work on dialogue with people of other living faiths was not significantly advanced at Mexico City, and although the conference endorsed the idea of "Joint Action for Mission," the official history records a slow response and "inadequate attention at Geneva" to this emphasis. The conference was, however, significant in establishing the understanding that, in LESSLIE NEWBIGIN's words, "the home base of the world mission is worldwide, and that the mission field is also worldwide." Accordingly the conference broke new ground in the attention it gave to missionary endeavor in the secular world of North America and Europe.

JOHN H. Y. BRIGGS

SEE ALSO World Council of Churches Conferences.

Bibliography. R. K. Orchard, *Witness in Six Continents. Records of the meeting of the commission on World Mission and Evangelism of the World Council of Churches, Held in Mexico City, December 8th to 19th 1963;* N. Lossky et al., *DEM,* p. 330; L. Newbigin, *The Ecumenical Advance: A History of the Ecumenical Movement,* 2:193–95.

Mexico *(Est. 2000 pop.: 102,410,000; 1,958,201 sq. km. [756,061 sq. mi.]).* Mexico is Latin America's third largest country in land mass. A civil war *la Revolución* took place from 1910 to 1917, and ended the long dictatorship of Porfirio Díaz ushering in a new period of equality and democracy. Nevertheless, the *Partido Revolucionario Institucional* (PRI) has dominated politics throughout the century, frequently resorting to fraud and corruption.

Catholicism was introduced into the country through the Spanish conquerors. This resulted in many distortions of the faith and much SYNCRETISM. Nevertheless, there were many sincere missionaries, including the famous BARTOLOMÉ DE LAS CASAS. Almost 90 percent of Mexicans are Roman Catholics, although fewer than 10 percent participate in weekly services. The Catholic Church has had a stormy relationship with the government, including a violent civil war which claimed over a million lives (1916–29). Due to the current vulnerability of both institutions, they are seeking a mutually beneficial relationship. The four main factions within the church are the conservative traditionalists loyal to the Vatican, the nationalists, a socially concerned *comunidad de base* sector led by a few progressive bishops, and a growing charismatic wing.

The history of the Protestant Church in Mexico can be understood as a series of "waves," each one building on and going beyond the previous one. The first wave consisted of European immigrants who arrived in New Spain. Usually these were subjects of Charles V and Phillip II but were from countries other than Spain. The earliest was Andrés Moral, a Moravian lapidary, arrested in Mexico City in 1536 for ten Lutheran heresies. So many followed in his footsteps that a special tribunal of the Holy Inquisition was established in Mexico City in 1571. Almost every year "Lutheran and Calvinist heretics" were tried and sentenced. The last two condemned to death by the Inquisition in Mexico were Catholic priests Hidalgo and Morelos, the founding fathers who led the war of independence from Spain beginning in 1810.

The second wave was more intentional and took place in independent Mexico. JAMES "DIEGO" THOMSON was the representative of the British and Foreign Bible Society and of the British and Foreign School Society. He had traveled extensively throughout Latin America establishing Lancaster Schools (schools that utilized the more advanced students to teach the younger ones and used the Bible as one of the principal texts). He arrived in Mexico in 1827 with the same purpose. Political liberals in Mexico became thoroughly committed to his cause, such that on his departure in 1830, José María Luis Mora, a very influential statesman and author, became the official representative of the Bible Society in Mexico and promoted the translation of the Scriptures into the Spanish, Náhuatl, Tarasco, Otomí, and Huasteco languages.

The third wave was perhaps the most important and has rightly been called Mexico's own "Protestant Reformation." In 1857 President Benito Juárez and his cabinet implemented the Laws of Reform, which separated church from state and, in effect, granted religious liberty in Mexico. Although the Roman Catholic hierarchy condemned the new Constitution and the liberal politicians that promoted it, a significant number of priests were supportive of these initiatives. These *Padres Constitucionalistas* were expelled from the Catholic Church and formed an independent church with Juárez's support. They underwent their own "Reformation" without much foreign influence. Although this *Iglesia Mexicana de Jesús* did not survive much past 1870, many of its leaders, such as Arcadio Morales and Sóstenes Juárez, became the founders and leaders of the Presbyterian, Methodist, and Anglican churches in the following decades.

The fourth wave was the arrival of foreign missionaries sent out by denominational mission organizations, primarily based in the United States, beginning in the 1870s. The Methodist, Baptist, Presbyterian, and other denominations experienced slow but steady growth during the long Porfirian dictatorship. Perhaps their most significant contribution was the 614 schools that they started throughout the country. Evangelical participation in the Revolution (1910–17) was widespread, especially in the military, ideological, educational, and political arenas. Nevertheless, after the Revolution, Protestant denominations abandoned the public sphere due to legal and theological factors.

Pentecostals constitute the fifth wave. Mexican migrant workers in the United States returned to Mexico after the Revolution and many brought with them "Pentecostal fire." Not only denominations like the Assemblies of God and the Church of God (Cleveland) were begun, but entirely autonomous movements sprouted, such as the *Iglesia de Dios en la República Mexicana*, the *Iglesia Interdenominacional de Portales*, the *Iglesia de Pachuca*, the *Movimiento de Iglesias Evangélicas Pentecostés Independientes* (MIEPI), and others. Currently, each of these movements has more than five hundred member churches.

Over the past twenty years, a sixth wave has burst on the scene, the Neo-Pentecostals. With many of their numbers coming from the middle and upper classes, these groups are much less traditional than other evangelicals. Utilizing lively music by Marcos Witt, Miguel Cassina, and others, these groups emphasize vigorous praise and worship more than doctrine and biblical exposition. Groups such as *El Castillo del Rey* (Monterrey), *Amistad Cristiana,* and *Calocoaya* (Mexico City) minister to tens of thousands in their weekly services.

Comprising about 10 percent of the current population, Mexican evangelicals are involved in creative social ministries and venturing more and more into the political arena. Religious persecution continues in Chiapas, Oaxaca, Hidalgo, and other states, but this persecution has resulted in even greater growth.

The most rapid and extensive growth of Protestantism in Mexico has occurred during the last forty years in the southern states of Chiapas, Oaxaca, Tabasco, Veracruz, Quintana Roo, and Yucatán. Large people movements among Mayan tribal peoples have been common. In Chiapas, Tabasco, and Yucatán over 25% of the population is reportedly evangelical Portestant or Pentecostal.

LINDY SCOTT

Bibliography. L. Scott, *Salt of the Earth: A Socio-Political History of Mexico City Evangelical Protestants (1964–1991).*

Micronesia. POLYNESIA, MICRONESIA, and MELANESIA comprise the three major divisions of the large Pacific Ocean. It is located north of the equator in the western part of the Pacific. Geographically, Micronesia includes the large island nation of KIRIBATI (formerly Gilbert Islands, a British protectorate) located in the easternmost part and straddling the equator. Then, spread from east to west are the islands of the former U.S. Trust Territory of the Pacific—the MARSHALL ISLANDS, the FEDERATED STATES OF MICRONESIA of Kosrae, Pohnpei, Chuuk (Truk), Yap; and PALAU (Belau); and the NORTHERN MARIANAS ISLANDS (Rota, Tinian,

Saipan). In the westernmost part, the island of GUAM, an unincorporated territory of the United States, completes the list of Micronesian islands. It is an island world composed of over 2,000 islands scattered over 3 million square miles of the Pacific with a population of over 260,000.

In 1852, AMERICAN BOARD OF COMMISSIONERS FOR FOREIGN MISSION (ABCFM) missionaries, assisted by newly trained Hawaiian couples, entered the eastern part of Micronesia (Marshalls, Kosrae, and Pohnpei) and established small island churches. Within the first twenty years missionaries on Pohnpei reached farther west to the Chuuk Islands with the help of local servants of Christ. Roman Catholic missionaries reached the western parts of Micronesia (Guam and the Northern Marianas) in the late seventeenth and the early part of the eighteenth centuries. They eventually established churches on Yap and Palau, and throughout the rest of the Micronesian islands.

ABCFM missionaries and Hawaiian co-workers evangelized the northern islands of Kiribati (Gilberts) in 1857, while the southern islands were reached by English missionaries of the LONDON MISSIONARY SOCIETY as the islands had become part of an English Protectorate and later an English Crown Colony.

In 1898, after Spain lost the Spanish-American War, the United States took over Guam. The rest of the Micronesian islands became a colonial possession of Germany. Thus, in 1906, German Protestant missionaries of the Liebenzeller Mission (former German branch of the CHINA INLAND MISSION) entered the eastern part of Micronesia in place of the American missionaries. They proceeded to strengthen the existing churches and to evangelize the unreached islands west of Chuuk. During World War I, Japan took over Micronesia from Germany. They replaced German missionaries with workers from the Protestant Church of Japan. In the 1920s and 1930s the Japanese government allowed German missionaries to return to the islands, but they placed them under severe restrictions as the islands were fortified for war. The U.S. liberation of Micronesia during World War II ended the Japanese control and initiated an American administration in the islands as the U.S. Trust Territory of the Pacific Islands. This allowed missionaries from the original American Board to return to the eastern part of Micronesia. Further, German missionaries who had survived the war were allowed to continue their work under the auspices of the American Board. These missionaries joined their efforts to regather island Christians and to rebuild their lives and their churches.

The United States brought its educational, monetary, and postal system to the islands of Micronesia. They also provided health care and a political program that led the war-torn islands into a period of restoration and growth. Vigorous training programs by the United States equipped islanders with needed skills to rebuild the islands and explore new forms of democratic government. With proper training, they wrote their own Constitutions and democratically elected their own forms of governments at the municipal, state, and national levels. In the early 1960s, elected leaders from each island group formed the Congress of Micronesia and a national government in cooperation with the U.S. administration. However, over the past twenty years, each island group has elected its own style of government, thus ending a united Micronesia and resulting in the various island nations: the Republic of the Marshall Islands, the Federated States of Micronesia (FSM) made up of the four Island States of Kosrae, Pohnpei, Chuuk, and Yap; the Republic of Belau (Palau); and the Commonwealth of the Northern Marianas.

All of these young island nations, except the Northern Marianas, have chosen to maintain their close ties with the United States through a unique arrangement with the United States, called the "Compact of Free Association." Under this compact, the United States provides the island nations with needed funding for their internal development. They also have freedom to deal with their internal affairs and are allowed to enter the United States without a visa. In exchange, the United States receives options on land use for United States military purposes. The United States also assumes the responsibility for the defense of the area. The people of Northern Marianas elected an even closer bond with the United States, the status of a "commonwealth," allowing them to receive greater benefits, especially U.S. citizenship.

The island of Guam, "unincorporated territory" of the United States and located within the western part of Micronesia, provides the United States with one of the most forward bastions of defense in the vast Pacific Ocean. There is a large U.S. military presence on Guam. The Organic Act of Guam (1950) by the U.S. Congress designated the island as an "unincorporated territory" of the United States, giving its people, the Chamorros, U.S. citizenship without the privilege of voting for the president of the United States. As the "Hub of the Pacific," Guam has become the home for many Micronesians, Asians, and U.S. citizens. The island has also become the "honeymoon capital" for Japanese newlyweds. In recent years, Chamorros have been seeking to change their island status from a U.S. territory to a commonwealth.

During this crucial transition period, the missionaries assisted the island churches in developing their leadership through local training programs, centralized pastoral schools, as well as overseas education in Bible colleges and seminaries. This has resulted in self-governing and self-supporting island churches in the past twenty-five years. The mission boards (American Board/UCC and Liebenzell) still assist with some funding and personnel at the request of the churches.

The traditional island churches are also challenged by other Christian organizations establishing their ministries. The Assemblies of God, the Seventh-Day Adventists, the Independent Baptists, Youth with a Mission, Campus Crusade, and more recently the Salvation Army have become active on various island centers. The Jehovah's Witnesses, the Mormon Church, and the Baha'i are also offering their services to the Micronesians.

Over the past twenty-five years, enormous changes have challenged the island traditions and cultural values. Subsistence farming and fishing is giving way to a cash economy. Communal living and sharing of resources is being taxed by a greater emphasis on the individual. Overseas travel and education, movies, TV (cable, CNN), videos, and other mass media bring incredible challenges to the island people and their cultural values. Elementary and high school education for all island young people adds to the culture change facing families, communities, and churches. Drugs, alcohol, and a promiscuous lifestyle challenge the island communities.

Rural–urban drift due to education, jobs, and adventure has drawn the young educated elite from their islands to the crowded administration centers of Micronesia, often leaving the very young and the older ones back on their islands. Guam, within easy access of most of the islands, has become the most attractive urban center for islanders from the central and western part of Micronesia. Since the "Compact of Free Association" was ratified in the early 1980s, Micronesian citizens have unrestricted entry into the United States. Thus, Guam, Hawaii, and the United States have become home to many Micronesians. For example, a recent estimate claims that over 9,000 Chuukese have migrated to Guam. Chuukese churches have attempted to provide pastoral care for their people on Guam. In addition, many Chuukese have settled in Hawaii and various parts of the United States. They have become a significant people group, among whom evangelistic and pastoral work is being done.

The continuous cultural change over the years has also sparked the rise of "nativistic movements" (Palau and Chuuk) that urge a return to cultural values and practices rejected and neglected by generations of island Christians. These movements have challenged the churches to become more sensitive to the unmet needs of islanders. Also, the persistent animistic practices, involving local medicine and magical assistance of various kinds through contact with ancestral spirits and traditional powers, challenge island

Christians to demonstrate the all-sufficiency of Jesus Christ.

One of the most important roles for the island churches in Micronesia today is to be the prophetic voice of God to the elected leaders of the island nations; to provide a cohesive community of faith and values for island Christians in the face of rapid cultural change; and to demonstrate to many islanders in meaningful POWER ENCOUNTERS the all-sufficiency of the Lord Jesus Christ and the power of the gospel.

HERMAN BEUHLER

Micronesia, Federated States of (*Est. 2000 pop.: 144,000; 702 sq. km. [271 sq. mi.]*). Comprised of more than six hundred islands in four main groups (Truk [Chuuk], Pohnpei, Yap, and Kosrae), in 1993 the population was estimated to be 90 percent Christian (40% Protestant, 48% Catholic, and 2.1% marginal Christian), with 14.5 percent being evangelical. The largest Protestant denominations included the Protestant Church of East Truk, Protestant Church of the Caroline, United Church of Pohnpei, and the Assemblies of God. Mormons and Jehovah's Witnesses are also active.

A. SCOTT MOREAU

SEE ALSO Micronesia.

Middle East. Since World War II, the lands from the eastern Mediterranean Sea to the Persian Gulf have been called the Middle East. Other designations include the Levant and Near East. Though the geographic perimeters vary, the Middle East consists of the states or territories of the Arabian Peninsula, Cyprus, Iran, Iraq, Israel, Jordan, Lebanon, Palestine, Syria, and Turkey. At the core, religiously, it is a largely Islamic world. However, more than 8 million Christians live in the region. Despite the fact that massive emigration of Christians has eroded the strength of Christianity in some areas, notably Palestine, overall the Christian population is growing.

Christian presence in the region goes back to establishment of the first church in Jerusalem on Pentecost, when the Holy Spirit came upon the disciples of Jesus (Acts 1–2). From that epicenter the gospel was to spread to Judea, Samaria, and the ends of the world (Acts 1:8). Earliest Christianity in the Middle East thus had a missionary dynamic. Within the lifetime of Jesus' first followers, Christianity spread to Africa, where notable Christian populations have continued to thrive in Egypt and Ethiopia despite the rise of Islam in the seventh century; to Europe; and eastward. Christians were first so-named at Antioch (Acts 11:26). Although surviving documents provide too slender a base to support some claims made about the expansion of Christianity in Asia during the lifetimes of Jesus' apostles, an early tradition is that Thomas carried the gospel to India and established seven congregations along the Malabar coast.

Christianity spread through the Hellenistic world, largely tending to follow trade lines and attracting converts in the great urban centers of the Roman Empire such as Antioch, Ephesus, Corinth, and Rome. Although conversion to the new faith was uneven, by the end of the third century Armenia had became the first Christianized kingdom followed, early in the fourth century, by the Roman Empire. Within two hundred years after the death of Christ, Syrian Christians were carrying the faith into the Persian Empire and across the steppes of Central Asia. In addition to the tradition that St. Thomas visited South India, there is another account, dating to the third century, of his visit to northwest India (what is now Pakistan). Earliest evidence of Nestorian missionary activity in the ancient Chinese capital Chang'an dates to 635.

Missionary dynamism did not endure. Contributing to this decline was the internal political and theological splintering of Christianity. However, in terms of the transformation it brought to the religious geography of the Middle East, the major factor was the rise of ISLAM. During the period from the *hijrah*, or emigration of the Prophet and his family from Mecca to Medina in 622 to his death in 632, Muhammad created a religious community held together by his personal presence and authority. Though it lasted only ten years, Muhammad's public mission had an impact similar to that of Jesus. After his death, his family and closest relatives by marriage transformed this community into a political and military empire. Within thirty years, the rule of the patriarchal caliphate stretched west through the richest provinces of North Africa halfway to the Atlantic Ocean, east into Asia, and north to the eastern shores of the Black Sea. Except for Asia Minor, Muslims ruled all of the ancient Christian Roman Empire in Asia.

Nonetheless, there remained a significant Christian minority population throughout the Middle East. Especially where large Arab Christian populations were involved, notably in what is now Egypt, Palestine, Lebanon, Syria, and Yemen, Muhammad's successors granted immunity from forcible conversion. For non-Arabs, in what is now Iran or Turkey, Christianity remained as a tolerated minority, often in a sort of religious ghetto and subject to special taxes.

Gradually over the next three centuries Christianity in Asia went into decline. Under the Umayyad Caliphate (661–750) and 'Abbasids (750–1258), a numerically large body of Christians persisted faithfully, but its missionary possibilities were curtailed and its long-term survival was in doubt. The world of Islam also experienced splintering, and ancient centers of civilization came under the sway of new Islamic political empires. These forced conversion to Islam all across Asia with the exception of the Middle East. The Nestorians in China disappeared, and the Thomas Christians of southern India were isolated as a minority-caste community.

Still Christianity survived under medieval Islamic rule. From the perspective of Asian history as a whole, the most distinguishing feature of the period was the fall of the Arabs and triumph of the Turks. There are, of course, other perspectives, most notably that of European history which tends to highlight the brief, failed intervention known as the CRUSADES. The first crusade began in 1095 with a call by Pope Urban II to the Christian rulers of western Europe to rescue the Holy Land from the Turks. This led to creation of a Latin kingdom of Jerusalem, which lasted in various forms from 1099 until the fall of Jerusalem in 1187. Properly speaking, the story of the succession of Crusades to restore Christian control of the Holy Land belongs to the history of the Western church. However, they did leave their mark on the churches of the Middle East. Negatively, they heightened the breach between Eastern and Western Christianity, and tended to unite Eastern Christians, Jews, and Muslims in their disenchantment with arrogant Western Christians. Positively, they contributed to the renaissance of European life, in part through the introduction of new architectural forms and learning to Europe. They also contributed to the emergence of two new Catholic missionary orders, the Dominicans and Franciscans.

The Castillian Dominic (1170–1221) sent preaching friars to the Middle East with a sense of mission shared by the Franciscans, to strive to heal the divisions of Christianity and to reach out in faithful evangelistic witness to Muslims. Among the early Dominican missionaries, Raymond Martin (1230–84) became a notable scholar of Islam. FRANCIS OF ASSISI (1182–1226), never reached the Middle East. However, his personal mission to Egypt impressed Muslims. His model of sincere Christian witness inspired Islamic rulers to allow Franciscans to remain in the region, often as custodians of the Holy Sites.

Between the fourteenth and eighteenth centuries, Christian missionary activity in the Middle East was limited. Early in this period, the best-known missionary was the Spanish layman, RAYMOND LULL (c. 1235), who sought to convince the Western church of the vital need for peaceful missionary work among Muslims. During his preaching journeys to Tunis and Algeria in North Africa, and to Cyprus, he was attacked, arrested, and expelled many times. He met a martyr's death by stoning in Tunis.

The Reformation period of the sixteenth century, which witnessed the creation of new Roman Catholic missionary orders and some initial Protestant outreach, quickened the pulse of Christian evangelistic activity and awakened interest in work among Jews and Muslims. However, virtually no effort to evangelize in the Middle East followed from this. It remained for the evangelical awakening of the late eighteenth century to generate missionary activity in the region.

In the nineteenth century, Protestants undertook several initiatives. Animated by Paul's example of preaching first to the Jew (Rom. 1:16), the London Society for Promoting Christianity among the Jews (Church Mission to Jews, or Church's Ministry among the Jews), founded in 1808 as an offshoot of the LONDON MISSIONARY SOCIETY, was the first of some twenty-three such societies in Britain alone. Many of these continue to the present. The London Society sent the Reverend Joseph Wolff (1796–1862), a converted Jew, to undertake various exploratory journeys, leading to the start of a medical ministry in Jerusalem in 1824.

Elsewhere, in 1818, the CHURCH MISSIONARY SOCIETY (CMS) sent a party of five missionaries to Egypt. The AMERICAN BOARD OF COMMISSIONERS FOR FOREIGN MISSIONS (ABCFM) established work in Beirut in 1823. Notable work was done in the area of translation of the Bible into modern Arabic and establishment of the Syrian Protestant College, which became the American University of Beirut in 1920. The American Board also began work in Turkey in 1831. The Reverend William Gordell settled in Constantinople. The educational work gradually extended to other centers in Asia Minor and Armenia. In terms of conversions, however, numerical growth came from adherents of the ancient Eastern churches as, perhaps regretfully or unwisely, the mission formed a new Protestant denomination. In Iran, HENRY MARTYN, en route to England from service in Calcutta, India, between 1806 until 1811, worked on a Persian version of the New Testament until his death at age thirty-one, having baptized one convert. Missionaries with the ABCFM who opened a station at Urmia in 1835 concentrated on adherents of Eastern Christianity, with the same results as noted in Turkey. By contrast, Swiss missionaries of the BASEL MISSION, who settled in Tabriz in 1813, concentrated on contact with Muslims. Among its missionaries, KARL PFANDER completed in 1829 the *Mizan-al-Haqq* (Balance of Truth), a book which helped pioneer a more tolerant approach to Muslims, with an inner understanding of Islam not characteristic of earlier missionaries. This approach began to bear fruit under the ministry of an Irish Anglican Robert Bruce, who spent ten years in the Punjab and, like Martyn, obtained permission to spend a year in Iran on his way back from furlough in Britain to improve his knowledge of Persian and of Islam. His year's stay extended to two, and in 1871, as he prepared to leave for India, nine Muslims with whom he had studied Islam in Isfahan asked for baptism. He remained in Iran and was joined by another CMS missionary with a background in India, Edward Craig Stuart. Their ministry bore fruit when the first Persian, Hassan Barnabas Dehquni-Tafti, was consecrated Anglican bishop on April 25, 1961.

One additional nineteenth-century initiative is worthy of note. Even as Christianity arose in Jerusalem under the unitive ministry of the Holy Spirit, Jerusalem was the setting of an ecumenical initiative between 1841 and 1886. In 1841 the Church of England and Prussian Evangelical Union jointly established the Protestant bishopric in Jerusalem. The first bishop, Michael Solomon Alexander, was a converted Jewish rabbi. He served from 1842 to 1845. His successor, Samuel Gobat, a French-speaking Swiss Protestant who had served the Church Missionary Society in Ethiopia, was bishop for thirty-three years, from 1846 to 1879. His tenure proved controversial in such areas as liturgy, missionary strategy, and relations with local political and religious authorities. When his successor, Joseph Barclay, died suddenly after less than two years in office, the joint undertaking collapsed, and the British Archbishop of Canterbury appointed a successor on a purely Anglican basis. The demise of the Jerusalem episcopacy in 1886, due to conflict in Jerusalem and imperial politics in Europe, contributed to the continued breach between the Anglican and Lutheran churches and the splintering of the Christian community in the Holy Land. Proselytizing activities among Eastern Christians and failure to establish any viable Jewish Christian community among the local inhabitants further weakened Christian witness in the Holy Land. This initiative contributed in some measure to the continued failure on the part of Western Christians to rethink attitudes toward Eastern Christians and the people of Israel.

The religious awakening of interest in the Middle East coincided with the decline of the Ottoman Empire and an awakening of European imperial ambitions in the region. At times, ecclesiastical and political rivalries often contributed directly to conflict, starting with Napoleon Bonaparte's invasion of Egypt in 1798. In 1847, the Roman Catholic Church revived the Latin Patriarchate under French auspices. This in turn attracted Russian interest, allegedly in support of Orthodox authorities, and contributed in some measure to the outbreak of the Crimean War in 1854. Struggle among European imperial powers for control of the region intensified in the aftermath of the collapse of the Ottoman Empire after World War I.

The lands of the Bible have extraordinary significance for Christians, Jews, Muslims, and the tiny community of Samaritans as well as for other religious communities such as the BAHA'I and Druze. Interest in and care for the Holy Land have long characterized major streams of Christian spirituality. Pilgrimage has been a major manifestation. Another has been Christian ZIONISM, a phenomenon first expressed during the sixteenth century. Especially within the Anglican and Calvinist traditions, some Protestants began to read the Bible in such a way that they expected, as a prelude to Christ's second coming, that Jews would return to their ancient homeland. By the nineteenth century, many Christians, influenced by a dispensational hermeneutic (*see* DISPENSATIONALISM), expressed an accepting attitude toward the desire of many diaspora Jews to return to the Holy Land and initiated political activity promoting restoration of Jews to the Holy Land. In effect, Christian Zionism preceded the emergence of political Jewish Zionism, an ideological instrument for mobilizing international patronage for a Jewish homeland in the Holy Land. In Britain, Canada, and the United States, Christian Zionists have exhibited considerable activity and influence, anticipating Christ's second coming by the end of the second millennium of the common era. Christian Zionists welcomed the Balfour Declaration, which, on November 2, 1917, promised the Jews a national home in Palestine; capture of Jerusalem a few weeks later; establishment of the British mandate of Palestine after World War I; appointment of a Jew, Herbert Samuel, as the first High Commissioner; Jewish emigration to the Holy Land; organization of Jewish para-military forces; creation of the State of Israel in 1948; reunification of Jerusalem under Israeli control in 1967; and the response of the world community to Iraq's invasion of Kuwait in 1990. Christian Zionists still engender fervent support for the State of Israel. The intimate linkage between Christian Zionism and political decision-making remains a political factor in Western diplomacy related to the Israeli-Arab and Israeli-Palestinian conflicts.

As the era of Western influence in the region waned after mid-nineteenth century, involvement by indigenous Christians in the wider social and religious life of Middle East has increased. Despite the great diversity of the region, it is possible to make a few generalizations. On the whole, the social influence of Christians is disproportionate to their numbers throughout the region. Generally, they are better educated than the Muslim majority. They are prominent in commerce, education, and the professions. Christians fare relatively well economically and are less likely to number among the poorest of the poor. Where Islamic law prevails, and in the State of Israel, Christians are generally tolerated provided there is no missionary activity from outside. In countries where so-called Islamic fundamentalism is particularly strong, or religious nationalism particularly strident, as in Iran since 1979, Christians have suffered persecution. Christians exercise considerable political power of Cyprus, which remains partitioned, and in Lebanon, where they once formed a majority of the population. Religiously, the Christian churches remain fragmented, notwithstanding the longings of ordinary Christians to live as one body, including gestures to promote unity, such as the pilgrimage of the Roman Catholic Pope Paul VI in January 1964, and the encounters he had with Benedictos I, Greek Orthodox Patriarch of Jerusalem, and Athenagoras I, Ecumenical Patriarch of Constantinople.

PAUL R. DEKAR

Bibliography. Y. Ben-Arieh, *The Rediscovery of the Holy Land in the Nineteenth Century;* R. B. Betts, *Christians in the Arab East. A Political Study;* S. P. Colbi, *A History of the Christian Presence in the Holy Land;* J. S. Conway, *Holocaust and Genocide Studies* 1 (1986): 127–46; K. Cragg, *The Arab Christian. A History in the Middle East;* R. T. Handy, ed., *The Holy Land in American Protestant Life 1800–1948. A Documentary History;* N. A. Horner, *A Guide to Christian Churches in the Middle East;* S. M. Jack, *Journal of Religious History* 19 (December 1995): 181–203; S. H. Moffett, *A History of Christianity in Asia.*

Midway Islands. *See* MICRONESIA.

Migration. Migration is as old as the departure of Adam and Eve from the garden (Gen. 3:23–24). Its uprooting nature drove Cain in fear to the security of the city (Gen. 4:13–14, 17) and scattered the builders of Babel's city and tower (Gen. 11:9). Today, as of old, it has been motivated by famine and natural disaster, by the search for a better life, and by political conflict and war.

Migration Then and Now. Past or present, these migratory movements take many forms, some more peaceful in origin. The Berbers of Africa's past and today's Fulani demonstrate *nomadism*, a fixed lifestyle of wandering from place to place. *Immigration*, a relatively free movement of peoples within and across political boundaries, has a long history. With the passage of the 1793 Alien Bill in England its formal control was initiated and now has become the rule (Kritz, Keely, and Tomasi, 1983, xiii).

Out of the displacement of war and sociopolitical struggle have come the cause/effect patterns of *Invasion* and *Displacement Migration*. The mass intrusions into Israel's history by conquering Assyria and Babylonia are good examples. They were accompanied by deportation, resettlement, and assimilation. Things have not changed much. World War II saw the displacement of some 40 million people in Europe alone. Since the end of the Vietnam War in 1975, over 2 million people have fled from Southeast Asia.

But there are new twists also. Ease of travel has increased international migration. Currently an estimated 125 million people live officially

outside the countries of their birth, some permanently, others as a temporary labor force. Migration in the eighteenth and early nineteenth centuries flowed from richer countries to poorer ones; now the flow is from less developed regions to more developed ones. There is a growing feminization of both international and internal migration.

However, it is internal migration within the Third World countries that has deeply modified past patterns. That migration is from rural to urban areas, supporting a continuing trend toward ever-larger cities. Budgets are swamped by human needs and POVERTY has become the dominant social problem. Africa today resembles a "huge refugee camp" (Mieth and Cahill, 1993, 15).

Mission Response. Migration has been a major "bridge of God" for Christianity's spread in the past (Norwood, 1969). "Aliens and strangers in the world" (1 Peter 2:11), Christians have wandered in dispersion "among the nations" (Luke 24:47). Christian immigrants planted the church at Rome and in Gaul. Wandering monks crossed Europe and followed the ancient silk route through Central Asia into China. Even such brutal invasions as the CRUSADES and the colonial conquests of Africa, Asia, and Latin America opened pilgrim paths for a compromised Christianity. Christians were part of the transoceanic migrations to Australia and North America in the seventeenth and eighteenth centuries. Opportunities for skilled labor abroad today have opened CREATIVE ACCESS COUNTRIES to TENT-MAKING MISSIONS.

Migrants have also been the objects of evangelism and compassionate service. Christian ministries like the TEAR Fund, World Vision, and World Relief have become involved in social transformation and DEVELOPMENT projects for refugees and "children at risk." CHURCH PLANTING has had its successes among the mainline Chinese, relocating after 1949 in Taiwan. The church has not forgotten that the treatment of strangers and aliens is still a criterion of fidelity to God's covenant (Exod. 22:21; James 2:14–17). In caring for strangers, they care for Jesus (Matt. 25:36, 40).

HARVIE M. CONN

SEE ALSO Urbanization.

Bibliography. M. Kritz, C. Keely, and S. Tomasi, eds., *Global Trends in Migration: Theory and Research on International Population Movements;* D. Mieth and L. Cahill, eds., *Migrants and Refugees;* F. Norwood, *Strangers and Exiles: A History of Religious Exiles,* vols. 1–2.

Míguez Bonino, José (1924–). Argentinean Methodist theologian whose pastoral concern for the poor, coupled with his lifelong interest in theological and political ethics have been combined to make him one of the most outstanding Latin American Protestant theologians. Born in

Santa Fe, he has degrees from the Facultad Evangélica de Buenos Aires (1948), Emory University in Atlanta (1952), and Union Theological Seminary in New York (1960). His major contribution has been as a proponent of the theology of liberation, drawing heavily from Marxist principles of social analysis and praxis, yet rejecting parts of them on the basis of his view of Christian ethics. He makes this clear in his books *Toward a Christian Political Ethics* as well as in *Doing Theology in a Revolutionary Situation*. No less important has been his contribution in the field of ecumenism, both in his books and articles and in his participation in the WORLD COUNCIL OF CHURCHES, in the Protestant-Roman Catholic dialogue toward unity, and as the only Latin American Protestant observer at Vatican II. Another significant contribution has been in the field of theological education, as president of the Instituto Superior de Estudios Teológicos, in Buenos Aires and as a visiting professor in several institutions in the Americas and Europe. His pastoral heart has also led him to translate and arrange several hymns exalting Christ as Savior and Lord.

PABLO E. PÉREZ

Millennial Thought. Belief in the earthly reign of Christ before the end of the world and the eternal state. The most notable form of this doctrine is PREMILLENNIALISM, which claims that the Lord will return before the golden age and is based on certain key passages of Scripture, including Daniel 7–11, Ezekiel 37–39, Matthew 24, 1 Thessalonians 4, 2 Thessalonians 2, and especially Revelation 20. There are two other major views, POSTMILLENNIALISM, which states that the Lord will return after the millennium and AMILLENNIALISM, which states that the language of Scripture is too figurative to suggest that there will be a literal reign of Christ on earth.

Although these interpretations have never been without adherents in Western Christianity, in certain periods a particular outlook has predominated. During the first three centuries of the Christian era, premillennialism appears to have been the dominant eschatological interpretation. In the fourth century, when the Christian church was given a favored status under the emperor Constantine, the amillennial position was accepted. The millennium was reinterpreted to refer to the church. The famous church father, Augustine, articulated this position and it became the prevailing interpretation in medieval times.

Despite the fact that the Protestant Reformers accepted Augustinian eschatology, their emphasis on a more literal interpretation of the Bible and identification of the papacy with Antichrist called attention to the prophetic Scriptures. Later scholars especially in the Reformed tradition such as J. H. Alsted (1588–1638) and Joseph Mede (1586–1638) revived premillennialism. During the seventeenth century their view was shared by many of the leaders of the Puritan Revolution in England. However, with the restoration of the Stuart kings this opinion was discredited.

As premillennialism waned, postmillennialism became the prevailing eschatological interpretation, receiving its most important formulation in the work of Daniel Whitby (1638–1726). According to Whitby, the world was to be converted to Christ, after which the earth would enjoy universal peace, happiness, and righteousness for a thousand years. At the close of this period, Christ would return personally for the last judgment. Perhaps because of its agreement with the views of the ENLIGHTENMENT, postmillennialism was adopted by the leading Protestant theologians of the era. New England Puritans, continental pietists, and evangelical revivalists of the eighteenth century all encouraged the emphasis on millennialism. One of the most outstanding missionary spokespersons of this period, JONATHAN EDWARDS (1703–58), was a devoted postmillennialist.

During the nineteenth century, premillennialism again attracted attention. This interest was fostered by the violent uprooting of European political and social institutions caused by the French Revolution. Later in the century millennial enthusiasm found renewed support in the Plymouth Brethren Movement. J. N. Darby (1800–1882), an important Brethren leader, articulated the dispensationalist understanding of millennialism. Its name comes from the practice of dividing history into a series of ages, usually seven in number, which culminate in the millennium. A distinction is made between ethnic Israel and the church, and there is to be a tribulation period at the end of the church age caused by the Antichrist. After these events, Christ will return and rule the world for a thousand years with the help of the saints. This belief, popularized by the *Scofield Reference Bible*, the Bible Institute movement, popular evangelists, and mass media preachers, has become the dominant eschatology of American fundamentalists.

Despite the development of DISPENSATIONALISM, postmillennialism was the great dynamic for much of the missionary enthusiasm of the nineteenth century. America, many claimed, was the agent of God to bring in the last times. Timothy Dwight (1752–1817) anticipated the day when not a single Catholic cathedral, mosque, or pagoda would be left standing. Other spokespersons also merged the language of Manifest Destiny with millennialism and dreamed of the conquest of the world under the same laws and social characteristics as the Anglo-Saxons who would control all of North America. It was this confidence that led JOHN R. MOTT to publish *The*

Evangelization of the World in This Generation (1900) and inspired the famous WORLD MISSIONARY CONFERENCE in Edinburgh (1910).

However, the new age did not come and more of those involved in the missionary movement adopted a premillennial view. Rather than trying to bring God's kingdom to earth, they turned to winning individuals to Christ and preaching the gospel as witness to all nations so that Christ will return. Two world wars, genocide, economic depression, the rise of pluralism, the success of liberalism, and the privatization of religion in a secular society convinced them that only a supernatural, cataclysmic return of Christ would help the world. Yet changes in dispensational doctrine, a renewed emphasis on the Spirit of God by charismatic groups, and the concept of reaching whole groups of people with the gospel continue to encourage the postmillennial view. Despite the lively debate over the millennium there is no divergence of opinion among Christians as to the fact of Christ's coming.

ROBERT G. CLOUSE

SEE ALSO End Times; Eschatology.

Bibliography. R. G. Clouse, *The Meaning of the Millennium. Four Views;* R. G. Clouse, R. V. Pierard, and R. Hosack, *The Millennial Manual;* J. A. DeJong, *As the Waters Cover the Sea: Millennial Expectations in the Rise of Anglo-American Missions 1640–1819;* E. L Tuveson, *Redeemer Nation: The Idea of America's Millennial Role;* T. P. Weber, *Living in the Shadow of the Second Coming: American Premillennialism (1875–1925).*

Mills, Samuel John, Jr. (1783–1819). American mission promoter and organizer. Samuel Mills was a visionary, a motivator, and a tireless inspiration during the early days of mission organization in America. He is best remembered for organizing a prayer meeting for missions at Williams College which, afterward, led to further stimulus for mission at Andover Seminary. Finally, this Society of the Brethren, as it was called, indirectly led to the formation of the AMERICAN BOARD OF COMMISSIONERS FOR FOREIGN MISSIONS (ABCFM).

Mills, the son of a Congregational minister, was converted in the revivals that moved through the churches in New England at the end of the nineteenth century. Called to mission work, he attended Williams College (1806). While concerned with Asia and Africa, the Society of the Brethren did most of their planning around missions to the American Indians. It was during extended study at Andover Seminary that Mills with his friends, including ADONIRAM JUDSON, presented themselves for mission work, leading to the formation of the ABCFM.

Samuel Mills spent his life in far-reaching mission concerns. He planned to tour South America to open up missions. He worked among the poor in New York City. He worked tirelessly for the resettlement of freed slaves in West Africa, which helped form the American Colonization Society and, ultimately, the nation of Liberia. Mills died in June 1818 as he was returning from Africa after consulting about territories available for liberated slaves.

DEAN S. GILLILAND

Bibliography. D. N. Howell, *CDCWM,* p. 385; K. S. Latourette, *A History of the Expansion of Christianity,* vol. IV, pp. 70ff.; T. C. Richards, *Samuel J. Mills.*

Minjung Theology. Minjung theology is called "a theology of the mass of people *(minjung),*" or "the Korean version of liberation theology," or "a contextualized Korean theology of the poor." It began to appear in 1975 and made its theological impact upon the Korean church and the society in the late 1970s and early 1980s, during the oppressive governments of President Park Chung-Hee and President Chun Too-Hwan.

Historical Background. The massive student demonstrations on April 19, 1960, brought down the government of President Syngman Rhee; political confusion followed afterwards. General Park Chung-Hee was able to take over power through his military coup d'etat on May 16, 1961, and ruled the nation with an iron fist until his assassination on October 12, 1979. President Park's military government became oppressive and cracked down on any opposition to the government by limiting the freedom of speech and assembly. Many politicians, church leaders, professors, and students who opposed the military regime were imprisoned and severely tortured. There was a deep sense of *Han* (profound agony, sorrow, bitterness, resentment, and righteous indignation) in the souls of many Korean people.

There were three main reasons many pastors and theologians especially in the 1970s, voiced their opposition against the government: oppression, socio-economic injustice, and religious indifference. In 1974 the Korean National Council of Churches published "The Declaration of Human Rights in Korea," and sixty-six Korean theologians and pastors also produced "The Theological Statement of Korean Christians." In 1975 a renowned poet, Kim Chi-Ha, who was imprisoned for his writings against the military regime, wrote his "Conscience Declaration." On March 1, 1976, twelve prominent leaders produced "The Declaration for the Restoration of Democracy." Following that, a number of liberal theologians such as Suh Tong-Nam, Ahn Byung-Moo, Moon Hee-Suk, Kim Yong-Bock, Choo Chai-Yong, Hyun Yoon-Hak, and others began to introduce a new theology of liberation for the suffering masses in Korea, known as Minjung Theology.

Doctrines. Minjung theology is founded on other Western and Latin American theologies such as secular theology, theology of hope, liberation theology, process theology, and theology of history. It teaches that God is the co-liberator with the minjung in history, because God and the minjung are co-sufferers and co-operators in the history of liberation of humankind from suffering. God's reality in our experience occurs only in God's liberating activity in and with the minjung. Like liberation theologians in Latin America, Minjung theologians see the book of Exodus in the Old Testament as the Book of God's liberation of an exploited people (Exod. 1:11–14) and of God's human rights law (Exod. 20:22–23:19).

Minjung Christology begins with the *Han* experience of the oppressed people, and relates Jesus' messianic movement with socio-political and religious-cultural dimensions of the oppressed minjung's experience. Therefore, minjung theologians' interpretations of Jesus' ministry in Palestine and his cross and resurrection are all related to the liberation concept. Jesus as a social revolutionary dealt with the poor and oppressed but not with the rich. Jesus not only identified himself with the minjung, but himself became a minjung at a specific time in history. Therefore, he was the personification of the minjung.

Jesus was considered to be the liberator of minjung, and his cross was interpreted as a political event because of his uprising against the Jerusalem rulers who exploited the minjung in his time. Therefore, Jesus' death signified the death of suffering minjung. The RESURRECTION OF CHRIST was the resolution of *Han* and the restoration of God's righteousness. The historical aspect of Jesus' resurrection from the dead is not that important, because his resurrection is a social event or a rebirth into a new society with a spiritual body. Therefore, the resurrection faith is the will of humans in the expectation of a new society and messianic politics. There is neither the doctrine of eschatological JUDGMENT nor the hope of the New Heaven and New Earth. SALVATION is not by the GRACE OF GOD but is a person's self-achieved process of resolving the *Han* of the minjung.

Evaluation. There are both positive and negative elements in minjung theology. Positively, minjung theologians awakened both the church and society to the issues of political oppression and economic injustice in a society where there is an increasing gap between rich and poor. The Korean churches in particular, which had more interest in bigger church buildings and local church affairs, were challenged to have wider concerns for individual freedom of the oppressed minjung and economic and social justice in the nation.

Negatively, first, there is the problem of HERMENEUTICS. Although minjung theologians use many scriptural passages, their exegetical method is inadequate and produces a wrong interpretation of the original meaning of the texts. For example, their interpretation of the Book of Exodus in the light of Korean *Han* misses the messianic-redemptive aspects of the exodus.

Second minjung theologians' interpretations of major doctrines of the church such as Jesus' cross and resurrection, salvation, and eschatology have been severely criticized by evangelical theologians, for their doctrines are not in line with the biblical faith of the Christian church. The influence of minjung theology has greatly diminished in Korea since the civilian government of President Kim Yong-Sam was established in 1993.

BONG RIN RO

SEE ALSO Asian Theologies; Liberation Theologies; Missiology; AND Political Theologies.

Bibliography. Y. H. Hyun, *Minjung the Suffering Servant and Hope;* C. H. Kim, *Kim Chi-Ha Collection;* Y. B. Kim, ed., *Minjung Theology;* N. D. Suh, *In Search of Minjung Theology.*

Minority, Minority Populations. While the Bible teaches the basic unity of the entire human race because of our descent from the same original parents, it is obvious that there is tremendous diversity in the human race as well. This diversity opens the door for numerous minority groups.

It was God's will that humankind should spread out over the earth (Gen. 1:28; 11:9). While this diffusion was promoted by the rapid development of dialects and languages, once the groups became isolated from one another, their isolation encouraged still further diversity (or variety) of tongues.

It is more difficult to explain the variety in the physical appearance of people. Physical anthropologists who take an evolutionary view of human origins can describe this diversity, but can only speculate as to why it has occurred. It is best to say that our original parents, Adam and Eve, were created with genes that allowed for physical diversity over time, and that this diversity might very well have occurred whether or not humankind fell into sin.

Why, then, do we have minority groups all over the world? The basic reason is found in the age-old tendency of human beings to move. Some minorities have chosen to become minorities when they moved into the area of a majority group. Others became a minority group when a more dominant or larger group moved in on them. European expansionism, the slave trade, COLONIALISM, the desire for economic betterment—all these factors have contributed to the creation of more and more minority groups as history progresses.

Most minority groups are ethnic groups. That is to say, they have their own language and culture which is different from that of the majority group. There are also religious and social minorities, but the ethnic minorities tend to be the most prominent, especially when ETHNICITY is reinforced by differences in physical appearance.

The apostle Paul spoke of human diversity when he told the Athenians, "And he made from one man every nation [ethnic group] of men to live on all the face of the earth, having determined allotted periods and the boundaries of their habitation" (Acts 17:26). What he said next is also important: "That they should seek God, in the hope that they might feel after him and find him" (v. 27). Here Paul suggests that human diversity contributes to evangelism rather than detracting from it.

Many missionaries and evangelists have found this to be the case. Although occasionally a minority group is politically, socially, or economically dominant in a given society, usually the dominant group is the majority group. The minority group or groups are often considered inferior by the majority group. They are given inferior work with less pay, they are given inferior schools, they are denied access to decent housing, and the like.

If both the majority and the minority group(s) have the same religion, those in the minority position will likely be more open to religious change, including a change to Christianity.

Missionaries to India were surprised when during the early decades of the twentieth century the untouchables of India responded to the gospel in significant people movements even though no missionary was attempting to reach them. They saw in Christianity a release from their servitude and a rejection of the Hindu caste system that had permanently locked them into the lowest social status.

In recent years special efforts have been made to reach the Kurds of northern Iraq and surrounding nations precisely because they have been persecuted by their Muslim "brothers." It is thought that God might be using this persecution to prepare them to recieve the gospel. In ancient times it was the slaves and lower classes of Greco-Roman society that especially responded to the gospel. The spread of the gospel was not by a trickle-down diffusion but rather by a welling up from the bottom rungs of society.

The existence of various minorities in many societies and their alienation from the majority group might be God's provision for breaking the phalanx of unbelief that the gospel often encounters. But when minority groups have come to Christ and begin to form churches, new problems emerge. Within the walls of a church there is often a majority group and one or more minority groups. Will the majority group accept the appearance, the language, the dress, and the customs of the minority group? Or will they say, "We are all one in Christ," and use that thought as a club to enforce majority customs and language on all minority groups?

When the apostle Paul wrote, "There is neither Jew nor Greek, there is neither slave nor free, there is neither male nor female" (Gal. 3:28), he did not mean that Jews had lost their ethnic identity or that men and women lost their sexuality when they became Christians. He rather meant that those who are joined to Christ are also joined to one another. Christians should therefore respect the ethnic differences among themselves.

But sometimes a minority group prefers to give up its identity as much as possible and be amalgamated or assimilated to the majority group. They may even change their family name in order to hide their ethnic background. If that is their choice, it is to be accepted. Amalgamation of languages and peoples (as well as separation) has occurred since the dawn of history. The important thing is that it is not forced on a group that is not ready for it.

The best word on this whole subject was given by Paul: "Accept one another, then, just as Christ accepted you, in order to bring praise to God" (Rom. 15:7).

TIMOTHY MONSMA

Miracles in Mission. Contemporary mission endeavor cannot and should not seek to avoid the subject of supernatural power and the miraculous. Neither, on the other hand, should missions today become obsessed with or distressed over the power and activity of evil beings under Satan's control, nor over those who teach about them. The Bible teaches Christ's victory over all the POWERS (authorities), PRINCIPALITIES (rulers), dominions, and demons (1 Cor. 2:6; 15:24; Eph. 1:15–23; Col. 1:15–20, 2:15; 2 Thess. 2:8; Heb. 2:14). Mission today needs to rest assured that God still can and does work miracles.

Areas of Interface between the Miraculous and Mission. Missions interface with the miraculous in evangelism, healing, deliverance, and other areas.

The Miraculous and Evangelism. All evangelism is miraculous but in missions today individuals and groups are opened to the gospel in ways that can only be miraculous. The history of Christianity is replete with accounts of people movements that obviously were instigated and promoted by the Holy Spirit.

Some contemporary missionaries consider warfare prayer and the "binding" of territorial spirits as a major method in evangelistic activities. C. PETER WAGNER defines TERRITORIAL SPIRITS as members of the hierarchy of evil spirits who, delegated by Satan, control regions, cities, tribes, people groups, neighborhoods, and other social networks and inhibit evangelistic breakthrough. John Duncan and Edgardo Silvoso recount how, in Argentina, after prayer, fasting, confession, and confronting territorial spirits, the Lord granted a marvelous gospel breakthrough. John Wimber, who believes in "power evangelism" and miracles in evangelism, does not hold miracles necessary for evangelism. He sees proclamation of the gospel as the "heart and soul" of evangelism.

The Miraculous and Healing. God has used healing to reveal the truth of his message throughout history. The Lord has healed through the prophets (2 Kings 5:1–16), Jesus (Mark 1:40–41; John 4:46–54), the apostles (Acts 3:1–10), New Testament believers (Acts 14:3), and Christian missionaries today. God continues to perform miracles of healing, both to meet the physical needs of suffering people and to reveal the truth of his message.

Belief in divine healing in no way prohibits using modern medicine and using modern medicine does not indicate a lack of faith in God's power to heal. Missions today should allow God to speak both through modern medicine and God's direct healing action.

The Miraculous and Deliverance. Demons (evil spirits, powers) exist and harm, but do not possess in the sense of owning, human beings, whether believers or unbelievers. Jesus and New Testament Christians expelled demons from persons (Matt. 8:28–34; Mark 5:1–20; Acts 5:16; 16:16–18). Contemporary missionaries face expanding needs and opportunities to oppose evil spirits who demonize persons. Deliverance from evil spirits has become a growing phenomenon among evangelical missionaries. Demons who attack people can be expelled and rendered powerless through God's power (*see also* DEMONS, DEMONIZATION; EXORCISM; and SPIRITUAL WARFARE).

The Miraculous and Other Manifestations. Miracles today are evidenced in tongues, knowledge, visions, and other areas (1 Cor. 12–14). These manifestations, questioned by some, indicate to others the direct action of God. Missionaries must deal honestly and directly with these manifestations.

Principles Relating to Missions and the Miraculous. Several principles relate to miracles and missionary work. First, missionaries should welcome the aid of miracles and other manifestations of SIGNS AND WONDERS in missionary ministry. In regard to supernatural power and the miraculous, missionaries must be careful never to be materialists, disbelieving in supernatural powers, nor magicians, thinking supernatural powers can be controlled by ritual (*see* MAGIC).

Second, missionaries must affirm that miracles, signs, and wonders are not necessary for evangelism or other missionary work. The Holy Spirit continues to grant evangelistic fruit where there are no outward signs of miracles. Signs and wonders can, however, be instrumental in helping people become more willing to hear the gospel.

Third, missionaries must accept that healing is not always God's plan for every person. God speaks through suffering as well as through healing. Missionaries should not, therefore, promise healing as God remains sovereign in granting healing.

Fourth, missionaries must also remember that power resides in the gospel itself, not in miracles (Rom. 1:16; 1 Cor. 1:18). Missionaries must be certain never to make miracles seem imperative for missionary effectiveness. They must remember that miracles, like all other Christian deeds, must glorify God rather than calling attention to humans. When miracles are used to bring fame and notoriety to humans, these "signs" are not of God. Christians may be seen doing miracles but never be doing miracles to be seen.

Finally, missionaries should remember that miraculous events are not always of God. Pharaoh's magicians did signs (Exod. 7:10–22) as did Satan (2 Thess. 2:9). Jesus declared that false prophets would perform miracle (Matt. 24:24). Missionaries must beware of counterfeit miracles. Missionaries must remember that signs and wonders function to convey truth, especially divine compassion. The purpose of signs is that people apprehend the message the signs bring rather than dwell on the signs themselves.

EBBIE C. SMITH

Bibliography. C. E. Arnold, *Ephesians: Power and Magic;* idem, *Powers of Darkness;* D. Bridge, *Signs and Wonders Today;* J. Dawson, *Taking Our Cities for God;* N. Geisler, *Signs and Wonders;* P. G. Hiebert, *Anthropological Reflections on Missiological Issues;* D. Powlison, *Power Encounters;* E. Rommen, ed., *Spiritual Power and Missions;* T. M. Warner, *Spiritual Warfare;* C. P. Wagner, *Engaging the Enemy;* C. P. Wagner, and F. D. Pennoyer, eds., *Wrestling with Dark Angels.*

Missio Dei. Latin for "the sending of God," in the sense of "being sent," a phrase used in Protestant missiological discussion especially since the 1950s, often in the English form "the mission of God." Originally it was used (from Augustine on) in Western discussion of the Trinity for the *"sentness of God (the Son)"* by the Father (John 3:17; 5:30; 11:42; 17:18). Georg F. Vicedom popularized the concept for missiology at the CWME meeting in MEXICO CITY in 1963, publishing a book by this title: *The Mission of God: An Introduction to the Theology of Mission.*

Ecumenicals claim a comprehensive definition of *missio dei:* everything God does for the communication of salvation and, in a narrower sense, everything the church itself is sent to do. Historically, most evangelicals focused on the more immediate purpose of the Triune God in the sending of the Son: the task of world evangelization, the planting of the church among non-Christians, and the nurture of such churches. More recently, many have acknowledged the holistic nature of the task, though few give it an eschatological reference (*see* HOLISTIC MISSION).

The difference between the two approaches hinges on how the primary and fundamental human problem is defined—whether as a broken relationship with a transcendent God, or as suffering, oppression, and broken human relationships. Views of how the KINGDOM OF GOD is to be fulfilled now or eschatologically, how wide the scope of human salvation will prove to be, and basic assumptions about the authority and interpretation of Scripture are also critical (*see* BIBLE and HERMENEUTICS).

Missio Dei was first used in a missionary sense by the German missiologist Karl Hartenstein in 1934. He was motivated by Karl Barth's emphasis on the *actio Dei* ("the action of God"), over against the human-centered focus of liberal theology at that time; he was also inspired by Barth's 1928 lecture on mission, which related it to the Trinity. Hartenstein used the term again in his "Theological Reflection" on the IMC's WILLINGEN CONFERENCE (1952), published in the German report. Though the documents of the meeting itself grounded mission in the Trinity, it did not use the term *missio Dei*. Nevertheless, in its new, trinitarian-mission(ary) sense the phrase has been widely used since Georg F. Vicedom's book.

Missio Dei came to encapsulate an important change in IMC and WCC thinking, from the TAMBARAM CONFERENCE (1938) emphasis on the mission of the *church* to the Willingen stress on the mission of *God*. The latter meeting quite properly recognized that the true source of the church's missionary task lay "in the Triune God Himself."

The roots of the later, social gospel usage of the term lay in two things: first of all, Willingen's "A Statement on the Missionary Calling of the Church," which exhibited a common theological mistake. It properly defined the church's missionary obligation as "beseeching all men to be reconciled to God," and its concluding section rightly stressed God's sovereign rule even in the "war and tumult" of history, the growth of human knowledge, and in political and social movements. However, it failed to distinguish this preserving, common-grace exercise of God's power from his reconciling, special, redemptive-grace exercise in the history of salvation. Nor did it state the relationship either between preserving and redemptive grace, or between this present age and the age to come (*see* HOPE).

The second and not unrelated factor was the presence of the Dutch missiologist, JOHANNES C. HOEKENDIJK. Hoekendijk was zealous to have the true arena of God's saving action be recognized

as the world of human affairs and the human condition, instead of the church. The mission of God (what he sent Christ into the world to do) was to establish SHALOM—"peace, integrity, community, harmony and justice"—or humanization in this world. In other words, the goal was the realization of the kingdom of God on earth. He insisted on redefining the church as a function of the "apostolate," that is, the church as an instrument, of God's action in this world, a means in his hands, by which he will establish *shalom*. This was the basic concept with which the phrase *missio Dei* came to be identified in WCC circles.

At the world conference of the World Student Christian Federation in Strasbourg (1960), Hoekendijk urged that Christians identify with "man in the modern world," that the church become "open, mobile groups" (Bassham) to join the *missio Dei* and push for the realization of *shalom*.

These ideas dominated subsequent WCC reports: *Witness in Six Continents* (Mexico City, 1963), *World Conference on Church and Society* (Geneva, 1966), and especially the Studies in Evangelism report, *The Church for Others* (1967). These included the radical assertion of the thought-pattern expressed in "God-world-church." The latter formula meant that the church should act in partnership with the sending God, not by world evangelization and church planting, but by directly promoting political and economic human good. Since *shalom* is the goal of God's action in the world, and "the world sets the agenda," the church must therefore forsake its existing "heretical structures" and join in God's action. Traditional Christian missions were therefore merely "transitory forms of obedience to the *missio Dei*," and no longer appropriate.

The climax of the impact of Hoekendijk's version of God's mission was to be seen at the Uppsala Assembly, in 1968, which fiercely resisted the admission of words on the need to evangelize the non-Christian world.

Christians certainly ought to join with others in the common grace promotion of social justice, though not as the church, and not exclusively as Christians, but with others (Clowney). Evangelicals have been remiss in not acting strongly or broadly enough for social justice in this century. But the WCC adopted an almost purely sociopolitical concept of the *missio Dei*. It did so on the basis of broad, modern theological assumptions: universal salvation, through the "cosmic Christ"; the church's election being only for the purpose of serving what God was already doing in the world; the ideas of process theology, Tillich's "new being," and Bultmann's demythologizing of the New Testament. Taken together, these meant that the WCC could not affirm that indeed history must come to an end, with Christ's coming, in order to realize the kingdom/*shalom* in its fullness. It lacked (and still lacks) commitment to other vital teachings of the historic Christian faith: the transcendence of God (his distinctness from creation); the reality of an objective, substitutionary atonement to deal with the fundamental human problem, sin, and its forgiveness; and the necessity of proclaiming Christ as the only one to whom one must turn for true *shalom* in this world and the world to come.

In WCC circles today some are questioning the very usefulness of the term *missio Dei*, and are seeking a "new link" between mission and church (Hoedemaker). Evangelicals, on the other hand, have struggled so far to match the theological depth and sophistication of the WCC. They need to show that the church is called not merely to expansion, not to become a mere "collection of converts" (Hoedemaker). It is "sent" for a faithful ministry of witness summoning the disobedient to turn to God, looking for success only to the Spirit of God. It must do this from the context of its life, where God is truly worshiped, the faithful built up, and compassion demonstrated. This whole is the true *missio Dei*, and foreshadows the true *shalom* to be realized in full at the Lord's return.

JOHN A. MCINTOSH

Bibliography. N. Goodall, ed., *Missions Under the Cross; Uppsala Report* 1968; R. C. Bassham, *Mission Theology, 1948–1975*; E. P. Clowney, *The Church*; A. F. Glasser and D. G. McGavran, *Contemporary Theologies of Mission*; L. A. Hoedemaker, *IBMR* 19:4 (1995): 166–70; idem, *Missiology*, pp. 157–71; P. Potter, *Life in All Its Fullness*; H. H. Rosin, *Missio Dei*; J. A. Scherer, *The Good News of the Kingdom*, pp. 82–88; T. Stransky, *DEM*, pp. 687–89.

Missiology. Missiology is the conscious, intentional, ongoing reflection on the doing of mission. It includes theory(ies) of mission, the study and teaching of mission, as well as the research, writing, and publication of works regarding mission. Involvement in or the *doing* of mission, however, preceded by several centuries the *scholarly reflection* on mission. Apparently it was the passionate visionary Spanish activist, RAYMOND LULL (c. 1235–1315), who first critically reflected on missions, published his thoughts, and proposed the establishment of colleges for the linguistic and theological preparation of missionaries to Muslims and Jews. Though such a school was established at Majorca in 1276, Lull was unsuccessful in persuading Christian princes to establish similar chairs in the major European universities. No complete catalogue of Lull's voluminous writings exists, but the partial list contains more than 280 titles. Lull may be considered the first missiologist in Christian history.

More than two centuries later the Jesuit missionary to Mexico and Peru, JOSÉ DE ACOSTA (c. 1539–1600), published his treatise *On Procuring the Salvation of the Indians* (1588), a learned discussion of missionary theology and methodol-

ogy. Another significant missiological work of this period was *On Procuring the Salvation of All Men* (1613) by Thomas à Jesu (1564–1627).

The formal study of missions by Protestants can be traced to the colonial expansion of England, the Netherlands, and non-Iberian European powers. The year Pope Gregory XV created the Sacred Congregation of Propaganda of the Faith, 1622, a small Protestant college for the training of missionaries for Dutch colonies opened as a branch of the University of Leiden. Unfortunately, the college was short-lived. (Five years later the Roman Catholic College of Propaganda opened in Rome.) With their growing awareness of other continents and peoples, a few European Protestant professors of theology began manifesting serious interest in missionary questions. Hadrianus Saravia (1531–1613)—Dutch Reformed pastor-missionary and later professor, who after a period in England became an Anglican—published in 1590 his carefully reasoned challenge to the prevailing Protestant view that the words of Matthew 28:19–20 were meant only for the original apostles. The influence of Saravia is evident in the inaugural lectures of GISBERTUS VOETIUS (1589– 1676) at the University of Utrecht, lectures he entitled *De plantatoribus ecclesiasticus* ("On Church Planting"). Several other Dutch scholars helped pave the way for formal missiological studies, such as Justus Heurnius (1587–1651) and Johannes Hoornbeeck (1617–66), the latter a student of Voetius.

Though a number of missiological works were published in the seventeenth and eighteenth centuries, no professor of missions was named and the number of courses in missions was very limited. This was true in both Europe and North America until the last half of the nineteenth century.

The writings, correspondence, and widespread influence of the German Pietist leaders, August Herman Francke (1663–1727) and Philip Jacob Spener (1635–1705); the Moravian founder NICOLAUS LUDWIG VON ZINZENDORF (1700–60); the Reformed theologian and philosopher JONATHAN EDWARDS (1703–58); the Baptist missionary WILLIAM CAREY (1761–1834); and the renowned theologian Friedrich Schleiermacher (1768–1834)—contributed to a slowly changing attitude regarding missions as a scholarly endeavor. However, attempts to establish missionary training programs in European or American universities during the seventeenth and eighteenth centuries were seldom successful. Two serious histories of missions during this period do deserve mention: Robert Millar's *History of the Propagation of Christianity and the Overthrow of Paganism* (1723) and Petrus Hofstede's two-volume work on the history of Christianity in the Dutch East Indies (1779–80).

The nineteenth century brought tangible change. When Princeton Theological Seminary was founded in 1811, it was envisioned not only as a means to prepare young men to be pastors, but also as "a nursery for missionaries to the heathen," a place where students could receive "appropriate training" to fit them for missionary work. The first concrete step to make the study of missions an academic requirement, however, occurred in 1835 when John Breckenridge (1797–1841) was elected professor of pastoral theology and missionary instruction. Though Breckenridge can be regarded as the first Protestant professor of missions, his tenure at Princeton was brief, 1836–38, and it would have been uneventful except for the fact that the course he initiated continued as a part of the curriculum until 1854.

F. A. E. Ehrenfeuchter, professor of practical theology at Göttingen, was one of the earliest European Protestants to include the subject of missions in his lectures in the 1840s and 1850s, and he is credited with publishing the first thoroughgoing theory of mission in Protestant history, *Die praktische Theologie* (1859).

In Roman Catholic and Eastern Orthodox circles J. B. Hirscher (1788–1865) urged that the study of missions be made an integral part of the study of pastoral theology, and shortly thereafter N. I. Liminsky (1821–91) published what can be regarded as the first scientific analysis of mission in the Orthodox Church.

In 1864 KARL GRAUL (1814–64), director of the Leipzig Mission, proposed that missions be accepted as a legitimate academic discipline in itself. His memorable lecture, "On the Place and Significance of the Christian Mission in Scientific Studies of a University Considered as a Whole," qualified him to teach in the University of Erlangen. Graul's untimely death prevented his becoming Europe's first Protestant professor of missions, a distinction that was ALEXANDER DUFF'S (1806–78) when in 1867 he was named professor of evangelistic theology at the University of Edinburgh. Duff's legacy, however, was mixed. The installation of GUSTAV WARNECK (1834–1919) as professor of the science of missions at the University of Halle in 1896 signaled the momentous changes ahead, for by the turn of the century three other professorships of missions had been established, and in the decades preceding and following the WORLD MISSIONARY CONFERENCE (Edinburgh 1910), the study of missions became a part of the curriculum in an increasing number of schools in both Europe and North America.

The academic study of missions therefore inched its way into university and seminary curricula, first as a part of the study of practical theology and/or church history, and later as a separate department or course of study, partially a result of the growing interest in the history of religions. By the turn of the century the number of essays, books, and journals dealing with mission issues had expanded significantly.

During the first three decades of the twentieth century, the number of courses, professors, and chairs of mission increased dramatically, only to be followed by a leveling off and then a downturn. Since the 1950s the number of universities in Europe and the United States with professorships in missions has decreased, but the corresponding number of seminaries and other schools, professors, and courses in mission-related subjects has increased substantially in the Americas, Africa, and Asia.

Roman Catholic missiological studies have followed much of the same path as Protestants since the time of Hirscher. Yet the number of outstanding missiologists has steadily increased as can be seen in the life and work of such giants as Robert Streit (1875–1930), JOSEF SCHMIDLIN (1876–1944), Wilhelm Schmidt (1868–1954), PIERRE CHARLES (1883–1954), John J. Considine (1897–1983), and a host of contemporary scholars.

Not all mission scholars and thinkers, however, have been professors. Some of the most influential theorists have been administrators, such as HENRY VENN (1796–1873) and RUFUS ANDERSON (1796–1880). Others have been missionaries, such as WILLIAM TAYLOR (1821–1902), JOHN L. NEVIUS (1829–93), J. HUDSON TAYLOR (1832–1905), ROLAND ALLEN (1868–1947), E. STANLEY JONES (1874–1973), and HENDRIK KRAEMER (1888–1965). Some have been missionaries and later teachers, such as STEPHEN NEILL (1900–1984) and DONALD A. MCGAVRAN (1897–1990). Only during the last third of his life did McGavran become the founder, dean, and professor in the School of World Mission of Fuller Theological Seminary.

Scholarship in mission of course involves much more than theories, professorships, and courses in missions. Equally important are the societies established for the study and support of missions. Often these have been student-led groups such as the Society of Inquiry on the Subject of Missions founded in 1811 at Williams College and replicated at Princeton Seminary in 1815, as well as the Student Christian Movement and the STUDENT VOLUNTEER MOVEMENT (1886). Both the SCM and the SVM became international organizations, and both contributed to a steady stream of mission books and other educational material. The SVM helped shape Protestant missions from 1890 to 1940, recruited thousands of young people for missionary service, and was a major influence leading to the pivotal Edinburgh conference of 1910.

As already implied, much of the scholarly activity in mission resulted directly and indirectly from a number of international ecumenical conferences on world missions held in New York in 1954 and 1900, in London in 1878 and 1888, and in Edinburgh in 1910. The preparatory papers and the addresses delivered provided a wealth of material and insight into the thinking and doing of missions.

The number of annual missions lectureships established in colleges, seminaries, and divinity schools—such as the Student Lectureship on Missions inaugurated in 1891 at Princeton Seminary—increased steadily in the twentieth century. More recent are the Scherer Missions Lectures inaugurated in 1995 at the Lutheran School of Theology in Chicago and the Missiology Lectures at Fuller Theological Seminary.

During the 1960s some observers were lamenting the decrease in books dealing with missions. But in the last thirty years the quantity, variety, and scope of published works, books as well as other materials, have increased and the quality has improved significantly. Besides denominational publications, there are publishing houses that specialize in producing books about missions—Orbis Books and William Carey Press are examples. Moreover, a number of secular publishing houses such as Harper & Row/Collins, Lippincott, Viking Penguin, Macmillan, T & T Clark, Steyler Verlag, and E. J. Brill, as well as notable university presses such as Harvard, Chicago, Yale, Illinois, and California are publishing works on missions and missionaries. University publications include not only mission history and biography, but also studies of the role of missions and missionaries in anthropology, economics, and international relations.

Currently, there are scores of JOURNALS OF MISSION AND MISSIOLOGY being published throughout the world. These include *The International Bulletin of Missionary Research*, the *Evangelical Missions Quarterly*, the *International Review of Mission*, *Missiology*, *Missionalia* (Southern Africa), *Indian Missiological Review*, and the *South Pacific Journal of Mission Studies*.

Though there has been a steady stream of outstanding histories of missions, until the last twenty-five years there were hardly any reference works other than Edwin M. Bliss, *Encyclopedia of Missions* (1891, 1904) and B. L. Goddard, *The Encyclopedia of Modern Christian Missions* (1967). The publication of the *Concise Dictionary of the Christian World Mission* (1972) edited by STEPHEN NEILL, GERALD H. ANDERSON, and John Goodwin, was followed by David Barrett's *World Christian Encyclopedia* (1982), the "A.D. 2000 Series" which includes *World Class Cities* and *World Evangelization* (1986), *Evangelize! A Historical Survey of the Concept* (1987), and *Seven Hundred Plans to Evangelize the World* (1988). Gerald Anderson's comprehensive *Biographical Dictionary of Christian Missions* (1997) will soon be followed by this work, *The Evangelical Dictionary of World Missions*.

Several centers for mission research are functioning, some for decades, such as the Overseas Ministries Study Center in New Haven, Connecticut. Newer ones include the Mission Advanced Research Center in Monrovia, California, the Oxford Center for Mission Studies and the Center for the Study of Islam and Muslim-Christian Religions, both in England.

Besides the universities and seminaries that offer the Ph.D., Th.D., S.T.D., and Ed.D. in mission studies, a growing number of institutions now have programs leading to a D.Miss. or doctorate in missiology (*see also* DOCTORAL DEGREES IN MISSION). Moreover, in the past half-century some twelve hundred doctoral dissertations dealing with mission questions have been approved by schools in the United States and Canada.

Mention should also be made of the archival sources available to the serious scholar of mission. Stephen L. Peterson has analyzed those available in North America (IBMR 15 [October 1991]: 155–64), and Norman Thomas of the United Theological Seminary in Dayton, Ohio, is directing a massive international project on documentation, archives, and bibliography. Annotated bibliographies of no less than 10,000 volumes in missiology in all major European languages published from 1960 to 1990 will be available in printed form and on compact disks.

Clearly the bulk of what is noted here relates principally to what has been and is taking place in the West. But as Christians become more numerous in the Two-Thirds World and as they devote more personnel and resources to scholarly endeavors, they will make their own missiological contributions. Mission study centers, for example, already are functioning in such diverse countries as Japan, Papua New Guinea, South Korea, Peru, India, Bolivia, and Brazil.

A great deal of the aforementioned activity can be traced to the increasing impact of professional missiological societies such as the DEUTSCHE GESELLSCHAFT FÜR MISSIONSWISSENSCHAFT (1918), the ASSOCIATION OF PROFESSORS OF MISSIONS (1952), the EVANGELICAL MISSIOLOGICAL SOCIETY (1972), the INTERNATIONAL ASSOCIATION FOR MISSION STUDIES (1972), and the AMERICAN SOCIETY OF MISSIOLOGY (1973). These societies meet regularly and most produce their own journals.

ALAN NEELY

SEE ALSO Mission Theory.

Bibliography. G. H. Anderson, R. T. Coote, N. A. Horner, and J. M. Phillips, *Mission Legacies*; G. H. Anderson, *IBMR* 15 (October 1991): 165–72; O. G. Mykebust, *The Study of Missions in Theological Education* 1 & 2; A. Neely, *Toward the Twenty-first Century in Christian Mission*, pp. 269–83; S. Neill, et al., *CDCWM*; S. L. Peterson, *IBMR* 15 (October 1991): 155–64; B. R. Pierce, *Missiology* 4 (1976): 75–87; J. Verkuyl, *Contemporary Missiology*; A. F. Walls, *IBMR* 15 (October 1991): 146–55.

Missiometrics. Science of missions which applies the contemporary scientific method to the phenomena of missions, studying them in ways that are empirical, quantitative, and material. The term thus parallels a whole series of twentieth-century neologisms describing over two hundred new empirical sciences, ranging from econometrics ("the use of mathematical and statistical methods in the field of economics to verify and develop economic theories"), to biometrics, jurimetrics, and bibliometrics (analysis of the whole range of books, libraries, holdings, usages). Since each year churches and missions worldwide regularly measure well over three hundred numerical indicators of their life and progress, missiometrics is thus presented with a gold mine of annual data waiting for analysis.

Based upon biblical concerns and criteria, missiometrics starts from the fact that the Old Testament is a vast storehouse of censuses and statistical data, and that the New Testament contains a surprising number of empirical mandates such as "Count the worshipers!" (Rev. 11:1, NIV, REB), "Measure the temple!" (Rev. 11:1), "Work out the number!" (Rev. 13:18, REB). There are some 23 verbs found in the major English Bible versions, with another 53 close synonyms, which (together with the 40 Greek biblical words associated with these synonyms) delineate the domain of the science of missiometrics. Because the 23 verbs enable us to measure the phenomena of mission, they are therefore the basic dimensions (from the Latin *dimensio*, a measuring) of the science of missiometrics. These biblical imperatives suggest Christians thus have a significant new method—metrical investigation—assisting them in contemporary obedience to the GREAT COMMISSION.

Missiometrics measures anything and everything in any way relevant to world mission and global evangelization. Major variables measured each year by churches and missions include church membership, church growth, places of worship, church workers, clergy, women workers, home missionaries, foreign missionaries, preachers, colporteurs, evangelists, audiences, catechisms, catechumens, converts, baptisms, collections, finances, Scripture distribution, literature production, church administration, logistics, communications, broadcasting, computer usage, e-mail volume, networks, and the like. Each of the these provides voluminous annual series of data which, if seriously investigated, can result in highly effective mission strategies and tactics. A major concern in this respect is that Christians involved in world mission be effective and imaginative in utilizing the vast new areas of data and communications now available over the Internet. Today's world is an enormously complex entity—6 billion human beings grouped into 13,000 ethnolinguistic peoples speaking over 12,000 languages. Thus navigating through these massive new data sources becomes a missiological priority.

DAVID B. BARRETT

SEE ALSO Quantitative Research.

Mission and Missions. Derived from the Latin *mitto*, which in turn is a translation of the Greek *apostellō* (to send), the term "mission," as an English term with no direct biblical equivalent, has a broad range of acceptable meanings. *The Oxford Dictionary* gives the earliest occurrences of the English word in 1598. By 1729, use of the word in relation to the church focused on the GREAT COMMISSION: "Jesus Christ gave his disciples their mission in these words, 'Go and teach all nations, & etc.'" (E. Chambers, *Cyclopaedia; or an Universal Dictionary of Arts and Sciences*).

The contemporary secular definition of mission is simply "sending someone forth with a specific purpose." That purpose may be defined broadly (e.g., to represent the interests of the sender) or very narrowly (e.g., to hand-deliver a message written by the sender). With the broadness of the term, our concept of the mission of the church will to a large degree depend on our theological orientation rather than an etymological analysis.

Few would challenge the need for clarity in our definition, for, as Dyrness notes: "mission lies at the core of theology—within the character and action of God himself. There is an impulse to give and share that springs from the very nature of God and that therefore characterized all his works. So all that theologians call fundamental theology is mission theology" (p. 11). At the same time, however, the difficulty of defining mission cannot be overlooked or minimized. "Mission is never something self-evident, and nowhere—neither in the practice of mission nor in even our best theological reflections on mission, does it succeed in removing all confusions, misunderstandings, enigmas and temptations" (Bosch, 9).

Several questions among the many which could be asked illuminate the contemporary discussion and options: (1) Is mission, most broadly, the whole scope of God's intention in the world or, more narrowly, the God-given MISSIONARY TASK of the church? (2) If our focus is on the task of the church, is mission limited to one core component of the church's work or is it everything that the church does? (3) Is it possible to determine a focus or priority for mission, and, if so, what should that be? At least until the IMC WILLINGEN CONFERENCE in 1952, the answers to these questions for evangelicals appeared to be relatively straight forward. Missions was evangelism and the evidence of successful missions was the extension of the church through the crossing of cultural, geographic, and linguistic boundaries.

In this century, however, we have seen several developments, most of which were birthed in the ECUMENICAL MOVEMENT and brought into evangelical discussion by people involved in both groups. Two of these developments relate to the word mission. First was the recognition that God's mission was broader than the activities of his Church. MISSIO DEI, coined as a missiological term by Karl Hartenstein in 1934, was used in the 1952 WILLINGEN CONFERENCE to stress that mission is God's not the church's. Georg Vicedom popularized it in the MEXICO CITY CONFERENCE (1963) and in his text *The Mission of God* (1965). *Missio Dei* focuses on everything God does in his task of establishing his kingdom in all its fullness in all the world. While it includes what the church does, it is not limited to that, for God works both in and out of the church. Thus themes such as "Let the world set the agenda" were driven by a recognition that God is not limited to his work in and through the church and that his mission is seen wherever kingdom values (especially justice and mercy) are being promoted, fought for, or instituted.

The second important development was the dropping of the "s" from "missions" to reflect the unity of the total biblical task of the church. The dropping of the final "s" was formalized in ecumenical discussion when the *International Review of Missions* became the *International Review of Mission* in 1970. By 1972, George Peters, an evangelical teaching at Dallas Theological Seminary, wrote that mission, in contrast to missions, was "a comprehensive term including the upward, inward and outward ministries of the church. It is the church as 'sent' (a pilgrim, stranger, witness, prophet, servant, as salt, as light, etc.) in this world" (Peters, 11). He maintained that missions, on the other hand, is the actual work and the practical realization of the mission of the church. Some evangelicals voiced concerns that dropping the "s" might lead to the loss of commitment to, and action for, world evangelization and church planting.

Evangelical approaches to defining mission have not been unified. John Stott allowed the broadening of the discussion, as long as evangelism was seen as a leading partner in the missionary task. W. Harold Fuller proposed using mission for our purpose and passion, while ministry refers to all that we do. Arthur Johnston opposed any broadening of mission. Ron Sider argued that social transformation is mission. On a pragmatic level, the reality of the disagreement is seen in the titles used for introductory theology courses taught in 78 North American institutions: 31 drop the final "s" ("Theology of Mission") and 46 keep it ("Theology of Missions") (Siewert).

Multiple conferences organized from within the EVANGELICAL MOVEMENT have sought to address the issue of mission and the primacy of evangelism within it. The CONGRESS ON THE CHURCH'S WORLDWIDE MISSION (WHEATON CONGRESS, 1966) was organized to deal with theological and practical issues. Affirming the scriptural foundation for social justice, the declaration of the congress still proclaimed the primacy of evangelism. In the same year the WORLD CONGRESS ON EVANGELISM (BERLIN CONGRESS 1966) was also held. Focused primarily on responding to shifting definitions of evangelism, the integral relationship of evangelism and missions was maintained. In 1970, the FRANKFURT DECLARATION ON THE FUNDAMENTAL CRISIS IN CHRISTIAN MISSION was developed in response to ecumenical shifts in thinking about mission, and it promoted a return to the classic orientation of mission as the presentation of salvation through evangelism. Calls for broadening the evangelical perspective came at the Thanksgiving Workshop on Evangelicals and Social Concern (Chicago, 1973), which issued the "Chicago Declaration of Evangelical Social Concern." This was "essentially an affirmation of God's total claim on the lives of his people, a confession of failure in demonstrating God's justice in society, and a call for evangelicals 'to demonstrate repentance in a Christian discipleship that confronts the social and political injustice of our nation'" (Padilla, 242). At the LAUSANNE CONGRESS ON WORLD EVANGELISM (1974), John Stott pointed to the broadening of the definition of mission and indicated that he saw no reason to resist this development. Building his paradigm on John's version of the GREAT COMMISSION, he proposed that we see mission as the church "sent" into the world to serve just as Jesus served, including EVANGELISM AND SOCIAL RESPONSIBILITY as partners in the missionary task. He did not see fulfilling the Great Commission as completing the directive of the GREAT COMMANDMENT, maintaining both as integral to mission. Lausanne proved to be a critical juncture in this respect. By 1989, in fact, the role of the Lausanne Covenant would be noted in the official story of Lausanne II as follows: "It is a watershed in placing social justice within the purposes of the Church's mission (Articles 4 and 5)" (Nichols, 15).

Since Lausanne, three streams have solidified within evangelicalism. One emphasizes the historic orientation of mission as evangelism, and carried on in meetings such as the GLOBAL CONSULTATIONS ON WORLD EVANGELIZATION (GCOWE) organized in 1989, 1995, and 1997. The focus of this stream remains the development of thriving church movements among people groups around the world.

A second stream, following Stott, focuses on integrating a holistic approach to mission, incorporating evangelism and issues of social justice and reconciliation (*see* HOLISTIC MISSION). Consultations such as that in Wheaton in 1983, convened to discuss the nature of the church, gave voice to this group and "laid a sound theological basis for the mission of the Church, with no dichotomy between evangelism and social responsibility" (Padilla, 247).

The third stream, sometimes referred to as the radical discipleship group, and including evangelicals such as Ron Sider, Rene Padilla, and Samuel Escobar, considers social justice to be mission just as evangelism is, and does not give priority to either (*see also* OPTION FOR THE POOR) .

Representatives of the three streams have come together from time to time, perhaps most notably at the CONSULTATION ON THE RELATIONSHIP BETWEEN EVANGELISM AND SOCIAL RESPONSIBILITY (CRESR 1982), where the partnership of evangelism and social responsibility and the primacy of evangelism were both reaffirmed, though it was noted that "some of us have felt uncomfortable about this phrase, lest by it we should be breaking the partnership" (LCWE, p. 24). WHEATON '83 gave greater weight to the partnership stream, as well as opening discussion on transforming societies through structural intervention as an element of holistic mission. Finally, representatives of all three streams were also present at the LAUSANNE CONGRESS II ON WORLD EVANGELISM (MANILA, 1989). Again, the focus continued to give weight to the idea of partnership with evangelism being primary. Through the declaration and subsequent ongoing reflection, the second stream gained prominence in evangelical mission.

The debate continues and consensus over this complex issue remains a goal to be reached in the future rather than a present reality.

A. SCOTT MOREAU

Bibliography. D. Bosch, *Witness to the World: The Christian Mission in Theological Perspective;* W. Dyrness, *Let the Earth Hear His Voice;* LCWE, *Evangelism and Social Responsibility: An Evangelical Covenant;* W. H. Fuller, *Church in Africa Today and Tomorrow: Proceedings of the A.E.A.M. 4th General Assembly,* pp. 280–98; A. Johnston, *The Battle for World Evangelism;* A. Nichols, ed., *The Whole Gospel for the Whole World: Story of Lausanne II Congress on World Evangelization, Manila 1989;* R. C. Padilla, *The Best in Theology,* 1:239–52; G. Peters, *A Biblical Theology of Missions;* D. L. Robert, *IBMR* 18 (1994): 146–62; J. Siewert, *Directory of Schools and Professors of Mission,* rev. ed.; J. R. W. Stott, *Mission in the Modern World;* C. Van Engen, *Mission on the Way: Issues in Mission Theology;* G. Vicedom, *The Mission of God: An Introduction to a Theology of Mission.*

Mission Archives. *See* MISSION LIBRARIES.

Mission Atlases. Mission atlases help the church see more clearly the work of God, the "white harvests," and the neglected peoples. They open our eyes, touch our hearts, and leave us in wonder at what God is doing in the world. Mission atlases

spur on the church to ministry beyond its own immediate context. In the process, motivated by mission zeal, the church has often led the way in mapping new areas of the world and publishing new geographic information.

Definition. There are many excellent atlases (books of maps, usually with graphics and geographical information), both contemporary and historical. A mission atlas is one that focuses on the distinctive mission of the church. This contrasts with secular atlases (which may include some treatment of Christianity) as well as Bible atlases, the mission component of which is often limited to the journeys of Paul. In addition, much mission understanding can be gleaned from historical atlases of religion and Christianity, since the history of the expansion of the church is essentially missionary.

Early Publications. The church has always been informed by maps. Early mission atlases, with exquisite hand-drawn maps, can be found in mission archives. The first modern Protestant mission atlas to be widely distributed was the *World Atlas of Christian Missions* (1911), an outgrowth of the *Statistical Atlas of Christian Missions* issued in conjunction with the 1910 WORLD MISSIONARY CONFERENCE in Edinburgh, focusing on missionary work among non-Christian peoples.

This landmark atlas was followed by a wealth of more specialized and denominational publications, including *The Churchman's Missionary Atlas* (1912), *the Concise C.M.S. Atlas* (1913), *Atlas Showing Mission Fields of the Christian and Missionary Alliance* (1922), and *World Missionary Atlas* (1925), with a related article "On Making a Missionary Atlas" by Charles Fah appearing in the April 1925 issue of the *International Review of Missions.*

Mission mapping continued in the latter half of the twentieth century, with the Christian and Missionary Alliance leading the way with two versions of their substantial *Missionary Atlas* published in 1950 and 1964. Also significant is Worldwide Evangelization Crusade's *Atlas of W E C Mission Fields: The Second World Survey of the Areas of the World Unreached by the Gospel* (1961).

Recent Publications. The 1980s and 1990s brought a resurgence of interest in mission data and mapping, as well as a more holistic view. The first such volume was *Target Earth: The Necessity of Diversity in a Holistic Perspective on World Mission* (1989) with computer-generated maps, graphics, and data tables, along with commentary and photographs. Most recently, Bryant Myers through MARC/World Vision has produced two similar mission atlas booklets, *The Changing Shape of World Mission* (1993) and *The New Context of World Mission* (1996), which provide brief, easy-to-read descriptions of the world in which Christian mission takes place. While not strictly speaking a mission atlas, the new, full-color *Atlas* *of World Christianity* (1998), edited by Peter Brierley and Heather Wright, does an excellent job of covering many mission themes.

Computerization. As we approach the turn of the century, the widespread use of personal computers, connected via the Internet, has enabled unprecedented collaboration in mission research and mapping, using "geographic information system" (GIS) software. As a result, more contemporary mission atlas material can be found today on a computer rather than on a bookshelf.

The Global Ministry Mapping System (CD-ROM updated annually since 1995) provides GIS software with extensive global geographic and statistical databases, including the mapping of over seven thousand ethnolinguistic peoples. With such tools, practitioners, researchers, educators, and managers are producing their own specialized mission atlases on demand. The result is an explosion of tailor-made individual mission maps but a dearth of mission atlases.

The World Wide Web promises to provide a rich environment for missions mapping. New strategic alliances between mission agencies and institutions—with the partners maintaining their respective data sets and integrating them with the whole—give public access to vast amounts of updated, geographically based mission information via the Internet.

The interactive, multimedia mission atlases of the future will make it possible to "drill down" to the specific information desired, listen to sounds and voices of people from other countries, watch video clips, simulate "flying through" a three-dimensional map, and transparently combine local information with networked information from the Web, all on a personal computer anywhere in the world.

MIKE O'REAR

Mission Headquarters. The development of mission headquarters began with the original missionaries of the modern missionary movement. Individuals were burdened and called by God to go overseas. They needed help of people at home to pray for them and to send finances.

There are several philosophies of mission headquarters. Some headquarters are simply a conduit for money to the missionary and provide tax deductible receipts for the donors. In this case, minimal help or accountability is offered to the missionaries. Other mission agencies have developed headquarters that share in decision making with the missionaries on the field. Typically, in this approach, the mission headquarters or mission board will establish broad areas of policy and a doctrinal statement. Missionaries are allowed to develop individual strategy and occasionally even define the structural relationships on the field.

A third type of mission headquarters is significantly involved in the daily life and activity of the missionary. The home office may decide the strategies, procedures, goals, and even methods for individual fields. They can provide vision, help set goals, and encourage missionaries who might be facing obstacles in their ministry. They may also provide medical and psychological support, emotional care, and spiritual advice (*see also* MEMBER CARE IN MISSIONS).

Leaders in mission headquarters are often former missionaries, pastors, or key lay leaders from churches. The leaders may also consist of individuals or groups of people burdened for a particular type of ministry. Some headquarters are led by entrepreneurial leaders who have a vision for ministry but minimal cross-cultural experience.

Recently, larger churches have been bypassing mission agencies. They totally support their missionaries, believing that the expense and extra supervision of a missions organization is not needed. While in some cases this may be true, serving through a mission agency often provides greater long-term stability for the missionary, broader prayer support, and more experienced care.

GLENN KENDALL

Mission Libraries. The professionalization of information science, formerly known as library science, during the past century has been a boon to mission studies. The spread of Christianity around the world is considered important as an aspect of the history of Western civilization. Thus the resources documenting the history of missions are to be found in numerous secular and religious repositories. The modern researcher is also aided by the computerization of indexes and the catalogs of most collections, but printed guides are still useful as much of the older material remains accessible only in that form. The collections accessible by computer are often available through the Internet, making them potentially searchable from anywhere in the world.

In North America, mission collections are found in the libraries of most Christian colleges and seminaries. Denominational mission boards and large mission agencies often maintain focused collections related to their work. Regional libraries and historical societies often contain the mission history of the local area, and large public libraries also collect the records of local and historical figures. Only a few of the younger denominations in America are caring adequately for their materials. Examples of these are the Assemblies of God (Springfield, Missouri), The Missionary Church (Mishawaka, Indiana), and the Church of God (Cleveland, Tennessee). In the non-Western world, financial resources are inadequate for younger churches to consider preserving any of their historical records, let alone the records of their evangelistic outreach.

Many university libraries in Europe contain extensive mission collections. Protestant collections may be found at Uppsala, Hamburg, Tübingen, Marburg, Utrecht, Oxford, Cambridge, and Edinburgh. The most notable Roman Catholic collections are at Munster, Louvain, Lisbon, and Madrid.

Selly Oak Colleges Library in Birmingham, England, was established to train missionaries and houses the Harold Turner Collection in the Center for the New Religious Movements. ANDREW WALLS was instrumental in establishing the resources of the Center for the Study of Christianity in the Non-Western World at the University of Edinburgh. Partnership House Library in London has incorporated the collections of The Church Missionary Society and The Society for the Propagation of the Gospel. The Henry Martyn Mission Studies Library is a small but important research center on the campus of Westminster College, Cambridge. Other prominent European collections are found at the Vahls Missions Library in Denmark, the Egede Instituttet in Norway, Hackmannsche Bibliothek at Marburg, the Library of the Norddeutsche Mission at Bremen, the Rhenish Missionary Society in Wuppertal Barmen, and the Paris Evangelical Missionary Society.

The primary Roman Catholic mission libraries are the Pontificia Bibliotheca delle Missioni (Library of the Congregation for the Propagation of the Faith) and the library of the Pontificia Universita Gregoriana. Perhaps the most prominent Roman Catholic collection in America is to be found at the Maryknoll Seminary Library in New York.

National repositories such as the British Museum, the Bodleian Library at Oxford, and the Cambridge University Library in the U.K. and the Library of Congress in the U.S. are excellent sources of published materials on missions. At the beginning of the twentieth century, two libraries were established to support world evangelization: the Day Missions Library at Yale University and The Missionary Research Library in New York. A direct outgrowth of joint evangelistic outreach symbolized by the Edinburgh conference of 1910, these centers supported research and publishing efforts toward that end. As interest in evangelism waned in mainline Protestant churches, these publications were taken over by other agencies, but the collections were preserved for their historical value. Currently Yale Divinity School Library continues to collect mission studies extensively in support of the Day Missions Library. Union Theological Seminary Library in New York now houses the Missionary Research Library collection and remains the depository of missions material for the denominational members of the National Council of Churches.

The task of collecting information resources for world evangelization was taken over by evangelical missionary training centers. Theological seminaries such as Asbury, Dallas, Fuller, Gordon-Conwell, Southwestern Baptist, and Trinity (Deerfield, Illinois) were leaders in developing major missions collections. In 1975, the Billy Graham Center was established on the campus of Wheaton College complete with its evangelism library and archives. The records of North American evangelical ministries are combined with published evangelism and missions resources from around the world to supplement materials from the Billy Graham Evangelistic Association. Following in the tradition of the Day Missions Library and Missionary Research Library, the collections of the Billy Graham Center are intended to provide information resources that will enable the Christian church to undertake strategic research and planning in order to complete the GREAT COMMISSION.

Significant ecumenical collections include the WORLD COUNCIL OF CHURCHES Library in Geneva and the Interchurch Center in New York which holds the libraries of the United Presbyterian Mission and Board of Missions of the United Methodist Church. Other specialized collections are found in the YMCA Historical Library in New York, the World's Alliance of YMCA Library in Geneva, as well as the libraries of various Missionary Societies and Bible Societies.

In the non-Western world, resources for mission studies are scarcer. Some important collections can be found at the Morrison Library on China in Tokyo, Serampore University in India, and the United Theological College in Bangalore, India. The Missiology Project of the Research Institute for Theology and Religion at the University of South Africa (UNISA) is taking a leading role in collecting resources for the continent of Africa.

KENNETH D. GILL

Bibliography. S. Neill, G. H. Anderson, J. Goodwin, *CDCWM*, pp. 31–32; idem, *CDCWM*, p. 407; F. W. Price, *Library Trends* 9:2 (1960): 175–85; R. D. Shuster, *Researching Modern Evangelicalism: A Guide to the Holdings of the Billy Graham Center*; M. L. Smalley, ed., *The Day Missions Library Centennial Volume*, Occasional Publication, no. 2.

Mission on Six Continents. The COMMISSION ON WORLD MISSION AND EVANGELISM (CWME) of the WORLD COUNCIL OF CHURCHES held its first world conference at MEXICO CITY in December 1963. It affirmed that the old unidirectional model of Westerners sending and non-Westerners receiving missionaries was past. Disavowing the antiquated paternalistic structures, the CWME declared under the caption "mission in six continents," that the emphasis should be that God's mission could now originate from every part of the world. Every part of the world had been implanted with the church and therefore was capable of sending mission agents to any other part of the world. Mission belonged to the essence of the church, and the paganism (or neo-paganism) of the West constituted as much a mission challenge as the paganism of countries far away from the West ever did. Indeed, the Western world now needed to realize what non-Western Christians could do to help its people find meaningful faith in God.

The new theological emphasis alerted the church in every continent to recognize its missionary calling within its own environment. It challenged the traditional one-way traffic in mission and denied that Westerners were the most authentic representatives of Christian belief, life, and practice. As JOHANNES VERKUYL pointed out, it discarded the distinction between mission (in distant lands) and evangelism (in one's own land) and challenged churches everywhere to focus on the one world, which is in need of the gospel. An assumption here was that PARTNERSHIPS and reciprocity are to characterize relationships between Christians from all parts of the world.

The slogan was a milestone of twentieth-century mission theology. It maintained currency for a few decades in ecumenical circles.

A. CHRISTOPHER SMITH

Bibliography. R. K. Orchard, ed., *Witness in Six Continents: Records of the CWME of the WCC Mexico City 1963;* J. Verkuyl, *Contemporary Missiology: An Introduction.*

Mission Schools. Mission schools serve the missions community by providing the educational, social, and spiritual support desired by missionaries for their children. The number and variety of missions schools have grown dramatically in the past fifteen years. In the 1800s, several mission boarding schools were established in the sending countries as well as areas of high missionary concentration, such as China, Hawaii, and India. Today there are over 140 schools in approximately eighty nations that serve the educational needs of missionary children.

Mission schools vary significantly in their institutional purpose statements. Some serve the children of missionaries exclusively, while others accept students from the international business, diplomatic, and host country communities. Mission schools may admit students from outside the missions community either on a space-available basis, according to board-established percentages, or as an equally targeted student group.

The variety of mission school purpose statements and target student groups, as well as the problematic use of the word "missionary" in many locations has led some schools to prefer the term International Christian School (ICS), rather than "Mission," or "MK School." But the majority of mission schools, whether called an MK school or an international Christian school, see their function as twofold: serving the missions community with an educational program for their children that prepares them for tertiary education in their home country and reaching the expatriate community with the gospel through the provision of an educational program presented from a Christian worldview.

Many of the more established schools offer a variety of support services. These include ESL programs, programs for students with special educational needs, boarding services, and advanced studies programs. Many are now establishing programs to support missionaries choosing to home school their children. In a recent survey of 134 mission schools, 49 (or 36 percent) were found to offer boarding home services (*Overseas Schools Profiles*).

Mission schools, originally staffed by "field" missionaries with varying degrees of expertise in pedagogy, are now predominately staffed by fully trained educational professionals. Most of the larger mission schools are now accredited and offer university preparatory curricula. Most mission schools are interdenominational and increasingly multinational in student and faculty composition. Mission schools procure teachers through missionary sending organizations, although an increasing number are directly hiring staff and offering full or partial stipends.

Mission schools face significant challenges. Paramount is the recruitment and retention of professional staff. This perennial challenge is exacerbated by the proliferation of mission schools and the desire of mission agencies to place educators in nontraditional educational settings, such as with clusters of missionary families who would otherwise be HOME SCHOOLING their children without support.

Mission schools also face the challenge of developing culturally sensitive curricula appropriate for the multinational student body of the school. As the missionary force becomes increasingly multinational, so do the student bodies of mission schools. A pressing issue for schools is how best to prepare these students for tertiary education in their passport countries. Mission schools also face the ongoing challenge of responding to the increased expectations of missionary families for the educational preparedness of their children.

In spite of the educational, professional, and financial challenges facing mission schools, mission school personnel find the experience of serving in the international missions context to be both professionally stimulating and personally fulfilling as they contribute to the development and discipleship of missionaries' children, support the ongoing missionary effort of their students' parents, and experience the joy of seeing the lost come to know Jesus through their ministry in the mission school.

PHILIP RENICKS

Bibliography. J. Blomberg, *EMQ* 31:2 (1995): 210–17; *Overseas Schools Profiles*, 5th ed.; J. Plueddemann, *A CSI World Report*, 1995.

Mission Theory. "Mission theory" identifies principles which are held to be essential to the successful practice of mission. Over the years, the term has been used in an elastic manner to encompass beliefs, goals, policies, strategies, and procedures involved in the tasks of mission. Some argue that mission (or missionary) theory occupies an intermediate level between theology and policy, because it is shaped not only by theological convictions but also by the fruits of actual experience. In that case, "mission strategy" and "mission policy" are viewed as being nearly synonymous.

A comprehensive framework for mission theory has probably never been fully elaborated. In the Middle Ages, Franciscan and Dominican monks thought carefully about how to do mission effectively, while Roman Catholic thinkers such as JOSÉ DE ACOSTA (1540–1600) and Tomas à Jesu, wrote perceptively in this cross-cultural area in the sixteenth and seventeenth centuries. The Jesuit Acosta produced a monumental mission manual in Peru, under the title *De Procuranda Indorum Salute* (1577), which was translated *as Predicacion del Evangelio en las Indias* ("Preaching the Gospel in the Indies"). Vibrant Dutch Protestants, including Hadrianus Saravia (1531–1613) and Justus Heurnius (1587–1651), also pondered over the essentials of mission. However, Protestant mission leaders in the nineteenth century did not pay much attention to them, if at all. Mission leaders such as the SERAMPORE TRIO drew much more from MORAVIAN and German PIETIST precedents, from their own experience in pre-Victorian India and from the theological well of Jonathan Edwards (1703–58), in developing their mission approach and philosophy.

During Europe's ENLIGHTENMENT era, an Englishman named William Orme urged (1828) that there was a need to develop a theoretical framework for the mission enterprise. Another contemporary of William Carey, during the opening phase of Protestantism's "modern missionary movement," was the German theologian Friedrich E. D. Schleiermacher (1768–1834). Partly influenced by Moravians and German Pietists, Schleiermacher viewed the "theory of mission" as part of practical theology.

Subsequent pioneers of mission studies in Germany, such as the Protestant GUSTAV WARNECK

(1867–1944) and JOSEPH SCHMIDLIN (1876–1944), insisted that a full-blown theory of mission was essential to mission studies; but British mission thinkers did not respond to the challenge. As a debtor to the European Enlightenment, Schmidlin, the father of Catholic MISSIOLOGY, equated "practical mission theory" rather narrowly with "missiology" in 1925. He modeled his Catholic mission theory on Gustav Warneck's *Missionslehre* and defined "mission theory" comprehensively as "the scientific investigation and statement of the principles and rules which govern the work of spreading the faith. As the theory of the missionary art, it seeks to answer the questions as to why, whither, how and by whom missions should be undertaken." Probably the last missiologists to develop distinctively German mission theory were WALTER FREYTAG (1899–1959) and Georg Vicedom (b. 1903).

During the Victorian period, the key idea in Anglo-American mission theory came to be the concept of the INDIGENOUS CHURCH. This was developed simultaneously by two remarkable mission statesmen, an American, RUFUS ANDERSON (1796–1880), and an Englishman, HENRY VENN (1796–1873).

Anderson decried the popular idea that Christian faith and Christian civilization were inseparable. He identified the proper aims of mission as being the planting of self-governing, self-supporting, and self-propagating churches. In the 1860s, Henry Venn, called for the "the euthanasia" of missions as the final stage of the mission-to-church process. Since he saw "the raising up of a Native Church" as the great object of a mission, he viewed mission as the scaffolding to be removed once a self-responsible indigenous church had emerged. JOHN L. NEVIUS (1829–93), an American Presbyterian missionary to China and Korea, ROBERT E. SPEER (1867–1947) and the Scot, John Ritchie (1878–1952), did much to further general acceptance of "indigenous church principles" in theory and practice until the mid-twentieth century.

Important contributions to the development of missions theorizing have come from the pens of missiologists such as ROLAND ALLEN (1868–1947), a vigorous critic of the Anglo-American mission system who wrote among other classic works *The Spontaneous Expansion of the Church and the Causes Which Hinder It* (1927, reissued 1960); WILLIAM E. HOCKING (1873–1966), *Re-Thinking Missions* (1932); HENDRIK KRAEMER (1888–1965), *The Christian Message in a non-Christian World* (1938); J. C. HOEKENDIJK (1912–75), *Kerk en Volk in de Duitse Zendingswetenschap* (1967); DONALD A. MCGAVRAN (1897–1990), *Understanding Church Growth* (1969); and RALPH D. WINTER (1924–).

Jongeneel opines that the term "theory of mission(s)" was replaced by the term "theology of mission(s)," particularly after the Second World War. This appears to be corroborated by changes in the classification system of the *International Review of Missions* [IRM], the premier missiological journal in mission studies during the first two-thirds of the twentieth century. The IRM's classification system was set up by J. H. OLDHAM in 1912 and it operated until 1963, when its categories were radically changed by LESSLIE NEWBIGIN in line with the thinking of the CWME MEXICO CITY CONFERENCE (1963). Until then, the "Theory and Principles of Missions" had featured as one of its major classification categories. Thereafter, the term "theory of mission" or "mission theory" sank out of view. Only the term mission "principles" was retained in the bibliography field of mainstream mission. Thus "the concept of mission theory and what it symbolized" evidently disappeared from general usage by the mid 1960s.

In the face of such a trend, serious work has been done recently in the U.S. to develop a new level of scholarly discourse on mission theory. After giving decades of attention to the subject, Wilbert R. Shenk, in his presidential address to the AMERICAN SOCIETY OF MISSIOLOGY in June 1995, outlined seven elements necessary for development of "a general theory of mission." He argued that "a general conceptual framework" would have to do the following:

1. Situate the mission process historically and empirically as an inter-cultural movement, including the agents and agencies, and the host culture and peoples. . . .
2. Identify and critically evaluate the main model(s) by which mission has been and may be prosecuted. . . .
3. Account for the impact of the mission on the host culture and the impact of the culture on the mission, i.e., as reflected in modifications and innovations the mission makes in response to the cultural context.
4. Correlate the development of the modern world system with the development of the mission, especially the impact of modern communications and the economic system. . . .
5. Trace the influence the various strands of renewal, revival, and revitalization [not all necessarily Christian in nature] that touch the churches, often with long-range implications.
6. Maintain a dialectical relationship between mission praxis and the biblical theological foundation of mission. . . .
7. Hold in tension local mission and God's mission to all people so that theory geared to the local context will be developed that will draw forth the fullness and richness of the particular in light of God's ultimate saving purpose . . . (1996, 41).

In light of this, Shenk has distinguished very clearly between the development of "mission theory," which must involve deep theological insight, and the business of mission strategizing (or planning). Vividly aware that "a strategy always reflects the culture and historical moment in which it is formulated" (1993, 219), he has underscored the "ambivalence" that "has characterized discussion of strategy in mission studies." He reminded Christian thinkers that their best formulations still fall far short of representing God's ways of advancing his kingdom.

Such warning was not intended to deter God's people from exploring the unfathomable patterns and dimensions of God's mission. Rather, it is a prophetic spur to missiologists to be doubly alert to the significance of what God is doing in the world, and the world church, today.

During the last quarter of the twentieth century, major contributors to our understanding of the dynamics of effective, cross-cultural Christian witness and service have included the South African, DAVID J. BOSCH (1929–94), especially his *Transforming Mission: Paradigm Shifts in Theology of Mission* (1991); the Puerto Rican, ORLANDO E. COSTAS (1924–87), with his *Christ Outside the Gate: Mission Beyond Christendom* (1982); the Gambian, Lamin Sanneh, especially his *Translating the Message* (1989) and *Encountering the West* (1993); and the Scot, ANDREW F. WALLS, a compendium of whose influential writings has been published under the title *The Missionary Movement in Christian History* (1996), of which his essay "Missionary Societies and the Fortunate Subversion of the Church" deserves special mention. At the end of the twentieth century, international Christian leaders consequently find themselves challenged by new frameworks from which to address missional situations, under rubrics such as a missiology for the West, CONTEXTUALIZATION of the gospel, Two-Thirds World missions, mission in the city, and reaching the unreached.

A. CHRISTOPHER SMITH

Bibliography. R. Allen, *Missionary Methods: St. Paul's or Ours?;* G. Anderson et al., eds., *Mission Legacies;* R. P. Beaver, ed., *To Advance the Gospel. Selections from the Writings of Rufus Anderson;* J. B. Jongeneel, *Philosophy, Science, and Theology of Mission in the 19th and 20th Centuries,* Part I; D. A. McGavran, *Understanding Church Growth,* rev. ed.; J. L. Nevius, *Planting and Development of Missionary Churches;* J. M. Phillips and R. T. Coote, eds., *Toward the 21st Century in Christian Mission;* W. R. Shenk, *IBMR* 5:4 (1981): 168–72; idem, *Missiology* 24:1 (1996): 31–45; J. Verkuyl, *Contemporary Missiology. An Introduction;* A. F. Walls, *Evangelical Quarterly* 60:2 (1988): 141–55; M. Warren, ed., *To Apply the Gospel:* Selections from the Writings of Henry Venn.*

Missionary. Few terms within the evangelical missiological vocabulary generate more diverse definitions. For some, "everybody is a missionary," but STEPHEN NEILL is right in saying that if everybody is a missionary, nobody is a missionary. A few argue that a select category of persons are honored with this title; but still others discard it totally and substitute "apostolic messenger" instead.

The Biblical Root and Uses. In the New Testament the Greek term *apostellō* (with a related one, *pempō*) emerges in two major categories: as a broadly used verb, the sending in one form or another and by different senders (132 times), and as a more specifically used noun, the apostolic person (80 times). The senders (either verb or noun) include a variety of people (including a negative one, Herod; Matt. 2:16), God (John 20:21), Christ (Luke 9:2), the church (Acts 15:27), the Spirit (*pempō* in Acts 13:4). The sent ones include the Spirit (1 Peter 1:23), Christ (Matt. 10:40; John 20:21), the apostles (Mark 3:15; Luke 6:12–16), other authorized representatives of the churches (2 Cor. 8:23; Phil. 2:25; Rom. 16:7), angels (Rev. 1:1), and servants or employees (Acts 10:17). The core New Testament meaning clusters around ideas related to sending and or crossing lines, to those being sent, the sent ones—whether messengers or the Twelve, or the others who serve with some kind of apostolic authority or function. The New Testament affirms that the apostolic messenger (the missionary) becomes the person authoritatively sent out by God and the church on a special mission with a special message, with particular focus on the Gentiles/nations.

Other Jewish records show this term (a derivative of the Hebrew *saliah*) describing authorized messengers sent into the diaspora: to collect funds for Jewish uses; or taking letters from Jews or Jewish centers with instructions and warnings, including how to deal with resistance. The New Testament adopts some of these ideas, as well as a broader one from Greek culture with the concept of divine authorization. It then injects new meaning into the missionary apostles (life-long service, Spirit-empowered, with particular focus on the missionary task) referring to the original Twelve (plus Paul) as well as other authorized messengers. This is the core of the Christian apostolic person and function. There is no evidence of this office being authoritatively passed on from generation to generation.

The Term through Church History. Ironically as the Latin language takes over Bible use and church life, its synonym, *mitto*, becomes the dominant word. From *mitto* we derive the English word "missionary." Therefore an "accident" of linguistic history has replaced the original Greek concept with all of its richness and depth. In the immediate post-apostolic era, the term was used of itinerant ministers, and in that form was known to Irenaeus and Tertullian. James Scherer argues that there is no New Testament connection that would utilize apostolic concepts and functions in the corporate life of the churches of that later period. "The functions of the apostolate were merged into the corporate ministry of the church."

Roman Catholic usage emerged by 596 when Gregory the Great sent the Benedictine monk AUGUSTINE OF CANTERBURY to lead a missionary delegation to the British Isles. The Roman Church also used the term in reference to their orders (as sent ones), starting with the Franciscans in the thirteenth century, and later other orders. This was established in 1622 when the Congregation for the Propagation of the Faith was instituted. Hoffman writes, "According to the letters patent it gave to apostolic laborers overseas, missionaries were those sent to announce the Gospel of Jesus Christ, to teach the gentiles to observe whatever the Roman Catholic Church commands, to propagate the Catholic Faith, and to forewarn of the universal judgment." Today Catholics use the terms missionary, missioner, missionate, and mission apostolate in a variety of ways, including ". . . anyone engaged in some manner in the establishment of the Church where it had not been established," as well as teachers, medical personnel, agronomists and others serving holistically. Within Catholicism the broadest meaning is now also applied ". . . to all apostolic Christians collaborating with Christ in bringing about the total redemption of all mankind, and indeed of all created nature . . . in a word, all those engaging in the mission of bringing Christ to all being and all being to Christ."

The Protestant REFORMATION, partially in reaction to the Roman positions, minimized the term and concept of the missionary. It reemerged with greater significance within German PIETISM at Halle, itself a reaction to the Reformation excess. Thus the Moravians used the term for their broad-spectrum enterprise, and then it was adopted by CAREY, JUDSON, MORRISON, and LIVINGSTONE and their successors.

The Term Used Today. We have mentioned the diverse Catholic uses of this term. In secular circles the term "mission" still has a variety of uses: diplomatic, commercial, or military missions. Some Protestants have argued for their own particular coinage applied in the broadest way for all Christian activity as "mission" and subsequently all Christians are missionaries. Some evangelicals use the slogan "everybody is a missionary" to reject an apparent special category, but also because they desire to universalize missionary responsibility.

Singaporean Jim Chew encourages us to substitute "cross-cultural messenger." To him, this special servant " . . . is not a temporary but an abiding necessity for the life of the church, provided always that the movement of mission is multidirectional, all churches both sending and receiving." However, Chew sustains the position that "missionary" is simply a generic term for all Christians doing everything the church does in service to the KINGDOM OF GOD. We do a disservice to the "missionary" by universalizing its use. While all believers are witnesses and kingdom servants, not all are missionaries. We do not glamorize or exalt the missionary, or ascribe higher honor in life or greater heavenly reward, and neither do we create an artificial office.

This focused conclusion comes from a biblical theology of vocations (God has given us diverse vocations and all are holy, but not all the same); a theology of gifts (not all are apostles nor all speak in tongues—1 Cor. 12:29) and therefore not all Christians are missionaries; and a theology of callings (the Triune God sovereignly calls some to this position and task; *see* MISSIONARY CALL). These men and women are cross-cultural workers who serve within or without their national boundaries, and they will cross some kind of linguistic, cultural, or geographic barriers as authorized sent ones.

WILLIAM DAVID TAYLOR

Bibliography. D. Müller, *NIDNTT*; 1:126–35; J. Chew, *When You Cross Cultures;* T. Hale, *On Being a Missionary;* J. H. Kane, *Understanding Christian Mission*, 3rd ed.; R. Hoffman, *NCE* 9:907; G. W. Peters, *A Biblical Theology of Missions;* J. A. Scherer, *Missionary, Go Home!*

Missionary Affluence. A relatively unexamined element of recent missionary life and work has been the affluence of Western missionaries in comparison with the majority of the world's peoples among whom they work. The development of great personal wealth in the West over the past few centuries and the cultural assumptions inherent with that wealth have been paralleled by the development of like assumptions and expectations of appropriate missionary lifestyles and capabilities. Wealthy missionaries, as Bonk rightly points out, find it difficult at best to truly incarnate Christ among the destitute of the world, as the gap between them is simply too big and the wealthy have too much to lose by letting go of that to which they cling.

It does not matter that missionaries, by Western standards, are generally on the lower end of the socioeconomic scale. What does matter is that all too often those among whom they work see the missionaries as having access to personal and institutional wealth of which the indigenous population can only dream. Often, however, it is not just a question of the amount of income; even missionaries who live at low income levels can still communicate a materialistic worldview, and those who have wealth can communicate gen-

uine lack of materialism. Additionally, that the missionary may live a truly incarnate lifestyle does not remove the fact that such a lifestyle is by the *missionary's choice*, and such a type of choice is unavailable for the poor.

The fact of such disparity may subvert the very gospel message the mission agencies and missionaries bring, and often leads to hidden resentment and eventually open conflict. As the gap between the rich and the poor continues to grow, and as INDIGENOUS CHURCHES begin to find their own authentic voices, it will become an increasing problem that Western missionaries who work in areas of endemic poverty will of necessity have to face more realistically if they are to be true partners in the global missionary task.

A. SCOTT MOREAU

Bibliography. J. J. Bonk, *Missions and Money: Affluence as a Western Missionary Problem.*

Missionary Call, The. All Christians are called to the service of the church as witnesses for Christ in every part of their lives. But the missionary call is more than this. It is a special and unique call to full-time ministry. Simply put, the missionary call is the command of God and the setting apart by the Holy Spirit of an individual Christian to serve God in a culture, a geographical location, and, very likely, in a language different than the missionary's own. The personal recognition of this call comes with a growing conviction that God has set the recipient apart for this service. The result of this conviction is an intense desire to obey and to go wherever God leads.

"Missionary call" is an extrabiblical term, yet it refers to a sovereign act of God in the life of a person to bring that person to a point of decision to serve God in a missionary capacity. Since the phrase is not found in the Bible, there has been some confusion as to what a missionary call entails. In the history of missions, we observe that God's call of his people to missions is as diverse as the missionaries themselves. This means that one cannot generate a checklist which, if completed, would produce or prove a missionary call. However, such a call is based on concrete circumstances and experiences such that, after identifying the call in one's own life, one can look back and observe God's sovereign guidance and control in the process leading to the call and personal recognition of it.

What are proper foundations for receiving a missionary call? (1) Belief in and commitment to the lordship of Jesus Christ such that it produces unconditional love for him and obedience to his will. (2) A commitment to obey the will of God in our walk with him. It is understood that if we are not seeking to obey his will in general terms, then he will not reveal his specific will for us, as, for example, in a call to missionary service. (3) Openness to the leading of the Holy Spirit. The Spirit leads as he wills, according to the uniqueness of the individual's gifts and personality. Each Christian must be sensitive to the leading of the Holy Spirit in his or her own life, for the Spirit leads each person uniquely. (4) Belief in the Word of God as authoritative and a commitment to obey the principles and guidance laid down in it. (5) An understanding that the GREAT COMMISSION was given by Jesus to all Christians, and therefore each person should be involved in helping to fulfill this command. God works sovereignly in the normal issues and activities of life to lay these foundations of faith, obedience, and desire. Their reality in a believer's life is an act of God's sovereign grace.

Given the foundations for receiving a missionary call, there are certain attitudes and activities that help prepare one for receiving this call. These are normally developed over time as the Holy Spirit leads the potential missionary to the place in life in which he or she is able to respond positively and maturely to God's call.

One significant attitude is a hatred of sin. A person should strive to mortify sin, to put it to death in the life, and to bring every thought captive to make it obedient to Christ (2 Cor. 10:5). This attitude, with appropriate actions, shows a person's desire to obey God rather than self. Additionally, the one called should have open eyes, seeing beyond his or her own world of relationships and circumstances, seeing the world as God sees it, lost and without hope.

There should also be an open heart, a soft heart for the lost, like God's heart (John 3:16; 2 Peter 3:9). Jesus gave up his life because of God's love for the lost (Rom. 5:8), and believers are to have this same attitude (Phil. 2:5–8). There should be open ears, a sensitive listening to the Holy Spirit. This is developed through careful listening to the Word of God and obedience to its commands. As God's commands and guidance from the Word are carefully applied, we become more sensitive to the Spirit's quiet leading. And so we are able to hear when he calls. Christians must also have open hands demonstrated through an involvement in some kind of work for the Lord. Finally, we should have the attitude Isaiah demonstrated in his response to God's call. "Here am I, send me!" (Isa. 6:8). This shows willingness to go anywhere as the Lord commands.

As is clear from the above, there are obvious activities that will help prepare Christians for God's call and enable them to move rather than hesitate when such a call comes. These include: (1) praying for the lost of the world, for their countries, and for the church, the missionaries and the ministries in those countries; (2) giving to missionaries and to mission programs and ministries; (3) going on short-term ministry opportunities in a different culture away from the security and comfort of home; (4) reading missionary biographies and newsletters and books and journals on missions; (5) serving under the oversight and encouragement of a local body of believers who will help in the identification and development of spiritual gifts and ministry skills; and (6) gaining broad ministry experience, giving attention to ministry in areas in which God gives wisdom, fruit, and joy.

As revealed through many missionary testimonies, a person's missionary call may be impressed on the mind and heart as one listens to a message or a testimony, reads a passage of Scripture, prays for the lost, reads an article or book, hears of a particular or general need, or is personally challenged to go. God is not limited in the means or methods he will use to call his missionaries to serve him on the mission field. Complementary to this realization must be the recognition and confirmation of a local body of believers (Acts 13:2). The church is Christ's agent on this earth, and he will use the church to confirm the call and to send the missionary with the needed support.

The proof of the missionary call for any individual is that God has seen fit to allow the individual to serve him on the mission field. There are those who feel that they have received the call but are never able to go. This can be the result of such things as ill health, family obligations, or lack of resources. The Lord works his sovereign will to further his kingdom in many ways. Those who are prepared to go but are unable to may serve a vital part of the missionary endeavor through their work of support and spreading the vision for missions.

THOMAS L. AUSTIN

Bibliography. E. P. Clowney, *Called to the Ministry;* H. R. Cook, *An Introduction to Christian Missions;* J. H. Kane, *Understanding Christian Missions.*

Missionary Children. With an international mission force composed primarily of families, missionary children (better known as MKs—missionary kids; *see* THIRD CULTURE KIDS) become central players in this movement. Western missions focused on the needs of their own offspring; but with the globalization of mission, MKs now come from all nations and go to all nations—whether they want to or not. Missions leaders from the newer sending countries (non-Western, Two-Thirds World) now grapple with issues that formerly challenged leaders from the older sending nations (Europe, North America, Australia, New Zealand), such as MK educational needs and cultural identity. Korean missionaries in the Philippines offer a fascinating case study. Early on they sent their children to a boarding school shaped by U.S. curriculum and values.

However, they saw their children increasingly isolated from Korean culture, some grappling with tensions of internal identity and others unqualified for Korean universities. They finally responded by establishing a Korean school.

MKs are the youngest, and perhaps the most vulnerable of "God's chosen people who are living as foreigners in the lands. . . ." (1 Peter 1:1). Pollock has noted that MKs worldwide grapple with the following crucial issues, each with its own benefits and particular challenges. (1) Mobility: MKs are adaptable with rich memory banks, but also struggle with rootlessness and restless migratory drives. (2) Relationships: they can grow deep people-roots by themselves, but tend to protect themselves while some drift into insulation. (3) Cultural balance: they enjoy a broad knowledge of cultural diversity as global pilgrims, but they can become "hidden immigrants," off-balance in their own "passport" culture. (4) Language: many speak multiple languages, appreciate learning styles and linguistic nuances, many become excellent teachers, but they can also suffer from language limitation and confusion. (5) WORLDVIEW: they tend to have broad cultural paradigms, able to think laterally, but can appear arrogant, reflecting patriotic ambivalence toward their "passport" nationality. (6) Cross-cultural skills: MKs are keen observers, adaptable, less judgmental, cultural bridges, but can appear to lack in convictions, be "social chameleons" and socially undeveloped. (7) Leave-taking: MKs project sensitive empathy, but saying farewell is always a critical passage from nation to nation, school to school, people group to people group, grappling with closure, which on the negative side can generate unresolved emotional conflicts. (8) Development: most MKs reflect higher personal maturity in relational and communication skills, and are comfortable working cross-generationally; but some experience stunted maturation and delayed developmental transitions, and many grieve the inability to "return home"; and those whose entire education was done in Christian boarding schools run the risk of growing up in a sequence of unrealistic "bubbles," comfortable only in those missionary subcultures.

Adult MKs never cease being MKs, and this reality has generated serious analysis of their particular issues. A surprising percentage return to some aspect of cross-cultural ministry, enter the helping professions, or head into other aspects of the borderless marketplace—whether in business, education, governmental foreign service, or relief and development. As adults they grapple with the challenges of what it means to be an adult MK, including: (1) Processing their memories. Most MKs share a memory pool that weaves them together, but not all come to positive terms with their emotions and story. Many have been damaged in childhood and find it difficult to surmount these handicaps. Other idealize their backgrounds or families, though in time the unrealistic perceptions will crumble or they hopefully will develop a healthy understanding and acceptance of their past. (2) Transitioning through life. Some of these changes are not unique to MKs, but they experience many of them, requiring constant variation and adjustment. Those who studied in boarding schools present a different profile from those who studied in a national, private, or international school. The vast majority transition to their passport culture for the last stages of their education, and there they face ongoing significant challenges and change, both positive and negative. Transitions can be keenly anticipated or feared, either as stepping stones to maturity or fraught with uncertainty and laced with pain. (3) Decisions at diverse crossroads. MKs have little control over their early life. As dependents of God's global nomadic families, their parents determined where or how to live and how to school them. As dependents they live with the results of these choices. Entering adulthood the decisions become personalized and critical: What is their personal faith and value system? How will they live? Will they accept or reject their backgrounds and their parents' faith? (4) Processing throughout their lives. At different stages of their life they will work through process memories, transitions, and key decisions, and it is crucial that they be encouraged to process these key elements that have so shaped them. The adult processing of unresolved grief which can be a haunting element must be addressed reasonably and thoroughly. Again the critical faith factor emerges, and MKs reflect the spectrum of attitudes of the particular spiritual and organizational subculture in which they were raised.

The majority of MKs do quite well emotionally, psychologically, spiritually, and career-wise. A small percentage are brilliant or outstanding leaders. But many are troubled and problematic. The prime stakeholders in MK welfare include the following groups: MKs themselves, their parents and close family; home-sending churches and mission societies; member care (physical and mental) providers; and educators. Healthy MKs tend to come from healthy families; unfortunately some missionary families are seriously dysfunctional. New geography and cross-cultural ministry never compensate for these dysfunctions. Therefore church and mission leadership must be alert to and address the holistic welfare of their missionary families.

WILLIAM DAVID TAYLOR

Bibliography. A. Daugherty-Gordon, *Don't Pig Out on Junk Food: The MK's Guide to Survival in the U.S.*; D. Pollock, and R. Van Reken, *Global Nomads: Growing Up Among Worlds;* W. D. Taylor, *Too Valuable to Lose: Exploring the Causes and Cures of Missionary Attrition;*

D. Walters, *An Assessment of Reentry Issues of the Children of Missionaries.*

The Missionary Task. Defining the missionary task of the church is central to missionary reflection. But it is more than that. It is also a crucial responsibility of the church, for a church unsure or misdirected about its mission can hardly achieve it. And yet rarely in church history has there been agreement on what the missionary task of the church is.

Following the early expansion of the Western church, the Middle Ages saw centuries of introversion that all but eliminated missionary activity, including later, among the reformers. Then came the Moravians, followed by what has been called the GREAT CENTURY OF MISSION. Nineteenth-century Protestants in Europe and North America gained a new missionary vision and were, for the most part, united in what the missionary task was—specifically, they grounded it in the commission Christ gave the first great missionary, Paul as "Mission to the Gentiles, to whom I now send you, to open their eyes and to turn them from darkness to light, and from the power of Satan to God, that they may receive forgiveness of sins and an inheritance among those who are sanctified by faith in me" (Acts 26:17, 18). The twentieth century was, if anything, an even greater century for missions, but from the start the unity of vision began to disintegrate. As the conviction weakened that people without Christ were lost, the definition of mission began to change. "Missions" became "mission," meaning purpose, and the old passion for classical evangelistic missions was swallowed up by the other good things a church must do. Consequently, from Europe and mainline churches in North America the stream of missionaries began to dry up, until by the end of the century it was a mere trickle.

Upon the gradual withdrawal of traditional missionaries nondenominational agencies and newer denominations (like the Assemblies of God and the Christian and Missionary Alliance) took up the slack for what may be history's greatest surge of evangelism, following World War II. How did these forces of the last half of the twentieth century define the task? As the initial evangelistic thrust into new territories was successful, the focus of missionaries typically shifted to serving the new churches in pastoral, educational, and other helping roles until the de facto definition of "missions" became, "sending people away from the home church to serve God in some capacity elsewhere, especially cross-culturally." Thus the popular understanding of "missions" moved gradually in the same direction as the earlier drift, defining missions as "all the good things a church does," as DONALD MCGAVRAN so

aptly put it, but with this spin: all the good things a church does *away from home.*

An even broader definition of "missions" and "missionary" began to emerge. In the effort to get all disciples fully involved in witness, it was said that "everyone is either a missionary or a mission field." *All* disciples are sent as missionaries to their own world. Does it make any difference to define the missionary task one way or another? Is it helpful to distinguish clearly among the tasks of the church? Is it necessary? History would seem to teach that it does indeed make a great deal of difference. In fact, failure to focus clearly on the New Testament understanding of missions seems to have always marked the beginning of the end of missionary enterprise.

The original, basic missionary task of the church was to send certain evangelistically gifted members to places where Christ is not known to win people to faith and establish churches. That this is a biblical definition can be demonstrated in two ways: (1) the meaning of the term used for "missionary" and (2) the example of those who heard Christ's final instructions.

Apostles. The term "apostle" (literally "one who is sent") was used in several different ways in the New Testament (*see* APOSTLES). It was used in the historic root meaning of any messenger (John 13:16; Phil. 2:25). But another nuance was emerging in New Testament times, meaning "one sent as an authoritative representative of the sender." In this meaning it is used supremely of Jesus, sent for our redemption (Heb. 3:1). When Christ finished his apostleship he passed that role on to others, called variously "the disciples" (though the ones highlighted were among hundreds of other disciples), "the twelve" (though there were more than twelve, with Matthias, Paul, and Jesus' brother, James, added to the select group), and "the Apostles," those sent with divine authority to establish Christ's church. Thus the term referred to a unique office, the founders of the church. But the term was used of others, too, people like Barnabas (often included in the apostolate), Timothy and Silas, Andronicus and Junia (Rom. 16:7), Epaphroditus (Phil. 2:25) and, indeed, the whole missionary team (1 Thess. 2:6). In this use, "apostle" refers not to an *office* (the "twelve" founders), but to a *role,* the role of pioneering. Paul describes this role clearly when he describes his ambition to proclaim Christ where he has not yet been named (Rom. 15:20; Haldane, Hodge, Murray, and Calvin all clearly identify this apostolic role). "All who seemed to be called by Christ or the Spirit to do missionary work would be thought worthy of the title . . ." (Plummer, 84). Lightfoot wrote the seminal exposition of this meaning of "apostle" in his extensive footnote on Galations 1:27. We call these pioneer church-starting evangelists, "missionaries," from the Latin translation of the Greek *apos-*

tolos. They are sent by the home church to win people to faith and establish churches where there are none.

This apostolic role continued after the original apostles died. Eusebius, writing of the time from A.D. 100–150 speaks of "numberless apostles" or "Preaching Evangelists" who were living then. He described them:

> They performed the office of Evangelists to those who had not yet heard the faith, whilst, with a noble ambition to proclaim Christ, they also delivered to them the books of the Holy Gospels. After laying the foundation of the faith in foreign parts as the particular object of their mission, and after appointing others as shepherds of the flocks, and committing to these the care of those that had been recently introduced, they went again to other regions and nations, with the grace and cooperation of God. (Schaff, 68)

Thus, from the beginning, there was a missionary function distinct from other roles in the church. It was distinct from the witnessing responsibility all Christians have, even distinct from that of evangelistically gifted Christians winning non-Christians who live nearby. These, rather, are *sent* ones, sent to those out of reach of present gospel witness. And their role is distinct also from what other "sent ones" do. These are "missionaries" who pastor the young church and who assist it in various other ways, but they do not have the apostolic function of winning to faith and starting churches. Failure to distinguish this task from other tasks may have the appearance of elevating their significance but in historic perspective it only serves to blur and diminish the original missionary task of the church. A full team is needed to reach the unreached, of course—those at home who send and colleagues on the field who reinforce the apostolic thrust in supportive ministries. But the original missionary task of the church is fulfilled through pioneer apostolic church starting evangelists. The first evidence for this is the way the term "apostle" was used in the New Testament and in the years immediately following. But there is other, even stronger evidence.

The Acts of the Apostles. One function of the Book of Acts is to demonstrate clearly what the missionary task of the church is. Christ gave what we call the GREAT COMMISSION on at least three occasions, probably on four, and perhaps on five. This, along with the demonstration of his own resurrection, was the only theme to which he returned in his several encounters with the disciples in the six weeks before he ascended. Clearly this "sending" was uppermost in his mind. What did he intend that those sent should do? Acts gives the answer of how those who received the commission understood it. Evangelism begins with incarnating the transforming gospel as we see from the first commissioning on the night of the resurrection: "As the Father sent me, so send I you" (John 20:21). If there were any doubt as to the implications of this command, John himself gives a commentary in his first letter: "As he is, so are we in this world" (1 John 4:17). But demonstrating the love of God (1 John 4:7–17) does not exhaust the evangelistic assignment. In fact, to live a good life without telling how we do it is bad news, not good news. So the second element in the commission is proclamation and witness, explaining what one has experienced personally: "Go into all the world and preach the gospel . . ." (Mark 16:15). This gospel ". . . shall be proclaimed to all nations . . . and you are witnesses . . ." (Luke 24:47, 48), and "You shall be witnesses to me. . . to the uttermost parts of the world" (Acts 1:8). But on these four occasions Jesus says nothing about winning to faith and establishing churches. Only once does he do that: "Go therefore and make disciples of all the nations, baptizing them . . ." (Matt. 28:19). He even goes beyond evangelism to the final fruit of evangelism: ". . . teaching them to observe all things that I have commanded you . . ." (v. 20). Here the pastoral and teaching role is included! How tragic if obedient children gathered in his family were not the end result of the missionary task.

In this way, four of the great commissions don't even extend to winning people to faith—just incarnation, proclamation, and witness. The first step of evangelism, to be sure, but hardly the whole of it. And the fifth great commission goes far beyond the initial task of evangelism, encompassing all the church was meant to be. Thus, Christ is clear enough on the initial stage and the final stage, but how do we find out what he intends for the in between? That is where the example of the churches' obedience to that commission comes in: *The Acts of the Apostles.* The early history of the church was given, in part, to demonstrate what Christ intended. And the picture emerges clearly and quickly: a select few were sent out from home churches to places where Christ was not known to win people to faith and gather them into local congregations. And that is the missionary task of the church. Paul and his missionary band first of all lived authentic lives, demonstrating the power of the gospel. In that context they immediately and constantly talked about it, explaining the gospel, urging their hearers to accept it. Thus they won people to faith and organized churches. Soon the responsibility for pastoring and teaching was turned over to others and, once the missionary task in that place was completed, the missionary band pressed on to regions beyond.

We derive our definition of the missionary task, then, from the New Testament term used to define the role, and from the New Testament example of those who fulfilled that role: the missionary task is to go, sent as representatives of the home church, to places where Christ is not known, winning people to faith and establishing congregations of those new believers.

ROBERTSON MCQUILKIN

Bibliography. L. W. Caldwell, *Sent Out: Reclaiming the Spiritual Gift of Apostleship for Missionaries and Churches Today*; C. Clark, *ERT* 13 (October 1989): 344–82; J. B. Lightfoot, *The Epistle of St. Paul to the Galatians*; A. Plummer, *DAC*, 1:82–84; P. Schaff, *The Oldest Church Manual Called the "Teaching of the Twelve Apostles"*; W. Schmithals, *The Office of Apostle in the Early Church*.

Modality. *See* SODALITY AND MODALITY.

Modernity. A historical development generally regarded as arising in Europe in the seventeenth century, modernity is also associated with the ENLIGHTENMENT, which fundamentally altered society and economy. The Enlightenment, inspired by major developments in science and mathematics, emphasized the positive potential of human reason and the prospect of open-ended progress if Enlightenment thought were applied in all areas of life. The Enlightenment was imbued with a sense of a universal purpose and mission.

Modernity emphasized the contrast between traditional society and the emerging new culture. By its intensiveness and extensiveness modernity forcibly displaced traditional culture. Its intensiveness is seen in the way it penetrated all aspects of human life, while its extensiveness is evident in its spread worldwide. Traditional society typically focused inward; modernity has been markedly expansive.

In traditional society the production of goods depended largely on animal or human power; production in modern industrial society is dependent on inanimate sources of energy. The view of products and labor as commodities, the money economy, and urbanization are marks of modernity. Modernity also stimulated a range of institutional developments, including today's nation-states and political systems.

The dynamism and the globalizing thrust of modernity have been fostered by several developments that mark the transition from traditional society to modernity:

1. *The separation of time and space.* Each traditional culture had its own way of measuring time. Time was defined by the people in a particular place. The invention of the mechanical clock changed this. Time could be dealt with independent of place since the clock made possible a universal basis for measurement. (The latter addition of international time zones unified the world further.) In a relatively short period the new basis for measuring time was accepted worldwide, thereby breaking the traditional connection between time and space. Each element could now be dealt with without reference to the other. Time and space had become instrumental elements to be exploited.

2. *The disembedding of social systems.* Modernity severed the nexus between social relationships and the context in which they were formed. Traditionally, relationships were dependent on and remained embedded in a particular social matrix. Modernity disembedded social relations from local culture. Various mechanisms facilitated this process. (a) Money replaced barter as the means of exchange. The modern economy uses money (a symbolic token) to facilitate the exchange of goods and services. The global capital market moves vast sums of money electronically and instantaneously without any reference to relationships or place of origin. (b) Knowledge and training have become increasingly specialized, with each area of specialization controlled by experts and a body of knowledge. Expertise is the court of appeal in problem solving. In modernity daily life is dependent on vast systems based on expert knowledge; health care, electrical power, transportation, and commerce are all independent of social relations. Indeed, disembedding is understood as a necessary step in making the productive process as efficient and cost-effective as possible. Traditional culture emphasizes the role of fortune or fate; modern culture puts a premium on expert knowledge.

3. *Perpetual reflection and reordering.* All humans to some extent reflect on their actions; in modernity reflexivity and skepticism are core values. In making decisions, traditional culture prized and drew authority from the past. Modernity insists on gathering feedback from all relevant sources in order to determine the most efficient future course. The past is regarded as a drag on progress; innovation is encouraged in order to achieve greater productivity. The ideal is a process of continual critical reflection, evaluation, and reordering. No area or activity is spared this routine, which actually undermines stability and security, for the process never reaches a stable point. In the modern process, knowledge is always incomplete. The only recourse is to generate further information.

Modernity engendered optimism about the future. Industrialization and URBANIZATION promoted economic growth and created new wealth. Modern societies experienced a rising standard of living. Even though social scientists have consistently pointed to certain problems that the modern system creates, they generally assumed that these negative consequences would, in the long run, be more than offset by the positive potential. By the mid-twentieth century, however, the problems of modernity were increasingly emphasized, and pessimism supplanted the earlier optimism. Among the causes of this loss of confidence in modern culture are the consumption of nonrenewable sources of energy at an accelerating rate; despoliation of the ENVIRONMENT; the harnessing of TECHNOLOGY by police states to control entire populations; the failure to achieve a more equitable distribution of resources among the peoples of the world; the rapid growth in world POPULATION; the rise of TOTALITARIANISM; the violence of two World Wars and many regional or local conflicts sustained by the industrial-military complex; the rising incidence of VIOLENCE in industrial society; new diseases; the breakdown of social and family structures; and confusion about moral values.

The dynamics of modernity have been inherently globalizing. At the center of GLOBALIZATION is the modern economy. The traditional national economy that had systems of exchange with other national economies has been increasingly replaced by the global economy. In the global economy, manufacturing is a process of assembling components from all over the world. The capital markets operate globally through electronic hookups. In light of these new conditions, the meaning and function of the nation-state are being redefined.

In the late twentieth century, growing numbers of people asserted that modernity was being displaced by a new historical epoch, POSTMODERNISM, which involves a repudiation of certain Enlightenment values. Science is no longer regarded as the undisputed authority. Postmodern epistemology affirms that all knowing is based on faith. The modern split between public and private, objective and subjective, secular and religious, is increasingly rejected in favor of wholeness and reconciliation. This changing climate presents new opportunities for Christian witness. The postmodern attitude is more open to the religious dimension than was modernity. But a credible witness will begin with respect for modern people and an ability to narrate the gospel in contemporary language.

WILBERT R. SHENK

See also Modernization; Pluralism.

Bibliography. P. L. Berger, *The Sacred Canopy*; idem, *Facing Up to Modernity*; A. Giddens, *The Consequences of Modernity*; C. E. Gunton, *Enlightenment and Alienation*; D. Harvey, *The Condition of Postmodernity*; J. R. Middleton and B. J. Walsh, *Truth Is Stranger Than It Used to Be*; L. Newbigin, *The Gospel in a Pluralist Society*.

Modernization. The process whereby traditional society is transformed according to modern processes, values, and goals. Cultures are never static, but in the modern period innovation became a primary cultural value. One stimulus of cultural innovation is intercultural relations. In the preface to *Das Kapital* Karl Marx observed:

"The country that is more developed industrially shows to the less developed the image of its future." Modernization was a synonym for industrialization, and the modern was considered superior to traditional society.

The expansion of the colonial powers into other regions and continents coincided with modernity and the Industrial Revolution (*see* COLONIALISM). Each colonial government transmitted to its colonies a particular model of modernization—British, French, Dutch, Japanese. Colonies were encouraged to modernize according to the model of their colonial masters. The nations of Africa, Asia, and Latin America were Europeanized or Westernized. Following World War II the United States became the dominant Western power, and modernization was equated with Americanization. The Russian model was followed in the communist bloc. As modernization became a global phenomenon, the domination and control by foreign powers began to stir resentment. People wanted modernization without the label "made in . . . ," which implied dependence on or being within the political orbit of a foreign power.

The relationship of modernization and DEVELOPMENT must be noted. While the term "modernization" has largely fallen into disuse, a considerable literature developed around it following World War II. Modernization was understood to be a systemic process that encompassed all aspects of a society, including ECONOMICS. But the terms "modernization" and "development" were not applied consistently and frequently were used interchangeably. Today "DEVELOPMENT" is the preferred term.

Early studies of modernization drew a number of general conclusions. First, it was recognized that no theoretical models were at hand for studying this complex process of cultural change. One tack was to analyze the paths to modernization taken by developed societies. This focused attention on the variables influencing whether a traditional society remained intact or modernized: natural resources, educational systems, geopolitical relationships. These prerequisites for takeoff toward modernization were widely discussed in the early literature.

Second, early studies saw the economy as fundamental. An expanding economy that effectively tapped a country's human and natural resources was essential to modernization.

Third, early studies recognized that industrialization has been the powerful engine of cultural change in the modern period. Industrial development entailed the centralization of the means of production, especially labor, so that goods and services could be produced in the greatest quantity at least cost. Thus, URBANIZATION has been a necessary concomitant of modernization. Considerable controversy has arisen with regard to the emphasis to be given to industry vis-à-vis other sectors such as agriculture.

Fourth, the impact of SECULARIZATION on traditional society, including religion, proved difficult to assess. In the first phase of modernization studies, secularization was regarded as the indispensable ally. It was also assumed that traditional religio-cultural values were incompatible with modernization and impotent in the face of secularization. For a society to modernize, the shackles of tradition had to be broken. Traditional mentality, it was argued, must be replaced by a rationalist and positivist outlook. Gunnar Myrdal's *Asian Drama* (1968) revamped the discussion by emphasizing the important role of attitudes and values, including religion, in modernization. And yet as modernization accelerated in the 1960s, some of the strongest resistance was evident in societies controlled by a religious tradition that sensed the threat of secularization to its core values. The outstanding example was Iran, where a countermodernizing Islamic movement led by Ayatollah Khomeini overthrew the promodernizing monarchy in 1979 and installed a regime committed to restoring the country to its Islamic foundation.

According to Daniel Lerner, three interlocking conditions are required to sustain modernization. The first is geographical and social mobility. Traditional society is characteristically static. For a society to modernize, its population must be ready to relocate in response to new opportunities. Throughout the modern period people have been leaving the rural and agrarian world for urban and industrialized society. This mobility has various essential characteristics, but most important are openness to change and willingness to adapt to new situations.

The second condition is psychic mobility. Physical mobility is prerequisite to psychic mobility. Explorations in the fifteenth century began expanding the geographical horizon. This was augmented by the printing press and publication of books and maps detailing expeditions to various parts of the world. The mass MEDIA have greatly expanded and accelerated psychic mobility by making vicarious experience of diverse realities possible.

The third condition is the system of modernity with its dependence on the mass media (*see* MASS COMMUNICATION). Traditional society is an oral society with certain correlates: the socioeconomic sector is rural; the cultural sector is nonliterate; the political sector is designative. In modern media-dependent society the socioeconomic sector is urban, the cultural sector is literate, and the political sector is electoral.

The model of modernization thus comprises four elements: urbanization, LITERACY, media participation, and political participation. The relationships among the four elements will vary.

Urbanization tends to progress at a more rapid rate than literacy, but media participation is extremely high, extending even to rural areas. The media have grown in importance as the world economic system has evolved.

The modern mission movement was an important agent of modernization worldwide. Some caution and dissent would have been justified, for modernization has espoused a technical and rational approach; it has largely ignored the religious dimension. A sound missiology, to the contrary, is concerned with the whole person, a subject that began to be addressed by Christian development theorists and missiologists from the 1960s on.

WILBERT R. SHENK

Bibliography. W. G. Bragg, *The Church in Response to Human Need*, pp. 20–51; D. Goulet, *The Cruel Choice;* D. C. Korten, *Getting to the 21st Century;* D. Lerner, *The Passing of Traditional Society;* G. Myrdal, *Asian Drama*, 3 vols.; N. Wolterstorff, *Until Justice and Peace Embrace.*

Moe, Malla (1863–1953). Norwegian missionary to Swaziland. Moe's parents died when she was a teenager, and she and her sister moved from Norway to Chicago to live with an older married sister. In 1892 evangelist FREDERICK FRANSON, founder of the Scandinavian Alliance Mission, challenged her to go to South Africa, even though she had no formal Bible training. She set out as one of a band of eight pioneer missionaries whose numbers dwindled to three after a year. Moe began her ministry by visiting African homes and learning the language, and her dependence upon Africans became a hallmark of her ministry. She used evangelistic methods many colleagues found unorthodox, like her traveling "Gospel Wagon" which she had built at age sixty-five to go into new areas. She planted a great many churches, and founded a mission station at a place she named Bethel, which became her base of operations for over fifty years of ministry in Swaziland.

Colleagues and critics struggled to work with a woman who was so independent and domineering, but her personal characteristics grew from a singular focus: her life was totally devoted to soul winning, and she was impatient with any impediments that kept her from doing God's work. She died in Swaziland in 1953 at age ninety.

JUDITH LINGENFELTER

Moffat, Robert (1795–1883). Scottish pioneer missionary to Southern Africa. Born in East Lothian, Scotland, he trained as a gardener, but after conversion heard God's call to the mission field. In spite of little formal education he was accepted by the LONDON MISSIONARY SOCIETY (LMS), which made room for "godly men who understood mechanic arts." Moffat's arrival in

Cape Town in 1816 brought no welcome from a colonial government that distrusted "Nonconformist" preachers, nor from Boer farmers convinced that God had made them superior to nonwhite races. Delayed by red tape (he spent the time learning Dutch), Moffat in 1817 journeyed north, befriending an outlawed Hottentot chief whose conversion eased official prejudice against the LMS. Despite the obstacles he pressed on toward remote villages where Jesus' name was unknown. He settled at Kuruman (1826–70) in modern Botswana. There he evangelized, built stone houses, irrigated orchards, made soap and clothes, and opened a school. Moffat was a great thanksgiver, with a genius for winning the friendship of local chiefs, but as a product of his culture and time could also exhibit muscular Christianity in repelling threatening invaders.

He translated the Bible into Sechuana (1840–57). His *Missionary Labours* (1842) and *Rivers of Water* (1863) sold in large numbers. In England (1838–43) he captivated audiences by his arresting accounts, sought and got the support of Christian England when the missionary movement was gathering momentum, and recruited for the Bechuana mission the young David Livingstone, his future son-in-law. But Moffat still had twenty-seven crowded years traveling out from Kuruman with the gospel. Even after retirement he directed attention to Africa. Made D.D. of Edinburgh, the "Apostle of the Bechuanas" downplayed his success with "I simply did the work of the day in the day."

J. D. Douglas

Bibliography. J. S. Moffat, *The Lives of Robert and Mary Moffat;* W. C. Northcott, *Robert Moffat: Pioneer in Africa, 1817–1870;* E. W. Smith, *Robert Moffat, One of God's Gardeners;* J. P. R. Wallis, ed., *The Matabele Journals of Robert Moffat, 1829–1860.*

Moffett, Samuel A. (1864–1939), American pioneer missionary to Korea. Moffett was commissioned as one of the pioneer missionaries to Korea by the Northern Presbyterian Mission in the United States to Korea, arriving in Seoul on his twenty-sixth birthday (January 25, 1890).

After his arrival, while engaging in language study, he directed and upgraded into a school an orphanage for boys which had been founded by Horace G. Underwood in 1886. In 1893, he moved permanently into the northern provinces of Korea, establishing long-term residence in Pyongyang. Through strategic planning and wide itineration he raised up a growing network of village and city churches, established a Bible training class system for all believers, and served as pastor of the Central Presbyterian Church of Pyongyang until 1907. He was elected to be the first moderator of the Presbyterian Church of Korea at its organizing Presbytery in September 1907.

Moffett, a strong proponent of education for Christians, founded several hundred primary schools for the children of believers and in 1901 he started the Presbyterian Theological Seminary in his living room in Pyongyang with two students. The first seven graduates were ordained in 1907. He served as president of the seminary until 1924. Among many other early Christian institutions established by him and his missionary colleagues was a Christian Academy for young men which evolved into the first Christian college in Korea, Soongsil. Moffett served as president from 1918 to 1927.

Moffett was very sympathetic to the movement for Korean independence from Japan, which had annexed Korea in 1910. His well-known opposition to efforts by the Japanese colonialist powers to subjugate worship of the triune God to the deified Japanese emperor through forced attendance of Christians at the Shinto shrines led eventually to his being driven from Korea on four hours' notice in 1936 after forty-six years in Korea.

Bong Rin Ro

Bibliography. A. D. Clark, *A History of the Church in Korea;* E. N. Hunt, Jr., *Protestant Pioneers in Korea;* L. G. Paik, *The History of Protestant Missions in Korea, 1832–1910.*

Moldova (*Est. 2000 pop.: 4,510,000; 33,700 sq. km. [13,012 sq. mi.]*). Moldova is a landlocked, ethnically diverse republic of the former Soviet Union, nestled between Ukraine and Romania. Moldova was once part of Romania, and nearly two-thirds of its citizens are ethnic Romanians, while slightly more than a quarter of its people are Slavs, most of whom live in the troubled Transdniester region. The Orthodox Church claims the nominal allegiance of at least two-thirds of the population, while evangelicals—especially Baptists and Pentecostals—make up less than 2 percent of the population. Although strong Orthodox opposition has made evangelical outreach difficult at times, the evangelical movement is growing. Particularly encouraging has been a significant movement to Christ among the minority Gagauz people, a Turkic ethnic group.

Raymond P. Prigodich

See also Commonwealth of Independent States.

Monaco (*Est. 2000 pop.: 34,000; 1.95 sq. km. [0.75 sq. mi.]*). "Money is power" in Monaco, one of the world's smallest nations. Images of Grand Prix automobile racing and wealthy tax-dodging exiles stereotype this principality surrounded by France and the Mediterranean Sea.

Missionaries to Monaco face many challenges. Material distractions dull spiritual sensitivity; indeed, a focus on the power of money dominates relationships. Further, although Monaco boasts freedom of worship, public evangelism is forbidden. Institutional religion, in the form of the Roman Catholic Church, is deeply engrained. As in neighboring France, the occult is powerful. Finally, Monaco's population is highly transient, few being native Monegasque. Although some come to faith and then move on, becoming a blessing to others, the frequent turnover is an obstacle to evangelism and church development.

Monaco, however, has provided a base for an incredible contribution to missions. The name of Monte Carlo is synonymous in much of Europe, the Middle East, and North Africa with Trans World Radio and Radio Monte Carlo, established in 1960. Christian programming in over twenty languages is transmitted daily into countries where local Christian broadcasting is in large part prohibited.

DAVID GREENLEE

Bibliography. P. Freed, *Towers to Eternity,* rev. ed.

Monastic Movement. Most missionaries from the fourth to the eighteenth centuries were monks, even though mission was not part of the original purpose of monasticism. The movement developed in the late third century, drawing men and women into celibate communities of work and worship. Their primary focus was the achievement of personal salvation through prayer and ascetic practices. But some penetrated new areas, winning pagan peoples to the faith, reducing languages to writing, and translating the Scriptures.

In the West, Celtic monasticism, beginning in the fifth century, was intentionally missionary and played a great role in evangelizing the British Isles and parts of the Continent. In the thirteenth century the Franciscans initiated missions to Muslims and with the Dominicans established a chain of mission stations across Central Asia all the way to China. The Jesuits in the sixteenth century joined them as the primary missionary agencies of the Roman Catholic Church, especially in Latin America, India, and Japan.

In the East the NESTORIANS were ardently missionary, even though considered heretical. They moved across Central Asia, introduced literacy among illiterate tribes, and reached China in 635. Most of their work did not survive. Sent by Constantinope, CYRIL and METHODIUS went to the Slavic peoples in the ninth century, devised an alphabet that became the basis of modern Slavic languages, translated the Scriptures, and established the church. In the tenth century monks took Christianity to Kiev, then to Moscow. They also did heroic work among Aleuts in Alaska beginning in the eighteenth century. The monks from the East emphasized the use of vernacular languages in liturgy and Scripture, while the Western church insisted on Latin.

Even though evangelicals would not agree with all of their theology, this movement produced thousands of men and women of prayer and devotion, who were the most important ambassadors of the gospel for fourteen centuries.

PAUL E. PIERSON

SEE ALSO Celtic Missionary Movement.

Bibliography. D. Bosch, *Transforming Mission: Paradigm Shifts in Theology of Mission;* S. Neill, *HCM.*

Money. The fact and scale of Western money constitutes a major barrier to cross-cultural transmission of the gospel, all the more so because chains of affluence may prevent discernment of their evil effects. For example, a major cause of conflict according to the Epistle of James is covetousness. Historically, Western Christian missionary outreach was undertaken in tandem with an insatiable quest in the West to control global resources, a process which began during centuries of the slave trade and colonial expansion of the West, and which continues through multinational corporations and international agencies such as the World Bank and International Monetary Fund. These chains also lead to the worship of false gods. In a pastoral message to North American churches, Bishop Oscar Romero of El Salvador (1917–80) wrote in 1979 that the idolatry of wealth and private property inclines persons toward "having more" and lessens their interest in "being more." It is this absolutism that supports structural violence and oppression of people (*Voice of the Voiceless,* 173). Elsewhere Romero wrote that the god of money forces us to turn our backs on the God of Christianity. As people want the god of money, many reproach the church and kill movements that try to destroy false idols.

The analysis of James and the prophetic warnings of Romero are but two portrayals of how money is a problem to those throughout the world struggling to incarnate the gospel. Mission activity cannot take place without money, but money poses at least three challenges. First, the affluent, including those who live privileged lives among the poor, must take into account teachings of the Bible on the subject of the poor, the wealthy, and the consequences of acquisitiveness. Second, Western missionaries have worked from positions of power and MISSIONARY AFFLUENCE. The relative wealth of Western Christians engenders strategies which create dependency among younger churches and harm the poor. Finally, affluence leads the relatively wealthy Christians of the West to aid and abet the processes which have plunged poor nations into a succession of traumas and may contribute to future crises (*see also* WEALTH AND POVERTY).

Formidable as these challenges might seem, many Christians are attempting to surmount them. The following illustrations are suggestive. Individually, Christians coming to grips with the call to follow Jesus are simplifying their lifestyles and counting the benefits of self-denial. Mission boards have changed policies relating to how missionaries live. Church agencies have sought to be more responsible in investment and development policies. Whether as individuals or corporately, many Christians have articulated an understanding of Christian stewardship as servanthood, advocacy for justice, and empowerment of the poor. Since the onset of the Two-Thirds World debt crisis in the early 1980s, many Christians have advocated debt forgiveness for severely poor countries. Many Christian voices are calling for a recovery of the Jubilee tradition to free the poor from all debt without condition. There is a growing religious environmental movement which articulates the understanding that the earth has lost the capability of sustaining the material prosperity of the West and the aspirations of the world's poor and calls for a new biblical perspective on care of God's creation.

PAUL R. DEKAR

SEE ALSO Economics.

Bibliography. J. J. Bonk, *Missions and Money: Affluence as a Western Missionary Problem;* D. J. Hall, *The Steward. A Biblical Symbol Come of Age;* I. McCrae, *Global Economics. Seeking a Christian Ethic;* M. Meeks, *God the Economist. The Doctrine of God and Political Economy;* R. Sider, *Rich Christians in an Age of Hunger: Moving from Affluence to Generosity.*

Mongolia *(Est. 2000 pop.: 2,661,000; 1,566,500 sq. km. [604,826 sq. mi.]).* Mongolia is a landlocked nation surrounded by China to the south and Siberian Russia to the north, with an estimated population of roughly 3 million.

The story of the earliest mission work in Mongolia is shrouded from contemporary view, though it is known that NESTORIAN Christians contacted the Mongols in the seventh century. This initial Christian influence died out by the tenth century. Catholic missionaries began work among the Mongols in the thirteenth century. They included JOHN OF MONTECORVINO, who translated portions of the Bible and conducted Masses for them. Protestant missions did not begin until the early 1800s. The best-known Protestant missionary is JAMES GILMOUR, referred to by some as the "Apostle to Mongolia." Despite the title and the affection and respect he received from the Mongols, Gilmour failed to see even one baptism in his more than two decades of service. Early missionaries and converts of all stripes regularly faced the reality of martyrdom, especially in times of strife such as the Boxer Rebellion in 1900.

In 1990 the communist government was renounced and a new multiparty system was installed in 1992. With freedom of religion now guaranteed in the Constitution, spiritual revival has taken place. Many Mongols are returning to their Buddhist and Shamanist roots, but others are turning to Christ and Christian churches are appearing on Mongolian soil for the first time since the early 1900s. In less than a decade the church grew from less than ten known indigenous believers in the nation to an estimated two thousand, and the numbers continue to grow steadily. Recently Mongols have begun reaching out to their own people. Churches in the capital are adopting Aymags (Provinces) and using the JESUS FILM and other methods to share Christ with their countrymen. The New Testament is translated into Mongolian, but numbers are limited. Despite the history, the future presents open possibilities for the continuing growth of the Mongolian church.

JAMIE FLOWERS

Bibliography. C. Lacy, *CDCWM,* p. 419; *Mongolia, a Country Study,* Area Handbook Series; R. Lovett, *James Gilmour of Mongolia;* V. Mortenson, *God Made it Grow, Historical Sketches of TEAM's Church Planting Work.*

Moninger, (Mary) Margaret (1891–1950). American Presbyterian missionary to China. Moninger was born near Marshalltown, Iowa. While at Grinnell College she joined the STUDENT VOLUNTEER MOVEMENT for Foreign Missions. After graduating in 1913, she taught school and then applied to the Presbyterian Board of Foreign Missions.

Arriving on Hainan Island in 1915, Moninger began language studies and worked tirelessly for the cause of female education. During her years on Hainan she served at the Kiungchow, Nodoa, and Kachek stations and functioned as mission treasurer, secretary, and agent at various times. Violence forced the Hainan missionaries to flee to Haiphong in 1925 and to Hong Kong in 1927.

Moninger was a delegate to the Church of Christ in China conference and to the Presbyterian China Council at Shanghai. She published several anthropological articles on the aborigine Miao people of the island's interior. She collected botanical specimens for the National Arboretum of the Philippines and Harvard University. She also compiled a two-volume dictionary of the Hainanese dialect. Held under virtual house arrest at Nodoa by the Japanese in 1937–38, she and her colleagues at Kiungchow-Hoihow were again placed under house arrest after July 1941. Moninger was repatriated first to Shanghai and then home on the *Gripsholm* in 1942. Ill health forced her retirement, and she died at Marshalltown.

KATHLEEN L. LODWICK

Bibliography. K. L. Lodwick, *Educating the Women of Hainan: The Career of Margaret Moninger in China, 1915–1942;* idem, *Journal of Church and State* 36 (1994): 833–46; idem, *American Presbyterians: The Journal of Presbyterian History* 65 (1987): 19–28 and 70 (1992): 247–58.

Monism. Monism is the philosophical view that there is only one ultimate reality of which everything else is merely a part. In religion it is usually connected with a pantheistic view of the nature of God ("God is all and all is God"). There is considerable diversity among monistic systems.

Among Asian religions, Hinduism, especially according to the interpretation of the Upanishads by the eighth-century mystic philosopher Sankara, is monistic in that all reality is summed up in *Brahman* and the gods are manifestations of *Brahman*. Likewise, the New Age movement in the West, because of Hindu influence, adheres to pantheistic monism. Some forms of Buddhism appear to be monistic, especially in the emphasis upon *nirvana* or *sunyata* (emptiness) as the ultimate reality.

Western thinking includes several philosophical monists, from Parmenides and Democritus in ancient Greece to Plotinus in the third century and on to B. Spinoza and G. W. F. Hegel in the modern period. Spinoza, for example, defined reality as the one substance, calling it either God or Nature, while Hegel is the most influential monistic thinker in the modern West with his concept of the Absolute.

Christian theology opposes monism for at least two reasons. First, monism is incompatible with the biblical distinction between God the creator and the created order. Second, monism is incompatible with Scripture in its idea of evil as an inherent part of the universe rather than an alien intrusion into the perfect creation through human choice.

WILLIAM H. BAKER

SEE ALSO Religious Ultimacy.

Bibliography. F. Copleston, *Religion and the One: Philosophies East and West.*

Monotheism. Derived from the Greek *monos* (single, only) and *theos* (god), monotheism is the belief that there is only one God. Monotheism is thus contrasted with POLYTHEISM (belief in a plurality of deities), HENOTHEISM (worship of one deity as supreme without necessarily denying the reality of other deities), and ATHEISM (denial of the existence of any deity). Monotheism is also generally understood as involving belief in a personal, transcendent creator of all else that exists, and thus monotheism must be distinguished from the various forms of nonpersonal monism (ultimately there is only one reality) and PANTHEISM (identification of God with the universe).

Monotheism is usually associated with Judaism, Christianity, and Islam, all of which affirm that there is one eternal Creator God. However, the three faiths differ substantially in their respective understandings of the nature of the one true God. Central to Judaism is the *Shema*, the creedal statement found in Deuteronomy 6:4—"Hear, O Israel: The LORD our God, the LORD is One." Jesus reaffirmed this confession in Mark 12:29–30, and the unity of the one eternal God formed the foundation of the early Christian community as well (1 Cor. 8:4, 6; Eph. 4:6; 1 Tim. 2:5). Nevertheless, the early church came to recognize that within the unity of the one eternal God there is a fundamental distinction among the Father, the Son, and the Holy Spirit, resulting in the doctrine of the Holy Trinity. Both Judaism and Islam reject the doctrine of the TRINITY and the deity of Jesus Christ.

Sikhism is also monotheistic in its emphasis on worship of the one God, the "True Name," the sovereign Creator. Theistic traditions that call for worship of one supreme deity (e.g., Shiva, Vishnu) can be found in certain forms of Hinduism and Buddhism (Amida and the Pure Land schools). The High God of African traditional religions is sometimes characterized as a form of diffused monotheism as well.

The challenge for Christians missiologically is twofold: (1) to encourage those from polytheistic, pantheistic, or animistic worldviews to come to an understanding and acceptance of the biblical God as the one, eternal, sovereign God; (2) to encourage non-Christian monotheists to embrace a fully biblical understanding of the deity of Jesus Christ and the triune nature of the one God. This is particularly important for ministry among Muslims. Islam seriously misunderstands the orthodox teaching of the Trinity, accusing Christians of denying genuine monotheism. These misunderstandings need to be addressed in a clear and sensitive manner. In an effort to be faithful to the teaching of Scripture and to build on common ground, ministry among Muslims, Jews, and Sikhs should emphasize the oneness and unity of God. While remaining consistent with the teaching of Scripture, ministry among non-Christian monotheists should explore new terms and fresh formulations for communicating the biblical understanding of the Holy Trinity.

RICHARD D. LOVE

Bibliography. W. H. Albright, *From the Stone Age to Christianity;* J. Carman, *Majesty and Meekness;* M. P. Christanand, *The Philosophy of Indian Monotheism;* H. P. Owen, *Concepts of Deity.*

Montenegro. *See* YUGOSLAVIA.

Montgomery, Carrie Judd (1858–1946). American Pentecostal minister-teacher, editor, writer, and social worker. Born and raised in Buffalo, New York, Montgomery dedicated herself to Christian ministry and lifelong teaching about divine healing after her own healing. Her efforts to bridge denominational barriers included work in transdenominational ministries and affiliations with Pentecostal and Holiness healing movements, the CHRISTIAN MISSIONARY ALLIANCE (CMA), the Episcopal Church, and the SALVATION ARMY. Montgomery's book recording her testimony influenced A. B. SIMPSON in founding the CMA. She became the recording secretary of the first CMA board and later organized a CMA church in Oakland.

In addition to writing numerous books, Montgomery began and edited (for sixty-five years) the nonsectarian magazine, *Triumphs of Faith.* Montgomery combined holiness and divine healing to establish several homes throughout the United States where sick people could come for prayer, teaching, and support. She married after moving to Oakland, California, in 1890. Although her wealthy husband, George Montgomery, remained a layman, Carrie was ordained by the Churches of God in Christ and credentialed as an evangelist in the Assemblies of God. Together, they developed several ministries, including an orphanage, a campground, a missionary training school, a mission, and a missionary rest and ministry center. Montgomery also pastored Beulah Heights Chapel.

MARGOT EYRING

Bibliography. E. L. Blumhofer, *DCA*, pp. 767–68; W. E. Warner, *DPCM*, pp. 626–28.

Montgomery, Helen Barrett (1861–1934). American Bible translator, author, mission advocate, and licensed Baptist preacher. Born in Kingsville, Ohio, and raised in Rochester, New York, Montgomery attributed her success to the influence of her school administrator/Baptist minister father. She excelled at Wellesley College and began her career teaching school, receiving a master's degree from Brown University and three honorary doctorates. She and her husband, William A. Montgomery, a successful businessman, gave sacrificially to missions. Montgomery also raised huge amounts of money for cooperative mission efforts. She and LUCY PEABODY, both leaders of the Women's Missionary Movement, traveled extensively to research and promote international missions.

Montgomery served ten years as the first president of the combined Women's American Baptist Foreign Mission Society. She was also the first woman to translate the New Testament from Greek to English (the Centenary Translation), first woman president of a major denomination (Northern Baptist Convention), founder and first president of the Federation of Women's Boards of Foreign Missions, first woman on the Rochester school board, and president of the Women's Educational and Industrial Union for twenty years. Montgomery often preached and she filled her father's pulpit after his death. A prolific scholar, Montgomery wrote numerous books about missions and lectured in seminaries and churches. She taught the Barrett Memorial Bible class for forty-four years.

MARGOT EYRING

Bibliography. W. H. Brackney, *DCA*, p. 768; E. Deen, *Great Women of the Christian Faith;* R. A. Tucker, *GGC*.

Montserrat (United Kingdom Dependent Area) *(Est. 2000 pop.: 11,000; 102 sq. km. [39 sq. mi.]).* A British colony in the northern Leeward Islands of the Caribbean, Montserrat has a tiny population of only 14,000 people and restricted economic opportunity. Montserrat nevertheless has benefited from its natural beauty and rugged terrain to emerge as an attractive tourist site. The largely Protestant population is 20 percent evangelical, two-thirds of whom are Pentecostal.

EVERETT A. WILSON

SEE ALSO Caribbean.

Bibliography. A. Lampe, *The Church in Latin America, 1492–1992,* pp. 201–15; J. Rogozinski, *A Brief History of the Caribbean: From the Arawak and the Carib to the Present.*

Moody, Dwight Lyman (1837–99). American evangelist. Born in Northfield, Massachusetts, at age seventeen he began working in a Boston shoestore, where he was converted through the witness of his Sunday school teacher, Edward Kimball. He moved to Chicago in 1856 and developed a successful shoe business. In 1858, he organized a Sunday school, which eventually grew into what is now Moody Memorial Church. In 1860, he devoted himself full-time to city missionary work through the YMCA. During the Civil War he ministered to soldiers. Between 1865 and 1869, he served as the president of the Chicago YMCA. In 1871, following the great Chicago fire, he began his career as a traveling revivalist. He was joined by Ira Sankey and together they ministered effectively throughout Great Britain from 1873 to 1875, returning to America as celebrities.

Moody held evangelistic campaigns in virtually every major city in America. His influence was far-reaching, not only in evangelism but in education (founding three schools), conferences, and publishing. Saving souls was his highest aim in life. He said: "I look upon this world as a wrecked vessel. God has given me a lifeboat and said to me, 'Moody, save all you can.'"

TIMOTHY K. BEOUGHER

Bibliography. L. Dorsett, *A Passion for Souls: The Life of D. L. Moody;* S. N. Gundry, *Love Them In: The Life and Theology of D. L. Moody;* W. R. Moody, *The Life of Dwight L. Moody.*

Moon, Charlotte ("Lottie") (1840–1912). American missionary to China. Born into an aristocratic Southern family in Scottsville, Virginia, she and her younger sister, Edmonia, became the first single women missionaries to northern China for the Southern Baptist Mission (1873–1912). Converted in 1858 revivals, "Lottie" joined her lifelong Presbyterian friend, Anna Safford. They taught and, in 1871, established their own girls' school in Cartersville, Georgia. When opportunities for single women to become missionaries opened, both women changed careers and became Chinese missionaries. Moon arrived in the Shandong city of Tengzhou in 1873.

Personal discipline, institutional loyalty, and generous hospitality characterized her relatively stable missionary career. Competent in Chinese and sensitive to the Chinese cultural restraints on women's roles, she made friendship a means to evangelism. Working at first in girls' schools in Tengzhou (1873–85), Moon later moved to the town of Pingtu, and became the first single woman missionary to open a Chinese station without any other support. Her work in the area resulted in the development of over thirty independent Chinese congregations.

During the anti-Qing revolutionary years, the septagenarian Moon's unselfish generosity led her to suffer from malnutrition with those around her. Colleagues discovered her condition only too late. She died, emaciated and incoherent, during the initial days of a voyage to North America for medical treatment. She has been idealized among Southern Baptists for her sacrificial act of love; yearly Christmas offerings for foreign missions is taken in her name. One estimate claims that these offerings have come to nearly $1.5 billion by 1995.

LAUREN PFISTER

Bibliography. C. Allen, *The New Lottie Moon Story;* idem, *A Century To Celebrate: History of Women's Missionary Union;* I. Hyatt, *Our Ordered Lives Confess.*

Moral Development. The most cohesive body of research on moral development has been carried on within the framework of the cognitive stage theory conceived by Jean Piaget (1965) and extended by Lawrence Kohlberg (1984), James Fowler (1981), and others. Intercultural findings related to the work of these theorists are quite consistent. Although rates of development vary and growth may be arrested before higher stages are reached, the same developmental patterns are observed across cultures.

Jean Piaget, a Swiss "genetic epistemologist" (as he preferred to call himself), spent forty years studying the cognitive development of children at his Center for Genetic Epistemology in Geneva. He identified four developmental stages: the *sensorimotor* stage (to 2 years), during which rudimentary logical-mathematical operations such as hiding and finding, grouping and separating develop; the *preoperational* stage (2–7 years), when the child begins to retain mental images while objects are absent and to engage in activities such as playing, speaking, and looking at pictures; the stage of *concrete operations* (7–11 years), during which the child becomes able to conserve substances, weights, and numbers when their shape or position changes; to classify objects by color, size, and shape; and to seriate objects from short to long, light to heavy, and so on. Piaget's final stage, *formal operations* (12 years and over), involves complex "operations upon the operations," such as extrapolating what comes next from what is there, and holding some variables constant while others are manipulated. Some cross-cultural Piagetian studies suggest that some adults who have not had school-like experiences that require thinking from action are still functioning at a concrete operations stage.

Piaget (1965) also constructed a moral reasoning model, based on the child's developing concepts of respect, fairness, intentions, and punishment. He identified a two-stage model: *heteronomy,* characterized by unilateral respect for authority and conformity to rules; and *autonomy,* marked by mutuality, reciprocity, equality, and cooperation. In one study within this framework, Native American children were found to believe that rules in white persons' games could be changed, while rules in their tribal games could not.

Lawrence Kohlberg (1984) developed a more complex six-stage model that extended Piaget's moral development theory into adulthood. He identified two *preconventional* stages, during which moral decision making is based on a fear of consequences and egocentric need gratification; two stages of *conventional* morality, characterized by a desire to please others and live by social rules, and, finally, two *postconventional* stages in which contractual commitments and universal principles predominate. Kohlberg studied the reasons behind moral decisions, not the ethical implications growing out of them. Only in the final years of his life did he acknowledge that some kind of advocacy or indoctrination might be necessary in moral education (Snarey, 1992, 857).

Although extensive research supports the validity of Kohlberg's first four stages across cultures, questions have been raised about the cross-gender and cross-cultural validity of his model at postconventional levels. Some evidence suggest that women tend to base moral decisions on caring rather than on Kohlberg's justice categories, and, in some cultures, communalism rather than individualism dominates DECISION MAKING processes (Snarey, 1992).

James Fowler (1981) of Emory University has applied stage theory to faith development. He identifies six stages of faith, beginning with the intuitive-projective faith of early childhood, filled with vivid visual imagery, through progressive stages that enable children to separate reality from fantasy and begin systematizing their belief-systems. As faith development continues into adulthood, capacities for critical reflection, self-awareness, and openness to other faiths unfold, and ultimately give way to a universalizing faith where issues of love and justice become paramount.

Perry G. Downs (1986) provides a succinct summary and critique of Fowler's theory. For Fowler, faith is shared, universal experience of trusting something or someone. The focus is on moral structures, not on content. This is in stark contrast to Christian faith, which is based on the Scriptures and a life transforming commitment to Jesus Christ (Downs, 30).

Although the relativistic assumptions of stage theories must be questioned, the developmental processes they postulate appear to be cross-culturally valid. As such, they can provide a useful conceptual tool in helping persons who are engaged in intercultural ministries to attune their discipling and spiritual formation efforts to the cognitive, moral, and faith development of their learners.

Some educators suggest that growth and maturation are more likely to occur when teaching is direct and purposeful, the attitude or value is modeled, the leader maintains a low profile, the setting is informal, divergent views are encouraged, the group is heterogeneous and holistic methods—such as moral dilemmas, open discussion, music, drama, prayer, projects, simulations, case studies, role playing, and other simulated and real life experiences—are employed (McKinney, 1984, 316–17).

LOIS MCKINNEY DOUGLAS

Bibliography. P. G. Downs, *CT*, October, 1986, pp. 29–30; J. W. Fowler, *Stages of Faith: The Psychology Human Development and the Question for Meaning*; L. Kohlberg, *Essays on Moral Development*, vol. 2: *The Psychology of Moral Development*; L. McKinney, *Missiology* 12:3 (1984): 311–26; J. Piaget, *the Moral Judgment of the child*; J. Snarey, *Encyclopedia of Educational Research*, 6th ed., 3:856–60.

Morale. An emotional and mental quality entailing a strong sense of purpose, confidence in the future, and conformity with the standards set by one's peers. Closely related to esprit de corps or team spirit, the maintenance of morale is vital if missionaries on the field are to stay healthy and productive. There are various methods of maintaining good morale in the individual: stress management (regular breaks from one's work for family and rest); spiritual conditioning (personal time in daily prayer and Bible study enabling one to meet setbacks with perseverance); open communication (exchanging current news with family and friends on the home front); interactive field administration (cooperation between all missionaries and their leaders in order to build team spirit); and personal hygiene (regular exercise, healthy diet, weight control, prevention of disease).

JOHN EASTERLING

Moratorium. Since the mid-nineteenth century, a number of international Christian leaders became very concerned about paternalistic and authoritarian mission practices and the need for new churches in the southern continents to determine their own courses of action. One hundred years later, HENDRIK KRAEMER, MAX WARREN, and James A. Scherer argued that mission business should not continue "as usual." Patronizing missions from the West needed to be dismantled in favor of a new order of relationships. Reflecting this, Bishop Federico Pagura of Central America wrote a pithy challenge in 1964 entitled "Missionary, Go Home . . . Or Stay."

After appeals in 1971 from John Gatu of Kenya and Emerito Nacpil of the Philippines, a heated debate developed over the need for "mission," but not for Western missionaries. This occurred both in print and especially at international conferences in Bangkok (1973), Lusaka (1974), Lausanne (1974), and Nairobi (1975). Calls were issued by some for a transfer of "the massive expenditure on expatriate personnel in the churches in Africa [for example] to programme activities manned by Africans themselves."

In 1974, GERALD H. ANDERSON argued that while there were "situations in which the withdrawal of missionaries would be in the best interests of the Christian mission," such a general policy for all situations was "neither biblically sound nor in the best interests of the churches" anywhere. Instead, he urged the development of "mutuality in mission." Similarly, STEPHEN NEILL observed that different churches held rather divergent views on the "moratorium" issue, reflecting the fact that many of them were at different stages in life.

During the 1990s, questions were raised in evangelical circles on questions such as: "Are American [or Western] missionaries still needed overseas?" Alternatives have been suggested by mission organizations acting on the premise that twenty-five or more local believers (who are far more effective evangelists than are expatriates) can be supported for the cost of maintaining one American missionary overseas (K. P. Yohannan).

A. CHRISTOPHER SMITH

Bibliography. G. H. Anderson, *Mission Trends*, No. 1, pp. 133–41; idem, *DEM*, pp. 702–3; E. Castro, *IRM*, 64:254 (April 1975), pp. 117–217; F. Pagura, *Mission Trends*, No. 1, pp. 115–16; K. P. Yohannan, *Revolution in World Missions*.

Moravian Missions. The Moravians had their roots in a small band of refugees, spiritual descendants of the fifteenth-century Hussite movement, who settled on the estate of Count NICHOLAS VON ZINZENDORF near Dresden in 1722. They named their settlement *Herrnhut*, the "Lord's watch." Others from various church traditions joined them. Zinzendorf had been raised in a pietist home, and made a deep commitment to Christ as a youth. At the University of Halle he was a founder of the Order of the Mustard Seed, one of whose stated purposes was "to carry the gospel to those beyond the sea."

As the community grew, there was dissension over various issues, including its relationship to the State Lutheran Church. In 1727 Zinzendorf called them to unity with the principle that "Herrnhut shall stand in unceasing love with all children of God in all churches, criticize none . . . to preserve for itself the evangelical purity, simplicity, and grace."

After weeks of teaching from 1 John, prayer, and fasting, the group experienced its Pentecost on August 13, 1727, and was knit together by a mighty visitation of the Holy Spirit. In February 1728 Zinzendorf introduced plans for evangelism in the West Indies, Greenland, Turkey, and Lapland. Twenty-six people made a covenant to pray for the mission and to go forth immediately when called. A chain of prayer around the clock was inaugurated that lasted one hundred years. The Moravians became a unique fellowship of laity and clergy, men and women, with the spread of the Christian message the major objective of the whole group, not just a minority. While they married and had families, in many respects they were monastic in their discipline and obedience, willing to go anywhere in mission. Their purpose was twofold: to take the gospel to those who had not heard, and to bring renewal and unity to churches that had grown cold. This small community furnished over half the Protestant missionaries in the eighteenth century.

In 1732 LEONHARD DOBER and DAVID NITSCHMANN left on foot for Copenhagen, their meager possessions on their backs and thirty shillings in their pockets, on their way to the West Indies. The missionaries were expected to make their own way and support themselves. By 1740 68 had gone; by 1760 the number had grown to 226. A report in 1739 mentioned 16 locations where they served in Asia, Africa, North America, and Asia, in addition to several areas in Europe, including the Baltic states and Russia.

They often went to the hardest places and worked with the most oppressed people, persevering despite terrible suffering. Over fifty adults and children died the first few years in the West Indies and Surinam. Work with the slaves brought opposition from the planters and the Dutch clergy. When missionaries were imprisoned on St. Thomas, slaves gathered outside the prison to hear their message and sing with them. Eight hundred were converted.

Called a fool by the European settlers, GEORGE SCHMIDT established the first mission station in South Africa and in 1742 baptized the first black converts. Soon he was expelled by the Dutch.

After the first three missionaries to Greenland had experienced near starvation, sickness, and the hostility of the people, they signed a covenant, vowing never to leave their posts, adding, "We came hither resting on Christ our Saviour, in whom all the nations of the earth shall be blessed." Three years later as he heard the story of Jesus in Gethsemane, newly translated into his own language, the first native Greenlander was converted.

Moravians worked among a number of indigenous American tribes, often incurring the enmity of both European colonists and other Indians. At Gnadenhutten, Pennsylvania, a number of Indians and missionaries were massacred. Moravians went to the West Coast of Africa, Ethiopia, and Algeria, to Kurds in Persia, and to Laplanders in the far north. Several were imprisoned in St. Petersburg. Others went to Ceylon, hoping to establish missions to the East Indies, Mongolia, and Persia. Their vision was worldwide.

They studied medicine, geography, and languages, and were sent out only with a strong sense of call, validated by the community. Their message was clear. "Tell them about the Lamb of God till you can tell them no more," Zinzendorf exhorted. So was their motive. "May the Lamb receive His due reward for what He suffered on the cross," two Moravians shouted as they bade farewell to friends and family. They took whatever jobs were available and formed self-supporting communities. Their pattern of life commended the gospel and consequently won many. They were not to seek glory for themselves. The missionary was to be content to suffer, die, and be forgotten.

They taught slaves to read, cared for widows and orphans, nursed the sick, and translated the Scriptures and other Christian literature into many languages. They encouraged converts to become teachers and elders.

Moravian missions among people of existing churches in Europe and North America focused on renewal and unity but were usually met with suspicion and rejection by church leaders. Even so, Zinzendorf warned against establishing Moravianism, encouraging converts to remain in their own churches. In Latvia, for example, five thousand nominal Lutherans were converted, forming Herrnhutten fellowships in the existing church.

As part of the broader eighteenth-century movements of revival, the Moravians played a major role as a catalyst to revival and missions. They were the first church to recognize their obligation to the Jews. Their influence on the Wesleys is well known. Spangenburg met JOHN WESLEY in Georgia and asked if he knew Jesus Christ. Wesley could not answer with certainty. Back in London in 1738 prior to Wesley's "heart warming" experience, Peter Boehler taught that he could know the assurance of salvation. The BASEL and LEIPZIG MISSIONARY SOCIETIES, the Methodist missionary enterprise, and the LONDON MISSIONARY SOCIETY were all stimulated and to some extent guided by the Moravians. In 1792 WILLIAM CAREY cited their example when he proposed the formation of the Baptist Missionary Society. The Moravians continue as a relatively small denomination in the United States and Europe. Well over half their members are located in Africa and Latin America.

PAUL E. PIERSON

Bibliography. W. M. Beauchamp, *Moravian Journals Relating to Central New York, 1745–66;* J. T. and K. G. Hamilton, *History of the Moravian Church;* A. J. Louis, *Zinzendorf, The Ecumenical Pioneer.*

Mormons. The followers of the Church of Jesus Christ Latter-day Saints (LDS) have come to be called Mormons because of their belief in a sacred text, the *Book of Mormon,* which was allegedly revealed to and translated by their founder Joseph Smith, Jr., in Upstate New York in 1830. The text purports to be the record of the early peoples of the Americas and of a visit to them by Jesus Christ.

Professing to be Christian, Mormons differ from historic Christianity in these doctrinal beliefs: the preexistent soul, God's evolution as a man to godhood, the potential of Mormon men to evolve into gods of their own planets, three separate heavenly abodes, the necessity of post-death baptism for non-Mormons, the inclusion of three additional texts as Scripture that are more authoritative than the Bible, the restoration of the Aaronic and Melchizedek priesthoods, the need for a living prophet (understood to be the current President and Apostle of LDS), and that all other churches are an abomination to God. LDS redefines the Trinity by stating the Heavenly Father is Elohim, Jesus is Jehovah, and the Holy Ghost is a bodiless spirit. Their Christology includes the belief that Jesus is the biological brother of Lucifer and all humans, born from a physical relationship between God and Mary, that Jesus married at least three wives and fathered children, and that his death paid only for Adam's sin. The cross has little significance to Mormonism.

The LDS is headquartered in Salt Lake City, Utah, and reflects a strong hierarchical structure. Its membership exceeded 8 million in 128 countries in 1993 and is projected to reach 35 million by 2020. Young men (more recently women as well) are encouraged to spend two years as active missionaries, resulting in nearly fifty thousand missionaries serving at the end of the twentieth century.

Mormons can be challenged on the authenticity of the LDS version of its history. Since they are taught that new revelation supersedes old, it is helpful to present them with the historic reliability of the Bible and the principle that new revelation cannot contradict older revelation.

WENDY PETERSON

SEE ALSO Cults, Cultism.

Bibliography. C. M. Larson, *By His Own Hand: A New Look at the Joseph Smith Papyri;* D. M. Quinn, *The Mormon Hierarchy: Origins of Power;* G. and S. Tanner, *Mormonism: Shadow or Reality?*

Morocco *(Est. 2000 pop.: 29,637,000; 446,550 sq. km. [172,413 sq. mi.]).* The history of this northwest African country has been shaped by the interaction between the original Berber population and a succession of outside invading peoples: Phoenicians, Carthaginians, Romans, Vandals, Arab Muslims, Spanish, and French. Today it is estimated that 75 percent of the population are of Berber stock. In Morocco there are three main Berber tribal groups: the Riffians in the north, who speak the Rif dialect, the Berraber in the center, who speak Tamazight, and the Shluh in the southeast, who speak Tashilhait. However, Arabic is the official language.

Christianity entered Morocco in the second century, but the church was weakened by persecution, the Donatist schism, and the ravages of invaders. In the thirteenth century, six Franciscan friars came to serve as missionaries. Morocco was opened to Protestant missions through the tolerance of Sultan Moulay Hassan (1873–94). In 1875, the Church Mission to the Jews established a ministry to the large Hebrew community in Morocco. In 1884, the mission to the Kabyles and Other Berber Races began work. This mission later was renamed the North Africa Mission, and still later became Arab World Ministries. Many other missions followed.

After France occupied Morocco in 1912, Christians began holding public meetings and selling reading material. Orphanages were established. Medical work was developed, most notably through the North Africa Mission Hospital in Tangier. (This hospital was nationalized in 1974.) By the 1960s, there were several Christian bookstores and a thriving camp program, as well as widespread distribution of Bible correspondence courses. At one point forty thousand Moroccans were enrolled in these courses, writing from every city in the nation.

Arabic radio broadcasts were begun by North Africa Mission in 1961 and by Gospel Missionary Union in 1966. Soon Berber broadcasts were added. By 1967, both the Bible correspondence courses and the publishing programs had moved outside Morocco, incorporating the radio ministries. By 1970 increasing pressure and expulsions by the government had reduced missionary personnel by two-thirds from its peak of one hundred in the early 1960s. Now a vigorous program of evangelism is carried on from outside the country by means of radio, Bible correspondence courses, and publications.

The penal code of June 5, 1963, prohibits the "use of means" to "exploit" the weakness of Muslims and "seduce" them to convert to another religion. Since then, hundreds of Bible correspondence course students in at least eight cities have been interrogated by the police, pressured to stop the courses, and threatened. Some believers have suffered job losses, house arrests, or imprisonment. Nevertheless, several hundred Moroccan believers gather in house meetings in several cities. Since conversion from Islam to Christianity is forbidden by law, these national Christians are not recognized as such by the government.

MIRIAM ADENEY

Morris, William Case (1864–1932). British-born Argentine missionary educator. Born in England, Morris lost his mother when he was six; the following year he and his father emigrated to Argentina. After serving as a Methodist lay worker and pastor, Morris was ordained in the Church of England and joined the (Anglican) South American Missionary Society. Motivated by a natural compassion for poor and especially motherless children, in 1898 he founded a school in Buenos Aires primarily for the underprivileged. Under his direction and untiring effort, by 1930 the "Argentine Philanthropic Schools," including an orphanage, counted some 140,000 alumni and were providing over 6,500 students with academic and vocational training, books, clothing and shoes, and a sense of duty to God and country.

Despite charges of proselytism and opposition from Catholic authorities to the use of the New Testament and evangelical hymns in the curriculum, the "Morris Schools" received government subsidies along with support from many local institutions and individuals. Morris was also an outstanding writer and translator; he edited a magazine, *La Reforma*, to which notable literary figures of the day contributed. Highly respected by the authorities and society, Morris is the only Argentine evangelical to have a monument in Buenos Aires in his honor and streets and communities named after him.

STEPHEN R. SYWULKA

Bibliography. R. Shaull, *BDCM*, p. 473.

Morrison, Robert (1782–1834). English pioneer missionary to China. Born in Morpeth, England, he entered Hoxton Academy in London in 1803. The following year the LONDON MISSIONARY SOCIETY appointed him as a missionary. For the next two and a half years, he studied at the "Missionary Academy" at Gosport, as well as studying medicine, astronomy, and Chinese. He arrived in Canton on September 6, 1807.

Living in Canton and Macao for the next twenty-seven years except for two years in England, Morrison saw his main calling as preparing the way for future missionaries. He served as interpreter for the East India Company (beginning in 1809) and for two British government missions to China. But in fulfillment of his calling, Morrison and his colleague William Milne completed and published the Bible in Chinese in 1823. He also authored nearly forty other works in Chinese and English, plus many articles in periodicals. Other than the Bible, his best-known publication was his six-volume *A Dictionary of the Chinese Language* (1815–22).

Morrison and Milne also established the Anglo-Chinese College in Malacca in 1818, with the dual purpose of providing Chinese-language training for future missionaries and educating local boys, a number of whom played significant roles in later Chinese history.

Recognized by scholars as a leading Sinologue, Morrison remained at heart a missionary fulfilling his calling to prepare the way for others. His plea to the AMERICAN BOARD OF COMMISSIONERS FOR FOREIGN MISSIONS led to the appointment of Elijah Coleman Bridgman as the first American missionary to China. One of his earliest co-workers, Leang Afa [Liang Fa], became known as the "first Chinese evangelist." While he had fewer than a dozen converts directly attributable to his work, Morrison gave his life in the conviction that he was laying the necessary groundwork for later effective missionary work in China. Clearly, his attribution as "Father of Protestant Missions in China" is well deserved.

J. BARTON STARR

Bibliography. M. Broomhall, *Robert Morrison: A Master-Builder;* E. A. Morrison, *Memoirs of the Life and Labours of Robert Morrison, D.D.,* 2 vols.

Morton, John (1839–1912). Canadian missionary to Trinidad. Born in Pictou county, Nova Scotia, to Scottish immigrants, Morton was educated at the Presbyterian Free Church College in Halifax and ordained as pastor of a Presbyterian church, Bridgewater, Nova Scotia, in 1861. Visiting the West Indies for his health he was moved by the deplorable condition of East Indian indentured laborers working on the sugar plantations. Sent by the Synod of the Maritimes, from 1868 until his death he led the Canadian Presbyterian Mission to the East Indians in Trinidad. He and his wife had to learn Hindi and Urdu to communicate with the people. When other missionaries arrived, the work expanded to Guyana, St. Lucia, Grenada, and Jamaica, and by 1873 they were operating twelve schools, which produced civic as well as church leaders. The first indigenous pastors were ordained in 1882. Morton's missiological methodology effectively combined education with evangelism; he started day schools, a teachers' college, and a theological college. His work resulted in a continuing viable mission and small self-supporting churches. By 1925 there were 101 places of worship and almost 12,000 members in Trinidad alone. Today they are part of the Presbyterian Church in Trinidad and Grenada, related to the United Church of Canada.

ALBERT H. FREUNDT JR.

Bibliography. I. Hamid, *A History of the Presbyterian Church in Trinidad 1868–1968: The Struggles of a Church in Colonial Captivity;* S. E. Morton, ed., *John Morton of Trinidad;* G. S. Mount, *Presbyterian Missions to Trinidad and Puerto Rico.*

Mother Teresa (1910–97). Yugoslavian social worker and missionary in India. Mother Teresa has become one of the most accepted and celebrated missionaries in the modern world, having been honored with the inaugural John XIII Peace Prize (1971), the inaugural Templeton Prize (1973), and the Nobel Peace Prize (1979).

Born in Skopje, Yugoslavia, as Agnes Gonxha Bojaxhiu in 1910 into an Albanian peasant family, at eighteen she joined Loreto Nuns. She came to Calcutta, where she taught at Loreto Convent High School for seventeen years. God called her as she was traveling by train to a Himalayan retreat in 1946 to give up everything and follow him to the slums to serve him among the poorest of the poor. Two years later she left the convent and started the Missionary of Charity Order, which began its first children's home in 1955 and its first leprosarium in 1957. The ministry now includes schools, food distribution centers, and AIDS hospices worldwide.

By the 1960s, nine foundations were established in other countries, and by 1975 there were more than a thousand sisters spread out all over the world. After an interview with Malcolm Muggeridge for British Broadcasting, she became an international celebrity. In recent years Missionaries of Charity has grown to over three thousand sisters and four hundred brothers.

Mother Teresa is a true model of Christian love in action. She was well accepted by all religious and political groups. She did not make an issue about people getting converted, but she shared Christ through her life and mission. Her life and work was her testimony for Christ. After her death, she was honored by an Indian state funeral with dignitaries from around the world present.

SAKHI ATHYAL

Bibliography. J. L. Gonzalez-Balado and J. N. Play-foot, *My Life for the Poor;* E. LeJoly, *Mother Teresa of Calcutta: A Biography;* R. Serrou, *Teresa of Calcutta: A Pictoral Biography.*

Motive, Motivation. One's motives for seeking missionary service must be correct ones. Some Christians are fascinated with the romance of travel, the idea that missions is the highest form of Christian service, the intrigue of another culture, or the desire to do good. These are all inadequate motives, which pale when compared with the centrality of biblical motives.

The missionary is one who is "sent." Although humans are involved in the process, the missionary must sense that the Holy Spirit is sending him or her.

God's dealings with Abraham (Gen. 12:2–3) are an early biblical indication that God desires to call, bless, and send his people, so that "all peoples on earth will be blessed" through them. This is repeatedly indicated to Abraham (Gen. 18:18; 22:16–18), as well as to Isaac (Gen. 26:4) and Jacob (Gen. 28:13–14). It is apparent that God did not intend Israel to be the sole recipient of his grace and love. Rather, Israel was to be a channel and a conduit through which his love could flow "to all nations on earth." At high moments in Israel's history, this focus was renewed (1 Kings 8:43; Ps. 96:3).

The five GREAT COMMISSION passages of the New Testament give us strong motivation for mission. Even Jesus' disciples finally caught on. Peter, in Acts 3:25, points back to God's promise to Abraham: "Through your offspring all peoples on earth will be blessed." Paul echoes the same thought in Galatians 3:8. It is apparent that God's plan has always been to wrap his message up in his people and then send them to reach others. This is the bedrock motivation for mission. We go in obedience to his will.

Another motivation that has propelled Christians to missionary service has been the needs of the world. The number of UNREACHED PEOPLES is a stimulus to missionary activity. Other Christians have been moved to do missionary work because of the hunger, sickness, or poverty around the globe. Acts 13:1–4 indicates that leadership in the church has a role to play (under the direction of the Holy Spirit) in setting apart persons for missionary service.

God's guidance to individuals in the form of a MISSIONARY CALLING is also a powerful motivation for mission. As he did with Abraham, so God still speaks to individuals. The nature of a call is the subject of great debate. Certainly we may say that such a call varies among people. For some it may come as a thunderclap; for others, it comes like the gradual dawning of a new day. However it is defined, most churches and mission agencies desire that a person should have a clear sense that God is leading him or her to apply for missionary service. This motivation often is the only anchor that will hold the new missionary steady during the dark testing times of CULTURE SHOCK and other problems on the field.

Biblical motives must be central for missions. The needs of the world may beckon us, the romance of other cultures may intrigue us, but in the end the primary motivation for mission must be because "Christ's love compels us" (2 Cor. 5:14).

CHARLES R. GAILEY

Bibliography. P. A. Beals, *A People For His Name;* C. Van Engen, *Mission on the Way.*

Mott, John Raleigh (1865–1955). American missionary promoter and ecumenical leader. Born into a Methodist family in Sullivan County, New York, he graduated from Upper Iowa and Cornell universities, was converted during his student days, and pledged himself to missionary service (1886). He was a YMCA secretary (1888–1915), co-founder and chair of the STUDENT VOLUNTEER MOVEMENT (1888–1920), prime mover in establishing the World Student Christian Federation (1895), and chair of the WORLD MISSIONARY CONFERENCE (Edinburgh, 1910). Mott traveled two million miles enthusiastically, his motto, "With God anywhere, without him, not over the threshold." He acquired an immense knowledge of the missionary enterprise worldwide, encouraging students and fieldworkers and setting up national councils of churches. In 1923 a Japanese Christian leader called him "father of the young people of the world." John R. Mott was adept at spotting and nurturing recruits, was much respected by political heads at home and abroad (he once spoke to three U.S. presidents—Taft, Coolidge, Wilson—in a day), labored tirelessly for prisoners of war and ORPHANAGE MISSION WORK, and could extract large donations from the American rich (Rockefeller funds established the Missionary Research Library). He was chair of the INTERNATIONAL MISSIONARY COUNCIL (1921–41) and presided over the JERUSALEM MISSIONARY CONFERENCE (1928). In 1935 a future archbishop of Canterbury declared, "He led us then; he leads us still." In 1946 he shared the Nobel Peace Prize; in 1948 the newly formed WORLD COUNCIL OF CHURCHES named him honorary president. But the Methodist layman who had declined prestigious academic and political posts wanted to be remembered simply as an evangelist.

His many works included *The Evangelization of the World in This Generation* (1910) and *Addresses and Papers* (6 vols., 1946–47).

J. D. DOUGLAS

Bibliography. B. Mathews, *John R. Mott, World Citizen;* C. H. Hopkins, *John R. Mott, 1865–1955: A Biography.*

Mozambique *(Est. 2000 pop.: 18,991,000; 801,590 sq. km. [309,494 sq. mi.]).* Mozambique is a Portuguese-speaking nation in southern Africa. Located in the east side of the continent bordering the Indian Ocean, the country encompasses 38 ethnic groups and 24 major vernacular languages. Religiously, 42 percent profess Christianity, 40 percent are adherents of traditional religions, 13 percent follow Islam, and 5 percent are nonreligious.

After nearly five hundred years of Portuguese colonial rule, the country became independent in 1975, under a Marxist regime. As the Portuguese left the country, civil war broke out and the country experienced its worst drought of the century. All these factors combined brought the country to a virtual collapse with almost all infrastructure destroyed. By October 1992 a peace accord between the anti-communist guerrilla movement and the government was signed in Rome. The guerrilla movement became the opposition party. In the following year Mozambique had its first multiparty elections.

Catholicism was brought to Mozambique by Portuguese Dominicans in the early sixteenth century. Protestantism arrived in the form of ABCFM missionaries in 1879. Shortly thereafter Methodists and Presbyterians began their work. After World War I Baptists, Pentecostals, Nazarenes, and Adventists joined the effort. After independence all forms of religion were suppressed by the communist state. As a result of civil war, which was aggravated by a vicious cycle of drought and floodings, the country spiraled toward economic collapse. As foreign aid started pouring in from Christian and Muslim agencies, the government relaxed its pressure on all religious groups, and in fact, called on them for help. By 1990 there was general religious freedom.

Mozambique is a melting pot for the world of mission agencies. The missionaries, now around four hundred belonging to forty-seven agencies, have to compete with the growing number of cults such as the Jehovah's Witnesses. The Protestant mission agencies with the largest number of missionaries are African Inland Mission, Youth With a Mission, and Africa Evangelical Fellowship. Besides the strong Catholic presence, Islam is particularly viable in the northern part of the country. In addition to radio and the JESUS FILM, a major area for missionary activity has been that of relief work. The large number of orphans, people ravaged by war, and unemployed youth constitute an important mission field.

Mission agencies and missionaries have a great task before them in Mozambique. One factor is an 80 percent illiteracy rate, another the paucity of the Scriptures available in local languages. But the major force against Christianity is doubtless the ever increasing attempt by Muslims to Islamicize the country. Mosques are being built in many locations and by 1996 the Muslims had two official holidays in the national calendar. Finally, there is an urgent need for instilling a missionary vision among Mozambiquian Christians to reach out to their own people. To date only a handful of Mozambiquians have gone out as missionaries, and this remains an unrealized potential for the church in Mozambique.

JARBAS DASILVA

Bibliography. A. Helgesson, *Church, State, and People in Mozambique;* V. W. Macy, *Discovery Under the Southern Cross;* P. Thompson, *Life Out of Death in Mozambique.*

Müller, George (1805–98). German faith missions advocate and founder of orphanages. Born in Prussia, Müller was converted and awakened to missions while a university student at Halle. He went to England to do mission work among the Jews and there joined the renewal movement within British Protestantism that became the Plymouth Brethren. He ended his connection with the London Society for Promoting Christianity among the Jews and served as pastor in Teignmouth, where he established his lifelong practice of accepting no salary, instead trusting God for his needs. In 1832 he moved to Bristol, where he lived the rest of his life. In 1834 Müller founded the Scriptural Knowledge Institution for Home and Abroad with the purposes of establishing day schools, Sunday schools, and adult schools for teaching the Bible, distributing Bibles, and supporting mission work. Müller achieved fame for founding the Bristol ORPHANAGE MISSION WORK. His greater contribution, however, was the example of his life of faith and prayer. He determined not to ask for support and instead prayed for the needs of the orphan homes and missions, trusting that God would meet those needs without his prompting others to give. By the end of his life, Müller had built five orphanages; cared for 120,000 children; preached in forty-two countries; raised a quarter million pounds for missions; and raised almost 2.5 million pounds altogether—all by faith.

DONALD R. DUNAVANT

Bibliography. A. T. Pierson, *George Müller of Bristol and His Witness to a Prayer Hearing God.*

Murray, Andrew (1828–1917). South African devotional writer and promoter of missionary awakening. He was born in 1828 in Graaff-Reinet, South Africa, to a Scottish minister and his wife. The Christ-centered home in which he was reared proved to be a launching pad for his own life of ministry both in South Africa and around the globe. During his time of theological training at Utrecht University in Holland, he and his brother John helped form a student missionary society. Ordained at age twenty, Murray returned to South Africa in 1848, where he would serve as a pastor until 1906. His years of service were spent in Bloemfontein, Worcester, Cape Town, and Wellington, where he labored for thirty-five years. During his pastorates he was also an impassioned itinerant evangelist in the Transvaal and other locations along the Cape, where he ministered to immigrants.

In addition to speaking he was active in establishing centers for higher education. He helped found the University College of Orange Free State in 1856, the Stellenbosch Theological Seminary in 1857, the Huguenot Seminary in 1874, and the Wellington Missionary Training Institute in 1877. The establishment of the latter was a reflection of his belief that missions was "the chief end of the church." His desire to see the lost reached and the believer discipled led to his cofounding and appointment as the president of the South Africa General Mission (now AFRICA EVANGELICAL FELLOWSHIP) in 1889, a position he held until his death in 1917. In his final twelve years, he was also responsible for introducing the KESWICK spirit into South Africa and spent much of his time participating in evangelistic meetings in the Western world. Murray's 240 writings challenged and inspired many to a deeper walk with Christ. *With Christ in the School of Prayer* and *Abide in Christ* continue to do so today.

WENDY S. LARSON

Bibliography. W. M. Douglas, *Andrew Murray and His Message;* J. Du Plessis, *The Life of Andrew Murray of South Africa;* P. Hassing, *CDCWM,* p. 428.

Music. *See* ETHNOMUSICOLOGY; SOCIOLOGY OF MUSIC.

Muslim Mission Work. Muhammad, the prophet of Islam, died in A.D. 632. From that point on the conflict between the world's two largest monotheistic religions (Christianity and Islam) has raged on unabated. Each persuasion has a great commission to fulfill. Each is convinced it is the unique path to God. Each declares that truth is revealed only in its scriptures. Thus the stage is set for mutual antagonism.

Certain critical historical events have caused Muslims to be resistant to the Christian message. The CRUSADES of the twelfth and thirteenth centuries were a terrible violation of basic human rights. Even though these events took place hundreds of years ago, Muslims today are still angry concerning the outrages against their ancestors.

Between 1700 and 1960, colonialists from the so-called Christian West reigned over much of the Muslim world. Missionaries took advantage of friendly rulers to gain permission to preach Christianity. Muslims in these countries had no recourse to legal procedures by which to expel missionaries.

The issue of Palestine came to the fore in 1948 as the United Nations, with the stroke of a pen, mandated the new state of Israel into existence. Muslims had been living in Palestine for over thirteen hundred years. What right, they asked, did the world have to radically change the political status of their land? Jihad was their declared response.

Lastly, the antagonism between Christianity and Islam has been enhanced by the Muslims' perception of Christians as pig eaters, wine drinkers, and perpetual adulterers. Western media have presented a powerful depiction of moral depravity in countries where most of the citizens would declare themselves to be Christians.

Muslims do not generally make a distinction between nominal Christians and practicing Christians. They look upon the 1.8 billion as one community. Accordingly, Christians are to be indicted as a whole for all of the reasons we have listed. Thus the task of Muslim evangelism is made exceedingly difficult, quite apart from theological distinctives.

Historically, Christian outreaches among Muslims made little impact prior to the mid-1960s. A few names stand out as exceptions; RAYMOND LULL (c. 1235–1315); HENRY MARTYN (1781–1812); and SAMUEL ZWEMER (1867–1952). But even these giants of faith failed to see large numbers of Muslims come to Christian belief through their evangelistic efforts.

Indonesia, the country with the world's largest Muslim population (in excess of 170 million), has produced the greatest number of converts to Christianity. In the 1960s, as a result of an uprising against communism, hundreds of thousands of Muslims embraced Christianity. Even today there continues to be a significant rate of conversion, especially on the island of Java. Other countries where there have been large numbers of converts to Christianity include Bangladesh and Ethiopia. Overall, however, there are few conversions to Christianity. Countries like Saudi Arabia, Mauritania, Algeria, and Afghanistan have produced but a small number of converts.

Among the evangelical missions emphasizing outreach among Muslims are the Southern Baptist Foreign Mission Board, Frontiers, TEAM, SIM, and Interserve. Frontiers is unique in that the mission force of five hundred adults is totally focused on Muslim evangelism. Almost all of their personnel are engaged in tentmaker ministries that allow them opportunity for personal witness.

The Samuel Zwemer Institute was founded in 1978 by Don McCurry. This small organization has produced a number of research projects related to the world of Islam. Fuller Theological Seminary offers the master's and Ph.D. degrees in Muslim studies. Columbia International University inaugurated a master's program in Islamics in 1996. Other Bible colleges and seminaries offer specialized courses on Islam. International Missions, Inc., administers a practical-cum-academic summer program geared to Muslim outreach.

One of the more innovative departures from traditional evangelistic methodology was pioneered by International Christian Fellowship (ICF), which merged with SIM in 1989. In the mid-1970s an ICF team of twenty-seven missionaries from six nations introduced a contextualized style of Muslim evangelism in Bangladesh. Their threefold goal was to (1) see a large number of Muslims accept Christ, (2) disciple these believers within their social and cultural context, and (3) minimize financial assistance to the converts. The approach included wearing local Muslim-style clothing, living in simple rented accommodations, adopting certain Muslim vocabulary, following a general pattern of Islamic worship styles, writing and designing attractive literature that would be appreciated and easily understood by the target Muslim community, initially seeking to win male heads of families to Christ, avoiding ministries that required high-profile institutions, and engaging in discipleship of new believers who would be encouraged to remain within their own community. This style of outreach has produced thousands of Muslim converts to Christianity in Bangladesh. Various missions and church bodies working both in Bangladesh and in other Muslim countries have incorporated segments of this methodology into their evangelistic strategy. Critics have averred that such contextualization is extremely vulnerable to syncretism. Most advocates of the new paradigm would agree and have taken steps to minimize this possibility.

Islamic shari'a law has been partially implemented in a number of Muslim countries. This legal system strongly opposes conversion from Islam to Christianity. In certain nations converts have been sentenced to death. This strict interpretation of shari'a law generates fear and inhibits all but the most courageous from any serious investigation of Christian claims to truth.

Arab oil money has fueled a new ethos of excitement and optimism within the Muslim world. New mosques are being built in many countries. Muslim missionaries from Egypt and Pakistan can be found in remote villages of Asia. Jobs are being offered to poor Christians who are willing to convert to Islam. Muslim organizations are surfacing in much of the Two-Thirds World. Their goal is to propagate Islam while assisting the poor. Muslim spokespersons have attributed their recent successes in evangelizing to their having learned the techniques that Christians have been using for decades.

Those dedicated to Muslim outreach face many challenges in the contemporary world. Yet more Muslims have probably turned to Christ in the past three decades than in any similar period throughout all of history.

PHIL PARSHALL

Bibliography. N. L. Geisler and A. Saleeb, *Answering Islam;* G. Livingstone, *Planting Churches in Muslim Cities;* D. M. McCurry, ed., *The Gospel and Islam: A 1978 Compendium;* B. Musk, *The Unseen Face of Islam;* P. Parshall, *New Paths in Muslim Evangelism;* J. D. Woodberry, ed., *Muslims and Christians on the Emmaus Road.*

Muslim. *See* ISLAM, MUSLIM.

Myanmar *(Est. 2000 pop.: 51,539,000; 676,578 sq. km. [261,227 sq. mi.]).* Myanmar, known as Burma before 1989, is an ancient nation in the Indochina peninsula. It shares borders with five nations: Bangladesh, India, China, Laos, and Thailand. Its long southern coastal plain stretches along the Bay of Bengal and Andaman Sea. Until recently, it has been relatively insulated from its neighbors in political and religious development.

The population is comprised of some 135 ethnic groups speaking 106 languages. The eight major ethnic groups and their percentage of the total population are: Bamar (69), Shan (8.5), Kayin (6.2), Rakhine (4.5), Mon (2.4), Chin (2.2), Kachin (1.4), and Kayah (0.4). There are 314 townships and 13,751 villages. The urban population is 24.81%, and the literacy rate is 66.5%.

The major religions in Myanmar are Buddhism (89.4%), Christianity (4.9%), Islam (3.9%), Hinduism (0.5%), and animism (1.2%). Small numbers practice Confucianism, Judaism, and Laipianism, a local religion.

The nation's political history can be divided into the times of the monarchy (1044–1855), colonialism (1824–1947), parliamentary democracy (1948–62), and the socialist regime (1962–88). Foreign agents and missionaries were expelled in 1966, during the socialist regime. Since 1988, Myanmar has been under military rule called the State Law and Order Restoration Council.

Churches in Myanmar are indigenous and steadily growing. More than thirty denominations and some parachurch movements are carrying out the mission tasks through three main streams: Catholic, Conciliar, and Evangelical-Pentecostal.

Portuguese traders introduced Roman Catholic Christianity to Myanmar around 1500. A Franciscan priest arrived at Bago with the traders in 1554, but had no success in gaining converts among the local population. Evangelization began when priests Calchi and Joseph Vittoni came to Thanlyin in 1721 and obtained permission from King Taninganwe (1714–83) for the propagation of the gospel.

Protestant Christianity was introduced to Myanmar by English Baptist missionaries James Chater, Richard Mardon, and Felix Carey in 1807, followed by the American Baptist missionaries ADONIRAM and ANN JUDSON in 1813. Today the Baptist Conference is the largest single Christian denomination in Myanmar, with over one million members. Roman Catholics, with an estimated 520,000 members, are the second largest.

CHIN KHUA KHAI

Bibliography. D. Barrett, *WCE;* B. B. Grimes, *Ethnologue;* J. Guennou, *NCE,* 2:901–2; M. Shwe Wa, *Burma Baptist Chronicle;* R. Taylor, *The State in Burma;* S. Tin, *Statistical Year Book of Myanmar.*

Myanmar Mission Boards and Agencies. There are two major streams of Protestant missionary efforts in Myanmar. The first is that of conciliar mission work, which is a joint effort of eleven mainline Protestant churches united in the Myanmar Council of Churches related to the WORLD COUNCIL OF CHURCHES. The Regional Council for Burma was formed in 1914, and renamed the Burma Christian Council in 1949 and the Burma Council of Churches in 1975. Today, Myanmar Baptist Convention, Methodists, and Presbyterians, through their mission boards and societies, are sending missionaries to the unreached areas. Evangelistic efforts since the 1970s, such as "Chins for Christ in One Century" and "Kachin Gideon Band-3/330," have been the most dynamic. The Conciliar mission stream emphasizes ecumenicity, development, and theological education.

Under the Evangelical-Pentecostal stream are seventeen denominations and some parachurch movements, ranging in persuasion from fundamentalistic to charismatic. The Myanmar Evangelical Christian Fellowship was organized in 1984. Assemblies of God, the fastest growing and third largest denomination in the country with a membership of 67,648, began in 1930 and is a strong mission church. The other denominations in this stream have come into existence as the result of renewal, evangelism, and church planting. The renewal movement among the Zomi Chin during the past three decades has resulted in mission across cultures. Also, parachurch movements such as Campus Crusade, Witnessing for Christ, Every Home for Christ, God's Trio Partners, Gospel for the Nation, and Myanmar Church Planting Mission all help fulfill the evangelistic mandate. The churches in this stream emphasize evangelism, renewal, church planting, and theological education in their missionary efforts.

In addition to these streams, the Myanmar Bible Society, Christian Literature Society, and Myanmar Blind Mission Fellowship all work independently with their own mission boards.

CHIN KHUA KHAI

SEE ALSO Asian Mission Boards and Societies.

Bibliography. D. Barrett, *WCE;* W. C. B. Purser, *Christian Missions in Burma; Statistics of Churches in Myanmar* (1995–1996); M. Shwe Wa, *Burma Baptist Chronicle;* S. Tin, *Statistical Year Book of Myanmar.*

Mystic, Mysticism. Mystical experience is common to most religions, although it assumes various forms in different traditions. Mysticism occurs in theistic contexts (Judaism, Christianity, Islam, theistic Hinduism), monistic traditions (philosophical Taoism, some forms of Hinduism and Buddhism), pantheistic traditions (Shinto), and even naturalistic contexts (nature mysticism). Mystical experience occurs in explicitly atheistic traditions such as Jainism and Zen Buddhism as well.

Understood in a general sense, mysticism has a long history in Christianity. Mystics such as Bernard of Clairvaux (d. 1153), Meister Eckhart (d. 1327), Teresa of Avila (d. 1582), and John of the Cross (d. 1591) all in varying ways gave testimony to experiences of immediate awareness of a special intimacy with God transcending normal categories. A distinction is sometimes made between numinous experiences (the experience of "the Other" or "the Holy" in theistic contexts) and mystical experiences (contemplative experiences associated with Hinduism and Buddhism in which one realizes the transcendent or ultimate by "looking within"). Christian mysticism would fall in the former category.

There are some phenomenological similarities between mystical reports from various cultures and religious traditions, although significantly different doctrinal claims are made on the basis of these experiences within the relevant traditions. Mystical experiences are generally characterized by an emphasis on the inadequacy of human language and rational categories to communicate ultimate reality; a sense of unity between the subject and object of experience; and a noetic quality (one attains superior insight into reality as a result of the experience). Central to mysticism is the notion of a direct, unmediated encounter with the ultimate or transcendent. In Hinduism and Buddhism mystical experience is cultivated through rigorous physical/psychic discipline (*yoga*).

Thinkers such as A. Huxley and S. Radhakrishnan have popularized the notion that mystical experience is a common factor in all major religions and forms the essential core of true religion.

However, in spite of some similarities in language in mystical reports, it is clear that mystics tend to interpret their experiences in light of the religious and theological traditions in which they participate. Thus Christian mystics claim to encounter God the Holy Trinity; Advaita Vedanta Hindus seek the identity between the self and Brahman; and Zen Buddhists, denying the substantial reality of both the self and a transcendent Being, claim direct access to Emptiness *(sunyata)*. The ontological implications of these experiences are mutually incompatible: the triune God of Christianity is quite different from nirvana Brahman, and both are incompatible with the insubstantial nature of Emptiness in Buddhism.

There is something of significant value in the mystical traditions. Mysticism reminds us of the limits of human knowledge; there is much about God that remains mysterious and unknown. It also reminds us of the importance of a dynamic, experiential dimension to faith. However, mysticism also presents special challenges to the Christian church. Cultures impacted by mysticism tend to emphasize intuitive religious experience and to regard conceptual knowledge and verbal expressions of religious truth with suspicion. Intuitive experience takes priority over explicit beliefs and doctrines. But at the heart of Christian faith is belief that God has revealed himself definitively in an understandable manner in the Scriptures, and that what we believe has a direct bearing on our salvation. The challenge for the church in contexts impacted by mysticism, then, is to recognize human limitations and the need for profound personal experience of God while also maintaining that all that is necessary for salvation and godly living has been revealed to us in God's Word.

HAROLD A. NETLAND

Bibliography. W. Corduan, *Mysticism: An Evangelical Option?;* W. James, *The Varieties of Religious Experience;* S. Katz, ed., *Mysticism and Philosophical Analysis;* G. Parrinder, *Mysticism in the World's Religions;* W. Wainwright, *Mysticism: A Study of Its Nature, Cognitive Value and Moral Implications.*

Myth, Mythology. The word "myth" in popular parlance connotes fiction or untruth. However, for the majority of the world's people, just as for the people of biblical times, mythology acts as a root metaphor for reality. While not always based on fact as seen from a rationalist viewpoint, myth is truth from the perspective of people for whom it establishes identity—it is their scripture.

Every society has myths at some level: epics that proclaim cosmic origins; folklore depicting family, cultural or national events, and heroes; etiological stories to explain how some things came to be; and fairy tales that entertain while passing moral value to the next generation.

Mythology can serve as a people's history and a rationale for their beliefs and values. It provides intellectual edification by communicating particular cultural lessons or knowledge. Mythology may also be used to validate appropriate behavior or to chastise inappropriate behavior. Passed down through the generations as oral literature or ritual drama, myth provides a sense of identity and place. The message may be encased in a series of stories organized to present a moral (cultural objectives and values) in acceptable forms.

If missionaries understand a people's mythology, they can present biblical themes in a similar style that will catch people's attention and relate God's wisdom to daily living. A people's acquaintance with epic could be used to introduce Genesis: similarly, a variety of mythic forms offer parallels to the parables of Jesus. Just as people respond to the truth of myth, they may come to faith in God who approaches human beings in the context of their myth.

R. Daniel Shaw

Bibliography. A. Dunes, *The Study of Folklore;* B. Malinowski, *Myth in Primitive Psychology;* R. D. Shaw, *Practical Anthropology* 19 (1972): 129–32.

Nairobi Assembly (1975). *See* WORLD COUNCIL OF CHURCHES ASSEMBLIES.

Namibia *(Est. 2000 pop.: 1,752,000; 824,292 sq. km. [318,259 sq. mi.]).* Namibia is thinly populated, with just over two individuals per square mile. English is the official language, though Afrikaans is the common language for most of the population. The largest group is the Ovambo (50%); other groups are the Damara (9%); Okovango (about 7%); and the Herero (7%). Those of European descent include the Afrikaaner (8%), German (3%), and English (1%).

Only one percent of the hot, dry desert land is arable, though half of the population depend on subsistence agriculture, primarily livestock. There are abundant mineral resources, and rich fisheries on its Atlantic shore. The urban population is increasing at more than double the general population increase. About 40 percent of the people are in urban areas, primarily in the capital, Windhoek. The resulting urban slums create a challenge for the churches.

The gospel entered what was then known as Southwest Africa in 1842 through the Rhenish Mission (German Lutheran). In the first fifty years, about four thousand members were gained. The Finnish Lutherans entered in 1870; in its first forty years, its churches had two thousand baptized Christians. The great growth of both of these groups came under the colonial rule of Germany, then South Africa, in a pattern similar to much of sub-Saharan Africa.

COLONIALISM meant stability and security for development of a diverse and extensive ministry. The Finnish Mission developed a large missionary and African staff for its ministry through ten high schools, ninety elementary schools, nine hospitals, and eleven dispensaries. By 1955, there were over two hundred thousand members in its associated church. Despite the interruptions of World War I and its aftermath, the Rhenish Mission had comparable growth.

Nearing the end of the twentieth century, more than 50 percent of the population were members of the United Evangelical Church of Southwest Africa, formed in 1970 by union of the works related to the Rhenish Mission and the Finnish Lutheran Mission. Namibia is the only country in Africa with a Lutheran population majority. Another 20 percent of Namibians are members of the Anglican Church, several indigenous churches, and the predominantly white Dutch Reformed Church. Approximately 15 percent are Roman Catholics. As a nation, Namibia has the highest percentage of Christians in Africa, despite increasing nominalism in the last decades of the twentieth century.

A German colony from 1884 to 1919, Namibia was administered and then annexed by South Africa (1949). There was much unrest under South African rule. Opposition to apartheid was led by the churches of Namibia, though they were divided on the issue of support for the guerrilla movement fighting for Namibian independence.

In 1971, African leaders of the United Evangelical Church of Southwest Africa officially condemned apartheid, and later called for independence. They were supported by Anglican and Catholic leaders. SWAPO, the Southwest Africa Peoples' Organization, identified three necessary elements of a successful revolution: church workers and clergy, workers in the towns, and guerrillas fighting in the bush. The South African government responded by expelling some foreign Christian workers and refusing entry to others.

After a long war that left much unemployment and many refugees, independence was achieved in 1990. Because of their identification with the liberation struggle, the major churches have the wide acceptance necessary to lead Namibia's diverse groups to reconciliation after the ravages of apartheid and war. Each week, the secular government has given the churches sixty hours of radio time on the national network.

Since 1970, several North American-based evangelical and Pentecostal missions have begun work in Namibia. Together, their memberships are less than 3 percent of Namibians. Two evangelical seminaries and specialized ministries in radio and to children contribute to revitalizing witness in the major church bodies. There are at least three missions based in Namibia, sending personnel (30 to 35 in 1998) to various parts of Namibia and Belgium, South Africa, and Netherlands.

DONALD K. SMITH

Bibliography. J. L. De Vries, *Mission and Colonialism in Namibia;* R. J. Enquist, *Namibia: Land of Tears, Land of Promise;* P. Johnstone, *OW;* P. Katjavivi, P. Frostin, and K. Mbuende, eds., *Church and Liberation in Namibia.*

Nation, Nation-Building, Nationalism. A nation is a significant group of people who are so identified with one another in terms of common language, ancestry, history, religion, and culture that they are recognized by others as a distinct entity.

Nationalism is a term that can simply express such a people's sense of belonging together as a nation, with appropriate pride and loyalty to that nation's history and culture. More commonly, however, it is used to refer to the political perspective on international relationships and programs that places loyalty to one's nation as the highest of human virtues. It therefore describes the ideologies that nurture national self-consciousness and the desire for national self-determination.

Although people have always been devoted to their native soil and to the traditions of their ancestors, it was only in the eighteenth century that what we now call "nationalism" came to be recognized as a distinct and potent religiopolitical force with the rise of political units known as "nation-states." These came to supersede the church, city, or local lord as the focal points for the allegiance of increasing numbers of people. In other words, nations are really historical phenomena, arising out of a particular set of contexts, rather than what might be called natural expressions of human life. The American and French Revolutions are often held up as the first significant manifestations of nationalism in the Western world, and the nineteenth century is usually referred to as the age of nationalisms in Europe.

Of course, similar movements have arisen in Africa and Asia throughout the twentieth century. In its historical context, the rise of African nationalism came as part of a response to European imperialism. However, while it is possible to analyze the emerging non-Western nationalisms solely in terms of a drive toward political independence, economic viability, and cultural emancipation, this would be to vastly undervalue both the importance of the desire to establish personal and national dignity, and the influence of religious beliefs and values.

There are, of course, positive values that are bound up with the concept of nationality. The Bible teaches that God is responsible for the creation of nations (Acts 17:26), and therefore we must assume that to some extent it is right to identify with our nationality and to rejoice in it. It is also easier for properly appointed leaders to govern people who share a common commitment to the larger community. Values such as loyalty and self-sacrifice can be nurtured in a nation that takes a healthy pride in its history and identity. Each national group has developed its own culture, and has thereby made a unique contribution to the life and history of humanity. Countries such as Poland, the United Kingdom, South Africa, and the United States of America have also interwoven a deeply felt Christian conviction with nationalist ideals to produce a powerful, though not unambiguous, sense of mission in the modern world.

All of this can therefore be interpreted as a healthy expression of the inherent dignity of human culture. If individuals, as neighbors, are to love and respect one another, then surely nations should demonstrate the same mutual acceptance and encouragement. Many would see it as a Christian responsibility in the modern world to encourage the development of strong and stable democratic nations, each fully respecting and supporting the others. Such a democratic nationalism is held to benefit Christians in a pluralist world.

However, nationalism is ambivalent by nature. It can also lead to self-serving ideologies and an ambition to marginalize other nations. Nations can become so preoccupied with protecting their own interests that they disregard those of others. We should not neglect the words of Machiavelli, who epitomized the raising of the state to an end in itself: "Where it is an absolute question of the welfare of our country, we must admit of no considerations of justice or injustice, of mercy or cruelty, of praise or ignominy, but putting all else aside, must adopt whatever course will save its existence and preserve its liberty." Nationalism, when it reaches this level, leads to xenophobia. In our time, we have seen many examples of "ethnic cleansing" among peoples whose prime motive was the creation of a "pure nation."

All too often, there is a clear relationship between nationalism and racism. The National Front of Britain published a book in 1977 in which one of its leaders wrote that "racialism is the only scientific and logical basis for nationalism. We seek to preserve the identity of the British nation." Missiologists are deeply concerned about this nationalistic rationalizing of the desire to marginalize and dominate others, since sin and evil are woven into the fabric of human nature and relationships.

Christian countries and their governments have not been free from the potent interplay of religion and politics in the temptation to dominate other peoples, as in, for example, the marriage between the interests of Christian missions and governmental colonialists in the nineteenth century.

What is more, many Christians would claim, since all people are made in God's image, the fact of a common humanity should be more important than differences based on race or nationality. The Bible is clear that God's love and commitment are given to all people, regardless of nationality or any other human distinction, and it presents the eschatological context for redeemed humanity as a united congregation of people of every nation (Rev. 7:9). Every Christian has a double responsibility in terms of his or her call to mission: as a citizen, to be "the salt of the earth," and as an evangelist, to be "the light of the world" (Matt. 5:13–16). Our nations and their governments, like all authorities, are part of God's provision for his world (Rom. 13:1–7), but they are also accountable to him (Amos 1–2), and Christians must give absolute loyalty to God (Matt. 4:8–10; Acts 4:18–20; Rev. 13).

Missiology has the task of helping churches recognize this, and to clearly distinguish between the desire to obey the Great Commission and the desire to dominate or inappropriately influence others.

WALTER RIGGANS

SEE ALSO Church and State; Colonialism; Ethnocentrism; Human Rights; Racism.

Bibliography. F. Catherwood, *Christian Arena* 43 (1990); L. Holmes, ed., *Church and Nationhood;* E. Sahliyeh, ed., *Religious Resurgence and Politics in The Contemporary World;* M. H. Tanenbaum and R. J. Zwi Werblowski, eds., *The Jerusalem Colloquium on Religion, Peoplehood, Nation and Land;* J. Verkuyl, *Break Down the Walls.*

Nationalism. *See* NATION, NATION-BUILDING, NATIONALISM.

Nationalization. *See* INDIGENIZATION.

Native American Religions. *See* INDIGENOUS AMERICAN RELIGIONS.

Nativistic Movements. *See* NEW RELIGIOUS MOVEMENTS.

Nauru *(Est. 2000 pop.: 12,000; 21 sq. km. [8 sq. mi.]).* A single island in Oceania between the Solomon Islands and Kiribati, Nauru achieved independence in 1968 after being a German colony, an Australian territory, and a United Nations trust territory. In 1993 it was estimated that 90.4 percent of the population was Christian (60% Protestant, 30% Catholic, 0.4% marginal). The largest churches are the Nauruan Protestant (Congregational) Church (1888) and the Anglican Church, though the Pentecostal Nauru Independent Church is growing quickly through evangelistic tools such as the JESUS FILM.

A. SCOTT MOREAU

Nee, Watchman (Ni Tuo-sheng) (1903–72). Chinese preacher and author. Born in Swatow, China, Nee was converted while a student at Trinity College, Fuzhou. He was influenced by missionary Margaret Barber, and the writings of Jeanne de la Motte Guyon (1648–1717), G. M. Pember, Robert Govett, D. M. Panton, and Jessie Penn-Lewis. From 1926 to 1928 Nee wrote *The Spiritual Man,* a spiritual compendium based on the trichotomous view of man as body, soul, and spirit. In 1928 he moved to Shanghai, and there edited *The Revival, The Bible Record,* and in 1930, *The Little Flock Hymnal.* In 1933 the "London Group" Brethren invited Nee to visit Britain, but broke fellowship with him because Nee attempted to visit T. Austin-Sparks (who deeply influenced his theology) while in London. Nee built his movement of "Assembly Hall" congregations and evangelistic efforts known as "the work," which grew rapidly in the 1930s and 1940s. In 1938 he preached in Europe; his messages in Helsingor, Denmark, were later transcribed as *The Normal Christian Life.* His theology is characterized by a heavy emphasis on man as body, soul, and spirit; he calls Christians to be broken in spirit so that the Spirit of God may be released in them. He taught that there should be one church per location; denominational connections are antibiblical. He was later imprisoned by the communist government. He deeply influenced the life and witness of the house churches in mainland China, and numerous Christians outside China. One of his followers, Witness Lee, developed his thought further into the aberration known as the "Local Church Movement," based in the United States.

SAMUEL LING

Bibliography. B. V. James, *TCDCB,* p. 273; A. I. Kinnear, *Against the Tide: The Story of Watchman Nee.*

Neill, Stephen Charles (1900–1984). Scottish mission scholar and missionary to India. Born in Edinburgh to second-generation evangelical Bengal missionary parents, he was converted in 1914. Educated at Trinity College, he served as a CMS missionary in India from 1924 to 1944.

In India Neill mastered the Tamil language and literary culture. He engaged in evangelistic work, dialogue with Hindus, and theological education. Along with other Tamil scholars, he worked on the revision of the Tamil Bible and in other ways promoted production of Christian literature. He also participated in church union discussions leading to the formation of the Church of South

India. His greatest lasting contribution, however, was in his writing.

Author of more than sixty-five books as well as articles and reviews, he also coauthored or coedited several volumes and was the chief editor of the *World Christian Books* series. Among Neill's best-known contributions are *A History of the Ecumenical Movement, 1517–1948* (1954), *Christian Faith and Other Faiths* (1961), *A History of Christian Missions* (1965), *Colonialism and Christian Missions* (1966), and *Concise Dictionary of the Christian World Mission* (1970). A less-known little book, *Bhakti: Hindu and Christian* (1974), indicates something of the breadth of Neill's scholarship and is of particular interest in India. At the time of his death he was engaged in writing a three-volume history of Christianity in India.

ROGER E. HEDLUND

Bibliography. M. Conway, *DEM*, p. 720; E. Jackson, *IBMR* 19 (1995): 77–80; E. Jackson, ed., *God's Apprentice: The Autobiography of Bishop Stephen Neill*; C. Lamb, *ML*, pp. 445–51.

Neo-orthodox Theology. Neo-orthodoxy identifies a broad alliance of theologians, including Karl Barth (1886–1968), Rudolph Bultmann (1884–1976), and Emil Brunner (1889–1966), who were brought together in the wake of World War I by their rejection of nineteenth-century liberal theology's optimistic quest for God in reason, history, and culture. Over against liberalism, this movement reclaimed and reworked some of the Reformation distinctives—God's absolute transcendence and holiness, the sinfulness of humankind, and Jesus Christ as the singular and unique revelation of God—and so the name, "neo-orthodoxy."

However, within a decade this coalition began fragmenting. Bultmann separated, arguing that God's revelation provides faith's self-understanding, not a knowledge of God in himself. For Barth and Brunner, however, God so assumed flesh in Jesus Christ that he has definitely revealed his very being, making possible a knowledge of God himself. Later Barth and Brunner divided over the latter's use of natural theology. In the midst of his 1934 struggle against the "German Christian" movement, which used natural theology to support Nazism, Barth issued a thundering *Nein* to Brunner's proposal. For Barth, God cannot be known outside God's revelation in Jesus Christ; nor is there a valid theological understanding of creation or sin outside this Christological context. These once allies, Barth thought, were now reverting to the path of liberalism.

Karl Barth. Barth was the leading representative of neo-orthodoxy. Through his study of Anselm (1931), Barth argued that theology has its own inner rationality in God's revelation in Jesus Christ and does not need any external justification. This insight became the central theme in his massive *Church Dogmatics*. Jesus Christ is the realization in time of God's decision from all eternity to be God for and with humanity; so in God's Word, Jesus Christ, the crucified and risen one, is contained the meaning of creation, humanity, as well as God's reconciliation to himself of us rebels. A giant in twentieth-century theology, Barth's work has profoundly affected the theology of missions.

The Relation between Revelation and Religion. According to Barth, theology can only be grounded in the Word of God, the revelation of God in Jesus Christ, as found in Scripture. Moreover, this revelation is known only through God's own act, that is, the Spirit, not through some inherent human capacity. There is no way to get from sinful humanity to God. Only God can make himself known and this God saves by grace alone! So Barth concludes that the revelation of God is the "abolition of religion." Since religion is the universal human attempt to find God, all religions, including Christianity, are manifestations of unbelief and works-righteousness (*CD* I/2:280ff.). Barth is not denying the religions' impressive human achievements, but their value as God's revelation. This critique was further developed and promoted by HENDRICK KRAEMER (1888–1965).

In view of the opposition between revelation and religion, Barth insists that missionaries must not seek for a point of contact in other religions. For the Word of God does not supplement what one already knows, but overturns our prior knowledge by requiring repentance, and reveals what we can know in no other way. Similarly, Jesus' reconciling work does not perfect the good humans already possess, but bridges the infinite chasm between the holy God and the rebellious sinner. Faith is simply accepting this fact that Christ has done for us what we cannot do for ourselves. To combine the Word of God with other religions domesticates and subverts revelation. So missions must be pursued with a sincere respect and yet also an equally sincere lack of respect for the religions.

God's Election of Jesus Christ. For Barth election is the sum of the gospel. By electing Jesus Christ, the God-man, God from all eternity determines that he is for humanity and determines humanity for himself. In Jesus Christ, God elects to take on himself the judgment that is due humanity so that all sinners are elected for glory. Simply put, election is God's great "Yes" to all humanity in Jesus Christ (*CD* II/2:94ff.). Contra Calvin and Luther, Barth rejects the notion of a double predestination grounded in an inscrutable decree, for Jesus Christ is the self-revelation of a gracious God.

Barth acknowledges that Christ's reconciling work must be subjectively appropriated through the Spirit to bear fruit. He even concedes that the sinner continually evades Christ and thus lives in danger of being condemned (*CD* IV/3:465). So the possibility exists that one may reject Jesus Christ, and through this perverse choice involuntarily bear witness to Jesus' judgment as the rejected one (*CD* II/2:321). Yet Barth insists that the believer who knows God in Jesus Christ must not assume the ultimate rejection of sinners, and should even pray for God's gracious mercy in a future universal salvation.

The Church's Mission. After discussing Christ's salvific work in his priestly and kingly offices, Barth treats Jesus as the true witness who declares his work of reconciliation and thereby fulfills his prophetic office. God's work in Jesus Christ makes possible the church's mission (*CD* IV/3:830ff.). Through the Spirit's work the church fulfills the Lord's command, "be my witnesses" (Acts 1:8).

Just as Jesus' mission was for the world, so also the church must serve the world which God reconciled to himself in Jesus Christ (2 Cor. 5:19). However, the world does not define the church's ministry. Rather the church is always a witness to its Lord, Jesus Christ. Through the term "witness," Barth reconceives the church as a missionary community, in place of the traditional notion of the church as an end in itself or the institution of salvation. For salvation is God's work alone. As a witness to God's reconciling work in Jesus Christ, the church stands at the heart of human history awaiting Christ's final coming when this new reality of reconciliation will finally appear to all.

Barth elaborates the church's ministry of "witnessing" broadly under twelve basic forms: praise, preaching, teaching, evangelization, foreign missions, theology, prayer, the cure of souls, personal examples of a Christian life, service to the needy, prophetic action in the world, and fellowship among races and classes. Through these forms of witnessing the church is not simply proclaiming but also making disciples. Consequently, the Christian community is constantly renewed as converts themselves become new disciples and begin witnessing to the gospel.

TIMOTHY R. PHILLIPS

Bibliography. G. C. Berkouwer, *The Triumph of Grace in the Theology of Karl Barth;* G. Hunsinger, *How to Read Karl Barth: The Shape of His Theology;* W. Scott, *Karl Barth's Theology of Mission;* M. W. Stroope, *Eschatological Mission: Its Reality and Possibility in the Theology of Karl Barth and its Influence on Modern Mission Theology.*

Neopagan, Neopaganism. The term "neopagan" is attributed to Tim Zell, founder of the Church of All Worlds, who coined it to refer to all worshipers of the Mother Goddess who were not part of the WICCA movement. Followers of the neopa-

gan tradition tend to follow the basic rituals developed by Gerald Gardner, but have added a substantial degree of variety and diversity, depending on their emphasis. Some pagan groups focus on particular cultural religious traditions, such as Celtic, Druidic, Egyptian, or Norse rituals and practices.

Neopagans worship the Great Mother Goddess, who along with her consort the Horned God (Pan), represent the male and female principles basic to life. Through the use of magic neopagans seek to draw on the cosmic powers that underlie the universe in their own personal quest for blessing, success, fertility, and harmony. Worshipers are generally organized into small autonomous groups, often called "covens." Worshipers meet semimonthly at new and full moons to worship the Great Mother Goddess and to practice their magic. They generally observe eight major solar festivals, including Halloween (October 31), Yule (December 21), Candlemas (February 2), Spring Equinox (March 21), Beltane (April 30), Summer Solstice (June 21), Lammas (August 1), and Fall Equinox (September 21).

DOUGLAS J. HAYWARD

Bibliography. D. Cole and E. Fitch, *A Book of Pagan Rituals;* J. G. Melton, *Magic, Witchcraft and Paganism in America, A Bibliography;* J. B. Russell, *A History of Witchcraft.*

Nepal *(Est. 2000 pop.: 24,842,000; 140,797 sq. km. [54,362 sq. mi.]).* Officially Hindu, Nepal also has a considerable Tantric Buddhist influence. Popular Nepali religion is a mixture of Brahmanism and shamanism with elaborate healing rituals, belief in malignant spirits, and astrology. Given this background, it is not surprising that the Christian church in Nepal is of recent origin despite attempts by Catholics and others to plant the gospel in the region. In fact, the story of the church in Nepal is not so much a story of foreign missions and missionaries as it is a record of efforts by Nepali Christians to reach their own people. Nepal was closed to the outside world, but Nepali people managed to seep out into India where they came in contact with Christian missions. Here and there, some Nepali were converted. A number became active evangelists. Foreign-mission influence was secondary. These Nepali Christians organized their own Gorkha Mission. Contacts developed along the border, and there were excursions into Nepal as well.

Revolution in 1950 brought change and the first decade of the church in Nepal. A new democratic monarchical government began an era of reform. St. Xavier's School was started by the Catholics in 1951. Christian worship began in Kathmandu in 1953, and secret believers eventually were baptized. Three Mar Thoma missionaries founded the Christa Shanti Sangh ashram and took up residence in Kathmandu in 1953. In the same year the Nepal Evangelistic Band received permission to open a hospital at Pokhara. In 1954 Tir Bahadur became the first pastor in the Kathmandu Valley, and the United Mission to Nepal received permission to begin medical work. Other agencies followed: Mission to Lepers, National Missionary Society of India, Seventh-Day Adventists, The Evangelical Alliance Mission. Restrictions were in force, but the missions were wanted to help build a new Nepal. The role of missionary women is significant, but the story of the church in Nepal is primarily a record of Nepali Christians, many of them women, penetrating their country with the gospel.

The second decade, the 1960s, saw dynamic evangelistic expansion and the beginning of church growth in east Nepal and far west Nepal. A new hymnbook and a revised New Testament appeared. The stage was set for great growth in the 1970s and 1980s. Christian organizations such as Wycliffe, Youth for Christ, Operation Mobilization, Far East Broadcasting, Gospel Recordings, and Scripture Union came to Nepal during this time.

In spite of PERSECUTION, imprisonment, and other hardships (it was illegal to profess and preach Christ), the churches multiplied, especially since 1980. The church from its inception was indigenous in character and outlook with an emphasis on local leadership development. In the late 1970s and early 1980s discipleship schools and Bible schools came into existence to meet the need for training. Christian witness spread to various parts of the nation. Many people became Christians through healings and other miracles.

In 1990 a multiparty government system was reestablished. Christians in prison were released. Since 1990 churches have been growing more rapidly. In 1991 there were more than 50,000 baptized believers in Nepal. The exact number of Christians is not known, but in 1996 was estimated to be 200,000.

BAL KRISHNA SHARMA AND ROGER E. HEDUND

Bibliography. R. Khatry, in *The Church in Asia Today*, pp. 379–92; J. Lindell, *Nepal and the Gospel of God;* L. Stone, *Illness Beliefs and Feeding the Dead in Hindu Nepal: An Ethnographic Analysis.*

Nestorian Mission. The Nestorian movement took the name of Nestorius, who was appointed patriarch of Constantinople in 428 but deposed three years later at the Council of Ephesus over the issue of the relationship of the human and the divine in Christ. His Christology was probably orthodox, although perhaps not stated adequately. Ecclesiastical politics were also involved. The controversy was a factor in the breach between the East and the West, and the church in Persia became Nestorian.

For several centuries the Syriac-speaking Nestorians were one of the most passionately missionary branches of the church. A school was established in Nisibis with a strong focus on spiritual discipline, Bible study, and mission. In the sixth century it had over a thousand students. Nestorians spread their faith through merchants, accountants, bankers, and physicians, as well as missionary monks and priests and in some cases women who married chiefs of central Asian tribes. In the sixth century Nestorians arrived in India, while a mission to the Huns in central Asia evangelized, reduced the language to writing, and taught agriculture.

The best-known mission was to China. A monument discovered in 1623 described the arrival of Alopen, the first missionary, in 635. Churches and monasteries were established, Christian literature was produced, and the movement had the favor of the emperor. It even reached the border of Korea. It died out in the tenth century but experienced a resurgence from the eleventh to thirteenth centuries, when it disappeared again. The reasons for its demise in China appear to have been threefold: overcontextualization to the point of religious syncretism, with inadequate focus on the cross and resurrection; foreign leadership of the church; and strong dependence on the imperial house. The movement disappeared first when the T'ang dynasty fell in the tenth century, and again in the fourteenth century because of government persecution.

Nestorian Christianity reached several central Asian tribes, notably the Uighurs, whose language was reduced to writing in the eighth century. From there it was passed to the Mongols. By the thirteenth century the Keraits were considered Christian. Nestorians often coexisted with Islam and served its leaders as physicians and scholars, even translating a number of Greek philosophical works into Arabic. However, the Christian faith in Asia was eventually exterminated by a combination of Islamic pressure and the massacres of Tamerlane in the fourteenth century. Scattered Nestorian communities, often calling themselves Assyrian Christians, still exist in some areas of the Middle East and the United States.

PAUL E. PIERSON

Bibliography. S. H. Moffett, *A History of Christianity in Asia*, vol. 1; J. Stewart, *The Nestorian Missionary Enterprise.*

Netherlands Antilles (Netherlands Autonomous Area) *(Est. 2000 pop. 389,000; 961 sq. km. [371 sq. mi.]).* Consisting of two groups of islands separated by some 800 km. (500 mi.) in the Caribbean Sea, the primary economic generators are tourism and offshore finance. In 1993 the population was estimated to be 94.5 percent Christian (12.9%

Protestant, 78.3% Catholic, and 3.3% marginal). The Catholics trace their origin to missionary work in the sixteenth century, Protestants to Dutch immigration and settlement in 1650. The island of Bonaire is home to the Trans World Radio station transmitter, the largest in the Western hemisphere.

A. SCOTT MOREAU

Netherlands *(Est. 2000 pop.: 15,934,000; 40,844 sq. km. [15,770 sq. mi.]).* The Netherlands is an independent European country located on the North Sea with Germany to the east and Belgium to the south. It is often called Holland after a historic region now a part of the modern nation. The Netherlands is one of the smallest and most densely populated countries in Europe. The population is approximately 15.9 million; more than 40 percent live in the two western provinces of North and South Holland, which include the three largest cities, Amsterdam, Rotterdam, and The Hague. The population is primarily Dutch, with some Indonesians and Surinamese. The national language is Dutch, a Germanic language. English, German, and French are quite commonly studied in most secondary schools.

The Franks established a Dutch church at Utrecht in the seventh century. WILLIBRORD and BONIFACE significantly advanced the cause of Christianity in the eighth century. Until the rise of prominent local cities around the time of the Crusades, the country remained under the Holy Roman Empire. In the sixteenth century, Holland became a refuge for the followers of the Reformers. After eighty years of intermittent war with Spain from 1568 to 1648, the Protestant-led revolt finally won the Dutch their independence. In the years following, they built a vast overseas empire, becoming for a time the world's leading maritime and commercial power. In 1794, Napoleon led his French revolutionary forces to invade the Netherlands and set up the Republic of Batavia. The Congress of Vienna liberated the country from France in 1815 and reestablished the United Kingdom of the Netherlands, which included present-day Belgium. The government is a constitutional monarchy with a democratic parliament.

Religion has influenced Dutch history, society, institutions, and attitudes, and is closely related to political life, though to a diminishing degree. Although church and state are separate, a few historical ties remain (e.g., the royal family belongs to the Dutch Reformed Church). Dutch Catholics and Protestants constitute two of the four principal groups on which the three main political parties are based.

Approximately 65 percent of the population is Christian, with 35 percent Roman Catholic and 28 percent Protestant, though there is much secularized Christianity. Both Protestant and Roman Catholic churches have yielded ground to SECULARIZATION. The large Protestant churches, which are traditional and formal, have become quite liberal in their theology and have focused on theological disputes rather than on missions and evangelism. The Catholic Church is also in a spiritual decline.

Fortunately, many Christian agencies have made some progress within the country to reach people for Christ. For example, Youth with a Mission (YWAM) has reached many of the diverse populations found within Amsterdam. The various media are also proving successful in the proclamation of the gospel in the Netherlands. With such little progress being made in and by the formal churches, at least for now, the future hope for missionary work in the Netherlands appears to be through the various new agencies.

MARKUS WAGNER

Nevius, John Livingston (1829–93). American missionary to China and leading missions theorist. Born into a Presbyterian family in Upstate New York, he graduated from Union College, Schenectady, and responded to God's call to missionary service while studying at Princeton Theological Seminary. He spent forty years as a Presbyterian missionary in China (1853–93), where he was active as an itinerant preacher and evangelist, wrote tracts, and did famine relief. He died of a heart attack in China.

Late in his career, after being invited to speak to Presbyterian missionaries in Korea, Nevius devised the plan of missionary work for which he is best remembered. The so-called NEVIUS PLAN became the Three-Self Plan: self-propagation, self-government, and self-support. It was so well received that the Presbyterians in Korea formally adopted it as mission policy. His plan is credited with the subsequent church growth in Korea after World War II and the Korean War. It shaped the mission strategies of countless evangelical agencies after World War II. Similar theories were developed by HENRY VENN and RUFUS ANDERSON, and later by ROLAND ALLEN. His plan also included requiring thorough Bible teaching of all converts and wide itineration by missionaries accompanied by national helpers. This was a reversal of the usual mission approach of paying national evangelists to do the preaching. Nevius thought missionaries should spend their time in discipleship training. The issue of self-support seemed primary to Nevius. The traditional system provided money for early church development and then gradually withdrew funds. Nevius was more interested in self-support from the beginning. His plan also called for strict church discipline, cooperation with other missions, and relief help for churches. He did not consider his plan the final word, and thought it should be modified by local circumstances.

JIM REAPSOME

Bibliography. P. Beyerhaus and H. Lefever, *The Responsible Church and the Foreign Mission;* C. A. Clark, *The Korean Church and the Nevius Method;* H. S. Nevius, *The Life of John Livingston Nevius.*

Nevius Method. In June 1890 the Presbyterian Mission in Korea invited JOHN NEVIUS and his wife, missionaries in China, to give a series of messages on Nevius's book, *The Planting and Developing of Missionary Churches.* Though the Neviuses were only in Korea for the two-week missionary conference, the Nevius Method was adopted by the missionaries as the primary means to reach Korea for Christ. Many attribute the rapid growth of the Korean church to the consistent application of the Nevius Method in Korea.

There are nine principles of indigenous church development in the Nevius Method, including an emphasis on personal evangelism through wide itineration; the development of congregations that are self-supporting, self-propagating, and self-governing; the need for systematic Bible study for every Christian; strict discipline in the noninterference in lawsuits; and general help for those in economic need. The heart of the Nevius Method, the three-self formula of indigenous mission work, is well known in modern missions strategy (*see* INDIGENOUS CHURCHES and THREE-SELF MOVEMENT [CHINA]).

Resulting from consistent application of the Nevius Method, the Korean church has established itself as a church which places a high emphasis on personal evangelism, self-support (tithing), self-propagation (Christianization of Korea Movement), self-government (strong denominations), and systematic Bible study and prayer (cell-groups).

The Nevius Method is still valid, though not as well implemented as it should be. For example, many church leaders of the developing nations in the Third World are heavily dependent on financial assistance from foreign missionary agencies. This dependence does not help the growth of the national church. The principles of indigenous missions outlined by Nevius are needed today just as they were in the late 1800s in order to strengthen indigenous local churches and speed the evangelization of each nation.

BONG RIN RO

Bibliography. C. A. Clark and A. Charles, *The Korean Church and the Nevius Method;* L. G. Paik, *The History of Protestant Missions in Korea, 1832–1910;* B. R. Ro and M. Nelson, eds., *Korean Church Growth Explosion.*

New Age Movement. The New Age movement offers many challenges to missiology and missionary endeavors. Many in the West have rejected atheistic materialism and are openly embracing spiritual ideas and experimenting with spiritual practices that are not Christian, despite some superficial similarities to Christian terminology. Since those caught in this spiritual error must be reached with the gospel, it is imperative to understand their worldview and its weaknesses.

Sociologically, the "New Age movement" is a misnomer because it is neither a unified social movement nor an organized conspiracy, notwithstanding its common themes and emphases. Nevertheless, New Age perspectives are affecting vast segments of Western culture. The American counterculture of the 1960s and early 1970s served as a cultural magnet for a wide variety of non-Christian worldviews. Experimentation with mind-altering drugs was often combined with explorations into oriental religions such as Hinduism, Buddhism, various indigenous pagan traditions such as Druidism and Shamanism, and Western occult practices. Although the flamboyance of the hippie culture is largely gone, many of its animating ideas live on in the New Age movement.

In the late 1980s, many dropped the term "New Age" because of its associations with glitzy and glamorous elements—such as an occult fascination with crystals—that were not reckoned as central to the worldview. In the 1990s essentially New Age ideas are being presented as a "new spirituality," a generic orientation to life that draws on spiritual strength in a very individualized manner. Although the influence of the New Age movement is global, it is probably the strongest in North America and the West in general (since it appeals more to post-Christian cultures than to pre-Christian situations). The new spirituality is eclectic and syncretistic; however, several common elements emerge.

New Age thinking looks to the self for spiritual power. This orientation is often mixed with a messianic and apocalyptic mood emphasizing the urgent need for massive individual and social renewal to solve the personal, social, and international problems facing the planet. As one New Age slogan puts it, "The only way out is in." Individuals and societies can only evolve harmoniously and usher in the New Age by tapping into the power within. New Age luminary Deepak Chopra claims in his best-selling book *The Seven Laws of Spiritual Success* (1994) that we all have unlimited potential to create wealth and happiness, once we awaken from the illusion of limitation and inadequacy. Chopra claims that we are all gods and goddesses. PANTHEISM is at the heart of the New Age; its god is an impersonal and amoral field, force, principle, power, or substance that is the one true reality. God is not respected as a personal and moral Creator who is ontologically separate from his creation.

Second, this new spirituality stresses the unity of all things (MONISM). Humans are not separated from each other, from the planet, from the universe, or from God. All is one. Chopra uses pseudoscientific terms to dub this oneness a quantum field of pure potentiality. The theme of monism unites most New Age thinking, although the emphasis on the individual's unique spiritual journey contradicts the ancient monistic Hindu teaching that individuality is nonexistent and illusory. The New Age effort to accommodate Western individualism while retaining an essential monism is deeply problematic.

A third essential New Age belief is that our consciousness must be transformed if we are to harness the power of our divinity. A number of spiritual practices, such as YOGA, visualization, MEDITATION, hypnosis, and consciousness-raising seminars, are recommended as means to the end of self-realization or God-realization, which are viewed as synonymous. The Transcendental Meditation (TM) movement, for example, has been instrumental in the West since the late 1960s in initiating millions into a Hindu form of yoga, which has been disingenuously presented as a religiously neutral self-help method. Many New Age books and seminars also promote the spiritual benefits purportedly available through contact with angels or other spiritual entities, which are understood in unbiblical terms (see Isa. 8:19–20; Col. 2:18–19; 1 John 4:1–4).

A new slant on New Age ideas comes from the culture of computer networks known as "cyberspace." Some claim that the electronic connections achieved through the Internet form a type of mystical, unified consciousness. Visionaries speak of "technoshamanism" as an electrically enhanced tool for spiritual awareness. Timothy Leary, LSD guru of the counterculture, was influential in advancing these ideas.

Fourth, this new spirituality emphasizes a pleasant view of the afterlife, usually involving a benign view of REINCARNATION. Many accounts of near-death experiences speak of the peace and light of the afterlife where there is no hell to fear and no holy God to face. The categories of heaven and hell (Matt. 25:46) are rejected as rigid, negative, and dualistic.

Fifth, New Agers are syncretistic, which forces them to reject the exclusive and absolute claims of Christ (John 14:6; Acts 4:12). For them, the mystical essence of all religions is pantheistic monism. Therefore, Christ is viewed as a master or guru who taught that we could attain his status by tapping into the "Christ consciousness." The view that he is "God's only son" (John 3:16) is dismissed as parochial.

Sixth, since all is one and we are all divine, a sense of absolute, objective, universal, and transcendent moral authority vanishes for many New Agers. A phrase commonly heard is that "we create our own reality," which means we are under no higher ethical standard (see Isa. 5:20).

Missiologists, missionaries, and others must develop an APOLOGETIC and an evangelistic strategy adequate to refute the New Age worldview (1 Peter 3:15–16; Jude 3). This entails subjecting pantheism, monism, OCCULTISM, reincarnation, SYNCRETISM, and RELATIVISM to exacting critiques, both logically and theologically (2 Cor. 10:3–5). Such an endeavor will expose: (1) the hollowness of an impersonal and amoral deity that cannot possibly love anyone, since it is impersonal; (2) the illogic of a monism that denies the pluralities we presuppose in everyday life; (3) the dangers of occultism and the reality of Satan and his fallen angels; (4) the lack of evidence for and the illogic of reincarnation; (5) the fact that syncretism is false, since religions make contradictory truth-claims; and (6) the errors of RELATIVISM that deny the essential and objective ethical categories of morality.

Constructively, we must set forth the cogency of the Christian worldview, particularly with respect to the uniqueness and supremacy of Jesus Christ as the one mediator between sinful humans and a holy God (1 Tim. 2:5). This will demand sound EXEGESIS (since New Agers misinterpret Scripture) and historical argumentation concerning the reliability of the Bible and its superiority to other supposed revelations about Christ. It will also involve earnest prayer for the spiritual protection, wisdom, humility, and courage required to face a very seductive and influential spiritual counterfeit (2 Cor. 11:14; Eph. 6:10–18).

DOUGLAS GROOTHUIS

Bibliography. D. K. Clark and N. L. Geisler, *Apologetics in the New Age;* D. Groothuis, *Unmasking the New Age: Is There a New Religious Movement Trying to Transform Society?;* idem, *Confronting the New Age: How to Resist a Growing Religious Movement;* V. Mangalwadi, *When the New Age Gets Old;* E. Miller, *A Crash Course on the New Age;* J. W. Sire, *The Universe Next Door: A Basic World View Catalogue.*

New Apostolic Reformation Missions. The New Apostolic Reformation is an extraordinary work of God at the close of the twentieth century which is, to a significant extent, changing the shape of Protestant Christianity around the world. For almost 500 years, Christian churches have largely functioned within traditional denominational structures of one kind or another. Particularly in the 1990s, but with roots going back for almost a century, new forms and operational procedures are now emerging in areas such as local church government, interchurch relationships, financing, evangelism, missions, prayer, leadership selection and training, the role of supernatural power, worship and other important aspects of church life. Some of these changes are being seen within denominations themselves, but for the most part they are taking the form of loosely structured apostolic networks. In virtually every region of the world, these new apostolic churches constitute the fastest growing segment of Christianity.

One of the strong characteristics of the new apostolic churches is the conscious desire to reinstate the ministry and office of apostle, whether the term itself is used or not. Churches which characterize themselves as apostolic in nature have outreach built into their very fabric. This includes outreach and church planting in their own surroundings and social ministries as well as foreign missions. The strong desire to be directly involved in taking the gospel to the nations of the world is reminiscent of the upsurge of world missions among traditional evangelical churches after World War II.

During the last quarter of the twentieth century the more traditional Western missionary agencies have been in notable decline, while Third World-based missionary agencies have been strongly increasing (*see* NON-WESTERN MISSION BOARDS AND SOCIETIES). Many of these Third World agencies have emerged from the new apostolic churches in their midst. An important part of their methodology is to recognize apostolic leaders in foreign nations, build personal relationships with them, and encourage the formation and multiplication of apostolic networks which relate to each other in non-bureaucratic, non-controlling ways. The local congregation frequently becomes the principal launching pad for overseas missions, somewhat to the dismay of traditional mission agencies, both denominational and interdenominational. Ted Haggard, pastor of new Life Church of Colorado Springs, said this at a National Symposium on the Post-denominational Church held at Fuller Seminary in 1996: "[The New Apostolic Reformation] is the 'black market' of Christian ministry. Because the lost of the world are demanding prayer and the message of the Gospel, the demand is forcing us to work outside normally accepted missions methods to satisfy the cry for eternal life in the hearts of people."

A common characteristic of new apostolic churches is for the senior pastor to lead teams of lay people on at least one, and more frequently two or three, mission trips to different nations each year. These are usually facilitated through personal relationships with apostolic figures in the nations visited, and they last for a week or two. Stated immediate objectives of these trips vary greatly from supporting the preaching and teaching ministry of the senior pastor to undertaking a construction project, to street evangelism, to prayer journeys to social service projects to literature distribution to other similar activities. However, a more fundamental reason for this kind of an ongoing program is the benefit of a constantly increasing level of missions interest and commitment throughout the local church. Almost invariably the individuals who take these trips return as transformed persons. Missions is no longer peripheral to them, but an essential part of their personalities. And this permeates through their respective spheres of influence in the church. How much can one local church be involved in missions? A new apostolic church of 2,500 in Anaheim, California, Grace Korean Church, pastored by Kim Kwang Shin, has an annual church budget of $6.5 million, of which $5 million is spent on foreign missions in East Africa, Russia, mainland China, Vietnam, and other places.

David Shibley of Global Advance, one of the foremost trainers of new apostolic missionaries, lists six reasons why new apostolic churches are making such a significant contribution to world evangelization: (1) less bureaucracy; (2) a high view of Scripture; (3) the expression of signs and wonders for the verification of the gospel; (4) strategic-level spiritual warfare and advanced intercession; (5) advanced praise and worship; and (6) apostolic networking (*Ministry Advantage*, July–August 1996, p. 8).

C. PETER WAGNER

New Caledonia (French Overseas Territory) *(Est. 2000 pop.: 195,000; 18,700 sq. km. [7,220 sq. mi.]).* New Caledonia, a French Overseas Territory, is an island in the southwest Pacific Ocean east of Australia. Although the French are the most numerous ethnic group, representing about 25% of the population, there are nearly 50 other ethnic groups as well. The population is over 87% Christian, including over 71% Roman Catholic. Active evangelical groups include *Eglise Evangeliques Autonome* with over 20,000 members, *Eglise Evangelique Libre* with 9,000 members, and Assemblies of God with 2,600 members.

TODD M. JOHNSON

New Covenant. The term *new covenant* is usually used in contrast to the *old covenant* of Moses found in the Old Testament (John 1:17). But the Old Testament contains more than one covenant, and most are related to mission. God made a covenant with Noah (Gen. 8:21–9:17) on which Paul based his appeal to his audience at Lystra (Acts 14:14–18). This cosmic or Noahic covenant, made with human beings in creation, is one part of the salvation story (Rom. 1:19–20), incomplete in itself and yet of continuing validity in evangelism. God covenants not to destroy again sinful humankind by a flood, promises to sustain life on earth, warns against sin, and establishes the cycle of seasons. This state of humanity is an expression of God's will.

God's covenant with Abraham (Gen. 12:3; *see* ABRAHAMIC COVENANT), his election of Israel to be the mediator of his salvation to the nations (Exod. 19:5–8), and his covenant with David to establish his eternal kingdom through David's descendant (2 Sam. 7:11–16) all look forward to the new covenant. Jeremiah foretold of the coming of this new covenant, when external rules would be replaced by the internal control of the living Spirit of God (Jer. 31:33–37).

The choice of Abraham and the election of Israel do not mean that the peoples of the earth are ignored or rejected. Neither, however, do any of the old covenants require that Israel seek actively by specific missionary activity to proclaim God to the nations. God's movement toward the nations is always with reference to their relation to Israel as God's people. As the nations see God's action in judgment and salvation in Israel, they may then share in the blessing of the elect nation. (Ps. 67:1–2).

Karl Barth comments:

> . . . it is precisely the covenant of Yahweh with a unique Israel, of Israel with a unique God . . . far from being an end in itself . . . that has meaning, revelation, real and dynamic import for the relation between God and *all* peoples, *men* of all peoples. (Blauw, 1962, 28)

Jesus comes as the elect and covenanted Servant of God who will "restore the tribes of Jacob . . . (be) a light for the Gentiles . . . (and) bring my salvation to the ends of the earth" (Isa. 42:1; 49:6).

The early ministry of Jesus in the New Testament, with occasional exceptions, was focused on reaching and renewing the "lost sheep of Israel" (Matt. 10:6). But he was also building a new community—a community of the covenant. This becomes clear during the last week of his earthly ministry when he instituted the Last Supper. Two things are of particular importance in the Matthean account (Matt. 26:26–30). By speaking of the "blood of the covenant," Jesus was reminding his disciples how Moses ratified the old covenant by sprinkling the blood of bulls on the altar and the people (Exod. 24:6–8). The blood of the new covenant—of Jesus' pending sacrifice—was "poured out for *many* for the forgiveness of sins." This covenant then went beyond blessing for Israel. It was for the peoples of the world. As believers everywhere celebrate the Lord's Supper, they are reminded of Jesus' sacrifice and of the need to make him known everywhere until Christ's return.

Paul elaborates on this by pointing out how the sacrifice of Christ destroyed the barrier between Jews and Gentiles (Eph. 2:11–22). This truth became the theological foundation enabling the early church to break out of its Jewish cocoon and realize that no people were "impure or unclean"—all could receive salvation through trust in Jesus who is the Way, the Truth, and the Life.

The author of Hebrews repeatedly refers to the blood of Christ and his one sufficient sacrifice—the central content of the new covenant—as being far superior to every feature of the old covenant. He notes the redemptive aspects of this covenant: forgiveness of sins (7:27, 8:12), being redeemed from sin (9:15), freedom from guilt (10:2), cleansing from an unclean conscience (9:14), a living way into the presence of God (10:22), and an eternal inheritance (9:15). The blessings of the new covenant are to the end that "we may *serve* the living God" (9:14).

With the theological foundation established by the new covenant, Jesus summoned his disciples to the mountain top in Galilee. Here he reminded them that they, as the beginning of the new covenant community, had a weighty responsibility, to reach out in a centrifugal mission activity, making disciples of all peoples. He assured them of his total authority and his eternal presence for this task. This new ministry was not merely a matter of obedience. It required the activity of the Holy Spirit, the Spirit of the new covenant (John 29:22; 2 Cor. 3:6, 17–18).

With confidence, then, the disciples proclaimed that "God has made this Jesus, whom you crucified both Lord and Christ" (Acts 2:36). Initially uncertain of the cultural expectations to be placed upon Gentile believers, they finally concluded that God had no favorites (Acts 10:34) and salvation was only through the grace of Jesus Christ (Acts 15:11). God's chosen servant, with whom he had made a covenant (Isa. 42:6), was the only source of salvation (Acts 4:12) and the "one mediator between God and humans" (1 Tim. 2:5). Under this banner, the message of salvation was spread throughout the Roman Empire (Acts 1:8; 28:28–31).

The question "what about those who have never heard" was not raised explicitly by the early believers. They assumed that they and those to follow them would take the message everywhere. With great zeal and sacrifice missionaries through the ages have sought to complete Christ's GREAT COMMISSION. Now that we know the task may not be completed in the foreseeable future, some missiologists are rethinking the "cosmic covenant" that God made with Noah. Is there a wider hope by which the unevangelized may receive the blessings of the new covenant without explicitly naming the name of Jesus? Even as through God's common GRACE some in the Old Testament—Abel, Enoch, Melchizedek, Job, Naaman, Rahab—had a relationship with God, is this probable, or even possible, now?

Thinkers like John Hick and Paul Knitter have opted for radical PLURALISM or UNIVERSALISM which affirms that all the unevangelized will be saved. The traditional evangelical view is that there is no hope for salvation for those who have not heard the message of Jesus and placed their hope in him. The "wider hope," now espoused by a number of evangelicals, posits the possibility of evangelization at or after death or universally accessible salvation apart from evangelization. The latter view is called "inclusivism" by its adherents who believe that salvation comes only through Christ as God works through general revelation and providence. The unevangelized need not have explicit knowledge of Christ and the sacrifice of the new covenant in order to be saved. John Sanders states, "God's salvific will is universal, and that is clearly manifested in the universal covenants of Genesis, which were neither revoked nor replaced by later covenants" (1992, 218).

The more recent statements of these views, theoretical at best, cannot negate the call of Christ in the new covenant actively to make disciples of all the peoples of the world. "He is the atoning sacrifice for our sins, and not only for ours but also for the sins of the whole world" (1 John 2:2).

RALPH R. COVELL

Bibliography. J. Blauw, *The Missionary Nature of the Church;* H. Maurier, *The Other Covenant: A Theology of Paganism;* A. Richardson, *An Introduction to the Theology of the New Testament;* A. McCaig, *ISBE,* I:795–97; J. Sanders, *No Other Name.*

New Delhi Assembly (1961). The Third Assembly of the WORLD COUNCIL OF CHURCHES (WCC) met in New Delhi, India, in November 1961. Unlike the two previous assemblies (AMSTERDAM, 1948; Evanston, 1954), New Delhi was precisely planned, crisply administered, and pragmatically efficient. The location in India was in sharp contrast to the western cities of Amsterdam and Chicago. The assembly was composed of 577 voting members, with a total of 1,006 persons participating.

New Delhi avoided the speculative theological themes addressed earlier, and prepared reports on witness, service, and unity. Four developments give New Delhi its significance in ecumenical history.

First, the enlargement of membership was dramatic. Twenty-three different communions joined the Council. The Russian Orthodox Church, with its satellites from Bulgaria, Romania, and Poland, joined, making the Orthodox tradition the largest communion of the WCC. Two large denominations of Pentecostals from Chile also became members.

Next, the Roman Catholic Church sent five official observers, giving New Delhi a status that had never been achieved previously by an assembly of the WCC.

Third, the confessional basis of the WCC was theologically reinforced, emphasizing the deity of Christ and the authority of the Bible. The trini-tarian and biblical aspects of the basis were strengthened, which pleased the evangelicals and the orthodox.

Fourth, ecumenical history was made by the merger of the INTERNATIONAL MISSIONARY COUNCIL (IMC) with the WCC. Although the merger had been discussed during the formative years of the WCC, the IMC had decided to maintain its separate identity. After 1958, however, negotiations with the ecumenical councils, and tremendous pressure from the WCC, led to the incorporation of the IMC into the WCC. The work of the IMC consequently became the responsibility of the newly created COMMISSION ON WORLD MISSION AND EVANGELISM of the WCC. New Delhi marked the end of one era and the beginning of another in ecumenical missions history.

JUSTICE C. ANDERSON

SEE ALSO World Council of Churches Assemblies.

Bibliography. N. Goodall, *The Ecumenical Movement;* W. A. Visser 't Hooft, *New Delhi Speaks;* R. Rouse and S. Neill, *HEM.*

New Religious Movements. The term "New Religious Movement" (NeRM) lacks precise definition but has become the term of choice among scholars in a conscious attempt to eliminate the more sensational and pejorative connotations of "cult" or "deviant religion." In general, the term is used to identify religious groups that adhere to a theological perspective and a structure or pattern of religious behavior that is self-consciously distinct from the dominant society. The group may be "new" in the innovative sense in which distinctly original religious visions and structures are developed in the context of the existing religious milieu (MORMONISM in the United States and BAHA'I in Iran). The term may also apply to mainline or marginal subgroups within established religious traditions that are imported whole into a new social and religious setting (Hare Krishnas in the United States and Mormonism in Asia).

NeRMs share a set of characteristics. The relative force of each characteristic will vary, but in general NeRMs are marked by strong charismatic leadership, clear boundary markers between members of the group and society at large that reflect and intensify the necessity of a high level of commitment, a claim to have access to or possession of Truth that is not available to anyone outside the group, and a pronounced emphasis on personal needs and experience.

While the emergence of new religions is as old as history itself, the last half of the twentieth century has been a remarkably fruitful time for the development and growth of NeRMs. This is a worldwide phenomenon and reflects the power of broad social trends characteristic of the modern age that have given rise to the rapid increase and relative success of numerous NeRMs.

Cultural globalization has enhanced the potential for the success of NeRMs in several distinct ways. Mass communication has brought the world to our doorstep, raising the level of awareness and interest in a wide range of religious traditions. Modern migration movements have placed numerous societies in direct contact with a wide range of alternative religious traditions, greatly increasing opportunities for interpersonal religious interchange. Being confronted with a Buddhist neighbor is significantly different than being confronted merely with Buddhist philosophy.

The post–World War II era has seen a marked decline in the power of established institutions to retain broad-based loyalty and commitment. Political and social institutions also reflect this change, but it has become increasingly characteristic of the modern religious landscape. This breakdown in the power of institutions is tied to the rise of individualism. Individualism acts as a two-edged sword, at once freeing persons to seek individual choices outside the constraints of social conformity while also leaving persons isolated and alone, highly responsive to the message of communal wholeness characteristic of many NeRMs.

The rise of RELATIVISM as the dominant ethical ethos of modern life, when combined with the social changes noted, helps reinforce a climate of moral and spiritual confusion. The most successful religious responses to this general climate of confusion have been a call to return to the old paths (worldwide fundamentalism) and the quest for new paths to an unknown future (NeRMs).

Beyond these generalized characteristics of the modern age, there appear to be specific social and cultural conditions that are particularly conducive to the rise of NeRMs:

- Secularization—decline of the authority and status of established religious institutions for participation in public discourse
- Generational discontinuity—the loss of confidence among youth in the ability of the values, institutions, and mores of the mature generation to meet the political, economic, social, and religious needs of the future
- Religious freedom—the lack of political and social constraint on personal religious orientation and practice

Postwar Japan is a classic case where these factors have coalesced to form a very fertile field for NeRMs. There are over 11,000 distinct Buddhist groups in Japan, the great majority formed in the postwar era (*see also* JAPANESE NEW RELIGIOUS MOVEMENTS).

While the twenty-first century has every potential of being most hospitable to NeRMs, the fact remains that the vast majority of NeRMs do not succeed in attracting and holding a significant following. In the United States nearly 75 percent of persons who join such movements leave within the first two years. The Mormon experience is a rare exception. Even those movements that appear to succeed remain quite marginal. In the United States the Hare Krishna never numbered more committed disciples than the average Sunday morning attendance of one large evangelical church. However, there are factors that generally mark off the more successful movements:

- A balance between continuity and tension with the dominant culture. Successful NeRMs must provide an alternative, but they cannot be too different.
- Effective charismatic leadership that balances a new vision with sufficient organizational skill.
- Strong internal relationships and clear boundary lines that mark off the group as distinct, if not unique, but do not result in complete isolation.
- Sufficient socialization of children that limits defections and ensures continuity.

Evangelicals generally characterize and respond to NeRMs in terms of their distance or deviation from orthodox Christian belief and practice. This theological approach is centered on an analysis of truth claims and should be motivated by a concern for the truth and for persons. It is wise and prudent for evangelical Christians to learn about the theology, practice, and methods of expansion of NeRMs and be prepared to speak the truth of the gospel of Christ in love. However, considerable caution should be exercised in linking those efforts with the secular anticult movement that carries a strong antireligious bias, affirms the right of the state to control religion, and is not constrained by Christian ethical concerns.

JAMES D. CHANCELLOR

Bibliography. E. Barker, *New Religious Movements: A Practical Introduction;* D. G. Bromley and P. E. Hammond, *The Future of New Religious Movements;* D. Hesselgrave, ed., *Dynamic Religious Movements.*

New Testament Theology of Mission. The New Testament is first and foremost a missionary document in the sense that it details the carrying out of God's plan of salvation for the world. Perhaps the best single portrayal of this is the "chain of revelation" in the Gospel of John, in which God reaches the world first through Jesus as the Sent One. Then the Father and Son "send" the Holy

Spirit and finally the Godhead "sends" the disciples to encounter the world with the demands of God and thereby to force decision. The means by which this is accomplished is called "mission," which technically, in John, means the process of sending chosen heralds with the gospel message of salvation.

Theology of Mission in the Gospels and Acts. One positive result of redaction criticism is the realization that each Gospel contains its own portrayal of Jesus and its own theological emphasis (*see also* JESUS AND MISSION). We will begin with Mark because of the likelihood that Mark was the first Gospel. The centrality of mission in Mark can be seen in the framing of Mark's prologue with "gospel" (1:1, 15). Jesus comes as one proclaiming the "good news" about the "KINGDOM OF GOD," calling for "repentance" and "faith-decision" (1:14, 15). The kingdom refers to the inbreaking of God's rule into history. Jesus taught it as both present (Mark 3:27; cf. Matt. 12:28; Luke 17:20–21) and future (Mark 1:15; cf. Luke 21:31). The disciples are thus heralds of the kingdom message, calling the lost to God. In this sense there is a progression of agents, from the prophets (12:2–5) to John the Baptist (1:2–3; 11:32) to the disciples, who from the start are "apostles" or "sent ones" (3:13–15), to the Son himself (1:38; 9:37). The disciples are called from the start to be "fishers of men" and to leave everything to do so (1:16–20; 10:28). Jesus warns them to expect terrible opposition (13:9–13) in their mission to the nations (13:10) but tells them that their task is worldwide proclamation (3:14; 14:9). Jesus' way is one of suffering (8:31; 9:30–31; 10:33–34), and the disciples are called to imitate Christ by "bearing their cross" with Jesus (8:34). One of Mark's major themes is discipleship failure (6:52; 8:14–21; 9:14–32; 14:27, 32–41, 50–52; 16:8) but Jesus provides the answer when he promises to meet them as Risen Lord and overcome their weaknesses (14:28; 16:7). In the midst of failure to understand and remain faithful, the disciple in mission is promised the presence of the Risen Lord.

Matthew's mission theme is built upon Mark's but expands several emphases. At the outset, there is an antinomy. Matthew has the greatest emphasis on particularism, that the mission is only for the Jews (10:5, 6; 15:24). At the same time, the Gentile mission is given an important place from the start, as the Gentile Magi are the first to come (drawn by a divinely sent star) to worship the newborn Messiah (2:1f.). In short, Matthew is a salvation-historical chronicle of the movement of God's plan of salvation in three stages: from the mission of the prophets (23:37; cf. 21:34–36; 22:3–6) and John the Baptist (3:1–12; 11:7–14) to the mission of Jesus that is the core of the first Gospel to the mission of the disciples to the nations that concludes the Gospel

(28:18–20) . Each stage prepares for the following step. The Jewish mission is the core of the first two stages, and the universal mission is the goal of the third. In this sense "the gospel of the kingdom" called both Jews (4:23; 9:35) and "all nations" (24:14) to repentance. In fact, the mission to the Jews was in reality the first stage of the universal mission, which in Matthew is linked to the eschaton (13:24–30; 24:14). A major theme in mission is rejection, as the disciples must expect the same hatred and persecution as Jesus suffered (10:17–36; see vv. 24–26 on sharing Jesus' suffering). But the goal of it all is to bring the Jewish people and the nations to faith (a key element in the miracle stories) and obedience. (The ethical requirements of the kingdom are central to the Sermon on the Mount.)

Mission in Luke–Acts is at the heart of the New Testament emphasis. The two should be considered together, for they form two volumes of a single story, detailing the divine plan of salvation as it moves from Jesus to the early church. In fact, one of the major themes of Acts is that the church relives and carries on the life and ministry of Jesus, seen in parallels between Luke and Acts in miracle stories, the road to Jerusalem/Rome, and the trials of Jesus and Paul. The two points of continuity between the life of Jesus and the church's mission are the temple (inaugurating both volumes) and the Holy Spirit (central to both). Soteriology is the primary theme, with the three major aspects coming together in Luke 24:47—REPENTANCE (25 times in Luke–Acts vs. 10 total in the other Gospels), FORGIVENESS OF SINS (9 in Luke–Acts vs. 3 total in the rest of the New Testament), and proclamation of the gospel (the heart of Acts; *see* PROCLAMATION EVANGELISM). In Luke we have salvation procured for the world, and in Acts we have salvation proclaimed to the world. In preparation for Acts, the universal mission is even more emphasized in Luke than in the other Synoptic Gospels, as in: (1) Simeon calling Jesus "a light of revelation for the Gentiles" (2:32); (2) 3:4–6, Luke adds to the Isaianic "voice in the wilderness" (Isa. 40:3–4) the statement in 40:5, "And all mankind will see God's salvation"; (3) Jesus' inaugural address of 4:18–27, which concludes with a shift from the Jews to the Gentiles (vv. 25–27); (3) Jesus' deliberate ministry to Gentiles (7:1f.; 8:26f.; 17:11f.); (4) Jesus stressing Gentile openness (7:9; 11:30–32; 13:29).

All this comes to fruition in Acts, as the mission is launched in two stages, Jesus' resurrection command (1:8) and the coming of the Spirit to launch the mission (2:1–12). Yet it takes time for the church to understand God's will. They apparently understood Jesus in terms of the Old Testament centripetal approach (*see* OLD TESTAMENT THEOLOGY OF MISSION), for they remained in Jerusalem, seemingly waiting for the Gentiles to come to them. The Spirit had to force them out in a series of steps to the Gentile mission, first in the PERSECUTION following STEPHEN's manifesto (8:1–3), then Samaria (8:4–25) and the Ethiopian eunuch (8:26–40), followed by the conversion of Paul, the missionary to the Gentiles (ch. 9), and finally the conversion of Gentile Cornelius (ch. 10). At each stage, supernatural leading was evident. The missionary journeys demonstrated several themes: evangelism and follow-up; flexible methods demonstrating sensitivity to culture; home-based church planting methods; the CONTEXTUALIZATION of the gospel for both urban and rural settings; and primarily the centrality of the empowering presence of the HOLY SPIRIT. Acts might better be entitled "The Acts of the Holy Spirit through the Apostles." It is the work of the Spirit that is carried out by the church, and the Spirit sends, guides, and empowers the human agents in carrying out God's mission.

An important subsidiary element in Luke–Acts is the ministry of Jesus and the church to the outcasts. Luke wants to show that the kingdom completely reverses all earthly mores, and so shows that Jesus and the disciples are especially oriented to the poor and the oppressed, as in the quotation from Isaiah 61:1–2 in the inaugural address of Luke 4:18–19, "The Spirit of the Lord . . . has anointed me to preach good news to the poor. . . ." This continues throughout Luke's Gospel (1:51–53; 3:11–14; 6:20–26; 12:13–33; 16:8b–13, etc.) and Acts (2:44–45; 4:32–35, etc.). The debate between EVANGELISM and SOCIAL RESPONSIBILITY in modern missions would be a false one for Luke. For him, to have one without the other produces a truncated gospel.

Mission in John has often been overlooked. Several recent studies have shown that mission is at the heart of John's purpose, which was twofold—to bring unconverted Jews to Christ, and to involve the church in God's mission. Let us begin with the "chain of revelation" introduced above. (1) In the prologue Jesus is called the "Word" (1:1, 2, 14), which means he is the "living revealer" of the Father; to meet Jesus is to encounter the presence of God. As such he is also the "sent one" (stressed over thirty times in the Gospel), which means he is the *shaliach* or "envoy" of God to the "world" (105 of the New Testament's 185 occurrences are in John). His task is to call the world to faith-decision, stressed in three word groups—"believe" (98 times), "know" (two words used 141 times), and "see" (five verbs used 114 times). God's universal salvific love (1:4, 7, 9; 3:16) has brought salvation to the world and called it to respond to the new "life" (66 times in John) in Jesus. (2) In the farewell discourse, the Holy Spirit as the *paraclete* (the best translation is probably "Advocate") is also a "sent one," being given or sent twice by the Father (14:16, 25) and twice by the Son (15:26; 16:7). He will carry the "witness" of the

Father and the Son (15:26) into the new age begun by Christ. (3) The followers of Jesus become "sent ones" (17:18; 20:21) and continue the mission to the world. In the resurrection commission of 20:21–23, they are sent by the entire Godhead and filled with the divine presence. Furthermore, they continue Jesus' function as judge (5:22, 30; 8:15–16; 9:39) in verse 23, for as the world responds to their mission, "whatsoever sins you forgive are forgiven, and whatsoever sins you retain are retained."

Mission Theology in Paul (*see also* PAUL AND MISSION). It is difficult to capture the message of so voluminous and deep a thinker as Paul. Virtually everything in his ministry and writings touches on the concept of mission, so all we can do is highlight key aspects. Before the Damascus road experience, Paul was a committed Jewish particularist, and so his conversion completely reversed his direction in life and all that he stood for. Paul's commission to mission came in three stages—the voice of Christ (Acts 26:16–18; cf. Gal. 1:15–16), the confirmation of Ananias (9:15), and a later vision in the temple (22:21). From that time Paul viewed himself as a pioneer missionary with a global rather than local vision (2 Cor. 10:15–16) who sought to bring the gospel to "those who have not heard" (Rom. 10:14). Those brought to Christ were his "joy and crown" (1 Thess. 2:19) and "the seal of my apostleship in the Lord" (1 Cor. 9:2). Yet evangelism was not his sole purpose; he strongly felt the responsibility to disciple those converted (following the GREAT COMMISSION), so he followed up on his churches by visit and letter (in this sense all his epistles are "follow-up"!) and continually dealt with problems in his churches.

Paul's mission strategy begins with his concept of revelation. God has revealed his plan of salvation and enacted it in the sacrificial death of his Son. This message must now be proclaimed (Rom. 10:14–15). The gospel is not just a message to be preached; it is the light of God shining in a world of darkness (2 Cor. 4:3–6), an eschatological revelation of that "mystery" hidden from the foundation of the world (Rom. 11:25; 16:25–26; Eph. 3:2–6). Mission is thereby an eschatological unfolding, a culmination of the divine intent from eternity past. In its united mission the church manifests the "manifold wisdom of God" to the cosmic powers, telling them in effect that they have lost. This victory is based upon the sovereignty of God and upon the cosmic reconciliation of "all things in heaven and earth" achieved by Christ (Col. 1:19–20). According to Colossians 2:15 Christ achieved this victory after the cross when he "disarmed," "triumphed over," and "made public display" (imagery of the Roman triumph) of the evil POWERS. The church participates in this reconciling and triumphant work by "proclaiming" the "hope of the Gospel" to "every creature under heaven" (Col. 1:23). The universal mission is the great mystery of God, and it needs the focus and priority of the people of God.

For Paul eschatology, Christology, and soteriology intertwine. The redemptive-historical act of God in Jesus is the basis of mission. All of history points to the life and sacrificial death of Christ on the cross as its mid-point. The sin and guilt brought about by Adam have now been expiated by the gracious gift of Christ (Rom. 5:12–21), leading to the justification of the sinner (Rom. 3:21–26). The creeds and hymns of the early church reflect upon the humiliation/exaltation of Christ (Rom. 1:3–4; Eph. 1:3–14; Phil. 2:6–11; Col. 1:15–20; 1 Tim. 3:16), and the unbeliever participates in this via faith-decision and confession (Rom. 10:9–10). This gracious and merciful act of God provides the content of mission. Paul believed strongly in a contextualized message and strategy in which the missionary became "all things to all people" in any area not contrary to the gospel "in order to win some" (1 Cor. 9:19–23). He adapted his message to reach the people where they were, centering on fulfillment of Scripture for Jews (Acts 13:16–43) and upon natural revelation for Gentiles (see Acts 14:14–18; 17:22–31).

Mission Theology in the General Epistles. The General Epistles do not all center upon mission. Some are primarily pastoral, like James, 2 Peter–Jude, or the Johannine epistles. The two that contain mission principles are Hebrews and 1 Peter. Hebrews defines itself as a "word of exhortation" (13:22), a pastoral homily addressing a church tempted to return to Judaism due to persecution. There are two primary themes, christology (the superiority of Christ) and soteriology (the pilgrimage theme). God is the one who completes his revelatory acts by speaking through his Son, the culmination of his plan (1:1–3). Indeed, all of Scripture points to fulfillment in him. Thereby he is superior to the angels (1:4–2:18), to Moses and Joshua (chs. 3–4), to the priesthood (chs. 5–7), and to the covenant, sanctuary, and sacrifices (ch. 8–10). Christ is not only the Son exalted to the right hand of God (1:2–3; 8:1; 10:12) but also has authority over this creation (1:2, 8, 10) and the angelic orders (1:9). Christ alone has made salvation possible by his once for all sacrifice (9:12, 26–28; 10:10–14). Hebrews does not discuss a mission to the Gentiles, but there is a witness theme. Like the heroes of the faith in chapter 11, who witness with their sacrificial lives (12:1), and like Jesus, who is the final model of those who are willing to "resist to the point of shedding blood" (12:2–4), believers are called to a life of pilgrimage. They must run the "race" (12:1–2) and consider themselves "strangers" in this world (11:9, 13), oriented not to the present but to a future reality, "a better country—a heavenly one" (11:10, 16). This means a willingness to "bear the disgrace (Christ bore" (13:13). The contribution of Hebrews to a mission theology deals with the negative side, rejection and persecution, as the people of God witness through suffering.

First Peter is also written to a suffering church, and like Hebrews it calls for believers to consider themselves called by God to be temporary visitors and resident aliens on this earth (1:1, 17; 2:11). The message of this book is that the mission, when conducted in the midst of terrible hostility, calls upon the believers to witness via exemplary lives of goodness. The theme is given in 2:12: when the pagans slander you as being evildoers, let your conduct so shine that they observe your goodness, are convicted by it, and "glorify God in the day of visitation" (*see also* 2:15). "Glorify God" means they are converted and then glorify God at the last judgment. Peter then shows how this works out in the three primary relationships Christians have—to government (2:13–17), to master-slave (2:18–25) and then wife-husband (3:1–7) relationships. Christ is the model for a proper reaction to hostility, for he refused to retaliate and instead entrusted himself to God (2:21–24). So his followers must also become models of faith and goodness when the world turns against them (4:19). That is their mission. For Peter mission is an eschatological journey, done in light of the blessings of salvation (1:3–12; 2:4–10) and at all times looking forward to the culmination of mission in eternity (1:4; 3:22; 4:7). With this in mind, in spite of persecution the people of God are always ready to respond to queries with gentleness and a life that proves the validity of the gospel (3:15–16).

Mission Theology in Revelation. Many have said that there is no mission in this book, since it deals with cosmic war and the end of human history. However, a close study shows a distinct and profound message. The major theme of the book is the SOVEREIGNTY OF GOD, and in the cosmic war the sub-theme is the futility of SATAN. Divine control is subsumed in the verb "was given" which occurs often in two key passages, the four horsemen of the Apocalypse (6:2, 4, 8) and the coming of the Beast (13:5, 7). This verb tells us that God (the giver) is in control of the forces of evil. They can do nothing without his permission. Moreover, everything Satan does is merely a parody or great imitation of what God has already done perfectly, such as the mortal wound healed (= resurrection), the mark of the beast (= God sealing the saints), the false trinity of 16:13. Armageddon is not the great defeat of Satan. It is actually his final act of defiance, for the war was won by the "slain Lamb" on the cross (the predominant title of Christ in the book).

Mission is the outgrowth of the activity of the slain Lamb, and it is far more predominant than has often been thought. In fact, Richard Bauckham (1993; 238–337) has noted that "the conversion of the nations" is a major theme of the book. The "nations" are not just predestined to judgment but are called to repentance. In fact, 14:6–7 shows that one of the purposes of the seals, trumpets, and bowls is not just to pour out JUDGMENT but to prove God's sovereignty over the earthly gods (the trumpets and bowls are built upon the Egyptian plagues of Exodus) and thus to proclaim "the eternal gospel" and call the nations to "fear God and give him glory." The earthdwellers reject that offer and refuse to repent (9:20, 21; 16:9, 11, though the refusal shows the call to repentance was real), but apparently some do repent and give "glory to the God of heaven" in 11:13. Moreover, the nations produce those "purchased" by the blood of Christ (5:9), worshipers before God (15:4), the "multitude" standing before the throne in 7:9, and the saints who bring their glory and honor into the New Jerusalem (21:24–26).

The saints are militant during the Great Tribulation not by fighting back (13:10) but by witnessing through their perseverance and their proclamation of the one true God. The use of lampstands for the church (1:12, 20) may well symbolize its witnessing activity, and the WITNESS theme is central to the book. Jesus as the "faithful witness" (1:5; 3:14) is the model, and the saints are called to the interdependent perseverance and witness. As seen often above, witness leads to PERSECUTION, and the mission of the church via *martyria* ("witness") ends in MARTYRDOM, as in 12:11 where the believers "conquer" the dragon by "the word of their testimony" in that "they did not love their lives so as to shrink from death" (see also 6:9). It is clear that the people of God are pictured as engaged in missionary activity even as they are hunted down by the forces of the Beast, and that some respond to their witness and have their place in the eternal city.

GRANT. R. OSBORNE

Bibliography. R. Bauckham, *The Climax of Prophecy: Studies on the Book of Revelation;* D. J. Bosch, *Transformation Mission: Paradigm Shifts in Theology of Mission;* A. Glasser, *Kingdom and Mission;* F. Hahn, *Mission in the New Testament;* R. E. Hedlund, *The Mission of the Church in the World: A Biblical Theology;* A. Köstenberger, *The Mission of Jesus and the Disciples According to the Fourth Gospel;* W. J. Larkin and J. F. Williams, eds., *Mission in the New Testament: An Evangelical Approach;* P. T. O'Brien, *Gospel and Mission in the Writings of Paul;* D. Senior and C. Stuhlmuller, *The Biblical Foundations for Mission.*

New Tribes Mission. Paul Fleming, a zealous evangelist serving in Malaysia, returned reluctantly to the United States due to sickness in the early 1940s. This seeming setback resulted in the formation of New Tribes Mission (NTM) in 1942.

The purpose of the fundamental, nondenominational, faith mission: to "reach new tribes until the last tribe has been reached." Its goal: to "evangelize unreached tribal groups, translate the Scriptures, and plant indigenous New Testament churches." Fleming started NTM because other agencies refused to accept mission candidates he felt were qualified spiritually. Such agencies required a high level of formal education and monthly support, restricted the number of children, and placed age limits. Fleming felt God can use anyone and supply their economic needs "by faith," as long as they are "channels for Him to work through." Forged under Fleming's philosophy, including a strong sense of urgency, NTM offered spiritually qualified candidates opportunity to participate in holistic tribal ministries.

Presently, the international agency based in Sanford, Florida, is composed of 3,199 missionaries from 28 countries. Members work in 200 language groups in 27 countries. Translators have completed 26 New Testaments with over 100 in progress. Church planters have planted over 770 churches. Twenty-five training centers exist in 11 countries to motivate and mobilize missionary candidates. Two missiological contributions that have broadened beyond NTM include Steffen's phase-out exit strategy for church planting, and McIlwains's comprehensive Chronological Teaching story model used for evangelism and follow-up.

The agency has faced numerous trials over the years. In 1944, the death of five martyrs challenged the fledging agency. More martyrs, forest fires and lost lives, potential splits, plane crashes (one of which claimed the life of Fleming), criticisms from anthropologists, and recent captivities created a resolve to remain true to the stated purpose and goal. Today, as founding leaders pass the baton to others, a mission-wide evaluation is under way to discern training needs for reaching twenty-first-century tribal people.

TOM A. STEFFEN

Bibliography. J. D. Johnson, *God Planted Five Seeds;* K. J. Johnston, *The Story of New Tribes Mission;* T. McIlwain, *Firm Foundations: Creation to Christ;* T. A. Steffen, *Passing the Baton: Church Planting That Empowers.*

New York (1900). *See* ECUMENICAL MISSIONARY CONFERENCE.

New York Missionary Conference (1854). *See* UNION MISSIONARY CONVENTION.

New Zealand *(Est. 2000 pop.: 3,759,000; 270,534 sq. km. [104,453 sq. mi.]).* New Zealand consists of two large and many smaller islands in the southwest Pacific, similar in land area to Japan. The main islands run 1,000 miles from northeast to southwest and are very mountainous with active volcanoes in the North Island and the South

Island divided by the southern Alps. The population is 3.76 million. Thirteen percent are Maori, the indigenous settlers, nearly 80 percent are of European descent, the majority having British ancestry, 5 percent are Pacific Islanders, and there is a growing Asian population.

The first missionaries came from the Anglican CHURCH MISSIONARY SOCIETY in 1814 under the leadership of SAMUEL MARSDEN with the support of Ruatara, a Maori chief. After initially emphasizing civilization as a preparation for evangelism the mission concentrated on evangelization and peace-making. Methodists arrived in 1822 and initially worked closely with the Anglicans. The first official baptism was in 1826. Maori evangelists and the impact of LITERACY played a significant role in the expansion and acceptance of Christianity in the 1830s and 1840s. The translation of the New Testament was completed in 1837 and the whole Bible in 1868. Roman Catholic French Marist missionaries arrived in 1838 led by Bishop J. B. F. Pompallier. Protestant missionaries played a significant role in the signing of the Treaty of Waitangi in 1840 between Maori chiefs and the British Crown, which resulted in New Zealand becoming a British territory.

The rapid growth of European migration after 1840 brought considerable pressure on Maori land, resulting in the emergence of the King movement with its assertion of Maori sovereignty. War in the 1860s led many Maori to reject missionary Christianity and identify with new religious movements which drew heavily from the Old Testament and their own culture. The movement led by Te Whiti and Tohu in the 1870s and 1880s combined prophetic utterances with passive resistance. T. W. Ratana's healing movement after the First World War developed both religious and political dimensions and by 1926 claimed 20 percent of Maori. Anglicans appointed a Maori bishop in 1928 but he had limited powers. The churches operated along assimilationist lines. In the 1980s and 1990s Anglicans and Methodists, in particular, recognized greater Maori autonomy and committed themselves to bicultural PARTNERSHIP.

The settler churches, with Anglicans the largest, followed by Presbyterians, Roman Catholics, Methodists, and others such as Baptists, Congregationalists, and the Salvation Army, reflected their British and Irish origins. Colonial Christianity faced the challenges of pluralism, sectarianism, and secularization. Evangelicals were committed to the transformation of society through individual conversion and moral reformation with attention to prohibition, Sabbath observance, and religious education in schools. Overseas missionary interest has been a significant dimension of the New Zealand churches almost from the beginning. Christianity flourishes among Pacific Islanders and there is a vibrant presence among recent Asian migrants. Ecumenism has resulted in significant cooperation between denominations without achieving church union. The impact of Pentecostalism and the charismatic movement has reinvigorated evangelical Christianity while mainline church membership has declined overall since the mid-1960s. Despite the nominal Christian adherence of many New Zealanders the country is very secular.

ALLAN K. DAVIDSON

Bibliography. A. K. Davidson, *Christianity in Aotearoa: A History of Church and Society in New Zealand;* A. K. Davidson and P. J. Lineham, *Transplanted Christianity: Documents Illustrating Aspects of New Zealand Church History;* P. Donovan, *Religions of New Zealanders;* R. Glen, *Mission and Moko: Aspects of the Work of the Church Missionary Society in New Zealand 1814–1882;* P. J. Lineham, *Religious History of New Zealand: A Bibliography.*

New Zealand Mission Boards and Societies.

Anglican CMS, Wesleyan Methodist, and French Catholic Missions predate the annexation of New Zealand by Britain and the signing of the Treaty of Waitangi in 1840. The involvement of missionaries in the negotiations contributed to Maori acceptance of the treaty and to Christian concern about the abuse of Maori rights by the British settlers and government. Christianity developed in distinct settler and Maori streams, but sensitivity to issues of mission at home such as these increasingly informed convictions about Christian mission overseas.

In 1841 an error in Bishop Selwyn's letters of appointment gave him jurisdiction in the Pacific and led to the formation of the Melanesian mission. Interest in Chinese in the Otago gold fields from the 1860s led to Presbyterian mission in Canton. Presbyterians were also involved in Vanuatu and later in India and Southeast Asia, particularly in medicine and theological education. The New Zealand Baptist Missionary Society began in Dunedin in 1885 and still maintains work in Bangladesh. The Church Missionary Society of New Zealand was founded in 1892 and by 1992 had sent out 280 missionaries to 24 countries. Open Brethren missions began in Argentina in 1896. By 1996 some 800 Brethren missionaries had gone to over 50 countries. In 1922 the interdenominational Bible Training Institute was founded with an emphasis on missionary training. The period after World War II initially saw growth in overseas involvement, but over time there was a reduction in length of service, a tapering off of denominational missions, and the multiplication of evangelical agencies, many linked to international groups based in North America and Britain. Founded in 1982, Servants to Asia's Urban Poor provides a contrasting model of holistic mission as a New Zealand initiative.

New Zealand churches have shared in worldwide moves toward ecumenism and the realization that Christianity is now a global, multicultural religion without a dominant culture defining its theology. While older denominational boards have often been sensitive to the realities of a postcolonial world, including the complex demands of genuine PARTNERSHIP, some appear weaker in their commitment to evangelism. Many, but not all, evangelical societies have a commitment to social ministries, though few are comfortable with political issues.

Mission boards and societies generally no longer have a monopoly on firsthand stories about social need and religious change in remote societies. In an electronic age the power that such information gave has gone forever. Not surprisingly supporters of mission have a wide range of perceptions of the needs of the world.

Historically women have served in large numbers as missionaries, and as supporters through denominational groups such as the Presbyterian Women's Missionary Union. Today feminist concerns seek to redress the lack of recognition for women's contribution to world mission, and reject models which still reflect values of patriarchy and dominance.

In 1997 there were some seventy mission agencies involved in supporting Christian mission outside New Zealand, about ten of which were denominational. Roman Catholics participate internationally through missionary orders. New Zealand Pentecostals share in the spontaneous commitment of the worldwide movement. Anglican Partnership-in-Mission structures provide for diocese to diocese links throughout the world. The contribution of migrant Polynesian and Asian Christianity to mission from New Zealand is likely to prove important. New Zealand's role as a place of international theological and mission education is still developing. Influence is impossible to quantify, but anecdotal evidence points to greater awareness of what can be done with modest resources, a distrust of ideologies, a somewhat pragmatic theology still finding its own roots, an eclectic spirituality and a willingness to relate across boundaries which the New Zealand Christian experience regards as unimportant.

JOHN ROXBOROGH

Bibliography. A. K. Davidson, *'With All Humility and Gentleness': Essays on Mission in Honor of Francis Foulkes,* pp. 41–50; S. L. Edgar and M. J. Eade, *Toward the Sunrise. The Centenary History of the New Zealand Baptist Missionary Society;* R. Glen, *Mission and Moko. Aspects of the Work of the Church Missionary Society in New Zealand, 1814–82; Mission Internet (NZ) Directory of Mission and Training Agencies;* G. Trew, ed., *Looking Back/Forging Ahead. A Century of Participation In Overseas Mission by New Zealand Brethren Assemblies.*

Newbigin, (James Edward) Lesslie (1909–98). British churchman, culture scholar, and missionary to India. Lesslie Newbigin's work and accomplishments demonstrate leadership in mission theology and the ECUMENICAL MOVEMENT. After ordination and commissioning as a missionary in 1936 by the Church of Scotland (though English by birth and education), he served for almost four decades in India. An architect of the church union that resulted in the Church of South India (CSI), he became one of its initial bishops (1947). In 1959 he took the assignment to be the general secretary of the INTERNATIONAL MISSIONARY COUNCIL at the time it was heading toward integration into the WORLD COUNCIL OF CHURCHES. Upon integration in 1961 at New Delhi, he became associate general secretary of the WCC and director of the newly established Division (later Commission) of World Mission and Evangelism, serving, in that capacity, as the editor of the *International Review of Missions*. In 1965 he returned to India and served as the (CSI) bishop of Madras. In 1974, he returned to England to teach mission theology at Selly Oak Colleges in Birmingham until 1979, during which time he wrote his major work on mission theology, *The Open Secret*. Thereafter he fostered in the churches of the West a sense of the missionary encounter of the gospel with their own culture.

A prodigious author, Newbigin published numerous articles and more than thirty books. Half of the latter deal explicitly with his own engagements with the two primary mission contexts of his life, India and the West. The rest are critical reflections on the missional issues facing all churches. His major contribution was to articulate a rationale for mission in the culturally and religiously plural world of the late twentieth century. Grounding his reasoning in the biblical account of the character, actions, and purposes of God, he has been an apologist both for the gospel, defending belief within a postmodern context, and for the Christian mission, providing confidence to those who give witness to the unique revelation of God in Christ.

GEORGE R. HUNSBERGER

Bibliography. L. Newbigin, *The Household of God;* idem, *Unfinished Agenda: An Autobiography;* idem, *Foolishness to the Greeks: The Gospel and Western Culture.*

Nicaragua (*Est. 2000 pop.: 5,169,000; 130,000 sq. km. [50,193 sq. mi.]*). Nicaragua is the largest of the Central American countries. During much of the twentieth century Nicaraguans lived under the dictatorships of three generation of Somozas. In 1979 the Sandinistas gained control of the government after a bloody civil war. The 1980s saw the rise of U.S.-supported subversion in the form of the Contras. Violeta Chamorro won the presidential election in 1990 and governs the country, although the Sandinistas are still a strong political force.

The Roman Catholic Church makes up about 79 percent of the population, although many Catholics are quite nominal in their participation. There are three rival factions within the Catholic Church: the conservative traditionalists, the more politically active base communities, and the worship-centered charismatics.

Protestant influence in the eastern seaboard of Nicaragua dates back to the 1670s, when the British assumed a protectorate over the Miskito Indian kingdom. Moravian missionaries arrived at the town of Bluefields in 1849. By 1852 an "English Protestant Church" had been established in San Juan del Norte (Greytown)

The Central American Mission began work in Nicaragua in 1900 and encountered both opposition and success. As a result of COMIBAM, a COMITY agreement assigned Nicaragua to the Baptists, and they extended their work in Managua, Masaya, Diriamba, and León. In addition to their many churches, they also founded the "Colegio Bautista" (1916) and a hospital (1930).

There are more than 120 Protestant denominations working in the country, and they constitute about 22 percent of the population. The overwhelming majority of these evangelical Christians belong to Pentecostal denominations, such as the Assemblies of God, the Apostolic Church, the Church of God (Cleveland), and the Church of the God of Prophecy. The largest non-Pentecostal denominations are the Moravians, the Seventh-Day Adventists, various groups of Baptists, the Brethren in Christ, and the Nazarenes.

A major turning point in the growth of Protestant work in Nicaragua came after the earthquake that rocked the country on December 23, 1972. Evangelicals banded together under the CEPAD organization *(Comité Evangélica Pro-Ayuda a los Damnificados)* to minister to those who had lost homes and loved ones. As a result, an increasing number of Nicaraguans became evangelicals. For example, the Assemblies of God Pentecostal denomination entered the country in 1912 but only had fifty members in three congregations by the 1930s. They had grown to 150 churches in 1979, and during the following decade they began two hundred additional churches. Other denominations have experienced similar growth.

The civil strife of the past three decades has left the country polarized into different factions. The evangelical churches are no exception. Those churches sympathetic to the Sandinista goals are involved in EDPAD, CIEETS, and/or the Baptist Theological Seminary. Other churches have chosen to form more conservative coalitions. More recently, evangelicals have been influential in the formation of politically diverse parties, and movements such as the *Partido de Justicia Nacional* (PJN), founded in 1991, the short-lived *Partido Ecuménico de Rehabilitación al Agraviado*

(Pera), and *Grupo de Convergencia,* and the *Movimiento Evangélico Popular* (MEP), founded in 1992. The evangelical movement in Nicaragua is demonstrating its maturity in maintaining its emphasis on both evangelism and social concern.

LINDY SCOTT

SEE ALSO COMIBAM.

Nicholson, William Patteson (1876–1959). Irish international evangelist. Born in Bangor, County Down, he was an apprentice seaman at fifteen, then worked on a railway construction gang in South Africa before returning to Belfast. He was suddenly converted in 1899 and studied at Glasgow's Bible Training Institute (1901–3). He stayed in Scotland as an evangelist with the Lanarkshire Christian Union (1903–8). He then joined Chapman and Alexander in their Australian and North American missions (1908–10), settled with his family in Pennsylvania, was ordained as an evangelist in the Presbyterian Church (1914), and joined the staff of the Bible Institute of Los Angeles.

In 1920 he returned to Ireland and conducted a series of missions in Ulster that brought thousands into the kingdom at a time of serious intercommunal strife. A robust preacher haunted by "the thud of Christless feet on the road to hell," he was in 1926 an unlikely last-minute substitute at Cambridge for a sick missioner, but about one hundred students professed conversion. In his latter years "Willie Nic" preached on four continents, and died just before his projected retirement. He wrote *On Towards the Goal* (1925), *The Evangelist* (1937), and *God's Hell* (1938).

J. D. DOUGLAS

Bibliography. S. W. Murray, *W. P. Nicholson: Flame for God in Ulster.*

Nida, Eugene A. (1914–). American premier linguist and translation consultant. At an early age Nida committed his life to Christ and was called to missionary work. His first contact with modern linguistics and Bible translation came the summer of his graduation from U.C.L.A., when CAMERON TOWNSEND invited him to attend the Summer Institute of Linguistics (SIL). Each summer from 1937 to 1953 Nida returned to the SIL to teach. In 1943 he completed his Ph.D., was ordained, married, and joined the staff of the American Bible Society (ABS). He was the associate secretary for versions (1944–46) and then executive secretary for translations.

Nida's ABS work involved travel to more than seventy countries. The volume and significance of his writing are phenomenal, especially in the face of his grueling travel and lecture schedule. His writings fall roughly into four chronological phases: descriptive linguistics (1943–51; *Morphology,* 1949); cross-cultural communication (1952–60; *Message and Mission,* 1960); translation (1961–73; *Towards a Science of Translation,* 1964; and *The Theory and Practice of Translation,* 1969); and semantics (1974–).

One of Nida's greatest contributions to missions was the development and popularization of DYNAMIC EQUIVALENCE translation, which seeks to capture the meaning and spirit of the original without being bound to its linguistic structure. This approach to translation is highly influential in modern BIBLE TRANSLATION work.

STEPHEN HOKE

Bibliography. E. M. North, *On Language, Culture and Religion: In Honor of Eugene A. Nida,* pp. vii–xx.

Niger (Republic of Niger) *(Est. 2000 pop.: 10,805,000; 1,267,000 sq. km. [489,189 sq. mi.]).* Niger is a large, arid, landlocked country on the southern edge of the Sahara, a region called the Sahel. The Niger River passes through the capital city, Niamey. Consisting primarily of highlands and sandy plains, a southern strip of arable land supports 90 percent of the population (10.8 million). Currently, Niger's economy rests on animal husbandry and subsistence farming of the main staples: millet, sorghum, and rice. One of the world's poorest countries, Niger ranks last (of 165 countries) in International Monetary Fund economic stability.

Niger was once the largest net exporter of uranium until world demand plummeted in the 1980s. Devastating drought and famine in 1972–74 and 1984–85 (which significantly curtailed the nomadic tradition of the Fulani and Tuareg peoples) interrupted ambitious government development plans and rendered the country even more dependent upon foreign aid.

Niger's sixteen ethnic peoples are divided into five principal language groups: Tamajaq (Tuareg), Fulfulde (Fulani), Kanouri, Hausa, and Songhai-Djerma. Historically, much of western Niger was part of the vast Songhai Empire. Following earlier treaties, Niger joined French West Africa in 1922, becoming independent in 1960. The first president, Hamani Diori, was overthrown in 1974 whereupon a military government, primarily under the popular Col. Seyni Kountche, ruled until single-party presidential elections in 1989. A new multiparty Constitution was established in 1992 and a tenuous democracy governed until another military coup in January 1996 prompted most donor nations to suspend their aid indefinitely.

Though a constitutionally secular state, Niger is largely Islamic, with ISLAM claiming 90.5 percent of the population. Another 9 percent is animistic, .5 percent Christian, with evangelicals comprising 0.2 percent. Islam came to the sub-Sahara in the ninth century, and is essentially of the folk variety today. Ethnic diversity has diluted traditional Islamic solidarity, with government policy and society currently resisting militant Islam.

The more than one hundred evangelical churches are experiencing steady growth, in spite of a waning period of division. The SOCIETY FOR INTERNATIONAL MINISTRIES (SIM; 7 ethnic ministry teams) and the Evangelical Baptist Church have been in the country since the 1920s, while other missions have entered in recent decades. Recent directions in outreach include media, an indigenous missionary training center, community and youth centers, AIDS awareness, and new translation projects. Indigenous missions from Nigeria have made increasing commitments, now numbering more than 20 missionaries.

KENNETH J. BAKER

Nigeria *(Est. 2000 pop.: 128,786,000; 923,768 sq. km. [356,667 sq. mi.]).* The West African nation of Nigeria, a country comprised of some 250 ethnolinguistic groups, is the most populous country in Africa. The south is the most densely populated. While the majority live in rural areas, urbanization is increasing. Although the country is well-endowed with natural and human resources, it is among the world's twenty poorest countries. There are twenty-five universities with many Nigerians also trained overseas, yet the literacy rate remains at 30%. Though a secular state, Christianity (50%) and Islam (40%) are the major religions, with 10% still adhering to traditional religions. Evangelicals are 15% of the population.

Islam arrived via the north in the eleventh and fifteenth centuries. Modern Christianity was introduced on the coast in the early nineteenth century by Anglicans, Methodists, Baptists, Presbyterians, and Roman Catholics. Freed slaves were instrumental in securing this initial success. One of them, SAMUEL CROWTHER, became the first African to become an Anglican bishop. His method combined the gospel with education and commerce. Sudan Interior Mission, Sudan United Mission, and the Anglicans penetrated central and northern Nigeria in the late nineteenth century under the leadership of RONALD BINGHAM, KARL KUMM, and Walter Miller. A combination of medical work and education was employed, especially in central Nigeria, where indigenous converts were key agents in the further spread of the gospel in central and northern Nigeria.

Of Nigeria's thirty-seven years of independence only nine have been under civilian rule. The resulting political instability has led to economic depression due to mismanagement and corruption. In the process the nation acquired a $28 billion debt with little to show for it. To these factors one should add Islamic pressure and multiethnicity as major factors affecting the development of Christianity in Nigeria today. Nigerian Muslims are belligerent and pressure from Islam has had a significant effect on the color of Nigerian Christianity. During the constitutional review in 1978 Muslims struggled unsuccessfully to introduce Shari'a law into the Constitution. In the late 1980s Muslims went on successive rampages in the north, burning churches and killing many Christians. Muslim heads of state have collaborated with Islamic groups to clandestinely enlist Nigeria in the Islamic Conference Organization. Concern over such events led to the formation of Christian Association of Nigeria. This association unites all Christians against Islamic-oriented political domination.

Around independence in 1960 many of the mission churches came under indigenous leadership. Despite allegations by some church historians that the conversion of many is not genuine the subsequent growth of the church has averaged 8.33% per annum. The majority of new churches, such as the Deeper Life Bible Church, and Living Faith Ministries, are Pentecostal/charismatic in nature. There are also syncretistic groups which to varying degrees are more inclined to traditional religions than to Christianity. Such independent groups as the Aladura, Cherubim and Seraphim, and Celestial Church of Christ were born out of discontent with mainline denominations and their supposed inability to be contextually relevant.

Part of the new growth has been through Nigerian missionary societies. Denominational societies such as Evangelical Missionary Society (EMS) of the Evangelical Church of West Africa (formerly led by PANYA BABA), Church of Christ in Nigeria Community Mission (CCM), the United Missionary Organization (UMCA), Baptists, Foursquare Gospel Church, and non-denominational societies such as CAPRO, Christian Missionary Foundation (CMF), and Nations for Christ Missionary Organization (NCMO) have missionaries serving both within and outside Nigeria. New Life for All (NLFA), an interdenominational lay movement, led for many years by the late Paul Gindiri, is instrumental in spreading the gospel among Muslims in the north. The Great Commission Movement, the Nigerian IFES (the largest student movement in the world), the Fellowship of Christian Students (FCS, Scripture Union (SU), and others are working with students and creating mission awareness.

Some of the churches, including ECWA, COCIN, Roman Catholics, and Lutherans, are involved in holistic ministry. The role of the church in these areas is increasingly important with the collapse of national health and educational systems due to the economic depression. There are also Christian nongovernmental organizations such as Christian Rural and Urban Development Association of Nigeria (CRUDAN), People Ori-ented Development of ECWA, Almanah Rescue Mission (ARM), Urban Frontier Mission (UFM), and the Mennonite Central Committee who are working with the indigent.

Some churches are involved in theological education. Although education in Nigeria was started by missions the development of theological institutions has not kept pace with secular education. Of these theological institutions the majority offer a diploma. Very few offer master's degrees. No evangelical school awards a doctorate.

There are still foreign missionaries working alongside churches in theological education, medical work, and development where the church does not have enough specialized personnel. Foreign missionaries serving as partners will always be welcome, government policies permitting, because the church belongs to Christ.

Despite the number of Christians, churches, and organizations the church is not making much impact upon society. Corruption is rampant in society and many Christians in public life cannot be distinguished from unbelievers. Lack of theological depth in the church is another limitation. While the church is growing fast, it lacks maturity. The poor economic state and lack of biblical teaching contribute to the recent resurgence of witchcraft and syncretistic practices.

Nevertheless, Nigerian indigenous missions have many prospects. Some 120 unreached people groups still exist in the country. If Nigeria's resources were properly harnessed, evangelicals could effectively evangelize the nation and the entire continent. Evangelical churches need to cooperate with one another to advance the cause of Christ. Divisions are exploited by Muslims to advance Islam. The Nigeria Evangelical Fellowship could do more to bring evangelical Christians together.

Urban mission is a critical need in Nigeria. Lagos, with 11 million people, is the second most densely populated city in the world. There is a dearth of evangelical churches in many cities. Foreign missionaries could play a key role in evangelizing the growing international communities in Lagos, Abuja, Kano, and other metropolises.

The role of women's fellowship groups in the growth of the Nigerian church is indispensable. Traditionally Nigerian women have not been sent out as missionaries. In the future the church has to incorporate them. Men, however, need to be mobilized to action and young people deeply rooted so that they are not swayed by the latest heresies. There are great prospects for the church but we are at an historical watershed. The nature of the future depends on the decisions made today.

BULUS GALADIMA

Nigerian Mission Boards and Societies. In 1842 Protestant missions came to what was to become

Nigeria. From the beginning, it was recognized that most of the work would have to be done by Africans. The Anglican CHURCH MISSIONARY SOCIETY (CMS) got many workers from among the rescued slaves settled in Sierra Leone. The Methodists used Ghanaians, and the Presbyterians had West Indian missionaries. As local converts were won, most foreign missions trained and sent out local evangelists as quickly as possible. Many of these worked in cultures not their own.

Most notable among the early African missionaries working with the CMS was SAMUEL ADJAI CROWTHER. He set up and supervised the Niger Mission, which worked along the Niger River from the delta to the confluence with the Benue River, ministering to at least five language groups. He recruited rescued Africans from Sierra Leone as staff. Crowther worked within the framework of the CMS, and the Niger Mission developed into regular Anglican dioceses. Today the Anglican Church in Nigeria has its own mission-sending structure.

In 1949 the Sudan Interior Mission, now the SOCIETY FOR INTERNATIONAL MINISTRIES, helped the churches they had founded to set up their own missionary-sending body, the African Missionary Society. Its name was changed to the Evangelical Missionary Society (EMS) upon the organization of the Evangelical Churches of West Africa in 1953. The oldest and largest Nigerian mission agency, the EMS has over a thousand workers in several African countries, Britain, and the United States.

The Nigerian Baptists have been sending missionaries to Sierra Leone for many years. They have also worked in the less-reached areas of Nigeria. Other notable denominational missions are the mission departments of the Church of Christ in Nigeria, Assemblies of God, Gospel Faith Mission, and Deeper Life Bible Church. Deeper Life had seventy-two missionaries in thirty-two nations in 1992.

Campus revivals in the 1960s and 1970s led to the founding of Nigeria's first nondenominational mission societies. Calvary Ministries started with educated young people in Zaire in 1975. By 1996 they had over two hundred workers serving in nineteen Nigerian ethnic groups and ten other African countries. The Christian Missionary Foundation started in Ibadan in 1982, and by 1992 had fifty-five missionaries in at least eight Nigerian tribes and nine other countries. Many smaller mission agencies continue to be formed.

In 1982, nine Nigerian mission organizations banded together to form the Nigeria Evangelical Missions Association (NEMA). Their joint projects include raising mission awareness, research, and missionary training. There were over thirty-five agencies in NEMA by 1996. Members include independent agencies, denominational agencies, support agencies, and specialized ministries (e.g., children's and student work).

Today many of the independent agencies run their own missionary training programs. The larger denominations have tried to incorporate missionary training into their existing theological education.

The number of Nigerian missionaries continues to grow. In 1992 there were 2,873 missionaries from Nigeria, of whom 1,259 were doing cross-cultural work. Most Nigerian cross-cultural missionaries work in less-reached Nigerian tribes, though there are about 250 working in other countries.

The Roman Catholics have a college for training Nigerian missionary priests. Some of the less orthodox African Independent Churches of Nigeria send missionaries to the Nigerian communities in Western lands and some to non-Christian Nigerian peoples.

Nigeria has 50 percent of the population of West Africa and 85 percent of the region's evangelicals. This makes it a strategic sending nation for the evangelization of West Africa.

LOIS FULLER

Bibliography. L. D. Pate, *From Every People: A Handbook of Two-Thirds World Missions.*

Niijima, Jom (1843–90). Japanese educator and church leader. Born in Edo (later Tokyo), he left for Hakodate, and then became a stowaway on a ship headed for the United States, in order to further his knowledge of Western culture. This took courage, for it was a capital offense to go abroad without permission, since Japan had tried to seal itself off against foreigners. In America, Niijima was befriended by an American Christian businessman, Alpheus Hardy, who supported his studies at Phillips Academy, and in honor of whom he sometimes styled himself "Joseph Hardy Neesima." Becoming an ardent Christian, he prepared for the ministry at Amherst College and Andover Seminary. He was asked by the Japanese government to accompany the Iwakura Mission to study Western education as a translator, for which he would be absolved for breaking the law in leaving the country. From this trip, Niijima formed the goal of founding a Christian institution of higher education that would guide Japan's future course. Eventually supported in this by the American Congregational Church, he returned to Japan in 1874 and set about founding his Christian school, the Domshisha ("the common-purpose association"), in Kyoto, just north of the former Imperial Palace. Beset by ill health, Niijima continued to work for the strengthening of the new Japanese Congregational churches, and his struggling Domshisha, until his death in 1890.

JAMES M. PHILLIPS

Bibliography. J. D. Davis, *A Sketch of the Life of Rev. Joseph Hardy Neesima;* R. H. Drummond, *A History of Christianity in Japan;* A. S. Hardy, *Life and Letters of Joseph Hardy Neesima.*

Niles, Daniel Thambyrajah (1908–70). Indian church leader and evangelist. Born near Jaffna, Ceylon, as a fourth-generation Christian, Niles was an active churchman, ecumenical leader, and evangelist. As an Asian church leader Niles played a significant role in the development of the ecumenical movement in which he was active during four decades and to which he contributed a blending of Eastern and Western thought. From 1953 to 1959 he was executive secretary of the Department of Evangelism of the WORLD COUNCIL OF CHURCHES (WCC). At the time of his death he was executive secretary of the East Asia Christian Council (EACC—of which he was a founder), president of the Methodist Church of Ceylon, and one of six presidents of the WCC.

Niles was ever an evangelist and preacher, explicitly Christocentric in faith and practice, a pragmatic Methodist. He emphasized the proclamation of the gospel, not polemics. To Niles, the rationale for evangelism stems from the uniqueness of Christ. According to LESSLIE NEWBIGIN, Niles was above all an expositor of the Bible. He is best known today through at least seventeen books that he wrote as well as the EACC hymnal he edited. Among his better known books are *Preaching the Gospel of the Resurrection* (1953), *The Preacher's Task and the Stone of Stumbling* (1958), *Upon the Earth* (1962), *The Message and Its Messengers* (1966), *Buddhism and the Claims of Christ* (1967), *Who Is This Jesus?* (1968).

ROGER E. HEDLUND

Bibliography. C. L. Furtado, *The Contribution of Dr. D. T. Niles to the Church Universal and Local;* C. Lacy, *ML*, pp. 362–70; L. Newbigin, *DEM*, pp. 729–31.

Ninian (c. 360–c. 432). Early missionary to Britain and Scotland. Of his life and ministry among the Southern Picts surprisingly little is known for certain, and even the dates given above have been challenged. Bede the historian says Ninian went to Rome, where he received theological training, papal encouragement, episcopal consecration, and a commission to evangelize his homeland. His return trip reportedly took him through Gaul, where he was warmly welcomed by fellow bishop MARTIN OF TOURS, pioneer of monasticism in the Western Church, who gave Ninian both spiritual counsel and practical assistance.

Ninian established his base at what is now Whithorn in southwest Scotland. There he built a stone church known as Candida Casa ("the White House"). A monastery was founded, and from this training center Ninian and his preachers took the gospel not only northward to the Grampians, but also south to England and over the sea to Ireland. The work Ninian began was continued in the sixth century by COLUMBA and Mungo. Here, too, the chronology has been challenged, but we do know that by the Middle Ages Whithorn was well known as a place of pilgrimage.

J. D. DOUGLAS

Bibliography. W. D. Simpson, *Saint Ninian and the Origins of the Christian Church in Scotland.*

Nitschmann, David (1696–1772). German missionary to the Caribbean. Born in Zauchtental, Moravia, he and his family in 1724 joined a colony of refugees that was taken in by Count NIKOLAUS LUDWIG VON ZINZENDORF at his estate in Herrnhut, Saxony. In 1727 a revival broke out at Herrnhut, and out of it sprang the MORAVIAN missionary movement.

Nitschmann, thirty-five, and Leonard Dober, thirty-one, facing ridicule and opposition, walked to Copenhagen and then sailed for St. Thomas, West Indies, on October 8, 1732. Zinzendorf had simply told them to do everything in the spirit of Jesus. They had no prior examples to follow and no society behind them. On arrival they found the family of the slave Anthony, whose visit to Herrnhut had inspired the Moravians' missionary vision in the first place. They preached the gospel to the slaves who gathered around them. The Moravians labored fifty years in the West Indies and had baptized 13,000 converts before any other mission arrived there. As the first bishop of the Moravian Brethren in Germany (consecrated in 1735), Nitschmann was instrumental in the opening of twenty-eight fields by 1760. He died on one of those fields—Bethlehem, Pennsylvania.

JIM REAPSOME

Bibliography. K. Hamilton, *History of the Moravian Church, 1722–1957;* J. Weinlick and A. Frank, *The Moravian Church Through the Ages.*

Niue (New Zealand Dependent Area). *(Est. 2000 pop.: 2,000; 260 sq. km. [100 sq. mi.].)* Located 300 miles east of Tonga and 350 miles southeast of Samoa, Niue is an uplifted coral atoll 36 miles in circumference. Called by James Cook "Savage Island," its Polynesian inhabitants initially rejected European and missionary contacts. Declared a British protectorate in 1900 it was annexed to New Zealand in 1901 and in 1974 became a self-governing territory in free association with New Zealand. Three-quarters of its population belong to the Ekalesia Niue (formerly LMS), 10% are Mormons, and the remainder mainly Roman Catholics, Seventh-Day Adventists, and Jehovah's Witnesses.

ALLAN K. DAVIDSON

SEE ALSO Polynesia.

Bibliography. Institute of Pacific Studies, *Niue: A History of the Island.*

Nobili, Robert de (1577–1656). Italian missionary linguist in India. De Nobili was born into a wealthy family in Montepulciano, Italy, and in 1597 joined the Roman Catholic monastic order the Society of Jesus, despite resistance from his relatives.

De Nobili asked to be sent to India as a Jesuit missionary, arriving on the Fisher Coast in 1605. There he spent several months studying Tamil before moving on to Madura, the hub of Tamil culture. Few converts were being won in Madura, especially among the higher-caste Brahmins. De Nobili saw that the Hindus despised the Portuguese for their foreign customs of eating meat and drinking wine. The Indians equated Christian conversion with becoming Portuguese, a notion reinforced by the missionaries.

Probably aware of the innovative methods of fellow Jesuit Mattheo Ricci in China, de Nobili decided to assume the identity of a Brahmin, adopting the local wardrobe and diet as well as some of the customs. An outstanding linguist, he applied himself to mastering Tamil, Sanskrit, and Telugu, eventually writing more than twenty books and other materials in these languages. Perceiving him to be a European holy man, many locals began coming to his new dwelling in the city's Brahmin section, where he explained Christianity, debated religious issues, and discussed the errors he had found in Hinduism, as well as its similarities with Christianity. He died in Mylapore, penniless and nearly blind.

Notoriety continues to follow de Nobili. While some fault his theology and claim his contextualized approach perpetuated the class distinctions still blighting the church in India, many more rank de Nobili with Ricci and Francis Xavier as among the greatest missionaries of his era.

STANLEY M. GUTHRIE

Bibliography. M. Amaladoss, *BDCM*, pp. 498–99; J. H. Kane, *A Global View of Christian Missions;* S. Neill, *HCM;* R. Tucker, *FJIJ.*

Nominal, Nominal Christian. While nominality is usually described rather than defined, the Lausanne Committee has defined nominal Protestant Christians as "those who, within the Protestant tradition, would call themselves a Christian, or be so regarded by others, but who have no authentic commitment to Christ based on personal faith."

Nominality is an acknowledged problem in second and succeeding generations of Christians who have lost the joy and fervor of the new birth. E. Gibbs gives two pathways to nominality: those who belong to the church but no longer believe and those who believe but no longer belong. The Lausanne Committee identified five types of nominal Christians: Those who (1) attend church regularly, worship devoutly without any relationship with Jesus Christ; (2) attend church regularly, but for cultural reasons; (3) attend church only for major church events; (4) hardly ever attend church but maintain a church relationship for reasons of security, emotional or family ties, or tradition; (5) have no relationship to any specific church and never attend but consider themselves believers.

A nominal Christian may be unconverted according to biblical criteria. Reasons for nominality can be classified as theological (i.e., leadership, local church, and cultural misunderstandings) or historical (i.e., traditions taking precedence over vital faith). The missiological challenge is to move nominal Christians toward genuine conversion and a vibrant, personal relationship with Christ.

MIKEL NEUMANN

Bibliography. E. Gibbs, *In Name Only: Tackling the Problem of Nominal Christianity;* Lausanne Occasional Paper No. 23, *Thailand Report: Christian Witness to Nominal Christians Among Protestants.*

Nommensen, Ludwig Ingwer (1834–1918). Danish missionary to Indonesia. The son of a dike-lock attendant, Nommensen was born on the island of Nordstrand in Schleswig. Escaping injury despite a serious accident, he decided to become a missionary and joined the Rhine Missionary Society in Barmen. In 1862 he traveled to Barus on the northwest coast of Sumatra. In 1864 he began work among the Toba Batak, who were independent of the Dutch crown colony. His respect for indigenous social structures earned him trust, as did his desire to win the people in their own language with a humble and patient attitude.

In 1874 Nommensen translated Luther's Small Catechism into the Batak language, followed by the New Testament in 1878. He also allowed the Batak a church polity that was contextually oriented. In 1881 Nommensen became director of the Rhine Mission to the Batak. When he extended his efforts to include the southern coast of Lake Toba, church growth advanced so rapidly that entire clans were baptized. Nommensen was awarded an honorary doctorate by the theological faculty of the University of Bonn for his services as the leader of the Batak church, and in 1911 he received the Officer's Cross from the Royal Dutch Order of Orange-Nassau. Nommensen died in 1918 in Sigumpar in Sumatra.

ROLF HILLE

Bibliography. N. DeWaard, *Pioneer in Sumatra: The Story of Ludwig Nommensen;* L. Schreiner, *Mission Studies* 9:2 (1992): 241–51.

Non-Church Movement (Japan). One of the distinctly indigenous expressions of Protestant Christianity in Japan today is the Mukyokai or "non-church" movement. It was founded by KANZO UCHIMURA (1861–1930), a devoted follower of Jesus who was at the same time intensely Japanese in his loyalties. Inevitably he became a vocal critic of Western denominationalism because of what he regarded as its unwarranted elevation of human leaders, its promotion of factionalism, and its penchant for superimposing Western values on Japanese Christians. Uchimura was a Luther-like apologist for the biblical faith and a genuine promoter of social righteousness. Although his spiritual experience began within Western denominationalism, its sectarian and ecclesiastical rigidities soon drew him to possible association with Quaker simplicity and its non-sacramental view of church ordinances. This led him to abhor both congregational organization and formalism in liturgy and polity, creeds and dogmas. Eventually the Mukyokai movement emerged. It is significant that no form of Christianity has been more prolific in its literature and more relevant to the educated elite in urban Japan. It is devoid of anything approximating a local or national federation of assemblies. No Sunday schools or systematic instruction of youth are permitted, no offerings are taken, and no sacraments are administered. All public witnessing by an ordained or professional clergy is eschewed. The Mukyokai movement is devoid even of church buildings. Despite this, Uchimura produced a religion of the spirit that is distinctly Japanese through and through. In the mid-1950s Emil Brunner reported that he felt that the non-church movement represented the "cream of Japanese Christianity, vital and biblical in the very best sense." The movement has plateaued of late, and tends to be currently regarded as just another Christian sect.

ARTHUR F. GLASSER

Bibliography. W. H. H. Norman, *IRM* 46 (1957): 380–93.

Nonresidential Missionary. Strategic mission planners of bygone eras historically tended to neglect the sections of the world that were more resistant to the gospel, with a few notable exceptions. Antagonistic zones have become more impenetrable, especially since the end of World War II. A nonresidential missionary, however, has the responsibility of discovering ways to identify and evangelize historically resistant and UN-REACHED PEOPLE groups, or population segments, with the intent of establishing a viable movement of Christian churches among them.

In the wake of the Western colonial era, emerging national governments dissolved legal restraints on precolonial, indigenous religious movements. Blocs of Islamic, Hindu, Buddhist, and tribal peoples renewed and reasserted themselves against external religiosocial influences.

Introduction of Marxist ideologies in many countries created an unprecedented set of circumstances that often coerced peoples to resist the gospel and to accept, or at least practice, various forms of atheism.

Identifying the world's distinct religiosocial groupings of peoples, primarily by linguistic criteria, has aided researchers in specifying the nature of the task remaining for fulfillment of Christ's commission to preach the gospel to all the peoples of the world. Technological advances enable mission strategists to gather data more effectively, assess the implications of that data more precisely, and envision new ways and means of penetrating resistant blocs of peoples.

In 1986, a team of Southern Baptist Foreign Mission Board researchers coined the term "nonresidential missionary" to describe a radically new mission methodology. Nonresidential missionaries function in innovative ways in that they often begin their ministry outside the indigenous locale of a distinct people group, or designated population segment, that is historically resistant to, or perhaps even left untouched by, the gospel. While living outside the target area, they commit themselves to strategic research, language learning, and discovery of new avenues for establishing contact with decision makers inside the target area. They usually do not rely on the resources of just one agency or denominational sending structure to penetrate their resistant people or population segment. Instead, they coordinate like interests among various Christian entities and orchestrate a collective but focused strategy to establish legitimate humanitarian bases for entry into the targeted area.

Once the nonresidential missionary establishes a viable foundation for working in the targeted context, the host government may grant a long-term presence. Teams of qualified people able to render and administer humanitarian services indirectly engage in evangelism, discipleship, and church planting ventures through the web of social relationships they are able to establish with individuals from their assigned people group.

It is at this point that the term "nonresidential" may lose its meaning because of an indefinite presence in the targeted area. Because of this frequent occurrence, some mission agencies relabel the model to reflect more accurately the function a nonresidential missionary performs, namely, the coordination of various strategic initiatives among Christians aimed at reaching an unreached area or people with the gospel and establishing a viable Christian presence.

KEITH E. EITEL

Bibliography. D. B. Barrett and T. M. Johnston, *Our Globe and How to Reach It: Seeing the World Evangelized by AD 2000 and Beyond;* V. D. Garrison, *The Nonresidential Missionary: A New Strategy and the People It*

Serves; idem, *IJFM* 9 (1992): 67–69; M. S. Philemon, *IJFM* 8 (1991): 141–46.

Non-Western Mission Boards and Societies.

As people in countries around the world were evangelized and incorporated into a worshiping group of believers by missionaries, one of the natural results was the development of missionary outreach from these newer churches. Similar to their counterparts in Europe and North America, believers in Africa, Asia, Latin America, and Oceania developed their own missionary-sending vision and efforts. Like those of the Western countries, these efforts required missionary-sending organizations with explicit policies and procedures.

Terms. There have been several labels for this development. The phrase "Third World Missions" was borrowed from political economics (*see* THIRD WORLD). Many from Africa, Asia, Latin America, and Oceania felt, however, that "Third World Missions" implied third-class missions. As this was not the intention, "Non-Western Missions" was suggested, a particularly good replacement to describe those in Asia, since most of their cultures are non-Western. However, the peoples in Latin America consider themselves just as Western as those of North America, so this term also had its deficiencies.

"Emerging Missions" was used to describe the arising army of new missionaries from countries that traditionally had received missionaries, yet now sent workers as well. The term was not meant to imply that the emerging movement was completely new. For records as early as the 1820s tell of missionaries like Joshua Mateinaniu, who planted churches by traveling from one Pacific island to another. What the term actually intended to convey was that this phenomenon had recently become better documented and in this sense was emerging.

The current term is "Two-Thirds World Missions," a more accurate representation of the resource God is now mobilizing for his kingdom; the countries of Africa, Asia, Latin America, and Oceania constitute nearly two-thirds of the world's inhabited land mass and at least that fraction (if not more) of the world's population (*see* TWO-THIRDS WORLD). Although "Two-Thirds World Missions" is the more popular term today, the other labels continue to have some use in describing this extremely significant development.

Growth. In 1972, the first year the worldwide activity of the emerging missions was reviewed, there were an estimated 2,951 missionaries sent out by 368 agencies and organizations. Similar systematic research was carried out in 1980 and 1988 and coupled with various regional studies. The results indicated that non-Western missions and agencies were growing more than five times faster than their counterparts in the West. By the mid-1990s, there were an estimated 88,000 cross-cultural workers sent out by approximately 1,600 non-Western agencies or organizations in Africa, Asia, Latin America, and Oceania. This growth has continued, while in the West missionary recruitment and deployment have either plateaued or declined.

Types of Agencies. The missionary activities of the Two-Thirds World can be classified as structured or unstructured. The unstructured groups consist of believers who spontaneously proclaim the good news of Christ's love without any formal organization to define and direct their activity. The Quechua Movement for Christ in Bolivia, the Tzeltal Christians and Chol Indian Church of Mexico, the Apostolic Church of Ghana, and the Chinese Christians in Burma are examples of effective unstructured missionary endeavors. Receiving encouragement from colleagues and church leadership, those members of the group who have an evangelistic vision reach out spontaneously, often to a neighboring village or town of another culture. Finances come from friends or tentmaking activities; training and pastoral supervision are often minimal.

Within the Two-Thirds World, however, most of the missionary activity is structured. There are national officers or directors, a system for raising and maintaining financial support, and methods to coordinate the evangelistic outreach of workers hundreds of miles from the central office. The agencies vary greatly in character, but are united by the fact that they are formally organized. They are usually led by a charismatic communicator, while the vast majority of workers are from the ethnic group or nation conducting the outreach.

There are large denominational agencies, like the Burma Baptist Convention and the Diocesan Missionary Association of the Church of the Province of Kenya (Anglican). On the other hand, there are large nondenominational agencies, like the Friends Missionary Prayer Band in India and Mission Amen in Peru. There are agencies that maintain their main office close to the field of service rather than in the home country, for purposes of recruitment and fund raising, for instance, Project Magreb, a Latin American agency located in Spain. And there are hundreds of smaller agencies that operate along family lines: employees at the home office are family members, and the missionaries are either friends of the family or relatives.

Problems. In the Two-Thirds World, mission agency problems are virtually the same as those anywhere. Funding the work and adequately training workers remain critical concerns for prayer and resolve. One of the ways in which newer agencies have learned to handle some of these difficulties has been to participate in continent-wide or international conferences on global missions. Another way they have learned about mission structure and administration has been from nationalized structures that are related to international agencies. Youth with a Mission, Operation Mobilization, New Tribes, Wycliffe, and a host of other agencies of European or North American origin have been sources of encouragement and education for newer groups.

The future of global missions clearly lies with the Two-Thirds World agencies and missionaries. Like those that preceded them, they are not always without cultural bias and limitations. Yet if the gospel message is to continue to move into all nations, it will in large measure be the work of very committed missionaries from the churches and agencies of the Two-Thirds World.

LARRY E. KEYES

Bibliography. D. J. Cho, *New Forces in Missions;* D. E. Clark, *The Third World and Missions;* M. L. Nelson, *The How and Why of Third World Missions: An Asian Case Study;* idem, *Readings in Third World Missions: A Collection of Essential Documents*; L. D. Pate, *From Every People: A Handbook of Two-Thirds World Missions;* idem, *The Last Age of Missions: A Study of Third World Mission Societies;* J. Richard, *Asian Church Leaders;* T. Williams, *World Missions—Building Bridges or Barriers;* J. Wong, P. Larsen, and E. C. Pentecost, *Missions from the Third World: A World Survey of Non-Western Missions in Asia, Africa and Latin America.*

Norfolk Island (Australian Territories) *(Est. 2000 pop.: 35,000; 2 sq. km. [1 sq. mi.]).* Norfolk Island, an external territory of Australia since 1913, is an island in the Pacific Ocean off the east coast of Australia. The island was originally settled by descendants of the mutineers from the Bounty. Forty percent of the population are Pitcairnese with the rest split between Australians, British, and New Zealanders. Three-quarters are Christians and one-quarter are nonreligious. Most of the evangelicals are found in the Anglican and Methodist communities.

TODD M. JOHNSON

North American New Religious Movements. From the time of the earliest English settlements, North America has had two religious personalities. The primary personality has been broadly Christian, with the clear dominance of Protestant Christianity. The alter ego has been one of remarkable religious diversity, the home of the free and the innovative. NEW RELIGIOUS MOVEMENTS (NeRMS) have been part of the American character from the beginning. However, the last half of the twentieth century has been particularly rich in number and variety of NeRMS. The Institute for the Study of American Religion identifies 1,667 different religious groups in North America, of which 836 are classified as "unconventional." Of these nonconventional movements, nearly 500 arose after 1950. These figures do not include movements not defined as religious, such as *est* and primal therapy, nor does it include the many

groups that are too small or secretive to be studied. Thus, 1,500 to 2,000 is a reasonable estimate of the number of NeRMS in North America.

The term "NeRMS" lacks precise definition. The differences among NeRMS in North America are enormous and it cannot be assumed that a characteristic of one movement applies to others. However, these movements share at some level most, if not all, of the following general characteristics. NeRMS are innovative in doctrine, worldview, forms of religious expression, and social arrangements. They tend toward an emphasis upon subjective experience and focus upon meeting personal needs. NeRMS are characterized by strong charismatic leadership; the group attributes to the leader the capacity for extraordinary insight, revelation, and authority. NeRMS tend to be separatistic, aiming for not only a different vision of society but a different model for society. They tend to be more holistic than conventional religious bodies, with higher levels of conformity and commitment.

NeRMS in North America fall into three broad categories: the revival of ancient religious traditions, variations on traditional Christian themes, and movements flowing out of the more established religious traditions of the non-Christian world. Many movements represent a synthesis across these category lines.

Many NeRMS that fall within the broad definition of "NEW AGE" are not at all new, but rather represent a modern revival of ancient and folk religious traditions. ASTROLOGY, one of the oldest and perhaps the most universal human religious expressions, plays a major role in most of these groups. Gnosticism, or the belief that humans are capable of direct and transcendental knowledge of God through esoteric ritualism or symbolic interpretation of Scripture, undergirds the worldview of many NeRMS. NEO-PAGANISM, the calling back to life of ancient Egyptian, Greek, and European deities, is a growing phenomenon in North America. Some persons heavily invested in the modern feminist and ecological movements have found a religious home in the neo-pagan revival.

Many NeRMS in North America grow directly out of more conventional Christianity. In the late nineteenth and early twentieth centuries, a number of powerful forces swept through American Protestantism—adventism, the Holiness Movement, and Pentecostalism. These forces certainly do not constitute a new religious movement, but when one or more became highly intensified, particularly under strong charismatic leadership, groups emerged that are clearly and self-consciously outside the broad American Protestant tradition. Branhamism, JEHOVAH'S WITNESSES, and The World Wide Church of God are classic examples of this form of NeRM. In addition, there are a number of groups that began as a variant of the Christian tradition, but have so synthesized ancient or folk traditions that the "Christian" aspect is little more than an overlay.

The third broad category of NeRMS consists of groups that reflect the flow of established religions into North America. The religious heritage of India has been an influential component of the New Age phenomenon (*see also* HINDU NEW RELIGIOUS MOVEMENTS). Transcendental Meditation, the International Society for Krishna Consciousness (Hare Krishna), and ZEN BUDDHISM are the most widely known of these movements, although there are many others with origins in Asia, the Middle East, and Africa. While few movements have drawn significant numbers of indigenous Americans as committed disciples, their influence on the overall religious ethos of North America is growing in significance. The UNIFICATION CHURCH is especially significant. It has roots in Protestant Christianity, introduced into Korea in the nineteenth century. The founder, Sun Myung Moon (b. 1920), combined elements of Christianity with Korean folk shamanism and a Taoist worldview. (Such synthesis is not unusual in NeRMS. There are thousands of such movements in Africa alone; *see also* AFRICAN INITIATED CHURCH MOVEMENT.) However, in the 1970s Moon came to North America and introduced his vision as both a NeRM and the final stage in the evolution of Christianity.

Perhaps the most significant issue facing evangelical Christians is not the "what" but the "why" of NeRMS. Scholarly research has developed a general profile of the convert to a NeRM. The greater number of converts are young, usually in their late teens or early twenties. Most are isolated and unattached. The vast majority of converts are single, geographically disconnected from family and located in a new or unfriendly environment. With the exception of ethnically centered groups (BLACK MUSLIMS, SANTERIA), most converts are from middle-class or upper-middle-class families and are better educated than the general population. Converts generally have a "seeking spirit" but have experienced alienation from family, friends, or society as a whole. Many converts experienced alienation and disillusionment with conventional American religion. They are on a quest for meaning and value and the quest has not been satisfied by mainstream American Christianity. The growth of NeRMS is not simply the result of failure in the church, but it may be more productive to view NeRMS less as a threat and more as a challenge.

A number of factors should be borne in mind when dealing with someone involved in a NeRM. In North America adults enjoy religious freedom. Forcible "deprogramming" is illegal, unethical, based upon faulty assumptions about "mind control," and is much more likely to do harm than good. It is indisputable that the vast majority of converts leave NeRMS voluntarily and few suffer long-term damage or disabilities. While it is important to learn all one can about a particular movement, one should treat with skepticism information from the movement itself or from secular anti-cult organizations. It is important to maintain contact with the person involved in the NeRM, fostering a good relationship of trust, and manifesting love and care for the convert.

JAMES D. CHANCELLOR

Bibliography. R. Ellwood and H. Partin, eds., *Religious and Spiritual Groups in Modern America;* R. Kyle, *The Religious Fringe: A History of Alternative Religions in America;* R. A. Tucker, *Another Gospel: Alternative Religions and the New Age Movement.*

North Korea. See KOREA, NORTH.

Northern Ireland. *See* IRELAND and UNITED KINGDOM.

Northern Mariana Islands (United States Dependent Area) *(Est. 2000 pop. 51,000; 457 sq. km. [176 sq. mi.]).* A chain of 14 islands some 650 km. (400 mi.) north of Guam. The population consists of 31 percent indigenous islanders, 64 percent Asian immigrants, and 5 percent U.S. mainlanders. The economy is dependent on tourism (mainly Japanese) and U.S. aid. In 1993 it was estimated to be 83 percent Christian (10% Protestant, 70.8% Catholic, and 2.2% marginal), 10 percent Buddhist, 5 percent nonreligious, and 2 percent animist.

A. SCOTT MOREAU

SEE ALSO Micronesia.

Norway *(Est. 2000 pop.: 4,427,000; 323,895 sq. km. [125,056 sq. mi.]).* Christianity came to Norway in the ninth century from the British Isles and Germany. During the twelfth century the church was firmly established. The Reformation was formally introduced in 1537 when the Danish-Norwegian king decided that Lutheranism was to be the religion of the two countries. In the Constitution of 1814 Lutheranism was retained as the official religion of the state. The Church of Norway is still a state church, but has in many ways become a self-governing body in line with the general democratic development.

Under the lay preacher Hans Nielsen Hauge a period of revivals took place at the beginning of the nineteenth century. They had a particular effect on common people who then established what later became free lay organizations for mission at home and abroad. The revivals occurred within the state church as reform movements. As a result the lay organizations have in many ways functioned as have the free churches in other countries (e.g., Sweden).

The Church of Norway has 3.8 million members (of a total population of 4.4 million), divided into 1,350 geographical parishes and 11 dioceses. The General Synod was instituted as late as 1984, with 80 delegates meeting once a year. Even though the king remains head of the church, and the government and parliament decide on the budget, appointment of bishops, and church laws, the state church is enjoying an increasing amount of freedom and independence, especially at the local parish level. Nevertheless, there is growing opposition to the state church system among younger clergy and evangelical laypeople.

It is impossible to understand Norwegian church life without seeing the interwoven nature of its official and voluntary structures. This pattern has since the early nineteenth century released much spiritual energy for evangelism and mission at home and abroad. The first of the voluntary structures was the Norwegian Missionary Society (formed in 1842). The largest Lutheran lay movement today is the Norwegian Lutheran Mission, with 500 career missionaries abroad. The Norwegian Lutheran Home Mission is the oldest of the organizations evangelizing in Norway, with 2,800 fellowships and hundreds of "prayer houses." These prayer houses, of which 2,600 are still in existence today, were built by laypeople in response to the revivals in the early part of the nineteenth century. Their use is, however, today decreasing (less than one-third are used weekly). Overall, the voluntary lay organizations within the Church of Norway functioned during the twentieth century as a committed opposition and reform movement in defining doctrinal matters and in challenging the less committed sections of the church to mission and evangelism. The Church of Norway does not have its own specific mission board. Rather, the independent missionary societies together carry on the church's mission activity. Today these Lutheran missionary societies support more than 1,000 Norwegian missionaries.

Among the churches outside the state church we find Methodist, Baptist, Covenant, and Lutheran (there are three Lutheran free churches in the country). The largest independent churches are, however, the Pentecostals with 32,000 members and the Roman Catholic Church with 40,000 members (many of them immigrants from southern Europe, Asia, and Latin America). The total membership of the free churches is 200,000. Most of the free churches are evangelical in doctrine and support a strong mission movement with 500 missionaries (290 of them Pentecostals).

Approximately 93 percent of the population is affiliated with Christian churches and fellowships, while 2 percent (95,000) belong to other religions; 4.5 percent (195,000) have no religious affiliation. The proportion of people baptized and confirmed is, however, decreasing: 84 percent have been baptized and 76 percent confirmed in the Church of Norway. About one-third of the adult population say they believe in Jesus as Savior, and one-fifth consider themselves "personal Christians." However, fewer than 400,000 attend church at least once a month. On a weekly basis about 5 percent attend church and religious meetings (prayer houses). This number (220,000) constitutes what is termed the active members.

It is primarily this active membership that supports the missionary work abroad. Of the 1,500 Norwegian career missionaries (not including tentmakers and team ministries, both of which are growing) 60 percent are women. Norwegian mission is active in about 75 countries (19 in Europe, 14 in Latin America, 20 in Asia, and 21 in Africa). Of the 650 missionaries working in African countries, 260 are in Ethiopia and Kenya. Within the 10/40 WINDOW Norwegian mission is fairly weak. The focus on mission to Muslims is, however, increasing today.

Beginning in the early part of the eighteenth century with mission to the Lapps and to Greenland, mission work has also in modern times experienced a great expansion in numbers of missionaries and in new working areas. Following the closure of China new work was started in Japan, Taiwan, Tanzania, Indonesia, Thailand, Israel, and Ethiopia. In the period after 1961 new independent, American-inspired activities blossomed, including Aril Edvardsen's support of indigenous evangelists and Norwegian branches of the Navigators, Operation Mobilization, and Youth with a Mission. At the same time work behind the Iron Curtain began. Since 1974 the LAUSANNE MOVEMENT has been a strong inspiration for much Norwegian mission. Coupled with worry over the theological and missiological developments within the WORLD COUNCIL OF CHURCHES (when the INTERNATIONAL MISSIONARY COUNCIL did not join the new COMMISSION ON WORLD MISSION AND EVANGELISM), the Lausanne emphasis on evangelization, partnership, and UNREACHED PEOPLES (including Muslims) has influenced missiology and mission work in Norway. As a result new work has been started in Kenya, Mali, Ivory Coast, Azerbaijan, and Mongolia.

Traditionally, Norwegian mission organizations have maintained their independence of the official church structures for theological, missiological, and economic reasons. Since 1994, however, some of the Lutheran missionary organizations have joined with the Church of Norway in a Cooperative Council for Church and Mission. The aim is to promote a natural integration of mission in congregational work by overcoming the traditional tension between the official church and the independent movements. A major reason for this cooperation and integration is the decline in membership and resources within some of the major organizations (The Norwegian Missionary

Society and the Norwegian Santal Mission). The initiative has met with fairly strong criticism from parts of the lay movement.

KNUD JØRGENSEN

Bibliography. P. Brierley, ed., *Norwegian Handbook for Churches and Missions.*

Ntsikana (c. 1780–1821). South African pioneer evangelist, composer, prophet, and missionary. One' of the first Xhosa to come to Christ, Ntsikana grew up in a prominent traditional Xhosa family during an era in which white settler encroachment on Xhosa lands resulted in dislocation and stress. Prior to his conversion, he was known among the Xhosa for his singing, oratory, and dancing skills. Apparently as a child he heard the preaching of pioneer missionary J. T. Van der Kemp, though his conversion did not come until he received a vision as an adult (c. 1815). After the vision, he immediately began preaching, holding regular services in mornings and evenings, unique among the Xhosa in that they were not kinship-formed. Instruction under missionary Joseph Williams from 1816 to 1818 solidified his biblical orientation. Ntsikana attracted many hearers; the relatively few who became his disciples came from the Xhosa social elite. His message to lay down spears and take up spiritual armor through singing his hymns and then submitting to life's circumstances was a prophetic one in distressing times for the Xhosa.

He reportedly composed the first four Xhosa hymns. His continuing influence after death is seen in several ways, including the continuing influence of his "Great Hymn" (inscribed shortly after his death and still sung today) and the development of the Ntsikana Memorial Association (1909) and the Ntsikana Memorial Church (split from the United Free Church) in 1911.

A. SCOTT MOREAU

Bibliography. J. Hodgson, *Journal of Theology for Southern Africa* 58 (1987): 18–31; idem, *Religion in Southern Africa* 1: 2 (1980): 33–58; idem, *Missionalia* 12:1 (1984): 19–33; W. Saayman, *Christian Mission in South Africa.*

Nuñez, Emilio Antonio (1923–). Salvadorian theologian, educator, and writer. Born into a poor family in El Salvador, he struggled to obtain an education as a schoolteacher. Through the woman who later become his wife, Sara Echegoyen, he came to Christ and shortly after, in 1944, enrolled in the Central American Bible Institute in Guatemala City, where after graduating he began teaching, in 1947. He was also a pioneer radio speaker and helped found a school for children from poor Christian families, especially those in ministry. Going to the United States for further studies, he earned a B.A. from Southern Methodist University, a Th.M. from Dallas Theological Seminary in 1964, and a Th.D. from Dallas in 1969. He served as dean and president of his alma mater, which had become the Central American Theological Seminary, and continued to teach there after giving up administrative responsibilities in 1979. A founder of the Latin American Theological Fraternity, he has served WEF, the Lausanne Committee, the Bible Societies, and other entities in various capacities. The author of seven books in Spanish, he wrote *Liberation Theology* (1985) and *Crisis in Latin America: An Evangelical Perspective* (1989, with William D. Taylor) in English.

STEPHEN SYWULKA

Nuttall, Enos (1842–1916). English missionary and church leader in Jamaica. Nuttall grew up in a church-based family and came to faith early in life. Educated largely by personal study and tutoring, he was later granted honorary B.D. (1879) and doctoral degrees (1908) recognizing his exemplary life and service.

Appointed a lay preacher for the Wesleyan church at the age of seventeen, a growing interest in missions in the Fiji Islands led him to London where he sat under George Osborn's tutelage. After three years, Osborn asked Nuttall to go to Jamaica and serve the Wesleyan Missionary Society (WMS), and he set sail in 1862.

After three years as a WMS lay missionary, Nuttall's perception that the WMS bore an un-Wesley-like antagonism toward the Church of England (CoE) eventually resulted in his application as a candidate for ministry within the CoE. He was accepted in 1886, and ordained four months later. Consecrated Bishop of Jamaica in 1880 and Primate of the West Indies in 1893, Nuttall served a total of fifty-four years in Jamaica. He was a prolific writer, though the bulk of his work is in his journals (comprising 19 volumes, begun in 1866), letters (over 35,000 in all), articles, and papers.

Despite bouts with severe illness, Nuttall served tirelessly and played critical roles ranging from helping to organize the Church of Jamaica after disestablishment from the CoE to founding education, medical, housing, and agricultural works as well as providing a strong, stabilizing influence after a devastating earthquake in 1907.

A. SCOTT MOREAU

Bibliography. F. Cundall, *The Life of Enos Nuttall: Archbishop of the West Indies.*

Obedience. Obedience (literally, "hearing under") embodies the core essence of the Christian life. Christ's obedience, learned from suffering (Heb. 5:8), provides the model (Phil. 2:8) and stands in stark contrast to Adam's disobedience (Rom. 5:17–18). Genuine faith results in obedience (Rom. 1:5), and obedience convincingly demonstrates our love for Christ (John 14:21).

The Great Commission (Matt. 28:19–20) contains one command to obey ("make disciples") and then describes a disciple as one who is baptized and being taught to obey. Here baptism illustrates the theological realities of being identified with Christ (Rom. 6:3–7) and placed into Christ (1 Cor. 12:12, 13). Thus, a disciple has been incorporated into Christ, into the invisible, universal body of Christ (Gal. 3:26–28) and into a visible, local body of believers (Acts 2:41). Then, in the context of that local church, a disciple begins the lifelong process of being taught to obey everything that Jesus commanded. Discipleship involves teaching a lifestyle of obedience, not merely a list of facts and doctrines.

The issue of obedience raises a significant and legitimate missiological concern. When a person from one culture defines obedience for someone from another culture, there exists the danger of cultural imperialism. Cultural rather than biblical norms may be put forward to be obeyed (e.g., North American Evangelicalism's stance against drinking as opposed to many European believers' enjoyment of alcoholic beverages, or Western forms and styles of worship as opposed to the use of traditional African music and instruments). Obedience must always be presented in the context of supra-cultural principles, though separating the biblical from the cultural is often quite difficult.

Obedience may cost in every culture. The Western believer may face ridicule and social ostracism, the loss of a job or a friend. For others, obedience may carry a much higher price. In many restrictive cultures or countries, the obedience of the disciple might lead to expulsion from the family, imprisonment, torture, and even death (see Martyrdom). Whatever the cost, the truth remains that obedience is not optional for the believer.

RICHARD CRUSE

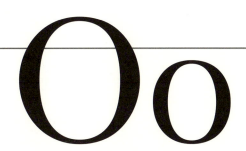

Occom, Samson (1723–92). Native American preacher and evangelist. Born in Mohegan (near New London, Connecticut) to a non-Christian family, Occom came to faith at seventeen during the Great Awakening. In 1743 he began tutelage under Eleazar Wheelock, a Congregational missionary to the Iroquois. He served the Montuak for twelve years as a teacher and minister, being ordained by the Long Island Presbytery in 1759.

In 1761 he traveled to central New York to work among the Oneida, and in 1765 he embarked on a highly successful two-year fund raising trip on behalf of Wheelock's Indian Charity School in Lebanon, Connecticut. His return to Connecticut brought reverse culture shock when his wife refused to adapt to British ways, and further personal shock when Wheelock moved the school to New Hampshire and opened it to whites, using the money raised by Occom to found Dartmouth College. The two separated, and Occom fell into poverty.

The last phase of Occom's life was spent working to develop a town where native Americans from diverse backgrounds would live and work in harmony. Brothertown was founded in Oneida territory after Occom secured a land grant in 1773. With the exception of the interruption of the Revolutionary War, Occom recruited people to move there, taking permanent residence himself in 1789. He published sermons, a hymn book, and one of the earliest Native American autobiographies (*A Short Narrative of My Life;* 1768). He is recognized by many as the best known Native American evangelist of the eighteenth century.

A. Scott Moreau

Bibliography. N. W. Bowden, *BCEB,* 2:840–41; M. G. Humphreys, ed., *Missionary Explorers among the American Indians;* W. D. Love, *Samson Occom and the Christian Indians of New England;* L. B. Richardson, *DAB,* 7:614–15.

Occultist, Occultism. The SHAMAN and other practitioners of the occult (the term comes from the Latin for "hidden" or "concealed") rely on secret techniques to gain access to the supernatural realm and obtain knowledge or power. Occult practices include ASTROLOGY, DIVINATION, reliance on charms or fetishes, fortune telling (tarot cards, tea leaf reading, Ouija board, palm reading), MAGIC, numerology (attaching special significance to numbers), automatic writing (and speaking), seances, witchcraft (*see* WICCA), and so on. The practices are as varied as the cultures in which they are found.

Practitioners typically separate what they consider good practices (white magic) from evil ones (black magic or SORCERY). Biblically, the two are inextricably intertwined, since the same techniques that are used for one may be used for the other. Occultic practices and practitioners of all types are judged harshly in the Bible (Deut. 18:9–14). Such practices are demonic in origin, however harmless they may appear to be on the surface, and are forbidden to the Christian.

Often in history people came to faith when missionaries successfully challenged the occult practitioners with the power of God (*see* POWER ENCOUNTER). At the same time the missionary must be aware not just of the practices but of the purposes they serve within the culture. For example, people rely on the occult for protection from spirits, sorcerers, evil people, bad luck, and so on. Those who come to Christ and give up occult protection need appropriate Christian substitutes to help them face their fears. Without such substitutes, they may return to the occult. Those who fear spirits or sorcerers need to know how to use prayer to exercise the authority they have in Christ. Those who fear bad luck need to understand God's sovereign and loving control over the universe. Creative application of the truths of God to the needs of the people is an important component of missionary work among occultists.

A. SCOTT MOREAU

Bibliography. D. Burnett, *Unearthly Powers*; R. Enroth, *NTCERK*, pp. 606–7; G. Van Rheenen, *Communicating Christ in Animistic Contexts*.

Oceania. Oceania is one of the most Christianized areas of the world. In a brief period of two hundred years, Christianity has spread across the vast expanse of the Pacific Ocean. Consisting of approximately 25,000 islands, Oceania extends from Easter Island on the east to Palau on the west; from Hawaii and the northern Mariana Islands on the north to Australia and New Zealand on the south.

Traditional society in Oceania is usually divided into four main cultural areas: POLYNESIA, MICRONESIA, MELANESIA, and Australia (Aborigines). The original hunting-and-gathering peoples of Australia and Melanesia came in the first of several major waves of migrations from Southeast Asia at least forty thousand years ago. Later, people with an agricultural way of living populated Melanesia, Micronesia, and Polynesia, as their boating skills allowed them to traverse immense distances of open waters. Beginning at the end of the eighteenth century, settlers and migrants from Europe and other parts of the world would soon form the majority of the populations of both Australia and New Zealand (whose original people, the Maoris, were Polynesian). Also, large numbers of indentured plantation laborers from India went to Fiji, and Filipinos, Japanese, and Chinese came to Hawaii.

The first organized mission work in Oceania itself was done by Catholic Spanish missionaries and Filipino catechists in Guam and other Mariana Islands in the seventeenth century, and by Spanish missionaries from Peru in Tahiti in the following century. However, the first major missionary movement was the fruit of the eighteenth-century evangelical revival in Britain—sparked by such great preachers as WHITEFIELD and WESLEY. Through his influence and financial support, Thomas Haweis convinced his fellow co-founders of the LONDON MISSIONARY SOCIETY (LMS) to establish their first mission in the Pacific. Their own ship, the *Duff*, carried thirty missionaries in 1797 to Tahiti, the Marquesas, and Tonga. Tahiti, although abandoned for a short time in 1808, would become the base for the LMS—"the first sustained Christian missionary activity in the South Sea islands" (Gunson, 1978, 12). JOHN WILLIAMS, their most famous missionary of this early period, and others sent out Polynesian evangelists, who "laid the foundation for the evangelization of Oceania" (Douglas, 1986, 23).

The LMS was soon joined by others. An evangelical Anglican mission was established in 1814 by the CHURCH MISSIONARY SOCIETY (CMS) in New Zealand under the direction of SAMUEL MARSDEN, who greatly influenced the early stages of evangelical missionary work throughout Oceania. CMS established the first mission among the Maoris of New Zealand and stimulated further missionary outreach by the Anglican churches of New Zealand and Australia.

Congregational missionaries from the AMERICAN BOARD OF COMMISSIONERS FOR FOREIGN MISSIONS in Boston arrived in Hawaii in 1820 and eventually expanded into Micronesia. English Methodists of the Wesleyan Missionary Society established a base in New Zealand in 1820, and contributed to the missionary movement from Tahiti and Hawaii westward across the Pacific into Tonga, Samoa, and Fiji. The MORMONS began in present-day French Polynesia in 1844, and the Seventh-Day Adventists came to the Pacific around 1890.

After recovering from the effects of the French Revolution and the Napoleonic wars, the Catholic Church in France began sending members of newly founded missionary societies to the Pacific in the 1830s. The Congregation of the Sacred Hearts of Jesus and Mary, or Picpus Fathers, worked in the eastern area of Oceania, and the Marists in the central. On many of the islands where Protestant missionaries had already begun working, there was competition between Catholics and Protestants. However, Christianity was established through the initial contacts of Catholic missionaries in such places as the islands of Mangareva and the Marquesas of present-day French Polynesia, and in Wallis and Futuna of western Polynesia.

The history of Christianity in Oceania in the nineteenth century is unfortunately scarred by tensions between Protestant and Catholic missionaries and churches. This situation was aggravated even further as competing colonial governments eventually began sweeping over the Pacific and in varying degrees favored "their own"—France the Catholics and Britain the Protestants.

Around 1850, primary missionary efforts began shifting to western Oceania, especially Melanesia. In contrast to Polynesia where Christianity was often accepted en masse with the conversion of their king or other hereditary leaders, missionaries faced a much different situation in Melanesia, consisting of many, smaller competitive social and linguistic units with a more fluid style of achieved leadership by elders, or "big men." In addition to these linguistic and cultural challenges, a number of missionaries died due to sickness and attacks by the islanders, who often identified the missionaries with the behavior of labor-recruiters, traders, and colonial officials—the great wave of outsiders "invading" their world and forcing them to jump directly from the Stone Age into modern times. While their intentions and approaches were very different, missionaries and Christianity admittedly played a significant role in the phenomenon of social change (cf. Whiteman).

Within this Melanesian context, the Anglican Church of New Zealand in 1849 initiated the successful Melanesian Mission under GEORGE SELWYN's innovative leadership. Presbyterian missionaries of the late evangelical revival in Scotland began in the 1850s in the Melanesian islands of New Hebrides (present-day Vanuatu). Due to his widely read autobiography, JOHN PATON became their most famous missionary. Around 1875, George Brown established the first missionary effort of Australian Methodists in the Bismarck Archipelago, with Fijian and Samoan Methodists also joining them. The Missionaries of the Sacred Heart (MCS), another Catholic congregation from France, came to this area in 1882. In that same year, the interdenominational Queensland Kanaka Mission began its work among Solomon Islands sugar plantation workers in Australia, and then in 1904 changed its name to South Sea Evangelical Mission and, based on the CHINA INLAND MISSION model, extended its missionary outreach to the Solomon Islands.

New Guinea, the largest island in Oceania, was the last to be approached by missionaries. By the end of the nineteenth century, only the coastal area had been touched. Appropriately the LMS, the pioneer missionaries of the Pacific, began on the south coast in 1871, and MSC on Yule Island in 1885. When the British established a protectorate on part of New Guinea in 1884, it was the first case in Oceania of a colonial government taking the initiative to invite missionaries—in this case, the Methodists and Anglicans from Australia. Germany annexed the northeastern part of the island in 1884 and one Catholic and two Protestant missionary agencies came from Germany: the Society of the Divine Word, Rhenish Missionary Society, and Neuendettelsau Mission Society.

By 1900, Christianity was just beginning in Melanesia, but in the rest of Oceania national churches for whole island groups were established and sent out their own missionaries. Pacific islanders played a major role in the world missionary movement (cf. Tippett), as did the young immigrant churches of Australia and New Zealand.

As for the issue of mission and politics, missionaries in eastern and central Oceania had arrived before the colonial powers and were very influential in precolonial political developments. Most missionaries did not initially favor colonial annexation, but many later changed this stance. Eventually, Tonga would be the only island nation to avoid colonial rule. In Melanesia, missionaries for the most part arrived after colonial annexation.

The years between 1900 and 1942 marked a period of relative stability for most island peoples and churches and it has even been called "the high point in the life and influence of South Pacific Christianity" (Forman, 1982, 11). Although colonial rule had somewhat curtailed the earlier influence of the church in island societies in eastern and central Oceania, other influences from outside the area were not too intrusive. Movements toward establishing independent churches began in Tonga, Samoa, and Fiji. At this same time, Christian missionary efforts were slowly but steadily making progress in Melanesia. The most significant newcomer to the missionary field during this period was the Assemblies of God.

This relative tranquility was shattered in 1942 as Oceania was engulfed in the turmoil of World War II. While some of the islands were only used as military bases, others became combat zones. A large number of islanders and missionaries died due to the war. Besides the upheaval to daily life (including missionary and church activities), events surrounding the war triggered shock waves of tumultuous social change throughout the Pacific, which often led to the dramatic phenomenon of adjustment movements (cf. Forman, 1982, 154–63; see also CARGO CULTS).

In the political arena, no sooner had colonial rule shifted in some islands through postwar negotiations, then there were initial steps toward political independence. A stronger call for church independence followed and missionaries in general took a more supportive backseat role. The Pacific Council of Churches was established in 1966. Also, many new religious groups were entering Oceania after World War II (cf. Ernst).

By 1980, most of the larger churches of Oceania had achieved independence and were sending missionaries to other parts of the world. For example, the churches with an LMS background are now joined together through the Council for World Mission. The Pacific is probably "the most solidly Christian part of the world" (Forman, 1982, 227), out of which "the regional concentration of evangelicals in the Pacific (17.6% of the Christian population) is the highest worldwide" (Ernst, 1994, 11). However, Pacific Islander Christians are facing new challenges today as each generation strives to respond to the continual call of God's mission.

ROGER SCHROEDER

Bibliography. J. A. Boutilier, D. T. Hughes, and S. W. Tiffany, eds., *Mission, Church and Sect in Oceania;* L. M. Douglas, ed., *World Christianity: Oceania;* M. Ernst, *Winds of Change: Rapidly Growing Religious Groups in the Pacific Islands;* C. W. Forman, *The Island Churches of the South Pacific: Emergence in the Twentieth Century;* J. Garrett, *To Live among the Stars: Christian Origins in Oceania;* idem, *Footsteps in the Sea: Christianity in Oceania to World War II;* N. Gunson, *Messengers of Grace: Evangelical Missionaries in the South Seas, 1797–1860;* C. Miller, ed., *Missions and Missionaries in the Pacific;* A. R. Tippett, *The Deep Sea Canoe: The Story of Third World Missionaries in the South Pacific;* D. L. Whiteman, *Melanesians and Missionaries: An Ethnohistorical Study of Social and Religious Change in the Southwest Pacific.*

Oceanic Mission Boards and Societies.

The island regions of the Pacific, or Oceania, can be divided into three general areas: Melanesia, Micronesia, and Polynesia. Over the past two centuries, the Christian faith has spread throughout these approximately 25,000 islands to make Oceania one of the most Christianized areas in the world. Indigenous missionaries have played an important role in the spread of the gospel throughout the Pacific, and more recently are contributing to worldwide gospel outreach as well.

Spanish Catholic missionaries saw a small measure of success in the seventeenth century. However, it was not until well after British, Protestant missions—such as the LONDON MISSIONARY SOCIETY (LMS), the CHURCH MISSIONARY SOCIETY (CMS), and the Wesleyan Methodist Missionary Society—started arriving around 1800 that Catholicism (increasingly French) started to grow significantly. Moreover, it has been primarily Protestant or independent efforts that have included the work of indigenous missionaries. For example, Tahitian missionaries first took Christianity to Fiji under the LMS; a missionary from Kiribati named Tabuia independently evangelized Nauru between 1888 and 1899; and, after a Samoan convert from Tonga had brought Christianity to Samoa in 1828, a Samoan missionary named Paulo helped lead two hundred to three hundred Niueans to faith by 1852. Other groups not long in coming to Oceania included the Presbyterians, the AMERICAN BOARD OF COMMISSIONERS FOR FOREIGN MISSIONS, the Seventh-Day Adventists, and the Liebenzell Mission.

A further illustration of the connection between Protestant (especially the LMS) and indigenous mission efforts was the Cook Islands Christian Church, begun by the LMS in the 1820s, which sent about seventy missionaries to Papau New Guinea between 1872 and 1896. Also, an LMS seminary established in 1844 trained numerous Samoans for evangelistic outreach. After Tahitians had helped evangelize Samoa in the 1830s, an LMS missionary named Murray trained Samoans in Tutuila, who in turn spread the gospel eastward to Manua.

Tahitian missionaries indeed have gone out all over the Pacific, as have Samoans: by 1972, over 210 Samoan Congregationalists had served as missionaries, introducing Christianity to Tokelau, Niue, the Gilbert and Ellis Islands (now Kiribati and Tuvalu), and Vanuatu. Moreover, new missionaries continue to be sent out throughout the Pacific and around the world. The Fijian church has been sending overseas missionaries for over one hundred years, and Tongan missionaries have gone out throughout the Pacific (e.g., to Samoa and Fiji in the nineteenth century), including Australia, Hawaii, and California.

Naming all of the missions and similar organizations operating in Oceania today would make a rather extensive list. Some of them are as follows, listed (where applicable) with their dates of establishment and grouped into identifiable categories: ecumenical agencies: Pacific Conference of Churches (PCC, 1966); Council for World Mission (formerly LMS, 1977); parachurch agencies for literature distribution: The Bible Society of the South Pacific, Lotu Pasifika Productions (1973); educational institutions: Pacific Theological College (associated with the PCC, 1965), Pacific Regional Seminary (Catholic, 1972), Christian Leaders Training Colleges; research and training organizations: The Micronesian Seminar, Pacific Churches Research Center (1976); student fellowships: Campus Crusade for Christ, Pacific Students for Christ; women's groups: YWCA (1974), The Girls' Brigade Asia-Pacific. The continuing presence of ex-patriate missionaries in leadership roles is perhaps best exemplified in the work of WYCLIFFE BIBLE TRANSLATORS, Mission Aviation Fellowship, and Christian Radio Missionary Fellowship in Papau New Guinea. Overall, however, the international missionary community in PNG and throughout Oceania works largely in supporting and cooperating roles with indigenous churches and missions in seeking to reach out to as yet unreached groups, as well as to countries throughout the world.

J. NELSON JENNINGS

SEE ALSO Non-Western Mission Boards and Societies.

Bibliography. L. M. Douglas, ed., *World Christianity: Oceania;* J. H. Kane, *A Global View of Christian Missions: From Pentecost to the Present;* K. Cragg, *CDCWM,* pp. 459–65.

Old Testament Prophets. The message and ministry of the Old Testament prophets focused primarily on Israel. At the same time, the commitment to communicating Yahweh's message to his people reflects an awareness of God's involvement in the history of other nations. Whether focusing on the various dimensions of life within the elect community or on the course of events in surrounding states, these spokespersons grounded their words in the person of Yahweh. This attention to the singularity of Yahweh must, therefore, be the starting point for any discussion of the mission of the people of God in the prophetic material.

The Uniqueness of God. The prophets repeatedly denounce the waywardness of Israel's penchant for seeking after other gods. The narrative of Elijah's confrontation with the prophets of Baal on Mount Carmel (1 Kings 18) might be the most impressive account of the continuous attack on IDOLATRY and SYNCRETISM, but the prophetic books are replete with passages underscoring that Yahweh alone is God and contrasting the reality of his person to the idols' lack of substance.

Isaiah, for instance, describes Yahweh as the sovereign Creator: he is not like the idols crafted by human hands (40:12–31; 44:6–20; 45:14–46:9), which can neither know nor bring to effect the things that are to come (41:22–23; 43:12–13; 44:7–8; 45:11, 21; 46:10; 48:3–5). Jeremiah and Ezekiel decry the presence of images in the sanctuary of Jerusalem and the pernicious presence of idolatry throughout Israel's history (Jer. 2, 10; Ezek. 8, 16, 23). Hosea powerfully presents the profound covenant love of Yahweh for his people through the parallel experiences of his own marriage (Hos. 1–3, 11) and angrily reproaches the Northern Kingdom for worshiping at the high places (4:10–5:7).

The social sciences and philosophical ETHICS can illuminate in part this diligence in highlighting the uniqueness of Yahweh (Carroll, 1992, 49–91, 122–34). Humans create and order their social worlds and cultures, and these contexts to a large extent determine self-understanding and perspectives on personal and communal life. RELIGION can play a significant role in this social construction of reality by providing answers to the ultimate questions of existence, detailing rules for life and welfare, and legitimizing (or challenging) social structures and practices through divine revelations, symbols, and rituals. In other words, a society's makeup, mores, and activities are impacted by its concept of God. The prophetic struggle to clarify the nature of the person of Yahweh and defend his demands, as well as their censure of inappropriate worship, is ultimately therefore a battle over Israel's self-definition and its vision of mission among the nations.

The Demand of Justice. The emphasis within the prophets on the person of God explains the all-encompassing breadth of their message (Birch, 1991, 240–69; Gossai). What the prophets seek is that the nation who calls itself by Yahweh's name reflect his person in every dimension of life. Thus, they speak to the actions and the ethos of the marketplace, judicial abuses, economic inequalities, and national foreign policy decisions. The persistent denouncing of religious ritual is not a call to definitively abolish sacrifice, but is rather a cry against religion divorced from justice and righteousness (e.g., Isa. 1; Hos. 4, 6; Micah 6; Amos 4–6).

This demand for worship of the one true God and for justice and compassion is not limited to God's people. It extends to every nation. Several prophetic books contain extensive sections of oracles directed against other nations' idolatry, cruelty in warfare, and unrestrained greed (e.g., Isa. 13–23; Jer. 46–51; Ezek. 25–32; Amos 1–2; Obad.; Nahum). In sum, mission within the prophetic corpus envisions that the people of God *be a blessing* among the nations in holiness and truth (cf. Gen. 12:1–9; *see* ABRAHAMIC COVENANT), yet these concerns are universalized to encompass all of humanity.

The Future Hope of the Prophets. The tone of the prophets is overwhelmingly negative. Most announce imminent and inevitable judgment. Yet, many also envision a future of peace, prosperity, and holiness beyond the coming divine chastisement. Most fundamentally, the prophetic hope centers around *the Messiah*. Different passages offer several pictures of the person and ministry of Yahweh's Anointed One (Kaiser, 1978,

182–261; Satterthwaite, Hess, Wenham). He will be a king and a shepherd, and he will be led by the Spirit of God. The Suffering Servant of Isaiah (Isa. 42; 49; 50; 52:13–53:12; 61), more than any other description, points to the extent of Yahweh's love and holy requirements: although meek, the Servant will persist even unto death to accomplish the task of bringing justice and salvation to the ends of the earth, for the glory of the Lord.

Another related dimension of the prophetic hope is *the eschatological role of Zion*. Its importance for mission lies in the belief that in the future the nations would stream to the mountain of God to learn of Yahweh and enjoy his bountiful provision (e.g., Isa. 2:2–4; 25:6–9; 66:17–24). Interpreters differ in their understanding of the fulfillment of the promises concerning the Messiah and Jerusalem, yet all agree that in some measure these hopes have been realized in the life and ministry of Jesus, at Pentecost, and in the history of the church.

Classic Prophetic Mission Passages Reconsidered. Those interested in missionary outreach and recruitment naturally go to the Old Testament seeking echoes of the New Testament mandates to take the good news of salvation to the ends of the earth. Two portions that have continually been appealed to are the call of Isaiah (Isa. 6, especially verse 8) and the Book of JONAH. The utilization of these passages, however, often does not reflect the textual data.

The charge to Isaiah is not to go to the nations with a word of hope. He is to announce irrevocable doom on his own people, without any expectation of repentance and escape from disaster (Isa. 6: 9–13). What is more, the words "Here am I, send me!" are not a response to an open-ended invitation to participate in God's plan for world evangelization, but instead reflect the willingness of the prophet to accept his difficult commission. He is the only human being present in this temple scene. Yahweh, although he has multitudes of seraphs ready to do his will (vv. 2–4), has decided to send someone from Judah. Isaiah apparently never leaves Jerusalem, and much of his ministry is directed at the monarchy. Nevertheless, a global element is present in the angelic proclamation that the whole earth is full of God's glory (v. 3). A careful reading of these lines in the context of the book, however, reveals that it will be Emmanuel, the Davidic king (Isa. 7, 9, 11, 32), who is also the Suffering Servant of later chapters, who will bring that universal glory to Yahweh through his righteous person and reign.

Warnings not to evade the touch of God to go to the nations sometimes point to the prophet Jonah for biblical support. The overriding sovereignty of God, it is said, will redirect the path of the disobedient to conform to the MISSIONARY CALL. The problem with this view is that the notion of going to the nations contradicts the Old Testament hope of their coming to Zion. In light of the vocabulary of 1:2 (cf. Gen. 4:10; 18:20), what one expects is that Jonah will go preach judgment against the sinful city. In fact, this is what he does when he finally arrives at Nineveh (3:4). It is not until chapter 4 that the prophet says why he ran away: he knew that the love of God extended beyond covenant boundaries (4:2, 11; cf. Exod. 34:6–7). He desired above all else the destruction of a violent empire, who was the enemy of Israel (3:8). The Book of Jonah, therefore, does not speak of obstinateness at obeying a missionary call. Perhaps a better application of its message resides in the realization that God's mercy must overcome all human prejudice and hatred, even if it is rooted in the memories of horrific suffering at the hands of the powerful.

In sum, the Old Testament prophets do not directly address world missions, as this is understood in the New Testament and the Christian church. Instead, their contribution lies in that they display the character of God, who, on the one hand, requires that his people accomplish the mission of being a holy people among the nations. On the other hand, this same Yahweh demonstrates that his love and justice are universal, both in the future judgment of all nations and in the worldwide ministry of Messiah.

M. DANIEL CARROLL R.

SEE ALSO Old Testament Theology of Mission.

Bibliography. B. C. Birch, *Let Justice Roll Down: The Old Testament, Ethics, and Christian Life*; M. D. Carroll R., *Contexts for Amos: Prophetic Poetics in Latin American Perspective*; H. Gossai, *Justice, Righteousness and the Social Critique of the Eighth-Century Prophets*; R. E. Hedlund, *The Mission of the Church in the World: A Biblical Theology*; W. C. Kaiser, Jr., *Toward an Old Testament Theology*; P. E. Satterthwaite, R. S. Hess, G. J. Wenham, eds., *The Lord's Anointed: Interpretation of Old Testament Messianic Texts*.

Old Testament Theology of Mission. Given that Israel was not sent out across cultural or geographical barriers, can one speak of mission at all in the Old Testament? Such a view, however, identifies mission too exclusively with the activity of human missionaries, whereas the Bible speaks first of all of the mission of God in God's world, and derives all human mission from that prior reality (*see* MISSIO DEI). From that point of view the Old Testament is fundamental for two reasons. First, it presents the mission and purpose of God with great power and clarity and with universal implications for all humanity. Second, the Old Testament shaped the very nature of the mission of the New Testament church, which, indeed, felt compelled to justify its mission practice from the Scriptures we now call the Old Testament.

The Manifesto: "The Gospel in Advance." Coming after the primal history of Genesis 1–11, in which the nations of humanity are portrayed as in rebellion against God, scattered and divided under his judgment, God's call of Abraham and the promise made to him, in Genesis 12, come as a radical new start in human history. After the three specific promises of posterity, blessing, and land comes the astonishing declaration of God's intention: "through you, all the families/nations of the earth will receive blessing" (Gen. 12:3, and cf. 18:18; 22:18; 26:4f.; 28:14; 35:11). Although the focus of attention from here on would be Israel as the descendants of Abraham, the ultimate mission of God is to bless the nations of humanity (*see* ABRAHAMIC COVENANT)—good news, indeed, in the light of the preceding chapters, and described as such by Paul, in defense of his own mission to the (Gentile) nations, in Galatians 3:8.

Missiologically the covenant with Abraham contains two balancing truths. First is the *universality* of God's purpose in the election of Abraham and Israel. They were called into existence only because of God's "missionary" purpose of ultimate blessing to all nations. Israel's election was not for the rejection of the nations, but for the sake of their salvation. Hence Paul's insistence that the in-gathering of the Gentiles in his day was not a contradiction of the promises made to Israel, but rather their eschatological fulfillment. Blessing the nations (which was the fruit of his mission) was the very reason for Israel's existence in the first place. Let those who wanted to make the Gentile converts into followers of Moses, "consider Abraham . . ." (Gal. 3:6–9).

Second is the *particularity* of the means God would use to bring about this universal blessing—"through you . . ." The instrument by which God would bless the nations would be the historical, particular, unique people he had created and called. Their uniqueness would ultimately be inherited by the Messiah, Jesus, as the one in whose name alone "repentance and forgiveness would be preached to all nations, beginning in Jerusalem" (Luke 24:47). It is important to hold these balancing truths together in a BIBLICAL THEOLOGY OF MISSION: the inclusive, universal goal (God's commitment to bless the nations); and the exclusive, particular means (the people, the Person, through whom God chose to do so).

The People: "A Light to the Nations." The nation of Israel was not, of course, physically sent out to the nations. Yet there are aspects of their identity and role that clearly have missional significance (*see* ISRAEL'S ROLE). First, there was the uniqueness of their historical experience of God's revelation and redemption (Deut. 4:32–40). No other nation experienced what they had of the knowledge or the saving power of God. This unique experience, however, was not an exclusive privilege, but a trust: "so that you might know that Yahweh is God in heaven above and on the earth beneath, and there is no other." The uniqueness of Israel's covenantal experience was the basis of their understanding of the uniqueness of Yahweh as God. This dimension of Israel's redemptive monotheism underlies the missionary nature of the New Testament proclamation of the UNIQUENESS OF CHRIST as Lord and Savior. (Note the way certain key Old Testament monotheistic texts are christologically expanded and quoted in the New Testament: e.g., Deut. 6:4, 4:35, 39 and 1 Cor. 8:5–6; Isa. 45:22–24 and Phil. 2:10–11).

Second, Israel was called to ethical distinctiveness, as part of what it meant to be "a light to the nations." As early as the patriarchal narratives, the link between the socioethical quality of life of the covenant community and the fulfillment of God's promise of blessing to the nations is made (Gen. 18:18–19). In Deuteronomy 4:6–8 Israel's visibility before the nations is put forward as a motivation for obedience to the law. Indeed, this missional perspective transforms a Christian understanding of the meaning of the law itself. Obedience was not only to be a matter of response to the grace of God's redemption (Deut. 6:20–25), but was to be for the purpose of attracting others to the light of God's presence among God's people (Isa. 58:6–10; 60:1–3; 62:1–2).

Third, Israel was given an identity (priestliness) and a task (holiness) in the foundational declaration at Sinai (Exod. 19:3–6). The priesthood in Israel stood between God and the rest of the people, both teaching God's law to the people and representing the people before God through sacrifice. Entrusted to Israel as a whole, the task of being God's priesthood in the midst of the nations is a mission in itself—to bring the knowledge of God to the nations, and to be the means of bringing the nations to God. Both centrifugal and centripetal dynamics are present in prophetic visions of this role (e.g., Isa. 2:2–5; 66:19–21). To be holy was to be fundamentally different (Lev. 18:3), and that difference was to be visible in social, economic, and political terms, not just in religion (Lev. 19). There is a correspondence between the desired visibility of Israel's distinctive ethic as a means of drawing the nations (Deut. 4:6–8) and the New Testament ethical exhortations that have the same missionary implications (Matt. 5:14–16; John 13:34f.; 1 Peter 2:9–12). As Luke observed, the social and economic life of the early Christian community was inseparable from the apostolic preaching in producing the growth and spread of the church (Acts 2:44–47; 4:34 [quoting Deut. 15:4]).

The Scope: The Totality of Human Need. Mission involves declaring and applying the redeeming work of God to the brokenness of the world. But what is the nature of that brokenness and what does redemption consist of? Again, it is the

Old Testament that provides so much of the fundamental WORLDVIEW that underlies the assumptions and practice of Christian mission. Its comprehensive analysis of the human predicament in terms of moral rebellion, the personal, social, historical, and ecological effects of sin, alongside the rich vocabulary through which this whole taxonomy of evil is expressed, all combine to forestall a shallow vagueness about what salvation needs to be and leaves us in no doubt that only God can accomplish it. An adequate understanding of the gospel depends upon an adequate appreciation of the radical effects of SIN. It is the Old Testament that provides this earthy realism.

Similarly, the Old Testament presentation of redemption offers a rich variety of models, all of which have influenced the Christian understanding of salvation through Christ and the MISSIONARY TASK of the people of God. The exodus, of course, stands as the key Old Testament model of redemption (and is celebrated as such, Exod. 15:13), with its comprehensive deliverance of Israel from political, economic, social, and spiritual bondage. The same holistic understanding of God's concern is found in the laws that the redeemed people were to follow in the land—perhaps focused most clearly in the Jubilee institution (Lev. 25), with its thrust toward restoration of people to meaningful participation in the community through access to fruitful resources. But it too is based on the theological roots of God's sovereignty and historical redemption (the exodus). The Jubilee strongly influenced Jesus' understanding of his own mission, and found eschatological echoes in the early missionary preaching of the church (Acts 3:21).

Then there is the sacrificial system, providing atonement and cleansing from sin. The cultic dynamics of Leviticus have been woven deeply into the Christian understanding of the death of Jesus, and in the hands of Paul, become, paradoxically, the language he uses to portray the power of the cross to unite Jew and Gentile in God's forgiveness (Rom. 3:25–31; Eph. 2:11–22 etc.). When Jesus declared, then, that "repentance and forgiveness would be preached in his name to all nations," the understanding of what those terms mean was already prepared for in the Scriptures (as indeed he was pointing out, Luke 24:45–47). Clearly, a holistic understanding of the nature of mission flows from a biblically holistic view of what redemption means and includes (see HOLISTIC MISSION). It is this breadth of understanding that the Old Testament contributes.

The Old Testament, however, has rich resources for mission which are not directly tied in to the redemptive-historical tradition of Israel. The wisdom literature, for example, with its strong creation base and its adaptation of the wisdom of other cultures to the faith of Yahweh, offers a WORLDVIEW and an approach to life and living that is perhaps the most cross-culturally bridge-building material in the Bible. Questions of what leads to a happy and successful life (Proverbs), how to wrestle with the problem of suffering (Job), and what to think in the face of futility and death (Ecclesiastes) are perennially and transculturally relevant, and provide an opening for the message of redemption from elsewhere in the canon.

And the worship of Israel at times rises to a breadth of universal vision in its faith imagination, in summoning all nations and all the ends of the earth to praise Yahweh (e.g., Pss. 47, 67, 96, 98, etc.)—a vision that is implicitly missionary in effect—as Paul realized when he quotes such material as the climax of his own missionary vision of the ingathering of the Gentiles (e.g., Rom. 15:7–12).

The Goal: "To Bring My Salvation to the Ends of the Earth." The eschatological vision of the Old Testament envisages the nations being brought in to share the blessings enjoyed by Israel. That was, of course, the very reason for Israel's election in the first place, and indeed "Israel" comes to be redefined and extended in a way that prophetically anticipates Paul's missionary theology in Romans 9–11.

In some contexts the nations are portrayed as summoned to celebrate what God had done in Israel, even when, paradoxically that included Israel's victory over them (cf. Ps. 47:1–4). The only justification for that must have been that the nations would somehow benefit from Israel's salvation history, unique as it was (cf. Pss. 22:27–28; 67; 96:1–3; 98:1–3). The Deuteronomistic history has some remarkable passages anticipating this universal blessing, most notably of all the prayer of Solomon at the dedication of the temple (1 Kings 8:41–43) in which God is asked to do for the foreigner whatever he asked in prayer (which had not even been promised to Israel!), so that God's name would be known and praised throughout the earth. Did those Gentiles who appealed so movingly to Jesus have any suspicion of the way they fulfilled this prayer (Matt. 8:5–13; 15:21–28)?

But in other contexts we find a more breathtaking vision that the nations would ultimately be included, along with Israel, as the extended people of God. Psalm 47:9 includes Gentile nobles "as the people of the God of Abraham." Isaiah 19:19–25 extends the privileged status of Israel ("my people, my inheritance, my handiwork") to their historical enemies. Isaiah 56:3–8 anticipates the joyful inclusion of certain categories of people previously excluded by the law (Deut. 23:1–3). Doubtless Luke intends us to see this text finding its first fulfillment in the salvation of the foreigner who was also a eunuch, and who was reading Isaiah at the time (Acts 8:26–39)! Significantly, though he had been to the temple in Jerusalem, the Ethiopian eunuch actually found joy when he believed in Jesus, the temple's fulfillment. A little later in Acts, James uses Amos 9:11–12 to clinch the theological (i.e., scriptural) justification for the amazing success of the Gentile mission (Acts 15:13–18).

This great Old Testament vision lies behind Paul's missiological theology of the multinational nature of the eschatological community being created in the Messiah, Jesus. Far from undermining in any way God's faithfulness to his promises to Israel, the ingathering of the nations was nothing less than the fulfillment of the very mission and raison d'etre of Israel.

The Servant of the Lord: "A Light to the Nations and the Glory of Your People Israel." The mission of Israel was also bound up with the identity and mission of the Servant, the mysterious figure in Isaiah 40–55 whose identity seems to oscillate between that of Israel and that of an individual yet to come. The mission of the Servant would be one of justice, gentleness, enlightenment, and liberation (Isa. 42:1–9). But it would also involve rejection and apparent failure (Isa. 49:4; 50:6–8) in the task of restoring Israel to God. In response to that, his mission would be extended to include the nations to the ends of the earth (Isa. 49:6). In that way, the mission of the Servant would be the fulfillment of the mission of Israel itself.

This dual nature of the Servant's mission—restoration of Israel and bringing salvation to the nations—lies behind the perception of the New Testament that the first task was Jesus' primary mission, while the second was entrusted to the church. This probably influenced the shape of Luke's two-volume work. His Gospel describes the mission of the servant to Israel, and Acts describes the fulfillment of Israel's scriptural mission in the ingathering of the Gentiles. This combined missiological understanding of Luke–Acts seems clearest in the "hinge" material of Luke 24:44–49 and Acts 1:6–8. It also seems that the dual nature of the servant's mission influenced the historical and theological shape of Paul's missionary strategy (Acts 13:46–48; Rom. 15:8–9), explaining among other things why one so conscious of his commission to the Gentiles believed it crucial that the gospel be preached "to the Jew first" (Rom. 1:16; 2:9–11).

The Scriptures of the Old Testament, then, not only provide the essential vision and themes of Christian mission, but also shape its initial and enduring theological structures.

CHRISTOPHER J. H. WRIGHT

SEE ALSO Jonah, Old Testament Prophets.

Bibliography. G. Anderson, *Theology of the Christian Mission;* D. Filbeck, *Yes, God of the Gentiles Too: The Missionary Message of the Old Testament;* A. F. Glasser, *Kingdom and Mission;* K. Gnanakan, *Kingdom Concerns: A Biblical Exploration Toward a Theology of Mission;* I. Hay, *Isaiah and the Great Commission;* R. Hedlund, *The Mission of the Church in the World: A Biblical Theology;* L. Newbigin, *The Open Secret;* G. W. Peters, *A Biblical Theology of Missions;* R. de Ridder, *Discipling the Nations;* D. Senior and E. Stuhlmueller, *The Biblical Foundations for Mission;* G. Van Rheenen, *Biblically Anchored Mission.*

Oldham, Joseph Houldsworth (1874–1969). Scottish ecumenical leader. Born in India to Scottish evangelical parents, he graduated from Oxford, where he had been JOHN MOTT's guide in 1891. He served the YMCA in India (1897–1901), then studied divinity at New College, Edinburgh, where he was to organize the WORLD MISSIONARY CONFERENCE (Edinburgh, 1910) and edit its nine-volume report. The diminutive Scot hailed by John Mott as "the deepest thinker and most influential worker in the British Student Movement," was named secretary (1910–21) of the continuation committee, not least because, sensitive to delicate situations, he was trusted both by the Germans and by the Anglo-Catholics. Oldham helped found and became joint secretary of the INTERNATIONAL MISSIONARY COUNCIL (1921–38) and founded and edited the *International Review of Missions* (1912–27). Concerned that missions might drift into a backwater, he begged Mott to concentrate exclusively on the IMC. He was also chief architect of the 1937 Oxford Conference and edited the *Christian News Letter* (1939–45), which sought to encourage Christian witness in secular life. His latter years were chiefly spent in improving the educational and social standards of the indigenous African peoples. He saw the importance of the future church in Africa, and persuaded missionary societies and the British government to devote more resources to Africa. Oldham's work was sometimes suspect in some American missionary circles whose continuing suspicion of colonialism led them to believe that his labors were only of value for the British Empire. He wrote *Christianity and the Race Problem* (1924) and *A Devotional Diary* (1929).

J. D. DOUGLAS

Oman (*Est. 2000 pop.: 2,626,000; 212,457 sq. km. [82,030 sq. mi.]*). The sultanate of Oman is one of the Gulf states in the southeast of the Arabian Peninsula. Oman is famous as an ancient trade center. In 1749, the dynasty of the al-Sa'id gained the Imanate with Ahmad bin Sa'id and established a sea empire. Trading in spices and slaves made Oman rich.

Although Oman's oil production started in 1967, the then Sultan Sa'id bin Taimur continued to isolate the country and forbade any innovation (no press, no media, no bikes, no glasses allowed; only three schools existed as well as twenty-five beds in a single hospital). Only after a coup d'etat in 1970 did the monarch's son, Sulan Qabus bin Said bin Taimur al-Said, gradually reform this medieval monarchy. Although he became the symbol of progress and development, he also paid respect to tradition. Today Oman remains an absolute monarchy (no political parties, no Constitution, no labor union, no Parliament), but with considerable freedom, political stability, and welfare for the average person. Still, much remains to be done for the approximately 60 percent illiterate with an annual growth of about 3.8 percent, since Oman's oil resources will probably be depleted by the year 2020.

Although open Christian witness is forbidden among the 65 percent Kbadi, 30 percent Sunni, and 5 percent Shi'i Muslims of Oman, there are 2.5 percent Christians of different denominations among the 530,000 foreign workers from the Philippines, Pakistan, India, Baluchistan, Europe, and the Near East. They worship in four centers in a number of churches. Foreign workers have been converted, and many of them are in daily contact with Omani people.

CHRISTINE SCHIRRMACHER

Omnipresence of God. God is infinite and therefore cannot be limited, measured, constrained, or contained in any particular space. Omnipresence speaks of God as infinite with respect to space. Though God is transcendent and wholly different from physical entities, he cannot be excluded from any part of his creation.

The omnipresence of God was fundamental to Paul's message and mission. He confidently proclaimed to his hearers that God is "not far from each one of us, for in him we live and move and have our being" (Acts 17:27–28). He affirmed that no one can escape God's presence, and could confidently assume that God preceded him and was present, even to his pagan hearers.

The omnipresence of God is personal. The psalmist extols the intimate presence of God that is for him a source of awe and strength, when he wonders: "Where can I go from your Spirit? Where can I flee from your presence?" (Ps. 139:7). God is infinitely and intimately present to humanity in time of need (Ps. 46:1). This is a source of profound assurance and hope: God is personally available to all who call on him—regardless of where they are. However dark the circumstances, God is there.

Those who speak and act in witness to Christ can be assured that God is never absent from a place, a people, or a person. The missionary never brings God, but rather announces and witnesses to the presence of God. The missionary is a witness to this reality and a catalyst by which it is awakened in the hearer's conscience.

Although God is completely present in all places and at all times, at times he is hidden and at other times revealed. At times God is obviously active; at other times God's presence is subtle or quiet.

We cannot assume that God is present where there are dramatic and visible signs. More often than not, God's presence is more difficult to discern. Elijah did not recognize God in the earthquake, wind, or fire, but in a still small voice (1 Kings 19). Discerning the presence of God begins with recognizing this principle.

GORDON T. SMITH

Bibliography. T. Oden, *The Living God.*

Omniscience of God. The omniscience of God describes God as all-knowing, an attribute of majesty that expresses God's transcendence (Weber, 1983, 403, 438). The fact that the merciful God (*see* GRACE OF GOD) wants to know us completely means that he accepts us and that he loves us. In the Bible the concept of knowing is broader and deeper than rational cognition of facts—it is intimate, loving relationship of care, commitment, and mutuality (e.g., Gen. 4:1; Prov. 1:7; John 8:19; 17:25–26).

Nothing in creation can be hidden from a God of love. The omniscience of God refers to God's knowing all things in terms of extent and scope, as well as in terms of penetration (God knows all things completely and deeply) and time (what has always been, is, and will be). "It is not merely an outer knowledge of its objects; it is also an inner knowledge. It is not partial; it is total" (Barth, II:1, 555; 1 John 15; Ps. 139:11–12). Thus God's foreknowledge is not time-bound, neither does it imply a mechanistic determinism as if God's foreknowledge meant his direct control or causation. Rather, God's foreknowledge is relational (John 1; Eph. 1; Col. 1).

Thus the Bible stresses God's intimate, relational knowing in love. God "knows" as creator. "By his knowledge the deeps were divided" (Prov. 3:20). God knows us in the womb before we are born (Pss. 103:14; 139:15–16). God knows our coming and going and even our thoughts (e.g., 1 Sam. 2:3; Pss. 44:21; 139:1). God knows our needs (Matt. 6:8) and he knows those who are his (2 Tim. 2:19). God knows us in choosing us "in him before the foundation of the world . . . to be adopted as his (children) through Jesus Christ" (Eph. 1:4–5). One of the ways in which the Gospels assert the deity of Jesus is to affirm that Jesus knows people's thoughts, yet does not control them (e.g., Matt. 12:25). He knows his sheep though they have not yet responded to him (e.g., John 10:14).

In cross-cultural missions, the omniscience of God has several implications. First, when we step into a new context of mission, there is an assurance of being accompanied by God in Jesus Christ, by the Holy Spirit. In fact, God has been there already, waiting for us. In the GREAT COMMISSION Jesus says that wherever his disciples go, he will be with them always. His omnipresence implies omniscience. Our Lord knows where we are going, knows us as we cross cultural barriers, and welcomes us when we get there. Second, as creator, sustainer, and lover of all people and all creation, God understands all cultures and all peoples in those cultures. He "knows his sheep," even sheep of another fold. Even while they were yet sinners, "Christ died for (them)" (Rom. 5:8). Thus, when we cross barriers to another culture, we can be assured that God understands the other persons though we may not. God knows their thoughts and their WORLDVIEWS and cares for those to whom we are sent. Third, God's omniscience implies that Christians in all cultures everywhere in the world are intimately known by God and therefore may be assured that they can read the Scriptures and hear God's Word in their own language and culture, and can know God in very special and unique ways in their particular worldview (Van Engen, 1996, 71–89).

CHARLES VAN ENGEN

Bibliography. K. Barth, *Church Dogmatics*; H. Berkhof, *Christian Faith*; S. Grenz, *Theology for the Community of God*; C. Van Engen, *Mission on the Way*; O. Weber, *Foundations of Dogmatics*.

OMS International. This mission society was founded by the Pilgrim Holiness missionaries to Japan, Charles E. and Lettie B. Cowman, in 1901. They were joined by Ernest E. Kilbourne whom they had come to know at God's Bible School in Cincinnati. Especially central to their success was their collaboration with Juji Nakada, who had been instrumental in their choice of Japan. Their goal was to establish self-supporting, self-governing, and self-propagating churches on the WILLIAM TAYLOR model. Among the results of this mission in Asia were the Japan Holiness Church and the Korean Holiness Church. The latter supports the largest seminary in Asia: Seoul Theological Seminary. The Korean Holiness Church is involved in mission throughout Asia, with special attention to Thailand, Siberia, and Japan.

During and after World War II, OMS spread into India, Taiwan, Hong Kong, Spain, and the Caribbean. Under the name of the Inter-American Missionary Society the group established denominations in Colombia, Brazil, and Equador. More recently OMS has sent missionaries to Indonesia, France, and the Philippines. OMS, Inc., maintains a close connection with Asbury College (where a study center for students and a missionary home are maintained) and Asbury Theological Seminary. The agency serves as a mission sending agency for Holiness members of the United Methodist Church as well as from the smaller Holiness churches. The international headquarters is in Greenwood, Indiana.

DAVID BUNDY

Bibliography. L. B. Cowman, *Charles E. Cowman: Missionary Warrior*; R. D. Wood, *In These Mortal Hands: The Story of the Oriental Missionary Society, the First Fifty Years*; T. Yamamori, *Church Growth in Japan: A Study in the Development of Eight Denominations*.

Option for the Poor. There has long been a recognition that the poor (economically, politically, and socially marginalized people) hold special attention and affection in God's eyes. The phrase "option for the poor" or "preferential option for the poor" is of relatively recent coinage. Roman Catholics began wrestling with issues related to poverty in the SECOND VATICAN COUNCIL (1962–65). Catholics in Latin America, who felt that the work at Vatican II did not go far enough, convened in Medellín, where the emphasis was changed from seeing the poor as the objects of the mercy of the church to seeing them as the subjects of their own history (González, 19). The actual phrase "preferential option of the poor" did not appear until the 1970s, reportedly used by Gustavo Gutiérrez in a lecture given in Spain in 1972 (ibid.). Since then the term has been used primarily in liberation and conciliar theological circles but also increasingly in evangelical missiology.

The concept behind the term is one that demands a radical paradigm shift. The poor are not to be seen as objects of mercy, but as people who are particularly gifted by God to represent his justice to the rest of the world. The "option" for the poor is not optional, but required by the very nature of God's compassion and incarnation in Jesus. Because Jesus came to preach liberty to the poor, they have an advantage in reading the Scriptures. They are not weighted down with the presuppositions and agendas of the rich and are freer to read and interpret the text as its primary audience. Such reading requires the recognition of structural issues that create and perpetuate poverty and new tools of analysis to understand and change those structures.

Evangelical use of the term traces its roots to the LAUSANNE CONGRESS ON WORLD EVANGELISM (1974) and the eventual wrestling of evangelicals over EVANGELISM AND SOCIAL RESPONSIBILITY (see Walker). A shift toward holism within the evangelical movement (*see* HOLISTIC MISSION), prompted in part by reflections from both non-Western evangelical theologians (e.g., Vinay Samuel, Rene Padilla, and Samuel Escobar) and Western evangelicals (e.g., Ron Sider and Jim Wallis), has resulted in greater empathy for the option for the poor (*see also* LIBERATION THEOLOGIES MISSIOLOGY). It is now not uncommon to see the phrase "option for the poor" across the spectrum of missiology. Evangelicals who have committed themselves to this agenda have in the past been referred to as radical evangelicals, though the language of opting for the poor has been gaining momentum in mainstream evangelical missiological circles in recent years.

What is God's view of the poor? They are people and part of his creation. They have oppressors who keep them poor. While they are sinners, they are also in significant ways sinned against by those who oppress and subvert justice against them. God does "opt" for them in the sense of siding with them in demanding impartiality and justice. He cares for their spiritual and material needs. The same attitude should be found in the church (e.g., James 2:2–6). That the poor teach us about God or enjoy special spiritual status is true in the sense that their humble circumstances force them to see more realistically their broken condition before God. That they are somehow automatically saved or members of God's church simply by virtue of their socioeconomic status, however, cannot be sustained in light of the overall biblical evidence. The poor are in need of having the Good News preached to them and thus the thrust of Jesus' statements about his mission in Luke 4:18–20.

A. SCOTT MOREAU

SEE ALSO Wealth and Poverty.

Bibliography. R. M. Brown, *Reading in the Bible Through Third World Eyes;* R. D. N. Dickinson, *DEM,* pp. 806–10; D. Dorr, *Option for the Poor: A Hundred Years of Catholic Social Teaching;* J. L. González, *Poverty and Ecclesiology,* pp. 9–26; F. Herzog, *DEM,* pp. 804–5; D. S. Walker, *Journal of Theology for Southern Africa* 79 (1992): 53–62.

Ordinances. *See* SACRAMENTS/ORDINANCES.

Oriental Missionary Society. *See* OMS INTERNATIONAL.

Original Sin. *See* FALL OF HUMANKIND and SIN, THE BIBLICAL DOCTRINE OF.

Orphanage Work in Christian Missions. Perhaps no other work in Christian missions has commanded so deep an emotional response to people as has care for children who have no place to call their home. The plight of Korean children during and after the Korean conflict (1949–51) and the work of Robert Pierce on their behalf not only raised the awareness of Western Christians to parentless children there, but also was the primary impetus for the establishment of World Vision International.

The beginnings of orphanage work in Christian missions, however, extend much farther back into the history of Christian missions. Indeed one could cite more than seven hundred references in Scripture concerning children as an indication of their importance to God, and hence to the religion that would spring from worship of him. A representative text of Jesus is known to many people. He said, "Let the little children come to me, and do not hinder them, for the kingdom of heaven belongs to such as these" (Matt. 19:14).

Throughout the early history of the church Christian compassion focused upon the plight of children. A representative sermon/essay by Cotton Mather reflects this emphasis and is likely the source for the term "orphanage." In his essay (c. 1711) he spoke of orphanages as "orphanotropheism," as "the care taken in the divine Providence for children when their parents forsake them." Need for such care was caused by the terrible conditions of the Industrial Revolution when parents were thrown into debtors' prisons and children were forced to work in crude factories, leaving many children without homes or parents (see Pierson, also Gaston).

Elsewhere on the globe, orphanages did not develop until the nineteenth century due in large part to the lack of any need for them. Asia, Africa, and Latin America were mostly nonindustrial regions, depending upon agriculture but with high infant mortality rates. The need for children and stable cohesive social structures provided a relatively secure social and family arrangement for them, except for conditions of war. This picture changed with the coming of industrial economies and the establishment of urban centers.

China is a case in point. There, feudal wars and terrible climatic conditions (famine, floods, etc.) left families economically impoverished and malnourished and children homeless. To meet these conditions missionaries, often women, took up the burden, established homes, or simply took in a wandering child, and then another and another, until finally an orphanage, de facto, was founded (see Wang).

The words "strategy" and "missionary method" seem oddly out of place when speaking of orphanages in missionary work. Such terms appear crass and manipulative, giving the appearance of "using" pain and loss for the purposes of proselytism. Nor do such terms reflect the spirit of such efforts. Mary Schauffler LaBaree writes with a keen intellect and deep feeling and conviction about the plight of children in Persia, and the significance of her work and ministry is unsurpassed. Yet, there is not a hint of missionary strategy in the book. The same can be said of Thomas Gamble's description of the establishment of George Whitfield's Bethesda (House of Mercy). Here you find no hint of winning people to Christ through philanthropy. Rather, you find work springing from the well of deep compassion for the plight of children and others.

THOMAS N. WISELY

Bibliography. T. Gamble, *Bethesda: An Historical Sketch of Whitefield's House of Mercy;* N. Gaston, *George Muller and His Orphans;* M. S. LaBaree, *A Child in the midst;* A. T. Pierson, *George Muller of Bristol;* M. Wang, *Precious Jewels.*

Orthodox Mission Movements. No comprehensive history of Eastern Orthodox missions exists today. Only studies of particular periods and personalities are available, especially in Russian Orthodox missions. Moreover, few "Departments of Missions" exist as distinct disciplines within Orthodox seminaries throughout the world. Only a handful of missiologists are qualified as specialists in this field, though the situation is gradually beginning to change. The subject, therefore, is a lacuna that needs to be aggressively filled in missiological studies today.

The history of Orthodox missions is made more difficult because the so-called Oriental Orthodox Churches (such as the Armenian, Syrian Jacobite, Coptic, and Ethiopian communities) rightly deserve to be included in the Orthodox family. Any treatment of Orthodox mission movements must view the church in light of its theological unity and complex administrative autonomies. Ideologically, throughout its history the Orthodox Church engaged in what may be termed "incarnational evangelism," that is, missionary enterprises that sought CONTEXTUALIZATION of the gospel for diverse nationalities out of faithfulness to the witness of the apostles. While this has had its obvious advantages, it also has tended to promote confusion among the uneducated between the gospel and NATIONALISM leading to "ethnic Christianity."

The history of Orthodox missions shows that there has been very few missionary institutions, organizations, or orders. After the apostolic age, Emperor Constantine in the fourth century was given the missionary titles "Equal to the Apostles" and "Overseer of the Things/People Outside" the empire. The emperor was called upon to be the political protector and promoter of the Christian faith in places where it had not yet been received. In the early Middle Ages, the Byzantine government frequently enlisted missionaries as agents of imperial policy. Military interventions and political diplomacy from the imperial throne were used to support the spread of Orthodox Christianity. Byzantine missions to Eastern Europe often implied the acceptance of both Orthodoxy and a political alliance with Constantinople. Some individuals were officially supported while others worked on their own. The principles of mission were incarnational: the Bible, liturgy, and the Church Fathers were translated into the vernacular; indigenous clergy were implemented to lead the flocks; and local autonomy was encouraged. By these methods, numerous races of the Russian plain, the Caucasus, Persia, Arabia, and Africa were baptized in the fourth, fifth, and sixth centuries. Some of these peoples have disappeared, though others still exist today (such as the Georgians, Armenians, Syrians, and Ethiopians).

The great age of Orthodox missionary activity began in the ninth and tenth centuries. Patriarch Photios dispatched a mission to Boris I of Bulgaria, and sent Sts. CYRIL and METHODIUS to the Moravians. The Great Moravian mission occasioned the first confrontation between Roman Catholic and Eastern Orthodox missions. Cyril and Methodius created a unique alphabet so they could preach the gospel and translate the liturgy into the native vernacular. Use of the vernacular in worship and mission polarized Rome and Constantinope in the ninth century and highlighted their different missiological principles. The greatest success of Byzantine missionaries was the conversion of Prince VLADIMIR I of Kiev in 988. Characteristically, missions in Russia worked from the top down by focusing first on the political leaders who then encouraged their people en masse to follow their example. People of the northern Caucasus region followed Russia's example. In the ninth century, systematic work in Serbia was undertaken by the followers of Cyril and Methodius, but it was not until the thirteenth century that Serbian attachment to the Eastern Church became final.

The history of missions from the fourteenth century is mainly the history of Russian Orthodox missions. This was due mostly to the Turkish captivity of the Greek Church under Islam. In Russian Orthodox missionary activity, the focus was on evangelism within the boundaries of the great Russian Empire itself. The progressive penetration of the gospel was carried on by monks who worked among the Finnish races in what is today northern Russia, and later in the Urals and Siberia. A special type of missionary, known as the "colonial monk," taught a new way of life without seeking to intentionally convert the heathen. These monks became bearers of Russian culture as well as the gospel. Examples of Russian missionary heroes are Sts. Sergius, STEPHEN OF PERM (both 14th century), and Seraphim of Sarov (17th and 18th centuries). Peter the Great, as part of his imperial strategy, also supported Russian missions, which extended as far as China in the eighteenth century. The nineteenth century was the "Great Century" of Russian Orthodox missions (though not comparable to the scope of Protestant and Catholic missions of the same period). In 1791, the Russian mission first arrived in Kodiak, Alaska, from the Valamo monastery in Finland under St. Herman. Possibly the greatest personality of the period was (John) INNOCENT VENIAMINOV, or "St. Innocent of Alaska" (1797–1879). Innocent followed the tradition of Cyril and Methodius by translating the

Gospels and liturgy into the Aleutian language and establishing a native priesthood.

East Asian missions in the nineteenth century included the Japanese Orthodox Church, founded by St. NICHOLAS KASATKIN, and the Korean mission founded by Russian clergy in 1898. In the twentieth century, at least two regions reveal modern missionary zeal: first, in Africa, an intensive enculturation of the Orthodox faith and worship has occurred under the Patriarchate of Alexandria, and in Asia under the Patriarchate of Constantinople; second, a significant emergence of new Orthodox communities has arisen in the so-called diaspora churches located especially in America, but also to a lesser degree in Canada, Western Europe, Australia, and Latin America. A new Pan-Orthodox mission board was recently founded in St. Augustine, Florida, as a means to promote Orthodoxy and serve the needs of the mother churches overseas. At present, the most active missionary group in North America is the Antiochian Orthodox Church, with approximately 50 percent of its pastoral staff comprised of converts from mostly Protestant and Catholic backgrounds. Advocates of American contextualization have called for indigenous new ways of incarnating the gospel in keeping with the church's past missiological practices. Such advocates highlight the missionary imperative of translating "Old World Orthodoxy" into the multicultural vernacular of an American audience through native creativity in liturgical, hymnographic, and iconographic expressions of the faith.

Documents for contemporary models and emphases in Orthodox missions have been hammered out largely in the context of the church's involvement in the WCC. The Orthodox have distinguished five contexts for their witness in the modern world: (1) traditional Orthodox countries, such as Greece, parts of Lebanon, and the Middle East; (2) postcommunist countries (closely overlapping the first), including Russia, Romania, Serbia, and Albania; (3) Islamic lands, such as Egypt; (4) churches of the so-called diaspora, such as America, Canada, and Western Europe; and (5) young missionary churches, including Africa and Korea. Renewal movements within the Orthodox Church itself—such as the Lord's Army in Romania, Zoe in Greece, the Orthodox Youth Movement in Lebanon, the Brotherhood of St. Symeon the New Theologian and the Antiochian Evangelical Orthodox Mission in America—have revived interest in Bible study, preaching, patristics, and liturgics. Moreover, mission organizations that build bridges between the Orthodox and evangelical traditions include the Society for the Study of Eastern Orthodoxy and Evangelicalism and Christians for Middle East Understanding. The greatest missiological challenge of global Orthodoxy at the dawn of the third millennium appears to be the need for "internal mission," for example, the reconversion of its own people to the saving gospel of Jesus Christ.

BRADLEY NASSIF

Bibliography. I. Bria, compiler and editor, *Go Forth in Peace: Orthodox Perspectives on Mission;* I. Bria and P. Vassiliades, *Orthodox Christian Martyria;* F. Dvornik, *Byzantine Missions among the Slavs;* G. Lemopoulos, *Your Will Be Done: Orthodoxy in Mission;* B. Nassif, ed., *New Perspectives on Historical Theology: Essays in Memory of John Meyendorff;* N. Nissiotis, *The Greek Orthodox Theological Review* 8 (1962): 22–52; I. Sauca, ed., *Orthodoxy and Cultures.*

Orthodox Theology of Mission.

The Eastern Orthodox Churches (EOC) are not generally thought of as missionary churches. In part, this stems from a lack of knowledge of the history of the Eastern Churches and also a misunderstanding of the theological framework of the Orthodox Church, which appears to be antithetical or at least indifferent to the missionary vision of both the Roman Catholic and Protestant experience. In spite of oppressive historical circumstances that have hindered the expression of missionary concern, Eastern Christianity, represented by both the Chalcedonian and non-Chalcedonian churches (also called Oriental Orthodox Churches [OOC] or occasionally lesser Orthodox Churches) share the same ethos as the mainline Eastern Orthodox Churches. The Nestorian Church had an impressive missionary thrust into China (*see* NESTORIAN MISSION). The Mar Thoma Church of South India has a very similar liturgy and theology, as do the other OOC. They are distinguished from the EOC in that the EOC are in communion with and recognized by the Ecumenical Patriarch of Constantinople.

For the EOC, the key elements of their theological framework revolve around the purpose of the incarnation. Often accused by Western theologians of having an inadequate doctrine of SIN, the EOC focus on the potential that humankind was created to achieve. The first human pair were created perfect but with the possibility and necessity for growth and development. This maturation would eventually lead to humans fully manifesting the image (but not the essence) of God. Evangelization therefore proceeds along the line of fulfilling God's purpose in creation. The goal is not justification of the sinner, but rather what would be termed in Western theological categories as justification and sanctification. The Orthodox call their understanding of the biblical meaning of salvation *theosis.* This Greek word is sometimes inadequately rendered *deification* in Latin, which has inherent pantheistic overtones, something not intended in the doctrine. The patristic phrase, "God became man, so that men might become god," does not convey a sharing of the divine essence. The intent is that to be fully human, one must become fully mature in the *imago Dei* (IMAGE OF GOD).

The goal of restoring humankind to the lost image of God has several implications for missions. In the first place, it highlights the importance of the liturgical community, which celebrates the incarnation and the death and resurrection of the Lord. It is in this community that the maturation and growth in grace occurs. Therefore it also elevates the importance of each culture because no language is inappropriate to worship God. Only in one's mother tongue can the true worship of God be expressed. The Orthodox see Pentecost as the reversal of the confusion of tongues at the Tower of Babel. The gospel must be preached in all the world and God worshiped in all the languages of the world. The entry of the Second Person of the Trinity into first-century Palestine is taken to be the model for the incarnation of the gospel into each people group so that each will be able to worship the Triune God. Indeed, the focus in the EOC is on the correct *(ortho)* praise *(doxia)*, and not merely on the correct doctrine. Great emphasis is placed on the use of the vernacular in the liturgy. The result is that where the Orthodox faith has been planted it has penetrated deeply into the soul of the nation. The transmission of the gospel into the culture has shaped the culture in many lands where the Eastern Church was the predominant Christian expression. This close identification of Orthodox Christianity and culture has led to the religious persecution of non-Orthodox Christians in traditionally Orthodox lands.

The pillars of the mission theology of the EOC have been the use of the vernacular, the deployment of indigenous clergy, the translation of the Bible into the vernacular and the selfhood of the national church. The goal was the creation of self-governing churches praising God in their own language and, to some extent, style which accounts for the minor differences in liturgical practice and theological emphasis throughout the EOC. These differences have been treated as either local traditions or under the category of *theolougemena* (theological opinion that does not contradict conciliar definitions). However, liturgical uniformity and allegiance to the creeds and councils bound the diverse linguistic groups into a whole.

To use the traditional Western categories of mission, the ultimate aim of mission is to restore all of humanity to a right relationship with God, which would issue in all of humankind correctly praising the Trinity. The motives for mission are obedience to God, love for God, and love for a fallen humanity. The method would be to have lives lived in accordance with the gospel and engaged in the worship of the true God. In Orthodox theory and practice, the liturgical expression of the church is a method of evangelistic outreach. In this, it mirrors the church of the early centuries, which allowed catechumens (those being instructed for baptism) to stay for all but the eucharistic portion of the liturgy. While the order of catechumens is no longer observed in the EOC, the warnings for them to depart before the Eucharist still form part of the liturgy of the EOC. However, the liturgical witness of the EOC is seen as a legitimate and appropriate form of evangelistic witness. Stories abound of the conversion of pagans once they had observed the liturgical ceremonies of the EOC. One of the traditional stories of the conversion of Prince VLADIMIR (989), founder of Russian Christianity, revolves around his envoys witnessing the liturgy celebrated in Constantinople.

A phrase used in EOC theology to describe the centrality of the liturgical rites is "the liturgy after the liturgy." This signifies the Orthodox view that engagement in the world is also an act of *leitourgia*. The word comes from the two Greek words *leitos* (public) and *ergon* (work). Traditionally the liturgy signified the celebration of the Eucharist by a local community, but this has been expanded to use "liturgy" to signify the Church's witness to the world. The other term used is *martyria* to signify the centuries of witness that led to MARTYRDOM. The EOC involvement in the ECUMENICAL MOVEMENT has led to a clearer articulation of a theology of mission that follows the traditional EOC theological perspective.

There are no independent mission societies in the EOC. All missionary work is undertaken under episcopal supervision. In 1870, Metropolitan Innocent, himself a former missionary to Russian Alaska, founded the Orthodox Missionary Society in Moscow. More recently, missionary interest in Greece was sparked by *Porethenes*, a missionary journal founded in 1959 and succeeded by *Pante ta Ethnes*. The Inter-Orthodox Missionary Centre was founded in Athens in 1961. The center supported the work of the African Orthodox Church, an African-initiated independent church located in East Africa. In North America, mission interest was stimulated by the Mission Committee of the Greek Orthodox Archdiocese of North and South America and the work of the Inter Orthodox Mission Center in St. Augustine, Florida. Orthodox missionaries are at work in Africa, Asia, Central Europe, and North America.

JAMES J. STAMOOLIS

Bibliography. I. Bria, *Martyria/Mission: The Witness of the Orthodox Churches Today*; idem, *The Liturgy after the Liturgy: Mission and Witness from an Orthodox Perspective*; A. Schmemann, *Church, World, Mission*; J. Stamoolis, *Eastern Orthodox Mission Theology Today*.

Overseas Missionary Fellowship (OMF). In 1964 the Overseas Missionary Fellowship succeeded the China Inland Mission (CIM), which had been founded in Great Britain in 1865 by JAMES HUDSON TAYLOR. Taylor had served as a missionary in China from 1835 to 1860 with the Chinese Evangelization Society. An international, inderdenominational organization, the CIM was a faith mission that eventually became the largest mission agency in China. It had its headquarters in Shanghai, as Taylor believed that decisions needed to be made in the country where the mission actually operated, not in the sending country. He firmly believed that God would provide the money necessary to run the organization and, accordingly, asked only for prayers and personnel for the work, never directly soliciting funds. Another unusual aspect is that Taylor insisted that his missionaries live as much as possible like those they sought to convert. All were required to adopt native dress, and, while the Qing dynasty was in power, the men were required to grow queues, pinning fake ones inside their hats until their own hair reached the proper length. As most of the CIM missionaries were married, the mission established a boarding school for their children at Chefoo.

While emphasizing belief in the whole Bible, the CIM encouraged its members to maintain their ties to the various denominational churches. CIM recruits were not required to be university graduates, and the organization sent unmarried women and unordained men to China as missionaries long before most other missions recognized the contributions they could make. In the first decades of its existence the CIM sent only British missionaries to the field, but in 1888 Taylor visited the United States to preach at various interdenominational mission conferences, and the CIM subsequently expanded its base to North America. The first North American recruits sailed from Canada that year. Henry W. Frost was appointed North American director and held the position for forty years.

Because Taylor was committed to the evangelization of China's unreached population, CIM missionaries often established themselves in remote locales and small towns overlooked by other mission groups. Notable among the CIM missionaries in China were the martyred John and Betty Stam, whose infant daughter escaped death and was carried in a basket by a Chinese convert to the nearest mission station. Taylor, who died in 1905, was succeeded as CIM director by D. E. HOSTE, George W. Gibb, Frank Houghton, J. O. SANDERS, Michael C. Griffiths, and James Hudson Taylor III, great-grandson of the founder. The CIM's major publication was the periodical *China's Millions,* which kept supporters at home informed of the work. When Christian missions were forced to withdraw from China in the early 1950s, the CIM removed its operations to other Asian countries including Japan, Hong Kong, Taiwan, Korea, the Philippines, Thailand, and Singapore.

KATHLEEN L. LODWICK

Bibliography. K. S. Latourette, *A History of Christian Missions in China;* P. Brierley, ed., *U.K. Christian Handbook,* 1983 ed.

Pp

Pacifist Theology. Christian pacifist theology grows from the conviction that Jesus meant it to be taken seriously when he said, "Love your enemies" and "Do not return evil for evil" (Matt. 5), even to the extent of laying down one's life rather than taking the life of another. Likewise, the theology of Christian missions stems from the conviction that Jesus' final words, "Go and make disciples of all people" (Matt. 28), were given to be obeyed, even to the extent of forsaking one's homeland so that others might hear the gospel.

Just as post-Constantinian obedience to the GREAT COMMISSION is rooted most clearly in the radical biblicism of such historic Christian movements as the Celts, the Franciscans, the Waldenses, Anabaptists, Moravians, Baptists, Wesleyans, and Pentecostals, so the Christian embrace of pacifism is most closely linked with these same expressions of renewal. In this broad historic sense there is a discernible connection between pacifist theology and mission.

However, many evangelical Christians with roots in the nineteenth- and twentieth-century missionary movement were unaware of these connections. Members of "historic peace churches" such as Quakers, Brethren, and Mennonites did, of course, maintain outspoken commitment to Christian pacifism, but they were somewhat less conspicuous at the forefront of the missionary movement, though they were certainly not absent. However, others such as Baptists and post–World War II Pentecostals almost forgot their pacifistic origins.

For example, the pre-1967 Assemblies of God official statement on war read in part, "We, as a body of Christians, while purposing to fulfill all the obligations of loyal citizenship, are nevertheless constrained to declare we cannot conscientiously participate in war and armed resistance which involves the actual destruction of human life, since this is contrary to our view of the clear teachings of the inspired Word of God, which is the sole basis of our faith" (Beaman, p. 24).

The engagement of these same groups at the forefront of global missions is a matter of historical record. For example, the Moravian revival of 1727 was rooted in a combination of contemporary German PIETISM and earlier European evangelical radicalism among the Hussites and Anabaptists. It was this same Moravian revival which, beginning immediately in its first decade, inaugurated the outpouring of missionary energy which resulted both in the conversion of JOHN WESLEY and the sending of Christian witnesses worldwide (*see* MORAVIAN MISSION). The link with pacifistic groups is clear, especially in their Reformation and pre-Reformation radical heritage. These historic connections between pacifism and missions are not accidental. They derive from a straightforward evangelical biblicism which affirms both "Go ye into all the world" and "Love your enemies." In each case, obedience requires sacrifice and suffering love.

Pacifist Christians maintain that the two are logically as well as biblically linked. The world is full of enemies, they say, and the only way to go to them with integrity is to go in love with a commitment to peace. Any other posture leads either to neglect of the missionary mandate (where the enemy is fought or ignored) or to compulsive proselytization of the kind which Jesus condemned.

Non-pacifist evangelical Christians, while maintaining commitment to love of enemies, argue that there are some circumstances in which Christians are permitted or even obligated to take up arms against others. These circumstances are usually defined as (1) times when the government which is ordained by God orders its citizens to arms or (2) when taking the life of another is necessary to protect the innocent. This position has been defended classically as "just war," although the use of mechanical war against citizen populations in the twentieth century and the threat of nuclear war after 1945 raised serious questions as to whether a traditional just war is any longer possible.

In summary, evangelical pacifists view the missionary movement since Pentecost as having been embedded in forms of biblical literalism and obedience which were either outright pacifistic or inclined in that direction, thus linking the two. Evangelical non-pacifists, in contrast, tend to see Christian pacifism either as an impossible ideal or as a failure to read Romans 13 correctly, thus denying significant connections between pacifism and missions.

Because various forms of evangelical non-pacifism have been predominant in twentieth-century evangelicalism and because most evangelical pacifists spend more time defending their view of peace biblically and philosophically than promoting it as intrinsic to a missiological stance, little has been written on missions and pacifism. It remains, however, a fertile field for investigation.

RICHARD SHOWALTER

Bibliography. J. Beaman, *Pentecostal Pacifism: The Origin, Development, and Rejection of Pacific Belief Among Pentecostals;* R. G. Clouse, ed., *War: Four Christian Views;* R. Ramseyer, ed., *Mission and the Peace Witness;* J. H. Yoder, *The Politics of Jesus.*

Padilla, Carlos René (1932–). Ecuadorian theologian, writer, and pastor. At an early age he started developing his writing and analytical skills and later took his training at Wheaton College Graduate School. Upon graduation he worked among university students, serving in Latin America with the International Fellowship of Evangelical Students (IFES). Almost simultaneously he earned a Ph.D. in New Testament from the University of Manchester, in Great Britain. Living and ministering primarily in a continent with deep social and economic problems and not fully satisfied with the solutions offered by either the theology of liberation or the evangelical movement as a whole, Padilla has written and spoken extensively throughout the world, calling for a hermeneutic not affected by ideology or traditional practices in the process of contextualizing the biblical message in order to communicate it effectively. This is the focus of a missionary theology, faithful to the gospel and relevant to the context. He has also written *Mission Between the Times,* and was the founder and editor of the magazine *Misión* from his headquarters in Buenos Aires, plus establishing "Kairós," a conference and retreat center for in-depth discussions of subjects pertinent to the times and situation in Latin America.

PABLO E. PÉREZ

Padwick, Constance Evelyn (1886–1968). English author and missionary in Egypt, Palestine, Sudan, and Turkey. Born in West Thorney, Sussex, England, to an Anglican family, Padwick was initially rejected from service abroad by the CMS for health reasons. She left CMS home office service to work in Egypt with the Nile Mission Press, but returned to the CMS when they agreed to accept her for work in the Middle East.

Gifted in communication and cultural observation, Padwick engaged in a successful literature ministry work throughout her career. In contrast to the polemic approach of literature written at that time for use in evangelization among Muslims, Padwick wrote so as to engage in "penitent love" by creating sensitive understanding of Islam. Her approach was to build bridges through loving understanding rather than to attack Islamic doctrines and beliefs. *Muslim Devotions* (1961), along those lines, is a compilation of devotions from various Sufi orders chosen to promote understanding among Christians of the deeply held religious faith of Muslims.

Writing biographies about missionaries such as HENRY MARTYN (1922) and W. H. TEMPLE GAIRDNER (1929), developing such works as *Muslim Devotions,* editing *Orient and Occident,* writing Arabic text books for Sudanese schools, and working with scholars such as HENDRIK KRAEMER, Padwick was a pioneer among women in bridging the gap between missionary service and missionary scholarship. She is rightly characterized by Ruth Tucker as one of the first great contemporary women missiologists.

A. SCOTT MOREAU

Bibliography. K. Cragg, *Muslim World* 49:1 (1969): 29–39; R. A. Tucker, *GGC;* idem, *Missiology* 15:1 (1987): 73–97.

Paganism. *See* NEOPAGAN, NEOPAGANISM.

Pakistan *(Est. 2000 pop.: 161,827,000; 796,095 sq. km. [307,372 sq. mi.]).* A token Christian presence from as early as the fourth century has been documented in the region of Pakistan. There is also a Thomas tradition, believable but not proven. Christian communities once existing in Baluchistan, Punjab, and Sindh became isolated, declined, and died out by the eleventh century, probably absorbed by Islam.

The earliest known missionary activity was initiated by Roman Catholics during the sixteenth and seventeenth centuries at the mouth of the Indus River. No continuing church resulted. A Jesuit mission to Akbar failed to gain the Moghul empire for Christianity. After the British annexed Sindh in 1843, and the Punjab in 1849, Roman Catholics arrived as chaplains of the British army and gradually extended their work to the local population.

The American Presbyterian Mission was the first Protestant agency, entering Punjab in 1849. CMS began its work in Sindh by 1850, and extended to Punjab by 1854. Then followed the United Presbyterians in 1855, the Church of Scotland in 1856, both in Punjab, and the Methodists in 1872 in Karachi. Three events had a lasting impact on the church. The first was a large-scale conversion movement in Punjab from 1880 to 1930. Two related developments were an indigenous Punjabi metrical paraphrase of the Psalms, and a spiritual revival that resulted in further conversions and a Christian Life Convention, which continues today at Sialkot.

After independence and separation from India in 1947, at least fifteen new mission agencies entered Pakistan. The 1951 census reported over 400,000 Christians, of whom more than half were Roman Catholics. In 1970 the Church of Pakistan was created by a union of Anglicans, Methodists, Church of Scotland Presbyterians, and Lutherans; the new church had a combined total of 200,000 members. The United Presbyterian Church, started in Sialkot in 1855, the largest single Protestant body in Pakistan, did not join the united church. Smaller groups included Baptists, Brethren, and Pentecostals.

The Islamic Republic of Pakistan has one of the largest Christian communities in the Muslim world. As of 1978 the churches in Pakistan claimed approximately 900,000 adherents—540,000 Protestants and 360,000 Roman Catholics. At least 90 percent are of Hindu background. The Christians are concentrated mainly in Punjab, 80 percent in rural areas. Muslims have been resistant, but there are signs of change.

The Christian Study Centre in Rawalpindi attempts to provide understanding between Christians and Muslims. The Pakistan Bible Correspondence School is active. In addition to hundreds of local schools, both rural and urban, that are operated by Christians, Pakistan has at least four Protestant seminaries, a large Roman Catholic seminary, and four Bible schools. Various Protestant and Catholic relief services are active. Catholics run twelve hospitals and Protestants twenty. Christians comprise only 2 percent of the population but provide 15 percent of the country's medical care.

ROGER E. HEDLUND

Bibliography. S. Athyal, ed., *The Church in Asia Today;* R. E. Hedlund, ed., *World Christianity: South Asia;* J. A. Rooney, *Shadows in the Dark (A History of Pakistan up to the 10th Century);* idem, *The Hesitant Dawn (Christianity in Pakistan 1579–1760);* idem, *On Heels of Battles: A History of the Catholic Church in Pakistan 1780–1886;* idem, *A History of the Catholic Diocese of Lahore, 1886–1986;* F. M. Stock, *People Movements in the Punjab;* *Survey Report of the Church in West Pakistan: A Study of the Economic, Educational and Religious Condition of the Church 1955–1959.*

Palau *(Est. 2000 pop.: 19,000; 508 sq. km. [196 sq. mi.].* A group of eight islands in Oceania, southeast of the Philippines. A constitutional government, Palau signed the Compact of Free Association with the United States in 1982, but took over a decade to ratify the agreement, which took effect on October 1, 1994. In 1993 it was estimated that the population was just over 96 percent Christian (25.4% Protestant, 39.7% Catholic, 3% foreign marginal) though 28.1 percent of that was indigenous marginal. For example, the Modekne movement, a syncretistic mix of Christianity and magic, has many adherents among the older population.

A. SCOTT MOREAU

SEE ALSO Micronesia.

Palau, Luis (1934–). Argentinian evangelist. Converted at an early age and discipled by British missionaries, he has become a global evangelist holding mass crusades in different parts of the world. He was trained in his native Buenos Aires and then completed his studies at Multnomah School of the Bible in Portland, Oregon. He first worked in Colombia under Overseas Crusades and as his ministry expanded, founded his own Luis Palau Evangelistic Team, with members from all of the Americas. Besides his main concern with the large cities of the world, which has included several large-scale crusades by satellite covering most of Latin America, he has endeavored to work with and through the church strengthening it and fostering church planting and church growth. He also has a daily radio program, as well as a newspaper column and has used television to enter many homes of the higher classes with his message. The fact that he is fluent both in Spanish and English has opened the doors to his ministry in the English speaking world, and has been an asset in his writing ministry. He has authored over thirty books in both languages, as well as a commentary on the Gospel of John. He also publishes a magazine for Christian leaders in Latin America, *Continente Nuevo.* Still committed to mass evangelism, he has shown special interest in reaching Muslims for Christ by emphasizing His love for them.

PABLO E. PÉREZ

Bibliography. S. R. Sywulka, *TCDCB*, pp. 291–92; T. Whalin, *Luis Palau.*

Palmer, Phoebe Worrall (1807–74). American revivalist. Phoebe Worrall was born in New York City to Methodist parents, her father having been converted under JOHN WESLEY's ministry. In 1827, she married Walter Palmer, a New York physician. She did evangelistic work in the slums of New York, founded the Hedding Church there, and in 1850 established the Five Points Mission, a forerunner of later settlement houses. In 1835, she began the "Tuesday Meeting for the Promotion of Holiness" and soon became a leading spokesperson for Holiness Theology. Her eighteen books include *Promise of the Father* (1859), and what was her most significant work, *The Way of Holiness* (1843). She also edited the *Guide to Holiness* periodical from 1864 to 1874. Palmer modified Wesley's doctrine of perfectionism by arguing that sanctification was instantaneous upon one's complete submission at the altar. God would then send a baptism of the Holy Spirit, which empowered the believer to live a life of holiness and witness effectively. She participated in over three hundred revival meetings throughout the United States, Canada, and Great Britain. She also was heavily involved in humanitarian causes and in the struggle for women's rights, but is best known for her emphasis on holiness.

TIMOTHY K. BEOUGHER

Bibliography. H. E. Raser, *Phoebe Palmer: Her Life and Thought;* C. E. White, *The Beauty of Holiness: Phoebe Palmer as Theologian, Revivalist, Feminist, and Humanitarian;* R. Wheatley, *The Life and Letters of Mrs. Phoebe Palmer.*

Panama Congress (1916). A watershed event in the life of the evangelical Protestant church, the Panama Congress drew attention to Latin America as a mission field and gave fresh impetus to the continent's small and struggling Protestant churches. The Congress came about largely as a reaction to the WORLD MISSIONARY CONFERENCE in Edinburgh six years earlier, where the organizers had excluded Latin America from the agenda. Considering it already Christian because of its Roman Catholic heritage, Edinburgh focused instead on "pagan" nations. During the Edinburgh conference, however, North American delegates laid plans for a special meeting to consider the unique missionary problems in Latin America.

The Panama Congress had a strong North American flavor, with representatives from several dozen agencies from the United States. World War I limited European representation. The proceedings were conducted in English, with ROBERT SPEER presiding at business sessions and Samuel G. Inman as executive secretary. Of the 304 participants, only 21 were native-born Latin Americans.

Nonetheless, the Panama Congress made a lasting impact on Latin Protestantism. It produced the first serious study of Protestant work on the continent. It also gave a sense of identity and solidarity to the small and struggling Protestant church, then numbered at 126,000 members, up from 50,000 in 1900. After the congress, Latin Protestants reportedly began identifying themselves as "evangelicals," since they were not "protesting" anything. The Panama Congress also gave rise to a series of follow-up regional conferences (Lima, Santiago, Rio de Janeiro, and San Juan), thus promoting efforts of evangelization.

JOHN D. MAUST

Bibliography. H. A. Johnson, V. M. Monterroso, and W. R. Read, *Latin American Church Growth;* E. A. Núñez and W. D. Taylor, *Crisis in Latin America.*

Panama *(Est. 2000 pop.: 2,856,000; 75,517 sq. km. [29,157 sq. mi.]).* Panama is the link between South America and the Central American isthmus. Panama seceded from Colombia in 1903, urged on by the United States in order to facilitate the construction of the Panama Canal. The canal is the primary source of income for the Republic as well as the cause of frequent foreign intervention. The Noriega military regime came to an end in 1989 when U.S. troops invaded the country. The resultant civilian government is weak.

The Catholic Church makes up about 72% of the population but the number of faithful participants is quite low. The Catholic leadership is perceived as weak and foreign, with 70% of the priests being non-Panamanians.

The Protestant Church dates back to the mid-nineteenth century, when Protestant North Americans came to Panama in order to build a railroad across the isthmus. In 1849 Episcopal services were being held in a hotel, and in 1864 "Christ Church by the Sea" was built by the Railroad Company. By 1884 the Methodists had a missionary presence as well. Protestantism has grown significantly in the past two decades, and now comprises some 18 percent of the population. Whereas there were thirty-eight Protestant congregations in 1935, there are close to two thousand at the present time.

The largest evangelical bodies are Pentecostal, led by the Assemblies of God, the International Church Four Square Gospel, and the Church of God (Cleveland). The largest non-Pentecostal groups are the Adventists, the Baptists, and the Methodists.

LINDY SCOTT

Panentheism. Panentheism, from the Greek *pan* (all), *en* (in), and *theos* (God), refers to a family of Western and non-Western religious perspectives on the relation between God and the world. In contrast to both classical theism (which maintains an ontological distinction between God and the world) and PANTHEISM (which identifies God with the world), panentheism both identifies God and the world in one sense while distinguishing between the two in another. The world exists in God, yet God is not exhausted by the world.

Panentheistic views are found in various schools of Hinduism, especially in the Visistadvaita-vedanta school of Ramanuja (*see* VEDANTA HINDUISM). Panentheistic themes can also be found in the Sufi mysticism of Islam. In the Christian context, panentheism is expressed in the process theism of John Cobb and Charles

Hartshorne, which finds its inspiration in the philosophy of Alfred North Whitehead. In contrast to classical theism, process theism holds that God himself is in a state of process and change. God is "dipolar"; in his moral character God is unchanging, but in his knowledge God is in process. God is limited both in power and knowledge, and God's knowledge grows in response to the changes brought about by free agents in the world.

In religious contexts influenced by the themes of panentheism, the effective missionary will be able to build upon those understandings of God which are compatible with biblical theism, but he or she must be careful to distinguish the biblical God from that of panentheism.

WILLIAM H. BAKER

Pantaenus (d. c. 194). Possible pioneer missionary to India. He was born in either Athens or Sicily; almost nothing is known of Pantaenus's childhood. He was head of a school in Alexandria from roughly 180 until his death, and was succeeded by Clement. While few details are known, Eusebius relates that Pantaenus responded to a call sent through the bishop of Alexandria and traveled to India. Jerome adds that his work was among the Brahmins. There he apparently met Christians who were familiar with Matthew's Gospel in Hebrew. The India mentioned by Eusebius may refer to South Arabia, and Pantaenus's work appears to have been little more than a visit.

A. SCOTT MOREAU

Bibliography. ODCC; G. Smith, *The Conversion of India;* M. Whittaker, *NCE,* 10:947.

Pantheism. The word "pantheism" is derived from the Greek *pan* and *theos* and means "all is God." Pantheism could also be described as the WORLDVIEW that individual human beings are not ultimately real as separate entities; what exists is a unified, ontological whole. The idea itself is at least as old as Hinduism, which teaches in the Vedas that all is Brahman, and as new as Alan Watts' pantheism in his New Age blend of Hindu, Buddhist, and Christian thought. But the name comes from the English writer John Toland (1670–1722) who held that the whole universe is God. The word "pantheism" has come to be used in contrast to "theism" which usually distinguishes God from the creation. It is also related to "monism" which teaches that everything is ultimately one.

There are many forms of pantheism. Among the more significant are *hylozoistic pantheism* which views God as immanent in the universe as its mover and changer; *absolute pantheism* in which God is identical with the universe; and *relativistic pantheism* which views the universe as

within God though he is changeless and unaffected by the world.

The Bible presents God as transcendent over the universe as its creator but at the same time immanent within its processes and active in history. Most significantly God is personality, providing a more satisfying cause for human personality and possibility for relationship.

WILLIAM H. BAKER

Papasarantopoulos, Chrysostom (1903–72). Greek Orthodox missionary to East Africa. He inaugurated a new period of mission endeavor within worldwide orthodoxy. Papasarantopoulos was born in Vasilitsion, Greece. Leaving home at fifteen, he joined the ascetic Panagoulakis, where he learned the disciplines of prayer, fasting, and the study of Scripture. Upon release from the Greek Armed Forces, Christos entered Marthakion Monastery, where he was tonsured a monk and renamed Chrysostom on August 4, 1925. Rising quickly, he was ordained a deacon and priest in May 1926; soon after he was appointed abbot of Gardikiou Monastery. After moving to the monastery of Chrysokellaris in 1935, where he founded catechism schools, he was called to Athens as archimandrite and appointed abbot of Fameromeni Monastery. Christos received his grammar and high school degrees at age fifty. Five years later, in 1958, he earned the Licentiate in Theology from the University of Athens.

Responding to the call to missions, Papasarantopoulos became the first twentieth-century Greek Orthodox missionary to Africa. During the following thirteen years, he worked in Uganda, Zaire, Tanzania, and Kenya, where he learned Swahili, built churches and schools, trained initiates for the priesthood, and translated liturgical books. His work and correspondence with individuals and organizations helped spawn a new period of missions within Greek Orthodoxy. Papasarantopoulos was laid to rest in 1972 at the Church of St. Andrew in Kananga, Zaire.

DIMITRIOS G. COUCHELL

Bibliography. L. Veronis, *TCDCB,* p. 293.

Papua New Guinea *(Est. 2000 pop.: 4,809,000; 462,840 sq. km. [178,703 sq. mi.]).* Due north of Australia, Papua New Guinea (PNG) is the eastern section of the second largest island in the world. PNG's 4.8 million people speak over 700 languages. While English is the official language, two local languages, Neo-Melanesian Pidgin (a creole of English) and Hiri Motu, are widely spoken. In addition to the cultural diversity, PNG's mainland and 600 islands extend from the equator to 11 degrees south. The mainland is divided by the central mountain range with peaks in excess of 12,000 feet and populated valleys at elevations up to 7,000 feet. The coastal lowlands are covered with tropical rain forests and savannas with rivers created from the high mountain rainfall. PNG is governed by the National Parliament with representatives from the 20 provinces. Port Moresby, the capital city, has a population of 193,000.

Although the earliest Christian contact came with the explorers during the sixteenth and seventeenth centuries, the first significant wave of missionaries was in the latter half of the nineteenth century. The early missionaries came from the LONDON MISSIONARY SOCIETY, the Methodists, Roman Catholics, Lutherans, and the Anglicans between 1870 and 1890. In addition to the missionaries from the colonial empires, a number of Pacific Island missionaries served sacrificially to establish the work in PNG. By the early 1890s, the major denominations had established their regional influence, which remains until the present. A second wave between 1890 and 1940 established new missions in PNG, particularly in the inland and coastal regions.

The post–World War II thrust included missions who targeted the isolated tribal peoples and those who concentrated on the growing urban populations. The large number of tribal groups and the geographic isolation, coupled with few government restrictions provided the ideal conditions for the multiplication of missions of all sizes and denominations. With more than 80 percent of the population living in rural areas, a defining characteristic of missions was their involvement in commerce, education, health, and transport.

From the early days of missionary work in PNG, local believers have served with expatriates as missionaries to other tribal groups. This tradition has matured with the churches and in many cases has led to local churches and denominations taking on the responsibility for evangelizing the unreached tribes within their region. During the past two decades, a mission movement has emerged among churches targeting the world outside of PNG. As a result, Papua New Guineans have joined international missions as part of their global outreach teams. The growing interest in missions has also given rise to at least one indigenous mission society with missionaries currently serving overseas.

The diversity of Christian traditions, churches, and missions has created a landscape of "mission pluralism," which has fostered a number of alliances. The mainline Protestant and Roman Catholic churches and missions have affiliated with the Melanesian Council of Churches to facilitate cooperative ventures and serve as a voice to the government. Due to the relative size of many of the evangelical missions and churches, an alliance (EA) was formed to provide training for church workers, teachers, and an evangelical voice to government bodies. The newest group is the Pentecostal Alliance, formed in the early 1980s by the rapidly expanding number of traditional and independent Pentecostal churches throughout PNG. With over 90 percent of the population claiming Christianity, missions have made one of the most significant contributions to the development of PNG.

DOUGLAS MCCONNELL

Bibliography. S. Dorney, *Papua New Guinea: People, Politics and History since 1975;* G. W. Trompf, *Melanesian Religion.*

Parachurch Agencies and Mission. Parachurch agencies appear at first glance to be a relatively recent phenomenon, by many accounts beginning their ministries shortly after the Second World War. But a closer look at the history of the church and its missionary enterprise will reveal a longer and deeper background. This background raises the question of defining these organizations, which relate in various ways to national denominations and local churches. Many would agree that the term "parachurch" is a convenient but imprecise term for these organizations. The term itself is a compound, indicating that such groups function "outside" the church, or at least parallel to it (from the Greek preposition *para*, meaning "beside" or "alongside"). These organizations specialize in a diverse array of Christian services and are self-supporting, drawing their funds from Christian churches and Christians within those churches. Further, parachurches see themselves for the most part as "arms of the local church" and not in competition with it. Although there are legitimate differences of opinion regarding just how such organizations come into being, many of them are born "in" the church and then sent out as functioning and healthy parts of the local or denominational body. Certainly it is beyond dispute that many, by the same token, are brought into being when a visionary Christian believes that either the church is not doing an adequate job in, for instance, reaching a particular segment of the community, or for whatever reason, the church is unable to do it.

History. Missiologist RALPH WINTER points out a distinction between stationary institutions (modalities) and mobile agencies (sodalities) that began in biblical times (*see* SODALITY AND MODALITY). In the next few centuries, the church became more institutionalized, heretical sects sprung up, and the church began to splinter into factions, sometimes resembling the denominations of the present century. Subsequent history records the significance of the councils of the church which gathered to sort out the lines of orthodoxy and to affirm and clarify precise statements by which the church would proceed. The early monastic movement and the subsequent orders of the Roman

Church indicated a useful paradigm for both spiritual formation as well as specialized ministry commitments. When these kinds of groups were formed, they were often made up of the laity "carrying on a personal ministry outside the direct authority and control of the church." The Reformation signaled a way in which a committed churchman like Martin Luther wanted to change the church from within but was prevented from doing so; the result (as in the later experience of JOHN WESLEY) was the formation of a new movement outside the church which developed into a full-fledged denomination. At the present time parachurch organizations almost defy description because of their proliferation throughout the Christian world. The main prerequisites seem to be an individual with a vision, a cadre of supporters who affirm that vision, and the courage to initiate ministry and raise the necessary capital to sustain the ministry. In the providence of God, many of these ministries have established themselves in such a way as to provide leadership for the church in areas where the church was either weak or where it lacked the incentive to undertake such bold initiatives in reaching out beyond the parameters of the local church. Foreign mission societies have enabled regional and national churches to specialize in meeting the needs of specific interest groups, and in so doing, they have enlarged the ministries of local congregations far beyond their ability to accomplish the same thing on their own.

Classification. Generally speaking, almost every conceivable area of mission has been addressed, with many of these, unfortunately, duplicating other ministries. By and large, these groups have been organized around GREAT COMMISSION and GREAT COMMANDMENT passages in the New Testament. EVANGELISM and DISCIPLESHIP, educational institutions, relief and community development (*see* RELIEF WORK and DEVELOPMENT), medical societies, Bible distribution and translation groups, media and communication agencies, and many specialized organizations too numerous to mention—these constitute a broad survey of the categories by which parachurch agencies can be identified.

Contributions of Parachurch Agencies in Missionary Activity. Parachurch organizations relate to missions by providing training and momentum for local churches and denominations. Some of the most creative initiatives in world mission have come from within these organizations, often working in tandem with local churches or denominations. Recently unique openings for the gospel have come from the almost universal screening of the life of Jesus from the Gospel according to Luke (*see* JESUS FILM); literally thousands of churches have been planted as a result of the follow-up and discipling of new believers. The ministry of the Bible translation has also resulted

in openings for the gospel in very remote areas of the globe, a ministry undertaken by WYCLIFFE BIBLE TRANSLATORS, INTERNATIONAL, a mission agency devoted to working in cultures with languages that had been without structured analysis and written materials. At the present time special emphasis is being given to reaching national and religious groups which traditionally presented great challenges to missionaries. The spread of communicable diseases, famine, earthquakes, floods, and national and international military conflicts have spurred the church into action, and often, the parachurch agencies (e.g., World Vision and World Relief) have responded quickly to relieve the immediate suffering, provide rescue operations, and in many cases have remained to provide supplies and aid in rebuilding the infrastructure destroyed in the struggle for peace and stability. Parachurch organizations have also pioneered strategic thinking in reaching unreached peoples (*see* PEOPLES, PEOPLE GROUPS), establishing cross-cultural training for both short-term and career missionaries, and exploring the potentially explosive CREATIVE ACCESS COUNTRIES through TENTMAKING MISSION strategies.

Hindrances to Parachurch Effectiveness in Missionary Activity. Parachurch agencies have always challenged the status quo in which religious culture can be found, and having pointed to their strengths it would be easy to overlook their weaknesses. Because of the tendency toward entrepreneurial leadership, there is often a lack of accountability outside the organization and particularly to the local church. From the churches' perspective, it is easy to ask for funds to meet a pressing need while at the same time not being sensitive to the counsel of godly leaders within the church, be it local or denominational. And even if it is not a stated policy, parachurch organizations have tended to hold their local church responsibilities rather loosely, sometimes scheduling events without coordinating with church calendars. Over the years, however, these issues have been addressed within the organizations themselves, and other agencies have been created expressly to assist in matters of financial integrity as well as in theological orthodoxy.

The Future. Few would deny that parachurch organizations have contributed greatly to the church's mission throughout the church's history. Indeed, the church has been enriched through the many ministries created by visionary Christians. But when the designation "parachurch" is used of such organizations, there is a clear expectation that these organizations will work more closely with national and local churches, always trying to achieve that unity which brings great delight to the heart of God (John 17:21–23; Eph. 4:1–13).

JOHN W. NYQUIST

Bibliography. Discipleship and Worship Program, The United Presbyterian Church in the U.S.A., *Para-Church Groups: A Report on Current Religious Movements;* K. S. Latourette, *Advance Through the Storm;* Lausanne Committee for World Evangelism, *Co-operating in World Evangelization, A Handbook on Church/Parachurch Relationships;* R. D. Winter, *Perspectives on the World Christian Movement,* pp. B45–B57; J. White, *The Church and the Parachurch: An Uneasy Marriage.*

Paraguay *(Est. 2000 pop.: 5,613,000; 406,752 sq. km. [157,047 sq. mi.]).* Paraguay is an inland, subtropical South American republic bordered by Bolivia, Argentina, and Brazil. The country is divided into two distinct areas by the Paraguay River, with 96 percent of the 5.3 million inhabitants living in the more fertile east. Although the capital of Asuncion (founded 1547) and its suburbs has a population approaching one million, over 50 percent of the total population is rural. The people are mostly of mixed Spanish and Guarani (the dominant indigenous people group) descent. As a result, although Spanish is the official language, 90 percent speak Guarani. Literacy is officially said to be 90 percent, but may be about 80 percent. There are two universities in the country, one of which is Catholic. The Guarani seem to have an innate gift for music and many are adept in the use of the Spanish guitar and harp accompanied by Guarani percussion instruments. Paraguayan painting and sculpture date from Jesuit mission art schools and often are found in the churches. The recent construction of two immense hydroelectric dams on the borders with Brazil and Argentina has provided high rates of employment as well as supplying the country with ample power.

The state religion is Roman Catholicism (92% of the population), which dates from the founding of Jesuit missions in 1609. In 1767 the Jesuits were expelled after supporting a Guarani revolt against the move to cede the country to Portugal. A disastrous 1865–70 war against Argentina, Brazil, and Uruguay resulted in the death of over half the population of one million. Less than 30,000 men survived. The territorial Chaco War against Bolivia from 1929 to 1932 added to Paraguay's land. There have been two hundred years of tyrannical dictatorships and government incompetence topped off by the oppressive presidency of Alberto Stroessner from 1954 until 1989. The country is well known for illegal commercialization (contraband) and its neighbors are happy to take advantage of it.

The earliest Protestant missionary came in 1817, and was the first of a number of traveling salesmen for the British Bible Society. Resident Methodist missionaries arrived in 1886. About 6 percent of the present population can be called Protestant, with slightly over 4 percent registered as evangelicals. Mennonites, who form the largest Protestant group, as well as other ethnic groups, live in self-contained colonies where European languages other than Spanish are dominant. Other denominations include the Assemblies of God (whose rapid growth after 1981 has resulted in 6,450 members in 172 churches), Southern Baptists (5,200 members in 73 churches), and various Pentecostal groups (8,200 members in 116 churches). Notable among social outreach is the Southern Baptist hospital founded in Paraguay in 1953. A recent high point in evangelical missions has been the increasing cooperative spirit among different Christian denominations.

DAVID SPRUANCE

Bibliography. P. Dostert, ed., *Latin America 1995;* J. O. Watson. *Baptist Ventures in Paraguay. The Commission.*

Paris Evangelical Missionary Society. *(Société des missions évangéliques de Paris)* [PEMS]. Established in 1822 after the pattern of other famous interdenominational missionary societies in the wake of the great religious revival of the nineteenth century, the PEMS began as a society of prayer in support of the LONDON MISSIONARY SOCIETY and the Evangelical BASEL MISSION. It soon established branches in France, Switzerland, Italy, and Holland, and won the support of many friends worldwide. At that time, long before the creation of the Evangelical Alliance in 1846, "evangelical" meant unifying Protestants in a common obedience to Jesus according to the gospel. The PEMS was always wary of doctrinal disputes, but actually followed the evangelical line when choices were necessary. A famous case was the refusal of ALBERT SCHWEITZER'S application as a missionary candidate for Lambarene in 1905 because of his alleged commitment to higher criticism. This evangelical line lost its visibility in 1948, when the PEMS was reorganized in the wake of the missiological ideal of merging church and mission. The PEMS was then almost completely integrated into the sending churches in France and Switzerland. Henceforth, final doctrinal and financial decisions were made by the respective synods.

The first missionaries of the PEMS went to Southern Africa in 1829, soon to be guided to Lesotho in 1833, where EUGENE CASALIS and Thomas Arbousset planted the Evangelical Church of Lesotho in close cooperation with the local king Moshoeshoe. From there new evangelistic ventures were launched with Esaïa Seele and other Sotho missionaries in 1863 and later with FRANÇOIS COILLARD and his party from 1877 along the Zambezi River, planting the church which is now a part of the United Church of Zambia. In the meantime the PEMS was asked by the LMS to take over some mission fields coming under attack by French colonialism and Roman Catholicism: Tahiti (1843, 1866), Madagascar (1897),

Loyalty Islands and New Caledonia (1883, Maurice Leenhardt as from 1902). The same pattern applied in West Africa. The PEMS took over the American Presbyterian field in Gabon (1892, Lambarene 1893), the German Baptist field and the Basel Mission field in French Cameroon (1917), and the German Lutheran field in Togo (1929). All these churches became formally independent in 1957–64, calling themselves "Evangelical Church" in Cameroon, in Madagascar, and in New Caledonia. These developments led the PEMS to decide on its own dissolution in 1971, giving birth to two new bodies, one common mission board of several French mainline Protestant Churches called *Département Français d'Action Apostolique* [DEFAP], and one international community of 47 Reformed, Lutheran, Methodist, and United churches (1997), called CEVAA (*Communauté Évangélique d'Action Apostolique* or Evangelical Community for Apostolic Action), both based in Paris.

The PEMS has been publishing since 1826 one of the oldest missionary magazines in the world, the *Journal des Missions Évangéliques*, until 1990 when the journal was renamed *Mission: Mensuel Protestant de Mission et de Relations Internationales* (monthly). The PEMS was also a publishing house, active in Bible translation and distribution (e.g., the Sotho Bible, 1879), promotional literature, and in-depth studies. Several periodicals in local languages were launched, including *Leselinyana* [The Little Light] (1863–), the second oldest periodical in Southern Africa (in Sotho) and *Ny Mpamafy* [The Sower] (1900–1958) (in Malagasy).

MARC R. SPINDLER

Parker, Peter (1804–88). American pioneer medical missionary to China. Born and raised in Framingham, Massachusetts, Peter Parker received his basic college education at Yale University. He then engaged in three years of intensive graduate studies at New Haven, receiving both his B.D. in theology and M.D. in medicine. After ordination as a missionary with the AMERICAN BOARD OF COMMISSIONERS FOR FOREIGN MISSIONS, he sailed for China as the first medical missionary to that country. In 1835 he opened the Ophthalmic Hospital in Canton. Three years later he assisted in founding the Medical Missionary Society for promoting medical missions in China.

During the political troubles at the time of the Opium War (1839–42) Parker returned to America, spoke extensively on medical missions, and strongly advocated to his government an American commission to China.

After his return to China in 1842, Parker served as interpreter in the 1844 Wanghsia treaty negotiations between the United States and China, became the American chargé d'affaires, and was ul-

timately appointed commissioner to China. His relationship with his mission board was terminated in 1847, both because of his political duties and because of disagreements over his role as a medical missionary. He left China in 1857 and lived in Washington, D.C., until his death in 1888.

RALPH R. COVELL

Bibliography. E. V. Gulick, *Peter Parker and the Opening of China.*

Parousia. Early Christians lived in the expectation of the prompt return of the Lord Jesus Christ (1 Thess. 4:16–18; 4:8; 2 Peter 3:3ff.). This belief flowed naturally out of their definition of the KINGDOM OF GOD as both a present reality and a future expectation. Both Judaism and Christianity are characterized as forward looking in their faith and practice. They believe human history cannot resolve the complex morass of human existence. Only God can. The parousia of Christ is for Christians the ultimate answer to death, evil, injustice, and chaos. What, then, is the relationship of the future appearance of Christ and world mission? Does a belief in the parousia encourage or paralyze the mission of the church?

The New Testament and the Parousia. While the parousia is uniquely Christian, some of the language and concepts in which it is couched are Jewish. During the Old Testament and intertestamental periods Jewish expectations of the kingdom became increasingly prominent. They believed the kingdom would appear in history as a gift from God. The Day of Yahweh was one of a number of phrases used to express this belief.

Jesus taught that the kingdom was present in his ministry and the New Testament writers believed that the kingdom had come through the incarnation, including the death and resurrection of Christ and the coming of the Holy Spirit (Matt. 12:28; Luke 2:17; 1 Cor. 15:23). Jesus also taught his disciples to expect a future coming of the kingdom (Luke 22:16, 18). Paul, the Gospel writers, James, and Peter taught explicitly that Jesus would appear a second time (Titus 2:13; John 21:22; James 5:8; 1 Peter 1:5). The word *parousia* means coming or appearance. The New Testament uses a number of words for the second advent such as coming, appearance, reveal, presence, and day (of Christ, God, Lord). Words such as appearance/coming *(parousia)* and day of the Lord were used to express this belief. At times the language and belief of Jesus and the early church was characterized by a note of imminence. But there was a uniform avoidance of date setting (Acts 1:7; Mark 13:32).

The Problem of the Delay. Modern critical study of the New Testament has in general been characterized by a belief that the delay of the parousia led to a crisis in early Christianity. When theology of imminence was followed by continued delay, so the argument goes, the church became disillusioned, resulting in an abandoning of the imminent expectation of the parousia. The hypothesis became a controlling presupposition of much twentieth-century scholarly study of the New Testament.

One of the obvious problems with this hypothesis is the notable absence of data in the New Testament and the early church fathers (2 Peter 3 and John 21:18ff.). The failure of these writers to talk about this problem seems to indicate there was no major problem in the delays of the parousia. That Jesus and the early Christians believed in imminence cannot be doubted. This being so, why did the delay of the parousia prove inconsequential?

Sociological studies show that movements that engage in date-setting, such as the Seventh-Day Adventists and Jehovah's Witnesses, may continue to grow and thrive in spite of eschatological disappointment. As for early Christianity it can be shown that although Jesus taught imminence, as did the apostles, their faith was deeply anchored in two things: a belief in present salvation and a total involvement in mission (Matt. 24:14; 28:20; Acts 1:6–11; Gal. 2:7–8; Rom. 1:14–16; 15:23–24). These early Christians were experiencing the "already" through the empowering presence of God in the resurrection and the outpouring of the Holy Spirit for life and witness. Any supposed delay of the parousia served a good purpose (2 Peter 3:9).

Mission and Parousia. There is a vital relationship between the parousia and mission. Alongside the church's belief in imminence was belief in worldwide mission. Jesus clearly and specifically called the Twelve and Paul to engage in mission to the world. The delay of the parousia caused no paralysis in mission, rather, as the church became universal its belief in the parousia was a motivating factor in mission (Matt. 24:14; Acts 1:6–11). The church engaged in mission, not to bring in the kingdom, but as an act of faithfulness to their king who was coming. World mission gives meaning to the church's life between the crucifixion/resurrection of Christ and the second coming of Christ. For those who had experienced the blessings of the age to come while living in this present age, their desire was to make this Good News known to the unreached while awaiting the completion of their salvation (Rom. 15).

While the place of the parousia in the life of the church has ebbed and flowed throughout the history of the church, the early church believed fervently in both imminence and world mission. Properly understood, the parousia of Christ motivates Christians for mission. Those who firmly believe that God will complete the not yet of the kingdom will be energized to preach the gospel to every people group in the world.

HAROLD E. DOLLAR

See also Eschatology; Millennial Thought.

Bibliography. O. Cullmann, *The Theology of the Christian Mission*, pp. 42–54; G. E. Ladd, *The Gospel of the Kingdom*; W. H. Mare, *Current Issues in Biblical and Patristic Interpretation*, pp. 336–45; A. L. Moore, *The Parousia in the New Testament*; S. P. Saunders, *Gospel in Context* 2:4 (Oct. 1979): 3–17; J. A. Scherer, *Missiology* 18:4 (1990): 395–413.

Parrish, Sarah Rebecca (1869–1952). American pioneer missionary physician in the Philippines. Born in Bowers, Indiana, Parrish developed a heart of compassion and an understanding of adversity from her early experience as an orphan. She received her medical training in the U.S. In 1906, Parrish was the first female physician sent to the Philippines under the auspices of the Methodist Episcopal Woman's Foreign Missionary Society. She combined medicine, evangelism, and social work in her efforts to ameliorate poverty and unsanitary conditions. Parrish began work in a one-room dispensary in Manila. Within a year, it had grown to two rooms with ten beds. Two years later, a generous donation from the Johnstons of Minneapolis enabled her to establish the Mary Johnston Hospital and School of Nursing in Tondo, a waterfront slum. Parrish maintained high credentialing standards at the hospital and it is still operating. She took few furloughs and worked in the Philippines for 27 years. Upon retirement, Parrish wrote her memoirs and lectured widely. In 1950, she received a citation and medal of honor from President Quirino and the Civic Assembly of Women for her pioneering efforts to inspire health and social welfare in the Philippines by ". . . bringing Christian love, healing, and enlightenment, and a better way of life."

MARGOT EYRING

Bibliography. G. H. Anderson, *CDCWM*, p. 472; G. J. Bekker, *DCA*, p. 869.

Participant Observation. *See* QUALITATIVE RESEARCH.

Partnership. The voices calling for the MORATORIUM of foreign mission agencies have grown silent. In their place new voices call for other options. As for church-mission relationships, these include, with numerous variations, at least four theories: (1) departure, (2) subordination, (3) parallelism, and (4) partnership.

Theory 1: Departure. Once the national church reaches maturity, the expatriates depart physically, although they may continue to send funds. HENRY VENN and RUFUS ANDERSON must be credited for this unrivaled mission theory of the nineteenth and first half of the twentieth centuries: the three-self INDIGENOUS CHURCH concept (self-propagating, self-supporting, self-governing). JOHN

NEVIUS, sensing the practicality of the three-selfs, instituted them in China and more effectively in Korea. Nevius's *The Planting and Developing of Missionary Churches* remains a classic. ROLAND ALLEN echoed Venn and Anderson's theory in the twentieth century, arguing that the three-selfs work not just because they are practical, as did Nevius, but because they are biblical. Allen makes the argument in his classic *Missionary Methods: St. Paul's or Ours?* Failure to ask the global questions, among other things, would eventually date this theory.

Theory 2: Subordination. Once the national church reaches maturity, expatriates work under national leaders while providing their own support. This unilateral theory transfers complete control to the national church. Some view this theory as ecumenism at its best while others see it as distorted partnership representing a kind of reverse paternalism.

Theory 3: Parallelism. Since the national church is mature, each party develops complementary, yet separate agendas while maintaining individual organizational structures, personnel, and budgets. This theory respects the unity, diversity, and autonomy of all the players. Proponents see the international body of Christ in action, utilizing the different parts to fulfill a unified goal. Opponents believe it stifles the Great Commission within the national church, leaving evangelism and mission to outsiders.

Theory 4: Partnerships. Luis Bush defines partnerships as: "an association of two or more Christian autonomous bodies who have formed a trusting relationship and fulfill agreed upon expectations by sharing complementary strengths and resources to reach their mutual goal." This theory advocates that institutions work not apart from each other [Theory 1], or under each other [Theory 2], or unified but separate [Theory 3], but as equal partners. Proponents argue this multilateral theory protects both the commission of the receiving national church and the sending institution or church. Opponents argue the complexity of ethnic relationships, economic levels, and so forth, make this theory extremely difficult to accomplish.

While the first three theories continue to receive endorsement, a growing number of nationals and expatriates, countering Henry Venn's "euthanasia of mission" strategy (also promoted by Roland Allen), support the fourth theory. They argue that in God's economy, inclusion, interdependence, and role changes should replace isolation, independence, or departure.

Partnership Fundamentals. Strategic partnerships today go far beyond mission agencies and national churches to include local churches, parachurch organizations, and academic training institutions. Participants may partner on the local, national, or international levels. On the in-

ternational level (often cutting across geography, theology, ethnicity, gender, generations, and income boundaries), participants may come from anywhere in the world and go anywhere in the world.

Motivations for forming strategic partnerships vary considerably. One is fear. The declining missionary population from the West in contrast to the increasing missionary population from the Third World (*see* NON-WESTERN MISSION BOARDS AND AGENCIES) raises control issues. The high cost of new start-ups, along with the maintenance of existing programs, creates tremendous competition for dollars in a shrinking support pool. The competitive search for dollars also influences job security. A second motivation is convenience. Seekers may find association with another group advantageous, whether for finances, personnel, training, facilities, technology, logistics, psychological security, linguistics, cultural or lifestyle nearness, name recognition, global access, or publicity. A more positive motivation is theology. The Bible calls for Christians to set aside unhealthy competition and instead create alternative complementary partnerships that utilize effectively the diversity represented, take seriously the stewardship of resources (human and material), and create liberated synergy, thereby credibility to witness.

Strategic partnerships deal with methodology, not with goals of what must be done. Central to the "what" should be the expansion of the church as a sign of God's kingdom. Wise partners will insist that the vision statement centers around selective components of the GREAT COMMANDMENT and the GREAT COMMISSION.

A common vision serves as the driving force behind effective strategic partnerships. Partners negotiate a vision statement, and the organizational structure to fulfill it. They agree upon assigned roles and rules that foster complementary participation. Every member shares in the risks without compromising their divine call or corporate values.

The duration of strategic partnerships varies depending upon the specified goals. Some are designed to field quick response teams for short periods. Others form for long-term activities or somewhere in between. Whatever the duration, partners will want to institute procedures for the graceful dismantling of the partnership, due either to the completion of the stated goals, to the completion of the original time frame for the partnership, or to unresolved conflicts that may arise.

Partnership Life Cycle Phases. Fundamental to the success of any strategic partnership is trust. Open communication facilitates trust-building and efficiency. During the exploration phase, potential partners will want to discuss their expectations in relation to the term "partnership." These expectations may include languages to be used, conflict resolution, goals and priorities, organizational structure (status and roles), decision-making, planning and evaluation, operation ethics, theological distinctives, mutual accountability contingency plans, finances, de-partnering, and how cultural distinctives influence the interpretation of each. During this phase they will seek to discover if there is a genuine mutual need, for herein lies the basis for healthy partnership.

The formation phase may involve a facilitator respected by all parties who demonstrates strong belief in the sovereignty of God, personal integrity, ability to network, an appreciation of diversity, ability to solve cross-cultural conflicts, live with ambiguity, and champion the vision. During the operational phase changes can be expected as adjustments are made to adapt to present realities. Participants will continually reevaluate personal relationships, the purpose, procedures, and performances. They will attempt to make necessary adjustments in culturally sensitive ways that reflect a Christian spirit. Once the partnership completes its goals, the dismantling phase begins.

TOM A. STEFFEN

Bibliography. R. Allen, *The Spontaneous Expansion of the Church;* L. Bush and L. Lutz, *Partnering in Ministry. The Directory of World Evangelism;* V. Gerber, ed., *Missions in Creative Tension: The Green Lake '71 Compendium;* W. D. Taylor, ed., *Kingdom Partnerships for Synergy in Missions;* C. P. Williams, *The Ideal of the Self-Governing Church: A Study in Victorian Missionary Strategy.*

Pastoral Counseling. Two major areas of concern exist with regard to pastoral counseling and missions. First is the provision of counseling services to missionaries themselves. Second is pastoral counseling provided by the missionary as part of his or her ministry.

Pastoral Counseling Services to Missionaries (*see also* MEMBER CARE). Commonly used measurements of stress reveal that the average missionary and family leaving for overseas faces significant stress before they even arrive to face the stressors of their placement. Gish (1983) identified nineteen areas of significant stress. The survey established the lack of pastoral care as significant stress for 35 percent of the missionaries surveyed. The following responses would assist in avoiding missionary BURNOUT.

Missions agencies must develop a commitment to provide supportive and caring environments. To form the foundation for this commitment, the ethos created by administrators and supervisors should value healthy and encouraging interpersonal relationships. Training for supervisory personnel should include basic courses in helping relationships and group/system dynamics. Additionally, mission agencies should employ or subcontract trained and experienced pastoral counselors, who themselves have served in cross-cultural settings long enough to adequately understand the missionary context. While requiring dual training will limit the number of available personnel, the dual training is necessary to effectively minister in this specialized context.

Missionary conscripts should receive preparation for spiritual and emotional stresses that will typically face them. Standard training should include stress management, identifying and coping with depression and anxiety, and cross-cultural conflict resolution.

A well thought out plan of pastoral care, based in careful and accurate studies of the points of vulnerability, should be put into action. For example, during their training period, new missionaries should establish a relationship with a pastoral counselor. The missionary should then receive an extended visit from this pastoral counselor after six months, and again after twelve months in the field.

Pastoral counselors serving missionaries should be allowed to maintain confidentiality (as is true of any licensed counselor) in order for the missionary to be assured that counseling content will not be shared with administrators without the missionary's permission.

As a standard, furloughs should include regular pastoral counseling for missionary and family. This counseling should focus on discovering how the individual and family are dealing with stress.

Last, continuing education seminars should be available on the field focusing on the areas identified in studies such as the one cited above. Extra time should be scheduled for seminar leaders to minister to missionaries. Other resources (i.e., literature, videos, audiotapes) can be provided as required.

Pastoral Counseling Provided by Missionaries. The goal of training missionaries to provide CROSS-CULTURAL COUNSELING as part of their ministry is simple: to better equip them in fulfilling their cross-cultural task. It is commonly accepted that missionaries must become deeply involved in the lives of those to whom they desire to bring God's Word. Since becoming deeply involved includes being involved with individual and family problems, training in cross-cultural counseling is essential. Attempting to minister to personal and family problems with an understanding of human behavior from an ethnocentric perspective can have extremely unfavorable results. Despite the best intentions, great harm can result.

Because effective counseling is based in understanding the feelings, cognitions, and behaviors of the culture being served, increasing importance must be given in mission and theological training centers to cross-cultural counseling.

DAVID WENZEL

Bibliography. D. Gish, *Journal of Psychology and Theology* 11:3 (1983): 236–43; D. J. Hesselgrave, *IBMR* 10:3 (1986): 109–13; M. Jones, *EMQ* 29:3 (July, 1993): 294–98; G. White, *EMQ* 25:3 (July, 1989): 304–9.

Pastoral Responsibilities. Pastoral responsibilities include guiding, comforting, correcting, encouraging, nurturing, protecting, healing, and worshiping. Caring for others, and being cared for by others, is not simply our biblical responsibility, but also a vital part of our evangelistic witness. Missionaries from Western countries are having less opportunities to serve as local-church pastors in Two-Thirds World countries. They still, however, find extensive opportunities for pastoral responsibilities.

The Methods of Pastoral Ministry. In regard to pastoral responsibilities, missionaries should remember that the biblical model for pastoral care and leadership clearly reflects the servant model. God called Abraham not just to become a great nation, but rather to become a blessing to the "nations" (Gen. 12:1–3). The Servant in Isaiah lived for the benefit of the people and not his own, and Israel was called to emulate this servanthood (Isa. 49:5–6; 53:4–6).

The incarnation remains the greatest example of the servant model (Luke 4:1–4; Phil. 2:5–11). Jesus explained his ministry as to serve rather than to be served (Mark 10:45; Luke 9:23–27). The Lord indicated that the pattern of leadership for people would not be that of the Gentile rulers who "lord it over" and "exercise authority over" those under their control. But, said Jesus, among his people the greatest would be the servant of all (Matt. 20:24–28).

Clear emphasis on the servant pattern of leadership and pastoral ministry comes through Jesus' teaching in John 12:20–28. Only the seed that falls into the ground and dies brings forth great fruit. The servant pattern produces fruitfulness; the absence of the servant pattern leads to the tragedy of fruitlessness.

All pastoral responsibilities for missionaries should be based on and patterned after this servanthood model. Genuine pastoral leadership eschews the authoritative, paternalistic, manipulative, controlling, leader-dominated patterns too often seen even among Christian leaders. Biblical ways in pastoral leadership and ministry follow the pattern of servanthood.

Servant leadership expresses itself through relationship rather than position. The missionary refuses to consider himself or herself as the one in a position of authority but as one in a relationship of helping. The servant pastor seeks to serve rather than control; this model of pastoral ministry recognizes that equipping is better than performing. Through properly expressing the servant pattern of pastoral ministry, the missionary can live out the example of Jesus in his or her pastoral duties.

The Goals of Pastoral Ministry. The goals of pastoral ministry center in efforts to equip people first for their own relationship with God and then for the ministries to which God has called them. Both missionaries and national leaders have opportunities for this equipping ministry. The goal of equipping others follows the proper interpretation of Ephesians 4:11–13 and remains a primary goal of pastoral work.

Pastoral responsibilities include guiding and correcting. Gentle, sympathetic guidance including correction are among the more imperative functions of missionary leaders, and should be carried out in ways that are in keeping with local, culturally accepted patterns.

One of the foremost opportunities for pastoral responsibilities in today's world relates to helping others develop pastoral skills, which multiplies the effectiveness of the missionary caregiver.

Pastoral responsibilities often include leading in worship. Worship leadership in cross-cultural situations demands sympathetic learning of the local ways in order that the worship will be done in culturally appropriate patterns rather than imported methods.

The Recipients of Pastoral Ministry. Missionaries engaged in pastoral responsibilities target different recipients for their ministries. One recipient group for pastoral ministry resides in the missionary's own family. The missionary finds abundant opportunity to be a pastor to spouse and children. Also, the families and individuals within the mission organizations often need pastoral care—in times of tragedy, stress, discouragement, and the like. A missionary pastoral worker makes full use of such opportunities for such ministries.

A second recipient group for pastoral ministries rests with the leaders of the national organization. Rather than allowing this relationship to become adversarial, the wise missionary will commit himself or herself to serving as pastor to these leaders. Ministry to national leaders is among the most fruitful of all pastoral roles for missionaries.

A third recipient group for pastoral ministries includes the members of the churches. Missionaries will often be called on to minister to church members and their families. Western missionaries will exercise care in rendering pastoral ministry in the cross-cultural setting. Acts that extend love and concern may be overlooked if the missionary does not take fully into account the cultural realities of the society.

Ebbie C. Smith

Bibliography. C. W. Brister, *Caring for the Caregivers: Caring for Ministers and Missionaries*; S. G. Lingenfelter and M. C. Mayers, *Ministering Cross Culturally;*

K. O'Donnell, ed., *Missionary Care: Counting the Cost for World Evangelization.*

Paternalism. In a generic sense, all that is positive in familial relationships, in particular that of father to child. When paternalism exists in adult or institutional (such as church-mission) relationships, however, the considerable literature shows it has negative connotations. Paternalism might be thought of as the use of coercion to achieve a good that is not perceived as such by those persons for whom it is intended.

Paternalism, the concept of intervening actively for the perceived well-being of another, has long existed in mission. People with knowledge, skills, funds, or power (the older missions) have used them to get new churches to follow their demands. An example of paternalism is a mission keeping control of a work because it feels that the locals are unqualified and would do themselves and the cause of Christ harm by taking leadership. Paternalistic attitudes assume superior knowledge, wisdom, and skills. While well intentioned in some cases, they fail to recognize the work of the Holy Spirit in young churches and their leaders.

While the connotations of paternalism are often negative, churches or missions sometimes develop rules (by-laws, covenants, mission and purpose statements) with the positive result of producing mature Christian behavior.

Paternalism is a complex issue. Mission leaders must face the tension involved in deciding how much or how little influence to exert, either actively intervening or passively withholding something, for the perceived good of emerging missions, churches, and their leadership.

MIKEL NEUMANN

SEE ALSO Partnership.

Bibliography. J. Kleinig, *Paternalism;* D. VanDeVeer, *Paternalistic Intervention.*

Paton, John Gibson (1824–1907). Scottish missionary to the South Pacific. Born near Dumfries, Scotland, and with little early education, he worked with the Glasgow City Mission (1847–56) while preparing himself for overseas service by undertaking studies in medicine and divinity. Ordained by the Reformed Presbyterian Church in 1858, he established a station on the New Hebrides island of Tanna. Incredible privations, chiefly caused by local hostility, coupled with the loss of his wife and infant son, forced his removal in 1862 to Australia. He extended the missionary challenge there, in New Zealand, and in Scotland, where his church elected him moderator in 1864 and where he recruited seven missionaries for the work in the New Hebrides. He settled on the island of Aniwa (1866–81) and most of its inhabitants professed Christianity.

Paton campaigned fearlessly against white men with vested interests that disregarded the welfare of the people, notably in arms, alcohol, and indentured labor. From 1881 Paton was based in Melbourne. His many missionary tours, including visits to the United States and Canada, produced vast sums for the work in the South Pacific region. He also translated parts of Scripture into the Aniwan tongue. Recipient of a Cambridge D.D. degree (1891), Paton was a simple but riveting speaker. At the ECUMENICAL MISSIONARY CONFERENCE in New York in 1900 he was hailed as a great missionary leader.

Paton died in Australia, but the family's missionary connection with the New Hebrides was to continue until 1970.

His best-selling autobiography was edited by his brother James (1907).

J. D. DOUGLAS

Bibliography. H. B. Genung, *John G. Paton: Missionary to "The Martyr Islands" in the South Seas;* A. K. Langridge and F. H. L. Paton, *John G. Paton: Later Years and Farewell.*

Paton, William (1886–1943). British missions statesman and author. The son of Scottish parents who had settled in England, he was educated at Oxford and Cambridge, and ordained in the Presbyterian Church of England ("to save him from [World War I] conscription," notes his biographer). He was missionary secretary of the STUDENT CHRISTIAN MOVEMENT (1911–21), combined with work for the YMCA under whose auspices he went to India. He returned there as general secretary of the newly formed National Christian Council of India, Burma, and Ceylon (1921–28) before appointment as joint secretary (with J. H. OLDHAM) of the London-based INTERNATIONAL MISSIONARY COUNCIL. Paton was an ecumenical pioneer, a champion of war-orphaned missions, an ardent pacifist, an indefatigable writer on a wide range of subjects, and the possessor of a wicked wit as seen in the parody (of Mott's famous watchword), "The Moon turned to Blood in our Generation." An ecumenical enthusiast who hung loose to denominational affiliations, Paton made a substantial contribution to the movement that in 1948 became officially the WORLD COUNCIL OF CHURCHES. His published works included *Jesus Christ and the World's Religions* (1916), *Christianity in the Eastern Conflicts* (1937), and *The Church and the New Order* (1941). For sixteen years he served as editor of the *International Review of Missions.*

J. D. DOUGLAS

Bibliography. E. Jackson, *Red Tape and the Gospel: A Study of the Significance of the Ecumenical Missionary*

Struggle of William Paton 1886–1943; M. Sinclair, *William Paton.*

Patrick (c. 389–461). Early British missionary; "Apostle of Ireland." Born in Roman Britain, he was captured at the age of sixteen by Irish raiders and carried into slavery in Ireland. After six years, he escaped and was eventually reunited with his family in Britain. Called in a dream to evangelize Ireland, he is said to have returned there as a bishop in 432, and from his base in Armagh carried out what he called his "laborious episcopate." He claims to have been the first to take the gospel to more remote regions of the island. Numerous legends have grown up around Patrick's life; he is said, for example, to have been trained in Gaul and to have had a close relationship with Martin of Tours (calling for a fourth-century Patrick).

Reliable data come only from his two short writings: *The Confession*, a spiritual autobiography; and a work denouncing the tyranny of a British chieftain who persecuted Christians. Patrick aimed first to convert the princes who would then give him safe conduct through their territories and access to the common people. He supported monasticism, refused all presents, broke the power of heathenism in Ireland, and typified the enthusiasm of the Celtic Church. He was known for remarkably clear statements of faith (he continually quoted Paul), and for a missionary heart that played a major part in sending monks to evangelize Europe during the following two centuries.

J. D. DOUGLAS

Bibliography. L. Bieler, *The Life and Legend of St. Patrick;* R. P. C. Hanson, *The Life and Writings of the Historical Saint Patrick.*

Pattaya Consultation (1980). *See* WORLD CONSULTATION ON WORLD EVANGELIZATION.

Patteson, John Coleridge (1827–71). English missionary in the South Pacific. Born in London, he was educated at Eton and Oxford. He took a curate in Alfington and was ordained in 1854. He was then recruited by Bishop GEORGE SELWYN for ministry in the South Pacific. Upon his arrival, Patteson noted the two influences of European civilization on the islanders: the immorality of the merchant sailors and the gospel. He was determined to make the latter stronger than the former, but gradually learned that for most of the indigenous population, Christianity and moral decadence were inextricably linked.

Education became his primary strategy. He made regular trips to the Solomon and New Hebrides Islands, selecting young men and women to be trained at St. John's College in Auckland, New Zealand. His plan was that upon returning to their homelands, the islanders would function as missionaries to their own people. The ministry was successful and on February 24, 1861, Patteson was consecrated bishop of Melanesia. By 1870 his school was training 145 students.

Danger to missionaries increased as a result of national reaction to the forced impressment of islanders by slave traders, and in September 1871 Patteson suffered a mortal blow to the head while visiting the island of Nukapu. He was buried at sea, earning the title "Martyr of the Islands."

LARRY POSTON

Bibliography. J. Gutch, *Martyr of the Islands;* C. M. Yonge, *The Life of John Coleridge Patteson, Missionary Bishop of the Melanesian Islands.*

Paul and Mission. The mission of the apostle Paul in the first century has functioned as a principal inspiration and paradigm for Christian witness during the millennia since. The modern missionary movement in particular has routinely attempted to take bearings from the apostle's missionary thinking and endeavors. Where this has been pursued at a scholarly level, such inquiries have not infrequently also proved suggestive for those engaged in the modern academic study of Paul. Among more familiar examples of such studies in the past century would certainly be those by Allen, Blauw, Senior and Stuhlmueller, and Bosch.

The modern academic study of Paul has had good reason, in any case, to devote considerable professional attention to Paul's mission, since that mission has functioned as a principal feature in the scholarly reconstructions of early Christian history and theology. In the process, contemporary Pauline research has sometimes proposed findings that challenge popular assumptions about the Pauline mission, serving thereby as a useful corrective for a too easy correlation between the Paul of history and the interests and requirements of the modern missionary movement. At the same time these modern academic inquiries have not always escaped their own accommodations to contemporary intellectual fashions.

Beginning with F. C. Baur of Tübingen in the mid-nineteenth century, and throughout the entire period of modern Pauline studies since, the history and literature of the Pauline mission have been continuously queried. For example, Baur counted only four of Paul's principal letters as authentic, and nonevangelical scholarship today tends conventionally to accept only seven as assuredly Pauline (excluding Ephesians, Colossians, 2 Thessalonians, and the Pastorals). Likewise the historical reliability of Acts, and of its account of the Pauline mission, has been repeatedly called into question. While fashionable opinion on the matter has oscillated over the years, the recent pattern has increasingly been to assume a sharp contrast between the Paul presented in the narrative of Acts and the historical Paul represented by his principal letters, and in consequence to discount the usefulness of Acts in assessing the history of the Pauline mission.

Such findings can often seem to have more to do with the predilections of the modern-day academic than with an even-handed scholarly assessment of the historical data. The problematic nature of many of the assumptions that undergird such findings has often been demonstrated. Nevertheless, a large segment of contemporary Pauline scholarship would doubt the traditional chronological reconstruction of Paul's mission, and in particular the "three tours" approach so characteristic of more popular presentations.

Yet it is noteworthy that in the alternative reconstructions being proffered, while the chronology of the Pauline mission is shifted, the pattern of Paul's geographical movement as presented in Acts is left largely intact. This anomaly within the modern inquiry arises from the fact that, whatever the chronology of events, the relevant data derivable from Paul's principal letters on the geographical pattern of his mission correlate remarkably well with the more detailed data available from Acts.

That is to say, in both the letters and in Acts Paul carries out his missionary endeavors in the same sector of the Mediterranean world, in the same provinces, and in the same general sequence. In both sources Paul works in the lands surrounding the northeastern Mediterranean, between Judea and the Adriatic; both sources show him progressing through this area generally from east to west; and both sources see him attending to Syria/Cilicia, Macedonia, Achaia, and Asia, in that order—and also Galatia at some point along the way.

Indeed, the Paul of the letters is explicitly conscious of such a geographical pattern in his mission. In a context in which he anticipates travel westward to Rome and beyond to Spain, he states that already "from Jerusalem all the way around to Illyricum I have fully proclaimed the gospel of Christ" (Rom. 15:19). The distinctiveness of this geographical dimension in the apostle's understanding of his mission can be obscured by its very familiarity. Paul clearly took his mission to be in part a geographically definable accomplishment.

A second distinguishing characteristic of the Pauline mission, evidenced both in the letters and in Acts, is the intentional focus on community formation. Paul saw his mission as more than gospel proclamation and conversion of individuals; through and beyond these endeavors he understood his missionary role to concern the establishment of settled, believing communities. This churchward orientation of his mission is ev-

ident not least in his surviving missionary letters, all of which are directed to the stabilization and maturation of newly planted churches. Paul pursued his geographical mission in terms of ecclesial achievement.

In the first decades of the twentieth century Pauline studies came increasingly under the influence of a history-of-religions approach, which emphasized the importance of the Greco-Roman religious context for understanding Paul. This approach affected the understanding of Paul's mission in at least two respects. First, it helped ignite a debate that continues to the present on the relationship of Paul's Damascus experience to his subsequent theology and to his Gentile mission preoccupation. For example, numerous studies attempted a religio-psychological interpretation of the Damascus experience, in which the sudden reorientation to Gentile mission of this erstwhile Pharisee was explained as the compensatory outworking of an uneasy conscience over the harsh exclusivism of Judaism. Such an approach is no longer in vogue, owing to the excessive degree to which modern assumptions must be interpolated into the historical data in order to render such psychological interpretations feasible.

It is now widely recognized that whatever led up to the Damascus event, the interpretive baseline for the event must begin with the fact that Paul experienced it as an encounter with the risen Jesus. And, in light of his own explicit testimony, it is also increasingly accepted that Paul experienced this encounter not as a conversion so much as a call, as a divine summons to a task on the model of OLD TESTAMENT PROPHETS (Gal. 1:15–16). No interpretation of the Damascus Road event and its consequences is likely to prove sustainable which does not recognize that the event was in the first place an encounter/call. That is to say, Paul understood his sense of commission not as derivative of his Damascus Road experience but as constituent to that experience. The complex ramifications of the event for Paul's subsequent life and thought are best accounted for as unfolding from this duality at the heart of the original experience. It was the christological encounter that set in motion Paul's theological reorientation, while it was the call to Gentile mission that determined the direction of the resulting theological development.

The history-of-religions phase within Pauline studies also stimulated considerable interest in the numerous examples of religious propaganda in the Greco-Roman world, and sought to reinterpret Paul's missionary efforts in light of this larger social phenomenon. Such studies highlighted not only the vigorous Jewish proselyte movement of the period, but also the wandering preachers then common in the Hellenistic world, and the rapid spread of the Eastern mystery religions throughout the empire at this time. Such studies have thrown much useful light on the patterns of religious propagation within Paul's world. At the same time, in attempting to trace a generalized phenomenon of the period, such investigations have tended to accent those characteristics common to all these efforts while obscuring the individual distinctives. In consequence, even today scholarly texts will speak with assurance of multiple first-century movements of religious propaganda, all functioning more or less on the familiar pattern of the Pauline mission.

Recent research has been severely undermining this projection. It is now being noted, for example, that the wandering preachers of Hellenism were not pursuing community formation. Neither was the spread of the mystery religions nor the Jewish proselyte movement furthered by individuals under a sense of divine calling to missionize. And none of these movements interpreted itself in terms of geographical progress. Even for Christianity itself in the initial postapostolic centuries, closer inquiry finds the evidence almost entirely lacking for the figure of the missionary evangelist seeking to plant churches in new geographical areas on the Pauline model. A significant result of this reassessment now in progress has been to clarify more adequately the distinctiveness of Paul's particular mission, and especially to clarify the extent to which the geographical framing of his mandate, and its ecclesial focus, represent exceptional characteristics for missionary perception and outreach in his day.

In the latter part of the twentieth century an increasingly influential sociological approach in New Testament studies produced illuminating contributions on the social dimensions of the early Christian mission. For example, a helpful distinction has been traced between the "itinerant charismatic" preachers of the early Palestinian Christian communities and the more orderly efforts of those like Paul who may be characterized as "goal-oriented community organizers." But more adventurous attempts to reinterpret Paul's missionary outreach itself in terms of modern sociological models for religious expansion, such as millennial, conversionist, or sectarian models, have thus far proved less than persuasive, owing to a general perception that these models are being inappropriately imposed upon the historical data. This field of inquiry is nevertheless promising, and more methodologically sensitive and disciplined studies along these lines should prove fruitful for a better understanding of the varied patterns of religious propagation in the Greco-Roman world.

The Bultmannian school of thought, which dominated Pauline studies in the middle decades of the twentieth century, transmuted the larger inquiry into existentialist categories in ways that rendered the essential issues of Paul's mission largely peripheral or irrelevant. By the last quarter of the century, this whole construct had been duly challenged and displaced, especially owing to the far-reaching reassessments in Pauline studies precipitated by E. P. Sanders in 1977, now mediated most prominently through work by J. D. G. Dunn in what is conventionally termed the "New Perspective" in Pauline studies. The result has been to move the dominant issues of Pauline inquiry at the commencement of the twenty-first century back into territory more congenial to acknowledging and addressing questions relating to Paul's mission and mission thinking.

In particular this shift of perspective has allowed renewed consideration of a significant but less dominant strand of inquiry in twentieth-century Pauline studies emphasizing and exploring the eschatological structuring of Pauline theology. The eschatological nature of Paul's thinking was first effectively accented in 1911 through an influential survey of Pauline studies by the New Testament scholar A. SCHWEITZER, who subsequently gained wide notice as a medical missionary in Africa. Beginning in 1936 O. Cullmann then directed attention to the eschatological nature of Paul's own self-understanding. Building on this, the Danish scholar J. Munck from 1947 on systematically worked out the proposition that all Paul's missionary thinking and endeavors are best interpreted in terms of his eschatological convictions.

Munck demonstrated that the salvation-historical framework in which all of Paul's theological reflection takes place also functions as the determinative framework for Paul's understanding and implementation of his mission. Paul took himself to be a participant in the end-time redemptive events of Old Testament prophetic expectation. More particularly, he understood himself to be a participant in the fulfillment of that part of Old Testament eschatology which expected the inclusion of the nations, the Gentiles, in the messianic blessing. Paul therefore took his own vigorous outreach to be part of the eschatological ingathering of the nations, and his Damascus experience to be a divine summons to participate in this outreach to the ends of the earth.

The historical characteristics of Paul's missionary outreach are then best understood as those practicalities implicit in seeking to implement such an eschatological assignment, given the realities of Paul's first-century world and his assumptions about that world. Paul sought to actualize the promised "blessing to the nations" by concrete efforts to help form believing communities province by province across his Roman world. This required deliberate travel to the population centers of these provinces. The little gatherings he formed center by center symbolize for him the incorporation of the Gentiles into the messianic community in fulfillment of Old Testament expectation. He recognizes that he is working between the "already" of Christ's redemptive act and the "not yet" of Christ's final triumph, bringing the life of the age to come into the present fallen world. And as a messenger of the Crucified One in this interim time, he knows that he must work amidst all the vicissitudes of the human condition, accepting toil and suffering and being vulnerable to conflict and disappointment. Yet he is sustained by the joyous assurance that God's eternal purpose, to unite Jew and Gentile together in the worship of Christ as Lord, will be fulfilled.

Of course the mission of the apostle Paul must not be used as an exclusive norm for appropriate Christian outreach. The biblical understanding of mission encompasses more than is represented by the particularities of the Pauline model. Yet within the larger scope of the biblical witness Paul does constitute a principal representative of evangelical outreach. And for those prepared to find in his mission a guiding point of reference for appropriate Christian witness in our own day, Paul can serve as an effective reminder of basic components of the biblical perspective on mission. This would include convictions such as:

(1) That Christian mission should be understood and implemented within a theological frame of reference; and that theological reflection may in turn discover a needed relevance, balance, orientation, and dynamic if pursued (as for Paul) within a missiological frame of reference.

(2) That within the eschatological structuring of God's redemptive purpose, the primal mandate for the time between Christ's first and second advents is gospel proclamation to the nations, that within the larger divine economy the core intention for the present interim period is the effecting of this mandate.

(3) That from among the recipients of redemption God may commission selected individuals to a singularly disciplined, proactive, and sustained collaboration in the proclamation to the nations.

(4) That the proclamation of the gospel is meant to be implemented, and its achievement measured, in part by geographical attainment, that a deliberately cross-cultural mission to the unreached peoples and nations of one's world functions under first biblical warrant.

(5) That through and beyond missionary proclamation and evangelism, the planting of believing communities and their nurture to settled maturity in Christ must remain a primary focus of any biblically validated missionary outreach.

(6) That God's redemptive purposes will assuredly be achieved, that he remains sovereign in the course of the missionary proclamation to the nations, and that he will triumphantly accomplish his intention to sum up all things in Christ.

W. PAUL BOWERS

Bibliography. R. Allen, *Missionary Methods: St. Paul's or Ours?;* J. Blauw, *The Missionary Nature of the Church;* D. Bosch, *Transforming Mission;* W. P. Bowers, *Novum Testamentum* 22 (1980): 316–23; idem, *JETS* 30 (1987): 185–98; idem, *DPHL,* pp. 608–19; D. Gilliland, *Pauline Theology and Mission Practice;* M. Green, *Evangelism in the Early Church;* F. Hahn, *Mission in the New Testament;* J. Munck, *Paul and the Salvation of Mankind;* D. Senior and C. Stuhlmueller, *The Biblical Foundations for Mission.*

Paul, Kanakarayan Tiruselvam (1876–1931). Indian church and mission leader. K. T. Paul was born at Salem, Tamil Nadu, in South India. He graduated from Madras Christian College, where he was a classmate of V. S. AZARIAH. With Azariah he was involved in the founding of the National Missionary Society of which Paul became secretary in 1907. In 1913 he was appointed national secretary of the Indian YMCA, and in 1916 became the first Indian to serve as general secretary of the YMCA in India. In this capacity Paul developed a program for rural construction and promoted adult education. The YMCA under Paul had a team of dynamic thinkers.

In 1930 Paul participated in the First Round Table Conference in London. He supported the idea that there were values in a continued British connection with India. Nevertheless, according to ROBERT SPEER, he heralded the demise of the colonial era of missions.

Paul was active in the negotiations for Church Union in South India. He was Moderator of the South India United Church from 1925 to 1927. He represented India at ecumenical conferences. Paul was the first Christian statesman of India and produced a theology of the church and its mission in the context of developing nationalism in a religiously pluralistic society.

ROGER E. HEDLUND

Bibliography. M. D. David, *The Y.M.C.A. and the Making of Modern India;* H. Lefever, *CDCWM,* pp. 475–76; S. Neill, *Colonialism and Christian Mission;* H. A. Popley, *K. T. Paul: Christian Leader;* M. M. Thomas and P. T. Thomas, *Towards an Indian Christian Theology.*

Paulinus of York (d. c. 644). Missionary to England. Sent to buttress the missionary work of AUGUSTINE OF CANTERBURY, Paulinus left Rome in 601. Nothing is recorded of his work between 601 and 625, when he was ordained as bishop and settled to work among the Northumbrians. King Edwin and his chiefs came to Christ two years later through the ministry of Paulinus, who then took up residence in York and began extensive travel throughout the region. After Edwin's defeat in battle and death in 632, however, Paulinus returned to Kent with Edwin's wife and took up the vacant bishopric of Rochester, where he ministered until his death.

A. SCOTT MOREAU

Bibliography. P. H. Blair, *England before the Conquest; ODCC;* R. D. Ware, *NCE,* 11:29.

Peabody, Lucy Whitehead McGill Waterbury (1861–1949). American missions advocate, teacher of deaf children, and missionary in India. Peabody was born in Belmont, Kansas, and raised in Rochester, New York. After three years teaching the deaf, she married Baptist missionary Norman Waterbury in 1881. They left for India within a month. Five years later, she and her two children returned to New York after her husband's death. There, at a missions meeting, she met her fellow advocate in the Women's Missionary Movement, HELEN BARRETT MONTGOMERY. In 1889, Peabody began work with the Women's Baptist Foreign Missionary Society in Boston and soon became its head. For over twenty years she served with the Central Committee for the United Study of Foreign Missions, a committee to educate and motivate women and churches about missions. Her second marriage to Henry Wayland Peabody was cut short by his death after two years. Peabody was a prolific speaker and writer and raised millions of dollars for missions. In 1920, Peabody and Montgomery formed the Joint Committee for Women's Union Christian Colleges in Foreign Fields which supported colleges for women overseas. She was also president of the Woman's National Committee for Law Enforcement, a vice president for the Woman's American Baptist Foreign Mission Society, founder and editor of the children's magazine *Everland,* and organizer of the World Day of Prayer for missions.

MARGOT EYRING

Bibliography. M. L. Hammack, *DWCH;* N. A. Hardesty, *Great Women of Faith: The Strength and Influence of Christian Women;* R. McHenry, ed., *Famous American Women: A Biographical Dictionary from Colonial Times to the Present.*

Peace. The word "peace" is multidimensioned, emotive, and capable of being misused. Peace can refer to inner tranquillity or tranquil relations between nations. Peace can also refer to war. Those who "fight for peace" may do so because they believe this is a way to ending conflict and moving toward a better world. For purposes of this entry, negative peace refers to the absence of war, or armed conflict. Positive peace refers to the absence of causes of war. In addition to practical efforts to make peace in personal and social relationships, peace is also a utopian idea. Throughout Christian history, followers of Jesus have looked forward to an end of time when God will intervene to bring about peace, "when nation shall not lift up sword against nation, neither shall they learn war any more" (Isa. 2:4).

Pacifism, principled opposition to all war, manifested itself early in Christian history (*see* PACIFIST THEOLOGY). The first Christians believed that military service and killing were contrary to Jesus' teaching. In the second and third centuries, prominent leaders such as Tertullian and Origen condemned war and military service. Gradually, however, the church accommodated itself to admitting soldiers into membership. A tradition known as just war theory, holding that Christians could sanction a war fought under certain conditions for a just cause and in a just manner, emerged. Pacifism did not disappear. In such forms as conscientious objection, it remains a way to witness as a Christian.

Apart from those in the historic peace churches (Anabaptists, Society of Friends [Quakers], and the Church of the Brethren), positive peace is implicit in the vocation of missionaries as ministers of reconciliation. During the nineteenth-century explosion of missionary activity, peacemaking often arose out of the encounter with religious practices and social structures missionaries regarded as barriers to personal religious and societal change. Missionaries often condemned evil and developed strategies to end practices perceived as immoral such as polygamy in Africa, the trans-Atlantic slave trade, opium trafficking in China, human rights violations in Macedonia, Armenia, and the Congo. In India, for example, missionaries focused on *sati,* the custom of burning of Hindu widows on the funeral pyres of their dead husbands; infanticide; and the caste system as barriers to the spread of the gospel.

While furloughed missionaries often found an audience for their attacks on *sati,* slavery, and other evils, they had a harder time developing models for mission sensitive to more durable cultural patterns. For example, it was nearly fifty years after the arrival of Protestant missionaries in India before several women missionaries pioneered *zenana* visitation as a strategy of effective evangelism among women, which entailed calling on caste women in the secluded quarters of their homes. They introduced potential converts to the rudiments of Christianity, identified families in need of food, clothing, or medicine, and recruited children for schools. Their vision of work among "neglected and despised" women of India led to formation of the Ludhiana Medical College.

Sometimes missionaries dealt directly with the issue of war. In the nineteenth century, for example, during the Burmese-British war in 1824–25, the Burmese government held ADONIRAM JUDSON (1788–1850) captive for eighteen months. After his release, he helped draft the Treaty of Yandabo which ended the war. Many missionaries joined peace societies, and successor organizations in the twentieth century such as the Fellowship of

Reconciliation of the Mennonite Central Committee. Some wrote for periodicals with titles such as *Peace and Goodwill.* In this century, perhaps the bloodiest in history, Christians have worked for positive and negative peace and reconstruction of war-torn regions.

Christian peacemaking is part of mission. Christian missionaries provide a comprehensive ministry of spiritual and physical healing. They incarnate Christ in a broken world among victims of sin, including war. They contribute to positive peace through a holistic sharing of the gospel of Jesus. When war has erupted, they number among martyr victims along with indigenous believers. Violent conflict serves as an impediment to mission, as experienced by the ancient eastern churches in the face of Islam, or churches around the world in the face of twentieth-century persecution. MARTYRDOM often proves a necessary form of witness.

PAUL R. DEKAR

SEE ALSO Shalom.

Bibliography. P. Dekar, *For the Healing of the Nations. Baptist Peacemakers;* R. G. Musto, *Catholic Peacemakers;* R. L. Ramseyer, ed., *Mission and the Peace Witness.*

Peace with God. Sharing the Good News that we have peace with God in Christ is the central mission task of gospel-bearers. Both the Old Testament and the New affirm that all peace is of God. Peace is an essential quality of God. The condition of peace is the presence of God. Peace with God is God's will for humanity (*see also* SHALOM).

In the New Testament alone, over ninety occurrences of the word "peace" (Greek: *eirēnē*) and its cognates attest that the gospel is a message of peace with God. A host of heavenly voices announced the birth of Jesus with promises of peace on earth (Luke 2:14). Through him we have peace with God (Rom. 5:1). According to Paul, Jesus proclaimed the gospel of peace to all who were estranged from God and from one another (Eph. 2:11–22). The life and teaching of Jesus, insofar as we can summarize them, have to do with restoring the fullness of God's image and likeness to us so that we, even though marred by sin, may participate in the divine nature through union with Jesus (2 Peter 1:4).

Jesus brought about a new reality in the divine-human relationship. Jesus also announced the in-breaking of God's realm to reorder earthly priorities (Luke 4:18–19). Yet people and social structures have never corresponded to God's purposes as the Bible reveals them. Jesus left tasks undone and dreams unfulfilled. Early Christians expected Jesus to return soon, drawing from a body of Jewish apocalyptic expectation about the impending end of history, a time when the world as it was known would disappear and God would usher in a new era of peace and righteousness. When this did not happen, they adjusted to living in the here-and-now. Jesus' disciples, the earliest missionaries, proclaimed in word and deed that Jesus Christ has made it possible for anyone to find peace with God. As followers of Jesus, they put on the sandals of peace (Eph. 6:15). While our Lord tarried, the ongoing mission of the church included proclamation of restored peace with God, the state which characterized humanity at the time of creation.

God in Christ engaged in the work of RECONCILIATION and then entrusted the Christian community with the "ministry of reconciliation" (2 Cor. 5:18–20). God forged this reconciliation with humanity, between estranged human beings, and with the entire created order (Eph. 2:14–16; Col. 1). When Christians engage in the ministry of reconciliation, they take part in God's mission as revealed in Christ. In these two passages, as well as Romans 5:1–11 and Colossians 1:15–23, Paul elaborates that God makes peace by the blood of the cross, and that Christ is the head of the church. In Christ all things hold together. Beginning with the cross, God has effected peace on earth and in heaven.

Jesus effected peace between Gentiles and Jews, males and females, free persons and slaves. In effect, he has made peace among all the nations. Announcing this human dimension is also part of the mission of the church. Jesus blessed peacemakers as God's children (Matt. 5:19) and warned disciples against hoarding material possessions and allowing themselves to be tempted by wealth and power (Matt. 6:19–21). A later writer affirmed that true justice is the harvest reaped by peacemakers from seeds sown in a spirit of peace (James 3:18); wealth and power represent the source of conflict and quarrels (James 4:1–5). Christian peacemakers reflect the very nature of the one known as the God of Peace (Rom. 15:33; 16:20; 1 Cor. 14:33; 2 Cor. 13:11; Phil. 4:9; 1 Thess. 5:23; Heb. 13:20).

In these few paragraphs, we have begun to lay the groundwork upon which a THEOLOGY OF MISSION is built from the biblical understanding that we have peace with God in Christ. Health, security, long life, healing of broken relations, salvation, wholeness, life in Christ: these have been the basic work of missionaries from the first century until our own. Through self-giving love, death, resurrection, and glorification, Jesus broke the cycle of death and made possible radiant living in peace. Peace with God, therefore, is the basis of all ministry and mission.

PAUL R. DEKAR

Bibliography. D. L. Buttry, *Peace Ministry;* G. Harkness, *The Ministry of Reconciliation;* J. Macquarrie, *The Concept of Peace;* D. Richardson, *Peace Child.*

Penman, David (1936–89). New Zealand missionary to Pakistan and Anglican Church leader. He was born on August 8, 1936, and raised in Wellington and Wanganui, New Zealand. While training as a teacher he was converted in a mission led by Howard Guinness, and in 1957 began training for the Anglican ministry, gained an MA from the University of Canterbury, and married Jean Newson. After a curacy in Wanganui, Penman was accepted in 1965 by the New Zealand Church Missionary Society as a missionary to Pakistan. He became a careful student of Muslim culture, and wrote a Ph.D. thesis on Islamic sociology while at the same time reaching out to students and young people. In 1968 he helped to found the Pakistan Fellowship of Evangelical Students. In 1972 Penman was invited by the International Fellowship of Evangelical Students to serve in Lebanon, and from 1974 to 1975 he served as regional director of IFES work in the Middle East. In 1976 he was invited to lead CMS missionary training at St. Andrew's Hall in Melbourne, but in 1979 accepted the invitation to serve as vicar of the large Anglican parish of All Saints, Palmerston North in New Zealand. In 1982 he returned to Melbourne first as an assistant bishop and then in 1984 as archbishop of the influential diocese. Here a lively administration with a reputation for liberal evangelicalism gave him strong political influence, particularly on Australia's policy toward the Middle East. He died on October 1, 1989, after leading Bible teaching at the LAUSANNE CONGRESS II ON WORLD EVANGELISM (MANILA, 1989). Ever an activist and a strategist, he did much to relate evangelical missions to the great questions of the age, in particular the racial and cultural tensions between Muslims and Christians.

PETER LINEHAM

Bibliography. A. Nichol, *David Penman, Bridge Builder, Peacemaker, Fighter for Social Justice.*

Pentateuch, Mission in the. Scholars have debated whether the concept of mission can be found in the Pentateuch. While there are no explicit examples of preachers being sent to other tribes or nations, still the five books of Moses do contribute to an understanding of mission. The Old Testament speaks about mission because Yahweh is a missionary God. The Pentateuch reveals this in several key passages.

Genesis 1–3 teaches that humanity is alike in two ways. All people are created in the IMAGE OF GOD (Gen. 1:26–27), and all people are affected by SIN and need redemption. Genesis 3 tells the tragic story of human sin, which leads to suffering and separation. It also reveals God as a missionary God who seeks to reconcile humanity to himself. God could have destroyed Eve and Adam because of their sin; but, instead, God sought

them in the Garden and provided for their needs. In this way God distinguished himself from all other deities in the world. In the world's religions people seek for gods, but in Christianity the true and living God seeks after fallen humanity.

Genesis 3:15 has been called the *protevangelium* because it provides the first mention of the gospel. Evangelical scholars have seen in this verse a foreshadow of the cross where Satan injured Jesus Christ, but Jesus crushed Satan and the power of sin (Rom. 16:20; Rev. 12:9; 20:2). God prefers to save people rather than judge them. God's holy nature makes the gospel necessary; his love motivated and provided it.

Genesis 12:1–3 speaks of God's call to Abram (*see also* ABRAHAMIC COVENANT). From this passage on, the history narrated in the Old Testament is the history of Israel, "and the history of Israel is the history of redemption" (Kane). God chose Abram and his descendants to fulfill his redemptive plan. Their election was not an end in itself, but the means to an end—world redemption.

In Genesis 12:1–3 God promised Abram several things: land, a name, and a nation; however, most important, God promised Abram that "all peoples on earth will be blessed through you." God repeated this promise to Abram (later Abraham) four more times (Gen. 18:17–19; 22:16–18; 26:2–5; 28:13–15). God's particular blessing of Abram resulted in the universal blessing of all peoples. People are blessed by Abram's example of faithfulness, but ultimately God blessed the peoples of the earth through Abram's descendant, Jesus Christ.

The NIV translates the Hebrew word *goyim* in verse 3 as "peoples," and that is superior to "nations," as some versions render it. God is not referring here to nations as political entities; rather, God is saying that through Abram every ethno/linguistic group on earth will be blessed. Surely this must be an encouragement to those who endeavor to discover and evangelize unreached people groups (*see also* PEOPLES, PEOPLE GROUPS).

In choosing Abram and his descendants God revealed a threefold purpose for Israel. First, Israel was to receive and guard God's special revelation to the world (Heb. 1:1–3). Second, Israel was to provide the door through which the Messiah would enter history. Third, Israel was to be God's servant and witness to the nations.

The Book of Exodus tells the story of God's deliverance of Israel from bondage in Egypt. The exodus is the pivotal event in the Old Testament, as central in the Old Testament as the cross is in the New Testament. Again, God's deliverance was not an end in itself, but a means to accomplish God's plan for world redemption. This becomes clear in Exodus 19:5–6. This passage records God's words to Moses and the nation of Israel. In these verses God made conditional promises to the Israelites. If the Israelites would obey God and keep his covenant, then God promised to make them a "treasured possession," a "kingdom of priests," and a "holy nation."

Of special interest here is the phrase "kingdom of priests." God intended for the people of Israel to become a nation composed of priests. Their role was to minister to the other nations. Old Testament priests were expected to teach the people God's law and mediate between God and the people. God wanted the Israelites to teach the other nations about his love and grace. They were to stand as a living testimony to the other nations. Unfortunately, Israel did not fulfill this role. Throughout their history they did little to fulfill God's intention for them. The Pentateuch, however, repeatedly emphasizes Israel's instrumental role in God's mission to the peoples of the earth.

JOHN MARK TERRY

Bibliography. D. Filbeck, *Yes, God of the Gentiles, Too;* H. Goerner, *All Nations in God's Purpose;* E. Hedlund, *The Mission of the Church in the World;* W. C. Kaiser, Jr., "Israel's Missionary Call," in *Perspectives on the World Christian Movement;* J. H. Kane, *Christian Missions in Biblical Perspective.*

Pentecostal Missions. A twentieth-century missions movement noted for its emphases on Spirit baptism, expectation of miraculous "signs and wonders" in gospel proclamation, utilization of indigenous church principles, pragmatism in communications and technology, and spectacular church growth.

Radical evangelicals on the fringe of the nineteenth-century missions movement anticipated the premillennial return of Jesus Christ and the outpouring of the Holy Spirit in the last days to spiritually equip believers with apostolic power for the world evangelization (Joel 2:28–29). Accordingly, miracles would witness to the power of the gospel as they had in the expansion of the Early Church. A. B. SIMPSON and A. J. GORDON, among others, believed that prayer for the sick and power encounters (exorcisms, etc.) would attract non-Christians to the gospel.

As the century drew to a close and statistics revealed the slow pace of conversions on the mission fields, some believed that God might also bestow xenolalic tongues (known human languages) on Spirit-baptized missionaries as happened on the Day of Pentecost (Acts 2:4). Hence, they could bypass lengthy language study and immediately begin preaching to bring swift closure to the GREAT COMMISSION. In varying degrees, Simpson, Gordon, and C. T. STUDD, with others such as W. B. Godbey, Frank W. Sandford, and the Kansas holiness preacher, Charles F. Parham, considered this possibility.

Parham concluded that speaking in tongues constituted the "Bible evidence" of Spirit baptism: he and most of his students at Bethel Bible School in Topeka, Kansas, experienced the phenomenon in January 1901. This event and particularly news of the later Welsh Revival (1904–5) prompted the Azusa Street Revival in Los Angeles, California, under the leadership of the African-American William J. Seymour. It became the most influential revival of the century in global perspective and marked the beginning of Pentecostal missions. Similar revivals followed in the wake of Topeka and Azusa Street including ones at Zion and Chicago, Ill.; Dunn, N.C.; Nyack, N.Y.; Winnipeg and Toronto, Canada; Sunderland, England; Oslo, Norway; and Stockholm, Sweden. From these arose a new diaspora of missionaries, reaching upwards of two hundred by 1910. In India, however, influenced in part by the Welsh Revival and the ministry of Minnie F. Abrams, the Pentecostal revival began autonomously in 1906.

Although robust in their faith, the early missionaries were often ill-prepared, traveling without salary or pledged support, and without cross-cultural preparation. Before 1908, most of them expected to preach with "missionary tongues," but subsequently understood them to be glossolalia or unknown tongues for prayer in the Spirit (1 Cor. 13:1; 14:2). Whereas in India, a significant contingent of veteran missionaries (e.g., CHRISTIAN AND MISSIONARY ALLIANCE [CMA], Methodists) became Pentecostal. Beginning in the 1920s, Bible institute graduates, particularly from North America and the United Kingdom, became the backbone for much of the mission enterprise.

Apart from glossolalia and belief that all of the gifts of the Spirit (1 Cor. 12:7–11) had been restored, Pentecostal missionaries initially differed little from their CMA and holiness contemporaries. As time passed, however, they continued to highlight miraculous signs and wonders more than their Wesleyan–holiness and Reformed revivalist brothers and sisters. Other evangelical missionaries virtually dismissed the notion of miracles. Nonetheless, because of their focus on the Spirit's work in mission, Pentecostals have willingly addressed the dark side of spirituality: Satanic power. This has helped them to effectively relate the gospel to peoples with non-Western worldviews. Because the Spirit's outpouring empowers seekers with spiritual gifts and for SPIRITUAL WARFARE (Eph. 6:12), Pentecostalism quickly becomes indigenous.

With ever-increasing numbers of missionaries, farsighted leaders recognized the need for organization. The earliest and most successful European mission agencies were in the United Kingdom the Pentecostal Missionary Union of Great Britain and Ireland (1909), Zaire Evangelistic Mission (1919); in Netherlands, the Pentecostal Mission Alliance (1920); and in Scandinavia, Missionaries sent out from Swedish and Norwegian Pentecostal congregations. In South Africa, the Apostolic Faith Mission (1913) sent missionaries to various people groups in that region.

North American agencies included the Pentecostal Mission in South and Central Africa (1910), Assemblies of God (1914), Pentecostal Assemblies of Canada (1922), Russian and Eastern European Mission (1927), Pentecostal Holiness Church (1911), and Church of God (Cleveland, Tenn.) (1902). Following the trinitarian dispute in the Assemblies of God (1913–16), many "Oneness" or "Jesus Name" missionaries joined organizations that eventually merged to form the United Pentecostal Church (1945). Still, a large number of independent missionaries served abroad, preferring the personal guidance of the Holy Spirit in their activities over the directives of mission boards.

With the delay in Christ's return, Pentecostals frequently borrowed the paternalistic practices of their Protestant counterparts to give permanence to their efforts. However, ALICE E. LUCE, formerly with the CHURCH MISSIONARY SOCIETY in India, influenced Pentecostal missions through her adaptation of ROLAND ALLEN'S teachings on the INDIGENOUS CHURCH in his *Missionary Methods: St. Paul's or Ours?* (1912) with Pentecostal distinctives. Reflecting the influence of Allen and Luce, Assemblies of God missiologist MELVIN L. HODGES penned his best-seller, *The Indigenous Church* (1953).

Growth in many countries accelerated after mid-century when missionaries, especially those from the Assemblies of God (U.S.A.) and the Pentecostal Assemblies of Canada, began moving away from paternal control to partnership with national church leaders. Scandinavian missionaries, rejecting any authority or agency above the local congregation, naturally supported indigenous church principles. Their successes in Brazil (and developments in Chile) first signaled the international progress of the movement. The unique combination of Pentecostal spirituality with the application of these principles accounts for the rapid growth. The Church of God (Cleveland, Tenn.) has also seen success but without formally embracing indigenous church principles; growth has also come in part through amalgamation with existing Pentecostal church bodies overseas. In recent years, mission churches have themselves begun sending out thousands of their own missionaries (e.g., Yoido Full Gospel Church in Seoul, Korea, pastored by David [formerly Paul] Yonggi Cho; Congregaçá Cristã do Brazil in São Paulo, Brazil, founded by Luigi Francescon; Calvary Charismatic Center in Singapore, pastored by Rick Seaward).

Since Pentecostals have always been more interested in the "doing" than "theorizing" of mission, they have produced few theologies of mission. The exceptions include: *The Baptism of the Holy Ghost & Fire*, 2d ed. (1906) by MINNIE F. ABRAMS, the first Pentecostal theology of mission; *Our Foreign Missions: A Biblical Guideline* (Vår Yttre Mission: Några Bibliska Riklinjer) ([Stockholm] 1937) by David Landin; *A Theology of the Church and Its Mission* (1977) by Melvin L. Hodges; *The Third Force in Missions* (1985) by Paul A. Pomerville; *The Liberating Spirit: Toward an Hispanic American Pentecostal Social Ethic* (1993) by Eldin Villafañe; and *Not By Might Nor by Power: A Pentecostal Theology of Social Concern in Latin America* (1996) by Douglas Petersen. In discussions on the mission of the Church (1990–95), Pentecostal scholars presented major papers on vital aspects of missiology at meetings of the fifth quinquennium of the international Roman Catholic and Classical Pentecostal Dialogue.

The emergence of Pentecostal missions represented a vibrant new thrust in evangelism at a time when the older missionary movement had begun to decline due in part to questions raised about the ultimate claims of the Christian faith. Without such hesitancies, Pentecostal missionaries have changed the landscape of Christianity in the twentieth century through their accent on the role of the Holy Spirit in the Christian world mission. Although contemporary statistics of worldwide church growth appear inflated, Pentecostals now represent one of the largest families of Christians. Pentecostalism has proven to be the most dynamic force of the century for Christian expansion.

GARY B. MCGEE

Bibliography. A. L. Clanton, *United We Stand: A History of Oneness Organizations;* E. L. Cleary and H. W. Stewart-Gambino, eds., *Power, Politics, and Pentecostals in Latin America;* M. W. Dempster, B. D. Klaus, D. Petersen, eds., *Called & Empowered: Global Mission in Pentecostal Perspective;* W. J. Hollenweger, *The Pentecostals;* J. A. B. Jongeneel, ed., *Pentecost, Mission and Ecumenism;* W. Ma and R. P. Menzies, eds., *Pentecostalism in Context;* L. G. McClung, Jr., ed., *Azusa Street and Beyond: Pentecostal Missions and Church Growth in the Twentieth Century;* G. B. McGee, *This Gospel Shall Be Preached: A History and Theology of Assemblies of God Foreign Missions,* 2 vols.; idem, "The Radical Strategy: The Linkage Between Paranormal Phenomena and Evangelism in Modern Christian Missions," in *The Holy Spirit and Mission Dynamics,* ed., C. D. McConnell; R. P. Spittler, Jr., "Implicit Values in Pentecostal Missions," *Missiology: An International Review* 16 (October 1988): 409–24; L. S. Vaccaro de Petrella, "The Tension Between Evangelism and Social Action in the Pentecostal Movement," IRM 75 (January 1986): 34–38; C. P. Wagner, *Spiritual Power and Church Growth.*

Pentecostal Movement. A restorationist and millenarian movement highlighting the baptism and gifts of the Holy Spirit that emerged from the broader holiness movement beginning in 1901. Branches of modern Pentecostalism include "Classical" (denominational) Pentecostals,

"Neo-Pentecostals" (charismatics), and so-called "Third Wave" evangelicals who view "signs and wonders" as essential for successful ministry (Acts 5:12).

Throughout the nineteenth century, Protestants from a broad spectrum of churches prayed for the outpouring of the Spirit (Joel 2:28–29) to divinely enable them to bring about moral and social reform and to evangelize the world. Among them, Wesleyan holiness advocates encouraged believers to seek for a postconversion experience of grace that would immediately bring "entire sanctification." Reflecting the influence of JOHN WESLEY, and more directly that of his associate John Fletcher, this experience became known as the "second blessing," the "double cure," or "eradication" of the sinful nature, and increasingly as the "baptism in the Holy Spirit." Writers such as PHOEBE PALMER and William Arthur taught that it would rid believers of the moral flaw in human nature. Late in the century, Benjamin H. Irwin's theology, which proposed a third work of grace— "fire baptism" for empowerment—played a crucial role in the development of Pentecostalism. Separating sanctification from Spirit baptism, however, generated questions about what distinguished them from each other. It was but a short step to arguing that speaking in tongues as found in the "pattern" of Spirit baptisms in the book of Acts (2, 8 [implied], 10, 19) provided definite evidence of the third work.

Reformed revivalists like CHARLES G. FINNEY, DWIGHT L. MOODY, A. B. SIMPSON, and REUBEN A. TORREY, as well as speakers at the annual Keswick conferences in England (see KESWICK CONVENTION), rejected the sinless perfection of the Wesleyans and taught that the second work brought the "fullness" of the Holy Spirit. Not only would it enhance personal holiness, but more importantly it would invigorate Christians for evangelism. In addition to the growing popularity of the doctrine of divine healing based on the atoning work of Christ (Isa. 53:5; James 5:13–15) and the dispensational premillennialism of the Plymouth Brethren, these beliefs crystallized together as the "full" or "fourfold gospel": Jesus Christ as Savior, Sanctifier (Baptizer in the Spirit), Healer, and Coming King.

Radical evangelicals from the holiness ranks wondered aloud with other premillennialists how humanity could be evangelized in the "last days" (Acts 2:17) before the imminent return of Christ. With a pessimistic appraisal of the future course of human history and discouraged by the slow pace of conversions in the mission lands, they prayed for the restoration of apostolic power. This "radical strategy" anticipated supernatural interventions of the Spirit's power in SIGNS AND WONDERS to reach every tribe and nation with the message of salvation (Matt. 24:14). For some, this meant praying for the sick and exorcising

demons, but others pondered the idea that God might restore the gift of tongues— "languages" (xenolalia). Through bypassing time-consuming language study, Spirit-baptized missionaries could expedite world evangelization by immediately preaching to their hearers. By 1890, this short-cut to cross-cultural evangelism had gathered considerable interest.

To prepare a special contingent of end-times missionaries, the Kansas holiness preacher Charles F. Parham opened Bethel Bible School in Topeka in the fall of 1900. Influenced by Irwin and convinced that tongues-speech represented the "Bible evidence" of Spirit baptism and afforded linguistic ability for gospel proclamation, he and his students prayed in early January 1901 to receive the gift and consequently testified to speaking in various languages. The "Apostolic Faith movement," as Parham called it, had begun and his insistence on tongues became the hallmark of Pentecostal doctrine.

In 1905, Parham started another Bible school in Houston, Texas. It was there that William J. Seymour, an African-American holiness preacher, met Parham and accepted his teachings. Leaving Houston in early 1906 and arriving in Los Angeles, he became the foremost leader of the Azusa Street revival (1906–9). The impact of this event brought global dimensions to the movement through the following revivals and others that it sparked: Toronto, Canada (1906); Oslo, Norway (1906); Dunn, North Carolina (1907); Memphis, Tennessee (1907); Nyack, New York (1907); Sunderland, England (1907); Stockholm, Sweden (1907); Calcutta, India (1907); South Africa (1908); Chile (1909); and Brazil (1910).

Yet among early Pentecostal revivals, Azusa Street was unique for its accent on racial reconciliation and the outpouring of the Spirit on the poor. Thus, while it shared the same concern for missions that marked Topeka, other aspects of the Spirit's work flowered, especially the fruit of the Spirit in human relationships as in the case of blacks, Hispanics, and whites in attendance. In addition to Seymour, prominent African-American leaders included Charles H. Mason (Church of God in Christ), Garfield T. Haywood (Pentecostal Assemblies of the World), L. M. Mason (United Holy Church of America), and Ida Robinson (Mount Sinai Holy Church of America). Pentecostal awakenings amid oppressed peoples (e.g., the victims of apartheid in South Africa) took inspiration from Azusa as a model of true Pentecostal blessing and liberation—the conferral of dignity and the Spirit's gifts upon the poor and oppressed.

News of the outpouring of the Holy Spirit spread through persons traveling from Los Angeles, in addition to printed reports in periodicals such as the *Apostolic Faith* (Los Angeles), published by the Azusa leaders. At the same time, believers schooled in holiness teachings in India began speaking in tongues in July 1906, though unaware of events in the United States and Parham's teaching on the evidential nature of tongues.

While there is little doubt that Pentecostalism attracted the poor and marginalized elements in society, this perception has also created an inaccurate stereotype. Recent research shows that while many Pentecostals came from the ranks of blue-collar workers; indeed, there were even some wealthy Pentecostals. In regard to their role in society and due to their biblicism and expectation of Christ's return, many were pacifists. As a result, some were jailed or ordered to do alternative service during World War I. As for women's involvement in ministry, many Pentecostals, like their holiness forebears, found justification for this in the Spirit's outpouring on women as well as men (Acts 2:17). Women, therefore, have made significant contributions as evangelists, missionaries, pastors, and Bible school administrators. Most notable among them were Anna Larssen Bjourner, Christine A. Gibson, AIMEE SEMPLE MCPHERSON, LILLIAN TRASHER, and Maria B. Woodworth-Etter.

Pentecostal dynamics in worship have included encouraging everyone to become involved in singing, giving testimonies to answers to prayer, playing musical instruments, clapping and raising hands in prayer, manifesting the gifts of the Spirit (1 Cor. 12:8–10), and praying for the sick, along with the preaching of the Word. The accent on the immanent presence of the Holy Spirit became the chief distinctive of their corporate worship.

Between 1906 and 1916, Pentecostals divided over three doctrinal issues. Beginning in late 1906, the first centered on the indispensable need of speaking in tongues as "initial evidence" of Spirit baptism. As the belief in "missionary tongues" failed, they increasingly considered speaking in "unknown" tongues *(glossolalia)* as prayer in the Spirit and the source of empowerment. Some emphasized tongues, but without insisting on them for Spirit baptism. However, the emerging Pentecostal denominations generally saw this as the entry into the Spirit-filled life.

The second division over the "Finished Work of Calvary" arose in 1910 when Pentecostals with Reformed backgrounds challenged the Wesleyan holiness notion of sanctification. The most prominent leader of the opposition, Chicago pastor William H. Durham, contended that Jesus finished the work of salvation and sanctification on the cross. The legacy of this controversy continues with the Wesleyan view retained by several "holiness-Pentecostal" organizations including the Church of God in Christ, Church of God (Cleveland, Tenn.), and International Pentecostal Holiness Church. The Assemblies of God, Pentecostal Assemblies of Canada, International Church of the Foursquare Gospel, Pentecostal Church of God, and United Pentecostal Church International (UPCI) represent "finished work" bodies.

The third division began in 1913 when a relatively small contingent of Pentecostals started teaching that water baptism in the name of Jesus Christ according to Acts 2:38 had precedence over the baptismal formula of Matthew 28:19. The restoration of another "pattern" in the book of Acts led Frank J. Ewart, Howard A. Goss, and others to replace the historic doctrine of the Trinity with a radical "Jesus-centrism." Dividing the Assemblies of God in 1916, "Jesus Name," "Apostolic," or "Oneness" Pentecostals left with many of them later joining together to form the UPCI in 1945.

Pentecostals have remained evangelical in doctrine, confessing belief in the Trinity (the large majority), the inspiration and infallibility of Scripture, justification by faith, substitutionary atonement of Christ, and other historic doctrines of the Christian faith. Nevertheless, they have differed on several vital points: the ordinances of the church, function of tongues in Spirit baptism, role of the Christian in society, attitudes toward women in ministry, and church polity.

Traditional Episcopal, Presbyterian, and Congregational polities are utilized with some Pentecostals claiming that the offices of apostle and prophet have been restored. Episcopal polity is evident in the Church of God (Cleveland, Tenn.), and even in circles that ostensibly appear Congregational (e.g., David Yonggi Cho's Yoido Full Gospel Church in Seoul, Korea). Hybrid Congregational/Presbyterian forms appear in such denominations as the Assemblies of God and Open Bible Standard Churches. Congregational polity dominates the continental European scene, Brazil, and many other sectors of the movement.

Evangelical recognition of American Pentecostals came with an invitation to several denominations to join the National Association of Evangelicals (NAE) at its founding in 1942. This close identification with the NAE and participation in its member agencies has led to a gradual "evangelicalization" of Pentecostalism, an adoption of issues and perspectives germane to the largely Reformed member organizations. NAE conferences also kindled interest in Pentecostal unity that led to the founding of the Pentecostal Fellowship of North America (1948), recently reorganized as the Pentecostal/Charismatic Churches of North America (1994). Concern for unity among Spirit-baptized believers had led earlier to the four meetings of the International Pentecostal Council in Europe prior to World War I. In 1939, the European Pentecostal Conference in Stockholm, Sweden, helped lay the basis for the founding of the Pentecostal World Conference in 1947. Pentecostal church bodies have also joined the WORLD EVANGELICAL FELLOWSHIP,

Lausanne Committee for World Evangelization, and WORLD COUNCIL OF CHURCHES.

Beginning with the charismatic renewal in the 1960s (*see also* CHARISMATIC MOVEMENT), "neo-Pentecostals" or "charismatics" appeared in the mainline Protestant churches, the Roman Catholic Church, and several of the Orthodox churches. This had actually begun in the Protestant churches in the 1950s and gained national press coverage in 1960 when Dennis Bennett, rector of St. Mark's Episcopal Church in Van Nuys, California, announced to his parishioners that he had been baptized in the Spirit and spoken in tongues. Several factors account for the renewal, including believers in the historic churches searching for a deeper work of the Spirit, the influence of the postwar faith healing movement, and the activities of the Full Gospel Business Men's Fellowship International.

The appearance of Pentecostal phenomena among Episcopalians, Presbyterians, Reformed, Mennonites, Methodists, Messianic Jews, Disciples of Christ, Baptists, Lutherans, and others prompted vigorous debate, but for the most part charismatics gained approval within their respective denominations. Official Catholic and Protestant doctrinal statements on the renewal can be found in *Presence, Power, and Praise* (1980) edited by Kilian McDonnell, O.S.B. In regard to theological reflection, Pentecostal and charismatic scholars have made important contributions in part through the conferences and journals of the Society for Pentecostal Studies and the European Pentecostal Theological Association.

The SECOND VATICAN COUNCIL (1962–65) laid the theological groundwork for the Catholic charismatic renewal, the largest of all the renewal movements. Beginning with the famous "Duquesne Weekend" retreat in the Pittsburgh, Pennsylvania, area in 1976, interest in the outpouring of the Spirit grew quickly, especially through the ministry of the Word of God community in Ann Arbor, Michigan, and major conferences at Notre Dame University in South Bend, Indiana. Leading figures have included Stephen Clark, Ralph Keifer, Ralph Martin, Edward D. O'Connor, C.S.C., Kevin and Dorothy Ranaghan, and Leon-Joseph Cardinal Suenens, the latter given oversight of the movement by Pope Paul VI.

David J. Du Plessis, a key leader in charismatic circles and sometime secretary of the Pentecostal World Conference, uniquely served as a bridge between classical Pentecostals and Protestant and Catholic charismatics. In response to the Catholic charismatic renewal and because of Pentecostal church growth in historically Roman Catholic countries, Du Plessis and McDonnell were instrumental in founding the Roman Catholic and Classical Pentecostal Dialogue that began in 1972.

Another path in the broader Pentecostal tradition came with the emergence of the "Third Wave" of the Holy Spirit by the early 1980s. According to this definition, the Pentecostal and charismatic movements represent the first and second waves of the Spirit in the twentieth century. Focusing their attention on prayer for the sick, exorcisms, and other spiritual manifestations, key proponents like C. PETER WAGNER and Charles H. Kraft have encouraged evangelicals to seek for supernatural power in ministry. Particularly influential has been John Wimber and the Vineyard movement. Speaking in tongues, however, has not been at the forefront of their thinking or deemed as a validation of Spirit baptism.

More recent developments have also impacted the world church, especially those at the Toronto Airport Vineyard in Canada beginning in 1994 and at Brownsville Assembly of God in Pensacola, Florida, a year later. Although not without controversy, these and continuing revivals in various parts of the world (e.g., Brazil, Argentina, Burkina Faso, Korea) have been influential in encouraging evangelism and revival elsewhere.

Classical Pentecostals alone constitute one of the largest families of Christians in the world today and along with charismatics and others in the Pentecostal/charismatic tradition enjoy an unusual grassroots ecumenicity in the Spirit rising above conciliar and creedal boundaries. Together, they represent the single most dynamic development in twentieth-century Christianity.

GARY B. McGEE

Bibliography. R. M. Anderson, *Vision of the Disinherited: The Making of American Pentecostalism;* S. M. Burgess, G. B. McGee, P. H. Alexander, eds., *DPCM;* E. L. Cleary and H. W. Stewart-Gambino, eds., *Power, Politics, and Pentecostalism in Latin America;* D. W. Dayton, *Theological Roots of Pentecostalism;* W. C. Fletcher, *Soviet Charismatics: The Pentecostals in the USSR;* D. E. Harrell, Jr., *All Things Are Possible: The Healing and Charismatic Revivals in Modern America;* P. Hocken, *The Glory and the Shame: Reflections on the 20th Century Outpouring of the Holy Spirit;* C. E. Jones, *Guide to the Study of the Pentecostal Movement,* 2 vols.; idem, *The Charismatic Movement,* 2 vols.; J. A. B. Jongeneel, ed., *Pentecost, Mission and Ecumenism;* R. Laurentin, *Catholic Charismatics;* K. Poewe, ed., *Charismatic Christianity as a Global Culture;* R. Quebedeaux, *The New Charismatics II;* J. L. Sandidge, *Roman Catholic/Pentecostal Dialogue (1977–82): A Study in Developing Ecumenism;* V. Synan, *The Holiness-Pentecostal Tradition;* G. Wacker, *Journal of Ecclesiastical History* 47 (July 1996): 505–28; C. P. Wagner, *The Third Wave of the Holy Spirit.*

Penzotti, Francisco (1851–1925). Italian missionary in South America. Born in Chaivenna, Italy, at the age of thirteen he emigrated to Uruguay, South America. In 1875 he heard the gospel and shortly thereafter became a Christian within the Methodist Church. He threw his heart into the spread of the Scriptures as a Bible distributor with the American Bible Society throughout Argentina, Bolivia, and Chile. Visits to Peru in 1884 and 1886 convinced Penzotti and the ABS of the need to establish a Bible Society agency to serve Peru, Ecuador, and the western part of Bolivia.

Penzotti moved his family to Callao, Peru, in 1888 to direct the ministry. During the following year Penzotti and his three colleagues, Juan Arancet, José Illescas, and Manuel Noriega, were able not only to distribute 4,500 Bibles or portions thereof, but also to explain the gospel to those who acquired them. Such receptivity was sure to cause concern among the Catholic hierarchy, especially at a time when public non-Catholic religious services were prohibited in Peru. Penzotti was taken to court, where his case attracted worldwide attention. He was imprisoned on July 26, 1890. After nine months in jail he was finally released on Easter Sunday in 1891. He continued his Bible distribution ministry in Peru, in Central America after 1896, and finally in Argentina, where this "Luther of Latin America" died in 1925.

LINDY SCOTT

Bibliography. A. M. Milne, *From Cape Horn to Quito with the Bible.*

People Movements. Phenomenon of a significant number of the people of one tribe, class, or caste converting to Christ together. The term is comparatively new in the annals of missions. J. Waskom Pickett reports that he searched a hundred volumes of reports from missions in which movements of this kind occurred without finding a single use of even the term "mass movement" until 1892 (1933, 21). There seems to have been no recognition of the need for a distinctive term to describe these movements, even on the part of those whose ministry precipitated them. Missionaries resorted to the word "REVIVAL" or whatever term was familiar to them on the basis of experiences in their home churches. When, belatedly, the term "mass movement" came into wider usage it was not without reservations. Picket himself adopted that term in writing his classic work *Mass Movements in India,* but he indicated that it obscured tribal, caste, and other types of unity shared by converts. In acceeding to the use of the term, he nevertheless acknowledged that the term "group movement" might have been preferable.

In a somewhat parallel but later development, DONALD A. MCGAVRAN became acquainted with Pickett and his work after his arrival in India. ALAN R. TIPPETT credits McGavran with coining the term "people movement" though he does so without complete confidence (1987, 253). In any case, it seems clear that McGavran has done more than anyone to popularize and promote this particular approach to mission strategy.

The history of the expansion of Christianity is replete with cases where numerous people sharing some common trait(s) have become Christians either simultaneously or within a short period of time. The Christian church began with the conversion of large numbers of Jews and Gentile God-fearers. From the time of Constantine through the Middle Ages, tribes and nations of southern, central, and then northern Europe were Christianized as missionaries preached the gospel message and sovereigns prescribed conversion to the Christian faith. People movement advocates readily admit that the conversion of Europe contains much that is repugnant to us today. Also that they will not be repeated in the modern world. Nevertheless, advocates insist that they were important to later advances evident in the ministry of people like Wycliffe, Knox, Luther, Fox, the Wesleys, and Carey.

As viewed by McGavran, Tippett, and others of the Church Growth school of thought, the typical missionary strategy that developed during the seventeenth, eighteenth, and nineteenth centuries was the "exploratory mission station approach" or the "exploratory gathered colony approach." Missionaries first acquired land and built suitable residences for themselves. Then they added churches, schools, orphanages, hospitals, residences for helpers, and so on. Since nationals who received the ministrations and message of the missionaries were often forced from their homes, many of them came to live at or near the mission station. Still others in the area became dependent on the mission station economy. This type of mission strategy grew out of the individualism of Western missionaries and the gap between the Western and non-Western worlds. It "fit" the times. But two additional things must be said about it. First, that pattern does not fit today's world in which the peoples of the world are determined to assert their own identity and resist the tutelage of foreigners. Second, though they have not been sought by missionaries in most cases, the history of modern missions as well as the history of the early church and Middle Ages reveals that the great majority of converts have come to Christ in people movements large and small. Mission accounts from a wide variety of cultures and areas around the world—Oceania, Indonesia, India, and Burma in Asia; and Ivory Coast and Gold Coast in Africa to name but a few—yield outstanding examples of Christward movements of this kind. Proponents of people movement strategy are quick to point out that they exemplify the strategy now required to evangelize the emerging world.

To test the validity of such claims, in the 1960s Marion Cowan undertook a study of a developing church among the previously resistant Tzotzil Indian tribe in Mexico. The gospel had entered the Tzotzil Indian tribe through a "chance" meeting between a neighboring Tzeltal Christian and an unbelieving Tzotzil. Cowan noted that most of the early Tzotzil believers were converted as a group. She then charted the various relationships that existed between the members of the believing group and attempted to discover the channels of effective initial communication (i.e., communication resulting in conversion). A detailed summary of her findings cannot be included here, but it is relevant to point out that, out of a total of eighty such cases, thirty-nine occurred between consanguineal kin and thirty-eight between affinal kin. Only three cases of effective communication occurred between persons not related by either blood or marriage, and these occurred between members of a small farmers' cooperative.

From a people movement point of view, the key to understanding the history of Christian missions and contemporary occurrences such as these is a recognition of the fact that they were not, and are not, simply movements of larger numbers of individuals acting on their own initiative and more or less independent of each other. Rather, they represent the way in which people actually communicate with each other and the way in which they "like" to come to Christ. People communicate and relate most often and effectively with their own kind of people. And they resist being wrenched out of the families, extended families, and other groupings with which they are most intimately associated (*see also* HOMOGENOUS UNIT PRINCIPLE).

Western Christians especially are inclined to take umbrage at the notion that social ties are—or, at least, should be—as consequential as people movement philosophy and strategy suggest. Numerous Scripture passages in both Old and New Testaments indicate that to please God one must be willing to leave father and mother or anyone standing in the way of obedience to God. Group conversion is often seen as entailing something less than the kind of personal decision that true commitment calls for. Moreover, in the church distinctions of race, class, and status are of no account. All are "one" in Christ.

These and other criticisms have occasioned various types of responses from people movement proponents, especially those of the Church Growth school of thought. First, terms and definitions have been modified in an effort to promote understanding. The term "mass movement" has been superseded by "people movement" and, in certain cases, "web movement." "Group decision" and "group conversion" have been explained as "mutually interdependent decision" and "multi-individual conversion." Changes and explanations of factors that occasion and characterize Christ-ward movements of this kind. Second, an effort

has been made to ground the strategy in Scripture—in the experience of the early church, the ministry of the apostle Paul, and, especially, in the requirements of the GREAT COMMISSION. The *ethnē* in Matthew 18:19 is understood as "people groups" rather than "nation-states" or even "Gentiles." Third, as indicated above, advocates are quick to point to the numerous instances of people movements in church and missions history, especially in the history of modern missions. Fourth, a case is made for concluding that the kind of group DECISION MAKING that is part and parcel of people movements results in more stability as well as more rapid church growth than does one-by-one gathered church extractionism. Fifth, advocates maintain that the kind of tribal-, race-, and class-consciousness that gives rise to a people movement is not permanent. Though it often is determinative of the way churches begin, it does not describe what churches will ultimately become as members grow in their understanding of God's way and will.

Efforts to quiet critics have met with varying degrees of acceptance. For example, the term "people group" now enjoys wide usage. But as originally defined by McGavran the term signified an "endogamous group." Subsequently it evolved through a series of modifications and now is usually thought of as an "affinity group." This latter definition, however, lacks the kind of precision necessary for sound strategic thinking. And the change process itself argues against equating "people group" with *ethnē* quite apart from a consideration of the biblical usage of the Greek word. Nevertheless, sound missiology is well informed by people movement thinking. Not only does it make a great contribution to our understanding of the ways in which people become Christians. It also arms us against the kind of cultural bias that overlooks the vital importance of group ties and the potential that often exists to both initiate and encourage whole groups of people to embrace and follow Christ.

DAVID J. HESSELGRAVE

Bibliography. M. Cowan, *PA* 9 (1962): 193–204; D. A. McGavran, *Bridges of God*; idem, *Understanding Church Growth*; J. W. Pickett, *Christian Mass Movements in India*; A. R. Tippett, *Introduction to Missiology*.

Peoples, People Groups. Way of perceiving humanity as being composed of identifiable cultural and/or sociological grouping. Mission is then seen as directed to such groups. Our Lord's mandate as recorded in Acts 1:8 made an early related strategic distinction: "You will be my witnesses, in Jerusalem, and in all Judea, and Samaria, and to the ends of the earth."

Later the Constantinian church, challenged from the north, sent missionaries to "barbarians." They in turn carried the gospel into pagan northern Europe and transformed other barbarian peoples into the entity that left its stamp on the definition of missions: Christendom. En route, mission was defined as directed toward the "heath men" or "HEATHEN."

When the modern missionary movement took shape, Europeans became aware, through travel and trade, of the vast reaches of whole "dark continents" without the gospel. There were the civilized inhabitants of Christendom, and there was the non-Christian world of the colonies. No further definition seemed necessary. Later, the historic flow of colonial contacts caused mission agencies and denominations to shift focus from the coastal port cities to the interior areas of these continents. Hence names like Africa *Inland* Mission, Sudan *Interior* Mission, China *Inland* Mission. "Interiors" now defined mission.

The surge of missionary effort subsequent to World War II took place in the context of newly independent nation-states, fifty-seven formed in Africa in a single decade. Mission agencies responded by focusing strategy on "national" boundaries and church bodies within them. Once a group, recognizable by denominational distinctives, was in existence, many agencies and strategists declared "mission" to be complete within the entire boundaries of these nation-states. Blindness to the possibility of mission on the part of the "Younger" churches took the next step of excluding from view countries from which Westerners were restricted. For a significant segment of mission sending, the day of mission was declared over. Supposed national churches existed, while whole segments of nations had no church or witness. A new definition was needed.

The often artificial nature of nation-state boundaries was missed. The consistent national experience, especially in Africa, was of near civil war, as truer identities surfaced and civil wars or unifying border strikes sought to reunite peoples through stronger tribal or ethnolinguistic identities. These natural units intruded themselves on the attention of mission strategists. Awareness of their reality forced, yet again, a redefinition of mission if the church was to express her universal, catholic nature. The simplest and most evident basis was ethnolinguistic.

Leslie G. Brierley of WEC began listing Remaining Unevangelized Peoples (RUPs) after 1941. CAMERON TOWNSEND led the identification of first *Two Thousand Tongues to Go* and later, through the *Ethnologue* (Grimes, 1988) which now describes about seven thousand language groups. DONALD MCGAVRAN, beginning in 1955, called attention in his writings to PEOPLE MOVEMENTS. R. PIERCE BEAVER chaired a 1972 conference on "The Gospel and Frontier Peoples." MARC listed certain people groups at the WORLD CONGRESS ON EVANGELISM (BERLIN CONGRESS 1966), and came to advocate the term "Un-reached" People Groups, first using the term for the LAUSANNE CONGRESS ON WORLD EVANGELISM (1974). These were popularized and defined in the *Unreached Peoples* MARC series from 1979 to 1987. The series included the Lausanne Committee for World Evangelization Strategy Working Group (SWG) definition of a people group as "a significantly large sociological grouping of people who perceive themselves to have a common affinity for one another. . . . From the viewpoint of evangelization, this is the largest possible group within which the Gospel can spread without encountering barriers to understanding or acceptance." Although Dayton and Wagner experimented with a definition of unreached as less than 20 percent Christian, the SWG moved to define unreached as the absence of a viable church capable of carrying on the group's evangelization. RALPH WINTER espoused the term "Hidden" or "Frontier" following his definitive paper presented at the 1974 Lausanne Conference. These semantic differences were resolved at a Chicago airport conference, when the SWG called together a set of missions leaders who agreed on a definition that would make "frontier" and "hidden" synonyms of the now prevailing "unreached," by which was meant any group that did not contain a contextualized church demonstrably capable of completing the evangelization of the group. Both are to be distinguished from the less precise "homogeneous unit" popularized by the CHURCH GROWTH MOVEMENT.

In practice, several definitional difficulties remained. 1. Was exhaustive and exclusive categorizing possible or necessary? 2. Most of the definitions remain to this day more serviceable for nonurban, traditional peoples. The intersective groups so common in sociological and urban analysis are confusing if shoe-horned into a classification that seeks to sort each and every inhabitant of earth into one and only one group. 3. The difference between evangelized peoples and unreached people groups seems to be that evangelization focuses on individuals and on external efforts made by others, while unreached deals with groups and with outcomes in church planting. The terms are unfortunately not used carefully. 4. Macro distinctions are used in attempts to simplify and communicate, but nomenclature remains a problem. Various authors have suggested solutions, including Wilson and Schreck: *Peoples vs. People Groups* (Schreck, 1987); Winter: *Macro-, Mega-,* and *Micro-spheres;* Johnstone: *Affinity Blocs* and *Gateway People Clusters* (Johnstone, 1996).

The basics of the definition for those who use the concept are these: 1. Strategic decision focuses on groups, not individuals. Strictly speaking, individuals are not unreached, but unevangelized. 2. The group must be real, not just a conceptual category. 3. Not all groups are of strategic interest. A group may be too small, that is, not large enough to require that a contextualized church become the vehicle of living out Christianity in sociocultural ways. The group must not be so large as to contain within itself segments that constitute barriers to evangelization. 4. The group is no longer unreached when a viable, contextualized church exists capable of carrying on effective witness. Thus, boundary-crossing mission is defined, and not merely the boundary between faith and unbelief. Evangelism is needed after mission is theoretically fulfilled.

Missiologists, particularly from South Africa, have objected to the use of the concepts on the grounds that it promotes racist church bodies. While this danger does exist, partisans respond that social divisions will and do already characterize branches of the church, and it is better to recognize and work against them, much as one would not reject the concept of caste or class, while still opposing their prejudicial effects (*see also* HOMOGENOUS UNIT PRINCIPLE).

The church of Jesus Christ is always missionary. The ways of defining missions sending in terms of units that are the focus of evangelism will continue to evolve. For the moment, real, intermediate groups without a contextualized church constitute our best working definition.

Recently, at least 1,746 large, ethnolinguistic groups have been identified which are verified as having no church among them capable of announcing Christ's Good News. Many have not a single believer. Such groups are truly aliens to grace. This eternal tragedy is a current and compelling call for continuing mission. The groups listed do not include intersective urban groups. The gospel has not been and does not go where a meaningful invitation to follow Christ is not given. Missionaries from both the north and south are necessary in order to bring a community of faith into existence which can speak the language and live the Christian life in every group. The integrity of each group's identity requires this of us. While "they" are unreached (i.e., no such church exists) the nature of our obedience calls us to obedient going. Until then, "they" are and will remain "unreached people groups."

SAMUEL WILSON

SEE ALSO Adopt-A-People; Ethnicity.

Bibliography. B. F. Grimes, ed., *Ethnologue*; P. Johnstone and M. Smith, eds., *The Unreached Peoples*; H. Schreck and D. Barrett, eds., *Clarifying the Task: Unreached Peoples*.

Periodicals. *See* JOURNALS OF MISSION AND MISSIOLOGY.

Perkins, Justin (1805–69). Pioneer American missionary to Iran. Perkins was born in West Springfield, Massachusetts, a descendant of John Perkins who arrived in the United States in 1631. At eighteen he came to Christ. He graduated with honors from Amherst, studied at Andover Theological Seminary, and then returned to Amherst to teach for one year.

Married and ordained in 1833, later that year he and his wife set sail for Persia. After six months in Constantinople, they set out for Tabriz via Russia on May 17, 1834. Bureaucratic problems delayed their arrival until August 23. When additional missionary help arrived, they moved and settled in Urumia, arriving on November 20, 1835.

Throughout his thirty-six-year missionary career, Perkins tirelessly worked in peaceful fashion among the Nestorian Christians in Iran. He opened schools, organized medical work, translated the Bible, Christian literature, and hymns into the Nestorian vernacular (Syriac), established a printing press which produced millions of pages of documents, contributed numerous articles for publications in journals, developed a Syriac lexicon, and wrote several books, including *Residence of Eight Years in Persia* (1843), *Missionary Life in Persia* (1861), and *Historical Sketch of the Mission to the Nestorians* (1862). A decline in health resulted in his return to Massachusetts, where he died the same year.

A. SCOTT MOREAU

Bibliography. M. Fackler, *WWCH*, p. 548; H. M. Perkins, *Life of Rev. Justin Perkins, D.D. Pioneer Missionary to Persia*; F. T. Persons, *DAB*, 7:475–76.

Persecution. Suffering experienced by those whose opinion or belief is being attacked by another group. For the first Christians who came from a Jewish heritage, SUFFERING and persecution were both part of their lot. Jews living under Roman rule could expect to be persecuted if they chose to follow Jesus (e.g., Matt. 5:10–12; 10:23; Luke 21:12; John 15:20).

The Jews as a people had been persecuted for centuries prior to Christ's birth. Christians who came out of Judaism still faced hostility from Rome. In addition, at least until A.D. 70, they faced persecution from the Jewish leaders. Such persecutions often had the opposite of the intended effect. The persecution of the church after Stephen's MARTYRDOM did not stop Christianity but spread the gospel beyond the confines of Jerusalem (Acts 8:1). Paul's conversion resulted from the Damascus road encounter with Jesus while he was traveling under Jewish authority to persecute the church in Damascus (Acts 9:1–31). In testimony and correspondence Paul frequently referred to his persecuting work (Acts 22:4; 26:11; 1 Cor. 15:9; Gal. 1:13; Phil. 3:6; 1 Tim. 1:13). James was martyred by Herod, and when the populace approved he had Peter arrested for the same purpose (Acts 12:1–11). Through God's intervention, the tables were turned and Herod lost his life, while Peter escaped and was able to continue sharing his faith. Jewish persecution of Paul for his evangelistic work led to his arrest and eventual transport to Rome under guard. In this, however, the Jews living in Rome as well as Paul's escorts and his guard detail all had the chance to hear the gospel (Acts 28:17–30; Phil. 1:12–14). Persecution, though violent and intended to shut down the church, often had the opposite effect.

The Roman rulers initially tolerated Christians as a subsect within Judaism, but Nero's scapegoating of them after the A.D. 64 fire in Rome started a pattern of persecution which continued for almost 250 years. With varying intensity, Christians were perceived as a threat to the state. Though not consistently applied throughout the Roman Empire, and with periods of hostility followed by temporary reprieves, the reality of Christianity's illegality as a religion remained part of the Christian experience until the Edict of Milan (A.D. 313) officially legalized Christianity in the empire. Though two relatively brief periods of persecution followed (under Licinius in 322–23 and Julian in 361–63), official toleration of Christianity across the Roman Empire was assured.

Contemporary Situation. While it is true that Christians have over the course of history persecuted others (e.g., Muslims during the CRUSADES; Jews during the Middle Ages and the modern era), including other Christians (e.g., the Donatists, Anabaptists, Puritans, and Huguenots), by and large it is accurate to say that Christians have been the recipients of hostility. Far from being only a thing of the past, persecution today continues to be a reality faced by many Christians, particularly those in militant religious states. It is estimated that more Christians have lost their lives through persecution in this century than all other centuries combined, though generally there has been little publicity of this in the secular press of free countries. David Barrett estimates that some 160,000 Christians were martyred in 1996 simply because they were Christians. Contemporary researchers have begun to speak out on behalf of the persecuted (e.g., Shea and Marshall), noting that the Western church and Western governments have been largely silent in the face of an increasingly well-documented reality.

A number of mission organizations have also been founded to investigate, publicize, and advocate on behalf of those at risk, including Brother's Keeper, Christian Solidarity International, International Christian Concern, and Voice of the Martyrs. Additionally, existing agencies are incorporating departments which emphasize the persecuted church, including Christian Life Commission of the Southern Baptist Convention, Open Doors, and World Evangelical Fellowship Religious Liberty Commission. The National Association of Evangelicals (U.S.) published a statement of conscience in 1996 reflecting "deep concern for the religious freedom of fellow believers, as well as people of every faith" and many agencies and churches have joined the WEF-sponsored International Day of Prayer for the Persecuted Church.

Missionary Implications. With the recent increase in interest in reaching the unreached, persecution of missionaries will likely grow rather than shrink in the coming decades, simply because so many of the unreached live under religious or political ideologies that suppress the spread of the Christian message. Additionally, Christians are often perceived as part of the West in general, and the official anti-Western tenor in these countries will exacerbate the potential problems.

Almost no missiological training in the West offered today will help future missionaries training face persecution, though it appears that house seminaries in China prepare their future pastors for interrogation. Missionaries, especially those going into at-risk situations, would benefit from realistic preparation for the possibilities they may face. In addition, having been trained, they may also be more able to offer both preparation and aid to indigenous Christians who suffer because of a choice to follow Christ in a hostile environment.

A. SCOTT MOREAU

Bibliography. G. W. Bromiley, *ISBE Revised*, 3:771–74; W. H. C. Frend, *ER* 11:247–56; P. Marshall, *IBMR* 22:1 (January 1998): 1–8; idem, *Their Blood Cries Out*; E. M. B. Green, *NBD*, pp. 913–14; H. Schlossberg, *A Fragrance of Oppression*; N. Shea, *In the Lion's Den*.

Person, Personhood. The divine persons of the Holy Trinity express themselves in human images. The essence of human personhood is our potential to image the ultimate personal being, the Lord God (*see also* IMAGE OF GOD). Scripture views all human beings as persons because we have the potential to rule and relate to God in God-like ways.

Adopting God's Stance. The answer to the question whether all humans are persons deserving to be treated with dignity and respect rests on our beliefs concerning the stance our Creator takes toward the wide variety of humans in sundry conditions. Throughout history, numerous people interpreted traits such as physical and mental capacities, gender, and race, as indicating less than full personhood. God takes the stance that the fetus and the profoundly impaired are fully human persons, created to image him. Like a flower in bud form, they are not yet all they will be, yet neither are believers (Ps. 139:13; 1 John 3:2).

Integral to human personhood is the experience of life in terms of role and STATUS. God assigns differing roles to men and women, having designed them physiologically for complementary functions (1 Cor. 11:3–12; *see also* GENDER ROLES). Male persons, with their physical capacity to implant "seed," symbolize God's initiating grace. Female persons, with their capacity to receive the "seed" and "bear fruit," symbolize believers' receptive faith. God saves and gifts each equally as co-heirs of the grace of life (1 Peter 2:7). Believers adopt God's stance and treat all men and women of all races and classes as potential brothers and sisters in Christ (Gal. 3:28–29).

Embodied Souls. Scripture summarizes persons as embodied souls. Into a figure made from dust God breathed the "breath of life" (Gen. 2:7). Paul utilizes the useful formula of spirit, soul, body in his prayer for believers to be preserved complete, without blame (1 Thess. 5:23; cf. Job 7:11, 15; Isa. 26:8, 9; Heb. 4:12), though he more typically writes in dual rather than tripartite language (e.g., 2 Cor. 7:1; 4:16; 1 Cor. 6:16, 17). The human soul synthesizes influences from the multiple systems in which it participates (body, personality structures, family, culture, society, spirituality) and offers creative influences back to those systems. Thus, the soul is a social reality that is always changing at new levels of organization, function, and value. Missionaries carry the message of a new birth for the whole person at all levels.

Five Aspects of Personhood. Human personhood may be described in a wide variety of ways. Some basic aspects of mature persons fulfilling their capacity to image God include rationality, consciousness, reciprocity, communication, and embodiment.

1. Rationality. People have the capacity to resist complete determination by their causal pasts, to say yes or no, to inject creativity into the chaos coming out of the past (LeFevre). Missionaries recognize that persons of all cultures decide the meaning of their life through creative choices, regardless of how their culture frames those choices. Our actions are more than mere events or happenings; they express our emotions and caring concerns, further forming those very emotions and potentially new concerns. Therefore, God tells us that he will judge people by their fruit (Prov. 24:12; James 2:24; Rev. 20:13).

2. Self-consciousness. A second aspect of mature human personhood emphasizes intentionality and self-motivated activity. Self-consciousness, including our awareness and concepts of our self, rests on learning our place in history (e.g. Isa. 1:3–4). We experience the GUILT of conscience and the relief of humor through reflection: we can stand apart from and enter into dialogue with our self. Self-motivated actions both delight God and determine just JUDGMENT for

each person (2 Thess. 1:11, 12). In executing JUSTICE, God deems a person's motives for his or her actions as of ultimate import, a matter of life and death (e.g., Josh. 20:3; 1 Thess. 2:3–4).

The unconscious and subconscious form our conscious identity as persons (Prov. 4:23). Mental and physical memories and the WORLDVIEW beliefs we integrate into those memory-stories constantly influence our emotional and physiological reactions and choices. Only through memory can a person maintain a relatively coherent, consistent identity over time.

3. Reciprocity. A person's life is social. Each person has been shaped by sociocultural interaction, by dialogue with others, and by the internal voice of community. Originally dependent on parents, the mature person continues those interdependent relations in appropriate ways. SIN defames God by proudly disregarding the interdependent nature of our relations. Conversely, we glorify God by submitting to him and to one another. God commands us to love him with all our heart, soul, mind, and strength (Mark 12:30–31). We demonstrate that love when we transcend ourselves by reaching out to others, entering imaginatively into their lives and into dialogue with them as persons. Thus we obey the command, "Love your neighbor as yourself."

God desires to use whole persons in healthy community to reconcile to himself fragmented persons in fragmented communities. Individuals who seek fulfillment in God become infinitely valuable to him for their potential impact on their community (Jer. 5:1; 9:23). Social ministry to whole persons in their community, not merely to "save souls," enables the churches to more clearly communicate the good news of the kingdom.

4. Communication. Fourth is the capacity for COMMUNICATION, especially verbal (cf. 2 Peter 2:16). Persons shape themselves and their world through LANGUAGE. Language makes possible the dialogue that gives birth to mind, self, and society. Language makes possible the distancing and the use of memory and imagination that grounds freedom (LeFevre) To the extent personhood rests on consciousness of contiguous stories, radical alteration in identity requires acquiring, integrating, and acting out new stories. The storying-approach to missions meets this need (*see* STORYTELLING).

5. Embodiment. A fifth aspect of human personhood is the integration of soul and body, mind and brain. Through our bodies we delight in pleasures that lift us close to divine joy (e.g., Song of Solomon). However, the passions of the flesh can deceive and overcome us, and drag us close to animalization (2 Peter 2:12). The FRUIT OF THE SPIRIT includes self-control (Gal. 5:16–26; cf. Mark 9:43–47; Rom. 6:13; 1 Cor. 9:27).

Missionaries proclaim the hope of resurrection: Christ removes the curse of death and reunites body and soul (Gen. 3:19; Acts 17:31; 1 Cor. 15:42–57; 2 Cor. 6:1–5; Phil. 3:21). Whole persons will stand before God to be judged for the deeds done "in the flesh" and angels will cast some "body and soul into hell" (Matt. 10:28).

Ideal Humanness. As J. I. Packer says, HOLINESS is simply human life lived as the Creator intended. Perfect and ideal humanness unites the aspects and systems of body and soul in a totally God-honoring and nature-fulfilling way.

DOUGLAS J. VARDELL

SEE ALSO Human Rights.

Bibliography. N. T. Anderson and R. L. Saucy, *The Common Made Holy: Being Conformed to the Image of God*; B. M. Ashley and K. D. O'Rourke, *Health Care Ethics: A Theological Analysis*, 4th ed.; R. Joyce, *What Is a Person?*, pp. 199–212; P. LeFevre, L. C. Allen, and L. H. Silberman, *Dictionary of Pastoral Care and Counseling*, pp. 883–93; L. K. Graham, *Care of Persons, Care of Worlds: A Psychosystems Approach to Pastoral Care and Counseling*; J. I. Packer, *Rediscovering Holiness*; A. Ross, *Creation and Blessing*; J. Sailhamer, *EBC*, 2:38.

Personal/Family Responsibilities. The obligations of the missionary to his or her own family are often sensitive and delicate issues. The goldfish bowl effect of public ministry, the education of children, and the care of aging parents in the home country are just a few of the dimensions of missionary life that can be stress-inducing. The missionary, like the pastor, often faces a tug-of-war between the care of family and commitment to ministry. Rightly understood, the tension between the two should be at a minimum.

Two persons who marry voluntarily take on certain obligations. The marriage covenant includes the vow "to love and to cherish." Missionaries are not exempt from this responsibility. When children are born into the family, an even more complex issue presents itself. Should the mother limit her missionary responsibility to care for the family?

The right perspective on these issues is a scriptural one. Guidelines such as Ephesians 5:21–6:4 are useful. Neither the family nor one's work should be ignored. Attitude is the key factor in successfully discharging family responsibilities. Many missionary children (including those sent to boarding school) testify that they did not feel deprived because their parents created a positive and supportive atmosphere in the home. The father may have to travel, but if the children sense that he really wants to stay at home, rather than go, they will be helped. Missionary parents should strive for a peaceful home that is characterized by mutual appreciation and kindness.

When considering missionaries' responsibilities to their families, there are few hard and fast rules. Varied situations obtain in different nations and cultures. There are a wide variety of personality types. An increasing number of mission agencies are providing personal and family counseling for their missionaries. Ultimately, prayer and the primacy of love (1 Cor. 13) provide the guideposts for the successful discharge of family responsibilities.

CHARLES R. GAILEY

SEE ALSO Missionary Children.

Bibliography. P. Echerd and A. Arathoon, *Understanding and Nurturing the Missionary Family*; M. Foyler, *Overcoming Missionary Stress*.

Peru (*Est. 2000 pop.: 26,082,000; 1,285,216 sq. km. [496,222 sq. mi.].*). An ethnically diverse South American country in whose vast territory is an ongoing process of cultural transformation. Its spiritual history is shaped by the syncretistic mixture of native animism with the medieval Catholicism brought by the Spanish after 1532. Christianization through Franciscans, Mercedarians, and Dominicans accompanied bloody military conquest. Writings by Jesuit JOSÉ DE ACOSTA (1539–1600) are evidence of unsuccessful efforts to correct early missionary practices. An established colonial church kept social control through the Inquisition, but after three centuries it was weakened by spiritual decline. It opposed political emancipation from Spain, barely accommodating to republican life after the war of independence (1821–24), but still managed to rule out religious toleration.

Scottish educator and colporteur JAMES "DIEGO" THOMSON arrived in Lima, the capital (1822–24), as the first of several agents of the BFBS (*see also* COLPORTAGE). He was hired by emancipation leader General San Martin to establish the first teacher training school. Thomson thought that the Roman Catholic Church could be reformed from the inside through popular education and Bible reading. The Anglican Church for foreign residents was allowed in 1849.

FRANCISCO PENZOTTI's arrival in Lima as a Methodist minister and agent of the ABS was a decisive step for evangelization. Between 1888 and 1896 Penzotti sold Bibles, preached, trained national colporteurs, and organized a Methodist church in 1889. Catholic reaction sent him to jail for nine months (1890–91). His case became an international scandal, gathering liberal forces to fight for a constitutional change. Religious toleration became a law in 1915. American Methodist Thomas B. Wood carried on intensive grassroots evangelism and founded schools. In the first three decades of this century, John Ritchie (RBMU) developed successfully an indigenous Peruvian Evangelical Church in the central and southern highlands. JOHN A. MACKAY (Free Church of Scotland) evangelized university students in Lima, and became influential among key political leaders. Ferdinand and Ana Stahl (Seventh-Day Adventist), through educational and health work, established strong churches among the Aymara natives around Lake Titicaca, the basis for what is today the largest non-Pentecostal denomination whose university and social agency OFASA are highly respected. Through COMITY agreements after 1916 Nazarene and Pilgrim Holiness missionaries worked in the northern and eastern jungles and Pentecostals in the Huaylas highlands north of Lima. In 1940 most Protestant churches and missions formed the National Evangelical Council, which in 1998 still continues to be the most representative Protestant institution.

After World War II a limited modernization process brought massive migration to Lima, and American missionary presence, both Catholic and evangelical, became stronger. Social activism of foreign missionaries living among the poor provoked a crisis of social awareness in Peruvian Catholicism and the beginnings of liberation theologies. FAITH MISSIONS and Southern Baptists have seen relatively little church growth. WYCLIFFE BIBLE TRANSLATORS made the Bible available in more than thirty tribal languages in the Amazonian jungle. Pentecostal churches such as Assemblies of God and Church of God have had the largest numerical growth, especially among the urban poor. Among the native Quechua- or Aymara-speaking population there has been lately significant evangelical growth, and sociological research has proven that conversion fosters economic and social development. A radio station started by THE EVANGELICAL ALLIANCE MISSION (TEAM) was influential in opening doors for significant growth of the CHRISTIAN AND MISSIONARY ALLIANCE among the middle and upper classes during the 1970s.

Failure of military attempts at social reform (1968–79) and inefficiency and corruption of center or left-oriented democratic regimes fostered a violent political climate. The ten-year war between Maoist guerrillas of the Shining Path and military forces (1980–90) affected especially isolated areas where missionary efforts had been successful. Presbyterian and Pentecostal leaders in Ayacucho became the target of communist terrorism and military repression, and more than seventy pastors were killed. This brought Protestants to public attention; relief and human rights work among the victims was followed by political activism. An estimated 8% of the population of Peru is evangelical and their vote was an important factor in the rise of Alberto Fujimori to power in 1990. Church growth at all levels has continued. Among thousands of Peruvian migrants for political or economic reasons, a significant number of evangelicals become active as lay missionaries, especially in Europe and the United States.

SAMUEL ESCOBAR

Bibliography. J. B. A. Kessler Jr., *A Study of the Older Protestant Missions and Churches in Peru and Chile;* J. Klaiber, *The Catholic Church in Peru, 1821–1985;* E. Dussel, ed., *The Church in Latin America 1492–1992.*

Peters, George W. (1907–88). Russian-born missiologist and professor of missions. The son of William Peters, a businessman and mayor of Orloff in southern Russia, Peters grew up in the tradition of the Anabaptist German-Dutch Mennonites. In the course of the Russian Revolution, he was an eyewitness to a massacre in which his own father was killed. Several of his older siblings died in the coal mines of northern Siberia. After finishing high school in 1924, Peters was denied entrance to medical school because he, out of his inner convictions, refused to join the communist youth movement *Komsomol*. So he participated in the mass emigration of Mennonites in 1925. Traveling via Moscow and Mexico, he finally ended up in Canada in 1926, where he earned his living as a farmer.

After an experience of faith Peters became a student at a Bible college in Herbert, Saskatchewan. He began his teaching career at Bethany Bible Institute in 1932. With the aid of colleagues he founded the Western Children's Mission, which was the first organized missionary movement in the Mennonite Brethren Church. The founding document of this organization envisioned an interdenominational, international, and evangelical evangelistic work.

After further studies at the Kennedy School in Hartford, Connecticut, Peters received his doctor's degree in 1947. In the same year he was called to lead the Pacific Bible Institute in Fresno, California, but stepped down from this position in 1952 because his spiritual service, effervescent creativity, and strong personality were hindered by administrative tasks. After two years of service in a pastorate in Buhler, Kansas, Peters took a professorship in missions at Dallas Theological Seminary, where his research concentrated on India, Indonesia, Japan, and South America. After retirement he continued his work in Germany, where he supported the establishment of the Free College of Missions in Liebenzell and later in Korntal. Peters was the first president of this school until 1987.

ROLF HILLE

Bibliography. H. Kasdorf and K. W. Muller, *Reflection and Projection: Missiology at the Threshold of 2001.*

Pfander, Karl Gottlieb (1803–66). German pioneer missionary to Armenia, India, and Turkey. Pfander was educated at Basel Evangelical Missionary Seminary, entering at the age of seventeen. There he was introduced to Islam and began Arabic and Qur'anic studies. He completed his studies in 1825, and was sent on his first missionary assignment to Shusha, a provincial capital in Russian Amenia. He focused his attention toward the Muslims, roughly two-thirds of the population. He wrote several tracts, including *Mizan ul-Haqq* (Balance of Truth; 1829), still considered a classic in evangelizing Muslims.

In 1833 Pfander took leave to find a wife, a quest in which he was successful. In 1835, however, his wife died on the mission field. Shortly after this, Protestant mission work was banned and the missionaries expelled from Armenia. After Urdu studies, and a lengthy application process, Pfander was sent in 1840 to Agra, India, under the CHURCH MISSIONARY SOCIETY (CMS). There he met Elizabeth Swinbourne and married for the second time.

Pfander's tracts, critical of Muhammad, received a wide reading resulting in sharp attacks by Islamic apologists. In 1854, Pfander was invited to a public debate, where he found himself unprepared and unable to successfully refute the European biblical criticism his Islamic opponent introduced.

Shortly after the debate, Pfander was transferred by the CMS to continue his work in Peshawar. In 1861, he was appointed to establish CMS work in Istanbul, Turkey. Eventually that work was shut down by Islamic authorities, and Pfander went to England, where he died in 1866.

A. SCOTT MOREAU

Bibliography. C. Bennett, *IBMR* 20:2 (1996), pp. 76–81; A. A. Powell, *BDEB*, pp. 879–880.

Phenomenology of Religion. In broad terms phenomenology (from the Greek, *phainomenon,* "that which appears" or "that which shows itself") is the study of "phenomena," or the ways in which "appearances" manifest themselves to human consciousness. Phenomenology of religion is the study of religious phenomena. It is helpful to distinguish phenomenology as a distinctive philosophical movement and methodology from phenomenology of religion, although the latter has been to some extent influenced by the former.

Philosophical Phenomenology. The term "phenomenology" was used as early as 1764 by J. H. Lambert, and it appears in the philosophical works of I. Kant (d. 1804) and G. W. F. Hegel (d. 1831). But its more modern meaning comes from the penetrating work of Edmund Husserl (d. 1938), founder of the phenomenological movement. Later philosophers who followed Husserl in phenomenology include M. Scheler (d. 1928), M. Heidegger (d. 1976), J. P. Sartre (d. 1980), and M. Merleau-Ponty (d. 1961). Phenomenology in philosophy is not so much a school with a clearly defined set of teachings as it is a broad methodological movement comprising diverse thinkers united by certain ideals and assumptions. Central to philosophical phenomenology is the investigation of phenomena that appear in immediate experience, allowing the distinctives of the phenomena themselves to control any description of the experiences.

Douglas Allen provides five characteristics of philosophical phenomenology. First, it is *descriptive in nature.* Philosophical phenomenology is concerned with classical issues in epistemology and ontology, but it holds that an indispensable element in dealing with such questions is a rigorous description of the phenomena of experience.

The concern with rigorous and accurate description leads to a strong *opposition to reductionism* in treatments of experience. Although philosophers such as Husserl, Heidegger, and Merleau-Ponty certainly went beyond mere description of experience, they exemplify phenomenology's reaction against earlier movements (empiricism, rationalism, idealism), which tended to reduce the elements of experience to more simple factors, thereby losing the richness of experience.

Third, phenomenology, under the influence of Franz Brentano (d. 1917) and Husserl, has characteristically emphasized *intentionality.* A careful investigation of experience, it is held, indicates that all consciousness is consciousness of something. All states of consciousness are directed toward something, the intentional object.

Fourth, in an effort to allow the phenomena to speak for themselves, phenomenologists advocate a method of *bracketing,* or what Husserl termed the *epoché.* Bracketing involves the methodological suspension of beliefs and judgments accepted by the phenomenologist, or the attempt to free oneself from unexamined assumptions that might interfere in the investigation of the phenomena. A totally "objective" stance that is not colored by any prior values or assumptions is, of course, impossible. But as a methodological ideal, bracketing enables one to minimize the distorting effects of such commitments.

Fifth, many phenomenologists also see the "intuition of essences," or the *eidetic vision,* as a major part of the task. Careful analysis is said to reveal the essences (or the "whatness") of the phenomena, uncovering essential features that enable us to identify and categorize the phenomena.

Phenomenology of Religion and Missions. Understood as an identifiable movement within the study of religion, phenomenology of religion can be traced back to Max Müller (d. 1900) and the *Religionswissenschaft* (history of religions) movement, which saw itself as a descriptive, objective science free from the biases of theology and philosophy. Among the more significant phenomenologists of religion was W. Brede Kristensen (d. 1953), who advocated a careful comparative approach to the study of religion that was rigorously descriptive and also sought an empathetic "feeling" for the data that reflected the stance of the believers themselves. Rudolf Otto (d. 1937) was concerned to recognize the irreducibly religious nature of religious experience, drawing attention to the "numinous" dimension that lies beyond the rational and conceptual elements. Gerardus vander Leeus (d. 1950) was enormously influential between 1930 and 1950, emphasizing in his work the special place of "power" in religion. Other notable phenomenologists include Friedrich Heiler (d. 1967) and Mircea Eliade (d. 1986).

Although there are significant differences in methodology and conclusions among the leading practitioners in the field, phenomenology of religion is generally characterized by its concern for a comparative, systematic, empirical, and rigorously descriptive approach to the study of religious phenomena. It has come to be understood in a loose sense as the descriptive study of religious phenomena, or as Ninian Smart puts it, "the procedure of getting at the meaning of a religious act or symbol or institution, etc., for the participant." It is an "attempt at value-free descriptions in religion" (*The Science of Religion*, pp. 20–21). It is antireductionistic, and seeks to preserve what is distinctively religious in the phenomena. Practitioners emphasize the importance of empathy or sympathetic understanding, and try to avoid (at least in principle) making judgments of value or truth about the phenomena under investigation.

Understanding religious worldviews is essential for those engaged in Christian mission, and the phenomenology of religion can be a useful tool toward that end. Phenomenology's concern with rigorous description of the phenomena can be helpful in understanding the religious symbols of a culture, and its emphasis on "bracketing" can help the missionary be aware of his or her prior assumptions, which might distort an understanding of such symbols.

It is also important, however, to recognize that phenomenology of religion has its limitations. Phenomenology of religion cannot stand alone and it should be combined with the related disciplines of cultural anthropology, ethnography, history, and so on in forming a comprehensive understanding of the religious worldview. Furthermore, the Christian missionary can never be content merely with a descriptive approach to religious phenomena. Questions of truth and compatibility with biblical values must be addressed, and doing so will involve going well beyond the phenomenology of religion. Evaluation of the religious phenomena is inevitable and, when conducted properly, is an essential part of engaging the culture in Christian witness. Evaluations should be made, however, only after careful study of the phenomena on their own terms and such assessment should

be based on clear biblical principles and values and not on one's own cultural biases.

HAROLD A. NETLAND

SEE ALSO Anthropology of Religion, Religion, AND Philosophy of Religion

Bibliography. D. Allen, *ER* 11:273–85; J. D. Bettis, ed., *Phenomenology of Religion: Eight Modern Descriptions of the Essence of Religion*; M. Eliade, *Patterns in Comparative Religion*; W. Brede Kristensen, *The Meaning of Religion: Lectures in Phenomenology of Religion*; N. Smart, *The Science of Religion and the Sociology of Knowledge*; idem, *The Phenomenon of Religion*; E. Sharpe, *Comparative Religion: A History*; G. van der Leeuw, *Religion in Essence and Manifestation*.

Philippine Mission Boards and Societies. Evangelical churches in the Philippines have been sending missionaries to peoples of other cultures since the beginning of the twentieth century. This movement may be due in part to the influence and example of the Western missionary movement. Perhaps a more significant reason, however, is the cultural diversity of the Philippine Islands. It is not uncommon for Filipinos to speak two or more languages. In one sense, one can say that cross-cultural communication is something Filipinos do as a matter of course in their daily lives. It is therefore not surprising, given the large Christian population and wide cultural diversity, that a strong indigenous missionary movement has grown and matured over the years. Generally, this movement focused at first primarily on CHURCH PLANTING and EVANGELISM within the Philippine Islands. Some worked cross-culturally while others called themselves missionaries as they worked among their own people group. Nevertheless, Tagalogs worked among the Samal and Badjao in the southern Philippines or among the Ifugao or Kalinga people of the north.

Two studies done in 1986 revealed that two-thirds of the mission agencies active at that time were founded in the 1970s and the first half of the 1980s, when Filipino missionaries could be found in Indonesia, Hong Kong, Singapore, the Middle East, Latin America, and Africa. Therefore, while the sending of missionaries is not a new phenomenon, the number of new mission agencies has grown significantly during the past two decades.

In 1986, Filipino national leaders, while considering how to evangelize their home country, set a goal of sending two thousand new Filipino missionaries by the year 2000. They further subdivided this goal by projecting that one thousand of these missionaries would be sent to minister cross-culturally within the Philippines and one thousand would be sent outside of the country.

Various modes of support for these missionaries have been used in their cross-cultural environments. Some Filipino missionaries have been sponsored by Western denominations. Others have served in TENT-MAKING MISSION, working as domestic or manual laborers, while serving Christ and giving witness to their faith in their newfound cultural contexts. Still others have been sent by local churches and supported through the sacrificial giving of the local church as full-time Christian missionaries. Those in this category have found missionary work difficult financially because the economic base for sending and supporting from the Philippines has not been strong enough to support the Western model. Also, it has been difficult to send local currencies abroad due to local government restrictions. Finally, several indigenous mission agencies are closely connected with Western or international mission agencies. The OMF Home Council is responsible for Filipino missionaries serving with Overseas Missionary Fellowship. New Tribes, Philippines, is also working closely with the New Tribes Mission of North America. Many agencies are beginning to develop their own international contacts without the benefit of Western involvement. This has been facilitated by the networking activity of the Missions Committee of the Evangelical Fellowship of Asia.

Three cooperative organizations are worthy of mention. AMNET, directed by Chito Navarro, is a loose association of independent churches which are cooperating to reach unreached peoples in the 10/40 WINDOW. In 1998, they were using one member mission agency, the Tribes and Nations Outreach, as their sending agency. But they have been effectively promoting a missions vision among their constituent churches. Another organization is a cooperative project of the Overseas Missionary Fellowship, SEND International, World Team, and the Alliance of Bible Christian Communities Philippines. They have called it the Global Alliance Philippines Ministries, Inc., or GAP. This new organization will be the sending agency for Filipino missionaries working with any of the participating international missions. They are currently considering the expansion of GAP to accommodate other mission agencies which can incorporate Filipino missionaries on their international missionary teams. Finally, there is the Philippine Missionary Society, which seeks to establish links between Filipino missionaries and local churches or denominations in other countries. For example, a local church in Guatemala may need a Christian worker for church planting or evangelism. PMA seeks to raise funds for travel and other costs for the Filipino missionary while the church in Guatemala takes on the support of that missionary when she or he arrives.

The growing number of mission agencies is an indication of a developing missions movement in the Philippines. Interest in serving in missions is high among university students and young professionals, but local churches are still reluctant to make the financial commitment to send. As this changes, further growth in number of mission agencies and the expansion of existing agencies can be expected.

ERIC D. SMITH, DEAN WIEBRACHT,
AND THOMAS N. WISELY

Philippines *(Est. 2000 pop.: 74,575,000; 300,000 sq. kkm. [115,830 sq. mi.]).* Christianity arrived in the Philippines with Ferdinand Magellan in 1521. Although Magellan died soon after his arrival, one of his ships managed to return to Spain. Its rich cargo convinced King Philip II, for whom the Philippines are named, to occupy the islands. Philip dispatched Miguel Legazpe to establish control. Father Andres de Urdaneta and five other Augustinian friars accompanied Legazpe. The Augustinians established their first church in Cebu and then followed Legazpe to Manila, where they established their second parish. Some historians believe that the Hispanization of the Philippines halted the northward spread of Islam, which had already gained a foothold on Mindanao and Sulu in the southern region.

The Spanish quickly gained control because of the fragmentation of the Philippines, which comprise 7,100 islands and coral atolls. Many of the islands are bisected by mountain ranges. The geography accounts for the fact that over one hundred languages are spoken in the islands.

Before the Spaniards arrived, most of the Filipinos adhered to their traditional animistic tribal religions. In 1594 the Council of the Indies in Spain assigned responsibility for specific regions in the islands to each of four religious orders: the Augustinians, Dominicans, Franciscans, and Jesuits. Later, the Jesuits agreed to share part of their region with the Recollects. All of the orders were allowed to establish churches and monasteries in Manila, the capital city. By 1898 almost 90 percent of the population had become Catholic, and the Philippines came to be called the only Christian nation in Asia.

Protestant Christianity first reached the Philippines when two representatives of the British and Foreign Bible Society arrived in Manila in 1873 and began to distribute Bibles. Their mission ended abruptly when they were poisoned. One man died, and the Spanish authorities imprisoned the other. Their efforts, though short-lived, must have borne some fruit. When the first Protestant missionaries arrived in 1898, they discovered thirty-five small evangelical congregations with about four hundred members.

The Protestant era began in 1898 when an American naval force under Commodore Dewey sank the Spanish fleet in Manila Bay. With American annexation came freedom for Protestant missionaries to evangelize. American denominations hastened to send missionaries to the Philippines: Methodists (1898), Presbyterians (1899), Northern Baptists (1900), United Brethren (1901), Disciples of Christ (1901), Episcopalians (1901), Congregationalists (1902), Christian and Missionary Alliance (1902), and Seventh-Day Adventists (1905). In 1901 several of the missions met in Manila and approved a comity agreement that divided the country into zones of responsibility. The comity agreement remained in force until World War II.

The Philippines became an independent country in 1946. While the Philippines struggled to overcome the destruction of the World War, civil war raged in China. The Communists' victory there forced many missionaries to relocate to other Asian countries. Thus the Philippines experienced an influx of evangelical missions. These included Southern Baptists, the Overseas Missionary Fellowship, Conservative Baptists, the Evangelical Free Church, the Far Eastern Gospel Crusade, Missouri Synod Lutherans, and the Baptist General Conference. The freedom of religion guaranteed by the Philippine Constitution made it possible for all these groups to enter and prosper.

Later, specialized mission agencies sent large numbers of missionaries to the Philippines. Included were the Summer Institute of Linguistics, New Tribes Mission, Missionary Aviation Fellowship, Campus Crusade for Christ, Youth with a Mission, and the Navigators. Several of these now deploy large numbers of Filipino Christians in cross-cultural ministry.

After World War II the government encouraged farm families to relocate to the southern island of Mindanao by offering them homesteads (free farm land). Many took advantage of the government's offer, and Mindanao became the frontier area of the country. Mindanao also offered opportunity to missionaries, and in 1980 it was described as the most responsive island in the world. Though Mindanao has only 20 percent of the nation's 74,575,000 people, 50 percent of the evangelical Christians in the Philippines live there.

As in Latin America, in recent years Pentecostal and charismatic groups have grown rapidly in the Philippines. The Assemblies of God entered the country in 1926, but their great growth came after World War II. Other denominations like the United Pentecostals and the Church of God began work in the postwar period. Charismatic Catholic fellowships have multiplied, and many independent charismatic fellowships are flourishing, particularly in urban areas.

Complete freedom of religion and the continued openness of the Filipino people bode well for the future. Many of the agencies named above are cooperating with the DAWN 2000 Movement, which has as its goal the planting of an evangelical church in every town and village in the Philippines. An increasing number of Filipino Christians serve as missionaries both domestically and internationally. Many of these intend to evangelize the unreached people groups found in remote areas of the country.

JOHN MARK TERRY

Bibliography. P. Gowing, *Islands under the Cross;* J. Montgomery, *New Testament Fire in the Philippines;* J. Phelan, *The Hispanization of the Philippines;* J. M. Terry, *An Analysis of Growth among Southern Baptist Churches on Mindanao 1951–1985;* R. Toliver, *Seeing the Church in the Philippines;* A. Tuggy, *The Philippine Church.*

Philosophy of Religion. The idea of philosophy of religion as a separate discipline is a relatively modern one that assumes a basic distinction between philosophy and religion/theology, a distinction that is accepted in the modern West but is more problematic in East Asian cultures. In the West, philosophy is regarded as the systematic, rational, and critical assessment of basic questions that perennially recur in human cultures. Philosophy of religion, in turn, can be thought of as the application of philosophical analysis to religious issues.

The Western Tradition. Philosophy is generally said to have emerged with Thales in Miletus, Greece, around 585 B.C. What distinguished philosophy was the attempt to answer fundamental questions about the cosmos through careful observation and reasoning rather than by simply resorting to the Homeric myths and prevailing views on the gods. Later Greek thinkers such as Plato (d. 347 B.C.) and Plotinus (d. A.D. 270) applied philosophical analysis to religious issues. Philosophy of religion—or, more accurately, philosophical theology—was practiced by devout Christian theologians in the Middle Ages such as Augustine (d. 430), Anselm (d. 1109), Thomas Aquinas (d. 1275), and John Duns Scotus (d. 1308). The Islamic tradition also produced some brilliant philosophical theologians, such as ibn-Sina (d. 1037) and ibn-Rushed (d. 1198), who grappled with many of the same issues addressed by Christian theologians. Indeed, medieval thinkers such as Aquinas were influenced in part by Islamic philosophical theologians.

In the eighteenth and nineteenth centuries the distinctions among philosophy, religious studies, and theology became more pronounced, with philosophy increasingly challenging theology. Epistemological difficulties with religious claims were given classic expression in the writings of David Hume (d. 1776) and Immanuel Kant (d. 1804), and much of modern theology and philosophy of religion has been a response to the agenda set by such critics. Although in the early twentieth century philosophers were generally hostile to religion (as exemplified by logical positivists), the 1980s and 1990s saw a remarkable resurgence of philosophy of religion, with some of the most influential and creative Anglo-American philosophers being outspoken Christians.

Philosophy of religion in the West has been conducted largely within the Jewish, Christian, and Islamic monotheistic tradition. Central issues thus include the existence of God, the nature of the divine attributes, the nature and limitations of religious language, divine sovereignty and human freedom, faith and knowledge, and religious experience. Ever since the ENLIGHTENMENT, and the critical views of Hume and Kant, philosophy of religion has been dominated by the question of the rational grounds for religious belief: Can we know whether God exists? What might constitute sufficient grounds for belief in God? Must one have adequate grounds for belief in order to be rational in believing in God? Some Christian philosophers, such as Richard Swinburne, have produced rigorous and sophisticated arguments for Christian theism, thus continuing in the tradition of natural theology. Others, such as Alvin Plantinga, have shifted the focus of the epistemological debate by maintaining that belief in God can be "properly basic"—that is, a Christian can be justified in believing in God apart from any supporting arguments. Creative and impressive work has also been done on the nature of the divine attributes and clarifying what is entailed by a Christian worldview.

The Eastern Tradition. Although the distinction between philosophy and religion is less clear in Asian cultures, philosophical reflection on religious themes in India goes back at least several centuries before the emergence of philosophy in Greece. The *Upanishads,* put into writing around the eighth century B.C., provided the material for the later systematization of the philosophical schools of HINDUISM. Recurring themes in the writings include the fundamental unity of the cosmos; the superiority of spiritual reality to the physical dimension; that the manifest universe is the product of divine agency; that proper works *(karma)* and special knowledge *(vidya)* are necessary for release from *samsara,* the wearisome cycle of rebirths. The later *Upanishads* spoke of Brahman as the sole reality, prompting the question of the relationship between the self *(atman)* and Brahman. An influential school of thought, Advaita VEDANTA, maintained the essential identity of the *atman* with Brahman.

BUDDHISM, emerging in sixth-century B.C. India, was as much a philosophical movement as a religious one. The central teachings of Buddhism were not regarded as products of divine revelation but rather the result of careful reflection and meditation, culminating in the Enlightenment of the Buddha. Buddhist writings in both the THERAVADA and MAHAYANA traditions have engaged in sophisticated philosophical discussions of epistemology and ontology, emphasizing the impermanence and insubstantiality of all things apart from *nirvana.* A recurring theme in much Buddhist literature, finding particular expression in ZEN, is the inherent inadequacy and limitations of reason and the need for direct experience of ultimate reality.

The distinction among ethics, philosophy, and religion is rather fluid in Chinese thought, particularly CONFUCIANISM. However, social and ethical concerns were typically placed within the broader context of the "heaven and earth relationship," which clearly had religious overtones. The TAOIST tradition, stemming from the *Tao Te Ching,* traditionally ascribed to Lao-Tzu (6th century B.C.) but perhaps put into writing several centuries later, emphasized the ultimate unity of the cosmos and the need to align the world of our experience with the ultimate Way, the Tao.

The philosophical/religious traditions of Asia manifest considerable diversity, some assuming THEISM, others embracing versions of MONISM, PANTHEISM, POLYTHEISM, and even naturalistic materialism. Some are explicitly atheistic. While broad generalizations are hazardous, we might note three recurring themes in much Eastern thought: (1) There is often a suspicion of human language and the capacity of rational categories to express higher levels of truth. The need for special intuitive insight, or direct experience, is emphasized. (2) Hindu, Buddhist, and Jain traditions have a strong "soteriological" concern—the philosophical perspectives are intended to provide release or liberation from the human predicament. (3) There is often concern for a comprehensive perspective that maintains that behind the plurality of the phenomenal world is a more wholistic and unified Reality.

Philosophy of Religion and Mission. Philosophy of religion can play a significant role in missiology. Particularly helpful is the emerging discipline of "cross-cultural philosophy of religion," or "worldview analysis" (Ninian Smart), which involves rigorous analysis of religious issues from multicultural and multireligious perspectives. The concern here is to understand various religious WORLDVIEWS as well as to clarify the basis on which claims to truth in various traditions can be assessed. For the Christian, philosophy of religion must always be subservient to God's unique and authoritative revelation in Scripture. But when properly conducted, philosophy of religion can assist missions in several ways.

First, it can help Christians understand their own tradition better. Whether for good or ill, at critical junctures throughout history major theological issues have been significantly influenced by contemporary philosophical movements. One cannot appreciate the christological discussions of the fourth and fifth centuries, or Aquinas's views on analogy in the thirteenth century, without some familiarity with Greek philosophy. Nor can one understand Schleiermacher in the nineteenth century apart from some grasp of Kantian philosophy.

Furthermore, while in no way removing the mystery of God, proper philosophical analysis can help Christians understand certain biblical teachings better. By clarifying relevant concepts, philosophical analysis can indicate what is and what is not entailed by biblical doctrines such as the Trinity, the deity of Jesus Christ, divine omniscience, or the relation of divine sovereignty to human freedom.

Philosophy of religion can also be an indispensable aid in APOLOGETICS by helping Christians understand the assumptions of the culture in which the gospel is to be presented and by removing some obstacles to faith and providing positive grounds for accepting the gospel.

Cross-cultural philosophy of religion can assist in understanding complex cultures such as India, China, and Japan, which have been shaped by centuries of sophisticated religious and philosophical traditions. The gospel has faced strong resistance in cultures dominated by Hinduism, Buddhism, and Taoism, as well as Islam. Part of the reason for this might be the failure of Christian missions to understand the religious worldviews adequately and to respond to them in an appropriate manner. Cross-cultural philosophy of religion can be an aid in developing an appropriate, culture-specific apologetic in such cultures.

HAROLD A. NETLAND

Bibliography. D. Allen, *Philosophy for Understanding Theology;* M. J. Charlesworth, *Philosophy of Religion: The Historic Approaches;* T. Dean, ed., *Religious Pluralism and Truth: Essays on Cross-Cultural Philosophy of Religion;* M. Peterson et al., *Reason and Religious Belief: An Introduction to the Philosophy of Religion;* N. Smart, *Reasons and Faiths;* idem, *Worldviews: Crosscultural Explorations of Human Belief.*

Pierson, Arthur Tappan (1837–1911). American minister, theological writer, and missionary spokesman. Hailed as the greatest popularizer of missions of his age and one who revolutionized missionary literature, he was born in New York City and educated at Hamilton College (1857) and Union Theological Seminary, New York (1860). After ordination in the Presbyterian Church, he served pastorates in Binghampton and Waterford (N.Y.), Detroit, and Philadelphia until 1889. An extended stay in Great Britain had him preaching at the Metropolitan Tabernacle of C. H. Spurgeon for a period of two years and lecturing at New College (Edinburgh). From 1895 to 1901, he was the president of A. J. GORDON's Missionary Training School (now Gordon College, Wenham, Mass.).

Pierson sustained a lifelong commitment to world evangelization. For twenty-four years he was the editor of *The Missionary Review of the World,* spoke at numerous conferences promoting missions, and wrote extensively on the subject. In 1886, at the D. L. MOODY sponsored conference in Mount Hermon, New York, Pierson gave a keynote address on missions to a group of 251 students from 89 colleges across the country. From this the STUDENT VOLUNTEER MOVEMENT arose in 1888, along with its watchword "the evangelization of the world in this generation." Pierson's address "God's Providence in Modern Missions" was later revised and published in volume 6 of *The Fundamentals.* Among Pierson's protégés were such mission giants as ROBERT E. SPEER, JOHN R. MOTT, AND SAMUEL ZWEMER.

Author of over fifty books, Pierson is best remembered as one of the original editors of the *Scofield Reference Bible* (1909), and author of such mission-related books as *George Müller of Bristol, The Crisis of Missions, The Miracles of Missions, Forward Movements of the Last Half Century,* and *God and Missions Today.*

WALTER A. ELWELL

Bibliography. D. L. Pierson, *Arthur T. Pierson;* J. K. Maclean; *Dr. Pierson and His Message;* D. L. Robert; *ML,* pp. 28–36.

Pietism. Along with Puritanism and the movements to which they gave birth, pietism led to the first Protestant missionary effort and became the catalyst for the wider Protestant missionary movement of the following centuries. An effort to continue and deepen the work of the REFORMATION, pietism focused on the renewal of the Christian life at a time when Lutheran orthodoxy emphasized belief in correct doctrine alone. Seeking the conversion of individuals, the renewal of the church, and the transformation of society, the movement had arisen in German Lutheranism shortly after the Thirty Years' War left the country in a disastrous situation physically, economically, and spiritually. Poverty, ignorance, and violence were common, and class distinctions were great.

Philip Spener (1635–1705) is generally considered the founder of pietism, but it had a number of roots in Germany and elsewhere. Johannes Arndt's *True Christianity* (1606–9) was significant, and as a student in Strasbourg, Spener was influenced by Puritan and Reformed writers. Appointed as senior pastor in Frankfurt in 1666, Spener found the church in a deplorable state. Drunkenness and immorality were common among the laity, who were expected to be passive listeners to erudite sermons that focused more on fine points of doctrine than edification. Spener encouraged the formation of small groups for prayer, Bible study, and the reading of devotional works. This concept of the church within the church, which was not intended to be divisive, spread widely within and beyond Germany despite bitter criticism. In 1675 Spener published an introduction to a new edition of Arndt's work. In *Pia Desideria* (Pious Desires) he called for the reform of Christian society through six means: (1) more extensive use of the Scriptures; (2) greater participation by the laity; (3) the practice of love in everyday life; (4) an attitude of love in controversies; (5) stress on piety as well as scholarship in theological schools; and (6) theological education that taught that preaching was to save souls, not just demonstrate scholarship. Thus pietism focused on the need for conversion, commitment, and personal trust in Christ, an authentic Christian life, and the ministry of the laity.

The Lutheran orthodoxy of the day denied that the GREAT COMMISSION was still in effect. Mission belonged to God, who needed no human helpers (*see* LUTHERAN MISSIONS). Furthermore, there was no place for mission structures. Thus missionary work was seen as unnecessary and even suspect. Earlier in the century Baron Justinian von Weltz had appealed to the Lutheran Church in Germany to undertake missionary work. He was called a fanatic and rejected. Pietism, on the other hand, reaffirmed the Great Commission as universally valid and taught that Christians must accept responsibility for proclaiming the gospel to all persons everywhere.

August Hermann Francke (1663–1727) became the second leader of the movement. Through the efforts of Spener he was appointed professor of theology at the University of Halle in 1691, and became pastor of the church in nearby Glaucha the following year. He believed that converted and transformed individuals would renew the church and society. He was instrumental in establishing schools for poor children including girls, as well as an orphanage. His vision also led him to focus on world mission. He established a Bible institute to print and distribute Bibles inexpensively. This was the first institution with the goal of bringing the Scriptures to every part of the world. His projects were supported by faith alone and became the model for the orphanages of GEORGE MÜLLER in Bristol, England, which then became the model for the faith principle of the CHINA INLAND MISSION.

Francke's mission involvement was extensive. He sent Henry Muhlenberg and others to the North American colonies, where they organized Lutheran churches among German immigrants. He sent missionaries to the Baltic states, where they worked for the renewal of Lutheran communities. Pietist influence was important in bringing a deeper life to the churches in the Scandinavian countries as well and would be the source of most Scandinavian mission societies.

In 1706, influenced by his pietist chaplain, King Frederick IV of Denmark decided to send missionaries to his colony in Tranquebar, India. Two young men from the University of Halle, BARTHOLEMAEUS ZIEGENBALG and Heinrich Plütschau, agreed to go. Plütschau returned in 1711, but Ziegenbalg remained, with one brief visit to Europe, until his death in 1719. This was the first Protestant missionary effort outside of Europe, with the exception of the Calvinist mission to Brazil in 1555. Despite the hostility of the Danish community and its chaplains, the higher Indian castes and Roman Catholics, and harassment from the governor, Ziegenbalg accomplished much during his short life. His missionary approach anticipated many methods that came later. He established schools to educate Christian children and develop leadership. In the belief that Christians needed the Scriptures in their own language, he translated the New Testament and part of the Old into Tamil before he died. He was convinced that missionaries needed to understand the WORLDVIEW and religious beliefs and practices of the people. Thus he wrote on aspects of Hinduism. As a pietist, his aim was personal conversion, but he also worked to establish an Indian church with its own pastors. The first Indian pastor was ordained in 1733. About sixty missionaries went from Halle to India during the eighteenth century, and the work was eventually taken over by the Anglican Society for the Propagation of Christian Knowledge.

The influence of pietism on the total missionary movement was great. Ziegenbalg's visit to Europe in 1714 resulted in the establishment of the College of Missions in Copenhagen, where Moravian missionaries would later study, and the founding at Halle of the first Protestant student mission movement, the Order of the Mustard Seed. This was led by NICOLAS LUDWIG VON ZINZENDORF, who later became the leader of the Moravians (*see* MORAVIAN MISSIONS). All of this activity built on Francke's vision for mission, which encompassed the whole world. He believed that the earth would eventually be transformed through godly people serving God and their neighbors, proclaiming Christ, and working to relieve poverty and oppression. His concern for the poor and emphasis on education as a means of social transformation were outgrowths of his theology. The intellectual and spiritual leader of missions, he was the first to inspire Christians in Europe to pray for and support missionaries, a radically new concept at that time.

Because of its focus on conversion and heart religion rather than theological controversies, pietism was broadly ecumenical. Francke corresponded with Anglicans, including the archbishop of Canterbury, and the New England Congregationalist leader Cotton Mather. Their correspondence went beyond denominational controversies and focused on the need for world evangelization. Anton Boehm, a court preacher in London, translated pietist writings and was influential in the expansion of the missionary vision of the Anglican Society for the Propagation of Christian Knowledge (SPCK). The SPCK made Ziegenbalg and Francke corresponding members, and a Copenhagen/London/Halle Alliance for Mission was formed. Francke also showed interest in mission to North American Indians. Thus pietism was the first Protestant movement that focused both on mission and on ecumenical relationships.

Further influence of pietism came through the Moravians, who served as an even wider catalyst for mission. Pietism along with Puritanism also laid the foundation for the eighteenth-century evangelical awakenings in North America, Britain, and the continent. These awakenings broadened the Protestant missionary movement (*see* GREAT AWAKENINGS). Theodore Frelinghuysen, a Dutch Reformed pietist, was the initial leader of the first Great Awakening, which began in New Jersey in 1726. That movement spread to New England in 1734 and up and down the Atlantic coast under its better-known leaders, JONATHAN EDWARDS, Gilbert Tennent, and GEORGE WHITEFIELD. It would eventually lead to the founding of the AMERICAN BOARD OF COMMISSIONERS FOR FOREIGN MISSIONS (ABCFM) in 1810. Susanna Wesley was motivated to a deeper Christian life through reading the accounts of the Danish-Halle missionaries in India. As a result, she began to spend an hour each week with her children, John and Charles among them, to nurture them in their Christian faith. The influence of the Moravians on the conversion and subsequent ministry of John and Charles Wesley is well known.

The wave of revivals on both sides of the Atlantic in the eighteenth century led to the establishment of a number of missionary societies and to the GREAT CENTURY OF MISSION. In Britain the BAPTIST MISSIONARY SOCIETY (1792), the LONDON MISSIONARY SOCIETY (1795), the Scottish societies in Edinburgh and Glasgow (1796), the CHURCH MISSIONARY SOCIETY (1799), the Religious Tract Society (1799), and the British and Foreign Bible Society (1804) were formed. On the Continent the Netherlands Society (1797), the BASEL MISSION (1815), and the BERLIN MISSIONARY SOCIETY (1824) were established. These early Protestant missionary societies could all trace their roots in one way or another back to the pietist impulse that came from Halle.

PAUL E. PIERSON

Bibliography. J. Aberly, *An Outline of Missions;* D. Brown, *Understanding Pietism;* G. Sattler, *God's Glory, Neighbor's Good;* J. A. Scherer, *Gospel, Church and Kingdom.*

Pike, Eunice (1913–). Missionary and Bible translator for Mexican Mazatecs. Shortly after receiving her nursing degree at Massachusetts General Hospital, Pike went to Mexico to do literacy and Bible translation work among the Mazatec tribes. She and her colleague Florence Hansen (Cowan) found mastering Mazatec, a tonal language, impossible until Pike's brother KENNETH PIKE shared his findings from working with another tonal language, Mixtec. With feedback from their native language helpers, Pike and Hansen immediately began translation of the New Testament, beginning with the book of 1 John. Pike soon began to focus on literacy, developing a series of Mazatec primers and teaching from her front window, while her partner and colleagues focused on translation. Once a book was completed, it was printed and Pike sold it in the markets. In 1961, the New Testament was completed as well as various passages from the Old Testament. In addition to translation and primers, Pike also authored hymns for the Mazatec church, wrote books on phonology, published several ethnographic and linguistic articles, and taught at the University of Oklahoma's branch of the Summer Institute of Linguistics during the summers. Pike also wrote a biography of her brother and three books describing her work among the Mazatecs.

GRACE L. KLEIN

Bibliography. E. Pike, *Words Wanted;* idem, *An Uttermost Part.*

Pike, Kenneth Lee (1912–). American pioneering linguistic scholar and missionary to Mexico. Born in Woodstock, Connecticut, Pike grew up in a pious Congregational family. At the age of 16, his country doctor father suffered complications from appendicitis, and Pike vowed to serve God if his father was healed. Eventually he was, and Pike began fulfilling his promise by attending Gordon College. Rejected by CHINA INLAND MISSION, Pike eventually became intrigued with phonetics, attended Camp Wycliffe (forerunner of SIL), and found his calling as a linguist.

Pike's accomplishments in linguistics over the next 60 years have been legendary. His first field assignment was among the Mixtec in Mexico. Work on his Ph.D. (1942), ongoing academic research and writing, and Wycliffe administrative responsibilities (Pike was president from 1942 to 1979) delayed the translation and printing of the Mixtec New Testament until 1951. In all, Pike wrote more than a dozen books, 200 articles, and 250 published poems. His pioneering work includes the development of the linguistic theory of *tagmenics* as well as the coining of the widely used terms *emic* and *etic*. Referred to as the greatest American descriptive-theoretical linguist of this century, Pike has been honored through ten honorary doctorates and fifteen nominations for the Nobel Peace Prize.

A. SCOTT MOREAU

Bibliography. E. V. Pike, *Ken Pike: Scholar and Christian;* K. L. Pike, *Language in Relation to a Unified Theory of the Structure of Human Behavior;* idem, *Intonation of American English;* idem, *Phonetics.*

Pilgrimages. Journeys to holy places undertaken to obtain supernatural help, to do penance, or to offer thanksgiving. Pilgrimages are a spiritual feature found among many of the world religions.

Within Islam, participation in the annual pilgrimage (hajj) to Mecca is one of the five essential requirements ("Pillars") of religious practice. Such a pilgrimage should be undertaken at least once during a Muslim's lifetime if at all possible. The hajj is very significant since Muslims believe that through it they will be freed from their sins if their pilgrimage is accepted by Allah. In Mecca the pilgrim makes seven circuits around the Kaaba and visits Arafat, Muzdalifah, and Mina.

Within folk Islam, the tombs of holy people also provide a focus for those seeking God's blessing. One of the most popular is that of Khwaja Muinud-din Chishti in Almer, India. While such shrines are looked down upon by Muslim purists, they attract the devotion of many visitors, particularly on the date commemorating the death of the saint.

There are many Hindu pilgrimage sites of local or national interest within India. Such sacred sites may be identified with a religious myth, a temple, a bathing place, or a geographical feature. The Kumbha Mela is the largest gathering of pilgrims and is held every twelve years at Allahabad, India, at the (supposed) confluence of the Ganges, Yamuna, and Saraswati rivers. Large numbers of pilgrims also bathe in the Ganges at Varanasi.

Some Christians have spiritual or educational reasons for visiting sites associated with the life of Christ. Within the Roman Catholic piety, pilgrimages are undertaken to various sacred places including Lourdes in France, which is associated with healing miracles.

PATRICK SOOKHDEO

Bibliography. *ODCC*, p. 1091; *ERE*, 10:10–28; B. Lewis and A J. Wensinck, *EI*, 3:31–38; C. W. Troll, ed., *Muslim Shrines in India.*

Pilkington, George Lawrence (1865–97). Irish missionary translator in Uganda. He attended Pembroke College, Cambridge, where in 1885 he was indirectly influenced by DWIGHT L. MOODY. He applied for missionary service with the CHINA INLAND MISSION, but delayed going to teach at Harrow School. When a call went out for university men to go to Uganda, Pilkington answered as a lay missionary with the CHURCH MISSIONARY SOCIETY of England.

Pilkington's translation work began within three months of his arrival in Uganda. In addition to the Bible, he translated hymns and pamphlets, and prepared a grammar and dictionary of Luganda. In 1893, discouraged by a lack of spiritual power, he retreated to the island of Kome, where he experienced a great baptism of power. Returning to Uganda, a revival broke out which included local Muslims. Soon after this, Pilkington led seventy-five Ugandan soldiers to Christ.

After a furlough to complete the printing of his translation work, Pilkington returned to Uganda in 1896. New hostilities caused the British governor to ask Pilkington to serve as a translator for the soldiers restoring British colonial control. While on this expedition, Pilkington was shot and soon died. His death was mourned on two continents.

MICHAEL SPRADLIN

Bibliography. C. F. Harford Battersby, *Pilkington of Uganda;* K. Ward, *BDCM*, p. 537.

Pioneer Mission Work. Work done from the first contact of an unreached area or population until a viable and indigenous local church is established. Frontier mission, a more recently coined term (see Winter), describes pioneer work in which the missionary crosses significant cultural boundaries. The types of activities done as part of pioneering work include such things as EVANGELISM and CHURCH PLANTING, LITERACY and TRANSLATION, RELIEF and DEVELOPMENT, and even establishing institutions (e.g., schools or hospitals). Such activities may be the full-time occupation of the missionary, or may be ancillary to some type of professional occupation (*see* TENT-MAKING MISSION).

In situations where countries grant missionary visas, missionaries are free to preach the gospel openly as their full-time job. While this was more generally the case in recent centuries (especially when Western missionaries worked under the protection of colonial empires), political autonomy and religious attitudes have today closed the doors of many nations to the traditional full-time pioneer missionary. Therefore, many involved in pioneer work today, especially in CREATIVE ACCESS COUNTRIES, can only attain residency as students, researchers, or professionals. When local residency is not possible, a base may be established outside the target country or culture from which periodic trips into the target area as a tourist are made to establish contacts or evangelize.

Since the goal of pioneer mission work is to plant an INDIGENOUS CHURCH, it must always include some form of evangelism. This evangelism, especially in sensitive areas, may be limited to small-scale or even covert work. Once people within the target area have come to Christ, pioneer missionaries need specific skills to gather them together in small fellowships and help them grow toward becoming a church.

While many pioneers have gone out as individuals, most have followed Paul's example of gathering a team to work together (*see also* TEAMS IN MISSION). In prior centuries a team was sometimes necessary simply to ensure survival, as missionaries came to harsh environments without the necessary survival skills or resistance to disease already possessed by the indigenous population. Further, a team approach makes it less imperative that any single individual possess each of the multiple gifts needed for church planting. It also provides a place of encouragement when the work is slow to develop.

The trend in contemporary evangelical missions discussion of pioneer work has been a switch from a focus on geo-political boundaries to ethnolinguistic ones (*see* PEOPLES, PEOPLE GROUPS) in conceptualizing the church-planting task of missions. The development of the related concepts such as the 10/40 WINDOW, unreached or hidden people groups, and the ADOPT-A-PEOPLE campaigns also reflect that shift. It is estimated today that there are some 12,000 ethnolinguistic people groups, and that some 2,000 of them have no viable witness or church and are therefore in need of pioneering mission work. Most of these groups, it is noted, lie in the 10/40 Window and—in part because they are the hardest to reach physically, politically, and religiously—less than one-tenth of the total missionary effort is actually concentrated on them.

Because frontier missions are focused on crossing significant cultural barriers to plant churches, it is a subset of pioneer mission work, which does not always involve the crossing of significant cultural barriers. The concept of pioneer mission work cannot be limited to settings where there has never been a gospel witness. It also includes evangelism in areas where there once was such a witness that is no longer viable. For example, secularized, post-Christian urban areas where the gospel is no longer proclaimed need missionaries with a pioneering outlook and commitment, and this should not be overlooked in considering the scope of pioneer mission work.

A. SCOTT MOREAU

SEE ALSO Reached and Unreached Mission Fields.

Bibliography. S. C. Neill, *CDCWM*, pp. 487–88; J. Piper, *Let the Nations Be Glad!*; T. Steffen, *Passing the Baton: Church Planting that Empowers*; R. W. Winter, *Perspectives on the World Christian Movement*, pp. B-176 to B-183.

Pitcairn (United Kingdom Dependent Area) *(Est. 2000 pop.: 100; 236 sq. km. [91 sq. mi.]).* Consist-

ing of four islands, with only one inhabited, the group is located 1,340 miles southeast of Tahiti. It was settled in 1790 by *Bounty* mutineers and Tahitians. The people were resettled on Norfolk Island in 1856 but some returned. In 1883 the islanders became Seventh-Day Adventists. Pitcairn has been administered as a British territory since 1898.

ALLAN K. DAVIDSON

SEE ALSO Polynesia.

Planning. Planning, whether of an ad hoc or strategic nature, is not new to the mission enterprise. Though current strategic planning for mission purposes increasingly emphasizes the SOCIAL SCIENCES and electronic technology, planning as a critical factor in Christian mission can be dated to certain events in the Book of Acts (e.g., the Jerusalem Council in Acts 15 or the hall of Tyrannus "campaign" in Acts 19). Monasticism, using music to teach Christian doctrine to the illiterate masses, and the development of mendicant orders are just a sampling of the resultant structures flowing from planning processes long before the modern mission era.

As we review the modern missions era, we see pioneers like WILLIAM CAREY who demonstrate key elements of planning in their writings. Carey's classic treatise *An Enquiry into the Obligation of Christians . . .* gives testimony to the strategic use of biblical information statistics, maps, organizational networking, and financial support structures in planning the mission enterprise. J. HUDSON TAYLOR's "Call to Service" also shows the evaluative processes and resultant planning necessary in the structural changes that occurred as missions headed "inland" in the mid-nineteenth century using the incipient structures of the faith mission model.

The work of RUFUS ANDERSON from the United States and HENRY VENN from England are representative examples of evaluative processes that led planned change in mission strategy during the latter part of the nineteenth century. Their planned change resulted in the famous "three-self" formula with its goal of planting and fostering the development of churches that were self-governing, self-sufficient, and self-propagating (*see* INDIGENOUS CHURCHES). This period of the nineteenth century also is an era in which women became increasingly assertive in organizing their own agencies for sending single women missionaries. The evaluation and subsequent strategic planning by valiant women opened the possibility of reaching women and children with the gospel in cultures where male missionaries had little access to the female and child population.

Consultations and conferences have been the contexts from which much planning and resultant strategic change have occurred. Mt. Hermon

(1886), Edinburgh (1910), Jerusalem (1928), Madras (1938), Berlin (1966), Lausanne (1974), and Lausanne II Manila (1989) are all examples of events that have not only resulted in planned change, but provided ongoing evaluation of mission endeavor. Centers like the U.S. Center for World Mission in Pasadena, California, Overseas Ministries Study Center in New Haven, Connecticut, or The Oxford Centre for Mission Studies in Oxford, England, exemplify the present commitment of the global mission enterprise to planning as an ongoing necessity.

Terms associated with the planning process are used differently. Words usually seen in planning literature include mission, purpose, vision, dream, goal, objective, and plan (action plan). These terms are used inconsistently, but with necessary definition become functional. Lyle Schaller suggests that all solid planning models must include a strong future orientation, an emphasis on action, realistic analysis of the context, participative agreement building, and challenge for participants to join in chosen course of action.

In the process of planning, terms like mission and purpose refer to the *why* of an organization or enterprise. Vision/dream refers to an image of a preferable future condition. Goals describe what we want to achieve with objectives, focusing on that which must be accomplished to reach a goal. Action plans describe the activities that will ultimately enflesh our conceptualizings.

The *mission–vision–goals–action plan* model or the *think–plan–act–evaluate* model exemplifies some current formats for the planning processes used in the mission enterprise.

BYRON D. KLAUS

Bibliography. R. R. Broholm, *The Power and Purpose of Vision: A Study in the Role of Vision in Exemplary Organizations*; J. M. Bryson, *Strategic Planning for Public and Nonprofit Organizations*; E. Dayton and D. Fraser, *Strategies for World Evangelization*; F. R. Kinsler and J. Emery, eds., *Opting for Change—Evaluating and Planning for TEE*; L. Schaller, *Effective Church Planning*.

Pluralism. Christianity exists and has always existed in the context of a plurality of competing and contrasting religions, but whereas in the past some Christians had an intellectual knowledge of those religions and fewer still an experiential encounter with them, today most Christians have both intellectual and experiential knowledge at least of the major non-Christian religions. This knowledge in turn tends to expel the merely prejudiced view of other religions as primitive and ignorant, with their adherents dissatisfied with their religions and open to conversion.

The question for mission is twofold: first the question of the salvific validity of other religions and second the question of the origins of those religions. The answer to this second question was in the past simplistic: they came from the devil.

Study of the histories of the religions, however, produces a different picture: Gautama in an earnest search for an explanation of human suffering, Muhammad in the cave Hira pondering the absurdities of Arab polytheism, even Marx, in the Reading Room of the British Museum, researching the causes of the miseries of the 'toiling masses' and some possible solution for them. There is today a general recognition that religions represent on the one hand a perverse human rejection of revelation (Karl Barth's 'principal preoccupation of godless humanity') and on the other hand a search, in the absence of revelation, for some understanding of the apparent meaninglessness of the human experience.

As to the salvific validity of other religions, there has been a spectrum of responses, ranging from the naive view that 'sincerity' in any religion is salvific to the denial that 'religion' can play any part at all in the process of salvation. This latter view is made untenable by the plethora of examples of those who have found the Traditional Religions, or Islam or Hinduism gateways to Christian faith. Broadly speaking four distinct views may be identified. There is the *inclusivist* view, that finds salvation somewhere in each religion, the *pluralist* view that the common root to all religions is precisely the salvific root, the *exclusivist* view that salvation is to be found in Christ alone or, more rigorously, that salvation depends on an overt acknowledgment of Christ as Lord, a view usually associated with HENDRIK KRAEMER, and the view that while salvation is necessarily based on Christ's Passion, an overt knowledge of Christ is not essential to salvation.

Each view has its own problems: John Hick's attempts to produce a Copernican Revolution, replacing Christianity as the center of the universe of religions by God, or the Absolute, or "the Real," adding epicycles to cycles, has served primarily to demonstrate the absence of a common center applicable to all religions, and the inevitability in any such exercise of the abandoning of core Christian theology, particularly incarnational theology. Karl Rahner's creation of Anonymous Christianity, which purported salvifically to identify sincere religionists as de facto Christians was crushingly labeled religious imperialism. As LESSLIE NEWBIGIN commented, the scheme was "vulnerable at many points." It must be said, however, that Rahner's view closely resembles the Constitutive Christocentrism of the SECOND VATICAN COUNCIL, with its generally positive stance respecting the universe of religions. However, Roman Catholic thinking has moved on, and Pope John Paul II in his 1995 *Crossing the Threshold of Hope* has gone some way toward restoring the 1442 Council of Florence Exclusive Ecclesiocentrism.

The traditional evangelical view has its own difficulty. The vast majority of humankind, through no fault of its own, never heard of Christ, and appears to be condemned for its sin, which (as a consequence of the fall), it could not resist and for which it had no remedy. The academic theologian has found this no particular problem, where the missiologist, with one foot firmly in the real world, most especially in the TWO-THIRDS WORLD, is, perhaps, touched with a greater compassion.

But the fourth view also is not without its difficulties, primarily because of the generally negative soteriological tenor of Bible texts such as Acts 17:24–28 and Romans 1:18–23 which speak of GENERAL REVELATION but apply it as a foundation for God's judgment while not explicitly discounting its salvific potential. It has been repeatedly suggested that any relaxing of the traditional exclusivist position must inevitably weaken missionary motivation. To this two replies must be made. First, that we seek and then follow biblical theology wherever it may lead us, and second, that the Christian mission is not merely response to command or obligation but is, or at least should be, ontological. The biblical imperative for mission is, of course, entirely clear. If the church is to be properly apostolic it must also be praxeologically apostolic, it must engage in mission. But to be effective in its praxis the church as a whole (not only its missionary representatives) must engage the religions by which it is confronted with a confident yet compassionate insistence on Jesus as the Way, the Truth, and the Life.

PETER COTTERELL

SEE ALSO Modernity; Theology of Religions.

Bibliography. K. Barth, *Christianity and Other Religions,* pp. 32–51; D. A. Carson, *The Gagging of God;* P. Cotterell, *Mission and Meaninglessness;* G. D'Costa, *Christian Uniqueness Reconsidered: The Myth of a Pluralist Theology of Religions;* B. Demarest, *General Revelation;* M. Erickson, *How Shall They Be Saved?;* P. F. Knitter, *No Other Name?;* J. Sanders, *No Other Name.*

Poland (*Est. 2000 pop.: 38,786,000; 323,250 sq. km. [124,807 sq. mi.]*). There has never been a developed Protestant foreign missionary movement from Poland, the major reasons being political. The Roman Catholic Counter-Reformation, using Polish nationalism, was successful in largely eliminating the strong Protestant churches that existed in the sixteenth century. The three Partitions of Poland among Russia, Prussia, and Austria in 1772, 1793, and 1975 removed the Polish state from the map of Europe. Only in 1918 did it reappear. Twenty-one years later it was again dominated and partly dismembered, this time by Nazi Germany and Soviet Russia. In 1945 its borders were moved westward to their present positions. The Roman Catholic Church has remained the main rallying point of Polishness for most of the past two centuries and is seeking at the present time to reassert its dominant position in the life of the nation. By reason of its international nature, the Roman Catholic Church has enabled Polish priests to take part in the missionary activity of the church. There are over one thousand Polish Catholics involved in various places in the Roman Church's worldwide mission. By contrast, Polish Protestant churches, all numerically small, have spent most of their energies in struggling to survive and maintain their congregational and denominational life under various adverse conditions. At the present time there is a small number of men and women sensing God's call to overseas missions. Some have come to the West to train, others are being prepared in the newer seminaries such as the Evangelical Seminary in Wroclaw. Contacts with Western evangelicals, which began before the demise of the Soviet empire, have been instrumental in this process. Western help, especially in the areas of information and financial support will continue to be needed if the movement is to achieve its full potential.

RONALD DAVIES

Political Elections. "The state," observes Sanders (1985, 273), "serves first as an institution to restrain the sinfulness of men by promoting social order." Secular historians Will and Ariel Durant confirm this observation in stating that "the prime task of government is to establish order" (1968, 68). The biblical data support this. God, who is the God of order (1 Cor. 14:33), ordained government and gave it authority (Rom. 13:1) to serve the good of the people and to punish "the wrongdoer" (Rom. 13:4). He commands rulers to do justice (Isa. 56:1), which is a precondition of peace. The government or the state, then, is not outside the sovereignty of God. Jesus is Messiah, and in him, Christians cannot escape their political vocation. As citizens of the state and of the KINGDOM OF GOD, their attitude to the state is a dual one, otherwise their "faith has either become sentimental or secularized" (Brunner, 1957, 60).

They are subject to authority (Rom. 13:1). They are to pray for rulers (1 Tim. 2:1–2) and to participate in the life of the city so that it may prosper (Jer. 29:7). In democratic countries, Christian involvement in political elections is critical because "the power of national leaders is derived from the populace which is the primary focus of God-given authority" (Mouw, 1973, 55). It is through this that Christians can serve their own people and share in God's work of redemption and preservation.

To elect governors is a privilege to be grateful for and a duty to be fulfilled. It is, first, a partnership with God in kingdom building in a world of rapid social change. As members of his church, they are to be "a responding community, a people whose task it is to discern the action of God in the world to join in His work" (Cox, 1965, 91). It is, second, to help put into office righteous people who are qualified for governance so that godless (evil) individuals will not rule, laying snares for people (Job 34:30). In righteousness a nation will be exalted (Prov. 14:34) or judged (Ps. 96:13).

Involvement in political elections also carries a number of correlative responsibilities. First, believers are to encourage others to vote for "capable men [and women] . . . who fear God, trustworthy men who hate dishonest gains" (Exod. 18:21) and who are committed to do what is just and right (Prov. 21:3). Second, Christians themselves may seek election for public office. The story of Jotham (Judg. 9:7–15) reminds us of the tragic consequences when qualified men and women reject the call to public ministry. Government is a "minister of God" (Rom. 13:4). Elected officials play a crucial role in value transformation. They teach ethics by their examples. They serve as role models and key arbiters of social values. "Morality," as Marshall points out, "must become concrete political morality" (Marshall, p. 16). Third, they are to help establish an electoral system that ensures an honest election. The will of the people expressed in their ballots must not be thwarted by fraud and violence.

Political elections are acts of faith that anticipate the future where "the kingdom of the world has become *the kingdom* of our Lord and of Christ; and he will reign forever and ever" (Rev. 11:15). This, obviously, will not be realized by legislation. Any social analysis that excludes sin in humanity and any solution that does not include the gospel will fail to achieve the kingdom. Justification by faith and justice are conjunctives of the kingdom of God. Weigle well summarized: "A state degenerates into tyranny if its citizens abandon conscience when they approach the polls, and forget God when they are in public office" (Weigle, 1947, 12).

AUGUSTIN "JUN" VENCER JR.

Bibliography. E. Brunner, *The Divine Imperative;* H. Cox, *The Secular City;* W. Durant and A. Durant, *The Lessons of History;* P. Marshall, *Thine Is the Kingdom;* R. J. Mouw, *Political Evangelism;* T. G. Sanders, *Protestant Concepts of Church and State;* L. A. Weigle, *Social Actions,* 13 (1947): 12–13.

Political Theologies. Today political theology is usually associated with various forms of liberation theology, such as that developed by Latin American thinkers. However, the theological roots of political theology can be traced to the work of postwar German theologians. In 1964 Jürgen Moltmann published his *Theology of Hope.* According to Moltmann, eschatology had become a sterile teaching of death and dying

rather than life and hope. Events such as the second coming were relegated to some future "last day" (*see also* MILLENNIAL THOUGHT AND MISSION). By divorcing these future events from our present experience, they are robbed of their impact on the present. The church is to live in the expectation of the future coming of God's kingdom (*see* KINGDOM OF GOD). Its primary role in this world is to announce the coming kingdom and by doing so to awaken hope. This is the missionary responsibility of the church—participating in the liberating sending of Jesus. This also includes the "other side of proclamation," Christianity's calling in society. The church has been called out to "creative discipleship" and simply cannot accept the obvious wrongs of society and its evil structures. Rather, it is to awaken hope by practicing a "present" eschatology which, in the expectation of God's coming kingdom, criticizes and changes society. In order for this biblical hope to be properly interpreted and applied to our world, a melding of the historical and contemporary horizons has to be achieved. Texts that come to us from our past should not be examined simply in terms of experiential possibilities offered within that particular situation, but should be interpreted in terms of their historical context—of their understanding of their own past, as well as their hope for the future. Only when the future horizon of the historical text is melded with the present horizon of the interpreter can the texts be understood and their truth applied.

A return to this kind of existential hermeneutic will help us concentrate on life itself rather than on vague and abstract theories. But in order to be of practical benefit it will have to be developed into a realistic political hermeneutic. Political theology represents an attempt to relate faith to society in general. Moltmann is initially interested in his own society. His analysis of postwar German culture revealed a political environment that left the country without a real capital, divided and cut off from its own history. He also discovered a religious climate which was essentially a form of civil religion, in which Christianity becomes an involuntary part of life devoid of decisions and community.

Several unsuccessful attempts have been made to adapt the gospel to that environment. Rudolf Bultmann sought to demythologize theology, but in the process left us with no absolute standards. Wolfhart Pannenberg developed a universal historical theology, which sought to provide objective orientation and reasons for faith. But it was, for that very reason, too narrow and even tended to support European prominence over other cultures and religions. Trutz Rendtorff's theory of Christianity attempted to integrate everything in the church. But that made it hard to distinguish between what is Christian what is modern European culture. Finally, there is what Moltmann calls the "Evangelical Apocalypse," which demands opposition to evil but operates in the "empty rooms of society, which are ignored by the ruling consciousness" (Moltmann, 1984, 21–26).

Moltmann's alternative is political theology, which is best understood as the field, the milieu, the context, and the stage on which Christian theology is to be done during this modern era. Looking to the cross as the crux of Christ's struggle with the public powers of his day, political theology seeks to use the cross as an instrument or symbol of criticism to be directed against what Moltmann calls political religion. This is the symbolic integration of a people and the unity of religion and society or civil religion. It leads to a number of modern idols, which oppress and subjugate people under a tyranny of arrogance and fear. Political religion is the focal point of political theology's criticism. Two fundamental assumptions underlie this activity. The first is that the Old Testament's ban on idol worship includes those forces that alienate and dehumanize people today. The second is that the theology of the cross represents the radical application of the Old Testament ban on idol worship in demythologization, in natural theology with its profanations of God, and in political theology through the fundamental democratization of power structures.

It is the Christian belief in a *Deus crucifixus* which liberates humanity from idol worship. Since the church (the community of believers) cannot identify itself with those idols (power structures), it must form its own fellowship. Having been liberated, it is no longer in need of self-confirmation (it has nothing to prove) and can (must) open itself to the others: the poor and oppressed. For that reason it cannot remain politically neutral. It must take a stand which works toward the democratization and the liberation of the oppressed. Hope is not only an open future but a future for the hopeless.

Political theology is above all a participation in history in order to understand history. It builds on traditional approaches in that it talks of promises made and fulfilled. But it goes beyond the traditional in that it views the future from the present and experiences the power of hope. For this reason it places emphasis on action and PRAXIS. This is not to be understood as a one-way exchange. Rather, it is a dialectic between reflection and action. It issues in a Christian passion for action that is not limited to the clergy. This is not a theology for priests and pastors, but for active laity.

It is not difficult to see how Moltmann's pioneering work served as a catalyst for similar theological models around the world. The basic themes of liberation and hope characterize almost every political theology, be it South African Black Theology (*see* AFRICAN THEOLOGIES), Latin American Liberation Theology (*see* LIBERATION THEOLOGIES), Philippine Theology of Struggle, Indian Dalit Theology, North American Black Theology, or Korean MING JUNG THEOLOGY.

EDWARD ROMMEN

Bibliography. J. Moltmann, *Theology of Hope.*

Politics. From New Testament times to the present, the relationship of Christian missions to government and politics has been ambivalent. On one hand, Jesus, Paul, and Peter all understood the legitimate claims of human government as an institution ordained by God for the restraint of evil and the promotion of good (Matt. 22:21; John 19:11; Rom. 13:1–7; 1 Tim. 2:1–2; 1 Peter 2:13–17). On the other hand, the New Testament also affirms that: (1) civil authority is subordinate to the sovereign God (Matt. 26:51–53; John 18:36); (2) there are times when the claims of the state interfere with the believer's obedience to God (Acts 4:19 and 5:29); and (3) government sometimes assumes an idolatrous and demonic character, as is evident throughout the Book of Revelation. Christian missionaries in all ages have had to function with an awareness of the biblical tension between the positive and negative traits of the political realm.

In the early church, Christian evangelists primarily faced circumstances where the Roman government was hostile and offered extremely limited possibilities for political engagement. Although persecution sometimes was sporadic, affording Christians the opportunities to utilize some of the benefits of the imperial system to spread the gospel, Christianity enjoyed no legal standing or protection. In the apostolic era, the apostle Paul did not hesitate to invoke his Roman citizenship when he was mistreated or when his life was in danger (Acts 16:37–39; 22:25–29; 25:7–12). It is not apparent, however, that Paul's example proved to be ultimately helpful for his own cause or for later generations of Christians who fell victim when the Roman state intensified its campaigns against the church. The initial evangelization of the Roman Empire occurred apart from any direct support or encouragement on the part of civil authorities. In fact, Christian refusal to participate in the emperor cult and state sacrifices provoked particularly aggressive attempts to exterminate the Christian movement between 250 and 311, thus highlighting an adversarial relationship between church and state that places major roadblocks in the path of Christian missionary advance (*see also* CHURCH/STATE RELATIONS).

Constantine's ascendancy to the imperial throne in the early fourth century set the stage for a whole new pattern of Christian expansion. The emperor's embrace of Christianity and his granting of favors to the institutional church held enormous implications for missions, which were reinforced later in the same century when Theodosius declared Christianity to be the one official state religion. These dramatic shifts created an alliance of throne and altar where, for several centuries, Christian missionary outreach would be significantly undergirded by the carnal weapons of "Christian" governments. In early medieval western Europe, for example, kings like Charlemagne in Saxon Germany and Olaf Tryggvason in Norway employed military force as a tactic in the Christianization of typically unwilling subjects. Later the CRUSADES illustrated the dangers of church-state coalitions aimed at the expansion of Christendom, whether directed at infidel Muslims who were attacked by European armies seeking to reclaim the Holy Land or at pagan Prussians who were compelled to be baptized by the victorious Teutonic Knights.

The Constantinian-Theodosian model persisted in some form into the REFORMATION and early modern periods. On the Roman Catholic side, Spain and Portugal built overseas empires with the blessing of Pope Alexander VI, who on the eve of the Reformation charged the monarchs of those countries with the evangelization of the lands that they conquered, thus creating a royal patronage system to support Catholic missionary endeavor. For their part, European Protestants almost universally accepted the state church tradition and the territorial conception of Christendom. These principles informed their early, sluggish mission efforts and eventually contributed to the linkage between colonization and Christianization that characterized the European missionary enterprise in the nineteenth and early twentieth centuries (*see* COLONIALISM). The common thread that ran through much of Christian missions from the fourth century on was an ecclesiastical willingness to rely on some measure of political assistance for fulfilling the GREAT COMMISSION.

Although the Constantinian impulse did not die quickly, it was struck a mortal blow by the ENLIGHTENMENT, which encouraged a division of the "religious" and the "secular." Enlightenment thought influenced the American political experiment, especially regarding the separation of church and state. Hence the American missionary movement developed without the baggage of the older European traditions; most mission agencies viewed themselves as nonpolitical, a perception that was not shared by European colonial authorities who sometimes feared American missionaries as subversives. In addition, the American missions enterprise did not entirely escape the clutches of Manifest Destiny and imperialism in the late nineteenth and early twentieth centuries, when missionary leaders often expressed facile sentiments that joined national and evangelical interests. In two notable cases, Protestant boards cooperated with the United States government in providing educational and social services for Native Americans at home and Filipinos overseas.

In the twentieth century, Christian missions encountered new challenges on the political front. Rising nationalism in Asia and Africa contributed to the collapse of colonial empires, which finally put to rest the antiquated notion of government-sponsored mission. At the same time, the emergence of totalitarian governments, particularly under the banner of communism, once again raised the issues of doing missions in the context of PERSECUTION. Similar concerns have been expressed in response to a resurgent Islam, since missionary activity in many Islamic nations is prohibited or severely curtailed. Beyond the problems inherent in relating to hostile governments, modern missionaries have been involved in many projects in the developing world that have political implications, including the encouragement of democracy, the operation of schools and hospitals, and the introduction of social reforms. Further, compelling evidence suggests that American missionaries have influenced the foreign policy of the United States in the Near East and China; more ominously, some have charged that the Central Intelligence Agency has used missionaries in its covert operations. Finally, political developments since 1989 in the former Soviet bloc have opened unexpected opportunities for ministry in areas that previously had been closed to missionaries.

JAMES A. PATTERSON

Bibliography. E. L. Frizen, Jr. and W. T. Coggins, *Christ and Caesar in Christian Missions;* C. W. Forman, *Missiology* 9 (October 1981): 409–22; J. H. Kane, *Missiology* 5 (October 1977): 411–26; S. Neill, *Colonialism and Christian Missions;* B. Stanley, *The Bible and the Flag: Protestant Missions and British Imperialism in the Nineteenth and Twentieth Centuries.*

Polity. See CHURCH POLITY.

Pollard, Samuel (1864–1915). English missionary to China. Born at Camelford in Cornwall of parents who were both preachers with the Bible Christian Church, Pollard was converted at eleven years of age. Initially prepared for a career with the civil service, he was influenced toward missions at a London conference in 1885 and sailed for China in 1887. After language study, he traveled to Zhaotong in Yunnan province, after which he was assigned to the provincial capital, now called Kunming.

During his early missionary years Pollard engaged in evangelism and a ministry of compassion among the Chinese. In 1907 a people movement to Christ among the Miao, a minority nationality, reached the Zhaotung area from its starting point in Anshun, and Pollard became its most famous missionary leader. Before his death in 1915, he established a center for the thousands of new believers in Shihmenkan across the Guizhou provincial border, itinerated widely, planted churches, trained leaders, obtained justice for Miao Christians from officials and landlords, developed the unique Pollard script, and used it to translate the New Testament into the Miao language.

RALPH R. COVELL

Bibliography. W. A. Grist, *Samuel Pollard, Pioneer Missionary in China;* R. E. Kendall, *Beyond the Clouds.*

Polyandry, Polygamy, Polygyny. *See* MARRIAGE, MARRIAGE PRACTICES.

Polygamy and Church Membership. The issue of what to do about believing polygamists has been a major concern in missionary circles from the beginning of Western missionary endeavor. With well over three-quarters of the societies of the world permitting plural marriages, and nearly half of them marriages with more than one wife as the ideal, Western missionaries encountered a major discrepancy between traditional custom and the Christian ideal. To this day the church has mainly responded by condemning the custom and reject for church membership any men who did not divorce their "extra" wives, no matter how sincere their faith might be.

Underlying this position were several largely unexamined Western worldview assumptions: (1) that Western-style monogamous marriage is the only form of marriage endorsed by God; (2) that God's patience with polygamy in the Old Testament has been replaced by condemnation of the custom as indicated by the "one wife" passages in 1 Timothy 2:1–13 and Titus 1:5–9; (3) that plural "marriage" is not really marriage at all but adultery; and (4) that all we have to do to change such a custom is to make rules and enforce them.

In spite the universality of the position that refused church membership to men with more than one wife, there have always been dissenting voices both within the missionary community and within the churches. Several conferences have been held through the years to discuss the issues raised by, on the one hand, the tenacity of the custom and, on the other, the intransigence of missionaries and the indigenous church leaders who followed them to change the church rules.

However, roughly since the 1950s a greater appreciation has arisen as to how God works with culture, even with customs that are less than ideal. This has brought a greater openness among missionary theorists and some mission leaders to rethink the church's position. Large numbers of indigenous leaders who are now in charge of the churches have, however, refused to change. Meanwhile, many church members either secretly engage in the custom while maintaining their church membership or they fall away. Or, they become members of the thousands of independent churches that have separated from the missionary churches (especially in Africa).

Behind these splits often lay the quest for a more culturally appropriate Christianity that allowed for an acceptance of centuries-old customs such as polygamy and the incorporation of indigenous approaches to Scripture and the church. Both the leaders of the splinter groups and mission theorists point out that God was patient for centuries with polygamy, even though it is not his ideal, and that Paul could not have had polygamy in mind when he wrote the passages in Timothy and Titus, since the custom did not occur in Greek society. Furthermore, in the societies where it occurs, polygamy is legal marriage, not adultery and, therefore, should not constitute a barrier to church membership for those who have come to genuine faith. Nor should the church continue to recommend divorce (which Jesus did condemn) as a way out of a custom about which both Jesus and the rest of Scripture are silent.

CHARLES H. KRAFT

SEE ALSO Marriage, Marriage Practices.

Bibliography. E. Hillman, *Polygamy Reconsidered;* C. H. Kraft, *Christianity in Culture.*

Polynesia. Polynesia covers a vast triangular area of the Pacific Ocean stretching from Hawaii in the north to New Zealand in the southwest and Easter Island in the east. The term "Polynesia" refers to the "many islands" settled by people who originated in Asia and began entering the Pacific from west to east c. 1000 B.C. Described as "Polynesians" by nineteenth-century scholars, the people were great seafarers who shared a common linguistic and cultural heritage which took on distinctive characteristics as they separated and migrated to different areas. Societies were ruled over by chiefs who inherited status and rank, although this varied from the significant kingdoms like Tonga and Hawaii, to large tribal units in Tahiti and small tribes in atoll settlements. Warrior traditions were strong and inter-tribal conflicts in the pursuit or defense of *mana*, prestige or power, were frequent. Religious beliefs varied with "departmental gods" prominent in eastern Polynesia while Tongans and Samoans gave more significance to local spirits. While there were common features and names within Polynesian mythology and cosmology, they were accented by particular emphases and influenced by geographical location. Rituals and practices were clearly defined and priests or specialists gave leadership in both spiritual and practical areas of life. Sacred spaces were set aside as places for rituals with, in some areas, special buildings. Concepts such as *tapu*, with its sense of holy or sacred, could be applied to people, places, and behavior and influenced the whole of life. Polynesians believed in an after-life where the spirits of the dead lived, although for Tongans this was limited to those of high rank. There was no sense of punishment and rewards. There was a close relationship between people, the land, and the sea.

The first European contact with Polynesia was made by voyagers such as Magellan (1521), Mendaña (1567–68, 1595), and Quiros (1606). Although motivated by Christian as well as materialistic ambitions their impact was limited. Dutch in the seventeenth century and French and British explorers in the eighteenth century, notably James Cook, mapped the Pacific and through their writings made its islands and people better known in Europe.

This new knowledge, combined with the eighteenth-century evangelical revivals in Great Britain, created considerable interest in the evangelization of the Pacific. The LONDON MISSIONARY SOCIETY, founded in 1795, chose the Pacific as its first sphere of work. In 1796 they dispatched the *Duff* with thirty missionaries, five wives, and three children to Tonga, Tahiti, and the Marquesas. Four were ordained and the rest were artisans, reflecting the influence of Thomas Haweis who believed Polynesians needed to be civilized in British ways as part of their evangelization. The missionaries were ill-prepared. Of the ten taken to Tonga in April 1797, three were killed, one "went native," and the remainder abandoned the mission in 1800.

In Tahiti, where they arrived on March 5, 1797, the missionaries were confronted by a society undergoing political and religious turmoil, in which they were valued for giving access to European goods rather than the Christian message. Progress in learning Tahitian was slow, most of the missionaries abandoned their work, and communication and support from England were difficult. Pomare II, a leading chief, requested baptism in 1812, but this was delayed until 1819 because of missionary anxiety about his behavior. LITERACY and the printed text, particularly the Bible, PEOPLE MOVEMENTS, POWER ENCOUNTERS, the surrender of idols, and the influence of chiefs were important in the rapid movement of Tahitians toward Christianity after 1815. Similar developments occurred elsewhere in Polynesia. Christianity spread through Tahiti and the surrounding islands, often through indigenous agency. Missionaries, in cooperation with the chiefs, attempted to control moral and political behavior through codes of law and were often disappointed at what they called "backsliding."

The expansion of Christianity throughout the Pacific owes a great deal to JOHN WILLIAMS who began at Moorea in 1817 and shifted to Raiatea in 1818. He emphasised morality and the acquisition of practical skills like carpentry and boat-building and attacked what he saw as Pacific indolence. Visitors from Rurutu were returned with two Raiatean teachers to their home island where they effected the conversion of their people. In 1821 Williams took two Raiateans, Papeiha and Vahapata, to Aitutaki in the Cook Islands where by 1823 they had achieved quick success. Papeiha was taken to Mangaia in 1823 but was withdrawn after a hostile reception. Williams then took him to Rarotonga and when Papeiha was visited in 1825, the missionary was astonished at the progress he had made. Two teachers were taken to Mangaia in 1824 and within a few months many had accepted Christianity. Williams, Charles Pitman, and their families went to reside in Rarotonga in 1827. Williams began translating the Bible into Cook Island Maori and introduced a code of laws. With limited resources he built the *Messenger of Peace* and with it was actively involved in visiting other islands, stationing islanders, and giving them support. Aaron Buzacott started a theological institution, Takamoa, on Rarotonga in 1839 to train "native agents."

In 1839 Williams visited the Wesleyan missionaries, Turner and Cross, in Tonga and it was agreed that the Methodists should concentrate on Tonga and Fiji and the LMS would take responsibility for Samoa. Accompanied by Fauea, a Samoan, Williams went to Samoa where he was well received by Malietoa, the leading Samoan chief. Tahitian teachers were left in Malietoa's care. When Williams returned to Samoa in 1832 with additional teachers, he was impressed with the progress. In 1834 the first Europeans, Platt and Wilson, were stationed in Samoa. A training institution was established at Malua in 1844. The New Testament in Samoan was completed in 1848 and the Old Testament in 1855.

Attempts by Williams to land teachers at Niue in 1830 resulted in the first of several rejections. In 1846 two Niueans, Peniamina and Fakafitiniu, who were converted in Samoa, returned to Niue and in 1849 Paulo, a Samoan, joined them. W. G. Lawes, the first European resident missionary, arrived in 1861 and by 1868 he had translated the New Testament. Initial LMS endeavors in the Tokelau islands in 1858 also met with opposition and the first missionaries, a Tokelauan converted in Samoa and two Samoan teachers, were accepted in 1861.

LMS teachers from Tahiti arrived in Tonga in 1822, the same year that Walter Lawry and his wife Mary, the first Methodist missionaries, settled on Tongatapu. Lawry abandoned Tonga in 1823, but in 1826 John Thomas and John Hutchinson resumed the Methodist work. The baptisms of leading chiefs, Aleamotu'a in 1830, Taufa'ahau in 1831, and Finau in 1832 and a revival in Vava'u in 1834 encouraged the rapid acceptance of Christianity. There was some resistance among rival families which resulted in civil war. Methodists promoted the first code of laws in 1839 and the recognition of Taufa'ahua, as King George Tupou I in 1845 consolidated the Methodist dominance in Tonga.

Despite the agreement with the LMS over Samoa, "Lotu Tonga," or Christianity in a Methodist form, had already reached Samoa through a chief who had been in Tonga before Williams' first visit. Peter Turner was sent to oversee Methodism in Tonga in 1835, but following LMS protests was withdrawn in 1839. Support from Tongans ensured the continuation of Samoan Methodism and in 1857 the Australasian Methodist Conference sent Martin Dyson to superintend this work. George Brown joined him in 1860 and made a notable contribution. A district training college was started in 1864 and in 1868 was transferred to Lufilufi and called Piula.

Protestant beginnings in the Pacific were marked by initial opposition but the rapid acceptance of Christianity in most areas resulted from indigenous evangelism, the impact of literacy, power encounters, people movements, and the significant role of chiefs. Missionaries introduced strict observance of Sunday, encouraged peacemaking between tribes, and codes of law which blurred the distinction between church and state. Indigenous movements such as Mamaia in Tahiti and Sio Vili in Samoa and the revival of traditional customs such as tatooing indicate that the acceptance of Christianity did not always meet the missionaries' expectations.

Catholic beginnings in Polynesia were closely associated with French missionary expansion and drew a hostile reaction from the Protestant missionaries. Eastern Polynesia was assigned to the Congregation of the Sacred Hearts of Jesus and Mary. Missionaries were landed at Tahiti in 1836, the Marquesas in 1839, the Cook Islands in 1894. The Society of Mary entered Western Polynesia under the leadership of Bishop J. B. F. Pompallier in 1837. Pierre Bataillon quickly converted Wallis (Uvea) and, after the murder of Pierre Chanel on Futuna in 1841, the people accepted Catholicism. Returning Tongan Catholics from Wallis and disaffected anti-Methodist families became the basis of "Lotu Popi," Tongan Catholicism, and their first resident priests arrived in 1842. The Vicariate of Western Oceania was set up in 1842. Catholic missionaries arrived in Samoa in 1845. Tokelauns were introduced to Catholicism at Wallis and took it back to their own people in 1861.

Missionary activity in Polynesia had ambiguous colonial connections. Only Tonga retained its independence. Shirley Baker, a Methodist missionary (1860–79) who drafted the country's Constitution, together with the King established the Free Church of Tonga in 1885 which separated from the Wesleyans who retained links with the

Australasian Conference until their reunion in 1924. The French protectorate accepted by Tahitian chiefs in 1842 emerged out of French naval intervention in support of Catholic missionaries. George Pritchard, British consul in Tahiti and former LMS missionary, was deported in 1844 because of his attempts to provoke Tahitian opposition to the French.

Seventh-Day Adventists and Latter Day Saints (Mormons) also entered Polynesia in the nineteenth century. Protestants throughout Polynesia, Samoa apart, maintained a COMITY policy trying to avoid competition. Anglican church members in Tonga, recruited by a disenchanted Shirley Baker, were taken over in 1902 by Alfred Willis, former Bishop of Hawaii, but their group remained small.

Some one thousand Polynesian missionaries, starting from Williams' visit to the New Hebrides (Vanuatu) in 1839, as catechists, teachers, and ministers, along with their wives, made significant contributions to the evangelization of Melanesia. Their training was limited, although Tupou College in Tonga under James Moulton reached high standards. Indigenous ministry was promoted by Protestant missions although control of the church remained in the paternalistic hands of European missionaries and missionary societies until well after the Second World War.

The LMS churches gained their independence in the Cook Islands in 1945, in Samoa in 1962, and in Niue in 1972. LMS work in French Polynesia was taken over by the PARIS EVANGELICAL MISSIONARY SOCIETY in 1863 and gained its full independence in 1963. Samoan Methodism became an autonomous Conference in 1964. Tongan Methodism separated from the Australian Conference in 1970 and its first indigenous president, Sione "Aminaki Havea," was elected in 1971. Samoa and Tonga became Catholic dioceses in 1967 and Pio Taofinu'u, a Samoan, bishop of Samoa in 1968 and a cardinal in 1973. Patelesio Finau, a Tongan, became bishop of his homeland in 1972.

Christianity has penetrated all aspects of life throughout Polynesia and in its different denominational forms contributes to the identity of both people and their country. Daily family worship, both morning and evening, and participation in services throughout the week and particularly on Sunday are the norm for village life in most parts of Polynesia. Churches have made notable contributions to education at the primary and secondary levels and through theological institutions.

Considerable pressure is placed on small Pacific societies by forces such as nuclear testing, external migration, secularization, the impact of television, economic pressures, and material values. The division of Christianity as a result of pentecostal and fundamentalist groups and the proliferation of groups such as Latter Day Saints and Jehovah's Witnesses challenge small communities. Polynesian Christianity, however, finds vibrant expression in song and dance and the language of Pacific peoples. Through migration Polynesian Christianity is significant in New Zealand, Australia and the west coast of the United States.

ALLAN K. DAVIDSON

Bibliography. C. W. Forman, *The Island Churches of the South Pacific;* J. Garrett, *To Live Among the Stars: Christian Origins in Oceania;* idem, *Footsteps in the Sea: Christianity in Oceania to World War II.*

Polytheism. The term originates from the Greek words *polus* (many) and *theos* (god), and refers to the recognition and worship of many gods. Popular nineteenth-century scholarship considered monotheism the apex of an evolutionary process in religious devotion. This evolution was thought to have moved from early primal awareness of supernatural powers to ANCESTOR WORSHIP to polydemonism to polytheism to MONOTHEISM (and, in the eyes of some, finally to ATHEISM). The Vienna School associated with Wilhelm Schmidt contrasted this view with the belief that monotheism was the original human creed, which later degenerated into polytheism; monotheism was then reintroduced at a later point in time. This is also the Judeo-Christian-Islamic worldview.

A consideration of the word "theism" automatically includes a belief in god *(theos)* to which "many" *(polus)* is added to account for the variety of human experiences (arts, fertility, industry, hunting, fishing, healing) and societal structures (families, clans, villages, cities, countries). That monotheism preceded polytheism is demonstrated (aside from the biblical revelation) in that society had to achieve some degree of compartmentalization (Gen. 5–11) in order to accommodate the personification of the various deities within the polytheistic structure. The monistic nature of Hebrew life (i.e., that life is one whole and God is One) automatically brought it into conflict with polytheism.

Polytheism relates to ANIMISM and polydemonism in that all three acknowledge superhuman powers as the creative forces. However, the clarity of thinking along theistic lines in polytheism is sharper than in animism or polydemonism. Additionally, unlike animism and polydemonism, the number of spiritual forces in polytheistic systems is generally limited. These deities may be viewed as friendly or unfriendly, and often take on some amalgam of human and creaturely form. They may be thought of as personifications of nature (e.g., Mithra, the Persian sun god; Thor, the Norse god of rain and storm) or of animals or plants (e.g., Kukulcan, the feathered serpent god of the Mayas).

The attributes of deity are sharply distinguished in polytheism and monotheism. Polytheism views the gods as immortal, though often with some type of beginning. Monotheism recognizes God as eternal, with no beginning or end. In polytheism, power is distributed among the various gods. In monotheism, God alone is all-powerful. Polytheistic gods are generally gods who act in this world, though some are perceived as remote (e.g., Zeus). Monotheism acknowledges God's transcendence (he is beyond all human events) as well as his immanence (he is involved in all human events, seen uniquely in the incarnation and person of Jesus Christ).

Where care is not taken to recognize and prevent the possibility of syncretistic thinking, a de facto polytheistic subsystem will exist in many expressions of Christianity. Often it results when the old gods are reduced to angels, demons, or saints within the Christian orbit. Therefore, great care must be taken to provide missiological and salvific responses to the belief in many gods that polytheism presents.

CLINT AKINS

SEE ALSO Gods and Goddesses.

Bibliography. E. O. James, *The Concept of Deity;* G. van der Leeuw, *Religion in Essence and Manifestation,* 2 vols.; R. J. Zwi Werblowsky, *ERE,* 10:435–39.

Poor. *See* POVERTY; OPTION FOR THE POOR.

Popular Religions. *See* FOLK RELIGIONS.

Population, Population Explosion, Population Planning. As the world enters the twenty-first century its population continues to grow at an alarming rate. In 1999, the projected population of the world reached 6 billion people, with the figure estimated to reach 10 billion by 2060. Rapid growth of the world's population impacts missions in a number of ways. In terms of sheer numbers it means that there are constantly increasing numbers of people who have yet to hear the gospel of Jesus Christ. Since the most rapid population growth tends to occur in some of the least evangelized sections of the world, this means that in spite of encouraging church growth in other sectors the task of world evangelization remains daunting. High birth rates tend to fall among those peoples who are also the poorest, compounding the problems of poverty, malnutrition, education, and general quality of life. For example, although the current doubling time for the world's population in general is 137 years, the doubling time for the poorer countries of the world is only 33 years (*New State of the World Atlas,* 1991). Finally, the population explosion raises ethical questions about stewardship of earth's natural resources, both in terms of preserving the limited resources for future generations and working toward a more equitable distribution of the use of existing resources among nations. There are those who say there is no cause for alarm, for there is plenty of food on this planet to feed everyone for many years. It is only a matter of a more equitable distribution of existing food supplies, or of using more fertilizer, or planting different types of crops, or the like.

Projected population data, however, will help bring reality to the discussion. If the 1999 world population was 6 billion and people in many nations of Asia and Africa are already suffering from either malnutrition or simple starvation, how will the world sustain a projected 10 billion people by the year 2060? If there is a surplus of food in Canada and there is need in India, who will pay to ship food from Canada to India on an indefinite basis? The economic realities and gigantic numbers involved all suggest that there is indeed a crisis, and that it will get worse before it gets better.

Demographers hope that the rate of growth will be slower during the twenty-first century due to greater use of birth control. Continued wars and the AIDS epidemic might also slow the growth. But even though it is slowing down, continued growth raises serious questions about the quality of life for most people during the twenty-first century and the continuing disparity in standards of living between the haves and the have-nots.

Some newspaper reporters and politicians in Africa have spoken out against population planning, suggesting that this is merely a Western device that is being promoted in order to keep Africa under Western domination. This argument overlooks the fact that many European nations are already setting the pace by holding their population growth to almost zero percent. Mainland China is also striving vigorously for zero population growth in spite of the felt hardships it creates for their people. It has been observed that regardless of what intellectual leaders may say, many Africans of moderate income desire to limit the size of their families because in a rapidly urbanizing world they no longer have the resources to support large families.

Ironically, population growth is greatest among the poor, who are those least able to sustain such growth. One way therefore to slow population growth is to raise living standards for the poor. But this will be difficult, for most poor people are already living in overcrowded areas where there is fierce competition for available resources.

In 1990 Luis Bush wrote, "More than eight out of ten of the poorest of the poor . . . live in the 10/40 Window" (5). He defined the 10/40 WINDOW as a rectangular block of land from the Atlantic to the Pacific from 10 to 40 degrees north of the equator. Inasmuch as most who live in this giant rectangle are Muslim, Hindu, or Buddhist, they are also unreached.

If the population explosion is taking place largely among the poor within the 10/40 Window, conversion to Christianity may be the only viable route to their physical betterment, for it has been observed time and again that when people turn to Christ, their standard of living tends to rise. And most wealthy nations of the world today have at least a Christian background although the majority of their citizens may not be practicing Christians.

The runaway population explosion, therefore, is added reason for missionary attention to the 10/40 Window. There is however another implication of this population explosion that the missionary world has been slower to grasp. As the population explodes, people are pushed off the farm and to the cities. There is direct correlation between the population explosion and the exploding growth of cities in the non-Western world (see URBANIZATION).

Attention to the 10/40 Window, therefore, should not simply identify the various ethnic groups so that missionaries and evangelists can be sent to them. It should also identify the various social groups in the giant cities of our world so that social groups that have been neglected may also receive missionary attention. Shantytown dwellers, street children, street vendors, and the unemployed are all legitimate targets for mission effort, as well as wealthy business people, government workers, soldiers, professional people, and all the social classes between these two extremes.

TIMOTHY MONSMA

Bibliography. E. Bos, M. T. Vu, E. Massiah, and R. A. Bulatao, *World Population Projections; 1994–95 Edition;* L. Bush, *Getting to the Core of the Core: The 10/40 Window; Human Development Report 1994; Population and Development; Implications for the World Bank.*

Portugal *(Est. 2000 pop.: 9,807,000; 92,389 sq. km. [35,671 sq. mi.]).* Traditionally Roman Catholic, Portugal severely restricted religious liberty for Protestants until 1910, when the monarchy ended and a republic was established. The nation was under a dictatorship from 1926 to 1974. That year a democracy was inaugurated, the African colonies given their independence, and religious liberty decreed. Portugal continues to be the poorest country in the European community, but it is now developing and modernizing quite rapidly with rising living standards.

Scottish Presbyterians began work in 1866. Brazilian Presbyterians and Baptists arrived in 1910. Brethren from England also began work early in the century, while the Assemblies of God, having arrived later, now constitute the largest evangelical movement in the country. Others include Seventh-Day Adventists, Methodists, Lusitanians (Anglicans), and various Pentecostal groups. Out of a population of approximately 10 million, only about 1.25 percent are evangelicals. Approximately 25 percent are practicing Catholics. Most of the rest are nominal Roman Catholics.

The changes in 1974 opened the door to religious pluralism and secularism despite an extremely conservative Roman Catholic Church. The evangelical movement, led by Pentecostals, is growing at approximately 5.7 percent per year, but MORMONS and JEHOVAH'S WITNESSES are growing at the same rate and constitute about 1 percent of the population. In 1993 there were 335 Protestant missionaries working in the nation, coming primarily from the United States, Brazil, and the United Kingdom, while Portuguese Protestant churches had sent 168 missionaries to other parts of the world.

Among the needs are greater unity of vision to reach the whole nation for Christ and increased CHURCH PLANTING, especially in the far north and south. With only one pastor for every three congregations, more full-time workers and lay leaders are needed along with adequate biblical and theological training. Groups needing greater focus are the 1.3 million Portuguese workers in other parts of Europe, the large number of marginalized youth, and immigrants from Africa and Macau.

There are nine theological seminaries and several programs of THEOLOGICAL EDUCATION BY EXTENSION; production of Christian literature and Bible distribution are growing, along with some Christian radio and television. The International Fellowship of Evangelical Students works in eight universities. Campus Crusade for Christ and Scripture Union are also present. As Portugal moves away from traditional Catholicism toward SECULARISM, there are significant challenges but also new opportunities.

PAUL E. PIERSON

Posselt, Wilhelm (1815–85). German missionary in South Africa. Born in Diekow (Neumark), Germany, he first was trained as a teacher and then attended the seminary of the BERLIN MISSIONARY SOCIETY. After completion of his studies and ordination in 1839, he arrived in South Africa in 1840 and served in the Berlin Mission's work in the Xhosa territory of the Eastern Cape Province (known at the time as Kafraria). During the British conflicts with the Xhosa he sought to establish closer relationship with the African peoples. In 1847 he began a work among the Zulu in Natal at Emmaus and in 1853 at Christianenburg, where he remained for the rest of his life. In his later years he served as the Berlin Mission's field director in Natal. He carried on an extensive pastoral ministry among the Zulu and Xhosa, and his station was a center for missionary endeavors in the region.

ULRICH VAN DER HEYDEN

Possession Phenomena. In almost every culture of the world the phenomenon of possession is known and experienced. Typical symptoms of possession include trance, trembling, sweating, groaning, screaming, speaking in a different voice or an incoherent language, taking on a new identity, inordinate strength, inexplicable knowledge, and prophecy. Often, but not always, those who have been possessed have no memory of the events of the possession after they are released (*see also* EXORCISM).

Explanations for possession can be classed in three categories: physical, psychological and social, and spiritual. Each generally offers alternative explanations for the same phenomena. However, the categories are not mutually exclusive; in many cultures possession first takes hold of a person as a result of an illness or emotional trauma, but is explained in spirit-related terms.

Physical explanations include fever, chemical imbalance, epilepsy, asthma, hypnosis, drug-induced hallucination, severe physical trauma resulting in shock, and sleepwalking. When possession is purely the result of a physiological state, it will be alleviated as soon as the physical problem is properly treated.

Psychological and social explanations include wish-fulfillment (as an attention-getting device), social stress and mob hysteria, and simulated possession (as a means of obtaining a desired goal). Anthropologists note the Taita of Kenya as an example. When Taita women are stressed because of their husbands' negligence, they may call for a community ceremonial dance. During the dance some become possessed, and spirits berate the husbands through the mouths of the wives. The husbands, fearing retribution from the spirit world for disobedience, obey the directions of the spirits. The Taita see this as actual possession, the anthropologists as a cultural phenomenon designed to alleviate social stress.

Spiritual explanations from a non-Christian perspective range from mystic states (e.g., a shaman's voyage) to beneficial mediumship. Non-Christian perspectives do not necessarily view possession as negative. For example, it may be a sign that ancestors or spirits have chosen a person as a channel through which they will communicate with the community. From the Christian perspective, however, all genuine possession (or demonization) is demonic control of the person and must be dealt with by exercising Christ's authority. It should be noted that some Pentecostal phenomena have a surface similarity to possession (e.g., slaying in the Spirit), but in those cases the explanation is that the Holy Spirit is at work.

The tendency of cross-cultural workers is to apply the explanation that makes best sense in light of their own cultural framework (*see* FLAW OF THE EXCLUDED MIDDLE). The missionary from a secular background may seek to explain possession purely in terms of physical or psychological categories. The missionary from an animistic culture will tend to explain all the phenomena as actual possession. The former must be aware that not all possession phenomena can be reduced to the physical and psychological, and the latter that not all that appears to be demonic possession is genuine demonization in the biblical sense (*see also* DEMON, DEMONIZATION). In terms of ministry, people will respond best when help is offered in categories that make sense to them culturally. Therefore the sensitive missionary will seek to develop contextualized ministry patterns that are faithful to the Scriptures and, as far as possible, in tune with cultural practices.

A. SCOTT MOREAU

Bibliography. D. W. Augsburger, *Pastoral Counseling across Cultures;* J. W. Montgomery, ed., *Demon Possession;* A. S. Moreau, *The World of the Spirits;* S. Walker, *Ceremonial Spirit Possession.*

Postmillennialism. Postmillennialists believe that the kingdom of God is already being realized in the present age through the proclamation of the gospel and the saving influence of the Holy Spirit. As a result, the whole world—the majority of the members of all nations including Israel, that is—will be christianized at a future, presently unknown time. Christ will return at the end of the millennium, an age of unknown duration marked by justice and peace. The new age will not be essentially different from the present and will come about as more people are converted to Christ. The postmillennialist view is the only one of the three significant eschatologies based directly on the charter of Christianity, the GREAT COMMISSION (Matt. 28:19–20), interpreting it not only as a command, but also as a promise and as prophecy.

The roots of modern Protestant world missions lie to a great extent in the work of Calvinist, Puritan, postmillennial preachers in England and America, as well as that of Lutheran, pietist, postmillennial pastors in Germany.

The first modern Anglo-Saxon missionaries (preaching to indigenous American Indians) were motivated by a Calvinist, postmillennial hope. That postmillennial expectations led to the establishment of practical missionary activity is true not only for Calvinist Anglicans, Presbyterians, and Congregationalists, but also for Calvinist Baptists such as WILLIAM CAREY whose major work, "An Enquiry into the Obligations of Christians . . ." (1792), initiated the final awakening of Protestant missions. Postmillennial expectations can be discovered in the sermons held at the founding of the LONDON MISSIONARY SOCIETY in 1795, of the New York Missionary Society in 1797, of the Glasgow Missionary Society in 1802, and to a certain extent of the CHURCH MISSIONARY SOCIETY in 1799. Many Calvinist mission leaders such as JOHN ELIOT, ALEXANDER DUFF, DAVID LIVINGSTONE, HENRY MARTYN, RUFUS ANDERSON, and HENRY VENN expressed a postmillennial hope.

American and British revival movements were seen as the first indications of a wider wave of conversion, expected to soon engulf the whole earth. Not only Jonathan Edwards, but also English (Isaac Watts, Philipp Doddridge) and Scottish theologians (John Willision, John Erskin) related postmillennial hope to revival and to the idea of missions.

The close relationship between postmillennialism and missions can be traced through the ideas of the Reformed Puritans of America and England back to the optimism of the Reformed theologians John Calvin, Ulrich Zwingli, Theoldor Bibliander, Martin Bucer, Peter Martyr, and Theodor Beza, even though none of them expressed a postmillennial system. This had, however, already occurred in the Reformation period in England, then by leading Puritan theologians such as John Cotton, John Owen, Matthew Henry, and Samuel Rutherford. For all of these Reformed thinkers since the Reformation, the kingdom of God still had a long period of time before it, in contrast to the immediate expectations of the end of the world of Lutheran orthodoxy.

It is therefore not surprising that postmillennialism, with its emphasis on reaching all peoples with the gospel, has been integrated only into Reformed confessions of faith (Calvin's Genevan Catechism, 268–270, Larger Catechism of Westminster, 191, Congregationalist Savoy Declaration 1658, art. 26.5). Postmillennialism offers the best explanation as to why the dogma of double predestination should not detract from missions but supports them.

Rufus Anderson was the first theologian to again emphasize the love for the lost as motivation for missions rather than postmillennial expectations, even though he clearly expressed a postmillennial belief. As late as 1909, W. O. Carver observed that the postmillennial view was still the most influential motivation for missions. Not until the end of the First World War did postmillennialism lose its preeminence. Following HUDSON TAYLOR it had, in the area of world missions, however, been gradually superseded by FAITH MISSIONS, which were strongly influenced by PREMILLENNIALISM.

A missionary-minded postmillennialism strongly emphasizing Old Testament Law became prominent in Calvinist circles since the 1970s through the Christian Reconstruction movement, best represented by Kenneth L. Gentry's book *The Greatness of the Great Commission*.

Similar developments can be observed in German-speaking evangelical missions, for Philipp Jakob Spener, and August Hermann Francke, the founders of German PIETISM and its growing missions movement, based their activities on postmillennial ideas. All of Spener's works, including his major work *Pia desideria* (pious wishes) are characterized by expectations of a better future. He radically rejected the pessimistic orthodox Lutheran interpretation of history including the expectation of Christ's immediate return. Postmillennialism maintained its dominant position in German pietism until Johann Albrcht Bengel began to combine premillennialism with postmillennialism by teaching the idea of two millennia. His pupils then completely rejected postmillennialism in favor of premillennialism and taught that missions should not be carried out until the millennium (for example, Johann Tobias Beck [1804–71]). Many state church mission societies, such as the BASEL MISSION (Theodor Oehler and Hermann Gundert, for example) continued to think in a postmillennial context.

THOMAS SCHIRRMACHER

SEE ALSO Millennial Thought and Mission.

Bibliography. C. L. Chaney, *The Birth of Missions in America;* K. L. Gentry, *The Greatness of the Great Commission;* I. Murray, *The Puritan Hope: Revival and the Interpretation of Prophecy;* P. Toon, ed., *Puritans, the Millennium and the Future of Israel: Puritan Eschatology 1600–1660.*

Postmodernism. A way of perceiving and explaining reality shared by thinkers in philosophy of language and science, sociology, the arts, architecture, management theory, and theology that arose in the West during the last half of the twentieth century in reaction to MODERNITY. At its most basic, postmodernism involves the realization of the ultimate bankruptcy of modern and premodern approaches to life.

Challenges to Modernity. Postmodernity's critique of modernity includes the issues of individualism, rationalism, scientific positivism, and technology. First, postmodernity has been critical of modernity's love for the autonomous individual. A more collective perspective is especially clear in postmodern philosophy of science, in which changes in scientific theory, called paradigm shifts, are seen as part of a corporate process in the discovery and use of new data.

Second, the modern myth of the autonomous individual elevated rationality to a point of near infallibility. One of postmodernity's strongest projects has been to call into question the modernist dependence on rationality by reconsidering the basic assumptions sustaining modernity's concept of rationality (and therefore of TRUTH). Postmodern philosophers and sociologists have pointed out that knowledge is in part socially constructed and draws from the whole person, not only from rational argument.

Third, at the heart of modernity lies a perspective of the world that reduces reality and truth to that which can be seen, tested, and verified through the inductive method of scientific materialism. Postmodernity has asked soul-searching questions about the assumptions of scientific positivism, demonstrating that such a scientific method tends to see only what it is looking for. Postmoderns want to assign equal validity to other sources of knowledge like experience, the emotions, the forces of social and personal psychology, and the spirit world.

Fourth, postmodernity has been rethinking the matter of technology. Clearly one of the most amazing and almost self-justifying aspects of modernity is the technological revolution it has produced. But modernists have been slow to reflect and evaluate the impact that technology has had on matters of value and belief. The reality of today's world has called the entire legitimating myth of technology into question. A threatened planet, the incurability of the AIDS epidemic, the use of technology in waging wars, and a deep fear of the cities that technology has produced are just a few examples of the reality that has stimulated a profound pessimism on the part of postmoderns with regard to technology.

Dangers. Postmodernity has helped us reexamine the world in which we live. Much of the world is simultaneously premodern, modern, and postmodern. Within two generations, societies like those in Korea, Malaysia, Indonesia, and Kenya have made significant progress in moving from being predominantly agricultural and rural to becoming industrial and now service-oriented. The postmodern critique offers us new vistas to understand how we may evangelize the peoples of the world, including those living in the West.

At the same time, evangelical missiologists must be aware of the dangers that postmodernity represents. Postmodernity advocates a degree of valuelessness and atomization of persons which is antithetical to the gospel. This relates not only to postmodernity's antifoundationalism, but also offers no solid footing on which to stand in seeking to transform a lost and hurting world so loved by God. Second, evangelical missiology must beware of postmodernity's elevation of RELATIVISM as the only acceptable alternative to rationality. The loss of any concept of truth undermines the message of the gospel and is unacceptable for evangelical missiology. Third, evangelical missiology needs to be careful with postmodernity's rejection of any referential use of LANGUAGE. Linguistically, postmodernity discards any sense that language refers to something beyond itself and affirms that language itself creates meaning. This leads to meaninglessness and ultimately to silence, since we are left with each person's exclamations of opinion. Such a direction is contrary to Christian notions of empathy and understanding. It represents a loss of commitment to truth and to the welfare of other persons, since all opinions are now just individual pronouncements of the person's own viewpoint. Fourth, postmodernity's rejection of concepts of purpose leaves little room for an evangelical to take seriously the metanarrative of the story of God's mission that is moving toward a final destiny. Instead, postmodernity creates a troubling paralysis that leaves Christians unable to participate actively in God's mission in the future.

Possible Contributions. In spite of the dangers, there are ways in which postmodernity can help us. First, postmodernity is helping us see that mission into the next century will be global and local rather than national and denominational. This is already evident in the rise of the mega-churches which are now increasingly involved in world evangelization directly as congregations, rather than working through denominational or mission structures. Second, postmodernity has reminded us that a biblical gospel is wholistic: the Holy Spirit comes to transform all of life and all relationships (*see* HOLISM, BIBLICAL). The church of the future needs to see itself as basically composed of relational networks of persons and groups rather than hierarchical organizations and structures. Third, postmodernity has offered us a new way to affirm that the church of Jesus Christ is a corporate body, not a gathering of isolated, autonomous individuals. Last, postmodernity has offered the church a new way of understanding and responding to the world of the unseen. Postmodern churches are providing a more realistic assessment of reality that understands that the world we live in includes not only the physical and the seen but the unseen world of spirits, demons, ancestors, and spiritual forces (*see* POWERS).

We are concerned about our non-Christian (and post-Christian) world that needs to know Jesus Christ as the only Way, the Truth, and the Life. We are called to respond to the nihilism, relativism, pluralism, and the loss of the concept of truth and sense of purpose that mark the foundationless character of postmodern society. We want to present an apology of the gospel as public truth and to do so in ways that a postmodern culture will be able to accept. We accept the challenge to be Christ's prophets who extend the word of hope in the midst of the hoplessness of a postmodern world.

CHARLES VAN ENGEN

Bibliography. D. Bosch, *Transforming Mission: Paradigm Shifts in Theology of Mission;* D. Dockery, ed., *The Challenge of Postmodernism: An Evangelical Engagement,* D. Harvey, *The Condition of Postmodernity: An Enquiry into the Origins of Cultural Change;* J. Hunter, *American Evangelicalism: Conservative Religion and the Quandary of Modernity;* N. Murphy and J. W. McClendon, Jr., *Modern Theology* 5:3 (April 1989): 191–214; J. Roxburgh, *Reaching a New Generation: Strategies for Tomorrow's Church;* P. Sampson, V. Samuel and C. Sugden, eds., *Faith and Modernity;* W. Shenk, *The Good News of the Kingdom,* pp. 192–99; H. A. Snyder, *Earth Currents: The Struggle for the World's Soul;* B. S. Turner, *Theories of Modernity and Postmodernity;* C. Van Engen, *Mission on the Way: Issues in Mission Theology.*

Potter, Philip A. (1921–). Dominican general secretary of the WCC and missionary to Haiti. After the 1930 hurricane destroyed Dominica's economy he came, as a boy, to understand that God in Christ assumed the human lot (Phil. 2).

After training for the Methodist ministry he served five years as a missionary to largely illiterate poor in Haiti. Later, while on the staff of the Methodist Missionary Society in London, he was involved in the INTERNATIONAL MISSIONARY COUNCIL (IMC). He did graduate studies in London University.

As a student he was active in the Student Christian Movement (SCM), and addressed the WCC assemblies of 1948 and 1954. He joined the WCC Youth Department in 1954, became chairman of the World Student Christian Federation (WSCF) in 1960, and director of Division of World Mission and Evangelism (DWME) in 1967. As general secretary of the WCC (1972–84) his influence included a threefold thrust: the fundamental unity of witness and service, the correlation of faith and action, and the inseparability of personal spiritual life from action in the world.

His thinking was strongly colored by Paul Tillich's and other modern theology. He defined *salvation* as liberation (from self-centeredness and self-assertion), both individual and corporate (structures, institutions), and *conversion* as "the realm of turning to each other in love as a result of being turned to the King" (the kingdom of God). The conversion from false gods to the true (cf. 1 Thess. 1:10), the objectivity of Christ's atoning work, and the root sin of worshiping the creature instead of the Creator were not in view.

JOHN A. McINTOSH

Bibliography. P. Potter, *Life in All Its Fullness.*

Poverty. *See* WEALTH AND POVERTY.

Power Encounter. The term "power encounter" was coined by Fuller missiologist ALAN TIPPETT to label an event commonly experienced by the peoples of the South Pacific as they converted to Christianity. Tippett noted that people usually had come to Christ in large groupings ("PEOPLE MOVEMENTS") soon after a major confrontation that tested the power of their ancestral gods against that of the Christian God, resulting in an obvious victory for the latter. These encounters were reminiscent of the scriptural encounters between Moses and Pharaoh (Exod. 7–12) and between Elijah and the prophets of Baal (1 Kings 18).

South Pacific peoples were (and are) keenly aware of the presence, activity, and power of spirits. Their leaders were openly committed to the gods of their islands. They credited these gods with providing protection, food, fertility, and all other necessities of life for them. But they also lived in great fear of their anger and vengeance. To challenge the ancestral gods was unthinkable for most South Pacific peoples. Nevertheless, in turning to Christ, often after years of weighing the consequences, it was chiefs and priests, those who knew the gods and their power best, who chose to challenge them. In doing so, they wagered that the Christian God had greater power than their gods and cast themselves completely on him for protection from the revenge of their gods.

A typical power encounter would involve a priest or chief, speaking on behalf of his people, publicly denouncing their allegiance to their god(s) in the name of Jesus and challenging the god(s) to do something about it. When the god(s) could not respond, the victory belonged to Jesus and large numbers of the people usually converted. As Tippett noted, power-oriented people require power proof, not simply reasoning, if they are to be convinced.

The value and validity of an approach to evangelism that involves power confrontations is widely accepted today in missiological thinking and practice, since it is recognized that most of the peoples of the world are power-oriented. Current theorists, however, have expanded Tippett's original concept to include healing and deliverance from demons as power encounters. They see Jesus' ministry as including numerous such power encounters. These encounters are usually less spectacular than those Tippett described but, it is argued, qualify as genuine power encounters since they involve the pitting of the power of God to bring freedom against the power of Satan to keep people in bondage. Furthermore, such "signs and wonders" frequently result in the conversion of families and even larger groups who accept the healing or deliverance as demonstrating the presence and power of God. There is, however, some difference of opinion over whether such encounters should be planned or simply taken advantage of when they occur.

It is important to note that conversion through power encounter does not assure that the movement will be stable and enduring. Throughout the Scriptures we see that people can observe God's mightiest demonstrations of power but soon go right back to the gods who were defeated. Thus it was both after Moses defeated Pharaoh and Elijah defeated the prophets of Baal. So it has been in many of the power events in the South Pacific and elsewhere. As always, the crucial dimension in conversion is what happens after the turning, whether people feed and grow in their new relationship with Jesus Christ or neglect it and let it die.

CHARLES H. KRAFT

Bibliography. C. H. Kraft, *Christianity With Power;* M. G. Kraft, *Understanding Spiritual Power;* A. R. Tippett, *People Movements in Southern Polynesia;* C. P. Wagner, *Confronting the Powers.*

Power Ministries. Proactive involvement in power ministries has not been characteristic of evangelical missions until recently. Two mind-sets which have been widespread among traditional evangelicals, including evangelical missiologists, have made them very cautious about participating in ministries that call upon the Holy Spirit to manifest outwardly the kinds of power ministries prominent in the Gospels and Acts. (1) The first mind-set is the doctrine of cessationism, which postulates that certain gifts of the Holy Spirit which were in use by the apostles and first-century church leaders had been given to the church only until the New Testament canon had been completed at the end of the apostolic age, at which time they ceased and are no longer to be expected in the church. The power ministries being introduced into evangelical missiology today would be included, for the most part, in the list of gifts which are thought to have ceased, and therefore cessationists could not accept the validity of contemporary power ministries. (2) The second mind-set among traditional evangelicals is a worldview suffering from what missiologist Paul G. Hiebert called the FLAW OF THE EXCLUDED MIDDLE. The Western worldview, strongly influenced by scientific rationalism, has a difficult time comprehending just how the supernatural powers of the invisible world can and do affect daily life of human beings. The non-Western worldview deals with such powers on a daily basis, and therefore is much more in tune with assumptions made by Old Testament and New Testament writers than are many Westerners. Exceptions to this among Third World leaders are generally those who have been trained by Westerners in Western-oriented institutions.

Both of these mind-sets were seriously challenged by evangelical leaders over the final two decades of the twentieth century. As a result cessationism has weakened in popularity. The major work reflecting this is Jack Deere's *Surprised by the Power of the Spirit* (1993). Changes in Western worldview are taking place more slowly except in circles influenced by the charismatic movement, by the New Apostolic Reformation, by missiologists, and by the New Age. The book which has been influential in helping evangelicals think through the paradigm shift is Charles H. Kraft's *Christianity with Power: Your World View and Your Experience of the Supernatural* (1989). A consequence of this is that evangelical mission leaders, although not in one accord, are much more open to power ministries as a component of mission strategies than they have been in the past. Of the many facets of power ministries now being advocated and used by evangelical missionaries, six may be noted as areas of particular significance.

Supernatural Signs and Wonders. Jesus sent his disciples out to preach the gospel of the kingdom of God accompanied by healing the sick, casting out demons, and raising the dead. He told them that, by the power of the Holy Spirit, they could expect to do even greater works than he did. In the framework of Third Wave thinking, John Wimber's *Power Evangelism* (1993) has been very influential in this area.

Prophecy. A frequent experience of the apostles was to hear God speaking direct words to them for instruction or admonition or comfort. The gift of prophecy is mentioned in the lists of spiritual gifts in Romans 12 and 1 Corinthians 12. Recently, beginning particularly in the 1980s, many evangelicals have begun to accept not only the gift of prophecy, but also the contemporary office of prophet. Two works have been particularly helpful in moving evangelicals out of the assumption that God does not exhibit any revelatory activity today, namely, Wayne Grudem's *The Gift of Prophecy in the New Testament and Today* (1988) and Jack Deere's *Surprised by the Voice of God* (1996).

Strategic-Level Spiritual Warfare. Taking seriously the biblical assertion that a major obstacle to world evangelization is the fact that Satan, the god of this age, has blinded the minds of unbelievers (*see* 2 Cor. 4:3–4), a number of evangelicals have argued that he does this by means of dispatching high-ranking demonic beings, sometimes referred to as TERRITORIAL SPIRITS, to keep cities, nations, people groups, religious blocs, and other social networks in spiritual darkness. They attempt to follow the lead of the apostle Paul, who asserts that we do not wrestle against flesh and blood but against principalities and powers of darkness (Eph. 6:12). Under the guidance of the Holy Spirit, they use the weapons of SPIRITUAL WARFARE, principally intercession, to neutralize these powers to the greatest extent possible in order to prepare the way for the harvesters who are the missionaries, the church planters, the pastors, and the evangelists. The major apologetic for strategic-level spiritual warfare is C. Peter Wagner's *Confronting the Powers* (1996), while the contrary position is expounded in Clinton Arnold's *3 Crucial Questions about Spiritual Warfare* (1997) (*see also* POWERS, THE) and Chuck Lowe's *Territorial Spirits and World Evangelization* (1998).

Spiritual Mapping. Prayer directed against the forces of the invisible world is seen to be more powerful if it is accurately targeted. The assumption is that the more we can discover about the devices of Satan (see 2 Cor. 2:11), the more vulnerable he and his forces become, and the less he will take advantage of us. Spiritual mapping is said to be to the intercessor what X-rays are to the surgeon. One of the leading figures in advocating spiritual mapping is George Otis Jr., whose principal works are *The Last of the Giants* (1991) and *The Twilight Labyrinth* (1997).

Identificational Repentance. Corporate repentance has been recognized as a principal weapon of spiritual warfare. The enemy frequently keeps people blinded to the gospel because unremitted corporate sins, both past and present, provide what is the equivalent of a legal right for the powers of darkness to afflict whole populations. Present generations can identify with and repent for corporate sins of their ancestors, removing the legal right of the enemy and opening the way for the healing of national wounds, and for the expansion of God's kingdom. The chief textbook describing this principle is John Dawson's *Healing America's Wounds* (1994).

Prayer Evangelism. While prayer has always played a role in the process of evangelization, some have felt that the potential power of prayer as a proactive evangelistic tool has been underutilized. The major work arguing that prayer can be used as an evangelistic methodology, rather than simply as a back up to other methodologies, is Ed Silvoso's *That None Should Perish* (1994).

C. PETER WAGNER

SEE ALSO Miracles in Mission; Signs and Wonders.

Power, Theology of. The power of God is a major theme of Scripture. Two central Old Testament metaphors graphically depict this power. First, God is the *Creator* who made from nothing what is. From the beginning of the world God is seen ruling over his creation by right of being its Creator. Humans, because they are made by God, should consider themselves to be "sheep of his pasture" (Ps. 100:3). Second, God is the *liberator* of covenant people elected to be in relationship to him. The Jewish confessional declares God's mighty acts of deliverance: "We cried out to the Lord, the God of our fathers, and the Lord heard our voice and saw our misery, toil and oppression. So the Lord brought us out of Egypt with a mighty hand and an outstretched arm, with great terror and with miraculous signs and wonders" (Deut. 26:7–8).

In both of these metaphors the power of God is not conveyed indiscriminately but *in relationship*.

Genesis 3 describes God the Creator searching for fallen humanity, calling, "Where are you?" This searching reveals the nature of God. He seeks to reestablish an intimate relationship between himself and his creation rather than merely exercise his power to punish. God's deliverance of the Israelites from Egypt was covenant deliverance: God delivered from oppression those with whom he had developed a relationship (Exod. 3:23–24). Based on this relationship (Exod. 20: 1), God called Israel into an exclusive relationship with him (Exod. 20:2–7). Throughout the Old Testament God is contrasted to the gods of the nations by the use of rhetorical questions demonstrating his incomparability. Moses, for example, praised God, asking, "What god is there in heaven or on earth who can do the deeds and mighty works you do?" (Deut. 3:24; cf. Pss. 77:13; 89:6).

In the New Testament God's power became incarnate in the person of Jesus Christ. His birth was by the power of God through the Holy Spirit so that he might be called "the Son of God" (Luke 1:35). As God's Son, Christ manifested "the power of the Spirit" in his ministry (Luke 4:14, 18, 36). The metaphors of creation and liberation can also be used to describe the power of God in Christ's life. As *re-creator*, Christ came "to seek and to save what was lost" (Luke 19:10). Sin separated humanity from God, but God in Christ has re-created those who believe to become new. As *deliverer*, Christ came "to destroy the devil's work" (1 John 3:8), to free those demonically oppressed and possessed. Christ was appointed "with the Holy Spirit and power" to heal "all who were under the power of the devil, because God was with him" (Acts 10:38). Finally, by his resurrection Christ is declared to be God's Son (Rom. 1:4) and has been exalted to God's right hand, where he stands above all principalities and powers (Eph. 1:18–23).

God's ministry in Christ was not an indiscriminate demonstration of power for the sake of power but rather power operating in divine relationship and through divine intention. Blind Bartimaeus, although chastised by the multitudes, continued to cry out in faith, "Son of David, have mercy on me!" (Mark 10:46–52). The Roman centurion demonstrated a remarkable faith in the power of Jesus to heal from a distance (Matt. 8:5–13). The father of the young boy possessed of an evil spirit responded to Jesus' statement that "Everything is possible for him who believes" by saying, "I do believe; help me overcome my unbelief!" (Mark 9:22–24). These works of power thus "presuppose faith both in him who does the work and in those on whose behalf they are done, so that a personal relationship is demanded" (Grundmann, 1985, 189).

Since the FALL OF HUMANKIND, God's rule has been challenged by SATAN. Satan, an angelic being cast down from heaven because of rebellion (Rev. 12:9; Van Rheenen, 1990, 264–66), created a dominion which stands in opposition to the KINGDOM OF GOD. The *gods* of the Old Testament, *demons* of the Gospels, and *principalities and powers* of Pauline literature are various terminologies describing the forces of Satan (*see also* POWERS, THE). Although described by these various terms, they all reflect the forces of the devil, who "has been sinning from the beginning" (1 John 3:8). Humans were created free to choose either the dominion of Satan or the kingdom of God (Gen. 2:16; 3:1–5).

Sometimes God's power is not apparent in a world largely controlled by Satan (1 John 5:19). Followers of God ask, "Why do you hide your face?" (Ps. 44) or "God, my Rock, why have you forgotten me?" (Ps. 42). Christians, participating in the sufferings of Christ (1 Peter 4:13), cry out in anguish, pleading for God to intervene (Rev. 6:9–11). During these times of suffering, Christians stand in faith, acknowledging God's ultimate sovereignty.

Not only is God's power quantitatively greater than Satan's, the quality is also different. Satan's power is debasing—contorting the disobedient who follow the cravings of their own sinful nature (Eph. 2:3). God's power, based on his great love, raises believers above these earthly cravings into heavenly realms (Eph. 2:4–6). Paul's prayer in Ephesians 3:14–21 interweaves God's power with his great love. Arnold writes, "Christ . . . roots and establishes the believer in his own love and strengthens the believer to follow the pattern of that love (3:16–17)." He succinctly contrasts Christian perspectives of power and love with pagan Ephesian perspectives: "In magic, many of the recipes and spells were used for the purpose of gaining advantage over people—winning a chariot race, attracting a lover, winning at dice, etc. God's power enables the believer to love after the pattern of Christ. The seemingly impossible demands of this kind of love require divine enablement in order for them to be fulfilled" (1989, 100).

Humans frequently misuse the power of God and contort it for their own selfish, egocentric purposes. The Willowbank Report says, "Power in human hands is always dangerous. We have to mind the recurring theme of Paul's two letters to the Corinthians—that God's power, seen in the cross of Christ, operates through human weakness (e.g., 1 Cor. 1:18–2:5; 2 Cor. 4:7; 12:9, 10). Worldly people worship power; Christians who have it know its perils" (Stott and Coote, 1980, 327). The power of God must never be used to give glory to human personalities or human institutions. Ultimate power is of God, and its use in defeating Satan must only give glory to God.

There is always significant distortion of the Christian message when Christianity is reduced to power. God's power must always be seen in a broad eschatological framework: God, who has already defeated Satan through the death and resurrection of Christ, will consummate his work at the end of time. Currently believers stand between the times: Christ, who has come, will return at the end of time.

These theological perspectives on power should guide Christians to understand both PRAYER and SPIRITUAL WARFARE. Prayer should never be understood primarily in terms of power but rather as relating to God who is the source of all power. The difference between the two is significant. If prayer is understood as power, Christians will readily seek power words or rituals rather than personally relating to a sovereign God and waiting for him to act in his own time. Likewise, these understandings help us comprehend the nature of spiritual warfare. Spiritual warfare is not about fighting Satan; he has been defeated by the triumphal resurrection of Jesus Christ. Spiritual warfare rather is standing firm in Christ's mighty power. It is accepting God's victory through Christ by faith and allowing God's redemptive power to work through Christ.

GAILYN VAN RHEENEN

Bibliography. C. E. Arnold, *Ephesians: Magic and Power*, W. Grundmann, *TDNT Abridged*, pp. 186–91; J. R. W. Stott and R. Coote, eds. *Down to Earth: Studies in Christianity and Culture*; G. Van Rheenen, *Communicating Christ in Animistic Contexts*; idem, *Missiology* 21:1 (January 1993): 41–53.

Powers, The. Given the reality of TERRITORIAL SPIRITS and their hostility to the gospel and to the people of God, some missiologists have been calling the church to take a direct and aggressive stance toward these supernatural powers. New strategies have been devised involving practices such as "spiritual mapping" (discerning the spirit powers) and "warfare prayer" to enable evangelists and Christian leaders to nullify the influence of territorial spirits and thereby enhance the receptivity of a people to the gospel. Many have wondered, however, whether these new practices are biblically rooted and, more importantly, whether believers have the authority to engage territorial spirits.

Since the mid-1980s numerous stories of Christians effectively battling territorial spirits have surfaced from all over the world, including the United States, Argentina, Korea, Japan, Canada, and elsewhere. More than anywhere else, Argentina became the focal point for the implementation of a strategy involving a direct attack against territorial rulers. Some evangelists and pastors in that country exercised authority in Jesus' name to cast out or bind the spirits over certain cities. According to the practitioners, the results have been dramatic. Once the territorial ruler has been identified and cast down, massive outpourings of people con-

verting to the gospel have followed and churches have grown exponentially.

Following the 1989 LAUSANNE CONGRESS II in Manila, an international group was formed to share and discuss ideas about battling the powers in the context of world mission. The "Spiritual Warfare Network" (SWN) has met annually under the leadership of C. PETER WAGNER, professor in the School of World Mission at Fuller Theological Seminary. The group officially became part of the prayer track of the AD 2000 and Beyond Movement. Wagner compiled many of the new insights and went public with a strategy for engaging high-ranking powers over cities and territories—a strategy he called "Strategic Level Spiritual Warfare" (SLSW). Wagner's numerous books on the issue have attracted significant attention as he has essentially become the principal spokesperson for SLSW.

At the heart of the new strategy is a threefold emphasis on (1) discerning the territorial spirits assigned to a city, (2) dealing with the corporate sin of a city or area, and (3) engaging in aggressive "warfare prayer" against the territorial spirits. "Spiritual mapping" is one method for discerning the territorial spirits. According to George Otis, Jr., the originator of the spiritual mapping concept, this task involves conducting an extensive spiritual analysis of a city or country especially focused on the religious history of the area. This information can provide specific clues for understanding the spiritual forces that are at work. This information is given to intercessors who can then pray with much more specificity and according to how the Spirit leads them.

Some advocates of SLSW have taken "spiritual mapping" much further and have sought information from pagan and occult contexts about spiritual forces. They have even understood mapping to be the attempt to uncover the demonic grids of power in a given city. This uncritical acceptance of information from occult or idolatrous contexts has led a number of critics to wonder whether some SLSW advocates are falling into a syncretistic form of Christian animism.

Since the mid-1990s, a strong emphasis in SLSW has been placed on the practice of "identificational repentance." In fact, the Philosophy of Prayer statement for the United Prayer Track of the AD 2000 and Beyond Movement states, "no aspect of warfare prayer is more important than identificational repentance." The assumption here is that corporate sin in a city or area has provided openings for high-ranking principalities and powers to establish spiritual strongholds. These must be dealt with through the corporate identification with the sins of a city and then confessing and repenting of these sins as a means of effecting reconciliation and thereby breaking Satan's grip on the city. The strongest advocate of this approach has been John Dawson.

Some advocates of SLSW believe that by engaging in identificational repentance they can "remit" the sins of others. But there is no sense in which one Christian can apply the atoning and forgiving work of Jesus to another person who has not personally exercised faith in Christ. What these proponents often mean, however, is that the intergenerational curse resulting from the sins of the ancestors can be lifted by identifying oneself with those sins and confessing them. But once again, there is no scriptural evidence supporting the notion that believers can vicariously confess the sins of other people and remove God's temporal penalty, or curse, on the corporate sin. Advocates of identificational repentance have also often inappropriately applied covenant promises given to the nation of Israel directly to contemporary nations and cities. Believers do not function in a priestly role between God and their nation in the sense that they bear a responsibility for confessing the sin of the unbelieving population to God. Their responsibility is to confess their own sins (perhaps even corporately) and proclaim a gospel that consists of the possibility for reconciliation between sinners and God.

The final aspect of battling territorial spirits—and perhaps the most controversial part—is the direct engagement with the territorial spirits. Some have called this "warfare prayer," but it is not properly prayer since it is not directed to God. Many proponents of SLSW would contend that there is a stage in the battle where one needs to take authority in the name of Jesus and command the ruling spirit(s) to leave. They contend that just as Jesus himself commanded Satan to leave after his temptation with the words, "Away with you, Satan!" (Matt. 4:10), believers have the responsibility to come against him in the cities and regions of their ministry.

There are difficulties with this last aspect of the strategy. Jesus was not evicting Satan from Jerusalem with his remarks, he was simply telling Satan to leave his person. In fact, there is no example in the Bible of any leader discerning a territorial ruler and commanding it to leave its territory. Jesus did not throw down the ruling spirit over Galilee or Judea; Paul did not command the spirit over Corinth to "be gone" nor did he bind the territorial ruler over Rome. Perhaps most instructive is the fact that in the most informative Old Testament account about territorial spirits, Daniel was not engaging in any kind of warfare prayer against the heavenly powers (Dan. 10:13, 20, 21). He was involved in praying and fasting on behalf of the people of Israel and actually had no awareness of the angelic struggle in the spiritual realm until he was told *after the fact* by the interpreting angel.

Debate still continues over the propriety of SLSW, but the current consensus remains to be that God has not given believers the authority or

responsibility to cast demons out of cities or territories. God himself will direct his angels to fight the battles against the high-ranking powers.

CLINTON E. ARNOLD

SEE ALSO Power Ministries.

Bibliography. C. E. Arnold, *Three Crucial Questions About Spiritual Warfare;* D. Greenlee, *Missiology* 22:4 (October, 1994): 507–14; E. Rommen, ed., *Spiritual Power and Missions. Raising the Issues;* C. P. Wagner, *Confronting the Powers: How the New Testament Church Experienced the Power of Strategic-Level Spiritual Warfare;* idem, *Warfare Prayer. How to Seek God's Power and Protection in the Battle to Build His Kingdom;* M. Wakely, *EMQ* 31:2 (April, 1995): 152–62.

Practical Missiology. The practical contours of the missionary role and task require consideration of CANDIDACY and training; field, home, and family responsibilities; and the contextual realities encountered abroad.

Screening of mission applicants should secure the highest calibre of personnel possible and preempt the financial cost and trauma of sending out persons who are not suitable for a missionary vocation. The MISSIONARY CALL should be pivotal to every applicant's testimony: a divine compulsion impelling the aspirant to communicate the reality of Jesus Christ across geographical and cultural frontiers. There should be a number of significant MOTIVES for mission service: a sense of obedience to God's mandate, a spirit of humility and gratitude as the recipient of God's grace, a zeal for Christ to be honored worldwide, an urgent desire to seize the particular moment in history, and a generous love for humankind. The applicant should meet the criteria of physical and mental health, evidencing an authentic spirituality, a mature personality, a flexible attitude, and a frontier spirit. Giftedness, previous theological training, and experience to match the assignment are other basic prerequisites. The goal of the selection process should be to confidently endorse the candidate as one who will meaningfully and effectively communicate the name and spirit of Christ in word, deed, and life in a cross-cultural environment.

Appointment to the field provides a poignant moment for the mission agency and local church both to promote the cause of world missions and to embrace prayerfully the departing missionary. This courier of the Good News is a gift from one church to another group of people and the missionary needs to recognize the importance of mediating and securing ongoing connection between the sending and receiving communities of faith.

On arrival, the missionary's first task is BONDING to the new culture as soon as possible. Acquisition of language and cultural skills will establish a sense of belonging and presence with the local people. Crossing the frontier of LANGUAGE,

CULTURE, and WORLDVIEW will generate excitement, apprehension, and the inevitable adjustment anxiety. CULTURE SHOCK touches every missionary at some point or other and is easily identifiable when the sent one begins to lament the fact that the cultural signs and guidelines from back home do not fit this new landscape.

It is imperative that the mission agency prepare their candidate to recognize the different stages of cultural ADJUSTMENT and how to cope with them. In the midst of the language learning "crisis" and cultural adjustment that creates natural feelings of vulnerability and homesickness, simply knowing that the feelings are normal helps the one persevere with Christian dignity, fortitude, and grace.

On the field the missionary will face strenuous demands and continuous expectations. A disciplined regimen will nourish the individual's spiritual life. A family altar should never be optional or discarded in the busyness of the day. Neglecting family for ministry is a travesty that God cannot endorse. The missionary home needs to be a haven of trust, love, humor, enrichment, and the forging of spiritual values and memories that become the talking points and strengths of this family for generations. Missionary parents will face hard decisions concerning their children in the areas of schooling, furloughs, and social dynamics (see PERSONAL/FAMILY RESPONSIBILITIES).

FURLOUGH times for the missionary are often a mixed blessing. The onerous DEPUTATION schedule, the competing expectations of relatives, and the disruptive lifestyle leaves many looking forward to a return to the mission field. On a more positive note, the leave of absence from the field provides opportunities for rest, recreation, reflection, and refitting (updating educational and professional skills).

The Christian missionary of the third millennium will not be able to adopt a neutral stance or bracket out faith convictions from the contextual realities of his or her place of service. Attitudes to life are cardinal and the missionary journey requires an INCARNATIONAL MISSION model that embraces compassion, servanthood, and the cross. Compassion prohibited both the Father and Son from noninvolvement and the bypassing of humankind. Jesus rolled up his sleeves and addressed the moral and social trouble spots of his day; the missionary is not exempt from walking the same path. Often the local context will provide an agenda for mission as the missionary addresses the spiritual and material plight in the area: endemic POVERTY caused by structural injustice and greed, corrupt political dispensations, rampant unemployment, competing truth claims of a secular and pluralistic society, and the anonymity and despair of the urban setting. The gospel's task is to confront and change people and circumstances. The missionary stands at life's cutting edge and must articulate clearly in word and deed the universality of God's activity in the world and the particularity of God's intervention in Jesus.

Servanthood requires diligence and hard work as it is inimical to human nature. The envoy for God comes with authority and conviction but must remember the divine enterprise of mission was birthed in servanthood and humility. Missionaries are guests in their new home and will have to contain the tendency toward cultural efficiency, aggression, and ecclesiastical colonialism. The local community makes the decisions, the missionary contributes when his or her advice is solicited. The national leaders shape their own churches in their image as they respond to the gospel. Identification with the local people presupposes self-denial on the part of the missionary that may at times require living with uncomfortable theological and ethical practices and symbols like polygamy and ancestral practices that contradict personal mores.

The cost of discipleship reminds every mission volunteer that MARTYRDOM is a reality in an era where terrorism, violence, and explosive brutality stalk the mission field. The propagation of the gospel afar is not some romantic adventure and quest in God's name but a provocative life-and-death struggle. The missionary must realize that the people who are to be won and saved always retain the possibility of crucifying the bearer of the good news.

David Bosch reminds both missionary and church of the pulsating eschatological dimensions that undergird modern missiology: Easter brought with it the dawn of the end time and the MISSIO DEI belongs to God—he retains the initiative, creates history, and guides it toward fulfillment. And we could add with wonderment and awe, ours is the privilege to be part of God's redemptive plan.

DAVID E. CRUTCHLEY

Bibliography. D. J. Bosch, *Transforming Missions;* J. H. Kane, *Life and Work on the Mission Field;* J. J. Kritzinger and W. Saaymen, *On Being Witnesses;* J. M. Phillips and R. T. Coote, eds., *Toward the 21st Century in Christian Mission;* N. Pirolo, *Serving as Senders.*

Praxis. Praxis is the outgrowth of a commitment to a dynamic hermeneutical methodology that interacts with the concrete historical reality on the one hand and the biblical text on the other. This dialectical process is foundational to respond adequately in an integral manner to the spiritual and physical needs of hurting people.

The motivation for such a contextual hermeneutic likely finds its roots in Aristotle's distinction between pure contemplation and human action which, expressed in concrete terms, forms the intention to put theory into action. Later, praxis was discussed as one of the early themes of LIBERATION THEOLOGY by theologians such as GUSTAVO GUTIÉRREZ and JUAN LUIS SEGUNDO. These two theologians, and others, enlarged the theme along two significant lines. First, practice should correspond with integrity to God's liberation of humankind. Fidelity to an interplay between theology and action provides the framework for Christian vocation. Second, praxis is rooted in efficacious love toward the poorest and most downtrodden. Praxis will unmask the unjust ideological basis for the existing social structures by promoting actions that are in accord with the authentic values of faith and theology. Thus liberation theology aimed to put praxis theology to the service of social transformation.

Theologians like Segundo candidly admit the debt that liberation theology and their perspective of praxis owe to Karl Marx. Most liberationists, however, shy away from the idea that they accepted wholesale use of Marxist categories. Still, the lurking presence of Marx in liberation theology frequently has caused evangelicals to understand this type of praxis as Marxism garbed in theological language. Several perceive unacceptable implications that generally accompany this process, including the poor being the initial and often the only point of involvement (see OPTION FOR THE POOR), and the use of SOCIAL SCIENCE analysis heavily influenced by Marxist categories. Evangelicals contend that insufficient emphasis has been placed upon the fallen nature of humankind. They may view the process as offering a situational hermeneutic that forces an application of the social context upon Scripture rather than seeking a theology produced by a reading of Scripture.

It is critical, then, to define carefully and precisely the way in which praxis may be used in evangelical theology. The underlying spiritual reality of a God who acts in human history provides a dynamic model which can and should be accepted as a legitimate point for theological reflection and basis for action on the part of evangelicals.

The purpose of praxis is to allow the Bible to speak to the ever-changing world in which action on behalf of others takes on concrete form. Further, the interplay between human action and theological reflection rooted in Scripture allows the Bible itself to stand as an authority over previous human-made interpretations of the Scripture and frees the Bible to shed fresh light on, and provide renewed motivation for, engaging in this dialectical process. Evangelicals can find a certain "praxis of faith" related to their social and personal conditions, a way of enacting or putting to work this faith experience nurtured by a constant reading of the Bible. Such faith is at the same time examined by the efficacy of what Christians do in everyday life. More specifically,

praxis cannot be seen as mere pragmatic action, nor a praxis that evaluates individual action as it solely relates to personal morality and holiness. Praxis moves beyond this limited though invaluable personal action to reflect theologically upon, and relate to, economic and social structures that sustain unacceptable conditions as well. Theology and practice are mutually supported, tested and corrected by the other. A praxis theology recognizes the need for a more distinctive ethic where the message of the biblical text and the compulsion of the Spirit directs one to respond creatively to the context in whatever form that may take.

It is possible that evangelicals can find in this praxeological hermeneutical method a way to keep their theological reflection integrally tied to concrete human experience, to the meaning of Scripture, and to pastoral action. Praxis moves beyond a theoretical agenda to the very essence of theological ethics.

DOUGLAS PETERSON

Bibliography. D. A. Carson, *Biblical Interpretation and the Church;* O. Costas, *Theology of the Crossroads in Contemporary Latin America;* idem, *Christ Outside the Gate;* C. B. Johns, *Pentecostal Formation;* J. B. Metz, *Faith in History and Society;* J. Miguez-Bonino, *Toward A Christian Political Ethics;* G. Osborne, *The Hermeneutical Spiral;* D. Petersen, *Not By Might Nor By Power.*

Prayer. Recently God has been awakening the church to the need for less talk about prayer and more actual prayer. Mission and denominational agencies have appointed full-time prayer coordinators whose sole job is to pray and organize prayer. Prayer and praise rallies have been held in urban centers around the world. Annual pilgrimages of praying through cities in the 10/40 WINDOW have been organized, with millions participating. The practice of walking through a target area and praying as prompted by the Spirit (known as prayer-walking) is being developed. More controversially, some advocate the engagement of TERRITORIAL SPIRITS in what has been called strategic-level warfare prayer as a new key to world evangelization. As signs of greater emphasis on prayer, all these efforts are welcomed in the missionary work of the church. At the same time, they must be evaluated not simply on the basis of reported effectiveness, but on fidelity to the scriptural picture of the prayer life of the church.

True prayer begins with God. It is the Lord who invited his disciples to pray (Matt. 7:7–11). It is also a command of God that people pray continually (1 Thess. 5:17). Prayer is the primary means that God uses to accomplish his work. God places prayer burdens on the hearts of his people in order to prompt prayer, through which he works. Historian J. Edwin Orr, after decades of researching revivals around the world, concluded that they both began and were sustained in movements of prayer. The missionary's prayer is not limited to the revival itself; Jesus commanded us to pray for the very laborers to work the fields that were ripe for harvest (Matt. 9:36–38).

Every individual Christian and every local church lives under the command to be devoted to prayer (Col. 4:2). As missionaries pray to the Lord of the harvest, we open ourselves to any attitudinal or behavioral adjustment that God wants us to make. Confessing sin is one important aspect of prayer (Ps. 66:18; Prov. 21:13; 28:9; 1 Peter 3:7). Our humility before God underscores that the purpose of prayer is not ultimately to achieve *our* agenda but the accomplishment of God's purposes in a way that honors his name (James 4:2). His ultimate purpose is the gathering of those who worship him at least in part in response to the missionary prayers and through the missionary efforts of his church.

Jesus' life was characterized by prayer. He prayed before and after the significant events in his life. He prayed when he was overwhelmed with the needs of people. He prayed when his life was unusually busy. His prayer aimed toward the Father's glory (John 17:1, 5), emphasized in the honoring of God's name as the first petition of the Lord's Prayer (Matt. 6:9). All of mission is to be driven by this supreme goal.

Characteristics of Prayer. Any activity that is stamped with God's full approval is to be motivated by love (1 Cor. 13:1). This will certainly include following Jesus' example by submitting our will to God's will (Matt. 26:39, 42, 44). It also involves imitating his fervency in prayer, and continually dealing with the anger and bitterness in our life and replacing it with forgiveness. This was taught by Christ in his instruction and by his example. It is for this reason that true prayer extends even to our enemies (Matt. 5:44). This type of loving prayer is foundational to the mission of the church, for through it our enemies may be won to Christ.

Of particular importance for the missionary's personal prayer life is the fact that prayer was never intended to be a mechanical discipline. It is an expression of an abiding relationship and of a life of communion with God undergirded by a heart of faith. This faith is placed in the revealed character of God, whose omniscience (Matt. 6:7–8) and goodness (Matt. 7:9–11) enable us to pray with confident expectancy in God's ability to accomplish his missionary purposes. Prayer is to be continual (1 Thess. 5:18) and to pervade all of our missionary work. The trials the missionary faces are not to hinder prayer life but to be used of God to deepen it (Acts 16:25).

Prayer and missions are inextricably intertwined in the Book of Acts. Prayer preceded the Spirit setting aside Paul and Barnabas as missionary candidates (13:2–3) and the missionary journeys themselves. Elders in newly established churches were prayed for and committed to God. The missionary trial of saying good-bye to loved ones is aided by committing them to the care of God in prayer (20:32).

Dynamics of Prayer. Missionaries and mission agencies have emphasized prayer throughout church history. At the same time, however, there is always a temptation to talk about prayer and state that it is important but not to actually pray. Mission agencies can fall into the trap of planning, organizing, leading, and then remembering to pray. Such prayer is really only asking God's blessing on our human efforts rather than seeking to align our organizational identity and plans with his ongoing work in the world and his call in our lives.

On the personal level, God aids the missionary in sustaining our prayer life through the crises we face. True prayer is exemplified by an attitude of helplessness and faith. God uses CULTURE SHOCK, LANGUAGE LEARNING difficulties, relational CONFLICTS, SPIRITUAL WARFARE, lack of RECEPTIVITY, and seemingly insurmountable obstacles to draw us to himself in prayer. He also has given us the HOLY SPIRIT to motivate, guide, and empower our prayer. In times of weakness the Holy Spirit prays for us (Rom. 8:26–27).

God ordained that our prayer be *persevering* to accomplish his sovereign work (Luke 11:5–8; 18:1–8). God uses persevering prayer to purify his church, prepare it for his answers, develop the lives of his people, defeat spiritual enemies, and give to his church the answer—intimacy with himself. This is especially important for missionaries working where the response to the gospel is limited.

WILLIAM D. THRASHER

Bibliography. P. E. Billheimer, *Destined for the Throne*; D. Bryant, *Concerts of Prayer*; D. A. Carson, *Teach Us to Pray*; W. L. Duewel, *Touch the World Through Prayer*; J. Edwards, *How to Pray for Missions*; O. Hallesby, *Prayer*; S. Hawthorne and G. Kendrick, *Prayer-Walking*; W. B. Hunter, *The God Who Hears*; A. Murray, *The Believer's School of Prayer*; R. A. Torrey, *How to Pray*; C. P. Wagner, *Warfare Prayer* and *Churches that Pray*.

Pre-evangelism. Many well-intentioned witnesses for Christ employ evangelistic strategies that assume every unbeliever is potentially ready to respond to the gospel upon first hearing. Such strategies encourage Christian witnesses to get right to the point to attempt to bring unbelievers, without delay, to repentance and faith in Christ, regardless of their background or lack of prior exposure to Christian truth.

In contrast to this direct approach, others prefer a more indirect style of evangelism, employing strategies that assume most unbelievers are initially not ready to respond meaningfully to the gospel. Proponents of the indirect approach are convinced that, in most instances, they need first to establish a relationship of trust with those to whom they are witnessing and to demonstrate their own credibility. They also argue that it generally takes time for unbelievers to become fully convinced that the gospel is true, relevant, and worth accepting, no matter what the cost. It is felt that unbelievers need first to process the new information they have received, to seek clarification, to abandon previously held views and presuppositions, and to weigh the potential ramifications of a decision to follow Christ. Otherwise, the new converts may make only a superficial, premature decision for Christ that fails to result in authentic conversion. Advocates of the indirect approach often characterize direct evangelism as a one-size-fits-all strategy that treats everyone essentially alike and thus fails to demonstrate appropriate respect for human dignity and individuality.

Over the past generation, James Engel had greater impact than any other person on evangelical thinking about the need for what is often called pre-evangelism. Elaborating on a model first advanced by Viggo Sögaard, Engel developed what has come to be known as the ENGEL SCALE, which sees conversion as an often lengthy process, only one part of which is the actual moment of regeneration. As Engel notes, recipients of Christian witness frequently begin their spiritual journey from a point at which they lack even an awareness of the existence of a supreme being. Then, often quite gradually and tentatively, they begin to move from initial exposure to Christianity to a vague awareness of their own personal spiritual need. Eventually, they may begin to develop at least a measure of interest in the gospel, but it often takes time for them to become fully aware, first of its essential details, and then of its implications for them personally. Typically, it takes additional time for unbelievers to develop a fully positive attitude toward the gospel and to recognize that it is indeed capable of meeting their deepest felt needs. It is only after they reach this point that they are ready to make a meaningful decision to repent and place their faith in Jesus Christ.

The Engel Scale helps us to see, therefore, that we really need to adjust the content and focus of our witness to persons as they are along the conversion continuum. Instead of immediately urging someone to make a definite decision for Christ, it is often more appropriate first to employ a variety of pre-evangelistic techniques, helping him or her gradually to move along the scale to the point where he or she is fully ready to follow Christ.

RAYMOND P. PRIGODICH

Bibliography. J. F. Engel, *Contemporary Christian Communications: Its Theory and Practice.* Nashville; J. F. Engel and W. H. Norton, *What's Gone Wrong with the Harvest? A Communication Strategy for the Church and World Evangelism.*

Predestination. *See* DIVINE ELECTION.

Preferential Option for the Poor. *See* OPTION FOR THE POOR.

Prejudice. *See* ETHNOCENTRISM.

Premillennialism. Belief that Jesus Christ will return to earth in glory, ushering in a thousand-year reign of peace, after which a new heaven and earth will replace the old ones, as foretold in the Book of Revelation. The exact nature of events such as the battle between the forces of righteousness and the forces of Satan (the battle of Armageddon), the "rapture" of believers to meet Christ in the air, and the features of the millennial kingdom vary according to different interpretations of the Bible. Although various interpretations of the second coming have existed throughout church history, modern premillennialism emerged during the mid-1800s from British and American movements to interpret biblical prophecies literally.

While millennialism of different types has encouraged missionary activity, premillennialism became a hallmark of evangelical missions from the late nineteenth century on. Prominent American pastors, including A. B. SIMPSON, A. T. PIERSON, A. J. GORDON, DWIGHT L. MOODY, Martin Wells Knapp, and C. I. Scofield, concluded from their study of the Scriptures that preaching the gospel worldwide was vital preparation for Christ's second coming. With the second coming believed imminent, believers felt compelled to evangelize non-believers, both to save all the souls they could before Christ's return cut off opportunities for salvation, and to fulfill the conditions outlined for his return in Matthew 24:14, "And this gospel of the kingdom will be preached in the whole world as a testimony to all nations, and then the end will come." Premillennial support for missions gained a wide audience through YMCA and Christian conventions, Bible studies, periodicals, and the best-selling book *Jesus is Coming* (1878) by Chicago businessman William E. Blackstone. *Jesus is Coming* sold over a million copies in forty-eight languages.

Premillennial thinking not only encouraged verbal proclamation in denominational missions like the Presbyterians and Baptists, but it caused the formation of numerous faith missions and independent agencies from the 1880s to the present. Premillennialists tended to focus their energies on evangelism rather than on teaching, medicine, or other aspects of Protestant missions. Nondenominational faith missions such as the

AFRICA INLAND MISSION and the Central American Mission stressed cross-cultural evangelism among specific groups such as Jews, the unreached interiors of Africa and Asia, or nominal Catholic lands. When Pentecostalism emerged in the early twentieth century, its adherents also adopted premillennial motivations for missions. Early Pentecostals believed that the Holy Spirit had endowed the gifts of tongues to complete the task of world evangelization in preparation for the second coming. For example, the Azusa Street Revival (1906–13) under pastor William J. Seymour sent Pentecostal missionaries around the world (*see* PENTECOSTAL MOVEMENT).

During the twentieth century, premillennialism remained a powerful motivation for world evangelization. For example, the Oriental Missionary Society (*see* OMS INTERNATIONAL) under Charles and then Lettie Cowman stressed house-to-house evangelism of every villager in Japan, and later "Every Creature Crusades" in Latin America, hoping to proclaim the gospel to the entire world before Jesus' return. CAMERON TOWNSEND, founder of the WYCLIFFE BIBLE TRANSLATORS, believed that translating the Bible into every language would help finish world evangelization and hasten the second coming. Founding student participants of the Urbana Missionary Conventions (1946) sought to complete the GREAT COMMISSION in preparation for the second coming. Premillennial motivations for mission received worldwide recognition when in 1974 three thousand evangelical leaders adopted the Lausanne Covenant, which became a basic statement of faith for evangelical missions. The last article of the Lausanne Covenant states, "We believe that Jesus Christ will return personally and visibly, in power and glory, to consummate his salvation and his judgment. This promise of his coming is a further spur to our evangelism, for we remember his words that the Gospel must first be preached to all nations. We believe that the interim period between Christ's ascension and return is to be filled with the mission of the people of God, who have no liberty to stop before the End" (*see also* LAUSANNE MOVEMENT).

As evangelicalism and Pentecostalism spread throughout the non-Western world, many indigenous Christians adopted premillennial motivations for missions, such as those expressed at the COMIBAM (*Congreso Missionero Ibero Americano*) missions conference of Latin American evangelicals in 1987. Just as in the late 1800s when many American evangelical Christians hoped to evangelize the world by the year 1900, an idea captured in the slogan "the evangelization of the world in this generation," so also in the late 1900s evangelicals worldwide sought to complete the task of world evangelization by the year 2000. Under international leadership, the AD 2000 and Beyond Movement held a series of global consultations to encourage "A Church for Every People and the Gospel for Every Person by the Year 2000." The idea of planting a church in every people group by the year 2000 carried premillennial overtones for many who believed that world evangelization was a prerequisite for the second coming.

DANA L. ROBERT

SEE ALSO Millennial Thought.

Bibliography. D. Bryant, *The Hope at Hand*; J. A. Carpenter and W. R. Shenk, eds., *Earthen Vessels. American Evangelicals and Foreign Missions, 1880–1980*; J. A. De Jong, *As the Waters Cover the Sea. Millennial Expectations in the Rise of Anglo-American Missions 1640–1810*; G. E. Ladd, *The Blessed Hope. A Biblical Study of the Second Advent and the Rapture*; T. Weber, *Living in the Shadow of the Second Coming. American Premillennialism 1875–1925*.

Presbyterian Missions. The first Presbyterian missionaries from the United States went to Syria and Lebanon under the AMERICAN BOARD OF COMMISSIONERS FOR FOREIGN MISSIONS in 1823. Others were appointed to India, Siam (Thailand), and Africa. In 1832 the Synod of Pittsburgh organized the Western Foreign Missionary Society and the following year sent a missionary to Liberia. In 1837 the General Assembly of the Old School Presbyterian Church (PCUSA) took over that society, forming its own board of foreign missions. At that time it had forty-four missionaries either overseas or under appointment. The United Presbyterian Church of North America (UPCNA), formed in 1858, soon began to send missionaries, especially to the Muslim world, and eventually sent more to that field than did any other Protestant denomination. The Southern Presbyterian Church (PCUS), having divided from the Northern Church in 1861, soon began its own work, sending missionaries first to China and then to Brazil. Among the countries where Presbyterians would have the greatest number of missionaries were China, India, Thailand, the Philippines, Korea, Japan, Brazil, Guatemala, Mexico, Ethiopia, Cameroon, the Congo (Zaire), Egypt, Sudan, Pakistan, and Lebanon.

The Presbyterian understanding of mission focused first of all on EVANGELISM and CHURCH PLANTING, with a strong emphasis on the preparation of indigenous LEADERSHIP. This was especially true in Korea, where the first national pastors were ordained twenty-two years after the arrival of the first missionary, and Brazil, where a seminary was established five years after the arrival of ASHBEL GREEN SIMONTON. The NEVIUS PLAN, which stressed the importance of an indigenous church from the beginning, would be a strong factor in the growth of the church in Korea, where today there are more Presbyterians than in any other country of the world.

Education was a second focus, seen as a means of preparing leadership for the church, evangelizing students, and aiding in the transformation of society (*see also* EDUCATIONAL MISSION WORK). Educational institutions from the primary through the university level were established in a number of countries. Yon Sei University in Seoul and McKenzie University in São Paulo are examples. Schools were important in most fields but especially in countries where there was little evangelistic success, especially the Middle East and Thailand. Some remained clearly Christian while others gradually became secularized.

A third focus was medical work, with clinics, hospitals, and eventually medical and nursing schools established. MEDICAL MISSION WORK was effective in ministering to women, who usually had no access to medical care until women physicians and nurses arrived. The ministry to women was carried on in other ways. Often mission schools provided the only opportunities for girls to study; eventually females would be encouraged to study through the university level and enter professions, especially nursing and medicine. Presbyterian missions employed Bible women in evangelistic work, and they became another factor in raising the status of women. Their ministry was especially significant in the Middle East, Korea, and China. A number of separate women's boards were established in the nineteenth century; these were absorbed into the male-dominated boards in the 1920s.

Presbyterian missionaries also established AGRICULTURAL MISSION projects designed to raise the economic level of the rural poor. The best known was the Allahabad Institute, established by SAM HIGGENBOTTOM, India's pioneer scientific agriculturist. At times missionaries clashed with colonial governments and commercial enterprises that exploited the indigenous peoples. This was especially true in the Congo, where the rubber companies and the Belgian government forced the people to work at a less than subsistence level to produce rubber and ivory. Presbyterian missionaries publicized the situation, leading to an international incident in which the missionaries were brought to trial and vindicated. This eventually resulted in some improvement of the conditions of the people.

Presbyterians had leadership roles in various cooperative movements. ROBERT E. SPEER, the greatest of the Presbyterian mission leaders, and JOHN MACKAY, a secretary of the board of foreign missions of the PCUSA and later president of Princeton Seminary, were leaders in cooperative efforts including the INTERNATIONAL MISSIONARY COUNCIL. Presbyterians encouraged church union in China, the Philippines, Thailand, and Japan. Presbyterian churches grew quite rapidly in some areas, notably Korea, Brazil, the Congo, and Guatemala. In other areas, for example, Japan, growth was slow.

Major changes came after World War II. In 1956 the PCUSA recommended the full integration of missions into the national churches within five years. In 1958 the PCUSA and the UPCNA merged to become the newly designated United Presbyterian Church in the U.S.A. (UPCUSA) and formed a Commission on Ecumenical Mission and Relations. This resulted from a major shift in thinking: the relationship between the sending and the receiving church should be direct, instead of through the mission of the American church. While this aided in ending missionary PATERNALISM, it often left the missionaries, now integrated into national church structures, without clearly defined roles, and was a contributing factor in the decline of the number of missionaries.

The PCUS merged with the UPCUSA in 1983, becoming once again the PCUSA; their mission boards merged in 1988, becoming the Worldwide Ministries Division.

The missionary strength of the Presbyterians peaked around 1927, with 1,606 workers under appointment by the PCUSA, 553 by the PCUS, and several hundred more by the UPCNA. This number had fallen to 425, serving in 56 countries, in 1996. Several smaller Presbyterian denominations are also involved in mission. The most important of these is the Presbyterian Church in America, which divided from the PCUS in 1973. By 1995 it had approximately 450 missionaries serving in 53 countries.

Up to the middle of the twentieth century, American Presbyterians were leaders both influentially and numerically in the missionary movement. At the end of the century the PCUSA, with a serious decline in numbers, was searching to rediscover its role in world mission. It was the only mainline denomination to affirm support of the AD 2000 Movement, which sought to plant churches among every people group by the end of the century.

PAUL E. PIERSON

Bibliography. A. J. Brown, *One Hundred Years: The History of the Foreign Missionary Work of the Presbyterian Church in the U.S.A.*; G.T. A. J. Brown, *Presbyterians in World Mission*; R. E. Speer, *Presbyterian Foreign Missions.*

Presence Evangelism. We often think of evangelism as consisting entirely of words, as being exclusively the verbal communication of a message. Frequently, however, the Christian message will have its intended impact only if our verbal communication of the gospel is accompanied and enhanced by our good deeds. Information alone is typically insufficient to persuade people that the gospel is true; it matters to them who is transmitting the information. Before accepting the message as credible, they must first be convinced of the credibility of the messenger. As Marshall McLuhan put it in the 1960s, in many respects the medium is the message. Christian presence, therefore, must accompany Christian proclamation.

In New Testament times, presence and proclamation typically functioned together to bring people to faith in Christ. As Jesus proclaimed the KINGDOM OF GOD, he "went around doing good" (Acts 10:38). The believers in Jerusalem sold their possessions in order that they might share with all who were in need; as a result, they "[enjoyed] the favor of all the people," and "the Lord added to their number daily those who were being saved" (Acts 2:45, 47). The apostle Peter counseled believers to live such good lives that, after seeing their good deeds, pagans would glorify God (1 Peter 2:12). New Testament evangelism, therefore, consisted not only of proclamation (kerygma), but also of fellowship (koinonia) and service (diakonia). And today, also, as Christians demonstrate love, unity, good works, and a commitment to justice, their witness becomes more convincing. The fruits of the gospel in the lives of Christians serve to authenticate the gospel. It is appropriate, therefore, that Christian missionary efforts have often included medical and educational components, as well as efforts to combat social injustice.

Presence alone, however, is insufficient. St. Francis of Assisi once said, "Preach the gospel at all times, and, if necessary, use words." But if people are to experience salvation in Christ, they must be told the way of salvation; it is always necessary, at least eventually, for words to accompany our good deeds. During the early part of the twentieth century large numbers of mainline Protestant missionaries began to opt for presence alone, apart from proclamation, which they equated with sectarian proselytization. Many in conciliar circles today similarly advocate humanization without proclamation. In reaction against this unbalanced approach to mission, evangelicals sometimes swing to the opposite extreme, advocating proclamation without presence, and accusing those committed to social concern of succumbing to theological liberalism. A consensus is growing among evangelicals, however, that, to be balanced, mission must include both dimensions. Paragraph 5 of the 1974 Lausanne Covenant declares that "we should share [God's] concern for justice and reconciliation throughout human society and for the liberation of [people] from every kind of oppression." It goes on to argue that, rather than being mutually exclusive, social concern and evangelism are both part of our Christian duty. An official commentary on this paragraph of the Lausanne Covenant argues that social involvement is both a bridge to evangelism and the partner of evangelism. "They

are like the two blades of a pair of scissors or the two wings of a bird." Jesus' words explained his work, and his works dramatized his words.

Gospel content, therefore, is most compellingly communicated within a context of credibility.

RAYMOND P. PRIGODICH

SEE ALSO Evangelism and Social Responsibility.

Bibliography. B. Bruce. *Bridging the Gap: Evangelism, Development and Shalom; Evangelism and Social Responsibility: An Evangelical Commitment. The Grand Rapids Report;* B. J. Nichols, ed., *In Word and Deed: Evangelism and Social Responsibility.*

Priesthood of Believers. Common identity of all Christians as priestly members of the church of Jesus Christ. In 1 Peter 2:4–5 believers are referred to as a "holy priesthood" whose task it is to offer "spiritual sacrifices acceptable to God through Jesus Christ." In virtue of their unity with Christ in his priestly ministry, all Christians are constituted priests (Rev. 1:5–6; 5:9–10). This is unlike the old covenant priesthood, in which a special priestly tribe was appointed to exercise a mediatorial ministry under the leadership of human high priests. Now, the new covenant priesthood is the privilege and responsibility of all the faithful under the headship of the one High Priest, Jesus Christ.

As a priesthood, believers are directed to offer various sacrifices, and each of these has important implications for the missionary enterprise: (1) The offering of oneself (Rom. 12:1) entails the sacrifice of all that one is and does: personal ambitions, life goals, and activities in surrender to God's design. This sacrifice constitutes the foundational step of missionary endeavor as a radical commitment is undertaken to go anywhere and do anything that God should command. (2) The offering of a "sacrifice of praise" to God (Heb. 13:15; 1 Peter 2:9) involves both confession of the majesty, sovereignty, goodness, power, and excellency of God, and thanksgiving to God for his wondrous acts of creation, providence, and redemption. The MISSIONARY TASK reaches, prepares, and mobilizes new priests who are dedicated to the worship of God through Jesus Christ. (3) The ministry of intercession, paralleling the intercessory ministry of Jesus the High Priest (Heb. 7:24–25), involves believers in prayer for family and friends, for the church, for missionaries already laboring in the harvest, and for those who need to be reached for Christ.

(4) The offering of service entails serving God and others through the faithful and responsible exercise of one's vocation in society. Whatever the job may be to which God has called a believer (including the most mundane, everyday tasks), work should be seen as an opportunity to live out one's priesthood in the world. In so doing, the believer is enabled to do good and share what he or

she possesses with others (Heb. 13:16). (5) Such service must be carried out in a spirit of cooperation, which entails valuing one another as fellow priests who enjoy equality in essence (Gen. 1:26–28), spiritual standing (Gen. 3:28), and endowments by the Spirit (1 Cor. 12), while recognizing the diversity of ministry and gifting of others, including the divine calling of some from among the priests to official ministry positions to strengthen and equip the priesthood and others to the missionary task to expand the priesthood. (6) One particular aspect of service to which all believers are called is the ministry of reconciliation (2 Cor. 5:18–21), which involves "ministering as priests the gospel of God" so that men and women "from every tribe and tongue and people and nation" may be presented to God as an "acceptable offering, sanctified by the Holy Spirit" (Rom. 15:16; Rev. 5:9).

GREGG R. ALLISON

Bibliography. C. Eastwood, *The Priesthood of All Believers;* idem, *The Royal Priesthood of the Faithful;* H. Kraemer, *Theology of the Laity;* M. Luther, *Luther's Works,* 40:3–44; idem, *Luther's Works,* 13:304–34.

Primal Religions. Primal religions are indigenous local traditional or tribal religions that are nonuniversal. They existed before the more widely practiced mainstream religious traditions such as Hinduism, Buddhism, Christianity, and Islam. They are also referred to as FOLK RELIGIONS, though that term encompasses local varieties of syncretistic mainstream religions (e.g., folk Islam, folk Buddhism, or folk Christianity). Primal religions lack sacred scriptures and are passed orally from one generation to another. They deal with the pragmatic considerations of daily life.

Primal religions are one expression of the desires and deep longings people have for a relationship with a power, a spiritual being, or someone beyond themselves. In primal religions, all of life is religious and it is not possible to separate it into distinct parts. There is no distinction between the sacred and the secular. Often there is no word in the language for "religion" per se; rather there are sacred traditions. Primal religion often has a sacred lore or metaphysic related to the natural environment. For example, *Nom* is the word for God in Ham (also known Jaba), an ethnic group in Nigeria. *Nom* translates as "sun" or "creator of the sun" (as well as creator of all else). The Bajju, a neighboring group, use *Kadza* for God, a word that means "rain" or the "one of the rain," "creator of the rain."

Such religions display an incredible diversity. They are best described locally or regionally of like religious systems rather than generically of things characteristic of all of them. For example, the Australian aborigines speak of the dreaming or dream time, which draws together linear time and the mythical time of their totemic animal ancestors.

In sub-Saharan Africa among speakers of Benue-Congo languages, including all the Bantu languages, there is widespread belief in God as the creator, with lesser spirits who traditionally were prayed to as intermediaries between humans and God. It also includes belief in other spirits who inhabit parts of nature, such as trees, snakes, rocks, rivers, and certain areas. This intermediate level includes the ancestral spirits who are believed to dwell with the living, watching over them and giving blessings or curses to people. People venerate or respect them and pray to them, pour libations and offer sacrifices to them (*see* ANCESTRAL PRACTICES). People's spirits live prior to birth and continue following death, with REINCARNATION purported to occur for many. These ancestral spirits appear from time to time as masquerades who speak to people and bless or punish people according to their deeds. Traditionally some groups, such as the Yoruba, believed in a pantheon of gods, while many others believed in one good god, the creator and sustainer of life.

The goodness of God in sub-Saharan Africa relates to a basic problem, namely, why people suffer misfortune, become ill, and die. The answer derives from their theology of God as being good. It deals with the widespread belief that individuals have an innate spiritual power that they can use to affect others in the supernatural realm, causing misfortunes, illnesses, and death. Evans-Pritchard, an early British social anthropologist, termed this explanatory system WITCHCRAFT. It is a system with its own internal logic. Use of *spiritual power* is a more accurate term, to distinguish it from Western definitions of witchcraft. There is a recognition both of the immediate cause (e.g., a person is hurt in an automobile accident) and an ultimate spiritual cause (e.g., someone is harming another in the spiritual realm). Diviners often use some form of divination to ascertain the spiritual cause of a problem (*see* DIVINATION, DIVINER).

The primal religion of Benue-Congo speakers contrasts with that of Nilotic language speakers, for whom the high god is of central importance with the ancestors and other spirits being insignificant. Speakers of Nilotic languages include the Maasai, Luo, Dinka, Nuer, and many others within the East African cattle complex of ethnic groups.

Most primal religions mark important times in the annual seasonal cycle, such as cultivating, planting, and harvesting (e.g., celebration of the first produce harvested). Religious rituals also mark RITES OF PASSAGE of individuals, such as birth, puberty, marriage, and death rituals. Other rites of passage are celebrated as well, depending on the culture. For example, in Kerala state in India there was the *tali* tying, an early marriage ceremony for a girl with a boy. He might or might not become her husband following puberty. In some cultures the first pregnancy was marked with religious celebrations (*see* RITUALS AND CEREMONY).

If we were to look for commonalties among different primal religions, we can use analytic categories such as beliefs, rituals, symbols, sacrifices, prayers, taboos, and trances (altered states of consciousness). Whereas from a Western perspective beliefs are central, from the perspective of many who hold primal religions practices are central. These religions are more often danced out than believed. Beliefs must be implied and extracted from religious practices.

Today there are revitalization movements in many primal religions worldwide. Some of these movements have received impetus from outsiders who encourage a resurgence of belief and practice of primal religions.

When missionaries come into an area, they need to understand the local religious system. Failure to do so results in traditional religion answering one set of questions and Christianity answering another set. The local Christians feel it necessary to retain both the primal religion and Christianity to address these differing issues, and thus Christianity becomes an overlay on the traditional religion. If Christianity is to become truly relevant and transformative, it must address the same issues as the primal religion. This means the Christian missionary must understand the local primal religion and its means of dealing with specific issues, then together with local Christians search the Bible for a Christian perspective on those issues.

People who practice primal religions are often open to the gospel of Jesus Christ. Their pragmatic approach to life allows them to try whatever religious system might help them solve their daily problems. Further, some will see a more mainstream religion as helping them integrate into the wider world, where such a religion is more acceptable then is their local religious system.

CAROL V. MCKINNEY

Bibliography. E. E. Evans-Pritchard, *Witchcraft, Oracles and Magic among the Azande;* R. C. Mitchell, *African Primal Religions;* H. Smith, *The World's Religions.*

Príncipe. *See* SÃO TOMÉ AND *PRÍNCIPE*.

Prison Mission Work. Ministry to prisoners in the United States has grown steadily during the last half of the twentieth century in numbers of ministries, volunteers, and participating churches. The estimated 15,000 volunteers in 1977 had grown to some 100,000 by 1997. The number of prison ministries of all sizes also increased substantially from 214 in 1977 to 1,200 in 1997, with some 30 of them serving nationwide.

The Impact of Prison Ministry. With over 100,000 active ministry volunteers evangelizing in jails and prisons, record numbers of inmates are making decisions to follow Jesus Christ. Yet the challenges are formidable, as there are over 1.5 million adults and 350,000 juveniles currently incarcerated.

Over 100,000 prisoners in the United States each year make a decision to follow Jesus Christ; 95 percent of them will be released within a three- to five-year period. When churches welcome these former inmates and help create a support system meeting practical needs, giving affirmation, and unconditional Christian love, 92 percent do not return to crime. Currently, however, 80 percent of the Christian ex-offenders do not find a church. Without a church support system, the "born again" ex-offenders' recidivism rate is 67 percent (compared to a normal 15% to 25%).

Of the 1,200 small organizations who faithfully visit local facilities, roughly 450 have an organizational structure. These ministries can be seen to fit into four basic categories: evangelistic, chaplaincy, discipleship, and aftercare.

Evangelistic. Clearly leading the evangelism forefront is former professional football player and prison ministry evangelist, Bill Glass. On weekends, Bill Glass Ministries (BGM) enters prisons with an average of 300 evangelist volunteers accompanied by special guests that include champion athletes. BGM now holds monthly evangelistic events in some 180 institutions. Heading the evangelistic effort to incarcerated juveniles is Bunny Martin, a friend of Bill Glass and former team member. His organization RAY (Reaching America's Youth) has focused efforts on the nearly 350,000 incarcerated juveniles in prisons and juvenile boot camps and detention centers nationwide.

Chaplaincy. Chaplains are essentially the "pastors" in prisons and are strategic in facilitating the presence of other ministries in institutions. They often serve as powerful witnesses for Christ among correction administrators and officers. Since 1961, Good News Jail and Prison Ministry has set the standard for professionalism in chaplaincy, and they currently have 116 chaplains in over 110 institutions across 25 states. The Federal Bureau of Prisons has approximately 70 chaplains with high professional and educational standards. Not all federal chaplains, however, are evangelical. Their numbers include chaplains of other faiths, as well as Roman Catholic priests.

Discipleship. The most significant discipleship ministry is Prison Fellowship, established in the early 1970s by former White House counsel, Charles Colson. Prison Fellowship presents seminars in prisons across American that help inmates in practical areas such as communication in marriage, life skills, and continuing education. Prison

Fellowship is represented in every state and is served by over 50,000 dedicated volunteers.

Aftercare. Aftercare, often the most neglected area in jail and prison ministry, relates to the needs of offenders after release. Frank Costentino, a former prisoner, began a network of aftercare facilities in Florida called The Bridge and a movement called Bridges Across America. He is also President of COPE (Coalition of Prison Evangelists). One goal of COPE is to assist the church in creating a support system for the Christian prisoners coming out of institutions. Prison Fellowship has also endorsed a model called *Koinonia House,* which began in Illinois, and is spreading nationwide as small residential facilities supported by local churches.

The International Perspective. Some prison ministries have a dynamic effect around the world. Prison Fellowship is chartered in over sixty countries worldwide; BGM is active in Mexico and the Caribbean; Good News Jail and Prison Ministry has chaplains in India, Thailand, Brazil, Africa, and the Baltics; COPE has an extensive evangelism in Eastern Europe in both Latvia and Estonia; and the late Chaplain Ray made many trips to Russia and Eastern Europe and his materials are used in Europe, Africa, the Middle East, and Russia.

Jail and prison ministries are largely evangelical and non-denominational FAITH MISSIONS, depending on the support of individuals and churches. Collectively, they are motivated by the need to bring the living gospel of Jesus to prisoners, and the mandate of sacred Scripture and not simply "well doing." They take their mandate for ministry from Matthew 25:36, where Jesus clearly identified with the incarcerated; Luke 4:18, where Jesus expresses his mission "to proclaim freedom for the prisoners . . . to release the oppressed"; and from Hebrews 13:3, which commands: "Don't forget about those in jail. Suffer with them as if you, yourself were there. Share the sorrow of those being mistreated, for you know what they are going through."

DON SMARTO

Problem of Evil and Mission, The. Religious worldviews all sense the need to explain suffering and moral evil, although some give greater attention to this than others. There is no single problem of evil that applies to all religions; the reality of suffering, combined with other beliefs about the cosmos, the religious ultimate, and the human person, produce distinctive problems within the various traditions.

Evil in World Religions. Monotheistic religions such as JUDAISM, Christianity, and ISLAM place evil in a subordinate relationship to God, the righteous Creator of all that exists. The task then is to account for evil without making God directly responsible for it. Islam, for example, recognizes evil as the product of human moral failure. But whereas in Christianity evil is a problem because it is perceived to conflict with God's love and goodness, in Islam it is a problem because it seems to conflict with God's omnipotence. Thus the QUR'AN and later Islamic theology stress that Allah is in control of all that occurs; in some sense, even suffering and evil come from him.

Religious traditions stemming from the Indian subcontinent (HINDUISM, BUDDHISM, JAINISM) look to *karma* as an explanation for present sufferings and evil. Living things are said to be continually being reborn. One's state in this life is determined by one's behavior and dispositions in previous existences, just as present actions will shape future lives. *Karma,* the impersonal principle that regulates such rebirths, is said to provide an explanation for the great disparity in our world—why some people suffer so much and others relatively little. On a popular level, dissatisfaction among Hindus and Buddhists with strictly philosophical explanations for suffering is reflected in the widespread belief in many demons, spirits, and gods who are responsible for our ills.

Common to the Hindu and Buddhist traditions is the view that evil and suffering are rooted in ignorance. This is related to an ontology that distinguishes between levels of reality and truth, ascribing evil and suffering to lower or penultimate levels. Thus in Advaita VEDANTA HINDUISM and ZEN BUDDHISM suffering and evil are regarded as the result of introducing a false duality into an essentially nondualistic reality. "Evil" dissolves when dualistic categories are overcome. But this relativizes evil by making the good–evil distinction applicable only on a lower level of reality; ultimately there is no duality between good and evil.

Perhaps no religion concentrates so directly upon the experience of suffering as does Buddhism. Although suffering seems to be a universal and inescapable phenomenon, Buddhism claims that there is a way to eliminate it. Suffering is rooted in desire or craving, and by eliminating desire suffering is eradicated as well. In Buddhism there is no problem of reconciling evil with an all good and all powerful God, for there is no such God in Buddhism. Both the problem and its solution are offered in strictly naturalistic terms of cause and effect.

In FOLK RELIGIONS worldwide evil is dealt with by invoking the realm of spirits, demons, ancestors, and gods—both as explanations for our problems and as powers for controlling evil and suffering.

The Problem of Evil in Christian Theism. The problem in Christian theism is to reconcile evil with the biblical picture of God as all good and all powerful: If God is perfectly good, he must want to abolish all evil. If he is limitlessly powerful, he must be able to abolish all evil. But evil exists. Therefore, either God is not perfectly good or he is not limitlessly powerful.

It is helpful here to distinguish several issues. The *existential* or *pastoral problem of evil* must be distinguished from strictly philosophical or theological problems. The pastoral problem is concerned with providing appropriate resources and support for one who is struggling with the reality of suffering or evil in his or her own experience.

The *logical problem of evil* maintains that there is an explicit or implicit contradiction among the following statements: (1) God is omnipotent, omniscient, and all good; (2) God exists; (3) God created the world; and (4) the world contains suffering and evil. If so, then orthodox Christian theism is falsified. But clearly the statements are not explicitly contradictory. The burden thus lies with the critic to provide missing premises which, when combined with the above, would produce clear contradiction.

Much more influential is the *evidential problem of evil*, which maintains that the mere presence of evil and suffering, or the amount of evil in our world, while not logically inconsistent with the existence of God, nevertheless provides strong evidence against the existence of God. Some critics claim that the mere presence of any evil in our world counts against THEISM; others hold that the degree of evil, or the apparently gratuitous nature of evil, counts against Christianity.

One can respond to the evidential problem in various ways. Some theologians are content with demonstrating: (1) that evil is not logically incompatible with Christian theism; and (2) that belief in God is not implausible or unreasonable given the reality of evil. Others go beyond this to offer a *theodicy*, which attempts to show why God allows evil, offering an explanation for evil and suffering within Christian theism.

It is important to note that evil and suffering are phenomena every WORLDVIEW—not simply Christian theism—must address. The viability of any worldview depends in part upon its ability to account for evil satisfactorily. Furthermore, in assessing the case for Christian theism, the problem of evil should not be treated in isolation. Evil is one of a large set of factors relevant to the question of God's existence. The reality of evil does provide negative evidence against theism, but this must be evaluated along with a variety of other factors providing positive evidence for God's existence.

Although the struggle with suffering is a recurring theme in Scripture (Job, Psalms, Habakkuk, Romans, 1 Peter, James), nowhere are we given a complete explanation concerning the origin of evil or why God chose to create a world in which such suffering would ensue. Scripture never denies the reality of evil or glosses over its horrible consequences. Yet God is righteous and is not the direct cause of evil. Ultimately, the origin of evil is hidden in God's sovereign will and the mystery of moral freedom.

Christian theologians have generally responded to the challenge of evil by emphasizing three themes. First, since the time of Augustine many have stressed that moral evil is due to the misuse of human free will. Evil and suffering are the result of sin, the abuse of freedom. Second, Christians hold that God permits evil for the sake of achieving a greater good. As Augustine put it, "God judged it better to bring good out of evil than to suffer no evil to exist." A world in which persons can make moral choices and mature spiritually, even if this results in significant evil and suffering, is better than a world without such freedom. Related to this is the "soul-making" theodicy, which emphasizes that God's purpose for his creatures is conformity to the image of Jesus Christ and that it is precisely an environment in which there are real moral choices and struggles with adversity that allows for such spiritual development.

Third, the heart of the gospel lies in the staggering claim that the power of evil has been broken in the incarnation, the cross, and the resurrection of Jesus Christ. The infinite and holy God has identified with evil humanity by becoming a man, suffering evil at the hands of sinful men, being put to death on the cross, and then demonstrating God's victorious power over evil through the resurrection of Jesus Christ (1 Cor. 15). The same power that raised Christ from the dead is available to believers today (Rom. 8:11).

The Problem of Evil and Missions. Central to Christian missions is leading others to Jesus Christ, the only one through whom there is victory over evil and suffering. It is only as persons are given new life in Christ and are liberated from the dominion of darkness and brought into the kingdom of God (Col. 1:13) that they can experience victory over evil. Evil is an enemy that already has been defeated at the cross (Col. 2:15), although for a limited time its influence continues.

The problem of evil is particularly acute today, after a century of unprecedented violence and suffering. Few criticisms of Christianity appear more frequently, or in as many diverse contexts, than the problem of evil. Secularists claim that evil falsifies Christianity. Hindus and Buddhists assert the superiority of their own traditions because of the alleged inability of Christianity to account for evil. A culturally sensitive apologetic that responds to the challenges presented by the problem of evil is essential to missions.

HAROLD A. NETLAND

SEE ALSO Apologetics.

Bibliography. J. Bowker, *Problems of Suffering in the Religions of the World;* J. Hick, *Evil and the God of Love;* M. Peterson et al., eds., *Reason and Religious Belief: An*

Introduction to the Philosophy of Religion; J. Wenham, *The Enigma of Evil.*

Proclamation Evangelism. Proclamation is at the very heart of New Testament evangelism. People need to be told the gospel. In the GREAT COMMISSION, Jesus sent his followers not only to be salt and light in the world, but to preach repentance and forgiveness of sins to all nations and to function as his verbal witnesses (Luke 24:47f.). And after asking, "How can [people] believe in the one of whom they have not heard? And how can they hear without someone preaching to them?" the apostle Paul replied that "faith comes from hearing the message, and the message is heard through the word of Christ" (Rom. 10:14, 17).

But what exactly is to be included in the message that we have been commissioned to proclaim? Paul preached that of first importance was the death of Christ for our sins, along with his burial and resurrection, as verified by his postresurrection appearances (1 Cor. 15:1ff.).

And how ought we to proclaim the gospel? Scripture makes it clear that there is no one best way to tell others about Christ. Rather, we need to look for the way that is best in each given situation. Jesus' approach was unique in each of the twenty-eight different evangelistic encounters recorded in the Gospel of John. The apostle Paul, too, regularly tailored his approach to fit his audience, becoming "all things to all [people] so that by all possible means [he] might save some" (1 Cor. 9:22). There simply is no "one-size-fits-all" evangelistic strategy that is equally effective in every situation and with all kinds of people. Our proclamation needs to be personalized, contextualized, and keyed to people's felt needs.

We often tend to associate proclamation especially with public preaching to large audiences. The New Testament, however, gives examples not only of mass evangelism, but also of small-group evangelism, household evangelism, and personal evangelism, each having its appropriate place. There are scores of additional methods and combinations of methods that we can utilize to proclaim the gospel, including the printed page, audio and video recordings, the MASS MEDIA, STORYTELLING, and drama. However, when deciding on a particular method or medium for the proclamation of the gospel, it is important that we assess its appropriateness for a given audience and its likely perceived credibility and degree of impact in a given context.

Much debate has taken place in recent years concerning the relative merits of confrontational versus relational evangelism (*see also* LIFESTYLE EVANGELISM). Research clearly indicates that unbelievers most often respond to the gospel within the context of a personal relationship with a Christian believer. The more impersonal and intrusional the WITNESS, the lower the rate of positive initial response and long-term followthrough. Actually, the function of an impersonal witness to the gospel tends often to be more pre-evangelistic than evangelistic; that is, seeds are planted which might only later bear fruit within the context of a more relational witnessing situation (*see* PRE-EVANGELISM).

Proclamation is frequently contrasted with two other approaches to evangelism: presence and persuasion. Evangelism is typically most effective when all three approaches are utilized consecutively. Before we ever open our mouths, it is often essential that we demonstrate by our lives and our good deeds what it means to be a Christian, establishing the credibility of both the message and the messenger. Then, having earned the right to be heard and having aroused people's interest, we can begin to proclaim to them the gospel of Christ. However, proclamation alone is insufficient. We want not simply to communicate truth on a take-it-or-leave-it basis, but to persuade people to act upon the truth. We want not only to be faithful in proclaiming the message, but to be successful in actually making disciples. Using the terminology of DONALD MCGAVRAN, we want our witness to be based not just on a theology of search, but on a theology of harvest. And this is where persuasion comes in.

In 2 Corinthians 5:11 Paul wrote, "Since we know what it is to fear the Lord, we try to persuade [people]." Then later in the same chapter he wrote, "We implore you on Christ's behalf: Be reconciled to God" (v. 20). We see in this passage that Paul accompanied his proclamation with passion. And we, too, need both to proclaim the gospel, so that people will hear and understand, and to engage in persuasion, so that people might actually believe and be converted.

We need to be careful, of course, that our persuasion does not become manipulation; that our pleading does not become coercion. We need always to respect the integrity of the person and not apply undue pressure in order to secure results at any cost. Also, although in our witness there is a place for emotion, we need to guard against allowing emotion to degenerate into shallow emotionalism, lest people make only superficial decisions for Christ, based strictly on the emotion of the moment, rather than on a deliberate, well-thought-out act of the will.

RAYMOND P. PRIGODICH

SEE ALSO Presence Evangelism.

Bibliography. J. C. Aldrich, *Life-Style Evangelism: Crossing Traditional Boundaries to Reach the Unbelieving World;* L. Ford, *The Christian Persuader;* M. Green, *Evangelism in the Early Church;* P. Little, *How to Give Away Your Faith;* J. Peterson, *Evangelism as a Lifestyle;* J. Stott, *Christian Mission in the Modern World;* C. Van Engen, *You Are My Witnesses.*

Profession of Faith. Public declaration of faith in someone or something. The word *profession* appears in the KJV as a translation for *homologia* (1 Tim. 6:12; Heb. 3:1; 4:14; 10:23). The term denotes "confession, by acknowledgment of the truth" (Vines). Hebrews 10:23 (KJV) provides the source for the phrase "profession of faith." Here it indicates the truth that the church has held to and should continue to hold.

The phrase may also be used interchangeably with "confession of faith" or "statement of faith." In this sense it is a concise written statement of belief. Therefore, to profess one's faith may mean simply a public recital or declaration of the accepted creed of a church or body of believers.

God's Word commands us to "hold fast the profession of our faith without wavering" (Heb. 10:14 KJV). The public declaration of faith should not be confused with a one-time event or regular recitation of a creed. Rather, it should be a continual demonstration unfolding from the life of the believer, and of the church.

This is important missiologically, because the CONTEXTUALIZATION of the gospel must consider what it looks like for a new believer in a specific context to publicly declare his or her faith. This will take on various forms, and may include public statements, demonstrations (baptism, walking to the altar), changed behavior, restitution, or charitable deeds. In whatever way it is expressed, it must not be limited in concept to a single event or a doctrinal statement, but must be evident in the daily life of the believer.

As a church, the faith we profess must be real and vibrant. The profession of our faith is the continual, personal, practical and public demonstration of our adherence to the unchanging truths found in the Word of God.

PAUL F. HARTFORD

SEE ALSO Confession.

Bibliography. P. G. Hiebert, *Anthropological Reflections on Missiological Issues*; C. Van Engen, *God's Missionary People*; W. W. Wessel, *BDT*, p. 422.

Prokhanov, Ivan Stepanovich (1869–1935). Russian evangelical church leader. Born into a family of Molokan (a Protestant denomination indigenous to Russia) believers who had recently moved to the Caucasus to avoid persecution, he was baptized in January 1887.

In 1888, he entered the St. Petersburg Institute of Technology to study mechanical engineering. Before graduating in 1893, he began to form his role as leader of the evangelical movement in Russia.

In 1889, he started clandestinely publishing and distributing *Beseda* (Symposium) to encourage Russian believers. This launched his prolific career in religious publishing, which included the periodicals *Khristianin* (Christian) and *Utrenni-* *aia Zvezda* (Morning Star), several hymnals (he wrote 614 hymns), and numerous other religious works.

He traveled to Europe to avoid exile and studied theology there from 1895 to 1898, but he was later arrested and imprisoned twice. In 1913, he formed a Bible School in St. Petersburg, but he is best known for his formation of the All-Russian Union of Evangelical Christians in 1910, which grew to over 30,000 members by 1923 and which later merged with the Baptists to form the All-Union Council of Evangelical Christians-Baptists in 1944. In 1928, Prokhanov heeded a warning from a kind government official and left the country never to return. He died having left behind a legacy that remains today.

JAMIE FLOWERS

Bibliography. I. S. Prokhanov, *In the Cauldron of Russia*; J. L. Wieczynski, *The Modern Encyclopedia of Russian and Soviet History*.

Promotion of Mission. In the New Testament we do not see the kind of promotion of the missionary enterprise we find today. The command of Christ and the working of the Holy Spirit in the local congregation were enough to make a church send and support missionaries—at least in Antioch. Jerusalem, however, needed some proactive promotion.

The strongest sending bodies among twentieth-century American churches were born as mission sending agencies in the nineteenth century: the Christian and Missionary Alliance and the Southern Baptist Convention. It takes less than 200 CMAers to send out a missionary, for example, while it takes 1,800 evangelicals in general to send one missionary. Probably no more than 10 percent of evangelical congregations in North America have a strong missions promotion program, such as an annual CHURCH MISSIONS CONFERENCE. Given this track record, God seems to have raised up other means of promoting his purposes of world evangelism—parachurch organizations, mission sending agencies, conventions, student movements, Bible colleges, and, of late, "mobilizers."

Of the hundreds of mission sending agencies, several have been so successful in recruiting that they dwarf the average denominational mission boards: WYCLIFFE BIBLE TRANSLATORS (6,000+), Campus Crusade for Christ (15,000+), Youth With a Mission (7,000+), and Operation Mobilization (2,000+). All these are specialized: translation, campus, or short-term. Conventions in this century have been the catalysts for mission promotion, beginning with Edinburgh (1910), continuing through the triennial URBANA student conventions under InterVarsity Fellowship (1946 and following), advanced by the congresses initiated by BILLY GRAHAM (BERLIN [1966] and LAU-

SANNE [1974]), and culminating in the great conventions in Korea in the 1980s and 1990s.

Student movements have energized the missions movement, beginning with the STUDENT VOLUNTEER MOVEMENT at the close of the nineteenth century and continuing through the Student Foreign Missions Fellowship (initiator of Urbana, merged with IVF), and, later in the century, smaller student movements like the Caleb Project.

In the great half century of North American missions advance following World War II, the Bible colleges led the way. It was said that 80 percent of American missionaries in that era had a Bible college background. It is interesting that the decline in missions interest in the churches and the decline of the Bible college movement in the latter quarter of the twentieth century have paralleled one another.

Since those traditional means of promoting missions have become less effective, a new breed has emerged, as yet unorganized, but who refer to themselves as "mobilizers." Advancing Churches in Missions Commitment (ACMC), The U.S. Center for World Missions, one of its many spinoffs, the Frontier Missions Movement, and the AD 2000 and Beyond movement are representative.

In the field of publishing there are several journals devoted to promoting missions, both mission agency journals and independent journals like *Frontiers*. Perhaps the most influential publication has been Patrick Johnstone's *Operation World*, a prayer guide with a distribution of hundreds of thousands.

The mysterious thing about promotion is that no matter what we may do, it is God's sovereign intervention that has been the successful promoter of missions. The surge of World War II veterans, who had seen a needy world firsthand, muscled the missions enterprise at midcentury. Then came the emergence of a powerful Third World mission initiative and, closing out the century, the mighty ingathering in China with no missionary assistance at all! God is still sovereign, and the sovereign God's method is still the church in which his Spirit is free to move.

ROBERTSON MCQUILKIN

Prophetic and Identity Movements. Social renewal movements through which people seek identity in the midst of dislocation. While the distinction between the two terms is typically blurred, generally speaking those that are dominated by charismatic and visionary prophets or prophetesses are called prophetic movements. They typically are seen in regions of the world newly impacted by the forces of MODERNIZATION or COLONIALISM. In traditional societies, modern change agents provoke an unavoidable need for social, cultural, and religious readjustment. In these times of great upheaval, prophets often emerge who are able to reinterpret the sociocultural and religious order.

These movements have been studied in such diverse locations as Brazil, Colombia, the Caribbean area, Melanesia, the Philippines, Indonesia, New Zealand, sub-Sahara Africa, Russian Asia, and among Native Americans in North America. Despite cultural differences, they usually manifest most or all of the following characteristics: (1) An individual possesses some familiarity with a major religious tradition (usually Christianity), receives a revelation (commonly in a dream or vision), and begins to proclaim this new message to a receptive population. (2) There is a dramatic break with some traditional ways, particularly those concerned with magic. (3) Rituals and symbols emerge that contain elements of both the traditional and modern religious systems. (4) The typical concerns of FOLK RELIGIONS, such as healing, protection from evil powers, and divine guidance, are retained. (5) The movement promotes moral reform, spiritual renewal, and identity-recovery for a people undergoing profound cultural change, often with political ramifications. (6) A remarkable missionary zeal propels the movement across tribal and national boundaries.

The great majority of prophetic movements has occurred in sub-Saharan Africa. Two of the continent's best-known and most influential prophets were WILLIAM WADE HARRIS of Liberia (1850–1929) and SIMON KIMBANGU of Congo (1889–1951). In 1910, Harris, in obedience to a vision, set off on a preaching tour that led him across coastal Cote d'Ivoire and Ghana. By 1914, an estimated 120,000 people had responded to his call to embrace the "one true and living God" by discarding fetishes and other religious traditions. The movement swelled the ranks of Methodist and Catholic missions alike, and spawned independent movements such as the Harrist Church and the Church of the Twelve Apostles. Kimbangu's faith was nurtured in a British Baptist mission, but after a cataclysmic three months of public ministry in 1921 he had gained nationwide renown as a healer who could even raise the dead. Masses flocked to hear him preach. Giving himself up for arrest to nervous Belgian officials after three months in hiding, Kimbangu spent the remainder of his life in prison. Meanwhile, his followers clandestinely diffused his message throughout Belgian and French Congos and Angola until legally recognized in 1959.

Early missionary response to prophetic movements was characteristically negative. Many of the churches and organizations they spawned, however, remain to this day. The Harrist Church in Cote d'Ivoire numbers over one hundred thousand; the Kimbanguist church numbers around 5 million. Their endurance has obligated missionaries and missiologists to assess whether to embrace them as true sister churches in Christ.

Some are clearly syncretistic and heretical, yet have moved significantly away from primal animism. Others could be labeled Hebraic by their ambivalence toward the New Testament gospel and their identity with the culture and prophetic themes of the Old Testament. Some, however, have emerged as independent Christian churches that confess the primacy of the Scriptures and the person of Jesus Christ. In the postcolonial age, church and mission leaders have increasingly voiced their conviction that the latter type of prophetic movements may indeed be culturally authentic expressions of the universal Church of Jesus Christ.

J. MICHAEL CONNOR

Bibliography. M. L. Martin, *Kimbangu: An African Prophet and His Church.*; D. A. Shank, *Prophet Harris, the "Black Elijah" of West Africa;* H. W. Turner, *Religious Movements in Primal Societies.*

Prophets. *See* OLD TESTAMENT PROPHETS.

Proselytism. The term "proselyte" derives from a Greek word, *proselutos,* often translated as "one who comes over." It is not a word from classical Greek, but is a Septuagintal term, being found more than seventy times there, translating the Hebrew term *ger.* This biblical word was originally used to describe non-Israelites who chose to live as residents within Israel, but it developed to mean someone who voluntarily converted to the religion of Israel.

References to proselytes began to multiply during the late Hellenistic and Roman periods, when multitudes of non-Jews, attracted by the radical monotheism and high moral standards of Judaism, began to convert to the Jewish faith and lifestyle. Many of these people, particularly among the men, stopped short of the final commitment of conversion but dedicated themselves as much as possible to the Jewish faith and practice. The term "proselyte" came to be used in a more technical sense for such people.

In more common usage, however, the term came to mean someone who converted from any one faith to another. Proselytism became a general term for the propagation of one's faith, and people and religions were referred to as proselytizing if they gave high priority to trying to persuade those of other faiths or ideologies to convert. In contemporary Judaism it is still used to describe non-Jews who convert to Judaism, and is employed without value judgments of any kind, although the Jewish people would not see themselves as a proselytizing community. In everyday Christian contexts, it has remained, more or less, a description of highly motivated, high-profile, and well organized EVANGELISM.

In the specific context of Christian missiology, however, the term has become one that is used in certain quarters to refer to unethical behavior in the attempt to persuade others. The first negative use of the word comes from post-Enlightenment eighteenth-century writers who associated it with those who, in their view, claimed to have a monopoly on truth. It was then associated with the type of person who aggressively tries to win converts to a cause or ideology (including religion). In the wake of the two World Wars of the twentieth century, and in particular since the 1960s, we have seen a further development of this use of the term in the writings of European and American theologians.

The documents of Vatican II include the following statement: "Proselytism is a corruption of Christian witness by appealing to hidden forms of coercion or by a style of propaganda unworthy of the gospel." The WORLD COUNCIL OF CHURCHES endorsed this same definition: "Proselytism embraces whatever violates the right of the human person, Christian or non-Christian, to be free from . . . whatever . . . does not conform to the ways God draws free men to himself."

In other words, in spite of the ongoing assumption by most Christians that proselytism is simply a synonym for evangelism, albeit of a planned and organized nature, it is now being used in a more technical sense by certain missiologists and others to refer only to a specific type of "evangelism." It refers to the abuse of people's freedom and the distortion of the gospel of grace by means of coercion, deception, manipulation, and exploitation. This type of "recruitment of members" does go on in a number of cults and NEW RELIGIOUS MOVEMENTS, and so there is clearly a need for some term to describe such unacceptable behavior, but confusion has certainly been created by the use of this existing and well-established word.

Christians need to be alert to this issue of appropriate and inappropriate methods of sharing their faith with others, but they must also be aware of the agenda of those who wish to present the very desire to share one's faith as unacceptable in principle. In particular, the church must resist the growing tendency in Western cultures to label all Christian evangelism as, by definition, an expression of the arrogance and insensitivity presupposed in this new understanding of proselytism.

A major task of missiology as we approach the twenty-first century is to facilitate a confident motivation to share the gospel that is scrupulously ethical in its every expression.

WALTER RIGGANS

Bibliography. E. Barker, *New Religious Movements;* M. E. Marty and F. E. Greenspahn, eds., *Pushing the Faith*; *The Ecumenical Review* 13 (1961): 79–89; G. Sabra, *Theological Review* 9 (1988): 23–36.

Providence of God. Christians everywhere confess, "And we know that in all things God works for the good of those who love him, who have been called according to his purpose" (Rom. 8:28). This simple conviction concerning God's sovereign control over us and our world reveals belief in what theologians have called the doctrine of God's providence.

The providence of God was long ago defined in the Westminster Shorter Catechism as "his most holy, wise and powerful preserving and governing all his creatures and all their actions." Scripture teaches that God is in sovereign control, yet not in an arbitrary or fatalistic way. His preservation and governing of all God's creatures is based on his unchanging nature of love, justice, wisdom and power (see Pss. 145:9, 17; 104:24; 103:19; 135:6; Rom. 11:36; Col. 1:16, 17). In his sovereign governing, God displaces neither the activity nor the responsibility of humans (see Acts 2:23; 1 Cor. 15:10; Gal. 6:7, 8; Phil. 2:12, 13). And though in control, he must never be conceived as the Author or Cause of evil (James 1:13, 14; 1 John 2:16), even though he may turn it for good (Gen. 50:20).

The truth of God's providential care over his children and world has strengthened missionaries through many trials. The following quotations (all from *World Shapers*) illustrate, in just three areas, how belief in God's providence has benefited missionaries.

Concerning Safety. "One cannot help feeling a deep, inward, peaceful consciousness that though we are absolutely shut off from every human help, yet we have protection more secure than any consul can afford—the omnipotent arm of Jehovah" (ALEXANDER MACKAY, 1991, 76).

"Safety does not depend on our conception of the absence of danger. Safety is found in God's presence, in the center of His perfect will" (T. J Bach, 1991, 73).

"The safest place for yourself and the children is in the path of duty" (JONATHAN GOFORTH, 1991, 73).

Concerning Mental Health. "The abiding consciousness of the presence and power of my Savior preserved me from losing my reason. . . . I had my nearest and dearest glimpses of the face and smile of my blessed Lord in those dread moments when musket, club, or spear was being leveled at my life" (JOHN G. PATON, 1991, 71).

"'If God be for us, who can be against us? We may boldly say, The Lord is my helper, and I will not fear what man shall do unto me' (Ps. 118:). The effect of these words at such a time was remarkable. . . . My soul seemed flooded with a great peace; all trace of panic vanished; and I felt God's presence was with us. Indeed, his presence was so real it could scarcely have been more so had we seen a visible form" (ROSLAND GOFORTH, 1991, 74).

Concerning Finances. "God's work done in God's way will never lack God's supplies" (J. HUDSON TAYLOR, 1991, 74).

"Wants are things we think we need; necessities are things God knows we need. God will supply our needs, not our wants" (T. J. Bach, 1991, 75).

"Financially, I have almost nothing to show for my 44 years of labor on behalf of the Indians. We own an automobile that you folks gave us two years ago, a home in the jungles of Peru, five hundred dollars in savings for the education of children and that's all. In the wealth of friendship, however, we are millionaires" (WILLIAM CAMERON TOWSEND, 1991, 76).

It is hard to conceive of the missionary enterprise, with all of its trials and victories, apart from a belief in God's providence. Knowing their sinfulness and weakness, together with the immeasurable opposition that confronts them, what missionary can long stand in the pathway of service without a firm conviction in the providence of God? Do missionaries ever despair? Yes. Why? One reason is that, like Peter, they take their eyes off of Christ, the reigning Lord to whom "all authority in heaven and on earth has been given" (Matt. 28:28; 14:22–33). They temporarily forget or doubt the wonderful truth of God's providential control. What can we do to help? First, pray that the work of Christian missions will be carried out with an unshakable faith in the providence of God. Then share with your missionary friends some verses from God's Word that will encourage them with the promises of God's constant love, support, and guidance (e.g., Prov. 3:5, 6; 16:9; 21:1; Dan. 4:34–37; 1 Cor. 10:13; Phil. 4:13; Heb. 13:5, 6; 1 Peter 1:6, 7).

ED GROSS

SEE ALSO Sovereignty of God.

Bibliography. V. Hampton and C. Pleuddemann, *World Shapers; The Shorter Catechism.*

Psychology. Mission agencies began utilizing the services of psychology in the late 1920s to assist with screening and CANDIDATE SELECTION. It was nearly another forty years, however, before they began discovering additional uses for applied psychology. During the later 1960s through the mid-1980s, the missions-psychology interdisciplinary focus broadened to include such concerns as preparation for CULTURE SHOCK, training in personal and family ADJUSTMENT TO THE FIELD, training in INTERPERSONAL COMMUNICATION and CONFLICT RESOLUTION, team development, crisis intervention in emergency situations, and personal and family counseling as needed (sometimes on the field, sometimes during home leave). This was the era in which a few psychologists began taking trips to various mission fields as short-term consultants, workshop leaders, and counselors. It was also a time in which a few master's level counselors began to go to various fields as short-term or career missionaries.

The 1980s saw an increasing number of Christian psychologists become aware both of the potential contributions they could make to missions and of the fact that as believers they, too, were under the mandate of the GREAT COMMISSION. There was also an increased awareness of new ways that psychologists could contribute to the work of missions. A major impetus to this awakening occurred in 1983 when two integrative journals *Journal of Psychology and Theology (JPT)* and *Journal of Psychology and Christianity (JPC)* each published an issue focusing entirely on psychology and missions. The *JPT* later produced two additional issues devoted to psychology and missions.

Another stimulus to the missions-psychology collaboration came by way of the three International Conferences on Missionary Kids (ICMK). The first was held in Manila in 1984, the second in Quito in 1987, and the third in Nairobi in 1989. These conferences were convened because of increasing interest in the uniqueness of the experience of THIRD CULTURE KIDS (TCKs) and particularly the missionary kids (MKs; *see* MISSIONARY CHILDREN). Missionary parents, mission personnel, school personnel, psychologists, and both adolescent and adult MKs came together to try to understand better both the blessings and the difficulties of being an MK/TCK and how to begin to address some of the difficulties.

From these conferences came an awareness of the need for research to try to answer important questions. Ten mission agencies linked up with six psychologists to form a research group: MKCART (MK Consultation and Resource Team). The missions prioritized the questions and the psychologists began the research. A major focus was on the boarding school experience, addressing questions such as the most important characteristics to seek in boarding school personnel to create healthy and positive experiences for the students.

Yet a third influence on the expansion of the psychology-missions alliance was the springing up of various interdisciplinary conferences such as the Mental Health and Missions Conference held each November since 1980 in Angola, Indiana. For the most part, such conferences have not been related to any specific organization but have simply been comprised of an informal network of mission leaders and mental health professionals who desire to interface with each other in order to stimulate each other, learn from each other, grow together, and work together to further the cause of missions.

Another influence in the growth of the missions-psychology alliance was the establishment of "care centers" to minister to bruised, broken, traumatized, or burned out missionaries—centers such as Link Care in Fresno, California, and Tuscarora Resource Center in Mount Bethel, Pennsylvania, where psychologists counseled missionaries in pain. As missionaries were restored to personal wholeness and effectiveness in ministry others took note, which resulted in greater openness on the part of missionaries and member care personnel to seek help when it was needed.

All of these influences worked together to bring about a rapid expansion of the missions-psychology interface in the 1980s and 1990s. Perhaps the greatest expansion took place in the area of member care (*see* MEMBER CARE IN MISSIONS). More missions began to place a higher priority on ministering to their missionaries' psychological needs, seeing the relationship between psychological and spiritual well-being and the relationship between such well-being and missionary effectiveness. In nearly all mission agencies, the personnel departments began to become increasingly sensitive to the psychological well-being of missionaries, as evidenced by the focus of discussion taken at the annual IFMA/EFMA Personnel Conferences. A number of mission agencies began to form member care departments or create new positions, such as member care director, to oversee the overall wellness of their missionaries. A few missions created intra-agency counseling departments to help care for their missionaries. One of the biggest concerns facing those involved in member care has been finding ways to provide for the needs of missionaries pioneering among the least evangelized people groups, missionaries who are in places where few member care resources are available or even feasible.

In the late 1980s and the 1990s, the collaboration of missions and psychology took on some new challenges. A few doctoral-level psychologists became overseas career missionaries to develop programs to provide more fully for the emotional health of missionaries on the field. Other psychologists went overseas as missionaries to utilize their professional skills to point people in pain to the Wonderful Counselor. Yet others went abroad to help establish Christian schools of psychology to train Christian counselors to provide biblically and psychologically sound counseling for their compatriots. These last two missionary efforts have highlighted the need to understand CROSS-CULTURAL COUNSELING and to help national believers develop counseling models that adequately reflect their culture while remaining thoroughly biblical. This challenge is especially great in non-Western cultures.

Another challenge in the international expansion of the missions-psychology partnership is working with the newer sending countries to incorporate member care into their mission practices. Helping multinational teams work together in a healthy and effective manner also remains a major endeavor. As they move into the twenty-first century, missions and psychology continue to inform each other in facing the challenges of the internationalization of their alliance.

JEANNE L. JENSMA

Bibliography. N. S. Duvall, *JPT* 21 (1993): 54–65; D. J. Hesselgrave, *JPT* 15 (1987): 274–80; W. F. Hunter and M. Mayers, *JPT* 15 (1987): 269–73; G. B. Johnson and D. R. Penner, *The Bulletin of the Christian Association for Psychological Studies* 7:4 (1981): 25–27; *JPT*, vols 11:3; 15:4; and 21:1; K. S. O'Donnell and M. L. O'Donnell, eds., *Helping Missionaries Grow: Readings in Mental Health and Missions.*

Psychology of Religion. Psychologists have been studying various dimensions of religious commitment for more than a century. Those with a vision for promoting the practice of evangelism and discipleship in every culture of the world might find it helpful to reflect on the growing consensus of thought emerging in the field about a number of relevant topics. As Paloutzian (1996, 2) has noted, a "small glance at the prevalence, scope, and effects of religion reveals how sweeping are its influences and how important it is to learn what psychological research has to say about it."

Definition. Broadly defined as the study of religious beliefs and behaviors from a social science perspective (Hood, Spilka, Hunsberger, and Gorsuch, 1996), the field raises many important questions that should especially interest those committed to the task of making Jesus Christ known, loved, and believed throughout the world. These include: (a) how do people differ in the ways in which they are religious? (b) what factors appear to facilitate the development of religion across the life span? (c) how can we best understand the process of religious conversion? and (d) how might religion relate to health and well-being? (see Malony, 1995).

Although the bulk of the empirical research in the psychology of religion has been limited to the broad Judeo-Christian tradition, scholars have differed widely in how they conceptualize or study religious beliefs and behaviors. Some have chosen to focus primarily on religion at the *personal* level (how an individual finds a sense of wholeness or completeness in life). Others prefer to study religion at the *social* or *societal* levels of analysis (the collective beliefs and practices of a group). Generally speaking, scholars tend to emphasize religious *function* (individual or group processes) rather than religious *substance* (individual beliefs or doctrinal statements). Further, researchers and theoreticians tend to emphasize one or more of the *dimensions of religious commitment* in their endeavors: (a) religious belief (ideological); (b) religious practice (ritualistic); (c) religious feeling (experiential); (d) religious knowledge (intellectual); and (e) religious effects (consequential). Unfortunately there is no widely agreed-upon definition of religion, nor is there widespread consensus on the best study approach (see Paloutzian, 1996 or Wulff, 1997 for helpful discussions).

Religious Orientation. Those who are deeply involved and invested in Christian ministry recognize that people have different expressive styles in their faith. Perhaps one of the most enduring distinctions in the field is between those individuals who appear to *live* their faith (truly informed and consistent believers), and those who seem to *use* it (belief and effects of religion in practical life are widely inconsistent). For decades, researchers have been comparing and contrasting *intrinsic* (committed) and *extrinsic* (consensual) religious orientations, especially as they relate to morally relevant attitudes and behaviors (*see* Kauffmann, 1991 or Clouse, 1993).

There is little debate now whether religious variables can be good (even powerful) predictors for some important human behaviors, including altruism, cognitive complexity, dogmatism, prejudice, and subjective experience (Hood, Spilka, Hunsberger, and Gorsuch, 1996). Numerous complex and highly sophisticated scales are now available that measure important dimensions of religious orientation or styles of faith (see Malony, 1995 for useful examples).

In light of the available evidence, it no longer seems helpful to merely state that someone is a Christian unless a concerted effort is made to clarify the precise manner in which that individual internalizes (incorporates) specific Christian beliefs and behaviors. Obviously, this can be a complex and even daunting challenge. As Malony (1995) has clearly demonstrated, it is certainly possible to show ways in which such diverse variables as age, gender, personality, and race can all significantly impact religious beliefs and behaviors without being condescending, patronizing, or reductionistic. Coupled with anthropological insights for missionaries (Hiebert, 1986) or overseas workers (Kohls, 1984), these useful social science findings have important implications for effective and sustained ministry.

Religious Development. Certain religious beliefs and behaviors appear to change considerably in the course of a person's life span. For example, the religion of children often develops from the vague to the concrete to the abstract, often following almost predictable stages of increasing cognitive and emotional sophistication (Paloutzian, 1996). In addition, more recent research on adolescents and young adults (Kauffmann, 1991) has raised important questions about the meaning of religious commitments in these formative years. Specifically, how can we best understand the ways in which emerging developmental capacities and significant life events potentially impact the striving for a sense of wholeness or completeness?

Astley and Francis (1992) offer many keen insights on faith development and spiritual formation from a Christian perspective. Adolescence, especially in highly industrialized societies, might best be viewed as a period of intense religious interest, experimentation, and doubt, moderated significantly by parental, peer, or other important socializing influences (e.g., religious education). Frequency of Bible reading and private prayer appears to increase with age beyond adolescence well into late adulthood. Many other important generational differences have been noted in this literature and possible explanations for those changes have been the focus of intense discussions and lively debates. In the course of development, particular religious practices may be performed for quite different reasons at different ages, reflecting complex and intertwined personal and social influences. Ideally, this development results in a more mature, holistic, and integrated Christian faith—where beliefs and behaviors are woven together in a manner that truly shapes the formation of Christian character, convictions, and community (see Garber, 1996). Our efforts to go and make disciples among all peoples will be significantly thwarted if we fail to consider the ways in which individual differences and developmental realities potentially impact the ability of people to hear and respond to all aspects of the Christian gospel (see Gangel and Wilhoit, 1994).

Religious Conversion. Probably no topic has received more careful attention in this literature during the last century than the study of religious CONVERSION. Generally speaking, three types of belief acquisitions have been described. The *sudden conversion type* occurs in a very brief time span (minutes, hours). Emotional factors are assumed to play an important role. Conversion is usually followed by a period of intense religious activity that gradually fades over time. The *gradual conversion type* occurs in a much longer period of time (days, months, years). Intellectual factors are assumed to be of the utmost importance. Involvement in religious activity is much slower and more deliberate, and never reaches the peak of the sudden type. Finally, the *religious socialization type* is related to an individual's entire life (she or he cannot recall a time of not believing). It is assumed to be related to learning, modeling, and reinforcement. Involvement in religious activity also tends to be gradual and seldom reaches the levels of either the sudden or gradual conversion types. In actual practice, the distinctions are often blurred, perhaps suggesting considerable overlap in the typology. What is clear, however, is the lingering suspicion in the literature that sudden conversions are highly vi-

olate, and more prone to recidivism and relapse (see Malony, 1991).

There are some helpful models of conversion that have been offered in recent decades (see Benner, 1988). It might be best to view conversion as an on-going process of holistic and integrated transformation, mediated by complex and intertwined affective, intellectual, and interpersonal variables. At a minimum, the existing typology might suggest more flexible and inclusive strategies for evangelism and discipleship that respect the mind, minister to the "heart," and seek to promote peace and justice. Finally, Paloutzian (1996) has offered some keen insights on the characteristics of cult leaders, on the process of "snapping" and brainwashing in new converts, and on ways to build immunity and resistance to the most destructive aspects of new religious movements (see pp. 163–73).

Health and Well-Being. There is little debate in the literature that religion has the potential for being an important resource when coping with the demands of everyday living—and especially so when an individual faces severe health difficulties or life-threatening situations (Hood et al., 1996). At their best, religious beliefs and behaviors offer people meaning, some measure of control, and a sense of self-esteem (efficacy). Prayer, ritual, and social support all have the potential to offer real hope in the midst of intense pain and suffering.

Attempts to demonstrate that there is a distinctive type of personality that lends itself to being religious have been largely unsuccessful. Furthermore, no consistent trends have emerged that would suggest that a general state of non-well-being or abnormality can be significantly correlated with religiosity (Paloutzian, 1996, 259). Only recently have significant efforts been made to determine whether or not distinctly Christian beliefs and behaviors significantly influence health and well-being (Wulff, 1997). A responsible conclusion in the interim would be that religious persons are generally neither better off nor worse off than other persons.

How we define health and well-being is extremely important. It is certainly possible for an individual to be a paragon of psychological wholeness as this is traditionally defined, and yet be living without faith in God through Jesus Christ. While it seems reasonable to assume that Christianity will enhance an individual's health and well-being, it would be hard to conclude from a more careful reading of the Scriptures that there could be any guarantees (see Jones and Butman, 1991).

Conclusion. The attempt to look for psychological processes that might underlie certain religious beliefs and behaviors has been a major emphasis in this field of scholarly endeavor for more than a century. To reduce Christian faith and experience to mere psychological dynamics—or to disillusion the faithful with an overly objective and dispassionate approach to the subject matter—is certainly unhelpful in our attempts to promote the Christian gospel. I would like to believe it is possible—perhaps even imperative—that we affirm and utilize the most helpful aspects of contemporary social science research.

Horace Fenton (1973), an outstanding Latin American missiologist and educator, offers us an unusually helpful perspective on this matter: "What we think is a direct, forthright message more often sounds to the unbelieving world like a complicated, confusing business—a message cluttered with qualifications and corrupted by footnotes and appendices. We too often give to cultural or social convictions—inherited or otherwise acquired—the same standing as the scriptural truths we have received from God by revelation. Sometimes people are kept from the Savior, not by the offense of the cross, but from the offense of the things we have added to the cross. God's true message is hidden by the accretions we have allowed to accumulate" (p. 14). These "barnacles," Fenton argues, greatly complicate the task of world mission. Perhaps a more careful reading of the literature in the psychology of religion might lessen our rather predictable tendency as evangelicals to add to the revelation of God.

RICHARD BUTMAN

Bibliography. J. Astley and L. Francis, *Christian Perspectives on Faith Development: A Reader;* D. Benner, *Psychology and Religion;* B. Clouse, *Teaching for Moral Growth;* H. Fenton, *The Trouble with Barnacles;* K. Gangel and J. Wilhoit, *Handbook of Spiritual Formation;* S. Garber, *The Fabric of Faithfulness: Weaving Together Belief and Behavior During the University Years;* P. Hiebert, *Anthropological Insights for Missionaries;* R. Hood, B. Spilka, B. Hunsberger, and R. Gorsuch, *The Psychology of Religion: An Empirical Approach,* 2nd ed.; S. Jones and R. Butman, *Modern Psychotherapies: A Comprehensive Christian Appraisal;* D. Kauffmann, *My Faith's O.K.—Your Faith's Not: Reflections on Psychology and Religion;* L. Kohls, *Survival Kit for Overseas Living;* 2nd ed.; H. Malony, *Psychology of Religion: Personalities, Problems, Possibilities;* idem, *The Psychology of Religion for Ministry;* R. Paloutzian, *Invitation to the Psychology of Religion;* D. Wulff, *Psychology of Religion: Classic and Contemporary.*

Pudaite, Rochunga (1927–). Indian Bible translator and president of Bibles for the World. Born in Senvor, Manipur, India, he was the son of an energetic Christian pastor and one of the first converts of the Hmar tribe. He received his early education at the Churachandpur Mission School, then attended St. Paul's College (Calcutta), and graduated from the University of Allahabad, Wheaton College (MA), and Northern Illinois University (MS, 1961). During this time, Pudaite accomplished one of his life's goals by translating the entire Bible into the Hmar language.

In 1958, Pudaite became the president of the Indo-Burma Pioneer Mission, which by 1970 had established 65 village schools, a high school, and a hospital and commissioned some 350 national missionaries. At one point, over 80 percent of the Hmar professed to be Christians.

In 1971, Bibles for the World was founded in Wheaton, Illinois. Its initial goal was to send copies of the Bible to everyone listed in the Calcutta and New Delhi phone books. The first fifty thousand copies sent out brought more than twenty thousand responses. Since that time over 14 million Bibles have been distributed throughout the world.

The original mission work (now called Partnership Mission) grew enormously until today it has 240 churches, established as the Evangelical Free Church of India, of which Pudaite was the moderator in 1996.

WALTER A. ELWELL

Puerto Rico (United States Dependent Area) *(Est. 2000 pop.: 3,825,000; 9,100 sq. km. [3,514 sq. mi.]).* The beginnings of Protestantism in Puerto Rico are identified with the liberalism of intellectuals and the Americanization of the island after the 1898 war with Spain. Thereafter, in the 1920s and 1930s, a large number of fundamentalist groups established a foothold, along with a number of Pentecostal churches. The largest of these, the *Iglesia de Dios Pentecostal,* was founded in 1916 by expatriate Puerto Ricans who had become involved with Pentecostals first in Hawaii and then in California before establishing congregations in their homeland. In turn, the Puerto Rican groups established Hispanic churches in the cities of the eastern seaboard of the United States. It is believed that 30 percent of the Puerto Rican population are evangelical Protestants, and an estimated 85 percent of the evangelical Protestants are Pentecostal. Baptist and Seventh-Day Adventists each account for an estimated 5 percent of the total, and Methodists 2 percent. Puerto Rican evangelicals have been responsible for sending missionaries throughout the Caribbean and the mainland Latin American countries. Puerto Rican preachers have been among the most effective evangelists in stadium crusades throughout the Latin American mainland republics in recent decades.

EVERETT A. WILSON

SEE ALSO Caribbean.

Bibliography. A. Lampe, *The Church in Latin America, 1492–1992,* pp. 201–15; J. Rogozinski, *A Brief History of the Caribbean: From the Arawak and the Carib to the Present.*

Pure Land Buddhism. Devotional schools of MAHAYANA BUDDHISM that focus on the Buddha

Amitabha and his transcendent realm known as the Pure Land. The origins of Pure Land Buddhism are in India, but it gained its largest following in East Asia, after the Pure Land scriptures were translated into Chinese. From China, where it was known as "Ching Tu," the Pure Land traditions passed on to Japan, where the largest schools are the "Jodo Shu" (Pure Land) and the "Jodo Shinshu" (Pure Land True Sect). The Pure Land schools are the most popular form of Buddhism in Japan today.

Three aspects of the Pure Land tradition are especially significant. First, Pure Land Buddhism teaches that rebirth in the Pure Land (culminating in *nirvana*) is attained by reliance on the grace and merit of the Buddha Amida (Japanese for Amitabha). Unlike other forms of Buddhism, Pure Land rejects "self-effort" in attaining liberation. Believers, while holding a rosary with 108 beads supposedly left by Amida, chant the "nembutsu," a prayer of faith and gratitude to Amida. The Japanese Shinran Shonin (1173–1263), founder of the Pure Land True Sect, emphasized that anyone could reach the Pure Land at death by relying solely on the merits of Amida Buddha. Amida, while still a Bodhisattva, had vowed that he would not become a Buddha until he had accumulated sufficient merit to save all who would call on him for rebirth in the Pure Land. Shinran, sometimes called the "Buddhist Martin Luther" for his doctrine of salvation by grace alone, composed the following hymn:

> Although the great chilliocosm may be filled with flames,
> Yet he who hears the Holy Name of the Buddha,
> Always in accord with steadfastness, Will freely pass to the Pure Land.
> Have ye faith in Amida's vow which takes us in eternally,

Because of him, of his great grace the light superb be thine.

However, there is a fundamental difference between Pure Land Buddhism and Christianity in that whereas Amida is understood to be a human being who attained divinity through his own efforts, and thereby earned sufficient merit to transfer to others, Christianity maintains that Jesus Christ is the incarnate Son of God. The grace of Amida, then, is fundamentally different from that of Jesus Christ, because true grace must originate from the almighty God himself.

Second, the notion of the Pure Land has some similarities to the concept of heaven or paradise in Christianity. Pure Land believers maintain that heaven (the Pure Land) is the destiny of believers and that hell awaits unbelievers. Closer inspection, however, reveals that the Buddhist Pure Land is substantially different from biblical eschatology and the scriptural accounts of heaven and hell.

Third, it is significant that Pure Land Buddhism has been most popular among the lower strata of society. Followers of the Pure Land traditions are aggressive in outreach to the common people. Thus the form of Buddhism that evangelicals in Asia are most likely to encounter is Pure Land Buddhism. Significant similarities between aspects of Pure Land Buddhism and Christianity offer possibilities for points of contact with Pure Land Buddhists, thereby facilitating evangelism. However, Christians must be careful to emphasize the very clear differences between Pure Land Buddhism and the gospel of Jesus Christ as well.

BONG RIN RO

Bibliography. A. Bloom, *Shinran's Gospel of Pure Grace;* E. A. Burtt, ed., *The Teachings of the Compassionate Buddha;* E. Conze, *Buddhism: Its Essence and Development;* P. O. Ingram, *Journal of the American Academy of Religion* 39 (1971): 430–47.

Qatar *(Est. 2000 pop.: 605,000; 11,000 sq. km. [4,247 sq. mi.]).* Qatar, a small protrusion jutting northward from the eastern edge of the Arabian Peninsula, is a barren desert not far from Bahrain. This peninsula was almost uninhabited for most of the Christian era. Nomadic Christian tribes passed through the area hundreds of years ago, such as the Ghasannid tribe. However, there was little of value there and the population was extremely small. Now there are perhaps fifty thousand people living in the country. Qatar, with the discovery of oil in 1939, became one of the leading producing areas of southwestern Asia. Its rainfall is less than four inches per year and there are few wells, which makes agriculture nearly impossible. Before oil was discovered people lived on the pearl industry or camel trading.

With the discovery of oil many from different nationalities flooded into the country to work in the oil fields. Among this group of workers were a number of Christians. They began small group meetings and in a quiet way have shared a witness. The Roman Catholic Church has a school there mostly for children of this outside work force and religious activities with it. A number of evangelical believers also have had employment and worship together in small groups or homes. At present a regular church is not permitted to exist. There are no resident missionaries working there. In addition any tent makers would be severely restricted and deported if they attempted an open witness. Some young men have studied abroad and been exposed to the Christian message. They are not permitted to express an opinion regarding their response to that message.

The several Arabic radio programs beamed in this direction may make an initial impact as well as the new Christian television satellite program. A number of people have written asking for the Bible and asking questions about Christianity. It is hoped that in the future the continued pressure on the peninsula by Qataris who have studied abroad, the regional democratization, and new concerns for individual rights and freedoms will lead to an easing of the restrictions and the possibility of opening up a regular church.

GEORGE E. KELSEY

Bibliography. R. B. Betts, *Christians in the Arab East;* S. Moffett, *A History of Christianity in Asia;* W. H. Storm, *Whither Arabia?;* J. S. Trimingham, *Christianity Among the Arabs;* S. M. Zwemer, *Heirs to the Prophets.*

Qualifications for the Missionary. The most important qualification for the missionary is an attitude of submission and obedience (Phil. 2:5–8). Spiritual disciplines (prayer, fasting, Bible study) are closely related to such an attitude, and thus are primary qualifications for missionary service. Ultimately, missions is a matter of the heart; spirituality is thus a bedrock necessity for one involved in the endeavor. The fruits of the Spirit (Gal. 5:22–23) have specific applications in cross-cultural ministry and are most essential.

In addition to spiritual qualifications, it is also important for the candidate to have sound physical and emotional health. The rigors and stresses of missionary ministry will usually heighten or increase weaknesses. This is especially true in the arena of interpersonal relationships.

In another era, physical hardships in various world areas may have been a formidable barrier to overcome, but in the twenty-first century, getting along with co-workers and working under indigenous leadership represent far greater hurdles. The leaders of many denominations and mission boards cite personal incompatibility as the number one cause of missionary failures. Versatility, humbleness, adaptability, good humor, and a willingness to take orders are especially needed when working in another culture. These psychological qualifications are indispensable.

Increasingly, churches and mission agencies recognize that there must be education for missionary service. This training is being provided at colleges and seminaries throughout the world. Anthropology is a discipline that is invaluable for the missionary. Knowledge about other cultures and customs and the ability to critique one's own culture are very important. Candidates learn about ETHNOCENTRISM (valuing other cultures by their own) and racism (the condemnation of other groups) and how harmful attitudes like these can devastate the growth of the church.

The prospective missionary should learn how to enter another culture (CULTURE LEARNING), learn another language (SECOND LANGUAGE ACQUISITION), and minimize CULTURE SHOCK. A global perspective should be developed, including a knowledge of WORLD RELIGIONS. A thorough understanding of the Christian faith and the ability to communicate that faith through culturally sensitive EVANGELISM are essential.

Some missionary training programs now include an internship component, in which the candidate is placed in a cross-cultural setting within the home nation. He or she is then guided by a mentor in adapting to different customs and language, while at the same time learning the proper missiological principles in the classroom.

Current strategy and sound doctrine learned in a suitable training program must be combined with submission to Christ and obedience to his will. Only then will "the sent one" be an effective conduit through which God's love can flow to a fractured world.

CHARLES R. GAILEY

SEE ALSO Candidate Selection.

Bibliography. P. Hiebert, *Anthropological Insights for Missionaries;* M. Jones, *Psychology of Missionary Adjustment.*

Qualitative Research. Qualitative research refers to the tradition that is concerned with human behavior and function as observed primarily in natural social situations. Eclectic in nature, qualitative research methods draw from the social and behavioral sciences. The common characteristic of qualitative research is an extended period of fieldwork. As applied to missiology, qualitative research is concerned with questions of meaning at the worldview level.

Qualitative Research Methods. Within the complex world of human interactions, qualitative research must begin with a research problem that is sufficiently narrow in focus. Common sources of research problems include: discussions with others who are working in the area; literature dealing with specific problems that require further research; and personal experience that raises concerns over specific issues. From the perspective of missiology, research problems often emerge from either personal or collective field experience. Once the problem has been identified, the researcher develops a research question that will determine the nature, boundaries, and method of the study. A practical consideration for missiology is the applicability of the potential findings to the wider missions community, which in turn justifies the allocation of resources.

In qualitative methods the researcher is the research instrument for the whole process. As such, the researcher becomes part of the lives of the participants, interacting with them in their social world. Accessibility and practical considerations must therefore be evaluated before the project begins to assure its viability. Beyond the issues of access are the ethical issues that are ultimately determinative, particularly in missiological research. Due to the nature of missionary work, determining the feasibility of a research project is a matter for careful consideration at many levels. Once a decision to conduct field research has been made, the researcher begins the process of gaining access to the context(s) required for the study. Again, this will be determined both by the nature of the research problem and by the sensitivities necessitated by the mission strategy. It is important to note that in most settings, a degree of reciprocity with participants is required to establish both cooperation and sustainable relationships.

The research problem and the role of the researcher generally determines the qualitative method used in the study. Four primary methods are used: (1) observational studies; (2) textual analysis; (3) interviews; and (4) recording and transcribing. While each method is distinct, they are often combined or used sequentially during the research process. In most cases, observation and interviews are used extensively. Data generated in the research are recorded as fieldnotes, which are analyzed for both linguistic and cultural categories. In addition to pencil-and-paper records, audio and video recording are increasingly used in qualitative research. Documents are another valuable source of data, including written records, minutes, correspondence, literature, and biographical material. The analysis and interpretation of data is an integral part of the research process that continues throughout the study. Although quantification of data may be used, the basic analyses of qualitative research are nonmathematical.

The final stage of research is the written or verbal reports that present the findings. The form of the report will vary depending on the audience, but usually includes a written document that may be published for internal or external use. The extent of the use of a research document has a direct bearing on the form and content of the report. This is particularly true of missiological research, where the nature of the missionary task goes beyond the acquisition of knowledge. Due to the nature of qualitative research, ethical considerations are crucial both at the level of research viability and in the distribution of the findings.

Contemporary Relevance. Interest in mission research has grown rapidly in the past several decades, as seen in publications such as the *Evangelical Missions Quarterly, Missionalia, Missiology, International Bulletin of Missionary Research,* and the publications of MARC. The statistical work of D. Barrett and the country profiles of P. Johnstone have been particularly influential at the level of stimulating missionary interest, prayer, and strategic planning. Among the other significant contributions have been qualitative studies by researchers combining their work with the pursuit of advanced degrees in seminaries and schools of world mission.

Missiological research is the interaction of at least four elements: the theological foundations of missionary praxis; the historical study of Christian missions; the strategic quantitative knowledge of social phenomena; and the qualitative understanding of contextual realities. As the fourth element, qualitative research makes its unique contribution through extensive contact with people in their own worlds. Through in-depth studies of specific contexts, researchers focus on meaning and the construction of social worlds. Hampered by the length and style of reporting, widespread use of qualitative research has been limited. However, as technology improves, qualitative information will be more accessible to missiologists in order to better interact with the other elements of missiological research.

C. Douglas McConnell

See also Ethnographic Research.

Bibliography. B. F. Crabtree and W. L. Miller, *Doing Qualitative Research;* B. Glaser and A. Strauss, *The Discovery of Grounded Theory;* C. Marshall and G. B. Rossman, *Designing Qualitative Research;* M. B. Miles and A. M. Huberman, *Qualitative Data Analysis;* S. L. Peterson, *Mission Studies Resources for the Future;* D. Silverman, *Interpreting Qualitative Data;* A Strauss and J. Corbin, *Basics of Qualitative Research;* J. Van Maanen, ed., *Qualitative Research Methods Series.*

Quantitative Missiology. Application of quantitative measurement and data analytic methods and modeling to understanding and applying missiological concepts in the practice of mission. The rightly celebrated advances in computer-assisted research, even if held in database format, are not by definition automatically quantitative.

Every major movement in modern missions has been associated with data gathering and analysis, however rudimentary. William Carey's *An Enquiry into the Obligations of Christians to Use Means for the Conversion of the Heathens* contained extensive world demographic data. The 1907 Egypt conference on Muslim evangelism led by Samuel Zwemer reviewed global data comparing Muslim and non-Muslim populations. The World Missionary Conference (Edinburgh 1910) preparatory materials included world survey data. Regional action flowing from Edinburgh expanded these data as a basis for cooperation. From just before the midpoint of this century, Leslie Brierley published the *World Christian Handbook* series, and this incubated the monumental *World Christian Encyclopedia (WCE),* edited by David Barrett. In between, the useful and informative prayer/data *Operation World (OW)* series edited by Patrick Johnstone has been a rich source of global information. The Missions Advanced Research and Communication (MARC) Division of World Vision published both the *North American Protestant Oversees Directory,* subtitled *The Mission Handbook,* begun by the Missionary Research Library, and the *Unreached Peoples* series, all containing some measure of raw data.

Extensive data are gathered yearly by churches, denominations, and mission agencies (Barrett, 1995). Several centers exist that have at least a part-time research function and that gather and report some implications of this raw data, although surprisingly little analysis is ever done on these rich sources.

In what sense are the above and other missions data research truly quantitative? Most initiatives have proceeded from the North, where activism has propelled intuitional rather than rigorous data reduction and analysis. Analysis does not move beyond variable measurement on the name and count level. Merely counting or ordering does not constitute quantitative analysis, even when the result is numeric.

Secular research, since 1939, has distinguished four levels of measurement that determine the appropriate use of data analysis and modeling techniques. And the simple truth is that very little has been done in missions that goes beyond the first two levels, namely, nominal, naming a category, unit of analysis, or phenomenon; or ordinal, ranking units (agencies, nations, etc.) in some ordered sequence. Further, very few attempts are made to relate variables to one another in conditional or causal hypotheses, even at these modest levels of measurement, usually referred to in research literature as qualitative methods. One reason for this is that the data collected are fodder for building dependent variables. Counting the results has absorbed missionary activists.

Missions researchers seldom collect data on explanatory variables. And, since the data collected rarely can be treated as interval or ratio scales, sophisticated correlation techniques and models or simulations are inappropriate or nonexistent. One exception to this rule is the almost unpublished research (Myers, 1996) in correlational analysis done by MARC in support of the development activities of World Vision International. Quantified relations among variables seldom appear in missions periodical literature. Even qualitative correlational analysis has been quite limited. The use of some limited data reduction techniques has occurred in missions periodicals and, in a rare case, inter-item correlation used to build variables. For example, most studies done in the church growth tradition have plotted growth against time, and then hypothesized about reasons for inflections in the plot, without introducing variable building measurement and analysis of possible conditional or causal variables with rigorous statistical models and tests. Seldom are data collected that could falsify the resulting speculation and conclusions. Data on nongrowing churches are rarely collected to compare with the growing congregations by means of even the simplest existing tests. The exclusion of the nongrowing congregations and comparative measurement on conditional or causal variables vitiates or at least leaves unsupported the conclusions advanced. Since data are not there, it may be that nongrowing churches are doing the things that allegedly are producing growth.

How much more helpful it would be if data were gathered and analyzed by correlation. This could thoroughly test whether and under what crisis conditions (for example, during recession or high unemployment, radical people displacement, such as migration, disaster, or refugeeism), accessions to the faith are affected.

Communications research surpasses other missions research in refining data to segregate markets and craft appropriate strategies utilizing the insights gained in the analysis. At its most straightforward, such research discovers what media are in use and therefore appropriate for the communication of the gospel. As practiced by James Engel, Viggo Søgaard, and their students, it may be the one instance of missions research that reasonably employs the possibilities of variable formation through data reduction tools. Such research may, therefore, qualify to be noted as quantitative. Other variable building seems to rely almost completely on face validity (i.e., I believe given items measure what I say they measure because they appear to me to do so).

Currently, the *WCE* is undergoing revision, as is *OW*. The AD 2000 Movement and related efforts continue the identification and adoption of people groups, as cooperation among researchers globally is promoted. In a spin-off from Global Mapping International and early MARC efforts toward cooperation, know-how is being widely disseminated and cooperation spurred toward greater information sharing.

In missions research, extensive data may exist, but sophisticated variable building, statistical hypothesis testing, modeling, and simulation are virtually nonexistent at this time.

SAMUEL WILSON

SEE ALSO Research.

Bibliography. D. B. Barrett, ed., *WCE;* idem, *IBMR,* 19:4 (1995): 154–60; W. Carey, *An Enquiry into the Obligations of Christians to Use Means for the Conversion of the Heatherns;* E. R. Dayton, S. Wilson, and J. Siewert, eds., *The Mission Handbook;* P. Johnstone, *Operation World;* B. L. Myers, *The New Context of World Mission.*

Quaque, Philip (c. 1741–1816). Ghanian pioneer Anglican missionary to Ghana. Quaque was chosen with two other Ghanaians to be sent to England in October of 1754 to be educated for the purpose of returning to Ghana as workers among their own people. One companion died of smallpox and the other of incurable madness.

In January of 1759, Quaque was baptized. With his ordination and appointment as "missionary, schoolmaster, and catechist to the Negroes on the Gold Coast" on May 17, 1765, he became the first non-European ordained in the Church of England.

Quaque arrived back home in February of 1766. He founded a school in his home, and thus began the work he would diligently perform until his death. Unfortunately, despite his ordination, he experienced continual opposition to his labors. He sought to perform his priestly duties among the European colonialists, but their debauchery and ridicule made his work difficult to carry out and, not surprisingly, also discouraged African response to his efforts. Another negative factor was that he had lost his first language while in England (a letter written in 1769 encouraged him to recover it).

Over his fifty years of ministry, Quaque baptized only a handful of people. Despite the relative paucity of results, his pioneering of African leadership and pastoral responsibilities stands as one of the early landmarks in missionary work in Africa.

A. SCOTT MOREAU

Bibliography. S. R. B. Attoh Ahuma, *Memoirs of West African Celebrities.*

Qur'an. The Qur'an (from an Arabic verb meaning "to read" or "recite") is regarded by Muslims as the word of God, sent down to the lower heavens during Ramadan and revealed from there to the Prophet Muhammad. Islamic theology declares that the Qur'an was not created; it is instead the earthly expression of the Well-Guarded Tablet *(al-lawh al-muhfuz),* which is with Allah. It is held to be untranslatable; one reads the Qur'an only in the original Arabic. The science of Qur'anic interpretation *(tafsir)* is extremely important in Islam.

Muslims believe that additional revelation became necessary after the *Tawrat* (the Torah, or Old Testament) and the *Injil* (the Gospels, or New Testament), revealed to Moses and Jesus respectively, were corrupted before their canonization was completed late in the fourth century A.D. The Qur'an is now considered to be the only reliable revelation of God, collected as it was within twenty years of Muhammad's death and allegedly transmitted through succeeding generations without alteration. Roughly equivalent to the New Testament in length, it is divided into 114 chapters, arranged from longest to shortest.

The Qur'an's major themes include the nature of God, the nature of humanity, the establishment of a worldwide Muslim community, the day of judgment, and the separation of humans into paradise and hell. A substantial amount of legal material is included as well, covering moral precepts, dietary regulations, and standards for community life.

Christians today are divided over whether specific portions of the Qur'an may be used to witness to Muslims. Some believe that certain narratives indicate the superiority of *'Isa* (Jesus) over Muhammad. That the second coming of *'Isa* rather than Muhammad forms a vital part of Islamic eschatology is a case in point. Presented properly, it is claimed, such passages may be used as a bridge to speaking of Christ's lordship. Others insist, however, that the overall teaching of Islam regarding the person and nature of Jesus (that he is merely a prophet and not part of a tri-une God) is so deeply ingrained in the Muslim mind-set that such an approach will inevitably fail. Further, it is claimed that to hold only certain passages as truthful runs the risk of raising the question why Christians accept only the passages with which they happen to agree, but consider the Qur'an as a whole to be the work of men, not a divinely inspired book.

Rather than attempting to show the similarities between Qur'anic teaching and biblical doctrine, it is perhaps best to emphasize the contrasts between the two. The Muslim scriptures display a sub-Christian view of Jesus, denying his divinity, crucifixion, and resurrection; they alter considerably the narratives dealing with the Hebrew patriarchs; and they substitute a work oriented soteriology for the biblical teaching of salvation by grace through faith alone.

LARRY POSTON

Bibliography. A. Y. Ali, *The Holy Qur'an: Text, Translation and Commentary;* F. Rahman, *Major Themes of the Qur'an;* A. A. Abdul-Haqq, *Sharing Your Faith with a Muslim.*

Rr

Race Relations. The reality of race and race relations has been central to the missions movement in the United States from at least the early nineteenth century. The combinations of increased scientific interest in race as a category (as evidenced in books as disparate as David Hume's *Of National Characters* in 1748 and Charles Darwin's *Origin of Species* in 1859) and the growing American dilemma of dealing with the enslavement of Africans and their descendants in this country helped focus the attention of people interested in missions, especially with respect to Africans and their descendants in the Western Hemisphere, on how to—and even whether to—evangelize people of other races.

Race as an ethnic designation has a rather recent history. By the dawn of the nineteenth century, Johann Friedrich Blumenbach's fivefold typology of races—Caucasian, Mongolian, Ethiopian, African, and Malayan—had not only gained ascendancy, but also reified racial categorization into a static, biological system, rather than a dynamic movement within human history. If race were to be seen as a static category, then race mixing could be rightly deemed "unnatural" and for Christians "sinful." Because of the presence of Africans and their descendants in the Western Hemisphere due to chattel slavery, these concerns took on special significance for black-white relations in the United States.

Christians engaged these issues in the early missions movement by (1) evangelizing Africans and African American slaves as equal members of the human family; (2) evangelizing Africans and African Americans slaves, but limiting their Christian freedom to the "spiritual realm" and denying their full human capacities and rights; (3) ignoring, denying, and even fighting against efforts to Christianize blacks out of a denial of their humanity and even fear of the power of the gospel to breed insurrection against the slavocracy. Of course, some slave missionary efforts reflected a basic compatibility between Christian faith and slavery, noting in a threefold defense of Christian slavery: "Abraham practiced it, Paul preached it, and Jesus is silent on the issue." Indeed, some missionary efforts to slaves revolved around the text "Slaves, obey your earthly master" (Eph. 6:5).

In the evangelization of Africa, race relations played a crucial role. Early efforts to send black Americans to Africa combined with efforts to repatriate freed blacks to Africa in colonization efforts was resisted by some free blacks who claimed America as their home. In the late nineteenth century, some missionary agencies declined to send blacks on African missions for fear of intermarriage with white missionaries. Others were concerned that blacks' interpretation of the recent Civil War in the United States as God's judgment against slavery would be dangerous baggage in evangelizing colonized Africans. As segregation became part of American denominational life, black denominations formed their own separate mission agencies and the work of missions became another reflection of American segregation.

The impact of the Civil Rights Movement and the changing patterns in American race relations affected missions work in bringing more blacks into the mainstream of home and foreign missions, and making visible to the larger society the steady stream of missionary activity sponsored by black churches at home and abroad. Contemporary efforts at racial reconciliation are building on the work of intergrationists in the 1950s and 1960s. The reconciliation accords reached between black and white Pentecostals in 1994 as well as ongoing conversations between the National Association of Evangelicals and the National Black Evangelical Association reflect the churches' sense that racial reconciliation is a part of kingdom work. Some missions organizations, such as Youth With a Mission, have even incorporated notions of identificational repentance and reconciliation as part of their missions strategies, noting the need for contemporary Christians to confess the sins of their forbears as part of the healing process.

HAROLD DEAN TRULEAR

Bibliography. G. Myrdal, *An American Dilemma: The Negro Problem in American Democracy;* T. Sowell, *Race and Culture: A World View;* W. Williams, *Black Americans and the Evangelization of Africa: 1877–1900*.

Racism. *See* ETHNOCENTRISM.

Radio Mission Work. Radio is used extensively in mission. The first wireless broadcast sent out to the world was an informal Christian program on Christmas Eve, 1906. The program included a solo, "O Holy Night," as well as a reading of the Christmas story from the Gospel of Luke. Christian radio broadcasting as such began on January 2, 1921, when a church service was broadcast in Pittsburgh.

The first missionary station, HCJB, "The Voice of the Andes," began broadcasting in 1931 from Ecuador. The Far East Broadcasting Company (FEBC) was founded in 1946, to be followed by Trans World Radio (TWR), Radio ELWA, and others. Today powerful Christian shortwave radio stations cover the world, broadcasting in numerous languages. There are also a few powerful medium-wave international stations, including TWR broadcasting from Monte Carlo in Southern Europe and FEBC from a powerful medium wave station covering a large section of China.

There are numerous local Christian stations, broadcasting on FM or medium wave to a single city or community. Some are commercial stations with professional staff, others are small and simple stations that depend on volunteers. For all, a high level of commitment is required.

Christian radio broadcasters are today on the air in some 200 different languages with 1,000 hours of transmitter time per week from major international broadcasters alone. This does not include local in-country stations, commercial time, and public broadcast time. The English (34%), Spanish (22%), Mandarin (8.6%), and Russian (6.4%) languages dominate on the international broadcasts; with the remaining 190 languages and dialects accounting for only 29% of the total. For example, there are eleven million English speakers in India, and a total of more than 102 hours of broadcasting each week is in English, but the fifty million Marathi speakers only get three hours a week, and the thirty-three million Urdu speakers get less than four hours per week.

In the hands of Christian communicators with the knowledge, means, and courage to use it creatively, radio has proven to be a powerful and effective tool in the task of world evangelization. Programs such as *The Old-Fashioned Revival Hour, Back to the Bible,* and others have made a significant contribution to the religious life of America. It is estimated that CHARLES E. FULLER had twenty million listeners a week up until his retirement in 1967.

In the international context, most of Southeast Asia's mountain-dwelling Hmong people have been almost completely cut off from any direct cross-cultural contact. Yet, on rare occasions when outsiders were able to visit, some reported strong indications of thousands of Hmong conversions to Christianity. In the early 1990s, the Vietnamese government conceded (somewhat regretfully) that hundreds of thousands of Hmong had become Christians. Far East Broadcasting Company's radio programs in the Hmong language offered the only available means by which most of these Hmong converts could have possibly heard the gospel. Indeed, in 1995 when two Hmong expatriates were able to conduct an extraordinary journey to several Hmong villages in northern Vietnam, they were greeted by multitudes of Hmong believers who welcomed them to impromptu open-air worship services which included original Christian songs exclusively featured on FEBC's Hmong broadcasts. Most had never met a Christian from outside their village, yet many were quite familiar with the Hmong songs heard only in FEBC's broadcasts.

In 1985, mindful of radio's potential impact among many of the world's hardest-to-reach peoples, the leaders of HCJB World Radio, Far East Broadcasting Company, Trans World Radio, and SIM (operator of radio station of ELWA in Liberia) launched the cooperative World by 2000 initiative to provide every man, woman, and child on earth the opportunity to hear Christian radio broadcasts in a language each can understand. Soon thereafter, broadcasters FEBA Radio and Words of Hope became active partners in the World by 2000 effort, which fostered an unprecedented level of cooperation among the various partner organizations.

The World by 2000 strategically targeted large language groups which had not been previously served by daily missionary radio broadcasts. These groups included many of the world's least evangelized peoples. By 1997, the World by 2000's list of megalanguages (each spoken by at least one million people) covered by Christian broadcasting increased by 80—raising up new groups of believers and planting new churches among many of these previously unreached peoples.

Because little or no broadcast media of any kind had been available in many of these languages, the sheer novelty factor of these newly launched programs attracts positive attention almost immediately. Although many of these peoples are relatively media-poor, the advent of regular radio broadcasts in their language has attracted considerable interest. Early on, listening among such media-starved peoples has tended to be avid, regular, and often a group experience. In northern Mozambique, for example, clusters of Lomwe listeners gather each night around one of the few radios to be found in their village. As the gospel message is thus regularly heard in a group setting, listeners often linger to discuss the program content after the conclusion of each Lomwe broadcast. In time, such a listening group can naturally become the nucleus for a new Christian congregation. As the Holy Spirit enables such newly formed fellowships to expand, each may blossom into a larger church, and/or start a daughter congregation. Evidence abounds that during the first seven years of Lomwe broadcasting from Trans World Radio/Swaziland to northern Mozambique, over 300 new churches were thus started by listeners. Church planting progress has since been reported among other Mozambican peoples who began receiving first-ever gospel broadcasts during the 1990s, including the Makhuwa, Makonde, and Sena.

Similarly, new churches have sprung up among listeners to many of the other pioneering radio broadcasts launched through the World by 2000 effort. The Banjaras of India, the Gypsies of central Europe, the Bariba of Benin, and the Chuvash of central Asia are just some of the notable examples. Although daily gospel broadcasts are still needed for dozens of megalanguage groups who remain unreached by Christian radio, steady progress continues to be made toward the World by 2000 goal. The accompanying examples of churches planted bear witness to the reliability of the Lord's promise that his Word will never return void. In addition, recent political developments such as the fall of communist regimes in Europe and the end of apartheid in South Africa have led to the added availability of many powerful international radio transmitters which had previously been used exclusively for the broadcasting of political propaganda. As a result, transmitters in Russia, Albania, Armenia, Poland, and South Africa have been added to the available inventory of super-powered international transmitters which are available for missionary broadcasting.

Radio can readily adapt to changing social and cultural conditions, and it has several advantages for Christian mission. It requires listening only, making it possible to reach all, including the more than one billion nonliterates. Radio uses sound only, which makes programming fairly inexpensive. It has wide coverage and can reach most people through the estimated 1.2 billion radio sets in use around the world. It crosses religious and political barriers. Furthermore, radio can handle a variety of program formats, limited only by the creativity of the producer.

Most Christian broadcasters ask for letter response from the listeners; in 1988, FEBC alone received approximately 615,000 letters from listeners. Unfortunately, most Christian radio ministries have not developed feedback systems that do not require mail, and thus non- and semi-literates are excluded.

VIGGO SØGAARD AND LEE DEYOUNG

Bibliography. E. G. Bowman with S. F. Titus, *Eyes beyond the Horizon;* F. A. Gray, *Radio in Mission.*

Ramabai, Pandita (1858–1922). Indian pioneer in educational and medical missions. Ramabai was one of the most popular native missionaries in India, an excellent example of indigenous mission to women in the Two-Thirds World. Having spent her early life in teaching pilgrimages with her family, once her parents and sister died, she and her brother continued their pilgrimages. She was called "Pandita" because of her knowledge in the Hindu scripture.

Married to a lower caste lawyer and widowed in her early twenties, she experienced the grief and agony of women in India. She went to England in 1883 to learn how to educate Hindu women and there came know Christ as her Savior.

Ramabai was involved in evangelism, education, Scripture translation, literature and social work, founding a mission, and organizing medical work. She ministered to women who were outcasts in society, giving them not only food and shelter, but also training for jobs and spiritual guidance. In addition to translating the Bible, she developed a Marathi concordance and lexicon and wrote many books. She was also deeply concerned to contextualize the gospel. For example, she utilized ideas from Hindu scriptures to communicate biblical truths, as well as Indian music and Indian forms of worship to make worship relevant to Hindu converts. In all of these ways God used Ramabai to bring many women of India from physical, emotional, mental and spiritual bondage into Christian freedom.

SAKHI ATHYAL

Bibliography. S. M. Adhav, *Panditha Ramabai;* C. Butler, *Panditha Ramabai Saraswathi: Pioneer in the Movement for the Education of the Child-widows of India;* H. S. Dyer, *Panditha Ramabai: The Story of Her Life.*

Rastafarian. *See* CARIBBEAN NEW RELIGIOUS MOVEMENTS.

Re-Entry Shock. *See* REVERSE CULTURE SHOCK.

Reached and Unreached Mission Fields. Since the mid-1970s intense debate has raged over what a mission field is and what it means for a field to be reached. In general, since the LAUSANNE CONGRESS ON WORLD EVANGELISM of 1974, the concept of a PEOPLE GROUP, defined by common language and culture, has displaced the older idea of a nation-state. There continues to be a discussion of whether the people groups to be evangelized should be defined more in terms of language or dialect (with over 12,000 in the world) or of culture (over 20,000). But leaving some latitude for those definitions, the chief ethnolinguistic groups have been identified.

But how do we determine when a group has been "reached"? In the mid-1980s there were said to be 12,000 unevangelized groups, but by 1990 that estimate was reduced to 6,000. With the advent of the AD 2000 and Beyond Movement, this was reduced to 2,000, then by 1995, to 1,600. Did the missionary enterprise advance that rapidly? No, the definition of "evangelized" or "reached" changed. Does "evangelized" mean that every person would hear with understanding the way to life in Christ as Mark 16:15 and Acts 1:8 seem to indicate? Or, as the objective set by some in recent years, does "evangelized" mean that every person would have access to the gospel? That is, when a church is near enough or there are radio broadcasts or book shops, the Bible has been translated into their language—everyone could hear the gospel if they wanted to. This greatly reduces the number of unevangelized people groups. Others opt to focus on Matthew 28:18–20 and Luke 24:47–48 and the goal of evangelism is said to be discipling the "nations" or people groups. But what is it to "disciple"? Some have said that when there is a witnessing church movement, the missionary task is complete. Others point out that a witnessing church movement in a tribe of 1,000 may mean the group is evangelized or "reached," but what if the group is 40 million in size? So others add the phrase, "capable of reaching its own people." If there is such a church movement, no more outside help would be needed to complete the task of evangelism, however defined. Still others define a reached people as those which are majority Christian. If Christian is used in an evangelical sense, however, no more than a handful of very small ethnic groups could be considered "reached" on that definition.

This debate is not academic nit-picking; it is very pragmatic, defining the task that remains and targeting those areas in which a church or mission should invest precious, limited resources. The consensus that seems to be emerging at the end of the twentieth century is to have a scale from "least reached" to "most reached." On this basis it can be said that there are at least 1,600 people groups larger than 10,000 in size in which there is no witnessing church movement capable of reaching its own people. If smaller groups are included, the number of unreached escalates to at least 6,000, including many with no gospel witness at all.

The majority of the least reached groups fall within the 10/40 WINDOW, a band of ethnic groups stretching east between the 10th and 40th degree latitudes (north) from the Atlantic Ocean to Indonesia in the Pacific. This embraces nations in northern Africa, the Middle East, and the Far East in which the least reached religious groups are concentrated: Islam, Hinduism, and Buddhism. These are not only the least reached,

they are the least reachable, the most resistant. In fact, because of religious, political, and cultural barriers, they are also the least accessible (see CREATIVE ACCESS COUNTRIES).

If "Christian" is defined as one who has a personal relationship with God through faith in Jesus Christ, and "mission field" is defined as any ethnolinguistic group in which there is no witnessing church movement capable of evangelizing that group, perhaps half the people groups of the world have been "reached." The other half need outside assistance, commonly called missionaries. If those groups with fewer than 10,000 were excluded from the tally, then the majority of the remaining people groups have been reached. If, on the other hand "reached" focuses on individuals rather than ethnic groups, and "access to the gospel" is the criterion, perhaps more than half the individuals of the world have been reached. If, however, "reached" means they have actually heard the gospel with understanding, far less than half could be considered reached.

The most succinct, reliable, and easily understood data on the reached or unreached status of each nation is found in *Operation World*. The most sophisticated composite of the efforts of the major research groups is found in *Status of Global Evangelization: Model and Database Design*, put out by Southern Baptist Convention, FMB and updated periodically.

ROBERTSON McQUILKIN

Receptivity. The dynamic state of a person or people in which, if presented with the Christian gospel in terms they can understand, they will respond favorably to this gospel.

Receptivity or responsiveness to the gospel is obviously demonstrated when people respond to the gospel by a faith commitment to Jesus Christ, are incorporated into congregations, and become responsible, reproducing believers. The degree of receptivity can be measured easily after a population has been presented with the gospel over time. However, it is more difficult to measure in advance.

The prediction of receptivity is one of the major concerns that faces missions in making decisions about either opening a new ministry or closing an existing one. Individual missions have developed research instruments for evaluating receptivity. Many of these instruments share a set of common assumptions. Two key assumptions include: (1) If some people in a community are responding to the gospel, others may be expected to respond as well. (2) If the people are experiencing significant WORLDVIEW change or worldview dissonance, or if they have experienced significant social, economic, or political changes, they may be expected to be receptive to the gospel (see also ANOMIE).

Receptivity is a dynamic condition that changes over time with a given person or a whole population. The variables that lead to one's being open to begin to move through the process of change to become a mature Christian vary over time. Two key sets of variables interact, but need to be assessed differently. The first set of variables relate to sociocultural concerns and the second to spiritual concerns.

Sociocultural concerns relate to a wide range of issues, including homogeneity/heterogeneity of the community, the rate of worldview change, previous knowledge of and attitude toward the Christian gospel, past experience with people who are perceived to be Christian, and the level of satisfaction/dissatisfaction with the present religious system.

Spiritual issues relate to the kinds of spiritual commitments the people have made. The history of the spiritual commitments of a person or a people sets the stage for the receptivity of the person or the people.

Receptivity affects the whole conversion process. David Krawthwol provides a descriptive sequence of the attitudinal change process. At each stage of the change process—receiving, responding, valuing, organization around values, and characterization by a set of values—the person or the community makes decisions (*see also* CHANGE, SOCIOLOGY OF). While the term "worldview" was not widely used when Krawthwol described this process, the process could be described as worldview change or the process of conversion. At each stage a person must be willing (receptive) to continue in the process. One may in the accepting of a new idea or in the acceptance of the gospel stop or stall the process, or may accelerate the process.

EDGAR J. ELLISTON

Bibliography. D. Krawthwol et al., *Taxonomy of Educational Objectives The Classification of Educational Goals Handbook II: Affective Domain;* D. McGavran, *Understanding Church Growth.*

Reconciliation. The Christian faith is fundamentally relational. It affirms that God has acted once and for all—decisively—in the life, death, and resurrection of Jesus Christ to bring the created order back to its original purposes. Pastor and homiletician Gardner C. Taylor argued that "the Bible has but one theme, that is, that God gets back what belonged to him in the first place."

This involves not merely the restoration of persons, the environment, and even the cosmos, but also the quality of relationships that they enjoyed at creation—the divine order in the heart of God as revealed in the Genesis account of beginnings.

In the beginning, God enjoyed full fellowship with humanity, unmarred by SIN. So too, there was harmony and PEACE in the relationships between humanity and CREATION, and between the first man and woman in the Garden of Eden. When sin entered the world, all of these relationships were damaged—sin separated humanity from a holy God. It also brought alienation between humanity and the ENVIRONMENT. Finally, it brought estrangement among people themselves, substituting blame and distrust for mutuality and complementarity (*see also* FALL OF HUMANKIND).

Reconciliation describes the process through which God works to restore these relationships. In the Book of Colossians, it is depicted as a cosmic process through which God in Jesus Christ reconciled "to himself all things, whether on earth or in heaven, making peace by the blood of his cross" (1:20). Here God brings nature into right relationship with himself through Christ, as well as showing his victory over demonic 'principalities and powers.' The souls of sinners are reclaimed as they trust the merits of Christ's blood.

The apostle Paul also depicts his ministry as a ministry of reconciliation. In 2 Corinthians 5:17–19 he affirms that there is new life in Christ, and that this life is "from God, who through Christ reconciled us to himself and gave us the ministry of reconciliation; that is, in Christ God was reconciling the world to himself, not counting their trespasses against them, and entrusting to us the message of reconciliation."

He goes on to describe his ministry as that of an AMBASSADOR OF GOD, representing him and pleading with persons on his behalf to be reconciled to God. In this sense, the missionary enterprise is one of representing Christ to a world in need of reconciliation to God, not merely the inculcation of doctrine or the spread of propositions. Rather it is the full-fledged acceptance of one's role as an ambassador for God's kingdom, preaching the gospel of reconciliation with God—the invitation to follow Christ as he brings all things into subjection to God. Missions at its core involves the proclamation and demonstration of the LOVE OF GOD for his creation, and the invitation to respond to his love through accepting his Son as Lord and Savior.

If reconciliation is a cosmic process, then missions involves the invitation to participate fully in the whole of the process. That is, the restoration of right relationships in the created order—the environment and surrounding interplanetary and interstellar space—and right relationships between human beings.

Paul recognizes this in pointing to the new fellowship created between Jew and Gentile in the body of Christ. This reconciliation in Christ he also calls "peace" (Eph. 2:14). Christ has "broken down the dividing wall of hostility by abolishing in his flesh the law of commandments and ordinances, that he might create in himself one new man in place of the two, so making peace." (vv. 14–15) To the Galatians, he wrote that in Christ "there is neither Jew nor Greek . . . slave nor free . . . male nor female" (3:28).

These latter passages have assumed great importance in contemporary conversations concerning missions because of the increased relevance of cultural CONTEXTUALIZATION in missions studies. As we have given greater weight to cultural contexts and become more clear about imperialism and power relationships, we have witnessed the need for a more sophisticated conversation about reconciliation across ethnic and cultural lines. Indeed, in the United States, missions organizations are looking at issues of cultural context not merely as a concern in overseas missions, but also working on how racial and ethnic reconciliation is to be sought within their own country.

At one level, the issue is, in the words of theologian Miroslav Volf, the "sacralization of cultural identity," the literal merger of cultural and religious commitments that gives people more of a sense of belonging to their cultural group than to Christ. Among racial and ethnic minorities, oppression can give the sense that loyalty to one's ETHNICITY is a stronger bond than that to other believers. And to those in the majority, the wedding of religion and culture often appears matter of fact, since they are the group in power and lack the critical distancing that comes from marginalization (*see* MARGINAL, MARGINALIZATION).

Some suggest that Christian faith is color-blind, in that God is "no respecter of persons." Others point to cultural difference as something to be celebrated—a rich diversity reflecting the creative genius of God. Few would opt for a segregated church which overemphasizes cultural or ethnic norms (*see also* HOMOGENOUS UNIT PRINCIPLE). Indeed, it may be that the ways in which Christians engage in the process of interpersonal and interethnic reconciliation within the church set an important agenda for worldwide missions on a planet beset by ongoing ethnic strife. Recent attempts at contextualizing theology, owning up to imperialistic cultural theologies, and the confession of our "ghettoization" of marginalized ethnic churches (by persons in both the majority and the minority) are steps in the right directions.

More radical ideas such as the recent practice of identificational or representational REPENTANCE (seeking the forgiveness of entire groups—such as the 1995 Southern Baptist apology for its attitudes on race and slavery—are still being debated (*see also* POWERS, THE). What cannot be debated is the ongoing work of God in Christ, as laid out in Scripture, to bring back what belonged to him in the first place.

HAROLD DEAN TRULEAR

Bibliography. R. P. Martin, *Reconciliation: A Study of Paul's Theology*; L. Sanneh, *Religion and the Variety of Culture: A Study in Origin and Practice*; M. Volf, *Exclusion and Embrace: A Theological Exploration of Identity, Otherness, and Reconciliation*; R. Washington and G. Kehrein. *Breaking Down Walls: A Model for Reconciliation in an Age of Racial Strife*.

Redemption and Lift. DONALD MCGAVRAN introduced the phrase "redemption and lift" to the field of missiology in his classic work, *Understanding Church Growth*. McGavran defined redemption as "Christ's saving activity in the human heart," in which Christ enters, makes a person a new creation, and leads the individual to repentance (1980, 296). This new life brings the person into church fellowship and mission activities, creating a secondary improvement, "lift." McGavran described lift as the great benefits new Christians gain from a congregation which provides medicine, education, technology, wealth, protection, and loving friendships. New Christians become middle-class members of the Christian community who "share in the general sense of well-being" even though they had not done so well in times past. This is what McGavran called "lift" (1980, 297).

McGavran warned of the danger of the "redeemed and lifted" becoming socially separated from former community relationships. While new converts may be persecuted and pressured by their former communities, McGavran warned that it is the church that often insists on a Christian's separation from the world. Having done mission work among people trapped in the Hindu CASTE system of India, McGavran seemed concerned about the dangers of a Christian caste system. On the mission field he observed that new Christians tended to become personally "cleaner" and acquire new attitudes toward germs, dirt, flies, and waste disposal. As they avoided civic affairs and non-Christian festivals, the gulf between Christians and former associates deepened to the point that effective communication ceased (1980, 298–99).

McGavran thus pondered: How might the church redeem and lift Christians without separating them from receptive sections of society? His solution was twofold: (1) Stress the open Bible and Spirit-filled life as essential aspects of redemption. Rather than rely on ivory tower specialists, put the Bible in the hands of people through literacy classes in churches. (2) View "lift" as a derivative aspect of redemption and, although a necessary derivative, the emphasis should be placed upon redemption (303).

McGavran described redemption and lift as a universal phenomenon not limited to the church geographically. David Barrett has since reported that about one-third of the world is made up of Christians who receive nearly two-thirds of the world's annual income and spend 97 percent on themselves (Barrett, 1983, 148). This trend continues as we approach the twenty-first century

(Barrett, 1995, 25), illustrating that redemption and lift remain crucial issues in missiology today.

PAUL HERTIG

SEE ALSO Church Growth Movement.

Bibliography. D. Barrett, *IBMR* 7:4 (October 1983): 146–51; idem, *IBMR* 19:1 (January 1995): 25; D. McGavran, *Understanding Church Growth*, rev. ed.

Redemption in Other Faiths. The common biblical words for "redemption" refer to deliverance from some evil by payment of a price. However, the Hebrew *pdh* and *g'l* occasionally seem to have a broader significance: God's deliverance from adversity without payment of a price (2 Sam. 4:9; 1 Kings 1:29). But while a wider sense of redemption is sometimes seen in the Hebrew Scriptures (e.g., in Ruth), the climactic event of redemption is the deliverance of Israel in the exodus. The New Testament develops this further. Although redemption still has a national application (Luke 24:21) and a wider meaning (e.g., Heb. 11:35), it refers primarily to the atoning work of Jesus Christ through his sacrificial death for the sin of the world. Other faiths contain parallels to the wider biblical concept of redemption, and even to some extent to the specific saving work of Christ at the price of his sacrificial death. But such parallels are only a shadow of the unique redemption in Jesus Christ.

Modern Judaism believes in the redeeming triumph of good over evil both nationally and individually. The Talmud uses *pdh* to speak of ransom, while *g'l* signifies redemption dependent on the covenant people's repentance and obedient good deeds. Thus a price is paid, deliverance is achieved for the nation and for the believer, God triumphs in his goodness over all evil.

In Islam the QUR'AN admonishes people to ask forgiveness for sin (40:55; 47:19; 48:2). The word for deliverance relates to the Hebrew for "cover" and thus to the atonement, which "covers" sins. Sura 37:107 talks of the sacrifice of Ishmael as a ransom; this is in keeping with the annual *qurban* sacrifice offered by Muslims on *Eid-ul-adha*, but seems to contradict 22:37 with its teaching that animal sacrifices are not propitiatory.

In Brahmanic Hinduism, sacrifice *(ajna)* generates cosmic power and plays a meaningful part in stimulating the gods to bring blessing to the cosmos. But *ajna* does not entail expiation of sin and bears little if any idea of propitiation of the righteous anger of God or the gods. Yet such sacrifices do deliver from the effects of evil, bringing blessings and material benefits to the world. Through animal sacrifices individual worshipers may also look to the gods to answer prayers, deliver from evil, and bring good things into their lives.

In Chinese and Japanese traditional religions sacrifices were propitiatory rather than expiatory; they were the means of approach to the gods and to the ancestral spirits of the nation. In Japan people also believed that sacrifices could supply the material needs of the gods and thus induce them to produce material blessings for the people. We may note in this a resemblance to earlier traditional religions in pre-Christian Europe, where the annual sacrifices of maidens satisfied the sexual needs of male deities and thus brought about increased fertility in humans and cattle as well as good crops. In contemporary traditional religions animal sacrifices may be used as a means toward reconciling opposing tribes or families. The shed blood delivers from the evil of hostility and brings the blessing of peace.

We conclude that parallels with Christian redemption do exist in other faiths (*see also* REDEMPTIVE ANALOGIES). Sacrifices are used to appease deities, just as propitiation is a means of access to the Christian God. And many peoples believe in a redemption that delivers from evils and brings blessings both nationally and individually. But Christian redemption is also unique. There is no equivalent in other faiths to the God-initiated atonement through his own Son. The Jesus Christ who serves as an effective vicarious sacrifice for sin and brings the fullness of salvation to God's people has no parallel.

MARTIN GOLDSMITH

Redemptive Analogies. A concept introduced in Don Richardson's *Peace Child* (1974) and further developed in his *Lords of the Earth* (1977) and *Eternity in Their Hearts* (1981). Richardson surmises that God, who ordained facets of Hebrew culture (e.g., animal sacrifice, the brazen serpent) to pre-figure Jesus as "the Lamb of God" and as one to be "lifted up," providentially plants Christ-foreshadowing elements in other cultures as well.

An example of this is found in John's Gospel, where Jesus personifies "Logos," a Greek philosophical name for a principle of constancy hidden behind all that is changing in the universe. In Acts 17, Paul links the biblical Elohim with "Agnosto Theo," the "unknown god" of pagan Athens.

Elohim historically has found numerous expressions of the Creator God in various cultures worldwide. For example, he who became "Deus" in Latin and "Dios" in Spanish became also "Gott" in German, "Shangti" in Chinese, and "Hananim" in Korean.

Redemptive analogies may be either *general* to many cultures or *special* to one culture. The apostle Paul, who constantly moved from one cultural context to the next, naturally favored general redemptive analogies: farmer/crop, athlete/prize, soldier/armor, teacher/pupil, and the like. General redemptive analogies communicate to a wider audience but are less potent cultural bridges.

John, ministering primarily to Jews and Greeks, chose analogies unique to Jewish and Greek culture respectively, such as those mentioned above. An analogy that people recognize as *special* to their own culture can have greater impact among them.

Special redemptive analogies occur in two categories: (1) those indigenous symbols linked to MONOTHEISM, that is, the nearly universal sky-god traditions which yield already familiar aliases for Elohim in Gentile languages worldwide, and (2) those pertaining to *indigenous ethics,* that is, requirements of Old Testament law that are found "written on the hearts" of Gentiles who have never heard of Torah. Richardson cites Yali places of refuge in Irian Jaya, Dayak "scapeboats" in Borneo, and the Chinese way of writing "righteous" using symbols which mean "I under the lamb."

Richardson finds that most writers on PEOPLE MOVEMENTS miss the role of redemptive analogy as the cultural catalyst God often uses to trigger such movements. Missionaries who know how to find and employ redemptive analogies, he claims, are more likely to experience the mass response a people movement brings. Many conservative theologians downplay the importance of GENERAL REVELATION. They credit it only with a negative role of bringing enough knowledge to condemn, but not enough to save. Richardson perceives redemptive analogies as evidence that God has been making a positive communication through general revelation. Indeed, Acts 14:17 and Romans 2:14, 15 clarify general revelation as the progenitor of gospel-foreshadowing redemptive analogies in cultures around the globe. Is general revelation's contribution ever so positive as to generate saving faith apart from knowledge of special revelation? That, Richardson maintains, is a separate question.

DON RICHARDSON

Bibliography. E. R. Nelson and R. E. Broadberry: *Genesis and the Mystery Confucius Couldn't Solve;* D. Marshall, *True Son of Heaven;* D. Kikawa, *Perpetuated in Righteousness;* J. Padinjarekara: *Christ in Ancient Vedas.*

Reed, Mary (1854–1943). American missionary to India. Born the second of nine children to a prosperous family in Lowell, Ohio, she came to Christ at age sixteen. Two years later she finished her education and then taught in public schools for ten years. At that time she sensed God's call on her life, and, with her parents' approval, applied to the Woman's Foreign Missionary Society of the Methodist Episcopal Church. She was accepted and appointed to India, where she arrived in November 1884. Shortly after her arrival, she became sick and was sent to the Himalayas to recover and give time to language studies. It was there that she first saw a leper colony and sensed that God wanted her to work among them. She recovered, and returned to the work to which she

had originally been assigned for the next five years. In January 1890 she again became ill, and this time was sent to the United States for diagnosis. The doctors in Cincinnati were baffled until God revealed to her that she herself had contracted leprosy. The diagnosis was confirmed by doctors in both New York and London. This cemented in her mind God's earlier call. She returned to India, not telling her parents her real condition out of fear that they might forbid her from going. Once she arrived, she informed them by mail and began her work as a leper among lepers. She served in a dual appointment with the Methodists and the British Mission to Lepers until 1898, when health issues forced her to give undivided service to the leper ministry. Under the sovereignty of God, the disease was held from its normal course, giving her more than fifty years of active service among the outcasts of society. She took one furlough in 1912, and then remained with her ministry until her death.

A. SCOTT MOREAU

Bibliography. J. T. Gracey, *Eminent Missionary Women;* J. Jackson, *Mary Reed: Missionary to the Lepers;* K. G. Sabiers, *Little Biographies of Great Missionaries.*

The Reformation and Mission. Sixteenth-century Lutherans and Calvinists have been criticized for showing little or no interest in mission, while their ANABAPTIST contemporaries have been praised for their missionary activity. This oversimplification distorts the true picture. Mission in the Reformation was complex, and its form depended primarily on one's understanding of the church. Luther adopted the medieval model of a territorial church, with the prince taking the leadership of its reformation. Thus mission was seen as the re-establishment of the church in a given area on the foundation of Reformation theology and structure (*see* LUTHERAN MISSIONS). Calvin's model was similar (*see* CALVINISM). The Anabaptist view of the church led to a different understanding: all, Catholics and Protestants alike, are called into communities of adult baptized believers that are separated from the state.

Another factor was the rejection of monasticism by Protestants for theological reasons, even though monastic communities had been the primary vehicle of mission since the fourth century (*see* MONASTIC MOVEMENT). This left Protestant churches with no adequate structure for mission beyond their own territories. As Lutheranism and Calvinism struggled to survive in the chaotic situation, the process of reformation and mission was mixed with politics and war. Many rulers accepted or rejected Protestantism for political motives, while others did so out of deep religious conviction.

The ideas of the Reformers were spread first of all through their writings, taken from one part of

Europe to another by scholars, but also by merchants and tradesmen who visited Reformation centers and spread the new ideas. The most significant missionary activity of Lutherans and Calvinists took place through former students at Wittenberg or Geneva. Lutheranism was established in areas where the rulers accepted it, and Bible translation was important in the process. This was true in the Scandinavian countries. Hans Tausen, a leader of the Reformation in Denmark, translated the New Testament in 1524. Johannes Bugenhagen led the reorganization of the Danish Church. The Reformation was introduced into Iceland by Oddur Gottskalkson, who translated the New Testament in 1540. Olaf and Lars Petersson were the leaders of the movement in Sweden. Michael Agricola led the Reformation in Finland, translating the New Testament, the Psalms, and some of the prophets. Matthias Devay began his ministry in Hungary in 1531, and along with Ganos Erdosy translated the New Testament into Magyar. Others took the Lutheran Reformation to Poland, Moravia, and the Baltic states. All of them had studied in Germany, most of them in Wittenberg.

Calvin was more intentional in encouraging mission. In some areas Calvinism became the religion of the state; in other areas local churches were established amidst PERSECUTION. Pastors were trained in Geneva and sent as missionaries; many were martyred. The 161 pastors who went from Geneva to the Reformed churches of France were a Protestant counterpart to the Society of Jesus. The movement was taken to the Low Countries by Protestants fleeing from persecution in France. In 1561 Guido de Brès, who had studied in Geneva, drafted the Belgic Confession, which bound together the congregations in the Low Countries. Calvinism exerted significant influence on English Protestantism through refugees who studied in Geneva and Zurich during the reign of Mary (1553–58) and then took Reformation ideas back to Britain after her death. John Knox established Presbyterianism in Scotland; others laid the foundations of Puritanism. The only Protestant mission outside of Europe in the sixteenth century was the Calvinist mission to Brazil in 1555, which eventually ended in betrayal and martyrdom.

The Anabaptists, beginning in Zurich in 1525, spread their faith as they fled from persecution. They also intentionally sent out missionaries to many areas of western Europe: southern Germany, upper Austria, Moravia, Hungary, and the Low Countries. Many of their greatest leaders, including Jacob Hutter and Balthaser Hubmaier, were burned at the stake. The Hutterites sent out scores of missionaries, some designated as servants of the Word, while others were ordinary brethren. Perhaps the most effective Anabaptist leader was Menno Simons, baptized as an adult in 1535; traveling widely in the Low Countries and northern Germany, he organized communities of believers. The Mennonite churches take their name from him.

Although the Reformers can be criticized for an inadequate ecclesiology with little place for mission in their church structure, they did lay the theological foundation for the later missionary movement. Calvin affirmed that God wills to offer the gospel to all peoples without exception. The Reformers also encouraged a considerable amount of missionary activity within western Europe even as they struggled for survival. With the exception of the Calvinist expedition to Brazil, Protestants would not be involved in mission outside of Europe until the Puritans went to Native Americans in the seventeenth century.

PAUL E. PIERSON

Bibliography. C. P. Clasen, *Anabaptism: A Social History, 1525–1618; New Cambridge Modern History,* vol. 2; H. J. Grimm, *The Reformation Era, 1500 to 1650;* J. T. McNeill, *The History and Character of Calvinism.*

Reformed Missions. Reformed missions encompasses the missiological reflection and action of churches with roots in the sixteenth-century Protestant Reformation who followed particularly the teaching of John Calvin (*see* CALVINISM). Reformed missions includes a Trinitarian perspective on the church's missionary call and action that is kingdom-oriented, concerned with all of life, and governed by Scripture alone. *Ecclesia reformata semper reformanda* (a Reformed church is continually reforming) is a Reformed principle that holds true for both church and society. Following this line of thought, Dutch Reformed missiologist JOHANNES VERKUYL defined missiology as "the study of the salvation activities of the Father, Son, and Holy Spirit throughout the world geared toward bringing the kingdom of God into existence. . . . (It) is the study of the worldwide church's divine mandate to be ready to serve this God who is aiming his saving acts toward this world. In dependence on the Holy Spirit and by word and deed the church is to communicate the total gospel and the total divine law to all (humanity)" (Verkuyl, 1978, 5).

Reformed theory of missions has its roots in the thought of Calvin and was subsequently articulated in the sixteenth and early seventeenth centuries by those who followed him: Dutch thinkers like Adrianus Saravia (1531–1613), GISBERT VOETIUS (1588–1676), J. Heurnius (1587–1651); and Americans JOHN ELIOT (1604–90), DAVID BRAINERD (1718–47), and JONATHAN EDWARDS (1703–58).

Gisbert Voetius was the first Protestant to develop a comprehensive "theology of mission." Dutch Reformed mission work began in Formosa in 1627. From 1622 to 1633 there was a seminary in Leyden for training missionaries (who were sent mostly to Indonesia and Ceylon). In 1648, J. Heurnius wrote *An Exhortation Worthy of Consideration, to Embark upon an Evangelical Mission among the Indians,* a work that would find surprising parallels in WILLIAM CAREY's *Enquiry* more than 170 years later. Heurnius himself went to Indonesia as a missionary.

In spite of the fact that Calvin was in touch with the establishment of a French colony in Brazil and that some German Reformed persons attempted something with the Slavs and the Turks, it would be a fair judgment to say that the Reformers did not have a missionary zeal like that exhibited by much of Protestantism in the eighteenth and nineteenth centuries. Yet there is much in Reformed theology that forms the foundation for all subsequent Protestant missions. SAMUEL ZWEMER asserted that "the very principles on which the modern missionary movement had its origin are to be found in Calvin's theology" (Zwemer, 1950, 207). Three major emphases of the sixteenth-century Reformation were the sovereignty of God, reality of grace, and a rediscovery of hope.

In the New England colonies, the best-known Protestant missionary pioneer was Puritan (and Reformed) John Eliot (1604–90), who ministered from the 1640s until his death among the Native Americans of Massachusetts. In developing his missionary theology, JONATHAN EDWARDS drew from the work and thought of JOHN ELIOT and the ministry and diary of DAVID BRAINERD, among others. Edwards was himself a missionary from 1751 to 1757 to a Native American settlement in Stockbridge, Massachusetts.

During the twentieth century, Western mission theory has been deeply affected by Reformed missiologists, including ABRAHAM KUYPER, J. H. BAVINCK, HENDRIK KRAEMER, J. C. HOEKENDIJK, Johannes Blauw, DAVID BOSCH, LESSLIE NEWBIGIN, JOHANNES VERKUYL, ARTHUR GLASSER, and Harvie Conn, to name a few.

Coupled with "the priesthood of all believers," a number of Reformed concepts have been essential in the construction of modern mission theory. Edmund Clowney suggested themes such as "the glory of God, the goal of missions; the grace of God, the source of missions; the Kingdom of God, the power of missions; and the Word of God, the message of missions" (Clowney, 1977, 128).

Reformed theology of mission affirms the sovereignty of God over all of life. This emphasis on God's sovereignty calls for a Trinitarian approach to mission that sees God the Father as the Creator and initiator of mission, Jesus Christ the Son as the Sent-one in whose mission the Body of Christ participates, and the Holy Spirit as the motivator, agent, and guide of the church's participation in God's mission. On the negative side, a rationalist and hyper-Calvinist stream of thought emerged that insisted that if God predestines individuals for salvation and others to perdition (double predestination), then Christians should leave it to him to save whom he wishes to save, according to his own pleasure. At times, this concept of predestination has had an unfortunate paralyzing effect on Reformed mission.

A second major aspect of Reformed mission is its strong christological emphasis. However, during the late seventeenth century a controversy arose between Theodore Beza, Calvin's successor in Geneva, and Adrian Saravia (1531–1613). Saravia contended that the GREAT COMMISSION had abiding validity for the church in all times, while Beza and much of Calvinism of the time affirmed that the Great Commission was a special labor uniquely given by Jesus to the apostles and limited to them and their time.

Third, Reformed mission stresses the unique and indispensable role of the church in mission: church-focused, but not church-centric. Seeing the church as a gathering of those who believe in Jesus Christ by grace through faith, Reformed mission perceives the whole church, including the laity, to be apostolic in its sentness and catholic in its universal extension. Negatively, sixteenth- and seventeenth-century Calvinism maintained a close, almost medieval, relationship between the church and the state, and thus mission was assumed to be the responsibility of civil government, as one can see, for example, in Article 36 of the Belgic Confession.

Finally, Reformed mission emphasizes the critical role of the Scriptures in evaluating and guiding mission. "The Church must in every generation be ready to brings its tradition afresh under the light of the Word of God. But not only must we examine our methods. The structures of the congregations; the relations between Western churches and those in Asia, Africa, and Latin America; the nature of the (missions of the churches) today; and the plans for future projects must also be (placed) under the examining light of God's Word" (Newbigin, quoted in Verkuyl, 1978, 5). Reformed mission seeks to be reformed and always in the process of reforming according to the Word of God.

On every continent there are churches that derive their histories from the efforts of Reformed missionary organizations and personnel. Today two of the most significant global fellowships of Reformed churches are the World Alliance of Reformed Churches (WARC) and the Reformed Ecumenical Synod. Both organizations seek to foster mission vision, initiative, and cooperation among Reformed and Presbyterian churches and mission organizations worldwide.

CHARLES VAN ENGEN

Bibliography. J. H. Bavinck, *An Introduction to the Science of Missions;* J. Blauw, *The Missionary Nature of* the Church; D. Bosch, *Witness to the World: The Christian Mission in Theological Perspective* (1980); idem, *Transforming Mission* (1991); E. Clowney in *Theological Perspectives on Church Growth*, pp. 127–49; Harvie Conn, *Eternal Word and Changing Worlds: Theology, Anthropology, and Mission in Trialogue*; R. De Ridder, *Discipling the Nations*; A. F. Glasser, *Kingdom and Mission*; J. Gort, *OBMR* 4 (1980): 156–61; J. C. Hoekendijk, *The Church Inside Out*; H. Kraemer, *From Mission-field to Independent Church*; *The Christian Message in a Non-Christian World*; D. McKim, ed., *Major Themes in the Reformed Tradition*; L. Newbigin, *Occasional Bulletin of Missionary Research* (November 1962): 1–9; idem, *The Household of God*; *The Open Secret*; C. Van Engen, *God's Missionary People: Mission on the Way*; J. Verkuyl, *Contemporary Missiology: An Introduction*; W. A. Visser 't Hooft, *No Other Name: The Choice Between Syncretism and Christian Universalism*; S. Zwemer, *Theology Today* 8 (1950): 206–16.

Reformed Theology. *See* CALVINISM.

Refugee Mission Work. Refugees are those who are displaced from their natural residence and who fear (for whatever reason) to return. They may be uprooted because of systematic genocidal campaigns, religious or political persecution, denial of fundamental civil rights, and so on. Refugees often lack the most basic necessities of food, water, and shelter. Typically defenseless, they are at the mercy of those in power over the territory in which they seek refuge. They often fear revealing what they have experienced because of repercussions from those in power. Even mission agencies working among them may be unable to publicize the stories since they depend on permission from governments to continue their work.

The Old Testament enjoins providing sanctuary for outcasts and refugees, including cities of refuge for those who commit accidental manslaughter (Num. 35:6–15). Israel became a nation of refugees because of Israel's apostasy (as promised in Deut. 28:63–68). Their repentance, however, resulted in a promise of being regathered and restored (Deut. 30:3–5; Isa. 11:11–12; Jer. 30:12–22). The nations around Israel also suffered as outcasts (Moab, Isa. 16:3 and Jer. 30:16). While the New Testament has no direct reference to refugees, we do see that Christians will be judged in light of our work on behalf of the poor and the oppressed (Matt. 25:31–46), which certainly includes refugees.

Prior to the twentieth century, with international travel relatively unrestricted, and the right of asylum taken for granted, there were generally less problems of dislocation. As the twentieth century progressed, however, new requirements (e.g., passports, visas, and qualifications for asylum), complicated the problems of repatriation and settlement. Today refugees are often people not only without a home, but like the Palestinians, they may also be without a country for decades. In emotional and physical shock at having to leave their homes, refugees often have nothing more than the clothing they wear. Typically by the time they are forced to evacuate they have been witnesses to incredible atrocities committed against friends, neighbors, and immediate family members. Women and children are particularly vulnerable and are all too often the favored targets of attack.

Since most displacement presently takes place in third world contexts, those fleeing are typically perceived by the countries of asylum as bringing unbearable demands on strained economies. Consequently, they may receive little if any assistance and may even be repelled (e.g., the boat refugees from Cambodia, China, or Cuba) or forcibly repatriated.

Four mission organizations directly working among and on behalf of refugee populations today may be noted. Christian Aid was founded in 1945 to help European refugees after Word War II, and is now active in over 70 countries. The World Council of Churches is also active. There were ecumenical efforts to help Jews escaping Nazi persecution even before the formation of the WCC in 1948; at one time refugee work was the single largest operation in the WCC, though now the work has been decentralized among regional (e.g., Action by Churches Together and Church World Service) and denominational (e.g., United Methodist Committee on Relief, Church of the Brethren Refugee/Disaster Services, Presbyterian Disaster Assistance, etc.) organizations. Refugees International was founded in 1979 in response to the Cambodian and Vietnamese refugee plight, and they actively promote refugee issues and situations in political circles in the United States. World Relief, founded in 1979 as the relief arm of the National Association of Evangelicals, is now working in more than 25 cities in the United States helping refugees cope with settling and gaining citizenship.

The total refugee population can fluctuate dramatically from year to year; the UN statistics show a decrease from 15.4 million refugees in 1995 to 13.2 million in 1996, primarily because of the repatriation of 1.6 million African refugees. The total number of UN recognized refugees, displaced, and at risk for 1996 was 22.7 million, of which only 11.7 million received assistance. Jesus' emphasis on the response to the naked, the thirsty, the hungry, the outcast, the sick, and the imprisoned (Matt. 25:31–46) still stands as a foundation for our moral obligation to participate in meaningful ways in the lives of refugees.

A. SCOTT MOREAU

SEE ALSO Relief Work.

Bibliography. G. Van Hoogevest, *DEM*, pp. 855–56; K. Win, *Asia Journal of Theology* 6:1 (1992): 83–92.

Regeneration. *See* Conversion.

Reincarnation and Transmigration. The hope for release from the world of travail and toils is as old as humanity since Adam's fall. The belief in transmigration is in part an expression of this aspiration. Even though the belief that the soul is repeatedly reborn in different bodies is found in many ancient cultures, the concept as we understand it today owes much to Hinduism, in particular the Upanishads and the Bhagavad Gita.

According to Hindu thought, the soul (Atman) is immortal. It has neither beginning nor end. It exists in one of three states: dormancy, incarnation, or liberation from the wheel of existence. The soul, though eternal, takes numerous transient physical bodies during its sojourn in order to realize its true spiritual nature. Once a body is dead, the soul then migrates to a higher or lower form of life depending on the law of karma, the principle of cause and effect, sowing and reaping. This process of rebirths can go on indefinitely until the karmic energy is stopped, that is, all the bad deeds have been recompensed by good ones. A person's present existence is not necessarily a direct result of actions from the immediate past, but most likely from unknowable previous incarnations. Salvation is not birth into a better life, but total release from the wheel of transmigration.

John D. L. Hsu

Bibliography. S. Radhakrishnan and C. A. Moore, *A Source Book in Indian Philosophy;* K. Sivaraman, ed., *Hindu Spirituality: Vedas through Vedanta;* R. C. Zaehner, *Hinduism.*

Relativist, Relativism. The term "relativism" is used in various ways. Descriptively, relativism merely indicates the fact of diversity. Thus "cultural relativism" is sometimes used to mean that various cultures have different beliefs, practices, and values, the function and significance of which must be appreciated from within the framework of the culture itself.

In a normative or ideological sense, relativism (whether cognitive, cultural, ethical, or religious) maintains that ultimately rationality norms, or truth, or criteria for assessing alternative perspectives all arise from particular contexts (sociocultural, historical, linguistic, conceptual) and thus are only applicable within those contexts. There are no universally valid truths or principles. This clearly conflicts with the Christian gospel, which affirms that there are truths that hold universally and apply to all people in all cultures.

Relativism in some form has always been an attractive option, especially at times when people are exposed to the great diversity in human cultures. It is a small and often easy step from the observation that people do in fact have different beliefs and values to the conclusion that there are no universally valid truths. In the modern West, relativism has been encouraged not only by increasing awareness of diversity but also by a pervasive skepticism concerning ethics and religion. Eastern traditions such as Hinduism and Buddhism have long emphasized the relativity and limited nature of human knowledge.

However, ever since the time of Plato it has been pointed out that relativism is a self-defeating position. Any statement of relativism, if intended to be more than "relatively true," implicitly appeals to the falsity of the central thesis of relativism. Furthermore, the price of accepting relativism is not only loss of the right to make universal truth claims but also forfeiture of the right to criticize any alternative perspective as false. The challenge for Christian missions is to maintain a proper appreciation for the great diversity in human cultures while maintaining truths, expressed in God's revelation, which are binding on all peoples in all cultures at all times.

Harold A. Netland

Bibliography. E. Hatch, *Culture and Morality: The Relativity of Values in Anthropology;* J. Meiland and M. Krausz, eds., *Relativism: Cognitive and Moral;* R. Trigg, *Reason and Commitment;* B. R. Wilson, ed., *Rationality.*

Relief Work. Mercy to and relief of the sufferer has been part of Christian practice from the early church to the present. Jewish culture, on which so many of the early church practices were based, structured acts of charity into the life of the people. The Old Testament contains numerous laws and practices regarding response to the poor and weak (Exod. 22:25–27; Deut. 15:7–11; 24:19–21). The conflicts that arise in Acts 6 really emerge out of the Jerusalem church's attempt to live compassionately in response to needy widows.

The history of Christianity from Francis of Assisi to Martin Luther, from the Wesley brothers to the modern missionary movement, is replete with accounts of outstanding men and women who have represented Christ by bringing relief and wholeness physically to the tragedies and crises of various societies. However, without serious reflection on the larger socioeconomic context in which poverty and crisis occur, well-intended compassionate efforts can really be nothing more than the phenomenon of "rice Christianity," which is the tendency to use efforts of compassion as a means to an end by dangling goods and services in front of people as a carrot for acceptance of the Christian faith.

A current definition of relief is "urgent provision of resources to reduce suffering resulting from a natural or human-made disaster." It is, in essence, immediate and temporary, prolonged only when self-reliance is impossible. The United States has over 250 Christian agencies which specialize in relief efforts around the world. These organizations are diverse theologically; some are governmentally subsidized and some are privately funded. Definitions of the term "relief" vary widely among these organizations.

While relief should never be completely distinct from DEVELOPMENT, these two related functions must be differentiated. Relief seeks to salvage human life and prolong survival in crisis circumstances. Development is a process that enables a community to provide for its own needs, above previous levels. Development must be indigenous, comprehensive, and aimed at improved self-reliance.

Christian relief work must ultimately rise above traditional reactive methods and plan proactively. Natural disasters and regional crises will inevitably impact POVERTY or frustrate the progress of the poor to reach self-reliance. Learning the method of contingency planning can dramatically reduce losses in crises necessitating relief intervention. The key to relief is to address potential needs before disaster occurs.

Relief from a Christian perspective is not just alleviating the effects of war, natural disasters, or tragedy. Christian relief involves the whole person who is introduced to new life under the rule of God's kingdom.

The following are some key objectives in a theology of relief: (1) Engagement in disaster relief must be efficient and effective, meeting real needs in a God-honoring way. (2) Relief efforts must be done with genuine care, compassion, and respect for a people and their culture. (3) The lifestyles and manner of relief workers must evidence that the Good News is true. (4) There should not be any attempt to proselytize, capitalize on tragedy, or discriminate in distribution of supplies. (5) The presentation of the Christian message must be adapted to the degree of knowledge and understanding of Jesus Christ in the context being served. (6) Finally, long-term effects on the people in their journey with Jesus Christ should always be considered.

BYRON D. KLAUS

Bibliography. A. Beals, *Beyond Hunger: A Biblical Mandate for Social Responsibility*; E. Elliston, ed., *Christian Relief and Development*; M. Meggay, *Transforming Society*; F. O'Gorman; *Charity and Change*.

Religion. Religion is a word/concept that attempts to cover a type of human experience as it relates to a transcendent reality. Religion is a familiar word that communicates a commonly recognized content. But for all its familiarity, it is a difficult word to define. This difficulty of definition has three main sources.

The first is a common and unavoidable one. As a word, "religion" is a Western creation from the Latin root, *religia*, meaning "to unite." As a West-

ern word, religion has accumulated meaning that is often more in concert with the structures of Western religions such as Judaism, Christianity, and Islam (where the task of religion is to "unite" the human and divine spheres), than with Eastern religions such as Hinduism and Buddhism (where the task of religion is to recognize the oneness of all being) or indigenous religions (where the task is to live in harmony with the god-imitating structures of tribe or ethnic group). Still, although the Westernization of the word/concept must be recognized, these origins have sometimes been overemphasized to the point that an essential idea is lost: some word must be used to describe this seemingly universal class of human experience and a word whose root means to join or unite is not that far off from the task of religions, be they Western, Eastern, or indigenous.

The second source of difficulty in defining religion stems from a general uncertainty over where exactly the essence of this common class of human experience is located. "Theologians" or professors of a particular religious tradition locate the essence of religion in the reality of the God, gods, or transcendental principle of their religious belief. For theologians, then, religion becomes the set of beliefs, and institutions that relate, identify, or explain that transcendence to human beings and the material realm. Others locate the essence of religion in a common human nature, although they tend to assign different aspects of human nature as the *locus classicus* of human religious experience. Some, like Anders Nygren, see religion as a function of rationality: "Religion is belief in divine beings." Frederich Schleiermacher, on the other hand, found religion's root in human emotions: "Religion is the feeling of absolute dependence." Still others locate religion in a set of volitions: "Religion is what the individual does with his own solitariness" (Alfred North Whitehead). Social scientists locate the essence of religion in a function of human social behavior, whether personal/psychological or social: "Religion is the feeling, acts, and experiences of individual men in their solitude, so far as they apprehend themselves to stand in relation to whatever they may consider the divine" (William James). "When a certain number of sacred things sustain relations of coordination or subordination with each other in such a way as to form a system, having a certain unity, but which is not comprised within any other system of the same sort, the totality of those beliefs and their corresponding rites constitutes a religion" (Emile Durkheim).

Each of these locations—transcendence, human nature, human society—produces valid and useful definitions of religion. Their diversity, however, means one must be clear in their use. Clearly stating the definitions one is using, and the purposes of those definitions, is mandatory. The diversity also points out the complexity of the word/concept. "Religion" is an attempt to bring under one broad umbrella an incredible diversity of religious ideas and practices.

The third source of the difficulty of defining religion is positing transcendence itself. Most definitions of religion recognize, if not the reality of, then the belief in, an entity that is above and beyond the mundane world of everyday existence. Yet by definition such an entity is beyond definition. When it comes to a definition of religion, this poses different yet related problems for all three of the approaches to religion we discussed in the last section. For the teachers of a particular religion, this transcendent principle is usually a presupposition, not only in terms of existence but in terms of qualities and nature. Any definition of religion in such a context, then, is heavily influenced by the nature of the presupposed transcendent. For those who locate religion in a common human nature, transcendence takes on a dual role of creator and created of the essential human nature. For social scientists, transcendence is reduced to a psychological or sociological construct, at least in so far as their study of religion is concerned. For all three, the reality of transcendence is lost as soon as it is defined.

For evangelicals, none of these three categories of definitions—and their attendant problems—should be considered out of bounds. Religion is ultimately a confessional enterprise, even for the a-religious. But religion may also with profit be viewed as a facet of human nature and an observable social construct. That the roots of each of these may be interpreted differently need not diminish their descriptive value.

TERRY C. MUCK

Bibliography. J. Hick, *An Interpretation of Religion;* R. Otto, *The Idea of the Holy;* E. Sharpe, *Understanding Religion;* N. Smart, *The Phenomenon of Religion.*

Religious Freedom. An attitude and conduct of tolerance for another person's or group's religious beliefs and practices. This involves respect for the opinion and practices of other faiths that may be in conflict with one's own. Diversity threatens the unity of orthodoxy and has been the foundation for such confrontations. The problem of religious freedom and Christian mission is prominent in church history.

Jesus and the early church suffered persecution by the Romans yet the spontaneous expansion of the Christian church flourished. Missionary bands traveled the Roman roads encountering sporadic and localized persecution. This continued until the fourth century because the church was seen to be politically subversive to the state and a threat to Roman unity (e.g., Acts 16:19–24). The situation was reversed when Constantine and the Edict of Milan (313) gave religious equality to Christianity. The church then became the persecutor and Christian mission faced new dangers. Instead of mission being guided by the Holy Spirit and penetrating culture, it became politically and militarily motivated and lost evangelistic force.

Through the Middle Ages the idea of the Christian state remained and became entrenched with the establishment of the Holy Roman Empire by Charlemagne in 800. Church membership and citizenship of the empire were inextricably connected. Thus, enemies of the church were enemies of the empire and were duly prosecuted, forcing the conversion of conquered peoples. This not only happened to non-Christians, but also to Christians who believed differently from the institutional church. Perhaps the most important renewal mission movement between the sixth-century Celts and the thirteenth-century Friars were the Waldensians. The people movement begun in France by Peter Waldo (1140–1218) sent out itinerant missionaries to preach the gospel and administer baptism and the Lord's Supper. They spread very rapidly to Italy, Austria, Bohemia, Moravia, Germany, Hungary, and Poland. The Waldensians were seen as heretics and suffered severe persecution because they had a different view of the gospel and the church.

In fourteenth-century England another Christian mission group to suffer under the hands of the established church was the Lollards. At the beginning John Wycliffe's biblical teaching formed a student movement as he sent out preachers to the common people to teach them the Scriptures in their own language. The church condemned Wycliffe in 1382, yet the Lollards continued sharing the truths of Scripture through the following century despite persecution. At the same time in Europe, John Huss (1373–1415) preached the centrality of Christ with a combination of nationalistic and religious passion. He was eventually burned at the stake by the Council of Constance for his attacks on the church's corruption.

Lack of religious freedom continued with the Protestant Reformation. Since the Christian state was still seen to be valid, Protestantism was not tolerated in Catholic countries and Catholicism was not tolerated in Protestant nations. Those who did not conform to either were seen as dissenters and were persecuted as heretics. Such a group was the Anabaptists, who did not believe that infant baptism was scriptural and so performed adult baptism. They felt that Luther and Calvin had not gone far enough in reforming the Catholic Church and rejected even more of the medieval church practices. Their understanding of mission was to win people to their way of viewing Christianity. Some of these evangelical Anabaptist groups were passionate missionaries and traveled all over Western Europe sharing their faith in areas of Moravia, Germany, Switzerland, Austria, Holland, and Belgium (*see* ANABAPTIST MISSIONS). Many were martyred since the wider society believed that religious uniformity was essential for social unity and that religious separatism would cause the disintegration of the social fabric.

Another Christian renewal movement that suffered a lack of religious freedom was Puritanism in sixteenth-century England. Influenced by the continental reformers, they wanted to reform the Church of England. In 1593 the Puritans were forced by a series of acts to submit to the Anglican Church. This eventually led to the Puritan Revolution, where Parliament and the Puritans fought against the monarch and the Church of England. This movement had a significant effect on PIETISM in Germany through its devotional writings. The first Western missionaries to the Native Americans of North America were the Puritans JOHN ELIOT and Samuel Mayhew. The pietists responded by sending the first Protestant missionaries from Europe to Asia—Heinrich Plutschau and BARTHOLOMAUS ZIEGENBALG who went to India.

Moravianism and Methodism were two similar reform movements that wanted to remain in the institutional church as a renewing element, but were rejected by the state church. Zinzendorf's Moravians mobilized for mission and went to the West Indies (1732), South Africa, Greenland, Labrador, Egypt, Surinam, Guiana, and twenty-one other countries in the same number of years (*see* MORAVIAN MISSIONS). Eventually Zinzendorf was banished from Saxony and the Moravians were forced to separate from the Lutheran Church. Moravianism became a major catalyst of the whole missionary movement and influenced JOHN WESLEY, the founder of Methodism. Again the Methodists suffered religious intoleration from the Anglican Church and wanted to remain within its borders. This was not to be the case and eventually Wesley was forced into a de facto relationship in 1784 by ordaining his own Methodist preachers and missionaries.

Religious freedom for modern missions has much to learn from church history. Such courage to share the gospel has weakened the bigotry of Western ecclesiastical authority and religious liberty is seen as a human right. However, current trends of religious FUNDAMENTALISMS in the Middle East, changes in the policies regarding religion of many European socialist states, and an increase in politico-religious conflict in Asia continue to make Christian missionary endeavors ever reliant on the guidance and strength of the Lord of the church.

ROBERT L. GALLAGHER

SEE ALSO Ideologies; Church and State.

Bibliography. M. S. Bates, *Religious Liberty;* J. Míguez Bonino, *Towards Christian Political Ethics;* R. Ellison, *AFER* 24 (1982): 106–15; D. J. Smit, *DEM*, pp., 607–10; A. J. Van der Bent, *Christian Response in a World of Crisis.*

Religious Scriptures. The word "scripture" comes from a Latin term meaning "that which is written." A vast amount of sacred literature (the BIBLE, QUR'AN, the Vedas, Tao Te Ching) is preserved in written form. Oral tradition (story, poem, song, proverb, etc.) also occupies a similar place among the sacred lore of certain societies. Scriptures are a powerful source of meaning, cohesiveness, and self-identity for a particular community, shaping its worldview and providing moral guidelines.

Nature of Sacred Scripture. Although there is considerable diversity among religious traditions concerning the nature and function of sacred scripture, some common themes emerge.

Sacredness. Religious scriptures are regarded as sacred due to their connection with the divine. Within oral traditions a special power is sometimes regarded as being inherent within the sounds of certain sacred words or symbols. The sacred power is said to be released through proper singing or incantation of the words (e.g., the mantra in Vedic HINDUISM).

Authority. Written scriptures are regarded as authoritative because of their connection with the divine or transcendent. But the nature of such authority varies: Christianity and ISLAM ascribe definitive authority to their scriptures, whereas some traditions of Hinduism and BUDDHISM have less strict understandings of authority for their scriptures. But for most traditions the scriptures are normative for worship, doctrine, and behavior.

Revelation. MONOTHEISTIC traditions regard their scriptures as specially revealed by God, although Christianity and Islam have very different views on the nature and content of such revelation. Hindus distinguish between *smrti* ("that which is remembered") and *sruti* ("that which is heard"), the latter being regarded as texts specially revealed to the sages. Buddhist scriptures are not regarded as products of divine REVELATION so much as the authoritative insights of "enlightened ones."

Inspiration. The sacred writings of most traditions are regarded as inspired in a general sense, although monotheistic traditions have more clearly defined notions of divine inspiration. For Islam divine inspiration of the Qur'an means there is no human contribution to the writing of the Qur'an; it was dictated in Arabic to Muhammad. Christians maintain that the Bible is fully inspired by God, but that God used the distinctives of human authorship in putting his Revelation in writing.

Canon. Most traditions have an authoritative list of sacred texts. In monotheistic traditions such as Christianity and Islam the canon (Bible, Qur'an) is clearly defined and is "closed" (material cannot be added to or subtracted from the authoritative canon). Some branches of Hinduism, Buddhism, and Shinto have less clearly defined notions of canonicity, and in some cases the canon is regarded as "open"—new authoritative scriptures can be recognized.

Content of Sacred Scripture. Religious texts reflect a wide range of content.

Story. Sacred narrative unfolds the nature of divine beings, the beginning of existence, the purpose of life, and the like. Narratives can include paradox, riddles, or parables, and can be presented in ways that are contrary to normal experience. Story has the capacity to communicate important truths and to move the believer toward the desired ideal.

Doctrine. Scriptures communicate certain beliefs, both explicitly and implicitly. The religious communities, reflecting upon scriptures, formulate authoritative teachings, dogmas, and systems that help transform believers, delineate sacred time and space, and provide explanation for the crises threatening human existence.

Ritual. Scripture also prescribes acceptable rituals and patterns of behavior relating to the sacred. Actions pertaining to sacrifice, purification rites, and pilgrimage are defined. Worship is encouraged through song, praise, prayer, chant, petition, meditation, and the like.

Experience. The dilemmas of human existence are expressed in scriptures in the form of confession of sinfulness; struggles with suffering, frailty, and ignorance; and descriptions of the precariousness and insignificance of human life. Human experience with evil is a common theme. The scriptures bring meaning to these struggles and hope for their resolution, here or in the hereafter.

Ethics. Models for proper behavior encompass the entire range of life, including private and public conduct, customs, standards of morality, regulations for purity, rewards for righteousness, punishments for error, and satisfaction or atonement for sin.

Sacred scriptures thus provide identity, authorization, and ideals for those of a particular religious tradition. Whether the Bible, Torah, Qur'an, Vedas, Tao Te Ching, Adi Granth, or the Avesta, the holy writ of a people tells how institutions were formed, covenants ratified, and the divine acted so that believers may have a charter for their history and an explanation for their existence.

ED MATTHEWS

Bibliography. F. F. Bruce and E. G. Rupp, *Holy Book and Holy Tradition;* L. Cunningham et al., *The Sacred Quest;* R. Ellwood, *Introducing Religion;* G. Lancgkowski, *Sacred Writings;* W. O'Flaherty, *The Critical Study of Sacred Texts;* W. Paden, *Interpreting the Sacred.*

Religious Typologies. A religious typology is a means of classifying different religious systems. A number of religious typologies have been proposed, including the following.

Auguste Comte (1798–1857) posited three stages in the evolution of thought: (1) the theological stage, with spiritual beings; (2) the metaphysical stage, with abstract invisible forces; and (3) the positivistic stage, where causes are sought in a scientific and pragmatic manner. E. B. Tylor (1832–1917) proposed five stages: (1) ANIMISM, belief in spiritual beings and an afterlife, (2) fetishism, (3) belief in demons, (4) POLYTHEISM, and (5) MONOTHEISM. Sir James Frazer (1854–1941) postulated that humans began with MAGIC. When they found magic ineffective, they turned to religion, and finally to science. This schema, especially the belief that science if pursued far enough will yield ultimate answers, is held by many today. R. R. Marett (1866–1943) believed animatism is basic to a religious system His theory is based on his learning about *mana*, supernatural power that is present in certain men, spirits, and natural objects, in some Pacific cultures, and similar concepts in other cultures. Karl Marx (1818–83) theorized that the disappearance of religion would result in a classless society. He viewed religion as a tool of exploitation of the people. He predicted that as cultures and societies become more modernized and industrialized, SECULARIZATION would eventually eliminate religion.

Each of the above theories has failed under reality checks. Fieldworkers found that people in technologically primitive cultures believe in God, the sustainer and creator of life. Thus many groups have been monotheists for centuries. Wilhelm Schmidt (1868–1954), who conducted field research in South America among people in Tierra del Fuego, in Africa (Rwanda), and on the Andaman Islands in the Indian Ocean, provided data that contradict these early theories.

Wallace proposed four typologies: (1) individual religious systems, (2) communal religions, (3) ecclesiastical institutions, and (5) universalistic religions. A possible fifth category is secularism, including secular humanism. Each of the more complex religious systems, with the possible exception of secularism, encompasses all that are below it. Traditionally the type of religious system often correlated with the level of sociopolitical complexity of the society. For example, hunter and gatherer societies tend toward individual and communal religious institutions while state societies tend to have ecclesiastical and universalistic religions.

In individualistic religious systems, individuals function as their own religious specialists (e.g., the vision quest by North American plains Indians). Communal religions have great diversity. Ecclesiastical religions have creeds, sacred scripture, and religious specialists who are organized hierarchically (e.g., the religions developed in Egypt, China, Mesopotamia, Rome, Greece, Mesoamerica, South America, and Africa; examples include the religions of the Aztec, Maya, and Inca). In universalistic religions, adherents claim that their religious messages apply to all of humanity (e.g., Judaism, Christianity, Islam, Hinduism, and Buddhism). These are known as the great religious traditions.

In secularization and accompanying individualism, religion becomes a private affair, separate from social, political, and economic institutions. Secular humanism is the dominant ideology in many modern states. One problem with this perspective is that it is not possible to abstract religion from the rest of culture. To do so undermines a culture's moral and ethical foundations. Religion, with its moral and ethical principles, is essential for a stable healthy society.

CAROL V. McKINNEY

SEE ALSO Religion.

Bibliography. M. Harris, *Magic, Witchcraft, and Religion: An Anthropological Study of the Supernatural*; J. R. Hinnells, ed., *A Handbook of Living Religions*; H. Smith, *The World's Religions*; E. B. Tylor, *Primitive Culture: Researches into the Development of Mythology, Religion, Language, Art, and Custom*, 2 vols.; A. F. C. Wallace, *Religion: An Anthropological View*.

Religious Ultimacy. Most religions identify a being or state as ontologically ultimate. The religious ultimate provides an explanation for the cosmos, gives life its meaning, and defines the spiritual goal of religion. Yet religions disagree on the nature of the religious ultimate.

Monotheistic traditions ascribe ultimacy to the one eternal God, a personal being who acts and is the Creator of all that exists. Christianity understands God to be a Holy Trinity, with Jesus Christ being God incarnate. JUDAISM and ISLAM both reject the deity of Jesus Christ, but they disagree over the nature of God's revelation to humankind. There are also theistic traditions within HINDUISM, focusing on Shiva or Vishnu, as well as in PURE LAND BUDDHISM, with its devotion to the Amida Buddha. SIKHISM regards the one God as the True Name.

Monistic traditions identify religious ultimacy with the one true reality. Advaita VEDANTA HINDUISM regards *nirguna* Brahman (Brahman beyond all attributes or dualism) as the sole reality; Vishisht-Advaita Vedanta holds that the one reality, Brahman, is a personal being with distinctions and attributes. In MAHAYANA BUDDHISM the religious ultimate is thought of as the *Dharmakaya* (the Buddha as the absolute, formless, ineffable reality underlying all phenomena) or as *sunyata* (Emptiness, the Void). Chinese TAOISM

regards the ultimate as the Tao (the Way), the source and pattern of the cosmos.

Some traditions are atheistic, denying the reality of any deities. Although Jainism recognizes higher beings on various celestial levels, they are finite beings subject to rebirth. Theravada Buddhism ascribes ultimacy to *nirvana*, which alone is unconditioned and permanent.

In polytheistic and animistic traditions there are many deities and supernatural beings, usually with no single ultimate deity. Japanese SHINTO holds that the many *kami* include phenomena of nature, ancestors, living persons, and animals. In some primal religions and African traditional religions there is recognition of a High God, a supreme deity who rules over all but who may be far removed from the affairs of daily life.

HAROLD A. NETLAND

Bibliography. S. G. F. Brandon, ed., *The Savior God*; J. Carman, *Majesty and Meekness*: *A Comparative Study of Contrast and Harmony in the Concept of God*; E. G. Parrinder, *Comparative Religion*.

Renewal Movements. Change is an inevitable part of life. All cultures and religions experience times of decline and decay. In order for them to survive, revitalization and renewal are necessary.

Cultural Revitalization. Revitalization movements are a deliberate effort to construct a more satisfying CULTURE. Though they may include religious elements, their major focus involves the entire cultural system. When reality provides no escape from the frustration of social deterioration, revitalization movements offer a way out.

The Ghost Dance of the American Indians, the Mau Mau of Africa, and the CARGO CULTS of Melanesia longed for the defeat of an enemy, freedom from slavery, and arrival of utopian riches. These dreams were nurtured by anxiety that reached an explosive intensity. In each case, the anticipated overthrow of an existing system—and inauguration of a replacement—was an attempt to reduce stress.

According to Anthony Wallace, a common sequence in revitalization movements involves: (1) the normal state in which needs are adequately met by existing components in the society; (2) a period of increased stress, where frustration is amplified by outside domination or lack of material goods; (3) a time of cultural distortion when normative methods of releasing tension are laid aside; and (4) the rise of a revitalization movement, a dynamic group within a community dedicated to overcoming degradation in their midst. Often these movements are out of touch with reality, doomed to failure from the start. Sometimes revitalization movements stir a latent power within a culture whereby satisfying correctives are generated. As a result, further decline is avoided, achieving a new normal state.

Spiritual Renewal. Religions remain viable only as they periodically experience renewal. The divine side of renewal is called revival. The human manifestation is labeled nativistic, messianic, millennial, or renewal movements. Though they differ in form and content from place to place and from time to time, renewal movements typically emerge when religions lose their vitality. Where renewal furnishes a system of meaningful beliefs and practices—a system useful in dealing with the realities of life—old beliefs and practices are altered or abandoned (depending on the extent and immediacy of the need for change). Under such circumstances, teachers, leaders, messengers, prophets, or messiahs provide supernaturally sanctioned reinterpretations of traditional ideologies, establish a new sect within the old religious system, or begin a new religion. Spiritual renewal usually involves both borrowing and inventing, a reworking of old and adding of new religious elements.

Renewal is instigated by various conditions and implemented through different processes. Religion grows stale when excitement, sacrifice, and commitment give way to cold, mechanical, and impersonal performance. What began as a vibrant movement hardens into a lifeless organization. Vision is lost. Focus shifts from people to programs, from flexibility to rigidity, from ministry to administration. The shell of religiosity no longer satisfies the human need to meet the holy. A seedbed for change, the conditions for renewal are present.

Religion should be an intensely personal matter expressed in a closely knit community. When these are absent, renewal will focus on individuals and organizations. Individual renewal is needed when religious fervor wanes. Spiritual refreshment comes from above (chants, sermons, prayer, meditations, songs, and pilgrimages help fan the dying embers of a sagging faith into the glowing warmth of a new life). Newness expresses itself in two areas. First, individual renewal will result in personal restoration. People will rededicate themselves to their religion, recommit themselves to their God or gods. A personal restoration includes abandoning an old life and adopting a new life that brings knowledge, healing, liberation, purity, salvation, or forgiveness. Second, individual renewal will express itself in ritual rejuvenation. Ritual is a way of acting out religion, a way of escaping the secular routine of daily living to enter spiritual realms. The solution to dead rituals is not rejecting but regenerating them. Renewal reinstills the sacred in worship. A confrontation with the holy restores a sense of awe, mystery, or respect for the divine.

Organizational renewal is needed when an institution imposes dehumanizing rules and procedures on its members. Since some sort of religious system is essential, the solution is not destroying but renewing organization. Reforming churches, monasteries, fellowships, orders, agencies, and movements will minimize their evil and maximize their good. Organizational renewal takes two forms. First, it manifests itself in para-institutions. Those organizations that stand alongside existing institutions address particular issues that have been neglected, lost, or deemphasized by the older organizations. Such groups attract talented people with high commitment. As older organizations lose members and resources, they either die, create rivalries, or renew themselves. Recent Christian para-institutions include Focus on the Family, Promise Keepers, InterVarsity Christian Fellowship, Christian Business Man's Club, Youth for Christ, Navigators, and Campus Crusade for Christ (*see* Parachurch Agencies). Non-Christian para-institutions include the Rastafarians, Radhasoami, Eckankar, Theosophy, and the Anthroposophical Society.

Organizational renewal reveals itself in new structures. When bureaucratic inertia and membership nominalism deaden an organization, those who retain the commitment of the "founding fathers" may begin anew. Reshaping the old seems hopeless. New structures become a viable option. Catholic orders and Protestant denominations are salient Christian examples of this phenomenon. Black Muslims, New Thought Movement, The Self-Realization Fellowship, Soka Gakkai, Great White Brotherhood, and the Bahai faith are new structures that grew out of non-Christian religious organizations.

Culture and religion provide a worldview that describes and explains the nature of the universe, humanity, and the holy. As circumstances render elements of Worldview impracticable, new beliefs and practices are required. Where change is slow, there is usually time for gradual adjustments. Where change is rapid, traditional beliefs and practices fail to help adherents adjust quickly enough. As a consequence, cultural revitalization and spiritual renewal often develop. When these adaptive efforts succeed, new cultural and spiritual expressions are born that will last until they also become irrelevant to the ever-changing ways of life.

Ed Mathews

See also Change, Sociology of; New Religious Movements.

Bibliography. P. Hammond, *An Introduction to Cultural and Social Anthropology;* P. Hiebert, *Anthropological Reflections on Missiological Issues;* C. Kottak, *Anthropology: The Exploration of Human Diversity;* A. Wallace, *An Anthropological View;* idem, *Culture and Personality.*

Repentance. Repentance is the central message that the church is to bring to the world (Luke 24:47). It is a characteristic of the life of the church, and is one of the primary goals of the church's mission.

The key terms in the Old Testament are *nâham* and *shûbh*. The former word carries the root idea of "to pant, sigh, or groan." It speaks of lamenting and grieving and when it is aimed at one's own character it has the idea of repenting. The latter word speaks of turning from sin to righteousness (2 Chron. 7:14). Through Israel, God calls all nations to repent.

The key New Testament terms are *metamelomai*, *metanoeō*, and *epistrephō*. *Metamelomai* stresses the emotional aspect of care, concern, and regret. It can refer to genuine repentance (Matt. 21:29, 32) and may also refer to a regret and remorse that is not accompanied by an abandonment of sin (Matt. 27:3). *Metanoeō* is used to note the need to "have another mind" by changing one's opinion and purposes (Matt. 3:2; Mark 1:15; Acts 2:38). The dominant idea of *epistrephō* is a change of mind that may result in accompanying emotions and consequent reformation.

Elements of Repentance. True repentance has intellectual, emotional, and volitional elements. Intellectually it involves a change of mind about God, sin, Christ, and oneself. The resultant change of mind views God as good and holy; sin as evil and injurious before God and people; Christ as perfect, necessary, and sufficient for salvation; and oneself as guilty and in need of salvation. Such repentance is an essential element of missionary proclamation.

Repentance involves a change of view, a change of feelings and a change of purpose. The emotional aspect may be seen in the passionate pleas found in David's repentance (Ps. 51:1, 2, 10, 14), and in Jesus' testimony of the tax-gatherer's feeling of remorse that led to faith (Matt. 21:32). However, when the emotional element stands by itself it is not true repentance (Matt. 27:3; Luke 18:23, cf. 2 Cor. 7:9–10). The sorrow that leads to repentance is a sorrow for *sin*, not only for its consequences. The volitional aspect of repentance is seen in the turning to God in faith (1 Thess. 1:9), and is an anticipated outcome of the church's mission among the nations.

Elaboration of Meaning. Repentance may be defined as a change of mind that is produced by the Holy Spirit leading to trust in God. Repentance is a part of true faith (Acts 20:21). It is not meritorious in itself, for Christ's death fully satisfies God's righteousness (Rom. 3:25). While repentance may lead to such outward acts as confession of sin and restitution, these are evidences of repentance and not the repentance itself. Repentance is an inward act that results in outward manifestations. Psalm 51 is an illustration of true repentance. The resulting attitude of repentance is reflected in Jesus' call to become like a child (Matt. 18:2–4) as well as in the first four Beatitudes (Matt. 5:3–6).

Subjects and Objects of Repentance. God has commanded the world to repent in order to avoid his judgment (Acts 17:30). His patience and kindness move him to be slow to wrath (Rom. 2:4; 2 Peter 3:9). God does not repent in the sense of changing his immutable perfection (1 Sam. 15:29), but his roused emotion may prompt him to a different course of action in carrying out his sovereign plan (Exod. 32:14; Jonah 3:10). It may imply God's sorrow or grief over humanity's sin (Jer. 6:6).

Unbelievers and believers may be appropriate subjects of repentance. The mission of the church is to carry out God's declaration to the world to repent and trust in Christ. The church is to exemplify a repentant lifestyle (Ps. 119:128). Jesus' command to take up one's cross is another way of describing this attitude, elaborated in Romans 6:11–13.

Repentance may have a variety of objects. Scripture speaks of repenting from trusting in money (Acts 8:22) as well as from a lack of trust in God's Word (Zech. 1:6). It also speaks of repentance from dead works (Heb. 6:1), idols (Ezek. 14:6), and leaving one's first love (Rev. 2:4–5). Repentance involves dealing with anything that hinders one from living under the authority of God (James 4:1–10) and being reconciled to other believers (Luke 17:3–4). Biblically, missionary proclamation must include a call to unbelievers to "repent and be baptized" (Acts 2:38; 3:19; 17:30; 26:20).

Preaching of Repentance. Repentance is a key theme in the proclamation of the church to a lost world that stands in need of the Savior. It was characteristic of the prophetic preaching (Jer. 8:6; Ezek. 14:6), John the Baptist (Matt. 3:2), Jesus (Matt. 4:17), the Twelve (Mark 6:12), Peter (Acts 2:38), and Paul (Acts 20:21). It is a message that is to be proclaimed to all peoples (Luke 24:47).

Reformed theology stresses the fact that repentance is a gift of God and a result of regeneration (Acts 5:31; 11:18; 2 Tim. 2:22). Arminian theology stresses the human element in repentance and regeneration. God is recognized in the latter as the primary cause and the person as the less principal cause. In both theologies the human responsibility of declaring God's Word is embraced as the means that God's Spirit uses to work repentance (Luke 10:30).

Results of Repentance. Christ's commission to the church to declare the message of repentance is motivated by God's kindness as God yearns for all peoples to taste the benefits that result from repentance. The Scriptures give the sad examples of the impenitent who refuse to live in agreement with God. Those who do repent become special objects of God's compassion. Repentance leads one to the experience of life (Acts 11:18), joy (2 Cor. 7:9), truth (2 Tim. 2:25), forgiveness (Acts

2:38), and the rule of God (Matt. 4:17). Repentance averts the wrath of God (Jonah 3:4–10) and leads to rejoicing in heaven (Luke 15:7, 10). An unrepentant church will no longer reflect the light of Christ (Rev. 2:5) that alone can lead the world to repentance.

WILLIAM D. THRASHER

Bibliography. J. Goetzmann and F. Laubach, *NID-NTT*, I:353–59; V. P. Hamilton, *TWOT*, II:909–10; O. Michel, *TDNT*, IV:626–29; E. Würthwein and J. Behm, *TDNT*, IV:975–1009.

Research. Disciplined inquiry suggesting a diligent search. Research involves investigating, inquiring, confirming, exploring, examining, inspecting, or collecting information about what can be known about a given topic. It goes beyond the casual observation or the ordinary human inquiry. Missiological research is a disciplined approach to collect data, analyze these data, and present them in service of the MISSIO DEI. Missiological research typically involves multiple academic disciplines because of the complexity and breadth of the issues involved.

Missiological research typically serves to develop theory, test theory, or employ theory to provide useful information for action or decision making. The development of theory allows one to explain what has been observed, predict what is likely to occur, provide bases for action, and provide means for validation of what is believed to be true. These theories depend on sets of assumptions or paradigms and ultimately on a person's WORLDVIEW. Paradigms provide the perspectives or assumptions from which one views. Theories differ from facts. Facts are observed phenomena whereas a theory is a systematic explanation of the facts. Theories also differ from laws that are "universal generalizations" about classes or categories of facts such as the "law of gravity" (Babbie, 51).

Types of Research. Research may be categorized in a variety of ways that depict differing aspects of its methods and purpose. *Descriptive research* seeks to describe what is or has been. The outcome is theory or a systematic explanation of what has been observed. Descriptions may range from perceptions or attitudes to behaviors and outcomes. Methods may arise out of history, sociology, anthropology, theology, or other academic disciplines and may be inductive or deductive.

Experimental research serves to test theory and is characterized by the control and manipulation of the variables and observation of the outcomes.

Evaluative research depends on the data collection methods of other approaches, but adds the element of values. The collection of data, the measurements of the data, and the interpretation of the data are all done in the light of a set of values. The outcome of this kind of research is useful information for decision making or value-based information.

Qualitative or Quantitative Research. Most simply the difference between qualitative and quantitative research is the difference between non-numerical and numerical data. That which can be counted is quantitative. That which cannot be counted is qualitative. One can count ten apples, for example—quantitative data. However, one cannot count another person's attitude toward those ten apples. That is qualititative data. Both kinds of research are important, but require different kinds of attention. Often the qualitative issues are the more significant and the more difficult to ascertain.

Inductive or Deductive Research. Inductive research moves from the particular to the general. Inductive research often does not explain the "why" but rather the "what" of the patterns of the phenomena being examined. Deductive research, on the other hand, typically moves from a generalization (a theory) to the particular or specific case. Deductive research moves from what would be expected to be observed to what actually happens. It begins with the "why" and moves to the "whether" or "what" of the occurrence. Both ways of doing research provide valid approaches.

Primary or Secondary Research. Primary research addresses the subject at hand by examining the original documents, observing the participant, and interviewing the actors. It treats the original information. Secondary research, on the other hand, searches what has already been studied about the topic. One might do primary exegetical research by reading a biblical text and then describing what the text means. Or, one may do secondary research about the same text to see what someone else has written about it. One might read an ethnography about the Maasai people as secondary research or go to observe and interview Maasai people directly as primary research.

Two primary issues arise when doing research. They appear in somewhat different ways, depending on the academic discipline and method from which one approaches the inquiry. These two issues are validity and reliability. Validity relates to the collection of the right information, whereas reliability has to do with consistency in the production of findings. One may be reliable, but miss the point. However, for one to have a valid study, it must also be reliable. One may accurately describe the pattern of aging among career missionaries (reliability), but that pattern will not answer the question about how many short-term missionaries will become career missionaries (a question of validity).

Significance for Missions. The usefulness of research for missions can hardly be overestimated. Biblical and theological research provides the "why" for missions as well as direction about the undergirding values, the how, who, where, when, why, how much, and in what social contexts. Several general points of significance may emerge from a single piece of missiological research, including: theory development, the testing of theory, value(s) identification, and ministry enhancement. Missiological research, like other research that depends in part on the social sciences, does not aim to "prove" anything in an absolute way, but rather to investigate and describe. These investigations may serve to provide useful information for decision making, strategic planning, and action, but not proof.

Missiological research does not aim to prove, but to investigate. Proof requires a standard of validity and reliability that is not possible with the kinds of issues treated in missiology. The limitations of the methods available reduce the kinds of conclusions (level of proof) that can be established. The "proof" level is different from a chemistry study in which timing, temperature, and other conditions may be held constant. Some of these missiological constraints include the complexity of the subject matter, particularly in intercultural contexts, as well as difficulties in observation. Motives, values, and attitudes are difficult to measure and assess even in one's own culture. When one crosses a cultural boundary, not only will these differ; their indicators will also differ. Exact replication is seldom if ever possible. Generally, one may expect interactions between the observer and the subjects. This interaction almost always colors the outcomes. Full control of the research situation is seldom if ever possible. Generally, the more significant the issues, the more difficult they are to measure. More trivial and insignificant issues are generally more easily quantified. One can easily count the people who live in a household, village, or city, but to describe their attitudes or to develop a full description of their worldview is very difficult. Even when all of the measures have been done, and done carefully, difficulties arise because each person's worldview perspectives will guide the way that person interprets the data and this will differ from another's. For example, when someone from the United States asks how old a person is, the responder will count from the time of birth. A Chinese will count from the time of conception. One's perspective makes a difference. With these kinds of complexities, one can hardly claim to "prove" anything.

Contemporary Missiological Research. In contemporary missiology, research may be typically divided into two broadly related, but differing arenas: academic missiology and applied missiology. Academic missiology generally seeks to broaden the theoretical bases of missiological research. Various forms of historical and theological research typically come in focus in this kind of missiological research. Broad encyclopedic studies often constitute major goals of this kind of research. Some outstanding examples of this would include works such as David Barrett's *World Christian Encyclopedia* and the annual updates to statistical estimates of the world Christian population published in *IBMR;* Patrick Johnstone's *Operation World,* in which current reasonable descriptions are given of individual countries, their Christian populations, and prayer needs; Kenneth Scott Latourette's monumental *A History of Christianity;* and J. Edwin Orr's works about the history of awakenings and revivals. David J. Bosch's *Transforming Mission* serves this genre from a theological perspective. All of these works have required an enormous amount of research leading to the development of missiological theory.

On the other hand, applied missiology takes on a much more immediate and practical sense. One could cite many outstanding examples of applied missiology. Linguistic research done by Wycliffe Bible Translators or developmental research done by World Vision would fit well in this genre. Applicational missiological research has focused on such diverse issues as church planting, curriculum improvement for leadership training, contextualizing theology, Bible translation, leadership emergence patterns, cross-cultural communication, and power ministries.

Both academic and application-oriented research have contributed to the other arena. However each researcher must clarify which of them is the researcher's focus. Each broad approach has developed a set of risks. A risk that commonly accompanies academic missiology is its occasional overemphasis on the theory with little thought to the application or relevance of the theory to real-life missiological situations. A parallel risk from the more applicational side of missiological research involves too strong an emphasis on contemporary action without a firm rooting in what could have been learned from other situations (theory).

Research continues to serve the *missio Dei.* Research does not replace the work of the Spirit but may be used as a means of discerning the leading and work of the Spirit. Research is not a substitute for prayer. It is a disciplined way of doing inquiry into the world around us and the revelation that God has provided.

EDGAR J. ELLISTON

Bibliography. E. Babbie. *The Practice of Social Research;* D. B. Barrett, *WCE;* P. Johnstone, *OW;* D. Bosch, *Transforming Mission: Paradigm Shifts in Theology of Mission.*

Restricted Access Countries. *See* CREATIVE ACCESS COUNTRIES.

Resurrection of Christ. The resurrection of Christ from the dead determines the nature of Christianity and defines its uniqueness. Of all religious systems, Christianity alone has made the bodily resurrection of an historical person the centerpiece of its message and faith. Mission as a centrifugal activity traces its dynamic directly from the resurrection. Resurrection and mission cannot be separated.

Resurrection and Scripture. The resurrection finds its origins deep in salvation history, even if there are very few verbal references to it in the Old Testament outside Daniel 12:2. Paul, as a Jewish scholar, was the first Christian to write about the resurrection. Paul's salvation experience, the mission to Jews and Gentiles, and discipling have their origins in his belief in and experience of the resurrection.

If the truth of the resurrection finds few verbal references in the Old Testament, how can Paul say that his preaching of the resurrection is "according to scripture" (1 Cor. 15:4)? For Paul and the early church the gospel is a salvation-history story, that is, the theme of resurrection is implicit in Israel's story of promise and fulfillment. The resurrection is at the heart of this story and gives the story significance and meaning.

Paul preached the crucifixion and resurrection of Jesus Christ. The longest chapter in all of Paul's epistles is on the resurrection (1 Cor. 15). His confidence in the resurrection was grounded in the testimony of numerous witnesses. Paul mentions witnesses such as Peter, the Twelve, James, the apostles, and more than five hundred, most of whom were still alive when he wrote. Finally, he was convinced of the resurrection because of having personally seen the risen Jesus (cf. 15:8 with 15:5–7). For Paul, an historical bodily resurrection was the bedrock of Good News. "If only for this life we have hope in Christ we are to be pitied more than all men" (1 Cor. 15:19).

All the New Testament writers agree with this emphasis on the resurrection. All of the Gospel writers conclude their accounts of the life and ministry of Christ with accounts of the resurrection of Jesus from the dead (Matt. 28; Mark 16; Luke 24; John 20–21). Luke takes the story one step further and recounts how the resurrection message was preached. For instance, Luke's summary of Peter's first sermon on the day of Pentecost gives more space to the resurrection than to any other subject (Acts 2:22–36).

The theme of resurrection is a dominant theme in Acts, finding its way into all parts of Luke's narrative (1:2, 25; 2:22–36; 3:15; 4:10, 33; 5:30; 7:56; 9:4; 10:40; 13:30–37; 17:3, 31–32; 22:7ff., 26:14ff., 23). Along with these explicit references to the resurrection are many other references where Luke ties the resurrection of Christ to hope as the center of the law and prophets and to Israel's general hope in the resurrection (23:6; 24:15; 21b; 26:22; and 28:20b).

Mission and Resurrection. For many the best proof of the historical resurrection is the existence of the Christian church. Within three centuries of the resurrection Christianity had become the dominant religion within the Roman Empire. This growth has continued unabated and today the Christian church numbers almost 2 billion, larger than Islam and Hinduism combined.

The biblical records intertwine resurrection and mission. The resurrection is both the green light for centrifugal missions and the impetus to carry out mission. Paul ties his apostolic commission as an apostle to the Gentiles with his experience with the resurrection of Christ (Gal. 1:16; 1 Cor. 15:8). John, Luke, and Matthew make it clear that mission was Jesus' central concern after his resurrection. Matthew shows the resurrected Jesus royally enthroned as the Lord of the nations, commissioning the apostles in Galilee with authority to engage in discipling the nations (Matt. 28:16–20). John reveals Jesus almost breathlessly rushing back to the upper room, and, after a hurried shalom says, "As the Father has sent me, I am sending you" (John 20:21).

Luke relates resurrection and mission in a number of ways. First, he shows its relationship to all of Scripture and to Jesus' incarnation (Luke 24:19–27, 37–44). Second, the resurrected Jesus blesses the commissioned apostles as he ascends to heaven (Luke 24:45–51). Third, Jesus appears to the apostles over a period of forty days, thereby confirming his resurrection as he expounds on their future mission. He concludes this period of time by giving as the fundamental consequence of the resurrection, not the founding of a kingdom with Israel as its center, but the founding of a worldwide mission with Spirit-empowered believers at the center (Acts 1:1–11). Finally, Luke concludes by showing that apostleship included preaching the resurrection and fulfilling the call of worldwide mission (Acts 1:12–26).

Scripture places the greatest importance on the relationship of resurrection and mission. Without the resurrection there is no gospel. Without mission the resurrection remains useless. The resurrection of Jesus makes mission and message possible.

HAROLD E. DOLLAR

Bibliography. D. C. Allison, *The End of the Ages Has Come;* H. Berkhof, *Christ the Meaning of History;* D. J. Bosch, *Transforming Mission;* O. Cullmann, *Salvation in History;* X. Leon-Dufour, *Resurrection and the Message of Easter;* P. Perkins, *Resurrection: New Testament Witness and Contemporary Reflection;* N. E. Thomas, ed., *Classic Texts in Mission and World Christianity.*

Return of Christ. *See* PAROUSIA.

Reunion (French Overseas Department) *(Est. 2000 pop.: 697,000; 2,510 sq. km. [969 sq. mi.]).* Reunion is a volcanically active island in the Indian Ocean, east of Madagascar. Reunionese Creole and Reunionese White make up 70 percent of the population. Tamils, at 15 percent, comprise a significant minority. Eighty-eight percent of the population is Christian with most of these being Roman Catholics. Assemblies of God, the fastest growing of all denominations, grew from only 800 members in 1970 to over 25,000 by 1995.

TODD M. JOHNSON

Revelation, General. Apart from revelation, there is neither genuine knowledge of God nor Christian faith. The core idea of revelation comes from the Hebrew *gamlah* and the Greek *apokalyptō*, whose basic meaning is "to uncover" or "to disclose." Revelation is the activity of God whereby he "uncovers" or discloses what was previously not known nor could be known.

The Scriptures speak of two kinds of revelation: general and special. General revelation is distinguished from special revelation in mode, content, and function. Special revelation is that divine activity whereby God discloses himself (knowledge, will, and purposes) to specific persons at particular times in history for the purpose of redemption. The inspired record of this is given in the BIBLE. On the other hand, general revelation is God's universal self-disclosure. Through general revelation a general knowledge of God has been made available to all humanity at all times. The main biblical passages which relate to general revelation are Psalm 19:1–6; Job 36:24–37:24; Romans 1:18–32; 2:14–15; Acts 14:15–17; and Acts 17:16–34 (many include John 1:9).

These passages speak of four ways (modes) in which general revelation is conveyed. First, the most evident mode of general revelation is the created order (Ps. 19:1–6; Rom. 1:19, 20). Something of the greatness, majesty, and nature of the Creator is disclosed by what he has made. Second, God's continuing care for what he has made testifies to his reality and goodness (Acts 14:17). Prayer and sacrifice during difficult times and thanksgiving during plentiful times have been a universal human experience, indicating a natural awareness of human dependence upon God. That God provides for human needs discloses his care and kindness. Third, human moral CONSCIENCE is another source of general revelation (Rom. 2:14, 15). God has created human beings with the ability to know moral right and wrong. This sense of right and wrong, at least partially, corresponds with God's moral nature. Fourth, the innate awareness of God, or what John Calvin called the *divinitatis sensum* (sense of divinity), is another way in which God is disclosed. This innate awareness is the seed of religion. Though this

seed has germinated differently in the many and diverse religions of the world, these religions testify to the internal awareness of the reality of God and the desire to know him. History is possibly a fifth mode of general revelation. Traditionally many have held that God discloses himself through the course and events of history. Certainly God acts in history and is directing the course of history. However, significant questions have been raised concerning our ability to discern God and his purposes in history. Even with the benefit of special revelation, the significance of particular historical events are often ambiguous and open to differing interpretations.

Dealing with the concrete content of general revelation is more problematic. The question of what can be known about God on the basis of general revelation alone (natural theology) has received considerable attention. The views of this have varied widely. Pluralistic theology, a contemporary form of liberal theology, contends that any knowledge or experience of God has its source in some form of general revelation only. It denies special revelation and rejects the uniquely inspired status of the Bible.

Thomas Aquinas is representative of a second approach that has had wide acceptance traditionally. Aquinas argued that God's existence could be proved and some knowledge of God attained through rational reflection on the created order. Such knowledge is not sufficient for salvation but was deemed to be adequate to prove the existence of God. The limitations of this view have become increasingly evident. The ability of these arguments to convince largely rests upon one's presuppositions and worldview.

A third approach is provided by John Calvin, who saw general revelation as having the ability to supplement and deepen the knowledge of God provided by special revelation, but only as general revelation was viewed through the "spectacles" of special revelation. Calvin insisted that because of sin it is not possible to develop a systematic and reliable knowledge of God. At best one gains bits and pieces of knowledge of God. In the twentieth century, Karl Barth's complete denial of general revelation represents the other extreme of the continuum of views. For Barth, the infinite qualitative distinction between God and humanity (God's total otherness), humanity's sinfulness, and Barth's tendency to equate any revelation with salvific experience of God led to a complete negation of the possibility of true knowledge of God, however minute, through general revelation. While this approach has appealed to many, it does contradict the testimony of Psalm 19, Romans 1:19f., and Romans 2:14–15.

Some of the difficulty in determining the precise content of general revelation rests in the fact that Scripture itself does not deal exhaustively with the issue. However, some indication is given of what can be known of God in general revelation. Psalm 19:1 states, "The heavens declare the glory of God; the skies proclaim the work of his hands." God intended creation itself to reveal the great intellect, wisdom, creativity, and ability of the One who made it all. Romans 1:20 declares that God's "eternal power and divine nature" can be known through that which he has made. It should be evident that he has the abilities and power necessary to effect that which he has made and that he possesses the attributes normally associated with deity.

Other considerations, however, mitigate against the attainment of concrete and consistent knowledge of God through general revelation. Human sinfulness (Rom. 1:21f.; 2 Cor. 4:4), human finitude (i.e., the natural limitations on human perception and understanding), and the fact that creation itself suffers under God's judgment (Rom. 8:20, 21), all contribute to the human inability to derive a natural theology. Special revelation is necessary to overcome these barriers to knowledge of God. Although general revelation potentially and in principle yields a definite knowledge of God, the actual attainment of such knowledge is severely limited and can only be attested through consistency in Scripture. General revelation points to God's abilities but is less clear on his character and purposes. The same creation that points to God's kindness because of his provision for human needs (Acts 14:17) also is the cause of great suffering through catastrophes, droughts, and the like. Calvin rightly asserted that we must look at general revelation through the "spectacles" of Scripture. Special revelation provides the necessary interpretive framework from which one can more clearly discern the abilities, character, and purposes of God witnessed to by general revelation.

What then is the function of general revelation for us today? Scripture suggests two ways in which it continues to serve God's purposes. On the one hand, it is an evidence of God's continuing love and mercy toward humankind. God continues to provide a witness to himself (Acts 14:17) and to stir humanity to seek him (Acts 17:27). On the other hand, general revelation serves God's redemptive purposes. Human rejection of general revelation demonstrates both God's justice in judging human sin (Rom. 1:19ff.; 2:12–16) and the need for special revelation and the gracious provision of redemption through his Son, Jesus Christ.

Implications for Missions. One's understanding of general revelation has important implications for several areas that pertain to the church's obligation to and practice of missions.

View of Other Religions. This is particularly true in relation to non-Christian religions. Religious PLURALISM presupposes that some form of a universal, general revelation is the ground of all religions, Christianity included. Karl Rahner's "Anonymous Christian" thesis represents an inclusivist approach which, while maintaining the superior and definitive nature of special revelation, allows for the possibility of true knowledge and redemption in other religions. As such, other religions are not hostile or in competition with Christianity. Rather, they are limited attempts to respond to God's general revelatory activity that need to be completed or corrected by special revelation. Evangelical theology's perspectives have ranged between seeing religions as well-intentioned but erroneous means of responding to God to being the product of active rebelliousness to what has been revealed by God in general revelation.

Religious expression is the consequence of the fact that God reveals himself and that humanity has both the innate ability and urge to know him. The only source of knowledge of God available to non-Christian religions is general revelation. However, the fallen state of creation and human nature results in the corruption of truth available in general revelation. Scripture's teaching on false worship, the inevitable and willful distortion of general revelation (Rom. 1:19ff.), Satan's deceptive activities, as well as redemption, all indicate that, whether well-intentioned or not (humanly speaking), non-Christian religions cannot attain true knowledge of God or accomplish reconciliation with God. Christianity must regard other religions as inadequate (at best) forms of worship which must be replaced by indigenous and culturally relevant forms of true worship based on special revelation (cf. Acts 17:22ff.).

Nature and Source of Salvation. Basing themselves on general revelation, many today hold that SALVATION is possible apart from the proclamation of the gospel. The pluralist maintains that all religions are equally ways of salvation and the source of knowledge for salvation (usually understood as some form of moral life) is general revelation, to which all people have equal access. Inclusivists maintain the necessity of Christ's atonement for salvation, but not the necessity of knowing and confessing Christ. If one responds to what knowledge of God is made known in general revelation, this faith is just as efficacious a saving faith as that faith which is consciously placed in Christ and the proclaimed gospel.

Scripture may permit an openness to the possibility that some may find full acceptance by God apart from the knowledge provided by special revelation or the gospel (e.g., Melchizedek). However, Scripture is silent concerning how such individuals came to faith so we must be careful about drawing conclusions from such exceptions. Scripture is more clear that humanity has willfully distorted what truth is given in general revelation and that the proclamation of the gospel is needed for salvation (cf. Rom. 10:14, 15). Therefore, an important element in the church's motivation for mission is the recognition that general revelation is not a sufficient source for salvation. In obedience to the Lord's command and in light of human estrangement from God because of SIN, the church is compelled to go to all the world with the gospel of salvation.

Contextualization. CONTEXTUALIZATION is concerned both with communicating the gospel to other cultures and with the development of culturally relevant theology. The universal nature of human beings, of their religious need and experience, and of general revelation make contextualization of theology possible. Therefore, we both expect to find areas of common ground from which to communicate the gospel and some points of truth and experience in other cultures which can deepen our understanding of God and help shape culturally relevant theologies. We should avoid the extremes of radical discontinuity between the gospel and culture, as in neo-orthodoxy, and radical continuity between gospel and culture, as in liberal and pluralistic theologies. The SYNCRETISM of the latter is avoided only by subjecting the ideas, insights, and practices of culture to the criteria and authority of Scripture. Those elements in culture that are consistent with Scripture can be utilized in contextualizing the gospel and theology.

Dialogue and Cooperation. The postmodern spirit and religious pluralism have been leading advocates of religious DIALOGUE. They presume the basic equality of all religious expressions and seek to grow in knowledge of God through mutual dialogue and cooperation. A biblical understanding of general revelation, Scripture, Christ, and salvation cannot approach other religions in this way. True worship and knowledge of God comes only through submission to Christ and the revelation provided in Scripture.

The doctrine of general revelation does allow for the possibility of interreligious dialogue in areas of mutual concern (moral, social, ecological, etc.). Further, dialogue is a legitimate way to gain mutual understanding and respect and may even cause the Christian opportunity to reflect differently on his or her faith in such a way as to gain new understanding. But Scripture is the sole authoritative and reliable source of knowledge of God. Truths gained through reflection upon general revelation are at best partial and must always be judged by Scripture.

WAYNE JOHNSON

Bibliography. E. Brunner, *Natural Theology;* B. Demarest, *General Revelation;* M. Erickson, *Christian Theology,* pp. 153–74; C. F. H. Henry, *God, Revelation and Authority,* vol. II, pp. 77–123; D. Hesselgrave and E. Rommen, *Contextualization;* C. Kraft, *Christianity and Culture,* pp. 169–253; H. Netland, *Dissonant Voices;* D. Okholm and T. Phillips, *More Than One Way?;* E. Rommen and H. Netland, *Christianity and the Religions.*

Revelation, Special. *See* BIBLE and REVELATION, GENERAL.

Reverse Culture Shock. The psychological, emotional, and even spiritual adjustment of missionaries who return to their home culture after having adjusted to a new culture. This shock is parallel to the CULTURE SHOCK experienced in initial adjustment to the mission field, but may be even more difficult because it can hit so unexpectedly. Also referred to as reentry shock, adjustment is necessary because both the missionary and the home culture have changed while the missionary was away. In addition, the home culture may have been idealized in the missionary's mind and no longer fits one's expectations.

The changes that have taken place in the missionary can be manifold. A major consideration here is that the nature of friendships and relationships varies dramatically from culture to culture. Missionaries who have crossed that divide often find that the way they look at relationships has fundamentally shifted, making readjustment to their home culture difficult. The missionary had to learn a host of new rules in the new culture; though initially strange, they have become comfortable ways of life that must be unlearned in the home culture.

The home culture (especially in the urban setting) also changes while the missionary is away. Changes may range from the relatively mundane (new television shows, new music, new stores) to deeper innovations (new church worship forms or even new religions, new expectations of toleration, new views on truth). All of these combined can make for a bewildering experience for one who is seeking security in what home was like before departure.

Reentry shock can be particularly acute for the children of missionaries (*see* THIRD CULTURE KIDS and MISSIONARY CHILDREN), some of whom may be entering the parents' home culture for the first time or have no real memories of that culture. Particular care should be taken to help them adjust to life in what for them was never really home at all.

A. SCOTT MOREAU

Bibliography. C. N. Austin, *Cross-Cultural Reentry: A Book of Readings.*

Revitalization Movements. *See* RENEWAL MOVEMENTS.

Revival, Revivals. The term "revival" means different things to different people. It has been used to describe renewed spiritual life, a series of evangelistic meetings, unbridled religious emotionalism, wild frontier religion, and fanaticism. How should the term be used?

Definition. The word "revival" means to wake up and live. The basic idea of revival is the returning of something to its true nature and purpose. It is a special movement of the Spirit of God in which he renews the hearts of believers. Earle Cairns defines revival as "the work of the Holy Spirit in restoring the people of God to a more vital spiritual life, witness, and work by prayer and the Word after repentance in crisis for their spiritual decline" (1986, 22).

The following points summarize this understanding of revival. First, revival comes from God. It is a work of the Holy Spirit. Second, revival primarily affects believers, those who have already experienced spiritual life. Third, revival presupposes declension. Fourth, prayer and the Scriptures are central in bringing and sustaining revival. Fifth, revival brings change, most specifically renewed spiritual life and witness. Isaiah's "revival" experience, described in Isaiah 6:1–8, serves as a paradigm for genuine revival. Isaiah encountered the presence of God and God's holiness overshadowed everything else. Isaiah recognized his sin and need for cleansing. This sense of brokenness in the presence of a holy God is an important characteristic of genuine revival. In Isaiah 5, we read of Isaiah pronouncing "woes" on others six different times. He could clearly see the sin in others' lives, and in his role as prophet he forthrightly said, "Woe to you." Yet when overcome by a deep awareness of God's holiness, Isaiah is not pointing his finger at anyone else. All he can say is, "Woe is me!"

When believers find themselves in the presence of a holy God during a time of revival, they become acutely aware of even the smallest sin. When God powerfully makes his presence known, anything out of keeping with his holiness is immediately brought to the surface. Sins which have been tolerated or excused as "little things" are suddenly brought to light and the fear of exposure pales in comparison with the need for confession and cleansing.

It is after conviction, repentance, and God's cleansing that joy comes (cf. Ps. 51). Conviction followed by confession and repentance leads to a freedom and joy in the experience of forgiveness. Joy comes through God's cleansing and ultimately leads to service.

The realization of being convicted and then cleansed by a holy God will make one eager to respond in gratitude to the Lord's call: "Here am I—send me!" Isaiah is available to God to be used however God chooses. When the burden of unconfessed sin is lifted there is freedom and willingness to serve.

Distinguishing between Revival and Revivalism. Revival, seen as a synonym for spiritual awakening, should be distinguished from revivalism, which is generally identified with prominent evangelists and mass evangelistic crusades focused on reaching the lost with the gospel. Despite a close relationship between revival and outreach, revival should not be seen as the same thing as EVANGELISM or revivalism. Confusion has resulted from using the terms "revival" and "revival meeting" for settings designed for preaching the gospel to the lost. One could drive by two different churches and see the following signs: "Revival every Sunday night!" and "Revival every night except Sunday!" Given this confused usage of the term "revival," one could be led to the absurdity of saying, "We had a revival, but no one was revived!"

Yet even though revival and evangelism are different in nature (as revival primarily deals with God's people whereas evangelism focuses on unbelievers), they both flow from the same source—the Holy Spirit. During times of revival, people call on the name of the Lord to be saved. Workers are raised up to go to the harvest fields of the world. An awakened church is an evangelistic church. An awakened believer is an evangelistic believer. When revival truly comes, evangelism will follow. Revival reminds us that methods, as important and helpful as they are, must always remain secondary in importance to the presence and power of the Holy Spirit in the life of believers.

Revival and Missions. Revival has had a profound impact on missions. First, tens of thousands have come to faith in Christ in great sweeping movements of the Holy Spirit around the globe. JOHN ELIOT'S ministry among Native Americans in Massachusetts and the Plymouth Colonies from 1647 to 1670 saw extraordinary results through periods of revival. From 1837 to 1843 a movement of revival swept Hawaii, with estimates as high as 20 percent of the population being converted to faith in Christ. The 1858 "Prayer Revival" saw scores of persons converted, with estimates as high as one million converts in the United States alone. Other countries which saw many come to faith in Christ during this period were Ireland, England, Scotland, Wales, South Africa, Scandinavia, Switzerland, Germany, and Canada.

The year 1860 saw revival in South India, the Ukraine, South Africa, and the Netherlands, while the following year a powerful awakening took place in Jamaica. The awakening of 1903 and following saw thousands converted in Wales, the United States, China, Denmark, Finland, Germany, Korea, Madagascar, Russia, Germany, and Sweden. East Africa had a tremendous period of revival from 1927 to 1935, as did China from 1927 to 1937, Ethiopia from 1936 to 1948, Indonesia from 1953 to 1971, and Canada in 1971–72.

This brief survey does not even begin to tell the full story. Numerous other examples could be cited of periods of awakening around the world.

During times of revival, thousands have come to faith in Christ. Second, revival also has impacted missions through the raising up of laborers to go to the harvest fields of the world. As the Isaiah 6 passage reminds us, a revived Christian is a Christian who has been reawakened to mission. One can point to several examples from church history to illustrate this point.

In the 1720s a powerful movement of revival began in Germany under the leadership of Count NICHOLAS VON ZINZENDORF that resulted in a major missionary thrust for decades to come. The Moravian missionary movement began in 1732 with the sending out of two missionaries. During the next 150 years the MORAVIANS would send out over two thousand missionaries to various foreign fields. Among those influenced by Moravian missionaries was JOHN WESLEY.

Wesley, along with GEORGE WHITEFIELD, became key leaders in the eighteenth-century evangelical awakening in Great Britain. In addition to thousands of persons being converted, many organizations were formed to promote Christian work in Great Britain and beyond. These groups included The Religious Tract Society (1799), The British and Foreign Bible Society (1804), the LONDON MISSIONARY SOCIETY (1795), the CHURCH MISSIONARY SOCIETY (1799), and THE BAPTIST MISSIONARY SOCIETY (1792), which sent out WILLIAM CAREY as its first missionary. The astonishing missionary advance in the late 1700s and early 1800s can be directly attributed to spiritual awaking.

In 1806, the famous HAYSTACK PRAYER MEETING took place at Williams College in Massachusetts. SAMUEL J. MILLS, a freshman at the college, helped lead a group of five students who were praying for revival on the campus. Being forced to seek shelter under the side of a large haystack during a storm, Mills challenged the others to join him in the task of taking the gospel to Asia. "We can do it if we will," he said. He led the group in prayer, providing the impetus for what would eventually become an unprecedented thrust in foreign missions. Mills would soon play a major role in the founding of the AMERICAN BOARD OF COMMISSIONERS FOR FOREIGN MISSIONS (1810), the American Bible Society (1816), and the American Colonization Society (1816). Thus, a plaque at the site of the Haystack Prayer Meeting bears the inscription, "The Birthplace of American Foreign Missions."

Other mission societies were formed during this period, including the New York Missionary Society (1798), the American Baptist Foreign Mission Society (1814), the Methodist Episcopal Foreign Mission Society (1819), the American Tract Society (1826), and the American Home Missionary Society (1826). Awakenings at numerous schools and colleges during this period resulted in large numbers of students going to the mission field under the auspices of these newly formed societies. Missionaries were sent to existing fields, and new works were started in places such as Hawaii, Indonesia, and Madagascar.

Following the 1858 Prayer Revival, a worldwide interdenominational student missionary movement began to flourish. In 1886, the STUDENT VOLUNTEER MOVEMENT was founded. This movement heightened missions awareness and over the next several decades helped recruit some 20,000 students who went forth to serve on the mission field. Other significant organizations that grew out of the 1858 Revival include the China Inland Mission (see OVERSEAS MISSIONARY FELLOWSHIP) and the AFRICAN INLAND MISSION.

The revival of 1904 and following brought the call of missions to many, including E. STANLEY JONES. Touched by a revival while a student at Asbury College in 1905, Jones committed himself to go to India as a missionary. Jones was not alone in sensing God's call to missions. As many as ten thousand missionaries went overseas from college campuses as a result of this awakening. This period also saw the beginnings of the PENTECOSTAL MOVEMENT with the Azusa Street Revival. Pentecostal and charismatic groups continue to have a growing impact on the scene of worldwide missions (see PENTECOSTAL MISSIONS). While many other examples could be cited, this brief survey demonstrates the significant impact revival has had upon the missionary enterprise. It would not be an exaggeration to characterize the history of the modern missions movement as the story of revival. When genuine revival comes, believers are reawakened to their evangelistic and social obligations. Mission efforts are a natural fruit of revival.

A Coming World Revival? Having briefly traced through history the impact of revival on missions, we now look to the role that revival might play in the future of missions. While some biblical scholars believe conditions in the world will continue to get worse and we cannot expect a great revival during the end times, others believe in the strong possibility of a coming world revival. This revival would result in multitudes of people responding to the gospel message and would raise up a host of workers for that great harvest of souls.

The Bible is clear that the GREAT COMMISSION will one day be fulfilled. There will be persons from "every nation, tribe, people and language" gathered around the throne, worshiping the Lamb of God (Rev. 7:9). While factors such as how one views the millennium, tribulation, and rapture will influence one's interpretation of these events (see ESCHATOLOGY), many believe the church will see a universal outpouring of the Holy Spirit in the days ahead. This coming world revival could take place in the midst of great suffering. The situation in the world and in the church would go from bad to worse. The conditions described in Matthew 24:5 and in Revelation 6–17 would become a reality. But out of this adversity people's thoughts would be turned to God. Many would acknowledge their need of a Savior.

The revival would sustain believers through their affliction and bring them to the true beauty of holiness. The church would be purified and empowered for ministry. There would be a great number of conversions as people cried out to the Lord. The revival would prepare the way for the return of Christ as Matthew 24:14 would be fulfilled (see END TIMES).

In summary, while there is no consensus on the likelihood of a coming world revival or on its timing in relation to other prophetic events, certainly the prospects of such a great revival is a summons to pray for such a work of revival around the world.

TIMOTHY K. BEOUGHER

Bibliography. E. E. Cairns, *An Endless Line of Splendor: Revivals and Their Leaders from the Great Awakening to the Present;* R. E. Coleman, *The Coming World Revival;* W. Duewel, *Revival Fire;* R. H. Glover, *The Progress of World-Wide Missions;* K. J. Hardman, *Seasons of Refreshing: Evangelism and Revivals in America;* I. Murray, *Revival and Revivalism: The Making and Marring of American Evangelicalism, 1750–1858;* J. E. Orr, *The Event of the Century: The 1857–58 Awakening;* R. O. Roberts, *Revival!*

Revolution. This term is generally associated with movements to overthrow existing governments through armed action and in that sense it is used to describe social processes as different as the American, French, and Russian Revolutions. The term may also be used to describe transformative processes that deeply affect cultural and social structures at their base in a slow and nonviolent way. The initial stage of Christian mission as recorded in the New Testament shows the transformative power of the gospel that upset existing structures and provoked reactions that ended in riots as in Philippi (Acts 16:11–40) or Ephesus (Acts 19:23–41). Roman authorities sometimes misjudged Jesus or Paul as political revolutionaries. Mission history at different moments records the revolutionary impact of the gospel, as in the transformation of the Roman Empire in the first two centuries, or the modernization of some Asian and African societies in our century. During the sixteenth century the Iberian Catholic mission in the Americas accompanied military conquest and the church became a symbol of the establishment and a defender of it against independence revolutions. Mission and empire were not so closely united in the Protestant missions of the nineteenth century, but missionaries still tended to support the imperial advance of their nation and worked within that frame (see also COLONIALISM). It is therefore understandable that theoreticians and leaders of revolutions such as Marx, Engels, or Lenin and their followers, would tend to see revolutionary movements as necessarily hostile to Christian mission. During the twentieth century, the revolt of Asian, African, and Latin American peoples against the European and North American colonial powers has been an important element of self-criticism for missions. Leaders of these revolutions were frequently inspired by Christian ideas of human dignity learned in missionary schools, but they adopted anti-Christian ideologies. The Marxist version of history that usually describes Christian mission as an ally of colonial powers should be matched with a more careful assessment of the liberating impact of mission work, such as that recorded by James Dennis in his three-volume *Christian Mission and Social Progress.* In spite of Western ethnocentrism the cultural transformation brought by Christian mission and Bible translation might be described as revolutionary. However, from the days in which Luke wrote Acts to the present situation, it has been necessary to state very clearly that the kind of deeply transformative social practice and proclamation of the gospel involved in mission does not imply the use of violent methods through which revolutionaries expect to change the world. This is a critical point because in some forms of liberation theology a theory of "just revolution" was developed adopting the medieval scholastic arguments in support of a "just war." On the other hand, there are presently places where oppressed ethnic minorities have been successfully reached by the gospel and have experienced church growth. Such is the case of Nagaland in India, the Karen and Chin communities in Myanmar, or the Mayan peoples in Chiapas, Mexico. The freedom and progress brought by Bible translation and proclamation of the gospel is considered something revolutionary and threatening for the dominant ethnic groups. Christian mission walks a rather tight rope in such situations.

SAMUEL ESCOBAR

Bibliography. J. Dennis, *Christian Missions and Social Progress: A Sociological Study of Foreign Missions;* S. Escobar and J. Driver, *Christian Mission and Social Transformation;* N. Goodall, *Christian Mission and Social Ferment;* B. Griffiths, ed., *Is Revolution Change?;* J. Míguez Bonino, *Toward a Christian Political Ethics;* S. Neill, *Colonialism and Christian Missions.*

Rhenish Mission Society *(Rheinische Missions Gesellschaft).* Representing pacesetting evangelical organizations, the Rhenish Mission Society is noted for its world missions emphasis, lay involvement, and cooperation with former mission fields.

In 1799 twelve Elberfeld, Germany laymen formed the Bergische Bible Society and the Wupperthal Tract Society. With the Barmen Mission Society (1815), these groups merged in 1828, forming the United Rhenish Missionary Society in Barmen. This organization focused on sending trained missionaries to non-Christian nations. Consisting mainly of Lutherans and Calvinists, their first missionaries arrived in South Africa in 1829.

The first Rhenish missionaries to South Africa worked with a broad range of people groups. By the twentieth century this area had 54 missionaries and over 11,800 communicants. Although the Rhenish missionaries have been accused of cooperating with Western colonialism in some of their work, their efforts culminated in 1957 when the Lutheran Church of South West Africa became independent.

Work in Borneo (now Malaysia), Dutch East Indies, began in 1842 (some sources list 1834). No converts were recorded for eight years and eventually insurrections and financial problems ended this Rhenish work. Two missionaries arrived in China in 1846 and the society's work there continued until 1951. The Chinese Rhenish Church, Hong Kong Synod, still exists today. In 1861 work began in Sumatra with the eventual rise of the Batak Protestant Christian Church. Work in eastern New Guinea began in 1885, but this effort was transferred to the American Lutheran Mission after World War I. By 1961 western New Guinea was added as a mission field.

In 1971 the Rhenish Mission Society and the Bethel Mission Society merged to form the United Evangelical Mission (German abbreviation VEM). In 1996 delegates from Asia, Africa, and Germany formed the "United Evangelical Mission—Community of Churches in Three Continents." Headquarters for this multinational society remained in Wuppertal, Germany. Current emphases include social ministries such as hunger aid and refugee relief.

MICHAEL R. SPRADLIN

Bibliography. Evangelical Church in Germany Bulletin, Sept. 1996; H. F. de Kline, *EMCM*, p. 563.

Ricci, Matteo (1552–1610). Italian Jesuit scholar and pioneer missionary to China. Ricci pioneered in Guangdong and Nanjing (1583–1601) before receiving permission to reside in Peking. Ricci mastered Chinese language, culture, literature, institutions, and government and further acculturated by adopting the prestigious attire of a Confucian scholar.

His books on Western science in Chinese were highly acclaimed and his "Great Map of Ten Thousand Countries," annotated in Chinese, opened the Chinese to globalism heretofore unknown.

Ricci rejected Buddhist notions of rebirth but accepted "original" Confucian thought as essentially monotheistic and consistent with Christian morality. His apologetic work, *The True Meaning of the Lord of Heaven* (1603), made use of Confucian terms to argue for and illustrate the Christian faith. In his view traditional ancestor worship was not idolatrous but this was sharply disputed by Dominicans and Franciscans, leading to the "Rites Controversy," which was finally decided by Clement XI (1704, 1715) against Ricci's position.

At his death advances were modest: eight foreign priests, eight Chinese lay brothers, missions in four cities, and 2,500 "neophytes." His grave was the gift of the emperor himself, a testimony to his stature as one of the most respected religious figures ever to come from the West.

JAMES F. LEWIS

Bibliography. A. C. Ross, *A Vision Betrayed: The Jesuits in Japan and China, 1542–1742.*

Rice Christian. *See* CULTURAL CONVERSION.

Richard, Timothy (1845–1919). British missionary to China. Born in Ffaldybrenin, South Wales, on October 10, 1845, Richard was baptized at age fifteen and soon thereafter decided to be a missionary. At age twenty he was admitted to Haverfordwest Theological Seminary, where he sensed a call to mission work in China. He was sent by the BAPTIST MISSIONARY SOCIETY to Shandong, North China, in 1869.

Once there, Richard realized that street evangelism and distributing Christian tracts were unfruitful. So he turned to writing on secular subjects such as modern science. He also raised funds and was the relief administrator for the famine in Shandong and Shanxi between 1876 and 1879. Among the Chinese literati, Richard established himself as a source of inspiration for reforms in education, agriculture, mining, transportation, and trade. After the Boxer Uprising in 1899–1900, Richard persuaded Qing officials to found Shanxi University. Throughout his career he had a deep interest in Chinese religions. His major publications include *Calendar of the Gods in China* (1906) and *Guide to Buddhahood: Being a Standard Manual of Chinese Buddhism* (1907). He died on April 17, 1919, three years after his retirement from China.

TIMOTHY MAN-KONG WONG

Bibliography. P. R. Bohr, *Famine in China and the Missionary: Timothy Richard as a Relief Administrator and Advocate of National Reform;* P. A. Cohen, *Papers on China* 11 (1957): 43–52; T. Richard, *Forty-five Years in China: Reminiscences.*

Richter, Julius (1862–1940). German missiologist. The son of a pastor, Richter was born near Osterburg in Brandenburg. His father died when he was young. After attending the Francke Stiftung, a private school in Halle, he went to Leipzig and then to Berlin to study theology. Having worked as a private teacher in Bad Boll following his theological examinations, he was accepted into the church seminary in Berlin (1886). Here he found an authoritative teacher in Rudolf Koegel. From 1887 to 1912 Richter pastored several different church parishes in the Brandenburg region. It was during these years that he began to write and publish articles concerning missions.

After receiving honorary doctorates from the Universities of Berlin (1908) and Edinburgh (1910), Richter began teaching at the University of Berlin, first as a private lecturer, then as a full professor of missiology (1914–30). He also served in official capacities at the Brandenburg Missionary Conference, the German Protestant Missionary Committee, and the GERMAN SOCIETY FOR MISSIOLOGY. Richter's numerous lecture tours took him across the world and opened to him distant relationships that allowed him to become one of the most significant ecumenical personalities of his day. In addition to his wish to serve his Lord alone, his varied work was characterized by a mentally sharp personality, tenacious industry, and a phenomenal memory.

ROLF HILLE

Ridderhof, Joy (1903–84). American missionary to Honduras and founder of Gospel Recordings. Ridderhof ranks among the major pioneers of twentieth-century missions. Gospel Recordings, which she founded in 1939, by 1997 provided the gospel message in almost five thousand languages. With a small band of volunteers and a handful of full-time staff, Gospel Recordings puts the good news in the heart language of more unreached people groups by far than anyone else in church history.

Ridderhof gained her hallmark perspectives on life as a young woman living in the home of ROBERT C. MCQUILKIN, first president of the fledgling Columbia Bible School (now Columbia International University): joy-filled faith and a passion for world evangelism. She testified of coming to Columbia from California a worried, fearful young woman and leaving as the first graduate of that institution, a new person. She went to Honduras as a pioneer missionary herself, but when illness kept her from returning there, she hit on the idea of sending her beloved people of Marcala "talking tracts"—recorded messages in Spanish. Within five years those recordings were being used over radio throughout Latin America. Invitations to record in Navaho and pleas from many missionaries catapulted her into a worldwide ministry. The rest is history. Averaging twenty new languages a year, more than half of all extant languages have now been recorded by teams sent out from over thirty countries by the Global Recordings Network.

ROBERTSON MCQUILKIN

Bibliography. S. M. Barlow, *Light is Sown;* P. Thompson, *Faith by Hearing;* S. B. Rossi, *Singing in His Ways.*

Riggs, Mary Ann Clark Longley (1813–69). American missionary to the Dakotas. The daughter of General Thomas Longley of Massachusetts, Riggs was educated to be a teacher by Mary Lyon, the founder of Mount Holyoke Seminary. After completing her studies, she was chosen to teach in a school in southern Indiana, where she met and married Stephen Return Riggs. The two departed for Bible translation and literacy work among the Dakota tribes of Minnesota in February 1837. The majority of their time among the Dakotas they lived and worked in Lac-qui-Parle, near Fort Rienville. Riggs taught the natives to read in Dakota and in English while her husband worked on translating the Bible. She also taught the women basic hygiene such as laundering clothing. The couple became involved in an experimental community, Hazelwood Republic, founded by the Dakotas, some of whom were the Riggs' converts, and ruled by an elected president. This experiment was cut short by an uprising, after which the Riggs moved to Beloit, Wisconsin. Mary died there on March 22, 1869. After her death, Stephen completed the translation of the entire Bible and wrote an autobiography of their work among the Dakotas using Mary's diary and letters.

GRACE L. KLEIN

Bibliography. S. R. Riggs, *Forty Years with the Sioux;* M. G. Humphreys, *Missionary Explorers Among the American Indians.*

Riis, Andreas (1804–54). Danish missionary of the Basel Mission Society to Ghana. Born in Luegumkloster, Denmark, and by trade a glassmaker, he studied at the Basel Mission's seminary and was posted as a chaplain to the Danish enclave at Christiansborg on the Gold Coast (modern-day Ghana) in 1832. Of the nine Basel missionaries sent there between 1828 and 1839, he was the only survivor. Dissatisfied with serving the European community and the unhealthy conditions on the coast, in 1835 he established (without mission permission) a station at Akropong in the hills 30 miles inland from Accra. Because of various difficulties he returned home, and the mission sent him to the West Indies to recruit Afro-Caribbean colonists. He chose 24 former slaves known for their religious devotion and technical skills as farmers and craftsmen, and returned to Akropong in 1843. He set up a mission plantation that became the nucleus of a Christian community in the Gold Coast. Because of allegations that he meddled in local politics, engaged in rum-running, and abused Africans under his supervision, Riis was recalled in 1845 and dismissed from the mission. He then accepted a pastorate in Norway and died shortly afterwards. Still, by his work at Akropong he essentially secured the Basel Gold Coast mission.

ULRICH VAN DER HEYDEN AND RICHARD V. PIERARD

Bibliography. P. B. Clarke, *West Africa and Christianity;* H. W. Debrunner, *The History of Christianity in Ghana;* C. Fyee, *DEB,* p. 940; J. Miller, *The Social Control of Religious Zeal.*

Rites Controversy. *See* ACCOMMODATION; ROMAN CATHOLIC MISSIONS.

Rites of Passage. Activities, usually rituals, marking culturally recognized transitions from one place to another, or from one stage of life to another. A rite of passage may mark any change of status—geographic place, condition of life, social position, or age. It gives public recognition to changed roles and relationships in the community, provides for readjustment of the society, affirms its values and beliefs, and helps the individual adjust to a new status.

Life transitions that commonly involve rites of passage are birth, initiation (admission into distinct groups of the society may occur several times, on entering different groups), marriage, parenthood, death.

Three phases of rites of transition are recognized: separation, transition, and incorporation, though these often overlap in the ritual activities (*see* RITUAL and CEREMONY). *Separation* marks withdrawal from a group and beginning the move to another place or status. *Transition* is the time between stages, having left one place or state and not yet having entered the next. It is also called the liminal phase of passage or segregation. Transitional people occupy ambiguous social positions, exempt from ordinary distinctions and expectations, and are frequently cut off from normal social contacts and behavior (*see* LIMINAL, LIMINALITY). Rites during the transition phase are often collective, building intense community spirit. A reversal of ordinary behavior may be a feature. Sometimes special conditions are imposed such as humility, poverty, obedience, sexual abstinence, or silence. *Incorporation* (also called integration or aggregation) is formally reentering society after completion of the rite. A new identity is recognized that establishes a changed social status. The missionary must consider if existing rituals can be given new meaning, or if a functional equivalent that is distinctly Christian can be introduced. Rites of passage can be a powerful medium for teaching and building Christian community.

DONALD K. SMITH

Bibliography. V. W. Turner, *The Ritual Process;* A. Van Gennep, *The Rites of Passage.*

Ritual and Ceremony. All religions have ways to attract the attention of supernatural beings and forces. These highly symbolic acts take many forms: MAGIC, supplication, SACRIFICE, or other means deemed necessary to restore and maintain balance between the supernatural and natural realms. Ritual brings MYTH to life and, though a performance invoking the action of powers that would otherwise not be present, allows for a display of beliefs and values. Such sacred drama is often performed by a religious practitioner who assists common people who are not equipped to approach these powers alone.

Anthropologists recognize three broad types of ritual. (1) Rites of transformation include ceremonies associated with stages of the life cycle (e.g., birth, naming, initiation, marriage, retirement, death), the recognition of conversion, and revivals or pilgrimages (*see also* RITES OF PASSAGE). (2) Rites of crisis are associated with healing, decision making, or dealing with calamity. (3) Rites of intensification answer the human need for order and identity (birthdays, planned festivals, and ancestral traditions). Ritual often takes place in stages that remove people from the mundane (e.g., ablution, removal of shoes, or silence upon entering a house of worship), bring them into the sacred (through worship), and return them to the mundane (e.g., putting on one's shoes before reentering the streets), better equipped to handle life.

Typically approaching religion as cognitive rather than experiential, Western missionaries have thereby rejected a holistic coincidence of supernatural and natural. This separation has created confusion for people who attempt to make God relevant to daily living. But by adapting Christian rituals to specific cultural contexts missionaries can demonstrate how God enters into relationship with people; for example, they might make use of the analogies between Christian baptism and pre-Christian initiation rites. However, care must be taken to ensure allegiance to God rather than to the ritual. The focus must be on God's intention to impact human affairs rather than on the power of a ritual to attract God's attention.

R. DANIEL SHAW

Bibliography. T. F. Driver, *The Magic of Ritual;* P. G. Hiebert, *Missiology* 10 (1982): 35–47; R. D. Shaw, *Missiology* 9 (1981): 159–65; A. R. Tippett, *Introduction to Missiology,* chap. 15; V. W. Turner, *The Ritual Process;* A. Van Gennep, *The Rites of Passage.*

Roberts, W. Dayton (1917–). American mission leader, author, and missionary in Costa Rica and Colombia. Born and raised by a missionary family in Korea, Roberts grew up deeply involved in the cause of mission.

After education at Wheaton College and Princeton Seminary, Roberts joined LAM in 1941. During his 41-year-tenure he spent five years in Colombia and the rest living or based in Costa Rica. A self-professed jack of all trades, Roberts' work included church planting, seminary teaching and leadership, and managing a radio station and a publishing house. He also directed Evangelism-In-Depth and facilitated the organization of CLAME (Latin American Community of Evangelical Ministries), a cooperative effort of several former LAM institutions. From 1982 he spent eight years before retirement working with World Vision in Monrovia, California, starting a journal, and directing MARC's publications program.

Roberts wrote no less than ten books, including *Revolution in Evangelism* (1967), *Strachan of Costa Rica* (1971), and more recently, *Patching God's Garment* (1994) and *One Step Ahead* (1996). His vision for mission is that of a holistic effort similar to a concert with a solo piano (*EMQ* 29:3 [July 1993]: 300–302). The piano is evangelism, and the rest of the orchestra the other elements of mission. While the piano is given the prominent role, all are needed for a successful performance.

A. SCOTT MOREAU

Bibliography. W. D. Roberts, *IBMR* 19:3 (July 1995): 110–12.

Rodgers, James Burton (1865–1944). American missionary to Brazil and the Philippines. Born in Albany, New York, Rodgers received degrees from both Hamilton College and Auburn Theological Seminary, and was ordained by the Presbyterian Church in the United States. He and his wife Anna were appointed as missionaries to Brazil, where they served for two terms.

Having acquired the Philippines as a result of its victory in the Spanish-American War, the United States opened the islands for the first time to Protestant missionaries. Eager to enter quickly, the Presbyterian Church transferred Rodgers to Manila before the fighting there was over. Leaving his family in Hong Kong, Rodgers arrived in Manila on April 21, 1899, began regular services on May 7, and baptized his first Filipino converts on October 22.

As a pioneer missionary, Rodgers warmly welcomed all new missionaries to the islands, often meeting them as they docked, and helping them to choose ministry locations. Deeply committed to COMITY and ecumenism, Rodgers was instrumental in the creation of the Evangelical Union of the Philippine Islands (1901). This body set up and governed the comity agreements between his denomination, the Methodists, the United Brethren, and other groups that joined later.

Rodgers helped to found the Union Theological Seminary in Manila in 1907 and taught there from 1908 to 1932. He also worked to found the United Evangelical Church (1929). Retiring in 1935, he continued to live in the Philippines until his death in 1944 during the Japanese occupation.

PAUL F. HARTFORD

Bibliography. G. J. Bekker, *DCA*, pp. 1023–24; K. J. Clymer, *Protestant Missionaries in the Philippines, 1898–1916.*

Role. *See* STATUS AND ROLE.

Roman Catholic Missions. *Roman Catholic Missions and Mission Theology Before Vatican II.* It was only in the context of the Counter-Reformation in the sixteenth century that the term " missions" came to be used to designate the Catholic Church's activity of preaching the gospel. The early Jesuits used the term to describe efforts (1) to revive and nurture faith among Catholics, (2) to win back Christians who had become Protestant, and (3) to convert to Christianity those who had not yet been baptized. During this period the political expansion of Europe to Asia and Latin America by the Roman Catholic kingdoms of Portugal and Spain was intimately linked to missions in the third sense of the term.

Augustinians, Dominicans, and Franciscans accompanied the explorers of the Philippines early in the sixteenth century, and relatively quickly and with little opposition the majority of the population was baptized. Missionaries saw little of value in Filipino culture, however, and imposed European doctrinal formulations and religious practices. Such a *tabula rasa* approach to evangelization was taken also in India, both with the "Thomas Christians" found there, and with new converts as well. The Jesuit FRANCIS XAVIER also shared this attitude, although, unlike other European missionaries, he stressed the importance of preaching and instruction in the local language. When Xavier traveled to Japan, however, he was so impressed by the level of civilization and natural goodness of the Japanese that he abandoned this *tabula rasa* approach in favor of one of ACCOMMODATION, wherever possible, to local customs. This more "inculturating" approach was also championed by ALESSANDRO VALIGNANO, who first came to Asia as a Jesuit visitor in 1579. Valignano strongly supported the work of MATTEO RICCI in China, who advocated the development of a Chinese Christianity, complete with the possibility of venerating ancestors. As missionaries from other orders began to work in China, however, such broad-minded acceptance of Chinese culture was opposed, and in 1742 any kind of adaptation was condemned at the conclusion of the famous "Rites Controversy."

By the mid-sixteenth century the conquest of Latin America was complete, and with conquest came Franciscan and Dominican—and eventually Jesuit—missionaries. While the missionaries were for the most part sincere, and made efforts to learn local languages and provide basic education, the success of their work was greatly hampered by the cruelty with which the indigenous peoples were treated by the conquerors. But the native people did have their champions in men like Antonio de Montesinos and especially BARTOLOMEW DE LAS CASAS, who worked for fifty years to convince the Spanish of the indigenous people's humanity and their need for basic human rights. Evanglization was also hampered by missionary attitudes that demeaned the local cultures and insisted that converts adopt a European lifestyle. In an effort both to protect the indigenous population from exploitation by the colonists and to form them in Christian living, villages or "reductions" were developed in which people could live in Christian community. These communities were developed especially by the Jesuits, who founded some twenty-three settlements in Paraguay in the seventeenth century. While life was peaceful in such communities, their weakness lay in failure to develop a sense of initiative and independence among the people. Until the system met its nemesis in the eighteenth century, not one candidate was brought forward for priesthood, nor one order of women religious founded.

In the sixteenth century, missions were directed by the Portuguese and Spanish monarchs and the missionary orders. While this had a number of advantages (royal protection, ready means of travel, financial assistance), the grave disadvantages of mixing political interests and trade with mission work, rivalry between the orders, and a limited pool of missionaries prompted Rome, as it was centralizing all of Catholicism in the wake of the Council of Trent, to place all missionary activity under a new curial body—the Congregation for the Propagation of the Faith. Established in 1622, its aims were to free missionary work from the stranglehold of Spain and Portugal, to create dioceses and promote local clergy, and to recruit diocesan clergy to balance personnel from the religious orders. In a famous set of instructions in 1659, the Congregation urged that missionaries should not destroy what is good in a culture: "What could be more absurd than to transport France, Spain, Italy, or some other European country to China? Do not bring these, but the faith."

It was in this spirit that ROBERT DE NOBILI ministered in India in the first half of the seventeenth century. Influenced by the methods of Ricci, he determined to immerse himself in Indian culture. He avoided eating meat and wearing leather shoes, wore the robe of the Indian holy man, mastered classical Tamil, and attempted to recast traditional Christian teaching with illustrations from the Indian classics. Anyone converting to Christianity need not abandon the many Indian cultural practices that de Nobili deemed inessential to Christian life. Although blessed with considerable success, de Nobili was not without his critics, and in 1703 all his methods were condemned by the Roman legate Charles Tournon.

In what is now Vietnam, Alexander de Rhodes made two significant contributions to missionary work. First, he formed a company of catechists, laymen whom he trained to give both religious instruction and medical assistance. In lieu of an indigenous Vietnamese clergy, such action assured that Christianity would be taught skillfully and accurately. Second, Rhodes developed a way to write Vietnamese using the Roman alphabet, and set Christian doctrine in the ordinary language of the people. By 1658 it was estimated that there were 300,000 Christians in Vietnam.

Between 1645 and 1700 the Capuchins baptized 600,000 people in the region of the Congo and Angola, and from 1700 on the average annual number of baptisms was 12,000. The reason for this, it seems, was a rather lax policy of baptism. Elsewhere in Africa, by 1624 the Jesuits had some twenty missionaries working in the Zambezi region, and the Dominicans and Augustinians had stations on Africa's east coast, but the involvement of the missionaries in various tribal wars slowed progress considerably and strengthened the impression that to become Christian was to accept the sovereignty of Portugal. Despite heroic efforts, no real commitment was made to learn local languages or cultures, and there was little attempt to follow easy baptism with extended catechesis.

In the seventeenth century, France began to exert its influence beyond Europe, particularly in North America. The first group of Jesuit missionaries was sent to Canada in 1632, and in 1639 Ursuline Marie de l'Incarnation and several companions were the first women missionaries to Canada. Work was slow and hard; the indigenous people treated each other and the missionaries with terrible cruelty, and many missionaries lost their lives, among whom were Jesuits Isaac Jogues and Jean Brebeuf and the layman Jean de la Lande. The Jesuit missionary Pierre Marquette is especially known for his explorations of the Upper Midwest.

The great effort of Roman Catholic mission work beyond Europe faltered gravely in the eighteenth century. The influence of Portugal and Spain began to diminish as Holland's and Britain's grew; the Roman decisions regarding Chinese ancestral rites precipitated a persecution in China; the suppression of the Jesuits in 1773 effected the withdrawal of several thousand missionaries from Asia and Latin America; the French Revolution and its persecution of the church virtually dried up the sources for French missionaries.

It is rather astonishing, therefore, that the nineteenth century was to see an amazing revival in the Catholic Church in general, and in its missionary efforts in particular. Napoleon's humiliation of the pope at the end of the eighteenth century ultimately created a movement of papal support and religious renewal throughout the whole church. In 1814 the Jesuits were reestablished, and other orders discovered new life. In addition, the nineteenth and early twentieth centuries saw the foundation of more new orders of men and women dedicated to missionary work than had any previous era. These included the Sisters of Saint Joseph of Cluny (1805), the Oblates of Mary Immaculate (1816), the Marists (1817), the Congregation of Mary Immaculate (1862), the Mill Hill Fathers (1866), the Comboni Missionaries (men, 1867; women, 1872), the Society of the Divine Word (1875), Sisters of the Precious Blood (1885), and the Catholic Foreign Mission Society of America (Maryknoll, 1911). The beginnings of large-scale lay participation in missionary work can be traced back to Pauline Jaricot, who in 1817 founded the Society for the Propagation of the Faith. The society solicited prayers, disseminated information, and collected funds for missionary support.

As the nations of Europe entered a new age of COLONIALISM, they welcomed, for the most part, missionaries of all sorts to help in education and health care. While Catholics and Protestants often pioneered in their own missionary areas, they occasionally competed, shamefully, against one another. Missionary efforts in Africa flourished, despite the hardships of the climate. Both China and Japan opened up once more for missionaries under the pressures of the colonial powers. Korean Catholicism struggled to grow, but was severely hampered by persecution at mid-century. Such legendary figures as Peter Chanel and Father Damien participated in the evangelization of the South Pacific.

In this great missionary era, however, there was little creative thinking. Nineteenth-century Catholic theology, with few exceptions, was inspired by the false universalism of Neo-Thomism. Loyalty to the papacy did indeed revitalize the church, but also made it Eurocentric and, like the colonial powers, derogatory of local culture. Any kind of adaptation was seldom considered, and local vocations to priesthood and religious life were, in the main, rarely encouraged.

A sign of renewal in Roman Catholic mission theology was the publication of five major mission encyclicals in the twentieth century, inspired no doubt by the emergence of the SOCIAL SCIENCES and the pioneering missiological work of JOSEF SCHMIDLIN, André Seumois, and PIERRE CHARLES. *Maximum illud* (Benedict XV, 1919) taught the need to be sensitive to local cultures and called for the training of local clergy; *Rerum ecclesiae* (Pius XI, 1926), while likewise calling for a local clergy, also affirmed the pope's role in global evangelization and enlisted bishops as primary agents in the task. In *Evangelii praecones* (1951) and *Fidei donum* (1957), Pius XII stressed the supranationality of the church, and called for the development in Africa. John XXIII's 1959 *Princeps pastorum* laid the groundwork for Vatican II.

From Vatican II to the Present. The SECOND VATICAN COUNCIL (1962–65), the most important event of the Catholic Church in the twentieth century, thoroughly rethought the theology and practice of mission. The "Dogmatic Constitution on the Church" (*Lumen gentium*, 1964) defines and describes the council's teaching on the church's identity, its organization, and its authority. In highlighting the universality of Christ, the Catholic Church is also defining itself as "the universal sacrament (sign) of salvation." It senses a "special urgency" in the task of "proclaiming the gospel of Christ to every creature."

The "Dogmatic Constitution" is noteworthy for two particular reasons, the first being the ways in which the Catholic Church continues to define itself in terms of a hierarchical structure (chap. 3) in spite of using the terms "mystery" (chap. 1) and "the People of God" (chap. 2) as controlling images of the contemporary church. The second is the way in which the Catholic Church identifies itself in relation to other religious and nonreligious realities. It is not clear whether the "Dogmatic Constitution" intends to identify the people of God with the Catholic Church exclusively, but it is clear that the traditional rubric "outside the church there is no salvation" is cited in a rather nuanced way. It is certainly ironic, at least from an evangelical point of view, that the groundwork is then laid for articulation of various ways in which members of non-Christian religions and even atheists can have a relationship with the church, even unconsciously (chaps. 14–16). It is encouraging to note, nevertheless, many statements of the GREAT COMMISSION and of the obligation of all disciples of Christ to use their individual abilities in the urgent task of global evangelization.

The biblical principles of a theology of mission are outlined in the council's "Decree on the Missionary Activity of the Church" (*Ad gentes*, 1965), the foundation of which is that "the pilgrim church is missionary by its very nature." The first paragraphs of the decree include a thoroughly biblical reflection on the trinitarian basis for mission, showing that the activity of preaching the gospel needs to be approached—even in Western culture—with different strategies. The evangelical will be uncomfortable with the juxtaposition of a particularist understanding of salvation and the assertion that "all people have a 'mysterious' relationship with the church (which) enlightens them in a way which is accommodated to their spiritual and material situation."

Some months after the publication of *Redemptoris Missio*, two Vatican congregations issued "Dialogue and Proclamation," a document which attempts to explain more fully the church's views of non-Christian religions and its efforts to interact with adherents of those faiths. The complexities of religious PLURALISM are to be explored by means of dialogue, a Christian message is not to be imposed in this situation, for sincere persons are "saved in Jesus Christ and thus already share in some way in the reality which is signified by the kingdom." Proclamation, on the other hand, is based on solid biblical material; here the integrity of the gospel demands avoidance of SYNCRETISM. Dialogue and proclamation must eventually come together. The gospel message needs to be included at some point in the practice of dialogue so as to provide the belief and faith called for in all Christians.

Contemporary Roman Catholic Mission Theology. Contemporary Roman Catholic mission theology revolves, then, around several interrelated themes. The first theme is that of proclamation, which holds the permanent priority in mission. Proclamation is rooted in the witness of Christian action and authentic Christian living, and blossoms into communication of the word (by a variety of media) only after discerning the presence of and listening to the Spirit in a particular context.

The second theme, interreligious DIALOGUE, is recognized today as an integral element of mission that finds its deepest justification in the dialogue with which God effects salvation. While proclamation is concerned with presenting Christ, dialogue seeks to discover him in other faiths, ideologies, and secular situations, and calls for mutual conversion and transformation. Dialogue is like proclamation, however, in that it entails both nonverbal and verbal witness to the reality of Christ.

Inculturation, the third theme, finds its theological roots in the doctrines of the incarnation, sacramentality, catholicity, and revelation. Like interreligious dialogue, inculturation looks for the presence of God in human life and culture—and so goes beyond the former models of adaptation; like proclamation, on the other hand, it calls for renewal and refinement of the human in the gospel's light—and so is always somewhat countercultural in intent. In theological articulation, liturgical expression, and questions of church order, not only the classical sources of Scripture and tradition need to be taken into account, but also those elements (culture, location, social changes) that make up present human experience. Pope John Paul II has characterized inculturation as the center, means, and aim of the new effort of evangelization.

In the last several decades the theme of liberation has emerged as central in theological reflection on the church's mission. While mission has almost always been involved in some kind of charitable or developmental work, current thinking would push beyond to ways of changing the underlying unjust and oppressive structures that keep people poor. Working for justice and integral liberation has been called constitutive of gospel proclamation, and inculturation is regarded as impossible without immersion in the reality of the poor and treating their religion—popular Christianity or non-Christian faith—with utmost seriousness and respect.

Finally, the church's mission is more and more recognized in contemporary theological reflection as trinitarian in both origin and aim. Mission is rooted in the God who is radically with and for humanity, and who calls humanity to become partners in the divine work of reconciling all of creation. God does this in the warp and woof of history (Spirit) and in the concreteness of history (Jesus); humanity does this most consciously by aligning with God's activity in the missional community of the church. The entire church is called to mission, and so laity as well as clergy and religious are to minister actively in the world.

Contemporary Roman Catholic mission theology is greatly influenced by contacts with other Christian churches, Orthodox, conciliar, and evangelical. "Christian Witness—Common Witness" (1980), a joint agreement between the Vatican and the WORLD COUNCIL OF CHURCHES, explores ideas for ecumenical cooperation in global evangelization and witness. A contribution to the ongoing discussions between conciliar Protestants and Roman Catholics, this document affirms certain perspectives on the church, defines the characteristics and results of effective witness, and even proposes various situations in which common witness can take place.

The Evangelical-Roman Catholic Dialogue on Mission (ERCDOM) took place over eight years (1977–84). The discussions demonstrated that evangelicals and Roman Catholics can talk together about issues of great importance without engaging in the usual polemics. The record of these meetings shows both integrity and candor regarding issues that have long divided the two groups. While there was considerable agreement on some of the basic points, there remains much that separates. "Evangelicals and Catholics Together" (1994) represents a more recent attempt in North America to identify areas of common concern to evangelicals and Roman Catholics and proposes strategies for future cooperation. The document demonstrates that there is much in common between the two groups, particularly when it comes to "cobelligerence," that is, a common commitment against, for example, RELA-

TIVISM, anti-intellectualism, nihilism, and social abuse. Although areas of disagreement are acknowledged, there is little theological reflection, with the unfortunate result of some oversimplification and confusion. In the main, three issues need further investigation and discussion: the significance of the Protestant Reformation, the criteria for membership in the body of Christ, and the scope of the GREAT COMMISSION as a mandate that engages all believers in Christ in all parts of the globe. It is certainly good and right that such discussions have taken place; in the future, however, provision should be made for the inclusion of those who can contribute significantly from the theological and biblical disciplines.

STEVEN B. BEVANS AND JOHN NYQUIST

Bibliography. W. M. Abbott, ed., *The Documents of Vatican II;* W. R. Burrows, *Redemption and Dialogue: Reading "Redemptoris Missio" and "Dialogue and Proclamation";* C. Carlen, ed., *The Papal Encyclicals, 1939–1958;* C. Colson and R. J. Neuhaus, eds., *Evangelicals and Catholics Together: Towards a Common Mission;* W. Jenkinson and H. O'Sullivan, eds., *Trends in Mission. Toward The 3rd Millennium: Essays in Celebration of Twenty-Five Years of SEDOS;* R. Latourelle, *Vatican II: Assessment and Perspectives 25 Years After (1962–1987),* 3 vols.; B. Meeking and J. Stott, eds., *The Evangelical-Roman Catholic Dialogue on Mission, (1977–1984);* K. Muller, *Mission Theology: An Introduction;* J. A. Scherer and S. B. Bevans, eds., *New Directions in Mission and Evangelization I: Basic Statements (1974–1991).*

Romania *(Est. 2000 pop.: 22,607,000; 237,500 sq. km. [91,699 sq. mi.]).* Romania is the largest country in the Balkans in southeastern Europe, bordering Ukraine, Moldovia, Hungary, Yugoslavia, Bulgaria, and the Black Sea. Although a socialist republic under Soviet influence, Romania became increasingly independent after 1974 under the dictatorial leadership of Nicolae Ceausescu. His regime collapsed amidst violent public unrest in 1989. Today the country is governed by an executive president and a bicameral legislature. Eighty percent of the population is Romanian in ethnic background, another 12 percent is Hungarian, and the remaining 8 percent is made up of several Gypsy groups and Eastern European communities including Bulgars, Croats, Czechs, Moldavians, Poles, Serbs, Slovaks, and Ukranians.

Despite the fact that manipulation and oppression of the churches was extreme before 1989, 89 percent of Romanians consider themselves Christian, with Orthodox representing nearly 85 percent of the country's population. Nonreligious and atheists made up over 15 percent of the population in 1970 but have fallen to less than 10 percent.

Even with numerous evangelistic crusades and Western-based outreach, evangelicals have grown slowly from 6.9 percent in 1970 to 8 percent by A.D. 2000. However, a major renewal movement called The Lord's Army is active within the Orthodox Church. Pentecostals, Christian Brethren, Baptists, and Seventh-Day Adventists are the largest evangelical groups. Much of the evangelical effort has been focused on Bucharest, the capital city. In recent years, many new groups, such as Calvary Chapels International (USA) have entered Romania for the first time, creating substantial followings. The JESUS FILM and RADIO MISSION WORK are two of the most effective means of evangelization.

TODD M. JOHNSON

Roseveare, Helen (1925–). English missionary to Zaire. After challenging medical tradition by training as a woman doctor at Cambridge, Roseveare turned her indomitable spirit toward the Congo in 1953. A pioneer in medical mission methods, she envisioned training centers where African nurses would be taught the Bible and basic medicine. Returning to their villages they would handle routine cases, teach preventive medicine, and function as evangelists. During her twenty-five years of service, Roseveare built two hospitals with training facilities plus the Evangelical Medical Centre in Nyankunde, Zaire. The center brought to fruition five outlying medical centers served by itinerating doctors with each center servicing ten to fifteen smaller rural hospitals.

Roseveare, who suffered countless setbacks through her misunderstood status as a single woman, is also known for her impregnable stance against physical brutality during the independence uprising of the early 1960s. Most significantly, her early flaunting of paternalistic attitudes toward nationals through her interaction with them as friends, colleagues, and spiritual advisors, remains one of her major achievements as she opened doors for their kingdom service. Leaving Zaire in 1973, she became an international speaker and writer for Christian missions.

ROBERTA R. KING

Bibliography. A. Burgess, *Daylight Must Come: The Story of a Courageous Woman Doctor in the Congo;* H. Roseveare, *Give Me This Mountain: An Autobiography; FJIJ.*

Rouse, Ruth (1872–1956). English evangelist, scholar, pioneer ecumenical leader, and missionary to India. Rouse was tireless in reaching students in countless universities and colleges throughout the world at a time when few took such a role. Educated at Bedford College (1891) and Girton College, Cambridge (1893), she was nurtured in Charles Spurgeon's Metropolitan Tabernacle, but converted to Anglicanism.

Missionary zeal marked Rouse's life. She traced her conversion to the Children's Special Service Mission. During college she signed the

STUDENT VOLUNTEER MOVEMENT (SVM) declaration, "I am willing and desirous, God permitting, to become a foreign missionary." After Girton, she spent one year studying Sanskrit at the British Museum in preparation for a missionary career in India.

During Rouse's professional career, which spanned thirty years, she was responsible for fostering missionary interest throughout the world. Her numerous roles included being editor of *The Student Volunteer*, traveling secretary for the American SVM, cofounder of the Missionary Settlement for University Women at Bombay, executive committee member of the British SCM and WSCF, head of European Student Relief, educational secretary of the Missionary Council of the National Assembly of the Church of England (then the highest position a woman could have in the Anglican Church), and executive committee member and president of the World YMCA. Rouse authored many articles and books, most importantly *The World's Student Christian Federation* (1948) and, with STEPHEN NEILL, *A History of the Ecumenical Movement, 1517–1948* (1955).

TOM RUSSELL

Bibliography. S. Bidgrain, *World* 50:1 (1957); R. Franzén, *ML*, pp. 93–101.

Russia and Kievan Rus

Russia and Kievan Rus *(for Russia, est. 2000 pop.: 145,552,000; 17,075,400 sq. km. [6,592,812 sq. mi.]).* Tradition says that in 988, Prince VALDIMIR of Kiev (Vladimir in Russian, Volodymyr in Ukrainian) chose Orthodoxy as the religion for his people after sending emissaries to investigate Orthodoxy, Catholicism, Islam, and the Jewish faith.

Orthodoxy remained the state religion for nearly a thousand years. During earliest periods of Russian history, the Orthodox patriarch had as much as, and sometimes more, political power than the czar. During the rule of Peter the Great, the patriarch and the Russian Orthodox Church were subjugated to the czar, but the church continued to exert great influence in society.

During the seventeenth century, a schism occurred in the Orthodox Church, resulting in the formation of the conservative Old Believers who split away from the state Orthodox Church. Later, sects such as the Dukhobors (Spirit-Wrestlers) and Molokans (Milk-Drinkers) emerged from Orthodoxy.

While Orthodoxy has always been and remains the predominant religion of Russia, in addition to the Old Believers and Orthodox sects, a small number of Catholics and Protestants entered Russia through emigration and acquisition of territory prior to the nineteenth century. Encouraged by the publication of the Bible in the vernacular, Protestantism flourished as an indigenous movement during the nineteenth century in the Caucasus, Ukraine, and St. Petersburg.

During much of this period before the Bolshevik Revolution in 1917, Protestants suffered reprisals from the state Orthodox Church. Following the overthrow of the czarist government in 1917, Lenin's Marxist followers instituted a policy of official atheism, and for the next seven decades, almost all religious believers suffered varying degrees of restrictions and repressions. Until 1929, the Bolsheviks restricted the state Orthodox Church most severely, allowing Protestants more freedom for expansion than they had experienced earlier.

With the ascendancy of Joseph Stalin in 1929, a campaign of terror closed most churches and brought imprisonment and death to millions of Christians of all confessions. However, during World War II Stalin permitted some churches to open in order to bolster the patriotism of religious citizens.

The rise to power of Nikita Khruschev in 1956 brought some cessation from the terror of Stalin. However, Khruschev unleashed a virulent antireligious campaign closing more than half the Orthodox and Protestant churches in the USSR.

Under the Communists, repression of religion continued until the rise to power of Mikhail Gorbachev and his policies of *glasnost* (openness) and *perestroika* (reconstruction). In October 1990, a new Law on Religion was enacted, providing full religious freedom.

Following the collapse of the Communist Party and dissolution of the Soviet Union in 1991, Orthodoxy, Protestantism, and Catholicism expanded in Russia, with thousands of new churches opening. Seminaries, missions, and other parachurch organizations, generally prohibited during the Soviet era, were started. Several thousand foreign missionaries, primarily evangelical Protestants, entered the former Soviet Union, including Russia, in the early nineties. Tensions rose between Orthodox and Protestants, with Orthodox hierarchy advocating legislation on religion that would restrict foreign missionaries and non-Orthodox Christian confession.

ANITA DEYNEKA

SEE ALSO Commonwealth of Independent States.

Bibliography. M. Bourdeaux, *Faith on Trial in Russia;* N. Davis, *A Long Walk to Church;* J. Ellis, *The Russian Orthodox Church: A Contemporary History;* D. Pospielovsky, *The Russian Church Under the Soviet Regime 1917–1982;* I. S. Prokhanoff, *In the Cauldron of Russia;* W. Sawatsky, *Soviet Evangelicals Since World War II;* P. D. Steeves, *Keeping the Faiths.*

Rwanda

Rwanda *(Est. 2000 pop.: 9,048,000; 26,338 sq. km. [10,169 sq. mi.]).* Dotted with beautiful lakes, terraced hillsides, and mountains, at times snow capped, Rwanda is known as the Switzerland of Africa. Tradition holds that the Twa or pygmy peoples were the first to migrate into Rwanda about 1,500 years ago. Some five hundred years later, the Hutu arrived, with the Tutsi coming roughly four hundred and fifty years ago. The Tutsi established a monarchy including a feudal system of nobles and landlords. Through contract, Hutu farmers pledged their services to Tutsi landlords. All three people groups live intermingled rather than in distinct tribal groups and speak the same language, which has facilitated the spread of Christianity.

In the early colonial era, Rwanda was part of German East Africa. After World War I it became a protectorate of Belgium in which the Tutsi dominated under colonial authority. In 1959, the Hutu tribesmen rebelled and massacred thousands of Tutsi in a bloody uprising. The king and more than 140,000 Tutsi fled to Uganda. The people then voted to make the country an independent republic and gave the Hutu control of the government. Independence came on July 1, 1962.

The White Fathers, a Catholic mission organization, arrived in 1889, but no permanent stations were established until 1900. The first Protestants were Lutheran missionaries, who arrived in 1907. They were followed by Anglicans and Seventh-Day Adventists. Though over half of the population is aligned with the Catholic Church, all of the early denominations experienced considerable growth and have had significant impact on the country. In 1927, the East African Revival broke out in Rwanda. It was characterized by confession of sin, repentance, and concrete salvation experiences, and the impact it left is still felt today throughout East Africa.

After World War II, additional evangelical mission groups from the United States and other countries arrived in Rwanda. Groups that stressed evangelism and worked in newly opened immigration areas grew rapidly. In the 1970s, the Catholic Church eased restrictions in Bible reading in Rwanda. This enabled a much greater emphasis on Bible reading and prayer within the Catholic Church.

In the early 1990s, as part of the government's effort of democratization, restrictions on the entry and registration of new church groups were eased. Many new groups arrived and splinter groups formed.

In October of 1990 the Tutsi in exile in Uganda invaded Rwanda. On April 6, 1994, the president of Rwanda, Juvinal Habyarimana, was killed when his plane was shot down. This set off massive killings of Tutsis and moderate Hutus by extremist Hutus. By the end of the summer, the Tutsi invasion, known as the RPF (Rwanda Patriotic Front), had routed the existing Hutu-dominated military. One million refugees were in Tanzania, almost two million were in Zaire. Somewhere between five hundred thousand and one million people died. Many church leaders fled along with the educated and businesspeople.

In light of ongoing animosity fueled by generations of anger and hatred, the future for Rwanda remains uncertain. The church still offers hope, but many no longer trust the church because of the involvement of church people in the killings.

GLENN KENDALL

Ryang, Ju Sam (1879–c. 1950). Korean evangelist, missionary, educator, and first Korean Methodist bishop. Ryang came to Christ from a Confucian background in 1902. He traveled to San Francisco in 1906, and started a Korean church there. Ordained as a Methodist minister in 1912, he returned to Korea in 1915 after studies at Vanderbilt and Yale. In Korea he took a teaching position at Methodist Union Theological Seminary, edited *The Theological World*, and served as a minister. For the rest of his career he promoted missionary work and tirelessly worked for the growth of the church. In 1921, he took oversight of the Siberia-Manchuria Mission, a Korean work in Siberia with which he maintained contact for the rest of his life. When the self-governing Korean Methodist Church was formed largely through his efforts in 1930, he was elected the first bishop. He served in this capacity until 1938. After North Korea took over Seoul in 1950, Ryang, then head of the Korean Red Cross, was abducted and never seen again.

A. SCOTT MOREAU

Bibliography. S. H. Moffett, *TCDCB*, p. 330; C. A. Sauer, *EWM*, 2:2061.

S s

Sabbath Observance. The Sabbath is the biblically mandated day of rest, specified in the Hebrew Bible as the seventh day of the week. Under the Mosaic Law, the penalty for nonobservance was being put to death, placed in parallel with being "cut off" from one's people, usually taken to refer to death directly at the hand of God (Exod. 31:14–15). The theological rationale for the Sabbath is found in the completion of creation (Exod. 20:11) and in the redemption from slavery in Egypt (Deut. 5:15).

The exact nature of Sabbath "rest" is not defined in Scripture, though we find examples of activity that desecrates the Sabbath. In contrast, by the time of Jesus, detailed *halakhah* (legal rules of behavior) were in the process of being formulated among various Jewish groups. By the time of the Mishnah (c. A.D. 200) and the Talmuds (c. A.D. 400–550), the rabbinic halakhah enumerated thirty-nine categories of prohibited work, each subdivided into additional categories. This became the basis of modern orthodox Jewish Sabbath observance.

In modern times, some Christians apply the term "Sabbath" to the first day of the week and advance reasons for regarding the Sabbath as having changed from the seventh day. Others worship and rest on the them, the Sabbath is no longer in effect because it was part of the Mosaic Law that has been done away in Christ. Some Christian groups advocate continued observance of the seventh-day Sabbath rather than Sunday as a particular mark of obedience to God.

Sabbath observance has traditionally been considered one of the most important Jewish distinctives, and remains so for the minority of observant Jews. With this in mind, in Jewish evangelism Sabbath observance is sometimes relevant.

Some Jewish Christians who are evangelical in doctrine may choose to participate in Sabbath observance with the understanding that the Law of Moses is no longer mandated and that any such observance is voluntary. Participating in such Jewish traditions becomes a way of maintaining ties to their Jewishness and testifying to nonbelieving Jews that faith in Christ and Jewish identity are not exclusive. Other Jewish believers in Jesus will not feel a need to observe the Sabbath. In contrast to the seventh-day Christian groups, Jewish Christians who contextualize their faith through Sabbath observance do not place a particular emphasis on the Sabbath over and above other points of behavior. The Sabbath can be a bridge of testimony even to nonobservant secular Jews, since it is a cultural as well as a religious institution. An exception to the general nonobservance of the Sabbath among Jewish people is the situation in Israel, where the Saturday Sabbath is officially and legally observed. Because Israelis are mostly secular, however, this observance does not necessarily extend into the personal lives of the citizens other than by necessity.

RICH ROBINSON

Bibliography. D. A. Carson, ed., *From Sabbath to Lord's Day.*

Sacraments/Ordinances. The spread of the Christian faith during the first centuries after Christ was attested by new believers not only by profession of faith in Jesus as Lord, but also by two visible rites—baptism and the Lord's Supper—both of which were rooted in Judaism. Though relatively simple acts as described in the New Testament, in succeeding generations they evolved into elaborate liturgical events. By the middle of the third century (or even earlier), infants born to Christian parents were being baptized; and after the conversion of Constantine, adults en masse were initiated into the Church by baptism, many whose lives did not necessarily evidence a spiritual transformation.

Disagreements over the rites occurred early in Christian history, and rather than serving as marks of unity, they became issues of intense debate and ultimately grounds for sectarian divisions. Christians have continued to differ, for example, as to what the rites should be called, sacraments or ordinances. Likewise they disagree as to the number of sacraments, whether they are means or symbols of grace, who is authorized to ministrate the rites, who are legitimate candidates for baptism, and what is the proper mode of baptism. Questions regarding re-baptism and the frequency for observing the Supper continue to divide Christians. While most Christian churches regard baptism as the sign and seal of one's incorporation into Christ—and thus include the baptism of infants in their liturgies—Mennonites, Baptists, Disciples of Christ, Brethren, and Pentecostals traditionally insist on the baptism of professed believers only. Anyone baptized as an infant who desires to be a Mennonite or Baptist, for example, traditionally has been required to submit to re-baptism, a practice Catholic, Reformed, and other historic churches view as a perversion or outright denial of the essential meaning of baptism as a sign of one's incorporation into Christ.

A striking example of non-Western Christians putting aside the traditional dissension over the sacraments can be seen in the mergers and formation of the Churches of South and North India, constituted respectively in 1947 and 1970.

One of the most serious and persistent problems evident in numerous mission areas, nevertheless, ensues from the insistence by many churches that the celebrant of the sacraments—particularly of the Eucharist—be an ordained clergyperson. The chronic insufficiency of ordained clergy, together with the vast and often growing number of believers, many of whom are dispersed over wide geographical areas, has often meant that new believers must wait inordinate periods of time for baptism, and congregants receive communion infrequently, if at all.

Despite the importance of baptism and the Eucharist, only occasional references to the rites are found in most histories of missions. Evangelical mission historians, for example, deplore the imposition of baptism on conquered "pagans" as a condition for peace exacted by European "Christian" conquerors during the Middle Ages. Equally troublesome, even for some Roman Catholic historians, is the baptism of hundreds, sometimes thousands of indigenous peoples, often in a single day and with little or no catechization, in sixteenth- and seventeenth-century Asia and Latin America. Also questioned is the clandestine baptism of infants in danger of death (*articulo mortis*) by Roman Catholic missionaries in nineteenth- and twentieth-century China.

In the Eastern Church, Orthodox missionaries, in keeping with their core theology, consider worship to be the essence as well as the purpose of mission. Consequently their task as they see it is to invite peoples everywhere to join in the continuing adoration of God the Father, Son, and Holy Spirit, with the central act of worship being the Eucharist, not the reading or the proclamation of the Word.

In some Asian and African churches today, indigenous elements such as rice cakes or bread made from potatoes, maize, and bananas are being substituted for wheat bread, and rice wine or honey and water for wine made from grapes.

ALAN NEELY

Bibliography. *Baptism, Eucharist and Ministry*; A. Harnack, *The Mission and Expansion of Christianity*, trans. James Moffatt; M. Takenaka, *God is Rice*, 1986; M. Ward, *The Pilgrim Church. An Account of the First Five Years in the Life of the Church of South India*, 1953.

Sacrifice. The call to follow Christ is a call to sacrifice because it involves a willing abandonment of self in favor of Christ. Christians should be willing to "give up everything they have" (Luke 14:33) as disciples of Jesus Christ (see Matt. 4:20, 22; Mark 10:21, 28, 52; Luke 5:28; John 1:43; 21:19, 22). In fact, on several occasions Jesus stressed that Christians are to give up their own life in deference to him (Matt. 10:37–39; Mark 8:34–38; Luke 17:33; John 12:25–26). Jesus is our hidden treasure and pearl of great value for which we willingly sell all that we have (Matt. 13:44–45). As such, forsaking everything else for Jesus is ultimately no sacrifice at all—it is the wisest choice. Missionary martyr JIM ELIOT understood this and said, "He is no fool who gives what he cannot keep to gain what he cannot lose" (Hampton and Plueddemann, 1991, 16).

Paul, the great missionary, spoke of "Christ Jesus my Lord for whose sake I have lost all things" (see Phil. 3:5–9). Paul was willing to sacrifice and suffer because Christ had become his Lord and Master. The lordship of Christ over us leads us to understand that we no longer belong to ourselves, but rather to him who bought us with his own blood (see Luke 6:46; Rom. 14:7–9; 1 Cor. 6:12–20; 1 Peter 1:18–19).

Paul expressed it well when he defined his identity in the following way: "the God whose I am and whom I serve" (Acts 27:33). He belonged to God so he had to serve him! Until the lordship of Christ becomes a central tenet in our WORLDVIEW, the call to sacrifice in his behalf will be extremely difficult. But once the knee bows to Christ and he is enthroned in our lives, sacrifice can become joyous service to our King! Even suffering for his sake can become something for which we "rejoice" (Rom. 5:3, see also Matt. 5:11–12; 2 Cor. 4:17; 11:23–33). Missionary pioneer J. HUDSON TAYLOR understood this and wrote, "What we give up for Christ we gain. What we keep back for ourselves is our real loss" (ibid., 119).

If a degree of sacrifice, then, is to be expected of all disciples, it should be even more so a hallmark of Christian missionaries. On behalf of the gospel, they are often called to forsake many things that are otherwise biblically allowable: cherished relationships, life-long dreams, comfortable living conditions, personal goals and plans, homeland cultures and models of ministry, relative anonymity, financial security, and many personal possessions. They do this willingly, while understanding that such sacrifice may not be appreciated even by those whom the Lord has called them to serve. Why endure such things? The worth of souls, the sanctification of sinners, and the example and glory of Christ are the reasons expressed by missionaries as being sufficient to counter whatever afflictions, persecutions, or deprivations they may face in their labors.

But where is the corresponding devotion to sacrifice for the missionary cause among Christian laypeople in our day? In a day of unparalleled affluence, many Western Christians are amassing luxury upon luxury and struggling to save for the future while millions of men and women made in God's image perish for lack of gospel knowledge. It is little wonder that non-Western missionaries are taking the place of Western missionaries in their Great Commission-centered living.

May the Holy Spirit break our hearts and bow us before Christ the Lord so that lives of sacrifice become the rule instead of the exception in our churches! Otherwise we will languish in our luxuries. As the psalmist cried out:

> "May God be gracious to us and bless us and make his face shine upon us, that your ways may be known on earth, your salvation to all nations" (Psalm 67:1–2).

ED GROSS

Bibliography. V. Hampton and C. Plueddemann, *World Shapers.*

Sacrifice in Other Faiths. Sacrifice (from the Latin *sacer*, "holy," and *facere*, "to make"), in some form, is a central element in most religious traditions, both ancient and modern. Sometimes, particularly in the context of biblical theology, a distinction is made between offering and sacrifice, with the latter being a special subcategory of the former. When dealing broadly with the phenomenology of religion, it is useful not to make a sharp distinction between the two concepts. In a general sense sacrifice is an intentional ritual offering of something valuable to one or more divine beings, spirits, or sacred powers.

Rituals of sacrifice have been characteristic of ancient religions such as those of Mesopotamia, Greece, and the Aztec and Mayan civilizations; primal religions; AFRICAN TRADITIONAL RELIGIONS; as well as HINDUISM and the religious traditions of China and Japan. Although early BUDDHISM discouraged popular sacrifices to supernatural beings or spirits, on the folk level offerings of flowers, food, or incense to exalted figures continued. In China and Japan Buddhism became closely identified with the ancestor cult and folk Buddhism today includes offerings and sacrifices to a wide range of figures. Islam is in principle opposed to sacrifice, although on the popular level of folk ISLAM veneration of the saints and offerings to ward off the evil effects of demons are widespread.

Nature of the Sacrifice. In many traditions any individual is able to make an offering or sacrifice for personal reasons. More common, especially in highly stratified societies, is the presence of a special person or group who performs sacrifices. In some cases, as in early Hinduism, the power and legitimacy of the priestly class are linked to their unique ability to perform the sacrifice in the requisite manner. Often a special individual will represent a larger group. Thus, in China the emperor represented the entire nation in offering sacrifices to Shang Di. In CONFUCIAN societies the father or eldest son represents the family in making offerings to spirits of the ancestors.

Inherent in the idea of sacrifice is giving up something of value to a superior being or power. The substance of the sacrifice may be something living or symbolic of life. Blood offerings have been characteristic of many traditions. Sheep, goats, cattle, pigs, fowl, reindeer, horses, dogs, and camels have all been used in sacrifices. Human sacrifice has been practiced in some earlier traditions. In the ancient Aztec civilization the hearts and blood of thousands of victims were sacrificed as a means of placating deities and maintaining the cosmic order. Forms of human sacrifice seem to have been practiced in ancient China, Africa, India, Korea, and Japan as well.

A variety of substitutes for animal or human life in sacrifices have also been used. Such "part-for-the-whole" sacrifices might include the offering of certain parts of the body such as fingers or hair, or blood drawn from one's own veins. In other cases representations of humans or animals (clay or paper figures) might be constructed and offered in place of living beings.

However, bloodless or nonliving things may also form the substance of the sacrifice. Vegetative materials and foodstuffs, such as fruit, grains, baked goods, oils, alcoholic beverages, and milk products, have been used. Of particular significance in early Hinduism was the libation of *soma*, a sacred and intoxicating juice used in sacrifice. In Japan today Shinto ceremonies include offerings of rice, *sake* (rice brandy), fish, fruit, or vegetables as well as money, jewels, or special clothing to the *kami* or ancestral spirits.

Recipients of sacrifice include, but are not limited to, various divine beings. MONOTHEISTIC traditions offer sacrifices to the one creator God.

African traditional religions that recognize a High God as the supreme deity nevertheless encourage sacrifices to intermediary beings and spirits who are considered more accessible. In POLYTHEISTIC and ANIMISTIC traditions recipients can include almost any being or power that inspires awe or fear, including not only deities but also various spirits, demons, animal guardians, natural objects (such as the sun or volcanoes), and spirits of departed ancestors.

Purpose of the Sacrifice. Some sacrifices seem to be intended as expressions of thanksgiving for benefits received, such as a bountiful harvest or victory in war. More common are sacrifices of supplication, in which a specific good is desired and the sacrifice is a means toward its realization. The desired benefit can be a material good (such as good crops, children, health, entrance into a desired school) or an immaterial blessing (forgiveness for some transgression, inner peace, courage). Sacrifice can assume the form of a transaction between the sacrificer and the recipient—*do ut des* ("I give so that you will give in return"). Skillful manipulation of the sacrifice thus ensures well-being for the individual or group.

Sacrifices can be used to ward off undesirable consequences of action in this life. In Chinese folk religion, for example, one must be careful in construction and land development not to offend the many demons or spirits identified with roads, mountains, and fields. Similarly, traditions that give prominence to the ancestor cult emphasize the importance of appeasing the spirits of the dead through ritual presentations of food, drink, or other valued objects.

Missiological Significance. While many of the rituals of sacrifice in non-Christian religions will be incompatible with the teachings of Scripture, the phenomenon of sacrifice itself can serve as a point of contact between indigenous beliefs/practices and Christian faith. The practice of sacrifice implicitly recognizes that our present lives are in an undesirable state and that something must be offered to a superior being or power in order to attain a better state. Building on this insight the missionary can lead the other persons to acknowledge their deepest need for a restored relationship with God and then introduce them to the only truly effective Sacrifice—Jesus Christ, the perfect Lamb of God.

HAROLD A. NETLAND

SEE ALSO Atonement; Soteriology in Non-Christian Religions.

Bibliography. J. van Baal, *Numen* 23 (1976), 161–78; J. Henninger, *ER,* XII:544–57; E. O. James, *Sacrifice and Sacrament;* D. Priest, *Doing Theology Among the Maasai.*

Saint Helena (United Kingdom Crown Colony) *(Est. 2000 pop.: 6,000; 412 sq. km. [159 sq. mi.]).* An island of volcanic origin in the southern Atlantic Ocean. It is well-known as the place of Napoleon's exile and death. Eurafrican Whites make up 80 percent of the population, the rest being British and Americans. The vast majority are Anglicans, with a significant evangelical movement among these. Smaller groups include Baptists, the Salvation Army, and Seventh-Day Adventists.

TODD M. JOHNSON

Saint Kitts and Nevis *(Est. 2000 pop.: 41,000 ; 261 sq. km. [101 sq. mi.]).* A former British colony in the northern Leeward Islands, Saint Kitts has an almost entirely Afro-Caribbean population. The island was dependent on sugar production until the collapse of world prices left it reliant on foreign aid and tourism. Isolated from the influences that have altered the culture of island groups like the Bahamas, the Caymans, and the Dutch island, Saint Kitts is 95 percent Protestant, but only 10 percent evangelical.

EVERETT A. WILSON

SEE ALSO Caribbean.

Bibliography. A. Lampe, *The Church in Latin America, 1492–1992,* pp. 201–15; J. Rogozinski, *A Brief History of the Caribbean: From the Arawak and the Carib to the Present.*

Saint Lucia *(Est. 2000 pop.: 152,000; 622 sq. km. [240 sq. mi.]).* Part of the British Caribbean Windward (southern) Islands, St. Lucia has close developmental ties to Saint Vincent and the Grenadines, but remains quite different religiously and linguistically. Although a British crown colony since the 1790s and officially an English-speaking population, a large proportion speak French Creole Patois, and three-quarters are Roman Catholic. Protestants constitute 18 percent of the population.

EVERETT A. WILSON

SEE ALSO Caribbean.

Bibliography. A. Lampe, *The Church in Latin America, 1492–1992,* pp. 201–15; J. Rogozinski, *A Brief History of the Caribbean: From the Arawak and the Carib to the Present.*

Saint Vincent and Grenadines *(Est. 2000 pop.: 117,000; 388 sq. km. [150 sq. mi.]).* A former British colony, Saint Vincent is located between Saint Lucia and Grenada at the southern end of the Windward Islands. The population is 85 percent Afro-Caribbean with a substantial East Indian minority. Less Protestant than a number of other former British possessions, the people are 20 percent Roman Catholic

EVERETT A. WILSON

SEE ALSO Caribbean.

Bibliography. A. Lampe, *The Church in Latin America, 1492–1992,* pp. 201–15; J. Rogozinski, *A Brief History of the Caribbean: From the Arawak and the Carib to the Present.*

Salvador Conference (1996). The 1996 Conference of the COMMISSION ON WORLD MISSION AND EVANGELISM (CWME), which convened in Brazil, had the theme "Called to One Hope—The Gospel in Diverse Cultures." The objective was to discuss the results of a worldwide five-year study of the ways in which cultures and the gospel have influenced each other over the centuries (*see also* GOSPEL AND CULTURE). Particular attention was given to authentic WITNESS within each culture, the gospel and cultural identity, local congregations in pluralist societies, and diverse expressions of the one gospel. The issue of religious PLURALISM was largely avoided.

After considerable debate the delegates (over six hundred from more than eighty countries) retained commitment to the document "Mission and Evangelism: An Ecumenical Affirmation," which had been adopted by the WCC Central Committee in 1982. Even so, some delegates and officials suggested that this document was now outdated and needed to be replaced. The keynote statement by Bishop LESSLIE NEWBIGIN that the specific responsibility of the church was "to bear witness to the reality of Jesus' victory who by his ministry, death and resurrection has broken the powers that oppress us" drew the largest ovation of the entire conference. This responsibility, he added, "has to be the center of our mission."

ARTHUR F. GLASSER

Bibliography. *IRM* 85 (1996): 336, 337; M. Pauw, *Reformed Ecumenical Council News Exchange* 34:1.

Salvation. The scriptural words for "salvation" in Hebrew and Greek refer to deliverance from any danger or distress. This article is concerned with salvation in its missiological context. So, it deals with salvation only as it relates to the rescue of humans from the cause and effects of SIN.

The History of Redemption. Sin entered the world through Satan's tempting of the first humans (Gen. 3; James 1:13). Adam and Eve yielded to Satan and chose to rebel against God by sinning. The effects of sin on Adam and Eve were: the loss of fellowship with God, the corruption of their entire being, their exposure to God's wrath and punishment including a life of misery, inevitable death and eternal separation from him (see Gen. 3:8, 24; Isa. 59:1–2; Gen. 6:5; Rom. 3:1–10; 8:7–8; Eph. 2:1–3; Job 5:7; Isa. 57:21; Rom. 5:14; 6:23; *see also* FALL OF HUMANKIND). Adam stood as the representative of all his descendants. The consequences of his decision not to follow God were to affect forever his

descendants and the world for good or for evil. All humankind has been affected by the consequences of the sin of its representative, and the fruit of which has been transmitted to each one through the process of birth (see Rom. 5:12; 1 Cor. 15:22; Ps. 51:5; 58:3; John 3:6). As a result, none of Adam's heirs are perfect. They are under God's righteous judgment (Ezek. 18:4; Rom. 1:18–20; 3:23).

The Bible, though, reveals from the very beginning God's response to sin as a gracious plan to reverse the horror of evil. Sin's instigator, Satan, would be crushed by one of Eve's male descendants (Gen. 3:15). Through subsequent revelations and the initiating of symbolic animal sacrifices, God taught the descendants of Adam that he loved them and would accept them if they dealt with their sins according to his will (Gen. 4:1–16; 6:8–9; Job 1:1–5; Heb. 1:1). His gracious plan of redemption has always been applied to sinners through the channel of FAITH (Gen. 15:6; Heb. 2:4; Rom. 1:17; 3:19–26; Eph. 2:8, 9). And true, saving faith was always distinguished from a temporary or merely intellectual faith—which could not save (Heb. 11; Luke 8:13; James 2:19).

Later in Moses' record of human history, God called Abraham and promised to produce a nation through him and through his descendants God would bless all the nations (Gen. 12:1–3; 15:1–6; 17:6–7; Rom. 4:18–22; *see also* ABRAHAMIC COVENANT). The rest of the Old Testament is a complex history of how God in his providence graciously fulfilled that promise in ways that teach, help, and encourage believers of all ages (Rom. 15:4; 1 Cor. 10:6, 11; 2 Tim. 3:14–16).

He gave to Abraham many children (see Gen. 12–50) who "were fruitful and multiplied greatly and became exceedingly numerous, so that the land [of Egypt] was filled with them" (Exod. 1:7). Though they were populous enough to be a nation, they needed to have their own land, culture, and leadership to become a lasting, viable nation (see Exodus through Joshua). God led them to the land of Canaan through Moses and established them in the Promised Land through a faithful and courageous leader: Joshua [whose name means "The Lord Delivers" and in Greek is the name Jesus]. Though warned of the consequences, the children of Israel rebelled against the Lord and his prophets and were sent into exile. In God's wonderful grace they were miraculously returned from exile into their own land, rebuilt their temple, and awaited the coming of the Promised One (see Judges through Malachi).

When the time was perfect "God sent his Son, born of a woman, born under law" (Gal. 4:4a). He was the reality toward which all the Old Testament animal sacrifices symbolically pointed. So upon seeing him, John declared, "Look, the Lamb of God, who takes away the sin of the world!" (John 1:29). Jesus was "the Lamb slain from the creation of the world" (Rev. 13:8). It was he who revealed his future coming to Abraham (John 8:56), to Moses (Deut. 18:15; Heb. 11:26), to the wandering Israelites (Heb. 4:2), to David (Acts 2:25–31), and to many others. Jesus taught that the Old Testament pointed to him (Luke 24:25–27, 44) and it was not until his followers understood this that they could understand the [OT] Scriptures (Luke 24:45) because "these are the Scriptures that testify about me," he claimed (John 5:39).

An angel told Joseph to name Mary's son "Jesus, because he will save his people from their sins" (Matt. 1:21). To accomplish salvation Jesus had to live perfectly under God's law as a human and then willingly substitute his own life as a payment for the penalty that sin demands (Heb. 2:14–15; 2 Cor. 5:21). So, Jesus lived perfectly under the law—without ever sinning (Heb. 4:15; 1 John 3:5). He alone could look at his enemies and say, "Can any of you prove me guilty of sin?" (John 8:46). And at the end of his perfect life, in the most amazing expression of love ever shown, he subjected himself to the wrath and curse of God on the cross, dying in the place of sinners (Rom. 5:8; Gal. 3:12–14; Matt. 27:45–46).

It was only through a perfect God-Man, substituting himself and paying the debt that sin demands from God's justice, that human sinners could be saved. There is no other possible way of salvation (John 14:6; Acts 4:12; Rom. 3:19–26; Gal. 2:21; 3:21). All that Jesus did, he did "to seek and to save what was lost" (Luke 19:10).

Following Jesus' substitutionary death, God raised him from the dead, proving to all that he accepted his Son's life and sacrifice, and forever establishing the truthfulness of all of Christ's claims (Rom. 1:4; Acts 2:22–24; Phil. 2:5–11). After appearing to hundreds of disciples over a period of several weeks, Jesus physically ascended into heaven. The apostles who saw all of these things were transformed by the Spirit into courageous witnesses who traveled throughout the world proclaiming the good news of salvation through Jesus and making disciples. They taught the disciples to do the same until the return of Jesus (Acts 1:1–11; 1 Cor. 15:1–8; Acts 2–4; 8:1–4; 14:21–23; 1 Cor. 10:31–11:1; Phil. 4:9; Matt. 24:14). As the Son of Man, Jesus is now seated at the right hand of God's throne where he sovereignly directs the affairs of all creation and represents his children until his return (Matt. 28:16–20; Heb. 7:22–26; 1 John 2:1; 1 Thess. 4:13–18).

This brief summary of the Old and New Testament story is given to show that the Bible is primarily a Book that reveals the history of salvation. Scripture is the story of God's saving love. It primarily depicts how God prepared the world for the First Coming of his Son and what he has done and is doing to prepare the world for the Second Coming of Jesus Christ.

Missiological Application. The term "salvation" in the Scriptures is a complex concept, not used solely of the conversion of individuals. Salvation in its broad scriptural use is something that has a past, present, and future sense. God's children have been saved (Rom. 8:24; Eph. 2:8; Titus 3:5), are being saved (1 Cor. 1:18; 2 Cor. 2:15), and shall be saved (Rom. 5:9–10; 13:11; 1 Thess. 5:8; Heb. 9:28; 1 Peter 1:4, 5). Western evangelicalism strangely stresses the past tense with almost no emphasis on the present and future. Missionaries and missiologists should question how significantly Western culture has influenced today's quick-and-easy, low commitment presentations of the gospel.

Scripture also speaks of salvation as impacting one's entire being forever. God's children have been, are being, and shall be saved from sin, self, and Satan. The process of salvation, then, is lifelong and consummated only when believers are perfected in the likeness of the Savior at the resurrection. This challenges the emphasis of some who equate salvation with merely "making a decision for Christ." It is far more than a simple decision to not want to go to hell sometime in the future. While it involves a personal choice, a true commitment to Christ is not merely a momentary, spiritual issue regarding one's eternal destiny and having little to do with here and now. True conversion will affect all of life. Its many implications should be articulated by the witness and understood by the hearer before a call for commitment is ever made.

Paul was concerned with some who misrepresented Jesus because the preaching of another Jesus also produced another gospel—one that could not save (see 2 Cor. 11:4; Gal. 1:6–9). Missiology must be greatly concerned with how Jesus is proclaimed today since it is only through him that salvation can occur. Jesus declared that the correct perception of him and his saving work was as the Messiah promised by God (Matt. 16:13–17).

According to the Old Testament, the promised Messiah would save his people by fulfilling three functions: he would be a divine Prophet (Deut. 18:15), Priest (Ps. 110:4; Isa. 53:4–12; Zech. 6:13) and King (Ps. 2; 2 Sam. 7:16; Ps. 89:3–4). The apostles used the messianic Old Testament passages to prove that Jesus was the Messiah and to describe the salvation that was offered through him (see Acts 2:29–31, 36; 3:17–18, 22–23; 4:25–27). Instead of saying, "Accept Jesus as your personal Savior," the apostles proclaimed that the multitudes should accept Jesus as their divine Prophet, Priest and King.

Is this an insignificant difference from the way evangelism is often done today? Not so if today's presentation carves away Christ's role as Prophet and King over his children. Many might gladly accept him as their sin-bearing Savior who might not be so quick to accept him as their Guide and submit to him as their King! Missionaries and missiologists should take a close look at who the Jesus is that is being proclaimed and what level of commitment is being made by those who are responding.

The GREAT COMMISSION involves salvation and is a command to make disciples (Matt. 28:18–20). In the early church every believer was expected to quickly become a disciple (Acts 6:1; 14:21–23). Summarizing how disciples are made, Jesus mentioned the importance of BAPTISM. Though it does not suit today's evangelical custom, the New Testament very closely relates conversion and baptism as linked together in the normal process of salvation (see Acts 8:12; 18:8; 22:16; Rom. 6:3; 1 Peter 3:21). When asked by a crowd what they should do to be saved, Peter responded, "Repent and be baptized . . . for the forgiveness of your sins" (Acts 2:38). Did Peter understand how to evangelize? The Holy Spirit thought he did and saved 3,000 people! Why did Peter combine baptism with repenting? Perhaps he was seeking to fulfill the Great Commission as he had been taught. Baptism in the New Testament, though not an *essential* component for salvation (*see* John 3:16, 36, etc.), was an *important* element of the process of true conversion and was normative in the early church. Missionaries and missiologists should explore much more fully the place of baptism, public confession, and church commitment as important elements of New Testament discipling. They should continually warn the church of the consequences of exporting Western styles of evangelism that do not follow apostolic patterns.

EDWARD N. GROSS

Bibliography. G. D. Congdon, *EMQ* 21:3 (1985): 296–99; M. Erickson, *BibSac* 152 (1995): 3–15; idem, *Southwestern Journal of Theology* 33 (1991): 5–15; idem, *Interpretation* 49 (1995): 255–66; E. Gross, *Christianity Without a King: The Results of Abandoning Christ's Lordship*; C. Hodge, *Systematic Theology*; H. Kasdorf, *Christian Conversion in Context*; J. Morikawa, *American Baptist Quarterly* 12 (1993): 122–26; B. Nicholls, *ERT* 15 (1991): 4–21; J. Orr, *ISBE*.

Salvation Army. The Salvation Army was created by WILLIAM (and Catherine) BOOTH in 1878 by restructuring an evangelistic mission they had started thirteen years before in London. The new movement stressed the reality of SPIRITUAL WARFARE, but it drew as well upon the contemporary popularity of military uniforms, parades, and brass bands. It developed rapidly in England over the next two years.

The Army's pioneer leaders were committed to evangelize among the "submerged tenth" of urban society, the marginalized and poverty-stricken who they believed had been overlooked by other forms of Christian outreach. Although their view of the activities of other Christians was too narrow, the early Salvationists were sincere and gave themselves completely to the crusade. From the start the Army's leaders supplemented their evangelistic appeal by small-scale charitable activities. This was partly in response to the teachings of Christ in passages like Matthew 7:12 and 25:34–40, and partly out of the conviction that persons attracted by the prospect of temporal relief would be available, and willing, to listen to the gospel. Some of these early programs achieved permanent success. The Army's Adult Rehabilitation Center program, for instance, is the world's largest residential rehabilitation program for homeless alcoholics. The Army's worldwide network of day-care centers, summer camps, and senior-citizen programs is efficient, popular, and respected by clients and professionals.

The Army took a worldwide view of its mission almost from the start. An early song proclaimed, "We'll march our Army thro' the world, And set the nations free." The first country outside the British Isles to be invaded by the Salvation Army was the United States (1880), where the Army eventually gained respect and popularity after struggling against public misunderstanding, a pattern seen in other countries as well. By the time of William Booth's death in 1912 the Army was established in nineteen countries and colonies of the British Empire and in twenty-one other countries, including Scandinavia, Germany, the Netherlands, France, and Switzerland.

Persons who are familiar only with the Salvation Army's local relief activities may be surprised by the scale of its present operations. As of 1996, the Army conducted its evangelistic and relief ministry in 103 countries, including in the former Soviet Union. The Army preached the gospel in 160 different languages—including 23 within the United States alone. The international organization included 17,389 officers (clergy, of whom 3,645 were American, including the current general, Paul A. Rader, chosen in July 1994) and 858,694 senior soldiers (full-time adult lay members, of whom 83,690 were American).

Because the Army requires a strict code of obedience and sacrifice of its officers and soldiers, their numbers are not large, considering the scale of the Army's worldwide religious and social service operations. General Rader has called for an international campaign to increase the number of soldiers to one million, a goal which will require great effort, but which Army leaders regard as essential if the movement is to expand its operations into new areas.

EDWARD McKINLEY

Bibliography. *The Salvation Army Yearbook;* E. McKinley, *Marching to Glory.*

Salvation in Non-Christian Religions. *See* SO-TERIOLOGY IN NON-CHRISTIAN RELIGIONS.

San Antonio Conference (1989). The WCC San Antonio conference had as its theme "Your Will Be Done: Mission in Christ's Way." It proved to be the most representative of CWME conferences, with solid numbers of women, Third World delegates, Catholic and evangelical observers, and an orthodox moderator.

Meeting six months before the Berlin Wall was dismantled, delegates from the Soviet Union were able to talk of the greater openness in their country and the importation of a quarter of a million Bibles. The conference was planned so that the voices of those not normally heard could be given maximum publicity. Worship and Bible study were integral parts of the conference, which divided into four sections that together reflected the fullness of the gospel. "Turning to the Living God" placed emphasis on the need to equip local congregations for the task of proclaiming the gospel and eliciting a search for personal faith, noting that the two-way relationship between mission and dialogue needed further study. The section on "Participating in Suffering and Struggle" sought to explore "the creative power of the Spirit in transforming people who suffer into those who struggle"; the question was raised as to how "resistance" could be part of mission in Christ's way. The section on "The Earth Is the Lord's" explored the reality that within many communities access to and ownership of the land was a key mission issue. "Towards Renewed Communities in Mission" emphasized the need to work out new patterns of PARTNERSHIP in mission that would be an authentic sign of gospel *koinonia.*

The conference affirmed that responding to the realities of the human struggle for justice as well as respect for God's creation was part of mission, "just as inviting people to put their trust in God is part of that mission." It affirmed a holistic view of the inseparability of the material and the spiritual, as seen in the ministry of Jesus, and that to withhold from the poor both justice and good news was to commit against them a "double injustice." In part because of the affirmation of the need to share the gospel, evangelical delegates met on several occasions during the conference to draft a letter of support from the San Antonio program to the Manila Conference sponsored by the Lausanne Committee for World Evangelization.

The San Antonio Conference seems to have proved a nourishing experience for those who attended, though it has been accused of so overloading the language of mission and evangelism that their particular meanings became submerged in a more general agenda. That said, a number of evangelicals were disappointed that more of San Antonio's concerns did not more obviously feed into the Canberra Assembly of the World Council.

JOHN H. Y. BRIGGS

SEE ALSO World Council of Churches Conferences.

San Marino *(Est. 2000 pop.: 27,000; 61 sq. km. [24 sq. mi.]).* The Republic of San Marino's area is mostly devoted to agricultural enterprises around Mount Titano. Two Italian regions, Emilia-Romagna and Marche-Montefeltro, surround the independent and neutral nation.

A stonecutter named Marinus, according to legend, founded the community about A.D. 301. He had fled Arbe in Dalmatia because of Diocletian's persecution of Christians. The district was a safe haven and has maintained that tradition. San Marino accepts refugees from any sort of tyranny or persecution.

The population is primarily Sammarinese and Italians. Roman Catholicism is dominant, but marginal groups like the Baha'i and Jehovah's Witnesses work in San Marino.

KEITH E. EITEL

Bibliography. D. B. Barrett, *WCE;* P. Johnstone, *OW.*

Sanctuary Movement. A sanctuary is a sacred place such as a temple, church, or mosque, which is recognized as a safe area for fugitives or criminals. Such places were known among the Greeks, Romans, and Hebrews (Num. 35:6–34). The right of sanctuary in a church was a common practice in medieval Europe, but with the growth of nation-states and more efficient systems of justice the tradition was discontinued.

The twentieth century witnessed the revival of this approach in the United States as many Christians felt that it was their mission to help illegal aliens escape from the injustices of global capitalism. These groups focused on aiding refugees who were fleeing their homelands in Central America. Due to the efforts of conservative governments to crush opposition and cooperate with multinational companies, these displaced people were forced to come to the United States to escape torture and death.

In 1982 Jim Corbett, a Quaker, and John Fife, pastor of the Southside Presbyterian Church in Tucson, joined with several others to start sanctuary churches. By 1986 over three hundred Protestant, Catholic, and Jewish groups had joined the movement and it had been recognized by such national bodies as the United Methodist Church and the Presbyterian Church, U.S.A. In addition to claiming religious and ethical precedents for their actions they cited the example of the "underground railroad" for escaped slaves as an example of civil disobedience. They also claimed that the immigration laws were unfairly enforced and that they contradicted the 1967 United Nations Protocol Relating to the Status of Refugees, which the United States had signed. On January 14, 1985, sixteen sanctuary workers were indicted for their assistance to illegal aliens and eight were later convicted but given suspended sentences. The trial of these individuals put the movement under considerable strain. Nevertheless it continued not only because it involved acts of compassion toward helpless people but also because it involved the relation of the Christian faith to nationalism and of individual conscience to the law.

ROBERT G. CLOUSE

Bibliography. I. Blau, *This Ground Is Holy: Church Sanctuary and Central American Refugees;* H. Cunningham, *God and Caesar at the Rio Grande;* R. Golden and M. McConnell, *Sanctuary: The New Underground Railroad;* R. Tomsho, *The American Sanctuary Movement.*

Sanders, J. Oswald (1902–92). New Zealand missionary leader. Sanders, first general director of the OVERSEAS MISSIONARY FELLOWSHIP, was born in Invercargill, New Zealand, on October 17, 1902. Converted in his childhood, he committed himself to Christian service at a convention, and attended the recently formed New Zealand Bible Training Institute in Auckland, where he made such an impression that he was invited onto its staff and eventually became its superintendent. In 1946 he was appointed as Australian representative of the China Inland Mission. That mission was soon thrown into disarray when its missionaries were expelled from China in the early 1950s. The appointment of Sanders in 1954 brought to its helm a calm and incisive leader, who reorganized the CIM into the OVERSEAS MISSIONARY FELLOWSHIP, sensitively expanded its ministry both on the field and in its "home countries," and pioneered the acceptance of Asians into the mission. He retired in 1969, but before his death in 1980 he served extensively in Bible College leadership, writing, and a worldwide preaching ministry. His first book was *The Divine Art of Soul Winning*, published in 1937. More than twenty-five books followed, including the well known *Spiritual Leadership* (1967), all combining strong faith with common sense. He was married first to Edith Mary Dobson in 1931, and after her death, to Mary Miller. He set the OMF on a path of preeminence among missions.

PETER LINEHAM

Bibliography. R. Roberts and G. Roberts, *To Fight Better: A Biography of J. Oswald Sanders;* J. O. Sanders, *This I Remember.*

Santería. See LATIN AMERICAN NEW RELIGIOUS MOVEMENTS.

São Tomé and Príncipe *(Est. 2000 pop.: 146,000; 964 sq. km. [372 sq. mi.]).* Two large and several smaller islands 200 km. (120 mi.) off the west coast of Africa. As early as the end of the fifteenth century, the main islands of São Tomé and Príncipe were used as supply posts for Portuguese ships en route to India. Catholic work was undertaken from 1534, and in 1993 the population was estimated to be 97 percent Christian (4.9% Protestant, 91.9% Catholic, 0.1% marginal). Protestant work was initiated indigenously by an Anglican exiled to São Tomé in 1930. Protestants in Angola (also a former Portuguese colony) sent missionaries in 1957 and 1960.

A. SCOTT MOREAU

Satan. The basic meaning of the word "satan" is "accuser"; the verb from which it derives is used six times in the Old Testament (Pss. 38:20; 71:13; 109:4, 20, 29; Zech. 3:1) with that meaning. The term can also mean "adversary" or "slanderer." In Zechariah it refers to an accusation made by Abishai against Shimei, which is true but not slanderous. However, in the five Psalm passages it is used of slander. Context determines its meaning.

The noun is used occasionally in the Old Testament of humans. David is the first human in the Old Testament called a "satan" (1 Sam. 29:4), meaning in context "an adversary." Others include Abishai (2 Sam. 19:22), Solomon's military enemies (1 Kings 5:4), Hadad of Edom (1 Kings 11:14), and Rezon of Syria (1 Kings 11:23, 25).

It is also used of celestial beings in the Old Testament. In Job 1 and 2, Satan is referred to fourteen times in the role of God's adversary in the discussion about Job. In Zechariah 3:1–2, Satan stands at the right hand of the angel of the Lord to accuse Joshua the high priest. Of the almost twenty celestial references to Satan as an adversary of God, every instance but one uses the article "the" with the word referring to "the Satan." This designates a particular adversary. The one case in which a celestial satan is not hostile to God is in Numbers 22:22, where that adversary is an angel (32) who is acting on God's behalf. Of the Old Testament references to celestial adversaries only once is the word used without an article and thus appears to be a proper name: "Satan stood up against Israel and incited David to number Israel" (1 Chron. 21:1).

Satan is referred to much more frequently in the intertestamental literature, the Apocrypha, and Pseudepigrapha, than in the Old Testament. This may be because of the feeling that God had abandoned the Jews because of their sin, destroying the temple with its Most Holy Place. The Jewish people thus transcendentalized God and allowed for much more evil activity between heaven and earth than in earlier religious belief.

Surrogate terms such as Asmodeus, Azazel, Belial, Satanail, Mastema, and Semjaza are commonly used in this literature to designate Satan.

The Hebrew (Old Testament) word "satan" never appears in the New Testament, which uses instead a transliterated form of the Aramaic word *satanas* in its thirty-five occurrences. However, the Aramaic term is usually translated Satan in English versions of the New Testament, the same as the Hebrew word in the Old Testament. Equally often in appearance in the New Testament is the Greek word *diabolos,* translated devil. This is not a different term, only a Greek translation in the Septuagint of the Hebrew word satan. Thus, its meaning is the same. In Revelation 12:9, both terms, Aramaic and Greek, are used to refer to the great dragon John saw in his revelation: "and the great dragon was thrown down, that ancient serpent, who is called the Devil and Satan." The word "devil" never appears in the Hebrew Old Testament.

Unlike the Old Testament, the New Testament always uses the word "satan" (adversary) to refer to Satan, the greatest enemy of God and Christ. Almost half (15) of the 35 occurrences of the word in the New Testament are in the Gospels. It appears only twice in Acts, 10 times in Paul's letters, and 8 times in Revelation.

The New Testament, like the intertestamental literature, uses other words for Satan (2 Cor. 12:7) and the devil (Matt. 4:1). These include Beelzebul (Mark 3:22), Belial (2 Cor. 6:15), and possibly Abaddon and Apollyon (Rev. 9:11). Additionally, metaphors are frequently used to describe Satan, including the terms Strong Man (Matthew 12:29), Evil One (Eph. 6:16), the Destroyer (1 Cor. 10:10), the Tempter (Matt. 4:3), the Accuser (Rev. 12:10), and the Enemy (1 Cor. 15:25).

Some animal metaphors are used of Satan: the Serpent (Rev. 12:9), the Dragon (Rev. 12:7), and the Lion (1 Peter 5:8; 2 Tim. 4:17). He is also referred to in cosmic terminology as the Prince of Demons (Matt. 9:34), the Ruler of this World (John 12:31), the Prince of the Power of the Air (Eph. 2:2), and the God of this World (2 Cor. 4:4).

The origin of Satan is never revealed in the Bible. Since dualism is not an acceptable biblical postulate for a co-eternal existence of God and Satan (Satan is referred to in the Bible only in male terminology, as are also the angels), Satan's origin must be accounted for as a created being. Isaiah 14:12 speaks of the "Day Star, son of Dawn" as "fallen from heaven" and Ezekiel 28:13 contains the phrase "you were in Eden, the garden of God . . . with an anointed guardian cherub . . . on the holy mountain of God . . . and the guarding cherub drove you out from the midst of the stones of fire . . ." Some see the origins of Satan in these passages. However, in the immediate context, Isaiah is writing a taunt against the king of Babylon, and Ezekiel is describing the fate of the king of Tyre. Whether these are allegorical allusions to Satan as well is debatable.

Somewhat parallel passages in the New Testament may provide some insight into the question of the origin of evil angels. Peter speaks of angels sinning and being "cast into hell committing them to pits of nether gloom to be kept until the judgment" (2 Peter 2:4). The expression "cast into hell" is literally in Greek "tartarize them." Jude writes: "And the angels that did not keep their own position but left their proper dwelling have been kept by him in eternal chains in the nether gloom until the judgment of the great day" (Jude 1:6 RSV).

Since Matthew refers to the devil and his angels, it is conceivable that the devil is himself a disobedient angel and the destiny of both is the "eternal fire" which is "prepared for them" (Matt. 25:41). Thus their destiny, if not their origin, is clear. However, Genesis has Satan present in the beginning of human creation tempting Adam and Eve in the Garden of Eden (Gen. 3:1; cf. 2 Cor. 11:3). He is in the form of a serpent on this occasion. That the serpent is indeed Satan is clearly stated in Revelation 12:9: "And the great dragon was thrown down, that ancient serpent, who is called the Devil and Satan, the deceiver of the whole world—he was thrown down to the earth, and his angels were thrown down with him" (cf. Rev. 20:2).

Satan's power has always been limited by the will of God. Job was allowed to be afflicted by Satan, but only to the extent allowed by God. Even though Satan has the power of death (Heb. 2:14), the use of that power is subject to the will of the Almighty. Even though Satan had the kingdoms of the world within his power and could deliver them to Jesus at his temptation (Matt. 4:9), that power was derived from God (Luke 4:6) and these kingdoms are under his influence only because they have chosen to sin and follow Satan rather than God. "The whole world is in the power of the evil one" (1 John 5:19 RSV). But, "The Evil One cannot touch" those who are born of God and do not "go on sinning" as a way of life but remain dedicated to serving him (1 John 5:18).

Satan is responsible not only for tempting humans to sin against God but also for leading cosmic powers to influence the church toward disunity which Jesus said would cause the world to disbelieve in him (John 17:21). Thus, Paul writes that through the church the manifold wisdom of God is made known to the principalities and powers in the heavenly places (Eph. 3:10). In the first four chapters of this Ephesian letter Paul is arguing for the unity of Jews and Gentiles in the body of Christ, among other reasons because of its comic implications. The price of a divided church is a disbelieving world.

Satan is popularly but erroneously called Lucifer. This name does not appear in the Bible. The English term Lucifer is a translation of the Hebrew and Greek words for "light bringer." The English word is actually a transliteration of the Latin word *luciforos* meaning "light bringer," which refers to the morning star or day star, Venus. The word appears in Isaiah 14:12 where Isaiah tauntingly calls the king of Babylon "Day Star, son of Dawn" because symbolically he has fallen from his position of power in the evening so soon after having arisen in the morning. In the history of biblical exegesis this passage was connected with Luke 10:18 in which Jesus said, "I saw Satan fall like lightning from heaven" and the word Lucifer came to be widely used as another name for Satan.

With the recent rise of interest in Satan and satanism in the West (*see* SATANIST, SATANISM), as well as an awareness of spiritual orientation of much of the rest of the world, it is crucial for missionaries from every culture to be aware of Satan and his schemes. Though there are excesses, the contemporary rise of the SPIRITUAL WARFARE movement is therefore a welcome development in mission. A mission theology of Satan and his work across cultural contexts is in the process of formation, and ensuring that it is biblically founded rather than experientially formed will remain a priority for missiologists in the future.

JOHN McRAY

Satanist, Satanism. The medieval church equated all forms of witchcraft and paganism with satanism and resorted to witchcraft trials to suppress such practices. During the twentieth century, a new form of revitalized paganism sought to differentiate between pagans, who worship the Mother Goddess, and satanists, who worship the Christian devil or at least the ideas that he represents.

Practices associated with satanism include celebration of the black Mass, the desecration of sacred objects, animal sacrifices, black magic, malevolent sorcery, and the reputed murder, mutilation, or rape of human victims. These rituals draw on the power of Satan to realize a worshiper's pragmatic and hedonistic purposes.

Followers of satanism fall into three categories. First are those who want to explore the realities of the so-called black arts, or those social rebels who want to shock others by embracing the forbidden world of Satan. The second consists of individuals who want to do evil and who draw on the metaphors and practices associated with malevolent sorcery and evil power. Such individuals usually act alone or in secret groups bent upon criminal or destructive activities. A third group are those who openly worship Satan and are members of a satanic church such as the Church of Satan founded by Anton LaVey or the Temple of Set.

Since the 1970s there has been widespread fear over the existence of a coordinated network of evil satanic cults that are rumored to engage in sexual orgies, cannibalism, blasphemy, and ritual murders of infants, some of which have been especially bred for this purpose. Members of this cult are alleged to be prominent citizens and well-placed leaders of the community who are involved in a nationally and internationally coordinated conspiracy dedicated to the subversion of society. They are believed to be responsible for the ritual deaths of tens of thousands of persons per year, but law enforcement agencies have never been able to uncover any credible evidence to support the existence of such an organization or their practices.

DOUGLAS J. HAYWARD

Bibliography. M. Bubeck, *The Satanic Revival;* R. D. Hicks, *In Pursuit of Satan;* J. S. Victor, *The Satanic Panic;* N. Wright, *The Satan Syndrome.*

Saturation Church Planting. Saturation church planting methodology takes seriously the GREAT COMMISSION's injunction to make disciples of all nations (Matt. 28:18–20). It adopts the strategy of mobilizing the entire body of Christ in whole countries in the effort to reach the goal of the Great Commission in each country by providing an evangelical congregation for every village, neighborhood, and kind and condition of people in the population.

The strategy recognizes that world evangelization can never be attained apart from providing viable congregations of redeemed people among every PEOPLE GROUP in the world. Saturation church planting recognizes that no single type of church can provide the needed resources for evangelizing an entire population. Jim Montgomery calls for a comprehensive, systematic plan in each country to mobilize the church to push toward the goal of evangelizing whole nations.

Saturation church planting also takes seriously the truth that every population, even in organized states, actually represents what Donald McGavran termed a "vast mosaic" of different groups of people, each with a different worldview and culture. Indonesia, for example, has some 360 distinct people groups among its millions of people. Even these groups can easily be subdivided.

To reach the people in all the groups demands a vast diversity of churches to match the vast diversity of peoples. Saturation church planting provides the strategy for providing this needed diversity.

The methodology understands that the evangelization of whole nations is rooted in the comprehensive purpose of God. This plan is seen in the

Old Testament (Gen. 18:18; 22:17–18; 26:4; 1 Kings 8:43; Ps. 102:15; Isa. 45:22) as well as in the New Testament (Matt. 28:18–20; Acts 26:16–18; Rom. 16:26; 2 Peter 3:9; Rev. 15:4). Saturation church planting takes seriously this plan for discipling whole nations and all nations.

The method is enunciated most thoroughly in Jim Montgomery's plan of DAWN (DISCIPLING A WHOLE NATION). This strategy calls for 7 million churches by A.D. 2000. If this goal is to be reached, the important place of house churches and unpaid workers must be stressed.

To evangelize the nations demands such a strategy as envisioned in DAWN and a commitment to a church among every people in order to bring whole nations to Christ. Every other strategy should be judged in relation to how it contributes to the goal of discipling whole nations and all nations.

EBBIE C. SMITH

Bibliography. B. Fitts, *Saturation Church Planting: Multiplying Congregations Through House Churches*; J. Montgomery, *DAWN 2000: 7 Million Churches to Go*; D. A. McGavran, *Understanding Church Growth*; E. C. Smith, *Balanced Church Growth*; C. P. Wagner, *Church Planting for a Greater Harvest*.

Saudi Arabia *(Est. 2000 pop.: 21,257,000; 2,149,690 sq. km. [829,995 sq. mi.]).* Saudi Arabia is the heart of the religious world of Islam and home of more than 21 million people. At Pentecost Arabic was one of the languages heard and this was soon followed by the apostle Paul's sojourn in Arabia. A despised nomadic tribe called the Salaiba is believed to be the remnants of an early Christian group. By the year 325 six bishops from Arabia attended the Council of Nicea. Shortly after 339 during the persecution by Sapor II, hundreds of Christians fled Persia seeking refuge in Saudi Arabia and established communities throughout the peninsula. The king of the Arabs in Hirtha, north of Qatar on the eastern coast, accepted Christianity in 512. By the year 525 Christianity was well established in Arabia.

However, a gradual decline began and in 570 when the prophet Mohammed was born chaos blanketed the area. A chaotic clash of religions including various Christian sects manifested itself in internal dissension, theological confusion, and lack of spiritual power. This marked the interaction of the Arians, Sabellians, and Nestorians. During the Caliphate of Omar even the tribute tax was no longer accepted. Nearly all who refused to adopt Islam were deported to Iraq. In the eleventh century the remaining Christians in the Hijaz section of Arabia who had not islamized migrated to Jordan and other countries in the north.

In 1811 HENRY MARTYN stopped for a time at Muscat on the southeast corner of Arabia and did some translation work. Ion Keith-Falconer started an independent work on the south coast at Sheik Othman in 1885 and then joined with the church of Scotland but died two years later. SAMUEL ZWEMER of the Reformed Church of America established work in Basrah in southern Iraq and from there penetrated towns along the perimeter of the coast as well as made tours into the interior.

Schools and medical clinics were established around the perimeter of the Arabian peninsula. The unification of the peninsula under the house of bin Saud has given absolute power over the minds of all. Economic standards have risen from abject poverty. Education is now available to nearly everyone and medical facilities are superb. Almost all of this is now firmly in the hands of the government. This has given new power to resist the entrance of missionaries, Bibles, and even tent makers.

Radio and satellite television transmission is penetrating in an amazing way and positive responses come from all parts of Arabia. The weakness of the chaotic Christian witness led to the eclipse of Christianity and the rapid rise of Islam. Now Islam has a nearly vise-like hold on the minds of people there. A large evangelical workforce is sprinkled throughout Arabia from emerging sending fields such as the Philippines, Korea and Brazil. Many young people have studied abroad and returned with new ideas of the dignity and freedom of the individual. The penetration of radio and TV and the increased number of students studying abroad as well as the large number of believers in the expatriate labor force who are believers there is hope for a change in this most resistant nation.

GEORGE E. KELSEY

Bibliography. R. B. Betts, *Christians in the Arab East*; S. Moffett, *A History of Christianity in Asia*; W. H. Storm, *Whither Arabia?*; J. S. Trimingham, *Christianity Among the Arabs*; S. M. Zwemer, *Heirs to the Prophets*.

Schaeffer, Francis (1912–84). American apologist and evangelist. Burdened to reach those with honest questions and doubts about Christianity, Schaeffer and his wife Edith founded the L'Abri Fellowship in Switzerland in 1948.

Schaeffer's prolific book-writing career began late in his life with the ground-breaking *The God Who Is There* (1968) and concluded with *The Great Evangelical Disaster* (1984). His writing flowed from his concern to communicate the cogency of the Christian worldview to the increasingly post-Christian culture of the West. Hailed as "a missionary to the intellectuals" (although not an academic), Schaeffer engaged the world of culture—literature, cinema, and philosophy—from a full-orbed, evangelical perspective. In this, he inspired many Christians to be more intellectually active in their profession of faith.

Schaeffer creatively combined a Reformed view of culture with an emphasis on cultural APOLOGETICS. Because Christ is Lord of all of life, Christians must endeavor to transform all of CULTURE for the glory of God. This entails not only exegeting the Bible, but also exegeting culture to discover its intellectual and existential weaknesses and areas of despair. This missiological strategy remains indispensable for the postmodern situation of the West.

DOUGLAS GROOTHUIS

Bibliography. L. T. Dennis, ed., *Francis Schaeffer: Portraits of the Man and His Work;* R. W. Ruegsegger, ed., *Reflections on Francis Schaeffer;* F. A. Schaeffer, *The Complete Works of Francis Schaeffer,* 5 vols.

Schereschewsky, Samuel Isaac Joseph (1831–1906). Russian-born missionary to China and Japan. Born into a Jewish family in Tauroggen, Russian Lithuania, Schereschewsky received Jewish education during his teenage years. He left for Frankfort in 1850 and later attended Breslau University, where he became fluent in German. In 1854 he moved to the United States, where he was baptized as a Christian and received theological education. His mastery of several languages, including Hebrew, Russian, German, and English, was deemed an advantage for missionary work in China because of the difficulty of learning Chinese.

In 1859, he left for China as a missionary of the Domestic and Foreign Missionary Society of the Episcopal Church. He stayed in China for more than two decades, and for almost a decade in Japan, where he died and was buried. He served as Bishop of China between 1877 and 1883. Throughout his missionary career, he made good use of his talent in linguistics for translation of the Bible and prayer books. Working with other China missionaries in Beijing, he completed translation of the Mandarin New Testament in 1872. He also worked with Joseph Edkins translating Matthew into Mongolian by 1872. In 1874 he completed the Old Testament in Mandarin. He also translated prayer books in Mandarin with John Burdon in 1872, and in 1881 he rendered them into the classical Chinese, popularly known as Easy Wenli by his contemporaries. He wrote also four short catechisms in Easy Wenli in 1881. He completed the New Testament in Easy Wenli in 1898, the Pentateuch in 1899, and the whole Bible in 1902. Furthermore, he helped found St. John's University in Shanghai, which proved to be a major place for nurturing prominent figures in modern China.

TIMOTHY MAN-KONG WONG

Bibliography. I. Eber, *Bulletin of School of Oriental and African Studies* 56:2 (1993): 219–21; J. A. Muller, *Apostle of China: Samuel Isaac Joseph Schereschewsky.*

Schmidlin, Josef (1876–1944). German pioneer of Roman Catholic missiology. Born on May 29, 1876, in Alsace, Schmidlin was ordained to the Catholic priesthood in 1899, and earned doctorates from Freiburg in philosophy (1901) and theology (1903). After ordination Schmidlin helped the noted historian Ludwig von Pastor with his monumental *History of the Popes,* and in 1906 was appointed the first private lecturer at the newly founded Catholic theological faculty in Strasbourg. Difficulties there, however, caused him to transfer to Münster, where in 1907 he was appointed lecturer in church history.

In 1910 Schmidlin lectured on Catholic missions in the German protectorates, but soon began the task (greatly helped by GUSTAV WARNECK's work, though perhaps, as a Catholic, more ecclesial in approach) of constructing a comprehensive Catholic missiology. Subsequently, a chair of Catholic missiology was established at Münster in 1914. A prolific writer, Schmidlin's best-known books are *Catholic Mission Theory* and *Catholic Mission History.* He was editor of *Zeitschrift für Missionswissenschaft* (1909–37) and a frequent contributor to many other journals.

Forced to resign his chair at Münster in 1934 because of outspoken opposition to the Nazi regime, Schmidlin was imprisoned and executed on January 10, 1944. He is remembered today as the father of Catholic missiology.

STEPHEN B. BEVANS

Bibliography. K. Müller, *ML,* pp. 402–9.

Schmidt, Georg (1709–85). German pioneer missionary to South Africa. Born in Kunewalde, Moravia, Schmidt went to Herrnhut after his conversion in 1725 to join the Moravian Brethren. He returned to his homeland to preach but was thrown in jail. After his release he responded to Count ZINZENDORF's request for a missionary to work among the migratory Khoikhoi people at the Cape of Good Hope. Having sailed in 1737 on a Dutch East India Company ship, he journeyed into the interior and settled at Baviaanskloof (later renamed Gernadendal).

Gathering a small band of followers, Schmidt taught them to read and write, established an agricultural community, and provided religious instruction in Dutch. As he had no support from home or European co-workers, he made his living by farming. In 1742 Zinzendorf ordained Schmidt by mail, and he baptized the first five Khoikhoi converts. Since the Dutch Reformed clergy at the Cape would not recognize his ordination and objected to the Moravian teachings, he closed the mission in 1744 and went to Amsterdam to seek official sanction for the work. His tiny congregation waited in vain for his return, as the Dutch East India Company barred the annoying missionary from its territories.

Schmidt spent his later years serving the Brethren in various capacities and finally settled in Niesky, Germany, where he continued to pray regularly for his flock at the Cape. Herrnhut missionaries restarted the work among the Khoikhoi in 1792. They followed Schmidt's precedent of gathering the congregation on a station, which eventually became the norm for missionary activity in South Africa.

ULRICH VAN DER HEYDEN AND RICHARD V. PIERARD

Bibliography. B. Krüger, *The Pear Tree Blooms;* K. Müller, *Georg Schmidt.*

Scholarship in Mission. *See* MISSIOLOGY.

Schreuder, Hans Paludan Smith (1817–82). Norwegian missionary to South Africa. Schreuder was born in Sogndal, Norway, the son of a lawyer. An orthodox Lutheran, he decided in 1836 to become a missionary and studied theology at the University of Oslo. In 1842 he published a widely discussed article that called on the Church of Norway to engage in overseas missions; this appeal resulted in the formation of the Norwegian Missionary Society (NMS). The following year he went to Natal, South Africa, as the society's first missionary to work among the Zulu. Denied entrance into the Zulu kingdom, he went to China in 1847 where he had no greater success, and after two years he was back in South Africa. King Mpande then allowed him to begin working in the Zulu lands, and within a few years he had founded several stations.

Schreuder was deeply interested in the Zulu language and produced a grammar in 1850. As he developed close ties with the Zulu king, he became involved in politics. In 1866 he was named bishop with responsibility over the NMS fields in Zululand and Madagascar. Feeling hampered by the NMS bureaucracy, he resigned his post in 1872, became an independent missionary, and founded a new society known as "The Church of Norway Mission by Schreuder." After his death the society established ties with Norwegian-American Lutherans who finally took over the field in 1927. Popularly known as the "Apostle of Zululand," he died at his station Untunjambile.

ULRICH VAN DER HEYDEN AND RICHARD V. PIERARD

Bibliography. J. du Plessis, *A History of Christian Missions in South Africa;* J. Simensen, ed., *Norwegian Missions in African History,* vol. 1.

Schrupp, Ernst (1915–). German mission scholar and advocate. Born into an Open Brethren family in Beyenburg close to Wuppetal (Rhineland), he became, after service in World War II and an experience of spiritual renewal, one of Germany's most influential evangelical mission leaders.

After release from the war Schrupp was one of the founders of the German IVF *(Deutsche Studentenmission).* In his spirituality he combined the Brethren's strong emphasis on the local congregation with the evangelical parachurch movements' emphasis on evangelism and missions.

In 1948 Erich Sauer called him to be a teacher at Wiedenest Bible School. This was an interdenominational Bible School based on the Brethren Movement in Germany. It was started in 1905 in Berlin as the Alliance Bible School to train Christian workers from and for Eastern Europe.

From 1952 on Wiedenest developed into a major mission sending agency. Schrupp developed his missiological concept of the "sending local church," combining insights from Brethren missiology with those from the interdenominational FAITH MISSIONS. In his concept, which was effectively applied in his Wiedenest Mission and influenced many other evangelical missions, the "sending congregation" was not only responsible for the "commissioning" of the missionary, but equally for continued material and spiritual support.

Beyond his own mission he was instrumental in the founding of several evangelical cooperative institutions, notably the *Arbeitsgemeinschaft Evangelikaler Missionen* (Evangelical Missionary Fellowship) in 1969.

KLAUS FIELDER

Schwartz, Christian Friedrich (1726–98). German pioneer missionary to India. Born in Sonneburg, Prussia, he was left without a mother at a very early age. He entered the University of Halle at twenty, where he was greatly influenced by a missionary who had returned from India. He was eventually chosen to reinforce the work of the Tranquebar Mission. Ordained in 1749, Schwartz and his companions reached South India on July 16, 1750.

Schwartz decided early in his attempts at evangelism that it would be vital for him to know the Indian sacred books. His superior language ability and his readiness to endure hardships paved the way for his ready acceptance both by the common people and at the palace.

In 1766, Schwartz took charge of the new station at Trichinopoly, where he served the rest of his career. He preached faithfully in the city and surrounding villages, quickly forming a congregation. In addition to preaching and teaching, Schwartz showed concern for the people's physical needs, distributing food to thousands in times of famine.

Schwartz died on February 13, 1798, forty-eight years after his arrival in India. It was said that prince and peasant, soldiers and civilians, Christian, Hindu, and Muslim alike mourned the friend they had lost. Schwartz never married, and when he died left nearly $50,000 to the Indian church. He and the other early Lutheran missionaries earned a reputation in South India for piety, wholehearted devotion to the Lord, and self-sacrificing love for the people.

STEPHEN HOKE

Bibliography. V. S. Azariah, *India and the Christian Movement;* H. H. Holcomb, *Men of Might in India Missions;* P. Thomas, *Christianity in India and Pakistan.*

Schweitzer, Albert (1875–1965). German theologian, musician, and missionary doctor. Born in Kayserburg, Alsace (at the time part of Germany), the son of a Lutheran pastor, he studied in Strasbourg, Paris, and Berlin. As a young man he had embarked on a successful academic career, with major works on Bach and Jesus, but he decided in 1906 while serving as a preacher in Strasbourg to become a missionary. He studied medicine, applied to the PARIS EVANGELICAL MISSION (which reluctantly accepted him because of his highly unorthodox views), and went to Gabon (French Equatorial Africa) in 1913 where he founded a hospital in Lambarene. During World War I he was interned and deported to Europe, where he lectured, gave organ recitals, and continued his writing. During this time he developed his famous "reverence for all life." In 1924 Schweitzer returned to Lambarene and continued his work as a missionary doctor. Through his writings and subsequent lecture tours he promoted his views on sharing suffering, atoning for crimes and injustice against Africa committed by European COLONIALISM, and striving for a better world that would be a "realm of harmony." He received the Nobel Peace Prize in 1952.

ULRICH VAN DER HEYDEN

Bibliography. J. Bentley, *Albert Schweitzer: The Enigma;* J. Brabazon, *Albert Schweitzer: A Biography;* G. Marshall and D. Poling, *Schweitzer;* A. Schweitzer, *On the Edge of the Primeval Forest;* idem, *African Notebook;* idem, *Out of My Life and Thought: An Autobiography;* idem, *Letters 1905–1965.*

Science and Missions. A classical view of science and mission identifies science as one of the main components of the culture of the West, namely, Europe and North America, and mission as reaching other peoples of the world with the Christian message. The relationship between science and mission is, in this view, one aspect of the relationship between Western culture, with its scientific worldview, and non-Western cultures, with their traditional forms of knowledge. This view has lost its dominance in recent times since the West is no longer seen as the exclusive possessor of rationality, and Christianity is losing its influence in the West while it is increasing in other regions of the world. However, mission can still be characterized as the enterprise that brings the light of the gospel to people who live in the darkness of not knowing the living God. And many Christians expect that the benefits of a rational order of life, which are in large measure created by science, will follow as part of the changes related to embracing the gospel.

At the same time, it is widely believed in the West that the ENLIGHTENMENT brought about by science has shown the irrationality of religion in general and of Christianity in particular. This claim has been debated for centuries, and the various responses to it have shaped Christian theology in a profound way. It is probably fair to say that the main question concerning the relation between science and religion, if we are to judge by the frequency with which it emerges, remains: Is it possible to be rational and have religious beliefs?

We are faced with a paradoxical situation. Science and mission seem to go hand in hand in winning over the non-Western and non-Christian world, while science and Christianity are at odds at the mission's home base. It is possible, of course, to maintain that the conflict is a consequence of a distorted view of both science and Christianity. For only scientism, an interpretation that grants science prerogatives beyond knowledge validation, condemns religion as the survival of ancient myths from a time of ignorance. However, no matter how well articulated and cogent the argument reconciling science and religion, the knowledge-intensive culture of what used to be the Christian world is not returning Christianity to the prominent place it once had.

There are two important consequences of this situation. First, the West is now a critical field of mission for Christianity. Of course, science is not the only reason, and may not even be the most important one, for the retreat of Christianity in the West. But as we articulate the message of the gospel for a post-Christian, knowledge-intensive society, we must broach anew the issue of the role and authority of science in the culture. In so doing, we must recognize that not only has the position of Christianity in this society changed, but science has also changed. The image of the individual genius wrestling with nature to uncover its secrets was never very accurate, but is much less so today. Science has grown to gigantic proportions and is carried out by large bureaucratic organizations in a complex web of relationships involving government, industry, the military, and the educational sectors. Most scientists are employees, many not even very highly ranked, and can hardly aspire to fill the role of guides of the unenlightened masses that the disputes with the clergy of earlier times suggest. Science or, more descriptively nowadays, technoscience is simply an aspect of production in a complex and differentiated economy. It does not receive its power from being true but from being effective, an outcome that is always contingent and perfectible. In such a context the perfectly legitimate question of the rationality of religious beliefs is hardly as pressing as how to be a witness for the power of the cross in a society where might makes right.

This leads to the second consequence of the paradoxical relationship between science and mission: the missionary enterprise, whether in the Western or non-Western world, must carefully consider the relationship between the means and ends of mission. For the most part, missionary work now involves the technical, communicational, and organizational means of scientific society. Effective use of these means requires some acquaintances with their technoscientific development. An important example is the use of the MEDIA for missionary purposes. The highly sophisticated techniques developed for effective commercial use of the media are applied to the communication of the gospel. However, much of this is done with very little critical assessment of how the sheer power of media communications affects the way people attribute meaning to the various aspects of the overall media experience. The ambiguity of the results of several decades of Christian media, with the well-known entanglements with political and financial agendas, contrasts sharply with the simplicity of the justification given for their use in the first place: to preach the gospel to as large an audience as possible with the shortest possible delay. The experimental methods of technoscience are central to the marketing techniques that govern effective use of the media. Thus it is not surprising that the gospel message undergoes not very subtle transformations. The tightly knit networks of contemporary technoscientific power reconfigure our own identities and goals. There is no necessity involved in this process. Given the contemporary societal arrangements, it is just the obvious and easiest way to do things. "But small is the gate and narrow the road that leads to life, and only a few find it."

JUAN D. ROGERS

See also Modernity AND Modernization.

Bibliography. I. Barbour, *Ethics in an Age of Technology*; B. Barry, *About Science*; D. Bosch, *Transforming Mission: Paradigm Shifts in Theology of Mission*; L. Newbigin, *Foolishness to the Greeks*; R. Padilla, *Mission between the Times*; Q. Schultze, *Televangelism and American Culture*; S. Shapin, *A Social History of Truth*; N. Stehr, *Knowledge Societies*.

Scotland *(78,000 sq. km. [30,116 sq. mi.]).* Scottish Christian identity reflects its Celtic roots and historic relationships with England and Ireland, and places farther removed (Norway, France, Germany, Geneva, Rome, the Americas, and the former British Empire). Internal divisions and tribal, geographical, political, economic, and the-

ological strife have left their mark. Scotland's sense of unity has been supported by democratic and egalitarian ideals, spiritual, educational, political, and economic interests, and negatively by antipathy toward the English.

There are traces of Christian presence from Roman times. Evangelization is associated with NINIAN around 500, and follows COLUMBA'S arrival in Iona in 563. Celtic Christianity was challenged by Roman practices at Whitby in 664, and suffered from Viking invasions around 800. It gave way to English and Roman forms under Queen Margaret (1046–93). Monastic orders and the diocesan organization were extended by her son David I (c. 1085–1153). The medieval period saw frequent wars with England, and an increase in nationalism.

The Reformation brought Scotland politically closer to England and theologically to Geneva. Documents of this period include John Knox's (1514–72) *History*, the *Scots Confession of 1560*, and the *First and Second Books of Discipline* (1560 and 1578). Presbyterian organization reflected a shift of power away from bishops and the crown. Royal attempts to anglicize the church met with resistance in the National Covenant of 1638, and helped draw Scotland into the English civil war. The influence of Scots on the Westminster Confession of 1646 was profound. After the Restoration of 1660, Covenanters were persecuted until the Presbyterian settlement of 1690.

The eighteenth-century Church of Scotland became polarized between a conservative, government-orientated, Moderate party, and Evangelicals, or Populars. This led to a number of secessions. Revivals were experienced in Cambuslang in 1742, and elsewhere. By 1834 Evangelicals had a majority in the General Assembly, but the "Ten Years Conflict" led to the Disruption of 1843 when a third left the Church of Scotland in protest at state interference. Many of the tensions in this period of intellectual ferment, economic growth, and social change, can be seen in the life of Thomas Chalmers (1780–1847). The nineteenth century saw growth in Catholic numbers and in Baptist, Episcopalian, and independent groupings. Christians as a whole responded to opportunities for mission around the world and in the growing cities and depleted Highlands.

Scotland today faces the forces of secularism and spirituality common to Western societies. Like others, Evangelicals share a commitment to the value of education and have their roots in the Reformation, the Covenants, revivals, Calvinism, English Puritanism, and the Disruption. Iona's place in the national spiritual heritage has been rediscovered since its reconstruction and the formation of the Iona Community in 1938.

Theological scholarship remains a strength, despite suspicion about creativity. Others take theological formulations for granted. The social implications of Christianity are generally accepted. Primal religion is often close to the surface. Robert Burns and Walter Scott are enduring humanitarian influences. From 2000, the challenges of political devolution will include the healing of ancient enmities, and for Scots to own responsibility for their future.

JOHN ROXBOROGH

Bibliography. J. H. S. Burleigh, *A Church History of Scotland;* G. Donaldson, *The Faith of the Scots,* N. M. de S. Cameron, ed., *Dictionary of Scottish Church History and Theology.*

Scott, Peter Cameron (1867–96). Scottish missionary to Kenya and founder of AFRICA INLAND MISSION. He was born near Glasgow on March 7, 1867, into a Christian family. They immigrated to the United States in November 1879. He became sick at age nineteen, and was sent back to Scotland to recover. While there, he visited the grave of a younger sister and vowed that if he was healed he would give his life to God's service. His health was restored, but after he returned to the United States he put aside his gravesite promise. Endowed with a gifted singing voice, Scott faced a crisis of the will when deciding whether to apply for an opera chorus position. Reminded of his promise, he rededicated his life to God's service.

He began a three-year training course, but was accepted by the Missionary Alliance before finishing the course. In November 1890 he sailed for West Africa, arriving in January 1891. There he was joined by an older brother who died within a few months. Scott was stricken with fever, and returned to the United States to recover. For the next two years, he studied Africa and determined that East Africa was in great need of mission work.

In 1894 he visited London, and at the grave of Livingstone God gave him a vision and commission for a chain of mission stations stretching across sub-Saharan Africa through which the continent could be reached. He returned to the United States, and formed the Africa Inland Mission (AIM). Its first missionaries departed for Africa in August 1895. The first station was planted on November 17, 1895, at Nzawi near Machakos, Kenya. Within ten months four stations had been planted. Scott died of complications from malaria on December 4, 1896, at the age of twenty-nine. By 1996 AIM had over eight hundred missionaries and was represented in fifteen African countries and several urban centers in the United States.

A. SCOTT MOREAU

Bibliography. C. S. Miller, *Peter Cameron Scott: The Unlocked Door.*

Scottish Mission Boards and Societies. Scotland's contribution to world mission is related to its experience of mission at home, the role of diaspora Scots in other parts of Britain and around the world, and its changing circumstances as a nation whose history is integral with that of Europe. It is also affected by its Celtic and Calvinist heritage and marked commitment to education.

The evangelization of Scotland was associated with Celtic monasticism and new orders in the medieval period. By the 1500s responsibility for mission had shifted to rulers. Scots had limited opportunities, rulers in no position to extend their territory, no missionary orders, and closed monasteries. Nevertheless the Confession of 1560, and the Westminster Confession and its catechisms, allowed for world mission. In 1698 a doomed attempt at colonization in Central America included Church of Scotland ministers with a missionary mandate. In 1723 Robert Millar of Paisley's *History of the Propagation of Christianity* called for mission to pagans. By the 1740s the Society in Scotland for the Propagation of Christian Knowledge (founded in 1709) supported work among North American Indians as well as charity schools in the Scottish Highlands. Education and a bias toward English were common to both. Its annual sermons show Scots thinking about mission into the 19th century.

In 1842 the Cambuslang Revival inspired a call for prayer which helped form the backdrop to the Baptist Missionary Society, founded in England in 1792. Scots were active in the formation of the Missionary Society in London in 1795 (*see* COUNCIL FOR WORLD MISSION) and provided many of its directors and some of its most notable missionaries including DAVID LIVINGSTONE, John Philip, and JAMES LEGGE. In 1796 the General Assembly of the Church of Scotland declined involvement, but theology students debated the needs of the non-Christian world. Local societies were formed in many places. The Glasgow and Edinburgh societies supported their own missionaries for a time. By 1800 there was little to show for the expenditure of money and lives. Later success depended on persistence, the lessons of experience, and the opening up of new opportunities, particularly after mission in India became legal in 1813. In the early 1820s student societies were founded in all four Scottish universities.

In 1824 the Church of Scotland took steps to engage in missions as the national church. By 1830 ALEXANDER DUFF was headmaster of the Church of Scotland's school in Calcutta. That year there were in Edinburgh, along with Bible societies, the Scottish SPCK and the Scottish Missionary Society, societies connected with the CMS, the LMS, Moravians, as well as others directed at Jews and for the abolition of slavery. Visiting missionaries, publications, correspondence, and systematic fund raising nurtured interest.

The 1830s were a peak of Scottish recruitment into the LMS. By the 1840s overseas mission was an accepted, though not central, dimension of Christian identity. After the Disruption of 1843 those who left the Church of Scotland for the Free Church were replaced. Livingstone's example as an explorer missionary calling for "Christianity, commerce and civilization" in Africa was widely heeded. The Edinburgh Medical Missionary Society began in 1841.

Duff's belief that a Christian worldview would demolish Hinduism captured people's imagination in Scotland at least, but Hinduism proved resilient. Missionaries who preferred vernacular education to English were vindicated in the long run. Duff's vision that missions were the chief end of the Christian church, and his occupancy of the first chair of mission studies anywhere, set up by the Free Church of Scotland in 1867, give him a place in history. The chair did not last. The elder Duff lacked the magic of his youth, mission was no longer in question, and future problems were not envisaged. Given the belief that mission should be integrated with other theological disciplines, it was not difficult to believe it could also be left to them. Scots missionaries offered the best of their own experience of salvation, and articulated theologies, which took other religions seriously. A proclivity for higher education often included an appreciation of artisan skills.

John Wilson engaged in polite debate with Hindus. James Legge became the most important Sinologist of the nineteenth century. J. N. Farquhar talked in terms of fulfillment—*Christ as the Crown of Hinduism*. MARY SLESSOR achieved in Africa what was still difficult for women in Britain. THE WORLD MISSIONARY CONFERENCE (EDINBURGH 1910) had a strong Scottish flavor. James Hastings' *Encyclopedia of Religion and Ethics* can be seen as a missiological statement. Today the Board of World Mission of the Church of Scotland maintains links with mission fields and offers training back in Scotland. The Council for World Mission, formerly the LMS, has links with the Congregational Union in Scotland and provides a model of post-colonial mission partnership. Roman Catholics share in mission overseas through Catholic orders and through the Scottish Catholic International Aid Fund.

JOHN ROXBOROGH

Bibliography. E. G. K. Hewat, *Vision and Achievement 1796–1956. A History of the Foreign Missions of the Churches United in the Church of Scotland;* D. Mackichan, *The Missionary Ideal in the Scottish Churches;* S. Piggin and J. Roxborogh, *The St. Andrews Seven;* A. F. Walls, *DSCHT*, pp. 567–94.

Scudder, Ida Sophia (1870–1960). American missionary to India from the Reformed Church in America. Born in India, she greatly resisted continuing in the tradition of her famous American missionary medical family yet became a renowned pioneer in medical mission work. What began in 1895 with a vision to meet the medical needs of women in India grew into an internationally acclaimed medical institution in Vellore. Initially establishing a hospital and medical training institution for women, Ida initiated "Roadside" clinics that grew into a highly organized system of mobile clinics. In 1959 alone, "roadside" treatment was extended to 92,756 patients. Gifted as a fundraiser, she founded a medical school for women in 1913 that was later transformed in 1938 into a coeducational institution. Her most daring challenge, the Christian Medical College and Hospital, stands among leading international institutions.

Besides the mobile dispensary, Scudder introduced a medical college for women, a college of nursing, mobile eye camps, neurology and neurosurgery departments, a cardiothoracic department, a rehabilitation center for leprosy patients, heart surgery, a mental health center, and a rural hospital. Her legacy of commitment to service, training, and research for the needs of India continues today. She died in 1960 greatly honored by the people whom she served.

ROBERTA R. KING

Bibliography. R. P. Beaver, *American Protestant Women in World Mission;* A. Brouwer, *Reformed Church Roots;* N. Hardesty, *Women Called to Witness;* D. Luidens, *Into all the World;* D. C. Wilson, *ML*, pp. 307–15; idem, *Dr. Ida: The Story of Dr. Ida Scudder of Vellore.*

Second Language Acquisition. From the time that God confounded the languages at Babel (Gen. 11:7–9) there has existed the necessity for people to learn other languages and cultures. Joseph, for example, learned the language of Egypt so well that when his brothers went to Egypt to get grain they did not realize that Joseph could understand them, since he was speaking that language fluently and using an interpreter to talk with them (Gen. 42:23). At the birth of the church God demonstrated the importance of language by communicating through the disciples in such a way that people heard the message each in their own language (Acts 2:6–12).

God's eternal plan is that people from all languages will worship and serve him (Dan. 7:13–14; Rev. 5:9–10). So, he sends his followers to the uttermost parts of the earth (Acts 1:8), to evangelize and disciple and teach all the peoples of the earth (Matt. 28: 19–20). This task that he has given the church necessitates that we be willing to reach people of all languages and that we be able to communicate clearly with the people in a language they understand in order to disciple and train them. Language learning is clearly part of our mandate.

Some, however, might assert that only those people gifted in languages should endeavor the task of learning another language. Although a high level of natural ability enables language learning to be more rapid and easier, lack of such ease in learning does not render a person ineffective in learning another language. Anyone who is motivated to learn and who decides to participate with the people of the language and submit to change can achieve at least functional bilingualism given normal aptitude and sufficient opportunity. Even a learner with low aptitude can achieve a good measure of success in the normal use of the language provided the person is well-motivated and has a good opportunity to learn the language (Larson and Smalley, 1974, 3, 51).

Learners with lower language aptitude need to plan to invest greater time, determination, discipline, and effort in language learning and should seek optimum opportunity and resources for learning. There are classes and training programs designed to help prepare potential learners for entry into another language and culture. These pre-field classes may include training in language learning strategy and tactics, phonetics, grammar, use of resources, applied linguistics, linguistic analysis, interpersonal skills, culture learning skills, and anthropology. While all learners would benefit from such training, it is especially helpful for those who face a challenging situation, whether through lower ability or lack of resources and programs in the language.

One of the key factors in learning a language is the learner's settled decision that he or she wants and needs to learn the language. For a missionary, this would be predicated upon a prior decision to follow the Lord's call to a particular people and to love the people who speak this language. Effective language learning necessitates a decision to learn the language and to involve oneself with the people of that language. Without such a firm decision it becomes easier to quit than to persevere in language learning.

Willingness to be a learner is a necessary corollary for effective language learning. A learner is one who recognizes a linguistic or cultural need and is willing to be vulnerable enough to expose that lack to others and allow others to help one learn. One who is a learner is willing to make mistakes and learn from them, willing to reach out to people who are different from oneself, willing to step outside one's own culture and begin to enter another's world, and willing to persevere in learning.

If the desire is to reach out to people and enter into life with them then the learner will make any life-style changes necessary to facilitate this involvement. The learner can take the effort to develop friendships with people who speak that language and spend time with them in learning activities as well as in relaxed social times, in order to hear the language, to practice speaking, and to experience the culture. The learner may choose to live in a neighborhood where the language is spoken so that there will be more opportunity to hear the language, to interact with people, and to form friendships. For greater and more intimate contact with the language and culture the learner should consider living for a period of time with a family who speaks that language. This will maximize involvement in the community, increase exposure to the language, enhance language learning, and give greater insights into the culture.

In addition to benefiting from contact with the community, the learner should take advantage of whatever other learning resources are available. In many languages, there are significant resources in the language such as written materials for learners (language text books, grammars, dictionaries, books for early readers, language analyses, dialect surveys), radio and television, tape recordings, videos, and computer programs. Use of these resources will enhance and facilitate learning.

Each learner should also seek a learning situation that corresponds with his or her needs, strengths, and learning style. In many languages there are excellent language schools, in others there are trained teachers or tutors. The learner should make appropriate use of this assistance. Lack of a school or program does not render language learning impossible but it does require more creativity and discipline from the language learner. If resources are scarce or unavailable, it behooves the learner to lean even more heavily on learning through contact with native speakers in the community.

Ideally, the language learner should plan on spending a minimum of a year in intense language learning focus with few if any other activities that would take one away from the language, and then spending at least some time daily on language learning for the next several years. The one who has learned how to learn can continue to learn as a way of life for the rest of his or her years in the language.

ELIZABETH S. BREWSTER

SEE ALSO Adjustment to the Field.

Bibliography. E. T. Brewster and E. S. Brewster, *Language Acquisition Made Practical;* idem, *Bonding and the Missionary Task;* H. D. Brown, *Principles of Language Learning and Teaching;* H. D. Brown, *Teaching by Principles;* L. Dickinson, *Self-Instruction in Language Learning;* D. L. Gradin, *Helping the Missionary Language Learner Succeed,* pp. 51–56; D. N. Larson and W. A. Smalley, *Becoming Bilingual, A Guide to Language Learning;* T. Marshall, *The Whole World Guide to Language Learning;* E. A. Nida, *Learning a Foreign Language;* H. Purnell, *Helping the Missionary Language Learner Succeed,* pp. 105–39; J. Rubin and I. Thompson, *How to be a More Successful Learner,* E. W. Stevick,

Success with Foreign Languages: Seven Who Achieved It and What Worked for Them; G. Thomson, *Helping the Missionary Language Learner Succeed,* pp. 241–57.

Second Vatican Council (1962–65). When in 1959 Pope John XXIII made the unexpected announcement of an ecumenical council, he called the leaders of the global Roman Catholic Church together for the first time since Vatican I, almost a hundred years earlier. His convocation of this council reflected his genuine desire to update and renew church life, and in particular to raise the question of the central mission of the Church. The Church needed to look outside as well as inside, attempting to come to terms with a world which had undergone deep and significant changes since the last council. Previous popes had addressed various problems facing the Church, but when Pope John called bishops from Africa, Asia, Latin America, and even from countries under the grip of totalitarian political systems, he was taking an unprecedented step. From the Catholic perspective, this would be the first truly ecumenical council.

The council's four sessions included two-month convocations in the Vatican with more than 2,500 bishops participating. Endless committees and subsequent reports stretched the hearts, minds, and bodies of the participants, and many of the documents reflect a sometimes rough summary of the attempt to blend the reports with finished papers. And although few of the bishops understood the impact those documents would have, we now have a much clearer picture of the ways and means of the Catholic Church. Not least in the catalogue of images was the understanding of the Catholic Church regarding world mission and evangelization.

Sixteen documents of uneven significance emerged from the council and a wide consensus of observers and interpreters recognizes six of those in a special way. Perhaps the most helpful observation of the council at this point in history—more than thirty-five years later—is to understand the tension during the council between theological conservatives and progressives. Changes are never easy and when one considers the nature of the Roman Catholic Church, the task of renewal might seem almost impossible. But when some of the bishops prevailed in their attempts to prod the church into engaging the modern world, the outcomes were less than predictable. And these winds of change were most obvious in the dialogue among the bishops relative to the meaning of the church and the gospel mandate "to make disciples of all nations."

The six documents which relate directly to world mission are as follows:

1. *Lumen Gentium* ("The Light of the Nations"), The Dogmatic Constitution of the Church;

2. *Dei Verbum* ("The Word of God"), The Dogmatic Constitution on Divine Revelation;

3. *Guadium et Spes* ("The Joys and Hopes"). The Pastoral Constitution on the Church in the Modern World;

4. *Ad Gentes* ("To All Nations"), The Decree on the Missionary Activity of the Church;

5. *Unitatis Redintegratio* ("Restoration of Unity"), The Decree on Ecumenism; and

6. *Nostra Aetate* ("In Our Times"), The Declaration on the Relationship of the Church to Non-Christian Religions. A seventh document on religious freedom (*Dignitatis Humanae)* is also significant but due to space limitations is omitted in this discussion.

Lumen Gentium ("The Light of the Nations") is a magisterial document which reflects an orthodox Catholic theology on the nature of the Church as well as the implications of these reflections for the Church's central mission. Essentially the CHURCH is pictured by the images of mystery, the People of God, and a hierarchical structure, displaying again the distinctives of both conservative and progressive ecclesiologies. Articles 13–17 represent the core of Catholic reflection on the universal nature of the Church's mission as it relates to its own, to non-Catholics, and to non-Christians. The ambiguities so characteristic of this document raise concerns about UNIVERSALISM and the nature of the gospel itself. Many Scriptures are brought to bear on the text and the GREAT COMMISSION passages are in abundance. Evangelicals would have welcomed even more reflection on the biblical texts, with more than what in many cases appear to be merely parenthetical references to texts.

Dei Verbum ("The Word of God") is an important document for evangelicals to study for several reasons, not least the obvious awareness of the evangelical tradition of biblical scholarship and church practice. The Scriptures are given prominence in this document, particularly in reference to the proclamation of the gospel. But it is unfortunate that some of the positive contributions of a fresh approach to the Bible are blunted by the traditional teaching of interpretations being subject to the magisterial office. Evangelicals can be encouraged to find the exhortation to the pastors of the Church to give much more attention to Bible study and sermon preparation, making the Scriptures more accessible to the entire Church universally. In the end, the traditional two-source theory of revelation prevails, even though it has been recast with God being the original source and Church tradition and Holy Scripture standing equally in the life of the Church.

Gaudium et Spes ("The Joys and Hopes") is the lengthiest of the sixteen documents, and although there is some ponderous repetition, the document itself bears a sympathetic reading. The culture of modernity is addressed and the document demonstrates the desire on the part of progressive Church leaders to interact with the secular and material world. This pastoral constitution is unique in that the discussion surrounding it arose during the council itself without following the protocol of pre-council preparations and paperwork. In the present situation where the Western church is struggling with its relationship with its own cultural developments, *Gaudium et Spes* pioneers in certain areas where the Church has avoided interaction with those outside the Church and perhaps even critical of it. The Preface, in fact, makes it clear: ". . . the Church now addresses itself without hesitation, not only to the sons of the Church and to all who invoke the name of Christ, but to the whole of humanity."

Ad Gentes ("To All Nations") is the most "evangelical" document in the way it addresses itself to the understanding of the Great Commission and the strategic implications in the life of the Church, locally and globally. The most quoted sentence in the entire document is the first of the doctrinal principles: "The pilgrim Church is missionary by her very nature" which represents a clear reflection of *Lumen Gentium* in the way that missionary activity was located within the center of the Church's life instead of on its periphery. It is also important to note that this document on missions is the final product of a long and arduous process that extended throughout most of the four years of the council. The several principles stated in *Ad Gentes* stem from a clear biblical understanding of the necessity of explicit gospel proclamation as the hallmark of missionary activity, incorporating those who respond into the local body, the church. Furthermore, this missionary effort pertains to the whole church, and not just the clergy or those orders of missionaries exclusively set aside for such ministry. It should not be forgotten that ten years after the conclusion of Vatican II, Pope Paul VI called another synod of bishops, after which he issued an even more carefully worded (and one might say "powerfully worded") statement, the Apostolic Exhortation, *Evangelii Nuntiandi* (Evangelization in the Modern World). This document, read alongside *Ad Gentes,* provides solid biblical and theological insights for missiologists and missionaries alike.

Unitatis Redintegratio ("Restoration of Unity") breaks new ground in the Roman Catholic understanding of its role in Christian dialogue with Protestants. Reflecting on the ECUMENICAL MOVEMENT begun earlier in the twentieth century, the bishops took some steps to recover lost ground since the schisms of the eleventh and sixteenth centuries. Vatican II began calling Orthodox and Protestant Christians "separated brethren" and looked for openings for bilateral discussions with various denominations. Four notable points can be observed which will highlight the contours of the document: (1) The Church's willingness to share blame for separations in past centuries; (2) the Church's affirmation of genuine Christianity as consisting in "all those justified by faith through baptism (being) incorporated into Christ"; (3) the calling attention to "an order of 'hierarchy' of truths (which) vary in their relationship to the foundation of the Christian Faith"; (4) the encouragement which the Catholic Church takes from their observation of the "love, veneration, and near cult of the sacred Scriptures (which) lead our brethren to a constant and expert study of the sacred text." These are significant movements which bear even more reflection for future conversations.

Nostra Aetate ("In Our Times") represents the shortest and, in the minds of many, the most controversial document. In our day of RELIGIOUS PLURALISM and political correctness, the "Declaration on the Relationship of the Church to Non-Christian Religions" makes an uncertain sound, particularly in the light of the high theology of *Ad Gentes*. The document places Hinduism, Buddhism, and Islam in the best possible light, mixing Scripture quotations in almost syncretistic fashion. There are two positive aspects of *Nostra Aetate:* (1) the lengthy section on the Jews addresses issues especially significant in light of World War II and correctly sees the strong biblical connection between Judaism and Christianity; (2) toward the conclusion of the document, the centrality of the cross of Christ for salvation is brought into focus, restating the necessity of the Church's preaching in proclaiming the "cross of Christ."

It is no exaggeration to say that when Pope John XXIII called for "a new Pentecost," few realized what kind of "depth charges" would be set off. It could also be said that Catholics living in the period even ten years prior to the council might not recognize the Church today. But in the end, the emphasis on proclamation to those who have not heard the gospel is biblical, and theological reflection is always required when attempting to carry out the Great Commission in the way the Lord of the Church, Jesus Christ, intended.

JOHN W. NYQUIST

SEE ALSO Roman Catholic Missions.

Bibliography. W. M. Abbott, ed., *The Documents of Vatican II;* D. J. Bosch, *Transforming Mission: Paradigm Shifts in Theology of Mission;* C. Butler, *The Theology of Vatican II;* H. Gensichen, *IRM* 56 (July 1967): 291–309; A. Glasser and D. A. McGavran, *Contemporary Theologies of Mission;* W. R. Hogg, *IRM* 56:223 (July 1967): 281–90.

Secondment. Practice of missionary personnel who have their primary identification with one particular mission agency or institution being "seconded," or assigned, to another institution in which to carry out their ministry. This can take a variety of forms and be undertaken for various reasons. A missionary serving with, for example, the Evangelical Free Church Mission might desire to work in a context in which the mission agency has no plans to establish a work. The missionary, while still remaining a Free Church missionary, might be seconded to a different agency (perhaps OMF International) which does have work in that context. The Free Church missionary would then work within the OMF structure in that ministry. Secondment often occurs with more specialized ministries (medical missions, theological education, relief and development, missions aviation, radio, etc.) so that a specialist can be assigned to ministry in institutions requiring his or her skills. Often such institutions are cooperative ventures, drawing on various denominational and missions organizations.

The practice of secondment reflects a healthy trend toward greater cooperation among various denominational and missions structures. Effectiveness in such contexts depends in part on a relationship of trust and open communication between the various partners, as well as clear lines of accountability between the missionaries and the various groups with which they are associated.

HAROLD NETLAND

Secular Humanism. *See* SECULARIST, SECULARISM.

Secularist, Secularism. A secularist is a person who has been secularized or who embraces secularism as a WORLDVIEW. The term "secular" is from the Latin *saeculum,* meaning "generation" or "age," signifying "belonging to this age or the world" rather than to a transcendent religious order. Secularism is a worldview which finds little if any place for the supernatural and the transcendent. It is often linked with philosophical naturalism, which holds that this world of matter and energy is all that exists. Secularism as a worldview must be distinguished from SECULARIZATION as an historical process in which religious beliefs, values, and institutions are increasingly marginalized and lose their plausibility and power. Secularization may result in the elimination of religion entirely, as in atheistic and agnostic societies. Or it may simply transform the nature and place of religion within society, resulting in "this worldly" secularized forms of religion. Secularization is often linked to modernization, so that as societies become increasingly modernized they also tend to become secularized.

In the West secularism has become identified with movement and ideology of secular human-ism. The ideology of secular humanism is expressed in the "Secular Humanist Declaration" (1981), which affirms ten points: free inquiry, separation of church and state, freedom, critical intelligence, moral education, religious skepticism, knowledge through reason, science and technology, evolution, and education. Underlying these points is a commitment to an agenda which will reduce the influence of religion in society and elevate the authority of a rationalism based upon reason and science.

As the world increasingly is influenced by modernization and secularization, missionaries in both the West and non-Western cultures will need to deal with secularists who have little interest in religion. Effective ministry will involve not only proclamation of the gospel but also exposing the inadequacies of secularism as a worldview.

WILLIAM H. BAKER

SEE ALSO Atheism AND Modernity.

Bibliography. S. Bruce, ed., *Religion and Modernization: Sociologists and Historians Debate the Secularization Thesis;* P. Sampson et al., eds., *Faith and Modernity;* R. Webber, *Secular Humanism: Threat and Challenge.*

Secularization. Secularism represents a philosophical viewpoint that began to germinate with the Renaissance and came to full flower during the ENLIGHTENMENT. It emphasizes the autonomy of the individual and the power of human reason, which provided the seed bed for the development of the scientific method. It maintains that the only real world is that of sensory experience and regards the universe as a closed system in which humankind operates without recourse to any real or imagined powers outside of itself. Another ramification is the denial of moral absolutes.

Based on the assumption that the world has evolved, secularism represents a significant epistemological shift away from the classical focus on design and purpose in a divinely created order, to an understanding of the universe as the product of chance and random relations that trigger chains of cause and effect. With God removed from the scene, either through the remoteness of DEISM or ATHEISM's denial of his existence, there is no appeal beyond the authority of science.

Secularism represents a rival, anthropocentric religion, an absolutizing of what were previously regarded as penultimate concerns. All religions are relativized, the products of particular historical and socioeconomic contexts. They represent the ways in which various cultures have tried to answer ultimate questions and provide ethical norms and moral sanctions. Their value is judged on their ability to provide coping mechanisms, and not on their truth claims in regard to the nature of God and his relationship to the created order.

Secularism the philosophical perspective should be distinguished from secularization the social phenomenon, the process through which successive sectors of society and culture are freed from the influence of religious ideas and institutions. On the positive side, secularization has effectively challenged the fatalistic attitudes and fear-inducing superstition of prescientific WORLDVIEWS, which discouraged intellectual creativity and social progress. But negatively it has compartmentalized life, leaving it without any sense of purpose or cohesiveness. Secularization relativizes and marginalizes religion to the extent that it is allowed into the public sphere only for the purpose of serving the interests of a secular society, whether by providing social cohesion (civil religion in the United States) or adding a splash of color and dignified pageantry (ceremonial religion in Europe). There is ambivalence toward religion as a source of ethical norms. Both historically and sociologically, its role is pervasive, and yet in the legislative and judicial process arguments based on religious convictions are excluded.

As to the future impact of secularization on religion, the social scientists of the 1960s were confidently predicting the demise of religion. A counter-position argued that the process of secularization in fact causes people to starve for the transcendent, and thus it may unwittingly be sowing the seeds for a revival of religion. The growing attraction of New Age religions, coupled with the impressive growth of many Christian churches that are worship- and experience-oriented, gives credence to the latter viewpoint. It is further strengthened by the crumbling of the Newtonian worldview in the wake of the findings of quantum physics regarding the random activity of subatomic particles, and the latest theories of astrophysicists regarding the origins of the universe.

When developing a mission approach to secularized persons, we should bear in mind that many are searching for meaning to life and have a desire for self-transcendence, even though they may not be able to articulate their deep-seated restlessness. They long for a sense of fulfillment in life and are baffled by the contradictory aspects of human nature, the inner struggle between knowing the good and doing the evil, and the need to find ways to balance personal freedom with mutual accountability and social justice.

EDDIE GIBBS

Bibliography. P. Berger, *The Sacred Canopy;* D. G. Bloesch, *Crumbling Foundations;* O. Guinness, *The Gravedigger File;* L. Newbigin, *Foolishness to the Greeks;* R. Stark and W. S. Bainbridge, *The Future of Religion: Secularization and Renewal and Cult Formation.*

Segundo, Juan Luis (1925–96). Uruguayan Roman Catholic theologian, one of the earliest and most prolific craftsmen of liberation theol-

ogy. Born in Montevideo, he spent most of his life in that city, but received his training under the Jesuits in San Miguel, Argentina, and Louvain, Belgium, and brilliantly defending two theses before a jury of the Sorbonne, being awarded the highest classification for the Doctorat ès Lettres in theology. These did not distract him from his major concerns as a pastor, delving deeply into whatever academic disciplines could help him defend the poor and oppressed as well as articulate for them a theology they could apply in their daily living. This he accomplished through his five-volume work *Theology for Artisans of a New Humanity.* Equally important was his contribution as the most original and most profound of the Latin American liberation theologians, with *The Liberation of Theology,* in which he emphasized the need to maintain the liberating character of theology by following the proper method to interpret the scriptural text to bring out its relevance to the needs of Latin America. A necessary corollary to this was his goal to formulate an authentic Christian theology and a true image of Jesus of Nazareth, which he accomplished through his five-volume work *Jesus of Nazareth Yesterday and Today.* His concern for his people would not allow him to accept teaching posts in many institutions in Europe and the Americas, but his short lectureships, as well as his books and articles, still stand as his testament to the world as a whole.

PABLO E. PÉREZ

Selywn, George Augustus (1809–78). English missionary and first Anglican bishop in New Zealand. Born at Hampstead, England, he was educated at Eton and St. John's College, Cambridge. Ordained a priest in 1834, he taught at Eton and was a curate at Boveney and Windsor. Consecrated bishop in 1841, Selwyn arrived in New Zealand in 1842 charged with oversight of the missionary work among Maori and the rapidly growing English settler population. His relationships with the CHURCH MISSIONARY SOCIETY and its missionaries were fraught with tension, in part because of evangelical suspicions of his sympathy with the Tractarians. Selwyn was a great visionary but his comprehensive educational institution at St. John's College in Auckland failed to achieve his expectations. The development of the Melanesian Mission from 1849 was innovative with his use of New Zealand as a base to bring Melanesian students for training as evangelists. His lasting achievement was the 1857 constitution of the church based on synodical government and lay participation. Selwyn attempted to defend Maori interests but his chaplaincy to the British troops in the wars of the 1860s destroyed his influence with Maori. He made a notable contribution to the first Lambeth

Conference in 1867 and the development of pan-Anglicanism. He returned to England in 1868 as Bishop of Lichfield.

ALLAN K. DAVIDSON

Bibliography. A. K. Davidson, *Selwyn's Legacy: The College of St. John the Evangelist, Te Waimate and Auckland, 1843–1992, A History;* J. H. Evans, *Churchman Militant: George Augustus Selwyn Bishop of New Zealand and Lichfield;* W. E. Limbrick, ed., *Bishop Selwyn in New Zealand 1841–68;* H. W. Tucker, *Memoir of the Life and Episcopate of George Augustus Selwyn,* 2 vols.

Senegal *(Est. 2000 pop.: 9,495,000; 196,722 sq. km. [75,954 sq. mi.]).* Despite a 90% Muslim majority, Senegal is a secular state with freedom of religion. Senegal's Islamic strength, mostly African Sunnis of the Malikite rite, is concentrated to the north. Portuguese explorers brought the Catholic Church to the Senegalese coast in 1445, baptizing the Senegalese chief Behemoi in 1486. By 1490 the first establishments were set up, and by 1514 the diocese of Funchal, including Senegal, was created. In 1840 three Senegalese priests were ordained. The vicariate of The Two Guineas became the vicariate of Senegambia in 1863 and later of Dakar in 1936. Dakar, Senegal's capital, became an archdiocese in 1955 with the first African archbishop consecrated in 1962, just two years after independence from France.

The Paris Mission's activity in 1863 resulted in the Protestant Church of Dakar, one of the two largest Protestant Churches whose membership is 60 percent European. With the government encouraging churches and religious groups to play a role in development, religious broadcasting has been accepted and used by the Assemblies of God, Catholic Church, Reformed Church, Conservative Baptists, and WEC INTERNATIONAL (first arrived from Britain in 1935).

GARY LAMB

Serampore Trio. A popular, shorthand term used by mission promoters and historians to refer to the close partnership of three English Baptists who codirected the Serampore Mission in Bengal between 1800 and 1823: WILLIAM CAREY, JOSHUA MARSHMAN, and WILLIAM WARD. Based at a tiny Danish colonial enclave thirteen miles up the Hooghly River from cosmopolitan Calcutta, the Serampore Mission grew out of the BAPTIST MISSIONARY SOCIETY'S (BMS) venture in Bengal, particularly as the pioneer triumvirate established financial and managerial independence of the administration in London.

The trio established the Serampore Union in 1807 as a way of regulating the internal affairs of their mission community. Some time around 1816 it became known as the Missionary Union at Serampore. This in turn was institutionalized informally to constitute what became known as the Baptist Mission at Serampore and later the Serampore Mission. Escalating disagreements with the BMS, especially over the founding (1818) and development of Serampore College, finally led to a costly split in 1827. The end of this schism began in 1837 with the death of the last member of the triumvirate. The Serampore Mission and college then limped along until an amicable settlement was reached with the BMS in 1855.

A. CHRISTOPHER SMITH

Bibliography. S. P. Carey, *William Carey, D.D., Fellow of Linnaean Society;* J. C. Marshman, *The Life and Times of Carey, Marshman and Ward: Embracing the History of the Serampore Mission;* E. D. Potts, *Baptist Missionaries in India, 1793–1837: The History of Serampore and Its Missions;* A. C. Smith, *IRM* 83 (1993): 451–75.

Serbia. *See* YUGOSLAVIA.

Serra, Junípero (1713–84). Spanish missionary to Mexico and California. Born José Miguel on the Spanish island of Majorca to a farming family, Serra joined the Franciscan Order and took the name of Junípero (1730). After his ordination (1738), Serra went on to receive a doctorate in theology at Lullian University, where he accepted a teaching post from 1743 until 1749.

Sensing God's call, he then sailed to Mexico to engage in mission and ministry among indigenous peoples there. He served in Mexico until 1767, and then took up work in Spanish-occupied lower California. Beginning in 1769, he accompanied the Spanish military expeditions north along the coast of California; by 1782 he had established nine missions across California including those in San Diego (1770), San Francisco (1776), and San Buenaventura (1782). At times frustrated with military treatment of the indigenous peoples, he wrote his *Representación* (1773) declaring to the Spanish viceroy in Mexico City thirty-two points of appropriate missionary conduct. Prior to his death it was calculated that he had baptized some six thousand and confirmed five thousand.

Contemporary assessments of Serra's work have been highly politicized, with appellations ranging from saint to sadist. The process of canonization and his inclusion as a figure on a U.S. postage stamp has raised many questions to the fore, with indigenous Americans and notable historians protesting that even Serra's treatment of local populations was inhumane and barbaric.

A. SCOTT MOREAU

Bibliography. D. Fogel, *Junipero Serra, the Vatican & Enslavement Theology;* K. M. King, *Mission to Paradise: The Story of Junipero Serra and the Missions of California;* J. J. Kortendick, *NCE,* 13:124–25; J. A. Sandos, *The Journal of Religious History* 15:3 (June 1989): 311–29; G. E. Tinker, *Missionary Conquest: The Gospel and Native American Cultural Genocide.*

Sexual Mores. The student of cross-cultural phenomena confronts a bewildering array of ideas about and practices of sexuality. Many of these ideas and practices will conflict with the cross-cultural worker's own socially conditioned beliefs and practices. Some of these ideas and practices may well conflict with biblical revelation.

The dual nature of this conflict sets the stage for missionary involvement in the sexual mores of the receptor culture. The cross-cultural worker may support mores that differ from his or her own socially conditioned views but that do not violate either biblical teachings or principles (i.e., bride price). The missionary may be compelled to advocate to local innovators changes in sexual mores that actually conflict with or violate biblical teachings or principles (i.e., female genital mutilation). In any case, the cross-cultural worker must seek to understand fully the meaning of the cultural practice and the biblical principles involved. Any proposed change in mores will proceed from this dual perspective.

EBBIE C. SMITH

Seychelles *(Est. 2000 pop.: 77,000; 455 sq. km. [176 sq. mi.]).* The 90-some granitic and coraline islands of the Republic of Seychelles stretch out over 154,000 square miles of the Indian Ocean, making their Sechellois people one of the most difficult to access in terms of physical geography. The outlying islands are isolated and consequently have not been given a clear challenge regarding the lordship of Christ.

Although the collapse of communism in other world areas has brought about political reform and multiparty elections, Seychellois youth have been hardened against biblical truth by a decade of Marxist orientation. The Catholics and Anglicans have openly opposed one-party rule but many of the members of the larger churches have syncretized the sacraments of baptism and confirmation with traditional beliefs and superstitions. Innovative outreach strategies to youth need to be developed and effective prayer teams challenged to pray that evangelical ministries will experience a strategic loosening of restrictions.

Christian radio has, in recent years, been effective in creating new opportunities for informing, educating, and challenging the Seychellois populace to the claims of Christ. Although almost all Seychellois claim to be Christians (97%), missiological strategies depend on new evangelical congregations challenging indigenous believers to develop ministries that answer the questions regarding traditional practices.

CLINT AKINS

Shalom. Hebrew word meaning wholeness. It is translated into English using such terms as completeness, soundness, peace, well-being, health, prosperity, and salvation. It implies a state of mind that is at peace and satisfied, and social relationships characterized by harmony and mutual support. It is based on three fundamental principles: this world and all in it belongs to God; all humans share equally in God's loving concern (God shows no favoritism to some people or nations); and the reign of God in creation and in human communities leads to peace, justice, and truly fulfilled lives. *Shalom* is a transcultural and timeless concept, but like other such symbols it finds its expression in the concrete situations of real life in real cultures and real history. In the Old Testament, the focus is more on earthly wholeness. In the New Testament, the dimension of eternal life comes into sharper focus.

One attribute of *shalom* is *agape*, the identification with and unconditional commitment to the other (*see* LOVE OF GOD). This is not a response to the desirable, lovable, or admirable, but to the needy, undesired, unloved, and enemy. *Shalom* initiates action, accepts vulnerability, bears suffering, and always hopes for the best. The supreme manifestation is Christ's crucifixion. A second attribute is righteousness. In Scripture, true *shalom* and righteousness flow from right relationships with God (Isa. 60:17), and reflect his character of righteousness, love, justice, peace, and perfection. There can be no *shalom* while one persists in sin and evil (Isa. 48:18; 54:13), and the renewal of righteousness is essential to the restoration of *shalom*. A third attribute is PEACE. This is not, as the modern world sees it, simply freedom from feelings of guilt, serenity, and peace of mind, nor merely the absence of war. It actively seeks harmonious, mutually edifying relationships in community life. A fourth attribute is the concept of health. *Shalom* communicates the sense of human well-being in which physical, emotional, mental, moral, and spiritual health are inextricably intertwined. Unlike the Western WORLDVIEW, which differentiates between spirit and body, spiritual and material realities, the Hebrew worldview views humans as whole beings in which spiritual, moral, mental, and physical attributes are inextricably intertwined. A fifth attribute is *koinonia*. *Shalom* speaks of social fellowship and communal harmony among friends, parties, and nations.

Shalom is an essential part of God's cosmic plan, and is one of the threads running through Scripture linking cosmic, human, and individual histories into a single, coherent story. It began at CREATION, when God saw all he had created and it was good. Only man by himself was not good (Gen 2:18), because he was not in community.

The fall shattered this harmony (*see* FALL OF HUMANKIND). In the biblical worldview, sin is at root the breaking of *shalom*, the severing of relationships. It began with the break in right relationships with God when humans put themselves as the center of their being and worshiped themselves. It led to broken human relationships between genders (Gen. 3:15), brothers (Gen. 4:8), and human communities (Gen 11:9). The result was jealousy, hatred, ethnocentrism, rivalries, injustice, violence, and war.

The establishment of *shalom* is at the heart of God's plan of SALVATION. In Christ, God reached out to save fallen humans and to reconcile them to himself. Salvation begins with forgiveness with God through Christ Jesus, and finds expression in the restoration of human relationships to God, and to one another in the church, the body of Christ. *Shalom* is associated with a peace covenant, in which this restoration of relationships and righteousness takes place (Num. 25:12; Isa. 54:7–8; Ezek. 34:5).

The final and full manifestation of *shalom* will occur when Christ returns and the kingdom of God is established over all creation. Then *shalom* and righteousness will reign in Zion (Isa. 60:17; Ps. 85:8–9), and violence and destruction will occur no more. *Shalom* is both a present reality in the life of the believer and the church, but also a future culmination in which all creation will be restored in harmony under the reign of Christ.

Shalom is of the essence of the KINGDOM OF GOD. It symbolizes the presence of God, who works to restore the entire creation to fulfill the purposes for which he created it. In the signs of this kingdom, such as salvation, reconciliation, and healing, people see the presence of God in this world, bringing life out of death, love and peace in the midst of hate and violence, and meaning to meaninglessness. Nature itself is included in God's salvation, for it will be a part of the new heaven and new earth that are essential in God's work to restore *shalom* throughout all his creation.

Shalom is to characterize the *ekklesia*, the CHURCH, the assembly or gathering of God's people. It is the test and hallmark of the church's divine nature as the outpost of the kingdom now on earth—the community that emerges when the covenant relationship between God and his people is restored, and that gives expression to the harmony intended by God. This church is not a social institution, although it finds expression in social forms. It is the community of the Spirit open to all who turn to God for reconciliation. At its heart is *koinonia*, the fellowship and harmony that give rise to a new saved and saving community based on the covenant of love that binds people together in mutual submission to one another. It is a new community that breaks down the walls of language, race, class, gender, and nationalism. It is also called to make peace, to seek social justice, provision for the needy, including widows, orphans, and the poor, and protection of the exploited and oppressed. Above all, it is apostolic, sent into the world with a divine commission to proclaim that the rule of God is at hand, that Jesus is Lord, and that people should change their ways and love in the light of the new reality and form new communities of followers.

Shalom is to characterize the life of the individual Christian, unlike the West, which sees autonomous, free individuals as the fundamental units of human reality, and differentiates between personal and social systems. Scripture sees individuals as fully human only as they are a part of communities of *shalom*, and healing as rooted in the community. Dan Fountain points out that "God's plan for the world is this: That all persons everywhere, in every nation, know God's saving health and be delivered from disobedience, disruption, despair, disease and all that would destroy our wholeness."

PAUL G. HIEBERT

Bibliography. B. Bradshaw, *Bridging the Gap: Evangelism, Development and Shalom;* D. E. *Fountain, Health, the Bible, and the Church;* S. Hauerwas and W. H. Williamon, *Resident Aliens: Life in the Christian Colony;* S. N. Kraus, *The Community of the Spirit;* C. Van Engen, *God's Missionary People.*

Shaman, Shamanism. Shamans are part-time religious specialists who serve as intermediaries between humans and the supernatural, and who seek spiritual remedies to individual problems. As such, they are said to live in the middle zone between humans and the supernatural. The word "shaman" comes from the Tungus, also called the Evenki, most of whom live in Russia, China, and Mongolia.

Shamans often invite spirits to possess their bodies in order to receive spiritual power, especially for curing. They are purported to be possessed by spirits in trances, also termed altered states of consciousness, which they enter through use of drugs (e.g., Yanomani shamans in southern Venezuela and northern Brazil), rapid drum beats (e.g., devotees during Hindu religious festivals in Malaysia), light flashes, and music. During trance they are either possessed by a spirit or their souls leave their bodies to ascend to the realm of the spirits (*see also* POSSESSION PHENOMENA).

The spirits, also termed "familiars" or "intermediaries," may be animal spirits (e.g., among some of the indigenous people of Siberia and the Yanomani, whose shamans are indwelt by the Jaguar spirit, among others). One Yanomami shaman stated,

> I'm a man of the spirit world, "shamans" we are called. The shaman is almost always the leader of his village. If he is a good shaman— I mean that if he can avoid the bad spirits and get the good ones—he can lead his village to good hunting, tell them when and where to plant, who to make war with—all the things that will make them into a great village (Ritchie, 1996, 18).

Shamans are clairvoyant, in that they can "see" in the spiritual realm. They claim to have perception, knowledge, or information about individuals that is received from a spiritual source, such that they are often aware of what is happening in their communities without having been told by another person. As one Yanomani shaman stated, "I just knew." One Bajju former shaman in Nigeria alleged that her ability to perceive in the spiritual realm came from "medicine" of special leaves in water with which she washed her face each morning.

Means of becoming a shaman include a visit by a spirit, a dream or vision, often following an illness, inheritance, an accident or unusual event, or a spontaneous call. People may recognize a change in behavior of a prospective shaman, such as hysteria, having prophetic visions or attacks that leave him or her unconscious. Such an individual then apprentices himself or herself to an established shaman to learn about shamanistic beliefs and practices, names and functions of spirits, techniques, and perhaps a special language. There are both men and women shamans, though gender is culture-specific.

The duties and religious obligations of shamans vary from culture to culture. However, their primary function is to cure illness by using the supernatural for the benefit of individuals and the community. Some treat illness by blowing smoke over patients. Others purportedly extract objects; others do cupping, placing animal horns or other containers over places on a patient's skin in order to bring heat to that part and perhaps to purportedly extract an object from it. Most shamans prescribe herbal medicines. The use of trance behavior, often accompanied by spirit possession, is common.

Since Western medicine rarely deals with spiritual causes of disease, shamanistic activities continue to be important to people in non-Western countries in the contemporary world. The services offered by shamans deal with a missing component of treatment. In Africa, a frequent diagnosis by shamans is that an individual has offended an ancestor, often one's deceased parents or grandparents, and thus is sick. In that case the usual prescribed remedy is sacrifice to the ancestor (*see* ANCESTRAL PRACTICES).

Some have referred to shamans as "witchdoctors," a derogatory term that fails to recognize the spiritual world to which these religious practitioners relate. Missionary and church teaching that their activities and beliefs are superstition begs the question of the reality of the spirit world, antagonizes those who know it is real, and serves to drive the activities of shamans underground. Shamans' motives often overlap with those of missionaries, local Christians, and health professionals—to bring healing and well-being to their people. Recognizing their impor-

tant role in the religious structure of a society should encourage missionaries to befriend them, share the gospel of Jesus Christ with them, and pray for them. Relating to shamans often involves SPIRITUAL WARFARE.

Shamans are distinct from priests, full-time religious specialists who are often organized and part of a sacred tradition. The term "diviner" refers to part-time religious specialists who deal with the spiritual realm with some divination involved. While diviners overlap with shamans in their activities, their use of divination to ascertain why people are ill, die, or suffer misfortune sets them apart (*see also* DIVINATION, DIVINER). Shamans also contrast with magicians, who use specific rituals to produce a specific result, and sorcerers, who use their powers for evil.

CAROL V. MCKINNEY

SEE ALSO Flaw of the Excluded Middle.

Bibliography. W. Howells, *Magic, Witchcraft, and Religion, an Anthropological Study of the Supernatural*, pp. 91–98; M. Ritchie, *Spirit of the Rainforest, A Yanomani Shaman's Story*.

Shame. In order to inculcate and motivate morality in its members, a society may seek to instill GUILT for violating persons or moral rules. Or it may seek to instill *shame* for moral failure. Rather than motivating by the threat of punishment, such a society motivates by threatening disapproval and shame to those who fail to exemplify desirable virtues, and by offering honor and respect to those who exemplify prescribed character traits.

While most societies cultivate and are attentive to shame, Western societies have tended to be much more attentive to guilt than to shame. Westerners typically see shame as a more superficial response to moral failure than guilt, wrongly assuming that shame is the tendency to feel bad only when caught. In consequence Western missionaries often go to non-Western societies with poorly developed understandings of shame, and with negative attitudes toward the way shame functions in people's lives. They mistakenly believe that their own inclination to stress guilt over shame is simply a reflection of biblical priorities. In fact, shame is the focal emotion in the Genesis creation account, and is a focal emotion throughout the Scriptures.

Shame involves seeing oneself as deficient with reference to certain character ideals. We often become aware of ourselves through the eyes of others. We suddenly see ourselves as others see us. While it is true that shame arises out of, and is in large part caused by, the disapproval of significant others, the source of the shame is our thoughts about our selves. Shame is not fully determined by the negative evaluation of others. What elicits shame is the acceptance of the negative evaluation of others as the correct one. Nor does shame require the presence of others. It is possible while alone to come to some shameful realization about the self which suffuses one with shame.

How then are guilt and shame to be distinguished? Guilt is tied to acts of transgression—acts that merit punishment or require compensation. Guilt is a feeling about one's *actions*. Shame, on the other hand, is a feeling about one's *self*—who one is. It is about not being good enough. I am guilt *for something*. I am ashamed *of myself*. A small lie, if treated as evidence of a person's true character, may trigger intense shame. We treat the guilt with indignation and demand punishment or restitution. We turn from the shameful with contempt. Guilt can be expiated. Shame, apart from transformation of the self, is retained.

Missionaries to those who stress shame would do well to stress relevant biblical imagery (of nakedness, covering, uncleanness, glory), the character of Christ as our model for the self, God as the ultimate significant other whose view of us ought to inform our view of ourselves, sin as falling short of the glory of God, and above all, the possibility of a new beginning (a rebirth, a new identity in Christ) where sins are covered and shame removed. Our end is glory.

ROBERT J. PRIEST

Bibliography. L. L. Noble, *Naked and Not Ashamed: An Anthropological, Biblical, and Psychological Study of Shame.*

Shedd, Russell Phillip (1929–). American missionary to Latin America. Born to missionary parents in Bolivia, he received degrees from Wheaton College and Graduate School, Faith Theological Seminary, and the University of Edinburgh. After short terms in U.S. pastorates, he taught for three years in the Leiria and Lisbon Portugal seminary, and then moved to Brazil where he has been for more than thirty years. As a New Testament professor he has taught mainly at the Baptist Theological Seminary in São Paulo, has been visiting professor at several U.S. seminaries, and has been the principal lecturer at numerous pastoral and youth conferences. Because of his pastoral experience in founding churches he has become known as a pastor to pastors. His writings include more than a dozen books and a variety of articles, mainly in Portuguese and most of which have to do with New Testament and the church. He is founder and visionary of the Nova Vida Publishers, as well as chief editor of *Biblica Nova Vida* (*New Life Bible;* 200,000 copies in print) whose commentary notes are written by him and others. His current special interests are Latin American cross-cultural missions, revival in the Brazilian

churches, and opening of traditional Protestant denominations to the charismatic movement.

DAVID SPRUANCE

Shellabear, William Girdlestone (1862–1947). English Bible translator, orientalist, and pioneer Methodist missionary in Malaysia and Singapore. As an English soldier in Singapore in 1887, Shellabear was impressed by Malays under his command. He learned their language and began what was to be his life's work of sharing his faith while striving to preserve Malay culture. He joined the American Methodist Mission and in 1890 founded the Methodist Publishing House. He was active in the leadership of the mission in Singapore and Malaya, and edited the *Malaysia Message* as well as classic Malay writings. His grammar, dictionary, and Bible translation remained in print for decades. In 1916 he left Malaya and studied Islam at Hartford, Cairo, and Leiden. From 1922 until his death he edited the *Muslim World* and in 1925 he became professor of Islamics at Hartford. He maintained his hope that Malay-speaking Christians would understand the religion of their Muslim neighbors, and that Muslim Malays would learn from their own scripture something of the Christian truth which impelled him to write. His respect for Muhammad combined with his commitment to Christ as the only known way of salvation marked him apart. His vision for a Malay-speaking church, and belief that Malay should be the unifying basis of Malayan society were long ignored.

JOHN ROXBOROGH

Bibliography. R. Hunt, *William Shellabear: A Biography.*

Shi'ite, Shi'ism. The Shi'ite branch of Islam comprises about 10 percent of all Muslims and is subdivided into three principal groups: the Zaydis (primarily in Yemen), the Isma'ilis (in Asia, Syria, and East Africa), and the Twelve-Imam Shi'ites or Twelvers. The Twelvers are by far the largest group, comprising most of the population of Iran, 50 percent of Iraq, and scattered communities in Lebanon, Pakistan, Syria, and the Gulf states. Shi'ism has been the official religion of Iran since the sixteenth century.

The term "Shi'ite" comes from the Arabic *shi'at Ali*, "party of Ali." The roots of Shi'ism go back to Muhammad's death and the ensuing leadership struggle. Shi'ites claim that Ali, as closest relative to Muhammad and husband to the Prophet's daughter Fatimah, was the rightful successor to Muhammad. Ali eventually became Caliph but was assassinated. His son, Husayn, raised a revolt and was killed at Kerbala in 680. This is the central event of Twelver Shi'ism.

The Shi'ites understand Muhammad and Ali to have possessed special status with God that gave them an absolute right to rule the Muslim community. This status was passed down through the descendants of Ali the Imams, who have both spiritual and political preeminence. They are said to possess secret knowledge, spiritual powers, and special favor with God. The Imams function as intermediaries between humankind and God and are necessary for the salvation of believers. Sunni Muslims, by contrast, have generally seen the claim of the Imams to all spiritual and temporal authority as an extension of the Persian "priest-king" paradigm and have rejected it.

In 873 the twelfth Imam, Muhammad, disappeared as a young boy. Until 940 he was represented by *wakils*, who claimed to be in communication with him. Since that time, Shi'ites have awaited his return as the Mahdi (or "guided one"). They believe he hears prayers and intercedes in human affairs. However, this situation left a considerable void in both political and religious leadership and authority.

Aside from the Imammate, Twelver Shi'ite theology and ritual do not differ greatly from the Sunni tradition. There are distinct shrines and pilgrimage sites associated with the Imams. Perhaps the greatest difference lies in the highly charged emotional climate of Shi'ite religiosity.

The major distinctive of Shi'ism is its understanding of religious leadership. For the past two hundred years, Shi'ite *mujtahids* (leading clerics) have gradually enhanced the level of their authority. They are much more tightly organized with a much more clearly defined hierarchy than their Sunni counterparts. All Shi'ites must identify with and then adhere personally to the superior authority of a *mujtahid*. Today, the top level of the Shi'ite Ulema, the *Ayatollahs*, function as the representatives of the Twelfth Imam on earth. This gradual rise to power culminated in the Iranian Revolution, in which the Ayatollahs seized both religious and temporal power in the name of the Hidden Imam. The hostility and tensions between Sunni and Shi'ite Muslims, which had been on the wane for much of the twentieth century, has again heated up due to the efforts of Iran to export its brand of Islamic revolution to other Muslim states.

The other divisions of Shi'ites play a significant role in some areas of the Islamic world. The Zaydis reject the doctrine of the Hidden Imam and hold that any adult male descendant of Ali can lead the community. They survive only in Yemen, where the Imams held political control until 1962. Doctrinally, the Zaydis are the closest Shi'ite branch to Sunni orthodoxy and have experienced far less tension with the Sunni majority.

Isma'ilism is essentially Islamic Gnosticism, holding that the Qur'an contains secret, hidden meanings. This superior, allegorical insight was secretly transmitted to Ali and down through the line of Imams. Only through initiation and graded secret teaching can one have access to this divine Truth, which is not accessible to other religions or the mass of Muslims.

JAMES DARRELL CHANCELLOR

Bibliography. D. M. Donaldson, *The Shi'ite Religion;* C. Glasse, ed., *The Concise Encyclopedia of Islam;* M. G. Hodgson, *The Venture of Islam: Conscience and History in a World Civilization,* 3 vols.

Shinto. The term "Shinto" covers a broad range of religious activities in Japan, from various types of FOLK RELIGION to the private rituals of the imperial family. Prior to World War II Shrine Shinto was officially the state religion. However, the new postwar Constitution clearly mandated the separation of religion and state, although the interpretation and implementation of this principle continues to be controversial. On a popular level, Shinto continues to be influential as folk religion, with many Japanese worshiping Shinto deities. As folk religion, Shinto includes various ritual festivals and ceremonies as well as ancestor worship organized along the lines of family or clan (*see* ANCESTRAL PRACTICES). The earliest archaeological and historical records indicate the presence of Shinto beliefs and practice. The traditions of Shinto, sometimes in a more pure form and other times more syncretistic, have been maintained continually until the present.

Of particular significance for Shinto are the *Kojiki* (Book of Ancient Traditions) from A.D. 712 and the *Nihonshoki* (Chronicles of Japan) from A.D. 720, the oldest literary works in the Japanese language. These ancient texts, along with their recensions, commentaries, and writings of scholars such as Kamono Mabuchi (d. 1769), Motoori Norinaga (d. 1801), and Hirata Atsutane (d. 1843), who worked for the revival of a purified Shinto, provide our primary sources on Shinto. The *Kojiki* is written in an entirely Japanese style, in terms of both language and content. The *Nihonshoki*, by contrast, includes many Chinese modes of expression and philosophical concepts. Both texts, however, present the same Japanese view of creation. "Creation" occurs without any Creator or first cause; matter appears before mind and deity has no existence apart from matter. The creation myths portray a process of evolution that continues until the gods themselves evolve into their final form.

According to the creation myths, the highest deity is the goddess Amaterasu, whose grandson Ninigi descended from heaven to earth. Ninigi's grandson, whose mother was a dragon in the form of a woman, was Jimmu, whom the myths present as the first emperor of Japan. The *Kojiki* and *Nihonshoki*, which form the foundation for all subsequent works of Shinto, depict Japan as the center of the earth and the Japanese emperor as the first of men and vicar of the gods.

Central to Shinto is reverence for the *kami* or gods. Shinto is explicitly polytheistic. Awe-inspiring or extraordinary things such as thunder, rocks, mountains, animals, certain human beings, departed ancestors, and the emperor all can be regarded as *kami*. Shinto contains no explicit moral codes. One's duty is to live in fear and reverence for the memory of the dead and to imitate noble examples of the gods and illustrious ancestors. All "sin" is viewed as a kind of pollution. Thus purification rites, in the form of ritual offerings, prayers for cleansing, and lustrations, are prominent in Shinto.

Shinto became influenced by Confucianism and Buddhism, which were introduced into Japan from China. In the late eighteenth and early nineteenth centuries Shinto scholars attempted to purge Shinto of foreign influences and to restore a purified Japanese Shinto. Included in this restoration was the tendency to view the military rulers of Japan *(shogun)* as political usurpers and the emperor as the sole legitimate ruler. A revitalized Shinto promoted reverence for the emperor, which soon grew into a zealous determination to restore the emperor to political rule and to eliminate foreign influences from Japan, including the "alien" religion of Buddhism. The Meiji Restoration of 1868 resulted in the restoration of the emperor to political rule. The nineteenth-century purificationists and restorationists thus set Japan on a course leading ultimately to World War II. Christians who refused to participate in Shinto rituals—not only in Japan but also in Korea, which Japan ruled as a colony—were often severely persecuted. The particular point of controversy usually concerned the worship of the emperor in state-sponsored Shinto shrines.

The postwar democratic Constitution of Japan has deprived Shinto of its special status, but it has also guaranteed it, along with all religious institutions, freedom of religion. Beginning in the 1960s, however, many politically conservative Japanese have pushed the government to support officially the Yasukuni Shrine, a Shinto shrine in which the spirits of soldiers who died in Japan's modern wars are worshiped. Despite widespread opposition from other religious groups due to the clear violation of the constitutional prohibition of such action, the government supported certain Shinto rites as part of the recent enthronement ceremony of Akihito, the current emperor. Thus both on the popular level of folk religion and in the public sector Shinto continues to exert considerable influence in Japan.

HISAKAZU INAGAKI

Bibliography. H. Hardacre, *Shinto and the State: 1868–1988;* D. C. Holtom, *The National Faith of Japan;* J. Kitagawa, *Religion in Japanese History;* S. Ono, *Shinto: The Kami Way.*

Short-term Missions. A term typically used to describe missionary service, normally involving cross-cultural immersion, that is intentionally designed to last from a few weeks to less than two years.

Short-term missions finds its roots in the Scriptures and, in a broad sense, can be understood through the words of Jesus in the GREAT COMMANDMENT (Matt. 22:37–39) and the GREAT COMMISSION (Matt. 28:18–20). In a sense Jesus establishes the guidelines for the early short-term mission experiences and demonstrates what is at the core of short-term missions in the sending out of the twelve (Matt. 10:1–42) and the seventy-two (Luke 10:1–20). He states quite clearly that those who are sent must love the Lord their God with all their heart, soul, and mind and then love their neighbor as themselves. From that posture, they must recognize that all authority has been given to him; therefore, they should go and make disciples of all nations.

Scope. As a modern-day phenomenon, the short-term missions movement has spanned the globe and has provided opportunities for thousands of individuals to experience, for a brief time, the world of missions. The length of service often varies from a week to several years. Mission agencies, churches, high schools, colleges and universities, parachurch ministries, families, and individuals are increasingly exploring and promoting short-term missions. The wide variety of people taking advantage of these opportunities include youth, college and university students, single adults, families, and seniors. The kinds of work that individuals and teams engage in include, but are not limited to, construction projects, teaching English, athletics and sports, drama and the arts, medical and health care, evangelism and discipleship, church planting, youth ministries, camp work, prayer and research, and general assistance.

Growth. The short-term missions movement has grown dramatically over the past several decades. Mission agencies, church denominations, and parachurch organizations as well as independent teams continue to contribute to the large numbers involved in the short-term missions enterprise. During the late 1990s, more than thirty thousand individuals joined forces each year with career missionaries and nationals to serve in urban centers, towns, and countries around the world. This rapid growth is due in part to modern travel that allows individuals to journey to the remotest areas of the world in a relatively short time. There continues to be a desire on the part of those who go to make themselves available in service without committing their entire lives to a missions career. There has been an overwhelming acknowledgment of short-term missions in recent years, and, though there is much discussion about the practice, it is obvious that short-term missions is a powerful and effective force in the modern missions movement.

The Critics. Many have been critical of short-term missions for numerous reasons. One of the main criticisms focuses on the motivation of those who go. Many career missionaries feel that short-term missionaries lack real commitment and endurance. Often the national church questions the presence of the short-term worker in their culture because it appears that the motivation of the short-termer is unclear. Some feel that the short-term workers provide a distraction for career missionaries. Other concerns focus on the perception that the results from short-term ministry are unreliable and there is little lasting fruit produced from the work of the short-term workers. Many suggest that the financial costs are too high and possibly take money away from career missionaries.

The Value. Despite the many criticisms, short-term missions is moving forward. The short-term missions movement definitely has been a key factor in the mobilization of world mission globally. The present generation of missionary candidates tends to make their decisions and commitments based on the knowledge gained through firsthand experience. As a result of short-term service a world vision can be developed that in turn affects the mobilization efforts of the church at large. In addition, many feel that short-term missions provides valuable respite for career missionaries, brings a fresh enthusiasm from the outside, and accomplishes practical projects as well as significant ministry. Obviously, many who serve in short-term missions are likely candidates for long-term service, and in fact, a significant number of career missionaries today have had a short-term mission experience. Those who return without making a commitment to long-term service are able to impact the churches that they are a part of with a global awareness and an expanded vision of God's work in the world. As a result, the prayer efforts and the giving patterns for missions are enhanced.

Needs. The short-term missions experience is valid, but there are some important components that must be put into place to ensure its effectiveness. A careful selection process should be established so that those who are being sent know the purpose for which they are being sent and are willing to go as learners and servants. Clear communication channels should be established with churches, nationals, and missionaries on the field in order to clarify expectations. Thorough preparation for those on the field, as well as the short-term workers, is essential. A clear understanding developed through training in the areas of spiritual formation, cultural issues, and interpersonal dynamics is necessary. Short-term workers should also understand the biblical basis of their service. Realistic expectations for the short-term

worker must be explored. Those expectations should assume a posture of learning and a desire to serve with the national leaders and career missionaries in a supportive partnership. One of the most important dimensions of any short-term mission is careful reflection at the end of the experience. Short-term workers must debrief and process their experience so that they can be responsible with what they have been allowed to experience. This will not only enable short-term workers to understand their mission experience better, but it will allow them to communicate their vision to others.

Conclusion. The short-term mission movement is rooted in the Scriptures and will continue to be a driving force for the advancement of the global cause of Jesus Christ. Short-term missions must continue to be tied to long-term missions. Partnerships must be forged between the ones who go, the national hosts, the career missionaries, the sending church, and those with whom the short-term workers serve. Training, preparation, and careful follow-up will be vital elements to the effectiveness of the work. As these areas intersect, short-term missions will fulfill its intended goals and will continue to enable people to develop a global missionary vision and make an impact for the cause of Christ.

DENNIS MASSARO

Bibliography. S. Barnes, *EMQ* 28:4 (1992): 376–81; B. Berry, *Mission Today 96 Special Report- Short-Term Missions;* idem, *The Short Term Mission Handbook;* S. Hawthorne ed., *Stepping Out;* J. Nyquist and P. Hiebert, *Trinity World Forum,* Spring 1995, pp. 1–4; L. Pelt, *EMQ* 28: 4 (1992): 384–88; M. Pocock, *EMQ* 23:2 (1987): 154–60; J. Raymo, *Marching to a Different Drummer;* B. Sjogren and B. Sterns, *Run with the Vision.*

Sierra Leone (*Est. 2000 pop.: 5,069,000; 71,740 sq. km. [27,699 sq. mi.].*). Established in 1787 as a by-product of philanthropic abolitionist efforts, for the dual purpose of a home for freed African slaves and the evangelization of Africa, Sierra Leone is Africa's oldest evangelical missionary station. It was here that the earliest experiments with an indigenous African church were conceived and aborted.

After the first European contact in 1462, "Serra Lyoa," meaning Lion Mountains, consisted of a twenty-mile square coastal strip of land which became a colony of freed slaves administered by a British chartered Company (1787–1807), then Crown Colony (1808–1961). The hinterland was annexed by Britain in 1896, to form what is today the home of about 5 million people comprised of 15 different ethnic groups.

Protestant missionary activities began in 1792, with the settlement of a Christianized group of freed slaves (The Nova Scotians). They organized and led Methodist, Baptist, and Huntingdom congregations even before evangelical Western missionaries visited the colony.

The CHURCH MISSIONARY SOCIETY (CMS) began work in Sierra Leone in 1804, followed by the Wesleyans in 1811. Many other missions operated in the country, but most remarkable was the policy of the CMS, which included a vision for an indigenous African church, led entirely by Africans.

This vision was enhanced by the arrival of the Recaptives. These were slaves rescued by British Naval Ships. They became the evangelistic target of the Nova Scotians and the CMS, with the goal of equipping them for the evangelization of their own people.

A typical product of this mission was SAMUEL ADJAI CROWTHER (1806–1892), who was rescued from a Portuguese slave ship in 1822. While in the custody of a CMS missionary, Crowther embraced Christianity and later became the first student of the CMS's indigenous missionary institution, Fourah Bay College, established at Freetown in 1828. He was consecrated as the first African Bishop of the Anglican Church in 1864.

Crowther was one of the CMS representatives on the first Niger expedition. After observing a remarkably high death toll among the European members (48 out of 150 died in six months), Crowther came to the conviction that Africans were best suited for the evangelization of Africa. Indeed, such was the swiftness with which Europeans generally succumbed to the dread malaria fever that Sierra Leone earned for herself the unenviable name of the "White Man's Grave." The Niger mission and later, the Delta Pastorate in 1892, were results of Crowther's vision. Both ventures were largely staffed by Africans (Creoles).

Despite their remarkable success in taking the gospel to other parts of Africa the Creoles unfortunately failed to evangelize the natives of their own country. Hence with the discovery of quinine, an effective antidote against malaria, evangelistic efforts were taken over by Western missionaries, eventually stifling Crowther's vision for an indigenous African Church.

Despite commendable efforts by foreign missions for over two centuries now, the Creoles are, by and large, only nominally Christian, while the indigenous people are still largely unreached. About 50 percent of the population are African traditional religionists. Islam claims about 30 percent. Christians are estimated at about 20 percent, of which 5 percent are evangelicals.

Frequent political unrest and economic instability have often led to the evacuation of all foreign missionaries, placing the responsibility of evangelization on national Christians. In a sense, this serves as a reminder of the value of Bishop Crowther's vision as a missionary strategy for Sierra Leone.

DAVID MUSA

Bibliography. L. G. A. Banbury, *Sierra Leone; Or the White Man's Grave;* C. P. Foray, *Historical Dictionary of Sierra Leone;* P. Falk, *The Growth of the Church in Africa;* J. Page, *The Black Bishop: Samuel Adjai Crowther.*

Signs and Wonders. Biblical expression that refers to God's powerful and miraculous interventions in creation. In Scripture, these acts were performed by God through his servants and included miraculous healings, demonic expulsions, control over natural phenomena, and POWER ENCOUNTERS. Signs and wonders usually occurred in conjunction with the proclamation of God's message in the Old Testament or with proclamation of the KINGDOM OF GOD in the New Testament. The purpose of the signs and wonders was to reveal the glory of God and his grace and power, to authenticate God's message and messenger, to confirm Jesus Christ as the promised Messiah, and to usher in the kingdom of God. The healings and demonic deliverances of Jesus and the disciples were considered part of the gospel itself. In the Book of Acts, signs and wonders followed the apostles and accompanied the verbal proclamation of the gospel. There is a pattern of growth and expansion of the church that followed these recorded miracles in Scripture. In many cases PERSECUTION followed the period of growth.

Records and references to different types of signs and wonders were prevalent in the writings of the early church fathers. From the fifth century until the twentieth century, reports of miracles, however, decreased, although there are numerous accounts of miracles and power encounters in conjunction with frontier missions. For example, power encounters, demonic deliverance, and healings are attributed to missionaries such as BONIFACE (680–754) and ULFILAS (c. 311–383).

In the nineteenth and twentieth centuries, the scientific, rational, Western WORLDVIEW shaped the missionary perspective of supernatural phenomena (*see also* ENLIGHTENMENT). Emphasis was placed on verbal proclamation without any distinctive manifestations of God's supernatural power, and supernatural phenomena were explained in nonsupernatural terms. Recently, however, many missionaries have found the need to combine the preaching of the gospel with some form of power manifestation to reach the people (*see also* POWER MISSION and POWERS, THE). This is most prominent in areas and cultures that adhere to some form of supernatural worldview. In many cases, these signs and wonders are followed by conversions and explosive church growth.

A renewed emphasis on signs and wonders brought forth by the charismatic and Third Wave movements has reestablished the need and place of signs and wonders in the evangelism process. This topic has become widely debated among theologians and missiologists. The two main questions in the discussion are: Do signs and wonders still exist today as they did in biblical times? What part should they play in evangelism and missions today?

On one end of the spectrum is the cessasionist view that signs and wonders ceased with the age of the apostles since their purpose was to confirm the message preached by the apostles. Signs and wonders may occur today at the initiative of God in areas were the gospel is introduced for the first time. However, such occurrences are very rare. Generally it is assumed that healings and other signs and wonders are no longer seen today and that verbal proclamation of the gospel is sufficient.

On the other end of the spectrum is the Pentecostal view that every Christian and church should experience and minister with signs and wonders. Healings, deliverance, and power encounters are part of the gospel message. Effective evangelism occurs where the gospel is proclaimed with power, and the signs and wonders that accompany such evangelism are the same as those in the New Testament. John Wimber popularized one expression of this position and played a key role in the increased use of signs and wonders among Western missionaries.

A third view affirms the presence of signs and wonders as important tools of evangelism and church growth, yet does not see them as normative. Proponents of this view affirm the need for signs and wonders in mission, but caution against an overemphasis and unbalanced view. They caution that in practice, signs and wonders have often taken center stage, at the expense of the verbal gospel message. Furthermore, they warn that it is easy to fall into a formula approach, an evangelical form of magic. Finally there is the concern that often miracles are reported and claimed where there are none. Signs and wonders are affirmed, but there is a need for an overall balance in the reliance on the miraculous in evangelism.

The debate remains as to the nature and place of signs and wonders in evangelism and mission. The conclusion of these questions is based primarily on the paradigm from which these issues are addressed. The evidence shows that many of those ministering with signs and wonders have and are experiencing conversion growth. This is especially the case among resistant peoples. The proclamation of the gospel in conjunction with signs and wonders has been the deciding factor for the conversion of many.

MARK WAGNER

SEE ALSO Flaw of the Excluded Middle; Miracles in Mission.

Bibliography. G. S. Greig and K. N. Springer, eds., *The Kingdom and the Power;* E. N. Gross, *Miracles, Demons, and Spiritual Warfare: An Urgent Call for Discernment;* P. G. Hiebert, *Anthropological Reflections on Missiological Issues;* C. P. Wagner, comp., *Signs and Wonders Today;* V. J. Sterk, *Missiology* 20 (July 1992): 371–84; D. Williams, *Signs, Wonders, and the Kingdom of God;* J. Wimber, *Power Evangelism.*

Sikh, Sikhism. Sikhism is a syncretistic religion combing the salient features of HINDUISM and ISLAM. The word "Sikh" is derived from its Pali origin "Sikka" or the Sanskrit word *Sishya,* meaning disciple. All Sikhs are the disciple of ten venerated "gurus" or teachers whose lives and teachings became the foundation of the doctrines and practices of Sikhism (*see also* GURU).

Beginnings and Growth. Sikhism had a twofold origin, one in the Hindu Bhakti (devotion) Movement, and the other in Sufi mysticism of Islam. Guru Nanak (1469–1539) the founder, lived in northwest India. Influenced by mysticism of both religions, he taught that there is only one God and he created all people equal. He rejected elaborate religious rituals, and the Brahmins' monopoly and authority in religious matters. After his time there were nine more great gurus.

Because of increasing Muslim opposition to the Sikhs, they grew into a militant sect and a political power. The tenth guru, Govind Singh, baptized five men from five different castes forming them into a fraternity called *Khalsa.* He gave them and himself the common surname Singh ("lion"), a surname used widely today. Women were given equal rights with men in worship and all affairs. Ranjit Singh united all Sikhs and established a kingdom as the Mogul power weakened.

Presently Punjab State has mostly a Sikh population. The Sikhs play a prominent role in agriculture, dairy industry, many business enterprises, and the military. One extremist segment of the Sikhs seeks autonomy and independence for their state through acts of violence.

Religious Teachings and Practices. A popular morning prayer of the Sikhs describes God as "The One, the Truth, the Creator, Immortal and Omnipresent." The belief in one God is strong. Many names of God taken from Hinduism and Islam are recited for the inner cleansing of the worshipers. Representation of God in images and idols is prohibited.

The Hindu cyclical theory of reincarnation and karma is upheld. If one lives faithfully in devotion and selfless service, after many births he/she will become one with God or achieve *moksha* or salvation. Though there are three broad ethnic groupings among the Sikhs, the CASTE system which is integral to the Hindu theory of transmigration of souls is clearly rejected. The most authoritative and the only canonical scripture is *Adi Granth*, the first book containing about 6,000 hymns. The scripture is often viewed as representing the deity.

Where there are five baptized Sikhs there is a *khalsa* or a "community of the pure" and regular reading of the scripture. Boys and girls are initiated into *khalsa* at the age of puberty. There is no professional priesthood. The place of worship is called *gurdwara*, or the gateway to the guru. The Sikhs observe several of the Hindu festivals and the birthdays of the main gurus.

In the communication of the gospel to the Sikhs, one main link is their strong belief in one God who is actively present in the world and who may be approached by personal devotion. In recent years, a significant member of Sikhs in the West have been open to the gospel of Christ.

SAPHIR ATHYAL

Bibliography. W. O. Cole and P. S. Sambhi, *The Sikhs: Their Religious Beliefs and Practices*; M. MacAuliffe, *The Sikh Religion: Its Gurus, Sacred Writings and Anthems*; G. Singh, *The Religion of the Sikhs*; K. Singh, *A History of the Sikhs*.

Simonton, Ashbel Green (1833–67). American pioneer Presbyterian missionary to Brazil. Named for the president of Princeton College, who was an advocate of mission, Simonton was dedicated to ministry by his parents, graduated from Princeton College, studied law, and professed conversion in a revival in 1855. Entering Princeton Seminary, he was motivated to missionary service through a sermon by Charles Hodge. He arrived in Rio de Janeiro in 1859, the second Protestant missionary resident in Brazil.

Simonton's accomplishments were impressive. He learned the Portuguese language extremely well, and in 1862 baptized his first Brazilian convert and organized the First Presbyterian Church of Rio de Janeiro. After his wife died in childbirth in 1864, he continued his ministry despite the loss. He established the first evangelical newspaper in Brazil in 1864, and the following year took part in the ordination of the first Brazilian Protestant minister, José Manuel da Conceiçaõ, a former Roman Catholic priest. Along with two other missionaries and Conceiçaõ he organized the first presbytery. He also established the first Protestant seminary with three candidates for the ministry. Worn out from his labors and ill with fever, he died on December 9, 1867.

PAUL E. PIERSON

Bibliography. H. T. Kerr, ed., *Sons of the Prophets: Leaders in Protestantism from Princeton Seminary*.

Simpson, Albert Benjamin (1844–1919). Canadian missions motivator and founder of the Christian and Missionary Alliance. Born of Scottish Presbyterian parents, he sensed a call to preach when he was a teenager, and went on to Knox College, Toronto. His first missionary interest sprouted during these years. During his ministry in Louisville, Kentucky, he maintained interest in overseas work through the Evangelical Alliance. In 1878 Simpson had a dream that drove him to commit himself to world missions. Unable to go overseas himself, he became a missions motivator and moved to Thirteenth Street Presbyterian Church in New York City. After he started an independent church, Simpson in 1887 founded the Christian Alliance as a home mission agency and the evangelical Missionary Alliance as a foreign society. Ten years later they formed the Christian and Missionary Alliance. Simpson's view of missions was simple: focus on Jesus Christ. Christ must be preached to the world, at home and abroad; Christ must be appropriated for Christian living and service. Simpson developed the Fourfold Gospel: Christ as savior, sanctifier, healer, and coming king. He stressed both the urgency of world evangelization and the cooperation of all Christians to do it.

JIM REAPSOME

Bibliography. A. B. Simpson, *Missionary Messages*; A. W. Tozer, *Wingspread: Albert B. Simpson—A Study in Spiritual Attitude*.

Sin. There is perhaps no concept more central and strategic to the Christian message than that of sin. The concept of sin is central to the biblical narrative of salvation history. It is central to the Christian explanation of suffering and death and is a crucial component of the meaning of the cross. It is key in any evangelistic presentation of the gospel and essential to the call for repentance and faith, in salvation, in sanctification, and in biblical eschatology. And it is foundational to the missionary mandate. It is because of sin and the eschatological consequences of sin, that missionaries go forth preaching a message of judgment and hope.

Missionaries cannot afford simply to take for granted their use of the concept of sin, for at least two reasons. On the one hand missionaries often go to societies in which a sense of sin, and a language for speaking of sin, seem to be markedly absent. On the other hand, many missionaries come from increasingly post-Christian societies where the concept of sin and judgment has come under attack and strong disapproval. Missionaries themselves are increasingly disapproved of as supposed purveyors of an unhealthy sense of sin and guilt. It is important, then, for missionaries to carefully reconsider their understanding and use of the concept of sin.

One might suppose that the concept of sin is simple, not complex, easy to translate and explain in other languages. Such is not the case. When accurately understood, sin carries a heavy load of meaning. Built into the meaning of that one word are ethical/moral, theological, anthropological, and eschatological implications.

Ethical/Moral. The language of sin presupposes a vigorous notion of good and evil, right and wrong, true moral obligations, normative ideals, and absolute standards. To violate what is ethical and good, to transgress against another person, to fail to exemplify the oral character traits one should, is to sin. Theft, murder, adultery, incest, slander, drunkenness, envy, and witchcraft are spoken of as sins.

At one level this is not a particular problem for missionaries, since all cultures have discourses of moral condemnation—discourses which presuppose notions of good and evil, right and wrong. At another level, missionaries face two distinct problems. First, cultures differ in terms of the ethical and moral norms and ideals which are recognized or stressed. Missionary messages about sin may thus presuppose notions of good and evil, right and wrong which contradict the consciences of those to whom they speak. This has many practical and profound implications for missionaries who hope to make the conscience of their listeners an ally rather than a foe (for a full treatment of such implications, see Priest, 1994).

Second, the biblical themes of God as the source of moral standards and of moral evil as disobedience to God, are implied by the biblical language of sin—but are not necessarily shared by the cultures of the world.

Theological. Dictionaries stress that "sin" is a religious term. "Sin" differs from "immorality," "evil," or "crime" in that it implies a vertical Godward dimension—a theological orientation. Sin is "against God." The Genesis 3 narrative of original sin focuses not on a horizontal relationship (theft, adultery, murder), but on the vertical one, relationship to God. The prohibition, "Don't eat the fruit!" was of a nature to factor out all other issues except the simple issue of relationship to God. The narrative is one a child can grasp. But the vertical and horizontal are linked. After God is rejected, then Cain kills Abel.

In Psalm 51 David cries out to God, "Against you, you only have I sinned. . . ." David has committed adultery, lied, and murdered faithful Uriah. He has sinned against many, but it is the horror of his failure toward God which grips him. In the Bible God is the central equation, the fundamental fact, the integrating factor of the universe. The ten commandments begin with God, and on that foundation move to the horizontal. ETHICS and morality are grounded in theology. Whatever else sin entails, it is rebellion against God.

Missionaries often discover that the society to which they go is more likely to link morality to the ancestors than to God. While many societies will have a vague notion of a high god, such a god is distant and not intimately concerned with people's ethical behavior. Instead of assuming a strong sense of God and a linkage between God and morality, missionaries must help to construct and re-articulate who God is, as well as the linkage of God and morality. The sense of sin is greatest where the sense of God is greatest (cf. Isa. 6). But the willingness to face God with our own sin will come only where a powerful message of love and grace makes such possible.

Missionaries in secular societies face their own difficulties. Here several centuries of effort have gone into denying that God is necessary to ethics and morality. As a result, the term "sin" has been moved to the margins of moral discourse. Nonetheless, as many philosophers have recognized, the effort to provide foundations for morality and ethics apart from a transcendent source, has utterly failed. The astute apologist will find it possible to present a persuasive witness that God is essential as the foundation of morality, and move from there to the gospel—including discussion of sin.

Anthropological. The concept of sin, as used in Scripture, implies truths about people. It implies, first of all, a high view of human personhood. It would not be meaningful to apply the word "sin" to a tornado, a snake, or a dog. People are active moral agents with free will. Sin is presented in Scripture as evil which is actively chosen by culpable human agents. Such agents are not simply products of heredity or environment. They are active in choosing between good and evil.

The concept of sin also implies a terrible truth about the human condition. Subsequent to the first primordial sin, all humans enter the world as sinners. "Sinful" is an adjective which applies not just to acts, but to people. It is not just that people occasionally commit sinful acts. They are themselves sinful. Sin is not simply episodic (like crime), but a pervasive on-going condition. People are sinful at the deepest levels. Repeatedly the Bible stresses that the outward acts simply reveal something about the inner state: the dispositions of the heart, such as lust, covetousness, and pride.

The concept of sin points to both freedom and captivity. People who actively and freely choose that which is wrong find themselves also to be "slaves" to sin. These twin themes are both important to any presentation of the biblical view of the human condition. Again, such a presentation must take into account what the relevant culture says about human nature, in order to more effectively articulate and communicate the biblical view. For example, one may have to counter the claim of human determinism—that humans are therefore not accountable—or the claim that humans are by nature good, and not sinful.

Eschatological. The word "sin" carries with it the idea of culpability and deserved punishment. "In the day that you eat of it, you shall die." "The wages of sin is death." The very language of sin carries with it the idea of deserved and future judgment. While the wicked may flourish in this life, the implication is that there is moral harmony and justice in this world, and the wicked will be punished. The concept of sin carries with it implicitly the notion of deserved and coming punishment. Sin points to the coming judgment. Sin points to HELL.

Missionaries often express frustration when they cannot find a word for "sin" in the language of the people with whom they work—little realizing the heavy load of meaning carried by that one word, and the unlikelihood of finding a single word with the same load of meaning in any culture except one heavily influenced by Christianity. Indeed there was no Hebrew or Greek word which carried the same range of meaning as our English word "sin." Instead there were many words drawn from everyday moral discourse with which to speak of sin. Dynamically equivalent vocabulary exists in every culture. Instead of looking for a single word and expecting that word to carry the full load of meaning, the missionary will need to pay attention to the meaning itself, and communicate that meaning into the language and culture. A deep knowledge of language and culture will discover fully adequate lexical and symbolic resources for communicating biblical truths concerning sin.

ROBERT J. PRIEST

SEE ALSO Human Condition in World Religions.

Bibliography. W. T. Dye, *Missiology* 4:1 (1976): 27–41; C. von Furer-Haimendorf, *Man (N.S.)* 9 (1974): 539–56; J. Grimes, *Notes on Translation* 22 (1945): 11–16; J. A. Loewen, *Culture and Human Values;* L. Noble, *Naked and Not Ashamed: An Anthropological, Biblical, and Psychological Study of Shame;* R. J. Priest, *Missiology* 22:3 (1994): 291–315.

Sin in World Religions. *See* HUMAN CONDITION IN WORLD RELIGIONS.

Singapore *(Est. 2000 pop.: 2,967,000; 618 sq. km. [239 sq. mi.]).* Singapore was founded as a British colony in 1819. British and American Protestants, and French and Portuguese Catholic missionaries were active from the 1820s, but most Protestant missionaries left for China after 1842. Nevertheless European, Eurasian, Chinese, and Indian Christian communities developed through the nineteenth century. Anglican churches were initially staffed by East India Company chaplains. Presbyterian churches were begun by Scottish expatriates, but present-day Presbyterianism owes most to the ministry of English Presbyterian missionaries, leadership from "Straits Chinese" Christian families, and links with South China. From 1885 American Methodists successfully engaged in education, publishing, and evangelism.

Since early times, expatriate missionaries have used Singapore as a center for outreach to the region. From the 1980s a fresh missionary impetus arose out of the Singapore churches themselves. Singapore is now a center for theological education and mission, assisted by excellent communications and a stable political situation. Increasing affluence, in what is still a religious society, accompanies an intense commitment to hard work. Singaporean culture finds some Christian values, including evangelical and Pentecostal emphases, congenial, though social criticism requires sensitivity. Formal ecumenical engagement has not flourished since independence. Its leadership was associated with expatriates during the colonial era, and pragmatic leadership today sees little point in trying to resolve differences in a dynamic situation where more seems to be gained by independent action. Singapore's strategic links, including with mainland China, will continue to have importance for Christian mission.

JOHN ROXBOROGH

Singh, (Sadhu) Sundar (1889–1929). Indian evangelist and missionary. Sundar Singh was born in a well-to-do, pious Sikh family in the Punjab area of North India in 1889. In 1904 a vision of Christ led to his conversion and expulsion from home. Shortly after his baptism on September 3, 1905, he began the life of a wandering renunciant *(sadhu)*. He remained loyal to the institutional church despite criticisms of it and refusal to take membership in any particular body. He was an itinerant evangelist among Hindus as well as a Christian conference speaker.

From 1917, visits to South India, the Far East, and finally Europe and North America brought Sundar to fame. The mid-1920s found him in seriously weakened health and the center of a storm of controversy. Sensationalist accounts of Sundar's preaching visits and amazing deliverances from persecution in Tibet, Nepal, and other Himalayan regions were the basis of attacks on his character and credibility. Claims made about an ancient Christian monk and a secret sannyasi mission still defy clear explanation.

Sundar saw visions of other worlds, and these lie behind a number of his small books written during the years of poor health. He is a striking example of viewing Christian life and faith from an Eastern perspective, and this gives enduring value to his writings. In broken health in 1929 he died attempting another visit to Tibet.

H. L. RICHARD

Bibliography. A. J. Appasamy, *Sundar Singh: A Biography;* F. Heiler, *The Gospel of Sadhu Sundar Singh;* T. E. Riddle, *The Vision and the Call: A Life of Sadhu Sundar Singh;* E. J. Sharpe, *IBMR* 14:4 (1990): 161–67; B. H. Streeter and A. J. Appasmy, *The Sadhu: A Study in Mysticism and Practical Religion.*

Single Missionary. Jesus lived his earthly life as a single man. The apostle Paul, who was probably single himself, encouraged others to adopt a single lifestyle (1 Cor. 7:35). Roman Catholic missionaries have almost always been single. Even with the increasing involvement of lay men and women in contemporary Catholic mission, the presence of the celibate religious remains the norm.

In contrast, modern Protestant missions have been largely led by married men. Early missionary societies sent single women overseas only in rare instances to help with household chores and to work with women and girls.

Then, during the last half of the nineteenth century, women's missionary societies began to appear. By 1907, 4,710 single women were serving with more than 40 foreign boards. Emerging FAITH MISSIONS also attracted single women. In 1882 CHINA INLAND MISSION reported 56 wives and 95 single women within its ranks. This was the period when women like ADELE FIELD developed the "Bible women" plan for training Asian women as evangelists, and MARY SLESSOR of Calabar exchanged a Victorian lifestyle for "up country" ministry in pioneer tribal areas.

As the twentieth century progressed, women's societies began to merge with denominational boards. Single women lost access to many leadership roles and their numbers began to decline. A 1996 survey of 61 agencies affiliated with INTERDENOMINATIONAL FOREIGN MISSION ASSOCIATION (IFMA) reported that only 11.4 percent of career missionaries were single women.

Although fewer in numbers and influence than they once were, these women are still making their presence felt in mission activities ranging from evangelism, church planting, and theological education to international development, medical work, Bible translation, literacy, communications, and the arts. A few have broken though a "glass ceiling" to serve on agency boards and in mission leadership positions.

Single men are having a missions impact as well, especially in remote frontier areas. Many more are needed. *The Mission Handbook: North American Protestant Ministries Overseas* (11th ed.) observed that the number of single men in missions dropped from 3,905 in 1938 to 903 in 1976. IFMA's 1996 survey reported 144 single men serving as career missionaries with their affiliated agencies.

Singles from the newer sending countries are joining the global missions force, perhaps in greater numbers than in the older countries. A 1994 survey of 64 Korean agencies reported 12.7 percent single women and 7.4 percent single men among their missionaries. A similar Brazilian survey reported 20 percent single women and 10 percent single men. These Two-Thirds World missionaries include persons like Kai-Yum Cheung,

founder of a lay school for evangelists in Hong Kong, and Najua Diba, Brazilian missionary to Albania, who has evangelized hundreds and planted at least three churches.

Journal articles about single missionaries tend to be problem-focused, examining issues such as loneliness, living arrangements, acceptance by missionaries and national co-workers, and communication with married couples. Discovering a cultural identity can be particularly difficult. Single men in parts of Africa are not considered adults until they marry. Single women in some situations have been mistaken for a missionary's second wife or mistress. Sometimes solutions to problems of this nature can be found in adopting a culturally understood role for a single, such as that of a religious person who has chosen not to marry.

More research related to single missionaries is needed. The extent of their involvement in missions needs to be described and compared in national and international studies. More biographies of missionaries from the newer sending countries need to be written. Attitudes toward singles require examination, along with theologies of singleness. Agency policies need to be evaluated. Mental health concerns among singles deserve more attention, as do issues related to housing needs, living allowances, and marriages to nationals.

Most important, factors contributing to the declining numbers of singles must be discovered and a concerted effort made to reverse a trend that is depriving the world missions movement of some of its choicest servants.

LOIS McKINNEY DOUGLAS

Bibliography. R. P. Beaver, *American Protestant Women in World Missions: History of the First Feminist Movement in North American.* 2nd ed.; T. Douglas, *EMQ* 24 (1988): 62–66; D. L. Robert, *American Women in Mission: A Social History of Their Thought and Practice;* R. A. Tucker, *GGC.*

Sisson, Elizabeth (1848–1934). American evangelist, author, and missionary to India. Born in New England, Sisson was converted in 1863 at New London, Connecticut, and joined Second Congregational Church. She subsequently felt called to ministry while attending an Episcopal ordination service and was later "sanctified" under the ministry of William S. Boardman, a prominent leader in the Holiness movement.

Sisson went to India in 1871 as a missionary with the AMERICAN BOARD OF COMMISSIONERS FOR FOREIGN MISSIONS and served in the Madura region of present-day Tamil Nadu. After becoming seriously ill, she returned to the United States in 1887. As a Holiness evangelist, she traveled to California in 1889 and met CARRIE JUDD MONTGOMERY, a prominent figure in the Christian and

Missionary Alliance. Sisson became associate editor of Montgomery's *Triumphs of Faith*, published many articles, and wrote several books. She identified with the Pentecostal movement after receiving baptism in the Holy Spirit at the campground at Old Orchard, Maine. In 1918 the Assemblies of God granted her ministerial credentials and she continued in evangelistic work until age eighty. Sisson's endeavors in India represent the contribution that single women have made to modern missions, while her evangelistic activities reflect the significant role that women played in the early expansion and self-understanding of the Pentecostal movement.

GARY B. MCGEE

Bibliography. E. Sisson, *Faith Reminiscences and Heart-to Heart Talks;* idem, *Foregleams of Glory: Resurrection Papers; Faith Reminiscences in Trinity College.*

Skepticism. *See* AGNOSTICISM.

Slavery. *See* ABOLITIONIST MOVEMENT.

Slessor, Mary (Mitchell) (1848–1915). Scottish missionary to Nigeria. Born in Aberdeen, Scotland, and raised in a one-room home in Dundee, she received only basic education and worked in a textile mill. Converted in her teens, she sought to reach the city's deprived youth. Her interest in the United Presbyterian Church's outreach in Calabar led her there after brief training in 1876, at a time when the region was a slave-trade center uncontrolled by any colonial power. Initially at the coast, she learned languages, customs, and religions, and how to cope without Western "necessities." After twelve years she went to join the Efiks, and in due course became an accepted insider among them. With her chief aim to win Africans for Christ she combined a deep concern for their moral and social welfare. She stoutly opposed slavery, witchcraft, trial by ordeal, human sacrifice, and twin-killing (rarely had she fewer than a dozen babies in her huts). The fifty churches and schools she set up were run by local Christians. When British rule extended over the territory she was made the first woman magistrate in the empire (in 1892). She encouraged commerce between the coast and inland areas, and in 1895 helped found the Hope Waddell Institute, which trained Africans in trades and medical work. From 1903 she worked at Itu among the Ibo people. Hailed affectionately as "the White Queen," she was a pioneer to the end, believing that "Every day's duties were done as every day brought them, but the rest was left with God."

J. D. DOUGLAS

Bibliography. J. Buchan, *The Expendable Mary Slessor;* C. Christian and G. Plummer, *God and One Redhead: Mary Slessor of Calabar;* W. P. Livingstone, *Mary Slessor of Calabar: Pioneer Missionary.*

Slovakia. *See* CZECH REPUBLIC AND SLOVAKIA. *(Est. 2000 pop.: 5,468,000; 49,035 sq km. [18,932 sq. mi.]).*

Slovenia *(Est. 2000 pop.: 1,945,00; 20,251 sq. km. [7,819 sq. mi.]).* Slovenia, a former republic of Yugoslavia, is a semi-mountainous state in central Europe bordered by Austria. Slovenes make up 90 percent of the population. Slovenia is over 91 percent Christian and 87 percent Roman Catholic. The Evangelical Christian Church in Slovenia, a Lutheran movement with over 25,000 members, is the largest evangelical group in the country. Baptists, Brethren, and Pentecostals all claim smaller numbers of adherents.

TODD M. JOHNSON

Small, Annie Hunter (1857–1947). Scottish educator and missionary to India. Annie Hunter Small was born in Falkirk, Scotland, on December 26, 1857. Her parents became missionaries to India, and Small spent her formative childhood years on Indian soil. After schooling in England, Small returned to India as a missionary in 1876, where she built upon her knowledge of Indian culture. Through watching her father she had learned how a Christian could best approach the Indian people.

In 1892, Small became seriously ill and was ordered to return to Scotland, but her impact on missions did not end. In 1894, she became the first principal of the Missionary College for Women in Edinburgh. Under Small's leadership, the college grew and attracted students from many different countries and churches. Small's experience as a missionary and her devotion to personal study and learning formed the basis for her teaching.

Throughout her career Small emphasized the missionary's call to a whole life of ministry. She continually emphasized the need for prayer and worship. Following her retirement in 1919, Small spent a great deal of time speaking, writing, and praying, which she regarded as her vocation. She continued to serve her Lord until her time on earth ended on February 7, 1945.

LAUREL PETERSON

Bibliography. O. Wyon, *The Three Windows: The Story of Ann Hunter Small;* A. H. Small, *Yeshu-Das: A Bondservant of Jesus.*

Small Groups. At the close of the twentieth century there were a significant number of excellent books about small group ministry, cell groups, home groups, growth groups, or the many other names by which this phenomena appears. Wuthnow states that 40 percent of Americans participate in a small group. The mega-churches of Asia, Latin America, Africa, and increasingly in Europe and North America are based on a small group model. While small groups are seen as enhancing church growth, Wuthnow says that they are more the result of a healthy church than the cause of it. Recent research in churches on five continents confirms that fact. Small groups often are introduced in a growing church to meet the needs of that growth. Small groups introduced into a stagnant church often have little effect.

A variety of names has sprouted many definitions. One such definition might be the following. A small group consists of five to fifteen people meeting together regularly to fulfill the one-another commands of Scripture, while being integrally related to a local church, and having an outward focus on the world with the overarching purpose of glorifying God.

Icenogle states that small group ministries find their roots in the Old Testament but in general they are patterned after New Testament concepts, especially the ministries of Jesus and Paul. In the early 1990s Carl George popularized the term "meta-church" to describe a structure for cell (small) group ministry. The meta (change) model denotes both a change of form as well as a change of mind. The model includes home-based groups, cell group leaders trained by senior leadership, and a large celebration service that brings the cell groups together for worship. This concept allows for a flexible model which can be applied to any size church. However, having a small group-based church does not guarantee flexibility.

Cell-based churches are those churches in which the principal life of the church is in the cell groups. The imagery comes from the living organism in which the cell is a small part of the body. Without the cell there would be no body. Yet together the cells combined to form the body. Small group-based churches worldwide have similarities which emphasize the important relationship between the small group and large group. (1) Senior leadership in each church has a dynamic vision of what the church is with small groups being a significant factor in that vision. (2) All small groups are integrally related to a local church's celebration. (3) Churches invest primarily in people not property. Many of these churches must rent facilities for the larger worship celebration. (4) Evangelism, modeled and facilitated by the leadership, is a key factor in the church's life. (5) Well-developed programs furnish an increasing supply of new leaders while enhancing the skills of growth. (6) Prayer strategies are proactive undergirding all of church life. (7) Worship is meaningful in both the small and large groups.

While small group churches have similarities, the small groups themselves have certain common characteristics. They present a high level of commonality. Members of the small group have a unifying characteristic that brings them together. The members have a group consciousness, a collective perception of unity whereby they identify with each other. They share a common purpose which may be either explicit or implicit, and demonstrate interdependence in satisfaction of needs. The members need to help one another to accomplish the purposes for which they joined the group. Additionally, members influence one another as a result of continuous interaction and communication. Finally, the small group shows an ability to work in a unitary manner, acting as a single organism (see Knowles, 1973).

Ralph Neighbour has pointed out that the small group model is effective for bringing people into the church and growing them in the faith. There are many reasons small groups are effective. Two of the most important may be noted.

First, church outreach moves along the natural networks in any society through interpersonal relationships with family, friends, and colleagues. These natural bridges link people together. Evangelism and Christian nurture occur through these social networks. Within the small group, community is built which strengthens the church, including the larger community celebration. Besides following the natural networks within a given society, small groups also have the ability to move into other societies through the weaker links members have with those groups that are more culturally distant.

Second, small group churches tend to be more relevant as they take advantage of cultural and social similarities of the group. The commonality is much higher in the small group than in the larger church celebration service so specific needs can be met within the group as the Bible is applied to daily life.

MIKEL NEUMANN

Bibliography. W. A. Beckham, *The Second Reformation, Reshaping the Church for the 21st Century;* J. Comiskey, *Home Cell Group Explosion;* C. George, *Prepare Your Church for the Future;* G. W. Icenogle, *Biblical Foundations For Small Group Ministry;* M. Knowles and H. Knowles, *Introduction to Group Dynamics;* R. W. Neighbour, Jr., *Do We Go From Here? A Guidebook for The Cell Group Church;* R. Wuthnow, *Sharing the Journey, Support Groups and America's Quest for Community.*

Smalley, William A. (1923–97). American translator, translation consultant, and missionary in Laos and Vietnam. Smalley was born in Jerusalem to William and Dorothy Smalley, CHRISTIAN AND MISSIONARY ALLIANCE (CMA) missionaries in Palestine. After graduating from Houghton College, he attended Columbia University, receiving his doctorate there in anthropological linguistics.

Smalley and his wife Jane went to Indochina in 1950 to serve under the CMA. In 1954 he accepted a post with the American Bible Society and for eight years his responsibilities encompassed many parts of the world. He also edited *Practical Anthropology* and directed the Toronto Institute of Linguistics. In 1962 Smalley and his family moved to Thailand where he served under the United Bible Societies as Translation Consultant and later as the Regional Translation Coordinator for Southeast Asia and the Pacific.

After leaving the Bible Society, Smalley took a teaching position at Bethel College in St. Paul, Minnesota. There he and his wife discovered themselves in a community with thousands of Hmong refugees from Southeast Asia among whom they could minister. Smalley retired in 1988 and has since focused his writings on holistic approaches to mission and promoting social justice.

Smalley's writings include edited compilations of articles from *PA* (*Readings in Missionary Anthropology I* [1967] and *II* [1978]); *Selected and Annotated Bibliography of Anthropology for Missionaries* (1962); *Manual of Articulatory Phonetics* (1963); as well as his more recent works *Translation as Mission* (1991); and *Linguistic Diversity and National Unity* (1994).

A. SCOTT MOREAU

Bibliography. W. A. Smalley, *IBMR* 15:1 (January 1991): 70, 72–73.

Smith, Amanda Berry (1837–1915). African American evangelist and missionary to India and Africa. Born a slave in Long Green, Maryland, she married in 1854 and was converted two years later. Following her husband's death during the Civil War, she took up residence in Philadelphia, where she married James Smith, an ordained deacon at the historic Bethel AME Church.

While visiting Green Street Methodist Episcopal Church, Smith was "sanctified" under the ministry of prominent Holiness leader John S. Inskip. After James' death in 1869, she became a popular Holiness evangelist known to many as the "Singing Pilgrim." Her twelve years of overseas ministry began with a visit to England in 1878. She then traveled to India as an independent faith missionary, where her endeavors earned the praise of Methodist bishop JAMES M. THOBURN, who also penned the introduction to her *Autobiography* (1893). After years spent in evangelism, she went to Africa and worked with William Taylor, Methodist bishop to Africa. Returning to the United States in 1890, she spent her remaining years caring for orphaned African American children in Harvey, Illinois. Her labors provided a role model for women ministers in AME and Methodist churches. Both African Americans and whites honored Smith's spiritual zeal, devotion to ministry at home and abroad, and calls for justice.

GARY B. MCGEE

Bibliography. M. H. Cadbury, *The Life of Amanda Smith;* N. A. Hardesty and A. Israel, *Spirituality & Social Responsibility;* M. W. Taylor, *The Life, Travels, Labors, and Helpers of Mrs. Amanda Smith, the Famous Negro Missionary Evangelist.*

Smith, Edwin Williams (1876–1957). Scholar and South African pioneer missionary to Zambia. Smith was born in the Cape colony (South Africa) of missionary parents, and educated in England. Returning to Africa in 1898 as a Primitive Methodist missionary, he labored in Lesotho and South Africa before doing pioneering work in northern Rhodesia (Zambia) among the Ila people. He reduced their language to writing and helped produce the first Ila New Testament. He returned to England during World War I, serving in France as a chaplain of the armed forces. After the war he joined the British and Foreign Bible Society, becoming secretary for Western Europe and, eventually, editorial superintendent (1933–39). From 1939 to 1943 he lectured as visiting professor at the Hartford Seminary Foundation in the United States, and in 1943 he became the head of the School of African Studies at Fisk University.

He wrote extensively on social, political, religious, biographical, and anthropological African themes. His writings display a remarkable combination of profound Christian faith, deep concern for the spiritual and general welfare of African peoples, and keen scholarly insight into the social and political problems of the day. They include *The Handbook of the Ila Language* (1907); *Robert Moffat: One of God's Gardeners* (1925); *The Golden Stool* (1926); *The Christian Mission in Africa* (1926); and *Aggrey of Africa* (1929).

KEVIN ROY

Smith, Nico (1929–). South African missiologist and pastor. Smith served as a missionary in South Africa to the Venda people. However it was not until later in his career when he was professor of missiology at the University of Stellenbosch that he began to see the corrosive effects of apartheid. His opposition to the system of separation of the races was based in his Christian beliefs. He edited *Storm-Kompass (Storm Compass)* a collection of essays by twenty-four Afrikaner intellectuals condemning apartheid. Resigning his chair at Stellenbosch, he pastored a black Dutch Reformed Church in Mamelodi near Pretoria. Convinced that Christians from the various racial groups in South Africa needed to have contact to be the church, he founded Koinonia, an organization dedicated to providing opportunities for Christians to visit across the racial divide. He was active in the negotiations with the ANC before the government opened talks. Convinced that unless God intervened, there would be genocide in South Africa, Nico spoke of the church being the buffer between the two sides of any racial conflict. It is in part because of the work of Nico and other Afrikaners that there was a peaceful transition to black African majority rule in the post apartheid era.

JAMES J. STAMOOLIS

Bibliography. R. de Saintouge, *Outside the Gate.*

Smith, Rodney ("Gipsy") (1860–1947). English evangelist. Born to gypsy parents in England, he was converted in 1876. In 1877, WILLIAM BOOTH heard him sing and pray in a meeting, and asked him to become an evangelist in the SALVATION ARMY, a position he held until 1882. He became known as "Gipsy Smith" and in 1889 made the first of many trips to the United States to hold evangelistic meetings. In 1892, he held services in Edinburgh, out of which grew the Gipsy Gospel Wagon Mission. He preached evangelistic crusades around the world from 1897 to 1912. His services were an alternation of singing and preaching, and he performed both tasks. He would preach for a while and then, without warning, launch into a song to reinforce his point. He was once asked in America if he would accept an honorary D.D. He inquired what that meant, and when told it stood for Doctor of Divinity, he replied, "My divinity don't need no doctor." He died while en route to America for another meeting. His legacy is seventy years of preaching the gospel throughout the world. He helped to popularize the practice of using decisions cards to keep records of the number of converts.

TIMOTHY K. BEOUGHER

Bibliography. D. Lazell, *From the Forest I Came;* H. Murray, *Sixty Years an Evangelist: An Intimate Study of Gipsy Smith.*

Smuggling. In missionary contexts this refers to carrying Bibles, books, videos, tapes, or other Christian items into a nation or region without the knowledge or approval of government officials. Smuggling activities have ranged from carrying a single copy of Scripture to shipping thousands of copies using trucks or airplanes to transporting whole printing presses for clandestine production and distribution. While no definitive numbers exist, one researcher estimates the presence of 2,000 groups or individuals involved, with perhaps a million Bibles smuggled annually in the Middle East and China alone (of a total of 64 million Bibles distributed worldwide, legally and otherwise). For most organizations, smuggling is just one ministry among many.

Some form of Bible smuggling has been done since at least the time of William Tyndale, who distributed copies of the Bible in vernacular English. Smuggling came to the fore in the latter half of the twentieth century in reaction to atheistic communist regimes that attempted to control or destroy evangelical churches. The most prominent smuggler has been BROTHER ANDREW, whose book, *God's Smuggler,* detailed his efforts behind the Iron Curtain and sparked widespread support for this kind of ministry. Brother Andrew founded the agency Open Doors. Other smugglers include Richard Wurmbrand of Romania, who came to prominence testifying to the U.S. Senate in 1966, and L. Joe Bass, founder of the controversial agency Underground Evangelism. Another prominent organization is The Bible League, which distributes Scriptures to the burgeoning but illegal house churches in China, which have a continuing Bible shortage despite the existence of the government-sanctioned Amity Printing Company.

While the church's need for Scriptures in communist and Islamic countries was and is extensive, smugglers have come under sharp scrutiny on a number of fronts. Christian critics have pointed out that some smugglers are more concerned with fighting communism than building the church, and that in fact some of their efforts hurt believers more than they have helped. High overhead costs are another target. Promotional literature, occasionally faulted for its sensationalism, has sometimes been accused of ignoring the needs of recipients. Other critics say smuggling is not needed in areas where governments allow Scripture distribution through government-sanctioned channels such as Amity.

Another ethical issue is whether disobeying governing authorities is right for the Christian (Rom. 13). Many smugglers, however, cite Peter's words before the Sanhedrin as justification for obeying God rather than people (Acts 4:19). They say God's command to spread the gospel takes precedence over any human law to the contrary. However, some Christians are troubled by the lying that sometimes accompanies smuggling. Brother Andrew in fact says he is against smuggling, which he defines as using any method necessary, including lying, to sell materials and make a profit from them. Andrew says his organization simply asks churches what they need and then supplies it.

While the former Soviet bloc countries have opened up and now allow more religious freedom, the situation is still unsettled. Nationalist-inspired religious protectionism from the dominant Orthodox and Islamic hierarchies will likely continue to make Christian smuggling an option in the future. In communist countries such as China and Vietnam, and in the Muslim world, smuggling will likely continue to be one way to provide the oppressed with God's word.

STANLEY M. GUTHRIE

Bibliography. D. Barrett, *IBMR* 21:1 (January 1977): 24–25; Brother Andrew, *God's Smuggler;* Editors, *Eter-*

nity, December, 1972, pp. 29–33; M. G. Maudlin, *CT* 39:14 (December 11, 1995), pp. 45–46; G. C. Studer, *Eternity*, December, 1972, pp. 24–29.

Social Ethics. *See* ETHICS.

Social Sciences. Specialization and integration in the social sciences are relatively recent developments in the larger academic disciplines in comparison with studies of the humanities (e.g., philosophy, literature) and the natural sciences (e.g., physics, chemistry). That they are *social* evidences the people component; that they are *sciences* shows commitment to certain methodological presuppositions across each of the fields. While there are several ways of classifying and categorizing disciplines in the social sciences, for the purposes of this article and in their relationship to mission and missiology they include ANTHROPOLOGY, COMMUNICATION, ECONOMICS, EDUCATION, LINGUISTICS, MODERNIZATION theory, POLITICS, PSYCHOLOGY, RELIGION, RESEARCH, and SOCIOLOGY. Anthropology is the study of humankind in individual and multiple cultural contexts; communication, the process of information flow among people; economics, the realities of exchange and use of exchange instruments in the world; education, the process of imparting information from one generation to the next, usually in formal contexts such as schools; linguistics, the development and use of language; modernization, a conglomeration of trends with social impact (from TERRORISM to URBANIZATION); politics, the study of political power within cultures and countries; psychology, the study of the mental processes and mechanisms of people; religion, the study of the various ways people express their faiths; research, the issues of how to uncover information concerning human societies (e.g., through QUALITIATIVE RESEARCH) and sociology the study of the way people associate and relate to each other. Obviously there are significant areas of overlap among each of these disciplines (e.g., ANTHROPOLOGY OF RELIGION, HISTORY OF MISSION, SOCIOLINGUISTICS, urban anthropology, psycholinguistics, and so on).

Until recently, evangelical Christians in general were suspicious of the social sciences. This stemmed at least in part from an association of these fields of study with sociocultural evolutionists such as Charles Darwin and Herbert Spencer, anti-Christian psychologists such as Sigmund Freud, and economic and sociopolitical theorists like Karl Marx. Additionally, many in the social science fields treat religion as only one aspect of human life, often a peripheral aspect, rather than recognizing it as being at the core of who we are as people.

The presumed conflicts between the social sciences and mission are not unfounded, for most schools of the social sciences rely on nonbiblical assumptions of knowledge and truth, methodology and measures, universe and humanity. Further, at least in the early developments of the disciplines, they often exhibited an unreserved optimism concerning human nature and future destiny.

Interaction of the Social Sciences within Mission. Following the pattern of formation and development of disciplines in the natural sciences, social scientists began by seeking to establish disciplinary distinctiveness for public recognition and after a period of formulation, flourishing, and full-blown growth, the current trend is interdisciplinary integration instead of isolationist specialization. Today social scientists learn from related disciplines, benefit from research done in other fields, borrow and exchange methodologies and techniques from one and another, and are beginning to collaborate in metadisciplinary projects.

For the past several decades, various disciplines and products of the social sciences have been accepted and utilized by Christians for mission. For example, many missions departments in Bible schools and seminaries have anthropologically trained faculty and offer courses in missionary anthropology. With increasing regularity, missionary candidates are screened by psychological testing prior to their acceptance by the organization and field appointments. Missionaries receiving language learning training are exposed to descriptive and applied linguistics. Many are trained in communication studies to enhance their ability to share Christ with non-Christians in culturally relevant ways.

The encouraging trend is that many godly Christian scholars with expertise in the social science disciplines are working toward integrating their academic excellence with Christian faith for mission purposes. As a result, and as mentioned above, an increasing number of Christian workers involved in mission receive basic training in mission-related subjects (e.g., anthropology, linguistics) as part of their ministry preparation. Though missiology has been a recognized academic discipline in Europe since the turn of this century, the first contemporary conservative evangelical institution in North America to have official degree programs in missiology was the School of World Mission at Fuller Theological Seminary, beginning in September of 1965. Increasingly higher level academic programs (Ph.D.s in particular) are utilizing intercultural studies as their guiding orientation, incorporating formal studies in the social sciences at the advanced level.

It is true that Christians are not of the world but are sent to the world to evangelize (John 17). Concerned Christians are utilizing knowledge and techniques of several related disciplines in the social sciences (ethnogeography, ethnohistory, statistics, communication science, etc.) to answer the following types of questions: What are the social structures and undergirding cultural values that drive people of a given culture? How do they see the world and communicate their thoughts and feelings about their perceptions to others? How do people associate with each other and what rules govern role and status in a given society? What social and cultural dynamics are involved in religious conversion? How are people motivated, and how do they make decisions? What are the means of social change in a culture? What is the impact of urbanization on traditional religion and WORLDVIEW? Many more such questions could be stated. All focus on the human realities with which every culture must grapple. The social sciences help missiologists understand the people of a culture and thus assist fostering SHALOM in a given community.

Theories and insights of the social sciences can enhance the Christian's knowledge of how to remove barriers and to build bridges in communicating the gospel to a given group of people. Factors of resistance to the gospel, which include religious background, cultural tradition, language limitations, social structure, and psychological orientations, are to be seriously considered as they impact the missionary task of sowing the gospel seed. Effective applications of the study of these and other important social issues should lead to programs and strategies in mission action. In the midst of seeing the importance of the social sciences, however, the missionary cannot lose sight of the fact that ultimately it is God who brings about the growth of his church. While through history he has chosen to honor careful and prayerful research, thought and planning in outreach ministry, it is still true that he alone draws people to himself and enables their response to Christ.

The interdisciplinary use of the social sciences in missiology has proven to be helpful and fruitful in the CHURCH GROWTH MOVEMENT, a driving force behind the use of the HOMOGENOUS UNIT PRINCIPLE, the understanding of ethnolinguistic peoples and MASS MOVEMENTS, the efforts to evangelize the UNREACHED PEOPLES, and the 10/40 WINDOW.

The current trend of interdisciplinary integration in the social sciences provides an excellent opportunity for Christians to benefit from their insights and implementation. The increasing number of professionally trained social scientists who are also productive workers for the gospel will contribute much to world evangelization, and missionaries will do well to be trained in the various disciplines of the social sciences in preparation for the task of calling those who do not yet know Christ to worship the King of kings.

ENOCH WAN

Bibliography. R. G. Clouse, ed., *Wealth and Poverty: Four Christian Views on Economics;* J. Engel, *Contemporary Christian Communications: Its Theory and Practice;* idem, *How Can I Get Them to Listen?;* K. Franklin, *Current Concerns of Anthropologists and Missionaries;* S. Grunlan, *Christian Perspectives on Anthropology;* S. Grunlan and M. Reimer, eds., *Christian Perspectives on Sociology;* D. J. Hesselgrave, *Planting Churches Cross-Culturally: A Guide for Homes and Foreign Missions;* idem, *Cross-Cultural Counseling;* P. G. Hiebert, *Anthropological Insights for Missionaries;* idem, *Anthropological Reflections on Missiological Issues;* P. Hiebert and E. H. Meneses, *Incarnational Ministry;* D. Kitagawa, *Race Relations and Christian Mission;* C. Kraft, *Christianity in Culture;* idem, *Communication Theory for Christian Witness;* idem, *Anthropology for Christian Witness;* A. Tippett, *Introduction to Missiology.*

Socialist, Socialism. A socialist is an advocate of an economic system based on the abolition of private ownership of the means of production and distribution. Socialism differs from COMMUNISM in the sense that socialism is a stage in the transition from capitalism to communism. Whereas socialism abolishes private *production*, communism abolishes private *ownership*, thus the principle of socialism would be "from each according to his abilities, to each according to his work," while communism would say "from each according to his ability to each according to his needs."

Originating with Henri de Saint-Simon's *Nouveau Christianisme* (1760–1825) which proposed that religion should guide society toward improving the conditions of the poor, Christian socialism developed through such men as John Stuart Mill and Friedrich Engels to the originator of the "social gospel," Walter Rauschenbusch, and eventually to theologians Paul Tillich and Reinhold Niebuhr.

The sharing of property and goods in Acts 2:43–44 should not be confused with socialism, because the Jerusalem Christians voluntarily liquidated their property to meet some extraordinary needs, and such extensive actions did not continue on into the apostolic age. The fatal flaw in socialism, so far as Christians are concerned, is in the biblical teaching on the depravity of humanity which ultimately causes pure socialism and communism to fail, because they are based on the supposed perfectibility of man and woman.

WILLIAM H. BAKER

Socialization. *See* ENCULTURATION.

Society for International Ministries (SIM). A missionary society founded in 1893 when Walter Gowans and ROWLAND BINGHAM of Canada and Thomas Kent of the United States landed in Nigeria determined to evangelize the Sudan region of Africa. Gowans and Kent died during the first year. Bingham, however, persisted and in

1901 the first station was established at Patigi on the banks of the Niger River.

In 1893 Benjamin Davidson, a Scotsman, began work on the island of Ceylon, while two Australians, Charles Reeve and Edward Gavin, established a base in Puna, West India. In South America, George and Mary Allen founded the Bolivian Indian Mission (later called Andes Evangelical Mission) in 1907.

Thus, missionaries from Australia, Canada, Great Britain, New Zealand, and the United States independently pioneered missionary work in Africa, Ceylon, India, and South America. Four different societies—Ceylon and India General Mission, The Puna India Village Mission, Bolivian Indian Mission, and the Sudan Interior Mission—resulted from their efforts. These four mission groups joined together in the 1980s to form the SIM.

As an international sending society, branches have been formed in Australia, Canada, East Asia, New Zealand, South Africa, Southern Europe, United Kingdom/Northern Europe, and United States of America, which together form the sending base for the 1,841 members (1995) serving in twenty-five countries.

The society is also an interdenominational faith mission. Each member is accepted on the basis of a personal relationship with Jesus Christ and agreement with the mission's evangelical doctrinal position. Each member must have total trust in God for the supply of all financial need, since the finances of the mission are all based on the proviso "as the Lord provides."

The objectives of the mission are twofold. On the one hand, it exists to develop and encourage interest in missions and to train and send out missionaries in keeping with the Great Commission. This focus is centered on local churches wherever they exist. It is a teaching and training role that assists recruits to fulfill the responsibility of their churches to be concerned both locally and for the whole world (Acts 1:8).

On the other hand, the mission also exists to fulfill the unfinished task of evangelism and to plant churches in parts of the world where the gospel has not been proclaimed adequately. Its goal is to begin, nurture, and equip churches and work in a loving, trusting, interdependent relationship with them.

The means to these objectives are multifaceted with a wide range of ministries in such things as aviation, evangelism and church planting, health care, relief and development, media, translation, linguistics, and literacy, along with theological and Christian education.

To this end, SIM has been blessed of God during the twentieth century in seeing more than ten thousand local churches brought into being. The mission believes the local church is God's plan for worship, witness, and the training of believ-

ers. The task of the mission, along with evangelism and church planting, is to provide leadership training that in turn enables those churches to train and send out their own missionaries.

These churches banded together in 1980 to form the Evangel Fellowship, which included member church associations comprising more than eight thousand local congregations from twelve non-Western countries. Under the leadership of PANYA BABA, in 1996 Evangel Fellowship formed the Evangelical Fellowship of Missions Association. The purpose of this new association was to stimulate mutual prayer for missions efforts of Fellowship members, encourage the formation and strengthen existing national movements, and coordinate joint mission efforts. The association enhances partnership and interdependence between these churches from the Third World and SIM. In this effort a fresh group of totally committed missionaries has been organized and mobilized to partner in the task of world evangelization.

IAN M. HAY

Bibliography. R. Bingham, *Seven Sevens of Years and a Jubilee;* W. H. Fuller, *Run While the Sun Is Hot;* idem, *Tie Down the Sun;* J. H. Hunter, *A Flame of Fire: The Life and Work of R. V. Bingham.*

Society for the Propagation of the Gospel in Foreign Parts (SPG). The SPG, the first Anglican missionary agency, was founded in London, England, in 1701 at the instigation of Thomas Bray and a group of landed gentry and clergymen upon Bray's return from a survey of colonial religious conditions. Their twofold intention emerged in a matter of weeks: to bolster Anglican Christianity among emigrants settled in the diversifying religious landscape of British colonies in North America and the Caribbean, and to secure "the conversion of heathens and infidels" in those colonies. The SPG was supported by voluntary subscriptions at the outset, but was firmly tied to established English institutions. It was incorporated by a royal charter and its first meeting was convened under the chairmanship of the archbishop of Canterbury. The ninety-six members of its original corporation envisioned the proper Protestant proclamation of the gospel to result in the creation of a self-supporting Anglican parish system and Prayer Book liturgy modeled on those of the mother country.

Under such competent missionary-clergy as the former Quaker George Keith, SPG clergy traveled throughout the colonies preaching, establishing congregations, recruiting missionaries, and sending reports to London. Typically, the congregation would provide the church a parsonage and a minimum salary; the SPG would outfit the missionary with a library, transatlantic fare, and a supplementary stipend. Success came soon. In the first forty years, seventy missionaries arrived and one hundred churches were built; by 1759 the Anglican Church in South Carolina was self-sufficient. But missions to indigenous people were few and unsuccessful (including those of a failed SPG missionary to Georgia, the young JOHN WESLEY), and SPG missionaries had to face the entrenched and hostile descendants of Puritan settlers the farther north they ventured.

At the turn of the century, driven from the colonies by the American Revolution, several problems burdened the SPG: a lax Georgian spirituality leading to a dependence on government grants, and from 1799 an Anglican competitor, the self-consciously evangelical and conversionistic CHURCH MISSIONARY SOCIETY. The SPG had to rethink its identity, theology, and strategy and compete for British resources. Renewal of the society came about in the shape of the "Hackney Phalanx," a distinctly high church group led by Joshua Watson with an incarnational and sacramental view of its overseas ministry. To that end it set up diocesan SPG committees, raised funds, sent off scores of missionaries, expanded the geographic scope of the Society to keep pace with growing British imperialism, widened the mission of the SPG to include educational and medical projects, and supported it all by its own institute, Canterbury College. These efforts were carried forward by the missionary thrust of a blossoming Anglo-Catholicism and the guidance of the energetic Ernest Hawkins, the first full-time general secretary. By 1900 SPG missionaries were working throughout the British Empire in 115 languages on their full range of projects, having helped create a significant number of autonomous Anglican dioceses.

The present century has been full of tremendous change for the SPG; it has felt the full weight of modernity bear down upon its mission and organization. Early in the century its faith in ecumenism, globalism, and indigenization drew it into the great Protestant optimism of the 1910 WORLD MISSIONARY CONFERENCE in Edinburgh. However, as the decades passed trends of all sorts, from postcolonialism to secularism and pluralism, challenged the self-concept of the Society. A drop in funds, recruitment, and projects prompted a merger of the SPG with the Universities' Mission in Central Africa (1965) and the Cambridge Mission to Delhi (1968). The new mission was called the United Society for the Propagation of the Gospel. Its new mandate has called its members to be "servants of the church" throughout the world, those that offer their experience and skills wherever needed, under the rubric of a compassionate and holistic gospel.

PAUL H. FRIESEN

Bibliography. M. Dewey, *The Messengers: A Concise History of the United Society for the Propagation of the Gospel;* C. F. Pascoe, *Two Hundred Years of the S.P.G.: An Historical Account of the Society for the Propagation of the Gospel in Foreign Parts, 1701–1950, Based on a Digest of the Society's Records.*

Sociolinguistics. The study of the many ways people use language in social interaction. Specialists in the discipline often distinguish between two major subdivisions, the *sociolinguistics of society* and the *sociolinguistics of language.* Each focuses primarily on one of the two ends of a continuum, with society at one extreme and language at the other.

The Sociolinguistics of Society. The sociolinguistics of society deals with the ways language and language-related decisions influence or shape groups of people, ranging from small subgroups within a society to entire nations. It includes the study of phenomena such as the attitudes of one group toward their own language and toward the languages of other groups, the survival and death of languages, the roles of individual languages in multilingual countries, and the spread of English as an international language.

Each of these areas of inquiry has practical implications for the members of a society. In multilingual countries, for example, the use of one language in government and/or education, usually elevates the status of its speakers while simultaneously marginalizing the speakers of other languages within the country. Likewise, in many nations the rapid growth of English as an international language has improved the financial status of those who can use it as the common language for conducting business transactions. Furthermore, the unprecedented growth in the number of speakers of English has fostered an increased sharing of ideas by researchers and practitioners in the various subfields of science and technology.

Mission agencies frequently draw on sociolinguistic data when they select the languages their personnel should learn, often encouraging the study of languages with the greatest numbers of speakers of the greatest perceived importance within the country or region. In addition, missionaries do sociolinguistic research when they conduct language surveys in order to make well-informed decisions about translation and literacy needs.

The Sociolinguistics of Language. The sociolinguistics of language addresses the ways various social factors and other variables influence or shape the language of its individual users. These include factors such as the speaker's social status, sex, and level of education, and for a given communicative exchange, the level of formality of the context, and the relationship of the participants.

When interacting with others, speakers who "know a language" employ more than the phonological, grammatical, and semantic patterns of that language. They also know how to produce utterances that are appropriate for a wide variety of social settings. For example, they know how to modify their speech or writing when addressing adults versus children, when addressing family members versus strangers. They generally know when to speak, how long to speak, and when it is more appropriate to remain silent. This often intuitive knowledge is part of their sociolinguistic competence (Savignon, 1983, 41–42).

Sociolinguistic competence refers to a person's knowledge of and ability to use the verbal and nonverbal social rules of language. That is, it includes the ability to produce language that is within a culturally acceptable range and to interpret the intended meaning from the language used for various *speech acts* (e.g., greetings, small talk, persuading, apologizing, complaining, sympathizing), *relationships or social roles* (e.g., friend/friend, stranger/stranger, insider/outsider, older person/younger person, person of higher status/person of lower status), *situations* (e.g., lady buying food in the market, elementary teacher telling a Bible story to children, doctor examining a patient, traveler inquiring about lost luggage at the airport), and *psychological roles* (e.g., formal/informal, happy/unhappy, patient/impatient, sensitive/insensitive, caring/indifferent, courteous/discourteous) (Canale and Swain; Dickerson; Larson).

This branch of sociolinguistics is highly relevant for missionary language learners. As Kindell (1995, 171) points out, "The missionary who wishes to communicate the Gospel effectively must learn . . . a range of appropriate [linguistic] behaviors for that society." She notes that for adults who are learning to represent Christ in a linguistically different and culturally distant society, the acquisition of sociolinguistic norms is one of the most important tasks of the language learner, as well as one of the most difficult.

LONNA J. DICKERSON

SEE ALSO Linguistics, Linguistic Theory.

Bibliography. M. Canale and M. M. Swain, *Applied Linguistics*, 1 (1980): 1–47; L. J. Dickerson, *Helping the Missionary Language Learner Succeed*; R. Fasold, *The Sociolinguistics of Society*; idem, *The Sociolinguistics of Language*; G. Kindell, *Helping the Missionary Language Learner Succeed*; D. N. Larson, *Guidelines for Barefoot Language Learning*; S. J. Savignon, *Communicative Competence: Theory and Classroom Practice*, 2nd ed.

Sociological Barriers. Jesus succeeded in breaking through social and economic barriers in order to reach people with the gospel. Huge crowds followed him. He accepted invitations from people from every strata of society, and ministered to the sick, the demonized, Gentiles, women, children, and other groups awarded little or no status in his day. Yet Jesus' approach was not merely a method; it reflected a genuine attitude of the heart that all creatures are equally precious in the sight of God. Paul, likewise, was concerned to remove legitimate obstacles in order to maximize people's opportunity to hear the gospel. While being careful never to compromise the offense of the cross itself, Paul sought to "become all things to all men" in order to at least "save some" (1 Cor. 9:19–23).

To this day, economic and sociological factors loom large in missionary proclamation. The CHURCH GROWTH MOVEMENT has advocated the HOMOGENOUS UNIT PRINCIPLE as well as a focus on receptive, responsive people groups to enhance the influx of new believers into the church (*see* RECEPTIVITY). Betty Sue Brewster has urged missionaries to bond with nationals rather than being submerged in a missionary subculture (*see* BONDING). Jonathan Bonk has recently examined disparities in living standards between Western missionaries and nationals. Roger Greenway and others have advocated a simpler lifestyle for missionaries. Proponents of the Church Growth Movement have alerted the missions world to the need to pay attention to sociological factors within the societies in which missionaries work. Mission work will be more effective if attention is paid to social stratification, homogeneous units, and webs of relationships. Homogeneous units are sections of society in which all the members have some characteristic in common, such as language or dialect, ways of life, standards, level of education, self-image, places of residence, and other characteristics. This insight has led later missiologists to define people groups as significantly large sociological groupings of individuals who perceive themselves to have a common affinity for one another (Lausanne Committee for World Evangelization).

DONALD MCGAVRAN observed that people like to become Christians without crossing racial, linguistic, or class barriers. He concluded that church planters who enable people to become Christians without crossing such barriers are significantly more effective than those who place them in people's way. Not merely rational, denominational, and theological elements play a significant role in conversion, but also environmental factors, be they economic (*see* ECONOMICS) or sociological. McGavran also noted that Americans are accustomed to a unified society and consequently do not like to face the fact that most human societies are stratified along socioeconomic and other class lines. Some contend that church growth advocates assess people's receptivity too optimistically and that its methods are largely products of Western pragmatism and utilitarianism. The rise of seeker-oriented churches in North America and elsewhere has demonstrated how the removal of socioeconomic obstacles and the targeting of specific segments of society with the gospel may lead to significant, even explosive, church growth. It has been objected, however, that even *necessary* obstacles to conversion and Christian growth, such as adequate instruction on the cost of discipleship, have occasionally been removed. Indeed, care must be taken not to sanction capitalistic, self-serving lifestyles and aspirations with the blessing of the gospel. Jesus' message to a similar audience may have been more confrontational and radical, rather than being directed primarily to meet people's needs while deemphasizing certain offensive elements of the Christian message.

Today mission has frequently become, not merely a calling from God, but a career. North American missionaries have grown more concerned about having incomes, health insurance, and retirement benefits comparable to professionals in their home country. Moreover, it has become increasingly common for missionaries not to serve for a lifetime but merely for a term, so that provision is made for circumstances conducive to their return home even before departure. Together with their dependence on foreign support while on the field and the frequent requirement for them not to engage in formal employment while serving with a missions agency, barriers are erected that set many missionaries up for failure from the very outset. This is not to minimize legal requirements for residency in the respective countries where missionaries serve or to belittle the needs of missionaries. It does, however, call for a conscious return to the attitudes modeled by Jesus, Paul, and the early church, and for a conscious effort to legitimately remove economic and social barriers for the sake of those who are to be reached with the gospel.

ANDREAS J. KÖSTENBERGER

SEE ALSO Conversion.

Bibliography. D. McGavran, *Understanding Church Growth;* G. W. Peters, *A Theology of Church Growth;* C. P. Wagner, *Church Growth and the Whole Gospel.*

Sociology. Study of human relationships and interaction. It employs methods of empirical and theoretical research in looking at group behavior, organizational life, and social problems. Sociologists look for patterns in human behavior in the attempt to both understand and predict forms of group, institutional, and social life.

The predictive function of sociology is often controversial. Taken to the extreme, it can result in sociological determinism, the notion that all human behavior is determined by social forces and location, and can be predicted through the assemblage of sufficient sociological data about a group or individual. But such rigid determinism is dangerous and antithetical to a biblical understanding of humanity and the sovereignty of God. Rather, the predictive function of sociology is best understood as a tool that helps discern patterns of human interaction in such a way that those engaged in significant roles within a given society will be able to plan, govern, negotiate, organize, and even evangelize within a given social order with some empirically verifiable idea of what is happening around them.

In doing sociological investigation, sociologists collect significant amounts of social data in order to establish some empirical basis for their conclusions. Quite often, the "common wisdom" of a society about a certain group, people, or behavior is based on stereotype, myth, or social location, rather than actual observation. Sociology serves an important function by exposing false ideas and beliefs about society and people, and giving accurate information that can aid in forming both public policy and social consensus.

There are two general areas of concern for the sociologist—the institutional life of a social group and the means of interpretation by which a group comes to understand its life together. The institutional life of a group is referred to as its social structure, or substructure. We can define the substructure as the system of shared relationships of the group. This would include patterns of behavior that are regularized by occupation (teacher, bus driver, nurse, mechanic, or musician) or family status (mother, father, cousin, son, grandparent) or religion (pastor, member, Baptist, Methodist) or political association (mayor, citizen, Republican, Democrat, ward leader, judge). Often, modern society is said to be composed of seven major institutions: family, government, economic/financial, religion, education, health/medical, and information/media.

The means of interpretation by which a social group understands its life together is called its culture, or superstructure. We can define the superstructure as the system of shared understandings of the social group. This includes patterns of ideas, values, beliefs, attitudes, and language that are common to the group. While ANTHROPOLOGY is the social science most often associated with the investigation of human CULTURE, sociologists are also concerned with questions of meaning and belief. Indeed, it is quite difficult to study the substructure and institutional life of a people without some basic understanding of how the group itself interprets its various forms of human interaction.

At one time, sociology was viewed with suspicion by orthodox Christians. This was due to sociology's strong reliance on empirical methodology, as well as the discipline's roots in nineteenth-century positivistic philosophy, which sought to place humanity at the center of the universe rather than God. However, the discipline has emerged as a helpful tool to the church in general and missionary movements in particular, as Christians have sought to contextualize sociological findings within a biblical-theological framework, and see how discerning patterns of human interaction have aided church leaders in negotiating the relationship between church and society. In his important text, *Sociology and the Human Image* (1982), British sociologist David Lyon shows how a Christian theological anthropology—an understanding of humankind as created in the IMAGE OF GOD, and in need of full restoration of that image through a personal relationship with Jesus Christ—is a necessary corrective to early excesses of sociological thinking about human interaction that rejected the idea of humanity-in-response-to-God and sought to establish the total autonomy of humanity and human will. While Lyon stops short of arguing for a "Christian sociology" he does aver that Christians can learn much from the empirical study of patterns of human interaction.

The problems of sociology's root are real, but clearly surmountable. Auguste Comte, the nineteenth-century French philosopher, coined the term by joining the Latin word *socius* (relationship) with the Greek word *logos* (study/knowledge) and deemed his new "sociology" a philosophy that would replace theology as the principal lens through which the human condition could be analyzed and understood. In his writings he called for the replacement of theologians by philosopher-entrepreneurs as the "new priests" of the emerging world order. While not as openly hostile to religion, Englishman Herbert Spencer also joined the rapidly growing sociological movement. His signal text *Principles of Sociology* (1882) drew from Darwinian philosophy, applying evolution, natural selection, and "survival of the fittest" to human social development. In these early years, sociology was as much a philosophy as a human science. It did, however, place increased emphasis on empirical research as the method of analysis. Indeed, much of Spencer's knowledge of so-called primitive societies, a knowledge base necessary for his theories of human social development, came from information collected from the missionaries of his time. As an empirical discipline, sociology began to look particularly at social problems, and became a primary tool in the hands of persons interested in political, social, and even religious solutions to the social ills of the day.

While French sociologist Frederic Le Play introduced the case study method of research (the study of a single group in great detail to discern social patterns and problems), the first major case study done in the United States was undertaken by African American social scientist W. E. B. Dubois beginning in 1896. Published as *The Philadelphia Negro* (1899), the study analyzed the problems of the black community and its environs and, consistent with the aims of the sociological research of the day, included specific recommendations for social policy and reform.

As sociology developed in the twentieth century, its methods became more varied and its subject matter more diffuse. Sociologists such as Talcott Parsons concentrated on general theories of society and social organization. Influenced by both the positivism of Comte and the functionalism of the German social thinker Max Weber, Parsons argued that society was held together by consensus—"equilibrium"—and that its varied parts were understood best in terms of their function in maintaining the stability of society as a whole. Others, such as W. I. Thomas and C. Wright Mills, looked at the smaller relationships within society to show how the simplest forms of human interaction could be the starting point for understanding the more broad patterns of human behavior.

There are two ways to look at field development in sociology. The first, related to method, divides social research and theory into several areas such as (1) general sociological theory—investigation into the general ordering of society and the interactions of its various institutions mentioned above; (2) community studies—the study of human life in and adaptation to the environments of neighborhood of geographical area such as the city, suburb, rural community, or exurb most often using case study method; (3) demography—the study of the distribution, movements, and changes of populations; (4) social organization—the study of institutional life: the ordering of social organizations and associations for common purpose in the social order; and (5) social change—the investigation of those forces in society that cause social change, and the processes through which a group moves in changing, such as assimilation, disintegration, conflict, and even war.

The second involves fields of investigation and data gathering, such as race and ethnicity, gender studies, religion, family studies, urban and rural sociology, and even political and economic life. In the case of the latter, cooperation with specialists in political science and economics can yield important insights concerning the nature of social organization. Indeed, all of the social sciences have roots in the quest for greater understanding of human society ushered in with the ENLIGHTENMENT. The study of RACE and ETHNICITY have been important as human societies have witnessed increased interaction between various ethnic groups within society in general, and in the United States, where race and ethnicity has long been a central interest to sociologists in particular. Gender studies have become increasingly important as social changes in the roles of women and interaction between women and men becomes evident in society.

The increased URBANIZATION of societies across the globe has yielded a significant increase in interest in urban sociology. As mission specialists become aware of the growing importance of cities in society, and the effect that urban ways of life are having on whole cultures, urban sociology becomes an important tool in mission studies. Sociologists and missions specialists look at the impact of cities on family organization, economic well-being, socialization patterns, and the interpretive schemes of a given culture, and offer church leaders important counsel in issues of evangelization and the CONTEXTUALIZATION of the gospel.

HAROLD DEAN TRULEAR

Bibliography. P. Berger, *Invitation to Sociology;* A. Comte, *The Positive Philosophy;* W. E. B. Dubois, *The Philadelphia Negro;* E. Durkheim, *The Rules of Sociological Method;* D. Lyon, *Sociology and the Human Image;* R. Merton, *Social Theory and Social Structure;* T. Parsons, *The Evolution of Societies;* R. Robertson, *Globalization: Social Theory and Global Culture;* B. Yorburg, *Sociological Reality: A Brief Introduction.*

Sociology of Music. Related to ETHNOMUSICOLOGY, the sociology of music may be broadly defined as the study of relationships between societies and the music they produce. Whereas traditional Western musicology focuses on individual composers and musical works, the sociology of music aims at understanding the social contexts that shape composers, performers, listeners, and their music.

The sociology of music begins in the later work of Max Weber. Weber saw Western music as broadly reflective of the gradual rationalization of society. Musical indications of this rationalization include the establishment of a notation system, the standardization of scales (particularly the well-tempered scale), and the development and acceptance of harmonic, melodic, and rhythmic patterns. These aspects of Western music provide the basis by which large and complex works may be performed by up to several hundred musicians working from the same score. Weber understood these results as neither intended nor predictable, but reflective of fundamental aspects of Western conceptual thought which shows deep influence from the Reformation.

T. W. Adorno supports Weber's position but asserts that the process of rationalization includes increasing controls that force Western artistry into bondage, either to totalitarianism or to capitalistic economic forces. Adorno identifies the Nazi use of German music (particularly the works of Richard Wagner) as a form of imperialism. However, he does not feel that Western free societies offer a liberating alternative. For Adorno, the capitalist free market is another form of tyranny that forces composers and musicians to write for the market, rather than from artistic inspiration. Both the totalitarian and the free market approaches include artistic subjugation, although the capitalist forms of control are more difficult to specifically identify. Adorno feels the genuine artist is one who breaks with either form of control in order to create from critical artistic motivation. His heroes include J. S. Bach, L. Beethoven, and A. Schoenboerg.

Investigation of music as a means to resist imperialism occupies a prominent place in writing since World War II. Of particular interest are several studies that explore the uses of music to support, maintain, and develop ethnic and religious identity—particularly when that identity is dominated or threatened. African American music and its social aspects provides much material for research in North American culture. Another example is the study of music in European Jewish communities under Nazi occupation.

In a recent work, P. J. Martin defends the socialization view of musical ideals and meanings. This position opposes views that advocate either the superiority of Western music (rooted in Social Darwinism) or the existence of musical deep structures (inspired by N. Chomsky's work in linguistics). According to Martin, musical ideals and meanings are entirely enculturated through socialization. These ideals may be observed through a given society's concepts of 'right' or 'wrong' musical patterns as well as meanings and associations commonly attributed to music styles and specific works.

Awareness of the general phenomenon of music socialization can greatly aid missionaries in the acculturation process. Arts of every kind provide windows into societies. Music, in particular, often expresses deeply held values, ideals, and myths. Careful research of a society's historic and contemporary artistic output is often beneficial in aiding missionaries in accurately acculturating into a host worldview.

In addition, a thorough understanding of the host culture's musical styles and associated meanings may give missionaries powerful tools for witness and Christian growth. Appropriate indigenous musical styles and texts address both the cognitive and affective dimensions, combining to create a medium that often overshadows the traditional spoken or printed word.

Finally, missionaries may significantly aid in the development of emerging Christian communities by encouraging critical appraisal of music from external sources. It is virtually impossible to impede outside music influences, but through thoughtful evaluation, local Christian communities can determine what aspects of style, content, and composer-performer intentions are appropriate. In addition, encouraging communities to create musical styles and works that express Christian convictions within their unique cultural contexts can enhance local identity as well as enrich the worldwide church.

STEVEN J. PIERSON

Bibliography. W. Adorno, *Introduction to the Sociology of Music*; G. Flam, *Singing for Survival: Songs of the Lodz Ghetto, 1940–45*; P. J. Martin, *Sounds and Society: Themes in the Sociology of Music*; M. Weber, *The Rational and Social Foundations of Music*.

Sociology of Religion. The study of religion has been attempted through the research paradigms and methodologies of the academic disciplines of theology, psychology, history, philosophy, and the twin disciplines of the social sciences—anthropology and sociology. While methodologically diverse a social science approach to the study of religion has traditionally been threefold: to identify, to describe, and to explain the diversity of practices and beliefs associated with human understandings regarding the nature and purpose of their existence, which generally includes their relationship to and understanding of the numinous. Social scientists have never been able to offer a universally agreeable definition for religion and those that have been proposed range from the parsimonious definition offered by E. B. Tylor, "the belief in spiritual beings," to the cumbersome definition of C. Geertz, "a system of symbols which acts to establish powerful, pervasive and long-lasting moods and motivations in men by formulating conceptions of a general order of existence, and clothing these conceptions with such an aura of factuality that the moods and motivations seem uniquely realistic."

While Geertz manages to avoid the use of such terms as supernatural, sacred, or spiritual, social scientists acknowledge that in spite of the inadequacies of language the sociological study of religion attempts to identify human understandings and responses to such phenomena. As such, the sociology of religion has encompassed such religiously associated topics as RITUAL AND CEREMONY, COSMOLOGY, social organization, MYTH and RELIGIOUS SCRIPTURES, religious practitioners, and any other associated beliefs, practices, or experiences (*see also* BELIEF SYSTEMS). At times social scientists have coined terminology to identify religious phenomena (such as ANIMISM, or the many terms that classify various divination techniques; *see* DIVINER, DIVINATION). At other times they have borrowed foreign terms from cultures under investigation (such as TOTEM, TABOO, and mana). One of the major challenges to the social sciences in respect to the task of identification of religious phenomena is the problem of similarity versus diversity. The broad diversity of religious beliefs and practices required careful ethnographic analysis of particular cultural practices prior to making cross-cultural comparisons or concluding that a given phenomenon is present in that culture.

With respect to the descriptive task of the social sciences, sociologists and anthropologists have discovered that some religious concepts are universal, that religious ideas and practices are intricately interwoven with other cultural concepts and institutions, that religious institutions reflect a culture's other social institutions, that religious sentiments constitute an important aspect of the social and cultural identity of a group, and that religion acts as a powerful motivation for behavior. They have further adopted what has come to be known as "an insider" or *emic* approach and "an outsider" or *etic* approach to describing cultural concepts.

In their attempts to explain religious beliefs and behavior social scientists do not have a unifying theory of religion on which they can agree, nor do they have a shared set of methodological tools by which to approach the study of religion in culture. At the heart of the problem associated with explanations of religious behavior is the issue of research bias, in which the theoretical or ideological presuppositions of the researcher influence the end results of the research.

Early sociological research sought to demonstrate that religion is the product of evolutionary development and forced a considerable amount of selected cultural data into their system until the whole theory collapsed under the weight of contrary data. Later functionalist and psychopathological theories sought to explain religious sentiments and practices as the product of ignorance, neurosis, false consciousness, or outright manipulation. Most such attempts to portray religion as irrational have not fared well and have in some instances reached ignominious dead ends.

In more recent years new and competing theories of religion have emerged that have sought to acknowledge a degree of legitimacy for religious beliefs and practices. While most social scientists continue to be skeptical or even hostile toward the subject matter of religion they have sought to record its implications in society. This has led them to inquire into such matters as the costs and benefits of religious behaviors, and the ecological and cultural consequences of any set of religious practices. The purpose of such studies has been to apply empirical testing, formulate falsifiable propositions, and demonstrate meaningful correlations between beliefs and social practices without at the same time becoming involved in the task of falsifying the doctrines or teachings of a given religious system. Critics of this approach to the study of religion accuse social scientists of confusing the benefits and sociocultural consequences of religion with the source or primal cause for the emergence and continuance of a religious system.

Postmodern social scientists have embraced a blend of humanist and interpretive approaches to conclude that the goal of a sociological study of religion ought to be that of recording and interpreting the meaning of religion in the lives of its believers. Such an approach rejects the notion that the sociological study of religious behavior can properly ascertain an objective and scientific description of cause and effect in religion because the supernatural cannot be subjected to such testing methods. Social scientists, they claim, should focus on the evocation and description of religious phenomena, and then, rather than trying to explain such behavior based on a secularist or ethnocentric theory, to interpret its meaning as perceived by the participants. This approach has sparked a lively debate within the discipline by those who see no logical guidelines to prevent researchers from flights of fantasy in their interpretive descriptions of religious experiences. In order to gain greater acceptance in the discipline this particular approach to the study of religion will have to ascertain commonly agreed hermeneutical guidelines for the legitimate interpretation of religious behaviors.

There has been a long history of antagonism between theology and the social sciences primarily because of the secularizing influences and critical scrutiny of the scientific community that has denied the epistemological validity of faith, revelation, and intuition. On the other hand scientists also recognize that science is not the perfect approach to truth and that all knowledge is at best tentative.

DOUGLAS J. HAYWARD

SEE ALSO Anthropology of Religion AND Phenomenology of Religion.

Bibliography. M. Banton, ed., *Anthropological Approaches to the Study of Religion;* R. N. Bellah, *Beyond Belief: Essays on Religion in Post-traditional World;* V. Turner, *The Forest of Symbols;* M. Weber, *The Sociology of Religion.*

Sodality and Modality. Roman Catholics have found the term *sodality* handy to refer to groups of younger and older women organized in a fellowship to handle some function within a parish. They apparently needed a word that did not include whole families but could refer to fellowships along age, sex, or task lines. The Protestant church historian, Latourette, employed the term in that same sense.

Cultural anthropologists came along and expanded the usage to include groups such as customary teams of young men who would together handle, say, irrigation duties. They have used it to refer to any coherent sub-group within a community which does not include entire families but only teams, task forces, or social groups of some kind. This has been the meaning when paired with the newly coined term, modality.

The very word *sodality* harks back to the Latin, meaning social group. But why would a term like this be in a dictionary of missions? And how did *modality* get connected to it? The author of this entry once wrote an article distinguishing between church communities and mission bodies, and needed a pair of general terms to do so. Jim Reapsome retitled that article (*Evangelical Missions Quarterly,* Oct. 1970), as "Churches need missions because modalities need sodalities." Later, in a much more detailed historical study, "The Two Structures of God's Redemptive Mission" (*Missiology* 2:1 [January 1974]: 121–39) this writer compared the synagogue as a modality to the sodalities constituted by Pharisaic mission bands that "traversed land and sea to make a proselyte," and, consequently compared the Antioch congregation as a modality related to, but not with authority over, the sodality of Paul's missionary band (which was not responsible to just one church). Then, in a major jump of time the parallel logically arose between the later Roman parishes as modalities when compared to the Roman orders which could be called sodalities along with what Protestants often call parachurch structures (*see also* PARACHURCH AGENCIES AND MISSION)—which normally do not count whole families as members. In a "missionary family," for example, usually only the adult members of the family are considered members of the mission. They are the ones who have made a *second adult decision* to become members. Some others have referred to the same distinction with the phrases *church structures* and *mission structures,* the difficulty being that it is important to insist that both structures are equally part of the church of Jesus Christ.

It is especially important to note that the sodality/modality distinction does not correspond precisely to the common church/parachurch terminology. One difference is that the sodality/modality terms in broad meaning may refer to secular entities, not just Christian entities. Even more specifically, many misunderstand the sodality/modality terminology to categorize denominational mission boards as modalities (just because they are closely allied with modalities) and fail to see that sodalities may (and should) track closely with one or more denominations, and often do, just as military structures are usually linked closely to civil modalities. Also, in America, a newly founded "church" fellowship is very much like a sodality if it is merely a "gathered" congregation of individual believers. It does not neatly fit into the modality category though it may be heading in that direction. The "churches" of the mission field and in the New Testament are often basically clusters of extended families and thus, like small towns and other civil entities, true modalities.

RALPH D. WINTER

Soga, Tiyo (1829–71). South African pioneer minister, missionary, writer, and translator. Son of a Xhosa leader, Soga was among the first of his people to receive an education. He attended a mission school, Lovedale. Taken to London in 1846 to escape war, he was baptized and returned to South Africa in 1848. He took a teaching post, but had to escape again in 1850, leaving for Scotland in 1851 to study at the University of Glasgow. He was the first South African ordained in the Presbyterian Church (1856). After marrying a Scottish woman in 1857, he returned to the Cape province in South Africa as a missionary among the Ngqika at Mgwali (1858–68) and Titura (Transkei; 1868–71). He preached and taught literacy, relying on indigenous helpers to spread the work. His translation of *Pilgrim's Progress* into Xhosa had a deep impact on the language.

Traditional missionary practice of the time was to separate converts from their traditional religious practices, about which Soga was ambivalent. For example, he generally accepted Xhosa customs, but specifically rejected circumcision in an encounter with church members in 1863 (he himself was circumcised). He fought against the dehumanizing colonialist attitudes while remaining within the Presbyterian Church, showing how to develop self-identity without a complete rejection of the colonial order. Long before political independence, he taught that the indigenous Africans had a rightful place in their political heritage. His life and teachings have resulted in his being regarded by some as the father of black nationalism in South Africa.

A. SCOTT MOREAU

Bibliography. J. Hodgson, *Journal of Religion in Africa* 16:3 (1986): 187–208; W. Saayman, *Christian Mission in South Africa;* idem *Missionalia* 17:2 (1989): 95–102; D. Williams, *Umfundisi: A Biography of Tiyo Soga 1829–1871.*

Solomon Islands *(Est. 2000 pop.: 444,000; 28,896 sq. km. [11,157 sq. mi.]).* A sparsely populated archipelago of densely forested, mountainous tropical islands about 1,000 miles northeast of Australia in the Pacific Ocean. The Kwaraae, at just under 9 percent of the population, is the largest ethnic group among at least 70 other groups. The people are 96 percent Christian but this is shared between Anglicans, Protestants, and Roman Catholics. The largest Evangelical movements are the South Sea Evangelical Church, planted in 1904 from Australia, and the Seventh-Day Adventists, each representing over 30,000 members.

TODD M. JOHNSON

Soltau, Henrietta Eliza (1843–1934). English missionary candidate assessor. Born into a fervent Brethren family, Soltau was the second of nine children. She came to Christ after months of anguish were answered with a vision in which she realized that she had not surrendered to him.

In 1866, she heard HUDSON TAYLOR speak and gave herself to God's service in China. Her father died in 1875, and she was finally free to apply to the CHINA INLAND MISSION (CIM). However, she was rejected from field service for health reasons and redirected to start a boarding school for missionary children in England. She ran the school for the next fourteen years without regular income, trusting God to meet their needs.

In 1889, Taylor asked her to found and direct a school in which the suitability of potential missionary candidates would be assessed. She carried on with the lessons learned in trusting God for the boarding school and ran the candidate school finances by faith. She directed the house from 1889 until 1916, assessing almost 550 of the single women who were accepted for service in China through CIM.

Her only visit to China came on a seventeen-month expedition in 1897 and 1898, when she toured forty-four mission stations. Soltau died of complications from a stroke, leaving a legacy of being instrumental in sending literally hundreds of women into the labor of the harvest.

A. SCOTT MOREAU

Bibliography. M. Cable and F. French, *A Woman Who Laughed.*

Somalia *(Est. 2000 pop.: 10,787,000; 637,657 sq. km. [246,199 sq. mi.]).* To be a Somali is to be a Muslim. Somalia, composed of one major language and ethnic group, the Somalis, has practiced the Islamic faith, brought by Arab and Persian traders, for nearly one thousand years. Entrenched in their Sunni or Sufi Islamic traditions, many of the 10 million Somalis have had the opportunity to hear the gospel, yet few have responded.

The lack of mission effectiveness is intricately linked with the history of the country. Both religious and political factors have worked together to make this nation highly resistant to Christianity. Modern Christian mission work, initiated by Swedish Lutheran missionaries, began in 1898. They claimed 350 converts by 1935 when Mussolini expelled them out of the country. In the 1880s the Roman Catholic Church founded schools, hospitals, and churches in association with the Italian colonial administration. Meanwhile, British colonial authorities forbade all mission work north in Somaliland where a revolt sparked by the conversion of Somali orphans to French Catholicism was led by fanatical Muslims from 1900 to 1920. Other evangelical mission work (SIM and Eastern Mennonite Board) continued up to and beyond independence in 1960, when Somaliland and Somalia became one independent country.

However, the socialist "revolution" of 1969, with the coming of Maxamed Siyaad Barre to power, expelled from the country virtually all Western organizations, including missionaries. In

895

1977, Somalia suffered a disastrous defeat at the hands of Ethiopia, opening up the country to foreign and Christian relief and development agencies working with refugees. Civil war broke out in northeastern Somalia in 1977 and 1982 in its bid for independence. This war eventually spread throughout the country by 1988. The infrastructure of the country was totally destroyed and the nation has disintegrated into warring clans. In 1992, the UN recognized Somalia as one of the world's worst humanitarian disasters. The outlook remains devastating with the wealthy, educated, and politically important having fled the country due to severe persecution.

Less than one thousand (.01%) of the 10 million Somali people, including those living in East Africa, the Middle East, Europe, North America, and other countries, are known to be Christian. The result of the civil war is no viable Christian church and total destruction of previous Christian work. Islam grows stronger with an increasing emphasis on fundamentalism. Hearts continue to harden. Outsiders who offer help are welcome but evangelism is perilously dangerous and not tolerated.

ROBERTA R. KING

Bibliography. *Somalia, A Country Study;* M. Delaney, *Somalia;* H. G. Marcus, *The Modern History of Ethiopia and the Horn of Africa: A Select and Annotated Bibliography.*

Sorcery. *See* WITCHCRAFT AND SORCERY.

Soteriology in World Religions. Religions generally assume that human beings are in some kind of undesirable condition and that a much better state can be attained, either through one's own efforts or through the intervention of some other power. Although generally used of salvation in Christian theology, soteriology (from Greek *soteria,* deliverance, salvation) can also refer to the common religious theme of deliverance from a present predicament. However, strikingly different views on the nature of and means for achieving the soteriological goal are found among the various religious traditions.

The Soteriological Goal. The soteriological goal of a particular tradition must be understood with reference to the tradition's diagnosis of the problem and its views on the nature of the religious ultimate.

Although they differ on particular issues, monotheistic religions generally understand the human predicament as the result of moral failure to live in accordance with God's righteous ways (sin). Accordingly, the soteriological goal is the restoration of a proper relationship with God and living eternally in the presence of God in heaven or paradise. Christianity, which emphasizes the radical corruption of human nature and its complete inability to save itself, views salvation as including not only eternal life with God in the future but also the possession of new life in Christ in the present.

Religious traditions from the Indian subcontinent view the human predicament in terms of *samsara,* the ongoing cycle of birth, death, and rebirth in which suffering is inevitable The religious goal thus is *moksha,* or liberation from the entire cycle of rebirths through overcoming the chains of *karma,* the principle regulating rebirths.

Both monistic and theistic traditions within Hinduism hold that BRAHMAN is the one ultimate reality, but they have rather different views on what liberation from *samsara* means. Theistic traditions claim liberation results in a blissful state of union with Brahman in which liberated souls retain distinct identities and consciousness. Monistic traditions understand liberation as the lifting of the veil of ignorance that prevents one from realizing the essential identity of the self with Brahman.

BUDDHISM originally identified the religious ultimate and the soteriological goal in nontheistic terms as *nirvana,* the paradoxical state characterized by release from the cycle of rebirths and elimination of passion and craving. As Buddhism moved into China and Japan, the religious goal tended to focus upon "enlightenment" or "awakening" in the present more than liberation from the cycle of rebirths. The ideal became harmony within the social and cosmic order, which is achieved through a penetrating insight into the true nature of things. There is also a strong theistic strain in Chinese and Japanese Buddhism, exemplified in the Pure Land traditions that view the Amida Buddha in theistic terms and anticipate future rebirth in the paradise of the Pure Land. On a folk level, many Hindus and Buddhists recognizes that complete liberation from *samsara* is impossible in this life and thus they are content with working toward a somewhat improved state in the next life.

Animistic and shamanistic traditions tend to identify salvation with deliverance from forces and powers causing suffering and misfortune in this life. Religious TAOISM is concerned not only with prosperity and well-being in this life, but also with achieving immortality beyond this life.

Means for Achieving the Goal. Religious traditions can be divided broadly into two classes: those that regard the soteriological goal as attainable solely through one's own efforts and those that hold that it is the result of assistance from some other power or being. Among monotheistic traditions, Protestant Christianity unequivocally maintains that salvation is entirely a gift of God's grace and rests upon the substitutionary and atoning death of Jesus Christ upon the cross (*see* ATONEMENT). Salvation is appropriated by an act of faith in which Jesus Christ is recognized as one's Lord and Savior. ISLAM, however, rejects the idea of substitutionary atonement. There is no need for a savior; each person is solely responsible for his or her own sins and will be judged impartially by Allah on the basis of faithfulness to Allah's precepts. Admittance to paradise is based upon an impartial weighing of one's conduct in this life.

The notion of salvation/liberation as a gift of grace is also found in theistic forms of Hinduism and Buddhism. The *bhakti* (devotion) tradition in Hinduism emphasizes passionate devotion and love to a particular deity (Shiva, Vishnu) in recognition of aid granted or anticipated. Similarly, the Pure Land sects of Buddhism stress that rebirth in the Pure Land is entirely the gift of the grace of Amida Buddha.

Other traditions explicitly link attainment of the soteriological goal with proper actions or insights that are cultivated through strict discipline. Thus, THERAVADA BUDDHISM holds that *nirvana* is attained solely through one's own efforts in carefully following the Noble Eightfold Path, and ZEN BUDDHISM, rejecting dependence upon the grace of another, maintains that enlightenment is gained through rigorous self-discipline. Similarly, Hinduism recognizes not only the way of devotion but also the way of works (proper compliance with one's duties as defined by one's position and stage in life) and the way of knowledge (proper insight attained through careful study of the sacred texts and rigorous discipline of the psychic/physical faculties) as effective paths to liberation. The eclecticism of Hinduism is reflected in the attitude that there are many different ways to approach the divine; there is no one way that is right for all people at all times.

Animistic and shamanistic traditions stress observing proper RITUAL so as to appease the spirits and forces that influence conditions in both this life and the afterlife. Religious Taoism seeks immortality through restored harmony with the Tao by means of moral conduct, alchemical techniques, and hygienic, dietary, and respiratory disciplines.

Significantly, most traditions emphasize that what one believes about reality directly affects whether one will attain the soteriological goal. This raises the inescapable question of truth: What is the cause of our present predicament and what is the proper cure for this problem? Scripture maintains that the root cause of all suffering and evil is sin, the deliberate rejection of a holy God and his righteous ways. The heart of the Christian gospel is the announcement that salvation—forgiveness for sin, new life in Christ, and a restored relationship with God both now and forever—is possible through repentance and faith in Jesus Christ to all who believe.

HAROLD A. NETLAND

Bibliography. S. G. F. Brandon, *Man and His Destiny in the Great Religions;* J. Hick, *Death and Eternal Life;* H. Netland, *Dissonant Voices;* E. J. Sharpe and J. R. Hinnells, eds., *Man and His Salvation.*

Soteriology. *See* SALVATION.

South Africa *(Est. 2000 pop.: 46,215,000; 1,221,037 sq. km. [471,442 sq. mi.]).* The present-day boundaries of South Africa date from 1910 when four British colonies were united to form the Union of South Africa. However, there has been a continual Christian presence in the region for about 350 years, which can be subdivided into three major periods: (1) the Dutch period (1652–c. 1800), (2) the British period (c. 1800–1910), (3) the modern period since 1910.

The Dutch Period. In 1652 the Dutch East India Company established a settlement at the Cape of Good Hope for the purpose of providing supplies for their ships trading in the East. The Company provided ministers of religion to care for the spiritual needs of the employees who were of the Reformed faith. Some of these ministers also attempted to evangelize the indigenous Khoikhoi people, resulting in the baptism of a few Khoikhoi before the end of the seventeenth century. To the original Dutch community were added settlers of German and French Huguenot extraction. Out of this community was to develop in time the Afrikaans-speaking people and the family of Dutch Reformed churches, which is today the largest Protestant community in South Africa.

The first full-time missionary to the Khoikhoi was the Moravian GEORG SCHMIDT, who arrived at the Cape in 1737. Authorized only to teach the Khoikhoi, his baptism of five converts in 1742 offended the Reformed ministers in the Cape who did not recognize him as an ordained minister competent to administer baptisms. Schmidt was obliged to withdraw from the Cape, and it was fifty years before the work of the MORAVIANS was resumed at Genadendal, where Schmidt had begun.

The British Period. In the political, spiritual, and social realms South Africa experienced momentous changes during the century of British rule. The closing decade of the eighteenth century saw a revival of missionary interest among Protestant churches in Europe and America, with the result that many agencies entered South Africa with the aim of spreading the gospel among the indigenous peoples there. In 1799 the LONDON MISSIONARY SOCIETY began its labors, which resulted in time in the United Congregational Church of Southern Africa. Van der Kemp, Philips, MOFFAT, and LIVINGSTONE are just some of the names of those who came to Africa through the LMS.

The arrival of British settlers in 1820 brought with them Methodists, Anglicans, Presbyterians, and Baptists, who all sought to establish their respective denominations and reach out to the African peoples. Under the dedicated leadership of men such as Barnabus Shaw and William Shaw (not related) the Methodists were especially successful in extending their church among the African peoples and today the Methodists are one of the largest Protestant bodies in South Africa. Presbyterian missionary efforts produced Lovedale, which was to become one of the foremost educational centers in South Africa. Under the vigorous leadership of their first bishop, Robert Gray, Anglicanism was placed on a sound organizational and pastoral footing and attention was given to missions. German and British Baptists came together to form the Baptist Union, characterized by evangelistic zeal.

Although Roman Catholics were the first to make contact with the original inhabitants of South Africa through explorers such as Bartholomew Diaz (1488), they had been excluded from the Cape under Dutch rule. The appointment of Raymond Griffith as Vicar Apostolic for South Africa in 1837 saw the extension of Catholic churches throughout the area. Missions were undertaken by many religious orders, including the Assumptionists, Jesuits, the Order of Mary Immaculate, and the Trappists. Perhaps the most famous of the Catholic missions in South Africa was Mariannhill in Natal, a work that led to the creation of a new religious order, the Religious Missionaries of Mariannhill. The Roman Catholic Church is the largest single denomination in South Africa today.

Discontent with British rule led many of the Afrikaans-speaking Boers to leave the Cape Colony and establish independent republics in the north, taking with them their Reformed faith and establishing churches in their new homelands. The Boers distrusted the British and their missionaries, favoring instead the German Lutheran missionaries. The Berlin, Rhenish, and Hermannsburg missionary societies helped establish Lutheranism in South Africa. Revival among the Dutch Reformed churches in the Cape and the able leadership of ANDREW MURRAY led to vigorous missionary efforts made by that denomination.

On the political front British military campaigns subdued the independent Xhosa and Zulu chiefs and defeated the Boer republics. All four British colonies were united in 1910 into the Union of South Africa and granted independence—under white rule.

The Modern Period. Out of the bitterness of the Boer defeat rose the Afrikaner nationalist movement, which was to culminate in the triumph of the Nationalist Party and the establishment of apartheid in 1948. This policy was defended by most Afrikaans-speaking white Christians as the only realistic solution to the problem of racial conflict and rejected by most other Christians as discriminatory and unjust. Opposition by the world, sustained criticism by the South African Council of Churches and other Christian bodies, as well as growing resistance offered by the ANC and other liberation movements eventually forced the Dutch Reformed Church and the Nationalist Party to concede that apartheid was both unworkable and unjust. Liberation movements were unbanned, apartheid legislation repealed, and elections were called for in 1994. The ANC won these elections and formed a government of national unity with other political parties.

On the spiritual front, the early twentieth century saw the beginnings and rapid rise of the Pentecostal movement as well as an explosive growth of African independent churches (see AFRICAN INITIATED CHURCH MOVEMENT). The latter usually represent an amalgam of Pentecostal, revivalist, ritualistic, and traditional African religious elements, with liturgies and ceremonies unique to southern Africa. Divided into over four thousand separate groups, African independent churches number some 10 million people (see also ZIONISM, AFRICAN CHURCH). Among the mainline churches the largest are the Roman Catholic, Reformed, Methodist, Anglican, and Lutheran. Recent years have seen a rapid increase of independent charismatic churches.

South African Christians have not only exerted themselves to evangelize their own country but have been involved in missionary outreach beyond their borders. In 1889 the South African General Mission was founded in Cape Town, later becoming the AFRICA EVANGELICAL FELLOWSHIP (AEF), which today is working in fourteen lands of southern Africa (including Madagascar, Mauritius, and Reunion). In the early decades of the twentieth century, the Dutch Reformed Church had established vigorous works in Nigeria (among the Tiv people), Malawi, and Zimbabwe. C. M. DOKE, a pioneer Baptist missionary to Zambia, translated the Bible into the Lamba language. He later taught African languages in the University of the Witwatersrand (Johannesburg), and today is honored as having been one of the greatest scholars in his field. Another South African scholar to achieve world renown was Dutch Reformed missiologist DAVID BOSCH.

At present there are about six hundred South African missionaries (mostly Protestant) serving in over fifty foreign countries through more than twenty-five missionary agencies. More than half of these are working in other African countries; the remainder serve in Asia, Latin America, Europe, and the Middle East.

Many challenges still face the Christian community in South Africa: the evangelization of millions of non-Christian fellow citizens (African traditionalists, Hindus, and Muslims); the promotion of peace and reconciliation in a deeply divided society; the need to bear witness to God's justice and righteousness in the face of massive crime, economic inequalities, and sexual permissiveness. "God's rainbow people" (the appellation coined by archbishop Desmond Tutu) stand poised also to make a greater contribution to the evangelization of all the nations of the world.

KEVIN ROY

Bibliography. J. D. Bosch, *Transforming Mission;* J. Du Plessis, *A History of Christian Missions in South Africa;* M. Froise, ed., *World Christianity: Southern Africa;* J. W. Hofmeyr and G. J. Pillay, eds., *A History of Christianity in South Africa;* idem, *Perspectives on Church History.*

South African General Mission. *See* AFRICA EVANGELICAL FELLOWSHIP.

South Korea. *See* KOREA, SOUTH.

Southern Baptist Convention, IMB. In 1845, because of mounting sectionalism in the United States due to the ABOLITIONIST MOVEMENT, the Baptist churches of the South split from the Northern churches and formed the Southern Baptist Convention (SBC). Two factors brought about the division. The slavery question was the occasion, but missiology was a factor. Baptists of the North had declared neutrality on the slavery question, but the Acting Board of their missionary society declared later, in response to an inquiry from Alabama Baptists, that it would not appoint a slaveowner as a missionary. Northern and Southern leaders agreed that further cooperation in missions was impossible. The Southern leaders, claiming they were prevented from fulfilling the GREAT COMMISSION, then called for a constitutional meeting that met in Augusta, Georgia, in May 1845, and founded the SBC.

The first action of the new SBC was to appoint a Foreign Mission Board (FMB). China was its first mission field. The FMB, in contrast to the missionary society of the Northern Convention, was a "board" of a centralized convention of churches, not a "society" of individuals. Therefore, the FMB pioneered a new type of missionary entity—a cooperative, comprehensive, denominational entity based on the voluntary cooperation of local congregations.

The FMB barely survived the agony of the Civil War and the Restoration period. After reacting to several wars, internal controversies, and financial debt, the FMB began to expand its work after the turn of the century. Since World War II its numerical growth has been phenomenal. In 1995 it had over 4,000 foreign missionaries working in 131 countries. In 1997 the name was changed to International Mission Board (IMB).

The IMB members are pastors and laymen representing the states of the SBC. They in turn monitor the staff of the IMB, which operates out of headquarters in Richmond, Virginia. The fields are divided into nine areas, each with its own area director. The IMB staff dictates the general philosophy of the IMB, but most of the missionary strategy is left to the area directors and their regional "missions." The "missions" work alongside national entities in the areas where they reside. Until World War II, most IMB missionaries were located in China, West Africa, and Latin America but since then the work has spread to Europe, Eastern and Southern Africa, and the Pacific Rim. Newly opened fields include the Commonwealth of Independent States and UNREACHED PEOPLES in the 10/40 WINDOW of North Africa and Central Asia.

The IMB defines its philosophy as "comprehensive"; therefore, there are all types of IMB missionaries—medical doctors, nurses, agricultural experts, administrators, engineers, maintenance men, teachers, musicians, and a host of other specialists—who complement the work of the field missionary, who is basically an evangelist and church planter.

The IMB missionaries count on a support system. Baptist State Conventions contribute through a Cooperative Program. About half the IMB budget comes from an Annual Christmas Offering in honor of LOTTIE MOON and by Woman's Missionary Union, an auxiliary of the SBC. The IMB has become one of the largest missionary sending bodies in the history of Christianity.

JUSTICE C. ANDERSON

SEE ALSO Baptist Missions.

Bibliography. W. R. Estep, *Whole Gospel Whole World: The Foreign Mission Board of the Southern Baptist Convention, 1845–1995;* J. C. Fletcher, *The Southern Baptist Convention: A Sesquicentennial History;* E. C. Routh, *ESB,* I:457–74.

Sovereignty of God. Though an emphasis on the sovereignty of God is frequently associated with Calvinism, God's sovereignty, or God's supreme power and authority, are conspicuous biblical themes in both the Hebrew and Christian Scriptures. Creation is the work of God (Gen. 1:1; Neh. 9:6; Ps. 102:25; Acts 14:15; and Heb. 11:3). God is the creator of all living things (Gen. 1:20–2:7; Ps. 8:3–8; Isa. 51:13; and Acts 17:28). God rules over all of God's handiwork (Job 12:17–25 and Prov. 21:1). God also rules over the nations of the world, not simply Israel (1 Chron. 29:11; Pss. 47:2; 83:18; 93:1; and Acts 17:24–31). God is the *only* God (Ps. 96:5). No one can interfere with God, "stay God's hand," or resist God's ultimate will (Deut. 4:39; Job 9:12; Dan. 4:35; Rom. 9:19). Finally, God's reign is eternal (Exod. 15:18; Ps. 10:16; Dan. 4:3).

In the New Testament, God's kingdom, not the church, is unquestionably the principal theme of Jesus' teaching and preaching (Matt. 3:2; 4:17; 5:3, 10; 6:33; 10:7; 11:11; 13:24, 31, 33, 44, 45, 47; 25:34–35; Mark 1:14; 9:1; 10:14, 23, Luke 4:43; 8:1; 9:2; 10:9; John 3:5; *see* KINGDOM OF GOD). But Jesus, according to the Gospels, also spoke of *his* kingdom (Matt. 16:28 and Luke 22:30), and he declared, "My kingdom is not of this world" (John 18:36), an indication that it was a radically different kind of order.

All this language is, however, symbolic. These are figures of speech, and we miss their authentic meaning and import when we literalize or attempt to historicize them. Furthermore, God as sovereign is a metaphor based on a regal model, namely, God as king, and all that God has created is subject to God: it is God's property. This kind of language was readily understandable in an age when earthly kingdoms were commonplace and when kings ruled absolutely. But that time has passed, and few kingdoms have survived the steady march toward democracy or more participatory forms of government. In this sense, the regal model for understanding God's authority is anachronistic. Furthermore, other paradigms of God's authority and relation with creation and with humanity are found in the Scriptures. More important, they are more easily comprehended— *God as parent*, for example (Ps. 68:5; Isa. 64:8; Matt. 6:9; 7:11; Luke 15:11–32; Rom. 8:15; 1 John 3:1); *God as friend* (James 2:23); *God as helper* (Heb. 13:16); *God as shepherd* (Ps. 23; Isa. 40:11; and Luke 12:32); *God as teacher* (Exod. 4:15; Ps. 25:12; Isa. 2:3; Jer. 32:33; and Micah 4:2); *God as redeemer* (Ps. 130:8; Jer. 50:34); *God as potter* (Isa. 64:8); *God as judge* (Gen. 18:25; Ps. 96:13; Matt. 25:31–46; and Heb. 12:23); and *God as fortress, refuge, and rock* (2 Sam. 22:2; Pss. 18:2; 91:2; 144:2). These last references from the Psalms also portray God as *stronghold, deliverance, shield, and savior.*

Even though the metaphor of God as sovereign is dated, it represents a valuable theological insight if it is not forced or literalized. Recognition of God's authority as the guiding principle for individual and collective living is sorely needed in our time. Yet when God's sovereignty is used to exalt some persons and degrade others, or when kingdom imagery is employed as *the* pattern for all human relationships, unfortunate results usually follow. Authoritarianism such as that exercised in hierarchically arranged families, churches, or governments may claim to be earthly manifestations of God's sovereign kingdom, but oppression is commonplace. Furthermore, when God's sovereignty is regarded as absolute, history is usually seen as predetermined, and the possibility of free will is nullified. The papacy in Rome and Geneva under Calvin are examples of God's sovereignty historicized.

Ecclesiastical authoritarianism, double-edged predestination, hyper-Calvinism, and the repudiation of all human efforts to engage in mission and evangelism are logical corollaries.

It is a mistake, however, to conclude that any emphasis on God's sovereignty inevitably undermines missionary and evangelistic passion. JONATHAN EDWARDS as well as WILLIAM CAREY were convinced Calvinists. They believed in God's sovereignty. But few in Christian history have been more passionate for the proclamation of the gospel and the salvation of the lost than were they.

In our time, the idea of God's sovereignty is probably best regarded not as a manifestation of power, but as an indicator of divine purpose. God is a God of purpose, and God's purpose is the salvation of the whole of creation. Israel and the new Israel are indispensable parts of that purpose.

ALAN NEELY

Bibliography. G. H. Anderson, *Witnessing to the Kingdom;* E. C. Blackman, *Canadian Journal of Theology* 11 (1965): 124–134; T. George, *The Life and Mission of William Carey;* A. Glasser, *Kingdom and Mission;* C. A. Smith, *Mission Legacies,* pp. 245–54; C. Van Engen, D. Gilliland, and P. Pierson, eds., *The Good News of the Kingdom.*

Spain *(Est. 2000 pop.: 39,848,000; 504,782 sq. km. [194,896 sq. mi]).* Bordered by France, Andorra, and Portugal, Spain is located at the western end of the Mediterranean Sea. Native ethnolinguistic groups speaking languages other than Spanish include Catalonians, Galicians, Basques, and Gypsies.

The earliest confirmed accounts of Christianity in Spain date to the third century. Earlier influence may have come through the apostle Paul (Rom. 15:24). But neither this nor the legend that the apostle James is buried at Santiago can be proven.

Christianity was strong enough in Spain to survive the Muslim advance from North Africa, which, after several centuries of conflict, was finally repelled in 1492. The Spanish Inquisition then eliminated most remaining Muslim and Jewish influences as well as those of the Reformation. Meanwhile, Spanish Roman Catholic missionaries joined with explorers and soldiers in conquering new territories in the Americas and Asia.

Modern Protestant missionary efforts in Spain date to the mid-1800s. Plymouth Brethren held house meetings as early as 1836. Churches were opened in Malaga, Granada, and Madrid in the 1860s. But Protestant growth remained slow in the ensuing decades; Roman Catholicism dominated the culture even when, at times, legal barriers were lowered.

With the end of the Franco regime (1939–75) Spain embarked on major change. With enhanced religious liberties came social changes that tended to deaden spiritual interest. Today one finds materialists, atheists, New Age adherents, and those who, especially during Holy Week, cling to conservative Catholic traditions. But rare is the Spaniard who demonstrates serious interest in the gospel. In 1993 evangelical Christians numbered only 78,000 out of the total population of 42,000,000.

Missionaries to Spain should work closely with the existing churches. Those displaying willingness to learn will find most Spanish churches eager for PARTNERSHIP. Missionary assistance is needed in various support ministries including pastoral counseling; youth, sports, and camping programs; and some teaching positions. Those with experience among Muslims may be able to reach the large population of resident and transient North Africans. Further, thousands of towns across Spain have no evangelical church and await persevering pioneer workers.

While Spaniards are sensitive to the needs of the world, not many evangelicals have become missionaries. Even as Spain receives Latin American evangelists, few of her well-trained Bible teachers serve to strengthen Latin American churches. Spain's historical and geographical links to North Africa suggest potential for a significant missionary contribution to that region even as the evangelization of Spain remains a daunting challenge.

DAVID GREENLEE

Bibliography. J. Morris, *Spain;* T. Wickham, *The Missionary in Spain: Adaptation or Interpretation?*

Special Revelation. *See* BIBLE.

Speer, Robert E. (1867–1947). American missions statesman and ecumenical leader. Born in Pennsylvania, he developed an interest in missions while he was a student at Princeton University. He traveled for a year during the heyday of the STUDENT VOLUNTEER MOVEMENT, spreading missions interest across the campuses of America. He went on to Princeton Theological Seminary, but left after a year to join the Presbyterian Board. However, Speer was much more than an administrator. He was a powerful speaker, keen writer, and perceptive analyst of missions affairs. He wrote sixty-seven books, the most notable of which was *The Unfinished Task in Foreign Missions,* based on his lectures at Union Seminary, Richmond, in 1926. Speer's travels kept him in close touch with field affairs. An avid reader, he combined mission and secular issues in his writings and lectures. He tried to look at contemporary trends in the light of world missions history. Whatever the issues, Speer maintained that the church's primary task was to bring Jesus Christ to the world. He also combined evangelism with concern for people's physical and social needs.

Speer took an active role in the early days of the ecumenical movement as seen in the old Federal Council of Churches (now the National Council of Churches of Christ) and the former INTERNATIONAL MISSIONARY COUNCIL, from which came the WORLD COUNCIL OF CHURCHES. In the face of those who diminished the uniqueness of Christ for the sake of interreligious dialogue, Speer stood firmly for Christ's supremacy and wrote extensively on the finality and incomparability of Christ. Along with keeping the proclamation of the gospel primary in missions, he foresaw the dangers of PATERNALISM and the demise of COLONIALISM.

JIM REAPSOME

Bibliography. R. E. Speer, *The Finality of Jesus Christ;* W. R. Wheeler, *A Man Sent from God: A Biography of Robert E. Speer.*

Spirit, Spirit Possession. *See* DEMON, DEMONIZATION and POSSESSION PHENOMENA.

Spiritual Formation. Spiritual formation is the driving force for world mission. Cross-cultural mission is the task of helping people in other cultures come to Christ and be formed in his image. The task of the missionary is teaching people to obey all Jesus commanded (*see* OBEDIENCE). The missionary Paul did not claim to have finished his task until the whole body attained to the whole measure of the fullness of Christ. The ongoing task of cross-cultural spiritual formation includes justification, sanctification, and glorification, and will not be finished in this world.

Spiritual formation is also the driving force for all aspects of human development. People who are not being formed in the image of Christ are not fully human, and thus in an important sense they are lacking in cognitive, social, and moral development. There should be no tension, then, between spiritual formation, community development, and meeting human need.

Spiritual formation is far more than mere behavioral change. People can memorize Bible verses, attend church five times a week, pray for an hour a day, and fast weekly, and still make no progress in spiritual formation. Of course, outward behavior is important, but only as a genuine indication of inner heart development. While we praise the Lord for the growth of churches around the world, numerical church growth is not necessarily an indicator of spiritual formation. Neither is spiritual formation the mere transmission of biblical or theological information. People with advanced degrees in theology have not necessarily made any progress in spiritual formation.

Spiritual formation is a process that takes place inside a person, and is not something that can be easily measured, controlled, or predicted.

Spiritual formation is a lifelong process and is not a precise task that will be finished by the year 2000 or even 3000.

A Plea for a Paradigm Shift in World Mission. The dominant current paradigm for mission is that of an efficient machine. Spiritual formation is neglected because it does not easily fit the assembly-line paradigm. The factory paradigm encourages missionaries to set objectives for mere outward behavior. It is primarily interested in quantities. How big is the church? What is the rate of growth? How many unreached people groups can we identify?

The factory paradigm does not fit the real world. Can you imagine the absurdity of a family trying to raise children with an assembly-line WORLDVIEW? Parents feeding the baby would be challenged to promote the most weight gain with the least amount of food. Child-rearing experts would challenge parents to set growth objectives for the child to grow six inches in the next eighteen months. Efficiency experts would suggest a ten-year plan to produce as many babies as possible with the least amount of cost. They might do computer projections on "baby growth" to the year 2000 and beyond.

The mechanistic paradigm makes an idol of efficiency, control, predictability, and measurement. Success is measured by how many people come forward, by the number of those who complete a discipleship booklet or by how many join a church. While all these things are good, they do not measure inner growth.

The mechanistic paradigm has contributed to the theologically anemic and lukewarm churches on so many mission fields. Mechanistic missiologists would count countries like Zaire, Liberia, and Rwanda as already "reached" because a certain percentage of people claim to be Christian. Could it be that a faulty paradigm is partly responsible for the massacres in these countries? Without a paradigm shift, we are merely going into all the world to make converts. Jesus' command was to make disciples. By aiming only for what can be predicted, we are by definition aiming at something temporal. Eternal, inward results cannot be predicted or easily measured.

We will do a better job of world evangelism when we better understand the process of cross-cultural spiritual formation (*see also* CROSS-CULTURAL MINISTRY). The plea for a paradigm shift in mission does not come from a desire to deemphasize evangelism. We may pray daily that we will win the world for Christ in this generation, but if we neglect spiritual formation we will be forced to reevangelize the world in *every* generation.

How to Facilitate Spiritual Formation. Spiritual formation comes by grace and is a mysterious process. The farmer in Mark 4:26 has a responsibility to scatter the seed faithfully and harvest it at the right time. But night and day,

whether he is asleep or awake, the seed sprouts and grows. He does not know how this happens. Just as the farmer cannot force growth by pulling on a stem of wheat, so spiritual formation cannot be forced.

Spiritual formation is a battle between evil and godly forces (*see also* SPIRITUAL WARFARE). PRAYER is a powerful force for spiritual formation. By prayer, the Spirit helps us see the relationship between the problems in our own lives and solutions from the Word of God. Prayer unleashes the power of the Holy Spirit to enable us to obey everything Jesus commanded.

The best way to facilitate spiritual formation is to make available the means of GRACE that God uses to promote the process of maturity. The primary means of grace are the Word of God, the Spirit of God, and the people of God. The Holy Spirit helps individuals understand and obey the Word of God as they are taught by people with spiritual gifts.

As Christ is being formed in people, they will progressively evidence the FRUIT OF THE SPIRIT, have a burden for the lost, and possess a passion for world mission. The goal of mission is to foster the life-long process of spiritual formation among every tribe, people, and language so that together we may sing the Hallelujah Chorus at the wedding feast of the Lamb. WORSHIP is both the motivation and the goal of spiritual formation in world mission.

JIM PLUEDDEMANN

SEE ALSO Moral Development and Spirituality.

Spiritual Gifts. *See* GIFTS OF THE SPIRIT.

Spiritual Mapping. *See* POWERS, THE.

Spiritual Warfare. Spiritual warfare is the Christian encounter with evil supernatural powers led by Satan and his army of fallen angels, generally called demons or evil spirits (*see* DEMON, DEMONS). The original battle was between Satan and God, but on the level of the heavenlies, the war has been won decisively by God (Col. 2:15; 1 John 3:8). On earth the battles continue, but the issue is to determine not who will win but whether God's people will appropriate the victory won for them by the cross and the resurrection.

The conflict began in the Garden of Eden as recorded in Genesis 3 and will continue until the fulfillment of the events predicted in Revelation 20. Scripture makes it clear that Satan leads the anti-God and anti-Christian forces as "the prince of this world" (John 12:31; 14:30; 16:11) or "the god of this world" (2 Cor. 4:4) and as a leader of the fallen angels (Matt. 25:41). It is also clear, however, that although Satan gained some measure of control through the events in the garden,

God retains ultimate sovereignty over his creation. God's people are assured of victory in the battle when they engage the enemy on the basis of faith and obedience—the conditions set by God in his covenant with Israel and the implications of submitting to God in James 4:7.

Every battle Israel fought in the conquest of Canaan was won or lost on spiritual considerations. When Israel obeyed God's commands and acted on the basis of faith, God gave them victory no matter what the military situation. The battle was ultimately between God and the gods. While idols are treated in the Old Testament with contempt as utterly devoid of spiritual power (Ps. 114:4–8; Isa. 40:18–20; 44:9–20; Jer. 10:3ff.), the god or spirit behind the idol was treated as real (cf. Deut. 32:17; Ps. 106:37; 1 Cor. 10:18–20). Yahweh was often compared to the gods (1 Kings 8:23; 1 Chron. 16:25; Pss. 86:8; 96:4; 135:5). That was not a comparison with nothing. It was the sovereign God compared to the angels who were in rebellion against him.

This battle is portrayed in the Gospels and in the rest of the New Testament. Paul states clearly that "our struggle is . . . against the powers of this dark world and against the spiritual forces of evil in the heavenly realms" (Eph. 6:12). These are real enemies, and resistance against them will involve spiritual warfare. While we are assured of victory in the battle, we are never assured that we will not have to fight in the battle.

The influence of the ENLIGHTENMENT and later the evolutionary hypothesis began a process which has resulted in the secularization of the Western worldview. As a result, biblical references to the role of spirit beings in the realm of the created world are often misinterpreted or ignored in dealing with the text, and many missionaries have gone to the field with a defective worldview, resulting in serious flaws in their approach to animistic belief systems.

At the other end of the spectrum, there is a tendency to overemphasize the role of spirits which produces a Christian SYNCRETISM with ANIMISM. People use the Bible as a good luck charm to protect one from evil spirits, prescribe certain words or expressions to be used in dealing with demons, or assume that knowing the name of a demon gives more power over it. People coming from animistic backgrounds also fall into syncretism, but that is usually because the Christians who introduce them to Christ do not help them understand the Christian worldview as it relates to issues of spiritual power.

Much of this confusion stems from the fact that Satan's primary tactic is deception. That does not mean that everything a demon says is a lie. Deception gains its power by concealing the lie in surrounding truth. What is needed is discernment, not simply in responding to what a demon may say but in dealing with the deceiving spirits that are constantly trying to confuse our belief system (Rev. 12:9; 1 Tim. 4:1).

The primary issue in deception is always truth, and Satan deceives especially concerning the source of power and of knowledge. God has provided all the power and knowledge we need to live as "more than conquerors" in Christ; but ever since the Garden of Eden, Satan has been trying to cause us not to trust God to provide the power we need and to doubt our ability to know God and to trust the Word of God.

Satan uses his power to cause us to fear him. For Christians to fear Satan they must first doubt the power and provision of God for victory over Satan. Thus he accomplishes two goals: to cause Christians to doubt God and to gain some measure of control over them through fear.

But Satan will also seek to entice people—believers or unbelievers—to take power from him rather than from God. He comes as an angel of light and makes his power seem desirable. This brings one into contact with a long list of occult practices such as fortune telling, magic, sorcery, and witchcraft. Satan has enough power to produce some striking results— "counterfeit miracles, signs and wonders" (2 Thess. 2:10). Some people only ask, "Does it work?" rather than "Is it from God; is it true?" Many people end up with a spiritual stronghold in their lives because they have fallen for Satan's deceptive use of power.

Ultimately spiritual warfare is the battle for the mind. Satan knows that people will always live what they really believe, even if they do not live what they profess to believe. Since one's belief about God is foundational to all other beliefs, Satan will almost always begin by trying to pervert one's belief about the character of God. It happened in Eden. Satan said that God's statement about dying if people ate of the fruit was a lie and that God could therefore not be trusted. He also implied that God could not love them and withhold that beautiful, desirable fruit from them. Once they began to question the integrity of God, they came under Satan's control.

It appears that Satan's great desire is to be God (Luke 4:5–7; 2 Thess. 2:3, 4). This is also seen in the Old Testament in the conflict between God and the gods. As noted above, the real power behind the "gods" in the Old Testament is Satan and his host of evil spirits. This same principle applies to all religious systems which set forth a god other than the Yahweh of Scripture. So the battle is still in process. Unfortunately, many missionaries have failed to help their converts make a thorough worldview change from an animistic view in which the spirit world is manipulable to a Christian view in which a sovereign God is in control. Not only can God not be manipulated by us, there is absolutely nothing we can do to commend ourselves to God. We are utterly dependent on his grace as a means of dealing with our sin and relating to him on a daily basis. The very definition of sin is dependent on one's view of the holiness and sovereignty of God. A low view of sin stems from a low view of God.

Thus winning in spiritual warfare always needs to begin with a right view of God and with a right view of what it means to be a child of God. If we say that we are children of God by faith but believe that we have to earn our daily standing with God, we become the victims of an impossible situation. By grace God makes us "co-heirs with Christ" (Rom. 8:17)—a standing which we could never earn by our own efforts. Believing that this is indeed our position "in Christ" provides the only viable position from which to resist the enemy. The battle looks very different from the vantage point of the throne of God than it does from the context of the circumstances of our lives on earth.

In missionary ministry this battle may well be more like a POWER ENCOUNTER than the battle for the mind which underlies it. Paul says that his call was "to open their eyes, to bring them from darkness to light, and from the power of Satan to God" (Acts 26:18). Thus evangelism is a kind of power encounter, and converts need to understand clearly that they are moving from one realm of spiritual power to another.

Often associated with conversion is the destruction of objects used in non-Christian religious practices. This is a visible renunciation of the old ways and old worldview, but it is also a challenge to the "gods" behind the objects to defend themselves if they are able.

Missionaries may well see overt demonic activity (see POSSESSION PHENOMENA), and they need to know how to minister with confidence in such a situation. Many places have been opened to the gospel through seeing a person set free from evil spirits. Spiritual practitioners in other religions may challenge Christians to demonstrate their power in a variety of ways. The missionary needs to be prepared to respond appropriately. Ultimately prayer may be the most important weapon in the Christian's arsenal against the enemy.

TIMOTHY M. WARNER

SEE ALSO Powers; Signs and Wonders.

Bibliography. N. Anderson, *How to Help Others Find Freedom in Christ;* M. Kraft, *Understanding Spiritual Power;* A. S. Moreau, *The Essentials of Spiritual Warfare;* E. Murphy, *The Handbook for Spiritual Warfare;* T. Warner, *Spiritual Warfare.*

Spirituality. Christian spirituality intersects the Christian mission at three critical points. First, the Christian mission is an extension of and an expression of authentic spirituality. True spirituality includes service in response to the call of God and the brokenness and alienation of the world. Christian spirituality includes sacrificial service for Christ. To walk with Christ is to respond to his mandate to make disciples.

The church in worship becomes the church in mission; a truly biblical spirituality will incorporate mission and one's participation in mission. If we are teaching people to walk in the Spirit under the authority of Scripture, then we will be teaching them and enabling them to participate in mission through sacrificial service and intercessory prayer.

Second, the spirituality of the church sustains Christian mission. Prayer and the disciplines of the spiritual life are an essential source of grace, wisdom, and emotional and spiritual strength in CROSS-CULTURAL MINISTRY. The awareness of call or a vocation to Christian mission arises from one's spirituality. But ideally we fulfill the whole of the missionary task in continuous response to the call of God and the prompting of the Spirit. Whether we speak of the individual missionary, the church engaged in mission, or the mission agency, the work of worship, prayer, meditation, and each of the spiritual disciplines enables the church to fulfill its mission with integrity, passion, and joy.

The dynamic relationship between spirituality and mission is obvious in the Book of Acts. For example, the elders in the church in Antioch were in prayer and fasting when they sensed the prompting of the Spirit to set aside two of their number for missionary service (Acts 13:1–2). It is also evident in the life of Jesus, whose confidence in his own call to preach "to the neighboring towns" arose directly out of his early morning prayer (Mark 1:35–38). And in the apostle Paul we see a dynamic connection, especially in 2 Corinthians, between his own journey of faith, prayer, and obedience, and his call to apostolic ministry.

Missionary endeavor is fruitless apart from a vital relationship to God in prayer—not just the prayer of intercession, but also the prayer of communion and contemplation.

Third, mission is calling the nations of the world to a true spirituality: a life lived in submission to Christ and a communion with Christ Jesus as Lord. Mission is more than evangelism; it includes enabling people to respond to the gospel and walk by faith in the fullness of the Spirit. Christian mission is incomplete if it does not include the introduction of new believers to the nature of the Christian experience in communion with Christ and in community with the church. This is part of what it means to make disciples (Matt. 28:16ff.).

But as Christian spirituality develops among a people, it will reflect the historical, geographical, and cultural background of these people, if it is truly an indigenous expression of their Christian faith (see INDIGENOUS CHURCHES).

We cannot demand or expect uniformity when it comes to spirituality. There will be certain normative elements, such as the centrality of Christ, the authority and priority of Scripture, the place of community and the church, and the critical place of personal and corporate holiness. But beyond certain common elements that are essential to a Christian spirituality, the work of the Spirit will be evident in remarkable diversity. In this regard, the Christian community in each land is well-advised to listen and learn from others. Those in the West can learn from those in Africa, who in turn might learn from the spiritual experience and journey of those in Latin America or Asia.

GORDON T. SMITH

SEE ALSO Spiritual Formation.

Bibliography. D. J. Bosch, *Spirituality of the Road;* M. Collins Reilly, *Spirituality for Mission.*

Sri Lanka *(Est. 2000 pop.: 19,504,000; 65,610 sq. km. [25,332 sq. mi.]).* Sri Lanka is an island located 50 miles southeast of the tip of India. Of the inhabitants, 74 percent are Sinhalese, 18.2 percent Tamil, and the rest are of various Asian or Eurasian extractions.

The *Chronicle of Mahavansa,* maintained by Buddhist monks from about the sixth century A.D., portrays a violent history of successive invasions and cultural upheaval. The Indian Hindu prince Vijaya conquered the land in 504 B.C. A sophisticated society developed after the third century B.C. when the Sinhalese officially adopted BUDDHISM. Tamil invaders dominated the island between the third and thirteenth centuries A.D. From 1517 to 1948, Portuguese, Dutch, and finally British colonialists ruled. Not until 1803 did ancient Kandy, in the interior of the island, succumb to invaders when the British occupied and finally annexed it. Sri Lanka became an independent Commonwealth member in 1948 and gained admission to the United Nations in 1955. In 1972, the name was changed officially from Ceylon to Sri Lanka.

Tensions have always been high between the Tamils in the north, the Buddhist majority in the south and central areas, and the Muslims. Ongoing ancient rivalries have been erupting since 1983 when civil war broke out between the Sinhalese and the Liberation Tigers of Tamil Eelam, a rebel faction desiring separate-nation status.

A tradition holds that Christianity entered Sri Lanka through the apostle Thomas. In A.D. 537 a Nestorian sojourner documented numerous churches and adherents. Later, the Portuguese introduced Roman Catholicism, the Dutch brought Reformed traditions, and the British established Anglicanism. Mission strategists document small unreached groups in Sri Lanka, namely, the Indo-Portuguese Burghers and the original inhabitants of the island, the Veddah people.

KEITH E. EITEL

Statistics. *See* QUANTITATIVE RESEARCH; MISSIOMETRICS.

Status and Role. When social scientists refer to status, the term is less freighted with implications of value than in more popular usage. Status, in SOCIOLOGY, refers to the position an individual occupies in a group or society. It is based on the common recognition within the group that the individual occupies the position, not the perceived value of the position. Status is distinguished from roles in sociological theory in that individuals occupy a status and play a role. Roles define the rights, functions, obligations, and interactions of persons. Status refers to the position from which individuals act out their roles.

A status will have wide recognition and group consensus over its definition. There are two types of status, ascribed and achieved. Social scientists define ascribed status as one that is given by society and over which we exercise little if any control, such as age, gender, or ETHNICITY. An achieved status is the result of some action on the part of the individual, such as teacher, student, shopkeeper, consumer, church member, or police officer.

Understanding status and role is significant in missions studies because they are important keys to understanding CULTURE. The statuses of parent, laborer, minister, and athlete all point to certain images of how we expect people to behave in a given social interaction. Sometimes these images are less clear than others, but it is the general consensus of the society or group around these images that enables us to understand them as statuses within a society. It is the action carried out by the person in a particular status that we call a role. For example, consumers in some cultures interact with the marketplace through bargaining over prices. Shopkeepers are expected to enter into a process of negotiation over prices. In other countries, such as the United States, prices generally are attached to goods, and consumers are expected to pay the marked price. In some cultures, university students are expected to learn by synthesizing and analyzing material, and then produce a relatively original final paper. In other cultures, students are expected to master the thought of the instructor and, in deference to the teacher's wisdom, replicate his or her thought as the mark of educational accountability. In all cultures, people learn the roles—specific behaviors, values, and skills—that are appropriate to a given status.

Also, making the distinction between achieved and ascribed status helps us in CROSS-CULTURAL

MINISTRY. For example, many cultures have rituals that make adulthood an achieved status (called RITES OF PASSAGE), whereas others follow laws that make adulthood ascribed (such as an eighteen-year-old voting age or individuals being tried in court as adults at a selected age). Knowing the difference can be crucial in developing cross-cultural ministries to adolescents and young adults.

What most people call status, social scientists call "social status." This refers to rank, honor, and esteem. Max Weber called it "social honor." In virtually all societies, relative prestige becomes a measuring stick for ranking individuals. In some societies, economic resources determine social status. In others, personal resources such as courage, intelligence, and leadership ability serve to determine social rank. In complex societies, a combination of ascribed (race, ethnicity, gender, age, even ancestry) and achieved (wealth, education, income) statuses determine social ranking.

HAROLD DEAN TRULEAR

Bibliography. H. Gerth and C. Wright Mills, eds., *From Max Weber: Essays in Sociology;* R. Merton, *Social Theory and Social Structure.*

Steidel, Florence (1897–1962). American missionary to lepers in Liberia. Born in Greenfield, Illinois, and reared in Missouri, Steidel responded to the call to missions in 1924 during prayer when she saw in a vision suffering people with no one to help them. Preparatory studies took her to a Bible institute in Chicago, Benton College of Law in St. Louis, Missouri, and nurse's training at Missouri Baptist Hospital from which she graduated in 1928. For additional studies in theology and missions, she enrolled at the Woman's Missionary Union Training School, Louisville, Kentucky, a Southern Baptist institution, and graduated in 1931.

Joining the Pentecostal movement, Steidel went to Liberia in 1935 as an Assemblies of God missionary. In 1942 she returned to the United States to recuperate from tuberculosis. Returning to Liberia two years later, she founded New Hope Town as a center for the care of lepers. There she supervised construction of more than seventy buildings, helped the community become self-sufficient, and established a school for the training of ministers. Steidel's contributions to the nation won the recognition of President William V. S. Tubman, who made her a Knight Official of the Humane Order of African Redemption in 1957—the first woman missionary in Liberia to be so honored. She continued working at New Hope Town until her death.

GARY B. MCGEE

Bibliography. I. Spence, *These Are My People: Florence Steidel.*

Stephen (d. c. 35). Early Christian martyr who inspired missionary activity. One of the seven men appointed to care for the needs of the widows of the early church (Acts 6), Stephen was a Jew who had apparently accepted a Hellenist (Greek) cultural outlook. The effects are seen in his defense before the Jewish council in Acts 7. He gave evidences that God's presence is not limited to a single place: God had appeared to Abraham in Mesopotamia, delivered Israel from Egypt, and gave the law at Mount Sinai—all outside the boundaries of Israel. He described the temple as *cheiropoētos* ("made with hands," v. 48), a term usually used of idols, thus implying that the contemporary Jewish view of the temple as a building to which the presence of the universal God was restricted was idolatrous. Israel's history, Stephen continued, was marked by unfaithfulness to God, culminating in her rejection and murder of "the just one" (v. 52). This term, along with "a prophet like Moses" (v. 37), "Son of man" (v. 56), the "Lord" (vv. 59–60) is one of four with which he referred to Jesus, the more-than-Jewish Messiah. Particularly important is the title "Son of man," the heavenly figure who comes to rule over all peoples and nations (Dan. 7:13–14).

Stephen's speech provides a theological basis and mandate for the world mission of the people of God, a mission that seeks to bring all peoples, nations, and languages under the domain of the suffering, glorified, ruling Son of Man/Messiah. Thus the Christian missionary movement had its genesis in (1) a proper understanding of the nature of God, (2) a realistic view of the history of the people of God, and (3) a presentation of the role played by Jesus Christ in the totality of God's saving work in history. It is significant that Acts presents the first Christian missionary activity as immediately following the account of Stephen's speech and death.

J. JULIUS SCOTT

Bibliography. M. Simon, *Saint Stephen and the Hellenists;* J. J. Scott Jr., *JETS* 21:2 (June 1978): 131–41.

Stephen, King of Hungary (975–1038). Founder of Hungary and initiator of Christianity among the Magyars. Born as Vajk, Stephen took a Christian name when he was baptized with his father Geza in 985. Inheriting the Magyar chieftainship in 997, he aggressively pursued a Christianizing program initiated by Geza. With a crown received at Stephen's request from Pope Sylvester II, he was enthroned as king on Christmas Day A.D. 1000. A strong supporter of the church, he invited the Benedictines to come and engage in the task of evangelizing the Hungarian population. Through them he organized bishoprics and abbeys and engaged in building churches throughout the kingdom. He also vigorously attacked pagan rites and symbols, seeking to eliminate them as an important step in the evangelization and the development of the political state of Hungary. Though later pagan kings sought to undo his influence, by the end of the eleventh century Christianity was generally accepted by the Hungarian population.

A. SCOTT MOREAU

Bibliography. EB; ODCC; S. Neill, *HCM;* D. Sinor, *NCE* 14:697–98.

Stephen of Perm (1340–96). Russian orthodox missionary to Siberia. Stephen of Perm was one of the founding fathers of Russian Orthodox missions. Born in 1340, he was part of a small Muscovite settlement in northwest Siberia surrounded by the pagan Zyrians of Perm. In 1365, on the day Stephen took monastic vows, he voiced to the bishop his desire to one day return to Perm and proclaim the gospel among the Zyrian people.

He spent his early years in the monastery cultivating a deep spiritual life of prayer, fasting, and continual study. He also began translating the Bible and liturgical services into Zyrian, even having to create a Zyrian alphabet.

In 1378, Stephen settled among the Zyrians and began to preach against their rampant idolatry and to show the impotence of their gods by destroying their idols and shrines. Eventually he challenged their main magician to a divine trial in which both were to walk through a burning hut and throw themselves into an opening in the ice of the Vichedga river. When the magician refused, the people turned against him and demanded his death. Stephen, however, preached God's mercy and called the magician to repent or be exiled. Stephen became the first bishop of Perm in 1383. His final words before his death were, "Live godly lives, read the Scriptures, and obey the Church."

LUKE A. VERONIS

Bibliography. J. J. Stamoolis, *Eastern Orthodox Mission Theology Today;* L. A. Veronis, *Missionaries, Monks and Martyrs: Making Disciples of All Nations.*

Stern, Henry Aaron (1820–85). German pioneer missionary among Jews in the Middle East. Born in Unterreichenbach to a Jewish family, Stern came to faith in Christ in 1840 through the influence of Dr. McCaul. Graduating from Hebrew College of the London Jew's Society, he was appointed a missionary to the Jews in the Middle East. He began his work among the Jews in Bagdad, which served as his base of itinerating operations until 1859. During his stay he made trips to Crimea and Arabia, evangelizing Jewish populations as he traveled. News of the Abyssinian Jewish populations in Ethiopia led to his transfer to Cairo and later Abyssinia. British mishandling of the Abyssinian King Theodore's request for closer relations resulted in Stern being imprisoned as retribution in 1863 until 1866. Reimprisoned shortly after, Stern was not finally freed until 1868, when Theodore was defeated by British troops. Stern immediately returned to England, and large audiences came to hear his story. In 1871 he was appointed senior missionary, continuing his work among the Jews in England. He wrote several books of his missionary journeys and his imprisonment.

A. SCOTT MOREAU

Bibliography. E. C. Dawson, *Henry A. Stern: Missionary Traveller and Abyssinian Captive;* N. Hillyer, *WWCH,* p. 638; R. M. A. Ibbotson, *Adventures of Missionary Explorers;* A. A. Isaacs, *Biography of Rev. Henry Aaron Stern, D. D.*

Stevenson, Marion Scott (1871–1930). Scottish missionary to Kenya. Daughter of a minister of the Church of Scotland, two of her uncles were missionaries in India. Her father died in 1877, and she was educated in Edinburgh, showing talent in languages. Although she suffered from ill health, she was active in encouraging mission projects in the Church. In 1903 she attended a Scottish "Keswick" and received spiritual blessing. After her mother's death in 1904 she felt free to pursue overseas work, and was passed as fit in 1905. After a course at Deaconess Hospital she sailed for Kenya in early 1907.

The Church of Scotland Mission in Kenya had then only one station, Kikuyu (Thogoto), fifteen miles from Nairobi. Marion was the first single woman to join the work, and had first to learn the difficult Kikuyu language. She began to visit the homesteads and was able to start a class, with boarding facilities for a few girls. In 1912, after her first leave in Scotland, she moved to a new center, Tumutumu, where she had to start again from the beginning, using a new dialect. Tumutumu was her home for the rest of her years in Kenya, though she also started a school at the third station, Chogoria. In 1929, after illness, she returned to Scotland, dying in Edinburgh in June 1930. A member of the United Kikuyu Language Committee, her main contribution had been her work for women and girls.

JOCELYN MURRAY

Bibliography. R. Macpherson, *The Presbyterian Church in Kenya: An Account of the Origins and Growth of the PCEA;* M. S. Stevenson, *A Saint in Kenya: A Life of Marion Scott Stevenson.*

Stewardship. In the parable of the talents (Matt. 25:14–30), Jesus teaches that we have been entrusted with certain special resources which belong to God, and we are responsible to use them wisely and for God's glory. If we approach stewardship and mission in this light, it appears that we will be held accountable before God as to how we manage and use the resources he has given to us and what we produce with them. These resources include not only the finances and what they will purchase but also the people of God, for they are our most valuable resource. Stewardship means that our resources must be invested wisely, with much prayer. This is especially so today due to the escalating cost of missions. Churches and mission agencies, therefore, must be responsible to choose missionaries, ministries, methods, and locations carefully.

This kind of stewardship is being seen as people in churches are holding mission agencies and missionaries accountable for the result of their work. This productivity is being measured not only in terms of the effectiveness of the ministry but also the cost of it. This means that churches are evaluating mission agencies in terms of their past performance, their specialty in ministry, their cost-effectiveness, the receptiveness of their ministry targets, their training programs, and the clarity and intent of their statement of faith. They are also evaluating missionaries in terms of their training, experience, ability, and their theological beliefs and practices. Many churches are responding to this responsibility by being more personally involved in training their missionary candidates and by sending their members to mission fields on vision trips and for SHORT-TERM MISSIONS. Churches are also finding alternatives by funding more cost-effective ministries such as FOREIGN FINANCING OF INDIGENOUS WORKERS, supporting TENTMAKING ministries, supporting ministries to internationals in the United States, and developing PARTNERSHIPS with local, established ministries around the world.

Mission agencies are responding to this need for increased stewardship with tighter controls through such means as specific and regular reporting to donors. Yet such mission leaders as DAVID HESSELGRAVE are calling for agencies to put less emphasis on statistics and more emphasis on effectiveness in their reporting. Also there is more emphasis on training and equipping missionaries. This is becoming one of the primary tasks of the mission agency. The stress on missionaries and their families is increasing because of the complex cultures emerging in the receiving countries due to MODERNIZATION and URBANIZATION and due to economic and political upheavals. Thus the agencies are finding that they must screen and develop their missionaries spiritually, theologically, emotionally, psychologically, and physically for cross-cultural ministry (*see also* CANDIDATE SELECTION). The agency is also paying more attention to the assignment and the management of the individual missionary in terms of location and task on the field. An unwise assignment match between missionary and ministry can end a potentially fruitful missionary career within one term. This is probably the greatest waste of all.

There are some very helpful programs being used to assist missionaries and their families. There are missionary training centers designed to prepare missionaries for cross-cultural life and ministry. There are missionary maintenance programs designed to counsel them and to keep them going back. There are programs for missionary children to help them adjust when they return to their home country for university. These have proven to be extremely helpful and should continue with the understanding that they are part of good stewardship (*see also* MEMBER CARE IN MISSIONS).

It is clear that there is tension in the matter of stewardship in mission. Many unreached areas are expensive and relatively unproductive, and yet we have the command to disciple the nations. This means that ultimately we cannot measure our success by the productivity of our effort or its cost-effectiveness but by our faithfulness to be good stewards of the gospel that God has also given to us and by our obedience to his Word. For in the final analysis, it is the words of our Lord, "Well done, good and faithful servant," that we long to hear.

THOMAS L. AUSTIN

Bibliography. D. J. Hesselgrave, *Today's Choices for Tomorrow's Missions;* P. Sookhdeo, ed., *New Frontiers in Mission*, pp. 176–90.

Stewart, Louisa (c. 1850–95). Irish missionary to China. Raised in Ireland under the influence of the Anglican Church, she first served with the Irish Missionary Society in her home country. She later married another Irish missionary in the Anglican Church, Robert Stewart. Noted for their evangelical zeal, promotion of missionary education strategies, and unselfish service to others, both became well recognized missionary representatives in Great Britain, Australia, and Canada.

The Stewarts left for China soon after their marriage, arriving in Fujian province in 1876. Using Christian materials as a major part of the curriculum in day schools for boys and girls, education became their major means for establishing INDIGENOUS CHURCHES.

The employment of single women missionaries to open many inland stations was another distinctive strategy. In addition, Louisa was a pioneer in training mature Chinese Christian women to become indigenous missionaries called "Bible women." Convinced that illiterate women could be taught to read more quickly through a romanized colloquial text, Louisa was also a major figure in the translation and publication of the romanized New Testament in the Fuzhou dialect.

By 1895 the Stewarts' educational strategies had proven immensely successful. During the Sino-Japanese war, a secret society called the Vegetarians publicly opposed their missionary enterprises. The chaos they incited in Fujian province led ultimately to the Stewarts' martyrdom on August 1, 1895.

LAUREN PFISTER

Bibliography. M. E. Watson, *Robert and Louisa Stewart—In Life and In Death.*

Stockton, Betsey (1798–1865). American missionary to Hawaii. The first single woman missionary to a foreign field from North America was a mulatto woman born to a slave mother in Princeton, New Jersey, in 1798. As a toddler Betsey Stockton was given to the family of a prominent Philadelphia clergyman, Ashbel Green, who later became president of the College of New Jersey (Princeton University). Green and his sons home-schooled Betsey in all the disciplines of religious instruction and general knowledge. She was an avid reader with a keen mind and sensitive spirit. After a conversion experience and official manumission in her late teens she became increasingly convinced that the Lord was calling her as a missionary. Under a unique appointment arranged by Ashbel Green through the AMERICAN BOARD OF COMMISSIONERS FOR FOREIGN MISSIONS she was sent in 1822 with the first reinforcements to the Sandwich Islands (Hawaii) attached to the family of Charles Stewart. There she and the Stewarts and another family opened the station at Lahaina on the island of Maui. Betsey Stockton started the first school in the islands for the children of commoners. Returning to the homeland after three years because of the illness of Mrs. Stewart, Betsey helped found schools for Indian children on Grape Island in Canada, later opening a school for black children in her native town of Princeton, which she served with distinction until her death in 1865.

EILEEN F. MOFFETT

Bibliography. E. F. Moffett, *IBMR* 19:2 (1995): 71–76.

Storytelling. No more powerful teaching or research tool exists than that of storytelling. Whether in cultural, psychological, or organizational analysis, preaching or teaching theology, and more recently, EVANGELISM and follow-up, this communication mode is trans-historical, trans-generational, trans-gender, trans-cultural, and trans-disciplinary. Stories move the world.

Since the 1980s, Christian workers began to (re)capture the significance of story in ministry. Fighting against a number of myths, such as assuming that stories are for children, stories focus on entertainment, stories are used by the unsophisticated, and stories compromise theology, this generation of pioneers fought to reinstate story as a legitimate communication tool.

The support for these pioneers came from numerous disciplines. Anthropologically, people define WORLDVIEW through stories and MYTHS. Stories of real and fictional characters and animals determine the soft boundaries of belief and behavior, distinguishing one people group from another. Researchers therefore analyze the lifestories of different generations and genders to understand better those they came to serve.

Psychologically, the use of narrative in the lifespan development of people through the use of case studies when presenting theories is sanctioned. The telling and hearing of stories can provide the emotional and therapeutic support necessary to cope with life's ups and downs.

Pedagogically, storytelling finds legitimacy in learning styles around the world. From children to grandparents, stories socialize listeners into new tasks, attitudes, and behaviors in informal, non-formal, and formal settings.

Organizationally, leaders tell stories of past and present heroes to define vision and values. They listen to the stories of workers and customers to pinpoint tension areas and find solutions.

Theologians and teachers have noted God's interest in narrative. Discovering that the Holy Spirit designed Scripture so that approximately 75 percent is in a narrative genre, and recognizing Jesus' preference for storytelling, they now promote the Bible as God's sacred Storybook.

Missiologically, the story format of God's sacred Storybook suggests that translators translate the Old Testament as well as the New, evangelists incorporate both Testaments in witness, and teachers ground fragmented theologies in the unified story of Scripture from which they derive.

TOM A. STEFFAN

Bibliography. P. G. Hiebert and F. F. Hiebert, *Case Studies in Missions*; L. Ryken, *How to Read the Bible as Literature*; B. Witherington, *Paul's Narrative Thought World: The Tapestry of Tragedy and Triumph*; T. A. Steffen, *Reconnecting God's Story to Ministry: Crosscultural Storytelling at Home and Abroad.*

Stott, John Robert Walmsley (1921–). English scholar, speaker, and mission advocate and son of Sir Arnold Stott, a notable physician. Rector of All Souls Langham Place, London, for twenty-five years. Honorary Chaplain to the queen 1959–91, Extra Chaplain from 1991. Director of the London Institute of Contemporary Christianity, but best known as an author and speaker of unusual clarity.

Of his more than thirty books probably the best known is *Basic Christianity* (1958), translated into some thirty-six languages.

His contribution to evangelical biblical and missionary scholarship is incalculable. More than any other he was responsible for displacing the negative and polemical character of early-twentieth-century evangelicalism, substituting a more patient and irenic, but still uncompromisingly biblical approach. He encouraged the highest possible levels of scholarship, especially in younger scholars. The Langham Trust and the Evangelical Literature Trust are practical expressions of that concern. The primacy of Scripture in formulating doctrine may be said to be the keystone to his thinking.

His influence went far beyond the Anglican communion. His influence on the formulation of the Lausanne Covenant is everywhere recognized, and his *Commentary* on it accepted as definitive. His 1975 *Christian Mission in the Modern World* is a further indication of his missiological concerns.

Over the years he has wrestled with such issues as the charismatic movement and the role of social action in Christian mission, and his balanced views on both have profoundly influenced evangelical thinking. More controversial was his debate with David Edwards which gave rise to *Essentials* (1988) and evidence that Stott was at least sympathetic to ANNIHILATION thinking with regard to the nature of hell. It must be added that Stott staunchly affirms his belief in hell and in eternal punishment (*ERT* 18:1 [1984]: 33).

F. PETER COTTERELL

SEE ALSO Lausanne Movement.

Bibliography. M. Eden and D. Wells, eds., *The Gospel in the Modern World: A Tribute to John Stott;* D. Edwards and J. Stott, *Essentials;* J. Stott, *Mission in the Modern World.*

Strachan, R. Kenneth (1910–65). American missionary to Costa Rica and founder of Evangelism-in-Depth. Born in Argentina, Strachan grew up in Costa Rica in the family that had founded the Latin America Mission, of which he became president when his father Harry died in 1945. He was thoroughly familiar with evangelistic crusades in many cities. But he felt something was missing: the involvement of lay people in prayer, door-to-door witnessing, and bringing people to hear the evangelists. He made a profound impact on the world of missions by applying the theory of total church mobilization to countrywide evangelism in Central America, South America, and the Caribbean. He coined the phrase "Evangelism-in-Depth" for this movement, which was used in eight countries. His plan called for all evangelical churches and missions to combine their efforts for nationwide campaigns that included a number of regional campaigns leading to one in the capital city. Strachan taught this concept widely and motivated many national church leaders to adopt it. Not all churches and agencies cooperated, and he was criticized by some. Strachan believed in using national evangelists as well. Thousands of Christians were trained and revitalized. Evangelical unity was demonstrated. More than one hundred thousand people were converted to Christ, in spite of opposition from Roman Catholic priests in many places.

JIM REAPSOME

Bibliography. E. Elliot, *Who Shall Ascend: The Life of R. Kenneth Strachan of Costa Rica;* W. D. Roberts, *Revolution in Evangelism: The Story of Evangelism-in-Depth.*

Strategic-Level Prayer. *See* TERRITORIAL SPIRITS.

Strategies in Mission. Many people moving out in mission do not seem to think much about strategy. At least the mainstream of missions at any given point in history has been what others are already doing. The constant element may have been a desire to share the riches of the gospel, but the actual technique at any point has usually been assumed.

One of the first major movements was the phenomenon of the highly individual initiatives of the Irish peregrini. They set out with the idea of monastic centers as a main strategy—the nature of the movement from which they derived. And it worked. The Benedictine movement gradually took over the Irish centers of biblical study, devotional life, and evangelistic outreach, adding so many Roman elements of industry and science that these centers became the nucleus of most of the major cities of Europe. Whole kingdoms came into the fold when strategically located wives influenced their husbands to adopt the faith, often from a variety of motives. Some groups were forced into the faith although contemporary writings denounced that approach. Some approaches represented CONTEXTUALIZATION so radical that they would not readily be conceived of today yet they went on with clear success. Can you imagine the orgy of a Spring goddess of fertility becoming an Easter sunrise service? But it worked. For that matter, can you imagine the entire Roman Empire deciding to become Christian? That event remarkably benefited the faith in many ways.

Much of the expansion of the faith in Europe—the overall phenomenon of the so-called conversion of barbarian Europe—was due to the prestige of the gospel representing the extension or renewal of the highly respected Roman civilization (minus its legions), much as modern missionaries have on their side whatever respect (or disrespect) people around the world have for the achievements of the West minus its colonial domination. That is, factors that are often unconscious, or not acknowledged, have given a gust of wind to strategies which might not otherwise have worked as well.

But behind what did or did not work lies the question about what it really is to do mission. Conscious strategy would have to build on basic concepts of what the goal is understood to be. What are we trying to do to people, their families, and societies? Is it merely a case of transmitting a message of hope and pardon? Do we demand that people repent and believe? Is it a case of bringing about "the obedience of faith" (Rom. 12:5; 16:26)? Is it something else to pray that his kingdom come (Matt. 6:10), and to "preach the kingdom" (Acts 28:31)? "As my father has sent me, so send I you." Are those marching orders? John records "the Son of God appeared for this purpose, that he might destroy the works of the devil." Have missionaries been doing this? They have fought ignorance, poverty, injustice, disease. Does that in itself clarify a strategy for mission? Somewhat. But missionaries have also carried disease with them. In North America in the early twenty-first century age stratification and family-dissolving individualism have progressed to the point that the American model for church planting consists to a great extent of the understandable concept of finding loose individuals and collecting them into fellowships which are like surrogate families. This does not work very well in a traditional society where natural families are already the basic structure. In that case the strategy sometimes becomes one of extracting people from real families in order to produce the expected fellowship.

Probably the strategy least likely to succeed is the one in which large, enthusiastic local congregations in the West send people out to reproduce the precise image of their Western fellowship, bypassing the mission agencies which over a period of many years have adjusted to some extent to the mixed realities of the field cultures and have accumulated wisdom rather than having to reinvent the wheel. Often an individual missionary family is less of a threat than a team, which often finds it more difficult to get close or much less inside a strange society.

God often has initiated a breakthrough by miracles and healings, and the very wording of Paul's summary in Acts 26:18–20 would seem to predict the early possibility of a POWER ENCOUNTER in which it is decided once and for all whether God or Satan has the upper hand within a given group. But can you plan this out? Turn it on? And, over the long haul is it proper to expect that the primary means of fighting rampant disease, for example, is to appeal to God for miracles? Do a thousand mission clinics and hospitals have a reason for existence? Are amazing new insights into microbial realities allowing and insistently requiring new strategies for destroying "the works of the devil"? Mercy ministries may be seen as bait; are they also essential to defining the very character of a loving God—and, by contrast, the character of our great enemy?

One of the most pursued strategies has been the planting of a string of "missions." Despite grumblings about "the mission station approach" the idea has prevailed of planting a complete community self-sufficient in food production, education, medicine, and even blacksmithing, masonry, and the importation of foreign building methods, materials, and patterns. Whether Roman Catholic, Moravian, or Protestant, this strategy has been, rightly or wrongly, one of the most enduring techniques, especially in frontier, pioneer, literally dangerous situations, where the "station" is in a certain real sense a fortress. The very opposite, say, that of a young, unarmed man going out and handing himself over to a tribal society for better or worse and becoming a functional part of that society has also worked. Somewhat similar, but not willingly, at first, would be the case of ULFILAS, who, as a captured slave in the fourth century was forced to become bilingual and was enabled eventually to contribute to the immensely influential Gothic Bible.

Much less frequently in the twenty-first century will we find conditions in which a lone individual might be the intended *method* as the *means* of significant mission. The world has changed beyond imagining, introducing obstacles and opportunities that can hardly be predicted from one day to the next. The very nature of the expanding kingdom of God is quite unclear in detail, but unquestionably it is a global phenomenon. And this certainly affects strategy.

For example, it is dramatically new that the Christian movement is leaping and abounding in the non-Western world without a parallel in the West. It is dramatically new that the former "mission fields" are now sprouting hundreds of mission societies of their own and thousands upon thousands of their own missionaries. Some of these new missionaries are often strikingly more able to fit in, while others are often embarrassingly less willing to adapt, just as Western missionaries have been known to be. In sheer number of agencies, associations of agencies, regional gatherings, global gatherings, scholarly gatherings, and scholarly societies, the situation is unprecedented.

When it comes to strategy one of the largest and yet most puzzling challenges is the emergence of a major phenomenon of indigenous movements that are neither fish nor fowl. In Africa at the turn of the millennium, the so-called AFRICAN INITIATED CHURCH MOVEMENT involves over thirty million people. Many of the leaders of this phenomenon are illiterate but quite intelligent, their movements fed by a few who read for the benefit of the rest. Their theologies range from what Westerners might approve to what staggers the imagination—such as the concept of divine persons as members. Few missions have developed a strategy for assisting these new churches to move in the right direction.

In India the very possibility of Hindus who continue to be Hindus in many cultural dimensions but who devoutly read the Bible, worship, and seek to follow Christ has many wondering. While no one knows how large this phenomenon is, some scholars estimate that it is as large as the explicitly Christian movement, and to some extent more earnest than those who, by now, are brought up culturally as Christians. Strategies being developed to reach out to assist and fellowship with people like this are likely to have as little initial acceptance as Paul's idea of uncircumcised Gentiles.

But parallel, if not similar, reasons for not identifying with Western Christians exist in both China and the world of Islam, and in both cases millions are profoundly impressed by the person of Jesus Christ and the strange power of the Judeo-Christian Bible. Strategies at the beginning of the Third Millennium must take into account the possibility that far more of what we call Christianity is simply reflective of a particular cultural background of one portion of the globe. And, the way things are going, Western Christianity now incorporates many detestable, even demonic, elements such as radical age segregation, the temporary family structure, and the world's highest divorce rate, delinquency rate, and prison population. Meanwhile, many other non-Christian societies exhibit stable family life. It already appears to be true that the faith of the Bible is now out of the control of the West. Just as the Roman tradition eventually lost control of European Christianity, the non-Western world is growing without adopting all of the features Westerners might expect or desire. What strategy can we develop in this situation? Missionaries have traditionally been willing to put up with deviations that might startle people back home. But probably the greatest obstacle to the development of effective new ways of working on the field may be the very fact that we have not been willing to employ mission field perspectives in our own backyards. Outgoing missionaries have no missiology to follow. Who among us has been able to know what to do with the burgeoning Mormon movement or the New Age movement?

Undoubtedly new strategies will be developed both through the inherent creativities of isolation and the methodical comparison of notes. The world is both bigger, more fluid, and more complex than ever. It is also smaller and more amenable to nearly constant interchange between workers who were once far more isolated from each other all across the world.

Some of the most pregnant possibilities, undreamed of before, are arising out of strategic PARTNERSHIPS and dozens of other ways in which workers are able to encourage and enlighten one another. Conversation and interchange have become virtually instantaneous compared to the need for endless months for travel or even for mail to get around the globe. Working closely together has always been a marvelous phenomenon in the world of overseas missionaries, and new levels of collaboration are now well established, possibly leading to new innovations in mission strategy in the future.

RALPH D. WINTER

Studd, Charles Thomas (1863–1931). English pioneer missionary to China, India, and Africa. Son of a wealthy planter, Studd was converted under D. L. MOODY (1876), educated at Cambridge, and played cricket for the English national team. He was one of the famous "Cambridge Seven" who sailed for China in 1895 with the CHINA INLAND MISSION. While there, he adopted a Chinese lifestyle and gave away his considerable inheritance to Christian causes, preferring to trust God completely. Ill health brought him home in 1894, and following several years working among students in America, he served as pastor of the Union Church at Ootacamund, South India (1900–1906). Despite continued health problems he founded in 1912 the Heart of Africa Mission (later the WORLDWIDE EVANGELIZATION CRUSADE), working in Congo until his death. He gave himself unreservedly to spreading the gospel, reducing local languages to writing, and translating the Scriptures. His motto was, "If Christ be God and died for me, then no sacrifice can be too great for me to make for him."

J. D. DOUGLAS

Bibliography. E. S. Buxton, *Reluctant Missionary;* N. J. Grubb, *C. T. Studd, Cricketer and Pioneer;* J. C. Pollock, *The Cambridge Seven: A Call to Christian Service.*

Student Mission Work. Ever since Daniel and his three friends were taken from their homeland and placed in the court of King Nebuchadnezzar of Babylon, students have had an active role in being missionary witnesses in foreign cultures. Students often have the enthusiasm and freedom to move easily into other cultures with the gospel. Furthermore, as in Daniel's time, students have the abilities and educational qualifications that make their presence in a foreign culture both acceptable and desirable to the host culture. Consequently it is not surprising that many of the great missionary initiatives in the last few hundred years have come from students.

In the early seventeenth century, seven law students from Lubeck, Germany, committed themselves to world missions while studying in Paris. At least three of them went to Africa, including Peter Heiling, who spent twenty years in Abyssinia (Ethiopia) where he translated the Bible into

Amharic and eventually died as a martyr for the cause of Christ.

The great MORAVIAN missionary movement began in the student days of Count NIKOLAUS LUDWIG VON ZINZENDORF, who, while studying, formed the Order of the Grain of Mustard Seed, which had as one of its purposes "to carry the gospel of Christ to those overseas who had never yet heard the message." Much of modern worldwide missionary movement can be traced to the hearts of those students who gathered together to pray for world evangelism.

Charles Wesley helped form the "Holy Club" at Christ Church College in Oxford in 1726. This group became involved in reaching out to the poor and those in prison. Subsequently in 1735, Charles and his brother, John, joined in a missionary effort among indigenous Americans in Georgia. It was a continuation of their desire to know God better which began in their student days at Oxford.

One of the most influential pastors in England during the early 1800s was Charles Simeon. He had become a believer in Christ during his student days at Cambridge. After graduation he was ordained to the ministry and served at Holy Trinity Church in Cambridge for fifty-four years. It was during these times that he influenced hundreds of students to know Christ and to serve him throughout the world. The British and Foreign Bible Society began in Cambridge in 1811 and the strongly missions-oriented Inter-Varsity Fellowship of England traces its roots directly to Simeon and student work at Cambridge.

Students in America were also key to missionary vision and commitment. In 1806 a group of students at Williams College in western Massachusetts met two afternoons each week to pray. One such meeting was particularly dedicated to pray that students would have an increased interest in foreign missions. However, the students got caught in a thunderstorm and sought refuge under a haystack. There they prayed and the result was the first student missionary society in America. According to KENNETH SCOTT LATOURETTE "It was from this HAYSTACK MEETING that the foreign missionary movement of the churches of the United States had an initial main impulse."

Later in that century, in 1883, the Princeton Foreign Missionary Society was formed by students and in 1885, 251 students from eighty-nine colleges in the United States attended a conference at Mt. Hermon with D. L. MOODY. A direct result of this conference was the formation of the STUDENT VOLUNTEER MOVEMENT for Foreign Missions in 1888. Its famous watchword was "the evangelization of the world in this generation." It is estimated that in the next fifty years more than twenty thousand students became active missionaries as a result.

In 1936 a new missionary thrust developed among students with the leadership of Robert McQuilkin, founder and president of Columbia Bible College. This new movement became the Student Foreign Missions Fellowship and spread rapidly to scores of primarily Christian colleges in the United States. Later, in 1945, the SFMF became the missionary arm at Christian schools for InterVarsity Christian Fellowship. This merger formed the backdrop for the first IVCF–SFMF international student missions convention held at the University of Toronto in 1946. Two years later the convention was held at the University of Illinois at Urbana, where it has been held since then on a triennial basis and become known simply as "URBANA." During the fifty-year history of Urbana, nearly 200,000 delegates have attended these missionary conventions and approximately 125,000 of these delegates have made commitments to be actively involved in the world mission of the church.

In the 1950s other organizations focused on students came into being. Campus Crusade, The Navigators, The Fellowship of Christian Athletes, Youth for Christ, Youth With a Mission, Operation Mobilization, and many other parachurch groups are actively involved in student missions projects. Church groups and most Christian colleges send thousands of young people overseas in short-term missions teams every summer.

One other dimension of student missions is the tremendous impact on world missions of campus revivals in the United States. JONATHAN EDWARDS observed that the First Great Awakening had its greatest impact "chiefly among the young." DAVID BRAINERD was one such young person at Yale who committed his life to the evangelization of Native Americans. In the revival of 1904–8, E. STANLEY JONES was a student at Asbury College who committed his life to going to India in missionary service. It has been estimated that perhaps as many as 10,000 to 15,000 students went overseas from this awakening.

In 1950, revivals at places like Asbury College and Wheaton College were dramatic. At Wheaton 39 percent of the class of 1950 devoted at least part of their lives to full-time Christian ministry. Another wave of revivals took place in 1970 with at least 130 colleges, seminaries, and Bible schools being touched by unusual spiritual activity and commitment. The Wheaton revival in 1995 has had a significant impact on students praying for greater involvement in world missions.

It is difficult to fully assess all of the dimensions of student mission work. However, it is not difficult to observe that students have had and will continue to have a significant role in world missions. In our current "information age," student status provides access to all parts of the world. The most endearing qualities of students, though, are their spiritual commitment and zeal for the kingdom of God. They are not yet entrenched in institutions and genuinely share the freshness of their faith with those who do not yet know Jesus. They accept the multicultural realities of the world without the prejudice of previous generations. They have great passion and compassion for those in need and are ready for a full commitment to career missionary service.

ROBERT A. FRYLING

Bibliography. T. Beougher and L. Dorsett, *Accounts of a Campus Revival;* R. Coleman, *The Coming World Revival;* D. Howard, *Student Power in World Evangelism;* D. McKenna, *The Coming Great Awakening.*

The Student Volunteer Movement for Foreign Missions (SVM). The Student Volunteer Movement was organized in 1888, the result of a student conference held in July 1886 at Northfield, Massachusetts. It had several roots. One was the Society of Brethren, which had been established to stimulate mission interest at Williams College (*see* HAYSTACK MEETING) and then spread to at least forty-nine other institutions by mid-century. A second was the college ministry of the YMCA, led by Luther Wishard, who was deeply committed to foreign missions. Third was the Princeton Foreign Missionary Society; it was led by Robert Wilder, the son of a retired missionary to India who in his own student days had been a member of the Society of Brethren. Wilder at Princeton and his sister Grace at Mount Holyoke College were both committed to motivate students to missionary service, then made a covenant to pray for a thousand missionary volunteers. Concerned for revival and mission, Robert formed groups that met daily for prayer. Another influence was the visit of J. E. K. Studd, brother of one of the Cambridge Seven, who spoke at a number of American colleges. This was significant in the life of JOHN R. MOTT, a student at Cornell.

The major speakers at the Northfied conference, which was attended by 251 students, were D. L. MOODY and A. T. PIERSON, a Presbyterian minister and well-known advocate of missions. Wilder attended while his sister prayed. She had faith that there would be a hundred volunteers enlisted at the conference. Midway into the conference students asked for permission to speak on various areas of the world and their needs, and to encourage others to sign a commitment to missionary service. At the final prayer meeting the one hundredth student signed the pledge. Wilder and John Forman were appointed traveling secretaries and visited 162 educational institutions the following year. In 1888 SVM was formally organized under the sponsorship of the YMCA, the YWCA, and the Interseminary Missionary Alliance, with Mott as its chairman. The motto of the SVM was "the evangelization of the world in this generation." Stressing urgency and purpose, the motto was sometimes criticized as being too American and too activist. However, it was not meant to be a prophecy; rather, it stressed the responsibility of Christians in each generation to proclaim the gospel to the whole world. Each volunteer signed a statement: "It is my purpose, if God permits, to become a foreign missionary." The SVM gave strong emphasis on the authority of Scripture, prayer, and the need for the power of the Holy Spirit. It taught that the needs of the world constituted the imperative for mission, and that no other special call was needed. Succeeding Wilder as traveling secretary in 1889, ROBERT E. SPEER visited 110 institutions and gathered 1,100 new volunteers. SAMUEL ZWEMER was another early leader.

Almost 600 volunteers from 159 institutions attended the quadrennial convention in 1891. The following year Wilder traveled to Britain, and the movement was launched in a number of European countries. It grew rapidly until after World War I. The 1920 convention was attended by 6,890 people from 949 schools, and that year 2,783 new volunteers enrolled. By 1940 at least 20,500 missionaries had sailed from North America and Europe to various mission fields. The movement more than tripled the number of missionaries from North America. They served primarily under the Methodist, Baptist, Presbyterian, and Congregational churches. The majority went to Asia, with smaller numbers going to Africa, Latin America, and the Middle East. In addition, an educational program to study missions spread rapidly. At one time over 40,000 students at 700 institutions were involved. Thus the movement not only multiplied the number of missionaries from the West, but also greatly increased the number of those at home who supported missions. The SVM was instrumental in forming the World Student Christian Federation in 1895, laid much of the groundwork for the 1910 WORLD MISSIONARY CONFERENCE, and contributed significant leadership to the early ECUMENICAL MOVEMENT.

After World War I the SVM began to decline. By 1940 it had ceased to be a decisive factor in students' religious life and in the promotion of mission in the churches. This was due first to the loss of a clear theological focus. After World War I theological liberalism and doubts about the validity of Western culture led to a turning inward. A desire to tackle the problems of Western society coupled with doubts about the validity of world evangelization. The generation of leadership that succeeded Mott and Speer had considerably less ability. The economic depression of the 1930s was another negative factor, along with a decline in missionary education. The movement no longer had much impact by 1940 and, after merging with other organizations in the 1950s, was officially terminated in 1969.

PAUL E. PIERSON

Bibliography. D. Howard, *Student Power in World Evangelism*; J. R. Mott, *Addresses and Papers*, vol. 1; M. Parker, *The Kingdom of Character: The Student Volunteer Movement for Foreign Missions, 1886–1926*; C. P. Shedd, *Two Centuries of Student Christian Movements*; T. Wallstrom, *The Creation of a Student Movement to Evangelize the World*; R. P. Wilder, *The Great Commission*.

Sudan *(Est. 2000 pop.: 32,079,000; 2,505,813 sq. km. [967,494 sq. mi.]).* Sudan, a land often referred to throughout the Old Testament as either Kush, Nubia, and Ethiopia, has long thirsted to know the living God. Isaiah 18 pronounces a prophecy against Cush, the Upper Nile region, but also proclaims "people tall and smooth-skinned, from a people feared far and wide" (v. 7) will come to worship the Lord Almighty.

Historically, the blooming of a Christian church began in the sixth century with the Byzantium/Egyptian missionary thrust. It had withered out by the sixteenth century. The key factor for this demise was the coming of Islam, a long process that began in the tenth century. The destabilization of Nubian states in the twelfth and thirteenth centuries by Mamluk warlords led to Islamic conversion of Nubia. Sudanese Islam follows Sufism, a mystic form of Islam.

The modern missionary period first saw the Catholics establishing a mission in Khartoum in the mid-nineteenth century. Daniel Comboni with his perceptively innovative mission strategy, "A Plan for the Regeneration of Africa by Means of Africans," of 1864 is regarded as the founder of the Catholic Church in Sudan. Comboni's method included buying slaves, educating them in Italy and Khartoum, and commissioning them for the work of the church in Sudan. Comboni also founded the Verona Fathers, a mission society, to carry out the plan.

Following the Anglo-Egyptian Conquest of 1898, three main strands dominated twentieth-century missions. The Verona Fathers, the CHURCH MISSIONARY SOCIETY of the Anglican Church, and the United Presbyterian Church of America each attempted to make inroads into Sudan. The Anglo-Egyptian administration feared Islamic rebellions and dictated the missions' agendas. Thus, the Conventions of 1899 forbade all direct evangelism but allowed educational and medical work. The strategy became holistic, seeking to minister predominantly through education, medical ministries, and Bible translation.

Independence in 1956 sparked civil war. The Islamic north wanted to impose Islam and arabization on the Christian south. The war continues until this day. Since 1956, there have been two main phases of rapid church growth. The churches of Equatoria, the southern belt, saw revival from 1960 to 1972. The second phase experienced an unprecedented, totally indigenous movement among the Dinka and Nuer beginning in 1983. In response to the need for an African identity as Christians, the church placed a strong emphasis on cultural forms—healing, prayer, dance with mime, and singing—that gained a high impact for the gospel.

Missiological challenges for today include the overwhelming need for leadership training in order to baptize and train thousands of new converts. Hundreds of evangelists, mostly women and young boys, are leading churches with minimal or no training. Literacy and theological education through open learning are imperative. One young pastor, for example, returned from training and baptized nine thousand converts his first year. The Sudan is experiencing a devastating war, a profound destruction of traditional life, horrible ethnic clashes (one million Christians killed), and failure of the economy and social systems. Yet the gospel is moving forward, in isolation from Western influence, with great responsiveness. The Sudan is thirsting to know the true, living God.

ROBERTA R. KING

Bibliography. G. Vantini, *Christianity in the Sudan*; A. Wheeler, *The Church in Sudanese History: Theological Education by Extension Programme*.

Sudan Interior Mission. *See* SOCIETY FOR INTERNATIONAL MINISTRIES.

Suffering. The universal symbol of Christianity is the cross, a symbol of suffering, specifically, the suffering of Jesus. To reflect upon the life of Jesus is to remember his suffering. As the Servant Songs of Isaiah anticipated, Jesus "was despised and rejected, . . . *a man of suffering* and acquainted with infirmity" (53:3 NRSV, see also 50:6 and 53:4–5, 7–12). Likewise, it has been the fortune of those who follow Jesus to experience suffering. "Remember the word I said to you," Jesus reminded his disciples, "'Servants are not greater than their master.' If they persecuted me, they will persecute you" (John 15:20). No sooner did the church begin to flourish then the apostles were arrested and threatened. They and others were imprisoned and murdered (Acts 4:1–22; 5:17–33; 7:54–60). But their suffering was seen not as an affliction; it was rather a means of witness. "They rejoiced that they were considered worthy to suffer dishonor for the sake of the name" (Acts 5:41). Though the words of the writer of 1 Peter were addressed to first-century Christian slaves, they have been regarded, and rightly so, as applicable to all of Jesus' disciples: "For to this you have been called, because Christ suffered for you, leaving you an example, so that you should follow in his steps" (1 Peter 2:21).

The Christian mission—if it is Christian, that is, Christ-like—is a replication of the mission of

Jesus, and in due time will involve suffering. In his second letter to the church at Corinth, Paul recounts his own suffering in the spreading of the gospel (11:23–28), and he reminds his readers that though suffering is a part of being a disciple, it also is a form of witness. "We are afflicted in every way," he writes, "but not crushed; perplexed, but not driven to despair; persecuted, but not forsaken; struck down, but not destroyed; always carrying in the body the death of Jesus, *so that the life of Jesus may also be made visible in our bodies*" (4:8–10).

It is important to remember, as Douglas Webster observes, that the Greek word for WITNESS, *martus*, soon acquired a new meaning, *one who died for the faith*, and it has been transliterated as *martyr*, thus "combining the ideas of mission and suffering" (1966, 104). To be a witness will therefore result in suffering, sometimes in death. This has been particularly true for missionaries. For some, mission has meant violent death, for example, JOHN WILLIAMS, ELEANOR CHESTNUT, and Archbishop Oscar Romero. For others it has meant harassment, arrest, and months or years in prison, for example, ADONIRAM JUDSON and WILLIAM WADE HARRIS. How many have suffered the loss of spouses and/or children, for example, GEORGE SCHMIDT, E. R. Beckman, and Carie Sydenstricker? Who knows the number who have experienced terribly unhappy marriages because of abusive or mentally ill spouses, for example, WILLIAM CAREY, ROBERT MORRISON, and Martha Crawford? Abandonment by colleagues or supporters has pushed some to the brink of despair, for example, ROWLAND BINGHAM and C. T. STUDD. Oppression of the poor and the defenseless invariably weighs heavily on compassionate missionaries and missionary bishops, for example, BARTHOLOMEW DE LAS CASAS and FESTO KIVENGERE. Significant, therefore, is the apostle Paul's conclusion following his recitation of personal suffering. He says, "And besides other things, I am under daily pressure because of my anxiety for all the churches" (2 Cor. 11:28). Many of the sufferings experienced in mission stem from apprehension and pain for Christ's people.

To be involved in the mission of Jesus Christ, therefore, is to experience suffering, and one of the most vivid reminders of this fact is when we as Jesus' followers gather for the celebration of the Eucharist, a reenactment of the sufferings of our Lord. Whether we hold to the real or symbolic presence in the elements, we should always remember that "the breaking of the bread" and the "drinking of the cup" happens repeatedly outside as well as inside the walls of the church.

ALAN NEELY

SEE ALSO Martyrdom AND Persecution.

Bibliography. A. J. Gittins, *Bread for the Journey;* J. S. Pobee, *Mission in Christ's Way;* R. A. Tucker, *FJIJ;* D. Webster, *Yes to Mission.*

Sufi, Sufism. Sufism is the mystical dimension of Islam. The term most likely comes from the Arabic *suf* (wool): the early Sufis wore plain woolen clothing to symbolize their commitment to poverty and simplicity. Sufism is the Islamic expression of the broad religious movement that seeks direct knowledge of God; it is the inward path to union with God that complements the outward, formal religious tradition. Sufism derives its doctrines and methods from the Qu'ran and Islamic traditions, though it reflects influences of Greek and Persian philosophy, Christianity, and even Hinduism.

The ultimate goal of the Sufi is to experience the oneness or unity of God. The movement toward this goal is termed the Way or the Path. The Path is subdivided into three basic steps: *makhafah*, the way of purification; *mahabbath*, the way of love; and *ma'rifah*, the way of knowledge. Aspects of the Sufi way include the disciplines of poverty, servanthood, subjugation of the self, and above all the remembrance of God. The remembrance of God is enhanced through meditation, sacred dance, and the constant repetition of the divine name. The final goal of the Sufi quest is *fana*, best translated as annihilation or extinction. Through annihilation first in the *shayk*, or religious leader then in the Prophet, and finally in Allah, one is able to die to self and this world and to exist in God alone.

In the early centuries of Islam, Sufism was a "movement without a name," a diverse spiritual movement within the broader tradition. In time, distinct brotherhoods or orders formed around particular teachers or saints, *shayks*, all of whom traced their spiritual lineage back to the Prophet. These brotherhoods came to dominate the religious landscape of many parts of the Islamic world. They also functioned as the principal missionary arm of Islam in Africa, Central Asia, and the Indian subcontinent.

The twelfth through the fourteenth centuries were the golden age of Sufism. Sufi masters such as Suhrawardi, Ibn 'Arabi, Jalal ar-Rumi, and al-Ghazali were known throughout the Islamic world for their poetry and religious insight. However, as the Orders increased in fame, influence, power, and wealth they fell prey to many of the temptations that accompany power and wealth. They were also subject to political manipulation. In some places, hundreds of thousands of persons found their primary religious identity in a local *shayk* or brotherhood. This gave rise to popular devotional Sufism, with an emphasis on psychic phenomena, communication with the spirit world, magic, and extraordinary physical feats as demonstration of spiritual power. In the past two hundred years, organized Sufism has been in marked decline throughout the Islamic world, with the possible exception of some parts of Africa and Asia. Modernists have tended to make Sufism the scapegoat for the technological lag of Muslim nations. Orthodox Muslims, both traditionalists and fundamentalists, have generally viewed Sufism as a threat to the purity of Islam and the establishment of a genuine Islamic society. The Orders were legally suppressed in modern Turkey and today they play little role in the religious life of most Muslims.

JAMES DARRELL CHANCELLOR

SEE Islam.

Bibliography. M. G. Hodgson, *The Venture of Islam: Conscience and History in a World Civilization;* M. Lings, *What Is Sufism?;* A. Schimmel, *Mystical Dimensions of Islam.*

Suh Sang-Yun (So Saw) (c. 1849–1926), Korean evangelist. Suh Sang-Yun, known as the "literary evangelist" in early Korean church history, led many Koreans to Christ prior to the coming of American missionaries to Korea in 1884. He was born in the elite "Yangban" class in the city of Uijoo in northwest Korea (near China). His parents died when he was fourteen years old, and he began a trade business in Manchuria. In 1878 he and his younger brother, Kyung-Cho, crossed over to Manchuria to sell red ginseng root used for medicinal purposes. When he became seriously ill in Manchuria, he was able to receive help from a Scottish missionary, John McIntye, who led him to a hospital in which a British doctor operated on him. Through this incident he became a Christian and began to be associated with two Scottish missionaries in China for the translation of the Bible into the Korean language, several years before the actual arrival of Western missionaries in Korea in 1884.

Suh Sang-Yun and other Koreans assisted John Ross and his brother-in-law John McIntyre in Manchuria to publish the Gospel of Luke (1882), the Gospels of Matthew and Mark and the Book of Acts (1883), and the entire New Testament (1887) in the Korean language. Suh Sang-Yun took Bibles secretly back to Korea during his business trips, distributed them, and witnessed quietly to many Koreans in Uijoo, Sorae (in Hwang Hae province), and Seoul.

There was a small Christian community of approximately 70 believers in Sorae where his brother Kyung-Cho was ministering before the arrival of American missionaries to Korea. HORACE G. UNDERWOOD, who arrived in Korea in 1885, was requested to baptize these believers. Suh Sang-Yun played a very important role by laying the foundation for the ministry of Western missionaries later in Korea.

BONG RIN RO

Bibliography. A. D. Clark, *A History of the Church in Korea;* L. G. Paik, *The History of Protestant Missions in Korea, 1832–1910.*

Sunday Observance. *See* SABBATH OBSERVANCE.

Sunday, William Ashley ("Billy") (1862–1935). American evangelist. A native of Iowa, he played professional baseball from 1883 to 1891. He was converted through the ministry of the Pacific Garden Mission (Chicago) in 1886, married Helen ("Nell") Thompson in 1888, and a few years later left baseball to work with the YMCA (1891–93). He assisted J. Wilbur Chapman in the planning and promotion of evangelistic crusades from 1894 to 1895 before launching out on his own. Sunday was a master of organizing citywide meetings and preached revival meetings in churches, tents, and large wooden tabernacles throughout America until his death in 1935. His able assistant, song leader, and soloist was Homer A. Rodeheaver. His crusade ministry was characterized by advanced planning, detailed organization, massive publicity, and passionate evangelistic preaching. He also preached often on morality, the evils of alcohol, and American patriotism. His animated style drew huge crowds and generated large love offerings, which eventually led to Sunday being criticized for an ostentatious lifestyle. Sunday popularized the phrase "hitting the sawdust trail," referring to those who responded by coming to the front during the invitation time. His legacy is the many converts (estimated as high as one million) who responded to his invitations.

TIMOTHY K. BEOUGHER

Bibliography. L. Dorsett, *Billy Sunday and the Redemption of Urban America;* W. G. McLoughlin, *Billy Sunday Was His Real Name.*

Sundkler, Bengt (1910–95). Swedish missiologist and missionary to Africa. From 1937 to 1945 Sundkler was a missionary in East and Central Africa before moving to South Africa. His work in South Africa led to his pioneering study of African Independent Churches, *Bantu Prophets in South Africa* (1948). In 1949 he became professor of missiology at the University of Uppsala in his native Sweden. He interrupted his academic work briefly to become Lutheran bishop of Bukoba, Tanzania. In 1974, after retiring from Uppsala, Sundkler returned to his study of African independent movements in Zulu Zion (1976). This more mature work represented an increasingly positive evaluation of independent movements although he remained alert to instances where the African zionist prophet attempted to eclipse the centrality of Christ (*see also* ZIONISM, AFRICAN CHURCH)

His career as a keen observer of African Christianity culminated in a two-volume study of the history of African Christianity, *Africa: A Church History.* His death in 1995 preceded its publication in 1998.

Sundkler's emphasis in all his work was the need to translate Christianity into the categories of African culture and thought without losing the essence of the message which he saw in terms of Luther's theology of the cross. While he commended those who had translated the Bible into Africa's vernacular languages he believed that "another and no less important work of translation remains to be tackled." The challenge of theological translation remains one of Sundkler's most important legacies to African Christianity.

MARK SHAW

Bibliography. B. Sundkler, *The Christian Ministry in Africa;* idem, *The Church of South India: The Movement Towards Union, 1900–1947;* idem, *The Christian Mission.*

Sung, John (1901–44). Chinese evangelist. Sung was born in Hinghwa (Xinghua), Fujian province, the sixth child of a Methodist minister. He was impacted by the Hinghwa revival of 1909, and began assisting his father in preaching. He received his Ph.D. in chemistry from Ohio State University. Upon self-evaluation he gave his life to the ministry, and attended Union Theological Seminary in New York. In February 1927 he had a deep spiritual experience of repentance from sin. He was sent to a mental institution for six months, after which he returned to China. He was a highly effective evangelist, often using eccentric methods of illustration. From 1932 to 1934 he joined the Bethel Evangelistic Band, traveled 54,823 miles, preached at 1,199 meetings, and spoke to over 400,000 people. Over 18,000 were converted. He began traveling in Southeast Asia in 1935. His preaching was centered on the need for thorough repentance. Numerous Christians in China and Southeast Asia can trace their conversion or total consecration to the preaching of John Sung.

SAMUEL LING

Bibliography. C. Lee, *TCDCB,* p. 732; L. T. Lyall, *John Sung.*

Sunni, Sunnism. The Islamic world is divided into two broad traditions, the Sunni and the Shi'ite. The Sunni tradition stretches from West Africa and Central Europe to East Asia. Approximately 85 percent to 90 percent of all Muslims are Sunni. The Sunni tradition accommodates a wide range of cultural expressions and intensity of religious commitment, but remains centered on a set of core beliefs and practices.

The full name of the Sunnis is *ahl as-sunnah wa-l-ijma,* "the People of the *Sunnah* and the Consensus." This fuller term for the Sunnis points to the centrality of the legacy of the Prophet Muhammad and primary role of the community of faith. The term "Sunni" comes from the Arabic *Sunnah,* the "custom of the Prophet." Sunnis often refer to themselves as "the orthodox." They recognize the validity of the first four Caliphs (the Righteous Caliphs), after Muhammad, as the founding figures of the Islamic community. The caliphs are said to have succeeded to Muhammad's authority as head of the community, but not to his function as prophet "Messenger of Allah." In this recognition, they at once affirm that ultimate authority in Islam rests with the *umma,* or Islamic community, and deny any unique or special religious or political authority to the physical descendants of Muhammad or Ali, his cousin and son-in-law. The Sunni tradition holds strongly to Muhammad as model human, the Qur'an and Hadith as normative scripture, the Five Pillars as normative for religious practice, and the Law of God as complete guide for all human endeavors.

There are four schools of law among the Sunnis: the Hanbali, Maliki, Hanafi, and Shafi'i. These schools emerged in the eighth and ninth centuries and over time each came to dominate general geographic regions. The Maliki school is found primarily in Africa and the Arab West; the Hanafi school dominates most areas formerly part of the Ottoman Empire. The Hanbali school is found in the Gulf region, and the Shafi'i school is observed in East Asia. While Sunnis regard each school as "orthodox," each individual Muslim is expected to adhere to one school.

For Sunni Islam, the center point of the faith is the Community of Believers. A few observations about the Ulema, the professional class of religious leaders, will bring this in focus. The Ulema are the custodians of knowledge about the QUR'AN, the Prophet, and the *Shari'ah.* They serve as teachers, prayer leaders, and preachers in mosques, Qur'an reciters, and professors of religion and sacred law in universities. They are very loosely organized in any institutional sense and draw their authority only from their ability to reach consensus themselves and bring that consensus to bear on the larger community. They do not constitute a priesthood, and in small or rural communities most of the functions of the Ulema are performed by lay Muslims.

JAMES DARRELL CHANCELLOR

Bibliography. M. G. Hodgson, *The Venture of Islam: Conscience and History in a World Civilization;* R. C. Martin, *Islam: A Cultural Perspective.*

Suriname (*Est. 2000 pop.: 447,000; 163,265 sq. km. [63,037 sq. mi.]*). Located on the north shore of South America, Suriname (formerly Dutch Guiana) is bounded on the west by Guyana, on the east by French Guiana, and on the south by

Brazil. The country was visited early in the sixteenth century by Spanish explorers who were not attracted to the region because there was no apparent source of wealth. The Dutch came as early as 1613, and the British in 1630. Finally the Dutch acquired Suriname from Britain in 1667 in exchange for their colony in New York. These two colonial powers, however, competed with each other to establish a foothold in the region. In 1799 the colony was conquered by the British and remained under their rule until 1802, when it was restored to the Netherlands. It became a British colony in 1804 and a Dutch colony (1814). In 1954, the Dutch colony was recognized at a level of equality with the Netherlands; independence finally was granted in 1975.

The most important religions include the Dutch Reformed Church, Moravianism, Roman Catholicism, Hinduism, and Islam. Against the prevailing point of view of the Dutch Reformed Church at his time, Justinian von Welz (1621–68) was of the conviction that the command of Christ to preach the gospel to all the world was still valid. He went as a missionary to Suriname, where he eventually lost his life. The Roman Catholic Church has not been very influential; it was not until 1842 that they created a vicariate apostolate. The most remarkable mission, however, has been that of the Moravians among the Indians and later extended to the maroons (known as "Bush Negroes," the descendants of escaped slaves), and to other blacks on the plantations on the coast. The maroons of Suriname have long been the hemisphere's largest maroon population. The Moravian testimony began in 1738, in the midst of many sufferings. Six years passed before the first convert was baptized. From that time on, the work spread and grew, and has continued until the present day. Moravian missions brought education and medical care to some remote areas. They also produced a good deal of missionary ethnography, especially about the Saramaka, the most important of the six Bush Negro tribes of Suriname. A major problem for church growth today in Suriname is the fact that immigration to the Netherlands has been very heavy. As a result, the total population of the country has persistently declined in the last two decades. Many Protestants among the Bush Negroes are now living, working, and continuing their education in the Netherlands.

PABLO A. DEIROS

Bibliography. J. T. Hamilton, *A History of the Missions of the Moravian Church During the Eighteenth and Nineteenth Centuries;* idem, *Protestant Missions in South America;* J. Holmes, *Historical Sketches of the Missions of the United Brethren;* J. E. Hutton, *History of the Moravian Missions.*

Swain, Clara A. (1834–1910). American pioneer missionary physician in India. Born in Elmira, New York, and raised in Castile, New York, Swain attended seminary and taught public school before beginning her medical apprenticeship in 1865. She received her M.D. in 1869 from the Woman's Medical College of Pennsylvania. The Woman's Foreign Missionary Society of the Methodist Episcopal Church sent her as the first female medical missionary to the Orient. She and ISABELLA THOBURN, an educator, left to work with women and orphans in India in 1869. In addition to her medical practice, Swain established a course of medical training for young Indian women. Because she did an effective job of respecting caste and working with women and children from all parts of society, she was given 40 acres by a Muslim prince in 1871. There she established the first hospital for women in India. She needed a three-year furlough from 1876 to 1879 to regain her health.

In 1885, she was invited by the Rajah of Khetri, Rajputane to become the palace physician for his wife. Her condition for acceptance was that she be allowed to evangelize in conjunction with her medical work. Because his wife responded so well to Swain's treatment, the Raj invited her to provide medical care for other women in the area and enabled her to open a dispensary. Swain effectively used music to share the gospel with many under her care. She retired in 1896 and returned to New York.

MARGOT EYRING

Bibliography. E. Deen, *Great Women of the Christian Faith;* M. L. Hammack, *DWCH;* R. McHenry, ed., *Famous American Women: A Biographical Dictionary from Colonial Times to the Present.*

Swaziland *(Est. 2000 pop.: 980,000; 17,364 sq. km. [6,704 sq. mi.]).* Swaziland, the smallest nation in the southern hemisphere, is wedged between the Republic of South Africa and Mozambique. It gained its independence from Britain in 1968. The Swazi originated from several different clans in Mozambique, but were eventually amalgamated into one nation to withstand the onslaughts of the warring Zulus.

The gospel first came to Swaziland as a fulfillment of a vision King Somhlolo had in the mid-1830s in which people with straight hair and strange-colored skin would come. Almost a decade later Somhlolo's son, King Mswati, heard about white men among neighboring people. He sent a delegation to them and, in 1844, two Methodist missionaries arrived, bringing two Basotho evangelists whom they left to begin the work.

Today, with 80 percent claiming to be Christian, Swaziland could be considered a country saturated with the gospel. There is, however, a high degree of nominalism and of those who claim to be Christian, only one in four recognizes a need to be an active member in a local church and only one in three is a faithful church attender.

Key church leaders are currently praying for renewed spiritual awakening among the nation's churches. While the church is involved in many areas, major hindrances to the spread of the gospel still remain. These include traditional religion, polygamous values, the universalistic views promoted by some African independent churches, syncretism, the institutional approach of mission societies and parachurch organizations, and churches that do not understand the changing society.

Major challenges confront the Swazi church. There still remain many targets for evangelism. Solid biblical principles concerning family life, the selection and training of church leaders, the proper stewardship of money, and meaningful prayer urgently need to be taught and modeled. AIDS-related ministries are required to care for both children and parents.

Because the church is not keeping up with the population growth the Swaziland Evangelism Task recommended the church in Swaziland strive to have 30 percent of the population as active members by the year 2015. Additionally, there is the growing conviction that it is time for the Swazi churches to involve themselves in God's global purposes to reach all nations with the gospel.

THOMAS J. KOPP

Bibliography. M. Froise, ed., *Swaziland Christian Handbook 1994;* idem, *World Christianity: Southern Africa;* P. Johnstone, *OW;* P. M. Kopp, *Fulfilling the Vision: A Report of the Swaziland Evangelism Task.*

Sweden *(Est. 2000 pop.: 8,972,000; 449,964 sq. km. [173,731 sq. mi.]).* The largest and most populous of the Scandinavian countries, Sweden exercises significant international influence in science, manufacturing, and politics. The Nobel Prize, instituted by Swedish inventor Alfred Nobel, is considered the premier scientific award in the world. Natural resources and careful management produce internationally known products such as Volvo automobiles, SKF bearings, and Hasselblad cameras. Swedish democratic socialism seems based on a dominant cultural value of equality. Other principal values include a love of untamed nature and individualism. The latter sometimes clashes with socialism, yet apparently functions to maintain political and social balance. Prominent Swedish politicians include former UN secretary general Dag Hammarsköld and prime minister Olaf Palme.

The most common Swedish philosophies find roots in naturalism, pragmatism, and existentialism (first conceived in Scandinavia). Naturalism prevails in the universities and science, pragmatism in industry and politics, and existentialism in personal choice and experience. Once rooted in Christian THEISM, Swedes have recently turned away from organized Lutheranism toward ATHEISM, AGNOSTICISM, or personal religious experience, the first two finding basis in naturalism, the latter in existentialism. Recent prosperity movements have attracted a number of adherents among Christian youth, perhaps stemming from the movement's combination of theistic pragmatism and existentialism.

The Swedish approach to existentialism can be readily observed in literature (Strindberg, Lagerquist) and film (Bergman). Special artistic attention is often given to existential angst, which may be described as an overwhelming hopelessness. The tendency toward loneliness and angst may also contribute to ongoing concerns over depression and alcohol misuse.

Swedish Christianity, once dominated by Lutheranism, currently displays a variety of convictions. Led by King Gustav Vasa and Luther student Olavus Petri, Lutheranism began to replace Catholicism in 1524. Until the twentieth century, Swedish Lutheranism tended toward the traditional. More recently, liberalism has pervaded the Swedish Lutheran theology, philosophy, and practice.

Seventeenth-century pietist and Moravian movements significantly influenced the formation of the free church movement, started in the 1830s by English Methodist missionary George Scott. Although Scott was forced to leave Sweden, the movement survived, gaining strength toward the end of the nineteenth century. Since the 1930s, however, membership in nearly all denominations has diminished. The free church is currently defined by the government as anything not related to the state church. Included are various Baptists, Mission Covenant, Methodists, evangelical Lutherans, Pentecostals, Holiness Union, Swedish Alliance, and the Salvation Army. Together, active free church members comprise under 10 percent of the total population. War and political refugees, however, have significantly added to the numbers of Catholics and Muslims. A recent vote (1995) called for a separation of the state–church relationship after the year 2000, Sweden being the first Western European country to do so.

Swedish Christianity has provided many influential evangelical leaders. Included are evangelist C. O. Rosenius, Mission Covenant leader and theologian P. P. Waldenström, Pentecostal leader Levi Petrus, and The Evangelical Alliance Mission founder FREDERIK FRANSON. Swedish mission efforts are considerable, especially when considering the relatively small number of evangelicals. Included are substantial (often tax supported) programs for hunger and development that stand beside traditional efforts in evangelism, church planting, and Bible translation.

STEVEN J. PIERSON

Bibliography. M. J. Gannon, *Understanding Global Cultures: Metaphorical Journeys through 17 Countries;* G. Hofstede, *Cultures and Organizations: Software of the Mind;* R. Murray, *A Brief History of the Church of Sweden;* H. W. Norton, *European Background and History of Evangelical Free Church Missions 1887–1955;* E. Torjesen, *Frederik Franson, a Model for Worldwide Evangelism.*

Swedish Mission Boards and Societies. Sweden, the most populous of the Scandinavian countries, has also made by far the largest contribution to the worldwide mission of the church. Like the others, at least 90 percent of its people are (for the most part nominally) related to the national Lutheran Church. But whereas in Denmark there are seven times as many parishes of the national church as in all other Protestant denominations combined, and in Norway and Finland the parishes greatly outnumber the total of free churches, in Sweden the situation is reversed. There are over twice as many free church congregations as parishes of the national church. Moreover, unlike in many countries, the free churches have been concerned almost since their beginnings not only with national revival but also with worldwide mission. However, it is now widely recognized that the pervasive SECULARIZATION of Sweden is affecting not only the dominant church (where attendance rarely reaches 5 percent of the membership), but even the free churches which, whether Pentecostal or not, have also been declining lately in active participants. The implications for future missionary effort are therefore ominous unless this is reversed.

From the early 1970s into the 1990s, the number of foreign missionaries sent out through some thirty agencies has been about 1,800. Probably less than a fifth of these have been through either of the two larger and some smaller Lutheran agencies; about half of them have been Pentecostals. Since 1912, in the wake of the Edinburgh WORLD MISSIONARY CONFERENCE, there has been a national missions council, but the work is still basically carried on by the individual agencies and denominations.

Within the framework of the national church there are two main agencies, quite distinct in how they relate to it. The older is usually translated as the Evangelical National Missionary Society, founded in 1856. It is basically a voluntary and lay initiative to promote renewal within the church and so most of its efforts are within Sweden. However, it also sent its first foreign missionaries, in 1865, to Africa, and then in 1877 to India. In the 1960s it had 120 foreign workers, five-sixths of them in eastern Africa.

Unlike many national churches, in Sweden it was decided, through confessional pressure, to make missions an endeavor of the official structures of the whole body, and so in 1874 the Church of Sweden Mission was organized. An earlier initiative dating from 1835 was soon incorporated, but the intention of soon drawing in the above society was not achieved. In 1876, the church sent its first missionaries to South Africa and also to India. In 1918 it entered China. Missionaries spread elsewhere in Africa, especially in Tanzania after the Germans had to leave because of World War I. By the 1960s there were nearly two hundred missionaries, all but 15 percent in southern Africa.

Pentecostalism came to Sweden early in the twentieth century and by 1907 the first missionaries left for China. The key leader, Lewi Pethrus, not only built up the huge Philadelphia Church in Stockholm (which was expelled in 1912 from the Baptists), but also promoted foreign missions. In 1916 the first missionaries were officially sent out to Brazil, and this vast country has been a major and successful field for them ever since. In 1920, outreach was begun elsewhere in Europe. Pentecostal missions have been distinguished from the Lutheran and even some other free church missions by their eagerness to witness in Latin America and elsewhere in Europe. However, the more common areas of China and Africa were also entered. In the latter, a major field was the eastern Congo, from which they spilled over into the deeply troubled countries of Burundi (where the Swedish Pentecostals built the largest Protestant denomination) and Rwanda (where they were second only to the Anglicans). A crucial feature of Swedish Pentecostalism, typically not shared by many other Pentecostal movements, is its strong congregational nature. Perhaps this is a reaction to the connectionalism of the state church. The coordination of the movement is maintained through conferences and voluntary cooperation and various specialized agencies. The mission agency, the Swedish Free Mission, upholds this pattern. For missions this has meant that a large degree of responsibility has been accepted by the individual congregations in sending out missionaries and a close personal attachment is felt toward them. The result was that by 1945 there were some three hundred Pentecostal missssionaries with a 50 percent increase by 1960, and currently there are about three times as many as in 1945.

The smaller free churches have generally maintained more centralized structures than the Pentecostals. The older Baptist Union has had Congo as its main field, having entered in 1914, and had thirty-five workers there in the 1960s with only a few elsewhere. The Oerebro Mission goes back to the 1890s and a split with the Baptists that would now probably be called charismatic in nature. They are now roughly as large as the older Baptists in Sweden, and also seem to be much more foreign missions-minded (from which interesting conclusions are obvious). Their first missionaries went to India in 1908, to Brazil in 1912, and to Congo in 1914. By the mid-1960s they had at least 160 foreign workers divided fairly evenly over Brazil, Africa, and Asia. Like Oerebro, the Swedish Alliance Mission is also a denomination as well as a sending agency, though it apparently began in the last century just to be the latter. By the mid-1960s it had about eighty-five missionaries mostly in South Africa and Asia.

DONALD TINDER

Swiss Mission Boards and Societies. Swiss mission boards and societies take shape according to the complex linguistic and political divisions of the country. An authority of coordination is the Swiss Council of Evangelical Missions, which includes three categories of members, while being itself a corporate member of the World Council of Churches Unit on Mission and Evangelism.

The first category is the mission board of the established Reformed churches of French-speaking Swiss cantons. It is called *Département Missionnaire*, with headquarters in Lausanne. Half of its budget supports the Evangelical Community for Apostolic Action in Paris. Together with other groups including evangelicals, it publishes a review of missiology, *Perspectives Missionnaires*.

The second category is the umbrella organization of German-speaking missions, known as KEM [*Kooperation Evangelischer Kirchen und Missionen*]. This council acts on behalf of several established churches and mission boards in sixteen Swiss cantons. Its most famous member is the BASEL MISSION, established in 1815 as a German-Swiss missionary society, presently in process of fundamental restructuring, aiming at sharing missionary power with its overseas partners. It publishes, together with the GERMAN SOCIETY OF MISSIOLOGY, a missiological quarterly, *Zeitschrift für Mission*. KEM includes other old missionary societies, like the Moravian Mission, the East-Asia Mission, the Evangelical Methodist Mission Board, the South-Africa Mission, the Nile Mission, and the Kwango Mission in Congo-Zaire.

The third category includes associated members without voting rights, belonging to non-denominational groups and evangelical free churches. Among them are the SALVATION ARMY, the Foundation for Church and Judaism, the Swiss Bible Society, the Blue Cross, the YMCA/YWCA, Scripture Union, the Evangelical Braille Mission, the International Missionary Alliance, and the Evangelical Missionary Service.

The last named is in itself a significant French-speaking network, acting on behalf of forty evangelical free church assemblies. It continues the Laos Mission founded in 1902, having a particular concern for Asian diasporas in Europe while accepting new partnerships in Asia and Africa. It is a member of the Federation of Francophone Evangelical Mission.

Well-known international missionary societies are represented in Switzerland: WYCLIFFE BIBLE TRANSLATORS, SOCIETY FOR INTERNATIONAL MINISTRIES, Sudan United Mission, OMF INTERNATIONAL, Open Doors, WEC INTERNATIONAL, TEMA [The European Missionary Association], CHRISTIAN AND MISSIONARY ALLIANCE, and Leprosy Mission International. Some coordination is provided in German-speaking Switzerland by the Working Group of Evangelical Missions, acting on behalf of 30 missions representing 900 missionaries.

Geneva is also the seat of the WORLD COUNCIL OF CHURCHES Unit on Mission and Evangelism, which implies significant interaction with Swiss missionary societies. It publishes the well-known *International Review of Mission*.

Roman Catholic missionary societies (except the Jesuits, prohibited until 1973) first worked for Catholic expansion in Switzerland, before joining fields overseas. The Bethlehem Foreign Missions is the only Swiss-founded society (1921). They publish the scholarly quarterly *Neue Zeitschrift für Missionswissenschaft/Nouvelle Revue de Science Missionnaire*. It is to be noted that the Orthodox Church with its center at Chambésy, near Geneva, is increasingly mission-oriented.

MARC R. SPINDLER

Switzerland (*Est. 2000 pop.: 7,494,000; 41,293 sq. km. [15,943 sq. mi.]*). Switzerland is a confederation of twenty-three almost autonomous cantons, each having its unique religious and political structure. Freedom of religion is guaranteed by the federal Constitution but without strict separation between church and state. In the sixteenth century, a majority of cantons and cities voted for the Reformation. Among other Reformers, Huldrych Zwingli (1484–1531) and his successor Heinrich Bullinger (1504–75) in German-speaking cantons, John Calvin (1509–64) and his successor Théodore de Beza (1519–1605) in French-speaking cantons, successfully shaped the Swiss Reformation with its distinct Presbyterian polity and its concern for intellectual development. The supreme authority of the Bible was proclaimed. A doctrinal agreement on Bible interpretation was formulated in 1566 in the Second Helvetic Confession.

A minority remained in the fold of the ancient Roman Catholic Church, with its peculiar love for cloisters and holiness. The cities of Fribourg and Lucerne have been ever since the centers of Swiss Catholicism. The Catholic University of Fribourg, created in 1889, grew rapidly as a center of excellence in theology, including missiology and other sciences. In the twentieth century it was committed to the renewal of Thomism (the philosophy and theology inherited from Thomas Aquinas) with Cardinal Charles Journet, a friend of Jacques Maritain. He was very vocal in his political fight against Nazi and communist totalitarian ideologies, while the Catholic hierarchy stuck to the principle of neutrality, very dear to Switzerland.

The independent spirit of Swiss Catholicism manifested itself in a spectacular way after the First Vatican Council (1870) when some Catholic bishops refused the new dogma of papal infallibility and created the Old Catholic Church (1874), which joined other non-Roman Catholic Churches mainly in Holland to form the Union of Utrecht (1889). Meanwhile the Catholic population increased through natural demographic growth and immigration from neighboring Catholic countries such as Italy, France, and Austria, later from Spain and Portugal. Geneva, once the symbol of Protestantism, now has a Roman Catholic majority.

In 1858 Protestant churches formed a national conference that became in 1920 the Swiss Federation of Evangelical Churches, including national as well as free churches (above five thousand members), with an efficient interchurch aid and relief network.

In spite of lingering traditions, every canton is now confronted with the problem of the coexistence of several Christian persuasions, from no-church movements in the wake of theosophy or akin to the Moral Rearmament, to all kinds of fundamentalism. Religious pluralism is still augmented by foreign adherents or indigenous converts belonging to world religions and new religious movements, not to mention agnostics.

Influential theological currents emerged in Swiss history, like the Enlightened Pietism of Jean Frédéric Ostervald (1663–1747), a kind of second reformation, the Free Church movement with Alexandre Vinet (1797–1847), the so-called modern theology, the religious socialism of Leonhard Regaz (1868–1945), the dialectic theology of Karl Barth (1886–1968) and Emil Brunner (1889–1966).

With its multilingual population (German, French, Italian, Romansch, Spanish, Portuguese) and its neutrality, Switzerland is a privileged location for international organizations, philanthropy, and ecumenical relations. The International Red Cross was founded by Henri Dunant (1863); the WORLD COUNCIL OF CHURCHES was established in Geneva in 1948.

MARC R. SPINDLER

Symbol, Symbolism. A symbol is something used to stand for something, such as an olive branch representing peace. Recent studies in human cognition have demonstrated that when we categorize objects in a taxonomy, there is one level that is more basic than the others. This "basic level" is the most abstract level at which we can form images. We can form an image of a *dog* or a *cat,* but not of the more abstract concept of an *animal.* The basic level is also the level at which we experience life. We interact with our pets as *dogs* and *cats,* not as *animals.* That we experience life at the basic level underlies our need to use the imagery of symbols to express more abstract concepts.

This need to use symbols for abstract concepts also makes us prone to IDOLATRY. We have a propensity to visualize the object of our worship, to create images of our gods. It is quite possible, therefore, that when God responded to Moses' request for a name to give to the idolatrous Egyptians, he gave Moses "I AM" so as to preclude them from representing him by an image (Rom. 1:23). Therefore, we need to keep in mind that the symbols we use to represent gospel truths have the potential of replacing those truths.

When people create a symbol to represent an object, the symbol usually bears a resemblance to that object. When a symbol closely resembles an object, however, it is a small step to the belief that the symbol mirrors the real world, that it exists apart from human creativity, and that it has inherent meaning.

The belief that symbols have inherent meanings that must be discovered underlies the practice of magic, divination, numerology, and astrology. It may also underlie the behavior of those who forbid others to use certain symbols because they regard those symbols as inherently evil. A recent example in the United States is the public pressure put on Procter and Gamble to drop their logo of the woman and the stars.

Many people regard symbols as having assigned meanings agreed on by a given society. The fact that the meanings are assigned by a given community not only allows a symbol to serve in communication within a society but also militates against the casual use of symbols for INTERCULTURAL COMMUNICATION. In one case, the introduction of baptismal names to symbolize new life in Christ was reinterpreted as a ruse to elude Satan, because Satan recognized people only by their prebaptismal names, but their new, baptismal names were the secret ones written in the Lamb's book of life (Rev. 2:17; 3:5). Therefore, we need to exercise care in using symbols to communicate gospel truths interculturally.

That the swastika arouses strong emotions points out that symbols are powerful because they are interpreted holistically as a gestalt. The sight of a swastika by a victim of the Holocaust transcends anti-Semitism to invoke the gestalt of the Holocaust with all the experiences and emotions of the perpetrators, the victims, and the complacent third parties. The viewers' emotional responses are grounded in the associations the symbol brings to their minds. Therefore, we need to keep in mind that simple symbols can represent very complex gestalts.

KENNETH A. McELHANON

Bibliography. J. Heisig, *ER*, 13:198–208; P. G. Hiebert, *Cultural Anthropology*; G. Lakoff, *Women, Fire, and Dangerous Things: What Categories Reveal about the Mind.*

Syncretism. Blending of one idea, practice, or attitude with another. Traditionally among Christians it has been used of the replacement or dilution of the essential truths of the gospel through the incorporation of non-Christian elements. Examples range from Western materialism to Asian and African animistic beliefs incorporated into the church. Syncretism of some form has been seen everywhere the church has existed. We are naive to think that eliminating the negatives of syncretism is easily accomplished.

To examine practices for syncretistic tendencies, we must first use a phenomenological approach in which we simply uncover what is actually happening or being taught. Built on that, we use theological and cultural analysis to understand what is happening. Finally, we evaluate what we have discovered in light of biblical truth. As a replacement of essential elements of the gospel with alternative religious practices or understanding, syncretism must be exposed and challenged. The means by which this is done are critical, and must be culturally informed.

Biblical Discussion. Case studies of syncretism are found throughout the Bible. Israel, forsaking the command to love God alone (Deut. 5:1–6:5), borrowed from the Canaanites ideas such as idolatry (Judg. 2:19; Ps. 106:35–39), shrine prostitution (1 Kings 14:24), and witchcraft (2 Kings 17:16–17). The attitude of syncretism is captured in 2 Kings 17:41: "Even while these people were worshipping the LORD, they were serving their idols." Old Testament exemplars who fought syncretism include the prophets as well as David, Hezekiah, Josiah, Nehemiah, and Ezra.

At the time of the New Testament, the domination of Rome intensified the possibilities of syncretism. Perhaps the most significant issue dealt with in the early church was that of the nature of Gentile inclusion in the Christian community (Acts 15; Gal. 2). The author of Hebrews wrote to Christians who were tempted to return to the Law (Heb. 5:11–6:12; 10:19–39). We also see warnings against syncretistic tendencies throughout the Epistles (e.g., 1 Cor. 10:20; 2 Cor. 11:13–15; Gal. 1:6–9; 3:1–6; Col. 2:8–23; 1 Tim. 1:3; 6:3; 2 Peter 2:1; 1 John 4:1–6).

Throughout the centuries since the New Testament era, the church has constantly wrestled over the issues of culture in relationship to Christian commitment (Visser 't Hooft).

Modern Discussion. Many scholars today challenge the need to define syncretism in its negative traditional sense. The meaning of the term has broadened to a more neutral concept of interpenetration of two or more paradigms. In this sense, since all churches are culture-based, every church is syncretistic. Such a broad definition, however, results in a term that loses useful analytic meaning.

A second significant issue is that the person or people who define syncretism are those who are in power. Practices which are threatening may be labeled syncretistic simply because they threaten the established order. This highlights the need for hermeneutical communities comprised of people of various cultures who together examine the contemporary phenomena under question in light of the biblical worldview.

A final issue is that all churches *are* in some sense syncretistic. The human heart regularly manufactures idols which find homes in the churches of the people who generate them. No church in any culture is free of the accretions of culture, and none of us is as objective in seeing syncretism within our own culture as we would like to think we are.

Suggested Guidelines. While "syncretism" does not appear in the Bible, it expresses a biblical concept. The broadening of discussion on syncretism in scholarly discussion has resulted in some observing that the Bible itself is syncretistic. Such use of the term masks the biblical concept of gospel truth relevant to all cultures being normative for all Christians at all times.

Biblically speaking, syncretistic ideas and practices are wrong because they violate the first commandment. In saying this we are not ignoring the complexities raised by recent hermeneutical discussions. There are convoluted interpretive issues which the worldwide church must tackle, but we cannot do so if we turn from the normative nature of the Bible as the cornerstone for discussion of the faith.

Because of the convoluted nature of culture, the declaration of syncretism in a particular setting cannot be simply left in the hands of expatriate missionaries. The local community must be empowered to biblically evaluate their own practices and teachings. Missionaries must learn to trust that indigenous peoples are able to discern God's leading and trust God to develop and maintain biblically founded and culturally relevant FAITH and PRAXIS in each local context. Finally, Christians of every culture must engage in genuine partnership with Christians of other cultures, since often the outsider's help is needed to enable local believers, blinded by culture and familiarity, to see that which contravenes scriptural adherence to the first commandment.

A. SCOTT MOREAU

SEE ALSO Christo-Paganism.

Bibliography. C. Colpe, *ER* 14:218–27; J. D. Gort, H. M. Vroom, R. Fernhout, A. Wessels, eds., *Dialogue and Syncretism: An Interdisciplinary Approach;* H. Kraemer, *Religion and the Christian Faith;* R. J. Schreiter, *IBMR* 17:2 (1993): 50–53; W. A. Visser 't Hooft, *No Other Name.*

Syria *(Est. 2000 pop.: 17,329,000; 185,180 sq. km. [71,498 sq. mi.]).* Syria experienced some of the earliest missionary efforts in the first century. Antioch became a leading sending center and an important area producing many of the earlier church fathers. One only needs to think of the tremendous influence of John Chrysostom on modern commentaries to see the scope of influence of Syria. From Edessa, modern Urfa, the church moved east to Afghanistan, China, and Mongolia as well as south through Iraq to Saudi Arabia.

Much theological controversy weakened the witness of the church in Syria. In addition she was always restive under Byzantine rule. Many Christian villages as well as leaders welcomed and even plotted with the Arab Muslim armies whom they felt would liberate them. That freedom was short lived as the development of Muslim thinking led to rather stringent policies that deprived them of many basic rights. Christian communities exist all over Syria embracing the various theological positions apparent in the struggles of the early centuries of the church's presence.

In the latter part of the nineteenth century the Presbyterians came to Damascus and established branches throughout the country. The CHRISTIAN AND MISSIONARY ALLIANCE sent a number of excellent missionaries and there remain many groups in that communion. A group of British women started a mission that for nearly a century sent out only women missionaries. This has now expanded to include men. These groups stressed schools, camps, and evangelistic outreach through literature and personal contacts. With the change of government in the latter half of the twentieth century most Westerners had to leave the country. By then some Baptist, Nazarene, and other groups had been started. A strong church exists in Damascus and good branches of several denominations are able to continue to function. It is nearly impossible for a typical Western missionary to be granted permission to work because of political factors more than religious factors. Yet during the last decade of the twentieth century many keen expatriates have had excellent opportunities for witness and ministry. Some are students, while others are teachers. With the strong impact of both radio and TV as well as Bible distribution, Theological Education by Extension and general interaction with Arab believers in adjacent countries, there is promise of real expansion and development in the immediate future.

GEORGE E. KELSEY

Bibliography. R. B. Betts, *Christians in the Arab East;* S. Moffett, *A History of Christianity in Asia;* W. H. Storm, *Whither Arabia?;* J. S. Trimingham, *Christianity Among The Arabs;* S. M. Zwemer, *Heirs to the Prophets.*

Systematic Theology. The foundational, organized, and comprehensive reflection by Christians on the faith of the church; systematic theology seeks to answer questions like "What do we believe?" "Why do we believe that and not something else?" "On what grounds is our belief justified?" "What is the relationship between the various concepts that we believe?" and "How do we articulate that belief so that it may have appropriate meaning in today's contexts?" Wayne Grudem gives a concise definition: "Systematic theology is any study that answers the question, "What does the whole Bible teach us today about any given topic?" (1994, 21). Stanley Grenz emphasizes the missional aspect of systematic theology: "Theology (is) a practical discipline. It is the intellectual reflection on the faith we share as the believing community within a specific cultural context. But it has as its goal the application of our faith commitment to living as the people of God in our world" (1993, 17–18).

Systematic theologians differ in their approach to the discipline. Some see God himself as the object of study, while others understand their work as reflection on the knowledge of God's revelation. They may differ in the sources they draw from for that knowledge: the Bible, Christ, the church, the history of dogma, or the preaching of the church.

Systematic theology builds on biblical theology and historical theology. Biblical theology has to do with the identification and understanding of the theology of the authors and books of the Bible in their cultural and historical contexts. Historical theology has to do with knowing the development of the church's doctrines in the way they were formed during the history of the church. Systematic theology seeks to find a way to bring together the testimony of the biblical authors with the contemporary questions of Christians in their contexts. Different traditions and various systematic theologians have built their systematic theologies upon a number of different foundations: the teachings of the church, the Bible, concepts of God's revelation, the Holy Spirit, or (especially, since Schleiermacher) humanity and its intellectual abilities. "None of these can serve as foundation and norm in abstraction from the others" (Berkhof, 1985 , 74–86).

During the first three centuries after Christ, systematic theology was inherently missional. The theologians of the church were primarily involved in APOLOGETICS, that is, the carefully reasoned presentation of the truth of the gospel to people in their contexts who were not yet Christians. By the fifth century, however, the missional character of theology began to be lost and systematic theology became increasingly an introverted activity, used to justify why the church's doctrine was right and why options offered by other Christians were wrong. The disciples and followers of the sixteenth-century Reformers essentially followed a similar dynamic, using theology as a tool to prove why their church was right and other traditions were wrong. Thus the missionary dimension of systematic theology—the presentation of the truth of the gospel to those who were not yet Christian—was lost. Lately, the missionary aspect of systematic theology is being recovered through a movement known as CONTEXTUALIZATION.

Since the 1960s there has been a growing realization that all theology is influenced by the context in which the theologians find themselves. Thus all theologies are seen as contextual. Harvie Conn says, "The contextual character of all theology . . . has been misplaced, buried under the weight of the Western respect for the expert (in this case the theologian). . . . The pastoral dimensions of theology are befogged by the church's understanding of theology as a schooling science, abstract, done by experts, yielding universal principles applicable to all times and cultures. The concrete relation of theology to the life of the people of God remains obscured. Inevitably, the focus of such theology remains fixed around the traditional (themes) of anthropology, Christology, soteriology, etc., (themes) reflecting thematic arrangements for the study of theology as it has, in its past, addressed Western contexts and Western worldviews. . . . To what part of the historical tradition . . . will (Christians in the Two-Thirds World) go to find answers for such problems as ancestor worship, the power structures of animism, (matters of spiritual power encounter), and the Muslim misconstructions of Jesus as the Son of God" (Conn, 1984, 299–300)?

During the past hundred years or so theologians and missiologists have struggled over where to place mission in the curriculum of traditional theological reflection. Jongeneel asks, "Does mission, *dogmatically*-speaking, belong to the doctrine of God the Father, of God the Son, and/or of God the Holy Spirit (in relation to the three major parts of the Apostles' Creed)? Or is mission merely an appendix to the doctrine of vocation? Or is it an important issue in ecclesiology? Does mission *ethically*-speaking, belong to the so-called general part of the discipline (principles of ethics): is it good, a virtue, and/or a duty? . . . Or does it belong to a particular part (for instance, social ethics)" (Jongeneel, 1997, 11)? One thing is clear: systematic theology that is not missional is not true to the biblical portrayal of a loving, self-revealing, covenanting God who "so loved the world that he gave his only Son" (John 3:16). And missiology that does not reflect carefully, deeply, and systematically on the nature, mission, and purpose of God may be church extension or expansion of empire—but it is not participation by the church of Jesus Christ in God's mission through the empowerment of the Holy Spirit.

Orlando Costas suggested a way to preserve the missionary dimension of theology: build it into one's definition. "Theology is the reflective activity of the Christian Church that tries to understand the mystery of faith, describe its implications for life, and make visible its mission in the world" (cited in Kirk, 1996, 7).

CHARLES VAN ENGEN

SEE ALSO Theological Method AND Theological Systems.

Bibliography. K. Barth, *Church Dogmatics;* H. Berkhof, *Christian Faith* (1979); idem, *Introduction to the Study of Dogmatics* (1985); D. Bloesch, *A Theology of Word and Spirit;* G. C. Berkouwer, *Studies in Dogmatics;* H. Conn, *Eternal Word and Changing Worlds;* G. Lewis and B. Demarest, *Integrative Theology;* T. Finger, *Christian Theology;* S. Grenz, *Revisioning Evangelical Theology* (1993); idem, *Theology for the Community of God* (1994); W. Grudem, *Systematic Theology: An Introduction to Biblical Doctrine;* P. Jewett, *God, Creation and Revelation;* J. A. B. Jongeneel, *Philosophy, Science, and Theology of Mission in the 19th and 20th Centuries: A Missiological Encyclopedia,* Part II: *Missionary Theology;* J. A. Kirk, *The Mission of Theology and Theology as Mission;* H. Küng and D. Tracy, eds., *Paradigm Change in Theology;* A. McGrath, *Christian Theology;* O. Weber, *Foundations of Dogmatics.*

Szabó, Aladá (1862–1944). Hungarian revivalist and missions promoter. Born in a countryside village, Szabó never lost his passion for inflaming the hearts of the grassroot masses of people who were of ordinary heritage. In 1880 he entered the Reformed Theological Academy at the University of Budapest. One year later he met Andrew Moody, a Scottish missionary working among the Jewish population in Hungary. Moody took Szabó under his care and fanned into flame the passion for mission which was to characterize Szabó's ministry.

During his life, Szabó sought renewal of the Hungarian church through crossing three barriers: nationalism, confessionalism, and feudalism. Nationalism kept the church focus geographically inward, seeking nation building as inextricably tied to kingdom building; Szabó encouraged a vision for the entire world. Lutheran and Reformed confessionalism vied competitively for the hearts of the Hungarian people; Szabó worked interdenominationally. As a result of a feudalistic mentality the clerical leaders ignored the needs of the masses, who were increasingly being attracted to sects; Szabó compassionately reached out to them and mobilized them for the missionary effort.

Though never himself a missionary, he is a key figure in the history of Hungarian missionary work. Kool relates, "Szabó became the herald of the [Hungarian] 20th century foreign mission movement by 'contextualizing' the Scottish Puritan and German Pietistic traditions and making them part of Hungarian theological thinking" (1993, 157).

A. Scott Moreau

Bibliography. A. M. Kool, *God Moves in a Mysterious Way: The Hungarian Protestant Foreign Mission Movement (1756–1951).*

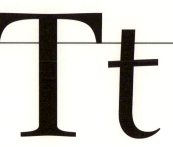

Taboo. The word "taboo" is of Tongan origin *(tabu)* and designates a person, thing, or action that is forbidden due to its sacred or supernatural character. The primary function of the category of taboo is that of protection, and this usually occurs on three levels: social, economic, and religious. Taboos possess functional purpose rather than moral value.

On the social level, chiefs and rulers, along with their property, are designated taboo to protect the monolithic social structure of the tribe or group. Economically, certain animals are designated taboo to protect them from misuse by the people (conservation). For instance, the Maori of New Zealand declared digging up sweet potatoes before they were ready to be cooked and eaten a taboo to counter greed and waste. On the other hand, certain foods (pork and shellfish) have been declared taboo to protect people from disease through improper preparation of the foods.

Religiously, taboos have often been created to accommodate fear of the unknown, such as the birth of twins in animistic settings (namely, only animals have multiple offspring). A dualistic worldview is often characteristic of a taboo-oriented belief system. Thus, taboo is not so much concerned with what is morally right or wrong but rather with what functions to keep away offense. Such worldviews are often related to ancestor or spirit worship, and the offense associated with the taboo can extend to the nonphysical spirit world as well. While unquestioning loyalty with respect to the taboo is required of the tribal members, great responsibility rests with the SHAMAN or religious leader not to lead the group into error that might result in the negative effects of the offense upon the group. "Salvation" then consists in maintaining a healthy balance (tension) between "good" and "bad" taboos.

It is essential that missionaries working in cultures in which taboos are prominent understand the nature and function of the taboos. Such understanding and sensitivity will not only prevent unnecessary offense, but it will provide valuable insights into the basic values and fears of the culture. Biblical answers to the fears underlying taboos can then be suggested.

CLINT AKINS

SEE ALSO Primal Religions.

Bibliography. S. Ruud, *Taboo*.

Taiwan. *See* CHINA (Taiwan).

Tajikistan *(Est. 2000 pop.: 6,973,000; 143,100 sq. km. [55,251 sq. mi.]).* In Central Asia, Tajikistan is the southernmost republic of the former Soviet Union and also the poorest. Unlike most other Central Asian peoples, the ethnic Tajiks, who make up 60 percent of the population, are of Iranian rather than Turkic stock. There is also a sizable Uzbek minority, making up nearly 25 percent of the population. While over 80 percent of the population is nominally Sunni Muslim, animistic practices and ancient Zoroastrian traditions dominate the people's everyday lives. Evangelicals make up well under 0.5 percent of the population, with most being Slavic or German. However, several hundred Tajiks have come to Christ, and a number of Tajik congregations have been established, especially in and around the northern city of Khojent.

RAYMOND P. PRIGODICH

SEE ALSO Commonwealth of Independent States.

Tambaram Conference (1938). By the time the INTERNATIONAL MISSIONARY COUNCIL met at Tambaram (Madras), India, in 1938, the global spread of the Christian church had become clear for all to see, for representatives of the younger churches provided more than half the official delegates for the first time at an ecumenical conference. As they discovered one another, more than one delegate also discovered what it was to become a world Christian.

The location of the conference, which received wide publicity, had to be moved from China to India because of the outbreak of war in China. Within the conference, however, fellowship between the Chinese and Japanese delegations offered a powerful witness to how the Christian faith can overcome barriers of nationalism. With many delegates experiencing the movement from mission to church, it was not unnatural that they should seek a major discussion of the nature of the church. The report of the conference was, in fact, entitled "The World Mission of the Church." But there was a context to that mission. Thus the hopeful signs in the life of the church were set over against a world that seemed to be on the edge of catastrophe. This was recognized by the conference in its identification of the rise of a militant "new paganism" demanding quasi-religious devotion from its followers. Out of pastoral concern for Christians in the Soviet Union, the Axis countries, and Japan, no specific situation was identified. The need to complete the evangelistic task and to relate it to the new world situation came together in the conference message: evangelism was the task "of the whole church for the whole world. . . . Nothing in the present world situation invalidates the gospel. . . . World peace will never be achieved without world evangelization." It has been said that "while the JERUSALEM CONFERENCE (1928) put the center of mission in Christ, the Madras [Tambaram] Conference took the logical step of calling on the whole church, as the Body of Christ, to be through all its members the bearer of the gospel in every place."

Formally the sections of the conference were concerned with the authority of the faith; the growing church; evangelism; the life of the church; the economic basis of the church and church–state relations. The first section was heavily influenced by the work of a professor of the sociology of religion from Leiden. HENDRIK KRAEMER's *The Christian Message in a Non-Christian World*, with its insistence on "biblical realism," commissioned by the Council, had been published just prior to the conference. *The Economic and Social Environment of the Younger Churches*, edited by J. Merle Davis, influenced other aspects of the conference.

A clear christocentric focus enabled the conference to tackle difficult issues of COLONIALISM and NATIONALISM, the relations between Western mission agencies and the emerging Asian churches, and the attitude of the churches to Asian SYNCRETISM. The need for some formalization of the link between the IMC and the about-to-be formed WORLD COUNCIL OF CHURCHES was already becoming obvious.

JOHN A. Y. BRIGGS

SEE ALSO World Council of Churches Conferences.

Bibliography. Conference Papers: The Church Faces the World, The World Mission of the Church; IMC Meeting at Tambaram, Madras, [The Madras Series]; K. S. Latourette, *HEM* I:366–69.

Tanzania *(Est. 2000 pop.: 34,074,000; 945,087 sq. km. [364,898 sq. mi.]).* The United Republic of Tanzania lies just south of the Equator on the east coast of Africa. Its central plateau, averaging over a half mile in altitude, sustains magnificent herds of African wildlife but due to aridity and insect-borne diseases, large areas are not suitable for modern agriculture. Therefore the more than 34 million people are clustered in the fertile lands in highland regions, around the great lakes of Victoria and Tanganyika, and in the cities, notable Dar Es Salaam on the Indian Ocean and Mwanza on Lake Victoria. Only 5 percent of the land is productive, tilled by 85 percent of the population.

Prior to the coming of Bantu peoples from the Congo basin, the area was inhabited by an aboriginal people referred to as Khoisans. They were hunters and gatherers, employing a unique click language. Over a thousand years ago Cushitic-speaking herders and Nilotic peoples from the north entered the region, inhabiting areas suitable for cattle grazing. About the same time the great migration of Bantu-speaking agriculturists from the Congo basin settled in lands suitable to their lifestyles. Today 90 percent of the population is Bantu, 6 percent Cushitic and Nilotic, with Khoisans a mere fraction of a percent.

Prior to the coming of Christianity over a hundred years ago the groups followed ancient folk religions in which the ancestral spirits played a pivotal role. A small minority of coastal people embraced Islam. Muslims from the Arabian region settled along the coast and in the offshore island of Zanzibar in the seventeenth century where they plied their trade in ivory, slaves, and cloves. Around these Arabic settlements grew a culture that spoke a Bantu language with many Arabic words and concepts. This is the Swahili language, which is now widespread across eastern Africa. Islam and the Kiswahili language spread along the trade routes, as far inland as the great lakes of Tanganyika and Victoria.

Tanzania was not impacted by the Portuguese or Spanish mission efforts of the sixteenth and seventeenth centuries, probably because Tanzania was under the sovereignty of the Arab rulers and traders. Because it was an important center of the slave trade which sold African slaves in Eastern nations, Zanzibar became the focus of modern Christian missions. British and German missionaries aided in the ABOLITIONIST MOVEMENT. After a series of meetings of European nations (1895, 1900), Germany assumed political control over Tanzania, which it held until the conclusion of World War I. The League of Nations then requested the United Kingdom to hold Tanzania as a Protectorate, not a colony. The United Kingdom fulfilled its mandate and granted independence to Tanzania in 1961. In 1963 the former Tanganyika and Zanzibar (which also gained independence) joined, thus the name Tanzania.

While under German control, Tanzania received missionaries from the German Lutheran Church, the Anglican Church, a variety of Roman Catholic orders, and Scandinavian and American evangelical missions. These mission agencies utilized medical services, education, and development efforts to spread Christianity. Almost all of the 120 plus ethnolinguistic peoples in Tanzania received some services from the mission agencies and in many groups the church flourished. Today only a few pockets, mainly aboriginal peoples, are considered "unreached." The Bible had been translated in 18 of the 131 languages but vast sections of the population can speak and read Kiswahili. Almost all of the citizens of the land use both their tribal language and Kiswahili. Tanzania is now about 50 percent Christian, 30 percent Muslim, and 20 percent followers of AFRICAN TRADITIONAL RELIGIONS. Tanzania has begun to send out missionaries of their own. Christian youth movements thrive and the evangelical unity is commendable. The church confronts poverty, disease, and lack of essential services.

Tanzania, one of the poorest nations in Africa, embraced a modified form of socialism, Ujamaa, from 1969 to 1992, which served to further impoverish the nation. The nation has experienced steady but painful economic growth since 1992, utilizing open-market policies to stimulate investments and local development. The nation is seeking to exploit, once again, its vast resources of gold and diamonds while increasing food production.

DONALD R. JACOBS

Bibliography. P. Collier, S. Radwan, and S. Wangwe, *Labor and Poverty in Rural Tanzania: Ujamaa and Rural Development in the United Republic of Tanzania;* M. Hodd, *East Africa Handbook: With Kenya, Tanzania, Uganda and Ethiopia,* 4th ed.; T. P. Ofcansky, R. Yeager, and L. S. Kurtz, *Historical Dictionary of Tanzania;* S. Rugumamu, *Lethal Aid: The Illusion of Socialism and Self-Reliance in Tanzania;* A. M. Tripp, *Changing the Rules: The Politics of Liberalization and Urban Informal Economy in Tanzania.*

Taoist, Taoism. Taoism, along with Confucianism and Buddhism, is one of the three major philosophical and religious systems in China. Although his historicity has been questioned, Lao-tze, a sixth-century B.C. contemporary of Confucius, is regarded as the founder of Taoism. Lao-tze had no interest in Confucian teachings on social conventions and ethical principles, advocating instead a return to the primitive simplicity of nature.

The *Tao-te-ching,* the key text of Taoism and traditionally said to be authored by Lao-tze, presents the Tao as the ultimate principle and source of all things. The Tao is utterly transcendent and defies all linguistic description, for "the Tao that can be described is not the eternal Tao" (*Tao-te-ching,* ch. 1). It is formless and impersonal, yet eternal and present everywhere. Immaterial, it is nevertheless the fountainhead of all material things. "The Tao engenders the one, the one engenders the two, the two engenders the three, the three engenders the myriad things" (ch. 42). All things flow from the Tao and return ultimately to the Tao. The Tao is both one and many, transcendent and immanent, being and nonbeing, action and nonaction, strong and weak. All opposites and contrasts are harmonized in the Tao.

Epistemologically, philosophical Taoism stresses inner intuitive enlightenment more than discursive reasoning. Thus a person with deep understanding can fathom the entire universe without leaving home. When one is in tune with the Tao, one sees that becoming and change happen only within the phenomenal world. Ultimately all differentiation between the universe and the individual disappears as the two are essentially one. This leads to the search for a mystical union with nature characteristic of religious Taoism.

Taoism emphasizes a return to a state of primitive simplicity and spontaneity, an original state of innocence. It assumes a latent goodness inherent in human nature [*te*]. What is, is good. Chuang-tse, a fourth-century B.C. Taoist, advocated following the heart's natural inclination since it reflects an originally good nature. The heart is to be one's teacher. Since one is born with a good nature, there is no need to strive to be good—the moment one consciously strives to be good, one deviates from the Tao. "It is only when one has lost the Tao that he would settle for virtue, it is only when one has lost virtue that he would settle for humanity [*jen*], it is only when one has lost humanity that he would settle for righteousness [*yi*], it is only when he has lost righteousness that he would settle for propriety [*li*]" (ch. 58). Rejecting common social principles and conventions, Lao-tze advocated nonstriving, contentment, meekness, modesty, and simplicity as ethical ideals.

Taoism called for an extreme laissez-faire approach to government, stressing noninterference. The analogy with water was used. Although water is gentle and passive, it is the strongest and most resilient force in nature, opening passages in the hardest rock and accomplishing difficult tasks without brute force. Similarly, the best government is that which rules through noninterference, just "letting it be." For it is by following natural inclinations that original goodness is achieved.

Although philosophical Taoism had influenced Chinese culture for centuries, it was not until the second century that religious Taoism became an institutional religion. A blend of Taoist philosophy, ying-yang, and folk religion, religious Taoism emphasizes mysticism, personal freedom, and the yearning for immortality. Adherents seek freedom from all restraints—whether physical, social, or mental—culminating in an immortality that transcends life and death. Chang Tao-ling (2nd cent.), credited as the founder of religious Taoism, claimed for himself the title "Heavenly Master." He held that there is a supreme god ruling over the pantheon of deities, a heavenly system somewhat similar to the earthly governmental bureaucracy.

The immediate objective of Taoist religion is to obtain health, longevity, and well-being in this life, whereas the ultimate goal is to become one with nature, living as the immortals. The immortals are said to be beings who have obtained total freedom from all restraints of the physical world. Free from even the law of gravity, they float in the air like feathers, wandering among scenic mountains and streams without a care in the world.

The basic means for attaining immortality is through internal and external alchemy along with other occult practices. Internal alchemy regulates the vital forces [*ch'i*] through yoga and breathing exercises so that harmony is achieved between the individual and the universe. External alchemy involves taking elixirs such as pure cinnabar. On a popular level, religious Taoism involves elaborate ceremonial rituals, exorcism, seances, *fengsue* (lit. wind and water, and attempt to harmonize with nature), fortune telling, astrology, and belief in deities who can bring good fortune or inflict harm, depending on their treatment.

As an institutional religion Taoism has today lost much of its status due to corruption within the priesthood as well as the impact of modernization. But one should not conclude that it is no longer significant in Chinese culture. Its influence has permeated many aspects of daily life, and in recent years there appears to be a resurgence of religious Taoism, especially among the educated classes in Taiwan, Hong Kong, and Southeast Asia.

JOHN D. L. HSU

Bibliography. J. Ching and H. Kung, *Christianity and Chinese Religions*; W. T. de Bary, W. Chan, and B. Watson, *Sources of Chinese Tradition*, vol. 1; Y. Fung, *History of Chinese Philosophy*; Y. Lin, ed., *The Wisdom of Laot-se*; K. Lo, *History of Chinese Philosophy*; B. H. Wang, *Philosophy of Lao-tse*.

Taylor, (James) Hudson (1832–1905). English missionary to China and founder of the China Inland Mission (now OVERSEAS MISSIONARY FELLOWSHIP). Born in Barnsley, England, where his pharmacist father was a Methodist local preacher, he was converted at age seventeen and set his heart on going to China. He even interrupted medical studies at the London Hospital to go there in 1854 under the short-lived China Evangelization Society, but soon committed himself to an independent ministry. Failing health forced him to return to England in 1860. There he worked on Bible translation, completed medical studies, and in 1865 published *China: Its Spiritual Needs and Claims.* Having found no society willing to sponsor him, he established the China Inland Mission, its candidates selected less for educational than for spiritual qualifications. In 1866 sixteen of them sailed with Taylor for itinerant work in a land where "a million a month [were] dying without God."

Taylor's fervor was matched by pioneering audacity. He adopted Chinese dress and customs, paired foreign missionaries with national Christians, directly solicited no funds ("Jehovah-jireh" was a favorite word), and saw the establishment of churches as less important than the task of presenting the gospel to as many as possible before the Lord's return. No distant board controlled the Mission; decisions were taken on the field. By 1891 Taylor led some 640 workers, but his influence and his principles extended far beyond CIM. He mobilized and motivated people for worldwide mission.

He lost two wives and four children to disease and famine. Soon after seeing seventy-nine colleagues and children slain in the 1900 Boxer Rebellion, ill health led to his retirement. In 1905 he undertook a last visit to his beloved China, and died there at Changsha.

J. D. DOUGLAS

Bibliography. D. Bacon, *The Influence of Hudson Taylor on the Faith Missions Movement*; A. J. Broomhall, *Hudson Taylor and China's Open Century*; J. C. Pollock, *Hudson Taylor and Maria: Pioneers in China*; R. Steer, *J. Hudson Taylor: A Man in Christ.*

Taylor, John Vernon (1914–). English author, missionary statesman, and missionary to Uganda. After taking a degree in English at the University of Cambridge, Taylor studied theology and was ordained an Anglican priest: his subsequent career has been spent entirely in the service of the Anglican Church. He taught at Bishop Tucker Theological College in Uganda for ten years, then took on the role of general secretary of the evangelical CHURCH MISSIONARY SOCIETY (1963–75), and finished his formal career as bishop of Winchester (1975–85) in Britain. He has published prolifically, from the 1950s to the 1990s, often on missions topics; *The Growth of the Church in Buganda* (1958), *Christians of the Copperbelt: the Growth of the Church in Northern Rhodesia* (1961), *The Primal Vision: Christian Presence Amid African Religions* (1963), and his widely read *The Go-Between God* (1972) are among these books. Taylor is most significant perhaps, to the development of Protestant missionary thought, as an evangelical spokesman for genuine openness to God's ongoing work in human society. Thus in a period of rapid global change and conservative reaction he has advocated the search for divine truths in other religions and the benefits of Pentecostalism; he has also argued for the formation of countercultural Christian communities of witness, the creation of a just world economy, and a broader interpretation of mission and missionaries—all without sacrificing the uniqueness of the Christian gospel or the distinctness of the missionary enterprise. "True theology," he wrote in 1994, "must inevitably be incarnational."

PAUL H. FRIESEN

Bibliography. J. V. Taylor, *The Go-Between God: The Holy Spirit and the Christian Mission;* T. Yates, *IBMR* 12 (1988): 11–15.

Taylor, Kenneth Nathaniel (1917–). American Bible translator and publisher. Born in Portland, Oregon, he received his education at Wheaton College, Illinois (BS, 1938), Dallas Theological Seminary (1943), and Northern Baptist Theological Seminary (ThM, 1944). Although ordained by the Central Bible Church, Portland, in 1944 for pastoral work, Taylor's lifelong interest in communicating the gospel in print was with him from the beginning. He served as editor of *His* Magazine, worked with Good News Publishers, directed Moody Bible Institute's Literature Mission, as well as the Moody Press, until founding his own publishing company, Tyndale House Publishers, in 1963.

Taylor is best remembered for his paraphrase of the Bible, begun in 1962 as *Living Letters* and completed in 1971 as the *Living Bible*. This was later totally revised as the *New Living Translation* (1996), by a team of ninety evangelical scholars under Taylor's direction. Taylor has also written numerous popular and children's books.

Taylor's interest in missions was also lifelong, and he was instrumental in founding Evangelical Literature Overseas (1953) and Short Terms Abroad (1965). His current involvement is by way of the Tyndale House Foundation and Living Bibles International, an organization whose purpose is to create Living Bibles in the major languages of the world for more effective communication of the gospel. Taylor's personal involvement has him connected in one capacity or another with Euroevangelism of Canada; Daystar, Nairobi; Hellenic Missionary Union, Athens, Greece; Middle East Media, North America; Fellowship of Christian Unions, Kampala, Uganda; and the Ethiopian Evangelical Christian Association.

WALTER A. ELWELL

Bibliography. K. N. Taylor, *My Life: A Guided Tour.*

Taylor, William (1821–1902). American author and missionary in Africa and Latin America. Taylor served as the second Methodist Episcopal missionary in California (1849–56) before embarking on a global career, during which crucial roles were played in the development of Methodism in Australia, India, England, the Caribbean, Latin America, and Africa. On the basis of his experience in South Africa, he developed (1866) the theory of "Pauline Missions." The central themes of the theory were that the results of mission were equal with all of the sending churches and that they should be self-supporting, self-governing, and self-propagating (*see* INDIGENOUS CHURCHES). The most complete statement of this theory was *Pauline Methods of Missionary Work* (Philadelphia, 1879).

After being forced by the Methodist Episcopal Missionary Society to cease functioning as a missionary, he went to Chile, where he established the Methodist Episcopal Church. Seeing the need for more "Self-Supporting" missionaries, he established a sending agency, the "Building and Transit Fund," to help Wesleyan/Holiness missionaries get to the mission field. Despite the antagonism of the Missionary Society, he was elected "Missionary Bishop" in 1884 and sent to Africa, where he established churches in Liberia, Congo, Angola, and Mozambique. Taylor became a model and inspiration for much of Wesleyan/Holiness missions. Many of the "Taylor" missionaries became Pentecostal after 1906, and he served as a theorist for early Pentecostal missions, especially in Europe.

DAVID BUNDY

SEE ALSO Wesleyan/Holiness Missions.

Bibliography. D. Bundy, *Methodist History* 27:4 (1989): 197–210; idem, *Methodist History* 28:1 (1989): 2–21; idem, *ML*, pp. 461–68; J. Paul, *The Soul Digger: or The Life and Times of William Taylor.*

Teaching English to Speakers of Other Languages (TESOL). The worldwide demand for English language instruction has made the teaching of English as a foreign or second language a significant strategy in contemporary missions. This demand is due to a number of factors, including the influence of English-based media and technological information, the widespread use of English for conducting international trade, and the desire for higher education in English-speaking countries. Since, in one estimate, 80 percent of the world's scientific and technical information is published in English, the language has become important in many countries as a means to modernization and participation in the global community.

Mission organizations have responded to the demand for English instruction in a variety of ways. English language teaching has allowed Christian workers (often referred to as tentmaking missionaries) to gain access to areas of the world where it is difficult for missionaries to obtain visas. In countries with fewer restrictions,

English language specialists often work in tandem with missionaries and national Christians to conduct evangelism and establish churches. In addition, the increase in non-Western missionaries has created a demand within the missions community for English language instructors to work in contexts such as theological institutions and missionary training centers.

In general, teaching English as a foreign language (TEFL) refers to instruction in countries where English is not the native language, while teaching English as a second language (TESL) refers to instruction in English-speaking countries. A common umbrella acronym is TESOL, "teaching English to speakers of other languages."

History. The association of TEFL with missions became prominent during the second half of the nineteenth century with the establishment of educational institutions in areas under British colonial influence. In countries such as India, Myanmar (Burma), Egypt, and China, these mission-based schools provided English instruction in several different forms. Some schools were English-medium, with English serving as the language of instruction, while in others English was taught primarily as a foreign language. In late-nineteenth-century Japan, where evangelism was prohibited but English was in great demand, English language instruction in mission-sponsored schools became an important means for missionary access.

A large-scale survey conducted prior to the 1910 WORLD MISSIONARY CONFERENCE in Edinburgh found that English language instruction was widespread in mission-sponsored educational institutions across the Far East, the Indian subcontinent, sub-Saharan Africa, and the Middle East. Nevertheless, the teaching of English was heatedly debated at Edinburgh and other early missionary conventions. The greatest concerns were that English language instruction would tend to associate Christianity with Anglo-Saxon culture, and that graduates of mission schools would become culturally separated from their own peoples.

During the second half of the twentieth century TEFL became associated with the tentmaking model of missions described by J. CHRISTY WILSON JR., who was himself initially an English instructor in Afghanistan in the early 1950s. A global survey in 1957 located 257 missionaries teaching English in 24 countries, with the largest number working in Japan. During the subsequent three decades, political change in China, Southeast Asia, the former Soviet Union, and central Europe created the opportunity for thousands of Christian EFL teachers to work in countries which were, to varying degrees, closed to traditional missionary work. In the 1980s several Christian agencies responded to this demand by specializing in training and sending short-term English teachers, while a number of established mission boards and agencies added TEFL to their global strategy. A 1996 survey of 250 mission organizations found that 65 had EFL-teaching openings or anticipated openings in the near future.

Concurrent with the rise in demand for TEFL in Europe, Asia, and Latin America was an increase in immigration to North America in the decades following the 1960s. Government funding of English instruction for immigrants led to the establishment of ESL classes in public schools, college, and adult education programs. This in turn stimulated the development of TEFL/TESL as a specialized field, with its own professional organization (TESOL, Inc., initiated in 1966), a growing body of research, scholarly and pedagogical journals, and professional preparation programs at the master's and doctoral levels.

Mission Strategy. As a strategy for evangelical mission, TEFL takes a variety of forms which are often related to the needs and limitations of a particular context. In countries which prohibit missionaries, such as communist and Islamic nations, English language teaching allows Christian workers to gain entry. These workers may include professional teachers who are unconnected with any Christian organization as well as missionaries who teach English primarily to maintain their visa status. In restricted locations, EFL teachers frequently work within secular schools and institutions. In some countries, most notably China in the 1980s and 1990s, the demand for English instruction is strong enough to make it possible to send large numbers of teachers for short term (ranging from one month to two years), with a limited amount of preservice training.

Less restricted contexts allow a broader range of options for the use of TEFL as a mission strategy. In nations such as Japan and Thailand, the ranks of English instructors include professional Christian teachers in secular institutions as well as career missionaries who use TEFL as a means of making evangelistic contacts. The latter approach often involves strategies such as short-term English camps, private tutoring, and informal classes using a Bible-based approach.

Another major use of TEFL occurs within evangelical contexts such as theological institutes, schools for missionary children, and missionary training centers. English has become the lingua franca of an increasingly diverse missionary population. In parts of the world which have a limited number of theological texts in the local languages, EFL instruction may be provided to allow seminary students and pastors to read the broad range of works published in English.

The rise of TEFL as a mission strategy has been paralleled by an increase in the availability of professional training programs and curricular materials. Some mission agencies have responded to the demand for English instruction by providing in-house training programs, while others send prospective teachers to one of the dozens of teacher education programs available at secular and Christian colleges and universities. Major publishing houses such as Cambridge University Press offer a variety of EFL textbooks ranging from basic "life skills" English for refugees and immigrants to English for professionals in the fields of medicine and engineering.

The association of English with Western culture continues to be a concern for missionaries and mission agencies. However, the character of English instruction and the nature of the English language itself have both changed since the 1910 Edinburgh conference. In the postcolonial era, English instruction is provided in response to demand rather than imposed by a foreign power. By providing this instruction, the missionary teacher often fills a role which is perceived by nationals as acceptable for a foreign worker. In addition, the rise of indigenous dialects of English—in India, Nigeria, and many other countries—has broadened the language beyond its Anglo-Saxon base. English is one of the few major languages with more second-language speakers than native speakers.

With the passage of time, increasingly varied forms of English will evolve—a process accelerated, perhaps, through the use of computer technology. As it adapts to international demand by taking increasingly varied and specialized forms, TEFL is likely to remain a significant avenue for missionary outreach.

ALAN A. SEAMAN

Bibliography. B. Baurain, *EMQ* 28:2 (1992): 164–73; B. Camenson, *Opportunities in Teaching English to Speakers of Other Languages;* L. Dickerson, *Handbook for Christian EFL Teachers;* P. Lakin, ed., *The ELT Guide;* D. Snow, *More than a Native Speaker: An Introduction for Volunteers Teaching Abroad.*

TEAM. *See* THE EVANGELICAL ALLIANCE MISSION.

Teams in Mission. A ministry strategy and organizational structure that uses a small-group format and emphasizes interdependent relationships in order to accomplish a given task. Applied to the missionary context, the term has been used to describe a wide variety of structures and strategies, including short-term teams, evangelistic teams, church-planting teams, strategic-ministry teams, and structures in wider interagency partnerships.

The concept of team mission has found increasing popularity in recent years. Parallel to current management trends that emphasize employee empowerment and group decision-making, it also reflects a deeper understanding of community within the body of Christ by stressing interdependent relationships, mutual care and nurture, and the balance of spiritual gifting.

Team structures are therefore seen as providing a more biblically correct model of the nature of the church. When team members develop and use their own SPIRITUAL GIFTS and natural abilities and, in their areas of weakness, depend on the gifts and abilities of others, the newly planted church gains valuable insight into the interdependence necessary if it is to survive and prosper. Team structures are also an advantage in the process of CONTEXTUALIZATION, for theology is seen as belonging to the church collectively, and not to individuals or professionals. New contextual theologies grow out of the mutual efforts of many Christians to understand and apply the gospel to the specific context.

The emphasis on team structures is not entirely new. It has been suggested that Paul's missionary journeys involved a team structure that was both fluid and mobile. Several individuals are mentioned in Acts as ministering alongside of Paul and Barnabas (or Paul and Silas).

Team structures in mission have the advantages of providing companionship, continuity, and balance as well as strength and a greater objectivity in decision making. Weaknesses include increased potential for disagreement and disharmony, concentration of power, stifling of individuality and initiative, inflexibility, and the fostering of dependency. In some PIONEER MISSION WORK, concentrated team structures may be impractical. In such settings a sense of community and teamwork can usually be achieved on a wider scale rather than through immediate physical proximity. Healthy missionary teams strive to balance these advantages and disadvantages.

Teams should be formed before departure to the field. It is also recommended that teams include experienced as well as inexperienced missionaries, and that they have a realistic view in regard to continuity. Not all of the initial members will remain with the team, and new members should be added, especially where the goal is to create a structure that will readily include national members and eventually become the local ministry team.

Lastly, it should be pointed out that a true sense of team does not come with an organizational structure, but with dynamic interaction and the development of relationships over time and, most notably, through crisis and conflict resolution. People working in the same place may be a group, but it takes commitment and mutuality in the face of the task at hand to weave the fabric of a team.

PAUL F. HARTFORD

Bibliography. M. S. Harrison, *Developing Multinational Teams;* J. R. Katzenbach and D. K. Smith, *The Wisdom of Teams;* S. L. Mackin, *EMQ* 28:2 (April 1992):

134–40; D. A. McGavran, *Readings in Third World Missions*, pp. 187–89; K. O'Donnell, ed., *Missionary Care*; D. W. Shenk and E. R. Stutzman, *Creating Communities of the Kingdom;* R. D. Winter, *Crucial Dimensions in World Evangelization*, pp. 326–44.

Technology. Missionaries and mission agencies use technologies both for internal functioning and to accomplish their primary external mission.

Communicational Technologies. The range and decreasing cost of communications technologies are placing virtually every missionary worldwide within an almost instantaneous interactive situation. Cellular and satellite phones in urban and rural areas have opened telecommunications to local missionaries who in the past have had no access to phone communications. E-mail provides a wide range of communicational opportunities. Through internet links one can not only have text-based communications, but graphics and audio as well. It is anticipated that interactive audio and video connections will soon not only be possible (as they now are), but will also be very practical and economical.

With the commitment of missions like Mission Aviation Fellowship (MAF) to link what they describe as the "telephone disadvantaged world" with the rest of the world through radio-based E-mail, the possibility of easily accessible two-way communication through E-mail is now being realized. By 1996 MAF had established approximately fifty "hubs" worldwide through which people could have access to internet-based E-mail. While often these connections are based on a relay system, the delay is hours rather than days or weeks. Some of these connections are phone-based and others are high-frequency radio-based.

With the rise in accessibility to the missionaries some questions have arisen related to the new forms of communication. Whereas in the past missionaries have often been distant in terms of time and geography, with E-mail they are just a click of a mouse button away. Some churches and individuals have sought to communicate more often with the missionaries and expect more and "better" reporting from them with less delay. With the current "faddishness" of E-mail some missionaries find themselves swamped with E-mail requests awaiting immediate response. The senders of E-mail and faxes, knowing that their messages arrive virtually as they send them, often expect answers back in the same way and in the same day.

Mission administrators then raise several crucial questions: Do the benefits justify the investment in the equipment and training costs? Are the technologies contextually appropriate? Will the use of the new technologies facilitate the reaching of the mission field or not? Many technologies are available and affordable, but irrelevant or distracting.

Access to information about new technologies is often available through shared databases available publicly in either electronic bulletin boards or internet connections or privately through a fee structure. Through the worldwide web one can access any of several search "engines" to identify information sources. If one does not have access to these databases, most research libraries have facilities to search a wide range of databases that touch on virtually any topic that has been put either in print or in an electronic medium.

New and useful technologies are becoming available in every arena of mission activity whether evangelism and church planting, leadership development, or relief and development. One could cite the software that Wycliffe Bible Translators is developing in morpheme parsing as a significant technological step forward in linguistic analysis. It facilitates a more rapid and accurate translation process as well as helping with literacy development. Or, one could mention some newly discovered "technologies" in the area of church growth that facilitate the wholistic growth of the church. One could show the new technologies being used in mission aviation to make flying safer. The application of new electronic technologies to education and the equipping of leaders generates much excitement and anticipation across the mission community. It will be helpful to briefly address some of the concerns about technologies in the arena of education for leadership development (*see also* Educational Mission Work).

Educational Technologies. Whether one lectures using a chalkboard or satellite-based teleconferencing, the primary purpose of using different technologies in leadership education is to enhance learning. The use of different technologies extends the potential range of learning experiences, and provides the opportunities for more appropriate response and the contextualization of the learning. The use of technology may increase the potential access to the learning by reducing the constraints of time, cost, and venue.

The appropriate selection of the technologies requires sensitivity to and knowledge about the local situation, learners, the people the learners will be working with, and the agency using the technologies. The following issues must be taken into account: purpose of learning; objectives for content; control (who makes/participates in the decision making?); characteristics of the learner (e.g., learning style, competence in subject area, familiarity with the technology, relevant experience, motivation, relevant skill level, spiritual maturity); overall educational delivery system, including the balance of formal, nonformal, and informal modes, and the administrative support system; costs to learner, agency, and community; available resources to the learner and for production, delivery, and support; instructors' competence, commitment both in the subject area and with the technology; skill objectives; and spiritual formation objectives.

In addition to an in-depth understanding of the community to be served, the students, the teachers, the agency providing the technology, and the technology's local application should also be understood before a significant commitment is made. Any change in the technological sphere of an educational enterprise can be expected to bring unpredictable changes in every part of the community. A change in technology may be expected to bring changes in the WORLDVIEW of the community, including its assumptions, values, forms, and expected ways of behavior. A technological change will result in a change in culture. The more technological change is introduced, the more cultural change can be expected. The more quickly it is introduced, the more one can expect cultural dissonance around the technology.

When selecting an educational technology the following values should be considered: the use of multiple sensory channels; the immediate use of the proposed learning in which analogous or equivalent immediate feedback is provided; active rather than passive participation by the learner; an employment of variety, suspense, and humor; opportunity for the learner to use his or her own experience to discover what is to be learned; building on prerequisites without repeating them and transferability of the learning.

Given the expectation of culture change when any new technology is introduced, the wise planner will ask about the kinds of culture change that will need to be addressed in advance. What assumptions need to be challenged? What values need to change? What behaviors will be affected? These kinds of questions of each of the involved constituencies should be addressed (e.g., learners, communities to be served, educational/training agency). It should not be assumed that instructors who are familiar with one set of technologies will automatically be skilled in the use of another. Similarly, the support of one set of technologies may require a change in one's "philosophy of education." For example, one may have to move from a teacher-directed, content-focused kind of education to a more student-directed, interactive, function-focused kind of education.

In anticipation of the required or expected cultural changes a wise planner will begin initiating the steps to facilitate these changes in the community. As new technologies are becoming available some educators are suggesting changes in interdisciplinary organization. Missiology often requires multidisciplinary research. Planners should then organize the information along less strict disciplinary lines or more multidisciplinary lines.

Educators also suggest that we implement design learning flexibility with both administrative and delivery structures more contextually designed. In some cases they would be more individually structured and in other cases more community/cooperatively structured. Different technologies lend themselves to this kind of flexibility. Some technologies serve individuals better whereas others serve groups well. For example, audiotapes tend to serve the individual better, whereas videorecordings may be used as well with groups. Retraining faculty and students about the new technologies provides skills and reduces fear.

Additionally, timing issues need to be designed more flexibly. Such issues include duration, beginning and ending points, and when a person can begin in terms of personal experience/prerequisites and allowance of self-pacing. Further, constraints related to venue, student selection, and class size may be treated more flexibly with the use of new technologies.

The use of computer-mediated courses has generated much interest in training circles. Computer-mediated courses are now available in missiology from the United States and one would expect in some other countries very soon. As areas develop access to the internet, these courses will become available. Other missiological information is becoming increasingly available on CD-ROM.

Missionaries and mission agencies should and will continue to explore and use an increasingly broad variety of technologies. However, the selection of the technologies to be used should be based on considered criteria, especially that of cultural sensitivity and availability, rather than just contemporary faddishness.

EDGAR J. ELLISTON

Bibliography. I. Babour, *Ethics in an Age of Technology;* F. Ferré, *Hellfire and Lightning Rods;* A. S. Moreau and M. O'Rear, *EMQ* 33:4 (1997): 464–66; idem, *EMQ* 35:1 (1998): 84–87; idem, *EMQ* 35:2 (1998): 212–15; N. Postman, *Technopoly;* R. Rowland, *Missiology and the Social Sciences,* pp. 84–101.

Tekla-Haymanot (c. 1215–c. 1313). Ethiopian evangelist and monastic innovator. Tekla-Haymanot is a legendary figure in evangelistic renewal of the Ethiopian church. He was born into a Christian family and came to know Christ at an early age. After joining a monastery and studying for ten years, he moved to Tegré as part of an attempted pilgrimage to Jerusalem. The attempt never came to fruition, but Haymanot remained in Tegré another twelve years before returning to his home area, which was predominately non-Christian at the time. He began to preach the gospel, and disciples gathered around him. He founded a small community, which became a significant learning center and from which most of the monastic communities in Ethiopia derive their origin. Unconfirmed stories abound concerning Haymanot's exploits, including reports of many miracles that greatly assisted his evangelistic efforts.

A. Scott Moreau

Bibliography. E. A. Budge, *The Life and Miracles of Tekla Haymanot;* T. Tamrat, *Church and State in Ethiopia 1270–1527.*

Television Evangelism. Today, television watching is the primary way in which people in many countries spend their free time; the average household watches several hours of television daily. Unlike radio, which can be listened to while driving, washing dishes, or looking at each other, television requires everyone to face in the same direction and pay full attention.

From the beginning, the United States opted for commercially based television, and noncommercial public broadcasting has had difficult times. In Europe, led by such agencies as the BBC in Britain, television has been financed by a license fee paid by all owners of television sets; but with the advent of satellite-based broadcasting the commercial model is advancing rapidly all over the world.

For the Christian evangelist, television has a number of strengths. It is a medium that reaches a large group of people at the same time. It can utilize numerous types of presentation: lecture, dialogue, drama, dance, music. On the other hand, television is very expensive and, given the size of the audience, tends to cater to the lowest common denominators. Furthermore, it usually operates in an entertainment environment. Such problems may seem insurmountable for Christian churches, but the medium is too powerful to be left exclusively in the hands of those who have no Christian interest and concerns. We should note that Christian use of television in the United States is already a billion-dollar enterprise.

The church will have to learn that television writes its own rules. Television communicates in the living rooms of the audience, and here the Christian communicator will be judged on equal terms with other television producers as to skills and mastery of the medium. The screen has to be filled with scenery, people, motion, and visual effects, and not just a talking head.

The electronic church is basically an American phenomenon. We have seen the rise of the televangelists, the superstars of American religious television. They have been the topic of many books and articles, ranging from horror stories to unreserved praise. The misbehavior of a few has had significant influence on the perceived credibility of all television preachers.

Ben Armstrong, former chairman of the National Religious Broadcasters, has come out strongly in favor of the electronic church as a revolutionary new form of the worshiping, witnessing church. Malcolm Muggeridge, on the other hand, claimed that Jesus would decline the offer, treating it as the fourth temptation. He was concerned about the fact that television centers on violence, sex, and deceit. There are times, Muggeridge conceded, when television can communicate true life, as was the case of the television program he made with Mother Teresa of Calcutta. True life and testimony seem to be well suited for television.

Other parts of the world have seen the development of low-cost city stations serving a limited community. There are also major developments in the area of satellite television. SAT-7 is a new initiative broadcasting into the Arab world, and a new Thai operation is giving space to a Christian channel that will cover most of East Asia.

Among the potential program formats, we should mention the big worship service—a church service actually produced for television. A good example would be the *Hour of Power,* the Sunday morning service of the Crystal Cathedral in California with Robert Schuller. This program has been on the air since 1970. Other formats include talk shows, such as the *700 Club* with Pat Robertson. Still others have experimented with short programs or spots. There are many children's shows. A real potential would be to develop new forms of teaching the Bible, for biblical illiteracy is becoming a serious issue in both church and society.

The challenge is to integrate television with other forms of evangelism, in particular with the outreach of the local church. To do that, the issue of financial support will need to be solved. There is also a need to find ways to minimize the negative impact of television on family life. Initiatives in this direction have been made by the Lutherans in Japan.

Viggo Søgaard

See also Media.

Bibliography. B. Armstrong, *The Electric Church;* W. F. Fore, *Television and Religion: The Shaping of Faith, Values, and Culture;* M. Muggeridge, *Christ and the Media;* V. B. Søgaard, *Media in Church and Mission: Communicating the Gospel.*

ten Boom, Corrie (1892–1983). Dutch missions advocate. The daughter of a watchmaker in Haarlem, Corrie ten Boom lived the first four decades of her life in her father's home. When Germany invaded Holland during World War II, she joined in the resistance movement by providing a hiding place for Jews. Corrie and her family were betrayed to the Gestapo by fellow countrymen in 1944. Her father Casper and sister Betsie died in prison, but Corrie was released from Ravensbruck concentration camp after eleven months. Almost immediately she began sharing with her fellow countrymen the lessons of hope and forgiveness that she had learned in Ravensbruck.

When the war ended, Corrie began sharing her message around the world, presenting the gospel at every opportunity. She gave special attention to Germany, opening a home of healing for those who had been traumatized in the concentration camps. She traveled extensively throughout Europe, made trips to Vietnam during the Vietnamese War, delighted in smuggling the gospel into Soviet Russia with BROTHER ANDREW, and visited prisons where she was warmly welcomed. Her special love for Jews took her often to Israel. She also wrote several books, made several films, and worked with the Billy Graham Association. In August of 1978, Corrie suffered a stroke that kept her housebound until she died in 1983.

GRACE L. KLEIN

Bibliography. C. Carlson, *Corrie ten Boom: Her Life and Her Faith;* C. ten Boom, *The Hiding Place.*

10/40 Window. The term "10/40 Window" has been used to describe a rectangular-shaped window 10 degrees by 40 degrees north of the equator spanning the globe from West Africa to Asia, including over 60 countries and more than 2 billion people. The majority of the unreached peoples of the world—those who have never heard the gospel and who are not within reach of churches of their own people—live within this window (*see* PEOPLES, PEOPLE GROUPS).

At the LAUSANNE CONGRESS ON WORLD EVANGELIZATION (1974), RALPH WINTER rocked the evangelical world with the challenge of unreached peoples. At the LAUSANNE CONGRESS II in Manila (1989), Luis Bush gave the ethnic orientation of unreached peoples a new geographical focus. There, during a plenary session of the congress, he presented the strategic concept of the 10/40 Window for the first time.

There are three major reasons for the dire spiritual state of the 10/40 Window. First of all, the 10/40 Window is the home of the world's major non-Christian religions: Islam, Hinduism, and Buddhism. Over 1 billion Muslims, and more than 1 billion Hindus and almost 240 million Buddhists live in this region.

Second, the poorest of the poor live in the 10/40 Window. The remarkable overlap between the fifty poorest countries of the world and the least evangelized countries of the world is no coincidence. After observing that the majority of the unreached people live in the poorest countries of the world, Bryant Myers concludes, "the poor are lost and the lost are poor."

Third, there has been a lack of missionaries serving among the peoples of the 10/40 Window. Only about 8 percent of the missionary force presently focuses on this needy and neglected area. Historically, the three religious blocs of this region (Muslim, Hindu, and Buddhist) have been considered resistant. But lack of fruit among these people may not be due to resistance so much as neglect. Generally, the church has made little effort to reach these peoples. The Bible is clear that little sowing leads to little reaping.

For these three reasons, the 10/40 Window represents what some missiologists describe as Satan's stronghold. From a careful analysis of the 10/40 Window, it appears that Satan and his forces have established a unique territorial stronghold that has restrained the advance of the gospel into this area of the world. In this region of the world, Paul's description of Satan as "the god of this age who has blinded the minds of unbelievers" (2 Cor. 4:4) can be clearly seen. Clearly the forces of darkness stand behind the overwhelming poverty and spiritual bondage of this region.

Therefore, the 10/40 Window serves as an important and strategic tool for the completion of the GREAT COMMISSION. It helps the church visualize its greatest challenge and focuses the church on its final frontier. The 10/40 Window calls for a reevaluation of the church's priorities, a refocusing of its energies, and a redeployment of its missionaries. Luis Bush, the international director of the AD 2000 and Beyond Movement, sums it up well: "If we are to be faithful to Scripture, obedient to the mandate of Christ, and if we want to see the establishment of a mission-minded church planting movement within every unreached people and city . . . so that all peoples might have a valid opportunity to experience the love, truth and saving power of Jesus Christ, we must get down to the core of the unreached—the 10/40 Window."

RICHARD D. LOVE

Bibliography. C. P. Wagner, S. Peters, and M. Wilson; eds., *Praying through the 100 Gateway Cities of the 10/40 Window;* J. D. Douglas, ed., *Proclaim Christ Until He Comes: Lausanne II in Manila,* F. K. Jansen, ed., *Target Earth.*

Teng, Philip (1922–). Chinese churchman and mission advocate. Born in Shandong province, China, the son of a Presbyterian minister, Teng was converted in 1939 and dedicated his life to full-time ministry in 1940. He graduated from National Northwest University in 1946, having majored in foreign languages. He attended New College, Edinburgh, Scotland (1947–50), and received the bachelor of divinity there. He arrived in Hong Kong in December 1950 and taught at Bethel Bible Seminary and the Evangelical Free Bible Institute. In 1956 he began teaching at The Alliance Bible Seminary, and in 1957 he accepted the call to pastor the North Point Alliance Church, which experienced tremendous growth and planted seven churches by 1979. He edited the Chinese edition of *Decision* magazine (1973–77), and became the founding honorary president of China Graduate School of Theology in 1975. In 1976 he became the first chairman of the Board for the Chinese Coordination Center of World Evangelism, and worldwide network of Chinese churches promoting unity and missions. He has promoted missionary endeavors since 1961, and became a missionary in East Kalimantan (southern Indonesia) in 1978. His writings emphasize the centrality of a vital personal relationship with Jesus Christ and the challenge of evangelism and missions in the contemporary context. Since retiring he continues to speak, teach, and write for a broad audience worldwide.

SAMUEL LING

Tent-Making Mission. The apostle Paul witnessed while he earned a living by making tents in the city of Corinth (Acts 18:3). This is how tent-making got its name. Tent-making mission has gained prominence in recent years, but tent-makers are not new. They are as old as Abraham, Isaac, and Jacob. While being semi-nomadic cattle-ranchers, they became witnesses to the living God, Yahweh, before the Canaanites. In the early church, persecution scattered believers from Jerusalem to Antioch and beyond. Those scattered went about bearing testimony as they worked their trades. The modern missionary movement sent out people as medical missionaries, social work missionaries, educational missionaries, and agricultural missionaries. They pursued their missionary calling while utilizing their professional skills.

Why has tent-making gathered considerable attention among the missionary strategists during the past decade? The reason is simple: missionaries as missionaries have not been permitted to go where the majority of non-Christian people are. During the past decades, missionaries have gradually been ousted from the countries of their service as communism, totalitarianism, and Islamic regimentation began to spread. Despite the collapse of Eastern European countries, the Berlin Wall, and the Soviet Union, the number of non-Christians in "closed" countries has been on the rise due to the resurgence of traditional religions and ideologies. The movement for reaching the unreached has added value to the acceptance of tent-making as a mission strategy.

Who, then, are these tent-makers? They may be defined as cross-cultural workers with a secular identity called to make disciples within "closed" countries. This understanding is more exclusive than other definitions. They are "cross-cultural workers," not mono-cultural workers. Christian witnessing to people of the same cultural background is the duty of all believers, and not to be categorized as something extraordinary. "With secular identity" refers to one's witnessing through one's occupation. "Called to make disciples" refers to one's sense of calling as a tent-maker with the *intentionality* to make disciples. Finally, tent-makers as defined here serve "within closed countries" (*see* CREATIVE ACCESS COUNTRIES).

There are two main areas of dispute among those favoring the tent-making strategy. First, the matter of tent-makers serving "within closed countries." The preference here for exclusivity is one of strategic concern. It is imperative that tent-makers receive special training with a focus on a special people group. Reaching those behind closed doors stipulates special preparation. Learning the language and culture of the people requires time and discipline. The success of their ministry depends on it. Their service as tent-makers may be prolonged rather than short-lived. Obviously tent-making is applicable in "open" countries. Second is the issue of support methods. We should not make this an issue to divide those who are advocates of the tent-making strategy.

In Acts 18:1–5, we see Paul supporting himself by teaming up with Aquila and Priscilla as tent-makers. Later when Silas and Timothy arrived in Corinth from Macedonia, Paul devoted himself exclusively to preaching. Paul vehemently defended fully-funded spiritual ministry (1 Cor. 9:1–14). There are various ways of doing ministry. On his part, he opted not to receive church support, *not on principle but for a pragmatic reason.* For he has indeed successfully argued for the legitimacy of accepting church support for his ministry.

What are the qualifications of tent-makers? The tent-makers must be (1) physically, emotionally, and spiritually self-reliant; (2) adaptable; (3) biblically literate; (4) alert to the emerging mission context; (5) trained in meeting needs vital to the people group they seek to penetrate; (6) trained in long-term and low-profile evangelistic skills; (7) equipped with broad new strategic thinking; and (8) prepared with a special strategy for responding to opportunities presented by need.

How does one go about finding a tent-making job across cultures? One must be creative and persistent in job hunting like anyone else. One may consult sources such as InterCristo, the International Placement Network, and the International Employment Gazette. One may look for international employment on the Internet. One may inquire regarding job availability through one's professional association or examine the job listing in a professional journal. Possibilities abound in high-tech fields. Foreign embassies are worth checking. Potential tent-makers may latch on to government or intergovernmental assignments. They may go to work with humanitarian relief and development organizations. TEACHING ENGLISH TO SPEAKERS OF OTHER LANGUAGES (TESOL) is in high demand all over the world. One can serve as a teacher in most fields and at all levels, as a medical doctor, as a nurse, as an engineer, as a farmer, and as a "professional" student.

There are some problems associated with tent-making. For security reasons, the "success" stories are in short supply. Often we hear only of failures, tent-makers coming home due to their inability to adjust to the culture of the host country, family reasons, or inadequate preparation. It is difficult to do the required balancing act between job and ministry successfully. There is often not enough time for ministry because of the job pressures. Tent-makers are to witness through their occupations, but some employers prohibit such witnessing activities. Despite these difficulties, tent-making missions must continue to be explored. The future context of mission as a whole demands it. Tent-makers are the agents of strategic missions for tomorrow as well as today.

TETSUNAO YAMAMORI

Bibliography. D. Hamilton, *Tentmakers Speak: Practical Advice from Over 400 Missionary Tentmakers;* J. Lewis, ed., *Working Your Way to the Nations: A Guide to Effective Tentmaking;* J. C. Wilson, Jr., *Today's Tentmakers;* T. Yamamori, *Penetrating Missions' Final Frontier: A New Strategy For Unreached Peoples.*

Territorial Spirits. The Bible speaks of evil angels or spirits that exercise significant influence and control over people groups, empires, countries, and cities. These perverse powers not only work to bring harm and misery, but more importantly, they strive to keep people from coming to a knowledge of the one true God. Since the mid–1980s, some evangelists and missiologists have begun advocating an aggressive strategy for doing spiritual battle with these so-called territorial spirits as a means of more effective evangelism (*see* POWERS AND MISSION, THE).

Although there is not extensive information in the Bible about territorial spirits, there is sufficient discussion to affirm their reality and provide some insight into their nature and activities. In a passage that highlights God's sovereignty over the nations, God is said to have divided humanity "according to the number of the sons of Israel" or, as the Septuagint and a scroll of Deuteronomy from Qumran put it, "according to the number of the sons of God"—a reference to angels (Deut. 32:8). The passage thus appears to be teaching that the number of the nations of the earth is directly proportional to the number of angels. This passage was widely understood in Judaism to mean that certain angels are associated with particular countries and peoples.

Some of these angelic rulers evidently have rebelled against God. Rather than direct the people's worship to the one true God, they have sought veneration for themselves and have falsely presented themselves to the people as "gods" (Ps. 82:1–8). The prophet Isaiah foretells the future judgment of these patron angels of the nations: "In that day the LORD will punish the powers in the heavens above and the kings on earth below" (Isa. 24:21).

These powers who have masqueraded as gods are, in reality, demonic spirits. The same chapter that reveals the allotments of humanity to angelic guardianship (Deut. 32:8) speaks of Israel provoking God to jealousy by embracing foreign gods (Deut. 32:16). Israel actually "sacrificed to demons" (Heb. = *shedim;* Greek = *daimonia*) (Deut. 32:17). They forsook the one true almighty God and gave their devotion to fallen angels, to demonic spirits. Of course they did not realize that they were worshiping evil spirits. These principalities and powers pulled off an effective hoax by deceiving people into thinking that they were the omnipotent rulers of heaven and earth.

The Septuagint version of Psalm 96:5 also unmasks the true identity of the various gods of the nations: "For all the gods of the nations are demons, but the LORD made the heavens." All of the rituals, prayers, sacrifices, and worship offered to the gods of other nations were not really offered to "gods" at all. They were accorded to angelic imposters usurping the rightful place of the one true God.

A particularly appalling aspect of this grand demonic deception is the horrific sacrifices that these rebellious angels demanded of the people as their "gods." They went so far as to elicit human sacrifice. The psalmist laments one of these sad chapters in the history of Israel: "They worshipped their idols which became a snare to them. They sacrificed their sons and their daughters to demons. They shed innocent blood, the blood of their sons and daughters, whom they sacrificed to the idols of Canaan, and the land was desecrated by their blood" (Ps. 96:36–38). The GODS AND GODDESSES of the Canaanites were, in reality, demonic spirits. They tempted the people of Israel and solicited their worship under the guise of local deities. They were what many are calling today "territorial spirits."

The most well known and illustrious passage about territorial spirits is Daniel 10. Since the text describes angelic powers that have specific connections to the successive empires of Persia and Greece, they might more appropriately be called "empire spirits." These evil angels are mentioned to Daniel by an interpreting angel, perhaps Gabriel (see Dan. 9:21), who came to explain a vision God had given to him. Gabriel reveals that there was a heavenly struggle that hindered his coming to Daniel for three weeks: "*The prince of the Persian kingdom* resisted me twenty-one days. Then Michael, one of the chief princes, came to help me, because I was detained there with the king of Persia" (Dan. 10:13). Later,

Gabriel informs Daniel that the heavenly warfare would continue, but would not include a struggle with another angelic prince: "Soon I will return to fight against *the prince of Persia,* and when I go, *the prince of Greece* will come. . . . No one supports me against them except Michael, your prince" (Dan. 10:20–21). Both the prince of Persia and the prince of Greece in these passages are not references to the human rulers, but to angelic forces. There is a clear consensus among Bible scholars on this foundational point. This interpretation is strongly suggested by the fact that the archangel Michael is also referred to as a "prince." The Septuagint (Theodotian) translation of the Hebrew term *sar* is *archon,* a word that was used by Paul (see Eph. 2:2; 1 Cor. 2:6, 8), John (John 12:31), and other first-century and early Christian writers for angelic powers.

The New Testament gives us little direct teaching about angelic patrons over cities, territories, regions, or nations. Jesus says nothing about these higher-level spirits. Neither does the Book of Acts contain explicit teaching about them. Paul's references to the "principalities and powers" are not directed toward issues surrounding regional or city spirits. His teaching is focused on the variety of ways evil spirits directly oppose believers. Some interpreters have seen territorial dimensions in his list of principalities and powers in Ephesians 6:12, but the whole context of this passage has to do with the believers' daily direct struggle with the demonic (*see* SPIRITUAL WARFARE). Paul's most pertinent teaching is his comment in 1 Corinthians 10:20 that "the sacrifices of pagans are offered to demons, not to God." Here he reaffirms the Old Testament notion that idolatry and false religion are animated by the demonic as part of their attempt to subvert the plan of God and seek worship for themselves.

Throughout the Bible there is never any intimation that these powers rival God in any way or present a serious threat to the fulfillment of his plan and purposes. God is sovereign and is infinitely more powerful than any of the spirits or angels. The Father earnestly seeks the full devotion of his people. He wants believers to call directly on him for wisdom, strength, and help.

CLINTON E. ARNOLD

Bibliography. C. E. Arnold, *Three Crucial Questions About Spiritual Warfare;* S. Page, *Powers of Evil. A Biblical Study of Satan and Demons;* E. Rommen, ed., *Spiritual Power and Missions. Raising the Issues;* C. Wagner, Confronting the Powers: How the New Testament Church Experienced the Power of Strategic-Level Spiritual Warfare; idem, Warfare Prayer: How to Seek God's Power and Protection in the Battle to Build His Kingdom.*

Terrorism. In the two years following June 1991, in the southern Philippines there were four missionaries killed, two raped, and six kidnapped. In addition, thirty-five were injured in a terrorist bombing. This is but one example of the risks missionaries are confronting as they propagate the Christian message of peace in a world of violence. Other areas of ongoing instability include Colombia, Peru, Liberia, Sudan, and Afghanistan.

Two of the main sources of terroristic activity are fundamentalist Muslims and communist guerrillas. These fringe groups have no affinity with Christianity. Therefore, the foreign missionary becomes a high profile person through whom they may make a religious or political statement. Missionaries are also usually unarmed and thus totally vulnerable as a "soft target."

Evacuation of missionary personnel from areas of danger is an emotional topic in mission circles. One side holds to a "stay at all costs" position. They demand the right to make an individual decision on the field level without reference to home base directives or to local embassy advisories. The other extreme represents those who are ready to evacuate at the first sign of danger. Most missionaries would be positioned between these two extremes.

Nationals in Bangladesh, Liberia, and Ethiopia expressed serious reservation as to how the missionaries fled their countries in times of danger. The local people felt forsaken by their spiritual guides. It would seem imperative that major decisions regarding evacuation be taken in tandem with these national believers.

One of the few evangelical organizations that is working with mission boards in risk assessment as well as in assisting in the release of kidnapped missionaries is Contingency Preparation Consultants. This group has held seminars in a number of countries for mission leaders.

Biblically, one finds the apostle Paul enduring extreme hardships as well as purposefully walking into dangerous situations. However, on at least seven occasions he fled from those who threatened his life, almost always upon the advice of the local people. This subject remains one of the most difficult areas with which missionaries and missions boards have to deal.

PHIL PARSHALL

Bibliography. L. Accad, *EMQ* 28:1 (1992): 54–56; R. Klamser, *EMQ* 28:1 (1992): 48–52; P. Parshall, *EMQ* 30:2 (1994): 162–66.

TESOL. *See* TEACHING ENGLISH TO SPEAKERS OF OTHER LANGUAGES.

Testimony. *See* WITNESS.

Thailand *(Est. 2000 pop.: 61,909,000; 513,115 sq. km. [198,114 sq. mi.]).* Thailand is a country whose 62 million people have accepted Christianity reluctantly and slowly. The origins of Christianity are attributed to the coming of the Portuguese Catholic missionaries in 1498, followed by Protestant missionaries in 1828, more than 300 years later. The arrival of both Protestant and Catholic missionaries was met initially by disinterest, followed soon by sporadic regional hostility. Few martyrs can be counted among those early missionaries, but that fact should not be viewed as any positive regard for Christianity. It was seen as the religion of Western hegemony in Southeast Asia and thereby regarded as a threat to Thai nationalism. From those early days Christianity has been regarded as a "foreigner's" religion and those that embrace it as *luuk farang,* the "child of the foreigner."

Several factors can be cited for that phenomenon. First among these is a tightly knit blend of conservative Theravadic Buddhism and animism, a pervasive form of religion that Christianity has found very difficult to penetrate. In their naiveté, the early missionaries, and many up to the present time, assumed that animistic phenomena were simply the residue of superstition and that Western science and education would dispel or replace indigenous or traditional perceptions of reality. Roman Catholics and conciliar Protestants believed in large part that long-term ENCULTURATION or Christianization via education would achieve that end, while evangelical and fundamentalist Protestants believed the "new birth" and "growth in Christ" would accomplish it.

Another important factor for the slow acceptance of Christianity in Thailand is the influence of NATIONALISM and a "scientific worldview." Added to that is the impact of GLOBALIZATION on Thai culture coupled with a more positive national self-image based primarily on economic development and education.

It is difficult to evaluate other factors such as the loss of influence of Christianity due to the popular notion that the West, and its religion by association, is "morally decadent." The strengthening of ASEAN ties also contributes to this, as does the influence of Eastern religions in the West. Generally, Thai people view Christianity as being a "foreigner's religion," though the intensities of that view are differently perceived.

A variety of methods and strategies have been employed throughout the history of Christianity in Thailand. Each strategy mirrors the unique purposes and theological distinctives of the respective mission agencies. Some methods resemble "Jesus, meek and mild," while others reflect the authoritative powerful Christ with the demoniac (Matt. 8:31). One might assume that because of this broad variety of Christian expression there is also a corresponding diversity in the strategic methods employed. The interesting fact is that most mission organizations used similar strategies (mission station, itinerant evangelism, preaching points, church structure, schools, hospitals, etc.). Any differences are primarily in the manner, intensity,

and applications in which similar strategies were employed (see Wisely, 144–64).

Christianity in both its Catholic and Protestant forms remains a struggling religious minority, its most significant obstacle not being syncretistic Buddhism, but its Western form of Christianity.

New approaches that take seriously traditional indigenous worldviews and that seek to devise relevant cultural practices are at work. The extent to which these new approaches will be effective in moving the percentage of Christians beyond the one percent barrier is not known, nor predictable.

THOMAS N. WISELY

Bibliography. A. Smith, *Siamese Gold;* T. N. Wisely, *Dynamic Biblical Christianity in the Buddhist/Marxist Context: Northeast Thailand.*

The Evangelical Alliance Mission (TEAM).

Based in the United States and Canada, the Evangelical Alliance Mission is an interdenominational mission agency whose purpose is "to help churches send missionaries to plant reproducing churches" in lands where awareness of the gospel is minimal. Forty percent of its missionaries are deployed in the 10/40 WINDOW. Reflecting the globalization of the Christian mission, TEAM missionaries partner with missionaries from evangelical agencies based in Australia, France, Germany, Holland, Japan, Sweden, Switzerland, Taiwan, Thailand, the United Kingdom, and Venezuela.

Founded in 1890 by evangelist FREDRIK FRANSON, TEAM was a product of the nineteenth-century spiritual renewal that swept the Scandinavian countries and produced the free evangelical churches of Europe and North America. The mission's character was shaped by a compelling belief in the necessity of personal conversion, by a commitment to start visible churches of earnest Christians, by a premillennial expectation of the "any day" return of Jesus Christ, and by the bold and direct evangelistic methods of D. L. MOODY, in whose campaigns Franson worked.

In 1889, when J. HUDSON TAYLOR called for one thousand missionaries to evangelize China, Franson, who was preaching in Germany at the time, informed Taylor of his determination to recruit and send one hundred of them. Before his death in 1908, the Scandinavian Alliance Mission of North America (as it was then called) had suffered its first martyrs in China and Mongolia and had expanded its work into six countries. Today, nine hundred TEAM missionaries serve in some forty areas; in addition, fourteen mission agencies and church fellowships in Europe and North America were either founded or early influenced by Franson.

The mission's general directors, after Franson, have been J. H. Hedstrom, T. J. Bach, David H. Johnson, Vernon Mortenson, Richard M. Winchell, and George W. Murray. After World War II, the mission changed its name to TEAM to reflect the broadening of the missionary force beyond the original Scandinavian constituency. The mission also joined the Interdenominational Foreign Mission Association (IFMA). In the years to follow, several smaller, specialized agencies merged with it, including Tibetan Frontier Mission (1946), Door of Hope Mission (1959), Caribbean Broadcasting Company (1963), Sudan United Mission, North American Branch (1969), Peruvian Gospel Fellowship (1975), Orinoco River Mission (1980), Japan Evangelical Mission (1982), and Bible Christian Union (1994).

The largest bloc of TEAM missionaries work directly in starting new churches, while the rest engage in leadership training, community development, radio and television production, Bible translation, literature production and distribution, education, and health ministries that support the church-planting effort. More than one hundred years after its founding, the aims of the mission echo the instructions given by Franson to his early recruits: "Our common goal must in every case be the salvation of souls and their continuing both in grace and in the work until the Lord returns. The essential task thus will not be to set up stations, but to get living congregations into being, whose continuing joy it will be to send out new missionaries from their own midst."

DAVID BROUCEK

Bibliography. V. Mortenson, *God Made It Grow;* P. H. Sheetz, *The Sovereign Hand;* E. Torjesen and F. Franson, *A Model for Worldwide Evangelism.*

Theism. *See* MONOTHEISM.

Theodicy. *See* PROBLEM OF EVIL.

Theodore of Tarsus (c. 602–690). Early English Christian leader. This key man in English history can best be described in relation to others such as Wilfrid, Willibrord, and Boniface—all of them part of a single, major transition in the long story of the British Isles.

The Celtic peoples were a tribal group in Paul's day that ranged from Ireland through England and the Continent, across a belt that stretched clear to Paul's Galatia. By Paul's day they had been overrun in southern Britain by what would become four centuries of Roman domination of literacy and civil order.

When Rome was threatened by invasion from the East it began to withdraw its legions from Southern England, allowing "the coming of the Anglo-Saxons," tribal peoples whose successive invasions would return England to illiteracy for the next two centuries. However, by the end of the Romano-Celtic period of British history the Irish, Welsh, and Scottish Celts (today's names) had already begun to develop a very scholarly

and unusually mission-minded version of Christianity that was considerably different from the Latin-Roman forms, being tied more closely with the Greek-Roman tradition.

The power vacuum created by the withdrawal of the Roman legions from England (c. A.D. 440) left Irish and Scottish Celtic Christianity to try to bring a semblance of order. Meanwhile, with the fall of the Western Roman Empire, Latin Christianity became a stable and influential Christian tradition no longer tied to a menacing empire and, by the time of Theodore's birth 150 years later, had sent AUGUSTINE OF CANTERBURY to reach out to the Anglo-Saxons settlers in England. After another sixty years the conflict between Celtic and Roman traditions was superficially solved by the Synod of Whitby, led by a young man named WILFRID. Supposedly this event (c. 664) brought the Celtic tradition into the (Latin) Roman rite, but it was a tenuous achievement.

A master stroke of the Western Roman church leaders was achieved when they appointed Theodore of Tarsus Archbishop of Canterbury. Theodore hailed from the eastern end of the Roman Empire, the source of much of what was Celtic Christianity. Thus, just as the Jerusalem Council asked Barnabus (who was both Greek and Jewish in culture) to go to Antioch to see to things there, Theodore was asked to go to Britain. Firm but patient, an organizer, scholarly, keen to disciple, in the next thirty years he was able to somehow gain the acceptance of those on both sides of the divide that had become both a Celtic-Anglo divide and then a Celtic-Roman polarization. According to Bede, Theodore was the first real Christian leader of all England.

By being even-handed, however, Theodore incurred the wrath of the younger, wealthy, and royally connected Wilfrid, who felt he ought to have been much more pro-Roman.

As late as Theodore's century, to people living in the forests of what we today call England, Rome was still an impressive word. The Mediterranean church (still bridging Latin and Greek) was the most durable institution, surviving the fall of the Roman Empire, and remained more nearly intact than any other institution. Understandably, in the British Isles, the virile, earlier Celtic form of Christianity characterized by some Eastern (Greek) Christian customs (Easter date, tonsure, the penitentials, Egyptian art, etc.) would eventually conflict with the imported Latin tradition. Theodore's significance in this story is that more than any other one person he was the firm hand affecting a melding of the virile Celtic Christianity and the prestigious Latin Roman version, a contextualization which was to last for many centuries.

RALPH D. WINTER

SEE ALSO Celtic Missionary Movement.

Theological Education by Extension. Theological education by extension (TEE) is a term that describes a method and a movement that appeared in the missions world in the early 1960s. Responding to the rapidly changing patterns of the church, the ministry, and leadership training, TEE revolted against the residence type of theological education. It espoused a new form of education, "which yields to the life cycle of the student, that does not destroy or prevent his productive relation to society, and does not make the student fit into the needs of a residential school." It was theological education *for* church growth.

Brief History of the Movement. TEE was born in Latin America, occasioned by the general needs of Latin American evangelicals, particularly by the Presbyterians in Guatemala in 1962. They had an excellent seminary of the traditional type in Guatemala City with a highly qualified faculty. But a survey revealed that in twenty-five years the seminary had prepared only ten pastors who were actively serving the denomination. At that time only six students were enrolled—hardly sufficient to serve two hundred rapidly growing churches in one of the most fertile fields of all Latin America. Something was radically wrong.

Providentially, a trio of highly qualified, unusually creative, and evangelically concerned missionary professors made up their faculty. RALPH WINTER, Jim Emery, and Ross Kinsler all had multiple degrees in engineering, anthropology, and theology. They moved from the city to the rural area where most of the churches were, but this did not solve the problem. A radical change in structure was necessary.

The church leaders could not come for training if it required residence away from their homes. From this sprang the idea of a decentralized seminary. If the potential students could not come to the seminary, the seminary would go to them! Regional centers were established. Courses on three levels were adapted to the schedules of the students. Textbooks were put into programmed instruction. Care was taken to maintain academic excellence. Enrollment immediately increased from six to fifty students—and the TEE movement was born.

Five advantages of the new TEE program were noted by the missionaries. First, the door was opened for leaders who desired to reach a higher level of training. Second, the leaders could receive theological training in the context of their own subculture. Third, the system permitted those students who had low motivation to leave without losing face. Fourth, instead of lowering academic levels, the extension student learns better and develops better study habits in his or her home. Finally, extension is much more economical than the conventional seminary, and it saves much time for the professor.

Thus a radical new form of theological education arose in a tiny country of Central America. Soon it became more widely known and its leaders went on the road to respond to requests from other fields with the same problems. The new method spread to Bolivia, Colombia, Brazil, Mexico, and Argentina during the 1960s and into most Latin American countries in the 1970s. From there it has spread to Asia and Africa, maintaining its basic principles while assuming different forms. TEE's adaptability has been one of its strong points. It targets established leaders instead of prospective leaders.

For almost a decade the TEE Movement met different degrees of opposition from traditional theological educators. This was due to some unmerited criticism of residential forms by TEE proponents. However, after realizing that TEE was not necessarily a substitute for, but a complement to, resident theological education, the two sides have gradually fused and see each other as mutually beneficial.

Methodology of the Movement. TEE can better be understood when one keeps in mind that it does not espouse the *extermination* of resident structures, but only their *extension*. TEE suggests that the seminary become student-centered instead of institution-centered. The seminary simply extends its theological education in several ways. Geographically, the seminary goes to the student in his or her natural habitat. Chronologically, the schedules of classes are drawn up *after* consulting the students. Seasonal classes and schedules must be considered. Culturally, the course material may be the same, but the Center adapts the content to the needs, customs, language, and thought patterns of the Center area. Academically, courses may have to be offered at several different levels, geared to the local environment. TEE is apt to reach people of different social and economic classes and prepare bivocational ministers. Finally, economically TEE avoids the enormous expense of maintaining institutional buildings and salaried faculties.

The TEE Movement has spread to all areas of the world of mission. Most missiologists agree that it is not a substitute for resident theological education, but a needed complement, especially in theological education on cross-cultural mission fields.

JUSTICE C. ANDERSON

SEE ALSO Bible Education by Extension.

Bibliography. R. Covell and P. Wagner, *An Extension Seminary Primer;* V. Gerber, ed., *Discipling Through Theological Education by Extension;* F. R. Kinsler, *The Extension Movement in Theological Education;* R. Winter, ed., *Theological Education by Extension.*

Theological Education Fund. *See* THEOLOGICAL EDUCATION IN NON-WESTERN CONTEXTS.

Theological Education in Non-Western Contexts. Theological education refers to the intentional and supervised equipping of the church's leadership. As such, theological education is and always has been an essential element of the task of missions. From the apostolic band of the New Testament age and the catechetical schools of the postapostolic period to graduate seminaries scattered throughout the contemporary world, theological education is the most compelling and prominent form of EDUCATIONAL MISSION WORK. Nevertheless, Johnstone (1993) reports that an inadequate supply of trained leaders—a failure of theological education—hobbles the vitality and expansion of the church in nearly every nation of the world at the close of the twentieth century.

The present failure does not reflect a lack of attention or effort. As Roman Catholic missionaries of the sixteenth century followed the Conquistadors to the New World and beyond, they established universities for training indigenous priests on the model of those in Europe. Early Protestant missionaries took apprentices, whom they trained as "evangelists." During the nineteenth and twentieth centuries, other missionaries founded hundreds of Bible schools in the non-Western world, beginning with Carey's College of Serampore. Lacking the skills needed to design culturally appropriate educational programs, Protestant missionaries, like Catholics of an earlier era, replicated (with minimal adjustments) the Western schools in which they trained. The results of this effort are mixed. On the one hand, we observe the tragic lack of effective leadership that Johnstone reports. On the other hand, the vast majority of leaders in non-Western churches today are products of these schools.

The most concentrated modern effort to reshape theological education in the non-Western world was launched in 1958 by the Theological Education Fund (TEF), which came under the WORLD COUNCIL OF CHURCHES in 1961. In three "mandate periods," stretching from 1958 to 1977, TEF channeled substantial resources from the West into theological education in the non-Western world. Twenty-seven theological schools in Africa, Asia, and Latin America received grants of $100,000 or more, further grants were made to develop libraries at three hundred theological schools, and programs were established to write, translate, and publish theological texts. More than four hundred Third World nationals received scholarships for graduate and postgraduate theological studies in the West.

The impact of TEF on non-Western theological education was enormous. Unfortunately, sensitivity to contextual issues surfaced late, and even then the appropriateness of Western educational models went largely unchallenged. Since Third World educators received scholarships to liberal theological schools in the West, perhaps the

TEF's most enduring legacy is promotion of Western liberal and postliberal theology among Latin American, African, and Asian churches.

THEOLOGICAL EDUCATION BY EXTENSION (TEE) also has dramatically impacted the training of the church's leadership in the non-Western world. In 1963, the faculty of a traditionally Western seminary in Guatemala faced the ineffectiveness of their training programs and determined to change. TEE emerged as an attempt to make ministry training accessible to functioning church leaders without disrupting their productive social, economic, and ministry relationships. This was achieved through self-instructional textbooks and frequent (often weekly) "seminars" led by a "center leader" or "tutor."

Dialogue between TEE educators and faculty at "residential" schools sometimes has turned acrimonious. Nevertheless, TEE has brought significant benefits to theological schools and the churches they serve. Although no firm statistics exist, thousands—perhaps hundreds of thousands—of church leaders in Latin America, Africa, and Asia have received some biblical or ministry instruction through TEE and BEE (see BIBLICAL EDUCATION BY EXTENSION) which they could not have obtained otherwise. Furthermore, many theological educators in "residential schools" have been sensitized to educational issues and methods that challenge them to rethink their approach to ministry training.

As part of TEF's Second Mandate, regional associations of Conciliar theological schools were organized to regulate academic standards. Evangelical educators founded the INTERNATIONAL COUNCIL OF ACCREDITING FOR EVANGELICAL THEOLOGICAL EDUCATION (ICAA—now ICETE) in 1980. Just as missionaries modeled schools on their alma matters in the West, so the regional accrediting agencies established during the 1960s and 1970s borrowed heavily—sometimes wholesale—from North American accrediting structures. Many theological schools have been challenged by ACCREDITATION to improve facilities and strengthen faculty qualifications and instructions. Nevertheless, assumptions underlying Western theological education and relationships between the theological school and its constituent church have all too often gone unexamined.

In 1983, ICAA adopted a "Manifesto on the Renewal of Evangelical Theological Education," which pledged to "introduce and reinforce" twelve critical aspects of theological education. The stirring rhetoric of the ICAA "Manifesto" has been grist for faculty discussions in many theological schools, but educators must tap their own creativity to discern how advocated commitments can be implemented. As a result, in most nations theological schools and churches continue to await a renewal of ministry training that will yield an adequate supply of leaders equipped for effective ministry in church and society.

ROBERT W. FERRIS

Bibliography. P. Bowers and R. Kemp, eds., *ERT*, 19:3 (1995): 211–315; R. W. Ferris, *Renewal in Theological Education: Strategies for Change*; P. Johnstone, *OW*; C. Lienemann-Perrin, *Training for a Relevant Ministry: A Study of the Contribution of the Theological Education Fund*.

Theological Method. Theology has traditionally been the exclusive domain of the cultures of Europe and to a lesser degree in North America. But as a result of successful missionary work theologizing is no longer limited to one cultural context. Churches have been established in almost every region of the world and many potentially different types of theology do, or certainly will, co-exist in the world church. This, however, should not be viewed with indifference since the interdependence of all theological activity makes each ethnotheology equally responsible for the truth and unity of the faith of the whole worldwide church. Each theology should be pursued and practiced within the framework of this universal continuity as well as the local context of its own culture. What does this mean for theological method?

Theology does not derive its unity, that is, internal structure, from any particular method or from practical concerns, but rather from the object of theological investigation, namely, God. Accordingly theology is best understood as the study of God in which the unique nature of its various subdisciplines is determined by the foundational principle *sub ratione Dei* (attempt to relate all data to God). This is what distinguishes theological activity from all other disciplines (e.g., anthropology) which concern themselves with the same or similar issues. The universality of theological activity grows out of several assumptions about the nature of the human and the divine as well as the nature and task of theology.

Since there is one God, and since the plight of humanity is the same in all societies, and since our yearning for release is answered in the sacrificial death of Christ, these essential elements of God's self-revelation will correspond to universally known elements of the human dilemma. On the basis of this fundamental continuity it seems reasonable to assume that all people and languages possess the thought categories to understand and accept those elements of the Christian message which have salvific import.

Assuming that God is the all-determining sustainer of reality (Heb. 1:1–4) and that his self-revelation is mediated through that reality, it follows that divine reality must be viewed as a universally present concept. Thus, theological activity, which seeks to ascertain and systematize knowledge about that reality (God) can, by definition, never be limited to any one of the many cultural contexts which comprise the whole of human reality. In other words, theological activity is universal, in terms of both its appropriateness and its potential fruitfulness.

The nature and the task of theology remain the same across all cultural and linguistic barriers. This can be summarized in terms of a threefold definition of theology adapted from interaction with John Feinberg.

First, theology is the inductive discovery of truth from any and all sources concerning the being, acts, and relationship to God. The data needed by the theologian are available from a variety of sources and can be grouped into two general classes: (1) Divine Revelation, that is, the self-revelation of God as evident in creation, in the life and work of Christ, and in Scripture; (2) the human situation, that which is observable (experiential) including both the negative and the positive, and the contemporary and historical aspects of human existence. As used here, the positive aspects are seen to issue from God's creative involvement with humans and are reflected in individually expressed rational, emotional, and social traits as well as their cumulative expressions, that is, philosophy, science, art, community, and tradition. The negative aspects give evidence of sin and its effects and confront us with questions of evil, injustice, death, and the like. This categorization is not intended to imply parity between the two sources of data, but some degree of correlation. The cultural context of the theologian influences preunderstandings as well as the fundamental questions. Not in the sense that the questions in any way dictate the content of revelation, but rather in the sense that revelation is sufficient.

Second, theology is the analytic penetration of the meaning of each portion of inductively discovered truth. Each of these must in turn be keyed to pertinent biblical data. Exegetical tools (*see* EXEGESIS) and hermeneutical principles (*see* HERMENEUTICS) are used to determine the meaning of a given passage. This provides a basis for evaluating inductive conclusions and enables further refinement or, where necessary, reformulation.

Finally, the theologian must synthesize each portion of truth into an internally consistent and logically ordered system which speaks to the issues of one's day. This provides a framework for a deductive process that allows valid derivation of additional conclusions.

All Christian theologies, regardless of where or by whom they are constructed, are related to one another by virtue of: (1) both positive (knowledge about God) and negative (sin) elements of the human situation; (2) a common context, the church; (3) common theological task; and (4) an essentially similar methodology. Since theological method is determined by the nature of the theological task and its raw material, the methods needed for determining the meaning of a given biblical text, formulating its principles, systematizing the concepts, and interpreting collective Christian experience (tradition) are going to demonstrate a degree of similarity from culture to culture.

The question arises as to whether we can or should have some kind of standardized methodology, "a fixed base, an invariant pattern, opening upon all further developments of understanding" (Crowe). If our definition of the theological task is correct and if the basic methodological framework is going to remain relatively unchanged from culture to culture, then we are still left with the problem of how to formally incorporate cultural differences in both our definition of doing theology, as well as our theological treatment of locally informed topics, like ANCESTRAL PRACTICES. Perhaps it would be useful to distinguish between method and model (Schökel).

A method is a defined and controllable way of proceeding. A model is a system of elements constructed to give a unified explanation of a set of observed data, or it is a system already known and tested in one field which is transferred to a new field of investigation. In both cases the model contains a surplus meaning which it puts at the service of the research. Once it is accepted it guides subsequent observation and explanation of data. It becomes an a priori form of the research and its methods. We commit ourselves to models, but we make use of methods. For example, historians make use of the same sources, use similar methods, but the different results reveal the ideological bias (model) of the historian. The model then is an a priori form of the method, which is chosen and assimilated, but the method is determined by the nature and data of the theological task.

EDWARD ROMMEN

SEE ALSO Contextualization AND Systematic Theology.

Bibliography. J. F. Crowe, *Method in Theology: An Organon for our Time;* L. A. Schökel, "Of Methods and Models." *Congress Volume: Salamanca, 1983.*

Theological Systems. What is the connection between theology and missions? Where is the intersection between organized, integrated reflection on the Bible, the world, and the church and the global, border-crossing mandate that both flows from and into that reflection? Why do missions and theology sound sometimes like partners, sometimes like strangers, and sometimes like enemies?

Mission Marginalized. In the pre-Constantinian centuries of the church, the dialogue between mission and theological formulation was invigorating. Theology's agenda was shaped by the church's mission in the world. And a mission motivation to reach the Greco-Roman world drove the church's theologians to in-depth study. Was Justin Martyr's apologetic with the Jews a missionary theology or a theological mission? Which label would fit the interplay of Origen and Clement of Alexandria with Greek philosophy? The church had not yet become a world-conquering, empire-approved majority. In this situation mission was "the mother of theology" (Bosch, 1991, 489).

In the years that followed, the two began to drift apart. As Europe become "Christianized," the "regions beyond" horizon of mission began to recede and theology isolated itself in the church world of Christendom. Missions increasingly looked like the religious arm of politics, the bearer of power and culture. And theology lost more and more of its "on-the-road" quality.

With the division of the western and eastern churches in 1054, the Eastern Orthodox Church shifted its understanding of mission and theology to the church as the community in worship. The eucharistic liturgy became a "missionary event." And the theology of the church became a search, not for the outsider, but for Christian unity limited by the boundary of the pre-Schism seven ecumenical creeds (Stamoolis, 1986, 110).

Theology Abstracted. Reinforcing the diminishing role of mission in the Western church was a new shift of emphasis in understanding theology. In its earliest form, theology was seen as *habitus,* the cultivation of a spiritual, reflective habit or disposition in the believer (Farley, 1983, 31).

But with the coming of the universities in the twelfth century, a new emphasis began to grow—theology as a theoretical discipline *(scientia).* Thomas Aquinas (1225–74) used the newly discovered works of Aristotle to build a climactic synthesis of philosophy and theology as the crown of human knowledge that was to dominate future centuries. His split-level view of grace as a supplement to natural law left philosophy to roam widely as the rational basis for faith. The practitioners of theology began to narrow—from believer to scholar, from lay people to clergy. And with this emerging paradigm the gap between the rational systematizing of theology and mission widened.

The ENLIGHTENMENT skepticism over supernatural revelation in the seventeenth and eighteenth centuries structured and modified the two definitions of theology again. It reinforced further the isolation of theology from mission. Theology as cognitive *habitus,* as the individual quest for the wisdom of redemption, became the practical know-how necessary for ministerial work. Theology as disciplined *scientia* became a technical and specialized scholarly undertaking; it was to be undertaken like any other pure science—systematically, rationally, and without the necessity of any accompanying faith in the supernatural character of its objects of study. Theological systems were thought to be freed to become a Neo-Platonic search for abstract, rational essences, unhindered by historical, geographical, or social qualifiers.

Interruptions. The springtime of missions in the thirteenth century saw the formation of the Franciscan and Dominican orders and their missionary thrusts into places like China and Mongolia. By the beginning of the sixteenth century, the sea routes to Africa, Asia, and the Americas had been discovered. "God and gold" drove explorers and evangelists into a larger new world. The fledgling Jesuit order was born.

But, with notable exceptions, the significance of that larger world for systematic, theological reformulation was lost. In contextual response to the Reformation movement the Council of Trent (1543–63) standardized a rigid liturgical and theological uniformity on the Catholic Church. The Catholic world of theology and mission was Latinized (Shorter, 1992, 146–47).

Protestantism's response to an expanding world was also mixed. Calvin and Luther restricted their understanding of mission largely to the reform of the existing church. Their affirmation of the global witness of the church to the Triune God remained a rich but untested potential (Scherer, 1987, 54–66). It was the Anabaptist movement that broke through the links between the territorial church and society and sought to liberate once more the outsider orientation of missions and theology. Pietists and Moravians followed that same direction in the seventeenth century.

At the same time, the missionary dimensions of REFORMATION—and then Puritan—theologizing was fashioning a delayed entrance. The creeds of the sixteenth and seventeenth centuries rejected the path of scholastic abstractionism and saw themselves as *habitus*, a revived church's reflections on God's mission in the world. The Reformation focus on *sola scriptura* and *sola gratia* turned theology from a metaphysical science of ontological speculation to a systematic search for God's wisdom that would speak pastorally to a Catholic context.

The polemical roles of those creeds as a teaching instrument for the instruction of church members and teachers expanded as the crisis demands of the time faded. Theological systems, properly committed to discerning the full teaching of Scripture, found themselves dividing into Calvinist versus Remonstrant (Arminian), everybody versus Anabaptist.

Compartmentalization Confronted. During the first two centuries after the Reformation, that missionary dimension of theology seldom became intentional. In abandoning monasticism, the Reformers had abandoned the prime missionary agency of the past. Without international contact with non-Christian peoples, they were torn by endless disputes, battling for sheer survival, and impacted by their own forms of scholasticism. Protestants, like Catholics, affirmed their theology as universals, bottom-line systems whose centuries-old cultural, social, or historical influences had become invisible in the context of mutual confrontation and self-definition.

The explosion of the territorial boundaries of Christianity that came with the missionary movement of the nineteenth and twentieth centuries was to change that isolation of missions from theology for both Catholic and Protestant. Christian theological systems, long embedded in the Anglo-Saxon world, began their gospel dialogue with very different cultures. As they did so, their own cultural conditioning slowly became visible.

The long confusion of "Christianizing" with Western "civilizing" came more and more to the surface in the missionary confrontation. The universal message of the gospel had not been carried in a vacuum across the globe. In the providence of God, the reflective task of the Western church also had been shaped, both for good and ill, by a cultural, social, historical, and linguistic context (Muller, 1991, 201–14). Once again, missions had become the instrument calling for a new look at theological systems.

A New Partnership of Missions and Theology. In the closing decades of the twentieth century the hermeneutical task behind theology's systematic constructions is becoming consciously global. There is a new sensitivity to how understanding takes place when the gospel's meaning is carried across social, ethno-cultural boundaries and speaks to different needs. More are recognizing now the impact of the human context "as part of the interpretive task of the church throughout the ages" (Muller, 1991, 202).

From the maturing world church are emerging theological reflections that bear the title of their geographical origins—ASIAN THEOLOGIES, AFRICAN THEOLOGIES. Others have originated in Anglo-Saxon contexts and speak to ethnic and gender-based issues of power and powerlessness—HISPANIC EVANGELICAL THEOLOGIES, BLACK THEOLOGIES, FEMINIST THEOLOGIES. Still others respond to issues of wealth and poverty, of political oppression—LIBERATION THEOLOGIES and Korean MINJUNG THEOLOGY.

Many of these new explorations remain deeply touched by a Neo-Enlightenment skepticism regarding the full integrity of the Scriptures. Such formulations too frequently place context above biblical text and minimize the hermeneutical priority of exegesis in their search.

These limitations create nervous concerns in the Anglo-Saxon evangelical community. Old expectations of a theology without context return: if the REVELATION of God is transcultural, shouldn't we expect the human exercise of theological reflection to sound the same across time and space, a *theologis perennis?* Legitimate fears of SYNCRETISM arise: are these new paths falling into a theological pluralism that cannot draw boundaries between TRUTH and error?

Expectations appear more positive in "Third World" settings where mission and theology have closer ties. Christian humility acknowledges its partnership debt to Western theological systems borrowed from the missionary. Christian hopes for the global progress of doctrine asks, "How can we do justice both to the absoluteness of Scripture's united testimony and to the uniqueness of our context in which it must speak again?" And Christian zeal for the gospel makes sure the question asked has a missionary intention and a missionary dimension.

HARVIE M. CONN

SEE ALSO Systematic Theology.

Bibliography. D. Bosch, *Transforming Mission: Paradigm Shifts in Theology of Mission;* E. Farley, *Theologia: The Fragmentation and Unity of Theological Education;* W. Jaeger, *Early Christianity and Greek Paideia;* R. Muller, *The Study of Theology: From Biblical Interpretation to Contemporary Formulation;* J. Scherer, *Gospel, Church, and Kingdom: Comparative Studies in World Mission Theology;* A. Shorter, *Toward a Theology of Inculturation;* J. Stamoolis, *Eastern Orthodox Mission Theology Today.*

Theology of Mission. A discipline that reflects on the presuppositions, assumptions, and concepts undergirding mission theory. Prior to the 1960s, a number of important people like GISBERTUS VOETIUS, JOSEF SCHMIDLIN, GUSTAF WARNECK, Karl Barth, Karl Hartenstein, Martin Kähler, WALTER FREYTAG, ROLAND ALLEN, HENDRIK KRAEMER, J. H. BAVINCK, W. A. Visser t'Hooft, MAX WARREN, Olav Myklebust, BENGT SUNDKLER, Carl F. H. Henry, and Harold Lindsell reflected theologically on mission. As a separate discipline with its own parameters, methodology, scholars, and focuses, theology of mission really began in the early 1960s with the work of GERALD ANDERSON. In 1961, Anderson edited what many consider to be the first text of the discipline, a collection of essays entitled *The Theology of Christian Mission.*

Ten years later, in *The Concise Dictionary of the Christian World Mission,* theology of mission was defined as "concerned with the basic presuppositions and underlying principles which determine, from the standpoint of Christian faith, the motives, message, methods, strategy and goals of the Christian world mission."

Theology of mission is multidisciplinary. Missiology is a multidisciplinary discipline that draws from many cognate disciplines. Within missiology, theology of mission examines the various cognate disciplines and clarifies their proximity to or distance from the center, Jesus Christ, asking whether there is a point beyond which the cognate disciplines may no longer be helpful or biblical. Theology of mission integrates who we are, what we know, and how we act in mission. It brings together our faith relationship with Jesus Christ, our spirituality, God's presence, the church's theological reflection throughout the centuries, a constantly new rereading of Scripture, our hermeneutic of God's world, our sense of participation in God's mission, and the ultimate purpose and meaning of the church and relates all these to the cognate disciplines of missiology. Theology of mission serves to question, clarify, integrate, and expand the presuppositions of the various cognate disciplines of missiology. As such, mission theology is a discipline in its own right, yet is not one of the related disciplines alongside the others, for it fulfills its function only as it interacts with all of them.

Theology of mission is integrative. When mission happens, all the various cognate disciplines occur simultaneously. So missiology must study mission not from the point of view of abstracted and separated parts, but from an integrative perspective that attempts to see the whole together. Theology of mission has to do with three arenas: (1) biblical and theological presuppositions and values are applied to (2) the ministries and mission activities of the church, set in (3) specific contexts in particular times and places.

First, theology of mission is *theology* because fundamentally it involves reflection about God. It seeks to understand God's mission, his intentions and purposes, his use of human instruments in his mission, and his working through his people in his world. Thus theology of mission deals with all the traditional theological themes of SYSTEMATIC THEOLOGY, but it does so in a way that differs from how systematic theologians have worked. The differences arise from the multidisciplinary missiological orientation of its theologizing.

In addition, because of its commitment to remain faithful to God's intentions, perspectives, and purposes, theology of mission shows a profound concern about the relation of the Bible to mission, attempting to allow Scripture not only to provide the foundational motivations for mission, but also to question, shape, guide, and evaluate the missionary enterprise itself (*see also* BIBLICAL THEOLOGY OF MISSION).

Second, theology of mission is *theology of.* In contrast to much systematic theology, here we are dealing with an applied science. At times it looks like what some would call pastoral or practical theology, due to this applicational nature. This type of theological reflection focuses specifically on a set of particular issues—those having to do with the mission of the church in its context. Theology of mission draws its incarnational nature from the ministry of Jesus, and always happens in a specific time and place.

Such contextual analysis facilitates a better understanding of the concrete situation, an understanding that helps the church hear the cries, see the faces, understand the stories, and respond to the living needs and hopes of the persons who are an integral part of that context. Part of this theological analysis today includes the history of the way the church's missions interfaced with that context down through history. The attitudes, actions, and events of the church's missional actions in a context will influence subsequent mission endeavors there.

Thus some scholars who deal with the history of theology of mission may not be especially interested in the theological issues as such, but may be concerned about the effects of that mission theology on mission activity in a context. They will often examine the various pronouncements made by church and mission gatherings (Roman Catholic, Orthodox, Ecumenical, Evangelical, Pentecostal, and charismatic) and question the impact of these on missional action. The documents resulting from these discussions become part of the discipline of theology of mission.

Third, theology of mission is specially oriented toward and for *mission*. Reflection in this arena is found in books, journals, and other publications dealing with the theory of missiology itself. However, neither missiology nor the theology of mission can be allowed to restrict itself to reflection only. As JOHANNES VERKUYL stated,

> Missiology may never become a substitute for action and participation. God calls for participants and volunteers in his mission. In part, missiology's goal is to become a "service station" along the way. If study does not lead to participation, whether at home or abroad, missiology has lost her humble calling. . . . Any good missiology is also a *missiologia viatorum*—"pilgrim missiology'" (1978, 6, 18).

Theology of mission is praxeological. Theology of mission, then, must eventually emanate in biblically informed and contextually appropriate missional action. The intimate connection of reflection with action is through a process known as PRAXIS. Although there have been a number of different meanings given to this idea, ORLANDO COSTAS's formulation is one of the most constructive.

"Missiology," Costas says, "is fundamentally a praxeological phenomenon. It is a critical reflection that takes place in the praxis of mission. . . . (it occurs) in the concrete missionary situation, as part of the church's missionary obedience to and participation in God's mission, and is itself actualized in that situation. . . . In reference to this witnessing action saturated and led by the sovereign, redemptive action of the Holy Spirit,

. . . the concept of missionary praxis is used. Missiology arises as part of a witnessing engagement to the gospel in the multiple situations of life" (1976, 8).

The concept of praxis helps us understand that not only the reflection, but profoundly the *action* as well is part of a "theology-on-the-way" that seeks to discover how the church may participate in God's mission in the world. The action is itself theological, and serves to inform the reflection, which in turn interprets, evaluates, critiques, and projects new understanding in transformed action in a constantly spiraling pilgrimage of missiological engagement in a context.

Because of the complexity of the inter- and multidisciplinary task that is theology of mission, mission theologians have found it helpful to focus on a specific integrating idea that serves as a hub through which to approach a rereading of Scripture. This "integrating theme" is selected on the basis of being contextually appropriate and significant, biblically relevant and fruitful, and missionally active and transformational.

Clearly we are trying to avoid bringing our own agendas to the Scripture and superimposing them on it. Rather, what is being sought is a way to bring a new set of questions to the text, questions that might help us see in the Scriptures what we had missed before. This new approach to Scripture is what DAVID BOSCH called "critical hermeneutics."

In 1987, the ASSOCIATION OF PROFESSORS OF MISSION said,

> The mission theologian does biblical and systematic theology differently from the biblical scholar or dogmatician in that the mission theologian is in search of the "habitus," the way of perceiving, the intellectual understanding coupled with spiritual insight and wisdom, which leads to seeing the signs of the presence and movement of God in history, and through his church in such a way as to be affected spiritually and motivationally and thus be committed to personal participation in that movement. . . . The center, therefore, serves as both theological content and theological process as a disciplined reflection of God's mission in human contexts. The role of the theologian of mission is therefore to articulate and "guard" the center, while at the same time to spell out integratively the implications of the center for all the other cognate disciplines (Van Engen, 1987, 524–25).

Thus we find that theology of mission is a process of reflection and action involving a movement from the biblical text to the faith community in mission in its context.

Theology of mission is definitional. One of the most interesting, significant, yet frustrating tasks of mission theology is to assist missiology in defining the terms it uses, including a definition of "mission" itself. By the way of illustration, the following may be offered as a preliminary definition of mission

Mission is the People of God
intentionally crossing barriers
from Church to non-church, faith to non-faith
to proclaim by word and deed
the coming of the Kingdom of God
in Jesus Christ,
through the Church's participation
in God's mission of reconciling people
to God, to themselves, to each other, and to the
world,
and gathering them into the Church
through repentance and faith in Jesus Christ
by the work of the Holy Spirit
with a view to the transformation of the world
as a sign of the coming of the Kingdom
in Jesus Christ.

Theology of mission is analytical. Theology of mission examines the theological and theoretical assumptions, meanings, and relations that permeate mission. To do this, mission theologians have found it helpful to partition the task into smaller segments. We noticed earlier that Gerald Anderson used the terms "faith, motives, message, methods, strategy, and goals." Jim Stamoolis studied *Eastern Orthodox Mission Theology Today* by analyzing "the historical background, the aim, the method, the motives, and the liturgy" of mission as that took place among and through the Eastern Orthodox.

Following this method, some mission theologians organize their questions around the fact that mission is MISSIO DEI, it is God's mission. So one finds a number of mission theologians asking about "God's mission" *(missio Dei)*, mission as it occurs among humans and utilizes human instrumentality *(missio hominum)*, missions as they take many forms through the endeavors of the churches *(missiones ecclesiae)*, and mission as it draws from and impacts global human civilization *(missio politica oecumenica)*.

So theology of mission is prescriptive as well as descriptive. It is synthetic (bringing about synthesis) and integrational. It searches for trustworthy and true perceptions concerning the church's mission based on biblical and theological reflection, seeks to interface with the appropriate missional action, and creates a new set of values and priorities that reflect as clearly as possible the ways in which the church may participate in God's mission in a specific context at a particular time.

When theology of mission is abstracted from mission practice it seems strange and can be too far removed from the concrete places and specific people that are at the heart of God's mission. Theology of mission is at its best when it is intimately involved in the heart, head, and hand

(being, knowing, and doing) of the church's mission. Theology of mission is a personal, corporate, committed, profoundly transformational search for a trinitarian understanding of the ways in which the people of God may participate in the power of the Holy Spirit in God's mission in God's world for whom Jesus Christ died.

CHARLES VAN ENGEN

Bibliography. G. H. Anderson, *The Theology of Christian Mission;* idem, *CDCWM*, pp. 594–95; J. H. Bavinck, *An Introduction to the Science of Missions;* H. Berkhof and P. Potter, *Keywords of the Gospel;* D. Bosch, *Transforming Mission: Paradigm Shifts in Theology of Mission;* A. Glasser and D. McGavran, *Contemporary Theologies of Mission;* H. Lindsell, *A Christian Philosophy of Missions;* R. Padilla, *Mission Between the Times: Essays on the Kingdom;* J. Scherer, *Gospel, Church and Kingdom: Comparative Studies in World Mission Theology;* W. Shenk, ed., *The Transfiguration of Mission: Biblical Theological & Historical Foundations;* W. Scott, *Bring Forth Justice: a Contemporary Perspective on Mission;* C. Van Engen, *Mission on The Way: Issues in Mission Theology,* idem, *God's Missionary People, Rethinking the Purpose of the Local Church;* C. Van Engen, P. Pierson and D. Gilliland, eds., *The Good News of the Kingdom: Mission Theology for the Third Millennium;* J. Verkuyl, *Contemporary Missiology: An Introduction;* G. Vicedom, *The Mission of God: An Introduction to a Theology of Mission.*

Theology of Religions. The wide range of Christian theological response to the existence of other world faiths has, for convenience if not total adequacy, been classified into three broad positions: exclusivism, inclusivism, and pluralism.

Exclusivism. The word is not being used in a personal, attitudinal, or social sense, that is, pride, superiority, and a desire to exclude others. Rather the word is theologically concerned only with the matter of where truth and salvation are to be found. It is the view that, if Jesus Christ is uniquely the truth, and the only way of salvation for humanity, then that excludes the possibility of other faiths being true in the same way, or being ways of salvation.

Exclusivism affirms that there is one living God, the Creator, who, in response to the radical fall of humanity, has taken action to reveal himself and to save his creation through the particular historical events recorded in the Bible, namely, the history of Israel and the Gospel story of Jesus of Nazareth. Jesus was the unique and final incarnation of God in a single historical human life. He both completed God's self-revelation and achieved God's work of salvation on the cross. Through his resurrection and ascension God vindicated him as Lord and so he is rightly to be worshiped as such. Salvation is therefore to be found only in and through Jesus Christ. Adherents of other faiths, in common with all human beings, are made in the image of God and share in the benefits of GENERAL REVELATION in

CONSCIENCE and nature. But other faiths as such cannot be ways of salvation, for that is only in Christ. There is therefore a radical discontinuity between the revelation and salvation of God in Christ and the tenets and claims of other religions. Exclusivism maintains that the central claims of Christianity are true, and that where the claims of Christianity conflict with those of other religions the latter are to be rejected as false. Salvation is not to be found in the structures of other religious traditions (*see also* UNIQUENESS OF CHRIST).

Though clearly identified with the evangelical theological tradition, exclusivism has a variety of views within it and questions to face. One major divide relates to the fate of the unevangelized—those who never in their lifetimes hear of Jesus Christ. Granted that salvation is only in Christ (the *ontological* necessity of Christ for salvation), is salvation also restricted to those who come to know him explicitly (the *epistemological* necessity of Christ)? Those who affirm that it is so restricted (labeled "restrictivists" by others) point to key texts such as John 14:6 and Acts 4:12. Others (nonrestrictivist exclusivists) are cautiously optimistic that God will save some who, while unreached by Christian evangelism, turn in some way from sin to God in repentance and faith. They point to the fact that Old Testament believers were saved but had no knowledge of the gospel of Jesus Christ in its New Testament form. Still others (advocates of "the wider hope") affirm that through Christ God will save multitudes who had no earthly opportunity to know and trust him. They point to the "pagan saints" of the Old Testament (non-Israelites who became believers) as examples of a wide phenomenon, not exceptions, and to texts such as Revelation 7:9 as implying a very wide optimism of salvation (*see* THE UNEVANGELIZED).

Exclusivism also has to wrestle with the extent to which it recognizes general revelation in other religions, and with the phenomenon of the actual worship of their adherents. In what sense is the living God active in the context of another faith if it includes some elements of truth that would be biblically valid, and what is the spiritual status of the prayers and devotion of human beings who have no knowledge of Christ?

Inclusivism. The one all-important point that exclusivism and inclusivism have in common is their commitment to the centrality of Jesus Christ. They are in agreement that Christ is the supreme and final revelation of God and that he is the one through whom ultimately people can and will be saved. However, whereas the exclusivist says that if Christ alone is the truth and the Savior, then that excludes all other faiths as vehicles of truth or salvation, the inclusivist argues that ultimately all truth is God's truth, wherever it is found. So Christ, who is the Truth, must therefore include all that is true in other faiths, elements of truth which must ultimately be from and through Christ. Christ is thus in some way present and active within other faiths, though in hidden ways, but is clearly and fully known only within the Christian faith. Inclusivism speaks, therefore, of continuity (rather than the exclusivist's discontinuity) between other faiths and Christianity, or it sees Christianity as the fulfillment of what is looked for, or hidden, or being prepared for, in other faiths.

Mainline Protestant inclusivism tends to give a high value to the existence of general revelation within other faiths, but to stop short of allowing that other religions can be salvifically effective. Roman Catholic inclusivism, however, since the work of Karl Rahner, and especially Vatican II, has been willing to affirm that the grace of God operates salvifically in other religions, but that it is grace in Christ. Those who genuinely respond to God's grace as experienced in another religion are implicitly responding to Christ and may therefore be called "anonymous Christians." They will be saved by Christ, but through the "sacraments" of their own religion, unless and until they are confronted with the gospel. So Christ remains definitive and normative, but salvation is somehow available through other faiths. Those who advocate inclusivism obviously want to steer between the rocks of narrowly dogmatic exclusivism (especially restrictivism), and the whirlpool of relativism and pluralism, which they equally strongly reject. They want to hold on to the uniqueness of Christ, and yet to find legitimate theological space within an understanding of God's sovereignty for the existence of non-Christian religions.

Inclusivists wrestle with the question as to whether other religions can be means of salvation, even if ultimately salvation depends on the work of Christ. But actually, the very question itself, "Is there salvation in other religions?" is strange, when considered from a biblical point of view. It seems to take for granted, as the premise on which the question rests, that salvation is something you get through a religion. But the radical biblical affirmation is that there is salvation in no religion. Religion does not save anybody. God does. And the Bible tells the story of what God has done in history to save his whole creation, including humanity. Salvation is the achievement of God on our behalf, not the end result of religious activity on our part. It is this fundamental fact about the Christian gospel—that it is the declaration of historical events by which God has intervened in Christ to save us from our sin—which exposes the inadequacy of all other religions. There is no salvation in them, not because they have nothing in common with Christianity in their beliefs (some do), but because they do not recount these events and therefore do not put people in touch with what God has already done to save them.

Pluralism. It is important to distinguish between pluralism as an ideological or theological stance and the simple fact of the social plurality of religions in many countries. It is one thing to respond to the latter with respect, love, and tolerance; it is quite another to accept the relativist philosophy that underlies theological religious PLURALISM.

Both exclusivism and inclusivism wish to be "Christocentric"—to preserve the centrality of Christ himself, whether in exclusive or inclusive terms. Christ is the center and the standard (norm) for all other faiths. Pluralists advocate a "theocentric" theology of religions, which places God *(theos)* at the center of the religious universe, not Christ or Christianity. All human religions (including Christianity) can then be understood as valid but different culturally and historically conditioned human responses to this one "Ultimate Divine Reality." Each response is partial and incomplete, but has its own element of truth and saving validity for those who follow it. Salvation is thus to be found in any or all faiths, including, but not confined to, Christianity. Christ and Christianity, instead of being the center of the saving and revealing work of God, "go into orbit" along with other faiths, as just one among many planetary responses to the gravitational pull of the sun of "transcendent reality" (another pluralist term) at the center. Or, to change the metaphor, the different religious names for the divine, are like the masks worn by classical actors. Each "face" may look very different, but the reality behind is single. The religious "ultimates" of the world faiths are the *personae*, or *impersonae* of the truly ultimate, which actually transcends all their partial (and mutually contradictory) insights and is "itself" beyond our knowledge (*see also* RELIGIOUS ULTIMACY).

Among the criticisms of the pluralist agenda in the theology of religions the following seem particularly serious. First, pluralism conceals an epistemological arrogance. It relativizes all the truth claims of the world faiths (not just those of Christianity) to a penultimate status while absolutizing its own stance as arbitrator. It fails to justify the epistemological grounds on which it claims sure knowledge about something ("the real") of which all religions have no ultimate knowledge. Second, it is subject to the self-destructive weakness of all radical relativisms, in claiming absolute truth for its own claim that all truth claims are relative. Third, it renders "God" abstract and impersonal, since "he/she/it" cannot be named, defined, or characterized in terms of any of the great religious traditions. The real, as it is in itself, is not to be identified with Yahweh, Allah, Jesus, Brahman, or any other. The rich biblical personal characterization of God is thus discounted as a mask, with no ultimate truth attaching to it. Fourth, it relativizes and diminishes Jesus, rejecting the classical incarnational Christology of the church as being only confessional or functional language with no ontological referential value. Thus, fifth, it requires a mythical reading of the New Testament in order to retain a semblance of using Christian vocabulary, but without historical realism. And finally, it renders Christian worship idolatrous and Christian mission invalid, inasmuch as pluralism requires that Christians, although they may continue to revere Jesus as their own saving point of contact with God, must surrender any claim to his absolute deity, Lordship, or claim on all people.

For these reasons, although pluralists tend to preserve the vocabulary and concepts of the Christian tradition, it is highly questionable whether pluralism can be regarded as a valid option for Christian theology of religions.

CHRISTOPHER J. H. WRIGHT

Bibliography. D. Carson, *The Gagging of God: Christianity Confronts Pluralism;* J. Hick, *An Interpretation of Religion: Human Responses to the Transcendent;* P. Knitter, *No Other Name: A Critical Survey of Christian Attitudes Towards the World Religions;* H. Netland, *Dissonant Voices: Religious Pluralism and the Question of Truth.*

Theravada Buddhism. Theravada Buddhism is one of the three main branches of Buddhism, along with Mahayana and Vajrayana. Unlike Vajrayana, the relatively homogeneous branch of Buddhism centered in Tibet (*see* TIBETAN BUDDHISM), Theravada is a relatively diverse collection of traditions connected as much by geography and culture as teachings. Theravada is the main tradition of the southeast Asian countries of Sri Lanka, Burma, Thailand, Laos, and Cambodia. MAHAYANA is the Buddhism of China, Japan, and Korea.

The name Theravada is the movement's self-chosen designation, meaning "the way of the elders *(theras).*" It has been called other things. In the first and second centuries A.D., when Mahayana Buddhism was growing in India and later China, Mahayanists called Theravadins Hinayana or the Lesser Vehicle. Mahayana, of course, means Greater Vehicle and this little bit of name-calling was the Mahayanists' way of claiming greater depth and profundity for their teaching.

Both Theravadins and Mahayanists trace their roots back to the sixth century B.C. and the life and teachings of a man named Siddharta Gautama (566–486 B.C.) who came to be known as the Buddha or the Enlightened One. It is almost impossible to tell whether Theravada or Mahayana is prior. The best reconstruction of Theravada history begins about 110 years after the Buddha's death when a major schism took place over the rules of discipline which the Buddha left to guide the monastic community, the *Sangha*. One group, the Sthaviravadins (the Sanskrit variant of the Pali Theravada) favored keeping the rules of discipline static while the Mahasamgikas favored change as cultural conditions warranted. Through numerous other splits (eighteen eventual sects is the usual number given), this traditional group, the Sthaviravada, seemed to maintain an identity, and when an early Indian king Asoka (272–236 B.C.) decided to send missionaries to carry the Buddha's teachings to neighboring countries, Theravada was the variant that stuck in southeast Asia, particularly Sri Lanka and Burma.

Despite its variety, we might identify seven distinctives of Theravada Buddhism:

1. Theravadins tend to emphasize the monastic life and the *arahat* ideal. *Arahats* are mostly monks, spiritually accomplished and on the way to Enlightenment, the goal of Buddhism.
2. Theravadins use Pali as their liturgical and philosophical language. Pali was probably the language of the Buddha.
3. Theravadins, more than other schools of Buddhism, emphasize the historical life events of Gautama Buddha. Like other Buddhists, they recognize that there have been many other Buddhas, but for Theravadins, Gautama, especially his life in India, is central.
4. Theravada Buddhism is located geographically in southeast Asia.
5. Theravada is distinguished by its emphasis on Pali commentaries (*atthakathas*) written to elucidate the many volumes of the Pali canon, the main scriptural books of the Theravada Buddhists. The commentaries were put in their final written form in Sri Lanka in the fifth century A.D. by Buddhaghosa, Theravada Buddhism's greatest scholar and intellect.
6. Although most of the sections of the Theravada Pali canon have similar books in other Buddhist traditions, one section, the scholastic Abhidhamma Pitaka, is unique, emphasizing the signature doctrines of Theravada Buddhism, *anatta* (no-self) and *anicca* (impermanence).
7. Throughout history, most Theravada Buddhist cultures have had a distinctive symbiotic relationship between monastery and monarchy. In general, southeast Asian Buddhist kings have seen themselves as supporters, protectors, and, upon occasion, purifiers of the order of the monks, the Sangha. The monks, in turn, have tended to see themselves as spiritual and sometimes political advisors to the kings.

In many ways, Theravada Buddhism occupies a similar place in the overall scheme of Buddhism as evangelical Christianity does in Christianity. Both place a heavy emphasis on a specific scriptural tradition, although their concepts of the authority of those scriptures differ. Both place a heavy emphasis on the historicity of their founders, Gautama and Jesus. Both are missions oriented, with similar "Great Commission" charges from their founders to go and preach the *dhamma*/gospel. Both have a vision of each individual being on a spiritual journey to escape the shortcomings of this life in anticipation of a better state to come, and that a life of moral purity is an important foundation for taking that journey.

It is this last point, however, that most clearly illustrates some of the sharpest differences between the two paths. Theravada Buddhists do not see a god or gods as being central figures in helping the spiritual seeker. Theravada Buddhism has sometimes been called a non-theistic religion because of its insistence on the ultimate aloneness of each of us. Although the Buddha did not deny that the gods of the Hindu pantheon are helpful at certain lower levels of the journey, he was adamant that when it comes to final Enlightenment each of us must "come and see" *(ehi passako)* for him or herself. And in the end it is an ironic journey, because the "self" that successfully "comes and sees" turns out to be an illusion, swallowed up in the oneness of Nirvana.

TERRY C. MUCK

SEE ALSO Buddhism, Mahayana Buddhism, AND Tibetan Buddhism.

Bibliography. S. Collins, *Selfless Persons: Imagery and Thought in Theravada Buddhism;* K. L. Hazra, *History of Theravada Buddhism in South-East Asia;* W. King, *Theravada Meditation;* R. C. Lester, *Theravada Buddhism in Southeast Asia;* B. L. Smith, *Religion and Legitimation of Power in Sri Lanka* and *Religion and Legitimation of Power in Thailand, Laos, and Burma;* D. K. Swearer, *Buddhism and Society in Southeast Asia.*

Third Culture Kids (TCK). A "third culture kid" (or TCK) is an individual who, having spent a significant part of the developmental years in a culture other than that of the parents, incorporates elements of his or her parents' culture with elements from the culture of the host country to form a personal combination of cultures or "third culture." Third culture kids are not only children of missionaries but also children of diplomatic, international business, military, and other personnel who have lived overseas.

The factors that most significantly influence the TCK's life and WORLDVIEW are the mobility and cross-cultural experience that characterize the developmental period. There are both significant benefits related to being raised in a country other than that of one's parents during this time of life, as well as accompanying challenges. For example, TCKs show mixed levels of maturity, often exhibiting outlooks and understandings of life beyond what would normally be expected by monocultural peers. In addition, TCKs often demonstrate an advanced ability to communicate with adults and are generally comfortable and capable of getting around in the world, even moving from one country to another. At the same time, however, such common tasks as writing a check or using new phone systems may seem daunting. As a result, TCKs often subjectively experience being "out-of-phase" with monocultural peers, feeling they don't fit in.

There are other issues related to the dimensions of mobility and cross-cultural experience. Leave-taking is one; relationships another. Because the average TCK moves eight times by the age of eighteen and may have to deal with people of many cultures, he or she often becomes quite adaptable, unshaken by change, and may be quite adept at building relationships and empathizing sensitively with others. A strong sense of independence and realistic views about loss and death are also developed. During adulthood, however, the TCK may experience a deep sense of rootlessness, a tendency to have too many relationships to manage, and difficulty planning. The pain associated with leave-taking as children often results in survival responses such as a "get close quickly, detach quickly" response in relationships, and there may be issues of unresolved grief from the many separations. Consequently, guardedness in relationships, almost automatic withdrawal from intimacy, and a flattening of emotions are common.

Because of the variety of experiences developmentally, TCKs have to deal with issues of cultural balance and skills as well as a unique worldview. While on the one hand they often have an understanding of different cultures and may move easily and comfortably between them, they also may experience the sense of being a "hidden immigrant"—appearing to others as if they should fit into a culture while not feeling as if they do. In addition, with their exposure to different cultural value systems and resultant ability to see differing points of view, TCKs often experience the challenge of personal values being unsettled and in constant flux. The unique and expanded worldview of TCKs often leads to a desire to become involved in the international arena where they often display exceptional linguistic skills. An associated challenge is the fact that the TCK feels deeply the pain of the real world. At the same time he or she may become impatient with those less knowledgeable and discerning and may be perceived as being critical and arrogant.

DAVE WICKSTROM

SEE ALSO Missionary Children.

Bibliography. D. Pollock, *The TCK Profile;* R. Van Reken, *Letters Never Sent;* D. Walters, *An Assessment of Reentry Issues of the Children of Missionaries.*

Third Wave. *See* PENTECOSTAL MOVEMENT.

Third World. The term, Third World, refers to those nations primarily in Africa, Asia, Latin America, and the Pacific which emerged from the colonial era after World War II. Having its origin in the commercial class of the French Revolution (third estate), the term Third World was coined first by the French intellectuals in the late 1940s and later by leaders of the nonaligned nations movement at a conference in Indonesia in 1955. Popular usage of the term has shifted from the political connotations with its emphasis on opposition to the colonial powers and the cold war nuclear threats of the first (capitalist) and second (communist) worlds, to a focus on the issues which are common to the Third World nations. Because the Third World represents approximately 4 billion of the world's population (6 billion), attempts have been made to change the term to the TWO THIRDS WORLD. Despite these efforts, the Third World remains a primary term of identification.

History. The emergence of the Third World may be viewed as the product of two major forces—external forces linked to the era of imperialism and internal forces linked to nationalism and REVOLUTION (Gheddo; Isbister). The period of Western imperialism began with the explorations of the fifteenth and sixteenth centuries. The discovery of new lands under the thrones of Europe gave rise to a period of rapid expansion of empires and the establishment of colonial rule (*see* COLONIALISM). Along with colonial rule came the inevitable access to the resources of the colonies and the economic advantage for the "mother country." The massive impact included the systems of education, economics, healthcare, justice, and government which were established as part of the process of colonization. Perhaps the most virulent import were the languages of the colonial empires. Although the colonial landscape changed with the Industrial Revolution, it continued unchallenged through the end of the nineteenth century with the rapid colonization of Africa and parts of Asia by the Western nations. World War I marked the end of the era of imperialism and the foreshadowing of the period of NATIONALISM which would follow World War II.

Beginning with the independence of India (1947) and China (1949), the political map began its most radical change in history. The spread of nationalist movements was fueled by the economic recovery in the West, the cold war tensions, and the social climate brought about by the formation of the United Nations. Nationalist leaders emerged from within the colonies with the momentum born of promises of a better world. While in some cases armed revolutions ensued, for the most part the nationalist movements pressured the already weakened governments of the West, resulting in the formation of newly independent nations. By the 1980s, the majority of the world had won or been granted political independence. Due in large part to the rapid political upheaval, the promises of better times have largely gone unachieved. Forces such as the vestiges of colonial structures, a global economy with advantages to the industrialized nations, unstable political climates, armed conflicts, and the population explosion contribute to a staggering array of challenges for the newly formed states of the Third World.

Third World Issues. Although the nations of the Third World represent the widest possible diversity of cultures, religions, and lifestyles, there are common issues which distinguish them from the more developed nations. The foremost issue facing the Third World is widespread POVERTY (Isbister). While poverty is to some extent relative and occurs in every nation, the extreme effects of poverty are experienced to a disproportionate degree in the Third World. In an attempt to avoid overstating the gap between rich countries and the Third World, the World Bank uses a "purchasing power parity" which in its estimates of per capita income reveal that U.S. incomes vary from 3 times higher than the richer countries of the Third World to 20 times higher than the poorest countries (Isbister). Another way of understanding poverty is in absolute terms or income levels at which people are unable to afford food which is nutritionally adequate and essential non-food items. Using an absolute standard, the United Nations Development Program estimates that one-third of the Third World lives in poverty with even higher proportions in Asia (60%) and Africa (50%).

The problems which cause or result from poverty are complex; however, a number of critical issues surround the extreme poverty of the Third World. The issues of health and physical well-being are of primary concern. Diseases which are linked to the shortage of potable water and inadequate nutrition plague the Third World. While the capacity to produce food and essential non-food items varies among nations, the difficulties of distribution and generation of sustainable income to purchase available supplies are common problems of the Third World. Added to these critical issues are the challenges of establishing appropriate education, sustainable development, healthcare, adequate housing, and equitable economic growth. Along with the debt crises, these issues are shaping the agenda of the Third World and to an escalating extent that of the industrialized world.

Missiological Considerations. One of the spin-offs of the independence movements among Third World nations has been an increasing attitude among Western Christians that missions to the Third World should be from the Third World. In other words, independence for the church is akin to that of the nations. While it is true that an increased partnership must be realized, it is also true that the church in the Third World cannot address the problems alone (*see* GLOBALISM). As Johannes Verkuyl put it, "interdependence is not only a necessity of life but also a calling with which we have been charged." Interdependence demands a "vision of transformation" which includes not only the generous sharing of resources, but a sustained commitment to the concerns of both evangelism and sociopolitical involvement (Samuel). The commitment was summarized well in the theme of Lausanne II, "calling the whole Church to take the whole Gospel to the whole world." The precarious position of the Third World raises major concerns for missiological reflection which include an ongoing commitment to "teaching them to observe" and "love your neighbor as yourself" (Matt. 22:39; 28:20).

C. DOUGLAS MCCONNELL

Bibliography. P. Gheddo, *Why Is the Third World Poor?;* J. Isbister, *Promises Not Kept: The Betrayal of Social Change in the Third World;* Lausanne Congress on World Evangelization, *The Lausanne Covenant;* V. Samuel, *Serving with the Poor in Asia,* pp. 145–54; United Nations Development Program, *Human Development Report;* J. Verkuyl, *To Break the Chains of Oppression,* pp. 85–103.

Third World Mission Boards and Societies. *See* NON-WESTERN MISSION BOARDS AND SOCIETIES.

Third World Women. Wherever Christianity has spread women have been deeply involved in that spread in a variety of ways. In recent discussion, the term THIRD WORLD (or TWO-THIRDS WORLD) has been used to describe the non-Western population. The simple truth is that throughout the history of the church, everywhere the vast majority of the women involved have been marginalized socioeconomically and culturally.

Focusing on the more recent historical context, Western women were involved in educational, medical, and social ministries, many of these among Third World women themselves. Gradually the recipients have become partners in mission, even though they often lack access to the economic resources of their Western counterparts.

Often separated from men in their social life, Third World women typically focused their own mission work among other women. Examples of women from indigenous churches engaged in mission include the Mar Thoma Church of India, who deployed women missionaries in 1919.

Third World women have been engaged in a wide variety of missionary endeavors. Many evangelists serve as missionaries within their own borders. Aleyamma Ommen of India, for example, traveled to different parts of the country with a band of people singing and preaching. Medical work was also started among women in India, China, and Africa, where culture forbade women from having male doctors. Medical and nursing colleges were started and women were trained as doctors and nurses to meet this need. A similar situation evolved in social work. Missionary women wrote and fought against social injustices, including widow burning, temple prostitution, foot binding, and so-called female circumcision. By the 1950s, many Third World women had taken up the responsibility to engage in this work. In the late 1800s and early 1900s, PANDITA RAMABAI was a pioneer in social development for women. Many of the Third World churches followed the Western example of organizing women's auxiliaries and organizations. The Mar Thoma Church, for example, started a women's voluntary Evangelistic Society *(Sannadha Savika Sangam)* in 1919. Even though women's participation in official church leadership positions was limited, they were still vitally involved in witnessing, social work, raising funds for churches, and training women to be models in their Christian lifestyle.

Formal theological education for women in Third World settings started with the development of training centers. By the 1960s many such centers had developed into theological colleges. Though many women were trained, formal leadership positions in the church were often unobtainable. More recently, however, some of the mainline churches in India have begun ordaining women. Generally most evangelical churches have not yet followed this practice, though many of them are debating the issue.

When we look at the missiological theories applied in mission work by Third World women, we can see several gradual changes taking place. Initially their work was confined to ministry among women and children. Later, in conciliar circles, Third World women were deeply involved in theological reflection and cooperation in different evangelical and non-evangelical organizations, including the WORLD COUNCIL OF CHURCHES (WCC), the Ecumenical Association of Third World Theologians (EATWAT), various National Christian Councils, the LAUSANNE MOVEMENT, and the WORLD EVANGELICAL FELLOWSHIP (WEF).

Slowly the emphasis has been changing to focus on both men and women in mission. Women's leadership in the churches became an important issue in the ECUMENICAL MOVEMENT of the 1970s, when the word "sexism" was used to describe gender discrimination. Throughout this time, Third World women maintained a strong biblical emphasis, rarely questioning the authority of the Bible. However, they were struggling to change some of the misunderstandings of the teachings of the Bible in relation to women's leadership. Many feel that unnecessary restrictions were put on women because of these misunderstandings. Following the UN "Decade of Women" (1976–85), on Easter Day in 1988 the WCC launched a decadal emphasis on the empowerment of women to participate in the decisions which affect them. Numerous activities promoting women's development and empowerment were organized in churches and church assemblies around the world.

Third World women have also become more actively involved among the evangelical organizations such as Lausanne Committee for World Evangelization, and the WEF. In 1980 only 9 percent of the participants were women, but by 1989 about 25 percent of the conferees at LAUSANNE CONGRESS II in Manila were women. Many of these were from the Third World and a few were involved as committee chairs and speakers, including Juliet Thomas and Sakhi Athyal. One result has been that women's role as leaders in the churches is increasingly discussed and accepted.

In their opportunity for mission women from the Third World have come a long way. But change is still needed in many areas. While the process of change has already started, it is important to recognize the possibilities of the critical importance of women as responsive entry points to resistant people groups in evangelism and community development. In China, the house church movement has grown largely through the ministry of women. Of the fifty thousand prayer cells in Paul Cho's church in Korea only three thousand of the leaders are men. So in many countries women's leadership in mission is crucial. There is an urgent need to recruit, train, and support far more women if we are to reach the unreached. It is not a matter of competition between men and women, but of necessity of sharing the load together: men and women need to work together as a community of believers in the Third World for the purpose of God's mission and the church's commission.

SAKHI ATHYAL

Bibliography. S. Athyal, *Indian Women in Mission;* V. Febella M. M. and M. A. Oduyoye, eds., *With Passion and Compassion: Third-World Women Doing Theology;* J. S. Pobee and B. Von Wartenberg-Potter, *New Eyes for Reading: Biblical and Theological Reflections by Women* *from the Third World;* J. Webster and E. Webster, *The Church and Women in the Third-World.*

Thoburn, Isabella (1840–1901). American pioneer missionary educator in India. The sister of the well known Methodist Bishop of India, JAMES THOBURN, she was sent to India by the Women's Foreign Missionary Society of the Methodist Church as one of the first single women sent out for educational work. During her thirty years in Lucknow, India, she proved to be an excellent teacher, administrator, and true friend to the students. She started a school with six Christian girls which grew to twenty-five in a month and eventually became a nine-acre complex for both boys and girls.

Convincing Indian parents about educating girls was a difficult task. One of the issues she struggled against was the caste system. She believed in educating all the caste girls and boys equally, but at the same time she wanted to respect the Indian culture. Her success in establishing a girls school for elementary and secondary education led her to attempt to start college education for women. She wrote articles and spoke out for their cause. In 1887 she opened a Christian College for women in Lucknow, India. That college produced many women leaders and scholars.

Thoburn was a deaconess missionary. Her mission theory came from the ideology of "women's work for women," based on the idea that education was the key for the liberation of women around the world. She also believed in creating the best leadership for women in India, and in this she succeeded.

SAKHI ATHYAL

Bibliography. R. P. Beaver, *American Protestant Women in World Mission: A History of the First Feminist Movement in North America;* J. M. Thoburn, *Life of Isabella Thoburn;* D. L. Robert, *American Women in Mission: A Social History of their Thought and Practice.*

Thoburn, James Mills (1836–1922). American Methodist bishop and missionary in India, Myanmar, and Singapore. Thoburn has been called "Methodism's missionary expansionist par excellence." He was raised in Ohio and later attended Allegheny College in western Pennsylvania. Coming to personal faith in Christ as a teen, he soon heard a distinct call from the Lord to "go preach my gospel." Within three years he was on his way to North India. After an initial tour, Thoburn took the advice of fellow-missionary WILLIAM TAYLOR and transferred to the teeming city of Calcutta, where he had great success in revival/evangelistic meetings.

From Calcutta, Thoburn moved to Burma and ministered to an Anglo-Burmese community in Rangoon. Within a few years he transferred to

Singapore and successfully planted a passion for missions in the English-speaking church of that city. Within fifteen years Methodist work began in Sarawak, Sumatra, Java, the Philippines, and the Malay Peninsula. Thoburn's insistence of self-government and self-support in these fledgling communities did much to assure their internal strength and durability. Thoburn's call for resident bishops in foreign fields initially caused a sensation, yet at length became the standard, quite fruitful approach of Methodist missions worldwide.

J. MICHAEL CONNOR

Bibliography. C. T. Copplestone, *Twentieth-Century Perspectives: The Methodist Episcopal Church, 1896–1939.*

Thomas, Madathilparampil Mammen (1916–96). Indian theologian, thinker, and ecumenical leader. Born in Kerala, India, in 1916, he gave leadership to many local, national and international organizations such as the World Student Christian Federation, East Asia Christian Council, Christian Institute for the Study of Religion and Society (1962–76), and WORLD COUNCIL OF CHURCHES (of which he was the Moderator 1968–75). He also served as the governor of the State of Nagaland.

He taught as a visiting professor in numerous centers of learning such as Union Theological Seminary (New York), Princeton, Perkins School of Theology, the Selley Oaks Colleges, and the University of Hamburg. During the last years of his life until his death in 1996 he wrote prolifically, and encouraged several forums dealing with human rights. It is estimated that the articles, book reviews, booklets, and books he wrote number over 1,500. The scores of books he wrote include *The Acknowledged Christ of the Indian Renaissance, The Christian Response to Asian Revolution, Salvation and Humanism,* and *My Ecumenical Journey.* His approach was to use the rich values in different ideologies such as Marxist thought, Gandhi's teachings, and Hindu spirituality for christocentric action and reflection. This may be termed "Christ-centered syncretism" or "spirituality for combat."

According to him in Christ only we find the ideal humanness, in his death limitless love, and in his lordship the unity of all humankind. The church's mission is to see the presence of Christ and his work in all peoples' search for full humanity in their God-given liberty and freedom.

SAPHIR ATHYAL

Thompson, Elizabeth Maria Bowen (1794–1869). English missionary to Lebanon. Born in England and raised in a Christian home, Elizabeth Bowen came to Christ as a child. Called early to the mission field, she joined the Syro-

Egyptian Mission. While in Syria she met and married James Thompson, a medical doctor.

From early on Bowen devoted her energies to opening schools and teaching women who longed for access to education. This work was cut short when her husband offered his medical services during the Crimean War. He came down with malignant fever shortly after their arrival, and soon died. After his death, Bowen returned to England.

In 1860 she joined the efforts of the Syrian Temporal Relief Fund, which helped Marionite Christian widows who escaped to Beirut after Syrian persecution. Her desire for a more hands-on ministry led her to Beirut, where she opened up her home to the widows and taught them basic skills that enabled them to support themselves and their children.

Her ministry expanded dramatically. Within three months, five schools were operating. Invitations began to come to open schools in other villages. Thompson traveled throughout the country, opening and staffing new schools. By 1864 a total of eighteen schools were founded. She dedicated the rest of her life to ministering to those decimated by war, opening schools for the disabled as well as the widows.

PENNY GUSHIKEN

Bibliography. E. C. Dawson, *Missionary Heroines in Many Lands;* E. R. Pitman, *Missionary Heroines in Eastern Lands: Women's Work in Mission Fields.*

Thompson, Muriwhenua (1930–92). New Zealand evangelist. Thompson was born in Mamaranui in northern New Zealand. While his own hopes centered on playing in a band, his mother's dream of him working as a member of the clergy led her to enroll him for boarding at the United Maori Mission while he attended school in Auckland. It was there that the influence of missionary Charlie Bennett played a crucial role in his coming to Christ.

Born with a heart problem, Thompson was often bedridden. After coming to Christ, he used those times to read about evangelists and preachers. Increasingly influenced through their lives to follow the path of an evangelist, he eventually joined Open Air Campaigners, a group promoting open-air evangelism and giving Thompson freedom to express his personality.

For the next several decades, Thompson's fiery preaching was heard throughout New Zealand. He was instrumental in kindling a revival in the Solomon Islands during a tour in 1970. On his return to New Zealand he was the chief speaker for the Marches for Jesus held in twelve major cities from 1972 on.

Throughout the years he also played a key mediatorial role between Maori activists and European conservatives, always hoping for reconciliation and redressing of grievances over issues of land, politics, and power.

A. SCOTT MOREAU

Bibliography. D. Stewart, *AFC,* pp. 200–204.

Thompson, Thomas (1708–73). English pioneer missionary to America and Ghana. In 1745 Thompson left a promising position as fellow and dean of Christ's College, Cambridge, to become a missionary under the SOCIETY FOR THE PROPAGATION OF THE GOSPEL (SPG) to New Jersey in America. There he came in contact with slaves and this inspired in him a desire to take the gospel to Africans in West Africa. The SPG agreed to send him and Thompson arrived in what is today Ghana in 1752 as the first Anglican missionary to any part of Africa. Due to ill health, Thompson was able to stay in Africa less than five years and he returned to England in 1756.

During his brief time in Africa he engaged in evangelism and teaching and baptized a number of African converts. Three converts, African boys under the age of twelve, were sent to England for further education. Two died but one, PHILIP QUAQUE, survived and was ordained in 1765 as the first African (and the first non-European since the Reformation) to receive Holy Orders in the Church of England. Quaque in turn returned to the Gold Coast under the SPG, where he served as a missionary until his death in 1816.

HAROLD A. NETLAND

Bibliography. T. Thompson, *An Account of Two Missionary Voyages.*

Thomson, James "Diego" (1788–1854). Innovative Scottish pioneer missionary to Latin America. Born in Scotland, Thomson was one of the first Protestant missionaries to Latin America, arriving in Argentina in 1818 as an agent of the British and Foreign Bible Society. He also represented the Lancastrian Educational Society, which promoted schools in which older students helped teach the younger ones and the Bible was the primary textbook. The liberal political climate in the newly independent South American countries and discreditation of conservative Catholic clergy from Spain opened the door for amazing success. Thomson established some one hundred Lancastrian schools in Buenos Aires alone and was made an honorary citizen of Argentina and of Chile, where he was invited by the government in 1821. In 1822 he went to Peru at the request of the Liberator, San Martin, and then to Ecuador, distributing Bibles everywhere. In Colombia he founded a national Bible Society whose directors included ten Catholic clergy. Sadly, a conservative political reaction and Vatican pressure undid most of Thomson's work in South America, although seeds remained. In

1827 Thomson was sent by the Bible Society to Mexico, and later worked in the Caribbean. After another attempt in Mexico in 1842, he spent the rest of his ministry in the evangelization of Spain.

STEPHEN SYWULKA

Three-Self Movement (China). After the People's Republic of China (PRC) was established (1949), a group of 40 Chinese Christian leaders met in Beijing in July 1950 to draft a manifesto calling for the end of all Chinese church ties with Western denominations and mission agencies. A year later (April 1951) about 150 representatives of China's larger denominations met in Beijing and formed the Chinese Christian Three-Self Reform Committee. The designation "Three-Self" was taken from RUFUS ANDERSON's definition of the aim of missions as "the planting of churches which would be self-governing, self-supporting, and self-propagating" (see INDIGENOUS CHURCHES). This committee was charged to replace the National Christian Council (formed in 1922) as the voice of Chinese Protestantism, since the council's "cultural imperialism" (Western ties) and theological liberalism (conservative churches refused to join) were regarded as unsuited to the new era. In 1954, with the official endorsement of the government the committee formed the Chinese Christian Three-Self Patriotic movement (TSPM) to represent Chinese Protestantism before the PRC authorities. By 1958 this organization had established branches in every province under the direct control of the national Religious Affairs Bureau. Separate Protestant denominations ceased altogether, and soon almost all churches in China closed down.

Then followed the Cultural Revolution; madness overtook the nation, and Christians suffered unbelievably. Fortunately, the coming of Deng Xiaoping to national leadership and his stress on "New Realism" eventually brought political relaxation. The TSPM reappeared and began to encourage and oversee the reopening of churches along with the restoration of their properties. By 1990 more than 6,000 churches were functioning, and over 15,000 other meeting points were registered for religious use. At least fourteen TSPM seminaries reopened and renewed former patterns of pastoral and lay biblical training, although no deviation was permitted from a pro-government political posture. Even so, during those most difficult years, a growing "Christianity fever" throughout the countryside was widely admitted by both political and TSPM authorities. This brought into being a "house church" movement that functions beyond TSPM control (see CHINESE HOUSE CHURCH MOVEMENT). Christians are currently estimated at about 35 million. Whether all congregations will eventually regis-

ter with the TSPM largely depends on the power struggle in Beijing between reactionaries and progressives.

ARTHUR F. GLASSER

Bibliography. D. H. Adeney, *China: The Church's Long March;* A. Hunter and K.-K Chan, *Protestantism in Contemporary China.*

Three-Self Churches. See INDIGENOUS CHURCHES.

Tibetan Buddhism. See VAJRAYANA (TIBETAN) BUDDHISM.

Tilak, Narayan Vaman (1862–1919). Indian poet, hymn writer, and contextualizer. Narayan Vaman Tilak was born in a Brahmin family in 1862 in a village in what is now Maharashtra state in western India. His mother and her father introduced him from infancy to the devotional *(bhakti)* piety of popular Hinduism. He was a gifted writer who is acknowledged as one of three poets responsible for a rebirth of Marathi poetry at the turn of the twentieth century.

Tilak was baptized in 1895 and his gifts were immediately employed for Christ; the many hymns he composed continue in wide use wherever Marathi is spoken. Some ten years after his baptism he intentionally adopted the poetic style (and even religious content to a large extent) of the Hindu *bhakti* poets, adding immensely to the power of his lyrics. He performed *kirtans* (recitation/song performances in traditional Hindu style) to present Christ appropriately to Hindus. He is most widely quoted for his claim to have come to Christ over Tukaram's bridge, Tukaram being generally acknowledged as the greatest of the medieval Marathi *bhakti* poets.

In the two years prior to his death, Tilak struggled toward a truly fresh expression of Christian faith that would impact the Hindu world. He concluded that he was called to be a Tukaram and a St. Paul combined in one, and began a brotherhood of both baptized and unbaptized disciples of Christ. His early death ended this striking effort, one of the few attempts in Protestant mission history to respond seriously to the demands of resistant Hindu contexts.

H. L. RICHARD

Bibliography. P. S. Jacob, *The Experiential Response of N. V. Tilak;* H. L. Richard, *Christ-Bhakti: Narayan Vaman Tilak and Christian Work among Hindus;* L. Tilak, *I Follow After An Autobiography;* idem, *From Brahma to Christ: The Story of Narayan Vaman Tilak and Lakshmibal his Wife;* J. C. Winslow, *Narayan Vaman Tilak: The Christian Poet of Maharashtra.*

Ting, Li-Mei (c. 1875–1937). Chinese evangelist and missions mobilizer. Born in Shandong province, Ting was deeply affected by the Boxer Uprising of 1900. He preached to students in

China, challenging them to devote their lives to full-time ministry. In 1909, more than one hundred students responded during a revival in Shandong province. In 1910 the Chinese Student Volunteer Movement was formed, with guidance from the YMCA Student Department. Ting resigned from his pastorate to give leadership to the movement. In twelve years 1,570 enlisted, 530 for full-time ministry. He is remembered for his insights into the Scriptures, intensive zeal for evangelism, and compelling presentation of China's need for educated pastors.

SAMUEL LING

Tippett, Alan R. (1911–88). Australian missiologist and missionary to Fiji. Tippett, the son of a Wesleyan pastor, spent his childhood in Victoria, Australia. After studies at Queen's College of Melbourne University, Tippett was ordained in the Methodist Church and with his wife, Edna, served in rural Victoria. The Tippetts were appointed to Fiji in 1941, where they served for twenty years. Tippett held many positions distinguishing himself as a pastor, church leader, and educator. Tippett's commitment to the Fijians led him to learn the local language, giving his first sermon in Fijian some two months after his arrival, and to regularly minister in the villages. During his last furlough from Fiji, Tippett pursued an M.A. from the American University in Washington, D.C. Tippett's early writings caught the attention of DONALD MCGAVRAN, who invited Tippett to join him at the newly founded Institute of Church Growth in Oregon in 1961. Tippett taught at the Institute and pursued a Ph.D. in anthropology at the University of Oregon. In 1965 he joined McGavran in establishing the School of World Mission at Fuller Theological Seminary. During the following twelve years, Tippett greatly influenced missiology and church growth through his interdisciplinary approach in teaching and writing. Tippett's scholarly contributions included his role as the founding editor of the journal, *Missiology.* Tippett retired in 1977 and returned to Canberra, Australia, where he continued to be influential through his writings.

DOUGLAS MCCONNELL

Bibliography. A. R. Tippett, *Solomon Islands Christianity;* idem, *Church Growth and the Word of God;* idem, *Introduction to Missiology;* D. Whiteman, *IBMR,* 16:4 (1992): 163–66.

Tithe, Tithing. Tithing (the giving of one-tenth of one's income) was an Old Testament ordinance designed by God primarily for the maintenance of the temple service (Deut. 12:2–7; 17–19; 14:22–29) and for charitable purposes to support widows, orphans, aliens, and the Levites (those who had inherited no property in Israel) (Deut. 26:12). It was an ancient custom (Abraham had paid tithes to Melchizedek; Gen. 14:20) and the underlying principle was that God owned everything and had given us of his bounty. In recognition of that, we should return something to him to be used for the purposes of ministry.

In the New Testament, except for one casual reference to Abraham (Heb. 7:2), tithing is mentioned only critically, and that by Jesus, because tithing had become a source of spiritual pride and abuse among the religious legalists of his day. Complex regulations were in the process of being developed regarding the tithing of virtually everything, rules that were later codified in the Mishnah. Jesus points out that such meticulous calculation was hypocritical when used as a cloak to cover neglect of what really mattered— "the weightier matters of the law, justice, mercy and faithfulness" (Matt. 23:23; Luke 11:42). The Old Testament prophets also recognized that following the letter of the tithing laws was meaningless apart from a sincere heart committed to the Lord (Amos 4:4). The self-righteous Pharisee mentioned by Jesus in his parable, who included tithing as one of his noblest virtues, epitomized this attitude (Luke 18:9–14).

Although tithing was open to abuse, the fundamental principle that God's people should support the ministry is maintained in the New Testament. Jesus accepted financial support for his ministry from those who followed him (Luke 8:1–3) and even maintained a surplus, necessitating a treasurer (John 13:29), the money being used for charitable purposes. Jesus was operating on the principle that was later taken up by the early church that "the worker is worth his keep" (Matt. 10:9–10) and should therefore not need to make excessive provision for himself because the ministry should be supported by those who are able to provide. This became the rule laid down by the apostle Paul, one that he traces directly back to Jesus, that "those who preach the gospel should make their living from the gospel" (1 Cor. 9:14). Paul sees it as a privilege that we can share in the work of the ministry by giving, and he uses Jesus as an example—he was rich and became poor for us, so that we through his poverty might become rich (2 Cor. 8:1–15). So Paul gratefully received gifts for his ministry (Phil. 4:14–18) and accepted contributions for the needs of others (Rom. 16:25–27), but he also worked with his own hands (as a tentmaker) to provide for himself (Acts 18:3; 1 Cor. 4:12). He had learned through this to trust the Lord who can supply all our needs according to his riches in glory through Christ Jesus (Phil. 4:19).

The New Testament teaches that everything belongs to God and we owe everything to him. We are to engage in honorable work, support our families, cheerfully support the ministry from our means, give as we are able, and more if necessary, counting it a privilege to participate in the work of God in this way. If God leads us to give a tithe of our income to such work, that would certainly be acceptable to him. If God should lead us to give in other ways and according to other formulas, that would also be an acceptable procedure. In the end we should know that we brought nothing into this world and we can take nothing out (1 Tim. 5:7), that an inordinate grasping of our money brings nothing but trouble (1 Tim. 4:10), and we should be building up treasures in heaven, not on earth, by the way we handle our finances.

WALTER A. ELWELL

SEE ALSO Stewardship.

Bibliography. R. de Vaux, *Ancient Israel;* G. F. Hawthorne, *NIDNTT,* III:851–55; B. K. Morley, *EDBT,* pp. 779–80; H. Lansdell, *The Sacred Tenth: Studies in Tithe-Giving Ancient and Modern;* L. Vischer, *Tithing in the Early Church.*

Togo *(Est. 2000 pop.: 4,818,000; 56,785 sq. km. [21,925 sq. mi.]).* Togo is a small country located in West Africa along the Gulf of Guinea between Benin and Ghana. It has a 32-mile (56 kilometers) coastline on the Atlantic Ocean and extends 320 miles (540 kilometers) inland. Its main ethnic groups include the Ewe, Mina, and Kabye.

The introduction of Christianity to the area is directly related to the presence of Europeans. The Portuguese came in the late fifteenth century and by the nineteenth century the coast area was competed over mainly by the French, British, and Germans who wanted the area's trade especially in slaves. In 1884 the Germans claimed a protectorate over the territory through a treaty with a village chief. The Germans lost this colony in World War I when it was divided among the British and French. In 1957 the British section was joined with Ghana and the French Togo became an independent state in 1960.

While Catholic mission work along the coast began early, a permanent chapel in the area was not established until 1835, primarily for Brazilian families who had returned. This work was led by the Sacred Heart of Mary headquartered in Gabon. The Catholic community was only firmly established when the Society of the Divine Word assumed responsibility in 1892 through the end of German colonial rule. Togo was made a separate vicariate in 1914. Evangelism in the north was slow and not encouraged by the colonial governments. In fact, missions was prohibited in the north until 1912 because of local opposition and a Muslim presence. After WW II the Catholic community grew rapidly and presently is the largest church in Togo.

Protestant work began in Togo at an early date. The Moravian Brothers under Count NIKOLAUS VON ZINZENDORF's leadership sponsored a number of early missionary efforts to Africa. Especially prominent was Jacob Protten, son of a Danish soldier and African princess, who began to evangelize the area around Togo from 1737 to 1769, including educating local children despite opposition from European officials.

The Bremen Missionary Society *(Norddeutsche Missiongesellschaft)* led the first sustained Protestant evangelizing effort beginning in the 1850s and later joined by the BASEL MISSION. They were very successful in creating a Protestant community in the south, but were forced to leave at the end of German rule.

As a result of the expulsion of German missions in WW I, the Protestant churches in Togo eventually created an autonomous church, later known as the *Eglise Evangelique du Togo,* under indigenous leadership. This church has been active in evangelizing and in education and is one of the major indigenous churches in West Africa and the largest Protestant church in Togo today. The Methodist Church is the oldest major Protestant church in Togo today. Its founding goes back to the evangelization of Africans by THOMAS BIRCH FREEMAN and Thomas Joseph Marshall in the mid-nineteenth century. In the twentieth century it lost many members to the Prophet Harrist movement, but continues to be a major religious presence in the coastal areas.

The Assemblies of God have had the most active Protestant work in the north beginning after WW II. In the 1970s the Togo government became less hospitable to religious groups and in 1978 limited recognition to Muslims, Catholics, and five Protestant churches. In 1990 greater religious freedom was granted to other churches and missions.

CHUCK WEBER

Bibliography. P. B. Clarke, *West Africa and Christianity;* H. Debrunner, *A Church Between Colonial Powers: A Study of the Church in Togo;* S. Decalo, *Historical Dictionary of Togo.*

Tokelau *(Est. 2000 pop.: 2,000; 10 sq. km. [4 sq. mi.]).* Three coral atolls, Fakaofo, Nukunonu, and Atafu, make up Tokelau, a non-self-governing territory under New Zealand, located north of Samoa between 8 and 10 degrees south of the equator in the central Pacific. Seventy percent of the population of two thousand are members of the Congregational Christian Church (formerly LMS), and 25 percent Roman Catholics.

ALLAN K. DAVIDSON

SEE ALSO Polynesia.

Bibliography. A. Hooper and J. Huntsman, eds.; *Matagi Tokelau: History and Traditions of Tokelau.*

Tonga *(Est. 2000 pop.: 102,000; 747 sq. km. [288 sq.mi.]).* The Kingdom of Tonga comprises three major groups and many smaller islands in the central south Pacific, east of Fiji. The majority of the population of 102,000 belong to one of the four Methodist churches with the Free Wesleyan Church the largest and most dominant. Roman Catholics and Mormons each have fifteen percent of the population and Seventh-Day Adventists five and one half percent.

ALLAN K. DAVIDSON

SEE ALSO Polynesia.

Bibliography. N. Rutherford, ed., *Friendly Islands: A History of Tonga.*

Torrey, Reuben Archer (1856–1928). American evangelist and educator. Born in New Jersey, he graduated from Yale College and Yale Divinity School, and later studied at German universities in Leipzig and Erlangen. He was ordained to the ministry in the Congregational Church in 1883 and served churches in Ohio and Minnesota. In 1889, D. L. MOODY named him superintendent of the Chicago Evangelization Society (now Moody Bible Institute), a position he held until 1908. From 1894 to 1906, he also served as pastor of the Chicago Avenue Church (later renamed Moody Memorial Church). He traveled worldwide from 1902 to 1906, carrying out evangelistic crusades throughout Canada, Europe, Asia, Australia, and New Zealand, as well as in major cities in the United States. He founded the Montrose (Pennsylvania) Bible Conference in 1908. From 1912 to 1924, he served as dean of the Bible Institute of Los Angeles (BIOLA). He also served as pastor of the Church of the Open Door in Los Angeles from 1915 to 1924. He wrote over forty books, including *How to Work for Christ* (1901) and *The Person and Work of the Holy Spirit* (1910). He also wrote many articles for *The Fundamentals* (1910–15), a work that mirrored Torrey's conservative theological beliefs.

TIMOTHY K. BEOUGHER

Bibliography. R. Martin, *R. A. Torrey: Apostle of Certainty;* G. T. B. Davis, *Torrey and Alexander.*

Totalitarianism. "Totalitarian" refers to ". . . a system of government which tolerates only one political party to which all other institutions are subordinate and generally demand total subservience of the individual to the state" (*Oxford English Dictionary,* 2nd ed). Possony quotes Gurian's definition as "the deification of a power system—the power system directed by that group which came into being as its creator and claims to act as its realizer." When applied to Christian missions, it points to the life of the church and its expanding/growing movement being realized under and in spite of oppressive political and religious systems. The related term, "authoritarian," also supports complete submission to authority, perhaps without some of the strongly pejorative values of totalitarianism.

Throughout biblical and church history, God's people have been forced to grapple with life under totalitarian regimes. The Old Testament provides a catalogue of diverse conditions: under the Egyptian oppression, the young nation of Israel under various shorter-lived oppressive regimes of closer neighbors, the destructive/transforming captivities to Assyria and Babylon, and the later servitude under the Roman Empire. Christ emerges to minister in the context of Roman imperial totalitarianism, the GREAT COMMISSION is given to the early church very familiar with political and religious oppression. Throughout church history, God's global people have found peace and prosperity an uncommon commodity, with the reality being more a context of poverty, weakness, violence, and oppression.

A contemporary typology of totalitarian regimes offers two major categories with their own subsets and variants: (1) secular state totalitarianism (Marxist, tribal, extreme nationalistic); (2) theocratic state totalitarianism and other religious totalitarianisms (Islamic, Hindu, Buddhist, Roman Catholic, Orthodox, and even Protestant). The subtle Western spirit of "political correctness" is nurtured by a ideological/cultural totalitarian virus.

Contemporary mission and church history finds the church engaging a spectrum of oppositions as it struggles to exist and thrive in diverse political and religious contexts. Following the collapse of Russian and European Marxism, an unwarranted euphoria swept the world, and idealists heralded a new era of global peace, justice, and democracy. That did not happen, and today nearly 120 nations restrict, in part or totally, open church life or access to foreign missions. Totalitarianism is inherently structured into the heart of humanity individually and collectively as well as in all created political and religious systems. One of the prime reasons we still have so many unreached nations and people groups is simply because they are difficult to reach—and the difficulty is often directly related to the specter (and spectrum) of totalitarianism found in these regions.

WILLIAM DAVID TAYLOR

SEE ALSO Church and State.

Bibliography. J. Ellul, *Violence: Reflections from a Christian Perspective;* E. L. Frizen Jr., and W. T. Coggins, eds., *Christ and Caesar in Christian Missions;* T. Lambert, *The Resurrection of the Chinese Church;* P. Marshall, with L. Gilbert, *Their Blood Cries Out: The Untold Story of Persecution Against Christians in the Modern World,* S. T. Possony, *NCE,* 14:210–11; N. Shea, *In the Lion's Den: A Shocking Account of Persecution and Martyrdom of Christians Today and How We Should Respond,* T. Yamamori, *Penetrating Missions' Final Frontier.*

Totem, Totemism. Totemism is a culturally constructed system of identifying kin groups by postulating a special relationship between human beings and nature, whereby each kin group in a society takes the name of an animal or plant species. Such an identification may lead to sympathetic relationships between human beings and their corresponding totems, which may mean that human beings are prohibited from killing or eating an animal or plant that bears their own name.

Totemic representations serve, among other things, to legitimate social groupings, explain certain behavioral patterns, support exogamous marriage practices, and establish an orderly system for classifying humanity and nature. The term "totem" is derived from the North American Ojibwa word *ototeman*, which was used to designate the various clans including Eagle, Reindeer, Otter, Bear, Buffalo, Beaver, and Catfish. The practice of naming kinship groups in this manner has been recorded in North American cultures, among the Australian Aborigines, and globally, where it may be found in various adaptations.

Totemism has been one of the most abused cultural concepts in anthropology. Anthropologists in the nineteenth century interpreted totemism from a cultural evolutionary perspective and identified the concept of totemism as an early stage in the evolution of religious belief. Durkheim, who has become famous for his argument that God and religion are the product of culture, made totemism a key element in his argument, focusing particularly on the totemic practices of the Australian Aborigines, who it was believed "had the most primitive and simple religion which it is possible to find."

Sigmund Freud added to the confusion regarding the true nature of totemism by fantasizing that the totem animal is in reality a substitute for the father and that morality, religion, and family concepts find their origins in this primitive concept. All this, in spite of dubious data and the lack of historical evidence.

Studies in totemism continue to attract the interest of anthropologists from various theoretical perspectives, including structuralists following the lead of Levi-Strauss, and cultural materialists following Marvin Harris, as they seek to both interpret the cultural significance of totemism and to reinforce their own theoretical perspectives.

Inasmuch as totemism has social, epistemological, ecological, and religious implications, sensitive missiologists need to be aware of the role totemism plays in forming the self-identity, social structure, and perceptions of the world of a given people.

DOUGLAS J. HAYWARD

Bibliography. F. Boas, *Race, Language and Culture;* E. Durkheim, *The Elementary Forms of the Religious Life;* E. E. Evans-Pritchard, *Theories of Primitive Religion;* R. Firth, *Tikopia Ritual and Belief;* S. Freud, *Totem and Taboo: Some Points of Agreement Between the Mental Lives of Savages and Neurotics;* A. Hultkrantz, *The Religions of the American Indians;* A. Kuper, *The Invention of Primitive Society.*

Townsend, William Cameron (1896–1982). American missionary to Guatemala and founder of WYCLIFFE BIBLE TRANSLATORS.

"Uncle Cam" Townsend was born in southern California. He worked tirelessly to see the Bible translated into minority languages. He founded the Summer Institute of Linguistics (1936), the Wycliffe Bible Translators (1942), and JAARS (1948).

Townsend went to Guatemala in 1917 to sell Spanish-language Bibles. In 1919 he was challenged by the fact that the Indian population did not understand Spanish well enough to benefit from the Spanish translation of the Bible. With his wife, Elvira, he learned the complex Cakchiquel language. By 1931 the Cakchiquel New Testament was completed.

When Townsend returned to the United States, he decided to train others to translate Scriptures for indigenous groups of Latin America. In 1934 Townsend taught two students at what he called "Camp Wycliffe." Townsend founded the Summer Institute of Linguistics in 1936 and the Wycliffe Bible Translators in 1942. In 1944 Townsend's first wife died; he married Elaine Mielke in 1946.

Townsend was convinced that the heart language was the most effective tool for evangelism. He emphasized the use of linguistics and modern technologies such as airplanes and radios. He also promoted a nonsectarian strategy of service to all.

PETER JAMES SILZER

Bibliography. J. Hefley and M. Hefley, *Uncle Cam;* H. Stevens, *A Thousand Trails: Personal Journal of William Cameron Townsend 1917–1919;* idem, *Wycliffe in the Making: The Memoirs of W. Cameron Townsend 1920–1933.*

Training of Missionaries. Jesus and Paul placed high priority on training people for ministry (Matt. 4:19; 2 Tim. 2:2) with the goal of producing effective workers with servant hearts capable of expanding Jesus Christ's rightful reign over his creation, leaving future generations a legacy to emulate. Training curriculum includes the "what," "who," "where," "when," "why," and "how" in praxis.

Preferred cross-cultural training begins with conceptualizing the product. What will it take to accomplish the end goal? This calls for a ministry profile, that is, a comprehensive picture that addresses long-term training needs from the perspectives of *character, commitment, competence,* and *culture.*

Just as Jesus and Paul placed great emphasis on *character,* so must the trainees' profile. How have the trainees' spiritual pilgrimages prepared them for cross-cultural ministry? What scaffolds exist? What gaps remain? Trainers will also want to know the trainees' level of *commitment* to God, the ministry team, and the task. Do track records demonstrate staying power? What must be done to improve these? *Competency* addresses the trainees' needs in relation to exegeting and communicating Scripture, the use of spiritual gifts, cross-cultural tools to exegete the community, skills in team development, conflict resolution, planning and problem solving, support maintenance, ministry, and contextualization. *Culture* refers to the trainees' grasp of the target culture, mental, emotional, and physical adjustment, flexibility, and empowerment. Such a profile discerns the gaps between the trainees' present state and the training path trainees must traverse to minister competently cross-culturally.

Profile-based training can take place through three forms of education: formal, nonformal, and informal. Formal education tends to take place in designated locations, be expert-centered and sequenced, focuses on individual achievement, covers topics broadly and in depth, and takes extended amounts of time, making it costly. Nonformal education tends to be held in locations of convenience, be participatory in nature, addresses specific topics in depth, focuses on individual or group improvement, and tends to be short in duration, making it more affordable. Informal education happens any time, any place, without cost, as people dialogue about a host of personal or ministry topics. Wise trainees will take advantage of the distinctives that each educational mode offers.

Cross-cultural training should reflect much more than the acquisition of cognitive knowledge. Whenever possible, it should be field-based, mentor-intensive, and team-oriented; require immediate application; and include constructive feedback that addresses the cognitive, affective, and behavioral domains.

Like much Bible training, most receive their missionary training piecemeal. A little theology here, a little character development there; a little experience here, a little cross-cultural communication there; a little evangelism here, a little follow-up there; a little prayer here, a little spiritual warfare there. A more systemic profile-based training model geared to the whole family is needed to counteract such fragmented, individualized training. Such a model will address training long term, covering pre-field, on-field, and post-field (furloughs) training. This training model recognizes the need for ministry-long training that addresses character, commitment, competence, and culture. Such comprehensive training will require international partnerships among assemblies, agencies, and academics.

Profile-based training calls for evaluation benchmarks. Such evaluation helps ensure that trainees continue to lessen the gap between inadequate and adequate training.

Effective cross-cultural workers trained throughout ministry will seek to exemplify high Christian morals in word and deed, all in a contextual manner. They will resist the temptation to import materials and methods that cannot be reproduced readily by the hearers/readers. Rather they will seek to empower responsibly the new community of faith, remembering Jesus' words: "anyone who has faith in me will do even greater things than these" (John 14:12).

TOM A. STEFFEN

Bibliography. A. B. Bruce, *The Training of the Twelve;* R. W. Ferris, *Establishing Ministry Training;* W. D. Taylor, ed., *Internationalizing Missionary Training: A Global Perspective.*

Tranquebar Mission. *See* DANISH-HALLE MISSION.

Transcendence of God. In WORSHIP and mission the church celebrates and proclaims the transcendence of the Creator, described by Walter C. Smith in his classic hymn as "Immortal, Invisible, God only Wise, In Light Inaccessible, hid from our eyes."

The idea of transcendence communicates not so much the idea of space—that God is high above the created order—but rather the idea of otherness. God is completely different, not of the same quality of being as his creation. God is spirit, not limited by space or time, not subject to sin, decay, death, or change. As such, God is the source and ground of all that is created.

God is alone and thus unique in his transcendence. God is not the highest order of being, but is alone in another sphere of existence. Thus, the transcendence of God speaks of the unknowability of God. God is never fully known; human wisdom or comprehension can never take in all that it means to be God.

God's transcendence does not mean that he is not present with his creation. He is both infinitely present and one with the created order and infinitely different from and apart from the creation. The same one before whom we bow in humble adoration is also the Good Shepherd. Indeed, we only know of the transcendent God because he has chosen to be present with us.

In Holy Scripture, the transcendence of God is fundamental to the Judeo-Christian faith and worship: "Great is the Lord and greatly to be praised; his greatness is unsearchable" (Ps. 145:3); "we offer to God an acceptable worship with reverence and awe; for our God is a consuming fire" (Heb. 12:28, 29). For the prophet Isaiah, the vision of the transcendent God left him speechless before the glory of one who was "high and lofty" (Isa. 6:1). In Isaiah we are also reminded that God is so completely different and other that he cannot be compared with anything in the created order. "To whom then will you compare me, or who is my equal? says the Holy One."

The danger in both worship and mission is the temptation to control God or confine God to ideas or spaces. An appreciation of God's transcendence sustains humility and frees us from the pettiness of idolatry. Christian worship depends on symbols and words, but always with a recognition that nothing we say or see can ever fully contain all of God. In mission we proclaim God through words, through analogies and pictures, but always recognizing that these point to a reality that cannot be contained by human language.

The confidence of Christian mission is that deep within every human heart there is a longing for transcendence, a recognition in each conscience that there is One who is wholly other, who cannot be constrained by things or explained by words. And mission attempts to draw men and women to the transcendent God who is known through immanence of the Incarnation in the person, words, and work of Jesus Christ.

GORDON T. SMITH

Bibliography. T. Oden, *The Living God;* A. W. Tozer, *The Knowledge of the Holy.*

Transformational Development. The term "transformational development" was coined to recognize the contribution of DEVELOPMENT work to Christian mission. As an expression of Christian mission, transformational development seeks to change the spiritual assumptions that form the basis of a survival strategy in a particular CULTURE. The change is from belief in the culture's existing spiritual milieu to faith in the Triune God as the Creator, Redeemer, and Sustainer of the world. A survival strategy is the combination of agricultural, medical, religious, educational, commercial, construction, and household activities that contribute to human welfare in a particular culture. A survival strategy reflects the WORLDVIEW assumptions of a community.

In most cultures, the activities that comprise a survival strategy have a spiritual foundation. For example, farmers and medical practitioners in traditional African cultures often make SACRIFICES to their ANCESTORS. They believe the sacrifices foster the blessings of spirits or deceased ancestors. In many Asian cultures, construction workers place the heads of sacrificed animals in the foundations of the buildings and bridges. They believe sacrificed animals appease the spiritual beings who control human destiny. The spiritual beings will prevent the bridges and buildings from collapsing if they accept the sacrifices.

Hindus have a variety of gods from whom they seek blessings of health, fertility, rain, land, money, and other necessities of life. In contrast, people in secularized Western cultures are prone to believe their survival does not have a spiritual basis. This, too, is a spiritual assumption. It assumes the spiritual realm does not exist, or that it does not interact with the physical realm.

The biblical basis for transformational development is Colossians 1:15–20. This passage has three key points. First, Christ is supreme in all of creation. Development that is transformational points toward the supremacy of Christ, and affirms that the development activities that improve human welfare bear witness to the character and activity of God through Christ.

Second, God reconciles the seen and unseen elements of creation to himself through Christ. This reconciliation is critically important to transformational development. The Greek term in the passage, *apokatallassō,* meaning *to reconcile,* is a unique expression of *katallassō,* the common word meaning to reconcile. The apostle Paul seems to have coined *apokatallassō* to communicate a comprehensive view of RECONCILIATION, particularly things that might not otherwise be reconciled. He used the term on two occasions. On one occasion, Paul used it to affirm that God fosters a relationship with the entire creation. God reconciles the seen and unseen elements of creation to himself through Christ (Col. 1:20), affecting every area of life.

Third, PEACE is the result of God's reconciling work through Christ. Peace, meaning a sense of harmony in creation, results when communities of people realize that they, through the empowerment of God, can meet their physical, social, emotional, and spiritual needs. By integrating and addressing these needs, transformational development affirms that God's reconciling work through Christ brings the fullness of peace to a fallen creation.

BRUCE BRADSHAW

Bibliography. B. Bradshaw, *Bridging the Gap: Evangelism, Development and Shalom;* P. G. Hiebert, *Anthropological Reflections on Missiological Issues;* R. Sider, *One Sided Christianity?*

Transgression. *See* SIN, THE BIBLICAL DOCTRINE OF.

Translatability. A concept introduced and explored by Lamin Sanneh, the notion of translatability indicates the process by which the Christian message shows its capacity to enter each cultural idiom and commence there a challenging and enduring dialogue. This deepens the notion of translation to something more than merely substituting words or grammar from one language for words and structures from another.

It suggests that there is something inherent in the Christian faith, evident from the New Testament onwards, that renders it compatible with all cultures. The genius of the Christian religion is its ability "to adopt each culture as its natural destination and as a necessity of its life." By entering the vernacular of each culture, the gospel provides the resources for self-realization and cultural fulfillment on the one hand, and it promotes the possibility of change on the other.

Translatability has two important implications. One consequence is that every culture is relativized. None may be justifiably absolutized as the final form of Christian faith and life. The missionary church has no monopoly on the form of faith required in the receptor culture, just as the early Judaic church could make no claim upon Gentiles that they be circumcised. The other consequence is that every culture is revitalized by its hearing of the gospel in its vernacular. It is destigmatized. It is treated not as inferior or untouchable but as the proper instrument for the expression of the divine message.

GEORGE R. HUNSBERGER

Bibliography. L. Sanneh, *Translating the Message: The Missionary Impact on Culture*; P. R. Satari, *The Church Between Gospel and Culture*, pp. 270–83.

Translation. Transmission of a message from one language to another whether in written or oral (interpretation) form. Nida and Taber define translation as "reproducing in the receptor language the closest natural equivalent of the source language message, first in terms of meaning and secondly in terms of style." Translation seeks to accurately convey the meaning of the original message via clear and natural linguistic forms in the receptor language. Translation is thus based on a correct understanding of the original message set as it is in particular forms in the source language; it is also subject to the available structures of the receptor language. Translation does not occur unless the original meaning is communicated. A translation can then be evaluated in terms of how faithfully it conveys the original message, how clearly it conveys that message to speakers or hearers in the receptor language, and how naturally the message is expressed in the receptor language. Accurately conveying the meaning of the original message is paramount, style secondary.

Translation is based on the premise that every language is capable of expressing human thought. A speaker or an author expresses a given message in a given social and physical context using particular words and phrases based on his or her intent (e.g., to inform, to persuade), assumptions about what the hearer or reader will understand, couched in the linguistic and rhetorical tools he or she controls (e.g., rhetorical questions, metaphors). The translator must understand this original message before beginning translation. Thus, language analysis or exegesis is an initial step in the translation process. Since languages are distinct and have different ways of expressing meaning, a particular word or phrase in a language may have numerous meanings. "Chris's house" expresses a different relationship between Chris and the house than "Chris's spouse" or "Chris's hand." A "hand" on an arm is different than a "hand" on a clock or a "hand" of bananas. To "give someone a hand" may involve physical assistance or applause, depending on the context. Linguistic forms convey different meanings in different contexts.

In addition to the referential sense of words, translation must also consider connotative meaning. A speaker or author may choose words with strong negative or positive connotations. These meanings must be understood in their temporal and cultural context.

Transferring the message from the source language to another language involves determining which forms in the receptor language will adequately convey the original meaning. Very rarely will the same form be appropriate for the multiple senses of a word in the source language. The source language may have multiple senses for a particular word that demand separate forms in the receptor language (the English noun "key" is translated *llave* in Spanish if it is for a lock, *clave* if it is for a code, and *tecla* if it is on a keyboard). Conversely, the source language may have separate lexical items that are appropriately translated with one word in the receptor language, (Indonesian *padi, beras,* and *nasi* are all "rice" in English.) The lack of simple one-to-one correspondences between languages motivates the translator to seek the most appropriate way to express the meaning of the receptor language in words and phrases understood well in the receptor language.

The receptor language also determines the grammatical form of the translation; if words are simply translated one by one from the source language the result is merely a glossed text, not a translation. Interlinear translations of texts provide helpful insights about the source language. but are not properly called translations as such.

Translation and interpretation are one task with two modes of expression. In both tasks, the meaning of an original message must be conveyed accurately, clearly, and naturally in another language. Interpreters provide oral expression of the original message within moments of hearing it. Translators typically have a relatively extended period of time to study the original message before providing a written form in the receptor language. In Bible translation especially translators enjoy the benefit of detailed studies of the original message to aid them in their analysis.

Translation is modeled in Scripture as a means to convey a message to people who do not understand the language of the original message (Mark 5:41; 15:34; John 1:38). The postexilic Jews may have used interpreters to bridge the gap from the classical Hebrew of the Torah to the Aramaic of the audience (Neh. 8:8).

Agencies such as the United Bible Societies and the WYCLIFFE BIBLE TRANSLATORS (along with the Summer Institute of Linguistics) have focused on translation as a missionary tool, specifically for Bible translation. Translation theory has been advanced by Christian authors; EUGENE A. NIDA wrote several seminal works on the theory and practice of translation. Countless other agencies around the world rely heavily on interpreters and translators to convey their message to people who speak a language not mastered by their missionaries. Mission interpreters and translators need to be well trained to translate accurately, clearly, and naturally.

PETER JAMES SILZER

SEE ALSO Bible Translation.

Bibliography. M. L. Larson, *Meaning Based Translation: A Guide to Cross-Language Equivalence;* E. A. Nida, *Toward a Science of Translating;* E. A. Nida and C. R. Taber, *The Theory and Practice of Translation.*

Translation Theory. Translation is the process whereby a message is transferred from one lexico-cultural context to another in such a way that the receptors respond as though the original communication had been in their context. Because the biblical authors in general, and God in particular, intended to be understood and have an impact on those who received the message, a translation of Scripture, like the original communication, must make sense, that is, it must be coherent. Furthermore, the parts of the text must interact and present the author's intent. Just like the original, a translation must communicate within its own linguistic and cultural context. The problem in translating is to convey through the chosen medium both the verbal and nonverbal elements. For the assumptions and concerns of both the author and original receptors are for the most part not those of an audience in another time and place with different communicational expectations.

While EUGENE NIDA's "code model" of communication with its focus on the author's message was effective for EXEGESIS, the more recent theories focus on relevance and the area of HERMENEUTICS, for the receptors must necessarily make inferences about an author's intent. Both exegesis and hermeneutics are essential for meaningful communication. Hence the basic question for a translator is not "How do I translate this?" but "How would the author have communicated this message in the present-day linguistic and cultural

context?" There must be faithfulness both to the source and to the receptor. If both are not taken into account, the translation runs the risk of miscommunication.

Translation theory today is increasingly emphasizing the process of translation as well as the end product. Translators need a thorough understanding of the contexts of both source and receptor (*see* BIBLE TRANSLATION). Also stressed is the impact of the translators' own LANGUAGE and CULTURE upon their understanding of the languages and cultures of source and receptor. The perspectives of source, receptor, and translator combine to create the translation context. Keeping all these perspectives in view will help translators ensure relevance through their exegetical and hermeneutical endeavor.

Another development in recent years is an increased interest in discourse theory. Textual linguistics enables a translator to understand the author's organization of a text. This discourse analysis illuminates the author's logic—the way the parts go together to create a whole. Why was a particular subject, argument, or procedure presented at a particular point in the text? How does one maintain that logic to impact the new audience? An appreciation of the genre or style of text will also enable translators to use the available linguistic and cultural elements in such a way as to ensure communication.

Along with discourse analysis is the necessity to understand the semantic elements chosen by an author for a particular context. How are these elements employed in order to convey a particular message? Appreciation of both the macrostructure (discourse analysis) and the microstructure (semantic analysis) is essential for effective and relevant communication. Once the elements of a text are isolated (exegesis), they can be meaningfully presented so that receptors can reconstruct the author's intent as it applies to their circumstances (hermeneutics).

The process of analyzing and then transferring discourse and semantic structures and meanings to another context creates many translation problems. Transferring the meaning of figures of speech that are highly specific to the original language and culture is difficult, particularly if no such idiom appears in the receptor context. In addition, each language introduces and then recalls referents to mind in its own way, thereby creating a huge problem of pronominal reference. Furthermore, the matters of order, introductions and conclusions, and quotations must be handled to ensure communication of the message. Each translation context poses different problems and requires specific solutions.

This raises the question of how much latitude can be allowed in making adjustments. To determine the answer, translators must have knowledge of the entire translation context. Such knowledge will help them determine how the receptors will interpret the message and the extent to which it must be adjusted to ensure communication of the author's intent and meaning to the new context. Unless all cultural and linguistic adjustments necessary for relevant communication are made, the translation is not complete.

The objective of a translation, then, is effective and relevant communication of what the original author intended. To the extent possible, receptors should have no doubt as to what the author meant. Discussion should pertain not to the meaning, but to the application of that meaning in the new context. So when a message is encased in Scripture (what God said to all human beings), we must first discern God's intent and the eternal nature of the message (that which transcends all specific human contexts), and then present God's meaning for a particular situation. Both the generality and the particularity are essential for translation. Translation that meets these criteria serves the cause of mission by enabling people to understand and apply God's message to their lives without depending on someone else to tell them what it means.

R. DANIEL SHAW

Bibliography. R. de Beaugrande and W. Dressler, *An Introduction to Text Linguistics;* E. A. Gutt, *Translation and Relevance;* E. A. Nida and C. Taber, *Theory & Practice of Translation;* R. D. Shaw, *Translation Review* 23 (1987): 25–29; D. Sperber and D. Wilson, *Relevance Theory.*

Transmigration. *See* REINCARNATION AND TRANSMIGRATION.

Trasher, Lillian (1887–1961). American missionary to orphans in Egypt. In denying her personal aspirations and desires, Lillian Trasher marveled at God's multiplication of her original plans at the end of her life. Her dream for a family of twelve children had grown to the birth and establishment of an orphanage in Egypt that housed some 1,400 children and widows at the completion of fifty years of ministry. After hearing the call to "be a missionary to Africa," Trasher broke her engagement to a pastor and within months found herself on board a ship with no mission board or financial backing.

Although she initially lived with a missionary family and began language study, Trasher soon found herself wanting to look after every neglected child she saw. Her missionary colleagues found this unacceptable. Stepping out in faith, she rented a house and founded the orphanage that became her distinguishing mark in ministry. By 1916 the Assemblies of God officially accepted her as one of their own missionaries. Spiritual victories were sparse in the first sixteen years of ministry, yet in 1927 she witnessed the greatest revival she had ever seen. At the time of her death, her ministry of compassion had touched more than eight thousand orphans.

ROBERTA R. KING

Bibliography. L. Trasher, *Letters from Lillian;* R. Tucker, *GGC.*

Trent. *See* COUNTER-REFORMATION.

Trinidad and Tobago (*Est. 2000 pop.: 1,380,000; 5,130 sq. km. [1,981 sq. mi.]*). The Republic of Trinidad and Tobago reflects both a strong Protestant Christian tradition and a strong Asian religious influence. Afro-Caribbeans constitute about 40 percent of the population, as do East Indians. The Protestant community is made up largely of mainline groups with 10 percent of the population considered evangelical. A quarter of the population is Hindu, with another 6 percent Muslim.

EVERETT A. WILSON

SEE ALSO Caribbean.

Bibliography. A. Lampe, *The Church in Latin America, 1492–1992,* pp. 201–15; J. Rogozinski, *A Brief History of the Caribbean: From the Arawak and the Carib to the Present.*

Trinity. Whereas in recent decades much scholarly thought about God has been drawn toward process theology or to some form of universalism, a small but healthy list of books has probed classic Trinitarianism, and some of this work has sketched the missiological implications.

Rejecting the speculative and frequently postmodern argumentation of the former, the latter approach anchors itself in what the Bible says about God's dealings with his covenantal people, and with the world, across the centuries, culminating in his gracious self-disclosure in Christ. While the biblical witness strenuously insists on the oneness of God, this one God is not *simplex:* the biblical material cries out for the kind of elaboration that issued in the doctrine of the Trinity. If the later elaborations (e.g., technical distinctions between "person" and "substance") should not be read back into the pages of Scripture, it does no harm to apply the term "Trinity" to what the Bible discloses of God, provided anachronism is avoided.

Even the Old Testament includes hints of the non-*simplex* nature of the one God (see, e.g., Erickson). But the biblical furnishing of the elements that called forth the doctrine of the Trinity comes to clearest focus in its treatment of Jesus the Messiah. Already in the Old Testament, one stream of prophetic expectation pictures Yahweh coming to rescue his people, while another stream pictures him sending his servant David. When these streams occasionally merge (e.g., Isa.

969

9; Ezek. 34), they do so in the matrix of anticipated mission.

Selected features of New Testament witness to God as triune become clear when their missiological bearing is articulated.

First, the kind of monotheism disclosed in the Bible is far more successful at portraying God as a loving God than any *simplex*-monotheism can ever be. A unitarian God may be thought to love his image-bearers in the space-time continuum. But it is very difficult to imagine how such a God could be said to be characteristically a God of love before the universe was created, unless the word "love" is stretched to the breaking point. Although little is said in the Bible regarding the intra-Triune relationships before creation, there are important hints. The Son enjoyed equality with God before the incarnation, but, far from wishing to exploit his status, in obedience to his Father's commission emptied himself, became a servant, and died the odious death of the cross (Phil. 2:6–11). In John's Gospel, the Son's love for the Father is expressed in unqualified obedience (e.g., John 8:29; 14:31). The Father's love for the Son is displayed both in withholding nothing from him and in "showing" him all that he does, including commissioning him with a mission that ensures all will honor the Son as they honor the Father (John 3:35; 5:16–30). Embedded deeply in Paul's thought is the conviction that the Father's giving over of the Son to death on the cross is the ultimate measure of God's love for us (Rom. 8:32; cf. 1 John 4:9). The love of God that ultimately stands behind all Christian mission is grounded in, and logically flows from, the love of the Father for the Son and of the Son for the Father. As much as the Son loved the world, it was his love for the Father which drove him to the cross (hence the cry in the Garden, Mark 14:36). The Father loved the world so much that he sent his Son (John 3:16). Thus it was the Father's love for the Son that determined to exalt the Son and call out and give to him a great host of redeemed sinners.

Second, the doctrine of the Trinity stands behind the incarnation. If God were one in some unitarian sense, then for God to become a human being the incarnation would either so exhaust God that the incarnated being would have no one to pray to or the notion of God would have to shift from his transcendent personhood and oneness to some ill-defined pantheism. Incarnation in the confessional sense is possible only if the one God is some kind of plurality within unity. The Word who was with God (God's own companion) and who was God (God's own self) became flesh, and lived for a while among us (John 1:1, 14). The Lion of the tribe of Judah comes from God's own throne (Rev. 5).

For God to become human, something other than a *simplex* monotheistic God was necessary.

This is more than a technical point. The high point of revelation is the coming and mission of Jesus Christ (cf. Heb. 4:1–4). His disclosure of God (cf. John 14:7) not only through instructive words and deeds of justice and mercy, but supremely in the cross, depends on the incarnation, which itself is dependent on biblical Trinitarianism. Conversely, if it were not for the incarnation of Jesus Christ, if it were not for what the incarnate Lord accomplished, it would be difficult to assign any sense at all to the conviction that believers come to "participate in the divine nature" (2 Peter 1:4).

Moreover, the sending of the Son becomes the anchor for the sending of the disciples (John 20:21). As he has had a mission from his Father, so we receive our mission from him. Indeed, in this sense the Christian mission is nothing more than a continuation of the mission of the Son, the next stage as it were. None of this would be particularly coherent if unitarianism replaced Trinitarianism.

Third, although orthodox Trinitarianism insists that all three persons of the Godhead are equally God, it insists no less strongly that each does not perform or accomplish exactly what the others do. The Father sends the Son, the Son goes: the relationship is not reciprocal. After his death and exaltation, the Son bequeaths the Spirit: the reverse is not true. The Spirit is given as the "down payment" of the ultimate inheritance: that cannot be said of the Father or the Son. When the exalted Christ has finally vanquished the last enemy, he turns everything over to his Father: once again, the two persons of the Godhead mentioned in this sentence could not have their roles reversed without making nonsense of the biblical narrative.

The bearing of these observations on missiological thought is twofold. First, God discloses himself to the ideal community, the archetypical community, "a sort of continuous and indivisible community," as the Cappadocians taught (the words are attributed to Basil of Caesarea). This stands radically against the isolated individualism espoused by many forms of liberal democracy. It is an especially important component of our vision of God in all attempts to evangelize and disciple societies less enamored with individualism than are many Western nations (*see also* INDIVIDUALISM and COLLECTIVISM).

Yet the Persons of the Godhead are not three indistinguishable godlets, like three indistinguishable peas in a pod. They interact in love, and, in the case of the Son to the Father and of the Spirit to the Son and to the Father, in obedience, they each press on with distinctive tasks in their unified vision. In confessional trinitarianism, the three Persons of the Godhead are equally omniscient, but they do not think the same thing, that is, the point of self-identity with each is not the same as with the other. The Father cannot think, "I went to the cross, died, and rose again." Each is self-defined over against the others, while preserving perfect unity of purpose and love. This observation, lightly sketched in Calvin, has been probed more thoroughly in recent times. It preserves the individual person without succumbing to individualism. This stands radically against a collectivity in which individuals are squeezed into conformity or submerged in the community, no longer a community of free persons.

It is within such a framework, then, that the church should pursue the unity for which Jesus prayed (John 17). This unity is in fact precisely what has been lived out among countless Christians over the centuries, in fulfillment of Jesus' prayer: a oneness in love, in shared vision, despite all the diversity—mirroring, however imperfectly, the oneness of God. The oneness of the collective, or of a unified ecumenical structure, is a poor reflection of this glorious reality. Indeed, this oneness in love becomes a potent voice of witness to the world (John 13:34–35). We love, not only because he first loved us, but because God is love (1 John 4:7–12).

Fourth and finally, full-orbed reflection on the significance of the doctrine of the Trinity for mission demands extended meditation on how the Triune God pursues a lost and rebellious race of those who bear his image, on the distinctive roles of the Father and the Son, on the part played by the Holy Spirit in this mission. The Holy Spirit convicts the world of sin, righteousness and judgment (John 16:7–11), enabling the person without the Spirit to see and understand what would otherwise remain closed off (1 Cor. 2:14). The Holy Spirit also strengthens believers for every good work, conforming them to Christ in anticipation of the consummation of the last day. His is the initiative in explosive evangelism in the Book of Acts; his is still the regenerating power that transforms men and women when the word of the gospel is heralded today.

DONALD A. CARSON

SEE ALSO Image of God.

Bibliography. L. Boff, *Trinity and Society;* C. E. Braaten, *Missiology* 18 (1990): 415–27; G. H. Clark, *The Trinity;* J. S. Connor, *Missiology* 9 (1981): 155–69; T. Dunne, *TS* 45 (1984): 139–52; M. J. Erickson, *God in Three Persons;* C. E. Gunton, *The Promise of Trinitarian Theology;* R. W. Jenson, *The Triune Identity;* E. Jüngel, *The Doctrine of the Trinity;* D. H. Larson, *Times of the Trinity;* J. Moltmann, *The Trinity and the Kingdom;* L. Newbigin, *Open Secret;* idem, *Trinitarian Faith and Today's Mission;* J. Piper, *The Pleasures of God;* K. Rahner, *The Trinity;* J. Thurmer, *A Detection of the Trinity.*

Trotman, Dawson E. (1906–56). American evangelist and founder of The Navigators. Born in Bisbee, Arizona, he moved to Lomita, California, where at the age of twenty he came to faith in Christ, largely by memorizing Bible verses. He began to do evangelism, both on the streets and in the churches. He continued to memorize Bible verses and within three years could recite one thousand verses. After Trotman introduced Bible memorization to a sailor in Los Angeles in 1933, he organized his ministry to sailors, calling it The Navigators—"A Bible Club for Service Men." During World War II it grew significantly. Trotman never completed college and remained a layman. He built the work of The Navigators on strict personal discipline and Scripture, as well as a passion for people.

After the war, The Navigators spread across U.S. campuses, churches, and communities, and then overseas. The mission emphasized Bible memory, small-group Bible study, evangelism, and discipleship. Philosophically and strategically, Trotman built his work on 2 Timothy 2:2. This self-reproducing ministry was soon taken up by many mission agencies. By 1994 The Navigators had some 3,300 workers in 90 countries.

Trotman drowned in upstate New York while saving the life of a girl who had been pitched overboard from a powerboat. Two of Trotman's sermons have been published: "Born to Reproduce" and "The Need of the Hour."

JIM REAPSOME

Bibliography. B. Foster, *The Navigator;* B. L. Skinner, *Daws;* L. E. Tift, *Valiant in Flight.*

Trotter, Isabelle Lilias (1853–1928). English missionary to Algeria and founder of the Algiers Mission Band. Born in London and brought up in comfortable circumstances, she was educated at home by French and German governesses, and showed talent in languages and in water-color painting. Living with her widowed mother (who died in 1879), she undertook voluntary Christian work and was influenced by speakers she heard at Holiness conventions. Feeling called to work in North Africa, she spent some time in preparation at the Mildmay Mission (East London), and in 1888 traveled to Algeria, with three women companions. She was able to speak in French to local people immediately, and Algiers was her home for the rest of her life.

Work had been started in several North African countries by Edward Glenny (North Africa Mission) and others, and in Egypt by the Egypt General Mission. Eventually the Algiers Mission Band united with the North Africa Mission (now known as Arab World Ministries). Other women joined Trotter; she spent a good deal of time in Egypt writing and translating material for the Nile Mission Press, started in 1905. She also wrote and illustrated several devotional books about her work. She died in Algiers in 1928. As founder of the Algiers Mission Band, her life typifies the initiatives taken by women to "proclaim the Good News" at a time when their gifts and calling were often ignored.

JOCELYN MURRAY

Bibliography. A. F. Pigott Blanche, *I. Lilias Trotter, Founder of the Algiers Mission Band;* K. Fiedler, *The Story of Faith Missions: From Hudson Taylor to Present Day Africa.*

Trumbull, David (1819–89). American pioneer missionary and journalist in Chile. Born to a well-to-do family in Elizabeth, New Jersey, Trumbull studied at Yale College and Princeton Seminary. While at Yale he came to Christ (1839), having been deeply impacted during the Second Great Awakening by CHARLES FINNEY's preaching. In 1845 he was ordained by the Congregational Church and appointed by the Foreign Evangelical Society as a chaplain to sailors from a base in Port of Valparaiso, Chile. Out of his work came the planting of Union Church, organized to meet the needs of the expatriate residents. On his first furlough (1850), he married Jane Fitch. Upon their return, she organized and directed a girl's school for the daughters of English families in Valparaiso, the first Protestant school in Chile.

Chile's population was controlled by the Spanish-descended Roman Catholic ruling class who used the Constitution to maintain Catholic domination. In this context, Trumbull was a powerful and persuasive advocate for religious freedom. His persistent efforts were rewarded with legal and eventually constitutional reform, starting with the passage of the interpretive Law in 1864 which prohibited public non-Catholic worship, thereby implying that private worship was legal and giving the first opportunity for evangelization among Spanish-speaking Chileans.

Trumbull's influence grew throughout his career. He founded two schools, a Bible Society, and two newspapers. The latter served as the platforms for his advocacy. After forty years of service in Chile, in 1886 Trumbull applied and was accepted for Chilean citizenship; he is acknowledged to be among the most significant Protestant missionaries to ever serve in Latin America.

A. SCOTT MOREAU

Bibliography. M. Daniels, *Makers of South America;* H. M. Goodpasture, *Journal of Presbyterian History* 56:2 (1978): 149–65; I. Paul, *A Yankee Reformer in Chile: The Life and Works of David Trumbull.*

Truth. In common use truth refers to that which is correct, actually exists, or has occurred. Philosophers investigate the nature of truth itself in the areas of knowledge, beauty, and morals. From the ENLIGHTENMENT (early eighteenth century) onward they have sought a truth which can be verified by science with accuracy. Immanuel Kant (1724–1802) raised the question of whether truth in itself is knowable or only as the knower perceives it. He opened the way to extensive questioning of even the existence of truth. Relativists may deny its existence in any objective, absolute sense in favor of a "truth" which is dependent upon knower and circumstances. Existentialists and their successors argue that truth emerges from experience. Postmodernists hold to a PLURALISM of many different "truths," whatever is true for a particular person or group is correct for them, even if it contradicts the truths held by others.

Throughout the Bible one can detect different nuances concerning truth. The common connotations of correctness and accuracy are assumed. The Old Testament frequently stresses faithfulness, reliability, and morality whereas in the New the emphasis is more upon true statements and teachings and attitudes and actions consistent with God's nature and will.

In both Testaments truth is a quality of God, at times almost becoming a personification of him. Speaking of God both the psalmist (119:160) and Jesus (John 17:17) affirm, "Your word is truth." The Holy Spirit is "the Spirit of truth" (John 14:17; 15:26; 16:13; cf. 1 John 5: 7). Hence, God's communication of truth is in complete harmony with his nature (he does not lie, Num. 23:19; 1 Sam. 15:29); God's revelation of his person, works, and will are accurate and trustworthy. Ultimately, Jesus Christ himself is truth. "I," he said, "am the way, the truth and the life, no one comes to the Father but by me" (John 14: 6). He himself is the embodiment of truth—truth that is both personal and absolute, eternal and relational, objective and experiential. What philosophers, kings, sages, scientists, common people, priests, prophets, shamans, and diviners seek is found in him. In Jesus all things find their form, function, relation, and meaning. As the truth itself, Jesus reveals the truth about God, the universe, and their relationship. He is also the only way to the reestablishment of a right, accepting relationship with God.

God's servants and representatives are to be people of truth. They are to reflect and point to the truth which is Jesus Christ. They are to report, to bear testimony to the Truth. The facts and implications they report must be accurate, even when they might be threatening or irritating, or bring hostility. In their own lives and activities they are to tell the truth and be characterized by faithfulness and dependability as they live the truth.

This is the background and presupposition for "truth and missions." Missions and missionaries must be committed to truth and be characterized by it. They must proclaim the pure truth of the gospel. God's truth, which is sure (Titus 1:9), absolute, changeless, and "committed once and for all to the saints" (Jude 3) may come in cultural dress and cannot be separated from the persons who proclaim it. Nevertheless, it transcends culture, time, and messenger. One must be careful neither to add to nor subtract from God's truth, nor to diminish his requirements or expectations. It is often difficult to distinguish between preference stemming from the missionary's culture and background and that which is a genuine part of God's saving message—its implications, and manners of life that comport with it. It usually requires conscious effort. It was in a cross-cultural situation that Paul employed the phrase "truth of the gospel" in a way which seems to equate the gospel and truth (Gal. 2:4, 14; 4:16; 5:7). For him to add, subtract, or act contrary to "the truth of the gospel" was to deny that the death of Christ and justification by faith produced their intended results (Gal. 2: 16–21).

Missions and missionaries struggle with truth in other ways. How information and attitudes are communicated differ from culture to culture. What seems to be correct, proper, or honest may be related or interpreted differently by different groups and raise questions about truthfulness. The missionary must never regard as inferior the persons or traditions of another group which do not impinge upon the content or the demands of God's message or of his will. Furthermore, God's cross-border, cross-cultural servants must neither glamorize nor exaggerate the successes, difficulties, or hardships of their tasks.

Truth is not only the believers' lives but our mission. It is our proclamation, life-style, operating principle, objective, and love. For God is truth, his word and revelation is truth, his standard is truth, his intent is truth, and he relates to and calls people to and in truth.

J. JULIUS SCOTT JR.

Tsizehena, John (c. 1840–1912). Malagasy evangelist in Madagascar. Tsizehena represents the host of indigenous Christian leaders of the early missionary era, whose almost unknown labors contributed much to the eventual establishment and expansion of the Christian church.

As a young man, Tsizehena had contact with Anglican (CMS) missionaries in Vohemar in the north of the island. He came to faith in Christ following a deathbed vision which also marked his dramatic restoration to health. Later, with other Christians, he moved to a part of the northeastern coast remote from the rest of the Anglican community. Here, determined not only to evangelize the surrounding region, but also to remain faithful to Anglican worship and liturgy, Tsizehena took the pragmatic step of declaring himself "The Right Reverend Lord Bishop of the North, D.D." Wearing appropriate home-spun attire, with no administrative or financial help from outside, he moved out from his base at Namakia with others of like zeal and evangelized the surrounding region, baptizing new converts, founding churches, and ordaining priests and deacons. For litany, Tsizehena followed closely the Book of Common Prayer; for certain special ceremonies (such as the consecration of a new church building) he improvised his own liturgies.

Just prior to his death Tsizehena agreed with an Anglican missionary bishop from the capital Tananarive that all the churches in his diocese would form part of the Anglican Communion in Madagascar, a communion that now numbers sixty to seventy thousand members.

GORDON MOLYNEUX

Bibliography. D. B. Barrett, *CDCWM*, pp. 608–9; G. L. King, *A Self-made Bishop: The Story of John Tsizehena, 'Bishop of the North, D.D.' CDCWM.*

Tucker, Alfred Robert (1849–1914). English missionary to Uganda. An artist and an athlete from the Lake District of England, Tucker felt a call to the Anglican ministry. Ordained at the age of thirty-three, he was soon moved to take up evangelism among the peoples of Eastern Equatorial Africa (Kenya and Uganda), was accepted by the evangelical CHURCH MISSIONARY SOCIETY in 1890, and was promptly consecrated bishop of that diocese. His task was daunting: the missionaries there were few and disheartened; their first bishop had been executed recently, and the second had died en route from England to the diocese. Tucker took up his charge with great enthusiasm, even impatience, in three key areas, often returning to England in order to accomplish his goals. He helped negotiate a stable and just political environment in the midst of wrangling between German and English imperial officials, and in spite of tensions among Muslim, Roman Catholic, Protestant, and indigenous religious adherents, frequently butting heads with authorities of all groups. He fought vigorously for the land claims of local chiefs and against forced labor, making enemies in the British government as a result. Above all, he campaigned tirelessly for a self-governing Anglican diocese, traveling thousands of miles throughout his diocese, preaching and ordaining indigenous priests in great numbers, and then promoting schools and hospitals. He can be recollected in his own *Eighteen Years in Uganda and East Africa* (1908). He was greatly loved by Ugandans and so has been best memorialized in their establishment of Bishop Tucker Theological College.

PAUL H. FRIESEN

Bibliography. B. H. Hansen, *Missionary Ideologies of the Imperialist Era: 1880–1920,* 104–16; A. P. Shepherd, *Tucker of Uganda: Artist and Apostle.*

Tucker, Charlotte (1821–1893), English missionary in India. Tucker was born on May 8, 1821, to a father who was a Bengal civilian who became the chairperson of the East India Company called "John Company." She loved to work with the poor. When she was at the age of fifty-four she heard the call from God to go to India and joined the Zenana Mission. She began her language study before she sailed to India and was prepared to begin her work of communicating the gospel as soon as she arrived.

Tucker's work focused on women in bondage. Known by some as "the Lady of England," she was a popular author and a woman of some means. She devoted eighteen years of her life to trying to win women in bondage to Christ, giving them medical care and educating them.

In addition to the Zenana work, Tucker also helped with boys in a boarding school and wrote some 68 books. Her best known title was *The Bee and the Butterfly*. Because of her close identification with the poor and downtrodden, she earned their love and respect, being given the nickname "Aunti Dear." On December 2, 1893, she passed away, a missionary who faithfully served the Lord in India even though she never saw significant results from her labors.

SAKHI ATHYAL

Bibliography. A. R. Buckland, *Women in the Mission Field;* R. A. Tucker, *GGC.*

Tunisia. (*Est. 2000 pop.: 9,694,000; 163,610 sq. km. [63,170 sq. mi.]*). Tunisia lies at the heart of North African church history, having been the earliest to receive the church, the last to release itself to its Islamic invaders, and the slowest to embrace the Christian message again in the twentieth century. From this center of early Christian influence during the Roman era, Tunisian giants were among the ranks of early Christian leadership. Men such as Tertullian and Cyprian made their mark. Today, however, church growth is minimal. Tunisian Christians are monitored closely by the government and restricted to informal groups meeting in homes. Islamic fundamentalism is present and vocal but under strong state control, and the neighboring countries of Libya and Algeria provide pressure for Islamization.

Tunisia is one of the more progressive and politically stable states of North Africa. Education is highly valued and the literacy rate is 63 percent, the highest in North Africa. The population growth is moderate, with 37 percent aged under fifteen, and the Human Development Index is one of the highest in the region.

While general religious tolerance for expatriates is moderate, the toleration of Christian witness is low, with many reports of government intimidation and interference. Even so, Christian media is pervasive with radio, video, and satellite TV all providing witness of the gospel.

J. RAY TALLMAN

Bibliography. R. Daniel, *This Holy Seed.*

Turkey (*Est. 2000 pop.: 67,748,000; 779,452 sq. km. [300,946 sq. mi.]*). The earliest recorded missionary expansion of the Christian church beyond the borders of the Jewish community itself took place in what is today modern Turkey (Acts 11:20). Antioch of Syria, where followers of Jesus were first called "Christians" and where a lively Hellenistic Christian congregation was nurtured by Barnabas and Saul (Acts 11:19–30), is at the beginning of the third millennium a bustling Turkish provincial capital called Antakya.

The "first missionary journey" of Barnabas and Saul (Acts 13–14) had its origin in Antioch, and most of their destinations on that first apostolic mission were also located in modern Turkey, places such as Perga, Pisidian Antioch, Iconium, Lystra, and Derbe. For Saul, who became known as Paul on this trip, it was entirely natural to begin his apostolic labors in these regions, for his birthplace had been Tarsus, another city of modern Turkey that still carries the same name.

By the end of the first century, the Christian church was strongly rooted in all the areas of what is modern Turkey, having been blessed by the apostolic witness not only of Paul but also of John and probably other apostles as well. The letters to the seven churches (Rev. 1–3) were all written to locations in western Turkey.

For the next millennium, the Byzantine blend of Christianity and Greek-Roman culture dominated the area until the Western Christian crusaders sacked Constantinople in 1204 and the Ottoman Turks took it in 1453 to make it their imperial capital. For the next five hundred years Christians were a tolerated minority in a great Muslim empire.

So at the beginning of the third millennium after Christ Turkey is one of the most totally Muslim nations of the world, with only a few tiny remnants of the ancient apostolic churches left after massive population changes following the breakup of the Ottoman Empire after World War I and the creation of the modern state of Turkey under the brilliant leadership of Kemal Ataturk. Modern evangelical witness through the work of the ABCFM had begun in the mid-nineteenth century, but after stiff opposition from Ottoman authorities to Christian witness among Turks sealed by a number of Turkish Christian martyrs, the nineteenth-century missionaries turned their efforts toward the traditional Christian communities of Armenian, Chaldean, Assyrian, and Greek origin. In these communities there had been significant evangelical renewal for more than fifty years, through the beginning of World War I.

The political and military settlements after World War I left the new nation-state of Turkey with scarcely any evangelical Christian witness. By the mid-1960s, however, Christian tentmakers from various nations began to find their way into Turkey, and in the next thirty years a small Turkish evangelical community began to emerge, by the end of the century numbering perhaps one thousand in a nation of more than 67 million.

RICHARD SHOWALTER

Turkmenistan *(Est. 2000 pop.: 4,551,000; 488,100 sq. km. [188,455 sq. mi.])*. Turkmenistan is a Central Asian republic of the former Soviet Union that is 80 percent desert. More than 85 percent of the population is of Turkic stock, with ethnic Turkmen alone making up about 70 percent. Turkmenistan is quite poor and has been particularly slow to experience any significant economic development. More than three-quarters of the population is at least nominally Sunni Muslim, and religious liberty is restricted. Evangelicals make up a lower percentage of the population than in any of the other ex-Soviet Central Asian republics, accounting for a meager 0.01 percent, most of whom are Slavs. Outreach efforts are few, and only a handful of people have so far come to Christ.

RAYMOND P. PRIGODICH

SEE ALSO Commonwealth of Independent States.

Turks and Caicos Islands (United Kingdom Dependent Area) *(Est. 2000 pop. 17,000; 500 sq. km. [193 sq. mi.])*. Uninhabited when discovered by Ponce de León in 1512, and consisting of two groups of thirty islands in the Caribbean, the economy of Turks and Caicos is dependent on tourism, offshore finances, and fishing. In 1993 the population was estimated at 99 percent Christian (84.5% Protestant, 12% Catholic, and 2.5% marginal). Protestant work has been primarily Baptist (since the mid-nineteenth century), Methodist (since the turn of the twentieth century), and Anglican (since the eighteenth century).

A. SCOTT MOREAU

Turner, Harold (1911–). New Zealand pioneering religious scholar and educator. Born in Napier, New Zealand, Turner was called into mission after the first year of an engineering curriculum in New Zealand. Following initial academic and pastoral work in New Zealand, he took a position at Goldsmith's College, London, as a means of making his way to Africa. This was realized with an appointment to the Faculty of Theology at Fourah Bay College in Sierra Leone. It was there, through a chance meeting with a member of the Church of the Lord Aladura on a beach in 1957, that he was exposed to the dynamic nature of the AFRICAN INITIATED CHURCH MOVEMENT. Transferring to the University of Nigeria (Nkassa), where he taught religious studies, he came across the works of Eliade and began to build a phenomenological orientation toward religious studies (*see* PHENOMENOLOGY OF RELIGION), reflected in *Profile through Preaching* (1965), his ground-breaking two-volume *History of an African Independent Church* (1967), and *From Temple to Meeting House: The Phenomenology and Theology of Places of Worship* (1979), which he considered his most relevant (and overlooked) contribution to missiology. During his career, he pioneered the phenomenological study of NEW RELIGIOUS MOVEMENTS, in the process building a significant collection of resources related to their study housed at the Centre for New Religious Movements (Selly Oaks) and represented in *Bibliography of New Religious Movements in Primal Societies* (6 vols.).

A. SCOTT MOREAU

Bibliography. W. R. Shenk, *BDCM*, pp. 684–85; H. W. Turner, *IBMR* 13 (1989): 71–74; A. F. Walls and W. R. Shenk, *Exploring New Religious Movements.*

Tuvalu *(Est. 2000 pop.: 10,000; 26 sq. km. [10 sq. mi.])*. Comprised of nine atolls in Oceania, Tuvalu was formerly known as Ellice Islands. Independence from Great Britain was achieved in 1978. In 1993 it was estimated that 96.6 percent of the population was Christian (93.8% Protestant, 1.1.% Catholic, and 1.7% marginal). Christianity came to the islands when Samoan pastors began preaching there in 1861, and the resulting Tuvalu Church (Congregationalist) is the largest denomination.

A. SCOTT MOREAU

Two-Thirds World. Synonym for terms such as "THIRD WORLD,""Non-Western World," and "The South." It is intended to avoid any connotation of "third-rate" and instead to point to the poverty and size of the Third World. In practice its use is mainly associated with Western discussion of non-Western theologies, and the increase in evangelical missionaries from the continents of Africa, Asia, and Latin America.

"Two-Thirds World" has been in greater use since 1982, but it is not universally preferred. While the Ecumenical Association of Third-World Theologians (EATWOT) is a representative group that continues to own "Third World" as a self-designation, others are hesitant about either term. Both relate to common experiences of COLONIALISM, poverty, and Christianity as a minority religion, usually in a multireligious context. That history needs to be explored comparatively and from the inside. However, it is not surprising that in particular countries, nationality and local culture are stronger influences on

Christian identity. Nobody sees themselves as primarily "Two-Thirds World." At most they see this as a designation they share with others over against the West.

The features that "Two-Thirds World" and "Third World" highlight are becoming less valid as points of commonality and differentiation. Increasingly poverty, riches, and world religions are global realities. Indigenous peoples and regional minorities have Third World/Two-Thirds World experiences with First World countries. Western theologies are now recognized as local enculturated theologies with the same processes of formation as theologies of the Two-Thirds World. Christian mission as a characteristically Western activity refers only to a limited period of history, and even then it was only partially true.

"Third World" and "Two-Thirds World" will remain useful while Western Christians adjust to changing global realities and Non-Western Christians discover what they can learn from one another. They are as necessary as the term "Western" to discuss important features of a recent era, but they are just as inadequate.

JOHN ROXBOROGH

Bibliography. V. Samuel and C. Sugden, eds., *Sharing Jesus in the Two Thirds World;* L. E. Keyes and L. D. Pate, *Missiology* 21:2 (1993): 187–206; L. D. Pate, *From Every People.*

Two-Covenant Theory. This theory contends that because God made an everlasting covenant with Abraham and the patriarchs (Gen. 18:19, etc.) and ratified it with all Israelites at Sinai, and because Jesus made a second covenant with the Gentile world in mind, his gospel should be theologically understood as intended for non-Jews only. This means that Judaism should be regarded by the followers of Jesus, whether Jews or Gentiles, as a divinely guided religion that is parallel to Christianity, "neither superseded by it, nor fulfilled within it" (Myers, 1990). This perspective allegedly has validity even though it is readily granted that the New Testament gives no endorsement to this radical reconceptualization of the significance of the new covenant instituted by Jesus in fulfillment of the prophecy made by Jeremiah (31:31–34). Hans Joachim Schoeps is often quoted in its support: "The continuous existence of Israel almost 2000 years *post Christum natum,* still undisturbed in its consciousness of being God's covenant people, is testimony that the old covenant has not been abrogated, that as the covenant of Israel it continues to exist alongside the wider human covenant of the Christian Church" (1961, 256, 7). Evangelicals rejoice that the Jewish people continue to exist due to God's faithfulness (Jer. 31:35–37), despite all efforts to destroy them. This is the great fact that makes certain the coming of their Golden Age. Then, re-

united to Jesus the Messiah, they shall be as "life from the dead" to the Gentile nations (Rom. 11:1–16, 25–36).

According to this theory Jews do not now need to believe in Jesus in order to be saved (despite the Jewish witness before the Sanhedrin to the exact opposite in Acts 4:12). The evangelization of the Jewish people is unwarranted and should cease. Jewish religious leaders should be heeded when they contend that the hostility between Christianity and Judaism generated over the centuries by the church's persistent efforts to evangelize their people should give way to mutual acceptance and friendly religious dialogue between their separate religious communities.

In this connection the words of Franz Rosenzweig (1886–1929), an Austrian Jewish philosopher, are often quoted: "We are wholly agreed as to what Christ and his church mean to the world: no one can reach the Father save through him. But the situation is quite different from one who does not have to reach the Father because he is already with him. And this is true of the people of Israel (though not of individual Jews)" (Glatzer, 1953).

The probability is that Rosenzweig's words would have never gained their widespread credence had he not been just about the first Jewish scholar to speak appreciatively of Christianity, the Christian church, and her significant success in world mission. In his famous book, *The Star of Redemption,* Rosenzweig contends that Jews are born Jews, born into the faith community instituted between God and Israel at Sinai. By this natural phenomenon, they do not have to undergo any form of spiritual rebirth. In contrast, since no Gentiles are born Christians, a rebirth is essential if they desire to become spiritual children of Abraham (Rom. 4:9–12). Inevitably, Rosenzweig's position generated much debate, pro and con in Jewry. Arthur A. Cohen argued that this "heady doctrine—provides the Jew at last with a means of explaining to the Christian, in essentially Christian terms, why it is that the promise of Jesus to the Jews isn't really interesting. Jews do not need redemption in the same way as Christians. Eternal life, as the Sabbath liturgy affirms, is already planted in our midst" (1971, 210).

Mainline Protestantism largely endorses the two-covenant theory. But this has not always been the case. In 1948 when the WORLD COUNCIL OF CHURCHES convened its first international assembly, it was agreed that despite the tragedy of Auschwitz and the failure of churches worldwide to protest the German destruction of European Jewry (1939–45), the Word of God must be upheld: "The fulfillment of the church's commission requires that we include the Jewish people in our evangelistic task" (WCC Publications, Document 1). By 1988 the drift from obedience to Scripture had gained such momentum that the WCC openly suggested to its member churches that "the next step may be to proscribe all proselytism of Jews on the theological ground that it is rejection of Israel's valid covenant with God" (1988, 186). Forgotten is Jesus' admonition to Nicodemus, "a ruler of the Jews," that no one can see, much less enter the KINGDOM OF GOD unless he is born anew (John 3:1–21).

Evangelicals readily agree with Axel Torm, the former chairman of the Danish Israel Mission, who stated: "In earlier times the church downgraded Judaism in order to exalt Christ. It was a sin that the church committed. Today, people downgrade Christ in order to exalt Judaism. Is that better?" (quoted by Kjaer-Hansen, 1994, 81).

ARTHUR F. GLASSER

Bibliography. A. A. Cohen, *The Myth of the Judeo-Christian Tradition;* N. N. Glatzer, "Introduction" in *One Star of Redemption;* K. Kjaer-Hansen, MISHKAN, 21:2 (1994); H. J. Schoeps, *Paul—The Theology of the Apostle in the Light of Jewish Religious History;* WCC Publications, *The Theology of the Churches and the Jewish People.*

Uu

Uchimura, Kanzō (1861–1930). Japanese evangelist, Christian thinker, and social critic. Uchimura's career can be summed up as an ellipse with the foci of "2 Js, Jesus and Japan." Born in a warrior family and reared in Confucianism, he became a Christian while studying at the Sapporo Agricultural School. After briefly serving the Japanese State he left for the United States in 1884, and studied at Amherst College where he experienced conversion, but his short stay at seminary ended in disillusionment with institutional Christianity. His autobiographical account, "How I Became a Christian" (1855), detailed his life until his return to Japan in 1888. Two later incidents seemed to indicate that he was an outsider to both mainline Christianity and the State and foretold the unique development of his "Christ-nationalism." One was his resignation in 1888 from a mission-school over the issue of evaluating the Japanese (vis-à-vis Christian) virtues, and the other was his forced resignation from a public school when he questioned the Emperor's divinity in 1891. Throughout his turbulent and prophet-like life, he was associated with such movements as weekly Bible lectures, adventism, and *Mukyokai* (NON-CHURCH MOVEMENT) as well as Christian pacifism and social reforms. The missiological question he posed, namely, relating Christianity and Japan, remains valid today.

TADATAKA MARUYAMA

Bibliography. H. Miura, *The Life and Thought of Kanzo Uchimura, 1861–1930.*

Uemura, Masahisa (1858–1925). Japanese church planter and mission advocate. Uemura, like many of the other early Christian leaders in Japan, grew up in a family which had relatively high status in the government which was deposed in the Meiji Restoration of 1868. Finding their old world shattered and their families almost destitute, some of these young men looked to non-traditional sources for education and a new worldview. Uemura studied with missionaries James Ballagh and S. R. Brown, was baptized in 1873, and became a member of Japan's first Protestant congregation in Yokohama. In 1877 he entered seminary, was ordained in 1879, and began a new congregation in his home neighborhood in Tokyo, the first congregation in Japan begun by a Japanese without missionary help. Uemura insisted throughout his life that the church in Japan must be independent of both foreign aid and foreign control.

Uemura's work and faith were located entirely in the classically orthodox Presbyterian/Reformed tradition, particularly in his emphasis on the person and work of Christ and on the church as the body of Christ. In 1886 he established what is now known as the Fujimicho Church which reached 1,600 members, one of the largest congregations in Japan. As a church leader Uemura actively promoted Japanese Christian mission activity in Taiwan and on the Asian mainland. In addition to pastoring, Uemura taught in the theology department of Meiji Gakuin University until he began an independent seminary in 1904. He was on the committee for translating the Old Testament and also was known as a gifted translator of hymns. He published a number of journals and his complete works run to eight volumes. He is best known, however, as a gifted preacher and church builder, one of the greatest leaders of the Church of Christ in Japan (Nihon Kirisuto Kyokai).

ROBERT L. RAMSEYER

Bibliography. R. A. Drummond, *BDCM*, pp. 687–88; A. Katsuhisa, *Dr. Masahisa Uemora: A Christian Leader.*

Uganda (*Est. 2000 pop.: 24,618,000; 241,038 sq. km. [93,065 sq. mi.]*). Having fulfilled his primary quest in finding David Livingstone, Henry Stanley traveled northwards to Uganda and met Kabaka (King) Mutesa I of the Buganda in 1874. Mutesa had become a Muslim in 1854, but Stanley convinced Mutesa to profess Christ and to request that Christian teachers be sent from Britain and teach his people about Christianity.

978

Stanley wrote a passionate appeal (Van Rheenen, 1976, 16) published in the *London Daily Telegraph* which was widely read. Eventually the appeal and a resulting anonymous donation resulted in eight volunteers for the mission to Uganda. Only two, ALEXANDER MACKAY and C. T. Wilson, managed to reach their destination, the rest dying en route.

Mutesa's conversion and character eventually proved to be dubious, and he began to request guns rather than teaching. Evan so Wilson and MacKay's influence grew, eventually arousing Muslim opposition. A further complicating factor was the arrival of French Catholics in March of 1879. Protestants, Catholics, and Muslims vied for Mutesa's approval, and he played them off against each other.

After his death in 1884, Mutesa was succeeded by his inexperienced eighteen-year-old son, Mwanga, who reverted to traditional religion and began persecuting Christians, eventually killing more than 200. Even so, Mackay toiled on until 1890, when he died of overwork. The same year, after several failed attempts to send more missionaries to Uganda, ALFRED TUCKER finally arrived to help with the work. His career in Uganda was characterized by the development of an indigenous leadership for the church.

Another key missionary in the early period was GEORGE PILKINGTON, a brilliant linguist remembered for his work (together with E. C. Gordon and W. A. Crabtree) in the translation of the Bible into Luganda. Pilkington believed that Bible reading was foundational to true conversion to Christianity: "The power to read the Bible is the key to the Kingdom of God. With the exception of one case, I have never known anyone profess Christ who could not read" (Harford-Battersby, 1898, 256). Pilkington was also a firm believer in and advocate of indigenous missions. "The natives are more qualified to evangelize than we missionaries are," he said. "The evangelization of Africa must be carried out by Africans . . ." (ibid.).

Perhaps nothing has had greater impact on the Ugandan church than the East African Revival. Its origins can be traced to two men: Joe Church, young British medical doctor and a missionary at Gahini, Rwanda; and Simeon Nsibambi, a health inspector. Together these two studied their Bibles, prayed, and confessed their sins for three days. After this they went their separate ways and God used them to begin the revival which spread throughout Uganda, Kenya, and Tanzania.

While other mission groups have worked to evangelize Uganda, none have been as successful as the Anglicans and Catholics. The Seventh-Day Adventists (SDA) began their work in 1926 and concentrated other efforts among the Buganda and BaAkonjo. The Southern Baptists entered in 1954, concentrating their efforts in the rural areas of eastern Uganda, among the Bagisu, Teso, and other areas where the Anglicans and Catholics were weakest. The Conservative Baptists went to Uganda in 1961 when the Congolese uprisings drove out some of their missionaries from Zaire (now the Democratic Republic of Congo).

The Pentecostals began their missionary work in 1959 with three mission groups: Glad Tidings Missionary Society of Canada, Pentecostal Assemblies of God (Canada), and the Elim Missionary Assemblies. However, internal friction over personal disagreements led to fragmentation in their efforts.

Uganda was generally slow in developing African independent church movements. By 1960, for example, there were only 66 denominations in Uganda compared to 296 in neighboring Kenya. Indigenous church groups continue to be formed in the recent years, some having local congregations of as many as 4,000 worshipers.

During the reign of Idi Amin (1971–79), Christians in Uganda experienced severe PERSECUTION. Twenty-eight Protestant denominations and organizations were banned and restrictions were placed on the preaching of the gospel. Hundreds of thousands, including prominent leaders such as Anglican Archbishop, Janani Luwum, were martyred for their faith.

More recently Uganda has enjoyed relative political and economic stability. However, even though the church is estimated to be just over 83% of the 24.6 million people, Uganda has been plagued with a crisis of AIDS spread by heterosexual promiscuity in epidemic proportions. While church and state have begun to cooperate on educational programs, and the HIV infection rate is reportedly stationary, AIDS still represents one of the biggest challenges Uganda has faced to date, affecting church and state alike.

LAZARUS SERUYANGE

Bibliography. C. F. Harford-Battersby, *Pilkington of Uganda;* J. Murray, *Proclaim the Good News: A Short History of the C.M.S.;* M. L. Pirouet, *Black Evangelists;* J. V. Taylor, *The Growth of the Church in Uganda: An Attempt at Understanding;* T. Tuma and P. Mutibwa, *A Century of Christianity in Uganda: 1877–1977;* G. Van Rheenen, *Church Planting in Uganda: A Comparative Study;* D. Wooding and R. Barnett, *Uganda Holocaust.*

Ukraine (*Est. 2000 pop.: 50,974,000; 603,700 sq. km. [233,089 sq. mi.]*). Ukraine, long known as the breadbasket of the Soviet Union, is one of three predominantly Slavic republics of the former Soviet Union. Ethnic Ukrainians make up 73 percent of the population, with Russians accounting for another 21 percent. Eastern Orthodoxy was first introduced into Ukraine in A.D. 988, and well over half the population still identifies at least nominally with Orthodoxy. Roman Catholics, particularly of the Uniate variety, are strong in the west and make up 15 percent of Ukraine's population. Ukraine is also known as

979

the "Bible belt" of the former Soviet Union; evangelical Christianity is stronger there than in any of the other ex-Soviet republics, making up at least 3 percent of the population. Ukraine enjoys full religious liberty, churches are growing, and a large number of indigenous mission societies have sprung up there.

RAYMOND P. PRIGODICH

See also Commonwealth of Independent States.

Ulfilas (c. 311–82). Early missionary to Germany; "Apostle to the Goths." A Cappadocian captured by the Germanic tribe that posed a constant threat to the Roman Empire, he had been brought up by them beyond the Danube. There was evidently a sizable Christian community among the barbarians, and Ulfilas was consecrated bishop by Eusebius of Nicomedia, whose Arian views he had espoused. He worked initially among the Goths of what is now Romania, many of whom turned to Christianity. Others resisted, seeing in the Christian missionary a device to bring them under Roman domination. After seven years Ulfilas in 348 obtained permission for himself and his converts to settle south of the Danube, and there he continued his work until his death.

His great monument, after creating an alphabet, is his Gothic translation of the Bible, the oldest written work in a Germanic language. It is said he omitted the books of Samuel and Kings to prevent the Goths' military appetite being further whetted by bloodthirsty narratives. More likely his translation was incomplete when he died, and that he had postponed parts of Scripture he regarded as least important for inculcating Christian behavior in his flock. His Arianism was later modified in a more orthodox direction, probably due to the influence of Emperor Theodosius the Great.

Many of his translations of the Gospels survive with the Pauline epistles and fragments of Nehemiah.

J. D. DOUGLAS

Bibliography. G. Friedrichsen, *The Gothic Version of the Gospel;* C. A. A. Scott, *Ulfilas, Apostle of the Goths.*

Umbanda. *See* LATIN AMERICAN NEW RELIGIOUS MOVEMENTS.

Underwood, Horace G. (1859–1916). English missionary educator in Korea. Underwood was born in London, England, though his family immigrated to the United States in 1872 when he was thirteen. He graduated from New York University in 1881 and from Dutch Reformed Theological Seminary in New Brunswick, New Jersey, in 1884.

Underwood was commissioned as a single young missionary by the Northern Presbyterian Church and sent to Korea, landing in Inchon on April 5, 1885. He was the first Presbyterian clergyman to enter Korea as a missionary. After assisting a medical missionary for a short time, he opened an orphanage for boys in Chong Dong in 1886 which later developed into the Kyong Shin Boys High School.

In 1887 Underwood organized the first Protestant church in Korea with 14 charter members. A tireless evangelist who itinerated widely, he was also deeply engaged in literacy work and in the translation of the Scriptures with other missionary colleagues.

At the First General Assembly of the Korean Presbyterian Church in 1912, Underwood was elected the moderator. In 1915 he founded Chosen Christian College (now Yonsei University), where he served as president until his death in 1916. After his death, his son, Horace Horton Underwood, succeeded his father as president of the college. Today the third and fourth generations of the Underwood family carry on a faithful missionary heritage in Korea. The Underwood family is one of the most widely known and most distinguished Presbyterian missionary families in Korea.

BONG RIN RO

Bibliography. A. D. Clark, *A History of the Church in Korea;* E. N. Hunt, Jr., *Protestant Pioneers in Korea;* L. G. Paik, *The History of Protestant Missions in Korea, 1832–1910;* L. H. Underwood, *Underwood of Korea.*

Unevangelized. The large segment of the world's population that lives without a viable witness of the gospel or a valid opportunity to accept or reject Jesus Christ as Lord and Savior. They have never heard the gospel with sufficient cultural relevance to allow them an informed response to Christ. The unevangelized are those who do not know or hear about Christ; who do not have an indigenous church with the resources to reach them; who do not have meaningful contacts with Christians; who do not have the Bible available to them; who live isolated from the gospel because of cultural, geographical, political, or linguistic barriers; and who will not be evangelized unless someone is sent to cross those barriers with the gospel. Some distinguish between evangelized and unevangelized people groups by insisting that a people group is evangelized when it has an indigenous church with the resources to evangelize the group without outside (cross-cultural) assistance.

Other related terms include "the lost" (those outside of Christ, separated from God, and living in spiritual darkness), "HEATHEN" (an older term for those outside Christ, especially in non-Christian countries), "hidden peoples" (those who live places where they are unseen and unreached by

Christians). In recent years, one of the terms most commonly used in the context of the unevangelized is "UNREACHED PEOPLES"—ethnolinguistic groups with a significant group identity and affinity which do not have their own indigenous witness or church and in which the majority of the members are unevangelized. The Lausanne Committee for World Evangelization uses a scale of terms to identify unevangelized peoples. The scale includes "hidden people" (no known Christians within the group), "initially reached" (less than one percent of the group are Christians), "minimally reached" (one to 10 percent of the group are Christians), "possibly reached" (10 percent to 20 percent of the group are Christians), and "reached" (over 20 percent of the group are Christians).

Unreached people groups became a serious focus of mission strategy with RALPH WINTER's address, "The Highest Priority—Cross-Cultural Evangelism," presented at the LAUSANNE CONGRESS ON WORLD EVANGELIZATION (1974). Winter challenged the notion that the gospel had been preached to all the world and drew attention to hidden or unreached peoples who are not culturally near to any Christians.

Winter asserted that these peoples can be reached only by a specialized CROSS-CULTURAL EVANGELISM. This innovation in thinking about the world in terms of unreached peoples and defining the unfinished task of missions as reaching the unreached profoundly impacted both the concept of missions and strategies of missions (*see also* MISSIONARY TASK, THE). It infused the missionary enterprise with a renewed sense of purpose and a new spirit of urgency.

Research organizations such as the U.S. Center for World Missions and World Vision's Mission Advanced Research Center (MARC) with its Unreached People Database were formed for the express purpose of identifying and mapping unreached people groups and motivating a movement of GREAT COMMISSION agencies, churches, and individuals to focus on reaching the unreached. Organizations such as the AD 2000 and Beyond Movement emerged with the vision of reaching all the people groups of the world as soon as possible. Major missions agencies added divisions or components to focus on the unreached and to develop creative approaches to penetrate them with the gospel. Greater cooperation has resulted between Great Commission missions agencies and organizations in the targeting of specific people groups (*see also* PEOPLES, PEOPLE GROUPS).

The estimate of the number of unreached people groups varies with the criteria used to identify them. In his Lausanne message, Winter spoke of 16,750 such groups. This number has often been quoted. Patrick Johnstone, compiler of *Operation World*, projects the number as approximately 12,000. Regardless of the different estimates, seeing the world in terms of unreached people groups accentuates the magnitude of the unfinished task of world evangelization.

There are general implications of the unreached peoples approach to missions strategy. It helps clarify the demands of world evangelization. It moves the focus of missions away from the geographic borders of nation-states. A church may be planted in a nation but not be indigenous to all the peoples of that nation. People groups transcend the borders of nations, and multiple groups live within a nation. It is reasonable, therefore, to see the task of world evangelization not as reaching nations but as reaching those unevangelized people groups wherein individuals have their primary identity.

The unreached peoples approach helps target those specific groups that are still to be evangelized. The concept of the 10/40 WINDOW, for example, has helped focus personnel, planning, and praying on that area of the world where the majority of the unevangelized live.

The unreached peoples approach helps communicate that the goal of world evangelization is achievable. The number of people groups is not infinite. The challenge is not to win every individual. It is instead to plant INDIGENOUS CHURCHES within each people group which, in turn, are able to evangelize the group. Thus, this approach provides a standard to measure progress in the task.

The unreached peoples approach underscores the growing need for specialized cross-cultural missionaries. The unevangelized peoples will not hear the gospel or have a church unless such workers penetrate their group with the gospel. A majority of the unevangelized live in either closed or CREATIVE ACCESS COUNTRIES. Traditional missionaries cannot gain entry in most of these situations. To reach them requires a force of missionaries with specialized training and specialized skills that are both relevant and necessary to the people group and will provide the means for residency (*see also* TENT-MAKING MISSION).

The unreached people approach has stimulated strategic innovations in missions planning and methods for accomplishing world evangelization. Among these are creative access strategies, the NONRESIDENTIAL MISSIONARY, targeting of people clusters, missionary specialists who utilize a vocation to establish residence, the increased number of Third World missionaries comprising the global missionary force (*see* NON-WESTERN MISSION BOARDS AND SOCIETIES), culturally sensitive models of church planting, specialized missionary training, reaching students and other members of particular groups abroad and training them to return to evangelize their group (*see* STUDENT MISSION WORK), utilizing development projects as points of entry and bridges to evangelism, and coordination and cooperation among Great Commission organizations to maximize spiritual, human, financial, and technical resources.

DONALD R. DUNAVANT

SEE ALSO Reached and Unreached Mission Fields.

Union Missionary Convention (New York Missionary Conference, 1854). Union Missionary Convention, held on May 4–5, 1854, at the Broadway Tabernacle in New York City. While touring the United States in 1854, ALEXANDER DUFF, missionary to Calcutta, India, gave an address in February in Philadelphia on the need to recruit more missionaries. Leaders of evangelical churches, inspired by his missionary vision and prompted by layman George H. Stuart of Philadelphia, resolved to hold a "general missionary conference" three months later in May. Two committees, one in New York and the other in Philadelphia, planned the Union Missionary Convention to promote unity among Protestants to advance the cause of missions. One hundred and forty-two church leaders, ministers, missionaries, and members registered for the convention, including such notables as RUFUS ANDERSON, Nathan Bangs, and William E. Dodge. The list does not mention the names of any women.

Duff gave the major speech of the convention, a stirring plea for modern missions. Eight questions were placed before the convention, but time limited the discussions to six. In response, six major resolutions passed with five being offered by Duff, centering on the need to convert the world to Christ; use all available means to evangelize; concentrate personnel in fields where non-Christian religions had long prevailed; avoid duplication of efforts through COMITY arrangements; and keep before church members and ministers the importance of the missionary calling. Seminaries were encouraged to offer courses in missions and evangelism. The sixth motion proposed by N. Murray won approval for the planning of another missionary convention in New York City in 1855. The Union Missionary Convention anticipated later ecumenical gatherings which dealt with varying issues facing missionaries and mission agencies. The spiritual unity and concern to evangelize the world demonstrated by the Convention's actions reflected the evangelical unity underlying the nineteenth-century mission movement.

GARY B. McGEE

Bibliography. Proceedings of the Union Missionary Convention held in New York, May 4th and 5th, 1854.

Uniqueness of Christ. Many discussions about the significance of Jesus Christ within the context of world religions virtually cut Jesus off from his historical and scriptural roots and speak of him as the founder of a new religion, whereas certainly Jesus had no intention of launching another "religion" as such. The coming of Jesus was prepared for through God's dealings with Israel and their Scriptures. It was from the Hebrew Bible that Jesus drew his identity and his motivating mission. Two major unique aspects of Old Testament revelation combined in the uniqueness of Christ: the uniqueness of Israel and the uniqueness of Yahweh. Both lie at the heart of a biblical understanding of mission (*see also* OLD TESTAMENT THEOLOGY OF MISSION).

The Uniqueness of Israel. The Bible presents God's redemptive answer to the human problem (comprehensively portrayed in Gen. 1–11) through the call of Abraham and the creation of Israel as God's people. God's covenant with Abraham concludes with God's commitment to the mission of blessing all nations (Gen. 12:3). God chose to achieve that universal goal through a particular historical means—the nation of Israel. Israel's unique election thus stands in integral connection to its place in the mission of God for the nations. The New Testament, from Matthew's opening genealogy, affirms that Jesus completed what God had already begun to work out through Israel. The mission of Jesus has to be understood against the background of a historical, particular people (*see also* JESUS AND MISSION). His uniqueness is linked to theirs. The Hebrew Bible is clear that God's action in and through Israel was unique. This does *not* mean that God was in no way involved in the histories of other nations. On the contrary, Israel boldly claimed that Yahweh was sovereign over all nations (e.g., Amos 9:7; Deut. 2:20–23; Exod. 9:13–16; Isa. 10:5–19; Jer. 27:5–7; Isa. 44:28–45:13). It does mean that only in Israel did God work within the terms of a covenant of redemption, initiated and sustained by his grace (e.g., Amos 3:2; Deut. 4:32–34; Ps. 147:19f.; Isa. 43:8–13; Exod. 19:5–6; 20:26; Num. 23:9; Deut. 7:6). Israel only existed because of God's desire to redeem people from every nation. While God has every nation in view in his redemptive purpose, in no other nation did he act as he did in Israel, for the sake of the nations. No other nation experienced what Israel did of God's revelation and redemption.

The New Testament presents Jesus as the *Messiah,* Jesus the Christ. And the Messiah "was" Israel. That is, he represented and personified Israel. The Messiah was the completion of all that for which Israel had been placed in the world— God's self-revelation and his work of human redemption. For this reason, Jesus shares in the uniqueness of Israel; indeed he was the point and goal of it. What God had been doing through no other nation he now completed through no other person than the Messiah, Jesus of Nazareth. The paradox is that precisely through the narrowing down of his redemptive work to the unique particularity of the single man, Jesus, God opened the way to the universalizing of his redemptive grace to all nations, which was his purpose from the beginning. It was this connection between the "mystery" of Israel's existence for the nations in the Old Testament and the significance of the gospel of Jesus' messiahship that formed the basis of Paul's mission theology in relation to the Gentiles (Gal. 3:14, 26–29; Eph. 2:11–13; 3:4–6). The fulfillment of Israel's *historical particularity* in Jesus was at the same time the fulfillment of Israel's *eschatological universality*. In this way the uniqueness of Christ is inseparable from the mission of God's people.

The Uniqueness of Yahweh. There can be no more powerful affirmation in the Old Testament than the claim that Yahweh alone is truly and uniquely God (e.g., Deut. 4:32–40). This monotheistic thrust was not simply the singularity of deity, but rather sought to define the one God in terms of the nature, character, and actions of Yahweh (e.g., Isa. 40:12–31; 43:10–12; 45:5, 22–24). Yahweh is unique in character, and deity.

An important ingredient in Old Testament Israel's eschatology was the conviction that Yahweh would come bringing both redemption and judgment. Several of these texts were applied by Jesus to himself, or to the circumstances surrounding his ministry (e.g., Isa. 35:4ff.; Matt. 11:4–6; Ezek. 34; John 10:11, 14; Matt. 22:41–46; Mal. 2:1; 4:5; Matt. 11:14). The implication was that, in the person of Jesus, Yahweh had indeed come, as the birth title "Emmanuel" also signified, to inaugurate the new age of his salvation and reign.

Similarly, soon after the death and resurrection of Jesus we find the early church referring to him and addressing him in terms which had previously been applied only to Yahweh in their Scriptures. They called him Lord, the Greek word *Kyrios* being the one regularly used in the Greek version of the Old Testament for the divine name Yahweh. They "called on his name" in worship and prayer (cf., Ps. 116:12f., 17). Stephen saw Jesus standing at the right hand of God sharing in his divine glory (Acts 7:55). Paul transferred the saving name of Yahweh to Jesus in his evangelism (Acts 16:31; cf. Joel 2:32; Rom. 10:13). In possibly his earliest letter, 1 Thessalonians, Paul speaks of Jesus in remarkable ways, given that it was written within about a decade of the crucifixion and that the Thessalonians obviously accepted the claims as basic elements in their new faith. He speaks of "the Lord Jesus Christ" in the same breath as "God the Father" (1:1, 3). He addresses prayer to both together (3:11–13). Jesus is "God's Son," who will come to bring in the final act of judgment and salvation (1:10). "The Day of the Lord (Yahweh)" (e.g., Joel 1:15; 2:11, 28–32; 3:14 etc.) has been transformed, in the light of the expected coming of Jesus, into "the Day of the Lord Jesus" (4:16–5:2).

The heartbeat of Old Testament monotheism can also be felt in the way Paul expanded the credal *shema* of Deuteronomy 6:4–5 into a declaration of the uniqueness of Jesus in relation to the world of Greco-Roman polytheism in 1 Corinthians 8, and in the way Peter converted the Deuteronomic affirmation that Yahweh is God "and there is no other" (Deut. 4:35–39), into the exclusive claim that salvation was to be found in the name of Jesus, and in "no other name" (Acts 4:12).

Possibly the most remarkable identification of Jesus with Yahweh comes in Philippians 2:5–11, probably part of an early Christian hymn which Paul incorporates here to make his point. Jesus has been given "the name above every name" (v. 9)—which in the light of the Hebrew Scriptures could only mean the name of Yahweh. Verse 10 then clinches this affirmation by applying to Jesus words taken from Isaiah 45:22f. which were originally spoken by Yahweh about himself, declaring his uniqueness as God and his unique ability to save. The uniqueness of Jesus is thus founded unmistakably on the uniqueness of Yahweh, and specifically to his action in salvation. It thus has a direct connection with the central dynamic of Christian mission.

In Jesus, then, the uniqueness of Israel and the uniqueness of Yahweh flow together, for he embodied the one and incarnated the other, climactically fulfilling the mission of both.

CHRISTOPHER J. H. WRIGHT

Bibliography. L. Hurtado, *One Lord, One God: Early Christian Devotion and Ancient Jewish Monotheism;* C. J. H. Wright, *Knowing Jesus through the Old Testament;* idem, *Thinking Clearly about the Uniqueness of Jesus;* N. T. Wright, *Who was Jesus?*

United Arab Emirates (*Est. 2000 pop.: 2,107,000; 83,600 sq. km. [32,278 sq. mi.]*). Home to no indigenous Christian community after the Arab conquest of the seventh century, Abu Dhabi became headquarters of the Roman Catholic vicariate of Arabia in 1974, which serves immigrant Eastern rite Catholics (Maronites, Melkites, Chaldeans, and others) attracted there by development of the region's oil fields. Various Orthodox and non-Chalcedonian Christians, including Armenians and Indian Mar Thomists, also help form the Christian community of the United Arab Emirates and other Persian Gulf principalities. At the time of writing, exact figures of their strength are unavailable. Christians may number over 150,000, or are estimated around 8 percent of the 2.1 million people of the United Arab Emirates.

Until April 1975, the United Arab Emirates permitted the building of churches. Authorities welcomed personal visits by Western missionaries of various traditions. Christians worked openly and freely. In April 1975, however, the sheikdoms forbade any further proselytizing activity by non-Muslims among Muslims. Christians exercise influence covertly, through two Catholic schools, or by Christian broadcasts in Arabic heard over international stations.

PAUL R. DEKAR

Bibliography. R. Betts, *Christians in the Arab East. A Political Study;* A. Horner, *A Guide to Christian Churches in the Middle East.*

United Bible Societies. *See* BIBLE SOCIETIES.

United Kingdom *(Est. 2000 pop.: 59,022,000; 244,100 sq. km. [94,247 sq. mi.]).* The origins of Christianity in the British Isles are not clearly identified: suffice it to say that missionary endeavor had established a Celtic church by the second, or at the latest, the third century. By the fourth century it was well enough established to send delegates to the Synod of Arles (314), though there is some evidence that in these early years Christianity was a religion of the poor, rather than of the army or wealthier or better organized parts of the population. In the fifth century, that Christian Celtic culture was pushed to the extremities of the British Isles by Saxon invasions, where it was maintained, isolated from continental influences, not least through the endeavor, in the late sixth and early seventh centuries, of monks of the caliber of COLUMBA and AIDAN, and their followers. This isolation meant that when Augustine was sent from Rome in 596 to reestablish the English church, there was a difference in emphasis between the churchmanship that he brought from Rome and the spirituality of the old Celtic Christians in the north and the west, though an accommodation was achieved at Whitby in 664. By the beginning of the next century, Britain was sending missionaries to Europe, among the most famous of whom was the Devon monk, BONIFACE, whose missionary endeavors extended as far east as Thuringia and Bavaria. Until the time of Wycliffe, the Scriptures were only partially available in English but the Wycliffite reforms stimulated the production of an English text even if it was not approved by the official church. Subsequently it became one of the achievements of the Renaissance to nurture critical awareness of the documents that lay behind the Vulgate, and, from those improved sources, to secure those reliable vernacular translations which did so much to encourage the work of the REFORMATION. Thus the importance of Miles Coverdale, who in 1535 produced on the Continent the first complete English Bible. His predecessor, William Tyndale, produced an English New Testament in 1526 but never published the whole Bible before his early death in exile in 1536. Surprisingly the renewed biblical scholarship of the Reformation did not immediately lead

to renewed missionary activity from the new reformed churches: some churches were too busy establishing their new identity as over against the claims of the COUNTER-REFORMATION. Elsewhere an exaggerated Calvinism paralyzed the church's outreach. At the end of the seventeenth century, Thomas Bray was influential in founding both the Society for Promoting Christian Knowledge (1698), part of whose function was to disperse religious literature overseas. Bray also founded the SOCIETY FOR THE PROPAGATION OF THE GOSPEL IN FOREIGN PARTS (1701), which, though partly focused on a ministry among expatriates, provided for evangelizing the non-Christian races of the world, a task taken up some thirty years later by the Moravians.

At the end of the eighteenth century, the Evangelical Revival began to produce a new concern for overseas missions. In 1783 THOMAS COKE, a close associate of JOHN WESLEY, published his *Plan of the Society for the Establishment of Missions among the Heathen,* nine years before WILLIAM CAREY'S *An Enquiry into the Obligations of Christians, to use Means for the Conversion of the Heathen,* which led to the founding that same year of the BAPTIST MISSIONARY SOCIETY (1792), the first of the new evangelical societies, followed in 1795 by the founding of the LONDON MISSIONARY SOCIETY. Originally called simply The Missionary Society, it was initially a pan-evangelical initiative though it subsequently became de facto a Congregational agency, as other denominations founded their own societies. Four years later, in 1799, what was to become the CHURCH MISSIONARY SOCIETY was founded. Later came the Wesleyan Methodist Missionary Society (1818). Not until 1824 did the Church of Scotland began to undertake work on its own account.

Typical of the new missionary theology which emerged in the 1780s was ANDREW FULLER'S *The Gospel Worthy of All Acceptation* (1781–85), which translated into an English context some of the new thinking about classical Calvinism that was circulating in North America from the pen of JONATHAN EDWARDS. Fuller's work sought to correct, where it existed, that hyper-Calvinism which Joseph Ivimey cruelly depicted as the "non-application, non-invitation system," when preachers, paralyzed by the idea of God's sovereign determination of the numbers of the elect, feared to preach seeking a human response to the gospel message. Edward Williams, twenty years later, was to serve a similar purpose for Congregationalists. This new understanding of God's purposes rather than the increased English knowledge of Africa, Asia, and the Pacific explains the timing of the founding of the modern missionary movement, putting it in a wider theological context than just a spin off from the abolition movement. Thus it provoked an interest in domestic as much as overseas missions. The two together were the fruit of a prayerful search among evangelical dissenters in the 1780s for an outpouring of the gifts of the Holy Spirit. Thus the missionary societies should not be separated from the founding of the great interdenominational adventures such as the Religious Tract Society (1799), the British and Foreign Bible Society (1804), and the London City Mission (1835).

By the 1830s the missionary idea had become nationalized into the view that Britain was a Christian nation which, in the context of her increasing power worldwide, imposed upon her the responsibilities of taking the Christian faith to all nations. Such mission endeavor was not at the behest of imperial pro-consuls but very often despite them because they feared that missionary enthusiasm would upset an easy tolerance of other living faiths and their religious practices. Thus the British Baptists in India initially had to seek Danish patronage because of the hostility of the East India Company. It was not until after the First World War that the imperial government came to realize that if it was to extend educational opportunities within the empire then mission agencies offered the most economical possibilities. Thus it came to be that an association developed between British missions and an emerging educated elite that soon began to speak in nationalist tones.

For the first thirty years of the great Victorian era of missions, new developments in missionary strategy generally came by way of denominational initiatives. HUDSON TAYLOR's founding of the CHINA INLAND MISSION in 1865 again proposed an interdenominational mission adventure. In so doing he developed the prototype of modern FAITH MISSION, not directly soliciting funds from supporters, investing control of mission operations in the decision making of missionaries in the field, and encouraging missionaries to identify with those to whom they ministered in dress and culture.

In 1846 international cooperation found an instrument for its nurture through the establishment of the Evangelical Alliance, an alliance of individual Christians rather than of churches. Even this body found it difficult to reconcile their differences over slave-holding and it was not until 1867 that an American branch was established. Two years prior to the establishing of the Evangelical Alliance, George Williams had begun what became the YMCA, an international organization for evangelism among young men. Lay, interdenominational, and international it, like the Evangelical Alliance, sought to bring together Christians of different traditions. A third initiative in this area was the founding in 1886 of the Student Volunteer Missionary Union, under whose influence many of the ablest young people offered themselves for service overseas, under the urgent slogan "The evangelization of

the world in this generation." Both their missionary vocation and their university experience argued against the denominational straitjacket that had emerged in Victorian England. To surmount such barriers, in the interests of global mission, the Edinburgh WORLD MISSIONARY CONFERENCE was convened. Whatever their meanings in Europe and North America, most denominational differences meant little or nothing in the South, and served only to impede the effective implementation of missionary strategies worldwide. Thus the missionary agenda gave birth to the ecumenical agenda.

JOHN H. Y. BRIGGS

SEE ALSO Scotland.

United States of America *(Est. 2000 pop.: 275,119,000; 9,363,520 sq. km. [3,615,255 sq. mi.]).* Missionary activity to North America, before and after the American Revolution, cannot be separated from attempts at conquest and then the many waves of immigration, first from Europe, later from other continents.

The earliest activity was by various Roman Catholic orders. They engaged in mission from Florida to California, sponsored at first by the governments of Spain and France. Three Spanish Franciscans, accompanying a military expedition, entered the American Southwest in 1540, remaining when the soldiers left in 1542. At least one was martyred, the others were never heard from again. Spanish Dominicans and Jesuits worked among Native Americans in Florida later in the century, while French priests moved into what is now New York State and down into the Mississippi valley in the mid-seventeenth century. A number of them were tortured and martyred. In the later half of the eighteenth century JUNÍPERO SERRA established a chain of missions in California, which led to the baptism of 100,000 native people. English Jesuits entered the colony of Maryland in 1634, working with Native Americans as well as English immigrants. Roman Catholic missionary activity continued through the succeeding centuries, directed both toward immigrants and Native American groups farther west.

Robert Hunt, pastor of the first Jamestown colony in 1606, went to minister to the colonists and to win "savages" to Christ. His successor, Alexander Whitaker, who baptized Pocahontas, wrote in 1613 that they were planting the KINGDOM OF GOD in the New World. Money was raised in England to establish a college to educate Native American youth in the Christian faith but the massacre of 1622, which killed 382 settlers, put an end to such attempts in Virginia.

In New England one aspect of the "Errand into the Wilderness" was to evangelize the "Indians." The charters of the Plymouth and Massachusetts Bay colonies both called for the conversion of the "savages" and in 1636 a law was passed calling for the preaching of the gospel to them. JOHN ELIOT, a Cambridge graduate, arrived in Boston in 1631, going to Roxbury as teacher in 1632, where he stayed until his death in 1690. He preached his first sermon in the Algonquin language in 1646, in 1653 he published a catechism, the first book printed in a North American language, and in 1663, the entire Bible was published. The first "Indian" church was established in 1660.

Four generations of the Mayhew family worked on Martha's Vineyard, beginning in 1646 and the Gospel of John and the Psalms were translated into the local language. By 1674 there were 1,800 native Christians on the island and 2,000 on the mainland, several having been ordained as pastors. Much of this work was destroyed in King Philip's War.

Johan Campanius, a Swedish Lutheran, worked among settlers and Native Americans on the lower Delaware River, beginning in 1643. He learned the local language, translated Luther's Small Catechism, and formed a congregation.

The Anglican Society for the Propagation of the Gospel in Foreign Parts (SPG), established by Thomas Bray in 1701, was active in North America up to the American Revolution. By 1785, when virtually all its personnel left, it had employed 310 ordained missionaries in North America. John and Charles Wesley served under the SPG briefly in Georgia. Its missionaries worked with immigrants, seeking to win them to strict Anglicanism, as well as with Native Americans and with Negroes. In 1741, the Rector in Albany reported he had 500 "Indians" under his care, and that year the SPG counted sixteen missionaries working among Native Americans and Negroes in New York. Despite the opposition of slaveholders, the Society established four schools for Negroes. Although there was less work among slaves than Native Americans, the Presbyterian, Samuel Davies, also preached to Negroes and admitted them to communicant membership in his church in Virginia.

Perhaps the most impressive work with Native Americans was done by MORAVIANS. While Count ZINZENDORF ministered to German and other immigrants, seeking to bring unity to the divided churches, Christian Henry Rauch began work in New York in 1740, but was forced to take his flock to an area near Bethlehem, Pennsylvania, where the community of Gnadenhutten was established with 500 believers. After almost all of them, including the missionaries, were massacred in 1755, the mission settled in what is now Ohio, where a large number were won to the Faith.

The First Great Awakening brought new missionary efforts. John Sargent established a mission at Stockbridge, Massachusetts, in 1734, later to be occupied by JONATHAN EDWARDS. Eleazer Wheelock founded an "Indian" school at Lebanon, Connecticut, which became Dartmouth College (see OCCAM, SAMSON), while the ministry of DAVID BRAINERD from 1744 to 1747 is well known and would become a catalyst for the worldwide missionary movement.

Another category of mission activity was directed toward the European immigrants, mainly by the more vital branches of their mother churches in Europe. Francis Makemie formed a Presbyterian church in Snow Hill, Maryland, in 1684 and worked for religious liberty. John Boehm began to minister to German Reformed colonists in 1720, Michael Schlatter to the Swiss in 1746, and Henry Muhlenberg came from Pietist Halle in 1742 to organize Lutheran churches among German settlers. The Quakers, ardently missionary in their first generation, ministered mainly to English colonists but were early leaders in the movement against slavery.

JOHN WESLEY sent a number of preachers to North America but most left when the Revolution began. FRANCIS ASBURY, who became their best known early leader, remained, and led the Methodists as they ministered effectively to newly arrived immigrants seeking land, especially across the Southeast. Their flexible style of leadership selection and training, their evangelistic zeal, and their constant travel combined to make them the largest American Protestant church by 1850. Their membership included large numbers of Black slaves and a smaller number of Native Americans.

Mission to the United States today is coming from former "mission fields" as churches from Asia, Latin America, and, to a lesser extent, Africa, send personnel to minister to immigrants who have come here. The largest group are the Koreans, who have established at least three thousand churches in the United States, and in some cases are beginning to reach out to non-Koreans. The effectiveness of their work is seen in the fact that while 25 percent of the population in Korea is Christian, it is estimated that between 65 percent and 75 percent of Koreans in the United States are Christians. Other groups come from Taiwan, Hong Kong, and Singapore. From the Philippines the newer churches are primarily involved in mission rather than the more traditional church extension. Among them are the charismatic Bread of Life Church, and the Iglesia Ni Cristo, a rapidly growing group with Arian Christology. Some Pentecostal as well as "mainline" groups from Latin America send missionaries to work with Spanish and Portuguese speakers. The Universal Church of the Kingdom of God, which originated in Brazil, has planted a number of churches among Hispanics in the United States. And the Nigerian Evangelical Church of West Africa, originally established by

SIM, now has a couple working with Nigerians in Chicago.

As the Christian missionary movement becomes increasingly international and intercultural, we can hope that some of the newer mission movements to the United States will reach the increasingly secularized population more effectively than the traditional churches.

PAUL E. PIERSON

Bibliography. C. Chaney, *The Birth of Missions in America;* J. T. Ellis, ed., *Documents of American Catholic History;* C. E. Olmstead, *History of Religion in the United States;* W. W. Sweet, *The Story of Religion in America.*

United States Mission Boards and Societies. Intercultural mission activities supported by church groups in the United States were already underway among Native Americans in the late 1700s. The first organization established in the United States for overseas mission work was initiated in 1810 by the General Association of Congregational Churches in Massachusetts and was called the AMERICAN BOARD OF COMMISSIONERS FOR FOREIGN MISSIONS (ABCFM). This action was taken, not without some misgivings, in response to a petition presented by several students, including SAMUEL J. MILLS, ADONIRAM JUDSON, and Luther Rice, from Andover Seminary. These and several other students also volunteered to be ABCFM's first missionaries.

In 1816 the first specialized service mission agency not part of a denomination, The American Bible Society, was formed. It united several local societies by pastors and laymen representing several denominations "to disseminate the Gospel of Christ throughout the habitable world." Most of the organizations in this period, however, were denominational, with the Methodists (1820), Episcopalians (1821), Dutch Reformed (1823), Presbyterians (1837), and others mounting overseas mission efforts. The missionaries of these agencies usually worked in the coastal areas.

During this early period "auxiliaries" began to be formed by women to supplement financially and in other ways encourage missionaries. Initially only married women, whose primary duty was to be that of a "missionary wife," were sent out. But by 1835 the Baptists had sent three single women missionaries to Burma. However, after one of them died of jungle fever in less than eighteen months, the board was reluctant to send more single women. In 1861 the Woman's Union Missionary Society was founded. Its board consisted of women from several evangelical denominations and its focus was sending single women to be missionaries among women. Following this, separate women's boards were organized by

many denominations and in less than thirty years women constituted 60% of the missionary force.

By the 1880s new agencies came on the scene desiring to go beyond the more accessible coastal regions to reach those who had not yet heard. For example, the U.S. branch of the China Inland Mission (now OMF INTERNATIONAL) followed its British counterpart in focusing on the inland territories of China. The movement that became the CHRISTIAN AND MISSIONARY ALLIANCE sent out over three hundred workers within a five-year period to regions without churches. Many missions started in the later 1800s were not related to a single denomination but drew personnel and support from churches of different denominations.

In 1886 DWIGHT L. MOODY conducted a month-long Bible study for 251 students from 89 colleges. The gathering was organized by Luther Wishard, the national secretary of the YMCA who possessed a world vision. From that conference grew the STUDENT VOLUNTEER MOVEMENT (SVM) which began asking college students to sign a declaration card stating "It is my purpose, if God permit, to become a foreign missionary." By 1891, the year of the SVM's first national student missionary convention, 321 had responded and sailed overseas.

In the early 1900s there was a renewed emphasis on the work of the Holy Spirit by Pentecostal and other believers. In 1914 the General Council of the Assemblies of God was organized with one of the purposes being a united effort for world evangelism. By 1918 there were 73 overseas missionaries on the roster of the General Council. They and other Pentecostal mission agencies continued to grow and had a significant impact in Latin America and other areas.

The first Roman Catholic organization in the United States to send missionaries overseas was founded in 1911 in Maryknoll, New York. Prior to that the United States was regarded as a receiving mission field by the Roman Catholic Church and attention was focused on providing churches for recently immigrated Catholics from Europe. The Orthodox Christian Mission Center, the official mission and evangelism agency of all Canonical Orthodox churches in North America, was established in 1994. Prior to that some missionaries had been sent by individual Orthodox bodies.

In 1934 an additional dimension in missions led to the formation of the WYCLIFFE BIBLE TRANSLATORS. This specialized service mission agency was co-founded by W. CAMERON TOWNSEND, whose earlier experiences in Latin America had convinced him that the Bible needed to be translated into the vernacular languages spoken by the tribal groups to overcome language barriers. At the same time missionaries, such as DONALD MCGAVRAN in India, recognized that social barriers also needed to be seriously considered for successful evangelism and church planting to take place. This set the stage for viewing world evangelization in terms of ethnolinguistic peoples and sociologically defined people groups (*see* PEOPLES, PEOPLE GROUPS).

At the end of World War II in 1945, mission boards and societies remobilized. Also new forms of missionary and mission support organizations appeared. Recruitment at the college student level was again a significant factor. As the SVM turned inward, an ongoing student mission convention was organized by the InterVarsity Christian Fellowship under the direction of J. Christy Wilson Jr. in 1946. Student ministries of Campus Crusade for Christ, The Navigators, and others also presented the challenge of world evangelization. This resulted in thousands becoming missionaries.

In 1974, the people group approach became widely known after the Lausanne Congress on World Evangelization. There an *Unreached Peoples Directory* was made available as a start in the needed worldwide research and a plenary presentation called for continuing the transition to an unreached peoples approach.

In the late 1990s the long-term Protestant mission force sent overseas by U.S. boards and agencies stands at a little over 33,000 men and women. Short-term personnel serving terms of 1 to 4 years is around 6,500. With the opening of Eastern Europe and the former Soviet Union, personnel involved in short-term service of less than a year grew dramatically to over 63,000 by 1996.

JOHN A. SIEWERT

Bibliography. B. L. Goddard, *The Encyclopedia of Modern Christian Missions;* D. J. Hesselgrave, *Today's Choices for Tomorrow's Mission;* D. M. Howard, *Student Power in World Missions;* G. B. McGee, *Called and Empowered,* pp. 203–24; D. L. Robert, *American Women in Mission;* J. A. Siewert and E. G. Valdez, eds., *Mission Handbook 1998–2000;* R. D. Winter, *Perspectives on the World Christian Movement,* pp. B33–B44.

Unity. The subject of Christian unity immediately evokes several basic questions: "With whom?" "By whom?" and "For whom?" In response, the meaning of Christian unity can be stated in objective terms as a foundational New Testament truth. It is first and foremost an understanding about Christ and salvation. Second, it is an attitude of belonging, respect, and fellowship. Third, it is an action that expresses union with Christ and with others of his body. Succinctly, biblical Christian unity is a supernatural reality based on the ontological truth of the union of believers with Christ. Since all true believers have been united to Christ through the new birth, they have likewise been united to one another as members of his body, the church.

The outworking or implications of Christian unity are expressed in a variety of New Testament references. In John's Gospel, Christ speaks of believers being one, as the Father and the Son are one. In 1 Corinthians, Paul likens the unity of the human body to the unity of Christians. Again, in Ephesians, he speaks of the true unity of Christians as a reflection of the unity of the Holy Trinity. Each of these descriptions is linked with a causal clause, which shows a consistent call for visible evidence of the spiritual reality of union with Christ for the purpose of witness and outreach. The reality of Christian unity is a fundamental spiritual truth, tied together with the foundational purpose of the church's mission in the world.

What does the absence of reference to organizational or ecclesiastical forms in the New Testament texts indicate about unity? Surely, it eliminates any basis for dogmatic imposition of structures. At the same time, all Christians are called to make the practical expression of Christian unity a high priority, or suffer the consequences of ineffective witness and outreach.

DARYL PLATT

Universalism. Universalism proposes that salvation is universal in its nature and scope; salvation is not only available to all, it is applicable to all and ultimately will be realized by all. Thus, universalism does not divide the human race into two groups, the saved and the lost. Instead, in various ways it maintains that all will be actually saved. Among the advocates of universalism there are great differences both in their conceptualization of the doctrine and in the degree of their dogmatism. The common denominator shared by all universalists is the belief that in the end all humans will be saved. This premise is based primarily on the goodness and sovereignty of God's love. Universalists, following the logic of God's omnipotent love, argue that since God is love, he saves people, and since God is omnipotent love, he will necessarily save all people.

The history of universalism is complex because it is interconnected with other theological issues such as the nature of God, the relationship between his love and justice, the deity of Christ, the nature of the atonement, the authority of the Bible, eternal punishment, and predestination and free will.

In the early church, universalism appeared in the Greek East. The most influential proponent of *apokatastasis* (universalism) was Origen. With his Platonic logic and allegorical hermeneutical method, he maintained that all intelligent beings (humans, angels, and devils) were created good and equal and with a free will. Those who sinned were restored to God by a process of discipline and punishment that could continue after death. To Origen, punishment was remedial; given unlimited time, it would result in all souls being united to God, including Satan and the devils.

Origen's univeralism was condemned at the Council of Constantinople in 543. While advocates of universalism are found throughout church history, it was not until the nineteenth and twentieth centuries that the doctrine found wide acceptance and popularity among liberal and neo-orthodox theologians. During the nineteenth century Darwinian evolution provided the worldview for some universalists to envision the soul's upward progress toward God.

The nineteenth-century German theologian F. D. E. Schleiermacher constructed his universalism on predestination and the all-determining will of God. In contrast to double predestination (some humans elected to salvation and others to lostness), Schleiermacher asserted that all people are elected to salvation in Christ and that the purposes and omnipotence of God cannot fail. In nineteenth-century England a less dogmatic universalism appeared with an uneasiness about HELL, a conditional mortality, and a "wider hope" for universal salvation.

A more dogmatic universalism took root during the twentieth century. C. H. Dodd constructed his universalism from the Bible based on the idea of development in the thought of Paul in Scripture. He concluded that the mercy of God will be as universally effective as sin has been. John A. T. Robinson asserted that hell is the existential reality of humans challenged by the gospel (judgment is the only way in which sinful persons can hear grace) and that universal salvation is the reality which God wills. For Robinson universalism was a necessity because of God's omnipotent love. Any final judgment would be a frustration of God's purposes and love. Robinson overcame the difficulty of human freedom with a paradigm of freedom being freely overcome and constrained by divine love.

Since the 1970s, the locus of universalism has been the plurality of religions. Advocated by such theologians as John Hick and Paul Knitter, PLURALISM denies the exclusiveness or even the superiority of Christianity over other religions. The pluralist insists, on the basis of historical relativism, that the various religions are attempts to conceptualize the Mystery. Thus, God reveals himself to some degree and provides salvation through the different religions of the world.

There are several important missiological implications of universalism and its alternative views of ANNIHILATION, conditional immortality, postmortem salvation, pluralism, and inclusivism. First, universalism redefines the meaning of missions. If all ultimately will be saved and lostness is merely an existential situation, then the only purpose of missions is to better the lives of people in this world and not to affect their destiny in the world to come. In contrast, the impetus of evangelical missions is rooted in the belief in life after death, the judgment of all people, and the eternality of heaven and hell.

Second, universalism alters the message of missions. In the universalist construct all exclusive language, in which truth claims are asserted about the UNIQUENESS OF CHRIST or the soteriological necessity of faith in Christ, is regarded as arrogant and divisive in relationship to other faiths. In place of the proclamation of the normativeness and finality of Christ, universalism promotes DIALOGUE with other faiths that both acknowledges their legitimacy and affirms that love embraces all peoples of all times. While acknowledging the place of dialogue and respect, evangelical missions insists on a biblically rooted CHRISTOLOGY and the attendant confession of the supremacy of Christ in salvation.

Third, universalism strikes at the heart of the urgency of missions. If explicit knowledge about the person and work of Christ and personal faith in Christ as a definitive decision in this life are not necessary for salvation, then the pressing motivation to take the gospel to all the world is eliminated. Evangelical missions, however, maintains that the proclamation of the unique gospel of Jesus Christ is the only means whereby people can be saved.

Fourth, universalism begs the question of the unreached multitudes of the world. If all will be saved then there is no imperative to take the gospel to those who have never heard the Good News. In contradistinction, evangelical missions is compelled by the conviction that the only hope of the UNEVANGELIZED is through a viable witness of the gospel.

DONALD R. DUNAVANT

SEE ALSO Justice of God, Judgment, Love of God, AND Mercy of God.

Universality of Mission. The universality of mission is the mandate of mission that the gospel be proclaimed to all the peoples of the world. It includes providing all peoples with the opportunity to hear with understanding the message of salvation found only in Jesus Christ, the opportunity to accept or reject him as Lord and Savior, and the opportunity to serve him in the fellowship of a church.

The impetus of the universality of mission arises from the nature of the GOSPEL itself. The universality of the gospel, in turn, is inextricably linked to its uniqueness, a uniqueness found in its CHRISTOLOGY (see also UNIQUENESS OF CHRIST). The incarnation, crucifixion, and resurrection of Jesus is the message of the presence of the eternal God providing in Christ the only way of salvation for all those living in spiritual darkness and death. The biblical witness is that "God was pleased to have all his fullness dwell in him [Jesus], and through him to reconcile to himself all things whether things on earth or things in heaven, by making peace through his blood, shed on the cross" (Col. 1:19–20). It is only in this unique gospel of Jesus Christ that the world is confronted with the reality of the redemption of God. Thus, the gospel is for all the world because it is about all the world. It alone reveals the alienation of all humans from God and the hope of their reconciliation to God.

The religious pluralist objects that such a particular and exclusive claim of salvation in Christ is a barrier to genuine relationship with those of other faiths (see PLURALISM and UNIVERSALISM). But if the uniqueness of the gospel is denied, how is one to affirm God's intention to provide the means of salvation for the world and the historical event that actualized salvation? It is the uniqueness of the gospel that requires that all the peoples of the world hear the content and condition of God's provision of salvation in Christ and be given the opportunity to believe in Jesus. Thus it is out of the unique message of the gospel that the necessity, urgency, obligation, and self-sacrifice of global mission emerge in their fullest implications (see also MISSIONARY TASK, THE).

Further, in the GREAT COMMISSION, the Lord Jesus commands the universal dissemination of the gospel. Matthew 28:18–20, Mark 15:16, Luke 24:46–47, and Acts 1:8 restate the intent of the commission in different words with the same effect—the gospel is to go to "all nations," "all the world," "all the nations," and to "the uttermost parts of the earth." In the Matthew passage Jesus prefaces his commission with the assertion of his absolute authority in heaven and on earth. To fail to take the gospel to all the world is tantamount to disobedience to the lordship of Christ.

The Matthew passage also provides added dimension to the scope of the commission. DONALD MCGAVRAN proposed that "all nations" (panta ta ethnē) refers to all the peoples of the world; that is, all humanity, all who live on earth, all the ethnolinguistic groups of the world (see also PEOPLES, PEOPLE GROUPS). The mandate of the Great Commission is to make disciples in all the world through evangelism, church planting, and instruction.

The importance of every individual, moreover, is related to the universality of mission. John 3:16 clearly declares God's intent that the message of his loving provision of salvation be universally communicated. "For God so loved the world that he gave his one and only Son, that whoever believes in him shall not perish but have eternal life." Each person, as a special creation of God, deserves the occasion to have his or her spiritual need and hunger met by God's redemptive love.

The universality of mission also has eschatological implications. Our Lord appears to link global evangelization with his return (see also MILLENNIAL THOUGHT AND MISSION). In Matthew 24:14 he declares, "And this gospel of the kingdom will be preached in the whole world as a testimony to all nations, and then the end will come." In Revelation 5:9 praise is ascribed to the enthroned Lord Jesus because with his blood he bought people "for God from every tribe and language and people and nation."

The ultimate impetus of the universality of mission is the glory of God. That is, global mission is driven by God's intention to redeem to himself a people to love and praise him out of all the nations and people groups of the world (see also WORSHIP).

DONALD R. DUNAVANT

Unreached Mission Fields. See REACHED AND UNREACHED MISSION FIELDS.

Unreached Peoples. See PEOPLES, PEOPLE GROUPS.

Uppsala Assembly (1968). See WORLD COUNCIL OF CHURCHES ASSEMBLIES.

Urban Churches. The apostle Paul, as he journeyed from city to city to help start new churches, clearly understood the importance of reaching cities. Cities are centers of power and influence spreads from the city outward. If the gospel took hold in the cities, it would naturally spread to areas surrounding the cities.

The Reformation also was an urban movement. It began in the cities of Europe and was established there, only later moving to the countryside.

Despite this early urban history, the church today is handicapped by an anti-urban bias that has been very difficult to reverse. While the world is urbanizing at a very rapid rate, the church has been slow to respond. Two exceptions in the United States are the African American Churches and the Roman Catholic Church. Both these churches have been far more at home in the city than the Anglo Protestant Church. Mission movements that have originated with the latter churches have exported this anti-urban bias to other continents, even while thousands flock daily to the cities of the Southern world. Thus while cities continue to grow, the percentage of Christians in these cities continues to decrease.

Many challenges face the urban church if the church is to be taken seriously in the urban world at the end of the twentieth century. Old wineskins will need to give way to new ones. Although there are many different forms of the church in the city, clearly they must be forms that break with traditional ways of being church. Many rural-oriented groups that begin work in the cities start by planting essentially rural churches in the city. While these churches may be successful with recent migrants to the city whose WORLDVIEW was formed in villages and nonurban areas, these rural models do not work for those who have lived in the city for many years.

One question often raised is whether these newcomers to the city are more open to the gospel, or whether the city instead has a secularizing effect. Evidence can be found for both views. Moving to the city begins the breakdown of traditional worldviews, thus people are more open to new ideas, including Christianity. Others come to the cities having been active in local churches, yet are lost to the church because of the drive to survive or the lure of consumerism. Materialism easily becomes the new religion. In either case, the church does well to respond quickly to reach out to recent migrants whose needs are great at all levels.

To become truly rooted in urban soil, the church must contextualize to the urban way of life. One prominent characteristic of that way of life is diversity. While churches may still choose to target certain populations, the church must realize that many true urbanites value this diversity of cultures, classes, backgrounds, and sexual orientations. This diversity can even be seen within the same immigrant group. The needs of the youth raised in the city are often very different from those of their parents. Korean churches in Los Angeles have services and youth programs in English as they attempt to keep their youth in the church.

Since many urban people consider the church irrelevant or foreign to their lives, another challenge of the church in the city is the mission of the church beyond the walls of the church building. If people will not come to the church, the church must find ways to go to where people are. This may be in homes, but it may also mean taking the church to public places where life is lived for many urbanites. The church does not live only for itself but to be a witness to the reign of God. This witness needs to take place both within the church and in the public sphere.

Although not all churches in the city are poor churches (despite stereotypes to the contrary), the church in the city needs to take seriously the plight of the poor. Whether they live in inner cities or squatter settlements on the edges of the cities of the Southern world, the systems of the city easily exploit the poor and the powerless. Yet poverty is not only a problem for the poor but also for the affluent. Despite efforts to scapegoat inner cities as problems, these areas are reflections of larger societal problems that affect everyone. Although they are very difficult to achieve, creative, non-paternalistic partnerships are needed between affluent and poorer churches that will lead to mutual understanding and transformation.

Other characteristics of cities also provide challenges—rapid change, increasing consumerism, the spirit of individualism, the systemic nature of the city. While one church might be overwhelmed by such challenges, urban churches are realizing the value of networking. Around the world church leaders are gathering in prayer networks to work together and encourage each other. They are realizing that the city is the place God wants to grow his church and demonstrate his transforming power in the lives of people and their communities.

JUDE TIERSMA WATSON

Bibliography. H. Conn, ed., *Planting and Growing Urban Churches;* P. Hiebert and E. H. Meneses, *Incarnational Ministry: Planting Churches in Band, Tribal, Peasant and Urban Societies;* L. Schaller, *Center City Churches;* C. Van Engen and J. Tiersma, eds., *God So Loves the City.*

Urbana Missions Conferences. In 1945 the InterVarsity Christian Fellowship (IVCF) and the Student Foreign Missions Fellowship (SFMF) merged, and SFMF became the missions department of IVCF. In the aftermath of World War II it was decided to experiment with a student missions conference. Thus in December 1946 IVCF/SFMF sponsored a conference at the University of Toronto that was attended by 575 students from across Canada and the United States. The response was overwhelmingly positive. So IVCF/SFMF decided to hold another convention in a more geographically central location.

In 1948 a second convention was held at the University of Illinois in the city of Urbana. This time nearly 1,300 students attended. It was so successful that it was decided to give every college student at least one opportunity to attend. Thus conventions have been held triennially from December 27 to 31 at Urbana. At Urbana 1976 the capacity of 17,000 seats in Assembly Hall at the University of Illinois was reached, and IVCF had to turn away students for the first time. Since then, most of the conventions have been filled to capacity. Today IVCF accepts up to 19,000 students, using closed-circuit television in other campus locations.

The purposes of the convention traditionally have been fourfold: (1) to present the biblical basis of world missions, helping students to understand what the Bible says about God's concern and plan for the world; (2) to present the contemporary situation, exposing students to what God is doing in world missions and what remains to be done; (3) to challenge students to respond to God's claims on their lives, to commit themselves to whatever he wishes for them in fulfilling the GREAT COMMISSION; and (4) to challenge students to return to their campuses and share the vision for world missions that God has given to them. The focus of Urbana is the college and university world. While some high school seniors have usually been allowed to attend, the major purpose is to reach college students for missions. Missionaries, pastors, and college professors are also encouraged to attend, in order to be resource personnel to help the students. Mission agencies set up displays of their work, giving students opportunity to interact directly with mission representatives.

The program is very full. Students begin the day with small-group Bible studies in their dormitory. Plenary sessions in Assembly Hall occupy most of the morning. Afternoons are given to several hundred workshops or seminars from which students may choose; there is opportunity at this time for personal conversations with mission representatives at their display booths. Additional plenary sessions fill the evening. Music and prayer play a major role in these sessions as do speakers from many nations and cultures. The day closes with small prayer groups.

Decision cards give the students several options for responding to God's claims on their lives. Half the card is kept as a personal prayer reminder. The other half is turned in to IVCF, so that follow-up materials can be sent to help the student fulfill the commitment made. It is probably safe to say that in the second half of the twentieth century the Urbana conferences were the greatest single factor challenging students in North America to commit themselves to world missions.

DAVID M. HOWARD

Urbanization. Wandering Cain's move to a city (Gen. 4:17) and the call for volunteers to live in a rebuilt Jerusalem (Neh. 11:1–2) point to urbanization's most familiar side: the process of people migrating to cities and the growth of those centers of power. Often associated with that definition is still another dimension—the impact of the city on humanity.

Changes in Research. Past discussions in SOCIOLOGY and cultural ANTHROPOLOGY have placed emphasis on the target of urbanization, the city as a place of population density, size, and social heterogeneity. Propelling these studies was an anti-urban bias that argued urbanization led to stress, estrangement, dislocation, and anomie (Gullick, 1989, 5–20).

This static, deterministic path has not helped missions; it has reinforced stereotypes of the church's often negative view of the city. Urbanization as a common grace provision of God loses its remedial role in human and social change.

All this is changing. Current urban research still recognizes that population size and density are common to virtually all definitions of the city. But scholarship is also recognizing that such criteria are minimal and threshold in nature, not all-or-nothing characteristics. Attention is turning from the city as place to the city (and to urbanization) as process. Other dimensions—religious, institutional, social, cultural, behavioral—must also be examined.

Alongside this shift is coming new attention to urban mission. In the wake of massive global urbanization since World War II the church is seeing the process as a "bridge of God" and the city as the stage for evangelization in the twenty-first century. Research and strategy planning are speaking of "gateway cities." New holistic partnerships of church planting, evangelism, and social transformation are being formed (Conn, 1997, 25–34, 193–202).

Missions and History's Urban Waves. The church's awareness of the city is not a recent development in world history. Missions has made use of each of the three great waves of urbanization that have preceded ours. In the first wave the city as the symbol of civilization shifted from its place as a religious shrine to a city-state to a military and socio-political center. And in the midst of the Greco-Roman world that was its climax the church was born. Along the roads that led to Rome, the church, following Paul and the early Christian community, carried the gospel to the far corners of the empire.

By the middle of the third century seven missionary bishops had been sent to cities in Gaul (including Paris). In southern Italy there were over a hundred bishoprics, all centered in cities. One hundred years after it became a licensed religion of the empire in A.D. 313, it numbered 1,200 bishops in the urban centers of North Africa. The church's urban orientation had transformed the Latin term *paganus*, originally meaning rural dweller, into the word used to describe the unbeliever.

With the decline of the empire, the impact of barbarian invasions, and an expanding Islam, once great western cities became isolated hamlets and autonomous villages. From the fifth to the eleventh centuries the urban world reverted to a rural mosaic. And the church in its administration and architecture became the preserver of Rome's urban political past in its borrowed patterns of parish and diocese (Mumford, 1961, 265–66).

God and gold introduced the second great urban wave as it did the third. Cities found new identities as permanent marketplaces; commerce became urbanization's new partner. THE CRUSADES (1096–1291) were more than holy wars; they expanded trade routes linking Europe and the Middle East. The bubonic plague of the fourteenth century struck a devastating blow to urbanization but Europe recovered. By 1500 the continent numbered 154 cities each with at least 10,000 inhabitants. By 1800 there were 364 such cities.

Increasingly shaping this new movement of urbanization was the Renaissance mentality of the fifteenth and sixteenth centuries. Medieval ideals of Christian knight and Christian prince were replaced. The institutional church was marginalized. Cities were seeing Christianity, represented by its clergy, more and more tied to another world, outsiders to the city.

Interrupting this time of urban transition came the REFORMATION. Under leaders like Martin Luther, Menno Simons, and John Calvin its urban impact was widespread. Fifty of the sixty-five imperial cities subject to the emperor officially recognized the Reformation either permanently or periodically. Of Germany's almost 200 cities with populations exceeding 1,000 most witnessed Protestant movements. Geneva under Calvin became the Jerusalem of Europe. Its impact stretched far and wide.

Ultimately the Reformation remained a parenthesis. It had hoped the city would be the urban exhibition of God's righteousness in Christ. But it could not stop the growing Renaissance emphasis on the SECULARIZATION of the city. The urban citizen transformed the Reformation call to the obedience of faith into freedom from religious superstition and nominalist uncertainty. A new ethic of urban service arose outside the institutional church.

The third great urban wave centered in the machine and the Industrial Revolution. The city turned for its symbol from the temple, the castle, and the marketplace to the factory.

Europe's colonial expansion and "new world discoveries" prefaced that revolution with previews of future urban patterns. Greed bypassed the indigenous cities of Africa, Asia, and Latin America to found colonial port cities as collection points for gathered wealth and natural resources. European racism harvested Africa's "black gold" of slaves from those same ports. Christian missions used those urban paths opened by COLONIALISM, promoting a growing pattern of "civilizing and Christianizing."

Industrialization in Europe, following the fatigue of the Napoleonic wars, gave a renewed lease on life to global expansionism and internal urbanization. England led the way. By 1790–1810 it was "the workshop of the world." London, followed by Liverpool and Manchester, grew from nearly 900,000 in 1800 to nearly 3 million in 1861.

The emerging United States turned quickly to industrialization. And urbanization followed (Conn, 1994, 49–58). In the one hundred years between 1790 and 1890 its total population grew sixteenfold and its urban population 139-fold. By contrast, the non-Anglo-Saxon world remained basically rural.

Soon colonialism shifted to a territorial form as it sought for political, social, and economic leverage. And Protestant missions, fed by the GREAT AWAKENINGS and the Anglo-Saxon power base of the "industrial age," turned the nineteenth-century global expansion of Western powers into the "Great Century" of church growth.

By 1900, the number of urban Christians totaled 159,600,000 (Barrett, 1997, 25). But they were located largely in the cities of Europe and North America. Missionary strategy had focused wisely on the rural world that still made up the vast bulk of global population. As it did, the West was becoming overwhelmed by urban poverty and immigrant needs; a strong anti-urban spirit began to emerge, fed by Anglo ethnocentrism (Lees, 1985).

Missions and the Fourth Urban Wave. Since World War II massive urban growth has shifted into high gear everywhere except North America and Europe. The number of city dwellers in 1985 was twice as great as the entire population of the world in 1800 (Abu-Lughod, 1991, 53). Africa's urbanization rate is the most rapid. Its urban population, 7 percent in 1920, more than quadrupled in 1980. Asia's urban population will likely hit 40 percent by 2000, a 665 percent growth over 1920. Seventy-four percent of Latin American and Caribbean populations lived in urban areas by 1997.

A unique feature of this urban wave is the trend toward ever-larger urban agglomerations. In 1900 there were 18 cities in the world with populations over one million; thirteen were in Europe and North America. At the turn of the twenty-first century, that figure will surpass 354. And 236 of the total will be found in developing countries (Barrett, 1986, 47). In 1991 there were 14 so-called mega-cities (exceeding 10 million inhabitants). Their number is expected to double by 2015, when most of them will be in developing countries. By contrast, the large cities of the West (London, New York, Paris) are not expecting much growth. The world's urban center of gravity is moving from the northern to the southern hemisphere.

Two realities of great significance for the future of the Christian mission are emerging out of this shift. First, the growth of the cities in non-Christian or anti-Christian countries, combined with the erosion of the church in the northern hemisphere, is multiplying the non-Christian urban population. In 1900 the world greeted 5,200 new non-Christian urban dwellers per day; by 1997, that figure had reached 127,000 (Barrett, 1997, 25). Out of the ten largest cities in the world in 1995, seven are located in countries with only minimal Christian impact. Increasingly, to speak of those outside of Christ is to speak of the urban dweller.

And, second, to speak increasingly of the urban lost is to speak of the poor. It is estimated that half the urban population in the southern hemisphere live in slums or shantytowns. In the year 2000, 33.6 percent of the world will be in cities in less developed regions. Forty percent of that number will be squatters (846 million). The last frontier of urban evangelism and ministry has become the "unmissionaried" urban poor (Conn 1997, 159).

HARVIE M. CONN

SEE ALSO Urban Churches.

Bibliography. J. Abu-Lughod, *Changing Cities: Urban Sociology;* D. Barrett, *IBMR* 21:1 (January 1997): 24–25; idem, *World-Class Cities and World Evangelization;* H. Conn, *The American City and the Evangelical Church;* idem, ed., *Planting and Growing Urban Churches: From Dream to Reality;* J. Gullick, *The Humanity of Cities: An Introduction to Urban Societies;* A. Lees, *Cities Perceived: Urban Society in European and American Thought, 1820–1940;* L. Mumford, *The City in History: Its Origins. Its Transformations, and its Prospects.*

Uruguay *(Est. 2000 pop.: 3,274,000; 177,414 sq. km. [68,500 sq. mi.]).* Uruguay is a small republic on the southeast coast of South America, bordered by Brazil on the north and Argentina on the south and west. Uruguay is noted for its temperate climate, rolling grassy hills, and vacation beaches along the Atlantic coast. Its population is predominantly European (Spanish and Italian) with no extant pure indigenous peoples. Spanish is the official language and the literacy rate is 95 percent. Forty percent of Uruguayan exports come from stock raising, which is the principal agricultural activity although only 8 percent of the population lives in rural areas. There is a two-party political system that maintains the long-standing advanced social welfare programs. The first European discoverer came in 1516 and the first permanent settlement was established in 1624. In 1726 the Spanish forced the Portuguese out and founded Montevideo, which is now the nation's capital.

Uruguay became independent in 1828 after obtaining freedom from Spain and shaking off years of subjection to Brazil. After a decline in the widespread benefits of a welfare state, there was an unfortunate eleven-year experiment (1973–84) with military governments. At the end, massive social unrest returned the country to two-party civilian rule.

The nineteenth-century Uruguayan patriot, Jose Artigas, set the tone for the Uruguayan society when he said that "We can expect nothing except from ourselves." In 1918 the government legislated a strict separation of church and state.

Uruguay is one of the most secularized societies in Latin America where, for example, Christmas is celebrated as Family Day and Easter Holy Week is called Tourism Week. This society has witnessed the results of SECULARIZATION, with two out of every three marriages resulting in divorce and reputedly Latin America's highest abortion rate. A Gallup Poll in the 1980s revealed that 37 percent of the population claimed to be atheist. While the government does nothing to promote religion, it does nothing to inhibit it, resulting in complete freedom and a general indifference to religion especially among the well-educated.

About 60 percent of Uruguayans are registered as Roman Catholics, but those who are practicing their religion are more likely 20 percent. Those who call themselves Protestants total less than 4 percent (church members: 47,000 in 72 denominations). Members of evangelical churches are slightly over 2 percent (32,000). Sectarianism is one of the problems faced by the churches of Uruguay. The latest figures indicate there are over 200 foreign missionaries in the country. The number of Mormon church members is roughly 50 percent more than that of evangelical churches. Other marginal Christian churches show as much growth as or more than the evangelicals. There is a large influx of Brazilian spiritists (over 200,000 in the capital), who have more centers in the country than there are Protestant churches. There are about 20 seminaries and Bible schools for Christian leaders. The largest Protestant denomination is the Assemblies of God. Since its initiation in 1946, the Assemblies have grown to 63 churches with a large number of outstations for a total of 6,500 members. At the end of 1995 the Assemblies' field director reported that although revival had reached other nations in the region, "Uruguay remains resistant." Uruguay has the notoriety of being labeled the "cemetery of missions."

DAVID SPRUANCE

Bibliography. P. E. Dostert, ed., *Latin America 1995; Latin American Press,* March 1, 1984; *Latin America Evangelist* 68, no. 2; *Field Focus—Uruguay.*

Uzbekistan *(Est. 2000 pop.: 25,383,000; 447,400 sq. km. [172,741 sq. mi.]).* Uzbekistan is the most densely populated of the Central Asian republics of the former Soviet Union. At least 83 percent of the population is of Turkic stock, with ethnic Uzbeks alone making up about 70 percent. Roughly two-thirds of the population is officially Sunni Muslim, although most practice a strongly animistic variety of folk Islam. Uzbekistan is considered to be the Islamic heartland of ex-Soviet Central Asia, and Muslim missionaries from abroad have been very active in strengthening Islam there. Evangelical Christians are few, making up less than 0.25 percent of the population, most being ethnic Slavs or Koreans; few Uzbeks have come to Christ. Although the government has banned all missionary activities, creative efforts are being carried out by a number of Christian organizations.

RAYMOND P. PRIGODICH

SEE ALSO Commonwealth of Independent States.

Vv

Vajrayana (Tibetan) Buddhism. Introduced to Tibet from India in the eighth century, MAHAYANA BUDDHISM of the Vajrayana (Tantric) tradition, in combination with Bon, the indigenous religious tradition of Tibet which was highly animistic and shaministic, has exerted great influence upon subsequent Tibetan life and culture.

In common with other forms of Buddhism, Tibetan Buddhism seeks release from the suffering inherent in the ongoing cycle of rebirths *(samsara)*. Liberation from rebirth—*nirvana*—is to be found in a confluence of proper insight into the nature of ultimate reality, emptiness *(sunyata)*. This comes only through rigorous discipline of the psychic faculties, and reliance upon the compassion of *bodhisattvas*, who although themselves liberated from rebirth have delayed *nirvana* so as to assist others. The influence of Tantrism can be seen in its adoption of sexual imagery as symbolic of metaphysical truths (including the notion that sexual union can be a way of experiencing the non-duality of ultimate reality, or Emptiness) and the use of esoteric magical formulas for releasing unusual powers. Tibetan Buddhism also provides one of the most intellectually sophisticated philosophical and psychological traditions in Buddhism.

There are four major schools of Tibetan Buddhism—the Nyingmapa, the Kargyupa, the Saskyapa, and the Gelugpa. Special monks, or lamas ("one who is superior"), provide leadership within the monastic community and are regarded as reincarnations of previous lamas. The Dalai Lama (currently Tenzin Gyatso) is traditionally the head of the Gelugpa school, and was originally regarded as an incarnation of the *bodhisattva* of compassion, Avalokita. Whereas prior to Chinese occupation of Tibet in 1951 there were about six thousand monasteries and a monkhood comprising one-fifth of the male population, after 1959 virtually all of Tibet's monasteries were destroyed and the monks exiled or executed. The Dalai Lama was forced into exile in India. Religious activity in Tibet remains under strict control by the Chinese authorities.

Although the primary significance of Tibetan Buddhism lies in its cultural and religious impact upon the Tibetan people, many of whom are now in exile in India and Nepal, it is significant that Tibetan Buddhism has attracted a considerable following among artists and intellectuals in the West. This is due not simply to its sophisticated metaphysics but also to the enormously attractive personality of the Dalai Lama, who has become a highly visible symbol of peace and tolerance in a world of deep divisions. The Dalai Lama was awarded the Nobel Peace Prize in 1989.

HAROLD A. NETLAND

Bibliography. H. V. Guenther, *Tibetan Buddhism in Western Perspective;* T. Gyatso, *Freedom in Exile;* H. Hoffman, *The Religions of Tibet;* G. Tucci, *The Religions of Tibet.*

Valignano, Alessandro (1539–1606). Italian missionary to Asia. Valignano, an Italian Jesuit, was the Jesuit Visitor to the East, in charge of all Jesuit missionaries in East Asia. After spending some time in what is now India, Indonesia, and Malaysia, Valignano concentrated upon Japan and China. He was the dominant figure in Jesuit missions in Asia during the last quarter of the sixteenth century.

In an era of Christian missions characterized by insensitivity to local cultures, Valignano crafted and implemented a missions policy that encouraged adaptation to Japanese and Chinese cultures. Valignano insisted that missionaries to Japan master the language and observe local customs. He promoted training of the Japanese for the priesthood, established theological training centers for the Japanese, facilitated the translation of Christian writings into Japanese, and wrote the *Japanese Catechism of Christian Faith*, a work in theology and apologetics that interacts with Buddhism.

Valignano's missions policy was also implemented in China with remarkable success by MATTEO RICCI, but was later opposed by Franciscans and Dominicans who attacked it for allegedly excessive accommodation to Chinese cultural and religious influences. After an extended controversy, Rome ruled against the Valignano–Ricci approach in 1715. Valignano's general approach has been vindicated by twentieth-century missiology in its emphasis on proper CONTEXTUALIZATION of the gospel.

HAROLD A. NETLAND

Bibliography. J. F. Moran, *The Japanese and the Jesuits: Alessandro Valignano in Sixteenth Century Japan;* A. Ross, *A Vision Betrayed: The Jesuits in Japan and China, 1542–1742;* J. Schutte, *Valignano's Mission Principles for Japan.*

Van der Kemp, Johannes Theodorus (1747–1811). Dutch missionary in South Africa. Born in Rotterdam and son of a theology professor, he became an army officer but gave up his commission when he married a working-class woman in 1780. He went to Edinburgh, obtained a medical degree in 1782, and published a well-regarded philosophical work. In 1791 he had an evangelical conversion experience after the accidental death of his wife and daughter, and became interested in missionary service. He joined the LMS and helped found a sister society in his native land, the Netherlands Missionary Society. He arrived in Cape Town in 1799 with four other LMS pioneers, helped found a South African Missionary Society, and began working among the Khoi Khoi. His successes among the Khoi in the Graaff-Reinet region and efforts to establish a Xhosa mission gained him the animosity of the white settlers. In 1803 he established the missionary settlement at Bethelsdorp, which whites derisively labeled a "Hottentot heaven." His marriage to a Madagascan slave girl further alienated him from the whites. He campaigned for just treatment of the Khoi and mixed race people and increasingly identified himself with the Africans and their culture. Although he maintained a strict ecclesiastical order and chose church members carefully, the Xhosa saw him as different from the other Europeans. He died in Cape Town in 1811.

ULRICH VAN DER HEYDEN

Bibliography. Memoir of the Rev. J. T. Van der Kemp. M.D., Late Missionary in South Africa; I. H. Enklaar, *Life and Work of Dr. Th. van der Kemp;* A. C. Ross, *DEB,* p. 1133.

Vancouver Assembly (1983). The Sixth Assembly of the WORLD COUNCIL OF CHURCHES met in Vancouver, Canada, on the campus of the University of British Columbia. Under the theme of "Jesus Christ—the Life of the World," 847 delegates representing 301 member churches gathered from July 24 to August 10, 1983.

Broad representation marked the Vancouver Assembly. Almost half of the voting delegates were laypersons, nearly a third were women, and more than a tenth were under the age of thirty. Up to 4,500 persons a day participated in assembly activities in one way or another.

Issue groups addressed eight areas of concern: witnessing in a divided world; taking steps toward unity; moving toward participation; healing and sharing life in community; confronting threats to peace and survival; struggling for justice and human dignity; learning in community; and communicating credibly.

Worship reflected conclusions contained in a text on baptism, Eucharist, and ministry formulated by the Faith and Order Commission in its 1982 meeting in Lima, Peru.

In affirming life in response to the threats posed by the forces of death, Vancouver called for engagement in the struggle for justice, peace, and ecological integrity as integral to the faith of the church. An all-night vigil was held to mark the atomic bombing of Hiroshima and Nagasaki.

Missiologically, Vancouver exhibited a Christocentric emphasis coupled with a keen awareness of the social, cultural, and religious context of witness. For the first time in the history of the WCC, representatives of religious faiths other than Christianity addressed the assembly. This appeared to some to soften the exclusiveness of Christ's claims and seemed incongruent with the 1982 COMMISSION ON WORLD MISSION AND EVANGELISM (CWME) document, "Mission and Evangelism: An Ecumenical Affirmation."

Some evangelicals, encouraged by what they perceived to be a vigorous trinitarian theology, a stronger scriptural focus, and increased emphasis on supernatural life in Christ, signed an open letter urging fellow evangelicals to engage actively in the ecumenical process. However, others remained unconvinced due to what they perceived as the acceleration of tendencies toward SYNCRETISM as well as the low priority Vancouver appeared to place on evangelistic activity and pioneer church planting among non-Christian populations.

KEN MULHOLLAND

SEE ALSO World Council of Churches Assemblies.

Bibliography. D. Gill, ed., *Gathered for Life.*

Vanuatu *(Est. 2000 pop.: 192,000; 12,189 sq. km. [4,706 sq. mi.]).* Vanuatu is an island chain in the southwest Pacific Ocean. Detribalized Vanuatuans are the largest group, but represent less than 14 percent of the population. There are at least an additional 120 peoples in the island chain. Nearly 95 percent have become Christians since the mid-nineteenth century when the gospel was first introduced by Presbyterians and Anglicans. The former are the largest denomination today with over 50,000 members. Apart from evangelicals found in the larger denominations, more recent inroads have been made by the Assemblies of God and the Seventh-Day Adventists.

TODD M. JOHNSON

Vatican City. *See* HOLY SEE.

Vatican II. *See* SECOND VATICAN COUNCIL (1962–65).

Vedanta Hinduism. The term "Vedanta Hinduism" (literally "end of the Vedas") refers to several related systems of Hindu philosophy that can also be classified as theology, for they are based on exegesis of the Upanishads (sacred scriptures also known as Vedanta because they conclude the Vedas). Vedanta is sometimes called *Uttara Mimamsa* ("Further Enquiry") because it was linked to and succeeded Mimamsa, another of the six classical schools of thought. The formative text is the Brahmasutra of Badarayana, who in the second century B.C. attempted a synthesis of Upanishadic theologies by investigating the nature of Brahman as the source of creation, the goal of enquiry, and the focus of worship. His ideas were further developed by Bhartrhari, who saw Brahman as the first principle embodied in the Divine Word *(Om)*. All things have being because of their being named by God, a belief also found in Platonic philosophy and the medieval Christian theology of nominalism. This teaching led to Vedantism.

The most important Vedantic traditions are Advaita ("nondualist") Vedanta, first expounded in about the fifth century A.D. by Gaudapada, from whom the greatest Indian philosopher, Sankara, derived his inspiration; the Visistadvaita ("qualified nondualist") Vedanta of Ramanuja (d. 1137); and the Dvaita ("dualist") Vedanta of Madhva (thirteenth century A.D.).

Sankara (c. 788–820), a Nambudiri Brahman from Kerala, who composed popular devotional songs in Sanskrit, not only provided the intellectual framework for a rebuttal of Buddhism by his teaching, but also created the first Hindu order of monks. He taught absolute MONISM—there is only one reality, Brahman (God); thus all distinctions and subject-object divisions are illusory. Utterly transcendent and beyond all worlds, Brahman, the Supreme Being, is nevertheless the ground of all being because the Atman ("breath") in human beings, and indeed in all transient beings, is identical with him. Hence the many are in fact One. The individual self *(jiva)* is a combination of Atman, which is based on pure consciousness, and transient individuality. When, like a dreamer awaking from sleep, one realizes one's essential identity with Brahman (the Upanishadic cry "Thou art That!"), one attains the experience of *satchitananda* ("existence, knowledge,

bliss") and hence liberation from the cycle of rebirth. Yet the phenomenological world is real enough for those still asleep. While Brahman is essentially without attributes *(nirguna)*, in the world of conventional limited reality he is a personal Creator, like a potter making pots, and therefore has attributes *(saguna)*.

Ramanuja felt that Sankara was too selective with the texts and that there were serious philosophical flaws in his system as well. Despite the nonduality in the Upanishads—the Oneness of God, the atmans, and the world—the multiplicity of the world is nevertheless real; it is not, as Sankara maintained, an illusion superimposed on the true order of things. The world is real because nature and souls are evolved from Brahman, who is the "soul" of the world, his "body." The world is a mode of God, who is in no way affected by its imperfections. The human spirit comes into the world as a consequence of turning away from God. Ramanuja also criticized the Advaita view of illusion and ignorance, which are not identical at all. And because Brahman has attributes *(saguna)*, Ramanuja could develop a meaningful theism as the basis of *bhakti marga*, liberation by way of loving devotion through the grace of God. Madhva taught a dualist system closer to Christian THEISM.

Significantly, these systems of thought inspired the movement known as neo-Hinduism or neo-Vedantism and the philosophy of modern leaders such as Vivekananda (1863–1902), founder of the Ramakrishna Mission and the Vedanta Society of the West; Aurobindo Ghose (1872–1950), who attempted to reconcile religion and science; and Sarvepalli Radhakrishnan (1888–1975), educator and president of the Republic of India.

A number of Christian thinkers such as Abhishiktananda, Bede Griffiths, John Hick, Raimundo Panikkar, and Keith Ward have explored points of congruence between Vedanta philosophy and Christian theism. In spite of some similarities, for example, with Pseudo-Dionysius the Areopagite, there are also important differences between Vedanta philosophy and Christian theism, especially with regard to the ontological relationship of God and creation, human history and the future destiny of the individual soul, and the nature of divine intervention in a wayward creation. Yet Ramanuja's exposition of the love of God, derived from the concluding chapters of the *Bhagavad Gita*, provides a bridge to the Christian understanding of God's love and grace as well as human unworthiness and failure.

E. M. JACKSON

SEE ALSO Hinduism.

Bibliography. Abhishiktananda, *Saccidananda: A Christian Approach to Advaitic Experience;* J. Carman, *Theology of Ramanuja;* N. K. Devarajah, *Hinduism and* the Modern Age; P. T. Raju, *The Philosophical Traditions of India.*

Veenstra, Johanna (1894–1933). American pioneer missionary to Nigeria. The third of six children born in Patterson, New Jersey, to Norwegian immigrants, she lost her father when she was five, and her mother ran a general store to meet family needs. Veenstra accepted secretarial work in New York at the age of fourteen.

As a sixteen-year-old, she gave her life to Christ. Three years later she entered Union Missionary Training Institute (UMTI) in Brooklyn. Between school years, at a missions conference, she heard Karl Kumm speak of Sudan United Mission (SUM) work. She surrendered to God's call to serve with SUM. Three years later, having completed additional training in Bible and midwifery, Veenstra sailed for Nigeria, arriving in January 1920.

Following one year of language study, she moved to Lupwe to pioneer work among the Kutep. Eight years later the first Kutep church was planted. As one example of Veenstra's goal of developing an indigenous church, local workers were paid only through local contributions.

Veenstra died on Palm Sunday of 1933 from heart complications after an appendectomy. She had inspired many in Christian Reformed Church circles through the various articles she wrote for denominational journals and the speaking tours she engaged in while on furlough. Her own account of her work, *Pioneering in the Sudan*, was published after her second furlough.

A. SCOTT MOREAU

Bibliography. H. Beets, *Johanna of Nigeria;* G. L. Zandstra, *Daughters Who Dared: Answering God's Call to Nigeria.*

Venezuela *(Est. 2000 pop.: 24,170,000; 912,050 sq. km. [352,143 sq. mi.]).* Venezuela became an independent nation in 1821 but was not free of rule by dictators until 1958 when it joined the free world with its own democratic experiment. The unparalleled rise in oil prices beginning in 1973 made Venezuela one of the richest countries in South America, but because of the AAA credit rating their oil reserves guaranteed, the country began borrowing additional money to launch itself into the modern world within one generation. When the price of oil began to drop back in 1983, Venezuela suddenly found itself facing interest payments that were disproportionately high, creating a budget crisis which led to devaluation of the local currency and the beginning of an inflationary spiral. Continued government corruption has hampered attempts to halt the economic slide.

Culturally, Venezuela is a collective society (Hofstede, 1984). Seen from the inside by a Venezuelan, belonging to a group is far more important than achieving personal independence. In contrast to an individualistic society, Venezuelans are parts of a whole, not whole parts (Hiebert, 1991). This does not deny individuality, but individuality is most likely to be expressed by trying to change status in the group to which a person belongs, not by achieving independence from the group.

The positive side of this is that people find support and help from other members of their group. The negative side can lead to racism, nationalism, and what Venezuelans are fond of describing as *facilismo* or "easyism." Just as a child in a family should not be expected to work in order to earn his or her place at the table, so the Venezuelan expects to share in the resources of the country to which he or she belongs without having to work for it. The oil bonanza converted this belief into reality for many Venezuelans, often destroying initiative and productivity.

This cultural trait has many implications for mission in Venezuela. First, the Venezuelan sense of group identity is probably much closer to what Paul described in Romans and Ephesians as a spiritual Body rather than churches that are seen only as composed of individuals who have decided to gather in the same place on Sunday morning for worship without necessarily celebrating relationship. Missionaries need to be willing to create new church patterns which promote relationships rather than simple attendance at church programs.

Second, missionaries would do well to become accepted in the Venezuelan collectives that already exist, rather than immediately expecting Venezuelans to want to join them in a new collective. In the cities, a good way for missionaries to do this would be through secular employment, where they would spend enough time with Venezuelans in their work collectively for natural emotional affinity to rise.

Third, the Venezuelan church must constantly guard against legalism, a natural result of sociocentric reasoning true of most collective cultures. Because of the desire to be appreciated and esteemed by those in one's group, the Venezuelan will intuitively grasp what pleases or displeases others. This can quickly lead to legalism if those in leadership insist on patterns of behavior instead of Spirit-directed transformation.

CHARLES A. DAVIS

Bibliography. G. Hofstede, *Culture's Consequences, International Differences in Work-related Values;* J. Ewell, *Venezuela: A Century of Change;* J. V. Lombardi, *Venezuela: The Search for Order, the Dream of Progress.*

Veniaminov, Innocent (1797–1878). Russian Orthodox missionary to Siberia and Alaska and founder of the Russian Orthodox Mission Society. Innocent Veniaminov established a legacy unmatched by any other missionary figure in Russian history. He worked for forty-five years as missionary priest and bishop in Alaska and Eastern Siberia, translated the Bible and liturgical services into Aleut and Thlingit, founded the Russian Orthodox Mission Society, and became metropolitan of the church in Russia.

Innocent was born in a small village of Siberia. As a married priest, he journeyed with his family to the new lands of Alaska in 1823. Early on he mastered and created an alphabet for the Fox-Aleut language. His Aleut catechetical book, *Indication of the Way into the Kingdom of Heaven*, became a classic and was translated into Russian and Slavonic, going through forty-seven printings. This book sparked spiritual renewal and missionary awareness in Russia. After ten years among the Aleuts, Innocent repeated the same effort of new translations among the Thlingit Indians.

In 1839, after the tragic death of his wife, Innocent was elevated as bishop of Kamchatka, the Kuril and Aleutian Islands. He served as a missionary bishop for the following twenty-seven years in this diocese; and three new ones later created in eastern Siberia.

In 1868, Innocent became metropolitan of Moscow and achieved a lifelong dream of founding the Russian Orthodox Mission Society. Over the following decades, this Society sent hundreds of missionaries throughout Siberia, Alaska, Japan, China, and Korea.

LUKE A. VERONIS

Bibliography. P. D. Garrett, *St. Innocent, Apostle to America;* M. Oleksa, *Alaskan Missionary Spirituality;* L. A. Veronis, *Missionaries, Monks, and Martyrs: Making Disciples of All Nations.*

Venn, Henry (1796–1873). English missions administrator and theorist. He was born in Clapham, where his father, John, was rector of Clapham parish, active in the Clapham Sect and a founder of the CHURCH MISSIONARY SOCIETY (CMS, 1799). Educated at Queens' College, Cambridge (M.A., B.D.), Venn served parishes at Hull and Upper Holloway, London. He became honorary clerical secretary of the CMS in 1841, serving until 1872. Together with RUFUS ANDERSON, Venn is recognized for his contribution to the theory of mission with the concept of the "three-selfs" and the "INDIGENOUS CHURCH." Venn also lobbied the British government on colonial policies (curbing slave trade, vernacular education, trade) and worked to accommodate the Anglican Church's archaic episcopal system to the needs of the growing churches throughout the world. As a leading evangelical he sought to moderate trends such as the millennial views that gained popularity after 1830 while resisting Anglo-Catholic and Broad Church influences. But mission was his main preoccupation. A prodigious worker, he conducted correspondence with hundreds of missionaries all over the world, drafted scores of policy statements, and was the dominant influence in the work of the CMS, the largest British society, for a generation.

WILBERT R. SHENK

Bibliography. W. Knight, *Memoir of the Rev. H. Venn—the Missionary Secretariat of Henry Venn, B.D.;* W. R. Shenk, *Henry Venn—Missionary Statesman;* M. Warren, ed., *To Apply the Gospel—Selections from the Writings of Henry Venn;* T. E. Yates, *Venn and Victorian Bishops Abroad.*

Verbeck, Guido Fridolin (1830–98). Dutch-born American pioneer missionary educator and statesman in Japan. Born in a staunch Moravian family in Zeist, Holland, Verbeck came to Christ early in life. Trained as an engineer at Utrecht, he emigrated to the United States at the age of 23. While ill, he promised to become a missionary if God intervened. Once he was restored to health, he attended Auburn Seminary and then accepted a call with the Reformed Church of America. He arrived in Nagasaki on November 7, 1858.

At that time Japan was closed to outsiders, and Nagasaki was the only port accessible. Verbeck began teaching English (using the Bible and the Constitution of the United States as his texts) and started a small Bible study. Working diligently on understanding the language and the culture, he was careful in sharing his faith, seeing posted everywhere the official edicts against Christianity. The first two converts did not come until 1866.

Verbeck developed a sterling reputation among the Japanese. Over the course of his career he worked as a teacher, preacher, statesman, and Bible translator. He played a significant role in founding what later became the Imperial University of Japan, and helped the Japanese develop relationships with the rest of the world. He was also instrumental in removing the ban on Christianity in Japan (1873). The Japanese emperor recognized his services by bestowing on him the decoration of the third class of the Order of the Rising Sun.

A. SCOTT MOREAU

Bibliography. G. K. Chapman, *CDCWM*, pp. 636–37; C. C. Creegan, *Pioneer Missionaries of the Church;* J. I. Good, *Famous Missionaries of the Reformed Church;* W. E. Griffis, *Verbeck of Japan, a Citizen of No Country;* K. S. Latourette, *DAB*, 19:248–49.

Verkuyl, Johannes (1908–). Dutch Reformed missiologist and missionary in Indonesia. Verkuyl was born into a Calvinst farm family. While he studied at the Free University of Amsterdam he was influenced by JOHAN BAVINCK, HENDRIK KRAEMER and W. A. Visser 't Hooft and pastored Indonesian university students in the Netherlands before going to Indonesia as a missionary in 1939.

Interned in a Japanese prison camp in 1942, Verkuyl continued his missionary work as a prisoner until the end of World War II. He lived in Jakarta from 1945 to 1963, where his mission service included reconciliation ministry in the conflict between the Netherlands and Indonesia, teaching social ethics in an interdenominational seminary, and writing extensively in Indonesian on the processes of nation- and church-building in the new state.

Verkuyl returned to the Netherlands in 1963 and served several years as general secretary of the Netherlands Missionary Council and president of the Interchurch Coordinating Committee for Development Projects. From 1968 until his retirement in 1978, he was professor of missiology and evangelism at the Free University of Amsterdam. Along with his teaching and writing, Verkuyl worked closely with Beyers Naudé and others in the South African Council of Churches and similar organizations in other countries involved in the struggle for socioeconomic, political, and racial justice.

Known best for his magnum opus, *Contemporary Missiology: An Introduction* (1978), a foundational textbook in the field, Verkuyl's contribution in the 1970s and 1980s to a wholistic, ecumenical, kingdom-oriented, sociopolitically transformational and deeply evangelical missiology cannot be underestimated. He was the mentor of ORLANDO COSTAS.

CHARLES VAN ENGEN AND NANCY THOMAS

Bibliography. J. Verkuyl, *Break Down the Walls; The Message of Liberation in Our Age;* idem, *IBMR* 10:4 (October, 1986) 150–54; idem, *The Good News of the Kingdom,* pp. 71–81.

Vicelin of Oldenburg (c. 1090–1154). German missionary to the Wends. Educated in Germany and France, Vicelin responded to a call to reach the Slavs to the east for Christ and was commissioned to the work in 1125 by Adalbert of Bremen. The military and political successes and failures of the Germans in subduing the Wend population were reflected throughout Vicelin's ministry. His initial successes during a peaceful period were all but wiped out in a Wend uprising in 1137 in which the monasteries and churches were burned and all missionaries expelled. The Germans eventually regained control, and reestablished abandoned posts. However, the disastrous German crusades against the Wends in 1147 once again set back Vicelin's work. Even though the culmination of his career was his appointment as bishop of Oldenburg in 1149, due to continuing Wend unrest, he was never able to

settle permanently. He died in 1154 after a long illness including two years of paralysis.

A. SCOTT MOREAU

Bibliography. G. F. MacLear, *Apostles of Medieaval Europe; ODCC;* R. H. Schmandt, *NCE,* 14:643.

Vietnam (*Est. 2000 pop.: 82,648,000; 331,689 sq. km. [128,065 sq. mi.]*). Located on the Indochinese peninsula, it is estimated that Vietnam is 9.8 percent Christian. Less than one percent of the total population is evangelical. In A.D. 939 the Vietnamese overthrew the Chinese, who had dominated the region from 111 B.C. The blending of Buddhism, Confucianism, and Taoism instilled during the Chinese period still marks the religious orientation of the country.

The first missionaries were Catholic Franciscans sent from the Philippines in the 1580s. The most important early missionary, however, was Alexander de Rhodes, who arrived in Vietnam in 1626 after spending time in Japan and Macao. He was instrumental in giving the Vietnamese people their written language. By developing friendly relations with the imperial court, he was successful in developing an independent church early in his work. Despite the rise of persecution in 1645, by 1639 there were as many as 130,000 followers. The first Catholic priests were ordained in 1668. Continuing, sporadic persecutions eventually resulted in French intervention and imposition of religious liberty in 1882. Two years later the country was declared a French protectorate. It was estimated in 1980 that the persecutions had resulted in 130,000 Catholic martyrs during Vietnam's history.

Protestant missionary recruiting efforts began in the late 1890s through the CHRISTIAN AND MISSIONARY ALLIANCE (CMA). Though two missionaries visited in 1895, it was not until 1911 that the French authorities granted permission for Protestant missionary activity and ROBERT JAFFRAY arrived as the first long-term Protestant missionary to Vietnam. In 1921, the Tourane Bible School was established to train indigenous workers, and in 1927 the Evangelical Church of Vietnam (ECVN) was granted autonomy. By 1940, there were 123 local congregations, 86 of which were fully self-supporting. All of them were self-supporting by the end of World War II.

Shortly after World War II, Ho Chi Minh led the Vietnamese to independence. In 1954, the country split in two, with Communists controlling the North and Americans the South. This brought an influx of American missionaries to South Vietnam and the migration of over five hundred thousand Christian (both Catholic and Protestant) refugees from North Vietnam. The Vietnam War, beginning in 1959 and escalating through the 1960s, devastated the country. The ECVN, which had previously focused solely on spiritual issues, was forced both by the war and the humanitarian efforts of mission agencies to pay more attention to the physical needs of the people. In 1975, when North Vietnam won the war, all missionaries were expelled. One hundred evangelical churches were closed and ninety pastors sent to reeducation camps.

One church leader in North Vietnam reported that by November 1975 the Protestant church numbered 13,000 in the North and 130,000 in the South. The government expressed the desire to have one Protestant Church for all of Vietnam, but the ECVN resisted efforts to unification and paid dearly for their resistance. Today there is evidence of revival in several places in Vietnam, with signs of a growing house church movement similar to that in China.

VIOLET JAMES

Bibliography. J. Buttinger, *The Smaller Dragon.*

Village Evangelism. Much of the world's population still lives in village settings, especially in developing countries. Even when the men and (less often) the women leave to find work in urban centers, they maintain unbreakable ties to their village. The village is home, the place to which they will return, retire, and be buried.

Several elements make village life unique. Normally, a village rests on a single economic base, most often, subsistence farming. Villages have significantly less access than urban centers to a nation's resources, technologies, schools, and wealth. Therefore, village life remains largely unchanged despite progress and change elsewhere.

Frequently, the village consists of an extended family or clan which has lived together in one place for an extended period of time. These people are bound together by similar beliefs, attitudes, expectations, and values. They share a culture, a language or dialect, and a history. Outsiders, though often greeted with gracious hospitality, are viewed with suspicion and remain outsiders.

A village often has a recognized leader (or leaders) appointed by traditional guidelines, by the government, or by both. While modernization and the economically inspired exodus of youth and men to the urban areas has introduced powerful influences, the village remains a strong and slowly changing element in many societies.

The gospel can be introduced into village life through a variety of methods: radio broadcasts, itinerant evangelists, the showing of movies like THE JESUS FILM, open-air evangelistic crusades, health programs (midwifery, clinics, immunization programs), community development programs (education, agriculture, water resources), and literature.

Often, those in a village setting hear the gospel through one of their own who has heard it in the city where he or she works. In parts of Africa, the weddings and funerals of believers provide key opportunities to proclaim the gospel in the village setting. Everyone from the village (and nearby villages) gathers, providing a powerful occasions to share the good news.

Experience shows, however, that proclamation alone is inadequate for effective evangelism. Fruit seemingly born out of any of the various methods mentioned often disappears over time. Practically and biblically, the most strategic method for reaching a village with the gospel is church planting. The church thus started must be culturally and linguistically relevant, sustainable in terms of local finances, and HOLISTIC in its approach to ministry (*see* INDIGENOUS CHURCHES). Such a church is the fulfillment of the GREAT COMMISSION as it conserves evangelistic fruit, provides for growth in spiritual maturity, and enables believers to stand against ever-present heresies and cults as well as other aggressively evangelistic religions like Islam. In the final analysis, villages in rural areas can be successfully reached through a variety of methods so long as the final outcome is the planting of a church.

RICHARD K. CRUSE

Virgin Islands of the United States (United States Dependent Area) *(Est. 2000 pop.: 108,000; 352 sq. km. [136 sq. mi.]).* A former Danish colony lying to the southeast of Puerto Rico, the Virgin Islands were purchased by the United States in 1917. Although tourism and oil refining have brought prosperity to a large sector of the population, a wide gap separates the largely foreign-born Afro-Caribbean laboring class from the better-established groups. A third of the population is Roman Catholic; half of the Protestant majority are considered to be only nominal Christians.

EVERETT A. WILSON

SEE ALSO Caribbean.

Bibliography. A. Lampe, *The Church in Latin America, 1492–1992,* pp. 201–15; J. Rogozinski, *A Brief History of the Caribbean: From the Arawak and the Carib to the Present.*

Visions. *See* DREAMS AND VISIONS.

Vladimir (956–1015). Russian prince responsible for the founding of Russian Orthodox Christianity. Vladimir came to be known as the Constantine of Russia for his Christianization of Russia. The details of Vladimir's conversion are shrouded in legend. Some accounts paint the prince as a saint who led his nation into righteousness while other accounts tell of Vladimir's sordid past and his own need for conversion before he could lead his people out of darkness into light.

Before his conversion, he killed his brother, Jaropolk, and then had a son by Jaropolk's widow, whom he took as one of his hundreds of wives. He also maintained hundreds of concubines.

After listening to the testimonies of Muslims, Roman Catholics, Jews, and Greek Orthodox Christians in 986, Vladimir sent his nobles to see how each of these religions worshiped. The legendary report from St. Sophia's Cathedral in Constantinople: "We knew not whether we were in heaven or on earth for there is not a similar sight upon earth, nor is there such beauty," convinced Vladimir to be baptized into the Greek Orthodox Church.

In 988 Vladimir was baptized as well as the nation at his command. Though the details of Vladimir's conversion from paganism to Christianity are subjectively recorded and his motives less then pure, on Vladimir's decision God has built his church in Russia.

JAMIE FLOWERS

Bibliography. F. Butler, *Images of Missionaries and Innovative Rulers in East Slavic Literature from Early Times Through the Reign of Peter the Great*; P. L. Garlick, *Pioneers of the Kingdom: Biographical Sketches From New Testament Days to Modern Times*.

Voetius, Gisbert (1589–1676). Dutch professor of theology and Oriental languages; early missiological thinker. Voetius was an active member of the Synod of Dord (1617–19), chief proponent of Calvinistic orthodoxy, and the most influential Dutch theologian of the seventeenth century. At the same time, he was one of the spokesman of the emerging mission-oriented Reformed pietism in the Netherlands and had personal contacts with English Puritans. His book *Disputations on Atheism* (1639) and other books against philosophies of his time show him to be an evangelist to the well educated. Voetius is also the founder of the comparative study of religions for missionary purposes. Nearly all his books and tracts contain long sections on missions, which do not appeal and call to mission work but discuss all major problems of missions scientifically as a fourth part of systematic theology 'Theologica elenctica' beside exegetical, dogmatic, and practical theology. Thus Voetius designed the first comprehensive mission theology written by a Protestant. He was well-read in Catholic mission literature. Following a distinction made in Reformed ethics, Voetius combines double predestination as God's absolute will with the conviction that God's moral will is world missions under biblical promises.

THOMAS SCHIRRMACHER

Bibliography. J. H. Bavinck, *Science of Missions*, p. 155; D. Bosch, *Witness to the World*, pp. 126–27; J. Verkuyl, *Contemporary Missiology: An Introduction*, p. 21.

Volunteer, Volunteerism in Mission. Voluntary association with or participation in the missionary activity of the church, Christians choosing on their own to become involved in intercultural missionary outreach.

Biblical Background. In the Old Testament, the renewal of the Mosaic covenant at Shechem under Joshua was an early demonstration of collective voluntarism (Josh. 24:1–4). Other examples include the prayer association of the Nazarites and the Jews organized by Nehemiah to rebuild the walls of Jerusalem.

In the New Testament, Jesus invited people to follow him, signifying a willing commitment. The basic ethic of Jesus' ministry was based on a willing, voluntary response and service. DISCIPLESHIP, in essence, was an act of one's own choosing. The cost of discipleship was a voluntary commitment (Luke 9:23; 12:32ff.). In his encouragement to prayer, Jesus again taught a voluntary principle: "Ask . . . seek . . . knock . . ." (Matt. 7:7).

The early church of the first century expanded through the voluntary acts of the disciples and apostles. The apostles followed a voluntary pattern, including the economic support of the community (Act 2:37–47). The concept of doing loving acts (charity) for others in the early church soon evolved into a more formal structure of good works in the imperial church.

The Emerging Theological Basis of Christian Voluntarism. During the period of medieval monasticism, Christians practiced voluntarism on a highly intense level. Thomas Aquinas (1226–74) provided a theological rationale for such effort by defining charity as "the mother of all virtues" because "it initiates the action of other virtues by charging them with life." FRANCIS OF ASSISI (1181–1226) and his followers serve as one of the great examples of this newly found collective Christian activism that catalyzed change in society.

The Launching of a New Era. Two important roots link the eighteenth-century religious awakenings and the rise of religious voluntarism. First, the GREAT AWAKENINGS in North America unleashed spiritual forces among large numbers of common people in the colonies. The mass meetings of GEORGE WHITEFIELD (1714–70) attracted thousands to his sermons of evangelism and discipleship, and led to the establishment of orphanages, academies, and pro-revival churches. Similarly, JONATHAN EDWARDS (1703–58) is connected with the English Prayer Call movement and other renewal forces in the colonies, and unleashed spiritual energy that led naturally to tangible forms of Christian service, typically in the form of new voluntary associations.

The Wesleyan movement was the second impetus that led Methodism to create numerous avenues of Christian service for its followers. JOHN WESLEY pioneered outdoor preaching and itinerant evangelism, and modeled a burden for the working classes and underprivileged.

By the 1780s the basic voluntary paradigms were in place. The catalyst that ignited the general cultural outbreak of voluntarism was WILLIAM CAREY, who pioneered a strategy whereby large numbers of people with modest resources could be involved in the work of missions.

The Evangelical Century. The voluntary association was the primary vehicle for the growth of the evangelical movement during the nineteenth century. Four emphases marked evangelical voluntarism in the latter half of the century: the holiness movement, the conservative/liberal debate, evangelistic missions in the empire, and humanitarian concerns. The perfectionist theology of CHARLES G. FINNEY (1792–1875) had a direct influence on the holiness tradition in Britain as well, and found institutional expression in several kinds of voluntary associations such as the KESWICK CONVENTION (1875). Various voluntary associations also grew up in response to the challenge to biblical authority from liberal theologians. In universities and among the churches, missionary and study societies, such as the Intercollegiate Christian Union (1877) and the Bible League (1892), grew up in support of the new evangelical concerns. The expansion of the British Empire provided a further field of interest for Victorian evangelicals. In India, a dozen associations were formed between 1848 and 1876, with at least ten more formed in China.

North American Developments. The earliest forms of voluntarism in the United States were denominational, and this was followed by cooperation among the denominations. THE AMERICAN BOARD OF COMMISSIONERS FOR FOREIGN MISSIONS was formed in 1813 and became the parent of all the cooperative voluntary mission associations at the national level.

The positive experience of churches with voluntary associations quickly lent itself to other forms of Christian endeavor. During and after the Civil War Christian voluntarism was especially concerned with the American South, fostering education societies, missionary bodies, and literacy bands. American cities also provided a fruitful arena for a variety of voluntary ministries dealing with housing shortages, poor sanitation, inadequate schools, crime, and unemployment. No other area of voluntary expansion better illustrates the pulse beat of American religious life in the late nineteenth century than women's work. Over two dozen associations of women for missions were formed to send women to mission work at home and abroad.

New Directions for a New Century. The twentieth century witnessed ecumenical voluntarism, particularly in the area of student missions. In 1886, the STUDENT VOLUNTEER MOVEMENT for foreign missions was formed and spread quickly to Britain and Europe. Out of this emerged InterVarsity in the United States in 1941. Similar to InterVarsity are the Navigators (1943), Youth for Christ (1930), Pioneer Clubs (1939), Young Life (1941), and Campus Crusade for Christ (1951).

In the later decades of the twentieth century new forms of religious voluntarism have arisen in the United States. One type is related to translating a religious perspective into political activism: the National Association of Religious Broadcasters and the Moral Majority. Another form is the organizational network centered on mass evangelism. Both radio and television evangelists have established vast networks of voluntary "prayer partners" and supporters.

The turn of the century calls the future of voluntarism into question. Does global change and increasing complexity threaten voluntarism as the primary means of doing Christian mission? Is voluntarism declining in the West as some suggest? What about the generation of aging Baby Boomers nearing retirement? Will they step into the gap as second-career mission volunteers? Will voluntarism spread from the West to the emerging churches in the majority world who venture to missions frontiers? Historians summarize the enduring values of Christian voluntarism as empowerment for groups of people, experimental spontaneity to respond to needs as they arise, the creation of new leadership, and its singularity of purpose—various types of Christian mission. To the extent that voluntarism continues as a values-driven movement it will survive.

STEVE HOKE

Bibliography. W. H. Brackney, *Christian Voluntarism in Britain and North America: A Bibliography and Critical Assessment;* idem, *Christian Voluntarism: Theology and Praxis.*

Von Zinsendorf. *See* ZINZENDORF, NIKOLAUS LUDWIG VON (1700–1760).

Voodoo. *See* CARIBBEAN NEW RELIGIOUS MOVEMENTS.

Waddell, Hope Masterton (1804–95). Irish missionary to Jamaica and Nigeria. Called to missionary service in 1822, and ordained by the United Succession Church, Waddell was sent to Jamaica by the Scottish Missionary Society in 1829. Together with other USC ministers, Waddell organized a presbytery in Jamaica in 1836. Within a few years an opportunity to minister among freed slaves arose, and the missionaries were galvanized into action. By 1841 the presbytery began discussing sending its own missionaries to West Africa. A letter from Calabar (Nigeria) sent to the Church of Scotland requesting missionaries was forwarded to the Jamaican church in 1843. By September of the following year, a mission society was formed. Reliant on Jamaican funding, Waddell was sent to Scotland to raise any additional funds he could secure. He arrived in Calabar (on the coast of the east side of Nigeria) in 1846 with five Jamaican companions. They established a school and began translation, preaching, and teaching. His strong authoritarian attitude eventually led in 1854 to the Mission Council forcing his resignation, after which he traveled inland to continue his own work among the Efik. In spite of his method of strong attacks against local customs he found repulsive, Waddell was still able to gain a hearing and win people to Christ. By 1858 ill health forced his return to Ireland, where he wrote of his experiences and was active in a missionary church.

A. SCOTT MOREAU

Bibliography: H. Goldie, *Calabar and its Mission;* G. Johnston, *BDCM,* p. 711; H. O. Russell, *BDEB,* pp. 1148–49; H. M. Waddell, *Twenty-nine Years in the West Indies and Central Africa.*

Wagner, Charles Peter (1930–). American missiologist, Church Growth Movement leader, and missionary to Bolivia. Educated at Rutgers University, Fuller Theological Seminary, and the University of Southern California, he served three missionary terms totaling sixteen years in Bolivia. It was there that Wagner began reading church growth works by DONALD A. MCGAVRAN that prompted him to return to the United States to study under McGavran.

Wagner took McGavran's missiological concepts in India and applied them to the American church. Whereas McGavran is considered the father of the CHURCH GROWTH MOVEMENT, Wagner would be rightly called the father of the American Church Growth Movement.

The American missiological impact of Wagner can be discerned in many ways. He has written some forty books, many of which have become classics in the field of American church growth. He has taught church growth to nearly two thousand pastors and denominational executives through the Fuller Seminary Doctor of Ministry program. Wagner was also the founding president of the North American Society for Church Growth (now the American Society for Church Growth) in 1984.

Wagner returned to his alma mater, Fuller Seminary, in 1971 to become a full-time faculty member. He continues to serve today as the Donald A. McGavran Professor of Church Growth. His most recent emphases in church growth have been spiritual warfare, the prayer movement, and postdenominational structures.

THOM S. RAINER

Bibliography. T. S. Rainer, *The Book of Church Growth: History, Theology, and Principles;* E. L. Towns, ed., *Evangelism and Church Growth: A Practical Encyclopedia.*

Wake Island. *See* MICRONESIA.

Wales. *See* UNITED KINGDOM.

Wallis (Uvea) and Futuna (French Overseas Territory) *(Est. 2000 pop.: 15,000; 274 sq. km. [106 sq. mi.]).* Two islands 125 miles apart with Futuna 150 miles northeast of Fiji. They were settled respectively by Tongans and Samoans. Protectorate agreements were signed on behalf of France in 1842 with local chiefs but these were not ratified until 1887, and together Wallis and Futuna became an overseas territory of France in 1961. All of the islanders are Roman Catholics.

ALLAN K. DAVIDSON

SEE ALSO Polynesia.

Walls, Andrew Finlay (1928–). Scottish Methodist historian of mission. He was educated at Exeter College, Oxford (M.A., B.Litt.; hon. D.D., Aberdeen, 1993).Walls taught theology in Sierra Leone (1957–62) and Nigeria (1962–65) and was then appointed lecturer in church history at Aberdeen University. He founded the Department of Religious Studies (1970) and drew a growing number of research students from Africa, Asia, and the Americas. All the while Walls continued to write seminal essays that reinterpreted the historical and ecclesiological significance of mission, the indigenizing principle, Christianity's changing center of gravity from north to south, new religious movements, and Africa's place in Christian history.

Walls challenged the insularity of the Western theological academy and its failure to take account of the growing Christian reality that extended beyond historical Christendom. He was founding editor of *Bulletin of the Society for African Church History* and *Journal of Religion in Africa*. In 1986 Walls relocated the Centre for the Study of Christianity in the Non-Western World to Edinburgh University. He retired as director in 1995, continuing as honorary professor and curator of the Centre's collections. In recognition of his numerous contributions to academic and public life, Walls was named to the Order of the British Empire (OBE) in 1987.

WILBERT R. SHENK

Bibliography. J. Thrower, ed., *Essays in Religious Studies for Andrew Walls;* A. F. Walls, *The Missionary Movement in Christian History: Studies in the Transmission of Faith.*

Wang, Leland (1898–1975). Chinese evangelist and founder of Chinese Foreign Missionary Union. Born in Fuzhow, China, he was led to Christ by his wife in 1920. Obedient to the Bible and sensing a call to ministry, Wang left his Navy career as a gunboat officer in 1921. He rented a hall in his native Fuzhow and began ringing a handbell to draw a crowd.

In 1928 he formed the Chinese Foreign Missionary Union, committed to the task of evangelism and mission endeavor to the scattered Chinese in the South Seas of Asia. From the 1940s to the 1960s Wang extended his preaching ministry to the United States, Canada, Europe, and the Middle East. He evangelized the Chinese diaspora and stirred Western Christians in holy living and ardent outreach to Asia. Wang received the Doctor of Divinity degree from Wheaton College in recognition of his labors on behalf of Christ.

His mission board, consisting at one time of twenty-six Chinese nationals working in thirteen mission stations and countries, was the first of its kind. Its breadth was amazing; its focus on church planting and pastoral training was unique at the time.

Wang, often referred to as the Moody of China, established his life and mission on the Scriptures. He lived by a self-imposed rule, "No Bible, no breakfast." He read the Old Testament through once a year, the New Testament twice a year, and the Psalms and Proverbs once a month.

HOOVER WONG

Wang, Thomas Yung-hsin (1925–). Chinese evangelist and international missions leader. Wang was born into a Christian home in Beijing. He was converted under the ministry of evangelist JOHN SUNG in 1936, and joined the Christian Tabernacle in Beijing pastored by Wang Mingdao. He served as a liaison officer between China and the U.S. Navy in Saipan Islands (1946–48), and worked for the Civil Air Transport in Hong Kong (1949–52), before attending the Presbyterian seminary in Tainan, Taiwan (1955–57). After a year of itinerant preaching in Europe (1957–58), he received training at Central Bible Institute in the United States (1959–60). He started the Chinese Christian Mission in Detroit in 1961, evangelizing the Chinese through preaching, literature, and the media. At the URBANA Student Missionary convention (1960) he launched the North America Congress of Chinese Evangelicals, which convened December 1972. At the LAUSANNE CONGRESS (1974) he led in the launching of the Chinese Congress on World Evangelism, which convened in Hong Kong in 1976. He served the Chinese Coordination Center of World Evangelism (1976–79) and the Lausanne Committee on World Evangelization (1987–89), being the director of the LAUSANNE CONGRESS II in Manila, 1989. Since 1989 he has led the AD 2000 and Beyond Movement and the Great Commission Center, pioneering preaching and church planting in the former Soviet Union and elsewhere.

SAMUEL LING

Ward, William (1769–1823). English pioneer missionary to India. Ward was an enterprising young Englishman who developed interesting professional skills before becoming a leader of the British Baptist mission in pre-Victorian India. In Bengal, he served with distinction as a peacemaker, personnel manager, pastoral counselor, and budding missiologist.

Born in Derbyshire, he was apprenticed to a printer who edited *The Derby Mercury,* a regional weekly newspaper. After functioning as a social and political commentator in the English Midlands during Europe's revolutionary years (1789–97), he decided to train for full-time Christian ministry among England's Particular Baptists. While studying in Yorkshire under John Fawcett, he was discovered by his denomination's mission, later known as the BAPTIST MISSIONARY SOCIETY. It needed a missionary printer in Bengal. Ward responded to its invitation to service in the spirit of Matthew 28:18–20. He was set apart for the work of a Christian missionary in Olney in May 1799. As one of a group of mission recruits, he sailed into the Hooghly estuary near Calcutta early in October 1799, only to run into a storm of official indignation from the British East India Company. To escape it, the would-be-missionaries fled for refuge upriver to a Danish settlement that served as a haven for Europeans anxious to evade the British law as known in Serampore.

Ward became indispensable to the Serampore Mission between 1800 and 1823 as practical administrator, printing press manager, irenic trouble-shooter, mentor to indigenous evangelists, and cross-cultural counselor. One of WILLIAM CAREY'S closest colleagues, he produced Serampore's strategic "Form of Agreement" (1805), a classic on Hindu mythology, and various missiological documents. After returning from a two-year furlough in Britain and North America (1819–21), he died suddenly from cholera near Calcutta. He was survived by his wife, Mary, herself already a one-time widow, and two daughters.

A. CHRISTOPHER SMITH

SEE ALSO Serampore Trio.

Bibliography. A. C. Smith, *American Baptist Quarterly* 10 (1991): 218–44; S. Stennet, *Memoirs of the Life of the Rev. William Ward;* W. Ward, *A View of the History, Literature, and Mythology of the Hindoos: Including a Minute Description of Their Manners and Customs, and Translations from Their Principal Works.*

Warneck, Gustav (1834–1910). German missiologist and first mission professor. Though he was not the first German missiologist, Warneck is called the "Father of German missiology" because he held the first chair of missions at a German university (Halle, 1896), wrote the first comprehensive German theology of missions (Gotha, 1892–1903), and even influenced strongly nascent German Catholic academic missiology (*see* JOSEPH SCHMIDLIN). Born in Naumburg, Warneck studied theology, but weak health prevented him from becoming a missionary. He became an inspector for the RHENISH MISSION, then parish minister. Together with devoted colleagues like Grundemann, CHRISTLIEB, and Zahn, he developed missiology by publishing the *Allgemeine Missionszeitschrift* (1874) and by starting Mis-

sionskonferenzen for the study of missions (1897). He furthered cooperation between missions through the Continental Mission Conferences (1866) and the German Missions–*Ausschuss* (1885). Warneck, much indebted to the GREAT AWAKENING and even to the Holiness Revival (Brighton, 1875), took the *Volkshirche* (folk-church, territorial church) as the goal of all missionary work (though it would start with individual conversions). Although Warneck actively opposed the early FAITH MISSIONS, not appreciating their ecclesiology and arguing that they would further split an already fragmented German mission landscape, he is today respected by many evangelical missiologists.

KLAUS FIEDLER

Bibliography. G. Warneck, *Gustav, Outline of the History of Protestant Missions;* idem, *Modern Missions and Culture: Their Mutual Relations.*

Warren, Max Alexander Cunningham (1904–77). Irish ecumenist and missionary statesman. Warren was born in Dun Laoghaire, Ireland, while his parents were on furlough from India. He was educated at Jesus College, Cambridge (M.A.), after which he spent a short term in Nigeria. He was awarded honorary doctorates by various universities, including Glasgow (D.D., 1963). He was appointed a canon of Westminster in 1963. Warren became secretary of CMS during World War II and served from 1942 to 1963.

His keen insight into the rapidly changing sociopolitical relationships and their implications for missions quickly won respect. In addition to some thirty books, Warren exerted wide influence through the 232 issues of the CMS *Newsletter* that he wrote during his tenure, treating a wide range of contemporary missiological themes. Warren sought to help missions adapt to the new situation. In retirement he wrote two important historical interpretations of the modern missionary movement: *The Missionary Movement from Britain in Modern History* (1965) and *Social History and Christian Mission* (1967). An Anglican evangelical, Warren was prominent in the INTERNATIONAL MISSIONARY COUNCIL. He opposed integration of the IMC with the WORLD COUNCIL OF CHURCHES (formally approved at New Delhi in 1961) on grounds this would result in the eclipse of mission.

WILBERT R. SHENK

Bibliography. F. W. Dillistone, *Into all the World: A Biography of Max Warren;* M. Warren, *Crowded Canvas: Some Experiences of a Life-time.*

Wars. War is one of the great social problems, along with poverty and racism, with which the missionary movement has had to struggle. It is difficult to formulate the Christian position on war because of the problem of harmonizing the Old Testament with the New Testament and the difficulty of applying the teachings of Jesus to society. In the Old Testament, many passages endorse armed conflict, such as Deuteronomy 7 and 20 and the war narratives of Joshua, Judges, and Samuel. Although these are used by some Christians to justify their participation in war, others point out that Israel was a theocratic state, and that in New Testament times there is no state where God is king, but he deals with humanity through an international body, the church. Another problem arises, however, over the directions that Jesus gave to his followers. He seems to indicate that they be nonviolent, in such statements as "But I tell you, do not resist an evil person. If someone strikes you on the right cheek, turn to him the other also" (Matt. 5:39) and "But I tell you, love your enemies and pray for those who persecute you" (Matt. 5:44). Because Christians are citizens of national states in addition to being members of the church, it has seemed to most of them that these words should be interpreted in a way that allows them to fight for their country. In an attempt to apply these Scriptures to world affairs, Christians have responded in a variety of ways, ranging from nonviolent pacifism to advocating a just war theory. The early church, certain Christian humanists, and the majority of Anabaptists have taken a nonresistant or pacifist stance (*see* PACIFIST THEOLOGY). The majority, however, have followed Augustine and claimed that certain wars are just. Denominations, including the Church of the Brethren, Quakers, and Mennonites, maintain a position of nonresistance, but the larger groups such as Lutherans, Presbyterians, Baptists, Roman Catholics, Methodists, and Reformed adhere to the just war interpretation. In certain rare instances Christians have even supported crusades. The medieval popes urged such action against the Turks, and in the twentieth century some Christians have maintained such an attitude toward Communists.

During the nineteenth century, from the defeat of Napoleon to the outbreak of World War I, there was a global expansion of Western Christian missionary efforts accompanying European imperialism and colonialism. These later movements depended on superior military power. Western Europe since medieval times had been the world leader in technology and now this skill was applied more completely to warfare. Challenged by the Napoleonic victories, a Prussian military instructor, Karl von Clausewitz, articulated the theory of "total war." He believed that it is necessary to push conflict to its "utmost bounds" in order to win. At the time he expressed these ideas the Industrial Revolution began increasing the power of armaments so that an enemy could be totally defeated in a manner never before possible.

Christians in the nineteenth century responded to the danger caused by new armaments by encouraging international cooperation and humanitarian endeavors. These attempts led to international gatherings, including the Hague Conferences of 1899 and 1907. But the forces that worked toward harmony and peace failed, and with World War I Clausewitz's view moved closer to reality. The two sides used mines, machine guns, poison gas, submarines, and aerial bombardment, thus taking the conflict to land, sea, and air. The churches supported the war. The rhetoric of leaders such as Woodrow Wilson made them feel that they were involved in a crusade to help humankind.

On the eve of World War I, thousands of missionaries were serving all over the world. During the nineteenth century numerous missionary societies had been founded in Europe and North America, many of which encouraged an interdenominational approach. Although the differences among the sending churches might be great, these did not seem so important on the mission field, because workers possessed the common purpose of preaching the gospel to people of other faiths. World War I had an enormous impact on this international Christian enterprise. Mission properties were seized and hundreds of workers were forced to leave the field and did not return. More serious than these physical losses was the spiritual damage done to the entire Protestant missionary movement. The conflict demonstrated that the ultimate loyalty of most of those who preached the gospel was not to Christ and his church but to the nation-state. The war also shattered the postmillennial hopes of the Anglo-American missionary enterprise. Although some of this optimism continued in the postwar years and led to the founding of the WORLD COUNCIL OF CHURCHES, the dynamic force in international outreach shifted to the conservative evangelical groups that followed a more individualistic approach to missions. These organizations, mostly premillennial, had little interest in promoting Christian unity or extending Christian culture to other parts of the world.

The damage done to the missionary cause by World War I included a change in the attitude of non-Western populations toward the Christian cause. In many instances missionaries had brought to such people modern medicine, peace among warring tribes, the abolition of the slave trade, and justice for those who were too weak to secure it for themselves. But now the European claims to a monopoly of religious truth and civilization were shattered as they waged what amounted to a civil war that left them bankrupt economically and spiritually. In World War I for the first time many Indian, African, and Japanese troops fought very effectively against the white men. The natural consequence of this was the awakening of nationalism among the peoples of Asia and Africa. This reaction was furthered by World War II. Although nationalism can be a positive force, it often becomes a narrow, arrogant intolerance toward members of other groups. This hurt the missionary movement in the many instances where it could not adjust to an indigenous church organization and ministry.

World War II, however, had many positive effects on the North American church and this encouraged missionary outreach. Many of those involved in the armed services experienced "fox-hole religion" and returned with the gospel to the places where they had fought. They also stirred the churches to give to missions, used new methods such as aeronautical technology, and founded interdenominational mission groups such as the Inter-Varsity Christian Fellowship that recruited and sent out missionaries. With the end of the Cold War and the resulting reduction of global tension, perhaps armed conflict will become a more isolated phenomenon as it was during the nineteenth-century period of missionary expansion.

ROBERT G. CLOUSE

Bibliography. R. H. Bainton, *Christian Attitudes Toward War and Peace;* R. G. Clouse, ed., *War: Four Christian Views;* R. V. Pierard, *Earthen Vessels, American Evangelicals and Foreign Missions, 1880–1980,* pp. 155–79; idem, *IBMR* 22:1 (1998): 13–19; M. Walzer, *Just and Unjust Wars: A Moral Argument With Historical Illustrations;* and R. A. Wells, ed., *The Wars of America.*

Waterston, Jane Elizabeth (1843–1932). Scottish missionary doctor to South Africa and Malawi. Born in a comfortable home, with affiliations to the Free Church of Scotland, and educated in Scotland, she sailed in 1867 to South Africa to take charge of the girls' school at Lovedale, in Kaffraria. She spent eighteen months learning Xhosa and then worked at Lovedale until 1873, gaining a reputation of being hard-working and enterprising. She then returned to Europe and studied medicine in Dublin, qualifying in 1879. The Free Church of Scotland Mission appointed her to Blantyre, Nyasaland (Malawi). Finding insufficient work there, she went back to Lovedale in 1880, but in an unofficial capacity. Here she had plenty of medical work, but finances were always precarious. In 1883, in order to help her family in financial difficulties (since the Free Church Mission would not accept her as a salaried missionary), she was obliged to take a better-paying position so that she could help them. She left Lovedale to practice in Cape Town as South Africa's first woman doctor.

Initially her way was difficult, but she soon built up a large and successful practice, winning respect and affection. She took a lead in public service enterprises, especially in providing better maternity services for women, and in medical work for the poor, including migrant laborers from the Transkei. During the Second Anglo-Boer War she was active in organizing relief for refugees. In her later years she received public appreciation for her years of service, and the example she had set for other women.

JOCELYN MURRAY

Bibliography. L. Bean and E. van Heyningen, eds., *The Letters of Jane Elizabeth Waterston 1866–1905;* S. M. Brock, *The Enterprising Scot: Scottish Adventure and Achievement,* pp. 75–89.

Wealth and Poverty. One of the great social problems that faces those who would bear witness to the Christian faith in a global manner is that of distributive justice. There is an extreme divergence between the rich and poor of today's world, a contrast often described in terms of the North–South divide. Experts in demographics estimate that early in the third millennium, the world's population will be 6.3 billion, and by 2025 it may reach 8.5 billion. Moreover, 95 percent of the global population growth over this period will be in the developing countries of Latin America, Africa, and Asia. By 2025, Mexico will have replaced Japan as one of the ten most populous countries on the earth, and Nigeria's population will exceed that of the United States.

Despite progress made in economic growth, public health, and literacy in the third world, at least 800 million live in "absolute poverty." This is defined as a condition of life where malnutrition, illiteracy, disease, squalid housing, high infant mortality, and low life expectancy are beyond any reasonable definition of human decency. The stark reality is that the North (including Eastern Europe) has a quarter of the world's population and 80 percent of its income, while in the South (including China) three-quarters of the world's people live on one-fifth of its income. Also, approximately 90 percent of the global manufacturing industry is in the North. While the quality of life in the North rises steadily, in the South every two seconds a child dies of hunger and disease.

Still the contrast between wealth and poverty does not correspond exactly with the North–South division. Many OPEC countries are rich, while poverty is found in North America and Europe. In the United States 14 percent of people and 30 percent of children are beneath the poverty line. In Britain over 10 percent live below the legal definition of poverty, and another 10 percent to 15 percent are close to this point. A great disparity between wealth and poverty is found not only between nations but also within them.

On the other hand, one-fifth of the world's population lives in relative affluence and consumes approximately four-fifths of the world's income. Moreover, according to a recent World Bank report, the "total disbursements" from the wealthy nations to the THIRD WORLD amounted to $92 billion, a figure less than 10% of the worldwide expenditures on armaments; but this was more than offset by the "total debt service" of $142 billion. The result was a negative transfer of some $50 billion from the third world to the developed countries. This disparity between wealth and poverty is a social injustice so grievous that Christians dare not ignore it.

God has provided enough resources in the earth to meet the needs of all. Usually it is not the fault of the poor themselves, since for the most part they were born into poverty. Christians use the complexities of economics as an excuse to do nothing. However, God's people need to dedicate themselves not only to verbal evangelism but also to relieving human need as part of sharing the good news (Luke 4:18–21), both at home and to the ends of the earth.

This explains why Christians in the two-thirds world place issues of poverty and economic development at the top of their theological agendas. Some Christians in the North have difficulty understanding why "liberation" is so central to the thinking of their counterparts in Latin America, Africa, and Asia, but they have never faced the stark, dehumanizing reality of grinding poverty (*see also* LIBERATION THEOLOGIES).

The Western missionary movement reflects an affluence that has developed as a result of the threefold revolution that has given Europe and North America a standard of living that is the envy of the world (*see also* MISSIONARY AFFLUENCE). Since the sixteenth-century the scientific, industrial, and political revolution has unleashed an avalanche of material goods that has raised the West from poverty. Most of the world has not shared in this achievement. When missionaries from the West went to preach and minister in other lands during the nineteenth century, they often believed that God favored them materially and scientifically so that they could overawe the heathen. As recently as the 1970s a missionary could observe that "Economic power is still the most crucial power factor in the western missionary movement. It is still the most important way that the Western missionary expresses his concept of what it means to preach the gospel" (Bernard Quick). The fact that most Protestant missionaries serve in some part of Africa, Latin America, or Oceania, those parts of the world where most of the poor reside, indicates that missionaries are economically superior in the social contexts of their ministry.

There have always been a few individuals who have pointed out that Western missionaries can take for granted a level of material security, lifestyle, and future options that are beyond the wildest dreams of the people among whom they work. As the twentieth century progressed others

joined in calling attention to the unforeseen and unwelcome effects of this economic disparity. At the TAMBARAM CONFERENCE (1938) a report was presented that clearly showed the dilemma between the comparatively "wealthy" missionaries and the "poor" people to whom they ministered. By the very nature of the situation missionaries were looked upon as the representatives of a wealthy and powerful civilization who introduced a new standard of economic values. The people that they served looked upon them not as proclaimers of a new faith, but as sources of potential economic gain. The problem of the personal affluence of Western missionaries when compared to the indigenous peoples was spelled out more explicitly in books such as *Ventures in Simple Living* (1933) and *Living as Comrades* (1950) written by Daniel Johnson Fleming, professor of missions at Union Theological Seminary (N.Y.). Writers like Fleming pointed out that the wealth of the West obscured the message of Christ, and led to feelings of helplessness and inferiority on the part of those to whom the missionaries ministered.

However, the problem of global economic disparity was once again obscured in the post–World War II period, when the North American missionary rank increased from less than 19,000 in 1953 to over 39,000 in 1985. These new missionaries were mostly from evangelical missionary groups who tended to neglect the work of the denominational agencies and focused on personal conversion, often ignoring economic and material problems.

Yet the work of authors such as Viv Grigg and Jonathan Bonk as well as a number of contributors to the *Evangelical Missions Quarterly* and *Missiology* focused attention on the obstacle to Christian witness inherent in the issues of wealth and poverty. Many of these writers counsel Christians in the more developed lands to share their material means with others. This can be done by supporting public and private efforts to aid the poor, by scaling down their standard of living, and by working for the empowerment of those who do not have the ability to represent themselves.

ROBERT G. CLOUSE

SEE ALSO Option for the Poor.

Bibliography. J. Bonk, *Missions and Money, Affluence as a Western Missionary Problem;* R. G. Clouse, ed., *Wealth and Poverty: Four Christian Views of Economics;* V. Griff, *Companion to the Poor;* K. Koyama, *Waterbuffalo Theology;* J. A. Scherer, *Global Living Here and Now;* J. V. Taylor, *Enough Is Enough: A Biblical Call for Moderation in a Consumer-Oriented Society.*

Webb, Mary (1779–1861). American founder of the Boston Female Society for Missionary Purposes. Born in Boston, Mary Webb contracted a childhood illness that left her a paraplegic at age five. Confined to a wheelchair in a society that disregarded the disabled, she determined not to be incapacitated by her handicap. Baptized at age nineteen, she joined a Baptist church pastored by Thomas C. Baldwin. At his urging, she organized seven Baptist and six Congregationalist women into the Boston Female Society for Missionary Purposes. This organization was revolutionary in that women assumed leadership. In addition, it crossed denominational bounds at a time when most shunned ecumenical activity; and, while emphasizing evangelism, it encouraged humanitarian ministry.

During her fifty years of service as secretary-treasurer, Webb's enthusiasm and influence spawned similar organizations, including the Female Cent Society (1803), the Children's Cent Society (1812), the Corban Society (1811), the Fragment Society (1812), as well groups that ministered to ethnic minorities and prostitutes. Her voluminous correspondence promoted cooperation and communication between women's missionary societies. This was difficult at best in an era characterized by strong denominational bounds; the women eventually separated to support their own denominations. Remembered as a visionary founder and social activist, Mary Webb died at age eighty-two of breast cancer.

GARY LAMB

Bibliography. R. A. Tucker, *GGC;* A. L. Vail, *Mary Webb and the Mother Society.*

WEC International. Worldwide Evangelization for Christ (formerly Worldwide Evangelization Crusade), WEC International was founded by C. T. STUDD in Britain in 1913. Studd was one of the "Cambridge Seven" who went out to China with the CHINA INLAND MISSION in 1885. He also played a significant role in the development of the STUDENT VOLUNTEER MOVEMENT. An interdenominational faith mission, WEC International has a primary focus on pioneer evangelism and church planting and in 1996 had 1,693 workers of 42 nationalities serving in 63 countries. There are an estimated 500,000 affiliated with WEC-related or founded churches today.

History. WEC was one of the later pioneer missions targeting the inland areas of unevangelized continents. Beginning as the Heart of Africa Mission in northeast Zaire, it extended to Amazonia in 1922, Arabia in 1924, and Central Asia in 1926. Studd's brusque actions, bold language, radicalism, and uncompromising dedication together with a breakdown of relationships with the Home Council almost led to the demise of the mission around the time of his death in 1931. Yet the principles and vision he imparted became the foundation for later fruitfulness.

Norman Grubb, Studd's son-in-law, rebuilt WEC with a distinctive structure and leadership principles which gave a high degree of flexibility and initiative to fields. Grubb was earlier instrumental in founding the Inter-Varsity Fellowship. By 1953 WEC had 550 workers in 24 countries. During Grubb's leadership the mission became more international with sending bases in North America, Australasia, South Africa, and Europe.

The emphasis on the least evangelized continues to be maintained. By 1996 nearly 70 percent of WEC's front-line personnel were in countries in the 10/40 WINDOW area with 63 percent serving Muslim, Hindu, and Buddhist peoples. These efforts required innovative methods and structures for residence and ministry.

Principles. WEC's foundational spiritual principles are known as the Four Pillars—faith, sacrifice, holiness, and fellowship. In terms of *structure*, fields and sending bases are self-governing. Wider issues are handled in fellowship with all relevant teams. The ultimate governing body in WEC is the Leaders Council comprised of all field, regional, and international leaders. All leaders are accountable to those they lead. After seeking God, decision-making is by consensus, including all those implicated in the decision. Women are eligible for leadership positions and couples are appointed together to leadership. In terms of *faith*, members seek to come to a common mind concerning God's will and then to act, trusting God for the supply of personnel, enablement, and finances. In terms of *commitment to work with others*, through partnership with churches and other agencies in the body of Christ, WEC seeks to effectively work for the completion of the task of world evangelization. The ministry of the book *Operation World* to the whole body of Christ is an example of this commitment. Finally, in terms of *internationalization*, WEC is committed to be international and multicultural. The rapid increase of non-Westerners to 15 percent of the front-line missionaries has been the result, with an increasing number of sending bases in Latin America, Asia and Africa.

PATRICK J. JOHNSTONE

Bibliography. N.Grubb, *C. T. Studd, Cricketer and Pioneer;* H. Roseveare, *Living Sacrifice.*

Wesley, John (1703–91). English missionary to North America. "The world is my parish," declared John Wesley. Born in Epworth, England, to an Anglican parish priest, Wesley would not be limited by ecclesiastical boundaries or a narrow doctrine of election.

Wesley's own missionary experience, before his evangelical conversion, involved two frustrating years in America as a chaplain in Georgia. After his return to England his heart was "strangely warmed" on May 24, 1738. The fire spread through his preaching and that of numerous workers Wesley sent across Britain, Ireland, the

American colonies, and the Caribbean. In individualistic frontier America, Wesleyan doctrine, personal evangelistic zeal, and ecclesiological innovations (for example, itinerant circuit riders) contributed to Methodism's dramatic rise. In the 1800s Methodist missionaries spread farther, planting national churches that today include millions of adherents worldwide.

Wesley remains relevant to missions today. His organizational genius was key to the spread of the Wesleyan revival, his emphasis on holiness vital to its sustained growth. Wesley's simple lifestyle and concern for slaves and the poor coupled with his evangelical message produced radical changes in English society. Finally, his charitable attitude toward other Christians in spite of harsh opposition, diverse experiences, or disagreement on secondary doctrines remains a model for Christian unity.

DAVID GREENLEE

Bibliography. R. E. Coleman, *Nothing to Do but Save Souls;* H. A. Snyder, *The Radical Wesley and Patterns for Church Renewal;* R. G. Tuttle, *John Wesley: His Life and Theology.*

Wesleyan/Holiness Missions. Wesleyan/Holiness missions are those missions that took place initially on the revivalistic edges of the Methodist Episcopal Church and within the contexts of the denominations that grew out of that church with "personal and social holiness" as major themes as articulated by JOHN WESLEY; many groups became Pentecostal after 1906 and are known as Wesleyan, Holiness, or "Sanctified" Pentecostal Churches. There are three primary methods of mission work: (1) mission based on the itinerary model of John Wesley; (2) the "Board" method of mission modeled on the AMERICAN BOARD OF COMMISSIONERS OF FOREIGN MISSION (ABCFM); and, (3) "self-supporting missions" on the basis of ideas developed by WILLIAM TAYLOR. The Wesleyan/Holiness denominations began to develop during the 1840s and now number in the hundreds, most of which have their own mission agencies on one of the above models and their own spheres of influence around the world among the approximately 12 million Wesleyan/Holiness believers worldwide, about half of which are associated with the SALVATION ARMY. An important part of the story of Wesleyan/Holiness missions is the role of women in establishing, supporting, and serving in mission.

Early History. The initial missions which may be described as "Holiness" were of the "itineracy model." Primary among these were the peripatetic labors of Lorenzo Dow in the U.S. and his trips to England, beginning in 1805, which resulted in the creation of the Primitive Methodist Church. He was part of that "Errand of the World" through which the Americans wished to transform the church in the "Old World." During the antebellum period much missionary fervor was devoted to the westward expansion of the Methodist Episcopal Church. Holiness revivalistic Methodists signed on as missionaries to the Native Americans and were sent to Oregon and California; others joined the American Missionary Association or were sent by the Wesleyan Methodist Church to the American South. The Methodist Episcopal Church Missionary Society was founded in 1819 in New York on the model of the ABCFM. Many of the early recruits of the society were from the Holiness or revivalistic movements of Methodism. The same is true for the Evangelical Association (later EUB), which eventually merged into the United Methodist Church active in German-speaking Europe, Africa, and Latin America.

William Taylor was the second Methodist Episcopal Church missionary to California (1849–56), sent by the bishops and not by the Missionary Society. He would develop the "self-supporting" or "Pauline" missions theory and would be instrumental in the global development of Methodism, the Holiness Movement, and later, Pentecostalism (*see* PENTECOSTAL MISSIONS). Other important independent mission work was carried on (1840–47) by James Caughey in Canada and England, Walter and PHOEBE PALMER in the British Isles (1860–65) as well as non-Methodists who were self-consciously Wesleyan/Holiness, including CHARLES FINNEY, Asa Mahan, William Boardman, and Robert and Hannah Whitall Smith, who spent time in England or on the Continent.

In Britain the efforts resulted in the Brighton Conventions. Many converts from these conventions would merge into the Church of the Nazarene. In Germany the *Gemeinschaftsbewegung* (1888) was organized out of the earlier *Heiligungsbewegung;* the Swedish Holiness Union was organized in 1885.

Denominational Missions. The Wesleyan/Holiness denominational board was that of the Wesleyan Methodist Church (WM, 1862) which, beginning in Sierra Leone (1889), established an important presence in Colombia, Japan, Haiti, Puerto Rico, Honduras, Mexico, the Philippines. It was through the Pilgrim Holiness (PH) Church that Charles E. and Lettie B. Cowman were appointed missionaries to Japan. The Cowmans withdrew to found the independent Oriental Missionary Society, now OMS INTERNATIONAL. The PH-WM merger produced the Wesleyan Church mission program, which is now located in Indianapolis, Indiana.

The second denominational Wesleyan/Holiness mission effort was by the Salvation Army (1878) founded by WILLIAM BOOTH and his wife Catherine. The Booths had been forced to leave the Methodist churches in England to work with the poor and to enable Catherine Booth to have a ministry as a woman. Because of this experience, women have full ministerial and leadership roles in the Salvation Army and the ministry to the poor continues to be the focus of the organization. Beginning in the U.S., and continuing in Europe and the rest of the world, the Salvation Army has become a global church. Its periodical, *War Cry* is published in forty-three languages. The international headquarters are in London.

THE CHRISTIAN AND MISSIONARY ALLIANCE, founded by A. B. SIMPSON (1887), was intended to expedite missionary activity. He maintained close contacts with the Free Methodists and Vanguard missionaries as well as the William Taylor missionaries in Latin America. The motto of the Fourfold Gospel, that is "Christ our Savior, Sanctifier, Healer, and Coming King," summarized the Holiness theological vision. The Alliance quickly established missions in India, China, Taiwan, Japan, the Philippines, Vietnam, Cambodia, Thailand, Indonesia, Argentina, Chile, Colombia, Equador, Peru, Puerto Rico, Brazil, Congo, and the Ivory Coast as well as in Europe. The denomination supports several educational institutions. The international headquarters are in Colorado Springs, Colorado.

The Free Methodist Church organized a mission board in 1881 after initially encouraging mission on the Taylor model. Beginning with India, the Free Methodist Church has had significant success in Central Africa (where it merged with the [Pentecostal] Congo Gospel Mission), Japan, Brazil, the Philippines, Egypt, Mozambique, South Africa, and Paraguay. Many of these areas have become independent or quasi-independent churches in "fellowship" with the North American churches. Missionaries who made major contributions and are either the authors or subjects of numerous books include E. F. Ward (India), Jacob DeShazer, Paul Kakihara, and Frank Kline. The international headquarters of the Free Methodist Church is in Indianapolis, Indiana.

The Church of the Nazarene mission program began with the effort of Hiram Reynolds while he served in one of the constituent denominations of the Church of the Nazarene, the Association of Pentecostal Churches in America. This began (1896) as a "self-supporting" mission project but soon evolved to the ABCFM model. When the denomination was nationally established in 1908, Reynolds became the mission leader of the denomination. The major areas of influence were in India, South Africa, Swaziland, Korea, Latin America, Brazil, and China, including the overseas Chinese. The denomination merged with groups in Britain, Switzerland, and Germany to establish a European presence. The Church of the Nazarene is the third largest global Wesleyan/Holiness denomination. Its international headquarters is in Kansas City, Missouri.

Founded in the 1880s, the Church of God (Anderson) already had congregations in seventeen countries when the mission board was established in 1909. These included Germany, England, Russia, Latvia, Switzerland, Sweden, and Denmark. Extensive and successful efforts were made in Mexico, India, and Kenya. Numerous periodicals have been published in different languages, which together with the very important *Church of God Missions* chronicle the mission efforts, policies, and personnel. The international headquarters of this agency is in Anderson, Indiana.

The Church of God in Christ organized a mission department in 1926 although the denomination had been sending missionaries for decades. The primary foci of mission have been Europe, Africa, the Caribbean, and Brazil. Special attention has been given to cooperating with indigenous churches of the African diaspora. The headquarters of the mission is in Memphis, Tennessee.

Also beginning in 1926, the Church of God (Cleveland) consolidated a mission program active since 1910 into a mission board. Mission was undertaken initially on the William Taylor model. This entrepreneurial style especially suited J. H. Ingram, who was responsible for establishing churches and recruiting missionaries for Bermuda, Mexico, Guatemala, Costa Rica, and Panama. From this beginning the Church of God (Cleveland) has spread throughout Europe, Asia, Africa, and Latin America. It maintains a number of educational institutions. This second largest global Wesleyan/Holiness denomination has transformed itself into a "democratic" church with the majority of the members outside North America. This has moved the "board" model back to an understanding of mission and ecclesiology more like that of Taylor.

Independent Mission Agencies. In addition to OMS International, three additional independent mission agencies were particularly important. The first was the Vanguard Mission, St. Louis, composed primarily of Free Methodist adherents of "self-supporting" missions of which the primary organizer and theorist was ANNA ABRAMS. The Vanguard mission, which included a mission training school, a transit and building fund to assist missionaries, and a monthly mission magazine, maintained close connections with the Pentecostal bands.

The Pentecostal Bands were founded by Free Methodist Vivian Dake (1882). These adapted the methods of William Taylor to evangelism initially in North America, and then throughout the world. Small groups were sent out to do evangelism, organize congregations, and then move on. After an evangelistic trip through Europe, Dake died in Africa (1892). The Bands were expelled from the Free Methodist Church (1896) and organized as Pentecostal Bands of the World with missions in at least ten countries and evangelistic efforts in several more. These merged with the Wesleyan Methodist Church in 1958.

The National Association for the Promotion of Holiness created the National Holiness Missionary Society (now World Gospel Mission) in 1910. The initial efforts of this society were focused on China, led by Cecil Troxel. After the foreign missionaries were expelled from China, the group expanded, first into India and then into other areas. It also serves smaller Wesleyan/Holiness denominations as a mission service agency. It supports theological education efforts in Colombia, Brazil, Japan, and India. It maintains an international headquarters in Marion, Indiana.

Other Mission Sending Agencies. Among the Wesleyan/Holiness and Holiness/Pentecostal Churches with active mission programs not discussed above are: Africa Evangelistic Band, Bethel Mission of China, Bible Methodist Missions, Bolivian Friends Holiness Mission, Brethren in Christ Mission, Church of Christ (Holiness), Church of God (Holiness), Church of God (Seventh Day), Church of God in Christ, Church of God of Prophecy, Churches of Christ in Christian Union, Congregational Holiness Church, Congregational Methodist Church, Emanuel Association, Emanuel Bible College, Emanuel Holiness Church, Evangelical Bible Mission, Evangelical Friends Association, Evangelical Methodist Church, Evangelistic Faith Missions, Fire Baptized Holiness Church, Friends Africa Gospel Mission, Great Commission Crusades (Haiti), Immanuel Gospel Mission, Immanueru Sogo Dendo Dan, India Evangelistic Association, Japan Holiness Church, Korean Holiness Church, Metropolitan Church Association, Mission Society for United Methodists, Missionary Church, Nihon Nacaren Kyodan, Nippon Jiyu Mesojisuto Kyodan, Peniel Missions, Pentecostal Holiness Church, Pillar of Fire, Swedish Holiness Union, Union Bible Seminary, United Brethren in Christ, Voice of China and Asia, World Gospel Crusades, World-Wide Missions, and Zainichi Beikoku Uesureyan Mesojisuto Senkyodan.

DAVID BUNDY

SEE ALSO Methodist Missions.

Bibliography. D. Barrett, WCE; D. Bundy, *Modern Christian Revivals*, pp. 188–44; idem,. *Methodist History 27* (1989): 197–210; idem, *Methodist History 28* (1989): 3–21; W. Cary, *Story of the National Holiness Missionary Society;* H. Conn, *Where the Saints Have Trod: A History of Church of God Missions;* R. Sandall, *History of the Salvation Army;* Taylor and R. DeLong, *Fifty Years of Nazarene Missions.*

Western Samoa *(Est. 2000 pop.: 187,000; 2,831 sq. km. [1,093 sq. mi.]).* Western Samoa consists of two large and six small islands 1,800 miles northeast of New Zealand and 2,300 miles southwest of Hawaii. British, German, and American strategic interests and complex Samoan rivalries culminated in German annexation of Western Samoa in 1899. In 1914 New Zealand troops occupied Western Samoa and it was administered by New Zealand until it became independent in 1962. Forty-two percent of its population of 187,000 are members of the Congregational Church (formerly LMS), 21 percent are Roman Catholic, 17 percent are Methodists, 10 percent Mormons with Seventh-Day Adventists, and Assemblies of God also prominent.

ALLAN K. DAVIDSON

SEE ALSO Polynesia

Bibliography. M. Meleisea, *Lagaga. A Short History of Western Samoa.*

Weston, Frank (1871–1924). English missionary to Africa and bishop of Zanzibar. Born in London, he graduated from Oxford, was ordained in 1894, ministered in London, and then, in 1898, joined the Universities' Mission to Central Africa (UMCA) in Zanzibar. He became principal of St. Andrew's Training College, Kiungani, in 1901, and was consecrated bishop of Zanzibar in 1908. He opposed a scheme for church reunion in East Africa, yet promoted reunion generally at the 1920 Lambeth Conference. Weston further drew attention by his "excommunication" of the bishop of Hereford for making liberal scholar B. H. Streeter a canon, and by his *Serfs of Great Britain* (1920), which attacked forced labor in Africa. As an impressive chair of the second Anglo-Catholic Congress in London (1923) he reminded delegates, "You cannot claim to worship Jesus in the Tabernacle, if you do not pity Jesus in the slum." The incarnational theology developed earlier in *The One Christ* (1907) was matched by Weston's concern for an East African church with its own trained clergy. After his death from blood poisoning he was mourned as a European who had a unique understanding of the African mind.

J. D. DOUGLAS

Bibliography. H. M. Smith, *Frank, Bishop of Zanzibar.*

Whately, Mary Louisa (1824–89). Irish missionary to Egypt. Born into the family of the archbishop of Dublin, she was early on attracted to a ministry among the poor because of her father's work in establishing a school for them. This desire was fostered during the Irish famine of 1846–51, and she began to visit the poor and work with the Irish Church Mission. The Whately family also opened their home to Italian refugees fleeing from the Crimean War.

Whately's commitment to cross-cultural missions did not come until she visited Cairo for medical reasons. While in Egypt, she was greatly troubled by the large number of children selling water without knowing the source of living water.

A second trip to Egypt in 1860 cemented her determination to remain in Egypt, where she started a school to teach women basic skills such as sewing and reading. Circumstances forced her to go back to Ireland for two years before she was able to return to Egypt and reopen the school. This time she was able to stay, and the school began to accept men and women who were destitute. For the next twenty-seven years, in addition to her school, she was deeply involved in village evangelism, traveling along the Nile, and distributing Bibles to literate people she met in the villages. She became ill in March 1889 while on one of her trips, and died after returning to Cairo.

PENNY GUSHIKEN

Bibliography. C. F. Hayward, *Women in the Mission Field*; E. R. Pitman, *Missionary Heroines in Eastern Lands: Women's Work in Mission Fields*.

Wheaton '83. Sponsored by the WORLD EVANGELICAL FELLOWSHIP and held as a continuation of the work done in the WHEATON CONGRESS (1966), the BERLIN CONGRESS (1966), the LAUSANNE CONGRESS (1974), the PATTAYA CONSULTATION (1980), and the GRAND RAPIDS CONSULTATION (1982), Wheaton '83 gathered 336 participants from 59 nations, with 60 percent coming from the non-Western world. The Consultation's theme was "I will build my Church," with each element in the agenda stressing the role of the local church as the central expression of God's kingdom in the world. There were three tracks within the consultation, with the following foci: (1) the biblical nature of the church and its mission; (2) the nature and mission of the church in new frontiers; (3) the nature of mission as involving both evangelism and social concerns.

Wheaton '83 continued the discussion with evangelical ranks on the nature of mission and the roles of evangelism and discipleship within mission. Within that debate, the tenor at Wheaton '83 was the recognition that alleviating poverty, bringing justice and transforming people and societies are all part of *MISSIO DEI*.

A. SCOTT MOREAU

Bibliography. M. L. Branson, *Theological Students Fellowship Bulletin* 7:1 (Sept.–Oct. 1983): 11–26; R. Covell, *Missiology* 11:4 (1983): 531–33; A. F. Glasser, *IBMR* 9 (1985): 9–13; R. C. Padilla, *The Best in Theology*, 1:239–52; T. Sine, ed., *The Church in Response to Human Need*; P. Sookhdeo, *New Frontiers in Mission*; Wheaton '83, *Wheaton '83: An International Evangelical Conference on the Nature and Mission of the Church: June 20–July 1, 1983, Wheaton, Illinois*.

Wheaton Congress 1966. *See* CONGRESS ON THE CHURCH'S WORLDWIDE MISSION.

Wheaton Declaration. *See* CONGRESS ON THE CHURCH'S WORLDWIDE MISSION.

Whitby Conference (1947). Located near Toronto, Whitby was the site of the first full meeting of the committee of the INTERNATIONAL MISSIONARY COUNCIL since 1938–39. On July 5–24, 1947, 112 persons from forty nations met to survey the state of the global church. Under the general theme "Christian Witness in a Revolutionary World" three major subjects were treated: partnership in obedience; the "supernationality" of missions; and the functions of the International Missionary Council.

The Whitby conference was characterized by deeply experienced unity despite the separation occasioned by the war. The percentage of representatives from younger churches was higher than at previous gatherings. The emphasis on "expectant evangelism" exhibited continuity with the vision of the WORLD MISSIONARY CONFERENCE at Edinburgh (1910) and the thrust of the MADRAS CONFERENCE (1938). Communism was recognized as a rival faith.

Whitby underscored that primary loyalty must be to Christ and his church universal rather than to nation, race, or denomination. In so doing, it laid the foundation for mutuality in the task of world evangelization, an emphasis later called "Joint Action for Mission." The delegates also declared worldwide evangelism to be central to the task of the church, but blurred its focus by broadening its definition to encompass all aspects of life.

The emphasis on PARTNERSHIP in obedience was prominent. The younger national churches of Asia, Africa, and Latin America were recognized as the principal agents of evangelization in their respective areas. Delegates to Whitby wrestled with issues related to the coordination and deployment of resources in mission strategy. In the process they downplayed the structural difference between mission societies and church bodies. Responsibility for mission initiative was placed in the hands of established national churches to the neglect of vast unevangelized populations beyond the influence of existing church bodies. This led increasingly to an understanding of unity that had no definitive commitment to global evangelization.

KEN MULHOLLAND

Bibliography. K. S. Latourette and W. R. Hogg, *Tomorrow Is Here*.

White, John (1866–1933). English missionary to Zimbabwe. Born as the oldest son in an English farming family of seven children, White came to Christ at age sixteen. Sensing a call to foreign ministry early in life, he attended Didsbury College in Manchester, where his call to Africa was confirmed. He arrived in South Africa in 1888, but suffered a nervous breakdown after two years of work there. In 1894, after delays due to political unrest and White's own recurring health issues, he was able to respond to the call to move and work among the Shona in Zimbabwe (then Southern Rhodesia); he gave nearly forty years in service to the people there.

Shortly after his arrival White developed the reputation of being a champion of national rights. He was especially incensed by the excesses and privileges of white colonialism, and fought against it throughout his career. His battle for land rights of Africans made him very unpopular among the settler population of Zimbabwe. This was exacerbated by his bypassing the local press and presenting the indigenous perspective in letters and articles published in Britain. Personal acts such as the purchase of three hundred bags of maize meal to give to people during the 1922 famine characterized his unselfish and giving spirit and endeared him to the Shona. As a missionary, he is perhaps best remembered for the pivotal role he played in founding and developing Waddilove Institution, one of the most important facilities for African academic, pastoral, and vocational education in the country. Several times during his career health issues forced him to return to England for treatment. He was finally diagnosed with cancer in 1931; he returned to England, where he died on August 7, 1933.

A. Scott Moreau

Bibliography. C. F. Andrews, *John White of Mashonaland.*

Whitefield, George (1714–70). Scottish evangelist and missionary to the United States. George Whitefield began preaching at the age of twenty-one. When he died at fifty-six it is estimated that he had preached more than 18,000 sermons. He was constantly on the move throughout England, Scotland, Ireland, Wales, and America. Dressed simply in a black gown, and standing on a table or hill Whitefield could project his voice clearly to crowds of 20,000 people.

Whitefield was converted through a book that Charles Wesley gave him, entitled *The Life of God in the Soul of Man.* His friendship with the Wesleys endured to the end, even though Whitefield and JOHN WESLEY had a difficult conflict over predestination and free grace. John Wesley preached the funeral sermon for Whitefield in London.

Whitefield made his first journey to America when he was only twenty-three years old. Much like the Wesleys, he did missionary work in Georgia. On the first journey to Georgia in 1737 he took 300 pounds Sterling to distribute to the poor. His frequent appearances in America caused Spurgeon to say, "Whitefield was alive. Other men seem to be only half alive but Whitefield was all life, fire, wing and force."

Though always an Anglican, Whitefield became very interdenominational. His unwavering insistence on conversion, his evangelizing across cultural boundaries, his deep concern for the poor, prisoners, and orphans are among Whitefield's contributions to missions.

DEAN S. GILLILAND

Bibliography. *George Whitefield's Journals;* J. P. Gledstone, *George Whitefield, M.A., Field Preacher;* S. C. Henry, *George Whitefield: Wayfaring Witness.*

Whitman, Leroy Frederick (1904–92). American pioneer missionary in Jordan. Born in the Congo, Jordan lived for a brief four years on Martha's Vineyard before studying in boarding school and Bible school in England. He arrived in Jerusalem in 1925 and only visited the United States two or three times in the next sixty-seven years. After brief associations with WEC and the Bible Evangelistic Mission, in 1927 he began working alone and for the rest of his life he lived frugally, often supported by sporadic gifts of Arab believers.

When he arrived on the east bank in the land of Transjordan from Jerusalem in 1926, there were almost no known evangelical believers. Through his pioneering efforts when he died in 1992 there were over forty churches and thousands of believers. In addition camps, schools, bookstores, and a seminary were being run by Jordanian believers. Not only was he instrumental in opening the barren desert kingdom to the gospel, but he gave constant encouragement and guidance to the five recognized evangelical groups now working there. God also used him in the north Palestine revival, in Lebanon, Syria, Iraq, Kuwait, and the Gulf states.

He stressed the importance of the local church and insisted that a church could function without the presence of an ordained clergy. He introduced the "magic lantern," films, Bible distribution and house meetings. He and Dora, his British wife for 59 years, founded the only evangelical relief society to deal with the repeated waves of refugees pouring into the country. People stoned him, shot at him, and abused him in different ways. Never discouraged, he spent much time in prayer. As a result of that prayer the man who tried to shoot him was converted and asked Roy to perform his wedding. Though he tried several times to retire he continued ministry in Jordan until a few days before his death on Christmas day, 1992.

GEORGE E. KELSEY

Wholism. *See* HOLISM, BIBLICAL.

Wholistic Mission. *See* HOLISTIC MISSION.

Wicca, Wiccan. A highly diversified group of worshipers of the Mother Goddess. They are followers of ideas popularized by Gerald Gardner, who, inspired by the arguments of Margaret Murray, taught that before Christianity there was an old religion that focused on issues of fertility and magical control over nature. Gardner blended selected elements of this supposed old fertility religion with the spiritualism and magic of Aleister Crowley to create a new nature-oriented faith.

Followers may refer to themselves as "witches" (depending on the group and, in some cases, only among themselves). They worship the Great Mother Goddess, sometimes identified as Diana, Isis, or Demeter, and celebrate the natural cycle of the seasons. Professing to do no evil, they claim to practice magic solely for good. They believe the effects of magic return threefold on the person who works it, including evil for those who depart from their creed. They have a deep love for nature and natural things and therefore a parallel interest in ecology, natural foods, and alternative healing practices.

While Wiccans worship in small "covens'" they may choose to associate with a larger national organization such as the Church of Circle Wicca, the Covenant of the Goddess, the Georgian Church, Feminist Wicca, or one of the Gardnerian Wiccas.

DOUGLAS J. HAYWARD

SEE ALSO Neopagan, Neopaganism.

Bibliography. G. Gardner, *Witchcraft Today;* S. Leek, *The Complete Art of Witchcraft;* M. Adler, *Drawing Down the Moon.*

Wilfrid (634–709). English pioneer church leader. Born of wealth and social position in the northern part of England (itself a backwoods to the Romanized south), he was educated as a boy in an even farther-north Celtic monastery (Lindisfarne). Wilfrid gained the earnestness, zeal, and evangelistic fervor of the Celtic tradition, but soon figured out that South and Rome were the path to prestige and power. He came to disdain the Celtic form of faith and became a life-long proponent of politically correct Latin-Roman Christianity. Presiding at age thirty over the overblown Synod of Whitby (664), which was a superficial but widely acclaimed victory of Roman over Celtic practice, he was riding high until Theodore, 32 years his senior, arrived in England with superior credentials from the pope himself, and, with a much keener insight and sympathy for the Celtic tradition. Wilfrid did many good things as both a bishop and missionary but could see no reason to compromise with Celtic practice. Theodore, who came from the Eastern Roman cultural source of most of the Celtic novelties, found many ways in which the two traditions could live together within an overt Roman structure. As a result Wilfrid and Theodore ran into conflict again and again over the next twenty years. Theodore succeeded in achieving functional unity of the two traditions employing "contextualized" insights. His work created a powerful English Christian tradition with an eventual worldwide impact. Wilfrid, for many centuries, was better known, and has been hailed as the one who was more faithful to Rome.

RALPH D. WINTER

Williams, Channing Moore (1829–1910). American pioneer missionary to China and Japan. Born in Richmond, Virginia, Williams completed his theological studies in 1855 and sailed for Shanghai, China, as a missionary under the Mission Board of the American Episcopal Church. Early in 1859 Williams and a colleague, John Liggins, were reassigned to begin mission work in Japan, which had just opened up to foreigners after two centuries of self-imposed isolation from the outside world. Williams and Liggins were the first Protestant missionaries in Japan. In 1866 Williams was made bishop of both China and Japan for the Episcopal Church. In 1874 another bishop was assigned to China and Williams continued as bishop of Japan until 1889. Williams continued to be active in missionary work in Japan until 1908, when he returned to America.

Williams was active in a variety of ministries in Japan, including evangelism (the first convert was baptized in 1866), education, and translation. He constructed the first Protestant church building in Japan, founded Rikkyo University and St. Luke's Hospital in Tokyo, and translated the Book of Common Prayer into Japanese. He was widely respected by Japanese and missionaries alike, not only for his accomplishments as a pioneer missionary but also for his pious and unpretentious manner.

HAROLD A NETLAND

Bibliography. O. Cary, *A History of Christianity in Japan;* C. W. Iglehart, *A Century of Protestant Christianity in Japan;* M. Minor, *Pioneer Missionary in Japan: Channing Moore Williams.*

Williams, John (1796–1839). English missionary to the South Pacific. John Williams was born in London and trained as a blacksmith. Aware of Captain Cook's adventures, Williams responded to a missionary challenge to the Pacific Islands. John and his wife Mary were commissioned by the LONDON MISSIONARY SOCIETY in 1816. Arriving on the island of Eimeo, they studied the Tahitian language and taught the gospel to a responsive people. At the invitation of the king, Williams sailed to Raiatea, where he built a cathedral, established a legal code, improved agricultural practices, and developed the sugarcane industry. Williams' concern for the unreached led him to form an indigenous missionary association dedicated to reaching the Pacific Islands. Accompanied by local missionaries, Williams sailed to other islands, including Rarotonga and the Somoan Islands, where the impact of the gospel again transformed the people. In assessing the work Williams said, "There is not an island of importance within two thousand miles of Tahiti to which the glad tidings of salvation have not been conveyed." After a furlough in England, Williams and a group of missionaries from Samoa and England decided to reach the people toward the west. It was on their arrival in Erromanga, New Hebrides, that Williams, the "Apostle to Polynesia," and other missionaries were martyred on November 20, 1839.

DOUGLAS McCONNELL

Bibliography. J. Gutch, *Beyond the Reefs: The Life of John Williams, Missionary.*

Willibald (700–786). English pioneer missionary in Germany. Like BONIFACE, and perhaps a relative of his, Willibald did not hail from Northumbria, but did become another Anglo-Saxon missionary resource, spending time in the Eastern Mediterranean, and then ten years at the original center of the Benedictine tradition, Monte Cassino, before being sent by the pope as a missionary bishop to Germany to carry on the splendid record of English missionaries in northern Europe. The leaders in Rome may have clearly sensed the strategic value of people with Anglo-Saxon background being missionaries to their linguistic cousins in the Germanic area. The English languages and dialects at this point in history had not yet suffered the extensive Latinization that began to occur when William the Conqueror took over England three hundred years later.

This moment of history allowed the extensive scholarly and literary tradition of the Celtic Christians to be influentially cross-pollinated by Christianized Germanic Anglo-Saxons in England and by the Germanic tribal societies on the Continent during a critically significant window of time just prior to the massive upheaval that would soon be initiated by yet another invading power. While earlier *pagan* Anglo-Saxons had invaded a settled, literate Romano-Celtic society, now, pagan Scandinavians would be invading a literate and *strongly Christian* Anglo-Saxon society—laced with outstanding scholars—a social force which in timely fashion had already contributed hugely to the survival of the faith in Europe

RALPH D. WINTER

Willibrord (658–739). English pioneer missionary in Frisia. Willibrord was a pupil of WILFRID at the monastic center Wilfrid established at Ripon, and later became one of a number of outstanding Northumbrian missionaries to the Continent, specifically following up work Wilfrid had begun in Frisia, and laying important groundwork for BONIFACE, an Anglo-Saxon scholar-missionary. Beyond Boniface, then, we have WILLIBALD, and Alcuin, other Northumbrians, and through them eventually a large contribution to bringing Northern Europe into the sway of the Latin-Roman Christian tradition.

Earlier missionaries like COLUMBAN had been ethnically Celtic, and stood for a crusading emphasis on morality and spirituality. They were ethnically and linguistically more remote than this later Anglo-Saxon group which combined both Celtic and Roman (Gregorian) missionary zeal, and, most of all, had impeccably Roman credentials to influence the people at the top, not just antagonizing them with a kind of John the Baptist preaching.

Thus, this series of sturdy Anglo-Saxon missionaries, reached their distant cousins, spread Celtic zeal and Roman order, championed the Benedictine rather than the more austere Irish monastic model, and furnished a crucial biblical and spiritual foundation for the later role of Charlemagne in the expanding Frankish kingdom and the entire Carolingian Renaissance.

RALPH D. WINTER

Willingen Conference (1952). Located in Germany, Willingen was the site of the second-to-last World Missionary Conference of the INTERNATIONAL MISSIONARY COUNCIL (IMC). One hundred ninety delegates met from June 5 to 17, 1952, to consider the theme "The Missionary Obligation of the Church" in light of the emerging realities of the postwar world.

Although missions had established beachheads worldwide, the rise of nationalism, the loss of China to communism, the resurgence of non-Christian religions, and the emergence of the WORLD COUNCIL OF CHURCHES posed new challenges. Thus, delegates sought to examine the theological foundation of mission and to reformulate mission policy.

Willingen located the source of mission not in the church, but in the nature of the Triune God. However, as a result of the emphasis on the activity of God in all of history, disagreement as to the precise relationship of the church to its mission and to the KINGDOM OF GOD characterized much of the proceedings.

Continuing in the tradition of the WHITBY CONFERENCE (1947), Willingen affirmed the concept of PARTNERSHIP in obedience, but interpreted it in such a way that unity among the churches appeared to receive higher priority than the unevangelized world.

By defining the missionary obligation of the church as the proclamation of Christ's reign on the part of every believer in every moment and every situation of human life, Willingen generated much subsequent reflection and debate about the missionary nature of the church.

KEN MUHOLLAND

Bibliography. N. Goodall, ed., *The Church under the Cross*.

Wilson, J. Christy (1891–1973). American clergyman, educator, and missionary to Iran. Born in Columbus, Nebraska, in 1891, Wilson received an M.A. degree from Princeton University in 1919, the M.Th. from Princeton Theological Seminary in 1926, and honorary D.D.'s from Emporia College and Lafayette College in 1934.

Wilson was ordained into the ministry of the Presbyterian Church in 1918 and served as an evangelistic missionary with the Presbyterian Board of Foreign Missions from 1919 to 1939 in Tabriz, Iran. From 1921 to 1923 he was chairman of the Near East Relief Committee for Persia and from 1937 to 1940 chairman of the Near East Christian Council.

Wilson returned to the United States in 1939, having accepted a position at Princeton Theological Seminary, where from 1941 to 1961 he was director of field work and associate professor of ecumenics. From 1942 to 1956 he was also the director of the Princeton Institute of Theology. He pioneered the development of field work in seminaries and was editor of the first basic text on the subject of *Ministers in Training* (1957). He also authored several books and tracts in Persian; articles and books in English, including *Apostle to Islam*, a biography of Samuel Zwemer; and the missionary column in *The Presbyterian* from 1935 to 1948.

PATRICK SOOKHDEO

Wilson, John Leighton (1809–75). American missionary to Liberia and mission executive. Born in Sumter County, South Carolina, he was educated at Union College, Schenectady, New York (1827–29), and, after a year of teaching, at Columbia Theological Seminary, South Carolina (1830–33). He was ordained by Harmony Presbytery, 1833, and he and his wife were sent by the AMERICAN BOARD OF COMMISSIONERS FOR FOREIGN MISSIONS to Cape Palmas, Liberia (1834–42). He wrote grammars, dictionaries, and translations of Scripture. One of his pamphlets published in England helped end the slave trade on the western coast of Africa. He was a missions secretary in New York City (1853–60), editor, and author of the encyclopedic *Western Africa: Its History, Condition and Prospects* (1854). Lafayette College, Pennsylvania, gave him a D.D. (1854). When the Civil War began he became the Foreign Missions Secretary of the Southern Presbyterian Church (1861–85) and, for a while, the Home Missions Secretary (1863–82). In 1876 his office was transferred from Columbia, South Carolina, to Baltimore. He died in retirement at his South Carolina home. Highly respected for his wisdom, humility, evangelistic spirit, and administrative skill, he led the Southern Presbyterians missions enterprise from their beginning in 1861 and helped give them the strong missions emphasis that marked the years of their separate existence.

ALBERT H. FREUNDT JR.

Bibliography. H. C. DuBose, *Memoirs of Rev. John Leighton Wilson, D.D., Missionary to Africa and Secretary of Foreign Missions*; J. M. Wells, *Southern Presbyterian Worthies*; H. A. White, *Southern Presbyterian Leaders*.

Wilson, Margaret Bayne (1795–1835). Scottish missionary to India. Born in Greenock, Scotland, she received a quality education and dedicated herself to teaching Sunday school and working with the Female Benevolent Society of Scotland. She became acquainted with John Wilson, a man nine years her junior, who aspired to work in India as a missionary. They were married on August 12, 1828, and left for India a few weeks later.

The Wilsons spent one year in language training and arrived in Bombay in 1829. Wilson quickly discovered that girls were considered intellectually inferior and unworthy of education. She was determined to challenge this notion and within six months of her arrival, organized six schools for girls from lower-caste families. She handled the administration of the schools, trained teachers, and wrote many textbooks. She eventually opened the first boarding school for girls in western India.

Wilson persuaded her sisters, Hay and Anna, to join her in India. She was convinced that the presence of capable females would provide beneficial role models for the Indian women. After only a few years her health began to fail and she died in Bombay. Her sisters continued her work. Inspired by her effort, the Edinburgh Association of Ladies for the Advancement of Female Education in India was formed in 1837. Wilson had succeeded in demonstrating that Indian girls could be educated and that women could contribute substantially to the mission effort.

KENNETH D. GILL

Bibliography. E. G. K. Hewat, *Christ and Western India*; D. P. Thomson, *Women of the Scottish Church*; J. Wilson, *A Memoir of Mrs. Margaret Wilson*.

Wilson, Mary Ann (Cooke) (1784–1868). English missionary educator in India. Born in England, Mary Ann Cooke had worked as a governess before going in 1820 to Calcutta under the British Foreign Schools Society. When their funds failed she was taken up by the CHURCH MISSIONARY SOCIETY (1822), and in 1823 she married a CMS missionary, Isaac Wilson. She founded and built up a school for girls, and her initiatives led to the founding, in England, of the Society for Promoting Female Education in the East (SPFEE) (1834). Widowed in 1828, she continued her work for Indian girls during and after her marriage. During a time of famine she established a female orphanage at Agarpura, north of Calcutta. She even won praise from Bishop Daniel Wilson of Calcutta, but became dissatisfied with the support she received, and after encountering the Brethren evangelist, Anthony Norris Groves, she left the Church of England in 1842. CMS continued to run the Agarpura institution.

Wilson appears to have then left India and to have taught in the Middle East, but she continued to encourage other women to set up Christian schools in India, through articles in the SPFEE's magazine. Truly a missionary pioneer, it was many years before any other woman served for any length of time, and she proved the usefulness of women's work in the Indian context.

JOCELYN MURRAY

Bibliography. M. Weitbrecht, *The Women of India and Christian Work in the Zenana;* E. Stock, *History of the Church Missionary Society: Its Environment, Its Men and Its Work,* vol. 1.

Winter, Ralph D. (1924–). American missiological thinker and missionary to Guatemala. One of the most innovative missiological thinkers of the twentieth century, Winter served from 1956 to 1966 as a Presbyterian missionary to the Mam Indians of Guatemala following the completion of his education at Cal Tech (B.S.), Columbia (M.A.), Cornell (Ph.D.), and Princeton (B.D.).

While in Guatemala, Winter was one of those instrumental in launching the THEOLOGICAL EDUCATION BY EXTENSION movement throughout Latin America. Traveling widely, he disseminated extension concepts and helped forge a continental network of extension educators. His work *Theological Education by Extension* provided historical perspective and practical guidelines for the movement.

Called to the School of World Mission of Fuller Theological Seminary, Winter taught in the areas of mission history and leadership training. In 1968, he and his wife Roberta founded the William Carey Library to publish missionary literature. In 1972, he helped establish the AMERICAN SOCIETY OF MISSIOLOGY and later the International Society of Frontier Missiology. His 1974 address to the LAUSANNE CONGRESS ON WORLD EVANGELIZATION helped awaken the global church to the presence of people groups beyond the reach of established churches and mission efforts (*see* UNREACHED PEOPLES). In 1976, he and his wife founded the United States Center for World Mission and in 1977 the William Carey International University to provide for and coordinate thinking, training, and services needed to establish Christian movements among the remaining unreached people groups.

KEN MULHOLLAND

Bibliography. R. D. Winter, ed., *Theological Education by Extension;* R. D. Winter and S. C. Hawthorne, eds., *Perspectives on the World Christian Movement,* rev. ed.

Witchcraft and Sorcery. Most of the peoples of the world assume that spiritual power can be directed toward others with the express aim of harming them. We label such concepts witchcraft and sorcery. Though technically sorcery is conscious and deliberate, while witchcraft is considered to be unconscious, the term "witchcraft" is commonly used to cover both conscious and unconscious malevolent spiritual activity done by specialists.

Shamans, diviners, and other purveyors of spiritual power are regularly sought by people who feel they have been wronged to conduct rituals designed to harm those against whom they wish to take revenge. In addition, the spirits of witches are believed to leave their bodies at night to go to other people and places to cause harm, often to the innocent.

In many societies it is assumed that illness, accident, and death are never natural occurrences. Commonly, then, it is assumed that when a person dies, becomes ill, or has an accident it is the result of witchcraft (including sorcery). It is then the task of a diviner or a "witch doctor" to ascertain who has caused the death and why. Various forms of divination and ordeal are used to identify the culprit. People often wear charms to protect themselves against witchcraft.

The fear of witchcraft is a major factor in most societies and an important concern of many churches and witch-finding organizations. Since witches are supposed to harm people unconsciously, those accused by such groups are often quite unaware of their supposed guilt.

A common form of witchcraft is the evil eye. This is the belief that some people, whether consciously or unconsciously, can direct evil power toward others, especially children, simply by looking at them. Looks plus compliments directed toward children are considered especially dangerous. Parents will, therefore, make their children less attractive to avoid drawing attention from those believed to have the evil eye.

Missionaries who ignore or summarily dismiss witchcraft and sorcery beliefs and practices often drive them underground. The practices and beliefs do not change; they are only removed from public scrutiny. Missionaries must find sensitive ways to understand and deal not only with the beliefs and practices, but with the functions such beliefs and practices serve within the societies in which they are found.

CHARLES H. KRAFT

Bibliography. D. Burnett, *Unearthly Powers;* A. C. Lehmann and J. E. Myers, *Magic, Witchcraft, and Religion: An Anthropological Study of the Supernatural;* A. S. Moreau, The World of the Spirits; P. Steyne, *Gods of Power.*

Witchdoctor. *See* SHAMAN, SHAMANISM.

Witness. A witness is one who bears testimony about a person, place, or event. While the modern term frequently is associated with seeing (e.g., an eyewitness), the underlying Hebrew and Greek terms focus more on testifying than on observing. Throughout the Bible the term is used in forensic contexts to indicate one who is able to explain what has happened due to personal experience of an event or issues related to the event being investigated. The purpose of such testimony is to establish truth so that appropriate judgment may be determined. To do so, however, two or more independent witnesses were necessary to establish accusations against the accused (Deut. 19:15). Bearing false witness against someone was forbidden (Exod. 20:16), and punishable by giving the false witness the punishment due the accused (Deut. 19:16–21).

In addition to the legal concept, a witness may authenticate accounts of an event or meaning outside of legal proceedings. Paul, for example, calls God himself as a witness of Paul's commitment to pray for the Christians in Rome (Rom. 1:9). The Spirit also bears witness with our spirit that we belong to God (Rom. 8:16).

The term also develops a nonlegal but technical sense of bearing testimony about Christ. John the Baptist bore such a testimony (John 1:7, 15). The word signifies lifestyle and verbal testimony about Christ before non-Christians in the hope of persuading them to respond to the gospel. (Acts 1:8). Jesus promised the power of the Spirit for such witness and in Acts 4:33 the apostles showed the fulfillment of Jesus' promise. In Paul's vision, Jesus encouraged Paul that he would bear witness of Christ in Rome just as he already had in Jerusalem (Acts 23:11).

Contemporary Issues. In many evangelical circles, *witnessing* refers to the act of evangelism. Typically it is used of verbal proclamation of the gospel and may be divorced from lifestyle.

Lifestyle witness (see also LIFESTYLE EVANGELISM) refers more specifically to our testimony to the truth through the concrete way we live. If detached from some type of truth proclamation (verbal, written, etc.), however, lifestyle witness will inevitably be read through the WORLDVIEW of the observer (*see also* PRESENCE EVANGELISM). In cross-cultural settings, the observers' worldviews may have little or no Christian orientation, and the lifestyle they see will be interpreted in categories that make sense to the observers rather than to the witness. While it is true that our lives bear witness for good or ill, lifestyles without corresponding sensitive and appropriate explanation to the receptor will always be read in light of the receptor's categories.

In ecumenical circles, witness refers to "the total evangelizing presence and manifestation of the church" (Bria, 1067), and is all that the church is and does. *Common witness* was popularized in ecumenical circles from the 1970s, and refers to the joint witness of the universal church in all of its efforts. It was built on the theological reflection that no single church fully manifests Christ to the world; it takes a universal effort to achieve such global witness. Particular attention in this understanding is given to cooperative efforts which display UNITY in mission, however imperfect they may be. Such efforts stand as a witness before the world of our unity in Christ and God's love for humankind. Common witness is broader than just cooperative efforts, however. It is also reflected when we live lives which honor our Christian commitments and display an accepting, ecumenical attitude toward Christians who are from different ecclesiological backgrounds.

A. SCOTT MOREAU

Bibliography. I. Bria, *DEM,* pp. 1067–69; H. D. Buckwalter, *EDBT,* pp. 765–69; F. W. Danker, *ISBE Revised,* pp. 1086–87; T. Stransky, *DEM,* pp. 197–200; A. Trites, *The New Testament Concept of Witness.*

Women in Mission. Women have a long history of responding to God's desire to use them in carrying out his purposes on earth. From Miriam, the sister of Moses (Exod. 15:20; Micah 6:4), Deborah, a judge chosen by God to rule (Judg. 45), and Huldah, a prophet carrying God's message (2 Kings 22:14–20; 2 Chron. 34:11–33) to Catherine Booth of the Salvation Army, MOTHER TERESA in her ministry to the poor of India, and ELISABETH ELLIOT, the great missionary writer, God has chosen and empowered women to do his bidding through the ages.

In Jesus' day, women traveled from town to village with Jesus and the disciples, helping support them out of their own means (Luke 8:13). They remembered Jesus' words concerning his death and resurrection and were ready for their first assignment of telling the disciples the Good News that Jesus had risen from the dead.

In the early church, women were active in the mission of the church. In Philippi, the Lord opened Lydia's heart in response to Paul's words and, after she and her household were baptized, she opened her home for believers to meet and grow in their faith (Acts 16:1415, 40). Priscilla was used by God to touch people in at least three different nations: Rome, Greece, and Asia Minor (Rom. 16:35; 2 Tim. 4:19). Priscilla's name is usually listed before her husband's in the biblical record and, since this is not common for that day, it most probably indicates her importance in the minds of the New Testament writers and her prominence in the church.

Many women were martyred for their love for Jesus in the first two centuries of Christianity. Santa Lucia of Sicily, who lived about A.D. 300, was involved in Christian charitable work. After marrying a wealthy nobleman, she was ordered to stop giving to the poor; she refused and was sent to jail. There she was persecuted and condemned to death. Melania, coming from a wealthy family in Rome with estates all around the Mediterranean, used her resources to give to the poor and build monasteries and churches for both men and women in Africa and in Jerusalem. Her missionary journeys started as she fled from Rome during the invasion by the Goths in A.D. 410. As a refugee, she and many other women played an important role in this great missionary movement. Some women were taken as hostages to northern Europe, where they later married their captors and evangelized them (Malcolm, 1982, 99–100). Clare, who lived and worked in the early thirteenth century, was a reformer where Christianity had forgotten the poor. She founded the Franciscan order of barefoot nuns in Italy (ibid., p. 104). Women who chose to remain single served God through living the cloistered life and were given the opportunity through the accepted ecclesiastical framework to proclaim the gospel.

In the Catholic tradition, priests, bishops, and nuns built churches and hospitals and founded schools and orphanages to establish the faith. Women who experienced a call to mission first had to join a celibate religious order. Catholic mothers were to have families as their primary responsibility. Not until the mid-twentieth century could lay women freely participate in official foreign missions with the full sanction of the Church. Catholic sisters were the first trained nurses in the United States. They nursed the wounded during the Revolutionary War and founded some of the first American hospitals for the poor in the early nineteenth century. Mother Mary Joseph in the 1920s founded the Maryknoll Sisters, who focused on direct evangelism, seeing themselves fully participating in the church's apostolic work. Six of the Maryknoll Sisters went to China as missionaries in 1921.

The Protestant Reformation in the sixteenth century brought about changes in the role of women in Christianity. The Reformers reemphasized that women's role is in the home and supportive of men. ARTHUR GLASSER writes: "The re-

formers also subjected women to the confining perspective that their only recognized vocation was marriage. With the dissolution of the nunneries women lost their last chance of churchly service outside the narrow circle of husband, home and children" (1979, 91). Within Protestantism the problem then arose as to whether women had the right to respond to the promptings of the Holy Spirit to proclaim the Word of God.

Ruth Tucker emphasizes that because women were restricted in serving in leadership within the institutional church, they were attracted to responding to serving God in mission work, where the limitations were less restrictive (1988, 9). This was due to the fact that mission leaders focused on reaching a lost world for Christ. Though male leadership within the church has limited how women can use their God-given gifts at home, the urgency of fulfilling the GREAT COMMISSION has required all available assistance.

In the early days of the Protestant mission advance, most women who went to the field were wives of missionaries. Many men even began looking for a wife to accompany them after they were appointed as missionaries. Women often felt a deep commitment to missions, but were required to marry before they could fulfill their own missionary calling. Discerning male missionaries recognized that contact with women in most non-Western societies was impossible. So it was that the missionary wives not only managed the home and children but developed programs to reach local women and girls. ANN JUDSON, wife of Adoniram, demonstrated how wives not only cared for the family and ran a household in a foreign country, but developed their own ministry as well. Ann ran a small school for girls, did evangelistic work with the women, was a pioneer Bible translator in two languages, and was the leading female missionary author of the early nineteenth century. Her letters and journals of their work with the Burmese inspired many in the homeland to support missions and consider missions as a vocation.

Single women were first sent to the field to care for missionaries' children and serve alongside the missionary family. Little by little as opportunities arose, single women missionaries began to supervise women's schools for nationals (Beaver, 1980, 59–86). Quietly they helped reach out to the local women who were secluded from society. In 1827, CYNTHIA FARRAR responded to a field request from India for a single woman to supervise the schools for national girls that had been started by the mission and was appointed by the American Board, the first unmarried woman sent overseas as an assistant missionary by any American agency. In 1839, ELIZA AGNEW went to Ceylon to serve as principal at an established boarding school for girls. She held that post until she retired forty years later. Many of her students became Christians. She endeared herself to her students and visited former students in their homes.

By 1837, when it became recognized by evangelical missions that female missionaries needed a more advanced level of training, Mount Holyoke Female Seminary was founded by Mary Lyon. The five basic areas of education included: (1) religious, (2) benevolence, (3) intellectual, (4) health, and (5) service. Students at the seminary were guided to develop a spirituality of self-sacrifice for the sake of the gospel and others. By 1887, Mount Holyoke had sent out 175 foreign missionaries to eighteen countries (Robert, 1996, 93–104). Soon graduates from Mount Holyoke were involved in starting similar training schools for women in many parts of the world.

The Civil War in the United States became a catalyst for change in women's role. Women were mobilized into benevolent activity on behalf of the soldiers. The death of the largest number of men in American history created an entire generation of single women. Since denominational mission boards were still dragging their feet on sending single women to the field and the supply of committed women was greater than ever, the Women's Missionary Movement was born. The first women's sending board was the Women's Union Missionary Society, an interdenominational board founded by Sarah Doremus in 1861. In quick succession, women of many denominational boards founded their own female missionary organizations.

A. B. Simpson, founder of the Christian and Missionary Alliance in 1887, held and promoted an open policy for women in ministry. He saw the issue as "one which God has already settled, not only in His Word, but in His providence, by the seal which He is placing in this very day, in every part of the world, upon the public work of consecrated Christian women" (Tucker and Leifeld, 1987, 287–88). When criticized for his views, he strongly suggested, "Let the Lord manage the women. He can do better than you, and you turn your batteries against the common enemy" (ibid, 288). This mission, along with many other Faith Missions in their zeal to reach the unreached and focus wholly on evangelism, attracted women who were usually restricted from regular theological education and ordination, but who felt strong calls to ministry and service and were willing to live in poverty and insecurity for the sake of the gospel. For the task of world evangelization, the whole church was mobilized and women were welcomed to serve as evangelists.

By 1900, over forty denominational women's societies existed, with over 3 million active women raising funds to build hospitals and schools around the world, paying the salaries of indigenous female evangelists, and sending single women as missionary doctors, teachers, and evangelists (Robert, 1996, 129). By the early decades of the twentieth century, the women's missionary movement had become the largest women's movement in the United States and women outnumbered men on the mission field by a ratio of more than two to one (Tucker, 1988, 10).

The fifty-year Jubilee of the founding of separate women's mission boards was celebrated in 1910–11. College-educated women were leading the woman's missionary movement at this time. Results of the Jubilee included the collection of over $1 million for interdenominational women's colleges in Asia, the founding of the World Day of Prayer, and the founding of the Committee on Christian Literature for Women and Children in Mission Fields (Robert, 1996, 256–71). The latter provided reading material from a Christian perspective, often in the form of magazines that encouraged indigenous Christian artists and writers. The Jubilee also spearheaded the most successful ecumenical mission publication series in American history. Of the twenty-one mission study texts produced by the Central Committee on the United Study of Foreign Missions from 1900 to 1921, fourteen were written by women and one by a married couple (ibid., 257). Summer schools of missions were offered for training leaders in the textbook material for teaching during the year. "In 1917, for example, nearly twelve thousand women and girls attended twenty-five summer schools around the country. Mission study, Bible study, pageants, and fellowship marked the summer schools" (ibid., 261).

Gradually from around 1910 to the time of the Second World War, the institutional basis of the women's missionary movement was eroding through the forced merger of women's missionary agencies into the male-dominated denominational boards. Because of reduced giving from the local churches in the 1920s and pressure within denominations, the women's missionary movement was dismantled and the male-controlled general boards took the money raised by the women (ibid., 305). Though women have since had less place of genuine influence and participation in administrative offices, board membership, and policymaking, the trend now is to include women. R. Pierce Beaver writes, "The big problem is that of personal and congregational commitment, involvement, and participation in world mission. The greatest loss consequent to the end of the distinctive, organized women's world mission movement has been the decline of missionary dynamism and zeal in the churches" (1980, 201).

Women have played an outstanding role in the modern missionary movement. Dana Robert shows that women's mission theory was holistic, with emphasis on both evangelism and meeting human needs (1996, xviii; *see* HOLISTIC MISSION). Women in mission have shown a deep commitment to and concern for women and children. Education, medical work, and struggles against foot binding, child marriage, female infanticide, and oppressive social, religious, and economic structures were commonly the focuses of their work. With their holistic approach to missions, women were committed to healing. Thus MEDICAL MISSIONS were dominated by women for many years. Women have been permitted great latitude in Christian ministry with their work ranging from EVANGELISM and CHURCH PLANTING to BIBLE TRANSLATION and teaching in seminaries. Since women were less involved in denominational activities and more focused on human need, it was easier for them to be ecumenically-minded and risk cooperation for common purposes. Women therefore often took the lead in founding ecumenical mission organizations.

MARGUERITE KRAFT

SEE ALSO Gender Roles AND Third World Women.

Bibliography. M. Adeney, *Missiology* 15 (1987): 323–37; R. P. Beaver, *American Protestant Women in World Mission: A History of the First Feminist Movement in North America*; A. Glasser, *Women and the Ministries of Christ*, pp. 88–92; K. T. Malcolm, *Women at the Crossroads: A Path Beyond Feminism and Traditionalsim*; D. L. Robert, *American Women in Mission: A Social History of Their Thought and Practice*; R. A. Tucker, *Guardians of the Great Commission: The Story of Women in Modern Missions*; R. A. Tucker and W. Liefeld, *Daughters of the Church: Women and Ministry from the New Testament Times to the Present*.

Women's Missionary Societies. *See* WOMEN IN MISSION.

World Congress on Evangelism (Berlin, 1966). An international gathering of evangelicals to promote the cause of missions, the Berlin congress had its roots in a burden BILLY GRAHAM had over the worldwide lack of clarity and agreement on evangelism. It was the decision of the staff of *Christianity Today* to celebrate their tenth anniversary by dealing with this burden. They invited 1,200 delegates from virtually all Protestant denominations in a hundred countries, as well as Roman Catholic and Jewish observers, to participate in a ten-day congress under the rubric "One Race, One Gospel, One Task." The response was positive, and delegates came from the oldest Christian church (the first-century Mar Thoma Syrian of India) and from the beginnings of the Auca church whose members a few years before had participated in the slaying of evangelical missionaries in Ecuador. With the precedent of the 1910 WORLD MISSIONARY CONFERENCE at Edinburgh, where approximately the same number (1,206) of delegates pledged to carry to comple-

tion the evangelization of the world, the Berlin Congress called the leaders of the WORLD COUNCIL OF CHURCHES to rekindle the dynamic zeal for world evangelization that had characterized Edinburgh fifty-six years previously.

Plenary sessions were devoted to reaffirming the divine authority and theological justification for world evangelization as well as exposing the internal hindrances and external obstacles standing in the way of its achievement. Serious attention was also given to reviewing how the biblical methods of evangelism could be adapted to the various situations facing churches throughout the world. Finally, "acting voluntarily, personally, and in wholesome unity, without committing their churches," the delegates pledged "to bring the Word of Salvation to the human race in this generation, by every means God has given to the mind and will of men." There were complaints that the congress failed to arrive at consensus on crucial issues such as the relation of EVANGELISM AND SOCIAL RESPONSIBILITY. But it did define clearly the biblical nature of evangelism and was later seen as an essential step in the movement of evangelicals worldwide to the launching of the LAUSANNE CONGRESS FOR WORLD EVANGELIZATION in 1974.

ARTHUR F. GLASSER

Bibliography. C. F. H. Henry and W. S. Mooneyham, eds., *One Race, One Gospel, One Task: World Congress on Evangelism, Berlin 1966*, 2 vols.; *Christianity Today* 10 (Oct. 14, 1966): 34; (Oct. 28): 67–93, 96–97; (Nov. 11): 131–39, 142–58, 177–79; (Nov. 25): 24–25, 34–36.

World Consultation on World Evangelization (Pattaya 1980). Held June 16–27 in Pattaya, Thailand, this Lausanne Committee on World Evangelization sponsored consultation gathered almost nine hundred people from around the world to consider strategic issues of reaching the unreached. Chaired by Leighton Ford and directed by DAVID HOWARD, Pattaya's primary focus was the seventeen miniconsultations included within the conference. Pattaya's five goals included: "1) to seek fresh vision and power for the task Christ has given to his church until he comes; 2) to assess the state of world evangelization, its progress and hindrances; 3) to complete an extended study program on theological and strategic issues related to world evangelization and to share the results; 4) to develop specific evangelistic strategies related to different unreached people groups; and 5) to review the mandate of the LCWE" (Scott, 1981, 60–61). While a larger statement was produced ("The Thailand Statement"), most of the consultations produced more voluminous reports, which became Lausanne Occasional Papers and were published separately. Organized to advocate a people group approach to mission strategy (*see* PEOPLES, PEOPLE GROUPS), Pattaya exhibited the lack of unanimity over the concept of "people" found within evangelicalism at that time in that the consultations were focused on religious, ideological, or socioeconomic distinctions rather than ethnolinguistic ones.

While Pattaya did have good representation of non-Western participants, the lack of women in positions of prominence was evident and a point of contention for some in attendance (see Sand). Coming within a month of the WCC-sponsored MELBOURNE CONFERENCE (1980), if nothing else Pattaya highlighted the difference between the evangelical and the ecumenical orientation to the missionary task (see Bosch). Pattaya focused on evangelizing unreached peoples, while Melbourne focused on the establishment of the KINGDOM OF GOD through acts of justice and liberation.

A. SCOTT MOREAU

Bibliography. D. J. Bosch, *Journal of Theology for Southern Africa* 36 (1981): 43–63; *How Shall They Hear? Consultation on World Evangelization Official Reference Volume: Thailand Reports;* F. A. Sand, *Missiology* 9:1 (1981) : 93–98; W. Scott, *Missiology* 9:1 (1981): 57–76.

World Council of Churches (WCC). The rise of the WCC may be seen historically through the ecumenical conferences of the twentieth century. From the WORLD MISSIONARY CONFERENCE (Edinburgh, 1910) three streams of the ECUMENICAL MOVEMENT developed. The first stream, the INTERNATIONAL MISSIONARY COUNCIL (IMC), whose roots can be traced directly to Edinburgh, was officially formed in 1921. The second stream, the Faith and Order Movement, came from the vision of cooperation generated at Edinburgh and held its first conference at Lausanne in 1927. The third stream, the Life and Work Movement, came largely as a result of the work of the World Alliance for Promoting International Friendship and held its pioneering conference in Geneva in 1925. The last two streams merged when delegates from 147 churches and denominations constituted the WCC at the AMSTERDAM ASSEMBLY in 1948. After much debate during the 1950s, the IMC was merged into the WCC at the NEW DELHI ASSEMBLY in 1961.

The WCC is composed of over 330 member churches and denominations from more than 120 countries and a broad variety of ecclesiastical traditions. More than two-thirds of those members are from the non-Western world. Since its inception the WCC has convened world assemblies at intervals of roughly seven years (*see* WORLD COUNCIL OF CHURCHES ASSEMBLIES). In addition to the assemblies, the three streams of the ecumenical movement (and more recently their related WCC program units) have held numerous conferences (*see also* WORLD COUNCIL OF CHURCHES CONFERENCES).

All member churches agree to hold to the basics of the WCC: "The World Council of Churches is a fellowship of churches which confess the Lord Jesus Christ as God and Savior according to the Scriptures and therefore seek to fulfill together their common calling to the glory of the one God—Father, Son, and Holy Spirit." This statement is not intended to be a confession of faith, but a framework of convictions that all members share.

Over the years many evangelicals, a number of whom have been active within the WCC, have raised several issues of concern. The four most significant are (1) a perceived lack of commitment to full biblical authority, (2) an undue influence of PLURALISM, as seen in the implicit UNIVERSALISM and lack of commitment to the traditional understanding of evangelism, (3) social and political biases and agendas that have tended to exclude emphasis on personal salvation, and (4) linguistic imprecision in WCC documents, allowing an unacceptably broad range of interpretation. Accordingly, evangelical opinion has been divided over cooperation with the WCC. Some people and organizations participate fully, hoping to steer it in a more biblical direction. Some organizations maintain a working relationship with the WCC but not official membership. Finally, many evangelical individuals and organizations advocate separation from the WCC altogether. Attempts have been made by both the WCC and a variety of evangelicals to find common ground, but the concerns run so deep that at present the prospect of widespread cooperation of evangelicals with the WCC remains remote.

A. SCOTT MOREAU

Bibliography. H. E. Fey, ed., *The Ecumenical Advance: A History of the Ecumenical Movement*, vol. 2; A. Johnson, *The Battle for World Evangelism;* R. Rouse and S. C. Neill, *A History of the Ecumenical Movement*, vol. 1; M. Van Elderen, *Introducing the World Council of Churches;* N. Yri, *Quest for Authority*.

World Council of Churches Assemblies. At the AMSTERDAM ASSEMBLY in 1948 the WCC came into being as a nonlegislative fellowship of churches united by their commitment to a common confession of "our Lord Jesus Christ as God and Savior." The assembly itself is the WCC's principal authority; a central committee representing the member churches proportionately meets twice annually.

The theme selected for the First Assembly was "Man's Disorder and God's Design." Since this was directly related to the mission concern of the INTERNATIONAL MISSIONARY COUNCIL (IMC), many were encouraged that the WCC agreed that evangelism must be on the constant imperative for all Christians, and that the struggle to express the unity of Christians for the sake of effective witness must continue. It unconditionally affirmed:

"All of our churches stand under the commission of our common Lord: 'Go ye into all the world and preach the gospel to every creature.'" Even so, two of Amsterdam's key perspectives aroused a measure of concern within IMC circles: (1) the older pattern of missionary activity identified with mission agencies was coming to an end; and (2) participating churches should awaken to their societal responsibilities and the ways in which lay ministries might be stimulated and augmented to this end.

The Second WCC Assembly was convened at Evanston, Illinois (1954), with the theme "Christ, the Hope of the World." The theme's eschatological implications stirred up a measure of public discussion, particularly among Jewish leaders who had earlier reacted against Amsterdam's call to the churches to engage in Jewish evangelism. The attention called to "the hope of Israel" (Rom. 9–11) provoked discord. In the end political as well as theological considerations forced the issue to be dropped. In addition, given the ferment generated at Amsterdam that the function of mission agencies should be carried out centrally by the church in mission, at Evanston the legitimacy of the IMC was inevitably questioned. Should not the IMC with its regional church councils seek merger with the WCC? As for evangelism, Evanston enlarged the call to dialogue with people of other faiths. This was regarded as more congenial to the spirit of the age than was recourse to "outdated, conversionary forms of evangelistic mission."

The Third WCC Assembly took place in New Delhi (1961) with the theme "Jesus Christ, the Light of the World." Agreeing that the IMC had become redundant, WCC leaders welcomed the petition from the IMC Accra Conference (1958) seeking merger with the WCC. This request was heralded as the only way to bring the concerns of mission and unity to the heart of the Ecumenical Movement. Evangelicals reacted with much misgiving. They contended that the witness of church history is virtually unanimous in demonstrating that church leaders invariably were so preoccupied with maintaining present structures that they rarely had the interest, energy, and time to launch frontier mission efforts. Even so, the WCC-IMC merger was enthusiastically welcomed, though it marked the beginning of the eclipse of missionary outreach in the WCC.

New Delhi should be particularly remembered for adopting a solid biblical basis to define itself: "The World Council of Churches is a fellowship of churches which confess the Lord Jesus Christ as God and Savior according to the Scriptures and therefore seek to fulfill together their common calling to the glory of the one God—Father, Son, and Holy Spirit." This promotion of the Trinity coupled with the ferment generated by the view of Jesus as "the Light of the World"

meant that henceforth the WCC would be caught up in exploring the implications of his uniqueness, especially as the ecumenical movement seemed to be entering ever more directly into the context of non-Christian religions. A hopeful addition to the growing WCC interest in the Theology of Mission was the call for a trinitarian basis that could be related to all aspects of the church's focus on mission, service, and unity. But there was a growing tendency to use "mission" to represent everything the churches were called upon to do in the world, a tendency promoted by the slogan "The Church Is Mission" (*see also* Mission and Missions). The inevitable result was further devaluation of the traditional understanding of the specific evangelistic role of missionaries and mission societies.

The Fourth Assembly at Uppsala (1968) marked the beginning of widespread evangelical disenchantment with the direction of the WCC. Although the theme was eschatological, "Behold, I Make All Things New!" this dimension was not given primary focus. Actually, preassembly documents provoked such concern among evangelicals that Donald A. McGavran raised the question, "Will Uppsala Betray the Two Billion?" He reflected the heightened sense of impatience among many evangelicals over the efforts of some WCC leaders to reconceptualize the Christian mission. The evangelicals determined to defend mission as biblically defined. Two major conferences in 1966 (the Congress on the Church's Worldwide Mission in Wheaton and the World Congress on Evangelism in Berlin) reflected their impatience and spelled out their concern. Both gatherings not only reflected the dramatic growth of evangelicals and charismatics throughout the postwar world, but produced documents marking the end of passivity regarding the WCC. Whereas they agreed that many of the concerns discussed at Uppsala were valid and worthy of serious attention, they were troubled when an undefined "Christian Presence" and interreligious dialogue, not gospel proclamation, were heralded as the means of lifting up "humanization" as the goal of mission. This imprecision of language and absence of biblical categories provoked concern as to the direction of the WCC. Its truncated call to social and political activism needed to be supplemented with the Berlin document "One Race, One Gospel, One Task" and with the biblical urgency behind Wheaton's reaffirmation of the watchword of the SVM.

The Fifth Assembly was convened at Nairobi in 1975 with the theme "Jesus Frees and Unites." The delegates had been greatly influenced by two conciliar gatherings of significance: the Geneva Conference on Church and Society (1966), which sought to define a "Christian response to the challenges of revolutionary changes in our time"; and the Commission on World Mission and Evangelism's BANGKOK CONFERENCE (1973), with its stress on celebrating salvation rather than seeking agreement on its meaning. The thesis that all peoples were already one in the cosmic Christ, thus denying any frontier between church and world—the frontier biblically crossed in mission—made mission redundant. Accordingly, WCC's emphasis on DIALOGUE with representatives of other living faiths was intensified. Although prominent evangelical leaders participated in Nairobi's discussions and their contributions were respected, Nairobi is remembered for its earnest call for the visible unity of all Christians, but provided no definition of the factors uniting them. It advanced two separate definitions of evangelism (biblical and existential), but seemed reluctant to grant Scripture the determinative role in defining the mission of God's people in the world. Nairobi divided evangelicals. Some (PETER BEYERHAUS) said that the parting of the ways had taken place with the conciliar movement. Others noted Nairobi's use of the covenant that arose from the LAUSANNE CONGRESS ON WORLD EVANGELISM (1974).

The many evangelicals who attended the Sixth WCC Assembly at Vancouver (1983) were filled with hope. This had been generated by the release in 1982 of the long-awaited "Mission and Evangelism—An Ecumenical Affirmation." Evangelical counsel had been widely sought in its preparation, and many expected it would be openly related to the assembly theme "Jesus Christ—the Life of the World." Strangely, no speaker referred to it. The focus was on the familiar issues of Christian unity, evangelism, and what was described as "world affairs in ecumenical perspective." WCC pronouncements on the Soviet invasion of Afghanistan and on Marxist oppression in Central America were so selective in their indignation that many voices in the religious and secular press were outraged. Was liberation theology still the council's reigning doctrine for church and society? Was the WCC controlled by the political and theological left? Despite these aberrations Vancouver gave evidence of vigorous evangelical currents within its worship and prayer, its biblical expositions, and trinitarian theology. The emphasis on sin as causing social alienation, was accompanied by emphasis on sin as spiritual alienation from God. During the assembly about two hundred evangelicals caucused from time to time and eventually produced a statement encouraging evangelicals worldwide to add their prayers and gifts to the process of working for the renewal of the people of God.

The Seventh WCC Assembly was convened at Canberra (1991) with a prayer as its theme: "Come, Holy Spirit—Renew the Whole Creation." This was appropriate. Many of the delegates feared that the war in the Persian Gulf would dominate discussion; others feared that the issue

of the suffering people in the Middle East would not be adequately addressed. All agreed, however, to expressing the council's concern with a peace march through Canberra followed by a prayer vigil and liturgical celebration. Only then did the assembly feel free to deal with its crowded agenda. Unfortunately, not much time was given to serious discussion of the Baptism, Eucharist and Ministry document (BEM) that had been years in preparation as well as enthusiastically heralded at Vancouver as the greatest achievement of the Faith and Order Commission. Time also prevented reviewing in detail "Mission in Christ's Way," a document from the SAN ANTONIO Conference (1989).

The Gulf war did not dominate the assembly. Rather, the convention was unexpectedly set on fire by the issue of SYNCRETISM, given prominence by Chung Hyun Hyung of Ewha Women's University in Seoul. Reflecting Korean folk culture, she developed an innovative presentation with music, dance, and symbols, invoking the spirits of the dead in such a way as to magnify the spirit world and largely ignore all biblical categories. The presentation drew both a standing ovation and severe condemnation of syncretism and paganism.

Needless to say, Canberra (1991) marked a decisive turning point in the history of the WCC and the ecumenical movement as a whole. In the years that followed, serious concern grew among orthodox churches as to whether further association would be congenial with their theological heritage. The desire of evangelicals to continue to serve began to diminish. Financial considerations forced drastic reduction in budget and staff. Questions were raised as to the future of the WCC. The adoption of the landmark document "Mission and Evangelism: An Ecumenical Affirmation" at the SALVADOR CONFERENCE (1996) demonstrated that mission, unity, and service continue to command WCC attention and response. But uncertainty surrounded prospects for future assemblies.

ARTHUR F. GLASSER

Bibliography. *A History of the Ecumenical Movement*, vol. 1, ed. R. Rouse and S. C. Neill, and vol. 2, ed. H. E. Fey; A. F. Glasser and D. A. McGavran, *Contemporary Theologies of Missions*; J. A. Scherer, *Gospel Church and Kingdom*; K. Raiser, *Ecumenism in Transition*; M. Reuver, et al., eds., *The Ecumenical Movement Tomorrow*; J. A. Scherer and S. B. Bevans, eds., *New Directions in Mission and Evangelization*, vols. 1–2.

World Council of Churches Conferences. The

usual starting point in discussions of Conferences that played a critical part in the development of the ecumenical movement is the great Edinburgh WORLD MISSIONARY CONFERENCE of 1910, which revealed how closely related were the subjects of the mission and the unity (disunity) of the church. After Edinburgh there developed two principal strands in the ecumenical movement. Life and Work conferences were held at Stockholm (1925) and Oxford (1937), while Faith and Order conferences were held at Lausanne (1927) and Edinburgh (1937). A third strand was that of the INTERNATIONAL MISSIONARY COUNCIL, which was formally constituted in 1921 and held conferences at JERUSALEM (1928), TAMBARAM (1938), WHITBY (1947), WILLINGEN (1952), and ACCRA (1958).

All three streams continued to organize conferences after the founding of the World Council of Churches in 1948, and indeed other ecumenical focuses were added. A major methodology for advancing the concerns of this worldwide body has been the convoking of conferences that have proper representation by region, confession, and status. Prepared for by well-worked-out study programs, these conferences seek to produce consensus documents.

The Faith and Order conferences have searched for unity, though not uniformity, in church life. For example, in 1952 the so-called Lund principle was accepted: the churches would seek to act together on all matters except those on which deep differences of conviction compelled them to act separately. At Louvain (1971), Accra (1974), and Bangalore (1978) the emphasis was not on analyzing past differences, but defining the hope at the center of Christian witness and discipleship. The Lima conference of 1982 addressed the relationship between the historic theologies of East and West and the newer contextual theologies of the south. It also sent to the churches the text *Baptism, Eucharist and Ministry* to find out how far they could make common affirmations in these areas. On the basis of an emerging consensus the conference also offered to the churches the "Lima liturgy," a eucharistic service for use by the churches as they wished, especially on ecumenical occasions. More recently Faith and Order conferences have been concerned with the interrelationship between ecclesiology and ethics (an attempt to bring together the old dichotomy between Faith and Order and Life and Work). The conference at Compostela in 1993 focused on koinonia as a gift and calling as a way of advancing unity.

The thrust of the conferences concerned with Inter-church Aid, Development, and Diakonia has been to eschew all forms of PATERNALISM in favor of developing genuine PARTNERSHIPS of mutual respect. Churches have also been encouraged to consider their responsibilities not simply in terms of relief, but increasingly in terms of nurturing and enabling DEVELOPMENT. The confidence of the 1960s that development was the solution to the economic problems of the TWO-THIRDS WORLD had become less certain by the 1980s. A conference at El Escorial in Spain in 1987 reinforced the need for the ecumenical sharing of resources, not simply in terms of economic wealth, but of spirituality, faith, and testimony to faithfulness in suffering.

The World Conference on Church and Society convoked in Geneva in 1966 provided the first opportunity for ecumenical leaders representing all the regions of the world to give comprehensive consideration to the social and political context of Christian witness. Because that context was in a state of dynamic flux, the subject of Christian attitudes to the ambiguities of revolution was placed on the ecumenical agenda. Following Geneva, conferences at Bucharest (1974) and the Massachusetts Institute of Technology (1979) considered the social significance of advancing scientific knowledge and technological competence, both of which were seen at that time as developments to be welcomed. There were, however, warnings that unequal access to technological power could be an instrument of injustice. Moreover, consumption of unrenewable resources, the pollution of seas and skies, and the creation of the greenhouse effect appeared to put ecology and life itself at risk. Hence the MIT theme "Faith, Science and the Future" in turn led the WCC to its emphasis upon "Justice, Peace and the Integrity of Creation." Behind this lies the belief that issues of justice, war and peace, especially in their nuclear dimension, and ecology all belong together. The interrelationship was most fully explored in the world convocation at Seoul in 1990.

JOHN H. Y. BRIGGS

Bibliography. H. E. Frey, ed., *The History of the Ecumenical Movement*, vol. 2, *The Ecumenical Advance, 1948–68;* J. H. Y. Briggs, M. A. Oduyoye, and G. Tsetsis, eds., *The History of the Ecumenical Movement*, vol. 3.

World Evangelical Fellowship (WEF). The first half of the nineteenth century saw a growing desire among evangelical Christians in Europe, North America, and elsewhere for some visible expression of unity within the body of Christ. During the 1840s several consultations were held, primarily in Great Britain, to consider how best to pursue this vision. As a result, in August 1846, eight hundred Christian leaders gathered in London and formed the Evangelical Alliance. The establishment of an organization for the purpose of expressing unity among Christians belonging to different churches was an innovation in church history. Its goal was to be worldwide in scope.

However, the worldwide vision foundered over the issue of slavery. England had abolished slavery following the noble work of evangelical statesmen such as William Wilberforce (*see* ABOLITION), so its delegates adamantly opposed admitting slaveholders to an evangelical alliance. Most North American delegates agreed. However, the social situation in the United States was such that some southern Christians still held slaves, and a few even tried to justify the practice on biblical grounds. Consequently, no consensus was reached for a worldwide fellowship. This would have to wait for another century. In the meantime evangelical alliances, loosely knit together in fellowship but with no organizational ties, were formed in many countries.

Following World War II a renewed desire for a visible expression of unity among evangelicals led again to a series of consultations both in Europe and in North America. In August 1951, leaders of the Evangelical Alliance of Great Britain and of the newly formed National Association of Evangelicals (U.S.) met with delegates from twenty-one countries near Zeist, Holland. After a week of fellowship, prayer, and careful consideration, they formed the World Evangelical Fellowship. Key leaders were Sir Arthur Smith, Roy Cattell, and A. J. Dain of the United Kingdom, and Harold J. Ockenga and J. Elwin Wright of the United States.

The purposes of the WEF were expressed in three phrases taken from Philippians 1: "fellowship in the gospel" (v. 5), "defense and confirmation of the gospel" (v. 7), and "furtherance of the gospel" (v. 12). The desire was to unite Christians around the world in true fellowship, in defending the gospel against constant attacks, and in mission outreach to those without the gospel. Following the example set since 1846 by the Evangelical Alliance of Great Britain, the WEF emphasized spiritual unity, an annual week of prayer, encouragement and help to Christians suffering persecution, and revival. A doctrinal statement was agreed upon, which has never been altered.

Gilbert Kirby of the United Kingdom, who was general secretary from 1966 to 1970, coined a phrase that expresses well the ministry of the WEF, "Spiritual Unity in Action." To implement this goal the WEF has formed various commissions composed of men and women from around the world: Theological Commission, Missions Commission, Communications Commission, Commission on Women's Concerns, Religious Liberties Commission, Youth Commission, Commission on Church Renewal, International Council for Evangelical Theological Education, and International Relief and Development Alliance. The WEF has also taken an active role in leadership training, especially in developing countries. Its Leadership Development Institute has held training sessions throughout the world.

The WEF has two types of membership. Full members are the regional and national evangelical fellowships or alliances from more than 115 countries of the world. They are composed of the local churches, denominations, and evangelical agencies in each country. Associate membership is open to denominations, mission agencies, and parachurch agencies. The WEF is governed by

the International Council, which is composed of men and women representing each region of the world and elected by the General Assembly, which is held every four to six years. Delegates to the General Assembly are elected by the full members. The International Council appoints the international director.

From its founding in 1951 all of the international directors (previously called the general secretary or general director) of the WEF were from the United Kingdom, Canada, or the United States; likewise, the international office was located in Europe or the United States. But in 1987 the WEF took a major step by moving the international headquarters to Singapore. This move helped greatly to change the mistaken image that the WEF was a Western organization. In 1992 a further significant step was taken at the General Assembly in Manila, when Augustin (Jun) Vencer of the Philippines was installed as the first non-Western international director.

In its desire for Christian unity the WEF has attempted to work closely with other international evangelical movements. When the INTERNATIONAL CONSULTATION ON WORLD EVANGELIZATION was held in Lausanne in 1974, the WEF requested that, in the interests of evangelical unity, no new international body be formed, but that the WEF by made responsible for following up the vision of that conference. Although this request was not granted, the WEF has worked closely with the Lausanne Committee for World Evangelization that grew out of the 1974 meeting (see LAUSANNE MOVEMENT). The AD 2000 and Beyond Movement and DAWN (DISCIPLING A WHOLE NATION) are both associate members of the WEF.

The WEF has set a goal that an evangelical alliance or fellowship be formed in every country of the world and linked with other such bodies through membership in the WEF. This vision, first proposed in 1846 and renewed and expanded in 1951 is stronger today than ever before, as the WEF seeks to help the church reach the world for Jesus Christ.

DAVID M. HOWARD

Bibliography. H. Fuller, *People of the Mandate;* D. M. Howard, *The Dream That Would Not Die.*

World Gospel Mission. Founded in 1919 by the National Association for the Promotion of Holiness (now the National Holiness Association) as the Missionary Bureau of the National Association for the Promotion of Holiness, WGM was developed as an interdenominational organization in the Wesleyan-Armenian tradition. The first field of service was Shantung province in northern China (1910). Today there are over 330 missionaries from more than 20 denominations serving in more than 20 fields, including Kenya (1929), India (1937), Burundi (1939), Bolivia

(1944), Japan (1952), Tanzania (1986), and Hungary (1992). Throughout its history, WGM's primary focus has been evangelism, the training of Christians through work in Bible training schools and TEE, and church planting. In addition to this, medical work and, more recently, community health and development and relief ministries have been undertaken to ensure that the needs of the whole person are being met.

A. Scott Moreau

Bibliography. W. W. Cary, *Story of the National Holiness Missionary Society;* L. Trachsel, *Kindled Fires in Africa;* idem, *Kindled Fires in Asia;* R. Warner, *EMCM,* pp. 699–700.

World Missionary Conference (Edinburgh, 1910). The World Missionary Conference held in Edinburgh in 1910 was one of those pivotal events whose significance is more clearly seen in its impact on subsequent events. It was a watershed event, building on a long series of missionary antecedents, and it stimulated a confluence of influences that greatly affected Christian expansion and ecumenicity. It was the outgrowth of earlier gatherings through which Protestants had been uniting in their purpose to give the gospel to the world (New York, 1854; Liverpool, 1860; London, 1888; and New York, 1900). Its various movements—pietism, revivalism, volunteerism—came together and were given a fresh impetus.

Edinburgh became the capstone of previous missionary conferences, but also the foundation stone of the modern Protestant ecumenical movement. Here the INTERNATIONAL MISSIONARY COUNCIL (IMC) was born, and the movement which was to give birth to the WORLD COUNCIL OF CHURCHES was initiated.

The Conference was composed of official representatives of missionary societies and denominations. Not all missionary societies were invited; only those operating among non-Christian peoples. This brought an ecclesiastical comprehensiveness to the Conference. Earlier meetings had been made up of those groups from the Evangelical Awakenings who were emphatically Protestant. Edinburgh, however, brought in the Anglo-Catholics as well.

Edinburgh was primarily a consultative assembly with a working agenda. Unlike other missionary conferences, it did not try to inform, impress, or educate the public. It aimed to analyze the Christian mission and to make plans to carry it to fruition by cooperation. The literature produced enhanced the growing field of missiology. The topics of the studies all treated the matter of Christian unity as a requirement for mission.

At Edinburgh 1910 the "younger churches" (today's Third World churches) came into their own. Nationals from several churches, seventeen in number, were given prominent participation on the program. Some were named to the Continuation Committee.

Edinburgh 1910 was the training ground for many of the future leaders of the missionary-ecumenical movement. J. R. Mott, Joseph Oldham, Charles Brent, and V. S. Azariah head a long list of outstanding churchmen, theologians, and lay leaders who continued the spirit of Edinburgh. J. R. Mott was made chairman of Edinburgh 1910's Continuation Committee.

Three movements emanated from the work of the Continuation Committee of Edinburgh 1910. First and foremost was the organization of the INTERNATIONAL MISSIONARY COUNCIL (IMC) in 1921, which continued the original purpose of Edinburgh 1910. It sponsored significant missionary conferences in Jerusalem 1928, Madras 1938, Whitby 1947, Willingen 1952, and Ghana 1958, before becoming a department of the WCC in 1961.

The other two movements were the Life and Work Movement (Stockholm 1925) and the Faith and Order Movement (Lausanne 1927). Both held second conferences in 1937. After much discussion, both Conferences approved plans for the formation of a World Council of Churches (WCC), organized in Amsterdam in 1948. The central missionary motif of Edinburgh 1910 is seen today in a myriad of evangelical missions associations and movements, such as the WORLD EVANGELICAL FELLOWSHIP, the LAUSANNE MOVEMENT, and the EVANGELICAL FELLOWSHIP OF MISSION AGENCIES.

Justice C. Anderson

See also Centenary Conference on the Protestant Missions of the World; Ecumenical Missionary Conference; Liverpool Missionary Conference; Union Missionary Convention; World Council of Churches Conferences.

Bibliography. W. R. Estep, *Baptists and Christian Unity;* N. Goodall, *The Ecumenical Movement;* R. Rouse and S. Neill, *HEM.*

World Religions. It is a remarkable fact of human history that cultures worldwide have characteristically included a religious dimension. With the emergence of the modern era, particularly in the nineteenth and twentieth centuries, significant numbers of people began to identify themselves explicitly as nonreligious or atheistic (*see* ATHEISM, SECULARIZATION, and SECULARISM); but even so the vast majority of peoples continue today to adhere to religious traditions of one kind or another. But people in various cultures have not all been religious in the same ways. As far back as recorded history takes us, our world has been characterized by diversity in religious beliefs and practices.

Categorizing Religious Traditions. In order to understand the many diverse ways in which people are religious it is helpful to group together traditions which have significant characteristics in common. In this way we come to have broad categories of traditions which are linked together under labels such as HINDUISM, BUDDHISM, ISLAM, CHRISTIANITY, and so on. It is best to think of each of these not simply as a single homogenous religious tradition but as a broad family of distinctive traditions which nevertheless share certain essential elements. Thus, Hinduism, for example, is not one clearly defined tradition but rather an enormous family of sometimes remarkably different traditions. But in spite of the great variety among Hindu traditions, there are certain commonalities which bind them together, such as recognition of the authority of the Vedas and belief in REINCARNATION.

In the modern era, with the beginnings of the disciplines of cultural ANTHROPOLOGY and COMPARATIVE RELIGION, it became common to think in terms of several major religious traditions which were identified as "world religions." It is helpful here to distinguish various kinds of religions. Terry Muck has distinguished among indigenous religions, world religions, and modern religions. *Indigenous religions* are the religions of the tribes and nations that occupied most lands before the impact of modern nationalism. Native American religious traditions and AFRICAN TRADITIONAL RELIGIONS are examples of this category.

World religions are those religions, many of which arose sometime around the fifth century B.C., which emphasize the individual's or group's standing before the gods or the transcendent, and which focus upon attainment of a better set of conditions beyond this present world. World religions are also generally those broad families of traditions which have established themselves through their acceptance by large numbers of people over a long period of time in a variety of geographical areas. Hinduism, Buddhism, Islam, and Christianity thus are clearly world religions. Somewhat more problematic are religions such as JUDAISM or SHINTO, which although clearly meeting some of the above criteria nevertheless are closely linked to a particular people (the Jews and the Japanese respectively) and thus are not widely accepted by different ethnic and cultural groups. Or we might think of world religions as those religions which have spread worldwide through deliberate and aggressive missionary endeavors. On this criterion Christianity, Buddhism, and Islam are clearly world religions but Hinduism, which traditionally has not had an aggressive missionary agenda, might not be. Generally, however, world religions do make at least implicit claims to universal validity, so that Buddhism, for example, does not regard itself as simply one religious perspective among others but holds that in a significant sense it is "privileged" or normative in its understanding of the human

predicament and the path to liberation from this predicament.

Finally, there are the *modern religions,* or those religions which emerged in times of particular social and intellectual upheaval during the past several centuries. BAHA'I, Theosophy, Christian Science, the NEW AGE MOVEMENT, and the many NEW RELIGIOUS MOVEMENTS are examples of such modern religions. Although many of these movements and traditions are having a significant impact upon people worldwide, they have not yet established themselves in the above sense as genuinely world religions. The one modern religion which is perhaps closest to being recognized as a world religion is Mormonism (*see* MORMONS).

There are other ways in which religions can be classified as well. We might distinguish between those religions which include belief in an eternal sovereign Creator who has created everything else that exists (Judaism, Christianity, and Islam) and those which do not (Buddhism); or between those which base their religious claims upon the authority of a divine revelation (Islam, Christianity) and those which do not (Buddhism). Another useful distinction is that between "high religion" and FOLK RELIGION. High or formal religion refers to the religious beliefs, practices, and institutions of the "orthodox" tradition, the religious elite or intellectuals, the authority figures within the particular religion. Folk religion, by contrast, refers to the set of beliefs, practices, and values of the common people, most of whom have little knowledge of the specialized doctrines and history of their own traditions. On the folk level one often encounters practices and beliefs which are inconsistent with the official teachings of the formal religion, but which have become widely accepted on the popular level. Folk religious practices are often highly syncretistic, combining elements from several distinct religious traditions (*see* SYNCRETISM).

Finally, mention must be made of the problem of definition in studying religion (*see* RELIGION). It has been notoriously difficult to provide a single definition of religion which adequately encompasses all of the relevant phenomena. Sometimes it is difficult to know just what is religious and what is not. SECULAR HUMANISM and MARXISM, for example, share many features of the world religions although they are explicitly atheistic and claim not to be religious. But belief in God by itself cannot be a criterion for being religious since some major traditions in Buddhism, Hinduism, and JAINISM are also atheistic. Nevertheless, secular humanism and Marxism are generally not included among the religions.

The Study of World Religions. Given the intimate relationship between religion and culture, if we are to understand the various peoples and cultures of the world we must have some grasp of major religions such as Hinduism, Buddhism,

Jainism, Islam, Shinto, and Judaism. The student today has unprecedented access to the basic tools for the study of religions. The past century has seen the development of several distinct disciplines—such as the PHENOMENOLOGY OF RELIGION, ANTHROPOLOGY OF RELIGION, COMPARATIVE RELIGION, SOCIOLOGY OF RELIGION, and PHILOSOPHY OF RELIGION—which can be very helpful in understanding other religions. Most of the sacred scriptures of the major religions are available in European languages. Most universities have departments which offer programs of study focusing upon one or more of the religions.

It is tempting for Christians studying other religions to concentrate solely upon the doctrines or beliefs of the religions. While this clearly is a significant element, it is by no means the only aspect of religion. A more adequate understanding of the nature of religion and its impact upon culture and individuals is obtained by considering religion as a multidimensional set of phenomena. Ninian Smart, for example, has suggested seven distinct dimensions for understanding religion. First is the *ritual dimension,* which includes the many rites, ceremonies, and institutions which are used in a carefully prescribed manner by the believers. Religious services, prayers, sacrifices, and baptisms can be examples of this dimension. The *experiential dimension* refers to that aspect of the religious tradition in which the believer actively participates in the various rites and appropriates for oneself the relationship with the divine or transcendent. The *narrative dimension* includes the prominent place that sacred stories and narratives play within a tradition. The *doctrinal or philosophical dimension* involves the attempts by intellectuals within a tradition to clarify, integrate, and systematize central beliefs of that tradition. The *ethical dimension* addresses the moral values and precepts which are to guide the religious community in its relationship with the transcendent realm, while the social or *institutional dimension* goes beyond the ethical to include the broader expectations which guide social relationships as well as the structures and institutions for the community. The social or institutional dimension tends to express itself in certain visible forms in the *material dimension,* as for example, in certain buildings (temples, mosques, churches) works of art, and icons.

A Theology of Religion. The Christian missionary of course should not be content merely with studying and understanding other religions on a phenomenological level. It is essential that one have an adequate THEOLOGY OF RELIGIONS which is shaped by the teachings of Scripture. While elements of truth and value in other traditions can be affirmed, a biblical perspective will also insist that God's special revelation of himself is not available equally through all religions but is to be found exclusively in the Old and New Testaments. Furthermore, Scripture does not allow for the perspective that the major religions are all equally legitimate alternative paths to God but rather insists that there is only one sovereign God and that all persons are to repent and come into a saving relationship with God through Jesus Christ alone (*see* RELIGIOUS PLURALISM and UNIQUENESS OF CHRIST). In faithful obedience to their Lord, Christians are to share the gospel of salvation through Christ with devout adherents of other religions.

It is significant that in spite of centuries of missionary effort, with a few notable exceptions, the Christian church has experienced little growth in cultures dominated by Islam, Hinduism, or Buddhism. Peoples shaped by the WORLDVIEWS of these three religions have proven to be remarkable resistant to the gospel. Perhaps part of what is needed in the coming decades is a much more serious engagement with the sophisticated worldviews underlying these religious traditions and more creative ways of expressing the gospel in these very challenging contexts.

HAROLD A. NETLAND

SEE ALSO Religious Typologies.

Bibliography. T. Muck, *The Mysterious Beyond: A Basic Guide to Studying Religion;* S. Neill, *Christian Faith and Other Faiths;* D. Noss and J. Noss, *A History of the World's Religions,* 9th ed., N. Smart, *The World's Religions;* idem, *Worldviews: Crosscultural Explorations of Human Beliefs,* 2nd ed.

World's Parliaments of Religions (1883 and 1993). The World's Parliament of Religions convened in Chicago, Illinois, in September 1893. A century later, August 28–September 5, 1993, the Parliament of the World's Religions met in the same city. Some 400 delegates attended the 1893 gathering. The 1993 meeting was not based on official delegates. It attracted an estimated 7,000 participants.

The major difference between the two parliaments was not simply in the number who attended. It was in the number of different religious faiths represented. At the 1993 parliament, Native Americans received the most enthusiastic response of any group at the opening ceremony. They were not invited in 1893. Likewise, the Baha'is were not represented in 1893. Islam had one representative in 1893, Mohammed Webb, a former U.S. ambassador to the Philippines who had been a Presbyterian before he converted to Islam. No Sikhs were at the 1893 parliament. Wiccans were highly visible in 1993, but not in 1893. Two hundred representatives of pagan groups attended. The 1993 gathering showed that religious pluralism is now a major factor of life in the United States, compared to 1893.

Also absent in 1893 were the Anglicans, who disapproved of the parliament because "the

Christian religion is the one religion." However, if this was not an issue for the Anglicans who participated in 1993, it was for a number of evangelical church leaders, theologians, and scholars, who refused parliament invitations to give papers. In 1893, Chicago evangelist DWIGHT L. MOODY strongly protested the parliament, but in 1993 public protests were limited to a number of fringe groups.

The 1993 parliament was not sponsored by any interfaith organization, but was a grassroots movement led by a dozen Chicago Bahai's, Buddhists, Hindus, and Zoroastrians. They were later joined by influential Roman Catholics and Protestants. The parliament's purpose was to promote religious understanding and cooperation, and to develop interfaith groups and programs for the twenty-first century. The program was built around sixteen plenary meetings and 750 seminars, led by speakers from all major and minor world religions—125 groups and organizations. However, David Ramage, chair of the parliament, said he was disappointed that both liberal and evangelical Protestants ignored it. The Orthodox came and left, as did the Jews.

JIM REAPSOME

Bibliography. A. Neely, *IBMR* 18:2 (1994): 60–64; H. M. Goodpasture, *Missiology* 21:4 (1993): 403–411.

Worldview. In popular usage the expression "worldview" often refers to nothing more than a particular point of view, a way of looking at something. But a worldview represents much more; it represents a whole constellation of assumptions and beliefs about what is real, how things fit together, and how things happen. Before considering a definition, however, it is useful to recognize two traditions in our understanding of worldview: the philosophical/theological and the cultural/societal.

The expression "worldview" (from *Weltanschauung*) has its origins in eighteenth-century German philosophy in the sense of ideology or system of thought, and this is the sense in which contemporary theologians use it. For most evangelical theologians a worldview constitutes a systematic approach to theology. Their focus is on the fundamental beliefs about the nature of God as Creator and Redeemer and the nature of humanity in its fallen state in need of a redeemer. They regard the Christian (biblical) worldview as in opposition to such ideologies as empiricism, humanism, naturalism, positivism, scientism, and secularism, as well as world religions such as Buddhism, Hinduism, and Islam. The religions of technologically primitive societies are often regarded collectively under labels such as ANIMISM or PRIMAL RELIGIONS.

In contrast, those who study the world's cultures use worldview to refer to how the peoples of different cultures conceive of the world, how they categorize the things in the world and structure their knowledge, and how they interpret life experience so as to live fulfilling lives.

No one cultural group can claim to have the correct worldview; rather, each group's worldview stands on its own. Consequently, we can only speak of particular worldviews such as those of the Amish, Navaho, Sioux, or Maasai societies.

A definition that satisfies both of these approaches is that of Nash (1992): "A worldview, then, is a conceptual scheme by which we consciously or unconsciously place or fit everything we believe and by which we interpret and judge reality." Nevertheless, the philosophical/theological and cultural/societal traditions differ substantially in what they include in the concept of worldview and in how they apply it.

Worldview as a Corrective Concept. Those who adopt theological approaches begin with a single, unifying principle which structures the rest of the worldview. Nash (1992) reduces the principle to a single statement: "Human beings and the universe in which they reside are the creation of the God who has revealed himself in [the Christian] Scripture." Working out a single principle, however, results in a "whole range of systematic theology" (Holmes).

Evangelical theologians generally present the Christian worldview as a systematic theology for the defense of the Christian faith or as an instrument to confront and dismantle opposing worldviews. In so doing they use philosophical and logical argumentation, and their approach is more corrective than interpretive. Those who adopt such an approach regard the CONTEXTUALIZATION of the gospel as a method for discovering the weaknesses of opposing worldviews and convincing their proponents of the superiority of the Christian faith.

Worldview as an Interpretive Concept. On the other hand, many evangelical Christian missionaries who adopt cultural approaches begin with both the Bible and the language and culture of the people they wish to reach. Because a command of the language is the key to understanding a worldview, they learn the language, how the people use the language to categorize the things they regard as important, and how they use it to interpret their life experiences. Thus their approach is more interpretive than corrective. They regard the contextualization of the gospel as an expression of the Christian faith through culturally appropriate concepts which are compatible with biblical truth. Accordingly, they speak of societal worldviews which have a Christian basis: thus American Christian, Navaho Christian, Maasai Christian or Zulu Christian worldviews. When, however, such Christian societal worldviews express biblical truth with categories which are unusual in comparison to those of the

European languages, Western theologians often suspect that those categories represent a fusion of Christian and heathen concepts (*see* SYN-CRETISM).

Overview of Worldview. A worldview may be thought of as having four integrated components: words, categories, patterned life experiences (i.e., schemas), and themes. Each of these contributes to the distinctiveness of a worldview and to how that worldview governs people as they live out their lives.

People generally do not think about their worldview; in fact most assume that peoples of other cultures think and reason in much the same way (*see* ETHNOCENTRISM). However, when they encounter another worldview with different assumptions and values they become aware of worldview differences.

To illustrate how a worldview integrates various concepts, we will consider some aspects of the worldview of the Selepet people of Papua New Guinea, a worldview which is radically different from those of Western societies, but which is typical of Melanesian societies. The Selepet people use the word *tosa* for a wide range of behavior. If a person steals someone's chicken, she or he acquires a tosa, which may be translated as "sin." To become free of the *tosa* requires that she or he give something of equivalent value to the chicken's owner. This item is known as a *matnge* and serves as restitution. A person may also acquire a *tosa* by destroying another person's property or physically abusing a person. The offender may remove the *tosa* with a *matnge* which serves as compensation. Or the offended party may exact their own *matnge* by an act of vengeance or by a demand for retributive punishment. To borrow something also incurs a *tosa*, and the repayment serves as the *matnge*. Finally, the acceptance of a gift incurs a *tosa*, which is best translated as "obligation," because one is obliged to remove the *tosa* by giving a *matnge* in the form of a comparable gift. What unifies all these examples is a dominant Selepet worldview theme that people have to maintain balance and harmony in their interpersonal relationships. Every *tosa* creates an imbalance which has to be rectified by a *matnge*.

Rather than focusing on the typical Western Christian concept of sin as falling short of God's standard or breaking God's law, this typically Melanesian worldview theme supports an equally Christian concept of sin as any action which disrupts a harmonious relationship. Adam and Eve's fundamental sin was to break their relationship with God by transferring their allegiance to Satan; disobedience was the outcome of that change. Therefore, one could regard the Melanesian Christian concept of sin as the more basic of the two.

If Melanesian Christians were to use their concept of sin to evaluate contemporary American culture, they would regard the development of the social security system and individual retirement accounts as fundamentally unchristian remedies for the elderly having to face retirement without family support. Moreover, they would strongly condemn the removal of the elderly from the family to nursing homes.

Many Western theologies emphasize that salvation is attained through repentance and faith (Acts 20:21) and maintained by an ongoing faith (Acts 13:43; Phil. 2:12). In many Melanesian worldviews, however, the concept of repentance is minimized. Rather, the process of salvation is seen to involve the giving of one's allegiance (John 1:12 NEB) which leads to reconciliation (Rom. 5:10; Col. 1:20) and adoption (Eph. 1:5), and is maintained by harmonious relationships (Eph. 4:30; Heb. 12:14). It is important to recognize that the Melanesian concept of sin and salvation can be consistent with biblical truth. Giving their allegiance to God results in their being adopted and entails that they stop doing those things which would harm that relationship. Thus, they repent even though they do not acknowledge it as such.

Worldview and Morality. The categories which a society creates are relevant to questions of morality. For example, Americans buy matches and regard them as personal property. Anyone who takes another person's matches is guilty of petty theft. However, in some technologically primitive societies fire belongs to everyone, just like water and air. So members of those societies may feel free to help themselves to an American's matches. Just because technology has captured fire, placed it on the end of a stick, and made it available for marketing does not remove matches from their category of things which belong to everyone, things not subject to being stolen. Rather, anyone who claims exclusive rights by withholding such a basic human resource as fire is regarded as morally deviant and exhibiting unchristian behavior.

In conclusion, it is important to recognize that the worldviews of different cultural groups need not be regarded as in opposition to a Christian worldview; rather they can become vehicles to express biblical truth just as did the classical Hebrew and Greek worldviews.

KEN A. MCELHANON

Bibliography. D. J. Hesselgrave, *Communicating Christ Cross-culturally: An Introduction to Missionary Communication.* 2nd rev. ed.; P. G. Hiebert, *Anthropological Insights for Missionaries;* A. F. Holmes, *Contours of a World View;* C. H. Kraft, *Anthropology for Christian Witness;* R. H. Nash, *Worldviews in Conflict: Choosing Christianity in a World of Ideas;* J. W. Sire, *The Universe Next Door.*

Worldwide Evangelization Crusade. *See* WEC INTERNATIONAL.

Worship. Today as throughout history, worship and mission are linked inextricably together, for God propels his mission through the drawing of worshipers to himself. God's call to worship him empowers us to respond with his passion to do mission. Thus, worship ignites mission; it is God's divine call-and-response strategy.

Indeed, the Scriptures resound with his global call to worship via mission. The prophet Isaiah, for example, responding in the midst of worship, takes up the call to go (Isa. 6:1–8). Likewise, the Samaritan woman encounters Jesus Christ, the incarnate God. He discloses that the Father is seeking authentic worshipers, people in relationship with him. The woman responds by immediately calling others to come see the man who told her everything she had done (John 4:26). Finally, the greatest call-and-response pattern surfaces when the disciples meet with the resurrected Jesus just before his ascension (Matt. 28:16ff.). Finally recognizing Jesus' true identity, they fall down and worship him. In the context of worship, Jesus gives his crowning imperative, the GREAT COMMISSION (Matt. 28:17–20). The missionary mandate flows out of an intimate relationship with God generated in worship. God's propelling call to go into all the world becomes our response of commitment and allegiance to him. We join him in his passion to call worshipers to himself.

Wherever we have seen meaningful, authentic worship, the church has experienced a new missions thrust. Yet, a radical separation of worship from mission has dominated mission methodologies. DONALD MACGAVRAN once claimed, "Worship . . . is good; but worship is worship. It is not evangelism" (1965, 455). The typical practice has been to call people to a saving faith in Jesus Christ with worship being a resultant by-product. While ignoring God's primary call to worship, missiologists have, however, recognized the need for relevant Christian worship to nurture a Christian movement. Thus, the model of "evangelism-before-worship" has dominated evangelical mission strategies.

Yet God's call to worship him is currently sweeping around the world in great, new revolutionary ways. Along with new openness to new forms and patterns of worship, there is greater recognition of the intimate relationship between worship and mission. Such winds of worship empowering mission have been building over the past few decades in relation to renewal movements. In 1939, for example, the Methodist Episcopal Church published a small manual, *A Book of Worship for Village Churches*, for the "great army of Christian pastors, teachers, and laymen who are leading the toiling villagers of India through worship to the feet of Christ" (Ziegler, 1939, 7). The manual resulted from a desire to see the church in India take root in its own soil in tandem with the vast treasures of two thousand years of Christian heritage. Research revealed that where dynamic worship was practiced, changed lives and growing churches resulted. On the other hand, weak, stagnant and ineffective churches existed where worship of God in Christ was neglected (ibid., 5).

More recently, as renewal movements grow in their experience with God, God calls them into mission. The common strategic link of each of these groups is their focus on worship with evangelism as the inclusive by-product: the "worship-propels-mission" model. French Benedictine monks, for example, have entered Senegal with the goal of creating a model of contextualized worship drawn from cultural musical traditions. They have adapted African drums and the twenty-one-string Kora harp to attract Muslims to Christ. Likewise, the Taizé Movement from France is growing through the development of contemplative, worship forms. Facilitated by the burgeoning impact of electronic media and new musical forms worldwide, the growth of a Worship and Praise Movement, originating from such streams as the Jesus People Movement through Marantha! Music and the Vineyard Movement, is forging an openness to new, global worship forms.

Among the most exciting developments are the new mission forces from Asia, Africa, and Latin America. Their distinctive approaches commonly revolve around worship. In Kenya, one of the most dynamic examples of church growth is found at the Nairobi Chapel. The Chapel bases much of its strategy on the development of meaningful worship (especially music) for effectively communicating the gospel to a predominantly university-student based church (Long). The vision does not stop with Kenya; they are reaching out to neighboring Tanzania. In West Africa, Senufo Christians of Cote d'Ivoire are reaching out to their neighbors through their distinctive worship form—song, dance, and drama (King). Christian Inca Indians from Peru are reaching out to Native Americans of North America. Through their deeper understanding of more culturally relevant worship forms, Inca Christians are preaching through the use of Indian storytelling styles. Asians are going to other Asians; Koreans to the Philippines and American Filipinos to Japan. In one case, Taiwans' Hosanna Ministries partnered with the Korean Tyrannus Team in initiating a series of Worship and Praise activities in 1989. This partnership brought forth a movement of renewal in Taiwan where unbelievers came to Christ and believers dedicated themselves to missions (Wong). They discovered "an intimate relationship between worship and mission" (1993, 3). Worship propelled both evangelism and commitment to do more mission.

With the growing surge of worship empowering mission, we must keep five factors in mind in order to achieve a lasting impact for the kingdom. First, worship must remain worship: we must, above all, seek encounter with God. Worship services should not serve as functional substitutes for evangelism. Rather, we must seek authenticity of interaction with God and developing relationship with him. Genuine worship of the Creator will attract and confront those who long to enter into the kingdom. Likewise, evangelistic programs must pursue evangelism. The two, worship and mission, must remain distinct, yet work hand-in-hand.

Second, we must allow God to transform and make anew his original creation. Contextualization of the gospel is not an option, but an imperative. Throughout the Scriptures and history, we see people worshiping God in ways that were formerly heathen but then transformed with radically new meaning. Service order, length, language, symbolism, prayer forms, songs, dance, bowing, speeches, Scripture reading, and artifacts must be captured to nurture believers and bring the peoples of the world into relationship with the living God.

Third, we are to pursue diversity within the unity of the body of Christ (Eph. 2; 1 Cor. 12): "Diversity (of worship forms) seems to coincide with the periods of effective mission efforts" (Muench, 1981, 104). Foundational mission goals must seek to make Christ understood and known within their own context. The Celtic church, for example, known as a strong mission church, encouraged each tribal group to develop its own worship service pattern. Likewise, worship patterns and forms must vary according to the cultural contexts—including multicultural settings. In order to know God intimately, peoples from differing contexts require the freedom to interact with him through relevant worship forms.

Fourth, there is a great need for research toward developing appropriate worship. We must allow dynamic worship to grow and change as relationship with God deepens. Worship forms are shaped by and reflect our relationship with God via appropriate, expressive cultural forms. There is great need for openness in pursuing, experimenting, exchanging, and documenting experiences in worship. Needed topics of research should include biblical models of worship that seek precedents for adapting cultural forms, comparative philosophical thought forms, historical models of worship from the Christian movement, uses and meaning of ritual (anthropology), verbal and non-verbal symbols (communication), and comparative cultural worship patterns.

Finally, we must train for worship and worship leading. In keeping with "spirit and truth" worship (John 4:23), missionaries must first of all be worshipers of the living God. Then they are empowered to take up God's passionate call to bring all peoples to worship him. Besides studying the nature of worship and the numerous patterns and forms that worship can embody, we must train people to lead worship and stimulate meaningful worship cross-culturally. Training for worship must become a major component in the formation of missionaries.

Authentic Christian worship brings people to encounter Jesus Christ. As one looks to God, God reveals his vision to us. We respond to his call. Thus, worship propels and empowers mission. Ultimately, God calls us to participate in achieving God's vision as entoned by the Psalmist: "All the nations you have made will come and worship before you, O Lord; they will bring glory to your name" (Ps. 86:9).

ROBERTA R. KING

Bibliography. P. B. Brown *In and For the World: Bringing the Contemporary Into Christian Worship;* J. G. Davies, *Worship and Mission;* R. R. King, *Pathways in Christian Music Communication: The Case of the Senufo of Cote d'Ivoire;* K. W. Long, *Worship and Church Growth: A Single Case Study of Nairobi Chapel;* S. Morgenthaler, *Worship Evangelism: Inviting Unbelievers into the Presence of God;* P. E. Muench, "Worship and Mission: A Review of Literature" M.A. Thesis, Fuller Theological Seminary; J. Piper, *Let the Nations Be Glad;* A. L. C. Wong, *The Dynamics of Worship and Praise in God's Mission in Taiwan;* E. K. Ziegler, *A Book of Worship for Village Churches.*

Wrath of God. The word "wrath" occurs in over two hundred places in the Bible and the concept is implied in many more. The overwhelming majority of these refer the attitude, activity, or response of God to human SIN. Wrath is the continuing reaction of the holy, pure, sovereign, personal God to anything which offends his moral nature and kingly rights. This includes rejection by the offender of his person, rule, will, and affronts to his holy being, whether it be conscious and direct or subconscious and indirect.

In Scripture God's wrath may be the threat of coming punishment and doom or of present or future judgment. In the absolute sense it is a synonym for eternal separation from God and punishment in HELL. Divine wrath may be directed toward a group or an individual. Those who do not acknowledge God, the HEATHEN, are under the wrath of God and will feel its full fury. God's people who turn away from him or refuse to live according to his will and law are also objects of his wrath. This is the primary way the term is used of Israel in the Old Testament. In the case of God's people there is the call to repent so that wrath may be averted and restitution offered, when the time of punishment is completed. The Old Testament also stresses that God is "merciful and gracious, slow to anger and abounding in steadfast love and faithfulness" (Ps. 86:15; 103:8; 145:8).

The precise phrase "wrath of God" appears only in the New Testament. Because the righteous visitation of wrath is a prerogative of divine sovereignty, God's people are not to avenge themselves (Rom. 12:19). Other references to the "wrath of God" fall into a number of categories. (1) It is the lot of those who reject Jesus Christ and refuse to obey God's will revealed in him. In John 3:36 the wrath of God is the opposite of having eternal life through believing in the Son and rests on those who do not obey the Son. Paul says wrath is being revealed against "all ungodliness and wickedness of men who . . . suppress the truth" (Rom. 1:18). He also insists that it comes "upon the sons of disobedience" who live immoral, frivolous, materialistic, idolatrous, ungodly lives (Eph. 5:6; Col. 3:6). (2) It is from wrath that we are saved in Christ. As Paul affirms, we are "justified by his blood, saved by him from the wrath of God" (Rom. 5:9). (3) The outpouring of the wrath of God is a central focus of the visions of judgment in Revelation (14:9; 15:1; 16:1; 19:15) and people seek refuge from it (6:16).

The Greek word *hilastērion*, translated "propitiation" in such passages as Romans 3:25 in the KJV and NASB, has a direct relation to "wrath." It refers to the sacrifice offered to appease the wrath of an offended deity. Either because propitiation is a word unfamiliar to moderns or because of a desire to dissociate the Judeo-Christian God with the vengeful, often irrational wrath of deities in pagan religions, most twentieth-century translations use some other rendering, such as "expiation" or "sacrifice of atonement." God is certainly not a vengeful, capricious being but wrath is his proper, just response to sin. However *hilastērion* and related terms are handled, one must not lose sight of the fact that Paul asserts that through the blood of Jesus God's wrath (note the occurrence of the term in the preceding context; Rom. 1:18; 2:5, 8; 3:5) is real but turned aside by God's grace received by faith.

The fact of God's wrath has often been a motivation for evangelism and mission. The threat of and warning against it is a frequent, legitimate part of the Christian message aimed at winning converts. It is also one of the appropriate stimuli for Christian behavior. It is, however, dangerous to sensationalize, dramatize, or overly emphasize wrath for it is only a part of God's nature. The prophet Habakkuk sought a balance when he cried, "In wrath remember mercy" (3:2).

JONATHAN EDWARD's sermon, "Sinners in the Hands of an Angry God," is sometimes cited as an example of extreme scare tactics. Edwards' concern was to show that although sinners do stand in danger of God's wrath, they are in the hands of one who is also compassionate, merciful, and loving to the repentant.

The heart of the Christian message is that God, against whom sin has been committed, rightly responds in wrath. His justice demands proper punishment for wrongdoers. However, God in love, mercy, and grace has, in Christ, acted to both satisfy his justice (Rom. 3:26) and to make forgiveness and salvation available in Christ. This is the balanced and correct impetus and message of the missionary enterprise.

J. JULIUS SCOTT. JR.

SEE ALSO Annihilation AND Judgment.

Bibliography. L. L. Morris, *The Apostolic Preaching of the Cross*; R. V. G. Tasker, *The Biblical Doctrine of the Wrath of God*; G. Van Groningen, *EDBT*, pp. 845–46.

Wycliffe Bible Translators, International.

Founded in 1934 by L. L. Legters and WILLIAM CAMERON TOWNSEND, Wycliffe Bible Translators (WBT) is a multinational organization dedicated to enabling all of the world's people to discover that God speaks their language. The founders envisioned making God's Word available through vernacular translations. WBT teams from over twenty nations have provided Scripture in over twelve hundred languages in seventy different nations.

Maintaining the founder's vision in the face of present-day sociopolitical and economic constraints has required new directions and strategies. Of central focus is the shift from serving as primary, pioneer translators to training national translators and consulting. Accordingly, the term "international" has been added to the organization's name (WBTI). Nationals trained in translation principles can build on their own linguistic and cultural heritage. Working in combination with consultants who have expertise in the source text enables them to provide Scripture for their own people. In partnership with missions, churches, and national entities, WBTI is continuing to adjust its training programs at all levels to meet field needs and to expand literacy and community-development projects. This has resulted in establishing national Bible translation organizations as well as mobilizing national churches to support and encourage translators. Once available, translations are used for evangelism and church growth.

To bring God's Word into the more than two thousand minority languages still in need of Scripture, Wycliffe, in conjunction with the Summer Institute of Linguistics (SIL), presently maintains training programs around the world. In cooperation with the Bible societies, missions and churches, increasing numbers of Wycliffe personnel are being assigned to work primarily in the areas of training and consultation. They assist missions and other translation organizations by providing a wealth of resources such as the *Ethnologue* (detailed linguistic, sociocultural, and spiritual data on each of the recorded languages of the world), *The Translator's Workplace* (a CD-ROM containing various translation materials and aids—journal articles, the biblical texts in Hebrew and Greek, and translations in twenty primary languages), *Lingua Links* (a computer database for anthropological, linguistic, and literacy research), and a plethora of technical, semitechnical, and popular books and articles. The development of aids for national translators is an increasing priority, as is partnership with colleges and seminaries that can help consultants to gain expertise in the source languages and biblical background. So while the founders' vision remains, the methods and means of realizing that vision have changed dramatically. WBTI continues to seek creative partnerships within the framework of their mission statement—communicating God's Word in "other words."

R. DANIEL SHAW

Bibliography. W. C. Townsend and R. S. Pittman, *Remember All the Way.*

Wynfrith of Crediton. *See* BONIFACE.

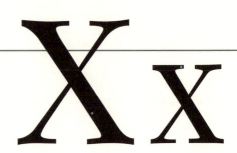

Xavier, Francis (1506–52). Spanish pioneer missionary in India and Japan. Born in a noble family of northern Spain, Xavier studied philosophy and theology in Paris, where he came under the influence of Ignatius Loyola and became a co-founder of the Society of Jesus in 1534. As the Society was approved by Pope Paul III in 1540, Xavier, a papal nuncio in the East and protected by the Portuguese king, embarked for Goa, India. His work in the Portuguese Indies (1542–49) resulted in establishing the mission apparatus and baptizing the natives up to an estimated 30,000 in Southern India. Through an encounter with a Japanese called Anjiro in Malacca, he fostered a vision for Japan and landed there in 1549. Two years of activity among "the best people yet discovered" marked a decisive entry of Christianity and counted 2,000 Christians. After returning briefly to India, he tried to enter China but died of fever on Sancian Island, off the Chinese coast.

Xavier pioneered modern missionary methods by advocating the study of the indigenous religions, customs, and languages, the use of educated national collaborators, and continuing pastoral care.

TADATAKA MARUYAMA

Bibliography. H. J. Coleridge, ed., *The Life and Letters of St. Francis Xavier*; L. Da Silva, *St. Francis Xavier: Apostle of the Indies*.

Xavier, Jerome (1549–1617). Spanish Catholic missionary to India. Born in Spain, he entered the Society of Jesus in 1568, and at that time adopted the name of his famous great-uncle, FRANCIS XAVIER. He arrived in India in 1581, serving first as rector of the college at Bassein and from 1586 at the college of Cochin.

Although initially Muslim, the Mogul emperor Akbar became disillusioned with Islam and adopted a tolerant and syncretistic approach to religions. He invited Jesuit missionaries to his court and gave some encouragement to the Christian faith. In 1594 Xavier was chosen to lead the third Jesuit mission to the Mogul court, arriving in Lahore in 1595. Xavier was to remain there almost continuously until 1615, at which time he returned to Goa, where he was given charge of the college of St. Paul. He died in 1617 in a tragic fire at the college.

Xavier's missiological approach was characterized by: (1) a careful study of the Persian language as well as the major religions of the empire, Islam and Hinduism; (2) sensitive adaptation to local religious and cultural distinctives; (3) an attempt to produce Christian literature in Persian; (4) extensive use of the liturgical ceremonies of the church to communicate Christian themes; and (5) use of rational argumentation for the truth of Christianity in dispute with Muslims. Xavier thus falls within the tradition of missionary apologists of the late Middle Ages. His most significant work is the *Fuente de Via* [Fount of Life], an apologetic work comparing the gospel of Jesus Christ with Islam and Hinduism.

HAROLD A. NETLAND

Bibliography. A Camps, *Jerome Xavier, S. J. and the Muslims of the Mogul Empire*; E. Maclagan, *The Jesuits and the Great Mogul*; S. Neill, *A History of Christianity in India: The Beginnings to 1707*.

Yannoulatos, Anastasios (1929–). Greek Orthodox missiologist and missions promoter. Born in Piraeus, Greece, as a young man he joined a spiritual renewal movement of the Church of Greece. In the late 1950s, he and several young theologians called for Orthodox churches worldwide to rediscover their great missionary tradition. In 1960, he founded the inter-Orthodox mission center "Porefthentes."

Following a bout with malaria, Yannoulatos was advised to abandon his desire to become an overseas missionary. Instead he pursued studies in missiology and world religions. In 1972, the University of Athens elected him professor of the history of religions. He established a center for missionary studies, which led to an eventual chair of missiology in 1976. His written work includes nine scholarly books, five catechetical books, over sixty treatises (fifty in foreign languages), and more than eighty articles.

Within ecumenical circles, Yannoulatos became the first Orthodox missiologist to serve as moderator of CWME from 1984 to 1991. From 1980 to 1991, Yannoulatos served as archbishop of East Africa, founding and running the only Orthodox seminary in Africa. In 1991, he was elected archbishop of Albania with the task of rebuilding a church devastated by atheistic rule.

LUKE A. VERONIS

Bibliography. L. A. Veronis, *Missionaries, Monks, and Martyrs: Making Disciples of All Nations;* A. Yannoulatos, *IRM* 54 (4): 281–97; idem, *Your Will Be Done, Orthodoxy in Mission.*

Yemen (*Est. 2000 pop.: 17,051,000; 527,968 sq. km. [203,848 sq. mi.]*). Early in Christian history, Nestorian missionaries evangelized North Yemen. A flourishing church suffered under Muslim rule. Home to no indigenous Christian community after the Arab conquest of the seventh century, Aden came under British control in 1839. Opening of the Suez Canal in 1869 highlighted the strategic importance of the area. Anglican chaplains began to serve the British community, followed by other Protestants. Perhaps the most important North American missionary to Muslims in this century, SAMUEL ZWEMER (1867–1952), of the Dutch Reformed Church in the United States, and his wife Amy Wilkes visited Aden in 1890 under auspices of the Arabian Mission. As for the Catholic Church, a Servite priest visited in 1841. This led to creation of the prefecture of Aden in 1854. From 1889 until 1974, a vicariate covering all of the Arabian Peninsula was headquartered there.

Over the past century, the area's strategic setting has attracted large numbers of Christian immigrants to North and South Yemen, notably Indian Mar Thomist Christians and, more recently, Palestinian Christians. Eastern rite Catholics (Maronites, Melkites, Chaldeans, and others) compose the largest single Christian community, followed by various Orthodox bodies and non-Chalcedonian Christians. At the time of writing, exact figures of their strength are unavailable; Christians number only a tiny percentage of Yemen's 17 million people.

Civil war during the 1960s, followed by creation of a Marxist state in South Yemen, led to expulsion of all missionaries. Christians exercise influence through educational and medical work, or by Christian broadcasts in Arabic heard over international stations.

PAUL R. DEKAR

Bibliography. R. Betts, *Christians in the Arab East. A Political Study;* A. Horner, *A Guide to Christian Churches in the Middle East.*

Yoga. A word derived from the Sanskrit *yuj* ("to control, to yoke") and cognate with the English word "yoke," yoga denotes a religious discipline or disciplines. By restraining one's mind and senses and focusing on a single point within, consciousness can be transformed, impurities such as greed or hate eradicated, and liberation of the soul attained. Adepts are called yogis, and their powers of concentration seem to give them the ability to defy the laws of nature and to cast spells. Yoga is in fact a very ancient tradition found in HINDUISM, JAINISM, and BUDDHISM, thus clearly antedating the evolution of separate world faiths. Iconographic evidence suggests a possible origin in the Indus Valley civilization of 2500–1500 B.C.

By the time of its classical formulation in the Yogasutras of Patanjali (who may be the Sanskrit grammarian of that name), yoga was evolving into one of the six orthodox schools of Hindu philosophical thought. Patanjali, who has been variously placed anywhere from the second century B.C. to the fifth century A.D., describes yoga as the cessation of mental fluctuation, a state of mind to be achieved not only by meditation, but also by a strictly moral life, control of one's bodily appetites, and posture. In his system, popularly known as Raja Yoga ("the best" or "royal" yoga), the pupil is taught to distinguish between ordinary awareness *(Citta)* and consciousness *(Purusha)* so that the latter, the essential self, can be released. The practical implications become clear when one reads the *Bhagavad Gita* ("The Song of the Lord"), where through Krishna's teaching him yoga Arjuna is enabled to resolve his ethical dilemma of pursuing his *dharma* ("religious duty") at the cost of his cousins' lives. It is Shiva, however, who is depicted as a yogi and emulated as such by devotees. The *Bhagavad Gita* in Sanskrit and in translation is enormously popular with all classes of Hindus, since they find in it a practical spirituality for everyday life. Yoga can also be assimilated to the Vedantic concept of a totally abstract divine principle to be sought through meditation.

In the Middle Ages more esoteric forms such as Hatha Yoga and Laya Yoga were developed. In the former the objective is to release *kundalini* ("the coiled one") believed to be a serpent sleeping at the base of the spine. This special force, which then rises through the *cakras* (mystical energy points in the body) to the brain, is sometimes identified with the goddess *(devi)* of Sakti Hinduism, who is said to seek her lord Shiva thus. Laya ("dissolution") techniques aim at the obliteration of individual awareness and personality prior to *samadhi*, the blissful absorption into the divine that all yogis seek.

Since the 1960s, yoga has been immensely popular in the West. This is not surprising because in India it has always been a layperson's self-help spirituality, though a teacher is advisable. Yoga is seen as beneficial to one's health, alleviating not just stress and angst, but heart conditions and hypertension as well, though the secularized Western version is of limited efficacy. Spiritual teachers from Asia have created organizations to propagate their particular disciplines, while some Christian theologians such as P. Chenchiah (1886–1959), a Madras lawyer, advocate a "Christian yoga" as a means of spiritual growth and authentic expression of Asian Christianity. For others, yoga is so closely identified with Hindu, Buddhist, or Jain assumptions that utilizing its techniques is inherently problematic.

ELEANOR M. JACKSON

Bibliography. T. Bernard, *Hatha Yoga—A Personal Experience;* E. Wood, *Yoga;* G. Flood, *Introduction to Hinduism.*

Young, Florence S. H. (1856–1940). New Zealand missionary to China and the Solomon Islands. Young was born in Motueka, in the Nelson province of the British Colony of New Zealand on October 10, 1856, the daughter of a former judge in the Bombay Presidency of the East India Company with aristocratic connections in England.

In 1882 she began a Bible class for Kanaks (indentured laborers from the Solomon Islands) working on the plantation. Out of this grew the Queensland Kanaka Mission. In 1890 she heard HUDSON TAYLOR speak in Sydney and volunteered to work with CHINA INLAND MISSION, serving in China for two terms. Meanwhile the Kanak Mission grew until it had eleven stations in Australia and nineteen European missionaries and one hundred indigenous teachers. In 1904 the Australian government introduced the White Australian policy which forced the Kanaks home, and so a branch of the mission was begun in the Solomons, and Young was asked to superintend the work. She established contacts with key converts of the previous era who had already begun Christian work in the islands. Annual trips to the Solomons enabled her to support an extensive indigenous work. A person of intense enthusiasm and spiritual conviction, she ran the mission firmly as Superintendent and Treasurer, working closely with her nephew-in-law, Northcote Deck. She died on May 28, 1940, directing the mission to the end. Out of it grew the South Seas Evangelical Church which has profoundly shaped the culture of Melanesia.

PETER LINEHAM

Bibliography. B. Burt, *Tradition & Christianity: The Colonial Transformation of a Solomon Islands Society;* J. Garrett, *Footsteps in the Sea: Christianity in Oceania to World War II;* F. S. H. Young, *Pearls from the Pacific;* idem., *In Memoriam: Emily Baring Deck 1842–1914.*

Yugoslavia *(Est. 2000 pop.: 10,696,000; 102,173 sq. km. [39,449 sq. mi.]).* The Federal Republic of Yugoslavia is a Balkan country in southeastern Europe stretching from the Adriatic Sea to the Danube River. It is comprised of the federal republics of Serbia and Montenegro. Sixty-two percent of the population is Serb, 17 percent Albanian, 4 percent Hungarian, and 4 percent Montenegrin. Nearly 70 percent of the population consider themselves Christians, with Orthodox Christians making up the largest percentage (63.7%). Muslims account for over 16 percent of the population, most of these being Albanians. Evangelicals have nearly tripled since 1970 (66,000 to 182,000). The largest of these are the Slovak Evangelical Christian Church, the Reformed Christian Church, and the Gypsy Evangelical Movement. Evangelical outreach has intensified since the collapse of communism. Of special concern to evangelicals is the Serbian province of Kosovo, which (prior to the events of 1999 was) 90 percent Albanian with a very small Christian presence. The flaring of ethnic tensions, resulting NATO campaign, and population displacements ensured that this will be a sensitive and needy region for the forseeable future.

TODD M. JOHNSON

Yun, Chi-ho (1865–1945). Korean Christian educator and church leader. Yun Chi-Ho was the first convert of the Southern Methodist Missions' ministry in Korea and the first theological student from Korea studying in the United States. He spent two years (1881–83) in Japan studying theology and English, and returned to Korea as the interpreter of the American envoy to Korea, L. H. Foote. During the political upheaval in 1884, Hun Chi-Ho left Korea for China and spent the next three and a half years in Shanghai, where he studied theology at the China-West Institute which was run by the Southern Methodist Missions in the United States. In 1887 he received baptism and became the first Korean Methodist member.

After studies at Vanderbilt and Emory Universities he returned to Shanghai in 1893 to teach English literature at the China-West Institute. While there, he held a number of important government and social positions.

He was a renowned Christian educator. In 1906 he became the founder and principal of the Korean American Study Institute in Kaesong. After three years in prison for his opposition to Japanese colonialism in 1911, he continued to be principal of the Institute under the new name of Songdo High School. He became the director of Korean Sunday School Association in 1908, worked as General Secretary of the Korean YMCA (1916–20) and president of Yonhui Technical School (1941–42). He is well remembered as a distinguished Christian educator and a strong promoter of the Korean Methodist Church.

BONG RIN RO

Bibliography. A. D. Clark, *A History of the Church in Korea.*

Zz

Zaire. *See* DEMOCRATIC REPUBLIC OF CONGO.

Zambia. (*Est. 2000 pop.: 10,754,000; 752,618 sq. km. (290,586 sq. mi.]*). The history of Protestant missions in Zambia began with the arrival of DAVID LIVINGSTONE in 1851. FREDERICK ARNOT, who had been a playmate of Livingstone's children, attempted work in Barotseland but after eighteen months of frustration moved on to Angola, where he is credited with beginning the Brethren's great mission endeavor in that country.

FRANCES COILLARD of the PARIS MISSIONARY SOCIETY who had been motivated by ROBERT MOFFAT led the first successful mission work in Zambia. In 1883, along with some Basotho evangelists, he built the first permanent missionary effort in northern Rhodesia. Within a twenty-year period the LONDON MISSIONARY SOCIETY, the Primitive Methodists, Plymouth Brethren (Arnot returned to greater success among the Lunda people), and Dutch Reformed Church Mission for the Orange Free State established works in various parts of the country.

One does not have to read between the lines to note the underlying assumption of European superiority. Robert I. Rotberg is one of many historians to reference several recorded instances which he is quick to conclude did not substantively slow the spread of mission work. It is not surprising to find the primary method of evangelism was to improve the lot of the "native" population through schools, hospitals, and clinics. By 1924 the Missionary Conference of northern Rhodesia reported less than 18,000 baptisms in a population of 1.5 million.

By the mid-1960s, however, many of the missions had begun to train and encourage national involvement in evangelistic activities, if not in organizational leadership. Nevertheless many of the country's national leaders, though educated in mission schools, left the mainline churches for the popular, African-run, separatist churches. The prominence of the church was not to be reestablished until the election of Fredrick Chiluba as president of October 1991. Though filled with intrigue, Chiluba's term has seen the rise of evangelistic activity. Declaring Zambia to be a Christian nation he stated in a 1995 *Christianity Today* article, "Where the Lord is there is unity. We are beginning to see order in our country."

Today there is a growing cooperation between missionary societies and churches as the church in Zambia goes through this time of transition. While the AFRICAN INITIATED CHURCH MOVEMENT continues to grow at the rate of 50 churches per year, the evangelical mission initiated churches now are adding some 350 churches annually. Unfortunately, even at this rate the church member-to-population ratio will decline from 24 percent to 22 percent by the year 2000.

Zambian Christians are faced with the challenge of AIDS (Zambia is one of the hardest hit by this epidemic) on the one hand and Islam on the other. Whether the push to get a Bible into the hands of every Zambian by President Chiluba will prove a turning point in either of these challenges will depend on the energy of the existing churches and their willingness to work together.

SHERMAN S. PEMBERTON

Bibliography. G. M. Anderson, *America*, 10:6 (Nov. 8, 1997), p. 177; D. P. Brierley, ed., *World Churches Handbook*; M. Froise, ed., *World Christianity: South Central Africa*; I. Phiri, *CT* (April 3, 1995), pp. 39, 94; J. P. Ragsdale, *Protestant Mission Education in Zambia, 1880–1954*; R. I. Rotberg, *Christian Missionaries and The Creation of Northern Rhodesia*; J. Weller and J. Linden, *Mainstream Christianity to 1980 in Malawi, Zambia, and Zimbabwe*.

Zamora, Nicolas (1875–1914). First Philippine ordained Protestant minister. Nicolas Zamora, one of three sons of Paulino Zamora, an outspoken critic of Spanish clerics, followed the family pattern of independence from Spanish and missionary domination. Nicolas followed the lead of his great uncle, Father Jacinto Zamora, who was executed in 1872 after being accused, probably falsely, of complicity in the Cavite Revolt.

Nicolas, the first Filipino ordained Protestant minister, led the division from the Evangelical

Methodist Church in 1909 that resulted in the *La Iglesia Evangelica Methodista en las Islas Filipinas* (IEMELIP). A leading nationalist and critic of Western missionaries, he sought self-identity and independence for Filipino ministers. He resisted the paternalism of the missionaries and their failure to acknowledge Filipino capabilities.

Following on the heels of the Aurora schism, Zamora's revolt became the most traumatic and influential of the Methodist encounters in the early 1900s. His movement exerted considerable influence, not only in the Methodist but in the Presbyterian churches as well.

Zamora was resisted and criticized by missionaries, who cited his ambition and supposed financial indiscretions. In spite of the missionary resistance, Zamora's life and teachings significantly influenced the independent efforts of Filipino churches.

EBBIE C. SMITH

Bibliography. M. S. Bernad, *The Christianization of the Philippines: Problems and Perspectives;* K. J. Clymer, *Protestant Missionaries in the Philippines, 1898–1916: An Inquiry into the American Colonial Mentality;* J. B. Rodgers, *Forty Years in the Philippines.*

Zen Buddhism.

Zen (Ch'an in Chinese) Buddhism is a form of Mahayana Buddhism developed indigenously in China and Japan. It teaches direct and sudden enlightenment (*satori* in Japanese, *dun-wu* in Chinese) through the discipline of meditation called *zazen*.

The idea of sudden awakening was first developed by Seng-chao (384–414) and Tao-sheng (360–434). However, it was Bodhidharma, a missionary from India, who emphasized the discipline of meditation as opposed to discourse on Buddhist scriptures. He did not meet with great success. It was Hui-neng (638–713), the Sixth patriarch, who brought Zen to prominence in China, and the 7th and 8th Century was the Golden Age. The flowering of Zen in Japan was brought about by the great Zen Master Dogen (1200–1253). It was he who made *zazen* (meditation with the right posture, sitting upright with legs crossed) the key to enlightenment.

Zen Buddhists believe that enlightenment does not depend on words and letters (scriptures). It comes when an insight points directly at a person's own nature. The deepest truth lies in the principle of identity. All *dharmas* have no reality of their own. All find their true nature in their unity and identity with the Absolute, which is Buddha. All differentiations have therefore to be recognized as illusion due to ignorance. All categories associated with differentiation are empty. Thus logic and knowledge built on differentiation and categories are all futile. The distinctions between the self and the world, subject and object are all misconceptions. All these must be transcended. Thus Zen is the art of attaining the wisdom of unknowing.

To achieve this, one has to practice contemplation in such a way as to expose the futility of concepts and thoughts, until one's mind becomes a clear mirror reflecting nothing but the Absolute. At that moment, not only are objects "melted" into the Void, even one's personal consciousness loses its own identity as it unifies with the Absolute Mind. The rejection of concepts is total, even the concept of nirvana or the concept of Buddha.

To facilitate illumination, a student of Zen is often confronted with riddles and paradoxical questions *(koans)*, until all preconceptions or understandings are cleared, and he or she is able to concentrate on the really real. By a sudden intuitive grasp, enlightenment can be achieved. In Japan, *zazen* was taught by Dogen as absolutely essential to the attainment of illumination. In *zazen*, one thinks of nonthinking, liberating oneself from all attachment to what seems to have differentiated identities. Then the world would reveal itself as the infinite world of Buddha, including one's self.

CARVER YU

Bibliography. H. Dumoulin, *A History of Zen Buddhism,* D. T. Suzuki, *Zen and Japanese Culture;* A. Watt, *The Way of Zen.*

Zenana Bible and Medical Missions. *See* INTERSERVE.

Ziegenbalg, Bartholomaeus

(1682–1719). Pioneer German missionary to India. The son of a grain seller, Ziegenbalg was orphaned at a very early age. Influenced by his pietist upbringing, he went as a young man to study in Halle under August Francke. In spite of his chronic stomach disorders and subsequent failure to complete his final examinations, he and Heinrich Plütschau were selected for service in the Danish Mission.

Following their ordination in Copenhagen, the two traveled to the Danish colony of Tranquebar, which they reached on July 9, 1706, after many dangers. As the first Lutheran missionaries in South India, they became pioneers in the missionary effort there. Only five years after their arrival Ziegenbalg completed his Tamil translation of the New Testament. In spite of the hostile attitude of the Danish governor, his work was richly blessed. Ziegenbalg compiled a Tamil grammar and wrote scholarly works on such topics as Indian philosophy, religion, and the caste system. He founded schools, orphanages, and a seminary to train native teachers.

Ziegenbalg's efforts are noteworthy in that he held great respect for the culture of the Hindus and stood for human dignity independent of race, status, and caste. Rejected for service as a deacon by the secretary of the Copenhagen Missionary Society, Ziegenbalg was dependent upon support from churches and friends. Having married during his European furlough (1714–16), he became the father of two sons and died in 1719 in Tranquebar.

ROLF HILLE

Zimbabwe. (*Est. 2000 pop.: 12,514,000; 390,759 sq. km. [150,872 sq. mi.]*). Before the occupation of the country that was to become Zimbabwe by the British South Africa Company (BSAC) in 1890, missionaries of various Christian denominations had been active in the area. Jesuits had come to Mashonaland through Mozambique in the sixteenth century. African and mixed race evangelists from South Africa had come independently to Mashonaland in the mid-twentieth century, and both the LONDON MISSIONARY SOCIETY (1859) and Jesuit missionaries (1879) initiated evangelistic work in Matabeleland.

With the BSAC occupation, Roman Catholic, Church of England, and Wesleyan Methodist missionaries established churches and schools throughout southern Rhodesia during Company (1890–1923) and colonial (1923–65) rule. Other Christian missions groups concentrated their efforts in particular regions of the country: the London Missionary Society in Matabeleland, Dutch Reformed Church missionaries in the southeast, and American Methodist missionaries in Manicaland in the northeast. Beyond these main missionary bodies there was an increasing proliferation of groups undertaking Christian mission work throughout the remainder of the twentieth century.

Most agencies used development institutions as their primary strategy. Both the Colonial and Smith governments were at first eager and later willing to delegate educational and health responsibilities for rural areas to mission agencies. They often allocated per capita funding to those willing to build and maintain schools and medical facilities as long as they followed government curriculum and regulations. By 1973 most mission agencies had abandoned this practice in place of nationalization. Many of the mission schools and hospitals remain, though now under national leadership.

Christian missions worked in partnership (though at times an uneasy one) with the white settler government during colonial times. The settler government's Unilateral Declaration of Independence in 1965 to avoid movement toward African political rights, and the subsequent campaign and war for independence fought by African nationalist groups, forced missionaries to reconsider their role in the country and how they were carrying out mission. The war years of the 1970s were also lean years for the churches.

Many missionaries left for other fields or went home, leaving the national leadership to pick up the slack, which they did admirably.

National evangelistic crusades such as the New Life For All Campaign helped create a sense of unity among the churches and add over two thousand congregations in those difficult years. Independence was expected to bring mission work to a halt due to the Marxist orientation of Prime Minister Mugabe. However, the churches saw the almost unprecedented government requirement that all children receive religious education along with the Marxist indoctrination as a challenge. Teachers were raised up from all denominations to teach the religious studies classes. An interdenominational council designed the first curriculum. The unity fostered during the war years carried into the next decade. Over twenty three seminaries and countless Christian printing shops have sprung up to continue the focus on leadership training and discipleship. According to the *World Churches Handbook* the Trinitarian churches (excluding Roman Catholic and indigenous churches) grew by over three thousand congregations in the decade following independence and are expected to double that growth by the year 2000.

Christian churches in Zimbabwe today, directed primarily by national leaders, exhibit considerable strength in numbers of congregations and members, as well as in sociocultural and educational influence. While the need for missionaries is reduced some of the major agencies are supporting national leadership in targeting neighboring people groups not yet churched. One example of this is the partnership of Central Africa Mission with the Christian Churches/Churches of Christ targeting the Shangaan in south central Mozambique.

SHERMAN S. PEMBERTON

Bibliography. N. Bhebe, *Christianity and Traditional Religion in Western Zimbabwe 1859–1923;* D. P. Brierley, ed., *World Churches Handbook;* A. J. Dachs, ed., *Christianity South of the Zambesi;* M. Froise, ed., *World Christianity: South Central Africa;* J. A. Siewert and E. G. Waldez, eds., *Mission Handbook 1998–2000;* J. Weller, and J. Linden, *Mainstream Christianity to 1980 in Malawi, Zambia, and Zimbabwe.*

Zinzendorf, Nikolaus Ludwig von (1700–1760). German father of MORAVIAN MISSIONS. Nikolaus Ludwig von Zinzendorf was a German Lutheran nobleman who, strongly influenced by the PIETISTIC movement, became the father of the eighteenth-century Moravian missionary movement. When he permitted a group of refugees from Moravia to settle on his estate in Saxony in 1722, he had no inkling that from them the gospel would spread to Greenland, the West Indies, North America, Central America, and Africa.

The movement began with a unique outpouring of the Holy Spirit at Herrnhut in 1727.

Zinzendorf's own missionary passion and vision melded with that of the Moravians. From initial benefactor he became the visionary, practical helper through his court connections, traveling missionary, and the second bishop of the Moravian church. All the while he maintained the intense personal piety and enthusiasm that grew out of his childhood faith. He was determined to cling to the doctrine of redemption by the blood of Christ, and to lay the atonement as the foundation of all other truth. His devotion flamed into missionary passion when he met a West Indian Christian servant, Anthony Ulrich, at the Danish court. His pleas for help ultimately were heard by the Moravians. Under Zinzendorf's leadership, they sent out their first missionaries in 1732.

JIM REAPSOME

Bibliography. J. R. Weinlick, *Count Zinzendorf;* J. R. Weinlick and A. Frank, *The Moravian Church Through the Ages.*

Zionism. A hill within Jerusalem, the ancient capital of Israel, Zion came to represent the temple, all Jerusalem, and even the entire Jewish people in their homeland. During their first scattering following the Babylonian destruction of Jerusalem (587 B.C.), Jews began to longingly remember the land in their prayers. When Herod's temple was destroyed (A.D. 70) and the Jews were later driven out of Jerusalem (A.D. 135), concern grew whether they would ever return.

The early nineteenth century witnessed the awakening of modern nationalism. At first this had little impact on Jewry as many identified with European national aspirations. However, with the increase in anti-Semitism, initial ideas of modern Jewish nationalism developed as some Orthodox Jews left Europe and settled in unoccupied parts of Palestine.

In 1886 Theodor Herzl, a Viennese journalist, wrote *The Jewish State*, which provided a platform for a new political movement that he called Zionism. Herzl's contention that the Jewish people needed a homeland was largely secular. Many of those at the First International Zionist Congress (1897) in Basel were adamantly secular and opposed to making Judaism the basis for Zionist ideology.

During World War I, Arthur J. Balfour, the British foreign minister, publicly expressed the gratitude of his government for Jewish military and scientific assistance. An official release declared that the government viewed with favor the establishment of a national home for the Jewish people in Palestine and would make efforts toward that end. Arabs were virtually powerless to oppose England, which had been granted the mandate for Palestine.

After World War II and the Holocaust, Jewish survivors poured into Palestine. England, tired of the expense of maintaining the mandate, withdrew. The United Nations assumed responsibility. On the day following the end of the British mandate, the plan for a Jewish and an Arab state was rejected by the Arabs, but accepted by the Jews. So on May 15, 1948, the state of Israel was born. Over the next twenty-five years five wars were fought between Israelis and Arabs. In 1975, under Arab influence, the United Nations declared Zionism to be a form of racism. Even though Israel has proved to be a disappointment to many, and the majority of Jews throughout the world do not want to return, it has to be noted that Judaism, the Jewish people, and the land now belong together.

ARTHUR F. GLASSER

Bibliography. H. Kung, *Judaism: Between Yesterday and Tomorrow;* R. M. Seltzer, ed., *Judaism: A People and Its History.*

Zionism, African Church. Of significance to missiologists is a form of Zionism that characterizes a church movement in South Africa. The term "Zion" was introduced to the context by missionaries from the Pentecostal apocalyptic church of Zion, Illinois. In this case the term does not refer to the literal mountain in Israel, but is a symbolic title for eternal life with Christ in a heavenly home. Especially during the apartheid era, it served as a rallying point for Africans who desired to secure their Christian identity despite the politically and socially oppressive environment. With several thousand registered churches and several million followers, the Zionists form the largest church movement in South Africa (*see also* AFRICAN INITIATED CHURCH MOVEMENT).

A. SCOTT MOREAU

Bibliography. P. M. Steyne, *Dynamic Religious Movements,* pp. 19–38.

Zoroastrian, Zoroastrianism. Around 1300 B.C. a man named Zarathushtra (Zoroaster) is believed to have taught a new religion to the Aryan people settled in what is now Iran. Its doctrines changed over centuries during which the people faced conquest by the Greeks, the spread of Christianity, and later the Arab conquest and Islam. In the ninth century A.D. some Zoroastrians sailed east in search of religious freedom, and settled in Gujarat where they were to become the Parsis. Today there are only a few small communities in Iran that are Zoroastrian (c. 30,000); the main traditions have passed to the influential Parsi communities in India and Pakistan (c. 100,0000).

The original teaching of Zarathushtra is found in the *Gathas* ("hymns") that are attributed to him and preserved in a diverse collection of writings called the Avesta (fourth to sixth century

A.D.). The primary innovation of Zarathushtra, which set his teaching apart from that of other Indo-European peoples of his time, was his emphasis on MONOTHEISM and a radical DUALISM. Ahura Mazda, the creator of heaven and earth, was good and just, but not all-powerful. He had an adversary, Angra Mainyu (the evil spirit), who was likewise uncreated. Ahura Mazda created the world as a battleground where they could meet. Human beings are therefore at the center of this struggle, and it is their duty to care for the God of creation and fight evil in all its forms. The PROBLEM OF EVIL and suffering is basic to Zoroastrian thought.

Zoroastrian cosmology focuses on three major events: the creation of the world, the revelation of good religion, and the final transfiguration. The ultimate aim of all virtuous striving is to bring about the salvation of the world. The last days will be marked by increasing suffering, and then the world savior will come in glory. A later tradition says that he is to be born of a virgin impregnated by the sperm of Zarathushtra while she bathed in a lake where it had been deposited and miraculously preserved. There will be a great battle between good and evil, ending in victory for the good. The bodies of those who died earlier will be resurrected and united with their souls, and the last judgment will take place. The kingdom of Ahura Mazda will then be established on earth.

A Zoroastrian has the duty to pray five times daily (at dawn, sunrise, noon, sunset, and midnight) in the presence of fire. In about 400 B.C. an ever-burning fire seems to have been instituted into the temple cult. There are three grades of fires: *farrbay*, the fire of the priests; *gushnasp*, the fire of the warriors; and *burzen mihr*, the fire of farmers. The symbolic role of fire led to the misconception, especially by Muslims, that the Zoroastrians were fire worshipers.

Boys and girls are initiated into the Zoroastrian community by being invested with a sacred shirt and cord. This usually takes place between the ages of seven and nine among the Parsis, and twelve and fifteen among the Iranians. On that day the young person bathes, drinks a consecrated liquid for inward cleansing, and puts on the sacred shirt. The priest then performs a simple ceremony, and the relatives dress the initiate in new clothes and give gifts. Ceremonies at death are equally important. The body is given into the charge of professionals, who wrap it in a cotton shroud and carry it on an iron bier to a stone tower. The polluting flesh is quickly eaten by vultures, and the bones bleached in the sun.

Prayers are made for the deceased on the fourth day, and regularly during the following year.

Zoroastrians do not proselytize. They favor marriage between cousins, with the result that they form close communities. From the ninth century the community in Iran has been separated from that in India, consequently, the teaching and ritual of the two groups differ. Although small in number, the Parsis have become an influential and wealthy community in India.

DAVID BURNETT

Bibliography. M. Boyce, *Zoroastrians: Their Religious Beliefs and Practices;* S. Insler, *The Gathas of Zarathustra.*

Zwemer, Samuel Marinus (1867–1952). American missionary to the Middle East. Born in Michigan of Dutch immigrant parents, he graduated from Hope College and New Brunswick Seminary before ordination by the Reformed Church in America. In 1890 he launched with James Cantine the Arabian Mission, working in a number of locations in Iraq and the Arabian Peninsula. From 1912 to 1928 he was based in Cairo, traveling extensively throughout the entire Muslim world. From 1929 until his retirement at the age of seventy-one he served as professor of the history of religion and Christian mission at Princeton Seminary. He continued an active schedule of writing and speaking right up to his death at age eighty-four.

A man of remarkable range and energy, Zwemer contributed to the missionary effort among Muslims and the wider Protestant missionary movement. In addition to his pioneering work in Arabia he was both scholar and motivator. His writings on Islamics ranged from historical studies to anthropological fieldwork on popular Islam; he founded and edited for thirty-seven years the important journal, *The Moslem World.* Along with academic writing he produced a variety of evangelistic, theological, and devotional literature. He played a leading role in international conferences devoted to Muslim evangelization, gathering and disseminating information and encouraging workers to increased effort. He richly deserved the title attributed to him as the Apostle to Islam.

TIMOTHY WIARDA

Bibliography. A. Neely, *BDCM,* p. 763; J. C. Wilson, *Flaming Prophet;* idem, *IBMR* 10 (1986): 117–21.

EDWM
Master Outline

This outline has been purposefully limited to three levels to avoid "a micro-organizational orientation" for the Dictionary. Many articles are listed in more than one area. Therefore, inclusion of an article under a certain area does not mean that the article's sole focus is on that area. Instead it means that at least one major focus in the article is of significance for the particular area under which the article is listed. Each set of articles at the third level is listed under the major heading alphabetically rather than logically. Italicized headings indicate logical division which are not actual articles; otherwise every entry (including headings) indicates an article.

1. History of Mission
    1.1 *Selected articles on missions topics covering eras prior to* A.D. *1792*
        1.101 Anabaptist Mission
        1.102 Celtic Missionary Movement
        1.103 Counter-Reformation
        1.104 Crusades, The
        1.105 Enlightenment
        1.106 Moravian Missions
        1.107 Nestorian Missions
        1.108 Monastic Movement
        1.109 Pietism
        1.110 Reformation and Mission, The
        1.111 Women in Mission
    1.2 *Selected articles dealing with the Great Century era (*A.D. *1792–1910)*
        1.201 Abolitionist Movement
        1.202 Centenary Conference on the 1.212 Protestant Missions of the World (London Missionary Conference, 1888)
        1.203 Clapham Sect
        1.204 Colonialism
        1.205 Comity
        1.206 Ecumenical Missionary Conference (New York, 1900)
        1.207 Faith Missions
        1.208 Great Awakenings
        1.209 Great Century of Mission (A.D. 1792–1910)
        1.210 Haystack Meeting
        1.211 Keswick Convention
        1.212 Liverpool Missionary Conference (1860)
        1.213 Nevius Method
        1.214 Parliaments of World Religions (1893 and 1993)
        1.215 Paternalism
        1.216 Pietism
        1.217 Revival, Revivals
        1.218 Serampore Trio
        1.219 Student Volunteer Movement for Foreign Missions (SVM)
        1.220 Union Missionary Convention (New York Missionary Conference [1854])
        1.221 Women in Mission
        1.222 World Missionary Conference (Edinburgh, 1910)
    1.3 *Articles related to the contemporary Ecumenical movement (see also several of the articles listed under 5.13, 5.14, and 5.15 below)*
        1.301 Accra Conference (1958)

1.302   Amsterdam Assembly (1948)
1.303   Bangkok Conference (1973)
1.304   Commission on World Mission and Evangelism
1.305   Dialogue
1.306   Ecumenical Movement
1.307   Foreign Missions Inquiry, Layman's
1.308   International Missionary Council (IMC)
1.309   Jerusalem Conference (1928)
1.310   Kairos Document
1.311   Melbourne Conference (1980)
1.312   Mexico City Conference (1963)
1.313   *Missio Dei*
1.314   Moratorium
1.315   New Delhi Assembly (1961)
1.316   Option for the Poor
1.317   World's Parliaments of Religions (1893 and 1993)
1.318   Praxis
1.319   Presence Evangelism
1.320   Salvador Conference (1996)
1.321   San Antonio Conference (1989)
1.322   Sanctuary Movement
1.323   Tambaram Conference (1938)
1.324   Third World Women
1.325   Vancouver Assembly (1983)
1.326   Whitby Conference (1947)
1.327   Willingen Conference (1952)
1.328   Women in Mission
1.329   World Council of Churches Conferences
1.330   World Council of Churches Assemblies
1.331   World Council of Churches
1.332   World Missionary Conference (Edinburgh, 1910)

1.4   *Articles related to the contemporary Evangelical movement (see also 1.2. above, and 1.6. below)*
1.401   Australian Evangelical Alliance
1.402   Chinese House Church Movement
1.403   Church Growth Movement
1.404   COMIBAM (Ibero-American Missionary Cooperation)
1.405   Congress on the Church's Worldwide Mission (Wheaton Congress, 1966)
1.406   Consultation on the Relationship between Evangelism and Social Responsibility (Grand Rapids, 1982)
1.407   Evangelical Fellowship of Mission Agencies (EFMA)
1.408   Evangelical Missionary Alliance (EMA)
1.409   Evangelical Missions Conferences
1.410   Evangelical Movement
1.411   Frankfurt Declaration on the Fundamental Crisis in Christian Mission
1.412   Global Consultations of World Evangelization (GCOWE '95 and GCOWE '97)
1.413   International Conference for Itinerant Evangelists (Amsterdam, 1983)
1.414   International Council of Christian Churches
1.415   Interdenominational Foreign Mission Association (IFMA)
1.416   Lausanne Congress on World Evangelism (1974)
1.417   Lausanne Congress II on World Evangelism (Manila, 1989)
1.418   Lausanne Movement
1.419   Mission and Missions
1.420   New Apostolic Reformation Missions
1.421   Panama Congress (1916)
1.422   Pentecostal Movement
1.423   Third World Women
1.424   Urbana Mission Conferences
1.425   Women in Mission
1.426   World Congress on Evangelism (Berlin Congress, 1966)

        1.427   World Consultation on World Evangelization (Pattaya, 1980)
        1.428   World Evangelical Fellowship (WEF)
        1.429   World Missionary Conference (Edinburgh, 1910)
    1.5   *Articles on selected denominational "families"*
        1.501   Anabaptist Missions
        1.502   Adventist Missions
        1.503   Anglican Missions
        1.504   Baptist Missions
        1.505   Brethren Missions
        1.506   Charismatic Missionaries, Independent
        1.507   Charismatic Missions
        1.508   Christian and Missionary Alliance Missions
        1.509   Christian Church Missions
        1.510   Friends' (Quakers) Missions
        1.511   Fundamentalist Denominational Missions
        1.512   Lutheran Missions
        1.513   Mennonite Missions
        1.514   Methodist Missions
        1.515   Moravian Missions
        1.516   Orthodox Mission Movements
        1.517   Pentecostal Missions
        1.518   Presbyterian Missions
        1.519   Reformed Missions Catholic Missions
        1.520   Roman Catholic Missions
        1.521   Salvation Army
        1.522   Second Vatican Council (1962–1963)
        1.523   Wesleyan/Holiness Missions
    1.6   Independent Non-Denominational Mission Agencies
        1.601   Africa Evangelical Fellowship
        1.602   Africa Inland Mission (AIM)
        1.603   American Board of Commissioners for Foreign Missions (ABCFM)
        1.604   Baptist Missionary Society (BMS)
        1.605   Basel Mission, The
        1.606   Berlin Missionary Society
        1.607   Bible Societies
        1.608   Church Mission Society (CMS)
        1.609   Danish-Halle Mission
        1.610   Faith Missions
        1.611   Friends Missionary Prayer Band (FMPB)
        1.612   India Evangelical Mission (IEM)
        1.613   International Fellowship of Evangelical Students (IFES)
        1.614   Interserve
        1.615   London Missionary Society (LMS)
        1.616   New Tribes
        1.617   OMS International
        1.618   Overseas Missionary Fellowship (OMF)
        1.619   Parachurch Agencies and Mission
        1.620   Paris Evangelical Mission Society
        1.621   Rhenish Missionary Society
        1.622   Society for International Ministries (SIM)
        1.623   Society for the Propagation of the Gospel in Foreign Parts (SPG)
        1.624   Southern Baptist Convention, IMB
        1.625   The Evangelical Alliance Mission (TEAM)
        1.626   WEC International
        1.627   Wycliffe Bible Translators, International
    1.7   *Selected articles on continental, regional, or national mission boards and societies (for scholarly mission groups and societies, see under 2.1)*
        1.701   African Mission Boards and Societies
        1.702   Argentine Mission Boards and Societies
        1.703   Asian Mission Boards and Societies
        1.704   Australian Mission Boards and Societies

1.705 Brazilian Mission Boards and Societies
1.706 Canadian Mission Boards and Societies
1.707 Chinese Mission Boards and Societies
1.708 Danish Mission Boards and Societies
1.709 Dutch Mission Boards and Societies
1.710 English Mission Boards and Societies
1.711 Finnish Mission Boards and Societies
1.712 French Mission Boards and Societies
1.713 Ghanaian Mission Boards and Societies
1.714 German Mission Boards and Societies
1.715 Indian Mission Boards and Societies
1.716 Japanese Mission Boards and Societies
1.717 Kenyan Mission Boards and Societies
1.718 Korean Mission Boards and Societies
1.719 Latin American Mission Boards and Societies
1.720 Myanmar Mission Boards and Societies
1.721 New Zealand Mission Boards and Societies
1.722 Nigerian Mission Boards and Societies
1.723 Non-Western Mission Boards and Societies
1.724 Pacific Ocean Mission Boards and Societies
1.725 Philippine Mission Boards and Societies
1.726 Scottish Mission Boards and Societies
1.727 Swedish Mission Boards and Societies
1.728 Swiss Mission Boards and Societies
1.729 United States Mission Boards and Societies
2. Missiology
   2.1 *Selected articles on academics, academic societies, research, and tools*
      2.101 Academic Associations of Missions
      2.102 American Society of Church Growth
      2.103 American Society of Missiology
      2.104 Association of Professors of Mission
      2.105 Atlases, Mission
      2.106 Bachelor's Degrees in Mission
      2.107 Biographies of Missionaries
      2.108 Cross-Cultural Research
      2.109 Degrees in Mission and Missiology
      2.110 *Deutsche Gesellschaft für Missionswisenschaft* (see German Society for Missiology)
      2.111 Dictionaries of Mission
      2.112 Directories of Missions
      2.113 Doctoral Degrees in Mission (Academic and Professional)
      2.114 Ethnographic Research
      2.115 Ethnography
      2.116 Evangelical Missiological Society (EMS)
      2.117 German Society for Missiology
      2.118 The Gospel and Our Culture Network
      2.119 Information Technology
      2.120 International Association for Mission Studies (IAMS)
      2.121 Intertestamental Studies
      2.122 Journals of Mission and Missiology
      2.123 Master's Degrees in Mission
      2.124 Missiology
      2.125 Missiometrics
      2.126 Mission Libraries
      2.127 Qualitative Research
      2.128 Quantitative Missiology
      2.129 Research
   2.2 *Selected articles on missiological theory*
      2.201 Accommodation
      2.202 Bridges of God
      2.203 Controversies in Contemporary Evangelical Mission

2.204   Cultural Conversion
2.205   Dialogue
2.206   Engel Scale
2.207   Evangelism and Social Responsibility
2.208   Evangelization, Measurement of
2.209   Extent of Missionary Identification
2.210   Fads in Mission
2.211   Flaw of the Excluded Middle
2.212   Foreign Financing of Indigenous Workers
2.213   Fraternal Workers
2.214   Globalization
2.215   Gospel and Culture
2.216   Holistic Mission
2.217   Homogenous Unit Principle
2.218   Incarnational Mission
2.219   Inculturation
2.220   Indigenization
2.221   Indigenous Churches
2.222   Liberation
2.223   Lifestyle Evangelism
2.224   Mass Movements
2.225   *Missio Dei*
2.226   Mission and Missions
2.227   Mission on Six Continents
2.228   Mission Theory
2.229   Missionary Calling
2.230   Missionary Task, The
2.231   New Covenant
2.232   Moratorium
2.233   Option for the Poor
2.234   Partnership
2.235   Peoples, People Groups
2.236   People Movements
2.237   Polygamy and Church Membership
2.238   Power Ministries
2.239   Proselytism
2.240   Reached and Unreached Mission Fields
2.241   Receptivity
2.242   Redemption and Lift
2.243   Redemptive Analogies
2.244   Sabbath Observance
2.245   Sociological Barriers
2.246   Sodality and Modality
2.247   Spiritual Warfare
2.248   Volunteerism in Mission
2.3   *Selected articles on missionary strategies, tools, and practice (see also 3.4)*
2.301   10/40 Window
2.302   Adopt-A-People
2.303   Bible Education by Extension (BEE)
2.304   Bible Translation
2.305   Bonding
2.306   Church Planting
2.307   Colportage
2.308   Comity
2.309   Contextualization
2.310   Creative Access Countries
2.311   Cross-Cultural Research
2.312   Crusade Evangelism
2.313   Discipling a Whole Nation (DAWN)
2.314   Educational Mission Work
2.315   Extent of Missionary Identification

2.316 Financing Missions
2.317 Foreign Financing of Indigenous Workers
2.318 Friendship Evangelism
2.319 Indigenization
2.320 Indigenous Churches
2.321 Information Technology
2.322 Itinerant Mission
2.323 Jesus Film
2.324 Literacy, Literature Mission Work
2.325 March for Jesus
2.326 Media
2.327 Nevius Method
2.328 Non-Residential Missionary
2.329 Pioneer Mission Work
2.330 Power Encounter
2.331 Pre-evangelism
2.332 Radio Mission Work
2.333 Saturation Church Planting
2.334 Short-Term Mission
2.335 Small Groups
2.336 Smuggling
2.337 Storytelling
2.338 Strategies in Mission
2.339 Teaching English to Speakers of Other Languages (TESOL)
2.340 Teams in Mission
2.341 Tent-making Mission
2.342 Theological Education by Extension (TEE)
2.343 Theological Education in Non-Western Contexts
2.344 Training of Missionaries
2.345 Urban Churches
2.346 Village Evangelism

3. Practical Missiology
  3.1 *Selected articles on administrating the task*
    3.101 Attrition
    3.102 Burnout
    3.103 Candidate Selection
    3.104 Church/Mission Relations
    3.105 Comity
    3.106 Contingency Plans
    3.107 Counseling of Missionaries
    3.108 Dropout
    3.109 Fund Raising
    3.110 Information Technology
    3.111 Interagency Cooperation
    3.112 Leadership
    3.113 Member Care in Missions
    3.114 Management
    3.115 Morale
    3.116 Mission Headquarters
    3.117 Planning
    3.118 Promotion of Mission
    3.119 Secondment
    3.120 Volunteerism in Mission
  3.2 *Selected articles on missionary life*
    3.201 Adjustment to the Field
    3.202 Bonding
    3.203 Candidacy
    3.204 Church Missions Conferences
    3.205 Church and State
    3.206 Commitment
    3.207 Creative Access Countries

	3.208	Deputation
	3.209	Divorce
	3.210	Evangelist
	3.211	Extent of Missionary Identification
	3.212	Family Life of the Missionary
	3.213	Field Appointment
	3.214	Field Responsibilities
	3.215	Furlough
	3.216	Health, Health Care
	3.217	Home Schooling
	3.218	Household Responsibilities
	3.219	In-service Education
	3.220	Language School
	3.221	Marriage, Marriage Practices
	3.222	Martyrdom
	3.223	Member Care in Missions
	3.224	Missionary
	3.225	Missionary Affluence
	3.226	Missionary Children
	3.227	Motive, Motivation
	3.228	Pastoral Counseling
	3.229	Persecution
	3.230	Personal/Family Responsibilities
	3.231	Qualifications for the Missionary
	3.232	Reverse Culture Shock
	3.233	Single Missionary
	3.234	Terrorism
	3.235	Third Culture Kids (TCKs)
	3.236	Training of Missionaries
3.3		*Selected articles on cross-cultural ministry*
	3.301	Apologetics
	3.302	Bible Translation
	3.303	Child Evangelism
	3.304	Christian Walk and Work in Mission
	3.305	Church Development
	3.306	Church Planting
	3.307	Cross-Cultural Counseling
	3.308	Cross-Cultural Evangelism
	3.309	Cross-Cultural Ministry
	3.310	Crusade Evangelism
	3.311	Disciple, Discipleship
	3.312	Extent of Missionary Identification
	3.313	Evangelism
	3.314	Evangelist
	3.315	Friendship Evangelism
	3.316	Homiletics
	3.317	Indigenization
	3.318	Indigenous Churches
	3.319	Invitation
	3.320	Lifestyle Evangelism
	3.321	Partnership
	3.322	Pastoral Counseling
	3.323	Pre-evangelism
	3.324	Presence Evangelism
	3.325	Proclamation Evangelism
	3.326	Spiritual Formation
	3.327	Television Evangelism
	3.328	Village Evangelism
	3.329	Witness
3.4		*Selected articles on types of missionary work and emphasis (see also 2.3 above)*
	3.401	AIDS and Mission

3.402   Agricultural Missions
3.403   Aviation Mission Work
3.404   Bible Education by Extension (BEE)
3.405   Bible Translation
3.406   Camping
3.407   Child Evangelism
3.408   Church Development
3.409   Church Planting
3.410   Colportage
3.411   Disaster Response
3.412   Educational Mission Work
3.413   Friendship Evangelism
3.414   Holistic Mission
3.415   Home Mission
3.416   Jewish Missions
3.417   Leprosy Mission Work
3.418   Literacy, Literature Mission Work
3.419   March for Jesus
3.420   Medical Mission Work
3.421   Mission Schools
3.422   Muslim Mission Work
3.423   Orphanage Mission Work
3.424   Pioneer Mission Work
3.425   Prison Mission Work
3.426   Short-Term Mission
3.427   Student Mission Work
3.428   Radio Mission Work
3.429   Refugee Mission Work
3.430   Relief Work
3.431   Tent-Making Mission
3.432   Teaching English to Speakers of Other Languages (TESOL)
3.433   Television Evangelism
3.434   Theological Education by Extension (TEE)

4. Social Sciences
  4.1   Anthropology
      4.101   Anthropology of Religion
      4.102   Behavior Patterns
      4.103   Biculturalism
      4.104   Cross-Cultural Research
      4.105   Culture
      4.106   Culture Learning
      4.107   Decision Making
      4.108   Enculturation
      4.109   Ethnographic Research
      4.110   Ethnography
      4.111   Ethnomusicology
      4.112   Individualism and Collectivism
      4.113   Inter-Cultural Competency
      4.114   Kinship
      4.115   Worldview
  4.2   Communication
      4.201   Art
      4.202   Intercultural Communication
      4.203   Interpersonal Communication
      4.204   Mass Communication
      4.205   Media
      4.206   Radio Mission Work
      4.207   Television Evangelism
      4.208   Storytelling
  4.3   Economics
      4.301   Bribery

4.302 Communism, Marxism
4.303 Consumerism
4.304 Debt
4.305 Dependence
4.306 Development
4.307 Missionary Affluence
4.308 Money
4.309 Transformational Development
4.310 Wealth and Poverty

4.4   Educational Mission Work
4.401 Accreditation
4.402 Bible Education by Extension (BEE)
4.403 Illiteracy
4.404 International Council for Evangelical Theological Education (ICETE)
4.405 Learning Theories
4.406 Literacy, Literature Mission Work
4.407 Mission Schools
4.408 Theological Education by Extension (TEE)

4.5   Linguistics, Linguistic Theory
4.501 Bible Translation
4.502 Dynamic Equivalence
4.503 Language
4.504 Language School
4.505 Second Language Acquisition
4.506 Sociolinguistics
4.507 Symbol, Symbolism
4.508 Translatability
4.509 Translation
4.510 Translation Theory

4.6   Modernization
4.601 Ecology, Ecological Movement
4.602 Environment
4.603 Marginal, Marginalization
4.604 Modernity
4.605 Pluralism
4.606 Postmodernism
4.607 Secularist, Secularism
4.608 Secularization
4.609 Terrorism
4.610 Third World
4.611 Two-Thirds World
4.612 Urban Churches
4.613 Urbanization

4.7   Politics
4.701 Church and State
4.702 Human Rights
4.703 Hunger
4.704 Ideologies
4.705 Land, Land Reform, Land Rights
4.706 Law, Legal Thought
4.707 Liberation
4.708 Martyrdom
4.709 Nation, Nation-Building, Nationalism
4.710 Paternalism
4.711 Political Elections
4.712 Population, Population Explosion, Population Planning
4.713 Religious Freedom
4.714 Revolution
4.715 Terrorism
4.716 Totalitarianism
4.717 Wars

       4.718   Wealth and Poverty
       4.719   Zionism
   4.8   Psychology
       4.801   Bonding
       4.802   Counseling of Missionaries
       4.803   Cross-Cultural Counseling
       4.804   Culture Shock
       4.805   Extent of Missionary Identification
       4.806   Guilt
       4.807   Learning Theories
       4.808   Moral Development
       4.809   Pastoral Counseling
       4.810   Reverse Culture Shock
       4.811   Shame
       4.812   Spiritual Formation
   4.9   Science and Mission
   4.10 Sociology
       4.1001 Alienation
       4.1002 Anomie
       4.1003 Association, Socio-Anthropology of
       4.1004 Bonding
       4.1005 Caste
       4.1006 Diaspora(s)
       4.1007 Enculturation
       4.1008 Ethnicity
       4.1009 Ethnocentrism
       4.1010 Gender Roles
       4.1011 Institutionalization
       4.1012 Leadership
       4.1013 Leadership Theory
       4.1014 Marriage, Marriage Practices
       4.1015 Migration
       4.1016 Minority, Minority Populations
       4.1017 Paternalism
       4.1018 Persecution
       4.1019 Population, Population Explosion, Population Planning
       4.1020 Race Relations
       4.1021 Reconciliation
       4.1022 Sociological Barriers
       4.1023 Sociology of Music
       4.1024 Sodality of Music
       4.1025 Status
       4.1026 Third World
       4.1027 Two-Thirds World
       4.1028 Zionism
5. Theology of Mission
   5.1   Bible
       5.101   Abrahamic Covenant
       5.102   Apostle, Apostles
       5.103   Babel
       5.104   Biblical Criticism and Mission
       5.105   Biblical Theology of Mission
       5.106   Creation
       5.107   Inerrancy, Infallibility of the Bible
       5.108   Jesus and Mission
       5.109   Jonah
       5.110   New Testament Theology of Mission
       5.111   Old Testament Prophets
       5.112   Old Testament Theology of Mission
       5.113   Paul and Mission
       5.114   Pentateuch, Mission in the

5.115   Religious Scriptures
5.116   Revelation, General
5.117   Revelation, Special (see Bible)
5.118   Truth
5.119   Two-Covenant Theory

5.2   Christology
5.201   Atonement
5.202   Christ and Culture
5.203   Christological Controversies
5.204   Great Commandment
5.205   Great Commission
5.206   Incarnational Mission
5.207   Resurrection of Christ
5.208   Uniqueness of Christ

5.3   Church
5.301   Church Discipline
5.302   Church Polity
5.303   Leadership
5.304   Pastoral Responsibilities
5.305   Priesthood of the Believer
5.306   Sacraments/Ordinance
5.307   Stewardship

5.4   Eschatology
5.401   Amillennialism
5.402   Annihilationism
5.403   Death
5.404   End Times
5.405   Hell
5.406   Hope
5.407   Judgment
5.408   Kingdom of God
5.409   Millennial Thought
5.410   Parousia
5.411   Postmillennialism
5.412   Premillennialism
5.413   Worship
5.414   Wrath of God

5.5   Ethics
5.501   Bribery
5.502   Church and State
5.503   Debt
5.504   Divorce
5.505   Human Rights
5.506   Hunger
5.507   Justice of God
5.508   Kingdom of God
5.509   Liberation
5.510   Love of God
5.511   Mercy of God
5.512   Missionary Affluence
5.513   Problem of Evil
5.514   Sexual Mores
5.515   Smuggling
5.516   Suffering
5.517   Stewardship
5.518   Tithe, Tithing
5.519   Wealth and Poverty
5.520   Wrath of God

5.6   God
5.601   Divine Attributes of God
5.602   Divine Deliverance

        5.603   Divine Election
        5.604   Divine Initiative
        5.605   Grace of God
        5.606   Immanence of God
        5.607   Immutability of God
        5.608   Justice of God
        5.609   Kingdom of God
        5.610   Love of God
        5.611   Mercy of God
        5.612   *Missio Dei*
        5.613   Omnipresence of God
        5.614   Omniscience of God
        5.615   Problem of Evil
        5.616   Sovereignty of God
        5.617   Transcendence of God
        5.618   Trinity
        5.619   Wrath of God
        5.620   Providence of God
    5.7   Holy Spirit
        5.701   Anointing
        5.702   Dreams and Visions
        5.703   Elenctics
        5.704   Fruit of the Spirit
        5.705   Gifts of the Spirit
        5.706   Miracles in Mission
        5.707   Power Encounter
        5.708   Power Ministries
        5.709   Signs and Wonders
    5.8   Humankind, Biblical Doctrine of (Anthropology, Biblical)
        5.801   Conscience
        5.802   Depravity of Humankind
        5.803   Fall of Humankind, The
        5.804   Image of God
        5.805   Human Rights
        5.806   Person, Personhood
        5.807   Priesthood of the Believer
    5.9   Salvation
        5.901   Assurance of Salvation
        5.902   Baptism
        5.903   Confession
        5.904   Conversion
        5.905   Divine Election
        5.906   Eternal Life
        5.907   Eternal Security
        5.910   Gospel, The
        5.911   Justification
        5.912   Liberation
        5.913   Peace with God
        5.914   Profession of Faith
        5.915   Reconciliation
        5.916   Repentance
        5.917   Sacrifice
    5.10 Sin
        5.1001 Apostasy
        5.1002 Blasphemy
        5.1003 Confession
        5.1004 Corruption
        5.1005 Depravity of Humankind
        5.1006 Doubt
        5.1007 Elenctics
        5.1008 Fall of Humankind, The

5.1009 Guilt
5.1010 Idolatry
5.1011 Shame
5.11 Spiritual Warfare
    5.1101 Curse, Curses
    5.1102 Demon, Demonization
    5.1103 Gifts of the Spirit
    5.1104 Miracles in Mission
    5.1105 Possession Phenomena
    5.1106 Power Encounter
    5.1107 Power Ministries
    5.1108 Powers, The
    5.1109 Satan
    5.1110 Satanist, Satanism
    5.1111 Signs and Wonders
    5.1112 Territorial Spirits
5.12 Spirituality
    5.1201 Commitment
    5.1202 Confession
    5.1203 Fruit of the Spirit
    5.1204 Gifts of the Spirit
    5.1205 Holiness
    5.1206 Honesty
    5.1207 Hope
    5.1208 Love
    5.1209 Joy
    5.1210 Motive, Motivation
    5.1211 Obedience
    5.1212 Peace
    5.1213 Prayer
    5.1214 Shalom
    5.1215 Spiritual Formation
    5.1216 Suffering
    5.1217 Unity
    5.1218 Worship
5.13 Theological Method
    5.1301 Accommodation
    5.1302 Adaptation
    5.1303 Contextualization
    5.1304 Ethnotheologies
    5.1305 Exegesis
    5.1306 Hermeneutics
    5.1307 Inculturation
    5.1308 Indigenization
    5.1309 Systematic Theology
    5.1310 Theological Systems
    5.1311 Translatability
    5.1312 Syncretism
5.14 Theological Systems
    5.1401 African Theologies
    5.1402 Arminian Theology
    5.1403 Asian Theologies
    5.1404 Black Theologies
    5.1405 Calvinism
    5.1406 Dispensationalism
    5.1407 Ethnotheologies
    5.1408 Evangelical Theology and Mission
    5.1409 Feminist Theologies
    5.1410 Hispanic Theologies
    5.1411 Liberal Theology
    5.1412 Liberation Theologies Missiology

5.1413 Minjung Theology
5.1414 Neo-Orthodox Theology
5.1415 Orthodox Theologies
5.1416 Pacifist Theology
5.1417 Political Theologies
5.1418 Theological Method
5.15 Theology of Mission
5.1501 Ambassador of God
5.1502 Christ and Culture
5.1503 Christian Walk and Work in Mission
5.1504 Church/Mission Relations
5.1505 Cultural Mandate
5.1506 Divine Initiative
5.1507 Evangelical Theology and Mission
5.1508 Evangelism and Social Responsibility
5.1509 Evangelist
5.1510 Gospel, The
5.1511 Gospel and Culture
5.1512 Great Commandment
5.1513 Great Commission
5.1514 Heathen, The
5.1515 Holism, Biblical
5.1516 Holistic Mission
5.1517 Incarnational Mission
5.1518 Israel's Role (as Light to the Nations)
5.1519 Jesus and Mission
5.1520 Justice of God
5.1521 Kingdom of God
5.1522 Liberation
5.1523 Martyrdom
5.1524 Miracles in Mission
5.1525 Mission and Missions
5.1526 Missionary Calling
5.1527 Missionary Task, The
5.1528 *Missio Dei*
5.1529 Mission and Missions
5.1530 Moratorium
5.1531 Motive, Motivation
5.1532 New Covenant
5.1533 New Testament Theology of Mission
5.1534 Old Testament Theology of Mission
5.1535 Option for the Poor
5.1536 Paul and Mission
5.1537 Power, Theology of
5.1538 Praxis
5.1539 Presence Evangelism
5.1540 Proclamation Evangelism
5.1541 Proselytism
5.1542 Shalom
5.1543 Theology of Religions
5.1544 Unevangelized
5.1545 Uniqueness of Christ
5.1546 Universality of Mission
5.1547 Witness
5.1548 Worship
6. World Religions
6.1 Belief Systems
6.101 Atheism
6.102 Agnosticism
6.103 Belief Systems
6.104 Communism, Marxism

6.105 Deism
6.106 Dualism
6.107 Henotheism
6.108 Ideologies
6.109 Monism
6.110 Monotheism
6.111 Polytheism
6.112 Panentheism
6.113 Pantheism
6.114 Relativist, Relativism
6.115 Secularist, Secularism
6.116 Socialist, Socialism
6.117 Universalism
6.2 *Selected articles on new religious movements*
6.201 African Initiated Church Movement
6.202 Asian New Religious Movements
6.203 Black Muslims
6.204 Cargo Cults
6.205 Hindu New Religious Movements
6.206 Islamic New Religious Movements
6.207 Japanese New Religious Movements
6.208 Jehovah's Witnesses
6.209 Kardecism
6.210 Latin American New Religious Movements (includes Macumba, Quimbanda, Santeria, Umbanda, Voodoo)
6.211 Mormons
6.212 Neopagan, Neopaganism
6.213 New Age Movement
6.214 New Religious Movements (NeRMs)
6.215 Non-Church Movement (Japan)
6.216 North American New Religious Movements
6.217 Prophetic and Identity Movements
6.218 Renewal Movements
6.219 Three-Self Movement (China)
6.220 Wicca, Wiccan
6.221 Zionism, African Church
6.3 *Selected articles on the study of religions*
6.301 Anthropology of Religion
6.302 Comparative Religion
6.303 Phenomenology of Religions
6.304 Philosophy of Religion
6.305 Psychology of Religion
6.306 Religion
6.307 Religious Typologies
6.308 Sociology of Religion
6.309 Theology of Religions
6.310 World's Parliaments of Religions (1893 and 1993)
6.4 *Selected articles on the world's religions*
6.401 Aboriginal Religions
6.402 African Traditional Religions
6.403 Astrology
6.404 Baha'i
6.405 Buddhist, Buddhism
6.406 Confucianism
6.407 Folk Religions
6.408 Fundamentalisms
6.409 Hindu, Hinduism
6.410 Indigenous American Religions
6.411 Islam, Muslim

6.412   Jain, Jainism
6.413   Jew, Judaism
6.414   Jewish Missions
6.415   Mahayana Buddhism
6.416   Muslim Mission Work
6.417   Neopagan, Neopaganism
6.418   Occultist, Occultism
6.419   Primal Religions
6.420   Pure Land Buddhism
6.421   Satanist, Satanism
6.422   Shi'ite, Shi'ism
6.423   Shinto
6.424   Sikh, Sikhism
6.425   Sufi, Sufism
6.426   Sunni, Sunnism
6.427   Taoist, Taoism
6.428   Theravada Buddhism
6.429   Totem, Totemism
6.430   Vajrayana (Tibetian) Buddhism
6.431   Vedanta Hinduism
6.432   Wicca, Wiccan
6.433   Yoga
6.434   Zen Buddhism
6.435   Zoroastrian, Zoroastrianism
6.5   *Selected articles on issues within and across in world's religions*
6.501   Ancestral Beliefs and Practices
6.502   Animism
6.503   Asceticism
6.504   Christo-Paganism
6.505   Cosmology
6.506   Cults, Cultism
6.507   Cultural Conversion
6.508   Curse, Curses
6.509   Death Rites
6.510   Divination, Diviner
6.511   Exorcism
6.512   Festivals, Religious
6.513   Folklore
6.514   Gods and Goddesses
6.515   Guru
6.516   Human Condition in World Religions
6.517   Initiation Rites
6.518   Liminal, Liminality
6.519   Magic, Magick, Magical Beliefs and Practices
6.520   Mystic, Mysticism
6.521   Myth, Mythology
6.522   Nominal, Nominal Christian
6.523   Pilgrimages
6.524   Possession Phenomena
6.525   Qur'an
6.526   Redemption in Other Faiths
6.527   Reincarnation and Transmigration
6.528   Religious Scriptures
6.529   Religious Ultimacy
6.530   Revelation, General
6.531   Rites of Passage
6.532   Ritual and Ceremony
6.533   Sacrifice in Other Faiths
6.534   Shaman, Shamanism

6.535   Soteriology in World Religions
6.536   Symbol, Symbolism
6.537   Syncretism
6.538   Taboo
6.539   Totem, Totemism
6.540   Truth
6.541   Uniqueness of Christ
6.542   Witchcraft and Sorcery
6.543   Zionism

Index

Abraham Mar Thoma, 28
Abrams, Anna, 28, 1012
Abrams, Minnie F., 29–30, 739
Acosta, José de, 33–34, 438, 633, 642, 749
Adalbert of Bremen, 34
Aedesius, 37, 322
Aggrey, J. E. Kwegyir, 48
Agnew, Eliza, 48, 1021
Aidan of Lindisfarne, 50, 984
Aitolos, Kosmas, 51
Aldersey, Mary Ann, 52
Allan, George, 53–54
Allen, Roland, 54, 194, 446, 484, 634, 642, 676, 726, 727, 739, 949
Anderson, Gerald H., 59, 635, 659, 949
Anderson, John, 60
Anderson, Rufus, 54, 55, 60, 183, 188, 194, 410, 483, 634, 642, 676, 726, 760, 772, 960, 982, 999
Andrews, Charles Freer, 60–61
Ansgar, 65–66
Argue, Andrew Harvey, 76
Armstrong, Annie Walker, 78
Arnot, Frederick Stanley, 62, 78, 239, 1042
Aroolappen, John Christian, 78–79, 417, 525
Arthington, Robert, 79–80, 110
Asbury, Francis, 80, 207, 986
Augustine of Canterbury, 95, 170, 644, 734, 943
Augustine of Hippo, 95, 176, 215, 440
Aylward, Gladys, 101
Azariah, Vedanayakam Samuel, 101–2, 181, 734, 1029

Baba, Panya, 44, 103, 690, 887
Baedeker, Friedrich Wilhelm, 104–5
Baker, Amelia Dorothea, 106
Baldwin, Mary Briscoe, 106–7
Barclay, Thomas, 114
Barth, Christian Gottlob, 114
Bavinck, Johan Herman, 115, 307, 321, 815, 949, 999

Bayne, Margaret. See Wilson, Margaret Bayne
Beach, Harlan Page, 115, 561
Beaver, Robert Pierce, 90, 115–16, 212, 745, 1022
Bell, Lemuel Nelson, 118
Bender, Carl Jacob, 118–19
Berntsen, Annie Skau, 120
Beyerhaus, Peter, 120, 371, 563, 1026
Bhengu, Nicholas Bhekinkosi Hepworth, 120
Bill, Samuel Alexander, 132, 504
Bingham, Hiram, 132, 160, 543, 886
Bingham, Rowland Victory, 41, 132–33, 690, 916
Birinus, 133
Bishop Abraham. See Abraham Mar Thoma
Bishop, Isabella Bird, 134
Bliss, Daniel, 136
Blyden, Edward Wilmot, 136, 576
Bompas, William Carpenter, 137–38
Boniface, 138–39, 170, 195, 330, 370, 388, 441, 676, 875, 984, 1017
Boone, William James, 139
Booth, Evangeline Cory, 139
Booth, Joseph, 139, 592
Booth, William, 139, 140, 205, 408, 850, 884, 1011
Bosch, David J(acobus), 31, 140, 643, 815, 898, 950
Braden, Charles Samuel, 141–42
Brainerd, David, 142, 301, 305, 395, 407, 444, 602, 814, 913, 986
Bridgman, Eliza Jane Gillett, 147
Bright, William, 147, 346, 519, 539
Brother Andrew, 147–48, 884, 938
Brown, Edith, 148
Buchman, Frank Nathan Daniel, 148

Bulu, Joeli, 151
Burns, William Chalmers, 152
Butler, Fanny Jane, 153

Cable, (Alice) Mildred, 154
Cabrini, Frances Xavier, 154
Calverley, Edwin Elliott, 154–55
Cámara, Helder Pessao, 156
Carey, Lott, 162, 576
Carey, Maude. See Cary, Maude
Carey, William, 58, 79, 83, 87, 97, 108, 110, 111, 124, 162–63, 209, 281, 289, 297, 304, 312, 313, 339, 379, 395, 408, 409, 410, 413, 444–45, 476, 479, 600, 602, 603, 611, 633, 644, 661, 760, 772, 803, 815, 832, 867, 900, 916, 984, 1003, 1006
Cargill, Margaret, 163
Carmichael, Amy Wilson, 168, 504, 537
Carver, William Owen, 168
Cary, Maude, 168–69
Casalis, Eugene, 169, 724
Castro, Emilio, 170, 213, 438, 614
Ch'eng, Ching-yi, 171–72
Chalmers, James, 172, 565
Chamberlain, Jacob, 172–73
Chambers, Oswald, 173
Chapman, J. Wilbur, 173, 247–48
Charles, Pierre, 176, 634, 839
Chestnut, Eleanor, 176, 916
Chi-Oang, 176
Chitambar, Jashwaut Rao, 181
Cho, (David) Paul Yonggi, 181–82
Christlieb, Theodor, 188, 1006
Clark, Charles Allen, 205–6
Clough, John Everett, 206
Codrington, Robert Henry, 184, 206
Coillard, Francois, 207, 724, 1042
Coke, Thomas, 88, 207, 984
Columba of Iona, 50, 170, 195, 211, 503, 693, 859, 984, 1017

Columbanus, 170, 195, 211, 330, 370, 384, 388, 503
Constantine. *See* Cyril
Coppin, Fanny Jackson, 232–33
Coppock, Grace Lydia, 233
Costas, Orlando E., 234–35, 642, 950, 1000
Cragg, Albert Kenneth, 238–39, 274
Crawford, Daniel, 239
Crawford, Isabel Alice Hartley, 239
Crowther, Samuel Adjai, 39, 201, 246–47, 690, 692, 875
Cyril, 259, 330, 442, 619, 654, 713

Das, Rajendra Chandra, 261
de Nobili, Robert. *See* Nobili, Robert de
Devanandan, Paul David, 271–72
Deyneka, Peter, Sr., 273–74
Dober, (Johann) Leonhard, 288, 660
Doke, Clement Martyn, 289, 898
Doremus, Sarah, 290, 1022
Duff, Alexander, 183, 293–94, 301, 304, 445, 589, 634, 772, 860, 982

Edwards, Jonathan, 275, 300, 304–5, 337, 379, 444, 627, 633, 758, 814, 815, 900, 913, 984, 986, 1002, 1036
Egede, Hans Povelsön, 305
Eliot, John, 160, 183, 308, 444, 772, 814, 820, 831, 845, 986
Elliot, Elisabeth Howard, 133, 308–9, 1020
Elliot, Philip James, 309
Emde, Johannes, 309
Evans, Helen E., 3
Evans, James, 347

Farrar, Cynthia, 355–56, 1021
Farrow, Lucy F., 356
Fearing, Maria, 356
Field, Adele Marion, 359, 880
Finkenbinder, Paul Edwin, 360
Finney, Charles Grandison, 247, 337, 361, 408, 746, 972, 1003, 1011
Fisk, Pliny, 362, 570
Fiske, Fidelia, 362
Fison, Lorimer, 362
Fjellstedt, Peter, 362–63
Flynn, John, 363–64

Forman, Charles W., 369
Forsyth, Christina nee Moir, 369
Francis, Mabel, 370
Francis of Assisi, 314, 370–71, 442, 598, 624, 1002
Franson, Fredrik, 371, 652, 920, 942
Fraser, Donald, 371–72
Freeman, Thomas Birch, 372–73, 390, 962
Freire, Paulo Reglus Neves, 273, 373, 568–69, 598
Freytag, Walter, 375, 389, 642, 949
Frumentius, 37, 38, 322, 378–79
Fuller, Andrew, 110, 379, 984
Fuller, Charles E., 379, 807

Gairdner, William Henry Temple, 383–84, 718
Gall, 211, 384
Gardiner, Allen Francis, 384–85
Geddie, John, 385
George, Eliza Davis, 386–87
Gih, Andrew, 180, 393
Gilmour, James, 393, 655
Glasser, Arthur F., 203, 223, 393, 815, 1021
Glegg, (Alexander) Lindsay, 394
Gloukharev, Makarius, 396, 443
Gobat, Maria, 396
Goforth, Jonathan, 400, 795
Goforth, Rosalind Bell Smith, 400–401, 795
Gordon, Adoniram Judson, 339, 401, 738, 756, 783
Gorham, Sarah, 401
Gossner, Johannes Evangelista, 404
Graham, William Franklin ("Billy"), 248, 302, 338, 346, 389, 394, 406, 458, 496–97, 537, 563, 604, 792, 1023
Graul, Karl, 406, 634
Greene, Elizabeth "Betty," 101, 415
Greene, Mary Jane Forbes, 415
Gregg, Jessie, 416
Gregory the Illuminator, 416
Grenfell, George, 41, 416
Grenfell, Sir Wilfred Thomason, 416–17
Groves, Anthony Norris, 417
Grubb, Sir Kenneth George, 417
Grubb, Wilfred Barbrooke, 417–18

Guinness, Henry Grattan, 420–21
Gutiérrez, Gustavo, 421, 598, 781
Gutmann, Bruno, 183, 421–22, 586
Gützlaff, Karl Friedrich August, 422, 445

Haining, Jane Mathison, 423
Hamer, Lilian, 423–24
Han, Chul-la, 424
Han, Kyung-Chik, 424
Harris, William Wade, 41, 235, 390, 424–25, 576, 793, 916
Harvey, Esther Bragg, 425
Haygood, Laura Askew, 425
Hepburn, James Curtis, 429–30, 513
Herman of Alaska, 430
Hesselgrave, David, 189, 281, 334, 432–33, 908
Hewat, Elizabeth G. K., 433
Heyling, Peter, 433
Hicks, Tommy, 433
Higginbottom, Sam, 434, 785
Hill, David, 434
Hinderer, Anna (Martin), 434
Hinz, Hansina, 437–38
Hocking, William Ernest, 366, 446, 572, 642
Hodges, Melvin Lyle, 194, 446, 484, 739
Hoekendijk, Johannes Christiaan, 446–47, 538, 572, 632, 642, 815
Hollenweger, Walter Jacob, 449
Honda, Koji, 456
Honda, Yoichi, 456
Hoover, James Matthew, 458
Hooever, Willis Collins, 458–59
Hoste, Dixon Edward, 459–60, 716
Howard, David Morris, 460, 1023
Huey, Mary Alice, 460–61
Hunt, John, 466
Hyde, John, 466

Ibiam (Sir Francis) Akanu, 467
Ignatius of Loyola, 238, 443, 469

Jackson, Sheldon, 511
Jaeschke, Heinrich Augustus, 511
Jaffray, Robert, 511–12, 1000
Javouhey, Anne Marie, 373, 515–16
Jessup, Henry Harris, 516–17
John, Griffith, 522

John of Montecorvino, 82, 178, 442, 522, 655

John XXIII, 522–23

Johnson, Richard, 523

Jones, David, 524

Jones, Eli Stanley, 28, 274, 524, 634, 832, 913

Jones, Lina Maude, 524–25

Joseph, Justus, 525

Judson, Adoniram, 55, 83, 111, 112, 209, 425, 445, 528–29, 544, 628, 644, 667, 735, 916, 987

Judson, Ann Hazeltine, 55, 112, 445, 528, 529, 667, 1021

Kagawa, Toyohiko, 533

Kalley, Robert Reid, 142, 533–34

Kane, J. Herbert, 281, 358, 534

Kasatkin, Nicholas, 444, 535, 714

Kato, Byang Henry, 45, 535–36

Keller, Mirian Wittich, 536

Kentigern, 536

Keysser, Christian, 183, 538, 586

Kil, Sun-Joo, 538

Kim, Helen, 410, 538

Kim, Joon-Gon, 538–39

Kimbangu, Simon, 41, 43, 267, 445, 539, 793

Kinsolving, Lucien Lee, 543

Kivebulaya, Apolo, 409, 543

Kivengere, Festo, 248, 329, 543–44

Ko Tha Byu, 445, 544

Kraemer, Hendrik, 194, 215, 216, 499, 547, 572, 634, 642, 659, 673, 718, 761, 929, 949, 999

Krapf, Johann Ludwig, 40, 536, 547

Krishna Pillai, H. A., 547–48

Kropf, Albert, 548

Kuhn, Isobel, 548

Kumm, Karl Wilhelm, 548–49, 690

Kunst, Irene, 549

Kuyper, Abraham, 549–50, 815

Las Casas, Bartholomew de, 553–54, 555, 620, 838, 916

Latourette, Kenneth Scott, 236, 331, 369, 561, 913

Laubach, Frank Charles, 562

Lavigerie, Charles Martial Allemand, 564

Lawes, William George, 565

Laws, Robert, 565, 592

Lee, Calvin, 570

Legge, James, 458, 570, 860

Lew, Timothy Tingfang, 571–72

Liddell, Eric Henry, 577

Little, Paul E., 581–82

Liu Tinfang. See Lew, Timothy Tingfang

Livingstone, David, 40, 78, 141, 209, 236, 239, 312, 409, 445, 565, 582, 592, 644, 772, 860, 897, 1042

Loewen, Jacob A., 66, 69, 582–83

Loyola, Ignatius. See Ignatius of Loyola

Luce, Alice Eveline, 585, 739

Lull, Ramon, 52, 71, 182, 442, 585, 624, 633, 666

Luzbetak, Louis J., 67, 69, 184, 587

Mabille, Adolphe, 588

Mackay, Alexander Murdock, 589, 795, 979

MacKay, George Leslie, 160, 179, 589

Mackay, John Alexander, 438, 499, 589–90, 749, 785

Macomber, Eleanor, 590

Mallory, Kathleen, 595–96

Marks, John Ebenezer, 598–99

Marsden, Samuel, 96, 600, 687, 702

Marshman, Joshua, 110, 444–45, 600–601, 867

Martin of Tours, 601, 693

Martin, Walter R., 601

Martin, William Alexander Parsons, 72, 601

Martyn, Henry, 444, 602, 624, 666, 718, 772, 855

Mayers, Marvin Keene, 67, 606–7

McDougall, Francis Thomas, 607

McGavran, Donald A., 56, 67, 69, 146, 194, 196, 199, 202, 229, 230, 333, 334, 351, 371, 379, 413, 446, 455, 484, 538, 563, 607, 634, 642, 648, 743, 745, 791, 811–12, 889, 961, 987, 990, 1004, 1025, 1034

McGeorge, Mary, 607–8

McLaren, Agnes, 608

McPherson, Aimee Semple, 608, 741

McQuilkin, Robert C., 608–9, 835

Mears, Henrietta Cornelia, 609

Merensky, Alexander, 617–18

Methodius, 259, 330, 442, 619, 654, 713

Miguez Bonino, José, 626–27

Mills, Samuel John, Jr., 425, 628, 832, 987

Moe, Malla, 652

Moffat, Robert, 141, 236, 312, 445, 652–53, 897, 1042

Moffett, Samuel A., 653

Moninger, (Mary) Margaret, 655–56

Montgomery, Carrie Judd, 656–57, 880–81

Montgomery, Helen Barrett, 657, 735

Moody, Dwight Lyman, 132, 173, 247, 302, 337, 408, 410, 417, 537, 556, 657–58, 740, 756, 759, 783, 912, 913, 914, 942, 963, 987, 1032

Moon, Charlotte ("Lottie"), 78, 352, 410, 658, 899

Morris, William Case, 662

Morrison, Robert, 52, 83, 124, 179, 236, 312, 445, 588, 603, 644, 662, 916

Morton, John, 662–63

Mother Teresa, 273, 663, 937, 1026

Mott, John Raleigh, 171, 300, 301, 302, 339, 498, 627, 664, 709, 756, 914, 1029

Müller, George, 371, 665, 757

Murray, Andrew, 40, 42, 665, 898

Nee, Watchman, 672

Neill, Stephen Charles, 111, 245, 274, 634, 635, 644, 659, 672–73, 842

Nevius, John Livingston, 194, 206, 351, 484, 547, 642, 676–77, 727

Newbigin, (James Edward) Lesslie, 32, 213, 402, 620, 642, 688, 693, 761, 815, 848

Nicholson, William Patteson, 689

Nida, Eugene A., 66, 67, 116, 124, 216, 245, 295, 499, 580, 689–90, 968

Niijima, Jom, 692–93

Niles, Daniel Thambyrajah, 693

Ninian, 693, 859

Nitschmann, David, 288, 660, 693

Nobili, Robert de, 32, 182, 238, 443, 694, 838

Nommensen, Ludwig Ingwer, 487, 694
Ntsikana, 700
Nuñez, Emilio Antonio, 438, 700
Nuttall, Enos, 700

Occom, Samson, 701
Oldham, Joseph Houldsworth, 210, 498, 516, 643, 709, 730

Padilla, Carlos René, 439, 563, 718
Padwick, Constance Evelyn, 718
Palau, Luis, 248, 346, 604, 719
Palmer, Phoebe Worrall, 337, 719–20, 740, 1011
Pantaenus, 346, 721
Papasarantopoulos, Chrysostom, 721
Parker, Peter, 55, 725
Parrish, Sarah Rebecca, 726
Paton, John Gibson, 300, 385, 703, 730
Paton, William, 730–31, 795
Patrick, 170, 195, 441, 503, 731
Patteson, John Coleridge, 206, 731
Paul, Kanakarayan Tiruselvam, 181, 734
Palau, Luis, 248, 346
Paulinus of York, 50, 734–35
Peabody, Lucy Whitehead McGill Waterbury, 657, 735
Penman, David, 737
Penzotti, Francisco, 299, 306, 556, 742–43, 749
Perkins, Justin, 746
Peters, George W., 281, 389, 563, 750
Pfander, Karl Gottlieb, 624, 750–51
Pierson, Arthur Tappan, 43, 300, 339, 413, 537, 756, 783, 914
Pike, Eunice, 758
Pike, Kenneth Lee, 67, 580, 758–59
Pikington, George Lawrence, 41, 759, 979
Pollard, Samuel, 765–66
Posselt, Wilhelm, 771
Potter, Philip A., 213, 774
Prokhanov, Ivan Stepanovich, 792
Pudaite, Rochunga, 799

Quaque, Philip, 390, 804, 959

Ramabai, Pandita, 28, 808, 957
Reed, Mary, 96, 813
Ricci, Matteo, 32, 72, 79, 178, 182, 222, 238, 330–31, 443, 481, 588, 694, 834, 837
Richard, Timothy, 110, 834
Richter, Julius, 834–35
Ridderhof, Joy, 604, 835
Riggs, Mary Ann Clark Longley, 835
Riis, Andreas, 835–36
Roberts, W. Dayton, 836–37
Rodgers, James Burton, 837
Roseveare, Helen, 611, 841
Rouse, Ruth, 841–42
Ryung, Ju Sam, 843

Sanders, J. Oswald, 716, 852
Schaeffer, Francis, 314, 563, 855–56
Schereschewsky, Samuel Isaac Joseph, 856
Schmidlin, Josef, 634, 642, 839, 856, 949
Schmidt, Georg, 39, 587, 660, 856–57, 897, 916
Schreuder, Hans Paludan Smith, 837
Schrupp, Ernst, 388, 837
Schwartz, Christian Friedrich, 78, 261, 857–58
Schweitzer, Albert, 41, 383, 724, 733, 858
Scott, Peter Cameron, 40, 42–43, 860
Scudder, Ida Sophia, 611, 861
Segundo, Juan Luis, 781, 866
Selwyn, George Augustus, 385, 613, 703, 731, 866–67
Serra, Junípero, 867, 985
Shedd, Russell Phillip, 871
Shellabear, William Girdlestone, 871
Simonton, Ashbel Green, 142, 784, 877
Simpson, Albert Benjamin, 160, 185, 339, 657, 738, 740, 783, 877, 1012, 1022
Singh, (Sadhu) Sundar, 61, 879
Sisson, Elizabeth, 880–81
Slessor, Mary (Mitchell), 41, 861, 880, 881
Small, Annie Hunter, 881
Smalley, William A., 66, 580, 882–83
Smith, Amanda Berry, 883
Smith, Edwin Williams, 66, 883
Smith, Nico, 883–84
Smith, Rodney ("Gipsey"), 884
Soga, Tiyo, 894–95
Soltau, Henrietta Eliza, 895

Speer, Robert E., 300, 340, 537, 642, 720, 734, 756, 785, 901, 914
Steidel, Florence, 906
Stephen, 405, 439, 906
Stephen (king of Hungary), 906–7
Stephen of Perm, 443, 713, 907
Stern, Henry Aaron, 907
Stevenson, Marion Scott, 907
Stewart, Louisa, 908–9
Stockton, Betsey, 909
Stott, John Robert Walmsley, 230, 274, 302, 339, 412, 413, 427, 439, 563, 909–10
Strachan, R. Kenneth, 910
Studd, Charles Thomas, 738, 912, 916, 1010
Suh Sang-Yun (So Saw), 917
Sunday, William Ashley ("Billy"), 173, 248, 917
Sundkler, Bengt, 917–18, 949
Sung, John, 918, 1005
Swain, Clara A., 410, 919
Szabó, Aladá, 926–27

Taylor, (James) Hudson, 52, 96, 300, 312, 331, 371, 408, 445, 458, 537, 634, 716, 760, 772, 795, 845, 895, 931, 942, 985
Taylor, John Vernon, 69, 201, 931–32
Taylor, Kenneth Nathaniel, 932
Taylor, William, 28, 634, 711, 932, 958, 1011
Tekla-Haymanot, 39, 936–37
ten Boom, Corrie, 937–38
Teng, Philip, 938–39
Theodore of Tarsus, 943
Thoburn, Isabella, 919, 958
Thoburn, James Mills, 300, 883, 958
Thomas, Madathilparampil Mammen, 89, 958
Thompson, Elizabeth Maria Bowen, 958–59
Thompson, Muriwhenua, 959
Thompson, Thomas, 959
Thomson, James "Diego," 208, 299, 556, 620, 749, 959–60
Tilak, Narayan Vaman, 960
Ting, Li-Mei, 960–61
Tippett, Alan R., 67, 69, 97, 184, 189, 484, 607, 743, 774, 961
Torrey, Reuben Archer, 247, 740, 963
Townsend, William Cameron, 580, 689, 745, 784, 795, 964, 987, 1036
Trasher, Lillian, 741, 969

Trotman, Dawson E., 971
Trotter, Isabelle Lillias, 52, 971–72
Trumbull, David, 972
Tsizehena, John, 973
Tucker, Alfred Robert, 973, 979
Tucker, Charlotte, 974
Turner, Harold, 69, 403, 975

Uchimura, Kanzō, 695, 978
Uemura, Masahisa, 979
Ulfilas, 442, 875, 911, 980
Underwood, Horace G., 653, 917, 980

Valignano, Alessandro, 837, 995–96
Van der Kemp, Johannes Theodorus, 996
Veenstra, Johanna, 998
Veniaminov, Innocent, 444, 713–14, 998–99
Venn, Henry, 39, 54, 55, 183, 194, 201, 247, 312, 410, 483, 484, 634, 642, 676, 726, 727, 760, 772, 999
Verbeck, Guido Fridolin, 513, 999
Verkuyl, Johannes, 235, 641, 814, 815, 950, 999–1000
Vicelin of Oldenburg, 1000
Vladimir, 442, 713, 715, 842, 1001–2
Voetius, Gisbert, 194, 633, 814, 949, 1002
Von Zinsendorf. *See* Zinzendorf, Nikolaus Ludwig von

Waddell, Hope Masterton, 1004
Wagner, Charles Peter, 55, 69, 199, 202, 455, 630, 742, 778, 1004
Walls, Andrew Finlay, 31, 640, 643, 1005
Wang, Leland, 180, 1005
Wang, Thomas Yung-hsin, 180, 1005
Ward, William, 110, 600, 603, 867, 1005–6
Warneck, Gustav, 183, 188, 389, 585, 634, 642, 856, 949, 1006
Warren, Max Alexander Cunningham, 201, 312, 417, 499, 659, 949, 1006
Waterston, Jane Elizabeth, 1008
Webb, Mary, 1009
Wesley, John, 39, 80, 207, 247, 312, 313, 337, 407, 507, 529, 618, 661, 702, 717, 719, 723, 740, 820, 832, 888, 984, 986, 1002, 1010–11, 1015
Weston, Frank, 1013
Whately, Mary Louisa, 1013–14
White, John, 1014–15
Whitefield, George, 247, 300, 313, 337, 407, 702, 758, 832, 1002, 1015
Whitman, Leroy Frederick, 1015
Wilfrid, 50, 943, 1016, 1017
Williams, Channing Moore, 1016

Williams, John, 409, 613, 702, 767, 916, 1016–17
Willibald, 1017
Willibrord, 170, 195, 676, 1017
Wilson, J. Christy, 933, 1018
Wilson, John Leighton, 1018
Wilson, Margaret Bayne, 1018
Wilson, Mary Ann (Cooke), 1018–19
Winter, Ralph D., 67, 205, 244, 351, 394, 414, 563, 642, 722, 745, 938, 944, 981, 1019

Xavier, Francis, 82, 238, 330, 443, 455, 487, 513, 694, 837, 1038
Xavier, Jerome, 1038

Yannoulator, Anastasios, 1039
Young, Florence S. H., 1040
Yun, Chi-ho, 1041

Zamora, Nicolas, 1042–43
Ziegenbalg, Bartholomaeus, 83, 260, 300, 444, 586, 757, 820, 1043–44
Zinzendorf, Nikolaus Ludwig von, 107, 259, 288, 300, 331, 339, 444, 511, 586, 633, 660, 693, 757, 832, 856, 913, 962, 986, 1044–45
Zwemer, Samuel Marinus, 106, 477, 503, 549, 666, 756, 803, 815, 855, 914, 1039, 1046